The Reader's Adviser

The Reader's Adviser
14th EDITION
Marion Sader, Series Editor

Volume 1
The Best in Reference Works, British Literature, and American Literature
David Scott Kastan and Emory Elliott, Volume Editors

Books About Books • Bibliography • Reference Books: General • Reference Books: Literature • Medieval Literature • Renaissance Literature • Shakespeare • Restoration and Eighteenth-Century Literature • The Romantic Period • The Victorian Period • Modern British and Irish Literature • British Literature: Popular Modes • Early American Literature: Beginnings to the Nineteenth Century • Early Nineteenth-Century American Literature • Middle to Late Nineteenth-Century American Literature • Early Twentieth-Century American Literature • Middle to Late Twentieth-Century American Literature • Modern American Drama • American Literature: Some New Directions • American Literature: Popular Modes

Volume 2
The Best in World Literature
Robert DiYanni, Volume Editor

Introduction to World Literature • Hebrew Literature • Yiddish Literature • Middle Eastern Literatures • African Literatures • Literature of the Indian Subcontinent • Chinese Literature • Japanese Literature • Korean Literature • Southeast Asian Literatures • Greek Literature • Latin Literature • Italian Literature • French Literature • Spanish Literature • Portuguese Literature • German Literature • Netherlandic Literature • Scandinavian Literatures • Russian Literature • East European Literatures • Latin American Literatures • Canadian Literature • Literature of the Caribbean • Australian Literature • New Zealand Literature • Comparative Literature

Volume 3
The Best in Social Sciences, History, and the Arts
John G. Sproat, Volume Editor

Social Sciences and History: General Reference • Anthropology • Economics • Geography • Political Science • Psychology • Sociology • Education • World History • Ancient History • European History • African History • Middle Eastern History • History of Asia and the Pacific • United States History • Canadian History • Latin American History • Music and Dance • Art and Architecture • Mass Media • Folklore, Humor, and Popular Culture • Travel and Exploration

Volume 4
The Best in Philosophy and Religion
Robert S. Ellwood, Volume Editor

Philosophy and Religion: General Reference • General Philosophy • Greek and Roman Philosophy • Medieval Philosophy • Renaissance Philosophy • Modern Western Philosophy, 1600–1900 • Twentieth-Century Western Philosophy • Asian and African Philosophy, 1850 to the Present • Contemporary Issues in Philosophy • Ancient Religions and Philosophies • Eastern Religions • Islam • Judaism • Early and Medieval Christianity • Late Christianity, 1500 to the Present • The Bible and Related Literature • Minority Religions and Contemporary Religious Movements • Contemporary Issues in Religious Thought

Volume 5
The Best in Science, Technology, and Medicine
Carl Mitcham and William F. Williams, Volume Editors

Science, Technology, and Medicine: General Reference • A General View: Science, Technology, and Medicine • History of Science, Technology, and Medicine • Philosophy of Science, Technology, and Medicine • Ethics in Science, Technology, and Medicine • Science, Technology, and Society • Special Issues in Science, Technology, and Society • Engineering and Technology • Agriculture and Food Technology • Energy • Communications Technology • Medicine and Health • Illness and Disease • Clinical Psychology and Psychiatry • Mathematics • Statistics and Probability • Information Science and Computer Science • Astronomy and Space Science • Earth Sciences • Physics • Chemistry • Biological Sciences • Ecology and Environmental Science

THE
Reader's Adviser®

14th EDITION

Volume 4

The Best in Philosophy and Religion

Robert S. Ellwood, Volume Editor

Marion Sader, Series Editor

R. R. Bowker®
A Reed Reference Publishing Company
New Providence, New Jersey

Published by R. R. Bowker
A Reed Reference Publishing Company
Copyright © 1994 by Reed Publishing (USA) Inc.

International Standard Book Numbers
0-8352-3320-0 (SET)
0-8352-3321-9 (Volume 1)
0-8352-3322-7 (Volume 2)
0-8352-3323-5 (Volume 3)
0-8352-3324-3 (Volume 4)
0-8352-3325-1 (Volume 5)
0-8352-3326-X (Volume 6)
International Standard Serial Number 0094-5943
Library of Congress Catalog Card Number 57-13277

ISBN 0-8352-3320-0

9 780835 233200

Contents

PREFACE   xiii
CONTRIBUTING EDITORS   xvii
ABBREVIATIONS   xix
CHRONOLOGY OF AUTHORS   xxi
INTRODUCTION   xxvii

1. **Philosophy and Religion: General Reference**   **1**
    General Histories and Surveys   2
    Encyclopedias and Dictionaries in Philosophy   2
    Encyclopedias, Dictionaries, and Atlases in Religion   3
    Handbooks, Sourcebooks, and Guides   5
    Indexes   7

PART ONE Philosophy   9

2. **General Philosophy**   **11**
    Encyclopedias, Dictionaries, and Indexes   12
    Histories of Philosophy   15
    Introductions to Philosophy   19
    Philosophy by Geographic Area   25
        Africa 26 *Europe* 27 *Latin America* 33 *United States* 33
    Comparative Philosophy   36
        East-West 37 *General Comparative* 37 *Ecophilosophy* 38
    Chronology of Authors   38
    AUTHORS (Main Entries)   38

3. **Greek and Roman Philosophy**   **44**
    General Works   46
        Histories and Texts 46 *Special Works* 47
    Pre-Socratics   49
        General Works 50 *The Milesian Philosophers* 51 *Parmenides
        and the Eleatics* 51 *The Pluralists and Atomists* 52
    The Sophists   53
        General Works 54
    Hellenistic Philosophies   54
        General Works 55 *Texts and Collections* 55 *The Stoics* 56
        The Skeptics 57
    Roman Philosophers   58
        General Works 59

Middle Platonism 59
    General Works 60
Neoplatonism 60
    General Works 61
Early Christian Thinkers 62
    General Works 63
Chronology of Authors 64
AUTHORS (Main Entries) 64

4. Medieval Philosophy 92
General Works 93
Collections of Medieval Philosophical Texts 94
Special Topics 95
    Problems of Method in the Study of Medieval Philosophy 95
    The History of Ideas and Medieval Thought 96 *Averroism and*
    Islamic Thought in the West 96 *Logic* 97 *Science* 97
    Politics 98
The Patristic Period 98
The Period of Recovery 100
The Twelfth and Thirteenth Centuries 101
The Later Middle Ages 103
    The Fourteenth Century 103 *The Fifteenth Century and After* 104
Chronology of Authors 105
AUTHORS (Main Entries) 105

5. Renaissance Philosophy 122
General Works 123
Chronology of Authors 132
AUTHORS (Main Entries) 133

6. Modern Western Philosophy, 1600–1900 157
General Bibliography 159
Chronology of Authors (Seventeenth Century) 163
AUTHORS (Main Entries) 163
Chronology of Authors (Eighteenth Century) 190
AUTHORS (Main Entries) 190
Chronology of Authors (Nineteenth Century) 219
AUTHORS (Main Entries) 219

7. Twentieth-Century Western Philosophy 259
General Works 262
Chronology of Authors 269
AUTHORS (Main Entries) 269

8. Asian and African Philosophy, 1850 to the Present 348
General Works 349
Chronology of Authors 350
Indian Philosophy 350
    General Works 351
    AUTHORS (Main Entries) 351

Tibetan Philosophy   355
  General Works 356
  AUTHORS (Main Entries) 356
Chinese Philosophy   357
  General Works 358
  AUTHORS (Main Entries) 359
Japanese Philosophy   363
  General Works 363
  AUTHORS (Main Entries) 363
African Philosophy   367
  General Works 368
  AUTHORS (Main Entries) 369
Islamic Philosophy   372
  General Works 372
  AUTHORS (Main Entries) 374

9. **Contemporary Issues in Philosophy**   **376**
General Works   378
The Present State of Traditional Philosophic Problems   379
The Nature of Mind   381
Current Philosophy of Science   383
Theories of Rights and Justice   385
Current Issues in Philosophical Ethics   387
Deconstruction and Postmodernism   390
Chronology of Authors   392
AUTHORS (Main Entries)   392

PART TWO Religion   **417**

10. **Ancient Religions and Philosophies**   **419**
Religions and the Study of Religions   420
  Problems of Definition and Origin 420 *Ways to Study*
  Religions 422 *General Topics* 427
Prehistoric Religions   431
  Paleolithic Period 432 *Neolithic Religion* 433 *Indo-European*
  Religions 434
Ancient Urban Civilizations: Religions of the Ancient
  Mediterranean World   438
  Ancient Mediterranean Civilizations 439 *Areas of Primary*
  Urbanization 440 *Secondary Centers of Civilization* 443
  The Mediterranean "Oikoumene": Religions of the Hellenistic
  World and the Roman Empire 448
Ancient Urban Civilizations: Religions of the New World   453
  Religions of Mesoamerica 454 *Inca Religion* 458
Indigenous Religions of Australia and Oceania, Africa, and
  the Americas   458
  Orality and Literacy 459 *Indigenous Religions of Australia*
  and Oceania 460 *Indigenous Religions of Africa* 462 *Indigenous*
  Religions of the Americas 463 *The Confrontation with the Modern*
  West 466
Chronology of Authors   468
AUTHORS (Main Entries)   468

11. Eastern Religions   495

South Asian Traditions   497
 Reference Works and Anthologies 497 *General Works* 498
 The Ancient Heritage: Pre-Vedic and Vedic Traditions 499
 Hinduism 502 *Jainism* 509 *Buddhism* 510 *Sikhism* 515
 Parsis (Zoroastrians in India) 517

Southeast Asian Traditions   518
 General Works 518 *Popular Religion* 518 *Buddhist*
 Traditions 519 *Vietnamese Traditions* 520

East Asian Traditions   520
 Chinese Traditions 521 *Japanese and Korean Traditions* 533

Central Asian Traditions   541
 Tibetan Traditions 542

Non-Islamic and Non-Jewish Traditions of the Middle East
 and North Africa   544
 Assyro-Babylonian and Semitic Traditions 544 *Persian*
 Zoroastrianism 546 *North African Traditions: Ancient Egypt* 548

Chronology of Authors   548
AUTHORS (Main Entries)   548

12. Islam   564

Dictionaries, Encyclopedias, and Literature   566
General Histories and Comparative Studies   567
Islamic Mysticism, Philosophy, and Theology   574
Islamic Society and Politics   577
Chronology of Authors   580
AUTHORS (Main Entries)   580

13. Judaism   591

General Works   592
 Judaism 595 *Judaism and Christianity through the Ages* 602

Ancient Judaism   603
 History of the Jews 603 *Literature* 607 *Material Evidence:*
 Art and Archaeology 613 *Religious Movements* 614

Medieval Judaism   622
 History of the Jews 622 *Jewish Thought* 626
 Religious Movements 630

Modern Judaism   633
 History of the Jews 633 *Jewish Thought* 645
 Religious Movements 650

Chronology of Authors   660
AUTHORS (Main Entries)   660

14. Early and Medieval Christianity   674

General References   675
 Reference Works 675 *Histories* 676 *Topical Studies* 678
 Source Collections 679

The Early Centuries (to circa A.D. 600)   681
 Special Histories 681 *Christianity in the World of the Roman*
 Empire 682 *Christian Doctrine and Heresies* 684
 Life in the Christian Church 687 *Church Fathers and Writers* 690

Medieval Christianity   690
   Special Histories 690   *Eastern Churches and Crusades* 692
   Emperors, Popes, and Councils 694   *Christian Thought and*
   Doctrine 695   *Christian Life and Culture* 698
Chronology of Authors   701
AUTHORS (Main Entries)   702

15. **Late Christianity, 1500 to the Present**   **715**
General Reference Works   716
Dictionaries, Encyclopedias, Handbooks   716
   The Church 716   *Ethics and Theology* 718   *Church History* 719
The Reformation of the Sixteenth Century: 1500–1560   720
   Background: Before the Reformation 721   *General Studies*
   of the Reformation 722   *The Radical Reformation: Anabaptists,*
   Spiritualists, and Evangelical Rationalists 723   *The English*
   Reformation: From Henry VIII to the Elizabethan Settlement 725
   The Catholic Reformation: From 1500 through the Council of
   Trent 727
The Reformation in Its Later Developments: 1560–1648   729
   Post-Luther Lutheranism in Germany and Scandinavia 730
   Reformed Struggle after Calvin 731   *The Radical Reformation*
   after the Death of Menno Simons, 1561 732   *The Reformation*
   in Great Britain: From the Elizabethan Settlement to 1700 733
   The Catholic Reformation after the Council of Trent 736
   Art and the Reformation 737
The Age of Reason: Christianity in the Eighteenth Century   738
The Age of Revolution: Christianity in the Nineteenth Century   740
Christianity in the Twentieth Century: 1914 to the Present   742
   General Religion and Theology 742   *Liberation Theologies* 747
Christian Religion in America   750
   Bibliographies 750   *General Studies* 751   *French and Spanish*
   Colonies 752   *Other Useful Books* 752
Eastern Orthodox Christianity   754
Chronology of Authors   756
AUTHORS (Main Entries)   757

16. **The Bible and Related Literature**   **792**
General Works   793
   Critical Editions of Original Texts 794   *Principal Access*
   Tools 794   *Bibliographies* 795
Texts and Versions of the Bible   796
   Ancient Versions 796   *English Versions* 797   *Chronology of*
   Principal Versions 799   *Textual Criticism* 805
Historical Background of the Bible   806
   Histories of Judaism and Early Christianity 806   *Biblical*
   Archaeology 808   *Biblical Geography* 809   *Biblical Backgrounds*
   and Extracanonical Materials 809
History, Method, and Examples of Modern Biblical Study   812
   Histories of Biblical Interpretation 813   *Methods and Principles*
   of Biblical Exegesis 814   *Introduction to the Two Testaments* 815
   Bible Dictionaries and Concordances 817   *Commentaries* 819
   Selected Masterworks on Biblical Topics and Authors 822
   Biblical Theologies 826

associations for me now that I pass 'Out of the stress of the doing, Into the peace of the done.' " Sadly, the United States's entry into World War II would soon interrupt that peace as well as the arrival of "future editions."

With the war near an end in June 1945, Bowker's Mildred Smith recommended Hester R. Hoffman, a bookseller with nearly 30 years' experience at the Hampshire Bookshop in Northampton, Massachusetts, to compile the next peacetime edition of Graham's *The Bookman's Manual*. Unfortunately, Hoffman's start was frustrated by more than a wartime paper shortage; Bowker's proposal reached her (as she later put it) while she was "lying flat in a room in a South Boston Hospital recovering from, of all things, a broken neck." Undaunted by her predicament, by the dearth of current titles on publishers' lists, and even by her typesetter's utter lack of foreign accents for the chapter on French literature, she succeeded in pulling together the sixth edition of *The Bookman's Manual* by 1948. The war, though, had taken its toll: despite a seven-year hiatus between editions, Hoffman's first effort was 62 pages *shorter* than Graham's last.

As the 1950s unfolded and the nuclear age cast a lengthening shadow, Hester Hoffman strove to keep *The Bookman's Manual* at the forefront of breaking literary and nonliterary events worldwide. A new chapter on science in the seventh edition of 1954 helped readers make sense of the profound legacy of such diverse theorists as Einstein and Freud. Thanks to Russian literature editors Helen Muchnic and Nicolai Vorobiov, anyone searching for contemporary Soviet novelists could have discovered the great Boris Pasternak (then known in the West only as a poet) fully three years before *Doctor Zhivago* made him an international sensation. In the eighth edition of 1958, the chapter on bibles updated readers who were eager to learn more about one of the seminal discoveries in Judeo-Christian history: a tattered collection of Hebrew and Aramaic parchments, concealed in pottery jars in caves near Qumran, that soon became known as the Dead Sea Scrolls.

Renamed *The Reader's Adviser and Bookman's Manual*, in 1960, the work continued to grow precipitously—struggling to reward the newfound postwar affluence, leisure, and cosmopolitan curiosity of American readers. With the baby boom at that time came a publishing boom, and, as Americans opened the New Frontier, they hungered for books about everything from rockets and space travel to parapsychology to segregation and the South. Indeed, just a glimpse of the new reading lists added during this heady and tumultuous era recaptures a time when readers were discovering ideas, arts, peoples, and places as perhaps they never had discovered before. There were books on the North American Indian and the opening of the West, Soviet history and policy, and the Civil War (as it reached its centenary); there were books by authors from Africa, Japan, China, India, Latin America, and, at long last, black America, as well as books about the lively arts of jazz, cinema, children's theater, and, yes, McLuhan's "cool medium," television.

By 1968, when Winifred F. Courtney guided the eleventh edition to press, one volume could no longer hold it all: It took two. The twelfth edition, published from 1974 to 1977, then blossomed to three volumes. As Bowker's own *Books in Print* continued to document a book market that was all but doubling in size every 10 years (from 245,000 titles in 1967 to 750,000 in 1987), the thirteenth edition, published in two installments, in 1986 and 1988, swelled to five volumes (plus a separately bound index). *The Reader's Adviser*, which always had been a reference tool built on the contributions of subject specialists, now had become virtually an encyclopedia—requiring separate editors for the set, for the individual volumes, for the sections . . . and even for the chapters!

As little as today's *Reader's Adviser* may resemble Bessie Graham's once modest *Bookman's Manual*, the work still adheres to tradition. More than ever the essential starting point for anyone who is setting out to read about the world of literary, artistic, philosophical, or scientific endeavor, the work's individual volumes are designed to carry users from the general to the specific—from overarching reference guides, critical histories, and anthologies about a genre or a field to the lives and works of its leading exemplars. As always, booksellers, reference and acquisitions librarians, lay readers, teachers, academics, and students alike can readily use it to identify the best of nearly everything available in English in the United States today, from the poetry of the ancients to Renaissance philosophy to meditations on the ethics of modern medicine.

Choosing what to include and what to leave out is never easy. As specialists, the volume and chapter editors know their field's most noted and popular figures, current and historic, and the body of literature on which the reputations of those individuals stand. Although I have asked each editor, when possible, to revise an "out of vogue" author's profile and bibliography rather than simply to eliminate it, paring is inevitable with any new edition. Then, too, the mere availability of an author's work can play its own editorial role. Although it is customary to list only titles published as books and (according to the latest monthly release of *Books in Print* on CD-ROM) currently for sale in the United States, exceptions are made for invaluable out-of-print works deemed likely to appear in the stacks of an established, modest-sized municipal library.

Revisions to the fourteenth edition have been judicious. Most noticeably, the set itself is longer and has a larger trim size—up from 6″ x 9″ to 7″ x 10″—to give the pages a more open look. As the heart of *The Reader's Adviser*, the bibliographies have been more extensively annotated than ever before, and the lists of "books by" that accompany each profiled author in Volumes 1 and 2 are now helpfully subcategorized into genres (fiction, nonfiction, poetry, plays, etc.). Furthermore, ISBNs have been added to the usual bibliographic data (again, drawn from the latest monthly release of *Books in Print* on CD-ROM) of publisher, price, and year of publication. In addition, on the sensible assumption that the author profiles preceding bibliographies should be a tantalizing appetizer for the entrée to come, the editors have done their best to season them all with rich, lively biographical detail. Finally, the reader should be aware that not all in-print editions of a work are necessarily listed but, rather, only those editions selected because of their quality or special features.

Another change in this edition is the addition of a "Chronology of Authors" section before the alphabetical arrangement of profiled authors in each chapter—a complement to the chronology that appears at the outset of each volume and a quick and easy means of placing each chapter's profiled entrants in historical perspective. Finally, to boost *The Reader's Adviser's* reference utility, the subject index of each volume has been greatly expanded, and the chapters on "Books about Books," "General Bibliography," and "General Reference" (which were previously split between Volumes 1 and 2) have been brought together and now appear at the beginning of Volume 1.

Of course, much about this new edition of *The Reader's Adviser* remains uniquely similar to the previous edition. The six-volume organization begun with the thirteenth edition continues: Volume 1 encompasses general reference works and American and British literature; Volume 2, world literature in translation; Volume 3, the social sciences, history, and the arts; Volume 4, the literature of philosophy and world religions; and Volume 5, the literature of science, technology, and medicine. Similarly, Volume 6 incorporates the name, title, and subject indexes of each of the previous volumes. Also retained are convenient cross-references throughout, which guide inquiring readers to related authors, chapters, sections, or volumes. A "see" reference leads the reader to the appropriate volume and chapter for information on a specific author. "See also" refers the reader to additional information in another chapter or volume. Within any sections of narrative, the name of an author who appears as a main listing in another chapter or volume is printed in large and small capital letters. If the chapter cross-referenced is to be found in a different volume from the one being consulted, the volume number is also given. Furthermore, to make basic research easier, the annotated bibliographies accompanying profiled individuals separately list works "by" and "about" those authors.

To assure that all volumes of the fourteenth edition are compiled concurrently and arrive together, I have relied on the contributions of countless authorities. Special thanks are due to both *The Reader's Adviser's* team of volume editors and the chapter contributors, whose names are listed in each volume. The book production experts at Book Builders Incorporated directed the almost Herculean task of coordinating the 110 chapters by 120 authors through numerous editing and production stages; to everyone's satisfaction, the system succeeded, as the reader can affirm from a glance at these six volumes. In particular, I must recognize Book Builders' Lauren Fedorko, president and guiding spirit, for her unfailing good spirits and intelligent decisions; Diane Schadoff, editorial coordinator; and Paula Wiech, production manager. Many thanks to them and their staffs for the extra hours and care that they lavished on our "magnum opus." Very special appreciation is due to Charles Roebuck, managing editor *extraordinaire*, whose concerns for accuracy, detail, and style made perfection almost attainable. Charles's contributions are countless, and much of the success of this edition is due to his tact and diplomacy in managing many people, many deadlines, and many pages of manuscript. Here at Bowker, I am especially grateful to my assistant, Angela Szablewski, who has had the monumental responsibility of coordinating all stages of the books' production.

In her 1938 article, Ms. Flexner wrote that "libraries are made up of good, old books as well as good, new books." In agreement with her view, I have continued in the *Reader's Adviser* tradition by including in this new fourteenth edition titles that are timeless, as well as those that are timely; the aim is to provide the user with both a broad and a specific view of the great writings and great writers of the past and present. I wish you all satisfaction in your research, delight in your browsing, and pleasure in your reading.

Marion Sader
Publisher
Professional & Reference Books
R.R. Bowker
September 1993

Contributing Editors

Gregory D. Alles, ANCIENT RELIGIONS AND PHILOSOPHIES
Associate Professor, Department of Philosophy and Religious Studies, Western
Maryland College

John P. Anton, GREEK AND ROMAN PHILOSOPHY
Distinguished Professor of Greek Philosophy and Culture and Director of the
Interdisciplinary Center for Greek Studies, University of South Florida

Alan J. Avery-Peck, JUDAISM
Kraft-Hiatt Professor of Judaic Studies, College of the Holy Cross

James J. Buckley, CONTEMPORARY ISSUES IN RELIGIOUS THOUGHT
Professor of Theology, Loyola College

Robert S. Ellwood, VOLUME EDITOR; MINORITY RELIGIONS AND CONTEMPORARY
RELIGIOUS MOVEMENTS; ASIAN AND AFRICAN PHILOSOPHY, 1850 TO THE PRESENT
Bishop James W. Bashford Professor of Oriental Studies with the School of Religion,
University of Southern California

W. Fred Graham, LATE CHRISTIANITY, 1500 TO THE PRESENT
Professor Emeritus of Religious Studies, Michigan State University

Leo Hamalian, ISLAM
Professor of English, The City College, City University of New York

John Heffner, CONTEMPORARY ISSUES IN PHILOSOPHY
Professor of Philosophy; Chair, Department of Religion and Philosophy, Lebanon
Valley College

Thomas P. Kasulis, ASIAN AND AFRICAN PHILOSOPHY, 1850 TO THE PRESENT
Professor of Comparative Studies in Humanities; Chair, East Asian Languages and
Literatures, The Ohio State University

J. Kenneth Kuntz, THE BIBLE AND RELATED LITERATURE
Professor of Religion, School of Religion, The University of Iowa

John L. Longeway, MEDIEVAL PHILOSOPHY
Associate Professor of Philosophy, University of Wisconsin at Parkside

Abbreviations

abr.	abridged
A.D.	in the year of the Lord
annot(s).	annotated, annotator(s)
B.C.	before Christ
B.C.E.	before the common era
B.P.	before the present
Bk(s)	Book(s)
c.	circa
C.E.	of the common era
Class.	Classic(s)
coll.	collected
comp(s).	compiled, compiler(s)
ed(s).	edited, editor(s), edition(s)
fl.	flourished
fwd.	foreword
gen. ed(s).	general editor(s)
ill(s).	illustrated, illustrator(s)
intro.	introduction
Lit.	Literature
o.p.	out-of-print
Pr.	Press
pref.	preface
pt(s).	part(s)
repr.	reprint
rev. ed.	revised edition
Ser.	Series
Supp.	Supplement
trans.	translated, translator(s), translation
U. or Univ.	University
Vol(s).	Volume(s)

Throughout this series, publisher names are abbreviated within bibliographic entries. The full names of these publishers can be found listed in Volume 6, the Index to the series.

Chronology of Authors

Main author entries appear here chronologically by year of birth. Within each chapter, main author entries are arranged alphabetically by surname.

1. Philosophy and Religion: General Reference

2. General Philosophy
Schilpp, Paul Arthur. 1897–

Copleston, Frederick Charles. 1907–

Hick, John Harwood. 1922–

Harding, Sandra G. 1935–

Singer, Peter Albert David. 1946–

3. Greek and Roman Philosophy
Pythagoras of Samos. c.582–c.507 B.C.

Heraclitus of Ephesus. fl. c.500 B.C.

Socrates. 469–399 B.C.

Xenophon. c.430–c.355 B.C.

Plato. 427?–347 B.C.

Aristotle. 384–322 B.C.

Theophrastus of Eresus. c.372–c.287 B.C.

Epicurus. 341–270 B.C.

Cicero or Tully. 106–43 B.C.

Lucretius. c.99–c.55 B.C.

Seneca, Lucius Annaeus. c.3 B.C.–A.D. 65

Marcus Aurelius. A.D. 121–180

Plotinus. A.D. 205–270

4. Medieval Philosophy
Origen. 185?–254?

Augustine of Hippo, St. 354–430

Boethius. c.480–c.524

Erigena, Johannes Scotus. c.810–c.877

Anselm of Canterbury, St. 1033?–1109

Abelard, Peter. 1079–1142

Bernard of Clairvaux, St. 1090?–1153

John of Salisbury. c.1115–1180

Grosseteste, Robert. c.1168–1253

Albert the Great. 1193–1280

Bacon, Roger. c.1214?–c.1294

Bonaventure of Bagnorea, St. 1221–1274

Thomas Aquinas, St. 1225?–1274

Duns Scotus, John. c.1265–1308

William of Ockham. c.1285–c.1349

5. Renaissance Philosophy
Petrarch. 1304–1374

Nicholas of Cusa. 1401?–1464

Valla, Lorenzo. c.1407–1457

Ficino, Marsilio. 1433–1499

Pomponazzi, Pietro. 1462–1525

Pico della Mirandola, Giovanni. 1463–1494

Erasmus, Desiderius. 1466?–1536

Cajetan, Cardinal. 1469–1534

Machiavelli, Niccolò. 1469–1527

Pico della Mirandola, Gianfrancesco. 1469–1533

More, Sir Thomas. 1478–1535

Agrippa of Nettesheim, Henry Cornelius. 1486–1535

Vives, Juan Luis. 1492–1540

Paracelsus, Philippus Aureolus. 1493?–1541

Bodin, Jean. 1530?–1596

Montaigne, Michel Eyquem de. 1533–1592

Bruno, Giordano. 1548–1600

Suárez, Francisco. 1548–1617

Galilei, Galileo. 1564–1642

Campanella, Tommaso. 1568–1639

6. Modern Western Philosophy, 1600–1900

Bacon, Francis. 1561–1626

Galilei, Galileo. 1564–1642

Hobbes, Thomas. 1588–1679

Gassendi, Pierre. 1592–1655

Descartes, René. 1596–1650

Arnauld, Antoine. 1612–1694

More, Henry. 1614–1687

Cudworth, Ralph. 1617–1688

Pascal, Blaise. 1623–1662

Conway, Anne. 1631–1679

Locke, John. 1632–1704

Pufendorf, Samuel. 1632–1694

Spinoza, Baruch. 1632–1677

Malebranche, Nicolas. 1638–1715

Newton, Sir Isaac. 1642–1727

Leibniz, Gottfried Wilhelm, Baron von. 1646–1716

Bayle, Pierre. 1647–1706

Vico, Giambattista. 1668–1744

Shaftesbury, Anthony Ashley Cooper, Third Earl of. 1671–1713

Clarke, Samuel. 1675–1729

Wolff, Christian. 1679–1754

Berkeley, George. 1685–1753

Montesquieu, Charles-Louis Secondat, Baron de. 1689–1755

Butler, Joseph. 1692–1752

Hutcheson, Francis. 1694–1746

Voltaire. 1694–1778

Reid, Thomas. 1710–1796

Hume, David. 1711–1776

Rousseau, Jean-Jacques. 1712–1778

Diderot, Denis. 1713–1784

Condillac, Étienne Bonnot de. 1715–1780

Price, Richard. 1723–1791

Smith, Adam. 1723–1790

Kant, Immanuel. 1724–1804

Burke, Edmund. 1729–1797

Lessing, Gotthold Ephraim. 1729–1781

Mendelssohn, Moses. 1729–1786

Herder, Johann Gottfried. 1744–1803

Bentham, Jeremy. 1748–1832

Fichte, Johann Gottlieb. 1764–1814

Schleiermacher, Friedrich Daniel Ernst. 1768–1834

Hegel, Georg Wilhelm Friedrich. 1770–1831

Schlegel, Friedrich. 1772–1829

Schelling, Friedrich Wilhelm Joseph. 1775–1854

Schopenhauer, Arthur. 1788–1860

Whewell, William. 1794–1866

Comte, Auguste. 1798–1857

Feuerbach, Ludwig Andreas. 1804–1872

Mill, John Stuart. 1806–1873

Kierkegaard, Søren. 1813–1855

Lotze, Rudolf Hermann. 1817–1881

Marx, Karl Heinrich. 1818–1883

Engels, Friedrich. 1820–1895

Dilthey, Wilhelm. 1833–1911

Green, Thomas Hill. 1836–1882

Brentano, Franz. 1838–1917

Sidgwick, Henry. 1838–1900

Peirce, Charles Sanders. 1839–1914

James, William. 1842–1910

Nietzsche, Friedrich Wilhelm. 1844–1900

Bradley, Francis Herbert. 1846–1924

Frege, Gottlob. 1848–1925

Royce, Josiah. 1855–1916

Bergson, Henri. 1859–1941

Dewey, John. 1859–1952

Husserl, Edmund. 1859–1938

7. Twentieth-Century Western Philosophy

Whitehead, Alfred North. 1861–1947

Mead, George Herbert. 1863–1931

Santayana, George. 1863–1952

McTaggart, John McTaggart Ellis. 1866–1925

Shestov, Lev. 1866–1938

Russell, Bertrand Arthur William. 1872–1970

Hocking, William Ernest. 1873–1966

Lovejoy, Arthur Oncken. 1873–1962

Moore, George Edward. 1873–1958

Berdyaev, Nikolai A. 1874–1948

Cassirer, Ernst. 1874–1945

Scheler, Max Ferdinand. 1874–1928

Gentile, Giovanni. 1875–1944

Cohen, Morris Raphael. 1880–1947

Aliotta, Antonio. 1881–1964

Teilhard de Chardin, Pierre. 1881–1955

Maritain, Jacques. 1882–1973

Schlick, Moritz. 1882–1936

Jaspers, Karl. 1883–1969

Lewis, Clarence Irving. 1883–1964

Ortega, y Gasset, José. 1883–1955

Bachelard, Gaston. 1884–1962

Gilson, Étienne. 1884–1978

Bloch, Ernst. 1885–1977

Broad, Charles Dunbar. 1887–1971

Collingwood, Robin George. 1889–1943

Heidegger, Martin. 1889–1976

Marcel, Gabriel. 1889–1973

Wittgenstein, Ludwig Josef Johann. 1889–1951

Carnap, Rudolf. 1891–1970

Gramsci, Antonio. 1891–1937

Blanshard, Brand. 1892–1987

Hartshorne, Charles. 1897–

Ryle, Gilbert. 1900–1976

Nagel, Ernest. 1901–1985

Weiss, Paul. 1901–

Adler, Mortimer J. 1902–

Hook, Sidney. 1902–1989

Feibleman, James Kern. 1904–1988

Sartre, Jean-Paul. 1905–1980

Merleau-Ponty, Maurice. 1908–1961

Ayer, Sir Alfred Jules. 1910–1989

Austin, John Langshaw. 1911–1960

Sellars, Wilfrid. 1912–1989

Grice, Paul. 1913–1988

Ricoeur, Paul. 1913–

Von Wright, Georg H. 1916–

Davidson, Donald Herbert. 1917–

Rawls, John. 1921–

Rescher, Nicholas. 1928–

Nozick, Robert. 1938–

Kripke, Saul. 1940–

8. Asian and African Philosophy 1850 to the Present

Rammohun Roy. 1772–1833

Ramakrishna. 1836–1886

Abduh, Muhammad. 1849–1905

K'ang Yu-wei. 1858–1927

Gandhi, Mohandas. 1869–1948

Nishida Kitarō. 1870–1945

Ghose, Aurobindo. 1872–1950

Iqbal, Sir Muhammad. 1876–1938

Tanabe Hajime. 1885–1962

Radhakrishnan, Sarvepalli. 1888–1975

Watsuji Tetsurō. 1889–1960

Hu Shih. 1891–1962

Mao Tse-tung. 1893–1976

Fung Yu-lan. 1895–1990

Nishitani Keiji. 1900–1990

Nkrumah, Kwame. 1909–1972

Takeuchi Yoshinori. 1913–

Abe Masao. 1915–

Yuasa Yasuo. 1925–

Oruka, J. Odera. 1930?–

Mbiti, John S(amuel). 1931–

Nasr, Seyyed Hossein. 1933–

Tenzin Gyatso, The 14th Dalai Lama. 1935–

Trungpa, Chögyam. 1939–1987

Tu Wei-ming. 1940–

Wiredu, Kwasi. 1940?–

Hountondji, Paulin J. 1942–

9. **Contemporary Issues in Philosophy**
Marcuse, Herbert. 1898–1979
Gadamer, Hans-George. 1900–
Popper, Sir Karl Raimund. 1902–
Adorno, Theodor W. 1903–1969
Arendt, Hannah. 1906–1975
Goodman, Nelson. 1906–
Quine, Willard Van Orman. 1908–
Chisholm, Roderick M. 1916–
Strawson, Peter F. 1919–
Kuhn, Thomas S. 1922–
Feyerabend, Paul K. 1924–
Hesse, Mary B. 1924–
Foucault, Michel. 1926–1984
Putnam, Hilary. 1926–
Habermas, Jürgen. 1929–
MacIntyre, Alasdair C. 1929–
Derrida, Jacques. 1930–
Rorty, Richard McKay. 1931–
Taylor, Charles. 1931–
Dennett, Daniel C. 1942–

10. **Ancient Religions and Philosophies**
Homer. fl. 8th century B.C.E.
Hesiod. fl. c.700 B.C.E.
Herodotus. c.490 B.C.E.–c.420 B.C.E.
Euripides. c.485 B.C.E.–c.406 B.C.E.
Apollodoros of Athens. c.180
    B.C.E.–?
Strabo. c.64? B.C.E.–after 21 C.E.
Plutarch. before 50 C.E.–after 120
    C.E.
Lucian of Samosata. c.120
    C.E.–after 180 C.E.
Apuleius. c.123 C.E.–after 161 C.E.
Pausanias. fl. c.150 C.E.
Smith, William Robertson.
    1846–1894
Harrison, Jane E. 1850–1928
Frazer, James George. 1854–1941
Otto, Rudolf. 1869–1937
Nilsson, Martin P. 1874–1967
Malinowski, Bronislaw. 1884–1942
Kerényi, Károly. 1897–1973
Dumézil, Georges. 1898–1986

Wach, Joachim. 1898–1955
Evans-Pritchard, Edward Evan.
    1902–1973
Nock, Arthur Darby. 1902–1963
Eliade, Mircea. 1907–1986
Vernant, Jean-Pierre. 1914–
Geertz, Clifford. 1926–
Burkert, Walter. 1931–
Smith, Jonathan Z. 1938–

11. **Eastern Religions**
Besant, Annie. 1847–1933
Vivekananda. 1863–1902
Gandhi, Mohandas K(laramchand).
    1869–1948
Suzuki, D(aisetz) T(eitaro).
    1870–1966
Paramahansa Yogananda.
    1893–1952
Krishnamurti, Jiddu. 1895–1986
Thich Nhat Hanh. 1926–
Tenzin Gyatso, the Dalai Lama.
    1935–

12. **Islam**
Muhammad. 570?–632
Avicenna. 980–1037
Ibn Hazm. 994–1064
Ghazālī, al-. 1058–1111
Ibn Tufayl. ?–1185
Averroës. 1126–1198
Ibn al-Arabi. 1165–1240
Rumi. 1207–1273
Ibn Khallikan. 1211–1281
Ibn Khaldun. 1332–1406
Jami. 1414–1492
Jalal al-Din al-Suyuti. 1445–1505

13. **Judaism**
Philo, Judaeus. c.20 B.C.–c.A.D. 50
Josephus, Flavius. c.A.D.38–100
Saadia Gaon. 882–942
Rashi. 1040–1105
Judah Ha-Levi. c.1075–1141
Maimonides. 1135–1204
Nahmanides. 1194–c.1270
Gersonides. 1288–1344
Ba'al Shem Tov. c.1700–1760

Nahman of Bratslav. 1772–1811

Hirsch, Samson Raphael.
  1808–1888

Cohen, Hermann. 1842–1918

Baeck, Leo. 1873–1956

Buber, Martin. 1878–1965

Kaplan, Mordecai Menahem.
  1881–1983

Rosenzweig, Franz. 1886–1929

Scholem, Gershom. 1897–1982

Soloveitchik, Joseph. 1903–

Heschel, Abraham Joshua.
  1907–1972

Fackenheim, Emil. 1916–

Borowitz, Eugene. 1924–

14. Early and Medieval Christianity

Apostolic Fathers. c.1st Century
  A.D.

Tertullian. c.160–c.230

Cyprian of Carthage, St. c.200?–258

Eusebius of Caesarea. c.260–c.340

Basil of Caesarea, St. c.330–379

Ambrose, St. 340?–397

Jerome, St. c.347–419

Chrysostom, St. John. c.354–407

Cassian, St. John. c.365–435

Patrick, St. c.390–460

Benedict of Nursia, St. c.480–540

Gregory the Great. c.540–604

Anselm of Canterbury, St.
  1033?–1109

Joachim of Fiore. c.1132–1202

Alan of Lille. d.1203

Francis of Assisi, St. c.1181?–1226

Eckhart, Meister. c.1260–c.1328

Wyclif, John. c.1330–1384

Julian of Norwich. c.1342–c.1416

Catherine of Siena, St. c.1347–1380

Hus, John. c.1372–1415

15. Late Christianity, 1500 to the Present

Luther, Martin. 1483–1546

Zwingli, Huldrych. 1484–1531

Cranmer, Thomas. 1489–1556

Ignatius of Loyola, St. 1491–1556

Menno Simons. 1496?–1561

Knox, John. c.1505–1572

Calvin, John. 1509–1564

Teresa of Avila, St. 1515–1582

Edwards, Jonathan. 1703–1758

Wesley, John. 1703–1791

Newman, John Henry, Cardinal.
  1801–1890

Berdyaev, Nikolai A. 1874–1948

John XXIII, Pope. 1881–1963

Barth, Karl. 1886–1968

Tillich, Paul Johannes. 1886–1965

Niebuhr, Reinhold. 1892–1971

Day, Dorothy. 1897–1980

Lewis, C(live) S(taples). 1898–1963

Bonhoeffer, Dietrich. 1906–1945

Weil, Simone. 1909–1943

Merton, Thomas. 1915–1968

Graham, William Franklin. 1918–

Daly, Mary. 1928–

Gutierrez, Gustavo. 1928–

Küng, Hans. 1928–

King, Martin Luther, Jr. 1929–1968

Ruether, Rosemary Radford. 1936–

Cone, James H. 1938–

16. The Bible and Related Literature

Gunkel, Hermann. 1862–1932

Moffatt, James. 1870–1944

Bultmann, Rudolf. 1884–1976

Dodd, Charles Harold. 1884–1973

Eichrodt, Walther. 1890–1978

Albright, William F. 1891–1971

Rad, Gerhard von. 1901–1971

Cullmann, Oscar. 1902–

Noth, Martin. 1902–1968

Bornkamm, Günther. 1905–

17. Minority Religions and Contemporary Religious Movements

Swedenborg, Emanuel. 1688–1772

Quimby, Phineas P. 1802–1866

Smith, Joseph, Jr. 1805–1844

Eddy, Mary Baker. 1821–1910

Blavatsky, Helena P. 1831–1891

Steiner, Rudolf. 1861–1925
Gurdjieff, G(eorge) I(vanovich).
    1872?–1949
Watts, Alan Wilson. 1915–1973
Moon, Sun Myung. 1920–
Malcolm X. 1925–1965

18. Contemporary Issues in Religious Thought
Rahner, Karl. 1904–1984

Levinas, Emmanuel. 1906–
Gustafson, James M. 1925–
Nasr, Seyyed Hossein. 1933–
Tenzin Gyatso, the Dalai Lama.
    1935–
Ruether, Rosemary Radford. 1936–

Introduction

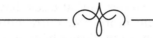

Through the years, *The Reader's Adviser* has changed and expanded to meet the needs and the changing character of the reading public. The main strength of the thirteenth edition of Volume 4 was its historical perspective. For general readers approaching the subjects of philosophy and religion, this approach was ideal. Moreover, the chapters and the information within them were authoritative, well organized by periods, and exceptionally complete. This new, fourteenth edition of Volume 4 preserves the strength of the earlier edition while updating the material to include works published since that last edition appeared in 1988. Throughout the volume, chapters that appeared in the thirteenth edition have been expanded with thousands of new, as well as revised, bibliographic entries, and the list of profiled authors has been greatly enlarged. Contributors should be commended for the skill and diligence they have employed in writing and revising their chapters. Faced with the challenge of reexamining their fields, they have succeeded in preserving the integrity of the volume while adding their own personal and professional insights. At the same time, contributors have also endeavored to supplement the thirteenth edition's strengths with two new virtues: more material on cross-cultural philosophy and religion, and thematic chapters on current issues in those two fields.

In today's pluralistic but interrelated world, cross-cultural understanding on the deep level undertaken by students of comparative religion and philosophy is increasingly recognized as essential. Furthermore, contemporary Asian and African philosophical work, like that of the "Kyoto School" in Japan or of contemporary Vedanta studies in India, are certainly no less sophisticated or significant than their Western equivalents. As a result, a new chapter has been added to this volume on Asian and African philosophy since 1850; and, additionally, the earlier chapter on Eastern religion and philosophy has been revised to focus primarily on religion. Together, these changes provide a greater multicultural perspective and help counter any tendency to focus on Western thought.

Philosophy and religion can be approached in two ways: historically and thematically; that is, they can be approached in terms of the sequence in which their important ideas appeared or in terms of the ideas themselves, ideas involving God, human nature, epistemology, aesthetics, ethics, and so on. Both approaches have merit, and the fourteenth edition of Volume 4 has attempted to retain the values of both. While the historical material could be sorted out thematically, our view is that the majority of readers will probably be most interested in current thought on contemporary debated issues (from the existence of God to ethical conundrums) yet will also appreciate an historical perspective on more traditional philosophical and religious issues and topics.

CHAPTER 1

Philosophy and Religion: General Reference

Mark Stover

> Of making many books there is no end, and much study wearies the body.
> —ECCLESIASTES 12:12

The primary sources in philosophy and religion are the ancient works of sacred scripture and the classical works of philosophy. The secondary sources are later commentaries on these literary and philosophical masterpieces, which sometimes become classics (and thus primary sources) in their own right (e.g., JOHN CALVIN's *Institutes of the Christian Religion*). The tertiary sources in philosophy and religion are reference books, which serve as guides and pointers to the primary and secondary texts. Without reference books, most of us never would be able to navigate the labyrinth of philosophical and religious literature.

It has been suggested that ARISTOTLE (see also Vol. 4) compiled the first dictionary of philosophy and that Moses wrote the first handbook of religion. In any event, reference works in these two disciplines certainly have existed for hundreds, if not thousands, of years. Although some older reference sources have taken on the status of classics, most of them become less helpful as they age. The books cited in this chapter have been chosen for their accuracy, currency, and usefulness.

Generally, encyclopedias are thought of as multivolume, exhaustive works in a particular field, whereas dictionaries are regarded as single-volume works with brief definitions of terms and concepts. However, many publishers have blurred the distinctions between these two types of reference works. For the purposes of taxonomy, we have listed encyclopedias and dictionaries together, but they have been divided into two categories; there is an additional section on handbooks, sourcebooks, and guides, as well as one on indexes.

Most reference books in philosophy are dictionaries or encyclopedias. These works define philosophical terms, list important figures of the past and present, and discuss key events and movements that have changed the way in which philosophers think.

Religion reference books, on the other hand, are more diffuse, because religion tends to be more interdisciplinary and, in some ways, more loosely defined than philosophy. Handbooks, directories, biographical reference sources, and atlases are some of the kinds of reference books in religious studies that are not found so frequently in philosophy.

The epigram at the beginning of this chapter suggests that book publishers are engaged in a Sisyphean task. If this is true—and even a superficial look at the exponential growth of libraries and bookstores hints that it is—readers must rely on reference sources to help them sort through the growing mountain of books and ideas. This chapter tries to provide a helpful step in that direction.

GENERAL HISTORIES AND SURVEYS

Copleston, Frederick. *The History of Philosophy*. Doubleday 1994 $15.00 ISBN 0-385-47041-X

Eliade, Mircea. *Essential Sacred Writings from around the World: A Sourcebook on the History of Religions*. Harper SF 1991 $17.00. ISBN 0-06-250304-9. Thematic overview of the history of religions; includes a cross-reference index to religions of the world.

———. *A History of Religious Ideas*. U. Ch. Pr. 1988 $27.50. ISBN 0-226-20404-9. Masterly chronological survey of religious ideas; includes a long and very useful bibliographic analysis.

Hamlyn, David W. *Being a Philosopher: The History of a Practice*. Routledge 1992 $29.95. ISBN 0-415-02968-6. Overview of Western philosophy that focuses on how philosophers have practiced their craft.

McAfee, Ward. *A History of the World's Great Religions*. U. Pr. of Am. 1983 $46.25. ISBN 0-8191-3394-9

McManners, John, ed. *The Oxford Illustrated History of Christianity*. OUP 1992 $25.00. ISBN 0-19-285259-0

Magill, Frank N., and John Roth, eds. *Masterpieces of World Philosophy*. HarpC 1990 $40.00. ISBN 0-06-016430-1. Contains 100 influential works spanning a range of time and thought from the Analects of Confucius to the present.

Noss, David S. *A History of the World's Religions*. Macmillan 1990 ISBN 0-02-388480-0. Surveys the origins, development, and divisions of the major religions of the world. Each chapter includes an extensive glossary.

Van Doren, Charles. *A History of Knowledge: Past, Present, and Future*. Ballantine 1992 $12.00. ISBN 0-345-37316-2. Provocative encyclopedic guide to great thinkers, concepts, and philosophical trends.

ENCYCLOPEDIAS AND DICTIONARIES IN PHILOSOPHY

Angeles, Peter A. *Dictionary of Philosophy*. HarpC 1981 $8.95. ISBN 0-06-43461-2. Emphasis is on terms, but an index of philosophers is included also.

Becker, Lawrence C., and Charlotte Becker, eds. *The Encyclopedia of Ethics*. 2 vols. Garland 1992 $150.00. ISBN 0-8153-0403-X. Contains 435 signed articles, all peer-reviewed, on historical and living ethicists and ethical concepts. Most articles are 1,000 to 5,000 words long, with bibliographies and cross-references. Includes general index as well as index of authors cited in bibliographies and a 13-part, multiauthored, 60,000-word history of ethics. Core is philosophical ethics in English-speaking countries.

Childress, James F., and John Macquarrie, eds. *Westminster Dictionary of Christian Ethics*. Westminster John Knox rev. ed. 1986 $35.00. ISBN 0-664-20940-8. Basic ethical concepts, biblical and theological ethics, philosophical traditions, and non-Christian ethics. Cross-references and signed articles. Some 40 percent of entries retained from first edition of 1967.

The Concise Encyclopedia of Western Philosophy and Philosophers. Ed. by J. O. Urmson and Jonathan Rée. Routledge Chapman & Hall 1990 $16.95. ISBN 0-04-445379-5. Updates the second edition, which was published in 1975.

Edwards, Paul, ed. *The Encyclopedia of Philosophy*. 4 vols. Free Pr. 1973 $425.00. ISBN 0-02-894950-1. This standard reference work consists of 1,450 signed articles by 500 authorities from 24 nations, under the direction of an editorial board of 153 international scholars. Articles vary in length from half a column to over 50 pages. Cross-referencing allows user to find topics easily.

Flew, Antony, ed. *A Dictionary of Philosophy*. St. Martin 1984 $24.95. ISBN 0-312-20924-X. Stressing the meanings of key words and phrases, the volume—with 34 contributors—also includes biographical entries, some running as long as 4,000 words.

Frolov, Ivan, ed. *Dictionary of Philosophy*. Intl. Pubs. Co. 1985 $8.95. ISBN 0-7178-0604-9. Translated from the Russian, this dictionary focuses on the Marxist tradition.

Grimes, John. *A Concise Dictionary of Indian Philosophy: Sanskrit Terms Defined in English*. State U. NY Pr. 1989 $49.50. ISBN 0-7914-0100-6. Brief definitions of many concepts in various Indian schools of thought, including Hinduism, Buddhism, Jainism, Yoga, and Vedanta. Devanagari script and Roman transliteration.

Lacey, A. R. *A Dictionary of Philosophy*. Routledge Chapman & Hall 1990 $13.95. ISBN 0-415-05872-4. Described by the author as "a pocket encyclopedia of philosophy," the work stresses meanings of philosophical terms and also provides suggested sources for additional reading.

Nauman, St. Elmo, Jr. *Dictionary of American Philosophy*. Littlefield 1973 $12.95. ISBN 0-8022-0275-X. Regional dictionary dealing with the figures and movements in the United States.

_____. *Dictionary of Asian Philosophies*. Littlefield 1978 o.p. Helps to fill the void in dictionary material on Asian philosophy.

_____. *The New Dictionary of Existentialism*. Littlefield 1971 o.p. Guide to the terminology of both philosophical and psychological existentialists. Bibliography appended.

Runes, Dagobert D., ed. *Dictionary of Philosophy*. Littlefield 1984 $14.95. ISBN 0-8226-0392-6. Aims to provide "clear, concise, and correct definitions and descriptions of the philosophical terms throughout the range of philosophic thought." Outstanding feature is the analysis of logic by Alonzo Church.

Wiener, Philip P., ed. *Dictionary of the History of Ideas*. 5 vols. Scribner 1980 $67.50. ISBN 0-684-16418-3. Cooperative study containing analyses of some 300 basic ideas by almost as many scholars representing various fields from art to science. Follows a philosophical history-of-ideas approach.

ENCYCLOPEDIAS, DICTIONARIES, AND ATLASES IN RELIGION

Barrett, David B. *World Christian Encyclopedia: A Comparative Survey of Churches and Religions in the Modern World, A.D. 1900 to 2000*. OUP 1982 $195.00. ISBN 0-19-572435-6. More than 500 scholars contributed to this major work covering Christian traditions, denominations, and organizations. Includes maps, illustrations, directories, indexes, and bibliography; international and ecumenical in scope.

Brandon, S. G. *A Dictionary of Comparative Religion*. Macmillan 1974 $60.00. ISBN 0-684-15561-3. Data on beliefs, deities, and practices of religions worldwide.

Choquette, Diane. *New Religious Movements in the United States and Canada: A Critical Assessment and Annotated Bibliography*. Greenwood 1985 $59.95. ISBN 0-313-23772-7. Covers the 1960s through 1983; includes indexes.

Crim, Keith, ed. *Abingdon Dictionary of Living Religions*. Abingdon 1981 $17.95. ISBN 0-687-00409-8. Defines over 1,600 key terms and provides major essays on important topics covering history, beliefs, and practices of major and minor world religions.

Davidson, Gustav. *A Dictionary of Angels: Including the Fallen Angels*. Free Pr. 1972 $19.95. ISBN 0-02-907050-3. Illustrated sourcebook containing 3,000 entries that identify and describe the angels of Judaism, Christianity, and Islam.

A Dictionary of Non-Christian Religions. Ed. by E. G. Parrinder. St. Mut. 1981 $90.00. ISBN 0-7175-0972-9. Very useful for quick reference on names; illustrated.

Douglas, J. D., ed. *New 20th-Century Encyclopedia of Religious Knowledge*. Baker 1991 $39.95. ISBN 0-8010-3002-1. Has its roots in the *Herzog-Hauck Realencyklopadie* published over 100 years ago. A total of 250 contributors wrote over 2,000 articles on church history, social issues, and the Bible. An evangelical Christian perspective.

Eliade, Mircea, ed. *Encyclopedia of Religion*. 16 vols. Macmillan 1986 $1,400.00. ISBN 0-02-909480-1. This massive work contains 2,750 signed articles (with bibliographies) by 1,400 scholars. Emphasis is on history of religions and cross-cultural religious thought.

Ellwood, Robert S. *Historical Atlas of the Religions of the World*. Ed. by Isma'il Ragi al Farugi. Macmillan 1974 o.p. Sixty-five maps highlighting geographic distribution of religions and the locations of significant temples and shrines.

Encyclopedia of Eastern Philosophy and Religion. Shambhala 1989 $39.95. ISBN 0-87773-433-X. Covers terminology and doctrine of Buddhism (including Zen), Hinduism, and Taoism; 4,000 entries. Intended for general readers.

Freedman, David N., ed. *The Anchor Bible Dictionary*. 6 vols. Doubleday 1992 $360.00. ISBNs 0-385-19351-3, 0-385-19360-2, 0-385-19361-0, 0-385-19362-9, 0-385-19363-7, 0-385-26190-X. Major work of international and interdenominational scope. Nearly 1,000 contributors from Catholic, Protestant, Jewish, and Muslim traditions; 6,000 entries covering diverse topics, from feminist hermeneutics to the new quest for the historical Jesus.

Gaskell, G. A. *Dictionary of All Scriptures and Myths*. Crown Pub. Group 1960 o.p. Deals with the sacred language of the various world religions—the origin, nature, and meaning of the scriptures and myths attached to them.

Glasse, Cyril. *Concise Encyclopedia of Islam*. HarpC 1989 $59.95. ISBN 0-06-063123-6. Persons and concepts in Islam, with several appendices including pictures, charts, chronologies, and bibliography.

Hastings, James, ed. *Encyclopedia of Religion and Ethics*. 13 vols. Bks. Intl. VA 1926 $1,250.00. ISBN 0-567-09489-8. Presents articles on all religions of the world and on all the great systems of ethics.

Hinnells, John R., ed. *The Penguin Dictionary of Religions*. *Reference Ser.* Viking Penguin 1984 $11.00. ISBN 0-14-051106-7. Contains brief entries on sects and practices, with a particularly good bibliography.

Komonchak, Joseph, ed. *New Dictionary of Theology*. Liturgical Pr. 1987 $59.95. ISBN 0-8146-5609-9. Signed articles focus on biblical, traditional, liturgical, and magisterial aspects of Roman Catholic theology. Some articles are short but most are more substantial, and each has a bibliography.

Lippy, Charles H., and Peter W. Williams, eds. *Encyclopedia of the American Religious Experience: Studies of Traditions and Movements*. 3 vols. Scribner 1988 $225.00. ISBN 0-684-18062-6. An authoritative and comprehensive work that consists of 105 long essays by leading scholars; arranged in nine broad subjects. Includes bibliographies and an extensive index.

Ludlow, Daniel, ed. *Encyclopedia of Mormonism*. 5 vols. Macmillan 1992 $750.00. ISBN 0-02-879606-3. History, scripture, doctrine, and procedure of Church of Jesus Christ of Latter-day Saints. The 1,500 signed articles, with bibliographies, are by 730 contributors. Vol. 5 includes all standard LDS works (Book of Mormon, etc.) except the Bible. Illustrated.

Macgregor, Geddes. *Dictionary of Religion and Philosophy*. Paragon Hse. 1990 $35.00. ISBN 1-55778-019-6. Primary focus is on religious concepts, movements, and historical figures, but philosophical implications and foundations of religion are discussed also. Emphasis on Judeo-Christian traditions. Short articles useful for desktop reference; cross-references; bibliography at end of volume.

Melton, J. Gordon, ed. *Encyclopedia of American Religions*. 3 vols. Gale 4th ed. 1991 $175.00. ISBN 0-8103-2841-0. Comprehensive and authoritative work, the standard reference in the field of American religions. Several indexes.

———, ed. *Encyclopedic Handbook of Cults in America*. Garland 2nd ed. 1992 $65.00. ISBN 0-8153-0502-8. Over 500 active cults (defined as nonmainstream religions) described in article format.

———, ed. *New Age Encyclopedia*. Gale 1990 $59.50. ISBN 0-8103-7159-6. More than 300 listings of organizations, personalities, practices, concepts, and terms of the New Age movement. Includes cross-references, bibliography, index, and addresses of organizations.

Mills, Watson, E., ed. *Mercer Dictionary of the Bible*. Mercer Univ. Pr. 1989 $35.00. ISBN 0-86554-402-6. The 225 contributors are all members of the National Association of Baptist Professors of Religion. Contains articles on every canonical and noncanonical book of the Bible, Apocrypha, and the Gnostic documents found at Nag Hammadi (Egypt), as well as most proper names and distinctive terms. Includes maps, pictures, outlines, and charts. Useful for beginning and advanced students.

New Catholic Encyclopedia. 15 vols. J. Heraty Assocs. 1989 repr. $750.00. ISBN 0-07-010235-X. Contains 17,000 signed articles by 4,800 contributors. Emphasizes English-speaking Catholic issues, although scope is worldwide.

Parrinder, Geoffrey. *A Dictionary of Non-Christian Religions*. St. Mut. 1973 $10.95. ISBN 0-7175-0972-9. "A timely and authoritative dictionary" (*Library Journal*). Three-volume supplement available at $80.00. ea.

Reid, Daniel G., ed. *Dictionary of Christianity in America*. InterVarsity 1990 $44.99. ISBN 0-8308-1776-X. Useful tool, with more emphasis on history, ideas, and personalities than on organized religious bodies. The 430 contributors have written 4,000 signed articles, with brief bibliographies.

Roth, Cecil, and Geoffrey Wigoder, eds. *Encyclopaedia Judaica*. 17 vols. Coronet Bks. 1982 repr. of 1972 ed. $895.00. ISBN 0-685-36253-1. The standard Jewish reference work. Contains over 25,000 signed articles, covering biographical, historical, theological, and cultural topics.

Shermis, Michael. *Jewish-Christian Relations: An Annotated Bibliography and Resource Guide*. Ind. U. Pr. 1988 $35.00. ISBN 0-253-33153-6. Comprehensive list of books, pamphlets, speeches, and articles, covering relations from antiquity to the present.

Wainwright, Geoffrey, ed. *Dictionary of the Ecumenical Movement*. Eerdmans 1991 $79.99. ISBN 0-8028-2428-5. A total of 650 signed articles (many of them biographical) on ecumenism. Illustrated.

Wigoder, Geoffrey. *Encyclopedia of Judaism*. Macmillan 1989 $75.00. ISBN 0-02-628410-3. Historical persons, places, events, literature, liturgy, theology, and practice. Literary excerpts and index, illustrations and charts, but no bibliographies.

Wright, David F., Sinclair B. Ferguson, and J. I. Packer, eds. *New Dictionary of Theology*. InterVarsity 1988 $29.99. ISBN 0-8308-1400-0. Over 200 scholars wrote 630 articles in systematic theology, biblical theology, and biography, from an evangelical and Reformed perspective.

Zaehner, Robert C., ed. *Concise Encyclopedia of Living Faiths*. Beacon Pr. 1967 o.p. Features scholarly and well-illustrated descriptions of the world's major religions.

HANDBOOKS, SOURCEBOOKS, AND GUIDES

Adams, Charles J., ed. *A Reader's Guide to the Great Religions*. Free Pr. 1977 o.p. Of the eight essays, Adams's long overview of Islam is among the best. Adams was director of Islamic Studies at McGill University, Canada.

Bahm, Archie J., Richard H. Lineback, and Mary M. Schurts, eds. *Directory of American Philosophers*. Bowling Green Univ. 16th ed. 1992 $99.00. ISBN 0-912632-90-9. Mostly faculty members in philosophy departments. A new edition comes out biannually.

Ballou, Robert O. *The Portable World Bible*. *Viking Portable Lib*. Viking Penguin 1977 $9.95. ISBN 0-14-015005-6. Contains sacred and traditional writing of the world's eight basic source religions, with excellent introductions to each section, plus glossary and index.

Bedell, Kenneth B. *Yearbook of American and Canadian Churches*. Abingdon 1993 $29.95. ISBN 0-687-46647-4. Annual, with current information. Includes names and addresses of church officers, denominational magazines, and statistical graphs.

Browne, Lewis, comp. *The World's Greatest Scriptures: An Anthology of the Sacred Books of the Ten Principal Religions*. Macmillan 1962 o.p. Historical introductions; interpretive comments; decorations and maps for the scriptures of Babylonia, Egypt, Hinduism, Buddhism, Confucianism, Jainism, Zoroastrianism, Judaism, Christianity, and Islam.

Burr, John R., ed. *Handbook of World Philosophy: Contemporary Developments since 1945*. Greenwood 1980 $85.00. ISBN 0-313-22381-5. Arranged by country; each chapter contains an essay and bibliography on various strands of philosophy within the specific area. Also includes directory of worldwide philosophical associations and name and subject indexes.

Bynagle, Hans E. *Philosophy: A Guide to the Reference Literature*. Lib. Unl. 1986 $35.00. ISBN 0-87287-464-8. Annotations on 421 reference works; chapters arranged by type of reference tool. Includes subject index and author-title index.

Cormier, Ramona, and Richard H. Lineback, eds. *International Directory of Philosophy and Philosophers, 1990–92*. Bowling Green Univ. 1990 $79.00. ISBN 0-912632-87-9. Covers philosophical organizations, educational and research institutions, journals, and individuals, classified by country. Indexes provided for individual philosophers, societies, universities, and publishers.

Dawsey, James. *A Scholar's Guide to Academic Journals in Religion*. Scarecrow 1988 $32.50. ISBN 0-8108-2135-4. Over 500 journals organized into 33 categories; each entry gives subject content of journals, editor's name and address, and submission requirements. Helpful source for authors.

Editors of *Life*. *The World's Great Religions*. Western Pub. 1957 o.p. Seeks to present religion and religious life "with enough reference to the contents of the holy books, the sacred legends and myths, and the traditional teachings that lie behind the various practices to make them intelligible."

Fieg, Eugene C. *Religion Journals and Serials: An Analytical Guide*. Greenwood 1988 $45.00. ISBN 0-313-24513-4. Around 400 journals related to religion are listed, described, and evaluated. Includes price, publisher, editor, and criteria for manuscript selection.

Gard, Richard A. *Great Religions of Modern Man*. 6 vols. Braziller 1961 o.p. Rituals, prayers, and dogmas with commentaries on the great world religions.

Inada, Kenneth K. *Guide to Buddhist Philosophy*. GK Hall 1985 $45.00. ISBN 0-8161-7899-2. Annotated bibliography; lists books, articles, and dissertations, arranged in broad categories.

Kepple, Robert J., and John R. Muether. *Reference Works for Theological Research: An Annotated Selective Bibliographical Guide*. U. Pr. of Amer. 3rd ed. 1992 $49.50. ISBN 0-8191-8564-7. Indispensable guide to the reference literature, focused primarily on Protestant Christianity. Part I organizes chapters by type of reference tool; Part II divides chapters by subject. Author and title index.

Kersey, Ethel M. *Women Philosophers: A Bio-Critical Source Book*. Greenwood 1989 $49.95. ISBN 0-313-25720-5. Short essays, with bibliographies, covering the life and work of women philosophers born before 1920. Lengthy introduction, name index, and helpful chart with name of philosopher, time period, country, and category of philosophy.

Koszegi, Michael A., and J. Gordon Melton, eds. *Islam in North America: A Sourcebook*. Garland 1992 $60.00. ISBN 0-8153-0918-X. Reprints of primary source documents, address directory of American Islamic organizations, and historical introduction to Islam in the United States, including the African American Muslim community. Extensive bibliography and indexes.

McCabe, James Patrick. *Critical Guide to Catholic Reference Books*. Lib. Unl. 1989 $47.00. ISBN 0-87287-621-7. Lists more than 1,500 reference books related to the Roman Catholic Church.

Mead, Frank S. *Handbook of Denominations in the United States*. Abingdon 1990 $13.95. ISBN 0-687-16572-5. History, beliefs, and statistics for 225 American religious groups.

Melton, J. Gordon. *Biographical Dictionary of American Cult and Sect Leaders*. Garland 1986 $50.00. ISBN 0-8240-9037-3. Sketches of 213 persons who founded or developed dissident minority religious groups in the United States; includes only those who died prior to 1983.

_____. *Religious Bodies in the United States: A Directory*. Garland 1992 $55.00. ISBN 0-8153-0806-X. Includes addresses, phone and fax numbers, and denominational magazines for a wide variety of religious groups in America; indexes, cross-references, and bibliography.

———. *Religious Leaders of America: A Biographical Guide to Founders and Leaders of Religious Bodies, Churches, and Spiritual Groups in North America.* Gale 1991 $79.95. ISBN 0-8103-4921-3. According to the introduction, treats "1,000 men and women who have shaped American religious life since 1865." Includes birth and death dates and places, affiliation, occupation, education, beliefs, and influence. Broad coverage of many religions and denominations. Bibliography and keyword index.

Melton, J. Gordon, and Michael A. Koszegi. *Religious Information Sources: A Worldwide Guide.* Garland 1992 $75.00. ISBN 0-8153-0859-0. Bibliographical and informational guide to world religions and religious organizations, including nontraditional spiritual movements. Several indexes.

Morreale, Don, ed. *Buddhist America: Centers, Retreats, Practices.* John Muir 1988 $12.95. ISBN 0-912528-94-X. Includes only selected groups that teach or promote meditation. Over 500 entries, with information supplied by each center; includes addresses, descriptions, and overview essays.

Payne, Wardell, J., ed. *Directory of African American Religious Bodies: A Compendium by the Howard University School of Divinity.* Howard U. Pr. 1991 $49.95. ISBN 0-88258-174-0. Religious organizations (including denominational colleges) that are primarily African American or have significant African American constituents. Also includes individuals who have played an important role in the religious life of the African American community. Several indexes and a bibliography.

Pritchard, James B., ed. *The Harper Atlas of the Bible.* HarpC 1987 $49.95. ISBN 0-06-181883-6. Color photographs, maps, and drawings, along with a chronology and glossary. Excellent resource.

Starkey, Edward D. *Judaism and Christianity: A Guide to the Reference Literature.* Lib. Unl. 1991 $42.00. ISBN 0-87287-533-4. Useful tool for beginning researchers. Part 1 describes various reference sources, and Part 2 reviews reference tools related to biblical studies.

Szonyi, David M. *The Holocaust: An Annotated Bibliography and Resource Guide.* Ktav 1985 $39.50. ISBN 0-88125-057-0. Bibliographies, filmographies, lists of survivor groups, research institutes, and other information on the Holocaust.

Vecsey, Christopher, ed. *Religion in Native North America.* U. of Idaho Pr. 1990 $22.95. ISBN 0-89301-135-5. Introductory resource handbook for Native American religious practices.

Who's Who in Religion, 1992–93. Marquis Who's Who 1992 $129.00. ISBN 0-8379-1604-6. More than 16,000 men and women, including clergy, religious educators, and lay leaders. Most data supplied by the biographees.

World Philosophy. 5 vols. Salem Pr. 1982 $250.00. ISBN 0-89356-325-0. Popular work, useful for representative essays on Western philosophy through 1971. Each volume covers a different time period.

INDEXES

The Catholic Periodical. 23 vols. Cath. Lib. Assn. 1969–1988. $45.00–$175.00. Bimonthly with two-year cumulations. Indexes 150 periodicals, as well as books, book reviews, and official Catholic documents.

Christian Periodical Index. 8 vols. Assn. Chr. Lib. 1956–. $40.00.–$75.00. Quarterly index of about 80 periodicals. Coverage is a mixture of popular and scholarly, with an evangelical focus.

Index to Book Reviews in Religion. American Theological Library Association 1986–. Quarterly, with annual cumulations. Access by author, title, reviewer, and series to book reviews from about 500 journals. Also available online and on CD-ROM.

Index to Jewish Periodicals. IJP $85.00 ea. 1963–. Semiannual. Indexes 44 English-
  language journals and magazines related to Judaism or Jewish thought. Covers
  articles and book reviews, indexed by author and subject.
New Testament Abstracts: A Record of Current Periodical Literature. Weston College
  School of Theology, 1956–. Selectively indexes and abstracts over 500 journals and
  briefly describes over 500 books each year. Three issues per year.
Old Testament Abstracts. Cath. U. Pr. 1978–. Indexes and abstracts over 200 journals as
  well as some books in 3 issues per year.
Philosopher's Index: An International Index to Philosophical Periodicals. 27 vols. Philos.
  Document. 1967–1992. Quarterly, with annual cumulations. The major tool for
  bibliographical research in philosophy. Indexes both English-language and foreign-
  language philosophy journals. Subject and author indexes, with article abstracts and
  book review coverage. Also available online and on CD-ROM.
Religion Index One: Periodicals. American Theological Library Association 1977–. Most
  important periodical index in religious studies. Semiannual, with annual cumulations. Broad coverage of over 400 journals, with several access points (author,
  subject, and biblical citation index). Also available online and on CD-ROM.
Religion Index Two: Multi-Author Works. American Theological Library Association
  1978–. Name and subject indexes to anthologies, *festschriften*, and other multiauthor
  works. Also available online and on CD-ROM.
Religious and Theological Abstracts. Religious and Theological Abstracts, Inc. 1958–.
  Quarterly index to over 200 journals, with an English-language and Protestant focus.
  Also available on CD-ROM.

PART ONE

PHILOSOPHY

CHAPTER 2

General Philosophy

Edward L. Schoen

Socrates: . . . the unexamined life is not worth living.
—PLATO, *Apology*

By "general philosophy" we mean that philosophical material either common to the historical periods into which we have divided philosophy in this volume, or pertaining to more than one of these periods. Such material includes dictionaries, encyclopedias, and general histories of philosophy, introductions to the field, and works describing the contributions of different regions or countries of the world.

One might have expected general philosophy to refer to the common features of philosophy or to what is agreed on by all philosophers; but, in fact, there is no consensus about these common features, nor anything that is agreed to by all philosophers. In this century, innumerable volumes have argued whether materialism, idealism, dualism, monism, naturalism, or phenomenalism—to name just a few of the possible "isms"—holds the truth. Through such disputes, the grand systems of the past have been thrown into serious question. Further, as the arguments developed, a somewhat curious result ensued. Each system became more subtle and sophisticated in response to criticism, and in doing so became more like its competitors in many ways. This raised the question as to whether the differences among these systems were ever real differences or whether they simply indicated a particular starting point preferred by a philosopher or a group. Some of the books in this chapter reflect that discussion and are included, at least partly, for the sake of completeness.

However, neither agreement nor difference is the point of philosophy. Today, many philosophers see their task as a cultural one, to revive, as we have shown in our Introduction, PLATO's (see also Vol. 3) "knowledge of the whole" approach. This requires that the technical philosopher study one or more of the other disciplines making up human culture in addition to philosophy. Yet the task of the individual person, whether professional philosopher or not, is self-definition. We have reached the philosophical moment when intellectual activity must include, as part of its task, the discovery of one's own position on a vast range of ultimate questions. At the moment Plato's insight—that the sovereigns of the world need "the spirit and power of philosophy"—made contact with the premise of Western social thought—that it is the people who are sovereign—it was clear that all of us must gain the spirit and power of philosophy.

This conclusion returns us to the position of SOCRATES, who philosophized everywhere with everyone, including slaves. Plato defined the goal of technical philosophy, and SOCRATES defined one of personal philosophy, and both are essential. The personal goal of philosophy is Socratic self-knowledge, and on this level the point of referring to other philosophers is to generate insight into one's own position. From this standpoint the systems of the great philosophers may be looked on as their own personal philosophies and as source material for developing one's own. The histories and other compendiums of philosophy here may thus be seen as the records of alternative approaches to self-knowledge in the Socratic manner. The extent to which publications in philosophy, both histories and introductions, are designed for initiating the reader into the activity of philosophizing reflects this point.

Although we have deemphasized the value of "isms," the reader will notice that different styles of philosophy—some with "ism" names—characterize different regions of the world. Many in Eastern Europe philosophize by means of a system called Marxism. The pragmatic element in American philosophy is unmistakable and has generated its own "ism"—pragmatism. The similarity between American and British philosophy in the contemporary world is so pronounced that one speaks of Anglo-American philosophy, and the name it bears is analytic philosophy. Analytic philosophers tend to be centered in logic and epistemology or use these disciplines as a kind of organon or instrument of analysis. The work is frequently rather technical and often disengaged from social issues. European philosophy, as opposed to Anglo-American philosophy, although it has no common name, is much more likely to be engaged with social issues, much more likely to be metaphysical and concerned about "isms." In both cases, the reasons are historical. American philosophy came from British empiricism—JOHN LOCKE (see Vol. 3), GEORGE BERKELEY, DAVID HUME. Later on, both were strongly influenced by the Vienna Circle's science-prone logical positivism and LUDWIG WITTGENSTEIN (turning philosophy increasingly toward the analysis of language). European philosophy came from its own seventeenth-century movement of rationalism—RENE DESCARTES (see also Vol. 5), BARUCH SPINOZA, GOTTFRIED VON LEIBNIZ—and the tradition that emerged from it, including the work of GEORGE HEGEL (see also Vol. 3), and KARL MARX (see also Vol. 3).

Although the dominant American tradition is analytic, European philosophizing has a following in the United States, just as the influence of analytic philosophy is felt in Europe. Furthermore, Eastern philosophy, which is not essentially separate from Eastern religion, exercises a continuing influence on Western philosophy. All of these tendencies will be evident in the following sections. One's philosophizing will almost certainly reflect one's region, in addition to one's own nature; yet, as our understanding of one another grows, there is an opportunity for regional differences to merge, so that those who announce the goal of world philosophy deserve careful consideration.

ENCYCLOPEDIAS, DICTIONARIES, AND INDEXES

Compendiums of philosophical ideas such as those in the books in this section have existed at least since the Roman period and play an important role in epitomizing philosophical work. SENECA (see also Vol. 2) was the author of one of these; VOLTAIRE (see also Vol. 2) was the author of another. Such aids exist in all major languages, directing the reader to the material in its original language.

Angeles, Peter A. *Dictionary of Philosophy*. HarpC 2nd ed. 1992 $13.00. ISBN 0-06-461026-8. Emphasizes terms, but also includes an index of philosophers.

Aristotle Dictionary. Ed. by Thomas P. Kiernan. Philosophical Lib. 1962 o.p. An alphabetical arrangement of topics. Provides insights into Aristotle's thought as well as quotable quotes. The first third of the book is an introduction to Aristotle.

Baldwin, James M. *Dictionary of Philosophy and Psychology.* 3 vols. in 4. Peter Smith 1960 $102.00. ISBN 0-8490-1721-1. Useful for philosophical material prior to 1900. The great American philosopher Charles Peirce was one of the major contributors.

Bales, Eugene F. *A Ready Reference to Philosophy East and West.* U. Pr. of Amer. 1988 $37.75. ISBN 0-8191-6640-4. A historical approach to major figures of Western philosophy, from ancient Greece to twentieth-century America, Britain, Europe, and Russia. Shorter sections are devoted to the history of Indian and Chinese philosophy.

Becker, Lawrence C., and Charlotte B. Becker. *Encyclopedia of Ethics.* 2 vols. Garland 1992 $150.00. ISBN 0-8153-0403-X. Contains over 400 signed articles on topics ranging from sexual harassment to suicide, bioethics, and friendship. Includes entries from more than 250 internationally recognized scholars.

Bynagle, Hans E. *Philosophy: A Guide to Reference Literature.* Libs. Unl. 1986 $35.00. ISBN 0-87287-464-8. Describes more than 300 philosophical reference works. Includes chapters covering major journals, research centers, and professional associations.

Collinson, Diane. *Fifty Major Philosophers: A Reference Guide.* Routledge Chapman & Hall 1987 $12.95. ISBN 0-7099-4871-9. Brief biographies, with lengthier expositions of important philosophers from the pre-Socratics to Wittgenstein and Sartre. Includes reading guides, lists of philosophical works, and a glossary of terms.

De George, Richard T. *The Philosopher's Guide to Sources, Research Tools, Professional Life, and Related Fields.* U. Pr. of KS 1980 o.p. A "guide to existing tools" in philosophy. Contains listings of histories, dictionaries (up through 1976), encyclopedias, journals, and bibliographies.

Dolan, Walter. *The Classical World Bibliography of Philosophy, Religion, and Rhetoric.* Garland 1978 o.p. A compendium of the sources for humanistic study in the classical period.

Edwards, Paul, ed. *The Encyclopedia of Philosophy.* 4 vols. Free Pr. 1973 $425.00. ISBN 0-02-894950-1. This standard reference work consists of 1,450 signed articles by 500 authorities from 24 nations under the direction of an editorial board of 153 international scholars. Articles vary in length from half a column to over 50 pages.

Flew, Antony, ed. *A Dictionary of Philosophy.* St. Martin 2nd rev. ed. 1984 $12.95. ISBN 0-312-20923-1. Stressing the meanings of key words and phrases, the 34 contributors also include biographical entries running on occasion to three or four thousand words.

Frolov, Ivan, ed. *Dictionary of Philosophy.* Intl. Pubs. Co. 1985 $8.95. ISBN 0-7178-0604-9. A dictionary paying special attention to the Marxist tradition.

Grimes, John A. *A Concise Dictionary of Indian Philosophy: Sanskrit Terms Defined in English.* State U. NY Pr. 1989 $49.50. ISBN 0-7914-0100-6. Cross-referenced, with terms in both Devanagari and roman script. Includes transliterations as well as translations of important technical terms.

Guerry, Herbert, ed. *A Bibliography of Philosophical Bibliographies.* Greenwood 1977 $55.00. ISBN 0-8371-9542-X. Attempts to list philosophical bibliographies published in all countries from the invention of printing through 1974. The first half of the work presents bibliographies on individual philosophers, the second half on philosophical topics.

Hetherington, Norriss S. *Encyclopedia of Cosmology: Historical, Philosophical and Scientific Foundations of Modern Cosmology.* Garland 1992 $125.00. ISBN 0-8240-7213-8. Includes discussions of Chinese, Egyptian, Native American, Arabian, and Mesopotamian cosmologies along with those of traditional Western scientists and philosophers from both ancient and modern times.

Jordak, Francis E. *A Bibliographical Survey for a Foundation in Philosophy.* U. Pr. of Amer. 1978 o.p. A research guide for undergraduates in philosophy, featuring in order dictionaries and encyclopedias in philosophy, philosophy journals with annotations and bibliographies on great philosophers, the history of philosophy and philosophical problems.

Kiernan, Thomas P. *The Who's Who in the History of Philosophy*. Philos. Lib. 1966 o.p. An alphabetically arranged dictionary of philosophical biography, including some twentieth-century figures.

Lacey, A. R. *A Dictionary of Philosophy*. Routledge 1990 $15.95. ISBN 0-415-05872-4. A pocket encyclopedia of philosophy, stressing discussion of the meanings of philosophical terms. Provides suggested sources for additional reading.

Lineback, Richard H. *Ethics: A Bibliography*. Garland 1976 o.p. A single-topic bibliography drawing on the extensive bibliographical resources on which Lineback has been engaged for many years.

——, ed. *The Philosopher's Index. 1990 Cumulative Edition*. Philos. Document. 1991 $144.00. ISBN 0-912632-52-6. Goes beyond dictionaries and encyclopedias to include philosophical analyses in more than 300 philosophy journals. Features subject, author, and book review indexes as well as author abstracts from 1940 to the present. Computer searchable through DIALOG.

——. *The Philosopher's Index Thesaurus*. Philos. Document. 1992 $19.00. ISBN 0-912632-20-8. A list of philosophical terms to supplement the information provided in the DIALOG program for computer search of the data contained in *The Philosopher's Index*.

Lucey, Kenneth, and Tibor Machan, eds. *Recent Work in Philosophy. Lib. of Philosophy*. Rowman 1983 $54.50. ISBN 0-8476-7103-8. Includes discussion of themes and literature on 11 central philosophical problems to about 1980. Henry E. Kyburg's essay on inductive logic is especially rich.

MacGregor, Geddes. *Dictionary of Religion and Philosophy*. Paragon Hse. 1991 $19.95. ISBN 1-55778-441-8. Primarily designed for students of religion; includes entries for both philosophical terms and philosophical authors of relevance to religious studies. Entries and bibliographies for Hinduism and Islam as well as for many modern religious movements.

Martin, Robert M. *The Philosopher's Dictionary*. Broadview Pr. 1991 $9.95. ISBN 0-921149-75-1. Concise dictionary of philosophical terms; includes entries for well-known philosophers.

Matczak, Sebastian A. *Philosophy: A Select, Classified Bibliography of Ethics, Economics, Law, Politics, Sociology. Philosophical Questions Ser*. Learned Pubns. 1970 $45.00. ISBN 0-912116-02-1. First volume in a projected series of study guides in philosophy. Concentrates on ethics and related disciplines, including material on histories, systematic studies, particular periods, and individuals. Brief descriptions of the point of view in question.

Nauman, St. Elmo, Jr. *Dictionary of American Philosophy*. Littlefield repr. of 1973 ed. $10.95. ISBN 0-8226-0275-X. A regional dictionary dealing with the figures and movements of philosophy in America.

——. *Dictionary of Asian Philosophies*. Carol Pub. Group 1978 $5.95. ISBN 0-8065-0617-2. Helps fill the void in dictionary material on Asian philosophy.

——. *The New Dictionary of Existentialism*. Carol Pub. Group 1972 $2.95. ISBN 0-8065-0281-9. A guide to the terminology of both philosophical and psychological existentialists. Bibliography appended.

Quine, W. V. *Quiddities: An Intermittently Philosophical Dictionary*. HUP 1987 $24.95. ISBN 0-674-74351-2. Short, lighthearted essays on topics ranging from philosophy, mathematics, and language to less-important matters.

Reese, William L. *Dictionary of Philosophy and Religion: Eastern and Western Thought*. Humanities 1980 $25.00. ISBN 0-391-00941-9. Named an "Outstanding Reference Work of 1980" by the American Library Association. Extensively cross-referenced, with over 3,500 alphabetically arranged entries. Significant body of material on both Western and Eastern thought.

Ruben, Douglas H., ed. *Philosophy Journals and Serials: An Analytical Guide. Annotated Bibliographies of Serials*. Greenwood 1985 $45.00. ISBN 0-313-23958-4. A bibliography of 335 entries, primarily of philosophy journals publishing articles in English. Archives, newsletters, and bulletins are included as well.

Runes, Dagobert D., ed. *Dictionary of Philosophy*. Littlefield rev. ed. 1984 $14.95. ISBN 0-8226-0392-6. The editor's announced aim is "clear, concise, and correct definitions and descriptions of the philosophical terms throughout the range of philosophic thought." Its outstanding feature is the analyses of logic by Alonzo Church.

———,ed. *Spinoza: Dictionary*. Greenwood 1976 repr. of 1951 ed. o.p. A dictionary related to the understanding of Spinoza, utilizing Spinoza's own discussions of his terms and ideas. The foreword is by Albert Einstein.

Sandeen, Ernest R., and Frederick Hale, eds. *American Religion and Philosophy: A Guide to Information Sources. Amer. Studies Information Guide*. Gale 1978 o.p. Concentrates primarily on the field of religion, but devotes 3 of its 21 chapters exclusively to philosophy. More than 1,600 entries. Books, articles, and bibliographical and other relevant source materials are referenced.

Steenbergen, G. J. *New Encyclopedia of Philosophy*. Trans. by Edmond Van Den Bossche. Philos. Lib. 1972 o.p. Contains entries on both terms and principal figures from the Dutch.

Tice, Terrence N., and Thomas P. Slavens. *Research Guide to Philosophy. Sources of Information in the Humanities Ser*. ALA 1983 o.p. A guide to the field of philosophy depicting, according to the authors, "the principal changes since the nineteenth century." Representative material is presented through carefully developed essays.

University of Southern California, Los Angeles. *Catalog of the Hoose Library of Philosophy*. 6 vols. G. K. Hall 1968 $655.00. ISBN 0-8161-0816-1. Catalog of one of the great libraries of philosophy, containing more than 37,000 volumes and representing all fields of philosophy (but with its greatest depth in classical and German philosophy). Very helpful for library development.

Urmson, J. O., ed. *Concise Encyclopedia of Western Philosophy and Philosophers*. Unwin Hyman 1990 $44.95. ISBN 0-685-46018-5. Short, descriptive summaries of standard topics, philosophical views, and major philosophers. Includes a few pictures of important past and contemporary philosophers.

Voltaire. *Philosophical Dictionary*. Trans. by Theodore Besterman *Penguin Class. Ser*. Viking Penguin 1984 $7.95. ISBN 0-14-044257-X. A wide-ranging compilation of essays by Voltaire that went through numerous editions during Voltaire's lifetime. A bestseller, it was also a target for book burnings.

Wiener, Philip P., ed. *Dictionary of the History of Ideas*. 5 vols. S&S Trade 1980 o.p. A cooperative study containing analyses of some 300 basic ideas by almost as many scholars from a variety of fields extending from art to science. Employs a philosophical history-of-ideas approach.

HISTORIES OF PHILOSOPHY

The books in this section deal with the material of philosophy chronologically, showing how a given period or philosophy arose from an earlier one. Encyclopedias and dictionaries epitomize knowledge; histories interpret it. Both derive from the writings of the philosophers. A considerable amount of the energy of the philosophical community is dedicated to the work of interpretation, most often showing how philosophical ideas interrelate as philosophies emerge from each other in history and from their cultures. Between the histories of philosophy and the introductions to philosophy, it is appropriate to mention a number of books that combine history and introduction. Preeminent among these is the much-maligned yet helpful *Story of Philosophy* (1926) by WILL DURANT (see Vol. 3). One of the features of the Durant book is its rather great stress on biography to interest readers in, as well as to help them understand, the philosophers. Another feature is the concentration on only the

greatest of the philosophers. Included below are books that do one or the other
of these things, as well as those that take a unique approach in some other
manner.

Alpern, Henry. *March of Philosophy*. Assoc. Faculty Pr. 1968 repr. of 1933 ed. o.p. One of
the older histories of philosophy. Well written.

Aquila, Richard E. *Rhyme or Reason: A Limerick History of Philosophy*. U. Pr. of Amer.
1981 o.p. Presents philosophy by combining rhyme with reason in 423 limericks.
Understanding the philosophy is often a condition for understanding the limerick.

Beiser, Frederick C. *The Fate of Reason: German Philosophy from Kant to Fichte*. HUP
1987 $34.95. ISBN 0-674-29502-1. Provides an introductory, general survey of the
major figures and controversies from Kant to Fichte. Individual chapters are devoted
to Jacobi, Mendelssohn, Herder, the Wolffians, Reinhold, Schulze, and Maimonides.

Bréhier, Emile. *History of Philosophy*. 7 vols. Trans. by Joseph Thomas and Wade
Baskine. U. Ch. Pr. Vol. 1 *The Hellenistic Age*. 1963 $5.00. ISBN 0-226-07217-7. Vol. 2
The Hellenistic and Roman Age. 1965 o.p. Vol. 3 *The Middle Ages and the
Renaissance*. 1967 o.p. Vol. 4 *The Seventeenth Century*. 1968 o.p. Vol. 5 *The
Eighteenth Century*. 1971 $5.00. ISBN 0-226-07227-4. Vol. 6 *The Nineteenth Century:
Period of Systems 1800-1850*. 1973 $5.00. ISBN 0-226-07229-0. Vol. 7 *Contemporary
Philosophy Since 1850*. 1973 $5.00. ISBN 0-226-07231-2. To a greater extent than
other historians, Bréhier places the philosophers in their cultural contexts, combin-
ing exposition and criticism.

Burley, Walter. *On the Lives and Characters of the Philosophers*. Ed. and trans. by Paul
Theiner. Garland 1981 o.p. An approach that is both philosophical and biographical.

Corbin, Henry. *History of Islamic Philosophy*. Trans. by Liadain and Philip Sherrard.
Routledge Chapman & Hall 1991 $65.00. ISBN 0-7103-0416-1. The full history of
traditional Islamic thought down to the present by a distinguished scholar.

De la Torre, Teodoro. *Popular History of Philosophy*. Lumen Christi 1988 $12.95. ISBN 0-
912414-48-0. Historical treatment of the full sweep of Western philosophical
development. Very brief treatments of major and minor figures and movements,
with numerous organizational charts and diagrams.

DeVries, Willem A. *Reality, Knowledge and the Good Life: A Historical Introduction to
Philosophy*. St. Martin 1991 $29.35. ISBN 0-312-03657-4. Collects classic writings of
major philosophers from the ancient Greeks to the present.

Dronke, Peter, ed. *A History of Twelfth Century Western Philosophy*. Cambridge U. Pr.
1988 $84.95. ISBN 0-521-25896-0. Chapters on Platonic, Stoic, and Arabic back-
ground to twelfth-century thought by a variety of authors. Major and minor figures
from this period are covered, as well.

Durant, Will. *Story of Philosophy*. S&S Trade 1961 $14.95. ISBN 0-671-20159-X. This
immensely successful volume combines philosophy and biography in an appealing
manner, but limits consideration to only the most famous philosophers.

Evans, G. R. *Philosophy and Theology in the Middle Ages*. Routledge 1993 $62.50. ISBN 0-
415-08908-5. Traces the complex interactions between Christian theology and
philosophy, beginning with Augustine. Also discusses the integration of scientific and
secular ideas.

Ferm, Vergilius, ed. *History of Philosophical Systems*. *Essay Index Repr. Ser*. Ayer 1950
$33.00. ISBN 0-8369-1923-8. Concentrates on metaphysical systems and the differ-
ences among them.

Frost, S. E., Jr. *The Basic Teachings of the Great Philosophers*. Doubleday 1980 repr. of
1942 ed. $9.00. ISBN 0-385-03007-X. A compendium of philosophical ideas, on the
order of a dictionary, but presented chronologically.

Hamlyn, D. W. *A History of Western Philosophy*. Viking Penguin 1989 $10.00. ISBN 0-14-
013752-1. An accessible, up-to-date explanation of major philosophers of the past,
with the focus on argumentation.

Hare, Peter, ed. *Doing Philosophy Historically*. Prometheus Bks. 1989 $39.95. ISBN 0-
87975-475-3. Collection of essays by various contemporary philosophers, grouped
into sections on ancient philosophy, Descartes, Kant, Hegel, the Scottish philosophy

of common sense, and recent American and European philosophy. Each grouping includes a critique of some or all of the essays in that group.

Hartshorne, Charles. *Insights and Oversights of Great Thinkers: An Evaluation of Western Philosophy*. Ser. in Systematic Philosophy. State U. NY Pr. 1983 $49.50. ISBN 0-87395-681-8. Confronts the history of philosophy from the standpoint of process philosophy, a position in contrast to the emphasis on substance used by Aristotle.

Hegel, Georg W. *Lectures on the History of Philosophy*. Trans. by E. S. Haldane and F. H. Simson. 3 vols. Humanities 1974 repr. of 1896 ed. $90.00. ISBN 0-685-55576-3. A work on the history of philosophy by the philosopher who, more than any other, made history a central philosophical consideration. Hegel applies his triadic method throughout.

Jaspers, Karl. *Socrates, Buddha, Confucius and Jesus: Taken from Vol. 1 of the Great Philosophers*. Trans. by Ralph Manheim. HarBraceJ 1966 $5.95. ISBN 0-15-683580-0. The only portion of Jaspers' multivolume history of philosophy now in print; exemplifies his method of concentrating on principal figures.

Jones, W. T. *A History of Western Philosophy*. 5 vols. HarBraceJ 1952. Vol. 1 *The Classical Mind*. $15.00. ISBN 0-15-538312-4. Vol. 2 *Medieval Mind*. $15.00. ISBN 0-15-538313-2. Vol. 3 *Hobbes to Hume*. $15.00. ISBN 0-15-538314-0. Vol. 4 *Kant and the 19th Century*. $15.00. ISBN 0-15-538316-7. Volume 5 *Twentieth Century to Wittgenstein and Sartre*. $15.00. ISBN 0-15-538317-5. Uses a principle of "concentration," since "it is better to understand a few theories than to recognize a great many." Concentrates on major figures, quoting generously from their writings.

Kellner, Douglas. *Jean Baudrillard: From Marxism to Postmodernism and Beyond*. Stanford U. Pr. 1989 $35.00. ISBN 0-8047-1738-9. Analyzes the thought of Baudrillard into three stages of development. Also discusses the influence of Marx, Freud, semiology, Bataille, Derrida, McLuhan, and Foucault.

Kenny, Anthony. *The Heritage of Wisdom: Essays in the History of Philosophy*. Blackwell Pubs. 1987 $34.95. ISBN 0-631-15269-5. A collection of essays, originally published from 1969 to 1986, on a variety of historical figures, including Aristotle, Thomas Aquinas, Sir Thomas More, and Descartes.

Kolenda, Konstantin. *Philosophy's Journey: From the Presocratics to the Present*. Waveland Pr. 1990 $15.95. ISBN 0-88133-509-6. Covers the full sweep of Western philosophy, providing a traditional grouping of standard figures who are explained at an introductory level.

Kreyche, Gerald F. *Thirteen Thinkers: A Sampler of Great Philosophers*. U. Pr. of Amer. 1976 $32.50. ISBN 0-8191-3888-6. An example of the history of philosophy studied through exemplary cases.

Lamprecht, Sterling P. *Our Philosophical Traditions: A Brief History of Philosophy in Western Civilization*. Century Philosophy Ser. Irvington 1980 repr. of 1955 ed. o.p. A durable standard history of philosophy, written in an even-handed yet lively manner. Avoids the faults of the usual history.

Lewes, George H. *The Biographical History of Philosophy, from Its Origins in Greece Down to the Present Day*. Gregg Intl. repr. of 1857 ed. $210.00. ISBN 0-576-29116-1. An approach to understanding philosophy through biography.

Lloyd, Genevieve. *The Man of Reason: Male and Female in Western Philosophy*. U. of Minn. Pr. 1985 $34.95. ISBN 0-8116-1381-8. Argues that, in the history of philosophy, reason has been regarded as a male attribute. Analyzes philosophers including Plato, Sartre, and Simone de Beauvoir, finding distortions that suggest that philosophy must proceed differently from now on.

Mahowald, Mary B., ed. *Philosophy of Woman: An Anthology of Classic and Current Concepts*. Hackett Pub. 1983 $34.95. ISBN 0-915144-49-2. Essays on the nature of woman, counterbalancing the male-dominated history of Western philosophy.

Marias, Julian. *A Biography of Philosophy*. Trans. by Harold C. Raley. U. of Ala. Pr. 1984 $19.95. ISBN 0-8173-0180-1. This "vitalist" Spanish philosopher finds prephilosophical problems in the common-sense world and traces their evolution into philosophical thought.

Oizerman, Theodor. *Problems in the History of Philosophy*. Beekman Pubs. 1975 $22.00. ISBN 0-8464-0763-9. Although many introductions to philosophy center on problems, this is one of relatively few histories to do so.

Ozmon, H. *Twelve Great Western Philosophers*. Oddo 1967 $9.95. ISBN 0-87783-046-0. Approaches the history of philosophy by way of a concentration on "great" figures.

Popkin, Richard H. *The Third Force in Seventeenth-Century Thought*. E. J. Brill 1992 $88.75. ISBN 90-04-09324-9. Includes 22 articles by Popkin on such figures as Hobbes, Henry More, Pascal, Spinoza, Cudworth, Isaac Newton, Hume, Condorcet, and Moritz Schlick.

Ree, J., M. Ayers, and A. Westoby. *Philosophy and Its Past*. Humanities 1978 o.p. A study in the philosophy of the history of philosophy, bringing historiography into the analysis of the discipline.

Ricoeur, Paul. *Main Trends in Philosophy. Main Trends in the Social and Human Sciences Ser.* Holmes & Meier 1979 $26.50. ISBN 0-8419-0506-1. This French philosopher applies his continental approach to the history of philosophy, using phenomenology and hermeneutics (an approach to philosophy that began with the interpretation of texts) as his tools.

Runes, Dagobert D. *Philosophy for Everyman: From Socrates to Sartre. Quality Pap. Ser.* Littlefield 1974 repr. of 1968 ed. $10.00. ISBN 0-8226-0276-8. Brief synopses of philosophers, arranged chronologically.

Russell, Bertrand, ed. *A History of Western Philosophy. Counterpoint Ser.* S&S Trade 1984 $8.95. ISBN 0-04-100045-5. One of the great histories of philosophy. Each philosopher is praised or criticized from Russell's own perspective. The book is characterized by Russellian humor, insight, and an occasional oversight.

Scharfstein, Ben-Ami. *The Philosophers: Life and Thought*. OUP 1980 $39.95. ISBN 0-19-520137-X. A psychoanalytically oriented study of the sources of philosophical systems.

Schlossberg, Edwin, and John Brockman. *The Philosopher's Game: Match Your Wits Against the One Hundred Greatest Thinkers of All Time*. St. Martin 1977 o.p. Of the many approaches to the history of philosophy, perhaps the most unusual is this one, in which philosophy is viewed as a game.

Stumpf, Samuel E. *Socrates to Sartre: A History of Philosophy*. McGraw 1988 $34.28. ISBN 0-07-062380-5. Explanations of the development of Western philosophy, in a clear and simple style. Offers a traditional coverage of main figures, issues, and movements.

Tarnas, Richard. *The Passion of the Western Mind: Understanding the Ideas That Have Shaped Our World View*. Crown Pub. Group 1991 $25.00. ISBN 0-517-57790-9. Beginning with the world view of the Homeric poems, traces the intellectual development of Western civilization through Greek and Roman times to the emergence of the domination of Christianity in the medieval world and down through the rise of modern science, ending with a consideration of postmodernism.

Ueberweg, Friedrich. *A History of Philosophy*. 2 vols. Trans. by George S. Morris. *Select Bibliographies Repr. Ser.* Ayer 1977 repr. of 1874 ed. $48.00. ISBN 0-8369-6788-7. A comprehensive history that begins with Thales and continues to the middle of the nineteenth century. Rich in references to philosophical literature in many languages and contains many scholarly footnotes.

Webb, Clement C. *A History of Philosophy*. Russell Sage 1985 repr. of 1984 ed. o.p. A brief history of philosophy written for the British Home University Library series (first ed., 1915), dealing with principal figures and movements in philosophy.

Wedberg, Anders. *A History of Philosophy*. 3 vols. OUP. Vol. 1 1982 $16.95. ISBN 0-19-824691-9. Vol. 2 1982 $45.00. ISBN 0-19-824640-4. Vol. 3 1984 $16.95. ISBN 0-19-824640-4. The coverage is from antiquity to Wittgenstein.

Windelband, Wilhelm. *A History of Philosophy*. Trans. by James H. Tufts. Greenwood 1979 repr. of 1938 ed. $42.50. ISBN 0-313-20872-7. One of the great nineteenth-century histories, extending from the Greeks to Nietzsche. Concentrates on prominent philosophers; relegates the less prominent to extensive footnotes.

INTRODUCTIONS TO PHILOSOPHY

There is, of course, a gradation from works in the history of philosophy to those that serve as introductions to philosophy. Indeed, there are two major strategies for introducing the reader to philosophy. One is through a discussion of problems, either by the author or by the philosophers themselves (excerpted in anthologies). The other is through the history of philosophy. Many of the previously mentioned works have also served as introductions to philosophy. Introductions, no less than histories, underline the extent to which philosophy is a teaching discipline. The introductions are most often ordered analytically in terms of problems, not chronologically. As suggested earlier, their deepest motivation is Socratic, although some stress an interest in choice among systems. Both strategies are to be found in the following list. Additional strategies are to be discerned here as well. One of these is the introduction to philosophy through literature. Another is to approach problems of philosophy through the eyes of a major philosopher; ST. THOMAS AQUINAS, for example, is sometimes so chosen: One of the works here is subtitled *A Sketch of Aquinate Philosophy*.

The problems approach typically includes consideration of seven or eight topics, among them ethics, epistemology, and the existence of God. Books with this approach differ, however, in that some emphasize questions of value (e.g., topics of ethics), whereas others stress questions of logic and epistemology. The same selection of emphasis is to be found in the philosophers writing or editing the books. When philosophy stresses logic and epistemology, it is often called analytic philosophy.

Although the philosophical strategy in use can often be read from the titles, the leaning toward analytic philosophy can seldom be determined in this way. The texts that are heavily analytic have sometimes been so identified; at other times, their preoccupation with questions of logic and epistemology, distinguishing marks of such philosophy, has been noted.

Abel, Reuben. *Man Is the Measure: A Cordial Invitation to the Central Problems of Philosophy*. Free Pr. 1976 $14.95. ISBN 0-02-900110-2. A book oriented to the problems of philosophy, consisting of analyses by the author.

Abelson, Raziel, and Michael Lockwood. *The Philosophical Imagination: An Introduction to Philosophy*. St. Martin 1977 o.p. An analytically oriented book of readings with introductions. The selections are in five areas, some from Eastern philosophers, some from literary sources.

Alston, William P., and Richard Brandt. *The Problems of Philosophy: Introductory Readings*. P-H 1978. ISBN 0-205-06110-9. Authors with contrasting views are included for each major problem, e.g., religious belief, value and obligation, free will and determinism, the mind-body problem, the foundations of knowledge.

Appiah, Anthony. *Necessary Questions: An Introduction to Philosophy*. P-H 1989. ISBN 0-13-611328-1. Includes chapters on logic, knowledge, science, language, morality, politics, and law. Provides historical background as well as biographical information for one major philosophical figure from each area covered. Glossary of philosophical terms as well as recommendations for further reading.

Beauchamp, Tom L., and Joel Feinberg. *Philosophy and the Human Condition*. P-H 1989. ISBN 0-13-662537-1. A standard anthology presenting contrasting selections on the basic problems of philosophy.

Beck, Robert N. *Perspectives in Philosophy: A Book of Readings*. H. Holt & Co. 1975 o.p. An approach to philosophy through the "isms." Readings on realism, materialism, idealism, positivism, linguistic philosophy, and existentialism.

Bedell, Gary. *Philosophizing with Socrates: An Introduction to the Study of Philosophy*. U. Pr. of Amer. 1980 o.p. Introduces one to philosophy by way of a study of the six early Socratic/Platonic dialogues (*Protagoras, Meno, Euthyphro, Apology, Crito, Phaedo*). An initial section on Socratic method; the two final sections on the nature of philosophy.

Berman, A. K., and James A. Gould, eds. *Philosophy for a New Generation*. Macmillan 1980 $12.95. ISBN 0-02-309640-3. A book of readings balanced between relevance and critical analysis of basic topics.

Bochenski, I. M. *Philosophy: An Introduction*. Trans. by William M. Newell. Kluwer Ac. 1963 o.p. A series of studies of selected philosophical problems and periods. An extensive bibliography of philosophy is included.

Bowie, G. Lee, Meredith W. Michaels, and Robert C. Solomon. *Twenty Questions: An Introduction to Philosophy*. HarBraceJ 1988 $20.00. ISBN 0-15-592388-9. A collection of brief readings from both classical and contemporary sources. Includes selections from literary and journalistic sources as well as from more traditionally philosophical writings.

Buford, Thomas O. *Personal Philosophy: The Art of Living*. H. Holt & Co. 1984 o.p. A problems approach, its sections initiated by case studies and followed by two opposed positions and then a mediating position—that of the author. The objective is to bring philosophy to bear on the issues of life.

Cahn, Steven M., ed. *Classics of Western Philosophy*. Hackett Pub. 1985 $45.00. 1985 ISBN 0-87220-106-6. The highlights of Western philosophy anthologized.

————, ed. *A New Introduction to Philosophy*. U. Pr. of Amer. 1986 repr. of 1971 ed. o.p. A reprint of one of the classic introductions to philosophy.

Capaldi, Nicholas. *An Invitation to Philosophy*. Prometheus Bks. 1981 $21.95. ISBN 0-87975-162-2. Combines discussions of the history of philosophy with discussion of basic problems. A chapter on Asian thought is included.

Capaldi, Nicholas, and others, eds. *Journeys Through Philosophy*. Prometheus Bks. rev. ed. 1982 $22.95. ISBN 0-87975-171-1. Standard readings from Plato to Russell (one-third of the selections are from Plato and Aristotle). A section of medieval philosophy is included; also, a guide to reading philosophy.

Cornman, James W., Keith Lehrer, and George S. Pappas. *Philosophical Problems and Arguments: An Introduction*. Hackett Pub. 4th rev. ed. 1992 $32.50. ISBN 0-87220-125-2. An analytical approach to philosophical arguments.

Davidson, Robert F. *Philosophies Men Live By*. H. Holt & Co. 1974 o.p. Interpretations of hedonism, rationalism, utilitarianism, naturalism, pragmatism, existentialism, and Zen Buddhism, with selected illustrative passages from their chief representatives.

Davis, Thomas D. *Philosophy: An Introduction through Original Fiction, Discussion and Readings*. Random 1986 $9.00. ISBN 0-394-32048-4. A problems approach to philosophy, each problem introduced by one or two fictional stories by Davis, followed by questions on the philosophical themes implicit in the stories, and finally an explicitly philosophical discussion of the topic.

Edwards, James C., and Douglas MacDonald. *Occasions for Philosophy*. P-H 1979 $10.95. ISBN 0-13-629262-3. Readings with the announced goal of Socratic self-knowledge. Begins with Socrates (the whole of *Euthyphro* and *Apology*), followed by critical discussions of Socrates' character and mission.

Edwards, Paul, and Arthur Pap, eds. *Modern Introduction to Philosophy*. Free Pr. 1973 $27.95. ISBN 0-02-909200-0. Analytic; substantial readings, placed in context by the editors. Each section ends with an elaborate annotated bibliography.

Ewing, Alfred C. *The Fundamental Questions of Philosophy*. Routledge Chapman & Hall 1985 $13.95. ISBN 0-7100-0586-5. A distinguished older text dealing with epistemology, matter, mind, space-time, freedom, and God.

Falcone, Vincent J. *Great Thinkers, Great Ideas: An Introduction to Western Thought*. North River 1988 $17.50. ISBN 0-88427-075-0. Written for high school students but also intended as an easy reference for college students or as an introduction to standard philosophical topics for beginning adults.

Feinberg, Joel. *Reason and Responsibility*. Wadsworth Pub. 8th ed. 1993. ISBN 0-534-19722-1. Mostly analytic in approach; deals with six problems, including the analytic-synthetic distinction. The selections are ample.

Flew, Antony. *Philosophy: An Introduction.* Prometheus Bks. 1980 $16.95. ISBN 0-87975-127-4. A standard introduction covering the customary topics of philosophy by a well-known British philosopher.

French, Peter A., and Curtis Brown, eds. *Puzzles, Paradoxes and Problems: A Reader for Introductory Philosophy.* St. Martin 1986 $29.35. ISBN 0-312-65720-X. Anthology of readings selected from both classical and contemporary sources. Includes such topics as backward causality and time travel, along with more conventional issues.

Geisler, Norman L., and Paul Feinberg. *Introduction to Philosophy.* Baker Bks. 1980 $15.95. ISBN 0-8010-3818-9. Subtitled "A Christian Perspective"; the Preface states that the book is "unashamedly" written from that perspective. After an initial section on the nature of philosophy, the volume deals with knowledge, reality, the ultimate, and ethics.

Gould, James A., ed. *Classic Philosophical Questions.* Macmillan 1989. ISBN 0-675-20849-1. Presents contrasting views from the history of philosophy. Each chapter concludes with study-guide questions and suggested readings.

Grassian, Victor. *Perennial Philosophical Issues.* P-H 1984 $26.95. ISBN 0-13-656769-2. A problems approach stressing enduring issues.

Hakim, Albert. *Historical Introduction to Philosophy.* Macmillan 1987. ISBN 0-02-348790-9. Designed for the beginning student of philosophy. Places philosophical problems in their historical settings and provides brief introductions to representative Western philosophers.

Halverson, William H. *A Concise Introduction to Philosophy.* McGraw 1981 $25.48. ISBN 0-07-554307-9. Consists of 64 chapters of 6- to 8-page arguing for various positions.
———. *Concise Readings in Philosophy.* McGraw 1981 $17.16. ISBN 0-07-554315-X. Sixty-four selections correlated to the chapters of the preceding work. Two-thirds are from historical sources.

Harris, William T. *Introduction to the Study of Philosophy.* Ed. by Marietta Kies. AMS Pr. 1976 repr. of 1889 ed. $21.00. ISBN 0-404-59166-3. A truly historic introduction to philosophy. Selected material from the work of William T. Harris, an idealist and Hegelian, for a course in philosophy at Mount Holyoke College, Massachusetts.

Hocutt, Max. *First Philosophy: An Introduction to Philosophical Issues.* Krieger 1986 repr. of 1980 ed. $26.00. ISBN 0-89874-898-4. An introduction to philosophy through metaphysics.

Hollis, Martin. *Invitation to Philosophy.* Blackwell Pubs. 1985 $8.95. ISBN 0-631-14226-6. Organized around various dichotomies; Hollis invites the student to think along with him about scientific and moral understanding, open and closed questions, vision and reason, inner and outer worlds, subjectivity and objectivity.

Honer, Stanley M., and Thomas C. Hunt. *Invitation to Philosophy.* Wadsworth Pub. 1982 $12.95. ISBN 0-534-16002-6. Presumes a use of primary reading sources; supplements them in concise discussions of basic philosophical concepts.

Jaspers, Karl. *Way to Wisdom: An Introduction to Philosophy.* Trans. by Ralph Manheim. Yale U. Pr. 1960 $9.95. ISBN 0-300-00134-7. A nonanalytic approach to philosophy by an important German existentialist philosopher. Discusses God, man, science, the world, and the Comprehensive.

Joad, Cyril E. *Guide to Philosophy.* Dover 1936 $12.95. ISBN 0-486-20297-6. One of the older introductions by a well-known British philosopher. Joad begins with a discussion of epistemology, which he then applies to metaphysical systems from Plato to Whitehead.

Johnson, Oliver A. *The Individual and the Universe: An Introduction to Philosophy.* HarBraceJ 1981 $29.50. ISBN 0-03-056888-9. A book of readings on the major fields and central issues of philosophy, beginning with Socrates and concluding with William James.

Klauder, Francis J. *The Wonder of Philosophy.* Philos. Lib. 1974 o.p. An outline of the principal positions of Thomistic philosophy, a brief survey of the main figures of Western philosophy, a very few pages on Eastern philosophy, and a glossary of terms.

Klemke, E. D., and others, eds. *Philosophy: The Basic Issues*. St. Martin 1985 $29.35. ISBN 0-312-02133-X. A standard anthology treating the problems of philosophy by way of contrasting selections.

Konecsni, Johnemery. *A Philosophy for Living: A Sketch of Aquinate Philosophy*. U. Pr. of Amer. 1977 $18.25. ISBN 0-8191-0138-9. An approach to philosophy through the system of Thomas Aquinas.

Lachs, John, and Charles E. Scott, eds. *The Human Search: An Introduction to Philosophy*. OUP 1981 o.p. A book of selections, with introductions of five to six pages, consisting of traditional philosophy, current applications to economics and morals, and literature with philosophic implications.

Ladd, George T. *Introduction to Philosophy: An Inquiry after a Rational System of Scientific Principles in the Relation to the Ultimate Reality*. AMS Pr. 1988 repr. of 1890 ed. $29.50. ISBN 0-404-59216-3. As the initial reviewer of this book wrote in 1891, this is a book to be read after, not before, "severe philosophical study." Treats philosophy as "the science of what is knowable by means of the special sciences."

Lazerowitz, M., and A. Ambrose. *Philosophical Theories*. Mouton 1976 $36.70. ISBN 90-2797-501-9. Deals with topics ranging from epistemology to ethics. Each chapter ends with a section on "doubts and queries." The suggestions for further reading direct one to the more analytic philosophers, such as Moore, Broad, Russell, Howe, and Malcolm.

Lehrer, Keith. *Theory of Knowledge*. Westview 1990 $52.50. ISBN 0-8113-0570-5. Though written as a textbook in the theory of knowledge, this volume defends a coherence theory of knowledge.

Levi, Albert W. *Varieties of Experience: An Introduction to Philosophy*. Bks. Demand repr. of 1957 ed. $134.30. ISBN 0-317-08882-3. A cultural approach to philosophy in Levi's own voice, combining readings and text.

McHenry, Leemon, and Frederick Adams, eds. *Reflections on Philosophy: Introductory Essays*. St. Martin 1993. ISBN 0-312-06777-1. Contemporary perspectives on 11 main areas of philosophy by 11 different authors.

MacKenzie, Patrick T. *The Problems of Philosophers: An Introduction*. Prometheus Bks. 1989 $18.95. ISBN 0-87975-486-9. Historically oriented introduction designed to interest beginners in philosophy.

Mandelbaum, Maurice, ed. *Philosophic Problems*. Macmillan 1967 o.p. Somewhat analytic.

Marias Aquilera, Julian. *Reason and Life: The Introduction to Philosophy*. Trans. by Kenneth S. Reid and Edward Sarmiento. Greenwood 1975 repr. of 1956 ed. o.p. Translated from the Spanish, and dedicated to the author's teacher, Ortega y Gasset, whose thought is followed in this analysis of philosophic problems, including Ortega's emphasis on a "vital reason."

Maritain, Jacques. *An Introduction to Philosophy*. Trans. by E. I. Watkin. Century Bookbindery 1983 repr. of 1930 ed. o.p. An approach to philosophy by a famous Catholic philosopher. Maritain combines the history of philosophy with analyses that are Aristotelian or Thomistic (following the thought of Thomas Aquinas).

Martinich, A. P. *Philosophical Writing: An Introduction*. P-H 1989. ISBN 0-13-664103-2. Offers guidance for writing undergraduate philosophical essays. Includes a detailed description of a simple model for an essay and chapters on logical concepts as well as on forms and styles of philosophical argumentation.

Mead, Hunter. *Types and Problems of Philosophy*. Irvington 1959 $37.95. ISBN 0-03-006240-3. A classic text presenting idealism and naturalism as the types of philosophy to be considered, and metaphysics, epistemology, ethics, and aesthetics as the problems. Also discusses the origin and development of life.

Minton, Arthur J., and Thomas A. Shipka. *Philosophy: Paradox and Discovery*. McGraw 1982 $29.00. ISBN 0-07-042413-6. Combines discussion of problems with readings.

Mourant, John A., and E. Hans Freund, eds. *Problems of Philosophy*. Macmillan 1964 o.p. A book of readings with ample selections. The authors have added philosophy of science to the more usual topics.

Munitz, Milton K. *The Ways of Philosophy*. Macmillan 1979. ISBN 0-02-384850-2. A standard introduction to philosophy by a well-known contemporary philosopher.

Nakhnikian, George. *An Introduction to Philosophy*. T.I.S. 1981 o.p. Concentrates on Plato, Descartes, and William James. Dealing with their views and arguments, it is designed to be read along with designated (but not included) readings from these thinkers.

Oizerman, T. I. *The Main Trends in Philosophy*. St. Mut. 1988 $70.00. ISBN 0-685-31609-2. Casts the traditional history of philosophical development in terms of a distinctively human spiritual quest.

Olen, Jeffrey. *Persons and Their World: An Introduction to Philosophy*. McGraw 1983 $23.72. ISBN 0-07-554311-7. A comprehensive introduction to the basic problems and fields of philosophy, with selections systematically including classical and contemporary philosophers dealing with the same problem.

Olscamp, Paul J. *An Introduction to Philosophy*. Bks. Demand repr. of 1971 ed. $130.80. ISBN 0-317-08892-0. A rigorous approach to the basic problems and fields of philosophy, using the techniques of ordinary language philosophers.

Perry, John, and Michael Bratman, eds. *Introduction to Philosophy: Classical and Contemporary Readings*. OUP 1986 $35.00. ISBN 0-19-503697-2. A collection of primary texts on topics ranging from the nature of philosophy to religion, knowledge and reality, mind and body, human values, puzzles and paradoxes.

Pojman, Louis P., ed. *Introduction to Philosophy: Classical and Contemporary Readings*. Wadsworth Pub. 1991. ISBN 0-534-14370-9. An anthology of standard readings about the nature of philosophy, theories of knowledge, religion, the mind, will, responsibility, and human values. Includes a section on how to read and write philosophy papers.

Popkin, Richard, and Avrum Stroll. *Philosophy and Contemporary Problems: A Reader*. H. Holt & Co. 1984 o.p. Includes classical and contemporary readings, but the latter are emphasized. The approach is problem centered, and contemporary issues, such as insanity and abortion, are included.

Purtill, Richard L. *A Logical Introduction to Philosophy*. P-H 1989. ISBN 0-13-539917-3. Includes an introduction to logic as well as to traditional philosophical problems.

Purtill, Richard L., and Peter J. Kreeft. *Philosophical Questions: An Introductory Anthology*. P-H 1985. ISBN 0-13-662305-0. Organized around the three Kantian questions—What can we know? What should we do? What can we hope?

Pustilnik, Jack, and Dale Riepe. *The Structure of Philosophy*. Littlefield 1966 o.p. A collection of readings on existence, method, and the ideal, combining selections from Asian philosophers, Western philosophers, and Marxist philosophers alongside the more usually non-Marxist ones.

Rader, Melvin. *The Enduring Questions*. HarBraceJ 1980 $25.00. ISBN 0-03-032949-3. One of the more durable texts. Provides unusually ample readings on epistemology, metaphysics, philosophy of religion, and ethics.

Richter, Peyton E., and Walter L. Fogg. *Philosophy Looks to the Future: Confrontation, Commitment and Utopia*. Waveland Pr. 1985 repr. of 1978 ed. $24.95. ISBN 0-88133-185-6. A future-oriented approach to philosophy.

Rogers, Jack B., and Forrest Baird. *Introduction to Philosophy: A Case Study Approach*. HarpC 1981 $14.95. ISBN 0-06-066997-7. A discussion-oriented approach to philosophy through contemporary issues, oriented toward ethics and theology.

Rosenberg, Jay. *The Practice of Philosophy: A Handbook for Beginners*. P-H 1984 $8.95. ISBN 0-13-687467-3. Discussions of the character of philosophy, the nature of argument, the joys and perils of dialectic, writing four kinds of philosophical essays, six ways to read a philosopher.

Russell, Bertrand. *An Outline of Philosophy*. Allen & Unwin 1979 o.p. A classic text dealing with learning, inference, the physical world, and a person's place in the universe.

————. *The Problems of Philosophy*. OUP 1959 repr. of 1912 ed. $6.95. ISBN 0-19-500212-1. A text from early in this century, discussing the nature of matter, knowledge by acquaintance and knowledge by description, and other epistemological questions.

Sanders, Steven, and David Cheny. *The Meaning of Life: Questions, Answers, and Analysis.* P-H 1980 $13.95. ISBN 0-13-567438-7. Twelve essays on life's meaningfulness (or its contrary) from Tolstoy, Stace, and Camus, as well as contemporary philosophers, including Kurt Baier, Paul Edwards, R. M. Hare, Kai Nielsen, and Richard Taylor.

Scherer, Donald, and Fred Miller. *Introduction to Philosophy: From Wonder to World View.* P-H 1979 o.p. A long introductory section on philosophy and logic. Deals with seven philosophical problems, each beginning with a piece of fiction; selections from classical philosophers, garnished with cartoons and photographs.

Scriven, Michael. *Primary Philosophy.* McGraw 1966 o.p. A hard-hitting discussion of philosophical problems. One major goal is to shift the focus of philosophy from God to man. The section on God is especially rigorous, Scriven argues strongly against the possibility of God's existence.

Snyder, William S., and Eugene A. Troxell. *Making Sense of Things: An Invitation to Philosophy.* St. Martin 1976 o.p. Conveys the message that the history of philosophy is a "storehouse of provocative ideas." Arranged by the nature and attractions of philosophy. Five ideas from the philosophical past. Includes perspectives from twentieth-century philosophy and a glossary.

Soccio, Douglas J. *Archetypes of Wisdom: An Introduction to Philosophy.* Wadsworth Pub. 1992. ISBN 0-534-14226-5. Integrates philosophical text materials, including the nontraditional and nonacademic, with commentary. Ranges beyond standard Western concerns to consider archetypically wise women, sages, iconoclasts, visionaries, and Buddhas.

——. *How to Get the Most Out of Philosophy.* Wadsworth Pub. 1992 o.p. A handbook for philosophy students that provides "how to" information on reading philosophical texts—everything from thinking and writing philosophically to speaking with philosophy professors and obtaining letters of recommendation.

Solomon, Robert C. *The Big Questions: A Short Introduction to Philosophy.* HarBraceJ 1985 $16.50. ISBN 0-15-505412-0. A problems-oriented approach to philosophy.

——. *Introducing Philosophy: A Text with Integrated Writings.* HarBraceJ 1993 $29.50. ISBN 0-15-500376-3. Combines Solomon's analysis with readings that are ample and well selected. A glossary of terms concludes each chapter. Biographies of the philosophers.

Sprintzen, David A. *The Drama of Thought: An Inquiry into the Place of Philosophy in Human Experience.* U. Pr. of Amer. 1978 o.p. An approach to philosophy that seeks its connections to the rest of life.

Stewart, David, and H. Gene Blocker. *Fundamentals of Philosophy.* Macmillan 1986. ISBN 0-02-417310-X. Includes standard topics in philosophy, such as metaphysics, epistemology, ethics, philosophy of religion, and social and political thought. Also covers philosophical themes from Hinduism, Buddhism, Confucianism, and Taoism.

Stroll, Avrum, and Richard Popkin. *Introduction to Philosophy.* HarBraceJ 3rd ed. 1979 $40.00. ISBN 0-03-021761-X. No readings, but a solid text on the basic problems of philosophy.

——, eds. *Introductory Readings in Philosophy.* HarBraceJ 1972 $32.00. ISBN 0-03-081288-7. A set of readings to accompany any text on the problems of philosophy.

Struhl, Karsten J., and Paula R. Struhl. *Philosophy Now.* McGraw 1980 $14.92. ISBN 0-07-553717-6. Combines classical and contemporary readings, with emphasis on the latter. Includes such topics as drug experience, the nuclear family, and world revolution, as well as the more usual ones.

Stumpf, Samuel E. *The Elements of Philosophy.* McGraw 1986 $35.16. ISBN 0-07-062309-0. Very short readings accompanying the author's text.

——. *Philosophical Problems.* McGraw 1983 $21.08. ISBN 0-07-062180-2. Substantial readings on five areas of philosophy, with alternative approaches to each, and a selected bibliography.

Titus, Harold, and Marilyn Smith. *Living Issues in Philosophy*. Wadsworth Pub. 8th ed. 1986. ISBN 0-534-05376-9. One of the very successful older books. The authors are interested in both problems and systems of philosophy.

Toulmin, Stephen. *Knowing and Acting: An Invitation to Philosophy*. Macmillan 1976 o.p. An epistemological approach to the issues of philosophy.

Trueblood, Elton. *General Philosophy*. *Twin Brooks Ser*. Baker Bk. o.p. Another of the very successful older books. The text is in the author's voice, with no accompanying readings. Two appendixes add biographical data on the philosophers discussed and provide a glossary of terms.

Van Croonenburg, Englebert J. *Gateway to Reality: An Introduction to Philosophy*. U. Pr. of Amer. 1982 repr. of 1963 ed. o.p. An introduction to philosophy from the phenomenological, existentialist point of view. Oriented to Gabriel Marcel and the Personalist tradition. Topics include personal vocation, fidelity, death and suffering, and the nature of religious faith.

Vesey, Godfrey, ed. *Philosophers Ancient and Modern*. Cambridge U. Pr. 1986 o.p. A critical exposition of standard Western philosophical texts. Designed for readers without extensive prior acquaintance with philosophy.

Wallace, William A. *The Elements of Philosophy: A Compendium for Philosophers and Theologians*. Alba 1977 $14.95. ISBN 0-8189-0345-7. A concept-oriented approach to philosophy.

Warburton, Nigel. *Philosophy: The Basics*. Routledge 1992 $59.95. ISBN 0-415-05385-4. Emphasizes ideas and the arguments for and against them, rather than major philosophical figures.

Westphal, Fred A. *Activity of Philosophy: A Concise Introduction*. *Philosophy Ser*. P-H 1969. ISBN 0-13-003608-0. An analysis of basic philosophical problems designed to be used along with one of the anthologies of philosophy.

Wilson, Margaret, and Dan W. Brock. *Philosophy: An Introduction*. P-H 1972 o.p. A standard introduction to philosophy.

Windt, Peter Y. *An Introduction to Philosophy: Ideas in Conflict*. West Pub. 1982 $38.25. ISBN 0-314-65587-5. Deals with nine problems of philosophy by means of readings, mostly modern. Includes appendixes giving advice on the writing of papers in philosophy, biographical notes, and a glossary of terms.

Wolff, Robert P. *About Philosophy*. P-H 1986. ISBN 0-13-005588-3. Classical readings and modern applications with respect to ethics, social philosophy, aesthetics, and philosophy of religion.

_____. *Philosophy: A Modern Encounter*. P-H 1976 repr. of 1973 ed. $17.95. ISBN 0-13-663385-4. A standard introduction stressing contemporary issues.

_____, ed. *Introductory Philosophy*. P-H 1979. ISBN 0-13-500876-X. A book of readings centering on seven problems, with selections from major philosophers. Questions end each selection.

Woodhouse, Mark B. *A Preface to Philosophy*. Wadsworth Pub. 1990. ISBN 0-534-12012-1. An analytical approach to recognizing philosophical subject matter and techniques in evaluating ideas and arguments. Provides appendixes on the lives and thoughts of great philosophers.

Young, John. *Reasoning Things Out*. Stella Maris Bks. 1982 $2.50. ISBN 0-909615-05-5

PHILOSOPHY BY GEOGRAPHIC AREA

This list consists of works that deal with one or another cultural area of the world. Since in this volume of *The Reader's Adviser* the philosophy and religion of the East have already been separated from those of the West, we shall refrain from mentioning works of Eastern philosophy here. To avoid interfering with the orderly progression from the Greek period to the present, the works of ancient Greek and Roman philosophy will also be avoided. This subsection therefore includes those general works that provide information about philosophy in various areas of the world. Philosophy tends toward universality, and yet, as noted in the Introduction with respect to the contrasts between Anglo-America and Europe, different styles of philosophizing characterize different areas of the world. Since geographic areas do not fit neatly into the historical periods of our division, the philosophy of geographic areas belongs to general philosophy, with some notable exceptions. One is that British and European philosophy are subject to discussion under the headings of both modern and twentieth-century philosophy. The other is that, because ancient philosophy is virtually identical to the philosophy of ancient Greece and Rome, coverage of these areas will be reserved for the relevant periods.

Africa

Apostel, L. *African Philosophy—Myth or Reality. Philosophy and Anthropology Ser.* Humanities 1981 o.p. Discusses the intermediate nature of African thought in terms of the religio-poetic structure of myth and the conceptual structure of philosophy.

Carman, John, and Vasudha Narayanan. *The Tamil Veda: Pillan's Interpretation of the Tiruvaymoli.* U. Ch. Pr. 1989 $49.95. ISBN 0-226-09305-0. Seeks insights into the thought of the major Hindu theologian, Ramanuja.

Gyekye, Kwame. *An Essay on African Philosophical Thought: The Akan Conceptual Scheme.* Cambridge U. Pr. 1987 $54.95. ISBN 0-521-32525-0. Provides clarification and interpretation of Akan ideas about God, persons, destiny, and morality by relating African philosophy to African cultural life. Argues for the legitimacy of genuinely African philosophy.

Hountondji, Paulin J. *African Philosophy: Myth and Reality. African Systems of Thought Ser.* Ind. U. Pr. 1983 o.p. Deals with the problem of moving from a mythical form of belief to philosophy. Two philosophies are treated, that of Amo (an eighteenth-century African philosopher) and the "consciencism" of Kwame Nkrumah. With an introduction by Irele Abiola.

Makinde, M. Akin. *African Philosophy, Culture and Traditional Medicine.* Ohio U. Pr. 1988 $13.00. ISBN 0-89680-152-7. Includes a general chapter on philosophy and culture as well as one on the nature of African philosophy. More specific chapters are devoted to the development of African philosophy, the social and political philosophy of Obafemi Awolowo, and African traditional medicine.

Nkrumah, Kwame. *Consciencism: Philosophy and the Ideology for Decolonization.* Monthly Rev. 1970 repr. of 1965 ed. $6.00. ISBN 0-85345-136-2. Adapting Marxism to the African reality, finds in socialism a modern equivalent to African communalism.

Okere, Theophilus. *African Philosophy: A Historico-Hermeneutical Investigation of the Conditions of Its Possibility.* U. Pr. of Amer. 1983 o.p. An application of hermeneutical techniques to the problem of the possibility of African philosophy.

Oruka, H. Odera, ed. *Sage Philosophy: Indigenous Thinkers and Modern Debate on African Philosophy.* E. J. Brill 1990 $74.50. ISBN 90-04-09283-8. Includes five chapters on the nature, methods, and history of African philosophy, with particular emphasis on the role of sages. Two chapters collect various texts from sages, while the last six chapters, written by a variety of scholars, are of a critical nature.

Serequeberhan, Tsenay. *African Philosophy: The Essential Readings.* Paragon Hse. 1991 $13.95. ISBN 1-55778-309-8. A collection of essays by scholars concerned with various aspects of African philosophy. Includes discussions of the roles of sagacity, myth, and reality in African thought. Also explores the nature, methods, and definition of distinctively African thought.

Teaching and Research in Philosophy: Africa. Studies on Teaching and Research in Philosophy throughout the World. UNIPUB 1985 $18.00. ISBN 92-3-102124-9. A report on philosophical teaching and writing in Africa.

Thompson, Robert F. *Flash of the Spirit: African and Afro-American Art and Philosophy.* Random 1984 $9.95. ISBN 0-685-04218-9. An examination of African culture,

including its influence on the West, through its art, religion, architecture, and
artifacts in general.

Wiredu, K. *Philosophy and an African Culture.* Cambridge U. Pr. 1980 o.p. A Ghanaian
philosopher, trained in the analytic tradition, finds a role for technical philosophy in
the modernizing nations of Africa. Warns that African philosophers must not lose
their African conscience. Also discusses the role of Marxist thought.

Wright, Richard A., ed. *African Philosophy: An Introduction.* U. Pr. of Amer. 1984 o.p.
Essays considering the possibility of an African philosophy, examining ancient
philosophy, social philosophy, and time and cause in an African context.

Europe

GENERAL

Bochenski, Innocentius. *Contemporary European Philosophy (Europaische Philosophie
der Gegenwart).* Trans. by Donald Nicholl and Karl Aschenbrenner. Greenwood 1982
repr. of 1956 ed. $38.50. ISBN 0-313-23490-6. A survey of contemporary British and
continental philosophy extending into the 1950s.

Chappell, Vere, ed. *Essays on Early Modern Philosophers: From Descartes and Hobbes to
Newton and Leibniz.* 12 vols. Garland 1992. Vol 1 *René Descartes.* $120.00. ISBN 0-
8153-0574-5. Vol. 2 *Grotius to Gassendi.* $54.00. ISBN 0-8153-0576-1. Vol. 3
Cartesian Philosophers. $60.00. ISBN 0-8153-0577-X. Vol. 4 *Port-Royal to Bayle.*
$60.00. ISBN 0-8153-0578-8. Vol. 5 *Thomas Hobbes.* $57.00. ISBN 0-8153-0579-6.
Vol. 6 *Seventeenth-Century British Philosophers.* $60.00. ISBN 0-8153-0580-X. Vol. 7
Seventeenth-Century Natural Scientists. $60.00. ISBN 0-8153-0581-8. Vol. 8 *John
Locke—Theory of Knowledge.* $90.00. ISBN 0-8153-0582-6. Vol. 9 *John Locke—
Political Philosophy.* $55.00. ISBN 0-8153-0584-2. Vol. 10 *Baruch de Spinoza.* $65.00.
ISBN 0-8153-0585-0. Vol. 11 *Nicolas Malebranche.* $69.00. ISBN 0-8153-0586-9. Vol.
12 *Gottfried Wilhelm Leibniz.* 2 vols. $140.00. ISBN 0-8153-0587-7. Following an
introduction by the editor, each volume collects a number of mostly recent, but
relatively technical, essays on relevant philosophers, issues, historical movements,
and background contexts.

Kearney, Richard. *Modern Movements in European Philosophy.* St. Martin 1988 $59.95.
ISBN 0-7190-1746-7. Provides a critical introduction to three major movements in
European philosophy: phenomenology, critical theory, and structuralism. Discusses
six major figures from each movement and provides comprehensive bibliographies
of both primary and secondary sources.

Perry, Ralph B. *Philosophy of the Recent Past: An Outline of European and American
Philosophy since 1860.* AMS Pr. 1982 repr. of 1926 ed. $29.00. ISBN 0-404-59295-3.
A survey of European and American philosophy from 1860 into the 1920s.

Stromberg, Roland N. *European Intellectual History Since Seventeen Eighty-Nine.* P-H
1986. ISBN 0-13-291998-2. A survey of European philosophy and letters from 1789 to
the present.

FRANCE

Akeroyd, Richard H. *Reason and Revelation: From Paul to Pascal.* Mercer Univ. Pr. 1991
$30.00. ISBN 0-86554-386-0. Beginning with the apostle Paul, traces the develop-
ment of the relation of reason to revelation through the ideas of the medievals up to
the time of St. Thomas Aquinas. Provides individual chapters on mysticism,
Montaigne, Descartes, and Pascal.

Alexander, Ian W. *French Literature and the Philosophy of Consciousness: Phenomenological Essays.* St. Martin 1985 $25.00. ISBN 0-312-30495-1. A phenomenological
approach to French literature and philosophy.

Appignanesi, Lisa, ed. *Ideas from France: The Legacy of French Theory.* Col. U. Pr. 1990
$14.50. ISBN 1-85343-113-3. A collection of essays by various scholars on Foucault,
structural Marxism, and the uses of history in French thought. Also discusses the
place of theory, particularly literary theory, in French philosophy.

Chiari, Joseph. *Twentieth-Century French Thought: From Bergson to Levi-Strauss.* Gordian 1975 $50.00. ISBN 0-87752-185-9. Interesting analyses giving the views of a dozen highly important French philosophers.

Leighton, Walter L. *French Philosophers—New England Transcendentalism.* Greenwood 1968 repr. of 1908 ed. $39.75. ISBN 0-8371-0143-3. Traces the influence of New England transcendentalism on such important nineteenth-century French philosophers as Cousin and Jouffroy.

Michaud, Regis. *Modern Thought and Literature in France. Essay Index Repr. Ser.* Ayer 1977 repr. of 1934 ed. $15.75. ISBN 0-8369-0707-8. Explores French thought— "philosophy" in a very general sense—through the work of three early twentieth-century French artists and writers.

Montefiore, Alan, ed. *Philosophy in France Today.* Cambridge U. Pr. 1983 $54.95. ISBN 0-521-22838-7. Essays by a dozen well-known French philosophers, interpreting their work to the English-speaking world.

Mortley, Raoul. *French Philosophers in Conversation: Levinas, Schneider, Serres, Irigaray, Le Doeuff, Derrida.* Routledge 1991 $42.50. ISBN 0-415-05254-8. A lively, interesting record of interviews; accessible to the nonspecialist.

Potts, D. C., and D. G. Charlton, eds. *French Thought since Sixteen Hundred.* Methuen 1974 o.p. The philosophical part of a multivolume work on French culture. Potts deals with the seventeenth- and eighteenth-century philosophers, Charlton with nineteenth- and twentieth-century French philosophy.

Smith, Colin. *Contemporary French Philosophy: A Study in Norms and Values.* Greenwood 1976 repr. of 1964 ed. o.p. A study of recent French thought by an Englishman who finds in it both an emphasis on values and a considerable amount of agreement.

Spink, John S. *French Free Thought from Gassendi to Voltaire.* Greenwood 1969 repr. of 1960 ed. $65.00. ISBN 0-8371-0663-X. A historical study of French thought from 1619 to 1751.

Wade, Ira O. *Intellectual Origins of the French Enlightenment.* Bks. Demand repr. of 1971 ed. $160.00. ISBN 0-8357-9501-2. An attempt to reveal the "true" Enlightenment. Concentrates on five freethinkers (Charron, La Mothe Le Vayer, Naude, Patin, and Sorbiere) and five philosophers (Malebranche, Leibniz, Locke, Newton, and Bayle).

GERMANY

Bubner, R. *Modern German Philosophy.* Trans. by Eric Matthews. Cambridge U. Pr. 1981 $19.95. ISBN 0-521-29711-7. The philosophers who stimulated the development of contemporary philosophy in Britain and America—Frege, Wittgenstein, the members of the Vienna Circle, Popper—also stimulated philosophy in Germany, influencing thought in numerous areas—phenomenology and hermeneutics, linguistic philosophy, dialectic, and theory of science, among others.

Christensen, Darrel E., and others, eds. *Contemporary German Philosophy.* 4 vols. Pa. St. U. Pr. 1982–85 o.p. Essays by contemporary German philosophers on topics of interest to them, including their predecessors. Includes reviews of book-length German philosophy.

Dewey, John. *German Philosophy and Politics. Select Bibliographies Repr. Ser.* Ayer repr. of 1915 ed. $12.50. ISBN 0-8369-5552-8. An analysis of German character occasioned by World War I, by a famous American philosopher. Argues for a dualism in the German psyche and in philosophy. Analyses of Kant, Fichte, and Hegel.

Mueller-Vollmer, Kurt, ed. *The Hermeneutics Reader: Texts of the German Tradition from the Enlightenment to the Present.* Continuum 1989 $19.95. ISBN 0-8264-0402-2. Selections from major figures, with a primary emphasis on the relation of hermeneutics to human language, art, history, and the human and social sciences.

Roberts, Julian. *German Philosophy: An Introduction.* Humanities 1988 $45.00. ISBN 0-391-03567-3. Includes chapters devoted to the thought of Kant, Hegel, Schelling, Schopenhauer, Feuerbach, Kierkegaard, Nietzsche, Lukacs, Heidegger, and Adorno.

———. *The Logic of Reflection: German Philosophy in the Twentieth Century.* Yale U. Pr. 1992 $30.00. ISBN 0-300-05207-3. Devotes major chapters to explicating the thought of Frege, Wittgenstein, Husserl, and Habermas.

Santayana, George. *Egotism in German Philosophy. Studies in German Lit.* Haskell 1971 repr. of 1916 ed. $75.00. ISBN 0-8383-1318-3. A polemic. Somewhat dubious philosophically. Occasioned, like Dewey's work (above), by World War I. Santayana finds German philosophy infected by what we would now term "megalomania."

Stegmueller, Wolfgang. *Main Currents in Contemporary German, British, and American Philosophy.* Kluwer Ac. rev. ed. 1969 $93.00. ISBN 90-277-0011-7. A careful and valuable work that assesses not only the contributions of German philosophy to the contemporary world—Kant, Brentano, Husserl, Scheler, Heidegger, Jaspers, N. Hartmann—but also the Austrian contribution—that of Wittgenstein, Carnap, and the Vienna Circle. American philosophy is discussed via Hempel, Oppenheim, Quine, Feigl, Goodman, Pap, and Stevenson; the British are represented by Russell, Broad, and Hare. Deepens one's appreciation of the debt contemporary philosophy owes to this part of its European background.

GREAT BRITAIN

Burtt, Edwin A., ed. *The English Philosophers from Bacon to Mill.* Modern Lib. 1939 $17.95. ISBN 0-394-60411-3. A well-crafted anthology, bringing together the principal works of the British empiricists, most of them in full.

Easthope, Anthony. *British Post-Structuralism: Since 1968.* Routledge 1988 $55.00. ISBN 0-415-00325-3. Considers not only philosophy but also film theory, musicology, art history, and literary theory. Also includes chapters on cultural studies, the social sciences, historical studies, and psychology. An appendix records an interview with Jacques Derrida.

Formigari, Lia. *Language and Experience in Seventeenth Century British Philosophy.* Benjamins North Am. 1988 $42.00. ISBN 90-272-4531-2. Beginning with Francis Bacon and the Renaissance linguistic tradition, focuses attention on the nature of language, the foundations of grammar, communication, semantics, semiotic logic, and the theory of meaning.

Grote, Harriet. *Philosophical Radicals of 1832.* B. Franklin 1967 repr. of 1866 ed. o.p. A classic, detailing the views of the utilitarian philosophers, especially in relation to the English Reform Bills of the 1830s.

Land, Stephen K. *The Philosophy of Language in Britain: Major Themes from Hobbes to Thomas Reid.* AMS Pr. 1986 $39.50. ISBN 0-404-61722-0. A study of eighteenth-century British approaches to language. Gives special attention to five theories of meaning that are of both historical and contemporary interest.

Levy, Paul. *Moore: G. E. Moore and the Cambridge Apostles.* OUP 1981 repr. of 1979 ed. o.p. A biography and analysis of the life and thoughts of the British philosopher G. E. Moore, including his relationship to the Apostles, a Cambridge intellectual society.

Morris, George S. *British Thought and Thinkers: From John of Salisbury and Roger Bacon to John Stuart Mill and Herbert Spencer.* Gordon Pr. 1977 $59.95. ISBN 0-8490-1557-X. A survey of British thought from the twelfth to the nineteenth century.

Muirhead, John H. *Platonic Tradition in Anglo-Saxon Philosophy. Muirhead Lib. of Philosophy.* Humanities repr. of 1931 ed. o.p. A discussion of the idealistic elements in British and American thought from the Cambridge Platonists through Bradley and Royce. Concludes with an assessment of "what is dead and what is alive in idealism."

GREECE (MODERN)

Cavarnos, Constantine. *Modern Greek Philosophers on the Human Soul.* Inst. Byzantine 1987 repr. of 1967 ed. $6.95. ISBN 0-914744-77-1. A contemporary Greek philosopher finds Platonic themes in modern Greek thought.

————. *Modern Greek Thought.* Inst. Byzantine 1986 repr. of 1969 ed. $5.95. ISBN 0-914744-11-9. An essay discussing the thought of Greek philosophers from the eighteenth century to the present.

ITALY

Baron, Hans. *In Search of Florentine Civic Humanism: Essays on the Transition from Medieval to Modern Thought.* 2 vols. Princeton U. Pr. 1988. Vol. 1 $37.50. ISBN 0-

691-05512-2. Vol. 2 $32.50. ISBN 0-691-05513-0. A collection of essays systematically examining the origins of important Florentine concepts and attitudes and the ways in which they evolved from the age of Petrarch to the time of Machiavelli.

Iorio, Dominick A. *The Aristotelians of Renaissance Italy: A Philosophical Exposition.* E. Mellen 1992 $69.95. ISBN 0-7734-9697-1. Beginning with a discussion of theological influences, traces a variety of medieval philosophical influences on both major and minor thinkers of the Italian Renaissance.

Kristeller, Paul O. *Eight Philosophers of the Italian Renaissance.* Stanford U. Pr. 1964 $25.00. ISBN 0-8047-0110-5. Concise discussions of the thought of eight major Renaissance humanists, from Petrarch to Bruno.

Vico, Giambattista. *On the Most Ancient Wisdom of the Italians: Unearthed from the Origins of the Latin Language.* Trans. by L. M. Palmer. Cornell Univ. Pr. 1988 $31.50. ISBN 0-8014-1280-3. An evaluation of the work of Descartes growing out of a discussion of the nature and truth of the sciences, followed by the author's own consideration of a full range of standard philosophical topics.

POLAND

Jordan, Z. A. *Philosophy and Ideology: The Development of Philosophy and Marxism-Leninism in Poland since the Second World War.* Sovietica Ser. Kluwer Ac. 1963 $84.50. ISBN 90-277-0054-0. Traces the rise, hegemony, and partial decline of Marxism-Leninism in Poland. Begins, despite the subtitle, with the development of Marxism from World War I. Part I, titled *Philosophy between the Two Wars*, details the rise of several schools of Polish philosophy that, following a political decree in 1956, were reduced to the single school of Marxism-Leninism. As the Polish logicians and philosophers criticized the shoddy logic of the official viewpoint, intellectual space appeared, allowing competing schools once more.

Walicki, Andrzej. *Philosophy and Romantic Nationalism: The Case of Poland.* OUP 1982 o.p. An assessment of the influence of Hegelian idealism and French revolutionary thought on mid–nineteenth-century Poland, leading to "romantic nationalism" by an expert on Russian and Slavic thought. The dissolution of this position after 1848 leads him to examine the views of Marx and Engels on the Polish question.

RUSSIA

Adelmann, F. J. *Philosophical Investigations in the U.S.S.R.* Boston College Studies in Philosophy. Kluwer Ac. 1975 $42.50. ISBN 90-247-1724-8. A compilation of the work of contemporary Soviet philosophers.

Bakhurst, David. *Consciousness and Revolution in Soviet Philosophy: From the Bolsheviks to Evald Ilyenkov.* Cambridge U. Pr. 1991 $49.50. ISBN 0-521-38534-2. Devotes major chapters to Vygotsky, Lenin, and Ilyenkov as well as to the relations among these and lesser figures.

Ballestrem, K. G. *Russian Philosophical Terminology.* Sovietica Ser. Kluwer Ac. 1965 $38.50. ISBN 90-277-0036-2. As a tool to aid in the interpretation of Russian philosophy, provides English, French, and German equivalents of Russian terms.

Blakeley, T. J. *Soviet Philosophy: A General Introduction to Contemporary Soviet Thought.* Sovietica Ser. Kluwer Ac. 1965 $38.00. ISBN 90-277-0036-2. Sets forth, often in catalog form, Soviet positions on matter, thought, psychology, logic, historical materialism, ethics, aesthetics, atheism, and the history of philosophy, in addition to the dialectical method.

———. *Soviet Scholasticism.* Sovietica Ser. Kluwer Ac. 1961 o.p. An analysis of Soviet philosophical method by a Western Sovietologist as not dialectic at all but hypothetico-deductive. Soviet positions become hypotheses from which testable consequences are to be deduced. The book was vigorously attacked in the Soviet press.

———, ed. *Themes in Soviet Marxist Philosophy: Selected Articles from the Sovietskaja Enciklopedija.* Sovietica Ser. Kluwer Ac. 1975 o.p. Philosophy articles selected from the *Soviet Encyclopedia*, providing an overview of Marxist philosophy.

Bochenski, I. M. *The Dogmatic Principles of Soviet Philosophy (as of 1958): Synopsis of Osnovy Marksistkoj Filosofii.* Trans. by T. J. Blakeley. *Sovietica Ser.* Greenwood 1963 $16.00. ISBN 0-313-23490-6. In 78 pages, summarizes the theses of the 1958 "official" text of Soviet-Marxist philosophy.

———. *Soviet Russian Dialectical Materialism.* Trans. by Nicholas Sollohub. Rev. by T. J. Blakeley. Kluwer Ac. rev. ed. 1963 o.p. A two-part analysis, the first historical, the second systematic.

Bochenski, I. M., and T. J. Blakeley, eds. *Studies in Soviet Thought. Sovietica Ser.* Kluwer Ac. 1961 o.p. Cooperative volume by the Bochenski "Sovietologists," surveying Marxist-Leninist views on logic, East-West ideological conflict, and the state of Polish and Czech philosophy in the post-World War II period.

Dobrolyubov, N. A. *Selected Philosophical Russian Contemporary Essays.* Inst. Econ. Pol. 1985 o.p. A volume extending the historical analyses of this section to the mid-1980s.

Edie, James M., and others. *Russian Philosophy.* 3 vols. U. of Tenn. Pr. 1976 repr. of 1965 ed. $14.95 ea. ISBNs 0-87049-200-4, 0-87049-715-4, 0-87049-716-2. A historical anthology of works of Russian thinkers especially translated for this publication.

Gavin, William J., and T. J. Blakeley. *Russia and America: A Philosophical Comparison. Sovietica Ser.* Kluwer Ac. 1976 $46.50. ISBN 90-277-0749-9. Finds Russia and America pragmatic as well as mystical, with a frontier mentality and a tolerance for ambiguity. Pairs the thinking of various Russian and American philosophers.

Laszlo, E., ed. *Philosophy in the Soviet Union: A Survey of the Mid-Sixties. Sovietica Ser.* Kluwer Ac. 1967 $41.50. ISBN 90-277-0057-5. Essentially an update of the material in the Bochenski and Wetter books; essays on Soviet thought by Western specialists connected with the Fribourg Institute of East European Studies.

Leatherbarrow, William J., and D. C. Offord, eds. *A Documentary History of Russian Thought: From the Enlightenment to Marxism.* Ardis Pubs. 1987 $18.95. ISBN 0-87501-019-9. A collection of readings grouped into sections on gentry revolutionaries and conservatives, early Russian idealism, Belinsky and Herzen, liberal Westernizers, polemics of the 1850s and 1860s, and revolutionary populism.

Lossky, Nicholas O. *History of Russian Philosophy.* Intl. Univs. Pr. 1969 repr. of 1951 ed. $45.00. ISBN 0-8236-2340-8. A history of Russian philosophy by a pioneer Russian theologian and philosopher.

Planty-Bonjour, G. *The Categories of Dialectical Materialism: Contemporary Soviet Ontology.* Trans. by T. J. Blakeley. *Sovietica Ser.* Kluwer Ac. 1967 $38.00. ISBN 90-277-0064-8. An examination of Soviet philosophy from the death of Stalin. Planty-Bonjour finds the dialectic a barrier preventing progress in Soviet thought.

Shein, Louis J., ed. and trans. *Readings in Russian Philosophical Thought.* Mouton 1977 $21.35. ISBN 90-279-2511-9. Includes notes and an introductory chapter by Shein.

Somerville, John. *Soviet Philosophy: A Study of Theory and Practice.* Greenwood 1968 repr. of 1946 ed. o.p. An introduction to Soviet philosophy by a sympathetic American philosopher. In addition to the usual topics, includes a chapter on the teaching of philosophy in the Soviet Union.

Swiderski, Edward M., ed. *Philosophical Foundations of Soviet Aesthetics. Sovietica Ser.* Kluwer Ac. 1979 $63.50. ISBN 90-277-0980-7. An analysis of Socialist realism both as a theory and as a guide to practice.

Wetter, Gustav A. *Dialectical Materialism.* Trans. by Peter Heath. Greenwood 1973 repr. of 1959 ed. o.p. An analysis of dialectical materialism by a German scholar who considers the doctrine apart from political implications, utilizing only Soviet writings.

———. *Soviet Ideology. Westview Encore Ed. Ser.* 1985 o.p. A study of Soviet philosophy considering the topics of dialectical materialism, historical materialism, and capitalism. As in the earlier work (above), Wetter's neo-Thomism is sometimes obtrusive.

SCANDINAVIA

Olson, Raymond E., and Anthony M. Paul, eds. *Contemporary Philosophy in Scandinavia.* Bks. Demand repr. of 1972 ed. $135.20. ISBN 0-318-34950-7. A set of essays by

Scandinavian philosophers detailing the contemporary situation in Scandinavian philosophy. The historical section goes back to Kierkegaard and includes the impact of Niels Bohr.

Skirbekk, Gunnar, ed. *Praxeology: An Anthology.* Universitet 1984 o.p. A collection of essays turning on the idea of practice by Scandinavian (mostly Norwegian) philosophers. Wittgenstein and philosophy of action are evident influences in these essays ranging from aesthetics to politics.

SCOTLAND

Broadie, Alexander. *The Tradition of Scottish Philosophy: A New Perspective on the Enlightenment.* Rowman 1990 $48.25. ISBN 0-389-20921-X. Attempts to link pre-Reformation thought with philosophical developments during the Enlightenment. The author finds Francis Hutcheson, David Hume, Thomas Reid, and Adam Smith to be dominant figures.

Bryson, Gladys. *Man and Society: The Scottish Inquiry of the Eighteenth Century.* Kelley 1968 repr. of 1945 ed. $37.50. ISBN 0-678-00373-4. Discussion of the eighteenth-century Scottish school of moral philosophers, including Adam Smith and David Hume, which led in the direction of social science.

Grave, S. A. *The Scottish Philosophy of Common Sense.* Greenwood 1973 repr. of 1960 ed. $35.00. ISBN 0-8371-6539-3. An exposition of the philosophy of common sense from its rise with Thomas Reid to its demise at the hands of John Stuart Mill. Topics treated are skepticism, common sense, natural signs, sensations, personal identity, morality, and free will.

Hope, Vincent, ed. *Philosophers of the Scottish Enlightenment.* Col. U. Pr. 1984 $24.00. ISBN 0-85224-477-0. A set of essays on Scottish philosophy in its best-known period, many by philosophers teaching in Scotland.

Johnston, G. A., ed. *Selections from the Scottish Philosophy of Common Sense.* Open Court 1915 o.p. Selections from Thomas Reid, Adam Ferguson, James Beattie, and David Stewart, all of whom were responding to David Hume.

Jones, Peter, ed. *Philosophy and Science in the Scottish Enlightenment.* Humanities 1988 $60.00. ISBN 0-85976-225-4. A collection of essays by a variety of scholars discussing figures from Thomas Reid to the Reverend John Walker and Sir James Stewart. Topics range from natural law, skepticism, and the philosophy of mind to the nature of scientific change and controversies over chemical reactivity and heat.

McCosh, James. *The Scottish Philosophy, Biographical, Expository, Critical, from Hutcheson to Hamilton. Philosophy in Amer. Ser.* AMS Pr. 1980 repr. of 1875 ed. o.p. A comprehensive and classic study of philosophy in Scotland from the end of the seventeenth century to the mid-nineteenth century.

Martin, Terence. *Instructed Vision: Scottish Common Sense Philosophy and the Origins of American Fiction.* Kraus repr. of 1961 ed. $16.00. ISBN 0-527-61950-7. (See under "United States" in this section.)

Robinson, Daniel S., ed. *The Story of Scottish Philosophy: A Compendium of Selections from the Writings of Nine Pre-eminent Scottish Philosophers, with Biobibliographical Essays.* Greenwood 1979 repr. of 1961 ed. $38.50. ISBN 0-313-21082-9. Selections from the writings of the luminaries making up the Scottish Enlightenment, with a foreword by Perry E. Gresham.

Seth, Andrew. *Scottish Philosophy. The Philosophy of David Hume Ser.* Garland 1983 $10.00. ISBN 0-8240-5417-2. A classic analysis accomplished through comparisons of Hume and Reid, Reid and Kant, Kant and Hamilton, Scottish philosophy and Hegel.

Stewart, M. A., ed. *Studies in the Philosophy of the Scottish Enlightenment.* OUP 1990 $79.00. ISBN 0-19-824967-5. Chapters on Francis Hutcheson, David Hume, and George Berkeley; general articles on the period; and essays tracing the development of the Aberdeen and Edinburgh schools of thought.

Markovic, Mihailo, and Gajo Petrovic, eds. *Praxis. Boston Studies in the Philosophy of Science.* Kluwer Ac. 1979 $101.50. ISBN 90-277-0727-8. Although ostensibly about the social sciences, these essays by members of a Yugoslavian group called "Praxis" discuss how to make philosophy practical—that is, a matter of practice (*praxis*).

Latin America

Davis, Harold E. *Latin American Thought: A Historical Introduction.* La. State U. Pr. 1972 $32.50. ISBN 0-8071-0249-0. A balanced analysis of Latin American thought, largely but not exclusively philosophical, from pre-Conquest to the present.

Gracia, Jorge J., and Mireya Camurati, eds. *Philosophy and Literature in Latin America: A Critical Assessment of the Current Situation.* State U. NY Pr. 1989 $59.50. ISBN 0-7914-0038-7. Discussions of the contemporary philosophical environment in a number of Latin American countries by various scholars, with particular attention to Argentina, Brazil, and Mexico. Most of this volume is devoted to literary figures and issues, however.

Haddox, John H. *Antonio Caso: Philosopher of Mexico. Texas Pan-Amer. Ser.* Bks. Demand repr. of 1971 ed. $37.00. ISBN 0-8357-7742-1. The life and thought of a major twentieth-century Mexican philosopher, with selections from his writings.

Lipp, Solomon. *Three Argentine Thinkers.* Humanities 1969 o.p. Analyses of the views of José Ingenieros, Alejandro Korn, and Francisco Romero.

_____. *Three Chilean Thinkers.* Humanities 1975 o.p. Analyses of the views of Francisco Bilbao, Valentin Letelier, and Enrique Molina.

Philosophical Thought in America. 3 vols. OAS 1971–76 o.p. Very brief overviews of major Latin American thinkers.

Romanell, Patrick. *Making of the Mexican Mind: A Study in Recent Mexican Thought. Essay Index Repr. Ser.* Ayer 1977 repr. of 1952 ed. $16.00. ISBN 0-8369-1189-X. Not only provides a history of Mexican thought, including analyses of Antonio Caso and José Vasconcelos, but also describes the impact on Mexico of such figures as Comte, Bergson, Ortega, and the existentialist philosophers. With a foreword by E. S. Brightman.

Vento, Arnold C. *El Hijo Prodijo: A Critical Index of Twentieth-Century Mexican Thought.* Pajarito Pubns. 1978 $5.00. ISBN 0-918358-06-X. A guide to the resources available in recent Mexican thought.

Weinstein, Michael A. *The Polarity of Mexican Thought.* Pa. State U. Pr. 1977 o.p. Finds in Mexican philosophy a polarity between instrumentalism and finalism, depending on whether values are viewed as means or ends. Along the way the major Mexican philosophers are discussed.

Zea, Leopoldo. *Latin American Mind.* Trans. by James H. Abbott and Lowell Dunham. U. of Okla. Pr. 1970 o.p. This important Mexican philosopher traces the rise of Latin American positivism, following Comte, as a reaction to earlier Latin American philosophies.

United States

American philosophy overlaps the periods of modern and contemporary philosophy. The originators of pragmatism, the principal figures of American philosophy, are treated in Chapters 6 and 7 in this volume. This section lists the general works dealing with the entire area.

Ames, Van Meter. *Zen and American Thought.* Greenwood 1978 repr. of 1962 ed. $35.00. ISBN 0-313-20066-1. An American philosopher discusses the similarities between Zen Buddhism and American thought, going back to Jonathan Edwards and proceeding as far as John Dewey.

Anderson, Paul R., and Max H. Fisch. *Philosophy in America from Puritans to James.* Hippocrene Bks. 1969 o.p. An anthology of American philosophy to 1900, accompanied by analyses and notes.

Beaumont, Ernest V. *The Intellectual Cowardice of the American Philosophers.* Am. Classical Coll. Pr. 1980 $69.75. A criticism of American philosophy based on its aloofness from social issues.

Bertocci, Peter A., ed. *Mid-Twentieth Century American Philosophy: Personal Statements.* Humanities 1974 o.p. Essays by 15 American philosophers in their sixties, invited to sum up their wisdom.

Caws, Peter, ed. *Two Centuries of Philosophy: American Philosophy since the Revolution—Papers from the Bicentennial Symposium. Amer. Philosophical Quarterly Lib. of Philosophy.* Rowman 1980 o.p. An overall assessment of American philosophy by a representative group of contemporary philosophers on the occasion of the nation's bicentennial.

Edwards, Rem B. *A Return to Moral and Religious Philosophy in Early America.* U. Pr. of Amer. 1982 o.p. An in-depth examination of the thought of Jonathan Edwards, Thomas Jefferson, and Ralph Waldo Emerson, with a view to rediscovering "America in its moral, religious and intellectual dimensions."

Farber, Marvin, ed. *Philosophic Thought in France and the United States: Essays Representing Major Trends in Contemporary French and American Philosophy.* Bks. Demand repr. of 1968 ed. $160.00. ISBN 0-317-09067-4. Nearly 40 well-known philosophers discuss the major trends in French and American philosophy.

Fisch, Max H., ed. *Classic American Philosophers.* P-H 1966 $26.95. ISBN 0-13-135186-9. A classic anthology of selected writings from the work of Peirce, James, Royce, Santayana, Dewey, and Whitehead. Introductory essays by Fisch, Burns, Henley, Kraushaar, Rice, Kennedy, and Lowe.

Gabriel, Ralph H. *American Values: Continuity and Change. Contributions in Amer. Studies.* Greenwood 1974 $35.00. ISBN 0-8371-7355-8. Believing the values of a people to be revealed in times of crisis, Gabriel seeks those expressed by American leaders. Writing in the 1950s and 1960s, he suggests that mid–twentieth-century America may represent the "New Enlightenment."

Gavin, William J., and T. J. Blakeley. *Russia and America: A Philosophical Comparison. Sovietica Ser.* Kluwer Ac. 1976 $46.50. ISBN 90-277-0749-9. (See under "Europe (General), Russia" in this section.)

Goodman, Russell B. *American Philosophy and the Romantic Tradition.* Cambridge U. Pr. 1990 $37.95. ISBN 0-521-39443-0. Gives primary attention to the thought of Ralph Waldo Emerson, William James, and John Dewey.

Hartshorne, Charles. *Creativity in American Philosophy.* State U. NY Pr. 1984 $49.50. ISBN 0-83795-816-0. From his own base in process thought, Hartshorne comes to terms with practically the whole of American philosophy. The final chapters deal with some of the younger philosophers, such as Rorty, Neville, and Nozick.

Hook, Sidney. *American Philosophers at Work: The Philosophic Scene in the United States.* Greenwood 1968 repr. of 1956 ed. o.p. A mid-century sampling of American philosophy, bringing together representative essays on logic, scientific method, metaphysics, theory of knowledge, ethics, and social philosophy.

Jones, Adam L. *Early American Philosophers.* Continuum 1958 o.p. Analysis of the initial stages of American philosophy.

Kallen, Horace M., and Sidney Hook, eds. *American Philosophy Today and Tomorrow. Essay Index Repr. Ser.* Irvington 1982 repr. of 1935 ed. $20.00. ISBN 0-686-79689-6. Twenty-five representative American thinkers present a cross section of American philosophical thought in the mid-1930s.

Kolenda, Konstantin, ed. *Person and Community in American Philosophy.* Rice Univ. 1981 o.p. A cooperative volume turning on themes of self, society, and community. Essays explicating the views of classical American philosophers, including Peirce, Royce, Santayana, William James, John Dewey, and G. H. Mead.

Kuklick, Bruce. *The Rise of American Philosophy.* Bks. Demand repr. of 1977 ed. $160.00. ISBN 0-8357-8310-3. Illuminates the "history of American thought as a whole" by means of the history of philosophy at Harvard "from the Civil War to the Great Depression." The writing is both lively and responsible.

MacKinnon, Barbara. *American Philosophy: A Historical Anthology*. State U. NY Pr. 1985 $59.50. ISBN 0-87395-922-1. A comprehensive anthology of American philosophy, its selections begin with the period of Puritanism and run to the present. Sections on Thomism, process philosophy, and phenomenology. Includes study questions.

Madden, Edward H. *Civil Disobedience and Moral Law in Nineteenth-Century American Philosophy*. U. of Wash. Pr. 1970 $9.00. ISBN 0-295-95070-6. An essay in ethics and politics. Madden demonstrates a tradition of civil disobedience theory in America long antedating Thoreau.

Martin, Terence. *Instructed Vision: Scottish Common Sense Philosophy and the Origins of American Fiction*. Kraus repr. of 1961 ed. $16.00. ISBN 0-527-61950-7. Argues that Scottish common sense philosophy, with its distrust of imaginative experience, influenced American fiction prior to the 1830s. Then the philosophical influence of Carlyle, Coleridge, Cousin, and Kant allowed an escape.

Miller, Perry G. *Errand into the Wilderness*. HUP 1956 $10.95. ISBN 0-674-26155-0. An interpretation of the sources of American life from the Puritans to Emerson by an expert in American studies.

———. *Nature's Nation*. HUP 1967 $24.95. ISBN 0-674-60550-0. A companion volume to the preceding entry. Discusses the building and development of America. The title refers to the nation's extension into the West.

Parrington, Vernon L. *Main Currents in American Thought*. 3 vols. U. of Okla. Pr. 1987 $32.95 ea. Vol. 1 *The Colonial Mind: 1620–1800*. ISBN 0-8061-2077-0. Vol. 2 *The Romantic Revolution in America: 1800-1860*. ISBN 0-8061-2078-9. Vol. 3 *The Beginnings of Critical Realism in America: 1860–1920*. ISBN 0-8061-2079-7. Detailed, extensive treatments of background influences on American thought. Includes discussions of both major and minor figures and movements.

Perry, Ralph B. *Philosophy of the Recent Past: An Outline of European and American Philosophy since 1860*. AMS Pr. 1982 repr. of 1926 ed. $29.00. ISBN 0-404-59295-3. A discussion of philosophy after Schopenhauer, extending into the 1920s. Organized around the positions of naturalism, idealism, pragmatism, and realism.

Philosophy in America. 204 vols. AMS Pr. 1982–86 o.p. A reprint series whose original publication dates reach from the latter part of the nineteenth century to the present. Covers psychology as well as philosophy. Includes works on such colonial figures as Jonathan Edwards and reprints of the British philosopher F.C.S. Schiller.

Riley, Isaac W. *American Thought from Puritanism to Pragmatism and Beyond: A Greenwood Archival Edition*. Greenwood 1970 repr. of 1923 ed. o.p. A history of American philosophy from Puritanism to critical realism, with a chapter on French influences—Cousin, Comte, and Bergson.

Rorty, Richard. *Consequences of Pragmatism: Essays 1972–80*. U. of Minn. Pr. 1982 o.p. Probes the interrelationships of established philosophies. Analytic philosophy loses its dominance, and pragmatism is America's most important contribution to human culture.

Schneider, Herbert W. *A History of American Philosophy*. Bks. Demand repr. of 1969 ed. $52.00. ISBN 0-8357-9065-7. A comprehensive history of American philosophy as part of cultural history.

———. *Sources of Contemporary Philosophical Realism in America*. Irvington 1964 $6.95. ISBN 0-672-60282-2. A discussion of critical realism in America. Includes a bibliography.

Shahan, Robert W., and Kenneth R. Merrill, eds. *American Philosophy: From Edwards to Quine*. U. of Okla. Pr. 1977 o.p. Selections from American philosophers from the eighteenth century until the present.

Smith, John E. *America's Philosophical Vision*. U. Ch. Pr. 1992 $39.95. ISBN 0-226-76367-6. Essays on the contributions of Peirce, James, Royce, and Dewey to important themes in American philosophical thought.

_____. *The Spirit of American Philosophy*. State U. NY Pr. 1982 o.p. Discusses Peirce, James, Royce, Dewey, and Whitehead. Santayana is omitted as "outside the main drift."

_____, ed. *Contemporary American Philosophy*. Bks. Demand repr. of 1970 ed. $88.00. ISBN 0-317-20049-6. A set of essays from 1970 by well-known American philosophers on their work.

Smith, Thomas V. *Philosophic Way of Life in America*. Assoc. Faculty Pr. 1968 repr. of 1943 ed. o.p. Appreciations of Royce, James, Dewey, and Santayana, to which is added Smith's own appreciation of legislative process and the way of compromise.

Stuhr, John J., ed. *Classical American Philosophy: Essential Readings and Interpretive Essays*. OUP 1987 $24.50. ISBN 0-19-504198-4. Offers general introductions to the thought of Peirce, James, Royce, Santayana, Dewey, and Mead as well as a variety of excerpts from their writings.

Townsend, H. G. *Philosophical Ideas in the United States*. 1934. Hippocrene Bks. 1968 $20.00. ISBN 0-374-97961-8. Surveys American philosophy from colonial times to John Dewey. Includes discussions of empiricism, pluralism, realism, and naturalism.

Weinstein, Michael A. *The Wilderness and the City: American Classical Philosophy as a Moral Quest*. U. of Mass. Pr. 1982 $22.50. ISBN 0-87023-375-0. Treating Royce, Peirce, James, Dewey, and Santayana, the author conducts an "inquest" into "what is still vital" in the American philosophical tradition. Argues for a "modern individualism" beyond that of pragmatism.

Werkmeister, William H. *A History of Philosophical Ideas in America*. Greenwood 1981 repr. of 1949 ed. o.p. A comprehensive history of American philosophy from Puritanism to logical empiricism, naturalism, and the humanism of the 1940s.

White, Morton. *The Philosophy of the American Revolution*. Amer. Social Thought Ser. OUP 1978 o.p. Reflections on the philosophy underlying the American Revolution. Includes such topics as self-evident truths, laws of nature, human rights, and "rebellion to tyrants." Discusses Locke, Hooker, Rousseau.

_____. *Science and Sentiment in America: Philosophical Thought from Jonathan Edwards to John Dewey*. OUP 1972 o.p. A history of philosophy relating philosophy to questions of general culture. Shows the extent to which American philosophers historically have gone far beyond philosophy as a technical pursuit.

_____, ed. *Documents in the History of American Philosophy: From Jonathan Edwards to John Dewey*. OUP 1972 o.p. Selections from American philosophers from the eighteenth through the middle of the twentieth century.

Wills, Gary, ed. *Values Americans Live By*. Ayer 1974 $25.00. ISBN 0-405-04166-7. A collaborative volume prospecting for American values.

Winn, Ralph B., ed. *Survey of American Philosophy*. Quality Pap. Ser. Littlefield 1965 repr. of 1955 ed. $7.25. ISBN 0-8226-0162-1. A cooperative volume on the fields and problems of American philosophy.

COMPARATIVE PHILOSOPHY

Some titles of this nature have already appeared: comparisons of American and British philosophy, for example, in the preceding section. In this section are works comparing three or more areas, as well as general comparisons of Eastern and Western philosophy. From that beginning there is the possible move toward world philosophy, an area pioneered by John Plott. And, in one way of looking at it, the most general area would be a philosophy relating to preservation of the ecosystem itself.

Recently, philosophers have begun to compare the Western philosophical tradition with perspectives that have been slighted, if not entirely ignored, by traditional thinkers. In this connection, SANDRA HARDING argues that Western patterns of thinking are dominated by a male bias, one that needs to be balanced by a feminist perspective; JOHN HICK, that Western philosophy has been influenced too exclusively by the Judeo-Christian tradition; and PETER SINGER, that Western thought is too anthropocentric.

East-West

Agera, Cassian R. *Faith, Prayer and Grace: A Comparative Study in Ramanuja and Kierkegaard.* South Asia Bks. 1987 $25.00. ISBN 0-8364-2347-X. Includes detailed expositions of faith as Bhakti; prayer as contemplation; and grace as availability, giving, and self-communication. Also discusses the relation of offense to commitment and piety to the awareness of presence.

Bowes, Pratima. *Between Cultures.* South Asia Bks. 1987 $24.00. ISBN 0-317-59369-2. Takes a contrasting world-views approach to the relation between Western and Indian philosophical perspectives. Includes discussions of logic, epistemology, philosophy of science, social and political values, ethics, and aesthetics.

Dilworth, David. *Philosophy in World Perspective: A Comparative Hermeneutic of the Major Theories.* Yale U. Pr. 1989 $28.00. ISBN 0-300-04357-0. Includes a general discussion of hermeneutics, followed by a consideration of themes from ancient Greek and Chinese thought. Major chapters are devoted to Confucian philosophy, modern Western philosophy, and world religions.

Herman, A. L., and R. T. Blackwood, eds. *Problems in Philosophy: West and East.* P-H 1975 o.p. An anthology of readings that can serve equally well as an introduction to philosophy in general and to comparative philosophy. Selections—on metaphysics, epistemology, theology, and ethics—pair readings from Western and Eastern sources.

Moore, Charles A. *Philosophy and Culture, East and West: East-West Philosophy in Practical Perspective.* UH Pr. 1962 o.p. A cooperative volume in which philosophers from East and West are paired in discussing the relation of philosophy and science to practice and the prospect for world understanding.

———. *Philosophy: East and West.* Essay Index Reprint Ser. Ayer 1977 repr. of 1944 ed. $24.50. ISBN 0-8369-1677-8. Essays by philosophers from East and West prospecting for a "world philosophy."

Nakamura, Hajime. *A Comparative History of Ideas.* Routledge Chapman & Hall 1986 $65.00. ISBN 0-7103-0122-7. An Asian perspective on key problems common to the history of both Eastern and Western thought.

Scharfstein, Ben-Ami, ed. *Philosophy East-Philosophy West: A Critical Comparison of Indian, Chinese, Islamic and European Philosophy.* OUP 1978 o.p. A cooperative but well-integrated volume by five experts in the field, making cross-cultural comparisons of India, China, and the West, followed by comparisons of Augustine, Descartes, and Shankara; al-Ashari and Spinoza; Kant and Nagarjuna; and others.

General Comparative

Burr, John R. *Handbook of World Philosophy: Contemporary Developments since 1945.* Greenwood 1980 $85.00. ISBN 0-313-22381-5. Provides information on philosophic thought and philosophers around the world since 1945.

Hatab, Lawrence J. *Myth and Philosophy: A Contest of Truths.* Open Court 1991 $34.95. ISBN 0-8126-9115-6. Interprets the historical relation of myth to philosophy in ancient Greece. Argues for the intelligibility of myth and for a pluralistic notion of truth.

Hutchison, John A. *Living Options in World Philosophy.* UH Pr. 1977 $16.00. ISBN 0-8248-0455-4. Argues for the possibility of a single world-context, and discusses philosophies from both the Western and Eastern worlds in pointing toward that possibility.

McDermott, Charlene, ed. *Comparative Philosophy: Selected Essays.* U. Pr. of Amer. 1983 $29.00. ISBN 0-8191-3487-2. A cooperative volume on the possibilities and problems of comparative philosophy.

Raju, P. T. *Introduction to Comparative Philosophy.* S. Ill. U. Pr. 1970 $9.95. ISBN 0-8093-0419-8. A comparative analysis of philosophy discussing similarities and differences in three great traditions—Western, Chinese, and Indian—by a well-known Indian philosopher who has long taught in the United States.

Ruf, Henry L. *Investigating Philosophy: A Holistic Introduction to Its Heritage, Traditions and Practices.* U. Pr. of Amer. 1987 o.p. Discusses Western as well as Eastern quests for metaphysically ultimate realities, epistemological foundations, and religious and social harmony.

Stunkel, Kenneth R. *Relations of Indian, Greek and Christian Thought in Antiquity.* U. Pr. of Amer. 1979 o.p.

World Philosophy. 5 vols. Salem Pr. 1982 $250.00. ISBN 0-89356-325-0. Analyses of 225 major works in philosophy, from East and West, to which are added reviews of scholarly discussions of these works. The analyses run three to five pages and the reviews one to two pages.

Zinn, William V. *The Global Philosophy.* Vantage 1983 o.p. Zinn considers the possibilities for an approach to philosophy in global terms.

Ecophilosophy

Skolimowski, Henryk. *Eco-Philosophy.* M. Boyars Pubs. 1981 o.p. Argues that both analytic philosophy and science have lost "values" while concentrating on fact. Promotes an ecological approach to the world, one sensitive to values and consistent with both the sciences and religious aspiration.

CHRONOLOGY OF AUTHORS

Schilpp, Paul Arthur. 1897–
Copleston, Frederick Charles. 1907–
Hick, John Harwood. 1922–

Harding, Sandra G. 1935–
Singer, Peter Albert David. 1946–

COPLESTON, FREDERICK CHARLES. 1907–

Born in Taunton, England, Frederick Copleston received his M.A. from Oxford University and his Ph.D. from the Pontifical Gregorian University in Rome. He entered the Society of Jesus in 1930 and became an ordained priest in 1937. Throughout his academic career, he has remained committed to his Roman Catholic faith, a commitment that is apparent, but not objectionably obtrusive, in his writing and his treatment of philosophical issues. Focusing primarily on the history of philosophy, Copleston has taught at various universities in England, Italy, and the United States. His published work includes individual volumes on such major philosophers as FRIEDRICH NIETZSCHE (see also Vol. 2) and ARTHUR SCHOPENHAUER. He also has written books devoted to particular movements, including logical positivism and existentialism, and has written on particular issues, including the relation of religion to philosophy and the relation of philosophy to culture. Sometimes he has concentrated his attention on specific geographical or social regions; his *Philosophy in Russia* (1988) reflects this latter approach. Not only has Copleston published numerous monographs, but also his writing has been excerpted and collected in everything from texts of introductory readings to volumes of essays about specialized, technical philosophical issues. Earlier in his career, Copleston sometimes found himself pitted in popular public debates against a famous advocate of atheism, BERTRAND RUSSELL (see also Vol. 5).

Among beginning philosophers and veterans alike, however, Copleston's most important academic contribution will forever remain his nine-volume *History of Philosophy* (1946–74). In his attempt to span the full sweep of Western philosophical development, Copleston starts with the pre-Socratics; in this, as in each successive volume, he devotes several hundred pages to a particular epoch in the history of Western philosophy, explaining dominant, representative figures as well as significant movements and covering each period and line of thought with extraordinary clarity. Generally, Copleston tries to reproduce the actual pattern of argument expressed in the writings of major philosophical figures, offering critical insights throughout the course of his exposition. Copleston's final volume brings his coverage of Western philosophy up through the writings of JEAN-PAUL SARTRE (see also Vol. 2).

Almost invariably, Copleston's discussions are fair, balanced, and faithful to the original text. Rarely innovative and never radical, his interpretations provide a standard, mainstream understanding of the growth of Western philosophy. Countless undergraduate philosophy majors and minors have used his work as their first toehold into the world of philosophy, shaping term papers and research projects by drawing on Copleston's interpretations and critiques. Because his understanding of the history of philosophy has been so widely respected for so long, even more advanced philosophers often find themselves checking their grasp of major figures or movements by reference to Copleston's work.

BOOKS BY COPLESTON

Aquinas. Viking Penguin 1956 $8.95. ISBN 0-14-02349-4. An exposition of the philosophy and theology of Thomas Aquinas. Includes a brief bibliography with notes.

A History of Medieval Philosophy. U. of Notre Dame Pr. 1990 $11.95. ISBN 0-268-01091-9. Includes chapters on Christian thought in the ancient world as well as on major medieval Christian writers. Additional chapters on Islamic and Jewish thought, political philosophy, and mysticism.

History of Philosophy. 1946–75. 9 vols. Vol. 1 *Greece and Rome.* Doubleday 1993 $15.00. ISBN 0-385-46843-1. Vol. 2 *Medieval Philosophy—Augustine to Scotus.* Doubleday 1993 $15.00. ISBN 0-385-46844-X. Vol. 3 *Ockham to Suarez.* Paulist Pr. 1976 $29.00. ISBN 0-8091-0067-3. Vols. 4–6 *Descartes to Leibniz, Hobbes to Hume, Wolff to Kant.* Doubleday 1985 $21.00. ISBN 0-385-23032-X. Vols. 7–9 *Fichte to Nietzsche, Bentham to Russell, Maine de Bira to Sartre.* Doubleday 1985 $24.95. ISBN 0-385-23033-8. Monumental and comprehensive look at philosophy and philosophers from the pre-Socratics to individuals and movements in twentieth-century Europe.

Medieval Philosophy. Bks. Demand repr. of 1952 ed. $50.00. ISBN 0-317-09453-X. A general survey that includes Islamic and Jewish thought as well as chapters on Thomas Aquinas and fourteenth-century philosophy. Devotes sections to Duns Scotus and Nicholas of Cusa.

Philosophies and Cultures. OUP 1980 $26.00. ISBN 0-19-213960-6. A comparative study of Western, Chinese, and Indian philosophy. Searches for patterns and laws in the history of philosophy.

Philosophy in Russia: From Herzen to Lenin and Berdyaev. U. of Notre Dame Pr. 1988 $15.95. ISBN 0-268-01569-4. Covers the development of Russian philosophical thought from the eighteenth century through the middle of the twentieth century. Emphasizes Marxism as well as religious thought.

HARDING, SANDRA G. 1935–

Born in San Francisco, Harding received her B.A. from Douglass College and both her M.A. and Ph.D. from New York University. She has held teaching positions in philosophy at the State University of New York at Albany and at the

University of Delaware, becoming director of women's studies at the University of Delaware in 1985. Early in her writing career, Harding's research was grounded in a fairly traditional approach to the philosophy of science. Over the years, however, she has become increasingly interested in the distorting influences of sexism and male bias. Although she is only one of a number of philosophers concerned with feminist issues and themes, Harding has ventured deeply into epistemological issues, offering a feminist critique of the very roots of Western thinking. Distinguished by a clear, forceful, and persuasive style, her more recent studies scrutinize the underlying motives driving the methods of the sciences.

BOOKS BY HARDING

Discovering Reality: Feminist Perspectives on Epistemology, Metaphysics, Methodology and Philosophy of Science. (ed.) Kluwer Ac. 1983 $19.00. ISBN 0-685-09564-9. A collection of feminist essays critical of the influence of masculine perspectives in philosophy. Suggests the possibility of developing alternative, feminist epistemologies and metaphysical positions.

The Science Question in Feminism. Cornell Univ. Pr. 1986 $11.95. ISBN 0-8014-9363-3. A survey of feminist critiques of science and scientific method. Discusses feminist empiricism and feminist postmodernism. Seeks more appropriate conceptions of scientific objectivity.

Whose Science? Whose Knowledge? Thinking from Women's Lives. Cornell Univ. Pr. 1991 $36.50. ISBN 0-8014-2513-1. Develops a feminist challenge to more traditional views of the natural sciences and epistemology.

HICK, JOHN HARWOOD. 1922–

Born in Scarborough, England, Hick received his D.Phil. from Oxford University. For several years he served as a Presbyterian minister in Northumberland, England, but soon moved to the United States, where he took a position teaching philosophy at Cornell University. He served as Stuart Professor of Christian Philosophy at Princeton Theological Seminary from 1959 to 1964. Since then he has held a variety of teaching positions in the United States and England. Throughout Hick's career, his main focus has remained on problems in the philosophy of religion. His numerous books, particularly those concerned with the epistemology of religious belief, are marked with a consistently clear and easily accessible style. For this reason, his writings have always been popular among professional philosophers and theologians, as well as among those who are more casually interested in the nature of religious belief or the place of religion in contemporary culture. In recent years, Hick has become more single-minded in his concern with the problem of religious pluralism. Convinced that Western philosophical and religious thought have been too narrowly shaped by preoccupation with the Judeo-Christian tradition, he argues for a broader, more ecumenical spirit.

BOOKS BY HICK

God Has Many Names. Westminster John Knox 1982 $10.99. ISBN 0-664-24419-X. A brief treatment of the recent rise of British pluralism. Discusses the influence on religious attitudes arising from Muslims, Hindus, Jews, Christians, and post-Christians trying to live and work together in British cities.

An Interpretation of Religion: Human Responses to the Transcendent. Yale U. Pr. 1989 $40.00. ISBN 0-300-04248-5. Surveys a variety of Eastern and Western religious traditions, seeking common bonds. Concludes that the world's major religions express different ways of affirming a transcendent reality.

Problems of Religious Pluralism. St. Martin 1985 $19.95. ISBN 0-312-65154-6. Argues for a
   pluralistic vision of the world's religions, whereby no single religious tradition
   represents the whole truth or the best way of approaching the transcendent.
Three Faiths—One God: A Jewish, Christian, Muslim Encounter. (coedited with Edmund
   S. Meltzer). State U. NY Pr. 1989 $59.50. ISBN 0-7914-0042-5. Twenty Christian,
   Jewish, and Muslim scholars contribute to topics ranging from the nature of God to
   earth and humanity. The significance of the land of Israel and the Christian doctrines
   of the Trinity and Incarnation are also considered.

SCHILPP, PAUL ARTHUR. 1897–

Born in Germany, Schilpp, in 1926, became a naturalized citizen of the United
States, where he was educated. He received his M.A. from Northwestern
University, his B.D. from Garrett Theological Seminary, and his Ph.D. from
Stanford University. After a few years as a Methodist minister, Schilpp served a
brief term as a professor of psychology and religious education at the College of
Puget Sound. From that time, however, he taught in the position of professor of
philosophy at various universities throughout the United States. From 1965 to
1980, he was Distinguished Research Professor in Philosophy at Southern
Illinois University at Carbondale.

Over the course of his career, Schilpp has published books on a diversity of
topics, including issues in higher education, theology, and the relation of
religion to science. Although he would like to be remembered as a teacher, his
most influential academic contribution has been his Library of Living Philosophers series, which now contains more than 20 volumes. Although the two most
recent volumes in this series, one on CHARLES HARTSHORNE and the other on SIR
ALFRED AYER, were edited by Lewis E. Hahn, Schilpp put together nearly all of
the earlier volumes without collaborative help.

The Library of Living Philosophers series was inspired by Schilpp's realization
that many past philosophers have been deeply misunderstood. In the hope of
fostering a better grasp of the thought of those prominent philosophers still
living, he planned each volume to include both expository and critical essays
written by scholarly academics about the work of some specific, active
philosopher. Then he asked the philosopher under discussion to formulate a
written reply to these interpretations and critiques. Whenever possible, Schilpp
also included an intellectual autobiography of the philosopher in question.
Finally, Schilpp prepared a relevant bibliography for each volume.

It may be debated, of course, whether Schilpp's strategy could ever provide
an effective antidote to the perennial penchant for misunderstanding among
practicing philosophers. Nevertheless, there can be little doubt that the
structured format of his Library of Living Philosophers series has been a fruitful
one. Schilpp's persuasive insistence that important philosophers interact within
an environment of carefully developed written exchanges has produced
permanent collections of valuable, and frequently innovative, philosophical
reflection.

BOOKS BY SCHILPP

Albert Einstein: Philosopher-Scientist. (ed.) *Library of Living Philosophers Ser.* Vol. 7 Open
   Court 1949 $54.95. ISBN 0-87548-133-7. Famous for his special and general theories
   of relativity, but also thought and wrote extensively on philosophical issues
   connected with the nature and development of scientific thought.
The Philosophy of Alfred North Whitehead. (ed.) *Library of Living Philosophers Ser.* Vol. 3
   Open Court 1951 $54.95. ISBN 0-87548-140-X. A major process philosopher who

wrote extensively in logic, epistemology, and the philosophy of science. His natural theology inspired the process theology of Charles Hartshorne.

The Philosophy of Bertrand Russell. (ed.) *Library of Living Philosophers Ser.* Vol. 5 Open Court 1971 $54.95. ISBN 0-87548-138-8. A British philosopher, mathematician, social critic, and pacifist. With Whitehead, he wrote *Principia Mathematica.*

The Philosophy of Brand Blanshard. (ed.) *Library of Living Philosophers Ser.* Vol. 15 Open Court 1980 $39.95. ISBN 0-87548-349-6. An American philosopher interested in questions of overlapping concern to philosophy and psychology. Wrote on ethical topics and challenged religious irrationalism.

The Philosophy of C. D. Broad. (ed.) *Library of Living Philosophers Ser.* Vol. 10 Open Court 1959 $54.95. ISBN 0-87548-128-0. An English epistemologist and historian of philosophy also concerned with the philosophy of science and the philosophical aspects of psychical research.

The Philosophy of C. I. Lewis. (ed.) *Library of Living Philosophers Ser.* Vol. 13 Open Court 1968 $54.95. ISBN 0-87548-135-3. An American epistemologist, logician, and moral philosopher who used an analytic, critical method. Explored various systems of modal logic in technical detail.

The Philosophy of Ernst Cassirer. (ed.) *Library of Living Philosophers Ser.* Vol. 6 Open Court 1949 $42.95. ISBN 0-87548-131-0. A German neo-Kantian particularly concerned with the nature of symbolic representation and the philosophy of culture.

The Philosophy of G. E. Moore. (ed.) *Library of Living Philosophers Ser.* Vol. 4 Open Court 1968 $54.95. ISBN 0-87548-136-1. A proponent of the philosophy of common sense. Emphasized the naturalistic fallacy in ethics and helped popularize an analytic style of philosophizing.

The Philosophy of Gabriel Marcel. (coedited with Lewis E. Hahn). *Library of Living Philosophers Ser.* Vol. 17 Open Court 1984 $54.95. ISBN 0-87548-369-0. A French philosopher, dramatist, and critic. A theistic existentialist, he was particularly concerned with the analysis and significance of mystery in all aspects of human life.

The Philosophy of Georg Henrik von Wright. (coedited with Lewis E. Hahn). *Library of Living Philosophers Ser.* Vol. 19 Open Court 1989 $99.00. ISBN 0-87548-372-0. Noted for his technical work in the interpretation of logical symbolisms. Worked tirelessly on contrary-to-fact conditionals and deontic logic, which concerns the logical structure of obligation and permissibility.

The Philosophy of George Santayana. (ed.) *Library of Living Philosophers Ser.* Vol. 2 Open Court 1952 $54.95. ISBN 0-87548-139-6. A philosopher proud of his Catholic and Spanish heritage. In his later writings, his naturalism shifted in the direction of platonism.

The Philosophy of Jean-Paul Sartre. (ed.) *Library of Living Philosophers Ser.* Vol. 16 Open Court 1981 $54.95. ISBN 0-87548-354-2. A French existentialist and novelist who wrote extensively about the imagination, human emotions, and self-consciousness.

The Philosophy of John Dewey. (ed.) *Library of Living Philosophers Ser.* Vol. 1 Open Court 1989 $54.95. ISBN 0-87548-132-9. An American philosopher, educator, and social critic often considered to be a leading proponent of pragmatism. With a new preface and expanded bibliography by Lewis E. Hahn.

The Philosophy of Karl Jaspers. (ed.) *Library of Living Philosophers Ser.* Vol. 9 Open Court 1981 $39.95. ISBN 0-87548-361-5. An early existentialist concerned with the careful description of the fringes of human existence. His metaphysics, fairly systematic and disciplined, led toward theology.

The Philosophy of Karl Popper. (ed.) *Library of Living Philosophers Ser.* Vol. 14 2 vols. Open Court 1974 $39.95. ISBN 0-87548-353-4. Often associated with logical positivism but rejected verifiability theories in favor of falsificationism.

The Philosophy of Martin Buber. (coedited with Maurice Friedman). *Library of Living Philosophers Ser.* Vol. 12 Open Court 1966 $54.95. ISBN 0-87548-129-9. A religious existentialist concerned with the personal dimension of religious experience. Emphasized the religious importance of the I-thou relationship.

The Philosophy of Rudolph Carnap. (ed.) *Library of Living Philosophers Ser.* Vol. 11 Open Court 1963 $56.95. ISBN 0-87548-130-2. A prominent logical positivist who wrote extensively in the philosophy of science and logic, developing formal systems of logic.

The Philosophy of Sarvepalli Radhakrishnan. (ed.) *Library of Living Philosophers Ser.* Vol. 8 Open Court 1952 $54.95. ISBN 0-87548-137-X. A Hindu apologist and philosopher. The foremost exponent of a modern version of Hinduism based on Vedanta. Interpreted and adapted the teachings of Shankara.

The Philosophy of W. V. Quine. (coedited with Lewis E. Hahn). *Library of Living Philosophers Ser.* Vol. 18 Open Court 1986 $54.95. ISBN 0-8126-9010-9. A philosopher who concentrated on issues connected with systems of symbolic logic and their relation to informal inference patterns. Quine also wrote extensively on the foundations of logic and the logical regimentation of ordinary language.

SINGER, PETER ALBERT DAVID. 1946–

Born in Australia, Singer received his B.A. and M.A. from the University of Melbourne and, in 1971, his B.Phil from University College, Oxford. During his teaching career, he has held positions in philosophy in England, the United States, and Australia. While a student at Oxford, Singer was deeply affected by a group of people who had become vegetarians for ethical reasons. Joining their commitment to the rights of animals, he wrote *Animal Liberation: A New Ethics for Our Treatment of Animals* (1975), a persuasively reasoned, yet clearly understandable defense of the rights of animals. Singer's vocal concern for the proper treatment of animals has triggered a new appreciation of the anthropocentric bias of traditional Western moral philosophy; other philosophers have followed his lead. Complaining that ethical theorists have focused too intensely upon the rights, responsibilities, and treatment of humans, Singer dubs this malady "speciesism" and calls for a broader moral perspective—one that includes a sensitivity to the needs and concerns of other sentient creatures.

BOOKS BY SINGER

Animal Liberation. Avon rev. ed. 1991 $9.95. ISBN 0-380-71333-0. A powerful, widely influential study of how animals are made to suffer in service to human purposes. Gives attention to animals used for scientific experimentation.

In Defense of Animals. HarpC 1986 $10.00. ISBN 0-06-097044-8. Contains a general prologue by Singer, with essays by other authors. Topics include animal rights, the strategies used by animal rights activists, and the place of animal suffering in scientific investigation.

CHAPTER 3

Greek and Roman Philosophy

John P. Anton

The truth is that we are far more likely to underrate the originality of the
Greeks than to exaggerate it, and we do not always remember the very short
time they took to lay down the lines scientific inquiry has followed ever since.
—JOHN BURNET, *Greek Philosophy*

Though the basis of the system of the Greeks was logic, they were not afraid of
applying it to ethics, politics, and religion, or of summoning faith to their aid
when argument had reached its limits and could do no more. Yet the strength
of Greek philosophy lies not so much in its range as in its assumption that
there is no problem which cannot be solved by hard and careful thought. It
assumes that the words are the instruments of thought and that thought is
about things, no matter how remote or impalpable or complex.
—C. M. BOWRA, *The Greek Experience*

Much of the thought of ancient philosophers has been lost over the course of
2,000 or more years. Indeed, only fragments have survived of what the early
Greeks produced as reflections of their thoughts about the world and the nature
of human existence. While there are a few exceptions, such as the writings of
PLATO (see also Vol. 3) and ARISTOTLE (see also Vol. 3), only a fraction of the
immense productivity of the ancient Greek mind exists—be it in philosophy,
epic poetry, drama, or history, not to mention art, sculpture, and architecture.
What is extant, however, is of superb quality and is worth studying not only for
the pertinence of these monumental achievements to all ages, but also for the
training of the mind they encourage and, perhaps even more, for the value they
possess in illuminating the problems of our own times.

Using the documents and other materials that have survived, scholars have
been able to piece together not the full story of the emergence and development
of philosophy, but what is probably a generally reliable account of developments in antiquity. Philosophers today distinguish between the cultural
developments that preceded the emergence of philosophical thinking itself and
the diverse phases that thinking exhibited in its development to the end of the
Hellenistic period and the appearance of Christian theology. A close study of
these phases permits scholars to divide ancient philosophy into periods. It is
customary to use SOCRATES as a landmark and divide the classical period of
Greek philosophy into the pre-Socratic age, the age of the Sophists and Socrates,
and the age of Plato and his pupil Aristotle.

Scholars refer to the post-Aristotelian developments in philosophy as the
Hellenistic Age, and this is usually divided into three periods. The early period
includes the Stoics, the Epicureans, the Skeptics, and those who continued the
traditions that Plato and Aristotle had started with the founding of their famous
schools. The middle period coincided with the expansion of the Roman Empire
and the migrations of ideas from East to West and vice versa; it led to the rise of

strong philosophical interest in Greek thought among the Romans and stimulated further explorations and revivals of older movements. The third period, known as the late Hellenistic Age, witnessed the rise of Neoplatonism— a complex, widespread, and influential movement that made Platonism palatable to the leaders of the growing Christian community, who were becoming increasingly preoccupied with the intellectual problems of their faith. Of importance in this blending of Greek speculation and Eastern religions was the role the writings of PHILO JUDAEUS played in the effort to bring the fruits of Greek logic to bear on the justification of religious beliefs.

In time, Greco-Roman civilization gradually was replaced with the steady advent of a culture centered on the fundamental beliefs of the Christian faith, and the initial ambivalent responses of the defenders of the new faith were succeeded by a more positive but selective attitude. Once fear and hostility toward this new faith subsided and Christianity became the official religion of the Roman Empire, the values and achievements of Greece and Rome (at least those that could fit more comfortably into the new way of the future) eventually were given due recognition. It was a long assimilative process, however, and it took centuries before the intellectual and administrative leaders of Christianity could accept the pre-Christian world in the positive light of a great heritage. The overcoming of initial resistance and the rediscovery and selective assimilation of the classical world of Greece and Rome have marked the phases of growth of the Western world and the passage from the medieval mind through the Renaissance to the great synthesis of the modern world.

What Greece and Rome bequeathed to humanity and to modern Western culture, in particular, is accepted now as a heritage of perennial value belonging to all humanity. To the Greek developments in philosophy, science, logic, the theater, tragedy, rhetoric, historiography, political freedom, and the idea of democracy the Romans added the results of their own genius in the great practical arts of administration, public service, and law and government; and although Rome did not produce original philosophies, it proved capable of adding to the spirit of Athens the glory of human virtue under the law of nations and universal peace. These philosophies continue to provide us today with the foundations and ideals of our humanities.

The bibliography below lists selections of texts in translation, general works covering whole periods or special periods, and works that are mainly treatments of fundamental problems or individual thinkers. Most of the extant texts of ancient works now are conveniently available in the Loeb editions, which contain the translation on facing pages. In the last few decades, a great number of translations by various hands have appeared in inexpensive editions. It would be burdensome to list all the translations of the writings of such philosophers as Plato and Aristotle that have appeared in paperback. New translations, aspiring to replace the older ones, continue to appear with unusual frequency. Certain venerable translations, of course, continue to hold their own for both elegance and faithfulness to the original. In the case of Plato and Aristotle, one still can recommend with confidence editions that probably will continue to grace any student's collection of masterworks, for instance, *The Collected Dialogues of Plato*, edited by Edith Hamilton and Huntington Cairns, and *The Basic Works of Aristotle*, edited by Richard P. McKeon.

GENERAL WORKS

Histories and Texts

Armstrong, A. H. *An Introduction to Ancient Philosophy. Quality Paper Ser.* Littlefield 3rd ed. 1981 $9.95. ISBN 0-8226-0418-3. Succinct account of the major thinkers and their ideas, at the introductory level.

Brumbaugh, Robert S. *Platonic Studies of Greek Philosophy: Form, Arts, Gadgets, and Hemlock.* State U. NY Pr. 1989 $21.95. ISBN 0-88706-898-7. Study of the ideas that received successful treatment in the systems of the leading Greek philosophers and proved influential in Western thought.

Cornford, Francis M. *Before and After Socrates.* Cambridge U. Pr. 1932 $34.95. ISBN 0-521-04726-9. Readable account of Greek philosophy; it consists of four lectures on early Greek science as the background to the chapters on Socrates, Plato, and Aristotle.

Diogenes Laertius. *Lives of Eminent Philosophers.* 2 Vols. *Loeb Class Lib.* HUP 1925 $15.50 ea. These biographies by a third-century Greek writer are particularly valuable for the quotations from earlier works not preserved by other ancient sources.

Easterling, P. E., and B.M.W. Knox, eds. *The Cambridge History of Classical Literature.* Vol. 1 *Greek Literature.* Cambridge U. Pr. 1985 $100.00. ISBN 0-5212-1042-9. Comprehensive survey of the literary record of Greece, including that of philosophy.

Gomperz, Theodor. *Greek Thinkers: A History of Ancient Philosophy.* 4 vols. Humanities 1964 repr. of 1901 ed. o.p. Offers a valuable interpretation of the main ideas in early Greek thinkers but presupposes considerable familiarity with individual philosophers and themes.

Guthrie, William K. *Greek Philosophers: From Thales to Aristotle.* HarpC 1960 $11.00. ISBN 0-06-131008-5. Brief course of lectures "designed for an audience of undergraduates."

———. *A History of Greek Philosophy.* 6 vols. Cambridge U. Pr. 1975-81 $69.50-$79.50 ea. Vol. 1 *The Earlier Presocratics and the Pythagoreans.* Vol. 2 *The Presocratic Tradition from Parmenides to Democritus.* Vol. 3 *The Fifth Century Enlightenment.* Vol. 4 *Plato, the Man and His Dialogues, Earlier Period.* Vol. 5 *The Later Plato and the Academy.* Vol. 6 *Aristotle: An Encounter.* Monumental multivolume study that brings together the results of classical scholarship and criticism in a synthetic work recognized as a landmark. Exhaustive bibliographies in each volume.

Irwin, Terence. *Classical Thought.* OUP 1989 $11.95. ISBN 0-1928-9177-4. ". . . An extremely useful survey of classical philosophy from Homer to Augustine" (*Library Journal*).

Jones, W. T. *A History of Western Philosophy.* 5 vols. HarBraceJ 2nd ed. Vols. 1–3 1969. $20.00 ea. ISBNs 0-15-538312-4, 0-15-538313-2, 0-15-538314-0. Vols. 4–5 1975 $20.00 ea. ISBNs 0-15-538316-7, 0-15-538317-5 Readable account of philosophers and schools, with frequent references to the cultural background.

McKirahan, Richard, Jr. *Philosophy before Socrates.* Hackett Pub. 1994 $12.95. ISBN 0-87220-175-9. Sourcebook and readable treatment of pre-Socratic philosophy and science, including the Sophistic movement and the controversies it generated.

Owens, Joseph. *History of Ancient Western Philosophy.* P-H 1959 $30.00. ISBN 0-13-389098-8. Learned and well-written account of the major figures, schools, and movements from the beginning of Greek philosophy to the death of Proclus in A.D. 485.

Reale, Giovanni. *A History of Ancient Philosophy.* 4 vols. Ed. and trans. by J. R. Catan. State U. NY Pr. Vol. 1 *From the Origins to Socrates.* 1987 $59.50. ISBN 0-8870-6292-X. Vol. 2 *Plato and Aristotle.* 1990 $74.50. ISBN 0-7914-0516-8. Vol. 3 *The Systems of the Hellenistic Age.* 1985 $59.50. ISBN 0-88706-027-7. Vol. 4 *The Schools of the Imperial Age.* 1989 $59.50. ISBN 0-7914-0128-6. Multivolume critical and comprehensive history of ancient philosophy from its origins to the revival of Platonism in the late Hellenistic period.

Robinson, John M. *Introduction to Early Greek Philosophy: The Chief Fragments and Ancient Testimony, with Connecting Commentary.* HM 1968 $22.95. ISBN 0-395-05316-1. Designed primarily as a student's handbook, useful to beginners. Emphasizing the unity of Greek thought, states the "main problem" formulated in the earlier stage and proceeds to the "solutions" worked out by the Pluralists and the Sophists.

Special Works

Adkins, Arthur W. *From the Many to the One: A Study of Personality and Views of Human Nature in the Context for Ancient Greek Society Values and Beliefs.* Constable 1970 o.p. Continues the work of Adkins' earlier book (listed below) and concentrates on the portrayal of human nature. Excellent on Plato.

_____. *Merit and Responsibility: A Study in Greek Values* Midway Repr. Ser. U. Ch. Pr. 1975 $20.00. ISBN 0-226-00728-6. Careful investigation covering the concepts of moral responsibility, moral errors, justice, and the logic of agreements, with extensive discussions on Plato and Aristotle as ethical philosophers.

Anton, John P., and George L. Kustas, eds. *Essays in Ancient Greek Philosophy.* Vol. 1 State U. NY Pr. 1971 o.p. Selection of the best papers presented at the meetings of the Society for Ancient Greek Philosophy (1954–67), covering all facets and periods of ancient thought.

Anton, John P., and Anthony Preus, eds. *Essays in Ancient Greek Philosophy.* Vol. 2 State U. NY Pr. 1983 $69.50. ISBN 0-87395-623-0. Selection of papers, from the pre-Socratics to post-Aristotelian thinkers, reflecting recent trends in scholarship.

Auden, W. H., ed. *The Portable Greek Reader. Viking Portable Lib.* Viking Penguin 1977 $11.00. ISBN 0-14-015039-0. Selections on significant topics and themes, some from the writings of philosophers, with a useful chronological outline of concurrent thinkers, works, and events.

Baldry, H. C. *The Unity of Mankind in Greek Thought.* Cambridge U. Pr. 1965 o.p. Very readable study, from the early Greek poets and the great philosophers to the thinkers after the conquests of Alexander and the rise of Rome.

Beare, J. I. *Greek Theories of Elementary Cognition from Alcmaeon to Aristotle. Classical Studies Ser.* Irvington 1980 repr. of 1906 ed. o.p. Discusses and documents the physiological and psychological theories of the Greeks on the elementary phenomena of perception, the five senses, and the faculty of sensation in general.

Boudouris, C., ed. *Ionian Philosophy. Studies in Greek Philosophy Ser.* Kardamitsas Pub. 1989 $40.00. A collection of research papers discussing issues related to the historiography, philosophy, cosmogony, political thought, and the impact of Ionian thought on culture.

Bowen, Alan C., ed. *Science and Philosophy in Classical Greece.* Garland 1991 $58.00. ISBN 0-8153-0214-2. Articles by specialists on the interaction of ancient philosophy and science.

Callahan, John F. *Four Views of Time in Ancient Philosophy.* Greenwood 1970 repr. of 1948 cd. $35.00. ISBN 0-8371-0337-1. Discusses time and the solutions to the problem of time as developed in the philosophies of Plato, Aristotle, Plotinus, and St. Augustine.

Cleary, John, and others, eds. *Proceedings of the Boston Area Colloquium in Ancient Philosophy.* 7 vols. U. Pr. of Amer. Vol. 1 1986 $28.00. ISBN 0-8191-5133-5. Vol. 2 1987 $28.00. ISBN 0-8191-5805-4. Vol. 3 1988 $59.50. ISBN 0-8191-6809-2. Vol. 4 1989 $53.00. ISBN 0-8191-7335-5. Vol. 5 1991 $65.50. ISBN 0-8191-7808-X. Vol. 6 1992 $88.00. ISBN 0-8191-8400-4. Vol. 7 1992 $60.00. ISBN 0-8191-8560-4. Papers and commentaries presented by invited scholars to the annual Boston Area Colloquium on individual classical philosophers.

Depew, David J., ed. *The Greeks and the Good Life.* Hackett Pub. 1980 $29.50. ISBN 0-937622-01-X. Essays by various scholars on basic ethical themes, mainly those in Plato and Aristotle.

Dicks, D. R. *Early Greek Astronomy to Aristotle.* Cornell Univ. Pr. 1985 $14.95. ISBN 0-8014-9310-02. Examines the main ideas that determined the development of astronomy in antiquity.

Dodds, Eric R. *The Greeks and the Irrational.* Peter Smith 1986 $23.75. ISBN 0-8446-6224-0. Landmark in the interpretation of Greek culture, thought, and literature, with frequent references to philosophy.

Edelstein, Ludwig. *The Idea of Progress in Classical Antiquity.* Johns Hopkins 1967 o.p. Important and well-documented analysis of the concept of "progress," which was familiar to the ancient Greeks before its late Hellenistic formulation.

Euben, J. Peter, ed. *Greek Tragedy and Political Theory.* U. CA Pr. 1986 $45.00. ISBN 0-520-05572-1. "Stimulating . . . attempts to show how tragic discourse—with its recognition of human contingency and particularity—can enrich political theorizing" (*Choice*).

Ferguson, John. *Moral Values in the Ancient World.* Ed. by Gregory Vlastos. Ayer 1979 repr. of 1958 ed. $21.95. ISBN 0-405-11542-3. Survey covering the subject of values in ethical pursuits from Homer to the late Hellenistic and early Christian times.

Frede, Michael. *Essays in Ancient Philosophy.* U. of Minn. Pr. 1987 $34.95. ISBN 0-8166-1274-9. Seventeen important papers on ancient philosophy, mostly on Aristotle and later thinkers.

Furley, David. *The Greek Cosmologists.* Vol. 1 *The Formation of the Atomic Theory and Its Earliest Critics.* Cambridge U. Pr. 1988 $34.50. ISBN 0-521-33328-8. Noted classicist discusses the Atomic theory and its early critics in the context of its logic and impact on scientific theory.

Gould, Thomas. *The Ancient Quarrel between Poetry and Philosophy.* Princeton U. Pr. 1990 $39.50. ISBN 0-691-07375-9. Critical survey of the celebrated polemic coupled with an assessment of the alleged effects of tragic drama.

Havelock, Eric A. *The Greek Concept of Justice: From Its Shadow in Homer to Its Substance in Plato.* HUP 1978 $35.00. ISBN 0-674-36220-9. Critical survey of justice from the moral function of the epic poets, the pre-Socratics, the lawgivers, and the tragic poets to Plato.

Jaeger, Werner. *Paideia: The Ideals of Greek Culture.* 3 vols. Trans. by Gilbert Highet. OUP 1943-45 $39.95 ea. ISBNs 0-19-500399-3, 0-19-500592-9, 0-19-500593-7. Excellent study of the cultural ideal as reflected in the writing of poets, historians, orators, and philosophers.

Lloyd, G.E.R. *Magic, Reason and Experience: Studies in the Origin and Development of Greek Science.* Cambridge U. Pr. 1979 $74.95. ISBN 0-521-22373-3. Complements other histories of Greek science, assessing the theoretical and practical sides of science and relating both to philosophy. Includes an especially valuable bibliography on the subject.

———. *Methods and Problems in Greek Science.* Cambridge U. Pr. 1991 $64.95. ISBN 0-521-37419-7. Collection of articles on Greek science, exploring its relation to Greek philosophy and culture.

McMullin, Ernan, ed. *The Concept of Matter in Greek and Medieval Philosophy.* Bks. Demand repr. of 1965 ed. $86.60. ISBN 0-318-34707-5. Of special interest are the essays dealing with the conceptions of the material world held by ancient Greek philosophers and scientists.

Murray, Gilbert. *Five Stages of Greek Religion: Studies Based on a Course of Lectures Delivered in April 1912 at Columbia University.* AMS Pr. repr. of 1925 ed. $19.50. ISBN 0-404-14577-9. First published in 1912 as *Four Stages of Greek Religion.* Famous for its chapter "The Failure of Nerve," portraying the breakdown of Greek rationalism in Hellenistic times under the impact of the Asian cults.

North, Helen. *Sophrosyne: Self-Knowledge and Self-Restraint in Greek Literature.* Cornell Univ. Pr. 1966 o.p. Outstanding treatment of the early meaning of sophrosyne in literature and philosophy and of its subsequent transformation into a Christian virtue.

Nussbaum, Martha C. *The Fragility of Goodness: Luck and Ethics in Greek Tragedy and Philosophy.* Cambridge U. Pr. 1986 $79.95. ISBN 0-521-25768-9. Draws from the original Greek sources to discuss the precarious elements of chance and the play of external forces on reason in pursuit of goodness.

Onians, Richard B. *The Origins of European Thought about the Body, the Mind, the Soul, the World, Time and Fate.* Ayer 1980 repr. of 1951 ed. $39.95. ISBN 0-405-04853-X. Traces the origins of European thought regarding these ideas back to Greek, Roman, Jewish, and Christian concepts and beliefs.

Osborne, Catherine. *Rethinking Early Greek Philosophy: Hippolytus of Rome and the Presocratics.* Cornell Univ. Pr. 1987 $49.95. ISBN 0-8014-2103-9. Reading of the available texts of Hippolytus, challenging current methods of reconstructing early Greek philosophy.

Owen, G.E.L. *Logic, Science, and Dialectic.* Ed. by Martha C. Nussbaum. Cornell Univ. Pr. 1985 $49.95. ISBN 0-8014-1726-0. "Owen's work reflects a combination of close philological argument, sophisticated philosophy, and immense erudition" (*Library Journal*).

Robb, Kevin, ed. *Language and Thought in Early Greek Philosophy.* Open Court 1983 $29.95. ISBN 0-914417-01-0. Discussions of the impact of orality on literacy, illumining the passage from myth to science and logic in Greek life.

Rohde, Erwin. *Psyche: The Cult of Souls and Belief in Immortality among the Greeks.* Select Bibliographies Repr. Ser. Ayer 1980 repr. of 1920 ed. $39.95. ISBN 0-8369-6749-6. A classic in the field of ancient views on life.

Sambursky, S. *Physical World of the Greeks.* Trans. by Merton Dagut. Methuen 1956 o.p. Study of the Greek conceptualization of the physical world and how it relates to the modern scientific method and its achievements.

Saxonhouse, Arlene W. *Fear of Diversity: The Birth of Political Science in Ancient Greek Thought.* U. Ch. Pr. 1992 $29.95. ISBN 0-226-73553-2. How the Greeks explained the diversity of the world by unveiling the unifying forces behind ordinary experience.

Snell, Bruno. *The Discovery of the Mind in Early Greek Philosophy and Literature.* Dover 1982 $7.50. ISBN 0-486-24264-1. Collection of essays on mythical thinking and the transition to logical thinking, explaining the relation of literary and intellectual movements to the rise of philosophy and poetry.

Vernant, Jean Pierre. *Myth and Thought among the Greeks.* Routledge 1983 $42.50. ISBN 0-7100-9544-9. When first published in 1965, immediately noticed as a pioneering approach to Greek studies, applying structuralist views to myth, the concept of space, personal identity, reason, work, and technology.

_____. *The Origins of Greek Thought.* Cornell Univ. Pr. 1982 $7.95. ISBN 0-8014-9293-9. "One of the most stimulating and thoughtful accounts of the invention of philosophy by the Greeks" (*TLS*).

PRE-SOCRATICS

The dominant characteristic of the early phase of Greek philosophy, conveniently called pre-Socratic, is an attitude of intellectual curiosity about nature—the things that change and the things that seem permanent. The early thinkers sought to find what comes first and how its priority offers an explanation, a beginning, in order to understand what comes after. They studied "nature" (*physis*), a general term for the "physical" phenomena and their causes. The latter, called principles, or *archai*, were considered whatever else they might be, the ultimate cause of all growth and change. Such principles, though not themselves subject to any alteration, warrant whatever order is observable in the universe. Thus it was that the early Greeks looked for the permanent elements in reality, and it should be of little surprise that they found them to be some type of ultimate matter, "Water" or "Air" or "Fire," even the "Boundless." Other principles, such as "Mind," "Number," and "Ideas," were added to the initial list as theoretical speculation reached higher levels of refinement.

The pre-Socratics in general were appealing strictly to the power of reason and a rationally controlled imagination to discover the nature of ultimate reality. The surviving records of the early Greek philosophers are scanty, but scholarship has recaptured much that is essential to understanding the beginnings of science and philosophy. The general quest for wisdom went through a sequence of phases tied together like the integral parts of a developing organism. The Greeks were the first to show what the power of intelligence, once distanced from unreflective belief, can accomplish. Thus it was that criticism and refinements of argument led to the opening of new theoretical vistas. The pre-Socratics had not only reflected on nature but also extended the quest for truth to include within its scope their practical concerns. Inquiries led to further investigations, and soon whole new reflective movements got under way. Great thinkers like HERACLITUS and Parmenides, and later, the Sophists, could be found in any major city from the coasts of Ionia and the Black Sea to Sicily and lower Italy, and finally, after the end of the Persian Wars, in Athens, the city that was destined to become the intellectual and cultural center of the Hellenic world. SOCRATES was the first Athenian philosopher.

General Works

Barnes, Jonathan. *The Presocratic Philosophers. Arguments of the Philosophers Ser.* Routledge 1982 $27.50. ISBN 0-7100-9200-8. Lively interpretive work on the rise and development of early Greek speculation on human beings and nature.

Burnet, John. *Early Greek Philosophy.* B&N Imports 4th ed. 1963 repr. of 1930 ed. o.p. One of the most discussed surveys of ancient thought in this century. Very readable and still challenging.

Cornford, F. M. *From Religion to Philosophy: A Study of the Origins of Western Speculation.* Princeton U. Pr. 1991 $12.95. ISBN 0-691-02076-0. First appeared in 1912, defending the view that science and philosophy could be traced to religious roots through the mythic beginnings of metaphysical concepts.

———. *Principium Sapientiae: The Origins of Greek Philosophical Thought.* Peter Smith o.p. Cornford's last work; brings together his lifelong research into prephilosophical thought, going back to Hesiod and parallel Babylonian sources, to discuss the "nonscientific" nature of early Greek philosophy, making the claim that it relied on inspiration rather than experimentation.

Furley, David J., and R. E. Allen, eds. *Studies in Pre-Socratic Philosophy. International Lib. of Philosophy and Scientific Method.* Humanities 1970 o.p. Essays on problems and interlacing themes, from the Milesians to the Atomists.

Heidegger, Martin. *Early Greek Thinking: The Dawn of Western Philosophy.* Trans. by Frank Capuzzi. Harper SF 1985 $12.00. ISBN 0-06-063842-7. Translation into English of four well-known and influential essays by Heidegger on Anaximander (one essay), Heraclitus (two essays), and Parmenides (one essay).

Hussey, Edward. *The Presocratics.* Macmillan 1982 $20.00. ISBN 0-684-17601-7. Popularized but competent introduction to early Greek thinkers, including the Sophists.

Hyland, D. *The Origins of Philosophy.* Humanities 1984 repr. of 1973 ed. $17.50. ISBN 0-391-03217-8. "Highly recommended to all undergraduate libraries" (*Choice*).

Jaeger, Werner. *The Theology of the Early Greek Philosophers: The Gifford Lectures, 1936.* Trans. by Edward S. Robinson. Greenwood 1980 repr. of 1947 ed. $62.50. ISBN 0-313-21262-7. Seeks to balance the widely held view of the pre-Socratics as scientists and allows them to surface as offerers of remarkable theological insights.

Jordan, William. *Ancient Concepts of Philosophy.* Routledge 1990 $45.00. ISBN 0-415-04834-6. A survey of ancient philosophy that includes a chapter on the pre-Socratics.

Kirk, G. S., J. E. Raven, and M. Schoenfield. *The Presocratic Philosophers: A Critical History with a Selection of Texts.* Cambridge U. Pr. 2nd ed. 1983 $27.95. ISBN 0-521-27455-9. Fresh interpretation of the early thinkers of Greece, down to the Atomists,

with long and illuminating introduction that takes into account the best of recent
scholarship; the extant texts are printed with new translations and commentaries.

Mourelatos, Alexander P. D., ed. *The Pre-Socratics: A Collection of Critical Essays.*
Doubleday 1974 o.p. Brings together a number of outstanding articles, some written
especially for this volume, examining fundamental issues in the pre-Socratic period,
with an emphasis on Heraclitus and Parmenides.

Navia, Luis E. *The Presocratic Philosophers: An Annotated Bibliography.* Garland 1993
$110.00. ISBN 0-8240-9776-9

Stokes, Michael C. *One and Many in Presocratic Philosophy.* U. Pr. of Amer. 1986 repr. of
1971 ed. $47.75. ISBN 0-8191-5528-4. Detailed analysis of the concepts of unity and
plurality in the early Greeks, with Xenophanes, Parmenides, and Zeno at the center
of the author's interest.

Sweeney, Leo. *Infinity in the Presocratics.* Nijhoff 1972 o.p. Largely on Anaximander's
apeiron (infinity) and literature on the subject, although attention is given to the
views of the other pre-Socratics.

Waterfield, Robin. *Before Eureka: The Presocratics and Their Science.* St. Martin 1990
$29.95. ISBN 0-312-04001-6. Straightforward introduction to pre-Socratic philoso-
phy from Thales to Democritus.

The Milesian Philosophers

The birthplace of conscious freedom of inquiry was Miletus, a flourishing city
in Ionia that had become a cultural and intellectual center. From its very start,
philosophic thought took the form of general theories about the nature and
origins of reality. The Greeks believed that the first philosopher was Thales of
Miletus (fl. 585 B.C.), who attracted others to his views and shared his theories
generously with his fellow citizens. What is indeed remarkable about Thales and
his immediate successors—Anaximander (c.610–546 B.C.), Anaximenes (fl. 545
B.C.), and others who came after them with the spread of philosophy to other
cities—is the appeal to human reason for explanations of all natural and human
events and the trust they put in reason to discover principles of unity behind the
multiplicity of phenomena.

Very few of the writings of these early philosophers have come down to us
directly; however, later thinkers put together whatever they knew about them
and made a commendable effort to preserve their theories. Thus a respectable
body of literature grew about the pioneer philosophers of Miletus, and as their
fame spread, so, too, did the spirit of critical thinking and the desire to come up
with better and sounder theories. The answers of later philosophers, however
different from one another, all were based on the firm belief that nature,
whatever it ultimately might be, is intelligible and accessible to human reason.

Kahn, Charles H. *Anaximander and the Origins of Greek Cosmology.* Col. U. Pr. 1964 o.p.
Treats Anaximander as the source of the early systems of cosmology; regarded as a
model of the study of the extant *testimonia.* The concluding chapter gives a
comprehensive view of the Ionian tradition.

Seligman, Paul. *The "Apeiron" of Anaximander: A Study in the Origin and Function of
Metaphysical Ideas.* Greenwood 1974 repr. of 1962 ed. o.p. Fine addition to the study
of early pre-Socratic philosophy and the interpretations of Anaximander's principle
of *apeiron* ("infinity" or "the indefinite").

Parmenides and the Eleatics

The Eleatic school was said to be founded by Parmenides (fl c.485 B.C.), a
citizen of the Greek city of Elea in southern Italy. However, it was actually
Xenophanes of Colophon, a teacher of Parmenides, who founded this school of

thought. Close in thought to the Milesians, Xenophanes made daring intellectual leaps in a direction of his own. He was exiled because of his criticisms of
popular religious beliefs, that is, for theorizing about the divine in the same way
that the Milesians theorized about nature. Parmenides, for his part, wrote a
famous philosophical poem that was destined to become influential and assure
him of being known as "the father of idealism." Ever since the time of PLATO
(see also Vol. 3), one of whose longest dialogues bears the title *Parmenides*,
numerous students of philosophy have essayed to explain Parmenides' doctrines. He saw the importance of HERACLITUS and sought to give a definitive
answer to the problem of change by denying that change is essential to
understanding being. According to Parmenides, reality is one—everlasting,
unchangeable, complete, determinate, a well-rounded sphere. His pupils Zeno
(fl. c.465–455 B.C) and Melissus (fifth century B.C.) defended the teachings of
their master and developed further the art of logical arguments, insisting that
unless one accepts Parmenides' teachings, one falls into paradoxical beliefs.

Austin, Scott. *Parmenides: Being, Bounds and Logic.* Yale U. Pr. 1986 $26.00. ISBN 0-300-
   03559-4. This "bold exploration of Parmenides' use of language and argument forms
   . . . a difficult but insightful work" (*Choice*).
Gallop, David, trans. *Parmenides of Elea: Fragments.* U. of Toronto Pr. 1984 $17.95. ISBN
   0-8020-2443-2. Includes a helpful introduction by the translator on basic issues
   related to understanding the extant fragments.
Lee, H.D.P. *Zeno of Elea: A Text with Translation and Notes.* Cambridge U. Pr. 1936 o.p.
   Collection of all the textual materials related to Zeno's paradoxes.
Lesher, J. H., trans. *Xenophanes of Colophon: Fragments.* U. of Toronto Pr. 1992 $45.00.
   ISBN 0-8020-5990-2. Scholarly work on an important pre-Socratic thinker, with a
   commentary by the translator.
Mourelatos, Alexander P. D. *The Route of Parmenides: A Study of World, Image and
   Argument in the Fragments.* Yale U. Pr. 1970 o.p. Well-known work explaining the
   grounds for considering the parts of the extant poem continuous and viewing
   Parmenides as "the father of Western rationalism."
Taran, Leonardo. *Parmenides: A Text with Translation, Commentary and Critical Essays.*
   Princeton U. Pr. 1965 o.p. Full as well as impressively technical discussion of the
   poem of Parmenides.

The Pluralists and Atomists

The fifth century B.C. produced a number of outstanding and original thinkers
who extended and deepened the work of previous generations. Although only
fragments of their writings have survived, scholars have enough to reconstruct
in broad outline their bold theories of nature. Empedocles of Acragas (fifth
century B.C.) won fame as a philosopher, physician, orator, and statesman. The
fragments of his two philosophical poems, "On Nature" and "Purifications,"
show a profound mind working to understand how the universe can be made
intelligible in all its stages when love and strife operate, alternately mixing and
unmixing the primordial elements of fire, air, water, and earth in order to
produce and dissolve nature as it is perceived.

Anaxogoras of Clazomenae (500–c.428 B.C.), who is said to have brought
philosophy to Athens, taught in that city for 20 years. He became a member of
the Periclean circle in the Golden Age of Greece, only to be accused of impiety
and forced to leave Athens to avoid execution. SOCRATES as a young man sought
out Anaxogoras as did many others who recognized the importance of his
theories, especially his views on cosmic reason and on how the interpenetration

of all elements creates a number of ordered "universes" through an ever-expanding vortex.

Leucippus (fifth century B.C.) and his pupil Democritus of Abdera (c.460–c.371 B.C.) won their places in the history of philosophy, as well as science, with their theory of Atomism, which argued that the building bricks of all things are atoms—indestructible, eternally mobile, endowed with size and shape, moving with different velocities in the void, colliding, hooking together, and separating to make and unmake things. EPICURUS accepted this theory and turned it into a lasting worldview.

Bailey, Cyril. *Greek Atomists and Epicurus: A Study*. Russell 1964 repr. of 1928 ed. o.p. The author wrote this "as a study of the development of Atomism in Greece and of its embodiment in the comprehensive system of Epicurus" (Preface).

Inwood, Brad, ed. and trans. *The Poem of Empedocles: A Text and Translation with an Introduction*. U. of Toronto Pr. 1992 $45.00. ISBN 0-8020-5971-6. Reexamines the thought of Empedocles, using a new rendition of the extant fragments.

Millerd, Clara E. *On the Interpretation of Empedocles*. Ed. by Leonardo Taran. *Ancient Philosophy Ser.* Garland 1980 o.p. Perceptive work making use of recent philology.

O'Brien, Denis. *Empedocles' Cosmic Cycle: A Reconstruction from the Fragments and Secondary Sources*. Cambridge U. Pr. 1969 o.p. Outstanding work on Empedocles' views, based on a firm grasp of the extant fragments, with a fresh interpretation of the role of love and strife.

Schofield, M. *An Essay on Anaxagoras*. Cambridge U. Pr. 1980 $34.95. ISBN 0-521-22722-4. Discussion centers on the doctrines of mind and includes a survey of current research on the fragments of Anaxagoras.

Teodorsson, Sven Tage. *Anaxagoras' Theory of Matter*. Humanities 1982 o.p. "Although Anaxagoras' theory of *Nous* has drawn few students in the twentieth century (and no separate study since von Fritz' of 1964), his theory of matter has been the object of study by an impressive series of scholars that begins with Paul Tannery in 1886. The serious student will work his way through this bibliography as diligently as through the original fragments and testimonia" (*Classical Journal*).

Wright, M. R. *Empedocles: The Extant Fragments*. Yale U. Pr. 1981 $52.50. ISBN 0-300-02475-4. Scholarly study with translation of the extant fragments and survey of recent interpretations.

THE SOPHISTS

The Sophists originally were itinerant teachers who wandered throughout Greece receiving fees for their lectures. In the second half of the fifth century B.C., certain representatives of the Sophist movement and SOCRATES of Athens were responsible for a gradual shift of philosophical interest toward the deepening of an inquiry into the problems of human values, human nature, and political institutions. There is evidence that the other pre-Socratics also kept in mind the problems of humanity and public conduct, law, and politics; but it is with the coming of the great Sophists—Gorgias of Leontini (c.480–380B.C), Protagoras of Abdera (c.490–420B.C.), Hippias, Prodicus, and others—that a method gradually emerged and became sufficiently refined for the critical analysis of ethical and social values and pursuits. The Sophists adopted different positions and theories, but the great issue that had to be decided was whether it was reasonable to say that universal values and standards for judging human actions could be found. The debate centered on the issue of teaching virtue and who was qualified to do so. The great Sophists took an early lead in this debate. Recognizing the importance of the art of persuasion in maintaining power and controlling public opinion, they developed rhetoric, furthered the logic of arguing in public, and became celebrated teachers. The challenge to their fame and teachings came from Socrates, a man of humble origins who made the future of his city his own cause. (See also the main entries for Socrates, Xenophon, Plato, Aristotle, and Theophrastus in this chapter.)

General Works

De Romilly, Jacqueline. *The Great Sophists in Periclean Athens*. Trans. by Janet Lloyd. OUP 1992 $75.00. ISBN 0-19-824234-4. Fresh assessment of the Sophistic movement as a major intellectual event, emphasizing its impact on the cultural outlook of Athenian society.

Guthrie, William K. *The Sophists*. Cambridge U. Pr. 1971 o.p. Originally published as Part I of *A History of Greek Philosophy*, Vol. 3 (1969), this covers "a series of standard topics—nature v. convention, rhetoric and skepticism, social compact theory, 'liberalism'—and then reviews these 'professors' one at a time, including some minor ones (Thrasymachus, Antisthenes, Lycophron)" (*Choice*).

Sprague, Rosamond Kent, and others, eds. and trans. *The Older Sophists*. U. of SC Pr. 1972 o.p. Complete translation of the part on the Sophists in *Die Fragmente der Vorsokratiker*. Brief introduction to each Sophist, including Antiphon and Euthedemus, citing extant fragments and *testimonia* in translation.

Versényi, Laszlo. *Socratic Humanism*. Greenwood 1979 repr. of 1963 ed. $35.00. ISBN 0-313-20716-X. Existentialist approach emphasizing the ideal of self-fulfillment and the unity of Socratic views.

HELLENISTIC PHILOSOPHIES

After the death of Alexander the Great in 323, a new cultural era began to emerge as a result of the fusion of various ideas and values. Until recently the originality of the philosophical works produced after PLATO (see also Vol. 3) and ARISTOTLE (see also Vol. 3) was seriously disputed. That judgment now has come under criticism and reexamination by philosophers, historians, and philologists who attempt to show that the Hellenistic Age, rather than being a period of long stagnation and decline, succeeded in making important advances in a number of philosophical and scientific fields. The Hellenistic period appears to divide into an early phase, during which the dominant quest was to secure practical wisdom, and a second phase, characterized by the gradual surge and prevalence of the search for salvational faiths and their justifications.

The changing fortunes of Hellenistic cultures, and the problems people faced as a result of wars and upheavals, proved too big for any of the intellectuals within the philosophical schools to handle; their theories were not philosophies of social salvation. The primary ethical doctrines that had emerged earlier had consolidated into three dominant outlooks. They nevertheless were open to anyone eager to seek the means to a more satisfactory kind of life beyond what the mores of the cities offered. The schools that had attracted followers outside the limits of Greece proper were Epicureanism (see the main entry for Epicurus in this chapter), Stoicism, and other doctrinal types like Eclecticism and Skepticism—schools that had worked out their own outlooks with materials borrowed from the teachings of Plato and Aristotle. During the later Hellenistic times, waves of revival of the older strands were mixed with beliefs and concerns originating in religious practices and rituals; the thinkers who responded finally emerged as the Neopythagoreans and Neoplatonists. They were the products of the age of syncretism.

General Works

Armstrong, Arthur H., ed. *The Cambridge History of Later Greek and Early Medieval Philosophy*. Cambridge U. Pr. 1967 $110.00. ISBN 0-521-04054-X. The work of several well-known specialists, offering a useful summary of this period—for example, Philip Merlan's "Greek Philosophy from Plato to Plotinus" and Henry Chadwick's "Philo and the Beginnings of Christian Thought."

Bevan, E. *Stoics and Skeptics*. OUP 1913 o.p. Stimulating and well-written summary on the rise and development of these schools.

Dudley, D. R. *A History of Cynicism from Diogenes to the Sixth Century A.D.* Gordon Pr. 1974 $250.00. ISBN 0-87968-137-3. Useful survey of the major phases of Cynicism as a philosophical attitude and way of life.

Erskin, Andrew. *The Hellenistic Stoa*. Cornell Univ. Pr. 1990 $39.95. ISBN 0-8014-2465-1. Examines the ideas of the Stoics in their historical context and explains the social and political environment in which they were first expressed.

Hahm, David E. *The Origins of Stoic Cosmology*. Ohio St. U. Pr. 1977 o.p. Examines critically the sources Stoic thinkers used and extended in creating their own cosmology.

Hicks, Robert D. *Stoic and Epicurean*. Russell 1962 repr. of 1910 ed. o.p. Three well-organized chapters on Epicurean hedonism, Atomism, and religion; also a fair treatment of Stoicism.

Inwood, Brad, and Lloyd Gerson, eds. *Hellenistic Philosophy: Introductory Readings*. Hackett Pub. 1988 $32.50. ISBN 0-87220-042-6. Consists of major texts of Epicureanism, Stoicism, and Skepticism.

Kristeller, Paul O. *Greek Philosophers of the Hellenistic Age*. Trans. by Gregory Woods. Col. U. Pr. 1993 $35.00. ISBN 0-231-07952-4

Long, A. A. *Hellenistic Philosophy: Stoics, Epicureans, Skeptics*. U. CA Pr. 1986 $45.00. ISBN 0-520-05808-9. Excellent treatment of these schools, with most attention given to Stoicism; the last chapter discusses the influence of Hellenistic philosophy on later developments and on modern thought.

More, Paul Elmer. *Hellenistic Philosophies*. Greenwood repr. of 1923 ed. o.p. General discussion, with a Platonic bias, of later Greek philosophy and its blending with Christian beliefs.

Randall, John H. *Hellenistic Ways of Deliverance and the Making of the Christian Synthesis*. Col. U. Pr. 1970 o.p. Excellent analysis of the Hellenistic schools of thought—Epicurean, Stoic, and Skeptic—as secular ways; the Roman philosophers; and the turning of Platonism into a religious way of deliverance, preparing the ground for the Christian assimilation of Greek philosophy.

Reale, Giovanni. *The Systems of the Hellenistic Age: A History of Ancient Philosophy*. Trans. by John R. Catan. State U. NY Pr. 1985 o.p. Reliable history of this period, from the minor Socratic schools, the Cynics, Cyrenaics, and Megarians, down to Cicero and Roman Eclecticism.

Texts and Collections

Annas, Julia. *Hellenistic Philosophy of Mind*. U. CA Pr. 1991 $35.00. ISBN 0-520-07554-4. Critical treatment of the Stoic and Epicurean philosophies, making frequent comparisons with modern approaches to similar problems.

Dillon, J. M. and A. A. Long, eds. *The Question of "Eclecticism": Studies in Later Greek Philosophy*. U. CA Pr. 1988 $40.00. ISBN 0-520-06008-3. Informative account of the emerging of the diverse contexts of the meaning of Eclecticism in Hellenistic times.

Inwood, Brad, and Lloyd Gerson, eds. and trans. *Hellenistic Philosophy: Introductory Readings*. Hackett Pub. 1988 $32.50. ISBN 0-8722-0042-6. Offers unexcerpted passages from the extant writings of Epicureanism, Stoicism, and Skepticism, with useful comments on textual and interpretive problems.

Long, A. A., and D. N. Sedley. *The Hellenistic Philosophers*. 2 vols. Cambridge U. Pr. 1987 $29.95 ea. ISBNs 0-521-25561-1, 0-521-25562-7. Vol. 1, translation of the sources, with commentary; vol. 2, comprehensive sourcebook of Greek and Latin texts from Stoic, Epicurean, and Skeptic philosophical schools.

Oates, W. J., ed. *The Stoic and Epicurean Philosophers*. Random 1957 o.p. Representative collection of the writings of Epicurus, Epictetus, Lucretius, and Marcus Aurelius in English translation, with an introduction and useful notes; included is Cleanthes' "Hymn to Zeus" and Matthew Arnold's essay on Marcus Aurelius.

Osler, Margaret J., ed. *Atoms, Pneuma, and Tranquility: Epicurean and Stoic Themes in European Thought*. Cambridge U. Pr. 1991 $49.50. ISBN 0-521-40048-1. Fine discussion of the influence of Epicurean and Stoic ideas on the development of modern European philosophy and science.

Schofield, Malcolm, Myles Burnyeat, and Jonathan Barnes, eds. *Doubt and Dogmatism: Studies in Hellenistic Epistemology*. OUP 1980 $24.95. ISBN 0-19-824601-3. Excellent introduction to the Skeptical tradition.

Schofield, Malcolm, and Gisela Striker, eds. *The Norms of Nature: Studies in Hellenistic Ethics*. Cambridge U. Pr. 1986 $59.95. ISBN 0-521-26623-8. One of the best collections of recent articles in Hellenistic ethical theory, interlacing discussions of the basic concepts and modes of reasoning.

Shapiro, H., and E. M. Curley. *Hellenistic Philosophy: Selections from Epicureanism, Skepticism, and Neoplatonism*. Modern Lib. 1965 o.p. Brief introductions and selections from Epicurus, Lucretius, Seneca, Epictetus, Marcus Aurelius, Sextus Empiricus, Lucian, Plotinus, and Cicero.

The Stoics

The Stoic philosophical school had a long and checkered career, from its founding by Zeno of Citium in Athens late in the fourth century B.C. to the Roman era, when Epictetus, a Greek slave, and the Roman emperor MARCUS AURELIUS held Stoic doctrines in the second century A.D. Thus Stoicism can be said to have two phases, a Greek phase and a Roman one, both of which held essentially the same principles and view of the universe but with different emphases on what the Stoic outlook means when applied to human problems. From the very start, the Stoics, from Zeno to Cleanthes, combined a revival of HERACLITUS's theory of nature and a creative extension of Aristotelian logic and they divided philosophy into three parts: logic, physics (mixing theology and psychology), and ethics. In certain ways, Stoicism is an eclectic position, but one not without considerable internal consistency. The extant fragments from Zeno's teachings make it difficult to achieve any coherent interpretation, but the situation improves with Cleanthes. The third head of the Stoa, Cleanthes is recognized as the system-builder of Stoicism, defending an ethical thesis that called for submission to the ways of nature, but a nature understood as thoroughly rational and determinate. The Stoics saw the world as being in process but unfolding a divine and necessary plan, totally logical and intelligible, with human beings capable of rising to ethical completion. Whereas humanity is a microcosmos of the universe, the universe is the macrocosmos of humanity. Human reason, being a particular manifestation of the cosmic mind, is a principle that secures the brotherhood and unity of humanity. Among the most important Stoics are Zeno of Citium (c.362/351?–264/259? B.C.), Cleanthes of Assos (c.300–232 B.C.), Chrysippus of Soli (281–201 B.C.), and Epictetus (A.D. 60–138).

Edelstein, Ludwig. *The Meaning of Stoicism*. HUP 1966 $8.95. ISBN 0-674-55850-2. The Martin Lectures presented at Oberlin; elliptical but worth reading and typical of the author's learning.

Edelstein, Ludwig, and I. G. Kidd, trans. *Posidonius: The Fragments*. Cambridge U. Pr. 1972 o.p. New edition of the extant fragments.

Epp, Ronald, ed. *Recovering the Stoics: The Spindel Conference 1984. The Southern Journal of Philosophy*. Vol. 23 (supplement). Memphis St. U. 1985 o.p. Articles on basic Stoic themes by specialists, with an exhaustive bibliography by the editor.

Erskine, Andrew. *The Hellenistic Stoa: Political Thought and Action*. Cornell Univ. Pr. 1990 $38.95. ISBN 0-8014-2463-1. Traces the development of the Stoic theory of politics in Zeno and the later Roman versions of Stoicism.

Gould, Josiah B. *The Philosophy of Chrysippus*. St. U. NY Pr. 1970 o.p. One of the best treatments of this leading Stoic and of the climate of opinion in the third century.

Hadas, Moses, ed. *The Essential Works of Stoicism*. Bantam 1961 o.p. Good selection of translated texts from Laertius, Cleanthes, Seneca, Epictetus, and Marcus Aurelius.

Mates, Benson. *Stoic Logic*. U. CA Pr. 1953 o.p. Offers a complete description of the propositional logic of the old Stoa; "the most accurate analytical study" (*Journal of Philosophy*).

Oldfather, W. A. *A Bibliography of Epictetus*. Holmes 1952 $20.00. ISBN 0-685-02325-7. Exhaustive list of publications of the writings of this Stoic thinker; a helpful guide.

———. *Contributions towards a Bibliography of Epictetus: A Supplement*. Holmes o.p. Covers additional philological work since the publication of the 1952 work above.

Reesor, Margaret E. *The Nature of Man in Early Stoic Philosophy*. St. Martin 1989 $45.00. ISBN 0-312-03579-9. Explains how ontology, knowledge, and language in the early Stoics determine their conception of human beings.

Rist, J. M. *Stoic Philosophy*. Cambridge U. Pr. 1969 $18.95. ISBN 0-521-07620-X. Close and clear examination of the major doctrines and the leading members of the Stoic school and their interlacing concerns and problems, with an emphasis on ethical theory.

———, ed. *The Stoics. Major Thinkers Ser*. U. CA Pr. 1978 o.p. Thirteen essays by leading authorities in Hellenistic philosophy, all commissioned for this volume, on topics ranging from Stoic grammar to theory of art.

Sambursky, Samuel. *Physics of the Stoics*. Princeton U. Pr. 1987 $39.50. ISBN 0-691-08478-5. Brings together all the sources available to construct a complete picture of the Stoic conception of nature.

Sandbach, F. H. *The Stoics*. Ed. by M. I. Finley. Norton 1975 o.p. One of the best introductions to the Stoic movement and its major themes, with discussion extending into the Roman phase of Stoicism.

Schofield, Malcolm. *The Stoic Idea of the City*. Cambridge U. Pr. 1991 $44.95. ISBN 0-521-39470-8. Thoughtful examination of the Stoic political theory as the cosmic city and the later conception of natural law.

Verbeke, Gerald. *The Presence of Stoicism in Medieval Thought*. Cath. U. Pr. 1982 o.p. Scholarly contribution showing how the views of the Stoics were adapted to medieval thought.

The Skeptics

Skepticism was a post-Aristotelian development that formulated its thesis alongside the more positive doctrines of the Epicureans and the Stoics, finally arriving at another version of "a way of life." From time to time, there appeared thinkers with subtle arguments claiming loyalty to the pursuit of truth but admitting that it was impossible to find. As a result, they declared that they had to withhold judgment and remain in intellectual suspension (in *aporia*) without a way out. Some actually advocated abandoning the desire to know, confident that complete knowledge was not within human reach. However, this was a conclusion arrived at only after long search and examination of the conditions of knowing; hence the name Skeptic, that is, a person who takes thinking seriously and accepts the negative consequence. One type of Skepticism originated with Pyrrho of Elis (365–275 B.C.), whose influence extended well into the third century A.D. Pyrrho concluded that because one cannot have confidence in any scientific theory, the wise man is really wise only when he preserves rational tranquility by becoming genuinely indifferent to all views. Another trend in Skepticism, less extreme, originated within PLATO's (see also Vol. 3) Academy and lasted two centuries (the fourth and third centuries B.C.); this period is known as the Middle Academy and the New Academy, and the main representatives are Arkesilaus and Carneades (sometimes called the "DAVID HUME" of antiquity). In the first century B.C., Aenesidemus of Crete revived Pyrrhonism but refined it along Academic lines. The last great Skeptic in the tradition of Pyrrho was Sextus Empiricus, a medical doctor who wrote extensively against the dogmatic teachings of the philosophers. The list given below is merely a selection of representative books on Skepticism and the Skeptics.

Annas, Julia, and Jonathan Barnes. *The Modes of Scepticism: Ancient Texts and Modern Interpretations*. Cambridge U. Pr. 1985 $39.95. ISBN 0-521-25682-8. Readable translation of the texts, with helpful commentary.

Barnes, Jonathan. *The Toils of Scepticism*. Cambridge U. Pr. 1990 $39.95. ISBN 0-521-38339-0. Analyzes the structure of Agrippa's "modes" and their role in later views on the nature of knowledge, especially those of Sextus.

Burnyeat, M. F., ed. *The Skeptical Tradition*. U. CA Pr. 1983 $47.50. ISBN 0-520-03747-2. "The originality of this book lies in that, for the first time, it gives a quite satisfactory view of the history of Skepticism as a tradition stretching from the fourth century B.C. up to Kant" (*Journal of the History of Philosophy*).

Galen. *Three Treatises on the Nature of Science*. Ed and trans. by R. Walzer and M. Frede. Hackett Pub. 1985 $27.50. ISBN 0-915145-91-X. In his introduction Frede offers an excellent discussion of the basic themes in the treatises: On the Sects for Beginners, An Outline of Empiricism, and On Medical Experience.

Hallie, Philip. *Scepticism, Man and God: Selections from the Writings of Sextus Empiricus*. Wesleyan U. Pr. 1964 o.p. Representative passages from the text illustrating the concepts involved, accompanied by carefully written annotations.

Patrick, Mary Mills. *The Greek Sceptics*. Col. U. Pr. 1929 o.p. Stimulating and reliable; mainly on the connection between later Skepticism and Alexandrian medicine.

Sextus Empiricus. *Against the Musicians (adversis Musicos)*. Trans. by Denise D. Greaves. U. of Nebr. Pr. 1986 $21.50. ISBN 0-8032-4168-2. Contains part of "Against the Mathematicians" and an analysis of the arguments of Sextus Empiricus for and against the nature and value of music.

Stough, Charlotte L. *Greek Skepticism: A Study in Epistemology*. U. CA Pr. 1969 $45.00. ISBN 0-520-01604-1. Systematic exploration of the epistemology of the Greek Skeptics, from Pyrrho to Sextus Empiricus.

Tarrant, Harold. *Scepticism or Platonism: The Philosophy of the Fourth Academy*. Cambridge U. Pr. 1985 $49.95. ISBN 0-521-30191-2. Scholarly reconstruction of the type of Platonism that arose in the first half of the first century B.C. from the mixture of various philosophical traditions, Stoicism, Platonism, and Skepticism.

ROMAN PHILOSOPHERS

While it is not possible to speak of a distinct philosophical school in the case of ancient Rome, the term *Roman* can be used comprehensively to cover the diverse character of interests and trends that Roman thinkers adopted and cultivated with evident fervor and taste. In general, it is fair to say that what determined the scope and quality of Roman philosophical activity was not the Hellenic passion for knowledge but the usefulness of knowledge for education and public policy. Thus it is no surprise to find that the most popular philosophies in ancient Rome were Epicureanism and Stoicism—but without any deep interest in their technical parts. The Epicureans were the first to venture to Rome, and their doctrines found a great poetic representative in LUCRETIUS. The political climate was such, however, that it made Stoicism more acceptable to the Roman intellectuals and poets, who added to it moral and religious sentiments of their own; the result was a world outlook that was more emphatically eclectic than it was internally coherent. In formulating their eclecticism, the Romans were aided by three Greek teachers of philosophy: Panaetius of Rhodes (180–111 B.C.), Posidonius of Apamea (c.135–c.51 B.C.), and Antiochus of Ascalon (128–68 B.C.), who was the teacher of CICERO (see also Vols. 2 and 3). A close reading of Cicero, SENECA, and MARCUS AURELIUS shows how the Romans' practical experience helped them form their own version of Stoicism, perhaps the only genuine Roman contribution to philosophy. In this one finds an explicit deification of nature, together with the idea of a universal reason, a view that reemerged strongly in the philosophies of the eighteenth century.

In seeking to make secure a world in which civilized humanity could be guided by law, duty, and loyalty, the Roman mind found no special appeal in the originality of Greek philosophy or in its devotion to the pursuit of theoretical knowledge. It is not surprising that a version of Stoicism finally prevailed, because it gave Roman intellectuals what they needed to reflect on the beliefs they already held.

General Works

Arnold, E. Vernon. *Roman Stoicism: Being Lectures. Select Bibliographies Repr. Ser.* Ayer repr. of 1911 ed. $27.50. ISBN 0-8369-5970-1. One of the best earlier attempts to discuss this phase of Stoicism and relate it to modern thought.

Clark, Martin L. *The Roman Mind: Studies in the History of Thought from Cicero to Marcus Aurelius.* Norton 1968 $7.95. ISBN 0-393-00452-X. "A quite admirable book, distinguished not only by its brevity and lucidity . . . but by an incisive historical judgment" (*TLS*).

MacKendrick, Paul, with Karen Lee Singh. *The Philosophical Books of Cicero.* St. Martin 1989 $49.95. ISBN 0-3120-3623-X. Brings together and analyzes the structure and purpose of key passages in Cicero's writings on philosophy and their relation to rhetoric.

Rosenmeyer, Thomas G. *Senecan Drama and Stoic Cosmology.* U. CA Pr. 1989 $39.95. ISBN 0-520-06445-3. Shows why a fuller understanding of the Stoic cosmology provides the proper background for the appreciation of Seneca's plots and characters.

Rutherford, R. B. *The Meditations of Marcus Aurelius: A Study.* OUP 1989 $29.95. ISBN 0-19-814879-8. Lucid introduction to the philosopher's ethical philosophy and its background.

Wood, Neal. *Cicero's Social and Political Thought: An Introduction.* U. CA Pr. 1988 $45.00. ISBN 0-520-06042-3. Concentrates on Cicero's views of the state and purports to show his conservatism in constitutional policy.

MIDDLE PLATONISM

The period from 80 B.C. to A.D. 220 was a time of great historical transitions in the Mediterranean World. The changes that occurred during these three centuries proved to be as decisive in the transformation of philosophical ideas as it was with regard to military, political, and cultural change. The philosophical activity of this period, known as Middle Platonism, is highly complex and should be reviewed carefully by those who want to undertake serious research into the movement known as Neoplatonism. Elements of Stoicism, Epicureanism, Skepticism, and Aristotelianism are all present in the writings of the Middle Platonists, but the dominant ideas that frame their outlooks and define their philosophical quest are fundamentally Platonic. The Middle Platonists —chief among them Antiochus of Ascalon; Eudorus and PHILO JUDAEUS of Alexandria; Plutarch of Chaeronia; the leaders of the Athenian School, Nicostratus, Atticus, and Harpocration—plus such thinkers as Gaius, Albinus, APULEIUS, and the Neopythagoreans Moderatus, Numerius, and others together form a wide spectrum of the Platonizing movement that broadened the era's conceptual apparatus to accommodate the claims of religious beliefs to philosophical credibility.

General Works

Billings, Thomas H. *The Platonism of Philo Judaeus.* 1919. Ed. by Leonardo Taran. *Ancient Philosophy Ser.* Garland 1979 o.p. Mainly useful for its careful listing of parallel textual references to Plato's works.

Dillon, John. *The Middle Platonists 80 B.C. to A.D. 220.* Cornell Univ. Pr. 1977 o.p. The best available treatment of a little-known but very influential period, especially as a formative force, with reference to early antecedents but mainly devoted to Philo, the Neopythagoreans, and Antiochus.

Filoramo, Giovanni. *A History of Gnosticism.* Trans. by A. Alcock. Blackwell Pubs. 1990 $39.95. ISBN 0-631-15756-5. English translation of a well-researched work on a complex religious movement and its contact with philosophy.

Gersh, Stephen. *Middle Platonism and Neoplatonism.* 2 vols. U. of Notre Dame Pr. 1986 $75.00. ISBN 0-268-01363-2. Fine, scholarly account of the Platonizing movement in the Hellenistic period and its influence on later development in the Middle Ages.

Goodenough, Erwin R. *An Introduction to Philo Judaeus.* Allenson 1962 o.p. Basic work on Philo's thought.

Sandmel, Samuel. *Philo of Alexandria: An Introduction.* OUP 1979 o.p. Covers the main idea of Philo as thinker and religious leader in Alexandria.

Winston, David, and John Dillon. *Two Treatises of Philo of Alexandria: A Commentary on De Gigantibus and Quod Deus Sit Immutabilis. Brown Class. in Judaica Ser.* Scholars Pr. GA 1983 $15.00. ISBN 0-89130-563-7. Makes accessible the two tracks of Philo's single treatise discussing the immutability of God.

Witt, R. E. *Albinus and the History of Middle Platonism.* Cambridge U. Pr. 1937 o.p. Challenging effort to place Albinus in Hellenistic thought.

Wolfson, Harry A. *Philo: Foundations of Religious Philosophy in Judaism, Christianity and Islam.* 2 vols. HUP rev. ed. 1962 $65.00. ISBN 0-674-66450-7. "We have here not only by far the best and most detailed treatise on Philo that has ever appeared but also an invaluable presentation of the subject matter of the philosophy of religion" (*AHR*).

NEOPLATONISM

During the third century A.D., philosophers and other thinkers embraced a new and intensified interest in Platonic thought that both assimilated certain elements from the complex tradition of the Middle Platonists and the teachings of the Stoics and tried to provide a philosophical alternative to the recurrent waves of religious movements. The result was Neoplatonism.

Neoplatonism is a modern term used to cover a very complex philosophical movement that occurred in later Hellenistic times, a movement that found adherents not only in Alexandria, where it had its beginnings, but also in many other places, including Athens. Neoplatonism embraced a comprehensive theory of the universe (its ultimate source and the cause of its development) as well as an attitude and a way of life. According to Neoplatonists, the divine origin of all things, including humanity, is the One, the perfect and eternal absolute Being or God. Human beings can return to the One only through the path of theoretical knowledge and purity by direct ecstatic experience. For the Neoplatonists, each level of reality requires the ascent to a higher place of inner consciousness until one finally is united in a timeless moment with the absolute One.

Insofar as Neoplatonism adopted the form of a definite system and made use of a philosophical method to articulate its basic thesis and develop distinct arguments to defend it, its real founder is PLOTINUS, the leading member of the Alexandrian type of Neoplatonism. Alexandrian Neoplatonism was the most influential of the Neoplatonic schools, the others being the Syrian school with I'amblichus its main representative, and the Athenian school led by Proclus (c.410–485), who also was head of the Academy of Athens. When the schools of philosophy were closed by order of the Emperor Justinian in 529 the Neoplatonism of Athens remained doctrinally alive. Revivals of Platonism, especially during the Renaissance, were actually in the guise of the Neoplatonism of Plotinus.

General Works

Blumenthal, H. J., and A. C. Lloyd, eds. *Souls and the Structure of Being in Late Neoplatonism—Syrianus, Proclus and Simplicius.* Humanities 1982 o.p.

Dodds, E. R. *Select Passages Illustrating Neoplatonism.* Ares 1980 $15.00. ISBN 0-89005-302-2. Collection of representative texts from the extant writings of Plotinus, Proclus, and other leading thinkers.

Evangeliou, Christos. *Aristotle's Categories and Porphyry.* E. J. Brill 1988 o.p. Systematic study exhibiting Porphyry's sympathetic treatment of the Aristotelian theory of categories as countering Plotinus's austere criticism of same.

Finamore, John. *Iamblichus and the Theory of the Vehicle of the Soul.* Scholars Pr. GA 1985 $14.95. ISBN 0-89130-883-0. "This monograph is an important, though naturally limited contribution to the larger topic of the relationship between philosophy and religion" (*Choice*).

Harris, R. Baine, ed. *The Significance of Neoplatonism.* St. U. NY Pr. 1967 $39.50. ISBN 0-87395-800-4. Collection of important papers sampling the significance of Neoplatonism in Western philosophy and culture; organized around three central themes: the sources, the interpretation, and the influence of Neoplatonism.

——, ed. *The Structure of Being: A Neoplatonic Interpretation. Neoplatonism: Ancient and Modern Ser.* St. U. NY Pr. 1981 $49.50. ISBN 0-87395-532-3. Collection of papers delivered at various meetings exploring the strands of logic and ontology in the Neoplatonic movement in contrast to the logic of other ways of philosophizing.

Hornum, M., trans. *Porphyry's Launching-Points to the Realm of the Mind: An Introduction to the Neoplatonic Philosophy of Plotinus.* Phanes Pr. 1988 $20.00 ISBN 0-933999-585. Reissue of the 1918 translation, with Hornum's discussion of Neoplatonism and Porphyry; introduction by K. Guthrie.

Lloyd, A. C. *The Anatomy of Neoplatonism.* OUP 1990 $55.00. ISBN 0-19-824229-8. Introduction to Neoplatonism emphasizing logic and semantics, often using Aristotle's writings and commentaries on his works.

Merlan, Philip. *From Platonism to Neoplatonism.* The Hague 2nd ed. 1960 o.p. Reliable, but deals often with fine philosophical points and technical matters.

Morewedge, Parviz, ed. *Neoplatonism and Islamic Thought.* State U. NY Pr. 1992 $59.50. ISBN 0-7914-1335-7. Christian, Jewish, and Islamic scholars explore how Neoplatonism became a framework for philosophical reflection in the Islamic world a few centuries after its origin.

Morrow, G. R., trans. *Proclus: A Commentary on the First Book of Euclid's Elements*.
    Princeton U. Pr. 1992 $19.95. ISBN 0-691-02090-6. Proclus's exposition of the
    Euclidean system, a fount of knowledge in the history of mathematics, offered now
    in an accurate scholarly translation with valuable comments; introduction by Ian
    Mueller.
Morrow, Glenn, and John M. Dillon, trans. *Proclus' Commentary on Plato's Parmenides*.
    Princeton U. Pr. 1992 $24.95. ISBN 0-691-02089-2. Excellent translation of Proclus's
    major work, which became the most important text of the Athenian school of
    Neoplatonism; introduction by John M. Dillon.
O'Meara, Dominick J., ed. *Neoplatonism and Christian Thought*. St. U. NY Pr. 1982
    $59.50. ISBN 0-87395-492-0. Nineteen specialists representing various fields discuss
    Neoplatonism and Christianity and the interaction between them.
Porphyry. *On Aristotle's Categories*. Trans. by Steven K. Strange. Cornell Univ. Pr. 1992
    $47.95. ISBN 0-8014-2816-5. Recent translation of an influential text.
_____. *Porphyry's Isagoge*. Trans. by E. W. Warren. Pontifical Inst. 1975 o.p. Excellent
    rendition of this influential handbook, with valuable observations in the translator's
    introduction and notes.
Proclus. *The Elements of Theology*. Trans. by E. R. Dodds. OUP 1992 $29.95. ISBN 0-19-
    82814-097-5. A work considered to be as important as Plotinus' *Enneads*; introduc-
    tion and commentary by the translator.
_____. *The Platonic Theology (Six Books of Proclus on the Theology of Plato)*. 2 vols. Ed.
    by Robert Navon. Trans. by Thomas Taylor. Selene Bks. Vol. 1 Bks. I-III 1985 repr. of
    1861 ed. $40.00. ISBN 0-9609866-7-7. Vol. 2 Bks. IV-VI 1986 repr. of 1816 ed. $40.00.
    ISBN 0-933601-05-0. With a preface by R. Blaine Harris.
Wallis, R. T. *Neoplatonism. Class. Life and Letters Ser*. Biblio NY 1972 o.p. Excellent and
    easily accessible introduction to the Neoplatonic schools from Plotinus to Damas-
    cius, written with mastery of the intricacies of the complex history of this movement.
Wallis, Richard T., and J. Bregman, eds. *Neoplatonism and Gnosticism*. St. U. NY Pr. 1992
    $59.50. ISBN 0-7914-1337-3. Informed interpretive papers on the interrelationship of
    these movements and their impact on philosophy and culture.
Whittaker, Thomas. *Neo-Platonists. Select Bibliographies Repr. Ser*. Ayer repr. of 1918 ed.
    $19.50. ISBN 0-8369-5305-3. General survey, still useful for its accounts of the
    background of Neoplatonism, religious developments in later antiquity, and the
    diverse schools within the movement and their influence on philosophy and
    theology.

EARLY CHRISTIAN THINKERS

When the religious reform of the Hebraic tradition assumed the form of
Christianity, Christian religious thinkers defended Jesus as *Christos* and mixed
Greco-Roman ideas with the new religion. The writings of Paul of Tarsus and
the fourth Gospel of John set the pace and gave direction to the movement,
which soon encountered rivalry and antagonisms. During the second century
A.D., there was a strong moral interpretation of Christianity aimed at purging the
religion of its mystical notions and elements of magical redemption. These
moral interpreters of Christianity are known as the Apologists, with Justin the
Martyr and Irenaeus as early spokesmen of this trend. The Alexandrian
Platonists—Athanasius, Clement, and ORIGEN—who espoused Christianity were
speculative theologians, interested in the philosophical interpretation of the
doctrine of the Trinity. Although the Western church fathers sought to build the
body of Christian doctrine on Paul's dualism and his rigorous moralism and on
ritual mystery, the Eastern church fathers stayed closer to the intellectual and
rationalist tradition of the Greek philosophers. Such Eastern thinkers as
Gregory of Nyssa (d.394), Basil the Great (d.379), and Gregory of Nanzianzen
(d.390) wrote treatises to explain the fundamentals of Christian faith with the

help of philosophical concepts and ideas. The first Westerner to introduce Platonism into Western Christianity was AUGUSTINE OF HIPPO (354–430), who synthesized Greek speculative thought, Hebrew morality, and Roman social experience into a coherent system of faith.

General Works

Balthasar, Hans Urs von, ed. *Origen: Spirit and Fire: A Thematic Anthology of His Writings.* Trans. by R. J. Daly. Cath. U. Pr. 1984 $34.95. ISBN 0-8132-0591-3. Representative selection of texts.

Bigg, Charles. *Christian Platonists of Alexandria: Eight Lectures.* AMS Pr. 1980 repr. of 1886 ed. $27.50 ISBN 0-404-00799-6. Still useful and informative on the philosophical ideas of Clement, Origen, and others.

Chadwick, H. *Early Christian Thoughts and the Classical Tradition.* OUP 1966 $19.95. ISBN 0-19-826673-1. By a scholar known for his contributions to the Cambridge *History of Greek Philosophy.*

Dodds, E. R. *Pagan and Christian in an Age of Anxiety: Some Aspects of Religious Experience from Marcus Aurelius to Constantine.* Cambridge U. Pr. 1991 $15.95. ISBN 0-521-38599-7. Judicious and penetrating examination of the conflict between Neoplatonism and Christianity.

Hatch, Edwin. *The Influence of Greek Ideas on Christianity.* Peter Smith 1970 $11.75. ISBN 0-8446-0683-9. A classic in its field, tracing the Greek antecedents of Christian thought; with a foreword by Frederick Grant.

Jaeger, Werner. *Early Christianity and Greek Paideia.* HUP 1961 $7.95. ISBN 0-674-22052-8. The Carl Newell Jackson Lectures at Harvard on the historical continuity and the tradition of Greek *paideia* in the centuries of late antiquity.

Jonas, Hans. *The Gnostic Religion.* Beacon Pr. 1958 $15.95. ISBN 0-8070-5799-1. Includes chapters on Gnostic and Neoplatonic worldviews; a good introduction to this complex religious movement.

Kerr, H. T. *The First Systematic Theologian, Origen of Alexandria.* Princeton U. Pr. 1958 o.p. Excellent introduction to the philosophical ideas of Origen.

Lilla, Salvatore R. *Clement of Alexandria: A Study in Christian Platonism and Gnosticism.* OUP 1971 o.p. Based on firsthand knowledge of the sources.

Louth, Andrew. *The Origins of the Christian Mystical Tradition.* OUP 1983 $19.95. ISBN 0-19-826655-3. Traces the tradition to Platonic and older origins, leading to a Neoplatonic formulation.

Osborn, E. F. *The Philosophy of Clement of Alexandria.* Kraus 1974 repr. of 1957 ed. $28.00. ISBN 0-8115-1716-0. Continues to be recognized as a useful introduction to Clement's thought.

Rorem, Paul. *Pseudo-Dionysius: A Commentary on the Texts and an Introduction to Their Influence.* OUP 1992 $39.95. ISBN 0-19-507664-8. Discusses the texts of the pseudonymous author who used Neoplatonic ideas to found Christian mysticism.

Scott, Alan. *Origen and the Life of the Stars: A History of an Idea.* OUP 1991 $49.95. ISBN 0-19-826462-3. Deals with the religious traditions Origen uses and extends to build his cosmology and biblical theology.

Tripolitis, Antonia. *The Doctrine of the Soul in the Thought of Plotinus and Origen.* Libra 1977 $15.00. ISBN 0-87212-061-9. Informative study tracing the background and different orientations of views on the nature of the soul in late antiquity.

Wallis, Richard T., and Jay Bregman, eds. *Neoplatonism and Gnosticism.* State U. NY Pr. 1993 $59.50. ISBN 0-7914-1337-3. Series of papers discussing how, in light of new historical evidence, Gnosticism was a phenomenon extending far beyond Christianity and displaying a strong Platonic influence.

Wolfson, Harry Austryn. *The Philosophy of the Church Fathers*: Vol. 1 *Faith, Trinity, Incarnation.* HUP 3rd rev. ed. 1970 $34.95. ISBN 0-674-66551-1. A classic in the field of early Christian theology and its relationship to religious and philosophical sources.

CHRONOLOGY OF AUTHORS

Greek Philosophers
Pythagoras of Samos. c.582–c.507 B.C.
Heraclitus of Ephesus. fl. c.500 B.C.
Socrates. 469–399 B.C.
Xenophon. c.430–c.355 B.C.
Plato. 427?–347 B.C.
Aristotle. 384–322 B.C.
Theophrastus of Eresus. c.372–
   c.287 B.C.
Epicurus. 341–270 B.C.

Roman Philosophers
Cicero or Tully. 106–43 B.C.
Lucretius. c.99–c.55 B.C.
Seneca, Lucius Annaeus. c.3 B.C.–
   A.D. 65
Marcus Aurelius. A.D. 121–180
Plotinus. A.D. 205–270

ARISTOTLE. 384–322 B.C.

One of the great thinkers of all times, Aristotle was born in Stagira in Chalcidice, northern Greece. His father, Nichomachus, was court physician to the king of Macedon. At the age of 17, Aristotle enrolled in PLATO's (see also Vol. 3) Academy and remained there for 20 years, first as a student and later as a teacher. After Plato's death, accompanied by several close associates, he went first to Assos and then to Lesbos, continuing his research and teaching. In 342 he accepted the invitation of King Philip of Macedon to be tutor to his son Alexander. In subsequent years he returned to Athens, where he opened his own school, the Lyceum, also known as the Peripatetic school. He remained there until after the death of Alexander, when the anti-Macedonian party in Athens accused him of impiety. He then fled Athens and died in 322 in the nearby city of Chalkis in Euboea.

Aristotle systematized the available knowledge of his times and added to it the results of his own original researches to become the founder of most of the sciences. He wrote on logic, rhetoric, literary theory, physics, botany, zoology, psychology, economics, ethics, politics, astronomy, and "first philosophy," or what was later to be named metaphysics. He laid the foundation of scientific methodology and developed further Plato's own ideal of science. Most of his surviving writings are genuine. They became very influential after the Roman conquest of Greece, when Greek scholars edited his manuscripts and wrote extensive commentaries. His philosophy never was eclipsed, although there have been periods of strong reaction against some of his principal doctrines. What has been written about Aristotle is enough to fill the wing of a modern library.

Aristotle sought to bring together within a logical scheme of explanation all the fields of human knowledge, be they about the elements, nature, life or human culture, and political activities. After criticizing his teacher, Plato, for holding that the forms of things are transcendent realities and ideal beings, he argued that forms can exist only as immanent in things and as functional structures determining their kinds and their purposes in each specific case. According to his general theory of life, the structures of living organisms become more complex, from plants to animals to human beings. Organisms develop as distinct individuals completing the cycle of their purpose in life, barring violence or other interruptive factors; but as members of species they remain what they are, untouched by what modern biology was to call evolution.

Human beings possess intelligence, and, as they form groups and societies, they establish institutions, which they seek to refine in an effort to perfect the ways of governing in civilized states. The purpose of human life for Aristotle is the completion of our potential through knowledge and enlightened habits to cope with our emotional and intellectual endowment and to promote cooperation to secure the common good. Thus, the highest art for Aristotle was that of intelligent politics and legislation that secures the conditions enabling citizens to live together in the pursuit of perfectibility and well-being through the habits of practical and intellectual excellence.

Aristotle, like his teacher, Plato, founded his own university and attracted a great number of students, who in turn undertook inquiries of their own with a real sense of intellectual independence. And like the Academy, this school appointed successors to lead it after the death of its founder. THEOPHRASTUS OF ERESUS, the first successor (from 323 to 287), initiated new investigations next to those of his contemporaries, for example, Eudemus in mathematics and astronomy, Aristoxenus in music, and Dikaiarchus in geography and political theory. The next successor, Strato (289–269), wrote on natural philosophy, but after Lyco's succession in 269, the school began to lose its impetus. Much later, after Aristotle's manuscripts were recovered by Tyrannion and Andronikus of Rhodes and new life was breathed into the school, the Peripatetics (as they were called) became concerned on the whole with editions and commentaries on the works of the master. The great scientific inquiries Aristotle had initiated followed for a while a path of their own. They were pursued by researchers at famous centers of learning, such as the Museum and the Library of Alexandria and the royal courts in other major cities.

BOOKS BY ARISTOTLE

As in the case of Plato's works, Aristotle's own have been translated and published as individual treatises, as groups of treatises, as the entire corpus, and in selections from representative treatises.

Aristotle's De Generatione et Corruptione. Ed. by C.J.F. Williams. OUP 1982 o.p. Translates as *On Generation and Corruption;* Aristotle's treatise on the constantly changing earthly, material bodies.

Aristotle's Eudemian Ethics. Ed. by M. J. Woods. OUP 1982 o.p. Argues that this work is less mature than the *Nicomachean Ethics;* a valuable commentary.

Aristotle's On the Soul (de Anima). Trans. by H. G. Apostle. Peripatetic 1982 $18.00. ISBN 0-9602870-8-6. Adequate translation with a brief introduction and comments.

Aristotle's Physics. Peripatetic 1980 repr. of 1969 ed. $21.60. ISBN 0-9602870-2-7. Conscientiously done translations that reflect the effort to remain faithful to the original.

The Basic Works of Aristotle. Ed. by Richard P. McKeon. Random 1941 $40.00. ISBN 0-394-41610-4

The Complete Works of Aristotle. Ed. by Jonathan Barnes. 2 vols Princeton U. Pr. 1984 $79.00. ISBN 0-691-09950-2. Revised edition of the standard Oxford translation of Aristotle's works, with a more comprehensive selection of the fragments.

De Partibus Animalium, Book I, and De Generatione Animalium, Book I, with Passages from Book II, 1–3. Ed. by D. M. Balme. OUP 1992 $24.95. ISBN 0-19-87128-1. Revised edition of two selected texts in which Aristotle sets forth his philosophy and methodology for the study of living beings.

Ethica Eudemia. Ed. by R. R. Walzer and J. M. Mingay. OUP 1991 $24.95. ISBN 0-19-814575-6. Revised text of the 1884 edition, with a critical apparatus and preface.

The Ethics of Aristotle. Ed. by John Burnet. Ayer 1974 repr. of 1900 ed. $40.00. ISBN 0-405-04833-5

Nicomachean Ethics. Trans. by Terrence Irwin. Hackett Pub. 1985 $34.95. ISBN 0-915145-65-0. Important among his more humanistic studies; Aristotle here tries to analyze happiness.

On Rhetoric. Trans. by George A. Kennedy. OUP 1991 $27.95. ISBN 0-19-506486-0. New translation, with an introduction offering an overview of the work.

The Poetics of Aristotle. Trans. by Preston H. Epps. U. of NC Pr. 1967 repr. of 1942 ed. $5.95. ISBN 0-8078-4017-3. Aristotle turns his attention to the arts, which he considers a dynamic principle of creativity.

The Politics. HUP $15.50. ISBN 0-674-99291-1

Prior Analytics. Trans. by Robin Smith. Hackett Pub. 1989 $36.00. ISBN 0-87220-065-5. Fine scholarship, with an introduction employing recent research in deductive models to interpret Aristotle's logic.

The Rhetoric and the Poetics of Aristotle. Trans. by W. Rhys Roberts and Ingram Bywater. *Modern Lib. College Ed. Ser.* Random 1977 $8.95. ISBN 0-394-60425-3. "Aristotle's analysis of the elements of rhetorical discourse (the speaker, the audience, the subject), the kinds of rhetorical discourse (forensic, deliberative, and epideictic), and the modes of persuasion (logical, ethical, and pathetic)" (*Thought*).

Works. Loeb Class. Lib. 23 vols. HUP 1926–70 $13.95 ea. Greek text with translation on the facing pages; competently done by various hands.

Works: The Oxford Translation. Trans. under the editorship of J. A. Smith and W. D. Ross by J. I. Beare, Ingram Bywater, and others. 12 vols. OUP 1908–52 o.p. Issued in parts over a period of years, this monumental translation supersedes all others and contains such great classics as the Jowett "Politics" and the "Poetics" by Bywater.

BOOKS ABOUT ARISTOTLE AND HIS SCHOOL

Ackrill, J. L. *Aristotle on Eudaimonia.* Longwood MA 1974 o.p. Discusses the arguments that seek to establish "happiness" as the highest value.

——. *Aristotle the Philosopher.* OUP 1981 $14.95. ISBN 0-19-289118-9. Stimulating general introduction emphasizing method, change, science, logic, metaphysics, and the ethics.

Adler, Mortimer J. *Aristotle for Everybody.* Bantam 1983 $4.95. ISBN 0-553-26776-0. Descriptive outline aimed at introducing Aristotle's philosophy to the casual reader.

Allan, D. F. *Philosophy of Aristotle.* OUP 2nd ed. 1970 o.p. Excellent introductory work on Aristotle's principal doctrines in metaphysics, ethics, logic, and politics.

Annas, Julia, Henry Blumenthal, and Howard Robinson, eds. *Aristotle and the Later Tradition.* OUP 1991 $65.00. ISBN 0-19-823965-3. Contributions to the study of Aristotle's treatment of his predecessors and the Neoplatonic and later uses of Aristotle.

Anton, John P. *Aristotle's Theory of Contrariety.* U. Pr. of Amer. 1987 $25.50. ISBN 0-8191-6526-3. Thorough study of a major theme in Aristotle's philosophical system that is present in all Greek thinkers.

Anton, John P., and Anthony Preus, eds. *Aristotle's Ontology: Essays in Ancient Greek Philosophy, V.* State U. NY Pr. 1992 $16.95. ISBN 0-7914-1028-5. Interpretations by specialists of fundamental issues in Aristotle's method, metaphysics, general theory of life, his treatment of property rights, and concept of persons.

——. *Essays in Ancient Greek Philosophy, IV: Aristotle's Ethics.* State U. NY Pr. 1991 $59.50. ISBN 0-7914-0654-7. Discussions by leading scholars on Aristotle's methodology and moral reasoning in ethics, virtue, and character.

Barker, Ernest. *Political Thought of Plato and Aristotle.* Dover 1949 $10.95. ISBN 0-486-20521-5. The second half of this classic work discusses in detail Aristotle's *Politics*.

Barnes, Jonathan. *Aristotle.* OUP 1982 $13.95. ISBN 0-19-287582-5. Recommended for undergraduates interested in Aristotle's views on science and logic.

Barnes, Jonathan, and Richard Sorabji, eds. *Articles on Aristotle.* 4 vols. St. Martin 1979 Vol. 1 $27.50. ISBN 0-312-05477-7. Vol. 2. $27.50. ISBN 0-312-05478-5. Vols. 3-4 o.p. Collections of scholarly contributions by specialists covering science (Vol. 1), ethics and politics (Vol. 2), metaphysics (Vol. 3), and psychology and ethics (Vol. 4).

Belfiore, Elizabeth. *Tragic Pleasures: Aristotle on Plot and Emotion*. Princeton U. Pr. 1992
    $45.00. ISBN 0-691-06899-2. Interprets the *Poetics* by relating it to the other
    Aristotelian works, especially the *Rhetoric* and the *Politics*.
Brentano, Franz. *Aristotle and His World View*. Trans. by Roderick Chisholm. U. CA Pr.
    1978 $27.50. ISBN 0-520-03390-6. Examines what Brentano found to be the essential
    features of Aristotle's worldview to show that they constitute a unified system.
_____. *On the Several Senses of Being in Aristotle*. Trans. by Rolf George. U. CA Pr. 1981
    repr. of 1975 ed. $35.00. ISBN 0-520-04420-7. Brentano's doctoral dissertation;
    important for the influence it had on Heidegger.
_____. *The Psychology of Aristotle: In Particular His Doctrine of the Active Intellect with
    an Appendix Concerning the Activity of Aristotle's God*. Trans. by Rolf George. U. CA
    Pr. 1977 $32.50. ISBN 0-520-03081-8. Of special interest because of the interpreta-
    tion Brentano attributes to Aristotle, particularly the doctrine in which Aristotle
    makes God an active principal in the creation of each human being.
Broadie, Sarah. *Ethics with Aristotle*. OUP 1991 $59.00. ISBN 0-19-506601-4. Discussion
    of the main concepts in Aristotle's ethical theory, particularly the status of *theoria* in
    relation to *eudaimonia*, with the help of recent analytical tools.
Butcher, S. H. *Aristotle's Theory of Poetry and Fine Art*. Dover 1955 $9.95. ISBN 0-486-
    20042-6. A standard work on the *Poetics*, prefaced by an essay on Aristotelian literary
    criticism by J. Gassner; with an introduction by Gassner.
Bywater, Ingram. *Aristotle on the Art of Poetry*. Ancient Philosophy Ser. Garland 2nd ed.
    1980 o.p. Readable and influential treatment of Aristotle's esthetics.
Charles, David. *Aristotle's Philosophy of Action*. Cornell Univ. Pr. 1984 $44.50. ISBN 0-
    8014-1708-2. Analyzes practical reason and incontinence, with frequent reference to
    recent ethical theorists.
Cherniss, Harold. *Aristotle's Criticism of Presocratic Philosophy*. Hippocrene Bks. 1964
    o.p. Great critical study, revolutionary and controversial, attacking Aristotle's
    historiographic method on the ground that Aristotle misunderstood the thought of
    Plato and thus made it an object of criticism.
Clark, Stephen R. *Aristotle's Man: Speculations upon Aristotelian Anthropology*. OUP 1983
    repr. of 1975 ed. o.p. "A unique interpretation of Aristotle . . . which makes the
    biological conception of devolution—opposed to evolution— crucial to Aristotle's
    biology" (*Choice*).
Cleary, John. *Aristotle on the Many Senses of Priority*. S. Ill. U. Pr. 1988 $15.95. ISBN 0-
    8093-1465-7. Significant exploration of the role of the concept of priority in
    Aristotle's metaphysical system, tracing its many aspects and uses from the *Topics* to
    the later works.
Cooper, John M. *Reason and Human Good in Aristotle*. Hackett Pub. 1986 repr. $30.00.
    ISBN 0-87220-115-5. Provides a unifying framework for Aristotle's views on virtue
    and practical intelligence, basing it on all his ethical writings.
Cooper, Lane. *Aristotelian Theory of Comedy*. Kraus repr. of 1922 ed. o.p. Experimental
    attempt to reconstruct the "lost" part of the *Poetics*.
_____. *Poetics of Aristotle*. Cooper Sq. 1963 repr. of 1930 ed. $45.00. ISBN 0-8154-
    0053-5. One of the best books on Aristotle's theory of poetry.
Dancy, R. M. *Sense and Contradiction: A Study in Aristotle*. Kluwer Ac. 1975 $67.00. ISBN
    90-277-0565-8. Outstanding discussion of Aristotle's logic as related to his metaphys-
    ics.
During, Ingemar, and G. E. Owens, eds. *Aristotle and Plato in the Mid-Fourth Century*.
    Humanities 1960 o.p. Excellent collection of essays by different authors setting high
    standards in Aristotelian scholarship.
Edel, Abraham. *Aristotle and His Philosophy* Bks. Demand repr. of 1981 ed. $128.00.
    ISBN 0-8357-3902-3. Comprehensive work on Aristotle's philosophy, with extensive
    discussion of its relationship to modern and contemporary systems and ideas.
Elders, L. *Aristotle's Theology: A Commentary on the Book of Metaphysics*. *Philosophical
    Texts and Studies Ser*. Humanities 1972 o.p. Extended analysis of the arguments and
    the conceptions of theology in Aristotle.

Else, Gerald Frank. *Aristotle's Poetics: The Argument*. HUP 1957 o.p. Monumental work on Aristotle's theory of tragedy, setting forth many original points of interpretation.
———. *Plato and Aristotle on Poetry*. Ed. by Peter Burian. U. of NC Pr. $32.50. ISBN 0-8078-1708-2. Comparative study of the Platonic antecedents of Aristotle's views on poetry.

Evans, J. D. *Aristotle's Concept of Dialectic*. Cambridge U. Pr. 1977 $32.95. ISBN 0-521-21425-4. Competent discussion of the difference between dialectic and demonstrative syllogism.

Ferejohn, Michael. *The Origins of Aristotelian Science*. Yale U. Pr. 1991 $32.50. ISBN 0-300-04649-9. Thorough treatment, based on direct acquaintance with Aristotle's theory of demonstration as the model of scientific knowledge and its indebtedness to Plato's method of division.

Ferguson, John. *Aristotle*. *Twayne's World Authors Ser*. G. K. Hall 1972 o.p. "There is no small compendium to Aristotle in English more useful than this one. It is not intended as a work for scholarly reference. It is written, nevertheless, for serious students in the style of a genial teacher, proceeding text by text, through the entire scope of Aristotle's work" (*Choice*).

Fine, Gail. *On Ideas: Aristotle's Criticism of Plato's Theory of Forms*. OUP 1993 $55.00. ISBN 0-19-823949-1. Full-length treatment of a major theme, with close attention to the text; relates the findings to contemporary philosophical interests.

Gill, Mary Louise. *Aristotle on Substance: The Paradox of Unity*. Princeton U. Pr. 1989 $35.00. ISBN 0-691-07334-1. Discusses Aristotle's arguments concerning the conceptual unity of form and matter to determine the consistency of his theory of substance.

Golden, Leon, and O. B. Hardison, Jr. *Aristotle's Poetics: A Translation and Commentary for Students of Literature*. U. Press Fla. 1981 $18.95. ISBN 0-8130-0720-8. Very useful handbook for advanced students in ancient views on tragedy.

Gotthelf, Allan, and James Lennox. *Philosophical Issues in Aristotle's Biology*. Cambridge U. Pr. 1987 $64.95. ISBN 0-521-31091-1. Well-planned collection of essays on Aristotle's biological works, examining the relationships of biology to the broader philosophical problems of scientific methodology and logic.

Graham, Daniel W. *Aristotle's Two Systems*. OUP 1988 $79.00. ISBN 0-19-824970-5. Responding to developmentalists like Jaeger and Owen, argues that Aristotle held two great yet incompatible systems, one based on the *Organon* and one on the *Physics* and *Metaphysics*.

Grene, Marjorie. *A Portrait of Aristotle*. U. Ch. Pr. 1979 o.p. Sympathetic account, with an emphasis on the scientific side of Aristotle, especially the biological investigations.

Grote, George. *Aristotle*. Ed. by Alexander Bain and C. Croom Robertson. Ayer 2nd ed. 1974 repr. of 1880 ed. $37.00. ISBN 0-405-04843-2. Classic, comprehensive study, still useful.

Halliwell, S. *Aristotle's Poetics*. U. of NC Pr. 1986 $30.00. ISBN 0-8078-1710-4. A contribution to the study of Aristotle's *Poetics* as theory of poetry and esthetics in general.

Halper, Edward C. *One and Many in Aristotle's Metaphysics: The Central Books*. Ohio St. U. Pr. 1989 $48.50. ISBN 0-8142-0456-2. Views substance (*ousia*) as a "one-and-many" problem encountered in Books 7–9 of the *Metaphysics;* proposes a solution after weighing the merits of recent interpretations.

Hardie, W. F. *Aristotle's Ethical Theory*. OUP 2nd ed. 1981 $39.95. ISBN 0-19-824633-1. Thorough study of Aristotle's ethics.

Heath, Thomas. *Mathematics in Aristotle*. *Ancient Philosophy Ser*. Garland 1980 o.p. Classic work that collects, translates, and discusses the passages on mathematics.

Hintikka, Jaakko. *Time and Necessity: Studies in Aristotle's Theory of Modality*. OUP 1973 o.p. Concentrates on the "logical modalities in Aristotle and their consequences for his ideas on time, determinism and infinity" (Frederick J. Crosson).

Irwin, Terence. *Aristotle's First Principles*. OUP 1988 $34.00. ISBN 0-19-824717-6. Comprehensive attempt to exhibit continuity of principles in Aristotle's metaphysical, ethical, and political views; focuses on two phases of dialectic and their implications.

Jaeger, Werner. *Aristotle: Fundamentals of the History of His Development*. OUP 2nd ed. 1962 o.p. A landmark in Aristotelian studies, seeking to trace the development of his basic ideas through a chronology of his works.

Joachim, H. H. *Aristotle: The Nicomachean Ethics: A Commentary*. Ed. by D. A. Rees. Greenwood 1985 repr. of 1951 ed. o.p. Reliable translation with insightful analyses of the major themes and cross-references.

Jones, John. *On Aristotle and Greek Tragedy*. Stanford U. Pr. 1962 $37.50. ISBN 0-8047-1092-9. Aims to discover what Aristotle really was saying about the drama in his *Poetics* and to test these discoveries on plays by Aeschylus, Sophocles, and Euripides.

Judson, Lindsay, ed. *Aristotle's Physics*. OUP 1991 $65.00. ISBN 0-19-824844-X. Fine collection of papers by experts exploring major themes in Aristotle's treatise on nature.

Keaney, John J. *The Composition of Aristotle's Athenaion Politeia*. OUP 1992 $39.95. ISBN 0-19-507032-1. Stimulating discussion of Aristotle's understanding of the Athenian constitution as cultural history and political record.

Kenny, Anthony. *The Aristotelian Ethics: A Study of the Relationship between the Eudemian and Nichomachean Ethics of Aristotle*. OUP 1978 o.p. Challenges the traditional view of the *Eudemian Ethics* as an immature Platonizing treatise written prior to the *Nicomachean Ethics*.

———. *Aristotle on the Perfect Life*. OUP 1992 $49.95. ISBN 0-19-824017-1. Reexamines the overall ideal in the *Nicomachean Ethics* and *Eudemian Ethics* for coherence and relevance in light of today's debates on the Aristotelian view of happiness.

Keyt, David, and Fred Miller, eds. *A Companion to Aristotle's Politics*. Blackwell Pubs. 1991 $63.95. ISBN 1-55786-200-1. Collection of articles by well-known scholars with a variety of viewpoints on philological, philosophical, and historical aspects of the *Politics*.

Kraut, Richard. *Aristotle and the Human Good*. Princeton U. Pr. 1989 $42.50. ISBN 0-691-07349-X. Close examination of the Aristotelian conception of happiness (*eudaimonia*); shows that Aristotle offers a consistent account arguing that the good resides exclusively in intellectual activity.

Lear, Jonathan. *Aristotle: The Desire to Understand*. Cambridge U. Pr. 1988 $47.95. ISBN 0-521-34523-5. Brings together salient representative texts from Aristotle's *Physics*, *Metaphysics*, *Ethics*, and *Politics* to discuss the intelligibility of the world.

———. *Aristotle and Logical Theory*. Cambridge U. Pr. 1986 $13.95. ISBN 0-521-31178-0. Scholarly approach describing the dual aspects of Aristotle's syllogistic in the broad sense of deductive logic and in the narrow sense of isolated formal inference.

Lewis, Frank A. *Substance and Predication in Aristotle*. Cambridge U. Pr. 1991 $44.50. ISBN 0-521-39159-8. Scholarly work examining basic issues in Aristotelian metaphysics, taking into account recent major writings.

Lloyd, Geoffrey E. *Aristotle: Growth and Structure of His Thought*. Cambridge U. Pr. 1968 $54.95. ISBN 0-521-09456-9. Good introduction to Aristotle's development, showing the unity and coherence of his philosophy.

Lord, Carnes. *Education and Culture in the Political Thought of Aristotle*. Cornell Univ. Pr. 1982 $31.50. ISBN 0-8014-1412-1. Argues persuasively for Lord's own interpretation of Aristotle's views on art and culture in the context of education.

Lord, Carnes, and David O'Connor. *Essays on the Foundations of Aristotelian Political Science*. U. CA Pr. 1991 $45.00. ISBN 0-520-06711-8. Emphasizing the beneficial side of human knowledge in Aristotle, reexamines a cluster of political issues—race, class, and gender—in the context of constitutional types.

Loux, Michael J. *Primary Ousia: An Essay on Aristotle's Metaphysics Z and H*. Cornell Univ. Pr. 1991 $39.95. ISBN 0-8014-2598-0. Close reading of two central books of the *Metaphysics*, comparing the mature version of primary substance to Aristotle's earlier views.

Lukasiewicz, Jan. *Aristotle's Syllogistic: From the Standpoint of Modern Formal Logic*. OUP 2nd ed. 1957 o.p. Standard work offering a modern interpretation of Aristotle's theory of syllogistic thinking.

Lynch, John Patrick. *Aristotle's School: A Study of a Greek Educational Institution*. U. CA Pr. 1972 o.p. Uses archeological, epigraphical, and literary *testimonia* to reconstruct the founding and history of Aristotle's Peripatetic school.

McKirahan, Richard D., Jr. *Principles and Proofs: Aristotle's Theory of Demonstrative Science*. Princeton U. Pr. 1992 $47.50. ISBN 0-691-07363-5. Discusses the theory of science as formulated in the *Posterior Analytics*, in all its intricate scope, with competence and genuine interest.

Modrak, Deborah K. W. *Aristotle: The Power of Perception*. U. Ch. Pr. 1987 $29.95. ISBN 0-226-53338-7. Examines Aristotle's psychology and views on reality to test the coherence of his theory of perception; argues that his philosophy of mind is tied to descriptive and methodological principles.

Monan, J. D. *Moral Knowledge and Its Methodology in Aristotle*. OUP 1968 o.p. Reexamination of the relationship between three ethical works—the *Protrepticus*, the *Eudemian Ethics*, and the *Nicomachean Ethics*—arguing that the *Eudemian* represents Aristotle's mature views.

Mulgan, R. G. *Aristotle's Political Theory: An Introduction for Students of Political Theory*. OUP 1977 $19.95. ISBN 0-19-827416-5. Useful introduction to Aristotle's political philosophy in conjunction with relevant parts of the *Ethics*.

Mure, G. R. *Aristotle*. Greenwood 1975 repr. of 1932 ed. Comprehensive study of Aristotle's contributions to all branches of knowledge.

Nussbaum, Martha C. *Aristotle's "De Motu Animalium."* Princeton U. Pr. 1985 $22.95. ISBN 0-691-02035-3. Reliable translation and excellent interpretive essays.

Nussbaum, Martha C., and Amelie Oksenberg Rorty, eds. *Essays on Aristotle's De Anima*. OUP 1992 $55.00. ISBN 0-19-824461-4. Excellent collection of essays on Aristotle's major work on his theory of life.

Oates, Whitney J. *Aristotle and the Problem of Value*. Princeton U. Pr. 1963 o.p. General treatment of the Aristotelian esthetic and conception of culture.

Organ, Troy W. *Index to Aristotle*. Gordian 1966 repr. of 1949 ed. $75.00. ISBN 0-87752-079-8. Lexicon of the English terminology, with references to particular key passages.

Owens, Joseph. *Aristotle: The Collected Papers of Joseph Owens*. Ed. by J. R. Catan. State U. NY Pr. 1981 $57.50. ISBN 0-87395-534-X. Brings together the author's representative essays on Aristotle since the 1951 publication of his major work on Aristotle's doctrine of being.

Pellegrin, Pierre. *Aristotle's Classification of Animals: Biology and the Conceptual Unity of the Aristotelian Corpus*. U. CA Pr. 1986 $50.00. ISBN 0-520-05502-0. Sets the standard in theoretical investigations of classification in antiquity, not as uncovering real taxonomic groups but as identifying homologous organs and behavior.

Randall, John H. *Aristotle*. Col. U. Pr. 1960 $50.00. ISBN 0-231-02359-6. Important book treating Aristotle as highly relevant to contemporary philosophical pursuits.

Reale, Giovanni. *The Concept of First Philosophy and the Unity of the Metaphysics of Aristotle*. Trans. by John R. Catan. State U. NY Pr. 1980 $59.50. ISBN 0-87395-385-1. Aims "to provide the unity of the *metaphysics* and speculative homogeneity" (Introduction); a major work.

Rhodes, P. J. *A Commentary on the Aristotelian Athenaion Politeia*. OUP 1981 $115.00. ISBN 0-19-814004-5. "Many scholars have agreed that Aristotle wrote the work . . . but P. J. Rhodes in the philological introduction to this excellent book decides against Aristotle. . . . As matters stand, uncertainties concerning the authorship do not diminish the significance of the text because, as Dr. Rhodes robustly declares, 'as a historian *A. P.* is mediocre (though by no means useless to us), but as a describer of constitutional practice he is first in the field'" (*Ancient Greece*).

Robinson, Daniel N. *Aristotle's Psychology*. Col. U. Pr. 1989 $31.50. ISBN 0-231-07002-0. Close examination of the pertinent work of Aristotle to show the full range of human faculties as organic unity and relate it to Greek culture.

Rorty, Amelie O., ed. *Essays on Aristotle's Ethics*. Major Thinkers Ser. U. CA Pr. 1980 $15.95. ISBN 0-520-04041-4. Collection of 21 essays by different authors on a broad range of themes on Aristotle's ethical philosophy.

_____. *Essays on Aristotle's Poetics*. Princeton U. Pr. 1992 $69.50. ISBN 0-691-06872-0. Collection of essays treating the major topics of the *Poetics* in relation to Aristotle's special works.

Ross, W. D. *Aristotle*. Routledge 1964 $17.95. ISBN 0-415-04306-9. Excellent one-volume introduction to Aristotle's works by one of his outstanding translators and editors in this century.

_____. *Aristotle's Prior and Posterior Analytics: A Revised Text with Introduction and Commentary*. Ancient Philosophy Ser. Garland 1980 o.p. Excellent work on the two logical treatises; a valuable contribution to scholarship.

_____. *Aristotle: Selections*. Scribner 1971 o.p. Representative texts in translation for students' use, with a general introduction.

Salkever, Stephen G. *Finding the Mean: Theory and Practice in Aristotelian Political Philosophy*. Princeton U. Pr. 1990 $35.00. ISBN 0-691-07803-3. Builds a cogent case to show that the proper understanding of ethical teleology is compatible with comparable modern views.

Schmitt, Charles. *Aristotle and the Renaissance*. HUP 1983 $18.50. ISBN 0-674-04525-4. Expert discussion of the postmedieval developments that emerge as novel trends in the encounter of Aristotelianism with new doctrines and the revived tradition.

_____. *John Case and Aristotelianism in Renaissance England*. Studies in the History of Ideas U. of Toronto Pr. 1983 $39.95. ISBN 0-7735-1005-2. This and the preceding title are among the best accounts of Renaissance Aristotelianism, written by a well-known authority in the history of ideas.

Simon, Yves. *The Definition of Moral Virtue*. Ed. by Vucan Kuic. Fordham 1985 $30.00. ISBN 0-8232-1144-4. Close discussion of the Aristotelian conception of the practical virtues.

Solmsen, Friedrich. *Aristotle's System of the Physical World*. Johnson Repr. repr. of 1960 ed. o.p. Detailed treatment by a leading classicist of Aristotle's physical, cosmological, chemical, and meteorological questions, including the connection between his scientific investigations and his theology. A major work.

Sorabji, Richard. *Aristotle on Memory*. U. Pr. of New Eng. 1972 $18.00. ISBN 0-87057-137-0. The best treatment of Aristotle's view on memory, with a translation of *De Memoria*.

_____. *Necessity, Cause and Blame: Perspectives on Aristotle's Theory*. Cornell Univ. Pr. 1983 $12.95. ISBN 0-8014-1162-9. Outstanding work on moral conduct to show that Aristotle was an indeterminist.

Stewart, J. A. *Notes on the Nicomanchean Ethics of Aristotle*. Ayer 1974 repr. of 1892 ed. $54.00. ISBN 0-405-04863-7. One of the best commentaries on the subject of ethical theory.

Stocks, John L. *Aristotelianism*. Cooper Sq. 1963 repr. of 1930 ed. $53.00. ISBN 0-8154-0220-1. One of the best short accounts of Aristotle's ideas and his influence.

Veatch, Henry B. *Aristotle: A Contemporary Appreciation*. Ind. U. Pr. 1974 $29.95. ISBN 0-253-30890-9. "Good books for undergraduates on classical philosophy are so rare that this book should probably be acquired by all college libraries" (*Choice*).

Von Fritz, Kurt. *Aristotle's Contribution to the Practice and Theology of Historiography*. U. CA Pr. 1957 o.p. Defends Aristotle's approach to historical events and theories.

Walsh, James J. *Aristotle's Conception of Moral Weakness*. Col. U. Pr. 1963 o.p. Very useful study of incontinence (*akrasia*) with reference to Socrates and Plato and in relation to Aristotle's own investigation as found in the *Nicomachean Ethics*.

Waterlow, Sarah. *Nature, Change and Agency in Aristotle's Physics: A Philosophical Study*. OUP 1982 $37.50. ISBN 0-19-824653-6. Uses the *Physics* to illumine the concept of change and to show how Aristotle constructs the metaphysics of nature.

Wedin, Michael V. *Mind and Imagination in Aristotle*. Yale U. Pr. 1988 $35.00. ISBN 0-300-04231-0. Discusses Aristotle's concept of *phantasia* and its role in the general theory of human intelligence, making Aristotle the founder of cognitive science.

Wilbur, J. B., and H. J. Allen, eds. *The Worlds of Plato and Aristotle*. Prometheus Bks. 1979 $18.95. ISBN 0-87975-116-9. Good selection brought together to illustrate the coherence of the systems; informative comments and notes.

Witt, Charlotte. *Substance and Essence in Aristotle: An Interpretation of Metaphysics VII–IX*. Cornell Univ. Pr. 1989 $24.50. ISBN 0-8014-2126-8. Concentrates on the middle books of the *Metaphysics* and arrives at a coherent account of sensible substance in relation to essence.

Woodbridge, Frederick J. *Aristotle's Vision of Nature*. Ed. by John H. Randall, Jr. Greenwood 1983 repr. of 1965 ed. $42.50. ISBN 0-313-24131-7. Overview of Aristotle's thought and his place in history, based on lectures edited posthumously.

CICERO or TULLY (MARCUS TULLIUS CICERO). 106–43 B.C.

Cicero, Roman orator and statesman, studied philosophy first at Rome under Greek tutors and later visited Greece and attended lectures at the Old Academy in Athens as well as those of Poseidonius, the Stoic. Cicero translated Greek philosophy into Latin and is responsible for much of the vocabulary transmitted to the West. The philosophical treatises *Academica* and *De Natura Deorum* and the moral writings *De Finibus* and *De Officiis* are renditions and paraphrasings of the Greek philosophies of the time. His most original work is to be found in the political texts *De Republica* and *De Legibus*.

BOOKS BY CICERO

De Officiis (On Duties). HUP 1930 $15.50. ISBN 0-674-99033-1. Fine edition, with a glossary and an index of names.

The Nature of the Gods. Trans. by C. P. McGregor. Viking Penguin 1975 $7.95. ISBN 0-14-044288-X. The best available edition, with a good introduction by J. M. Ross to Cicero's views on theology and his influence on later writers; glossary, bibliography, and index.

On Old Age and On Friendship. Trans. by Frank O. Copley. U. of Mich. Pr. 1967 $4.50. ISBN 0-472-06178-X

Select Letters. Ed by D. R. Shackleton Bailey. Cambridge U. Pr. 1980 $54.95. ISBN 0-521-22492-6. In addition to the letters, offers an informative introduction and useful appendixes.

Works. Loeb Class. Lib. 28 vols. HUP 1912–58 o.p. Standard text with translation on the facing page; introductions and useful notes supplied.

BOOKS ABOUT CICERO

Bailey, D. R. *Cicero*. Class. Life and Letters Ser. Biblio NY 1979 o.p. Reliable and readable treatment of Cicero's works and contributions.

Fuhrman, Manfred. *Cicero and the Roman Republic*. Blackwell Pubs. 1992 $34.95. ISBN 0-631-17879-1. Designed for a wide audience with little knowledge of this period. Exceptionally strong in its use of more than 800 Epistles of Cicero and of his extensive philosophical works, especially for the last decade of Cicero's life.

Habicht, Christian. *Cicero the Politician*. Johns Hopkins 1989 $28.00. ISBN 0-8018-3872-X. Reexamines the career, achievements, and failures of Cicero the statesman during Republican Rome's worst political crisis.

Mitchell, Thomas N. *Cicero, the Senior Statesman*. Yale U. Pr. 1991 $35.00. ISBN 0-300-04779-7. Lucid exposition of Cicero's idealistic political philosophy to illuminate the cruel realities and puzzling contradictions of his turbulent career.

Petersson, Torsten. *Cicero: A Biography*. Biblo 1920 $25.00 ISBN 0-8196-0119-5. One of the best standard accounts of Cicero's life.

Rawson, Beryl. *The Politics of Friendship: Pompey and Cicero*. Int. Spec. Bk. 1978 o.p. "That politics makes strange bedfellows is nowhere better illustrated than in the case of the political friendship between Pompey and Cicero during the last years of the dying Roman Republic. In her fine, scholarly scholarly study, Rawson . . . attempts to analyze and examine critically this case study of political friendship" (*Choice*).

Rawson, Elizabeth. *Cicero: A Portrait*. Cornell U. Pr. 1983 $39.50. ISBN 0-8014-1628-0. "A full and balanced life of Cicero is not to be written. To say that 'there are gaps in our knowledge particularly at the beginning and the end of his career, where the letters fail us,' flatters the biographer's predicament; for the correspondence [that] lures him to the enterprise scarcely begins until over two thirds of Cicero's life was over, leaving forty-five years of ascent and culmination in silhouette" (*TLS*).

Rolfe, John C. *Cicero and His Influence*. Cooper Sq. 1963 repr. of 1920 ed. o.p. Brief and concise account of Cicero's personal and political career.

Trollope, Anthony. *The Life of Cicero*. 2 vols. Ed. by N. John Hall. Ayer 1981 repr. of 1880 ed. $90.00. ISBN 0-405-14186-6

EPICURUS. 341–270 B.C.

Epicurus founded his philosophical school and lived with his friends in his "Garden" in Athens when the city was witnessing the rise of Macedonian dominance and Greek politics reflected the ongoing crisis in values and virtues. Many thinkers felt the growing need for intellectual conservatism and voluntary withdrawal to secure a life of imperturbability. That his school became a model followed in other cities, including Rome, for more than 500 years is both testimony to the strong appeal Epicurus's ethical doctrines exerted and a sign of the logical conviction the theory of Atomism generated in his followers. Epicurus, who knew the pre-Socratics well, revived and extended the Atomism of Democritus and Leucippus by finding broader applications for Atomism in psychology, physics, and ethics. Although the principles of the physical teachings of Epicurus were destined for a significant revival, and in certain ways, experimental confirmation in modern times, the special appeal of his philosophy was basically ethical. His physics remains the background to support a way of life aiming at the enhancement of pleasure and avoidance of pain. Epicurus's theories sought to reveal the causes of pain, especially fear— whether of death or of divine intervention. He taught that only the acquisition of knowledge helps in the effort to cope with fears and secure a happy life. His influence was felt strongly in Italy and it found in Rome an eloquent spokesman in LUCRETIUS, whose masterwork, *De Rerum Natura*, is by far the most complete exposition of Epicureanism.

BOOKS BY EPICURUS

Epicurea. Ed. by Herman Usener. Irvington 1981 repr. of 1887 ed. $69.00. ISBN 0-697-00059-1. The standard collection of sources.

Epicurus: The Extant Remain, with Short Critical Apparatus. Trans. by Cyril Bailey. Hyperion Conn. 1980 repr. of 1926 ed. o.p. Makes available the writings of Epicurus in English translation, with a guide to the text and the main ideas of Atomism.

The Philosophy of Epicurus: Letters, Doctrines, and Parallel Passages from Lucretius. Ed. by George K. Strodach. Northwestern U. Pr. 1962 o.p. Scholarly collection of Epicurus's writings.

BOOKS ABOUT EPICURUS

Asmis, Elizabeth. *Epicurus' Scientific Method*. Cornell Univ. Pr. 1983 $49.50. ISBN 0-8014-1465-2. "Offers on the whole judicious discussions of Epicurus's theory of perception and of the difficulties confronting his advocacy of the principle that all perceptions are true" (*TLS*).

Bailey, Cyril. *The Greek Atomists and Epicurus: A Study*. Russell 1964 repr. of 1928 ed. o.p. Still a leading study of Greek Atomism, with special attention to Epicurus's philosophy and its originality.

Clay, Diskin. *Lucretius and Epicurus*. Cornell Univ. Pr. 1983 o.p. Excellent and thorough comparative study of the two philosophers and of Lucretius's innovations.

De Witt, Norman W. *Epicurus and His Philosophy*. Greenwood 1973 repr. of 1954 ed. $65.00. ISBN 0-8371-6639-X. Strong defense of Epicurus's doctrines concerning "the injustice of the centuries." A very readable account of Epicureanism in antiquity.

Furley, David J. *Two Studies in the Greek Atomists*. Princeton U. Pr. 1967 o.p. Two excellent essays, one on indivisible magnitudes and the other a comparative critical analysis of voluntary action in Aristotle and Epicurus, with reference to the earlier Atomists.

Jones, Howard. *The Epicurean Tradition*. Routledge 1989 $39.95. ISBN 0-415-02069-7. Study of the philosophy of Epicurus and the impact of his epistemology and Atomism, especially on seventeenth-century science.

Mitsis, Phillip. *Epicurus' Ethical Theory: The Pleasures of Invulnerability*. Cornell Univ. Pr. 1988 $26.95. ISBN 0-8014-2187-X. Sympathetic yet critical approach to Epicurus's ethics, focusing on the concept of invulnerability and the originality of Epicurus's views on pleasure.

Panichas, George A. *Epicurus*. Twayne's World Authors Ser. G. K. Hall 1970 o.p. Good introduction to Epicurus's times and thought, written for the general reader; also discusses the fluctuations of Epicurus's influence throughout the centuries to recent times.

Rist, J. M. *Epicurus: An Introduction*. Cambridge U. Pr. 1972 o.p. Reliable introductory survey of Epicurus's life and doctrines, with attention to critical problems.

Sedgwick, Henry D. *Art of Happiness or the Teachings of Epicurus*. Essay Index Repr. Ser. Ayer repr. of 1933 ed. $17.00. ISBN 0-8369-1814-2. Balanced and sympathetic study of Epicurus's life and ethical goal of happiness.

Strozier, Robert M. *Epicurus and Hellenistic Philosophy*. U. Pr. of Amer. 1985 o.p. "Based on a reappraisal of Epicurus, this book argues that Epicurean thought underwent a significant development from Epicurus to Lucretius" (*Religious Studies Review*).

Wallace, William. *Epicureanism: Chief Ancient Philosophies*. Darby Pub. 1980 repr. of 1880 ed. o.p. Presents a sympathetic account of this movement and offers a number of still useful and valuable insights.

HERACLITUS OF EPHESUS. fl. c.500 B.C.

Heraclitus, an Ionian Greek, wrote the book *On Nature* and is credited with writing in a style so difficult that it earned him the reputation of the "dark" thinker. He posed with utter seriousness the problem of change and of an abiding unity that is the hidden "logic" of all reality, its hidden harmony. Although strife generates all processes, these are measured and orderly. Nature is basically the element of fire, as is soul. The extant fragments of his writings continue to perplex their readers, and recent philosophers of HEIDEGGER's (see also Vol. 5) stature have found in Heraclitus's vision of reality a source of inspiration and a place to start in the search for wisdom. "Little is known about his life, and the one book he apparently wrote is lost. His views survive in the short fragments quoted and attributed to him by later authors" (*Encyclopaedia Britannica*).

BOOKS ABOUT HERACLITUS

Heidegger, Martin, and Eugen Fink. *Heraclitus Seminar, 1966–1967*. Trans. by Charles H. Seibert. Northwestern U. Pr. 1992 repr. of 1979 ed. $14.95. ISBN 0-8101-1067-9. Preserves the record of a seminar on Heraclitus, the unifying theme of which was the distinction of "the one and the many"; fragmentary but interesting.

Kahn, Charles H., ed. *The Art and Thought of Heraclitus: An Edition of the Fragments with Translation and Commentary*. Cambridge U. Pr. 1981 $29.95. ISBN 0-521-28645-X. Discusses the thought of Heraclitus, emphasizing the place of logos-reason in nature and human beings, and offers also a new arrangement of the Diels-Kranz numbering of the fragments.

Kirk, G. S. *Heraclitus: The Cosmic Fragments*. Cambridge U. Pr. 1954 o.p. One of the most important books on Heraclitus to appear in English; especially valuable to readers who have a knowledge of Greek.

Robinson, T. M., ed. and trans. *Heraclitus: Fragments: A Text and Translation with a Commentary*. U. of Toronto Pr. 1991 $1995. ISBN 0-8020-6913-4. New rendition of the extant fragments, with a discussion on the unity of Heraclitus's vision of human beings and nature.

Sallis, John, and Kenneth Maly. *Heraclitean Fragments: A Comparison Volume to the Heidegger-Fink Seminar on Heraclitus*. U. of Ala. Pr. 1980 o.p. Contains essays on the fragments discussed by Heidegger.

Wheelwright, Phillip E. *Heraclitus*. Greenwood 1981 repr. of 1959 ed. $35.00. ISBN 0-313-23142-7. Stimulating account and guide to the extant fragments.

LUCRETIUS (TITUS LUCRETIUS CARUS). c.99–c.55 B.C.

We know little of the man. It is certain that he was a contemporary of CICERO and JULIUS CAESAR (see Vol. 3). He died at the age of 44, leaving only one work, *De Rerum Natura*, a long, didactic poem in six books in which he expounds the teachings of EPICURUS. Its stated purpose was to describe the real nature of the universe in order to help people learn the truth and thus rid themselves of fears and superstitions about punishments by the gods here or in an afterlife. The Atomic view of the universe and the theory of pleasure in Lucretius's poem reflect in close detail the writings of Epicurus. (See also Vol. 2.)

BOOKS BY LUCRETIUS

De Rerum Natura. 3 vols. Ed. by Cyril Bailey. OUP 1986 $210.00. ISBN 0-19-814405-9. Reissued in 1986; a classic in the field of Lucretian studies.

On the Nature of Things. Trans. by W.H.D. Rouse. *Loeb Class. Lib.* HUP rev. ed. 1975 $15.50. ISBN 0-674-99200-8. Offers text and translation on facing pages, with useful marginalia, informative notes, and a brief introduction.

BOOKS ABOUT LUCRETIUS

Clay, Diskin. *Lucretius and Epicurus*. Cornell Univ. Pr. 1983 o.p. Excellent and thorough comparative study of the two philosophers and of Lucretius's innovations.

Hadzsits, George D. *Lucretius and His Influence*. Cooper Sq. 1963 repr. of 1930 ed. o.p. "The author of this volume is to be congratulated on this sympathetic and perspicacious account of the thought and influence of the Roman poet . . . For him Lucretius lives not only because he turned out a noble collection of vigorous hexameters but also because he gave men a poetic reading of earth that has never been surpassed" (*The American Scholar*).

Minadeo, Richard. *The Lyre of Science: Form and Meaning in Lucretius's De Rerum Natura*. Wayne St. U. Pr. 1969 o.p. Emphasizes the literary and poetic features of Lucretius as having been neglected in favor of the philosophical side.

Nichols, James H., Jr. *Epicurean Political Philosophy: The "De Rerum Natura" of Lucretius*. Cornell Univ. Pr. 1976 o.p. Undertakes to offer a fuller view of Epicurean thought through a rigorous analysis of Lucretius's *De Rerum Natura*.

Santayana, George. *Three Philosophical Poets*. Cooper Sq. 1971 repr. of 1910 ed. o.p. Eloquent essay on Lucretius, stressing the poet's ethical naturalism.

Segal, Charles. *Lucretius on Death and Anxiety: Poetry and Philosophy in De Rerum Natura*. Princeton U. Pr. 1990 $29.95. ISBN 0-691-06826-7. Fine defense of Lucretius's Epicureanism and a masterful blending of poetry and philosophy, restating the master's answers to the problems of fear of death and sources of anxiety.

MARCUS AURELIUS (ANTONINUS). A.D. 121–180

Born in Rome, Marcus Aurelius was one of the most respected emperors in Roman history. When he was 17, Aurelius was adopted by emperor Antonius

Pius and succeeded him in A.D. 161. He ruled jointly with his adoptive brother, Lucius Verus, until 169, when he became sole emperor after Verus died. Aurelius was a humanitarian ruler who, nevertheless, accepted the view that Christians were the enemies of Rome. A stoic, his spiritual reflections, the *Meditations*, are considered a classic work of stoicism. Although a Roman, Aurelius wrote his *Meditations* in Greek, preferring that language for the "propriety and facility of his expressions," because "the Latin tongue in matter of philosophy comes as short of the Greek as the English doth of Latin." The *Meditations*, comprising 12 books, are Aurelius's only surviving work. They were written toward the end of his life, during a time when campaigns were being waged against tribes along the Danube. The work records his innermost thoughts, revealing his loneliness and also the fact that he was not embittered by the experiences of life. After he died, Aurelius was idealized as the perfect emperor whose reign contrasted sharply with the disastrous period, and reigns that followed.

BOOKS BY MARCUS AURELIUS

The following titles offer translations by different hands. The introductions vary in length and scope, but all are done by scholars with acknowledged competence.

Living Stoically: Selections from Marcus Aurelius. Ed. by Roy A. Lawes. St. Mut. 1985 $25.00. ISBN 0-7223-1848-0

Meditations. Ed. and trans. by G.M.A. Grube. Hackett Pub. 1984 repr. of 1963 ed. $21.50. ISBN 0-915145-78-2. "The student who is beginning to explore the humanities, the history of the late empire, and/or ancient philosophy will read the inspiring jottings of Marcus Aurelius and better understand the world in crisis in the second century A.D." (*Classical World*).

BOOKS ABOUT MARCUS AURELIUS

Bussell, Frederick W. *Marcus Aurelius and the Later Stoics*. Gordon Pr. 1976 $59.95. ISBN 0-8490-2207-X. "Dr. Bussell's learned and brilliantly able work, closely as it follows the text (all along with exact citations) both of Marcus Aurelius and (on a smaller scale) of his predecessors, Seneca and Epictetus, give in the end an estimate from a rather special and individual point of view" (*Intl. Journal of Ethics*).

Dole, Nathan H. *The Wisdom of Marcus Aurelius*. Found. Class. Reprints 1985 repr. of 1903 ed. $177.00. ISBN 0-89901-374-0

Farquharson, Arthur. *Marcus Aurelius: His Life and His World*. Greenwood 1975 repr. of 1951 ed. $35.00. ISBN 0-8371-8139-9. Good survey by the leading authority, who wrote a two-volume work on the *Meditations* (1944).

Oliver, James H. *Marcus Aurelius: Aspects of Civic and Cultural Policy in the East*. Am. Sch. Athens 1970 $15.00. ISBN 0-87661-513-2. Views the imperial philosopher in the context of his administration of the Roman Empire.

Rutherford, R. B. *The Meditations of Marcus Aurelius: A Study*. OUP 1989 $65.00. ISBN 0-19-814879-8. Study that manages to be both scholarly and accessible to nonspecialists. Examined in light of the contemporary intellectual and religious milieu.

Sedgwick, Henry D. *Marcus Aurelius: A Biography*. AMS Pr. 1974 repr. of 1921 ed. $21.00. ISBN 0-404-05691-1. Good account of the emperor's life and philosophical outlook.

PLATO. 427?–347 B.C.

Plato's real name was Aristocles. He was born into a wealthy, aristocratic Athenian family and was a blood relation to Pericles and other illustrious Athenians. In his early years he preferred poetry to politics. This changed when he met SOCRATES, a decisive encounter in his life. Plato, more than any other thinker (with the exception of his pupil ARISTOTLE [see also Vol. 3]), influenced profoundly the course of the intellectual history of the Western world. He witnessed the major events of the Peloponnesian Wars; he saw the defeat of Athens, the rise of the Thirty Tyrants in the wake of the Spartan victory and then the return of the Democratic party, and the trial and death of Socrates in 399. He wrote superb dialogues, unsurpassable for content and style, in which Socrates figures as the dominant speaker. The dialogues form three groups: the early, middle, and later dialogues. In the later dialogues, the dramatic setting loses intensity, and the logical and metaphysical themes receive special treatment. They put before the reader the ideal of the life of reason and of responsible discourse in a relentless pursuit of truth. Plato's philosophy is an outgrowth of basic Socratic teachings and covers just about every field of inquiry. His famous theory of the forms, which asserts the separate existence of transcendent values and universals, has been discussed and criticized or upheld by readers in every generation. We also have a number of letters stating his views in another style. The commentaries, books, and articles still being written on his works and the topics he treated constitute living testimony to the greatness of his thought and its relevance to Western culture.

Plato established the first school that could be called a real university, and it soon attracted a great number of students mature enough to continue Plato's ideas and extend his teachings in ethics, politics, and the special sciences, particularly mathematics. A succession of scholars presided over the activities of the Academy of Plato: Speusippus (399–347), Xenocrates (399–314), Polemo (314–270), and Crates (270–247), constituting the period known as the Old Academy. Arkesilaus, (247–241), introduced a skeptical philosophy of truth, marking the beginning of the period of the Middle Academy, which lasted about a century until around 129, when Carneades, as head of the Academy, initiated a period known as the Third or New Academy. Not until centuries later did a Neoplatonic trend in interpreting the teaching of Plato become fashionable; that approach eventually prevailed until the Academy, along with the other philosophical schools in Athens, was ordered closed by the Emperor Justinian in A.D. 529.

BOOKS BY PLATO

The translation of Plato's dialogues, many of them now available in paperback editions, have increased greatly in number in recent decades and continue to do so. The list given below, though far from being exhaustive, is intended only as a convenience to the interested student.

The Collected Dialogues of Plato. Ed. by E. Hamilton and H. Cairns. Trans. by various individuals. Princeton U. Pr. 1984 repr. of 1961 ed. $35.00. ISBN 0-691-09718-6. Includes the letters. The most convenient collection of Plato's dialogues in translation.

Opera. Ed. by John Burnet. 5 vols. OUP 1900–07. Vols. 1–4 $14.95 ea. Vol. 5 $24.95. The authoritative Greek text currently used by scholars.

Plato's Works. Loeb Class. Lib. 12 vols. HUP 1914–35 o.p. The Greek text, accompanied by translation into English. All volumes have introductions and notes; the translation is printed on the facing page.

Also recommended for their quality are the following translations of individual dialogues or groups of dialogues.

The Dialogues of Plato: Euthyphro; Apology; Crito; Meno; Gorgias; Menexenus. 2 vols. Trans. by R. E. Allen. Yale U. Pr. 1989–91 $17.00–$25.00. ea. ISBNs 0-300-04488-7, 0-300-04874-2. "Excellent individual introductions keyed to the translations" (*Choice*).

The Dialogues of Plato: The Symposium. Trans. by R. E. Allen. Yale U. Pr. 1991 $45.00.
ISBN 0-300-04874-2. Dependable new translation with original discussions on
religion, social morality, and philosophical argument and a commentary by the
translator.

Five Dialogues. Philosophical Class. Ser. Hackett Pub. 1981 $27.50. ISBN 0-915145-23-5.
With an introduction by Donald J. Zeyl.

Hippias Major. Trans. by Paul Woodruff. Hackett Pub. 1982 $27.95. ISBN 0-915145-25-1.
Translation and discussion of Plato's dialogue on the definition of the beautiful and
the refutation of Sophistic definitions.

The Last Days of Socrates. Trans. by Hugh Tredennick. Viking Penguin 1954 $4.95. ISBN
0-14-044037-2

The Laws: History. Viking Penguin 1970 $6.95. ISBN 0-14-044222-7. "Plato's longest and
most intensely practical work contains his ripest utterances on ethics, education,
and jurisprudence, as well as his one entirely nonmythical exposition of theology"
(*Encyclopedia Britannica*).

The Platonic Epistles. Trans. by J. Howard. *History of Ideas Ser.* Ayer 1976 repr. of 1932
ed. $19.00. ISBN 0-405-07330-5

Plato's Dialogue on Friendship: An Interpretation of the Lysis, with a New Translation.
Trans. by David Bolotin. Cornell Univ. Pr. 1979 $8.95. ISBN 0-8014-1227-7. ". . . A
novel interpretation of this dialogue, which must be seriously reflected on by anyone
who wishes to give an account of this work in the future" (*Review of Metaphysics*).

Plato's Euthyphro. History of Ideas Ser. Ayer 1976 repr. $13.00. ISBN 0-405-07313-5. With
an introduction by William A. Heidel.

Plato's Parmenides. OUP 1991 $35.00. ISBN 0-19-506445-3. Excellent work highly
recommended for content and argument.

Plato's Phaedo. Trans. by David Bostock. OUP 1986 $24.95. ISBN 0-19-824918-7.
Readable introduction to one of Plato's most influential dialogues, emphasizing
argument and basic themes.

Plato's Theaetetus. Trans. by David Bostock. OUP 1988 $24.00. ISBN 0-19-823930-4.
Section-by-section commentary and evaluation of Plato's examination of knowledge
as perception, frequently in response to recent interpretations.

Protagoras. Trans. by C.C.W. Taylor. OUP 1992 $55.00. ISBN 0-19-823970-X. "Designed
for the Greekless reader. It provides the biographical, historical, and linguistic
information requisite for understanding the setting of this important Dialogue,
whose themes cover a range of political, cultural, and ethical issues. . . . The
translation is in a comfortably modern idiom, with good notes on the more difficult
cross-cultural abstractions" (*Choice*).

The Republic. Trans. by A. Bloom. Basic rev. ed. 1991 $12.95. ISBN 0-4650-6934-7.
Includes an introduction and comments that make it a valuable alternative to other
approaches to Plato's political theory.

The Republic. Trans. by Robin Waterfield. OUP 1993 $16.95. ISBN 0-19-212604-0. One of
the major dialogues of Plato, in which he expounds his theories on the structure of
justice, of science, and of the soul.

The Symposium. Ed. by K. J. Dover. Cambridge U. Pr. 1980 $19.95. ISBN 0-521-29523-8.
Esthetic and mystical dialogue written at the height of Plato's dramatic power,
recording several banquet eulogies of *eros* (desirous love).

The Theaetetus of Plato. Trans. by M. J. Levett. Rev. by M. Burnyeat. Hackett Pub. 1990
$34.95. ISBN 0-915144-81-6. Extensive introduction by Burnyeat to a well-known
translation, with an updated bibliography at the end.

The Trial and Death of Socrates. Hackett Pub. 1975 $3.75. ISBN 0-915144-15-8

BOOKS ABOUT PLATO AND THE ACADEMY

Annas, Julia. *An Introduction to Plato's Republic.* OUP 1981 $29.00. ISBN 0-19-827428-9.
Especially insightful in discussing Plato's distinctions of types of consequences of
justice; identifies the dominant moral themes with analytical precision.

Anton, John P., and Anthony Preus, eds. *Essays in Ancient Greek Philosophy III: Plato.*
State U. NY Pr. 1989 $64.50. ISBN 0-87395-050-X. Essays reflecting how the study of

Plato in recent years has benefited from cross-fertilization between the analytic and the hermeneutic traditions.

Ast, Freidrich. *Lexicon Plantonicum Sive Vacum Platonicarum Index, 1835–1838*. 3 vols. B. Franklin 1969 o.p. The only available lexicon of Plato's technical vocabulary, with reference to key passages in each dialogue.

Barker, Ernest. *Political Thought of Plato and Aristotle*. Dover 1959 $10.95. ISBN 0-486-20521-5. Traces the origins of political thought in Greece and devotes the first four chapters to Plato and his Socratic predecessors.

Brandwood, Leonard. *The Chronology of Plato's Dialogues*. Cambridge U. Pr. 1990 $54.95. ISBN 0-521-39000-1. New attempt to decide the chronological order of Plato's dialogues, with critical discussion of recent scholarship on Plato's development as a writer.

Brumbaugh, Robert S. *Plato's Mathematical Imagination: The Mathematical Passages in the Dialogues and Their Interpretation*. Kraus 1954 o.p. Competent inquiry into Platonic mathematics "as it is revealed in mathematical imagery," with ample references to recent theories and views.

Burger, Ronna. *The Phaedo: A Platonic Labyrinth*. Yale U. Pr. 1984 o.p Interpretive reading of the dramatic structure of this dialogue to show that it corresponds to basic themes and the question of the duality of body and soul in particular.

Burnet, John. *Platonism*. Greenwood 1983 repr. of 1928 ed. $42.50. ISBN 0-313-23699-2. Sensitive account of Plato's thought by the eminent editor of the Oxford standard text of Plato's works.

Campbell, Lewis. *The Theaetetus of Plato*. Ayer repr. of 1861 ed. $19.00. ISBN 0-405-04837-8. Recognized as a landmark for laying the ground for the stylometric tests to decide questions about the chronological order of Plato's dialogues.

Chance, Thomas H. *Plato's Euthydemus: Analysis of What Is and Is Not Philosophy*. U. CA Pr. 1992 $40.00. ISBN 0-520-07754-7. Discusses Plato's views on the nature of philosophy as the major issue in this dialogue.

Cherniss, Harold F. *Aristotle's Criticism of Plato and the Academy*. Russell 1962 repr. of 1944 ed. o.p. Challenging work of high scholarship that analyzes the basis for Aristotle's "misguided" criticism of Plato's theory of ideas and numbers.

————. *The Riddle of the Early Academy*. Ancient Philosophy Ser. Garland 1982 o.p. The "riddle" is created by the discrepancy between what Aristotle reports and what Plato writes. Discusses the nature of studies in the Academy and explores the connection between the character of the school and the thought it produced.

Clegg, Jerry S. *The Structure of Plato's Philosophy*. Bucknell U. Pr. 1978 $25.00. ISBN 0-8387-1878-7. Close discussion of such central topics as Plato's metaphysics, theory of knowledge, psychology, theory of art, and politics, delineating a unifying structure and consistency in Plato's position.

Cobb, William S. *Plato's Sophist*. U. Pr. of Amer. 1991 $51.00. ISBN 9-8476-7652-8. Straightforward translation of the dialogue, with a useful summary of central topics and analysis of the relation between philosophy and Sophistry.

Cornford, F. M. *Plato and Parmenides*. Routledge 1939 o.p. Translation with running commentary tying the logical exercises of the *Parmenides* with that of Parmenides' poem, *Way of Truth*.

————. *Plato's Cosmology*. Routledge 1937 o.p. Translation with running commentary offering a comprehensive analysis of Plato's myth on the creation of the physical world.

————. *Plato's Theory of Knowledge: The Theateus and the Sophist of Plato*. Macmillan 1957 $3.50. ISBN 0-02-325160-3. Translation with running commentary, displaying the continuity of problems about knowledge and reality in the *Theaetetus* and the *Sophist*.

————. *The Republic of Plato*. OUP 1941 o.p. Translation with running commentary discussing Plato's political views and method of arguing in defense of their validity.

Crombie, I. M. *An Examination of Plato's Doctrines*. International Lib. of Philosophy and Scientific Method. 2 vols. Humanities Vol. 1 1962. Vol. 2 1963 o.p. Vol. 1, on Plato's theories of human nature and society; Vol. 2, a closely and well-argued analysis of his theories of reality and knowledge.

————. *Plato: The Midwife's Apprentice*. Greenwood 1981 repr. of 1965 ed. $42.50. ISBN 0-313-23243-1. In this shorter work Crombie brings together in highly readable form the conclusions of his two-volume study.

Cushman, Robert E. *Therapeia: Plato's Conception of Philosophy*. Greenwood 1976 repr. of 1958 ed. $59.50. ISBN 0-8371-8879-2. Challenging book based mainly on the view that Plato understood the problem of humanity as a plight for which a *therapeia* must be sought. Order in the realm of becoming was to be achieved through a way of life devoted to the search for good and being.

Dancy, R. M. *Two Studies in the Early Academy*. State U. NY Pr. 1991 $49.50. ISBN 0-7914-0632-6. Special annotated study of Eudoxus and Speusippus and Aristotle's reaction to their critiques of the Platonic forms.

Desjardins, Rosemary. *The Rational Enterprise: Logos in Plato's Theaetetus*. State U. NY Pr. 1990 $59.50. ISBN 0-88706-837-5. Novel interpretation of the argumentation employed in the *Theaetetus*, relating it to other dialogues to illustrate the underlying drama.

During, Ingemar, and G. E. Owen, eds. *Aristotle and Plato in the Mid-Fourth Century*. Humanities 1960 o.p. Excellent collection of essays by different authors, setting high standards in Platonic scholarship.

Elias, Julius A. *Plato's Defence of Poetry*. State U. NY Pr. 1984 $59.50. ISBN 0-87395-807-1. Argues that Plato restored the place of poetry in philosophy and political life—expelled in the *Republic*—by actually conjoining the value of poetry to high-minded myth.

Ferrari, G.R.F. *Listening to the Cicadas: A Study of Plato's Phaedrus*. Cambridge U. Pr. 1987 $49.95. ISBN 0-521-26778-1. Discussion of Plato as seasoned master of the literary arts, user of irony, and critic of rhetoric, as shown through artistic insights in the *Phaedrus*.

Ficino, Marsilio. *Commentary on Plato's Symposium on Love*. Trans. by Sears Jayne. Spring Pubns. 2nd rev. ed. 1985 $18.50. ISBN 0-88214-601-7. Translation from the Latin text of Ficino's celebrated and influential book on Platonic love.

Field, G. C. *Plato and His Contemporaries. Studies in Philosophy*. Haskell 1974 $75.00. ISBN 0-8383-1992-0. Written as a preliminary to the study of Plato, describes the times and climate of opinion in Plato's Athens and relates his writings to the literary, historical, and philosophical background.

Fowler, D. H. *The Mathematics of Plato's Academy*. OUP 1987 $98.00. ISBN 0-19-853912-6. Reconstruction of Greek mathematics, with Plato's philosophy at the center, introducing evidence from related ancient sources.

Friedlander, Paul. *Plato: An Introduction*. Ed. and trans. by H. Meyerhoff. Princeton U. Pr. 1973 $17.95. ISBN 0-691-0982-6. The first of a well-known three-volume work setting the pace for understanding Plato as philosopher, physicist, jurist, city planner, and seminal thinker.

Gadamer, Hans George. *Dialogue and Dialectic: Eight Hermeneutical Studies on Plato*. Yale, U. Pr. 1980 $32.50. ISBN 0-300-02126-7. Brings together several studies on basic Platonic topics: dialectic, immortality, truth, reason, poetry, and community, with an emphasis on the dialogue form and the dramatic situation. With an introduction by P. Christopher Smith.

————. *The Idea of the Good in Platonic-Aristotelian Philosophy*. Trans. by P. Christopher Smith. Yale U. Pr. 1986 $11.00. ISBN 0-300-04114-4. Series of lectures attempting to show a fundamental agreement between the two philosophers on the concept of the good; the agreement is explained on the basis of their common departure from the moral experience.

Gosling, J. C. *Plato. Arguments of the Philosophers*. Methuen 1984 o.p. Close analysis of Plato's thesis on method and the theory of forms.

Grene, David. *Greek Political Theory: The Image of Man in Thucydides and Plato*. U. Ch. Pr. 1965 o.p. In the second part, concentrates on Plato as a theorist of politics and a reflective teacher of the art of government.

Griswold, Charles L., Jr. *Self-Knowledge in Plato's Phaedrus.* Yale U. Pr. 1986 $37.00. ISBN 0-300-03594-2. Closely knit discussion of self-knowledge as the unifying theme of Plato's *Phaedrus.*

Grube, G. M. *Plato's Thought.* Hackett 1980 repr. of 1935 ed. $29.50. ISBN 0-915144-79-4. Reissued with new introduction by Donald Z. Zeyl, and bibliographic essay. Written with sensitivity to the original texts and the demands of the philosophic issues. One of the best introductions available, with a high degree of faithfulness to Plato's thought.

Gulley, Norman. *Plato's Theory of Knowledge.* Greenwood 1986 repr. of 1962 ed. $41.50. ISBN 0-313-25209-2. Traces the development of this theory by discussing in detail Plato's concepts of perception, belief, reason, and sensation, going back to the *Meno* and the *Phaedo* but concentrating mainly on the later Platonic dialogues.

Gunnell, John G. *Political Philosophy and Time: Plato and the Origins of Political Vision.* U. Ch. Pr. 1987 repr. of 1968 ed. $12.95. ISBN 0-226-31079-5. Situates Plato's political vision in the philosophical need to place change within permanence and salvage the soul from the chaos of historical process.

Hall, Robert W *Plato. Political Thinkers Ser.* Allen & Unwin 1981 o.p. Deals with Plato's political and legal views as found in the *Republic,* the *Statesman,* and the *Laws;* also discusses Plato's influence on later thinkers. Lucidly written.

Hampton, Cynthia. *Pleasure, Knowledge, and Being: An Analysis of Plato's Philebus.* State U. NY Pr. 1990 $57.50. ISBN 0-7914-0259-2. Defends the unified structure of this dialogue by identifying "the knots" Plato provided to keep the themes and arguments together.

Hare, R. M. *Plato. Past Masters Ser.* OUP 1982 $14.95. ISBN 0-19-287586-8. Good general introduction to Plato's major themes.

Havelock, Eric A. *Preface to Plato.* HUP 1982 $10.95. ISBN 0-674-69906-8. Taking Plato as a point of departure, the discussion leads to early Greek thought to show that it is rooted in the oral tradition.

Joseph, Horace W. *Knowledge and the Good in Plato's Republic. Oxford Classical and Philosophical Monographs.* Greenwood 1981 repr. of 1948 ed. $39.75. ISBN 0-313-22762-4. Good account explaining the myth of the sun, the divided line, and the myth of the cave to show how they support the doctrine of the forms and the way they are interrelated.

Klein, Jacob. *A Commentary on Plato's Meno.* U. of NC Pr. 1965 $14.95. ISBN 0-226-43959-3. Step-by-step discussion exhibiting the dramatic structure of each section of the dialogue.

————. *Plato's Trilogy: Theaetetus, the Sophist, and the Statesman.* U. Ch. Pr. 1977 o.p. Rich discussion of the dramatic quality of the *Meno,* aiming to bring the reader into active participation to view the roles of the interlocutors of Socrates and their ways of embodying virtue.

Koyré, Alexandre. *Discovering Plato.* Trans. by Leonora C. Rosenfield. Col. U. Pr. 1960 o.p. Lively account of select Platonic works to illustrate the method of philosophical dialogue and the range of Plato's doctrines on politics.

Krämer, Hans Joachim. *Plato and the Foundations of Metaphysics: A Work on the Theory of the Principles and Unwritten Doctrines of Plato with a Collection of the Fundamental Documents.* Ed. and trans. by J. R. Catan. State U. NY Pr. 1990 $59.50. ISBN 0-7914-0433-1. Defends the claim that the Unwritten Doctrine best expresses Plato and reveals his philosophy at the highest level of thought.

Kraut, Richard. ed. *The Cambridge Companion to Plato.* Cambridge U. Pr. 1992 $59.95. ISBN 0-521-43018-6. Collection of recent writings by various scholars on a wide range of Platonic themes, from mathematics to poetry and religion.

Ledger, Gerald R. *Re-Counting Plato.* OUP 1989 $74.00. ISBN 0-19-814681-7. Offers new conclusions on the chronology and authenticity of the dubious dialogues by applying the statistical methods of stylometrics.

Lodge, R. C. *Plato's Theory of Art.* Russell 1975 repr. of 1953 ed. o.p. Uses art in the broadest sense to include the art of politics at the apex of human activity and shows that for Plato all arts function best in the integrated life of the ideal city.

————. *Plato's Theory of Education*. Russell 1970 repr. of 1947 ed. o.p. Defends the practical side of Plato's theory of education, first as vocational and professional, then leading to political and philosophical leadership.

————. *Plato's Theory of Ethics: The Moral Criterion and the Highest Good*. Shoe String 1966 repr. of 1928 ed. o.p. Extensive discussion of what Plato proposes as the moral criterion of the highest good as compared with that of the other values.

Lutoslawski, Wincenty. *The Origin and Growth of Plato's Logic: With an Account of Plato's Style and the Chronology of His Writings*. *Classical Studies Ser*. Irvington 1981 repr. of 1897 ed. $59.99. ISBN 0-697-00041-9. Expands and elaborates on the findings of Lewis Campbell (above), using the stylometric method of dating the dialogues.

Lynch, William F. *Approach to the Metaphysics of Plato through the Parmenides*. Greenwood 1968 repr. of 1959 ed. $47.50. ISBN 0-8371-4833-2. Offers a step-by-step interpretation of the hypotheses in this Platonic dialogue and argues ably that Plato's metaphysics is one of unity, in which each form participates in a one-many mode relationship.

Lyons, Kimon. *Plato on Justice and Power: Reading Book I of Plato's Republic*. State U. NY Pr. 1987 $59.50. ISBN 0-8870-6415-9. Special study analyzing the argument to show that Socrates' thesis is to make justice an internal principle of the soul and integral to the good society.

McKirahan, Richard D., Jr. *Plato and Socrates: A Comprehensive Bibliography, 1958–1973*. *Lib. of Humanities Reference Bks*. Garland 1978 o.p. "Containing 4620 entries culled from hundreds of periodicals and numerous books, the work is divided into 14 subject sections with six on Plato and five on Socrates. The subject arrangements are easy to use and will be a boon to scholars concerned with a specific dialogue or aspect of either philosopher's life and work" (*Library Journal*).

Malcolm, John. *Plato on the Self-Prediction of Forms*. OUP 1991 $55.00. ISBN 0-19-823906-8. Raises the problem of the Third Man Argument as it relates to those instances of self-prediction in the early dialogues taken to be cases of universal statements.

Meinwald, Constace C. *Plato's Parmenides*. OUP 1991 $35.00. ISBN 0-19-506445-3. Treats the second part of the dialogue, which then is used to resolve the logical difficulties in the first part.

Miller, Mitchell H., Jr. *Plato's Parmenides: The Conversion of the Soul*. Princeton U. Pr. 1986 $30.00. ISBN 0-271-00803-2. Clear, unified interpretation of the two parts of this dialogue, with extensive commentary on the theory of forms.

Moline, Jon. *Plato's Theory of Understanding*. U. of Wis. Pr. 1981 $27.50. ISBN 0-299-08660-7. "Moline's discussion is a rich one, moving from an examination of pre-Platonic philologica and philosophical usage of the term *Episteme* through closely and clearly argued accounts of Plato's dialectic, psychology, epistemology and theory of forms" (*Choice*).

Moravcsik, Julius. *Plato and Platonism*. Blackwell Pubs. 1992 $54.95. ISBN 1-55786-202-8. Well-argued treatment of the thesis that the principles on which all ideals rest, the forms, are essential to the genuine arts of life and function as ultimate explanatory factors.

Moravcsik, Julius, and Phillip Tmeko, eds. *Plato on Beauty, Wisdom and the Arts*. Rowman 1982 o.p. Six papers on Plato's theory of art and beauty, aiming at dissolving the paradox of Plato's love of beauty and expulsion of the artist.

More, Paul E. *Platonism*. AMS Pr. 3rd ed. 1973 repr. of 1931 ed. $12.75. ISBN 0-404-04417-4. Full survey of Plato's doctrines by a sympathetic follower of Plato in the early part of the twentieth century.

Morgan, Michael L. *Platonic Piety: Philosophy and Ritual in Fourth-Century Athens*. Yale U. Pr. 1990 $30.00. ISBN 0-300-04517-4. The Dionysian and Orphic religious traditions are seen as constituting the background for a fuller understanding of ancient wisdom and of the Platonic theory of piety.

Morrow, Glenn R. *Plato's Slavery in Its Relation to Greek Law*. Ayer 1976 repr. of 1939 ed. o.p. Recognized as an admirable study on the complex issues of Plato's views on slavery and how it compares to current laws in Athens and Attica.

Murdoch, Iris. *The Fire and the Sun: Why Plato Banished the Artists.* OUP 1977 o.p. The 1976 Romanes Lecture reexamines the celebrated question of whether Plato meant to banish all the artists and uses the occasion to discuss Plato's views on beauty in light of comparable theories in modern philosophy and literature.

Nettleship, Richard L. *Lectures on the Republic of Plato.* Folcroft 1975 repr. of 1897 ed. o.p. One of the classic treatments of Plato's great work, still studied for its balanced interpretation of Plato's conception of political philosophy.

Ophir, Adi. *Plato's Invisible Cities: Discourse and Power in the Republic.* U. Pr. of Amer. 1991 $52.00. ISBN 0-389-20930-9. Views Plato's political philosophy in the context of Athenian politics and with reference to drama, myth, dialectic, and the problem of utopian cities.

Pater, Walter H. *Plato and Platonism.* Greenwood 1970 repr. of 1910 ed. $62.50. ISBN 0-8371-1151-X. Essays based on a series of lectures to make Plato's doctrines accessible to the layperson by drawing a vivid portrait of the philosopher.

Patterson, Richard. *Image and Reality in Plato's Metaphysics.* Hackett Pub. 1985 $29.50. ISBN 0-91545-72-3. Examines the concepts of image and model with reference to the sensible world and in the context of the theory of the forms.

Pelletier, Francis Jeffry. *Parmenides, Plato and the Semantics of Not-Being.* U. Ch. Pr. 1990 $23.95. ISBN 0-226-65390-0. Discusses prediction, representation, and natural language in this dialogue and shows the relevance of Plato's views to contemporary problems.

Plochmann, George Kimball, and Franklin E. Robinson. *A Friendly Companion to Plato's "Gorgias."* S. Ill. U. Pr. 1988 $49.95. ISBN 0-8093-1404-5. Extensive and clear commentary on the arguments and substantive ethical position Plato defended in this dialogue.

Polansky, Ronald M. *Philosophy and Knowledge: A Commentary on Plato's Theaetetus.* Bucknell U. Pr. 1992 $38.50 ISBN 0-8387-5215-2. An attempt to construct a comprehensive view of the diverse strands of knowledge by unlocking Plato's strategy.

Price, A. W. *Love and Friendship in Plato and Aristotle.* OUP 1989 $49.95. ISBN 0-19-824964-0. Explores and relates, with varying results, Platonic views on the nature of erotic conduct to Aristotle's theory of types of friendship.

Prior, William J. *Unity and Development in Plato's Metaphysics.* Open Court 1985 $24.95. ISBN 0-8126-9000-1. Useful work for the Greekless reader; traces the unity of Plato's metaphysics through six dialogues, including the *Timaeus* and the *Sophist.*

Randall, John H. *Plato: Dramatist of the Life of Reason.* Bks. Demand 1973 repr. of 1970 ed. $72.00. ISBN 0-317-30468-2. Unconventional but challenging and illuminating interpretation of Plato and his philosophy. Presents the dialogues as "dramatic portrayals of the life of mind," setting forth a coherent and remarkably complete vision of life, which makes Plato the "dramatist of the life of reason."

Raven, J. E. Earle John. *Plato's Thought in the Making: A Study of the Development of His Metaphysics.* Greenwood 1985 repr. of 1965 ed. $49.75. ISBN 0-313-24958-X. Concentrating on the middle dialogues as the ones "of greatest potential to the nonspecialist," proceeds with a rigorous treatment of the metaphysical themes in Plato's later works to unravel their conceptual implications.

Robinson, Richard. *Plato's Earlier Dialectic.* OUP 2nd ed. 1984 repr. of 1953 ed. o.p. Excellent on the method of examination and refutation in the early and middle Platonic dialogues.

Robinson, T. M. *Plato's Psychology.* Bks. Demand repr. of 1970 ed. $53.80. ISBN 0-317-08828-9. Thorough discussion of the Platonic views on the human soul in light of what modern authorities have said on the subject. Discounts the late Neoplatonic interpretations.

Rosen, Stanley. *Plato's Sophist: The Drama of Original and Image.* Yale U. Pr. 1983 $17.00. ISBN 0-300-03761-9. Cogent and comprehensive study of Plato's understanding of the difference between the philosopher and the Sophist.

————. *Plato's Symposium.* Yale U. Pr. 1987 $17.00. ISBN 0-300-03762-7. Important contribution to the literature on this dialogue, using the concept of irony to scan the range of the significance of Plato's erotic doctrines.

Ross, W. D. *Plato's Theory of Ideas.* Greenwood 1976 repr. of 1951 ed. $35.00. ISBN 0-8371-8635-8. Advances the position that Plato's development is from the immanence of the forms toward their transcendence, although Plato himself never was convinced that his theory was completely satisfactory.

Ryle, Gilbert. *Plato's Progress.* Cambridge U. Pr. 1966 o.p. Raises anew the question of Plato's development by rejecting the division between "Socratic" and non-Socratic dialogues, a position that has been widely discussed.

Saunders, Trevor J. *Bibliography on Plato's Laws 1920–1970, with Additional Citations through May 1975. History of Ideas Ser.* Ayer 1976 $10.00. ISBN 0-405-07324-0. "A list of the books and articles on *Laws* [that] have appeared since the first publication of E. B. England's *Commentary.* Saunders' work is partially inspired by the reprint of *Commentary* in 1975 (Arno Press)" (*Classical World*).

————. *Plato's Penal Code.* OUP 1991 $98.00. ISBN 0-19-814893-3. Discussion of the background of penology, leading to Plato's formulation of the utility of punishment in the *Laws* and crediting him with important innovations.

Sayre, Kenneth M. *Plato's Analytic Method.* Bks. Demand repr. of 1969 ed. $67.90. ISBN 0-685-23870-9. Well-written study on the development of Plato's philosophical methodology as found in the middle dialogues and how it blossoms as the employment of analysis in the *Theaetetus* and the *Sophist.*

Shorey, Paul. *The Unity of Plato's Thought. Ancient Philosophy Ser.* Garland 1980 o.p. "The text of this book is a résumé of the entire body of the Platonic writings. The endeavor has been to omit no significant ideas and to give with every idea enough of the dramatic setting and the over- and undertones of feeling" (Preface).

Sinaiko, Herman L. *Love, Knowledge, and Discourse in Plato: Dialogue and Dialectic in "Phaedrus," "Republic," "Parmenides." Midway Repr. Ser.* U. Ch. Pr. 1979 o.p. Argues that Plato's conception of philosophy required the employment of the dramatic form and demonstrates this thesis by scrutinizing three dialogues of the middle and late periods, *Phaedrus, Republic,* and *Parmenides.*

Skemp, J. B. *The Theory of Motion in Plato's Later Dialogues.* Coronet Bks. repr. of 1942 ed. o.p. Comprehensive discussion of the problem of reality and how it should be viewed as including the immovable forms as well as movement and life. The thesis of this work is that things in motion and in rest as well as the forms of motion and rest all partake in being.

Solmsen, Friedrich. *Plato's Theology.* Johnson Repr. 1942 o.p. Careful study centered on Plato's view of the soul as self-moving, regarded here as the foundation Plato used for a new cosmic religion beyond civic forms of worship.

Stalley, R. F. *An Introduction to Plato's Laws.* Hackett Pub. 1983 $32.50. ISBN 0-915145-84-7. Discusses Plato's *Laws* topic by topic to give a unitarian interpretation of his political philosophy.

Stuart, J. A. *The Myths of Plato.* St. Mut. 1983 o.p. Collection of the major Platonic myths together with an interpretation of their significance from an idealistic point of view.

Taylor, A. E. *Commentary on Plato's Timaeus.* OUP 1928 o.p. Monumental work discussing every aspect of Plato's views on the creation of the physical universe without ignoring the feature of the *Timaeus* that gives warning of the provisional character of the many theories advanced there.

————. *Plato: The Man and His Work.* U. of Okla. Pr. 1993 $22.95. ISBN 0-8061-2524-1. Offers close analyses of all the dialogues, along with very useful commentary; notable for its influence on scholarship.

Tracy, Theodore J. *Physiological Theory and the Doctrine of the Mean in Plato and Aristotle. Studies in Philosophy.* Mouton 1969 $48.00. ISBN 0-686-27755-4. Explores in great detail the doctrine of the mean in Plato, Aristotle, and the Hippocratic writings to show how essential it is to health and intellectual exercise.

Versényi, Laszlo. *Holiness and Justice: An Interpretation of Plato's "Euthyphro."* U. Pr. of Amer. 1982 $46.00. ISBN 0-8191-2316-1. Takes the position that the *Euthyphro* offers a positive thesis on holiness and knowledge about it; written clearly and with awareness of contemporary literature.

Vlastos, Gregory. *Platonic Studies.* Princeton U. Pr. 2nd ed. 1981 repr. of 1973 ed. o.p. Brings together the author's major papers along with several new studies, covering fundamental issues in Plato's metaphysics, ethics, and social philosophy.

_____, ed. *Plato, One: Metaphysics & Epistemology; a Collection of Critical Essays.* U. of Notre Dame Pr. 1978 o.p. Both this and the next title contain representative essays by various hands that generated new approaches and explorations reflecting intense interest among European and Anglo-American specialists in ancient philosophy; of the 30 articles included in both collections, only 5 had their first publication here.

_____. *Plato, Two: Ethics, Politics, and Philosophy of Art and Religion; a Collection of Critical Essays.* U. of Notre Dame Pr. 1978 $12.95. ISBN 0-268-01531-7.

_____. *Plato's Universe.* U. of Wash. Pr. 1975 o.p. The John Danz Lectures on the Greek view of the ordered universe and Plato's theories of celestial motion and the constitution of matter.

Voegelin, Eric. *Plato and Aristotle.* Vol. 3 in *Order and History.* La. State U. Pr. 1957 $29.95. In Part 1, discusses the philosophy of Plato as a precise system of symbols advancing beyond the symbolic framework of the older myth and marking, with Aristotle's system, the high point of philosophy among the Greeks.

Wedberg, Anders. *Plato's Philosophy of Mathematics.* Greenwood 1977 repr. of 1955 ed. $38.50. ISBN 0-8371-9405-9. Attempts to bring Plato's philosophy of mathematics in line with Aristotle's interpretation of Plato; very technical.

White, David A. *Rhetoric and Reality in Plato's Phaedrus.* State U. NY Pr. 1992 $54.50. ISBN 0-7914-1234-2. Shows the structural unity of Plato's method and ontology related to views on psychology and rhetoric.

White, Nicholas P. *A Companion to Plato's Republic.* Hackett Pub. 1979 $32.50. ISBN 0-915144-56-5. Readable and reliable guide to the main philosophical issues in Plato's political thought.

_____. *Plato on Knowledge and Reality.* Hackett Pub. 1976 $32.50. ISBN 0-915144-22-0. Moves progressively through the key dialogues to identify and reconstruct Plato's views on human knowledge of authentic reality and the role of language.

Wild, John. *Plato's Theory of Man.* Hippocrene Bks. 1964 o.p. Places in perspective Wild's interpretation of Plato's political philosophy as being in accordance with a coherent theory of natural law.

Woodbridge, F. J. *The Son of Apollo: Themes of Plato.* Biblo 1972 repr. of 1929 ed. $24.00. ISBN 0-8196-0278-7. Imaginative and unorthodox view of Plato's writings that sees them as the dramatization of the life of reason and illustrates this approach with discussions of Plato's major themes—love, education, politics, and death.

PLOTINUS. A.D. 205–270

Plotinus studied under Ammonius Sakkas and later moved to Rome, where he continued to develop his views and created a circle of faithful disciples, among them Porphyry the Phoenician (232–304), who edited Plotinus's *Enneads* and wrote works of his own, including *The Life of Plotinus.* Plotinus has been recognized as the last representative of Greek rationalism and one of the great thinkers of all times, having built a system that includes theories of reality, knowledge, ethics, esthetics, and theology.

The main stock of Plotinus's ideas comes from the classical age of Greek philosophy, recast to counter problems that the winds of new doctrines ushered in along with the rising power of religious worship and the spreading expectation for salvation.

Plotinus appeals to intellectual purity, an aspect often misunderstood as a concession to mysticism that lacks redeeming logical features. His philosophical system provides two ways to meet the demands of a fulfilled life. The first deals with finding one's place in a universe that is the result of the creative procession from the One, the source of all reality; the second is designed to effect the soul's "return" in a union with the One. Whereas the first way is metaphysical, the latter is ethical. The first brings understanding, the second grants blessedness.

Plotinus's insights proved influential, and many of his disciples, chiefly Porphyry, sought to preserve and transmit them to subsequent generations of thinkers in other parts of the Roman world, Syria and Greece in particular. Iamblichus (died c.A.D.330), Syrianus (fl. c.431), and Proclus (410–485) worked out their own versions of Neoplatonism. The schools' activities ended when they were ordered closed in A.D. 529. Still, the ideas had taken on a life of their own and moved in new directions. Many of them already had been taken over by Christian intellectuals who were learning how to respond to the need to strengthen the rational side of their religion.

BOOKS BY PLOTINUS

The Essence of Plotinus: Extracts from the Six Enneads and Porphyry's Life of Plotinus. Ed. by Grace R. Turnbull. Trans. by Stephen Mackenna. Greenwood 1977 repr of 1934 ed. $37.50. ISBN 0-8371-9054-1. Brings together selections made readable by the editor's corrections of the free translation by Mackenna.

The Essential Plotinus: Representative Treatises from the Enneads. Trans. by Elmer O'Brien. Hackett Pub. 1975 $24.95. ISBN 0-915144-10-7. Useful introduction and appendixes, with information on readings, glossary, bibliography, and a guide to sources.

Opera: Enneades. 3 vols. Ed. by H. R. Schwyzer and Paul Henry. OUP 1964–82 o.p. Definitive text of the *Enneads*, giving precise information on the manuscript tradition and full recording of critical emendations.

Plotinus: Text and Translation. 7 vols. Trans. by A. H. Armstrong. *Loeb Class. Lib.* HUP 1966–67 o.p. Armstrong's translation of the *Enneads* supersedes all previous renditions of Plotinus's thought.

BOOKS ABOUT PLOTINUS

Armstrong, A. H. *The Architecture of the Intelligible Universe in the Philosophy of Plotinus.* Cambridge U. Pr. 1940 o.p. One of the standard treatments of Plotinus's philosophy, with an emphasis on the doctrine of the three hypostases.

Atkinson, M. J., ed. *A Commentary on Plotinus: Ennead. Classical and Philosophical Monographs.* OUP 1983 $75.00. ISBN 0-19-814719-8. Excellent and detailed commentary, translation, and bibliography.

Bréhier, Emil. *The Philosophy of Plotinus.* U. Ch. Pr. 1958 o.p. Comprehensive yet adequate summary of Plotinus's life, writings, method, and ideas by the distinguished editor of Plotinus's texts in the Budé series.

Bussanich, John. *The One and Its Relation to Intellect in Plotinus: A Commentary on Selected Texts.* E. J. Brill 1988 o.p. Scholarly treatment of a fundamental Plotinian problem, bringing together the most pertinent texts in the *Enneads*.

Emilsson, Eyjolfur Kjalar. *Plotinus on Sense-Perception: A Philosophical Study.* Cambridge U. Pr. 1988 $44.95. ISBN 0-521-32988-4. Systematic exposition of Plotinus's general theory of soul, with separate chapters on vision, sensory affection, the unity of the senses, and the nature of judgment.

Inge, W. R. *Philosophy of Plotinus: The Gifford Lectures at St. Andrews, 1917–1918.* 2 vols. Greenwood 3rd ed. 1968 repr. of 1929 ed. $67.50. ISBN 0-8371-0113-1. A landmark in Plotinian studies, still very useful for its comprehensive scope but with an idealist bias.

_____. *The Religious Philosophy of Plotinus and Some Modern Philosophies of Religion.* Gordon Pr. 1977 $59.95. ISBN 0-8490-2513-3. Pioneer interpretation of Plotinus, placing his thought in the context of modern views and religion.

Mead, G. R. *Plotinus*. Holmes Pub. 1983 repr. of 1895 ed. $6.95. ISBN 0-916411-01-X. Introductory work; mainly of historical interest.

O'Meara, Dominic J. *Plotinus*. OUP 1993 $39.95. ISBN 0-19-875121-4. Introduction to the *Enneads* relating Plotinus's thought to preceding philosophies and to religious ideas of his time.

Rist, John M. *Eros and Psyche: Studies in Plato, Plotinus, and Origen*. Bks. Demand repr. of 1964 ed. $63.50. ISBN 0-317-08094-6. Excellent and thorough treatment of the idea of Platonic love in antiquity.

———. *Plotinus: The Road to Reality*. Cambridge U. Pr. 1977 $39.50. ISBN 0-521-06085-0. Comprehensive account of Plotinus's philosophy, with valuable excursions into the broader movement of Neoplatonism and its implications; also argues that Plotinus was conscious of his departures from Platonism.

Schroeder, Frederic M. *Form and Transformation: A Study in the Philosophy of Plotinus*. U. of Toronto Pr. 1992 $34.95. ISBN 0-7735-1016-8. Approaches Plotinus's conception of form as fundamental to the intellectual vision that transcends distinctions, with special chapters on light, silence, science, and love.

PYTHAGORAS OF SAMOS. c.582–c.507 B.C.

Legend has it that Pythagoras of Samos coined the word *philosophia*, which literally means "love of wisdom." Whereas the Milesian philosophers sought a physical element as the origin of all things and proceeded from there to work out a cosmology, their younger contemporary Pythagoras, who was considered one of the wisest and ablest of all Greeks, introduced the idea that the world is made of numbers and that its mathematical structure makes it a harmonious system. He and his disciples—one cannot tell them apart—proposed a table of opposites, on which one finds form and matter, limited and unlimited, good and evil, odd and even. One of these Pythagoreans, Philolaus, actually taught that the earth rotates on its axis. Later on, another scientist and astronomer, Aristarchus of Samos, declared, in 281 B.C., that the sun is immobile and that all the planets, including the earth, revolve around it. Pythagoras advocated the pursuit of the "philosophical" life to purify the soul in hope of ending its transmigrations or reincarnations.

BOOKS ABOUT PYTHAGORAS OF SAMOS

Burkert, Walter. *Love and Science in Ancient Pythagoreanism*. Trans. by Edwin L. Minar, Jr. HUP 1972 o.p. An excellent critical study of what is legend and what is reliable evidence about the views held by this school.

Guthrie, K. S. *The Pythagorean Sourcebook and Library*. Comp. by K. S. Guthrie. Trans. by D. R. Fideler. Phanes Pr. 1987 $30.00. ISBN 0-933999-50-X. Comprehensive collection of ancient texts, including biographies of Pythagoras.

Minar, Edwin L., Jr. *Early Pythagorean Politics in Practice and Theory*. Ed. by Gregory Vlastos. Ayer 1979 repr. of 1942 ed. $17.95. ISBN 0-405-11563-6. A thoroughly documented account of the religious and political activities related to Pythagorean principles.

Philip, James A. *Pythagoras and Early Pythagoreanism*. Bks. Demand repr. of 1968 ed. $58.00. ISBN 0-317-08752-5. Drawing chiefly on Aristotelian references, argues whether Pythagoras was shaman or a philosopher.

Raven, J. E. *Pythagoreans and Elatics: An Account of the Interaction between Two Opposed Schools*. Area Pubs. 1981 $20.00. ISBN 0-89005-367-7. An authoritative account of the early phase of the Pythagorean movement and its impact on the rise of the school of Elea in southern Italy.

SENECA, LUCIUS ANNAEUS. c.3 B.C.–A.D. 65

The Roman philosopher, statesman, and tragedian Lucius Annaeus Seneca was born in Cordoba, Spain. Educated in rhetoric and philosophy for a career in law, he received instruction in current eclectic Stoicism. During his career he had the misfortune of being banished to Corsica by the Emperor Claudius on a charge of adultery with the emperor's niece. In A.D. 49 he was recalled to Rome through the influence of Agrippina, the third wife of Claudius and sister of Julia, the woman with whom Seneca was accused of adultery. After his return to Rome, Seneca became the tutor to Agrippina's son Nero, the future emperor, and he later became Nero's principal adviser. In 57, three years after Nero became emperor, Seneca was accused of involvement in a conspiracy against the emperor. As a result, Nero ordered him to commit suicide, and Seneca did so with dignity and composure. Seneca wrote moral essays and letters and also nine tragedies. He espoused Stoic doctrines advocating virtue as the only true good and abstinence from materiality and emotions: Life must be ordered to accord with reason and divine will.

BOOKS BY SENECA

Four Tragedies and Octavia. Trans. by E. F. Watling. 1966 $7.95. ISBN 0-14-044174-3. Excellent translation for a more advanced readership of Seneca.

Seneca, Vol. 1: The Tragedies. Trans. by David R. Slavitt. Johns Hopkins 1992 $12.95. ISBN 0-8018-4309-X. Contains *Trojan Women, Thyestes, Phaedra, Medea,* and *Agamemnon.* Translation for introductory readers.

The Stoic Philosophy of Seneca: Essays and Letters. Trans. by Moses Hadas. Norton 1968 $6.95. One of the best collections available; introduced by Hadas, a learned authority in Latin literature.

BOOKS ABOUT SENECA

Eliot, T. S. *Shakespeare and the Stoicism of Seneca.* Porter 1979 o.p.

Griffin, Miriam D. *Seneca: A Philosopher in Politics.* 1992 $39.95. ISBN 0-19-814774-0. Outstanding work on Seneca's career and philosophy; well documented.

Gummere, Richard M. *Seneca the Philosopher and His Modern Message.* Cooper Sq. 1963 repr. of 1930 ed. $28.50. ISBN 0-8154-0098-5. Sympathetic, brief account, useful for its references to how modern literature sees Seneca.

Henry, D., and E. Henry. *The Mask of Power: Seneca's Tragedies and Imperial Power.* Bolchazy-Carducci 1985 $22.50. ISBN 0-86516-119-4. Attempts to contrast Seneca's serene Stoic ideals with his view of a hopeless Roman world.

Motto, A. L. *Seneca.* Twayne 1973 o.p. Well-written general introduction to Seneca's life and works, with an annotated bibliography.

Rosenmeyer, Thomas G. *Senecan Drama and Stoic Cosmology.* U. CA Pr. 1989 $39.95. ISBN 0-520-06445-3. Argues that account must be taken of the Stoic cosmology for the fuller understanding of the dramas, which, in turn, allows for a greater understanding of Stoicism and its effect on Western civilization.

SOCRATES. 469–399 B.C.

Socrates of Athens developed to a high degree the method of dialectic, not only to refute the Sophists, but also mainly to advance the thesis that universal standards exist. He wrote nothing—his teaching were entirely oral—but he influenced many in his lifetime and those who came after him. Socrates introduced a new, personal approach to philosophy. "Know thyself" was his motto.

Socrates was born just a decade after the decisive naval battle of Salamis. He grew up during the Periclean Age and lived through the Peloponnesian Wars. His endurance, valor, and loyalty to his friends are described in detail by PLATO (see also Vol. 3) and XENOPHON. He associated with many of the leading members of the Periclean circle and attempted to train several of the youth in political responsibility although he himself shunned a political career. His criticism of public views and policies led to his indictment, and in 399 he was put to death on the charge of corrupting the youth and introducing new deities. To the last day, Socrates continued his quest for the examined life; he spent the morning hours with his followers, discussing the nature of the soul and the meaning of immortality.

Plato wrote four dialogues in which Socrates in the chief speaker, and these are known as the Socratic dialogues. The *Euthyphro* discusses holiness and piety; the *Apology* is Socrates' defense before his judges; *Crito* is Socrates's answer to a proposal that he attempt escape from jail; *Phaedo* is the story of how Socrates drank the hemlock and died.

Socrates's pupils took their clues from the master's method, using his ethical teachings to work out their own theories. The Megarian school, founded by Euclid of Megara (450–374), adopted the Eleatic philosophy of the Unity of Being and asserted that there can be but one virtue. It demands that the *good* be understood as the essence of all things and that nothing else is real being. The other two schools followed different features of Socrates's teachings about the good life. Thus the Cyrenaic school, founded by Aristippus (c.435) at Cyrene, emphasized the pleasure of the intellectual quest, making it the good. The thesis held firmly together until Hegesias, a later member, showed that the doctrine leads to pessimism, because the pleasure of absolute knowledge as the highest good remains forever beyond our grasp. The Cynics, a school founded by Aristippus of Athens (445–360) and later led by Diogenes of Sinope (412–323), overstated the Socratic views and made virtue identical with knowledge, to be pursued without interest in pleasures. Because the Cynic position on virtue was bound to exaggerate freedom, it came to preach an extreme practice of abstinence and indifference toward possessions; in fact, it cultivated contempt toward civilized modes and advocated a return to nature. The Cyrenaic view eventually led to the philosophy of EPICURUS, whereas the Cynic position of "virtue for virtue's sake" later was taken over by the Stoics.

BOOKS ABOUT SOCRATES

Allen, R. E. *Socrates and Legal Obligation*. Bks. Demand repr. of 1980 ed. $42.40. ISBN 0-7837-2981-2. Outstanding examination of the early dialogues of Plato on Socrates' trial.

Benardete, Seth. *The Rhetoric of Morality and Philosophy*. U. Ch. Pr. 1991 $29.95. ISBN 0-226-04240-5. Interprets morality, rhetoric, and eros in the *Gorgias* and the *Phaedrus* as treating a common philosophical theme.

Benson, Hugh H., ed. *Essays on the Philosophy of Socrates*. OUP 1992 $45.00. ISBN 0-19-506756-8. Collection of some of the best articles by analytical philosophers on the subject of Socrates' thought.

Brickhouse, Thomas C., and Nicholas D. Smith. *Socrates on Trial*. Princeton U. Pr. 1989 $14.95. ISBN 0-691-07332-5. Integrates the authors' recent research on sources of the *Apology*, combining commentary and historical scholarship.

Dannhauser, Werner J. *Nietzsche's View of Socrates*. Cornell Univ. Pr. 1974 o.p. "A useful and instructive addition to the growing critical literature on Nietzsche" (*Choice*); it underscores Nietzsche's ambivalent attitude towards Socrates.

Dawson, M. M. *The Ethics of Socrates: A Compilation*. Gordon Pr. 1972 $59.95. ISBN 0-8490-0133-1. Convenient sourcebook of *testimonia* bearing on Socrates' distinct ethical theory.

Guthrie, William K. *Socrates*. Cambridge U. Pr. 1971 o.p. Extracted from Vol. 3 of his *A History of Greek Philosophy*.

Kraut, Richard. *Socrates and the State*. Princeton U. Pr. 1984 $50.00. ISBN 0-691-07666-9. Close analysis of Socrates' position as a victim of politics and defender of the law.

Nichols, Mary P. *Socrates and the Political Community: An Ancient Debate*. State U. NY Pr. 1987 $59.50. ISBN 0-88706-395-0. Provocative reading of the views of the "political" Socrates by Aristophanes, Plato, and Aristotle.

O'Brien, Michael J. *The Socratic Paradoxes and the Greek Mind*. U. of NC Pr. 1967 o.p. Outstanding work examining closely the paradoxes attending the conceptualization of the relationship between knowledge and virtue.

Santas, Gerasimos X. *Socrates*. Routledge 1982 $15.95. ISBN 0-7100-9327-6. Detailed and absorbing account of views and arguments pertaining mainly to the Socratic method and ethics.

Seeskin, Kenneth. *Dialogue and Discovery: A Study in Socratic Method*. State U. NY Pr. 1986 $59.50. ISBN 0-88706-337-3. Concentrates on Socrates' method of refutation and on the high drama in the text as reflective of character.

Strauss, Leo. *Socrates and Aristophanes*. Midway Repr. Ser. U. Ch. Pr. 1980 repr. of 1966 ed. $18.95. ISBN 0-226-77691-3. Close reading and interpretation of the comedies of Aristophanes for the light they cast on Socrates' moral and political teachings.

Taylor, A. E. *Socrates*. Hyperion Conn. 1991 repr. of 1951 ed. $22.00. ISBN 0-88355-718-5. Socrates' biography reconstructed on the basis of various reports, especially Plato's.

Vlastos, Gregory. *Socrates, Ironist and Moral Philosopher*. Cornell Univ. Pr. 1991 $57.50. ISBN 0-8014-2551-4. Close analysis of the moral teachings of Socrates and of the paradoxical use of irony in his method of investigation for finding truth.

———, ed. *The Philosophy of Socrates: A Collection of Critical Essays. Modern Studies in Philosophy*. U. of Notre Dame Pr. 1980 repr. of 1971 ed. o.p. Brings together some previously published and five original essays by various scholars, examining once again the Socratic doctrines.

THEOPHRASTUS OF ERESUS. c.372–c.287 B.C.

Theophrastus assumed the leadership of the Lyceum after ARISTOTLE's (see also Vol. 3) death. He was industrious and learned but lacking in originality. His importance lies in the fact that he carried on the research Aristotle had firmly established and he attracted numerous students to the school. Diogenes Laertius preserved whatever we know about Theophrastus, especially the long list of his writings—220 titles. Only a few of his treatises survived: *Enquiry into Plants* and *On the Causes of Plants*, a brief philosophical essay known as "Metaphysics," fragments of his *Physical Opinions*, and a literary work titled *Characters*.

Other important members of the Peripatetic school and successors to its leadership were Dikaiarchos of Messene, Aristoxenus, Clearchus, Demetrius of Phaleron, Stration of Lampsakos, Herakleides Ponticus, and Eudemus of Rhodes; of special interest are Andronicus of Rhodes (first century B.C.), who edited the works of Aristotle, and Alexander of Aphrodisias (c. A.D. 200), who wrote important commentaries on Aristotle's *De Anima* and *Metaphysics*.

BOOKS BY THEOPHRASTUS

The Characters of Theophrastus. Ayer 1979 repr. of 1909 ed. $20.00. ISBN 0-405-11441-9. Makes available Theophrastus's collection of 30 brief delineations of typical characters illustrative of Aristotle's pictures of representative kinds of people discussed in the ethics.

Metaphysics. Ed. and trans. by W. D. Ross and F. H. Fobes. OUP 1929 o.p. Excellent and rare edition, the best available, with introduction and valuable commentary.

BOOKS ABOUT THEOPHRASTUS

Fortenbaugh, W., and R. Sharples, eds. *Theophrastean Studies, On Natural Science, Physics and Metaphysics, Ethics, Religion and Rhetoric*. Transaction Pubs. 1987

$49.95. ISBN 0-88738-171-5. Specialists on Theophrastus deal with basic themes and ideas current in the Peripatetic school.

Fortenbaugh, William W., ed. *Theophrastus of Eresus: On His Life and Work. Studies in Classical Humanities.* Transaction Pubs. 1985 $49.95. ISBN 0-88738-009-3. Results of recent work by specialists have been brought together in this collection of essays; an excellent work.

Stratton, G. M. *Theophrastus and the Greek Physiological Psychology before Aristotle. Classical Studies Ser.* Irvington 1981 repr. of 1917 ed. $52.00. ISBN 0-697-00017-6. Fine and dependable account of what has survived of Theophrastus's great work on the history of physics.

XENOPHON. c.430–c.355 B.C.

SOCRATES's influence grew and a number of "Socratic" schools were formed, each claiming to give an authentic interpretation of his teachings on virtue and dialectic—for example, the Megarians, the Cyrenaics, and the Cynics. Meanwhile, Xenophon, an admirer of Socrates who was more practical than intellectual, preserved a record of what he saw and understood from his association with the "teacher." His writings as historian of both military and cultural events have survived. Xenophon's *Memorabilia, Apology of Socrates,* and *Symposium* give a picture from the common person's point of view that complements that of ARISTOPHANES, the comic poet, whose caricature of Socrates colored the perception of his contemporaries in no small way, as PLATO (see also Vol. 3) reports in his own *Apology.*

BOOKS BY XENOPHON

Hellenika. I-II 3.10. Ed. by A. Krentz David Brown. 1989 $49.95. ISBN 0-85668-463-5. The first two books of the Hellenika are the only one of three known continuations of Thucydides' *History of the Peloponnesian War* to survive.

Memorabilia. Ed by W. R. Connor. Ayer 1979 repr. of 1903 ed. $23.00. Convenient and useful edition with informative notes.

BOOKS ABOUT XENOPHON

Anderson, J.K. *Xenophon. Class. Life and Letters Ser.* Biblio NY 1979 o.p. General introduction to the life and times of Xenophon.

Higgins, W. E. *Xenophon the Athenian: The Problem of the Individual and the Society of the Polis.* State U. NY Pr. 1977 $49.50. ISBN 0-87395-369-X. Discusses the social and political aspects of Xenophon's writings, especially as they relate to Socrates.

Hirsch, Steven W. *The Friendship of the Barbarians: Xenophon and the Persians.* U. Pr. of New Eng. 1985 $30.00. ISBN 0-87451-322-7. Examines the historical relationship between the Greeks and the Persians, whom Xenophon respected and admired. Full and up-to-date bibliography and beautifully useful notes.

Lander, Mary K. *Index of Xenophontis Memorabilia.* Johnson Repr. repr. of 1900 ed. Compilation of lexical uses and themes.

Morrison, Donald R., ed. *Bibliography of Editions, Translations, and Commentary on Xenophon's Socratic Writings, 1600 to Present.* Mathesis Pubns. 1988 $15.00. ISBN 0-935225-02-1. A wealth of information gleaned from resources not readily available.

Strauss, Leo. *Xenophon's Socratic Discourse: An Interpretation of the Oeconomicus.* Bks. Demand repr. of 1970 ed. $57.00. ISBN 0-685-20911-3. Chapter-by-chapter discussion of the dialogue to provide a guide to the understanding of Xenophon and the Socratic views he recorded; includes a foreword by A. Bloom.

Copleston, F. C. *A History of Medieval Philosophy*. U. of Notre Dame Pr. 1990 $11.95.
ISBN 0-268-01091-9. A good Catholic treatment, more accurate and more balanced
than Gilson, but also duller reading.
_____. *History of Philosophy*. 2 vols. Doubleday 1993. Vol. 1 *Greek and Rome*. $15.00.
ISBN 0-385-46845-8. Vol. 2 *Augustine to Scotus*. $15.00. ISBN 0-385-46844-X. A fuller
account than his other history (above), with the same virtues and the same vices.
Dronke, Peter, ed. *A History of Twelfth-Century Western Philosophy*. Cambridge U. Pr.
1988 $84.95. ISBN 0-521-25896-0. A first-rate treatment, with contributions by a
variety of experts and an excellent bibliography. Fills the gap between Armstrong
(above) and Kretzmann (below) quite nicely.
Edwards, Paul, ed. *The Encyclopedia of Philosophy*. 4 vols. Free Pr. 1973 $425.00. ISBN 0-
02-894950-1. The standard encyclopedia of philosophy in English, carrying articles
on all the major thinkers and movements of the Middle Ages. The articles are
generally quite good, philosophically sophisticated, and easy to read.
Gilson, Étienne. *History of Christian Philosophy in the Middle Ages*. Chr. Classics 1955 o.p.
Well written, with a wealth of information and very full bibliographical notes,
marred somewhat by Gilson's obsessive concern with Thomistic orthodoxy, but still
very much worth reading.
Knowles, David. *Evolution of Medieval Thought*. Cor. and updated by D. E. Luscombe and
C.N.L. Brooke. Longman 1989 $19.95. ISBN 0-582-49426-5. An intelligent brief
treatment, but densely written.
Kretzmann, Norman, and others. *The Cambridge History of Later Medieval Philosophy:
From the Rediscovery of Aristotle to the Disintegration of Scholasticism 1100–1600*.
Cambridge U. Pr. 1982 $85.00. ISBN 0-521-22605-8. Concentrates on secular
philosophy. Up to date and scholarly, with extensive bibliographies. An excellent
survey in the areas it covers.
Marenbon, John. *Early Medieval Philosophy, 480–1150: An Introduction*. Routledge 1988
$13.95. ISBN 0-415-00070-X
_____. *Later Medieval Philosophy (1150–1350). An Introduction*. Routledge 1987 $35.00.
ISBN 0-685-19266-0. An excellent and up-to-date treatment, quite readable.
Strayer, Joseph R., ed. *Dictionary of the Middle Ages*. 13 vols. Macmillan 1989 $990.00.
ISBN 0-684-19073-7. Contains 5,000 signed articles dealing with various aspects of
medieval study, c.500 to 1500. Emphasis is on English-language works.
Weinberg, Julius R. *Short History of Medieval Philosophy*. Princeton U. Pr. 1964 $13.95.
ISBN 0-691-01956-8. A very readable, philosophically sophisticated history, concen-
trating on the theory of knowledge and giving more favorable attention than usual to
the Ockhamist movement and skeptical tendencies. The best short treatment.

COLLECTIONS OF MEDIEVAL PHILOSOPHICAL TEXTS

All of the thinkers mentioned in the collections of texts listed here are
represented by sizable pieces in them. Often very little of their work is available
in English elsewhere.

Fairweather, Eugene R., and John T. McNeill, eds. *Scholastic Miscellany: Anselm to
Ockham. Lib. of Christian Class*. Westminster John Knox 1982 $14.99. ISBN 0-664-
24418-1. Attractive translations of theological works, mostly from the early scholastic period of the eleventh and twelfth centuries. Especially see the long pieces from
Anselm and the brief selections from Abelard's theological works.
Grant, Edward. *A Source Book in Medieval Science. Source Books in the History of
Science Ser*. Bks. Demand repr. of 1974 ed. $180.00. ISBN 0-7837-4152-9. A very
large collection, topically arranged, of selections from the entire period. Well
translated, with extensive explanatory material. Much of this material has bearings
on what we now call philosophy of science.
Hyman, Arthur, and James J. Walsh, eds. *Philosophy in the Middle Ages: The Christian,
Islamic and Jewish Traditions*. Hackett Pub. 1983 repr. of 1967 ed. $39.95. ISBN 0-

915145-80-4. An exceptionally wide-ranging collection, with a considerable representation of Jewish and Muslim authors, who are generally slighted in these
collections. See especially the "Decisive Treatise" of Averroës on the relation of
philosophy to religion. The translations are of uneven quality.

Kretzmann, Norman, and Eleonore Stump, eds. *The Cambridge Translations of Medieval
Philosophical Texts*. Cambridge U. Pr. 1988 $69.95. ISBN 0-521-23600-2. Vol. 1 *Logic
and Philosophy of Language*. The first of four volumes planned for the series.
Excellent translations of pieces not otherwise available in English, but the material is
rather technical, at least in this first volume. For the more advanced student.

Lerner, Ralph, and Muhsin Mahdi, eds. *Medieval Political Philosophy: A Sourcebook*.
Agora Pap. Cornell Univ. Pr. 1972 $16.95. ISBN 0-8014-9139-8. Long selections from
all the more notable works in the Islamic, Jewish, and Latin traditions. Very useful
for its Islamic and Jewish sources, many of them unobtainable elsewhere in English.

McKeon, Richard, ed. and trans. *Selections from Medieval Philosophers*. 2 vols.
Macmillan 1971 o.p. Accurate and readable, but wordy translations. A common
theme is the nature of Truth and the way in which it is known. Especially notable is a
selection from Abelard on universals.

Wippel, John F., and Allen B. Wolter, eds. *Medieval Philosophy: From St. Augustine to
Nicholas of Cusa*. Free Pr. 1969 $12.95. ISBN 0-02-93650-4. A well-translated
collection covering the whole period, with a strong Thomist emphasis. See
especially the early-fourteenth-century treatise on the Agent Intellect.

SPECIAL TOPICS

Bruyne, Edgar de. *The Esthetics of the Middle Ages*. Trans. by Eileen B. Hennessy.
Continuum 1969 o.p. Old, but the only general treatment in English, and certainly
interesting reading; accessible to those inexpert in philosophy.

Eco, Umberto. *Art: Beauty in the Middle Ages*. Yale U. Pr. 1988 repr. of 1986 ed. $7.95.
ISBN 0-300-04207-8. Written by one of the foremost semiologists in the field, as well
as an expert on the Middle Ages.

Potts, T. C. *Conscience in Medieval Philosophy*. Cambridge U. Pr. 1980 $47.95. ISBN 0-
521-23287-2. An introduction and collection of texts on conscience translated from
Jerome, Augustine, Peter Lombard, Phillip the Chancellor, Bonaventure, and
Aquinas.

Problems of Method in the Study of Medieval Philosophy

The study of medieval philosophy has raised a number of theologically potent
questions of method, echoing and extending medieval disputes over the nature
of philosophy and its relation to religious belief. Some works reflecting and
dealing with these questions are listed below.

Gilson, Étienne. *Spirit of Medieval Philosophy*. U. of Notre Dame Pr. 1991 $12.95. ISBN 0-
268-01740-9. Gilson argues that a true Christian philosophy limits its aims to a
philosophical understanding of Christian dogma, remaining faithful to the dogma
within the framework of purely rational speculation.

Harnack, Adolf. *History of Dogma*. Trans. by Neil Buchanan. 7 vols. in 4. Peter Smith o.p.
A classic work on the development of Christian doctrine, rooted in the notion that
theological doctrine has developed and changed since the beginnings of Christianity.

Lovejoy, Arthur O. *Great Chain of Being: A Study of the History of an Idea*. *William James
Lectures Ser.* HUP 1936 $13.95. ISBN 0-674-36153-9. Deals somewhat impressionisti-
cally with an interesting topic in Neoplatonic thought, tracing its development from
late antiquity through the Middle Ages and into modern thought.

Troeltsch, Ernst. *The Social Teaching of the Christian Churches*. Trans. by Olive Wyon.
2 vols. U. Ch. Pr. 1992 $29.99. ISBN 0-664-25320-2. The best statement of a

thesis, critical of Harnack and Lovejoy, that the development of Christian doctrine cannot be understood apart from its changing social and cultural setting.

The History of Ideas and Medieval Thought

The works listed below belong to the "history of ideas." They suffer somewhat from a lack of sophistication in philosophy, in which they are only secondarily interested. Because they are also committed to identifying a single well-defined view of the world characterizing the Middle Ages, they tend to misrepresent the actual variety in the period's thought. They are valuable, however, for their picture of the relation of philosophy to the worldview of the "ordinary" (i.e., upper-class, clerical) person.

Artz, Frederick B. *The Mind of the Middle Ages: An Historical Survey, A.D. 200–1500*. U. Ch. Pr. 1980 $17.95. ISBN 0-226-02840-2. An updating of Taylor (below). Like Taylor, Artz approaches the period more from the standpoint of literature and the arts than from that of philosophy.

Coulton, G. G. *Studies in Medieval Thought*. Russell Sage 1966 o.p. The most philosophically oriented of these works. Despite its title, the "studies" cohere in a unified account of the whole period.

Southern, R. W. *Medieval Humanism and Other Studies*. Blackwell Pubs. 1984 o.p. A collection of articles. Interest in "humanism" in the Middle Ages is in reaction to characterizations of the period as oriented exclusively to the supernatural.

Taylor, Henry Osborn. *The Medieval Mind*. 2 vols. HUP 1959 o.p. The classic work in this genre. Makes Dante's *Divine Comedy* the centerpiece exhibiting the fully developed medieval worldview.

Averroism and Islamic Thought in the West

Western speculation was strongly influenced by Islamic interpretations of ARISTOTLE (see also Vol. 3). The thought of AVICENNA, whose Neoplatonic reading of the Master provided the backbone for the conservative Franciscan approaches to Aristotle, was important from early on in the thirteenth century. The much more radical AVERROËS became important in the second half of the thirteenth century. He held that philosophy uncovered a truth that religious doctrine expressed only in metaphors. That was provocative enough, but he coupled this doctrine with a denial of the immortality of the individual soul and of the creation of the world in time. He was the devil himself to the conservative theologians, and the Latin Averroists, beginning with Siger of Brabant, were accused of holding to his heresies. They seem, in fact, to have held only that his results are what natural reason would prove, and so are "true" in philosophy but are known through revelation to be false, because God in His power has sometimes set aside the natural laws on which the philosopher relies. Averroist views became quite widespread in the fourteenth and fifteenth centuries, despite conservative Thomistic opposition.

Boethius of Dacia. *On the Supreme Good. On the Eternity of the World. On Dreams*. Trans. by John F. Wippel. Pontifical Inst. of Medieval Studies 1987 o.p. Arguments by a Latin Averroist, in the first treatise that, philosophically, the good of the intellect is the supreme good, and in the second that reason and philosophy are independent from theology.

Davidson, Herbert A. *Alfarabi, Avicenna and Averroës*. OUP 1992 $39.95. ISBN 0-19-507423-8. An impressive study of problems revolving around these Arabic thinkers' theories of the intellect.

Fakhry, Majid. *History of Islamic Philosophy*. Col. U. Pr. 1983 $44.50. ISBN 0-231-05532-3. A full account of historical developments in the Middle Ages, though it shows some lack of philosophical sophistication.

Leaman, Oliver. *An Introduction to Medieval Islamic Philosophy*. Cambridge U. Pr. 1985 $19.95. ISBN 0-521-28911-4. The most philosophically sophisticated discussion in English, but short on biographical detail, summaries of minor figures, and the like. Nicely supplemented by the work by Fakhry (above).

———. *Averroës and His Philosophy*. OUP 1988 $55.00. ISBN 0-19-826540-9. A philosophically sophisticated treatment of some central themes in Averroës: the existence and nature of God, soul and the intellect, and the relation of the divine law to human ethics.

MacClintock, S. *Perversity and Error*. U. of Ind. Pr. 1956 o.p. A study of the Averroists that takes Steenberghen's work (below) into account and extends its range to a consideration of the flourishing Averroism in Italy and France in the fourteenth and fifteenth centuries.

Steenberghen, F. van. *The Philosophical Movement in the Thirteenth Century*. Nelson-Hall 1955 o.p. This work is fundamental not only for the Averroists but also more generally for the introduction of Aristotle to the West. A first-rate scholarly study, but not inaccessible to the general reader who has a little background.

Watt, William Montgomery. *Islamic Philosophy and Theology*. Col. U. Pr. 1988 $12.50. ISBN 0-85224-552-1. An authoritative work of scholarship, but Leaman's (above) much less scholarly books are more enlightening on the philosophical issues and options.

Logic

Bochner, Philotheus. *Medieval Logic: An Outline of Its Development from 1250–1400*. Hyperion Conn. 1979 repr. of 1952 ed. o.p. The best general introduction to new, non-Aristotelian developments in medieval logic from the twelfth century on.

Kneale, William, and Martha Kneale, eds. *The Development of Logic*. OUP 1962 $56.00. ISBN 0-19-824183-6. Brief selections from works of logic in translation, including a considerable representation of medieval and ancient writers, with connecting commentary and explanation. A good book to examine after Boehner.

Nuchelmans, G. *Theories of the Proposition*. *Linguistics Ser.* 2 vols. Elsevier 1973–82 o.p. A sophisticated examination of theories of meaning in the ancient world and the Middle Ages, centering on the meaning of sentences rather than the meaning of words.

Science

Crombie, A. C. *Augustine to Galileo*. HUP 1979 $35.00. ISBN 0-674-05273-0. A good introductory treatment; brief, readable, and interesting, but necessarily superficial on many topics.

Duhem, Pierre. *Medieval Cosmology, Theories of Infinity, Place, Time, Void and the Plurality of Worlds*. Ed. and trans. by Robert Ariew. U. Ch. Pr. 1985 $19.95. ISBN 0-226-16923-5. Contributions by a distinguished philosopher of science of the beginning of this century; still of interest.

Grant, Edward. *Physical Science in the Middle Ages*. *History of Science Ser.* Cambridge U. Pr. 1978 $15.95. ISBN 0-521-29294-8. A well-written and well-informed brief treatment, suitable for the beginner.

Lindberg, David C., ed. *Science in the Middle Ages*. *Chicago History of Science and Medicine Ser.* U. Ch. Pr. 1979 $20.00. ISBN 0-226-48233-2. A collection of articles by some of the most significant modern scholars. Up to date and fascinating.

Maier, Anneliese. *At the Threshold of Exact Science: Selected Writings of Anneliese Maier on Late Medieval Natural Philosophy*. Ed. and trans. by Steven D. Sargent. U. of Pa. Pr. 1982 o.p. Maier's extensive German writings provide wonderful reading on all aspects of physical thought in the later Middle Ages. This selection provides an excellent introduction to medieval science.

Thorndike, Lynn. *The First Thirteen Centuries*. Vols. 1 and 2 in *A History of Magic and Experimental Science*. Col. U. Pr. 1923 $98.00 ea. ISBNs 0-213-08794-2, 0-213-08795-0. A monumental treatment of medieval science and many aspects of medieval philosophy. It is well worth checking the indexes for a particular philosopher or topic.

Politics

Burns, J. H., ed. *The Cambridge History of Medieval Political Thought, c.350–c.1450*. Cambridge U. Pr. 1988 $110.00. ISBN 0-521-24324-6. An up-to-date survey by multiple contributors. Much original scholarship, superseding earlier treatments. An excellent bibliography.

Johnson, Harold J., ed. *The Medieval Tradition of Natural Law*. Medieval Inst. 1987 $22.95. ISBN 0-918720-81-8. A fine collection of articles on natural-law theory from Aquinas to the early Enlightenment.

Kantorowicz, Ernst H. *The King's Two Bodies: A Study of Medieval Political Theology*. Princeton U. Pr. 1981 $19.95. ISBN 0-691-02018-3. On the theory of kingship in the Middle Ages.

Lewis, Ewart. *Medieval Political Ideas*. Cooper Square 1973 repr. of 1954 ed. o.p. A collection of translations from all the major writers, arranged by topic, with an introductory essay on each topic.

Morrall, John B. *Political Thought in Medieval Times*. *Medieval Academy Repr. for Teaching Ser.* U. of Toronto Pr. 1980 $8.95. ISBN 0-8020-6413-2. A brief introductory treatment.

THE PATRISTIC PERIOD

The period from the crystallization of orthodox Christian belief at the end of the first century to the twilight of Rome in the fifth century saw the domestication of philosophy within Christianity. The largely Platonic, and later Neoplatonic, thought of such "Fathers of the Church" as ORIGEN, AUGUSTINE OF HIPPO and BOETHIUS is the starting point for philosophy until the introduction of ARISTOTLE's (see also Vol. 3) works in the latter half of the twelfth century. In particular, Augustinian epistemology provided a model for later reflections, and the preservation of ancient elementary logic texts by Boethius provided the groundwork for rich developments in the twelfth century. However, the real strength of the Fathers is to be found in their philosophical consideration of religious themes, and here their thought remains influential even today.

Bauer, Walter. *Orthodoxy and Heresy in Earliest Christianity*. Bks. Demand repr. of 1971 ed. $88.00. ISBN 0-685-17039-X. An influential work. Argues that the application of later standards of orthodoxy in the discussion of early Christianity is anachronistic and misleading.

Campenhausen, Hans von. *The Fathers of·the Greek Church*. A. & C. Black 1963 o.p.
_____. *The Fathers of the Latin Church*. Trans. by Manfred Hoffmann. Stanford U. Pr. 1964 $39.50. ISBN 0-8047-0685-9. Another edition of this book appeared under the title *Men Who Shaped the Western Church*. Both *The Fathers of the Greek Church* and *The Fathers of the Latin Church* contain perceptive essays on the character, life, and thought of the major church fathers.

Cassiodorus. *An Introduction to Divine and Human Readings*. Trans. by L. W. Jones. Hippocrene Bks. 1966 o.p. Laid down the program for the preservation of the classical heritage of Rome and Greece as the chaotic barbarian centuries began, threatening the entire destruction of that heritage.

Chadwick, Henry. *Early Christian Thought and the Classical Tradition: Studies in Justin, Clement, and Origen.* OUP 1984 $19.95. ISBN 0-19-826673-1. A first-rate discussion of Justin Martyr and Clement of Alexandria (late second and early third century) on faith and reason, philosophy, and Christianity. Attractively written and accessible to the beginner.

Cochrane, Charles N. *Christianity and Classical Culture: A Study of Thought and Action from Augustus to Augustine.* OUP 1957 $12.95. ISBN 0-19-500207-5. A sophisticated discussion of the developments in philosophy of history, political philosophy, and the role and conception of the state in the transformation of the pagan to a Christian empire. Confined largely to Latin writers, but discusses both Christian and pagan authors, beginning with Virgil and Cicero.

Grant, Robert M. *The Early Christian Doctrine of God.* U. Pr. of Va. 1966 o.p. Covers some of the same ground as Norris (below), but chiefly interested in the Trinity, the humanity of Christ, and like concepts, rather than God's relation to the world He created.

———. *Miracle and Natural Law in Graeco-Roman and Early Christian Thought.* Elsevier 1981 repr. of 1952 ed. o.p. Part 1 is on the notions of natural law in late ancient thought; Part 2 is on the account of miracles in Christianity and its reflection on Christian notions of natural law.

Grant, Robert M., and David Tracy. *A Short History of the Interpretation of the Bible.* Augsburg Fortress 1984 $13.00. ISBN 0-8006-1762-2. On scriptural interpretation in general throughout the Middle Ages.

Hatch, Edwin. *The Influence of Greek Ideas on Christianity.* Peter Smith 1970 $11.75. ISBN 0-8446-0683-9. A classic work updated. Very much worth reading.

Justin Martyr. *Complete Writings.* Trans. by T. B. Falls. *Fathers of the Church Ser.* Cath. U. Pr. 1948 o.p. The first of the new Christian intellectuals to set himself up as a philosopher. His Platonism is superficial, but many of his themes persisted in Clement and Origen.

Lewis, Clive S. *The Discarded Image: An Introduction to Medieval and Renaissance Literature.* Cambridge U. Pr. 1968 o.p. A very readable introduction to the world picture inherited from the fifth century by the later Middle Ages. Nontechnical.

Norris, Richard A. *God and World in Early Christian Theology.* Seabury 1965 o.p. On the cosmological notions of later Greek antiquity and the Gnostic and Christian reactions to them. Discusses Justin Martyr, Irenaeus, Tertullian, and Origen.

O'Meara, Dominic J. *Neoplatonism and Christian Thought. Neoplatonism: Ancient and Modern Ser.* State U. NY Pr. 1981 $59.50. ISBN 0-87395-492-0. A collection of articles, most by Catholic scholars, on Neoplatonism in Christian thought from Origen to the twentieth century. For the more sophisticated reader.

Pannenberg, Wolfhart. *Basic Questions in Theology: Collected Essays.* Westminster John Knox 1983 repr. of 1971 ed. o.p. Contains a sophisticated discussion of the adoption into Christianity of the philosopher's notion of God. For someone who wants to go more deeply into the matter.

Pelikan, Jaroslav. *The Christian Tradition: A History of the Development of Doctrine.* 5 vols. U. Ch. Pr. 1971–85. $12.95–$15.95 ea. ISBNs 0-226-65371-4, 0-226-65373-0, 0-226-65380-3, 0-226-65375-7, 0-226-65377-3. A brilliant and comprehensive work. See especially Vol. 1, Chap. 1, on the conflict between Christianity and pagan philosophy. The best general treatment, and superbly written. Should be read first.

———. *The Shape of Death: Life, Death, and Immortality in the Early Fathers.* Greenwood 1978 repr. of 1961 ed. $38.50. ISBN 0-313-20458-6. Chapters on Tatian, Clement, Cyprian, Origen, and Irenaeus. Suggestive, brief sketches of their accounts of life after death. Pelikan's scholarship thoroughly informs his discussion.

Rand, Edward K. *The Founders of the Middle Ages.* Dover 1957 repr. of 1928 ed. o.p. A classic study of some early thinkers. Outdated now, but still provides a nice introduction to late antiquity, discussing the relation of the Church to pagan culture, Ambrose, Jerome, Boethius, Augustine, and Dante.

Roberts, Alexander, and James Donaldson, eds. *The Ante-Nicene Fathers*. 10 vols. Eerdmans 1951 o.p. A reprint, with additional material, of a major collection of early texts first published in the nineteenth century.

Sandmel, Samuel. *Philo of Alexandria: An Introduction*. OUP 1979 $9.95. ISBN 0-19-502515-6. Updates a classic work by the author's teacher, E. Goodenough, and attempts to clear up its obscurities. Rather more guarded than Wolfson (below) in its assessment of Philo.

Schaff, Philip, and others. *A Select Library of Nicene and Post-Nicene Fathers of the Christian Church*. 28 vols. Eerdmans 1952–56 o.p. A collection of translations first published in the late nineteenth century. The translations are often stuffy, and sometimes inaccurate, but these volumes are readily available in libraries.

Turner, Henry E. *The Pattern of Christian Truth: A Study in the Relations between Orthodoxy and Heresy in the Early Church*. AMS Pr. 1977 repr. of 1954 ed. $47.50. ISBN 0-404-161114-6. Criticizes, with some effectiveness, Bauer's view that there was no established orthodox tradition in the first two centuries of the Christian era.

Wilken, Robert L., ed. *The Christians as the Romans Saw Them*. Yale U. Pr. 1984 $27.00. ISBN 0-300-03066-5. An insightful work, arguing that early Christianity was seen as a secret and private religion in a society depending on a public civic religion for civil unity and moral training. Finds many later Roman objections to Christianity well founded and instrumental in stimulating Christian theological development.

Wolfson, Harry A. *Philo: Foundations of Religious Philosophy in Judaism, Christianity and Islam*. 2 vols. HUP 1962 $65.00. ISBN 0-674-66450-7. Argues that Philo first developed the medieval style of Jewish, Arabic, and Christian religious thought through his adaptation of Platonism to the Jewish faith.

———. *Philosophy of the Church Fathers: Faith, Trinity, Incarnation*. HUP 1970 $34.95. ISBN 0-674-66551-1. A classic discussion by a great scholar, often displaying philosophical sophistication but sometimes grumpy and idiosyncratic as well. Entertaining reading.

THE PERIOD OF RECOVERY

After BOETHIUS, chaos settled upon the West. It ended only when Charlemagne, who emerged in the latter part of the eighth century as the most powerful ruler in Europe, took an interest in reestablishing learning in his empire. At this time there was still considerable intellectual borrowing from the empire of Byzantium, which was to fade gradually as the West asserted its spiritual independence. The most important philosophical figures of the period are JOHANNES SCOTUS ERIGENA and ANSELM.

Hornell, W., ed. and trans. *The Rhetoric of Alcuin and Charlemagne*. Princeton U. Pr. 1941 o.p. A dialogue between Charles and Albinus. Interesting material on a variety of topics, including justice.

Laistner, Max, and H. H. King. *Thought and Letters in Western Europe, A.D. 500–900*. Gordon Pr. $59.95. ISBN 0-8490-1207-4. An excellent general account of medieval thought in the period of the Dark Ages and the recovery.

Marenbon, John. *From the Circle of Alcuin to the School of Auxerre: Logic, Theology, and Philosophy in the Early Middle Ages*. Cambridge U. Pr. 1981 o.p. A scholarly account of the period from the eighth to the eleventh centuries, with an especially full treatment of developments in philosophical semantics.

Wallach, Luitpold. *Alcuin and Charlemagne: Studies in Carolingian History and Literature*. Johnson Repr. repr. of 1959 ed. o.p. Interesting for the political side of Carolingian thought.

Wolff, Philippe. *The Awakening of Europe*. Trans. by Anne Carter. Viking Penguin 1968 o.p. A stimulating popular history of the cultural background to philosophy focusing on Alcuin, Gerbert, and Abelard. Alcuin was responsible for reestablishing learning in Charlemagne's kingdom. Gerbert was interested in scientific matters, and rose to become Pope.

THE TWELFTH AND THIRTEENTH CENTURIES

In the twelfth century, European philosophy came of age. The ancient texts it had inherited, elementary as they were, posed philosophical questions about the relation of language to reality that were explored in a way going beyond the texts themselves in depth and sophistication. Here ABELARD is the outstanding figure. With the introduction of ARISTOTLE's (see also Vol. 3) works to the West, along with the Aristotelian philosophies of the Islamic thinkers AVICENNA and AVERROËS, the philosophical scene was transformed. The urgent problem for theologians became the domestication of this foreign giant in the Christian context, and THOMAS AQUINAS's thought represents the culmination of efforts in this direction.

Aelred of Reivaulx. *Spiritual Friendship*. Cistercian Pubns. 1974 o.p. A charming writer, Aelred (d.1148) here adapts Cicero's *On Friendship* for Christians.

Burr, David. *The Persecution of Peter Olivi. Transaction Ser.* Am. Philos. Society 1976 o.p. A Franciscan, Olivi (1248–1298) is most noted for arguing that the soul, though joined to the body in a substantial unity by inferior forms, is not itself the form of the body. This position was condemned at the Council of Vienna (1311). A scholarly discussion of both the political and the philosophical-theological issues involved.

Bursill-Hall, G. L. *Speculative Grammars of the Middle Ages: The Doctrine of Partes Orationis of the Modistae. Approaches to Semiotics Ser.* Mouton 1971 $75.00. ISBN 90-2791-913-5. Speculative grammar, which is to medieval logic roughly what Chomskian depth grammars are to modern logic, has captured the interest of modern linguists. The best introduction to the subject in English.

Chenu, M. D. *Nature, Man, and Society in the Twelfth Century: Essays on New Theological Perspectives in the Latin West.* Trans. by Lester Little. U. Ch. Pr. 1979 o.p. Translations from an important French scholar. See especially the essays "The Renaissance of the Twelfth Century," "The Platonisms of the Twelfth Century," "The Symbolist Mentality," and "The Masters of the Theological Sciences."

Cobban, A. B. *The Medieval Universities.* Methuen 1975 o.p. A good, compact treatment updating the scholarship of Haskins (below).

Gracia, Jorge J. E. *Introduction to the Problem of Individuation in the Early Middle Ages: 500–1200 A.D.* Philosophia Pr. 1988 $105.00. ISBN 3-88405-075-3. A sophisticated examination of the problem of individuality in the Platonists—Boethius, Johannes Scotus Erigena, and the School of Chartres—and their Aristotelian critics—Abelard and John of Salisbury.

Haskins, Charles H. *The Renaissance of the Twelfth Century.* HUP 1971 $14.00. ISBN 0-676-76075-1. A classic, arguing that the twelfth century shares many of the characteristics of the fifteenth-century Renaissance and ushers in a period of high civilization. It has given rise to much controversy.

———. *The Rise of Universities.* Cornell Univ. Pr. 1957 $6.95. ISBN 0-8014-9015-4. The standard introduction to this medieval institution, which arose in the late twelfth and early thirteenth centuries and in whose context philosophy has since largely taken place.

Hugh of St. Victor. *Discascalicon: A Medieval Guide to the Arts.* Trans. by Jerome Taylor. Col. U. Pr. 1961 o.p. An introduction to the liberal arts and a guide to studies. Hugh of St. Victor (1096–1141) was a member of a notable school of mystical thought in the twelfth century.

John of Paris. *John of Paris on Royal and Papal Power.* Trans. by Arthur P. Monahan. Col. U. Pr. 1974 $42.00. ISBN 0-231-03690-6. A late-thirteenth-century defense of the secular power against claims that papal power should absolutely dominate. Suggests popular consent, rather than the bishop's annointment, is necessary to legitimize the rule of the king.

Kleinz, J. *The Theory of Knowledge of Hugh of St. Victor.* Cath. U. Pr. 1978 o.p. Provides a picture of the theory of knowledge in the West before Aristotle intruded on the scene.

Leff, Gordon. *Paris and Oxford Universities in the 13th and 14th Centuries: An Institutional and Intellectual History.* Krieger 1975 repr. of 1968 ed. o.p. An account of the origin and growth of the two universities and the development of their curricula. The split between Anglo-Saxon scientific empiricism and continental humanistic rationalism can be traced to the distinctive intellectual styles of these universities.

Llull, Ramon. *Selected Works of Ramon Llull (1232–1316).* Ed. and trans. by Anthony Bonner. 2 vols. Princeton U. Pr. 1985 $194.00. ISBN 0-691-07288-4. A collection of good translations, with ample aids for the reader. Llull's odd sort of logical calculus was intended to produce a deduction of every necessary truth from the fundamental concepts by which we can classify reality. Some of Leibniz's notions about logic are rooted in Llull's conceptions.

Lynch, John E. *The Theory of Knowledge of Vital du Four. Philosophy Ser.* Franciscan Inst. 1972 $17.00. ISBN 0-686-11546-5. An excellent survey of the status of theory of knowledge, in particular sense knowledge and knowledge of singulars, just before the great systems of Ockham and Scotus arose.

McKeon, C. K. *A Study of the "Summa philosophiae" of the Pseudo-Grosseteste.* Col. U. Pr. 1948 o.p. A kind of encyclopedia, giving a snapshot of the opinions of its time, attributed to Robert Grosseteste (c.1175–1253) but in fact written later by an unknown author. Discusses the work of theology in absorbing Arabian and Greek philosophy and making it Christian, along with treatises on a variety of other topics.

Peter of Spain. *Language in Dispute. An English Translation of Peter of Spain's "Tractatus."* Trans. by Francis P. Dinneen. Benjamins North Am. 1990 $58.00. ISBN 90-272- 4524-X. A favorite textbook in logic throughout the Middle Ages. Compare to the works of William of Sherwood (below).

Reeves, Marjorie. *The Influence of Prophecy in the Later Middle Ages: A Study of Joachimism.* OUP 1969 o.p. A study of Joachim of Fiore (c.1135–1202), a mystical philosopher of history who inspired apocalyptic expectations of a new age, often associated with heresy, as late as the sixteenth century.

Smalley, Beryl. *The Becket Conflict and The Schools: A Study of Intellectuals in Politics in the Twelfth Century.* Rowman 1973 o.p. Becket's murder is a dramatic tale often retold in modern literature. Smalley's study gives us another view of it, centered neither in politics nor in dramatic possibilities, but in the role of the intellectual in society.

Thorndike Lynn, trans. *University Records and Life in the Middle Ages. Columbia Univ. Records of Civilization Ser.* Norton 1975 o.p. A fascinating collection of documents bearing on every aspect of university life.

Tobin, Frank. *Meister Eckhart: Thought and Language.* U. of Pa. Pr. 1986 $40.95. ISBN 0-8122-8009-1. An excellent study of the philosophical underpinnings of Eckhart's mystical thought.

Wallace, William A. *Causality and Scientific Explanation: Medieval and Early Classical Science.* U. Pr. of Amer. 1981 o.p. Discusses Grosseteste, Aquinas, and a number of other medieval thinkers on philosophy of science, concentrating on their notions about the nature of scientific explanation and its connection to causal accounts of phenomena.

William of St. Thierry. *The Enigma of Faith.* Trans. by John Anderson. Cistercian Pubns. 1974 o.p. A consideration of the mystical vision and our knowledge of God, culminating in a discussion of the Trinity, by a contemporary of Bernard of Clairvaux and Abelard.

_____. *The Golden Epistle: A Letter to the Brethren at Mont Dieu.* Cistercian Pubns. 1971 o.p. A great Cistercian mystic's chief work. William provides here an account of the nature and destiny of human beings, discussing animal, rational, and spiritual ends and their relations to one another.

———. *The Mirror of Faith*. Trans. by Thomas X. Davis. Cistercian Pubns. 1979 o.p. William's letters concerning Abelard's errors in theology precipitated the condemnation of Abelard's works at Sens. This antiphilosophical tract reflects a conservative Augustinianism and emphasizes the need to subject reason to Scripture.

William of Sherwood. *Introduction of Logic*. Trans. by Norman Kretzmann. Greenwood 1975 o.p. Important work in the development of medieval logic.

———. *William of Sherwood's Treatise on Syncategorematic Words*. Trans. by Norman Kretzmann. U. of Minn. Pr. 1968 o.p. First-rate translations of William of Sherwood (mid-thirteenth century). The best introduction in English to the logic of reference and meaning, and to the analysis of the real logical form of a sentence, developed in the twelfth and thirteenth centuries.

Wippel, John F. *The Metaphysical Thought of Godfrey of Fontaines: A Study in Late Thirteenth-Century Philosophy*. Cath. U. Pr. 1981 o.p. Godfrey was a teacher at the University of Paris who defended the real distinction between being and essence against Henry of Ghent (d.1306?). A thorough and scholarly analysis, though it gives little attention to the interests of present-day secular philosophy.

THE LATER MIDDLE AGES

The fourteenth century presents us with philosophy in its vigorous maturity. The task in such thinkers as JOHN DUNS SCOTUS and WILLIAM OF OCKHAM was no longer to absorb and explicate ARISTOTLE (see also Vol. 3) but to deal, directly on one's own account, with the issues he raises. The period is marked above all by the final abandonment by Ockham's followers of even the most weakened forms of the theory of real universals, and all schools are impressed with the problem of explaining how knowledge of universal truths, natural laws, and the like can be extracted from our acquaintance with particulars. Ockham takes the most radical view, arguing that we know nothing except our own concepts. British empiricism is foreshadowed in this position, and the distinction between English and continental thought is becoming established. The fifteenth century marks the beginning of the Renaissance, but the old medieval schools continue to flourish.

The Fourteenth Century

Buridan, John. *Sophisms on Meaning and Truth*. Trans. by T. K. Scott. Irvington 1966 o.p. A fairly accessible translation with notes, but the topic is inaccessible, and the book is only for someone with a knowledge of logic.

Courtenay, William J. *Schools and Scholars in Fourteenth-Century England*. Princeton U. Pr. 1987 $55.00. ISBN 0-691-05509-0. Deals with the social context rather than the content of fourteenth-century thought. Useful background.

Daly, Lowrie J. *The Political Theory of John Wyclif*. Loyola 1962 o.p. An examination of the radical political thought of Wyclif (1330?–1384), tracing its roots in his intellectual and political background.

Giles of Rome. *De erroribus philosophorum*. Ed. by J. Koch. Trans. by J. O. Riedl. Marquette 1944 o.p. A work cataloging the errors of excessive Aristotelianism, but do not be fooled: Giles is more an Aristotelian, as well as more skeptical, than Thomas Aquinas.

———. *Giles of Rome on Ecclesiastical Power*. Ed. and trans. by R. W. Dyson. Boydell & Brewer Pr. 1986 $75.00. ISBN 0-85115-434-4. An important work written in 1301–02, presenting ideas similar to those of John of Paris.

———. *Theorems on Essence and Existence*. Trans. by M. V. Murray. Marquette 1952 o.p. Like Thomas Aquinas, Giles pins his metaphysical thought on a real distinction between essence and existence, but his view of the distinction is more extreme than Thomas's, emphasizing that only the individual really exists.

Gilson, Étienne. *Dante and Philosophy*. Trans. by David Moore. Peter Smith 1949 $12.75. ISBN 0-8446-0645-6. The foremost study of the topic. One point of controversy is Dante's relation to Averroism, given his praise of Thomas Aquinas's opponent, Siger of Brabant, in *The Divine Comedy*.

Henninger, Mark G. *Relations: Medieval Theories, 1250–1325*. OUP 1989 $55.00. ISBN 0-19-824444-4. A first-rate discussion of the problem of relations dealing with Aquinas, Scotus, and Ockham as well as other, lesser-known figures.

Kilvington, Richard. *The Sophismata of Richard Kilvington*. Trans. and with notes by Barbara Kretzmann and Norman Kretzmann. Cambridge U. Pr. 1990 $59.95. ISBN 0-521- 35419-6. Logical puzzles that raise fundamental issues both in philosophical semantics and in such topics as the analysis of the continuum. Expert translation and notes.

Kretzmann, Norman, ed. *Infinity and Continuity in Ancient and Medieval Thought*. Cornell Univ. Pr. 1982 o.p. A collection of articles in the treatment of infinite divisibility and space and time and the logical problems they give rise to. Somewhat technical, but accessible to the attentive amateur. Wilson (below) is concerned with similar problems.

Leff, Gordon. *Bradwardine and the Pelagians: A Study of His "De causa Dei" and Its Opponents*. Cambridge U. Pr. 1957 o.p. An interesting study of a recurrent theological dispute in Christianity, rooted in Augustine's account of the necessity of God's grace if a man is to do any good or praiseworthy action at all. It is viewed here in the context of the new currents of the fourteenth century.

_____. *The Dissolution of the Medieval Outlook: An Essay on Intellectual and Spiritual Change in the Fourteenth Century*. NYU Pr. 1976 o.p. A brief treatment of some of the main themes of fourteenth-century thought and their effect on the worldview of the Middle Ages. A useful introduction, though its emphasis on the more radical developments gives a false view of the age.

Nicholas of Autrecourt. *The Universals Treatise of Nicholas of Autrecourt*. Trans. by L. A. Kennedy and others. Marquette 1971 o.p. Places the views on causation of Nicholas, an Ockhamist characterized as the "Hume of the Middle Ages," in a wider context. See Weinberg's study (below) for Nicholas's skeptical side.

Robson, John A. *Wyclif and the Oxford Schools: The Relation of the "Summa de Ente" to Scholastic Debates at Oxford in the Later Fourteenth Century*. Cambridge U. Pr. 1961 o.p. Examines the philosophy and theology of a fascinating maverick who held to a form of ultrarealism in reaction to the Ockhamism of his time. He was also the founder of Wyclifism, a heretical reformist movement in Britain. For his political thought see Daly (above).

Spade, Paul Vincent. *Lies, Language, and Logic in the Late Middle Ages*. Ashgate Pub. Co. 1988 $83.95. ISBN 0-86078-220-4. A collection of papers, most dealing with medieval contributions to the logical problems associated with the liar paradox and self-reference and with the philosophical semantics of William of Ockham.

Weinberg, R. J. *Nicholas of Autrecourt*. Princeton U. Pr. 1948 o.p. An excellent study, especially of Nicholas's skepticism. Sophisticated but readable.

Wilson, Curtis. *William Heytesbury: Medieval Logic and the Rise of Mathematical Physics*. U. of Wis. Pr. 1956 o.p. An interesting survey of the writings on logic, mathematics, and the physical sciences by Heytesbury, who worked in Merton College from about 1330 (d.1372?–1373?). Somewhat technical, but accessible to the attentive reader.

The Fifteenth Century and After

Baudry, Leon. *The Quarrel over Future Contingents (Louvain, 1465–1475)*. Trans. by Rita Guerlac. Kluwer Ac. 1989 $129.00. ISBN 0-7923-0454-3. A classic French collection of texts for the advanced student, providing a good example of a notable university dispute.

Kennedy, Leonard A. *Peter of Ailly and the Harvest of Fourteenth-Century Philosophy*. E. Mellen 1986 $89.95. ISBN 0-88946-307. A good, accessible account of Peter of Ailly's thought plus a nice, brief introduction to the fifteenth century.

Oakley, Francis. *The Political Thought of Pierre D'Ailly*. Elliots Bks. 1964 $89.50. ISBN 0-685-69849-1. A good example of the radical strain in fifteenth-century theory that identified the consent of the governed as the source of political authority.

Oberman, Heiko A. *The Harvest of Medieval Theology: Gabriel Biel and Late Medieval Nominalism*. Labyrinth Pr. 1983 repr. of 1963 ed. $18.50. ISBN 0-939464-05-5. The Ockhamist thought of Biel (d.1495), beautifully presented in its full context. Scholarly but not technical. A useful introduction to the fifteenth century.

Shank, Michael H. *"Unless You Believe, You Shall Not Understand": Logic, University and Society in Late Medieval Vienna*. Princeton U. Pr. 1988 $39.50. ISBN 0-691-05523-8. An excellent discussion of the debate between Henry of Langenstein and Henry of Oyta over whether the doctrine of the Trinity could be explicated in terms of Aristotelian logic or must be believed, against all reason, on the basis of faith.

Skinner, Quentin. *The Foundations of Modern Political Thought: The Renaissance*. 2 vols. Cambridge U. Pr. Vol. 1 1978 $22.95. ISBN 0-521-29337-5. Vol. 2 $27.95. ISBN 0-521-29435-5. Offers a description of the principal texts of late medieval and early modern political thought; illustrates a general historical theme in political theory.

Suárez, Francisco. *The Metaphysics of Good and Evil according to Suárez: Metaphysical Disputations X and XI and Selected Passages from Disputation XXII and Other Works*. Trans. by Jorge J. E. Gracia and Douglas Davis. Philosophia Pr. 1989 $66.00. ISBN 3-88405-066-4. Deals with the philosophy of good and evil.

————. *On the Essence of Finite Being as Such*. Trans. by Norman J. Wells. Marquette 1983 o.p. Tackles the problem of essence and existence and the distinction between the two.

————. *On Formal and Universal Unity*. Trans. by J. F. Ross. Marquette 1964 o.p. Taken from the author's *Metaphysical Disputations*.

————. *On the Various Kinds of Distinctions*. Trans. by C. Vollert. Marquette 1947 o.p. A sample of Suárez's metaphysics; introduces his teaching on the modes.

————. *Suárez on Individuation*. Marquette 1982 o.p. Difficult but rewarding selections from the *Metaphysical Disputations* of Francisco Suárez (1548–1617), the most important of the sixteenth-century Thomists.

CHRONOLOGY OF AUTHORS

Origen. 185?–254?
Augustine of Hippo, St. 354–430
Boethius. c.480–c.524
Erigena, Johannes Scotus. c.810–c.877
Anselm of Canterbury, St. 1033?–1109
Abelard, Peter. 1079–1142
Bernard of Clairvaux, St. 1090?–1153
John of Salisbury. c.1115–1180

Grosseteste, Robert. c.1168–1253
Albert the Great. 1193–1280
Bacon, Roger. c.1214?–c.1294
Bonaventure of Bagnorea, St. 1221–1274
Thomas Aquinas, St. 1225?–1274
Duns Scotus, John. c.1265–1308
William of Ockham. c.1285–c.1349

ABELARD, PETER. 1079–1142

Peter Abelard is considered to be the founder of the University of Paris. He studied under the nominalist Roscelin de Compiègne and the realist William of Champeaux. Disagreement with William led him to withdraw to the provinces and set up his own school at Melun in 1104. He returned to Paris in 1116 to teach. His disastrous love affair with the brilliant and sensitive Héloïse followed in 1118. Abelard had been hired as her tutor, and, after the birth of their son, they were secretly married. They later separated, and Abelard became a monk and Héloïse a nun. Their correspondence during their years of separation is a literary classic. Abelard withdrew to Brittany after the separation and wrote the

Theologia summi boni, which was condemned at Soissons in 1121. When he returned once more to Paris in 1136–40 to teach, his theology was condemned at Sens, chiefly because of the influence of BERNARD OF CLAIRVAUX. Peter the Venerable of Cluny mediated the dispute between the two while Abelard was on his deathbed, and Abelard spent his last days peacefully and was buried near Héloïse.

BOOKS BY ABELARD

Abailard's Christian Theology. Trans. by James Ramsay McCullum. Richwood Pub. 1976 repr. of 1948 ed. o.p. McCullum includes a good deal of introductory material and commentary. The chief point of Abelard's work is to establish a purely rational understanding of the Trinity.

A Dialogue of a Philosopher with a Jew and a Christian. Trans. by Pierre J. Payer. Pontifical Inst. of Medieval Studies 1979 o.p. Not a diatribe against Jews, but a pair of discussions between a philosopher and, first, a Jew, then a Christian. The promised adjudication of the disputes is never reached in this incomplete work, but much of Abelard's ethics and theology emerges.

Ethics. Ed. and trans. by D. E. Luscombe. *Oxford Medieval Texts Ser.* OUP 1971 $89.00. ISBN 0-19-822217-3. A sophisticated argument that a sin resides in one's intention, not in the outward action violating the law.

The Letters of Abelard and Heloise. Trans. by Betty Radice. Viking Penguin 1974 $6.95. ISBN 0-14-044297-9. Includes a nice selection from the letters exchanged between Peter and Héloïse, Abelard's "Story of My Misfortunes" (*Historia calamitatum*), and the deeply affecting letters between Héloïse and Peter the Venerable on Abelard's death.

Sic et non: A Critical Edition. Ed. and trans. by Blanche Boyer and Richard McKeon. U. Ch. Pr. 1976 $130.00. ISBN 0-226-00066-4. Passages from the church fathers on a long list of issues in theology, in each case ranged for and against a stated position. Provides one of the foundations of the scholastic method, though the *Sentences* of Peter Lombard became the standard text of this sort in the universities.

BOOKS ABOUT ABELARD

Luscombe, D. E. *Peter Abelard.* Historical Assoc. 1979 o.p. A brief but excellent scholarly account of Abelard's life, well written and up to date. For those who wonder how much truth there is in Abelard's own rather querulous account of himself.

————. *The School of Peter Abelard: The Influence of Abelard's Thought in the Early Scholastic Period.* Cambridge U. Pr. 1969 o.p. Luscombe is able to argue that Abelard's influence was considerable, despite his trouble with Church councils. Especially good for Abelard's theology.

Sikes, J. G. *Peter Abailard.* 1932. Cambridge U. Pr. 1965 o.p. The best overall treatment of Abelard's life and thought.

Tweedale, M. *Abailard on Universals.* Elsevier 1976 o.p. Rather technical, but clearly written. A superb book for anyone interested in the problem of universals, making clear the attractiveness of Abelard's sophisticated and influential approach to the question. Full translations of most of the relevant material in Abelard's logical works.

Weingart, Richard E. *The Logic of Divine Love: A Critical Analysis of the Soteriology of Peter Abailard.* OUP 1970 o.p. A good account of Abelard's theology from the viewpoint of the Fall and salvation of humanity.

ALBERT THE GREAT. 1193–1280

Albertus Magnus, or Albert the Great, was a Dominican scholar noted as the teacher of THOMAS AQUINAS. He took roughly the same view of Aristotelianism as his student. His interests, however, extended in other directions. His reputation is based less on his philosophy than on his work as a naturalist, a dabbler in "natural magic," and an encyclopedic scholar determined to review the whole realm of learning on whatever topic he undertakes. His work is that of a great scholar who helped make the Aristotelian and Arabic traditions available in the West.

BOOK BY ALBERT THE GREAT

The Book of Secrets of Albert Magnus of the Virtues of Herbs, Stones, and Certain Beasts: Also a Book of Marvels of the World. Trans. by Michael R. Best and Frank H. Brightman. OUP 1973 $7.95. ISBN 0-19-519786-0. The source of Albert's reputation as a dabbler in "natural magic."

BOOKS ABOUT ALBERT THE GREAT

Kovach, Francis, and Robert Shahan, eds. *Albert the Great: Commemorative Essays.* U. of Okla. Pr. 1980 o.p. A collection of essays by Catholic scholars on Albert's metaphysics, including universals, time, being, our knowledge of God, action at a distance, and his opposition to the view of conservative Augustinian scholars of the Franciscan order that all created things are composed from matter and form.
Schwertner, Thomas M. *St. Albert the Great.* Norwood repr. of 1933 ed. o.p. An interesting biography of Albert.
Weisheipl, James, ed. *Albertus Magnus and the Sciences.* Pontifical Inst. of Medieval Studies 1980 o.p. A good collection of articles on Albert's treatment of the sciences and philosophy of science.

ANSELM OF CANTERBURY, ST. 1033?-1109

Anselm of Canterbury, far and away the best philosopher of the eleventh century, described his philosophical work as faith seeking understanding. Following AUGUSTINE OF HIPPO, he argues that without faith he could not find the convincing rational arguments that establish understanding and that convincing evidence of a contradiction to the faith would invalidate any argument. Nonetheless, faith with understanding is better than faith alone. He avoids the citation of authorities in his writings, using argument alone to establish his points (something for which his teacher Lanfranc chided him), and he insists on answering every possible objection to his views with clear reasons against it. He is but little interested in the task of reconciling authorities or finding a unity of doctrine in the thought of the various Church Fathers. However, Augustine is, in fact, his constant inspiration, providing him even with the dialogue form he uses in his works. Anselm's thought is rooted in dialectical and grammatical technique. He is particularly skilled at resolving difficulties by uncovering the true logical form of expressions with misleading grammatical forms. His writings are without exception a feast for the analytical mind, yet accessible even to a beginner.

BOOKS BY ST. ANSELM OF CANTERBURY

Anselm of Canterbury. 4 vols. Ed. and trans. by Jasper Hopkins and Herbert Richardson. E. Mellen 1974-76 $124.95. ISBN 0-88946-977-6. A translation of most of Anselm's important writings. Note especially the philosophical fragments in Volume 2.
The De Grammatico of St. Anselm: The Theory of Paronymy. Trans. by Desmond P. Henry. Bks. Demand repr. of 1964 ed. $47.00. ISBN 0-317-08123-3. Deals with the meaning and reference of names. Of interest to the philosopher of language.
A New, Interpretive Translation of St. Anselm's Monologion and Proslogion. Trans. by Jasper Hopkins. Banning Pr. 1986 $25.00. ISBN 0-938060-33-3. Latin and English on facing pages, with, in the introduction, a detailed discussion of recent work on the ontological argument in Anselm.

Proslogium. Trans. by M. J. Charlesworth. U. of Notre Dame Pr. 1979 repr. of 1965 ed. $7.00. ISBN 0-87548-109-4. An exemplary analytical and scholarly discussion for the serious student.

Saint Anselm: Basic Writings. Open Court 1974 o.p. Contains Anselm's most famous writings, including fascinating discussions of God's power, freedom of will, evil and its cause, justice and mercy, and a number of other topics. A masterpiece of Christian literature. Introduction by Charles Hartshorne.

Trinity, Incarnation and Redemption. Trans. by Jasper Hopkins and Herbert Richardson. HarpC 1970 o.p. Includes two letters on the Trinity written against the views of the nominalist Roscelin, who apparently held that, were custom to permit it, we could say there are three Gods.

Truth, Freedom, and Evil: Three Philosophical Dialogues. Trans. by Jasper Hopkins and Herbert Richardson. E. Mellen 1974 o.p. Includes *On Truth, On Freedom of Choice,* and *On the Fall of the Devil.* All are clever and fun to read, but the last, an examination of the cause of evil in the world and an attempt to excuse God of any blame, is the most fun.

Why God Became Man and the Virgin Conception and Original Sin. Ed. by Herbert Richardson. Magi Bks. 1982 $6.95. ISBN 0-87343-025-5. Concerned with aspects of the incarnation and atonement of Christ. Introduction by Joseph M. Colleran.

BOOKS ABOUT ST. ANSELM OF CANTERBURY

Barnes, Jonathan. *The Ontological Argument.* St. Martin 1972 o.p. A sophisticated discussion of Anselm's famous argument for the existence of God.

Evans, Gillian Rosemary. *Anselm.* Morehouse Pub. 1989 $15.95. ISBN 0-8192-1484-1. A good summary account of Anselm's theology.

Henry, D. P. *The Logic of St. Anselm.* OUP 1967 o.p. A general study of Anselm's theory of meaning and its deployment in argument. Rather technical, but rewarding to someone with a background in logic or in modern analytic philosophy.

———, ed. and trans. *Commentary on "De Grammatico": The Historical-Logical Dimensions of a Dialogue of St. Anselm's. Synthese Historical Lib.* Kluwer Ac. 1973 o.p. Both Henry's translation and commentary presuppose a reader with knowledge of modern symbolic logic and an interest in the analytic philosophy of language.

Hopkins, Jasper. *A Companion to the Study of St. Anselm.* U. of Minn. Pr. 1972 o.p. A great deal of useful information and a thorough bibliography.

Southern, Richard W. *Saint Anselm and His Biographer.* Cambridge U. Pr. 1963 o.p. A study of Anselm's thought as well as his life.

AQUINAS, ST. THOMAS. 1225?–1274

[SEE THOMAS AQUINAS, ST. in this chapter.]

AUGUSTINE OF HIPPO, ST. 354–430

Augustine was far and away the most important of the Western Church Fathers. His adaptation of Neoplatonic thought to Christianity and his forceful defense of his positions in a series of controversies cast a shadow over the entire Middle Ages and had a great deal to do with the Reformation. Two noteworthy positions, which define later Augustinianism, are that human knowledge occurs only as a result of the illumination of the intellect by God (who acts in this respect more or less like the Platonic forms) and that perception is an active process of judgment rather than a passive reception of forms. Augustine also held somewhat ambiguously to the view that the will could, in its natural state before original sin, act entirely from itself, without any outside influence. This contrasts with the view that the will is bound to will as it does by one's intellectual view of what is good. On faith and reason, he argues that understanding why a doctrine is true is better than mere belief on faith, and he is quite confident that such understanding is attainable by the healthy intellect, at least if it is guided by what it accepts through faith.

BOOKS BY ST. AUGUSTINE OF HIPPO

Against the Academicians. Trans. by Sister M. Patricia Garvey. *Medieval Philosophical Texts in Translation.* Marquette 1957 $7.95. ISBN 0-87462-202-6. Established an antiskeptical attitude in Christian philosophy that was to persist until the fourteenth century. Augustinians of the Middle Ages, notably St. Anselm, tended to believe that the propositions of the faith could be proved by reason.

Basic Writings of St. Augustine. Ed. by Whitney J. Oates. Baker Bk. 1993 $95.00. ISBN 0-8010-0164-1. A well-selected collection, including 12 early treatises, the *Confessions*, and extensive selections from *On the Trinity.*

The City of God against the Pagans. 413–426. 7 vols. HUP 1958 $15.50 ea. Discusses political philosophy, in which Augustine takes the radical position that state power is illegitimate, but rulers should be obeyed for the sake of the limited peace they can guarantee. Augustine's views of history, also laid out here, are a self-conscious departure from the cyclical theories implicit in the Platonic worldview.

The Confessions. Trans. by Vernon J. Bourke. OUP 1991 $24.95. ISBN 0-19-281779-5. A masterpiece of Western literature, the first introspective autobiography. See especially the famous discussions of time and eternity in Book XI, and of memory (that is, Platonic *anamnesis* of the forms) in Book X. Books XII and XIII provide a Platonistic account of creation.

De Dialectica. Ed. by Jan Pinborg. Trans. by B. Darell Jackson. *Synthese Historical Lib.* Kluwer Ac. 1975 $67.00. ISBN 90-277-0538-0. Thought inauthentic until recently but now generally accepted as Augustine's. This and *On Christian Doctrine* contain some interesting discussions of semantics. See also the articles on Augustine's doctrine of signs in Markus's collection of essays (below).

The Essential Augustine. Ed. by Vernon J. Bourke. Hackett Pub. 1974 $27.50. ISBN 0-915144-077. A topically arranged collection of brief selections. An excellent introduction to Augustine's thought in his own words.

Letters. Fathers of the Church Ser. Cath. U. Pr. 1989 $29.95. ISBN 0-8132-0081-4. Important discussions of doctrine and the relation of faith to reason. The best available translation of all the letters in English but, like most older translations of the Church Fathers, too often garbled and incorrect.

On Christian Doctrine. Trans. by D. W. Robertson, Jr. Macmillan 1958. ISBN 0-02-402150-4. Especially concerned with the interpretation of Scripture but also bears on the nature of our mystical knowledge of God.

On Free Choice of the Will. Trans. by A. S. Benjamin and L. H. Hackstaff. Macmillan 1964 $8.25. ISBN 0-02-308030-2. Often treated as Augustine's definitive and comprehensive treatment of philosophy. Its central question: how to establish that God is not responsible for evil.

The Teacher. The Free Choice of the Will. Grace and Free Will. Trans. by Robert P. Russell. Cath. U. Pr. 1968 $17.95. ISBN 0-8132-0059-8. *The Teacher* presents the doctrine that God's illumination of the soul through Christ is necessary for human knowledge, a position that characterizes Augustinianism throughout its history.

Works. Fathers of the Church Ser. 16 vols. Cath. U. Pr. 1960 o.p.

BOOKS ABOUT ST. AUGUSTINE OF HIPPO

Bonner, Gerald. *St. Augustine of Hippo: Life and Controversies.* AMS Pr. 1985 repr. of 1963 ed. $42.50. ISBN 0-404-62376-X. A learned and sympathetic survey of Augustine's career and literary productions. Especially good on Augustine and Manichaean dualism and in general on the contrasting religious viewpoints of the time.

Brown, Peter. *Augustine of Hippo: A Biography.* Dorset Pr. 1987 $22.50. ISBN 0-88029-098-6. The standard biography. Well written, thoroughly competent and scholarly, and unusually free from theological bias. Brown's treatment of Augustine's philosophy is nontechnical, concentrating on its religious meaning and its relation to his cultural background.

Chadwick, Henry. *Augustine. Past Masters Ser.* OUP 1986 $6.95. ISBN 0-19-287534-5. An excellent brief study and a good first book on Augustine.

Deane, Herbert A. *The Political and Social Ideas of Saint Augustine.* Col. U. Pr. 1966 $20.00. ISBN 0-231-08569-9. An honest and hard-working effort to come to terms with Augustine's views.

Evans, G. R. *Augustine on Evil.* Cambridge U. Pr. 1990 $15.95. ISBN 0-521-39743-X. A good complement to Hick's *Evil and the God of Love.*

Ferguson, John. *Pelagius: A Historical and Theological Study.* AMS Pr. 1979 repr. of 1956 ed. $27.00. ISBN 0-404-16107-3. An excellent short account of Augustine's chief opponent on matters concerning grace and free will, an English monk who held that men were capable of doing good of their own free will without God's aid.

Gilson, Étienne. *The Christian Philosophy of St. Augustine.* Hippocrene Bks. 1983 repr. of 1960 ed. o.p. The most thorough general account of Augustine's philosophy and one that comes to grips with the issues, though Gilson is often too concerned to preserve Augustine's orthodoxy to see his text clearly.

Kirwan, Christopher. *Augustine.* Routledge 1989 $75.00. ISBN 0-415-00812-3. A discussion of some central philosophical issues in Augustine's work: skepticism, language, free will, politics, the ethics of lying, and love and sex. Pays close attention to the arguments, though sometimes lacks historical perspective.

Markus, Robert A. *Saeculum: History and Society in the Theology of St. Augustine.* Bks. Demand repr. of 1970 ed. $68.70. ISBN 0-318-34820-9. About the best available study on Augustine's views of politics and history.

Markus, Robert A., ed. *Augustine: A Collection of Critical Essays.* Doubleday 1972 o.p. A first-rate collection of articles concentrating on philosophical, as opposed to theological, topics. Also offers a brief but intelligent discussion of the ways in which Augustine was led to consider philosophical issues.

Marrou, H. I. *Augustine and His Influence through the Ages.* HarpC 1957 o.p. An excellent brief study by a noted scholar of Augustine's immense influence on the Middle Ages.

O'Connell, Robert J. *Imagination and Metaphysics in St. Augustine.* Marquette 1986 $7.95. ISBN 0-87462-227-1. Attempts to reconstitute the three distinct worlds of St. Augustine's philosophy.

————. *The Origin of the Soul in St. Augustine's Later Works.* Fordham 1987 $40.00. ISBN 0-8232-1172-X. A groundbreaking work that explores how Augustine modified his conception of the soul and its origins as he developed his views on original sin in response to the Pelagians.

————. *St. Augustine's Early Theory of Man, A.D. 386–391.* Bks. Demand repr. of 1968 ed. $86.20. ISBN 0-7837-4173-1

————. *St. Augustine's Platonism.* Augustinian Institute 1984 o.p. Argues that Augustine's Neoplatonism was not as quickly modified in the direction of orthodoxy as has usually been supposed. First-rate studies free from presuppositions about what Augustine must have meant.

BACON, ROGER. c.1214?–c.1294

Roger Bacon, an Oxford Franciscan, is well known for proposing a grand reform of learning and theology and for his dabblings in natural science. His vision of science was intensely practical, and he talks much of observation and experiment; consequently he has been represented as a precursor of the scientific revolution. Although recent scholarship has considerably deflated his rather exalted view of himself and undermined the notion that he was some kind of empiricist anticipating the scientific revolution of the sixteenth century, he remains an interesting thinker. He is now viewed as something of an Avicennan conservative, who was impressed by Arabic scientific lore but began to look old-fashioned with the introduction of a stricter Aristotelianism in the second half of the century.

BOOKS BY BACON

Compendium of the Study of Theology. Ed. and trans. by T. S. Maloney. E. J. Brill 1987. ISBN 90-04-08510-6. Contains a great deal of discussion on the signification of terms and other topics in philosophy of language.

Opus Maius. 1267–68. Trans. by Robert Belle Burke. 2 vols. OUP 1962 o.p. Bacon's chief work, proposing his grand reform of learning and theology.

Roger Bacon's Letter Concerning the Marvelous Power of Art and of Nature and Concerning the Nullity of Magic. Trans. by Tenney L. Davis. AMS Pr. 1981 repr. of 1923 ed. $19.50. ISBN 0-404-18495-2. The source of Bacon's reputation as a proponent of natural science.

Three Treatments of Universals by Roger Bacon. Trans. by T. S. Maloney. MRTS 1989 $18.00. ISBN 0-86698-075-X. Selections from the first and second sets of questions on Aristotle's First Philosophy (i.e., the *Metaphysics*) and from the *Communia Naturalium*.

BOOKS ABOUT BACON

Bridges, John H. *The Life and Work of Roger Bacon: An Introduction to the Opus Majus.* Ed. by J. Gordon Jones. AMS Pr. 1983 repr. of 1914 ed. $21.50. ISBN 0-404-18450-2. A sound work in its time, but Bridges's praise of Bacon as a harbinger of scientific methods of investigation has been considerably moderated in more recent work.

Easton, Stewart C. *Roger Bacon and His Search for a Universal Science.* Greenwood 1971 repr. of 1952 ed. $38.50. ISBN 0-8371-3399-8. The most recent general treatment in English.

BERNARD OF CLAIRVAUX, ST. 1090?–1153

The foremost reformer of his age, Bernard of Clairvaux spearheaded the Cistercian movement, reestablishing serious discipline and spirituality in the corrupt Benedictine monasteries. His mystical thought is enormously influential, and deservedly so, but he was also, like many reformers, very much a conservative who opposed the progressive philosophical movement of his age. This was a time when philosophy was freeing itself from theology, with the establishment of schools of logic and the liberal arts that were no longer under the thumb of the theologians, where faculty interest centered on nontheological issues. Bernard is especially known for his attacks on PETER ABELARD and Gilbert de la Porrée (1076–1154).

BOOKS BY ST. BERNARD OF CLAIRVAUX

Letters. Ed. by Bruno S. James. AMS Pr. 1980 repr. of 1953 ed. $47.50. ISBN 0-404-17004-8. Entertaining reading full of wisdom, though there is little philosophy here. Bernard's letters make a nice complement to Abelard's complaint-filled autobiography.

Selected Works. Trans. by G. R. Evans. Paulist Pr. 1987 $15.95. ISBN 0-8091-0398-2. Works bearing on mystical prayer.

Treatises II: The Steps of Humility and Pride, on Loving God. Cistercian Pubns. 1974 o.p. Something of a masterpiece of psychological insight, chastening in its accurate vision of our strategies for avoiding surrender of ourselves to God.

BOOKS ABOUT ST. BERNARD OF CLAIRVAUX

Butler, C. *Western Mysticism: Neglected Chapters in the History of Religion.* Gordon Pr. 1973 $250.00. ISBN 0-87968-244-2. Concerned especially with the practice of mystical prayer and the monastic life. An excellent treatment dealing with St. Bernard at some length.

Evans, G. Rosemary. *The Mind of St. Bernard of Clairvaux*. OUP 1983 o.p. A biography
that gives due attention to Bernard's intellectual labors. Argues that Bernard's
motives and procedure expressed an understandable concern for the preservation of
the integrity of Christian doctrine in the trials of Abelard and Gilbert de la Porrée.
Gilson, Étienne. *The Mystical Theology of St. Bernard*. Trans. by A.H.C. Downes. Sheed &
Ward MO 1940 o.p. Concerned with Christian mystical thought from a theoretical
rather than a practical point of view.
Pennington, M. Basil, ed. *St. Bernard of Clairvaux: Commemorating the Eighth Centenary
of His Canonization*. Cistercian Pubns. 1977 o.p. A collection of studies by Catholic
scholars. One piece by Joseph Chu-Cong intelligently explores similarities between
Far Eastern and Christian mystical experience.

BOETHIUS, c.480–c.524

Born of a distinguished family, Boethius received the best possible education
in the liberal arts in Athens and then entered public life under Theodoric the
Ostrogoth, who ruled Italy at that time. He obtained the highest office, but in the
end he was accused of treason, imprisoned, and executed. His *Consolation of
Philosophy* was written while he was in prison. His philosophy, like that of all
the Church Fathers, was Platonistic, but he preserved much of ARISTOTLE's (see
also Vol. 3) elementary logic and reported in his commentaries the views of
Aristotelians even when they disagreed with his Platonism. Thus he created an
interest in Aristotle in subsequent centuries and provided a basis for the
introduction of Aristotle's works into Europe in the twelfth and thirteenth
centuries.

BOOKS BY BOETHIUS

The Consolation of Philosophy. Trans. by Martin F. Tupper. Viking Penguin 1976 $6.95.
ISBN 0-14-044208-1. One of the most popular classics in the Western world.
Translated into English first by King Alfred of England, later by Geoffrey Chaucer,
and again by Queen Elizabeth I. See especially the discussion of God's foreknowledge.
Tractates, De consolatione philosophiae. Ed. and trans. by E. K. Rand and H. F. Stewart.
Loeb Class. Lib. HUP 1973 $15.50. ISBN 0-674-99083-8. See especially the tractate on
the Trinity, which attempts to reconcile that difficult Christian doctrine with the
demands of logic.

BOOKS ABOUT BOETHIUS

Chadwick, H. *Boethius: The Consolations of Music, Logic, Theology and Philosophy*. OUP
1981 $26.00. ISBN 0-19-826549-2. The most thorough and authoritative work on
Boethius. Scholarly and sometimes a bit dry, but on the whole well written and
always well thought through. An excellent book.
Reiss, Edmund. *Boethius. Twayne's World Authors Ser.* G. K. Hall 1982 o.p. A good
biography providing a less technical consideration of *The Consolation*, as much from
a literary as from a philosophical point of view.

BONAVENTURE OF BAGNOREA, ST. 1221–1274

A conservative French Franciscan, Bonaventure was an active propagandist
in the campaign against radical Aristotelianism. He regarded even THOMAS
AQUINAS as too radical and was the first of a series of Franciscans to oppose the
new Aristotelian with an older, Avicennan-Augustinian, view. He has been a
favorite of his order, in part because of his early conservatism, which, in the
period following the Reformation, provided the Franciscans with a master free
from the modernist taint of the fourteenth century. Yet he is also a talented
allegorist and a perceptive spiritual and mystical thinker. His thought is rooted

in the Neoplatonic mystical tradition of the twelfth century, but it has been updated under the influence of thirteenth-century Aristotelianism, despite Bonaventure's opposition to the radical side of that movement.

BOOKS BY ST. BONAVENTURE OF BAGNOREA

Breviloquium. Trans. by Erwin E. Nemmers. Herder 1946 o.p. A brief summary of speculative theology, without much argument or discussion of alternative views.

De reductione artium ad theologiam. Trans. by Emma Therese Healy. Franciscan Inst. 1955 o.p. On the relation of the arts, in particular philosophy, to theology. The arts shall all be used in service of theology, which is the highest science.

Disputed Questions on the Mystery of the Trinity. Trans. by Zachary Hayes. Franciscan Inst. 1979 o.p. The best source for Bonaventure's proof of God's existence.

Holiness of Life. Ed. by F. Wilfrid. Trans. by Laurence Costello. Herder 1923 o.p. A work full of psychological insight concerning the practice of mystical piety. Discusses the mystical virtues: self-knowledge, humility, poverty, silence, prayer, the love of God as inspired by reflection on Christ's sacrifice, and perseverance.

The Mind's Journey to God (Itinerarium mentis in Deum). Trans. by Lawrence S. Cunningham. Franciscan Pr. 1979 o.p. Usually regarded as Bonaventure's chief work. A treatment of mystical theology, reconciling academic studies and philosophy to a mystical vocation.

BOOKS ABOUT ST. BONAVENTURE OF BAGNOREA

Gilson, Étienne. *The Philosophy of St. Bonaventure.* Franciscan Pr. 1965 o.p. A classic discussion of the philosopher from a Thomist viewpoint.

Spargo, Emma J. *The Category of the Aesthetic in the Philosophy of St. Bonaventure. Philosophy Ser.* Franciscan Inst. 1953 $8.00. ISBN 0-686-11541-4. An examination of a Platonic theme—God's beauty reflected in the world—in a great mystical thinker.

DUNS SCOTUS, JOHN. c.1265–1308

John Duns Scotus died at about 43 years of age. His thought represents a valiant and subtle effort to meet the new critical tendencies of his times, so apparent in the work of WILLIAM OF OCKHAM, while yet retaining a recognizable Augustinian realism. The result is a philosophy marked by distinctions sometimes too subtle to be convincing and a dialectical technique often too complex to follow without close study. Yet, Duns Scotus is by no means a sterile dialectician. His thought is motivated by genuine problems, and he is too much aware of the important considerations on all sides to try to make things appear simple. He lives in a new age, and his response to its contrary and perplexing currents is deep and considered. He is a philosopher worth mastering. Duns Scotus attempted to preserve his Augustinian heritage, particularly the preeminence of the will and its liberty. He argues that the will can command acts of understanding, providing a vision of the good to the intellect, and is not guided, as THOMAS AQUINAS would have it, entirely by a prior, intellectual conception of the good. The will is entirely free. Another important view holds that each individual has a *haecceitas*, a "thisness," which is its form as an individual. Thus, individuation is due not to matter or accidents but to the form of the individual itself. This *haecceitas* is the actuality of the substantial form, which becomes actual only by becoming individual. Duns Scotus is also known for his proof of God's existence, which is enormously complex because of his sensitivity to the problems with earlier, simpler proofs. It is probably the most sophisticated and complex argument for God's existence ever attempted.

Books by Duns Scotus

Duns Scotus on the Will and Morality. Ed. and trans. by Allan B. Wolter. Cath. U. Pr. 1986 $54.95. ISBN 0-8132-0622-7. A collection of texts on the relation of the will to the intellect, the moral law and its relation to God, goodness and the moral and intellectual virtues, and sin. Well selected and translated, with useful notes by the translator.

Duns Scotus's Political and Economic Philosophy. Trans. by Allan B. Wolter. Old Mission Santa Barbara 1989 o.p. Current interest in business ethics and economic justice has led to a rediscovery of the treatment of these topics in medieval thinkers. This piece from Scotus's *Ordinatio* concerns property rights.

God and Creatures: The Quodlibetal Questions. Trans. by Felix Alluntis and Allan B. Wolter. Princeton U. Pr. 1975 o.p. Well translated, with a very useful (and, for the technicalities of Scotism, necessary) glossary. Full of interesting discussion, but not for those lacking in courage.

Philosophical Writings. Trans. by Allan B. Wolter. Hackett Pub. 1987 $34.95. ISBN 0-87220-019-1. Selections from the Oxford Commentary on the Sentences, concerning the existence and unicity of God, human knowledge of God and the natural world, the immortality of the soul, and the metaphysical primacy of being.

Treatise on God as First Principle. Trans. by Allan B. Wolter. Franciscan Pr. rev. ed. 1985 $15.00. ISBN 0-8199-0860-6. The best place to study Scotus's proof of God's existence and the demonstration of His chief properties.

Books about Duns Scotus

Bonansea, Bernardino M. *Man and His Approach to God in John Duns Scotus*. U. Pr. of Amer. 1983 o.p. Discusses especially the primacy of the will and Scotus's opposition to intellectualism, his proof of God's existence, and his notions on predestination and the soul. An excellent treatment, to be studied before going on to more detailed work.

Day, Sebastian. *Intuitive Cognition: A Key to the Significance of the Later Scholastics*. Philosophy Ser. Franciscan Inst. 1947 o.p. An excellent study of theories of the knowledge of individuals in the fourteenth century, covering Ockham and others as well as Scotus. Essential for an understanding of later medieval epistemology.

Ryan, John K., and Bernardino M. Bonansea, eds. *John Duns Scotus, 1265–1965. Studies in Philosophy and the History of Philosophy*. Cath. U. Pr. 1966 o.p. A good collection of essays.

Wolter B. Allan. *The Philosophical Theology of Duns Scotus*. Ed. by Marilyn McCord Adams. Cornell Univ. Pr. 1990 $48.50. ISBN 0-8014-2385-6. A collection of articles by a foremost scholar of Scotus. Taken together, the articles constitute a sophisticated and comprehensive discussion of Scotus's philosophy.

ERIGENA, JOHANNES SCOTUS. c.810–c.877

Far and away the greatest thinker of his age, Johannes Scotus Erigena was born in Ireland and as a youth studied in an Irish monastery, where he learned some Greek. By 850 he had immigrated to the Continent and attached himself to the court of Charles the Bald, king of the West Franks (843–877) and, as Charles II, Holy Roman Emperor (875–877). His *On Predestination* (851) defended the reality of freedom of the will but incurred suspicion because of its original interpretation of Augustine of Hippo. He reintroduced the late classical Neoplatonism of Eastern Christianity to the West in translations of Pseudo-Dionysius and Maximus the Confessor as well as in his great treatise *On the Division of Nature* (c.865), which was condemned at the beginning of the thirteenth century when Amalric of Bene used it to support his reputed pantheism. Erigena's influence on medieval Platonism was nonetheless great, and his work forms an important point of departure for mystical thought.

BOOK BY ERIGENA

Periphyseon: The Division of Nature. Trans. by I. P. Sheldon-Williams, rev. by John O'Meara. Dumbarton Oaks 1987 $35.00. ISBN 0-88402-173-4. Provides only a partial translation, with summaries of large stretches of this protracted work, which takes nature to be the totality of what is, so that it includes God as well as creatures. Although he often explicitly denies that creatures are identical to God or any part of Him, he also often treats God as all-inclusive, pulling all reality somehow into Himself both as its source and its final end. With summaries by Jean A. Potter.

BOOKS ABOUT ERIGENA

O'Meara, John J. *Eriugena.* OUP 1988 $69.00. ISBN 0-19-826674-X. A useful summary of modern scholarship. Quite readable, though sometimes superficial in its analysis of the *Periphyseon.* A good introductory text.

Otten, Willemien. *The Anthropology of Johannes Scottus Eriugena.* E. J. Brill 1991 $51.50. ISBN 90-04-09302-8. A consideration of Erigena's metaphysics and theology from the viewpoint of human beings' place in the world.

GROSSETESTE, ROBERT. c.1168–1253

Robert Grosseteste was an important figure in the introduction of ARISTOTLE (see also Vol. 3) and the initiator of the Oxford tradition of science later exemplified in ROGER BACON. His thought, which brought a Neoplatonic reading to Aristotle, is old-fashioned by the standards of the latter half of the century. He held many important positions, being one of the first chancellors of Oxford University and, later, bishop of Lincoln, and was an influential advocate of the Franciscans.

BOOK BY GROSSETESTE

Robert Grosseteste on Light. Trans. by Clare C. Riedl. Marquette 1942 o.p. An intriguing blend of Neoplatonic metaphysics and the science of optics, of considerable influence. Grosseteste views light as a self-replicating form that spreads from the sun, losing strength gradually as it moves outward. The entire natural world is the expression of this light informing matter and space.

BOOKS ABOUT GROSSETESTE

Callus, D. A., ed. *Robert Grosseteste: Scholar and Bishop.* OUP 1955 $22.50. ISBN 0-19-821387-5. A groundbreaking study that is still useful.

McEvoy, James. *The Philosophy of Robert Grosseteste.* OUP 1982 $79.00. ISBN 0-19-824645-5. An excellent study of all aspects of Grosseteste's thought, but concentrating especially on his account of knowledge. Thoroughly informed, careful scholarship.

Marrone, Steven P. *William Auvergne and Robert Grosseteste: New Ideas of Truth in the Early Thirteenth Century.* Princeton U. Pr. 1983 $47.50. ISBN 0-691-05383-9. An excellent study of the difference the introduction of new works by Aristotle made in philosophical thought. William of Auvergne represents Western thought on the theory of knowledge just before the introduction of *Posterior Analytics.* Grosseteste was the first influential commentator on the newly introduced treatise.

JOHN OF SALISBURY. c.1115–1180

John of Salisbury learned about court life as secretary first to Thibaud, and then to Thomas à Becket, both archbishops of Canterbury. He later became bishop of Chartres. His books are urbane and clearly written, providing a cultured view of the upper-class society of the twelfth century.

BOOKS BY JOHN OF SALISBURY

The Metalogicon of John of Salisbury: A Twelfth-Century Defence of the Verbal and Logical Arts of the Trivium. Trans. by D. D. McGarry. Greenwood 1982 repr. of 1955 ed. $55.00. ISBN 0-313-23539-2. A major source for the philosophy of the twelfth century. Presents all sides to the disputes of the age without taking any, except to advance the suggestion that universals are in fact concepts, not words or things.

Policraticus: The Statesman's Book. Cambridge U. Pr. 1990 $54.95. ISBN 0-521-36701-8. Argues that a king becomes a tyrant if he does not rule in accord with justice and the law. Develops a sustained critique of courtly life that goes so far as to commend tyrannicide, but the chief aim is to reform court life so that the characters of rulers will be more virtuous.

BOOKS ABOUT JOHN OF SALISBURY

Webb, Clement C. J. *John of Salisbury.* Russell Sage 1971 repr. of 1931 ed. o.p. The standard biography of a fascinating man.

Wilks, Michael J., ed. *The World of John of Salisbury. Studies in Church History.* Blackwell Pubs. 1985 $65.00. ISBN 0-631-13122-1. A collection of articles, most in English, by first-rate scholars on all aspects of John's thought, but especially on his political views.

NICHOLAS OF CUSA (NICHOLAS CUSANUS). 1401?–1464

[SEE Chapter 5 in this volume.]

ORIGEN. 185?–254?

Origen is the foremost member of the School of Alexandria, the first school of genuinely philosophical Christian theology. His Platonism is of an older form, uninfluenced by the Neoplatonism of PLOTINUS, so his philosophy is quite distinct from that of AUGUSTINE OF HIPPO on a number of issues, but especially on the issue of original sin and freedom of will and on the justification of God's permitting evil in the world. Origen became a center of controversy because of his contention that even the Devil would in the end return to God, and he seems to have held that a person enjoys as many successive lives on earth as are needed to return to God after the Fall. However, all matters concerning the interpretation of his thought are controversial. The other members of the school are Clement of Alexandria (c.150–c.213) and Irenaeus of Lyons (died c.202).

BOOKS BY ORIGEN

Contra Celsum. Trans. by Henry Chadwick. Cambridge U. Pr. 1953 o.p. A fundamental source for Christian thought in the second century. Written against the anti-Christian polemic of the pagan philosopher Celsus.

On First Principles: Being Koetschau's Text of the De Principiis. Peter Smith 1973 repr. of 1966 ed. $12.25. ISBN 0-8446-2685-6. An exciting book, quite controversial in its day, dealing with, among other things, free will and its connection to rationality, the problem of evil, and Christ as the Platonic Logos, the Mind in which the forms reside. Presents a sweeping cosmological view of world history built around the Fall of God's creatures and their restoration. With an introduction by H. de Lobac.

BOOKS ABOUT ORIGEN

Bigg, Charles. *The Christian Platonists of Alexandria: Eight Lectures.* AMS Pr. 1980 repr. of 1886 ed. $27.50. ISBN 0-404-00799-6. Despite its age, perhaps the best single study of Clement and Origen of Alexandria. Argues that their theology is determined by their philosophical views, not the other way around.

Grant, Robert M. *The Letter and the Spirit.* Society for the Propagation of Christian Knowledge 1957 o.p. A good study of the techniques of scriptural exegesis used by the Alexandrians, who adapted allegorical methods of interpretation from pagan philosophical treatments of mythology.

Hick, John H. *Evil and the God of Love*. HarpC rev. ed. 1978 $18.00. ISBN 0-06-063902-4. Traces the development of Irenaeus's (2nd century) style of theodicy. An excellent book. Most of what it says about Irenaeus bears on Clement and Origen as well.

Trigg, Joseph W. *Origen: The Bible and Philosophy in the Third Century Church*. Westminster John Knox 1983 o.p. An excellent intellectual biography that uses Origen's commentaries and homilies as well as his *On First Principles* to place his thought in its cultural and historical context. Presents a somewhat less radically Platonistic Origen than is seen by those who rely solely on *First Principles*.

THOMAS AQUINAS, ST. 1225?–1274

Thomas Aquinas, the most noted philosopher of the Middle Ages, was born near Naples to the ruling family of Aquino. He was given a good education, and his family was disappointed when he entered the new Dominican order in 1244. He was a fairly radical Aristotelian, distinguished from the Augustinians by his rejection of any form of special illumination from God in ordinary intellectual knowledge, as well as by his view that the soul is the form of the body, the body having no form independent of that provided by the soul itself. He held that the "natural light" of the intellect was sufficient to abstract the form of a natural object from its sensory representations, and thus was sufficient for natural knowledge without God's special illumination. He asserts that the individual intellect is sufficient in itself for knowledge of the real natures of things, and he rejects the Averroist notion that natural reason might lead us correctly to conclusions that would turn out false when one takes revealed doctrine into account. He is distinguished from later Ockhamists by his "moderate realism": He believed that knowledge arises when the form of a natural object actually enters the intellect, taking on a new manner of being in doing so, so that we actually know the substantial form of a thing as it is in itself. The Ockhamists denied this, holding that we have at best a representation of the form, not the form itself, in the intellect, and had to face certain skeptical problems as a result.

BOOKS BY ST. THOMAS AQUINAS

An Aquinas Reader. Ed. by Mary T. Clark. Doubleday 1972 $5.95. ISBN 0-385-02505-X. Many short selections arranged by topic. Useful for its extensive selections from the commentaries on Aristotle and on Boethius's *On the Trinity*.

Basic Writings of St. Thomas Aquinas. Ed. by A. C. Pegis. 2 vols. Random 1945 o.p Extensive selections from the *Summa Theologiae* and *Summa contra Gentiles*.

The Divisions and Methods of the Sciences. Trans. by Armand Maurer. Pontifical Inst. of Medieval Studies 4th rev. ed. 1986 o.p. A translation of Questions V and VI of the commentary on Boethius's *De Trinitate*, concerning the nature and classification of scientific knowledge.

Faith, Reason and Theology. Trans. by Armand Maurer. Pontifical Inst. of Medieval Studies 1987 o.p. A translation of Questions I–IV of the commentary on Boethius's *De Trinitate*, concerning the relation between faith and reason, philosophy and theology.

Introduction to St. Thomas Aquinas. Ed. by A. C. Pegis. *Modern Lib. College Ed. Ser.* Random 1965 o.p. Selections from the two *Summae*, more abbreviated than those in the *Basic Writings* (above).

On Kingship to the King of Cyprus. Rev. by I. Th. Eschmann. Trans. by G. B. Phelan. Pontifical Inst. of Medieval Studies 1949 o.p. Develops a complete theory of kingship rooted as much in Aristotle as in Scripture.

On Law, Morality, and Politics. Ed. by William Baumgarth and Richard Regan. Hackett Pub. 1988 $32.50. ISBN 0-87220-032-9. A good selection of well-translated texts on conscience, natural and human law, justice, property, war, killing, sedition, church-state relations, and diplomacy.

On the Eternity of the World. Trans. by Cyril Vollert and others. Marquette 1964 o.p. Directed against Averroism. The issue here is whether natural reason leads us to a conclusion that must be rejected by theology (i.e., that the world is eternal).

On the Power of God. Trans. by L. Shapcote. Newman 1952 o.p. Especially interesting for its extensive consideration of the problem of evil.

On the Truth of the Catholic Faith. Trans. by A. C. Pegis and others. U. of Notre Dame Pr. 1975 o.p. An excellent summation of St. Thomas's thought, in a style more congenial to the modern reader than that of the bigger *Summa.*

On the Unity of the Intellect. Trans. by B. Zedler. Marquette 1968 o.p. Written against the Averroists. Argues that there is no common intellect for all men, so that nature permits individual survival of the soul after death.

On Truth. Trans. by R. W. Mulligan and others. 3 vols. Regnery Gateway 1952–54 o.p. Deals with all sorts of questions, but especially interesting for the way in which St. Thomas handles Augustinian views.

St. Thomas Aquinas: On Charity. Trans. by Lottie H. Kendzierski. Marquette 1960 $7.95. ISBN 0-87462-210-7. Argues that charity—that is, the love of God—is the most important of the virtues oriented toward the supernatural world rather than toward man's natural ends. Marks the division of St. Thomas's ethics from Aristotle's, since Aristotle takes no notice of the supernatural.

St. Thomas Aquinas: On Spiritual Creatures. Trans. by Mary C. Fitzpatrick and John J. Wellmuth. Marquette 1949 $7.95. ISBN 0-87462-205-0. Concerns the soul's nature and its immortality, the mind-body problem, and the nature of angels.

St. Thomas Aquinas: Philosophical Texts. Ed. by Thomas Gilby. Labyrinth Pr. 1982 o.p. (See *Theological Texts,* below).

St. Thomas Aquinas: Theological Texts. Ed. by Thomas Gilby. Labyrinth Pr. 1982 o.p. With *Philosophical Texts* (above), useful for an overview of St. Thomas's opinions. Much that is memorable and quotable, but not a good place to find his reasons or the more difficult and philosophically subtle points in his thought.

Selected Writings of Thomas Aquinas. Ed. by Robert P. Goodwin. Bobbs 1965 o.p. A good selection of texts, including *On Being and Essence,* to supplement the *Summae;* well translated.

Treatise on Separate Substances. Trans. by Francis J. Lescoe. St. Joseph College 1959 o.p. Poses a number of questions about how angels can be contingent, created things if they have no matter, and if they have no knowledge, how they can possess sense perception.

BOOKS ABOUT ST. THOMAS AQUINAS

Copleston, Frederick. *Thomas Aquinas.* B & N Imports 1976 repr. of 1955 ed. o.p. A brief Catholic treatment, clear and straightforward.

Eco, Umberto. *The Aesthetics of Thomas Aquinas.* Trans. by Hugh Bredin. HUP 1988 $16.95. ISBN 0-674-00676-3. An excellent treatment of the subject, providing considerable insight into the cultural ideals of the Middle Ages as well as Thomas's thought.

Gilby, Thomas. *The Political Thought of Thomas Aquinas.* U. Ch. Pr. 1958 o.p. An excellent, though complex, study of St. Thomas's theory of law and citizenship, tracing its roots in theology, in ecclesiastical and civil law, in the concerns of the Dominican monk with the status of his vows of poverty, and in Aristotle.

Gilson, Étienne. *The Philosophy of St. Thomas Aquinas.* Ayer repr. of 1937 ed. $26.50. ISBN 0-8369-5797-0. A good summary of St. Thomas's thought, scholarly and thoroughly referenced, though one should not expect a critical examination of St. Thomas here.

Hankey, W. J. *God in Himself: Aquinas's Doctrine of God as Expounded in the Summa Theologica.* OUP 1987 $45.00. ISBN 0-19-826724-X. Emphasizes the Neoplatonic elements in Thomas's thought, in contrast to older works, which often overstress Thomas's Aristotelianism. A careful analysis of the first 43 questions of *Summa Theologica* I.

Kenny, Anthony. *Aquinas. Past Masters Ser.* OUP 1980 $6.95. ISBN 0-19-287500. A brief treatment by a sympathetic analytic philosopher. The most sophisticated introduction philosophically and the best first book on Aquinas.

———. *The Five Ways: St. Thomas Aquinas' Proofs of God's Existence.* U. of Notre Dame Pr. 1980 o.p. A critical examination of the most famous of St. Thomas's arguments.

———, ed. *Aquinas: A Collection of Critical Essays.* U. of Notre Dame Pr. 1976 repr. of 1969 ed. o.p. A collection of essays, very nicely selected, bearing on various philosophical issues approached by St. Thomas. Many fine insights are to be found here.

Kretzmann, Norman, and Eleanore Stump. *The Cambridge Companion to Aquinas.* Cambridge U. Pr. 1993. ISBN 0-521-43769-5. A first-rate collection of essays by a variety of experts introducing the reader to the entire range of Aquinas's thought.

Lonergan, Bernard *Verbum: Word and Idea in Aquinas.* Ed. by David B. Burrell. U. of Notre Dame Pr. 1967 o.p. Touches on all the central topics in St. Thomas's thought. Difficult reading, but it reflects deep consideration and repays the effort.

McInerny, Ralph M. *Aquinas against the Averroists.* Purdue U. Pr. 1992 $27.00. ISBN 1-55753-028-9. A good discussion of Aquinas's theory of the human intellect and his opposition to the Averroist insistence on the unity of the possible intellect.

———. *Aquinas on Human Action.* Cath. U. pr. 1992 $39.95. ISBN 0-8132-0746-0. A good up-to-date treatment of Aquinas's theory of human action and the will.

———. *A First Glance at St. Thomas: A Handbook for Peeping Thomists.* U. of Notre Dame Pr. 1990 $19.95. ISBN 0-268-00976-7. A popular treatment, and fun to read, but also serious philosophy by a true scholar.

Maurer, Armand. *Being and Knowing. Studies in Thomas Aquinas and Later Medieval Philosophers.* Pontifical Inst. of Medieval Studies 1990 o.p. A collection of essays by a senior scholar on Thomas and his medieval critics, many of them focusing on Thomas's epistemological realism and on his distinction between essence and existence.

Roensch, Frederick J. *Early Thomistic School.* Allenson 1964 o.p. Discusses Thomism in England and France, with biographical information on the important Thomists in the 50 years after St. Thomas.

Steenberghen, F. van. *Thomas Aquinas and Radical Aristotelianism.* Trans. by Dominic J. O'Meara and others. Cath. U. Pr. 1980 o.p. A penetrating study that recasts the older view of the Aristotelian movement. An excellent survey of the period as well.

Weisheipl, James A. *Friar Thomas D'Aquino: His Life, Thought, and Work.* Cath. U. Pr. 1983 repr. of 1974 ed. $18.95. ISBN 0-8132-0590-5. An excellent up-to-date biography.

Wippel, John F. *Metaphysical Themes in Thomas Aquinas. Studies in Philosophy and the History of Philosophy.* Cath. U. Pr. 1984 $31.95. ISBN 0-8132-0578-6. A Catholic work that takes issue with Gilson's interpretation of Aquinas's position on Christian philosophy. Insightful, but never reaching outside the circles of Catholic scholarship.

WILLIAM OF OCKHAM (or OCCAM). c.1285–c.1349

William of Ockham was a Franciscan at Oxford. He came just short of receiving his theology degree; he was never able to undertake the necessary year of teaching because of the long list of those waiting and the opposition of his enemy, John Lutterel. From 1320 to 1324, he taught and wrote at the London *Studium*, the private school of his order. He was summoned to Avignon in 1324 on charges of heresy and became involved there in the dispute over Franciscan poverty. In 1328 Ockham fled with Michael of Cesena, general of his order, was excommunicated, and took refuge in Munich with Duke Ludwig of Bavaria, who had also been excommunicated. From there he engaged in an extensive polemic against Pope John XXII and his successors, writing numerous political works. Ockham's metaphysics and his logic are closely connected because of his deployment of "Ockham's razor," the notion that we should not suppose that more things exist than are needed to explain the meaning of true sentences. Very often his arguments hang on the logical analysis of a sentence, revealing its logical structure and making it clear that some questionable entity, something other than a word or an individual thing, is not referred to in it. His philosophy is marked by nominalism. He rejected the notion that we somehow or other get the forms of things themselves into our intellect, attacking especially Scotist attempts to hold on to this view using the "formal distinction." Instead, he held that our concepts were like mental words, with a natural capacity to signify their objects but in no way to be identified with their objects. This led to a strong skeptical current among his followers.

BOOKS BY WILLIAM OF OCKHAM

Ockham's Theory of Propositions: Part II of the Summa Logicae. 1488. Trans. by Alfred J. Freddoso and Henry Schuurman. U. of Notre Dame Pr. 1980 $20.00. ISBN 0-268-01495-7. With the volume above, presents the elementary part of Ockham's logic in good translations.

Ockham's Theory of Terms: Part I of the Summa Logicae. 1488 Trans. by Michael J. Loux. U. of Notre Dame Pr. 1974 $20.00. ISBN 0-268-00550-8

Predestination, God's Foreknowledge, and Future Contingents. Trans. by Marilyn McCord Adams and Norman Kretzmann. Hackett Pub. 1983 $24.50. ISBN 0-915144-14-X. The problem is one noted by Boethius in his *Consolation of Philosophy*, Book V: If God foreknows our actions, do we then act freely, or are our actions necessitated? It is deepened by a famous passage in Aristotle's *De Interpretatione* that asks if it can be true now that an event will happen in the future if it is not necessarily fixed already that it will happen. Logically fascinating.

Philosophical Writings. Ed. and trans. by Philotheus Boehner. Rev. by Stephen Brown. Hackett Pub. 1990 $32.50. ISBN 0-87220-079-5. Good brief selections, well translated, from Ockham's works, concentrating on logic and epistemology.

Quodlibetal Questions. Trans. by Frank E. Kelley and Alfred J. Freddoso. 2 vols. Yale U. Pr. 1991 $100.00. ISBN 0-300-04832-7. A relatively late work covering a broad range of topics in philosophy and theology.

BOOKS ABOUT WILLIAM OF OCKHAM

Adams, Marilyn McCord. *William Ockham.* 2 vols. U. of Notre Dame Pr. 1986 $90.00. ISBN 0-268-01940-1. The definitive general study, sophisticated in both the scholarly and the philosophical sense. Adams is especially interesting on Ockham's views in theology and philosophy of religion.

Boehner, Philotheus, and Eligius Buytaert. *Collected Articles on Ockham. Philosophy Ser.* Franciscan Inst. 1958 $23.00. ISBN 0-686-11542-2. The articles in the second half of this book, on truth and logic, metaphysics, and political thought, are accessible to the nonspecialist. Those in the first half are not.

Commemorative Issue. Franciscan Studies. 1984–86. Franciscan Inst. 1988 o.p. A collection of papers delivered at the conference on Ockham given upon completion of the Institute's Latin edition of his works. Essential papers on every aspect of Ockham's thought.

Freppert, Lucan. *The Basis of Morality According to William of Ockham.* Franciscan Pr. 1988 $8.95. ISBN 0-8199-0918-1. An excellent examination of Ockham's rooting of ethical obligation in God's arbitrary will, while holding that the divine will is revealed through reason, so that a rational examination of ethics is possible.

Fuchs, Oswald. *The Psychology of Habit According to William Ockham. Philosophy Ser.* Franciscan Inst. 1952 $8.00. ISBN 0-686-11538-4. *Habit* refers to any disposition that is reinforced by its exercise, and so to knowledge and virtues and vices, as well as habitual inclinations of the will. A competent study.

McGrade, A. S. *The Political Thought of William of Ockham. Studies in Medieval Life and Thought*. Cambridge U. Pr. 1974 o.p. A wide-ranging study of Ockham both as a political activist and a theorist. Essentially an exposition of Ockham's views, with only occasional references to his influence, sources, or relation to other thinkers.

Menges, M. C. *The Concept of Univocity Regarding the Predication of God and Creature According to William of Ockham. Philosophy Ser.* Franciscan Inst. 1952 $8.00. ISBN 0-686-11539-2. An examination of Ockham's contention that God exists in the same sense of the word that we do, opposing the Thomistic view that God is His own existence and so exists in a different manner.

Moody, Ernest Addison. *The Logic of William of Ockham*. Russell Sage 1965 repr. of 1935 ed. o.p. An excellent general treatment of Ockham's logic, which plays a greater role in determining his views than it does in those of any previous thinker.

————. *Studies in Medieval Philosophy, Science, and Logic*. U. CA Pr. 1975 o.p. Good essays on the Ockhamist tradition.

Shapiro, Herman. *Motion, Time and Place According to William Ockham. Philosophy Ser.* Franciscan Inst. 1957 o.p. A detailed discussion of Ockham's work on some topics in Aristotle's *Physics*, which aimed to give an account of motion, time, and place that would exclude any existents other than individuals.

Tachau, Katherine. *Vision and Certitude in the Age of Ockham: Optics, Epistemology and the Foundations of Semantics, 1250–1345*. E. J. Brill 1987 $89.25. ISBN 90-04-08552-1. A scholarly and sophisticated exploration of the theory of knowledge in Ockham and his contemporaries. Highly influential in current discussions.

Webering, Damascene. *Theory of Demonstration According to William Ockham. Philosophy Ser.* Franciscan Inst. 1953 $8.00. ISBN 0-686-11540-6. A very useful study of Ockham's treatment of scientific knowledge, which he conceived as knowledge through "demonstration," as laid out in Aristotle's *Posterior Analytics*. Valuable for Ockham's notions about knowledge of the existence of things and of causal laws.

CHAPTER 5

Renaissance Philosophy

Frederick Purnell, Jr.

> During the Renaissance, philosophical thought, without abandoning its
> theological connections, strengthened its link with the humanities, the
> sciences, and, we may add, with literature and the arts, thus becoming
> increasingly secular in its outlook.
> —PAUL OSKAR KRISTELLER, *Renaissance Thought and Its Sources*

Although the Renaissance—the era in Western cultural history that extended
roughly from 1350 to 1600—may be said not to have produced a philosopher of
equal importance to the greatest thinkers of the Middle Ages or the Enlightenment, it was nevertheless an important period in the history of philosophy. One
cannot fully appreciate the differences that separate a medieval thinker such as
THOMAS AQUINAS from a modern philosopher such as RENÉ DESCARTES (see also
Vol. 5) or JOHN LOCKE (see also Vol. 3) without giving due attention to the
philosophical changes that took place during the Renaissance, a period best
understood as one of transition or fermentation rather than major philosophical
synthesis.

One feature of Renaissance culture that influenced the philosophical literature of the period was the rise of humanism. The humanists (whose name
derives from an Italian university slang term for a teacher or student of the
studia humanitatis, or "humanities") shared an educational ideal founded on
the study of grammar, rhetoric, poetry, history, and moral philosophy.
Humanism was thus not a philosophical school or body of teaching akin to
Platonism or Stoicism but a broader cultural movement that profoundly
influenced many areas of Renaissance art, literature, and political and social
thought and practice.

Humanists displayed attitudes toward philosophy and philosophers ranging
from admiration and praise to criticism and outright ridicule, particularly of the
"sterile" disputes of the medieval scholastics. At the same time, the humanists'
interest in ethics led them to compose moral treatises of their own, in both
polished classical Latin and the vernacular languages, and to edit, publish,
translate, and comment on the works of ancient philosophers, many of whom
were unknown or only partially known in the Middle Ages. Although it would be
difficult to identify any single philosophical doctrine that all humanists shared,
their ethical writing generally tended to emphasize the individual and freedom
of the human will.

Stimulated in part by the new editions and translations of the humanists and
the increased emphasis given to the study of Greek during the fifteenth and
sixteenth centuries, Renaissance philosophers devoted their attention to
studying and adapting to their own purposes the philosophical heritage of
classical antiquity and the medieval period. Platonism had influenced much

medieval philosophical speculation, and its influence continued into the Renaissance, but the study of it was now grounded directly on the works of PLATO (see also Vol. 3) and the principal Platonists to a degree that had been impossible in the Latin world since late antiquity. MARSILIO FICINO's Latin translations of the works of Plato, PLOTINUS, and other important Platonic sources stimulated a resurgence of interest in Plato's thought that was to carry over into the modern period, and his attempt to reconcile Platonism with Christianity would influence the way in which Western philosophers interpreted the Platonic works for centuries.

In similar fashion, the Aristotelian tradition flourished during the Renaissance, giving rise to a multifaceted intellectual movement. Such medieval scholastic-Aristotelian traditions as Thomism and Scotism still found spirited defenders, but alongside these developed a secular Aristotelianism centered in the universities of northern Italy, which sought to interpret ARISTOTLE's (see also Vol. 3) teachings outside the framework of Christian faith. Such thinkers as PIETRO POMPONAZZI, Jacopo Zabarella, and Cesare Cremonini provided an analysis of Aristotle's teachings on such issues as immortality, freedom of the will, and divine providence, which challenged the medieval synthesis of faith and reason.

Besides the attempts to revive the classical philosophical traditions, the Renaissance witnessed efforts by some philosophers to provide an alternative to the authority of the ancients. New philosophies of nature appeared as competitors of the Aristotelian natural philosophy that remained largely dominant in the university faculties of philosophy. The writings of such innovative thinkers as Bernardino Telesio, PHILIPPUS AUREOLUS PARACELSUS (see also Vol. 5), Francesco Patrizi, TOMMASO CAMPANELLA, GIORDANO BRUNO, and GALILEO (see also Vol. 5) attacked the metaphysical and methodological assumptions underlying the Aristotelian approach to the study of nature, gave new relevance to such alternative ancient traditions as Stoicism, atomism, and skepticism, and prepared the way for the development of mathematical physics in the seventeenth century.

GENERAL WORKS

Allen, Don C. *Doubt's Boundless Sea*. Ayer 1979 $25.50. ISBN 0-405-10577-0. Deals with the revival of the ancient skeptical tradition in the Renaissance and its influence on religious thought.

Ashworth, E. J. *Language and Logic in the Post Medieval Period*. Kluwer Ac. 1974 $106.00. ISBN 90-277-0464-3. An important study of the development during the Renaissance of late medieval terminist logic, so-called from its emphasis on analyzing the use of terms in sentences.

———. *Studies in Post-Medieval Semantics*. Ashgate Pub. Co. 1985 $91.95. ISBN 0-86078-175-5. Additional studies on Renaissance logicians.

Baron, Hans. *Crisis of the Early Italian Renaissance: Civic Humanism and Republican Liberty in an Age of Classicism and Tyranny*. Princeton U. Pr. 1966 $21.95. ISBN 0-691-00752-7. This classic study has continued to influence Renaissance intellectual history for more than 30 years. Baron emphasizes the importance, for an understanding of Renaissance political ideals, of what he terms "civic humanism," whose chief proponent was the Florentine republican Leonardo Bruni.

———. *In Search of Florentine Civic Humanism: Essays on the Transition from Medieval to Modern Thought*. 2 vols. Princeton U. Pr. 1988. Vol. 1 $37.50. ISBN 0-691-05512-2. Vol. 2 $32.50. ISBN 0-691-05513-0. A collection of some of Baron's most important studies.

Becker, Reinhard P., ed. *German Humanism and Reformation: Selected Writings.* Continuum 1982 $27.50. ISBN 0-8264-0251-8. Valuable collection of texts dealing with German humanism.

Bentley, Jerry H. *Humanists and Holy Writ: New Testament Scholarship in the Renaissance.* Bks. Demand repr. of 1983 ed. $70.20. ISBN 0-7837-1429-7. Valuable analysis of the influence of humanist textual scholarship on Biblical studies.

Bernstein, Eckhard. *German Humanism. World Authors Ser.* G. K. Hall 1983 o.p. Treats the influence of the humanistic movement in the German-speaking lands.

Blau, Joseph L. *The Christian Interpretation of the Cabala in the Renaissance.* Kennikat 1965 o.p. Classic study of the employment of Jewish cabalistic literature by Christian Renaissance thinkers, such as Agrippa, Pico, and Bruno.

Boas, Marie. *The Scientific Renaissance 1450–1630.* HarpC 1962 o.p. A good, general introduction to the scientific achievement of the Renaissance, in which philosophers played a significant role.

Botero, Giovanni. *The Reason of State and the Greatness of Cities.* Routledge 1956 o.p. The two principal works of the great sixteenth-century political thinker who opposed Machiavelli's amoral view of politics with a defense of the art of the possible.

——. *A Treatise, Concerning the Causes of the Magnificence and Greatness of Cities.* Walter J. Johnson 1979 repr. of 1606 ed. $25.00. ISBN 90-221-0910-0. One of the two works listed above, in a currently available edition.

Bouwsma, William J. *Concordia Mundi: The Career and Thought of Guillaume Postel, 1510–1581. Historical Monographs Ser.* HUP 1957 $25.00. ISBN 0-674-15950-0. Excellent treatment of the stormy career of the learned French Orientalist and prophet of universal religious harmony.

——. *The Culture of Renaissance Humanism.* Am. Hist. Assn. 1973 o.p. A brief but illuminating introduction to the significance of humanism on Renaissance culture.

Bréhier, Emile. *The Middle Ages and the Renaissance.* Vol. 3 in *The History of Philosophy.* Trans. by Wade Baskin. U. Ch. Pr. 1965 $5.00. Contains an enlightening chapter on major Renaissance thinkers.

Brues, Guy de. *The Dialogues of Guy de Brues: A Critical Edition with a Study in Renaissance Scepticism and Relativism.* Ed. by P. P. Morphos. Johns Hopkins 1953 o.p.

Bruni, Leonardo. *The Humanism of Leonardo Bruni: Selected Texts.* Ed. and trans. by Gordon Griffiths, James Hankins, and David Thompson. *Medieval and Renaissance Texts and Studies.* MRTS 1987 $25.00. ISBN 0-86698-029-6. A fine selection of works by the great Florentine humanist (1370–1444). Excellent introductions evaluate his achievements as classical scholar, historian, political theorist, and philosopher.

Buckley, George T. *Atheism in the English Renaissance.* Sage 1965 repr. of 1932 ed. o.p. Classic study of atheistic tendencies in Renaissance thought and the reaction they provoked from English writers. Traces the influence of French and Italian debates on immortality and political ideas on such authors as Sidney, Bacon, Marlowe, and Walter Raleigh.

Burtt, Edwin A. *The Metaphysical Foundations of Modern Physical Science.* Humanities 1980 $15.00. ISBN 0-391-01742-X. A somewhat dated but still stimulating study of the relation between metaphysics and scientific theories. Discusses Copernicus, Kepler, and Galileo, as well as later figures.

Bush, Douglas. *The Renaissance and English Humanism.* U. of Toronto Pr. 1939 o.p. A brief, readable survey, stressing the literary aspects of the humanist influence.

Caponigri, A. Robert. *Philosophy from the Renaissance to the Romantic Age.* Vol. 3 in *A History of Western Philosophy.* U. of Notre Dame Pr. 1963 o.p. A good general introduction to a selection of the major thinkers of the period.

Cassirer, Ernst. *The Individual and the Cosmos in Renaissance Philosophy.* Trans. by Mario Domandi. U. of Pa. Pr. 1972 o.p. A famous study of Renaissance philosophy in relation to the development of modern thought. Places particular emphasis on Nicholas of Cusa's theory of knowledge as radically distinct from medieval positions, but tends to overstate his direct influence on later thinkers.

_____, and others, eds. *The Renaissance Philosophy of Man*. U. Ch. Pr. 1956 $12.95. ISBN 0-226-09604-1. Excellent selection of Renaissance philosophical texts in translation, with important introductory essays. Includes selections from Petrarch, Valla, Ficino, Pico, Pomponazzi, and Vives.

Charron, Jean D. *The Wisdom of Pierre Charron: An Original and Orthodox Code of Morality*. Greenwood 1979 repr. of 1961 ed. o.p. An important study of the sixteenth-century French skeptic.

Charron, Pierre. *Of Wisdome*. Walter J. Johnson 1971 repr. of 1612 ed. o.p. Charron (1541–1603) was a major figure in Renaissance skepticism. This is his most important philosophical work, first published in 1601.

Clulee, Nicholas H. *John Dee's Natural Philosophy: Between Science and Religion*. Routledge 1989 $55.00. ISBN 0-415-00625-2. Valuable study of Dr. John Dee, a sixteenth-century English occultist whose views on magic and philosophy gained a wide audience.

Copenhaver, Brian P. *Symphorien Champier and the Reception of the Occultist Tradition in Renaissance France*. Mouton 1978 $75.00. ISBN 90-279-7647-3. Best modern study of Champier, a humanist influenced by Platonism, Aristotelianism, and spurious sources of ancient wisdom.

Copenhaver, Brian P., and Charles B. Schmitt. *Renaissance Philosophy*. Vol. 3 in *A History of Western Philosophy*. OUP 1992 $62.00. ISBN 0-19-219203-5. Outstanding survey of major figures and movements in Renaissance thought. Excellent bibliography.

Copleston, Frederick. *History of Philosophy: Late Medieval and Renaissance Philosophy*. Vol. 3 in *History of Philosophy*. Paulist Pr. 1976 $19.95. ISBN 0-8091-0066-5. Long a standard history of philosophy in English. The treatment of the Renaissance is uneven, generally far better on northern European philosophers than on Italian thinkers. Clearly written and accurate.

Costello, Frank B. *The Political Philosophy of Luis De Molina, S. J.* Jesuit Hist. 1974 $18.00. ISBN 88-7041-338-1. Considers the political thought of the famous Spanish Jesuit theologian.

Couliano, Ioan P. *Eros and Magic in the Renaissance*. Trans. by Margaret Cook. U. Ch. Pr. 1987 $34.95. ISBN 0-226-12315-4. Important for the philosophical assumptions underlying the popularity of magic in the Renaissance.

Davis, J. C. *Utopia and the Ideal Society: A Study of English Utopian Writing, 1516–1700*. Cambridge U. Pr. 1983 $74.95. ISBN 0-521-23396-8. Utopian literature flourished during the later Renaissance, with many important philosophers contributing to the genre. This volume discusses English works, concentrating primarily on the seventeenth century.

Debus, Allen G. *Chemistry, Alchemy and the New Philosophy, 1550–1700. Studies in the History of Science and Medicine*. Ashgate Pub. Co. 1987 $83.95. ISBN 0-86078-197-6. A collection of articles by a distinguished historian of early modern science and philosophy.

_____, ed. *John Dee: The Mathematicall Preface*. Watson Publ. Intl. 1974 $17.00. ISBN 0-88202-020-X. Careful edition of Dee's influential introduction to Euclid's *Elements*.

_____. *Man and Nature in the Renaissance*. *History of Science Ser.* Cambridge U. Pr. 1978 $34.95. ISBN 0-521-21972-8. Fine general introduction to Renaissance science, particularly valuable for its attention to the role of philosophical and mystical patterns of thought in influencing the scientific practices of the day. Amply illustrated.

Dijksterhuis, E. J. *The Mechanization of the World Picture: Pythagoras to Newton*. Trans. by C. Dikshoorn. Princeton U. Pr. 1986 $19.95. ISBN 0-691-02396-4. An important and influential study of the emergence of modern physical science. Foreword by D. J. Struik.

Drake, Stillman, and I. E. Drabkin, eds. *Mechanics in Sixteenth-Century Italy: Selections from Tartaglia, Benedetti, Buido Ubaldo and Galileo*. Bks. Demand repr. of 1969 ed. $119.40. ISBN 0-7837-1657-5. Essential selection of sources illustrating the attacks on Aristotelian physics in the late sixteenth century. Excellent introduction.

Fallico, Arturo, and Herman Shapiro, eds. *Renaissance Philosophy.* 2 vols. Modern Lib. 1967–69 o.p. An extensive collection of texts in translation, with brief introductory essays. Particularly valuable for selections from Italian philosophers of nature and northern humanists.

Febvre, Lucien. *The Problem of Unbelief in the Sixteenth Century: The Religion of Rabelais.* Trans. by Beatrice Gottlieb. HUP 1982 $12.95. ISBN 0-674-70826-1. A justly famous analysis of skepticism and atheism in the Renaissance, particularly valuable for its treatment of French sources.

Field, Arthur. *The Origins of the Platonic Academy of Florence.* Princeton U. Pr. 1989 $50.00. ISBN 0-691-05533-5. Groundbreaking new study on the earliest influences of Platonism in fifteenth-century Florence.

Fierz, Markus, ed. *Girolamo Cardano, 1501–1576: Physician, Natural Philosopher, Mathematician, Astrologer and Interpreter of Dreams.* Trans. by Helga Niman. Birkhauser 1983 $37.95. ISBN 0-8176-3057-0. Cardano was an Italian polymath and physician, author of over 200 books on mathematics, philosophy, and the occult.

Figgis, John N. *Political Thought from Gerson to Grotius: 1414–1625.* AMS Pr. 1976 repr. of 1907 ed. $21.00. ISBN 0-404-14540-X. Long a standard history of Renaissance political philosophy.

Fox, Alistair, and John Guy. *Reassessing the Henrician Age: Humanism, Politics and Reform, 1500–1550.* Blackwell Pubs. 1986 $49.95. ISBN 0-631-14614-8. Valuable source on humanist influence in sixteenth-century England.

Friedman, Jerome. *The Most Ancient Testimony: Sixteenth Century Christian-Hebraica in the Age of Renaissance Nostalgia.* Ohio U. Pr. 1983 $26.95. ISBN 0-8214-0700-7. Masterful study of Christian thinkers' use of Hebrew sources in the search for ancient wisdom.

Funkenstein, Amos. *Theology and the Scientific Imagination from the Middle Ages to the Seventeenth Century.* Princeton U. Pr. 1989 $65.00. ISBN 0-691-08408-4. Emphasizes the interplay of science and theology in the formation of modern science.

Garin, Eugenio. *Astrology in the Renaissance: The Zodiac of Life.* Trans. by June Allen and Carolyn Jackson. Viking Penguin 1988 $10.95. ISBN 0-14-019259-X. A masterful study by the leading Italian historian of Renaissance thought. Focuses on the debate over the validity and implications of astrology carried on by such philosophers as Pico, Ficino, and Pomponazzi.

———. *Italian Humanism: Philosophy and Civic Life in the Renaissance.* Trans. by Peter Munz. Greenwood 1976 repr. of 1965 ed. $38.50. ISBN 0-8371-8578-5. Garin views humanism as a broadly philosophical movement, so that his studies embrace much more technical philosophical writing than those of scholars who define the movement more narrowly.

———. *Science and Civic Life in the Italian Renaissance.* Trans. by Peter Munz. Peter Smith 1969 $11.50. ISBN 0-8446-2110-2. Important work by the most renowned Italian scholar of Renaissance humanism.

Gilbert, Neal Ward. *Renaissance Concepts of Method.* Col. U. Pr. 1960 o.p. A very important study of a central problem—the development of the concept of *method* in the period leading up to the Scientific Revolution. An excellent survey of Renaissance views on method that traces them to their sources in classical antiquity.

Gilson, Étienne. *History of Christian Philosophy in the Middle Ages.* Random 1955 o.p. The most comprehensive history in English of the works of Christian medieval philosophers. Contains much that is useful for the study of Renaissance figures, particularly those working in the scholastic tradition. Tends to downplay the originality of Renaissance philosophy.

Gleason, John B. *John Colet.* U. CA Pr. 1989 $50.00. ISBN 0-520-06510-7. Basic study of the famous humanist, friend of More and Erasmus.

Grafton, Anthony, and Lisa Jardine. *From Humanism to the Humanities: Education and the Liberal Arts in Fifteenth- and Sixteenth-Century Europe.* HUP 1986 $36.00. ISBN 0-674-42300-3. Important work on the influence of humanism on education.

Grant, Edward. *Much Ado about Nothing: Theories of Space and Vacuum from the Middle Ages to the Scientific Revolution.* Cambridge U. Pr. 1981 $89.95. ISBN 0-521-22983-9.

Traces the influence of Stoic, atomistic, and Hermetic teachings (the doctrines attributed to the legendary Egyptian sage Hermes Trismegistus) on the development of early modern concepts of space.

Grassi, Ernesto. *Heidegger and the Question of Renaissance Humanism: Four Studies*. MRTS 1983 $18.00. ISBN 0-86698-062-8. Humanism from the perspective of the great modern existentialist philosopher Martin Heidegger.

———. *Renaissance Humanism: Studies in Philosophy and Poetics*. MRTS 1988 $18.00. ISBN 0-86698-035-0. Valuable collection of studies on the philosophical influence of humanism.

———. *Rhetoric as Philosophy: The Humanist Tradition*. Pa. St. U. Pr. 1980 $20.00. ISBN 0-271-00256-5

Gundersheimer, Werner L. *French Humanism: 1470–1600*. Peter Smith 1970 o.p. A series of essays on major topics in French humanism.

Hankins, James. *Plato in the Italian Renaissance*. 2 vols. E. J. Brill 2nd rev. ed. 1991 $171.50. ISBN 90-04-09163-7. Monumental analysis of the way the Renaissance read and adapted the works of Plato. Concentrates on Italian authors from the fifteenth century. Volume 2 provides a wealth of primary source material to support the conclusions presented in Volume 1. Outstanding.

Hathaway, Baxter. *The Age of Criticism: The Late Renaissance in Italy*. Greenwood 1972 repr. of 1962 ed. o.p. A basic study.

Heller, Agnes. *Renaissance Man*. Trans. by Richard E. Allen. Schocken 1981 o.p. How people altered their attitudes toward their place in nature during the Renaissance.

Howell, Wilbur S. *Logic and Rhetoric in England, 1500–1700*. Sage 1961 repr. of 1956 ed. o.p. Important for the philosophical background of the English Renaissance.

Hughes, Philip E. *Lefèvre: Pioneer of Ecclesiastical Renewal in France*. Bks. Demand repr. of 1984 ed. $57.80. ISBN 0-685-23456-8. Good study of Jacques Lefèvre d'Étaples (c.1460–1536), French humanist, philosopher, and theologian influenced by Platonic and Aristotelian sources.

Huppert, George. *The Idea of Perfect History: Historical Erudition and Historical Philosophy in Renaissance France*. U. of Ill. Pr. 1970 $24.95. ISBN 0-252-00076-5. Important for an understanding of the influence of humanism on the concept of history.

Kahn, Victoria. *Rhetoric, Prudence and Skepticism in the Renaissance*. Cornell Univ. Pr. 1985 $31.50. ISBN 0-8014-1736-8. Valuable on humanist ethics and the skeptical tradition.

Kelley, Donald R. *Renaissance Humanism*. Twayne 1991 $22.95. ISBN 0-8057-8602-3. "Masterly summations of the contributions of Kristeller, Baron, Garin, Cassirer, among others, and also profound original insights. . . . Highly recommended for undergraduates and general readers" (*Choice*).

Kennedy, Leonard A. *Peter of Ailly and the Harvest of Fourteenth Century Philosophy*. E. Mellen 1989 $89.95. ISBN 0-88946-307-7. Discusses the skeptical implications of the thought of Pierre d'Ailly (1350–1420), a French philosopher and theologian influenced by William of Ockham.

———, ed. *Renaissance Philosophy: New Translations of Lorenzo Valla, Paul Cortese, Cajetan, T. Bacciliere, Juan Luis Vives, Peter Ramus*. Mouton 1973 $23.35. ISBN 90-2797-193-5. A good selection of primary sources in translation.

Koenigsberger, Dorothy. *Renaissance Man and Creative Thinking: A History of Concepts of Harmony 1400–1700*. Humanities 1979 o.p. "Provides interesting insights for the scholar who has already developed his own perception of the Renaissance" (*Renaissance Quarterly*).

Kohl, Benjamin G. *Renaissance Humanism 1300–1550: A Bibliography of Materials in English*. Reference Lib. of the Humanities. Garland 1985 o.p. A basic bibliographic source useful for the study of humanists with philosophical interests.

Kohl, Benjamin G., and Ronald G. Witt. *The Earthly Republic: Italian Humanists on Government and Society*. U. of Pa. Pr. 1978 $19.95. ISBN 0-8122-1097-2. Excellent introduction to humanist contributions to political and social philosophy.

Koyré, Alexandre. *From the Closed World to the Infinite Universe*. Johns Hopkins 1968 repr. of 1956 ed. $13.95. ISBN 0-8018-0347-0. An important and influential study of the development of the doctrine of an infinite universe. Penetrating accounts of premodern cosmologies.

Kristeller, Paul Oskar. *Eight Philosophers of the Italian Renaissance*. Stanford U. Pr. 1964 $25.00. ISBN 0-8047-0110-5. Fundamental study by the master historian of the Renaissance philosophy. Balanced biographical and expository essays on Petrarch, Valla, Ficino, Pico, Pomponazzi, Telesio, Patrizi, and Bruno.

_____. *Medieval Aspects of Renaissance Learning: Three Essays*. Ed. by Edward P. Mahoney. Col. U. Pr. 1992 $40.00. ISBN 0-231-07950-8. Three important essays on medieval intellectual influences on Renaissance thought.

_____. *Renaissance Thought and Its Sources*. Ed. by Michael Mooney. Col. U. Pr. 1981 $55.00. ISBN 0-231-04512-3. An anthology of some of Kristeller's most important studies, including essays on Renaissance humanism, Platonism and Aristotelianism, and Renaissance concepts of man.

_____. *Renaissance Thought and the Arts: Collected Essays*. Princeton U. Pr. 1990 $29.50. ISBN 0-691-07253-1. More classic studies, including a famous consideration of the development of the modern concept of the arts during the Renaissance.

Kuntz, Marian Leathers. *Guillaume Postel, Prophet of the Restitution of All Things: His Life and Thought*. Kluwer Ac. 1981 $75.50. ISBN 90-247-2523-2. Best modern study of Postel (1510–1581), heterodox orientalist and philosopher of history.

Levi, A. *French Moralists: The Theory of the Passions 1585–1649*. OUP 1964 o.p. Considers the importance of the passions in late Renaissance ethical thought.

Lindberg, David. *Theories of Vision from al-Kindi to Kepler*. U. Ch. Pr. 1981 $10.00. ISBN 0-226-48235-9. The authoritative study of the topic. Essential for an understanding of philosophical discussions of perception in the early modern period.

Lindhardt, Jan. *Martin Luther: Knowledge and Mediation in the Renaissance*. E. Mellen 1986 $89.95. ISBN 0-88946-817-6. Considers Luther as a representative of Renaissance humanism.

Lockwood, Dean P. *Ugo Bénzi, Medieval Philosopher and Physician 1376–1439*. U. Ch. Pr. 1951 o.p. Fundamental study of the famous Italian physician, important for understanding the development of medical methodology in an era when philosophy was an integral part of a doctor's training.

Mahoney, Edward P., ed. *Philosophy and Humanism: Renaissance Essays in Honor of Paul Oskar Kristeller*. Col. U. Pr. 1976 o.p. Wide-ranging anthology of essays in intellectual history by leading American authorities on Renaissance thought.

Manuel, Frank E., and Fritzie P. Manuel. *Utopian Thought in the Western World*. HUP 1979 $41.00. ISBN 0-674-93185-8. Standard study, valuable for Renaissance utopianism.

Martindale, Joanna, ed. *English Humanism: Wyatt to Cowley*. Longwood 1984 o.p. An anthology of essays that "does much to elucidate . . . the influence of Erasmus on English men of letters" (*Times Educational Supplement*).

Matsen, Herbert S., ed. *Alessandro Achillini (1463–1512) and His Doctrine of Universals and Transcendentals*. Bucknell U. Pr. 1975 $38.50. ISBN 0-686-85741-0. A detailed study of an Italian Aristotelian whose logic and metaphysics show the influence of William of Ockham's teachings.

Merkel, Ingrid, and Allen G. Debus, eds. *Hermeticism and the Renaissance: Intellectual History of the Occult in Early Modern Europe*. Folger Bks. 1988 $68.50. ISBN 0-91806-85-1. Papers assessing the influence of the spurious philosophical and alchemical works attributed to the ancient Egyptian priest Hermes Trismegistus.

Noreña, Carlos G. *Studies in Spanish Renaissance Thought*. Kluwer Ac. 1975 $88.50. ISBN 90-247-1727-2. "*The* required introduction into this difficult area of the history of philosophy" (*Journal of the History of Philosophy*).

Oberman, Heiko A. *Forerunners of the Reformation: The Shape of Late Medieval Thought*. Trans. by Paul Nyhus. Bks. Demand repr. of 1981 ed. $86.80. ISBN 0-685-17052-7. Emphasizes the importance of late medieval philosophy and theology for an understanding of later controversies.

————. *The Harvest of Medieval Theology: Gabriel Biel and Late Medieval Nominalism.* Labyrinth Pr. 1983 repr. of 1963 ed. $18.50. ISBN 0-939464-05-5. Biel was a fifteenth-century German philosopher deeply influenced by the writings of predecessors in the nominalistic tradition, such as William of Ockham. Oberman's influential works have stressed the transitional role of late medieval thought in preparing the way for the Protestant Reformation.

Oberman, Heiko A., and Frank M. James III, eds. *Via Augustini: Augustine in the Later Middle Ages, Renaissance and Reformation. Studies in Medieval and Reformation Thought.* E. J. Brill 1991 $65.75. ISBN 90-04-09364-8. Authors discuss the extensive influence of St. Augustine on theological and philosophical thought during the Renaissance.

Oestreich, Gerhard. *Neostoicism and the Early Modern State.* Ed. by B. Oestreich and H. G. Koenigsberger. Trans. by D. McLintock. *Studies in Early Modern History.* Cambridge U. Pr. 1982 $64.95. ISBN 0-521-24202-9. Documents the revival of interest in Stoicism during the Renaissance and its influence on political thought.

Ong, Walter J. *Ramus, Method, and the Decay of Dialogue: From the Art of Discourse to the Art of Reason.* HUP 1983 $!1.95. ISBN 0-674-74802-6. Masterful study of the fiercely anti-Aristotelian French Calvinist whose attempt to replace traditional logic in the university curriculum aroused heated opposition during the sixteenth century.

Overfield, James H. *Humanism and Scholasticism in Late Medieval Germany.* Princeton U. Pr. 1984 $50.00. ISBN 0-691-07292-2. Illustrates the interplay of humanism with medieval scholasticism in the German Renaissance.

Ozment, S. *The Age of Reform, 1250–1550: An Intellectual and Religious History of Late Medieval and Reformation Europe.* Yale U. Pr. 1980 $17.00. ISBN 0-300-02760-5. Excellent general introduction to the period.

Padley, G. A. *Grammatical Theory in Western Europe 1500–1700.* Cambridge U. Pr. 1985 Vol. 1 $69.95. ISBN 0-521-22307-5. Vol. 2 1988 $84.95. ISBN 0-521-33514-0. Detailed study of grammatical theory in the sixteenth and seventeenth centuries.

Pagel, Walter. *Religion and Neoplatonism in Renaissance Medicine.* Ed. by Marianne Winder. Ashgate Pub. Co. 1985 $89.95. ISBN 0-86078-174-7. Outstanding analysis of the influence of philosophy on Renaissance medicine by a leading authority.

Partee, Charles, ed. *Calvin and Classical Philosophy.* Heinman 1977 o.p. Analyzes Calvin's utilization of ancient philosophical doctrines.

Paul of Venice. *Logica Magna. Part I Fascicule 8: Tractatus de Necessitate et Contingentia Futurorum.* Ed. and trans. by C. J. F. Williams. *Classical and Medieval Logic Texts.* OUP 1991 $45.00. ISBN 0-19-726101-9. Paul (c.1369–1429), an Augustinian hermit, was one of the greatest of the long series of logicians who taught at Padua during the fifteenth and sixteenth centuries. This section of his *Great Logic* deals with the issue of whether future events are predetermined.

————. *Logica Magna. Part II Fascicule 3: Tractatus de Hypotheticis.* Ed. and trans. by Alexander Broadie. *Classical and Medieval Logic Texts.* OUP 1990 $59.00. ISBN 0-19-726095-0. *Part II Fascicule 4: Capitula de Conditionali et de Rationali.* Ed. and trans. by G. E. Hughes. *Classical and Medieval Logic Texts.* OUP 1990 $59.00. ISBN 0-19-726094 2. Two additional selections from the *Great Logic* dealing with hypothetical and conditional reasoning.

————. *Logica Magna, Tractatus De Suppositione.* Ed. and trans. by Alan R. Perreiah. Franciscan Pr. 1971 $16.00. ISBN 0-686-11560-0. A careful edition and translation of Paul's analysis of supposition, the section of logic that deals with the ways in which terms function in sentences.

————. *Logica Parva.* Trans. by Alan R. Perreiah. Cath. U. Pr. 1984 o.p. Paul's "short logic" became a standard textbook and played an important part in the introduction of late medieval terminist logic—the analysis of the role of terms in sentences—into Italy. It offers a fine example of the approach to logic rejected and ridiculed by the humanists. This careful translation is provided with excellent notes and introductory essays that interpret Paul's work in the light of modern discussions in semantics and the philosophy of language.

Perreiah, Alan R., ed. *Paul of Venice: A Bibliographical Guide.* Philos Document 1986
$28.50. ISBN 0-912632-83-6. A thorough listing of works by and about Paul of
Venice.

Popkin, Richard H. *The History of Scepticism from Erasmus to Spinoza.* U. CA Pr. 1979
$13.95. ISBN 0-520-03876-2. "Certain to remain the standard work on the history of
early modern scepticism" (*Renaissance Quarterly*).

———, ed. *Philosophy of the Sixteenth and Seventeenth Centuries.* Free Pr. 1966 $12.95.
ISBN 0-02-925490-6. A good anthology of texts in translation. Renaissance thinkers
treated include Vespucci, Erasmus, Luther, Copernicus, Kepler, Galileo, and
Montaigne.

Rabil, Albert, Jr., ed. and trans. *Knowledge, Goodness and Power: The Debate Over
Nobility Among Quattrocento Italian Humanists. Texts and Studies.* MRTS 1991
$30.00. ISBN 0-86698-100-4. Good selection of texts on a favorite humanist theme.

———, ed. *Renaissance Humanism, Vols. 1–3: Foundations, Forms and Legacy.* 3 vols. U.
of Pa. Pr. 1992 $85.00. ISBN 0-8122-1400-5. Thorough treatment of humanism's
impact. The first volume treats humanism in Italy, the second outside Italy, the third
its influence on the scholarly and professional disciplines.

Randall, John Herman. *From the Middle Ages to the Enlightenment.* Vol. 1 in *The Career of
Philosophy.* Col. U. Pr. 1970 o.p. The strongest treatment of Renaissance thought in a
general history of philosophy in English. Randall argues that the rise of modern
scientific method was influenced by the logic of the secular Aristotelians teaching at
the University of Padua during the Renaissance.

Reinharz, Jehuda, and Kalman P. Bland, eds. *Mystics, Philosophers, and Politicians:
Essays in Jewish Intellectual History in Honor of Alexander Altman.* Duke 1982 o.p.
Contains several important essays on Jewish thinkers of the Renaissance.

Reuchlin, Johann. *On the Art of the Kabbalah (De Arte Cabbalistica).* Trans. by Martin
Goodman and Sarah Goodman. Abaris Bks. 1983 $20.00. ISBN 0-913870-56-0.
Reuchlin (1455–1522) was the leading Christian Hebraist of his day. His exposition of
the Jewish cabala was to prove influential on generations of Christian thinkers who
sought to employ its methods in biblical exegesis, philosophy, and magic.

Rice, Eugene F., Jr. *The Renaissance Idea of Wisdom.* Greenwood 1973 repr. of 1958 ed.
$35.00. ISBN 0-8371-6712-4. Traces the progressive secularization of the concept of
wisdom during the Renaissance, from Petrarch to Pierre Charron.

Riedl, John O. *A Catalogue of Renaissance Philosophers: 1350–1650.* Coronet Bks. repr.
of 1940 ed. o.p. A valuable listing of philosophers active during the Renaissance,
many little-known and overlooked in standard histories of philosophy.

Robb, Nesca A. *Neoplatonism of the Italian Renaissance.* Hippocrene Bks. 1968 o.p.
Although more than 50 years have elapsed since its first appearance, Robb's work
remains a valuable introduction to Renaissance Neoplatonism. He analyzes the
impact of Neoplatonic sources on Petrarch, Ficino and his Florentine circle, and
several important sixteenth-century poets, artists, and philosophers, demonstrating
particular sensitivity to the interplay between philosophy and the creative arts.

Rossi, Paolo. *Philosophy, Technology and the Arts in the Early Modern Era.* Trans. by
Salvator Attanasio, HarpC 1970 o.p. Lucid analysis of the change in attitude toward
the mechanical arts during the sixteenth and seventeenth centuries and how it
affected the modern view of science.

Santillana, Giorgio de, ed. *The Age of Adventure: The Renaissance Philosophers.* Ayer
repr. of 1956 ed. $22.95. ISBN 0-8369-1850-9. A good anthology of writings in
translation. Selections from Leonardo, More, Machiavelli, Michelangelo, Erasmus,
Copernicus, Montaigne, Kepler, Galileo, and Bruno.

Saunders, Jason L. *Justus Lipsius: The Philosophy of Renaissance Stoicism.* Liberal Arts
Pr. 1955 o.p. Lipsius (1547–1606), a Belgian, was one of the greatest humanist
scholars of the late sixteenth century. This careful study assesses his central role in
the revival of interest in classical Stoicism during the Renaissance.

Schmitt, Charles B. *The Aristotelian Tradition and Renaissance Universities.* Ashgate
Pubs. 1984 $89.95. ISBN 0-86078-151-8. An anthology of essays by a leading historian

of Renaissance Aristotelianism. These papers focus on the teaching of philosophy and science in the university curriculum.

_____. *Aristotle and the Renaissance*. HUP 1983 $18.50. ISBN 0-674-04525-4. An excellent introduction to the many forms of Aristotelianism that flourished during the Renaissance and the many areas of intellectual life they affected.

_____. *Cicero Scepticus: A Study of the Influence of the "Academica" in the Renaissance*. Nijhoff 1972 o.p. Traces the role played by Cicero's writings in the Renaissance revival of skepticism.

_____. *John Case and Aristotelianism in Renaissance England. Studies in the History of Ideas*. McGill CN 1983 $39.95. ISBN 0-7735-1005-2. Extensive study of a major English Renaissance philosopher.

_____. *Reappraisals in Renaissance Thought*. Ed. by Charles Webster. Ashgate Pub. Co. 1989 $83.95. ISBN 0-86078-245-X. An important collection of this distinguished historian's later articles.

_____. *Studies in Renaissance Philosophy and Science*. Ashgate Pub. Co. 1981 $91.95. ISBN 0-86078-093-7. An anthology of Schmitt's most important papers on the relation between philosophy and modern science.

Seigel, J. E. *Rhetoric and Philosophy in Renaissance Humanism: The Union of Eloquence and Wisdom*. Princeton U. Pr. 1968 o.p. Good general account of Renaissance humanism.

Skinner, Quentin. *The Foundations of Modern Political Thought: The Renaissance*. 2 vols. Cambridge U. Pr. 1978 Vol. 1 $21.95. ISBN 0-521-29337-5. Vol. 2 $24.95. ISBN 0-521-29435-5. The best introduction to the political philosophy of the Renaissance. Provides a lucid interpretation of the writings of all the major political theorists of the fourteenth to the sixteenth centuries and of many lesser-known figures.

Smith, Gerard, ed. *Jesuit Thinkers of the Renaissance*. Marquette 1939 $8.95. ISBN 0-87462-431-2. An anthology of studies of Jesuit scholastics, including Suàrez, Molina, Juan de Mariana, and Cardinal Bellarmine.

Tatarkiewicz, Wladislaw. *Modern Aesthetics*. Vol. 3 in *History of Aesthetics*. Mouton 1974 $64.00. ISBN 90-2793-943-8. This volume, from the most comprehensive modern history of the philosophy of art, concentrates on the early modern period to 1700.

Taylor, Henry Osborn. *Thought and Expression in the Sixteenth Century*. 2 vols. Continuum 1930 o.p. A venerable classic, still valuable for its portraits of leading Renaissance men of letters. Compelling account of the humanist influence in literature and philosophy.

Thorndike, Lynn. *A History of Magic and Experimental Science*. 8 vols. Col. U. Pr. 1923–58 $98.00 ea. ISBN 0-231-08801-9. A treasure trove of information on magic and the occult and their role in the history of science. Volumes 3 to 6 cover the Renaissance period.

_____. *Science and Thought in the Fifteenth Century*. Hafner 1967 repr. of 1929 ed. o.p. An introduction to Renaissance science by the renowned historian of magic.

Toffanin, G. *History of Humanism*. Trans. by E. Gianturco. Lat. Am. Lit. Rev. Pr. 1954 o.p. Controversial interpretation of humanism as a Catholic reaction to heretical tendencies in thirteenth-century theology and philosophy.

Trinkaus, Charles. *Adversity's Noblemen*. Hippocrene Bks. 1965 $15.00. ISBN 0-374-97999-5. Classic study by one of America's leading historians of humanism.

_____. *In Our Image and Likeness*. 2 vols. U. Ch. Pr. 1970 o.p. A masterful analysis of how the Renaissance humanists transformed the concept of human nature inherited from the medieval world. Detailed discussion of numerous thinkers and texts, including works by Petrarch, Salutati, Valla, Ficino, Pico, Manetti, and Pomponazzi.

_____. *The Scope of Renaissance Humanism*. U. of Mich. Pr. 1983 $39.50. ISBN 0-472-10031-9. A collection of essays from various sources.

Walker, D. P. *The Ancient Theology: Studies in Christian Platonism from the Fifteenth to the Eighteenth Century*. Cornell Univ. Pr. 1972 o.p. An indispensable collection of essays on the impact on Renaissance thought of ancient, often spurious, philosophical and theological sources, such as Orpheus, Hermes Trismegistus, and the Chaldaean Oracles.

————. *Music, Spirit and Language in the Renaissance*. Ed. by Penelope Gouk. Ashgate Pub. Co. 1985 $91.95. ISBN 0-86078-160-7. An essential collection of studies by one of the foremost historians of Renaissance occultism.

————. *Spiritual and Demonic Magic from Ficino to Campanella*. Kraus repr. of 1958 ed. o.p. A fine account of the theory and practice of magic among Renaissance philosophers.

Wallace, William A. *Causality and Scientific Explanation: Medieval and Early Classical Science*. U. Pr. of Amer. 1981 o.p. How theories of causation were related to the rise of modern physical science. Particularly sensitive to the importance of Renaissance philosophical sources in Galileo's intellectual development.

Waswo, Richard. *Language and Meaning in the Renaissance*. Princeton U. Pr. 1987 $42.50. ISBN 0-691-06696-5. Controversial analysis of theories of language in the works of Renaissance philosophers and humanists.

Weiss, Roberto. *Dawn of Humanism in Italy*. Haskell 1970 repr. of 1947 ed. $49.95. ISBN 0-8383-0336-6. An important work on the origins of humanism.

————. *Humanism in England during the Fifteenth Century*. OUP 1941 o.p. Documents the spread of humanism from the Continent to England, where it influenced the English Renaissance.

Witt, Ronald G. *Hercules at the Crossroads: The Life, Works, Thought of Coluccio Salutati*. Duke 1983 $49.95. ISBN 0-8223-0527-5. Definitive study of the great humanist (1331–1406) whose moral and political writings were of major influence.

Wolf, Albert. *A History of Science, Technology and Philosophy in the Sixteenth and Seventeenth Centuries*. 2 vols. Peter Smith o.p. Profusely illustrated history of the sciences and their philosophical background in the early years of the Scientific Revolution.

Woodward, William H. *Vittorino Da Feltre and Other Humanist Educators*. *Classics in Education Ser*. Tchrs. Coll. Pr. 1964 o.p. Classic study, first published in 1905, of Vittorino (1378–1446), who founded a famous humanist school in Mantua, and of humanist educational philosophy. Foreword by E. F. Rice, Jr.

Yates, Frances A. *Ideas and Ideals in the North European Renaissance*. *Collected Essays, Vol. 3*. Routledge Chapman & Hall 1984 $29.95. ISBN 0-7102-0184-2. Important anthology of studies by a great intellectual historian whose interests embraced art, literature, and the occult, in addition to philosophy.

————. *Occult Philosophy in the Elizabethan Age*. Methuen 1983 repr. of 1979 ed. o.p. Stimulating account of the influence of the Jewish cabala on Christian thinkers in the late fifteenth and early sixteenth centuries.

CHRONOLOGY OF AUTHORS

Petrarch. 1304–1374
Nicholas of Cusa. 1401?–1464
Valla, Lorenzo. c.1407–1457
Ficino, Marsilio. 1433–1499
Pomponazzi, Pietro. 1462–1525
Pico della Mirandola, Giovanni. 1463–1494
Erasmus, Desiderius. 1466?–1536
Cajetan, Cardinal. 1469–1534
Machiavelli, Niccolo. 1469–1527
Pico della Mirandola, Gianfrancesco. 1469–1533
More, Sir Thomas. 1478–1535

Agrippa of Nettesheim, Henry Cornelius. 1486–1535
Vives, Juan Luis. 1492–1540
Paracelsus, Philippus Aureolus. 1493?–1541
Bodin, Jean. 1530?–1596
Montaigne, Michel Eyquem de. 1533–1592
Bruno, Giordano. 1548–1600
Suárez, Francisco. 1548–1617
Galilei, Galileo. 1564–1642
Campanella, Tommaso. 1568–1639

AGRIPPA OF NETTESHEIM, HENRY CORNELIUS. 1486–1535

Born in Cologne, Henry Cornelius Agrippa of Nettesheim lived a life that combined action and adventure with scholarly pursuits. His early career was spent as a secretary and diplomat for the Holy Roman Emperor. Missions to Paris and London brought him into contact with new intellectual movements, and he immersed himself in the study of philosophy and theology, learning Hebrew in order to read the Jewish cabalistic literature. His first great written work, *The Occult Philosophy* (*De occulta philosophia*), completed 1509–10 but not published until 1531–33, is a compendium offering a mystical interpretation of nature through such arcane methods as cabalistic manipulation of Hebrew words and Pythagorean numerology. It quickly established itself as a major handbook of Renaissance magic and deeply influenced such thinkers as GIORDANO BRUNO.

In the years following the writing of *De occulta philosophia*, Agrippa served as a soldier, lawyer, physician, and theologian. A virulent critic of the clergy and of scholastic theology, he engaged in bitter exchanges with theologically conservative opponents over his religious attitudes. Agrippa's own position lay between the intellectual reformism of ERASMUS and the outright break with Catholicism represented by MARTIN LUTHER. However, Agrippa later moved away from his early confidence in the magical and mystical methods to an unquestioning biblical faith. His most important later work, *Of the Vanitie and uncertaintie of artes and sciences* (*De incertitudine et vanitate scientiarum et artium*), published at Antwerp in 1530, advocates a thoroughgoing rejection of learning and intellectual attainment in favor of a simple religious piety. It came to play an important role in the Renaissance revival of the skeptical tradition of antiquity. Shortly after the appearance of *De incertitudine*, Agrippa was imprisoned for heresy and died in exile in Grenoble, France.

BOOKS BY AGRIPPA

Of the Vanitie and uncertaintie of artes and sciences. 1530. Ed. by Catherine M. Dunn. Trans. by James Sandford. CSU Pr. Fresno 1974 o.p. The famous Renaissance translation, originally published in London in 1569.

The Philosophy of Natural Magic. Kessinger Pub. 1992 $27.00. ISBN 1-56459-160-3. A heady dose of Agrippa's magical theory and practice.

Three Books of Occult Philosophy or Magic. 1531–33. AMS Pr. 1981 repr. of 1898 ed. $39.50. ISBN 0-404-18401-4

BOOKS ABOUT AGRIPPA

Morley, Henry. *Cornelius Agrippa: The Life of Henry Cornelius Agrippa von Nettesheim.* 2 vols. Chapman & Hall 1856 o.p. A dated and somewhat unreliable account of Agrippa's life and works.

Nauert, Charles G., Jr. *Agrippa and the Crisis of Renaissance Thought.* Bks. Demand repr. of 1965 ed. $95.50. ISBN 0-8357-5273-9. The only comprehensive scholarly account of Agrippa's thought in English. A careful, well-documented study that places Agrippa's work within the intellectual climate of the times.

BODIN, JEAN. 1530?–1596

One of the most influential French philosophers of the sixteenth century, Jean Bodin is known today for his political thought. He received training in law at the University of Toulouse and became an advocate in Paris, where he won the favor of the royal family. His first major work, *Method for the Easy Comprehension of History* (*Methodus ad facilem historiarum cognitionem*), published in 1566, provides an overall introduction to his philosophical system. *The Six*

Bookes of a Commonweale, which appeared in French in 1576 and later in a Latin version, is in many respects his chief claim to fame as a political philosopher. It contains a strong defense of absolute sovereignty and of monarchy as the best form of government. His *Demonomania*, first published in 1580, is an elaborate account of witchcraft and sorcery intended to assist in the suppression of the black arts. *Theatre of Nature* (*Universale theatrum naturae*), printed in 1596, contains his cosmology and his speculations on the nature of the human soul, angels, and the spiritual world. *Colloquium of the Seven* (*Colloquium heptaplomeres*), composed in 1588, did not appear in print until the nineteenth century. It takes the form of a dialogue among seven sages of different religions and philosophical persuasions in search of a common creed. Although he was an active and, at times, controversial writer during the period of France's most bitter religious strife, Bodin seems to have avoided sectarian conflict while maintaining his loyalty to the Catholic church and the monarchy.

BOOKS BY BODIN

Bodin: On Sovereignty. Ed. by Julian H. Franlin. *Texts in the History of Political Thought.* Cambridge U. Pr. 1992 $15.95. ISBN 0-521-34992-3. A selection from Bodin's political works.
Colloquium of the Seven about Secrets of the Sublime. 1857. Ed. and trans. by Marion L. Daniels. Bks. Demand rpt. of 1975 ed. $159.90. ISBN 0-8357-3302-5
Method for the Easy Comprehension of History. 1566. Trans. by Beatrice Reynolds. Sage 1985 repr. of 1945 ed. o.p.
The Six Bookes of a Commonweale. 1576. Ed. by J. P. Mayer. Ayer 1979 repr. of 1962 ed. $66.50. ISBN 0-405-11680-2

BOOKS ABOUT BODIN

Franklin, Julian H. *Jean Bodin and the Rise of Absolutist Theory.* Cambridge U. Pr. 1973 o.p. An excellent account of Bodin's political thought.
————. *Jean Bodin and the Sixteenth-Century Revolution in the Methodology of Law and History.* Greenwood 1977 repr. of 1963 ed. $35.00. ISBN 0-8371-9525-X. Considers Bodin as legal theorist and philosopher of history.
King, Preston T. *The Ideology of Order: A Comparative Analysis of Jean Bodin and Thomas Hobbes.* HarpC 1974 o.p. Bodin's political ideas compared and contrasted with those of the author of *Leviathan*.
Mayer, J. P., ed. *Fundamental Studies of Jean Bodin: An Original Anthology. European Political Thought Ser.* Ayer 1979 $46.00. ISBN 0-405-11671-3. Important collection of basic studies on Bodin.

BRUNO, GIORDANO. 1548–1600

One of the most intriguing characters in late Renaissance thought, Giordano Bruno has long held a fascination for historians of science and philosophy. Revered in the nineteenth century as a martyr for the Copernican view of the universe, he has been shown in recent studies to have been far less "modern" in many of his key teachings than previously believed.

His life was a continuous series of conflicts and peregrinations. Born at Nola, near Naples, he entered the Dominican order as a youth but ran afoul of the authorities over the orthodoxy of his beliefs. He fled Italy in 1576 to avoid charges of heresy and made his way to Geneva, where he soon angered the Calvinists, then to Paris, where he lectured on philosophy for a time and published treatises on the art of memory. In 1583 he journeyed to London to join the household of the French ambassador to the English court. There he composed his most important early works, all written in Italian and published surreptitiously in London. The following four appeared in a single year, 1584:

(1) *The Ash Wednesday Supper* (*La cena de le ceneri*) contains Bruno's defense of Copernican heliocentrism, conceived as having enormous metaphysical and ethical, as well as merely astronomical, significance; (2) *On the Cause, Principle and One* (*De la causa, principio et uno*) expounds Bruno's metaphysics through the analysis of the notions of cause and principle; (3) *On the Infinite, the Universe and Worlds* (*De l'infinito, universo et mondi*) introduces Bruno's concept of the physical universe as infinite in extent, embracing innumerable finite world-systems; and (4) *The Expulsion of the Triumphant Beast* (*Lo spaccio de la betia trionfante*) puts forward a heavily symbolic proposal for a reconciliation of religious differences. Other works from the same period deal with Jewish cabala and poetic inspiration.

Bruno's published works reveal him as an innovative thinker who drew his inspiration from ancient philosophical sources as well as from the scientific works of his own time. His bold assertion of the infinity of the physical universe, for example, goes beyond the claims of COPERNICUS (see Vol. 5) or, later, GALILEO (see also Vol. 5), but it was not based on any empirical observations or mathematical calculations. Instead, it was a logical inference from Bruno's metaphysical assumption that an infinite devine principle could not but produce an infinite effect. His "modern" cosmological views must thus be seen against the background of his absorption with Hermeticism, Neoplatonism, demonic magic, and millenarianism, all of which found other spirited advocates during the Renaissance.

After his stay in England, Bruno traveled in central Europe, teaching and preaching his new vision of the universe to an often hostile audience. In 1591 he accepted an invitation to tutor a Venetian nobleman but was turned over to the Inquisition on charges of heresy. After a long imprisonment in Venice and Rome, he was burned at the stake on the Campo de' fiori in Rome on February 17, 1600. Although his love of magic and metaphysics may weaken his claim to be viewed as a forerunner of modern science, Bruno remains a legitimate martyr to the principles of free thought and expression.

BOOKS BY BRUNO

The Ash Wednesday Supper. 1584. Trans. by Stanley L. Jaki. Mouton 1975 $32.75. ISBN 90-2797-581-7

Cause, Principle, and Unity: Five Dialogues. 1584. Trans. by Jack Lindsay. Greenwood 1976 repr. of 1962 ed. $41.50. ISBN 0-8371-9040-1

The Expulsion of the Triumphant Beast. 1584. Ed. and trans. by Arthur D. Imerti. U. of Nebr. Pr. 1992 $12.95. ISBN 0-8032-6104-7

Giordano Bruno's "The Heroic Frenzies." 1585. Trans. by P. E. Memmo, Jr. U. of NC Pr. 1964 o.p. Another edition.

The Heroic Enthusiasts. 1585. Gordon Pr. 1976 $59.95. ISBN 0-8490-1947-8. One of Bruno's most important "moral" dialogues, dealing with poetic inspiration.

On the Composition of Images, Signs and Ideas. 1591. Trans. by Charles Dora. Willis Locker & Owens 1991 $39.95. ISBN 0-930279-18-2. Bruno's work on constructing images to be used in an artificial memory system.

BOOKS ABOUT BRUNO

Atanasijevic, Ksenija. *The Metaphysical and Geometrical Doctrine of Bruno as Given in his Work "De triplici minimo."* Trans. by George V. Tomashevick. Green 1972 $12.50. ISBN 0-87527-081-6. An analysis of Bruno's complex Latin philosophical poem, first published in 1591.

Gatti, Hilary. *The Renaissance Drama of Knowledge: Giordano Bruno in England.* Routledge 1989 $66.50. ISBN 0-415-03207-5. Careful study of Bruno's sojourn in Elizabethan England.

Greenberg, Sidney. *The Infinite in Giordano Bruno: With a Translation of His Dialogue "Concerning the Cause, Principle, and One."* Hippocrene Bks. 1971 o.p. An important study of the historical sources of Bruno's concept of the infinite, a central notion in his metaphysics and cosmology.

McIntrye, J. L. *Giordano Bruno.* Kessinger Pub. 1992 $24.95. ISBN 1-56459-141-7. One of the earliest attempts to analyze Bruno's philosophical works in a systematic way, first published in 1903.

Michel, Paul-Henri. *The Cosmology of Giordano Bruno.* Cornell Univ. Pr. 1973 o.p. Extremely important study of Bruno's account of the physical universe, which views his philosophy of nature as anticipating modern views.

Nelson, John C. *Renaissance Theory of Love: The Context of Giordano Bruno's "Eroici Furori."* Bks. Demand repr. of 1958 ed. $72.00. ISBN 0-317-09244-8. Places one of Bruno's most important "moral" dialogues in the context of Platonic treatises on love, a literary-philosophical genre that flourished during the Renaissance.

Paterson, Antoinette M. *The Infinite Worlds of Giordano Bruno.* C. C. Thomas 1970 o.p. "Succeeds on the whole in making Giordano Bruno relevant enough to our own time and engaging enough to students who might wish to look further into his work" (*Renaissance Quarterly*).

Singer, Dorothea W. *Giordano Bruno, His Life and Thought.* Greenwood 1968 repr. of 1950 ed. $35.00. ISBN 0-8371-0230-8. The best intellectual biography of Bruno. Contains a valuable translation of Bruno's dialogue "On the Infinite, Universe and Worlds."

Yates, Frances A. *The Art of Memory.* U. Ch. Pr. 1974 $18.95. ISBN 0-226-95001-8. Bruno's work seen in the context of the tradition of artificial memory systems, whose roots extend to classical antiquity.

———. *Giordano Bruno and the Hermetic Tradition.* U. Ch. Pr. 1990 $16.95. ISBN 0-226-95007-7. Groundbreaking study that places Bruno in the tradition of Hermetic philosophers, who accepted the authenticity of late ancient texts falsely attributed to the ancient Egyptian sage Hermes Trismegistus.

———. *Lull and Bruno: Collected Essays, Vol. 1.* Routledge Chapman & Hall 1982 $32.50. ISBN 0-7100-0952-6. A selection of Dame Frances Yates's most important studies of Giordano Bruno and Ramon Lull. Valuable for an understanding of Renaissance occultism and its influence in philosophy, art, and science.

CAJETAN, CARDINAL (THOMAS DE VIO). 1469–1534

The most able and eloquent of the Renaissance followers of the Thomist school of scholastic theology, Thomas de Vio took the name Cajetan from his hometown of Gaeta in Italy. As a youth he entered the Dominican order and, after a rigorous training in philosophy and theology, taught at the University of Padua, then a major center of Aristotelian philosophy, and later at Pavia and Rome. He became master general of the Dominican order in 1508 and a cardinal in 1517. A mission to Germany (1518–19) brought him into the forefront of the Church's confrontation with MARTIN LUTHER, with whom he engaged in a celebrated theological debate at Augsburg.

In addition to commentaries on works of ARISTOTLE (see also Vol. 3) and THOMAS AQUINAS, Cajetan composed theological treatises and essays on social philosophy. His most famous work is his massive commentary on Aquinas's *Summa Theologiae*, which played a major role in the development of scholastic theology during the sixteenth century. As a philosopher, Cajetan provided an influential exposition of the concept of analogy and came to reject the possibility of a philosophical proof of the soul's immortality.

BOOKS BY CAJETAN

The Analogy of Names and the Concept of Being. Ed. and trans. by E. A. Bushinski and H. J. Koren. Duquesne 1959 o.p. Cajetan's central metaphysical views are propounded in his analysis of the concepts of being and his development of the Thomist doctrine of analogy.

Aristotle on Interpretation: Commentary by St. Thomas and Cajetan. Trans. by J. T. Oesterle. Marquette 1962 o.p. Presents the comments of both Thomas Aquinas and his chief Renaissance expositor on the Aristotelian work *On Interpretation.*

Cardinal Cajetan Responds: A Reader in Reformation Controversy. Ed. and trans. by Jared Wicks. Bks. Demand repr. of 1978 ed. $75.00. ISBN 0-8357-7963-7. Presents a selection of the great cardinal's writings on theological issues.

Commentary on Being and Essence. 1508. Ed. and trans. by Lottie H. Kendzierski and Francis C. Wade, S.J. Marquette 1964 o.p. This is Cajetan's commentary on St. Thomas's *On Being and Essence.*

CAMPANELLA, TOMMASO. 1568–1639

A radical and innovative thinker, Tommaso Campanella lived a stormy life that was characterized by charges of political intrigue, imprisonment, philosophical speculation, poetic inspiration, and the practice of magic. Today he is best known as a political philosopher, author of the famous utopia, *The City of the Sun* (c.1602).

Like his older contemporary GIORDANO BRUNO, Campanella emerged from the intellectual milieu of the Dominican order in southern Italy with a philosophical orientation that authorities considered heretical and dangerous. Imprisoned at Naples in 1599 (the year before Bruno's execution) on charges of heresy and plotting against Spanish rule, he was not released until 1626. Following another period of imprisonment at Rome and an examination of his views by the Roman Inquisition, he fled Italy in 1634, taking refuge in Paris, where he lived his last years.

Before his imprisonment Campanella had been deeply influenced by Bernardino Telesio's defense of a naturalistic, empirically grounded philosophy of nature against the dominant Aristotelianism of the university curriculum. From Telesio he adopted the notions of heat and cold as active principles operative on matter, space, and time as prior to, and independent of, bodies and the concept of spirit as a corporeal power responsible for sensation and distinct from the intellective mind infused into humans by God. These doctrines gave a strongly naturalistic character to Campanella's concept of nature and humankind, but they were combined with an interest in magic that had its origins in ancient Neoplatonism and Hermeticism.

BOOKS BY CAMPANELLA

The City of the Sun: A Poetical Dialogue. 1623. Ed. by Daniel J. Donno. U. CA Pr. 1981 $35.00. ISBN 0-520-04034-1. Portrays a highly ordered communistic state in which political power and religious authority are united in a controlling priesthood. This beautifully presented bilingual edition includes a superb introduction.

The Defense of Galileo. 1616. Trans. by Grant McColley. Richwood Pub. 1976 repr. of 1937 ed. $16.00. ISBN 0-915172-20-8. Campanella's *Apologia* on behalf of the great scientist's defense of Copernicanism.

BOOK ABOUT CAMPANELLA

Bonansea, Bernardino M. *Tommaso Campanella: Renaissance Pioneer of Modern Thought.* Cath. U. Pr. 1969 o.p. "A balanced and informative discussion of three of the most important studies made by Campanella—epistemology, metaphysics, and ethico-political theory" (*Renaissance Quarterly*).

ERASMUS, DESIDERIUS. 1466?–1536

The most renowned scholar of his time, Desiderius Erasmus was a leading proponent of what has been termed "Christian humanism," the mastery of the humanities and classical studies coupled with a devotion to Christian piety. Born in Rotterdam, Holland, Erasmus received his early training at the famous school of the Brethren of the Common Life at Deventer, where NICHOLAS OF CUSA had studied earlier. He entered the Augustinian order and in 1492 was ordained a priest. A period at Paris devoted to the study of philosophy and theology was followed by a series of journeys to England and Italy, which brought him into contact with many of the leading humanists in Europe. During an extended visit in England (1509–14), he stayed for a time with SIR THOMAS MORE (see also Vol. 1), to whom he dedicated his *Praise of Folly* (*Moriae encomium*) in 1509; this witty satire on the foolishness of those in high places is Erasmus's most famous work. He was appointed professor of Greek and Divinity at Cambridge University where he prepared his influential edition of the New Testament. Returning to the Continent, he devoted the remainder of his life to his writing, editing, and correspondence.

A prolific writer, Erasmus is a prime example of the tremendous influence a Renaissance man of letters could attain through the medium of print. His editions of classical and early Christian authors formed the patrimony of generations of subsequent scholars. His open criticism of the hypocrisy and venality of the churchmen of his day sounded a chord that MARTIN LUTHER was to echo and doubtless aided in the progress of the Protestant Reformation. Erasmus himself was no Protestant, however. Though he advocated reform, he remained within the Catholic church, openly attacking Luther's position on the will in his treatise *On Free Will* (*De libero arbitrio*) of 1524.

Like many of his humanist contemporaries, Erasmus did not compose formal philosophical treatises but presented his thoughts on ethics, religion, and society in polished literary essays or in his voluminous correspondence. Particularly important for an understanding of his thought are the *Colloquies* (1516), *The Handbook of a Christian Soldier* (*Enchiridion militis christiani*) (1503), and *The Praise of Folly*.

BOOKS BY ERASMUS

Adages. 1508. Ed. and trans. by Margaret M. Phillips and Roger A. Mynors. *Collected Works of Erasmus.* 4 vols. U. of Toronto Pr. 1982–1992. Vol. 1 $75.00. ISBN 0-8020-2373-8. Vol. 2 $80.00. ISBN 0-8020-2412-2. Vol. 3 $100.00. ISBN 0-8020-5954-6. Vol. 4 $85.00. ISBN 0-8020-2831-4.

Christian Humanism and the Reformation: Selected Writings with the Life of Erasmus by Beatus Rhenanus. Ed. by John C. Olin. Peter Smith 1973 o.p.

Ciceronianus: Or, A Dialogue on the Best Style of Speaking. Trans. by Izora Scott. *Columbia Univ. Teachers College Contributions to Education.* AMS Pr. 1982 repr. of 1908 ed. $22.50. ISBN 0-404-55021-5. Important for an understanding of Erasmus's dedication to humanist rhetorical ideals.

Colloquies of Erasmus. 1516. Trans. by Craig R. Thompson. U. Ch. Pr. 1965 o.p.

Desiderius Erasmus Concerning the Aim and Method of Education. Ed. by William H. Woodward. *Classics in Education Ser.* Tchrs. Coll. 1964 $8.00. ISBN 0-8077-2347-9. A classic study of Erasmus's educational philosophy, accompanied by a selection of his writings on education. Extensive bibliography and a foreword by Craig R. Thompson.

Discourse on Free Will. 1524. Ed. and trans. by Ernst F. Winter. *Milestones of Thought Ser.* Continuum 1985 $8.95. ISBN 0-8044-6140-6. Contains selections from Erasmus's *De libero arbitrio* and Luther's *De servo arbitrio*.

Education of a Christian Prince. 1516. Trans. by Lester K. Born. Hippocrene Bks. 1965 o.p. An extensive introduction complements a careful translation of this classic of Christian humanism. Good bibliography.

Enchiridion of Erasmus. 1503. Trans. by Raymond Himelick. Peter Smith $16.50. ISBN 0-8446-0614-6

Erasmus on His Times: A Shortened Version of the Adages of Erasmus. Ed. by Margaret M. Phillips. Cambridge U. Pr. 1967 o.p.

The Essential Erasmus. Ed. and trans. by John P. Dolan. New Amer. Pr. 1964 $5.95. ISBN 0-452-00972-3. A handy selection of texts, including *The Praise of Folly* and *The Handbook of the Militant Christian.*

On Copia of Words and Ideas. Ed. and trans. by Donald B. King and H. David Rix. Marquette 1963 o.p. Erasmus's influential textbook for rhetorical training. It profoundly influenced Renaissance literary style and education.

The Praise of Folly. 1509. Ed. by Leonard F. Dean. Trans. by Betty Radice. Viking Penguin 1971 $7.95. ISBN 0-14-044240-5. Trans. by Hoyt H. Hudson.

Ten Colloquies. 1516. Trans. by Craig R. Thompson. Macmillan repr. of 1957 ed. ISBN 0-02-420620-2

BOOKS ABOUT ERASMUS

Allen, Percy S. *Age of Erasmus.* Russell Sage 1963 repr. of 1914 ed. o.p. *Age of Erasmus* and the following title are standard studies of Erasmus's life and times.

_____. *Erasmus: Lectures and Wayfaring Sketches.* OUP 1934 o.p.

Bainton, Roland. *Erasmus of Christendom.* Scribner 1969 o.p. Masterful intellectual biography.

Bouyer, Louis. *Erasmus and His Times.* Trans. by F. X. Murphy. Newman 1959 o.p. Translation of the French edition. A good general introduction to Erasmus's place in the history of Renaissance humanism.

Boyle, Marjorie O. *Christening Pagan Mysteries: Erasmus in Pursuit of Wisdom.* Bks. Demand repr. of 1981 ed. $49.50. ISBN 0-8357-4722-0. "Excellent, learned, and useful" (*Renaissance Quarterly*).

_____. *Erasmus on Language and Method in Theology.* Bks. Demand repr. of 1977 ed. $70.30. ISBN 0-317-26938-0. Masterful study of Erasmus's theological views.

_____. *Rhetoric and Reform: Erasmus' Civil Dispute with Luther.* Harvard Historical Monographs. HUP 1983 $25.00. ISBN 0-674-76870-1. Essential for an understanding of Erasmus's differences with Luther.

Dorey, T. A., ed. *Erasmus.* U. of NM Pr. 1970 o.p. "This volume by British and Canadian scholars "contains chapters on the importance of Erasmus as an interpreter of the Classics, as a satirist, and as a writer of letters. There is an account of his work as a Biblical scholar and religious reformer, an examination of his linguistic style, and a discussion of the Medieval background and the significance of Erasmus to our own times" (Introduction).

Huizinga, Johan. *Erasmus and The Age of Reformation.* HarpC 1957 o.p. "Excellent intellectual biography" (*Encyclopedia of Philosophy*).

Phillips, Margaret M. *Erasmus and the Northern Renaissance.* Rowman 1981 o.p. Excellent introduction to Erasmus's works, summarizing the results of recent scholarship.

Rabil, Albert. *Erasmus and the New Testament: The Mind of a Christian Humanist.* Bks. Demand repr. of 1972 ed. $51.50. ISBN 0-317-08044-X

Schoeck, Richard J. *Erasmus grandescens: The Growth of a Humanist's Mind and Spirituality.* Coronet Bks. 1988 $57.50. ISBN 90-6004-398-7. Fine intellectual biography.

_____. *Erasmus of Europe: The Making of a Humanist.* Rowman 1991 $49.75. ISBN 0-389-20953-8. Traces Erasmus's rise to prominence as a scholar and man of letters.

Screech, M. A. *Erasmus: Ecstasy and the Praise of Folly.* Viking Penguin 1989 $7.95. ISBN 0-14-055235-9. Valuable study of the *Moriae encomium.*

Smith, Preserved. *Erasmus: A Study of His Life, Ideals and Place in History.* 1923. Dover 1962 o.p. Standard biography.

_____. _The Renaissance, the Reformation and the Erratic Behavior of Desiderius Erasmus._ 2 vols. Am. Classical Coll. Pr. 1991 $298.50. ISBN 0-89266-705-2. Important studies by the great biographer of Erasmus.

FICINO, MARSILIO. 1433–1499

The leading figure in the Renaissance revival of Platonism, Marsilio Ficino profoundly influenced the philosophical thought of his own and following centuries. Born near Florence, the son of a physician, Ficino received his early training in philosophy, medicine, and theology and devoted himself to the study of Greek. His learning attracted the attention of one of his father's eminent patients, Cosimo de' Medici, of the powerful Florentine banking family, and in 1462 Cosimo established him at a villa and supplied him with Greek manuscripts for translation. Here Ficino set up his famous Florentine Academy, devoted to the study and celebration of PLATO's (see Vol. 3) teachings. He continued to receive the active support of the Medici until their expulsion from Florence in 1494.

Ficino's labors as a translator provided his Greekless contemporaries with access to the greatest works of the ancient Platonic tradition. His Latin version of the dialogues of Plato, published in 1484, made the entirety of Plato available for the first time in translation. Ficino also prepared translations of other important sources, such as the Neoplatonist PLOTINUS, Proclus, Iamblichus, Pseudo-Dionysius the Areopagite, and the Greek works attributed to Hermes Trismegistus (a fabled Egyptian priest supposedly contemporary with Moses).

To Ficino, the Platonic tradition represented an ongoing heritage of divinely inspired ancient wisdom reconcilable with Christian revelation. His reading of Plato in the light of late Neoplatonists, such as Plotinus and Proclus, survived long after the Renaissance and remained the prevalent interpretation of Plato's thought until comparatively recent times. His chief philosophical work, _Platonic Theology_ (1482), represents an attempt to demonstrate the immortality of the human soul on Platonic grounds in a way that was consistent with Christian doctrine. It represents reality as a hierarchy, from God down to material bodies, with rational soul, the level proper to man, as a mean that participates in the characteristics of both higher and lower beings. This scheme, derived with important modifications from Plotinus, was to influence many later Platonists, including Ficino's younger friend and colleague GIOVANNI PICO DELLA MIRANDOLA.

Ficino's devotion to Platonism must thus be seen within the context of his Christianity. He was ordained a priest in 1437 and later served as a canon of the Florentine cathedral. His intellectual synthesis of Platonism and Christianity, however, so powerfully appealing to the Medici circle, was a far cry from the reformist zeal of Savonarola, whose rise to power in 1494 saw Ficino enter into a quiet retirement until his death.

In addition to the titles listed below, see also the books by Garin, Hankins, Kristeller, Robb, and Walker in the "General Works" at the beginning of this chapter.

BOOKS BY FICINO

The Book of Life. Trans. and intro. by Charles Boer. Spring Pubns. 1980 $16.00. ISBN 0-88214-212-7. First English translation of Ficino's important treatise on medicine and natural magic.

Commentary on Plato's Symposium on Love. 1469. Trans. by Sears R. Jayne. Spring Pubns. 1985 $18.50. ISBN 0-88214-601-7. Careful translation of one of Ficino's most influential works, a classic in the rich Renaissance philosophical literature on love.

The Letters of Marsilio Ficino. 1495. 4 vols. Vols. 1–3 Schocken 1985 o.p. Vol. 4 Paul &
    Co. Pubs. 1989 $30.00. ISBN 0-85683-070-4. Carefully executed translation from
    Ficino's published correspondence, a rich source for his philosophical teachings.
Marsilio Ficino: The 'Philebus' Commentary. Ed. and trans. by Michael J. B. Allen. U. CA
    Pr. 1975 $50.00. ISBN 0-520-03977-7. Careful translation and study of Ficino's great
    commentary on Plato's *Philebus.*
Marsilio Ficino and the Phaedran Charioteer. Ed. and trans. by Michael J. B. Allen. U. CA
    Pr. 1981 $47.50. ISBN 0-520-04222-0. Masterly translation and introduction to the
    various texts in which Ficino discusses the enduring Platonic image of the rational
    soul as charioteer in the *Phaedrus.*
Three Books on Life: A Critical Edition and Translation with Introduction and Notes. Ed.
    and trans. by Carol V. Kaske and John R. Clarke. *Medieval and Renaissance Texts
    and Studies.* MRTS 1989 $32.00. ISBN 0-86698-041-5. Excellent new translation with
    valuable introduction and notes.

BOOKS ABOUT FICINO

Allen, Michael J. B. *Icastes: Marsilio Ficino's Interpretation of Plato's "Sophist."* U. CA Pr.
    1989 $40.00. ISBN 0-520-06419-4. Five masterful studies of Ficino's interpretation of
    this crucial dialogue, together with a critical edition and translation of Ficino's
    comments.
————. *The Platonism of Marsilio Ficino: A Study of His Phaedrus Commentary, Its
    Sources and Genesis.* U. CA Pr. 1984 $47.50. ISBN 0-520-05152-1. A rich and learned
    account of Ficino's Platonism, centering on the *Phaedrus* commentary. An essential
    work.
Collins, Ardis B. *The Secular Is Sacred: Platonism and Thomism in Marsilio Ficino's
    Platonic Theology.* Nijhoff 1974 o.p. Emphasizes Ficino's debt to Thomas Aquinas.
Eisenbichler, Konrad, and Olga Z. Pugliese, eds. *Ficino and Renaissance Neoplatonism.*
    MRTS 1985 $16.00. ISBN 0-919473-59-8. Valuable collection of studies.
Jayne, Sears R. *John Colet and Marsilio Ficino.* Greenwood 1980 repr. of 1963 ed. $35.00.
    ISBN 0-313-22606-7. Discusses Ficino's influence on English humanism.
Kristeller, Paul Oskar. *The Philosophy of Marsilio Ficino.* Peter Smith 1964 o.p. Long a
    classic, this is still the best general study of Ficino. The English version lacks the
    comprehensive annotation of the Italian and German editions.

GALILEI, GALILEO. 1564–1642

Galileo Galilei, the great astronomer and physicist whose researches played
so crucial a role in the history of science, also occupies an important place in
the history of philosophy for his part in overthrowing the predominant
Aristotelian concept of the nature of the universe. Galileo considered himself a
philosopher and referred to himself as such on the title pages of his most
influential works. Much recent research has been devoted to examining both
the philosophical background of Galileo's scientific achievements and the
philosophical implications of his scientific method.

Born in Pisa, the eldest son of a famous music theorist, Galileo entered on the
study of medicine at the University of Pisa but quickly shifted his interest to
mathematics. From 1589 to 1592, he taught mathematics at Pisa while studying
independently with Jacopo Mazzoni, a distinguished professor of philosophy.
His earliest scientific works, directed against ARISTOTLE's (see also Vol. 3)
account of freely falling bodies, date from this period. In 1592 he moved to
Padua, where he lectured on mathematics and astronomy, and by 1597 he was
defending the Copernican helicocentric theory of the universe in a letter to his
friend Mazzoni.

When in 1609, he learned of the invention of the telescope in Holland, Galileo
quickly designed an improved version of the instrument for his own astronomi-

cal observations. His startling discoveries—including the satellites of Jupiter—were revealed in 1610 in his *Starry Messenger* (*Sidereus nuncius*), which led to his appointment as mathematician and philosopher to the Grand Duke of Tuscany. On a visit to Rome in 1611, he demonstrated the power of his instrument and defended the Copernican worldview in learned circles.

Church authorities were divided on the question of whether the Copernican theory was consistent with scriptural accounts of the cosmos, and Galileo's position was attacked on theological grounds. He defended himself eloquently in his famous *Letter to the Grand Duchess Christina* (1615), arguing for the independence of scientific inquiry from theological constraints. Nevertheless, in the following year, he was forbidden to hold or teach the Copernican view. Retiring to Florence to pursue his scientific researches, Galileo let the Copernican question lie until a new pope, Urban VIII, seemed to offer a more favorable reception to his views. In 1632 he brought out his great *Dialogue Concerning the Two Chief World Systems*, a presentation of the Ptolemaic-Aristotelian and Copernican systems heavily weighted in favor of the scientific superiority of the latter. In spite of the support of his Florentine and Roman friends, Galileo was tried and forced to recant his defense of helicocentrism under the threat of torture; the *Dialogue* was placed on the *Index of Prohibited Books* and its author sentenced to house arrest for life. Galileo's last years were spent in scientific investigations that culminated in the publication of his *Discourses on Two New Sciences* (1638).

Galileo's legacy as a philosopher lies in his outspoken defense of the autonomy of scientific investigation from philosophical and theological authority, and his conviction that mathematical proofs can and should be sought in physical science, that celestial and terrestrial phenomena can be accounted for by a single set of scientific laws, and that scientific explanations cannot be divorced from direct empirical observation of phenomena.

In addition to the titles listed here, see also the books by Boas, Burtt, Dijksterhuis, Drake and Drabkin, Koyré, Randall, and Wallace in "General Works" at the beginning of this chapter.

BOOKS BY GALILEO

Dialogue Concerning the Two Chief World Systems, Ptolemaic and Copernican. 1632. Trans. by Stillman Drake. U. CA Pr. 1967 $15.95. ISBN 0-520-00450-7

Discoveries and Opinions of Galileo. Doubleday 1957 $7.95. ISBN 0-385-09239-3. Includes *The Starry Messenger* (1610), *Letter to the Grand Duchess Christina* (1615), and excerpts from *Letters on Sunspots* (1613) and *The Assayer* (1623).

Galileo's Early Notebooks: The Physical Questions. Trans. by William A. Wallace. U. of Notre Dame Pr. 1977 o.p. Reveals Galileo's early dependence on scholastic sources.

On Motion and On Mechanics. Ed. and trans. by I. E. Drabkin and Stillman Drake. *Publications in Medieval Science.* U. of Wis. Pr. 1960 o.p. Galileo's early treatise on motion (c.1590), criticizing Aristotle's theories, and his treatise on mechanics (c.1600), both with valuable introductions.

Operations of the Geometric and Military Compass. Trans. by Stillman Drake. Smithsonian 1978 $9.95. ISBN 0-87474-383-4

Two New Sciences: Including "Centers of Gravity" and "Force of Percussion." 1638. Ed. and trans. by Stillman Drake. Bks. Demand repr. of 1974 ed. $91.30. ISBN 0-317-55783-1

BOOKS ABOUT GALILEO

Blackwell, Richard J. *Galileo, Bellarmine and the Bible.* U. of Notre Dame Pr. 1991 $29.95. ISBN 0-268-01024-2. Outstanding study of the theological background to

Galileo's defense of Copernican cosmology. Includes translations of several major texts involved in the controversy.

Butts, Robert E., and Joseph C. Pitt, eds. *New Perspectives on Galileo.* Kluwer Ac. 1978 $80.00. ISBN 90-277-0859-2. An important collection of recent studies.

Clavelin, Maurice. *The Natural Philosophy of Galileo: Essay on the Origins and Formation of Classical Mechanics.* Trans. by A. J. Pomerans. MIT Pr. 1974 o.p. Influential study of the philosophical background of Galileo's scientific work.

Drake, Stillman. *Cause, Experiment and Science: A Galilean Dialogue Incorporating a New English Translation of Galileo's "Bodies That Stay Atop Water, Or Move in It."* U. Ch. Pr. 1985 $9.95. ISBN 0-226-16230-3. Provides a valuable introduction to Galileo's work on floating bodies.

_____. *Galileo. Past Masters Ser.* OUP 1980 $6.95. ISBN 0-19-287526-4. Good general introduction to Galileo's achievements.

_____. *Galileo: Pioneer Scientist.* U. of Toronto Pr. 1990 $40.00. ISBN 0-8020-2725-3. Latest contribution by the preeminent historian of Galileo's scientific practices.

_____. *Galileo at Work: His Scientific Biography.* U. Ch. Pr. 1978 o.p. Important, if somewhat controversial, portrait of Galileo's scientific career. Emphasizes the study of the great scientist's research techniques, rather than his finished works.

_____. *Galileo Studies: Personality, Tradition, and Revolution.* U. of Mich. Pr. 1970 o.p. Valuable series of papers on Galileo's scientific achievements, emphasizing his associates and opponents in his physical and astronomical investigations.

_____. *Telescopes, Tides and Tactics: A Galilean Dialogue about the "Starry Messenger" and Systems of the World.* U. Ch. Pr. 1983 $22.50. ISBN 0-226-16231-1. An introduction to Galileo's approach to defending Copernicanism.

Finocchiaro, Maurice A. *The Galileo Affair: A Documentary History.* U. CA Pr. 1989 $60.00. ISBN 0-520-06360-0. Very valuable collection of texts and documents relating to the condemnation of Galileo by Church authorities. Excellent commentary.

_____. *Galileo and the Art of Reasoning: Rhetorical Foundations of Logic and Scientific Method.* Kluwer Ac. 1980 $80.00. ISBN 90-277-1094-5. "Finocchiaro certainly succeeds in making his point that the *Dialogue* makes a splendid work-book for anyone who wants to see critical reason in action. . . . The book will be very useful for anyone who is working with the complex argument of the *Dialogue*" (*Renaissance Quarterly*).

Geymonat, Ludovico. *Galileo Galilei: A Biography and Inquiry into His Philosophy of Science.* Ed. and trans. by Stillman Drake. McGraw 1965 o.p. Influential intellectual biography of Galileo, carefully tracing the development of his scientific works and his ongoing battle with ecclesiastical authorities.

Golino, Carlo L., ed. *Galileo Reappraised.* U. CA Pr. 1966 $30.00. ISBN 0-520-00490-6. Five papers by leading Galileo scholars on a range of topics, including his role as a man of letters and his religious views.

Koyré, Alexandre. *Galileo Studies.* Trans. by J. Mephem. Humanities 1978 o.p. Discusses Galileo's achievement from a philosophical perspective. Koyré emphasizes the Platonic character of Galileo's view of reality.

McMullin, Ernan. *Galileo Man of Science.* Scholars Bookshelf 1988 $50.00. ISBN 0-945726-02-3. Includes a comprehensive bibliography of works on Galileo (1940–64).

Pitt, Joseph C. *Galileo, Human Knowledge, and the Book of Nature. Univ. of Western Ontario Ser. in Philosophy of Science.* Kluwer Ac. 1992 $87.00. ISBN 0-7923-1510-3. Stresses Galileo's importance as a theoretician of knowledge, developing a modern scientific methodology.

Redondi, Pietro. *Galileo Heretic.* Trans. by Raymond Rosenthal. Princeton U. Pr. 1990 $42.50. ISBN 0-691-08451-3. Extremely controversial but valuable study of the theological implications of Galileo's writings in Counter-Reformation Rome. Redondi makes use of an anonymous manuscript in the archives of the Holy Office to argue that the atomist views Galileo defended in his polemical work *The Assayer* were considered heretical long before the condemnation of his Copernicanism.

Ronan, Colin a. *Galileo*. Putnam Pub. Group 1974 o.p. Nicely illustrated, readable account of Galileo's overall achievement.

Santillana, Giorgio de. *The Crime of Galileo*. U. Ch. Pr. 1978 $14.00. ISBN 0-226-73481-1. Influential if dated account of Galileo's struggle with ecclesiastical authorities.

Shapere, Dudley. *Galileo: A Philosophical Study*. U. Ch. Pr. 1974 o.p. Fundamental study by a distinguished philosopher of science.

Shea, William R. *Galileo's Intellectual Revolution: Middle Period, 1610–1632*. Watson Pub. Intl. 1977 $8.95. ISBN 0-685-56651-X. "An informative and illuminating contribution to Galileo studies . . . concise and well written" (*Renaissance Quarterly*).

Wallace, William A. *Galileo and His Sources*. Princeton U. Pr. 1984 $52.50. ISBN 0-691-08355-X. Emphasizes Galileo's dependence on scholastic Aristotelian sources, showing his ties to thinkers such as Christopher Clavius and Jacopo Mazzoni.

———. *Galileo, the Jesuits and the Medieval Aristotle*. Collected Studies Ser. Ashgate Pub. Co. 1991 $87.95. ISBN 0-86078-297-2. Further research on the extent of Galileo's indebtedness to his teachers at the Jesuit Collegio Romano.

———. *Galileo's Logical Treatises: A Translation, with Notes and Commentary, of His Appropriated Latin Questions on Aristotle's "Posterior Analytics."* and *Galileo's Logic of Discovery and Proof: The Background, Content and Use of His Appropriated Treatises on Aristotle's "Posterior Analytics."* 2 vols. Kluwer Ac. 1992 $199.00. ISBN 0-7923-1579-0. A painstaking study of the manuscript questions on Aristotle's great treatise on scientific demonstration that Galileo employed in his own studies. Wallace contends that these documents were influential in the development of Galileo's own scientific method.

———. *Prelude to Galileo: Essays on Medieval and Sixteenth-Century Sources of Galileo's Thought*. Kluwer Ac. 1981 o.p. "Required reading for the expert, the early chapters particularly provide a lucid introduction to that cloudy world of science from the High Middle Ages through the 17th Century" (*Choice*).

MACHIAVELLI, NICCOLO. 1469–1527

Niccolo Machiavelli was a Florentine diplomat, political theorist, and man of letters whose name has become synonymous with political amorality and opportunism as a result of his candid and uncompromising portrayal of the effective ruler in *The Prince*. From 1498 to 1512, during the period of republican government in Florence, Machiavelli enjoyed successful career as public servant and diplomat, but on the reinstatement of the Medici he was dismissed and sent into exile. Frustrated by his enforced absence from political life, he turned his attention to a serious study of the classics. The perspective gained from this reading, coupled with his reflection on his own experiences and observations of political events, formed the basis for his writings.

The Prince, written in 1513 but published posthumously in 1532, was dedicated to Lorenzo de' Medici, ruler of Florence. It is a handbook for successful rule, predicated on the assumptions that human nature is constant, that the political skill (*virtù*) exhibited by successful rulers in the past in dealing with adverse fortune can be drawn on to instruct a contemporary prince in similar circumstances, and that only such a prince—able to be ruthless when necessary—will be strong enough to unite Italy and free her from foreign dominion. This represents a bold departure from the standard handbooks of the education of princes, which emphasized the moral improvement of the people through the example of a morally superior ruler.

Machiavelli's other works include the *Discourses on Livy* (1532), *The Art of War* (1521), *History of Florence* (1532), and a popular comedy, *La Mandragola* (1524). His correspondence is filled with witty and often irreverent reflections on contemporary events and personalities.

BOOKS BY MACHIAVELLI

The Art of War. 1521. Trans. by Ellis Farneworth. Introduction by Neal Wood. Da Capo 1990 $12.95. ISBN 0-306-80412-3. Machiavelli's learned treatise on the theory and practice of warfare.

The Chief Works and Others. Trans. by Allan Gilbert. 3 vols. Duke 1989 $100.00. ISBN 0-685-27155-2. The most comprehensive and accurate English edition.

The Discourses. 1532. Ed. by Bernard Crick. Viking Penguin 1984 $6.95. ISBN 0-14-044428-9. Machiavelli's masterly exposition and commentary on Livy, essential for an understanding of his political thought.

The Portable Machiavelli. Ed. by Peter Bondanella and Mark Musa. Viking Penguin 1979 o.p. Excellent selection from the full range of Machiavelli's writings.

The Prince. 1532. Ed. by Daniel Donno. Bantam 1984 $2.50. ISBN 0-553-21278-8

BOOKS ABOUT MACHIAVELLI

Gilbert, A. H. *Machiavelli's "Prince" and Its Forerunners.* B & N Imports 1968 o.p. Seminal study that views *The Prince* against the background of traditional "advice to princes" literature. Includes a detailed commentary on *The Prince*.

Gilbert, Felix. *Machiavelli and Guicciardini: Politics and History in Sixteenth Century Florence.* Norton 1984 $9.95. ISBN 0-393-30123-0. Places Machiavelli in the political context of his times.

Mansfield, Harvey C., Jr. *Machiavelli's New Modes and Orders: A Study of the "Discourses on Livy."* Cornell Univ. Pr. 1979 o.p. Controversial study that gives an unorthodox interpretation of the *Discourses*.

Parel, Anthony J. *The Machiavellian Cosmos.* Yale U. Pr. 1992 $30.00. ISBN 0-300-05169-7. Questions the modernity of Machiavelli's thought by examining his views on the nature of humans and the universe.

Pitkin, Hanna F. *Fortune Is a Woman: Gender and Politics in the Thought of Nicolò Machiavelli.* U. CA Pr. 1984 $45.00. ISBN 0-520-04932-2. "Wide-ranging and deep-reaching study on the psychological and political problem of 'autonomy.' . . . Filled with insights, broad learning, and wisdom" (*Renaissance Quarterly*).

Pocock, J. G. A. *The Machiavellian Moment: Florentine Political Thought and the Atlantic Republican Tradition.* Princeton U. Pr. 1975 $27.95. ISBN 0-691-10029-2. Valuable analysis of Machiavelli's influence as a defender of republican ideals. Essential for an understanding of the *Discourses*.

Ridolfi, Roberto. *The Life of Niccolò Machiavelli.* Trans. by C. Grayson. U. Ch. Pr. 1963 o.p. Comprehensive biography by a leading Machiavelli scholar.

Ruffo-Fiore, Silvia. *Niccolò Machiavelli. World Authors Ser.* G. K. Hall 1982 o.p. Good general introduction to Machiavelli's life and works.

Strauss, Leo. *Thoughts on Machiavelli.* U. Ch. Pr. 1984 $19.95. ISBN 0-226-77704-9. Original and controversial account of Machiavelli's politics.

MONTAIGNE, MICHEL EYQUEM DE. 1533–1592

Michel Eyquem de Montaigne, the great French essayist, was not a systematic philosopher. Yet his *Essays*, published in three editions between 1580 and 1595, exercised a powerful influence in philosophical circles with their acute reflections on customs, biases, and the human condition. Born to an aristocratic family near Bordeaux, Montaigne enjoyed a life of relative retirement, devoted to his writings. His tolerance and lack of dogmatism enabled him to avoid the religious controversies raging in France, and, apart from a visit to Italy and a period of service as mayor of Bordeaux, his time was largely given over to his intellectual pursuits.

The main subject of Montaigne's *Essays* was himself, with all his foibles. His preoccupation with himself reflects a tendency present in many Renaissance humanists, beginning with PETRARCH, to make the individual with his or her personal peculiarities an object of study. Yet with Montaigne this is no mere literary concern, but the starting point of a philosophical employment of introspection that would lead ultimately to DESCARTES's (see Vol. 5) method of doubt.

It cannot be said that a consistent philosophical position runs through the *Essays*. Knowing Montaigne, we should not expect one. Yet patterns of thought emerge, recurring themes from Stoic and Epicurean sources, as well as an abiding skepticism. The most sustained presentation of his skepticism may be found in his essay *Apology for Raymond Sebonde*, in which he expresses his concern for the inability of human reason to arrive at knowledge by its own devices.

In addition to the titles listed here, see also Popkin's *History of Scepticism* in the "General Works" at the beginning of this chapter.

BOOKS BY MONTAIGNE

The Complete Essays of Montaigne. 1580–95. Trans. by Donald M. Frame. Stanford U. Pr. 1958 $45.00. ISBN 0-8047-0485-6. Frame's great translation is a model of accuracy and eloquence.

The Complete Works of Montaigne: Essays, Travel Journal, Letters. Trans. by Donald M. Frame. Stanford U. Pr. 1957 $55.00. ISBN 0-8047-0484-8. Most accurate and readable modern English translation of Montaigne. "Contains Montaigne's famous 'Essays,' written from 1572 to 1592; the 'Travel Journal,' an account of his trip to Germany, Switzerland and Italy in 1580; and the thirty-nine 'Letters,' most of which were written when Montaigne was mayor of Bordeaux from 1581 to 1585" (*N.Y. Herald Tribune Bk. Review*).

BOOKS ABOUT MONTAIGNE

Brush, Craig. *Montaigne and Bayle: Variations on the Theme of Skepticism*. Nijhoff 1966 o.p. Evaluates Montaigne's role in the skeptical tradition. "[Brush] has succeeded marvellously well" (*Journal of the History of Philosophy*).

Frame, Donald M. *Montaigne: A Biography*. N. Point Pr. 1984 repr. of 1965 ed. o.p. Outstanding life by the leading American authority on Montaigne.

——. *Montaigne's Discovery of Man: The Humanization of a Humanist*. Greenwood 1983 repr. of 1955 ed. $39.75. ISBN 0-313-24120-1. Classic study of Montaigne's humanism.

Hallie, Philip P. *The Scar of Montaigne: An Essay in Personal Philosophy*. Wesleyan Univ. Pr. 1966 o.p. "Brings philosophical as well as literary discipline to bear primarily on the skeptical aspects of Montaigne's thinking. The result is a sympathetic and penetrating analysis" (*Choice*).

La Charité, Raymond. *The Concept of Judgment in Montaigne*. Nijhoff 1968 o.p. Provides a close analysis of Montaigne's use of the concept of judgment in relation to allied notions such as "understanding," "reason," and "knowledge."

——, ed. *"O un Amy!" Essays on Montaigne in Honor of Donald M. Frame*. French Forum 1977 $16.95. ISBN 0-917058-04-6. An important collection of studies dedicated to the great translator and interpreter of Montaigne.

Regosin, Richard. *The Matter of My Book: Montaigne's "Essais" as the Book of the Self*. U. CA Pr. 1977 $35.00. ISBN 0-520-03476-7. "One of the best recent books on Montaigne" (*Renaissance Quarterly*).

Sayce, R. A. *The Essays of Montaigne: A Critical Exploration*. Northwestern U. Pr. 1972 o.p. "This book takes as its starting-point . . . [Montaigne's] contradictions . . . and aims at a total picture of the Essais, their thought and form, which will not throw one side into relief by suppressing another. The contradictions are examined in detail and through them the elements of a final unity emerge" (Publisher's note).

Screech, M. A. *Montaigne and Melancholy: The Wisdom of the Essays*. Susquehanna U. Pr. 1984 $29.50. ISBN 0-941664-08-2. Excellent guide to the *Essays*.

MORE, SIR THOMAS. 1478–1535

Humanist, statesman, martyr, and saint, Sir Thomas More was one of the leading figures of the English Renaissance. Educated at Oxford University, he combined the study of law with a mastery of Greek and an interest in the humanistic disciplines. In 1497 he met and befriended ERASMUS, who later dedicated his *Praise of Folly* to him. More was also influenced by GIOVANNI PICO DELLA MIRANDOLA and composed a biography of the Italian Platonist that he published with a translation of some of his works.

More's most influential work was his *Utopia*, published in Louvain in 1516. It is a fanciful depiction of an island whose inhabitants practice community ownership, religious toleration, and control of their baser instincts. More's creation was intended both as a stinging critique of the social evils of contemporary England and as an image of the ideal state.

Like Erasmus, More was not led to religious dissent by his reformist ideas. His decision to engage in political life in a time of religious confrontation led to his martyrdom. While serving as lord chancellor under Henry VIII, More opposed the king's divorce of Catherine of Aragon, was removed from office, and later tried and executed for refusing to swear allegiance to the king as head of the Church of England. He composed *A Dialogue of Comfort against Tribulation* (1534) during his imprisonment.

In addition to the titles listed here, see also the books by Davis, Figgis, Manuel and Manuel, and Skinner in the "General Works" in this chapter.

BOOKS BY MORE

A Dialogue of Comfort against Tribulation. 1534. Ed. by Louis L. Martz and Frank Manley. Yale U. Pr. 1976 $80.00. ISBN 0-300-01609-3. More's consolatory piece penned during his imprisonment. The Yale edition is definitive.

Utopia. 1516. Ed. and trans. by George M. Logan and Robert M. Adams. Cambridge U. Pr. 1989 $37.95. ISBN 0-521-34573-1. Trans. by John Sheehan and John Donnelly. Marquette Univ. Pr. 1984 $4.95. ISBN 0-87462-448-7. Ed by John Dolan and James Greene. New Amer. Pr. 1984 $4.95. ISBN 0-452-00687-2. Ed. and trans. by Robert M. Adams. Norton 1991 $6.95. ISBN 0-393-96145-1. Trans. by Paul Turner. Viking Penguin 1965 $4.95. ISBN 0-14-044165-4. Trans. by Peter K. Marshall. Washington Square Pr. 1990 $3.95. ISBN 0-671-72653-6. Ed. by Edward Surtz. Yale U. Pr. 1964 $7.95. ISBN 0-685-42415-4

BOOKS ABOUT MORE

Chambers, Raymond W. *The Place of St. Thomas More in English Literature and History.* Haskell 1969 repr. of 1937 ed. $75.00. ISBN 0-8383-0523-7.

———. *Thomas More.* U. of Mich. Pr. 1958 o.p. A standard work, still valuable.

Fox, Alistair. *Thomas More: History and Providence.* Yale U. Pr. 1983 $35.00. ISBN 0-300-02951-9. Valuable study of More's intellectual outlook.

———. *Utopia: An Elusive Vision.* Twayne 1992 $21.95. ISBN 0-8057-9419-0. Excellent account of the place of More's famous book in the history of utopian literature.

Hexter, Jack H. *More's Utopia: The Biography of an Idea. History of Ideas Ser.* Greenwood 1976 repr. of 1952 ed. $39.75. ISBN 0-8371-8947-0. Justifiably famous analysis of the methods and motives that underlie More's great work.

Kautsky, Karl. *Thomas More and His Utopia.* Humanities 1980 o.p.

Kenny, Anthony. *Thomas More. Past Masters Ser.* OUP 1983 $6.95. ISBN 0-19-287573-6. Solid general introduction to More by a distinguished historian of philosophy.

Logan, George M. *The Meaning of More's Utopia.* Princeton U. Pr. 1983 $42.50. ISBN 0-691-06557-8. "This informed and humane work is . . . among the *optimi* I have seen on Utopia" (*Renaissance Quarterly*).

Marius, Richard. *Thomas More: A Biography*. Knopf 1984 o.p. Outstanding biography, essential to an understanding of a complex and often enigmatic figure.

Martz, Louis L. *Thomas More: The Search for the Inner Man*. Yale U. Pr. 1990 $16.95. ISBN 0-300-04784-3. Good intellectual analysis of More.

Surtz, Edward L. *The Praise of Pleasure: Philosophy, Education, and Communism in More's "Utopia."* HUP 1957 o.p. "The book is well worth the attention of readers who desire to penetrate beneath the surface of such a world-classic as 'Utopia' and the age which produced it" (*Library Journal*).

NICHOLAS OF CUSA (NICHOLAS CUSANUS). 1401?–1464

Churchman, humanist, and philosopher, Nicholas of Cusa was born in Kues (Latin, Cusa), Germany, and educated at the famous school of the Brethren of the Common Life in Deventer, Holland. Following university training in philosophy, theology, and canon law, he began a career as a legal adviser to church officials. He served on several important embassies as papal representative and was made a cardinal in 1448.

Nicholas's philosophical works are characterized by their concern with the problem of knowledge. *On Learned Ignorance* (*De Docta Ignorantia*) and *On Conjectures* (*De conjecturis*), both written in 1440, emphasize the limitation placed on human reason by its need to extend its knowledge through a comparison of the unknown with the known. Since absolute precision can never be attained by a finite comparative power, the absolute truth is unattainable by rational means. Wisdom thus consists in recognizing the approximate, conjectural character of all rational theories, and Nicholas was hopeful that reflection on the limits of rational investigation would serve to banish dogmatism from philosophical and theological disputes.

In his cosmological speculations, he asserted the indeterminacy of the physical universe, and hence denied that the earth could be located precisely at the center of the cosmos. He thus represents a step toward a more open-ended view of the universe and was doubtless influential on such later cosmologists as GIORDANO BRUNO.

BOOKS BY NICHOLAS OF CUSA

De ludo globi: The Game of Spheres. 1463–64. Trans. by Pauline W. Trinkaus. Abaris Bks. 1986 $20.00. ISBN 0-89835-068-9. Important for an understanding of Nicholas's later thought.

Idiota de mente (The Layman: About Mind). 1450. Trans. by Clyde Lee Miller. Abaris Bks. 1979 $20.00. ISBN 0-913870-65-X. Trans. by M. L. Fuhrer. MRTS 1989 $10.00. ISBN 0-919473-56-3

Nicholas of Cusa on God as Not-Other: A Translation and an Appraisal of De Li Non Aliud. 1462. Trans. by Jasper Hopkins. Banning Pr. 1987 $20.00. ISBN 0-938060-38-4. "Provide[s] students of Cusanus with the opportunity of studying his later philosophical ideas more fully than before" (*Renaissance Quarterly*).

Nicholas of Cusa on Interreligious Harmony: Text, Concordance and Translation of "De pace fidei." 1453. Ed. by James E. Biechler and H. Lawrence Bond. *Texts and Studies in Religion*. E. Mellen 1991 $69.95. ISBN 0-88946-736-6. A plea for religious harmony in the shadow of the fall of Constantinople.

Nicholas of Cusa On Learned Ignorance: A Translation and an Appraisal of De Docta Ignorantia. 1440. Trans. by Jasper Hopkins. Banning Pr. 1985 $23.00. ISBN 0-938060-30-9. Nicholas's most important early work, with a close philosophical commentary.

Nicholas of Cusa's Debate with John Wenck: A Translation and an Appraisal of De Ignota Litteratura and Apologia Doctae Ignorantiae. 1449. Trans. by Jasper Hopkins. Banning Pr. 1988 $23.00. ISBN 0-938060-40-6. Presents the attack on Nicholas's *On*

Learned Ignorance by John Wenck (a scholar at the University of Heidelberg), together with Nicholas's reply.

Nicholas of Cusa's Dialectical Mysticism: Text, Translation, and Interpretive Study of De Visione Dei. 1453. Trans. by Jasper Hopkins. Banning Pr. 1988 $25.00. ISBN 0-938060-39-2.

Nicholas of Cusa's Metaphysic of Contradiction. Trans. by Jasper Hopkins. Banning Pr. 1983 $23.00. ISBN 0-938060-25-2. Nicholas's *De dato patris luminum (On the Gift of the Father of Lights).*

On Learned Ignorance. 1440. Trans. by Germain Heron. Hyperion Conn. 1991 repr. of 1945 ed. $23.00. ISBN 0-88355-806-8

BOOKS ABOUT NICHOLAS OF CUSA

Bett, Henry. *Nicholas of Cusa. Great Medieval Churchmen Ser.* Richwood Pub. 1976 repr. of 1932 ed. o.p. Long a standard account of Nicholas's life and work.

Hopkins, Jasper. *A Concise Introduction to the Philosophy of Nicholas of Cusa.* Banning Pr. 1986 $20.00. ISBN 0-938060-32-5. "Offers . . . not only an introductory essay on Nicholas's life, some problems of interpretation, and some of his important philosophical ideas, but also an English translation of *De possest* (1460) alongside its Latin text" (*Renaissance Quarterly*).

Sigmund, Paul E. *Nicholas of Cusa and Medieval Political Thought.* HUP 1963 o.p. Considers the cardinal as a political philosopher against the background of his times.

Watts, Pauline Moffit. *Nicholaus Cusanus: A Fifteenth-Century Vision of Man.* E. J. Brill 1982 o.p. The best overall account of Nicholas's philosophy in English.

PARACELSUS, PHILIPPUS AUREOLUS (THEOPHRASTUS BOMBASTUS VON HOHENHEIM). 1493?–1541

Swiss physician, chemist, alchemist, and mystic, Philippus Aureolus Paracelsus spent his life traveling, healing, teaching, and writing. The son of a physician, he was attracted to the study of metallurgy, and his medical practice emphasized the use of chemical over herbal remedies. Paracelsus rejected the traditional medical authorities of Greek and Arabic science, such as Galen, AVICENNA, and Celsus (his name can be interpreted to mean "beyond Celsus"). Instead, he steeped himself in the alchemical and Hermetic literature (the body of works attributed to the fabled Hermes Trismegistus), developing a full-blown philosophy grounded on the alchemical theory of the human as the microcosm, and of the identity of the humors with the essential chemical principles of nature. Paracelsus's teachings thus juxtapose originality and innovation with acceptance of arcane and occult beliefs and practices, a combination encountered in many Renaissance thinkers.

In addition to the titles listed here, see also the books by Debus and Pagel in the "General Works" at the beginning of this chapter.

BOOKS BY PARACELSUS

The Archidoxes of Magic. c.1524. Kessinger Pub. 1992 $17.95. ISBN 1-56459-171-9. Originally entitled *Of the Supreme Mysteries of Nature.*

The Aurora of the Philosophers. Trans. by A. E. Waite. Holmes Pub. 1985 $3.95. ISBN 0-916411-50-8

Coelum Philosophorum: Or, the Book of Vexations. Trans. by A. E. Waite. Holmes Pub. 1984 repr. of 1894 ed. $2.95. ISBN 0-916411-13-3

The Hermetic and Alchemical Writings of Paracelsus. Trans. by A. E. Waite. 2 vols. Shambhala Pubns. 1976 repr. of 1894 ed. o.p. Old but still useful selection of works in translation. A glossary of alchemical terminology is appended.

Hermetic Astronomy. Trans. by A. E. Waite. Holmes Pub. 1983 $4.95. ISBN 0-916411-09-5

Selected Writings. Ed. by Jolande Jacobi. Trans. by Norbert Guterman. *Bollingen Ser.*
     Princeton U. Pr. 1958 $47.50. ISBN 0-691-09810-7. Basic collection of Paracelsus's
     most important works.

BOOKS ABOUT PARACELSUS

Debus, Allen G. *The Chemical Philosophy: Paracelsian Science and Medicine in the
     Sixteenth and Seventeenth Centuries.* Science History Pubns. 1977 o.p. A compre-
     hensive study of the ancient and medieval alchemical background to Paracelsus's
     work, his original contributions as chemist and philosopher, and the influence of his
     work on later figures. Illustrated.
_____. *The French Paracelsians: The Chemical Challenge to Medical and Scientific
     Tradition in Early Modern France.* Cambridge U. Pr. 1991 $59.95. ISBN 0-521-
     40049-X. Vivid account of the struggle between defenders of Paracelsian chemistry
     and medical traditionalists in France.
Pachter, Henry M. *Magic into Science: The Story of Paracelsus.* Arden 1982 repr. of 1951
     ed. o.p. Still useful.
Pagel, W. *From Paracelsus to Van Helmont: Studies in Renaissance Medicine and Science.*
     Ed. by Marianne Winder. Ashgate Pub. Co. 1986 $91.95. ISBN 0-86078-183-6. An
     important anthology of essays by a preeminent scholar of Renaissance medicine.
_____. *Paracelsus.* S. Karger 1982 $111.25. ISBN 3-8055-3518-X. Authoritative account
     of Paracelsus's work and its significance.
Stillman, John M. *Theophrastus Bombastus von Hohenheim Called Paracelsus.* AMS Pr.
     1982 repr. of 1920 ed. $34.50. ISBN 0-404-18491-X. Good introduction.

PETRARCH (FRANCESCO PETRARCA). 1304–1374

The great Italian poet and scholar Petrarch has been called the father of
humanism and the first modern man. Renowned today chiefly for his Italian
verses—the *Canzoniere*—Petrarch was famous in his own time for his Latin
writings, which included orations, letters, and moral treatises. Many of the
attitudes he expressed and the sources he cited exercised great influence on his
numerous humanist successors.

Petrarch rejected the scholasticism of the medieval period as sterile and
barbarous, preferring the elevated and refined classical works of such authors
as CICERO (see also Vols. 2 and 3) and SENECA (see also Vol. 2) to the empty
theological subtleties of the schoolmen. He admired ARISTOTLE (see also Vol. 3),
who was venerated by the scholastics, but he preferred PLATO (see also Vol. 3).
His favorite Christian author was AUGUSTINE OF HIPPO, from whom he adopted
the use of pagan learning and eloquence to support a Christian ideal of life. One
of his important treatises, *On the Secret Conflict of My Worries* (*Secretum*,
1358), takes the form of a dialogue between himself and the saint.

Petrarch was born in Arezzo but lived most of his life at Avignon until he
returned to Italy in 1353. Among his most important writings on philosophical
ideas are *On the Solitary Life* (1356), *On the Remedies of Good and Bad Fortune*
(1366), *On His Own Ignorance and That of Many Others* (1367), and *The Ascent
of Mount Ventoux.*

BOOKS BY PETRARCH

Letters on Familiar Matters: Rerum Familiarum Libri. Trans. by Aldo S. Bernardo. 3 vols.
     Johns Hopkins 1975–85 $135.00. ISBN 0-8018-2768-X. First full translation into
     English of 350 letters written by Petrarch between 1325 and 1366.
The Life of Solitude. 1356. Trans. by Jacob Zertlin. Hyperion Conn. 1985 repr. of 1924 ed.
     $29.50. Petrarch's famous defense of the solitary life, a reminder that not all
     humanists preferred the active life over the contemplative.

Petrarch's Remedies for Fortune Fair and Foul: A Modern English Translation of "De Remediis Utriusque Fortunae" with a Commentary. 1366. Trans. by Conrad H. Rawski. 5 vols. Indiana U. Pr. 1991 $395.00. ISBN 0-253-34844-7. Excellent edition.

Petrarch's Secret: Or, the Soul's Conflict with Passion. c.1358. Trans. by William H. Draper. Hyperion Con. repr. of 1911 ed. 1991 $24.00. ISBN 0-88355-596-4.

BOOKS ABOUT PETRARCH

Baron, Hans. *Petrarch's "Secretum": Its Making and Its Meaning.* Medieval Acad. 1985 $25.00. ISBN 0-910956-87-1. "Anyone who works on the *Secretum* in the future must take his start from Baron's careful and perceptive treatment of it" (*Renaissance Quarterly*).

Bergin, Thomas G. *Petrarch.* G. K. Hall o.p. Excellent introduction to the life and works by the eminent Italianist.

Boyle, Marjorie O. *Petrarch's Genius: Pentimento and Prophecy.* U. CA Pr. 1991 $34.95. ISBN 0-520-07293-6. Valuable analysis of Petrarch's thought.

Foster, Kenelm. *Petrarch: An Introduction to the Canzoniere.* Col. U. Pr. 1984 o.p. Provides a background to the study of Petrarch's poetic masterpiece.

_____. *Petrarch: Poet and Humanist.* Col. U. Pr. 1987 $10.00. ISBN 0-85224-548-3. Lucid account of Petrarch's literary interests and achievements.

Mann, Nicholas. *Petrarch. Past Masters Ser.* OUP 1984 $14.95. ISBN 0-19-287609-0. "An excellent introduction" (*Renaissance Quarterly*).

Trinkaus, Charles. *The Poet as Philosopher: Petrarch and the Formation of Renaissance Consciousness.* Yale U. Pr. 1979 $27.50. ISBN 0-300-02327-8. "Beginning with what has frequently been taken as Petrarch's solipsism, Trinkaus cogently describes how Petrarch generalized his own subjective experience. . . . The rich variety of secondary themes and striking insights cannot even be catalogued" (*Renaissance Quarterly*).

Wilkins, Ernest H. *The Making of the "Canzoniere" and Other Petrarchan Studies.* Folcroft 1977 repr. of 1951 ed. o.p. Important series of papers by the dean of American Petrarch scholars.

_____. *Petrarch's Eight Years in Milan.* Medieval Acad. 1958 $20.00. ISBN 0-910956-43-X. Covers the productive period from 1353 to 1361 when Petrarch lived under the patronage of the Visconti after his return to Italy.

_____. *Petrarch's Later Years.* Medieval Acad. 1959 $25.00. ISBN 0-910956-44-8. The continuation of Wilkins's masterly study of Petrarch's career.

_____. *Studies in the Life and Works of Petrarch.* Medieval Acad. 1977 repr. of 1955 ed. o.p.

PICO DELLA MIRANDOLA, GIANFRANCESCO. 1469–1533

Not to be confused with his celebrated uncle, GIOVANNI PICO DELLA MIRANDOLA (see his biography below), the Gianfrancesco Pico della Mirandola played a very different role in Renaissance thought. Deeply influenced by the zealous piety of Savonarola, he adopted a skeptical attitude toward the claims of reason and philosophy that stands in bold contrast to the intellectual optimism of his uncle. Pico's chief work, *On the Vanity of Pagan Learning* (*Examen vanitatis doctrinae gentium*), appeared in 1520. It defends a fideistic position—affirming the superiority of faith—and declares that only by depending on faith can human reason arrive at truth or wisdom. As the first Renaissance work to employ in a serious way the arguments of the great ancient skeptic Sextus Empiricus, it occupies an important place in the history of skepticism.

In addition to the title listed here, see also Popkin's *History of Scepticism* in the "General Works" at the beginning of this chapter.

152   THE READER'S ADVISER

BOOK BY GIANFRANCESCO PICO

On the Imagination. 1500. Ed. and trans. by Harry Caplan. Greenwood 1971 repr. of 1930
   ed. o.p. Gianfrancesco draws his inspiration in this work from Aristotle's discussion
   of imagination in his treatise *On the Soul.*

BOOK ABOUT GIANFRANCESCO PICO

Schmitt, Charles B. *Gianfrancesco Pico della Mirandola (1469–1533) and His Critique of
   Aristotle.* Nijhoff 1967 o.p. Only comprehensive account in English of Gianfrancesco's major work. Emphasizes his place in the skeptical tradition and his importance
   as a source of skeptical ideas in later thinkers. Comprehensive bibliography.

PICO DELLA MIRANDOLA, GIOVANNI. 1463–1494

The Count of Mirandola and Concordia, a small state not far from Florence,
Giovanni Pico was the exemplification of the brilliant Renaissance philosopher-
prince. As a youth he went to Florence and entered into the circle of MARSILIO
FICINO's Platonic Academy. He studied philosophy at the University of Padua, a
center of Aristotelian thought, and in Ferrara and Paris. As a result, his writings
show a more positive assessment of Aristotelianism and the scholastics than do
Ficino's, even though Pico was strongly influenced by the great Platonist's
theories. In 1486 Pico published at Rome his famous collection of 900
Conclusions, which he hoped to defend in a public disputation against all
comers. A papal commission found several of the conclusions of dubious
orthodoxy, however, and the debate was canceled. Pico composed an *Apology*
(1487) in defense of his views but was forced to flee to France in an attempt to
avoid arrest. Imprisoned briefly, he was released through the intervention of his
Florentine patron, Lorenzo de' Medici. Pico died in his thirty-second year in
1494, the year in which the Medici were expelled from Florence.

The most arresting statement of Pico's philosophical aims is found in the
famous *Oration* intended to open the defense of his 900 *Conclusions* in 1486.
Frequently referred to as the *Oration on the Dignity of Man,* the work begins
with a praise of humankind's miraculous nature. Against the background of a
Neoplatonic view of reality derived from Ficino, Pico singles out the human
being as unique in the universe, having been endowed by God with the seeds of
all sorts of beings, from the highest to the lowest, in the soul. Through free will,
people are able to adopt for themselves the nature they choose; by their choices
they can live the life of a beast, a rational thinker, or a god. No more eloquent
defense of the human capacity for self-perfection was penned during the
Renaissance.

Pico advocated an eclectic approach to the study of philosophy, refusing to
limit himself to a single school or tradition in his search for truth. He attempted
to reconcile the views of PLATO (see also Vol. 3) and ARISTOTLE (see also Vol. 3)
where they appeared to differ, and, though he accepted the validity of
Christianity, he did not hesitate to employ Islamic and Jewish sources in his
studies. His use of Jewish cabalistic writings was particularly significant. Among
his important works are the treatise *On Being and the One* (1491), *Heptaplus*
(1489), an allegorical interpretation of the biblical account of creation, and his
unfinished *Disputation against Astrology* (1496).

In addition to the titles listed here, see also the books by Blau, Garin, Walker,
and Yates in the "General Works" at the beginning of this chapter.

BOOKS BY GIOVANNI PICO

Commentary on a Canzone of Benivieni. 1486. Trans. by Sears R. Jayne. Peter Lang 1984
   o.p. An example of the way in which Florentine Platonists drew philosophical
   inspiration from poetic works.

Heptaplus, or Discourse on the Seven Days of Creation. 1489. Trans. by Jessie B. McGraw. Littlefield 1977 o.p. Pico's allegorical and philosophical interpretation of the creation reveals his dependence on ancient Platonic sources and Jewish cabala.

Of Being and Unity. 1491. Trans. by Victor M. Hamm. Marquette 1943 $5.95. ISBN 0-87462-203-4. The only surviving portion of Pico's attempt to reconcile the views of Plato and Aristotle. Reveals his originality within the Florentine Platonic Academy.

On the Dignity of Man, On Being and the One, Heptaplus. 1486–96. Trans. by Charles G. Wallis and others. Bobbs 1965 o.p.

Oration on the Dignity of Man. 1486. Trans. by A. Robert Caponigri. Regnery Gateway 1956 $4.95. ISBN 0-89526-925-2. The famous introduction to the ill-fated public defense of Pico's 900 *Conclusions*.

BOOKS ABOUT GIOVANNI PICO

Dulles, Avery. *Princeps Concordiae: Pico della Mirandola and the Scholastic Tradition.* HUP 1941 o.p. Stresses Pico's use of scholastic sources. He was more influenced by the Latin scholastics than was Ficino.

Kibre, Pearl. *The Library of Pico della Mirandola.* AMS Pr. 1977 repr. of 1936 ed. $17.50. ISBN 0-404-03667-8. This valuable reconstruction of Pico's library reveals his wide reading and eclectic tastes. Essential for an appreciation of his intellectual background.

Wirszubski, Chaim. *Pico della Mirandola's Encounter with Jewish Mysticism.* HUP 1988 $35.00. ISBN 0-674-66730-1. Important account of Pico's interest in the cabala and Hebrew sources of ancient wisdom.

POMPONAZZI, PIETRO. 1462–1525

The leading Aristotelian philosopher of his day, Pietro Pomponazzi is an excellent example of the new "secular" interpreters of ARISTOTLE (see also Vol. 3), who became influential during the Renaissance. These thinkers provided a distinctly different reading of Aristotle's views from that of the medieval scholastic theologians and were less hesitant in stressing the issues on which he differed from Christian doctrine.

A native of Mantua, Pomponazzi studied philosophy and medicine at the University of Padua and taught there from 1488 to 1509. In the latter year, he moved to the University of Ferrara, then to Bologna in 1512. In 1516 he published his controversial *Treatise on the Immortality of the Soul (Tractatus de immortalitate animae)*, which immediately gave rise to a storm of protest. In it he rejected the Thomistic defense of human immortality as inconsistent with the principles of Aristotle's philosophy. Although the immortality of the soul could be accepted on faith, it could not be defended by reference to Aristotle or human reason, both of which clearly argued that the soul dies with the body.

Pomponazzi's analysis in the *Tractatus* raised questions about his candor in professing to accept on faith what could be shown to be inconsistent with reason. Similar questions arise with regard to his other works, especially *On Enchantments (De incantationibus)* and *On Fate, Free Will and Predestination (De fato, libero arbitrio et praedestinatione)*, both of which, though composed around 1520, were published only posthumously—the former in 1556, the latter in 1567. In any case, his lead was followed by later secular Aristotelians, and his strict separation of the realms of faith and reason may be said to anticipate in some ways the philosophical attitudes of the Enlightenment.

Pomponazzi's works are generally unavailable in English; however, a translation of his *Tractatus* may be found in ERNST CASSIRER and others, *The Renaissance Philosophy of Man*, listed in the "General Works" at the beginning of this chapter.

BOOK ABOUT POMPONAZZI

Douglas, Andrew H. *The Philosophy and Psychology of Pietro Pomponazzi*. Ed. by C. Douglas and R. P. Hardie. Coronet Bks. repr. of 1910 ed. $57.50. ISBN 0-685-13727-9. An old classic; out of date in many respects, it is still valuable for the light it sheds on this important philosopher.

SUÁREZ, FRANCISCO. 1548–1617

Francisco Suárez, the leading Jesuit philosopher and theologian of the Counter-Reformation, was born in Granada, Spain, and studied law at the University of Salamanca. He joined the Jesuits in 1564 and pursued studies in philosophy and theology that led to his appointment as professor at several Spanish and Portuguese universities and the Jesuit College at Rome. His career centered on his teaching and writing until his retirement shortly before his death.

Suárez was a metaphysician of the first order, and his views influenced such later philosophers as DESCARTES (see also Vol. 5) and LEIBNIZ. His *Metaphysical Disputations* (*Disputationes metaphysicae*), 1597, shows the influence of THOMAS AQUINAS, although Suárez rejected key Thomistic doctrines, such as the real distinction between essence and existence in creatures. He showed his independence particularly in his philosophy of law, developing an account of legal obligation founded on the primacy of will rather than reason. His legal writings have won him a prominent place among theorists of international law.

BOOKS BY SUÁREZ

On Formal and Universal Unity. Trans. by J. R. Ross. Marquette 1964 o.p. Central to an understanding of Suárez's metaphysics and theology.

On the Essence of Finite Being as Such, on the Existence of the Essence, and Their Distinction. Trans. by Norman J. Wells. Marquette 1983 $24.95. ISBN 0-87462-224-7. Expounds Suárez's views on the key metaphysical problem of the relation of essence to existence in finite beings.

On the Various Kinds of Distinctions. Trans. by Cyril Vollert. Marquette 1947 $7.95. ISBN 0-87462-204-2. How Suárez applies distinctions to the solution of metaphysical problems.

Selections from Three Works of Francisco Suárez. 1612–21. Ed. by J. B. Scott. 2 vols. OUP 1944 o.p. Selections (Vol. 1 in Latin. Vol. 2 in English translation) from Suárez's chief works—*De legibus, Defensor fidei*, and *De triplici virtute theologica*—dealing with international law.

BOOKS ABOUT SUÁREZ

Fichter, Joseph Henry. *Man of Spain: A Biography of Francis Suárez*. Macmillan 1940 o.p. "An enthusiastic and very readable story of his life, written because the author thinks, not without reason, that the great Spanish scholar who was addressed even before his death by a Roman Pontiff as Doctor *eximius et pius* deserves of posterity a more popular place than has been accorded him" (*America*).

Mullaney, T. *Suárez on Human Freedom*. Johns Hopkins 1950 o.p. Valuable discussion of Suárez's conception of will.

VALLA, LORENZO. c.1407–1457

A distinguished historian, humanist, and classical scholar, Lorenzo Valla was also the author of several works of philosophical importance. Born in Rome, he counted among his teachers Leonardo Bruni and the great humanist educator Vittorino da Feltre. He was ordained a priest in 1431, taught rhetoric briefly, then traveled through northern Italy before accepting a position as secretary to

Alfonso I, King of Naples, with whom he remained for more than a decade. In 1448 he moved to Rome and accepted a position as a papal notary.

Valla's most renowned scholarly accomplishment was his exposure of the famous "Donation of Constantine" as a forgery. This document had long been cited in support of papal claims to temporal authority in Italy; Valla's careful analysis showed it to be spurious. His *Elegantiae*, composed between 1435 and 1444 and first published in 1471, set the standard of correct Latin style for generations. As a philosopher he is remembered for the dialogue *On Pleasure*, also known as *On the True Good* (c.1434), which defends pleasure—interpreted as the beatitude to be enjoyed by Christians in the life to come—as the highest good, rejecting the Stoic ideal of virtue. His *On Free Will* deals with the apparent conflict between divine foreknowledge and human freedom, rejecting the standard medieval solution derived from BOETHIUS and proposing Valla's own, which LEIBNIZ would later praise. He criticizes scholastic theology and expresses reservations about reason's capacity to provide answers to ultimate metaphysical questions. In his *Dialectical Disputations*, Valla mounted an attack on Aristotelian logic and put forward his own novel alternative based on classical Latin usage. Valla serves as an example of a Renaissance humanist whose philosophical interests carried him beyond a merely stylistic rejection of medieval scholasticism.

The Renaissance Philosophy of Man, edited by ERNST CASSIRER and others, contains a translation of Valla's *On Free Will*. (See "General Works" at the beginning of this chapter.)

BOOKS BY VALLA

De Voluptate (On Pleasure). c.1434. Trans. by Maristella Lorch and A. Kent Heiatt. Abaris Bks. 1977 $20.00. ISBN 0-913870-33-1. "The translators are to be commended both for treating the original faithfully and for rendering Valla's lively Latin into a brisk and idiomatic modern English" (*Renaissance Quarterly*).

"The Profession of the Religious" and the Principal Arguments from "The Falsely-Believed and Forged Donation of Constantine." Ed. and trans. by Olga Z. Pugliese. *Renaissance and Reformation Texts in Translation*. U. of Toronto Pr. 1985 o.p. Two of Valla's most famous works, his dialogue on the religious orders and his skillful unmasking of the forged "Donation of Constantine."

VIVES, JUAN LUIS. 1492–1540

Spanish humanist and outspoken critic of scholasticism, Juan Luis Vives spent most of his career in northern Europe. Born in Valencia, he left Spain as a youth to study at the University of Paris and then settled in Bruges, Belgium. Vives found the university faculty in Paris strongly dominated by adherents of late medieval terminist logic (devoted to the analysis of the use of terms in sentences). In his treatise *Against the Pseudo-Dialecticians (Adversus pseudodialecticos)* of 1520, he rejected their attempt to employ the methods and distinctions of logical analysis in treating philosophical and theological questions.

Vives taught for a time in Louvain, where he became friends with ERASMUS, whose aim of combining classical learning and Christian piety he shared. He also taught at Oxford University, and while in England served as adviser to Queen Catherine of Aragon, whom he supported during Henry VIII's divorce proceedings. Returning to Bruges, he devoted the remainder of his life to teaching and writing.

Vives shared the general humanist disdain for scholastic theology, though his objections went beyond questions of style. Like AUGUSTINE OF HIPPO, he preferred self-analysis and moral improvement to the scientific study of nature. His *On the Soul and Life* (1538) stressed the empirical study of the self. Although he rejected key elements of Platonism, Vives was thoroughly conversant with the writings of the Florentine Platonists. His delightful *Fable about Man* expresses, through allegory, GIOVANNI PICO's view of humans as uniquely capable of determining their own nature.

The *Renaissance Philosophy of Man*, edited by ERNST CASSIRER and others, contains a translation of Vives's *Fable about Man*. (See the "General Works" at the beginning of this chapter.)

BOOKS BY VIVES

De conscribendis epistolis. Ed. by Charles Fantazzi. E. J. Brill 1989 $37.95. ISBN 90-04-08896-2. An edition, with English translation, of Vives's influential treatise on writing letters.

Juan Luis Vives Against the Pseudodialecticians: A Humanist Attack on Medieval Logic. 1520. Ed. and trans. by Rita Guerlac. Reidel Pub. 1979 o.p. An excellent translation of one of Vives's most important attacks on scholasticism.

The Passions of the Soul: The Third Book of "De anima et vita." 1538. Trans. by Carlos G. Noreña. *Studies in Renaissance Lit*. E. Mellen 1990 $69.95. ISBN 0-88946-147-3. Vives's treatment of the passions, selected from his major philosophical work.

Somnium et vigilia in Somnium Scipionis: Commentary on the Dream of Scipio. Ed. and trans. by Edward V. George. *Lib. of Renaissance Humanism*. Attic Pr. 1990 $85.00. ISBN 0-87921-080-X. Vives's commentary on a famous fragment of Cicero's *De republica*, much beloved by Platonists since ancient times.

Tudor School Boy Life. Intl. Spec. Bk. 1970 $25.00. ISBN 0-7146-2279-6. Selections from Vives's works on education.

Vives on Education: A Translation of the "De Tradendis Disciplinis" of Juan Luis Vives. 1531. Rowman 1971 repr. of 1913 ed. o.p. Sets forth Vives's program for humanist education. With an introduction by Foster Watson and a foreword by Francesca Cordasco.

BOOKS ABOUT VIVES

Noreña, Carlos G. *Juan Luis Vives*. Nijhoff 1970 o.p. "This is an important book and clearly the best introduction to Vives" (*Renaissance Quarterly*).

———. *Juan Luis Vives and the Emotions*. S. Ill. Pr. 1989 $35.00. ISBN 0-8093-1539-4. Careful study of Vives's views on the emotions in his *De anima et vita*.

———. *A Vives Bibliography*. E. Mellen 1990 $49.95. ISBN 0-88946-148-1. Comprehensive listing of works by and about Vives.

Tobriner, Marian Leona. *Vives' Introduction to Wisdom: A Renaissance Textbook*. *Classics in Education Ser*. Tchrs. Coll. Pr. 1968 o.p. Contains a translation of Vives's handbook for the humanist seeker after truth, with a careful analytic introduction by the translator. Foreword by Lawrence A. Cremin.

CHAPTER 6

Modern Western Philosophy, 1600–1900

Allen W. Wood and Matthew Stuart

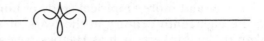

Wonder is not precisely knowing
And not precisely knowing not,
A beautiful but bleak condition
He has not lived who has not felt.
—EMILY DICKINSON

The growth of modern philosophy in Europe was closely intertwined with that of modern capitalism, the centralized coercive authority of the modern state, and, above all, modern physical science. The chief philosophers of the seventeenth century were all concerned with providing a general a priori rationale, usually in the form of a method based on a conception of human cognitive capacities, for the new natural philosophy, with its austerely mathematical and mechanistic program. In contrast to both medieval Scholasticism and philosophy since the Enlightenment, original philosophy in the early modern period was largely the work of people outside the universities. Chief among these was DESCARTES (see also Vol. 5), who provided the first comprehensive modern vision both of nature and of the human mind's mode of access to it. The form taken by the Cartesian concept of method was influenced by the recent rediscovery of ancient Greek skepticism.

The concerns of seventeenth-century science were also directly theological, strongly influenced by the conceptions of divine transcendence and divine sovereignty that had prevailed in the sixteenth century. The emerging picture of modern science was in some respects a cosmic idealization of the emerging modern political state: that of a world created and governed by a distant but almighty intelligence according to precise laws that regulated its operations down to the smallest detail. Cambridge Platonism, a countermovement emphasizing divine immanence, considerably influenced NEWTON's (see also Vol. 5) resistance to Cartesian and other European conceptions of nature, but the form of Newtonianism that eventually triumphed in the eighteenth century had already been thoroughly Cartesianized in those aspects that would have mattered most to Newton. In the eighteenth century, the application of mechanistic conceptions to human ideas, combined with LOCK's genetic theory of mental contents and operations, resulted in the influential empiricist theories of HUME and CONDILLAC.

A more successful attempt to rescue divine immanence took the form of the revolution in conceptions of causality, as philosophers became increasingly skeptical of the traditional notion that finite substances have causal power. The leading figure here was MALEBRANCHE, but the tendency to locate all true causal power in the Deity is strikingly present also in SPINOZA, BERKELEY, and LEIBNIZ. The gradual separation of the philosophy of nature from theological issues during the eighteenth century led in the direction of Humean skepticism about the whole idea of causal power in substances and the reduction of causal connections to observed regularities between events.

In moral and political thought the chief development was HOBBES's attempt to justify absolute state power on the basis of an atomistic theory of the modern political thought was therefore that of state sovereignty and its relation to individual rights and interests, often pursued through the idea of a social contract, sometimes in conjunction with traditional natural-rights theory, as in Locke. A richer and more empirical study of human culture and history began early in the eighteenth century in the work of VICO and MONTESQUIEU. It was later taken up by thinkers such as HERDER (see also Vols. 2 and 3), HEGEL (see also Vol. 3), MARX, (see also Vol. 3), and DILTHEY.

The emergence of the individual subject as knower in Cartesian epistemology was paralleled by the central place of individual moral judgment and motivation. At the end of the eighteenth century, the decline of theological ethics led philosophers to look for a basis for moral judgments within the world. The rationalist position followed SAMUEL CLARKE in seeking eternal and objective ethical truth in things or the relations of natural fitness or unfitness between them. Another tradition, begun by SHAFTESBURY and followed by HUTCHESON, HUME, and ADAM SMITH (see also Vol. 3), sought the basis of morality in human feelings. An intermediate position, pursued by JOSEPH BUTLER, grounded morality in human feelings but distinguished these from the capacity of reflection or conscience to judge feeling from the standpoint of principles. A revolutionary new moral rationalism took the form of KANT's theory that morality is autonomously legislated by human reason. A powerful variant of the Hobbesian program in ethical theory was BENTHAM's utilitarianism, emerging in the Enlightenment and later extending its influence over the moral philosophies of MILL and SIDGWICK.

The rise of the European middle class led to individualistic and democratizing tendencies in society. Social change and contact with non-Europeans through military and economic imperialism led to an awareness of historical and cultural plurality and the mutability of human ways of thinking and acting. The two tendencies are seen in the Enlightenment, the first philosophical movement to set for itself a self-consciously historical mission. Though the movement was centered in France, its greatest and most influential representative was Kant, whose philosophy led to the last great revolution in philosophy, that of German idealism, which began in the late eighteenth century and was manifest in the systems of FICHTE, SCHELLING, and Hegel. One symptom of the continuing power of this revolution is the persistent tendency to distort philosophy of the preceding period by assigning it to the categories of either "rationalism" or "empiricism," their opposition to be overcome only by the revolutionary Kantian synthesis.

By the end of the eighteenth century, the limits of the mechanistic program in natural science were becoming apparent. The age of German idealism saw a renewed emphasis on the idea of divine immanence as well as the replacement of mechanistic with organic and teleological conceptions. Philosophy in the nineteenth century radicalized the conception, developed during the Enlightenment, of philosophy's vocation as self-consciously historical and expressive of determinate cultural and social practices and institutions. This conception was developed by Fichte, perfected by Hegel, and united with radical political practice by Marx. The same impulses were given a different direction late in the nineteenth century by American pragmatism.

Another important development in the nineteenth century was the rise of an antiphilosophical scientistic materialism. Based on the recent separation from philosophy of the specialized empirical sciences, it paralleled the final break between science and religion, now seen either to be at war with each other or else badly in need of some kind of reflective reconciliation. The independence of natural sciences led to various philosophical attempts to comprehend the sciences as a whole or to provide a new philosophical foundation for them, as in the positivism of COMTE, in neo-Kantianism, and in the phenomenology of HUSSERL. The twentieth century's repeated radical questioning of the entire Western philosophical tradition—indeed of the whole enterprise of philosophy—was anticipated by NIETZSCHE (see also Vol. 2).

GENERAL BIBLIOGRAPHY

Aiken, Henry D., ed. *The Age of Ideology: The Nineteenth-Century Philosophers. Essay Index Repr. Ser.* NAL-Dutton 1989 $4.95. ISBN 0-452-00792-5. Selected readings from various nineteenth-century thinkers, such as Kant, Fichte, Hegel, Schopenhauer, Comte, Mill.

Beck, Lewis W., ed. *Eighteenth-Century Philosophy.* Frcc Pr. 1966 $13.95. ISBN 0-02-902100-6. Includes selections from Rousseau, Condillac, Holbach, Voltaire, Wolff, and Lessing as well as other major European philosophers of the time.

Becker, Carl. *The Heavenly City of the Eighteenth Century Philosophers.* Yale U. Pr. 1932 $11.00. ISBN 0-300-00017-0. Covers the utopian expectations of some of the leading eighteenth-century thinkers.

Beiser, Frederick C. *Enlightenment, Revolution and Romanticism.* HUP 1992 $38.00. ISBN 0-674-29502-1. German political thought from 1790 to 1800.

_____. *The Fate of Reason.* HUP 1987 $38.00. ISBN 0-674-29502-1. German philosophy from Kant to Fichte.

Bréhier, Emile. *History of Philosophy.* Trans. by Wade Baskin. U. Ch. Pr. Vols. 4–7 $5.00 ea. Vol. 4 *Seventeenth Century.* 1968 ISBN 0-226-0725-8. Vol. 5 *Eighteenth Century.* 1971 ISBN 0-226-07227-4. Vol. 6 *The Nineteenth Century: Period of Systems, 1800–1850.* 1973 ISBN 0-226-07229-0. Vol. 7 *Contemporary Philosophy since 1850.* 1973 ISBN 0-226-07231-2. Portions of a massive and comprehensive history of philosophy by a leading French authority.

Bronowski, Jacob, and Bruce Mazlish. *The Western Intellectual Tradition: From Leonardo to Hegel. Essay Index Repr. Ser.* Ayer repr. of 1960 ed. $37.00. ISBN 0-8369-2448-7. A general survey of the development of the modern intellectual world.

Burkhardt, Hans, ed. *Handbook of Metaphysics and Ontology.* 2 vols. Philosophia Pr. 1991 $380.00. ISBN 3-88405-080-X. An attempt to make available the results of recent scholarship in the history of philosophy as well as in analytic metaphysics.

Burtt, Edwin A., ed. *The English Philosophers from Bacon to Mill.* Random 1977 $17.95. ISBN 0-394-60411-3. Lengthy selections from Bacon, Hobbes, Locke, Hume, and Mill.

_____. *The Metaphysical Foundations of Modern Physical Science. International Lib. of Psychology, Philosophy, and Scientific Method.* Humanities 1982 $15.95. ISBN 0-391-01742-X. The mystical, metaphysical, alchemical, and astrological ideas that played a role in the rise of modern science.

Caponigri, A. Robert. *Philosophy from the Romantic Age to the Age of Reason.* Vol. 4 in *A History of Western Philosophy.* U. of Notre Dame Pr. 1971 o.p. "Its focus is . . . primarily on the 19th century. . . . While selective as any history must be, the volume is a good manual on 19th-century thought. Lists of readings, name index, and subject index" (*Choice*).

Cassirer, Ernst. *The Philosophy of the Enlightenment.* Trans. by J. Pettegrove. Princeton U. Pr. 1951 $14.95. ISBN 0-691-01963-0. An important, comprehensive survey by one of the leading historians of philosophy. Emphasizes the Enlightenment in Germany.

Cavalier, Robert, James Gouinlock, and James Sterba, eds. *Ethics in the History of Western Philosophy.* St. Martin 1989 $39.95. ISBN 0-312-02145-3. Central ideas in moral theory from Plato to Rawls.

Chappell, Vere, ed. *Essays on Early Modern Philosophers.* 12 vols. Garland 1992 $890.00. ISBN 0-8153-0573-7. A very valuable collection of the best papers on Descartes, Spinoza, Locke, Leibniz, Malebranche, Bayle, Newton, and other seventeenth-century thinkers.

Collins, James D. *God in Modern Philosophy.* Greenwood 1978 repr. of 1959 ed. $75.00. ISBN 0-313-20079-3. A study of how the conception of God changed in modern thought.

———. *Interpreting Modern Philosophy.* Princeton U. Pr. 1972 $17.95. ISBN 0-691-01985-1. An excellent exposition of the role of the history of philosophy in understanding philosophy.

Copleston, Frederick. *Modern Philosophy: The French Enlightenment to Kant.* Vol. 6 Pt. 2 in *A History of Philosophy.* Doubleday 1994 $15.00. ISBN 0-385-47043-6. Part of an important nine-volume comprehensive history of philosophy by a leading English Catholic thinker.

———. *Seventeenth and Eighteenth Century British Philosophers.* Vol. 5 in *A History of Philosophy.* Doubleday 1994 $15.00. ISBN 0-385-47042-8. "One of the volumes in a remarkable history of Western philosophy" (*Choice*).

Crocker, Lester G. *An Age of Crisis: Man and World in Eighteenth-Century French Thought. Goucher College Ser.* Johns Hopkins 1959 o.p. An overall interpretation of the Enlightenment by an important scholar of the history of ideas in France.

Edwards, Paul, ed. *The Encyclopedia of Philosophy.* 4 vols. Free Pr. 1973 $425.00. ISBN 0-02-894950-1. Contains articles on all of the main movements and thinkers of the period by a wide variety of scholars from the United States and Europe. The articles include basic bibliographical materials for further reading.

Feyeraband, Paul. *The Rise of Western Rationalism. Philosophy Now Ser.* Humanities 1978 o.p. A provocative picture of how modern thought developed.

Flower, Elizabeth, and Murray G. Murphey. *A History of Philosophy in America.* 2 vols. Hackett Pub. 1977 $50.00. ISBN 0-685-02034-7. A careful scholarly history; the most complete available.

Frankel, Charles. *The Faith of Reason.* Hippocrene Bks. 1969 repr. of 1948 ed. o.p. Important study on the idea of progress in the Enlightenment.

Funkenstein, Amos. *Theology and the Scientific Imagination from the Middle Ages to the Seventeenth Century.* Princeton U. Pr. 1989 $16.95. ISBN 0-691-02425-1. A brilliant interpretation of the role of theology in the rise of scientific ideas.

Gardiner, Patrick, ed. *Nineteenth-Century Philosophy.* Free Pr. 1969 $14.95. ISBN 0-02-911220-6. "One of an eight-volume series of readings covering the span of Western philosophy, it solves the problem of selection by limiting itself to 13 writers (Fichte, Hegel, Schopenhauer, Feuerbach, Stirner, Marx, Kierkegaard, Nietzsche, Comte, Whewell, Mill, Mach, Bradley) and choosing from each a series of short extracts on issues which are alive and moot in contemporary philosophy" (*Choice*).

Gay, Peter. *The Enlightenment: An Interpretation.* Norton 1977 $14.95. ISBN 0-393-00870-3. A major overall study by a leading intellectual historian.

Hacking, Ian. *The Emergence of Probability: A Philosophical Study of Early Ideas about Probability, Induction, and Statistical Inference.* Cambridge U. Pr. 1984 $12.95. ISBN 0-521-31803-3. An important, controversial monograph about how probability and induction developed as kinds of reasoning.

Hampshire, Stuart, ed. *Age of Reason: The Seventeenth-Century Philosophers.* NAL-Dutton 1984 $4.50. ISBN 0-452-00989-8. [A] "volume in the Great Ages of Western Philosophy Series. It includes a general introduction, and selections from the writings of Bacon, Galileo, Hobbes, Descartes, Pascal, Spinoza, and Leibniz" (*Jewish Social Studies*).

Hartshorne, Charles. *Insights and Oversights of Great Thinkers: An Evaluation of Western Philosophy*. St. U. NY Pr. 1983 $49.50. ISBN 0-87395-681-8. A discussion by a leading American philosopher of what we can learn from past thinkers.

Hazard, Paul. *European Thought in the Eighteenth Century: From Montesquieu to Lessing*. Peter Smith 1973 $16.50. ISBN 0-8446-2226-5. A survey of Enlightenment thought by one of the best French historians of ideas.

Hertzberg, Arthur. *The French Enlightenment and the Jews*. Col. U. Pr. 1968 o.p. A study of the conflict between the tolerant theoretical views of the *philosophes* and their actual views about Jewish emancipation.

Höffding, Harald, and B. E. Meyer. *A History of Modern Philosophy: A Sketch of the History of Philosophy from the Close of the Renaissance to Our Own Day*. 2 vols. Folcroft 1985 repr. of 1908 ed. o.p. A still basic history of modern thought, covering material through the nineteenth century.

Jones, W. T. *Hobbes to Hume*. Vol. 3 in *A History of Modern Philosophy*. HarBrace J 1969 o.p.

_____. *Kant and the Nineteenth Century*. Vol. 4 in *A History of Modern Philosophy*. HarBrace J 1975 o.p.

Kaufmann, Walter. *From Shakespeare to Existentialism*. Princeton U. Pr. 1980 $18.95. ISBN 0-691-01367-5

Kersey, Ethel. *Women Philosophers: A Bio-Critical Sourcebook*. Greenwood 1989 $55.00. ISBN 0-313-25720-5. A useful research tool in an area that is receiving increasing attention.

Koestler, Arthur. *Sleepwalkers*. Putnam Pub. Group 1963 o.p. "I think Mr. Koestler has two basic motives: (1) He wants to show that the great inventors were not rational, totally lucid minds, but passionate, confused, lyrical and, most often, religious. They were 'sleepwalkers,' in the sense that they stumbled forward, sometimes not even recognizing their most important discoveries. (2) He wants to heal the gap he sees between science and religious belief by arguing that the basic impulse behind the two phenomena is the same" (*20th Century*).

_____. *The Watershed: A Biography of Johannes Kepler*. U. Pr. Amer. 1985 o.p. The selection from *Sleepwalkers* containing the story of Kepler. "This is as entertaining as Nancy Mitford's account of Voltaire and Mme. Du Châtelet" (*20th Century*). Foreword by John Durston.

Koyré, Alexandre. *From the Closed World to the Infinite Universe*. Johns Hopkins 1968 repr. of 1956 ed. $13.95. ISBN 0-8018-0347-0. Important study of the philosophical assumptions involved in the beginnings of modern science.

Lamprecht, Sterling P. *Our Philosophical Traditions: A Brief History of Philosophy in Western Civilization*. Century Philosophy Ser. Irvington 1980 repr. of 1955 ed. o.p. A good general introductory history of philosophy.

Levi, Albert W. *Philosophy and the Modern World*. Midway Repr. Ser. U. Ch. Pr. 1977 repr. of 1959 ed. o.p. "The most interesting and informative general interpretation of seventeenth-century philosophy that has been written" (Huston Smith, *Saturday Review*).

Lewes, George H. *The Biographical History of Philosophy from Its Origin in Greece down to the Present Day*. Gregg Intl. 1968 repr. of 1857 ed. $210.00. ISBN 0-576-29116-1. A well-known mid-nineteenth-century work, giving the lives of famous philosophers.

Loeb, Louis E. *From Descartes to Hume: Continental Metaphysics and the Development of Modern Philosophy*. Cornell Univ. Pr. 1981 o.p. A history of seventeenth- and eighteenth-century thought seen from the perspective of contemporary analytic philosophy.

Lossky, Nicholas O. *The History of Russian Philosophy*. Intl. Univs. Pr. 1969 $50.00. ISBN 0-8236-2340-8. An excellent study of Russian thought by one of the leaders of the Russian Orthodox Seminary in Paris.

Lovejoy, Arthur O. *Great Chain of Being: A Study of the History of an Idea*. William James Lectures Ser. HUP 1936 $13.95. ISBN 0-674-36153-9. Traces a central metaphysical idea from antiquity to the nineteenth century.

Lukàcs, Georg. *History and Class Consciousness*. Trans. by Rodney Livingstone. MIT Pr. 1971 repr. of 1923 ed. $10.95. ISBN 0-262-62020-0. A major Marxist study of the rise of modern philosophy.

Mandelbaum, Maurice. *History, Man, and Reason: A Study in Nineteenth-Century Thought*. Johns Hopkins 1971 o.p. Available through University Microfilms. Important study by a leading authority on the development of the philosophy of history.

Mandrou, Robert. *From Humanism to Science, 1480 to 1700*. Trans. by Brian Pearce. *History of European Thought Ser*. Gordon & Breach 1992. ISBN 2-88124-568-4. A survey of modern thought by a leading French intellectual historian.

Marias, Julian. *History of Philosophy*. Dover 22nd ed. 1966 $9.95. ISBN 0-486-21739-6. Important history of philosophy from the pre-Socratics to Heidegger and Ortega by a leading twentieth-century Spanish thinker.

Merz, John Theodore. *A History of European Thought in the Nineteenth Century*. 4 vols. Peter Smith 1976 o.p. One of the finest histories of the period.

O'Connor, Daniel J., ed. *A Critical History of Western Philosophy*. Free Pr. 1985 $16.95. ISBN 0-02-923840-4. A collection of essays by British and American scholars on various philosophers. Their views are presented and examined in terms of analytic philosophy.

Parkinson, G.H.R., ed. *Handbook of Western Philosophy*. Macmillan 1988 $100.00. ISBN 0-02-949593-8. An up-to-date single-volume collection of short essays on philosophy. Combines the history of philosophical problems with the most recent attempts of analytic philosophers to answer them.

Popkin, Richard H. *The High Road to Pyrrhonism*. Ed. by R. A. Watson and J. E. Force. Hackett Pub. 1989 $28.50. ISBN 0-89690-002-9. A collection of essays on the role of skepticism in modern thought, written over 25 years. Deals with Bayle, Berkeley, Hume, and the development of modern racism.

———. *The History of Scepticism from Erasmus to Spinoza*. U. CA Pr. 1979 $15.00. ISBN 0-520-03876-2. Basic study of the revival of ancient skepticism in the Renaissance and Reformation and its influence on the development of modern thought.

———. *Philosophy of the Sixteenth and Seventeenth Centuries*. Free Pr. 1966 $14.95. ISBN 0-02-925490-6. Selected readings from Renaissance authors and Bacon, Descartes, Gassendi, Hobbes, Pascal, Spinoza, Malebranche, Leibniz, and Bayle.

———. *The Third Force in Seventeenth-Century Thought*. E. J. Brill 1992 $88.75. ISBN 90-04-09324-9. Twenty-two articles on subjects in the history of modern philosophy.

Randall, John H. *The Career of Philosophy*. 2 vols. Bks. Demand repr. of 1970 ed. $160.00. ISBN 0-8357-6048-0. Vol. 1 *From the Middle Ages to the Enlightenment*. Vol. 2 *From the German Enlightenment to the Age of Darwin*. A monumental history of modern philosophy that reinterprets most of the philosophers.

———. *The Making of the Modern Mind: A Survey of the Intellectual Background of the Present Age*. Col. U. Pr. 1976 $78.50. ISBN 0-231-04142-X. An important survey, written over 60 years ago, showing how the modern intellectual world began.

———. *Philosophy after Darwin: Chapters for the Career of Philosophy and Other Essays*. Ed. by Beth J. Singer. Col. U. Pr. 1977 $50.00. ISBN 0-231-04114-4. The unfinished remainder of Randall's history of modern philosophy.

Rée, Jonathan, Michael Ayers, and Adam Westoby. *Philosophy and Its Past*. Humanities 1978 o.p. Essays on the value of the history of philosophy.

Rosenfield, Leonora. *From Beast Machine to Man Machine: Animal Soul in French Letters from Descartes to La Mettrie*. Hippocrene Bks. 1968 o.p. Important study of the materialistic, biological, and psychological theories in France from Descartes to the mid-eighteenth century.

Russell, Bertrand. *A History of Western Philosophy*. *Counterpoint Ser*. S&S Trade 1984 $8.95. ISBN 0-04-100045-5. A lively, although not always accurate, survey by a leading twentieth-century thinker.

Sellars, Wilfrid. *Philosophical Perspectives: History of Philosophy*. Ridgeview 1979 $27.00. ISBN 0-917930-24-X. Essays on philosophical topics, using historical settings, by a leading contemporary American thinker.

Smith, Thomas V., and Marjorie Grene, eds. *Philosophers Speak for Themselves: Berkeley, Hume, and Kant.* Bks. Demand repr. of 1957 ed. $105.60. ISBN 0-8357-8983-7
———. *Philosophers Speak for Themselves: From Descartes to Locke.* U. Ch. Pr. 1957 $12.95. ISBN 0-226-76481-8
Spink, John S. *French Free-Thought from Gassendi to Voltaire.* Greenwood 1969 repr. of 1960 ed. $65.00. ISBN 0-8371-0663-X. A useful study of irreligious skeptical thought from 1650 to 1750 in France.
Ueberweg, Friedrich. *A History of Philosophy.* Trans. by George S. Morris. 2 vols. *Select Bibliographies Repr. Ser.* Ayer repr. of 1874 ed. o.p.
Waithe, Mary Ellen, ed. *A History of Women Philosophers.* Kluwer Ac. 1990 $108.00. ISBN 90-247-3571-8. A much-needed survey of women's philosophical contributions. Volume 3 is dedicated to women philosophers from 1600 to 1900.
Weinberg, Julius R. *Ockham, Descartes, and Hume: Self-Knowledge, Substance, and Causality.* Ed. by William J. Courtenay. U. of Wis. Pr. 1977 o.p. A collection of essays, by a leading American historian of philosophy, on medieval and modern thinkers, emphasizing epistemological themes.
Wiener, Philip. *Evolution and the Founders of Pragmatism.* Peter Smith 1972 $11.75. ISBN 0-84446-0964-1. The role of the theory of evolution in the development of pragmatic philosophy in the nineteenth century. Foreword by John Dewey.
———, ed. *Dictionary of the History of Ideas.* 5 vols. Scribner 1980 o.p. A topical collective work covering many important general themes about modern philosophy, such as modern skepticism and religious tolerance. Written by noted scholars from different disciplines.
Windelband, Wilhelm. *A History of Philosophy: With Especial Reference to the Formation and Development of Its Problems and Conceptions.* Trans. by James H. Tufts. Greenwood 1979 repr. of 1938 ed. $42.50. ISBN 0-313-20872-7. One of the most important nineteenth-century German histories of philosophy.
Yolton, John W. *Perceptual Acquaintance from Descartes to Reid.* U. of Minn. Pr. 1984 $39.95. ISBN 0-8166-1162-9. Theories about the role of perception in human knowledge in Descartes, the Cartesians, and the British empiricists up to Thomas Reid.
———. *Thinking Matter: Materialism in Eighteenth-Century Britain.* Bks. Demand repr. of 1984 ed. $68.10. ISBN 0-7837-2903-0. A scholarly study of the controversy over whether thinking can be a material process, and the implications of such a theory.

CHRONOLOGY OF AUTHORS
(Seventeenth Century)

Bacon, Francis. 1561–1626
Galilei, Galileo. 1564–1642
Hobbes, Thomas. 1588–1679
Gassendi, Pierre. 1592–1655
Descartes, René. 1596–1650
Arnauld, Antoine. 1612–1694
More, Henry. 1614–1687
Cudworth, Ralph. 1617–1688
Pascal, Blaise. 1623–1662

Conway, Anne. 1631–1679
Locke, John. 1632–1704
Pufendorf, Samuel. 1632–1694
Spinoza, Baruch. 1632–1677
Malebranche, Nicolas. 1638–1715
Newton, Sir Isaac. 1642–1727
Leibniz, Gottfried Wilhelm, Baron von. 1646–1716
Bayle, Pierre. 1647–1706

ARNAULD, ANTOINE. 1612–1694

The chief representative in Catholic theology of the Augustinian reform movement known as Jansenism, Antoine Arnauld was one of the seventeenth century's most important and influential writers on metaphysics, epistemology, and philosophy of mind. He was born in Paris into a wealthy family and educated at the Sorbonne, where he entered the priesthood and received a doctorate in theology in 1641. Invited to contribute a set of objections to DESCARTES's (see also Vol. 5) *Meditations on First Philosophy* (1641), he was the first to raise the problem of the "Cartesian circle." Arnauld, however, was deeply impressed by the Cartesian system and defended an essentially Cartesian position in his philosophical works, as well as in his later controversies with MALEBRANCHE and LEIBNIZ. Subject to lifelong persecution by the Jesuits for his theological views, Arnauld was admitted to the faculty of theology at the Sorbonne in 1643 only because of the death of Cardinal Richelieu, who had prevented his entry. When he was expelled in 1655, he took refuge at the monastery of Port-Royal near Paris, which his sister Angelique, the abbess there, had reformed according to Jansenist principles. Thereafter, although he was defended by such Jansenist friends as BLAISE PASCAL, Arnauld was effectively excluded from French academic life. He died in exile in Brussels.

Arnauld's most important philosophical work was *The Art of Thinking* (1662), nicknamed the "Port-Royal Logic," which he coauthored with Pierre Nicolet. Elaborating the Cartesian theory of clear and distinct ideas, it attempted to reform the theory of logic by using as its basis Descartes's *Regulae* rather than the traditional *Prior Analytics* of ARISTOTLE (see also Vol. 3). His treatise *On True and False Ideas* (1683) defended a representative theory of perception against Malebranche's view that the immediate objects of human thoughts are ideas in the mind of God. Several years later, in correspondence, Arnauld interrogated Leibniz over the latter's *Discourse on Metaphysics*, arguing that the Leibnizian theory of complete individual concepts is committed to an objectionable form of determinism.

BOOKS BY ARNAULD

The Art of Thinking. 1662. Trans. by James Dickoff and Patricia James. Bobbs 1964 o.p. The most recent translation of Arnauld's major work.
On True and False Ideas. 1683. Trans. by Stephen Gaukroger. E. Mellen 1990 $89.95. ISBN 0-88946-287-9. A new though not completely reliable translation of Arnauld's critique of Malebranche.

BOOKS ABOUT ARNAULD

Kilcullen, John. *Sincerity and Truth: Essays on Arnauld, Bayle, and Toleration.* OUP 1988 $55.00. ISBN 019-826691-X. Contains an essay on Arnauld's renunciation of "philosophic sin."
Nadler, Stephen. *Arnauld and the Cartesian Philosophy of Ideas.* Princeton U. Pr. 1989 $32.50. ISBN 0-691-07340-6. A study of Arnauld's epistemology and his account of perception.
Sleigh, Robert. *Leibniz and Arnauld.* Yale U. Pr. 1990 $30.00. ISBN 0-300-04565-4. A master study of the two men's philosophical correspondence.

BACON, FRANCIS (BARON VERULAM, VISCOUNT ST. ALBANS). 1561–1626

Best known in philosophy for his advocacy of modern science and the use of empirical methods of inquiry, Francis Bacon was an extremely versatile thinker who wrote on a variety of subjects. Born in London to a prominent family, Bacon was educated at Cambridge University and joined the civil service in 1584. He enjoyed a spectacularly successful political career, rising to the offices of solicitor general (1607), attorney general (1613), and finally lord chancellor (1618) before being driven from office in disgrace in 1621 for receiving bribes. Throughout his political career, he wrote prolifically, publishing his most important works on scientific method, the *Novum Organum* and *The Great Instauration*, in 1620.

Bacon's writings on natural science were an inspiration to generations of seventeenth- and eighteenth-century philosophers and empirical inquirers, perhaps most of all because of his criticisms of Scholasticism and, more generally, his rejection of authority and tradition. In matters of both politics and religion, however, Bacon was a conservative, siding with the Crown against Parliament and defending both the doctrines and the prerogatives of the Anglican church. Bacon's recommendations on scientific method are highly programmatic and have been given widely divergent interpretations. His contribution to modern science, powerful and significant though it was, is perhaps best appreciated if it is viewed as the contribution of neither a direct practitioner nor of a philosophical methodologist but rather of an enthusiastic and eloquent literary advocate, publicist, and cheerleader.

BOOKS BY BACON

The Advancement of Learning. 1605. Am. Classical Coll. Pr. 1993 $227.00. ISBN 0-89266-731-1. A statement of Bacon's plans for improving knowledge.

The Essayes or Counsels, Civill and Morall. Ed. by Michael Kiernan. HUP 1985 $39.95. ISBN 0-674-31740-8

Essays. 1597–1625. AMS Pr. 1988 repr. of 1940 ed. $31.50. ISBN 0-404-20015-X. Essays modeled on Montaigne's, dealing with a wide range of topics—literary, philosophical, political, and so on.

Francis Bacon: A Selection of His Works. Ed. by Sidney Warhaft. *College Class. in Eng. Ser.* Odyssey Pr. 1965 o.p.

Great Instauration and New Atlantis. 1617–1620. Ed. by J. Weinberger. *Croft Class. Ser.* Harlan Davidson 1980 o.p. Bacon's fundamental theory for changing the way of gaining knowledge and his utopian picture of how this would work out.

Novum Organum and Related Writings. Ed. by Thomas Fowler. Arden Lib. repr. of 1889 ed. 1979 o.p. Bacon's theory of knowledge, and his methodology.

Philosophical Works of Francis Bacon. Select Bibliographies Repr. Ser. Ayer repr. of 1905 ed. $38.00. ISBN 0-8369-5395-9

The Philosophy of Francis Bacon. Ed. by Benjamin Farrington. U. Ch. Pr. 1967 o.p. "Farrington has translated three works of Bacon available previously only in their original Latin for the classicists or in fragmented and inadequate translations. . . . The translations are felicitous. . . . The writing is clear, the thoughts penetrating, and no educated person can read these little-known pieces without recognition of Bacon's genius" (*Science and Society*).

The Physical and Metaphysical Works of Lord Bacon, Including the Advancement of Learning and Novum Organum. Scholarly 1976 $55.00. ISBN 0-403-06143-1

Works of Francis Bacon. 15 vols. Ed. by J. Spedding and others. Scholarly 1988 repr. of 1858–74 ed. $1,200.00. ISBN 0-403-00003-3. The only complete edition of Bacon's works.

BOOKS ABOUT BACON

Anderson, Fulton H. *Francis Bacon: His Career and His Thought.* Greenwood 1978 repr. of 1962 ed. $85.00. ISBN 0-313-20108-0. A standard intellectual biography.

Craik, George L. *Bacon: His Writings and His Philosophy.* Arden Lib. 1983 repr. of 1860 ed. o.p. A general survey, written in the 1840s, of Bacon's views.

Farrington, Benjamin. *Francis Bacon: Philosopher of Industrial Science. Eng. Biographies Ser.* Haskell 1973 o.p. An influential Marxist interpretation of Bacon's thought.

Jardine, Lisa. *Francis Bacon: Discovery and the Art of Discourse.* Cambridge U. Pr. 1975 o.p. An important study examining Bacon's theory of discovery in terms of Renaissance ideas.

Rossi, Paolo. *Francis Bacon: From Magic to Science.* Trans. by Sacha Rabinovitch. *Midway Repr. Ser.* U. Ch. Pr. 1978 repr. of 1968 ed. o.p. "A first-rate translation of what has become a Baconian classic . . . Rossi's study is also a compendium of rare titles and authors of the English and European Renaissance to which scholars and graduate students will refer again and again" (*Choice*).

Urbach, Peter. *Francis Bacon's Philosophy of Science: An Account and Reappraisal.* Open Court 1987 $34.95. ISBN 08126-9015-X. An important book that explodes many of the common misconceptions about Bacon's philosophy of science.

Vickers, Brian. *Francis Bacon and Renaissance Prose.* Cambridge U. Pr. 1968 $69.95. ISBN 0-521-06709-X. An important study by a scholar well versed in the intellectual background of the Renaissance.

————, ed. *Essential Articles for the Study of Francis Bacon. Essential Articles Ser.* Shoe String 1968 o.p. Brings together much important recent research and reinterpretation.

Wallace, Karl R. *Francis Bacon on the Nature of Man.* U. of Ill. Pr. 1967 o.p. A study of Bacon's views about human intellectual, volitional, and emotive faculties.

Weinberger, Jerry. *Science, Faith, and Politics: Francis Bacon and the Utopian Roots of the Modern Age.* Cornell Univ. Pr. 1985 $39.95. ISBN 0-8014-1817-8. A commentary on Bacon's *The Advancement of Learning.*

BAYLE, PIERRE. 1647–1706

Born at Carla-le-Comte (now Carla-Bayle) in southern France, Pierre Bayle was the son of a French Protestant minister. Forced to flee to Holland in 1681 because of the persecution of the Huguenots, he lived there the rest of his life. Bayle not only wrote a large number of works attacking all kinds of theological and philosophical theories and opposing all kinds of intolerance, but he also edited one of the first major philosophical journals. His most famous work is his immense four-folio *Historical and Critical Dictionary* (1697–1702), in which he developed a complete skepticism against "everything that is said, and everything that is done." This work, considered the "Arsenal of the Enlightenment," greatly influenced BERKELEY, HUME, and VOLTAIRE (see also Vol. 2).

BOOKS BY BAYLE

Historical and Critical Dictionary: Selections. Trans. by Richard Popkin. Macmillan 1965 $11.50. ISBN 0-672-60406-X

Selections from Bayle's Dictionary. Ed. by E. A. Beller and M. du P. Lee, Jr. Princeton U. Pr. 1952 o.p.

BOOKS ABOUT BAYLE

Kilcullen, John. *Sincerity and Truth: Essays on Arnauld, Bayle, and Toleration.* OUP 1988 $55.00. ISBN 019-826691-X. Contains a lengthy essay on Bayle on the rights of conscience.

Labrousse, Elizabeth. *Bayle.* OUP 1983 $14.95. ISBN 0-19-287541-8. A short introduction to Bayle's thought and influence by the leading scholar of his work.

Sandberg, Karl. *At the Crossroads of Faith and Reason: An Essay on Pierre Bayle.* Bks. Demand repr. of 1966 ed. $33.80. ISBN 0-8357-5827-3. An intriguing essay arguing that Bayle was a serious religious believer.

CONWAY, ANNE. 1631–1679

Born Anne Finch, this Cambridge Platonist philosopher became Viscountess Conway through her marriage in 1651 to Lord Edward Conway. Her father and husband were both high officials of state under Charles II. She was educated by tutors and shortly before her marriage began a correspondence with HENRY MORE, who remained her philosophical mentor. After a serious illness at the age of 12, Conway suffered the rest of her life from chronic and severe headaches that kept her in constant pain for months at a time. Before her marriage she was treated by William Harvey (discoverer of the circulation of the blood); later her doctor was Francis Mercury van Helmont (1618–98), a friend of LEIBNIZ, who also encouraged her philosophical labors. It was apparently through Helmont that Conway came into contact with Quakerism. She was influenced by Robert Barclay and corresponded with both George Keith and William Penn. Over More's disapproval, she joined Helmont in becoming a Quaker around 1675, and Quaker meetings were subsequently held at Ragley, the Conway estate. It was probably between 1677 and her death in 1679 that Conway composed her only extant work, *The Principles of the Most Ancient and Modern Philosophy*, which was finally published in 1690 through Helmont's efforts as editor and publicist.

Like More, Conway not only studied modern philosophers, such as DESCARTES, HOBBES, and SPINOZA, whose systems she critically discusses in the final chapter of her treatise, but also read extensively in Christian mystical literature. Her work also makes extensive reference to Jewish Cabalistic literature. The foundation of Conway's philosophical system is a natural theology based on an orthodox conception of God and an original interpretation of the Christian doctrines of the Trinity and the Incarnation. The second person of the Trinity, the Word or *Messias*, plays a significant role in her theory of cosmogony. Conway ascribes to God a liberty of indifference (ability to choose otherwise than He does) but agrees that He is nevertheless determined by His nature to create the best world. This is one in which space and time, which are infinite, are also filled infinitely with creatures.

Leibniz himself acknowledged Conway as a precursor of his view that there is "life and perception in all things." Conway's theory of created things is a metaphysics of *monads* (a term now associated with the name of Leibniz, which both he and Conway derived from More), which strikingly anticipates Leibniz's *Monadology* while also differing from it in a number of respects. For Conway the physical monad is the least part of matter, but each body is divisible infinitely into smaller creatures, though not (as Leibniz held) actually divided infinitely. Leibniz held that monads, or ultimate simples, were nonextended perceiving minds or spirits rather than extended material bodies. For Conway, however, only God is essentially incorporeal; all creatures have a common essence, in relation to which the difference between spirit and body is one of degree or mode; thus, bodies are naturally changed into spirits, and vice versa, and most things are simultaneously spiritual and corporeal.

BOOKS BY CONWAY

Conway Letters: The Correspondence of Anne Viscountess Conway, Henry More, and their Friends, 1642–1684. Ed. by Marjorie Nicolson. Elliots Bks. 1930 $100.00. ISBN 0-685-89745-1

The Principles of the Most Ancient and Modern Philosophy. 1690. Ed. by Peter Lopston. Nijhoff 1982 o.p.

BOOK ABOUT CONWAY

Merchant, Carolyn. *The Death of Nature.* Harper SF 1990 $12.00. ISBN 0-06-250595-5. Conway's philosophy contrasted with the mechanism of Leibniz and Newton.

CUDWORTH, RALPH. 1617–1688

The most systematic of the Cambridge Platonists, Ralph Cudworth was born at Aller in Somerset, educated at Emmanuel College, Cambridge, elected a fellow of the college in 1639, and appointed master of Clare College in 1645. In these turbulent revolutionary years, he made many enemies, a development that prompted his retirement from the university to become rector of North Cadbury in Somerset in 1650. Four years later, however, he returned to be master of Christ's College, where his friend HENRY MORE was a fellow. He married in the same year, and his daughter Damaris (1658–1708), later Lady Masham, was a significant philosopher in her own right as well as a friend and patron of JOHN LOCKE. Cudworth's chief work, *The True Intellectual System*, was published in 1678. It was an important work of scholarship on Greek philosophy as well as a metaphysical system based on theism and a dualist theory of mind. His theory of "spiritual plastic powers," which he ascribed to all living things, influenced the Encyclopedists. Two important posthumous works by Cudworth, *A Treatise Concerning Eternal and Immutable Morality* (published in 1731) and *A Treatise on Free Will* (published in 1838), are directed against both Calvinism and Hobbesian materialism, defending freedom of the will and a rationalist and realist conception of the good.

BOOKS BY CUDWORTH

The Cambridge Platonists. Ed. by Gerald Cragg. OUP 1968 o.p. Contains selections from Cudworth.

The Cambridge Platonists. Ed. by C. A. Patrides. Cambridge U. Pr. 1980 $52.50. ISBN 0-521-23417-4. Contains brief selections from Cudworth.

The True Intellectual System of the Universe. 2 vols. Hy Cohen 1977 repr. of 1678 ed. ISBN 3-487-06009-4. There is no twentieth-century edition of Cudworth's magnum opus.

BOOKS ABOUT CUDWORTH

Colie, Rosalie. *Light and Enlightenment: A Study of the Cambridge Platonists and the Dutch Arminians*. Bks. Demand repr. of 1957 ed. $44.00. ISBN 0-317-08829-7. Contains a chapter on Cudworth and the vitalist controversy.

Gysi, Lydia. *Platonism and Cartesianism in the Philosophy of Ralph Cudworth*. P. Lang Pubs. 1962 $21.00. ISBN 3-261-00648-X. Traces Cudworth's philosophical debts.

Passmore, John. *Ralph Cudworth: An Interpretation*. Cambridge U. Pr. 1951 o.p. A short introduction to Cudworth's philosophy.

DESCARTES, RENÉ. 1596–1650

René Descartes was born to a wealthy family in the village of La Haye (now called Descartes) in Touraine. He was educated at the newly founded Jesuit college of La Fleche. In 1619 he joined the army of Prince Maurice of Nassau. During most of the 1620s, Descartes lived in Paris, where he had become well known after his invention of the branch of mathematics known as analytic geometry. In 1628 Descartes moved back to Holland, where he continued to pursue his philosophical and scientific projects, remaining connected to the world chiefly through correspondence with his friend Marin Mersenne, a priest and Franciscan friar who had wide connections within the scientific and intellectual world. Descartes presented his philosophy first in the *Discourse on Method* (1637), then more fully in *Meditations on First Philosophy* (1641), which was published by Marin Mersenne, along with six sets of objections by Caterus, HOBBES, ARNAULD, GASSENDI, and others, together with Descartes's replies. Descartes developed his philosophy in textbook form in the *Principles of Philosophy* (1644). In 1649 he left his retirement in Holland to accept the invitation of Queen Christina of Sweden to join her court. The severe climate was too much for his always fragile state of health, and he died in 1650.

Descartes's method is ostensibly a means of establishing knowledge on a basis of unshakable certainty; he prefaces the *Meditations* with a statement of his intent to establish the existence of God and the immortality of the soul. Without denying the sincerity of these aims, recent scholarship has emphasized the close connection between Descartes's philosophical aims and his wide-ranging empirical scientific work, which encompassed physics, astronomy, and physiological psychology. Descartes developed the first systematic account of the motions of the solar system, based on modern physical principles. His system served in this way as a model for the Newtonian system, which was later to attack and supersede the Cartesian outlook. When we look at the methodological and antiskeptical procedure in the *Meditations* in this light, it becomes apparent that his way of replying to skepticism was meant all along to serve the deeper purpose of overthrowing both the Scholastic conception of scientific method and the traditional Aristotelian picture of the natural world so as to provide a basis for the emerging modern mechanistic physics. He thereby set the agenda for the philosophy of at least the next two centuries.

BOOKS BY DESCARTES

Descartes' Conversation with Burman. OUP 1974 o.p. Burman was a philosophy student who visited Descartes and asked him various questions about his philosophy. The text is Burman's, and if correct, gives some interesting answers to problems Descartes's views have raised.

Discourse on Method. 1637. Ed. and trans. by Donald A. Cress. Hackett Pub. 1980 $3.50. ISBN 0-91544-83-2. This was Descartes's systemization of how one arrives at truth. "The method which Descartes proposed to apply to every sphere of knowledge was that which was best exemplified in analytical geometry. The stages and procedure used in a geometrical problem could surely be made to yield results of equal certitude in the sphere of metaphysics, logic, and ethics" (E.W.F. Tomlin).

Meditations on First Philosophy. 1641. Trans. by Ronald Rubin. Arete Pr. 1986 $4.95. ISBN 0-941736-11-3. "Extensive metaphysical, heuristic work; his major opus" (Tice and Slavin, *Research Guide to Philosophy*, ALA, 1983).

Philosophical Letters. Ed. and trans. by Anthony Kenny. U. of Minn. Pr. 1981 o.p. A selection of important letters dealing with basic philosophical topics.

The Philosophical Writings of Descartes. 3 vols. Ed. by John Cottingham, Robert Stoothof, Dugald Murdoch, and Anthony Kenny. Cambridge U. Pr. 1985–1991. Vol. 1 1985 $69.95. ISBN 0-521-24595-8. Vol. 2 1985 $19.95. ISBN 0-521-28808-8. Vol. 3 1991 $69.95. ISBN 0-521-40323-5. A new translation that includes much not available in previous translations.

Principles of Philosophy. 1644. Trans. by Reese P. Miller and Valentine R. Miller. Kluwer Ac. 1983 $59.00. ISBN 0-685-46956-5. A new complete translation, with annotations of this statement of Descartes's system.

Treatise of Man. Trans. with commentary by Thomas S. Hall. *Monographs in the History of Science Ser.* HUP 1972 o.p. Descartes's posthumously published study on the human species as a biological entity.

BOOKS ABOUT DESCARTES

Balz, Albert G. *Descartes and the Modern Mind.* Shoe String 1967 repr. of 1952 ed. o.p. A by now classic study of Descartes and his role in the formulation of modern thought.

Beck, Leslie J. *The Metaphysics of Descartes: A Study of the Meditations.* Greenwood 1979 repr. of 1965 ed. o.p. A careful examination of this text by a well-known Descartes commentator.

Blom, John J. *Descartes: His Moral Philosophy and Psychology.* NYU Pr. 1978 $40.00. ISBN 0-8147-0999-0. A 100-page study of Descartes's moral and psychological views, plus translations of some of his letters from 1641 to 1649.

Chappell, V. C. *Twenty-Five Years of Descartes Scholarship, 1960–1984: A Bibliography*. Garland 1987 o.p.

Chomsky, Noam. *Cartesian Linguistics: A Chapter in the History of Rationalist Thought*. U. Pr. of Amer. 1983 repr. of 1966 ed. $14.00. ISBN 0-8191-3092-3. An attempt by one of the leading theorists in contemporary linguistics to show that the roots of his own nonbehavioral theory of linguistics go back to certain followers of Descartes at the end of the seventeenth century.

Cottingham, John, ed. *The Cambridge Companion to Descartes*. Cambridge U. Pr. 1992 $49.95. ISBN 0-521-36696-8. A generally helpful though uneven collection of papers covering the main aspects of Descartes's epistemology, metaphysics, and philosophy of science.

Curley, E. M. *Descartes against the Skeptics*. HUP 1978 $27.50. ISBN 0-674-19826-3. A careful examination of Descartes's arguments against skepticism, and an evaluation of his system in terms of contemporary analytic philosophy.

Doney, Willis, ed. *Eternal Truths and the Cartesian Circle*. Garland 1987 $20.00. ISBN 0-8240-4651-X. A collection of papers on two important and closely related topics in Descartes's philosophy.

Frankfurt, Harry. *Demons, Dreamers and Madmen: The Defense of Reason in Descartes's Meditations*. Macmillan 1970 o.p. A study devoted to Descartes's epistemology, focusing mainly on the First Meditation.

Garber, Daniel. *Descartes' Metaphysical Physics*. U. Ch. Pr. 1992 $60.00. ISBN 0-226-28219-8. A historically sensitive and long overdue book on Descartes's physics and its relation to his metaphysics.

Gaukroger, Stephen, ed. *Descartes: Philosophy, Mathematics and Physics*. History of Science and Philosophy Ser. B & N Imports 1980 o.p. An interesting collection of essays by leading scholars on Descartes's work in each of these fields. The emphasis is on his mathematical and scientific activities, which are too often neglected in considering his philosophy.

Gilson, Étienne. *Index Scholastico-Cartesian*. B. Franklin 1964 repr. of 1913 ed. o.p. First work to show significant similarities and differences between Descartes's work and the Scholasticism of his times.

Gueroult, Martial. *Descartes' Philosophy Interpreted According to the Order of Reasons: The Soul and God*. Trans. by Roger Ariew. U. of Minn. Pr. 1984 $39.95. ISBN 0-8166-1255-2. An interpretation by one of the most important Descartes scholars in France in recent years.

Hooker, Michael, ed. *Descartes: Critical and Interpretive Essays*. Bks. Demand repr. of 1978 ed. $83.30. ISBN 0-317-55760-2. "The Hooker collection emphasizes formal logical tools more than the other collections and it focuses on the concept of method in the *Meditations* and body-mind duality" (*Choice*).

Joachim, Harold L. *Descartes' Rules for the Direction of the Mind*. Ed. by Errol E. Harris. Greenwood 1979 repr. of 1957 ed. $35.00. ISBN 0-313-21263-5. A very careful commentary on this early work of Descartes.

Kenny, Anthony. *Descartes: A Study of His Philosophy*. Garland 1987 o.p. Includes a very useful introduction.

Rorty, Amélie, ed. *Essays on Descartes' Meditations*. U. CA Pr. 1986 $17.00. ISBN 0-520-05496-2. An excellent collection of 22 essays that follows the thematic development of the *Meditations*.

Rosenfield, Leonora. *From Beast Machine to Man Machine: Animal Soul in French Letters from Descartes to La Mettrie*. Hippocrene Bks. 1968 o.p. A study of how Descartes's theory about beasts and machines developed into a mechanistic theory of man.

Roth, Leon. *Descartes' Discourse on Method*. Folcroft 1975 repr. of 1937 ed. o.p. A careful examination by an important scholar of modern philosophy.

Sebba, Gregor. *Bibliographia Cartesiana: A Critical Guide to the Descartes Literature (1800–1960)*. Heinemann Ed. 1964 o.p. An indispensable guide to all of the literature on Descartes up to 1960. Covers materials in most languages, with evaluative comments.

Smith, Norman. *Studies in the Cartesian Philosophy.* Telegraph Bks. 1985 repr. of 1902 ed. o.p. Still valuable interpretation of Descartes's theory.

Spinoza, Baruch de. *The Principles of Descartes' Philosophy.* Trans. by Halbert Hains Britan. Open Court 1978 o.p. Spinoza's first published work, which is in part a commentary on Descartes's views.

Vendler, Zeno. *Res Cogitans: An Essay in Rational Psychology. Contemporary Philosophy Ser.* Cornell Univ. Pr. 1972 $29.95. ISBN 0-8014-0743-5. On Descartes's theory of the mind.

Voss, Stephen, ed. *Essays on the Philosophy and Science of Rene Descartes.* OUP 1993 $49.95. ISBN 0-19-507551-X. Essays by prominent Descartes scholars.

Watson, Richard A. *The Breakdown of Cartesian Metaphysics.* Humanities 1986 o.p. An expanded and revised version of an earlier study on what happened to Descartes's philosophy in the latter half of the seventeenth century.

――――. *Downfall of Cartesianism. International Studies in the History of Ideas.* Austin Hill Pr. o.p. "An intellectual history informed by analytic interests . . . explains the 'downfall of Cartesianism' . . . as due to the inability to handle an ontology of mind and extension" (Tice and Slavin, *Research Guide to Philosophy*, ALA, 1983).

Williams, Bernard. *Descartes: The Project of Pure Enquiry.* Viking Penguin 1990 $8.95. ISBN 0-14-013840-4. An interpretation and analysis by a leading present-day English thinker.

Wilson, Margaret. *Descartes.* U. of Minn. Pr. 1985 $16.95. ISBN 0-8166-1655-5. Excellent book on the *Meditations* by one of the best American Descartes scholars.

GALILEI, GALILEO. 1564–1642

Born in Pisa, Galileo Galilei studied medicine and mathematics at the University of Pisa and held the chair of mathematics there from 1589 to 1591, when he moved to Padua. For the next 20 years, he did groundbreaking work in mathematical physics and observational astronomy. Galileo's hostility to Aristotelianism, which in his writings frequently assumed the form of ridicule, his open espousal of the Copernican theory of planetary motion, and his published contention that the language of the Bible should be interpreted in the light of human knowledge about nature, made him a target of academic and ecclesiastical attacks. With the accession of Pope Urban VIII in 1623, Galileo thought he was safe, since as a cardinal the new pope had been one of Galileo's supporters and patrons. This emboldened him to publish his *Dialogue Concerning the Two Chief World Systems* in 1632, but five months later his printer was ordered to cease publication of the book, and Galileo was summoned to Rome to stand trial before the Inquisition. In June of the following year, he was ordered to recant his objectionable doctrines—which he did—and was sentenced to life imprisonment. He was, however, permitted to reside with the Archbishop of Siena, a former pupil, and he even managed to publish his final work on physics, *Two New Sciences*, by smuggling the manuscript to Holland.

Galileo's influence on modern science, and with it modern philosophy, has been enormous. There is, however, no consensus concerning his own philosophical views or the philosophical underpinnings of his scientific work. He has been variously read as an empiricist, a Platonist, and a problem-solving scientist with no particular philosophical views or commitments. He certainly did mount philosophical arguments against Aristotelianism, and he had definite views about scientific method, the use of language in science, the nature of sensible qualities, and the possible scope of our knowledge of nature. But whether these views can be synthesized into a determinate philosophical position to be laid alongside those of DESCARTES (see also Vol. 5), GASSENDI, and other seventeenth-century scientist-philosophers is still an open question.

BOOKS BY GALILEO

Dialogues Concerning the Two Chief World Systems, Ptolemaic and Copernican. Ed. and trans. by Stillman Drake. U. CA Pr. 1967 $16.00. ISBN 0-520-00450-7

Dialogues Concerning Two New Sciences. Trans. by Henry Crew and Alfonso de Salvio. Bks. Demand repr. of 1950 ed. $79.00. ISBN 0-8357-9453-9

Discoveries and Opinions of Galileo. Ed. by Stillman Drake. Doubleday 1957 o.p. A collection of shorter works, including the *Starry Messenger.*

BOOKS ABOUT GALILEO

Drake, Stillman. *Galileo: Pioneer Scientist.* U. of Toronto Pr. 1990 $40.00. ISBN 0-8020-2725-3. A study of Galileo's experimental work that draws heavily on his working papers.

————. *Galileo at Work.* U. Ch. Pr. 1978 o.p. A scientific biography.

————. *Galileo Studies: Personality, Tradition, and Revolution.* U. of Mich. Pr. 1970 o.p. A collection of papers by a leading Galileo scholar.

Finocchiaro, Maurice. *The Galileo Affair: A Documentary History.* U. CA Pr. 1989 $60.00. ISBN 0-520-06662-6. Correspondence and depositions connected with Galileo's trial and condemnation.

Geymonat, Ludovico. *Galileo Galilei: A Biography and Inquiry into His Philosophy of Science.* Trans. by Stillman Drake. McGraw 1965 o.p. Translation of a 1957 study.

Golino, Carlo. *Galileo Reappraised.* U. CA Pr. 1966 $30.00. ISBN 0-520-00490-6. Five essays on Galileo's science, religion, and precursors.

Kaplon, Morton, ed. *Homage to Galileo.* MIT Pr. 1965 o.p. Useful collection of papers.

Levinger, Elma. *Galileo, First Observer of Marvelous Things.* Messner 1952 o.p. Brief account of Galileo's life and work.

Shea, William. *Galileo's Intellectual Revolution.* Macmillan 1972 o.p. A study of Galileo's "middle period," from 1610 to 1632.

GASSENDI, PIERRE. 1592–1655

Born at Champtercier in southern France, Pierre Gassendi was educated at Digne, Aix, and Avignon, where he received a doctorate in theology in 1614 and was ordained a priest in 1616. He was professor of philosophy at Aix from 1617 to 1623, where he undertook an ambitious seven-part critique of Aristotelian philosophy that was never completed. In the 1620s Gassendi lived in Paris for several periods, associating with philosophers and scientists. After a brief period spent in the Low Countries, he divided his time between Paris and Provence, writing scientific works and skeptical critiques of the rationalist theologian Herbert of Cherbury and the Rosicrucian Robert Fludd, as well as his well-known objections to DESCARTES's (see also Vol. 5) meditations. He also familiarized himself with Epicurean Atomism, which strongly influenced his scientific work and later philosophical thought. In 1634 Gassendi was promoted to Provost of the Cathedral of Digne, and in 1645 he was named to the faculty of the Collège de France in Paris, but declining health led to his absence from this post after 1648.

Gassendi's philosophy anticipates many philosophical themes that were later developed under the heading of empiricism. He attempted to combine a moderate skepticism concerning the possibility of knowing the real nature of the world with a materialistic physical theory based on mechanistic Atomism. The relation of Gassendi's philosophical views to his religious profession is a subject of dispute, but he was always careful to formulate his ideas in such a way that they were consistent with church teachings. Gassendi's scholarly output was prodigious. He wrote a biography of EPICURUS (1647), a 1,700-page commentary on Book X of Diogenes (the *Animadversiones*) (1640), and his philosophical magnum opus, *Syntagma philosophicum* (published posthumously, 1658). Gassendi's influence on later philosophy is greater than is usually appreciated, perhaps largely because it was mediated through that of other seventeenth- and eighteenth-century thinkers such as BAYLE, LOCKE, and VOLTAIRE (see also Vol. 3).

BOOKS BY GASSENDI

Pierre Gassendi's Institutio Logica. 1658. Ed. by Howard Jones. Humanities 1981 o.p. A posthumous work of Gassendi, which is the best presentation of his theory of knowledge.
Selected Works. Trans. by Craig B. Brush. Johnson Repr. 1972 o.p. A collection of Gassendi's writings on philosophy, science, and religion.

BOOKS ABOUT GASSENDI

Brundell, Barry. *Pierre Gassendi: From Aristotelianism to a New Natural Philosophy*. Kluwer Ac. 1987 o.p. Argues that the major purpose of Gassendi's philosophy was the quest to bring about a revolution in the natural sciences.
Egan, Howard T. *Gassendi's View of Knowledge: A Study of the Epistemological Basis of His Logic*. U. Pr. of Amer. 1984 o.p. An examination of Gassendi's empiricism and his use of Cartesian methodological doubt.

HOBBES, THOMAS. 1588–1679

Thomas Hobbes was born at Malmesbury, England, during the attack of the Spanish Armada on England. He came from a poor family but received an education and taught Latin and Greek. After receiving his B.A. from Oxford University in 1608, he became a tutor to the son of William Cavendish, Earl of Devonshire. In this capacity he traveled in Europe and met GALILEO and many important scientists in France and Italy. Through the Earl of Devonshire, he also met leading English figures, including FRANCIS BACON.

During the Puritan Revolution, Hobbes fled to Paris, where he stayed from 1640 to 1651. He was part of the circle of philosophers and scientists around Marin Mersenne, a central figure in European intellectual life who corresponded with people all over Europe. While in Paris, Hobbes wrote and published *De Cive* (1642), his reply to DESCARTES (see also Vol. 5), and developed most of what appeared in the *Leviathan* (1651). In the late 1640s, he became tutor to the exiled son of the king, the future Charles II. The publication of his political theory in *Leviathan* led to his estrangement from the royalists and to his return to England, where he spent the rest of his long life. Hobbes was constantly engaged in quarrels with theologians, politicians, philosophers, scientists, and mathematicians and was regularly accused of antireligious and even atheistic views. In his later years, he wrote several controversial works defending himself against his many opponents. After the Restoration, Charles II awarded him a pension, but the religious establishment considered him a heretic. His political theory on the basis of sovereignty and political obligation has had great influence and is still much studied and debated.

BOOKS BY HOBBES

Behemoth: or the Long Parliament. U. Ch. Pr. 1990 $12.95. ISBN 0-226-39544-0
De Cive or the Citizen. 1642. Ed. by Sterling P. Lamprecht. Greenwood 1982 repr. of 1949 ed. $38.50. ISBN 0-313-23659-3. Warrender's version is the initial volume of the new Clarendon edition of the philosophical works of Hobbes. *De Cive* is Hobbes's first published version of his political theory, intended as one part of his overall philosophy dealing with the social body.

174   THE READER'S ADVISER

Dialogue between a Philosopher and a Student of the Common Laws of England. Ed. by
    Joseph Cropsey. U. Ch. Pr. 1971 o.p. "Cropsey has in effect given Hobbes scholars a
    new dimension in interpreting his theory of politics and has provided a lengthy and
    lucid introduction which students of politics, philosophy, and law should find
    provocative" (*Choice*).
Elements of Law: Natural and Politic. 1650. Ed. by Ferdinand Tonnies. Intl. Spec. Bk.
    1969 $35.00. ISBN 0-7146-2540-X. The earliest formulation of Hobbes's political
    theory.
The English Works of Thomas Hobbes. 11 vols. Ed. by William Molesworth. Adlers
    Foreign Bks. 1966 o.p. The only complete edition of Hobbes's works in English.
Leviathan. 1651. Ed. by Richard Tuck. Cambridge U. Pr. 1993 $54.95. ISBN 0-521-39492-
    9. A definitive critical edition.
Man. 1658. (and *Citizen.* 1651). Ed. by Bernard Gert. Peter Smith 1978 o.p. Hobbes's
    theory of living bodies, especially of man.
Thomas White's De Mundo Examined in First English Translation. Trans. by H. W. Jones.
    Beekman 1976 o.p. This is a hitherto unknown writing of Hobbes—probably his
    earliest philosophical work—discovered in manuscript in Paris in the 1950s.

BOOKS ABOUT HOBBES

Brown, K. C. *Hobbes Studies.* Blackwell Pubs. 1965 o.p. Contains articles by several
    leading scholars, including Leo Strauss, A. E. Taylor, and Keith Thomas.
Gauthier, David P. *Logic of Leviathan: The Moral and Political Theory of Thomas Hobbes.*
    OUP 1969 $12.95. ISBN 0-19-824616-1. A careful analytic study of Hobbes's basic
    argument.
Goldsmith, Maurice. *Hobbes's Science of Politics.* Col. U. Pr. 1966 $17.50. ISBN 0-231-
    02804-0. "Goldsmith's well written, lucid, sensible, and comprehensive analysis of
    Hobbes' political philosophy, his careful examinations of rival interpretations, and
    his full and useful bibliography and footnotes undoubtedly make his book the most
    valuable single work on Hobbes for the undergraduate library" (*Choice*).
Hampton, Jean. *Hobbes and The Social Contract Tradition.* Cambridge U. Pr. 1986
    $64.95. ISBN 0-521-36827-8. A sustained interpretation of Hobbes's argument in
    Leviathan for absolute sovereignty.
Hinnant, Charles H. *Thomas Hobbes.* Twayne's Eng. Authors Ser. G. K. Hall 1977 o.p.
    "The reader looking for a straightforward guide to Hobbes's life and doctrines will
    find this study of use" (*Library Journal*).
MacPherson, Crawford B. *The Political Theory of Possessive Individualism: Hobbes to
    Locke.* OUP 1962 $13.95. ISBN 0-19-881084-9. "MacPherson's Marxian presupposi-
    tions may discourage some readers from close study of his book. Yet the serious
    student of the Stuart period should not neglect this provocative and often
    penetrating analysis" (*American Historical Review*).
Oakeshott, Michael. *Hobbes on Civil Association.* U. CA Pr. 1975 o.p. Four essays by a
    leading Hobbes scholar on Hobbes and interpretations of him. "Oakeshott's
    measured admiration for Hobbes is expressed with the grace, buoyancy, and insight
    that make this essay required reading for all students of Hobbes, if not of modernity
    itself. . . . A classic in its field" (*Choice*).
Peters, Richard S. *Hobbes.* Greenwood 1979 repr. of 1956 ed. $41.50. ISBN 0-313-
    20799-2. "The author notes the manifold source of Hobbes' outlook: the Baconian
    concept of knowledge as the ability to manipulate nature to human goals; the
    Cartesian belief that a sound scientific method is the key which opens the secrets of
    man and nature; the then widespread belief in the values of the geometric approach
    as solving all problems from epistemology to ethics, i.e., an approach which started
    from self-evident deductive principles and concluded in a philosophy of civilization
    logically proceeding from such axioms" (*Science and Society*).
Raphael, D. D. *Hobbes: Morals and Politics. Political Thinkers Ser.* Allen & Unwin 1977
    o.p. "Intended as a handbook for students unfamiliar with the moral and political
    philosophy of Hobbes. . . . It provides an introduction to most of the major issues

raised in Hobbes's philosophy as well as . . . interpretations of some of those issues" (*Choice*).

Reik, Miriam. *The Golden Lands of Thomas Hobbes.* Wayne St. U. Pr. 1977 $34.95. ISBN 0-8143-1574-7. A study of Hobbes's development as a writer, historian, and political theorist.

Rogers, G. A. J., and Alan Ryan, eds. *Perspectives on Thomas Hobbes.* OUP 1988 $49.95. ISBN 0-19-824998-5. A useful collection of papers by a mix of new and established Hobbes scholars.

Rogow, Arnold A. *Thomas Hobbes: Radical in the Service of Reaction.* Norton 1986 o.p. "Rogow's thesis is that Hobbes's pessimistic depiction of man's state of nature as one of timidity, insecurity, distrust, and ambition has its psychological origins in Hobbes's own character, particularly as a result of his formative years in Malmesbury. . . . An informative work for scholars and students" (*Library Journal*).

Sacksteder, William. *Hobbes Studies Bibliography: 1879–1979.* Philos. Document 1982 $18.50. ISBN 0-912632-49-6. The most complete available bibliography on Hobbes.

Shapin, Steven, and Simon Schaffer. *Leviathan and the Air Pump: Hobbes, Bayle, and the Experimental Life.* Princeton U. Pr. 1985 $65.50. ISBN 0-691-08393-2. An attempt to place Hobbes in the development of the science of his time.

Sorrell, Tom. *Hobbes.* Routledge 1991 $15.95. ISBN 0-415-06366-3. This excellent book focuses mainly on Hobbes's philosophy of science.

Stephen, Sir Leslie. *Hobbes.* 1904. U. of Mich. Pr. 1961 o.p. "One cannot read Sir Leslie Stephen's book without appreciating that, apart altogether from the circumstance that English moral philosophy shaped itself—and, for the most part, frankly—as an answer to Hobbes' daring system, Hobbes for his own sake makes a charming study" (*International Journal of Ethics*).

Strauss, Leo. *Political Philosophy of Hobbes: Its Basis and Its Genesis.* Trans. by Elsa M. Sinclair. U. Ch. Pr. 1984 o.p. "The strengths of the book include the availability of the essays under a single cover, the systematic introduction, and the thorough chronological bibliography. [Hilail] Gildin's introduction is a valuable summary of Strauss' thought and contains some interesting observations on historicism and positivism" (*Choice*).

Tuck, Richard. *Hobbes.* OUP 1989 $6.95. ISBN 0-19-287668-6. An introduction to Hobbes's philosophy.

Von Leyden, W. *Hobbes and Locke: The Politics of Freedom and Obligation.* St. Martin 1982 o.p. Important comparative study by a leading authority on seventeenth-century English thought.

Warrender, Howard. *The Political Philosophy of Hobbes: His Theory of Obligation.* OUP 1957 o.p. A now classic study of Hobbes's thought. "Partly because of [the] wise limitation of his objective, but chiefly because of the natural clarity of Mr. Warrender's style and his high standards of exposition, this is probably the clearest and most readable account yet to appear of Hobbes's political philosophy" (*Hibbert Journal*).

Watkins, J.W.N. *Hobbes's System of Ideas.* Hilary Hse. Pubs. 1965 o.p. "Mr. Watkins suggests that while Hobbes did derive his prescriptions from factual premises, he did not commit a logical fallacy, because 'his prescriptions are not *moral* prescriptions—they are more like doctor's orders of a peculiarly compelling kind'" (*English Historical Review*).

LEIBNIZ (or LEIBNITZ), GOTTFRIED WILHELM, BARON VON. 1646–1716

Gottfried Wilhelm Leibniz, one of the last real polymaths, was born in Leipzig. Educated there and at the Universities at Jena and Altdorf, he then served as a diplomat for the Elector of Mainz and was sent to Paris, where he lived for a few years and came into contact with leading scientists, philosophers, and theologians. During a trip to England, he was elected to the Royal Society; he made a visit to Holland to meet SPINOZA. Back in Germany he became librarian to the

Duke of Brunswick, whose library was the largest in Europe outside the Vatican. From there he became involved in government affairs in Hanover and later settled in Berlin at the court of Queen Sophie Charlotte of Prussia. Leibniz was involved in the diplomatic negotiations that led to the Hanoverian succession to the English throne.

From his university days he showed an interest in mathematics, logic, physics, law, linguistics, and history, as well as theology and practical political affairs. He discovered calculus independently of NEWTON (see also Vol. 5), and had a protracted squabble about which of them should be given credit for the achievement. The developer of much of what is now modern logic, he discovered some important physical laws and offered a physical theory that is close to some twentieth-century conceptions. Leibniz was interested in developing a universal language and tried to master the elements of all languages.

Leibniz corresponded widely with scholars all over Europe and with some Jesuit missionaries in China. His philosophy was largely worked out in answer to those of other thinkers, such as LOCKE (see also Vol. 3), MALEBRANCHE, BAYLE, and ARNAULD. Although he published comparatively little during his lifetime, Leibniz left an enormous mass of unpublished papers, drafts of works, and notes on topics of interest. His library, which has been preserved, contains annotations, analyses, and often refutations of works he read. The project of publishing all of his writings, undertaken in the 1920s by the Prussian Academy, was delayed by World War II but was resumed thereafter. It is not likely that the project will be completed in the twentieth century.

BOOKS BY LEIBNIZ

Discourse on Metaphysics, Correspondence with Arnauld, Monadology. Ed. and trans. by George R. Montgomery. Open Court 1973 $6.50. ISBN 0-87548-030-6. Some of the best short statements of Leibniz's philosophy, and his defense and explanation of it in answer to Arnauld.

Discourse on the Natural Theology of the Chinese. Trans. by Henry Rosemont, Jr., and Daniel J. Cook. UH Pr. 1977 o.p. One of the first attempts by a Western thinker to understand Oriental philosophy and how it relates to the concerns of Western thinkers. Leibniz got most of his information from Jesuit missionaries.

The Leibniz-Arnauld Correspondence. Ed. and trans. by H. T. Mason. Garland 1985 o.p. An important discussion of some of Leibniz's key ideas in letters to one of his critics. Introduction by G. H. Parkinson.

Leibniz's Philosophical Writings. Ed. by G. H. Parkinson. Trans. by Mary Morris. Rowman 1973 o.p. Some basic essays on the metaphysics of Leibniz.

Logical Papers: A Selection. Trans. by G. H. Parkinson. OUP 1966 $56.00. ISBN 0-19-824306-5. Some of Leibniz's writings that relate to modern symbolic logic and mathematics.

The Monadology and Other Philosophical Writings. Ed. by Anne Schrecker and Paul Schrecker. Macmillan 1965. ISBN 0-02-406970-1. Edition of some of Leibniz's central metaphysical texts.

New Essays Concerning Human Understanding. Ed. by Peter Remnant and Jonathan Bennett. Cambridge U. Pr. 1981 o.p. A new translation of Leibniz's answer to John Locke.

Philosophical Essays. Ed. and trans. by Daniel Garber and Roger Ariew. Hackett Pub. 1989 $37.50. ISBN 0-87220-063-9. A valuable selection that especially illuminates Leibniz's relations to his contemporaries.

Philosophical Papers and Letters. Ed. by Leroy E. Loemker. Kluwer Ac. 1975 $102.00. ISBN 90-277-0008-7. The largest group of writings presently available in English.

Political Writings of Leibniz. Ed. by Patrick Riley. Cambridge U. Pr. 1988 $54.95. ISBN 0-521-35380-7. These writings are interesting in themselves and also in relation to

Leibniz's political activities in European dynastic politics and to efforts by the Lutherans to reunite the Christian churches.

Books about Leibniz

Adams, Robert M., and others, eds. *Essays on the Philosophy of Leibniz.* 1978 $10.00. ISBN 0-89263-234-8. A group of essays by a variety of contemporary scholars.

Barber, W. H. *Leibniz in France—From Arnauld to Voltaire: A Study in French Reactions to Leibnizianism, 1670–1760.* Ed. by R. C. Sleigh, Jr. Garland 1985 $20.00. ISBN 0-8240-6529-8. A reprint of an important study of Leibniz's personal activities in France and of his influence, positive and negative, in the Enlightenment.

Brown, Stuart C. *Leibniz.* U. of Minn. Pr. 1985 $15.95. ISBN 0-8166-1391-5. "The book proceeds by briefly discussing the important topics to be found in Leibniz's philosophy, and it sets these topics in a developmental framework. . . . Thus it concentrates on the *Discourse on Metaphysics* and the *New System* and does not more than mention the *New Essays on Human Understanding* or *Theodicy*" (*Choice*).

Hooker, Michael, ed. *Leibniz: Critical and Interpretive Essays.* Bks. Demand repr. of 1982 ed. $99.60. ISBN 0-8357-8939-X. A collection of essays by various scholars on Leibniz. "The essays are of high quality and deal with epistemological and logical issues. . . . also contains a useful and extensive bibliography by John Kish" (*Choice*).

Jolley, Nicholas. *Leibniz and Locke: A Study of the New Essays and Human Understanding.* OUP 1984 $47.00. ISBN 0-19-875066-1. An examination of Leibniz's critique of Locke's *Essay.*

Loemker, Leroy E. *Struggle for Synthesis: The Seventeenth-Century Background of Leibniz's Synthesis of Order and Freedom.* HUP 1972 o.p. "This substantial study of Leibniz goes beyond its title to consider many related topics and writers. . . . Not only is the author at home with the well-known theological, literary, and scientific works closely related to Leibniz, but he also introduces unfamiliar writers and works, adding to this study's value" (*Choice*).

Martin, Gottfried. *Leibniz: Logic and Metaphysics.* Ed. by R. C. Sleigh, Jr. Garland 1985 $15.00. ISBN 0-8240-6539-5. Translation of an important German study on Leibniz.

Merz, John T. *Leibniz.* Arden Lib. 1978 repr. of 1901 ed. o.p. A still valuable study of Leibniz's thought.

Meyer, R. W. *Leibniz and the Seventeenth-Century Revolution.* Ed. by R. C. Sleigh, Jr. Garland 1985 $20.00. ISBN 0-8240-6540-9. Leibniz seen in terms of the political, intellectual, and religious crisis of his time.

Mungello, David E. *Leibniz and Confucianism: The Search for Accord.* UH Pr. 1977 $14.00. ISBN 0-8248-0545-3. On Leibniz's interpretations of Chinese thought.

Ortega y Gasset, José. *The Idea of Principle in Leibnitz and the Evolution of Deductive Theory.* Norton 1971 o.p. "Although the matter is highly technical, the manner is brilliantly compelling even to the lay reader—in Ortega's own estimate, this is 'something presented as literature which results in philosophy.' Obligatory reading for all students of 20th-century thought" (*Library Journal*).

Parkinson, G. H. *Logic and Reality in Leibniz's Metaphysics.* Ed. by R. C. Sleigh, Jr. Garland 1985 o.p. An examination of the relation of logic to metaphysics and theology in Leibniz.

Rescher, Nicholas, ed. *Leibniz: An Introduction to His Philosophy.* U. Pr. of Amer. 1986 repr. of 1979 ed. o.p. A short technical presentation of Leibniz by a leading American philosopher.

Ross, G. MacDonald. *Leibniz.* OUP 1984 o.p. A comprehensive introduction to Leibniz's achievements in philosophy, science, and mathematics; includes a lengthy biographical introduction.

Russell, Bertrand. *A Critical Exposition of the Philosophy of Leibniz.* Humanities 1958 o.p. Russell, at the end of the nineteenth century, was one of the first to read Leibniz's mathematical-logical manuscripts and to see their relevance to contemporary thought. Russell became convinced there must have been two Leibnizes: one who wrote popular metaphysical theory and another who was a great mathematical logician far in advance of his time.

Sleigh, Robert. *Leibniz and Arnauld.* Yale U. Pr. 1990 $30.00. ISBN 0-300-04565-4. A masterful study of their philosophical correspondence.
Wilson, Catherine. *Leibniz's Metaphysics: A Historical and Comparative Study.* Princeton U. Pr. 1990 $42.50. ISBN 0-691-07359-7. An ambitious and valuable study.
Yost, Robert. *Leibniz and Philosophical Analysis.* Ed. by R. C. Sleigh, Jr. Bks. Demand repr. of 1954 ed. $55.00. ISBN 0-317-10243-5. A study of the relation of Leibniz's views and those of contemporary philosophical analysis.

LOCKE, JOHN. 1632–1704

Born at Wrington, Somerset, John Locke was the son of an attorney and sometime clerk. After receiving a master's degree at Christ's Church, Oxford University, he lectured there in Latin, Greek, and moral philosophy. Influenced by Thomas Sydenham (known as "the father of English medicine") and the chemist Robert Boyle, Locke became interested in medicine and experimental science and in 1675 received a medical degree. It was through medicine that Locke began his long association with the first Earl of Shaftesbury, at the time an influential government figure. Shaftesbury suffered from an abdominal abscess that threatened his life; Locke alleviated his pain by performing what was then (given the antiseptic practices of the era) a risky surgical procedure, the insertion of a silver drainage tube. After a miraculous recovery, Shaftesbury made Locke first his personal physician and later his secretary and adviser.

In 1671 Locke wrote two drafts of what was later to become his most important work, the *Essay Concerning Human Understanding.* In 1675 he made a protracted trip to France; when he returned in 1679, he found himself in the middle of dangerous political conflicts, Shaftesbury having fallen into disfavor. In 1683 these political pressures drove Locke to Holland, and it was there that he found the leisure to complete the works for which he is remembered. The year of his return to England, 1689, saw the publication of the *Essay* and of two anonymous works: the *Two Treatises of Government* and the *First Letter Concerning Toleration.*

Locke's philosophy is characterized above all by a spirit of moderation. According to his epistemology, very few of our beliefs count as knowledge rather than as opinion or belief, and yet he is never tempted by anything but the mildest skepticism. In politics, he believed that a constitutional monarchy was the best form of government, but he also admitted the people's right to rebel under extreme circumstances. He was a passionate advocate of religious toleration but did not favor extending this toleration so far as to include atheists or Catholics.

In 1691 Locke took up residence at Oates, the family home of his friend Damaris Cudworth Masham, the daughter of the Cambridge Platonist RALPH CUDWORTH and a philosopher in her own right. In 1693 Locke published *Some Thoughts Concerning Education* and in 1695 *The Reasonableness of Christianity.* Throughout the 1690s he was involved in a number of epistolary controversies; most notable was the correspondence with Edward Stillingfleet, the Bishop of Worcester, in which Locke clarified several key doctrines of the *Essay.* In his final years, Locke composed an essay on miracles and a commentary on the Epistles of St. Paul.

BOOKS BY LOCKE

Correspondence of John Locke. 8 vols. Ed. by E. S. De Beer and Gavin R. De Beer. OUP Vol. 1 *Letters 1–461.* 1976 $115.00. ISBN 0-19-824396-0. Vol. 2 *Letters 462–848.* 1976 $129.00. ISBN 0-19-824559-9. Vol. 3 *Letters 849–1241.* 1978 $125.00. ISBN 0-19-824560-2. Vol. 4 *Letters 1242–1701.* 1979 $135.00. ISBN 0-19-824561-0. Vol. 5 *Letters*

1702–2198. 1979 $135.00. ISBN 0-19-824521-9. Vol. 6 *Letters 2199–2664.* 1981
$145.00. ISBN 0-19-824563-7. Vol. 7 *Letters 2665–3286.* 1982 $135.00. ISBN 0-19-
824564-5. Vol. 8 *Letters 3287–3648.* 1989 $115.00. ISBN 0-19-824565-3. First
complete edition of Locke's letters, with translations of Latin ones.

Drafts for the Essay Concerning Human Understanding *and Other Philosophical Writings.*
Vol. 1 Ed. by Peter Nidditch and G.A.J. Rogers. OUP 1990 $98.00. ISBN 0-19-824545-
9. Contains material known as "Draft A" and "Draft B."

An Essay Concerning Human Understanding. 1690. Ed. by Peter H. Nidditch. OUP
$110.00. ISBN 0-19-824386-3

A Letter Concerning Toleration. Hackett Pub. 1983 $3.95. ISBN 0-915145-60-X. Locke's
important statement on the reasons for tolerating diverse opinions in religion.

The Reasonableness of Christianity and A Discourse of Miracles. Ed. by I. T. Ramsey.
Stanford U. Pr. 1958 $8.95. ISBN 0-8047-0341-8. Locke's moderate views on religious
questions.

The Second Treatise of Civil Government. Prometheus Bks. 1986 $4.95. ISBN 0-87975-
337-4. Locke's most important statement of his theory of democratic government.

Two Tracts on Government. Ed. by Philip Abrams. Cambridge U. Pr. 1967 o.p. A critical
edition of Locke's two main writings on political theory. "Readily intelligible to
undergraduate students of political philosophy. Most important and highly recommended" (*Choice*).

Two Treatises of Government. Ed. by Peter Laslett. Cambridge U. Pr. 1988 $49.95. ISBN 0-
521-35448-X. Laslett's erudite introduction is almost a book in itself.

Works. 10 vols. Adlers Foreign Bks. 1963 repr. of 1823 ed. $775.00. ISBN 3-571-02600-8.
A new edition of the works of John Locke is being prepared by scholars. This is to be
published by the Oxford Clarendon Press (John Locke, *A Paraphrase and Notes on
the Epistles of St. Paul,* ed. by Arthur W. Wainwright, 2 vols., 1987), based on much
new manuscript material, plus material from Locke's library.

BOOKS ABOUT LOCKE

Aaron, Richard I. *John Locke.* OUP 1971 $51.00. ISBN 0-19-824355-3. A basic commen-
tary on Locke's philosophy. "Although the book does not argue a revisionist or
reworked thesis, it remains, in its bibliographically updated edition, one of the best
surveys of Locke's general philosophy and impact. A fine introduction to Locke
which even the specialist will value" (*Choice*).

Alexander, Peter. *Ideas, Qualities and Corpuscles.* Cambridge U. Pr. 1985 $64.95. ISBN 0-
521-26707-2. An important study of Boyle's influence on Locke, although some of the
author's interpretations are idiosyncratic.

Ayer, Michael. *Locke.* 2 vols. Routledge 1991 $150.00. ISBN 0-415-06408-2. The most
ambitious book on Locke's epistemology and metaphysics ever written, this study is
historically sensitive but at times dogmatic.

Brandt, Reinhard, ed. *John Locke Symposium.* De Gruyter 1980 $45.50. ISBN 3-11-
008266-7. A series of important essays on Locke.

Christophersen, Hans O. *Bibliographical Introduction to the Study of John Locke.* B.
Franklin 1969 repr. of 1930 ed. o.p. Important bibliography, now somewhat out of
date.

Cranston, Maurice. *John Locke: A Biography.* Ed. by J. P. Mayer. *European Political
Thought Ser.* Ayer 1979 repr. of 1957 ed. $34.50. ISBN 0-405-11690-X. This is now the
standard biography.

Dewhurst, Kenneth. *John Locke: Physician and Philosopher.* Garland 1985 o.p. Emphasizes Locke's medical works and concerns. Includes Locke's medical notes.

Dunn, John. *Locke. Past Masters Ser.* OUP 1984 $7.95. ISBN 0-19-287560-4. "John Dunn
has done an excellent job in relating the different parts of Locke's writing to one
another and, in addition, his book is highly readable and has an agreeable reflective
melancholy of its own" (*The Listener*).

———. *The Political Thought of John Locke: An Historical Account of the Argument of the
Two Treatises of Government.* Cambridge U. Pr. 1983 $19.95. ISBN 0-521-27139-8. A

very careful attempt to place Locke's political writings in their historical setting; based on access to the Locke manuscripts.

Dworetz, Steven. *The Unvarnished Doctrine: Locke, Liberalism, and the American Revolution.* Duke 1990 $37.50. ISBN 0-8223-0961-0. Drawing on the sermons of New England clergy, this careful study contends that Locke's influence was a significant, radicalizing force in American revolutionary thought.

Franklin, Julian H. *John Locke and the Theory of Sovereignty: Mixed Monarchy and the Right of Resistance in the Political Thought of the English Revolution. Cambridge Studies in the History and Theory of Politics.* Cambridge U. Pr. 1981 $14.95. ISBN 0-521-28547-X. A study of Locke's unique contribution to the modern theory of sovereignty.

Fraser, Alexander C. *Locke.* Telegraph Bks. 1985 repr. of 1907 ed. o.p. Important nineteenth-century interpretation of Locke.

Grant, Ruth. *John Locke's Liberalism.* U. Ch. Pr. 1987 $24.95. ISBN 0-226-30607-0. A study of Locke's views on the powers of the state and the consent of the governed.

Gibson, James. *Locke's Theory of Knowledge and Its Historical Relations.* Bks. Demand repr. of 1968 ed. $88.00. ISBN 0-317-08834-3. A fundamental study of Locke.

Green, Thomas Hill. *Hume and Locke.* Peter Smith 1968 o.p. "A 19th-century philosopher, now much too neglected, offers a penetrating critique of the empirical tradition in British philosophy" (*N.Y. Times Book Review*).

Hall, Roland, and Roger Woodhouse. *Eighty Years of Locke Scholarship, 1900–1980: A Bibliographic Guide.* Col. U. Pr. 1983 $22.50. ISBN 0-85224-431-2. Basic bibliographical guide for twentieth-century writing on Locke.

Jenkins, J. J. *Understanding Locke.* Col. U. Pr. 1983 $15.00. ISBN 0-85224-449-5. An introduction to philosophy through Locke's *Essay.* "The book is full of arguments for and against Lockean positions, and the clear and lively style makes it a joy to read. . . . Excellent bibliography" (*Choice*).

Jolley, Nicholas. *Leibnitz and Locke: A Study of the New Essay and Human Understanding.* OUP 1984 $47.00. ISBN 0-19-875080-3. A study of Leibniz's critique of Locke.

Kendall, Willmoore. *John Locke and the Doctrine of Majority Rule.* Peter Smith 1965 o.p. "The work under review is heartily to be welcomed. For Professor Kendall is concerned, not simply with the theory of majority decision, but rather with a complex of ideas which together constitute the philosophy of majority-rule democracy" (*American Political Science Review*).

King, Peter. *The Life and Letters of John Locke, with Extracts from His Journals and Common-place Books.* Garland 1984 o.p. The earliest bibliographical work on Locke.

Lough, John. *Locke's Travels in France, 1675–1679: As Related in His Journals, Correspondence and Other Papers.* Garland 1984 o.p. Interesting in terms of the leaders in science and philosophy Locke met in France at the time.

Mackie, J. L. *Problems from Locke.* OUP 1976 $32.00. ISBN 0-19-824555-6. Discussion of several basic epistemological issues based on Locke's account of knowledge.

MacPherson, Crawford B. *The Political Theory of Possessive Individualism: Hobbes to Locke.* OUP 1962 $13.95. ISBN 0-19-881084-9. An important Marxist interpretation of Hobbes and Locke.

Morris, Charles R. *Locke, Berkeley, Hume.* Greenwood 1979 repr. of 1931 ed. $38.50. ISBN 0-313-22091-3. A significant study by a leading American pragmatist.

Norris, John. *Christian Blessedness, with Reflections upon a Late Essay Concerning Human Understanding.* Ed. by René Wellek. Garland 1978 repr. of 1690 ed. o.p. An evaluation of Locke by the leading English follower of Malebranche.

Schouls, Peter A. *The Imposition of Method: A Study of Descartes and Locke.* OUP 1980 $49.95. ISBN 0-19-824613-7. A comparison of the methodology employed by the two thinkers.

Sergeant, John. *Solid Philosophy: Asserted against the Fancies of the Idealists: Or, the Method to Science Farther Illustrated; with Reflexions on Mr. Locke's* Essay Concerning Human Understanding. Garland 1984 o.p. Important criticism of Locke by one of the leading Catholic philosophers of his time.

Squadrito, Kathleen M. *John Locke. Twayne's Eng. Authors Ser.* G. K. Hall 1979 o.p. Good general presentation of Locke's views on theory of knowledge, religion, ethics, education, and political philosophy.

Steinberg, Jules. *Locke, Rousseau, and the Idea of Consent: An Inquiry into the Liberal-Democratic Theory of Political Obligation. Contributions in Political Science.* Greenwood 1978 $42.95. ISBN 0-313-20052-1. A comparison and contrast of these two theoreticians of liberal democratic theory.

Vaughn, Karen I. *John Locke: Economist and Social Scientist.* U. Ch. Pr. 1980 o.p. A study of Locke's economic theory, which is usually ignored.

Von Leyden, W. *Hobbes and Locke: The Politics of Freedom and Obligation.* St. Martin 1982 o.p. A very good study by one of the leading scholars of seventeenth-century English thought.

Wood, Neal. *The Politics of Locke's Philosophy: A Social Study of* An Essay Concerning Human Understanding. U. CA Pr. 1983 $42.50. ISBN 0-520-04457-6. An attempt to interpret Locke's *Essay* in terms of the politics of the time. "Wood's work is an exploration of the social and political views of Locke and his age, based on Locke's *Essay*. Neither the subject matter nor the author's language will raise any difficulties for a typical undergraduate" (*Choice*).

Woolhouse, R. S. *Locke. Philosophers in Context Ser.* U. of Minn. Pr. 1983 o.p. An attempt to put the basic ideas of Locke's *Essay* in their historical context. "The background information and quotations are used judiciously and always with an eye toward illuminating the central ideas in Locke's *Essay*" (*Choice*).

Yolton, J. W. *John Locke: An Introduction.* Blackwell Pubs. 1985 o.p. A general presentation of Locke's views by a leading contemporary Locke scholar.

———. *John Locke and the Way of Ideas.* AMS Pr. 1987 repr. of 1956 ed. $29.50. ISBN 0-404-18076-0. Represents the same kind of historical-philosophical study as his *Locke and the Compass of Human Understanding.*

MALEBRANCHE, NICOLAS. 1638–1715

Known primarily as an exponent of Cartesianism, Nicolas Malebranche was a philosopher whose originality, depth, and historical influence are too often underappreciated. He was born in Paris, studied philosophy and theology at the College de la March and at the Sorbonne, and at the age of 22 was ordained a priest. Malebranche's most important work was his first and longest, *The Search after Truth* (1674–75). He revised it several times during his life and in later editions appended to it a series of responses to his critics under the title *Elucidations of the Search after Truth.*

In *The Search* Malebranche skillfully defended many of DESCARTES's (see also Vol. 5) metaphysical doctrines. His two chief innovations were his thesis that we "see all things in God" and his theory of occasionalism. Whereas Descartes maintained that all of our ideas are modifications of our minds, Malebranche argued that some of our mental representations—those that provide us with an accurate scientific picture of the world—are actually located in God's mind. This is a very literal philosophical interpretation of the Pauline dictum that it is in God that we live, move, and have our being. Occasionalism is the view that no created substance has any causal power. According to Malebranche, apparent cases of causal interaction between bodies are merely occasions for God to move the bodies himself. He held that created minds are also causally inefficacious, so that God is the true cause even of the voluntary movements of one's own body.

Malebranche published many other philosophical and theological works; most notable among them are the *Treatise on Nature and Grace* (1680) and the *Dialogues on Metaphysics and on Religion* (1688). His account of divine grace in the *Treatise* provoked a response from another Cartesian, ANTOINE ARNAULD. A vituperous controversy ensued, one that culminated in 1690, when Arnauld contrived to have the *Treatise* added to the Catholic church's Index of Forbidden Books.

Interest in Malebranche among English-speaking philosophers has been growing, partly as a result of a renewed appreciation of his immense historical influence. This was not limited to other Cartesian philosophers, or even to philosophers on the Continent; the British empiricists GEORGE BERKELEY and DAVID HUME also owed much to him.

BOOKS BY MALEBRANCHE

Dialogues on Metaphysics. Trans. by Willis Doney. Abaris Bks. 1980 o.p. A popular presentation of Malebranche's central theories.

The Search after Truth and Elucidations of the Search after Truth. 1674. Trans. by Thomas Lennon. Ohio St. U. Pr. 1980 $82.50. ISBN 0-8142-0246-2. This is Malebranche's first and major statement of his philosophy, along with his answers to some of his Cartesian opponents, who had attacked him for deviating from the master's views on some points. The first new translation since 1704.

Treatise on Nature and Grace. Ed. by Patrick Riley. OUP 1992 $55.00. ISBN 0-19-824832-6. An important work previously unavailable in English.

BOOKS ABOUT MALEBRANCHE

Connell, Desmond. *The Vision in God: Malebranche's Scholastic Sources.* Nauwelaerts 1967 o.p. Traces Malebranche's vision-in-God hypothesis to the teachings of St. Thomas, Duns Scotus, and Suarez on angelic knowledge.

Jolley, Nicholas. *The Light of the Soul: Theories of Ideas in Leibniz, Malebranche, and Descartes.* OUP 1990 $49.95. ISBN 0-19-824443-6. A lucid story emphasizing Malebranche's divergence from the Cartesian conception of the mind.

Luce, A. A. *Berkeley and Malebranche.* OUP 1934 $34.95. ISBN 0-19-824319-7. A classic early work showing Berkeley's great debt to Malebranche, and consequently challenging the myth that there was relatively little fruitful exchange between British rationalists and continental empiricists.

McCracken, Charles. *Malebranche and British Philosophy.* OUP 1983 o.p. Highly recommended, this sophisticated and lucid study contains a good general account of Malebranche's philosophy and then details his influence on the British empiricists.

Nadler, Steven. *Malebranche and Ideas.* OUP 1983 $39.95. ISBN 0-19-824664-1. A valuable study of Malebranche's epistemology.

Radner, Daisie. *Malebranche: A Study of a Cartesian System.* Van Gorcum 1978 o.p. Gave English-language Malebranche scholarship a much-needed boost.

Rome, Beatrice. *The Philosophy of Malebranche.* U. Ch. Pr. 1963 o.p. Ambitious and highly readable study of Malebranche's philosophy of science, his epistemology, his account of God, and his occasionalism.

Walton, Craig. *De la recherche du bien: A Study of Malebranche's Science of Ethics.* Kluwer Ac. 1972 o.p. An examination of a side of Malebranche's work that is too often neglected.

MORE, HENRY. 1614–1687

The best known of the Cambridge Platonists, Henry More was born at Grantham, Lincolnshire. His father was a strict Calvinist, but More's education at Eton College led him to abandon the doctrine of predestination. He entered Christ's College, Cambridge, in 1631, was elected to a fellowship in 1639, and remained there the rest of his life. Devoted to the study of philosophy, he took little part in public affairs or university administration. The focus of his interest was the relation between God and creation, especially the individual soul. He was influenced by the writings of Christian mysticism and by poetry, especially the writings of SPENSER (see als Vol. 2). His thinking is more in the spirit of

Renaissance Christian Neoplatonism than of either Scholastic Aristotelianism or the modern philosophy that was emerging in the seventeenth century.

Upon first acquaintance with the writings of DESCARTES (see also Vol. 5), More expressed great admiration for his philosophy; as time passed, however, and More began to appreciate the true character of Cartesian natural science, he became increasingly critical of Cartesian materialism and mechanism as a conception of the natural world, which he regarded as atheistic. His thought is believed to have influenced NEWTON's (see also Vol. 5) conception of space as God's "sensorium" and Newton's view that space, even where empty of matter, may be occupied by spiritual natures. More's chief works are *The Immortality of the Soul* (1659), the *Enchiridion Ethicum* (1667), the *Divine Dialogues* (1668), and the *Enchiridion Metaphysicum* (1671).

BOOKS BY MORE

The Immortality of the Soul. Ed. by A. Jacob. Nijhoff 1987 o.p. Contains More's criticisms of both Descartes and Hobbes.

Philosophical Poems of Henry More, Comprising Psychozozoia and Minor Poems. Ed. by Geoffrey Bullough. Manchester 1931 o.p.

Philosophical Writings of Henry More. Ed. by Flora Mackinnin. AMS Pr. repr. of 1925 ed. $26.00. ISBN 0-404-04409-3

BOOKS ABOUT MORE

Hutton, Sarah. *Henry More (1614–1687) Tercentenary Studies.* Kluwer Ac. 1990 o.p. A valuable collection of papers.

Lennon, Thomas. *Problems of Cartesianism.* U. of Toronto Pr. 1982 $39.95. ISBN 0-7735-1000-1. Contains essays on More's relation to Cartesianism and his opposition to mechanism.

NEWTON, SIR ISAAC. 1642–1727

Born at Woolsthorpe, England, Sir Isaac Newton was educated at Trinity College, Cambridge University, where he graduated in 1665. During the plague of 1666, he remained at Woolsthorpe, during which time he formulated his theory of fluxions (the infinitesimal calculus) and the main outlines of his theories of mechanics, astronomy, and optics, including the theory of universal gravitation. The results of his researches were not circulated until 1669, but when he returned to Trinity in 1667, he was immediately appointed to succeed his teacher as professor of mathematics. His greatest work, the *Mathematical Principles of Natural Philosophy*, was published in 1687 to immediate and universal acclaim. Newton was elected to Parliament in 1689. In 1699 he was appointed head of the royal mint, and four years later he was elected president of the Royal Society; both positions he held until his death. Personally Newton was shy, reserved, and humorless, as well as ambitious, jealous, and quarrelsome. He preferred to engage in polemics by proxy, as he did, for example, in the controversy with LEIBNIZ over who had first discovered the calculus. In later life Newton devoted his main intellectual energies to theological speculation and alchemical experiments. The latter were apparently without result, and the former were deliberately left in obscurity because of Newton's unorthodox anti-Trinitarian views.

The philosophical foundations of Newton's physical theory, as seen by its creator, have been a matter of speculation. From the eighteenth century onward, it was customary to interpret Newton as a modest empiricist: his remark in the *Mathematical Principles* that he "does not feign hypotheses" regarding the cause of gravity has usually been read in this way. But twentieth-century scholarship has suggested a different view. It appears that Newton was convinced that there had to be a mechanistic explanation of gravitational attraction but was frustrated in his attempts to provide one. However, like HENRY MORE, Newton opposed Cartesian physics because he thought it too materialistic; Newton denied the principle of conservation of energy, believing that divine design, and even direct divine influence in the world, was required to account for the origin and stability of the solar system and to prevent the stars from collapsing into a single mass under the influence of gravity. It was from More that Newton derived his view that space is a divine attribute and God's "sensorium," but More could not be described as a philosopher of an even remotely empiricist bent.

BOOKS BY NEWTON

Certain Philosophical Questions: Newton's Trinity Notebook. Ed. by J. E. McGuire and Martin Tamny. Cambridge U. Pr. 1983 $125.00. ISBN 0-521-23164-7. A careful scholarly edition of the notebook Newton kept when he first went to college, indicating the interest he had at the time in the theories of the Cambridge Platonists.

Newton's Philosophy of Nature. Trans. by H. Standish Thayer. *Lib. of Class. Ser.* Free Pr. 1974 $12.95. ISBN 0-685-43029-4. Excerpts from Newton's scientific writings that indicate his philosophy and that played an important role in Enlightenment thought.

Sir Isaac Newton's Mathematical Principles of Natural Philosophy and His System of the World. 1687. 2 vols. Trans. by Andrew Motte. U. CA Pr. 1962. Vol. 1 *The Motions of Bodies* $13.95. ISBN 0-520-00928-2. Vol. 2 *The System of the World* $60.00. ISBN 0-520-00929-0

BOOKS ABOUT NEWTON

Bricker, Phillip, ed. *Philosophical Perspectives on Newtonian Science.* MIT Pr. 1990 $37.50. ISBN 0-262-02301-6. A useful collection of papers on Newton's scientific methodology.

Christianson, Gale E. *In the Presence of the Creator: Isaac Newton and His Times.* Free Pr. 1984 $24.95. ISBN 0-02-905190-8. "While not the scholarly tour-de-force of Richard Westfall's definitive biography *Never at Rest*, Christianson's account . . . provides a reliable and captivating study" (*Library Journal*).

Dobbs, Betty J. *The Foundations of Newton's Alchemy: Or "The Hunting of the Greene Lyon."* Cambridge U. Pr. 1983 $24.95. ISBN 0-521-27381-1. "Dobbs's study of Newton's alchemical manuscripts now shows us yet another side of this complex genius. Through deep and careful research she has established that Newton was not only curious about alchemy but that he studied the subject intensely and believed he had succeeded in carrying through alchemical transformations" (*Choice*).

Force, James. *Essays on the Context, Nature, and Influence of Isaac Newton's Theology.* Kluwer Ac. 1990 $83.50. ISBN 0-7923-0583-3. A collection of essays showing that Newton's natural philosophy cannot be fully understood when divorced from his theological views.

Hurlbutt, Robert H. *Hume, Newton, and the Design Argument.* U. of Nebr. Pr. 1985 $27.50. ISBN 0-8032-2337-4. An examination of the design or teleological argument about the existence of God as presented by Newton and criticized by Hume.

Manuel, Frank E. *The Religion of Isaac Newton: The Fremantle Lectures 1973.* OUP 1974 $24.95. ISBN 0-19-826640-5. Attempts to give a psychological explanation of Newton's religious views; includes the publication of one of his manuscripts on religion.

Westfall, Richard S. *Never at Rest: A Biography of Isaac Newton.* Cambridge U. Pr. 1981 $105.00. ISBN 0-521-23143-4. A prize-winning work that attempts to give an overall interpretation of Newton as scientist, alchemist, and theologian.

PASCAL, BLAISE. 1623–1662

Blaise Pascal was born in Clermont-Ferrand, France, reared in Paris (where his father was a government official), and educated privately. Pascal discovered mathematics independently and as a child started working out mathematical theories. At the age of 16 he completed a work on conic sections, and at the age of 19 invented the first adding machine. (The principle on which his machine was based led to the development of the computer language called "Pascal.") Pascal next joined the contemporary scientific community, many members of which were friends of his father. In his early twenties, he wrote on the nature of the vacuum, and in 1648 made the crucial experiment of carrying an inverted tube of mercury (a barometer) up a mountain, thus obtaining measurements from which he evolved the theory of atmospheric pressure.

Pascal's family was involved with the reform movement within the Catholic church called Jansenism. After an overpowering mystical experience, Pascal devoted himself chiefly to religious writings and activities, often withdrawing to the Jansenist monastery at Port-Royal outside Paris. There he wrote his *Provincial Letters* (1656), a satirical defense of Jansenism against the Jesuit opposition, and also the fragments that comprise his masterpiece, the *Pensées* (*Thoughts*) (1670), which presents his views on philosophy, religion, and morality. Left unfinished at his death, this work is still being revised and reordered on the basis of continued scholarly examination of the actual fragments and new information about Pascal's last years.

Books by Pascal

Great Short Works of Pascal. Ed. and trans. by John Blackenagel and Emile Caillet. Greenwood 1974 repr. of 1948 ed. o.p. Pascal's scientific, mathematical, and short religious writings.

Pensées. 1670. Trans. by A. J. Krailsheimer. Viking Penguin 1966 $7.95 ISBN 0-14-044171-9. A translation based on the reordering of Pascal's text.

The Provincial Letters. 1656. Viking Penguin 1982 $7.95. ISBN 0-16-044196-4. Pascal's scathing, satirical attack on the Jesuits.

Books about Pascal

Coleman, Francis. *Neither Angel nor Beast: The Life and Work of Blaise Pascal.* Routledge 1986 $24.95. ISBN 0-7102-0693-3. A well-written but brief intellectual biography.

Davidson, Hugh M. *Blaise Pascal. Twayne's World Authors Ser.* Macmillan 1983 $22.95. ISBN 0-8057-6548-4. An overall presentation of Pascal's thought in science, religion, and philosophy, and an examination of him as a writer.

————. *The Origins of Certainty: Means and Meanings in Pascal's* Pensées. U. Ch. Pr. 1979 o.p. Attempt to elucidate Pascal's method and how it leads to religious certainty.

Goldmann, Lucien. *Hidden God.* Trans. by Philip Thody. *International Lib. of Philosophy and Scientific Method Ser.* Humanities 1976 o.p. An intriguing interpretation by a leading French Marxist thinker.

Rescher, Nicholas. *Pascal's Wager: A Study of Practical Reasoning in Philosophical Theology.* U. of Notre Dame Pr. 1985 $19.95. ISBN 0-268-01556-2. An examination of the kind of reasoning involved in Pascal's wager (his conclusion that since one cannot prove or disprove God's existence, one may lose by not believing and can only gain by believing) and an evaluation of what it establishes, by a leading contemporary thinker.

PUFENDORF, SAMUEL. 1632–1694

Born in Dorfchemnitz, Saxony, the son of a Lutheran pastor, Samuel Pufendorf was educated at Leipzig and Jena. At Jena he first read Grotius and Hobbes, and studied under Erhard Weigel. In 1658 he became a tutor in the household of the Swedish ambassador to Denmark; when war erupted between these two countries, he was imprisoned for eight months. It was during this time that Pufendorf wrote his first work in philosophy of law, the brief *Universal Elements of Jurisprudence* (1660). Subsequently he taught jurisprudence at the University of Heidelberg and the University of Lund (in Sweden); from 1688 onward he lived in Berlin as court historian to the Duke of Brandenburg. Pufendorf produced historical writings, such as his 1667 account of the Holy Roman Empire, as well as treatises on moral and legal philosophy. His greatest work was the *On the Law of Nature and Nations* (1672). Although Pufendorf is often described (accurately enough) as a natural rights theorist and also as the thinker who first introduced the ideas of Grotius and Hobbes into Germany, his true originality consisted in his view that a society's law and morality are a function of its culture considered as a determinate and living whole. He may thus be regarded as the inventor of the sociological approach to law. As a historian, he anticipated many of the views of nineteenth-century historicism.

BOOKS BY PUFENDORF

On the Duty of Man and Citizen According to Natural Law. Ed. by James Tully. Trans. by Michael Silverthorne. Cambridge U. Pr. 1991 $54.95. ISBN 0-521-35195-2
On the Law of Nature and Nations. Trans. by C. H. Oldfather and W. A. Oldfather. Oceana 1964 o.p. A reprint of the 1688 Latin edition with a translation.
On the Natural State of Men. Trans. by Michael Seidler. E. Mellen 1990 $69.95. ISBN 0-88946-299-2

BOOK ABOUT PUFENDORF

Krieger, Leonard. *The Politics of Discretion: Pufendorf and the Acceptance of Natural Law.* U. Ch. Pr. 1965 o.p. A survey of Pufendorf's contributions to moral and political philosophy, jurisprudence, history, and theology.

SPINOZA, BARUCH (or BENEDICT). 1632–1677

Baruch Spinoza was born in Amsterdam, the son of Portuguese Jewish refugees who had fled from the persecution of the Spanish Inquisition. Although reared in the Jewish community, he rebelled against its religious views and practices, and in 1656 was formally excommunicated from the Portuguese-Spanish Synagogue of Amsterdam and was thus effectively cast out of the Jewish world. He joined a group of nonconfessional Christians (although he never became a Christian), the Collegiants, who professed no creeds or practices but shared a spiritual brotherhood. He was also apparently involved with the Quaker mission in Amsterdam. Spinoza eventually settled in The Hague, where he lived quietly, studying philosophy, science, and theology, discussing his ideas with a small circle of independent thinkers, and earning his living as a lens grinder. He corresponded with some of the leading philosophers and scientists of his time and was visited by LEIBNIZ and many others. He is said to have refused offers to teach at Heidelberg or to be court philosopher for the Prince of Condé. During his lifetime he published only two works, *The Principles of Descartes' Philosophy* (1666) and the *Theological Political Tractatus* (1670). In the first his own theory began to emerge as the consistent consequence of that of DESCARTES (see also Vol. 5). In the second, he gave his reasons for rejecting the claims of religious knowledge and elaborated his theory of the independence of the state from all religious factions. After his death (probably caused by consumption resulting from glass dust), his major work, the *Ethics*, appeared in his *Opera Posthuma*, and presented the full metaphysical basis of his pantheistic view. Spinoza's influence on the Enlightenment, on the Romantic Age, and on modern secularism has been tremendous.

BOOKS BY SPINOZA

Algebraic Calculations of the Rainbow and the Calculation of Chances. Ed. by Michael Petry. Kluwer Ac. 1986 $80.00. ISBN 90-247-3149-6. A careful critical edition of a work that was believe lost.

The Collected Works of Spinoza. Ed. by Edwin Curley. Princeton U. Pr. 1985 $75.00. ISBN 0-691-07222-1. This is the first volume (of an expected two-volume set) in the complete new translation presently underway (the former one, more than a century old, is not complete). Volume 1 contains the *Ethics* and *On the Correction of the Understanding.* It is very carefully done, with much scholarly explanation of the problems involved.

Earlier Philosophical Writings: The Cartesian Principles and Thoughts on Metaphysics. Trans. by F. A. Hayes. Irvington 1973 repr. of 1963 ed. o.p. The first work published by Spinoza, not included in *Works.*

The Ethics and Selected Letters. Trans. by Samuel Shirley. Hackett Pub. 1982 o.p. A lively new translation of this portion of Spinoza's work.

The Works of Spinoza. 2 vols. Trans. by R. H. Elwes. Peter Smith 1951 $38.50. ISBN 0-8446-2986-3. Although it does not contain all the works, and the translation is no longer adequate, this is the most complete collection of Spinoza's writings presently available. Volume 1 includes the *Theological Political Treatise* and the *Political Treatise.* Volume 2 contains the *Ethics,* the *Improvement of the Understanding,* and selected letters.

BOOKS ABOUT SPINOZA

Allison, Henry E. *Benedict De Spinoza.* Yale U. Pr. 1987 $14.00. ISBN 0-300-03596-9. A good general introduction to the thought of Spinoza.

Balz, Albert G. *Idea and Essence in the Philosophies of Hobbes and Spinoza.* AMS Pr. 1983 repr. of 1918 ed. $17.00. ISBN 0-404-00489-X. A good basic study by an important American historian of philosophy.

Bennett, Jonathan. *A Study of Spinoza's Ethics.* Hackett Pub. 1984 $34.95. ISBN 0-915145-82-0. This provocative examination of Spinoza's text by a leading contemporary linguistic philosopher has stirred much debate.

Boscherini, Emilia Giancotti. *Lexicon Spinozanum.* Nijhott 1970 o.p. An immense 2-volume listing of all the words and terms that appear in Spinoza's writings; the terms are given only in their original languages.

Caird, John. *Spinoza. Select Bibliographies Repr. Ser.* Ayer repr. of 1888 ed. $21.00. ISBN 0-8369-5877-2. A still interesting presentation by a leading English historian of philosophy.

Collins, James, ed. *Spinoza on Nature.* S. Ill. U. Pr. 1984 o.p. One of the last works by this important historian of philosophy.

Delahunty, R. J. *Spinoza. Arguments of the Philosophers Ser.* Routledge 1985 $49.95. ISBN 0-7102-0375-6. A detailed presentation of the various aspects of Spinoza's thought.

Donagan, Alan. *Spinoza.* U. Ch. Pr. 1988 $34.95. ISBN 0-226-15569-2. A survey of Spinoza's philosophy, emphasizing his naturalism.

Duff, Robert A. *Spinoza's Political and Ethical Philosophy.* Kelley 1920 repr. of 1903 ed. $49.50. ISBN 0-678-00615-6. A classic study of Spinoza's views about man and society.

Feuer, Lewis S. *Spinoza and the Rise of Liberalism.* Greenwood 1983 repr. of 1958 ed. $52.50. ISBN 0-313-24250-X. One of the most stimulating books about Spinoza's political thought and its relation to historical developments.

Freeman, Eugene, and Maurice Mandelbaum, eds. *Spinoza: Essays in Interpretation.* Open Court 1975 $9.95. ISBN 0-87548-196-5. A collection of articles by 14 English and American scholars, with a most useful bibliography of E. M. Curley.

Giancotti, Emilia, ed. *Proceedings of the First Italian International Congress on Spinoza*. Humanities 1985 o.p. One of the three volumes resulting from congresses in commemoration of the three-hundred-fiftieth anniversary of Spinoza's birth. (The others were held in Amsterdam and in Wolfenbuttel, Germany, respectively.) These congresses brought together scholars from all over the world to share their interests and findings about Spinoza, and the resulting volumes contain some very worthwhile papers.

Grene, Marjorie, ed. *Spinoza: A Collection of Critical Essays*. Modern Studies in Philosophy. U. of Notre Dame Pr. 1979 repr. of 1973 ed. o.p. "These essays on Spinoza deal with his method, with his metaphysics, and with his views on man and society. . . . With a teacher's help the essays can provide undergraduates with a valuable source of critical commentary" (*Choice*).

Grene, Marjorie, and Debra Nails, eds. *Spinoza and the Sciences*. Kluwer Ac. 1986 $97.00. ISBN 90-277-1976-4. An important collection of articles by various Spinoza scholars on the connection between his work and the development of physical and social science in his time and now.

Hampshire, Stuart. *Spinoza*. Viking Penguin 1952 $5.95. ISBN 0-14-022778-4. One of the best introductions to and surveys of Spinoza's thought; by one of England's leading philosophers.

Harris, Errol E. *Spinoza's Philosophy: An Outline*. Humanities 1992 $35.00. ISBN 0-391-03736-6. Compared to many recent works, this has the advantages of clarity and style.

Hessing, Siegfried, ed. *Speculum Spinozanum: 1677–1977*. Methuen 1978 o.p. This collection of 32 essays, some by Hessing and others by an international group of scholars, issued for the three-hundredth anniversary of Spinoza's death, was the first of several such collective volumes that greatly revived interest in Spinoza's thought and have led to the publication of a journal of Spinoza studies, *Studia Spinozanum*. Hessing stresses the relation of Spinoza's thought to mysticism, Buddhism, and the cabala. Foreword by Huston Smith.

Jaspers, Karl. *Spinoza*. Trans. by Ralph Manheim. *Great Philosophers Ser*. Harcourt 1974 o.p. An exposition of Spinoza's thought by one of the leading German existentialists.

Kashap, S. Paul, ed. *Studies in Spinoza: Critical and Interpretive Essays*. U. CA Pr. 1973 $13.00. ISBN 0-520-02590-3. A collection of essays by 14 Spinoza scholars from Europe and America. "[This volume] will be welcomed by all serious Spinoza students, particularly so because, while some of these articles are frequently cited, the original publications are scattered and often difficult to obtain" (*Library Journal*).

Kennington, Richard, ed. *The Philosophy of Baruch Spinoza*. Studies in Philosophy and the History of Philosophy. Cath. U. Pr. 1980 o.p. A group of 16 studies on Spinoza by various scholars, including Paul Weiss, Michael Hooker, Willis Doney, José Benardete. "The titles [of the essays] give a fair indication of the topics treated, and as they show, the collection is balanced, first of all, in the obvious sense of including a cross section of major issues in Spinoza's philosophy" (*Review of Metaphysics*).

Kline, George L. *Spinoza in Soviet Philosophy: A Series of Essays*. Hyperion Conn. 1981 repr. of 1952 ed. o.p. A fundamental study of the importance of Spinoza's views in Russian Communist thought.

Lucas, Jean M. *The Oldest Biography of Spinoza*. Ed. by Abraham Wolf. Assoc. Faculty Pr. 1970 repr. of 1927 ed. o.p. This work, dating from the late seventeenth or early eighteenth century, is the first known biography of Spinoza and contains many stories about him that have become legendary. It, along with the first published biography (by Colerus), established the saintly image of Spinoza. Only in recent years has information come to light that makes one doubt some of the picture. The Lucas biography, first published in 1719, was presumably written by a follower of Spinoza. It circulated in manuscript, often together with a work called *The Spirit of M. Spinoza, Or the Three Imposters, Moses, Jesus, and Mohammed*, whose authorship is still unknown, although much of the text is drawn from Spinoza's published works.

Mark, Thomas C. *Spinoza's Theory of Truth*. Col. U. Pr. 1972 o.p. A prize-winning dissertation that gave rise to a reevaluation of Spinoza's epistemology.

McKeon, Richard. *The Philosophy of Spinoza: The Unity of His Thought*. Ox Bow 1987 $35.00. ISBN 0-8118024-47-1. A scholarly but accessible work that discusses the development of Spinoza's thought and relates him to other modern philosophers.

Naess, Arne. *Freedom, Emotion and Self-Substance: The Structure of a Central Part of Spinoza's Ethics*. Universitet 1975 o.p. A leading Scandinavian scholar stresses the importance of Spinoza's conception of humankind and the world of the environmentalist concerns of today.

Negri, Antonio. *The Savage Anomaly: The Power of Spinoza's Metaphysics and Politics*. U. of Min. Pr. 1990 $44.95. ISBN 0-8166-1876-3. For Negri, Spinoza is the anomaly— one who, in the century that saw the birth of bourgeois ideology and the bourgeois state, discovered an alternative mode of thought and practice, a nondialectial path to social organization and liberation.

Oko, Adolph S. *A Spinoza Bibliography*. G. K. Hall 1970 o.p. Oko built up the two great Spinoza collections that are at Columbia University and Hebrew Union College, Cincinnati. His bibliography is invaluable for doing research on Spinoza. A privately printed catalog exists of the Abraham Wolf Spinoza Collection, which is now in Special Collections at the University of California, Los Angeles.

Pollack, Frederick. *Spinoza: His Life and Philosophy*. Irvington 1981 repr. of 1880 ed. $47.00. ISBN 0-697-00055-9. This was the standard work on Spinoza available in English a century ago. Much of it is still interesting and useful.

Roth, Leon. *Spinoza*. Hyperion Conn. 1986 repr. of 1954 ed. $23.75. ISBN 0-88355-813-0. A clear, careful presentation of Spinoza's philosophy seen in terms of the ideas of his time.

———. *Spinoza, Descartes and Maimonides*. Russell Sage 1963 o.p. An important work, comparing these three philosophers on basic metaphysical and epistemological issues. Since Spinoza attacked Maimonides so often, it is interesting to see how their views actually compare.

Scruton, Roger. *Spinoza*. OUP 1986 $7.95. ISBN 0-19-287630-9. A general introduction to Spinoza's philosophy.

Strauss, Leo. *Spinoza's Critique of Religion*. Trans. by E. M. Sinclair. Schocken 1982 o.p. Written in Germany before Hitler, this study by one of the most stimulating political theorists of modern times attempts to show what Spinoza was really driving at in his *Tractatus Theologico-Politicus*. Erudite and provocative.

Wetlesen, Jon. *The Sage and the Way: Studies in Spinoza's Ethics of Freedom*. Humanities 1979 o.p. Interprets Spinoza in the light of Buddhist thought.

Wienpahl, Paul. *The Radical Spinoza*. NYU Pr. 1979 $45.00. ISBN 0-8147-9186-7. A strong statement of the view, first offered at the end of the seventeenth century by Pierre Bayle, that Spinoza's thought is a kind of Oriental philosophy.

Willis, R. *Spinoza: His Life, Correspondence and Ethics*. Gordon Pr. 1977 $76.95. ISBN 0-8490-2657-1. A work of a century ago, giving the background of Spinoza, information about his milieu, his influence to the mid-nineteenth century, and the text of his correspondence and *Ethics*.

Wolf, Abraham, ed. *Correspondence of Benedict De Spinoza*. Biblio Dist. 1966 o.p. The complete correspondence of Spinoza (except for a recently discovered additional letter), this volume also provides information about the various correspondents.

Wolfson, Harry A. *The Philosophy of Spinoza: Unfolding the Latent Processes of His Reasoning*. HUP 1983 $22.00. ISBN 0-674-66595-3. This masterful commentary tries to show how Spinoza developed his theory. Wolfson stresses the role of medieval arguments, especially among the Jewish commentators known to Spinoza, and claims that Spinoza was both the last of the medieval thinkers and the first of the modern ones.

CHRONOLOGY OF AUTHORS
(Eighteenth Century)

Vico, Giambattista. 1668–1744
Shaftesbury, Anthony Ashley Cooper,
    Third Earl of. 1671–1713
Clarke, Samuel. 1675–1729
Wolff, Christian. 1679–1754
Berkeley, George. 1685–1753
Montesquieu, Charles-Louis Secondat,
    Baron de. 1689–1755
Butler, Joseph. 1692–1752
Hutcheson, Francis. 1694–1746
Voltaire. 1694–1778
Reid, Thomas. 1710–1796
Hume, David. 1711–1776

Rousseau, Jean-Jacques. 1712–1778
Diderot, Denis. 1713–1784
Condillac, Étienne Bonnot de.
    1715–1780
Price, Richard. 1723–1791
Smith, Adam. 1723–1790
Kant, Immanuel. 1724–1804
Burke, Edmund. 1729–1797
Lessing, Gotthold Ephraim. 1729–1781
Mendelssohn, Moses. 1729–1786
Herder, Johann Gottfried. 1744–1803
Bentham, Jeremy. 1748–1832
Fichte, Johann Gottlieb. 1764–1814

BENTHAM, JEREMY. 1748–1832

Jeremy Bentham, the founder of English utilitarianism and leader of the Philosophical Radicals, was born in London and educated at Queen's College, Oxford University, entering at the age of 12 and graduating at 15. Bentham's father, a lawyer, had him trained at Lincoln's Inn, and he was called to the bar in 1767, before the age of 20. Bentham never practiced law, however, preferring instead to investigate and reform the foundations of English law, which he regarded as obscure and irrational in theory and brutal and cumbersome in practice. Bentham's reforms were based on the theory of utility, which held that the rightness of an action depends wholly on its consequences for the pleasure and pain of all those affected by it. On this basis he advocated numerous legal reforms aiming at making the law simpler, clearer, more coherent, and more humane.

Of his voluminous writings on the law, Bentham published only one major work, his *Introduction to the Principles of Morals and Legislation* (1789). But as leader of a group known as the Philosophical Radicals, he attracted an influential following and founded both the radical *Westminster Review* and University College, London.

Aside from his moral and legal thought, Bentham's chief contribution to philosophy is in the philosophy of language. He advocated an extreme nominalism, arguing that most words refer to "fictions" and that the meaning of all terms referring to qualities, relations, classes, time, place, motion, and substance require "definition by paraphrasis"—that is, reductive translation into terms referring to real entities.

BOOKS BY BENTHAM

The Collected Works of Jeremy Bentham. 8 vols. Ed. by J. H. Burns. Humanities 1968 o.p.
    A critical edition of the works and correspondence. Five volumes of correspondence
    and three of writings on jurisprudence were published before the project was taken
    over by Oxford University Press (see below).
Chrestomathia. Ed. by W. Burston. OUP 1983 $85.00. ISBN 0-19-822610-1
Constitutional Code. Vol. 1 Ed. by Frederick Rosen. OUP 1983 $140.00. ISBN 0-19-
    822608-X
Deontology. Ed. by Amnon Goldworth. OUP 1983 $98.00. ISBN 0-19-822609-8

BOOKS ABOUT BENTHAM

Crimmins, James. *Secular Utilitarianism*. OUP 1990 $74.00. ISBN 0-19-827741-5. An
    erudite study of Bentham's theory of social science and his critique of religion.

Dinwiddy, John. *Bentham*. OUP 1989 $7.95. ISBN 0-19-287622-8. A general introduction.
Harrison, Ross. *Bentham*. Routledge 1983 $45.00. ISBN 0-7100-9526-0. The best introduction to the whole of Bentham's philosophy.
Lyons, David. *In the Interest of the Governed*. OUP 1991 $45.00. ISBN 0-19-823964-5. An excellent study of Bentham's utilitarianism and his philosophy of law.
Mack, M. P. *Jeremy Bentham: An Odyssey of Ideas*. Col. U. Pr. 1963 o.p. An intellectual biography.

BERKELEY, GEORGE. 1685–1753

Born and reared in Ireland, George Berkeley studied at Trinity College, Dublin, and then taught as a fellow there, eventually becoming Dean of Derry (1724) and Bishop of Cloyne (1734) in the Irish branch of the Anglican church. His primary philosophical interests included metaphysics and epistemology, the psychology of perception, philosophy of science, and natural theology. But he is best known for his defense of metaphysical idealism and denial of the existence of matter. Berkeley's best-known writings were produced relatively early in his life, between the ages of 24 and 28: *Essay Towards a New Theory of Vision* (1709), *Treatise Concerning the Principles of Human Knowledge* (1710), and *Three Dialogues* (1713). In 1728 Berkeley made a voyage to America in an unsuccessful attempt to found a college in Bermuda. He lived for two years at Newport, Rhode Island, and had a significant influence on American education, chiefly through his association with and donation of books to Yale University and his correspondence with Samuel Johnson, the first president of what is now Columbia University.

BOOKS BY BERKELEY

Berkeley's Philosophical Writings. Ed. by David M. Armstrong. Macmillan 1965 $6.95. ISBN 0-02-064170-2. A collection of all the main philosophical works of Berkeley.
Philosophical Works Including the Works of Vision. Ed. by M. R. Ayers. C. C. Tuttle 1975 $8.95. ISBN 0-460-87119-6. Berkeley's main philosophical works, plus the works on vision, the philosophical commentaries, and his correspondence with Johnson.
Philosophical Writings. Ed. by T. E. Jessop. Greenwood 1983 repr. of 1953 ed. $47.50. ISBN 0-8371-1056-4. A collection of Berkeley's texts by one of the editors of his complete works.
Principles, Dialogues and Philosophical Correspondence. Ed. by Colin M. Turbayne. Macmillan 1965 o.p. Berkeley's two main philosophical works and his correspondence with Johnson.
Three Dialogues between Hylas and Philonous. 1713. Ed. by Robert M. Adams. Hackett Pub. 1979 $21.50. ISBN 0-915144-62-X
A Treatise Concerning the Principles of Human Knowledge. 1710. Ed. by G. J. Warnock. Open Court 1985 $6.00. ISBN 0-87548-446-8
Works of George Berkeley, Bishop of Cloyne. 9 vols. Ed. by T. E. Jessop. KRP 1990 $525.00. ISBN 0-8115-0322-4
Works on Vision. Ed. by Colin M. Turbayne. *Lib. of Liberal Arts*. Greenwood 1981 repr. of 1963 ed. $42.50. ISBN 0-313-23186-9. Relevant texts on vision, plus discussions of the topic from other works of Berkeley.

BOOKS ABOUT BERKELEY

Atherton, Margaret. *Berkeley's Revolution in Vision*. Cornell Univ. Pr. 1990 $53.50. ISBN 0-8014-2358-9. A reassessment of Berkeley's *New Theory of Vision* (1709).
Bracken, Harry M. *Berkeley*. St. Martin 1975 $19.95. ISBN 0-312-07595-2. A new interpretation of Berkeley by one of the most careful contemporary scholars.
_____. *The Early Reception of Berkeley, 1710–1733*. Kluwer Ac. 1965 o.p. A study of the first reactions to Berkeley's philosophy.

Broad, C. D. *Berkeley's Argument. Studies in Philosophy*. Haskell 1975 $59.95. ISBN 0-8383-0113-4. Examination of Berkeley's central epistemological arguments by one of England's expositors of philosophy.

Dancy, Jonathan. *Berkeley: An Introduction*. Blackwell Pubs. 1987 $26.95. ISBN 0-631-15509-0. An introduction to Berkeley's metaphysics and epistemology by a contemporary analytic philosopher.

Grayling, A. C. *Berkeley: The Central Arguments*. Open Court 1986 $36.95. ISBN 0-8126-9037-0. A sympathetic account of Berkeley's main philosophical doctrines.

Jessop, Thomas E. *Bibliography of George Berkeley. Bibliography and Reference Ser.* B. Franklin 1968 repr. of 1934 ed. o.p. Bibliography of Berkeley's published works and manuscripts, and writings about him. A revised, enlarged edition published by Nijhoff, The Hague, 1973.

Luce, A. A. *The Life of George Berkeley, Bishop of Cloyne*. Greenwood repr. of 1949 ed. o.p. The most complete biography yet done, by a leading interpreter and defender of Berkeley.

Moked, Gabriel. *Particles and Ideas: Bishop Berkeley's Corpuscularian Philosophy*. OUP 1988 $59.00. ISBN 0-19-824990-X. An examination of Berkeley's attitude toward the mechanistic science of his day. Moked argues that this attitude underwent a dramatic change in Berkeley's final work, *Siris*.

Rand, Benjamin. *Berkeley's American Sojourn*. AMS Pr. 1987 repr. of 1932 ed. $8.50. ISBN 0-404-59323-2. The information available about Berkeley's trip to America, whom he met, and what he did.

Sosa, Ernest. *Essays on the Philosophy of George Berkeley*. Kluwer Ac. 1987 $85.00. ISBN 90-277-2405-9. Essays on Berkeley's immaterialism, his epistemology, and his theory of perception.

Steinkraus, Warren E., ed. *New Studies in Berkeley's Philosophy*. U. Pr. of Amer. 1982 repr. of 1966 ed. o.p. A collection of articles by various scholars.

Turbayne, Colin M., ed. *Critical and Interpretive Essays*. Bks. Demand repr. of 1982 ed. $10.95. ISBN 0-737-2912-X. A variety of essays on Berkeley by 20 different scholars.

Urmson, J. O. *Berkeley. Past Masters Ser.* OUP 1982 $6.95. ISBN 0-19-287546-9. An exposition of Berkeley's thought by one of the best linguistic philosophers of English.

Warnock, G. J. *Berkeley*. U. of Notre Dame Pr. 1983 o.p. A survey of Berkeley's views by a leading English contemporary philosopher.

BURKE, EDMUND. 1729–1797

Born in Ireland of a Catholic mother and a Protestant father of modest means, Edmund Burke studied classics at Trinity College, Dublin. He moved to England, where he pursued a literary career and then a political one, entering the House of Commons in 1766 as a Whig. He favored both the Irish and the American independence movements on the grounds that British rule in both places represented an interference with traditional rights and customs. Burke supported freedom of the press and favored exempting dissenters from subscribing to the Thirty-Nine Articles (the creed of the Anglican faith). Throughout his life, however, he vigorously opposed extending the suffrage or any other democratizing parliamentary reforms. In philosophy Burke is best known for an influential early work in aesthetics, *On the Sublime and Beautiful* (1756), and for his famous attack on the ideals of the French Revolution in *Reflections on the Revolution in France* (1790). Burke's aesthetics, especially in its emphasis on the experience of sublimity, the infinity of imagination, and of what is obscurely suggested rather than explicitly stated, prefigures both nineteenth-century romanticism and late twentieth-century postmodernism. Burke's political thought is characterized by Christian pessimism about human nature; he opposes all attempts to reform social institutions on the basis of human reason or preference on the grounds that the corrupt nature of all reformers leads inevitably to the failure of their schemes. Tradition, he thinks, represents our only guide to what has been found tolerable and consistent with human nature.

BOOKS BY BURKE

The Burke-Paine Controversy. Ed. by Ray Browne. HarBrace J 1963 o.p.
The Correspondence of Edmund Burke. 9 vols. Ed. by Thomas Copeland. U. Ch. Pr. 1958–1978 $32.00 ea. ISBNs 0-226-11553-4, 0-226-11554-2, 0-226-11555-0, 0-226-11556-9, 0-226-11557-7, 0-226-11558-5, 0-226-11559-3, 0-226-11560-7, 0-226-11561-5. The definitive edition.
The Philosophy of Edmund Burke. Ed. by Louis Bredfold and Ralph Ross. U. of Mich. Pr. 1960 $14.95. ISBN 0-472-06121-6
Selected Works. Ed. by W. J. Bate. Greenwood 1960 $35.00. ISBN 0-8371-8122-4
The Writings and Speeches of Edmund Burke. Ed. by P. J. Marshall. OUP. Vol. 2 *Party, Parliament and the American Crisis 1766–1774.* Ed. by Paul Langford. 1981 $135.00. ISBN 0-19-822416-8. Vol. 5 *India, Madras and Bengal.* Ed. by P. J. Marshall. 1980 $130.00. ISBN 0-19-822417-6. Vol. 6 *India: The Launching of the Hastings Impeachment 1786–1788.* Ed. by P. J. Marshall. 1991 $129.00. ISBN 0-19-8217-88-9. Vol. 8 *The French Revolution 1790–94.* Ed. by L. G. Mitchell. 1990. $130.00. ISBN 0-19-822422-2. Vol. 9 *The Revolutionary War, 1794–1797.* Ed. by R. B. McDowell. 1992 $160.00. ISBN 0-19-821787-0. A new critical edition, including some previously unpublished material.

BOOKS ABOUT BURKE

Maccuun, John. *The Political Philosophy of Burke.* Edward Arnold 1913 o.p. Dated but still useful.
Macpherson, C. B. *Burke.* OUP 1980 $5.95. ISBN 0-19-287518-3. A brief introduction.
O'Gorman, Frank. *Edmund Burke: His Political Philosophy.* Ind. U. Pr. 1973 o.p. Deals with Burke's writings on the British constitution, imperialism, and the French Revolution.
Wilkins, Burleigh. *The Problem of Burke's Political Philosophy.* OUP 1967 o.p. Discusses the question of whether Burke should be considered a natural-law theorist.

BUTLER, JOSEPH. 1692–1752

Born at Wautage, Berkshire, of a Presbyterian family, Joseph Butler converted to the Church of England sometime before entering Oriel College, Oxford University. He was ordained a priest in 1718, later serving as Bishop of Bristol and then as Bishop of Durham. Butler's contributions to philosophy lie in his moral philosophy and moral psychology, set forth in his *Sermons* (1726) and in his natural theology, expressed in *The Analogy of Religion* (1736). Despite the overtly religious context in which Butler presented it, his moral philosophy seeks to find a foundation for morality not in the divine will but in human nature, in the interplay of self-love and benevolence, and in reflection or conscience—a faculty superior to particular affections that judges them and recommends actions as right or wrong independently of them. In moral philosophy Butler is well known for his acute criticisms of the psychological egoism of HOBBES and Mandeville and in natural theology for his defense of revealed religion against the English deists. In an appendix to the *Analogy*, he also presented an influential critique of LOCKE's theory of personal identity.

BOOKS BY BUTLER

The Analogy of Religion. Ibis Pub. VA 1986 $19.95. ISBN 0-935005-40-4
Fifteen Sermons. Ibis Pub. VA 1986 $18.95. ISBN 0-935008-45-5
Five Sermons. Ed. by Stephen Darwall. Hackett Pub. 1983 $19.50. ISBN 0-915145-61-8
The Works of Bishop Butler. Ed. by J. H. Bernard. London 1900 o.p.

BOOKS ABOUT BUTLER

Carlsson, Percy. *Butler's Ethics.* Mouton 1964 o.p.
Cunliffe, Christopher, ed. *Joseph Butler's Moral and Religious Thought: Tercentenary Essays.* OUP 1992 $72.00. ISBN 0-19-826740-1. Fourteen essays on his philosophy and theology.

CLARKE, SAMUEL. 1675–1729

Born at Norwich, England, the son of the parliamentary representative from that district, Samuel Clarke studied at Caius College, Cambridge University. There he became acquainted with the natural philosophy of NEWTON (see also Vol. 5), whose friend and associate he became. Clarke produced a Latin translation of Newton's optics and an improved Latin version of Rohault's *System of Natural Philosophy*, the standard Cartesian textbook on physics, to which he appended critical notes reflecting the Newtonian standpoint. Clarke, an Anglican priest, held a number of ecclesiastical positions, including chaplain to Queen Anne. His chief philosophical work is *A Discourse Concerning the Being and Attributes of God*, a redaction of the Boyle lectures he gave twice in 1704 and 1705. In the first set of lectures, Clarke advances the most influential modern version of the cosmological argument for God's existence; he is generally thought to have been the model for the dogmatic rationalist theologian Demea in HUME's *Dialogues Concerning Natural Religion*. The second set of lectures sets forth a naturalistic theory of ethics, providing a basis for moral principles independently of the divine will in the natural "fitness" or "unfitness" between things (e.g., between a human being and certain types of action). When Caroline, Princess of Wales, proposed to sponsor a correspondence between LEIBNIZ and the Newtonians on questions of physics and natural religion, Newton selected Clarke as the philosopher best suited to represent the English side of the controversy. The result was a highly influential series of epistolary exchanges, which came to an end only with the death of Leibniz in 1716.

BOOKS BY CLARKE

The Leibniz-Clarke Correspondence. Ed. by H. G. Alexander. Ayer repr. of 1956 ed. $50.00. ISBN 0-405-13865-2
The Works. 4 vols. Garland 1978 o.p. A reprint of the 1738 edition, containing the Boyle lectures in their entirety; the correspondence with Leibniz, Butler, and Collins; "Letters on Liberty and Necessity;" and the sermons and various other theological writings.

BOOKS ABOUT CLARKE

Ferguson, James. *The Philosophy of Dr. Samuel Clarke and Its Critics.* Vantage 1974 o.p. A study of Clarke's arguments for the existence of God, his controversy with Anthony Collins on the free will problem, and his moral theory.
———. *Dr. Samuel Clarke: An Eighteenth Century Heretic.* Roundwood 1976 o.p. The only biography.
Rowe, William. *The Cosmological Argument.* Princeton U. Pr. 1975 o.p. Contains several chapters dealing with Clarke's argument for the existence of God and some objections to it.

CONDILLAC, ÉTIENNE BONNOT DE. 1715–1780

Born in Grenoble, France, Étienne Bonnot de Condillac studied theology at Saint-Sulpice and the Sorbonne and was ordained a Catholic priest in 1740. He was, however, always less interested in pursuing his sacred calling than in the advancement of secular knowledge. In this he was supported and encouraged by his cousin, the *philosophe* Jean le Rond d'Alembert, who introduced him to the circle of the encyclopedists, so that he became acquainted with DIDEROT, Helvetius, Fontenelle, and ROUSSEAU. Like them, Condillac admired the philosophies of LOCKE and NEWTON (see also Vol. 5); he set out to develop an experience-centered epistemology founded on sensation, modeled on Locke's genetic account of human knowledge (which he knew in Coste's translation) and on the mechanistic paradigm of science embodied in nineteenth-century Newtonian physics, which he knew through VOLTAIRE's (see also Vol. 2) *Elements of the Philosophy of Newton* (1738). The result was that, along with HUME and at about the same time, Condillac invented modern empiricism. His first works were *A Treatise on Systems* and *An Essay on the Origin of Human Knowledge* (both 1746). The former was a critique of traditional metaphysicians (especially MALEBRANCHE, LEIBNIZ, and SPINOZA), and the latter a positive statement of Condillac's sensationalist psychology and epistemology. In response to DIDEROT's objection that his epistemology seemed to commit him to Berkeleyan idealism, Condillac composed his most influential work, the *Treatise on Sensations* (1754), in which he attempted to explain how through sensation the mind naturally arrives at the ideas of independent material objects. His later writings include *Commerce and Government* (1776), a defense of physiocratic doctrines, and the posthumously published *Logic* (1792).

BOOKS BY CONDILLAC

An Essay on the Origin of Human Knowledge. Ed. by Robert Weyant. Trans. by Thomas Nugent. Schol. Facsimiles 1971 $60.00. ISBN 0-8201-1090-6. Condillac intended this as a supplement to Locke's *Essay.*
Philosophical Writings of Étienne Bonnot, Abbe de Condillac. Trans. by Franklin Philip and Harlan Lane. Erlbaum Assocs. 1982 $69.95. ISBN 0-89859-181-3. Contains *A Treatise on Systems, A Treatise on Sensations,* and *Logic.*
Treatise on the Sensations. Trans. by Geraldine Carr. U. of S. Cal. Pr. 1930 o.p.

BOOKS ABOUT CONDILLAC

Hine, Ellen. *A Critical Study of Condillac's* Traite des Systems. Nijhoff 1979 o.p. A scholarly study of Condillac's attack on the metaphysical systems of the seventeenth century.
Schaupp, Zora. *The Naturalism of Condillac.* U. of Nebr. Pr. 1926 o.p.

DIDEROT, DENIS. 1713–1784

Born in Langres, France, the greatest of the *philosophes* distinguished himself as a boy in the local Jesuit schools and was sent to Paris, where he received a master's degree at the age of 19. He lived in poverty for several years, engaging in intellectual pursuits and refusing to adopt a regular profession, a course that cut him off from the support of his family. In 1746 he published his first philosophical work, *Philosophical Thoughts.* In the same year, through his association with Jean le Rond d'Alembert, he became editor-in-chief of the *Encyclopedia,* a project that consumed most of his time until its completion in 1772. Diderot found time, however, to write a number of essays—*The Dream of d'Alembert, Refutation of Helvetius, Jacques the Fatalist,* and *Rameau's Nephew*—many of which were not published until after his death. In 1773 he visited the court of Catherine the Great of Russia, who made him custodian of her library. His hope was that the empress would put him in charge of recodifying her laws. But in 1774, as a result of his support of the more radical position in the controversy between deists and atheists, Diderot lost the patronage of both Catherine and Frederick the Great of Prussia; he spent the remainder of his life in Paris.

Diderot studied and wrote on an amazing variety of subjects—metaphysics, epistemology, physiology, psychology, ethics, political philosophy, history, literary criticism, and aesthetics. He defended empiricism, materialism, and a version of compatibilism concerning free will. His ethical thought owes much to stoicism, but he was interested in moral differences among cultures; in works such as *Rameau's Nephew* he shows an acute awareness of the moral dilemma confronting modern culture. Diderot's writings display literary creativity and novelty in form. He viewed all his work as a means of effecting progressive social and political change that would enfranchise the middle class and abolish the privileges of the nobility.

Books by Diderot

Diderot, Interpreter of Nature: Selected Writings. Ed. by Jonathan Kemp. Trans. by Jean Stewart. Hyperion Conn. 1990 repr. of 1937 ed. $35.00. ISBN 0-88355-841-6. Fine translations of Diderot's chief philosophical works.

Diderot's Early Philosophical Works. Ed. by Margaret Jourdain. AMS Pr. 1981 repr. of 1916 ed. $15.00. ISBN 0-404-08219-X. Contains his *Philosophic Thoughts, Letter on the Blind* and its additions, and *Deaf and Dumb.*

Diderot's Thoughts on Art and Style. Trans. by Beatrix Tollemache. *Philosophy Monographs Ser.* B. Franklin 1971 repr. of 1893 ed. o.p. Diderot's writings on art criticism.

The Letter on the Blind for the Benefit of Those Who See. 1749. Amer. Class. Coll. Pr. 1983 o.p. An important scientific and epistemological study.

A Pictorial Encyclopedia of Trades and Industry. 1751–52. 2 vols. Ed. by Charles C. Gillespie. Dover 1959 o.p. Includes some of the articles from the *Encyclopedia* on these subjects.

Political Writings. Ed. and trans. by John Mason and Robert Wokler. Cambridge U. Pr. 1992 $54.95. ISBN 0-521-36044-7

Rameau's Nephew and D'Alembert's Dream. 1796. Viking Penguin 1976 o.p. Diderot's most famous philosophical stories.

Books about Diderot

Brenner, Geoffrey. *Order and Chance: The Pattern of Diderot's Thought.* Cambridge U. Pr. 1983 $54.95. ISBN 0-521-25008-0. Presents the central thread of Diderot's ideas.

Cru, R. Loyalty. *Diderot as a Disciple of English Thought.* Columbia Univ. *Studies in Romance Philology and Literature.* AMS Pr. 1981 repr. of 1925 ed. $33.75. ISBN 0-404-50613-5. Diderot's use of English ideas from Locke onward.

Fellows, Otis. *Diderot.* Macmillan 1989 $26.95. ISBN 0-8057-8225-7. A 150-page intellectual biography.

France, Peter. *Diderot. Past Masters Ser.* OUP 1983 $13.95. ISBN 0-19-287550-7. A general presentation of Diderot's thought.

Furbank, Philip. *Diderot: A Critical Biography.* Knopf 1992 $29.50. ISBN 0-679-41421-5. Likely to become the standard biography.

Gordon, Douglas H., and Norman L. Torrey. *The Censoring of Diderot's Encyclopedia and the Reestablished Text.* AMS Pr. 1981 repr. of 1947 ed. $15.00. ISBN 0-404-02865-9. An account of what the censors removed from the *Encyclopedia.*

Morley, John. *Diderot and the Encyclopedists.* 2 vols. Richard West 1975 repr. of 1878 ed. o.p. A classic study of Diderot's role in the Enlightenment.

Schwartz, Leon. *Diderot and the Jews.* Fairleigh Dickinson 1981 $27.50. ISBN 0-8386-2377-8. "This good, well-written, scholarly work focuses on Diderot's attitude to Jews and Judaism. Schwartz disagrees with the broad scholarly opinion that Diderot was anti-Semitic. . . . [Diderot's] occasional anti-Jewish remarks, Schwartz argues, are to be taken with consideration of an evaluation of Diderot's views toward toleration" (*Choice*).

Vartanian, Aram. *Diderot and Descartes: A Study of Scientific Naturalism in the Enlightenment.* Bks. Demand 1975 $85.80. ISBN 0-317-09015-1. A comparison of Diderot's and Descartes's biological views, showing what is new in Diderot.

Warner, Stephen. *Socratic Satire: An Essay on Diderot and* Le Neveu de Rameau. Summa Pubns. 1987 $18.95. ISBN 0-917786-59-9. A work on Diderot's satire and Socrates's irony.

FICHTE, JOHANN GOTTLIEB. 1764–1814

Born of a poor family at Rammenau in eastern Germany, Johann Gottlieb Fichte attracted the attention of a baron who had him educated at Pforta and then at the Universities of Jena, Wittenberg, and Leipzig with a view to a clerical career. Drawn to philosophy by the writings of Lessing and Spinoza, he was converted to Kantianism in 1790 and went to Koenigsberg to visit Kant, showing him the manuscript of a work on religion, his *Attempt at a Critique of All Revelation.* Kant helped him publish it in 1792; the work appeared anonymously, and reviewers thought it was the work of Kant himself. When the truth became known, Fichte won instant fame and was appointed a professor at Jena. Between 1794 and 1800, he taught at Jena, his *Theory of Science* (1794) laying the ground for the German idealist movement. Fichte was dismissed from his professorship, ostensibly on grounds of atheism but actually because of his notoriously Jacobin political views and his difficult personality. He was welcomed in Berlin as a victim of religious persecution and briefly held a professorship at Erlangen before being named rector of the newly founded university in Berlin in 1810. Personal conflicts once again led to his resignation, but he retained the prestigious chair of philosophy until his death. In 1813 Fichte's wife Johanna became ill with typhus when nursing soldiers in the struggle against Napoleon. She recovered, but Fichte caught the disease and died in 1814.

Fichte's influential Jena period system was founded on the principle of the I, the original human awareness of freedom. From this base Fichte attempted a transcendental deduction of all theoretical and practical categories, including the category of passivity or sensibility, thus rejecting the Kantian doctrine of the thing-in-itself, all with the aim of rendering Kantian transcendental idealism less vulnerable to skeptical objections. Fichte's 1794 system was developed in haste, under the pressures of teaching at Jena. Its aims and methods are obscure, and throughout his life Fichte attempted time and again to develop the basic ideas, shifting his position significantly over the years. During the Jena period Fichte also developed a system of natural right and ethics, providing for strong redistributive rights and responsibilities on the part of the state, with a view to insuring civil and economic equality of all citizens. After leaving Jena, Fichte's idealism became more metaphysical and religious in orientation, and his practical philosophy became more nationalistic, as exhibited in his inspirational *Addresses to the German Nation* (1808), reflecting his strong commitment to the cause of resisting the Napoleonic invasion. Fichte's Jena period system was decisive for the development of the speculative idealism of Schelling and Hegel (see also Vol. 3); it is therefore decisive for the development of all continental thought since Kant.

Books by Fichte

Addresses to the German Nation. Trans. by R. F. Jones and G. H. Turnbull. HarpC 1968 o.p. Fichte's call to German nationalism in resistance against the French.

Attempt at a Critique of All Revelation. Trans. by G. D. Green. Cambridge U. Pr. 1978 o.p. Fichte's first major work.

Early Philosophical Writings. Trans. by Daniel Breazeale. Cornell Univ. Pr. 1988 $19.95. ISBN 0-8014-8121-X. Excellent new translations of important texts from Fichte's Jena period.
Popular Works. 2 vols. Trans. by William Smith. J. Chapman 1848 o.p. Old translations of various lectures by Fichte, mostly postdating the Jena period.
The Science of Ethics. Trans. by A. E. Kroeger. Routledge 1897 o.p. Badly translated, but again the only English rendering of an important text.
The Science of Knowledge. Trans. by Peter Heath and John Lachs. Cambridge U. Pr. 1982 $24.95. ISBN 0-521-27050-2. A new translation of Fichte's main text of 1794, including the two Introductions of 1797.
The Science of Rights. Trans. by A. E. Kroeger. Lippincott 1869 o.p. A poor translation, but the only existing English version of a very important text.
The Vocation of Man. Trans. by William Smith. Rev. by Roderick Chisholm. Macmillan 1956 o.p. A popular exposition of Fichte's philosophy from 1800.
The Wissenschaftslehre nova methodo. Trans. by Daniel Breazeale. Cornell Univ. Pr. 1992 o.p. An excellent translation of Fichte's illuminating attempt to expound his system in lectures between 1796 and 1799.

BOOKS ABOUT FICHTE

Hegel, G.W.F. *The Difference between Fichte's and Schelling's System of Philosophy.* Trans. by H. S. Harris. State U. NY Pr. 1977 $44.00. ISBN 0-87395-336-3. Hegel's first published work in 1801 was a defense of Schelling's speculative idealism in contrast to Fichte's "philosophy of reflection."
Neuhouser, Fred. *Fichte's Theory of Subjectivity.* Cambridge U. Pr. 1990 $14.95. ISBN 0-521-39938-6. An excellent new study of some major themes in *The Science of Knowledge.*

HERDER, JOHANN GOTTFRIED. 1744–1803

Born at Mohrungen, East Prussia, Johann Gottfried Herder enrolled in the University of Koenigsberg in 1762. He was profoundly impressed by KANT, but also by J. G. Hamann ("the Magus of the North"), an original but idiosyncratic religious thinker who also lived in Koenigsberg. Herder's thought can be seen as a struggle to unite what he thought was true in each of these two sharply contrasting standpoints. He became a Lutheran pastor, and from 1764 to 1769 taught at a cathedral school in Riga. Herder's prize-winning 1771 treatise on the origin of language gained him appointment as court preacher at Bueckeberg and then at Weimar, where he was befriended by GOETHE (see Vol. 2). He remained at this post the rest of his life.

Herder's writings encompass philosophy, history, and literary criticism. His chief philosophical work was the four-volume *Ideas toward the Philosophy of History of Humanity* (1784–91). The first two volumes were critically reviewed by Kant, whose philosophy of art and history they nevertheless influenced. Perhaps the leading thinker of the "Sturm and Drang" school, Herder saw the Enlightenment's reliance on autonomous reason as tending toward cultural rootlessness and ethnocentric arrogance. He himself was an Enlightenment thinker insofar as he favored liberal political institutions (even to the point of apparently espousing a brand of naive anarchism at times) and believed in modern European culture as the fruit of a progressive historical process. But Herder insisted that each culture and each stage in history represents a unique aspect of humanity, and he thought that human reason goes astray when it operates in abstraction from a larger humanity rooted in poetic and religious experience. His approach to the study of human psychology and human society was holistic; he treated human beings and human societies as natural phenomena that nevertheless give evidence through their spirituality of a

supernatural destiny. Herder is the forerunner of nineteenth-century romanticism, historicism, and cultural pluralism, as well as of the tendency in
nineteenth- and twentieth-century religious thought that relates religion more
closely to aesthetic feeling than to science and rational metaphysics.

BOOKS BY HERDER

God, Some Conversations. Trans. by Francis Harrison. Macmillan 1962 o.p.
Reflections on the Philosophy of the History of Mankind. Trans. by T. O. Churchill.
    Bks. Demand repr. of 1968 ed. $111.60. ISBN 0-8357-7007-9
*Selected Works, 1764–1767: Early Addresses, Essays, and Drafts; Fragments on Recent
    German Literature.* Ed. by Ernest Menze and Karl Menges. Trans. by Ernest Menze
    and Michael Palma. Pa. St. U. Pr. 1992 $35.00. ISBN 0-271-00712-5

BOOKS ABOUT HERDER

Barnard, Frederick. *Herder's Social and Political Thought: From Enlightenment to
    Nationalism.* OUP 1965 o.p. A dependable study emphasizing the organic character
    of Herder's thought.
———. *Self-Direction and Political Legitimacy: Rousseau and Herder.* OUP 1989 $76.00.
    ISBN 0-19-827327-4
Berlin, Isaiah. *Vico and Herder: Two Studies in the Philosophy of History.* Viking Penguin
    1976 o.p. Contains a 65-page essay on Herder and the Enlightenment.
Clark, Robert. *Herder: His Life and Thought.* U. CA Pr. 1955 o.p. The standard English
    biography.
Gillies, Alexander. *Herder.* OUP 1945 o.p. A general introduction to Herder's life and
    work.
Koepke, Wulf. *Johann Gottfried Herder.* Macmillan 1987 $26.95. ISBN 0-8057-6634-0. A
    general account of Herder's life and philosophy for the nonspecialist.
McEachran, F. *The Life and Philosophy of Johann Gottfried Herder.* OUP 1939 o.p. An
    account of Herder's life and work; superseded by Clarke and Barnard.
Nisbet, Hugh Barr. *Herder and the Philosophy and History of Science.* Cambridge U. Pr.
    1970 o.p. A detailed examination of Herder's philosophy of science.

HUME, DAVID. 1711–1776

David Hume was born in Edinburgh to a minor Scottish noble family, raised
at the estate of Ninewells, and attended the University of Edinburgh for two
years until he was 15. Although his family wished him to study law, he found
himself unsuited to this. He studied at home, tried business briefly, and after
receiving a small inheritance traveled to France, settling at La Flèche, where
DESCARTES (see also Vol. 5) had gone to school. There he completed his first and
major philosophical work, *A Treatise of Human Nature* (1739–40), published in
three volumes. Hume claimed on the title page that he was introducing the
experimental method of reasoning into moral subjects, and further that he was
offering a new way of seeing the limits of human knowledge. Although his work
was largely ignored, Hume gained from it a reputation as a philosophical
skeptic and an opponent of traditional religion. (In later years he was called
"the great infidel.") This reputation led to his being rejected for professorships
at both Edinburgh and Glasgow. To earn his living he served variously as the
secretary to General St. Clair, as the attendant to the mad Marquis of Annandale,
and as the keeper of the Advocates Library in Edinburgh. While holding these
positions, he wrote and published a new version of his philosophy, the two
Enquiries, and many essays on social, political, moral, and literary subjects. He
also began his six-volume *History of England from the Roman Invasion to the
Glorious Revolution* (1754–62), the work that made him most famous in his
lifetime. Having now become well known in literary and political circles, he

was appointed secretary to the British ambassador in Paris, where he was for a time in charge of the embassy. He was on friendly terms with many of the leading figures in the French Enlightenment but had a disastrous friendship with ROUSSEAU (see also Vol. 3), who visited England under his sponsorship. Hume served as secretary of state in the British government in 1767–68 but lost his position when the government fell because of its policy toward the American colonies. After seeking other positions, Hume retired from public life and settled in Edinburgh, where he was the leading figure in Scottish letters and a good friend to many of the leading intellectuals of the time, including ADAM SMITH (see also Vol. 3) and BENJAMIN FRANKLIN (see Vol. 1). During this period, he completed the *Dialogues Concerning Natural Religion*, which he had been working on for more than 25 years. Hume first worked on the *Dialogues* in the middle of his career, but put them aside as too provocative. In his last years he finished them and they were published posthumously in 1779. They are probably his best literary effort and have been the basis for continuous discussion and debate among philosophers of religion. Toward the end of Hume's life, his philosophical work began to be taken seriously, and the skeptical problems he had raised were tackled by philosophers in Scotland, France, and finally Germany, where KANT claimed that Hume had awakened him from his dogmatic slumbers.

Hume was one of the most influential philosophers of modern times, both as a positive force on skeptical and empirical thinkers and as a philosopher to be refuted by others. Interpreters are still arguing about whether he should be seen as a complete skeptic, a partial skeptic, a precursor of logical positivism, or even a secret believer.

BOOKS BY HUME

Abstract of a Treatise of Human Nature, 1740: A Pamphlet Hitherto Unknown. Ed. by P. Sraffa. Shoe String 1965 o.p. A pamphlet by Hume, apparently his own review of his *Treatise of Human Nature.* Introduction by John Maynard Keynes.

Dialogues Concerning Natural Religion. 1779. Ed. by Richard H. Popkin. Hackett Pub. 1980 $22.50. ISBN 0-915144-65-X. The text in Popkin's edition has been checked against Hume's original manuscript and is accompanied by two of his other posthumously published essays, "On Suicide" and "On the Immortality of the Soul."

Enquiries Concerning Human Understanding and Concerning the Principles of Morals. 1751. Ed. by P. H. Nidditch. OUP 1975 $15.95. ISBN 0-19-824536-X. "It is the first edition of either Enquiry to contain extended scholarly annotations (40 pages worth) and it claims more accuracy than the modern American-style versions edited by C. W. Hendel. . . . authoritative and very readable" (*Choice*).

An Enquiry Concerning Human Understanding: And Letter from a Gentleman to His Friend in Edinburgh. 1748. Ed. by Eric Steinberg. Hackett Pub. 1977 $22.50. ISBN 0-915144-16-6. The *Letter from a Gentleman* is a recently discovered pamphlet in which Hume defended his views from charges made against them when he was being considered for a professorship at the University of Edinburgh. The pamphlet, apparently put together from letters Hume had sent to Lord Kames, may also be the basis of his revised presentation of his philosophy in *Enquiry.*

An Enquiry Concerning the Principles of Morals. 1751. Ed. by J. B. Schneewind. *Philosophical Class. Ser.* Hackett Pub. 1983 $22.50. ISBN 0-915145-46-4. "Though there may be some contradictions in Hume's philosophy (and in some cases he was well aware of them himself), there is more consistency in his approach to morals as related to his approach to cognizance than would seem on the surface. . . . In the analysis of moral judgment, Hume finds that it too is ultimately founded not on reason but on a sentiment. Though Hume refrains from referring to this statement as skeptical, we are entitled to conclude that in a sense it amounts to skepticism. On the other hand, this sentiment is a fundamental working factor in human life" (*Ethics*).

History of England: From the Invasion of Julius Caesar to the Revolution of 1688. 1754–62. Liberty Fund 1975 $120.00. ISBN 0-86597-020-3

The Letters of David Hume. 2 vols. Ed. by J. Y. Greig. Garland 1983 o.p. This is a reprint of the 1932 edition. Many letters have been discovered since this publication. Because the volume includes only Hume's letters and not those written to him, it is often difficult (without using Burton, listed below) to follow what is being discussed.

The Natural History of Religion. 1755. (and *Dialogues Concerning Natural Religion*). Ed. by H. E. Root. Stanford U. Pr. 1957 $8.95. ISBN 0-8047-0333-7. A critical edition of these two works with extensive annotations.

The New Letters of David Hume. Ed. by Ernest C. Mossner. Garland 1983 o.p. This volume includes letters discovered after Greig's edition. Other letters that have since been found appear in various journals. No complete edition of Hume's correspondence is in the offing.

Of the Standard of Taste and Other Essays. Ed. by John W. Lenz. Macmillan 1965 $7.97. ISBN 0-672-60269-5. Some of Hume's writings on aesthetics.

Philosophical Works. 4 vols. Ed. by Thomas H. Green and Thomas H. Grose. Adlers Foreign Bks. 1964 repr. of 1882 ed. $530.00. ISBN 3-511-01210-4. This, the closest there is to a "complete works" of Hume, does not include any of his *History of England*, the recently discovered works, or the philosophical correspondence. An edition of Hume's philosophical writings is presently being prepared for the Princeton University Press by David Fate Norton (4 volumes of text and 4 volumes of concordance are scheduled for completion by 1999).

A Treatise of Human Nature. 1739–40. Ed. by P. H. Nidditch. OUP 1978 $15.95. ISBN 0-19-824588-2. The Oxford edition is the best available one of Hume's first and fullest statement of his philosophy. Nidditch has included corrections found in Hume's hand in copies of the original printing; unfortunately, however, they are in an appendix and have not been integrated into the text.

Writings on Economics. Ed. by Eugene Rotwein. *Essay Index Repr. Ser.* Ayer repr. of 1955 ed. $22.00. ISBN 0-8369-2907-1. Hume's writings on banking, public credit, trade, and so forth.

BOOKS ABOUT HUME

Ayer, A. J. *Hume*. OUP 1980 $6.95. ISBN 0-19-287528-0. Sprightly presentation of Hume by one of the best-known English analytic philosophers.

Baier, Annette. *A Progress of Sentiments: Reflections on Hume's Treatise*. HUP 1991 $42.50. ISBN 0-674-71385-0. An attempt to show the *Treatise* as a unified argument against a limited, intellectualist notion of reason.

Beauchamp, Tom L., and Alexander Rosenberg. *Hume and the Problem of Causation*. OUP 1981 $32.50. ISBN 0-19-520236-8. A very carefully argued attempt to resolve the problem of causation as raised by Hume.

Berry, Christopher J. *Hume, Hegel and Human Nature*. Kluwer Ac. 1983 $80.00. ISBN 90-247-2682-4. A striking comparison of the views of Hume and Hegel considered in their contemporary settings.

Burton, John H. *The Life and Correspondence of David Hume*. Garland 1983 o.p. The first basic collection of data about Hume's life.

Capaldi, Nicholas. *David Hume: The Newtonian Philosopher. Twayne's World Authors Ser.* Macmillan 1975 o.p. A fine survey of Hume's views, presenting him in the traditional Newtonian experimental philosophy.

Church, Ralph W. *Hume's Theory of the Understanding*. Greenwood 1980 repr. of 1935 ed. $47.50. ISBN 0-313-20651-1. One of the first works of new scholarship about Hume's philosophy.

Flage, Daniel. *David Hume's Theory of Mind*. Routledge 1991 $65.00. ISBN 0-415-02138-3. An account of Hume's bundle theory of the mind, claiming that it provides the key for understanding Hume's own low opinion of his early *Treatise*.

Flew, Anthony. *David Hume: Philosopher of Moral Science*. Blackwell Pubs. 1986 $49.95. ISBN 0-631-13735-1. A comprehensive account of Hume's philosophy that sets it in the context of his life's work in the "moral sciences"—broadly defined to include history and literature.

Fogelin, Robert. *Hume's Skepticism in the Treatise of Human Nature*. Routledge 1985 $29.50. ISBN 0-7102-0368-3. A systematic study that gives more emphasis to Hume's naturalism than the title suggests.

Hall, Roland. *Fifty Years of Hume Scholarship*. Col. U. Pr. 1979 $15.00. ISBN 0-85224-337-5. This work supplements Jessop's bibliography (see below) and covers almost all the books and articles on Hume in the period. The bibliography is kept up to date by addenda published in journals.

Hendel, Charles W. *Studies in the Philosophy of David Hume*. Garland 1983 o.p. A reprint of one of the basic studies of the naturalist side of Hume's thought.

Hurlbutt, Robert H. *Hume, Newton, and the Design Argument*. U. of Nebr. Pr. 1985 $27.50. ISBN 0-8032-2337-4. A study of Newton's presentation of the design or teleological argument, and Hume's criticism of it.

Jessop, T. E. *A Bibliography of David Hume and of Scottish Philosophy from Francis Hutcheson to Lord Balfour*. Garland 1983 $36.00. Reprint of the basic bibliographical reference work about Hume.

Kemp Smith, Norman. *The Philosophy of David Hume*. Greenwood 1983 o.p. An interpretation of Hume as a naturalist rather than a skeptic, the dominant reading for many years.

Leroy, Andre L. *David Hume*. Trans. by J. P. Mayer. *European Political Thought Ser.* Ayer 1979 repr. of 1953 ed. $25.50. ISBN 0-405-11713-2. A presentation and interpretation of Hume's views by the leading French Hume scholar (and translator of Hume into French).

Livingston, Donald W. *Hume's Philosophy of Common Life*. U. Ch. Pr. 1985 $13.95. ISBN 0-226-48715-6. Shows that Hume's positive writings on moral and social topics are consistent with his skepticism.

Mackie, J. L. *Hume's Moral Theory*. *International Lib. of Philosophy and Scientific Method*. Methuen 1980 o.p. A good presentation and examination of Hume's moral theory.

Merrill, Kenneth R., and Robert W. Shahan, eds. *David Hume: Many-Sided Genius*. U. of Okla. Pr. 1976 $10.95. ISBN 0-8061-1387-1. A group of essays by Hume scholars in connection with the bicentennial of his death.

Mossner, Ernest C. *The Forgotten Hume, Le Bon David*. AMS Pr. 1967 repr. of 1943 ed. o.p. A groundbreaking study of Hume's role as a literary critic of his contemporaries.

––––––. *The Life of David Hume*. OUP 1980 $59.00. ISBN 0-19-824381-2. The most comprehensive biography of Hume to date.

Norton, David F. *David Hume: Common Sense Moralist, Sceptical Metaphysician*. Princeton U. Pr. 1982 $47.00. ISBN 0-691-07265-5. An attempt to reconcile Hume's positive naturalistic moral theory with his skeptical theory of knowledge.

Noxon, James. *Hume's Philosophical Development: A Study of His Methods*. OUP 1973 $39.95. ISBN 0-19-824398-8. An attempt to show how Hume's philosophy developed, against interpreters who say he had the same theory all his life.

Passmore, John. *Hume's Intentions*. Longwood 1980 repr. of 1968 ed. o.p. Examination of what Hume was trying to achieve, and the weakness of his reasoning in so doing.

Penelhum, Terence. *David Hume: An Introduction to His Philosophical System*. Purdue U. Pr. 1992 $27.00. ISBN 1-55753-012-2. Selected texts of Hume followed by liberal commentary.

Popkin, Richard H. *The High Road to Pyrrhonism*. Ed. by R. A. Watson and J. E. Force. Hackett Pub. 1980 $28.50. ISBN 0-89690-002-9. A collection of the author's essays, many on Hume, which started the modern interpretation of Hume as a complete skeptic.

Price, Henry H. *Hume's Theory of the External World*. Greenwood 1981 repr. of 1940 ed. $35.00. ISBN 0-313-22707-1. A very careful discussion of the texts in Hume dealing with our knowledge of the external world.

Seth, Andrew. *Scottish Philosophy*. Garland 1983 o.p. Important nineteenth-century survey of the eighteenth-century Scottish thinkers, including Hume.

Stove, D. C. *Probability and Hume's Inductive Skepticism*. OUP 1973 $27.50. ISBN 0-19-824501-7. Applies the modern theory of induction to Hume's analysis and argues that some of Hume's skeptical conclusions are not warranted.

Stroud, Barry. *Hume. Arguments of the Philosophers Ser.* Routledge 1981 $14.95. ISBN 0-415-03687-9. Presents Hume's skepticism in terms of contemporary analytic thought.

Strawson, Galen. *The Secret Connexion: Causation, Realism, and David Hume*. OUP 1989 $55.00. ISBN 0-19-824853-9. A challenging, philosophically sophisticated, revisionist account of Hume on causation.

Talmor, Ezra. *Descartes and Hume*. Pergamon 1980 o.p. Tries to show how Hume saved Cartesianism from its own contradictions.

Taylor, A. E. *David Hume and the Miraculous*. Folcroft 1927 o.p. Hume contended that the occurrence of miracles is inherently implausible and cannot be accepted by reasonable people. This work, which should be compared with C. S. Lewis's *Miracles*, claims that Hume's conclusion is unjustified.

Todd, William B., ed. *Hume and the Enlightenment: Essays Presented to Ernest Campbell Mossner*. U. of Tex. Pr. 1974 o.p. A *festschrift* volume.

HUTCHESON, FRANCIS. 1694–1746

The founder of moral sense theory was born in County Down, Ireland. Francis Hutcheson's father and grandfather were Presbyterian ministers, and he studied at the University of Glasgow from 1711 to 1717 in preparation for the Presbyterian ministry. For the next decade, he taught at an academy for dissenting clergy in Dublin, most of the time serving as its head. He was appointed professor of moral philosophy at Glasgow in 1730, a position he held until his death. Hutcheson's principal contributions to philosophy were in the fields of moral philosophy and aesthetics. His chief works are *Inquiry into the Original of Our Ideas of Beauty and Virtue* (1725), *Philosophiae Moralis Institutio* (1742), and the posthumously published *System of Moral Philosophy* (1755). Against the English rationalists SAMUEL CLARKE and RICHARD PRICE, Hutcheson rigorously developed SHAFTESBURY'S suggestion that moral distinctions are made by our sensitive rather than our rational nature. In aesthetics he gave an analogous account of our sense of beauty. Hutcheson's theories profoundly influenced HUME and also had a significant impact on KANT in his precritical period.

BOOKS BY HUTCHESON

Illustrations on the Moral Sense. Ed. by Bernard Peach. HUP 1971 $27.50. ISBN 0-674-44326-8

An Inquiry Concerning Beauty, Order, Harmony, Design. Schol. Facsimiles 1969 o.p. A reprint of the 1742 edition.

A Short Introduction to Moral Philosophy. AMS Pr. repr. of 1747 ed. $34.50. ISBN 0-404-17194-X

BOOKS ABOUT HUTCHESON

Blackstone, William. *Francis Hutcheson and Contemporary Ethical Theory*. U. of Ga. Pr. 1965 o.p. Contains an exposition of Hutcheson's moral sense theory and an account of the controversy with Richard Price.

Jensen, Henning. *Motivation and the Moral Sense in Francis Hutcheson's Ethical Theory*. Nijhoff 1971 o.p. Focuses on problems arising from the conjunction of Hutcheson's moral sense theory and his theory of motivation.

Kivy, Peter. *The Seventh Sense*. B. Franklin 1976 o.p. A study of Hutcheson's aesthetics and its influence in eighteenth-century Britain.

Raphael, D. D. *The Moral Sense*. OUP 1947 o.p. An excellent 200-page study of the school
of moral philosophy, which included Hutcheson, Hume, Price, and Reid.

KANT, IMMANUEL. 1724–1804

The greatest of all modern philosophers was born in the Baltic seaport of
Königsberg, East Prussia, the son of a humble saddler; the outstanding
representative of Enlightenment cosmopolitanism never left the vicinity of his
remote birthplace. Through his family pastor, Immanuel Kant received the
opportunity to study at the newly founded *Collegium Fredericianum*, proceeding
to the University of Königsberg, where he was introduced to Wolffian
philosophy and modern natural science by the philosopher Martin Knutzen.
From 1746 to 1755, he served as tutor in various private households near
Königsberg; he then received his master's degree and began teaching as an
unsalaried lecturer. Between 1755 and 1770, Kant published treatises on a
number of scientific and philosophical subjects, including a 1755 treatise in
which he originated the nebular hypothesis of the origin of the solar system.
Some of Kant's writings in the early 1760s attracted the favorable notice of
respected philosophers such as J. H. Lambert and MOSES MENDELSSOHN, but a
professorship eluded Kant until he was over 45. He published virtually nothing
for the next decade, apparently disappointing those who had seen such promise
in him.

Then in 1781 Kant finally published his great work, the *Critique of Pure
Reason*. The early reviews were hostile and uncomprehending, and Kant's
attempt to make his theories more accessible in his *Prolegomena to Any Future
Metaphysics* (1783) was largely unsuccessful. Then, partly through the influence
of his former student J. G. HERDER, whose writings on anthropology and history
challenged his Enlightenment convictions, Kant turned his attention to issues in
the philosophy of morality and history, writing several short essays on the
philosophy of history and sketching his ethical theory in the *Foundations of the
Metaphysics of Morals* (1785). Kant's new philosophical approach finally began
to receive attention in 1786 through a series of articles in a widely circulated
Göttingen journal by the Jena philosopher K. L. REINHOLD. The following year
Kant published a new, extensively revised edition of the *Critique*, following it up
with the *Critique of Practical Reason* (1788), treating the foundations of moral
philosophy, and the *Critique of Judgment* (1790), an examination of aesthetics—
rounding out his system through a strikingly original treatment of two topics
that were widely perceived as high on the philosophical agenda at the time: the
philosophical meaning of the taste for beauty and the use of teleology in natural
science. From the early 1790s onward, Kant was regarded by the coming
generation of philosophers as having overthrown all previous systems and as
having opened up a whole new philosophical vista.

During the last decade of his philosophical activity, Kant devoted most of his
attention to applications of moral philosophy. His two chief works in the 1790s
were *Religion Within the Bounds of Plain Reason* (1793–94) and *Metaphysics of
Morals* (1798), the first part of which contained Kant's theory of right, law, and
the political state. At the age of 74, most philosophers who are still active are
engaged in consolidating and defending views they have already worked out.
Kant, however, had perceived an important gap in his system and had begun
rethinking its foundations. These attempts went on for four more years until the
ravages of old age finally destroyed Kant's capacity for any further intellectual
work. The result was a lengthy but disorganized and obscure manuscript that
was first published in 1920 under the title *Opus postumum*. It displays the

impact of some of the more radical young thinkers Kant's philosophy itself had inspired (notably SCHELLING).

Kant's philosophy focuses attention on the active role of human reason in the process of knowing the world and on its autonomy in giving moral law. Kant saw the development of reason as a collective possession of the human species, a product of nature working through human history. For him the process of free communication between independent minds is the very life of reason, the vocation of which is to remake politics, religion, science, art, and morality as the completion of a destiny whose shape it is our collective task to frame for ourselves.

BOOKS BY KANT

The *Cambridge Edition of the Writings of Immanuel Kant* is a projected comprehensive edition of all his principal works in 14 volumes, under the general editorship of Paul Guyer and Allen W. Wood. At this writing three volumes have appeared:

Lectures in Logic. Ed. and trans. by J. Michael Young. Cambridge U. Pr. 1992 $85.00. ISBN 0-521-36013-7

Opus postumum. Ed. by Eckart Foerster. Trans. by Eckart Foerster and Michael Rosen. Cambridge U. Pr. 1993 $49.95. ISBN 0-521-26511-8

Theoretical Philosophy 1755–1770. Ed. and trans. by David Walford and Ralf Meerbote. Cambridge U. Pr. 1992 $75.00. ISBN 0-521-39214-4

Other translations:

Anthropology from a Pragmatic Point of View. Trans. by Mary Gregor. Nijhoff 1974 o.p.

Conflict of the Faculties. Trans. by Mary Gregor. U. of Nebr. Pr. 1992 $12.95. ISBN 0-8032-7775-X

Critique of Judgment. Trans. by Werner Pluhar. Hackett Pub. 1987 $13.95. ISBN 0-87220-025-6

Critique of Practical Reason. Trans. by Lewis White Beck. Macmillan 1992. ISBN 0-02-307753-0

Critique of Pure Reason. Trans. by Norman Kemp Smith. St. Martin 1969 $17.35. ISBN 0-312-45010-9

Foundations of the Metaphysics of Morals. Trans. by Lewis White Beck. Macmillan 1959 o.p.

The Kant-Eberhard Controversy. Trans. by Henry Allison. Bks. Demand repr. of 1973 ed. $53.00. ISBN 0-317-30115-2

Kant on History. Ed. by Lewis White Beck. Trans. by Lewis White Beck, Robert Anchor, and Emil Fackenheim. Macmillan 1963 o.p.

Lectures on Ethics. Trans. by Louis Infield. Hackett Pub. 1980 $7.95. ISBN 0-915144-26-3

Lectures on Philosophical Theology. Trans. by Allen W. Wood and Gertrude M. Clark. Cornell Univ. Pr. 1978 $31.50. ISBN 0-8014-1199-8

Metaphysical Foundations of Natural Science. Trans. by James Ellington. Macmillan 1965 o.p.

Metaphysics of Morals. Trans. by Mary Gregor. Cambridge U. Pr. 1991 $54.95. ISBN 0-521-30372-9

Philosophical Correspondence. Trans. by Arnulf Zweig. U. Ch. Pr. 1986 $18.95. ISBN 0-226-42361-1

Political Writings. Ed. by Hans Reiss. Trans. by H. B. Nisbet. Cambridge U. Pr. 1991 $54.95. ISBN 0-521-39185-7

Prolegomena to Any Future Metaphysics. Trans. by Lewis White Beck. 1985 $5.00. ISBN 0-87548-056-X

Religion Within the Limits of Reason Alone. Trans. by H. Hudson and T. M. Greene. HarpC 1960 $14.00. ISBN 0-06-130067-5

BOOKS ABOUT KANT

Allison, Henry. *Kant's Theory of Freedom*. Cambridge U. Pr. 1990 $17.95. ISBN 0-521-38708-6. A comprehensive, sympathetic treatment of Kant's concept of freedom and its relation to Kantian ethics.

Aune, Bruce. *Kant's Theory of Morals*. Princeton U. Pr. 1979 $35.00. ISBN 0-691-02006-X. An acute, critical exposition of Kant's ethical theory by a leading analytical philosopher.

Beck, Lewis White. *A Commentary on Kant's Critique of Practical Reason*. U. Ch. Pr. 1960 o.p. The classic discussion of this work.

———. *Studies in the Philosophy of Kant*. Greenwood 1981 $47.50. ISBN 0-313-23183-4. A collection of articles by a leading Kant scholar.

Bennett, Jonathan. *Kant's Analytic*. Cambridge U. Pr. 1966 $19.95. ISBN 0-521-09389-9. A philosophically acute critical discussion of Kant's positive theory of knowledge.

———. *Kant's Dialectic*. Cambridge U. Pr. 1974 $21.95. ISBN 0-521-09849-1. A companion volume critically discussing the various problems raised in the Transcendental Dialectic of the *Critique of Pure Reason*.

Bird, Graham. *Kant's Theory of Knowledge*. Routledge 1962 o.p. A brief but classic study, breaking with the standard early twentieth-century interpretation of Kant.

Cassirer, Ernst. *Kant's Life and Thought*. Trans. by James Haden. Yale U. Pr. 1981 $50.00. ISBN 0-300-02358-8. The best intellectual biography of Kant available in English.

Crawford, Donald. *Kant's Aesthetic Theory*. Bks. Demand repr. of 1974 ed. $50.00. ISBN 0-317-12976-7. One of the best treatments of Kant's aesthetic theory.

Friedman, Michael. *Kant and the Exact Sciences*. HUP 1992 $45.00. ISBN 0-674-50035-0. The best existing study of Kant's philosophy of mathematics and natural science.

Guyer, Paul. *Kant and the Claims of Knowledge*. Cambridge U. Pr. 1987 $27.95. ISBN 0-521-33772-0. The best recent study of Kant's theoretical views, tracing their development and providing a critical reconstruction of the arguments for them.

———. *Kant and the Claims of Taste*. HUP 1979 $32.00. ISBN 0-674-50020-2. Difficult reading, but the best existing treatment of Kant's theory of taste.

———. *Kant and the Experience of Freedom*. Cambridge U. Pr. 1993 $59.95. ISBN 0-521-41431-8. Essays investigating the relation between aesthetics and morality in Kant's philosophy.

———, ed. *The Cambridge Companion to Kant*. Cambridge U. Pr. 1992 $59.95. ISBN 0-521-36768-9. A comprehensive anthology of excellent, informative articles.

Heidegger, Martin. *Kant and the Problem of Metaphysics*. Trans. by James Churchill. Bks. Demand repr. of 1962 ed. $72.80. ISBN 0-685-44463-5. A famous and original twentieth-century philosopher's most useful piece of historical scholarship.

Hill, Thomas E., Jr. *Dignity and Practical Reason*. Cornell Univ. Pr. 1992 $38.50. ISBN 0-8014-2514-X. A collection of insightful papers by a leading scholar of Kant's ethics.

Kemp Smith, Norman. *A Commentary on Kant's Critique of Pure Reason*. Macmillan 1923 o.p. A classic commentary.

Kitcher, Patricia. *Kant's Transcendental Psychology*. OUP 1990 $38.00. ISBN 0-19-505967-0. An informed, original study of central themes in Kant's *Critique of Pure Reason* and their bearing on contemporary psychology and philosophy of mind.

Martin, Gottfried. *Kant's Metaphysics and Theory of Science*. Trans. by P. G. Lucas. Greenwood 1974 $42.50. ISBN 0-8371-7154-7. The author was the most influential Kant scholar in Germany in the generation after World War II.

McFarland, J. D. *Kant's Concept of Teleology*. Col. U. Pr. 1971 $22.50. ISBN 0-85224-070-8. The best book-length treatment of this topic in English.

Melnick, Arthur. *Kant's Analogies of Experience*. U. Ch. Pr. 1973 o.p. A good discussion of Kant's theory of substance and causality.

Mulholland, Leslie. *Kant's Theory of Rights*. Col. U. Pr. 1990 o.p. The most thorough treatment of Kant's Doctrine of Right available in English.

O'Neill, Onora. *Acting on Principle*. Col. U. Pr. 1975 $41.00. ISBN 0-8357-5083-3. The most influential interpretation of Kant's formula of universal law in the last generation.

Paton, H. J. *The Categorical Imperative*. HarpC 1947 o.p. The classic mid-century commentary on Kant's *Foundations of the Metaphysics of Morals*.
_____. *Kant's Metaphysics of Experience*. 2 vols. Humanities 1984 $50.00. ISBN 0-391-00673-8. A painstaking classic commentary on the first half of the *Critique of Pure Reason*.
Pippin, Robert. *Kant's Theory of Form*. Yale U. Pr. 1982 $35.00. ISBN 0-300-02659-5. An insightful study of Kant's theory of pure intuition and the forms of thinking.
Rosen, Allen. *Kant's Theory of Justice*. Cornell Univ. Pr. 1993 $28.50. ISBN 0-8014-2757-6. The most philosophically acute discussion of Kant's political philosophy available in English.
Ross, Sir David. *Kant's Ethical Theory*. Greenwood 1978 $38.50. ISBN 0-8371-9059-2. A succinct critical exposition by a leading twentieth-century moral philosopher.
Schaper, Eva. *Studies in Kant's Aesthetics*. Col. U. Pr. 1979 $16.50. ISBN 0-85224-359-6. A collection of papers by one of the century's leading scholars of Kant's aesthetics.
Strawson, P. F. *The Bounds of Sense*. Routledge 1966 $17.95. ISBN 0-415-04030-2. An influential, independent-minded exposition of Kant's theoretical philosophy by a leading British philosopher.
Sullivan, Roger. *Kant's Moral Theory*. Cambridge U. Pr. 1989 $19.95. ISBN 0-521-36908-8. A comprehensive, readable exposition of Kant's ethical thought.
Van der Linden, Harry. *Kantian Ethics and Socialism*. Hackett Pub. 1988 $32.00. ISBN 0-87220-028-0. A sympathetic, historically informed discussion of the relation of Kantian ethics to the traditions of neo-Kantian and Marxist socialism.
Velkley, Richard. *Freedom and the End of Reason*. U. Ch. Pr. 1989 $29.95. ISBN 0-226-85260-1. An original, historically informed discussion of the ethical roots of Kant's philosophy.
Walker, Ralph. *Kant*. Routledge 1978 $13.95. ISBN 0-415-04297-6. The best recent exposition of Kant's philosophy as a whole.
Wood, Allen W. *Kant's Moral Religion*. Cornell Univ. Pr. 1970 o.p. The most thorough discussion available of Kant's moral arguments for God's existence.
_____. *Kant's Rational Theology*. Cornell Univ. Pr. 1978 $35.00. ISBN 0-8014-1200-5. The best discussion of Kant's conception of God and critique of traditional theistic proofs available in English.
_____, ed. *Self and Nature in Kant's Philosophy*. Cornell Univ. Pr. 1984 $13.95. ISBN 0-8014-9268-8. An anthology of excellent papers by various authors on topics ranging over Kant's theory of the self, moral freedom, metaphysics, and philosophy of science.
Yovel, Yirmiahu. *Kant and the Philosophy of History*. Princeton U. Pr. 1980 $55.00. ISBN 0-691-07225-6. The best book-length treatment of the topic in English.

LESSING, GOTTHOLD EPHRAIM. 1729–1781

Born at Kamenz in Saxony, this son of a Lutheran pastor studied theology at the University of Leipzig, where he absorbed the rationalistic philosophy of Christian Wolff and read the English deists. More a man of letters than a philosopher in the strict sense, Lessing was nevertheless an influential critic and aesthetician, and his theological views—far from orthodox, open-minded and restless, rationalistic yet undeniably pious in a highly personal way—had an impact well into the next century (on Kierkegaard, for example). Lessing's most important work in aesthetics was *Laocoon, or the Bounds of Painting and Poesy* (1766). It altered his era's perception of Greek culture, defended the autonomous value of the aesthetic, and suggested a theory of the interconnection between theme and medium in works in art. Lessing's publication in 1773 of the "Wolfenbüttel Fragments," a set of highly unorthodox historical commentaries on scripture by the deist Hermann Samuel Reimarus (1694–1768), involved him in a heated controversy with Johann Melchior Goeze. His essay *On the Proof by Spirit and Power* (1777) argued that historical events and religious truth belong to separate categories, so that the latter can never be inferred from the former. Lessing's drama *Nathan the Wise* (1779)—the title character was modeled on his friend MOSES MENDELSSOHN—was an eloquent plea for religious toleration. His essay *The Education of the Human Race* (1780) conceived religious belief as part of the process through which the human race reaches historical maturity. In later years Lessing was greatly attracted to the philosophical system of SPINOZA. Five years after his death, the controversy between F. H. Jacobi and Moses Mendelssohn over the extent and character of Lessing's Spinozism served to bring Spinoza's philosophy back into currency, which proved to be an important factor in the development of post-Kantian German idealism.

BOOKS BY LESSING

Laocoon, Nathan the Wise, Minna von Barnhelm. Ed. by William Steel. Dent 1970 o.p.
Lessing's Theological Writings: Selections in Translation. Ed. by Henry Chadwick. Stanford U. Pr. 1967 $9.95. ISBN 0-8047-0335-3. Contains nine of Lessing's essays on revealed and rational theology and the philosophy of history.

BOOKS ABOUT LESSING

Allison, Henry. *Lessing and the Enlightenment.* Bks. Demand repr. of 1966 ed. $57.50. ISBN 0-317-08206-X. The best study in English of Lessing's philosophy of religion.
Batley, Edward. *Catalyst of the Enlightenment: Gotthold Ephraim Lessing.* P. Lang Pubs. 1990 $63.80. ISBN 3-261-04193-5. An account of Lessing's life, his aesthetics, and his theology.
Ugrinsky, Alexej, ed. *Lessing and the Enlightenment.* Greenwood 1986 $39.95. ISBN 0-313-25313-7. A collection of 17 essays on Lessing's writings and philosophy.

MENDELSSOHN, MOSES. 1729–1786

Moses Mendelssohn was born at Dessau in Anhalt, the son of a poor Jewish copyist of sacred scrolls. He first studied the Torah, the Talmud, and the philosophical and theological writings of the medieval Jewish philosopher MAIMONIDES. Mendelssohn went to Berlin in 1745, where he learned German and Latin while living in severe poverty. In 1750 he was hired as a tutor in the household of Isaak Bernhard, a wealthy Jewish textile manufacturer, and eventually became a bookkeeper and then a partner in Bernhard's firm. He soon made the acquaintance of prominent Berlin intellectuals, including Thomas Abbt, C. F. Nicolai, and G. E. LESSING (who became his close friend). Despite the fact that Mendelssohn was in his teens before he became acquainted with German, his writing style in the language is exemplary in its evocativeness, directness, and lucidity.

Mendelssohn's first important philosophical writings appeared in 1755 and gained him an immediate reputation as "the Jewish Socrates." In 1764 his treatise on evidence in the metaphysical sciences won a prize from the Berlin academy. Perhaps the philosophical work best known in his lifetime was *Phaedo, or on the Immortality of the Soul* (1767), an attempt to bring the Socratic defense of immortality up to date in a dialogue similar to PLATO's (see also Vol. 3). Mendelssohn's great work *Jerusalem*, a political-religious discourse on Judaism and its position in history, is a rationalist plea for religious and political tolerance, advocating the political disestablishment of religion and the political and civil equality of all citizens regardless of religion.

Mendelssohn was one of the leading philosophers of the German Enlightenment and the most able of the Berlin "popular philosophers" of the 1770s and 1780s. Although he and KANT were on opposite sides of many issues in metaphysics and never met, they greatly respected each other's work. In 1764, in a review of one of Kant's metaphysical essays, Mendelssohn predicted that Kant would become one of the most important philosophers in German—a prediction that was fulfilled over 20 years later. Mendelssohn's *Morning Hours* (1785) is an attempt to defend the traditional metaphysical proofs for God's existence against Kant's criticisms. In 1786 Mendelssohn became involved in a literary controversy with F. H. Jacobi, replying to the latter's accusations that Lessing (who had died in 1781) had been a Spinozist, and to Jacobi's more general philosophical allegations that only faith, not reason, can provide us with religious conviction and a humanly tenable outlook on the world. Mendelssohn's defense of religious rationalism was cut short when he suddenly fell ill and died. The controversy itself, by bringing SPINOZA's philosophy into current discussion and raising issues about the scope of reason, had a far-reaching influence on the development of post-Kantian philosophy in Germany. The great romantic composer FELIX MENDELSSOHN (see Vol. 3) was Moses Mendelssohn's grandson.

BOOKS BY MENDELSSOHN

Jerusalem; or, on Religious Power and Judaism. Ed. by Alexander Altmann. Trans. by Allan Arkush. U. Pr. of New Eng. $35.00. ISBN 0-87451-263-8
Moses Mendelssohn: Selections from His Writings. Edited by Alfred Jospe. Viking Penguin 1975 o.p.
Phaedon; or, the Death of Socrates. Ayer repr. of 1789 ed.

BOOKS ABOUT MENDELSSOHN

Altmann, Alexander. *Moses Mendelssohn: A Biographical Study.* B'nai Br'ith Bk. 1973 $57.00. ISBN 0-19-710015-5. A massive, detailed intellectual biography.
Beck, Lewis White. *Early German Philosophy: Kant and His Predecessors.* Bks. Demand repr of 1969 ed. $153.10. ISBN 0-7837-1670-2. Includes an excellent discussion of Mendelssohn and the German Enlightenment.
Beiser, Frederick C. *The Fate of Reason: German Philosophy from Kant to Fichte.* HUP 1987 $38.00. ISBN 0-679-2502-1. Contains a lively, informative, and original discussion of Mendelssohn, the controversy with Jacobi, and the intellectual milieu of the German Enlightenment.

MONTESQUIEU, CHARLES-LOUIS SECONDAT, BARON DE. 1689–1755

Born to a noble but impecunious family near Bordeaux, Montesquieu inherited his title from his uncle and achieved financial security through a prudent marriage to a wealthy Protestant woman. He also inherited the office of president of the Bordeaux parliament, a position he held for 12 years before going to Paris and then traveling abroad to gather material for writing projects. Montesquieu achieved literary renown with his *Persian Letters* (1721), a satire on French manners, religion, and politics presented in the form of letters sent home by two Persians visiting France. In 1734 he published a treatise on Roman history. Montesquieu's greatest and most influential work was *The Spirit of the Laws* (1748). In it he argued that although the law is a product of universal human reason, laws vary with and are naturally adapted to the geographical and cultural circumstances of different nations. Although a monarchist, he argued for constitutional rule and originated the doctrine of separation of powers into legislative, executive, and judicial.

BOOKS BY MONTESQUIEU

Selected Political Writings. Ed. and trans. by Melvin Richter. Hackett Pub. 1990 $32.50. ISBN 0-87220-091-4

The Spirit of the Laws. Ed. by Anne Cohler and others. Cambridge U. Pr. 1989 $59.95.
ISBN 0-521-36183-4. Fully annotated and thorough treatment of this central
eighteenth-century text.

BOOKS ABOUT MONTESQUIEU

Baum, Alan. *Montesquieu and Social Theory.* B. Franklin 1979 $80.00. ISBN 0-08-024317-
7. Discusses Montesquieu's contribution and relevance to the origins of sociology.
Durkheim, Emile. *Montesquieu and Rousseau: Forerunners of Sociology.* U. of Mich. Pr.
1960 o.p.
Hampson, Norman. *Will and Circumstance: Montesquieu, Rousseau and the French
Revolution.* U. of Okla. Pr. 1983 $26.95. ISBN 0-8061-1843-1. A study of Montesquieu
and Rousseau's influences on major figures of the French Revolution such as
Robespierre, Marat, and Saint-Just.
Mason, S. M. *Montesquieu's Idea of Justice.* Nijhoff 1975 o.p.
Pangle, Thomas. *Montesquieu's Philosophy of Liberalism: A Commentary on* The Spirit of
the Laws. U. Ch. Pr. 1974 $25.00. ISBN 0-226-64543-6
Shackleton, Robert. *Montesquieu: A Critical Biography.* OUP 1961 $29.95. ISBN 0-19-
815339-2. The standard biography in English.

PRICE, RICHARD. 1723–1791

Born in the Welsh town of Llangeinor, Price was the son of a dissenting
preacher and was himself ordained as one at age 21. He is best known for his
moral philosophy but also wrote on financial and political subjects. His writings
on life expectancy and life insurance claims led to sweeping changes in the
actuarial and benefit policies of insurance companies and benefit societies; an
article by him on public debt convinced William Pitt, the prime minister, to
establish a fund to extinguish the English national debt.

Price's chief philosophical work is *A Review of the Principal Questions in
Morals* (1758, revised editions 1769 and 1787). Price was a moral realist and
rationalist, a critic of HUTCHESON's moral sense theory and an adherent of
SAMUEL CLARKE's view that there is an immutable standard of right and wrong
discerned by reason. Price's *Four Dissertations* (1767) contains a defense of his
religious convictions, including a reply to HUME's essay on miracles. Against
JOSEPH PRIESTLEY (see Vol. 5) he defended freedom of the will in *A Free
Discussion of the Doctrines of Materialism and Philosophical Necessity* (1778).

Price's political views were progressive. In addition to urging political
reforms in England, he wrote a widely circulated pamphlet defending the
American cause against the British crown; the pamphlet is said to have
encouraged the colonists' decision to declare independence. Price later became
a friend of BENJAMIN FRANKLIN (see Vol. 1). He was offered American citizenship
by the Continental Congress if he would emigrate and serve as a financial
adviser to the American government, an offer he gratefully declined. Price also
welcomed the French Revolution; in fact, it was in reply to a 1790 treatise by
Price that EDMUND BURKE wrote *Reflections on the Revolution in France.*

BOOKS BY PRICE

The Correspondence of Richard Price. Ed. by D. O. Thomas and Bernard Peach. Duke
1992 $52.95. ISBN 0-8223-1203-4
A Review of the Principle Questions in Morals. Ed. by D. D. Raphael. OUP 1975 $21.95.
ISBN 0-19-824518-1
*Richard Price and the Ethical Foundations of the American Revolution: Selections from his
Pamphlets.* Ed. by Bernard Peach. Duke 1979 $37.50. ISBN 0-8223-0400-7

BOOKS ABOUT PRICE

Aqvist, Lennart. *The Moral Philosophy of Richard Price*. Gleerup Lund 1960 o.p.

Hudson, William. *Reason and Right: A Critical Examination of Richard Price's Moral Philosophy*. Freeman Cooper 1970 o.p.

Laboucheix, Henri. *Richard Price as Moral Philosopher and Political Theorist*. Trans. by Sylvia Raphael and David Raphael. OUP 1982 o.p.

Thomas, David. *The Honest Mind: The Thought and Work of Richard Price*. OUP 1977 o.p.

REID, THOMAS. 1710–1796

The founder and greatest representative of Scottish commonsense philosophy was a Presbyterian minister who was born in Aberdeen and studied at Marischal College, Aberdeen. In 1751 he was made regent at King's College, Aberdeen, and after 1764 was professor of moral philosophy there. Reid's chief works are *An Inquiry into the Human Mind on the Principles of Common Sense* (1764), *Essay on the Intellectual Powers of Man* (1785), and *Essay on the Active Powers of Man* (1788). Reid was greatly influenced by HUME's empiricist skepticism, to which his whole philosophy may be seen as a systematic reply, although he also devoted attention to answering BERKELEY's antimaterialism and LOCKE's theory of personal identity. He attacked the theory of ideas and the representative theory of perception common in modern philosophy, arguing that it was based on false analogies between mental and physical objects, and led to a series of unwarranted conclusions repugnant to common sense. He maintained that mental perceptions are "natural signs" of things, analogous in their function to words, though their meaning is innate rather than learned. In moral philosophy, Reid was a realist, holding that moral properties are not merely the projections of our feelings but possess genuine objectivity and a unique content. Reid's "commonsense" philosophy is based not on an uncritical acceptance of what most people believe but rather on a set of principles that he thinks do a better job of accounting for the use of our mental powers than the principles appealed to by previous philosophers. Reid's approach to philosophy was taken up by other Scottish philosophers, among them James Beattie, Dugald Stewart, and William Hamilton. He also had an important influence on several later philosophical defenders of common sense, including Pierre Royer-Collard, CHARLES SANDERS PEIRCE and GEORGE EDWARD MOORE.

BOOKS BY REID

Essays on the Active Powers of the Human Mind. MIT Pr. 1969 o.p. Introduction by B. Brody.

Essays on the Active Powers of Man. 1788. Ibis Pub. VA 1986 repr. of 1788 ed. $25.95. ISBN 0-935005-63-3. This and the preceding title are Reid's lectures, which he organized in these two works after he retired from teaching.

Practical Ethics. Ed. by Knud Haakonssen. Princeton U. Pr. 1990 $65.00. ISBN 0-691-07350-3

Thomas Reid's Inquiry and Essays. Ed. by Ronald E. Beanblossom and Keith Lehrer. *Philosophical Class. Ser.* Hackett Pub. 1983 repr. of 1975 ed. o.p.

BOOKS ABOUT REID

Dalgarno, Melvin, and Eric Matthews, eds. *The Philosophy of Thomas Reid*. Kluwer Ac. 1989 $102.00. ISBN 0-7923-0190-0. A collection of 27 essays on Reid's philosophy of mind, epistemology, moral philosophy, and historical context.

Daniels, Norman. *Thomas Reid's Inquiry: The Geometry of Visibles and the Case for Realism*. Stanford U. Pr. 1989 repr. of 1974 ed. $37.50. ISBN 0-8047-1712-5. A study of Reid's theory of perception and its relation to present-day realist theories.

Gallie, Roger. *Thomas Reid and the "Way of Ideas."* Kluwer Ac. 1989 $82.50. ISBN 0-7923-0390-3. A sympathetic treatment of Reid's philosophy, contrasting his views with those of Locke, Arnauld, and Hume.

Grave, S. A. *The Scottish Philosophy of Common Sense.* Greenwood 1973 repr. of 1960 ed. $35.00. ISBN 0-8371-6539-3. A basic study of the philosophical basis of the Scottish commonsense philosophy.

Hope, Vincent, ed. *Philosophers of the Scottish Enlightenment.* Col. U. Pr. 1984 $24.00. ISBN 0-85224-477-0

Jessop, T. E. *A Bibliography of David Hume and of Scottish Philosophy from Francis Hutcheson to Lord Balfour.* Garland 1983 o.p.

Lehrer, Keith. *Thomas Reid.* Routledge 1989 $22.50. ISBN 0-415-06390-6. A complete account of Reid's philosophical system based on the published works, emphasizing his nativist accounts of the understanding and of the moral faculty.

McCosh, James. *The Scottish Philosophy, Bibliographical, Expository, Critical, from Hutcheson to Hamilton.* AMS Pr. 1980 repr. of 1875 ed. $41.50. ISBN 0-404-59254-6. An exposition of Scottish commonsense philosophy by one of its best adherents.

Marcil-Lacoste, Louise. *Claude Buffier and Thomas Reid: Two Common Sense Philosophers. Studies in the History of Ideas.* U. of Toronto Pr. 1982 $39.95. ISBN 0-7735-1003-6. Comparative study of a French and Scottish version of the commonsense theory of philosophy.

Priestley, Joseph. *An Examination of Dr. Reid's Inquiry into the Human Mind.* Ed. by René Wellek. Garland 1978 repr. of 1774 ed. o.p.

Rowe, William. *Thomas Reid on Freedom and Morality.* Cornell Univ. Pr. 1991 $27.95. ISBN 0-8014-2557-3. An account of Reid's moral theory and his arguments for libertarianism, set against the background of the philosophies of Locke, Clarke, and Collins.

ROUSSEAU, JEAN-JACQUES. 1712–1778

Born in Geneva to an irresponsible father and a mother who died giving birth to him, Jean-Jacques Rousseau had little formal education, living for a time with an uncle and then becoming apprentice to an engraver, whose brutal and tyrannical treatment drove him to seek his fortune in France. He converted from Calvinism to Catholicism and lived an unsettled life, educating himself and ingratiating himself with various people of wealth and influence while working as a servant, a tutor, and a music copier. He developed a new system of musical notation and set out to Paris to gain success by means of it. Though Rousseau's scheme was a failure, he made the acquaintance not only of powerful patrons but also of intellectuals, including DIDEROT, d'Alembert, and other *philosophes*. In 1743 he became secretary to the French ambassador to Venice but was dismissed after quarreling with his employer. About 1745 Rousseau began a liaison with Thérèse Levasseur, an illiterate servant girl by whom he had several illegitimate children, all of whom he turned over to a foundling home.

Rousseau began his literary career with *Discourse on the Sciences and Arts* (1750), which won a prize from the Academy of Dijon. He composed an opera, *Le Devin du village*, which received the favor of Louis XV; Rousseau, however, forfeited any hope of advancement from it by refusing to be presented to the king. In 1754 he journeyed to Geneva and readopted Protestantism but soon returned to Paris to continue his writing. His relations with Diderot and the encyclopedists cooled, but he entered on the most productive period of his career, producing *Discourse on the Origin of Inequality* (1755), *The New Héloise* (1761), *Emile* (1762), and the *Social Contract* (1762).

The condemnation of *Emile* on religious grounds forced Rousseau to leave France for Neuchatel, Switzerland, and then to flee Switzerland as well. He took refuge for a time with DAVID HUME in Scotland, but the two men were of incompatible temperaments and soon quarreled violently: Rousseau regarded Hume as an unprincipled scoundrel, while Hume regarded Rousseau as mentally unbalanced and expressed his deep disappointment with the religious views for which Rousseau had been persecuted, saying that he had proved to be "little better than a Christian." Rousseau then returned to France but had to keep moving and was in constant fear of persecution. His later writings, most of them published posthumously, were increasingly personal and concerned with self-justification: *Confessions, Rousseau, Judge of Jean-Jacques*, and *Reveries of a Solitary Walker*.

Rousseau's thought was immensely influential in the late eighteenth and early nineteenth centuries. His moral earnestness, religious unorthodoxy, eccentric individuality, and uncompromising critique of all social privilege and unjust political authority fascinated thinkers throughout the Enlightenment and the Romantic period. In the twentieth century, it has remained a matter of vigorous debate whether his political thought is fundamentally liberal or totalitarian in its import. His strange life and personality and the fruits of his literary and philosophical genius are still a fertile ground for reflection on what human life has come to mean in modern culture.

BOOKS BY ROUSSEAU

The Collected Writings of Rousseau. 3 vols. Ed. by Roger Masters and Christopher Kelley. Trans. by Judith Bush, Roger Masters, and Christopher Kelley. U. Pr. of New Eng. 1990–93 $40.00 ea. ISBNs 0-8745-1603-X, 0-8745-1580-X, 0-8745-1495-X. The first two volumes of this new edition contain *Rousseau, Judge of Jean-Jacques; The Discourse on the Sciences and Arts (First Discourse)*; and *Polemics*.

Confessions. Ed. by P. N. Furbank. Knopf 1992 $20.00. ISBN 0-679-40998-X

Emile. Trans. by Barbara Foxley. NAL-Dutton 1974 o.p.

The Miscellaneous Works of Mr. J. J. Rousseau. B. Franklin 1972 o.p.

The Reveries of the Solitary Walker. Ed. and trans. by Charles Butterworth. Hackett Pub. 1992 repr. of 1979 ed. $29.95. ISBN 0-87220-163-5

Rousseau: Selections. Ed. by Maurice Cranston. Macmillan 1988. ISBN 0-02-325521-8. Contains some lesser-known writings important for understanding his philosophy.

Social Contract and Discourses. Trans. by G.D.H. Cole. C. E. Tuttle 1991 $6.95. ISBN 0-460-87041-6

BOOKS ABOUT ROUSSEAU

Cranston, Maurice. *Jean-Jacques: The Early Life and Works of Jean-Jacques, 1712–1754.* U. Ch. Pr. 1983 $17.95. ISBN 0-226-11862-2. A wonderfully written intellectual biography based on manuscript sources.

———. *The Noble Savage: Jean-Jacques Rousseau, 1754–1762.* U. Ch. Pr. $32.50. ISBN 0-226-11863-0. Covers the most productive years of Rousseau's life.

Dent, N.J.H. *Rousseau: An Introduction to His Psychological, Social and Political Theory.* Blackwell Pubs. 1989 $55.00. ISBN 0-631-15883-9. An assessment of Rousseau's main ideas in psychology and political theory.

France, Peter. *Rousseau: Confessions.* Cambridge U. Pr. 1986 $29.95. ISBN 0-521-32803-9. Sets the work in the context of Rousseau's life.

Gildin, Hilail. *Rousseau's Social Contract: The Design of the Argument.* U. Ch. Pr. 1983 $22.50. ISBN 0-226-29368-8. A careful and stimulating study.

Grimsley, Ronald. *Jean-Jacques Rousseau.* B & N Imports 1983 o.p. A study of Rousseau's philosophy as it is revealed in both his fiction and his nonfiction.

———. *The Philosophy of Rousseau.* OUP 1973 o.p. A short survey by a well-known Rousseau scholar.

Masters, Roger. *The Political Philosophy of Rousseau.* Bks. Demand repr. of 1968 ed. $126.90. ISBN 0-685-44420-1. A classic study of Rousseau's system.

Miller, James. *Rousseau: Dreamer of Democracy*. Yale U. Pr. 1984 $32.00. ISBN 0-300-03044-4. Analyzes the argument of the social contract and explores Rousseau's influence.

Perkins, Merle. *Rousseau and the Religious Quest*. OUP 1968 o.p.

Viroli, Maurizio. *Jean-Jacques Rousseau and the Well-Ordered Society*. Cambridge U. Pr. 1988 $54.95. ISBN 0-521-33342-3. A study of Rousseau's conception of the ideal society; also explores his debt to Machiavelli.

SHAFTESBURY, ANTHONY ASHLEY COOPER, THIRD EARL OF. 1671–1713

Born in London, Shaftesbury was the grandson of the Whig leader who was JOHN LOCKE's chief patron; he was also a direct ancestor of the Seventh Earl of Shaftesbury, who worked successfully for important labor reforms, such as the Ten Hours Bill, in nineteenth-century England. Locke supervised Shaftesbury's early education. Elected to Parliament in 1695, he served for three years before a serious asthmatic condition forced him to retire. Succeeding to the earldom in 1699, he faithfully attended the House of Lords and was a productive writer despite constant illness. After marrying in 1709, he retired from public life and moved to Italy for reasons of health.

Shaftesbury's writings are erudite, elegantly crafted, and often original and suggestive, but they are not systematic or rigorous enough to attract most philosophical scholars. His main works are collected in a single three-volume magnum opus: *Characteristics of Men, Manners, Opinions, Times*, which was first published as a whole in 1711. Shaftesbury argues for freedom of thought and an enlightened attitude toward religion and for the independence of morality from religion. He criticizes the egoism of HOBBES and presents a theory of human nature aimed at showing that human sentiments provide a sufficient foundation for virtue. In the course of doing so, he anticipated the moral sense theories of HUTCHESON and HUME and was the first philosopher to use that phrase.

BOOKS BY SHAFTESBURY

Anthony Ashley Cooper, Earl of Shaftesbury (1671–1713) and 'Le Refuge Français' Correspondence. Ed. by Rex Barrell. E. Mellen 1989 $89.95. ISBN 0-88946-466-9. Shaftesbury's correspondence with Pierre Bayle, Jacques Basnage, Jean LeClerc, Pierre Coste, and Pierre des Maizeaux.

Characteristics of Men, Manners, Opinions, Times. Ed. by John Robertson. Bobbs 1964 o.p.

BOOK ABOUT SHAFTESBURY

Grean, Stanley. *Shaftesbury's Philosophy of Religion and Ethics*. Bks. Demand repr. of 1967 ed. $80.00. ISBN 0-317-09231-6. A study of Shaftesbury's *Characteristics*.

SMITH, ADAM. 1723–1790

The father of classical political economy first became known as a moral philosopher. He was born in Kircaldy, Scotland, and studied at the University of Glasgow under FRANCIS HUTCHESON before entering Balliol College, Oxford University. From 1748 to 1751, Smith lived in Edinburgh, where he became friends with HUME and Lord Kames. In 1751 he was appointed professor of logic and moral philosophy at Glasgow, a post he held for 10 years. His widely acclaimed *Theory of Moral Sentiments* (1759) brought him an invitation to be tutor to the Duke of Buccleuch, with a pension for life. He resigned his professorship and served in this capacity, traveling much of the time on the

Continent, until 1766. For the next 10 years Smith used the leisure gained by his pension to research and write *The Wealth of Nations* (1776). In 1778 he was appointed commissioner of customs for Scotland.

Most of Smith's *Theory of Moral Sentiments* deals with moral psychology, which he sees as resting on the feeling of sympathy, which he argues has different effects when directed to another's situation, feelings, or judgments. On this basis Smith develops a theory of moral merit and propriety, which, when subjected to general rules, accounts for our sense of duty and justice. Smith rejected the moral sense theory of his teacher Hutcheson, formulating a theory of moral judgment based on his conception of the considered feelings of a "rational, impartial spectator." His empiricist and individualist approach to psychological and sociological observation in moral psychology may also be seen in his approach to economic theory.

BOOKS BY SMITH

Adam Smith's Moral and Political Philosophy. Ed. by Herbert Schneider. Hafner 1948 o.p.

Early Writings of Adam Smith. Ed. by J. Ralph Lindgren. Augustus Kelley 1967 o.p.

Essays on Philosophical Subjects. Ed. by W. P. Wightman, J. C. Bryce, and I. S. Ross. OUP 1980 $69.00. ISBN 0-19-828187-0. A reprint of the 1795 edition with a biographical introduction by the eighteenth-century Scottish philosopher Dugald Stewart.

Essential Adam Smith. Ed. by Robert Heilbroner with Laurence Malone. Norton 1987 $8.95. ISBN 0-393-95530-3

The Glasgow Edition of the Works and Correspondence of Adam Smith. Ed. by R. H. Campbell, A. S. Skinner, and W. B. Todd. OUP 1976 o.p.

Theory of Moral Sentiments. Ibis Pub. VA 1971 $24.95. ISBN 0-935005-66-8. A reprint of the 1759 edition.

The Wisdom of Adam Smith. Ed. by Benjamin Rogge. Liberty Fund 1977 $7.95. ISBN 0-913966-21-5. Selected by John Haggarty.

BOOKS ABOUT SMITH

Campbell, T. D. *Adam Smith's Science of Morals.* Humanities 1971 o.p. A comprehensive study of Smith's philosophy and social theory.

Lindgren, J. Ralph. *The Social Philosophy of Adam Smith.* o.p. A historically sensitive study of the full range of Smith's writings.

Muller, Jerry. *Adam Smith in His Time and Ours.* Free Pr. 1992 $22.95. ISBN 0-02-922234-6. Partly intellectual biography, partly a study of the contemporary relevance of Smith's philosophy of economics.

Raphael, D. D. *Adam Smith.* OUP 1985 $13.95. ISBN 0-19-287559-0. A succinct introduction to Smith's thought, devoted mainly to his economics.

Skinner, Andrew, and Thomas Wilson, eds. *Essays on Adam Smith.* Col. U. Pr. 1992 $55.00. ISBN 0-7486-0346-8. A bulky collection of essays on Smith's moral and political philosophy and his economics.

Wood, John, ed. *Adam Smith: Critical Assessments.* 4 vols. Rothman 1984 o.p. A total of 150 papers on Smith's life and work.

VICO, GIAMBATTISTA. 1668–1744

The son of a book dealer, Giambattista Vico was born in Naples and attended a Jesuit college, but he was largely self-educated through reading his father's wares. He served as tutor to the nephews of the Bishop of Ischia and was appointed professor of rhetoric at the University of Naples in 1695, a post he held until 1735, when he became royal historiographer to the court of Naples.

Vico's first important work was *On The Study Methods of Our Time* (1709). After writing works on Italian intellectual history, Vico began his greatest work, *The New Science* (1728), which went through two revised editions (1730, 1744).

The Complete Tales of Voltaire. 3 vols. Trans. by William Walton. Fertig 1990 $95.00.
    ISBN 0-86527-393-6
Philosophical Dictionary. Trans. by Theodore Besterman. Viking Penguin 1984 $7.95.
    ISBN 0-14-044257-X
Philosophical Letters. Trans. by Ernest Dilworth. Macmillan 1961. ISBN 0-02-330610-6
Philosophy of History. Carol Pub. Group 1965 $3.45. ISBN 0-8065-0078-6. A reprint of the
    1766 edition. Preface by Thomas Kiernan.
Portable Voltaire. Ed. by Ben Ray Redman. Viking Penguin 1977 $12.50. ISBN 0-14-
    015041-2

BOOKS ABOUT VOLTAIRE

Brooks, Richard. *Voltaire and Leibniz.* Librairie Droz 1964 o.p. A study of the problem of
    theodicy in the work of these two philosophers.
Gay, Peter. *Voltaire's Politics.* Yale U. Pr. 1988 $18.00. ISBN 0-300-04095-4. Reprint of an
    influential 1959 study of Voltaire's political views, their historical context, and their
    influence.
Lanson, Gustav. *Voltaire.* Trans. by Robert Wagner. Wiley 1960 o.p. A classic introduc-
    tion to Voltaire by a French scholar.
Lauer, Rosemary. *The Mind of Voltaire.* Newman Pr. 1961 o.p. A study of Voltaire's views
    about human freedom, morality, God, and humanity's place in nature.
Mason, H. T. *Pierre Bayle and Voltaire.* Russell & Russell 1947 o.p. A study of Voltaire's
    debt to the earlier philosopher.
Orieux, Jean. *Voltaire.* Trans. by Barbara Bray and Helen Lane. Doubleday 1979 o.p. The
    standard biography.
Schwartzbach, Bertram. *Voltaire's Old Testament Criticism.* Librairie Droz 1971 o.p. A
    fairly sympathetic assessment of Voltaire's criticism of the Bible.
Torrey, Norman. *Voltaire and the English Deists.* Yale U. Pr. 1930 o.p. A study of
    Voltaire's religious views and his influence on such English thinkers as Collins and
    Bolingbroke.
Wade, Ira. *Intellectual Development of Voltaire.* Bks. Demand repr. of 1969 ed. $160.00.
    ISBN 0-317-08701-0. An intellectual biography.
————. *Studies on Voltaire.* Russell & Russell 1947 o.p. Essays on Voltaire's philosophy,
    together with some unpublished papers of Mme. du Chatelet.
Waterman, Amy. *Voltaire, Pascal, and Human Destiny.* Col. U. Pr. 1942 o.p. A detailed
    analysis of Voltaire's criticisms of Pascal.

WOLFF, CHRISTIAN. 1679–1754

The most influential German philosopher of the early and mid-eighteenth
century was born at Breslau. He studied mathematics at the University of Jena
and, after a period at Leipzig, was appointed professor of mathematics at the
University of Halle. On the recommendation of LEIBNIZ, he was elected to the
Berlin Academy in 1711. Wolff's rationalist views in theology and his defense of
causal determinism (albeit a version that was supposed to be compatible with
freedom of the will) made him enemies among pietists in both the university
and the Prussian court. In 1723 they prevailed upon the brutal, ignorant
militarist King Frederick William I to deprive Wolff of his professorship and put
a price on his head, giving him only 48 hours to leave Prussian domains under
penalty of death. He was welcomed at the Calvinist university of Marburg,
where he remained until 1740. Upon Frederick William's death, he was recalled
in triumph by the new Prussian king, Frederick the Great. Wolff was made not
only professor of law at Halle but also chancellor of the university, a privy
counselor to the crown, and a baron of the Holy Roman Empire.

Wolff's early works at Halle were written in German, but he produced most of
his writings at Marburg, where it was more suitable that they be in Latin. He was
an extremely prolific writer of encyclopedic scope, combining Leibnizian

metaphysics and physics with Scholastic Aristotelianism, and creating a vast philosophical system that encompassed theories of metaphysics (or ontology), psychology, cosmology, theology, ethics, and natural right. In the first half of the eighteenth century, Wolff's system was dominant throughout the German universities, and his influence was perpetuated through the work of his many students and followers, including A. G. Baumgarten, H. F. Meier, and Martin Knutzen, KANT's teacher. Soon after Wolff's death his views were challenged by C. A. Crusius and criticized by the popular Enlightenment philosophers centered in Berlin, though some of them (including the leading philosopher among them, MOSES MENDELSSOHN) always remained in substantial agreement with Wolffian doctrine. Wolff's influence finally ended in the last years of the eighteenth century, when German philosophy was swept up in the revolution made possible by Kant.

BOOK BY WOLFF

Preliminary Discourse on Philosophy in General. Trans. by Richard Blackwell. Bobbs 1963 o.p.

BOOKS ABOUT WOLFF

Beck, Lewis. *Early German Philosophy: Kant and His Predecessors.* Bks. Demand repr. of 1969 ed. $153.10. ISBN 0-7837-1670-2. A masterful study.
Burns, John. *Dynamism in the Cosmology of Christian Wolff: A Study in Pre-Critical Rationalism.* Norris World 1966 o.p. Discusses Wolff's treatment of substance, body, and the elements.

CHRONOLOGY OF AUTHORS
(Nineteenth Century)

Schleiermacher, Friedrich Daniel Ernst. 1768–1834
Hegel, Georg Wilhelm Friedrich. 1770–1831
Schlegel, Friedrich. 1772–1829
Schelling, Friedrich Wilhelm Joseph. 1775–1854
Schopenhauer, Arthur. 1788–1860
Whewell, William. 1794–1866
Comte, Auguste. 1798–1857
Feuerbach, Ludwig Andreas. 1804–1872
Mill, John Stuart. 1806–1873
Kierkegaard, Søren. 1813–1855
Lotze, Rudolf Hermann. 1817–1881
Marx, Karl Heinrich. 1818–1883

Engels, Friedrich. 1820–1895
Dilthey, Wilhelm. 1833–1911
Green, Thomas Hill. 1836–1882
Brentano, Franz. 1838–1917
Sidgwick, Henry. 1838–1900
Peirce, Charles Sanders. 1839–1914
James, William. 1842–1910
Nietzsche, Friedrich Wilhelm. 1844–1900
Bradley, Francis Herbert. 1846–1924
Frege, Gottlob. 1848–1925
Royce, Josiah. 1855–1916
Bergson, Henri. 1859–1941
Dewey, John. 1859–1952
Husserl, Edmund. 1859–1938

BERGSON, HENRI. 1859–1941 (NOBEL PRIZE 1927)

Born in Paris of Jewish parents, Henri Bergson received his education there and subsequently taught at Angers and Clermont-Ferraud before returning to Paris. He was appointed professor of philosophy at the Collège de France in 1900 and elected a member of the French Academy in 1914. Bergson developed his philosophy by stressing the biological, evolutionary elements involved in thinking, reasoning, and creating. He saw the vitalistic dimension of the human species as being of the greatest importance. His various writings received great acclaim both in France and throughout the learned world, and in 1927 he was awarded the Nobel Prize for literature (there is no Nobel Prize for philosophy). In defiance of the Nazis after their conquest of France, he insisted on wearing a yellow star to show his solidarity with other French Jews; shortly before he died, he gave up all his positions and renounced his many honors in protest at the discrimination against Jews by the Nazis and the Vichy French regime.

BOOKS BY BERGSON

Creative Evolution. 1907. Trans. by Arthur Mitchell. U. Pr. of Amer. 1984 repr. of 1911 ed. $23.00. ISBN 0-8191-3553-4. Bergson's most famous work on the development of humanity and the cosmos.

The Creative Mind: An Introduction to Metaphysics. 1934. Carol Pub. Grp. 1992 $8.95. ISBN 0-8065-0421-8. On the role of humans in the evolutionary world.

Laughter: An Essay on the Meaning of the Comic. 1901. Trans. by Cloudesley Brereton and Fred Rothwell. Richard West 1977 repr. of 1921 ed. o.p. One of the few philosophical works on this subject.

Matter and Memory. 1896. *Muirhead Lib. of Philosophy.* Zone Bks. 1988 $28.95. ISBN 0-942299-05-1. Bergson's theory of mind and body.

Time and Free Will. 1889. *Muirhead Lib. of Philosophy.* Humanities 1971 o.p. Bergson's development of the notion of real duration and its relation to human freedom.

The Two Sources of Morality and Religion. 1932. U. of Notre Dame Pr. 1977 $12.95. ISBN 0-218-01835-9. Bergson's attempt to develop an evolutionary ethics and religion.

BOOKS ABOUT BERGSON

Capek, M. *Bergson and Modern Physics: A Reinterpretation and Reevaluation. Synthese Lib.* Kluwer Ac. 1971 $93.00. ISBN 90-277-0186-5. A careful consideration of Bergson's views by a philosopher of science, who relates them to the changes in physics in the twentieth century.

Dodson, George R. *Bergson and the Modern Spirit.* Gordon Pr. 1976 $59.95. ISBN 0-8490-1489-1

Grogin, R. C. *The Bergsonian Controversy in France, 1900–1914.* Calgary 1988 o.p. Places Bergson at the center of controversies about science, religion, and politics; claims that he cannot be understood apart from the occult revival of pre-1914 France.

Kolakowski, Leszek. *Bergson.* OUP 1985 $14.95. ISBN 0-19-287644-9. A very brief introduction.

Lacey, A. R. *Bergson.* Routledge 1989 $39.95. ISBN 0-415-03007-2. A critical but not wholly unsympathetic survey of Bergson's thought from the standpoint of contemporary analytical Anglo-American philosophy.

Maritain, Jacques. *Bergsonian Philosophy and Thomism.* Greenwood 1968 repr. of 1955 ed. $47.50. ISBN 0-8371-0559-5. A consideration of Bergson's views by the leading French Catholic philosopher of the twentieth century.

Pilkington, A. E. *Bergson and His Influence.* Bks. Demand repr. of 1976 ed. $67.90. ISBN 0-8357-7137-7. Attempt to evaluate Bergson's impact.

Russell, Bertrand. *The Philosophy of Bergson.* Folcroft 1980 repr. of 1914 ed. o.p. Russell's very interesting critique of his contemporary.

BRADLEY, FRANCIS HERBERT. 1846–1924

The leading British idealist philosopher was born in Clapham, son of an evangelical clergyman, and educated at University College, Oxford University. In 1870 he was elected to a lifetime research fellowship at Merton College, Oxford University, and he devoted his life to philosophical writing. His chief works are *Ethical Studies* (1876), *Principles of Logic* (1883), and *Appearance and Reality* (1893). Bradley's analytical acuteness as a thinker, and perhaps even more his polemical brilliance as a writer, made him the most prominent representative of the British idealist movement in the late nineteenth and early twentieth centuries. Like his contemporary Bernard Bosanquet, Bradley was influenced by T. H. Green, and like them Bradley is also often described as a Hegelian. In fact, however, Bradley's views were less Hegelian than Bosanquet's; politically, for example, Green and Bosanquet were liberals, while Bradley was a Tory. It is ironic that because of Bradley's prominent controversies with BERTRAND RUSSELL (see also Vol. 5) and G. E. MOORE, his philosophy determined the image of Hegelian philosophy in Britain. Bradley's philosophy is monistic, tending in ethics to a social holism and in metaphysics defending the idea that true reality consists of a Parmenidean absolute, in relation to which all else constitutes a realm of self-contradictory appearances. Bradley's critique of traditional logic, with its emphasis on a sharp distinction between logical form and grammatical form, did much to prepare the way for the development of twentieth-century logic, even though the form it eventually took was very different from Bradley's theory.

BOOKS BY BRADLEY

Appearance and Reality: A Metaphysical Essay. 1893. OUP 1930 repr. of 1897 ed. o.p.
Collected Essays. 2 vols. Ayer 1968 repr. of 1935 ed. $40.00. ISBN 0-8369-0244-0. Some of the articles on philosophical subjects Bradley published in different journals.

BOOKS ABOUT BRADLEY

MacNiven, Don. *Bradley's Moral Psychology.* E. Mellen 1987 $89.95. ISBN 0-88946-306-9. A sympathetic study of Bradley's ethical theory, showing its foundation in his idealistic metaphysics.
Manser, Anthony. *The Philosophy of F. H. Bradley.* OUP 1987 $26.00. ISBN 0-19-824972-1. The best available study of Bradley.

BRENTANO, FRANZ. 1838–1917

The nephew of the poet Clemens Brentano and the author Bettina von Arnim was born at Marienburg, in what is now Poland, and was ordained a Catholic priest in 1864. He then taught philosophy and psychology at the Universities of Würzburg and Vienna. Brentano wrote voluminously on a variety of philosophical subjects, including philosophy of mind and psychology, logic, epistemology, moral philosophy, and philosophical theology. He was also a distinguished scholar of classical Greek philosophy, especially ARISTOTLE (see also Vol. 3). His influence was reflected in his many distinguished students, who included EDMUND HUSSERL, Alexius Meinong, Carl Stumpf, Tamas Maszaryk, and Anton Marty. His best-known philosophical contribution is his theory of intentionality, which characterizes mental events as involving the "direction of the mind to an object." This doctrine was taken up in different ways by Meinong and Husserl. Brentano, objecting to the doctrine of papal infallibility, left the Catholic church in 1873.

BOOKS BY BRENTANO

Aristotle and His World View. Trans. by George Rolf. U. CA Pr. 1978 $27.50. ISBN 0-520-03390-6
On the Existence of God. Ed. and trans. by Susan Krantz. Nijhoff 1987 o.p. Lectures given at the Universities of Würzburg and Vienna from 1868 to 1891.
On the Several Senses of Being in Aristotle. Trans. by George Rolf. U. CA Pr. 1981 repr. of 1975 ed. $35.00. ISBN 0-520-04420-7

The Origin of Our Knowledge of Right and Wrong. Trans. by Roderick Chisholm and
  Elizabeth Schneewind. Routledge 1969 o.p.
Psychology from an Empirical Standpoint. 1874. Ed. by Linda McAlister. London 1973
  o.p.
The Theory of Categories. 1911. Trans. by Roderick Chisholm and Norbert Guterman.
  Nijhoff 1981 o.p.

BOOKS ABOUT BRENTANO

Bergmann, Gustav. *Realism: A Critique of Brentano and Meinong*. U. of Wis. Pr. 1967
  $25.00. ISBN 0-299-04330-4. A difficult work with a minimum of exposition of
  Brentano's philosophy.
Chisholm, Roderick. *Brentano and Intrinsic Value*. Cambridge U. Pr. 1986 $37.95. ISBN
  0-521-26437-5. Attempts to make Brentano's philosophy comprehensible to those
  from the English-speaking analytic philosophical tradition.
_____. *Brentano and Meinong Studies*. Atlan. High. Hum. Pr. 1982 o.p. Nine papers by a
  well-known scholar.
_____. *Die Philosophie Franz Brentanos*. Rodopi 1978 o.p. Contains some contributions
  in English.
McAlister, Linda, ed. *The Development of Franz Brentano's Ethics*. Atlan. High. Hum. Pr.
  1982 o.p. Brentano's later moral philosophy was not published, and this book draws
  heavily on his unpublished manuscripts and letters.
_____. *The Philosophy of Franz Brentano*. Duckworth 1976 o.p. A collection of 19 papers
  on the entire span of Brentano's philosophy, together with a complete bibliography
  of writings about him.
Srzednicki, J. *Franz Brentano's Analysis of Truth*. Nijhoff 1966 o.p. A discussion of
  previously unpublished manuscripts; the manuscripts and translations are included
  in several appendices.

COMTE, AUGUSTE. 1798–1857

Auguste Comte, born at Montpellier, France, began and developed the
philosophy called "positivism." He held that all previous philosophies could be
described and classified according to which of three historical stages they
belonged to—the supernatural, the metaphysical (or abstract), or the positive
(or scientific) stage. The positive or scientific stage allowed for a science of
human society—sociology—that described human development from the
primitive or religious to the positive stage. Comte is often considered the
founder of sociology. To replace the supernatural and metaphysical religions,
Comte introduced a religion of humanity, which had some of the trappings of a
church but was devoted to humanistic approaches to human problems.

BOOKS BY COMTE

Auguste Comte and Positivism: The Essential Writings. Ed. by Gertrud Lenzer. HarpC 1975
  o.p. Selections that give a picture of Comte's views.
A General View of Positivism. Reprints in Sociology Ser. Irvington 1971 repr. of 1848 ed.
  $39.50. ISBN 0-697-00214-4. An overall presentation of Comte's philosophy.
Introduction to Positive Philosophy. Trans. and ed. by Frederick Ferre. Hackett Pub. 1988
  repr. of 1970 ed. $19.50. ISBN 0-87220-051-5
The Positive Analysis of Social Phenomena. Am. Classical Coll. Pr. 1983 $154.50. ISBN 0-
  89266-426-6. One of Comte's systematic statements of his philosophy.
Positive History of the New Social Order and Historical Analysis of Social Phenomena.
  Found. Class. Reprints 1990 $227.75. ISBN 0-89901-428-3
Positive Philosophy. Trans. by Harriet Martineau. AMS Pr. 1977 repr. of 1855 ed. $67.50.
  ISBN 0-404-08209-2. The central statement of Comte's theory. A condensation of
  Comte's six-volume French presentation.

System of Positive Polity. 1851. 4 vols. B. Franklin 1973 repr. of 1875 ed. o.p. A late massive formulation of Comte's views.

BOOKS ABOUT COMTE

Caird, Edward. *Social Philosophy and Religion of Comte.* Kraus Repr. 1968 repr. of 1885 ed. o.p. A Victorian evaluation of Comte.

Levy-Bruhl, Lucien. *The Philosophy of Auguste Comte.* Gordon Pr. 1976 repr. of 1903 ed. $59.95. ISBN 0-8490-2430-7. A presentation of Comte's views by one of the leading French social theorists of the following generation.

Mill, John Stuart. *Auguste Comte and Positivism.* U. of Mich. Pr. 1961 o.p. Still one of the best presentations and analyses of Comte's system.

Pickering, Mary. *Auguste Comte, Vol. 1: An Intellectual Biography.* Cambridge U. Pr. 1993 $49.95. ISBN 0-521-43405-X

Sokoloff, Boris. *The Mad Philosopher: Auguste Comte.* Greenwood 1975 repr. of 1961 ed. o.p. Stresses the eccentricities of Comte and his philosophy, as well as its antidemocratic tendencies.

DEWEY, JOHN. 1859–1952

John Dewey, one of the most important philosophers and educators of the United States, was born in Vermont. He studied at Johns Hopkins University and taught at the Universities of Michigan and Minnesota before settling at the University of Chicago in 1894. During his 10 years there, Dewey began to publish a series of works on human psychology and reasoning and on the ways people learn. These works put him quickly in the forefront of philosophers and psychologists of education. He developed a kind of social pragmatic theory that he called "instrumentalism," showing how people learn by doing. In 1904 he moved to Columbia University, where he remained for the rest of his academic career—the dominant figure in the philosophy department and its chairman for many years, and the guiding influence on Teachers College, Columbia's school of education. In a very full series of works, Dewey sought to show how his instrumentalist theory could explain the thinking process, the way in which people deal with problems, and how both could be improved by the application of scientific methods and knowledge. Dewey's program included both educational reform (he was the theoretician of the progressive education movement that children should learn by doing) and reform of the intellectual process. His books *The Quest for Certainty* and *Reconstruction in Philosophy*, both from the 1920s, showed how intellectuals had tried to achieve too much in the quest for unattainable goals, and how, by restricting the intellectual quest to attainable goals, the growing results of science could be continuously applied to the solution of human problems. For Dewey, the pragmatic interpretation of human intellectual activity was more a social matter than an individual one, as WILLIAM JAMES (see also Vols. 3 and 5) had construed it. Dewey stressed the social needs and the social goals that could be achieved. Society would be improved and better able to deal with its problems through a better educated citizenry. Society itself, as Dewey saw it, should be organized to best deal with problem solving. Such an organization would involve a thoroughly democratic political structure emphasizing social needs.

Dewey was an important figure in movements to develop social democracy and to strengthen democratic institutions. Throughout his long career, he emphasized the importance of the practical and the role of theory as an aid to solving practical problems. He was opposed by those adhering to various metaphysical traditions and by the logical positivists and analytic philosophers, who thought that he had grossly underestimated the role of abstract thinking and that his theory could not really encompass the results of modern logic. Dewey's thought was extremely influential in the first half of this century but has gradually been eclipsed by interest in other philosophical theories, especially analytic philosophy and recent Continental philosophy.

Dewey was one of the most prolific writers in philosophy. The project of publishing his complete works in chronological order is now nearing completion.

BOOKS BY DEWEY

A Common Faith. Yale U. Pr. 1934 $6.95. ISBN 0-300-00069-3. Dewey's philosophy of religion.

Democracy and Education: An Introduction to the Philosophy of Education. 1916. Free Pr. 1966 $13.95. ISBN 0-02-907370-7. The role of an improved educational process in a democratic society.

The Early Works of John Dewey, 1882–1898. 5 vols. Ed. by Jo Ann Boydston. S. Ill. U. Pr. 1967–72 $50.00 ea. ISBNs 0-8093-0349-3, 0-8093-0282-9, 0-8093-0402-3, 0-8093-0496-1, 0-8093-0540-2. This collection and the subsequent volumes listed below are sponsored by the Cooperative Research on Dewey Publications Program at Southern Illinois University.

Experience and Education. Peter Smith 1983 $17.50. ISBN 0-8446-5961-4. A lecture by Dewey.

Experience and Nature. 1925. Dover 1958 repr. of 1929 ed. $8.95. ISBN 0-486-20471-5. The Carus Lectures, Dewey's "metaphysics."

How We Think: A Restatement of the Relation of Reflective Thinking to the Educative Process. 1909. Heath 1933 $19.50. ISBN 0-669-20024-7. Early study in the psychology of logic.

Human Nature and Conduct. 1922. S. Ill. U. Pr. 1988 $14.95. ISBN 0-8093-1437-1. One of Dewey's basic works on ethics.

The Influence of Darwin on Philosophy and Other Essays. Peter Smith 1951 o.p. Some of Dewey's early influential essays.

Knowing and the Known. (coauthored with Arthur F. Bentley). Greenwood 1976 repr. of 1949 ed. $47.50. ISBN 0-8371-8498-3. Dewey's last work, on epistemology.

The Later Works of John Dewey, 1925–1953. 17 vols. S. Ill. U. Pr. 1981–90 $50.00 ea. ISBNs 0-8093-0986-6, 0-8093-1131-3, 0-8093-1132-1, 0-8093-1162-3, 0-8093-1163-1, 0-8093-1199-2, 0-8093-1200-X, 0-8093-1246-8, 0-8093-1266-2, 0-685-48744-X, 0-8093-1267-0, 0-8093-1678-1, 0-8093-1425-8, 0-8093-1426-6, 0-8093-1535-1, 0-8093-1537-8, 0-8093-1661-7

Logic: Theory of Inquiry. 1938. Irvington 1982 $49.50. ISBN 0-89197-831-3. Dewey's mature examination of the reasoning process.

The Middle Works of John Dewey, 1899–1924. 15 vols. Ed. by Jo Ann Boydston. S. Ill. U. Pr. 1976–83 $50.00 ea. ISBNs 0-8093-0753-7, 0-8093-0754-5, 0-8093-0775-8, 0-8093-0776-6, 0-8093-0834-7, 0-8093-0835-5, 0-8093-0881-9, 0-8093-0882-7, 0-8093-0933-5, 0-8093-0934-3, 0-8093-1003-1, 0-8093-1004-X, 0-8093-1083-X, 0-8093-1084-8, 0-8093-1085-6

On Education. U. Ch. Pr. 1974 o.p. A reprint of one of Dewey's important statements on his views.

Philosophy of Education. 1946. *Quality Pap. Ser.* Littlefield 1971 repr. of 1958 ed. o.p.

Problems of Men. 1946. Greenwood 1968 repr. of 1946 ed. $47.50. ISBN 0-8371-0382-7. A collection of essays and addresses.

The Public and Its Problems: An Essay in Political Inquiry. Swallow 1954 $7.95. ISBN 0-8040-0254-1. Dewey's instrumentalism applied to the political process.

Reconstruction in Philosophy. 1920. Beacon Pr. 1957 $14.00. ISBN 0-8070-1585-7. Lectures Dewey gave in Tokyo, presenting his survey of modern philosophy and how it can be saved.

The School and Society. 1899. S. Ill. U. Pr. 1980 $9.95. ISBN 0-8093-0967-X. Early statement of Dewey's philosophy of education.

Studies in Logical Theory. AMS Pr. 1975 repr. of 1903 ed. $34.50. ISBN 0-404-59129-9. One of Dewey's first examinations of the psychology of logic.

The Theory of Moral Life. Irvington 1980 repr. of 1960 ed. o.p. Another statement of Dewey's ethical views.

Theory of Valuation. Foundations of the Unity of Science Ser. U. Ch. Pr. 1939 o.p. Dewey's instrumentalist explanation of values.

BOOKS ABOUT DEWEY

Bernstein, Richard J. *John Dewey.* Ridgeview 1981 repr. of 1966 ed. $30.00. ISBN 0-917930-35-5. Focuses on Dewey's views on experience and nature, his metaphysics.

Blewett, John, ed. *John Dewey: His Thought and Influence.* Greenwood 1973 repr. of 1960 ed. $47.50. ISBN 0-8371-6543-1. A collection of essays by various Catholic scholars, including James Collins. Foreword by John S. Brubacher.

Boydston, Jo Ann, ed. *A Guide to the Works of John Dewey.* S. Ill. U. Pr. 1972 o.p. An indispensable research tool for studying Dewey's philosophy.

Coughlan, Neil. *Young John Dewey: An Essay in American Intellectual History.* U. Ch. Pr. 1975 o.p. A study of Dewey's early intellectual life.

Dykhuizen, George. *Life and Mind of John Dewey.* S. Ill. U. Pr. 1973 o.p. The most complete scholarly intellectual biography of John Dewey, representing many years of careful research. Introduction by Harold Taylor.

Gouinlock, James. *John Dewey's Philosophy of Value.* Humanities 1972 o.p. An important study of this aspect of Dewey's thought.

Handlin, Oscar. *John Dewey's Challenge to Education: Historical Perspectives on the Cultural Context.* Greenwood 1972 repr. of 1959 ed. $38.50. ISBN 0-8371-5602-5. Interesting pictures of Dewey's role written by one of the best American social and intellectual historians.

Hickman, Larry A. *John Dewey's Pragmatic Technology.* Ind. U. Pr. 1992 $29.95. ISBN 0-253-32747-4. A comprehensive overview of Dewey's logic, metaphysics, aesthetics, philosophy of history, and social thought with the aim of showing the centrality of technological concerns to them.

Hook, Sidney. *John Dewey: An Intellectual Portrait.* Greenwood 1976 repr. of 1939 ed. $47.50. ISBN 0-8371-3951-1. A picture of Dewey by one of the next generation of American pragmatists.

Lamont, Corliss, ed. *Dialogue on John Dewey.* Horizon Pr. 1981 o.p. A tribute by some of Dewey's friends and students.

Moore, Edward C. *American Pragmatism: Peirce, James and Dewey.* Greenwood 1984 repr. of 1961 ed. $52.50. ISBN 0-313-24740-4. Basic comparative study of the three leading American thinkers.

Morganbesser, Sidney. *Dewey and His Critics.* Hackett Pub. 1977 $37.50. ISBN 0-931206-00-6. A collection of articles raising critical points about Dewey's philosophy.

Nathanson, Jerome. *John Dewey: The Reconstruction of the Democratic Life.* Continuum 1967 o.p. An excellent summary of Dewey's ideas in his role as philosopher, psychologist, educator, and social theorist.

Paringer, William. *John Dewey and the Paradox of Liberal Reform.* State U. NY Pr. 1990 $59.50. ISBN 0-7914-0253-3. Addresses Deweyan philosophy in relation to contemporary liberal reform movements in education.

Rockefeller, Steven C. *John Dewey: Religious Faith and Democratic Humanism.* Col. U. Pr. 1991 $50.00. ISBN 0-231-07348-8. Exhaustive study that examines Dewey's thought from the perspective of its religious meaning and value.

Sleeper, R. W. *The Necessity of Pragmatism: John Dewey's Conception of Philosophy.* Yale U. Pr. 1986 $30.00. ISBN 0-300-03538-1. Challenges recent interpretations of Dewey's philosophy and attempts to show the systematic character of his thought.

Thayer, Horace S. *Logic of Pragmatism: An Examination of John Dewey's Logic.* Greenwood 1970 repr. of 1952 ed. $38.50. ISBN 0-8371-2409-3. A study of Dewey's views on logic and the reasoning process.

Thomas, Milton H. *John Dewey: A Centennial Bibliography.* Bks. Demand repr. of 1962 ed. $73.00. ISBN 0-8357-9646-9. This bibliography of writings about Dewey first appeared in 1929. A second edition was published 10 years later, and the third, in 1962, carried the project up to 1960.

Tiles, J. E. *Dewey*. Routledge 1989 $39.50. ISBN 0-415-00908-1. Discusses Dewey's philosophy both in its historical context and in light of more recent philosophers.

Westbrook, Robert B. *John Dewey and American Democracy*. Cornell Univ. Pr. 1993 $16.95. ISBN 0-8014-8111-2

White, Morton G. *Origin of Dewey's Instrumentalism*. Hippocrene Bks. 1964 o.p. A reprint of this prize-winning work, which traces the roots of Dewey's philosophy.

DILTHEY, WILHELM. 1833–1911

Born in Biebrich, Germany, the son of a Reformed clergyman, Wilhelm Dilthey studied theology in Wiesbaden and Heidelberg but then moved to Berlin, where he turned to history and philosophy. He held professorships at Basel (1866), Kiel (1868), and Breslau (1871) before becoming Lotze's successor in Berlin (1882), where he taught until 1905. Dilthey wrote many essays on history, the history of philosophy, and the foundation of the human sciences (or *Geisteswissenschaften*, "sciences of spirit"), his contribution to which is the main source of his lasting influence. He is associated with the idea of "philosophy of life"—that lived experience is both the source and the sole subject matter of philosophy. He argued that the human sciences have an aim and method that differs from the natural sciences because they are founded not on causal explanation but on "understanding," which leads to interpretation of the meaning of lived experience. Dilthey's approach to the human studies is holistic, and he is concerned about the problem of historicism, raised by incommensurability of the life experiences and understanding of different ages. He is regarded as one of the chief sources of the "hermeneutical" tradition in German philosophy, whose best-known twentieth-century representatives are MARTIN HEIDEGGER (see also Vol. 5) and HANS GEORG GADAMER.

BOOKS BY DILTHEY

The Essence of Philosophy. Trans. by Stephen A. Emery and William T. Emery. AMS Pr. 1976 repr. of 1954 ed. $27.00. ISBN 0-404-50913-4. The first work of Dilthey's to appear in English.

Introduction to the Human Sciences. Ed. and trans. by Ramon J. Betanzos. Wayne St. U. Pr. 1988 $49.95. ISBN 0-8143-1897-5

Poetry and Experience. Vol. 5 in *Selected Works of Dilthey*. Ed. and trans. by Rudolf A. Makkreel and Frithjof Rodi. Princeton U. Pr. 1985 o.p. The first edition of Dilthey's selected works, giving a good indication of his method of analysis.

BOOKS ABOUT DILTHEY

Hodges, Herbert A. *The Philosophy of Wilhelm Dilthey*. Greenwood 1974 repr. of 1952 ed. $35.00. ISBN 0-8371-7112-1. The first attempt to explain Dilthey's philosophy in English.

Makkreel, Rudolf A. *Dilthey: Philosopher of the Human Studies*. Princeton U. Pr. 1993 $18.95. ISBN 0-691-02097-3. A comprehensive reinterpretation of Dilthey's philosophy as well as a study of its development.

Rickman, H. P. *Dilthey Today: A Critical Appraisal of the Contemporary Relevance of His Work*. Greenwood 1988 $45.00. ISBN 0-313-25933-X. A reassessment of Dilthey's thought in the light of the recent publication of his later collected works.

ENGELS, FRIEDRICH. 1820–1895

Son of a textile manufacturer, Friedrich Engels was born at Barneu, in the Rhineland. His hopes for a career in literature were thwarted by his father, who insisted that he work in the family business. Engels was already an adherent of the Young Hegelian and radical working-class movements when he first made the acquaintance of KARL MARX (see also Vol. 3) in Berlin in 1842. Some two years later in Paris the two men became friends, beginning a lifetime of extraordinarily close collaboration. It was Engels who introduced Marx to both the working-class movement and the study of political economy. After participating in the unsuccessful revolution of 1848, Engels moved to Manchester, where he worked in the family business for 20 years. Until Marx's death in 1883, he produced a series of writings on history, politics, and philosophy; he devoted the last 10 years of his life to the posthumous publication of the second and third volumes of Marx's *Capital*. Engels's own principal writings include *Condition of the Working Class in England* (1844), *Eugen Duhring's Revolution in Science* (1875), *The Origins of the Family, Private Property and the State* (1884), and the posthumously published *Dialectics of Nature* (written 1875–76, published 1925).

Always acknowledging Marx's mind to be more original and profound than his own, Engels nevertheless was an able writer of encyclopedic learning, whose writings cover a much broader range of topics than Marx's. Because Engels popularized the thought of his friend and extended it to the realms of science and philosophy, the philosophy of dialectical materialism owes far more to his writings than to Marx's. Some of the major doctrines with which Marxism is identified owe more to Engels than to Marx. Chief among them are the notions that Marxism socialism is *scientific* (in contrast to the "utopian" socialism of earlier theorists) and that the world outlook based on materialist dialectics should view nature as operating according to dialectical laws.

BOOK BY ENGELS

Marx Engels Collected Works. 50 vols. Intl. Pubs. Co. 1975–present. $24.95 ea. This comprehensive edition, nearing completion, contains all of the principal writings of Engels.

BOOKS ABOUT ENGELS

Carver, Terrell. *Friedrich Engels: His Life and Thought.* St. Martin 1990 $39.95. ISBN 0-312-04501-8. The best intellectual biography of Engels in English.
———. *Marx and Engels: The Intellectual Relationship.* U. of Ind. Pr. 1983 o.p. A reliable account of a subject often mishandled.
McLellan, David. *Friedrich Engels.* Viking Penguin 1977 o.p. A good, brief, readable intellectual biography.
Rigby, S. H. *Engels and the Formation of Marxism.* St. Martin 1992 $69.95. ISBN 0-7190-3530-9. A new study of Engels's thought.
Ruben, David-Hillel. *Marxism and Materialism.* Humanities 1977 o.p. The best discussion of the issues in Marxist philosophy treated by Engels.

FEUERBACH, LUDWIG ANDREAS. 1804–1872

Born in Landshut, Bavaria, Ludwig Andreas Feuerbach was the son of the influential jurist and legal reformer Anselm Feuerbach. He studied theology at Heidelberg and Berlin, transferring to philosophy in 1825 after hearing the lectures of HEGEL (see also Vol. 3). He received a doctorate at Erlangen in 1828, where he assumed a teaching position. In 1830 he published anonymously *Thoughts on Death and Immortality*, which charged that Christianity is an egoistic and inhumane religion. The essay caused a scandal, and when the identity of its author became known in 1837, Feuerbach was dismissed. He lived the remainder of his life on a small pension from the Bavarian government, the income from his writings, revenues from his wife's investments, and in later years on the generosity of his friends. Between 1836 and 1843, he collaborated with Arnold Ruge on a journal published in Halle, in which many of his writings first appeared. He broke with Ruge in 1844, when the latter joined KARL MARX (see also Vol. 3) in publishing the *German-French Annals*, though Feuerbach contributed to the first issue. While the young Marx admired Feuerbach and his work, Feuerbach's political views were liberal rather than radical. Feuerbach's chief writings are *The Essence of Christianity* (1841), *Principles of the Philosophy of the Future* (1843), *The Essence of Religion* (1846), and *Theogony* (1857). He maintained an extensive correspondence with admirers of his work throughout Europe.

Feuerbach, a leading representative of the "Young Hegelian" or "Left Hegelian" philosophical movement, interpreted Hegel's philosophy in a radically humanistic way. He held that metaphysics, including Hegelian speculative philosophy, is only a later and more intellectualized version of religious consciousness, which must be seen through and abolished if humanity is to be free. According to Feuerbach, the real object of our idea of God is the human essence—the human species considered ideally and collectively as a social whole. In primitive religion this idea is grasped intuitively but naively projected outward in the form of one or more separate beings. In later and less innocent stages of human history, the alienated idea of a divine lawgiver and judge is used to confirm the tyrannical power of rulers and priests over human beings. Like other Young Hegelians, Feuerbach advocated the abolition of religious consciousness, maintaining that doing so would liberate humanity from alienation and point the way to a reformed society of equals; in such a society self-denial would be replaced by the affirmation of life, and the human (especially sexual) love that is repressed by religion would be recognized as sacred in its own right.

BOOKS BY FEUERBACH

The Essence of Christianity. 1841. Peter Smith 1958 $24.50. ISBN 0-8446-2055-6. Feuerbach's most influential text, arguing for a completely humanistic interpretation of Christianity. Foreword by H. Richard Niebuhr.
Thoughts on Death and Immortality. Trans. by James A. Massey. U. CA Pr. 1980 $45.00. ISBN 0-520-04051-1. Feuerbach's first work, which treated Christianity as an egoistic and inhumane religion.

BOOKS ABOUT FEUERBACH

Engels, Friedrich. *Ludwig Feuerbach and the Outcome of Classical German Philosophy.* AMS Pr. repr. of 1934 ed. $18.00. ISBN 0-404-15369-0. On the role played by Feuerbach in influencing the philosophy of Marx and Engels.
Marx, Karl, and Friedrich Engels. *Feuerbach: Opposition of Materialistic and Idealistic Outlook*. Beekman Pubs. 1970 $12.95. ISBN 0-8464-0409-5. Evaluation of Feuerbach's view from a Marxist perspective.
Wartofsky, Marx. *Feuerbach*. Cambridge U. Pr. 1982 $59.95. ISBN 0-521-21257-X. Important contemporary reexamination and reevaluation of Feuerbach.
Wilson, Charles. *Feuerbach and the Search for Otherness*. P. Lang Pubs. 1989 $56.95. ISBN 0-8204-0894-8. An analysis of the university writings from 1824 to 1832.

FREGE, GOTTLOB. 1848–1925

The creator of modern logic was born in the Pomeranian town of Wismar. His father was headmaster at a school for young ladies, which Frege's mother took over after her husband's early death. Frege studied mathematics at the University of Jena. His studies were encouraged by Ernst Abbe, who encouraged him to obtain a doctorate at Göttingen and then helped him secure a position as lecturer at Jena in 1874. Although trained as a mathematician, Frege also studied with LOTZE at Göttingen, and his work shows the influence of both LEIBNIZ and KANT. After the publication in 1879 of Frege's first important work, the *Begriffschrift* (*Conceptual Notation*), he was promoted to professor, and he remained at the University of Jena the rest of his life. The *Begriffschrift* was the basis of his new system of logic, which he then sought to apply to the task of deriving number theory entirely from logic, via the theory of classes. This he did in *The Foundations of Arithmetic* (1884).

The next decade saw several of Frege's other important papers on the philosophy of logic and language, including "Function and Concept" (1891), "Concept and Object" (1892), and "Sense and Reference" (1892). Frege was an extreme critic of "psychologism" in logic, mathematics, and philosophy of language—that is, of any view that attempts to treat logic or other sciences pursuing necessary truth as sciences whose subject matter is the actual functioning of the human mind as it can be empirically observed. His critique of psychologism had a far-reaching impact on philosophy in the twentieth century, strongly influencing the development not only of logical positivism and analytical philosophy in English-speaking countries, but also of neo-Kantianism and the phenomenological movement on the continent.

After the publication of the *Foundations*, Frege became aware of certain deficiencies in the logical basis of his theory, which he attempted to remedy in his two-volume *Fundamental Laws of Arithmetic* (1893–1903). Shortly thereafter, Frege received a letter from BERTRAND RUSSELL (see also Vol. 5), which pointed out a contradiction in his theory, since it allowed classes to include themselves as members. Take the class of all classes that are not members of themselves, Russell said; if you assume it is a member of itself, then it follows that it is not, and if you assume it is not, then it follows that it is. Frege attempted to evade the Russell Paradox in a hastily composed appendix, but it was ad hoc and has generally been viewed as unsuccessful. Even apart from this, he later became convinced that the whole project of founding mathematics on logic was doomed to failure.

BOOKS BY FREGE

Conceptual Notation and Related Articles. Ed. and trans. by Terrell Ward Bynum. OUP 1980 o.p. Contains reviews of the *Conceptual Notation* by Frege's contemporaries, as well as a bibliography of Frege's works.

The Foundations of Arithmetic. Trans. by J. L. Austin. Northwestern U. Pr. 1968 $14.95. ISBN 0-8101-0605-1

Logical Investigations. Ed. by P. T. Geach. Trans. by P. T. Geach and R. H. Stoothoff. Yale U. Pr. 1977 o.p.

Translations from the Philosophical Writings of Gottlob Frege. Ed. by Peter Geach and Max Black. Blackwell Pubs. 1980 o.p.

BOOKS ABOUT FREGE

Baker, G. P., and P.M.S. Hacker. *Frege: Logical Excavations.* OUP 1984 $49.95. ISBN 0-19-503261-6. The authors contend that the neglected *Begriffschrift* provides the key to Frege's philosophy.

Bell, David. *Frege's Theory of Judgment.* OUP 1979 o.p. A careful, scholarly treatment of this aspect of Frege's philosophy of language.

Dummett, Michael. *Frege: Philosophy of Language.* HUP 1993 $19.95. ISBN 0-674-31931-1. A huge, magisterial study.

———. *Frege: Philosophy of Mathematics.* HUP 1991 $34.95. ISBN 0-674-31935-4. A long-awaited volume by the best-known Frege scholar.

Grossman, Reinhardt. *Reflections on Frege's Philosophy*. Bks. Demand repr. of 1969 ed. $52.70. ISBN 0-8357-9468-7. Commentary on Frege's major works.

Haaparanta, Leila, and Jaakko Hintikka, eds. *Frege Synthesized*. Kluwer Ac. 1986 $115.00. ISBN 90-277-2126-2. Papers on Frege's semantics, epistemology, logical theory, and philosophy of mathematics.

Resnik, Michael. *Frege and the Philosophy of Mathematics*. Cornell Univ. Pr. 1980 $29.95. ISBN 0-8014-1293-5. Especially sensitive to the historical context of Frege's philosophy of mathematics, relating his work to Mill, Hilbert, and others.

Sluga, Hans. *Gottlob Frege*. Routledge 1980 $29.50. ISBN 0-7100-0474-5. A general introduction to Frege's philosophy and its historical setting.

Weiner, Joan. *Frege in Perspective*. Cornell Univ. Pr. 1990 $32.50. ISBN 0-8014-2115-2. A careful reassessment of Frege's philosophy of language and mathematics.

GREEN, THOMAS HILL. 1836–1882

Born in Birkin, Yorkshire, the son of an Anglican clergyman, Thomas Hill Green entered Balliol College, Oxford, in 1855 and was elected a fellow in 1860. His early efforts at an academic career were unsuccessful, and in 1865–66 he worked on a royal commission investigating the British educational system. He then returned to Balliol as a tutor. When Benjamin Jowett became master in 1870, Green took over many of the college's administrative duties; he was finally elected a professor of moral philosophy in 1878. Throughout his career Green was active in politics as a Liberal, supporting the temperance movement and the local Oxford school system. Green's chief works are his critique of empiricism in his long introduction to his and T. H. Grose's edition of HUME's works (1874) and his *Prolegomena to Ethics* (published posthumously, 1883). The remainder of his writings, including his lectures on political philosophy, were published in three volumes between 1885 and 1888. Green's interests centered on ethics and political philosophy. He was one of the leading "British idealists," critical of empiricism and naturalism and sympathetic to the metaphysical position of KANT and HEGEL (see also Vol. 3).

BOOKS BY GREEN

David Hume: The Philosophical Works. (coauthored with T. H. Grose). 4 vols. Scientia Verlag Aalen 1964 repr. of 1886 ed. o.p. Green's famous 300-page "introduction" to this edition of Hume's works is a brilliant idealist attack on the empiricism of Locke and Hume.

Freedom and Politics in Ethical Behaviour. 2 vols. Found. Class. Reprints 1985 repr. of 1883 ed. $227.50. ISBN 0-89901-237-X

Free Will and the Theory of the Moral Desire. 2 vols. Found. Class. Reprints 1987 repr. of 1883 ed. $287.50. ISBN 0-89901-332-5

Lectures on the Principles of Political Obligation. U. of Mich. Pr. 1967 o.p.

The Political Theory of T. H. Green: Selected Writings. Appleton 1964 o.p.

Prolegomena to Ethics. Ibis Pub. VA 1986 repr. of 1883 ed. $24.95. ISBN 0-935005-57-9

Works of Thomas Hill Green. Ed. by R. L. Nettleship. 3 vols. AMS Pr. repr. of 1894 ed. $135.00. ISBN 0-404-02910-8

BOOKS ABOUT GREEN

Cacoullos, Ann. *Thomas Hill Green: Philosopher of Rights*. Twayne 1974 o.p. A short introduction to his life and work.

Richter, Melvin. *The Politics of Conscience: T. H. Green and His Age*. HUP 1964 o.p. A study of Green's philosophy, its milieu, and its influence.

Thomas, Geoffrey. *The Moral Philosophy of T. H. Green*. OUP 1988 $79.00. ISBN 0-19-824788-5. The best book on this subject.

HEGEL, GEORG WILHELM FRIEDRICH. 1770–1831

Born in Stuttgart, Georg Wilhelm Friedrich Hegel, the son of a middle-class civil servant, was educated at the Tübingen theological seminary, where the friends of his youth included the philosopher F.W.J. SCHELLING and the poet FRIEDRICH HÖLDERLIN (see Vol. 2). In 1794 he worked as a private tutor first in Bern, Switzerland, and then in Frankfurt am Main. A legacy following the death of his father in 1799 financed a university career at the University of Jena, the liveliest philosophical milieu in Germany, where Schelling (though five years Hegel's junior) had just been appointed professor. Hegel achieved the rank of professor in 1805, but a year later university life—and with it Hegel's academic career—were interrupted by Napoleon's victory at the battle of Jena (which Hegel nevertheless welcomed). His first major philosophical work, *The Phenomenology of Spirit*, was published in 1807, after his university career had apparently ended. Hegel spent a year as editor of a newspaper in Bamberg and then became headmaster of a secondary school in Nuremberg, where he continued his philosophical work, completing the first volume of his *Science of Logic* in 1812, the second volume in 1816. From this point, his rise to academic prominence was meteoric. In 1816 he was appointed professor at Heidelberg, publishing the *Encyclopedia of Philosophy* as a textbook to be used in his university lectures. Then in 1818 he was named to the prestigious chair of philosophy at the University of Berlin; its only previous occupant had been FICHTE.

Hegel was brought to Berlin by Karl von Altenstein, a representative of the reform-minded government of Prussia, which had been taking Prussia in the direction of constitutional and representative government since 1808. Hegel's moderately progressive political views were obviously one reason for his having been appointed to his prominent position. When he arrived in Berlin, Hegel probably had with him a draft of the textbook on right and political theory he expected to use for his lectures. But in the summer of 1819 there was a sudden reversal in Prussian politics; the policies of the reformers were decisively defeated by their reactionary adversaries within the Prussian nobility. Several prominent academics were deprived of their positions and censorship of politically sensitive publications was instituted. With several of his students the objects of political persecution, Hegel decided to postpone publication of his textbook, which did not appear until early in 1821. *Elements of the Philosophy of Right* still defends the constitutional state envisaged by the reformers, but in its preface, written in June 1820, Hegel made every effort to portray himself as anything but a subversive, declaring that a true philosophy of the state would be concerned solely with understanding it rationally rather than prescribing how it ought to be. He succeeded in appeasing the censors but enraged many intellectuals, who misinterpreted his philosophy as an apology for the reactionary status quo. This is an albatross Hegel's political philosophy has carried ever since, though since the mid-twentieth century a scholarly consensus has recognized its essentially progressive character. Hegel stayed at Berlin until his death, expanding the *Encyclopedia* to three volumes in 1827 but producing no major new philosophical works. He lectured extensively on world history, aesthetics, religion, and the history of philosophy during the 1820s, however, and detailed, edited transcriptions of his lectures were included in the first collected edition of his writings in 1833.

From its inception in the philosophy of Fichte, the German idealist movement saw itself as a philosophy in process, trying to complete the revolution that KANT had begun. Hegel's system, which encompassed an enormous range, came to be generally recognized as the consummation of this movement. Hegel's students tended to dominate the German university system into the 1840s. Thereafter Hegel's reputation declined sharply; despite its revival in England toward the end of the nineteenth century, it remained relatively low until after World War I. Since then, however, Hegel's repute has enjoyed a remarkable renaissance, first on the continent of Europe and more recently in English-speaking countries.

Books by Hegel

The Difference Between Fichte's and Schelling's System of Philosophy. 1801. Trans. by W. Cerf and H. S. Harris. State U. NY Pr. 1977 $44.50. ISBN 0-87395-336-3. Hegel's published work, a critique of Fichte and defense of Schelling.

Early Theological Writings. 1794–1800. Trans. by T. M. Knox. U. of Pa. Pr. 1971 repr. of 1948 ed. $18.95. ISBN 0-8122-1022-0. A selection from Hegel's writings in the 1790s, not published until 1920.

Elements of the Philosophy of Right. 1821. Ed. by Allen W. Wood. Trans. by H. B. Nisbet. Cambridge U. Pr. 1991 $59.95. ISBN 0-521-34438-7. An exemplary new translation of Hegel's famous text on right, ethics, and the state, with informative editorial notes.

The Encyclopedia Logic. 1817. Trans. by T. F. Geraets and others. Hackett 1991 o.p. The Berlin *Encyclopedia*, Volume 1.

Hegel's Aesthetics. Trans. by T. M. Knox. OUP 1975 o.p. Lecture transcriptions from the Berlin period.

Hegel and the Human Spirit. Trans. by L. Rauch. Bks. Demand repr. of 1986 ed. $50.00. ISBN 0-7837-3655-X. Notes from Hegel's last series of Jena lectures, 1805–06.

Lectures on the History of Philosophy. 3 vols. Trans. by Robert Brown. U. CA Pr. 1990 $55.00. ISBN 0-520-06812-2. Lecture transcriptions from the Berlin period.

Lectures on the Philosophy of Religion. 3 vols. Trans. by P. Hodgson and R. F. Brown. U. CA Pr. 1984–87 $65.00–$75.00. ISBNs 0-520-04676-5, 0-520-05513-6, 0-520-05514-4. Lecture transcriptions from the Berlin period.

Lectures on the Philosophy of World History: Introduction. Trans. by H. B. Nisbet. Cambridge U. Pr. 1975 o.p. The best introduction to Hegel, a transcription of the first part of Hegel's 1830 Berlin lectures.

Letters. Trans. by C. Butler and C. Seiler. U. of Ind. Pr. 1984 o.p. Hegel's philosophical correspondence, with commentaries.

Natural Law. 1802. Trans. by T. M. Knox. U. of Pa. Pr. 1975 o.p. An important essay from Hegel's Jena period.

Phenomenology of Spirit. 1807. Trans. by A. V. Miller. OUP 1977 o.p. Hegel's first major work, a continuing object of intense study.

The Philosophical Propaedeutic. 1812. Ed. by M. George and A. Vincent. Trans. by A. V. Miller. Blackwell Pubs. 1986 $45.00. ISBN 0-631-15013-7. Notes from Hegel's lectures in Nuremberg.

Philosophy of Mind. 1817. Trans. by A. V. Miller. OUP 1971 $18.95. ISBN 0-19-875014-5. The Berlin *Encyclopedia*, Volume 3.

Philosophy of Nature. 1817. 3 vols. Trans. by M. J. Petry. Allen & Unwin 1970 o.p. An excellent, annotated version of the Berlin *Encyclopedia*, Volume 2.

Philosophy of Subjective Spirit. 1817. 3 vols. Trans. by M. J. Petry. o.p. An excellent, annotated version of the first part of the Berlin *Encyclopedia*, Volume 3.

Political Writings. Trans. by T. M. Knox. OUP 1942 o.p. A collection of Hegel's shorter essays on political subjects from 1800 to 1831.

Science of Logic. 1812. Trans. by A. V. Miller. Humanities 1989 $49.95. ISBN 0-391-00675-4. One of Hegel's most important works.

Books about Hegel

Avineri, Shlomo. *Hegel's Theory of the Modern State.* Cambridge U. Pr. 1974 $49.95. ISBN 0-521-08513-6. The most readable book-length account of Hegel's political thought.

Beiser, Frederick C., ed. *The Cambridge Companion to Hegel*. Cambridge U. Pr. 1993 $59.95. ISBN 0-521-38274-2. An excellent, comprehensive anthology on Hegel's philosophy.

Burbidge, John. *On Hegel's Logic*. Humanities 1981 o.p. Probably the best philosophical interpretation of Hegel's logic.

DeVries, Willem. *Hegel's Theory of Mental Activity*. Cornell Univ. Pr. 1988 $31.50. ISBN 0-8014-2133-0. An excellent study of Hegel's contribution to the philosophy of mind.

Dickey, Laurence. *Hegel: Religion, Economics and Politics of the Spirit, 1770–1807*. Cambridge U. Pr. 1989 $21.95. ISBN 0-521-38912-7. An informed original interpretation of Hegel's early thought.

Forster, Michael. *Hegel and Skepticism*. HUP 1989 $29.50. ISBN 0-674-38707-4. The best available account of Hegel's epistemology, based on his treatment of ancient skepticism in the Jena period.

———. *Hegel's Idea of a Phenomenology of Spirit*. HUP 1993 o.p. The best available treatment in English of Hegel's method in the *Phenomenology*.

Foster, M. B. *The Political Philosophies of Plato and Hegel*. OUP 1935 o.p. An old but still useful and interesting account of Hegel's political thought.

Hardimon, Michael. *The Project of Reconciliation*. Cambridge U. Pr. 1993 o.p. A critical examination of Hegel's attempt rationally to reconcile the reflective modern individual with modern society.

Harris, H. S. *Hegel's Development: Night Thoughts*. o.p. A continuation of *Toward the Sunlight* in the Jena period, 1801–1806.

———. *Hegel's Development: Toward the Sunlight*. OUP 1972 o.p. A detailed intellectual biography of Hegel's early life, 1770–1801.

Houlgate, Stephen. *Hegel, Nietzsche and the Criticism of Metaphysics*. Cambridge U. Pr. 1987 $54.95. ISBN 0-521-32255-3. A defense of Hegelian philosophy against criticisms of metaphysics in the existentialist tradition.

Inwood, Michael. *Hegel*. Routledge 1984 $61.50. ISBN 0-7100-9509-0. The most thorough, philosophically sophisticated critical survey of Hegel's philosophy available.

———, ed. *Hegel*. OUP 1985 $13.95. ISBN 0-19-875066-8. A valuable anthology of articles on various aspects of Hegel's thought.

Kojève, Alexandre. *Introduction to the Reading of Hegel*. Trans. by J. H. Nichols. Cornell Univ. Pr. 1980 $13.95. ISBN 0-8014-9203-3. Famous and influential lectures on the *Phenomenology*; imaginative but highly unreliable as interpretation of Hegel.

Mure, G.R.G. *An Introduction to Hegel*. Greenwood 1982 repr. of 1940 ed. $42.50. ISBN 0-313-23741-7. One of the most useful introductions to Hegel.

Pippin, Robert. *Hegel's Idealism*. Cambridge U. Pr. 1989 $54.95. ISBN 0-521-37026-4. A philosophically subtle and informed account of the development of Hegel's system out of the problems set by Kant and Fichte.

Rosen, Michael. *Hegel's Dialectic and its Criticism*. Cambridge U. Pr. 1985 $34.50. ISBN 0-521-24484-6. An interpretation of the Hegelian dialectic in light of late twentieth-century philosophy.

Smith, Steven. *Hegel's Critique of Liberalism*. U. Ch. Pr. 1991 $14.95. ISBN 0-226-76350-1. A valuable assessment of Hegel's contribution to modern political theory.

Taylor, Charles. *Hegel*. Cambridge U. Pr. 1977 $27.95. ISBN 0-521-20679-0. The most influential interpretation of Hegel's philosophy as a whole.

Toews, John. *Hegelianism*. Cambridge U. Pr. 1980 o.p. The best treatment in English of Hegel's immediate followers and his influence on German philosophy in the mid-nineteenth century.

Westphal, Kenneth. *Hegel's Epistemological Realism*. Kluwer Ac. 1989 $82.50. ISBN 0-7923-0193-5. An original, provocative interpretation of Hegel's theory of knowledge.

Wood, Allen W. *Hegel's Ethical Thought*. Cambridge U. Pr. 1990 $54.95. ISBN 0-521-37432-4. A lucid critical exposition of Hegel's contribution to ethical theory.

HUSSERL, EDMUND. 1859–1938

Born to Jewish parents in what is now the Czech Republic, Edmund Husserl began as a mathematician, studying with Karl Theodor Weierstrass and receiving a doctorate in 1881. He went on to study philosophy and psychology with FRANZ BRENTANO and taught at Halle (1887–1901), Göttingen (1901–16), and Freiburg (1916–29). Because of his Jewish background, he was subject to persecution by the Nazis, and after his death his unpublished manuscripts had to be smuggled to Louvain, Belgium, to prevent their being destroyed. Husserl is the founder of the philosophical school known as phenomenology.

The history of Husserl's philosophical development is that of an endless philosophical search for a foundational method that could serve as a rational ground for all the sciences. His first major book, *Philosophy of Arithmetic* (1891), was criticized by GOTTLOB FREGE for its psychologism, which changed the whole direction of Husserl's thinking. The culmination of his next period was the *Logical Investigations* (1901). His views took an idealistic turn in the *Ideas Toward a Pure Phenomenology* (1911). Husserl wrote little from then until the late 1920s, when he developed his idealism in a new direction in *Formal and Transcendental Logic* (1929) and *Cartesian Meditations* (1932). His thought took yet another turn in his late lectures published as *Crisis of the European Sciences* (1936), which emphasize the knowing I's rootedness in "life world." Husserl's influence in the twentieth century has been great, not only through his own writings, but also through his many distinguished students, who included MARTIN HEIDEGGER (see also Vol. 5), MAURICE MERLEAU-PONTY, JEAN-PAUL SARTRE (see also Vol. 2), Eugen Fink, Emmanuel Levinas, and Roman Ingarden.

BOOKS BY HUSSERL

Cartesian Meditations: An Introduction to a Phenomenology. 1932. Kluwer Ac. 1988 $14.50. ISBN 0-317-67317-3. These are lectures Husserl gave in Paris, introducing his views to the French philosophical public. They are published in the phenomenology series started by the Dutch publisher Martinue Nijhoff (now part of Kluwer Academic), originally edited by L. Van Breda, who, along with several of his students had helped save Husserl's papers. The series contains a great many works by and about Husserl in German, French, and English.

The Crisis of European Sciences and Transcendental Phenomenology: An Introduction to Phenomenological Philosophy. Trans. by David Carr. Northwestern U. Pr. 1970 $39.95. ISBN 0-8101-0255-2. This work was written two or three years before Husserl's death and contains the final version of his view.

Ideas Pertaining to a Pure Phenomenology and to a Phenomenological Philosophy. 1913. Trans. by Fred Kersten. Kluwer Ac. 1982 $126.50. ISBN 90-247-2503-8

Phenomenology and the Foundation of the Sciences. Trans. by Ted Klein and William Polin. Kluwer Ac. 1980 $50.50. ISBN 90-247-2093-1. Part of the continuing publication of Husserl's writings in English.

BOOKS ABOUT HUSSERL

Bachelard, Suzanne. *Study of Husserl's Formal and Transcendental Logic.* Trans. by Lester E. Embree. *Studies in Phenomenology and Existential Philosophy Ser.* Northwestern U. Pr. 1990 repr. of 1968 ed. $16.95. ISBN 0-8101-0859-3. By one of France's most brilliant logicians.

Bell, David. *Husserl.* Routledge 1992 $16.95. ISBN 0-415-07045-7. A critical study of the major themes in Husserl's thought, from the foundations of arithmetic to intentionality and consciousness.

Carr, David. *Interpreting Husserl: Critical and Comparative Studies.* Kluwer Ac. 1987 $117.00. ISBN 90-247-3505-X. Contains essays falling into three categories: tensions within Husserl's thought, comparisons of Husserl with other thinkers and approaches, and less historical treatments of time and existence.

Dreyfus, Hubert L., and Harrison Hall, eds. *Husserl: Intentionality and Cognitive Science.* MIT Pr. 1982 o.p. A collection of writings by various authors.

Edie, James. *Edmund Husserl's Phenomenology: A Critical Commentary*. Bks. Demand 1987 $45.40. ISBN 0-7837-1749-0. A collection of papers by a well-known Husserl scholar.

Gurwitsch, Aron. *Studies in Phenomenological Psychology*. Northwestern U. Pr. 1966 o.p. By one of the first members of the phenomenological movement to come to the United States.

Ingarden, Ramon. *On the Motives Which Led Husserl to Transcendental Idealism*. Kluwer Ac. 1975 o.p. Ingarden developed an important center of phenomenological thought at the University of Krakow.

Kockelmans, Joseph J. *Edmund Husserl's Phenomenological Psychology*. Psychology Ser. Humanities 1978 repr. of 1967 ed. o.p. A study of Husserl's psychology, its role and influence.

Levinas, Emmanuel. *The Theory of Intuition in Husserl's Phenomenology*. Studies in Phenomenology and Existential Philosophy Ser. Northwestern U. Pr. 1985 repr. of 1973 ed. $12.95. ISBN 0-8101-0708-2. Levinas was one of Husserl's most important and original students.

Natanson, Maurice. *Edmund Husserl: Philosopher of Infinite Tasks*. Studies in Phenomenology and Existential Philosophy Ser. Northwestern U. Pr. 1973 $35.95. ISBN 0-8101-0456-3. A presentation of Husserl's ideas by a leading American phenomenologist.

Sokolowski, Robert. *Husserlian Meditations: How Words Present Things*. Studies in Phenomenology and Existential Philosophy Ser. Northwestern U. Pr. 1974 $22.95. ISBN 0-8101-0440-7. An exposition and commentary on Husserl's work.

Spiegelberg, Herbert. *The Context of the Phenomenological Movement*. Kluwer Ac. 1981 o.p. A collection of studies by Spiegelberg on Husserl and his influence.

_____. *The Phenomenological Movement*. Kluwer Ac. 1981 $165.50. ISBN 0-90-247-2577-1. An all-important history of the phenomenological movement by one of its early members.

Willard, Dallas. *Logic and the Objectivity of Knowledge: Studies in Husserl's Early Philosophy*. Ser. in Continental Thought. Ohio U. Pr. 1984 $29.95. ISBN 0-8214-0715-5. A scholarly exposition of Husserl's early philosophical writings.

JAMES, WILLIAM. 1842–1910

William James, the leading figure of the movement in American philosophy called pragmatism, was born in New York. He was the son of Henry James, Sr., a minor New England transcendentalist who was one of the leading advocates of Emmanuel Swedenborg's Church of the New Jerusalem (a movement to which the English poet WILLIAM BLAKE [see Vol. 1] also belonged). William James was also the brother of HENRY JAMES (see Vol. 1), and it was often said that William wrote philosophy books as if they were novels, and Henry wrote novels as if they were philosophy books. Thus, the easy style of William is contrasted with the ponderous one of Henry. William was educated in the United States and Europe. He studied painting, science, and medicine, earning a medical degree at Harvard University in 1869. He took part in LOUIS AGASSIZ's (see Vol. 5) expedition to Brazil and also did advanced scientific and medical study in Germany. He was then appointed an instructor in anatomy and physiology at Harvard in 1872, moved on to become an assistant professor of psychology, and from 1880 a professor of philosophy. He gave the Gifford Lectures in Edinburgh in 1901 and 1902.

James's first major publication was his *Principles of Psychology* (1890). Building on his psychological researches and his discussions in a philosophy club with CHARLES SANDERS PEIRCE and Chauncey Wright, he began developing a theory about how human beings think and what forms the bases for their beliefs. He called this theory pragmatism, a term he borrowed from Peirce. As James devoted more and more of his time to developing his philosophical approach, and to teaching philosophy, he expounded the pragmatic theory in a series of books and essays that have provided the fundamental statement of the view. James, possibly from his parental upbringing, had a religious temperament, unlike many of his tough-minded scientific colleagues. Using both his pragmatic method and his psychological researches, he sought to defend some kind of religious attitude in his essay "The Will to Believe" (1897) and in his book *The Varieties of Religious Experience* (1902). As the leading spokesman for pragmatism, he defended this theory against idealistic opponents in the United States and against more positivistic thinkers like BERTRAND RUSSELL (see also Vol. 5).

BOOKS BY JAMES

Collected Essays and Reviews. Ed. by Ralph B. Perry. Russell Sage 1969 repr. of 1920 ed. o.p. Thirty-nine articles from 1869 to 1910.

Essays in Pragmatism. Ed. by Alburey Castell. Free Pr. 1974 $9.95. ISBN 0-317-30538-7. Seven of James's best-known philosophical essays.

Essays in Psychology. Ed. by Frederick Burkhardt, Fredson Bowers, and Ignas K. Skrupskelis. HUP 1983 $45.00. ISBN 0-674-26714-1. This is Volume 13 of *The Works of William James.*

Essays in Radical Empiricism and a Pluralistic Universe. 1912. Rprt. Serv. 1992 repr. of 1912 ed. $75.00. ISBN 0-7812-3483-2. Two of the most basic statements of the pragmatic theory of knowledge and the nature of the world.

Essays in Religion and Morality. HUP 1982 $35.00. ISBN 0-674-26735-4. Collection of essays on these subjects.

The Letters of William James. Ed. by Henry James. 2 vols. Kraus Repr. 1920 o.p. James's correspondence edited by his son.

The Meaning of Truth: A Sequel to Pragmatism. 1909. Ed. by Frederick Burkhardt, Fredson Bowers, and Ignas K. Skrupskelis. Rprt. Serv. 1992 $75.00. ISBN 0-7812-3480-8. Reissue of James's defense of pragmatism against such early critics as Bradley and Russell.

Memories and Studies. 1911. Ed. by Henry James. Greenwood 1968 repr. of 1911 ed. $47.50. ISBN 0-8371-0496-3. Fifteen popular essays and addresses, chosen by his son, Henry James.

A Pluralistic Universe. 1909. HUP 1977 $40.00. ISBN 0-674-67391-3. James's criticism of idealism challenges Hegel, Fechner, and Bergson.

Pragmatism. 1907. Ed. by Ralph Barton Perry. Rprt. Serv. 1992 $75.00. ISBN 0-7812-3477-8. Edited by one of James's leading students.

Pragmatism: A New Name for Some Old Ways of Thinking. 1907. Ed. by Frederick Burkhardt. Bks. Demand repr. of 1978 ed. $107.80. ISBN 0-7837-3856-0. Reissue of James's immensely popular and influential work. "In addition to the 'clear text,' it provides a splendid historical, philosophical, and biographical introduction by H. S. Thayer, notes on the text with full bibliographical data, a complete account of the textual history and critical apparatus (including four appendixes of documents related to the text), and a complete index" (*Choice*).

Pragmatism and Other Essays. Ed. by J. L. Blau. WSP 1983 o.p. A collection of some of James's essays edited by a leading historian of American philosophy.

Pragmatism and The Meaning of Truth. Intro. by A. J. Ayer. HUP 1978 $11.95. ISBN 0-674-69737-5. Two of James's essays edited by a leading historian of American philosophy.

The Principles of Psychology. 1890. 2 vols. Peter Smith 1950 $43.00. ISBN 0-8446-2310-5. James's first major work. "This critical text of the preeminent classic of American psychology incorporates the results of the highest standards of textual scholarship to present James's intentions in a definitive edition. . . . Awarded the Seal of the Center for Scholarly Editions" (*Choice*).

Some Problems of Philosophy: A Beginning of an Introduction to Philosophy. Greenwood 1968 repr. of 1911 ed. $42.50. ISBN 0-8371-4464-7. James's last work, unfinished, contains his theory of perception.

The Varieties of Religious Experience: A Study in Human Nature. 1902. Random 1993 $17.50. ISBN 0-679-60075-2. James's major work on the study of religion, its effect on people, and its value.

William James on Psychical Research. Ed. by Gardner Murphy and Robert Ballou. Kelley 1979 repr. of 1960 ed. $37.50. ISBN 0-678-03164-9. "This book, ably compiled and edited, contains lectures, articles, letters, and a detailed account of sittings with the medium Mrs. Piper, in whom James was interested from 1885 right up to the time of his death in 1910" (*New Statesman*).

The Will to Believe and Human Immortality. 1897. Dover 1956 $7.95. ISBN 0-486-20291-7. A pragmatic defense of some kind of religious belief.

The Works of William James. 17 vols. HUP 1975–88 o.p.

The Writings of William James. Ed. by John M. McDermott. U. Ch. Pr. 1978 $19.95. ISBN 0-226-39188-4. A collection of selections from James's main works.

BOOKS ABOUT JAMES

Ayer, Alfred J. *Origins of Pragmatism: Studies in the Philosophy of Charles Sanders Peirce and William James.* Freeman Cooper 1968 $12.50. ISBN 0-87735-501-0. A lively discussion of the two philosophers and of pragmatism in general by one of England's leading analytic philosophers.

Barzun, Jacques. *A Stroll with William James.* U. Ch. Pr. 1984 $25.00. ISBN 0-226-03865-3. An interesting and witty appreciation of James as a person and as a thinker by one of America's best intellectual historians and literary critics.

Bird, Graham. *William James.* Routledge 1987 $39.95. ISBN 0-7100-9602-X. This book does not offer a chronological account of James's development but instead outlines his central doctrines, comparing him with such later philosophers as Grice, Parfit, and Wittgenstein.

Bjork, Daniel W. *William James: The Center of His Vision.* Col. U. Pr. 1988 $47.00. ISBN 0-231-05674-5. A fine reconstruction of James's intellectual and creative life.

Cotkin, George. *William James, Public Philosopher.* Johns Hopkins 1989 $34.00. ISBN 0-8018-3878-9. A fair and succinct portrait of James's intellectual, professional, and personal life.

Flournoy, T. *Philosophy of William James. Select Bibliographies Repr. Ser.* Aycr 1978 repr. of 1917 ed. $22.00. ISBN 0-8369-5087-9. A presentation of James's philosophy by a Swiss philosopher.

Ford, Marcus P. *William James's Philosophy: A New Perspective.* U. of Mass. Pr. 1982 o.p. "This book is concerned with James's thought overall. . . . [Ford] believes that James's theory of truth is a confused form of the correspondence theory of truth and that James was, for the most part, a panpsychist" (Publisher's note).

James, William, ed. *In Commemoration of William James, 1842–1942.* AMS Pr. 1981 repr. of 1942 ed. $18.00. ISBN 0-404-03550-7. A volume of addresses made by various scholars in honor of the one-hundredth anniversary of James's birth at celebrations held by the Conference on Methods in Philosophy and the Sciences, the Eastern Division of the American Philosophical Association, and the Western Division of the American Philosophical Association.

Johnson, Michael G., and Tracey B. Henley, eds. *Reflections on the Principles of Psychology: William James after a Century.* L. Erlbaum Assocs. 1990 $49.95. ISBN 0-8058-0205-3. Series of essays examining the impact of James on psychology as a human experience; includes bibliographic references.

Kallen, Horace M. *William James and Henri Bergson: A Study in Contrasting Theories.* AMS Pr. 1975 repr. of 1914 cd. $30.00. ISBN 0-404-59209-0. Kallen was one of the best pragmatists trained at Harvard in James's time.

Levinson, Henry S. *The Religious Investigations of William James. Studies in Religion.* U. of NC Pr. 1981 $32.50. ISBN 0-8078-1468-7. "A first-class analysis of James, sustaining the high level in making clear relations with other systems and figures of James's lifetime and the implications of positions and currents" (*Choice*).

Marcell, David W. *Progress and Pragmatism: James, Dewey, Beard and the American Idea of Progress. Contributions in Amer. Studies.* Greenwood 1974 $47.95. ISBN 0-8371-

6387-0. A comparative study of these three thinkers in relation to the American view of progressive development.

Moore, Edward C. *American Pragmatism: Peirce, James and Dewey.* Greenwood 1984 repr. of 1961 ed. $52.50. ISBN 0-313-24740-4. This volume has become one of the standard presentations and evaluations of the subject.

Myers, Gerald. *William James: His Life and Thought.* Yale U. Pr. 1986 $19.95. ISBN 0-300-04211-6. A monumental intellectual biography.

Perry, Ralph B. *Annotated Bibliography of the Writings of William James.* Folcroft 1972 repr. of 1920 ed. o.p.

———. *The Thought and Character of William James.* 2 vols. Greenwood 1974 repr. of 1935 ed. o.p. An excellent intellectual biography by one of James's leading students.

Reck, Andrew J. *Introduction to William James: An Essay and Selected Texts.* Bks. Demand repr. of 1967 ed. $41.80. ISBN 0-317-09895-0. A fine essay on James, plus some important texts; "gives the broad outline of James's philosophy . . . [stressing its] contemporary relevance" (*Library Journal*).

Seigfried, Charlene H. *William James's Radical Reconstruction of Philosophy.* State U. NY Pr. 1990 $59.50. ISBN 0-7914-0401-3. Reconceptualizes James's writings and methodologies, providing a fresh approach to many of the problems raised over the years.

Vanden Burgt, Robert J. *The Religious Philosophy of William James.* Nelson-Hall 1981 o.p. "On the whole Vanden Burgt's study . . . makes a unique and valuable contribution. [He] has written in clear, nontechnical language an introduction to the religious philosophy of James and has done it in such a way as to set James within the context of contemporary discussions in theology and the philosophy of religion" (*Christian Century*).

Wild, John D. *The Radical Empiricism of William James.* Greenwood 1980 repr. of 1969 ed. $41.50. ISBN 0-313-22641-5. The relation of James's thought to modern Continental philosophy and such philosophers as Heidegger, Merleau-Ponty, and Husserl.

KIERKEGAARD, SØREN. 1813–1855

Born in Copenhagen, Denmark, Søren Kierkegaard was the son of a wealthy middle-class merchant. He lived all his life on his inheritance, using it to finance his literary career. He studied theology at the University of Copenhagen, completing a master's thesis in 1841 on the topic of irony in SOCRATES. At about this time, he became engaged to a woman he loved, but he broke the engagement when he decided that God had destined him not to marry. The years 1841 to 1846 were a period of intense literary activity for Kierkegaard, in which he produced his "authorship," a series of writings of varying forms published under a series of fantastic pseudonyms. Parallel to these, he wrote a series of shorter *Edifying Discourses*—quasi-sermons published under his own name. As he later interpreted it in the posthumously published *Point of View for My Work as an Author*, the authorship was a systematic attempt to raise the question of what it means to be a Christian. Kierkegaard was persuaded that in his time people took the meaning of the Christian life for granted, allowing all kinds of worldly and pagan ways of thinking and living to pass for Christian. He applied this analysis especially to the speculative philosophy of German idealism (particularly the system of HEGEL [see also Vol. 3], which was then current in the intellectual life of Denmark as well as Germany). After 1846, Kierkegaard continued to write, publishing most works under his own name. Within Denmark he was isolated and often despised, a man whose writings had little impact in his own day or for a long time afterward. They were translated into German early in the twentieth century and have had an enormous influence since then, on both Christian theology and the existentialist tradition in philosophy

BOOKS BY KIERKEGAARD

Attack upon "Christendom." 1854–55. Trans. by Walter Lowrie. Princeton U. Pr. 1944 $13.95. ISBN 0-691-01950-9. These are Kierkegaard's polemical writings against the religious establishment and the comfortable believers, written at the end of his life.

Christian Discourses. 1848. Trans. by Walter Lowrie. Bks. Demand repr. of 1971 ed. $110.50. ISBN 0-7837-1945-0. Some religious discussions on various themes.

The Concept of Anxiety. Trans. by Howard V. Hong and Edna H. Hong. Princeton U. Pr. 1980 $39.50. ISBN 0-691-07244-2. A psychological study of sin.

The Concept of Irony: With Constant Reference to Socrates. 1841. Trans. by Lee M. Cappel. Princeton U. Pr. 1991 $69.50. ISBN 0-691-07354-6. This is Kierkegaard's master essay. Cappel's introduction is illuminating.

The Concluding Unscientific Postscript. 1846. Trans. by Walter Lowrie. 2 vols. Princeton U. Pr. 1992 $99.50. ISBN 0-691-07403-8

Kierkegaard Anthology. Princeton U. Pr. 1973 $14.95. ISBN 0-691-01978-9. A well-rounded collection of selections from the various aspects of Kierkegaard's writing.

Philosophical Fragments. 1844. Ed. by Niels Thulstrup. Trans. by David Swenson. Princeton U. Pr. 1985 $55.00. ISBN 0-691-07273-6. In addition to many notes, this edition contains a commentary on the work.

Purity of Heart. Trans. by Douglas Steere. HarpC 1956 $12.00. ISBN 0-06-130004-7. On the nature of spiritual life.

The Sickness unto Death: A Christian Psychological Exposition for Upbuilding and Awakening. 1848. Trans. by Howard V. Hong and Edna H. Hong. Princeton U. Pr. 1980 $37.50. ISBN 0-691-07247-7. Discussion of the meaning of life.

Søren Kierkegaard's Journals and Papers. Trans. by Howard V. Hong and Edna H. Hong. 7 vols. Ind. U. Pr. 1967–78 $44.95–$69.95. ISBNs 0-253-18240-9, 0-253-18241-7, 0-253-18242-5, 0-253-18243-3, 0-253-18244-1, 0-253-18245-X, 0-253-18246-8. An all-important source for following Kierkegaard's development and interpreting his ideas.

Three Discourses on Imagined Occasions. Princeton U. Pr. 1993 $35.00. ISBN 0-691-03300-5

Training in Christianity. 1850. Trans. by Walter Lowrie. Bks. Demand repr. of 1967 ed. $78.80. ISBN 0-8357-4650-X. One of the major "indirect" statements of Kierkegaard's theology.

Two Ages: The Age of Revolution and the Present Age. Trans. by Howard V. Hong and Edna H. Hong. Princeton U. Pr. 1978 o.p. This work started out as a book review and became an important essay about literature.

Upbuilding Discourses in Various Spirits. Princeton U. Pr. 1993 $45.00. ISBN 0-691-03274-2

Works of Love: Some Christian Reflections in the Form of Discourses. 1847. Trans. by Howard V. Hong and Edna H. Hong. HarpC 1964 $13.00. ISBN 0-06-130122-1. Kierkegaard's important discussion of Christian ethics.

BOOKS ABOUT KIERKEGAARD

Arbaugh, George E., and George B. Arbaugh. *Kierkegaard's Authorship: A Guide to the Writings of Kierkegaard.* Augustana College 1968 o.p. A useful guide to unraveling the various pseudonyms used by Kierkegaard.

Collins, James. *The Mind of Kierkegaard: With a New Preface and Updated Bibliographical Notes.* Princeton U. Pr. 1983 repr. of 1965 ed. $12.95. ISBN 0-691-02027-2. Important study of Kierkegaard by the leading Catholic historian of philosophy in America.

Elrod, J. W. *Being and Existence in Kierkegaard's Pseudonymous Works.* Bks. Demand repr. of 1975 ed. $72.60. ISBN 0-8357-6037-5. A very careful examination of a key thread in Kierkegaard's thought.

_____. *Kierkegaard and Christendom.* Bks. Demand repr. of 1981 ed. $89.20. ISBN 0-8357-6176-2. A study of Kierkegaard's actual relation to the Christian world.

Gardiner, Patrick. *Kierkegaard.* OUP 1988 $32.50. ISBN 0-19-287643-0. A short, accessible introduction to Kierkegaard's thought.

Kirmmse, Bruce. *Kierkegaard in Golden Age of Denmark.* Ind. U. Pr. 1990 $35.00. ISBN 0-253-33044-0. The only comprehensive intellectual biography of Kierkegaard in any language.

Lebowitz, Naomi. *Kierkegaard: A Life of Allegory.* La. State U. Pr. 1985 $32.50. ISBN 0-8071-1186-4. A very sensitive analysis by a literary critic.

Lowrie, Walter. *Kierkegaard.* 2 vols. Peter Smith 1970 $28.50. ISBN 0-8446-0778-9. Lowrie's complete biography, plus his interpretation of Kierkegaard's thought. This was the first work to give the English language audience a large picture of Kierkegaard's philosophy.

_____. *Short Life of Kierkegaard.* Princeton U. Pr. 1942 $12.95. ISBN 0-691-01957-6. The first biography available in English.

McKinnon, Alastair, ed. *Computational Analysis of Kierkegaard's Samlede Vaerker.* 6 vols. Princeton U. Pr. 1979 $495.00. ISBN 0-686-75220-1. A concordance of all the words that appear in Kierkegaard's writings, done by computer analysis. Very helpful if one wants to follow Kierkegaard's use of certain concepts.

Pattison, George. *Kierkegaard: The Aesthetic and the Religious.* St. Martin 1992 $49.95. ISBN 0-312-06836-0. An account of Kierkegaard's aesthetics and its role in his own authorship; draws on contemporary Danish sources.

Perkins, Robert L., ed. *Kierkegaard's Fear and Trembling: Critical Appraisals.* U. of Ala. Pr. 1981 o.p. A collection of evaluations of this great work of Kierkegaard by different scholars.

Sontag, Frederick. *A Kierkegaard Handbook.* Westminster John Knox 1980 o.p. A reference guide for leading ideas in Kierkegaard. "Rather than presenting an overall systematic development of Kierkegaard's thought, Sontag concentrates on complementary categories such as 'happy/unhappy,' 'inwardness/communication,' 'necessity/possibility,' 'repetition/freedom,' which nevertheless lead to a unifying comprehension of Kierkegaard's total work" (*Library Journal*).

Stack, George J. *Kierkegaard's Existential Ethics.* Ashgate Pub. Co. 1992 $49.95. ISBN 0-7512-0018-2. An attempt to find a central focus in Kierkegaard's thought.

Thompson, Josiah. *Kierkegaard.* Knopf 1973 o.p. This is one of the best surveys of Kierkegaard's views.

_____. *Kierkegaard: A Collection of Critical Essays.* Doubleday 1972 o.p. An excellent collection of articles on Kierkegaard by several scholars, dealing with many aspects of Kierkegaard's thought.

Thulstrup, Niels. *Kierkegaard's Concluding Unscientific Postscript.* Trans. by Robert J. Widenmann. Princeton U. Pr. 1984 $72.50. ISBN 0-691-07180-2. The commentary is most helpful with this central and difficult text of Kierkegaard.

_____. *Kierkegaard's Relation to Hegel.* Trans. by George Stengren. Bks. Demand repr. of 1980 ed. $108.20. ISBN 0-8357-6177-0. An important study. One of the key focuses of Kierkegaard's point of view.

LOTZE, RUDOLF HERMANN. 1817–1881

Born at Bautzen and educated at Leipzig, Rudolf Hermann Lotze studied mathematics and physics before taking doctorates in both medicine and philosophy. He began teaching in the medical faculty at Leipzig in 1841, becoming professor of philosophy there in 1844. Lotze's main work is the three-volume *Mikrokosmos* (1856–64), although later he planned a more comprehensive account of his philosophy in three volumes, of which two, *Logic* (1874) and *Metaphysics* (1879), were completed. Lotze argued that it is not the function of metaphysics to ground empirical science by deducing its basic categories but only to analyze and clarify the concepts of the particular sciences, grounding itself on them and hence always remaining open to revision. This was to be a highly influential view in neo-Kantian, logical positivist, and analytical philosophy in the late nineteenth and twentieth centuries. But Lotze's conception of philosophy also includes the idea that human beings have an impulse, founded on ethics, to go beyond what science can warrant in the interests of knowing and achieving the ultimate good. Thus, for Lotze philosophy leads to religion, which is ultimately not so much a matter of knowledge as of feeling, one that seeks a unified relation to the world and to human life as a meaningful whole.

BOOKS BY LOTZE

Logic in Three Books: Of Thought, Of Investigation, and Of Knowledge. Ed. and trans. by
    Bernard Bosanquet. OUP 1888 o.p.
Metaphysics in Three Books: Ontology, Cosmology, and Psychology. Ed. and trans. by
    Bernard Bosanquet. OUP 1887 o.p.

BOOKS ABOUT LOTZE

Santayana, George. *Lotze's System of Philosophy.* Ed. by Paul Kuntz. Bks. Demand repr.
    of 1971 ed. $71.50. ISBN 0-317-08898-X. A survey of Lotze's thought by an important
    twentieth-century American philosopher.
Thomas, E. E. *Lotze's Theory of Reality.* London 1921 o.p. A critical exposition of Lotze's
    metaphysics.

MARX, KARL HEINRICH. 1818–1883

Born in Trier—the son of a Jewish lawyer who converted to Christianity during his childhood—Karl Marx studied law at the Universities of Bonn and Berlin before switching to philosophy and completing his doctorate in 1841. As a member of the Young Hegelian movement, Marx had no chance at an academic career after the accession of the conservative Prussian king, Friedrich Wilhelm IV, in 1840, so he worked as a radical journalist in the Rhineland. Marx's acquaintance with both political economy and the working-class movement date from 1844 and the beginning of his lifelong association with FRIEDRICH ENGELS. Both were active in the revolution of 1848, after which Marx and his family lived the rest of his life in exile in London, much of it under conditions of extreme want. Marx founded the International Workingmen's Association in 1864. The first volume of *Capital*, his great systematic work on political economy, was published in 1867. The remaining two volumes, left in manuscript at his death, were edited and published by Engels.

The prevailing notion today is that Marx's thought has been discredited by the disintegration of the Soviet system of state-controlled commodity production. This view, however, is extremely shortsighted. To begin with, one would look in vain in Marx's writings for the advocacy of any such system. The prevailing idea would make sense only if one made the highly dubious assumption that the Soviet system offered the only conceivable alternative to the capitalist system Marx attacked, so that its failure constituted a final practical refutation of his entire critique of capitalism. This issue aside, there is no question that Marx changed the course of social thought, especially the way in which political, philosophical, and other ideas are viewed in relation to social reality and social struggles. Furthermore, his thought continues to inspire radical movements oriented toward the abolition of racial, national, and sexual oppression. These Marxian revolutions continue to affect our world in ways that show no signs of diminishing, however ignominious the historical fate of the political movements most closely associated with Marx's name.

BOOKS BY MARX

Capital. 3 vols. Trans. by Ben Fowkes (Vol. 1) and David Fernbach (Vols. 2 and 3). Viking Penguin 1992–93 $13.95–$14.95. ISBNs 0-14-044568-4, 0-14-044569-2, 0-14-044570-6. An excellent translation of Marx's chief work.

Early Writings. Ed. by Lucio Colleti. Random 1975 $13.00. ISBN 0-344-72005-9. An excellent edition of Marx's writings before 1845.

The First International and After. Ed. by David Fernbach. Viking Penguin 1993 $11.95. ISBN 0-14-044573-0. An excellent edition of some of Marx's principal political writings after 1864.

Grundrisse. Trans. by Martin Nicolaus. Random 1973 o.p. A good translation of an important preliminary draft of *Capital*, written in 1857–58 but unpublished until 1939.

Marx Engels Collected Works. 50 vols. Intl. Pubs. Co. 1975– . This massive edition, which is nearing completion, will contain virtually all the writings of Marx and Engels in reasonably good English translations.

The Revolutions of 1848. Ed. by David Fernbach. Viking Penguin 1993 $10.95. ISBN 0-14-044571-4. A fine edition of some of Marx's best political writings.

Surveys from Exile. Ed. by David Fernbach. Viking Penguin 1993 $10.95. ISBN 0-14-044572-2. A fine edition of some of Marx's later political writings.

BOOKS ABOUT MARX

Althusser, Louis. *For Marx.* Trans. by Ben Brewster. Routledge Chapman & Hall 1985 $16.95. ISBN 0-902308-79-3. The influential book about Marx's early writings by an influential French Marxist philosopher.

Althusser, Louis, and Etienne Balibar. *Reading Capital.* Trans. by Ben Brewster. Routledge Chapman & Hall 1985 $16.95. ISBN 0-902308-56-4. The Althusserian reading of *Capital*.

Avineri, Shlomo. *The Social and Political Thought of Karl Marx.* Cambridge U. Pr. 1970 $54.95. ISBN 0-521-04071-X. A highly readable and historically informed discussion of Marx's thought.

Ball, Terence, and James Farr, eds. *After Marx.* Cambridge U. Pr. 1984 $54.95. ISBN 0-521-25702-6. A wide-ranging anthology of good articles on Marx and the implications of his thought.

Berlin, Isaiah. *Karl Marx.* OUP 1978 o.p. An influential intellectual biography.

Carver, Terrell. *The Cambridge Companion to Marx.* Cambridge U. Pr. 1991 $59.95. ISBN 0-521-36625-9. A comprehensive collection of articles on Marx's thought.

———. *Marx's Social Theory.* OUP 1983 $26.00. ISBN 0-19-219170-5. An exposition of Marx's social ideas by a leading scholar.

Cohen, G. A. *Karl Marx's Theory of History: A Defense.* Princeton U. Pr. 1980 $41.50. ISBN 0-691-07175-6. The most rigorous and influential treatment of Marx's historical materialism.

Draper, Hal. *Karl Marx's Theory of Revolution.* 4 vols. Monthly Rev. 1978–89 $14.00–$32.00. ISBNs 0-85345-461-2, 0-85345-439-6, 0-85345-673-9, 0-85345-797-2. A historically informative discussion of Marx's ideas.

Elster, Jon. *Making Sense of Marx.* Cambridge U. Pr. 1985 $24.95. ISBN 0-521-29705-2. A detailed, informative critical study of Marx's social thought.

Gilbert, Alan. *Marx's Politics.* Lynne Rienner 1988 $17.95. ISBN 1-55587-149-6. A very illuminating study of Marx's thought, with special attention to the light thrown on it by his own political practice.

Godelier, Maurice. *Rationality and Irrationality in Economics.* Trans. by B. Pearce. Monthly Rev. 1975 $7.50. ISBN 0-85345-349-7. The author is a leading French structuralist Marxist.

Hobsbawn, E. J. *The History of Marxism.* Vol. 1 Ind. U. Pr. 1982 $39.95. ISBN 0-253-32812-8. An informed, provocative treatment of Marx's thought and its relation to his own time.

Kamenka, Eugene. *The Ethical Foundations of Marxism*. Routledge 1972 o.p. An original and philosophically penetrating approach to ethical themes in Marx.

Korsch, Karl. *Marxism and Philosophy*. 1923. Trans. by F. Halliday. Bks. Demand repr. of 1970 ed. $47.30. ISBN 0-7837-3909-5. A historically important philosophical discussion of Marxism and its roots in Hegelian philosophy.

Little, Daniel. *The Scientific Marx*. U. of Minn. Pr. 1986 $44.95. ISBN 0-8166-1504-7. The best available discussion of Marx's philosophy of science.

Lukes, Steven. *Marxism and Morality*. OUP 1987 $36.00. ISBN 0-19-876101-5. An acute and earnest argument in favor of a moralistic reading of Marx's critique of capitalism.

McLellan, David. *Karl Marx: His Life and Thought*. HarpC 1973 o.p.

Mepham, John, and David-Hillel Rubin, eds. *Issues in Marxist Philosophy*. 4 vols. Harvester 1979–1981 o.p. A collection of articles on a wide variety of themes in Marxist philosophy.

Miller, Richard. *Analyzing Marx*. Princeton U. Pr. 1984 $47.00. ISBN 0-691-06613-2. An original and acute discussion of the lasting philosophical import of Marx's thought.

Roemer, John, ed. *Analytical Marxism*. Cambridge U. Pr. 1986 $59.95. ISBN 0-521-30025-8. An anthology of excellent articles on Marxian themes by a variety of philosophers and social scientists.

Schmitt, Richard. *Introduction to Marx and Engels*. Westview 1987 $17.95. ISBN 0-8133-0426-1. A highly readable and perceptive philosophical exposition of Marx.

Tucker, Robert C. *The Marxian Revolutionary Idea*. Norton 1970 o.p. A stimulating polemical encounter with Marx's thought.

Wood, Allen W. *Karl Marx*. Routledge 1985 $15.95. ISBN 0-7102-0390-X. A comprehensive discussion of Marx's thought from a philosophical standpoint.

MILL, JOHN STUART. 1806–1873

Son of James Mill—philosopher, psychologist, and leading disciple of JEREMY BENTHAM—John Stuart Mill was born in London and educated by his father according to an extraordinary scheme that had him reading Greek and Latin before he was 5 years old. Mill began publishing learned articles while in his teens, and by the age of 20 was one of the leading spokesmen for the utilitarian position on moral and political issues. At this point in his life, Mill underwent a psychological crisis, involving a sense of the utter meaninglessness of his existence, which he examines searchingly in his *Autobiography*. Mill attributed the crisis to his upbringing, which he thought had had a dehumanizing effect on him by concentrating too narrowly on the development of his scientific intellect and providing too little for the development of his feelings and his appreciation for art and literature. In 1823 Mill went to work for the British East India Company, where his father was a high official, continuing to work there until his retirement in 1858. By that time Mill had become chief of his department, a position of considerable influence and responsibility. In 1857 he wrote a defense of the company that led to a renewal of its charter by Parliament.

In 1831 Mill formed a strong attachment to Harriet Taylor, the wife of a successful merchant and a woman of extraordinary intellectual gifts and independence of mind. Defying the proprieties of Victorian society, the two spent as much time as possible in each other's company for nearly two decades, although their relationship during this time apparently involved no sexual intimacy whatever. Harriet Taylor's husband died in 1849, and she married Mill in 1852. The couple spent much time outside England, especially in the south of France. Harriet died at Avignon in 1858, and at his request Mill's remains were eventually placed next to hers.

The work that established Mill's fame was the *System of Logic* (1843), a comprehensive discussion, from an empiricist point of view, of scientific method, inductive logic, and the foundation of the human (or "moral") sciences. Mill's first important work in social and political philosophy was the *Principles of Political Economy* (1848). A year after his wife's death, Mill published *On Liberty*, and not long afterward he wrote *Considerations on Representative Government* (1861) and then his short masterpiece on ethical theory, *Utilitarianism* (1863). In 1865 Mill was elected to Parliament and joined the forces of electoral reform, but fell out with the movement because he refused on principle to support any extension of the suffrage that did not include giving the vote to women. He was turned out of office at the next election. Mill attributed both his feminism and his views about individual liberty to the influence of Harriet; it appears that she also influenced his political thought in the decidedly antidemocratic direction found in *Representative Government*. In later life, however, Mill came to describe himself as a democratic socialist.

Mill's devastating critique of Sir William Hamilton's philosophy, published in 1865, was extremely influential in establishing empiricism in Britain over the metaphysical turn commonsense philosophy had taken by midcentury. The last major work published in his lifetime was *The Subjection of Women* (1869), but three essays on religion and the *Autobiography* (both 1873) were published after Mill's death by his stepdaughter Helen Taylor.

BOOKS BY MILL

The Autobiography of John Stuart Mill. 1873. Col. U. Pr. 1960 $15.50. ISBN 0-231-08506-0

Collected Works. Gordon Pr. 1972 $600.00. ISBN 0-87968-893-9. This scholarly edition is still in progress; several volumes have already appeared. Includes letters, autobiographies, and literary essays.

An Examination of Sir William Hamilton's Philosophy. Ed. by J. M. Robson. U. of Toronto Pr. 1979 $60.00. ISBN 0-8020-2329-0. Mill's careful discussion of the philosophy of common sense.

On Liberty. 1859. Ed. by Currin V. Shields. Viking Penguin 1982 $6.95. ISBN 0-14-043207-8

Representative Government and the Degeneration of Democracy. 2 vols. Inst. Econ. Pol. 1985 o.p. Important study of the theory of representative governments, and their faults in practice.

The Subjection of Women. (coauthored with Harriet Taylor Mill). 1869. Ed. by Sue Mansfield. Hackett Pub. 1988 $22.50. ISBN 0-87220-055-8. One of the seminal works showing the condition of women, the supposed justifications of that condition, and needed reforms.

System of Logic: Ratiocinative and Inductive. 1843. Ibis Pub. VA 1986 repr. of 1872 ed. $31.95. ISBN 0-93005-29-3

Three Essays on Religion. AMS Pr. 1974 repr. of 1874 ed. $23.45. ISBN 0-404-04325-9. These essays are one of the best statements of agnosticism.

Utilitarianism. 1863. Ed. by Oskar Piest. NAL-Dutton 1974 $9.95. ISBN 0-452-00970-7. Mill's statement and defense of a modified version of Bentham's original theory.

BOOKS ABOUT MILL

Bain, Alexander. *John Stuart Mill: A Criticism with Personal Recollections.* Kelley 1969 repr. of 1882 ed. $29.50. ISBN 0-678-00468-4. An important intellectual biography of Mill by an empiricist of the following generation in England.

Duncan, G. *Marx and Mill: Two Views of Social Conflict and Social Harmony.* Cambridge U. Pr. 1973 o.p. A comparative study of these two contemporary political philosophers.

Ellery, John B. *John Stuart Mill.* Eng. Authors Ser. G. K. Hall 1970 o.p. A good general presentation of Mill's contributions in philosophy and politics.

Halevy, Elie. *The Growth of Philosophical Radicalism*. Faber & Faber 1972 o.p. The best history of the philosophical movement that runs from Bentham to Mill.

Hayek, Friedrich A. von, ed. *John Stuart Mill and Harriet Taylor: Their Friendship and Subsequent Marriage*. Kelley 1969 repr. of 1951 ed. o.p. A study by one of the leading economic theorists of the twentieth century.

Lane, Michael. *Bibliography of the Works of John Stuart Mill*. U. of Toronto Pr. 1982 o.p.

Marcuse, Herbert. *A Critique of Pure Tolerance*. Beacon Pr. 1969 $11.00. ISBN 0-8070-1559-8. One of the strongest attacks on Mill's view of civil liberties by a leading Marxist thinker.

Neff, Emery. *Carlyle and Mill*. Hippocrene Bks. 1964 $26.00. ISBN 0-374-96042-9. An interesting picture of these two brilliant intellectuals who were originally friends and became advocates of completely opposing philosophies.

Rees, John. *John Stuart Mill's "On Liberty"*. OUP 1989 $19.95. ISBN 0-19-824237-9. These essays, some previously unpublished, were viewed by the author as drafts of chapters for a book that he had been planning to write for some years before his death.

Skorupski, John. *John Stuart Mill*. Routledge 1991 $22.50. ISBN 0-415-06270-5. An excellent full-length study emphasizing Mill's philosophy of science and his philosophy of language.

Spencer, Herbert, and others. *John Stuart Mill: His Life and Works*. Folcroft 1976 repr. of 1873 ed. o.p. Twelve essays by scholars who considered themselves Mill's disciples, written shortly after his death.

Stephen, Leslie. *The English Utilitarians: Jeremy Bentham, James Mill, John Stuart Mill*. 3 vols. Peter Smith 1950 $24.00. ISBN 0-8446-1422-X. An excellent study of these thinkers by a leading intellectual historian.

NIETZSCHE, FRIEDRICH WILHELM. 1844-1900

The son of a Lutheran pastor, Friedrich Wilhelm Nietzsche was born in 1844 in Roecken, Prussia, and studied classical philology at the Universities of Bonn and Leipzig. While at Leipzig he read the works of SCHOPENHAUER, which greatly impressed him. He also became a disciple of the composer RICHARD WAGNER (see Vol. 3). At the very early age of 25, Nietzsche was appointed professor at the University of Basel in Switzerland. In 1870, during the Franco-Prussian War, Nietzsche served in the medical corps of the Prussian army. While treating soldiers he contracted diphtheria and dysentery; he was never physically healthy afterward. Nietzsche's first book, *The Birth of Tragedy Out of the Spirit of Music* (1872), was a radical reinterpretation of Greek art and culture from a Schopenhaurian and Wagnerian standpoint. By 1874 Nietzsche had to retire from his university post for reasons of health. He was diagnosed at this time with a serious nervous disorder. He lived the next 15 years on his small university pension, dividing his time between Italy and Switzerland and writing constantly. He is best known for the works he produced after 1880, especially *The Gay Science* (1882), *Thus Spake Zarathustra* (1883-85), *Beyond Good and Evil* (1886), *On the Genealogy of Morals* (1887), *The Antichrist* (1888), and *Twilight of the Idols* (1888). In January 1889, Nietzsche suffered a sudden mental collapse; he lived the last 10 years of his life in a condition of insanity. After his death his sister published many of his papers under the title *The Will to Power*.

Nietzsche was a radical questioner who often wrote polemically with deliberate obscurity, intending to perplex, shock, and offend his readers. He attacked the entire metaphysical tradition in Western philosophy, especially Christianity and Christian morality, which he thought had reached its final and most decadent form in modern scientific humanism, with its ideals of liberalism and democracy. Nietzsche expounded a vitalistic metaphysics of the will to power, which he applied psychologically to undermine traditional conceptions of mind as well as moral, religious, and philosophical ideas. At the same time he attacked systematic thinking as a whole, maintaining the nihilistic view that there is no such thing as truth, but only an endless variety of equally false views of life held from variously interested perspectives. Although for a long time English-speaking academic philosophy tended to dismiss Nietzsche's philosophy as irresponsible (merely "literary"), it has become increasingly clear that his writings are among the deepest and most prescient sources we have for acquiring a philosophical understanding of the roots of twentieth-century culture.

BOOKS BY NIETZSCHE

The Antichrist. Ayer 1972 repr. of 1930 ed. $9.95. ISBN 0-405-03799-6

Basic Writings of Nietzsche. Ed. and trans. by Walter Kaufmann. Random 1977 $20.00. ISBN 0-394-60406-7. The best available collection of some of the most important of Nietzsche's writings.

Beyond Good and Evil. 1886. Gordon Pr. 1974 $300.00. ISBN 0-87968-207-8. A more didactic presentation of Nietzsche's thought.

The Birth of Tragedy. Trans. by Walter Kaufmann. Random 1967 o.p. Nietzsche's first important work.

The Birth of Tragedy (and *The Genealogy of Morals*). Trans. by Francis Golffing. Doubleday 1956 $8.95. ISBN 0-385-09210-5. Nietzsche's first works, which combined his philology and philosophy.

Complete Works. Ed. by Oscar Levy. 18 vols. Gordon Pr. 1974 $300.00. ISBN 0-87968-173-X. The only complete edition in English.

Ecce Homo. 1908. Trans. by R. J. Hollingdale. Viking Penguin 1992 $7.95. ISBN 0-14-044515-3. Nietzsche's autobiography.

The Gay Science. Trans. by Walter Kaufmann. Random 1974 $9.00. ISBN 0-394-71985-9. Nietzsche's enthusiastic evolutionary study of values.

The Joyful Wisdom. Gordon Pr. 1974 $300.00. ISBN 0-87968-205-1. This is the same work as *The Gay Science.*

Nietzsche: A Self-Portrait from His Letters. Ed. by Peter Fuss and Henry Shapiro. HUP 1971 o.p. This out-of-print work is available through University Microfilms. The letters give remarkable insight into Nietzsche's personality and his final collapse into insanity.

A Nietzsche Reader. Trans. by R. J. Hollingdale. Viking Penguin 1978 $8.95. ISBN 0-14-044329-0. A good collection of texts.

On the Genealogy of Morals. 1887. Trans. by Walter Kaufmann. Random 1989 $10.00. ISBN 0-679-72462-1. Nietzsche's great work on how values developed.

The Portable Nietzsche. Ed. and trans. by Walter Kaufmann. Viking Penguin 1977 $12.00. ISBN 0-14-015062-5. Contains translations by Kaufmann of some of the major works: *Thus Spake Zarathustra; Twilight of the Idols; The Antichrist; Nietzsche Contra Wagner.*

Thus Spake Zarathustra. 1883–91. Gordon Pr. 1974 $300.00. ISBN 0-87968-206-X. Nietzsche's best-known work set forth his philosophy in literary parables.

The Will to Power. 1901. 2 vols. Gordon Pr. 1974 $600.00. ISBN 0-87968-209-4. Very influential on antidemocratic forces in the twentieth century.

BOOKS ABOUT NIETZSCHE

Ackerman, Robert. *Nietzsche: A Frenzied Look.* U. of Mass. Pr. 1990 $25.00. ISBN 0-87023-722-5. A short survey of Nietzsche's philosophy, attempting to explain its unity and coherence.

Allison, David, ed. *The New Nietzsche.* MIT Pr. 1985 $11.95. ISBN 0-262-51034-0. A collection of writings about Nietzsche that have had some impact on subsequent thought.

Brandes, Georg. *Friedrich Nietzsche.* Haskell 1972 repr. of 1914 ed. $75.00. ISBN 0-8383-1463-5. By the first critic to recognize Nietzsche's importance and his genius.

Clive, Geoffrey. *The Philosophy of Nietzsche*. NAL-Dutton 1984 $4.95. ISBN 0-452-00699-6. A good presentation of Nietzsche's views by a leading interpreter of nineteenth-century thought.

Copleston, Frederick. *Friedrich Nietzsche: Philosopher of Culture*. B & N Imports 1975 o.p. An interesting appreciation of Nietzsche by the leading English Catholic historian of philosophy.

Danto, Arthur. *Nietzsche as Philosopher*. Col. U. Pr. 1980 repr. of 1963 ed. $15.50. ISBN 0-231-05053-4. A lively, critical evaluation by a leading contemporary analytic philosopher.

Gilman, Sander, ed, and David Parent, trans. *Conversations with Nietzsche: A Life in the Words of His Contemporaries*. OUP 1987 $32.50. ISBN 0-19-504961-6. A fascinating collection of letters and memoirs.

Guppy, Robert, ed. *Index to Nietzsche*. Trans. by Paul V. Cohn. Gordon Pr. 1974 $300.00. ISBN 0-87968-212-4

Higgins, Kathleen. *Nietzsche's Zarathustra*. Temple U. Pr. 1987 $39.95. ISBN 0-87722-482-X. An analysis of Nietzsche's magnum opus.

Jaspers, Karl. *Nietzsche: An Introduction to His Philosophical Activity*. 1936. Trans. by Charles F. Wallrof and Frederick J. Schmitz. Regnery Gateway 1969 o.p. One of Germany's leading thinkers presents Nietzsche's basic theories.

Kaufmann, Walter. *Nietzsche: Philosopher, Psychologist, Antichrist*. Princeton U. Pr. 1975 $14.95. ISBN 0-691-01983-5. A well-written presentation by a scholar who devoted many years to comprehending Nietzsche's achievements.

Lampert, Laurence. *Nietzsche's Teaching: An Interpretation of* Thus Spoke Zarathustra. Yale U. Pr. 1987 $15.00. ISBN 0-300-04430-5. A chapter-by-chapter commentary on Nietzsche's most famous work.

Magnus, Bernd. *Nietzsche's Existential Imperative. Studies in Phenomenology and Existential Philosophy Ser.* Bks. Demand repr. of 1978 ed. $66.10. ISBN 0-8357-6686-1. "Although not meant as an introduction to Nietzsche's thought, the book is more insightful than Walter Kaufmann's general overview ([in his translation of Nietzsche's] *Beyond Good and Evil*, 1966), though less detailed than Karl Jaspers's work (*Nietzsche*). Its attention to both logical and existential aspects should make it a touchstone for future studies" (*Library Journal*).

Mann, Heinrich. *The Living Thoughts of Nietzsche*. Ed. by Arthur O. Mendel. Trafalgar 1981 o.p.

Mencken, Henry L. *The Philosophy of Friedrich Nietzsche*. Noontide 1982 $11.00. ISBN 0-939482-24-X

Morgan, George A., Jr. *What Nietzsche Means*. Greenwood 1975 repr. of 1943 ed. $35.00. ISBN 0-8371-7404-X. An early attempt to make clear that Nietzsche was not the philosopher the Nazis had made of him.

Nehemas, Alexander. *Nietzsche: Life as Literature*. HUP 1985 $25.00. ISBN 0-674-62435-1. Emphasizes Nietzsche's perspectivism and tries to show that it is neither self-defeating nor equivalent to relativism.

Peters, Hans F. *Zarathustra's Sister: The Case of Elizabeth and Friedrich Nietzsche*. Wiener Pub. Inc. 1985 repr. of 1977 ed. $9.95. ISBN 0-910129-37-1. The role Nietzsche's sister played in the editing and publishing of his works.

Rosenberg, Alfred. *Nietzsche*. Gordon Pr. 1975 $250.00. ISBN 0-8490-0732-1. The Nazi theoretician's version of the philosopher's thoughts.

Salomé, Lou A. *Nietzsche*. Trans. by Siegfried Mandel. *Austrian-German Culture Ser.* Black Swan CT 1986 $22.50. ISBN 0-933806-31-0. Lou Andreas-Salomé was a young Finnish woman who played a fateful part in Nietzsche's life; she was interested in his intellectual pursuits but not in marriage to him.

Schacht, Richard. *Nietzsche. Arguments of the Philosophers Ser.* Routledge 1983 $39.95. ISBN 0-7102-0544-9. A good sympathetic presentation.

Shestov, Lev. *Doestoevsky, Tolstoy and Nietzsche*. Trans. by Bernard Martin and E. Spencer. Ohio U. Pr. 1969 o.p. A leading thinker of the Russian Orthodox Church compares and evaluates the religious views of the three thinkers.

Solomon, Robert C., ed. *Nietzsche: A Collection of Critical Essays. Modern Studies in Philosophy*. U. of Notre Dame Pr. 1980 repr. of 1973 ed. o.p. "Contains 21 interpretive and evaluative essays, seven of which were written especially for this volume. There are original pieces by Philippa Foot, Ivan Soll, Arnold Zuboff, the editor, et al., and excerpts from works by Walter Kaufmann, Martin Heidegger, Karl Jaspers, Thomas Mann, G. B. Shaw, Herman Hesse, et al." (*Library Journal*).

Solomon, Robert, and Kathleen Higgins, eds. *Reading Nietzsche*. OUP 1988 $32.50. ISBN 0-19-506858-X. Informative and entertaining essays aimed primarily at students and non-Nietzsche scholars.

Steiner, Rudolf. *Friedrich Nietzsche: Fighter for Freedom. Spiritual Science Lib.* Garber Comm. 1985 repr. of 1960 ed. $16.00. ISBN 0-89345-033-2. By the leading twentieth-century theosophist. Introduction by Paul M. Allen.

Stern, J. P. *A Study of Nietzsche. Major European Authors Ser.* Cambridge U. Pr. 1979 o.p. A good overall presentation of Nietzsche's views.

Young, Julian. *Nietzsche's Philosophy of Art*. Cambridge U. Pr. 1992 $44.95. ISBN 0-521-41124-6. The first book-length study of Nietzsche's philosophy of art, which is traced chronologically from *The Birth of Tragedy* to *Ecce Homo*.

PEIRCE, CHARLES SANDERS. 1839–1914

Charles Sanders Peirce was the son of the eminent mathematician and Harvard professor Benjamin Peirce. The young Peirce attended Harvard University, where he studied science, mathematics, and philosophy. For 30 years he worked for the U.S. Coast and Geodetic Survey. Because of personal difficulties—he was overbearing and eccentric—he taught only briefly as a lecturer at Harvard (1864–65, 1869–71) and at Johns Hopkins University (1879–84). Peirce greatly influenced such contemporaries as WILLIAM JAMES (see also Vols. 3 and 5) and JOSIAH ROYCE. He wrote no books and published very little during his lifetime—mostly articles and encyclopedia entries—but many collections of his articles and unpublished papers have appeared. Peirce was a brilliant logician and creative metaphysician. His papers, many published long after his death, are of great importance in the philosophical literature.

BOOKS BY PEIRCE

Chance, Love, and Logic. Century Bookbindery 1980 repr. of 1923 ed. o.p. A collection of essays on various subjects.

Collected Papers of Charles Sanders Peirce. 8 vols. Ed. by Charles Hartshorne, Paul Weiss, and Arthur Burks. Bks. Demand repr. of 1966 ed. Vols. 1–2 *Principles of Philosophy and Elements of Logic*. $180.00. ISBN 0-7837-1682-6. Vols. 3–4 *Exact Logic and the Simplest Mathematics*. $180.00. ISBN 0-7857-1508-0. Vols. 5–6 *Pragmatism and Pragmatism and Scientific Metaphysics*. $180.00. ISBN 0-7837-1683-4. Vols. 7–8. *Science and Philosophy and Reviews, Correspondence and Bibliography*. $180.00. ISBN 0-787-1509-9. This edition is arranged by topics.

Philosophical Writings of Peirce. Ed. by Justus Buchler. Dover 1940 $7.95. ISBN 0-486-20217-8. A selection of 28 essays on a wide range of topics.

Reasoning and the Logic of Things. Ed. by Kenneth Ketner. HUP 1992 $45.00. ISBN 0-674-74966-9. The Cambridge Conference lectures of 1898.

Selected Writings. Ed. by Philip P. Wiener. Dover 1966 o.p. Subtitled "Values in a Universe of Chance."

Writings of Charles S. Peirce: A Chronological Edition. 4 vols. Ind. U. Pr. 1982–9. Vol. 1 $57.50. ISBN 0-253-37201-1. Vol. 2 $57.50. ISBN 0-253-37202-X. Vol. 3 $57.50. ISBN 0-253-37203-8. Vol. 4 $67.50. ISBN 0-253-37204-6. Vol. 5 $65.00. ISBN 0-253-37205-4. A new edition undertaken to place Peirce's writings in their proper chronological sequence.

BOOKS ABOUT PEIRCE

Apel, Karl-Otto. *Charles Sanders Peirce: From Pragmatism t Pragmaticism. Der Denkweg von Charles Sanders Peirce.* Trans. by John M. Krois. U. of Mass. Pr. 1981 $30.00. ISBN 0-87023-177-4. An evaluation by a leading contemporary European philosopher.

Ayer, Alfred J. *Origins of Pragmatism: Studies in the Philosophy of Charles Sanders Peirce and William James.* Freeman Cooper 1968 $12.50. ISBN 0-87735-501-0. An insightful examination of these two major American thinkers by one of the leading British analytic philosophers.

Bernstein, Richard J., ed. *Perspectives on Peirce: Critical Essays on Charles Sanders Peirce.* Greenwood 1980 repr. of 1965 ed. $38.50. ISBN 0-313-22414-5. Essays by Paul Weiss, Rulon Wells, Norwood Hanson, R. Bernstein, and John E. Smith.

Buchler, Justus. *Charles Peirce's Empiricism.* Hippocrene Bks. 1966 o.p. A basic study by an important American pragmatist.

Freeman, Eugene, ed. *The Relevance of Charles Peirce.* Hegeler Inst. 1983 $39.95. ISBN 0-914417-04-5. A collection of essays by present-day scholars on Peirce's importance today.

Gallie, W. B. *Peirce and Pragmatism.* Greenwood 1975 repr. of 1966 ed. $35.00. ISBN 0-8371-8342-1. One of the basic studies of Peirce's thoughts.

Hookway, Christopher. *Peirce.* Routledge 1985 $17.95. ISBN 0-415-08780-5. A general discussion of the central themes in Peirce's philosophy, including treatments of his work on truth, perception, signs and language, and mathematics.

Ketner, Kenneth, and Christian Kloesel, eds. *Peirce, Semiotic, and Pragmatism: Essays by Max H. Fisch.* Ind. U. Pr. 1986 $45.00. ISBN 0-253-34317-8. A collection of the principal essays on Peirce and related topics.

Moore, Edward C. *American Pragmatism: Peirce, James and Dewey.* Greenwood 1985 repr. of 1961 ed. $52.50. ISBN 0-313-24740-4. "A discussion of American pragmatism as it is found in the writings of its three major advocates" (Preface).

Murphey, Murray G. *Development of Peirce's Philosophy.* HUP 1961 $83.60. ISBN 0-8357-9155-6. Basing his book on unpublished Peirce manuscripts, Murphey sought insight into Peirce's thought through the events of the philosopher's life.

Tursman, Richard. *Peirce's Theory of Scientific Discovery: A System of Logic Conceived as Semiotic.* Bks. Demand repr. of 1987 ed. $46.20. ISBN 0-7837-1762-8. An account of the system of logic Peirce worked on in his later years.

ROYCE, JOSIAH. 1855–1916

Josiah Royce was the leading idealistic philosopher in the United States during the period of the development of American pragmatism. Born in Grass Valley, California, he was educated in San Francisco and at the University of California. After his graduation in 1873, he studied in Germany for a year at Heidelberg, Leipzig, and Göttingen. He then returned to the United States and took a doctorate at Johns Hopkins University. He taught English composition at the University of California and in 1882 was invited to Harvard University to "fill in" for WILLIAM JAMES (see also Vols. 3 and 5). He was appointed to an assistant professorship at Harvard in 1885 and remained there for the rest of his career. Influenced by HEGEL (see also Vol. 3), Royce developed his own philosophy of absolute or objective idealism, in which it is necessary to assume that there is an "absolute experience to which all facts are known and for which all facts are subject to universal law." He published his major works from 1885 onward, including his Gifford Lectures, *The World and the Individual* (1900–01). Along with James, Royce had a great influence on the advanced students who were to become the next generation of American philosophers.

BOOKS BY ROYCE

Basic Writings of Josiah Royce. 2 vols. Ed. by John J. McDermott. Bks. Demand repr. of
1969 ed. Vol. 1 $160.00. ISBN 0-8357-5991-1. Vol. 2 $152.50. ISBN 0-8357-5992-X.
"Stresses the relevance for today of Royce's belief that true individualism is possible
only as part of life in a community" (*Library Journal*).

The Conception of Immortality. 1900. Greenwood 1968 $59.00. ISBN 0-7812-0089-X.
Discusses what can be permanent in human existence.

Fugitive Essays. 1920. *Essay Index Repr. Ser.* Ayer repr. of 1920 ed. $21.50. ISBN 0-8369-
0840-6. A wide range of essays on various philosophers and philosophical problems,
and on religion.

The Philosophy of Josiah Royce. Hackett Pub. 1982 repr. of 1971 ed. $34.95. ISBN 0-
915145-41-3. Selections from representative works, with a good introduction by
John K. Roth.

The Philosophy of Loyalty. Hafner 1971 repr. of 1908 ed. o.p. Royce's basic moral theory.

The Problems of Christianity. 1913. U. Ch. Pr. 1968 o.p. A fuller development of the
themes in *The Philosophy of Loyalty.* Royce's last major work.

The Religious Philosophy of Josiah Royce. Ed. by Stuart G. Brown. Greenwood 1976 repr.
of 1952 ed. $35.00. ISBN 0-8371-8810-5. Excerpts from Royce's major works, with a
brief introduction.

The Spirit of Modern Philosophy. 1892. Dover 1983 $10.95. ISBN 0-486-24432-6. Royce's
evaluation of some of the many thinkers from Spinoza onward, and the problems
they were dealing with.

The World and the Individual. 1900–01. 2 vols. Peter Smith 1976 $21.50. ISBN 0-8446-
2842-5. The Gifford Lectures, containing the most extended presentation of Royce's
views.

BOOKS ABOUT ROYCE

Buranelli, Vincent. *Josiah Royce. Twayne's U.S. Authors Ser.* NCUP 1964 $10.95. ISBN 0-
8084-0194-7. A presentation of Royce not only as a philosopher but as a novelist,
essayist, and social critic as well.

Clendenning, John. *The Life and Thought of Josiah Royce.* U. of Wis. Pr. 1985 $27.50.
ISBN 0-299-10310-2. A genuinely comprehensive intellectual biography of Royce,
from his family background to his intellectual struggles at Harvard. An excellent
scholarly work.

Fuss, Peter L. *The Moral Philosophy of Josiah Royce.* HUP 1965 o.p. This first full-scale
study of Royce's ethics carefully and critically expounds Royce's views and traces
their development.

Marcel, Gabriel. *Royce's Metaphysics.* Trans. by Gordon Ringer. Greenwood 1975 repr. of
1956 ed. $22.50. ISBN 0-8371-7978-5. A presentation, interpretation, and evaluation
of Royce's philosophy and religious views by one of the leading French Catholic
existentialist thinkers.

Oppenheim, Frank. *Royce's Mature Philosophy of Religion.* U. of Notre Dame Pr. 1987
$34.95. ISBN 0-268-01633-X. An account of Royce's work from 1912 to 1916,
drawing on biographical information.

Robinson, Daniel S. *Royce and Hocking: American Idealists.* Chris Mass 1968 o.p. An
introduction to the philosophy of these two American idealists, with selected letters.

_____, ed. *Royce's Logical Essays.* Chris Mass 1971 o.p. A collection of the essays on
traditional and symbolic logic.

Singh, Bhagwan B. *The Self and the World in the Philosophy of Josiah Royce.* C. C.
Thomas 1973 o.p. Royce's thought compared with Indian philosophy.

Smith, John E. *Royce's Social Infinite: The Community of Interpretation.* Shoe String 1979
repr. of 1950 ed. $35.00. ISBN 0-208-00729-6. Important study of this aspect of
Royce's view by one of the leading historians of American philosophy.

SCHELLING, FRIEDRICH WILHELM JOSEPH. 1775–1854

The son of a Lutheran pastor, Friedrich Wilhelm Joseph Schelling was born at
Leonberg, in southwestern Germany. He entered the theological seminary at

Tübingen at the age of 15, where his fellow students included HEGEL (see also Vol. 3) and the poet HÖLDERLIN (see Vol. 2). While serving as tutor to the sons of a noble family between 1794 and 1798, Schelling began to produce a series of philosophical writings reflecting the radical post-Kantian idealism of FICHTE. Schelling, however, was never happy with what he saw as the one-sided subjectivism of Fichte's position; he showed an equal interest in the "philosophy of nature," the speculative attempt to construct the results of the natural sciences from a purely philosophical standpoint. Both sorts of writings brought him early fame, and when Fichte was dismissed from his professorship at Jena in 1799 on grounds of "atheism," Schelling—whose religious views at the time were, if anything, even less orthodox than Fichte's—was named his successor. The culmination of Schelling's philosophy to this point was his *System of Transcendental Idealism* (1800). But at Jena his philosophy developed into the so-called system of identity: Absolute reality, Schelling argued, must be conceived neither as the I nor as the not-I, neither as subject nor as object, but as an unrepresentable identity that precedes their separation in any possible consciousness. He developed this idea most fully in his philosophical dialogue *Bruno* (1802).

Schelling left Jena in 1803 after an affair with Caroline Schlegel, wife of AUGUST SCHLEGEL (see Vol. 2), who divorced her husband and went with Schelling to a new life at the University of Würzburg. Schelling later held professorships at Munich and Erlangen, before finally being named HEGEL's (see also Vol. 3) successor at Berlin in 1841. Schelling had broken with Hegel as early as 1807, and he had watched in dismay as Hegel's system had come to be accepted as the definitive version of German idealist philosophy. Over the years Schelling's views, both religious and political, had also become much more conservative. For this reason the new Prussian king, Friedrich Wilhelm IV, upheld Schelling's philosophy in order to counteract the powerful influence still exerted by Hegel's (though the latter had died 10 years previously). Schelling lectured at Berlin until his retirement 5 years later.

Together with Fichte and Hegel, Schelling is one of the major German idealist philosophers. Along with his development of Fichte's idea of a system of transcendental idealism and Hegel's conceptions of a dialectic of thought and a history of culture, Schelling's unique philosophical achievements lie in his idea of a speculative philosophy of nature and his conception of art as yielding the highest kind of philosophical insight. Where Hegel defended the primacy of reason and conceptual thinking in opposition to the romantics, Schelling inspired philosophical romanticism through his theories of art and his emphasis on religious experiences and conceptions.

BOOKS BY SCHELLING

The Ages of the World. 1854. Trans. by Frederick D. Bolman. AMS Pr. 1981 $21.00. ISBN 0-404-05586-9. Schelling's posthumous study in the philosophy of history.

Bruno, or On the Natural and Divine Principle of Things. 1802. Ed. and trans. by Michael Vater. State U. NY Pr. $64.50. ISBN 0-87395-793-8. The fullest account of Schelling's "system of identity," presented in dialogue form.

Ideas for a Philosophy of Nature. 1797. Trans. by Errol Harris and Peter Heath. Cambridge U. Pr. 1988 $19.95. ISBN 0-521-35733-0. Schelling's principal work on the philosophy of nature.

Of Human Freedom. 1809. Trans. by James Gutmann. Open Court 1985 $7.00. ISBN 0-87528-025-X. The last major work Schelling published during his lifetime, a metaphysical-theological study of the problem of evil.

On University Studies. Ed. by Norbert Guterman. Trans. by E. S. Morgan. Ohio U. Pr. 1966
     o.p. An exposition of Schelling's system in lectures of 1803.
The Philosophy of Art. 1859. Ed. and trans. by D. W. Stott. U. of Minn. Pr. 1989 $44.95.
     ISBN 0-8166-1684-1. Schelling's lectures of 1802–03, published posthumously,
     contain the best exposition of his aesthetic theory.
System of Transcendental Idealism. 1800. Trans. by Peter Heath. U. Pr. of Va. 1978
     $28.50. ISBN 0-8139-0780-2. One of Schelling's most important works.
The Unconditioned in Human Knowledge: Four Early Essays, 1794–1796. Ed. and trans.
     by Fritz Marti. Bucknell U. Pr. 1976 o.p. Essays from Schelling's most Fichtean
     period, including his aphorisms on natural right.

BOOKS ABOUT SCHELLING

Brown, Robert F. *The Later Philosophy of Schelling: The Influence of Boehme on the
     Works of 1809–1815.* Bucknell U. Pr. 1976 $29.95. ISBN 0-8387-1755-1. Interesting
     study of the influence of the seventeenth-century German mystic on Schelling's later
     works.
Esposito, Joseph L. *Schelling's Idealism and Philosophy of Nature.* Bucknell U. Pr. 1978
     $29.50. ISBN 0-8387-1755-1. A good exposition of Schelling's metaphysical system.
Heidegger, Martin. *Schelling's Treatise on the Essence of Human Freedom.* Trans. by Joan
     Stambaugh. *Continental Thought Ser.* Ohio U. Pr. 1985 $15.95. ISBN 0-8214-0691-4.
     An evaluation of one of Schelling's great works by a leading German thinker of the
     twentieth century.
Marx, Werner. *The Philosophy of F.W.J. Schelling: History, System, and Freedom.* Trans.
     by Thomas Nenon. Ind. U. Pr. 1984 o.p. The most complete examination of
     Schelling's thought available in English.
Tillich, Paul. *Mysticism and Guilt-Consciousness in Schelling's Philosophical Develop-
     ment.* Trans. by Victor Nuovo. Bucknell U. Pr. 1975 $22.50. ISBN 0-8387-1493-5. An
     examination of religious themes in Schelling by an important twentieth-century
     theologian.
White, Alan. *Schelling: An Introduction to His System of Freedom.* Yale U. Pr. 1983 o.p. An
     accessible introduction to Schelling's philosophical development.

SCHLEGEL, FRIEDRICH. 1772–1829

     More a literary figure than a philosopher, Friedrich Schlegel nevertheless
interacted with German idealist philosophy in his time and made significant
contributions to aesthetics, political philosophy, and the history of philosophy;
his thought had considerable influence on the subsequent course of philosophy.
Born at Hanover, Schlegel studied law at Leipzig and Göttingen, but he was
more interested in literature and classical Greek culture, studies that he
pursued in Dresden before moving to Jena as a lecturer in 1796. There he came
under the influence of FICHTE, whose philosophy decisively influenced him.
Schlegel moved to Berlin in 1797, where he soon became the leader of the
romantic movement in philosophy, aesthetics, and literary studies through his
editorship of the journal *Athenaeum.* In 1798 he began an affair with Dorothea
Veit, daughter of the philosopher MOSES MENDELSSOHN and wife of a Berlin
banker. The autobiographical references in his short novel *Lucinde* (1799),
celebrating illicit love and attacking conventional notions about the relations
between the sexes, were well known; the scandal occasioned by the book
followed Schlegel through life, even after he had become grotesquely obese and
politically reactionary.
     Schlegel lectured in Paris in 1802, and in later years taught at Cologne. In the
beginning, Schlegel's romanticism was politically progressive, favoring republi-
canism rather than monarchy and offering a communitarian alternative to
liberalism. But his growing conservatism was marked by his conversion to

Catholicism in 1808 and his political activities in the service of Metternich and the Viennese court. Among Schlegel's contributions to aesthetics are the distinction between the "classical" and "romantic" styles of art and his theory of irony. These are embedded in a philosophy of culture, history, and society that regarded the Christian Middle Ages as its ideal of community.

BOOKS BY SCHLEGEL

The Aesthetic and Miscellaneous Works. Trans. by E. J. Millington. London 1860 o.p.
Dialogue on Poetry and Literary Aphorisms. Ed. and trans. by Ernst Behler and Roman Struc. Pa. St. U. Pr. 1968 $28.50. ISBN 0-271-73136-2
Lucinde and Fragments. Trans. by P. Firchow. U. of Minn. Pr. 1971 $15.00. ISBN 0-8166-0624-2. An abridged translation of Schlegel's scandalous novel and some of his early writings.
Philosophical Fragments. Trans. by P. Firchow. U. of Minn. Pr. 1991 $11.95. ISBN 0-8166-1901-8. An expanded edition of aphorisms from *Athenaeum* and *Lyceum* and other early writings, with a new foreword by Rodolphe Gasche.
Philosophy of History. Trans. by James Robertson. AMS Pr. 1976 $18.00. ISBN 0-404-05606-7. A reprint of the 1873 edition. A course of lectures delivered in Vienna.
The Philosophy of Life, and Philosophy of Language, in a Course of Lectures. Trans. by A. J. Morrison. AMS Pr. 1973 $27.50. ISBN 0-404-08249-1. A reprint of the 1847 edition.

BOOKS ABOUT SCHLEGEL

Bullock, Marcus. *Romanticism and Marxism*. P. Lang Pubs. 1989 $37.95. ISBN 0-8204-0317-2. The development of literary theory in Schlegel and Walter Benjamin.
Eichner, Hans. *Friedrich Schlegel*. Twayne 1970 o.p. The best exposition in English of Schlegel's philosophical views.

SCHLEIERMACHER, FRIEDRICH DANIEL ERNST. 1768–1834

The son of a devout Reformed clergyman, Friedrich Schleiermacher was born at Breslau, studied theology at Halle, and was ordained in 1790. In 1796 he became a preacher in Berlin, where he came under the influence of Fichtean idealism through his close association with FRIEDRICH SCHLEGEL. Schleiermacher became famous through the publication of what is still his best-known work, *On Religion: Speeches to Its Cultured Despisers* (1799). In this he argued that religion is not a matter of theoretical knowledge (whether metaphysical or historical) but rather of the "feeling of absolute dependence" through which the individual self relates itself to the whole of existence. During the next decade he produced a series of works on religion and ethics, and a translation of PLATO's (see also Vol. 3) dialogues. He held professorships in theology at Halle (1804–10) and Berlin (after 1810). Schleiermacher's greatest theological work was *The Christian Faith* (1821–22).

His philosophical works are some of the best products of the romantic movement. His ethical theory is, broadly speaking, in the Kantian tradition but argues for a more flexible conception of ethical norms than KANT's, making allowances both for cultural diversity and for the idiosyncrasies of the individual personality. His religious thought is characterized by an emphasis on feeling and an attempt to show the affinity of religious with aesthetic feeling. His theology makes the person of the Redeemer central to Christian doctrine. Schleiermacher's theological writings not only emphasize the importance of pious feeling but also show great sensitivity to the empirical history of Christianity and rigorous scriptural scholarship. Through the latter, Schleiermacher made important original contributions to the theory of textual interpretation, and can be considered a forerunner of DILTHEY in the "hermeneutic" tradition in philosophy.

BOOKS BY SCHLEIERMACHER

Hermeneutics: The Handwritten Manuscripts. Scholars Pr. GA 1978 $19.95. ISBN 0-89130-186-0

The Life of Jesus. Ed. by Jack Verheyden. Trans. by S. Maclean Gilmour. Fortress Pr. 1975 o.p.

On the Glaubenslehre: Two Letters to Dr. Leucke. Trans. by James Duke and Francis Fiorenza. Scholars Pr. GA 1981 $14.95. ISBN 0-89130-420-7

On Religion: Speeches to Its Cultured Despisers. Ed. and trans. by Richard Crouter. Cambridge U. Pr. 1988 $16.95. ISBN 0-521-35789-6

Schleiermacher's Soliloquies. Trans. by Horace Friess. Hyperion Conn. $25.50. ISBN 0-88355-712-6

BOOKS ABOUT SCHLEIERMACHER

Barth, Karl. *The Theology of Schleiermacher.* Bks. Demand 1982 $79.90. ISBN 0-8357-4353-5. Lectures given at Göttingen in the winter semester of 1923–24.

Brandt, Richard. *The Philosophy of Schleiermacher: The Development of His Theory of Scientific and Religious Knowledge.* HarpC 1941 o.p. The author is a well-known moral philosopher.

Dawson, Jerry. *Friedrich Schleiermacher: The Evolution of a Nationalist.* U. of Tex. Pr. 1966 o.p. A political biography.

Gerrish, B. A. *A Prince of the Church.* Fortress Pr. 1984 o.p. A 70-page introduction.

Niebuhr, Richard. *Schleiermacher on Christ and Religion.* Scribner 1964 o.p. The best study in English of Schleiermacher's theology.

Speigler, Gerhard. *The Eternal Covenant: Schleiermacher's Experiment in Cultural Theology.* HarpC 1941 o.p. A study of Schleiermacher's *Dialektik.*

SCHOPENHAUER, ARTHUR. 1788–1860

Born in Danzig (now Gdansk) to a father who was a successful businessman and a mother who was a successful novelist, Arthur Schopenhauer traveled in childhood throughout Europe and lived for a time in GOETHE's (see Vol. 2) Weimar, where his mother had established a salon that attracted many of Europe's leading intellectuals. As a young man, Schopenhauer studied medicine, first at the University of Göttingen and then in Berlin, where he attended the lectures of FICHTE and SCHLEIERMACHER (which, however, greatly disappointed him).

Schopenhauer's first work was *The Fourfold Root of the Principle of Sufficient Reason* (1813), followed shortly by a treatise on the physiology of perception, *On Vision and Colors* (1816). When Schopenhauer wrote his principal work, *The World as Will and Idea* (1819), he was confident that it was a work of great importance that would soon win him fame, but in this he was badly disappointed. In 1819 he arranged to hold a series of philosophical lectures at the same time as those of the newly arrived professor HEGEL (see also Vol. 3), whom Schopenhauer despised (calling him, among other creative epithets, an "intellectual Caliban"). This move resulted only in further humiliation for Schopenhauer, since no one showed up to hear him.

Schopenhauer continued to be frustrated in repeated attempts to achieve recognition. In 1839 and 1840 he submitted essays on freedom of the will and the foundation of morality to competitions sponsored by the Royal Danish Academy but he won no prize, even when his essay was the only entry in the competition. In 1844 he published a second volume of *The World as Will and Idea*, containing developments and commentaries on the first. Around 1850, toward the end of his life, Schopenhauer's philosophy began to receive belated recognition, and he died in the confidence that his long-awaited and deserved fame had finally come.

Schopenhauer's philosophy exercised considerable influence in the late nineteenth and early twentieth centuries, not only among academic philosophers but even more among artists and literati. This may be in part because, unlike his German idealist contemporaries, Schopenhauer is a lucid and even witty writer, whose style consciously owes more to HUME than to KANT (whose philosophy he nevertheless revered as far greater than that of his successors). Among those who acknowledged his influence on their work were WAGNER (see Vol. 3), TOLSTOY (see Vol. 2), PROUST (see Vol. 2), RILKE (see Vol. 2), HARDY (see Vol. 1), THOMAS MANN (see Vol. 2), and the artist Max Beckmann.

Schopenhauer's philosophy is founded on the idea that reality is Will–a single, insatiable, objectless striving that manifests itself in the world of appearance as a vast multiplicity of phenomena, engaged in an endless and painful struggle with one another. He saw the same vision in the texts of Indian religions—Vedanta and Buddhism—which he regarded as vastly superior to Western monotheism. Schopenhauer's theory of the empirical world is an idealism, in which the doctrines of Kant are identified with those of BERKELEY.

In aesthetic enjoyment Schopenhauer saw a form of knowledge that is higher than ordinary empirical knowledge because it is a disinterested contemplation of the forms or essences of things, rather than a cognition of causal connections between particulars driven by the will's interest in control and domination. True salvation, however, lies in an intuitive insight into the evil of willing, which in its highest manifestations is capable of completely extinguishing the will in a state of *nirvana*. In his perceptive development of the psychological consequences of his theory, Schopenhauer gives particular emphasis to the way in which our knowledge and behavior are insidiously manipulated by our unconscious volition; this stress, plus the central role he gives to sexuality in his theory of the will, contains much that is found later in FREUD (see Vol. 3) (who acknowledged that Schopenhauer had anticipated his theory of repression). Schopenhauer's main influence on twentieth-century philosophy, however, was mediated by NIETZSCHE (see also Vol. 2), whose theory of the will to power added a poignant twist by committing itself to the affirmation of the will while still conceiving it in essentially the same way—insatiable, painful, predatory, deceptive, and subversive of rational thought—which it had been in Schopenhauer's metaphysical pessimism.

BOOKS BY SCHOPENHAUER

Counsels and Maxims. Scholarly 1981 repr. of 1899 ed. $39.00. ISBN 0-8369-2820-2. Schopenhauer's epigrams and advice.

On the Basis of Morality. 1841. Ed. by E.F.J. Payne. Macmillan 1965 o.p. Schopenhauer's attack on Kantian ethics, which the author said on the title page was *not* awarded a prize by the Royal Danish Society of Scientific Studies.

On the Fourfold Root of the Principle of Sufficient Reason. 1813. Trans. by E.F.J. Payne. Open Court 1974 $10.00. ISBN 0-87548-201-5

Parerga and Paralipomena: Short Philosophical Essays. 1851. 2 vols. Trans. by E.F.J. Payne. OUP 1974. Vol. 1 $56.00. ISBN 0-19-824508-4. Vol. 2 $63.00. ISBN 0-19-824527-0. A collection of essays and aphorisms by Schopenhauer.

Religion: A Dialogue, and Other Essays. Trans. by T. Bailey Saunders. *Essay Index Repr. Ser.* Ayer 1980 repr. of 1891 ed. $13.00. ISBN 0-8369-2820-2. Another collection of some of Schopenhauer's most negative views.

Studies in Pessimism. Scholarly repr. of 1903 ed. $49.00. ISBN 0-403-00044-0. Some of
Schopenhauer's most pessimistic essays.
The Will to Live: Selected Writings of Arthur Schopenhauer. Ed. by Richard Taylor.
Continuum 1967 o.p. A collection of representative texts by Schopenhauer.
The Wisdom of Life: Being the First Part of Aphorismen zur Lebenswiesheit. Ayer 1972
repr. of 1890 ed. $12.00. ISBN 0-8369-2821-0. One of the first works of Schopenhauer
to be widely read in English.
The World as Will and Representation. 1818. 2 vols. Trans. by E.F.J. Payne. Peter Smith
1966 $42.00. ISBN 0-8446-2885-9. Another translation of Schopenhauer's major
work, *The World as Will and Idea.*

BOOKS ABOUT SCHOPENHAUER

Copleston, Frederick. *Arthur Schopenhauer: Philosopher of Pessimism.* B & N Imports
1975 repr. of 1946 ed. o.p. By a leading English Catholic historian of philosophy.
Dauer, Dorothea W. *Schopenhauer as Transmitter of Buddhist Ideas. European Univ.
Studies.* P. Lang Pubs. 1969 $9.55. ISBN 3-261-00014-7. A brief study of Schopen-
hauer's role in making Europe aware of Buddhism.
Hamlyn, D. W. *Schopenhauer. Arguments of the Philosophers Ser.* Routledge 1985 $15.95.
ISBN 0-7102-0543-0. An examination of Schopenhauer's main philosophical
writings.
Janaway, Christopher. *Self and World in Schopenhauer's Philosophy.* OUP 1989 $78.00.
ISBN 0-19-824969-1. An ambitious and scholarly study of Schopenhauer's
philosophy, which places it in its historical context.
Magee, Bryan. *The Philosophy of Schopenhauer.* OUP 1983 $35.00. ISBN 0-19-824673-0. A
new general presentation of Schopenhauer's views for a contemporary audience.
Mann, Thomas. *The Living Thoughts of Schopenhauer.* Arden Lib. repr. of 1939 ed. o.p. A
selection of Schopenhauer's ideas by one of the greatest twentieth-century German
novelists.
Nietzsche, Friedrich. *Schopenhauer as Educator.* Regnery Gateway 1965 o.p. Nietzsche
was originally very impressed by Schopenhauer but then decided that his views were
too negative. Schopenhauer is also attacked in Nietzsche's *Human, All Too Human.*
Safranski, Rudiger. *Schopenhauer and the Wild Years of Philosophy.* Trans. by Ewald
Osers. HUP 1990 $30.00. ISBN 0-674-79275-0. An intellectual biography.
Wallace, William. *Life of Arthur Schopenhauer.* Scholarly 1971 repr. of 1890 ed. $59.00.
ISBN 0-403-00196-X. One of the first works to make the English public aware of
Schopenhauer.
Young, Julian. *Willing and Unwilling: A Study in the Philosophy of Arthur Schopenhauer.*
Kluwer Ac. 1987 $66.50. ISBN 90-247-3556-4. A study of Schopenhauer's philosophy
and its relations to that of Kant.

SIDGWICK, HENRY. 1838–1900

Born at Skipton, Yorkshire, Henry Sidgwick studied at Trinity College,
Cambridge University, where he was appointed a fellow in 1859. In 1869 he
resigned his fellowship when growing religious doubts led him to decide that he
could no longer subscribe to the Thirty-Nine Articles of the Anglican church (as
fellows were required to do). He was subsequently reappointed when the
religious requirements were abolished, becoming professor of moral philosophy in 1883 and continuing to teach at Trinity College until his death. Sidgwick
was active in many fields: education, classics, literature, political theory, and
history as well as philosophy. He was interested in the cause of women's
education and was instrumental in the founding of Newnham College for
women at Cambridge. Sidgwick's most important contributions to philosophy
lie in the field of ethics, and his most important work is *Methods of Ethics*
(1874). In ethical theory, he was a proponent of utilitarianism; he is generally
regarded as the third great representative of that position, along with BENTHAM

and John Stuart Mill (see also Vols. 1 and 3). He rejected the empiricism on which earlier utilitarians had grounded their theory and displayed much greater complexity and sophistication in treating the psychology of moral motivation. In political theory, Sidgwick was more conservative than either Bentham or Mill.

Books by Sidgwick

Lectures on the Ethics of T. H. Green, Herbert Spencer, and J. Martineau. Kraus 1968 o.p. A reprint of the 1902 edition.

Lectures on the Philosophy of Kant and Other Philosophical Lectures and Essays. Kraus 1968 o.p. A reprint of the 1905 edition.

The Methods of Ethics. Hackett Pub. 1981 $35.00. ISBN 0-915145-28-6. Foreword by John Rawls.

Outlines of the History of Ethics. Hackett Pub. 1988 $24.50. ISBN 0-87220-060-4

Books about Sidgwick

Havard, W. C. *Henry Sidgwick and Later Utilitarian Political Philosophy.* U. of Fla. Pr. 1959 o.p. Traces Sidgwick's views on politics and economics and their basis in his ethics.

James, D. G. *Henry Sidgwick: Science and Faith in Victorian England.* OUP 1970 o.p. Three short lectures totaling 60 pages.

Schneewind, Jerome. *Sidgwick's Ethics and Victorian Moral Philosophy.* OUP 1977 $55.00. ISBN 0-19-824931-4. An analytical history of nineteenth-century moral thought, centering on Sidgwick's *Methods of Ethics.*

Schultz, Bart. *Essays on Henry Sidgwick.* Cambridge U. Pr. 1990 $65.00. ISBN 0-521-39151-2. Thirteen essays on Sidgwick's moral philosophy.

WHEWELL, WILLIAM. 1794–1866

Born the son of a builder in Lancaster, England, William Whewell soon revealed his intellectual gifts, which opened the doors to an education at Trinity College, Cambridge University. Whewell is remembered chiefly for having been an extraordinary polymath. His earliest studies were in mathematics, with his first publications being two very successful textbooks on mechanics. In 1826 he was ordained a priest and two years later became professor of mineralogy at Trinity. In a few short years he revolutionized British crystallography with the introduction of a new system of nomenclature and taxonomy. At the same time he was writing a work on the architecture of German churches; he soon resigned the professorship to continue his architectural studies.

Whewell next turned to astronomy, natural theology, and a mathematical study of the tides. In 1837 he published his *History of the Inductive Sciences*, which served as the foundation for his magnum opus, *The Philosophy of the Inductive Sciences* (1840). This work is strikingly modern in its insistence that the philosophy of science be sensitive to the history of science, but Whewell's Kantianism and the religious setting of his philosophy of science may strike the modern reader as somewhat anachronistic.

Whewell's later works included a book arguing for the likelihood of extraterrestial life, translations of Plato (see also Vol. 3) and of various poets, and several works on moral philosophy, most notably the *Elements of Morality Including Polity* (1845). In 1838 he became professor of moral philosophy at Trinity College. He soon resigned his second professorship and in 1841 was made master of Trinity.

BOOKS BY WHEWELL

History of the Inductive Sciences. 3 vols. Intl. Spec. Bk. 1967 $85.00. ISBN 0-7146-1149-2.
   A reprint of the 1857 edition.
The Philosophy of the Inductive Sciences. 2 vols. Intl. Spec. Bk. 1967 $95.00. ISBN 0-
   7146-1156-5. A reprint of the 1847 edition.
Selected Writings on the History of Science. Ed. by Yehuda Elkana. U. Ch. Pr. 1984 $15.00.
   ISBN 0-226-89434-7
William Whewell's Theory of Scientific Method. Ed. by Robert Butts. Pittsburgh U. Pr.
   1968 o.p.

BOOKS ABOUT WHEWELL

Fisch, Menachem. *William Whewell, Philosopher of Science.* OUP 1991 $59.00. ISBN 0-
   19-824240-9. A critical and historiographical study.
Fisch, Menachem, and Simon Schaffer, eds. *William Whewell: A Composite Portrait.* OUP
   1991 $105.00. ISBN 0-19-824900-4. Thirteen papers on Whewell's life and works.

CHAPTER 7

Twentieth-Century Western Philosophy

Andrew J. Reck

Whereof one cannot speak, thereof one must be silent.
—LUDWIG WITTGENSTEIN, *Tractatus Logico-Philosophicus*

Philosophy is a persistent, resolute, self-critical, speculative adventure seeking to encompass the whole of things, free from irrelevancy and error; it is an inquiry concerned with achieving an ordered knowledge of the world and of the conditions and principles involved in an adequate grasp of it.
—PAUL WEISS, *Modes of Being*

At the beginning of the twentieth century, philosophy was divided into two main schools of thought: idealism and naturalism. Idealism was closely allied to religion, specifically spirituality and the belief in an everlasting Being. Proponents of idealism held that the objects of sense perceptions are actually ideas that the mind knows directly, and are not the objects themselves. In contrast, naturalism favored logical thought and science, which had achieved dramatic success at the turn of the twentieth century. The proponents of naturalism equated reality with sense perceptions that could be interpreted using logic and science concepts. They believed that natural objects and phenomena, known and experienced scientifically, is all that exists; there is no supernatural or spiritual creation, control, or significance in the world. In the nineteenth century, the leading champion of idealism was GEORG HEGEL (see also Vol. 3). He maintained that the key to understanding the nature of reality was by observing characteristic features and operations of the human mind; it favored a spiritualistic interpretation of the world. The dominant form of idealism in the nineteenth century was absolute idealism; it posited the existence of an absolute mind. But some idealists rose up on behalf of the primacy of finite personal selves. In the twentieth century, JOHN MCTAGGART and Edgar Sheffield Brightman are distinct but exemplary representatives of personalism. In contrast, naturalism was inspired by the great progress the sciences were making. Measuring the impact of Darwinian evolution on the inherited conceptions of human beings and human values, philosophical naturalism was initially a deterministic materialism. However, it differed from its antecedents by assuming the form of evolutionism, and it underscored the employment of the scientific method as the sole route to reliable belief or knowledge.

In the early 1900s, two movements began to challenge the reigning schools of idealism and naturalism. Realism had its roots in earlier philosophy, especially the Scottish commonsense realism of THOMAS REID in the eighteenth and James McCosh in the nineteenth century. Idealism had stated that the object of cognition does not exist independently of the knowing mind while realism

259

asserted its independent reality. At the end of the nineteenth century, the leading idealists, such as F. H. BRADLEY at Oxford University and JOSIAH ROYCE at Harvard University, were criticized by a broad spectrum of thinkers on this epistemological thought. GEORGE EDWARD MOORE at Cambridge University and the new realists in America, such as R. B. Perry at Harvard, led the assault against idealism on behalf of realism. Subsequently new realism was challenged by critical realism. Although the critical realists concurred with the new realists in affirming the independent existence of the objects of knowledge, they affirmed that knowledge of them is indirect, that it is mediated by mental representations. In time, critical realists divided into two camps. One camp led by GEORGE SANTAYANA argued that mind is directly cognizant of essences, which have a distinct ontological status. Others such as Roy Wood Sellars and ARTHUR ONCKEN LOVEJOY maintained that the mental representations of objects consist of sense data, which are located in the mind.

Pragmatism, originating in the thought of CHARLES SANDERS PEIRCE and popularized by WILLIAM JAMES (see also Vols. 3 and 5), developed in the late nineteenth century, but it flourished in the first quarter of the twentieth century, fed by the works of JOHN DEWEY (see also Vol. 3), GEORGE HERBERT MEAD (see also Vol. 3), C. I. LEWIS, and SIDNEY HOOK. Whatever the differences among the pragmatists, and these differences were considerable, their common theme was that thought is intimately linked to action and that meaningful theory is grounded in experience and practical results.

Meanwhile, the naturalism inspired by science began to split up and move in almost opposite directions. Attention to the development of the categories of natural science (particularly in the wake of the acceptance of the Darwinian principle of evolution in biology and of the quantum theory and relativity in physics) inspired speculations in philosophical cosmology, represented by John Elof Boodin and by ALFRED NORTH WHITEHEAD. Indeed, Whitehead offered the last great speculative system to receive a wide hearing. Although Whitehead called his system the philosophy of organism, it is now referred to as process philosophy. The most recent expression of process philosophy, with special reference to theology, has been in the works of CHARLES HARTSHORNE. A characteristic theme of process philosophy in its most influential recent formulation is theism, in contradistinction to the ruling scientific naturalism, which is sometimes atheistic and professedly humanist.

Process philosophy grew out of naturalism, in particular evolutionism, to propose a doctrine of God in opposition to atheism and secular humanism. Another school of thought widespread in the mid-twentieth century developed under the aegis of the Roman Catholic church. In 1879, Pope Leo XIII urged the devoted study of the philosophy and theology of St. THOMAS AQUINAS. But, Leo XIII explicitly admonished that the revival of Thomism be consistent with the discoveries made since the saint's time. Neo-Thomism became a major intellectual force from World War I until well after World War II, persuasively presented in the works of JACQUES MARITAIN, ETIENNE GILSON, and, in a singular way, by MORTIMER J. ADLER, since he is not a professed Roman Catholic. In recent decades neo-Thomism has receded, persisting in Roman Catholic thought in the guise of transcendental Thomism, articulated by the Jesuit Bernard Lonergan.

In the twentieth century, science, not religion, has been the most prestigious cultural institution. Early in the century, the investigations of BERTRAND RUSSELL (see also Vol. 5) and Alfred North Whitehead on the nature of mathematics bore fruit with the presentation of the formalist theory. This theory maintained that the foundations of mathematics are in logic; it consequently transformed logic so that it came to resemble mathematics in its symbolic representation. Further investigations into the nature of formal statements in logic and mathematics led to the theory, advocated by LUDWIG WITTGENSTEIN, that these statements say nothing about the world, that they are tautologies. This conception, allied with the scientific method that requires concepts and theories to be testable experimentally or within experience in order to be cognitively meaningful, constituted the core of the movement known as logical positivism, originating in Vienna in the 1920s and spreading to the English-speaking world. Logical positivism broadened into logical empiricism, perhaps the dominant philosophical attitude in American philosophical thought today, which poses an antimetaphysical stance; it is nonetheless fundamentally naturalistic. Logical empiricism is the movement out of which a whole generation of leading American philosophers has sprung, including W. V. QUINE, NELSON GOODMAN, WILFRID SELLARS, and RODERICK CHISHOLM.

During the 1930s, in Great Britain, Wittgenstein had begun to turn his attention from investigations into the formal languages of logic and mathematics exclusively. These investigations had been the focus of his early work and had proved to be central to logical positivism. They continued to be pursued in the United States with vigor by RUDOLF CARNAP. Wittgenstein, on the other hand, then inspired the examination of ordinary language. Carried on at Oxford by GILBERT RYLE, JOHN AUSTIN, and P. F. STRAWSON, to a degree independently of each other, these investigations gave rise to a kind of analytic philosophy that, in contrast with the emphasis of logical empiricism on formal language, has been termed "linguistic analysis."

Logical empiricism and linguistic analysis constituted the movement of analytic philosophy that most academic philosophers embraced, mainly in the English-speaking world. However, events outside the academy had shaken the foundations of Western culture. Many philosophers addressed themselves to the problems of value and the philosophy of culture, including ERNST CASSIRER, JOSÉ ORTEGA Y GASSETT, and MIGUEL DE UNAMUNO (see also Vol. 2).

Even more pervasive was the movement of philosophers toward a renewed emphasis on subjectivity that led to the rise of existentialism. Foreshadowed by SOØREN KIERKEGAARD's religious and cultural investigations and by FRIEDRICH NIETZSCHE's (see also Vol. 2) poetic, aphoristic essays concerning man, morals, and culture in the nineteenth century, existentialism dominated philosophical thought in the mid-twentieth century on the European continent and in literary circles everywhere. Existentialism had found its philosophical method in the phenomenology of EDMUND HUSSERL. In the hands of MAX SCHELER, MARTIN HEIDEGGER (see also Vol. 5), KARL JASPERS, and later JEAN-PAUL SARTRE (see also Vol. 2) and MAURICE MERLEAU-PONTY, phenomenology has been extended to examine value-laden areas of human experience and action beyond simply the cognitive states of consciousness. This expanded line of exploration, concentrating on the moral and social problems and breakdowns in twentieth-century Western civilization, naturally led existentialists to confront the challenges of Marxism.

As long as the Soviet Union survived as a political force, it advocated Marxism as its official ideology. Its influence compelled intellectuals in the West to study Marxism with a radical seriousness. They tended to find the humanistic character of the early KARL MARX (see also Vol. 3) more appealing than the historical or economic determinism of his later pronouncements. Their Marxism consequently took on a different guise, attending more to matters of art and culture than to economics. Thus, critical theory was formulated, associated with the Frankfurt School. With the collapse of the Soviet Union, Marxism has retreated from the center of study, although themes critical of private corporate capitalism and of imperialism persist in contemporary philosophical discussions.

Current philosophy is reflected by the rivalry of all these schools, further complicated by the existence of independent minds. Although the speculative system building exemplified by the works of Whitehead and Santayana in the first third of this century has receded, it still is represented by the prodigious work of a singular thinker, such as PAUL WEISS. However, the preoccupation with philosophical method, conspicuous in the writings of analytic philosophers at midcentury, remains a prevalent trait of current philosophical thinking. But it has taken a "postanalytic" turn with the emergence of the hermeneutics of HANS-GEORG GADAMER and the deconstructionism of MICHEL FOUCAULT (see also Vols. 2 and 5) and JACQUES DERRIDA.

GENERAL WORKS

Aune, Bruce A. *Rationalism, Empiricism, and Pragmaticism: An Introduction.* Random 1970 $10.12. ISBN 0-07-553543-2. A textbook in theory of knowledge that translates classical theories in modern philosophy into the contemporary idiom of analytic philosophy.

Ayer, Alfred Jules. *Logical Positivism.* Free Pr. 1966 $14.95. ISBN 0-317-3052-3. "A well-selected collection of 17 very important essays . . . plus a valuable historical orientation in the form of an introduction by the editor" (*Guardian*).

_____. *Philosophy in the Twentieth Century.* Random 1983 $22.50. ISBN 0-394-50454-7. Presents "brief explanations of some main issues in this century's critical and speculative Western philosophy, primarily of the Anglo-American varieties" (*Library Journal*).

Barnes, Hazel E. *Existentialist Ethics.* 1967. U. Ch. Pr. 1985 $19.95. ISBN 0-226-03729-6. A "highly critical work" (*Library Journal*).

Barrett, William. *The Illusion of Technique: A Search for Meaning in a Technological Civilization.* Doubleday 1978 $8.95. ISBN 0-385-11202-5. "In this survey of twentieth-century philosophy, Barrett concentrates on the thought of Ludwig Wittgenstein, Martin Heidegger, and William James" (*Book Review Digest*).

_____. *Irrational Man: A Study in Existential Philosophy.* Doubleday 1962 $9.95. ISBN 0-385-03138-6. Barrett is very clever and clear in following the thread of [existentialism] down through the ages but is at his best in the chapters in which he describes the individual contributions of such men as Kierkegaard, Nietzsche, and Heidegger" (*Kirkus*).

Bernstein, Richard J. *The New Constellation: The Ethical-Political Horizon of Modernity—Postmodernity.* MIT Pr. 1992 $35.00. ISBN 0-262-52166-0. On the cutting edge in defining the contrast between the modern and the postmodern.

_____. *Philosophical Profiles: Essays in a Pragmatic Mode.* U. of Pa. Pr. 1986 $36.95. ISBN 0-8122-7995-6. Penetrating essays on leading contemporary European thinkers by a brilliant American commentator.

Bertocci, Peter A., ed. *Mid-Twentieth Century American Philosophy: Personal Statements.* Humanities 1974 o.p. Intellectual creeds of 15 prominent American philosophers including Brand Blanshard, Charles Hartshorne, Stephen Pepper, Roy Wood Sellars, and Paul Weiss.

Blackham, Harold John. *Six Existentialist Thinkers.* Routledge Chapman & Hall $13.95. ISBN 0-7100-4611-1. A trustworthy handbook.

Bochenski, Innocentius Marie. *Contemporary European Philosophy.* Trans. by Donald Nicholl and Karl Aschenbrenner. Greenwood 1982 repr. of 1956 ed. $38.00. ISBN 0-

313-23490-6. A selective survey of twentieth-century philosophy. Distinguishes seven main systems; empiricism, idealism, life, philosophy, phenomenology, existentialism, and the philosophy of being.

Boyer, David L., and others, eds. *The Philosopher's Annual*. Rowman. Vol. 1 1978 o.p. Vol. 2 1979 $35.00. ISBN 0-8476-6202-0. Ridgeview Vol. 3 1980 $32.00. ISBN 0-917930-38-X. Vol. 4 1981 $32.00. ISBN 0-917930-75-4. Vol. 5 1982 $31.00. ISBN 0-917930-77-0. Selection of outstanding articles by distinguished philosophers published during the year.

Brown, S. C., and Wolf Mays, eds. *Linguistic Analysis and Phenomenology*. Bucknell U. Pr. 1972 $32.50. ISBN 0-8387-1025-5. "An attempt . . . to find a bridge between linguistic philosophy and phenomenology and to see if these two styles of philosophy could be unified" (*Book Review Digest*).

Burr, John R., ed. *Handbook of World Philosophy: Contemporary Developments since 1945*. Greenwood 1980 $85.00. ISBN 0-313-22381-5. One-volume survey attempting to provide an internationally representative sample . . . of the character, directions, wealth, and varieties of the reflections and activities called "philosophic'" (*Library Journal*).

Butler, Christopher. *Interpretation, Deconstruction, and Ideology: An Introduction to Some Current Issues in Literary Theory*. OUP 1984 $19.95. ISBN 0-19-815791-6. "Useful to those who feel they have not yet grasped the grounds of the various oppositional modes in criticism, and the differences in their oppositions" (*Times Literary Supplement*).

Callinicos, Alex. *Marxism and Philosophy*. OUP 1989 $14.95. ISBN 0-19-285151-9. "An overview of Marxist philosophy, especially its status as a philosophy." (*Choice*).

Caton, Charles E. *Philosophy and Ordinary Language*. Bks. Demand 1963 $65.00. ISBN 0-317-09788-1. "An anthology presenting 12 essays on language by philosophers of the 'ordinary-language' movement" (*Library Journal*).

Chiari, Joseph. *Twentieth Century French Thought from Bergson to Levi-Strauss*. Gordian 1975 $50.00. ISBN 0-87752-185-9. An assessment of such French philosophers as Merleau-Ponty, Sartre, Marcel, Lavelle, Maritain, Camus, Weil, Teilhard de Chardin, Bachelard, Foucault, and Althusser.

Chisholm, Roderick M., ed. *Realism and the Background of Phenomenology*. Ridgeview 1981 $30.00. ISBN 0-917930-34-X. An anthology of such thinkers as Brentano, Husserl, Prichard, the American new realists, Samuel Alexander, Russell, Lovejoy, and G. E. Moore.

Christensen, Darrel E., and others, eds. *Contemporary German Philosophy. Contemporary German Philosophy Ser*. Pa. St. U. Pr. Vol. 1 1983 $28.50. ISBN 0-271-00336-7. Vol. 2 1983 $28.50. ISBN 0-271-00352-9. Vol. 3 1984 $28.50. ISBN 0-271-00365-0. Vol. 4 1985 $28.50. ISBN 0-271-00381-2. ". . . devoted to making available in English contributions to philosophical comprehension originating in German" (*The Philosopher's Index*).

Cobb, John B., Jr., and W. Widick Schroeder, eds. *Process Philosophy and Social Thought*. Ctr. Sci. Study 1981 $31.95. ISBN 0-913348-18-X. Eighteen essays that explore the influence of process philosophy on social and political thought.

Copleston, Frederick Charles. *Bergson to Sartre*. Vol. 9, Part 2 in *History of Philosophy*. Doubleday 1977 $3.50. ISBN 0-385-06532-2. The second half of the final volume of Copleston's monumental history of philosophy is devoted to French philosophy in the twentieth century.

Cunningham, Gustavus W. *Idealistic Argument in Recent British and American Philosophy. Essay Index Repr. Ser*. Ayer 1977 repr. of 1933 ed. $27.50. ISBN 0-8369-0356-0. "An excellent statement of the development of idealistic philosophy in England and America since 1800" (*Journal of Religion*).

Dilworth, David. *Philosophy in World Perspective: A Comparative Hermeneutic of the Major Theories*. Yale U. Pr. 1989 $28.00. ISBN 0-300-04357-0. A pioneering metaphilosophical essay.

Durfee, Harold A. *Foundational Reflections: Studies in Contemporary Philosophy.* Kluwer Ac. 1987 $93.00. ISBN 90-247-3504-1. Explorations of the fundamentals of analytic philosophy and phenomenology.

Feigl, Herbert and Wilfred Sellars, eds. *Readings in Philosophical Analysis.* Ridgeview 1981 $33.00. ISBN 0-917930-29-0. An anthology that introduced a generation of American students to logical empiricism.

Flew, Antony G., ed. *Logic and Language Second Series.* Blackwell Pubs. 1973 $11.95. ISBN 0-631-17300-5. An anthology on later developments in Anglo-American analytic philosophy.

Floistad, Guttorn, ed. *Contemporary Philosophy: A New Survey.* Kluwer Ac. 1987 $112.50. ISBN 90-247-3422-3. A continuation of two earlier series of chronicles, *Philosophy in the Midcentury* (1958–59) and *Contemporary Philosophy* (1968).

Friedman, George. *The Political Philosophy of the Frankfurt School.* Cornell Univ. Pr. 1981 $39.95. ISBN 0-8014-1279-X. Treats the ideas of the German scholars and social critics associated with the Frankfurt School (Benjamin, Adorno, Horkheimer, Marcuse).

Friedman, Maurice, ed. *The Worlds of Existentialism: A Critical Reader.* Humanities 1991 $19.95. ISBN 0-391-03700-5. "A lively introduction. . . . versatile, cosmopolitan and exhaustive. . . . Recommended generally" (*Library Journal*).

Garcia, Jorge J., and others, eds. *Philosophical Analysis in Latin America.* Kluwer Ac. 1984 $115.00. ISBN 90-277-1749-X. An anthology of articles by Latin American analytic philosophers demonstrating the interest in "scientific philosophy" in Latin America.

Geuss, R. *The Idea of a Critical Theory: Habermas and the Frankfurt School. Modern European Philosophy.* Cambridge U. Pr. 1981 $12.95. ISBN 0-521-28422-8. "An excellent discussion of the various meanings attributed to the concept of ideology. . . . Strongly recommended for scholars" (*Choice*).

Grene, Marjorie. *Introduction to Existentialism.* U. Ch. Pr. 1984 $11.95. ISBN 0-226-30823-5. A lucid exposition and critical evaluation of existentialism by an expert in the history of philosophy.

———, ed. *Philosophy in and out of Europe.* U. Pr. of Amer. 1987 $14.75. ISBN 0-8191-6324-4. A collection of essays on current research concerning continental philosophy.

Hanfling, Oswald. *Logical Positivism.* Col. U. Pr. 1981 o.p. "Attempts to delineate the philosophical problems, and preferred solutions to those problems, that gave rise to . . . logical positivism" (*Choice*).

———, ed. *Essential Readings in Logical Positivism.* Blackwell Pubs. 1981 $16.95. ISBN 0-631-12566-3. Basic writings by the logical positivists whom Hanfling treated in his book.

Harlow, Victor E. *Bibliography and Genetic Study of American Realism.* Kraus repr. of 1931 ed. $15.00. ISBN 0-527-38000-8. A pioneer historical, critical, and bibliographic account of new realism and critical realism in American philosophy.

Held, David. *Introduction to Critical Theory: Horkheimer to Habermas.* U. CA Pr. 1980 $47.50. ISBN 0-520-04121-6. Distinguishes "(1) the Frankfurt School, which includes Horkheimer, Adorno, and Marcuse, and (2) Jürgen Habermas" (*The Philosopher's Index*).

Holt, Edwin B., and others. *New Realism: Cooperative Studies in Philosophy.* Kraus repr. of 1912 ed. $36.00. ISBN 0-527-66900-8. The classic cooperative volume containing the program of and essays by the American new realists.

Hook, Sidney, ed. *Art and Philosophy: A Symposium.* NYU Pr. 1966 o.p. Proceedings of a conference consisting of brief addresses, followed by comments and replies on the part of leading experts in aesthetics and philosophy of art, organized by the editor.

———. *Determinism and Freedom in the Age of Modern Science: A Philosophical Symposium.* NYU Pr. 1958 o.p. In the same format as above, a profound record of the issues of freedom and determinism at the cutting edge of contemporary philosophical research.

_____. *Human Values and Economic Policy: A Symposium.* 1967. NYU Pr. 1988 o.p. In the same format as above, a good starting point for persons interested in situating economic value in the general scheme of values.

_____. *Language and Philosophy: A Symposium.* NYU Pr. 1969 o.p. A valiant effort to bring together leading philosophers on the nature and function of language.

_____. *Law and Philosophy: A Symposium.* NYU Pr. 1964 o.p. An early symposium on the philosophy of law.

_____. *Philosophy and History: A Symposium.* NYU Pr. 1963 o.p. Leading philosophers reflect on history and on each other's views.

_____. *Psychoanalysis, Scientific Method and Philosophy: A Symposium.* Transaction Pubs. 1990 $19.95. ISBN 0-88738-834-5. A tough-minded series of examinations and critiques on whether psychoanalysis is scientifically valid.

_____. *Religious Experience and Truth: A Symposium.* NYU Pr. 1961 $12.50. ISBN 0-8147-3393. This is one of the volumes, some listed above, that reprint the proceedings of a series of important symposia held under the auspices of New York University's Institute of Philosophy.

Joergensen, Joergen. *Development of Logical Empiricism. Foundations of the Unity of Science Ser.* U. Ch. Pr. 1951 $2.50. ISBN 0-226-5799-3. A monograph in the *Encyclopedia of Unified Science*, this work traces the development of logical empiricism, focusing on the Vienna Circle.

Kallen, Horace M., and Sidney Hook, eds. *American Philosophy Today and Tomorrow.* Irvington 1982 repr. 1935 ed. $20.00. ISBN 0-686-79689-6. Twenty-five representative American thinkers on the problems with which the times confront the American philosopher, and the solutions which Americans must find for tomorrow" (*Boston Transcript*).

Kaufmann, Walter. *From Shakespeare to Existentialism: Essays on Shakespeare and Goethe; Hegel and Kierkegaard; Nietzsche, Rilke, and Freud: Jaspers, Heidegger, and Toynbee.* Princeton U. Pr. 1980 $18.95. ISBN 0-691-01367-5. Lucid and witty, Kaufmann uncovers the "hidden meanings" in Heidegger.

Kingston, Frederick T. *French Existentialism: A Christian Critique.* Bks. Demand 1961 $59.30. ISBN 0-317-08761-4. A sensible and sensitive essay favoring Marcel over Sartre.

Krikorian, Yervant H., ed. *Naturalism and the Human Spirit.* Col. U. Pr. 1944 $56.00. ISBN 0-231-01424-4. A collection of 15 original essays, including one by John Dewey, articulating the philosophy of naturalism.

Kuklick, Bruce. *The Rise of American Philosophy: Cambridge, Massachusetts, 1860–1930.* Bks. Demand 1977 $160.00. ISBN 0-8357-8310-3. A gossipy history of the Harvard philosophy department, which included such greats as James, Royce, Santayana, C. I. Lewis, and A. N. Whitehead, as well as such lesser figures as Ralph Barton Perry and William Ernest Hocking.

Laszlo, Ervin. *Introduction to Systems Philosophy—Toward a New Paradigm of Contemporary Thought.* Gordon & Breach 1972 $108.00. ISBN 0-677-03850-X. A zealous advocacy of a holistic systems approach in contradistinction to the allegedly outmoded atomistic approach of modern science.

_____. *Philosophy in the Soviet Union: A Survey of the Mid-Sixties.* Kluwer Ac. 1967 $41.50. ISBN 90-277-0057-5. Describes Marxist philosophy when the Soviet Union was at high tide.

Lucey, Kenneth, and Tibor Machan. *Recent Work in Philosophy.* Rowman 1983 $54.50. ISBN 0-8476-7103-8. Slanted to social, political, and economic philosophy, with a libertarian bias.

Lyotard, Jean F. *The Postmodern Explained: Correspondence 1982–85.* Ed. by Don Barry. Trans. by Julian Pefanis and Thomas Morgan. U. of Minn. Pr. 1992 $29.95. ISBN 0-8166-2210-8. A leading French philosopher defines postmodern thought and practice.

Macquarrie, John. *Existentialism.* Viking Penguin 1973 $7.95. ISBN 0-14-021569. An "adequate, comprehensive view of existentialism eminently useful" (*Christian Century*).

————. *Twentieth Century Religious Thought: The Frontiers of Philosophy and Theology, 1900–1980*. Trinity Presbyterian International 1989 $19.95. ISBN 0-334-01709-2. A perceptive and scholarly survey by a leading theologian.

Magill, Frank N., ed. *World Philosophy: Essays and Reviews of 225 Major Works*. 5 vols. Salem Pr. o.p. Volumes 4 and 5 cover the period 1896–1971; each major work is summarized, followed by a summary of leading critical works on it and a selective annotated bibliography.

Mehta, Ved. *Fly and the Fly-Bottle: Encounters with British Intellectuals*. Col. U. Pr. 1983 $50.00. ISBN 0-231-05618-4. "A report of the author's interviews with British historians and philosophers. These include discussions with Bertrand Russell, Ernest Gellner, A. J. Ayer, Iris Murdoch, A.J.P. Taylor, Lewis Namier, and others. The material in the book originated in *The New Yorker*" (*Book Review Digest*).

Merrell, Floyd. *Deconstruction Reframed*. Purdue U. Pr. 1985 $18.50. ISBN 0-911198-72-5. A scholarly study of deconstruction, mainly for literary criticism.

Montefiore, Alan, ed. *Philosophy in France Today*. Cambridge U. Pr. 1983 $54.95. ISBN 0-521-22838-7. Original essays by 11 contemporary French philosophers: Pierre Bourdieu, Jacques Bourveresse, Jacques Derrida, Jean-Toussaint Desanti, Vincent Descombes, Claude Lefort, Emmanuel Levinas, Jean-François Lyotard, Pierre Macherey, Louis Maren, and Paul Ricoeur."

Morris, Charles. *Logical Positivism, Pragmatism and Scientific Empiricism*. AMS Pr. 1979 repr. of 1937 ed. $20.00. ISBN 0-404-59273-2. A lucid exposition and evaluation of the common features of three main tendencies in twentieth-century philosophy.

————. *The Pragmatic Movement in American Philosophy*. Braziller 1970 o.p. "The clearest explanation of American pragmatism ever written" (Robert Ginsburg, *Annals of the American Academy*).

Mortley, Raoul. *French Philosophers in Conversation*. Routledge 1991 $42.50. ISBN 0-415-05254-8. Appealing introduction to contemporary Parisian intellectual life.

Norris, Christopher. *The Contest of Faculties: Deconstruction, Philosophy and Theory*. Routledge Chapman & Hall 1985 $35.00. ISBN 0-416-39930-4. A brilliant study of deconstructionism by a leading expert in literary criticism and philosophy.

————. *Deconstruction: Theory and Practice*. Routledge rev. ed. 1991 $13.95. ISBN 0-415-06174-1. "A clear and critical picture of central issues without jargon and partisanship" (*Library Journal*).

————. *Deconstruction and the Interests of Theory*. U. of Okla. Pr. 1989 $34.95. ISBN 0-8061-2208-0. Good discussion of controversial issues in critical theory.

————. *The Deconstructive Turn: Essays in the Rhetoric of Philosophy*. Routledge Chapman & Hall 1984 $12.95. ISBN 0-416-36140-4. "Tries to show the superiority of Derrida's reading of the theory of philosophy" (*Choice*).

Passmore, John. *A Hundred Years of Philosophy*. Viking Penguin 1967 o.p. Restricts 'philosophy' to epistemology, logic and metaphysics; mainly from an English point of view.

————. *Recent Philosophers*. Open Court 1985 $19.95. ISBN 0-87548-488-4. A worthy successor to *A Hundred Years of Philosophy*; with discussions of Chomsky, Davidson, Dennett, Derrida, Dummet, Feyerabend, Goodman, Mary Hesse, Kripke, David Lewis, Montague, Putnam, and Rorty.

Perry, Ralph Barton. *Philosophy of the Recent Past: An Outline of European and American Philosophy since 1860*. AMS Pr. 1980 repr. of 1926 ed. $29.00. ISBN 0-404-59245-3. "Treats post-Schopenhauerean thought, English, American and Continental, with special regard to the development of its four main tendencies: naturalism, idealism, pragmatism, and realism" (*Literature Review*).

————. *Present Philosophical Tendencies*. 1910. Greenwood 1968 repr. of 1955 ed. $49.75. ISBN 0-8371-0191-3. Presents accounts of idealism, naturalism, pragmatism, and realism.

Poster, Mark. *Critical Theory and Poststructuralism: In Search of a Context*. Cornell Univ. Pr. 1989 $11.95. ISBN 0-814-9588-1. Concludes with a study of the family in Orange County, California, as the test of crucial social theory in relation to electronically mediated communication.

_____. *Essential Marxism in Postwar France: From Sartre to Althusser.* Bks. Demand 1975 $111.30. ISBN 0-8357-8874-1. The scholarly classic on the topic.

_____. *The Mode of Information: Poststructuralism and Social Context.* U. Ch. Pr. 1990 $39.95. ISBN 0-226-67595-5. Pioneering examination of how critical theory and social situation are related to electronic information and communication.

Rajchman, John, and Cornell West, eds. *Post-Analytic Philosophy.* Col. U. Pr. 1985 $52.50. ISBN 0-231-06066-1. "There is a diversity in philosophy today that contrasts with the uniformity of logical positivism and analytic philosophy, the programs which formed these philosophers, but from which, in various ways and to various degrees, they have all departed" (Preface). Among the philosophers included are Richard Rorry, John Rawls, and Richard J. Bernstein.

Randall, John H., Jr. *Philosophy after Darwin: Chapters for the Career of Philosophy and Other Essays.* Ed. by Beth J. Singer. Col. U. Pr. 1977 $50.00. ISBN 0-231-04114-4. "The volume is remarkable for its lucid, penetrating taxonomy of what Randall deems the chief ingredients of 'modern philosophy.' It is essential for all graduate and undergraduate libraries" (*Choice*).

Reck, Andrew J. *The New American Philosophers: An Exploration of Thought since World War II.* La. State U. Pr. 1968 o.p. Treats C. I. Lewis, Stephen Pepper, Brand Blanshard, Ernest Nagel, John Hermann Randall, Jr., Justus Buchler, Sidney Hook, F.C.S. Northrop, James Kern Feibleman, John Wild, Charles Hartshorne, and Paul Weiss.

_____. *Recent American Philosophy: Studies of Ten Representative Thinkers.* Pantheon 1964 o.p. "Will likely remain standard for some time. Recommended for colleges and large city libraries" (*Library Journal*).

Ricoeur, Paul. *Main Trends in Philosophy. Main Trends in the Social and Human Sciences Ser.* Holmes & Meier 1979 $26.50. ISBN 0-8419-0506-1. A leading French philosopher's interpretive survey.

Rorty, Richard McKay, ed. *The Linguistic Turn: Recent Essays in Philosophical Method.* U. Ch. Pr. 1971 $17.95. ISBN 0-226-72568. A total of 37 selections from twentieth-century philosophers and an erudite 40-page introduction by the editor.

Ryan, Michael. *Marxism and Deconstruction: A Critical Articulation.* Johns Hopkins 1982 $12.95. ISBN 0-8018-3248-3. Compares deconstruction and marxism in an attempt to relate deconstruction to the dialectical tradition in philosophy and demonstrate how deconstruction can be used in the critique of ideology.

Schneider, Herbert W. *Sources of Contemporary Philosophical Realism in America.* Irvington 1964 $6.95. ISBN 0-672-60282-2. A survey of American realism, new and critical, discussing the issues and the figures, and providing bibliography, by the historian of American philosophy.

Sciacca, Michele F. *Philosophical Trends in the Contemporary World.* Trans. by Attilio M. Salerno. Irvington 1964 $49.50. ISBN 0-268-00210-X. A survey of the main trends in philosophy in midcentury by a leading Italian philosopher.

Silverman, Hugh J., and Don Ihde, eds. *Hermeneutics and Deconstruction: Selected Studies in Phenomenology and Existential Philosophy.* State U. NY Pr. 1985 $59.59. ISBN 0-87395-979. An anthology of essays by academic experts on the subject.

Smith, John E. *America's Philosophical Vision.* U. Ch. Pr. 1992 $39.95. ISBN 0-226-76367-6. Provides a powerful case for the continuing relevance and vitality of a philosophical tradition.

_____, ed. *Contemporary American Philosophy: Second Series.* Humanities 1971 o.p. "Contains contributions from teachers of philosophy in American universities . . . [discussing] their own work and that of their teachers and colleagues" (*Choice*).

Solomon, Robert C. *Existentialism.* Random 1974 $7.00. ISBN 0-685-16614-2. An excellent selection of writings by a leading scholar on existentialism.

_____. *Introducing the Existentialists.* Hackett 1981 $17.50. ISBN 0-915144-47-6. Imaginary interviews with Sartre, Heidegger, and Camus.

Spiegelberg, Herbert. *The Phenomenological Movement: An Historical Introduction.* Kluwer Ac. rev. ed. 1982 $164.60. ISBN 90-247-2393-0. The classic survey of the main figures and topics in phenomenology.

Stegmueller, W. *Main Currents in Contemporary German, British and American Philosophy.* Kluwer Ac. rev. ed. 1969 $93.00. ISBN 90-277-0011-7. A thorough and demanding survey of the main figures and significant philosophical theories in twentieth-century philosophy.

Taylor, Mark C., ed. *Deconstruction in Context: Literature and Philosophy.* U. Ch. Pr. 1986 $45.00. ISBN 0-226-79139-4. A collection of critical essays for the advanced student.

Thayer, H. S. *Meaning and Action: A Critical History of Pragmatism.* Hackett 1981 $38.75. ISBN 0-915144-73-5. "For any collection on American philosophy this volume will be an essential addition, because of its comprehensiveness, scholarly competence, and sound judgments. The bibliography is most scholarly" (*Library Journal*).

———, ed. *Pragmatism: The Classic Writings.* Hackett 1982 $22.50. ISBN 0-915145-38-3. An anthology to match the book listed above.

Urmson, J. O. *Philosophical Analysis: Its Development Between the Two World Wars.* OUP 1956 o.p. A survey of the genesis of linguistic analysis from the earlier twentieth-century forms of analytic philosophy represented by G. E. Moore, Bertrand Russell, C. D. Broad, and the early Wittgenstein.

Wachterhauser, Brice R., ed. *Hermeneutics and Modern Philosophy.* State U. NY Pr. 1986 $57.50. ISBN 0-88706-295-4. A collection of scholarly essays for the advanced student.

Wahl, Jean A. *A Short History of Existentialism.* Greenwood 1972 repr. of 1949 ed. $38.50. ISBN 0-8371-5570-6. A facile but insightful sketch of the development of existentialism by a leading French philosopher.

Warnock, Geoffrey J. *English Philosophy since 1900.* Greenwood 1982 repr. of 1969 ed. A concise but reliable history.

Warnock, Mary. *Ethics since Nineteen Hundred.* OUP 1978 $19.95. ISBN 0-19-289108-1. Concise, lucid standard work.

———. *Existentialism.* OUP 1970 $10.95. ISBN 0-19-888052-9. "This useful and modest little book . . . guides the nonspecialist through existentialism, shows that this philosophy is really no more difficult than any other serious intellectual movement, and that the problems of these thinkers have much in common with those of other philosophic schools" (*Modern Language Journal*).

Wedberg, Anders. *A History of Philosophy: From Bolzano to Wittgenstein.* OUP 1984 $16.95. ISBN 0-19-824693-5. "This third and final volume of Wedberg's *History of Philosophy* traces the development of European philosophy from the beginning of the nineteenth century through the mid-twentieth century. Like its predecessors, its scope is limited to logical, epistemological, and ontological questions presented from an analytical perspective" (*Choice*).

Weitz, Morris. *Twentieth-Century Philosophy: The Analytic Tradition.* Free Pr. 1966 $14.95. ISBN 0-02-934990-7. A useful anthology.

West, Cornel. *The American Evasion of Philosophy: A Genealogy of Pragmatism.* U. of Wis. Pr. 1989 $16.95. ISBN 0-299-11964-5. Charts the emergence, development, decline, and recent resurgence of American pragmatism.

White, Morton. *Pragmatism and the American Mind: Essays and Reviews in Philosophy and Intellectual History.* OUP 1973 o.p. This "collection of essays and critical reviews by one of America's most able analytic philosophers [treats] a wide range of topics in American intellectual history" (*Choice*).

———. *Toward Reunion in Philosophy.* Atheneum 1963 o.p. A brilliant attempt by one of America's leading philosophers to uncover the common ground of pragmatism and analytic philosophy.

———, ed. *Age of Analysis: Twentieth Century Philosophers.* 1955 Ayer $19.00. ISBN 0-8369-1853-4. "It is not simply an anthology. It is an anthology plus. . . . The 'plus' consists in the introduction to the collection and to each of the thinkers presented" (*N.Y. Herald Tribune*).

CHRONOLOGY OF AUTHORS

Whitehead, Alfred North. 1861–1947
Mead, George Herbert. 1863–1931
Santayana, George. 1863–1952
McTaggart, John McTaggart Ellis.
  1866–1925
Shestov, Lev. 1866–1938
Russell, Bertrand Arthur William.
  1872–1970
Hocking, William Ernest. 1873–1966
Lovejoy, Arthur Oncken. 1873–1962
Moore, George Edward. 1873–1958
Berdyaev, Nikolai A. 1874–1948
Cassirer, Ernst. 1874–1945
Scheler, Max Ferdinand. 1874–1928
Gentile, Giovanni. 1875–1944
Cohen, Morris Raphael. 1880–1947
Aliotta, Antonio. 1881–1964
Teilhard de Chardin, Pierre.
  1881–1955
Maritain, Jacques. 1882–1973
Schlick, Moritz. 1882–1936
Jaspers, Karl. 1883–1969
Lewis, Clarence Irving. 1883–1964
Ortega, y Gasset, José. 1883–1955
Bachelard, Gaston. 1884–1962
Gilson, Étienne. 1884–1978
Bloch, Ernst. 1885–1977
Broad, Charles Dunbar. 1887–1971

Collingwood, Robin George.
  1889–1943
Heidegger, Martin. 1889–1976
Marcel, Gabriel. 1889–1973
Wittgenstein, Ludwig Josef Johann.
  1889–1951
Carnap, Rudolf. 1891–1970
Gramsci, Antonio. 1891–1937
Blanshard, Brand. 1892–1987
Hartshorne, Charles. 1897–
Ryle, Gilbert. 1900–1976
Nagel, Ernest. 1901–1985
Weiss, Paul. 1901–
Adler, Mortimer J. 1902–
Hook, Sidney. 1902–1989
Feibleman, James Kern. 1904–1988
Sartre, Jean-Paul. 1905–1980
Merleau-Ponty, Maurice. 1908–1961
Ayer, Sir Alfred Jules. 1910–1989
Austin, John Langshaw. 1911–1960
Sellars, Wilfrid. 1912–1989
Grice, Paul. 1913–1988
Ricoeur, Paul. 1913–
Von Wright, Georg H. 1916–
Davidson, Donald Herbert. 1917–
Rawls, John. 1921–
Rescher, Nicholas. 1928–
Nozick, Robert. 1938–
Kripke, Saul. 1940–

ADLER, MORTIMER J. 1902–

Born in New York City, Mortimer Adler was educated at Columbia University, where as a philosophy instructor he taught in a program focused on the intellectual foundations of Western civilization. Called to the University of Chicago in 1927 by President ROBERT MAYNARD HUTCHINS, he played a major role in renovating the undergraduate curriculum to center on the "great books." His philosophical interests, committed to the dialectical method, crystallized in a defense of neo-Thomism, but he never strayed far from concerns with education and other vital public issues.

From 1942 to 1945, Adler was director of the Institute for Philosophical Research, based in San Francisco, California. Since 1945 he has served as associate editor of Great Books of the Western World series, and in 1952 he published *Syntopicon*, an analytic index of the great ideas in the great books. In 1966 he became director of the editorial planning for the fifteenth edition of the *Encyclopaedia Britannica*, and in 1974, chairman of its editorial board.

Adler has been devoted in recent years to expounding his interpretations of selected great ideas and to advocating his *Paideia Proposal*, a program that would require that all students receive the same quantity and quality of education and that would concentrate on the study of the great ideas expressed in the great books, a study conducted by means of the dialectical method.

BOOKS BY ADLER

The Angels and Us. Macmillan 1988 $7.95. ISBN 0-02-016021-6. Adler takes angels
  seriously and indicates why.

Aristotle for Everybody. Macmillan 1978 $12.95. ISBN 0-02-064111-7. A lucid introduction to the difficult philosophy of Aristotle, which Adler espouses.

Art and Prudence. Ed. by Garth S. Jowett. Ayer 1978 repr. of 1937 ed. $49.50. ISBN 0-405-11126-6. A comprehensive and penetrating study of the authority of morals over art.

The Capitalist Manifesto. (coauthored with Louis O. Kelso). Greenwood 1975 repr. of 1958 ed. $45.00. ISBN 0-8371-8210-7. The case for capitalism, an antidote to communism and socialism.

Desires, Right and Wrong: The Ethics of Enough. Macmillan 1991 $22.95. ISBN 0-02-500281-3. An investigation into moral philosophy "often simplistic . . . sometimes dogmatic, but its clear exposition and concrete examples should help the reader separate the good from the bad in it" (*Library Journal*).

Freedom: A Study of the Development of the Concept in the English and American Traditions of Philosophy. Magi Bks. 1968 $00.50. ISBN 0-87343-007-7. An example of dialectic applied to the idea of freedom.

Great Books of the Western World. (coedited with Robert Hutchins). 1952. 54 vols. o.p. A collection of the great books in well-bound standard editions in the English language.

The Great Ideas: One Hundred Two Essays. Macmillan 1992 $40.00. ISBN 0-02-500573-1. Concise, lucid essays on the ideas presented in the *Syntopicon*.

The Great Ideas Anthologies. (coauthored with Robert Hutchins). 4 vols. Ayer 1976 $84.00. ISBN 0-405-07170-1. The 100 great ideas illustrated by selections of passages in which they are expressed.

Great Treasury of Western Thought: A Compendium of Important Statements on Man and His Institutions by the Great Thinkers in Western History. (coauthored with Charles Van Doren). Bowker 1977 $49.50. ISBN 0-8352-0833-8. A selection of passages of wisdom on all the fundamental topics that concern human beings.

Have Without Have-Nots: Six Essays on Democracy and Socialism. Macmillan 1991 $21.95. ISBN 0-02-500561-8. Wise assessment of practical problems from a theoretical framework.

How to Read a Book. (coauthored with Charles Van Doren). S&S Trade rev. ed. 1972 $10.95. ISBN 0-671-21209-5. A useful, unrivaled guide.

How to Speak, How to Listen. 1983. Macmillan 1985 $7.95. ISBN 0-02-079590-4. A useful guide.

How to Think about God: A Guide for the Twentieth-Century Pagan. 1980. Macmillan 1991 $9.00. ISBN 0-02-016022-4. A provocative, but very clear, essay.

The New Capitalists. (coauthored with Louis O. Kolso). Greenwood 1975 repr. of 1961 ed. $38.50 ISBN 0-8371-8211-5. Additional investigations of how capitalism flourishes.

Paideia Problems and Possibilities. Macmillan 1983 $7.95. ISBN 0-02-013050-3. A continuation of the discussion posed by *The Paideia Proposal.*

The Paideia Program: An Educational Syllabus. Macmillan 1984 $8.95. ISBN 0-02-013040-6. The proposal for implementing *The Paideia Proposal.*

The Paideia Proposal: An Educational Manifesto. Macmillan 1982 $5.95. ISBN 0-02-064100-1. A proposal for an educational program based on great ideas and dialectic.

Philosopher at Large: An Intellectual Autobiography. 1974. Macmillan 1992 $9.00. ISBN 0-02-0010011-7. Witty, informative account of the author's life and works in and out of academe.

Reforming American Education. Macmillan 1989 $19.95. ISBN 0-02-500551-0. Timely constructive response to critiques of American education on behalf of the great books tradition.

St. Thomas and the Gentiles. Marquette 1938 $8.95. ISBN 0-87462-102-X. A concise statement of neo-Thomism.

A Second Look in the Rear-View Mirror: Further Autobiographical Reflections of a Philosopher at Large. Macmillan 1992 $22.00. ISBN 0-02-500571-5. Continues the author's intellectual and professional odyssey.

Six Great Ideas: Truth, Goodness, Beauty, Liberty, Equality, Justice. Macmillan 1984 $7.95. ISBN 0-20-072020-3. A clear and concise discussion of these ideas.

Some Questions about Language. Open Court 1991 $12.95. ISBN 0-8126-9178-4. Raises
  questions about the validity of linguistic philosophy.
Ten Philosophical Mistakes. Macmillan 1985 $7.95. ISBN 0-02-064120-6. A facile, but
  illuminating, philosophical essay.
Truth in Religion: The Plurality of Religions and the Unity of Truth. Macmillan 1992
  $10.00. ISBN 0-02-064140-0. Defends Western religions' adherence to a coherent
  doctrine of truth, in contrast to Eastern religions.
We Hold These Truths. Macmillan 1988 $6.95. ISBN 0-02-061430-3. Incisive analysis and
  defense of the principles that underlie the American political system, focused on the
  Constitution.

Book about Adler

Torre, Michael E., ed. *Freedom in the Modern World: Jacques Maritain, Yves R. Simon,
  Mortimer J. Adler*. U. of Notre Dame Pr. 1990 $15.00. ISBN 0-268-00978-3. Scholarly
  critical essay on three neo-Thomists' variations on the theme of freedom.

ADORNO, THEODOR W. 1903–1969

[See Chapter 9 in this volume.]

ALIOTTA, ANTONIO. 1881–1964

Born in Salerno, Antonio Aliotta taught at the Universities of Padua and
Naples in Italy. After publishing studies in experimental psychology, he wrote in
1912 a vast critical analysis of contemporary philosophy in which he defended a
theistic idealism. This work was translated into English and published in 1914.
As the neo-Hegelian idealism of Benedetto Croce (see Vol. 2) and Giovanni
Gentile became ascendant in Italy, Aliotta sided with its opponents, drawing for
his support on philosophical developments outside Italy; in particular he
embraced pragmatism, realism, and relationism.

Book by Aliotta

The Idealistic Reaction against Science. 1912. Trans. by Agnes McCaskill. *History,
  Philosophy and Sociology of Science*. Ayer 1975 repr. of 1914 ed. $37.50. ISBN 0-405-
  06576-0. "Vast critical analysis of contemporary philosophy . . . which defended a
  monadological spiritualism with a theistic tendency" (*Encyclopedia of Philosophy*).

ARENDT, HANNAH. 1906–1975

[See Chapter 9 in this volume.]

AUSTIN, JOHN LANGSHAW. 1911–1960

Born in Lancaster, England, and educated at Shrewsbury School and Balliol,
Oxford University, John Langshaw Austin became a fellow at Oxford in 1933,
where he taught until his death in 1960. During World War II, Austin served as a
chief organizer for military intelligence of the Allied armies. For his wartime
contributions, he received the Order of the British Empire, French Croix de
Guerre, and the American Legion of Merit. At Oxford he was appointed White
Professor of moral philosophy in 1952. A prominent figure in the development
of British analytic philosophy, Austin was greatly influenced by the thought of
Ludwig Wittgenstein. Austin emphasized the value of ordinary language in
illuminating and resolving philosophical problems. He preferred to do philosophy by attending to the way words function in ordinary language.
    Austin pioneered the analysis of speeches and led the linguistic-analysis
approach to philosophy, which attempted to resolve philosophical problems by
analyzing and clarifying the meanings of words. His methods and results are

contained in numerous papers and two succinct books. His major achievements in the school of linguistic analysis include (1) his theory of elocutionary forces in language usage, which overhauled the distinctions between performatives and constatives, and (2) his critique of sense-datum theory in the light of his linguistic discoveries.

BOOKS BY AUSTIN

How to Do Things with Words. OUP 1962 o.p. An introduction to Austin's theory of language and his method of linguistic analysis.
Philosophical Papers. 1961. Ed. by James Urmson and Geoffrey Warnock. OUP o.p. A collection of Austin's published articles; for advanced scholars only.
Sense and Sensibilia. Ed. by Geoffrey Warnock. OUP 1964 $9.95. ISBN 0-19-500307-1. Austin's devastating critique of the sense-datum theory in epistemology.

BOOKS ABOUT AUSTIN

Fann, K. T., ed. *Symposium on J. L. Austin. International Lib. of Philosophy and Scientific Method.* Humanities 1979 repr. of 1969 ed. o.p. A collection of 28 essays by prominent Anglo-American analytic philosophers on Austin's conception of philosophy, on specific points raised in his papers, on his critique of sense-datum theory, and on his theory of linguistic meaning and speech acts.
Warnock, Geoffrey. *J. L. Austin.* Routledge 1989 $33.00. ISBN 0-415-02962-7. Terse critical exposition of Austin's philosophy by a disciple.

AYER, SIR ALFRED JULES. 1910–1989

After attending Eton School and Oxford University, Sir Alfred Jules Ayer studied philosophy at the University of Vienna, where he affiliated with the Vienna Circle, the school of logical positivism led by MORITZ SCHLICK. On his return to England, he accepted an appointment in 1933 as lecturer at Oxford, and, except for his military service during World War II, he wrote and taught philosophy until his death. During World War II, Ayer was commissioned into the Welsh Guards, and in 1945 was an attaché at the British Embassy in Paris. In 1946 he was appointed Grote Professor at the University of London and in 1959 Wykeham Professor of logic at Oxford.

Ayer's fame was established with the publication of his first book, *Language, Truth and Logic*, in 1936. This work introduced logical positivism to the English-speaking world in a clear, vigorous, and persuasive style. Building on the thought of BERTRAND RUSSELL (see also Vol. 5) and LUDWIG WITTGENSTEIN, Ayer sharpened their theses, boldly revealing the affiliations of logical positivism with traditional British empiricism, particularly the work of DAVID HUME. Ayer claimed that only verifiable statements are true or false. He considered statements of religion or art as merely emotional expressions.

For his contributions to philosophy, Ayer was knighted by the British Crown. He has provided an account of his life, at least of its professional and philosophical sides, in two autobiographies listed below.

BOOKS BY AYER

Bertrand Russell. U. Ch. Pr. 1988 $9.95. ISBN 0-726-03343-0. An intellectual portrait by a disciple who had moved beyond his master.
Freedom and Morality and Other Essays. OUP 1986 $19.95. ISBN 0-19-824691-6. A collection of Ayer's previously published essays, mostly on moral and practical topics.
Hume. OUP 1980 $6.95. ISBN 0-19-287528-0. A critical appreciation of the Scottish empiricist.

Language, Truth and Logic. 1936 Peter Smith 1952 repr. of 1946 ed. $17.25. ISBN 0-8446-1571-4

Logical Positivism. Greenwood 1978 repr. of 1959 ed. $75.00. ISBN 0-313-20462-4. Readings from the logical positivists with an introduction by the editor.

The Meaning of Life: Essays by the Author of Language, Truth and Logic. Macmillan 1990 $19.95. ISBN 0-684-19195-4. Attempts to reflect upon ultimates without being confined to logically strict criteria of meaning.

More of My Life. OUP 1984 o.p. The second volume of memoirs.

Origins of Pragmatism: Studies in the Philosophy of Charles Sanders Peirce and William James. Freeman Cooper 1968 $12.50. ISBN 0-87735-501-0. Commentaries on themes in the philosophies of Peirce and James relevant to logical empircist issues.

Part of My Life. OUP 1978 o.p. The first volume of Ayer's autobiographical reflections.

Philosophical Essays. Greenwood 1980 repr. of 1954 ed. $35.00. ISBN 0-313-20902-2. A collection of Ayer's previously published essays on epistemology and the philosophy of mind.

Philosophy in the Twentieth Century. Random 1982 $22.50. ISBN 0-394-50454-7. A critical history.

Problem of Knowledge. Viking Penguin 1957 $6.95. ISBN 0-14-020377-X. An elementary presentation of the epistemology of logical positivism.

Russell and Moore: The Analytical Heritage. William James Lectures Ser. HUP 1971 $17.50. ISBN 0-674-78103-1. Appreciative but critical account of the contributions of Russell and Moore.

Thomas Paine. Macmillan 1989 $19.95. ISBN 0-689-11996-8. An appreciation of the eighteenth-century revolutionary and freethinker.

Voltaire. Random 1986 o.p. A critical appreciation of the French *philosophe*, with excerpts from his writings.

Wittgenstein. U. Ch. Pr. 1986 $12.95. ISBN 0-226-03337-6. A critical appreciation of the contributions of this major twentieth-century philosopher.

BOOKS ABOUT AYER

Foster, John. *Ayer.* Routledge Chapman & Hall 1985 $35.00. ISBN 0-7102-0602-X. Sharply focused critical study in *The Arguments of the Philosophers Series.*

Griffiths, A. Phillips, ed. *Memorial Essays.* Cambridge U. Pr. 1992 $18.95. ISBN 0-521-42246-9. Evaluations by Anglo-American philosophers, originating in *The Royal Institute of Philosophy Supplements Series.*

Hahn, Lewis E., ed. *The Philosophy of A. J. Ayer.* Open Court 1991 $49.95. ISBN 0-8126-9172-5. A well-organized collection of scholarly essays in *The Library of Living Philosophers Series;* examines all aspects of Ayer's thought.

BACHELARD, GASTON. 1884–1962

Born in Bar-sur-Aube, France, Gaston Bachelard received his doctorate in 1927, became professor of philosophy at the University of Dijon in 1930, and held the chair in the history and philosophy of science at the University of Paris from 1940 to 1954.

In epistemology and philosophy of science, Bachelard espoused a dialectical rationalism, or dialogue between reason and experience. Rejecting the Cartesian conception of scientific truths as immutable, he insisted on experiment as well as mathematics in the development of science and described the cooperation between the two as a philosophy of saying no, of being ever ready to revise or abandon the established framework of scientific theory to express the new discoveries.

In addition to his contributions to the epistemological foundations of science, he explored the role of reverie and emotion in the expressions of both science and more imaginative thinking. His psychological explanations of the four elements—earth, air, fire, water—illustrate this almost poetic aspect of his philosophy.

BOOKS BY BACHELARD

Air and Dreams: An Essay on the Imagination of Movement. Trans. by Joanne H. Stroud. Dallas Inst. Pubns. 1988 $25.00. ISBN 0-91005-11-0. Foreword by Edith and Frederick Furrell.

The Flame of the Candle. Trans. by Joni Caldwell. Dallas Inst. Pubns. 1989 $18.00. ISBN 0-911005-14-5

Fragments of a Poetics of Fire. Trans. by Kenneth Hultman. Dallas Inst. Pubns. 1991 $25.00. ISBN 0-91105-17-X

Lautreamont. Trans. by Joanne H. Stroud. Dallas Inst. Pubns. 1986 $20.00. ISBN 0-911005-08-0. Foreword by Robert S. Dupree.

The New Scientific Spirit. 1934. Beacon Pr. 1985 o.p. The introduction to his dialectical interpretation of science, in which experiment and imagination are as significant as reason.

On Poetic Imagination and Reverie. Trans. by Colette Gaulin. Spring Pubns. 1987 $12.50. ISBN 0-88214-331-X. Revised edition with an introduction by the translator.

Poetics of Reverie: Childhood, Language and Cosmos. Beacon Pr. 1971 $12.00. ISBN 0-8070-6413-0. A late work tracing Bachelard's themes back to the mental life of children.

Poetics of Space. Trans. by Maria Jolas. Beacon Pr. 1969 $13.00. ISBN 0-8070-6439-4. The geometry of space approached and construed as imaginative poetry.

Psychoanalysis of Fire. 1932. Trans. by A. C. Ross. Beacon Pr. 1964 $12.00. ISBN 0-8070-6461-7. The first of his imaginative psychological explanations of the elements.

The Right to Dream. Trans. by J. A. Underwood. Dallas Inst. Pubns. 1989 $17.00. ISBN 0-911005-16-1

Water and Dreams: An Essay on Imagination of Matter. 1942. Trans. by Edith R. Farrell. Dallas Inst. Pubns. 1983 $25.00. ISBN 0-91005-01-3. An exploration of the role of dreams in the formation of the scientific theory of matter.

BOOKS ABOUT BACHELARD

Jones, Mary M. *Gaston Bachelard, Subversive Humanist.* U. of Wis. Pr. 1991 $37.50. ISBN 0-299-12790-7. Selected texts and readings in the *Science and Literature Series.*

McAllester, Mary, ed. *The Philosophy and Poetics of Gaston Bachelard.* U. Pr. of Amer. 1989 $38.50. ISBN 0-8191-7471-8. A collection of scholarly essays in the *Current Continental Research Series* under the auspices of the Center for Advanced Research.

Smith, Roch C. *Gaston Bachelard.* P-H 1982. An informative introductory study.

Tiles, Mary. *Bachelard: Modern European Philosophy.* Cambridge U. Pr. 1985 $44.95. ISBN 0-521-24803-5. This introduction to Bachelard's basic ideas discusses his theory of conceptual change and compares his approach to that characteristic of analytic philosophers.

BERDYAEV, NIKOLAI A. 1874–1948

The great Russian Orthodox religious philosopher Nikolai A. Berdyaev was born into an aristocratic family in Kiev. At the turn of the century, the Czarist government exiled Berdyaev for his Marxist views. After the revolution he founded the Free Academy of Spiritual Culture and was given the chair of philosophy at the University of Moscow. He was imprisoned for his defense of religion and was driven into exile, first to Berlin (1922), then to Paris (1934). In Berlin, Berdyaev founded the Academy of the Philosophy of Religion, which he later moved to Clamart—near Paris.

Although Berdyaev's early interest was in Marxism, "it was a deviation from orthodox Marxism in that it insisted that only transcendental critical idealism can solve the problem of truth" (Louis J. Shein, *Readings in Russian Philosophical Thought*). He later became interested in mystical and religious ideas, and developed a process cosmology and theology.

His last testament, *The Realm of Spirit and the Realm of Caesar*, found after his death and put into publishable form by a group of his friends, shows "no sign of decay of mental power or spiritual force." His "lucid thought and luminous style give his work an almost compulsive force." Berdyaev was strongly committed to freedom and individualism, which caused him great difficulty with ecclesiastical and political authorities.

BOOKS BY BERDYAEV

The Beginning and the End. Trans. by R. M. French. Greenwood repr. of 1948 ed. $37.50. ISBN 0-313-20968-5. A profound essay on the eschatological aspects of cosmology and theology.

The Destiny of Man. 1954. Trans. by Natalie Duddington. Hyperion Conn. 1991 repr. of 1954 ed. $32.00. ISBN 0-88355-775-4. A process metaphysics of humanity's nature, status, and function in the cosmos.

Leontiev. 1940. Academic Intl. 1968 $20.00. ISBN 0-87569-004-1. A concise critical biography.

The Realm of Spirit and the Realm of Caesar. 1953. Trans. by Donald A. Lowrie. Greenwood 1975 o.p. Posthumously published work exhibiting Berdiaev's final struggles with the political and religious conflicts of his life and times.

The Russian Idea. 1948. Trans. by R. M. French. Greenwood 1979 $37.50. A probing attempt to elicit the essence of Russia.

The Russian Revolution. 1933. U. of Mich. Pr. o.p. Perceptive explanation of the world-shaking event by an ambivalent Russian émigré.

Solitude and Society. Trans. by George Reavey. Greenwood 1976 repr. of 1938 ed. $35.00. ISBN 0-8371-3250-9. An exemplary presentation of the reflective nature of this intensely religious but heterodox philosopher.

BOOKS ABOUT BERDYAEV

Attwater, Donald, ed. *Modern Christian Thinkers.* Ayer repr. of 1947 ed. $23.00. ISBN 0-8369-2304-9. A facsimile edition of an essay on Berdyaev's Christian philosophy.

Lowrie, Donald A. *A Rebellious Prophet: A Life of Nicolai Berdyaev.* Greenwood 1960 o.p. The author was a close associate of Berdyaev during the Russian thinker's 24-year exile in Paris. "Utilizing unrivaled opportunities for an intimate knowledge of his subject, Lowrie has produced a book which may be confidently regarded as Berdyaev's definitive biography—at least for a long time to come" (*Christian Century*).

Seaver, G. *Nicolas Berdyaev.* Gordon Pr. 1973 $59.95. ISBN 0-8490-0730-5. A reliable critical biography.

BLANSHARD, BRAND. 1892–1987

Born in Fredericksburg, Ohio, the son of a minister, Brand Blanshard was an American philosopher who studied at Oxford University as a Rhodes scholar. The Oxford method of education and the philosophical school of idealism (or rationalism) that flourished there during the period around World War I profoundly influenced his career as a teacher and philosopher in the United States. He received a B.A. from the University of Michigan (1914), an M.A. from Columbia University (1918), and Harvard University (1921).

Blanshard taught at Swarthmore College for twenty years (1925–1945) before becoming Chair of the department of philosophy at Yale University. His two-volume work *The Nature of Thought* (1939) is a critical survey of the theories of mind and knowledge that prevailed during the first half of the twentieth century and is also a constructive argument for the nature of reason as sovereign. Blanshard is widely known for his "coherence" theory of truth, i.e., truth is apprehended as a whole or gestalt, rather than piecemeal. In his Gifford lectures at St. Andrews and his Carus lectures before the American Philosophical Association, Blanshard argued against what he considered the detractors of reason—moral relativism and noncognitivism, existentialism, and analytic philosophy in its various forms. He published these lectures in expanded and revised form in the trilogy on reason listed below.

BOOKS BY BLANSHARD

Education in the Age of Science. Essay Index Repr. Ser. Ayer 1959 $20.00. ISBN 0-8369-2144-5. A collection of essays defending liberal education.

Four Reasonable Men: Aurelius, Mill, Renan, Sidgwick. U. Pr. of New Eng. 1984 $14.95. ISBN 0-8195-6102-9. Beautifully written studies of four moralists whose lives and works exemplify the significance of reason.

The Nature of Thought. Muirhead Lib. of Philosophy. 1939 2 vols. Humanities 1964 o.p.

On Philosophical Style. Greenwood repr. of 1954 ed. $39.75. ISBN 0-8371-1975-8. An elegant essay on the importance of clarity in philosophy.

Reason and Analysis. Paul Carus Lecture Ser. Open Court 1964 $14.95. ISBN 0-87548-104-3. A critique of analytic philosophy and defense of a systematic philosophy based on a holistic rationalism.

Reason and Belief. Gifford Lectures. Bks. Demand repr. of 1974 ed. $160.00. ISBN 0-8357-8755-9. A rationalist critique of irrationalisms in the philosophy of religion and theology, concluding with a constructive reformulation of a rationalist theory of the world.

Reason and Goodness. Gifford Lectures. Open Court 1961 o.p. Criticizes and refutes moral theories that deny the role of reason; systematically reconstructs the ethics of self-realization on rational grounds.

BOOK ABOUT BLANSHARD

Schilpp, Paul Arthur, ed. *The Philosophy of Brand Blanshard. Lib. of Living Philosophers.* Open Court 1980 o.p. Blanshard's autobiography, 30 critical essays, Blanshard's replies to his critics, and a bibliography.

BLOCH, ERNST. 1885–1977

Ernst Bloch ranks as a major German Marxist philosopher. Beginning his career as author and teacher during World War I, he moved in the orbit of Marxist thought during the 1920s. In 1933 he left Germany and eventually found his way to the United States, where he created his major work, *The Principle of Hope.* After World War II, he settled in East Germany, where from 1948 to 1957 he was professor at the University of Leipzig. His work eventually aroused the hostility of the authorities, and in 1961 he was granted political asylum in West Germany.

Bloch departed from orthodox Marxism by attending to the problem of intellectual culture and refraining from treating it merely as superstructure determined by the materialist elements of political economy. Stressing the role of hope—as an inner drive or hunger in human beings—for a possible ideal future order, Bloch's thought may be described as utopian, involving the realization of a religious community, akin to the kingdom of God, where people are no longer exploited but are free. His style echoes recent expressionism and is also rich in mystical overtones of biblical origin.

BOOKS BY BLOCH

Essays on the Philosophy of Music. Trans. by P. Palmer. Cambridge U. Pr. 1985 $69.96. ISBN 0-521-24873-6. A collection of essays.

Heritage of Our Times. Ed. by Martin Jay and Anton Kaes. Trans. by Melville Plaice and Stephen Plaice. U. CA Pr. 1991 $40.00. ISBN 0-520-70757-7. German cultural criticism during the Weimar Republic.

Natural Law and Human Dignity. 1960. Trans. by Dennis J. Schmidt. MIT Pr. 1987 $14.95. ISBN 0-212-52129-6

The Principle of Hope. 1954–59. Trans. by Nelville Plaice and others. 3 vols. MIT Pr. 1986 $95.00. ISBN 0-262-002248-6. A major work in the history of philosophy.

The Utopian Function of Art and Literature: Selected Essays. Trans. by Jack Zipes and Frank Mecklenberg. MIT Pr. 1989 $14.95. ISBN 0-0262-52139-3. Further studies in German social thought and culture criticism.

BOOKS ABOUT BLOCH

Hudson, C. Wayne. *The Marxist Philosophy of Ernst Bloch.* St. Martin 1982 $29.95. ISBN 0-312-51860-9. Scholarly study of a basic strand in Bloch's philosophy.

Kushner, David Z. *Ernst Bloch.* Garland 1988 $63.00. ISBN 0-8240-7789-X. A guide to research.

Nordquist, Joan, ed. *Ernst Bloch: A Bibliography.* Ref. Rsch. Serv. 1990 $15.00. ISBN 0-937855-37-5. Pamphlet number 19 in the bibliographic series on social thought.

Roberts, Richard H. *Hope and Its Hieroglyph: Critical Decipherment of Ernst Bloch's Principle of Hope.* Scholars Pr. GA 1990 $20.95. ISBN 1-55540-369-7

West, Thomas H. *Ultimate Hope Without God: The Atheistic Eschatology of Ernst Bloch.* P. Lang Pubs. 1992 $46.95. ISBN 0-8204-1488-3. A specialized monograph in the American University series of theology and religion.

BROAD, CHARLES DUNBAR. 1887–1971

Born in a suburb of London and educated at Cambridge University, Charles Dunbar Broad taught at several universities before returning to Cambridge, where he reluctantly became Knightbridge Professor of moral philosophy in 1933. During the period between the two world wars, Broad was the clear and meticulous advocate of the traditional academic philosophy. In epistemology he defended the doctrine of representative perception; in metaphysics, the doctrine of mind-body dualism; and in moral philosophy, the objectivity of value and the cognitive character of moral judgments.

BOOKS BY BROAD

Berkeley's Argument. Studies in Philosophy. Haskell 1975 $59.95. ISBN 0-8383-0113-4. A concise but probing essay on the Irish philosopher's idealism.

Ethics. Ed. by C. Lewy. Kluwer Ac. 1985 $109.00. ISBN 90-247-3088-0. A collection of papers for advanced students.

Ethics and the History of Philosophy: Selected Essays. Hyperion Conn. 1986 repr. of 1952 ed. $24.00. ISBN 0-88355-777-0. Impeccably lucid philosophical scholarship.

Examination of McTaggart's Philosophy. 3 vols. Hippocrene Bks. repr. of 1933 ed. o.p. Intensive commentary of the singular metaphysical idealism of the Cambridge philosopher.

Five Types of Ethical Theory. 1920. Humanities 1978 o.p. Lucid analyses of great ethical theories, such as those of Spinoza, Kant, and John Stuart Mill.

Induction, Probability and Causation: Selected Papers. Kluwer Ac. 1968 o.p. A collection of technical papers for the advanced student.

BOOK ABOUT BROAD

Schilpp, Paul Arthur, ed. *The Philosophy of C. D. Broad. Lib. of Living Philosophers.* Open Court 1959 $34.95. ISBN 0-87548-128-0. Contains Broad's autobiography, critical essays on his work by various philosophers, his reply to his critics, and a bibliography.

CARNAP, RUDOLF. 1891–1970

Born in Ronsdorf, Germany, Rudolf Carnap studied at the Universities of Freiburg and Jena from 1910 to 1914. He received his doctorate from Jena, where he had studied under *Gottlob Frege*, who, along with LUDWIG WITTGENSTEIN and BERTRAND RUSSELL (see also Vol. 5), profoundly influenced his thought. In 1926, on the invitation of MORRIS SCHLICK, he joined the faculty of the University of Vienna. An active participant in the discussions of the Vienna Circle, he soon rose to eminence in the movement of logical positivism, or logical empiricism. From Vienna he went to Prague, and in 1930 he founded, with HANS REICHENBACH in Berlin, the journal *Erkenntnis*, the main organ for the publications of the logical positivists and empiricists. In 1935, with the rise of Nazism, he moved to the United States, where he occupied teaching and research positions at the University of Chicago, Columbia University, the University of Illinois, and the University of California in Los Angeles. When he died, he was the most famous of the logical empiricists.

His 1928 book, *The Logical Structure of the World*, established the basic project of logical empiricism. Carnap sought to demonstrate that, by the method of construction from elementary experiences, all the objects in the world that were also objects of knowledge could be attained. As a consequence, unless a statement could be validated either by rules of logic or by experimental testing in experience, it could be dismissed as devoid of knowledge. Carnap thus proceeded to dismiss most of traditional philosophy and metaphysics as consisting of pseudo-problems.

Carnap maintained that the genuine task of philosophy was the logical analysis of the language of science. In his 1934 book, *The Logical Syntax of Language*, he introduced basic distinctions, such as object-language and meta-language, formal mode and material mode of expression, that were to be widely accepted in philosophy. However, neither his symbolism nor his restriction of philosophy to the logical analysis of syntax—i.e., the purely formal features of language—endured. Influenced by Alfred Tarski, Carnap came to appreciate the need to take account of nonformal meanings (those involving external reference). This led to his publication of *The Introduction of Semantics* (1942), a work restricted to exclusively extensional logic, as was the subsequent volume, *Formalization of Semantics* (1943). However, he moved on to consider non-extensional logics in *Meaning and Necessity*.

A leader in the unity of science movement, Carnap also wrestled with the empirical verification principle of meaning and the problems of induction and probability theory. His last major treatise was the book *Logical Foundations of Probability* (1950).

BOOKS BY CARNAP

Introduction to Symbolic Logic and Its Applications. Dover 1958 $5.95. ISBN 0-486-60453-3. A textbook for beginners.
The Logical Structure of the World and Pseudoproblems in Philosophy. Trans. by Rolf A. George. U. CA Pr. 1967 $14.95. ISBN 0-520-0147-0
Meaning and Necessity: A Study in Semantics and Modal Logic. U. Ch. Pr. 1988 $17.95. ISBN 0-226-09347-6
Philosophy and Logical Syntax. AMS Pr. repr. of 1935 ed. $11.50. ISBN 0-404-14518-3
Two Essays on Entropy. Ed. by Abner Shimony. U. CA Pr. 1978 $40.00. ISBN 0-520-02715

BOOKS ABOUT CARNAP

Butrick, Richard, Jr. *Carnap on Meaning and Analyticity.* Mouton 1970 $12.00. ISBN 0-686-22409-4. A technical monograph.

Quine, Willard V., and Rudolf Carnap. *Dear Carnap, Dear Van: The Quine-Carnap Correspondence and Related Work.* U. CA Pr. 1990 $34.95. ISBN 0-520-06847-5. Introduction by Richard Creath.

Schlipp, P. A., ed. *The Philosophy of Rudolf Carnap. Lib. of Living Philosophers Ser.* Open Court 1963 $44.95. ISBN 0-87548-130-2. Contains Carnap's illuminating autobiography, 26 critical essays on various aspects of his philosophy, his reply to his critics, and an exhaustive bibliography.

CASSIRER, ERNST. 1874–1945

Ernst Cassirer, a German neo-Kantian philosopher, taught at several European universities before moving to the United States and teaching at Yale (1941–44) and Columbia universities. A prolific historian of philosophy, Cassirer was influenced by IMMANUEL KANT and GEORG HEGEL (see also Vol. 3) but originated his own distinctive doctrine. The centerpiece of Cassirer's thought is his theory of symbolic forms. He construed representation, the ground of symbolic form, to be essentially symbolic, fusing perceptual materials with conceptual meanings. The human species, he taught, is essentially a symbolizing animal. He maintained that symbolic forms are manifest in different modes—language, myth, art, science, and religion. Cassirer utilized his theory of symbolic forms in the elaboration of a flexible philosophy of culture.

BOOKS BY CASSIRER

An Essay on Man: An Introduction to a Philosophy of Human Culture. Yale U. Pr. 1962 repr. of 1944 ed. $12.95. ISBN 0-300-00034-0. Philosophical anthropology elucidated within the framework of symbolic form theory.

Kant's Life and Thought. 1918. Trans. by James Haden. Yale U. Pr. 1981 $50.00. ISBN 0-300-02358-8. An influential intellectual biography.

Language and Myth. 1925. Trans. by Susanne K. Langer. Dover 1953 repr. ot 1946 ed. $2.95. ISBN 0-486-20051-5. A concise, lucid theory of language and myth with reference to symbolic form.

The Myth of the State. Ed. by C. W. Hendel. Yale U. Pr. 1961 repr. of 1946 ed. $12.00. ISBN 0-300-00036-7. A timely and provocative theory of politics.

The Philosophy of the Enlightenment. 1932. Trans. by F. Koelin and J. Pettegrove. Princeton U. Pr. 1951 $14.95. ISBN 0-691-01963-0. One of the great works of scholarship on the Enlightenment.

The Philosophy of Symbolic Forms. 1923–29. Trans. by Ralph Manheim. 3 vols. Yale U. Pr. 1953–57. Vol. 1 *Language.* $14.95. ISBN 0-300-00035-7. Vol. 2 *Mythical Thought.* $14.95. ISBN 0-300-00038-3. Vol. 3 *The Phenomenology of Knowledge.* $14.95. ISBN 0-300-00039-1. Cassirer's comprehensive masterwork, presented with unsurpassed philosophical scholarship and brilliance.

The Platonic Renaissance in England. 1932. Gordian 1970 repr. of 1954 ed. $45.00. ISBN 0-87752-128-X An engaging historical study of an intellectual episode in E gland.

The Problem of Knowledge: Philosophy, Science, and History since Hegel. 1906–20. Trans. by W. H. Woglom and C. W. Hendel. Yale U. Pr. 1950 $14.00. ISBN 0-300-01098-2. Cassirer's presentation of the problem of knowledge by means of historical studies.

The Question of Jean Jacques Rousseau. Yale U. Pr. 1989 $7.95. ISBN 0-300-04329-5. A critical essay of lasting interest to intellectual historians and literary theorists.

Renaissance Philosophy of Man. (coedited with others). U. Ch. Pr. 1956 $12.95. ISBN 0-226-09604-1. A collection of essays and selections from original sources.

Substance and Function and Einstein's Theory of Relativity. 1910. Trans. by W. C. Swabey and M. C. Swabey. Dover 1953 $8.95. ISBN 0-486-20050-7. A probing and speculative philosophical examination of scientific concepts.

Symbol, Myth, and Culture: Essays and Lectures by Ernst Cassirer 1935–1945. Ed. by Donald P. Verene. Bks. Demand repr. of 1979 ed. $82.20. ISBN 0-8357-3742-X. A collection of previously unpublished essays with an erudite introduction by the editor.

BOOKS ABOUT CASSIRER

Itzkoff, Seymour W. *Ernst Cassirer: An Annotated Bibliography*. Garland 1986 o.p. The standard Cassirer bibliography.

―――. *Ernst Cassirer: Scientific Knowledge and the Concept of Man*. Bks. Demand 1971 $74.50. ISBN 0-317-08062-8. "An exposition and extension of the philosophy of Ernst Cassirer, especially as that philosophy is set forth in the philosophy of symbolic forms" (*Choice*).

Krois, John M. *Cassirer, Symbolic Forms and History*. Yale U. Pr. 1985 $30.00. ISBN 0-300-03746-5. Well-written and well-researched interpretation.

Schilpp, Paul Arthur, ed. *The Philosophy of Ernst Cassirer. Lib. of Living Philosophers*. Open Court 1973 $42.95. ISBN 0-87548-131-0. A critical survey of Cassirer's life and thought, containing 23 essays by contemporary philosophers, an essay by Cassirer, and a bibliography of his work.

Sundaram, K. *Cassirer's Conception of Causality*. P. Lang Pubs. 1987 $26.00. ISBN 0-8204-0405-5. A specialized monograph in the *American University Studies Series* in philosophy.

CHISHOLM, RODERICK M. 1916–

[SEE Chapter 9 in this volume.]

COHEN, MORRIS RAPHAEL. 1880–1947

Morris Raphael Cohen, who taught philosophy at the City College of New York and who began life as the son of Russian-Jewish immigrants, was one of the foremost Jewish intellectuals in America during the first half of the twentieth century. He expounded a philosophy of rationalism and realism in step with contemporary science and relevant to the social issues of his times and, through his books and teaching, had a widespread influence. His book, *Reason and Nature* (1931), offered a clear exposition and critique of the central concepts in science and sought to demonstrate that the scientific method required rational elements (mathematics and formal logic) no less than experimental procedures that appealed to sense experience.

In a review of *A Dreamer's Journey* (1949), Cohen's autobiography, Perry Miler wrote in *The Nation*: "It is both ironic and fitting that with the posthumous publication of his autobiography, even though it was left unfinished and the last chapters are fragments, there appears the book by which Morris Cohen will be longest and most widely remembered. It will demand a permanent place among the classics of immigrant narrative, and one not too far behind the greater classics of intellectual biography. And because it reveals in human terms, with humility and yet with a touch of vanity, the sources from which his strength is gathered, it explains why he conspicuously succeeded in writing philosophy that can be read as literature."

BOOKS BY COHEN

A Dreamer's Journey: The Autobiography of Morris Raphael Cohen. Modern Jewish Experience. Ayer 1975 repr. of 1949 ed. $30.00. ISBN 0-405-06702-X

The Faith of a Liberal. Ayer repr. of 1946 ed. $26.00. ISBN 0-8369-1598-4. Persuasively written political and social creed of an American Jewish intellectual of the first rank.

Law and the Social Order: Essays in Legal Philosophy. Social and Moral Thought Ser. Transaction Pubs. 1982 $21.95. ISBN 0-87855-876-4. Supplemented by Cohen's

Moral Aspects of Criminal Law. An early investigation of legal theory by an American philosopher.

The Meaning of Human History. 1947. *Paul Carus Lecture Ser.* Open Court 1968 $5.95. ISBN 0-87548-101-9. Unfinished treatise on the philosophy of history.

Reason and Nature: An Essay on the Meaning of Scientific Method. Dover 1978 $8.95. ISBN 0-486-23633-1. Clear exposition and critique of the central concepts in science by a proponent of the parity of reason with experiment.

BOOK ABOUT COHEN

Delaney, Cornelius. *Mind and Nature: A Study of the Naturalistic Philosophies of Cohen, Woodbridge and Sellars*. U. of Notre Dame Pr. 1969 o.p. A work of outstanding scholarship accessible to readers who are not advanced students of philosophy.

COLLINGWOOD, ROBIN GEORGE. 1889–1943

Robin George Collingwood was a remarkable thinker who sought to bridge the gulf that CHARLES DARWIN's (see Vol. 5) discoveries appeared to have set up between science and religion in the nineteenth century. He began to study Latin at age 4, Greek at 6, and the natural sciences shortly afterward. He attended Oxford University, where he studied philosophy, classics, archeology, and history: later he taught philosophy there. Participation in numerous archeological excavations allowed him to see, he said, "the importance of the questioning activity in life," and he became a respected scholar on the subject of Britain under the Roman conquest. In fact, Collingwood's sense of history was unparalleled among his contemporaries. His first-rate work in archeology resulted in a number of books—*Roman Britain* (1921), *The Archaeology of Roman Britain* (1930, with Ian Richmond), *Roman Britain and the English Settlements* (1937, with J. N. Myres), and *Roman Inscriptions of Britain* (1965, with R. P. Wright)—testifying to his excellence in the field.

He was also an artist by nature—a fine, disciplined writer who was actively interested in music and the pictorial arts. He deplored the diversiveness of increasing specialization and sought a philosophy that would harmonize all knowledge and a religion "scientific" in nature in which faith and reason each played a role. He felt that the Renaissance had mistakenly separated the various disciplines of study and that a close unity existed among them.

He began as an idealist, and his thought reflects the influence of individual idealists, in the case of art, for example, the influence of BENEDETTO CROCE (see Vol. 2). But more important than recent philosophers to the shaping of his thought were PLATO (see also Vol. 3) and GEORG HEGEL (see also Vol. 3), especially as regards the dialectical method. In his mature period, Collingwood sought to ground all the special sciences on idealist foundations, to ascertain within the dialectical function of mind the unity of religion, science, history, art, and philosophy. In his last years, however, Collingwood became critical of idealism. His ethical and political views grew somber, and pessimism seemed to overwhelm him.

BOOKS BY COLLINGWOOD

An Autobiography. OUP 1939 $19.95. ISBN 0-19-824694-3. The author's intellectual development concisely and wittily related.

An Essay on Metaphysics. U. Pr. of Amer. 1984 o.p. A critical theory of metaphysics as the study of presuppositions.

An Essay on Philosophical Method. OUP 1933 o.p. A lucid, concise presentation of Collingwood's critical method.

Essays in the Philosophy of History. Ed. by Robin W. Winks. Garland 1985 o.p. A
    collection of essays of interest to the specialist.
Essays in Political Philosophy. Ed. by David Boucher. OUP 1990 $55.00. ISBN 0-19-
    824823-7 A collection of essays written mainly during the period between the two
    world wars.
Human Nature and Human History. Studies in Philosophy. Haskell 1972 repr. of 1936 ed.
    $59.95. ISBN 0-8383-0312-0. An essay on philosophical anthropology marking the
    author's shift from idealism to pessimism.
The Idea of History. Ed. by T. M. Knox. OUP 1946 $11.95. ISBN 0-19-500205-9. A novel
    philosophy of history elaborated systematically, with studies of historians and
    philosophers and their methods.
The Idea of Nature. 1960 repr. of 1945 ed. $9.95. ISBN 0-19-500247-2. An imaginative,
    critical, and speculative survey of the idea of nature in the history of thought.
The New Leviathan: Man, Society, Civilization and Barbarism. 1942. OUP rev. ed. 1992.
    ISBN 0-19-823981-5. A gloomy treatise on the state of politics and civilization,
    provoked in part by the times. With an introduction by David Boucher.
Outlines of a Philosophy of Art. Somerset Pub. repr. of 1925 ed. $39.00. ISBN 0-403-
    07231-X. A useful guide to the basic principles and problems in the field.
The Principles of Art. OUP 1958 repr. of 1938 ed. $11.95. ISBN 0-19-500209-1. Basic work
    on the philosophy of art; highly readable.
Speculum Mentis, or The Map of Knowledge. Greenwood 1982 repr. of 1924 ed. $41.50.
    ISBN 0-313-23701-8. Original idealist treatise on the branches of human knowledge
    and cultural fields, magisterially composed.

BOOKS ABOUT COLLINGWOOD

Donagan, Alan. *The Later Philosophy of R. G. Collingwood.* U. Ch. Pr. 1986 $20.00. ISBN
    0-226-15568-4. A critical study attributing Collingwood's later pessimism to his
    mental condition.
Ketner, Kenneth L. *An Emendation of Collingwood's Doctrine of Absolute Presupposi-
    tions. Graduate Studies.* Tex. Tech. Univ. Pr. 1973 $5.00. ISBN 0-89672-011-X. A
    narrow, technical essay on a central topic in Collingwood's methodology.
Kraus, Michael, ed. *Critical Essays in the Philosophy of Robin George Collingwood.* OUP
    1972 o.p. "[A] useful volume, one which ought to introduce Collingwood to readers
    in many fields other than philosophy" (*Virginia Quarterly Review*).
Mink, Louis O. *Mind, History, and Dialectic: The Philosophy of R. G. Collingwood.* U. Pr. of
    New Eng. 1987 $15.00. ISBN 0-8195-6178-9. Lucid, erudite critical monograph on
    Collingwood's philosophical method in the interpretation of history.

DAVIDSON, DONALD HERBERT. 1917–

Born in Springfield, Massachusetts, the son of an engineer (Clarence),
Davidson is among the most influential analytical philosophers of the last 25
years. He was educated at Harvard University, where he received his Ph.D. in
1948, and has held teaching and research positions at the City University of New
York, Stanford University, Princeton University, Rockefeller University, and the
University of Chicago. Currently, Davidson is professor of philosophy at the
University of California at Berkeley. He has won numerous honors in the United
States and abroad for distinguished work in philosophy. In 1963, he received a
senior research fellowship from the National Science Foundation, and was
awarded a Guggenheim Fellowship in 1973. Through his writings and his
teaching, he has been in the forefront of the linguistic turn in philosophy during
the second half of the twentieth century. His work continues the line of thinking
associated with his mentor, W. V. QUINE, but goes further, reflecting on
language, logic, and the history of philosophy. He is esteemed as a founder of
the philosophical field of action theory. Davidson's work combines two
antagonistic approaches to propositional content, one that goes with the causal

theory of action and anomalous monism (the idea that phenomena can be explained by a single unifying principle), and one that goes with the more hermeneutic approach on radical interpretation and the principle of charity. Thus, Davidson synthesized the analytic approach to textual interpretation and the more charitable, traditional, and continental method.

BOOKS BY DAVIDSON

Essays on Actions and Events. OUP 1980 $65.00. ISBN 0-19-824529-7. Highly sophisticated, technically rich work fundamental to the field of action theory.

Inquiries into Truth and Interpretation. OUP 1984 $65.00. ISBN 0-19-824617-X. "[A] collection of 18 closely interrelated essays in which it is argued that formal theories of truth can serve as theories of meaning for natural languages, the theories being fitted to linguistic behavior by a process of radical interpretation" (*The Philosopher's Index*).

Plato's Philebus. Harvard Dissertations in Philosophy Ser. Garland 1990 $103.00. ISBN 0-8240-3201-2. An early work showing Davidson's mastery of a classic in the history of philosophy.

BOOKS ABOUT DAVIDSON

Eynine, Simon. *Donald Davidson. Key Contemporary Thinkers Ser*. Stanford U. Pr. 1991 $32.50. ISBN 0-8047-1852-0. An introduction and critical evaluation.

LePore, Ernest, ed. *Truth and Interpretation: Perspectives on the Philosophy of Donald Davidson*. Blackwell Pubs. 1986 $60.00. ISBN 0-631-14811-6. Essays by contemporary scholars on Davidson's epistemology; for specialists.

LePore, Ernest, and Brian McLaughlin, eds. *Actions and Events: Perspectives on the Philosophy on Donald Davidson*. Blackwell Pubs. 1988 $24.95. ISBN 0-631-16187-2. A collection of essays on Davidson's metaphysics and action theory; for specialists.

Malpas, J. E. *The Mirror of Meaning: Donald Davidson and the Theory of Interpretation*. Cambridge U. Pr. 1992. ISBN 0-521-41721-X. The most thorough critical examination of Davidson's theory of interpretation, intended for advanced scholars.

Vermazen, Bruce, and Merrill B. Hintikka, eds. *Essays on Davidson: Actions and Events*. OUP 1985 $39.95. ISBN 0-19-824749-4. This collection of essays focuses on Davidson's metaphysics and action theory.

DERRIDA, JACQUES. 1930–

[SEE Chapter 9 in this volume.]

FEIBLEMAN, JAMES KERN. 1904–1988

Born in New Orleans, James Feibleman is a prolific philosophical author who has published nearly 50 books of poetry, novels, autobiography, but mostly serious philosophy. He attended the University of Virginia for several years, but did not graduate. From 1925 to 1929, Feibleman was the assistant manager of a department store. He then resumed his education in Europe during the 1930s. During World War II, he was a professor of English at Tulane University, later becoming Chair of the department of philosophy from 1952 to 1969. His major endeavor was formulating a system of philosophy that rested on the ontological foundations of realism harking back to PLATO (see also Vol. 3) (the idea that there is an a priori argument for existence) but that incorporated modern science. The outline of Feibleman's system was expounded in his massive *Ontology* (1951) but was elaborated in a number of volumes in special areas such as aesthetics, ethics, political philosophy, and legal philosophy. Feibleman also published several books on popular philosophy.

In addition to his active career in philosophy, Feibleman was a successful businessman. From 1930 until 1954, he was vice-president and general manager of James K. Feibleman Realty Company. And, he was a major partner in the Leopold Investment company (1954–71).

BOOKS BY FEIBLEMAN

Adaptive Knowing. Kluwer Ac. 1977 $59.00. ISBN 90-247-1890-2. A technical work on the philosophy and epistemology of cognition in a naturalistic setting.

Christianity, Communism, and the Ideal Society. A Philosophical Approach to Modern Politics. AMS Pr. 1978 repr. of 1937 ed. $38.00. ISBN 0-404-59149-3. Reflective assessment of the promises and the defects of rival ideologies.

The Destroyers: The Underside of Human Nature. P. Lang Pubs. 1987 $26.00. ISBN 0-8204-0609-0. A misanthropic examination of the dark side of human behavior.

Education and Civilization. Kluwer Ac. 1987 o.p. Philosophy of education with thoughtful applications.

Justice, Law, and Culture. Kluwer Ac. 1985 $28.00. ISBN 9-02-473105-4. Realistic philosophy of law.

Ontology. Johns Hopkins 1951 o.p. This technical work presents three domains of being: actuality, possibility, and destiny.

Philosophers Lead Sheltered Lives: A First Volume of Memoirs. AMS Pr. 1979 repr. of 1952 ed. $27.50. ISBN 0-404-59150-3. Sensitive autobiography of the philosopher's early years.

Religious Platonism. Greenwood 1971 repr. of 1959 ed. $39.75. ISBN 0-8371-6184-3. Insightful scholarly monograph on the references to religion in Plato and their subsequent uses in the history of thought.

Understanding Oriental Philosophy. New Amer. Pr. 1984 repr. of 1976 ed. $9.95. ISBN 0-452-00710-0. A compact handbook introducing Oriental philosophies.

BOOK ABOUT FEIBLEMAN

Whittemore, Rober C., ed. *The Reach of Philosophy, Essays in Honor of James Kern Feibleman.* Tulane Univ. Pr. 1977 o.p. This festschrift consists of 10 essays by scholars who discuss all areas of Feibleman's thought. It also contains a bibliography of his philosophical writings through 1976.

FOUCAULT, MICHEL. 1926–1984

[SEE Chapter 9 in this volume.]

GADAMER, HANS-GEORG. 1900–

[SEE Chapter 9 in this volume.]

GENTILE, GIOVANNI. 1875–1944

Born in Castelvetrano, Sicily, Giovanni Gentile was one of the major figures in the rise of idealism in Italy during the early twentieth century. Gentile was a professor of philosophy for more than 40 years at various Italian universities, including Naples (1898–1906); Palermo (1906–14); and Pisa (1914–17), where he was Chair of the philosophy department. His longest tenure was at the University of Rome, where he was a professor from 1917 until his death during World War II. Gentile formulated a neo-Hegelian philosophy referred to as actual idealism in which the present act of thinking was the foundation of all behavior. His idealism was therefore absolutely subjective, although he preferred to regard it as an actualism. In 1922, Gentile was appointed minister of education in Benito Mussolini's cabinet and in 1924 the first president of the National Fascist Institute of Culture. He also was the Minister of Public Instruction in Italy from 1922 until 1924. He remained a loyal Fascist to the end, serving as the ideological spokesman for Mussolini. When Mussolini fell, Gentile retired briefly, then actively supported the Fascist Social Republic that

the Germans had established. He was killed in Florence on April 15, 1944, by
Italian Communist partisans. Perhaps Gentile's most significant accomplishment was planning the *Encyclopedia Italiana*, from 1929 to 1936. It consisted of
35 volumes and became the showpiece of Mussolini's regime.

BOOKS BY GENTILE

Genesis and Structure of Society. Trans. by H. S. Harris. U. of Ill. Pr. 1966 $12.50. ISBN 0-
    252-74519-1. Philosophical sociology on an authoritarian basis; excellent translation.
Reform of Education. Trans. by Dino Bigongiari. *Studies in Fascism: Ideology and
    Practice*. AMS Pr. 1981 repr. of 1922 ed. $25.00. ISBN 0-404-16935-X. The classic
    document delineating and establishing the Fascist theory and system of education.
Theory of the Spirit and the Egocentric Propensities of Man. 2 vols. Found. Class. Reprints
    1986 $237.45. ISBN 0-89901-264-7. Original statement of Gentile's idealism systemat-
    ically presented.

BOOKS ABOUT GENTILE

Holmes, Roger W. *The Idealism of Giovanni Gentile*. *Studies in Fascism: Ideology and
    Practice*. AMS Pr. repr. of 1937 ed. $29.50. ISBN 0-404-16948-1. "A clear and
    competent account of Gentile's technical philosophy and those seeking knowledge
    of the Italian's thought will find this book a useful introduction" (*The Nation*).
Romanell, Patrick. *Croce versus Gentile: A Dialogue on Contemporary Italian Philosophy*.
    Studies in Fascism: Ideology and Practice. AMS Pr. repr. of 1947 ed. $18.00. ISBN 0-
    404-16979-1. Polemical contrast of the views of two influential twentieth-century
    thinkers, exposed by a leading scholar in the field.
Smith, William A. *Giovanni Gentile on the Existence of God*. Ed. by S. A. Matczak.
    Philosophical Questions Ser. Learned Pubns. 1970 $18.00. ISBN 0-912116-04-8. A
    careful study of a central theological theme in Gentile's thought.

GILSON, ÉTIENNE. 1884–1978

Born in Paris, Étienne Gilson was educated at the University of Paris. He
became professor of medieval philosophy at the Sorbonne in 1921, and in 1932
was appointed to the chair in medieval philosophy at the Collège de France. In
1929 he cooperated with the members of the Congregation of Priests of St.
Basil, in Toronto, Canada, to found the Pontifical Institute of Medieval Studies
in association with St. Michael's College at the University of Toronto. Gilson
served as professor and director of studies at the institute.

Like his fellow countryman JACQUES MARITAIN, Étienne Gilson was a neo-
Thomist for whom Christian revelation is an indispensable auxiliary to reason,
and on faith he accepted Christian doctrine as advocated by the Roman Catholic
church. At the same time, like ST. THOMAS AQUINAS, he accorded reason a wide
compass of operation, maintaining that it could demonstrate the existence of
God and the necessity of revelation, with which he considered it compatible.

Why anything exists is a question that science cannot answer and may even
deem senseless. Gilson found the answer to be that "each and every particular
existing think depends for its existence on a pure Act of existence." God is the
supreme Act of existing. An authority on the Christian philosophy of the Middle
Ages, Gilson lectured widely on theology, art, the history of ideas, and the
medieval world.

BOOKS BY GILSON

The Arts of the Beautiful. 1965. Greenwood 1982 $75.00. ISBN 0-8371-9294-3. "Very
    difficult, original, highly stimulating book . . . for libraries with holdings in the fields
    of art, philosophy, and aesthetics" (*Library Journal*).

Dante the Philosopher. Trans. by David Moore. Peter Smith $12.75. ISBN 0-8446-0645-6. Contends that "Dante was a pure Thomist" (*Saturday Review*).

Elements of Christian Philosophy. Greenwood 1979 repr. of 1960 ed. $35.00. ISBN 0-313-20734-8. A handbook of essentials.

God and Philosophy. Yale U. Pr. 1941 $9.00. ISBN 0-300-00097-9. Incisive narration of the leading early Christian, Muslim, and medieval conceptions of the basis of theological beliefs.

Heloïse and Abelard. U. of Mich. Pr. 1960 $13.95. ISBN 0-472-06038-4. The scholarly study of a legendary relationship that has excited the imaginations of romantics for centuries.

History of Philosophy and Philosophical Education. Aquinas Lecture. Marquette 1947 $7.95. ISBN 0-87462-112-7. Lucid demonstration of the role of the history of philosophy in philosophical understanding.

Methodical Realism. Trans. by Phillip Trower. Christendom Pr. 1990 $8.95. ISBN 0-93188-36-0

The Mystical Theology of St. Bernard. Trans. by A. H. Downeo. *Cistercian Studies Ser.* 1940. Cistercian Pubns. 1955 $9.95. A major scholarly interpretation of the thought of the twelfth-century theologian.

The Philosophy of St. Bonaventure. 1938. Franciscan Pr. 1965 $15.00. ISBN 0-8199-0526-7. A major scholarly work.

The Philosophy of St. Thomas Aquinas. 1919. Ed. and trans. by G. A. Ebrington and Edward Bullough. Ayer 1982 repr. of 1937 ed. $26.50. ISBN 0-8369-5797-0. Sympathetic exposition of Aquinas's thought, lucidly presented.

The Spirit of Medieval Philosophy. 1932. U. of Notre Dame Pr. 1991 $12.95. ISBN 0-268-01740-9. Magisterial interpretation.

Thomist Realism. Trans. by A. Mark Wauck. Ignatius Pr. 1986 $12.95. ISBN 0-89870-094-9. Systematic presentation of neo-Thomist philosophy.

Wisdom and Love in St. Thomas Aquinas. Aquinas Lecture. Marquette 1951 $7.95. ISBN 0-87462-116-X. Scholarly elucidation of central themes in Thomas Aquinas's thought.

BOOKS ABOUT GILSON

O'Neil, Charles J., ed. *An Étienne Gilson Tribute.* Bks. Demand repr. of 1959 ed. $88.80. ISBN 0-317-09021-6. "Twenty-one contributions on 21 phases of philosophical thought . . . an expression of the esteem held for Étienne Gilson by his students from the Pontifical Institute of Medieval Studies over 30 years" (Publisher's note).

Shook, Lawrence K. *Étienne Gilson.* Humanities 1984 o.p. An invaluable introductory survey of Gilson's life and works.

GOODMAN, NELSON. 1906–

[SEE Chapter 9 in this Volume.]

GRAMSCI, ANTONIO. 1891–1937

Founder of the Italian Communist party in 1921, Antonio Gramsci was a man of action who also ranks as a man of thought. Imprisoned by the Fascists in 1926 and not released until a week before his death, Gramsci overcame oppressive prison conditions to write thousands of pages on philosophy and politics. After World War II, selections from his writings were published and widely read by those who formed the New Left in Western Europe, contributing immeasurably to the development of neo-Marxism.

Gamsci rejected the idea that the Communist revolution could be achieved by political action alone, without philosophy. The task, he felt, was to transform Marxist theory from ideas in individual minds into mass beliefs. The philosophy that could effectuate this task was for him tantamount to a new ethic. Seeking to construct a philosophy appropriate to the intellectual and cultural forms dominant in the Italy of his time, Gramsci blended Crocean idealism with Marxism. While he defended Leninism and the importance of political organization and action, he held that the adoption of the new ethic, reinvigorating Marxist philosophy, was necessary if the revolution was to be achieved.

BOOKS BY GRAMSCI

The Modern Prince and Other Writings. Intl. Pubs. Co. 1959 $4.95. ISBN 0-7178-0134-9. Gramsci's renovation of Machiavellianism and his critique of Fascism.

Prison Notebooks. Vol. 1. Col. U. Pr. 1992 $45.00. ISBN 0-231-06082-3. A scholarly edition introduced by Joseph Buttigieg; illustrated.

Prison Notebooks: Selections. Trans. by Quentin Hoare and Geoffrey N. Smith. Intl. Pubs. Co. 1971 $9.95. ISBN 0-7178-0397-X. Selections from voluminous politico-philosophical writings composed during his imprisonment, inspired by his expressed purpose: "It would be important to do something for eternity."

Selections from Cultural Writings. Ed. by David Forgacs and Geoffrey N. Smith. Trans. by William Boelhower. HUP 1985 $25.00. ISBN 0-674-79985-2. "[W]ritings by Gramsci on such topics as theatre criticism, literary criticism, aesthetics, language, popular literature, journalism, Italian Catholic writers, Dante, Pirandello, and Manzoni" (*Review of Metaphysics*).

Selections from Political Writings, 1910–1920. Ed. by Quintin Hoare. Trans. by John Mathews. 1978. U. of Minn. Pr. 1990 $14.95. ISBN 0-8166-1841-0. Collection of articles, many of which had appeared in the Socialist newspaper *Avanti.*

Selections from Political Writings, 1921–26. Ed. and trans. by Quintin Hoare. U. of Minn. Pr. 1990 $14.95. ISBN 0-8166-1842-9

BOOKS ABOUT GRAMSCI

Boggs, Carl. *Gramsci's Marxism.* Longwood 1976 o.p. Critical evaluation of Gramsci's renovated Marxism.

———. *The Two Revolutions: Antonio Gramsci and the Dilemmas of Marxism.* South End Pr. 1984 $35.00. ISBN 0-89608-226-1. Appreciation of Gramsci's role in neo-Marxism and the theory of revolution.

Cammett, John M. *Antonio Gramsci and the Origins of Italian Communism.* Stanford U. Pr. 1967 $37.50. ISBN 0-8047-0141-5. A substantial contribution to the growing body of literature dealing with a critical phase of modern European history.

Entwistle, Harold. *Antonio Gramsci: Conservative Schooling for Radical Politics.* Methuen 1979 o.p. "[R]eadable and should be of interest for students of educational, political, and social theory" (*Choice*).

Fernia, Joseph V. *Gramsci's Political Thought: Hegemony, Consciousness, and the Revolutionary Process.* OUP 1981 o.p. Expert analysis of Gramsci's political theory and its practical application; indispensable for the understanding of Gramsci.

Joll, James. *Antonio Gramsci.* Modern Masters Ser. Viking Penguin 1978 o.p.

Sassoon, Anne S. *Approaches to Gramsci.* Writers & Readers 1982 $14.95. ISBN 0-906495-55-5. An elementary guide to a complex thinker.

———. *Gramsci's Politics.* U. of Minn. Pr. 1988 $44.95. ISBN 0-8166-1647-7. A scholarly exposition and critique of the political theory and praxis of perhaps the most important European communist thinker since Lenin.

GRICE, PAUL. 1913–1988

Paul Grice was a fellow and a tutor at St. John's College, Oxford University, from 1938 to 1967. He then taught philosophy at the University of California, Berkeley, until his death. Approaching philosophy in the post-Wittgensteinian mode through the study of ordinary language, Grice has been esteemed by the Anglo-American community of philosophers as "a miniaturist who changed the way other people paint big canvases" (*Times Literary Supplement*). Most of Grice's books are collections of articles. They have been influential among professional philosophers not only because they present important theories but also because they "scintillate" (HILARY PUTNAM's word), stimulating other philosophers to pick up the themes. The number of articles focused on Gricean themes has increased with each passing year.

BOOKS BY GRICE

The Conception of Value. OUP 1991 $45.00. ISBN 0-19-82449-9. A metaphysical defense of absolute values; considered the beginning of a new phase in philosophy.
Intentions and Uncertainty. 1972 o.p.
Studies in the Ways of Words. HUP 1989 $32.50. ISBN 0-674-85270-2. A carefully arranged and framed sequence of essays emphasizing not a certain set of ideas but a habit of mind, a style of philosophizing.

HABERMAS, JÜRGEN. 1929–

[SEE Chapter 9 in this volume.]

HARTSHORNE, CHARLES. 1897–

Charles Hartshorne was educated at Harvard University, where he coedited with PAUL WEISS the first six volumes of *The Collected Papers of Charles Sanders Peirce* (1931–36) and became associated with ALFRED NORTH WHITEHEAD. He has taught at Harvard, the University of Chicago, Emory University, and the University of Texas-Austin. Hartshorne is the undisputed leader in the development of process philosophy and theology since the death of Whitehead.

A consummate metaphysician, Hartshorne has resurrected the ontological argument for the existence of God, reframing it in terms of contemporary modal logic. He has espoused a doctrine of panpsychism, according to which mind (with feeling) permeates all things, and has defended the compatibility of this doctrine with contemporary physics. A pantheist, Hartshorne has proposed a complex theory of God, which views divinity as a relative, processional kind of being, with an abstract eternal nature and a concrete nature subject to change and suffering. He has presented his process theology in his widely read book *The Divine Relativity.*

In addition to his labors as teacher and philosophical author, Hartshorne is an avid birdwatcher and has written a prizewinning book, *Born to Sing: An Interpretation and World Survey of Bird Song.*

BOOKS BY HARTSHORNE

Anselm's Discovery: A Re-Examination of the Ontological Proof for God's Existence. Open Court 1973 $14.95. ISBN 0-87548-217-1. Readable interpretation of Anselm's profound and obscure argument for the existence of God.
Aquinas to Whitehead: Seven Centuries of Metaphysics of Religion. Aquinas Lectures Ser. Marquette 1976 $7.95. ISBN 0-87462-141-0. Insightful elaboration of a central theme in philosophy and religion.
Beyond Humanism: Essays in the Philosophy of Nature. Peter Smith 1975 repr. of 1937 ed. $11.50. ISBN 0-8446-5116-8. A collection of essays demonstrating that the twentieth-century revolution in science supports a new natural theology.
Born to Sing: An Interpretation and World Survey of Bird Song. 1973. Ind. U. Pr. 1992 $35.00. ISBN 0-253-32729-6
Creativity in American Philosophy. State U. NY Pr. 1985 $49.50. ISBN 0-87395-816-0. Original and controversial interpretation of American philosophy and its essential themes.
The Darkness and the Light: A Philosopher Reflects upon His Fortunate Career and Those Who Made It Possible. State U. NY Pr. 1990 $49.50. ISBN 0-7914-0337-8. "[V]ery informal autobiography . . . liberally laced with philosophical reflection" (*Choice*).

The Divine Relativity: A Social Conception of God. The Terry Lectures Ser. Yale U. Pr. 1982 $10.00. ISBN 0-300-02880-6. The basic text of process theology.

Insights and Oversights of Great Thinkers: An Evaluation of Western Philosophy. Suny Ser. in Systematic Philosophy. State U. NY Pr. 1983 $49.50. ISBN 0-87395-681-8. Idiosyncratic but illuminating interpretations of the history of philosophy.

The Logic of Perfection and Other Essays in Neoclassical Metaphysics. Open Court 1973 $8.95. ISBN 0-87548-037-3. Remarkable for its reformulation of the ontological argument for the existence of God in the symbolic calculi of mathematical logic.

A Natural Theology for Our Time. Open Court 1967 $9.95. ISBN 0-87548-239-2. Sketch of process theology and its ground in the science of nature.

Omnipotence and Other Theological Mistakes. State U. NY Pr. 1984 $34.50. ISBN 0-87395-770-9. Acute critique of conventional features of traditional conceptions of God.

Philosophers Speak of God. (coedited with William L. Reese). *Midway Repr. Ser.* 1953. U. Ch. Pr. 1976 $29.00. ISBN 0-226-31862-1. Selections from the history of thought on the nature of God; comprehensive and readable.

The Philosophy and Psychology of Sensation. Telegraph Bks. 1985 o.p. Comprehensive general theory of sensation, carefully constructed, supporting the claims of panpsychism.

Whitehead's Philosophy: Selected Essays, 1935–1970. U. of Neb. Pr. 1972 o.p. Essays by one of Whitehead's leading followers and commentators.

Wisdom as Moderation: A Philosophy of the Middle Way. SUNY Ser. in Philosophy. State U. Pr. 1987 $49.50. ISBN 0-88706-472-8. Hartshorne's "penultimate book on philosophy," of interest to his "more ardent fans" (*Choice*).

BOOKS ABOUT HARTSHORNE

Boyd, Gregory A. *Trinity and Process: A Critical Examination and Reconstruction of Hartshorne's Du-Polar Theism Towards a Trinitarian Metaphysics. Amer. Univ. Studies.* P. Lang Pubs. 1992 $56.95. ISBN 0-8204-1660-6. Profoundly interpretive monograph in process theology.

Cobb, John B., Jr., and Franklin I. Gramwell, eds. *Existence and Actuality: Conversations with Charles Hartshorne.* U. Ch. Pr. 1985 $20.00. ISBN 0-226-11122-9. [A] collection "containing Hartshorne's short autobiographical sketch, 'How I Got That Way,' and nine critical and appreciative essays, with his response to each" (*Ethics*).

Devaney, Sheila G. *Divine Power: A Study of Karl Barth and Charles Hartshorne. Harvard Dissertations in Religion Ser.* Fortress Pr. 1986 $16.95. ISBN 0-8006-7072-8. Scholarly comparative study of two outstanding twentieth-century theologians.

Goodwin, George L. *The Ontological Argument of Charles Hartshorne.* Scholars Pr. GA 1978 $14.95. ISBN 0-89130-288-X. Limited but thorough examination of Hartshorne's favorite argument for the existence of God.

Hahn Lewis E., ed. *The Philosophy of Charles Hartshorne. The Lib. of Living Philosophers.* Open Court 1991 $49.94. ISBN 0-8126-9147-4. Contains Hartshorne's intellectual autobiography, specialized essays by expert scholars, his responses, and a complete biography of Hartshorne's publications to the date of publication.

Morris, Randall C. *Process Philosophy and Political Ideology: The Social and Political Thought of Afred North Whitehead and Charles Hartshorne.* State U. NY Pr. 1991 $57.50. ISBN 0-7914-1415-3. A comparative exposition and critique of the sociopolitical ideas and implications of the two leading twentieth-century process philosophers.

Moskop, John C. *Divine Omniscience and Human Freedom: Thomas Aquinas and Charles Hartshorne.* Mercer Univ. Pr. 1984 $14.95. ISBN 0-86554-123-X. Dissertation comparing and critizing the doctrines of rival theologians set apart by the centuries.

Viney, Donald W. *Charles Hartshorne and the Existence of God. Philosophy Ser.* State U. NY Pr. 1985 $49.50. ISBN 0-87395-907-8. A critical interpretation of a central question in Hartshorne's philosophy.

Whitney, Barry L. *Evil and the Process God: The Problem of Evil in Charles Hartshorne's Thought. Toronto Studies in Theology.* E. Mellen 1985 $89.95. ISBN 0-88946-160-8. Dissertation on a crucial theme in Hartshorne's thought.

Wood, Forrest, Jr., and Michael DeArmey, eds. *Hartshorne's Neo-Classical Theology*. Tulane Studies in Philosophy 1986 o.p. Proceedings of a conference on Hartshorne held at the University of Southern Mississippi in 1985.

HEIDEGGER, MARTIN. 1889–1976

Although Martin Heidegger's early education was in scholastic philosophy, he became interested in EDMUND HUSSERL's phenomenology. Whereas Husserl's phenomenological investigations centered on cognition and bracketed existence, Heidegger expanded the subject matter for phenomenology, examining such noncognitive states as anxiety. Moreover, he employed the phenomenological method to illuminate ontology and resolve questions of existence.

After teaching at Marburg University, Heidegger went to Freiburg University as successor to Husserl. In 1933 he became the first National Socialist rector at Freiburg. Esteemed by many as the foremost twentieth-century philosopher, Heidegger has been tainted by his association with the Nazis. At Freiburg he concluded his lectures with the declaration: "Hell Hitler!" Nevertheless, during his final years, he was described in the *New York Times* as "everyman's conception of a German philosopher: ascetic, withdrawn, a trifle eccentric and virtually impossible to understand . . . [a] mixture of scholar and Black Forest peasant and he still favors breeches and heavy woolen stockings. From time to time he shows up at the University of Freiburg to hold crowd-attracting lectures. . . . Almost a recluse, Heidegger has been known to abuse callers who have gotten him on the phone, and to follow it up with an unfriendly letter. This does not happen often, because Heidegger has no phone of his own."

Heidegger's *Sein und Ziet*, first published in 1927, is one of the great classics of modern philosophy and a basic work in existentialism. It is a very difficult book even for a German reader, "full of coined expressions, puns, and resurrected obsolete terms" (*Library Journal*). Yet it found early acceptance by students in Germany, its doctrines gradually spreading to the rest of Europe.

Heidegger distinguished *Sein* (Being) from *Dasein* (Being there). *Dasein* implies that "man is possibility, he has the power to be. His existence is in his choice of the possibilities that are open to him, and since this choice is never final, once for all, his existence is indeterminate because not terminated. . . . The mode of existence of the human being . . . is being-in-the-world . . . the being of a self in its inseparable relations with a not-self, the world of things and other persons in which the self always and necessarily finds itself inserted" (H. J. Blackham, *Six Existentialist Thinkers*). This stark view of the individual confronting absolute nothingness has been paradigmatic for twentieth-century atheistic existentialism. The later Heidegger, with his mystical references to the concealment of Being, opened the door to theism.

Heidegger's philosophy has been advanced by means of a reinterpretation of the entire Western philosophical tradition since the pre-Socratics. Despite the opposition of specialist scholars, his work has been received as an achievement of contemporary hermeneutics. Meanwhile, his own mode of expression, intermixing philosophical jargon with the German slang of his time, has inspired countless commentaries. No twentieth-century philosopher has been the subject of as many books, monographs, and articles.

BOOKS BY HEIDEGGER

The Basic Problems of Phenomenology. Trans. by Albert Hofstadter. *Studies in Phenomenology and Existential Philosophy*. Ind. U. Pr. 1982 $45.00. ISBN 0-253-17686-7. Authoritative, if abstruse, work in excellent English translation.

Basic Writings. Ed. by David F. Krell. Harper SF 2nd rev. ed. 1977 $13.95. ISBN 0-06-063845-1. An anthology of selections that offers a good place to begin.

Being and Time. 1927. Trans. by John Macquarrie and Edward Robinson. Harper SF 1962 $26.00. ISBN 0-06-063850-8. The first translation into English of *Sein und Zeit*, "reflect[ing] the original style and spirit as well as the substance, with a marked consistency of vocabulary aided by a glossary of German expressions and several indexes" (*Library Journal*).

Discourse on Thinking. Trans. by John M. Anderson and E. Hans Freund. HarpC 1969 $10.00. ISBN 0-06-131459-5. "Can be recommended to the lay reader who wants a brief introduction to Heidegger" (*Library Journal*).

Early Greek Thinking: The Dawn of Western Philosophy. Trans. by David F. Krell and Frank A. Capuzzi. Harper SF 1985 $9.95. ISBN 0-06-063842-7. Controversial interpretation of the pre-Socratics.

Existence and Being. Regnery Gateway 1949 $8.95. ISBN 0-89526-935-X. A collection of essays that, in English translation, introduced Heidegger to an Anglo-American audience.

Hegel's Phenomenology of Spirit. Trans. by Parvis Emad and Kenneth Maly. *Studies in Phenomenology and Existential Philosophy.* Ind. U. Pr. 1988 $29.95. ISBN 0-253-32766-0. "[T]he text of Heidegger's 1930–31 university lectures on the opening chapters of Hegel's first major work . . . represent[ing] Heidegger's most sustained treatment of Hegel" (*Library Journal*).

Heraclitus Seminar. (coauthored with Eugen Fink). Trans. by Charles H. Seibert. *Studies in Phenomenology and Existential Philosophy.* Northwestern U. Pr. 1992 $14.95. ISBN 0-8101-1067-9

History of the Concept of Time: Prolegomena. Studies in Phenomenology and Existential Philosophy. Ind. U. Pr. 1992 $45.00. ISBN 0-253-32730-X

An Introduction to Metaphysics. 1953. Trans. by Ralph Manheim. *Master Works of Literature Ser.* Yale U. Pr. 1959 $12.00. ISBN 0-300-01740-5. This reworked text of lectures delivered at the University of Heidelberg in 1935 contains two favorable allusions to Nazism.

Kant and the Problem of Metaphysics. Trans. by Richard Taft. *Studies in Continental Thought.* Ind. U. Pr. 1990 $35.00. ISBN 0-253-32719-9

The Metaphysical Foundations of Logic. Trans. by Michael Heim. *Studies in Phenomenology and Existential Philosophy.* Ind. U. Pr. 1992 $29.95. ISBN 0-253-33783-6. Obscurantist critique of logic in good translation.

Nietzsche. 1961. Trans. by David F. Krell. Pt. One, Vols. 1 and 2. 2 vols. Harper SF 1991 $16.95. ISBN 0-06-063841-9. Pt. Two, Vols. 3 and 4. 2 vols. Harper SF 1991 $16.95. ISBN 0-06-063794-3. Voluminous investigations that convey more about the thinking of the author than of his subject.

On the Way to Language. Ed. by J. Glenn Gray and Fred D. Wieck. Trans. by Peter Hertz. HarpC 1982 $10.95. ISBN 0-06-06-3859. Preliminary to the understanding of language in the Heideggerian mode.

On Time and Being. Trans. by Joan Stambaugh. HarpC 1978 $10.00. ISBN 0-06-131941-4. "[C]ontains four items: a 1962 lecture, 'Time and Being'; a seminar report on it by Alfred Guzzani; a 1969 lecture, 'The End of Philosophy and the Task of Thinking'; a 1963 festschrift essay, 'My Way to Phenomenology'" (*Library Journal*).

Parmenides. Studies in Continental Thought Ser. Trans. by Andre Schuwer and Richard Roycewicz. Ind. U. Pr. 1992 $29.95. ISBN 0-253-32726-1

Poetry, Language, Thought. Trans. by Albert Hofstadter. HarpC 1975 $11.00. ISBN 0-06-090430-5. "Indispensable addition to Heidegger in English and required reading for anyone interested in philosophy" (*Choice*).

The Principle of Reason. Studies in Continental Thought Ser. Trans. by Reginald Lilly. Ind. U. Pr. 1992 $27.50. ISBN 0-253-32724-5. "Heidegger's important and influential 1955–56 seminar . . . in an accurate and readable English translation" (*Choice*).

The Question of Being. Trans. by William Kluback and Jean T. Wilde. *Master Works of Literature Ser.* 1958 $7.95. ISBN 0-8084-0319-2. Basic ontology with a tendency to obscurantism.

The Question Concerning Technology and Other Essays. Trans. by William Lovitt. HarpC
    1982 $12.00. ISBN 0-06-131969-4. Influential work contributing to the current
    hostility of humanistic intellectuals toward technology.
Schelling's Treatise on the Essence of Human Freedom. Trans. by Joan Stambaugh.
    Continental Thought Ser. Ohio U. Pr. 1985 $26.95. ISBN 0-8214-0690-6. Heideggerian
    hermeneutics exercised on the nineteenth-century German romantic idealist's most
    coherent major tract.
What Is Called Thinking? Trans. by J. Glenn Gray and Fred D. Wieck. HarpC 1972 $12.00.
    ISBN 0-06-090528-X. "A translation of lectures from 1952 that are as near a
    definitive statement of Heidegger's new period that can be found" (*Library Journal*).
What Is a Thing? Trans. by W. B. Barton, Jr., and Vera Deutsch. Regnery Gateway 1968
    $5.95. ISBN 0-89526-979-1. "[I]mportant in its own right, without reference to the
    clarification of the history of Heidegger's thought which it can provide: . . .
    investigates . . . tools, man, works of art, the state, and the world" (*Library Journal*).
What Is Philosophy? Trans. by William Kluback and Jean T. Wilde. *Master Works of
    Literature Ser.* NCUP 1956 $7.95. ISBN 0-8084-0319-2. Metaphilosophy in the
    puzzling mode of questioning.

BOOKS ABOUT HEIDEGGER

Ballard, Bruce W. *The Role of Mood in Heidegger's Ontology.* U. Pr. of Amer. 1990 $32.50.
    ISBN 0-8191-7978-7. A specialist's treatment of a crucial aspect of Heidegger's
    philosophy.
Behler, Ernest. *Confrontations: Derrida-Heidegger-Nietzsche.* Trans. by Steven Taube-
    neck. Stanford U. Pr. 1991 $35.00. ISBN 0-8047-1945-4. A difficult but rewarding
    interpretation of three thinkers at the crossroads of modernity/postmodernity by a
    prominent German critical theorist.
Bernasconi, Robert. *The Question of Language in Heidegger's History of Being.* Humani-
    ties 1985 $39.95. ISBN 0-391-03093-0. "[C]haracterizes Heidegger's account of the
    history of Being and differentiates it from Hegel's history of spirit" (*The Philosopher's
    Index*).
Bernstein, Richard J. *The New Constellation: The Ethical-Political Horizons of Modernity-
    Postmodernity.* MIT Pr. 1992 $35.00. ISBN 0-262-02337-7. More than a book on
    Heidegger, a brilliant interpretation of the intellectual scene in the late twentieth
    century by a leading philosopher with a mastery of American and European thought.
Bonsor, Jack A. *Rahner, Heidegger and Truth: Karl Rahner's Notion of Truth, The
    Influence of Heidegger.* U. Pr. of Amer. 1987 $40.75. ISBN 0-8191-6159-4. Primarily
    on the twentieth-century Catholic theologian's intellectual debt to Heidegger.
Bourdieu, Pierre. *The Political Ontology of Martin Heidegger.* Trans. by Peter Collier.
    Stanford U. Pr. 1991 $22.50. ISBN 0-8047-1698-0. "[U]ses sociological and linguistic
    insights to challenge readings of Heidegger's philosophy which either ignore
    politics, or, alternatively overinterpret . . . [his] Nazi sympathies" (*The Philosopher's
    Index*).
Bruns, Gerald L. *Heidegger's Estrangements: Language, Truth, and Poetry in the Later
    Heidegger.* Yale U. Pr. 1989 $28.00. ISBN 0-300-64420-8. "[A] very important study of
    Heidegger's 'later' views on language, poetry, and thinking as they are found in
    Poetry, Language, Thought (1971) and *On the Way to Language* (1971)" (*Choice*).
Caputo, John D. *The Mystical Element in Heidegger's Thought.* Ohio U. Pr. 1978 $28.95.
    ISBN 0-8214-0372-9. Splendid disquisition on Heidegger's mysticism.
Dallmayr, Fred. *Between Frieburg and Frankfurt: Toward a Critical Ontology.* U. of Mass.
    Pr. 1991 $35.00. ISBN 0-87023-764-0. Focuses on "two continental schools of
    thought: [t]he 'Freiburg School' represented chiefly by Heidegger and the 'Frankfurt
    School' of critical theory represented chiefly by Habermas and Adorno" (*The
    Philosopher's Index*).
Dreyfus, Hurbert L. *Being-in-the-World: A Commentary on Heidegger's Being and Time,
    Division I.* MIT Pr. 1990 $16.95. ISBN 0-262-54056-8. Helpful guide by a leading
    American thinker.

Farrias, Victor. *Heidegger and Nazism*. Ed. by Joseph Margolis and Tom Rockmore. Trans. by Paul Burrell and Gabriel R. Ricci. Temple U. Pr. 1989 $29.95. ISBN 0-87-722-640-7. Exposition of Heidegger's Nazism, which led to an explosion of publications.

Ferry, Luc, and Alain Renault. *Heidegger and Modernity*. Trans. by Franklin Philip. U. Ch. Pr. 1990 $16.95. ISBN 0-226-24462-8. "A lively and brisk book, with a good summary of the issues (concerning Heidegger's relations to Nazism), well written and translated" (*Choice*).

Foti, Veronique M. *Heidegger and the Poets: Poiesis/Sophia/Techné*. Humanities 1992 $35.00. ISBN 0-391-03720-X. "[Guides us through Heidegger's lectures and seminars on Hölderlin, Mörike, Trakl, and Rilke" (*Choice*).

Fynsk, Christopher. *Heidegger: Thought and Historicity*. Cornell Univ. Pr. 1986 $29.95. ISBN 0-8014-1879-8. Lucid and coherent monograph on Heidegger's conception of history and its relation to philosophical thought.

Gelven, Michael. *A Commentary on Heidegger's Being and Time*. N. Ill. U. Pr. rev. ed. 1989 $30.00. ISBN 0-87580-145-5. "[A] section-by-section commentary on *Being and Time* which has been well received for twenty years because it is clearly written" (*The Philosopher's Index*).

Graybeal, Jean. *Language and the "Feminine" in Nietzsche and Heidegger*. Ind. U. Pr. 1990 $24.95. ISBN 0-253-32628-1. "[A]rgues that the writings of Nietzsche and Heidegger are important for contemporary discussions about what it means to be women and men" (*The The Philosopher's Index*).

Guignon, Charles B. *Heidegger and the Problem of Knowledge*. Hackett 1983 $32.50. ISBN 0-915145-21-9. Perceptive discussion of the epistemological problems in Heidegger's philosophy.

Halliburton, David. *Poetic Thinking: An Approach to Heidegger*. U. Ch. Pr. 1982 $22.50. ISBN 0-226-31372-7. Engrossing approach through poetry and the German philosopher's use of language, of special interest to students of literary criticism.

Hans, James S. *The Question of Value: Thinking Through Nietzsche, Heidegger, and Freud*. S. Ill. U. Pr. 1989 $24.95. ISBN 0-8093-1506-8. "[W]eaves together key ideas of Nietzsche, Heidegger, and Freud in an engaging essay in nondeconstructionist cultural criticism" (*Choice*).

Kaelin, E. F. *Heidegger's Being and Time: A Reading for Readers*. U. Press Fla. 1988 $34.95. ISBN 0-8130-0865-4. "[A] careful and insightful commentary on Heidegger's magnum opus" (*Choice*).

Kockelmans, Joseph J. *Heidegger's Being and Time: The Analytic of Dasein as Fundamental Ontology*. Current Continental Research Ser. U. Pr. of Amer. 1989 $51.50. ISBN 0-8191-7599-4. A profoundly critical examination of a difficult subject.

_____. *On the Truth of Being: Reflections on Heidegger's Later Philosophy*. Studies in Phenomenology and Existential Philosophy. Ind. U. Pr. 1985 $29.95. ISBN 0-253-34245-7. Reflective investigations of key elements in Heidegger's post-World II thinking.

Kolb, David. *The Critique of Pure Modernity: Hegel, Heidegger, and After*. U. Ch. Pr. 1988 $25.00. ISBN 0-226-45031-7. Scholarly interpretation of the responses to modernity by the dominant modes of idealism and existentialism in recent thought.

Krell, David F. *Daimon Life: Heidegger and Life-Philosophy*. Studies in Continental Thought. Ind. U. Pr. 1992 $39.95. ISBN 0-253-33147-1. A distinguished addition to the canon.

_____. *Intimations of Mortality: Time, Truth, and Finitude in Heidegger's Thinking of Being*. Pa. St. U. Pr. 1986 $22.50. ISBN 0-271-00427-4. Probing examination of Heideggerian ethics.

Lacoue-Labarthe, Phillippe. *Heidegger, Art and Politics: The Fiction of the Political*. Trans. by Chris Turner. Blackwell Pubs. 1990 $49.80. ISBN 0-631-16702-1. A perceptive interpretation of Heidegger's political theory and affiliations—with, for example, National Socialism—by a contemporary French intellectual.

Langan, Thomas. *The Meaning of Heidegger: A Critical Study of an Existentialism Phenomenology.* Greenwood 1983 repr. of 1959 ed. $43.75. ISBN 0-313-24124-4. Brilliant introductory exposition and commentary.

Llewelyn, John. *The Middle Voice of Ecological Conscience: A Chiasmic Reading of Responsibility in the Neighborhood of Levinas, Heidegger and Others.* St. Martin 1991 $45.00. ISBN 0-312-06173-0. Highly interpretive work threading together themes centering on the environment.

McWhorter, La Delle. *Heidegger and the Earth: Issues in Environmental Philosophy.* TJU Pr. 1990 $35.25. ISBN 0-943549-08-6. Develops the implications of Heidegger's thought for environmental ethics.

Mulhall, Stephen. *On Being in the World: Wittgenstein and Heidegger on Seeing Aspects.* Routledge 1990 $52.50. ISBN 0-415-014416-2. "[A]ttempts to do several things, with mixed success. . . . For graduate audiences with some knowledge of Wittgenstein's philosophy" (*Choice*).

Neske, Gunther, and Emil Kettering. *Martin Heidegger and National Socialism: Questions and Answers.* Trans. by Lisa Harries. Paragon Hse. 1990 $29.95. ISBN 1-55778-310-1. Contains "contributions pro and con concerning the extent of Heidegger's association with Nazism] by more than a dozen distinguished scholars (including Hannah Arendt, Hans-George Gadamer, Jacques Derrida, Karl Lowith, Hans Jonas)" (*Library Journal*).

Nicholson, Graeme. *Illustrations of Being: Drawing upon Heidegger and upon Metaphycis. Contemporary Studies in Philosophy and the Human Sciences.* Humanities 1992 $49.95. ISBN 0-391-03738-2. A foray into fundamental ontology.

Nordquist, Joan, ed. *Martin Heidegger: A Bibliography. Social Theory: A Bibliographic Ser.* Ref. Rsch. Serv. 1990 $15.00. ISBN 0-937855-33-2. An indispensable research tool.

Okrent, Mark. *Heidegger's Pragmatism: Understanding Being and the Critique of Metaphysics.* Cornell Univ. Pr. 1987 $30.00. ISBN 0-8014-2094-6. Argues for "the essentially pragmatic nature of the early Heidegger's discussion of understanding . . . [and] shows that Heidegger's subsequent critique of metaphysics follows directly from his long-held pragmatic understanding of intentionality" (*The Philosopher's Index*).

Parkes, Graham, ed. *Heidegger and Asian Thought.* UH Pr. 1990 $12.95. ISBN 0-8248-1312-X. Essays by 12 scholars (from 7 countries), who discuss Heidegger's thinking in relation to Vedanta, Taoism, Zen, and Tibetan Buddhist philosophy.

Rapaport, Herman. *Heidegger and Derrida: Reflections on Time and Language.* U. of Nebr. Pr. 1989 $32.50. ISBN 0-8032-3887-8. "[F]ocuses on the convergence of literature and ontology and their divergence" (*The Philosopher's Index*).

Richardson, Joseph. *Heidegger. Phaenomenologica Ser.* Kluwer Ac. 1974 $76.00. ISBN 90-247-0246-1. Monumental commentary, second to none in the field.

Robinson, James M., and John B. Cobb, Jr., eds. *The Later Heidegger and Theology.* Greenwood 1979 repr. of 1963 ed. $38.50. ISBN 0-313-20783-6. A collection of scholarly essays examining Heidegger's early atheism and later theism.

Rockmore, Tom, and Joseph Margolis, eds. *The Heidegger Case: On Philosophy and Ethics.* Temple U. Pr. 1992 $49.95. ISBN 0-87722-907-4. A collection of critical essays centering on Heidegger's Nazism.

Rorty, Richard. *Essays on Heidegger and Others: Philosophical Papers.* Vol. 2 Cambridge U. Pr. 1991 $42.95. ISBN 0-521-35370-X. "[C]ontends that the European philosophers who rank as Nietzsche's principal successors, most notably Heidegger and Derrida, can be viewed as quite similar to the American pragmatists" (*Library Journal*).

Sallis, John. *Echoes: After Heidegger. Studies in Continental Thought Ser.* Ind. U. Pr. 1990 $27.95. ISBN 0-253-35058-1. "[M]obilizes the figure of echo, used by Heidegger to characterize ordinary thinking, as the motif around which to organize a radical reading of Heidegger's most important texts" (*The Philosopher's Index*).

———, ed. *Reading Heidegger: Commemorations. Studies in Continental Thought.* Ind. U. Pr. 1992 $45.00. ISBN 0-253-35053-0. A collection of perceptive essays edited by the Vanderbilt philosopher.

Schmidt, Dennis J. *The Ubiquity of the Finite: Hegel, Heidegger, and the Entitlements of Philosophy. Studies in Contemporary German Social Thought.* MIT Pr. 1990 $9.95. ISBN 0-262-69139-6. "[A]sks how Heidegger can claim to have destroyed metaphysics despite Hegel's claim to have perfected its possibilities" (*The Philosopher's Index*).

Schrift, Alan. *Nietzsche and the Question of Interpretation.* Routledge 1990 $39.95. ISBN 0-415-90311-4. "A fine addition to Nietzsche scholarship [via a discussion of] Heidegger's and Derrida's methods of interpretation through an exegesis of their respective interpretations of Nietzsche" (*Choice*).

Schurman, Reiner. *Heidegger on Being and Acting: From Principles to Anarchy. Studies in Phenomenology and Existential Philosophy.* Ind. U. Pr. 1986 $39.95. ISBN 0-253-32721-0. "[A] comprehensive interpretation of Heidegger from the perspective of the question, 'What is to be done at the end of metaphysics?'" (*The Philosopher's Index*).

Shahan, Robert W., and J. N. Mohanty, eds. *Thinking about Being: Aspects of Heidegger's Thought.* U. of Okla. Pr. 1984 $23.95. ISBN 0-8061-1780-X. A collection of articles originally published in the *Southwestern Journal of Philosophy.*

Stambaugh, Joan. *The Finitude of Being. SUNY Ser. on Contemporary Continental Philosophy.* State U. NY Pr. 1992 $44.50. ISBN 0-7914-1105-2. Penetrating metaphysical essay inspired by Heideggerian thoughts.

Standish, Paul. *Beyond the Self: Wittgenstein, Heidegger, and the Limits of Language. Ser. in Philosophy.* Ashgate Pub. Co. 1992 $59.95. ISBN 1-85628-271-6. An unusual reflection on the philosophical implications of two giants of twentieth-century thought.

Steiner, George. *Martin Heidegger.* U. Ch. Pr. 1987 $10.95. ISBN 0-226-77232-2. Brilliant interpretation by a stellar literary critic.

Tamineaux, Jacques. *Heidegger and the Project of Fundamental Ontology.* Ed. and trans. by Michael Gendre. *SUNY Ser. in Contemporary Continental Philosophy.* State U. NY Pr. 1991 $49.50. ISBN 0-7914-0685-7. Lucid and basic study.

Tropea, Gregory. *Religion, Ideology and Heidegger's Concept of Falling. Amer. Academy of Religion Ser.* Scholars Pr. GA 1987 $20.95. ISBN 1-55540-041-8. A dissertation for advanced students.

Versenyl, Laszlo. *Heidegger, Being, and Truth.* Bks. Demand $54.50. ISBN 0-317-09090-9. A classic early study on Heidegger's theory of truth.

White, David A. *Heidegger and the Language of Poetry.* U. of Nebr. Pr. 1989 $25.00. ISBN 0-8032-4703-6. Of particular interest to students of poetry and literary criticism.

————. *Logic and Ontology in Heidegger.* Ohio U. Pr. 1986 $36.75. ISBN 0-8142-0396-5. Insightful specialized monograph on major Heideggerian concerns.

Wolin, Richard. *The Politics of Being: The Political Thought of Martin Heidegger.* Col. U. Pr. 1990 $29.50. ISBN 0-231-07314-3. "[A]rgues that Heidegger's 'decision for National Socialism, though hardly a necessary outgrowth of his philosophical texts, cannot be understood apart from the most fundamental categories of his philosophy'" (*The Philosopher's Index*).

Wyschogrod, Edith. *Spirit in Ashes: Hegel, Heidegger, and Man-Made Mass Death.* Yale U. Pr. 1990 $12.95. ISBN 0-300-04622-7. Sensitive assessment of the great philosophers and the implications of their thinking for the Holocaust.

Zimmerman, Michael. *Heidegger's Confrontation with Modernity: Technology, Politics, and Art. The Indiana Ser. in Philosophy of Technology.* Ind. U. Pr. 1990 $39.95. ISBN 0-253-36875-8. Profound examination and critique of Heidegger's thought in regard to crucial contemporary concerns.

HOCKING, WILLIAM ERNEST. 1873–1966

Influenced by both WILLIAM JAMES (see also Vols. 3 and 5) and JOSIAH ROYCE, as well as by early initiation into science and engineering, William Ernest Hocking described his philosophical thinking as composed of "realism . . . mysticism . . . idealism also, its identity not broken." He once said, "I wish to discern what character our civilizations, now unsteadily merging into a single

world civilization, are destined to take in the foreseeable future, assuming that
we have a foreseeable future."

The Harvard "President's Report" (1965–66) said of him that he was "a
scholar who bridged the years from the admired era of SANTAYANA, Palmer,
Royce and James to our own times. His school of thought has been called
objective idealism, or in his own words 'non-materialistic realism,' a kind of
blend of the pragmatic and the idealistic. His first book, *The Meaning of God in
Human Experience* (1912), which drew on James's pragmatism and Royce's
idealism, established his reputation and became a classic in the region between
philosophy and theology. This was the beginning of a long line of books and
articles that for half a century brought his characteristic 'warmth, clarity and
insight' (in the worlds of a colleague) to a variety of human problems ranging
from ethics to education. A sampling of [his] titles will suggest the reach of his
ecumenical temper. . . . Mr. Hocking graduated from the College in 1901 and
took his doctorate in 1904. After a period at Berkeley and at New Haven, he
returned here as Professor of Philosophy in 1914 and five years later was elected
to the Alford Chair. Although he became *Emeritus* in 1943, he remained active
and intellectually alert to the end of his life, conducting a large and lively
correspondence with friends, colleagues and students the world over and
lending the kindly sagacity of a great teaching mind to countless admiring
younger men and women."

BOOKS BY HOCKING

Freedom of the Press. Civil Liberties in Amer. History. Da Capo 1974 repr. of 1947 ed.
    $29.50. Comprehensive treatment of the topic.
Human Nature and Its Remaking. 1923. AMS Pr. 1982 repr. of 1929 ed. $37.00. ISBN 0-
    404-59187-6. Highly original philosophy stressing the primacy of will.
The Lasting Elements of Individualism. AMS Pr. 1980 repr. of 1937 ed. $14.00. ISBN 0-
    404-59188-4. Vigorous defense of liberalism against the then ascendant totalitarian-
    isms.
Living Religions and a World Faith. Hibbert Lecture Ser. AMS Pr. 1980 repr. of 1940 ed.
    $28.50. ISBN 0-404-59189-2. Comparative studies in search of common religious
    ground.
Man and the State. Elliots Bks. 1958 repr. of 1926 ed. $37.50. ISBN 0-686-83615-4.
    Elegantly written, systematic idealist political philosophy.
The Meaning of God in Human Experience. Yale U. Pr. 1912 o.p. Influential work in the
    philosophy of religion drawing on James's pragmatism and Royce's idealism.
The Meaning of Immortality in Human Experience, Including Thoughts on Life and Death.
    Greenwood rev. ed. 1982 $45.00. ISBN 0-8371-6621-7. Imaginative metaphysical
    essays, containing proofs of man's immortality.
Present Status of the Philosophy of Law and of Rights. Rothman 1986 repr. of 1926 ed.
    $22.50 ISBN 0-8377-2234-9. Critical monograph of contemporary legal theory as
    bearing on rights.
The Self, Its Body, and Freedom. AMS Pr. 1980 repr. of 1928 ed. $13.00. ISBN 0-404-
    59191-4. Idealist metaphysics, clearly written but profound in content.
What Man Can Make of Man. AMS Pr. 1980 repr. of 1942 ed. $18.00. ISBN 0-404-59192-2.
    Concise essay on human possibilities optimistically appreciated.

BOOKS ABOUT HOCKING

Furse, Margaret. *Experience and Certainty: William Ernest Hocking and Philosophical
    Mysticism. Studies in Religion*. Scholars Pr. GA 1988 $16.95. ISBN 1-55540-164-3.
    "[A]n exposition of the thought on the subject of mysticism . . . [examining concepts
    of] . . . experience, doubt, certainty, and the ideas of William James and Josiah
    Royce" (*The Philosopher's Index*).

Rouner, Leroy S. *Within Human Experience: The Philosophy of William Ernest Hocking*. HUP 1969 o.p. "[T]he essence of Hocking's 17 books and 270 essays. . . . a fairly readable introduction to this Weltanschauung" (*Choice*).

HOOK, SIDNEY. 1902–1989

Sidney Hook was born and educated in New York City and taught, very early in his career, in the city's public schools. MORRIS COHEN was among his teachers at City College; he later studied under JOHN DEWEY (see also Vol. 3) at Columbia University, where he received his Ph.D. in 1927. He immediately began teaching at New York University, where he subsequently served as chairman of the philosophy department at the Washington Square College, head of the graduate department, and head of the all-university department, retiring from this post in May 1968. At his retirement ceremony, one of his colleagues recalled Hook's remark, "I've had a wonderful week, a fight every day." BRAND BLANSHARD called Hook "that inexhaustible geyser of books, lectures, and essays, a philosopher who scents the smell of battle from afar and is soon in the midst of it, giving as well as he gets, and usually somewhat better."

An early Marxist in his fervent desire for social reform, Hook was deeply impressed by his teachers Cohen and Dewey. He continued to espouse a form of Marxism that he termed "democratic socialism." Hook was an early anti-Communist, denouncing communism as practiced in the Soviet Union. Hook opposed all intolerant ideologues. For example, he was an early critic of Joseph Stalin, but bitterly opposed the American senator Joseph McCarthy, a major anti-Communist politician of the early 1950s. During the 1960s and 1970s, Hook advocated extremely conservative views on foreign policy and domestic issues. He opposed affirmative action and preferential hiring of minorities.

"As a philosopher, Hook's most distinctive contribution is his theory of democracy. . . . On occasions too numerous to count, Hook has attempted to elucidate the objective meaning of democracy, to canvas the objections raised against it, to marshal the arguments in its behalf, and, as behooves the philosopher, to examine the kinds of theoretical justifications that from time to time come forth in its support. . . . His early books, *Towards the Understanding of Karl Marx* and *From Hegel to Marx*, are by far the best expository, interpretive, historical, and critical studies of KARL MARX's (see also Vol. 3) thought ever written by an American philosopher. . . . Persistently criticizing the historical determinism of orthodox Marxism, Hook argues that history contains the contingent and the unforeseen and, further, that individual men play important roles in the making of history" (Andrew Reck, *The New American Philosophers*). *The Hero in History* features this idea.

The *New York Times* said of him: "a pragmatist who believes that all viable reform must come from within, he has had few rivals in his ability to launch and sustain a dialogue on the great issues of our time. He has made those dialogues memorable for their fireworks, whether the subject was nuclear physics or psychoanalysis, civil disobedience or the Bill of Rights—or a new form of tyranny over the mind of man." He defended the right of the scholar to remain "disengaged" in his search for truth, and attacked HERBERT MARCUSE for what Hook considered a new dogmatism.

Hook received Guggenheim Fellowships in 1928 and 1953 to study European philosophy, traveling to Russia and Germany, and was granted a Ford Foundation Fellowship in 1958 to study Asian philosophy and culture. As founder of New York University's Institute of Philosophy, he edited a series of volumes recording the symposia it conducted, symposia on the cutting edge of philosophical research (see above under "General Works." Hook also served as Thomas Jefferson Lecturer at the Library of Congress, the most distinguished appointment in the humanities to be offered by the federal government of the United States.

BOOKS BY HOOK

Common Sense and the Fifth Amendment. Constructive Action 1963 repr. of 1957 ed. $1.75. ISBN 0-911956-10-7. Polemic tract during the McCarthy era that criticized those who invoked the Fifth Amendment when questioned by congressional committees.

Convictions. Prometheus Bks. 1990 $25.95. ISBN 0-87975-473-7. Profession of a naturalist, humanist creed.

From Hegel to Marx: Studies in the Intellectual Development of Karl Marx. U. of Mich. Pr. 1962 repr. of 1936 ed. $14.95. ISBN 0-472-06066-X. In-depth essays on the German thinkers who led up to Marx from Hegel, organized around the theme of Marx's own development.

The Hero in History: A Study in Limitation and Possibility. Transaction Pubs. 1991 $29.95. ISBN 0-88738-428-5. A concise critical examination of the great man theory of history.

John Dewey: An Intellectual Portrait. Greenwood 1973 repr. of 1939 ed. $45.00. ISBN 0-8371-3951-1. A readable interpretation of Dewey's philosophy by a disciple who emphasized its affinity to Marxism.

Marx and the Marxists: The Ambiguous Legacy. Krieger 1982 repr. of 1955 ed. $9.50. ISBN 0-87874-443-1. Probes ways the humanism of Marx was betrayed by Soviet communism.

The Metaphysics of Pragmatism. AMS Pr. 1982 repr. of 1927 ed. $20.00. ISBN 0-404-59196-5. Dissertation on the fundamental categories implicit in Deweyan pragmatism.

Out of Step: An Unquiet Life in the Twentieth Century. Carroll & Graf 1988 $14.95. ISBN 0-88184-399-7. Intellectual autobiography.

The Paradoxes of Freedom. Prometheus Bks. 1987 $9.95. ISBN 0-87975-410-9. Provocative essay by an American Marxist-pragmatist who became the favorite intellectual of conservatives during the Nixon administration.

Philosophy and Public Policy. S. Ill. U. Pr. 1980 $13.95. ISBN 0-8093-1041-4. Pioneering investigation of the interplay of philosophy and public affairs.

The Quest for Being and Other Studies in Naturalism and Humanism. Prometheus Bks. 1991 $11.95. ISBN 0-87975-700-0. A materialistic naturalist objects to fashionable modes of metaphysical thinking, illustrated by Heidegger.

BOOKS ABOUT HOOK

Kurtz, Paul. *Sidney Hook and the Contemporary World: Essays on the Pragmatic Intelligence.* HarpC 1968 o.p. A collection of essays in honor of Hook on his sixty-fifth birthday, edited by a disciple who is also the leading American humanist.

————. *Sidney Hook: Philosopher of Democracy and Humanism.* Prometheus Bks. 1982 $29.95. ISBN 0-87975-300-5. A collection of essays in honor of Hook's eightieth birthday. 20 contributors, including Richard Rorty, Lewis Feuer, Ernest Nagel, David Sidorsky, Anthony Flew, Marvin Kohl, and Nicholas Capaldi.

JASPERS, KARL. 1883–1969

Karl Jaspers was one of the originators of German existentialism. He began his career as a psychiatrist but was increasingly concerned about philosophical and moral issues. His was "a lucid and flexible intelligence in the service of a genuine and passionate concern for mankind." Removed from his professorship at the University of Heidelberg by the Nazis in 1937, he was reinstated in 1945 on the approval of the American occupation forces. In 1949 he went to the

University of Basel. The *New York Times* wrote of him in his lifetime: "Jaspers shows himself . . . to be one of the most diligent and sensitive students of contemporary history. He has a good eye for the present because he knows what to fear in it—particularly the loss of individual freedom."

Jaspers was deeply concerned about the human condition, and in his book *The Future of Mankind* (1957), entitled in its updated edition *The Atom Bomb and the Future of Man* (1961), he attempted to arouse conscience in the face of the deadly danger of atomic warfare "at the same time . . . attempt[ing] to apply the principles of his philosophy to a new field, and to lay the foundations of a political philosophy" (*Times Literary Supplement*). After the German publication of this book, Jaspers was awarded the German Peace Prize at the 1958 Frankfurt Book Fair. HANNAH ARENDT (see also Vol. 3), who had been his student and a translator of some of his works, made the presentation.

Jaspers's multivolume work, *The Great Philosophers*—edited by Hannah Arendt, translated by Ralph Manheim, and published in English from 1962 to 1966—was hailed by the *Library Journal* as "a major work, a brilliant book . . . Jaspers defends the unity of philosophy and his aim is to make philosophy available to all, to provide the serous reader with a guide 'to the thinking of the great philosophers and to a personal encounter with them.'"

The obituary of Jaspers in the *New York Times* commented on his great personal courage: "As professor of philosophy at the University of Heidelberg he was outspoken against Hitlerism. The Nazis retired him in 1937, but they could not silence him short of killing him. And this they planned to do. Indeed, on the eve of the departure of Jaspers and his wife for a concentration camp, they were saved by the American Army's capture of Heidelberg in 1945. Restored to his professorship after the war, he was unsparing in criticism of Germans for their war guilt and for their genocidal campaigns against Jews and other minorities. . . . As for moral guilt, he argued that every individual is morally accountable for his deeds. 'It is never simply true that orders are orders,' he declared. . . . Dr. Jaspers' wife was Gertrud Mayer, whom he married in 1910. She was a Jew, and her husband's refusal to part from her was among the Nazis' indictments of Dr. Jaspers." The *Times* said in assessing him: "With SØREN KIERKEGAARD, MARTIN HEIDEGGER [see also Vol. 5], and JEAN-PAUL SARTRE [see also Vol. 2], Karl Jaspers was one of the makers and shapers of existentialist philosophy. For almost 50 years, in books, essays and lectures, he strove to give a personalist answer to modern man's questions about his own nature and the nature of existence."

BOOKS BY JASPERS

The Atom Bomb and the Future of Man. Trans. by E. B. Ashton. U. Ch. Pr. 1984 o.p.

General Psychopathology. 1922. Trans. by J. Hoenig and W. Hamilton. U. Ch. Pr. 1963 o.p. Authoritative textbook for its time.

The Great Philosophers. 2 vols. HarBraceJ 1962–66 o.p.

Kant. Trans. by Ralph Mannheim. HarBraceJ 1966. $7.95. ISBN 0-15-646685-6. Taken from *Great Philosophers*, Volume 1, pt. 3.

Karl Jaspers: Basic Philosophical Writings. Ed. by Leonard Ehrlich and others. Ohio U. Pr. 1986 $55.00. ISBN 0-8214-0712-0. A worthwhile anthology, selecting representative writings, recommended as the text for a seminar on Jaspers.

Man in the Modern Age. 1931. AMS Pr. 1978 repr. of 1933 ed. $28.50. ISBN 0-404-14558-2. Incisive critique of civilization in the aftermath of World War I; early analysis of alienation.

The Origin and Goal of History. Trans. by Michael Bullock. Greenwood 1977 repr. of 1953 ed. $41.50. ISBN 0-8371-8983-7. Perplexing but profound metaphysics of history.

Philosophy. Trans. by E. B. Ashton. Vol. 2 1970 $21.00. ISBN 0-226-3949. Vol. 3 1971 $14.00. ISBN 0-226-39494-8. Jaspers "takes his place among the major expositors of existential philosophy on the American scene" (*Choice*).

Philosophy of Existence. Trans. by Richard F. Grabau. U. of Pa. Pr. 1971 $15.95. ISBN 0-8122-1010-7. Excellent translation of basic work on existentialism.

Philosophy and the World. Trans. by E. B. Ashton. Regnery Gateway 1989 $10.95. ISBN 0-89526-757-8

Plato and Augustine. Trans. by Karl Manheim. HarBraceJ 1966 $4.95. ISBN 0-15-672035-3. Taken from *Great Philosophers* Volume 1, pt. 2.

Socrates, Buddha, Confucius and Jesus. Trans. by Ralph Manheim. HarBraceJ 1966 $5.95. ISBN 0-15-683580-0

Truth and Symbol. Masterworks of Lit. Ser. NCUP 1959 $7.95. ISBN 0-8084-0303-6. Surprisingly readable monograph on meaning and knowledge.

The Way to Wisdom: An Introduction to Philosophy. Trans. by Ralph Manheim. Yale U. Pr. 1954 $9.95. ISBN 0-300-00134-7. A summary of his philosophical beliefs, "a beautiful and puzzling book" (*Library Journal*).

BOOKS ABOUT JASPERS

O'Connor, Bernard F. *A Dialogue Between Philosophy and Religion: The Perspective of Karl Jaspers*. U. Pr. of Amer. 1988 $18.25. ISBN 0-8191-6863-7. A scholarly dissertation.

Schilpp, Paul Arthur, ed. *The Philosophy of Karl Jaspers. Lib. of Living Philosophers*. Open Court 1981 $39.95. ISBN 0-87548-361-5. Consists of Jaspers's philosophical autobiography, 24 essays by prominent philosophers on different aspects of Jasper's thought, his reply to comments and criticism, and a bibliography.

Wallraff, Charles F. *Karl Jaspers: An Introduction to His Philosophy*. Bks. Demand 1970 $65.00. ISBN 0-8357-6173-8. An accessible overview of Jaspers's philosophy, perhaps the best intellectual biography of the German philosopher in English.

Walters, Gregory J. *Karl Jaspers and the Role of "Conversion" in the Nuclear Age*. U. Pr. of Amer. 1988 $48.25. ISBN 0-8191-6836-X. A dissertation focused on Jaspers's religious response to the atomic bomb.

Young-Bruehl, Elisabeth. *Freedom and Karl Jaspers' Philosophy*. Yale U. Pr. 1981 o.p. "[A] scholarly, demanding work—in keeping with its subjects—and very worthwhile" (L. H. Brody).

KRIPKE, SAUL. 1940–

Born in Bay Shore, New York, the son of a rabbi (Myer Samuel) and a writer (Dorothy Karp), Saul Kripke demonstrated his genius to his startled parents when he was only 3 years old. He not only drew the logical consequences of ordinary beliefs, but also solved intricate problems in mathematics. As a child prodigy, he was presented by his father to distinguished mathematicians and philosophers, who were overwhelmed by his talents. His father introduced him at the age of 15 to a group of eminent mathematicians, headed by Haskell B. Curry. From his debut grew his first published article, "A Completeness Theorem in Modal Logic," which appeared in the *Journal of Symbolic Logic*.

Kripke's boyhood genius did not flicker out in the 1960s, when he studied at Harvard, Oxford, Princeton and Rockefeller University or, more accurately, when he worked independently at these institutions and had occasional contact with his surroundings. His academic training was unique. He ascended directly to full professorships, without ever earning a doctorate. In fact, his highest academic degree was a B.A. from Harvard University, which he received in 1962. Kripke never earned a doctorate, because no academician could be found to teach him. Consequently, the universities let him alone and admitted him to their faculties when he said he was ready.

Slow to publish his lectures, Kripke nonetheless released a few articles, which he published exclusively in technical journals of philosophy and mathematics. So far his work has extended the boundaries of the most abstruse field of analytic philosophy, modal logic. He is esteemed for having invented the quantitative formulations of modality and for having opened up the ontological territory of possible worlds. At the age of 36, he was appointed James McCosh Professor of Philosophy at Princeton University. Kripke's awards include a Fulbright Fellowship (1962), Guggenheim Fellowship (1968), and a Fellowship from the American Council of Learned Societies (1981). His work, esoteric as it may seem to a public acquainted with such "social" philosophers as John Dewey (see also Vol. 3) or Jean-Paul Sartre (see also Vol. 2), has created new fields in mathematical set theory and modal logic, which will generate Ph.D. theses for years to come.

Books by Kripke

Naming and Necessity. HUP 1980 $17.50. ISBN 0-674-59845-8. A landmark work on the theory of proper names.
Wittgenstein on Rules and Private Language. HUP 1982 $8.95. ISBN 0-674-95401-7. A penetrating if idiosyncratic monograph on the philosophy of the founder of linguistic analysis.

LEWIS, CLARENCE IRVING. 1883–1964

C. I. Lewis ranks among the most influential American academic philosophers. He spent most of his long career at Harvard University, guiding the education of many graduate students who later held faculty positions at American colleges and universities. As a very young professor, first at the University of California, at Berkeley and later at Harvard, Lewis established a national and international reputation in symbolic logic, to which he had been introduced in the early years of the century by his mentor Josiah Royce. Lewis wrote one of the early histories of symbolic logic, *A Survey of Symbolic Logic* (1918). Of more importance his dissatisfaction with the principle of material implication presented by Bertrand Russell (see also Vol. 5) and Alfred North Whitehead in *Principia Mathematica* inspired him to construct a system of strict implication, one of the earliest forms of modal logic. He presented this theory in a book he coauthored with Cooper Harold Langford, *Symbolic Logic* (1932).

Lewis is most famous for his articulation of a form of pragmatism known as conceptual pragmatism. A close student of Immanuel Kant, he was impressed with the role of a priori concepts in the interpretation of experience and the formation of knowledge. Critical of what he regarded as the neglect of formal conceptual structures by such philosophers as William James (see also Vols. 3 and 5) and John Dewey (see also Vol. 3) he upheld a doctrine of the a priori, but, unlike Kant, he stressed its pragmatic character. His epistemology of conceptual pragmatism was unfolded in his book *Mind and the World-Order* (1929).

When the American Philosophical Association met in 1945 for the first time after World War II, Lewis was invited to deliver its most prestigious lectures— the Paul Carus lectures. He addressed himself to the epistemological and valuational issues raised by the rising tide of logical positivism. He defended and elaborated a theory of meaning that denied its reducibility to the syntax of language. He drew sharp distinctions between the analytic and synthetic and articulated a theory of formal and empirical judgments. Against the noncognitivists he expounded a naturalistic theory of value judgments, published under the title *Analysis of Knowledge and Valuation*. Lewis's lectures prompted discussions in the professional journals of a quantity and quality that had never before been equaled in American philosophy.

BOOKS BY LEWIS

Analysis of Knowledge and Valuation. 1947 *Paul Carus Lecture Ser*. Open Court 1981 o.p.

Collected Papers of Clarence Irving Lewis. Ed. by John D. Goheen and John L. Mothershead. Stanford U. Pr. 1970 o.p. Scholarly edition of Lewis's papers, published for the most part in technical journals.

Mind and the World-Order: Outline of a Theory of Knowledge. Dover 1990 $9.95. ISBN 0-486-26564-1

Values and Imperatives: Studies in Ethics. Ed. by John Lange. Stanford U. Pr. 1969 $27.50. Lewis's writings on ethics; cogent and Kantian.

BOOKS ABOUT LEWIS

Rosenthal, Sandra. *The Pragmatic*. Fireside Bks. 1975 o.p. Dissertation on Lewis's theory of necessary knowledge.

Schilpp, Paul Arthur, ed. *The Philosophy of C. I. Lewis*. *Lib. of Living Philosophers*. Open Court 1968 $29.95. ISBN 0-87548-131-0. [C]ontains Lewis's philosophical autobiography, essays in various aspects of his philosophy by distinguished philosophers, his reply to his critics, and a bibliography.

LOVEJOY, ARTHUR ONCKEN. 1873–1962

Arthur Oncken Lovejoy, who was educated at the University of California at Berkeley and at Harvard University, taught at several American universities before going in 1910 to Johns Hopkins University, where he taught until his retirement in 1938. His major contributions were in epistemology and the history of ideas; he also helped organize the Association of American University Professors.

Lovejoy's earliest philosophical interests were in epistemology and metaphysics. In metaphysics he was a temporalist, and many of his writings are devoted to the nature of time and to the doctrines of philosophers and scientists on time. He firmly believed in the reality of time, including the reality of past time.

Epistemologically, Lovejoy was a critical realist. In this regard he was one of seven philosophers who contributed to *Essays in Critical Realism* (1920), a major cooperative effort signaling a school of thought that held that knowledge is about an independent reality but is mediated by representations or ideas. This view involves an epistemological dualism, and Lovejoy's book *The Revolt against Dualism* (1930) is the most penetrating critique of such philosophers as ALFRED NORTH WHITEHEAD and BERTRAND RUSSELL (see also Vol. 5), who attempted to supplant dualism with monism. It also presents a systematic defense of epistemological dualism and, further, of mind-body, or psychophysical, dualism.

Lovejoy was a pioneer in the field of intellectual history. Indeed, he was founding editor of the *Journal of the History of Ideas*. Lovejoy defined ideas as unit principles that persist through history and that ramify in a variety of fields, requiring cross-disciplinary studies. He himself was an expert practitioner of the method, his own book *The Great Chain of Being* remaining a classic of which contemporary scholars in the field must still take account.

BOOKS BY LOVEJOY

Essays in the History of Ideas. Greenwood 1978 repr. of 1948 ed. $35.00. ISBN 0-313-20504-3. Collection of previously published essays illustrating Lovejoy's unsurpassed erudition.

The Great Chain of Being: A Study of the History of an Idea. William James Lectures Ser. HUP 1936 $12.95. ISBN 0-674-36155-9. Classic interpretation of a major theme in Western philosophy.

The Reason, the Understanding, and the Time. Bks. Demand 1961 $56.00. ISBN 0-317-20645-1. Inimitable exploration of metaphysical themes in philosophy during the eighteenth and nineteenth centuries, illuminating Kant, Hegel, and Bergson.

Reflections on Human Nature. Johns Hopkins 1961 $12.95. ISBN 0-8018-0395-0. Study of moral philosophy during the seventeenth and eighteenth centuries as the background for understanding the works of the American founding fathers.

The Revolt against Dualism: An Inquiry Concerning the Existence of Ideas. 1930. *Paul Carus Lecture Ser.* Open Court 1960 $26.95. ISBN 0-87548-107-8

The Thirteen Pragmatisms and Other Essays. Greenwood 1963 o.p. A collection of scholarly essays by Lovejoy, published mainly during his early period when pragmatism was the primary target of his criticism.

Three Studies in Current Philosophical Questions. AMS Pr. repr. of 1914 ed. ISBN 0-404-59237-6

BOOKS ABOUT LOVEJOY

Kuntz, Paul G., and Marion Kuntz. *Jacob's Ladder and the Tree of Life: Concepts of Heirarchy and the Great Chain of Being.* Amer. Univ. Studies. P. Lang Pubs. 1987 $58.00. ISBN 0-8204-0233-8. Erudition on a theme developed by Lovejoy confirming, and comparable to, his own.

Wilson, Daniel J. *Arthur O. Lovejoy: An Annotated Bibliography.* Garland 1982 o.p. Useful and authoritative; indispensable to research on Lovejoy.

————. *Arthur O. Lovejoy and the Quest for Intelligibility.* 1980. A biography that focuses on Lovejoy's intellectual development and on the connections among the facets of his career.

MCTAGGART, JOHN MCTAGGART ELLIS. 1866–1925

John McTaggart was a British metaphysician who taught at Cambridge University from 1897 to 1923. He was one of the main figures in the school of Hegelianism that flourished in Great Britain from the third quarter of the nineteenth century well into the first quarter of the twentieth century. Though he ranks beside F. H. BRADLEY and Bernard Bosanquet, McTaggart espoused a peculiar brand of Hegelian idealism. On GEORG HEGEL (see also Vol. 3) he was a superb commentator, but never a slavish expositor. While he believed that reality is essentially spiritual, his idealism retreated from conjuring up absolutes. Rather, he insisted on the primacy of finite individual persons. His denial of the existence of time has continued to intrigue philosophers, and his *Nature of Existence* has incited the extensive critique of CHARLES DUNBAR BROAD, in what is perhaps the most celebrated instance in twentieth-century philosophy of an exceptionally prominent and influential thinker painstakingly and at length commenting on the work of another.

BOOKS BY MCTAGGART

Commentary on Hegel's Logic. Ibis Pub. VA 1968 repr. of 1910 ed. $14.00. ISBN 0-935005-50-1. Clearest introduction to Hegel's "greater logic" ever written.

Human Immortality and Pre-Existence. Kraus 1964 repr. of 1916 ed. $28.00. ISBN 0-527-59950-6. Idiosyncratic but cogent case for the transmigration of souls and reincarnation.

The Nature of Existence. 2 vols. 1921–27. Cambridge U. Pr. 1988. Vol. 1 $21.95. ISBN 0-521-35768-3. Vol. 2 $24.95. ISBN 0-521-35769-1. Systematic treatise on metaphysics, clearly expounded and cogently argued, containing such startling theses as the unreality of time.

Philosophical Studies. Ed. by S. V. Keeling. Ayer 1977 repr. of 1934 ed. $17.75. ISBN 0-
    8369-0660-8. Posthumously published collection of essays on a variety of topics.
Some Dogmas of Religion. Kraus 1968 repr. of 1906 ed. $23.00. ISBN 0-527-60000-8.
    Highly original, beautifully composed essays undermining the foundations of
    Christian theism.
Studies in Hegelian Cosmology. Ibis Pub. VA 1986 repr. of 1918 ed. $21.95. ISBN 0-
    935005-59-5. Brilliant, innovative interpretations of Hegel's philosophy, replacing
    the notion of the Absolute with the idea of the all-inclusive spiritual community.
Studies in Hegelian Dialectic. Russell 1964 o.p. Further original commentary on Hegel,
    focused on the German's methodology.

BOOKS ABOUT MCTAGGART

Broad, Charles Dunbar. *Examination of McTaggart's Philosophy.* 3 vols. 1933 o.p. The
    most intensive critique of one twentieth-century philosopher by another.
Geach, P. T. *Truth, Love, and Immortality: An Introduction to McTaggart's Philosophy.* U.
    CA Pr. 1979 $37.50. ISBN 0-520-03755-3. Keenly analytical monograph on perplex-
    ing themes in McTaggart composed subtly by a prominent British philosopher with
    the intention of providing an introduction.
Rochelle, Gerald. *The Life and Philosophy of J. McT. E. McTaggart, 1866–1925. Studies in
    the History of Philosophy.* E. Mellen 1991 $69.95. ISBN 0-7734-9692-0. A succinct
    overview and critique.

MARCEL, GABRIEL. 1889–1973

Gabriel Marcel has been described as a theistic or Christian existentialist.
Born in Paris of Protestant parents, he converted to Roman Catholicism in
1924. Prior to his conversion, he had immersed himself in idealism, as his first
book, a study of ROYCE's metaphysics, reveals. Before JASPERS and HEIDEGGER
(see also Vol. 5) were known to French intellectuals, Marcel had written about
themes central to existentialism, but with a religious twist. He had acknowledged concern for the vitality and pervasiveness of religious experience, and,
like MARTIN BUBER, he had pointed to the sociality of human experience, which
bears witness to the presence of the Divine.

For Marcel, Being involves participation. No one can be separated from the
whole of Being to which he or she is related. Nor can a person be reduced to
merely a facet of Being; for he or she is a concrete individual, with experience
that is immediate, spontaneous, unpredictable. Though entranced by the
mystery of existence, a person may illuminate it by means of philosophical
reflection.

BOOKS BY MARCEL

Being and Having: An Existentialist Diary. 1935. Trans. by Katherine Farrer. Peter Smith
    1949 o.p. The intimate record of one man's experience of his personal participation
    in fundamental Being.
Homo Viator: Introduction to a Metaphysic of Hope. Trans. by Emma Craufurd. Peter
    Smith 1962 repr. of 1951 ed. $16.75. ISBN 0-8446-2529-9. Christian existentialist
    theory, stressing hope instead of despair; an inspiration.
The Mystery of Being. Trans. by René Haugue. *Gifford Lectures.* 2 vols. in 1. AMS Pr. 1976
    repr. of 1951 ed. $44.50. ISBN 0-404-60504-4. Ontology demonstrating the limits of
    reason and the need for faith.
Philosophical Fragments: 1901–1914 and the Philosopher and Peace. U. of Notre Dame Pr.
    1965 $3.95. Early philosophical reflections that throw light on the philosopher's
    development from idealism to existentialism.
Philosophy of Existence. Trans. by Manya Harai. *Essay Index Repr. Ser.* Ayer 1978 repr. of
    1949 ed. $15.95. ISBN 0-8369-1094-X. Introduces existentialism from the Christian
    standpoint.

The Philosophy of Existentialism. Carol Pub. Group 1961 $4.95. ISBN 0-8065-0901-5. Restatement of Marcel's "philosophy of existence," contrasted with opposing or rival types of existentialism.

Royce's Metaphysics. Trans. by Virginia Ringer and Gordon Ringer. Greenwood 1981 repr. of 1956 ed. $39.75. ISBN 0-8371-7978-5. A profound dissertation on idealism.

Tragic Wisdom and Beyond. Trans. by Stephen Jolin and Peter McCormick. *Studies in Phenomenology and Existential Philosophy Ser.* Northwestern U. Pr. 1973 $14.95. ISBN 0-8101-0614-0. Excellently translated treatise on the interconnection of the moral and the metaphysical in human existence.

BOOKS ABOUT MARCEL

Cain, Seymour. *Gabriel Marcel.* Regnery Gateway 1979 $4.50. ISBN 0-89526-905-8. Readable, reliable portrait of Marcel's thought.

Gallagher, Kenneth T. *The Philosophy of Gabriel Marcel.* Fordham rev. ed. 1975 $14.00. ISBN 0-8232-0471-5. Approving foreword by Marcel.

McCown, Joe. *Availability: Gabriel Marcel and the Phenomenology of Human Openness.* Scholars Pr. GA 1978 $14.95. ISBN 0-89130-144-5. A dissertation on a central theme in Marcel's philosophy.

Schilpp, Paul Arthur, and Lewis E. Hahn, eds. *The Philosophy of Gabriel Marcel. Lib. of Living Philosophers.* Open Court 1984 $39.95. ISBN 0-87548-369-0. Marcel's reply to some of his major critics. . . . [and] also includes a bibliography of Marcel's writings prepared by François Lapointe and an intensely personal intellectual autobiography" (*The Philosopher's Index*).

MARCUSE, HERBERT. 1898–1984

[SEE Chapter 9 in this volume.]

MARITAIN, JACQUES. 1882–1973

T. S. ELIOT (see Vol. 1) once called Jacques Maritain "the most conspicuous figure and probably the most powerful force in contemporary philosophy." His wife and devoted intellectual companion, Raissa Maritain, was of Jewish descent but joined the Catholic church with him in 1906. Maritain studied under HENRI BERGSON but was dissatisfied with his teacher's philosophy, eventually finding certainty in the system of ST. THOMAS AQUINAS. He lectured widely in Europe and in North and South America, and lived and taught in New York during World War II. Appointed French ambassador to the Vatican in 1945, he resigned in 1948 to teach philosophy at Princeton University, where he remained until his retirement in 1953. He was prominent in the Catholic intellectual resurgence, with a keen perception of modern French literature. Although Maritain regarded metaphysics as central to civilization and metaphysically his position was Thomism, he took full measure of the intellectual currents of his time and articulated a resilient and vital Thomism, applying the principles of scholasticism to contemporary issues.

In 1963 Maritain was honored by the French literary world with the national Grand Prize for letters; he learned of the award at his retreat in a small monastery near Toulouse where he had been living in ascetic retirement for some years. In 1967 the publication of *The Peasant of the Garonne* disturbed the French Roman Catholic world. In it, Maritain attacked the "neo-modernism" that he had seen developing in the church in recent decades, especially since the Second Vatican Council. According to Jaroslav Pelikan, writing in the *Saturday Review of Literature*, "He laments that in avant-garde Roman Catholic theology today he can 'read nothing about the redeeming sacrifice or the merits of the Passion.' In his interpretation, the whole of the Christian tradition has identified redemption with the sacrifice of the cross. But now all of that is being discarded, along with the idea of hell, the doctrine of creation out of nothing, the infancy narratives of the Gospels, and belief in the immortality of the human soul."

Maritain's wife, Raissa, also distinguished herself as a philosophical author and poet. The project of publishing *Oeuvres Completes* of Jacques and Raissa Maritain has been in progress since 1982, with seven volumes now in print.

BOOKS BY MARITAIN

Approaches to God. Trans. by Peter O'Reilly. Greenwood 1978 repr. of 1954 ed. $45.00. ISBN 0-313-20606-6. Persuasive, clear-headed descriptions of how God can be reached.

Art and Scholasticism: With Other Essays. Trans. by J. F. Scanlon. *Essay Index Repr. Ser.* Ayer 1980 repr. of 1930 ed. $13.00. ISBN 0-8369-2241-7. Influential, insightful, informed account of the status, nature, and functions of art in neo-Thomist perspective.

Bergsonian Philosophy and Thomism. Greenwood 1968 repr. of 1955 ed. $45.00. ISBN 0-8371-0559-5. English translation of Maritain's doctoral dissertation, in which he rejected the temporalist, evolutionist philosophy of his teacher, Bergson, for the Roman Catholic philosophy of St. Thomas Aquinas.

A Christian Looks at the Jewish Question. Ayer 1981 repr. of 1939 ed. $17.00. ISBN 0-405-05280-4. An attack on antisemitism.

Christianity and Democracy. Trans. by Doris C. Anson. *Essay Index Repr. Ser.* Ayer 1972 repr. of 1944 ed. $15.00. ISBN 0-8369-7243-0. (and *Rights of Man and Natural Law*) Ignatius Pr. 1986 $12.50. ISBN 0-89870-030-2. Delineates clearly the Christian bases of democracy.

Creative Intuition in Art and Poetry. Bollingen Ser. Princeton U. Pr. 1952 $60.00. ISBN 0-691-09789-5. Brilliant philosophy of aesthetics.

Education at the Crossroads. Terry Lectures Ser. Yale U. Pr. 1943 $9.00. ISBN 0-300-00163-0. The case for neo-scholasticism forcefully argued.

The Education of Man: Educational Philosophy. Ed. by Donald Gallagher and Idella Gallagher. Greenwood 1976 repr. of 1967 ed. $38.50. ISBN 0-8371-8479-7. A collection of Maritain's essays on the theory of education.

Freedom and the Modern World. Trans. by Richard O'Sullivan. Gordian 1971 repr. of 1936 ed. $35.00. ISBN 0-87752-147-6. A tract for the times when totalitarianisms were on the rise threatening all freedom and when the liberal democracies mistook individual license for genuine freedom.

An Introduction to Philosophy. Trans. by E. I. Watkin. Century Bookbindery 1930 o.p. A basic textbook for neo-Thomism.

The Living Thoughts of St. Paul. Arden Lib. 1942 o.p. A thoughtful selection with illuminating comments.

Man and the State. 1951. U. Ch. Pr. 1956 $9.95. ISBN 0-226-50552-9. Received the Catholic Literary Award (1952); neo-Thomist political philosophy on the grand scale.

Notebooks. Trans. by Joseph W. Evans. Magi Bks. 1984 $12.95. ISBN 0-87343-050-6. A saintly man's jottings lovingly translated and posthumously published.

On the Church of Christ: The Person of the Church and Her Personnel. Trans. by Joseph W. Evans. U. of Notre Dame Pr. 1973 $24.95. ISBN 0-268-00519-2. Roman Catholic interpretation of Christianity.

On the Philosophy of History. Kelley 1979 repr. of 1957 ed. $27.50. ISBN 0-678-02760-9. A lecture transformed into a monograph presenting the Roman Catholic theory of history harking back to St. Augustine's *City of God*.

On the Use of Philosophy: Three Essays. Greenwood 1982 repr. of 1962 ed. $39.75. ISBN 0-313-23199-0. Persuasive arguments for the importance of philosophy.

The Person and the Common Good. U. of Notre Dame Pr. 1966 $5.95. ISBN 0-268-00204-5. Essential to an understanding of Maritain's neo-Thomist social thought and his concern for social justice.

A Preface to Metaphysics: Seven Lectures on Being. Ayer 1983 repr. of 1939 ed. $16.95. ISBN 0-8369-5807-1. Readable, concisely written introduction to Maritain's neo-Thomism.

Ransoming the Time. Trans. by Harry L. Binsse. Gordian 1972 repr. of 1941 ed. $50.00. ISBN 0-87752-153-0. Sensitively composed essay on the temporalism of modernism and the Catholic remedy.

Reflections on America. Gordian 1975 repr. of 1958 ed. $35.00. ISBN 0-87752-166-2. An optimistic tribute to the American way.

The Responsibility of the Artist. Gordian 1972 repr. of 1962 ed. $20.00. ISBN 0-87752-145-X. On the relationship between art and morality.

Rights of Man and Natural Law. Gordian 1971 repr. of 1943 ed. $25.00. ISBN 0-87752-146-8. Human rights interpreted in the framework of natural law; a classic in the field.

Saint Thomas and the Problem of Evil. Marquette 1942 $7.95. ISBN 0-87462-106-2. Stimulating lecture on a contemporary problem pertinent to the philosophy of St. Thomas.

Scholasticism and Politics. Essay Index Repr. Ser. Ayer 1983 repr. of 1940 ed. $15.00. ISBN 0-8369-2805-9. Political philosophy in a neo-Thomist framework directed against the causes of World War II.

Science and Wisdom. Telegraph Bks. o.p. Profound, abstruse, technical treatise on his theory of knowledge, intended for advanced students.

The Things That Are Not Caesar's. Telegraph Bks. 1930 o.p. Persuasive lecture on the supreme matters of morals and religion.

Three Reformers: Luther, Descartes, Rousseau. Greenwood 1982 repr. of 1950 ed. $35.00. ISBN 0-8371-2825-0. In-depth studies of three major modern thinkers, who are sympathetically but critically examined by one who rejected modernity.

True Humanism. Trans. by M. R. Adamson. Greenwood 1983 repr. of 1941 ed. $41.50. ISBN 0-8371-2902-8. Emphasis on religion and spirituality to distinguish Maritain's humanism from secular humanism.

BOOKS ABOUT MARITAIN

Allard, Jean-Louis. *Education for Freedom: The Philosophy of Education of Jacques Maritain.* Trans. by Ralph C. Nelson. U. of Notre Dame Pr. 1982 $8.95. ISBN 0-268-00909-0. Scholarly monograph on a practically significant aspect of Maritain's thought.

Bars, Henry, and Eric Jourdan, eds. *The Story of Two Souls: The Correspondence of Jacques Maritain and Julien Green.* Trans. by Bernard Doering. Fordham 1988 $50.00. ISBN 0-8232-1190-8. "[O]ffers the reader a glimpse of the inner workings of the creative mind of Julien Green, novelist and convert to Catholicism, more than they do to Maritain, philosopher, spiritual godfather to Green and, like him, a convert to Catholicism" (*Choice*).

Doering, Bernard. *Jacques Maritain and the French Catholic Intellectuals.* U. of Notre Dame Pr. 1983 o.p. Investigative reconstruction of Maritain's French milieu.

Griffin, John H., and Yves R. Simon. *Jacques Maritain: Homage in Words and Pictures.* Magi Bks. 1974 $19.95. ISBN 0-87343-046-8. Celebratory collection; primarily of human interest.

Hudson, Deal W., and Matthew J. Maucini, eds. *Understanding Maritain: Philosopher and Friend.* Mercer Univ. Pr. 1988 $39.95. ISBN 0-86554-279-1. A collection of appreciative essays.

Jung, Hwa Jol. *The Foundation of Jacques Maritain's Political Philosophy. Univ. of Florida Social Sciences Monographs.* U. Press Fla. 1960 $7.95. ISBN 0-8130-0124-2. Scholarly monograph focused critically on Maritain's political philosophy.

McInerny, Ralph. *Art and Prudence: Studies in the Thought of Jacques Maritain.* U. of Notre Dame Pr. 1988 $21.95. ISBN 0-685-44086-9. An insightful, appreciative monograph by a disciple.

Redpath, Peter, ed. *From Twilight to Dawn: The Cultural Vision of Jacques Maritain*. U. of
   Notre Dame Pr. 1991 $15.00. ISBN 0-268-00979-1. Essays memorializing Maritain's
   life and works.
Torre, Michael D., ed. *Freedom in the Modern World: Jacques Maritain, Yves R. Simon,
   Mortimer J. Adler*. U. of Notre Dame Pr. 1990 $15.00. ISBN 0-268-00978-3. Essays
   focused on the political philosophy of three twentieth-century neo-Thomists.

MEAD, GEORGE HERBERT. 1863–1931

George Herbert Mead was a leading figure in the development of pragmatism.
He joined the faculty of the University of Chicago at the invitation of JOHN
DEWEY (see also Vol. 3) and, after Dewey's departure for Columbia University,
became chairman of its philosophy department.

Mead's influence extended beyond philosophy to psychology and sociology.
He presented a theory of the emergence of the human mind in the evolutionary
social process and of the development of individual personality that is known as
social behaviorism. He also probed the metaphysical issues raised by pragmatism and the advances of science in regard to evolution and relativity physics as
well as in regard to the formulation of scientific method. He proposed a
philosophy of the present according to which the past is interpreted (construed)
from the standpoint of the present. At the time of his death he was at work on a
cosmology in which the act is the central category. During his lifetime Mead
published numerous articles articulating every aspect of his thought but never
published a book-length work. He was nevertheless esteemed as a seminal
thinker of the first rank, and his lecture notes were posthumously published as
books.

BOOKS BY MEAD

George Herbert Mead on Social Psychology. Ed. by Anselm Strauss. U. Ch. Pr. 1964 $13.95.
   ISBN 0-276-51665-2. A selection from Mead's published writings intended as an
   introductory text.
The Individual and the Social Self: Unpublished Work of George Herbert Mead. Ed. by.
   David L. Miller. U. Ch. Pr. 1982 $26.00. ISBN 0-226-51668-7. New light is cast on the
   development of Mead's social psychology by this collection prepared by a devoted
   disciple.
Mind, Self, and Society: From the Standpoint of a Social Behaviorist. 1934. Ed. by Charles
   W. Morris. U. Ch. Pr. 1967 $11.95. ISBN 0-226-51668-7. Splendidly edited lecture
   notes from Mead's famous course on social psychology.
The Philsophy of the Act. 1938. Ed. by Charles W. Morris and David L. Miller. U. Ch. Pr.
   1972 o.p. Lecture notes and other notes and papers by Mead on his fundamental
   philosophy.
The Philsophy of the Present. Ed. by Arthur E. Murphy. *Paul Carus Lecture Ser*. U. Ch. Pr.
   1980 $5.95. ISBN 0-226-5167-7. Unpublished Carus lectures, supplemented by
   published papers, presenting Mead's novel theory of time.
Selected Writings. Ed. by Andrew J. Reck. U. Ch. Pr. 1981 $10.95. ISBN 0-226-31671-7. A
   representative selection of 25 articles Mead published in his lifetime.

BOOKS ABOUT MEAD

Aboulafia, Mitchell. *The Mediating Self: Mead, Sartre, and Self-Determination*. Yale U. Pr.
   1986 $22.50. ISBN 0-300-03523-3. Imaginative and suggestive scholarly monograph.
_____. *Philsophy, Social Theory, and the Thought of George Herbert Mead*. SUNY Ser. in
   the Philsophy of the Social Sciences. State U. NY Pr. 1991 $57.50. ISBN 0-7914-
   0359-9. An anthology that "includes noteworthy examples of recent work on Mead
   by Europeans and Americans" (*The Philosopher's Index*).

Baldwin, John D. *George Herbert Mead: A Unifying Theory for Sociology. Masters of Sociological Theory Ser.* Russell Sage 1986 $34.95. ISBN 0-8039-2321-X. Readable account of Mead for sociologists.

Corti, Walter R. *The Philosophy of George Herbert Mead.* Alders Foreign Bks. 1977 $31.75. ISBN 3-7873-0353-7. Proceedings of an international conference on Mead.

Cronk, George. *The Philosophical Anthropology of George Herbert Mead. Amer. Univ. Studies Ser.* P. Lang Pubs. 1987 $26.00. ISBN 0-8204-0404-7. A scholarly investigation of Mead's conception of language and mind.

Gunter, Pete A., ed. *Creativity in George Herbert Mead.* Foun. Phil. Great 1990 $31.00. ISBN 0-8191-7916-7. A symposium on the role the concept of creativity plays in Mead's thought.

Hamilton, Peter. *George Herbert Mead: Critical Assessments.* Routledge 1992 ISBN 0-415-03759-X. A tightly written critique.

Kang, W. *G. H. Mead's Concept of Rationality: A Study of the Use of Symbols and Other Implements. Approaches to Semiotics.* Mouton 1976 $42.70. ISBN 90-2793-165-8. Probing but sympathetic critique of Mead's Theory signs.

Miller, David L. *George Herbert Mead: Self Language and the World.* U. Ch. Pr. 1980 $7.95. ISBN 0-226-52613-5. A comprehensive and sympathetic interpretation of Mead's thought by a former student.

Pfuetze, Paul. *Self, Society, Existence, Human Nature and Dialogue in the Thought of George Herbert Mead and Martin Buber.* Greenwood 1973 repr. of 1961 ed. $45.00. ISBN 0-8371-6708-6. A penetrating, although sometimes pedestrian, comparative study.

Rosenthal, Sandra B., and Patrick L. Bourgeois. *Mead and Merleau-Ponty: Toward a Common Vision.* State U. NY Pr. 1991 $49.50. ISBN 0-7914-0789-6. "[U]nites George Herbert Mead and Maurice Merleau-Ponty in a shared rejection of substance philosophy as well as a spectator theory of knowledge in favor of a focus on the ultimacy of temporal process and the constitutive function of social praxis" (*The Philosopher's Index*).

Schellenberg, James A. *Masters of Social Philosophy: Freud, Mead, Lewin, and Skinner.* OUP 1978 $9.95. ISBN 0-19-502622-5. An excellent book to begin the study of Mead's contribution in relation to those of other prominent twentieth-century psychologists.

MERLEAU-PONTY, MAURICE. 1908–1961

Appointed professor at the Collège de France in 1952, Maurice Merleau-Ponty was a highly esteemed professional philosopher because of his technical works in phenomenology and psychology. He was also an activist commentator on the significant cultural and political events of his time, as well as a collaborator with JEAN-PAUL SARTRE (see also Vol. 2) and SIMONE DE BEAUVOIR (see Vol. 2) in the founding and editing of *Les Temps Modernes* in Paris immediately after World War II.

Besides being influenced by EDMUND HUSSERL and MARTIN HEIDEGGER (see also Vol. 5), Merleau-Ponty assimilated the contributions of experimental philosophy and Gestalt psychology to focus on perception and behavior. His work *The Structure of Behavior*, although centering on the body, presented an interpretation of the distinctions among the mental, the vital (biological), and the physical that ruled out the reductionist inclinations of behaviorism. With the appearance of his work on the phenomenology of perception in 1945, his position as a philosopher ranking beside Heidegger and Sartre was established. He unveiled a theory of human subjectivity similar to theirs but with greater technical precision. From the standpoint of an existentialist thinker whose conception of subjectivity stressed the primacy of freedom, he examined Marxism and the political factions and movements fostered in the name of KARL

MARX (see also Vol. 3). The resulting studies, always insightful and provocative, satisfied neither the right nor the left.

In the foreword to the English translation of Merleau-Ponty's inaugural lecture at the Collège de France, *In Praise of Philsophy*, John Wild and James Edie praised him for having made "important contributions to the phenomeno-logical investigation of human existence in the life-world and its distinctive structures. He was a revolutionary, and his philosophy, even more than that of his French contemporaries, was a philosophy of the evolving, becoming 'historical present.' Merleau-Ponty views man as an essentially historical being and history as the dialectic of meaning and non-meaning which is working itself out through the complex, unpredictable interaction of men and the world. Nothing historical ever has just one meaning; meaning is ambiguous and is seen from an infinity of viewpoints. He has been called a philosopher of ambiguity, of contradiction, of dialectic. His search is the search for 'meaning.'"

BOOKS BY MERLEAU-PONTY

Adventures of the Dialectic. 1955. Trans. by Joseph J. Bien. *Studies in Phenomenology and Existential Philsophy Ser.* Northwestern U. Pr. 1973 $26.95. ISBN 0-8101-0404-0. Incisive critique and interpretation of Hegelian and Marxist themes.

Consciousness and the Acquisition of Language. Trans. by Hugh J. Silverman. *Studies in Phenomenology and Existential Philsophy Ser.* Northwestern U. Pr. 1973 $21.95. ISBN 0-8101-0597-7. A "strange blend of philosophy and psychology" (*Choice*).

Humanism and Terror: An Essay on the Communist Problem. 1947. Beacon Pr. 1969 $15.95. ISBN 0-8070-0277-1. "Merleau-Ponty has a faith in the proleteriat that is beautiful in the abstract but that sees in the revolutionary reality what simply isn't there" (*America*).

In Praise of Philsophy. Trans. by John Wild and others. Northwestern U. Pr. 1988 $12.95. ISBN 0-8101-0796-1

The Phenomenology of Perception. 1945. Trans. by Colin Smith. Humanities 1981 $29.95. ISBN 0-391-02551-1. Conceptually complex and original synthesis of Gestalt philoso-phy and experimental psychology in conformity with the phenomenological method.

The Primacy of Perception. Ed. by James M. Edie. Trans. by William Cobb and others. *Studies in Phenomenology and Existential Philsophy Ser.* Northwestern U. Pr. 1964 $24.95. ISBN 0-8101-0165-3. Reexamine[s] the basis of humanity. . . . Of special significance is the correlation which Merleau-Ponty finds between the linguistic phenomenon and the emergence of the sense of self-identity" (*Library Journal*).

The Prose of the World. Ed. by Claude Lefort. Trans. by John O'Neill. *Studies in Phenomenology and Existential Philsophy Ser.* Northwestern U. Pr. 1973 $24.95. ISBN 0-8101-0412-1. Posthumously published work that illuminates Merleau-Ponty's understanding and employment of language.

Sense and Non-Sense. 1948. Trans. by Hubert L. Dreyfus. Northwestern U. Pr. 1964 o.p. Seminal work on the meaning of meaning and meaninglessness.

Signs. 1960. Trans. by Richard C. McCleary. *Studies in Phenomenology and Existential Philsophy Ser.* Northwestern U. Pr. 1964 $14.95. ISBN 0-8101-0253-6. "Leaves no important area on inquiry untouched—the philosophical, political, anthropological, the sociological or the artistic—in his search for that which can be understood from within even as 'personal intentions' are tending toward progresses which are themselves 'mediated by things'" (*Library Journal*).

The Structure of Behavior. 1942. Trans. by Alden Fischer. Duquesne 1983 $19.95. ISBN 0-8207-0163-7. Shows "that man relates to his own existence as a totality which moves from this wholeness in ways which favor his own particular growth tendencies rather than as a mere reactor to the world as an imposer of determined responses" (*Library Journal*).

Texts and Dialogues. Ed. by Hugh Silverman and Barry James. *Contemporary Studies in Philsophy and the Human Sciences.* Humanities 1992 $45.00. ISBN 0-391-03702-1

The Visible and the Invisible. Trans. by Alphonso Lingis. *Studies in Phenomenology and Existential Philosophy Ser.* Northwestern U. Pr. 1969 $26.95. ISBN 0-8101-0026-6. Foray into fundamental metaphysics.

BOOKS ABOUT MERLEAU-PONTY

Barral, Mary R. *The Body in Interpersonal Relations: Merleau-Ponty.* U. Pr. of Amer. 1984 $23.00. ISBN 0-8191-3755-3. Scholarly monograph focused on Merleau-Ponty's theory of the body in psychology; for the advanced student.

Cooper, Barry. *Merleau-Ponty and Marxism: From Terror to Reform.* Bks. Demand $62.50. ISBN 0-8357-3635-0. Accurate evaluation of the French philosopher's relation to Marxism.

Dwyer, Philip. *Sense and Subjectivity: A Study of Wittgenstein and Merleau-Ponty. Studies in Epistemology, Psychology, and Psychiatry.* E. J. Brill 1990 $57.25. ISBN 90-04-09205-6. A specialized comparative study of the possibility of private language according to Wittgenstein and Merleau-Ponty.

Gill, Jerry H. *Merleau-Ponty and Metaphor.* Humanities 1991 $35.00. ISBN 0-391-03713-7. Focuses on his use of metaphor and its implications for his thought in general.

Hadreas, Peter J. *In Place of the Flawed Diamond: An Investigation of Merleau-Ponty's Philsophy of Perception. Amer. Univ. Studies* P. Lang Pubs. 1986 $30.30. ISBN 0-8204-0211-7. An examination of Merleau-Ponty's phenomenology of perception for specialists.

Johnson, Galen A., and Michael B. Smith, eds. *Ontology and Alterity in Merleau-Ponty. Studies in Phenomenology and Existential Philsophy.* Northwestern U. Pr. 1990 $39.95. ISBN 0-8101-0872-0. A collection of scholarly essays.

Low, Douglas B. *The Existential Dialectic of Marx and Merleau-Ponty. Amer. Univ. Studies.* P. Lang Pubs. 1987 $36.00. ISBN 0-8204-0435-7. A perceptive interpretive monograph.

O'Neill, John. *Perception, Expression and History: The Social Phenomenology of Maurice Merleau-Ponty. Studies in Phenomenology and Existential Philsophy.* Northwestern U. Pr. 1970 $12.95. ISBN 0-8101-0299-4. Highly interpretive but rewarding monograph.

Rosenthal, Sandra, and Patrick L. Bourgeois. *Mead and Merleau-Ponty: Toward a Common Vision.* State U. NY Pr. 1991 $49.50. ISBN 0-7914-0789-6. "[U]nites George Herbert Mead and Maurice Merleau-Ponty in a shared rejection of substance philosophy as well as a spectator theory of knowledge, in favor of a focus on the ultimacy of temporal process and the constitutive function of social praxis" (*The Philosopher's Index*).

Whiteside, Kerry H. *Merleau-Ponty and the Foundation of an Existential Politic. Studies in Moral Legal and Political Philsophy.* Princeton U. Pr. 1989 $45.00. ISBN 0-691-07781-9. A rich and reliable source of information on his political thought.

MOORE, GEORGE EDWARD. 1873–1958

George Edward Moore was one of the giants in the formation of analytic philosophy in the English-speaking world. During most of his professional life, he was affiliated with Cambridge University—as a student and as a fellow at Trinity College, from 1892 to 1896 and from 1898 to 1904, respectively; as a university lecturer from 1911 to 1925; as a professor of mental philosophy and logic from 1925 until his retirement in 1939.

Moore's philosophical contributions touch on three areas: philosophical method, moral philosophy, and theory of knowledge. His philosophical method is exhibited in his unrelenting effort to discover and elucidate the meanings of philosophical concepts and in his appeal to common sense. This method is evident in his work in ethics and epistemology. *Principia Ethica* (1903) established him as the foremost critic of ethical naturalism; his conceptions of goodness as an indefinable quality and of intrinsic value as organic unity were influential not only in philosophical circles but also among the artists and writers of the Bloomsbury group. Moore's work in epistemology was expressed in a large number of articles distinguished for their nicety of analysis. They span six decades, revealing a thinker who moved out of idealism into realism and then moved back and forth among the varieties of realism on such questions as the status of sense data, that is, whether they exist, and if they exist, whether they are physical parts of things or are mental representations only.

BOOKS BY MOORE

Early Essays. Ed. by Tom Regan. Temple U. Pr. 1986 $37.95. ISBN 0-87722-442-0. An excellent edition of Moore's early writings, mainly on epistemology and ethics.

The Elements of Ethics. Ed. by Tom Regan. Temple U. Pr. 1991 $54.95. ISBN 0-87722-770-5. A series of 10 previously unpublished lectures presented by Moore at the London School of Ethics and Social Philsophy.

Philsophical Papers. Muirhead Lib. of Philsophy. Humanities 1977 o.p. "Included are 'A Defence of Common Sense' and 'Proof of an External World,' two works essential to an understanding of Moore's thought, and Moore's careful notes on the 1930–33 lectures of Wittgenstein" (*Ethics*).

Principia Ethica. Cambridge U. Pr. 1903 $44.95. ISBN 0521-05753-1. Most influential work in the English language on ethics in the twentieth century.

BOOKS ABOUT MOORE

Ayer, Alfred J. *Russell and Moore: The Analytical Heritage. William James Lectures Ser.* HUP 1971 $17.50. ISBN 0-674-78103-1. Critical estimations of the works of two of England's most famous twentieth-century philosophers by an equally famous one.

Baldwin, Thomas. *G. E. Moore. Arguments of the Philosophers' Ser.* Routledge 1990 $89.95. ISBN 0-415-00904-8. Tightly written, closely reasoned critique.

Cavarnos, Constantine. *A Dialogue on G. E. Moore's Ethical Philsophy: Together with an Account of Three Talks with Moore on Diverse Philsophical Questions.* Inst. Byzantine 1979 $7.95. ISBN 0-914744-43-7. Aims "to point out and clarify some basic ideas contained in Moore's *Principia Ethica*, by posing and answering certain questions, commenting on Moore's views and comparing them with those of two other eminent English philosophers, C. D. Broad and W. D. Ross" (*The Philosopher's Index*).

Hochberg, Herbert. *Thought, Fact, and Reference: The Origins and Ontology of Logical Atomism.* U. of Minn. Pr. 1978 $39.95. ISBN 0-8166-0867-9. Technical philosophy relevant to an understanding of Russell and Wittgenstein as well as Moore.

Klemke, E. D. *Epistemology of G. E. Moore.* Northwestern U. Pr. 1969 $15.95. Solid critical monograph.

O'Connor, David. *The Metaphysics of G. E. Moore.* Kluwer Ac. 1982 $67.00. ISBN 90-277-1352-9. Systematic interpretation and commentary.

Regan, Tom. *Bloomsbury's Prophet: G. E. Moore and the Development of His Moral Philsophy.* Temple U. Pr. 1986 $34.95. ISBN 0-87722-446-3. Well-researched interpretation of Moore's moral philosophy in connection with the famous Bloomsbury circle, which included Virginia Woolf.

Rohatyn, Dennis. *The Reluctant Naturalist: A Study of G. E. Moore's Principia Ethica.* U. Pr. of Amer. 1987 $37.00. ISBN 0-8191-5767-8. Pioneering investigation of the ambiguities and contradictions in Moore's work concluding that he "is not the all-destroyer, but creates and grounds a new axiology" (*The Philosopher's Index*).

Schilpp, Paul Arthur, ed. *The Philsophy of G. E. Moore. Lib. of Living Philosophers.* 2 vols. Open Court 1968 $29.95. ISBN 0-87548-136-1. Collection of original critical essays by prominent thinkers on Moore and his replies; a scholar's treasure.

Sylvester, Robert D. *The Moral Philsophy of G. E. Moore.* Ed. by Ray Perkins and R. W. Sleeper. Temple U. Pr. 1990 $44.95. ISBN 0-87722-645-8. Argues that criticism of Moore's work in moral philosophy has been based on misinterpretations of his unified position.

White, Alan R. *G. E. Moore: A Critical Exposition.* Greenwood 1979 repr. of 1969 ed. $38.50. ISBN 0-313-20805-0. Thoughtful and well-written critical study.

NAGEL, ERNEST. 1901–1985

Born in Czechoslovakia, Ernest Nagel emigrated to the United States and became a naturalized American citizen. In 1923 he graduated from the City College of New York, where he had studied under MORRIS COHEN, with whom he later collaborated to coauthor the highly successful textbook, *An Introduction to Logic and Scientific Method* (1934). Pursuing graduate studies at Columbia University, he received his Ph.D. in 1930. After a year of teaching at the City College of New York, he joined the faculty of Columbia University, where in 1955 he was named John Dewey Professor of Philosophy. In 1966 he joined the faculty of Rockefeller University.

Nagel was one of the leaders in the movement of logical empiricism, conjoining Viennese positivism with indigenous American naturalism and pragmatism. In 1936 he published in the *Journal of Philosophy* the article "Impressions and Appraisals of Analytic Philosophy," one of the earliest sympathetic accounts of the works of LUDWIG WITTGENSTEIN, MORITZ SCHLICK, and RUDOLF CARNAP intended for an American audience.

Nagel was esteemed for his lucid exposition of the most recondite matters in logic, mathematics, and natural science, published in essays and book reviews for professional journals, scientific periodicals, and literary reviews. Two of his books, now out of print, consisted of collections of his articles: *Sovereign Reason and Other Studies in the Philosophy of Science* (1954) and *Logic Without Metaphysics and Other Essays in the Philosophy of Science* (1957). He also wrote a monograph, *Principles of the Theory of Probability* (1939), which appeared in the *International Encyclopedia of Unified Science*. In his major book-length work, *The Structure of Science*, Nagel directed his attention to the logic of scientific explanations—in his own words, "with their logical structure, their mutual relations, their functions in inquiry, and their device for systematizing knowledge."

BOOKS BY NAGEL

Godet's Proof. (Coauthored with James R. Newman). NYU Pr. 1958 $7.50. ISBN 0-8147-0325-9

The Structure of Science. Hackett Pub. 1979 $37.95. ISBN 0-915144-72-7

Teleology Revisited and Other Essays in the Philosophy and History of Science. Col. U. Pr. 1982 $18.50. ISBN 0-231-04505-0

NOZICK, ROBERT. 1938–

Educated at Columbia and Princeton universities, Robert Nozick is Arthur Kingsley Porter Professor of Philosophy at Harvard University. He rose to eminence in the last quarter of the twentieth century as a creative philosopher who has expressed philosophical truths beyond the reach of analytic argumentation. Honed in the technical intricacies of analytic philosophy, he has nonetheless restored meditation to its proper place in the philosophical canon.

Nozick's first book, *Anarchy, State and Utopia* (initially published in 1974), won the National Book Award in 1975 and became the fundamental text of the Libertarian movement. *The American Scholar* acclaimed Nozick for his "ability to surround a subject, to anticipate objection, to see through weakness and pretense, to extract all the implications of a contention, to ask a huge number of relevant questions about a seemingly settled matter, to enlarge into full significance what has only been sketched by others." Nozick's book and JOHN RAWLS's *Theory of Justice* are considered the two most influential recent American works on social and political philosophy.

Nozick's second book, *Philosophical Explanations*, was given the Ralph Waldo Emerson Award of Phi Beta Kappa in 1982. It covers a wide range of basic philosophical topics: the question why there is something rather than nothing, the identity of the self, knowledge and skepticism, free will, the foundation of ethnics, and the meaning of life. The English philosopher Bernard Williams hailed it as "the great American novel in philosophy."

Nozick abandons philosophical proof or argumentation as too coercive and opts instead for methods of explanation that promote understanding. This approach has culminated in his third book, *The Examined Life*, where, taking off from SOCRATES's statement, he "probes the topics of happiness, dying, immortality, creativity, religious faith, sexuality, good and evil, wisdom, and the gap between the ideal and the actual" (Publishers note).

BOOKS BY NOZICK

Anarchy, State and Utopia. Basic 1977 $15.00. ISBN 0-465-09720-0
The Examined Life: Philosophical Meditations. S&S Trade 1990 $10.95. ISBN 0-671-72501-7
The Normative Theory of Individual Choice. Harvard Dissertations in Philosophy Ser. Garland 1990 $82.00. ISBN 0-8240-3207-1
Philosophical Explanations. HUP 1981 $33.00. ISBN 0-674-66448-5

ORTEGA Y GASSET, JOSÉ. 1883–1955

Essayist and philosopher, a thinker influential in and out of the Spanish world, José Ortega y Gasset was professor of metaphysics at the University of Madrid from 1910 until the outbreak of the Spanish Civil War in 1936. *The Revolt of the Masses*, his most famous work, owes much to post-Kantian schools of thought, especially to FRIEDRICH NIETZSCHE (see also Vol. 2) and HENRI BERGSON. Ortega's predominant thesis is the need of an intellectual aristocracy governing in a spirit of enlightened liberalism. Although Franco, after his victory in the civil war, offered to make Ortega Spain's "official philosopher" and to publish a deluxe edition of his works—with certain parts deleted—the philosopher refused. Instead, he chose the life of a voluntary exile in Argentina, and in 1941 he was appointed professor of philosophy at the University of San Marcos in Lima, Peru. He returned to Spain in 1945 and died in Madrid.

Ortega's reformulation of the Cartesian *cogito* displays the fulcrum of his thought. While RENÉ DESCARTES (see also Vol. 5) declared *"Cogito ergo sum"* (I think, therefore I am), Ortega maintained *"Cogito quia vivo"* (I think because I live). He subordinated reason to life, to vitality. Reason becomes the tool of people existing biologically in a given time and place, rather than an overarching sovereign. Ortega's philosophy consequently discloses affinities in its metaphysics to both American pragmatism and European existentialism in spite of its elitism in social philosophy.

BOOKS BY ORETAGA Y GASSET

History as a System, and And Other Essays toward a Philosophy of History. 1924 Greenwood 1981 repr. of 1961 ed. $38.50. ISBN 0-313-23112-5. Ortega's suggestive existentialist statement.
An Interpretation of Universal History. Trans. by Mildred Adams. Norton 1984 $8.95. ISBN 0-393-00751-0. Philosophy of history in the grand manner, seeking to delineate patterns of meaning in the plethora of events.
Man and Crisis. 1922. Trans. by Mildred Adams. Norton 1958 $8.95. ISBN 0-393-00121-0. "This book will not only be widely read. It will also be remembered" (*N.Y. Times*).

Man and People. 1957. Trans. by Willard R. Trask. Norton 1963 $8.95. ISBN 0-393-00123-7. A "vivid recounting of some of the chief features of the topography, flora and fauna of live human experience" (*N.Y. Herald Tribune*).

Meditations on Hunting. Macmillan 1986 $10.95. ISBN 0-684-18630-6

The Modern Theme. 1923. Trans. by James Cleugh. Darby Pub. 1981 o.p. Vitalistic interpretation of intellectual and cultural tendencies in the early decades of the twentieth century.

The Origin of Philosophy. Trans. by Tony Talbot. Norton 1968 $6.95. ISBN 0-393-00128-8. Contends that "philosophy was a fruit of the entrance of Greece into a period of freedom, that freedom involves enlargement of the circle of possibilities beyond immediate needs, that contact with foreigners expands the circles of one's choices, that 'vital wealth' results in part from emancipation from myth and tradition" (*Library Journal*).

Psychological Investigations. Trans. by Jorge Garcia-Gomez. Norton 1987 $19.95. ISBN 0-393-02401-6

The Revolt of the Masses. 1930. Ed. by Kenneth Moore. Trans. by Anthony Kerrigan. U. of Notre Dame Pr. 1985 $25.95. ISBN 0-268-01609-7. Most famous and influential work; required reading for persons interested in the nature of civilization.

What Is Philosophy? 1958. Trans. by Mildred Adams. Norton 1964 $7.95. ISBN 0-393-00126-1. Charming if biased essay.

BOOKS ABOUT ORTEGA Y GASSET

Dobson, Andrew. *An Introduction to the Politics and Philosophy of José Ortega y Gasset.* *Cambridge Iberian and Latin Amer. Studies* Cambridge U. Pr. 1989 $49.95. ISBN 0-521-36068-4. General survey of his life and work.

Gray, Rockwell. *The Imperative of Modernity: An Intellectual Biography of José Ortega y Gassett.* U. CA Pr. 1989 $45.00. ISBN 0-520-06201-9. Scholarly interpretation of Ortega's philosophical odyssey.

Marias, Julian. *The Structure of Society*. Trans. by Harold C. Raley. U. of Ala. Pr. 1986 $23.95. ISBN 0-8173-0181-X. Ortega's social philosophy superbly presented by his leading Spanish disciple in an excellent translation.

Ourmette, Victor. *José Ortega y Gasset. Twayne's World Authors Ser.* G. K. Hall 1982 o.p. Straightforward portrayal of Ortega's principal works.

Raley, Harold. *José Ortega y Gasset: Philosophy of European Unity*. U. of Ala. Pr. 1971 o.p. Scholarly monograph on a major theme in Ortega's thought.

POPPER, SIR KARL RAIMUND. 1902–

[SEE Chapter 9 in this volume.]

PUTNAM, HILARY. 1926–

[SEE Chapter 9 in this volume.]

QUINE, WILLARD VAN ORMAN. 1908–

[SEE Chapter 9 in this volume.]

RAWLS, JOHN. 1921–

John Rawls, professor of philosophy at Harvard University, had published a number of articles on the concept of justice as fairness before the appearance of his magnum opus, *A Theory of Justice* (1971). While the articles had won for Rawls considerable prestige, the reception of his book thrust him into the front ranks of contemporary moral philosophy. Presenting a Kantian alternative to conventional utilitarianism and intuitionism, Rawls offers a theory of justice that is contractual and that rests on principles that he alleges would be accepted by free, rational persons in a state of nature, that is, of equality. The chorus of praise was loud and clear. Stuart Hampshire acclaimed the book as "the most substantial and interesting contribution to moral philosophy since the war." H. A. Bedau declared: "As a work of close and original scholarship in the service of the dominant moral and political ideology of our civilization, Rawls's treatise is simply without a rival." Rawls historically achieved two important things: (1) He articulated a coherent moral philosophy for the welfare state, and (2) he demonstrated that analytic philosophy was most capable of doing constructive work in moral philosophy. *A Theory of Justice* has become the most influential work in political, legal, and social philosophy by an American author in the twentieth century.

BOOKS BY RAWLS

Justice as Fairness. Irvington Repr. Ser. in Philosophy. Irvington 1991 $1.00. ISBN 0-8290-2601-0. Reprint of an early article.
A Theory of Justice. Belknap Pr. 1971 $30.00. ISBN 0-674-88010-2
Two Concepts of Rules. Irvington Repr. Ser. in Philosophy. Ivrington 1991 $1.00. ISBN 0-8290-2601-1. Reprint of an article.

BOOKS ABOUT RAWLS

Baynes, Kenneth. *The Normative Grounds of Social Criticism: Kant, Rawls, and Habermas.* State U. NY Pr. 1991 $57.50. ISBN 0-7914-0867-1. Critical theory (Habermas) and contractarian liberalism (Rawls) studied historically and comparatively in favor of the former.
Blocker, H. Gene, and Elizabeth H. Smith, eds. *John Rawls' Theory of Social Justice: An Introduction.* Ohio U. Pr. 1980 $29.95. ISBN 0-8214-0445-8. A collection of essays for the serious student.
Corlett, J. Angelo, ed. *Equality and Liberty: Analyzing Rawls and Nozick.* St. Martin 1991 $39.95. ISBN 0-312-06018-1. A collection of scholarly essays examining the two men's theories of fundamental democratic values.
Kukathas, Chandran, and Philip Petit. *Rawls: A Theory of Justice and Its Critics. Key Contemporary Thinkers Ser.* Stanford U. Pr. 1990 $22.50. ISBN 0-8047-1768-0. Discusses "a historical interpretation of Rawls's *A Theory of Justice*, moral individualism, contractarian theory, as well as libertarian and communitarian critiques of Rawls's theory" (*The Philosopher's Index*).
Pogge, Thomas W. *Realizing Rawls.* Cornell Univ. Pr. 1989 $39.95. ISBN 0-8014-2124-1. Defends Rawls's social philosophy against his major critics, Nozick (libertarian) and Sandel (communitarian), arguing that it "yields plausible priorities for global institutional reform and can help move international relations from modus vivendi toward overlapping consensus on values" (*The Philosopher's Index*).

RESCHER, NICHOLAS. 1928–

Born in Germany, Nicholas Rescher moved to the United States with his parents in 1939 and became a naturalized American citizen in 1944. He attended Queens College in New York City and he received his Ph.D. from Princeton University in 1951. Rescher served in the U.S. Marine Corps from 1952 to 1954 and was employed by the Rand Corporation from 1954 to 1956. He resumed his academic career in 1957 and in 1961 joined the faculty of the University of Pittsburgh, where he is now Research Professor of Philosophy. He played a major role in propelling Pittsburgh into the very top rank among graduate schools in philosophy in the United States.

Rescher is the most prolific living American philosophical author, as the list of his books in print reveals. He is also the founding editor of three major philosophical journals: *American Philosophical Quarterly*, *History of Philosophy Quarterly*, and *Public Affairs Quarterly*. Approaching philosophy with a solid background in mathematics and science, he has also specialized in the history of philosophy, with a doctoral dissertation and early articles on Leibniz and, later, with pioneering scholarship on medieval Arabic logic. Rescher's experiences led him to seek practical applications for his philosophical expertise, and he ventured beyond academic philosophy to draw upon empirical research as well as logical method to produce significant works in social thought. He has also sought to formulate a coherent philosophical system in the great tradition. His thinking has moved in the direction of philosophical idealism as he increasingly emphasized the role of mind in constituting its objects.

Of his philosophy Rescher has said: "I unhesitatingly view myself as a specifically American philosopher—for three reasons: (1) the methodology I favor is a fusion of analytical techniques with historical concerns, an approach characteristic of the tradition of those modern American philosophers I admire most (from C. S. Peirce to Clarence I. Lewis and W. V. Quine); (2) my philosophical ambience in terms of close personal and professional contacts runs heavily towards my American colleagues; and (3) the tenor of my thinking is oriented markedly towards pragmatism, which is generally—and, I think, rightly—regarded as the quintessentially American philosophy."

Books by Rescher

Baffling Phenomena: And Other Studies in the Philosophy of Knowledge and Valuation. Rowman 1990 $42.50. ISBN 0-8476-7638-2

Cognitive Economy: The Economic Dimension of the Theory of Knowledge. U. of Pittsburgh Pr. 1989 $29.95. ISBN 0-8229-3617-8

The Development of Arabic Logic. Bks. Demand $65.00. ISBN 0-317-08129-2

Dialectics: A Controversy-Oriented Approach to the Theory of Knowledge. State U. NY Pr. 1977 $39.50. ISBN 0-87395-372-X

Ethical Idealism: An Inquiry into the Nature and Function of Ideals. U. CA Pr. 1987 $37.50. ISBN 0-520-05696-5

Forbidden Knowledge. Kluwer Ac. 1987 $73.00. ISBN 90-277-2410-5

Human Interests: Reflections on Philosophical Anthropology. Stanford Ser. in Philosophy. Stanford U. Pr. 1990 $29.50. ISBN 0-8047-1811-3

Induction. U. of Pittsburgh Pr. 1981 $34.95. ISBN 0-8229-3431-0

Introduction to Value Theory. U. Pr. of Amer. 1982 $17.75. ISBN 0-8191-2474-5

Leibniz's Monadology: An Edition for Students. U. of Pittsburgh Pr. 1991 $39.95. ISBN 0-8229-3670-4

The Limits of Science. Pittsburgh Ser. in Philosophy and History of Science. U. CA Pr. 1984 $42.50. ISBN 0-520-05180-7

The Logic of Decision and Action. Bks. Demand $59.00. ISBN 0-317-08258-2

Mid-Journey: An Unfinished Autobiography. U. Pr. of Amer. 1983 $46.25. ISBN 0-8191-2522-9. Inspiring story of a life until age 47.

Moral Absolute: An Essay on the Nature and Rationale of Morality. Studies in Moral Philosophy. P. Lang Pubs. 1989 $29.00. ISBN 0-8204-0797-6

Ongoing Journey. U. Pr. of Amer. 1986 $23.25. ISBN 0-8191-5591-8. Contains *Mid-Journey* and continues to age 57.

Pascal's Wager: A Study of Practical Reasoning in Philosophical Theology. U. of Notre Dame Pr. 1985 $19.95. ISBN 0-268-01556-2

Peirce's Philosophy of Science: Critical Studies in His Theory of Induction and Scientific Method. U. of Notre Dame Pr. 1979 $6.95. ISBN 0-268-01527-9

Rationality: A Philosophical Inquiry into the Nature and Rationale of Reason. Clarendon Lib. of Logic and Philosophy. OUP 1989 $49.95. ISBN 0-19-824435-5

Reason and Rationality in Natural Science: A Group of Essays. U. Pr. of Amer. 1985 $45.25. ISBN 0-8191-4763-X

Risk: A Philosophical Introduction to the Theory of Risk Evaluation and Management. Nicholas Rescher Ser. U. Pr. of Amer. 1983 $20.75. ISBN 0-8191-2270-X

Scientific Progress: A Philosophical Essay on the Economics of Research in Natural Science. U. of Pittsburgh Pr. 1977 $26.95. ISBN 0-8229-1128-0

Skepticism: A Critical Appraisal. Rowman 1980 $42.00. ISBN 0-8476-6240-3

The Strife of Systems: An Essay on the Grounds and Implications of Philosophical Diversity. U. of Pittsburgh Pr. 1985 $34.95. ISBN 0-8229-3510-4

Studies in the History of Arabic Logic. Bks. Demand $27.00. ISBN 0-317-08256-6

A System of Pragmatic Idealism. Vol. 1 *Human Knowledge in Idealistic Perspective.* Princeton U. Pr. 1991 $37.50. ISBN 0-691-07391-0

A System of Pragmatic Idealism. Vol. 2 *The Validity of Values—A Normative Theory of Evaluative Rationality.* Princeton U. Pr. 1993 $37.50. ISBN 0-691-07393-7

Temporal Modalities in Arabic Logic. Foundations of Language Supplementary Ser. Kluwer Ac. 1966 $32.50. ISBN 90-277-0083-4

Unpopular Essays on Technological Progress. U. of Pittsburgh Pr. 1980 $12.95. ISBN 0-8229-3411-6

Unselfishness: The Role of the Vicarious Affects in Moral Philosophy and Social Theory. U. of Pittsburgh Pr. 1975 $12.95. ISBN 0-8229-3308-X

A Useful Inheritance: Evolutionary Aspects of the Theory of Knowledge. Rowman 1990 $43.50. ISBN 0-8476-7615-3

Welfare: The Social Issues in Philosophical Perspective. Bks. Demand $49.50 ISBN 0-317-26659-4

RICOEUR, PAUL. 1913–

Professor of philosophy at the University of Paris and the University of Chicago, Paul Ricoeur has been described as "possibly the only younger philosopher in Europe whose reputation is of the magnitude of that of the old men of Existentialism—MARCEL, JASPERS, HEIDEGGER [see also Vol. 5] and SARTRE [see also Vol. 2]. . . ." His work has been characterized as "the most massive accomplishment of any philosopher of Christian faith since the appearance of Gabriel Marcel."

A practitioner of the phenomenology of EDMUND HUSSERL mediated by a return to IMMANUEL KANT—in that things in themselves, though unknowable, are not excluded by bracketing existence but are acknowledged as the necessary conditions for the possibility of human experience—Ricoeur has examined those parts of experience—faulty, fallible, and susceptible to error and evil—that other phenomenologists, interested primarily in the cognitional, have neglected. In this respect he follows in the footsteps of Heidegger and Sartre, but he goes beyond them in his discovery of principles transcending human subjectivity that are amenable to spiritual interpretation. Here Ricoeur steps within the contemporary hermeneutic circle of Heidegger and HANS-GEORG GADAMER, on whom he has written. Ricoeur's hermeneutical method, however, has much in common with the methods of biblical exegesis, and in this respect his works should be especially appealing to seminarians and the clergy.

BOOKS BY RICOEUR

The Conflict of Interpretations: Essays on Hermeneutics. Ed. by Don Ihde. *Studies in Phenomenology and Existential Philosophy Ser.* Northwestern U. Pr. 1974 $34.95. ISBN 0-8101-0442-3. This collection contains 22 essays written from 1960 to 1969 in "an attempt at redefining the Greek and Biblical hermeneutic patterns by 'grafting' them onto phenomenology" (*Choice*).

Essays on Biblical Interpretation. Ed. by Lewis S. Mudge. Bks. Demand $50.00. ISBN 0-685-24168-8. Especially recommended for clergy.

Fallible Man: Philosophy of the Will. 1966. Fordham rev. ed. 1986 $35.00. ISBN 0-8232-1150-9. The first part of Ricoeur's *Philosophie de la volonté* to be translated into English.

Freedom and Nature: The Voluntary and Involuntary. Trans. by E. V. Kohak. *Studies in Phenomenology and Existential Philosophy Ser.* Northwestern U. Pr. 1966 $42.95. ISBN 0-8101-0208-0. Advanced phenomenology pertinent to the problem of free will versus scientific determinism.

Freud and Philosophy: An Essay on Interpretation. Trans. by Denis Savage. *Terry Lectures Ser.* Yale U. Pr. 1970 $18.00. ISBN 0-300-02189-5. Examines "the validity of the psychoanalytical interpretation of culture, particularly as expressed in Freud's writings on art, morality, and religion" (*Times Literary Supplement*).

From Text to Action. Trans. by Kathleen Blamey and John Thompson. *Studies in Phenomenology and Existential Philosophy.* Northwestern U. Pr. 1991 $42.95. ISBN 0-8101-0978-6

Hermeneutics and the Human Sciences. Ed. by John B. Thompson. Cambridge U. Pr. 1981 $54.95. ISBN 0-521-23497-2

History and Truth. Studies in Phenomenology and Existential Philosophy Ser. Northwestern U. Pr. 1965 $32.95. ISBN 0-8101-0207-2. Deeply metaphysical treatise in quest of transcendent principles within the course of events.

Husserl: An Analysis of His Phenomenology. Trans. by Edward G. Ballard and Lester Embree. *Studies in Phenomenology and Existential Philosophy Ser.* Northwestern U. Pr. 1967 $14.95. ISBN 0-8101-0530-6. By "the foremost authority of all French commentators on Husserl" (*Journal of Philosophy*).

Interpretation Theory: Discourse and the Surplus of Meaning. Tex. Christian 1976 $8.00. ISBN 0-912646-59-4. A monograph to make hermeneutics plain.

Lectures on Ideology and Utopia. Ed. by George Taylor. Col. U. Pr. 1988 $52.50. ISBN 0-231-06048-3. Rewarding reflections on politics.

Main Trends in Philosophy. Main Trends in the Social and Human Sciences. Holmes & Meir 1979 $26.50. ISBN 0-8419-0506-1. An overview of philosophy in midcentury.

Oneself as Another. Trans. by Kathleen Blamey. U. Ch. Pr. 1992 $29.95. ISBN 0-226-71328-8

The Philosophy of Paul Ricoeur: An Anthology of His Work. Ed. by Charles E. Reagan and David Stewart. Beacon Pr. 1978 $16.00. ISBN 0-8070-1517-2. Ricoeur's hermeneutic writings on the will, phenomenology, religion, faith, philosophy of language, and Freud.

The Reality of the Historical Past. Aquinas Lecture Ser. Marquette 1984 $7.95. ISBN 0-87462-152-6

The Ricoeur Reader: Reflection and Imagination. Ed. by Maris J. Yaldes. U. of Toronto Pr. 1991 $60.00. ISBN 0-8020-5880-9

The Rule of Metaphor: Multi-Disciplinary Studies of the Creation of Meaning in Language. Trans. by Robert Czerny. U. of Toronto Pr. 1977. $22.50. ISBN 0-8020-6447-7. An examination of the philosophy of metaphor from Aristotle to the present.

Symbolism of Evil. Trans. by Emerson Buchanan. Beacon Pr. 1969 $7.00. ISBN 0-8070-1569-9. Compelling interpretation; hermeneutics at its best.

Time and Narrative. Trans. by Kathleen Blamey and David Pellauer. 3 vols. U. Ch. Pr. Vol. 1 1990 $12.95. ISBN 0-226-71332-6. Vol. 2 1990 $12.95. ISBN 0-226-71333-4. Vol. 3 1988 $29.95. ISBN 0-226-71335-0. "[I]ntroduces Ricoeur's theory of the interdependence of temporality and narrative order" (*Library Journal*).

BOOKS ABOUT RICOEUR

Jervolino, Domenico. *The Cogito and Hermeneutics: The Question of the Subject in Ricoeur.* Kluwer Ac. 1990 $74.00. ISBN 0-7923-0824-7. Comprehensive review of Ricoeur's thought.

Klemm, David E. *The Hermeneutical Theory of Paul Ricoeur: A Constructive Analysis.* Bucknell U. Pr. 1983 $29.50. ISBN 0-8387-5041-9. Analyzes "Ricoeur's hermeneutical method of textual understanding and the possibility that Ricoeur's philosophy is equivalent to theological hermeneutics" (*The Philosopher's Index*).

McCormick, Thomas W. *Theories of Reading in Dialogue: An Interdisciplinary Study.* U. Pr. of Amer. 1988 $56.50. ISBN 0-8191-7168-9. Compares and contrasts philosophical and psychological theories of reading.

Vanhoozer, Kevin J. *Biblical Narrative in the Philosophy of Paul Ricoeur: A Study in
  Hermeneutics and Theology*. Cambridge U. Pr. 1990 $59.95. ISBN 0-521-34425-5.
  Creative interpretation of Ricoeur's hermeneutics, relating it to his earlier work in
  philosophical anthropology.
Webb, Eugene. *Philosophers of Consciousness: Polanyi, Lonergan, Voegelin, Ricoeur,
  Girard, Kierkegaard*. U. of Wash. Pr. 1988 $35.00. ISBN 0-295-96621-1. Probing
  studies stitched together by a single topic.

RORTY, RICHARD MCKAY. 1931–

[SEE Chapter 9 in this volume.]

RUSSELL, BERTRAND ARTHUR WILLIAM, 3RD EARL RUSSELL
1872–1970 (NOBEL PRIZE 1950)

Of Bertrand Russell his publishers have written: "It has been said that his
admirable and lucid English style may be attributed to the fact that he did not
undergo a classical education at a public school." As an English stylist, Russell
had the extraordinary gift of understanding and pioneering in the most abstruse
fields of human knowledge and of being able to make at least their broader
outlines crystal clear to the layperson. Though a mathematical logician, Russell
lived a life that was political and passionate. In the first volume of his
Autobiography, he said: "Three passions, simple but overwhelmingly strong,
have governed my life: the longing for love, the search for knowledge, and
unbearable pity for the sufferings of mankind."

After a lonely childhood, Russell went to Cambridge, the university with
which he was chiefly associated throughout his long, productive life. Although
he succeeded to an earldom in 1931 and then took his seat in the House of
Lords, he was imprisoned during World War I as a pacifist.

Russell wrote his greatest work, *Principia Mathematica* (1910–13), in collaboration with ALFRED NORTH WHITEHEAD. It demonstrated that mathematics rests
on logical foundations, and it formulated logical expressions in a symbolic
calculus to reveal logical structures concealed by ordinary grammar. The
impact of this work was to transform logic as a philosophical discipline. The
subject-predicate form and the syllogism discovered by ARISTOTLE (see also
Vol. 3) yielded center stage to a symbolic logic of relations and quantification.
The "unofficial parts" of *Principia* (the parts written in English) are attributed to
Russell, while Whitehead is credited with composing the symbolic calculi.
These "unofficial" parts introduce key notions such as material implication,
existential quantification, descriptions, and the theory of types. Discussions of
these notions dominated philosophy of logic and epistemology for a half century
thereafter, and Russell's theories, presented in articles and books, were the
normal starting point for these discussions.

Russell's serious philosophical works after *Principia* were in epistemology
and philosophy of mind. He strove to overcome the Cartesian dualisms of both
the epistemological and the psychophysical kinds. His theory of knowledge then
was very close to new realism, although in his later work he lapsed into
phenomenalism. On the mind-body dualism he expounded a neutral monism,
mind and matter being functional distinctions drawn in regard to a stuff that
was in itself neither mental nor physical.

After World War I, Russell came under the influence of WITTGENSTEIN, whose
Tractatus Logico-Philosophicus he introduced to English readers. During this
period, Russell expounded a theory of logical atomism. In 1940 he lectured at
the University of Chicago, Harvard University, and the University of California;

that year he was appointed professor of philosophy at the College of the City of New York, but the appointment was later revoked by a Supreme Court justice on the ground that certain passages in his books carried moral contamination for the youth of New York City. (See Dewey and Kallen's *Bertrand Russell Case*, listed below). He returned to England in 1944 as fellow and lecturer at Trinity College, Cambridge University. Here he completed his "philosophical testament," *Human Knowledge* (1948), a book of enormous scope." As Sidney Hook described it: "All the central issues in contemporary philosophy, from the theory of meaning to the nature of space-time are discussed with . . . characteristic incisiveness, technical skill and imagination." A rationalist, a materialist, a great mathematician, to him science was truth. His books were always provocative and highly personal, reflecting his immense knowledge and zest for life. He was awarded the 1950 Nobel Prize for literature, sharing it with the novelist William Faulkner (see Vol. 1)

Always a crusader for pacifism, he dreaded nuclear war, and this attitude colored most of his later writings. In *Unarmed Victory* (1963) he tried to influence leaders and public opinion in both the Soviet and Western blocs. In 1967 Russell sponsored, but did not attend, a "Vietnam war crimes tribunal," which he declared to be in the legal tradition of the international trials at Nuremberg after World War II. This tribunal criticized the American role in the war and accused the United States of genocide. Russell's own articles on the subject, *War Crimes in Vietnam*, were published in 1967. Early in 1969 a conference called by the Bertrand Russell Peace Foundation (again without the philosopher in attendance) found the Soviet Union similarly blameworthy for its 1968 invasion of Czechoslovakia.

The first two volumes of Russell's *Autobiography* have sometimes been found frivolous and "scrappy" but are admired by most critics as the eminently readable—and often very funny—outline of an incredibly rich experience of a fearless iconoclast, in constant contact with the great and near-great, who often found himself discharged or willingly let go for his unorthodox activities and opinions—particularly in this country—and often in financial straits as a result. Russell wrote an average of a letter every 30 hours of his life, and some 100,000 of these (mostly to other great or powerful men of his age) were privately sold in 1967, together with some 400 manuscripts. This treasure trove has yet to be published; books by Russell, therefore, may be expected to appear for a generation or more to come. Because of his longevity, his acquaintances spanned nearly a century. As George Steiner put it: "He debated philosophy with Wittgenstein and fiction with Conrad (see Vol. 1) and D. H. Lawrence (see Vol. 1), he . . . argued economics with Keynes (see Vol. 3) and civil disobedience with Gandhi, his open letters . . . provoked Stalin (see Vol. 3) to a reply and Lyndon Johnson to exasperation."

In 1983 Russell's publisher launched the publication of all his writings. *The Collected Papers of Bertrand Russell*, projected to run to 28 volumes when completed, was under the editorship of the Macmaster University Group, including Kenneth Blackwell and others. Peter F. Strawson, reviewing the first volumes in *The Times Literary Supplement*, wrote: "The editorial task has been discharged with exemplary thoroughness and efficiency. The entire series of volumes, when completed, will be indispensable to a thorough study of the intellectual development of one whose influence on the philosophy of his and our time has perhaps been greater than that of any other single individual."

BOOKS BY RUSSELL

The ABC of Relativity. 1925. NAL-Dutton 1985 $4.50. ISBN 0-451-62738-5. Philosophical analysis of the scientific theory; good exposition.

The Analysis of Mind. Humanities 1978 o.p. Profound but lightly written theory demolishing the substance concept of mind.

The Art of Philosophizing and Other Essays. Quality Paperback Ser. Littlefield 1977 $8.95. ISBN 0-8226-0273-3

Atheism: Collected Essays, 1943–1949. Atheist Viewpoint Ser. Ayer 1972 repr. of 1971 ed. $19.95. ISBN 0-405-03808-9

Authority and the Individual. 1949. Unwin Hyman 1977 $9.95. ISBN 0-04-170031-7. Reith lecture, vaunting individual freedom.

The Autobiography of Bertrand Russell. Unwin Hyman 1978 $16.95. ISBN 0-04-921022-X. Vol. 2 *1914–1944.* Unwin Hyman 1968 $34.95. ISBN 0-04-921009-02. Vol. 3 *1944–1967.* Unwin Hyman 1981 repr. of 1970 ed. $34.95. ISBN 0-04-921010-6

The Basic Writings of Bertrand Russell 1903–1959. Ed. by Robert E. Egner and Lester E. Dennon. S&S Trade 1967 $17.95. ISBN 0-671-20154-9. "[A]nthology, authorized and introduced by the author himself, consist[ing] of 81 essays and chapters or passages from longer works and . . . selected to represent Lord Russell as philosopher, mathematician, man of letters, historian and analyst of international affairs" (*Library Journal*).

Bertrand Russell. Living Philosophies Ser. Ed. by Ann Redpath. Creative Ed. 1986 $18.50. ISBN 0-88682-012-X. Readable selections providing a partial picture of Russell's educational theory.

Bertrand Russell Speaks His Mind. Greenwood 1974 repr. of 1960 ed. $35.00. ISBN 0-8371-7445-7. Selection of Russell's provocative statements on the issues of the day.

Bertrand Russell's Best. Ed. by R. E. Egner. 1958 $3.95. ISBN 0-451-62508-0. Selection of Russell's witticisms.

Bolshevism: Practice and Theory. Ayer 1978 repr. of 1920 ed. $17.00. ISBN 0-405-04587-5. Journalistic account of the Soviet Union in its early days by a sympathetic visitor who turned critical.

Cambridge Essays 1888–1889. Ed. by Kenneth Blackwell and others. Unwin Hyman 1988 $130.00. Volume 1 of *The Collected Papers of Bertrand Russell.*

Common Sense and Nuclear Warfare. AMS Pr. repr. of 1959 ed. $18.00. ISBN 0-404-05465-X. A "Better Red Than Dead" tract.

The Connection between Scientific Method and Metaphysics, or Logic and Mysticism. 2 vols. Found. Class. Reprints 1991 $257.85. ISBN 0-89901-432-1

The Conquest of Happiness. 1930. Liveright 1971 $8.95. ISBN 0-87140-244-0. Ethics intended for the educated layperson.

Consciousness, Introspection and the Operation of the Mind. Am. Inst. Psych. 1985 $217.00. ISBN 0-89920-081-8

Essays on Language, Mind and Matter, 1919–1926. Ed. by Bernd Frohmann and John G. Slater. Unwin Hyman 1988 $150.00. ISBN 0-04-920075-5. Volume 9 of *The Collected Papers of Bertrand Russell.*

Has Man a Future? Greenwood 1984 repr. of 1962 ed. $38.50. ISBN 0-313-24382-4

A History of Western Philosophy. 1945. S&S Trade 1967 $5.95. ISBN 0-671-20158-1. Classic yet popular work; the best history of philosophy written by a great twentieth-century philosopher.

If I Could Preach Just Once. (coauthored with others). Ayer repr. of 1929 ed. $17.00. ISBN 0-8369-2457-6

Impact of Science on Society. AMS Pr. repr. of 1953 ed. $15.00. ISBN 0-404-05466-8

In Praise of Idleness and Other Essays. 1935. Unwin Hyman 1981 $7.95. ISBN 0-04-304006-3. Imaginative popular essays.

An Inquiry into Meaning and Truth. 1940. Unwin Hyman 1980 $7.95. ISBN 0-04-121019-0. Technical work in philosophical semantics during the early period of the field's development.

Introduction to Mathematical Philosophy. 1919. S&S Trade 1971 o.p. Elementary
   restatement of the theory of mathematics based on logic.
Justice in Wartime. English Lit. Ser. Haskell 1974 $75.00. ISBN 0-8383-1738-3
Logic and Knowledge: Essays 1901–50. Ed. by Robert C. Marsh. Unwin Hyman 1988
   $21.95. ISBN 0-04-440267-0. A selection of Russell's most significant essays on the
   technical subjects of logic and epistemology, prepared for the serious student.
Logical and Philosophical Papers, 1909–1913. Ed. by John G. Slater and Bernd
   Frohmann. Routledge 1993 $185.00. ISBN 0-415-08446-6. Volume 6 of *The Collected
   Papers of Bertrand Russell.*
Marriage and Morals. Liveright rev. ed. 1970 $11.95. ISBN 0-87140-211-4
Mathematics, Metaphysics and the Power of the Scientific Mind. Found. Class. Reprints
   1991 $277.85. ISBN 0-89901-429-1
The Metaphysics of Education. 2 vols. Found. Class. Reprints 1986 repr. of 1922 ed.
   $198.75. ISBN 0-88901-257-4
My Philosophical Development. 1959. Unwin Hyman 1975 $9.95. ISBN 0-04-192030-9. An
   intellectual autobiography—beginning when he was 16 and written with his usual
   clarity and wit. With an appendix, "Russell's Philosophy," by Alan Wood.
Mysticism and Logic and Other Essays. 1918. B & N Imports 1981 o.p. A collection of
   stimulating essays that have been influential beyond the limited circle of academic
   philosophers.
The Nature of Man and His Relation with the Universe. 2 vols. Am. Classical Coll. Pr. 1992
   $337.00. ISBN 0-685-55455-4
Our Knowledge of the External World. 1926. Humanities 1972 o.p. Original theory of
   knowledge unfolding the perspectival theory of perception.
Philosophical Papers 1896–1899. Ed. by Nicholas Griffin. Unwin Hyman 1990 $140.00.
   ISBN 0-04-920068-2. Volume 2 of *The Collected Papers of Bertrand Russell.*
The Philosophy of Atomism and Other Essays, 1914–1919. Ed. by John G. Slater. Unwin
   Hyman 1988 $125.00. ISBN 0-04-920074-7. Volume 8 of *The Collected Papers of
   Bertrand Russell.*
The Philosophy of Leibniz. Hollowbrook 1989 $27.50. ISBN 0-89341-548-0
Political Ideals. Unwin Paperback Ser. Unwin Hyman 1980 $9.95. ISBN 0-04-320120-2
Power. 1938. Norton 1969 o.p. Ambitious though superficial endeavor to plumb the root
   principle of politics.
Principia Mathematica. (coauthored with Alfred North Whitehead.) 1910–13. 3 vols.
   Cambridge U. Pr. 1927 $500.00. ISBN 0-521-06791-X. Monumental treatise on the
   foundations of mathematics; a classic for all time, though accessible only to the
   expert.
The Principles of Mathematics. 1903. Norton 1964 repr. of 1930 ed. $12.95. ISBN 0-393-
   00249-7. Introductory work presenting Russell's revolutionary theory that logic is
   the basis of mathematics.
The Problems of China. Unwin Hyman 1922 o.p. Journalistic account of post-World War I
   China from an enlightened visitor.
The Problems of Philosophy. 1912. OUP 1959 $6.95. ISBN 0-19-500212-1. Classic
   introduction to philosophy for the educated layperson.
Religion and Science. OUP 1961 $9.95. ISBN 0-19-50028-8
Roads to Freedom: Socialism, Anarchism and Syndication. Unwin Paperbacks. Unwin
   Hyman 1966 $9.95. ISBN 0-04-335033-X
The Role of the Emotions and the Will in the Process of Mental Phenomena. Gloucester Art
   1985 $198.00. ISBN 0-86650-145-2
Sceptical Essays. 1928. Unwin Hyman 1960 $19.95. ISBN 0-04-104803-1. Popular and
   stimulating.
Sensations and Images and the Strange Deviations of the Mind. Am. Inst. Psych. 1987
   $247.00. ISBN 0-89920-156-3
Theory of Knowledge: The 1913 Manuscript. Ed. by Elizabeth R. Eames and Kenneth
   Blackwell. Routledge 1992 $16.95. ISBN 0-415-08298-6
The Totality of Man's Philosophical System. 2 vols. Found. Class. Reprints 1992 $327.45.
   ISBN 0-685-53614-9

War Crimes in Vietnam. Bks. Demand $44.50. ISBN 0-317-08492-5
What I Believe. Darby Pub. 1983 o.p. A credo for the humanist, the naturalist, the empiricist, and the liberal.
Why I Am Not a Christian and Other Essays on Religion and Related Subjects. S&S Trade 1967 $9.95. ISBN 0-671-20323-1
Why Men Fight: A Method of Abolishing the International Duel. Ayer repr. of 1917 ed. $20.00. ISBN 0-8369-5906-X
Wisdom of the West. Outlet Bk. Co. 1989 $17.99. ISBN 0-517-69041-1

BOOKS ABOUT RUSSELL

Ayer, A. J. *Bertrand Russell.* U. Ch. Pr. 1988 $9.95. ISBN 0-226-03343-0. Sympathetic interpretation of Russell by a leading English philosopher.
_____. *Russell and Moore: The Analytical Heritage. William Jones Lectures Ser.* HUP 1971 $17.50. ISBN 0-674-78103-1. Brilliant comparative study illuminating the background of Russell's thought.
Clark, Ronald. *The Life of Bertrand Russell.* Da Capo 1990 $17.95. ISBN 0-306-80397-6. Outstanding, comprehensive biography by an accomplished author.
Dewey, John, and H. M. Kallen, eds. *The Bertrand Russell Case.* Da Capo 1941 o.p. The report on Russell's academic freedom case against the City College of New York prepared by two famous American philosophers.
Grattan-Guinness, I., ed. *Dear Russell—Dear Jourdain: A Commentary on Russell's Logic Based on his Correspondence with Jourdain.* Col. U. Pr. 1977 $44.00. ISBN 0-231-04460-7. Easy access to abstruse theories through casual letters.
Griffin, Nicholas. *Russell's Idealist Apprenticeship.* OUP 1991 $98.00. ISBN 0-19-824453-3. Well-researched monograph on Russell's philosophy when, as a Cambridge University student and young don, he espoused the idealism of the period and wrote his book on Leibniz.
_____, ed. *The Selected Letters of Bertrand Russell, Vol. 1: The Private Years, 1884–1914.* HM 1992 $35.00. ISBN 0-395-56269-4. Masterful editorial work quietly illuminating the formative years in Russell's intellectual and emotional development.
Hardy, Godfrey H. *Bertrand Russell and Trinity: A College Controversy of the Last War.* Ed. by Walter P. Metzger. Ayer 1977 repr. of 1942 ed. $14.00. ISBN 0-405-1022-1. An investigative record of Russell's loss of his position at Cambridge during World War I because of his pacifism, including accounts of the villianous role played by McTaggart.
Hendley, Brian. *Dewey, Russell, Whitehead: Philosophers as Educators.* S. Ill. U. Pr. 1985 $14.95. ISBN 0-8093-1243-3. An informative study comparing the educational theories of the three philosophers.
Hill, Claire O. *Word and Object in Husserl, Frege, and Russell: The Roots of Twentieth Century Philosophy. Ser. in Continental Thought.* Ohio U. Pr. 1991 $34.95. ISBN 0-8214-1002-4. Rewarding but demanding monograph on Russell's theory of reference in relation to the work of his predecessors.
Kilmister, C. W. *Russell.* St. Martin 1984 $27.50. ISBN 0-312-69613-2. A critical evaluation of Russell's work.
Kuntz, Paul G. *Bertrand Russell. Twayne's Eng. Authors Ser.* Macmillan 1986 $19.95. ISBN 0-8057-6916-1. Well-researched, well-written study prepared by an outstanding scholar that is an excellent place to start the study of Russell.
Sainsbury, Mark. *Russell. Arguments of the Philosophers Ser.* Routledge Chapman & Hall 1979 $36.00. $15.95. ISBN 0-7102-0536-8. Acute analytic critique of Russell's thought for the advanced student.
Savage, C. Wade, and C. Anthony Anderson, eds. *Rereading Russell: Essays on Bertrand Russell's Metaphysics and Epistemology. Minnesota Studies in the Philosophy of Science.* U. of Minn. Pr. 1989 $39.95. ISBN 0-8166-1649-3. A collection of critical essays on Russell's thought, including Anderson's "Russell on Order in Time" and Savage's "Sense Data in Russell's Theory of Knowledge."
Schilpp, Paul A., ed. *The Philosophy of Bertrand Russell. Lib. of Living Philosophers.* Bks. Demand repr. of 1971 ed. $160.00. ISBN 0317-09085-2. Collection of original critical

essays, preceded by Russell's intellectual biography and followed by his responses to his critics. The volume closes with a bibliography of Russell's writings.

Vellacott, Jo. *Bertrand Russell and the Pacifists in the First World War.* St. Martin 1981 $26.00. ISBN 0-312-07705-X. Careful reconstruction of an important moment in Russell's life; very readable social history.

RYLE, GILBERT. 1900–1976

Gilbert Ryle exerted an influence over academic philosophers in the English-speaking world almost without equal at midcentury. As Waynefleet Professor of Philosophy at Oxford University and as G. E. MOORE's successor to the editorship of *Mind*, the most prestigious philosophical journal in Great Britain, Ryle shaped the orientation of philosophical discussion for more than a decade. Independently of LUDWIG WITTGENSTEIN, he invented a philosophical method of linguistic analysis, maintaining indeed that systematic confusions in theory stemmed from misleading grammatical expressions.

Ryle's most remarkable contribution to philosophy, however, was in the area of philosophy of mind. His crowning achievement was *The Concept of Mind* (1949). Utilizing his method of linguistic analysis on a discourse about mind and the mental, he maintained that the radical distinction between mind and body, Cartesian dualism, stemmed from category mistakes. A felicitous writer with a distinctively colloquial style free of jargon, Ryle invented phrases—such as "the ghost in the machine" to indicate supposed Cartesian mental substance—that still reverberate in the literature of philosophy and psychology.

BOOKS BY RYLE

The Concept of Mind. 1949. U. Ch. Pr. 1984 $11.95. ISBN 0-226-73295-9. Most influential work in the philosophy of mind by a British author to appear after World War II.

Dilemmas. Cambridge U. Pr. 1954 $13.95. ISBN 0-521-09115-2. "From the first page to the last the argument is easily followed and brilliantly illustrated by example" (*New Statesman and Nation*).

Plato's Progress. Bks. Demand repr. of 1966 ed. $79.80. ISBN 0-317-08852-1. "Professor Ryle presents an original indeed revolutionary account of Plato's development" (*Times Literary Supplement*).

On Thinking. Rowman 1980 o.p. A monograph displaying Ryle's characteristic conceptual verve.

BOOKS ABOUT RYLE

Kolenda, Konstantin, ed. *Studies in Philosophy: A Symposium on Gilbert Ryle.* Rice Univ. 1972 o.p. A collection of original critical essays by prominent philosophers.

Lyons, William. *Gilbert Ryle: An Introduction to His Philosophy.* Humanities 1980 o.p. "[L]ays bare the central themes in Ryle's work, shows how they knit together, and critically discusses his arguments when pursuing those themes (*The Philosopher's Index*).

SANTAYANA, GEORGE. 1863–1952

A gentle philosopher-poet, born and reared in Spain, educated at Harvard University and later professor of philosophy there, George Santayana resided in England, France, and Italy after 1914. At the beginning of World War II, he entered the nursing home in Rome managed by nuns known as the Blue Sisters and remained there until his death. His last book, *The Poet's Testament* (1953), contains a few unpublished lyrics, several translations, and two plays in blank verse. The title comes from the poem read at his funeral, which begins: "I give back to the earth what the earth gave/All to the furrow, nothing to the grave."

Santayana wrote philosophy in an inimitable prose, enriched with imagery and metaphor. His meanings were always complex and often ironic. In this style, so untypical of the professionalized philosophy common in the English-speaking world during his lifetime, Santayana nevertheless articulated an epistemological critical realism and an ontology of essence and matter that drew the attention and admiration of philosophers and scholars.

His first published philosophical book, *The Sense of Beauty* (1896), was an important contribution in aesthetics, a classic text that is still in use. His multivolume work *The Life of Reason* expresses his naturalistic philosophy of history and culture. It states the essence of his attitude toward nature, life, and society. *Scepticism and Animal Faith* (1923) presents his theory of knowledge and also serves as an introduction to his system of philosophy, *Realms of Being* (1927–40). The titles of the separate volumes of this remarkable work, now out of print, reveal the lineaments of his system: *Realm of Essence* (1927), *Realm of Matter* (1930), *Realm of Truth* (1937), and *Realm of Spirit* (1940). His ideas were "popularized" in his only novel, *The Last Puritan*, which became a surprise bestseller overnight. According to the *New York Times*, "He came into a changing American scene with a whole group of concepts that enormously enriched our thinking. He gave a moving vitality to what had often been obscure abstractions . . . he made the whole relationship of reason and beauty, each to the other, come alive and stay alive." Although Santayana's *Complete Poems* (1975) is out of print, several volumes of his poetry are available and are listed below.

Publication of *The Complete Works of George Santayana*, under the general editorship of Herman J. Saatkamp, Jr., is in progress. Conforming to the guidelines of a critical edition, *The Complete Works* is a long-range multivolume project of which a few volumes have already appeared to critical acclaim.

Books by Santayana

Birth of Reason and Other Essays. Ed. by Daniel Cory. Col. U. Pr. 1968 $42.00. ISBN 0-231-03169-6. Excellent collection of Santayana's essays introducing his thoughts, prepared by his former secretary.

Character and Opinion in the United States 1920. Transaction Pubs. 1991 $19.95. ISBN 0-88738-890-6. Contains acidic views of the philosophies of Josiah Royce and William James, Santayana's mentors and colleagues at Harvard.

Dominations and Powers: Reflections on Liberty, Society and Government. 1951. Kelley 1975 repr. of 1954 ed. $45.00. ISBN 0-678-02775-7. Masterful political philosophy with comments relevant to the international situation immediately after World War II.

Egotism in German Philosophy. Haskell 1971 repr. of 1916 ed. $75.00. ISBN 0-8383-1318-3. Polemical monograph against German idealism as causative of World War I.

The Genteel Tradition at Bay. 1931. Haskell 1977 $75.00. ISBN 0-8383-2154-2. Collection of incisive essays on literature and culture.

The Hermit of Carmel, and Other Poems. AMS Pr. repr. of 1901 ed. $27.50. ISBN 0-404-59340-2

The Idea of Christ in the Gospels; or God in Man, a Critical Essay. AMS Pr. 1979 repr. of 1946 ed. $30.00. ISBN 0-404-59341-0. Santayana's critical interpretation of Christianity.

The Idler and His Works. Ed. by Daniel Cory. Ayer 1975 repr. of 1957 ed. $15.00. ISBN 0-8369-0052-2. Scintillatingly popular.

Interpretations of Poetry and Religion: Critical Edition. Ed. by Herman J. Saatkamp, Jr., and William G. Holzberger. *Complete Works of George Santayana.* MIT Pr. 1990 $37.50. ISBN 0-262-19286-1. First published in 1900, this original work demonstrated the symbolic affinity of art and religion.

The Last Puritan: A Memoir in the Form of a Novel. The Scholarly Edition of the Complete Works of George Santayana Ser. MIT Pr. 1992 $45.00. ISBN 0-262-19328-0. Best-selling 1936 novel expressing Santayana's evaluation of America.

The Life of Reason. Macmillan 1981 $30.00. ISBN 0-684-16831-6. One-volume, revised and reduced edition of the 1905–06 multivolume work, consisting of Vol. 1 *Reason in Common Sense*; Vol. 2 *Reason in Society*; Vol. 3 *Reason in Religion*; Vol. 4 *Reason in Art*; Vol. 5 *Reason in Science.*

Little Essays Drawn from the Writings of George Santayana. Ed. by L. P. Smith. Ayer 1978 repr. of 1920 ed. $20.00. ISBN 0-8369-0848-1. Excerpts from Santayana's writings, especially from *The Life of Reason*; very well done.

Lotze's System of Philosophy. Ed. by Paul G. Kuntz. Bks. Demand repr. of 1971 ed. $71.50. ISBN 0-317-08898-X. Santayana's Harvard doctoral dissertation. With an introduction by the editor.

Lucifer: A Theological Tragedy. Irvington repr. of 1899 ed. $36.00. ISBN 0-8398-1850-5

Persons and Places: The Autobiography of George Santayana. Ed. by Herman J. Saatkamp, Jr., and William G. Holzberger. MIT Pr. 1986 $47.50. ISBN 0-262-19238-1. Critical edition of the first volume of Santayana's autobiography.

Physical Order and Moral Liberty. Ed. by John Lachs and Shirley Lachs. Vanderbilt U. Pr. 1969 $17.95. ISBN 0-8265-1131-7. Previously unpublished essays.

The Poet's Testament: Poems and Two Plays. AMS Pr. repr. of 1953 ed. $22.00. ISBN 0-404-59424-7

Reason in Art. Dover 1982 $5.95. ISBN 0-486-24358-3. Volume 4 of *The Life of Reason* as originally published.

Reason in Science. Dover 1983 $6.95. ISBN 0-486-24439-3. Volume 5 of *The Life of Reason* as originally published.

Reason in Society. Dover 1980 $5.95. ISBN 0-488-24003-7. Volume 2 of *The Life of Reason* as originally published.

Scepticism and Animal Faith: Introduction to a System of Philosophy. 1923. Dover 1955 $7.95. ISBN 0-486-20236-4. The best formulation of the theory of knowledge of critical realism, and a sketch of the realms of being.

Selected Critical Writings of George Santayana. Ed. by Norman Henfrey. 2 vols. Bks. Demand. repr. of 1968 ed. Vol. 1 $87.00. ISBN 0-317-28141-0. Vol. 2 $64.30. ISBN 0-317-26410-9

The Sense of Beauty: Critical Edition. Ed. by Herman J. Saatkamp, Jr., and William Holzberger. *The Complete Works of Santayana Ser.* MIT Pr. 1988 $37.50. ISBN 0-262-19271-3. The outline of an aesthetic, first published in 1896, that influenced the course of thought in the field.

Soliloquies in England and Later Soliloquies. Rprt. Serv. 1992 $79.00. ISBN 0-7812-6853-2

Some Turns of Thought in Modern Philosophy. Ayer 1972 repr. of 1933 ed. $11.00. ISBN 0-8369-0849-X. Collection of inimitable essays interpreting recent philosophy.

Three Philosophical Poets. Cooper Sq. 1971 o.p. Dante, Shakespeare, and Goethe are construed in terms of the philosophies they project.

BOOKS ABOUT SANTAYANA

Arnett, Willard Eugene. *Santayana and the Sense of Beauty.* Peter Smith 1984 repr. of 1955 ed. $12.00. ISBN 0-8446-0458-5. A discerning analysis of Santayana as artist-philosopher.

Ashmore, Jerome. *Santayana, Art, and Aesthetics.* Bks. Demand $38.30. ISBN 0-317-08999-4. Lucid, scholarly monograph on Santayana's aesthetics.

Dawidoff, Robert. *The Genteel Tradition and the Sacred Rage: High Culture vs. Democracy in Adams, James and Santayana. Cultural Studies in the United States.* U. of NC Pr. 1992 $32.50. ISBN 0-8078-2017-2. Polemical literary theory used to investigate intellectual history.

Kirkwood, Mossie M. *Santayana: Saint of the Imagination.* Bks. Demand $65.60. ISBN 0-8357-6382-X. Appealing, sensitive portrait of the philosopher and his thought.

Levinson, Henry S. *Santayana, Pragmatism and the Spiritual Life.* U. of NC Pr. 1992 $39.95. ISBN 0-8078-2031-8. Brilliant original interpretation of Santayana's philosophy in relation to the philosophical pragmatism he publicly despised.

McCormick, John. *George Santayana: A Biography.* Paragon Hse. 1988 $12.95. ISBN 1-55778-010-2. The best account of Santayana's life and thought, comprehensive and penetrating, informative and interesting; eminently readable.

Munson, T. N. *The Essential Wisdom of George Santayana.* Bks. Demand $59.00. ISBN 0-317-09248-5. Scholarly interpretation of Santayana's thought, stressing the doctrine of essence.

Saatkamp, Herman J., Jr. and John Jones. *George Santayana: A Bibliographical Checklist, 1880–1980.* Philos Document 1982 $25.50. ISBN 0-912632-75-5. Authoritative bibliography indispensable to the serious researcher.

Singer, Beth. *The Rational Society: A Critical Reading of Santayana's Social Thought.* Bks. Demand $38.80. ISBN 0-317-08959-5. Invaluable analytic monograph on a central aspect of Santayana's work.

Sprigge, Timothy. *Santayana: An Examination of His Philosophy. Arguments of the Philosophers Ser.* Routledge Chapman & Hall 1974 $29.50. ISBN 0-7100-7721-1. Penetrating critical evaluation of Santayana, insightfully rendered.

Woodward, Anthony. *Living in the Eternal: A Study of George Santayana.* Vanderbilt U. Pr. 1988 $22.50. ISBN 0-8265-1227-5. "[A]n intellectual portrait, encompassing art, politics, religion, as well as philosophy, and aims to show that the philosophical synthesis of Santayana's later writing is best viewed as the imaginative expression of a personal disposition" (*The Philosopher's Index*).

SARTRE, JEAN-PAUL. 1905–1980 (NOBEL PRIZE 1964)

Jean-Paul Sartre was the chief prophet of atheistic existentialism, that bleak philosophy of despair that grew from the defeat of France. When the intellectuals of the Left Bank felt abandoned and helpless, it offered both a personal and a social answer. There are two types of existentialists—those who follow the mystical Danish pastor of the nineteenth century, SØREN KIERKEGAARD, and Sartre's atheistic followers, who reject Kierkegaard's belief in God but accept his idea of human existence in a hostile, disordered world, trying to make the best of things, fulfilling life and achieving final freedom. In *Existentialism*, Sartre denied that his philosophy is one of despair, and said: "Man is nothing else but what he makes of himself. You're free, choose, that is, invent." However, many find his formula full of paradoxes. *Being and Nothingness* (1943), *Search for a Method* (1957), and *Critique of Dialectical Reason* (1960) provide the core of his thought and its development. In the latter two volumes he answered his critics by setting the existentialist "man alone" in his social and world context.

Sartre initially subscribed to the phenomenological movement that originated with EDMUND HUSSERL, but he departed from pure phenomenology when he followed MARTIN HEIDEGGER (see also Vol. 5) in the quest for an ontology. His 1937 work, *The Transcendence of the Ego*, marks his departure from Husserlian phenomenology and his movement in the direction of the existentialist ontology expressed in *Being and Nothingness*.

In the decade after World War II, Sartre's thinking moved to the left, and his high esteem for Marxism, manifest in his journalistic publications, is evident in his thick, almost impenetrable work, the *Critique of Dialectical Reason*.

For 13 years Sartre was an obscure teacher of philosophy. Mobilized as a private at the beginning of the war, he was taken prisoner and spent nine months in a German war prison. When released, he returned to Paris to take an active part in the Communist resistance organization. He abandoned teaching for writing and formulated his philosophy. In Paris he was the leader of a brilliant and creative group of writers that included MAURICE MERLEAU-PONTY, ALBERT CAMUS (see Vol. 2), and SIMONE DE BEAUVOIR (see Vol. 2).

In 1964 Sartre published the autobiography of his early years, *The Words*, and in the same year was offered the Nobel Prize for literature, which he refused. Sartre's achievements as a man of letters rival his contributions to philosophy. He is known for such novels as *Nausea* (1938), *The Age of Reason*, and *Troubled Sleep*, the plays *No Exit* (1944), *The Flies* (1943), and the short story "The Wall." He also wrote penetrating works of literary and philosophical criticism on JEAN GENET (see Vol. 2), GUSTAVE FLAUBERT (see Vol. 2), and CHARLES BAUDELAIRE (see Vol. 2).

BOOKS BY SARTRE

Anti-Semite and Jew. 1948. Schocken 1965 $12.00. ISBN 0-8052-0102-5. Controversial existentialist analysis of anti-Semitism.

Being and Nothingness. 1943. Trans. by Hazel E. Barnes. PB 1983 $6.99 ISBN 0-671-49606-9

Critique of Dialectical Reason. 1960. 2 vols. Routledge Chapmann & Hall Vol. 1 *Theory of Practice Ensembles*. Ed. by Jonathan Ree. Trans. by Alan Sheridan. 1984 $18.95. ISBN 0-86091-757-6. Vol. 2 Trans. by Hoare Quintin. 1991 $49.95. ISBN 0-86091-311-2

The Emotions: Outline of a Theory. Trans. by Bernard Frechtman. Carol Pub. Group 1984 $3.95. ISBN 0-8065-0904-X. Influential phenomenological study.

Essays in Aesthetics. Trans. by Wade Baskin. Ayer 1963 $12.00. ISBN 0-8369-1104-0. A collection of Sartre's essays on art and philosophy, some having appeared in *Les Temps Modernes*, which he founded and edited with Simone de Beauvoir and Maurice Merleau-Ponty.

Essays in Existentialism. Ed. by Wade Baskin. Carol Pub. Group 1967 $7.95. ISBN 0-8065-0162-6. A useful collection of readable essays.

Existentialism and Human Emotions. Carol Pub. Group 1971 $4.95. ISBN 0-8065-0902-3. Contains *Existentialism* as well as parts of *Being and Nothingness*.

Existentialism and Humanism. 1947. Haskell 1977 $49.95. ISBN 0-8383-2148-8. Defines existentialism as humanism.

Existential Psychoanalysis. 1953. Trans. by Hazel E. Barnes. Regnery Gateway 1962 $8.95. ISBN 0-89526-940-6. A new psychoanalysis based on the principles of existentialism.

Imagination: A Philosophical Critique. Trans. by Forrest Williams. U. of Mich. Pr. 1962 o.p. Of great importance to philosophers and psychologists and of interest to the informed layperson.

Literature and Existentialism. 1962. Trans. by Bernard Frechtman. Carol Pub. Group 1980 $4.95. ISBN 0-8065-0105-7. Reiteration of paramount value of commitment on the part of the author for significant literature.

Notebooks for an Ethics. Trans. by David Pellauer. U. Ch. Pr. 1992 $49.95. ISBN 0-226-73511-7

Psychology of Imagination. Greenwood 1978 $35.00. ISBN 0-313-20498-5. Significant phenomenological investigation.

Search for a Method. 1957. Trans. by Hazel E. Barnes. Random 1968 $7.95. ISBN 0-394-70464-9. An introduction to Sartre's second great philosophical work after *Being and Nothingness*—the *Critique of Dialectical Reason*—demonstrating how he reconciled his existentialism with Marxism as aspects of the same worldview.

The Transcendence of the Ego: An Existentialist Theory of Consciousness. 1937. Ed. and trans. by Forrest Williams and Robert Kirkpatrick. FS&G 1957 o.p. A "brilliant polemic against the pure Ego" (*Journal of Philosophy*).

Truth and Existence. Trans. by Adrian Yan Den Hoven. U. Ch. Pr. 1992 $18.95. ISBN 0-226-73522-2

What Is Literature? 1947. Peter Smith 1958 $18.50. ISBN 0-8446-2867-0. Stresses the importance of the commitment of the writer.

The Writings of Jean-Paul Sartre. (coauthored with Richard C. McCleary). 2 vols. *Studies in Phenomenology and Existential Philosophy.* Northwestern U. Pr. Vol. 1 *A Bibliographical Life.* 1974 $42.95. ISBN 0-8101-0430-X. Vol. 2 *Selected Prose.* 1974 $12.95. ISBN 0-8101-0709-0

BOOKS ABOUT SARTRE

Aronson, Ronald. *Sartre's Second Critique.* U. Ch. Pr. 1987 $13.95. ISBN 0-226-02805-4. An explanation and critique.

Barnes, Hazel E., *Sartre and Flaubert.* U. Ch. Pr. 1982 $25.00. ISBN 0-226-03720-7. Scholarly, literary study by Sartre's translator.

Boschetti, Ann. *The Intellectual Enterprise: Sartre and Les Temps Modernes.* Trans. by Richard McCleary. Northwestern U. Pr. 1988 $42.95. ISBN 0-8101-0755-4. Cultural study of Sartre and the influential review he founded.

Brosman, Catherine. *Jean-Paul Sartre. Twayne's World Authors Ser.* Macmillan 1983 $20.95. ISBN 0-8057-6544-1. Concise, comprehensive treatment of Sartre's life and work; a good introduction.

Busch, Thomas W. *The Power of Consciousness and the Force of Circumstances in Sartre's Philosophy. Studies in Continental Thought.* Ind. U. Pr. 1990 $19.95. ISBN 0-253-31283-3. Profound monograph.

Cannon, Betty. *Sartre and Psychoanalysis: An Existentialist Challenge to Clinical Metatheory.* U. Pr. of KS 1991 $35.00. ISBN 0-7006-0445-6. Assesses Sartre's contributions to existentialist psychoanalytic theory.

Catalano, Joseph S. *Commentary on Jean-Paul Sartre's Being and Nothingness.* U. Ch. Pr. 1985 $17.95. ISBN 0-226-09699-8. Helpful critical reading of Sartre's obscure masterpiece in existential ontology.

————. *A Commentary on Jean-Paul Sartre's Critique of Dialectical Reason: Theory of Practical Ensemble.* U. Ch. Pr. 1987 $40.00. ISBN 0-226-09700-5. Useful guide to the understanding of Sartre's systematically dialectical work on Marxism and existentialism.

Caws, Peter. *Sartre. Arguments of the Philosophers Ser.* Routledge Chapman & Hall 1979 $26.95. ISBN 0-7102-0233-4. Acute elucidation and critique of the cogency of Sartre's philosophy.

Cohen-Solal, Annie. *Sartre: A Life.* Pantheon 1988 $12.95. ISBN 0-394-75662-2. This "long, careful and loving portrait of Sartre turns a remote and puzzling mandarin into a true existential being, warts and all" (*Time*).

De Beauvoir, Simone. *Adieux: A Farewell to Sartre.* Trans. by Patrick O'Brian. Pantheon 1985 $8.95. ISBN 0-394-72898-X. Loving personal salute, sometimes bittersweet, from Sartre's lifelong lover.

Detmer, David. *Freedom as a Value: A Critique of the Ethical Theory of Jean-Paul Sartre.* Open Court 1988 $29.95. ISBN 0-8126-9082-6. "[A]ttempts to provide a critical exposition of the ethical theory of Sartre . . . and also defends Sartre's concept that freedom is the highest and most important value and shows how these two themes are intertwined" (*The Philosopher's Index*).

Fell, Joseph P., III. *Emotion in the Thought of Sartre.* Col. U. Pr. 1965 $42.00. ISBN 0-231-02756-7. Based mainly on Sartre's *The Emotions: Outline of a Theory* and *Being and Nothingness.*

Greene, Norman N.. *Jean-Paul Sartre: The Existentialist Ethic.* Greenwood 1980 repr. of 1960 ed. $35.00. ISBN 0-313-22422-6. Capable critical study focused on ethical themes.

Hartmann, Klaus. *Sartre's Ontology: A Study of Being and Nothingness in the Light of Hegel's Logic. Studies in Phenomenology and Existential Philosophy Ser.* Northwestern U. Pr. 1966 $14.95. ISBN 0-8101-0610-8. "An outstanding interpretation of Sartre for specialists" (*Library Journal*).

Harvey, Robert. *Search for a Father: Sartre, Paternity, and the Question of Ethics.* U. of Mich. Pr. 1991 $34.50. ISBN 0-472-10225-7. Psychological investigation to illuminate moral philosophy.

Hayman, Ronald. *Sartre*. S&S Trade 1987 $19.95. ISBN 0-671-45942-2. Intellectual biography.

Hendley, Steve. *Reason and Relativism: A Sartrean Investigation*. State U. NY Pr. 1991 $44.50. ISBN 0-7914-0723-3. Penetrating, scholarly interpretation.

Hyim, Gila J. *The Existential Sociology of Jean-Paul Sartre*. U. of Mass. Pr. 1982 $10.95. ISBN 0-87023-381-5. Exposition of the Sartrian principles of social groups.

Kerner, George C. *Three Philosophical Moralists: Mill, Kant, and Sartre*. OUP 1990 $49.95. ISBN 0-19-824227-1. A sophisticated essay on the concepts of moral freedom in three giants of modern thought.

Lapointe, Francis, ed. *Jean-Paul Sartre and His Critics: An International Bibliography, 1938–80, with Annotations*. Philos Document 1981 $42.50. ISBN 0-912632-44-5. A useful research tool.

Light, Stephen. *Shuzo Kuki and Jean-Paul Sartre: Influence and Counter-Influence in the Early History of Existential Phenomenology*. S. Ill. U. Pr. 1987 $13.95. ISBN 0-8093-1271-9. A monograph in the history of philosophy.

McBride, William L. *Sartre's Political Theory*. Ind. U. Pr. 1991 $37.50. ISBN 0-253-33621-X. Insightful monograph on Sartre's politics from his resistance to Nazism to his modified acceptance of Marxism.

Manser, Anthony. *Sartre: A Philosophic Study*. Greenwood 1981 repr. of 1966 ed. $38.50. ISBN 0-313-22827-2. "[S]erious, painstaking study, into which the reader is carefully drawn" (*Choice*).

Morris, Phyllis S. *Sartre's Concept of a Person*. U. of Mass. Pr. 1976 $22.50. ISBN 0-80723-185-5. An analytic approach to an existentialist theory.

Murdoch, Iris. *Sartre: Romantic Moralist*. Viking Penguin 1989 $6.95. ISBN 0-14-010143-8. A subtle intellectual portrait by the distinguished English philosopher-novelist.

Natanson, Maurice. *A Critique of Jean-Paul Sartre's Ontology*. *Studies in Philosophy*. Haskell 1972 repr. of 1950 ed. $75.00. ISBN 0-8383-1412-0. Careful exposition and criticism, highly compressed, good to have at hand when reading *Being and Nothingness*.

Poster, Mark. *Sartre's Marxism*. Cambridge U. Pr. 1982 $19.95. ISBN 0-521-24559-1. Positively merits being the last word on the subject.

Schilpp, Paul A., ed. *The Philosophy of Jean-Paul Sartre*. *Lib. of Living Philosophers*. Open Court 1981 $34.95. ISBN 0-87548-354-2. A collection of original essays by leading experts on all aspects of Sartre's thought.

Scriven, Michael. *Sartre's Existential Biographies*. St. Martin 1984 $29.95. ISBN 0-312-69968-9. An Australian analytic philosopher of science changes course and comes up with a winner.

Suhl, Benjamin. *Jean-Paul Sartre: The Philosopher as a Literary Critic*. Col. U. Pr. 1973 $16.00. ISBN 0-231-08319-X. "One of the best books on Sartre" (*Choice*).

SCHELER, MAX FERDINAND. 1874–1928

Born in Munich, Max Ferdinand Scheler was a pupil of Rudolf Eucken. Afterward he taught at the Universities of Jena, Munich, and Cologne. In 1910 he retired from teaching to live in Berlin and pursue an independent career as a philosophical writer. Under the influence of EDMUND HUSSERL, he adopted the phenomenological method, which he used to examine value experiences such as those involved in social institutions and religion. Scheler's main contributions were to the fields of philosophy and sociology. He is credited with having influenced MARTIN HEIDEGGER, ERNST CASSIRER, GABRIEL MARCEL, and JOSÉ ORTEGA Y GASSET.

Scheler has been viewed as a symbol of European intellectual unrest before and after World War I. His personal life was stormy. Yet in the midst of internal and external unrest and turmoil, Scheler persisted in his philosophical labors. Between 1913 and 1916, he published what is regarded as his major work,

Formalism in Ethics and Non-Formal Ethics of Values, an ambitious attempt to articulate a phenomenology of ethical values. Scheler's conversion to Roman Catholicism in 1920 was widely interpreted as a manifestation of the spiritual and intellectual vitality of the church. An account of his conversion is given in his book *On the Eternal in Man* (1921). This book has been acclaimed as "one of the clearest and most comprehensive discussions of the approach to theistic philosophy, a work that shows "a remarkable combination of observation with metaphysical acumen."

BOOKS BY SCHELER

Formalism in Ethics and Non-Formal Ethics of Values: A New Attempt Toward the Foundations of Ethical Personalism. Trans. by Manfred S. Frings and Roger L. Funk. 1913–16 *Studies in Phenomenology and Existential Philosophy Ser*. Northwestern U. Pr. 1973 $18.95. ISBN 0-8101-0620-5

Man's Place in Nature. Trans. by Hans Meyerhoff. 1928. FS&G 1962 o.p. Philosophical anthropology in the service of the metaphysically transcendent, stirringly eloquent for a philosopher's work.

On the Eternal in Man. Trans. by Bernard Noble. 1921. Shoe String 1972 o.p.

On Feeling, Knowing, and Valuing: Selected Writings. Heritage of Sociology Ser. U. Ch. Pr. 1992 $41.00. ISBN 0-226-73670-9

Problems of a Sociology of Knowledge. Ed. by Kenneth Strikkers. Trans. by Manfred S. Frings. *International Lib. of Sociology*. Routledge Chapman & Hall 1980 $32.50. ISBN 0-7100-0302-1. Scheler's pioneering writing in a field that came into existence, partly through his efforts, after his death.

Selected Philosophical Essays. Trans. by David Lachterman. *Studies in Phenomenology and Existential Philosophy Ser*. Northwestern U. Pr. 1973 $15.95. ISBN 0-8101-0619-1. Essays based largely on *Formalism in Ethics and Non-Formal Ethics of Values*.

BOOKS ABOUT SCHELER

Nota, John H. *Max Scheler: The Man and His Works*. Franciscan Pr. 1983 $12.00. ISBN 0-8199-0852-5. An appreciation.

Perrin, Ron. *Max Scheler's Concept of the Person: An Ethics of Humanism*. St. Martin 1991 $10.00. ISBN 0-87842-275-1. "A critical study of Max Scheler's personalist ethics grounded in Scheler's attempt to overcome the limitations of Kant's formalism" (*The Philosopher's Index*).

Staude, J. R. *Max Scheler, 1874–1928: An Intellectual Portrait*. Free Pr. 1967 $14.95. ISBN 0-02-930770-8. "A good introductory study" (*Choice*).

SCHLICK, MORITZ. 1882–1936

Moritz Schlick studied at Berlin under MAX PLANCK (see Vol. 5) and received his Ph.D. in physics in 1904. He taught at Rostock and Kiel before joining the faculty at Vienna in 1922. His early work, *General Theory of Knowledge* (1918), reveals his commitment to realism and to the experimental method in scientific and philosophical knowledge. At Vienna he led the Vienna Circle of logical positivism and was instrumental in recruiting RUDOLF CARNAP. The publication of LUDWIG WITTGENSTEIN's *Tractatus Logico-Philosophicus* (1921) influenced radically the subsequent development of his thought. Increasingly he stressed the empirical verification criterion for truth and meaning and became severely critical of statements in philosophy and elsewhere that could not meet this criterion. Hence the logical positivists whom he led became notorious for their thesis that metaphysics in non-sense. His mature epistemology was presented in the publication of the second edition of his *General Theory of Knowledge* (1925). He also advanced a noncognitivist theory of ethical statements in his book *Problems of Ethics* (1939).

BOOKS BY SCHLICK

General Theory of Knowledge. 1925. Trans. by A. E. Blumberg. *Lib. of Exact Philosophy.*
   Open Court 1985 $12.00. ISBN 0-87548-442-5
The Problems of Philosophy in Their Interconnection. Ed. by Henk L. Mulder and others.
   Kluwer Ac. 1987 $122.50. ISBN 90-277-2465-2

BOOK ABOUT SCHLICK

McGuinness, Brian, ed. *Morritz Schlick.* Kluwer Ac. 1985 $55.00. ISBN 90-277-2096-7. A
   collection of scholarly articles that originally appeared in a special number of the
   publication *Synthese* that was devoted to Schlick.

SELLARS, WILFRID. 1912–1989

Wilfrid Sellars taught at the University of Minnesota, Yale University, and the
University of Pittsburgh. The son of the American philosopher Roy Wood
Sellars, he won early fame at Minnesota as the coeditor of two volumes, one on
logical analysis, the other on ethical theory, that introduced a generation of
American students to the problems and issues of analytic philosophy. *Readings
in Philosophical Analysis* (1949) was immediately adopted as the major textbook
on analytic philosophy used in American colleges and universities, and his
Readings in Ethical Theory (1952) was equally influential. E. W. Hall, reviewing
the first edition for *Ethics,* declared that "This reviewer finds the volume
intellectually exciting. . . . This result was achieved by a rigorous restriction in
the range of material used and in a happy and entirely rational collection of it.
The selections are uniformly high level: they reveal competent ethicists at work,
writing for philosophically literate readers."

Sellars's early articles, influenced by the logical atomism of LUDWIG
WITTGENSTEIN and BERTRAND RUSSELL (see also Vol. 5), reveal an inquisitive
metaphysician who was also a careful student of the great figures in the history
of philosophy. As Sellars matured, his work took a turn in the direction of
IMMANUEL KANT and C. S. PEIRCE. From Kant he derived his sense of the role of
conceptual structure—in the contemporary term, language—in shaping experience, so that there is no absolute given. From Peirce he gained insight into the
normative aspect of all beliefs, including science. However, Sellars did not
merely follow his sources. A profoundly original metaphysician, he transformed
all these conceptions in the articulation of a philosophical system distinctively
his own. His major book, *Science and Metaphysics: Variations on Kantian
Themes* (1968), received great acclaim. The reviewer for the *Times Literary
Supplement* noted: "Although Professor Sellar's philosophical writings make
difficult reading, their content is rewarding. . . . What distinguishes [his]
scientific realism from older and modern versions of scientism is his emphasis
on the normative aspects of both practical and theoretical thinking."

BOOKS BY SELLARS

The Metaphysics of Epistemology: Lectures by Wilfred Sellars. Ridgeview 1989 $35.00.
   ISBN 0-917930-94-0. Introduced by P. V. Amaral.
Naturalism and Ontology. Ridgeview 1980 $27.00. ISBN 0-917930-36-3. A treatise on
   metaphysics.
Philosophical Perspectives: History of Philosophy. Ridgeview 1979 $27.00. ISBN 0-917930-
   24-X. Collection of essays on important philosophers and topics.
Philosophical Perspectives: Metaphysics and Epistemology. Ridgeview 1979 $27.00. ISBN
   0-917930-25-8. Collection of essays on philosophy.
Pure Pragmatics and Possible Worlds: The Early Essays of Wilfrid Sellars. Ed. by Jeffrey
   Sicha. Ridgeview 1980 $32.00. ISBN 0-917930-26-6

Readings in Ethical Theory. (coedited with John Hospers). 1952. P-H 1970 o.p.
Readings in Philosophical Analysis. (coedited with Herbert Feigl). 1949. Ridgeview 1981
   $33.00. ISBN 0-917930-29-0
Science and Metaphysics: Variations on Kantian Themes. 1968. Humanities 1982 o.p.
Science, Perception and Reality. Ridgeview 1991 $39.00. ISBN 0-924922-50-8

BOOKS ABOUT SELLARS

Delaney, C. F., and others. *The Synoptic Vision: Essays on the Philosophy of Wilfrid
   Sellars.* U. of Notre Dame Pr. 1977 $17.95. ISBN 0-268-01596-1. "[A] general
   introduction to the philosophy of Wilfrid Sellars."
Evans, Joseph Claude, Jr. *The Metaphysics of Transcendental Subjectivity: Descartes,
   Kant and W. Sellars.* Benjamins North Am. 1984 $35.00. ISBN 90-6032-256-8. "The
   last chapter deals with Sellars' transformation of Kant" (*The Philosopher's Index*).
Pitt, Joseph C. *Pictures, Images and Conceptual Change: An Analysis of Wilfrid Sellars'
   Philosophy of Science.* Synthese Lib. Kluwer Ac. 1981 $53.50. ISBN 90-277-1276-X.
   "[A]n analysis of the problems undermining an adequate account of conceptual
   change as found in the work of W. Sellars, Goodman and Quine" (*The Philosopher's
   Index*).
Siebt, Johanna. *Properties as Processes: A Synoptic Study of Wilfred Sellars' Nominalism.*
   Ridgeview 1990 $38.00. ISBN 0-917930-99-1. "[T]he only nominalist approach that
   does justice to each dimension of a nominalist stance" (*The Philosopher's Index*).

SHESTOV, LEV. 1866–1938

Lev Shestov belongs in the stream of the religious existentialists and was
deeply interested in the work of FRIEDRICH NIETZSCHE (see also Vol. 2) and
SØREN KIERKEGAARD; he knew and was close to NIKOLAI BERDYAEV and in touch
with EDMUND HUSSERL, MARTIN HEIDEGGER (see also Vol. 5), and MARTIN BUBER.
In his own strong voice, however, deeply reliant not on the God of the
conventional churches but on the Old Testament as he interpreted it, he
denounced conventional metaphysics and the domination of a rigidly structured worldview in which we are governed by necessity. He believed that we
have fettered ourselves with crutches and limits and made ourselves puny; we
must seek a new God—with God "all things are possible." His most important
early "existential" work, an attack on traditional metaphysics, was *The
Apotheosis of Groundlessness* (1905, entitled in English translation *All Things
Are Possible*), to which D. H. LAWRENCE (see Vol. 1) provided the introduction.
The novelist wrote: "'Everything is possible,' this is his really central cry. It is
not nihilism. It is only a shaking free of the human psyche from old bonds. The
positive central idea is that the human psyche, or soul, really believes in itself. . . . No ideal on earth is anything more than an obstruction, in the end, to
the creative issue of the spontaneous soul." In a brilliant introduction to *Athens
and Jerusalem* (1938), Bernard Martin says, "Shestov suggests . . . that modern
man can perhaps reach the God of the Bible only by first passing through the
experience of his own nothingness, and by coming to feel, as Nietzsche did, that
God is not. . . . 'Sometimes [says Shestov] this is the sign of the end and of death.
Sometimes of the beginning and of life. As soon as man feels that God is not, he
suddenly comprehends the frightful horror and the wild folly of human
temporal existence . . . [and] awakens. . . . Was it not so with Nietzsche, SPINOZA,
PASCAL, LUTHER, AUGUSTINE, even with St. Paul?'"

The son of Jewish parents, Shestov studied at Kiev and the University of
Moscow. He received the title candidate of laws from the University of Kiev, but
was denied the doctor of law title because his dissertation on the Russian
working class was judged "revolutionary" by the Committee of Censors in

Moscow. Working for awhile in his father's textile firm, he began writing for avant-garde periodicals in Kiev. In 1898 his first book appeared: *Shakespeare and His Critic Brandes*, in which he attacked the positivism and skeptical rationalism of the famous Danish critic and essayist in the name of a vague moral idealism.

Shestov spent a number of years abroad—in Switzerland or Germany—before World War I. In 1918–19 he taught Greek philosophy at the People's University of Kiev, but, dissatisfied with the Bolshevik regime, he settled in Paris in 1920, where he taught at the Sorbonne and moved in a circle of Russian émigrés, including Berdyaev. He became increasingly interested in religion and the work of the great religious philosophers. Shestov was deeply concerned philosophically with Russian literature—particularly FYODOR DOSTOEVSKY (see Vol. 2) and ANTON CHEKHOV (see Vol. 2)—and wrote many essays on the subject.

BOOKS BY SHESTOV

All Things Are Possible and Penultimate Words and Other Essays. Ohio U. Pr. 1977 $16.00. ISBN 0-8214-0237-4. A collection of the most important of Shestov's essays; an excellent introduction to his thought.

Athens and Jerusalem. Trans. by Bernard Martin. Ohio U. Pr. 1966 o.p.

Chekhov and Other Essays. 1908. Bks. Demand $58.30. ISBN 0-317-09970-1. Contents: "Anton Chekhov"; "The Gift of Prophecy [Dostoyevsky]"; "Penultimate Words"; "The Theory of Knowledge."

Dostoyevsky, Tolstoy and Nietzsche. Trans. by Bernard Martin and Spencer E. Roberts. Ohio U. Pr. 1969 o.p. Literary criticism in the service of religion.

In Job's Balances: On the Sources of Eternal Truths. Trans. by Camilla Coventry and C. A. Macartney. Ohio U. Pr. 1975 $20.00. ISBN 0-8214-0143-2. Profoundly mystical.

Potestas Calvium. 1919. Trans. by Bernard Martin. Ohio U. Pr. 1978 o.p. A "striking assault on rationalist metaphysics" (*Publishers Weekly*).

Speculation and Revelation. Trans. by Bernard Martin. Ohio U. Pr. 1982 $32.95. ISBN 0-8214-0422-9. Singular mystical response to the time-honored controversy between reason and revelation or faith.

BOOKS ABOUT SHESTOV

Shein, Louis J. *The Philosophy of Lev Shestov, 1866–1938: A Russian Religious Existentialist. Toronto Studies in Theology.* E. Mellen 1991 $39.95. ISBN 0-7734-9662-9

Wernham, James C. *Two Russian Thinkers: An Essay in Berdyaev and Shestov.* Bks. Demand 1968 $33.00. ISBN 0-317-08859-9. "[S]hows Shestov as having had the sharper critical faculty" (*Library Journal*).

STRAWSON, PETER FREDERICK. 1919–

[SEE Chapter 9 in this volume.]

TEILHARD DE CHARDIN, PIERRE. 1881–1955

Born in Sarcenat, France, Teilhard de Chardin was the son of a landowner and was educated at a Jesuit school. In 1911 he was ordained a Jesuit priest, but also became interested in geology and paleontology. In 1918 Teilhard de Chardin became professor of geology at the Institut Catholique in Paris. Between 1923 and 1946, he went on paleontological and anthropological expeditions to China and Central Asia, where he helped discover Peking Man in 1929. His work in Cenozoic geology and paleontology earned him widespread recognition, including the French Legion of Honour (1946). *Early Man in China*, one of his writings from his period as a scientist, is still available.

Teilhard de Chardin's lively mind moved beyond science to speculative cosmology. He ranks as an interpreter of naturalistic evolution within a broadened framework of spirituality. During his lifetime his writings were disapproved by the authorities in his order and the church; however, their posthumous publication in the wake of Vatican II catapulted Teilhard into the very center of attention, by intellectuals and philosophers throughout the world. Although his views seem insupportable to many more cautious minds, they have been taken seriously and have stimulated considerable discussion.

Teilhard's system on philosophy has been ably epitomized by J. E. Bruns in his review of *Phenomenon of Man*: "'The story of life is not more than a movement of consciousness veiled by morphology.' These words of the author, referring to consciousness as related to organic structure, express the essential theme of his book. . . . Evolution has not run its course. Geogenesis led to biogenesis, 'which turned out in the end to be nothing else than psychogenesis. . . . Psychogenesis has led to man. Now it efficaces itself, relieved or absorbed by another and a higher function—the engendering and subsequent development of all the stages of the mind, in one word *noogenesis*.' Noogenesis implies the production of a 'superabundance of mind' and looks forward to the ultimate earth, a 'universe of conscious substance.' Teilhard envisions mankind, through an ever increasing psychosocial unity, concentrating on the transcendent center of this psychic convergence—God—until it reaches the 'Omega point,' the 'fulfillment of the spirit of the earth,' a detachment of the mind from its material matrix and an abandonment of its organoplanetary foothold" (*Catholic World*).

BOOKS BY TEILHARD DE CHARDIN

Activation of Energy. 1971. Trans. by René Hague. HarBraceJ 1972 $6.95. ISBN 0-15-602860-3. Spiritualistic theory of the source of physical energy.

Christianity and Evolution. 1971. HarBraceJ 1974 $6.95. ISBN 0-15-611740-4. Synthesis of traditional religion and biological science.

Divine Milieu: An Essay on the Interior Life. HarpC 1975 $10.00. ISBN 0-06-090487-9. Almost mystical rhapsodic description and speculation on the pervasiveness of the divine mind.

Early Man in China. AMS Pr. 1975 repr. of 1941 ed. $22.00. ISBN 0-404-16688-1. Scientific record of the discovery of Peking man.

Future of Man. 1964. HarpC 1969 o.p. Visionary hypothesis of where evolution leads.

The Heart of the Matter. Trans. by René Hague. HarBraceJ 1980 $7.95. ISBN 0-15-640004-9. Confession of the primacy of the spiritual in all union and affection.

Human Energy. 1971. HarBraceJ 1972 o.p. Plumbs the spiritual depths of human effort.

Hymn of the Universe. 1965. HarpC 1976 $12.00. ISBN 0-06-131910-4. Poetic prose on the spiritual unity of the universe.

On Love and Happiness. HarpC 1984 o.p. Lucid moral essay grounded in the principles of a cosmic religion.

Phenomenon of Man. Trans. by Bernard Wall. HarpC 1975 $12.00. ISBN 0-06-090495-X. Philosophical anthropology within a spiritual cosmic framework; the key to Teilhard's thought.

Toward the Future. HarBraceJ 1975 $4.95. ISBN 0-15-690780-1. Hopeful and aspiring essay.

BOOKS ABOUT TEILHARD DE CHARDIN

Birx, H. James. *Pierre Teilhard de Chardin's Philosophy of Evolution.* C. C. Thomas 1972 o.p. Scholarly monograph restricted to a critical interpretation of Teilhard on evolution.

Dodson, E. O. *The Phenomenon of Man Revisited: A Biological Viewpoint on Teilhard de Chardin.* Col. U. Pr. 1984 $38.00. ISBN 0-231-05850-0. Outstanding work of scholarship; the best yet to appear on Teilhard.

Farcy, Robert S. *The Spirituality of Teilhard de Chardin.* HarpC 1981 o.p. Sympathetic introduction to Teilhard's religiosity.

Grau, Joseph A. *Morality and the Human Future in the Thought of Teilhard de Chardin: A Critical Study.* Fairleigh Dickinson 1976 $32.50. ISBN 0-8386-1579-1. Narrow scholarly monograph, useful for an understanding of Teilhard's moral philosophy.

Gray, Donald P. *A New Creation Story: The Creative Spirituality of Teilhard de Chardin.* Anima Pubns. 1979 $3.00. ISBN 0-89012-014-5. Uncritical laudatory essay.

Grim, John, and Mary E. Grim. *Teilhard de Chardin: A Short Biography.* Anima Pubns. 1984 $3.00. ISBN 0-89012-038-2. Concise, covers the basic facts.

King, Thomas H. *Teilhard de Chardin. The Way of the Christian Mystics Ser.* Liturgical Pr. 1988 $12.95. ISBN 0-8146-5631-5. Appreciative biographical essay.

Kraft, R. Wayne. *Reason to Hope: A Synthesis of Teilhard de Chardin's Vision and Systems Thinking.* Intersystems Pubns. 1983 $13.95. ISBN 0-914105-14-0. Special plea for a dubious synthesis.

Kropf, Richard W. *Teilhard, Scripture and Revelation: Teilhard de Chardin's Reinterpretation of Pauline Themes.* Fairleigh Dickson 1980 $35.00. ISBN 0-8386-1481-7. Excellent but limited scholarly monograph.

Lukas, Mary, and Ellen Lukas. *Teilhard.* McGraw 1981 o.p. Worthy intellectual, spiritual portrait.

Lyons, J. A. *The Cosmic Christ in Origen and Teilhard de Chardin.* Ed. by Maurice Wiles. OUP 1982 $59.00. ISBN 0-19-826721-5. Invaluable contribution to the history of Christology.

Neilson, Francis. *Teilhard de Chardin's Vision of the Future.* Revisionist Pr. 1979 $39.50. ISBN 0-685-96640-2. Sympathetic, persuasively written work.

Overzee, Anne H. *The Body Divine: The Symbol of the Body in the Works of Teilhard de Chardin and Ramanuja. Studies in Religious Traditions.* Cambridge U. Pr. 1992 $49.95. Penetrating interpretive scholarship in comparative religion.

Sethna, K. D. *The Spirituality of the Future: A Search Apropos of R. C. Zaehner's Study in Sri Aurobindo and Teilhard de Chardin.* Fairleigh Dickinson 1981 $37.50. ISBN 0-8386-2028-0. Scholarly monograph, commenting on a commentator.

Tucker, Mary E. *The Ecological Spirituality of Teilhard.* Anima Pubns. 1985 $3.00. ISBN 0-89012-040-4. A follower's sympathetic account.

UNESCO Colloquium. *Science and Synthesis: An International Colloquium Organized by UNESCO on the Tenth Anniversary of the Death of Albert Einstein and Teilhard de Chardin.* Trans. by B. M. Crook. Spr-Verlag 1971 o.p. Record of the proceedings, containing the addresses and comments of leading scholars in the field.

TOYNBEE, ARNOLD JOSEPH. 1889–1975

[See Volume 3.]

UNAMUNO, MIGUEL DE. 1864–1936

[See Volume 2.]

VON WRIGHT, GEORG H. 1916–

Born in Helsinki, Finland, von Wright is a philosopher and logician, who has mainly taught at the University of Helsinki (1946–61) and Cornell University (1965–77). He also has been a visiting lecturer at Columbia University, Oxford University, and Cambridge University. Arriving at Cambridge in 1939, he soon came under the spell of Ludwig Wittgenstein. Nevertheless, he is a most original neo-Wittgensteinian, associated with the Vienna Circle of logical positivists in the 1940s. Famous for his pioneer work in the development of deontic logics, he has investigated in original ways other philosophical topics, such as the epistemological distinction between explanation and understanding and the significance of this distinction for such problems as the nature of causation and the differences between the natural and the social sciences.

BOOKS BY VON WRIGHT

Explanation and Understanding. Contemporary Philosophy Ser. Cornell Univ. Pr. 1971 $31.50. ISBN 0-8014-0644-7. Original treatise in theory of knowledge, basic to the conception of the division between natural sciences and "social sciences."
Logic and Philosophy. Kluwer Ac. 1980 $46.50. ISBN 90-247-2271-3
Philosophical Papers. 2 vols. Cornell Univ. Pr. 1983 Vol. 1 *Practical Reason.* $33.50. ISBN 0-8014-1673-6. Vol. 2 *Philosophical Logic.* $33.50. ISBN 0-8014-1674-4. A collection of Von Wright's previously published papers.
A Portrait of Wittgenstein as a Young Man: From the Diary of David Hume Pinsent 1912-1914. Blackwell Pubs. 1990 $29.95. ISBN 0-631-17511-3
Truth, Knowledge, and Modality: Philosophical Papers. Vol. 3. Blackwell Pubs. 1985 $45.00. ISBN 0-631-13367-4
Wittgenstein. U. of Minn. Pr. 1982 $34.95. ISBN 0-8166-1210-2. A memoir of the great philosopher by a devoted student.

BOOK ABOUT VON WRIGHT

Hahn, Lewis E., and Paul A. Schilpp. eds. *The Philosophy of Georg Henrik von Wright. Lib. of Living Philosophers.* 2 vols. Open Court 1986 Vol. 1 $99.95. ISBN 0-87548-372-0. Vol. 2 $99.95. ISBN 0-685-07273-8. Contains original critical essays by prominent scholars, preceded by Von Wright's intellectual autobiography and followed by his reply to his critics. Concludes with a bibliography.

WEISS, PAUL. 1901–

Born in New York City, the son of a laborer (Samuel), Weiss was educated at the City College of New York and Harvard University, where he prepared his doctoral dissertation in the late 1920s under the supervision of ALFRED NORTH WHITEHEAD. Paul Weiss has taught at Bryn Mawr College, Yale University, and the Catholic University of America. Founding editor of the *Review of Metaphysics* and founding first president of the Metaphysical Society of America, Weiss has been the leading advocate of speculative philosophy in the English-speaking world since World War II. He received a Guggenheim Fellowship in 1938 and the Townshend Harris Medal in 1964.

His work may be divided into three stages. During the first stage, Weiss labored as a logician whose earliest publications were devoted to the nature of systems as logical wholes. During this period, he coedited with CHARLES HARTSHORNE *The Collected Papers of Charles Sanders Peirce* (1931–58). As he matured, however, he became increasingly interested in metaphysical and ethical questions, as manifest in his books *Reality* (1938), *Nature and Man* (1947), and *Man's Freedom* (1950). The concern with ethical questions caused him to revise radically his early metaphysics. This led to the second stage of his development, capped with the publication of *Modes of Being* (1958). In his modal philosophy Weiss presented and justified dialectically four modes of being: actuality, ideality, existence, and God. Thereafter he explored the concrete manifestations and interplay of these modes in history, art, education, sport, and so forth.

As Weiss progressed in these investigations, he entered the third stage of his development—the postmodal phase in which he revised his four-mode metaphysics by acknowledging additional principles. His books *Beyond All Appearances* (1974), *First Considerations* (1977), and *Creative Ventures* (1992) are landmarks, in this final stage. Weiss now acknowledges seven ultimate principles. These include the two modes of being, actuality and existence, and their five finalities or conditions: substance, being, voluminousness, ideality, and God. His recently discovered seventh principle is the dunamis, a cosmic dynamic creativity. During Weiss's latest period, he has further advanced his investigation into the realities and norms for persons and the social order.

Weiss's multivolume *Philosophy in Process*, a remarkable document, in which the philosopher reveals how he thinks about the topics and themes as he writes the books on them, shows the intellectual wrestlings of an important thinker at work.

BOOKS BY WEISS

Beyond All Appearances. S. Ill. U. Pr. 1974 o.p. Penetrating postmodal metaphysics, marking change in Weiss's ontology.

Cinematics. S. Ill. U. Pr. 1975 $9.95. ISBN 0-8093-0671-9. Philosophy of the cinema; of universal interest.

Creative Ventures. S. Ill. U. Pr. 1992 $45.00. ISBN 0-8093-0671-9. A dense metaphysical essay, ostensibly devoted to the study of creativity but actually unveiling Weiss's mature system of actualities, the final finalities, and the dunamis.

First Considerations: An Examination of Philosophical Evidence. S. Ill. U. Pr. 1977 $13.85. ISBN 0-8093-0797-9. Stresses "the transition from appearances and actualities to ultimate conditioning realities—finalities" (Weiss). Contains comments by critics and Weiss's replies.

God We Seek. S. Ill. U. Pr. 1964 $10.95. ISBN 0-8093-0133-4. Profound, original work, indispensable to the theologian or the clergy.

History: Written and Lived. S. Ill. U. Pr. 1962 $6.95. ISBN 0-8093-0067-2. Philosophy of history as an application of a metaphysics.

Making of Men. S. Ill. U. Pr. 1967 $7.95. ISBN 0-8093-0405-8. Lucid philosophy of education.

Man's Freedom. 1950. *Arcturus Bks. Paperbacks.* S. Ill. U. Pr. 1967 $8.95. ISBN 0-8093-0277-2. Theory of human freedom in a distinctly novel metaphysical framework.

Modes of Being. Arcturus Bks. Paperbacks. S. Ill. U. Pr. 1958 $19.95. ISBN 0-8093-0012-5. A dialectical classic of ontology, depicting the modes of actuality, ideality, existence, and God.

Nature and Man. 1947. U. Pr. of Amer. 1983 $21.00. ISBN 0-8191-3590-9. Naturalistic theory of man as the basis for an ethics.

Our Public Life. 1959. S. Ill. U. Pr. 1966 $10.95. A concise and original theory of law and of politics.

Philosophy in Process. 7 vols. 1966–1978. S. Ill. U. Pr. $25.00 ea. Vol. 1 June 24, 1955–December 25, 1960. ISBN 0-8093-1090-3. Vol. 2 December 26, 1960–March 6, 1964. ISBN 0-8093-0231-4. Vol. 3 March–November 1964. ISBN 0-8093-0329-9. Vol. 4 November 26, 1964–September 2, 1965. ISBN 0-8093-0401-5. Vol. 5 September 3, 1965–August 27, 1968. ISBN 0-8093-0465-1. Vol. 6 August 28, 1968–May 22, 1971. ISBN 0-8093- 0678-6. Vol. 7 April 13, 1975–June 21, 1976. ISBN 0-8093-0821-5

Philosophy in Process. 6 vols. 1985–88. State U. NY Pr. Vol. 7, pt. 2 $76.95. ISBN 0-88706-080-3. Vol. 8 $76.95. ISBN 0-87395-824-1. Vol. 9 August 16, 1980–March 15, 1984 $76.95. ISBN 0-88706-293-8. Vol. 10 April 15, 1984–January 18, 1986 $76.95. ISBN 0-88706-497-3. Vol. 11 January 19, 1986–May 27, 1987 $76.95. ISBN 0-88706-762-X. This remarkable series records Weiss's daily thinking as he grapples with the themes he presents in his books. It is a singular effort of open thinking done in private but made available to the reading public.

Privacy. S. Ill. U. Pr. 1983 $30.00. ISBN 0-8093-1066-X. Probing investigation of interior humanity.

Reality. 1938. *Arcturus Bks. Paperbacks.* S. Ill. U. Pr. 1967 $8.95. ISBN 0-8093-0244-6. Original metaphysics of the highest quality, influenced by Aristotle and Whitehead.

Religion and Art. Marquette 1963 $7.95. ISBN 0-87462-128-3. Lecture on the interplay of two major cultural institutions.

Right and Wrong: A Philosophical Dialogue between Father and Son. (coauthored with Jonathan Weiss). *Arcturus Bks. Paperbacks.* S. Ill. U. Pr. 1974 $5.95. ISBN 0-8093-0658-1. "Its only precedent may be *De Magistro* (*On Teaching*), a dialogue recorded in A.D. 389 between St. Augustine and his brilliant fifteen-year-old illegitimate son, Adeodatus" (*Time*).

Sport: A Philosophic Inquiry. S. Ill. U. Pr. 1969 $24.95. ISBN 0-8093-0358-2. Philosophy of sport; original but readable by anyone.

Toward a Perfected State. State U. NY Pr. 1986 $59.50. ISBN 0-88706-9. Addresses "the metaphysical principles that underlie social and political philosophy" and "traces the interconnections of particular practical issues with speculative topics in ontology and epistemology" (*Ethics*).

World of Art. Arcturus Bks. Paperbacks. S. Ill. U. Pr. 1964 $10.95. ISBN 0-8093-0112-1. Philosophy of art, unfolding the basic categories.

You, I, and the Others. S. Ill. U. Pr. 1980 $29.95. ISBN 0-8093-0923-8. "Studies the fundamental dimensions and roles of the individual human actuality" (Krettek).

Book about Weiss

Krettek, Thomas, ed. *Creativity and Common Sense: Essays in Honor of Paul Weiss.* State U. NY Pr. 1987 o.p. This collection makes a significant contribution to the development of Weissian scholarship and to the growing appreciation of the significance of his thought for the discussions of contemporary philosophy.

WHITEHEAD, ALFRED NORTH. 1861–1947

Alfred North Whitehead, who began his career as a mathematician, ranks as the foremost philosopher in the twentieth century to construct a speculative system of philosophical cosmology. After his graduation from Cambridge University, he lectured there until 1910 on mathematics. Like BERTRAND RUSSELL (see also Vol. 5), his most brilliant pupil, Whitehead viewed philosophy at the start from the standpoint of mathematics, and, with Russell, he wrote *Principia Mathematica* (1910–13). This work established the derivation of mathematics from logical foundations and has transformed the philosophical discipline of logic. From his work on mathematics and its logical foundations, Whitehead proceeded to what has been regarded as the second phase of his career. In 1910 he left Cambridge for the University of London, where he lectured until he was appointed professor of applied mathematics at the Imperial College of Science and Technology. During his period in London, Whitehead produced works on the epistemological and metaphysical principles of science. The major works of this period are *An Enquiry Concerning the Principles of Natural Knowledge* (1919), *The Concept of Nature* (1920), and *The Principles of Relativity* (1922).

In 1924, at age 63, Whitehead retired from his position at the Imperial College and accepted an appointment as professor of philosophy at Harvard University, where he began his most creative period in speculative philosophy. In *Science and the Modern World* (1925) he explored the history of the development of science, examining its foundations in categories of philosophical import, and remarked that with the revolutions in biology and physics in the nineteenth and early twentieth centuries a revision of these categories was in order. Whitehead unveiled his proposals for a new list of categories supporting a comprehensive philosophical cosmology in *Process and Reality* (1929), a work hailed as the greatest expression of process philosophy and theology. *Adventures of Ideas* (1933) is an essay in the philosophy of culture; it centers on what Whitehead considered the key ideas that have shaped Western culture.

BOOKS BY WHITEHEAD

Adventures of Ideas. 1933. Macmillan 1933 $12.95. ISBN 0-02-935170-7. Breezy philosophy of civilization by elucidation of key ideas.

The Aims of Education. 1928. Free Pr. 1967 $12.95. ISBN 0-02-931518-4. Theory of education; invaluable for educators.

The Concept of Nature. Cambridge U. Pr. 1971 repr. of 1920 ed. $18.95. ISBN 0-521-09245-0. Brilliant but technical attack against dualism.

The Dialogues of Alfred North Whitehead. Greenwood 1977 repr. of 1954 ed. $72.50. ISBN 0-8371-9341-9. Recorded from conversations with Whitehead by a former student, Lucien Price.

An Enquiry Concerning the Principles of Natural Knowledge. 1919. Dover 1982 o.p. Original investigation into the cognitive grounds of science.

Essays in Science and Philosophy. Greenwood 1968 repr. of 1947 ed. $37.50. ISBN 0-8371-0268-5. A collection of Whitehead's essays.

The Function of Reason. 1929. Beacon Pr. 1958 $9.95. ISBN 0-8070-1573-3. Beautifully written and profound monograph on the speculative and practical uses of reason.

Introduction to Mathematics. 1911. OUP rev. ed. 1959 $8.95. ISBN 0-19-500211-3. For the intelligent reader, who need not be a mathematician.

Modes of Thought. 1938. Free Pr. 1968 $12.95. ISBN 0-02-935210-X. Abstruse but fundamental.

Nature and Life. Greenwood 1970 repr. of 1934 ed. $35.00. ISBN 0-8371-0751-2. Brief presentation of the basic categories in Whitehead's system of process metaphysics.

The Organization of Thought, Educational and Scientific. Greenwood 1974 repr. of 1917 ed. $35.00. ISBN 0-8371-3448-X. Systematically illuminating work.

Principia Mathematica. (coauthored with Bertrand Russell). 3 vols. 1910–13. Cambridge U. Pr. 1925–27 $500.00. ISBN 0-521-06791-X. Classic work demonstrating the logical foundations of mathematics; for the expert only.

Process and Reality: An Essay in Cosmology. 1929. Free Pr. rev. ed. 1978 $19.95. ISBN 0-02-934580-4. Greatest and most influential work in English on speculative systematic philosophy in the twentieth century.

Religion in the Making. 1926. New Amer. Pr. 1960 o.p. Process philosophy of religion; recommended to theologians and clergy.

Science and the Modern World. 1925. Free Pr. 1967 $12.95. ISBN 0-02-935190-1. History of science at the highest level of suggestiveness; most widely read of Whitehead's books.

Symbolism: Its Meaning and Effect. 1927. Fordham 1985 $20.00. ISBN 0-8232-1137-1. Whitehead's basic principles of knowledge and meaning, concisely presented.

Whitehead's American Essays in Social Philosophy. Ed. by A. H. Johnson. Greenwood 1975 repr. of 1959 ed. $35.00. ISBN 0-8371-7716-2

BOOKS ABOUT WHITEHEAD

Alfred North Whitehead: A Primary-Secondary Bibliography. Philos Document 1977 $23.50. ISBN 0-912632-34-8. A good place for the researcher to start.

Barineau, R. Maurice. *The Theory of Alfred North Whitehead: A Logical and Ethical Vindication.* U. Pr. of Amer. 1991 $39.75. ISBN 0-8191-8167-6. A scholarly defense of Whitehead's process theology by an adherent.

Blyth, John W. *Whitehead's Theory of Knowledge.* Kraus 1973 repr. of 1941 ed. $18.00. ISBN 0-527-09100-6. A doctoral dissertation.

Brumbaugh, Robert S. *Whitehead, Process Philosophy, and Education.* U. of Amer. Pr. 1992 $14.75. ISBN 0-8191-8484-5. Monograph on process philosophy of education by a Whiteheadian.

Christensen, Darrell E. *Hegelian-Whiteheadian Perspectives.* U. Pr. of Amer. 1989 $24.25. ISBN 0-8191-7079-8. Essays on phenomenology examining the perspectives of Hegel and Whitehead on temporal realities.

_____. *The Search for Concreteness-Reflections on Hegel and Whitehead: A Treatise on Self-Evidence and Critical Method in Philosophy.* Susquehanna U. Pr. 1986 $50.00.

ISBN 0-941664-22-8. Intends "to set forth a methodological basis for a . . . philosophy of concrete reality as such, and . . . breaks new ground in its mediation between two varied traditions of process philosophy" (*The Philosopher's Index*).

Christian, William A. *An Interpretation of Whitehead's Metaphysics.* Greenwood 1977 repr. of 1959 ed. $41.50. ISBN 0-8371-9638-8. Based mainly on the later writings, beginning with *Science and the Modern World* (1925), this work discusses theological implications.

Eisendrath, Craig R. *Unifying Moment: The Psychological Philosophy of William James and Alfred North Whitehead.* HUP 1971 $25.50. ISBN 0-674-92100-3. Imaginative endeavor to demonstrate common ground for Whitehead and James.

Emmet, Dorothy. *The Passage of Nature.* Temple U. Pr. 1991 $39.95. ISBN 0-87722-896-5. An original metaphysical theory in which creativity in the passage of nature comes through the activities of things and persons sustaining processes; by a British philosopher who acknowledges the influence of an early interest in Alfred North Whitehead's philosophy of process.

Ford, Lewis S. *The Emergence of Whitehead's Metaphysics, 1925–29.* State U. NY Pr. 1985 $45.50. ISBN 0-87395-856-X. Careful historical reconstruction by a disciple of Whitehead's preparation for *Process and Reality.*

Ford, Lewis S., and George L. Kline, eds. *Explorations in Whitehead's Philosophy.* Fordham 1983 $40.00. ISBN 0-8232-1102-9. Collection of essays by experts.

Hall, David L. *The Civilization of Experience: A Whiteheadian Theory of Culture.* Fordham 1973 $35.00. ISBN 0-8232-0960-1. Brooding speculative essay on any aspect of Whitehead's thought; highly recommended.

Hartshorne, Charles. *Whitehead's Philosophy: Selected Essays, 1935–70.* U. of Nebr. Pr. 1972 o.p. Collection of insightful essays on Whitehead by the leading process theologian.

Hendley, Brian. *Dewey, Russell, Whitehead: Philosophers as Educators.* S. Ill. U. Pr. 1985 $14.95. ISBN 0-8093-1243-3. Informative.

Kuntz, Paul G. *Alfred North Whitehead. Twayne's Eng. Authors Ser.* G. K. Hall 1984 o.p. Excellent intellectual portrait by a distinguished scholar.

Lango, John W. *Whitehead's Ontology.* State U. NY Pr. 1972 $49.50. ISBN 0-87395-093-3. Analysis of Whitehead's basic categories.

Lawrence, Nathaniel. *Whitehead's Philosophical Development.* Greenwood 1968 repr. of 1956 ed. $35.00. ISBN 0-8371-0139-5. Exceptional scholarly investigation, indispensable to an understanding of Whitehead.

Lowe, Victor. *Alfred North Whitehead: The Man and His Work, Vol. I: 1861–1910.* Johns Hopkins 1985 $39.95. ISBN 0-8018-2488-5.

———. *Alfred North Whitehead: The Man and His Work, Vol. II: 1910–1947.* Johns Hopkins 1990 $39.95. ISBN 0-8018-3960-2. The second volume of Lowe's comprehensive biography, edited by J. B. Schneewind.

———. *Understanding Whitehead.* Johns Hopkins 1962 $14.95. ISBN 0-8018-0400-0. "[R]emarkably successful in helping the more general reader to understand Whitehead's philosophy" (*Library Journal*).

Lowe, Victor, and others. *Whitehead and the Modern World: Science, Metaphysics, and Civilization. Essay Index Repr. Ser.* Ayer 1977 repr. of 1950 ed. $15.00. ISBN 0-8369-7281-3. A collection of original essays.

Lucas, George R. *Two Views of Freedom in Process and Thought.* Scholars Pr. GA 1979 $14.95. ISBN 0-89130-304-9. Specialized commentary.

Mack, Robert D. *Appeal to Immediate Experience. Essay Index Repr. Ser.* Ayer 1976 repr. of 1945 ed. $14.00. ISBN 0-8369-0085-5. Scholarly monograph on the method of Bradley, Dewey, and Whitehead.

Nobo, Jorge L. *Whitehead's Metaphysics of Extension and Solidarity.* State U. NY Pr. 1986 $74.50. ISBN 0-88706-261-X. Scholarly commentary on difficult topics.

Ross, Stephen D. *Perspective in Whitehead's Metaphysics.* State U. NY Pr. 1983 $59.50. ISBN 0-87395-658-3. Buchler's creative disciple has prepared an enlightening interpretation of Whitehead.

Schilpp, Paul A. *The Philosophy of Alfred North Whitehead. Lib. of Living Philosophers Ser.*
1971 Bks. Demand $160.00. ISBN 0-317-09081-X. Contains the only existing
Whitehead autobiography, critical essays, and bibliography of his works.
Sherburne, Donald W., ed. *A Key to Whitehead's "Process and Reality".* U. Ch. Pr. 1981
$13.95. ISBN 0-226-75293-3. Useful handbook.
Wallack, F. Bradford. *The Epochal Nature of Process in Whitehead's Metaphysics.* State U.
NY Pr. 1980 $49.50. ISBN 0-87395-404-1. Scholarly monograph on a crucial point.

WITTGENSTEIN, LUDWIG JOSEF JOHANN. 1889–1951

Born in Vienna, Ludwig Josef Johann Wittgenstein was educated at Linz and
Berlin University. In 1908 he went to England, registering as a research student
in engineering at the University of Manchester. There he studied BERTRAND
RUSSELL's (see also Vol. 5) *Principles of Mathematics* by chance and decided to
study with Russell at Cambridge University. From 1912 to 1913, he studied
under Russell's supervision and began to develop the ideas that crystallized in
his *Tractatus*. With the outbreak of World War I, he returned home and
volunteered for the Austrian Army. During his military service, he prepared the
book published in 1921 as the *Tractatus*, first translated into English in 1922 by
C. K. Ogden. Wittgenstein emerged as a philosopher whose influence spread
from Austria to the English-speaking world.

Perhaps the most eminent philosopher during the second half of the twentieth
century, Wittgenstein had an early impact on the members of the Vienna Circle,
with which he was associated. The logical atomism of the *Tractatus*, with its
claims that propositions of logic and mathematics are tautologous and that the
cognitive meaning of other sorts of scientific statements is empirical, became
the fundamental source of logical positivism, or logical empiricism. Bertrand
Russell adopted it as his position, and A. J. AYER was to accept and profess it 15
years later.

From the end of World War I until 1926, Wittgenstein was a schoolteacher in
Austria. In 1929 his interest in philosophy renewed, and he returned to
Cambridge, where even G. E. MOORE came under his spell. At Cambridge
Wittgenstein began a new wave in philosophical analysis distinct from the
Tractatus, which had inspired the rise of logical positivism. Whereas the earlier
Wittgenstein had concentrated on the formal structures of logic and mathematics, the later Wittgenstein attended to the fluidities of ordinary language. His
lectures, remarks, conversations, and letters made lasting imprints on the
minds of his most brilliant students, who have long since initiated the unending
process of publishing them. During his lifetime Wittgenstein himself never
published another book after the *Tractatus*. However, he was explicit that the
work disclosing the methods and topics of his later years be published. This
work, *Philosophical Investigations* (1953), is esteemed to be his most mature
expression of his philosophical method and thought.

BOOKS BY WITTGENSTEIN

The Blue and Brown Books: Preliminary Studies for the Philosophical Investigations. 1958.
HarpC 1969 $12.00. ISBN 0-06-131211-8. Notes of Wittgenstein's lectures, circulated
originally among his students, revealing his shift of methods.
Culture and Value. Ed. by G. H. Von Wright. Trans. by Peter Winch. U. Ch. Pr. 1984
$7.95. ISBN 0-226-90435-0. Remarks on the language of anthropology.
Last Writings Vol. 1: Preliminary Studies for Part III of Philosophical Investigations. Ed. by
G. H. Van Wright and Heikki Nyman. Trans. by C. G. Luckhardt and A. E. Aue, U. Ch.
Pr. 1989 $18.95. ISBN 0-226-90429-6. Posthumously published incomplete second
part of *The Philosophical Investigations*.

ideas found in the *Tractatus Logico-Philosophicus* and *Philosophical Investigations* and traces Wittgenstein's influences on the schools of logical positivism and analytical philosophy and some contemporary British philosophers" (*Library Journal*).

Hodges, Michael P. *Transcendence and Wittgenstein's Tractatus*. Temple U. Pr. 1990 $39.95. ISBN 0-87722-692-X. "[A] finely spun argument, which is intricately complex and admirable lucid" (*The Modern Schoolman*).

Hunnings, Gordon. *The World and Language in Wittgenstein's Philosophy*. State U. NY Pr. 1988 $59.50. ISBN 0-88706-585-6. An investigation of Wittgenstein's philosophy of language across the periods of its development.

Hunter, J. M. *Understanding Wittgenstein: Studies of Philosophical Investigations*. Col. U. Pr. 1985 $30.00. ISBN 0-85224-497-5. Probing and insightful.

Kenny, Anthony. *The Legacy of Wittgenstein*. Blackwell Pubs. 1986 $14.95. ISBN 0-631-15063-8. Assessment of Wittgenstein's influence on philosophy.

Kerr, Fergus. *Theology after Wittgenstein*. Blackwell Pubs. 1986 $49.95. ISBN 0-631-14688-1. Assessment of the post-Wittgensteinian status of theology.

Lapointe, François H., comp. *Ludwig Wittgenstein: A Comprehensive Bibliography*. Greenwood 1980 $49.95. ISBN 0-313-22127-8. A good place for the serious researcher to begin.

McDonough, Richard. *The Argument of the "Tractatus": Its Relevance to Contemporary Theories of Logic, Language, Mind, and Philosophical Truth*. State U. NY Pr. 1986 $59.95. ISBN 0-88706-152-4. Good on tracing the implications of Wittgenstein's early thought.

McGuinness, Brian. *Wittgenstein: A Life: Young Ludwig, 1889–1921*. U. CA Pr. 1988 $80.00. ISBN 0-520-06476-3. A perceptive biography.

——, ed. *Wittgenstein and His Times*. U. Ch. Pr. 1982 $15.00. ISBN 0-226-55881-9. Excellent collection illuminating Wittgenstein's background.

Malcolm, Norman. *Nothing Is Hidden: Wittgenstein's Criticism of His Early Thought*. Blackwell Pubs. 1989 $16.95. ISBN 0-631-16024-8. Penetrating subtle interpretation of the philosopher's self-criticism.

Monk, Ray. *The Duty of Genius*. Free Pr. 1990 $29.95. ISBN 0-02-921670-2. Psycho-biographical work.

Mounce, H. O. *Wittgenstein's Tractatus: An Introduction*. U. Ch. Pr. 1989 $12.95. ISBN 0-226-54321-8. No better work on Wittgenstein's *Tractatus* in print.

Mulhall, Stepen. *On Being in the World: Wittgenstein and Heidegger on Seeing Aspects*. Routledge 1990 $52.50. ISBN 0-415-04416-2. Compares and contrasts the metaphysics of two twentieth-century philosophical greats.

Nieli, Russell. *Wittgenstein: From Mysticism to Ordinary Language: A Study of Viennese Positivism and the Thought of Ludwig Wittgenstein*. State U. NY Pr. 1987 $59.50. ISBN 0-88706-397-7. An exploratory monograph on a neglected aspect of Wittgenstein's philosophy.

Pears, David. *The False Prison: A Study of the Development of Wittgenstein's Philosophy*. 2 vols. OUP. Vol. 1 1987 $15.95. ISBN 0-19-824770-2. Vol. 2 1988 $45.00. ISBN 0-19-824487-8. A thoroughly researched, and carefully constructed, work on the development of Wittgenstein's thinking on the central concepts and problems in his philosophy.

Peterson, Donald. *Wittgenstein's Early Philosophy: Three Sides of the Mirror*. U. of Toronto Pr. 1990 $40.00. ISBN 0-8020-2770-9. A rewarding commentary on the *Tractatus*.

Rhees, Rush, ed. *Ludwig Wittgenstein: Personal Recollections*. Rowman 1981 $49.00. ISBN 0-8476-6253-5. Recollections of Wittgenstein by prominent disciples.

Richardson, John T. *The Grammar of Justification: An Interpretation of Wittgenstein's Philosophy of Language*. St. Martin 1976 $25.00. ISBN 0-631-17198-3. A major contribution to the understanding of Wittgenstein.

Rundle, Bede. *Wittgenstein on Language: Meaning, Use, and Truth*. Blackwell Pubs. 1990 $54.95. ISBN 0-631-17198-3. Investigates Wittgenstein's identification of meaning with use and a range of other concepts in philosophy of language and philosophy of mind.

Schulte, Joachin. *Wittgenstein: An Introduction*. Trans. by William H. Brenner and John F. Holley. State U. NY Pr. 1992 $29.50. ISBN 0-7914-1081-1. An indication of how German philosophers understand Wittgenstein.

Shanker, S. G. *Wittgenstein and the Turning Point in the History of Mathematics*. State U. NY Pr. 1987 $59.50. ISBN 0-88706-482-5. "[C]hallenges the currently prevailing interpretations that Wittgenstein was engaged in an 'anti-realist' critique of the foundations of arithmetic, and that he was interested in a 'full-blooded conventionalist' or 'radical constructivist critique'" (*The Philosopher's Index*).

———, ed. *Ludwig Wittgenstein: Critical Assessments*. 4 vols. Routledge Chapman & Hall 1986 $525.00. ISBN 0-7099-2384-8. Massive collection of critical articles on Wittgenstein.

Stenius, Erik. *Wittgenstein's Tractatus: A Critical Exposition of Its Main Lines on Thought*. Greenwood repr. of 1964 ed. $35.00. ISBN 0-313-23246-6. Classic commentary.

Suter, Ronald. *Interpreting Wittgenstein: A Cloud of Philosophy, a Drop of Grammar*. Temple U. Pr. 1990 $44.95. ISBN 0-87722-664-4. "[A] general, problem-oriented overview of the later philosophy of Wittgenstein . . . non-technical, well written, and nicely organized" (*Choice*).

Tighgman, B. R. *Wittgenstein, Ethics and Aesthetics: The View from Eternity*. State U. of NY Pr. 1991 $49.50. ISBN 0-7914-0594-X. "[E]xplores Wittgenstein's views about ethics and aesthetics and argues that the works of the *Philosophical Investigations* made these notions intelligible in a way that the *Tractatus* could not" (*The Philosopher's Index*).

Weiner, David A. *Genius and Talent: Schopenhauer's Influence on Wittgenstein's Early Philosophy*. Fairleigh Dickinson 1992 $28.50. ISBN 0-8386-3441-9. A well-researched monograph on Wittgenstein's intellectual debt to Schopenhauer.

Werhane, Patricia H. *Scepticism, Rules, and Private Languages*. Humanities 1992 $35.00. ISBN 0-391-03750-1. A scholarly examination of Wittgenstein on language, knowledge, and solipsism.

Westphal, Jonathan. *Colour: Some Philosophical Problems from Wittgenstein*. Blackwell Pubs. 1987 $45.00. ISBN 0-631-14937-6. Carefully wrought analytic commentary.

CHAPTER 8

Asian and African Philosophy, 1850 to the Present

Thomas P. Kasulis and Robert S. Ellwood

> We must first thoroughly study Western logic, but at the same time we must have a critical attitude toward it. What we call the study of the Orient today has meant only taking the Orient as the *object* of study. What we must still do is reflect profoundly about the Oriental way of thinking, so we can evolve a new *method* of thinking.
>
> —NISHIDA KITARŌ, *The Problem of Japanese Culture*

The story of modern philosophy in Asia and Africa is a story framed around the encounter with the West. The nature and timing of that encounter varies from one geographical region to the next, but modern Asian and African philosophical movements generally were spawned in the period between the mid-nineteenth and mid-twentieth centuries. In short, the Asian and African traditions of modern philosophy grew out of the problem of modernization, which, in effect, was also Westernization.

The impact of the West on Asian and African philosophies typically has been made via three institutions, each with its own distinctive intellectual framework: Western science or technology, Christianity, and Marxism. Most often these institutions themselves functioned under the broader rubric of colonialism. Hence, modern Asian and African philosophies were often responses to, and eventually against, colonial rule by the Western powers. Because of the political, social, economic, and cultural changes brought by the foreign invaders, however, it has been virtually impossible for Asian and African cultures to return to their precontact conditions. Thus, the Westernization process has been inevitable and permanent, and the only viable option has been to manage or limit it. It is within this broad social, political, and cultural reality that modern Asian and African philosophies often have developed.

A culture might take one of three basic stances vis-à-vis the influx of Western ideas and values. First, the culture simply might give itself over to the Westernizing processes, assimilating Western thought as rapidly and wholeheartedly as possible. A second alternative might be to resist all change, to cultivate an ethnic consciousness as a vaccine to protect against the contamination from outside. After all, why should one adopt the ways of one's former oppressor? The third alternative might be to avoid either extreme and to constitute somehow a new alternative that draws on both the traditional and the Western. That is what NISHIDA KITARŌ called a "new *method* of thinking." The theoretical purity of the first two options usually fails in the reality of practicalities. It simply is not always possible either to cut off one's traditional roots or to turn the clock back on the process of modernization once it has been set in motion. Pragmatic considerations force the exploration of the third alternative, which is, however, the most complex and frustrating option from the theoretical standpoint, because it demands coherence and consistency. As such, it gnaws away at anyone who possesses intellectual sensitivity, not just the philosophers in their ivory towers.

It is not surprising, therefore, that we might have to look for modern African and Asian philosophical developments in a variety of places: Some certainly might occur in academic settings, but we must look to political and religious movements as well. Not every political or religious movement is philosophical, but, insofar as it reflects on its intellectual origins, articulates its values, and argues for its correctness in words, whether written or spoken, it has a philosophical dimension. The story of modern philosophy in these regions of the world is necessarily dialogic: modern (Western) versus traditional values, populist versus elitist goals, scientific versus religious orientations, collective versus individual identity, and so forth. There are complex intellectual trade-offs to negotiate, and philosophers, whether professional academicians or not, often have played an important role in the cultural negotiations.

Despite the similarities we have noted, we also should pay heed to the differences among the various thought-worlds covered here: Indian, Tibetan, Chinese, Japanese, African, and Islamic. Each tradition is distinctive enough that it requires its own brief introduction. The generalities, however universal in theory, must be exemplified in the concrete conditions of each cultural region. Philosophizing might be a global phenomenon, but the character of every philosophical expression ultimately is informed and shaped by local circumstances. Even when there are common concerns, it is not surprising to find different philosophical strategies for addressing those concerns.

GENERAL WORKS

Bonevac, Daniel, and Stephen Phillips. *Understanding Non-Western Philosophy: Introductory Readings*. Mayfield Pub. 1992 $14.95. ISBN 1-55934-077-0. Good sampling of short philosophical readings from Africa and Asia, both traditional and modern.

Deutsch, Eliot, ed. *Culture and Modernity: East-West Perspectives*. UH Pr. 1991 $48.00. ISBN 0-8248-1370-7. Thirty-six essays on a variety of topics related to modernity by major philosophers from around the world.

Fu, Charles Wei-hsun, and Gerhard E. Spiegler, eds. *Movements and Issues in World Religions: A Sourcebook and Analysis of Developments since 1945—Religion, Ideology, and Politics*. Greenwood 1987 $95.00. ISBN 0-313-23238-5. Twenty-one brief essays by a broad representation of scholars describing the relationship between religion and politics in today's world. Includes useful bibliographies.

Jaspers, Karl. *Socrates, Buddha, Confucius, and Jesus: Taken from Vol. I of The Great Philosophers*. Trans. by Ralph Manheim. HarBraceJ 1966 $5.95. ISBN 0-15-683580-0. Pioneering work in which a major Western philosopher tries to understand philosophy as a global phenomenon. Originally published in German.

Koller, John M. *Oriental Philosophies*. Macmillan 2nd ed. 1985. ISBN 0-02-365810-X. Textbook explaining the fundamental philosophies of India, China, and Buddhism. Includes some brief discussion of modern developments.

Larson, Gerald James, and Eliot Deutsch, eds. *Interpreting across Boundaries: New Essays in Comparative Philosophy*. Princeton U. Pr. 1988 $44.50. ISBN 0-691-07319-8. Sixteen essays on East-West philosophy by important Asian and Western philosophers.

Nakamura, Hajime. *A Comparative History of Ideas*. Routledge rev. ed. 1986 $65.00. ISBN 0-7103-0122-7. Broad survey of Western and Asian philosophy. Includes a large section on modern developments.

_____. *Ways of Thinking of Eastern Peoples: India, China, Tibet, Japan*. Trans. by Philip P. Wiener. UH Pr. rev. ed. 1964 $16.95. ISBN 0-8248-0078-8. Classic, though sometimes overgeneralized, study of philosophical differences among different Asian cultures as reflected by changes in Buddhist thought from one culture to the next.

Parkes, Graham, ed. *Heidegger and Asian Thought*. UH Pr. 1987 $12.95. ISBN 0-8248-1312-X. Thirteen perceptive essays by a variety of Asian and Western philosophers concerning the impact of Martin Heidegger on modern Asian philosophy and of East Asian philosophy on Heidegger's own philosophizing.

_____. *Nietzsche and Asian Thought*. U. Ch. Pr. 1991 $27.50. ISBN 0-226-64683-1. Fourteen essays on Friedrich Nietzsche's view of Asian (primarily Indian) thought and his later impact on modern Indian, Chinese, and Japanese philosophers.

Radhakrishnan, Sarvepalli, ed. *History of Philosophy: Eastern and Western*. 2 vols. Allen & Unwin 1957 o.p. Focuses on Indian and Western philosophy, with a good discussion of later Indian thought. Not as broad as the title suggests.

Scharfstein, Ben-Ami, ed. *Philosophy East/Philosophy West: A Critical Comparison of Indian, Chinese, Islamic, and European Philosophy*. Blackwell Pubs. 1978 o.p. Four essays on the theoretical complexities of cross-cultural philosophical comparison. Includes five specific case studies.

CHRONOLOGY OF AUTHORS

Indian Philosophy
Rammohun Roy. 1772–1833
Ramakrishna. 1836–1886
Gandhi, Mohandas. 1869–1948
Ghose, Aurobindo. 1872–1950
Radhakrishnan, Sarvepalli. 1888–1975

Tibetan Philosophy
Tenzin Gyatso, The 14th Dalai Lama. 1935–
Trungpa, Chögyam. 1939–1987

Chinese Philosophy
K'ang Yu-wei. 1858–1927
Hu Shih. 1891–1962
Mao Tse-tung. 1893–1976
Fung Yu-lan. 1895–1990
Tu Wei-ming. 1940–

Japanese Philosophy
Nishida Kitarō. 1870–1945
Tanabe Hajime. 1885–1962
Watsuji Tetsurō. 1889–1960
Nishitani Keiji. 1900–1990
Takeuchi Yoshinori. 1913–
Abe Masao. 1915–
Yuasa Yasuo. 1925–

African Philosophy
Nkrumah, Kwame. 1909–1972
Oruka, J. Odera. 1930?–
Mbiti, John S(amuel). 1931–
Wiredu, Kwasi. 1940?–
Hountondji, Paulin J. 1942–

Islamic Philosophy
Abduh, Muhammad. 1849–1905
Iqbal, Sir Muhammad. 1876–1938
Nasr, Seyyed Hossein. 1933–

INDIAN PHILOSOPHY

With the intrusion of the European colonialists into India during the early nineteenth century, the seed for modern Indian philosophy was planted. The Western ways brought challenges and opportunities to India's philosophical thinkers. Certainly, there was much to say for modernization and the adoption of certain Western ways, but how could traditional philosophical ideals be preserved? Initially, contact with the West brought a heightened sense of the need for social reform and improved technology. For some, this reform was embedded in Christian principles introduced by missionaries. As time passed, however, there was an increasing tendency to see these principles as also inherent in traditional Hindu virtues, and forms of Hindu utopianism flourished. By the mid-twentieth century, India already had accomplished what it had done so often before: It had begun to integrate originally disparate elements into a greater unity. Hence, in social reform, in the nationalist movement, in mystical experience, and in philosophical systematization, Western and Indian ideals were drawn on for common inspiration.

General Works

Basham, A. L. *The Wonder That Was India*. Macmillan 1954 o.p. Highly readable, far-reaching overview of traditional Indian culture.

Dasgupta, Surendranath. *A History of Indian Philosophy*. 5 vols. Cambridge U. Pr. 1975 $56.00. ISBN 0-8426-0963-6. Excellent historical survey of Indian philosophy up to, but not including, the modern period.

Koller, John M. *The Indian Way*. Macmillan 1982. ISBN 0-02-365800-2. Good textbook that treats both classical and modern traditions of Indian thought, including Hindu, Buddhist, Muslim, Jain, and Sikh.

Moore, Charles A., ed. *The Indian Mind: Essentials of Indian Philosophy and Culture*. UH Pr. 1967 o.p. Interesting collection of 19 essays on a variety of themes central to Indian philosophy, mostly by contemporary Indian philosophers.

Radhakrishnan, Sarvepalli. *Indian Philosophy*. 2 vols. Routledge Chapman & Hall 1989 $49.95 ea. ISBNs 0-04-181009-0, 0-04-181010-4. Renowned philosopher's comprehensive study of the positions taken by the major traditional schools of Indian thought.

Radhakrishnan, Sarvepalli, and Charles A. Moore, eds. *A Source Book in Indian Philosophy*. Princeton U. Pr. 1957 $18.95. ISBN 0-691-01958-4. Excellent collection of short readings representing most of the major classical and modern philosophers.

Radhakrishnan, Sarvepalli, and John Henry Muirhead, eds. *Contemporary Indian Philosophy*. Macmillan 2nd ed. 1952 o.p. Excellent selection of essays by some of India's most prominent philosophers.

Wolpert, Stanley A. *A New History of India*. OUP 4th cd. 1993 $39.95. ISBN 0-19-507659-1. Highly respected and up-to-date general history of India.

Zimmer, Heinrich. *Philosophies of India*. Ed. by Joseph Campbell. Princeton U. Pr. 1969 $18.95. ISBN 0-691-01758-1. Classic thematic study of Indian philosophies, including an evaluation of their relevance today.

GANDHI, MOHANDAS (MAHATMA). 1869–1948

Mohandas Gandhi is well known as a political activist and pacifist who played a key role in achieving India's independence from Great Britain. Although born in Porbandar, India, to parents of the *Vaisya* (merchant) caste, he was given a modern education and eventually studied law in London. After returning briefly to India, Gandhi went to South Africa in 1893, where he spent the next 20 years working to secure Indian rights. It was during this time that he experimented with and developed his basic philosophy of life.

Philosophically, Gandhi is best known for his ideas of *satyagraha* (truth-force) and *ahimsa* (nonharming). Intrinsic to the idea of truth-force is the correlation between truth and being; truth is not merely a mental correspondence with reality but a mode of existence. Hence, the power of the truth is not what one argues for but what one is. He developed this idea in conjunction with the principle of nonviolence, showing in his nationalist activities that the force of truth, expressed nonviolently, can be an irresistible political weapon against intolerance, racism, and social violence. Although his basic terminology and conceptual context were Hindu, Gandhi was impressed by the universal religious emphasis on the self-transformative power of love, drawing his inspiration from Christianity, Western philosophy, and Islam as well.

BOOKS BY GANDHI

Autobiography: The Story of My Experiments with Truth. Trans. by Mahadev Desai. Greenlf Bks. 2nd ed. 1983 $12.00. ISBN 0-934676-40-2. Gandhi's fascinating telling of his own story and how he came to his spiritual and political insights.
Gandhi on Christianity. Ed. by Robert Ellsberg. Orbis Bks. 1991 $12.95. ISBN 0-88344-756-8. Gandhi's reflections on the nature and practical message of Christianity.
Gandhi on Non-Violence: Selected Texts from Gandhi's Non-Violence in Peace and War. Ed. by Thomas Merton. New Dir. Pr. 1965 $4.95. ISBN 0-8112-0097-3. Some of Gandhi's classic statements on pacifism in short excerpt form. Chosen and introduced by an American pacifist and Christian mystic.
Gandhi's Essential Writings. Ed. by Raghavan Iyer. OUP 1991 $28.00. ISBN 0-19-562543-9. Good selection of readings, with a useful bibliography.
The Moral and Political Writings of Mahatma Gandhi. Ed. by Raghavan Iyer. 3 vols. OUP. Vol. 1 *Civilization, Politics and Religion.* 1986 $115.00. ISBN 0-19-824754-0. Vol. 2 *Truth and Non-Violence.* 1987 $105.00. ISBN 0-19-824755-9. Vol. 3 *Non-Violent Resistance and Social Transformation.* 1987 $125.00. ISBN 0-19-824756-7. Comprehensive collection of Gandhi's writings related to politics and morals, edited by a noted scholar in the field.

BOOKS ABOUT GANDHI

Ashe, Geoffrey. *Gandhi.* Stein & Day 1968 o.p. Reliable biography presenting a balanced account of the man and his deeds.
Bondurant, Joan V. *Conquest of Violence: The Gandhian Philosophy of Conflict.* Princeton U. Pr. 1988 $11.95. ISBN 0-691-02281-X. Perceptive analysis of Gandhi's *satyagraha* as a political instrument for justified change.
Chatterjee, Margaret. *Gandhi's Religious Thought.* U. of Notre Dame Pr. 1986 $11.95. ISBN 0-268-01011-0. Important study by a first-rate philosopher of religion.
Iyer, Raghavan Narasimhan. *The Moral and Political Thought of Mahatma Gandhi.* OUP 1973 o.p. Highly regarded study of Gandhi's politics, based in his spiritual insight.

GHOSE, AUROBINDO. 1872–1950

Born in West Bengal, but educated from childhood through college in Great Britain, Aurobindo Ghose returned to India in 1893 and took a position as a teacher of English and French. Although he had virtually no knowledge of traditional Indian thought, he became involved in national politics, leading a Bengal revolutionary group against British rule. When he was imprisoned in 1908 for his activities supporting Indian nationalism and independence, he became interested in yoga and had a spiritually transformative experience. After his release in 1910, he retreated to Pondicherry in the former French India, where he founded his Ashram and remained until he died in 1950. It was during this time that he developed his philosophy and practice of "integral yoga." In his major work, *The Life Divine* (1955), Ghose set forth a comprehensive theory of universal consciousness and its evolution to higher states through yogic meditation. Unlike many traditional theories of yoga, Ghose's theory ended, not with a spiritual release from this world but, rather, with an active reinvolvement in it. Hence, he had a utopian vision of an ideal community that became a model for his followers around the world.

BOOKS BY GHOSE

The Essential Aurobindo. Ed. by Robert A. McDermott. Lindifarne Pr. 1987 $16.95. ISBN 0-940262-22-3. Good selection of Aurobindo's key writings, selected, introduced, and edited by a noted Aurobindo scholar.

The Life Divine. Lotus Light 2nd ed. 1990 $39.95. ISBN 0-941524-62-0. Aurobindo's most comprehensive and technical work, explaining his overall vision of reality.

The Message of the Gita: With Text, Translation and Notes. Ed. by Anilbaran Roy. Auromere 1979 $7.95. ISBN 0-8071-225-5. Notes from Aurobindo's essays on the *Bhagavad Gita* attached to relevant sections of the original text in Sanskrit and English translation.

BOOKS ABOUT GHOSE

Bruteau, Beatrice. *Worthy Is the World: The Hindu Philosophy of Sri Aurobindo.* Fairleigh Dickinson 1975 $25.00. ISBN 0-8386-7872-6. Fine study of Aurobindo's evolutionary theory of reality.

Chattopadhyaya, D. P. *Sri Aurobindo and Karl Marx: Integral Sociology and Dialectical Sociology.* South Asia Bks. 2nd ed. 1988 $38.50. ISBN 81-208-0388-4. Interesting comparative study of the social theories developed by Aurobindo and Marx.

Heehs, Peter. *Sri Aurobindo: A Brief Biography.* OUP 1989 $12.95. ISBN 0-19-562307-X. Trustworthy account of Aurobindo's life, action, and thought.

McDermott, Robert A., ed. *Six Pillars: Introduction to the Major Works of Sri Aurobindo.* Conococheague Assoc. 1974 o.p. Six insightful essays by major Western scholars on various aspects of Aurobindo's philosophy and practice.

O'Connor, June. *The Quest for Political and Spiritual Liberation: A Study in the Thought of Sri Aurobindo.* Fairleigh Dickinson 1976 $16.50. ISBN 0-8386-1734-4. Illuminating study of the relationship between Aurobindo's politics in his younger years and his later spirituality.

Phillips, Stephen H. *Aurobindo's Philosophy of Brahman.* E. J. Brill 1986 $41.25. ISBN 90-04-07765-0. Philosophical analysis of the technical aspects of Aurobindo's philosophy of the ultimate.

RADHAKRISHNAN, SARVEPALLI. 1888-1975

A philosopher and scholar, Sarvepalli Radhakrishnan was also a statesman, even to the extent of serving as India's president from 1962 to 1967. Brought up as a devout Hindu but also educated in Christian missionary schools, Radhakrishnan's philosophy often was comparative, finding lines of convergence and divergence between East and West. Based in Vedantic idealism, Radhakrishnan affirmed the necessity of an experience of the absolute as the basis of any truly profound grasp of reality. In this regard, he focused his scholarship on the great classical texts of the Indian tradition: the *Upanishads*, the *Bhagavad Gita*, the *Brahma Sutra*, and the various Vedantic commentaries.

However, Radhakrishnan's fundamentally mystical, idealistic dimension did not lead him to renounce the material world. On the contrary, he affirmed action in the world as the expression of the transformative power of the absolute itself. Unlike many traditional Vedantists, Radhakrishnan did not view the material world with all its differentiation as unreal; rather, it is simply not absolute in itself. Spiritual and moral value ultimately derives from something deeper. In this way, he established a metaphysical ground for religious tolerance, an openness he brought to his own activities in the political sphere.

BOOKS BY RADHAKRISHNAN

Brahma Sutra: The Philosophy of Spiritual Life. Trans. by Badarayana. Greenwood 1968 repr. of 1960 ed. $55.00. ISBN 0-8371-0291-X. More than a translation, commentary shows Radhakrishnan's sophistication as a modern philosophical interpreter of an ancient Hindu classic.

Eastern Religions and Western Thought. OUP 1990 $9.95. ISBN 0-19-562456-4. Noted work in comparative philosophy.

An Idealist View of Life. AMS Pr. repr. of 1932 ed. $37.00. ISBN 0-404-60425-0. Readable but not overly technical, expression of Radhakrishnan's philosophical perspective based on his 1929 Hibbert Lectures.

The Principal Upanishads. Humanities 1992 $35.00. ISBN 0-391-03479-0. Fine translation, with excellent philosophical commentary on these fundamental texts of Hindu religious thought.

BOOKS ABOUT RADHAKRISHNAN

Gopal, Sarvepalli. *Radhakrishnan: A Biography.* Unwin Hyman 1989 $39.95. ISBN 0-04-440449-2. Extensive biography, with detail not found elsewhere.

Minor, Robert Neil. *Radhakrishnan: A Religious Biography.* State U. NY Pr. 1987 $59.50. ISBN 0-88706-554-6. Biography emphasizing the development of Radhakrishnan as a religious thinker and leader.

Murty, K. Satchidananda, and Ashok Vohra. *Radhakrishnan: His Life and Ideas.* State U. NY Pr. 1990 $49.50. ISBN 0-7914-0343-2. Good general study of Radhakrishnan's philosophy.

Organ, Troy Wilson. *Radhakrishnan and the Ways to Oneness of East and West.* Ohio U. Pr. 1989 $22.95. ISBN 0-8214-0936-0. Analysis of Radhakrishnan's monistic thought in light of his comparative philosophy.

Schilpp, Paul Arthur, ed. *The Philosophy of Sarvepalli Radhakrishnan. Living Philosophers Ser.* Bks. Demand repr. of 1952 ed. $160.00. ISBN 0-317-08813-0. Valuable critique of various aspects of Radhakrishnan's thought by noted authorities. Includes Radhakrishnan's response.

RAMAKRISHNA. 1836–1886

Although not a philosopher in the technical sense, Ramakrishna developed a philosophical perspective that has had a lasting influence on Hindu religious thought and has been the foundation for a worldwide religious movement. Born in Bengal to a Brahman family, early in his life he showed a tendency to ecstatic trances and visions. Out of these devotional experiences, he established a theory that reality was, on the one hand, formless and, on the other, the playful expression of the Divine Mother, to whom he was religiously devoted. In his later years, his practice extended to the visualization of Muslim and Christian realities as well. Thus, based on his experience, he developed a metaphysical view that all religions are manifestations of the Divine Mother. Led initially by his most famous disciple, Vivekananda, the Ramakrishna Mission gradually established centers around the world.

BOOKS BY RAMAKRISHNA

The Condensed Gospel of Sri Ramakrishna. Ed. by M (pseud.). Vedanta Pr. 1979 $5.95. ISBN 0-87481-489-8. The best anthology currently available.

The Gospel of Sri Ramakrishna. Trans. by Swami Nikhilananda. Ramakrishna 1974 o.p. Although Ramakrishna himself never wrote any works, this collection of conversations with visitors and disciples gathered by Mahendranath Gupta are considered authentic.

BOOKS ABOUT RAMAKRISHNA

Isherwood, Christopher. *Ramakrishna and His Disciples.* Vedanta Pr. 1980 $10.95. ISBN 0-87481-037-X. Engaging and useful biography not only of Ramakrishna, but also of his early followers.

Mueller, Friedrich Max. *Ramakrishna: His Life and Sayings.* AMS Pr. repr. of 1899 ed. $22.00. ISBN 0-404-11452-0. Early and insightful study by one of the great pioneering scholars of Indian religion.

Olson, Carl. *The Mysterious Play of Kali: An Interpretive Study of Ramakrishna*. Scholars Pr. GA 1990 $29.95. ISBN 1-55540-339-5. Fine critical study of the religious impulse in Ramakrishna's life.

Sharma, Arvind. *Ramakrishna and Vivekananda: New Essays*. Apt. Bks. 1989 $18.95. ISBN 0-685-22941-6. Insightful essays on various aspects of the religious philosophy of Ramakrishna and his major disciple.

Vivekananda, Swami. *Ramakrishna and His Message*. Comp. by monks of the Ramakrishna Order. Vedanta Pr. 1971 $1.95. ISBN 0-87481-126-0. Good example of the devotional approach to Ramakrishna taken by Vivekananda in his missionary work.

Whitmarsh, Katherine. *Concordance to the Gospel of Sri Ramakrishna*. Ed. by Mary Dresser. Vedanta Pr. rev. ed. 1990 $24.95. ISBN 0-87481-046-9. Useful reference for the serious study of Ramakrishna's writings; explains the deities, incarnations, and historic figures.

RAMMOHUN ROY (ROY, RAM MOHAN). 1772–1833

Ram Mohan Roy, or as he was better known to the West, Rammohun Roy, was a precursor of modern Indian thought, establishing the foundation for much of what was to follow. Raised by a devoutly Hindu Brahman family, he was educated in his early years in Patna, a center of Islamic learning. In his youth he also traveled widely, encountering a variety of religions, including Buddhism and Christianity. After a successful career with the East India Company, he retired to become an intellectual and a political activist. Impressed by the Christian critiques of Indian society (he was particularly close to the Unitarians), Roy argued for similar reforms. Yet he based his political and social arguments on the classic texts of Hinduism, arguing that many unsavory aspects of Indian society, such as the oppression of women (including *sati*, the self-immolation of widows on their husband's funeral pyres), were as anathema to true Hinduism, as they were to Christianity. He established the Brahmo Samaj religious society, which was highly influential on many of the reformers of the next generation, such as SIR RABINDRANATH TAGORE (see Vol. 2) and Keshab Chandra Sen.

BOOK BY ROY

The English Works of Raja Rammohun Roy. Ed. by Jogendra Ghose. AMS Pr. repr. of 1906 ed. $49.50. ISBN 0-404-14738-0. Standard collection of Roy's major writings.

BOOKS ABOUT ROY

Crawford, S. Cromwell. *Ram Mohan Roy: Social, Political, and Religious Reform in 19th Century India*. Paragon Hse. 1987 o.p. Important study of the ethical influence of Roy on his society.

Kopf, David. *The Brahmo Samaj and the Shaping of the Modern Indian Mind*. Princeton U. Pr. 1979 $60.00. ISBN 0-691-03125-8. Excellent study of Roy as a major figure in Indian modernism and as the founder of an important intellectual movement.

Sankhdher, B. M. *Ram Mohan Roy, The Apostle of Indian Awakening: Some Contemporary Estimates*. South Asia Bks. 1989 $44.00. ISBN 81-7013-051-4. Evaluations of Roy's role in India's transition into modernity.

TIBETAN PHILOSOPHY

Tibetan philosophy in the latter twentieth century has been a Diaspora tradition. Until the Chinese invasion of Tibet in 1959, Tibetan philosophical tradition generally was isolated from the outside world and developed according to the needs of its own society. With the Communist takeover and the subsequent attempts to destroy the fabric of traditional Tibetan culture, many of Tibet's major religious leaders (who were also the most educated in the native philosophical traditions) relocated outside the country. The goal of the Diaspora intellectuals has been the preservation of the Tibetan Buddhist tradition for its own people and the adaptation of the traditional teachings as a spiritual and philosophical inspiration to the outer world, especially Europe and North America. Through this sequence of events, Tibetan Buddhist philosophy suddenly has found itself in the midst of the Western crises of modernity and postmodernity. Two Tibetan intellectuals most involved in this philosophical process of redefinition and adaptation have been The 14th Dalai Lama, TENZIN GYATSO (also spelled Bstan-'dzin-rgya-mtsho), and CHÖGYAM TRUNGPA.

General Works

Hopkins, Jeffrey. *The Tantric Distinction: An Introduction to Tibetan Buddhism.* Ed. by Anne C. Klein. Wisdom MA 1984 $8.95. ISBN 0-86171-023-1. Perceptive and nontechnical explanation of basic principles in Tibetan Buddhism, based on public lectures for nonspecialists.
Shakabpa, W. D. *Tibet: A Political History.* Potala 1984 repr. of 1967 ed. ISBN 0-9611474-1-5. The most definitive study of the political history of Tibet.
Snellgrove, David L., and Hugh E. Richardson. *A Cultural History of Tibet.* Shambhala Pubns. 1980 $15.95. ISBN 0-685-43283-1. Excellent overview, including a good, although somewhat dated, bibliography.
Stein, Rolf A. *Tibetan Civilization.* Trans. by J. E. Driver. Stanford U. Pr. 1972 $45.00. ISBN 0-8047-0806-1. Well-respected study of Tibetan culture and history.
Tucci, Giuseppe. *Religions of Tibet.* Trans. by Geoffrey Samuel. U. CA Pr. 1988 $35.00. ISBN 0-520-03856-8. Basic overview of Tibetan religious traditions by a noted Tibetologist.

TENZIN GYATSO, THE 14th DALAI LAMA. 1935– (NOBEL PRIZE 1989)

Born of peasants, at the age of 4 Tenzin Gyatso was identified as the reincarnation of the previous Dalai Lama and was taken to the capital, Lhasa, to be trained for his future role as the political, spiritual, and cultural leader of Tibet. After the Chinese crushed an uprising against their occupation of the country in 1959, the Dalai Lama fled to India, where he established a government in exile. As time passed, however, the Dalai Lama became more visible as a citizen of the world, arguing for the peaceful return of his country's sovereignty, the preservation of Tibetan culture, and the relevance of traditional Tibetan Buddhist teachings to the problems of today. For his efforts in this regard, he was awarded the Nobel Peace Prize in 1989.

BOOKS BY TENZIN GYATSO

The Buddhism of Tibet. Ed. and trans. by Jeffrey Hopkins. Snow Lion repr. of 1975 ed. $12.95. ISBN 0-937938-48-3. Overview of the basic philosophical orientation of Tibetan Buddhism as understood and practiced by the Dalai Lama.
Freedom in Exile: The Autobiography of the Dalai Lama. HarpC 1990 $22.95. ISBN 0-06-039116-2. Recent autobiography paying special attention to events after 1960.
Gentle Bridges: Conversations with the Dalai Lama on the Sciences of Mind. Ed. by Jeremy Howard and Francisco J. Varela. Shambhala Pubns. 1992 $15.00. ISBN 0-87773-517-5. Nonsystematic, but insightful, comments about the Tibetan Buddhist understanding of epistemology and psychology. Consists of intriguing and provocative discussions with Western scientists, psychologists, and philosophers.
My Land and My People. Potala 1983 repr. of 1962 ed. $6.95. ISBN 0-9611474-0-7. Earlier autobiography, from childhood to the escape from Tibet and the beginning of his

exile. Includes a fascinating account of the Dalai Lama's traditional religious and philosophical training as a child.

The Nobel Peace Prize and the Dalai Lama. Snow Lion 1990 $4.50. ISBN 0-937938-86-6. Background material about the awarding of the Peace Prize, including the Dalai Lama's acceptance speech and comments.

BOOK ABOUT TENZIN GYATSO

Goodman, Michael Harris. *The Last Dalai Lama: A Biography.* Shambhala Pubns. 1986 o.p. Sympathetic telling of the Dalai Lama's story, focusing on his years of exile from Chinese Communist-controlled Tibet.

TRUNGPA, CHÖGYAM. 1939–1987

Chögyam Trungpa was one of the most visibly active of the Tibetan Buddhist refugees to come to the West and to lay the foundation in Europe and North America for the study of the Tibetan traditions. Born the son of a farmer and considered the eleventh incarnation of Trungpa Tulku, he was given a traditional training in religious philosophy but in his teens had to be hidden from the invading Chinese. Fleeing in 1959 when the Communists invaded Tibet, he ultimately moved to Great Britain, where he studied comparative religion at Oxford University and established a Tibetan meditation center in Scotland. He moved to the United States in 1970 and established the Buddhist university, Naropa, in Colorado. Naropa became the center for seminars, many of which he cotaught with prominent American artists, scholars, and scientists. His philosophical goal was to present traditional Tibetan Buddhist teachings in a new manner that would help them take root in Western soil. In that way, he would both preserve the insights of his culture and bring Buddhist philosophy to the benefit of humanity at large.

BOOKS BY TRUNGPA

Born in Tibet. Random 1985 $9.95. ISBN 0-394-74219-2. Autobiographical account of Trungpa's escape from Tibet to India, giving unusual insights into his childhood training.

Cutting through Spiritual Materialism. Ed. by John Baker and Marvin Casper. Shambhala Pubns. 1987 $14.00. ISBN 0-87773-050-4. Trungpa's most successful effort at adapting traditional Tibetan Buddhist thought to the situation of interested Westerners. Focuses on the danger of ego-enhancement as a motivation for undertaking Buddhist practice.

Meditation in Action. Shambhala Pubns. 1991 repr. of 1985 ed. $60.00. ISBN 0-87773-550-6. Introductory collection of Trungpa's early lectures on basic Buddhist principles, intended for his audience of Western followers.

Orderly Chaos: The Mandala Principle. Ed. by Sherab Chodzin. Shambhala Pubns. 1991 $13.00. ISBN 0-87773-636-7. Analysis of the mandala as symbolic of both nonessentialism (chaos) and creative, spontaneous expression (order).

Transcending Madness: The Experience of the Six Bardos. Shambhala Pubns. 1992 $15.00. ISBN 0-87773-637-5. The traditional states of existence after death reinterpreted as an analysis of states of psychological turmoil in this world. Includes useful short biographical sketch of Trungpa's career.

CHINESE PHILOSOPHY

Modern philosophy in China began in the first and second decades of the twentieth century. The increased presence of Western colonialism created ever greater tensions between the imperial system and the young intellectuals who wanted to modernize the country. With the overthrow of the imperial system and the rise to power of the nationalists, the new breed of philosophers set to work building a new China. Traveling abroad, receiving their education in Europe or the United States, the young intellectuals brought new methods and new democratic visions to what was still, in many respects, a premodern state.

After the May Fourth Incident of 1919, the reformers found themselves divided into two camps: the liberal nationalists and the Communists. Both shared a desire to overcome the stultified traditions that prevented modernization, and both shared a desire for national independence free from either Western or Japanese encroachment; yet their vision of the means to achieve those ends differed radically. With the Communist victory in 1949, the Maoist era began. Philosophy increasingly became a tool in the service of the socialist revolution and the evolution of the pure Maoist state.

At the same time, a Diaspora tradition of philosophical liberalism continued in the refugees who fled to Hong Kong, Taiwan, or the West. New formulations of Confucian values, radically altered to fit the modern situation, have been developing quietly outside the Communist sphere of influence. Whether these philosophical reformulations will find their way back into China during a time of intellectual openness and freedom remains to be seen.

General Works

Brière, O. *Fifty Years of Chinese Philosophy 1898–1950*. Trans. by Laurence Thompson. Greenwood 1965 repr. of 1956 ed. $39.75. ISBN 0-313-20650-3. Important study of modern, pre-Communist philosophy in China.

Chan, Wing-tsit. *A Source Book of Chinese Philosophy*. Princeton U. Pr. 1963 $18.95. ISBN 0-691-01964-9. Comprehensive selection of excerpts from the great philosophers of Chinese history. Includes a short section on modern thought.

Creel, Herrlee G. *Chinese Thought: From Confucius to Mao Tse-tung*. U. Ch. Pr. 1971 repr. of 1953 ed. $10.95. ISBN 0-226-12030-9. Readable and useful overview of basic ideas in Chinese philosophy.

de Bary, William Theodore, Wing-tsit Chan, and Burton Watson. *Sources of Chinese Tradition*. 2 vols. Col. U. Pr. 1960. Vol. 1 $19.50. ISBN 0-231-08602-4. Vol. 2 $18.00. ISBN 0-231-08603-2. Comprehensive selection of brief excerpts from the writings of major literary and intellectual figures. Vol. 2 concentrates on the modern period.

Fairbank, John King, Edwin O. Reischauer, and Albert Craig. *East Asia: The Modern Transformation*. HM 3rd ed. 1989 $51.96. ISBN 0-395-45023-3. Excellent overview of the political, social, and economic development of modern East Asia.

Fu, Charles Wei-hsun, and Wing-tsit Chan. *Guide to Chinese Philosophy*. G. K. Hall 1978 o.p. Basic bibliography; somewhat dated but still useful.

Fung Yu-Lan. *A History of Chinese Philosophy*. 2 vols. Trans. by Derk Bodde. Princeton U. Pr. Vol. 1 1952 $25.00. ISBN 0-691-02021-3. Vol. 2 1953 $35.00. ISBN 0-691-02022-1. Classic treatment of the great philosophers of traditional China. Includes a short section on early modern developments.

———. *The Spirit of Chinese Philosophy*. Trans. by E. R. Hughes. Greenwood 1970 repr. of 1947 ed. o.p. Readable, nontechnical history portraying Chinese philosophy in broad strokes.

Gernet, Jacques. *A History of Chinese Civilization*. Trans. by J. R. Foster. Cambridge U. Pr. 1985 $74.95. ISBN 0-521-24130-8. Excellent one-volume survey of Chinese history to the early 1970s.

Louis, Kam. *Critiques of Confucius in Contemporary China*. St. Martin 1980 o.p. Survey of anti-Confucianist movements in China from the turn of the century to the 1970s.

Moore, Charles A., ed. *The Chinese Mind: Essentials of Chinese Philosophy and Culture*. UH 1967 $12.95. ISBN 0-8248-0075-3. Good selection of 15 essays by contemporary Chinese philosophers on both traditional and modern topics.

Munro, Donald J. *The Concept of Man in Contemporary China.* U. of Mich. Pr. 1977 o.p.
Outstanding analysis of the understanding of human nature and society as developed
in Maoist China by thinkers from various disciplines.

Schwartz, Benjamin I. *Communism and China: Ideology in Flux.* Bks. Demand repr. of
1968 ed. $70.20. ISBN 0-7837-1721-0. Insightful essays by one of America's premier
specialists in modern Chinese thought.

FUNG YU-LAN (FENG YOU-LAN). 1895–1990

Fung Yu-lan's philosophical works, which developed under the influence of
American pragmatism and Neo-Realism, as well as Confucianism and Marxism,
show a marked transition from traditional interpretations to radical Maoist
thinking.

After receiving his B.A. from Beijing University, Fung went to Columbia
University to complete his doctorate in philosophy. Still sympathetic to
Confucianism, he returned to China in the late 1920s and set to work applying
his newly learned pragmatic methods to the study of classical Chinese
philosophy. The development of this comparative East-West perspective can be
seen in both his *Philosophy of Life* and his two-volume *A History of Chinese
Philosophy* (1931, 1934). In attempting to overturn many traditional interpretations, he soon earned a reputation for himself, not only in China, but also in the
West.

By the late 1930s, Fung had started to formulate his own philosophical
system—a rational formalism that reinterpreted the apparently ontological
categories of Neo-Confucianism (such as *dao, li,* and *qi,* also romanized as *tao,
li,* and *ch'i*) into logical functions. Of his works at this time, *New Li Hsüeh* (*The
New Rational Philosophy*) was his most important and famous expression of
Neo-Confucianism in light of modern philosophy.

With the Communist Revolution, Fung's ideas came under attack as being
overly idealistic. This led to the rethinking of his former historical and logical
positions more in light of dialectical materialism.

Fung eventually became a supporter of MAO TSE-TUNG's anti-Confucian
campaign during the 1970s and served as intellectual consultant to Mao's wife,
Chiang Ch-ing. Nevertheless, Fung never quite fit the paradigm of the Maoist
philosopher, and until his death his philosophy periodically underwent official
criticism as being overly "abstract" and "idealistic." His "philosophical career"
ended when Chiang's group fell from power shortly after Mao's death.

BOOKS BY FUNG YU-LAN

*Chuang Tzu: A New Selected Translation with an Exposition of the Philosophy of Kuo
Hsiang.* Krishna Pr. $250.00. ISBN 0-87968-187-X. Translation of Fung's commen-
tary accompanies this translation of the classic Taoist text.

A History of Chinese Philosophy. 1931, 1934. 2 vols. Trans. by Derk Bodde. Princeton U.
Pr. Vol. 1 1952 $25.00. ISBN 0-691-02021-3. Vol. 2 1953 $35.00. ISBN 0-691-02022-1.
Classic treatment of the great philosophers of traditional China. Includes a short
section on early modern developments.

The Spirit of Chinese Philosophy. Trans. by E. R. Hughes. Greenwood 1970 repr. of 1947
ed. o.p. Readable, nontechnical history portraying Chinese philosophy in broad
strokes.

BOOK ABOUT FUNG YU-LAN

Masson, Michel C. *Philosophy and Tradition: The Interpretation of China's Philosophic
Past: Fung Yu-lan 1939–1949.* Institut Ricci 1985 o.p. Focused appraisal of Fung's
historical writings before the Revolution by an intellectual historian.

HU SHIH. 1891–1962

In 1910 Hu Shih traveled to the United States to receive his college education, completing his undergraduate work at Cornell University and his doctoral work in philosophy under JOHN DEWEY (see also Vol. 3) at Columbia University. After returning to China in 1917, Hu tried to apply Dewey's pragmatism and theories of education to the Chinese context. Hu argued for the elimination of classicist elitism and worked toward modernization on various fronts, including the development of a writing style based on the contemporary spoken, rather than archaic literary, forms. He also applied Western scholarly methods to the reading of Chinese history, overturning many of the accepted, but inaccurate, perceptions of the past. Following the May Fourth Incident of 1919, Hu found himself more or less allied with the liberal intellectuals against the radical activists and served for a time as the ambassador to the United States. After the Communist Revolution in 1949, Hu moved to New York, where he lived out the final years of his life.

BOOKS BY HU SHIH

China's Own Critics: A Selection of Essays. (coauthored with Lin Yu-tang). Hyperion Conn. 1986 repr. of 1931 ed. $22.00. ISBN 0-8305-0006-5. Includes five short essays by Hu Shih on matters of practical reform in China and on breaking free of China's "sterile inheritance."

The Chinese Renaissance. Paragon Hse. 1963 repr. of 1934 ed. o.p. Series of lectures outlining Hu Shih's pragmatic vision for a new China—one free of the more constricting conditions of class and formality.

The Development of Logical Method in Ancient China. Krishna Pr. 1973 $79.95. ISBN 0-87968-524-1. Historical study attempting to show the functional roots of classical Chinese thinking.

BOOK ABOUT HU SHIH

Chou, Min-chih. *Hu Shih and the Intellectual Choice in Modern China.* U. of Mich. Pr. 1984 $34.50. ISBN 0-472-10039-4. Important study of Hu Shih's liberalizing vision for the development of modern China.

K'ANG YU-WEI. 1858–1927

Best known as the leader of the 1898 Hundred Days' Reform, K'ang Yu-Wei was an intellectual historian, social reformer, and utopian philosopher. Educated in traditional Confucianism, Buddhism, and Taoism, K'ang's readings of Western authors in his early twenties sparked his interest in progress and the establishment of ideal societies, as well as his ambition to reform Chinese society. In his theory of historical progress, K'ang argued that the versions of the texts traditionally taken to be the authentic classics of Confucianism were, in fact, forged 2000 years ago for political purposes. This claim marked him as a central figure in the "New Text School," which considered a different version of the texts as authentic. In making this transition, he shook the foundations of established exegesis and elaborated an interpretation of CONFUCIUS as a reformer. This served his second purpose, the modern reform of China, in which he was an active figure. After being exiled for 16 years, he returned to China in 1912, opposing the policies of Sun Yat-sen and advocating the adoption of Confucianism as the state religion.

Philosophically, he is most noted for his utopian elaboration of the "three ages" found in early Confucian texts: the Age of Chaos, the Age of Small Peace, and the Age of Great Unity. According to K'ang, in the final age, humanity is governed strictly by an ideal benevolence or love, people no longer suffer, and they are treated as equals: There are no longer nations, classes, or even families. Even religion no longer will be needed. K'ang argued that social reform would bring about the second, and ultimately the third, age. His *Book of the Universal Concord*, in which he fully expanded his utopian vision, was considered so radical that it was not published until eight years after he died.

BOOK BY K'ANG YU-WEI

Ta T'ung Shu, The One-World Philosophy of K'ang Yu-Wei. Trans. by Laurence G. Thompson. Allen & Unwin 1958 o.p. Good translation of K'ang's philosophical *magnum opus*.

BOOKS ABOUT K'ANG YU-WEI

Chang, Hao. *Chinese Intellectuals in Crisis: Search for Order and Meaning (1890–1911)*. U. CA Pr. 1987 $47.50. ISBN 0-520-05378-8. Outstanding study of this critical period in Chinese intellectual and social history. Special attention is given to K'ang, Tan Ssu-Tung, Chang Ta-yen, and Liu Shih-pei.

Hsiao, Kung-Chuan. *A Modern China and a New World: K'ang Yu-wei, Reformer and Utopian, 1858–1927*. U. of Wash. Pr. 1975 $40.00. ISBN 0-295-95385-3. Comprehensive study of K'ang's thought, its historical context and social impact.

Lo Jung-pang, ed. *Kang Yu-wei: A Biography and a Symposium*. Bks. Demand repr. of 1967 ed. $149.90. ISBN 0-7837-0028-8. Collection of excellent papers and a useful biography.

MAO TSE-TUNG (also MAO ZEDONG). 1893–1976

Mao Tse-tung is known primarily, of course, as a Communist revolutionary and statesman. Although lacking his more scholarly contemporaries' sophistication and thorough knowledge of the history of Western philosophy, Mao's thinking is important for understanding the influence of Marxism and Leninism on Chinese philosophy today.

Born in Hunan province to a former peasant family that had become relatively affluent as grain traders, Mao eventually left home to pursue his higher education in Beijing. There he became part of the student movement arising out of the May Fourth Incident, turning his allegiance from the liberal nationalists to the Communist revolutionaries. Leader of the Chinese Communist party from 1931, he led the revolution and came to power as chairman in 1949. Until his death, he served as either head of state or head of the party.

The late 1930s constituted his most active period of philosophizing. In those years he formulated his interpretation of theory and practice, best expressed in his 1937 lecture "On Practice." Here Mao argued that theory and practice are in a symbiotic, cyclical relationship such that one always must lead inevitably to the other. He later developed more fully his revisions of Marxist theory to fit the Chinese situation, especially his emphasis on the rural peasantry instead of the urban proletariat as the primary agents for revolutionary change.

Since Mao's death, with the development of a more tolerant attitude toward the West and traditional thought, Maoist philosophy has been greatly criticized, yet it remains a creative attempt to blend Marxist and traditional Chinese viewpoints. (See Volumes 2 and 3 for additional information on Mao Tse-tung.)

BOOKS BY MAO TSE-TUNG

Five Essays on Philosophy. China Bks. 1977 $5.95. ISBN 0-8351-0451-6. Central philosophical essays outlining Mao's theory of revolutionary change.

Mao's Road to Power: Revolutionary Writings 1912–1949. Ed. by Stuart R. Schram. M. E. Sharpe 1992 $100.00. ISBN 1-56324-049-1. Wide selection of writings relevant to Mao's early years and the planning of the revolution.

Mao Zedong on Dialectical Materialism: Writings on Philosophy, 1937. Ed. by Nick Knight. M. E. Sharpe 1990 $49.95. ISBN 0-87332-682-2. Writings from Mao's theoretical period, during which he developed his philosophy of history and change.

Quotations from Chairman Mao Tse-tung. China Bks. 1990 $7.95. ISBN 0-8351-2388-X. Version of the "Little Red Book" with aphorisms and short excerpts useful for sloganizing.

Selected Works. 5 vols. Franklin 1977 repr. of 1954–62 ed. $216.00. ISBN 0-08-022984-0. The standard edition of Mao's works.

The Writings of Mao Zedong, Sept. 1949–Dec. 1955. Ed. by Michael Y. M. Kau and John K. Leung. M. E. Sharpe 1986 $115.00. ISBN 0-87332-391-2. Mao's writings from the early years following the success of the revolution.

BOOKS ABOUT MAO TSE-TUNG

Lawrance, Alan. *Mao Zedong: A Bibliography*. Greenwood 1991 $59.50. ISBN 0-313-28222-6. The most up-to-date and definitive bibliography currently available.

Schram, Stuart R. *The Thought of Mao Tse-tung*. Cambridge U. Pr. 1989 $49.95. ISBN 0-521-32549-8. Balanced and insightful overview of the development of Mao's political and social theories, written by a major authority in the field.

Starr, John Bryan. *Continuing the Revolution: The Political Thought of Mao*. Princeton U. Pr. 1979 $50.00. ISBN 0-691-07596-4. Fine study of Mao's theoretical adjustments as he moved from the revolution to the dictatorship of the proletariat to the classless society.

Wakeman, Frederic E. *History and Will: Philosophical Perspectives of Mao Tse-tung's Thought*. U. CA Pr. 1973 $13.95. ISBN 0-052-02907-0. Major study evaluating the presuppositions and rationale of Mao's philosophy.

Womack, Brantly. *The Foundations of Mao Zedong's Political Thought, 1917–1935*. UH Pr. 1982 $17.50. ISBN 0-8248-0752-9. Excellent study of the early twentieth-century intellectual context of Mao's thinking.

TU WEI-MING. 1940–

Receiving his graduate training at Harvard University, Tu Wei-ming has spent most of his academic career as a professor in the United States. His basic philosophical position has been to argue for a Confucian-based humanism as a response to the alienation, nihilism, and mechanization of modern society in the West, as well as in East Asia. His essays are collected in such books as *Centrality and Commonality (1989), Humanity and Self-Cultivation* (1980), and *Confucian Thought: Selfhood as Creative Transformation* (1985). In each case, he draws on the classical Confucian tradition, adapting its message in creative ways to argue toward a revision of personhood in today's society.

BOOKS BY TU WEI-MING

Centrality and Commonality: An Essay on Confucian Religiousness. State U. NY Pr. rev. ed. 1989 $48.95. ISBN 0-88706-927-4

Confucian Thought: Selfhood as Creative Transformation. State U. NY Pr. 1985 $49.50. ISBN 0-88706-005-6

Humanity and Self-Cultivation: Essays in Confucian Thought. Asian Human. Pr. 1980 $30.00. ISBN 0-89581-600-8

Neo-Confucian Thought in Action: Wang Yang-ming's Youth. U. CA Pr. 1976 $35.00. ISBN 0-520-02968-2. Scholarly study of an important early sixteenth-century Neo-Confucian figure who advocated the unity of knowledge and action.

JAPANESE PHILOSOPHY

Unlike most other non-Western traditions, contemporary Japanese philosophy did not develop under the influence of Western colonialism. Because it maintained its sovereignty until 1945, Japan had the opportunity to develop its modern philosophy without the burden of values and ideas imposed from abroad. This does not mean that modern Japanese thought has been isolated from the West. On the contrary, Commodore Perry's demand in 1853 that Japan open its doors to trade left the country with two alternatives: the option of eventual dominance by Western expansionism or the option of a sustained effort at self-determinism backed by military and economic strength. The latter choice was pursued, leading to a period of intense industrialization and remaking of the national social, economic, and educational systems. In this process, Japan's brightest and most creative thinkers studied Western ideas as possible models for its internal transformation. Part of this effort was the study of Western philosophies.

Having seen itself for centuries as the receptor of the best of Asian mainland cultural traditions, Japanese philosophers consciously tried to adopt the best of Western thought as well. In the early decades of the twentieth century, they developed their own schools of thought, representing, for example, Western pragmatism, existentialism, and process philosophy. The result has been an extraordinarily rich and complex philosophical tradition—one that is as likely to draw on KANT as on CONFUCIUS, on ARISTOTLE (see also Vol. 3) as on Buddha, and on HEIDEGGER (see also Vol. 5) as on Lao Tzu. A recurring concern for modern Japanese thinkers has been how to integrate these various philosophical strands into a coherent and comprehensive philosophical vision. This has been an especially strong theme in the development of philosophy within the Kyoto School, the most widely known of the modern Japanese philosophical traditions and the one that has attracted increasing attention from the West in recent years as works have become available in translation.

General Works

Franck, Frederick, ed. *The Buddha Eye: An Anthology of the Kyoto School.* Crossroad NY 2nd ed. 1982 $14.95. ISBN 0-8245-1071-2. Seventeen readable essays from a variety of important modern thinkers, not all of whom are philosophers or members of the Kyoto School.

Holzman, Donald, and Yukihiko Motoyama. *Japanese Religion and Philosophy.* Greenwood 1975 repr. of 1959 ed. $35.00. ISBN 0-8371-7910-6. Dated bibliographical work containing some citations not found elsewhere.

Moore, Charles A., ed. *The Japanese Mind: Essentials of Japanese Philosophy and Culture.* UH Pr. 1967 $8.50. ISBN 0-8248-0077-X. Collected essays by an eminent group of contemporary Japanese thinkers. Many are written for nonspecialists.

Piovesana, Gino K. *Contemporary Japanese Philosophical Thought.* St. John's U. Pr. 1969 o.p. Pioneering, but still unsuperseded, study of movements and key figures from 1862 to 1960.

ABE MASAO. 1915–

A student of D. T. SUZUKI, Hisamatsu Shin'ichi, and NISHITANI KEIJI, Abe Masao is the member of the Kyoto School who has been most active in personally interacting with Western philosophers and theologians. His essays draw on a variety of sources in an effort to make East and West more intelligible to each other and to push both traditions to new philosophical and religious insights.

BOOKS BY ABE MASAO

A Study of Dōgen: His Philosophy and Religion. Ed. by Steven Heine. State U. NY Pr. 1991 $39.50. ISBN 0-7914-0837-X. Six-essay study of the thirteenth-century philosophies of Dōgen and Shinran in light of Abe's own philosophical orientation.
Zen and Western Thought. Ed. by William R. LaFleur. UH Pr. 1989 $24.94. ISBN 0-8248-0952-1. Sixteen essays on a variety of themes selected from different times in Abe's career. Good introduction to his thought.

NISHIDA KITARŌ. 1870–1945

Generally considered Japan's first major modern philosopher, Nishida Kitarō was the founder of an approach to philosophy that usually is identified as the Kyoto School. Born near Kanazawa, where he was a childhood friend of D. T. SUZUKI, Nishida attended Tokyo University and upon graduation became a country high school teacher. During this time, he was drawn to Zen Buddhism as both a philosophy and a way of life. Simultaneously, he deepened his readings in Western philosophy, especially German idealism, psychology, and American pragmatism. In 1910 he took an appointment at Kyoto University, where he taught until his retirement in 1928. His first work, *Zen-no-kenkyū (A Study of Good)* (1911), features his early ideas, explaining the relationships among thought, reality, ethics, and religion. He continued to write books, mainly in the form of related essays, until his death in 1945.

Nishida's philosophy often is classified into three periods. In the early period (1910–1917?), he emphasized the analysis of "pure experience"—borrowing WILLIAM JAMES's (see also Vols. 2 and 3) term—attempting to show a common drive to unity in the experiences underlying the formation of science, art, morality, and religion. In his second, transitional period (1917–1927?), he studied the philosophies of the German Neo-Kantians and turned to an interest in the logical structure of judgment instead of the psychological roots of experience. Fine-tuning his ideas in *Intuition and Reflection in Self-Consciousness* (1917) and *The Problems of Consciousness* (1920), he concluded that the ultimate basis of consciousness is "absolute free will." This shift led to his third period (1927–45), during which he developed his "logic of place," a systematic attempt to characterize the contextual structures within which judgments (empirical, idealistic, and ethical-aesthetic-religious) are formed. He later extended this view to cover the historical world. Although sometimes criticized for his artificiality, and, despite various twists and turns in his philosophical career, Nishida consistently strove to articulate a philosophical system that would incorporate the insights of both Western and Asian thought.

BOOKS BY NISHIDA KITARŌ

Art and Morality. Trans. by David A. Dilworth and Valdo H. Viglielmo. Bks. Demand repr. of 1973 ed. $59.30. ISBN 0-8357-6026-X. Essays focusing mainly on the nature of religion and aesthetics. Represents Nishida's middle period.
Fundamental Problems of Philosophy. Trans. by David A. Dilworth. Sophia U. Pr. 1970 o.p. Six broad-reaching technical essays from Nishida's mature period.
An Inquiry into the Good. Trans. by Abe Masao and Christopher Ives. Yale U. Pr. 1990 $25.00. ISBN 0-300-04094-6. Nishida's maiden work of 1911.
Intelligibility and the Philosophy of Nothingness. Trans. by Robert Schinzinger. Greenwood 1973 repr. of 1958 ed. $35.00. ISBN 0-8371-6689-6. Three essays from the late 1920s and 1930s. Includes a good philosophical analysis by the translator.

Intuition and Reflection in Self-Consciousness. Trans. by Valdo H. Viglielmo with
Takeuchi Yoshinori and Joseph S. O'Leary. State U. NY Pr. 1987 $74.50. ISBN 0-
88706-368-3. Edited version of Nishida's published journals (1913–17), dealing with
his critical readings of German Neo-Kantian philosophers.

Last Writings: Nothingness and the Religious Worldview. Trans. by David A. Dilworth. UH
Pr. 1987 $18.00. ISBN 0-8248-1040-6. Two of Nishida's last essays explaining his final
view of the logic of religious experience. Includes two useful commentarial essays by
the translator.

BOOKS ABOUT NISHIDA KITARŌ

Carter, Robert E. *The Nothingness beyond God: An Introduction to the Philosophy of
Nishida Kitarō.* Paragon Hse. 1988 $22.95. ISBN 1-55778-072-2. Good overview of
Nishida's philosophy, especially its ramifications for East-West philosophical and
theological dialogue.

Keiji, Nishitani. *Nishida Kitarō.* Trans. by Yamamoto Seisaku and James Heisig. U. CA Pr.
1991 $19.95. ISBN 0-520-07364-9. Ten essays on Nishida's life and thought by one of
his disciples.

NISHITANI KEIJI. 1900–1990

A student of both NISHIDA KITARŌ in Japan and MARTIN HEIDEGGER (see also
Vol. 5) in Germany, Nishitani Keiji has become one of the most influential of
modern Japanese philosophers, both in Japan and in the West. His work focuses
on the nihilism inherent in the failure of modern Western philosophy and the
global culture it has produced. Nishitani's position was that only by facing that
nihilism can one encounter a more profound nothingness at the core of human
experience. Rather than a merely negative nihility, this nothingness is the
wellspring of religious insight and creative expression.

BOOKS BY NISHITANI KEIJI

Nishida Kitarō. Trans. by Yamamoto Seisaku and James Heisig. U. CA Pr. 1991 $19.95.
ISBN 0-520-07364-9. Ten essays on Nishida's life and thought by one of his disciples.

Religion and Nothingness. Trans. by Jan Van Bragt. U. CA Pr. 1982 $45.00. ISBN 0-520-
04329-4. Highly influential series of essays from the late 1940s and early 1950s in
which Nishitani develops his philosophy of religion and its application to understanding Christianity as well as Buddhism.

The Self-Overcoming of Nihilism. Trans. by Graham Parkes and Setsuko Aihara. State U.
NY Pr. 1990 $57.50. ISBN 0-7914-0437-4. Provocative, readable collection of essays
written from 1949 to 1972 analyzing and evaluating the tradition of nihilism from
Hegel to Sartre to postwar Japan.

BOOKS ABOUT NISHITANI KEIJI

Unno, Taitetsu, ed. *The Religious Philosophy of Nishitani Keiji.* Asian Human. Pr. 1989
$60.00. ISBN 0-89581-870-1. Collection of essays written primarily by Western
philosophers, theologians, and scholars. Addresses various aspects of Nishitani's
Religion and Nothingness.

Waldenfels, Hans. *Absolute Nothingness: Foundations for a Buddhist-Christian Dialogue.*
Trans. by J. W. Heisig. Paulist Pr. 1980 o.p. Theological response to aspects of
Nishitani's thought as a basis for Buddhist-Christian philosophical interaction.

TAKEUCHI YOSHINORI. 1913–

A member of the Kyoto School who primarily studied philosophy under
TANABE HAJIME, Takeuchi Yoshinori also trained as a scholar of Buddhism. After
his detailed study of modern German philosophy, Takeuchi applied Western
philosophical thought to the articulation of traditional Buddhist ideas. The
result is a reading of the Buddhist tradition that springs from existential

concerns much like those found in such Christian theologians as RUDOLF BULTMANN or PAUL TILLICH.

BOOK BY TAKEUCHI YOSHINORI

The Heart of Buddhism: In Search of the Timeless Spirit of Primitive Buddhism. Ed. and trans. by James W. Heisig. Crossroad NY 1991 repr. of 1983 ed. $12.95. ISBN 0-8245-1070-4. Seven essays relating his analysis of the basic Buddhist worldview to his broader analysis of human existence.

TANABE HAJIME. 1885–1962

Born and raised in Tokyo, Tanabe Hajme shifted his college training at Tokyo University to philosophy, after an initial interest in mathematics and science. As he progressed in the field, he became keenly interested in the work of NISHIDA KITARŌ, who brought him to Kyoto University in 1919 to teach; Tanabe's early works reflect their close association. From 1922 to 1924, Tanabe studied in Germany, primarily under Alois Reihl and EDMUND HUSSERL, and upon returning to Kyoto, he worked in earnest to develop his own philosophical theory.

Although he was an important figure in establishing the Kyoto School, his philosophy increasingly diverged from Nishida's. Influenced by HEGEL's (see also Vol. 3) work, Tanabe formulated his own "absolute dialectic" in *Elements of Philosophy* (1933). In opposition to Nishida's viewpoint, Tanabe next focused on what he called the "logic of species," a system that attempts to privilege neither the universal nor the individual, but rather to see both as polar mediations within a single state. In his later thought, developed during and shortly after World War II, Tanabe turned to the analysis of the limitations and dangers of modern rationalism. Philosophy's true role, he argued, was to be *metanoetio*—to use reasoning as a tool to criticize itself and its inherent tendencies to substantialize, overstructure, and control—all from the standpoint of a reified ego. This marked a shift in the content of his logic and a return to religious philosophy.

BOOK BY TANABE HAJIME

Philosophy as Metanoetics. Trans. by Takeuchi Yoshinori. U. CA Pr. 1987 $55.00. ISBN 0-520-05490-3. Detailed technical analysis of the human situation and the need for philosophy to take a "metanoetic" role.

BOOK ABOUT TANABE HAJIME

Unno, Taitetsu, and James W. Heisig, eds. *The Religious Philosophy of Tanabe Hajime.* Asian Human. Pr. 1990 $60.00. ISBN 0-89581-872-8. Twenty critical essays by American and Japanese scholars on various aspects of Tanabe's thought.

WATSUJI TETSURŌ. 1889–1960

Born in Himeji, Watsuji Tetsurō graduated from Tokyo University with a specialization in Western philosophy. While studying philosophy, he wrote several short novels and plays, and his lifelong interest in Japanese history and culture resulted in the publication of three books on the subject: *Nihon Kodai Bunka* (*Ancient Japanese Culture*) (1920) and the two-volume *Nihon Seishin-shi Kenkyū* (*Studies on the History of the Japanese Spirit*) (1926).

In 1925 he received an appointment at Kyoto University and became de facto a member of the Kyoto School. Yet he was not as directly influenced by NISHIDA KITARŌ as were other, more central figures in the movement. Watsuji spent the years 1927–29 in Europe, following up his earlier works concerning SØREN

KIERKEGAARD and FRIEDRICH NIETZSCHE (see also Vol. 2), as well as studying the history of Western ethical theory. During that time, he also was profoundly influenced by MARTIN HEIDEGGER's (see also Vol. 5) recently completed book, *Being and Time*.

After returning to Japan, Watsuji became increasingly dissatisfied with Western existentialism, seeing it as too individualistic and overly fixated on temporality to the virtual exclusion of spatiality. He began in earnest to focus on developing his own ethical theory, first in his pioneering 1934 work, *Ethics as Philosophical Anthropology (Ningengaku To Shite No Rinrigaku)*, and then in his monumental three-volume work *Ethics (Rinrigaku)*, published between 1937 and 1949. His basic position was that human existence emerges out of a "betweenness," a middle ground between the poles of individualism and collectivism. His critique was that the West too often had emphasized exclusively the former pole, and East Asian thought (such as Confucianism), the latter. Watsuji argued that ethics is possible only through a "double negation." First, one must break away from the inherited values as established by the group mentality into which one is born in order to establish one's own values. Then, one must voluntarily relinquish some of those individualistic values for the common good. His postwar works, such as *History of Japan's Ethical Thought (Nihon Rinri Shisō-shi)* (1952), centered on Japanese ethical thinking and social behavior, continuing to reflect this philosophy.

BOOK BY WATSUJI TETSURŌ

Climate and Culture: A Philosophical Study. Trans. by Geoffrey Bownas. Greenwood 1987 repr. of 1961 ed. $45.00. ISBN 0-313-26558-5. Somewhat idiosyncratic but popular work arguing for an intimate connection between climatic environs (spatiality) and thought. In part a response to Heidegger's emphasis on time in *Being and Time*.

YUASA YASUO. 1925–

Yuasa Yasuo studied ethics under WATSUJI TETSURO at Tokyo University and developed a broad background in Western philosophy, psychoanalytic theory, Asian thought, and Japanese cultural history. His many books in Japanese span the range of these interests. Since the late 1970s, his work increasingly has focused on theories of the body in Asian and Western philosophy, religion, and medicine. His own theorizing has been toward discovering a model of mind-body function true to the insights of these varied traditions.

BOOKS BY YUASA YASUO

The Body: Toward an Eastern Mind-Body Theory. Ed. by T. P. Kasulis. Trans. by Nagatomo Shigenori and T. P. Kasulis. State U. NY Pr. 1987 $49.50. ISBN 0-88706-469-8. Provocatively constructive philosophical theory that analyzes and draws on Japanese philosophy, Western phenomenology, depth psychology, and Eastern and Western medicine.
Science and Comparative Philosophy: Introducing Yuasa Yasuo. (coauthored with Nagatomo Shaner). E. J. Brill 1989 $91.50. ISBN 90-04-08953-5. Includes two important long essays by Yuasa on contemporary science and spiritual self-cultivation. Also contains useful introductory materials on Yuasa's life and thought.

AFRICAN PHILOSOPHY

African philosophy became a field of study only with the ethnographic work of Placide Tempels in his 1945 classic, *Bantu Philosophy*. Until then, the colonial ideology typically maintained that the Africans were intrinsically different from Europeans and incapable of the higher, abstract functions of thought. Tempels claimed that his research with the Bantu indicated that there was at least an implicit philosophical worldview at work in the Africans' communal life. Still, he found fundamental differences between traditional African belief systems and those of the Europeans.

Tempels's work raised as many problems for African consciousness as it solved, however. Now that it was established that Africans were capable of "higher thought," should their thinking be brought increasingly into line with European philosophical assumptions? Does modernization necessarily imply the death of traditional values and ways of thinking? As the African nationalist and independence movements blossomed in the ensuing decades, these became issues no longer of colonialist policy but of national or even Pan-African self-determination. Africa would have to define African philosophy for itself.

This process is still very much in its emergent form, and there is little common agreement on how to proceed. In general, there are three centers of influence tugging at the burgeoning tradition. First, there are those who wish to analyze and articulate the traditional values of African cultures. They argue that whatever Africa is to become will have to be rooted in its own traditions. Furthermore, those traditions, if they are to be preserved and cherished, must be articulated in as philosophically clear a manner as possible before they become enmeshed in outside influences resulting from modernization. Second, there are those who argue that philosophy is philosophy, no matter where it might be practiced. Philosophy is a technical, reflective, critical enterprise that can interact with tradition as its focus but that itself is not limited or colored by any cultural tradition. Last, there are those who see philosophy as a tool for generating a social and political consciousness, the means for exposing the inner dynamics of colonialism, imperialism, racism, classicism, and capitalism that have endangered Africa's past and continue to threaten its future if unchecked. Despite the attempts of the various factions to label each other, probably no individual African philosopher is attracted to only one of these focal points. Yet these views do serve as useful parameters by which the different individuals tend to locate their distinctive positions.

General Works

Asante, Molefi Kete. *The Afrocentric Idea*. Temple U. Pr. 1987 $29.95. ISBN 0-87722-483-8. Provocative analysis maintaining that an Afrocentric, rather than Eurocentric, view should be taken in order to study Africa as a self-determining agent instead of as the passive receptor of European analysis and cultural invasion.

Bodunrin, P. O., ed. *Philosophy in Africa: Trends and Perspectives*. U. of Ife Pr. 1985 o.p. Good collection of 17 essays on a variety of philosophical themes, both generally and specifically related to Africa.

Diop, Cheik Anta. *The African Origin of Civilization: Myth or Reality*. Ed. and trans. by Mercer Cook. L. Hill Bks. 1974 $11.95. ISBN 1-55652-072-7. Controversial book arguing that Eurocentric historians have repressed the evidence concerning Egypt as the source of ancient Greek civilization and that Egypt was a black African culture at the time.

Ghadegesin, Segun. *African Philosophy: Traditional Yoruba Philosophy and Contemporary African Realities*. P. Lang Pubs. 1991 $27.95. ISBN 0-8204-1770-X. Powerful analysis of traditional Yoruba social and political assumptions in Nigeria and the application of that analysis to a constructive philosophy addressing the social issues of Africa today.

Gyekye, Kwame. *An Essay on African Philosophical Thought: The Akan Scheme.* Cambridge U. Pr. 1987 $54.95. ISBN 0-521-32525-0. Sophisticated ethnophilosophical work analyzing the epistemological, ethical, metaphysical, and anthropological dimensions within the traditional Akan culture of West Africa.

Kwame, Safro, ed. *Readings in African Philosophy: An Akan Collection.* Hollowbrook 1992 $37.50. ISBN 0-89341-718-1. Collection of readings representing the ethnophilosophical study of the Akan.

Makinde, Akin M. *African Philosophy, Culture, and Traditional Medicine.* Ohio U. Ctr. Int. 1988 $13.00. ISBN 0-89680-152-7. Analysis of African indigenous worldviews, especially in relation to ethnomedicine and science.

Mudimbe, V. Y. *Invention of Africa: Gnosis, Philosophy, and the Order of Knowledge.* Ind. U. Pr. 1988 $39.95. ISBN 0-253-33126-9. Probing historical criticism analyzing how the idea of "Africa" is constructed by the European mind.

Okere, Theophilus. *African Philosophy: A Historico-Hermeneutical Investigation of the Conditions of Its Possibility.* U. Pr. of Amer. 1983 o.p. Technical philosophical study analyzing the relationship between culture and philosophy, with special consideration given to the future of African philosophy.

Ruch, E. A., and K. C. Anyanwu. *African Philosophy: An Introduction to the Main Philosophical Trends in Contemporary Africa.* Catholic Bk. Agency rev. ed. 1984 o.p. Early, influential attempt at characterizing the nature of modern African philosophy.

Serequeberhan, Tsenay. *African Philosophy: The Essential Readings.* Paragon Hse. 1991 $13.95. ISBN 1-55778-309-8. Excellent collection of 11 essays by African philosophers, representing a range of perspectives. Useful bibliography included.

Tempels, Placide. *Bantu Philosophy.* Presence Africaine 1969 o.p. Pioneering ethnophilosophical study treating Africans as having rational structures for ordering reality, albeit different from those of Europeans. First published in French in 1945.

Wright, Richard A. *African Philosophy: An Introduction.* U. Pr. of Amer. 3rd ed. 1984 o.p. Balanced textbook approach to the range of issues involved in the study of African philosophy.

HOUNTONDJI, PAULIN J. 1942–

A student of Louis Althusser, Paulin J. Hountondji is one of the most outspoken Francophone critics of the ethnophilosophy movement. For Hountondji, philosophy is primarily a highly refined, critical mode of analysis that is ultimately personal and not collective. For this reason, he thinks that the ethnophilosophers (a term he coined) are looking in the wrong place for African philosophy. Indeed, according to Hountondji, their assertion that Africa already has an indigenous philosophical tradition, one that is fundamentally different from European rationality, only reinforces the claims of "otherness" originally imposed by the colonialists. Rather than generating an African sense of racial or ethnic pride, ethnophilosophy hampers the process of modernization.

Hountondji's emphasis on philosophy as an individual, reflective, and theoretical enterprise also pits him against the Marxists, who see philosophy as simply a means to revolutionary change. For Hountondji, it is just as corrupting to use philosophy to serve ideology as it is to use it to support ethnic or racial distinctiveness.

Very active in developing the field of philosophy in an African context, Hountondji was one of the founders of the important bilingual journal *Cahiers Philosophiques Africains* in 1972.

BOOK BY HOUNTONDJI

African Philosophy: Myth and Reality. Trans. by Henri Evans with Jonathan Ree. Hutchinson & Co. UK 1983 o.p. Eight highly provocative essays addressing several critical issues in African philosophy, including Hountondji's critiques of ethnophilosophy and "Nkruma ism." Includes an excellent introductory essay by Abiola Irele outlining the basic controversies in African philosophy and Hountondji's relation to them.

MBITI, JOHN S(AMUEL). 1931–

John Mbiti was born in Kitui, Kenya, and received his education in Africa and abroad. Trained as an Anglican priest, he went on to be both professor and parish minister in Switzerland, where he later settled. As a philosopher and Christian theologian, Mbiti became one of the early African authorities on African religions. Using his philosophical skills, he focuses on deriving a representation of a coherent philosophical worldview from the indigenous traditions. One of his projects, for example, has been to articulate a view of temporality in indigenous African thought different from that of the modern West.

Mbiti's goal, however, has not been simply to develop ethnophilosophical analyses. Concerned with the future of Africa, he has argued that certain traditional African values should be preserved, but also—for the sake of modernization and reform—that other values (based often in Christianity) should be assimilated into the culture. This latter orientation has made him the subject of some controversy among other African philosophers.

BOOKS BY MBITI

African Religions and Philosophy. Heinemann Ed. 2nd ed. 1990 $20.00. ISBN 0-435-89591-5. Classic, ground-breaking study for which Mbiti is most famous.
Introduction to African Religion. Heinemann Ed. 2nd rev. ed. 1992 $18.50. ISBN 0-435-940023-3. Textbooklike approach to the study of African religions.

NKRUMAH, KWAME. 1909–1972

Born on the Gold Coast (present-day Ghana), the son of a goldsmith and market trader from the Nzima tribe, Kwame Nkrumah was educated in the United States and Great Britain. His earlier degrees were in economics, sociology, and theology, but he also received an M.A. and did doctoral work in philosophy. In 1945 he put aside the academic career for which he had been training under SIR ALFRED AYER and became a Marxian political activist for the cause of Africans at home and abroad. He returned to the Gold Coast in 1947 and led the nationalist movement, for which he was jailed by the British. He was released in 1952, became prime minister, and helped effect independence in 1957, renaming the country Ghana. He served as president until 1966, when he was deposed by a military coup. He died in Bucharest, Rumania, while undergoing treatment for cancer.

A distinctive dimension to Nkrumah's political impact was his contribution to Marxist socialist theory, with particular application to today's Africa. In this regard, his theory of "consciencism" is the most central. Nkrumah saw Africa pulled by the three religious value systems represented by indigenous tradition, Islam, and European Christianity. This is what Nkrumah saw as the crisis of African "conscience." Ultimately, according to Nkrumah, the solution lies in the qualified acceptance of Marxist socialism, but a socialism adapted to the cultural context of Africa.

BOOKS BY NKRUMAH

Africa Must Unite. Intl. Pub. Co. 1970 o.p. Nkrumah's reflection on the African situation and his call to Pan-Africanism. Includes bibliography.
Autobiography. Humanities 1973 $9.95. ISBN 0-901787-34-5. Nkrumah's own story of his life, rise to power, and exile.

Consciencism—Philosophy and Ideology for Decolonization and Development with Particular Reference to the African Revolution. Monthly Rev. 1970 repr. of 1965 ed. $6.00. ISBN 0-85345-136-2. Nkrumah's most developed statement of his social philosophy and vision of consciencism.

BOOK ABOUT NKRUMAH

Okadigbo, Chuba. *Consciencism in African Political Philosophy.* Four Dimension Pub. 1985 o.p. Critique of Nkrumah's social philosophy from Okadigbo's own Marxian socialist perspective.

ORUKA, J. ODERA. 1930?–

J. Odera Oruka is a Kenyan philosopher best known for his development of the concept of "sage philosophy." This is a form of ethnophilosophy emphasizing the special role of elders or sages in traditional African communities. Oruka distinguishes sages who merely reflect the accepted wisdom of the community from those who take a critical, reflective stand on that body of knowledge, making their role "philosophical" in a sense much like that found in the West. Oruka emphasizes that the oral tradition is irrelevant to its philosophical nature.

In taking this position, Oruka is critical of the ethnophilosophers who look to the assumptions of ordinary people in daily life as the basis for defining a distinctively "African" philosophy. He also rejects the idea that the only legitimate kind of philosophy is that defined in the tradition of Western philosophy.

BOOK BY AND ABOUT ORUKA

Sage Philosophy: Indigenous Thinkers and Modern Debate on African Philosophy. E. J. Brill 1990 $74.50. ISBN 90-04-09283-8. Balanced study of Oruka's "sage philosophy" approach to ethnophilosophy. Includes five essays by Oruka, two chapters of conversations with living sages, and six chapters by other African philosophers critiquing Oruka's approach.

WIREDU, KWASI. 1940?–

Kwasi Wiredu is a Ghanaian trained in the British tradition of logic and philosophy of language. Some of his philosophical work is directly in the analytic tradition and has no special focus on African issues. In his own view, these works represent "African philosophy" only in the sense that he is an African involved in philosophy.

Antoher aspect of Wiredu's writings more directly addresses the issue of identifying African philosophy as either a tradition or a tradition in the making. Wiredu's basic thesis is that, as Africa inevitably modernizes, philosophy can play a key role in its development. For Wiredu it is not enough to identify a traditional set of African beliefs and call it philosophy; rather, philosophy is a critical, reflective, rational enterprise. Indigenous belief systems can be the starting point of African philosophy, but they will truly become a philosophical tradition only insofar as they become the grist for critical philosophizing. In this way, there can be a blend of traditional beliefs and modern, Western critical reflection.

BOOKS BY WIREDU

Person and Community: Ghanaian Philosophical Studies I. (coedited with Kwame Gyekye). Coun. Res. Values 1992 $45.00. ISBN 1-56518-005-4. Collection of essays representing a broad spectrum of philosophical opinion.

Philosophy and an African Culture. Cambridge U. Pr. 1980 o.p. Excellent sampling of
Wiredu's philosophy. Includes essays on African philosophy, two on his liberal
socialist critique of Marxism, and six technical essays on the nature of truth from an
analytic standpoint.

ISLAMIC PHILOSOPHY

Recent and contemporary Islamic philosophy has confronted issues similar to
those faced by all traditional religions in the nineteenth and twentieth centuries:
the many-faceted question of how to reconcile an older belief system with the
spirit of modernity in science, democracy, and individualism in a highly
skeptical world. There is pressure to accept a religious outlook compatible with
modern individualism and a rational view of the world—one in which faith
depends less on miracles, supernatural revelations, and traditional institutions
than on an inward relation to God. Against this pressure, however, is the
perhaps agonizing awareness of meaninglessness and anomie experienced by
many moderns in light of these conflicts.

These problems have been even greater for Islam than for some other
traditions, because Islam had to face them first. In the world of nineteenth- and
early twentieth-century European imperialism, almost all of the Islamic world
was either under the rule of non-Islamic European overlords (British, French,
Dutch, Russian) or part of the Ottoman or Persian Empire, both of which also
were subservient to the West in innumerable ways. Thus, the "modern" came to
Islam in the guise of foreign, but seemingly more powerful, political and
cultural forces. For Islamic thinkers of this period, philosophy had to develop in
the context of sometimes wrenching decisions about whether, or how much, to
accept Western ideas and values, or how much to resist them in the name of
Islam—and under what vision of the meaning of Islam.

By the twentieth century, Islamic nationalism in the modern style was
decisively on the rise, and philosophers often engaged in these debates with
thoroughly practical concerns. Questions of the need for modernization versus
the need for affirmation of the traditional ways often resulted in painful splits
between liberal and "fundamentalist" views of Islam and became crucial
matters "on the street" as well as in the academy.

The issues were complicated further by the long-standing interconnection of
metaphysics with law and society in the Islamic world. Among important
modern Islamic philosophers, therefore, one seldom sees "pure" philosophy
discussed apart from its implications for society and the task of nation building.
For Islamic thinkers, the basics of God and revelation usually are, in some way,
assumed; the question is what they mean here and now, in the context of
struggles to make a better world.

General Works

Ahmad, Aziz. *An Intellectual History of Islamic India.* Col. U. Pr. 1967 $13.00. ISBN 0-
85224-057-0. Excellent overview, giving the modern philosophical situation and its
background.

Ali, Ameer. *The Spirit of Islam.* South Asia Bks. 1990 repr. of 1923 ed. $18.50. ISBN 81-
85395-91-8. Classic but now dated presentation of Islam as representing the best of
modern Western values.

Azad, Abu-l-Kalam. *Islam and Nationalism.* New Delhi, Kala Prakashan 1969 o.p. Holding
that Islam above all affirmed the unity of humanity, Azad rejected the nationalistic
interpretation of the faith.

Baqir As-Sadr, Muhammad. *Our Philosophy*. Routledge Chapman & Hall 1987 $57.50. ISBN 0-71030179-0. Major work by a leading Iranian thinker. Criticizes Western philosophy and presents Islamic alternatives in both method and content, particularly in philosophy of knowledge. Comparable to the thought of Seyyed Hossein Nasr, who provides a foreword.

Cragg, Kenneth. *Counsels in Contemporary Islam*. Col. U. Pr. 1965 o.p. Splendid survey of modernity throughout the Islamic world, with extensive bibliography.

Dabashi, Hamid. *Theology of Discontent: The Ideological Foundations of the Islamic Revolution in Iran*. NYU Pr. 1993 $75.00. ISBN 0-8147-1839-6. Valuable exploration of the intellectual background of the most publicized Islamic revolution.

Donahue, John J., and John L. Esposito, eds. *Islam in Transition: Muslim Perspectives*. OUP 1982 $39.95. ISBN 0-19-503022-2. Good selection of original sources in translation. Includes introductions.

Fakhry, Majid. *History of Philosophy in Islam*. Col. U. Pr. 1987 o.p. Excellent survey, including material on the modern period.

Fyzee, A. A. *A Modern Approach to Islam*. Asia Pub. Hse. 1963 o.p. Vision of Islam based on faith and experience rather than on legalistic authority. Holds that the Koran must be reinterpreted to meet modern conditions.

Gibb, Hamilton. *Modern Trends in Islam*. U. Ch. Pr. 1947 o.p. Critical discussion of Muhammad Abduh, Sayyid Amir Ali, Iqbal, and other Islamic modernizers who have tried to argue the benefits of Islam in terms of modern values. One of the first Western books to explore this world.

Gokalp, Ziya. *Turkish National and Western Civilization: Selected Essays of Ziya Gokalp*. Greenwood repr. of 1959 ed. $45.00. ISBN 0-313-23196-6. Basic work of the modernizing philosopher who deeply influenced Kamal Ataturk, the father of modern Turkey.

Hamidullah, M. *Islam, Philosophy and Science*. UNIPUB 1981 $14.00. ISBN 92-3-101951-1. Four lectures offering an accessible survey of past and present Islamic positions on these topics.

Hourani, Albert. *Arabic Thought in the Liberal Age 1798–1939*. Cambridge U. Pr. 1983 $21.95. ISBN 0-521-27423-0. The best overview of this era.

Malik, Charles. *God and Man in Contemporary Islamic Thought*. Amer. U. of Beirut 1972 o.p. Valuable collection of papers by a spectrum of leading contemporary Muslim philosophers.

Mutahhari, Ayatollah M. *Fundamentals of Islamic Thought: God, Man and the Universe*. Mizan Pr. 1985 $19.95. ISBN 0-933782-14-4. The perspective of a leading Shi'ite thinker, summarizing Islamic doctrine in the context of philosophical discourse.

Noer, Deliar. *The Modernist Muslim Movement in Indonesia, 1900–1942*. OUP 1973 o.p. Modernism in the most populous Islamic country. Mostly political but contains intellectual background of modern movements.

Quadir, C. A. *Philosophy and Science in the Islamic World*. Routledge Chapman & Hall 1988 $69.50. ISBN 0-89633-054-0. Scholarly approach clarifying the sources of arguments that Islam is especially receptive to rational and scientific thought.

Rahman, Fazlur. *Islam and Modernity: Transformation of an Intellectual Tradition*. U. Ch. Pr. 1984 $10.95. ISBN 0-226-70284-7. Major modernist positions are explored and critically assessed by one of the world's leading Islamic intellectuals.

Schuon, Fritjof. *Understanding Islam*. Unwin Hyman 1976 $9.96. ISBN 0-04-297035-0. Somewhat personal expression by a Western philosopher and convert to Islam who has helped many non-Islamic people to understand Islam in a deeply spiritually way. By the author of the now out of print *Islam: The Perennial Philosophy* and *Dimensions of Islam*.

Watt, William Montgomery. *Islamic Fundamentalism and Modernity*. Routledge 1988 $35.00. ISBN 0-85224-552-1. Valuable survey of Islamic intellectual currents by a major Western scholar of Islam.

ABDUH, MUHAMMAD. 1849–1905

Considered the father of modernistic Islamic thought, Muhammad Abduh was born in Mahallat Nasr in Egypt and received his traditional education in Tanta. In 1866 he entered al-Azhar, the major seat of Islamic learning at that time. There he became disillusioned with the antiquated methods of teaching, especially in relation to philosophy and theology, and later inaugurated the reformation of this university.

Greatly influenced by the Persian revolutionary thinker al-Afghānī, Abduh held that science and religion cannot conflict and that the truth of Islam can be subjected to scientific analysis. This, he claimed, was enjoined by the Koran, which urges believers to use intelligence and study nature, replete with signs of the presence of God. As put forth in his treatise *Risalāt al-Tauhīd* (*The Theology of Unity*) (1897), Abduh contended that Islam is the only religion that calls upon humans to use reason and science in exploring truth. Islam, therefore, must be open to new ideas and modern knowledge generally.

BOOK BY ABDUH

The Theology of Unity. Trans. by I. Musa'ad and K. Cragg. Allen & Unwin 1965 o.p. The major statement in English by the original voice behind Islamic modernism.

BOOKS ABOUT ABDUH

Adams, Charles C. *Islam and Modernism in Egypt.* London 1933 o.p. Important early study centered on Muhammad Abduh.

Husain, Taha. *A Student at the Azhar.* Trans. by Hilary Wayment. London 1958 o.p. Fascinating autobiographical account by a blind theological student in Abduh's time.

Kerr, Malcolm H. *Islamic Reform: The Political and Legal Theories of Muhammad Abduh and Rashid Rida.* U. CA Pr. 1966 o.p. Good scholarly study.

IQBAL, SIR MUHAMMAD. 1876–1938

A very influential poet and philosopher, Muhammad Iqbal was born in the Punjab, where he received his early education. He also studied philosophy in England and in Germany but returned to India three years later to practice law. Although he noted that European civilization was materially advanced, he also found it hypocritical and lacking in support of true human values. Islam, on the other hand, though somnolent, was at once both truly creative and able to give humanity moral direction. It was this, the true Islam of MUHAMMAD and the Koran, that Iqbal sought to help Muslims recover.

As evidenced in his six lectures on *The Reconstruction of Religious Thought in Islam* (1928–29), he interpreted the dynamic of Islam in Bergsonian vitalistic terms, as a leading extension of the fully developed self. In line with his attempt to rethink the problems of Islam in terms of modern categories, Iqbal advocated that the solidly Muslim portions of northwest India be given autonomy so that they could be governed in accordance with Islamic ideals, a position that led to the emergence of the state of Pakistan. He was knighted in 1922.

BOOKS BY IQBAL

The Mysteries of Selflessness. Trans. by Arthur J. Arberry. London 1953 o.p. Attempts to show how the role of individuals must harmonize with their social role in a dynamic society.

The Pilgrimage of Eternity. Trans. by Shaikh Mahmud Ahmad. Lahore 1961 o.p. Describes the poet's journey through the universe with the great Persian mystic Jalal al-Din as his guide.

The Reconstruction of Religious Thought in Islam. Kazi Pubns. repr. of 1934 ed. $15.00.
   ISBN 0-685-55584-4. Basic statement of the author's religious position.
Secrets of the Self. Orient Bk. Dist. 1979 $12.15. ISBN 0-89684-083-2. Literary work
   expounding Iqbal's view of the self as capable of "extension" and taking part in the
   ongoing unfoldment of life.

Books about Iqbal

Bakhtiar, Laleh. *Iqbal: Manifestation of the Islamic Spirit.* Abjad Bk. 1989 $10.00. ISBN 1-
   871031-20-6. Sympathetic study, translated from Persian.
Masud, Muhammad K., and M. Muntaz Liaqat, eds. *Iqbal through Western Eyes.* Apt. Bks.
   1992 $35.00. ISBN 81-207-0891-1. Studies by non-Muslims of the great poet and
   thinker.
Schimmel, Annemarie. *Gabriel's Wing: A Study into the Religious Ideas of Sir Muhammad
   Iqbal.* E. J. Brill 1963 o.p. Fine study of Iqbal's life and work by a prominent scholar
   of Islamic mysticism.

NASR, SEYYED HOSSEIN. 1933–

Born in Tehran, Seyyed Hossein Nasr, the son of an educator, received a
Ph.D. from Harvard University in 1958, after which he returned to Iran to teach
and eventually to become a university chancellor. He was compelled to leave
his native country after the revolution of 1979 and since then has taught in
universities in the United States.

Deeply influenced by the mystical Sufi tradition, Nasr—of a later generation
than Abduh or Iqbal—is less concerned with reconciling the faith with
modernism and is more concerned with presenting a traditionalist, though
mystical, interpretation of religion that offers a way out of the contradictions of
modernity. Through authentic spiritual experience, Nasr holds, one can
penetrate the superficiality of modern scientific and other knowledge to find
eternal truth. He is associated with the neotraditionalist school of philosophy,
along with such writers as Fritjof Schuon, Ananda Coomeraswamy, René
Guénon, and Huston Smith. Undoubtedly, Nasr has had more general influence
in the Western philosophical world than any other contemporary philosopher in
the Islamic tradition. (See Chapter 18 for additional information on Seyyed
Hossein Nasr.)

Books by Nasr

The Essential Writings of Fritjof Schuon. Element MA 1991 $29.95. ISBN 1-85230-260-7.
   Basic works of this noted Western philosopher of Islam presented in a mystical-
   traditionalist vein comparable to Nasr's view.
Ideals and Realities of Islam. Beacon Pr. 1972 o.p. Philosophical explication of Islam,
   containing a profound view of time, history, and eternity in Islam.
Islam and the Plight of Modern Man. Longman 1975 o.p. Modern people are "between the
   axis and the rim," unable fully to experience the core of reality yet dissatisfied with
   living merely on its surfaces. The Islamic tradition provides a way of knowing that
   there is a core and that it can be known.
Knowledge and the Sacred. State U. NY Pr. 1989 $44.50. ISBN 0-7914-0176-6. Scathing
   indictment of the superficiality of modern thought and life combined with an appeal
   for exploration of the inner significance of consciousness as a key to the meaning of
   the universe.
Traditional Islam in the Modern World. Routledge Chapman & Hall 1987 $49.50. ISBN 0-
   7103-0177-4. Islam as a continuing witness to the spiritual significance of human life.

CHAPTER 9

Contemporary Issues in Philosophy

John Heffner

. . . philosophy is the critic of abstractions.
—ALFRED NORTH WHITEHEAD, *Science and the Modern World*

As a discipline, philosophy always has been polyphonic, and its voices generally engage their own past. Thomistic philosophy, for example, has enjoyed an unbroken history from the thirteenth century to the present, and it was informed originally by earlier medieval thought and by the Western rediscovery of ARISTOTLE (see also Vol. 3). When historians look for patterns of development, and when they characterize an age by what is new to it, they might tend to overlook survivals and ongoing dialogue. This makes the delineation of any era more arbitrary than one would like. Nevertheless, about 1975, give or take a few years, what we might call the classical period of twentieth-century philosophy drew to a close as the discipline began to move in new and largely unanticipated directions.

The classical period was dominated in English-speaking countries by analytic philosophy and on the continent of Europe by phenomenology and existentialism. It was marked by a sense that earlier methods of philosophical inquiry had failed and that no improvement could occur without an absolutely rigorous examination of what was unique, whether in content or in method, to philosophy. The discipline thus withdrew from its traditional role of producing large-scale accounts of the true, the good, and the beautiful. Analytic philosophy, for example, restricted itself by taking what RICHARD MCKAY RORTY calls the linguistic turn. Given a statement, concept, or theory, according to this view, philosophy would ask no longer about its truth but about its meaning. Questions of truth or falsehood, rather, would be relegated to the various sciences. Philosophy would be devoted to discovering the conditions under which something could be said to be meaningful. On the Continent, the search for precision and boundaries took a rather different form in the work of EDMUND HUSSERL and MARTIN HEIDEGGER. All agreed, however, that philosophy should remain aloof from the sciences and that the sciences in turn, whether natural or human, have nothing to contribute to philosophy.

More recent work views these constraints as arbitrary. These new directions are marked by a renewed interest in questions of truth and by extensive cross-fertilization with other disciplines. Along with the proliferation of work in philosophy of art, of history, of religion, of science, of literature, and so forth, has come a vastly increased willingness on the part of philosophers to draw on the specific content of these other fields. Although some of the old guard has complained that this reverses the proper order of epistemology, virtually all of the authors profiled in this chapter illustrate this sense of connectedness, to be found in cognitive science, in the sociology of knowledge, and in the critiques of art, literature, and culture developed by critical theory and the postmodern movement. This new spirit is less concerned with disciplinary boundaries than with sources of insight—wherever they are found.

Philosophy is the critic of abstractions. As ALFRED NORTH WHITEHEAD explains it, this role has two aspects. The first gives perspective to other areas of knowledge. It locates them within the larger view, reveals the influences that shaped them, sharpens their theory and methodology, and tries to prevent an overstepping of their conceptual limits. Much classical twentieth-century philosophy focused its considerable critical energy upon itself. Newer work has expanded the criticism in general directions that Whitehead might have approved, if not always producing the results he might have preferred.

Critical theory provides a good example of this newly expanded scope for philosophy. It has developed an impassioned critique of both totalitarian government and capitalist society. Although it has done so by interpreting KARL MARX (see also Vol. 3), its interpretation owes little to the dogma of dialectical materialism and still less to the parody of Marx that too often was taught in American civics classes during the cold war. Rather, it relies on philosophy's own critical tools. By contrast, analytic philosophy, especially as it has turned to applied ethics, seems bland. However, it has produced a large literature, which at its best has greatly clarified our understanding of many crucial concrete issues in medicine, ecology, and justice.

The second aspect of philosophy as the critic of abstractions is speculation. This aspect has had a decidedly bad reputation for much of the twentieth century; in fact, it was expressly repudiated by analytic philosophy. Whitehead, however, saw it as a constructive, synthesizing, and creative activity. Much of the work profiled in this chapter represents a renewed interest in the great questions of philosophy—of reason and knowledge, of how well we know the world and our place in it, of human nature and society, of ethics and the good life. In the resulting array, agreement is not to be sought, let alone valued, for contemporary work is steeped in pluralism. The surprise is that philosophy should address these questions at all.

In beginning to explore these issues, philosophers do what they often have done in times of transition: They turn to the past. Thus, the last few decades have produced an unparalleled surge of scholarship in the history of philosophy.

Other potentially important sources of philosophic insight have proven less influential. Non-Western philosophy in general, and the great Asian traditions in particular, have been slow to affect the contemporary scene. One reason is the apparent strangeness to most Western minds of Asian categories of thought; another is the tendency of scholarship on the Asian traditions to be concentrated in religious studies.

Although many histories have overemphasized the separation between Anglo-American and Continental work, there is nevertheless much truth in the assertion that the two have had relatively little to say to each other. In recent years, however, this has begun to change. If we look for the important voices of the classical period, we find them in BERTRAND RUSSELL (see also Vol. 5) and LUDWIG WITTGENSTEIN in England and America, and in Heidegger, KARL JASPERS (see also Vol. 5), and JEAN-PAUL SARTRE (see also Vol. 2) elsewhere in Europe. Excepting Wittgenstein, much of whose reputation was posthumous, they died respectively in 1970, 1976, 1969, and 1980. If we take 1975 as a rough median of these years, we can use it as a milestone for the "marriage" of the two traditions. A less morbid choice of milestone might be 1979, when Rorty's book *Philosophy and the Mirror of Nature* brought postmodernism into the American mainstream.

Although the new directions of contemporary philosophy are due largely to new ideas, they also are due in part to demographics. Many organizations—religious congregations, social clubs, political parties—enjoy more or less prolonged periods of relative harmony, after which they experience friction from new concepts or new members. As a first response, they stiffen their standards and guard their boundaries. The upstarts, thus excluded, form their own organizations, which gradually earn respect. Finally, the older organizations expand their horizons and begin to accommodate the new.

So it is, too, in philosophy. The twentieth century has marked a cyclical return of the discipline to the academy, and, during its classical period, there was a rough match between practitioners and teaching positions. The giants were elected by consensus. Leading philosophers usually held prestigious chairs, wrote the books, edited the journals, and were featured as speakers at professional meetings. Aspirants with unorthodox views were told, in effect, not to apply. With deplorable frequency, their work was rejected as inferior, and they were so notified in condescending and even degrading terms.

During the 1970s, the number of candidates began to outrun the supply of teaching positions. At the same time, many institutions attempted to raise their faculty standards by increasing their demands that professors write for publication. One result was an annual battle, which continued for several years and was loud enough to make the news sections of *The New York Times*, over the membership of the watchdog program committees of the American Philosophical Association. Another was the proliferation of journals and organizations. The profession no longer can be measured by a few associations, a dozen journals, or a handful of prestigious graduate programs. Contemporary philosophy, to quote John Passmore, is "tumultuous, ill defined, immensely variegated in aspiration and methods" (*Recent Philosophers*).

Finally, two notes of caution. The first is that no survey of this kind can possibly hope for completeness. The careful reader will understand that the issues and authors profiled are to be taken as a representative sample rather than as a comprehensive survey. Much recent work has been published in journals; other work, although published in books, is accessible only to highly trained specialists. For each author included in this chapter, two or three more could claim inclusion with equal justification.

The second warning is that surveys of this kind never age well. Amusing examples from the past rest undisturbed on the shelves of every college library. Writing in the present inevitably reduces perspective, so that the result soon will seem to be myopic. The difficulty has been increased in recent years by the sheer volume of material and by the rapidity with which it goes out of print. Nobody can read more than a tiny fraction of it, and it often disappears, so it would seem, almost before it can be reviewed in professional journals.

GENERAL WORKS

Baynes, Kenneth, James Bohman, and Thomas McCarthy, eds. *After Philosophy*. MIT Pr. 1986 $16.95. ISBN 0-262-52113-X. Significant overview of current authors and topics.

Bernstein, Richard J. *Beyond Objectivity and Relativism*. U. of Pa. Pr. 1983 $16.95. ISBN 0-8122-1165-0. Excellent and accessible critical review of contemporary work;

includes extended discussions of Arendt, Feyerabend, Gadamer, Habermas, Kuhn, Popper, and Rorty.

————. *Philosophical Profiles*. U. of Pa. Pr. 1986 $34.95. ISBN 0-8122-7995-6. Further discussions of most of the authors reviewed in *Beyond Objectivity and Relativism*, plus treatments of MacIntyre and Marcuse; an important survey.

Bürger, Peter. *The Decline of Modernism*. Trans. by Nicholas Walker. Pa. St. U. Pr. 1992 $35.00. ISBN 0-271-00889-X. Reflections on the context of modern aesthetics; includes discussions of Adorno and Foucault.

Callinicos, Alex. *Marxism and Philosophy*. OUP 1983 $12.95. ISBN 0-19-285151-9. Overview of contemporary Marxism; includes treatments of materialism, ideology, and language.

Christensen, Darrel E., and others, eds. *Contemporary German Philosophy*. 4 vols. Pa. St. U. Pr. $28.50 ea. Vol. 1 1983 ISBN 0-271-00336-7. Vol. 2 1983 ISBN 0-271-00352-9. Vol. 3 1984 ISBN 0-271-00365-0. Vol. 4 1985 ISBN 0-271-00381-2. Presents English translations of recent German work.

Cobb, John B., and W. Widick Schroeder, eds. *Process Philosophy and Social Thought*. Ctr. Sci. Study 1981 $18.95. ISBN 0-913348-18-X. Eighteen essays on social theory, ethics, and liberation theology.

Garcia, Jorge J., and others, eds. *Philosophical Analysis in Latin America*. Kluwer Ac. 1984 $115.00. ISBN 90-277-1749-4. Anthology of articles by Latin American authors.

Montefiore, Alan, ed. *Philosophy in France Today*. Cambridge U. Pr. 1983 $54.95. ISBN 0-521-22838-7. Eleven original essays by contemporary French philosophers, surveying the present climate.

Nagel, Thomas. *The View from Nowhere*. OUP 1986 $18.95. ISBN 0-19-503668-9. Discussion of how to reconcile subjective and objective perspectives; accessible to the general reader.

Passmore, John. *Recent Philosophers*. Open Court 1985 $19.95. ISBN 0-87548-448-4. Essential survey of the contemporary scene, especially strong on some of the leading analytic philosophers not profiled below.

Rajchman, John, and Cornell West, eds. *Post-Analytic Philosophy*. Col. U. Pr. 1985 $52.50. ISBN 0-231-06066-1. Study of the diversity of current work, including work by Bernstein, Rawls, and Rorty.

Wilson, John. *What Philosophy Can Do*. B & N Imports 1986 $23.50. ISBN 0-389-20622-9. Plea for the importance of philosophy and its relevance to justice and education.

THE PRESENT STATE OF TRADITIONAL PHILOSOPHIC PROBLEMS

For most of the twentieth century, logic was dominated by the development of symbolic logic, the work of BERTRAND RUSSELL (see also Vol. 5) and ALFRED NORTH WHITEHEAD being the foremost examples. Most recent work can be sketched by imagining logic as a spectrum of topics, with mathematics at one end, epistemology and ordinary speech at the other, and symbolic logic somewhere in the middle. Of the authors profiled, WILLARD VAN ORMAN QUINE and HILARY PUTNAM are the most important contributors to symbolic logic. At the mathematical end, more work is done now by mathematicians than by philosophers, and the subject itself, of interest mainly to specialists, is fading as a central concern of philosophy.

At the other end, however, logic has remained of interest. One of its important topics is the nature and uses of argument—what a proof is, how implication and entailment are related, and how fallacies are defined. PETER STRAWSON amplifies this topic to include a full discussion of the relation between logic and ordinary language. That such topics are debated at all would surprise an earlier generation of more dogmatic logical positivists.

Other work, which again is illustrated by Quine and Putnam, examines the relation between logic and ontology. This relation remains a topic of controversy. Quine holds a minimalist view of logic, dividing it from mathematics but holding that ontology is relative to it, whereas Putnam sees logic as part of a larger epistemological whole, which might be subject to change.

By 1975 it was clear to many that the foundations of analytic philosophy had been laid by the middle decades of this century. Analytic work continues in epistemology, illustrated by many of the books cited below and especially in the work of Donald Davidson, Alvin Goldman, and David Lewis. This work has become highly technical and is virtually inaccessible except to specialists. Just as technical has been the extension of analytic philosophy into modal logic, which attempts to systematize the relations among statements qualified by logical operators, such as "necessarily" or "possible," as in "two plus two are necessarily four" or "tomorrow it might possibly rain." Possible-worlds ontology, which is an amazing extension of this work, sees our world as only one of infinitely many possible worlds. Its critics, NELSON GOODMAN to name one, regard this field as the Disneyland of metaphysics. Although not much is said about God in Disneyland—a fact that might please for more than one reason—theological topics *are* discussed in philosophy of religion.

Consistent with the pluralizing tendency of current philosophy as a whole, philosophy of religion draws on a variety of sources. One aspect of the field, illustrated in the book by John Hick cited below, is concerned with world religions and their comparison. It explores various dimensions of religious thought and experience, as expressed by the various traditions, as a way to examine whether philosophy can discover common ground or whether world religions must necessarily be interpreted individually.

Another aspect of philosophy of religion, illustrated in the book cited below by Michael Petersen and others, draws on science. Using methods of scientific inference, it addresses anew some of the traditional issues of natural theology.

Aune, Bruce. *Metaphysics*. U. of Minn. Pr. 1985 $25.00. ISBN 0-8166-1412-1. Clear introduction to contemporary analytic metaphysics; minimal jargon.

———. *Rationalism, Empiricism, and Pragmatism*. McGraw 1970 $10.12. ISBN 0-07-553543-2. Basic textbook of epistemology that discusses traditional problems in a contemporary analytic idiom.

Bonjour, Laurence. *The Structure of Empirical Knowledge*. HUP 1985 $27.95. ISBN 0-674-84380-0. Detailed examination of the case for a nonfoundational view of knowledge.

Coburn, Robert C. *The Strangeness of the Ordinary*. Rowman 1990 $34.50. ISBN 0-8476-7606-7. Accessible introduction to contemporary metaphysics and "a delightful invitation to conceptual puzzles" (*Choice*).

Davidson, Donald. *Inquiries into Truth and Interpretation*. OUP 1984 $65.00. ISBN 0-19-824617-X. Excruciating essays arguing that theories of truth can serve as theories of meaning for natural languages.

Double, Richard. *The Non-Reality of Free Will*. OUP 1990 $32.50. ISBN 0-19-506497-6. Argues that the terms *free will* and *moral responsibility* express attitudes rather than coherent concepts; useful treatment of recent literature.

Goldman, Alvin. *Epistemology and Cognition*. HUP 1986 $27.50. ISBN 0-674-25895-9. Difficult but widely cited book that links epistemology with cognitive science.

Harman, Gilbert. *Change in View*. MIT Pr. 1986 $19.95. ISBN 0-262-08155-5. Argues that improved coherence is a basis on which human beings change their beliefs.

Hick, John. *Disputed Questions in Theology and the Philosophy of Religion*. Yale U. Pr. 1993 $22.50. ISBN 0-300-05354-1. Updated assessment by one of the leading scholars in the field.

Kirkham, Richard L. *Theories of Truth*. MIT Pr. 1992 $35.00. ISBN 0-262-11167-5. Nontechnical; a critical comparison and evaluation of contemporary views, including Davidson, Dummett, Kripke, and Tarski.

Lehrer, Keith. *Theory of Knowledge*. Westview 1990 $35.00. ISBN 0-8133-0570-5. Clear survey of issues; advocates a standard of coherence and argues against skepticism.

LePore, Ernest, and Brian McLaughlin. *Actions and Events*. Blackwell Pubs. 1986 $45.00. ISBN 0-631-14451-X. Critique and companion volume to Donald Davidson's work of the same title.

Lewis, David K. *On the Plurality of Worlds*. Blackwell Pubs. 1986 $39.95. ISBN 0-631-13993-1. Difficult discussion of Lewis's modal realism; an example of possible worlds ontology.

Margolis, Joseph, Michael Kraussz, and Richard Burian, eds. *Rationality, Relativism and the Human Sciences*. Kluwer Ac. 1986 $86.00. ISBN 90-247-3271-9. Collection of papers by important contemporary philosophers.

Michalos, Alex C. *Improving Your Reasoning*. P-H 1986. ISBN 0-13-453465-4. An introductory text.

Petersen, Michael, and others. *Reason and Religious Belief*. OUP 1990 $17.95. ISBN 0-19506155-1. Excellent introductory survey of recent work; includes the contributions of conservative Christians.

Rosen, Stanley. *The Limits of Analysis*. Yale U. Pr. 1985 $13.00. ISBN 0-300-03327-3. Critique of the basic assumptions of analytic philosophy.

Taylor, Richard. *Metaphysics*. P-H 1991. ISBN 0-13-567819-6. Excellent starting point.

Walton, Douglas. *The Place of Emotion in Argument*. Pa. St. U. Pr. 1992 $45.00. ISBN 0-271-00833-4. Argues that appeals to emotion are not necessarily to be rejected as fallacious.

Wegener, Charles. *The Discipline of Taste and Feeling*. U. Ch. Pr. 1992 $24.95. ISBN 0-226-87893-7. Defense of the traditional view of "cultivated taste" as a background for aesthetics and art criticism.

THE NATURE OF MIND

Under the influence of GILBERT RYLE and other followers of LUDWIG WITTGENSTEIN, philosophy of mind is taken to be a subdivision of philosophy of language. It sees its main task as understanding the language of mental imagery. The statement "I changed my mind," for example, although superficially clear to speakers of English, is nevertheless highly figurative. When we examine its precise meaning, we discover additional questions of whether mind is something we *possess* or something we *are*, whether it is nothing but a short label for various categories of behavior, something of a misnomer. Similar questions arise for many other terms—*consciousness, belief, intention, desire,* and the like—all of which concern mind or mental states.

Analytic philosophy approaches these terms through a detailed study of the linguistic connections by which they are expressed. This effort has produced a large and growing literature. Most of it is critical of mind-body dualism, which generally is regarded as a mistaken direction inspired by RENÉ DESCARTES (see also Vol. 5). Interestingly, this aspect of analytic philosophy makes little or no reference to empirical psychology.

Cognitive science begins with a different approach. It attempts to forge an inclusive science of mind by combining material from philosophy, computer science, and experimental psychology. Among its central theoretical issues is the "identity theory" of the mind-brain relation: an attempt to show that each mental event is identical to a corresponding neurophysical event in the brain. Under the encouragement of philosophically sophisticated psychologists, such as Richard Gregory, many philosophers now are much more willing than they were during the classical period to consider experimental studies of perception and cognition as useful in their own work. Of the authors profiled in this chapter, DANIEL C. DENNETT is the outstanding example of philosophers making use of science. At the same time, experimental psychology has expanded its own conceptual horizons, perhaps because, as a maturing science, it is no longer an adolescent needing to prove itself and perhaps also because its methodology has outgrown some of the more arbitrary strictures of behaviorism.

Artificial intelligence explores parallels between human thinking and computer activity. Apart from the enormous complexity of the task, it might seem no more problematic to build a machine that thinks than to build one that hammers nails or computes invoices; that is to say, if a machine can imitate one form of human behavior, why rule out another? One reason is that much of Western philosophy has used "mind," or "reason," or "consciousness," or some similar concept to differentiate humans from the rest of nature. Would a machine that thinks also be accorded legal status or moral responsibility?

Artificial intelligence approaches this question by asking what the criteria would be for a machine that thinks. One such criterion holds that a computer is thinking if, through a keyboard and screen, it can carry on a conversation with a human, such that the human is unable to tell that the other participant is a machine. This criterion is reasonably well met by actual programs. In view of this achievement, new questions can be asked about the use of language as a standard and about what, if anything, we can learn of human cognition by building machines that imitate it.

Carruthers, Peter. *Introducing Persons*. State U. NY Pr. 1986 $34.50. ISBN 0-88-706378-0. Accessible introduction to behaviorism, language, mind-body dualism, life after death, and other issues.

Churchland, Patricia Smith. *Neurophilosophy*. MIT Pr. 1986 $42.00. ISBN 0-262-03116-7. Attempts to develop a unified science of mind and brain; includes philosophy of mind, neuroscience, cognitive theory, and philosophy of science.

Copeland, Jack. *Artificial Intelligence*. Blackwell Pubs. 1993 $44.95. ISBN 0-631-18384-1. Introduction to the philosophical implications of artificial intelligence, including whether the human brain can be regarded as a computer.

Dummett, Michael. *The Logical Basis of Metaphysics*. HUP 1991 $34.95. ISBN 0-674-53785-8. Revision of Dummett's William James lectures; metaphysics via an analytic philosophy of language.

Elgin, Catherine Z. *With Reference to Reference*. Hackett Pub. 1983 $29.50. ISBN 0-915145-52-9. Lucid survey of various kinds of symbolic meaning.

Flanagan, Owen. *Concerning Consciousness*. MIT Pr. 1992 $24.95. ISBN 0-262-06148-1. Clear explanation of philosophical naturalism and what it can contribute to understanding the mind-body relation.

————. *The Science of the Mind*. MIT Pr. 1991 $15.95. ISBN 0-262-56056-9. Excellent introduction to cognitive science.

Graham, George. *Philosophy of Mind*. Blackwell Pubs. 1993 $39.95. ISBN 0-631-17955-0. The concepts of the mind-body problem, personal identity, consciousness, intentionality, and freedom of will—introduced for the general reader.

Gregory, Richard L., and O. L. Zangwill, eds. *The Oxford Companion to the Mind*. OUP 1987 $49.95. ISBN 0-19-866124-X. An essential, comprehensive, and thoroughly delightful reference book.

Haugeland, John. *Artificial Intelligence*. MIT Pr. 1986 $11.95. ISBN 0-262-58095-0. Highly recommended review of computers, what has and has not been done with them, and their philosophical implications.

Hookway, Christopher, ed. *Minds, Machines, and Evolution*. Cambridge U. Pr. 1985 $49.95. ISBN 0-521-26547-9. Essays on artificial intelligence as it relates to biological evolution and epistemology.

Kitchener, Richard F. *Piaget's Theory of Knowledge.* Yale U. Pr. 1986 $35.00. ISBN 0-300-03579-9. Piaget's genetic epistemology, related to psychology and education.

Martin, Robert M. *The Meaning of Language.* MIT Pr. 1987 $19.95. ISBN 0-262-13224-9. Introduction to contemporary analytic philosophy of mind and language, accessible to the general reader.

Searle, John. *Intentionality.* Cambridge U. Pr. 1983 $59.95. ISBN 0-521-27302-1. Technical study of mind via analytic philosophy of language, written by a giant in the field.

Shaffer, Jerome A. *Philosophy of Mind.* P-H 1968. ISBN 0-13-663724-8. Brief and accessible introductory survey from a materialist perspective.

Smith, Peter, and O. R. Jones. *The Philosophy of Mind.* Cambridge U. Pr. 1986 $44.95. ISBN 0-521-32078-X. Introductory account, including historical background.

Whiten, Andrew. *Natural Theories of Mind.* Blackwell Pubs. 1991 $49.95. ISBN 0-631-17194-0. Cognitive science related to developmental psychology and philosophy of mind.

CURRENT PHILOSOPHY OF SCIENCE

If a single event were designated a watershed in philosophy of science, it surely would be the publication of THOMAS S. KUHN's (see also Vol. 5) *The Structure of Scientific Revolutions* (1962). This book has shifted the focus of attention within the field and also has proved to be highly influential in other areas, including literature, religious studies, and the social sciences. What might be called the classical philosophy of science—before Kuhn—began as a specialized discipline in the nineteenth century and evolved into a cluster of relatively well-defined issues. Two of them, which will serve as examples, concerned methodology and the status of theories.

Methodology was concerned with such issues as criteria for scientific observations and inductive logic. The former dealt with standards for data, whereas the latter treated the ways in which generalizations were related to their supporting evidence. Both were topics for debate. On generalizations, for example, CARL GUSTAV HEMPEL (see Vol. 5) and like-minded colleagues attempted to develop methods for the positive confirmation of theories, whereas Popperians sought a standard in the absence of refutation; nevertheless, both groups tended to agree on the basic terms of the debate.

The status of theories considers the interpretation of abstract concepts. SIR ISAAC NEWTON's (see also Vol. 5) law of gravity, for example, provides an elegant explanation of many apparently unrelated phenomena, but it also introduces the concept of universal gravitation. It thus becomes necessary to ask whether *gravitation* names a part of nature or whether it is merely a convenient and more or less arbitrary label for part of a mathematical equation. As science develops, its theories introduce concepts further and further removed from the furniture of day-to-day life. When theories introduce "black holes" in the universe or subatomic particles with "charm," it is difficult to know whether we are dealing with abstract mathematics, esoteric nature, science fiction, or combinations of the three.

Discussion of these issues has continued, but with Kuhn's work a new group of issues has been added. Kuhn argues that science cannot be understood apart from its history and practice—indeed, that its history and practice *are* its methodology. Some readers of Kuhn have seen this view as a challenge to scientific objectivity, whereas others have seen it more as a broadening of epistemology to include a social dimension. At the very least, his work has incorporated the transformative nature of history into mainstream philosophy of science, so that history no longer can be seen mainly as a source of examples used to illustrate an otherwise timeless methodology.

Along with the interest in Kuhn, work in philosophy of the biological and social sciences has expanded greatly. In part, this expansion has been occasioned by a rising consciousness of how much science, especially big corporate science, is shaped by its own social structure. In part, it has been occasioned also by an increased skepticism about the traditional hierarchy of the sciences, which placed physics at the top and scarcely allowed room at the bottom for psychology, sociology, and economics. A more positive and perhaps more significant reason for the expansion of the philosophy of science, however, has been the explosion of material within the various sciences themselves. Molecular genetics, for example, has produced important discoveries so rapidly that it is difficult to remember just how new the field is. To keep up with the new developments in science, the related philosophy has had to stretch as well.

Aaronson, Jerrold L. *A Realist Philosophy of Science.* St. Martin 1984 $25.00. ISBN 0-312-66474-5. Scientific theories explained as descriptive of the underlying nature of things.

Bechtel, William. *Philosophy of Science.* L. Erlbaum Assocs. 1988 $24.95. ISBN 0-89859-695-5. Introductory survey that relates recent developments in the philosophy of science to cognitive science.

Böhme, Gernot. *Coping with Science.* Westview 1992 $34.95. ISBN 0-8133-1237-X. Critique of science emphasizing its conceptual limitations and its negative impact on the quality of life.

Brown, Hanbury. *The Wisdom of Science.* Cambridge U. Pr. 1986 o.p. Addresses the relevance of science to religion, society, and culture; argues that their relation has been misconstrued and supports a rapprochement.

Brown, Harold I. *Observation and Objectivity.* OUP 1987 $24.95. ISBN 0-19-504825-3. A clear exposition arguing that theory plays analogous roles in epistemology and science.

Friedman, Michael. *Foundation of Space-Time Physics.* Princeton U. Pr. 1983 $19.95. ISBN 0-691-02039-6. Reexamination of space, time, and geometry in the perspective of the general theory of relativity.

Fuchs, Stephan. *The Professional Quest for Truth.* State U. NY Pr. 1992 $59.50. ISBN 0-7914-0923-6. A sociologist examines the practice of large-scale science.

Griffin, David Ray, ed. *Physics and the Ultimate Significance of Time.* State U. NY Pr. 1986 $59.50. ISBN 0-88706-113-3. Collection of papers that develop a philosophy of science from the perspective of process philosophy.

Harre, Rom. *An Introduction to the Logic of the Sciences.* St. Martin 1983 $22.50. ISBN 0-312-42911-8. Good overview of scientific reasoning written for nonspecialists.

_____. *The Philosophies of Science.* OUP 1986 $13.95. ISBN 0-19-289201-0. Accessible, serviceable, and somewhat pedestrian introduction to the field.

Hempel, Carl. *Philosophy of Natural Science.* P-H 1966. ISBN 0-13-663823-6. Short and lucid account by one of the great positivists; no technical background required to appreciate it.

Himsworth, Harold. *Scientific Knowledge and Philosophic Thought.* Johns Hopkins 1986 $24.00. ISBN 0-8018-3316-7. Emphasizes the similarities between scientific and philosophical methods.

Hull, David. *Philosophy of Biological Science.* P-H 1974 o.p. Introduction to basic issues in biology and their philosophical implications; sketchy and a bit demanding for the reader with no familiarity with science; teaches "all the perennial issues" (*Science*).

_____. *Science as a Process.* U. Ch. Pr. 1988 $39.95. ISBN 0-225-36050-4. Overview of the history of biology developed by analogy with evolutionary theory.

Kitchen, Philip. *Vaulting Ambition*. MIT Pr. 1985 $35.00. ISBN 0-262-11109-8. Penetrating critique of sociobiology.

Little, Daniel. *Varieties of Social Explanation*. Westview 1991 $55.00. ISBN 0-8133-0565-9. Accessible introduction to the philosophy of social science; presents a variety of models of explanation.

Medawar, Peter. *The Limits of Science*. 1985. OUP 1988 $9.95. ISBN 0-19-505212-9. Argues that science is constrained by its own methods, and that therefore, though not limited within its proper domain, it is unable to contribute to larger philosophical issues.

Moravscik, Michael. *How to Grow Science*. Universe 1980 $12.50. ISBN 0-87663-3440. Lucid discussion of how science actually works; issues in funding and public policy.

Nagel, Ernest. *The Structure of Science*. Hackett Pub. 1979 $37.95. ISBN 0-915144-72-7. After 40 years, still an essential work and a classic treatment.

O'Hear, Anthony. *Introduction to the Philosophy of Science*. OUP 1989 $14.95. ISBN 0-19-824813-X. Excellent review of recent work on key issues, including scientific realism, the relation between observation and theory, inductive logic, falsification, and probability.

Reichenbach, Hans. *The Rise of Scientific Philosophy*. U. CA Pr. 1951 $10.95. ISBN 0-520-01055-8. Beautifully written discussion of basic themes by one of the hardest of all hard-line positivists.

Rescher, Nicholas. *The Limits of Science*. U. CA Pr. 1984 $42.50. ISBN 0-0520-05180-7

Rosenberg, Alexander. *Philosophy of Social Science*. Westview 1988 $58.50. ISBN 0-8133-0616-7. Study of scientific criteria applied to the social sciences; a standard work.

Ruse, Michael. *Philosophy of Biology Today*. State U. NY Pr. 1988 $29.50. ISBN 0-88706-911-8. Outstanding and accessible survey by a leader in the field.

Scheffler, Israel. *Science and Subjectivity*. 1967. Hackett Pub. 1982 $27.50. ISBN 0-915145-31-6. Important defense of objectivity, as attainable and essential to science, against its recent critics.

Sorensen, Roy A. *Thought Experiments*. OUP 1992 $45.00. ISBN 0-19-507422-X. Nontechnical comparison of the role played by thought experiments in science and other disciplines.

THEORIES OF RIGHTS AND JUSTICE

Twenty years ago, discussions of rights and justice were divided more or less by their genealogy. One line, which derived from the nineteenth-century utilitarians, especially JOHN STUART MILL (see Vol. 3), continued the development of political liberalism. The other line, which was represented particularly by GEORG HEGEL (see also Vol. 3) and KARL MARX (see also Vol. 3) in the nineteenth century, emphasized community as a cohesive structure and evolved into a critique of capitalist institutions. In recent years these lines have tended to merge.

The line of political liberalism begins with the individual person and models social organization as a contract. This view is forward-looking and sees institutions as more or less voluntary associations dedicated to a common good. The most important expression of this view has been JOHN RAWLS's *A Theory of Justice* (1971), which of all books since World War II has been the most widely discussed American work on the foundations of law. Rawls reworks social contract theory and utilitarian ethics to argue for justice as represented by the aims of the modern welfare state. Although his work stresses rights, it also sees justice in economic terms and thus supports redistribution of wealth in the interest of a greater good. Political conservatives, needless to say, are deeply suspicious of such a role for government. They tend to support the tradition of

Mill, which attempts to minimize the role of government in economic matters and to limit the legitimate scope of government to protection.

The conservative movement also has opposed utilitarian views of punishment—those theories that, as a forward-looking measure, emphasize deterrence, restitution for damages, and the rehabilitation of criminals. By contrast, conservatives have developed pragmatic arguments offering evidence that rehabilitation simply does not work very well, and theoretical arguments, which, based in ethics, see punishment as deserved payment for past wrong.

The philosophic line that has developed from Hegel and Marx views the social contract as a dangerous myth. It assumes that wealth and power are partners and that disparities of either nullify the basic assumption of a contract, which is that the various parties to the contract meet on more or less equal terms. The work of THEODOR W. ADORNO, JÜRGEN HABERMAS, and HERBERT MARCUSE has been deeply concerned with power as a corrupting influence in culture.

If the sovereignty of the individual is rejected, the basic human unit is taken to be the community itself. This assumption requires a new interpretation of justice, focusing on the treatment of individuals within a group. Yet justice cannot be understood solely as a convention within the society, because totalitarian governments routinely redefine justice to serve their own ends. But to identify justice as whatever a society decides is to forestall any critique of atrocity. The Holocaust is the paramount example; Holocaust studies have greatly expanded our understanding of justice. The communitarian line of political theory has developed profound critiques of authoritarian and totalitarian government that are every bit as important as its critiques of capitalism. The work of HANNAH ARENDT is an outstanding example.

Bedau, Hugo. *Death Is Different*. Northwestern U. Pr. 1987 $25.00. ISBN 1-55553-008-7. Important argument against capital punishment; includes case studies of varying state laws.

Dworkin, Ronald. *A Matter of Principle*. HUP 1985 $28.00. ISBN 0-674-55460-4. Essays on law and its relation to current ethical controversies.

Feinberg, Joel. *The Moral Limits of the Criminal Law*. 4 vols. OUP. Vol. 1 *Harm to Others*. 1987 $13.95. ISBN 0-19-504664-1. Vol. 2 *Offense to Others*. 1983 $36.00. ISBN 0-19-503449-X. Vol. 3 *Harm to Self*. 1989 $15.95. ISBN 0-19-505923-9. Vol. 4 *Harmless Wrongdoing*. 1990 $36.00. ISBN 0-19-504253-0. Essential series of essays that examine the proper limits of individual freedom with respect to injury, privacy, paternalism, and informed consent.

Gewirth, Alan. *Human Rights*. U. Ch. Pr. 1983 $35.00. ISBN 0-226-28877-3. Collection of essays on the concept of rights as applied to both specific issues and theory.

Greenawalt, Kent. *Discrimination and Reverse Discrimination*. McGraw 1983 $10.52. ISBN 0-07-554392-3. Textbook relating law and ethical judgments to problems of discrimination.

Harris, Leonard. *Philosophy Born of Struggle*. Kendall-Hunt 1983 $27.95. ISBN 0-8403-3328-5. Collection of essays by twentieth-century African American philosophers exploring issues of race, class, and justice.

Kenny, Anthony. *The Ivory Tower*. Blackwell Pubs. 1985 $45.00. ISBN 0-631-13985-0. Analysis of the concept of murder with specific applications to nuclear war.

Lucey, Kenneth, and Tibor Machan, eds. *Recent Work in Philosophy*. Rowman 1983 $54.50. ISBN 0-8476-7103-8. Collection of essays emphasizing a libertarian approach to social, political, and economic philosophy.

Narveson, Jan. *The Libertarian Idea*. Temple U. Pr. 1988 $34.95. ISBN 0-87722-569-9. Application of social contract theory to libertarian perspectives on issues of public policy.

Neilsen, Kai. *Equality and Liberty*. Rowman 1986 $56.00. ISBN 0-8476-6758-8. Social justice developed from a perspective of radical equality.

O'Neill, Onora. *Faces of Hunger*. Allen & Unwin 1986 o.p. Study of justice related to poverty and world hunger; concludes that these issues are better understood from a Kantian than from a utilitarian perspective.

Primoratz, Igor. *Justifying Legal Punishment*. Humanities 1989 $40.00. ISBN 0-391-03574-6. Lucid moral defense of the retributive view of justice and punishment.

Shapiro, Ian. *The Evolution of Rights in Liberal Theory*. Cambridge U. Pr. 1986 $54.95. ISBN 0-521-32043-7. Study of how the concept of rights has come to be central in Western political thought.

Thomson, Judith J. *The Realm of Rights*. HUP 1990 $35.00. ISBN 0-674-74948-0. Analytic discussion of the concepts and limits of rights.

———. *Rights, Restitution, and Risk*. Ed. by William Parent. HUP 1986 $11.95. ISBN 0-674-76981-3. Essays on rights as applied to current ethical issues.

Wertheimer, Alan. *Coercion*. Princeton U. Pr. 1988 $34.50. ISBN 0-691-00759-2. The use of coercion related to ethics and justice; an excellent discussion suited to a wide audience.

White, Alan R. *Rights*. OUP 1984 o.p. Detailed analysis of concepts related to rights, by an important analytic philosopher of law.

CURRENT ISSUES IN PHILOSOPHICAL ETHICS

The most significant theoretical development in ethics has been a resurgence of normative ethics. Normative ethics attempts to articulate standards that identify specific behavior as right or wrong, thus providing concrete and prescriptive guidelines for conduct. Because such standards were offered by the great ethical theories of the past, much recent work has begun with a second look at IMMANUEL KANT and the utilitarians. ALASDAIR MACINTYRE, whose *After Virtue* (1981) has been the most influential work in this area, argues for the essential failure of ethical theories of the modern period. He recommends, instead, a renewal of ethics based on a classical Greek understanding of character and virtue.

This development is surprising, because analytic philosophy typically emphasizes "meta-ethics." This branch of ethics is concerned not so much with guidelines for behavior as with abstract criteria for recognizing what is distinctive about ethics. Meta-ethics generally treats history, social concerns, and moral psychology as irrelevant. Although this work continues, much of the emphasis in analytic ethical theory has shifted to applications in medicine, business, the environment, and issues of war and peace. The analytic emphasis on clarity and precision has greatly advanced the discussion of these topics.

Philosophical treatments of medical ethics have attempted to clarify many of the issues that are prominent in current national affairs. In addition to debates about euthanasia and abortion, philosophers have conducted important discussions on standards for medical experimentation; about the extent to which medical technology impedes the humane treatment of patients; and about the distribution, accessibility, and rationing of health care. Philosophers trained in medical ethics are widely consulted in actual cases, whether of institutional policy or of individual patients, and their families are confronted with difficult decisions.

Although "business ethics" still is regarded in some circles as an oxymoron, interest in the area has greatly increased since the scandals of the 1980s. Few would accept MILTON FRIEDMAN's (see Vol. 3) principle that business has only two responsibilities—to turn a profit and to obey the law—if only because it has become clear just how much effort business makes to bend the law to its other goal. Nevertheless, philosophers have developed no general consensus about the extent of corporate responsibility. Specific issues that are widely discussed cover economic justice, including taxation, fair profits, and compensation; protection of consumers and the environment, including government regulation and the morality of advertising; information rights, including trade secrets and employee privacy; and the general rights and duties of employers and employees, including discrimination, workplace safety, loyalty, and whistle-blowing.

Human beings unquestionably bear responsibility for the degradation of the environment. Ethical discussions of this issue focus on where the responsibility lies, with what combination of government and the private sector. Although a variety of views are represented in the literature on this topic, the preponderance leans toward environmental activism. Among the issues under discussion are economic development as related to the wise use of natural resources; animal rights; and sustainable techniques in agriculture.

Discussions of the military have been concerned both with the role of the individual in a military force and with the use of force itself. Modern warfare has become so destructive and so unpredictable that the traditional doctrine that war is the continuation of diplomacy by other means has been seriously questioned. Few current authors show great nostalgia for nineteenth-century imperialism, if only because it resulted in two world wars of unimaginable destruction. At the same time, there is much practical skepticism of the opposing view that military intervention is seldom or never warranted. At the theoretical level, therefore, there has been renewed discussion of the standards for justifiable war, as they have been developed in Western thought by ST. THOMAS AQUINAS and others. Transcending any special pleading that prostitutes the doctrine to serve the cause of the moment, this discussion has focused on the question of whether modern warfare is so ugly that all standards for "just" wars have been superseded.

Axinn, Sidney. *A Moral Military*. Temple U. Pr. 1989 $34.95. ISBN 0-87722-615-6. The most important recent book on ethics related to the role of armed forces; well informed, sensitive to the issues.

Barbour, Ian. *Ethics in an Age of Technology*. HarpC 1992 $35.00. ISBN 0-06-060934-6. Splendid survey; Barbour tends to locate himself in the middle of the spectrum on most issues.

Bowie, Norman, and Ronald Duska. *Business Ethics*. P-H 1990 $22.00. ISBN 0-13-095910-3. Excellent introduction; examines both the individual within organizations and the practices of organizations themselves.

Brodie, Howard. *The Healer's Power*. Yale U. Pr. 1992 $30.00. ISBN 0-300-05174-3. Study of medical ethics with careful attention to how the practice of health care actually works.

Campbell, Robert, and Diane Collinson. *Ending Lives*. Blackwell Pubs. 1988 $34.95. ISBN 0-631-15329-2. Accessible but carefully argued discussion of suicide and euthanasia.

Cox, Gary. *The Ways of Peace*. Paulist Pr. 1986 $11.95. ISBN 0-8091-2797-0. Activist view of peace surveying the work of recent philosophers on this topic.

Daniels, Norman. *Am I My Parents' Keeper?* OUP 1988 $19.95. ISBN 0-19-505233-1. Supports, with due qualification, the rationing of health care on the basis of age.

———. *Just Health Care*. Cambridge U. Pr. 1985 $54.95. ISBN 0-521-23608-8. Equal access as the basis for a fair distribution of medical services.

DeGeorge, Richard R. *Business Ethics*. Macmillan 1989. ISBN 0-02-328011-5. College textbook that discusses corporate practice as related to moral theories.

Flanagan, Owen. *Varieties of Moral Personality*. HUP 1991 $34.95. ISBN 0-674-93218-8. Excellent study relating ethics to recent work in psychology.

Fletcher, George P. *Loyalty*. OUP 1993 $21.00. ISBN 0-19-507026-7. Stimulating discussion; draws on Kant, utilitarianism, and Rawls to engage contemporary political and moral issues.

Fox, Michael Allen. *The Case for Animal Experimentation*. U. CA Pr. 1985 $35.00. ISBN 0-520-05501-2. A justification for using animals for experimentation, argued in terms of the benefits to humans.

French, Peter A., and others. *Corporations in the Moral Community*. HarBraceJ 1992 $16.95. ISBN 0-03-030782-1. Views on whether corporations themselves have ethical responsibilities or whether such responsibilities are limited to their individual members.

Gervais, Karen G. *Redefining Death*. Yale U. Pr. 1987 $22.50. ISBN 0-300-03616-7. Separates philosophical, biological, and clinical issues; defines death as the permanent cessation of consciousness.

Griffin, James. *Well-Being*. OUP 1987 $48.00. ISBN 0-19-824903-9. Creative, sophisticated, yet accessible version of utilitarianism.

Holmes, Robert L. *On War and Morality*. Princeton U. Pr. 1989 $35.00. ISBN 0-691-07794-0. Argues that modern methods of warfare cannot be morally justified; "excellent" (*Choice*).

Humphrey, Derek, and Ann Wickett. *The Right to Die*. Hemlock Soc. 1990 o.p. Historical survey and review of recent controversies concerning euthanasia.

Kekes, John. *The Examined Life*. Bucknell U. Pr. 1988 $29.50. ISBN 0-8387-5132-6. Discussion of normative ethics, emphasizing "virtues of self-control, self-knowledge, moral sensitivity, and wisdom" (*Review of Metaphysics*).

McCloskey, H. J. *Ecological Ethics and Politics*. Rowman 1983 o.p. Argument for liberal democracy as the best long-range hope for balancing human needs and natural resources.

Martin, Mike W. *Self-Deception and Morality*. U. Pr. of KS 1986 $19.95. ISBN 0-7006-0297-6. Clear and balanced examination of hypocrisy, self-betrayal, and other forms of self-deception.

Midgley, Mary. *Animals and Why They Matter*. U. of Ga. Pr. 1984 $18.00. ISBN 0-8203-0704-1. Argues that discussions of the ethics of humans' treatment of animals are best viewed through the continuity of human with other life forms.

————. *Can't We Make Moral Judgments?* St. Martin 1993 $16.95. ISBN 0-312-0872608. Critique of the attitude that we no longer need ethics for daily life.

Miller, Richard W. *Moral Differences*. Princeton U. Pr. 1992 $16.95. ISBN 0-691-02092-2. Argues that our access to moral truth and our view of justice are developed in light of contributions from philosophy and the social sciences.

Regan, Tom. *The Case for Animal Rights*. U. CA Pr. 1983 $30.00. ISBN 0-520-04904-7. Examination of animal rights focusing on justice, cruelty, and human responsibility.

————, ed. *Just Business*. Temple U. Pr. 1983 $32.95. ISBN 0-87722-335-1. Broadly based collection of introductory papers.

Regan, Tom, and Peter Singer. *Animal Rights and Human Obligations*. P-H 1989 $20.00. ISBN 0-13-036864-4. Updated survey.

Rescher, Nicholas. *Ethical Idealism*. U. CA Pr. 1987 $37.50. ISBN 0-520-05696-5. Study of ethics as requiring a commitment to ideals; an important analysis of optimism and pessimism; written by one of the foremost (and amazingly prolific) contemporary American philosophers.

Slote, Michael. *From Morality to Virtue*. OUP 1992 $38.00. ISBN 0-19-507562-5. Technical and foundational examination of the ethics of virtue, contrasted with the ethics of Kant and utilitarianism.

Steinbeck, Bonnie. *Life before Birth*. OUP 1992 $29.95. ISBN 0-19-505494-6. Balanced treatment of legal and ethical issues concerning abortion, embryo research, and prenatal care.

Wenz, Peter S. *Environmental Justice*. State U. NY Pr. 1988 $49.50. ISBN 0-88706-644-5. Useful review of theories of distributive justice applied to environmental issues.

Wilson, John. *A Preface to Morality*. B & N Imports 1987 $27.50. ISBN 0-389-20749-7. Clear discussion of ethics as applied to virtue, justice, relativism, and absolutism.

DECONSTRUCTION AND POSTMODERNISM

Because postmodernism resists the rationalizing habits of Western philosophy, it defies any brief definition. It defines itself by its opposition to rationalism, particularly to the rationalism epitomized by the Enlightenment, which it views as an imperialism of the mind. Postmodernism regards philosophical theories as practical failures and conceptual illusions. It sees theory building not as an unbiased effort to attain an objective truth but as a self-serving mask for power. It thus aims to reveal the forces of history and wealth that shape the conceptual outlook of any culture. Although Protagoras (fifth century B.C.E.) is arguably the first postmodern philosopher, more recent ancestors of this movement are MARTIN HEIDEGGER (see also Vol. 5) and FRIEDRICH NIETZSCHE (see also Vol. 2).

Of the authors profiled in this chapter, JACQUES DERRIDA, MICHAEL FOUCAULT, and RICHARD MCKAY RORTY are consciously postmodern. THEODOR W. ADORNO, HANS-GEORG GADAMER, JÜRGEN HABERMAS, and HERBERT MARCUSE also deserve mention, however, even though they began to write well before the postmodern label came into use. For although they see their work as standing in the long tradition (indeed, as its culmination—hardly as its negation), they nevertheless develop postmodern themes. All seven are concerned with political and cultural forces that combine to make objective knowledge impossible. And whether by philosophical hermeneutics, as developed by Gadamer, or by critical theory, as developed by the philosophers of the Frankfurt School, the conviction is voiced that any hope for culture must begin with a thorough examination of its implicit assumptions.

Deconstruction, which is associated particularly with Derrida, began as a movement in literary criticism. Like postmodernism, it has ancestors in Nietzsche and Heidegger. Protagoras, claiming that humanity is the measure of all things, can be seen as the first postmodern philosopher; his contemporary, Gorgias, saying that we cannot know anything and that, if we do, we cannot express it, is in a sense the first deconstructionist. Although deconstruction emphatically shares the postmodern critique of rationalism, it is more specifically concerned with written language, that is, with "texts" and how they acquire meaning. Instead of locating *the* meaning of a text in the intention of the author, which cannot be known, or in a single and definitive interpretation, which cannot be expressed, deconstructionists see a text as producing many meanings, depending upon whatever assumptions the reader imports. Deconstructionists delight in exhibiting these assumptions, the "subtexts" of power, which manipulate the unsuspecting interpreter. At their extreme, deconstructionists deny any restriction of the meaning of a text beyond what the reader supplies; less controversially, they emphasize the reader as one factor among others. Despite the opinions of some observers that its tide has begun to ebb, deconstruction is finding new applications in social issues and philosophical topics beyond language.

Women's studies are growing rapidly as one branch of this literature. Although feminists contribute to every branch of philosophy, they are included here, and not dispersed throughout the chapter, for three reasons. First, feminists have been somewhat slower to influence philosophy than other disciplines, particularly literature and religious studies. In logic and epistemology, for example, they have made relatively slow headway in entering the mainstream. A focused placement will reduce the impression of fragmentation and will help the reader also to appreciate the feminists' scope and to utilize their resources. Second, most feminist philosophers are consciously post-modern, sharing postmodernism's themes of how power is submerged in rationalistic theories. Third, many feminist writers have drawn on deconstruction, explicitly addressing its issues and authors.

Barth, Else M. *Women Philosophers*. Philos Document 1992 $39.00. ISBN 0-912632-91-7. Complete bibliography through 1990, with a helpful analytic table of contents.

Butler, Christopher. *Interpretation, Deconstruction, and Ideology*. OUP 1984 $19.95. ISBN 0-19-815791-6. Useful introduction to recent criticism.

Callinicos, Alex. *Against Post-Modernism*. St. Martin 1990 $49.95. ISBN 0-312-04224-8. A Marxist critique.

Carr, David. *Time, Narrative, and History*. Ind. U. Pr. 1986 $25.00. ISBN 0-685-43536-9. A philosophy of history in relation to societies, their narratives, and how they are used to interpret time.

Code, Lorraine. *What Can She Know?* Cornell Univ. Pr. 1991 $42.50. ISBN 0-8014-2476-3. Feminist critique of analytic philosophy; interprets the subjectivity and relativity of the knower.

Dews, Peter. *Logics of Disintegration*. Routledge Chapman & Hall 1988 $39.95. ISBN 0-86091-105-5. Balanced, informative treatment of the major figures of Continental philosophy.

Diamond, Irene, and Lee Quinby, eds. *Feminism and Foucault*. Northwestern U. Pr. 1988 $37.50. ISBN 1-55553-032-X. Collection of essays.

Duran, Jane. *Toward a Feminist Epistemology*. Rowman 1991 $42.00. ISBN 0-8476-7635-8. An advanced survey; draws on contemporary feminism and analytic philosophy; argues that there are distinctively feminine ways of knowing.

Garry, Ann, and Marilyn Persall, eds. *Women, Knowledge, and Reality*. Unwin Hyman 1987 $39.95. ISBN 0-04-445221-7. Essays collected from other sources.

Griffiths, Morwenna, ed. *Feminist Perspectives in Philosophy*. Ind. U. Pr. 1988 $35.00. ISBN 0-253-32172-7. Accessible survey with an extensive bibliography.

Grimshaw, Jean. *Philosophy and Feminist Thinking*. U. of Minn. Pr. 1986 $16.95. ISBN 0-8166-1546-2. Rich in critical insight and widely cited.

Harding, Sandra. *The Science Question in Feminism*. Cornell Univ. Pr. 1986 $11.95. ISBN 0-8014-9363-3. Survey of feminist critiques of science.

Harvey, Elizabeth D., and Kathleen Okruhlik, eds. *Women and Reason*. U. of Mich. Pr. 1992 $39.50. ISBN 0-472-10220-6. Feminist critique of classical issues in the history of science, philosophy, and literature; requires familiarity with these subjects.

Llewelyn, John. *Beyond Metaphysics?* Humanities 1985 $15.00. ISBN 0-391-03619-X. Critical though obscure treatment of hermeneutics.

Manning, Rita. *Speaking from the Heart*. Rowman 1992 $49.00. ISBN 0-8476-7733-8. Feminist perspective on current moral issues; develops an ethics of caring.

Merrell, Floyd. *Deconstruction Reframed*. Purdue U. Pr. 1985 $18.50. ISBN 0-911198-72-5. Scholarly study emphasizing deconstruction as related to literary criticism.

Mills, Patricia J. *Women, Nature, and Psyche*. Yale U. Pr. 1987 $26.50. ISBN 0-300-03537-3. An essential contribution to feminist philosophy, especially as related to Marcuse and Adorno.

Neville, Robert Cummings. *The Highroad around Modernism*. State U. NY Pr. 1992 $59.50. ISBN 0-7914-1151-6. Classical American philosophers as an alternative to postmodernism.

Noddings, Nel. *Caring*. U. CA Pr. 1984 $27.50. ISBN 0-520-05043-6. Feminist ethics; care as a basis for decisions and moral education.

Norris, Christopher. *The Contest of Faculties*. Routledge Chapman & Hall 1985 $35.00. ISBN 0-416-39930-4. Brilliant study of deconstruction focusing on its relation to philosophy and literary criticism.

_____. *Deconstruction: Theory and Practice*. Routledge Chapman & Hall 1982 $13.95. ISBN 0-416-32070-8. A clear and balanced presentation.

————. *The Deconstructive Turn*. Routledge Chapman & Hall 1984 $12.95. ISBN 0-416-36140-4. Essays that compare deconstruction and analytic philosophy, to the advantage of deconstruction.

Nye, Andrea. *Feminist Theory and the Philosophies of Man*. Routledge 1988 $44.95. ISBN 0-7099-1852-6. An essential work; feminism related to Marxism, psychoanalysis, and deconstruction.

Ryan, Michael. *Marxism and Deconstruction*. Johns Hopkins 1982 $12.95. ISBN 0-8018-3248-9. Deconstruction related to Marxist dialectics and ideology.

Silverman, Hugh J., and Don Ihde, eds. *Hermeneutics and Deconstruction*. State U. NY Pr. 1985 $59.50. ISBN 0-87395-979-5. Collection of advanced essays.

Taylor, Mark C., ed. *Deconstruction in Context*. U. Ch. Pr. 1986 $45.00. ISBN 0-226-79139-4. Advanced essays on literature and philosophy.

Wachterhauser, Brice R., ed. *Hermeneutics and Modern Philosophy*. State U. NY Pr. 1986 $49.50. ISBN 0-88076-295-4. Advanced essays by major authors; excellent introductory survey.

Wyschogrod, Edith. *Saints and Postmodernism*. U. Ch. Pr. 1990 $40.00. ISBN 0-226-92042-9. Difficult but rewarding critique of the failure of ethical theories; draws on an impressive range of postmodern literature; saints' lives used as ethical models.

CHRONOLOGY OF AUTHORS

Marcuse, Herbert. 1898–1979
Gadamer, Hans-Georg. 1900–
Popper, Sir Karl Raimund. 1902–
Adorno, Theodor W. 1903–1969
Arendt, Hannah. 1906–1975
Goodman, Nelson. 1906–
Quine, Willard Van Orman. 1908–
Chisholm, Roderick M. 1916–
Strawson, Peter F. 1919–
Kuhn, Thomas S. 1922–

Feyerabend, Paul K. 1924–
Hesse, Mary B. 1924–
Foucault, Michel. 1926–1984
Putnam, Hilary. 1926–
Habermas, Jürgen. 1929–
MacIntyre, Alasdair C. 1929–
Derrida, Jacques. 1930–
Rorty, Richard McKay. 1931–
Taylor, Charles. 1931–
Dennett, Daniel C. 1942–

ADORNO, THEODOR W. 1903–1969

Theodor W. Adorno is the progenitor of critical theory, a central figure in aesthetics, and the century's foremost philosopher of music. He was born and educated in Frankfurt, Germany. After completing his Ph.D. in philosophy, he went to Vienna, where he studied composition with ALBAN BERG (see Vol. 3). He soon was bitterly disappointed with his own lack of talent and turned to musicology. In 1928 he returned to Frankfurt to join the Institute for Social Research, commonly known as The Frankfurt School, which began as a privately endowed center for Marxist studies but later was merged with Frankfurt's university under Adorno's directorship in the 1950s. As a refugee from Nazi Germany during World War II, he lived for several years in Los Angeles before returning to Frankfurt. Much of his most significant work was produced at that time.

Critics find Adorno's aesthetics to be rich in insight, even when they disagree with its broad conclusions. Although Adorno was hostile to jazz and popular music, he advanced the cause of contemporary music by writing seminal studies of many key composers. To the distress of some of his admirers, he remained pessimistic about the prospects for art in mass society.

Critical theory emphasizes the ways in which power corrupts the mind. In developing what traditionalists call "first" philosophy, it provides techniques for objective analysis that eliminate biases and false assumptions. It is most centrally concerned with social theory and with the social dimensions of knowledge. A neo-Marxist, Adorno thought that the only hope for democracy was to be sought in an interpretation of Marxism that is opposed to both positivism and dogmatic materialism. His opposition to positivisim and advocacy of a method of dialectics grounded in critical rationalism propelled him into intellectual conflict with GEORG HEGEL, MARTIN HEIDEGGER, and Heideggerian hermeneutics.

BOOKS BY ADORNO

Aesthetic Theory. 1970. Trans. by G. Lenhardt. Methuen 1984 o.p. Adorno's most comprehensive work on the philosophy of art.

Against Epistemology—A Metacritique. 1956. Trans. by Willis Domingo. MIT Pr. 1983 o.p. A major contribution to phenomenology and epistemology.

Alban Berg: Master of the Smallest Link. 1968. Trans. by C. Hailey and J. Brand. Cambridge U. Pr. 1991 $39.95. ISBN 0-521-33016-5. A critical study of the composer.

The Authoritarian Personality. (coauthored with Else Frenket-Brunswick.) 1950. Norton 1983 $12.95. ISBN 0-393-30042-0. A basic work on the subject; treats the personality traits of American immigrants.

Dialectic of Enlightenment. 1947. Trans. by John Cummings. Continuum 1975 $16.95. ISBN 0-8264-0093-0. A critique of the Enlightenment from the standpoint of critical theory.

In Search of Wagner. 1952. Trans. by R. Livingstone. Routledge Chapman & Hall 1991 $13.95. ISBN 0-86091-796-7. A study of philosophy of music and the composer, showing Wagnerian influences on Nazism.

Introduction to the Sociology of Music. 1962. Trans. by E. B. Ashton. Continuum 1988 $12.95. ISBN 0-8264-0403-0. A basic work in this field, hostile to jazz and popular music.

The Jargon of Authenticity. 1965. Trans. by Knut Tarnowski and Fredcrick Will. Northwestern U. Pr. 1973 $10.95. ISBN 0-8101-0657-4. A difficult, dialectical study of the language of morals.

Kierkegaard: Construction of the Aesthetic. 1933. Trans. by Robert Hullot-Kentor. U. of Minn. Pr. 1989 $39.95. ISBN 0-8166-1186-6. A critical study of the philosopher.

Mahler: A Musical Physiognomy. 1960. Trans. by Edmund Jephcott. U. Ch. Pr. 1992 $27.50. ISBN 0-226-00768-5. A study of the composer.

Minima Moralia. Trans. by Edmund F. Jephcott. 1951. Routledge Chapman & Hall 1985 $15.95. ISBN 0-86091-704-5. A difficult but profound treatment of ethical issues confronting twentieth-century living; a collection of aphorisms.

Negative Dialectics. 1966. Continuum 1982 $19.95. ISBN 0-8264-0132-5. Dialectics as a method of inquiry.

Notes to Literature. 1958–74. Trans. by Shierry Nicholsen. 2 vols. Col. U. Pr. Vol. 1 1991 $35.00. ISBN 0-231-06332-6. Vol. 2 1992 $39.00. ISBN 0-685-53215-1. Literary criticism.

Philosophy of Modern Music. 1949. Continuum 1980 $10.95. ISBN 0-8264-0138-4. An original study that praises Schoenberg and criticizes Stravinsky.

The Positivist Dispute in German Sociology. 1970. Ashgate Pub. Co. 1981 $22.95. ISBN 0-435-82656-5. A critique of Popper and other positivists who emphasize determinism in the social sciences.

Prisms. 1955. Trans. by Samuel Weber and Shierry Weber. MIT Pr. 1982 $10.95. ISBN 0-262-51025-1. Essays on aesthetics and culture; one of Adorno's most widely read books.

Quasi Una Fantasia: Essays on Music and Culture. 1963. Routledge Chapman & Hall 1992 $29.95. ISBN 0-86091-360-0. A collection of essays.

BOOKS ABOUT ADORNO

Friedman, George. *The Political Philosophy of the Frankfurt School*. Cornell Univ. Pr.
    1981 $39.95. ISBN 0-8014-1279-X. A critical review of the major themes of Adorno's
    work as related to Marcuse and others.
Jay, Martin. *Adorno*. HUP 1984 $20.00. ISBN 0-674-00514-7. A useful account of Adorno's
    aesthetic modernism, cultural conservatism, and anticipation of deconstruction.

ARENDT, HANNAH. 1906–1975

A cultural critic and eminent political theorist, Hannah Arendt is best known
for her pioneering studies of anti-Semitism and totalitarianism. Before leaving
Germany for France in 1933 as a refugee from the Nazis, she studied with KARL
JASPERS (see also Vol. 5) and MARTIN HEIDEGGER (see also Vol. 5). She came to
the United States during World War II. She taught at the University of Chicago
and Princeton University, where she was the first woman to be appointed to the
rank of full professor. Her last 12 years were spent as a distinguished faculty
member of New York City's New School for Social Research. Throughout her
later years, she was an advocate of many Jewish social causes.

Arendt's first major work in English, *The Origins of Totalitarianism* (1951), has
become a classic. It examines the social and psychological factors that support
totalitarian governments. Her subsequent books explore historical dimensions
of political theory; issues in culture, mind, and morals; and, most famously, the
roots of anti-Semitism. She coined the phrase "the banality of evil" to express
her controversial thesis that Nazi culture flourished more because of its
ordinary bureaucratic machinery than because of its sinister leadership.

BOOKS BY ARENDT

Between Past and Future. 1961. Viking Penguin 1977 $10.00. ISBN 0-14-004662-3. An
    exploration of issues in political theory and practical politics.
Crises of the Republic. 1972. HarBraceJ 1978 $15.00. ISBN 0-15-123095-1. A collection of
    articles on violence, revolution, and other political topics.
Eichmann in Jerusalem. 1963. Viking Penguin 1977 $8.95. ISBN 0-14-004450-7. A widely
    read profile, in which she originated the phrase "the banality of evil."
The Human Condition. 1958. U. Ch. Pr. 1970 $13.95. ISBN 0-226-02593-4. A profound
    study of social philosophy; less demanding than *The Life of the Mind*.
Lectures on Kant's Political Philosophy. 1982. Ed. by Ronald Beiner. U. Ch. Pr. 1989
    $9.95. ISBN 0-226-02595-0. Posthumously published university lectures.
The Life of the Mind. 1978. HarBraceJ 1981 $12.95. ISBN 0-15-651992-5. A posthumously
    published, unfinished, and difficult work of systematic philosophy.
Men in Dark Times. 1968. HarBraceJ 1970 $8.95. ISBN 0-15-658890-0. Studies of
    individuals confronting difficult political situations.
On Revolution. 1963. Viking Penguin 1977 $7.95. ISBN 0-14-021681-2. A philosophical
    theory of revolution contrasting the American, French, and Russian revolutions.
The Origins of Totalitarianism. 1951. HarBraceJ 1973 $14.95. ISBN 0-15-670153-7. A
    study of psychological and social factors supportive of dictatorship; originally
    published in three volumes: *Anti-Semitism*, *Imperialism*, and *Totalitarianism*; the
    work that established Arendt's reputation.
Rachel Vernhagen: The Life of a Jewish Woman. 1957. Trans. by Richard Winston and
    Clara Winston. HarBraceJ 1974 o.p. A biography illustrating feminism and struggles
    against anti-Semitism.

BOOKS ABOUT ARENDT

Bowen-Moore, Patricia. *Hannah Arendt's Philosophy of Natality*. St. Martin 1989 $24.95.
    ISBN 0-312-02831-8. A sympathetic reconstruction of Arendt's themes; "fresh,
    coherent, and comprehensive" (*Review of Metaphysics*).

Bradshaw, Leah. *Acting and Thinking: The Political Thought of Hannah Arendt.* U. of Toronto Pr. 1989 $45.00. ISBN 0-8020-2625-7. A scholarly monograph basic to studies in the field.

Canovan, Margaret. *Hannah Arendt.* Cambridge U. Pr. 1992 $59.95. ISBN 0-521-41911-5. A study of Arendt's political philosophy, arguing that other interpretations are flawed by "a failure to see her work in its proper context."

Kaplan, Gisela, and Clive Kepler, eds. *Hannah Arendt: Thinking, Judging, Freedom.* Unwin Hyman 1989 $39.95. ISBN 0-04-820041-7. A collection of critical essays.

Kateb, George. *Hannah Arendt.* Rowman 1984 $21.00. ISBN 0-8476-7558-0. A sympathetic exposition and critique.

Nordquist, Joan. *Hannah Arendt: A Bibliography.* Ref. Rsch. Sv. 1989 $15.00. ISBN 0-937855-26. A good reference tool for further study.

Young-Bruehl, Elisabeth. *Hannah Arendt.* Yale U. Pr. 1983 $17.95. ISBN 0-300-0309-1. A biographical study based on the author's personal acquaintance with Arendt, Arendt's personal papers, and interviews with her family and friends.

CHISHOLM, RODERICK M. 1916–

An analytic philosopher, Roderick M. Chisholm is a meticulous epistemologist, although he also addresses historical figures and basic issues in metaphysics. He was born in Massachusetts, educated at Brown and Harvard universities, and in 1947 returned to Brown, where, with the exception of many visiting appointments, he has spent his academic career. His work is influenced by THOMAS REID, FRANZ BRENTANO, and GEORGE MOORE, to whose close attention to detail he owes something of his own style. All three were deeply concerned with perception, which is a major theme of Chisholm's work. His 1957 book, *Perceiving*, is a discussion of philosophical puzzles of perception and an attempt to resolve them. He also has written important studies of Brentano and of abstract concepts in philosophy of mind.

BOOKS BY CHISHOLM

Brentano and Intrinsic Value. Cambridge U. Pr. 1986 $37.95. ISBN 0-521-26437-5. A critical study of the nineteenth-century philosopher and psychologist.

Brentano and Meinong Studies. Humanities 1982 o.p. Advanced, scholarly treatment.

The First Person. Open Court 1979 o.p. Treats reference and intentionality; a major contribution to contemporary metaphysics and philosophy of mind.

The Foundations of Knowing. U. of Minn. Pr. 1982 $29.95. ISBN 0-8166-1103-3. A technical, analytic study of essential issues in epistemology.

On Metaphysics. U. of Minn. Pr. 1989 $29.95. ISBN 0-8166-1767-8. An abstract treatment of substance, mind, and individuality; includes many references to Plato and Aristotle.

Perceiving. Cornell Univ. Pr. 1957 o.p. The detailed analytic study that made Chisholm's reputation.

Person and Object. Open Court 1979 $16.95. ISBN 0-87548-341-0. The Paul Carus lectures; a defense of the metaphysical concept of substance.

The Problem of the Criterion. Marquette 1973 $7.95. ISBN 0-87462-138-0. A carefully wrought lecture in the analytic vein on a central theme in classic theory of knowledge.

Realism and the Background of Phenomenology. Ridgeview 1981 $30.00. ISBN 0-917930-34-7. An anthology, with a scholarly introduction by Chisholm.

Theory of Knowledge. 1966. P-H 1988. ISBN 0-13-914177-4. A good introduction to epistemology from an analytic standpoint and a good introduction to Chisholm.

BOOKS ABOUT CHISHOLM

Bogdan, Radu J., ed. *Roderick M. Chisholm.* Kluwer Ac. 1986 o.p. An autobiographical sketch of Chisholm, a bibliography of his work, and a collection of original critical essays.

Davidson, Donald. *Essays on Actions and Events.* OUP 1980 $18.95. ISBN 0-19-824637-4.
   A collection of short but very difficult essays by a highly regarded epistemologist.

DENNETT, DANIEL C. 1942–

   An American philosopher of mind and a pioneer in the cognitive science
movement, Daniel C. Dennett was born in Boston and educated at Harvard and
Oxford universities. He is Distinguished Professor of Arts and Sciences and
director of the Center for Cognitive Studies at Tufts University, where he has
taught since 1971.
   His work is notable for its inclusion of empirical psychology and computer
science as these fields bear on the mind-body problem. Although not a
traditional dualist, Dennett rejects a purely physical analysis of mind as brain
states. He argues that the terms of psychology, particularly those expressing
intentionality, can be understood scientifically without their necessarily having
physical reference. Among the topics that receive detailed treatment in his work
are consciousness, belief, and freedom, and their relevance to ethics and moral
responsibility.

BOOKS BY DENNETT

Brainstorms. MIT Pr. 1980 $14.95. ISBN 0-262-54037-1. Essays on psychology and the
   philosophy of mind; even a beginner can read the last chapter with pleasure.
Consciousness Explained. Little 1991 $27.95. ISBN 0-316-18065-3. According to *The New
   York Times,* "brilliant . . . a science book aimed at both professionals and general
   readers . . . in the hands of a master explicator, the richness and power of the
   computer metaphor of the mind comes shining through."
Content and Consciousness. Routledge Chapman & Hall 1986 $13.95. ISBN 0-7102-
   0846-4. A study of brain mechanisms as related to the mind-body problem.
Elbow Room. MIT Pr. 1984 $11.95. ISBN 0-262-54042-8. A lucid, well-informed analysis
   of various interpretations of free will and what follows from them; defends a
   naturalistic view of reason and responsibility.
The Internal Stance. MIT Pr. 1987 $32.50. ISBN 0-262-04093-X. A study of mind as
   related to artificial intelligence, computer science, and biology; 10 papers.
The Mind's I. (coauthored with Douglas R. Hofstadter). Bantam 1982 $13.95. ISBN 0-553-
   34343-2. A delightful and undogmatic piece subtitled *Fantasies and Reflections on
   Self and Soul.*

BOOK ABOUT DENNETT

Dahlbom, Bo, ed. *Dennett and His Critics.* Blackwell Pubs. 1993 $49.95. ISBN 0-631-
   18549-6. A collection of essays; covers all of Dennett's work but concentrates on
   Consciousness Explained; includes viewpoints by critics from the fields of philosophy, biology, and computer science.

DERRIDA, JACQUES. 1930–

   Jacques Derrida is a leading proponent of the movement in philosophy and
literary criticism known as deconstructionism. Born in Algeria, he has lived in
Paris and taught at the École Normale Supérieure for many years. His work is
deeply informed by MARTIN HEIDEGGER (see also Vol. 5) and by EDMUND HUSSERL
and phenomenology. From these sources, which he takes to be the culmination
of Western philosophy, Derrida draws the theme of "presence." Presence is
explained as the self-authenticating experience that reveals meaning—an
experience whose possibility Derrida denies.
   Derrida arrives at this position by a critique of language, especially written
language, which requires a reader if it is to have any meaning. Because written
language is mediated by physical signs—for example, inscriptions on paper or

stone—the difference between the sign and its object eliminates the possibility of "presence." Thus, deconstruction dismantles the pretensions of metaphysics and literature by revealing their presuppositions. These presuppositions, which were submerged prior to the deconstruction, are revealed as contradictory. On the one hand, they require that the language of the text be taken as a transparent medium, fully able to represent thought; at the same time, they depend upon difference by assuming the presence of the reader.

BOOKS BY DERRIDA

Acts of Literature. Ed. by Derek Attridge. Routledge 1991 $49.95. ISBN 0-415-90056-5

The Archaeology of the Frivolous. Trans. by John P. Leavey. U. of Nebr. Pr. 1987 $7.95. ISBN 0-8032-6571-9. An extended essay on Condillac; how his apparent break with metaphysics nevertheless left him captive.

Cinders. Trans. by Ned Lukacher. U. of Nebr. Pr. 1991 $25.00. ISBN 0-8032-1689-0

Dissemination. Trans. by Barbara Johnson. U. Ch. Pr. 1983 $14.95. ISBN 0-226-14334-1. A work of "jungle-like obscurity" (John Passmore, *Recent Philosophers*); includes comments on Plato.

The Ear of the Other. Trans. by Peggy Kamuf. U. of Nebr. Pr. 1988 $9.95. ISBN 0-8032-6575-1

Edmund Husserl's "Origin of Geometry." Trans. by John Leavey. U. of Nebr. Pr. 1989 $9.95. ISBN 0-8032-6580-8. An important commentary on Husserl's essay; technical; Derrida's first presentation of deconstruction.

Glas. Trans. by John Leavey and Richard Rand. U. of Nebr. Pr. 1990 $80.00. ISBN 0-8032-1667-X. A huge, obscure work that defeats any effort at brief characterization.

Limited, Inc. Trans. by Samuel Weber and Jeffrey Mehlmann. Northwestern U. Pr. 1988 $10.95. ISBN 0-8101-0788-0. A biting critique of Searle and his analytic philosophy of language.

Margins of Philosophy. Trans. by Alan Bass. U. Ch. Pr. 1984 $13.95. ISBN 0-226-14326-0. Confronts philosophy with its own prejudices; discusses Heidegger, Nietzsche, and Sartre; more systematic than Derrida's other books.

Memories for Paul de Man. Trans. by Cecile Lindsay and others. Col. U. Pr. 1986 $33.00. ISBN 0-685-209529-X. Art commentary dedicated to the controversial critic, with a warm account of his relation to Derrida.

Of Grammatology. 1967. Trans. by Gayatri Spivak. Johns Hopkins 1977 $14.95. ISBN 0-8018-1879-6. A theory of language developed by extended comments on Rousseau; explores why we find the figurative interpretation of written language more compelling than the literal.

Of Spirit: Heidegger and the Question. Trans. by Geoffrey Bennington and Rachel Bowlby. U. Ch. Pr. 1989 $19.95. ISBN 0-226-14317-1. A 1987 lecture on Heidegger's early avoidance and later ambiguous use of the term *spirit*.

The Other Heading. Trans. by Pascale-Ann Brault and Michael Nass. Ind. U. Pr. 1992 $19.95. ISBN 0-253-31693-6. Reflections on current figures in Continental thought.

Positions. Trans. by Alan Bass. U. Ch. Pr. 1982 $5.95. ISBN 0-226-14331-7. A brilliant essay arguing that there are no firm connections between reality and representations of it.

The Post Card. Trans. by Alan Bass. U. Ch. Pr. 1987 $19.95. ISBN 0-226-14322-8. A "playful, self-reflective, and somewhat narcissistic" comparison of speech and writing (*Choice*); fictional, mock-scholarly account of Plato and Socrates.

Signeponge-Signeponge. Trans. by Richard Rand. Col. U. Pr. 1985 $40.50. ISBN 0-231-05446-7. Literary exercises, sometimes exasperating, sometimes obfuscating, but always rewarding.

Speech and Phenomena. Trans. by David B. Allison. Northwestern U. Pr. 1973 $24.95. ISBN 0-8101-0397-4. A collection of essays on Husserl's theory of language; analyzes the impossibility of determinate meaning.

Spurs: Nietzsche's Styles. Trans. by Barbara Harlow. U. Ch. Pr. 1981 $7.95. ISBN 0-226-14333-3. A collection of puzzling essays.

The Truth in Painting. Trans. by Geoffrey Bennington and Ian McLeod. U. Ch. Pr. 1987
$19.95. ISBN 0-226-14324-4. More readable than *Glas*; contains a critique of
traditional work in aesthetics.
Writing and Difference. Trans. by Alan Bass. U. Ch. Pr. 1980 $13.95. ISBN 0-226-14329-5.
A basic work on deconstruction; explores the ethical as transcending reason, what a
text is, and Freud.

BOOKS ABOUT DERRIDA

Coward, Harold, and Toby Foshay, eds. *Derrida and Negative Theology.* State U. NY Pr.
1992 $49.50. ISBN 0-7914-0963-5. A collection of scholarly essays on the intersection
of deconstruction and theology.
Gasche, Rodolphe. *The Tain of the Mirror* $32.95. HUP 1986 ISBN 0-674-86700-9. An
important critique; locates historical antecedents and shows how to read Derrida.
Harvey, Irene E. *Derrida and the Economy of Difference.* Bks. Demand repr. of 1986 ed.
$81.00. ISBN 0-7837-1754-7. A critical survey of Derrida's main ideas that locates
him within the Continental tradition.
Kamuf, Peggy, ed. *A Derrida Reader: Between the Blinds.* Col. U. Pr. 1991 $68.50. ISBN 0-
231-06658-9. An anthology with introduction and commentary by the editor.
Llewelyn, John. *Derrida on the Threshold of Sense.* St. Martin 1986 $12.95. ISBN 0-312-
19409-9. A perceptive commentary on meaning and truth.
Martin, Bill. *Matrix and Line: Derrida and the Possibilities of Postmodern Social Theory.*
State U. NY pr. 1992 $49.50. ISBN 0-7914-1049-8. A scholarly monograph in radical
social and political theory.
Megill, Allan. *Prophets of Extremity.* U. CA Pr. 1985 $45.00. ISBN 0-520-05239-0. Derrida
against the background of nineteenth-century thought, the assumptions of which he
turns on themselves.
Nordquist, Joan. *Jacques Derrida: A Bibliography.* Ref. Rsch. Serv. 1986 $15.00. ISBN 0-
937855-02-2. A useful reference work.
Norris, Christopher. *The Contest of Faculties.* Routledge Chapman & Hall 1985 $35.00.
ISBN 0-416-39930-4. Insights of deconstruction applied to epistemology, philosophi-
cal semantics, narrative theory, and legal interpretation.
_____. *Derrida.* HUP 1988 $25.00. ISBN 0-674-19823-9. An excellent introduction,
valuable for readers at all levels.
Percesepe, Gary J. *Future(s) of Philosophy: The Marginal Thinking of Jacques Derrida.* P.
Lang. Pubs. 1989 $36.00. ISBN 0-8204-0804-2. Raises interesting questions about the
meaning of philosophy for Derrida and his distancing himself from the deconstruction "industry."
Sallis, John, ed. *Deconstruction and Philosophy.* U. Ch. Pr. 1989 $24.95. ISBN 0-226-
73438-2. Twelve essays on Derrida and one by Derrida himself.
Silverman, Hugh J., ed. *Derrida and Deconstruction.* Routledge 1989 $40.00. ISBN 0-415-
03093-5. A collection of specialized essays, including one by the editor entitled
"Derrida, Heidegger, and the Time of the Line."
Staten, Henry. *Wittgenstein and Derrida.* U. of Nebr. Pr. 1984 $21.50. ISBN 0-8032-
4138-0. A specialized comparison of the two authors; for experts.
Wood, David ed. *Derrida: A Critical Reader.* Blackwell Pubs. 1992 ISBN 0-631-16102-3.
An anthology for academics.

FEYERABEND, PAUL K. 1924–

A controversial and influential voice in philosophy of science, Paul K.
Feyerabend was born and educated in Vienna. After military service during
World War II and further study at the University of London, he returned to
Vienna as a lecturer at the university. In 1959, having taught for several years at
Bristol University in England, he came to the United States to join the faculty of
the University of California at Berkeley, from which, after numerous visiting
appointments elsewhere, he retired in 1990.

Since the 1970s, Feyerabend has devoted much of his career to arguing that science as practiced cannot be described, let alone regulated, by any coherent methodology, whether understood historically, as in THOMAS KUHN's (see also Vol. 5) use of paradigms, or epistemologically, as in classical positivism and its offspring. He illustrates this stance on the dust jacket of one of his books, *Against Method* (1975), by publishing his horoscope in the place usually reserved for a biographical sketch of the author. In his entry in the *Supplement to Who's Who in America*, he is quoted as saying, "Leading intellectuals with their zeal for objectivity . . . are criminals, not the liberators of mankind."

BOOKS BY FEYERABEND

Against Method. 1975. Routledge Chapman & Hall 1988 $50.00. ISBN 0-86091-222-1. Feyerabend's best-known work; develops his anarchistic view of knowledge and history of science.

Farewell to Reason. Routledge Chapman & Hall 1988 $49.95. ISBN 0-86091-184-5

Philosophical Papers. 2 vols. Cambridge U. Pr. 1981. Vol. 1 $69.95. ISBN 0-521-22897-2. Vol. 2 $59.95. ISBN 0-521-23964-8. Considers problems of empiricism, realism, rationalism, and scientific method.

Science in a Free Society. New Left Bks. 1978 o.p. A development of his views "in large part by way of a series of unprecedentedly lengthy and vitriolic replies to reviewers" (Passmore, *Recent Philosophers*).

Three Dialogues on Knowledge. Blackwell Pubs. 1991 $42.95. ISBN 0-631-17917-8. "A stimulating ice-breaker" (*Choice*) that reiterates themes developed in *Against Method.*

BOOKS ABOUT FEYERABEND

Couvalis, George. *Feyerabend's Critique of Foundationalism.* Ashgate Pub. Co. 1989 $52.95. ISBN 0-566-07043-X. A study that requires prior acquaintance with the issues.

Munevar, Gonzalo. *Beyond Reason.* Kluwer Ac. 1991 $135.00. ISBN 0-7923-1272-4. A collection of specialized essays.

FOUCAULT, MICHEL. 1926–1984

Michel Foucault is a principal representative of the postmodern movement. Born in Poitiers, France, he was educated at the Sorbonne and held a number of important university positions. He was one of the reigning intellectuals of Paris, and, for the last 14 years of his life he was professor of the history of systems of thought at the Collège de France.

Influenced by FRIEDRICH NIETZSCHE (see also Vol. 2) and KARL MARX (see also Vol. 3), Foucault emphasized the cultural and historical factors that condition knowledge. Because such factors are generally opaque to persons living in a given era, Foucault believed that it is impossible to achieve anything like the objectivity traditionally prized by conventional scientific methodology.

Foucault's wide-ranging work includes detailed case studies, which in his earlier work were used to develop what he called the "archaeology" of the sciences: a look at how the defining assumptions of a subject are shaped by history. According to Foucault, these assumptions can be exposed by patiently uncovering the hidden concepts that shape thought and practice over time.

Foucault's later work shifted the emphasis to the "genealogy" of knowledge, a designation reminiscent of Nietzsche's genealogy of morals. In this work Foucault also utilized case studies in order to emphasize the submerged relationships of power that condition all other claims.

BOOKS BY FOUCAULT

The Archaeology of Knowledge. Trans. by A. M. Sheridan-Smith. Irvington 1972 $29.50. ISBN 0-394-47118-0. An attempt to discover how society manipulates language for political purposes; why some linguistic constructions survive in time.

Birth of the Clinic. Random 1974 $9.00. ISBN 0-394-71097-5. A history of medicine, illustrating Foucault's thesis about concealed power relations.

Death and the Labyrinth. Trans. by Charles Ruas. U. CA Pr. 1987 $10.95. ISBN 0-520-059990-5. Art criticism, subtitled *The World of Raymond Roussell.*

Discipline and Punish. Trans. by Alan Sheridan. Random 1979 $11.00. ISBN 0-394-77767-3. The evolution of penal institutions shown as symptomatic of society's need to maintain surveillance and control of all of its members—not just its "criminals."

The History of Sexuality. Trans. by Robert Hurley. Vol. 1 *Introduction.* Random 1990 $10.00. ISBN 0-679-72469-9. Challenges conventional views of sexual history as repression.

The History of Sexuality. Trans. by Robert Hurley. Vol. 2 *The Uses of Pleasure.* Pantheon 1985 $17.95. ISBN 0-394-54349-1. Greek views of sexuality.

The History of Sexuality. Trans. by Robert Hurley. Vol. 3 *The Care of the Self.* Pantheon 1986 $18.95. ISBN 0-394-54814-0. A comparison of Roman and early Christian attitudes toward sexuality.

Language, Counter-Memory, Practice. Ed. by Donald F. Bouchard. Cornell Univ. Pr. 1980 $12.95. ISBN 0-8014-9204-1. Selected essays and interviews with Foucault.

Madness and Civilization. 1973. Random 1988 $11.00. ISBN 0-679-72110-X. A history of how the concept of insanity evolved as an instrument of control during the so-called Age of Reason.

Mental Illness and Psychology. U. CA Pr. 1986 $8.95. ISBN 0-520-05919-0. Contains three chapters on the psychology of mental illness with regard to evolution, individual history and existence, and two chapters on the history and structure of madness in relation to culture.

The Order of Things. Random 1973 $10.00. ISBN 0-394-71935-2. Foucault's most important presentation of his concept of the archeology of knowledge.

Politics, Philosophy, Culture. Routledge 1990 $14.95. ISBN 0-415-90149-9. A collection of interviews and dialogues from 1977 to 1984; features Foucault's repeated efforts to question what is regarded as self-evident.

Power-Knowledge. Pantheon 1980 $14.00. ISBN 0-394-73954-X. A brilliant selection of provocative remarks.

Remarks on Marx. Autonomedia 1991 $6.00. ISBN 0-936-756-33-0

This Is Not a Pipe. Trans. by James Harkness. U. CA Pr. 1982 $25.00. ISBN 0-520-04916-0. A playful, imaginative, exciting work whose title is taken from Réné Magritte's paradoxical painting.

BOOKS ABOUT FOUCAULT

Arac, Jonathan, ed. *After Foucault Humanistic Knowledge, Postmodern Challenges.* Rutgers U. Pr. 1988 $29.00. ISBN 0-8135-1329-4. "Nine excellent essays. . . [on] the importance of Foucault's work for research in a wide range of humanistic disciplines." (*Choice*)

Bernauer, James W. *Michel Foucault's Force of Flight.* Humanities 1990 $49.95. ISBN 0-391-03635-1. An excellent introduction and sympathetic critique.

Bernauer, James W., and David Rasmussen, eds. *The Final Foucault.* MIT Pr. 1988 $10.95. ISBN 0-262-52132-6. A valedictory anthology prepared by disciples.

Cooper, Barry. *Michel Foucault: An Introductory Study of His Thought.* E. Mellen 1982 $79.95. ISBN 0-88946-867-2. An illuminating exposition for the advanced reader.

Deleuze, Gilles. *Foucault.* Trans. by Sean Hand. U. of Minn. Pr. 1988 $29.50. ISBN 0-8166-1674-4. A study of one of the major figures of postmodern philosophy, by one of his most prominent colleagues.

Dreyfus, Hubert L., and Paul Rainbow. *Michel Foucault: Beyond Structuralism and Hermeneutics.* U. Ch. Pr. 1983 $25.00. ISBN 0-226-16311-3. An advanced interpretation of Foucault's major works, emphasizing his treatment of human discourse and history.

Eribon, Didier. *Michel Foucault*. Trans. by Betsy Wing. HUP 1991 $27.95. ISBN 0-674-57287-4. An important intellectual biography.

Gutting, Gary. *Foucault's Archaelogy: Science and the History of Reason. Modern European Philosophy Ser.* Cambridge U. Pr. 1989 $47.95. ISBN 0-521-36619-4. A penetrating critique of Foucault's epistemology, intended primarily for specialists with a knowledge of his thought.

Hoy, David C., ed. *Foucault: A Critical Reader*. Blackwell Pubs. 1986 $45.00. ISBN 0-631-14042-5. An excellent collection of 13 essays by important critics.

McNay, Lois. *Foucault and Feminism*. Northeastern U. Pr. 1993 $37.50. ISBN 1-55553-152-0. A feminist critique of Foucault's later work; arguing that he stands in the tradition of the Enlightenment and is not purely postmodern.

Miller, James. *The Passion of Michel Foucault*. S&S Trade 1993 $27.50. ISBN 0-671-69550-9. A deconstruction of Foucault's life.

Nordquist, Joan, ed. *Michel Foucault: A Bibliography*. Ref. Rsch. Serv. 1992 $15.00. ISBN 0-937855-53-7. An important reference work.

Rajchman, John. *Michel Foucault: The Freedom of Philosophy*. Col. U. Pr. 1986 $15.50. ISBN 0-231-06071-8. Perceptive, informative, sometimes obscure commentary.

Sawicki, Jana. *Disciplining Foucault: Feminism, Power, and the Body. Thinking Gender Ser.* Routledge 1991 $42.50. ISBN 0-415-90187-1. "[V]aluable both as a contribution to feminist theory and a clarification of Foucault's approach." (*Choice*)

Shumway, David R. *Michel Foucault*. Twayne 1989 $24.95. ISBN 0-8057-8252-4. A clear, accurate presentation of Foucault's major ideas.

GADAMER, HANS-GEORG. 1900–

Hans-Georg Gadamer is the father of contemporary philosophical hermeneutics. He was born and educated in Marburg, Germany, where he studied under MARTIN HEIDEGGER (see also Vol. 5). Shortly after World War II, he was appointed professor of philosophy at Heidelberg University, a position that he held for almost 20 years, until he retired in 1968. His work seeks a recovery of the Greek sense of a comprehensive and coherent worldview, which he believes has been lost in the fragmentation of modern industrial culture. Gadamer has written major studies of PLATO (see also Vol. 3), ARISTOTLE (see also Vol. 3), and GEORG HEGEL (see also Vol. 3). He is known for opposing science as it is developed and valued in Enlightenment thought.

Gadamer's major contribution has been his work in hermeneutics, an approach that seeks to liberate the humanistic interpretation of experience from the strictures of science and technology, challenging the doctrine that truth is correspondence between an external fact and an idea in the mind of a subject. In place of mechanistic perspectives that regard nature as nothing but raw material for human manipulation, philosophical hermeneutics aims to develop a broader interpretation of experience by showing that all experience is conditioned by history. Thus, various investigations of the same subject can lead to different conclusions. Only interpretation provides the means to understand how this can occur and also to open culture once again to the voices of art. As developed by Gadamer, hermeneutics engages tradition critically so that culture can become alert to its own moral horizons and thereby restore a continuity of thought and practice.

BOOKS BY GADAMER

Dialogue and Dialectic. 1968. Trans. by P. C. Smith. Yale U. Pr. 1980 $32.50. ISBN 0-300-02126-7. A major hermeneutical interpretation of Plato.

Hegel's Dialectic. 1971. Trans. by P. C. Smith. Yale U. Pr. 1982 $11.00. ISBN 0-300-02842-3. Interpretations of important themes in Hegel.

The Idea of the Good in Platonic-Aristotelian Philosophy. Yale U. Pr. 1988 $11.00. ISBN 0-300-04114-4. ". . . how it is that Aristotle offers serious criticisms of Plato's theory of ideas, and yet essentially accepts . . . the idea of the good . . ." (*Review of Metaphysics*).

Philosophical Apprenticeships. 1977. Trans. by Robert R. Sullivan. MIT Pr. 1987 $25.00. ISBN 0-262-07092-8. Hermeneutical investigations of philosophical influences.

Philosophical Hermeneutics. 1967. U. CA Pr. 1976 $12.95. ISBN 0-520-03475-9. Gadamer's theory of interpretation; a good introduction to his method.

Plato's Dialectical Ethics. 1968. Trans. by Robert M. Wallace. Yale U. Pr. 1991 $27.50. ISBN 0-300-04807-6. An interpretation of Plato's Philebus.

Reason in the Age of Science. 1976. Trans. by Frederick G. Lawrence. MIT Pr. 1982 $10.95. ISBN 0-262-57061-0. A critique of scientific method.

The Relevance of the Beautiful. Ed. by Robert Bernasconi. Cambridge U. Pr. 1987 $14.95. ISBN 0-521-33953-7. Essays on aesthetics, which combine to form a review of Gadamer's work.

Truth and Method. Ed. by Donald G. Marshall and Joel C. Weinsheimer. Continuum 1993 $19.95. ISBN 0-8264-0585-1. Profound epistemological inquiry into the status of truth as regards science and humanistic scholarship.

BOOKS ABOUT GADAMER

Palmer, Richard E. *Hermeneutics.* Northwestern U. Pr. 1969 $12.95. ISBN 0-8101-0459-8. An advanced study; relates Habermas to Heidegger and to his nineteenth-century influences.

Silverman, Hugh J., ed. *Gadamer and Hermeneutics.* Routledge 1991 $45.00. ISBN 0-415-90373-4. A collection of essays by various scholars, including one by the edtor entitled "Interpreting the Interpretive Text."

Sullivan, Robert R. *Political Hermeneutics: The Early Thinking of Hans-Georg Gadamer.* Pa. St. U. Pr. 1990 $22.50. ISBN 0-271-0670-6

Warnke, Georgia. *Gadamer: Hermeneutics, Tradition, and Reason. Key Contmporary Thinkers Ser.* Stanford U. Pr. 1987 $35.00. ISBN 0-8047-1433-9. A good systematic account of Gadamer's views.

Weinsheimer, Joel. *Gadamer's Hermeneutics.* Yale U. Pr. 1988 $13.95. ISBN 0-300-04135-7. A controversial exposition; accessible to nonspecialists.

Wright, Kathleen, ed. *Festivals of Interpretation.* State U. NY Pr. 1990 $44.50. ISBN 0-7914-0377-7. A collection of papers presenting an interdisciplinary interpretation of Gadamer's work.

GOODMAN, NELSON. 1906–

Nelson Goodman's work develops themes in philosophy of science, mind, art, and language. Born in Massachusetts, he was educated at Harvard University and had an early career as an art dealer. After military service during World War II, he chose the academic life and taught at the University of Pennsylvania and Brandeis University before returning to Harvard in 1968.

Goodman's early work grows out of logical positivism. His paradox presents a difficulty for inductive logic. It is developed by showing that an empirical statement can be expressed by more than one set of words and that its degree of confirmation can depend on the words used to express it—not solely on its content or the supporting evidence. Scientific method thus intersects the philosophy of language. On this basis, Goodman develops a sophisticated nominalism (a view stressing the power of language to determine meaning), which remains solidly within the analytic tradition. His philosophy of language also develops themes of construction and simplicity.

Goodman's later work contains an original treatment of representation. In asking how an original can be represented in perception, language, or art, he argues that there is no straightforward relation between the original and its representation. Understanding a photograph as a representation, for example, is neither simple nor intuitive. Representations, to be understood as such, must be interpreted instead within a network of more or less conventional rules.

BOOKS BY GOODMAN

Fact, Fiction and Forecast. 1954. HUP 1983 $14.50. ISBN 0-674-29070-4. Goodman's important original work on inductive logic.

Languages of Art. 1968. Hackett Pub. 1976 $32.50. ISBN 0-915144-35-2. Analytic philosophy of art at its best.

Of Mind and Other Matters. HUP 1984 $19.50. ISBN 0-674-63125-0. A collection of essays on philosophy of mind and other metaphysical, epistemological, and aesthetic themes, elaborated with unmatched logical precision.

Problems and Projects. Hackett Pub. 1973 $37.95. ISBN 0-915144-37-9. Issues at the frontier of analytic philosophy.

The Structure of Appearance. 1951. Kluwer Ac. 1977 $80.00. ISBN 90-277-0773-1. A technical treatise on phenomenalism and ontology written from the perspective of Carnap's philosophy of language.

Ways of Worldmaking. Hackett Pub. 1978 $24.50. ISBN 0-915144-52-2. A pluralistic theory of philosophical systems.

BOOKS ABOUT GOODMAN

Elgin, Catherine Z. *With Reference to Reference.* Hackett Pub. 1983 $29.50. ISBN 0-915145-52-9. ". . . weaves Goodmanian insights into a comprehensive extensional theory of reference. . . shows how . . . aesthetic contexts can account for the ways symbols function elsewhere" (*The Philosopher's Index*).

Martin, Richard M. *Pragmatics, Truth, and Language.* Kluwer Ac. 1979 $75.00. ISBN 90-277-0992-0. A technical critique of Goodman's epistemology presented by a prominent analytic philosopher.

HABERMAS, JÜRGEN. 1929–

Jürgen Habermas believes that a comprehensive assessment of epistemology can be done only by locating the analysis within its wider social and historical context. Habermas was born in Düsseldorf, Germany, was educated at Marburg and Bonn universities, and has held several important university positions in Germany, most notably the chair of philosophy at Frankfurt University. He is a leading advocate of critical theory as it grew out of the work of THEODOR ADORNO, HERBERT MARCUSE, and the Frankfurt School.

His treatment of critical theory observes that epistemology, taken as an independent discipline, cannot achieve the objectivity it seeks because it labors under subjective conditions. In attempting to reestablish the lost connections between philosophy and social practice, Habermas has developed a negative assessment of positivism, doctrinaire Marxism, and technological society. He thinks that contemporary higher education, with its emphasis on technology, is the servant of capitalism and that it will be unable to contribute to the growth of knowledge until it becomes independent.

BOOKS BY HABERMAS

Communication and the Evolution of Society. Trans. by Thomas McCarthy. Beacon Pr. 1979 $16.00. ISBN 0-8070-1513-X. The role of language in society, a forerunner of the *Theory of Communicative Action.*

Jürgen Habermas on Society and Politics: A Reader. Ed. and trans. by Steven Seidman. Beacon Pr. 1989 $18.00. ISBN 0-8070-2001-X. An anthology that brings together, in one volume, Habermas's most important writings on society, the state, and social theory.

Knowledge and Human Interests. Trans. by Jeremy Shapiro. Beacon Pr. 1971 $15.00. ISBN 0-8070-1541-5. A difficult but essential discussion of epistemology; Habermas's most widely cited book.

Legitimation Crisis. Trans. by Thomas McCarthy. Beacon Pr. 1975 $13.00. ISBN 0-8070-1521-0. A critique of the establishment and its claims of authority.

Moral Consciousness and Communicative Action. Trans. by Christian Lenhardt and Shierry Nicholsen. 1983. MIT Pr. 1990 $27.50. ISBN 0-262-08192-X. Habermas attempts to refute skepticism in ethics, discussing MacIntyre, Rawls, Strawson, and others.

The New Conservatism. Trans. by Shierry W. Nicholsen. MIT Pr. 1990 $27.50. ISBN 0-262-08188-1. Essays and interviews, cultural criticism, and history.

On the Logic of the Social Sciences. Trans. by Shierry Nicholsen and Jerry Stark. MIT Pr. 1988 $29.95. ISBN 0-262-081776. Methodology and critique of the social sciences.

The Philosophical Discourse of Modernity. Trans. by Frederick G. Lawrence. MIT Pr. 1990 $15.95. ISBN 0-262-58102-7. Twelve lectures on Habermas's view of the rise and fall of rationalism in Western thought.

Post Metaphysical Thinking. MIT Pr. 1992 $22.50. ISBN 0-262-08209-8. Philosophy and twentieth-century civilization.

The Structural Transformation of the Public Sphere. Trans. by Thomas Burger. MIT Pr. 1991 $14.95. ISBN 0-262-58108-6. Subtitled "An Inquiry into a Category of Bourgeois Society," this is a seminal work of broad interest to social theorists, political theorists, and others.

Theory and Practice. Trans. by John Viertel. Beacon Pr. 1973 $14.00. ISBN 0-8070-1527-X. After *Knowledge and Human Interest*, Habermas's most widely cited work; a hermeneutics of philosophy of action.

The Theory of Communicative Action. Trans. by Thomas McCarthy. 2 vols. Beacon Pr. $40.00 ea. Vol. 1 *Reason and the Rationalization of Society.* 1985. ISBN 0-8070-1506-7. Vol. 2 *Lifeworld and System.* 1989. ISBN 0-8070-1400-1. Habermas's most significant mature work; quite obscure.

Toward a Rational Society. Trans. by Jeremy Shapiro. Beacon Pr. 1970 $11.00. ISBN 0-80780-4177-7. A short book that uses critical theory to discuss the student movement of the 1960s.

BOOKS ABOUT HABERMAS

Benhabib, Seyla. *Critique, Norm, and Utopia.* Col. U. Pr. 1987 $18.00. ISBN 0-231-06165-X. Habermas and critical theory related to Hegel, Kant, and social ethics.

Bernstein, Richard, ed. *Habermas and Modernity.* MIT Pr. 1985 $25.00. ISBN 0-262-02227-3. Essays by experts, with a good introduction.

Braaten, Jane. *Habermas's Critical Theory of Society. Philosphy of the Social Sciences Ser.* State U. NY Pr. 1991 $44.50. ISBN 0-7914-0759-4. A good introduction to his work.

Calhoun, Craig, ed. *Habermas and the Public Sphere.* MIT Pr. 1992 $45.00. ISBN 0-262-03183-3. A collection of scholarly essays on the relationship between civil society and public life.

Geuss, R. *The Idea of a Critical Theory.* Cambridge U. Pr. 1981 $12.95. ISBN 0-521-28422-8. An indispensable but advanced critical study; study of the ideology of Habermas and the Frankfurt School.

Held, David. *Introduction to Critical Theory.* U. CA Pr. 1980 $47.50. ISBN 0-520-04121-6. The historical context of Habermas's philosophy, along with a critical review of its themes.

Holub, Robert C. *Jürgen Habermas.* Routledge 1991 $49.95. ISBN 0-415-02208-8. Habermas as social critic and social philosopher.

Ingram, David B. *Habermas and the Dialectic of Reason*. Yale U. Pr. 1987 $35.00. ISBN 0-300-03680-9. A critique of critical theory.

Keat, Russell. *The Politics of Social Theory*. U. Ch. Pr. 1981 $9.00. ISBN 0-226-42876-1. An assessment of critical theory in its relation to positivism and psychoanalysis.

McCarthy, Thomas A. *The Critical Theory of Jürgen Habermas*. MIT Pr. 1978 $17.50. ISBN 0-262-63073-7. A standard work; the first major study of Habermas in English and still one of the best.

Rasmussen, David M. *Reading Habermas*. Blackwell Pubs. 1990 $47.95. ISBN 0-631-15273. A comprehensive survey, with extensive bibliography by Rene Gortzen.

Thompson, John B. *Studies in the Theory of Ideology*. U. CA Pr. 1985 $47.50. ISBN 0-520-05411-3. An advanced examination; hermeneutics, ideology, and Habermas related to social structure, violence, and other topics.

Thompson, John B., and David Held, eds. *Habermas: Critical Debates*. MIT Pr. 1982 $37.50. ISBN 0-262-20043-0. Essays on Habermas's social theory, with his reply.

White, Stephen K. *The Recent Work of Jürgen Habermas*. Cambridge U. Pr. 1988 $42.95. ISBN 0-521-34360-7. Emphasizes Habermas's treatment of reason, justice, and modernity.

HESSE, MARY B. 1924–

As a philosopher of science, Mary B. Hesse defends scientific methods and objectivity against their recent critics. Her work is particularly informed by the historical and social dimensions of science and by its differences from ideology.

Educated in London, Hesse taught mathematics at Leeds University and taught history and philosophy of science in London before receiving a faculty appointment at Cambridge University in 1960. A fellow of the British Academy, she has been president of the Philosophy of Science Association and a Gifford lecturer.

Concerned with the differences between science and other forms of thought, Hesse argues that science, at least in its limited and practical contexts, approximates truth. According to this view, the natural sciences produce convergent, if provisional, descriptions of nature. Thus, they stand in contrast to social sciences, which tend to incorporate moral assumptions in their methodology.

BOOKS BY HESSE

Applications of Inductive Logic. (ed.) OUP 1979 o.p. A collection of technical essays.

The Construction of Reality. (coauthored with Michael A. Arbib). Cambridge U. Pr. 1986 $47.95. ISBN 0-521-32689-3. Gifford lectures; advanced, analytical treatment of traditional philosophical issues.

Forces and Fields. 1962. Greenwood 1970 $38.50. ISBN 0-8371-3366-1. History of science viewed as a succession of conceptual frameworks; engages Kuhn's *The Structure of Scientific Revolutions*.

Models and Analogies in Science. U. of Notre Dame Pr. 1966 o.p. Addresses the role of models and analogies in the construction of scientific theories.

Revolutions and Reconstructions in the Philosophy of Science. Ind. U. Pr. 1980 o.p. Further considerations of history of science, with particular reference to Kuhn and Feyerabend.

Science and the Human Imagination. TPI PA 1953 o.p. A discussion of creativity in science.

The Structure of Scientific Inference. U. CA Pr. 1974 o.p. A treatise on the relation between scientific observations and the credibility of hypotheses.

BOOKS ABOUT HESSE

Hollis, Martin, and Steven Lukes, eds. *Rationality and Relativism*. MIT Pr. 1983 $15.95. ISBN 0-262-58061-6. A far less pedestrian collection of papers than the typical anthology; relates Hesse's themes to the social sciences.

Mulkay, M. J. *Science and the Sociology of Knowledge.* Ind. U. Pr. 1991 $39.95. ISBN 0-253-33933-2. Hesse's work as applied to sociology of knowledge.

KUHN, THOMAS S. 1922–

Thomas S. Kuhn's work is best described as a normative historiography of science. He was educated at Harvard University, where in 1949 he completed a doctorate in physics. As a student, he was impressed by the differences between scientific method, as conventionally taught, and the way science actually works. Before moving to the Massachusetts Institute of Technology in 1979, he taught at Harvard University, the University of California at Berkeley, and Princeton University.

Kuhn's most celebrated contribution to the philosophy of science is his controversial idea of paradigms and paradigm shifts. A paradigm is understood as a widely shared theoretical framework within which scientific research is conducted. According to Kuhn, science normally develops more or less smoothly within such a paradigm until an accumulation of difficulties reduces its effectiveness. The paradigm finally breaks down in a crisis, which is followed by the formation of a radically new paradigm in a so-called scientific revolution. The new paradigm is accepted, even though it might neither resolve all of the accumulated difficulties nor explain the data better than the older paradigm that it replaces. We find examples of paradigm shifts in the work of COPERNICUS, (see Vol. 5), GALILEO (see also Vol. 5), ISAAC NEWTON (see also Vol. 5), CHARLES DARWIN (see Vol. 5), and others. Since its original publication in 1962, *The Structure of Scientific Revolutions* undoubtedly has been the single most influential book in the philosophy of science.

BOOKS BY KUHN

Black-Body Theory and the Quantum Discontinuity, 1894–1912. 1918. U. Ch. Pr. 1987 $18.95. ISBN 0-226-45800-8. An important historical study of the early development of modern physics.
The Copernican Revolution. 1957. HUP 1959 $10.95. ISBN 0-674-17103-9. An historical study of how astronomy has influenced Western thought.
The Essential Tension. U. Ch. Pr. 1979 $13.95. ISBN 0-226-45806-7. A collection of essays.
The Structure of Scientific Revolutions. 1962. U. Ch. Pr. 1970 $19.95. ISBN 0-226-45803-2. Kuhn's most important book; the most influential recent book in the philosophy of science.

BOOKS ABOUT KUHN

Barnes, Barry. *T. S. Kuhn and Social Sciences.* Col. U. Pr. 1982 $40.50. ISBN 0-231-05436-X. An important study of the influence of Kuhn's work on the social sciences, written by a leading sociologist of knowledge.
Gutting, Gary, ed. *Paradigms and Revolutions.* U. of Notre Dame Pr. 1980 o.p. An excellent collection of papers that survey the scope of Kuhn's work and trace its applications to other fields.

MACINTYRE, ALASDAIR C. 1929–

Although he is most widely known for his book *After Virtue* (1981), with its critique of reason and ethics, Alasdair MacIntyre writes in other areas of philosophy as well, including philosophical psychology, political theory, and philosophy of religion. Born in Scotland, he was educated at Manchester, London, and Oxford universities. In 1969 he went to the United States, where he has taught at Brandeis, Boston, and Vanderbilt universities. Since 1988, when he also delivered the Gifford lectures, MacIntyre has taught at the University of Notre Dame.

After Virtue is one of the most widely discussed of all recent books on moral philosophy. It is the culmination of MacIntyre's deep engagement with the history of ethics. In it he argues that modern ethical theory, as it has developed since the seventeenth century, has been exposed by FRIEDRICH NIETZSCHE (see also Vol. 2) as conceptually bankrupt. To find an alternative, he looks to ancient Greece and especially to ARISTOTLE's (see also Vol. 3) concept of virtue. Although his critics consider this alternative to be something of an impossible dream, MacIntyre argues that it is central to a recovery of ethics.

BOOKS BY MACINTYRE

After Virtue. 1981. U. of Notre Dame Pr. 1984 $11.95. ISBN 0-268-00611-3. The most widely discussed recent book on ethics.

Against the Self-Images of the Age. U. of Notre Dame Pr. 1978 $11.95. ISBN 0-268-00587-7. A collection of critical essays on ideology and its relation to philosophy.

Herbert Marcuse. Viking Penguin 1970 o.p. A sharp but brilliant portrait of a major contemporary social critic and philosopher.

Marxism and Christianity. 1953. U. of Notre Dame Pr. 1984 $7.95. ISBN 0-268-01358-6. A critical comparison.

Secularization and Moral Change. OUP 1967 o.p.

A Short History of Ethics. Macmillan 1966 $9.95. ISBN 0-02-087260-7. Perhaps the best short book on the history of ethical theories.

Three Rival Versions of Moral Enquiry. U. of Notre Dame Pr. 1990 $24.95. ISBN 0-268-01871-5. Gifford lectures; MacIntyre's view of what intellectual life in the academy should be.

The Unconscious. Humanities 1958 o.p. A critique of psychoanalysis.

Whose Justice? Which Rationality? U. of Notre Dame Pr. 1989 $22.95. ISBN 0-268-01942-8. A major study, historically oriented, but not as innovative as *After Virtue*.

MARCUSE, HERBERT. 1898–1979

Herbert Marcuse is the foremost American interpreter of KARL MARX (see also Vol. 3). Born in Berlin, he was educated at the Universities of Freiburg and Berlin. He migrated to the United States in 1934 as a refugee from the Nazis and became a U.S. citizen in 1940. During World War II, he served the U.S. government as a consultant. Before moving to the University of California at San Diego in 1965, Marcuse taught at Columbia and Brandeis universities. During the student movements of the 1960s and 1970s, he was regarded as a hero by many members of the New Left. In a 1968 interview in *The New York Times Magazine*, he was quoted as saying, "I am optimistic, because I believe that never in the history of humanity have the resources necessary to create a free society existed to such a degree. I am pessimistic because I believe that the established societies—capitalist society in particular—are totally organized and mobilized against this possibility."

Marcuse condemned totalitarian government while openly embracing class struggle and revolution—a position that provoked censure from both ends of the political spectrum. His interpretation of Marxism, influenced by critical theory and the Frankfurt School, opposed blind ideology. At the same time, Marcuse saw the pervasive force of power and wealth as self-serving and corrupting influences. Artistic expression, for example, is tamed by the dead hand of the status quo, which turns it into an avant-garde commodity with its celebrity of the moment. Art thus loses its prophetic voice to a homogenized and safe mass-produced culture. Modern technological society thus reduces the richness of human experience to the ideological flatness of "one-dimensional man"—a key Marcuse concept.

BOOKS BY MARCUSE

The Aesthetic Dimension. Beacon Pr. 1978 $11.00. ISBN 0-8070-1519-9. A rather difficult book on art and aesthetics that offers a Marxist interpretation of this subject.

Counterrevolution and Revolt. Beacon Pr. 1972 $10.95. ISBN 0-8070-1533-4. Aesthetics and philosophy of nature related to prospects for world revolution.

A Critique of Pure Tolerance. (coauthored with Robert Paul Wolff). Beacon Pr. 1965 o.p. Marcuse's essay "Repressive Tolerance" is a short and clear starting point for those familiar with liberalism mostly in the tradition of John Stuart Mill.

Eros and Civilization. Beacon Pr. 1974 $14.00. ISBN 0-8070-1555-5. A synthesis of Freud and Marx; a basic text for the American New Left.

An Essay on Liberation. Beacon Pr. 1969 $11.00. ISBN 0-8070-0595-9. An explosive critique of conservative capitalism and a utopian vision of a free society.

From Luther to Popper. Routledge Chapman & Hall 1983 $15.95. ISBN 0-86091-781-9. Essays on intellectual history; uneven.

Hegel's Ontology. MIT Pr. 1987 $37.50. ISBN 0-262-13221-4. Historicity and metaphysics in Hegel; a more technical work than *Reason and Revolution*; less ideological than much of Marcuse's work.

One-Dimensional Man. 1964. Beacon Pr. 1966 $10.95. ISBN 0-8070-1575-X. A brilliant book, which considers the social sciences, logic, linguistics, literature, and the arts; Marcuse's most widely read work.

Reason and Revolution. 1941. Humanities 1954 $17.50. ISBN 0-391-02999-1. An influential study of Hegel, seeing Hegel as a positive force in social theory.

Revolution or Reform. (coauthored with Karl Popper). 1974. Transaction Pubs. 1976 $14.95. ISBN 0-89044-020-4. A polemical exchange between the two philosophers.

Soviet Marxism. Col. U. Pr. 1985 $17.00. ISBN 0-231-08379-3. A critical study.

BOOKS ABOUT MARCUSE

Alford, C. Fred. *Science and the Revenge of Nature.* U. Press Fla. 1985 $29.95. ISBN 0-8130-0817-4. Scholarly critique of science as interpreted by Marcuse and Habermas.

Freidman, George. *The Political Philosophy of the Frankfurt School.* Cornell Univ. Pr. 1981 $39.95. ISBN 0-8014-1279-X

Kellner, Douglas. *Herbert Marcuse and the Crisis of Marxism.* U. CA Pr. 1985 $38.50. ISBN 0-520-05176-9. A sympathetic critique of Marcuse's goal of a free and humane society.

Lind, Peter. *Marcuse and Freedom.* St. Martin 1985 $27.50. ISBN 0-312-51445-X. A study of Marcuse's treatment of liberation.

Lipshires, Sidney. *Marcuse's Dilemma.* Schenkman Bks. Inc. 1974 $11.95. ISBN 0-87073-677-9. An intellectual portrait emphasizing the background of Marcuse's thought.

Lukes, Timothy J. *The Flight into Inwardness.* Susquehanna U. Pr. 1985 $24.50. ISBN 0-941664-04-X. A highly interpretive but lucid summary of Marcuse's relation of art to freedom.

MacIntyre, Alasdair. *Herbert Marcuse.* Viking Penguin 1970 o.p. A brilliant critical portrait.

Pippin, Robert, and others. *Marcuse: Critical Theory and the Promise of Utopia.* Greenwood 1987 $47.95. ISBN 0-89789-106-6. A collection of specialized essays.

Schoolman, Morton. *The Imaginary Witness.* 1980. NYU Pr. 1984 $20.00. ISBN 0-8147-7833-X. A judicious evaluation of Marcuse's critical theory.

POPPER, SIR KARL RAIMUND. 1902–

Although he writes widely in philosophy, Sir Karl Raimund Popper is best known for his thesis that an empirical statement is meaningless unless conditions can be specified that could show it to be false. He was born and educated in Vienna, where he was associated with, although not actually a member of, the Vienna Circle. Two years after the German publication of his *Logic of Scientific Discovery* (1935), he left Austria for New Zealand, where he was senior lecturer at the University of Canterbury. In 1945 he moved to England and began a distinguished career at the London School of Economics and Political Science.

According to Popper, there is no "method of discovery" in science. His view holds that science advances by brilliant but unpredictable conjectures that then stand up well against attempts to refute them. This view was roundly criticized by more dogmatic positivists, on the one hand, and by FEYERABEND and KUHN, on the other. In 1945 he published *The Open Society and Its Enemies*, which condemns PLATO (see also Vol. 3), GEORG HEGEL (see also Vol. 3), and KARL MARX (see also Vol. 3) as progenitors of totalitarianism and opponents of freedom. The scholarship that underpins this book remains controversial. Popper's later works continue his interest in philosophy of science and also develop themes in epistemology and philosophy of mind. He is particularly critical of historicism, which he regards as an attitude that fosters a deplorable tendency toward deterministic thinking in the social sciences.

BOOKS BY POPPER

Conjectures and Refutations. HarpC 1968 o.p. An original treatise on scientific method and the growth of knowledge.

In Search of a Better World. Routledge 1992 $25.00. ISBN 0-415-087740-0. A collection of Popper's essays and lectures; Popper's view of himself as a public philosopher.

The Logic of Scientific Discovery. 1935. HarpC 1968 o.p. Popper's first major work; an essential book in the development of logical empiricism.

Objective Knowledge. OUP 1972 $16.95. ISBN 0-19-875024-2. A good introduction to evolutionary and realistic epistemology.

The Open Society and Its Enemies. 1945. 2 vols. Princeton U. Pr. 1966 $16.95 ea. Vol. 1 *The Spell of Plato.* ISBN 0-691-01968-1. Vol. 2 *The High Tide of Prophecy.* ISBN 0-691-01972-X. A controversial but widely read work.

The Open Universe. Rowman 1982 $21.00. ISBN 0-8476-7388-X. A collection of essays adding to *The Logic of Scientific Discovery* and supporting free will against philosophical determinism.

Popper Selections. Ed. by David Miller. Princeton U. Pr. 1985 $57.50. ISBN 0-691-07287-6. A good starting point for an understanding of Popper.

The Poverty of Historicism. 1961. HarpC 1977 o.p. Popper's criticism at its destructive best.

Quantum Theory and the Schism in Physics. Ed. by W. W. Bartley. Rowman 1984 $21.00. ISBN 0-8476-7389-8. A collection of Popper's technical essays.

Realism and the Aim of Science. Ed. by W. W. Bartley. Rowman 1983 $55.00. ISBN 0-8476-7015-5. Another collection of Popper's essays, covering probability, induction, scientific inference, and Popper's replies to critics.

The Self and Its Brain. (coauthored with Sir John Eccles). Springer-Verlag 1985 $67.00. ISBN 0-387-08307-3. A discussion of the mind-body problem that attempts to incorporate an understanding of the brain and its functions; idiosyncratic.

The Subtle Connection between the Theory of Experience and the Logic of Science. 2 vols. Found. Class. Reprints 1985 $167.50. ISBN 0-89901-227-2. A specialized work in the philosophy of science.

Unended Quest. Open Court 1982 $12.95. ISBN 0-87548-366-6. A revision of Popper's inspiring intellectual biography; first published in *The Library of Living Philosophers*.

BOOKS ABOUT POPPER

Berkson, William, and John Wettersten. *Learning from Error.* Open Court 1984 $16.95. ISBN 0-912050-74-8. A specialized application of Popper's work to educational psychology.

Burke, T. E. *The Philosophy of Popper*. 1983. St. Martin 1988 $22.95. ISBN 0-7190-0911-1.
   A critical study of Popper's ideas "on philosophy, science, pseudo-science, historicism, freedom" (*The Philosopher's Index*).
Magee, Bryan. *Philosophy and the Real World*. Open Court 1985 $12.95. ISBN 0-87548-
   436-0. A brief, accurate introductory guide.
Munz, Peter. *Our Knowledge of the Growth of Knowledge*. Routledge 1986 $34.95. ISBN
   0-7102-0460-4. A defense of Popper's philosophy of science; requires prior familiarity
   with his work.
O'Hear, Anthony. *Karl Popper*. Methuen 1982 o.p. ". . . concerned mainly with Popper's
   epistemology . . . clearly written and competent" (*Library Journal*).
Schilpp, Paul A., ed. *The Philosophy of Karl Popper*. 2 vols. Open Court 1974 $39.95. ISBN
   0-87548-353-4. An essential book; Popper's intellectual biography, original essays on
   his work, Popper's reply, bibliography; in *The Library of Living Philosophers* series.
William Douglas E. *Truth, Hope, and Power*. U. of Toronto Pr. 1989 $35.00. ISBN 0-8020-
   2643-5. An excellent critique; requires familiarity with Popper's work.

PUTNAM, HILARY. 1926–

According to John Passmore, Hilary Putnam's work is a "history of recent
philosophy in outline" (*Recent Philosophers*). He adds that writing "about
'Putnam's philosophy' is like trying to capture the wind with a fishing-net."
Born in Chicago and educated at the University of Pennsylvania and the
University of California at Los Angeles, Putnam taught at Northwestern
University, Princeton University, and the Massachusetts Institute of Technology
before moving to Harvard University in 1965. In his early years at Harvard, he
was an outspoken opponent of the war in Vietnam.

Although he writes in the idiom of analytic philosophy, Putnam addresses
major themes relating science to ethics and epistemology. If these themes are
reminiscent of DAVID HUME—as, for that matter, is much of analytic philosophy—his treatment of them is not. Putnam's work is far more profoundly
shaped by recent work in logic, foundations of mathematics, and science than
would have been possible for Hume; Putnam has contributed to each. He differs
from Hume and stands more in the tradition of WILLARD QUINE and American
pragmatism in his treatment of the crucial distinctions between analytic and
synthetic statements and between facts and values. Both distinctions, sharply
made by Hume, are claimed by Putnam not to be absolute. He attempts to show,
for example, that basic concepts of philosophy, science, and mathematics all are
interrelated, so that mathematics bears more similarity to empirical reasoning
than is customarily acknowledged.

BOOKS BY PUTNAM

Many Faces of Realism. Open Court 1988 $8.95. ISBN 0-8126-9043-3. Lectures, accessible
   by comparison to other works by Putnam; builds an argument for metaphysical
   relativism.
Philosophical Papers. 3 vols. Cambridge U. Pr. Vols. 1 and 2 1979 $24.95 ea. ISBN 0-521-
   29551-3. Vol. 3 1981 $42.95. ISBN 0-521-23035-7. Technical, but an essential
   collection of Putnam's work on mathematics, philosophy of mind, metaphysics,
   methodology, and epistemology.
Philosophy of Logic. HarpC 1971 o.p. An important but technical contribution.
Philosophy of Mathematics. Ed. with Hilary Benacerraf. Cambridge U. Pr. 1984 $74.95.
   ISBN 0-521-22796-8. A collection of papers.
Realism with a Human Face. HUP 1990 $37.50. ISBN 0-674-74950-2. Profound restate-
   ment and argument on behalf of philosophical realism.
Renewing Philosophy. HUP 1992 $25.00. ISBN 0-674-76093-X. Gifford lectures; evolu-
   tionary biology as irrelevant to philosophy of language; a general critique of what

Putnam sees as the undue deference given to science by recent philosophy; assumes
some reader familiarity with recent work.

Representation and Reality. MIT Pr. 1988 $26.00. ISBN 0-262-16108-7. Technical; a
further development of Putnam's pragmatic realism, with a critique of his own
earlier work.

Books about Putnam

Boolos, George, ed. *Meaning and Method.* Cambridge U. Pr. 1990 $59.95. ISBN 0-521-
36083-8. A collection of papers; assumes familiarity with Putnam's work.

Salmon, Nathan U. *Reference and Essence.* Princeton U. Pr. 1981 o.p. A study of
Putnam's realism and philosophy of language.

QUINE, WILLARD VAN ORMAN. 1908–

Willard Van Orman Quine has made lasting contributions to epistemology,
ontology, and mathematical logic. Born in Akron, Ohio, he graduated from
Oberlin College and proceeded to Harvard University, where he completed his
doctorate under the eminent philosopher and mathematician Alfred North
Whitehead. A traveling fellowship took Quine to the universities of Warsaw and
Vienna, then great European centers for logic, and included work with Rudolph
Carnap (see also Vol. 5) at the University of Prague. He returned to a teaching
career at Harvard University, from which he retired in 1978.

Using the rigorous tools of formal logic, Quine expresses himself in a fine, if
spare, prose style. In analyzing language, he finds defects in the epistemological
underpinnings of logical positivism. He undermines the distinction between
analytical and synthetic statements, and he questions the reduction of empirical
statements to unequivocal reports of sensory experience. He shows, instead,
that empirical statements can be meaningful only within the larger conceptual
structures to which they belong. This holistic approach to what Quine calls "the
web of belief" is accompanied by a nominalistic view of ontology.

Books by Quine

Elementary Logic. HUP 1981 $11.00. ISBN 0-674-24450-8. A terse introduction to the
subject.

From a Logical Point of View. 1961. HUP 1980 $16.95. ISBN 0-674-32350. Nine essays on
logic and philosophy, including Quine's famous "Two Dogmas of Empiricism."

Mathematical Logic. 1940. HUP 1982 $12.95. ISBN 0-674-55451-5. An advanced work and
a key contribution.

Methods of Logic. 1950. HUP 1982 $12.95. ISBN 0-674-57176-2. A technical treatment.

Ontological Relativity. 1969. Col. U. Pr. 1977 $16.00. ISBN 0-231-08357-2. An important
collection of papers on the relation of language to metaphysics.

Philosophy of Logic. 1969. HUP 1986 $7.95. ISBN 0-674-66563-5. A good introduction to
Quine and the subject; accessible to the patient general reader.

Pursuit of Truth. HUP 1990 $17.50. ISBN 0-674-74351-2. A continuation of Quine's
themes and a good general introduction to more specialized topics than are found in
Philosophy of Logic and *The Web of Belief.*

Quiddities. HUP 1987 $9.95. ISBN 0-674-74352-0. Quine's views on 83 topics; "compact,
quick-witted, quirky" (*Choice*).

The Roots of Reference. Open Court 1973 $27.95. ISBN 0-87548-123-X. The Carus
lectures; treats basic ideas of language and meaning.

Set Theory and Its Logic. 1963. HUP 1969 $10.95. ISBN 0-674-80207. A technical
treatment.

Theories and Things. 1981. HUP 1986 $8.95. ISBN 0-674-87926-0. A restatement of
Quine's views on language and ontology.

The Time of My Life. MIT Pr. 1986 $30.00. ISBN 0-262-17003-5. An autobiography that reveals little of Quine's intellectual development; said by *Choice* to be "a dry chronicle."

The Ways of Paradox. HUP 1976 $22.50. ISBN 0-674-94835-1. A collection of specialized essays collected from professional journals.

The Web of Belief. (coauthored with J. S. Ullian). Random 1978 $10.50. ISBN 0-394-32179-0. A good introduction to Quine and epistemology; accessible to the general reader.

Word and Object. MIT Pr. 1960 $12.95. ISBN 0-262-67001-1. A classic of analytic philosophy; Quine's most systematic work.

BOOKS ABOUT QUINE

Dilman, Ilham. *Quine on Ontology, Necessity, and Experience.* State U. NY Pr. 1984 $54.50. ISBN 0-87395-761-X. A negative review of Quine's metaphysics.

Gibson, Roger F. *The Philosophy of W. V. Quine.* U. Press Fla. 1982 $19.50. ISBN 0-685-05101-3. A sympathetic introduction.

Gochet, Paul. *Ascent to Truth.* Philosophia Pr. 1986 $39.00. ISBN 3-88405-050-8. A scholarly monograph by a leading European interpreter of Quine.

Hahn, Lewis E., and Paul Arthur Schilpp, eds. *The Philosophy of W. V. Quine.* Open Court 1986 $44.95. ISBN 0-8126-9010-9. An essential work; a collection of original essays by leading experts, Quine's intellectual autobiography, Quine's response to his critics, and a bibliography of Quine's writings.

Hookway, Christopher. *Quine: Language, Experience, and Reality.* Stanford U. Pr. 1988 $35.00. ISBN 0-847-1386-3. A good introduction to Quine for readers with limited background.

Kirk, Robert. *Translation Determined.* OUP 1986 $42.00. ISBN 0-19-824921-7. A rejection of Quine's thesis that rival linguists working independently could produce mutually incompatible translations of the same text.

Shahan, Robert G., and Chris Swoyer, eds. *Essays on the Philosophy of W. V. Quine.* U. of Okla. Pr. 1979 $19.50. ISBN 0-8061-1516-5. A collection of journal articles.

RAWLS, JOHN B. 1921–

[SEE Chapter 7 in this volume.]

RORTY, RICHARD MCKAY. 1931–

Richard McKay Rorty is the principal American voice of postmodern philosophy. He was born in New York City and educated at the University of Chicago and Yale University. After having taught philosophy at Princeton University for more than 20 years, Rorty became a university professor in humanities at the University of Virginia in 1982. He has been awarded fellowships by the Guggenheim and MacArthur foundations.

In 1967 Rorty published *The Linguistic Turn*, an anthology of twentieth-century philosophy that opens with his 40-page introduction. This work has become a standard introduction to analytic philosophy, and its title names an era.

Despite his early hope for the future of analytic philosophy, Rorty came to doubt its foundations. This doubt prodded him to master American pragmatism as well as continental European work in hermeneutics and deconstruction. This work, in turn, led Rorty to question the entire tradition of Western philosophy.

These doubts are expressed in his second book, *Philosophy and the Mirror of Nature* (1979), which is one of the most widely discussed of all recent American works in philosophy. It announces the death of philosophy as a kind of higher knowledge but recommends its continuance as edification and as a branch of literature. *Choice* proved prophetic in stating that "this bold and provocative book is bound to rank among the most important of the decade."

BOOKS BY RORTY

Consequences of Pragmatism: Essays 1972–1980. U. Minn. Pr. 1982 o.p. Consists of 12 essays that show how Rorty drew upon Nietzsche, Heidegger, Foucault, and Derrida to blend European thought with American pragmatism.

Contingency, Irony and Solidarity. Cambridge U. Pr. 1989 $42.95. ISBN 0-521-35381-5. A difficult but exciting book; argues for the radical contingency of beliefs and values.

The Linguistic Turn. (ed.) 1967. U. Ch. Pr. 1992 $17.95. ISBN 0-226-72569-3. An excellent anthology, the introduction to which established Rorty's reputation as an analytic philosopher.

Objectivity, Realism, and Truth: Philosophical Papers. Cambridge U. Pr. 1990 $42.95. ISBN 0-521-35359-6. Contains 14 papers published between 1980 and 1989. Contends that "Knowledge, including scientific knowledge, is not a matter of truth or falsity, but of acquiring useful habits of action for coping with reality" (*Library Journal*).

Philosophical Papers. 2 vols. Cambridge U. Pr. $42.95 ea. Vol. 1 1990. ISBN 0-521-35369-6. Vol. 2 1991. ISBN 0-521-35370-X. Essays on objectivity, truth, relativism, Heidegger, and other major authors.

Philosophy and the Mirror of Nature. Princeton U. Pr. 1979 $16.95. ISBN 0-691-02016-7. Humorous, subtle, and revolutionary, this book established Rorty's reputation as a postmodern philosopher.

BOOKS ABOUT RORTY

Bhaskar, Roy. *Philosophy and the Idea of Freedom.* Blackwell Pubs. 1991 $47.95. ISBN 0-631-15911-8. A discussion of Rorty's views on realism and ethics as applied to Marxism and the social sciences.

Hollinger, Robert, ed. *Hermeneutics and Praxis.* U. of Notre Dame Pr. 1985 $12.95. ISBN 0-268-01081-1. A collection of papers that examine Rorty, Heidegger, and Gadamer.

Kolenda, Konstantin. *Rorty's Humanistic Pragmatism.* U. Press Fla. 1990 $22.95. ISBN 0-8130-0970-7. A rather demanding critical review.

Malachowski, Alan, ed. *Reading Rorty: Critical Response to Philosophy and the Mirror of Nature.* Blackwell Pubs. 1990 $48.95. ISBN 0-631-16148-1. A collection of scholarly essays.

Nielsen, Kai. *After the Demise of the Tradition.* Westview 1991 $40.00. ISBN 0-8133-8044-8. A study of Rorty as related to critical theory and the future of philosophy.

STRAWSON, PETER F. 1919–

Although the ordinary-language branch of analytic philosophy began as an effort to dissolve philosophy, Peter F. Strawson, who has been one of its major voices, has shown that this approach can be enlarged to address many of the great themes of the Western tradition. Strawson was born in England and educated at Oxford University. After military service during World War II and a brief period of teaching in Wales, he returned to Oxford, where he has remained.

Strawson's *Introduction to Logical Theory* (1952) shows that symbolic logic does not capture the complexity of ordinary language. He therefore argues for a logic of everyday discourse that can capture the conditions under which we use logical construction to express ourselves. He tries to show that some classes of valid arguments are not recognized as such within formal systems and that Aristotelian logic can be defended as preferable to modern logic.

Strawson's emphasis on language continues in his later work, in which he uses linguistic structures to address metaphysics and epistemology. His book on IMMANUEL KANT, for example, uses language to rework a priori knowledge.

Individuals (1959) begins his work in descriptive metaphysics by proposing that the concept of the person be taken as philosophically primitive. This, he believes, would avoid two equally incoherent views, the first being Cartesian dualism, the second being the view that states of consciousness can be discussed without reference to a knowing subject.

BOOKS BY STRAWSON

Analysis and Metaphysics. OUP 1992 $42.50. ISBN 0-19-875117-6. Assumes some background, but an excellent introduction to Strawson; argues against a reductive concept of philosophical analysis and in favor of respecting interconnections among concepts.

The Bounds of Sense. Routledge Chapman & Hall 1966 $7.95. ISBN 0-415-04030-2. Less a commentary on Kant, as it claims, than a treatment, from Strawson's perspective, of their common themes.

Freedom and Resentment. Methuen 1976 o.p. Collection of 12 essays.

Individuals. 1959. Routledge Chapman & Hall 1964 $16.95. ISBN 0-415-05185-1. Strawson's pioneering study, taking ordinary-language philosophy into the field of descriptive metaphysics.

Introduction to Logical Theory. 1952. Methuen 1963 o.p. "Nowhere before have the problems of interpreting as opposed to doing formal logic been so fully and so seriously treated. "(*New Statesman and Nation*)

Logico-Linguistic Papers. Methuen 1974 o.p. Collection of essays on logic and language.

Skepticism and Naturalism. Col. U. Pr. 1985 $28.50. ISBN 0-231-05916-7. Strawson's Woodbridge lectures; a defense of naturalism against skepticism.

Subject and Predicate in Logic and Grammar. Methuen 1974 o.p. Discussion of predication, naming, and the requirements for rules of grammar.

BOOKS ABOUT STRAWSON

Tiles, J. E. *Things That Happen.* Humanities 1981 o.p. A denial of "Strawson's claim that a language could be used to talk about material objects without its speakers having the capacity to talk about events" (*The Philosopher's Index*).

Van Straaten, Zak, ed. *Philosophical Subjects.* OUP 1980 $59.00. ISBN 0-19-824603-X. A collection of 12 original essays covering many aspects of Strawson's work.

TAYLOR, CHARLES. 1931–

Charles Taylor works creatively with material drawn from both analytical and Continental sources. He was born in Montreal, educated at McGill and Oxford universities, and has taught political science and philosophy at McGill since 1961. He describes himself as a social democrat, and he was a founder and editor of the *New Left Review.*

Taylor's work is an example of renewed interest in the great traditional questions of philosophy. It is informed by a vast scope of literature, ranging from PLATO (see also Vol. 3) to JACQUES DERRIDA. More accessible to the average reader than most recent original work in philosophy, Taylor's *oeuvre* centers on questions on philosophical anthropology, that is, on how human nature relates to ethics and society. Taylor develops his themes with an engaging, historically accurate insight.

BOOKS BY TAYLOR

The Ethics of Authenticity. HUP 1992 $17.95. ISBN 0-674-26863-6

The Explanation of Behavior. Humanities 1964 o.p.

Hegel. Cambridge U. Pr. 1977 $27.95. ISBN 0-521-29199-2. An important commentary on the great philosopher.

Hegel and Modern Society. Cambridge U. Pr. 1979 $14.95. ISBN 0-521-29351-0. Partly a condensation of *Hegel* but adds new material on subjectivity and freedom.

The Malaise of Modernity. HUP 1992. ISBN 0-674-54384-X

Multiculturalism and "The Politics of Recognition." Princeton U. Pr. 1992 $14.95. ISBN 0-691-08786-5

Pattern of Politics. Firefly Bks. Ltd. 1970 o.p.

Philosophical Papers. 2 vols. Cambridge U. Pr. 1985. Vol. 1 $59.95. ISBN 0-521-26752-8. Vol. 2 $54.50. ISBN 0-521-26753-6. The importance of values in social science and self-understanding; argues against the reduction of human nature to mechanistic psychology; "indispensable" (*Choice*).

Sources of the Self. HUP 1989 $39.95. ISBN 0-674-82425-3. A splendid discussion of values as they relate to concepts of the self; analyzes the historical development of this concept in Western thought.

Book about Taylor

Wright, Larry. *Teleological Explanations.* U. CA Pr. 1976 o.p. A specialized study of Taylor's *The Explanation of Behavior*, examining the origins and causes of goals in behavior.

PART TWO

RELIGION

CHAPTER 10

Ancient Religions and Philosophies

Gregory D. Alles

The real history of man [humanity] is the history of religions.
—F. MAX MÜLLER

This device was the silliest in all history, especially because the Greeks have
been from very ancient times distinguished from the barbarians by superior
sagacity and freedom from foolishness.
—HERODOTUS, *Histories*

In the sentence quoted immediately above, HERODOTUS (see also Vol. 3) is
preparing the reader for a strange story. He is about to tell how Pisistratus
became tyrant of Athens for the second time (mid-sixth century B.C.). Pisistratus,
the story goes, entered into an alliance by marrying the daughter of his former
enemy, Megacles. Once allied, these two crafty rogues set to work. They hunted
up a beautiful woman six feet tall, dressed her in full armor, and placed her in a
chariot with Pisistratus at her side. Then they sent heralds ahead of the chariot
to proclaim that Athena herself, the patroness of Athens, was escorting the
former tyrant back to her city. The ruse is supposed to have worked. "The
rumor spread throughout the countryside that Athena was bringing back her
favorite, and those in the city, convinced that the woman really was the goddess,
worshiped her and welcomed Pisistratus" (Herodotus 1.60).

Herodotus's tale and his preface to it are in a way analogous to the materials
covered in this chapter and the average reader's likely reaction to them. This
chapter discusses what may loosely be called "ancient religions and philosophies." It contains three main blocks of material: (1) prehistoric religions and
philosophies (from the rise of humanity to the invention of writing); (2) the
religions and philosophies of the ancient urban civilizations of the Mediterranean region and of Middle and South America; and (3) the religions and
philosophies of the indigenous peoples of Australia, Oceania, Africa, and the
Americas.

In part, the chapter title has been adopted for editorial convenience. First, it
is rarely necessary to distinguish philosophy from religion for any of these
peoples. Among them, philosophy as a major, autonomous tradition of thought
is found only in ancient Greece and its cultural legacy (see Chapter 3, "Greek
and Roman Philosophy," in this volume). Ordinarily, the chapter will simply
speak of religion. Furthermore, prehistoric and indigenous religions are not
usually considered "ancient religions," but these religions are extremely
important, and they deserve a place in *The Reader's Adviser*. As a result, the
religions in this chapter are ancient only in a rather vague sense: They do not as

419

such play major roles in what Europeans and North Americans call "the
modern world."

It is futile to try to identify common traits that distinguish these religions from
the kinds of religions discussed in other chapters. What they share the most is
perhaps the analogy to Herodotus and his story. Unlike many of the religions of
Asia, or Judaism, Christianity, and Islam, these ancient religions do not often
convey to the average American reader the metaphysical profundity—moral
rigor or emotive intensity—that evokes our admiration, if at times our confused
admiration. Moreover, the social, economic, political, cultural, and psychological circumstances in which these religions flourished are, unlike those of
minority religions in the United States, usually too remote for us to have a
ready, possibly intuitive grasp of the needs that these beliefs, practices, and
institutions satisfied. It is easy to admire Egyptian or Greek or Aztec "advances"
in science or politics or literature. The average reader is likely to look on the
religions of these people—the worship of the sun or heart sacrifice—as
foolishness and superstition.

This chapter begins with a section on the study of religions. It ends with a set
of individual authors who contribute substantially to knowledge about religions,
either as ancient witnesses or as modern scholars. Several books in these two
sections do not discuss ancient religions at all. Nevertheless, discerning readers
can learn from them strategies and techniques that they can use to make sense
of the religions that follow. They will discover that these are the same strategies
and techniques that the best books on ancient religions—and other religions—
employ.

RELIGIONS AND THE STUDY OF RELIGIONS

In many cases, the ways in which different scholars study religions reflect the
history of their disciplines, especially from the Enlightenment to the present.
There is no entirely satisfactory history of these developments, but several
books are helpful.

DeVries, Jan. *Perspectives in the History of Religions.* U. CA Pr. 1977 $9.95. ISBN 0-520-
03300-0. A confirmed romantic's history of significant movements; screeches to a
halt in the mid-twentieth century.

Jordan, Louis Henry. *Comparative Religion: Its Genesis and Growth.* Scholars Pr. GA
1986 $26.95. ISBN 1-55540-014-0. Often verbose and vapid; a wealth of information
on the nineteenth century for the more serious reader.

Preus, J. Samuel. *Explaining Religion: Criticism and Theory from Bodin to Freud.* Yale U.
Pr. 1991 $45.00. ISBN 0-300-05134-4. Insightful examination of those who would
rather explain religion than understand it; concentrates on representative thinkers,
some of whom are not commonly discussed.

Sharpe, Eric J. *Comparative Religion: A History.* Open Court 1987 $33.95. ISBN 0-8126-
9032-X. Interesting stories about influential persons, as well as summaries of their
ideas.

Strenski, Ivan. *Four Theories of Myth in Twentieth-Century History: Cassirer, Eliade, Levi-
Strauss and Malinowski.* U. of Iowa Pr. 1987 $27.00. ISBN 0-87745-181-8. Examines
four scholars in their historical context to argue that "myth" is an artifact of recent
historical processes.

Problems of Definition and Origin

Nonspecialists occasionally ask scholars of religions two basic questions that
they cannot answer: What is religion, and where does—or did—religion come
from?

Many different definitions of religion have been proposed. Some suggest that scholars should work with a commonsense notion of religion. Others formulate definitions that reflect more sophisticated theories about religion and culture. Still others advocate describing the "family resemblances" that most religions more or less share.

None of these proposals is entirely satisfactory. *Religion* is an English word that grew up in the climate of Judaism, Islam, and especially Christianity. It is in many ways well suited to express the kinds of phenomena that are encountered in these traditions, but cultural phenomena in other parts of the world often do not conform to the Judeo-Christian-Islamic model. Traits that English-speaking people are accustomed to associate with religion may be entirely lacking elsewhere, and many languages do not even have a word for religion. As a result, scholars generally find it more fruitful *not* to define religion. Instead, they use religion as a rough label and develop categories that are appropriate to the purposes and materials they are studying.

Every now and then, the question of the definition of religion gives a little kick. The question of the origin of religion seems to have died. The last half of the nineteenth century was a time of intense fervor about evolution. At that time several theories of the origin of religion were born. The names of some of these theories are still well known. Occasionally they put in an appearance in introductory textbooks, but the theories themselves lost their power to animate scholarly discussions long ago.

"Animism" (formulated by E. B. Taylor) suggested that religion began with the belief that spirits hidden in all sorts of objects were responsible for life and events. "Preanimism" (formulated by R. R. Marett) focused on the emotional encounter with *mana*, a fluid, nonpersonal, powerful but dangerous substance that early humans found they could not manipulate with magic. "Totemism" (formulated by J. F. McLennan) centered on the relations between social groups and animal species that were thought to be their eponymous ancestors. JAMES GEORGE FRAZER conceived of religion as a response of submission before natural phenomena when attempts at magical control had failed.

One occasionally reads that speculations about the origin of religion ceased when scholars discovered they could not refute a very surprising theory, the theory of "original monotheism" (formulated especially by Wilhelm Schmidt beginning in 1912). What actually happened was that scholarly presuppositions and concerns changed. Scholars began to write about particular cultures instead of "culture" and particular religions instead of "religion." They also began to search for complex sociological and psychological forces hidden beneath the surface of appearances that were responsible for religious ideas and behavior. At the same time, many who specialized in the study of religion became fascinated with ideas first developed by FRIEDRICH SCHLEIERMACHER in the early nineteenth century. They looked on each religion as expressing a unique and incomparable experience of the sacred, to be understood and respected in its own right. Finally, prehistorians became increasingly suspicious of the methods their predecessors had used: assuming that a logical sequence from the simplest to the most complex described actual events, and drawing conclusions from contemporary peoples who were "still living in the stone age." Prehistorians began to insist on a critical explication of tangible evidence from the past, but what evidence we have reveals little about religion.

As a result of all these shifts, the question of the origin of religion gradually went out of fashion. Since the 1960s, however, interest has grown in the science of ethology (the study of animal behavior). Scholars have begun to note parallels between patterned animal behavior and human religious rituals. There may be seeds here for a new theory of the origin of religion, but a sustained and vigorous argument has not yet been published.

Baird, Robert D. *Category Formation and the History of Religions*. Mouton 1991 $19.95. ISBN 3-11-012821-7. Eventually endorses Tillich's "ultimate concern"; philosophical discussion probably too complex for the average reader.

Banton, Michael, ed. *Anthropological Approaches to the Study of Religion*. Routledge 1968 $15.95. ISBN 0-422-72510-2. Contains two now classic definitions: Melford Spiro's definition of religion in terms of culturally postulated superhuman beings and Clifford Geertz's notion of religion as a cultural system.

Bellah, Robert N. *Religious Evolution*. Irvington 1991 $1.90. ISBN 0-8290-2641-X. A reprint from *American Sociological Review* (1964), attempting to develop a model of religious evolution cognizant of common twentieth-century criticisms of the approach.

Sharpe, Eric J. *Understanding Religion*. St. Martin 1984 $19.95. ISBN 0-312-83208-7. Proposes a fourfold alternative to Smart's six dimensions.

Smart, Ninian. *The Religious Experience of Mankind*. Scribner 1991. ISBN 0-02-412735-2. An introductory textbook; toward the beginning gives Smart's now well-known "six dimensions of religion."

Smith, Wilfred C. *The Meaning and End of Religion*. Augsburg Fortress 1990 $14.95. ISBN 0-8006-2475-0. Useful discussion of the term *religion* and the problems with it; Smith's solution—"faith" and "cumulative tradition"—has its own drawbacks.

Tillich, Paul. *Systematic Theology*. 3 vols. U. Ch. Pr. 1967 $55.00. ISBN 0-226-80336-8. A major work in philosophical theology that advances a popular definition—religion as the state of being grasped by an "ultimate concern"—in the opening pages to volume one.

Ways to Study Religions

For a general introduction to the many different ways of studying religions, the following anthologies are helpful.

Morris, Brian. *Anthropological Studies of Religion: An Introductory Text*. Cambridge U. Pr. 1987 $54.95. ISBN 0-521-32794-6. Descriptive introduction to modern theories— mostly sociological, psychological, and anthropological—from G.W.F. Hegel and Karl Marx to Claude Lévi-Strauss and other structuralists.

Paden, William E. *Interpreting the Sacred: Ways of Viewing Religion*. Beacon Pr. 1992 $24.95. ISBN 0-8070-7706-2. A useful, readable introduction that discusses the different perspectives from which scholars view religion: psychological, sociological, comparative, theological, and critical.

Waardenburg, Jacques. *Classical Approaches to the Study of Religion: Aims, Methods and Theories of Research*. 2 pts. Mouton 1973–74 pt. 1 $60.00. ISBN 90-279-7226-5. pt. 2 $74.00. ISBN 90-2797-971-5. First part contains small selections from a wide variety of influential scholars of religions, beginning in the mid-nineteenth century; part 2 is a bibliography.

Whaling, Frank, ed. *Contemporary Approaches to the Study of Religion*. 2 vols. Mouton 1984 vol. 1 $59.95. ISBN 3-11-009834-2. vol. 2 $39.95. ISBN 3-11-009836-9. Intended as a companion to Waardenburg (above); a survey of current scholarship.

THEOLOGICAL (CHRISTIAN)

Within a particular religious tradition, there are many possible approaches to other religions. They form a spectrum between two extremes: assimilating one religion to another (because they are thought to be complementary or identical) and polemics (attacking other religions as erroneous and threatening). In the ancient Mediterranean world, the first extreme was by far the more common. The second was the approach that Christians preferred. Christianity made claims that were usually exclusive. At most its ancient adherents considered non-Christian beliefs and practices to be "preparation for the gospel."

Today, many practicing Christians still engage in polemics. As a result, some denominational publications on non-Christian religions are misleading or simply erroneous. But many thinkers in mainline Protestant denominations and in the Roman Catholic church have adopted more moderate positions. For example, the well-known Catholic theologian KARL RAHNER called devout adherents of other religions "anonymous Christians"—Christians who had not heard the name of Christ. (This term often irritates adherents of other religions. It refuses, they say, to recognize who they really are.) In the late nineteenth and twentieth centuries a movement arose within Christianity that strove to overcome the divisions between the various Christian bodies. This "ecumenical" movement has now spilled over into more open relations with and a genuine interest in other religions. The basic method, "interreligious dialogue," assumes many forms but it is not without detractors. Some non-Christians, and some Christians, too, are convinced that "dialogue" is just another veil behind which Christian propagandists lurk.

The most consequential theological movement of the last 25 years has been liberation theology in a variety of dimensions, including African American, Latin American, and feminist (womanist/mujerista) theologians. These theologians have critiqued not just patriarchal, racist, and colonial religious structures and practices but also the manner in which earlier scholars examined religions. Feminist theologians have also offered alternative accounts of "ancient" matriarchies and goddess religions that allegedly predate patriarchal oppression.

Daly, Mary. *Gyn/ecology: The Metaethics of Radical Feminism.* Beacon Pr. 1990 $16.00. ISBN 0-8070-1511-3. Perhaps the leading book of theological radical feminism, presenting a needed criticism of past scholarship and its presumptions, but with all the nuance of saturation bombing.

Ingram, Paul O., and Frederick J. Streng, eds. *Buddhist-Christian Dialogue: Mutual Renewal and Transformation.* U.H. Pr. 1986 $10.00. ISBN 0-8248-0829-0. An introduction to one of the most vibrant and thoughtful interreligious conversations taking place today.

Kung, Hans, and others. *Christianity and World Religion: Paths to Dialogue with Islam, Hinduism and Buddhism.* Trans. by Peter Heinegg. Orbis Bks. 1993 repr. of 1986 ed. $19.95. ISBN 0-88344-858-0. How not to engage in dialogue; a prominent Catholic theologian talks with three scholars rather than adherents of non-Christian religions.

Rahner, Karl. *Concerning Vatican Council II.* Vol. 6 in *Theological Investigations.* Crossroad NY 1973 o.p. Contains Rahner's essay "Anonymous Christians."

Smith, Wilfred Cantwell. *Towards a World Theology: Faith and the Comparative History of Religion.* Orbis Bks. 1990 $16.95. ISBN 0-88344-646-4. Attempts to formulate a theological view rooted in the unity that the author perceives in all human religious history.

Swidler, Leonard, ed. *Death or Dialogue? From the Age of Monologue to the Age of Dialogue.* TPI PA 1991 $15.95. ISBN 0-334-02445-5. Four scholars at the forefront discuss the coming "age of dialogue"; a good introduction to this approach.

SOCIAL-SCIENTIFIC

The social sciences represent a different approach to religions that has at times been openly antagonistic. This approach seeks to explain certain religious phenomena, and sometimes all religion, in terms of psychological and/or sociological forces. Those who wrote groundbreaking studies at the beginning of the twentieth century are still highly influential: for the psychology of religion, SIGMUND FREUD (see Vols. 3 and 5), CARL G. JUNG (see Vol. 5), and

WILLIAM JAMES (see also Vols. 1, 3, and 5); and for the sociology of religion, KARL MARX (see also Vol. 3), MAX WEBER (see Vol. 3), and EMILE DURKHEIM (see Vol. 3). All of these thinkers belong to what might be called the "grand theoretical tradition" of the social sciences. Much less grand, much more concrete, but no less indispensable are those social scientists who use statistical methods to address specific problems.

PSYCHOLOGICAL

Downing, Christine. *The Goddess: Mythological Images of the Feminine.* Crossroad NY 1984 $9.95. ISBN 0-8235-0624-3. Mixes the mythology of Greek goddesses with autobiography; written by a therapist who is also past president of the American Academy of Religion.

Freud, Sigmund. *The Future of an Illusion.* Ed. by James Strachey. Norton 1989 $10.95. ISBN 0-393-01120-8. Freud's analysis of the conscious and unconscious personality led him eventually to diagnose religion as a neurotic illusion.

———. *Moses and Monotheism.* Random 1955 $8.00. ISBN 0-394-70014-7. A psychological explanation of the origins of monotheism.

———. *Totem and Taboo.* Trans. by Abraham A. Brill. Buccaneer Bks. 1989 $26.95. ISBN 0-89966-634-5. Contends that religion derives from the guilt brothers feel when, in the primal horde, they kill the father who has been keeping all women for himself; terrible history, more interesting as psychology.

Homans, Peter. *Theology after Freud: An Interpretive Inquiry.* Irvington 1970 $29.50. ISBN 0-672-51245-9. Uses neo-orthodox Protestant theology and Freud's psychoanalysis to explore the relations of theology and psychology and more generally the problems of secularization.

James, William. *The Varieties of Religious Experience: A Study in Human Nature.* HUP 1985 $48.00. ISBN 0-674-93225-0. A leading, early American psychologist examines extreme manifestations of religious experience.

Jung, Carl G. *Collected Works by C. G. Jung.* No. 9, Pt. 1: *The Archetypes and the Collective Unconscious.* Ed. by Gerhard Adler, and others. Trans. R. F. Hull *Bollingen Ser.* Princeton U. Pr. 1968 $60.00. ISBN 0-691-09761-5. Essays on Jung's concept of the archetype and analyses of examples.

——— *Psyche and Symbol: A Selection from the Writings of C. G. Jung.* Princeton U. Pr. 1990 $12.95. ISBN 0-691-01903-7. A reasonable selection of essays that can serve as an introduction to Jung, who sought to identify the shared images, or "archetypes," that constitute the collective unconscious.

Kakar, Sudhir. *The Analyst and the Mystic: Psychoanalytic Reflections on Religion and Mysticism.* U. Ch. Pr. 1992 $15.95. ISBN 0-226-42283-6. A brief attempt to approach mysticism, especially the Hindu mystic Ramakrishna, "as a psychoanalyst approaches a subject in a clinical encounter."

Obeyesekere, Gananath. *Medusa's Hair: An Essay on Personal Symbols and Religious Experience.* U. Ch. Pr. 1984 $9.95. ISBN 0-226-61601-0. Discusses ecstatic priests and priestesses at Katagarama, Sri Lanka, mixing sociological and psychological analysis, Weber and Freud, and questions about the division between cultural and personal symbols.

Van Herik, Judith. *Freud on Femininity and Faith.* U. CA Pr. 1982 $42.50. ISBN 0-520-04368-5. An exploration that finds misogyny and androcentrism underlying Freud's critical thought; focuses on Freud's critique of religion in *Moses and Monotheism* and *Totem and Taboo.*

SOCIOLOGICAL

Bellah, Robert. *Beyond Belief: Essays on Religion in a Post-Traditional World.* U. CA Pr. 1991 $12.95. ISBN 0-520-07394-0. Essays on religion in modern society and the problems of modernization in the Western and non-Western world.

Berger, Peter L. *The Sacred Canopy: Elements of a Sociological Theory of Religion.* Doubleday 1990 $8.95. ISBN 0-385-07305-4. Religion in terms of a society's "world-construction" and "world maintenance," with a close look at secularization.

Blasi, Anthony J., and Michael W. Cuneo, eds. *Issues in the Sociology of Religion: A Bibliography*. Garland 1984 o.p. More than 3,500 unannotated titles under three main headings—structures, processes, disciplinary conceptualizations—with many divisions; provides little specific guidance.

Durkheim, Emile. *The Elementary Forms of the Religious Life*. Trans. by Joseph W. Swain. Free Pr. 1965 $14.95. ISBN 0-02-908010-X. Uses Australian "totemism" to discuss religion as the objectification of cohesive social forces.

Marx, Karl. *On Religion*. Scholars Pr. GA 1982 repr. of 1964 ed. $24.95. ISBN 0-89130-599-8. A useful anthology; for Marx, religion is part of an ideological superstructure built on the ground of an economic infrastructure characterized by class struggle.

Weber, Max. *The Protestant Ethic and the Spirit of Capitalism*. Harper SF 1985 $8.95. ISBN 0-00-302070-3. Perhaps the most accessible way to approach Weber's thought on religion; stands Marx on his head to examine the ways in which economic systems are conditioned by religious ethics.

Wilson, Bryan. *Religion in Sociological Perspective*. OUP 1982 $14.95. ISBN 0-19-826664-2. By a modern-day Weberian who has been especially interested in sectarianism.

HISTORICAL-INTERPRETIVE

The social-scientific and theological approaches are most often applied to contemporary religions. Those who study ancient religions usually take an approach that can be called "historical-interpretive." It is possible to distinguish three broad historical-interpretive disciplines on the basis of the "interpretive framework" that each uses to understand religions.

1. History in the narrow sense—critical history—examines documents in order to construct both narratives about past events and accounts of past structures. Occasionally history is informed by insights from psychology, sociology, and other reflective disciplines, but many historians who have written about ancient religions think that simple accuracy is their goal. As a result, their accounts are often informative but unsophisticated. The operative interpretive framework for such historians is generally an "area" defined by the limits of space and time, for example, Republican Rome.

2. Anthropology has tended to explore contemporary indigenous peoples through the method of ethnography. It interprets religious phenomena as one component of human culture, the interpretive framework it employs. Anthropologists write accounts of cultural structures and of the forces that impel them to change. During the twentieth century, anthropological studies have become increasingly sophisticated, and anthropologists frequently invoke insights developed in the social sciences. In the early days, anthropologists studied ancient religions intensely. More recently, leading scholars of ancient religions have once again tried to incorporate anthropological theories into their work.

3. A third discipline, the "history of religions," technically investigates religious structures and events in terms of a different interpretive framework: religion as a global phenomenon. Historians of religions have tended to be suspicious of the social sciences, accusing them of "reducing" (or ignoring) what makes religion distinctive. In recent usage, the term *history of religions* has almost become synonymous with the ideas of a single, influential scholar, MIRCEA ELIADE (see also Vol. 2).

The historical-interpretive study of religions has passed through various phases, as have all humanistic studies, for during different periods scholars use different models or "paradigms" to help them study and make sense of religions. After World War I, scholars of religions tended to look on religions as sets of meanings. In the neoromantic view, these meanings were conceived of as expressions of religious experiences. More recently, they have been derived from the place that religious phenomena occupied in language-like codes. In an extreme form, the investigation of these codes became known as "structuralism."

Today, much creative scholarship is taken up with redressing deficiencies in classical developments of the paradigm of meaning. Some conceive of their activities as filling out that paradigm. Others see themselves struggling to replace it. Studies written in the 1980s have often focused on topics such as religious change, religions of women and oppressed minorities, religion and power, and the place of the physical body in religion. Anthropologists in particular have reflected as well in a postmodern style on the nature of their enterprise as a mode of writing.

Bell, Catherine. *Ritual Theory, Ritual Practice.* OUP 1992 $35.00. ISBN 0-19-506923-4. Sophisticated reflection among religious scholars on recent interest in ritual and where it might lead.

Clifford, James, and George E. Marcus, eds. *Writing Culture: The Poetics and Politics of Ethnography.* U. CA Pr. 1986 $42.50. ISBN 0-520-05652-3. Selected essays that reflect on anthropology as writing; a good place to begin exploring this theme.

Fernandez, James W., ed. *Beyond Metaphor: The Theory of Tropes in Anthropology.* Stanford U. Pr. 1991 $39.50. ISBN 0-8047-1940-3. Essays that attempt to broaden anthropological inquiry from metaphor to all the traditional rhetorical tropes.

Haddad, Yvonne Yazbeck, and Ellison Banks Findly, eds. *Women, Religion, and Social Change.* State U. NY Pr. 1985 $59.50. ISBN 0-88706-068-4. Essays on women and social change with a global perspective.

Lessa, William A., and Evon Z. Vogt. *Reader in Comparative Religion: An Anthropological Approach.* HarpC 1990 $45.00. ISBN 0-06-043991-2. For years and through successive editions, a very useful anthology of the study of religion primarily by anthropologists.

Lévi-Strauss, Claude. *Structural Anthropology.* Basic Bks. 1974 $17.00. ISBN 0-465-09516-X. Outlines Lévi-Strauss's structuralist method in several famous essays.

————. *Tristes Tropiques.* Viking Penguin 1992 $15.00. ISBN 0-14-016562-2. A delightful, autobiographical account of ethnological experiences, primarily in South America; with a few hints of its author's theories.

Lincoln, Bruce. *Death, War, and Sacrifice: Studies in Ideology and Practice.* U. Ch. Pr. 1991 $45.00. ISBN 0-226-48199-9. Broad collection of insightful essays, charting the author's course through subjects usually labelled Indo-European, along with a political critique of Georges Dumézil.

Long, Charles H. *Significations: Signs, Symbols, and Images in the Interpretation of Religion.* Augsburg Fortress 1986 $13.95. ISBN 0-8006-1892-0. Collected essays on religious meanings informed by both hermeneutical ("interpretive") and critical thought.

Marcus, George, and Michael F. J. Fischer. *Anthropology as Cultural Critique: An Experimental Moment in the Human Science.* U. Ch. Pr. 1986 $10.95. ISBN 0-226-50449-2. Anthropology's function as criticizing implicit assumptions in our own culture by means of examining the cultures of others.

Ricoeur, Paul. *Interpretation Theory: Discourse and the Surplus of Meaning.* Tex. Christian 1976 $8.00. ISBN 0-912646-59-4. A short, difficult book by the leading contemporary philosopher of interpretation.

Rosaldo, Renate. *Culture and Truth: The Remaking of Social Analysis.* Beacon Pr. 1991 $12.95. ISBN 0-8070-4609-4. Questions the symbolic approach of Geertz, taking seriously the criticism of anthropological theorizing by those who have been its object.

Smart, Ninian. *Concept and Empathy: Essays in the Study of Religion.* Ed. by Donald Wiebe. NYU Pr. 1986 $45.00. ISBN 0-8147-7851-8. Collected essays on the philosophy and comparative study of religion by a leading British-American thinker who prefers to label his subject of study "worldviews."

Smith, Wilfred Cantwell. *Belief and History.* U. Va. Pr. 1977 $9.95. ISBN 9-8139-1086-2. Argues that belief has only recently become important in religion; written by a scholar who made a career of historicizing deconstruction.

Strenski, Ivan. *Religion in Relation: Method, Application, & Moral Location.* Ed. by Frederick M. Denny. U. of SC Pr. 1992 $34.95. ISBN 0-87249-866-2. Examines religion and religious studies in relation to other areas of life and other studies, focusing on Mircea Eliade, René Girard, Martin Heidegger, Claude Lévi-Strauss, and the school of Émile Durkheim.

Van der Leeuw, Gerardus. *Religion in Essence and Manifestation.* Trans. by J. E. Turner. Princeton U. Pr. 1986 $80.00. ISBN 0-691-07272-8. A classical "phenomenology" of religion, discussing no particular religion but, rather, religious "phenomena," such as prayer and sacrifice, in a universal setting.

General Topics

Certain general topics in the study of religions have been so important as to give rise to bodies of literature devoted to their comparative and theoretical examination. Four such topics are especially significant for the religions discussed in this chapter: myth, sacrifice, rites of passage, and shamanism. The bibliographies that follow will introduce the reader to the major lines of inquiry in these four areas.

MYTH

Readers who are not academics are likely to look upon myth in one of two ways: as either pleasant stories with little religious importance and no truth, or as attempts to explain events for which a people's scientific knowledge was simply inadequate. Nevertheless, in the twentieth century, scholars of religions of every disciplinary persuasion have begun to take myths very seriously. If we define myth as a sacred narrative that expresses the most profound religious truth, regardless of historical accuracy or logical consistency, it is possible to call the creation stories in Genesis and the stories about the life of Jesus myths, regardless of our personal convictions.

Views on and theories about myth are as varied as the different sorts of scholars who study religions. Among the more important have been studies in the early part of this century that explored the relations between myth and ritual; the work of MIRCEA ELIADE (see also Vol. 2), which emphasizes the cosmogonic myth as a means to return to and re-create the original conditions of the cosmos; the structuralist school of CLAUDE LÉVI-STRAUSS (see Vol. 3) and his successors, which reads myths in terms of embedded codes based on binary oppositions (yes/no; black/white; and so on); psychological interpretations based either on the work of CARL G. JUNG (see Vol. 5) (myths as expressions of unconscious archetypes) or SIGMUND FREUD (see also Vols. 3 and 5) (myths as projections of repressed psychological tensions); and sociological interpretations informed by ÉMILE DURKHEIM's (see Vol. 3) notion of collective representation, especially seen in the comparative mythology of Georges Dumézil.

COLLECTIONS

Leeming, David A. *The World of Myth: An Anthology.* OUP 1991 $24.95. ISBN 0-19-505601-9. A selection of myths from around the world, with unobtrusive comments, organized according to archetypes: the cosmos, the gods, heroes, and places and objects.

Long, Charles H. *Alpha: The Myths of Creation.* Scholars Pr. GA 1983 repr. of 1963 ed. $19.95. ISBN 0-89130-604-8. A seminal study of cosmogonic myths.

Sproul, Barbara C. *Primal Myths: Creating the World.* HarpC 1979 $14.95. ISBN 0-06-067501-2. More myths than Long's book, but much less insightful analysis.

STUDIES

Austin, Norman. *Meaning and Being in Myth.* Penn St. U. Pr. 1990 $28.50. ISBN 0-271-00681-1. A psychological study inspired by Freud, in which ancient myths reveal the quest for the self.

Bonnefoy, Yves, ed. *Mythologies.* Trans. by Wendy Doniger. 2 vols. U. Ch. Pr. 1991 $250.00. ISBN 0-226-06453-0. Global in scope but not exhaustive, presents 395 articles by roughly 100 authors centering on the relationship between myth and society.

Campbell, Joseph. *The Masks of God.* Viking Penguin 4 vols. 1991 $12.95. ISBN 0-14-019440-1. $13.00. ISBN 0-14-019441-X. $13.00. ISBN 0-14-19442-8. $13.00. ISBN 0-14-019443-6. A major collection by a well-known American thinker, applying Jungian insights in a rather eclectic fashion.

Doty, William G. *Mythography: The Study of Myths and Rituals.* U. of Ala. Pr. 1986 $17.50. ISBN 0-8173-0398-7. An extensive discussion of the various approaches to mythology; good orientation.

Dundes, Alan, ed. *Sacred Narrative: Reading in the Theory of Myth.* U. CA Pr. 1984 $47.50. ISBN 0-520-05156-4. A selection of readings from a wide range of scholars of myth, both classical and contemporary.

Kramer, Samuel Noah, ed. *Mythologies of the Ancient World.* Doubleday 1961 $8.95. ISBN 0-385-09567-8. Useful essays on mythology throughout the ancient world.

Lévi-Strauss, Claude. *From Honey to Ashes: Introduction to a Science of Mythology.* Trans. by John and Doreen Weightman. U. Ch. Pr. 1983 $13.00. ISBN 0-226-47489-5. Applies Lévi-Strauss's ideas to South American mythology.

_____. *From Honey to Ashes*, Vol. 2: *Mythologiques.* Trans. by John and Doreen Weightman. U. Ch. Pr. 1990 $13.00. ISBN 0-685-48382-7

Liszka, James J. *The Semiotic of Myth: A Critical Study of the Symbol.* Ind. U. Pr. 1990 $35.00. ISBN 0-253-33513-2. A case for myth as transvaluation, for readers who can tolerate heavy doses of twentieth-century theorizing, especially involving semiotics and structuralism.

O'Flaherty, Wendy D. *Other People's Myths: The Cave of Echoes.* Macmillan 1988 $19.95. ISBN 0-02-896041-6. An energetic, engaging presentation with special focus on Hindu mythology, addressing in succession seven questions that arise when scholars look at other people's myths.

Reynolds, Frank E., and David Tracy, eds. *Myth and Philosophy.* State U. NY Pr. 1990 $59.50. ISBN 0-7914-0417-4. Essays aimed at laying the foundation for a more global philosophy of religion by exploring the interface between philosophy and myth.

Strenski, Ivan. *Four Theories of Myth in Twentieth-Century History: Cassirer, Eliade, Levi-Strauss and Malinowski.* U. of Iowa Pr. 1987 $27.00. ISBN 0-87745-181-8. Examines four scholars in their historical contexts to argue that "myth" is an artifact of recent historical processes.

SACRIFICE

Sacrifice, or the ritual killing of animals, has largely disappeared from the world's three major monotheistic traditions—Judaism, Christianity, and Islam. In fact, the practice has become so unusual that religions, such as Santería, that still practice sacrifice, have sparked public controversy. In the early 1990s, the U.S. Supreme Court decided that a law that specifically forbids sacrifice is unconstitutional.

The two oldest theories of sacrifice are the gift theory and the communion theory. Both were given classical form toward the end of the nineteenth century. The gift theory (expressed by the British anthropologist E. B. Tylor) is encapsulated in an old Latin saying addressed to the god: *do ut des*, "I give so that you will give." The communion theory, as formulated by WILLIAM ROBERTSON SMITH, envisions sacrifice as originating when members of a clan celebrated their common ancestry by killing and eating the animal that represented their ancestor (their "totem"). Two French sociologists, Henri Hubert and Marcel Mauss, formulated a more sophisticated notion of sacrifice as communion. Through the consecration and mediation of the victim, the sacrificer comes into contact with the world of the sacred.

More recent scholars have formulated other theories to account for sacrifice. One theory, working with the interaction of myth and ritual, sees sacrifice as the ritual expression of a mythical view according to which the world or life derived from the division of a primal being. Another theory suggests that sacrifice is a means to redirect social aggression from members of society onto a harmless victim. Still another more psychological theory views sacrifice as a ritual means of dealing with the anxiety that accompanies the act of killing.

None of these theories has achieved universal acclaim, but the last two, being more recent, are probably receiving the most attention.

Burkert, Walter. *Homo Necans: The Anthropology of Ancient Greek Sacrificial Ritual and Myth.* Trans. by Peter Bing. U. of CA Pr. 1983 $13.95. ISBN 0-520-05875-5. A study by a brilliant master that uses primarily Greek material to advance the notion of sacrifice as a reaction to anxiety.

De Heusch, Luc. *Sacrifice in Africa: A Structuralist Approach.* Trans. by Linda O'Brien and Alice Martin. *African Systems of Thought Ser.* Ind. U. Pr. 1985 $30.00. ISBN 0-253-35038-7. An account of African sacrifice that contains a critique of the views of René Girard.

Detienne, Marcel, and Jean-Pierre Vernant, eds. *The Cuisine of Sacrifice among the Greeks.* Trans. by Paula Wissing. U. Ch. Pr. 1989 $39.95. ISBN 0-226-14351-1. Insightful essays on Greek sacrifice by several French scholars, with a full (but not comprehensive) bibliography on the subject.

Girard, Rene. *Violence and the Sacred.* Trans. by Patrick Gregory. Johns Hopkins 1977 $13.95. ISBN 0-8018-2218-1. The sacrifice as a social mechanism redirecting violence onto a scapegoat—for Girard, the source of the sacred itself.

Hamerton-Kelly, Robert G., ed. *Violent Origins: Walter Burkert, Rene Girard, and Jonathan Z. Smith on Ritual Killing and Cultural Formation.* Stanford U. Pr. 1987 $39.50. ISBN 0-8047-1370-7. Papers by the subtitled authors, including introduction, comment, and discussions; a wonderful, stimulating book.

Hubert, Henri. *Sacrifice: Its Nature and Function.* Trans. by W. D. Halls. U. Ch. Pr. 1964 $15.95. ISBN 0-226-35679-5. A classic study of Hebraic and Vedic sacrifice; application to tribal peoples questionable.

Jensen, Adolf E. *Myth and Cult among Primitive Peoples.* Bks. Demand 1963 $93.40. ISBN 0-8357-8960-8. Traces the origin of sacrifice to the ritual reenactment of myths among early planters; a difficult but worthwhile book.

RITES OF PASSAGE

Rites of passage are the very common rituals that accompany transitions through significant stages of life, especially birth, puberty, marriage, and death. Since 1909, the common model for understanding these rituals has been the sequence of events proposed by Arnold van Gennep. Van Gennep applied this schema to both rites of passage and rites marking transitions in the course of the year (new year, solstices, equinoxes). According to him, these rites take place in three stages: (1) preliminal rites, or rites of separation; (2) liminal rites, or rites of transition; and (3) postliminal rites, or rites of reintegration. (The word *liminal* derives from Latin *limen*, meaning "threshold.")

Since van Gennep's time, several scholars have expanded on certain facets of his schema. The most influential of these attempts was the work of anthropologist VICTOR TURNER (see Vol. 3). Turner utilized the "liminality" found at the center of Arnold van Gennep's analysis to explore all sorts of "antistructural" conditions and situations, such as groups on the fringes of societies.

In recent years, scholars have begun to devote more attention to women's rites of passage, which had been unduly neglected. Rites of passage have also become the focus for much popular religiosity, both in women's and New Age movements.

Bettelheim, Bruno. *Symbolic Wounds: Puberty Rites and the Envious Male*. Free Pr. 1954 o.p. Well-known psychological study of mutilation, a common facet in rites of passage.

Eliade, Mircea. *Rites and Symbols of Initiation: The Mysteries of Birth and Rebirth*. HarpC 1966 $11.00. ISBN 0-06-131236-3. Explores religious significance of rites of passage.

Gennep, Arnold van. *The Rites of Passage*. Trans. by Monika B. Vizedon and Gabrielle L. Caffee. U. Ch. Pr. 1961 $6.95. ISBN 0-226-84849-3. The classic study.

Herdt, Gilbert H., ed. *Rituals of Manhood: Male Initiation in Papua New Guinea*. U. CA Pr. 1982 $49.95. ISBN 0-520-04448-7. Essays by a group of scholars on a classic rite of passage.

Lincoln, Bruce. *Emerging from the Chrysalis: Studies in Rituals of Women's Initiation*. OUP 1991 $12.95. ISBN 0-19-506910-2. Women's initiation in several societies, with an assessment of van Gennep's theory.

Metcalf, Peter, and Richard Huntington. *Celebrations of Death: The Anthropology of Mortuary Ritual*. Cambridge U. Pr. 1979 $49.50. ISBN 0-521-41312-5. Two anthropologists with experience in Borneo and Madagascar consider death rituals and two influential theorists, Robert Hertz and Arnold van Gennep.

Turner, Victor W. *The Ritual Process: Structure and Anti-Structure*. Cornell Univ. Pr. 1977 $9.95. ISBN 0-8014-9163-0. The most accessible source for Turner's notions of liminality and *communitas* (the social correlate to liminality, where people encounter each other directly rather than in roles defined by status).

SHAMANISM

Several types of religious specialists are found among the religions discussed in this chapter, including priests and sacred kings. One type of specialist that has received intense scholarly scrutiny is the shaman.

The word *shaman* is derived from the Tunguz language in Asia. Defined strictly, shamanism is a phenomenon of Siberia and central Asia, but, in this narrow sense, it has strong affinities to rituals and beliefs found in other parts of the globe, especially among the indigenous peoples of North and South America.

Significant shamanic traits include an ecstatic, trancelike state, at times induced by drugs, that is interpreted as the wandering of the shaman's soul from his or her body; dramatic rituals (and magic tricks) that allow the community to participate in the shaman's wanderings and to receive their benefits; the invocation of spirits, at times in animal form, as the shaman's assistants; and severe initiatory experiences, often associated with physical and mental illness, conceived in terms of death and rebirth.

In Siberia and central Asia, the shaman is primarily a healer. Shamans are also said to meet with the celestial gods, escort the souls of the dead to their new homes, and gain esoteric knowledge from their travels in the spirit world.

Balzer, Marjorie M., ed. *Shamanism: Soviet Studies of Traditional Religion in Siberia and Central Asia*. M. E. Sharpe 1990 $42.50. ISBN 0-87332-624-5. Four writers taking a Marxist-Leninist perspective provide sensitive and significant accounts of shamanism.

Duerr, Hans P. *Dreamtime: Concerning the Boundary between Wilderness and Civilization*. Blackwell 1987 pap. $14.95. ISBN 0-631-15548-1. A wide-ranging and provocative essay, with voluminous notes, on general phenomena, such as witchcraft and shamanism.

Eliade, Mircea. *Shamanism: Archaic Techniques of Ecstasy*. Trans. by Willard R. Trask. *Bollingen Ser*. Viking Penguin 1989 $10.95. ISBN 0-14-019155-0. Full discussion of what Eliade calls the "shamanic ideology" over a wide expanse of the globe; full bibliography to date of composition.

Ginzburg, Carlo. *Ecstasies: Deciphering the Witches' Sabbath*. Viking Penguin 1992 $14.00. ISBN 0-14-015858-8. Intriguing and perhaps too bold a study, tracing European witchcraft back to prehistoric shamanism.

Lewis I. M. *Ecstatic Religion: An Anthropological Study of Spirit Possession and Shamanism*. Routledge 1989 $14.95. ISBN 0-415-00799-2. A comparative sociology that starts from the distinction between central and marginal cults, a distinction in which gender distinctions are often at work.

Taussig, Michael. *Shamanism, Colonialism, and the Wild Man: A Study in Terror and Healing*. U. Ch. Pr. 1987 $29.95. ISBN 0-226-79012-6. Something of a *tour de force*, replete with detail from history and the author's experience in Colombia.

PREHISTORIC RELIGIONS

The term "prehistoric religions" embraces the immense expanse of religious activity that extends from the rise of humanity over 1 million years ago to the founding of the first major urban civilizations in the Ancient Near East around 3500 B.C.E. The designation identifies not so much a coherent group of religious beliefs, practices, and institutions as it does the problem researchers face when trying to study these religions. The mute, physical remains that survive from this period provide little definite information about prehistoric beliefs and institutions or even about the particular rituals of which they are the remnants. In fact, there is no evidence at all for religion throughout most of prehistory. Some date evidence for religious beliefs and practices back as early as 100,000 years ago, but such a date is highly speculative and probably much too early.

In trying to overcome these difficulties, scholars have traveled one of two roads. Some prefer a high road that others find too airy and unsure. They assume that there is a clear and uniform relationship between cultural patterns, especially means of livelihood, and certain religious beliefs, practices, and institutions. Then they try to elucidate the religions of prehistoric peoples through analogies with similar contemporary or near-contemporary peoples. These scholars usually associate the religion of hunters and gatherers with some sort of "otiose" supreme being and a quasi-divine master of animals. The next major stage is the religion of agriculturalists, with its themes of sexuality and death. Then, at the end of the prehistoric period, come cities with their gods, temples, and perhaps sacred kings.

The alternate approach to prehistoric religions avoids speculation and stays much closer to the actual, physical remains. Those who travel this "low road" provide us with detailed and occasionally interesting descriptions of artifacts and the locations where they were found. Unfortunately, all too often they can tell us very little about the religious significance of these artifacts. Still, many prefer an honest admission of ignorance to bolder and less certain speculations.

The following titles are useful for studying the entire prehistoric period.

Bonser, Wilfrid. *A Prehistoric Bibliography*. Ed. by June Troy. Blackwell Pubs. 1976 $85.00. ISBN 0-631-17090-1. Nine thousand books and articles, but unfortunately now over a decade and a half old.

Dahlberg, Frances. *Woman the Gatherer*. Yale U. Pr. 1983 $30.00. ISBN 0-300-02572-6. Eight contributors attempt to redress the androcentric orientation of many books on prehistory.

Daniel, Glyn, and Colin Renfrew. *The Idea of Prehistory*. Columbia U. Pr. 1986 $45.00. ISBN 0-85224-532-7. Chronicles European interest in prehistory over roughly the last 200 years.

Fagan, Brian M. *World Prehistory: A Brief Introduction*. HarpC 1993 $20.50. ISBN 0-673-52262-8. For a quick overview of human origins and the prehistory of Old and New Worlds; unfortunately, little on religion before the advent of "civilization."

Hawkes, Jacquetta, ed. *Atlas of Ancient Archaeology*. McGraw 1974 o.p. A useful tool designed for the general reader. Maps and drawings with commentary region by region; Europe predominates.

Jensen, Adolf E. *Myth and Cult Among Primitive Peoples*. Trans. by Marianna Choldin and Wolfgang Wiessleder. Bks. Demand repr. of 1963 ed. $93.40. ISBN 0-8357-8960-8. Heavy reading, tightly theoretical; very significant in critiquing categories often applied to prehistoric religions.

Maringer, Johannes. *The Gods of Prehistoric Man*. Knopf 1960 o.p. Older but useful period-by-period survey of evidence, with a synthesis on religions of hunters and early farmers.

Renfrew, Colin, and Paul Bahr. *Archaeology: Theories, Methods and Practice*. Thames Hudson 1991 $29.95. ISBN 0-500-27605-6. A thick, up-to-date, well-illustrated textbook, organized around the questions archaeologists ask.

Wenke, Robert J. *Patterns in Prehistory: Mankind's First Three Million Years*. OUP 1990 $45.00. ISBN 0-19-506848-3. An account from the beginnings to the complex civilizations of the Old and New Worlds, which portrays a deterministic, evolutionistic picture.

Paleolithic Period

The Paleolithic period (the "Old Stone Age") ended in Europe about 10,000 years ago. It provides several kinds of evidence that are suggestive of religion but by no means definitive. All dates are only approximate.

Burials, which begin in the Middle Paleolithic (50,000 B.P.?), form part of the earliest evidence. (B.P. stands for "before the present.) Certain features hint at a belief in life after death: careful placement and orientation of the body, the use of red ocher (perhaps as a symbol of life), and the presence of grave goods, which become increasingly numerous toward the end of the Paleolithic period.

Some scholars see evidence of animal sacrifice in deposits of bones near burial sites and of hunting rituals in what would appear to be the careful treatment of bear skulls and longbones (from about 50,000 B.P.). Closer investigation, however, reveals that the "cult of the cave bear" actually existed only in the archaeological imagination as it examined natural deposits of bones.

Much more suggestive of religion are various forms of representational art. Cave paintings begin about 30,000 years ago. They are found in an area that stretches from the Ural Mountains to the Atlantic, but they are concentrated in southern France and northern Spain. The most frequent subjects are carefully drawn animals, such as reindeer. Some features suggest shamanistic practices. For example, one famous drawing portrays a supine, ithyphallic man with what appears to be a bird-headed staff by his side.

Slightly later (28,000 B.P.?) female figurines began to appear. Some are stylized carvings of bone, others slightly more realistic, but all emphasize powers of regeneration and nurture: the hips, belly, and breasts. These figurines seem to be connected with some sort of fertility cult, but their religious significance remains obscure.

Breuil, Henri, and Raymond Lantier. *The Men of the Old Stone Age: Palaeolithic and Mesolithic*. Trans. by B. B. Rafter. Greenwood 1980 repr. of 1965 ed. $38.50. ISBN 0-

313-21289-9. Careful introduction to a wide range of material; good discussion of art. Final chapters on funerary customs and religious practices.

Clark, J. G. *Mesolithic Prelude: The Paleolithic-Neolithic Transition in Europe and the Near East*. Columbia U. Pr. 1980 $16.00. ISBN 0-85224-365-0. Questions the usefulness of sharply dividing prehistory into Paleolithic and Neolithic periods.

Dickson, D. Bruce. *The Dawn of Belief: Religion in the Upper Paleolithic of Southwestern Europe*. U. of Ariz. Pr. 1990 $29.95. ISBN 0-8165-1076-8. $14.95. ISBN 0-8165-1336-8. Daring in that it attempts to reconstruct and interpret Paleolithic religious practice from material remains; many scholars would reject it on principle.

LeRoi-Gourhan, André. *The Dawn of European Art: An Introduction to Palaeolithic Cave Painting*. Cambridge U. Pr. 1982 o.p. Beautiful, color illustrations and artistic analysis by one of the world's leading authorities.

Soffer, Olga. *The Upper Paleolithic of the Central Russian Plain*. Acad. Pr. 1985 $61.00. ISBN 0-12-654270-8. For those who want to see detailed archaeology in action; conclusions are readable.

Wymer, J. J. *The Paleolithic Age*. St. Martin 1984 $12.95. ISBN 0-312-59477-1. A detailed, but still readable, discussion of evidence, for those who want more than a general survey of trends.

Neolithic Religion

The Neolithic period began with a revolution: the discovery of agriculture in Europe and Southeast Asia about 10,000 years ago. Other significant discoveries gave this period a distinctive character: the domestication of animals, such as dogs, sheep, and goats; the development of pottery and metallurgy; and a shift to a sedentary way of life. Toward the end of the period, the Neolithic gives way to large-scale urbanization and the invention of writing, that is, to the historic civilizations of the Ancient Near East that came into existence about 3500 B.C.E..

The shift to agriculture may have resulted in significant religious developments, such as a new concern for the symbolic significance of the earth. Nevertheless, there was no uniform Neolithic religious complex. When the Neolithic began around 8000 B.C.E., there were only isolated settlements. During the next 3,000 years, Neolithic cultures were active and expanding in the Near East and southeast Europe. After about 5000 B.C.E., intense Neolithic activity began in other parts of the globe, such as North Africa and southwest Europe.

The best known Neolithic religious complexes are those of the Near East (for example, Jericho and Catal Huyuk) and of southeast Europe (for example, Lepenski Vir). The religion of the Neolithic Near East centered on the sexual aspects of agriculture, chthonic cults, death, and ancestor cults. It had distinctive house shrines that became completely separated from dwellings by the end of this period. The religion of Neolithic southeast Europe appears to have been somewhat different. Sites there show little concern for death, ancestor cults, and few indisputable shrines. Instead, the cult seems to have centered on the domestic hearth, which was carefully laid out. Southeast Europe has also provided scholars with a large number of very suggestive Neolithic figurines.

One feature of Neolithic religious practice consistently attracts the attention of nonspecialists. About the fifth millennium B.C.E., processes began that led eventually to the construction of impressive megaliths in west and northwest Europe. The best known of these monuments is, of course, Stonehenge, first built about 3800 years ago during the Late Neolithic in Britain.

Gimbutas, Marija. *The Civilization of the Goddess: The World of Old Europe*. Harper SF 1991 $60.00. ISBN 0-06-250368-5

———. *Language of the Goddess: Unearthing the Hidden Symbols of Western Civilization*. Harper SF 1991 $24.95. ISBN 0-06-250418-5. Both of Gimbutas's books are fully and beautifully illustrated and discuss "pre-Indo-European" Europe and its cult of "the Goddess." Skeptics might call the treatment of religion speculative.

Hodder, Ian. *The Domestication of Europe: Structure and Contingency in Neolithic Societies*. Blackwell Pubs. 1990 $54.95. ISBN 0-631-17413-3. In a more contemporary idiom: "domestication as a discourse of power"; not specifically a book in religious studies, but one with many applications.

Krupp, E. C., ed. *In Search of Ancient Astronomies: Stonehenge to Von Daniken, Archaeoastronomy Discovers Our Sophisticated Ancestors*. McGraw 1979 $6.95. ISBN 0-07-035556-8. Articles on the "astronomy" of Neolithic Britain, along with other areas and periods, including North America, Mesoamerica, and Egypt.

Marshack, Alexander. *The Roots of Civilization: The Cognitive Beginnings of Man's First Art, Symbol, and Notation*. Moyer Bell 1992 $49.95. ISBN 1-55921-041-9. A reflective, speculative encounter with the evidence.

Mellaart, J. *The Neolithic of the Near East*. Thames Hudson 1975 o.p. An unfortunately out-of-print study of sites such as Catal Huyuk.

Michell, John. *Megalithomania: Artists, Antiquarians and Archaeologists at the Old Stone Monuments*. Cornell Univ. Pr. 1982 $29.95. ISBN 0-8014-1479-2. Profusely illustrated account of modern humanity's love affair with the megaliths, by one of the lovers.

Nissen, Hans. *The Early History of the Ancient Near East, 9000–2000 B.C.* U. Ch. Pr. 1988 $34.95. ISBN 0-226-58656-1. An innovative, up-to-date history for the serious reader, downplaying the significance of the invention of writing and attentive to the role of environment.

Renfrew, Colin. *The Megalithic Monuments of Western Europe: The Latest Evidence*. Thames Hudson 1983 $9.95. ISBN 0-500-27307-3. The "latest evidence" is becoming increasingly dated, but Renfrew is a reliable scholar.

Thomas, Julian. *Rethinking the Neolithic*. Cambridge U. Pr. 1991 $54.50. ISBN 0-521-40377-4. Instead of the Neolithic as an economic period, proposes an alternate model in which Neolithic is a way to look at the world ("an integrated conceptual and classificatory system").

Indo-European Religions

"Indo-European" is the name of the set of related languages whose speakers inhabited lands that stretched from the west coast of Europe to Iran, South Asia, and through central Asia to a small portion of the Asian Pacific coast. At least, that is where Indo-European speakers lived before modern European colonial expansion began in earnest about 500 years ago.

To account for the wide geographical distribution of these languages, scholars have customarily used a model of mass migrations. They supposed that initially the members of a community or a set of related communities spoke the language from which all the classical and modern Indo-European languages had descended, a hypothetical language known as "proto-Indo-European." Over time, various groups left the original home and started on great treks of conquest, some to central Europe and Scandinavia, some to western Europe, some to Italy and Greece, some to Turkey, some to Iran, yet others to India, to central Asia and the Pacific coast of Asia. Just where to situate the original home has been a matter of dispute. Marija Gimbutas has argued vigorously that the proto-Indo-Europeans appear in the archaeological record as a culture she calls "Kurgan," after the local name for the kinds of mounds these people built. The Kurgan people originally lived in the South Russian steppe between the Dneper

River and the Ural Mountains, north of the Caucasus. They began expanding outward during the first half of the fourth millennium B.C.E.

Recently, the British archaeological theorist Colin Renfrew has proposed a different model to account for the geographical spread of Indo-European languages. He suggests that the language spread through contact rather than migration. To be specific, it accompanied the spread of an agricultural complex based on wheat and other domesticates from the region of eastern Turkey and the Iranian rim. Far from being conveyed by wandering armies, words and linguistic features spread more or less peacefully as people gradually adopted the manner of livelihood with which the linguistic features were associated. This model, if accepted, will require scholars to rethink radically many of the claims that they have made for Indo-European mythology and religion.

In addition to the hypothetical Proto-Indo-Europeans, this section discusses Celtic and Germanic religions. For the religions of other Indo-European speakers, see below under "Ancient Urban Civilizations: Religions of the Ancient Mediterranean World" and Chapter 11 "Eastern Religions," in this volume.

PROTO-INDO-EUROPEANS

Scholars have tried to reconstruct both the society and the religion of the Proto-Indo-Europeans by comparing the vocabulary, myths, and institutions of people who speak Indo-European languages. The most important contribution has been made by the French scholar GEORGES DUMÉZIL.

According to Dumézil, the Proto-Indo-Europeans were seminomadic pastoralists whose most important herds consisted of cattle. Both their pantheon and their society were stratified in a three-tiered hierarchy that resembled the three upper classes (the three twice-born *varnas*) in traditional Hindu society. Dumézil has described this system of classification as an ideological structure, independent of social and religious organizations, but with an order. The ideology is composed of three functions (hence its common designation, "the tripartite ideology").

A few writings have explored aspects of Indo-European religion that stand outside Dumézil's model. Among the most interesting is the notion, first articulated by Bruce Lincoln and Jaan Puhvel, that the Indo-Europeans shared a cosmogony, according to which the world came into existence through the division of a primal person, as in the famous Indian *Purusha-sukta* (*Rigveda* 10.90). The model has several possible implications, among them the potential for elucidating the practice of sacrifice common among Indo-European speakers and the frequent myths of the periodic disintegration and reconstitution of the universe.

Colin Renfrew's recent criticism of common views on the spread of Indo-European languages takes particular exception to the assumptions underlying Dumézil's views and raises questions about most study of Proto-Indo-European religion. Readers should be at least aware of Renfrew's criticisms.

Benveniste, Emile. *Indo-European Language and Society*. Trans. by Elizabeth Palmer. U. of Miami Pr. 1973 o.p. Indispensable study of Indo-European institutions through comparative philology.

Lincoln, Bruce. *Myth, Cosmos, and Society: Indo-European Themes of Creation and Destruction*. HUP 1986 $25.50. ISBN 0-674-59775-3. Insightful study by an author always worth reading; sensitive to religious issues.

_____. *Priests, Warriors and Cattle: A Study in the Ecology of Religions*. U. CA Pr. 1981 $49.95. ISBN 0-520-03880-0. Argues for a common religious structure for Indo-

European and East African peoples, resulting from a way of life centered on cattle herding.

Polome, Edgar C. *Language, Society, and Paleoculture: Essays by Edgar C. Polome.* Ed. by Anwar S. Dil. Stanford U. Pr. 1982 $49.50. ISBN 0-8047-1149-6. Essays by a leading thinker on the reconstruction of ancient cultures from languages.

Puhvel, Jaan, ed. *Myth and Law among the Indo-Europeans.* U. CA Pr. 1970 o.p. ISBN 0-520-01587-8. Scholarly essays by a number of contributors; an old standby.

Renfrew, Colin. *Archaeology and Language: The Puzzle of Indo-European Origins.* Cambridge U. Pr. 1990 $18.95. ISBN 0-521-38675-6. Advances a new model of Indo-European diffusion and in the process a severe critique both of Dumézil's assumptions and his conclusions.

Skomal, Susan S. and Edgar C. Polome, eds. *Proto-Indo-European: The Archaeology of a Linguistic Problem.* Inst. Study Man 1987 $60.00. ISBN 0-941694-29-1. In honor of Marija Gimbutas, scholars from many specialties contribute essays attempting to link archaeology and the linguistic study of Proto-Indo-European.

CELTIC RELIGION

The Celts were Indo-European inhabitants of the continent of Europe and the British Isles. Their civilization climaxed during the fourth century B.C.E. Later, they were displaced from much of continental Europe and England by their distant Germanic cousins. Our knowledge of Celtic religions is based on Celtic literature from Ireland, descriptions of Celtic beliefs and practices by Greek and Roman writers (especially JULIUS CAESAR [see Vol. 3], who called them "Gauls"), some sculpture, and a few inscriptions.

The religious ideas and the deities of the Celts remain somewhat obscure. Their great god, known in Ireland as Lug Lamfota (called Mercury by Caesar), was a patron of the arts. Other gods included Taranis/Jupiter, a god of the sky and thunder; Teutates/Mars, perhaps a tutelary god of the tribe; and the horned Cernunnos, some of whose representations recall the Indian god Shiva Pasupati as well as the "horned god" from Indus Valley seals, who seems to have been a sort of Master of Animals.

The details of Celtic worship are also obscure. There are many references to human sacrifice. Irish sources tell us that the year was divided in half by major festivals on May 1 (Beltine) and November 1 (Samain). These days are, of course, still associated with celebrations, such as Mayday and Halloween. Before the Roman period, the Celts seem to have worshiped in forest sanctuaries rather than in temples. Their priests were the well-known Druids, who preserved their lore by committing verses to memory, refusing to write it down. The Celts also made use of seers, both men and women, who practiced their art by interpreting the flights of birds and the bodies of slain animals.

Daniel, Glyn, and Paul Bahn. *Ancient Places: The Prehistoric and Celtic Sites of Britain.* Hippocrene Bks. 1989 $30.00. ISBN 0-09-467210-5. Black-and-white photos of 33 sites, arranged alphabetically, with a short introduction and comments.

MacCana, Proinsias. *Celtic Mythology.* Bedrick Bks. 1991 $14.95 ISBN 0-87226-242-1. A brief, illustrated survey.

Nagy, Joseph Falaky. *The Wisdom of the Outlaw: The Boyhood Deeds of Finn in Gaelic Narrative Tradition.* U. CA Pr. 1985 $42.50. ISBN 0-520-05284-6. Uses modern mythological theory to explore an important Irish cycle; for the dedicated student.

Piggott, Stuart. *The Druids.* Thames Hudson 1985 $10.95. ISBN 0-500-27363-4. An accessible account of the Celtic priests.

Powell, T. G. E. *The Celts. Ancient People and Places Ser.* Thames Hudson 1983 repr. of 1980 ed. $14.95. ISBN 0-500-27275-1. A readable, illustrated overview of the Celts, with one of the four chapters on religion.

Thomas, Charles. *Celtic Britain*. Thames Hudson 1986 $22.50. ISBN 0-500-02107-4. An
   update of *Celtic Britain* by Nora Chadwick which covers Britain after the Romans,
   including Cornwall, Scotland, Wales, then Christianity and art, and a little on Celtic
   religion.

GERMANIC RELIGION

The Germanic peoples inhabited the broad expanse of land and islands
between the Black Sea and Greenland just prior to the Christianization of
northern Europe. Features of their religion are described by classical and
medieval Latin authors, such as TACITUS (see Vol. 3). Their religion is also
known for archaeological remains in Scandinavia and runic inscriptions that
begin about the first century C.E. The best sources of information, especially
about myths are lengthy Old Norse compositions that originated in Iceland from
the twelfth to fourteenth centuries, the Eddas and the scaldic poems.

At the center of the Germanic world was the world tree, an evergreen ash
known as Yggdrasil. Beneath it was a well—the well of wisdom. The gods were
divided into two major families that at one time had done battle with one
another: the Aesir, for the most part gods of battle, and the Vanir, gods of
fertility and riches. Among the former were several well-known deities: Odin
(god of occult wisdom), Thor (god of order), Balder (in West Norse, the
innocent, suffering god), and Loki (a shape changer who deceived and cheated
the gods). The Germans also knew a host of other beings, including elves,
dwarfs, spirits, and guardians.

The Germans seem to have had no universal beliefs about the afterlife. Many
modern readers will be familiar with the notion of Valhalla, but it does not seem
to have been widespread among the Germanic peoples. Another distinctive and
familiar notion is that of the *Ragnarok*, a time in the future at which the gods
and demons will fight to mutual annihilation, resulting in the world's
destruction. Some traditions suggest that a new world will arise after this
destruction, but this may result from Christian influence.

Many sagas, Eddas, and other texts are conveniently available in English
translation from Penguin Classics.

Bauschatz, Paul C. *The Well and the Tree: World and Time in Early Germanic Culture*.
   U. of Mass. Pr. 1982 $27.50. ISBN 0-87023-352-1. A scholarly exploration of early
   Germanic cosmology.

Davidson, Hilda R. Ellis. *Gods and Myths of Northern Europe*. Viking Penguin 1965 $9.95.
   ISBN 0-14-020670-1. Readable, informative account of Germanic mythology, but
   occasionally unreliable.

Dumézil, Georges. *Gods of the Ancient Northmen*. Trans. by Elinar Haugen. U. CA Pr.
   1974 $12.95. ISBN 0-520-03507-0. The Germanic gods in comparative perspective
   (for Dumézil, see under "Proto-Indo-Europeans," above).

Sturluson, Snorri. *The Prose Edda of Snorri Sturluson: Tales from Norse Mythology*.
   Trans. by Jean Young. U. CA Pr. 1964 $8.95. ISBN 0-520-01232-1. Selected
   translations of an 800-year-old work intended to preserve the traditional art of
   poetry; it preserved mythology, too, although not always the most ancient traditions.

Terry, Patricia, trans. *Poem of the Elder Edda*. U. of Pa. Pr. 1990 $39.95. ISBN 0-8122-
   8235-2. Important mythological texts in a translation that is readable as well as loyal
   to the conventions of Eddic poetry.

Turville-Petre, E. O. G. *Myth and Religion of the North*. Greenwood 1975 repr. of 1964 ed.
   $66.50. ISBN 0-8371-7420-1. A full and reliable account of Germanic religion.

ANCIENT URBAN CIVILIZATIONS: RELIGIONS OF THE ANCIENT MEDITERRANEAN WORLD

The word *civilization* does not imply increased mental capabilities or more complex thought. It refers instead to innovations in patterns of settlement and technology. In general, civilizations are characterized by urbanization, technological progress, occupational specialization, social stratification, complex political organization, and literacy.

The development of civilizations and city life is a complex and debated question. The best case for the role of religion has been made by geographer Paul Wheatley. According to Wheatley, the ceremonial center was the focus around which urbanization first occurred. But many other competing views of the origin of civilization, urbanization, and complex societies attribute little weight to religion as a casual factor.

Urbanization seems to have arisen independently in several areas that are here called areas of "primary urbanization," among them Egypt, Mesopotamia, Mesoamerica, and the Peruvian highlands. Areas that adopt "civilized" ways of life as the result of diffusion are here called "secondary centers of civilization."

Although the religions of ancient urban civilizations show considerable variation, some rough characterizations are possible. The idea of a separation between religion and government was unknown in the ancient world. All early civilizations had official religions. In fact, for any given people these are usually the earliest religions we know about. Official religions were often localized around temples, as they were in Mesopotamia, Egypt, Israel, Greece, Rome, and Mesoamerica. The gods were believed to reside at temples, most often in images enshrined there. Specialized functionaries attached to temples attended to divine needs for sustenance, entertainment, and daily service. Together, religion and government were responsible for the flourishing of society and the cosmos.

In time, other religious practices came into view, although they probably existed earlier. These practices include the veneration of deceased ancestors, rituals centering on the life cycle, and rituals of healing. The growth of transregional empires had an impact on religion in both the Old and New Worlds. In the Mediterranean this move deemphasized the religions of local states and encouraged religious exchange and assimilation. A gradual shift also occurred from locative to utopian religions, in the terms of JONATHAN Z. SMITH, from religions connected with specific places to unlocalized ones. The early centuries C.E. saw the emergence of a concern with life after death and resurrection from the dead among several Mediterranean religions, including Christianity.

This chapter discusses the ancient urban civilizations of both the ancient Mediterranean world and the Americas. For the ancient civilizations of India and China, see Chapter 11, "Eastern Religions" in this volume.

Adams, Robert. *Evolution of Urban Society: Early Mesopotamia and Prehispanic Mexico.* Aldine de Gruyter 1966 $28.95. ISBN 0-202-33016-8. A fascinating account that uses anthropological categories to draw parallels.

Childe, V. Gordon. *New Light on the Most Ancient East.* Norton 1969 $4.95. ISBN 0-393-00469-4. No longer all that new, but by a leading materialist theorist of the development of civilization; looks at Egypt, Mesopotamia, and the Indus valley.

Fustel de Coulanges, Numa Denis. *The Ancient City.* Gordon Pr. 1972 $59.95. ISBN 0-87968-624-3. A nineteenth-century classic; this edition contains a helpful foreword by Arnaldo Momigliano and S. C. Humphreys, two outstanding modern scholars.

Hammond, Mason. *The City in the Ancient World.* Ed. by Lester Bartson. Harvard U. Pr. 1972 $38.00. ISBN 0-674-13180-0. The city in the ancient Mediterranean from its emergence to the early medieval period, with an extensive annotated bibliography.

Lamberg-Karlovsky, C. C., and Jeremy A. Sabloff. *Ancient Civilizations: The Near East and Mesoamerica.* Waveland Pr. 1987 repr. of 1979 ed. $19.95. ISBN 0-88133-301-8. An informed account from a materialist, archaeological perspective that recounts theories rather than reports supposed facts.

Wenke, Robert J. *Patterns in Prehistory: Humankind's First Three Million Years.* OUP 1990 $45.00. ISBN 0-19-506848-3. Written from a materialist-evolutionistic perspective, discusses the origin of complex societies and individual societies with an eye fully open to the literature; treatment of religion, however, is spotty.

Wheatley, Paul. *Pivot of the Four Quarters: A Preliminary Inquiry into the Origins and Character of the Ancient Chinese City.* Beresford Bks. 1971 o.p. A remarkable study of immense comparative breadth, looking well beyond the Chinese city.

Ancient Mediterranean Civilizations

Scholar Cyrus H. Gordon has sought to identify the common features of the ancient Mediterranean civilizations or to be more precise, the civilizations of the Ancient Near East. Gordon's syntheses are fascinating for the general reader, but in the scholarly world he has remained something of a lone wolf. Most scholars find his characterizations both too vague and too general to be genuinely distinctive and too inattentive to differences between various regions and religions. They prefer to limit their investigations to various aspects of particular times and places.

A few books and sets, however, are very useful in studying several or all of the religions of the ancient Mediterranean. The reader may find the following titles especially useful or provocative.

Doria, Charles, and Harris Lenowitz. *Origins: Creation Texts from the Ancient Mediterranean.* AMS Pr. 1976 $32.50. ISBN 0-404-14849-2. A brief introduction, then a wide variety of translated texts, arranged topically by methods of creation (rising, falling, dividing, creation through verbal proclamation).

Finegan, Jack. *Archaeological History of the Ancient Middle East.* Westview 1979 o.p. Concentrates on Egypt and Mesopotamia, ignoring other peoples; peculiarly deferential to traditions about Israel.

Frankfort, Henri, and William A. Irwin. *The Intellectual Adventure of Ancient Man: An Essay on Speculative Thought in the Ancient Near East.* U. Ch. Pr. 1977 repr. of 1946 ed. $13.95. ISBN 0-226-26008-9. Brilliant interpretive essays on the mythic worldviews of Egyptians, Mesopotamians, Hebrews, and Greeks.

Gaster, Theodor H. *Thespis: Ritual, Myth, and Drama in the Ancient Near East.* Gordian 1975 $75.00. ISBN 0-87752-188-3. An impressive, speculative account of seasonal rituals and myths and their literary survivals; not to everyone's taste.

Gordon, Cyrus H. *Ancient Near East.* Norton 1965 $9.95. ISBN 0-393-00275-6. Now a dated book, but it communicates some of Gordon's distinctive views.

Grant, Michael, and Rachel Kitzinger, eds. *Civilization of the Ancient Mediterranean.* 3 vols. Macmillan 1988 set $195.00. ISBN 0-318-32911-5. Three massive tomes actually limited to Greece and Rome, with articles by first rank scholars; vol. 2 discusses religion at length.

Kramer, Samuel Noah, ed. *Mythologies of the Ancient World.* Doubleday 1961 $8.95. ISBN 0-385-09567-8. Useful essays on mythology throughout the ancient world.

Ochshorn, Judith. *The Female Experience and the Nature of the Divine.* 1981. Bks. Demand n.d. $71.50. ISBN 0-685-16314-8. Vulnerable but useful; stresses Israelites as unusually misogynistic.

Pritchard, James B., ed. *Ancient Near East in Pictures with Supplement.* Incl. *Ancient Near Eastern Texts Relating to the Old Testament with Supplement.* Princeton U. Pr.

1969 set $89.50. ISBN 0-691-03503-2. Standard collection from texts in less than fluent translations from all over the Near East.

Saggs, H. W. F. *Civilization Before Greece and Rome.* Yale U. Pr. 1991 repr. of 1989 ed. $18.00. ISBN 0-300-05031-3. General topic-by-topic survey of the region from Egypt to the Indus, 3500–500 B.C.E.; the last chapter discusses religion.

Seltzer, Robert, ed. *Religions of Antiquity.* Macmillan 1989 $12.95. ISBN 0-02-897373-9. Essays from the *Encyclopedia of Religion*; perhaps useful for those without ready access to or interest in the whole encyclopedia.

Areas of Primary Urbanization

MESOPOTAMIAN RELIGIONS

Ancient Mesopotamia (the land between the Tigris and Euphrates rivers; modern Iraq) confronts the modern reader with a bewildering array of different peoples. Among them, the most important were the Sumerians, the early inhabitants of the regions where the rivers flow into the Persian Gulf, and Semitic invaders, who spoke Akkadian and eventually exercised control over the entire region. The Semites eventually divided into two major groups: the Babylonians in the south and the Assyrians in the north. At different times in the second and first millennia B.C.E., the Assyrians and Babylonians managed to conquer and rule the entire region.

Mesopotamian gods generally represented the forces and objects of nature. They dwelt in temples, where their presence was usually symbolized with a sacred image. Temple complexes often included a stepped pyramid, or ziggurat, but the precise significance of the ziggurats is disputed.

At the temples, human servants tended to the god's daily needs. They fed, clothed, bathed, and entertained the god; took him or her out for walks; woke the god up and put him or her to bed. On special occasions, such as the famous Akitu festival, the god might be carried in procession through the town or from one residence to another. Mesopotamian myths often attribute human existence to the gods' desire for servants so that they themselves would not have to work.

The Mesopotamians developed complex arts of astronomy and divination through dreams and hepatoscopy (the examination of livers of sacrificed animals). Remnants of a well-developed literature survive in cuneiform writing on clay tablets that include fragments of the well-known epic Gilgamesh and the cosmogonic hymn *Enuma Elish*, sung in praise of Marduk, god of Babylon. Some writings, such as the *Enuma Elish*, have distinct similarities to accounts familiar from the Bible.

TEXTS

Gilgamesh. Trans. by John Gardner and John R. Maier. Random 1985 $13.00. ISBN 0-394-74089-0. An author and a scholar team up to produce a readable, tablet-by-tablet translation of this famous epic.

Heidel, Alexander. *The Babylonian Genesis: The Story of Creation.* U. Ch. Pr. 1963 $6.50. ISBN 0-226-32399-4. Translations of *Enuma Elish* and other creation texts; with commentary and remarks on parallels with the Hebrew Bible.

Jacobsen, Thorkild. *The Harps that Once: Sumerian Poetry in Translation.* Yale U. Pr. 1987 $40.00. ISBN 0-300-03906-9. A veritable treasure of accessible translations by a master Sumerologist, including myths, hymns, and lovesongs.

Wolkstein, Diane, and Samuel Noah Kramer. *Inanna: Queen of Heaven and Earth.* HarpC 1983 $12.00. ISBN 0-06-090854-8. Illustrated, poetic retelling of the myths and hymns of Inanna, with commentary; scholars may fret, but very good for the nonspecialist.

STUDIES

Frankfort, Henri. *Kingship and the Gods: A Study of Ancient Near Eastern Religion as the Integration of Society and Nature.* U. Ch. Pr. 1978 repr. of 1948 ed. o.p.

Hooke, S. H. *Babylonian and Assyrian Religion.* U. Okla. Pr. 1975 o.p.

Jacobsen, Thorkild. *The Treasures of Darkness: A History of Mesopotamian Religion.* Yale U. Pr. 1976 $14.00. ISBN 0-300-02291-3. The best recent, general survey; outlines by millennia successive stages through which Mesopotamian religion passed.

Kramer, Samuel Noah. *From the Poetry of Sumer: Creation, Glorification, Adoration.* U. CA Pr. 1979 $40.00. ISBN 0-520-03703-0. An overview, with excerpts, of Sumerian literature, organized around the three themes of the subtitle.

———. *History Begins at Sumer: Thirty-Nine Firsts in Man's Recorded History.* U. of Pa. Pr. 1981 $19.95. ISBN 0-8122-1276-2. A survey of Sumerian life and achievements; the rhetorical device—"first achievements"—is at times strained.

———. *In the World of Sumer: An Autobiography.* Wayne St. U. Pr. 1986 $37.50. ISBN 0-8143-1785-5. A personal look at the life of the century's leading Sumerologist.

———. *Sumerian Mythology: A Study of Spiritual and Literary Achievement in the Third Millennium B.C.* Greenwood repr. of 1972 ed. $55.00. ISBN 0-313-26363-9. An examination of important Sumerian texts with many lengthy quotes.

Nissen, Hans. *The Early History of the Ancient Near East, 9000–2000 B.C.* U. Ch. Pr. 1988 $34.95. ISBN 0-226-58656-1. An innovative and up-to-date history for the serious reader. Downplays the significance of the invention of writing; attentive to the role of environment.

Oppenheim, A. Leo. *Ancient Mesopotamia: Portrait of a Dead Civilization.* U. Ch. Pr. 1977 $15.95. ISBN 0-226-63187-7. Features an essay on the dangers of trying to write an overview of Mesopotamian religion.

Pallis, Svend A. *The Babylonian Akitu Festival.* AMS Pr. 1982 repr. of 1926 ed. $42.50. ISBN 0-404-18203-8. Older scholarly study of perhaps the most famous Babylonian ritual.

Ringgren, Helmer. *Religions of the Ancient Near East.* Trans. by John Sturdy. Westminster John Knox 1972 o.p. Survey of Sumerian, Babylonian-Assyrian, and Canaanite religions, with an eye to Old Testament parallels.

EGYPT

The religion of ancient Egypt is remarkable on several accounts. First, it persisted for a very long time relatively undisturbed by foreign influences. Second, at its center stood several distinctive concepts. The world was considered to be an eternal unity; it presided over the king (in later times called the pharaoh) as the living embodiment of the god; the king's primary function was to ensure the continuance of order (*ma'at*) against chaos by performing the daily and seasonal rituals. (In actual practice the king delegated these responsibilities to the priests of various temples.)

Despite the major position of funerary texts and monuments in our knowledge of ancient Egypt, the Egyptians were hardly morbid pessimists. The texts reveal an optimistic attitude toward life, of which death was simply an inevitable part.

The Egyptian gods readily combined the animal and the human, the material and the abstract. For example, the falcon-headed Horus was identified with the reigning king. Each locality had its own system of gods, whose personalities were somewhat fluid.

During the Old Kingdom (dynasties 3–6, roughly 2700–2200 B.C.E.), Egyptian religion was primarily a state religion with little interest in the private concerns of individuals. During this periods the famous pyramids were built as funerary monuments to the king. Later, in less stable times, the Egyptians began to discuss such topics as human responsibility and the possibility of an afterlife for others besides the king. During the New Kingdom (dynasties 18–20, roughly

1600–1100 B.C.E.), the supremacy of the Egyptian empire under the watchful eye of Amon-Re was celebrated in stone with massive, impressive temples at Thebes.

One series of events has long fascinated modern readers. Amenhotep IV (1360–1344 B.C.E.) changed his name to Akhenaton, moved his capital to Amarna, and imposed what to some was a monotheism centered on the sun, Aton. Akhenaton's attempt was as much a political as a religious maneuver; in Egypt the two were hardly distinct. His movement died with the pharaoh himself, and later generations obliterated Akhenaton's name from Egypt's monuments.

TEXTS

Faulkner, Raymond O. *The Ancient Egyptian Book of the Dead.* Ed. by Carol Andrews. U. of Tex. Pr. 1990 $22.95. ISBN 0-292-70425-9. Reliable, readable translations of almost all the spells, together with beautiful photographs depicting many spells from British Museum manuscripts.

Lichtheim, Miriam. *Ancient Egyptian Literature: A Book of Readings.* Vol. 1: *The Old and Middle Kingdoms.* U. CA Pr. 1973 $13.00. ISBN 0-520-02899-6. Vol. 3: *The Late Period.* U. CA Pr. 1980 $37.50. ISBN 0-520-03882-7. Good translations from a wide variety of texts plus brief commentary.

Simpson, William K. *The Literature of Ancient Egypt: An Anthology of Stories, Instructions, and Poetry.* Trans. by R. O. Faulkner, et al. Yale U. Pr. 1973 $16.00. ISBN 0-300-01711-1. Selected translations by leading scholars.

STUDIES

Cerny, Jaroslav. *Ancient Egyptian Religion.* Greenwood 1979 repr. of 1957 ed. $55.50. ISBN 0-313-21104-3. Popular treatment; general but useful.

David, A. Rosalie. *The Ancient Egyptians: Religious Beliefs and Practices. Religious Beliefs and Practices Ser.* Routledge 1982 $19.95. ISBN 0-7100-0878-3. A history of Egyptian religion from the earliest times to the end of the New Kingdom.

El Madhy, Christine. *Mummies, Myth and Magic: In Ancient Egypt.* Thames Hudson 1991 $15.95. ISBN 0-500-27579-3. A profusely illustrated and well-written account of a perennially fascinating topic; more descriptive than analytical.

Frankfort, Henri. *Ancient Egyptian Religion: An Interpretation.* HarpC 1961 $12.00 ISBN 0-06-130077-2. Speculative treatment of selected topics, emphasizing themes of unity and static eternality.

———. *Kingship and the Gods: A Study of Ancient Eastern Religion as the Integration of Society and Nature.* U. Ch. Pr. 1978 repr. of 1948 ed. o.p.

Hornung, Erik. *Conceptions of God in Ancient Egypt.* Cornell Univ. Pr. 1982 $36.50. ISBN 0-8014-1223-4. Insightful study of the interaction of polytheism and unity in the Egyptian view of god.

———. *The Valley of the Kings: Horizon of Eternity.* Trans. by David Warburton. Timken Pubs. 1990 $50.00. ISBN 0-943221-07-2. Features visions of life beyond death in the royal tombs of New Kingdom Egypt; lavishly illustrated; a beautiful book.

Morenz, Siegfreid. *Egyptian Religion.* Cornell Univ. Pr. 1973 $49.95. ISBN 0-8014-0782-6. The best recent, general survey.

Redford, Donald B. *Akhenaton: The Heretic King.* Princeton U. Pr. 1984 ed. $52.50. ISBN 0-691-03567-9. A careful study of the pharaoh and his movement by a scholar thoroughly familiar with the evidence.

Romer, John. *Ancient Lives: Daily Life in Egypt of the Pharaohs.* H. Holt & Co. 1990 $16.95. ISBN 0-8050-1244-3. From a television series; centers on daily life in a village of Egyptian artisans.

Shafer, Byron E. *Religion in Ancient Egypt: Gods, Myths, and Personal Practice.* Cornell Univ. Pr. 1991 $36.95. ISBN 0-8014-9786-8. Accounts by three leading scholars of Egyptian deities, cosmogonies, and religious practice; one of the few recent, comprehensive volumes originally in English.

Secondary Centers of Civilization

IRANIAN RELIGIONS

The religious traditions of Iran prior to the advent of Islam in the seventh century C.E. have been extremely influential in the history of the world's religions. Unfortunately, the available literary sources are fragmentary, not infrequently inconsistent, and at times written in a language that is tremendously difficult to construe.

In origin, the Iranians are Indo-European peoples with close affinities to the Aryans in India. From hints in later writings and from comparative evidence, it seems that these people worshiped a multitude of gods, divided into ashuras and daevas (cp. Sanskrit *asura* and *deva*), through libations and animal sacrifices administered by a class of priests. Followers of GEORGES DUMÉZIL have detected his tripartite ideology in the old Iranian pantheon: the first function represented by Mithra and Ahura Mazda (cp. Sanskrit Mitra and, perhaps, Varuna), the second by Verethraghna (cp. Sanskrit Vritrahan, an epithet of Indra), the third by Anahita, Nanhaithya, and Atar.

The major event in Iranian religions was the reform of Zarathustra, who lived in the eastern part of the region sometime during the first half of the first millennium B.C.E. Zarathustra rejected the sacrifice of animals and formulated an ethical monotheism focused on Ahura Mazda, the "wise lord." The choice between good and evil was reflected in two opposed spirits, twin sons of Ahura Mazda: Spenta Mainyu and Aura Mainyu.

The religion of Zarathustra's followers—Zoroastrianism—is characterized by several distinctive traits: fire rather than animal sacrifice, a dualistic struggle between good and evil in which human beings participate, an apocalyptic vision in which God intervenes at the end of history to vindicate the good, the belief that upon death human beings must successfully negotiate the "bridge of the requiter," and the exposure of corpses to be stripped of their flesh by vultures and other animals, a practice taken from the Magi (pre-Zoroastrian and then Zoroastrian priests of the Medes in western Iran). The Zoroastrian scriptures, the Avesta, contains poems (*Gathas*) attributed to Zarathustra.

Significant features of Judaism, Christianity, and Shi'ite Islam resemble Iranian religions, and scholars have often tried to derive them from Iranian influence. In addition, Iran contributed significant movements to the Hellenistic and Roman worlds: Mithraism (a mystery religion) and Manichaeism (a gnostic religion of salvation). Zoroastrianism still thrives today. Its most numerous representatives are the Parsis, an influential community in India. In recent years, Zoroastrians have also founded institutions in the United States.

TEXTS

Avesta. The Hymns of Zarathustra. Trans. by M. Henning. Hyperion Conn. 1985 repr. of 1952 ed. $23.00. ISBN 0-88355-826-2. Readable translation of the Gathas attributed to Zarathustra.

Boyce, Mary. *Textual Sources for the Study of Zoroastrianism.* U. Ch. Pr. 1990 $12.95. ISBN 0-226-06930-3. Texts from a variety of periods and sources.

Duchesne-Guillemin, Jacques. *Hymns of Zarathustra: Being a Translation of the Gathas Together with Introduction.* C. E. Tuttle 1992 $12.95. ISBN 0-8048-1810-X. An older translation by a once-leading scholar, fortunately back in print.

Malandra, William W. *An Introduction to Ancient Iranian Religions: Readings from the Avesta and Achaemenid Inscriptions.* U. of Minn. Pr. 1983 $29.95. ISBN 0-8166-1114-9. A wide range of readings, organized by topic, with an introduction.

STUDIES

Boyce, Mary. *A History of Zoroastrianism*. Brill 1982 o.p. The now-standard English-language history of the movement, with material on pre-Zoroastrian background.

———. *Zoroastrians*. Ed. by John Hinnels. Routledge 1986 $17.95. ISBN 0-7102-0156-7. A popular account of medieval and modern Zoroastrianism.

Duchesne-Guillemin, Jacques. *The Western Response to Zoroaster*. Greenwood 1973 $47.50. ISBN 0-8371-6590-3. A critical survey of much of Western Zoroastrian scholarship by a leading figure in the field.

Hinnells, John R. *Persian Mythology*. P. Bedrick Bks. 1985 $24.95. ISBN 0-87226-017-8. A useful presentation of both pre-Zoroastrian and Zoroastrian mythology; tastefully illustrated with black-and-white and some color photographs.

———. *Zoroastrianism and the Parsis*. St. Mut. 1985 o.p. A popular, informative account of the Parsis.

HITTITE AND CANAANITE RELIGIONS

The best-known religion of ancient Asia Minor (Turkey) is that of the Hittites. The Hittites were Indo-European peoples who settled in the center of the region and ruled from about 1700 to 1200 B.C.E. Their archives have been discovered at Bogazkoy (ancient Hattusa).

Literary remains are too fragmentary to provide any full information on the myths of these people. Their gods, who were treated as monarchs or masters, lived in temples, from which they occasionally departed if they were displeased. The causes of divine displeasure were discerned through divination. Archaeologists have uncovered prayers by Hittite kings that confess faults to the gods and seek to make expiation. Among the Hittite gods were Tarhum, a weather god associated with a sacred bull, and his wife, the sun goddess Arinnitti. The Hittite goddess Kubaba appears to have become the Hellenistic Cybele, but the precise manner in which this transformation took place is not known.

Of ancient Syria and Palestine, the best-known religion (apart from the religion of ancient Israel) is the religion of the Canaanites. The Canaanites were Semitic-speaking, allegedly pre-Israelite inhabitants of Palestine, with close cultural affinities to ancient Syrian peoples. They are known from the Hebrew Bible and from texts discovered at the site of ancient Ugarit (fl. c.1450–1200 B.C.E.; north coast of Syria). Excavations at Ebla (fl. especially c.2600–2250; northwest Syria) during the last quarter century have also provided us with texts, but the interpretation of these texts is hotly disputed.

The Canaanites worshiped a variety of deities, among them El, king and creator; Asherah, the consort of El; Dragon, an obscure god associated with fertility; Baal ("Lord") Hadad, a storm god who figures in myths of death and resurrection; Anath, the consort of Baal, who resembles the Indian goddess Kali; and Astarte, goddess of love and war. Canaanite myths from Ugarit show strong affinities to the narratives of the Hebrew Bible. Canaanite sacrificial rituals are little known, but seem to have resembled those of ancient Israel. Similarly, it is presumed that the Canaanites had three agricultural festivals similar to the festivals to which the later Israelites gave a historical interpretation: *Pesach* (Passover), *Shavuot* (Weeks or Pentecost), and *Sukkot* (Booths).

Many scholars approach Canaanite religions from the perspective of later Judaism and Christianity. Even with the best of intentions, they often reflect the much too exaggerated distinction between Canaanites and Israelites that was propounded by the Hebrew Bible after the fact and for ideological reasons.

HITTITES—STUDIES

Alexander, Robert L. *The Sculpture and Sculptors of Yazilikava*. U. Delaware Pr. 1986 $35.00. ISBN 0-87413-279-7. An architectural historian, whose primary interest is

America, examines a major, late, Hittite outdoor sanctuary (fourteenth century to twelfth century B.C.E.).

Gurney, O. R. *The Hittites*. Viking Penguin 1991 $11.00. ISBN 0-14-012601-5. A classic account, thankfully back in print.

————. *Some Aspects of Hittite Religion*. OUP 1977 $24.95. ISBN 0-19-725974-X. One of the very few book-length studies of Hittite religion written in English; discusses pantheon, cult, magical formulae.

McMahon, Gregory. *The Hittite State Cult of the Tutelary Deities*. Oriental Inst. 1991 $30.00. ISBN 0-918986-69-9. An analysis of all texts pertinent to the subject; too technical for most readers, but accessible literature, specifically on Hittite religions, is hard to come by.

Macqueen, J. G. *The Hittites and Their Contemporaries in Asia Minor*. Thames Hudson 1986 $22.50. ISBN 0-500-02108-2. Illustrated and readable account of several aspects of Hittite life, including religion.

CANAANITES—TEXTS

Cassuto, Umberto. *The Goddess Anath: Canaanite Epics of the Patriarchal Age*. Eisenbrauns 1971 repr. of 1951 ed. $30.00. ISBN 965-223-482-6. The "sub-subtitle" is *Texts, Hebrew Translation, Commentary, and Introduction*; primarily for scholars, but perhaps useful for the serious reader undeterred by the trappings of scholarship.

Coogan, Michael D., ed. and trans. *Stories from Ancient Canaan*. Westminster John Knox 1978 $8.99. ISBN 0-664-24184-0. Translations of a variety of Ugaritic texts, with introductions; intended for the general reader. A valuable tool.

Driver, G. R. *Canaanite Myths and Legends*. A. R. Allenson 1950 o.p.

CANAANITES—STUDIES

Albright, William F. *Yahweh and the Gods of Canaan: An Historical Analysis of Two Contrasting Faiths*. Eisenbrauns 1990 repr. of 1968 ed. $23.50. ISBN 0-931464-01-3. See especially its Chapter 3, "Canaanite Religion in the Bronze Age."

Gerstenblith, Patty. *The Levant at the Beginning of the Middle Bronze Age*. Eisenbrauns 1983 $17.50. ISBN 0-89757-105-3. Good for archaeological data.

Pettinato, Giovanni. *Ebla: A New Look at History*. Trans. by C. Faith Richardson. Johns Hopkins 1991 $38.95. ISBN 0-8018-4150-X. By the epigrapher of the expedition; a lot of pots and plans, but a few pages on religion, too.

Ringgren, Helmer. *Religions of the Ancient Near East*. Trans. by John Sturdy. Westminster John Knox 1972 o.p.

Sandars, Nancy K. *The Sea Peoples: Warriors of the Ancient Mediterranean 1250 to 1150*. Thames Hudson 1985 o.p.

Young, Gordon Davis, ed. *Ugarit in Retrospect: Fifty Years of Ugarit and Ugaritic*. Eisenbrauns 1981 $22.50. ISBN 0-931464-07-2. Collected articles, mostly in English and mostly technical.

GREEK RELIGION

During the second millennium B.C.E., two different cultural traditions inhabited mainland Greece and the Aegean. The Cretan-based Minoans dominated during the first half of the millennium. They are well known for frescoes depicting a sport of bull-jumping and for a great female deity, depicted with bare breasts, flounced skirt, and snakes in her hands. Although some writers have recently revived the earlier notion that Minoan society was matriarchal, others regard this claim as largely motivated by ideology and lacking sufficient evidence. The mainland-based Mycenaeans dominated during the second half of the millennium. They were Greek-speaking people whose tablets, in a script known as Linear B, have revealed the names of many later Greek gods: the supreme male god Zeus, Hera, Potnia (Athena), and several others, including Dionysus.

"Classical Greece" (more accurately, archaic and classical Greece) refers to the civilization associated with Greek-speaking city-states (*poleis*) and peoples or regions (*ethnē*) in the eastern and central Mediterranean prior to the conquests of Philip II and his son Alexander "the Great" of Macedon (mid-fourth century B.C.). The religious patterns of classical Greece were established in the eighth and early seventh centuries B.C.E., when the polis and Greek literacy developed.

Normative religious structures included activities on three levels: (1) cults of the individual household; (2) the festivals of the polis; and (3) celebrations at pan-Hellenic sanctuaries such as Delphi, Dodona, and Delos. The activities of poets such as HOMER (see also Vol. 2) and HESIOD (see also Vol. 2) systematized the Greek pantheon and myths to some extent, but each polis had its own deities, myths, and festivals. Those of Athens are the best known.

In addition, the Greeks knew several religious practices that stood at more or less distance from the normative observances. Mysteries were secret, initiatory rituals connected with agriculture rather than social structures. The worship of Dionysus celebrated the sacred as destructive of normal order, often in images of bands (*thiasoi*) of raging women (*maenads*) ripping apart animals and eating raw flesh (*omophagia*). Orphism, a nebulous movement, stood at the opposite extreme from Dionysiac movements. It promised a blessed destiny for the soul after death through a life of purification and vegetarianism.

At times the polis appropriated the first two types of observance for itself. The best examples are the mysteries of Eleusis and the festivals of Dionysus at Athens. Orphism remained the preserve of itinerant, charismatic ascetics.

TEXTS

Rice, David G., and John E. Stambaugh, eds. *Sources for the Study of Greek Religion.* Scholars Pr. GA 1979 $13.95. ISBN 0-89130-347-2. Topically arranged selections with brief commentary.

STUDIES

Bernal, Martin. *Black Athena.* Vol. 1: *The Afroasiatic Roots of Classical Civilization: The Fabrication of Ancient Greece, 1785–1985.* Vol. 2: *The Archaeological & Documentary Evidence.* Rutgers U. Pr. 1987, 1991 $60.00 ea. ISBN 0-8135-1276-X, 0-685-48854-3. A controversial account that accuses European scholars of obscuring the African and Asiatic roots of Greek civilization; use with caution, check the reviews.

Boardman, John, and David Finn. *The Parthenon and Its Sculptures.* U. of Tex. Pr. 1985 $45.00. ISBN 0-292-76498-7. A highly readable and visually pleasing treatment of this famous Greek temple by a leading authority.

Caldwell, Richard. *The Origin of the Gods: A Psychoanalytic Study of Greek Theogonic Myth.* OUP 1989 $39.95. ISBN 0-19-505504-7. The succession of the Greek gods provides a likely target for psychoanalytic investigation.

Chadwick, J. *The Mycenaean World.* Cambridge U. Pr. 1976 $59.95. ISBN 0-521-21077-1. A readable, well-illustrated account of the Mycenaeans on the basis of the Linear B tablets, by one of the scholars who deciphered them; a chapter on religion.

Detienne, Marcel. *The Creation of Mythology.* U. Ch. Pr. 1986 o.p.

Dodds, E. R. *The Greeks and the Irrational.* Peter Smith n.d. $23.75. ISBN 0-8466-6224-0. A classical study of Greek psychology.

Ferguson, John. *Among the Gods: An Archaeological Exploration of Ancient Greek Religion.* Routledge 1989 $55.00. ISBN 0-415-02953-8. An extensive and readable account of Greek religious life that relies on archaeological data as much as possible.

Fontenrose, Joseph. *Didyma: Apollo's Oracle, Cult, and Companions.* U. CA Pr. 1988 $47.50. ISBN 0-520-05845-3. By a careful scholar, who has made a career of studying Greek oracles; includes a catalog of oracular responses.

Garland, Robert. *Introducing New Gods: The Politics of Athenian Religion.* Cornell Univ. Pr. 1992 $48.95. ISBN 0-8014-2766-5. A fascinating study exploring by what process new gods and cults were accepted as part of Athenian religion; stops at 399 B.C. (the trial of Socrates).

Lefkowitz, Mary R. *Women in Greek Myth.* Johns Hopkins 1990 repr. of 1986 ed. $10.95. ISBN 0-8018-4108-9. Written for nonspecialists by a respected scholar, aware of modern trends of thought but not bound to them.

Linforth, Ivan M. *The Arts of Orpheus.* Ayer 1977 repr. of 1941 ed. $24.50. ISBN 0-405-04847-5. Hypercritical; refreshing for an occasional shot of academic sobriety.

Parke, H. W. *Festivals of the Athenians. Aspects of Greek and Roman Life Ser.* Cornell Univ. Pr. 1977 $12.95. ISBN 0-8014-9440-0. A reliable, month-by-month survey; little interpretation.

Pomeroy, Sarah B. *Goddesses, Whores, Wives and Slaves: Women in Classical Antiquity.* Schocken 1976 $16.00. ISBN 0-8052-0530-6. The first book to read on women in the ancient world.

Vidal-Naquet, Pierre. *The Black Hunter: Forms of Thought and Forms of Society in the Greek World.* Trans. by Andrew Szegedy Maszak. Johns Hopkins 1986 $48.50. ISBN 0-8018-3251-9. Assorted essays, challenging but stimulating, by a leading French scholar.

ROMAN RELIGION

Rome is said to have been founded April 21, 753 B.C.E. as a Latin settlement on the Palatine Hill. It was governed by a king until 509, when a republic was established. The power of the Roman Republic gradually expanded to encompass much of the Mediterranean world, but republican government collapsed during civil wars in the mid-first century B.C.E. It was replaced by an empire, established about 30 B.C.E. under the beneficent tutelage of Augustus, its "first citizen" or princeps.

Roman religion can be characterized by three distinctive traits. First, the Roman gods were identified not by mythology, which Rome essentially lacked, but by their distinctive functional activities. At times, functional specialization produced a great number of minor deities, each of whom presided over one minute aspect of an entire endeavor. Second, the Romans were religiously conservative. They carefully preserved the ways of the past, even when they had forgotten their meaning or purpose. Third, the Romans readily supplemented their own traditions with the gods and rituals of others. They rarely, however, allowed these new cults inside the sacred boundary of the old city, the pomerium.

The Romans worshiped their gods as necessary to success in any endeavor. During the Republic, several significant developments took place in this worship. Through Greek influence, the Roman gods were given human-like personalities and identified with Greek gods (Jupiter-Zeus; Juno-Hera; Minerva-Athena). Greek influence also led to the adoption of new kinds of rituals for these gods.

Religious functionaries held prominent positions in Roman society and during the Republic importance gradually shifted away from the old functionaries of the monarchy (the *rex sacrorum*—"king of the rites"—and the flamines) toward the *pontifex maximus* (the "highest priest") and several priestly associations or "colleges," such as the college of augurs, from whom officials had to secure divine sanction before undertaking any official act. Originally these offices were the prerogative of the aristocratic or patrician class, but gradually they became open to the people (the "plebs").

TEXTS

Grant, Frederick C., ed. *Ancient Roman Religion*. Macmillan 1957 $6.50. ISBN 0-672-61171-6. A very useful collection of sources, divided more or less by historical periods; scanty on commentary.

STUDIES

Bettini, Maurizio. *Anthropology and Roman Culture: Kinship, Time, Images of the Soul*. Trans. by John van Sickle. *Ancient Society & History Ser*. Johns Hopkins 1991 $36.95. ISBN 0-8018-4104-6. Part 3, by far the shortest, discusses bees, moths, and bats as images of the postmortem soul.

Connor, W. R. *Roman Augury and Etruscan Divination*. *Ancient Religion and Mythology Ser*. Ayer 1976 $14.00. ISBN 0-405-07273-2

Fowler, W. Warde. *The Roman Festivals of the Period of the Republic*. Gordon Pr. 1977 $59.95. ISBN 0-8490-2532-X. A turn-of-the-century, month-by-month account; helpful for data, but depends on outmoded notions of early religion and society.

Henig, Martin. *Religion in Roman Britain*. St. Martin 1984 $29.95. ISBN 0-312-67059-1. Roman religion in a province where remains are very accessible.

Liebeschuetz, J. H. W. G. *Continuity and Change in Roman Religion*. OUP 1979 $79.00. ISBN 0-19-814822-4. A very scholarly study of the interaction of political and religious change.

Ogilvie, R. M. *The Romans and Their Gods in the Age of Augustus*. Norton 1970 $8.95. ISBN 0-393-00543-7. Religion at a time when Romans were conservatively turning to the ways of the past; depends heavily on literary evidence.

Scullard, H. H. *Festivals and Calendars of the Roman Republic*. Cornell Univ. Pr. 1981 $38.95. ISBN 0-8014-1402-4. Month-by-month, day-by-day; more up to date than Fowler, but the weight of sheer description is often overwhelming.

The Mediterranean "Oikoumene": Religions of the Hellenistic World and the Roman Empire

By the time Alexander the Great died in 323 B.C.E., he had overrun the Persian Empire and territories to the east as far as the Indus River. When Rome annexed Egypt almost 300 years later, it had no control over the eastern parts of Alexander's territories, but it joined the rest of Alexander's land to its own holdings to form a unified, civilized world (in Greek, an *oikoumene*) that filled the entire Mediterranean basin. The result was a common, hybrid culture, shared by diverse peoples who were united by two linguae francae, Greek in the east and Latin in the west.

In this oikoumene, the old religious orders—religions of particular peoples and places—remained, but they merely existed, they did not thrive. Several changes overwhelmed them: (1) The new oikoumene dispersed peoples and their religions throughout the "world," and distinctions born from local conceit—Greek/barbarian, Jew/Gentile—gave way to a sophisticated cosmopolitanism. (2) Religions tended to address the needs not of communities but of individuals; as religions of conviction, they promised converts individual rewards, such as a blessed afterlife. (3) The dominant form of religious society was not the community of one's birth but the voluntary association.

A general tolerance marked most of the religious movements and trends of the period, and this tolerance often led to accommodation. Romans adopted Greek rituals and Greek names for their gods. Magical formulae frequently linked the god of the Greeks and the god of the Jews, Zeus and Yahweh (YHWH). Only two exclusive movements violated the general rule of tolerance while otherwise conforming to "ecumenical" patterns: rabbinical Judaism and orthodox-catholic Christianity.

The conversion of the emperor Constantine to orthodox Christianity (c.313 C.E.) marked the beginning of the end of this vibrant period in the history of religions. On November 8, 392, the emperor Theodosius outlawed all pagan practices. The last institution actually to succumb was the temple of Isis at Philae, which ceased to operate during the reign of the emperor Justinian (527–565 C.E.). It is generally supposed, however, that many local practices survived in the cults of saints. Later heresies, such as the Albigensians in southern France, display remarkable similarities to earlier practices, such as Gnosticism.

TEXTS

Austin, M. M. *The Hellenistic World from Alexander to the Roman Conquest: A Selection of Ancient Sources in Translation.* Cambridge U. Pr. 1981 $29.95. ISBN 0-521-29666-8. Includes 279 selections, many from ancient historians, organized by geography and chronology; suggested readings, but few comments.

Bagnell, Roger, and Peter Derow. *Greek Historical Documents: The Hellenistic Period.* Scholars Pr. GA 1981 $15.95. ISBN 0-89130-496-7. Inscriptions and papyri, organized topically with a heavy emphasis on Egypt; 20 documents on religion in Greek cities and Ptolemaic Egypt.

Kraemer, Ross S., ed. *Maenads, Martyrs, Matrons, Monastics: A Sourcebook on Women's Religion in the Greco-Roman World.* Augsburg Fortress 1988 $19.95. ISBN 0-8006-2071-2. Properly ignores the divide between "pagan," Jewish, and Christian to present sources within about 400 years either direction from the turn of the era; very useful.

MacMullen, Ramsay, and Eugene N. Lane, eds. *Paganism and Christianity, 100–425 C.E.: A Sourcebook.* Augsburg Fortress n.d. $14.95. ISBN 0-8006-2647-8. A collection designed to elucidate the religious world that Christianity eventually came to dominate; organized by themes and important historical events.

STUDIES

Brown, Peter. *Society and the Holy in Late Antiquity.* U. CA Pr. 1982 $40.00. ISBN 0-520-04305-7. Masterful essays on both method and selected topics of late antiquity; highly recommended.

Chuvin, Pierre. *A Chronicle of the Last Pagans.* Trans. by B. A. Archer. HUP 1990 $25.00. ISBN 0-674-12970-9. A scholarly and accessible examination of how Christianity took over and what happened.

Dodds, E. R. *Pagan and Christian in an Age of Anxiety: Some Aspects of Religious Experience from Marcus Aurelius to Constantine.* Norton 1991 repr. of 1965 ed. $15.95. ISBN 0-521-38599-7. Attempts to look at psychological causes for the material and spiritual changes that occurred roughly in the third century A.D.

Ferguson, John. *The Religions of the Roman Empire. Aspects of Greek and Roman Life Ser.* Cornell Univ. Pr. 1985 $39.95. ISBN 0-8014-0567-X. Discursive description of Roman religion around the year 200 A.D.

Koester, Helmut. *History, Culture and Religion of the Hellenistic Age.* Vol. 1: *Introduction to the New Testament.* 1982 Mouton 1987 $19.95. ISBN 0-89925-351-2. A full survey of the times, but with less on Hellenistic religions than one might imagine or desire.

Kraemer, Ross S. *Her Share of Blessings: Women's Religions among Pagans, Jews, and Christians in the Greco-Roman World.* OUP 1992 $24.95. ISBN 0-19-506686-3. Not only an account of women's' religions but a reflection on what those religions mean for scholarship; written by a feminist historian, not a theologian.

MacCormack, Sabine. *Art and Ceremony in Late Antiquity.* U. CA Pr. 1981 $15.95. ISBN 0-520-06966-8. Detailed, readable, and intelligent study of the art and ceremony of the imperial court after Diocletian; illustrated, but not so well as one would like.

MacMullen, Ramsay. *Paganism in the Roman Empire.* Yale U. Pr. 1981 $12.00. ISBN 0-300-02984-5. By a scholar who has been pioneering new approaches to the subject.

Martin, Luther H. *Hellenistic Religions: An Introduction.* OUP 1987 $24.95. ISBN 0-19-504390-1. The best, book-length introduction to the subject available.

MYSTERIES

Mysteries derive their name from the manner in which their most sacred rituals and narratives were performed: in secret celebrations to which only initiates were admitted. They also often included other acts, such as processions, that were performed publicly. Many but not all mysteries had their roots in seasonal, agricultural celebrations. By Hellenistic and Roman times they had been individualized and interiorized. Their common concern was with the fate of the individual after death, generally the fate of the individual soul.

There were many different mystery religions, each with its own deity, rituals, and class of worshipers. In them, feminine images of the divine often predominated. The Great Mother of Phrygia, Cybele, was worshiped particularly by craftsmen. Her priests publicly castrated themselves in imitation of her young lover Attis. The most popular mysteries were the mysteries of Isis, originally connected with the funerary rites of the dead Egyptian king. Her mysteries were practiced especially by the lower classes in seaport and trading towns. Especially popular with Roman soldiers and administrators was the god Mithras, originally an Indo-Iranian god, who created life by capturing and slaying a bull. The mysteries of Sol Invictus, the Syrian sun-god whose birthday was celebrated on December 25, were eventually assimilated with the mysteries of Mithras. They were very popular during the third century C.E., and for a time they were promoted as the official religion of the Roman Empire.

During the second century Christianity came to be practiced as a mystery cult; for example, only initiates were allowed to be present at the celebration of the Eucharist. Christianity still retains many features derived from the mysteries, such as occasional liturgical references to Christ as the Sun (Sol) and the celebration of his birth on December 25. Many Gnostic movements also adopted the trappings of the mystery cults.

Burkert, Walter. *Ancient Mystery Cults. Carl Newell Jackson Lectures Ser.* HUP 1987 $8.95. ISBN 0-674-03387-6. Not a description, but an interpretation that begins with the mysteries as personal religion then discusses organization, "theology," and experience.

Cumont, Franz. *The Mysteries of Mithra.* Trans. by Thomas J. McCormack. Dover 1956 repr. of 1911 ed. $6.95. ISBN 0-486-20323-9. An older, useful account of the growth of Mithraism and its teachings, practices, and institutions.

Godwin, Joscelyn. *Mystery Religions in the Ancient World.* Harper SF 1981 $9.95. ISBN 0-06-063140-6. Probably the best introduction for the average reader; illustrated.

Meyer, Marvin, ed. *The Ancient Mysteries: A Sourcebook.* Harper SF 1987 $14.95. ISBN 0-06-065576-3. Essential sources for studying the mysteries, with some introductory material.

Nilsson, Martin P. *The Dionysiac Mysteries of the Hellenistic and Roman Age. Ancient Religion and Mythology Ser.* Ayer 1976 repr. of 1957 ed. $15.95. ISBN 0-405-07261-9. A readable, illustrated essay with occasional terms in Greek, by a reliable and respected scholar.

Ulansey, David. *The Origins of the Mithraic Mysteries: Cosmology and Salvation in the Ancient World.* OUP 1991 repr. of 1989 ed. $7.95. ISBN 0-19-506788-6. Elucidates the relationship between the mysteries of Mithras and ancient astronomical lore.

HEALERS, MAGICIANS, AND DIVINE MEN

Even before the oikoumene, the peoples of the Mediterranean were familiar with the arcane arts of the Middle East. Etruscan haruspicy seems to have been indebted to Babylonian divination, while the skills and lore of the Magi, priests of the Medes, had become legendary among the Greeks. The cosmopolitan culture of the oikoumene gave the practitioners of arcane arts a wide territory in which to display their talents. In the first two centuries of the Roman Empire, charismatic individuals of all sorts—prophets, magicians, and healers—abounded.

Astrology was extremely fashionable during this period. In fact, it was during the Hellenistic period that astrology as ordinarily practiced—with signs of the zodiac, planets and their houses, and correspondences between the heavens and the human body—was invented.

During the same period, the resort to magicians and magical formulae was common on every level of society. Disease was often attributed to the influence of demons. As a result, magicians were often summoned to identify the offending demons and order them to depart. The ability to perform magical acts might not simply be a sign of special skills. Those who performed wonders were at times endowed with an aura of divinity. They were "divine men."

These last characteristics have, of course, a certain affinity to the person of Jesus. A more pagan example might be Apollonius of Tyana, a wandering ascetic and teacher in the neo-Pythagorean tradition. Apollonius is alleged to have performed miracles of healing, including resuscitating the dead.

In the early twentieth century, scholars tried to explain these similarities by saying that Christian stories of Jesus had imitated pagan myths. Later, scholars suggested that pagans have borrowed from Christians. Recently, JONATHAN Z. SMITH has suggested what may more closely approximate the truth: Neither borrowed from the other; instead, both went through the same developmental process.

Betz, Hans Dieter, ed. *The Greek Magical Papyri in Translation, including the Demotic Spells.* U. Ch. Pr. 1992 $45.00. ISBN 0-226-04446-7. Translation, with full scholarly apparatus, of very important documents for the study of ancient magic.

Corrington, Gail Peterson. *The "Divine Man": His Origin and Function in Hellenistic Popular Religion.* P. Lang Pubs. 1986 $35.00. ISBN 0-8204-0299-0. Sees divine men against a popular rather than literary or philosophical background.

Cumont, Franz. *Astrology and Religion among the Greeks and Romans.* Dover 1912 $4.50. ISBN 0-486-20581-9. The best book on Greek astrology is even older and in French, but this provides a good introduction.

Faraone, Christopher A., and Dirk Obbink, eds. *Magika Hiera: Ancient Greek Magic and Religion.* OUP 1991 $42.50. ISBN 0-19-504450-9. Essays by ten scholars who consider both new data and new methods of working with them; for serious readers.

Hadas, Moses, and Morton Smith. *Heroes and Gods: Spiritual Biographies in Antiquity. Essay Index Repr. Ser.* Ayer repr. of 1965 ed. $19.00. ISBN 0-8369-1880-0. General study of "aretalogies" (accounts of miraculous deeds) from the Greek heroes to Christian martyrs; includes translations and summaries of more notable texts (including the Gospel of Luke).

Luck, Georg. *Arcana Mundi: Magic and the Occult in the Greek and Roman Worlds.* Johns Hopkins 1985 $14.95. ISBN 0-8018-2548-2. Primarily literary texts, a few formulaic papyri, with sometimes lengthy introduction, pertaining to magic, miracles, demonology, divination, astrology, and alchemy.

IMPERIAL CULT

The modern secular state is a new star that arose on the horizon of history during the Enlightenment. Before then, religion and politics were generally intertwined, often in very complicated ways.

In the first two centuries of the Roman Empire, the relation between religion and politics took a form that we are likely to misread as a cheap political trick: worship of the emperor. Alexander the Great, never given to modesty, had earlier had himself proclaimed the son of Zeus Ammon. The practice offended his Greek soldiers but not the conquered peoples, who were accustomed to associate their rulers with the divine. The cult of the ruler continued among Alexander's successors. As Rome expanded, victorious generals and provincial governors found themselves accorded divine honors in the east. When JULIUS CAESAR (see Vol. 3) was apotheosized by the Senate, his adopted son, the emperor Augustus, erected temples dedicated to both Rome (whose protective spirits had long been worshiped) and the divine Julius.

The cult of the emperor took many forms: cults fostered by the imperial government, cults granted by individual municipalities, and cults established by private individuals and corporations. In the Augustan period, worship was directed to Rome and Augustus jointly—in Italy, to the genius (life spirit) of Augustus and the guardians of the crossroads. Later emperors were worshiped in association not with Rome but with the collective body of emperors, or else simply individually. In Rome, an emperor generally did not receive divine honors until after his death. Recent scholarship has begun to note that the emperor, although divine, was not given quite the same honor or status as the other, traditional gods.

The imperial cult waned in the third century. It was replaced by the view that the emperor ruled on the basis of divine appointment.

Fears, J. Rufus. *Princeps A Diis Electus: The Divine Election of the Emperor as a Political Concept at Rome.* Am. Acad. Rome 1977 o.p. Religious and historical assessment—for the serious student.

Millar, Fergus. *The Emperor in the Roman World. Aspects of Greek and Roman Life Ser.* Cornell Univ. Pr. 1992 $21.95. ISBN 0-8014-8049-3. General discussion, with occasional references to religious aspects.

Price, S. R. F. *Rituals and Power: The Roman Imperial Cult in Asia Minor.* Cambridge U. Pr. 1985 $21.95. ISBN 0-521-31268-X. A careful study that reassesses the nature of the emperor's divinity in Asia Minor; difficult for the average reader, but worth it.

Schowalter, Daniel N. *The Emperor and the Gods: Images from the Time of Trojan. Harvard Dissertations in Religion Ser.* Augsburg Fortress 1993 $14.95. ISBN 0-8006-7082-5. Uses a panoply of evidence from Trojan's time (98–117 A.D.) to argue that the emperor and his relation to the gods were portrayed in many different ways.

Taylor, Lily R. *The Divinity of the Roman Emperor.* Scholars Pr. GA 1981 $22.50. ISBN 0-89130-702-8. An older account, in its own way a classic, the general reader may find useful and accessible.

GNOSTICISM

The name *Gnosticism* derives from the Greek word *gnosis*, "knowledge." It refers to a variety of movements in the late ancient world that shared one fundamental trait: in them, a person was said to be saved by esoteric knowledge. The origins of Gnosticism and its precise relation to Christianity—was it a heresy or an independent movement?—are disputed. In any case, Gnosticism was flourishing by the second century C.E.

Gnosticism never had an organized hierarchy to insist on a uniform set of beliefs or practices. The typical organization was that of an elite teacher with a select band of followers. Gnosticism also did not have a universally accepted set of sacred writings. Instead, Gnostics wrote their own rather obscure compositions and used allegory to read the scriptures of many different religions in a peculiarly gnostic manner. Similarly, Gnostics often borrowed and adapted cultic observances from other religious traditions, although they considered some practices, such as baptism and the Christian Eucharist, suspect.

The Gnostics were dualists. They sharply distinguished light from darkness and spirit from matter. In their view, the world was not created by the supreme God, the absolute good spirit. Rather, the world was basically a mistake that came into existence through division, a fall, or the agency of a lesser demiurge, often identified with the Jewish god Yahweh (YHWH). But Gnosticism also taught that human beings were intrinsically related to the supreme "unknown God." They contained a certain divine spark, and it was the purpose of Gnosticism to liberate this divine spark through knowledge revealed by a divine emissary or redeemer. Gnostic myths often invert images familiar from the Bible. As a result, Gnostic texts make plentiful use of feminine figures.

For centuries Gnosticism was known primarily from the writings of its Christian enemies. In 1945 a large number of writings, many of them Gnostic, were discovered at Nag Hammadi in Egypt. Scholars are still assessing their implications. One Gnostic sect, the Mandaeans, may still reside in southern Iraq, although scholars who study them have been unable to establish contact after the Persian Gulf War.

TEXTS

Grant, Robert M., ed. *Gnosticism: A Source Book of Heretical Writings from the Early Christian Period*. AMS Pr. 1961 $32.50. ISBN 0-404-16108-1. A convenient selection from Gnostic texts.

Layton, Bentley. *The Gnostic Scriptures: A New Translation with Annotations*. Doubleday 1987 $35.00. ISBN 0-385-17447-0. A very useful, highly recommended collection, organized according to Gnostic school, with extremely helpful supporting material.

Robinson, James M., ed. *The Nag Hammadi Library in English*. Harper SF 1990 repr. of 1978 ed. $18.00. ISBN 0-06-066935-7. Updated translations of the Nag Hammadi Codices; indispensable for the study of Gnosticism.

STUDIES

Hedrick, Charles W., and Robert Hodgson, eds. *Nag Hammadi, Gnosticism, and Early Christianity*. Hendrickson MA 1986 $14.95. ISBN 0-913573-16-7. Collection of articles by leading scholars.

Jonas, Hans. *The Gnostic Religion: The Message of the Alien God and the Beginnings of Christianity*. Peter Smith 1961 $27.75. ISBN 0-8446-2339-3. For years the standard book with which to begin studying Gnosticism.

King, Karen L., ed. *Images of the Feminine in Gnosticism. Studies in Antiquity and Christianity Ser.* Augsburg Fortress 1988 $44.95. ISBN 0-8006-3103-X. Collected essays on an important facet of Gnosticism and one that distinguishes it from orthodox Christianity.

Pagels, Elaine. *The Gnostic Gospels*. Random 1989 $9.00. ISBN 0-679-72453-2. A scholarly study that has not met with uniform assent.

Pearson, Birger A. *Gnosticism, Judaism, and Egyptian Christianity*. Augsburg Fortress 1990 $29.95. ISBN 0-8006-3104-8. Collected essays intended for a scholarly audience; general readers may benefit from the essays on Seth, Norea, Cain, and Melchizedek.

Rudolph, Kurt. *Gnosis: The Nature and History of Gnosticism*. Trans. by P. W. Coxon, K. H. Kuhn, and R. M. Wilson. Harper SF 1982 $18.00. ISBN 0-06-067018-5. The best, current, comprehensive survey, discussing the sources, general structure, and history of Gnosticism.

ANCIENT URBAN CIVILIZATIONS: RELIGIONS OF THE NEW WORLD

For years many scholars of prehistoric America believed that human beings had lived in the New World much earlier than the available evidence indicated.

In recent years, dramatic discoveries have begun to confirm that suspicion. An example from North America is the Meadowcroft Rock Shelter in Pennsylvania, with finds datable roughly to 20,000 years ago.

But compared with the Old World, civilizations in the New World arose rather late, for the American environment posed different challenges from those of Europe, Asia, and North Africa. For example, the inhabitants of the Americas needed to develop to a high degree the cultivation of several different crops (corn, beans, squash) that they could plant concurrently before a large population could be sustained in a small area. As early as 6500 B.C.E., inhabitants of the New World began to domesticate plants, but two important crops, maize and then beans, appear not to have been domesticated until about 3,000 years later. Village settlements began to appear in Mesoamerica and Peru sometime around 2000 B.C.E. We can begin to detect the rise of civilizations in these regions from about 1200 B.C.E. from the remains of monumental traditions of temple architecture and sculpture.

Carrasco, David. *Religions of Mesoamerica.* Harper SF 1990 $10.00. ISBN 0-06-061325-4. A beginning college text that emphasizes especially cosmology and the ceremonial center; highly recommended.

Dixon, E. James. *Quest for the Origins of the First Americans.* U. of NM Pr. 1993 $24.95. ISBN 0-8263-1406-6

Fagan, Brian M. *Kingdoms of Gold, Kingdoms of Jade: The Americas Before Columbus.* Thames Hudson 1991 $24.95. ISBN 0-500-05062-7. Beautifully illustrated account of the cultural riches and diversity of pre-Columbian Americas, with much attention to religion; for the general reader.

Hill, Jonathan D., ed. *Rethinking History and Myth: Indigenous South American Perspectives on the Past.* U. of Ill. Pr. 1988 o.p.

Lamberg-Karlovsky, C. C., and Jeremy A. Sabloff. *Ancient Civilizations: The Near East and Mesoamerica.* Waveland Pr. 1987 repr. of 1979 ed. $19.95. ISBN 0-88133-301-8. More on the Old than the New World, but the discussion is insightful and acquaints the reader with different scholars and their theories, although it tends to downplay religious influences.

Miller, Mary E. *The Art of Mesoamerica. World of Art Ser.* Thames Hudson 1986 $12.95. ISBN 0-500-20203-6. A beautiful and insightful account of Mesoamerican art, from the Olmecs to the Aztecs; this book is a must.

Religions of Mesoamerica

THE MAYAN REGION

In Mesoamerica, civilization first developed in the alluvial lowlands of Tabasco and the Yucatan peninsula. The earliest civilization is associated with people known as the Olmecs, whose remains have been found at such sites as San Lorenzo, La Venta, and Tres Zapotes (late second to first millennium B.C.E.). The Olmecs were succeeded by the Maya, who flourished in the Yucatan lowlands especially from 300 to 900 C.E. After this "classical period," the Maya did not disappear. Their descendants survive to this day, practicing a variety of Christianity that integrates many native elements.

The interpretation of Olmec religious monuments is a particularly vexing problem. Religion seems to have centered on complex rites performed in temples for the sake of both cosmic and sociopolitical well-being. On one account, Olmec iconography utilized especially two different figures: a Dragon (crocodile-eagle-jaguar-human-serpent) as a deity of an elite, and a Bird Monster (eagle-mammal-reptile) associated with agriculture and mind-altering substances. There is some evidence that the Olmecs knew the sacred ballgame characteristic of later Mesoamerican religions. A stela at Tres Zapotes also makes it look as if the so-called Maya calendar was actually an Olmec invention.

The Mayan religion continued features found earlier among the Olmecs: temples as the ceremonial centers of settlements, elaborate rituals performed by a priesthood, and perhaps the androgynous creator god known to the Maya as Itzamna. The Maya divided their world into four directions, with a "first tree" at the center. Above the earth were several layers of "heaven," below was the realm of Xibalba. Bloodletting played an important role in ritual, helping establish a relationship of reciprocity between human beings and the gods.

Perhaps the most impressive religious achievement of the Olmecs and Maya is the calendar. It consisted of two separate, concurrent cycles, a 260-day cycle of 20 13-day "weeks" and a 365-day cycle of 18 20-day "months," supplemented by 5 intercalary days. Specific conjunctions of the two cycles recurred after an interval of 52 years. The great 52-year "Calendar Round" began on the conjunction of the first days of both cycles. It marked the periodic dissolution and re-creation of the world. The Maya also recorded dates with a system known as the "Long Count," a set of numbers whose longest unit stood for 400 360-day years. The first day of the Long Count referred to a date in 3114 B.C.E. If it were still in use, the Long Count would end on December 23, 2012.

OLMECS

Bernal, Ignacio. *The Olmec World*. Trans. by Fernando Horcasitas. U. CA Pr. 1969 $16.95. ISBN 0-520-02891-0. A general cultural survey, with some illustrations, that includes a brief section on Olmec religion.

Coe, Michael D., and Richard A. Diehl. *In the Land of the Olmec*. U. of Tex. Pr. 2 vols. 1980 $100.00. ISBN 0-292-77549-0. Volume 1 is a report on excavations at San Lorenzo; volume 2 is an ethnography of the people of the region, together with the region's history.

Nicholson, H. B., ed. *Origins of Religious Art and Iconography in Preclassic Mesoamerica*. U. of S. CA Lat. Amer. Ctr. 1976 o.p. Contains a definitive paper on the Dragon and Bird Monster by Peter Joralemon.

Piña Chan, Román. *The Olmec: Mother Culture of Mesoamerica*. Ed. by Laura Laurencich Minelli. Rizzoli 1989 o.p.

Sharer, Robert J., and David C. Grove, eds. *Regional Perspectives on the Olmec. School of American Research Advanced Seminar Ser.* Cambridge U. Pr. 1989 $59.95. ISBN 0-521-36332-2. Scientific and humanistic archaeologists—explainers and interpreters—examine many topics, including religion; questions Olmec influence on all later Mesoamerican cultures.

Soustelle, Jacques. *The Olmecs: The Oldest Civilization in Mexico*. Trans. by Helen R. Lane. U. of Okla. Pr. 1985 $12.95. ISBN 0-8061-1962-4. An up-to-date synthesis.

MAYA

Aveni, Anthony F. *Skywatchers of Ancient Mexico. Texas Pan-Amer. Ser.* U. of Tex. Pr. 1983 $22.95. ISBN 0-292-77578-4. Something of a classic text by a leader in the study of archaeoastronomy; well worth reading.

Fash, William L. *Scribes, Warriors and Kings: The City of Copan and the Ancient Maya*. Thames Hudson 1993 $19.95. ISBN 0-500-27708-7. By a participant in recent, significant, and innovative archaeological work at Copan, Honduras, in the Southern Mayan Lowlands.

Hammond, Norman. *Ancient Maya Civilization*. Rutgers U. Pr. 1982 $15.00. ISBN 0-8135-0906-8. A recent survey for the general reader of Mayan history and way of life; includes a short chapter on religion.

Henderson, John S. *The World of the Ancient Maya*. Cornell Univ. Pr. 1983 $18.95. ISBN 0-8014-9257-2. An illustrated survey, organized more or less chronologically, with a nice chapter on the Maya worldview.

Sabloff, Jeremy A. *The New Archaeology and the Ancient Maya*. W. H. Freeman 1989 $32.95. ISBN 0-7167-5054-6. The latest that archaeology has to offer about the Maya; readable and beautifully illustrated; highly recommended, even if religion only appears sporadically.

Scarborough, Vernon L., and David R. Wilcox, eds. *The Mesoamerican Ballgame*. U. of Ariz. Pr. 1991 $45.00. ISBN 0-8165-1180-2. Sixteen scholarly essays on the ballgame in different locations, as well as on its symbolism and iconography.

Tedlock, Barbara. *Time and the Highland Maya*. U. of NM Pr. 1992 $14.95. ISBN 0-8263-1358-2. Divination and the calendar among contemporary Maya.

Tedlock, Dennis. *Popol Vuh: The Definitive Edition of the Mayan Book of the Dawn of Life and the Glories Gods and Kings*. S&S Trade 1986 $10.95. ISBN 0-671-61771-0. An important Mayan text, with notes, glossary, and an extensive introduction.

Thompson, J. Eric S. *Maya History and Religion. Civilization of the Amer. Indian Ser*. U. of Okla. Pr. 1970 o.p. In-depth but readable accounts of such topics as the use of tobacco, patterns of worship, the major and lesser gods, and creation myths.

THE MEXICAN HIGHLANDS

Civilization in the drier highlands of central Mexico began later than in the moister lowlands, but it followed similar patterns, perhaps inherited from the Olmecs.

The most significant early settlement was the city of Teotihuacan, about 30 miles northeast of Mexico City. The city flourished especially between 100 and 650 C.E.; it was later regarded as a mythical, perfect city by both Toltecs and Aztecs. Teotihuacan is especially notable for the care with which it was laid out. The city was divided into quarters by two broad avenues that crossed at right angles. The Avenue of the Dead, the major north-south avenue one-and-a-half miles long, connected the pyramid of the moon at its north with the temple of Quetzalcoatl at its south. Along the east side of the avenue was a complex containing the massive pyramid of the sun.

After the decline of Teotihuacan, the Toltecs were the next major group to dominate the region. They founded the city of Tula about 50 miles north of Mexico City. One of their most fateful contributions was the mythological figure, Topiltzin Quetzalcoatl. Tales of his early life included accounts of a miraculous birth, rigorous training, and a vision of the cosmic pair, Omoteotl. After ascending the throne of Tula, Topiltzin forbade human sacrifice, but he lost his throne in dispute with a rival. Dying in exile, he was transformed into the Morning Star. Legend said he would return one day from the east, and when Cortez appeared, apparently some Aztecs believed he had.

The last of the great civilizations of the Mexican highlands was that of the Aztecs, who called themselves Mexica. At the direction of their patron deity, the Aztecs built their city, Tenochtitlan, in 1325 on an island in the center of a lake, today the site of Mexico City.

The Aztecs preserved the elaborate spatial and temporal arrangements of their Mesoamerican predecessors. They worshiped several gods in anthropomorphic form, who show iconographical similarities with the gods of earlier peoples. Among their gods were Huitzilopochtli, their patron; the celestial androgyne Omoteotl; and his/her four offspring: Tezcatlipoca (the archsorcerer), Quetzalcoatl (the feathered serpent god), Xiuhtecuhtli (the sacred fire), and Tlaloc (god of rain and fertility).

Aztec religion attempted to maintain the orders of the universe and of society by imitating the creative sacrifice of the gods. The most notorious and typical of Aztec rituals was the heart sacrifice, practiced primarily for the purpose of nourishing the sun. A major site of that practice was the immense Templo Mayor, the remains of which were recently unearthed in Mexico City.

TEOTIHUACAN

Berlo, Janet C., ed. *Art, Ideology, and the City of Teotihuacan: A Symposium at Dumbarton Oaks, 8th and 9th October 1988.* Dumbarton Oaks 1993 $38.00. ISBN 0-88402-205-6. Scholarly essays that represent a tremendous increase in knowledge of the distinctive site of Teotihuacan; contains a survey of research 1950–1990.

Berrin, Kathleen, and Esther Pazstory, eds. *Teotihuacan.* Thames Hudson 1993 $45.00. ISBN 0-500-23653-4. Profusely illustrated with interpretive essays by scholars and published in conjunction with an exhibit at The Fine Arts Museum of San Francisco.

Moctezuma, Eduardo M. *Teotihuacan: The City of Gods.* Rizzoli Intl. 1990 $75.00. ISBN 0-8478-1198-0. Beautiful photographs with a brief text by a highly respected Mexican archaeologist; a brief section specifically on religion.

TOLTECS

Davies, Nigel. *The Toltec Heritage: From the Fall of Tula to the Rise of Tenochtitlan.* U. of Okla. Pr. 1980 $34.50. ISBN 0-8061-1505-X

_____. *The Toltecs, Until the Fall of Tula.* U. of Okla. Pr. 1987 $18.95. ISBN 0-8061-2071-1. Both volumes by Davies immerse the reader in the many problems that arise in studying the Toltecs. The first is a close look at a very obscure period.

Diehl, Richard A. *Tula: The Toltec Capital of Ancient Mexico.* Thames Hudson 1983 $29.95. ISBN 0-500-39018-5. A profusely and beautifully illustrated book, discussing the excavations at Tula and the Toltec culture, by the director of the excavations; little specifically on religion.

Healan, Dan M., ed. *Tula of the Toltecs: Excavations and Survey.* U. of Iowa Pr. 1989 $47.95; incl. computer disk. ISBN 0-87745-209-1. For those whose interest in Tula is serious enough to wade through archaeological reports.

AZTECS

Aveni, Anthony F. *Skywatchers of Ancient Mexico.* Texas Pan-Amer. Ser. U. of Tex. Pr. 1983 $22.95. ISBN 0-292-77578-4. Something of a classic text by a leader in the study of archaeoastronomy; well worth reading.

Broda, Johanna, David Carrasco, and Eduardo Moctezuma. *The Great Temple of Tenochtitlan: Center and Periphery in the Aztec World.* U. CA Pr. 1988 $42.50. ISBN 0-520-05602-7. Three interpretive articles on the great, central temple of the Aztecs; including information on history and symbolism, ritual, and myth.

Brundage, Burr C. *The Fifth Sun: Aztec Gods, Aztec World.* Texas Pan-Amer. Ser. U. of Tex. Pr. 1979 $13.95. ISBN 0-292-72438-1. Perhaps the best book with which to start; focuses on myths and worldview.

_____. *The Jade Steps: A Ritual Life of the Aztecs.* U. of Utah Pr. 1985 o.p.

Carrasco, David, ed. *To Change Place: Aztec Ceremonial Landscapes.* Univ. Pr. Colo. 1991 $29.95. ISBN 0-87081-194-0. Brings together scholars of many backgrounds to explore the ceremonial disposition and transformation of space.

Clendinnen, Inga. *Aztecs: An Interpretation.* Cambridge U. Pr. 1991 $29.95. ISBN 0-521-40093-7. A remarkable attempt "to discover something of the distinctive tonalities of life . . . in the early 16th century"; much to say on ordinary people and human sacrifice.

Conrad, Geoffrey W., and Arthur A. Demarest. *Religion and Empire: The Dynamics of Aztec and Inca Expansion.* Cambridge U. Pr. 1984 o.p.

Davies, Nigel. *The Aztecs: A History.* U. of Okla. Pr. 1980 repr. of 1973 ed. $16.95. ISBN 0-8061-1691-9. For those who want a general, historical overview.

Leon-Portilla, Miguel. *Aztec Image of Self and Society: An Introduction to Nahua Culture.* Ed. by J. Jorge Klor de Alva. U. of Utah Pr. 1992 $27.50. ISBN 0-87480-360-8. By a preeminent Mexican scholar who interweaves Nahua and Spanish accounts with modern reflections.

Inca Religion

When the Spaniards first came to the Andes in 1527, the Incas were the dominant power. Their empire was relatively new. They had started to expand about a century earlier, and they had been preceded by several civilizations in the region. Unfortunately, we have no written records from the Incas or any other pre-Columbian Andean peoples (as we do for the Maya and Aztecs in Mesoamerica). Knowledge of their religion is limited.

Among the gods of the Incas were Viracocha, a creator and culture-hero; Inti, the sun, the supreme god; Apu Illapu, the giver of rain; and Mama-Kilya, the goddess of the moon. The Incas built temples for these gods, often in the form of stepped pyramids, the most famous of which is the temple of the sun at Cuzco. In addition, there were many smaller shrines and sacred places.

The temples housed not only the images of the gods but also priests and "chosen women" dedicated to temple service. Typical Inca religious practices included sacrifice, in times of extreme need human sacrifice, and (like the Romans) the resort to divination before every official activity. The Inca calendar had 12 months of 30 days each. It identified both religious and agricultural occasions.

Cobo, Bernabe. *Inca Religion and Customs*. Ed. and trans. by Roland Hamilton. U. of Tex. Pr. 1990 $25.00. ISBN 0-292-73854-4. An account by a Jesuit active among the Inca in the early 1600s; dependent upon earlier, written sources.

MacCormack, Sabine. *Religion in the Andes: Vision and Imagination in Early Colonial Peru*. Princeton U. Pr. 1991 $39.50. ISBN 0-691-09468-3. How both Inca imperial religion and the non-Inca local religions were remembered, represented, and practiced in the first 200 years after the arrival of the Spanish.

Moseley, Michael E. *The Incas and their Ancestors: The Archaeology of Peru*. Thames Hudson 1992 $35.00. ISBN 0-500-05063-5. An account of the Inca, then of the steps that produced their civilization; sporadic, scant attention to religion.

Silverblatt, Irene. *Moon, Sun and Witches: Gender Ideologies and Class in Inca and Colonial Peru*. Princeton U. Pr. 1987 $45.00. ISBN 0-691-07726-6. The construction of gender distinctions and hierarchies, including the role of religion.

Urton, Gary. *At the Crossroads of the Earth and the Sky: An Andean Cosmology*. U. of Tex. Pr. 1988 repr. of 1981 ed. $11.95. ISBN 0-292-70404-6. Fieldwork among a contemporary Andean people (at Misminay) reveals astronomical beliefs and practices strongly reminiscent of the ancient Incas.

Zuidema, R. Tom. *Inca Civilization in Cuzco*. Trans. by Jean-Jacques Decoster. U. of Tex. Pr. 1990 $19.95. ISBN 0-292-73850-1. The way the Inca organized the world, centering on kinship but with an eye toward the whole cosmos.

INDIGENOUS RELIGIONS OF AUSTRALIA AND OCEANIA, AFRICA, AND THE AMERICAS

The religions of the indigenous peoples of Australia and Oceania, sub-Saharan Africa, and the Americas are ancient religions only in a very loose sense of the term. For example, one might say that a native American ritual belongs to "the religion of the ancients," but such a phrase is misleading. It tempts us to view indigenous practices as both age-old and irrelevant to modern life. The truth is that indigenous religions have never been static. They are not fossils preserved from the Stone Age. Like the religions of urban civilizations, they can and do change with time, sometimes dramatically. Furthermore, inherited indigenous traditions still can and do influence contemporary life, even in "modern" settings.

The number of different indigenous religions is immense. For example, some estimate that there are as many as 700 different indigenous religions in sub-Saharan Africa alone. Obviously, this chapter cannot begin to provide references to them all, but indigenous religions tend to show regional similarities. Therefore, this section is divided along broad geographical lines: the religions of Australia and Oceania, of Africa, and of the Americas.

There is danger in this approach. In some sense, continental regions are still too broad. The best works on indigenous religions tend to be focused much more narrowly. They usually deal only with the beliefs, practices, and institutions of a particular people.

One of the most important recent developments in writing on the indigenous religions of North America, Africa, and to a lesser extent Australia is the appearance of books by indigenous people themselves. It is understandable and salutary that these writers vigorously insist on the dignity of their beliefs and practices in confrontation with those who in their eyes have misrepresented and ravaged them, including many scholars, and work hard to recover a heritage from which they feel forcibly distanced. It often remains to be seen what sort of critical distance these indigenous writers will bring to their own traditions.

Two other topics deserve special attention in this section. Indigenous religions have often been called "nonliterate religions," for the peoples who practice them have not traditionally had means of writing. Scholars have discussed the implications of orality and literacy extensively, not just in relation to the indigenous peoples on whom this section focuses but also in relation to the ancient Mediterranean world. Some of the more important contributions are listed below. In addition, the modern West has had an immense impact on most indigenous societies, including their religions. The confrontation with the West forms the last topic of this section.

Orality and Literacy

Discussions of the peculiar nature of oral traditions are at least as old as 1762. In that year, the Scottish poet James MacPherson published what he claimed were translations of orally transmitted poems by the Scottish Gaelic poet Ossian (third century C.E.). For the next century, MacPherson's claim sparked debate all over Europe. At roughly the same time, Europeans developed a great deal of interest in collecting folklore of all sorts. Much of the impetus came from the ideas of JOHANN GOTTFRIED VON HERDER (see also Vols. 2 and 3), who insisted that poetry derived from feelings human beings had when they encountered the world and that these feelings were best expressed not in literate poetry but in oral folk songs.

In the last few decades, discussions have focused on the conditions that orality imposes on nonliterate cultures. One major hypothesis suggests that oral compositions, especially poetry, are constructed from a traditional store of formulaic phrases and themes. This hypothesis was developed by Milman Parry and his student, Albert Lord, on the basis of contemporary Yugoslav and ancient Homeric poetry. A bolder theory suggests that the technology of communication (oral, literate, electronic) inevitably conditions the nature of thought. This suggestion was made most notoriously by MARSHALL MCLUHAN (see Vol. 3); among more professional scholars the view has been advanced best by the anthropologist Jack Goody and among students of antiquity by Eric Havelock. Both theories are suggestive, but neither has found universal assent. It has become clear that the distinction between orality and literacy is complex and related to many other distinctions, for example, that between elite and popular.

Especially during the last 15 years, scholars have begun to think not only about conditions orality imposes on the societies they study but also about the conditions it imposes on their own work. There has been a particular interest in the possibility of using oral sources to write history, as well as or even instead of using written documents.

Finnegan, Ruth. *Oral Poetry: Its Nature, Significance and Social Context*. Ind. U. Pr. 1992 $35.00. ISBN 0-253-32200-6. The best single-volume introduction to oral poetry.

Goody, Jack, ed. *The Domestication of the Savage Mind*. Cambridge U. Pr. 1977 $15.95. ISBN 0-521-29242-5. The effects of literacy on an oral culture edited by the leading anthropological theorist.

Havelock, Eric A. *The Muse Learns to Write: Reflections on Orality and Literacy from Antiquity to the Present*. Yale U. Pr. 1988 repr. of 1986 ed. $8.95. ISBN 0-300-04382-1. A leading Greek scholar of the subject ties together over thirty years of work.

Henige, David. *Oral Historiography*. Longman 1982 o.p. On gathering historical materials through oral interrogation; good bibliography.

Lord, Albert B. *The Singer of Tales*. HUP 1981 $12.95. ISBN 0-674-80881-9. The classic statement of the Parry-Lord hypothesis.

Olson, David R. and Nancy Torrance, eds. *Literacy and Orality*. Cambridge U. Pr. 1991 $54.50. ISBN 0-521-39217-9. Papers from a 1987 conference that explore orality and literacy with regard to forms of discourse, cognition, and human culture.

Ong, Walter J. *Orality and Literacy: The Technologizing of the World*. Routledge 1982 $13.95. ISBN 0-415-02796-9. A concise statement of the view that orality and literacy produce certain structures of consciousness.

Parry, Milman. *The Making of Homeric Verse*. Ed. by Adam Parry. OUP 1987 $21.00. ISBN 0-19-520560-X. Collected papers with an extensive introduction from a scholar who died young but left as a legacy the building blocks of the oral-formulaic theory.

Sweeney, Amin. *A Full Hearing: Orality and Literacy in the Malay World*. U. CA Pr. 1988 $45.00. ISBN 0-520-05910-7. Oral and written composition as they interact in Malay, the official language of Indonesia, Malaysia, and Brunei and sixth in the world in total number of speakers.

Thomas, Rosalind. *Literacy and Orality in Ancient Greece*. Cambridge U. Pr. 1992 $16.95. ISBN 0-521-37742-0. Examines written and oral communication in ancient Greece with an eye both to contemporary, theoretical discussions and the Greek social and historical background.

Indigenous Religions of Australia and Oceania

Central to and distinctive of all Australian religions is the way in which Australians conceive of the sacred: "the Dreaming." The Dreaming is the time when mythical beings first emerged from the formless chaos and created the world as it is today. When these beings departed, they left some of their sacredness behind, especially in particular sacred places.

The religious life of the Australians consists essentially of the interrelations between people and the sacred as manifested in the Dreaming. At times these relations occur naturally. For example, conception and birth result when a spirit animates a new human being. These relations also occur in rituals, some of which are open to all members of the community, others restricted to one sex or the other. Because the other spectacular rituals are performed by men in secret, earlier scholars concluded that women had no secret, sacred knowledge or activities. Later research, especially by women in the field, has proved them wrong.

Australian rituals often recreate the myths of the Dreaming, using special vehicles to indicate the presence of deities, such as the bull-roarer (an object that is attached to a string and whirs as it is swung in a circle) or the *tjurunga* (a sacred, decorated board).

The religions of Oceania (the islands of the southwest Pacific) present several common features. The behavior of the peoples in this region is governed to a great degree by status or rank (expressed in Polynesian by the terms *mana* and *tapu*). Status derives in turn largely from owning and successfully tending plots of land.

The peoples of Oceania account for the objects and events of the world by invoking two classes of beings: (1) gods who have never been human, among them an "otiose" creator and culture heroes who are active in cosmogonic myths; and (2) the sacred dead, who inhabit a distant, often indistinct land. As a result, most of these peoples have careful and elaborate rituals for disposing of corpses. The inhabitants of this region conceive of the divine as being able to take up temporary residence in small, carved, human-shaped figurines (*tiki*). In cases of need, they frequently have recourse to diviners, often women.

The indigenous religions of Australia still flourish in the northern and central parts of the continent. Most of Oceania is now nominally Christian, but traditional features are often evident beneath a very thin Christian veneer.

AUSTRALIA

Bell, Diane. *Daughters of the Dreaming.* 2nd ed. U. of Minn. Pr. 1993 $16.95. ISBN 0-8166-2398-8. A descriptive account of women and their rituals from fieldwork in north-central Australia.

Berndt, Ronald M, and Catherine H. Berndt. *Man, Land and Myth in North Australia: The Gunwinggu People.* Mich. St. U. Pr. 1970 $10.00. ISBN 0-87013-165-6. Explicates the manner in which religion, especially myth, links the Gunwinngu, a people of western Arnhem Land, to the land and identifies their places in the traditional world.

Charlesworth, Max, and Kenneth Maddock, eds. *Religion in Aboriginal Australia: An Anthology.* U. of Queensland Pr. 1984 $22.95. ISBN 0-7022-2008-6. Essays by fieldworkers on a wide range of topics.

Eliade, Mircea. *Australian Religions: An Introduction.* Ed. by Victor Turner. *Symbol, Myth and Ritual Ser.* Cornell Univ. Pr. 1973 o.p. An influential historian of religions reflects on Australian religions.

Kaberry, Phyllis M. *Aboriginal Women, Sacred and Profane.* Gordon Pr. 1972 $300.00. ISBN 0-87968-056-3. A groundbreaking study of aboriginal women, including their religion.

Swain, Tony. *Aboriginal Religions in Australia: A Bibliographical Survey.* Greenwood 1991 $55.00. ISBN 0-313-26044-3. More than a bibliography; surveys the history of scholarship to 1990, as well as major themes and regions in Australian religions.

OCEANIA

Alpers, Anthony. *The World of the Polynesians Seen through Their Myths and Legends, Poetry, and Art.* OUP 1987 $11.95. ISBN 0-19-558142-3. An attractive collection of Polynesian bits and pieces with some introduction; fun to browse.

Bateson, Gregory. *Naven: A Survey of the Problems Suggested by a Composite Picture of the Culture of a New Guinea Tribe Drawn from Three Points of View.* Stanford U. Pr. 1958 $42.50. ISBN 0-8047-0519-4. Theoretically, ground-breaking ethnographic account that begins with a study of a ritual known as *naven*; for the serious reader.

Firth, Raymond. *The Work of the Gods in Tikopia.* Humanities 1967 $48.50. ISBN 0-485-19501-1. Descriptive account with some theorizing of an important ritual cycle from the Solomon Islands by a master ethnologist.

Meigs, Anna S. *Food, Sex and Pollution: A New Guinea Religion.* Rutgers U. Pr. 1984 $30.00. ISBN 0-8135-0968-8. Fascinating study of a religion of the New Guinea highlands not in terms of gods, spirits, and beliefs but as a "religion of the body."

Obeyesekere, Gananath. *The Apotheosis of Captain Cook: European Myth-Making in the Pacific.* Princeton U. Pr. 1992 $24.95. ISBN 0-691-05680-3. Argues that the vulgate image of James Cook is not biographical truth but a version of the European myth of conquest, imperialism, and civilization.

Oliver, Douglas L. *Oceania: The Native Cultures of Australia and the Pacific Islands.* 2 vols. UH Pr. 1988 set $90.00. ISBN 0-8248-1019-8. Only ten of over 1,000 pages are headed "religion," but diligent searching will turn up useful information elsewhere (e.g., beliefs about death and what lies beyond).

Sahlins, Marshall. *Island of History.* U. Ch. Pr. 1987 repr. of 1985 ed. $19.95. ISBN 0-226-73358-0. A sophisticated reflection on history, using Hawaii as the example; a stimulating book, but only for the serious reader.

Indigenous Religions of Africa

Several traits characterize most, if not all, of the indigenous religions of sub-Saharan Africa. These people generally know a supreme god, but this god is usually remote from human beings and their concerns. As a result, he receives no cult. Instead, the events of daily life are the preserve of various kinds of lesser deities and of the ancestors who receive the appropriate ritual attention.

African religions take a great deal of interest in misfortunes. Human sickness and suffering are attributed to one of two causes: (1) they are either caused by spirits or ancestors offended by a person's actions or inattention or (2) they are the result of sorcery practiced by one's personal enemies.

In the case of either of these events, the sufferers and their families will consult a specialist: a priest or diviner or medium. These specialists identify the cause of the misfortune and prescribe its ritual cure. Offended spirits or ancestors are generally palliated by an offering, usually animal sacrifice.

For most Africans, the individual person is a composite of many souls. A person's life proceeds along several fixed stages, generally marked by rites of passage. The last stage of life occurs after death, when the once living person becomes an ancestor.

Bascom, Willian. *Ifa Divination: Communication Between Gods and Men in West Africa.* Ind. U. Pr. 1991 repr. of 1969 ed. $24.95. ISBN 0-253-20638-3. A relatively brief account of Ifa divination among the Yoruba, followed by over 400 pages of divination verses; for those who want a good, hard look.

Booth, Newell, S. *African Religions: A Symposium.* NOK Pubs. 1977 $21.50. ISBN 0-88357-012-2. Articles on various aspects of African religions, including African religions in the Americas and Christianity and Islam in Africa.

Deng, Francis Mading. *Dinka Folktales: African Stories from the Sudan.* Holmes & Meier 1974 $39.50. ISBN 0-8419-0138-4. A collection of tales with a brief introduction.

Karp, Ivan, and Charles S. Bird, eds. *Explorations in African Systems of Thought. African Systems of Thought Ser.* Smithsonian 1987 repr. of 1980 ed. $19.95. ISBN 0-87474-591-8. Essays on a variety of topics, loosely organized as modes of thought, images of social experience, cultural dynamics, and comparison.

Lienhardt, Godfrey. *Divinity and Experience: The Religion of the Dinka.* OUP 1988 $21.00. ISBN 0-19-823405-8. Fieldwork classic from the Sudan; organized in terms of types of divinities and techniques for controlling experience.

MacGaffey, Wyatt. *Religion and Society in Central Africa: The Bakongo of Lower Zaire.* U. Chi. Pr. 1986 $45.00. ISBN 0-226-50029-2. A readable account, from the perspective of the anthropology of religion, of cosmology, ritual and power, and continuity and change.

Mbiti, John S. *Introduction to African Religion*. Heinemann Ed. 1992 $18.50. ISBN 0-435-94002-3. A topical overview intended for general readers with no previous knowledge of the subject.

Olupona, Jacob K., ed. *African Traditional Religion in Contemporary Society*. Paragon Hse. 1991 $24.95. ISBN 0-89226-077-7. Wide-ranging essays representing exchanges between well-known scholars and equally well-known practitioners of traditional religions.

Parrinder, Geoffrey. *African Mythology*. P. Bedrick Bks. 1986 $24.95. ISBN 0-87226-042-9. A topic-by-topic discussion (e.g., the origin of the cosmos, of human beings, etc.) intended for the most general audiences.

———. *African Traditional Religion*. Greenwood 1976 $48.50. ISBN 0-8371-3401-3. Popular for years; discusses African worldviews, gods, rituals, sociological aspects, sorcery, and the fate of the soul.

Ray, Benjamin C. *Myth, Ritual, and Kingship in Buganda*. OUP 1991 $42.50. ISBN 0-19-506436-4. Reflects on kingship as the most important cultural institution in Buganda from a perspective that sees religion, myth, ritual, and the sacred as "irreducible categories of human experience."

Turner, Victor. *The Forest of Symbols: Aspects of Ndembu Ritual*. Cornell Univ. Pr. 1970 $13.95. ISBN 0-8014-9101-0. A study of ritual symbolism by one of the most influential anthropologists of recent decades.

Zahan, Dominique. *The Religion, Spirituality, and Thought of Traditional Africa*. Trans. by Lawrence M. Martin. U. Ch. Pr. 1979 repr. of 1970 ed. $9.95. ISBN 0-226-97778-1. A stimulating attempt to discover the principle that animates African life; not to everyone's taste.

Zuesse, Evan. *Ritual Cosmos: The Santification of Life in African Religions*. Ohio U. Pr. 1985 $14.95. ISBN 0-8214-0814-3. Attempts to combine anthropology and religious studies to elucidate the spiritual universe underlying African symbols and practices.

Indigenous Religions of the Americas

Indigenous American religions differ according to several distinct regions. Inasmuch as these differences are likely to be of more immediate interest to the North American readers, it seems best to comment not on the indigenous religions of the Americans as a whole but briefly on each regional section.

The indigenous religions of North America (often called "Native American Religion") know a variety of gods and spirits. Among them the most common are a sky-god as the supreme deity; a trickster figure who, as a culture hero, is prominent in myths; and among hunting peoples, animal-shaped guardians that are obtained in visions, often brought on by severe fasting. Rituals in this region tend to be very elaborate, consisting of long sequences of prayers, offerings, and dances. Their goal is to maintain a balance in relations with gods and spirits. A common figure in North America is the medicine man, or shaman, a visionary who, along with other powers, has the power to heal.

Mesoamerica has as a region been heavily Christianized from the days of the Spanish conquest, but as mentioned above, the Christianity of the Indian peoples often retains many pre-Columbian elements. Among the strongest of these elements are an intense concern with cosmology that sees earthly order as a replication of heavenly order; shamans who often use hallucinogens—still indispensable but now outside the bounds of acceptable society; and the ancient cult of the dead. Perhaps the best example of Mesoamerican syncretism is the widespread veneration of the Virgin of Guadalupe. The story is that the Virgin Mary manifested herself in Indian form in Guadalupe in December 1531, and since that time she has been venerated, in a form distinct from the Spanish Catholic Mary, under the name of the Aztec goddess Tonantzin.

South America has a wide variety of religious traditions, ranging from the descendants of the ancient Andean civilizations to simpler tribes in the eastern lowlands. As in many other tribal religions, most indigenous peoples of this region know of a supreme creator god, but this god remains without a cult, except in the Andes. Of more direct significance, especially among hunting peoples, are different types of masters of animals. A common religious symbol in this region in the jaguar, and the jaguar is in turn connected at times with the shaman. In South America shamans were very widespread, and they frequently used mind-altering drugs to supplement their other arts.

The best known of the pre-Columbian Caribbean religions are those of two peoples: the Island Arawak and the Island Carib. Both peoples knew a high god who was of little practical importance. Rituals were generally directed instead to spirits (*zemii*), often embodied in conical objects, and among the Arawak to the ancestors. Both peoples made ritual use of tobacco, narcotics, and stimulants, but the Caribbean region is most noted for one ritual that was certainly practiced and for another that may be only legendary. The Caribs practiced a ritual known as couvade: in imitation of their wives' labor, new fathers were isolated for 40 days and nights. From the word *Carib* (in Spanish, *Caribal*) derives the English word "cannibal." Some have suggested that the Caribs never practiced cannibalism. If they did, they would have done so on infrequent ritual occasions.

NORTH AMERICA

Brown, Joseph E., and Black Elk, eds. *The Sacred Pipe: Black Elk's Account of the Seven Rites of the Oglala Sioux. Civilization of the American Indian Ser.* U. of Okla. Pr. 1989 $26.95. ISBN 0-8061-0272-1. Recounts seven rituals as taught by (Nicholas) Black Elk, a famous Lakota (Sioux) visionary.

Deloria, Vine, Jr. *God Is Red: A Native View of Religion.* Fulcrum Pub. 1992 $22.95. ISBN 1-55591-904-9. A classic confrontation with religion by an indigenous American activist.

Dooling, D. M., and Paul Jordan-Smith, eds. *I Became Part of It: Sacred Dimensions in Native American Life.* Harper SF 1992 $15.00. ISBN 0-06-250235-2. Essays centered on religion by indigenous American writers seeking to reconnect with their cultural heritage.

Driver, Harold E. *Indians of North America.* U. Ch. Pr. 1969 $24.95. ISBN 0-226-16467-5. Comprehensive, comparative overview by topic; see especially its Chapter 8, "Social and Religious Aspects of Subsistence," and Chapter 23, "Religion, Magic, and Medicine."

Gill, Sam D. *Mother Earth: An American Story.* U. Ch. Pr. 1987 $24.95. ISBN 0-226-29371-8. A daring book that relates how European scholarship created an archetypal image of Mother Earth from the various female figures found in traditional stories and how indigenous peoples adopted that image.

———. *Native American Religions: An Introduction.* Wadsworth 1981 write for info. ISBN 0-534-00973-5. A good general introduction, tending to focus on the Southwest, the author's specialty.

———. *Native American Traditions: Sources and Interpretations. The Religious Life of Man Ser.* Wadsworth Pub. 1983 write for info. ISBN 0-534-01374-0. A broad range of sources to accompany the textbook.

Hultkrantz, Ake. *Belief and Worship in Native North America.* Ed. by Christopher Vecsey. Syracuse U. Pr. 1981 $30.00. ISBN 0-8156-2248-1. Collected essays on belief and myth, worship and ritual, ecology, and persistence and change.

———. *Native Religions of North America.* Peter Smith 1992 $20.00. ISBN 0-8446-6622-X. An introductory account of indigenous North Americans and their general worldview, followed by more specific considerations of the Wind River Shoshoni and the Zuni.

_____. *The Study of American Indian Religions*. Scholars Pr. GA 1983 $29.95. ISBN 0-685-06714-9. Six essays for those who want to put various scholars into historical perspective.

Loftin, John D. *Religion and Hopi Life in the Twentieth Century. Religion in North America Ser*. Ind. U. Pr. 1991 $19.95. ISBN 0-253-33517-5. Addresses the Hopi orientation to the world on two levels, mythical-traditional and historical.

Sullivan, Lawrence E., ed. *Native American Religions: North America. Readings from the Encyclopedia of Religion Ser*. Macmillan 1989 $12.95. ISBN 0-02-897402-6. One of many sets of articles from the *Encyclopedia of Religion*; useful for those who do not want to juggle sixteen heavy tomes.

Tedlock, Dennis, and Barbara Tedlock, eds. *Teachings from the American Earth: Indian Religion and Philosophy*. 1975. Liveright 1992 $10.95. ISBN 0-87140-146-0. Essays by important and respected authors, chosen because they allow the reader to learn from indigenous American religions, not just about them.

Underhill, Ruth M. *Red Man's Religion: Beliefs and Practices of the Indians North of Mexico*. U. Ch. Pr. 1972 $13.95. ISBN 0-226-84167-7. Readable study by a well-known scholar.

MESOAMERICA

Burns, Allan F., trans. *An Epoch of Miracles: Oral Literature of the Yucatec Maya. Texas Pan American Ser*. U. of Tex. Pr. 1983 $24.50. ISBN 0-292-72037-8. Bridges ancient and modern: "no other book for all of Mesoamerica . . . so brings the verbal arts to life . . . the way this one does" (Dennis Tedlock).

Dow, James. *The Shaman's Touch: Otomi Indian Symbolic Healing*. U. of Utah Pr. 1986 $15.95. ISBN 0-87480-257-1. A recent report on field experience; in places reads somewhat uneven.

Handbook of Middle American Indians. U. of Tex. Pr. 16 vols. and suppls. 1964–76 various prices. See especially Vol. 6, *Social Anthropology*, for articles on religion. 1967 $45.00. ISBN 0-292-73666-5

Markman, Roberta H., and Peter T. Markman. *The Flayed God: The Mythology of Mesoamerica*. Harper SF 1992 $30.00. ISBN 0-06-250528-9. Myths in words and pictures and analysis to assist in understanding.

Myerhoff, Barbara. *Peyote Hunt: The Sacred Journey of the Huichol Indians*. Cornell Univ. Pr. 1976 $9.95. ISBN 0-8014-9137-1. Well-known description of the peyote hunt and reflections on its significance.

Taggart, James M. *Nahuat Myth and Social Structure. Texas Pan-Amer. Ser*. U. of Tex. Pr. 1983 $25.00. ISBN 0-292-75524-4. A somewhat technical account of traditional cosmology and society in the valley of Mexico.

Tedlock, Barbara. *Time and the Highland Maya*. U. of NM Pr. 1992 $14.95. ISBN 0-8263-1358-2. Divination and the calendar among contemporary Maya.

Vogt, Evon Z. *Tortillas for the Gods: A Symbolic Analysis of Zinacanteco Rituals*. HUP 1976 $21.00. ISBN 0-674-89554-1. A sophisticated study of all sorts of rituals in Zinacanteco culture, aiming at a symbolic decoding.

SOUTH AMERICA

Brown, Michael F. *Tsewa's Gift: Magic and Meaning in an Amazonian Society*. U. CA Pr. 1993 price n/a. ISBN 0-520-08203-6. *Ethnographic Inquiry Ser*. Ethnographic account of the Aguaruna Jívaro of the Alto Río Mayo, Peru; very sensitive to symbolism.

Guss, David M. *To Weave and Sing: Art, Symbol, and Narrative in South American Rainforest*. U. CA Pr. 1989 $42.50. ISBN 0-520-06427-5. Uses basket weaving as an entrance into the ideological world of the Yekuana.

Lévi-Strauss, Claude. *From Honey to Ashes: Introduction to a Science of Mythology*. Trans. by John and Doreen Weightman. U. Ch. Pr. 1983 $13.00. ISBN 0-226-47489-5. Applies Lévi-Strauss's ideas to South American mythology.

Osborne, Harold. *South American Mythology*. P. Bedrick Bks. 1986 $24.95. ISBN 0-87226-254-5. The best general overview of the subject.

Sullivan, Lawrence E. *Icanchu's Drum: An Orientation to the Meaning in South America Religions*. Macmillan 1988 $33.65. ISBN 0-02-932160-3. Discusses archaeology (views of origins), cosmology, anthropology, and "terminology" (views of death and the end of the world).

Urton, Gary, ed. *Animal Myths and Metaphors in South America*. U. of Utah Pr. 1985 $20.00. ISBN 0-87480-205-9. Several authors use South American material to discuss a vexing anthropological problem: the relations other peoples postulate between themselves and animals.

Viveiros de Castro, Eduardo. *From the Enemy's Point of View: Humanity and Divinity in an Amazonian Society*. Trans. by Catherine V. Howard. U. Ch. Pr. 1992 $60.00. ISBN 0-226-85801-4. An ethnography of the Arawaté of Eastern Brazil, elucidating cosmology by discussing ideas of person, death, and divinities and institutions of shamanism and warfare.

Wilbert, Johannes, and Karin Simoneau, eds. *Folk Literature of the Tehuelche Indians*. UCLA Lat. Amer. Ctr. 1976–85 ea. $25.00–$37.00. Several volumes, all of whose titles begin *Folk Literature of*; for those who want collections of folklore.

CARIBBEAN

Alegria, Ricardo E. *Ball Courts and Ceremonial Plazas in the West Indies*. Yale U. Anthro. 1983 $12.50. ISBN 0-913516-15-5. Scholarly study of a very common ritual setting in the Americas.

Arens, W. *The Man-Eating Myth: Anthropology and Anthropophagy*. OUP 1979 $9.95. ISBN 0-19-502793-0. Takes a critical view—perhaps a too critical view—of all reports of cannibalism.

Kerns, Virginia. *Women and the Ancestors: Black Carib Kinship and Ritual*. U. of Ill. Pr. 1989 $16.50. ISBN 0-252-06077-6. How older Black Carib women preserve and pass down to their daughters the ceremonial component of their culture; from fieldwork in Belize.

Olsen, Fred. *On the Trial of the Arawaks. Civilization of the Amer. Indian Ser.* U. of Okla. Pr. 1975 o.p. A readable and well-illustrated account; occasionally rich in autobiographical narrative and reflection.

The Confrontation with the Modern West

In terms of material possessions, technological abilities, and the capacity for war, the European colonial powers had a distinct edge over the indigenous peoples of Australia and Oceania, Africa, the Americas, and Asia. In addition, Europeans brought many new diseases to the Americas with them that decimated the indigenous populations. Those who did survive the onslaughts of disease and human colonizers were severely disadvantaged economically, politically, and culturally under colonial rule. They were also subjected to intense pressures to adopt European Christianity that, whatever the intentions of the missionaries, were experienced as an extension of colonial policy. In this situation, traditional religions, which usually sought to provide well-being in the world, were severely strained.

Many indigenous peoples adjusted their traditions to the changing world, not infrequently in an attempt to do what sheer physical force could not do: drive out or destroy the white invaders or, failing that, preserve some amount of independent integrity. Among such movements are the Ghost Dances, Sun Dances, and Peyote movements of the indigenous North Americans, the neo-traditional movements in Africa, and neo-African movements in the Caribbean such as voodoo, Santería, and Shango.

Perhaps the most famous of these movements are the cargo cults of Melanesia. These cults attempt to induce the gods to send to the natives massive amounts of European goods, and they arouse in their followers the conviction that just such cargo is about to arrive. Political motives for the cargo cults cannot be discounted, but not all cargo cults have involved hostility toward Europeans. According to traditional beliefs, the gods are ultimately the source of all material well-being. Cargoists seem to be using these traditional beliefs to interpret and respond to the immense material disparity between themselves and the European colonizers.

Other indigenous peoples found the pressures to adopt Christianity irresistible, for a variety of reasons, but they often transformed the "white man's" religion drastically. Ecstatic-emotional Christianity (Pentecostal movements)—in some sense a critique of normative Christianity—has been popular among some North Americans and Australians. The Christianity of contemporary Mesoamerican Indians has preserved many traditional elements.

In Africa, many churches have seceded from the churches of their former rulers. Others have been founded independently by African prophets, such as Simon Kimbangu and Isaiah Shembe. Within Christianity powerful schools of thought have developed, which deal with liberating indigenous peoples as well as African Americans and women (liberation theology), but strictly speaking that topic belongs outside the purview of this chapter.

Aberle, David F. *The Peyote Religion among the Navaho.* U. of Okla. Pr. 1991 repr. of 1982 ed. $19.95. ISBN 0-8061-2382-6. A sound treatment of the peyote cult among a particular people.

Barrett, Leonard E. *The Rastafarians: Sounds of Cultural Dissonance.* Beacon Pr. 1988 $14.00. ISBN 0-8070-1027-8. For a look at the religiopolitical movement most familiar to American readers from its association with reggae (music of Jamaican origin).

Burridge, Kenelm. *New Heaven, New Earth: A Study of Millenarian Activities.* Blackwell Pubs. 1969 $16.95. ISBN 0-631-11950-7. A careful analysis of millennial movements that finds at the core a prophet who redresses imbalances created when a community living under one symbolic code moves to another.

Comaroff, Jean, and John L. Comaroff. *Of Revelation and Revolution, Vol. 1: Christianity, Colonialism, and Consciousness in South Africa.* U. Ch. Pr. 1991 $60.00. ISBN 0-226-11441-4. The results of interaction between nonconformist missionaries and the Tswana living on the border between Botswana and South Africa; attentive to issues of power and resistance.

Jorgenson, Joseph G. *The Sun Dance Religion: Power for the Powerless.* U. Ch. Pr. 1974 repr. of 1972 ed. $14.95. ISBN 0-226-41086-2. About an old hunting ritual that was transformed by the wretched experience of reservation life and continues as a dominant religious form to this day.

Kolig, Erich. *Silent Revolution: The Effects of Modernization on Australian Aboriginal Religion.* Inst. for the Study of Human Issues 1981 o.p.

LaBarre, Weston. *The Peyote Cult.* U. of Okla. Pr. 1989 $15.95. ISBN 0-8061-2214-5. For an introduction to the peyote cult in general.

Laitin, David D. *Hegemony and Culture: Politics and Religious Change among the Yoruba.* U. Ch. Pr. 1986 $30.00. ISBN 0-226-46789-9. The interaction of culture and politics in the Yoruba religious conflict; very self-conscious about the Western tradition of analyzing both.

Lawrence, Peter. *Road Belong Cargo: A Study of the Cargo Movement in the Southern Madang District New Guinea.* Waveland Pr. 1989 repr. of 1964 ed. $10.95. ISBN 0-88133-458-8. Emphasizes the role of the native view of the world in examining a particular cargo cult in Papua New Guinea.

MacGaffey, Wyatt. *Modern Congo Prophets: Religion in a Plural Society.* Bks. Demand repr. of 1983 ed. $78.30. ISBN 0-685-23906-3. A sensitive, sophisticated account.

Metraux, Alfred. *Voodoo in Haiti.* Schocken 1989 $12.95. ISBN 0-8052-0894-1. If you read only one book on voodoo, read this one; it is the best general introduction.

Simpson, George E. *Black Religions in the New World*. Columbia U. Pr. 1978 $62.50.
ISBN 0-231-04540-9. Black religions in the Caribbean, South America, and North
America, presented by an anthropologist who wrote on the subject for 40 years.
Sundkler, Bengt. *Bantu Prophets in South Africa*. Bks. Demand repr. of 1961 ed. $102.90.
ISBN 0-8357-3226-6. The price is outrageous, but the book is perhaps the classic
work on the subject.
Trompf, G. W., ed. *Cargo Cults and Millennarian Movements: Transoceanic Comparisons
of New Religious Movements*. Religion and Society Ser. Mouton 1990 $120.00. ISBN
0-89925-601-5. A wide-ranging collection of scholarly essays.
Turner, Harold W., ed. *Bibliography of New Religious Movements in Primal Societies*.
G. K. Hall Reference Ser. Macmillan 1992 $45.00. ISBN 0-8161-9089-5. Vol. 3:
Oceania. Macmillan 1990 $45.00. ISBN 0-8161-8984-6. Vol. 4: *Europe and Asia*.
Macmillan 1990 $45.00. ISBN 0-8161-7930-1. Vol. 5: *Latin America*. Macmillan 1991
$45.00. ISBN 0-8161-7929-8. Useful bibliographical entry into a massive literature.

CHRONOLOGY OF AUTHORS

Ancient Authors
Homer. fl. 8th century B.C.E.
Hesiod. fl. c.700 B.C.E.
Herodotus. c.490 B.C.E.–c.420 B.C.E.
Euripides. c.485 B.C.E.–c.406 B.C.E.
Apollodoros of Athens. c.180 B.C.E.–?
Strabo. c.64? B.C.E.–after 21 C.E.
Plutarch. Before 50 C.E.–after 120
C.E.
Lucian of Samosata. c.120 C.E.–after
180 C.E.
Apuleius. c.123 C.E.–after 161 C.E.
Pausanias. fl. c.150 C.E.

Modern Authors
Smith, William Robertson. 1846–1894
Harrison, Jane E. 1850–1928

Frazer, James George. 1854–1941
Otto, Rudolf. 1869–1937
Nilsson, Martin P. 1874–1967
Malinowski, Bronislaw. 1884–1942
Kerényi, Károly. 1897–1973
Dumézil, Georges. 1898–1986
Wach, Joachim. 1898–1955
Evans-Pritchard, E(dward) E(van).
1902–1973
Nock, Arthur Darby. 1902–1963
Eliade, Mircea. 1907–1986
Vernant, Jean-Pierre. 1914–
Geertz, Clifford. 1926–
Burkert, Walter. 1931–
Smith, Jonathan Z. 1938–

APOLLODOROS OF ATHENS. c.180 B.C.E.–?

Apollodoros studied with the renowned ancient scholar, Aristarchos, at
Alexandria, then worked at Pergamom and Athens, two other ancient centers of
learning. His most important writing, the *Histories* (*Chronika*), records in Greek
verse history from the fall of Troy (dated 1184 B.C.E.) to 144 B.C.E. He also
composed a philosophizing account of Greek religion under the title *On the
Gods* (*Peri theōn*).

Apollodoros's name appears here, however, because of a work he almost
certainly did *not* write, the *Library* (*Bibliotheka*). It is a compendium of Greek
mythology probably dating from the first to second centuries C.E. The work
begins with the birth of the gods and ends with the death of Odysseus in exile. It
is organized genealogically and includes accounts of such familiar figures as
Heracles, Europa, Minos, Cadmus, Atlas, Callisto, Theseus, and Pelops. Its last
section provides a complete summary of the Homeric cycle, from the moment
Zeus first decided to stir up trouble to the homecomings of various heroes,
including Odysseus. The *Library* does not exactly provide access to popular
Greek belief. Whoever wrote it seems to have followed literary sources fairly

slavishly and unimaginatively. Nevertheless, it is an extremely significant compendium.

BOOK BY APOLLODOROS

The Library. 2 vols. HUP $15.50 ea. ISBNs 0-674-99135-4, 0-674-99136-2. Greek on one side of the page, English on the other; translated with an introduction and lengthy appendix by Sir James G. Frazer.

APULEIUS. c.123 C.E.–after 161 C.E.

Apuleius was born in North Africa and educated at Carthage, Athens, and Rome. After a career in Rome, he was active in Carthage not only as a rhetorician but with some claims to being a Platonic philosopher as well. He eventually became a high priest of the province of Carthage. Many flamboyant speeches by Apuleius survive, but he is generally remembered for the work that makes him important to the study of ancient religions, the frolicking *Metamorphoses*, commonly known as "The Golden Ass."

The book's nickname derives from the unfortunate experiences of its main character. Lucius, too interested in the arts of magic for his own good, is accidentally transformed into an ass. He wanders the world in this form until, after many adventures, the goddess Isis takes pity on him. Initiated into her mysteries, he becomes one of her priests and regains human form.

Opinion on the *Metamorphoses* is mixed. Some see its framing narrative as only an excuse to present to its audience a good number of somewhat raucous tales, along the order of BOCCACCIO (see Vol. 2) or CHAUCER (see Vol. 1). Others consider it a serious attempt to convert its audience to the worship of Isis. Used judiciously, the work can be an important source for studying the mysteries of Isis and Osiris.

BOOKS BY APULEIUS

Apologia and Florida of Apuleius of Madaura. Trans. by H. E. Butler. Greenwood 1970 repr. of 1909 ed. $39.75. ISBN 0-8371-3066-2. For those who want to know a little about Apuleius's life and his rhetoric.

Cupid and Psyche. Ed. by M. G. Balme and J. H. Morwood. OUP 1976 $19.95. ISBN 0-19-912047-1. A much-loved and often repeated story, excerpted from Apuleius's *Metamorphoses.*

Metamorphoses. 2 vols. Trans. by Arthur J. Hanson. HUP 1989 $15.50 ea. ISBNs 0-674-99049-8, 0-674-99498-1. Latin text with a recent, facing-page English translation; the introductory material is unfortunately brief.

BOOKS ABOUT APULEIUS

Haight, Elizabeth H. *Apuleius and His Influence. Our Debt to Greece and Rome Ser.* Cooper Sq. 1963 repr. of 1930 ed. $30.00. ISBN 0-8154-0108-6. Basic and old, but perhaps still useful for cautious beginners.

Hijmans, B. L., Jr., and R. T. Van der Paardt, eds. *Aspects of Apuleius' Golden Ass.* Benjamins North Am. 1978 $53.50. ISBN 90-6088-061-7. By Dutch scholars who have also written commentaries on Books 3 and 6.

Schlam, Carl C. *The Metamorphoses of Apuleius: On Making an Ass of Oneself.* U. of NC Pr. 1992 $24.95. ISBN 0-8078-2013-X. Argues against Winkler that Apuleius wrote as a second century Middle Platonist and that a vision of cosmic order underlies the book's humor.

Tatum, James. *Apuleius and the Golden Ass.* Cornell Univ. Pr. 1979 o.p.

Winkler, John J. *Auctor and Actor: A Narratological Reading of Apuleius' Golden Ass.* U. CA Pr. 1985 $49.95. ISBN 0-520-05240-4. Uses modern narrative theory to examine

Apuleius's self-conscious tale; in the process transvalues the significance of the *Metamorphoses* for the history of religions.

BURKERT, WALTER. 1931–

German-born scholar Walter Burkert currently teaches at the University of Zurich. He is the leading active scholar of the religion of early and classical Greece.

Burkert's work proceeds through intense, meticulous historical and philological investigation, seeking to understand Greek religion in and of itself. In that regard it differs considerably from KÁROLY KERÉNYI's "theological" attempt to discern the spiritual meaning of Greek religion. At the same time, Burkert goes beyond the austere historical positivism of MARTIN P. NILSSON and ARTHUR DARBY NOCK to engage theoretical issues to their fullest. As a result, his studies wed philology and history with methods drawn from anthropology and resemble the work of JONATHAN Z. SMITH. But, unlike Smith, who seems to rule out diachronic considerations categorically in favor of synchronic taxonomies or "analogical comparisons," Burkert remains very interested in questions of long-term historical evolution and cross-cultural influence.

Burkert gives particular attention to psychological causation and the biological roots of human behavior as revealed by the science of ethology. For example, his study of Greek sacrifice, *Homo necans*, roots the practice of sacrifice in the biological necessity faced by prehistoric hunting groups that killed to survive. Burkert suggests that this necessary, aggressive behavior gave rise to anxiety, but through the practice of sacrifice the unavoidable aggression, which otherwise threatened to destroy society, was redirected to its promotion instead. In *Structure and History* Burkert's theoretical concerns are larger, including both myth and ritual. The precise relation between myth and ritual has been a vexing question for scholars of ancient religions; Burkert places them side by side and links them at a structural level. He thinks ritual is older than myth, because it is a form of behavior found even in animals. (In fact, Burkert appeals to the behavior of monkeys to interpret ithyphallic Greek terms.) Nevertheless, ritual and myth share several important features: Both depend upon "basic biological or cultural programs of action" (a concept Burkert adopts from Vladimir Propp), "both are detached from pragmatic reality, [and] both serve communication." Because myth and ritual are related in this way, it is possible for them to be found together.

Burkert's *Greek Religion* is the current, standard handbook on the religions of ancient Greece. His most recent work has been devoted to examining the influence of the ancient Near East on archaic Greek civilization.

BOOKS BY BURKERT

Ancient Mystery Cults. HUP 1987 $8.95. ISBN 0-674-03387-6. An interpretation that begins with the ancient mysteries as personal religion, then discusses organization, theology, and experience.

Greek Religion. Trans. by John Raffan. HUP 1985 $33.00. ISBN 0-674-36280-2. The current, standard reference handbook, organized according to kinds of religious phenomena.

Homo Necans: The Anthropology of Ancient Greek Sacrificial Ritual and Myth. Trans. by Peter Bing. U. CA Pr. 1983 $13.95. ISBN 0-520-05875-5. Burkert's important study of sacrifice, relating it to prehistoric hunting practice.

Lore and Science in Ancient Pythagoreanism. Trans. by Edwin L. Minar, Jr. Bks. Demand repr. of 1972 ed. $144.50. ISBN 0-7837-2230-3. A meaty investigation of the school of Pythagoras.

The Orientalizing Revolution: Near Eastern Influence on Greek Culture in the Early Archaic Age. HUP 1992 $29.95. ISBN 0-674-64363-1. Uses archaeological, textual, and historical evidence to reveal the contribution of the Orient to the emergence of Greek civilization 750–650 B.C.

Structure and History in Greek Mythology and Ritual. U. CA Pr. 1980 $37.50. ISBN 0-520-03771-5. An elaborate account much indebted to the structural analysis of Vladimir Propp and biological ethology.

DUMÉZIL, GEORGES. 1898–1986

Until his death, Georges Dumézil was the guiding light of the study of Indo-European civilizations. He taught at the Collège de France for many years, directed the Section des Sciences Religieuses of the Ecole des Hautes Études of the Sorbonne, and by the time he was elected to the Académie Français in the fall of 1978, Dumézil had extended his influence worldwide.

In essence, Dumézil's work effects a "paradigm shift" in the study of Indo-European mythology. Earlier scholars worked from a narrowly philological paradigm. Dumézil supplemented this approach with insights derived from functionalist sociology. His concern was not with isolated pieces but with systems. At its simplest, his basic idea is that Indo-European peoples share a "tripartite ideology"; they tend to think in specific groups of three.

Dumézil postulated that initially Indo-European society was arranged hierarchically into three distinct groups: priests, warriors, and herder-cultivators. Corresponding to each group was a specific function: sovereignty, physical (primarily military) prowess, and sustenance. Furthermore, each group was represented collectively by gods and goddesses who shared its function. The hierarchical division of society has been preserved only in India (the upper three *varnas*, or classes), but its effects are widespread in the mythologies and religions of Indo-European peoples, and occasionally, as at Rome, in their accounts of their histories as well.

Some scholars have always disputed Dumézil's theories. The most notable, recent critic has been British archaeological theorist Colin Renfrew. In the last few years, Dumézil, like many of his generation, has also been criticized for his politics.

BOOKS BY DUMÉZIL

Archaic Roman Religion. 2 vols. Trans. by Philip Krapp. U. Ch. Pr. 1971 $45.00. ISBN 0-226-16968-5. A reconstruction of the earliest religion of Rome that centers on the Capitoline triad of Jupiter, Mars, and Quirinus.

Camillus: A Study of Indo-European Religion as Roman History. Ed. by Udo Strutynski. Trans. by Annette Aronowicz, and others. U. CA Pr. 1980 $39.95. ISBN 0-520-02841-4. Relates the legend of Camillus to the mythology of dawn and the sun; a useful introduction sets the work in context.

Destiny of a King. Trans. by Alf Hiltebeitel. U. Ch. Pr. 1988 $15.00. ISBN 0-226-16975-8. Dumézil's three functions as they appear in legends of the "first kings," with special attention to the Indian figure Yayati.

From Myth to Fiction. Trans. by Derek Coltman. U. Ch. Pr. 1973 $22.00. ISBN 0-226-16972-3. An unusual case in Dumézil's massive engagement with myth and epic: the way Saxo Grammaticus used traditional mythology as literature.

Gods of the Ancient Northmen. Ed. and trans. by Einar Haugen. U. CA Pr. 1974 $11.95. ISBN 0-520-02044-8. An account of the Germanic gods in terms of Dumézil's tripartite ideology.

Mitra-Varuna: An Essay on Two Indo-European Representations of Sovereignty. Trans. by Derek Coltman. Zone Bks. 1988 $26.95. ISBN 0-942299-12-4. Develops Dumézil's idea that the first function is often divided among two complementary mythical figures.

The Stakes of the Warrior. Ed. by Jaan Puhvel. Trans. by David Weeks. U. CA Pr. 1983 $35.00. ISBN 0-520-04834-2. Another translated fragment of Dumézil's study of myth and epic; for others, see *Camillus* and *The Destiny of a King*.

BOOKS ABOUT DUMÉZIL

Belier, Wouter W. *Decayed Gods: Origin and Development of Georges Dumézil's 'Ideologie Tripartie'*. E. J. Brill 1991 $68.75. ISBN 90-04-09487-3. Somewhat plodding; eventually criticizes Dumézil's fully developed theory as inaccessible to either verification or falsification.

Lincoln, Bruce. *Death, War, and Sacrifice: Studies in Ideology and Practice*. U. Ch. Pr. 1991 $45.00. ISBN 0-226-48199-9. Broad collection of insightful essays charting Lincoln's own course through subjects usually labeled Indo-European; also includes a political critique of Dumézil.

Littleton, C. Scott. *The New Comparative Mythology: An Anthropological Assessment of the Theories of Georges Dumézil*. U. CA Pr. 1980 $12.95. ISBN 0-520-05103-8. Through successive editions the standard volume on Dumézil; perhaps read it before trying Dumézil's own works.

Polome, Edgar C., ed. *Homage to Georges Dumézil*. Inst. Study Man 1983 $25.00. ISBN 0-941694-28-3. Several scholars positively assess and continue Dumézil's project.

Renfrew, Colin. *Archaeology and Language: The Puzzle of Indo-European Origins*. Cambridge U. Pr. 1990 $18.95. ISBN 0-521-38675-6. Not specifically about Dumézil, but this book advances a new model of Indo-European diffusion and, in the process, a severe scholarly (rather than political) critique of Dumézil's assumptions and conclusions.

DURKHEIM, ÉMILE. 1858–1917

[SEE Volume 3.]

ELIADE, MIRCEA. 1907–1986

Mircea Eliade has been the single, most influential scholar on the general study of religions in the second half of the twentieth century. His wide-ranging works can be divided into five distinct types: (1) broad historical studies, initially of particular religious phenomena (*Shamanism, Yoga: Immortality and Freedom, History of Religious Ideas*); (2) explorations in what Eliade calls the "morphology" of religion, as seen in *Patterns in Comparative Religion*, which gave birth to many partial, popularizing restatements, including *The Sacred and the Profane*, a frequently used introductory text; (3) original works of fiction that often make free use of the religious patterns identified by Eliade's scholarly works; (4) reference materials for both students and scholars (for example, *From Primitives to Zen*); and (5) autobiographical reflections, published toward the end of his life at tedious length. Combined, these five kinds of writing make up a self-conscious corpus whose central theme was the manifestation of the Sacred ("hierophany") as a fundamental structure of human consciousness.

Born and educated in Rumania, Eliade spent several formative years (1928–32) in India, studying in Calcutta with Surendranath Dasgupta and living for several months in an ashram in the Himalayas. After his return, Eliade was extremely active in the literary and intellectual life of his homeland until the outbreak of World War II. From these early experiences, Eliade derived his intense appreciation for the religions of Asia, especially of India, and his fascination with "primal" or "archaic" religious phenomena, more or less equivalent to what Eliade saw as the fundamental, peasant substratum of southeast European culture. Eliade spent the war years with the Rumanian foreign office first in London, then in Lisbon. Afterward, he taught at the University of Paris and, from 1957, at the University of Chicago. At Chicago his influence came to dominate the field of the nontheological study of religions, through his students, his editorial activity, and his writing.

Eliade's thought has certain affinities to JUNG's (see also Vol. 5); for example, both discussed "archetypes" and noted some of the same patterns. But Eliade talked about structures of human consciousness, not a collective unconscious, and he interwove the various archetypes together to form a distinctive whole. At the center of his thought stands what he called the dialectic of the Sacred: the eruption of the Sacred into the world of profane existence. According to Eliade, anything at all can and probably has become a vehicle for the manifestation of the Sacred, but throughout history we can identify certain basic patterns or forms (hence "morphology") in nature (e.g., sun, moon, earth), in space (e.g., the center, the pivot of the universe [axis mundi], microcosmic imitation of macrocosmic order [imago mundi], and in time (the time-before-time of myth, the return to that original moment in ritual). Religion is the attempt to appropriate these manifestations of the Sacred and use them for human benefit. From these attempts a religious person (homo religiosus) strives for Being, Meaning, and Truth.

Eliade claimed that religion must be studied hermeneutically or interpretively rather than naturalistically or scientifically. After everything else, scholars of religions must deal with religious data within their own frame of reference; that is, they must seek to decipher and elucidate religious meanings. Never one to think in small terms, Eliade envisioned this work as the core of a "new humanism" that will create a revitalized, planetary culture. But Eliade also believed that the discovery of the unconscious has freed scholars from the need to verify their interpretations by referring to what religious people actually say and believe. This conviction led Eliade to interpretations that are problematical.

In recent years increasingly severe criticism of Eliade's methods, conclusions, assumptions, and even political loyalties has been voiced from a wide variety of perspectives. The most searching and convincing criticism from within the study of religions is that of JONATHAN Z. SMITH.

BOOKS BY ELIADE

Autobiography, Vol. 1 *Journey East, Journey West 1907–1937*. Trans. by Mac L. Ricketts. U. Ch. Pr. 1990 $15.95. ISBN 0-226-20407-3. Perhaps the most interesting of the many volumes of Eliade's autobiography and journals available.

Essential Sacred Writings from Around the World: A Thematic Sourcebook on the History of Religions. Harper SF 1991 $17.00. ISBN 0-06-250304-9. A reprint of *From Primitives to Zen*, a handy collection of texts anthologized from various sources and organized according to familiar Eliadean themes.

A History of Religious Ideas. 3 vols. Trans. by Willard R. Trask, and others. U. Ch. Pr. Vol. 1 *From the Stone Age to Eleusinian Mysteries*. 1981 $27.50. ISBN 0-226-20400-6. Vol. 2 *From Gautama Buddha to the Triumph of Christianity*. 1985 $18.95. ISBN 0-226-20403-0. Vol. 3 *From Muhammad to the Age of Reforms*. 1988 $16.95. ISBN 0-226-20405-7. A magisterial survey of the world's religions; the crowning achievement of Eliade's life's work.

Myth of the Eternal Return. Trans. by Willard R. Trask. Princeton U. Pr. 1954 $35.00. ISBN 0-691-09798-4. A short work on rejuvenation through a return to the origins, a significant Eliadean theme.

Ordeal by Labyrinth: Conversations with Claude-Henri Rocquet. Trans. by Derek Coltman. U. Ch. Pr. 1982 $14.95. ISBN 0-226-20387-5. To learn about Eliade's life and self-image, start here, not with his journal or autobiography.

The Quest: History and Meaning in Religion. U. Ch. Pr. 1984 $11.95. ISBN 0-226-20386-7.
An important collection of essays that reflect on the study of religions, including the
important essay on the history of religions as a "new humanism."
The Sacred and the Profane: The Nature of Religion. Peter Smith 1983 $18.75. ISBN 0-
8446-6080-9. A popular introductory text, perhaps the most accessible, comprehen-
sive statement of Eliade's ideas.
Shamanism: Archaic Techniques of Ecstasy. Trans. by Willard R. Trask. Princeton U. Pr.
1964 $16.95. ISBN 0-691-01779-4. A comprehensive account of shamanic techniques
around the globe.
Tales of the Sacred and the Supernatural. Westminster John Knox 1981 $9.99. ISBN 0-
664-24391-6. A brief collection of short stories and a good place to begin reading
Eliade's fiction.
Yoga: Immortality and Freedom. Ed. by Willard R. Trask. Princeton U. Pr. 1991 $14.95.
ISBN 0-691-01764-6. A classic account of perennially fascinating Indian techniques
to achieve liberation.

BOOKS ABOUT ELIADE

Altizer, Thomas J. *Mircea Eliade and the Dialectic of the Sacred.* Greenwood 1975 repr. of
1963 ed. $35.00. ISBN 0-8371-7196-2. An attempt to use Eliade to address the post-
Christian condition of modernity; written by a once famous (or infamous) "Death of
God" theologian.
Carrasco, David, and Jane M. Swanberg. *Waiting for the Dawn: Mircea Eliade in
Perspective.* U. Pr. of Colo. 1991 $14.95. ISBN 0-87081-239-4. A personable account
of a seminar at the University of Colorado, containing selections from Eliade, three
critical responses, and a number of pictures.
Cave, John D. *Mircea Eliade's Vision for a New Humanism.* OUP 1992 $29.95. ISBN 0-19-
507434-3. Examines Eliade's biography in order to elucidate the centrality of his
notion of a "new humanism."
Ricketts, Mac L. *Mircea Eliade: The Romanian Roots, 1907–1945.* 2 vols. East Eur.
Quarterly 1988 set $240.00. ISBN 0-88033-145-3. At 1,500 pages, this biography of the
first half of Eliade's life will probably appeal only to seriously afflicted Eliade
"groupies"; for them it will be a gold mine.

EURIPIDES. c.485 B.C.E.–c.406 B.C.E.

The last of the three canonical Athenian tragedians, Euripides is one of the
best-known authors in Greek literature, but his reputation in antiquity was less
than stellar. His personality was said to have been somewhat antisocial. His
attitude toward his mythological subjects struck some as irreverent and
cavalier. (For example, in the *Frogs,* ARISTOPHANES [see Vol. 2] has Euripides
confess that his tragedies mixed the high with the ordinary.) Furthermore, his
plays did not very often win first place when they were produced. Yet, of an
alleged total of 92 plays, some 19 survive, more than of his two Athenian rivals,
AESCHYLUS (see Vol. 2) and SOPHOCLES (see Vol. 2). All of the plays have
mythological subjects and in that sense are of some significance for the study of
ancient religion (and irreligion). Of particular interest is the *Bacchae,* first
produced after Euripides's death. Because the play represents a Dionysiac revel,
it is a major if not unproblematic source in the study of the mysteries of
Dionysos.

BOOKS BY EURIPIDES

Bacchae. Ed. by E. R. Dodds. OUP 1960 $19.95. ISBN 0-19-872125-0. An edition of the
Greek text, with classic introductory material by the editor.
Four Tragedies, nos. 1–4, Three Tragedies, no. 5. Ed. by David Grene and Richmond
Lattimore. U. Ch. Pr. 1955–69 $7.95 ea. ISBNs 0-226-30780-8, 0-226-30781-6, 0-226-

30782-4, 0-226-30783-2, 0-226-30784-0. All the plays of Euripides in the Chicago Complete Greek Tragedy set; perhaps the standard translations.

Works. 4 vols. HUP $15.50 ea. ISBNs 0-674-99010-2, 0-674-99011-0, 0-674-99012-9, 0-674-99013-7. The Loeb Classical Library edition; handy volumes for those who want to peek at the Greek text and read a translation.

BOOKS ABOUT EURIPIDES

Burian, Peter, ed. *Directions in Euripidean Criticism: A Collection of Essays.* Duke 1985 $29.95. ISBN 0-8223-0610-7. Selected, scholarly essays with a bibliography from 1945 to date of publication.

Foley, Helene P. *Ritual Irony: Poetry and Sacrifice in Euripides.* Cornell Univ. Pr. 1985 $32.95. ISBN 0-8014-1692-2. The way Euripides represents sacrifice, especially in four plays: *Iphigenia in Aulis, Phoenissae, Heracles,* and *Bacchae.*

McDermott, Emily A. *Euripides' Medea: The Incarnation of Disorder.* Pa. St. U. Pr. 1989 $19.75. ISBN 0-271-00647-1. Reads the *Medea* as a sustained assault on the most sacred of Greek values, climaxing in Medea's killing of her own children.

Meagher, Robert. *Mortal Vision: The Wisdom of Euripides.* St. Martin 1989 $29.95. ISBN 0-312-02720-6. Euripides, the theatre, and metaphysical and political order, tied together by a concentration on the ethical.

Segal, Charles. *Dionysiac Poetics and Euripides' Bacchae.* Bks. Demand repr. of 1982 ed. $98.60. ISBN 0-8357-8861-4. An interpretation of the *Bacchae* that explores the intersection of literary, social, ritual, and aesthetic structures.

Whitman, Cedric. *Euripides and the Full Circle of Myth.* HUP 1974 $13.00. ISBN 0-674-26920-9. *Iphigenia in Tauris, Ion,* and *Helen* as revealing struggles for spiritual wholeness.

EVANS-PRITCHARD, E(DWARD) E(VAN). 1902–1973

E. E. Evans-Pritchard was the leading British anthropologist of his generation. His best work is a model of precise and perceptive fieldwork, conducted in the southern Sudan. Two of Evans-Pritchard's books in particular changed assumptions underlying the anthropological study of religion, probably forever.

Up to Evans-Pritchard's day, it was common to view magic as the result of a muddled mode of thinking or apparently irrational behavior that met unexpressed social needs. Evans-Pritchard's careful account of *Witchcraft, Oracles, and Magic among the Azande* shows the significant limitations of both of these views. In this account, magical practices exhibit the same rational concern for causation that is present in ordinary life. Far from irrational, Azande beliefs about magic turn out to be systematic, logically coherent, and consistent with the social contexts in which they occur.

Just as Evans-Pritchard's book on the Azande made it impossible to speak of "primitive irrationality," his book on *Nuer Religion* made it impossible to speak simplistically of "primitive religion." This sympathetic, linguistically subtle account reveals a complex system of religious thought and behavior with well-formed notions of God, spirits, ghosts, and souls.

It would be difficult to underestimate Evans-Pritchard's impact on the study of religions. His two classic works should not be missed.

BOOKS BY EVANS-PRITCHARD

Nuer Religion. OUP 1956 $14.95. ISBN 0-19-874003-4. The third volume in a trilogy on the Nuer of the Sudan; a sensitive account of religious beliefs, practices, and institutions.

Theories of Primitive Religion. OUP 1968 $14.95. ISBN 0-19-823131-8. A very readable account that can still provide beginners with a clear and cogent introduction.

Witchcraft, Oracles, and Magic among the Azande. o.p. A classic study that led to important questions about rationality in various cultures.

FRAZER, JAMES GEORGE. 1854–1941

A classicist by training and an expert on the ancient world, James George Frazer became the leading anthropological theorist on religions in the early twentieth century, especially in the English-speaking world. His influence was so pervasive that it is even seen in many works of art from the time, the most prominent example being T. S. ELIOT's (see Vol. 1) poem, "The Waste-Land."

The book for which Frazer is justly famous is *The Golden Bough*, which he continued to amplify until it drew into 12 massive, erudite volumes. The project began as an attempt to account for a peculiar Roman custom. If a runaway slave could reach the grove of Nemi at the town of Aricia outside Rome and kill the priest who guarded it, he would be granted his freedom. But he also became the new guardian of the grove, threatened with death at the hands of the next runaway slave.

In *The Golden Bough*, Frazer explained this custom by referring to the beliefs and practices of what were known in his day as "primitives" and "savages." In doing so, he manufactured a full arsenal of ideas on comparative religion. Actually, these ideas become the real core of the book, and the story of Nemi is eventually only a frame within which to present them.

Central to Frazer's views is the assumption, common in his day, that the human mind has evolved from a state in which the dominant mode of thinking was magical through one dominated by religion to science. It is possible to recover earlier states of mind not just from ancient evidence but also from the views and practices of contemporary "primitives" and peasants. That is because similar practices and myths represent similar ways of thinking.

In the course of his exposition, Frazer developed several influential ideas. For example, he postulated that many communities were once ruled by priest-kings who embodied communal flourishing and so needed to be protected by taboos, magic, sacrifices, and ritual scapegoats. Perhaps most fateful for the study of ancient religions has been his notion of the "dying and rising god." In this view, the deities of the ancient eastern Mediterranean were spirits of vegetation, whose seasonal dying and rising was enacted in many ways, including ritual battle. Frazer gave special attention to Attis, Adonis, Osiris, and Dionysos, but left any comparison with Jesus implicit.

Today, anthropologists regard Frazer as outdated, although readers of popular literature often encounter his ideas. Among specialists, his ideas were soon replaced by more subtle and complex accounts developed by those who actually engaged in anthropological fieldwork, which Frazer never did.

BOOKS BY FRAZER

The Fear of the Dead in Primitive Religion. Ed. by Robert Kastenbaum. 3 vols. in 1. Ayer 1977 repr. of 1936 ed. $57.50. ISBN 0-405-09566-X. What one would expect: a massively documented account of the title subject.

The Golden Bough. 13 vols. St. Martin 1969 repr. of 1890 ed. $450.00. ISBN 0-312-33215-7. The complete masterpiece, weighing in at 5,230 pages.

The New Golden Bough. Ed. by Theodor H. Gaster. NAL-Dutton 1975 $6.95. ISBN 0-451-62208-1. An abridgement of Frazer's classic which, at 832 pages, is probably still enough Frazer for anyone.

Totemism and Exogamy. 1910 o.p. Almost 2,000 pages on totemism; when it was written, one of the most important topics in the anthropology of religion.

The Worship of Nature. AMS Pr. repr. of 1926 ed. $41.50. ISBN 0-404-11427-X. The Gifford lectures for 1924–1925 on a quintessentially Frazerian theme.

BOOKS ABOUT FRAZER

Ackerman, Robert. *J. G. Frazer: His Life and Work.* Cambridge U. Pr. 1987 $54.95. ISBN 0-521-34093-4. A literary historian relates Frazer's life.

Fraser, Robert. *The Making of "The Golden Bough": The Origins and Growth of an Argument.* St. Martin 1990 $39.95. ISBN 0-312-04205-1. How Frazer's masterwork achieved its massive size and how Frazer's thinking changed in the process.

———, ed. *Sir James Frazer and the Literary Imagination: Essays in Affinity and Influence.* St. Martin 1991 $45.00. ISBN 0-312-05321-5. Casts a much broader net than Vickery: more figures, more context; the final essay by A. S. Byatt is on postmodernist fiction.

Gaster, Theodore H. *Myth, Legend and Custom in the Old Testament: A Comparative Study with Chapters from Sir James G. Frazer's Folklore in the Old Testament.* 2 vols. Peter Smith $36.00. ISBN 0-8446-5189-3. Applies Frazer's ideas and methods to the Hebrew Bible; indeed, updates Frazer's *Folklore in the Old Testament* and is subject to the same criticism.

Manganaro, Marc. *Myth, Rhetoric, and the Voice of Authority: A Critique of Frazer, Eliot, Frye, and Campbell.* Yale U. Pr. 1992 $28.50. ISBN 0-300-05194-8. Argues that what gave evolutionary comparativism its authoritative voice was its "being everywhere," in distinction from ethnographers, whose authority derives from "being there" (Geertz).

Vickery, John B. *The Literary Impact of the Golden Bough.* Princeton U. Pr. 1973 $62.50. ISBN 0-691-01331-4. Frazer's influence on W. B. Yeats, T. S. Eliot, D. H. Lawrence, and James Joyce.

FREUD, SIGMUND. 1856–1939

[SEE Volumes 3 and 5.]

GEERTZ, CLIFFORD. 1926–

Since 1982 the Harold F. Linder Professor of Social Science at the Institute for Advanced Study in Princeton, New Jersey, Clifford Geertz is the leading exponent of symbolic or interpretive anthropology and arguably the leading anthropologist of the present day. He has done extensive fieldwork in Java and Morocco, and these two countries provide the significant exempla for his writings. His audience and influence extend well beyond the traditional boundaries of anthropology. Indeed, Geertz himself evinces a wide reading, having fought for years against a "provincialized" anthropology.

Influenced in part by earlier anthropologists and thinkers, such as RUTH BENEDICT (see Vol. 3), Clyde Kluckhohn, EDWARD SAPIR (see Vol. 3), and ROBERT REDFIELD (see Vol. 3), Geertz broke decisively with the functionalism that dominated anthropology in the 1950s. His move was paralleled at the time by other anthropologists, notably MARY DOUGLAS (see Vol. 3) and VICTOR WITTER TURNER (see Vol. 3).

Geertz insists that cultural institutions such as ritual, myth, and art should be seen not as reflections of social structure but as systems of symbols, and he defines the anthropological task accordingly. As Geertz states programmatically in *The Interpretation of Cultures*: "Believing with Max Weber that man is an animal suspended in webs of significance he himself has spun, I take culture to be those webs and the analysis of it to be therefore not an experimental science in search of law but an interpretive one in search of meaning." Geertz famously identified the analysis of those webs as "thick description."

Scholars of religions have found Geertz's approach very congenial, and his influence on the study of religions has been immense. One essay in particular has become a classic—"Religion as a Cultural System," conveniently reprinted in *The Interpretation of Cultures*. In this essay, Geertz elaborates at length a quinquipartite definition of religion: "A religion is (1) a system of symbols which acts to (2) establish powerful, pervasive, and long-lasting moods and motivations by (3) formulating conceptions of a general order of existence and (4) clothing these conceptions with such an aura of factuality that (5) the moods and motivations seem uniquely realistic."

In the time since Geertz began his career, anthropology has become very self-conscious and self-critical. Geertz's recent book, *Works and Lives*, addresses to some extent the relation between political imperialism and the discipline of anthropology that grew up concurrently with it.

Books by Geertz

Interpretation of Cultures. Basic 1977 $15.00. ISBN 0-465-09719-7. Collected essays that attempted to sum up Geertz's ideas about interpretive anthropology; see especially "Religion as a Cultural System."

Islam Observed: Development of Religion in Morocco and Indonesia. U. Ch. Pr. 1971 $6.95. ISBN 0-226-28511-1. Contrasts two very different styles of Islam, one activist and individualizing, the other aesthetic and dissolving of personality.

Local Knowledge: Further Essays in Interpretive Anthropology. Basic 1985 $14.00. ISBN 0-465-04162-0. Essays that continue the project of *Interpretation of Cultures*, some years later.

Negara: Theatre-State in 19th Century Bali. Princeton U. Pr. 1980 $45.00. ISBN 0-691-00778-0. For specialists and nonspecialists alike; constructs an image of political organization in nineteenth-century Bali, using history, archaeology, and ethnography.

The Religion of Java. U. Ch. Pr. 1976 $14.95. ISBN 0-226-28510-3. Three religious strands in the town of Modjokuto and how they interact: *abangan* (popular, peasant religion), *santri* (the Islamic religion of traders), and *prijaji* (the Hindu-Buddhist religion of upper classes).

Works and Lives: The Anthropologist as Author. Stanford U. Pr. 1989 $25.00. ISBN 0-8047-1428-2. Uses the lives and contexts of Claude Lévi-Strauss, E. E. Evans-Pritchard, Bronislaw Malinowski, and Ruth Benedict to reflect on the writing that is anthropology.

HARRISON, JANE E. 1850–1928

One of the first women to study classics at Cambridge University, Jane Harrison enjoyed a global reputation based on her writings about Greek religion. At a time when the study of texts was often seen as the only means to study ancient religions, Harrison helped break new ground by using materials and insights derived from archaeology, art history, and comparative anthropology.

In Harrison's view, religion is primarily something done; words and reflection come later. In writing on Greek religion, she made a sharp distinction between the cult of the Olympian deities, which she initially disvalued, and non-Olympian practices. She correlated this distinction with one between rituals of tendance and rituals of aversion, that is, rituals that venerate and those that seek to ward off potentially evil spirits. In accordance with views popular at the time, she also gave her classification an evolutionary twist, attributing the Olympian cult to invading Indo-European patriarchs from the north, and the non-Olympian practices to a matriarchal, pre-Indo-European, Mediterranean civilization.

Readers should approach Harrison's entirely speculative, historical reconstruction with extreme caution. As is true for virtually every scholar of Harrison's generation, the value of her writing consists in the potential elucidation that her questions and categories can provide, not in the results of her actual investigations. Together with James G. Frazer and the so-called Cambridge Ritualists, Harrison has recently been the object of intense biographical scrutiny.

Books by Harrison

Alpha and Omega. AMS Pr. repr. of 1915 ed. $27.50. ISBN 0-404-56753-3. A collection of highly personal, mostly autobiographical essays, with an "Epilogue on the War."

Epilegomena to the Study of Greek Religion. Holmes Pub. 1991 $7.95. ISBN 1-55818-179-2. Applies Harrison's views to then contemporary religious questions, advocating a variety of asceticism.

Prolegomena to the Study of Greek Religion. Princeton U. Pr. 1991 $18.00. ISBN 0-691-01514-7. Harrison's classic account of Greek religion, distinguishing rituals of tendance and aversion and rooting Greek religion in primitive action.

Themis: A Study of the Social Origins of Greek Religion. Humanities 1977 $19.95. ISBN 0-85036-229-6. An analysis of the "year-spirit" that revised the *Prolegomena* and shows the influence of Henri Bergson and Émile Durkheim.

Books about Harrison

Ackerman, Robert. *The Myth and Ritual School: J. G. Frazer and the Cambridge Ritualists.* Garland 1990 $34.00. ISBN 0-8240-6249-3. Traces the precursors and analyzes the works not just of Jane Harrison, the premier "Cambridge ritualist," but also of her associates, G. Murray, F. M. Cornford, and A. B. Cook.

Arlen, Shelley. *Cambridge Ritualists: An Annotated Bibliography of the Works by and about Jane Ellen Harrison, Gilbert Murray, Francis M. Cornford, and Albert Bernard Cook.* Scarecrow 1990 $42.50. ISBN 0-8108-2373-X. For those who want to start with a much fuller bibliography.

Calder, William M., ed. *Cambridge Ritualists Reconsidered.* Scholars Pr. GA 1991 $44.95. ISBN 1-55540-605-X. Papers from a scholarly conference of mostly classicists and ancient historians; three essays on Harrison, as well as her colleagues, her context, and her school.

Peacock, Sandra J. *Jane Ellen Harrison: The Mask and the Self.* Yale U. Pr. 1988 $30.00. ISBN 0-300-04128-4. Harrison's life, with special attention to her relations with Gilbert Murray and Francis Cornford; annoyingly refers to all the principal players by their first names.

HERODOTUS. c.490 B.C.E.–c.420 B.C.E.

Herodotus has often been called the Father of History. To the extent that this is true, he was also the first historian to study the religions of the ancient world.

Born at Halicarnassos on the west coast of what is now Turkey, Herodotus traveled to Athens before settling in the Athenian colony at Thurii in the old Greek area of the Italian peninsula. His writings testify that he was well-traveled in the eastern Mediterranean region, having firsthand knowledge of Egypt, Mesopotamia, Scythia, and the northern Aegean, although probably not Persia. The work for which he is renowned, the "History," also called "The Persian Wars," mentions no event later than the year 430 B.C.E.

In Greek, *historiē* means "inquiry." Herodotus tells us that he conducted his "inquiry" to preserve what is reported of the "great deeds" human beings have done and to record the reasons the Greeks and Persians came to fight. One should not imagine that Herodotus was a critical historian in the modern sense.

He reported what he heard with a minimum of sifting. If he knew more than one account of the same event, he presented more than one.

The "History" wends its way lazily from what Herodotus identifies as the ultimate cause of conflict between Greeks and Persians (the militant behavior of Croesus, king of Lydia) to the attacks on the Greek mainland under Darius in 490 B.C.E. and Xerxes in 480 B.C.E. Along the way, especially in the early books, Herodotus left himself much room for historical and ethnographical diversion. A master of prose narration, he loved a good story or joke. One example tells how Gyges found himself forced to kill his master Candaules, marry his master's widow, and thereby become king of Lydia. The oracle of Apollo at Delphi plays a major role in Herodotus's narrative. Indeed, Herodotus is largely responsible for the impression that the Delphic oracle gave its answers as poetic riddles. For example, he tells how Croesus received the advice, "If you go to war, you will destroy a great kingdom." Croesus went to war and lost his kingdom.

In describing his experiences in Egypt, Herodotus left the impression that he received special religious teaching there. At the same time, he was no theologian or philosopher. He was convinced that "everyone knows equally about divine things," that is, everyone knows equally little. Under cover of a commonsense piety, Herodotus provides splendid, if not always reliable, descriptions of religious life in many areas of the eastern Mediterranean.

BOOKS BY HERODOTUS

Histories. Trans. by Aubrey de Selincourt. *Classics Ser.* Viking Penguin 1954 $5.95. ISBN 0-14-044034-8. The translation of choice of almost forty years.
The History. Trans. by David Grene. U. CH. Pr. 1988 $30.00. ISBN 0-226-32770-1. The most recent and the best of the Herodotus translations; includes a strong introduction.
History of the Persian Wars. 4 vols. HUP $15.50 ea. ISBN 0-674-99130-3, 0-674-99131-1, 0-674-99133-8, 0-674-99134-6. The Loeb Classical Herodotos, for those who like to keep an eye on Greek while they are reading English (or vice versa).

BOOKS ABOUT HERODOTUS

Evans, J. A. S. *Herodotus, Explorer of the Past: Three Essays.* Princeton U. Pr. 1991 $24.95. ISBN 0-691-06871-2. Discusses Herodotus's way of thinking and working; a good place to get an idea of current scholarly thought.
Gould, John, *Herodotus.* St. Martin 1989 $24.95. ISBN 0-312-02855-5. On Herodotus's "mind": what does he mean by *historiē* (inquiry), how does he work, how does he perceive the world?
Hartog, Francois. *The Mirror of Herodotus: The Representation of the Other in the Writing of History.* Trans. by Janet Lloyd. U. CA Pr. 1988 $52.50. ISBN 0-520-05487-3. How Herodotus looked at others, especially the Scythians, raised questions about himself, and provided the mirror through which others would see the past.
Immerwahr, Henry R. *Form and Thought in Herodotus.* Scholars Pr. GA 1983 $27.00. ISBN 0-89130-278-9. Summarizes the histories and attempts to identify the unity of Herodotus's historical vision, including his religious convictions.
Lang, Mabel. *Herodotean Narrative and Discourses.* HUP 1984 $20.00. ISBN 0-674-38985-9. Argues for the oral composition of Herodotus with special attention to speeches and narrative transitions.
Shimron Binyamin. *Politics and Belief in Herodotus.* Coronet Bks. 1988 $29.50. ISBN 3-515-05240-2. Interrogates Herodotos's attitude toward the supernatural to determine his attitude toward history and political understanding; requires the ability to comprehend Greek words.

HESIOD. fl. c.700 B.C.E.

Along with HOMER (see also Vol. 2), Hesiod was the earliest of the Greek poets. From his works we learn that he spent his life at Ascra, a village near Mt. Helicon on mainland Greece. The only exception seems to have been a trip by boat to the neighboring island of Boeotia to participate in a poetic contest, an excursion Hesiod claimed he did not much enjoy. Hesiod also informed us of a dispute with his brother Perses over their inheritance. Indeed, this dispute, in which Hesiod accused Perses of bribing local officials, became the occasion for one of Hesiod's two great poems, the *Works and Days*. Hesiod ascribed his poetic gift to a visitation of the Muses.

The earlier of Hesiod's poems, the *Theogony*, is a sense, the first Greek attempt at systematic theology. It recounts the generations of the gods from the beginning of time to the ascendancy of Zeus. It opens with Chaos, Earth (Gaia), and Desire. Earth gives birth to Sky (Ouranos), Mountains, and Sea (Pontus), and then Sky rules the universe until he is castrated by his son Kronos. Kronos rules until he is in turn overthrown by his son Zeus. During the last 30 years, scholarship has emphasized the striking similarities between the *Theogony* and Near Eastern accounts of divine genealogy (Hurrian, Hittite, and Akkadian). Two centuries after Hesiod, at the earliest, a "Catalogue of Women" was appended to the *Theogony*. It traces the ancestry of heroes to the union of divine fathers and human mothers (cp. Gen. 6.4). Unlike the *Theogony*, the "Catalogue" survives only in fragments.

The *Works and Days* was Hesiod's attempt to persuade his brother to abandon the pursuit of wealth through unjust litigation and turn to hard work. In the process, he recounted the story of Prometheus, which also figured prominently in the *Theogony*, as well as tales of Pandora and of the devolution of the world (the five ages of gold, silver, bronze, the heroes, and iron). The latter part of the poem contains a calendar detailing agricultural tasks appropriate to each season, instruction on social and religious conduct, and an almanac of auspicious and inauspicious days. Clearly, all of this material is significant for the study of ancient religions, although scholars question whether the last parts of the *Works and Days* were originally part of the poem or added later.

BOOKS BY HESIOD

Hesiod: Theogony, Works and Days. Trans. by Apostolos Athanassakis. Johns Hopkins 1983 $9.95. ISBN 0-8018-2999-2. Translations that follow the original Greek closely but still flow; introduction and notes draw parallels with customs in modern Greece.

Hesiod, Homeric Hymns, Fragments of the Epic Cycle, Homerica. HUP $15.50. ISBN 0-674-99063-3. The works of Hesiod and a lot more in the Loeb Classical Library edition.

Theogony: Translated with Introduction, Commentary and Interpretative Essay. Trans. by Richard S. Caldwell. Focus Info. Gr. 1987 $6.95. ISBN 0-941051-00-5. Not only the "Theogony" but also the first part of the "Works and Days" in verse translation; the essay interprets myths as expressing repressed unconscious fantasies.

Theogony and Works and Days. Ed. by M. L. West. *The World's Classics Ser.* OUP 1988 $6.95. ISBN 0-19-281788-4. Translations by one of the world's foremost authorities on Hesiod.

The Works and Days. Trans. by Richmond Lattimore. U. of Mich. Pr. 1991 $12.95. ISBN 0-472-08161-6. English renderings by a translator whose renderings of Homer have been cherished for a generation. Bound with *Theogony; The Shield of Herakles*.

BOOKS ABOUT HESIOD

Hamilton, Richard. *The Architecture of Hesiodic Poetry*. Johns Hopkins 1989 $25.00. ISBN 0-8018-3819-3. Focuses on the poems and deliberately neglects their contexts in an attempt to identify Hesiod's poetic programs.

Lamberton, Robert. *Hesiod*. Yale U. Pr. 1988 $11.00. ISBN 0-300-04069-5. A little about
    Hesiod and his world, then analyses of the "Theogony" and "Works and Days";
    primarily focuses on literature, aimed at the nonspecialist.
Walcott, P. *Hesiod and the Near East*. Wales U. Pr. 1966 o.p. An older book comparing
    Hesiod's *Theogony*, the story of Pandora, and his didactic sections with Near Eastern
    materials, especially Hittite and Babylonian.

HOMER. fl. 8th century B.C.E.

Homer is the name of the alleged author of several ancient Greek poems. The
Iliad and the *Odyssey* are generally attributed to him today. At various times in
the past, he has also been credited with the other epics that tell the story of the
Trojan War (the "Homeric cycle") and with the "Homeric hymns," hymns to
various Greek gods in the meter of Homeric epic. According to legend, Homer
was blind and inhabited one of several cities in Asia Minor (today, the west coast
of Turkey); in reality, little is known about the author or authors of these poems.
Scholars have often attributed the *Iliad* and the *Odyssey* to two different authors.
Some have even argued that the author of the *Odyssey* was a woman, a
suggestion that is possible but not compelling.

Although modern readers tend to be interested in Homeric epic as literature,
in ancient Greece Homer functioned in many ways as a sacred text. The
Homeric epics were recited competitively at festivals, such as the Panathenaia
in Athens. PLATO (see also Vol. 3), who disliked the content of the poems,
recognized Homer as the "educator of Greece"; Homeric epic was memorized
by school students, and from it they learned essential values. The characters of
the epics were often worshiped in different locations as heroes, and Homer's
depiction of the gods provided a somewhat canonical picture of the deities as
worshiped in official state cults. As a result, Homeric epic is a major source for
the study of Greek religion.

The Homeric gods, however, present modern readers with severe interpretive
difficulties. They do not much resemble the God that Jews, Christians, and
Muslims worship. At the same time, they seem to "overdetermine" actions; that
is, they provide causal explanations for events when satisfactory natural
explanations are already at hand. Some writers have seen Homer's gods as
purely literary. One variant of this view derives Homeric epic from more primal
myths that have been demythologized. Others see Homer's gods as objectifica-
tions of psychological processes. It was once fashionable to credit Homer with
creating a bright, lucid, rational religion in contrast to the more superstitious
practices that had held sway earlier. The present author prefers instead to
connect Homer's deities with the active role religion played in the rise of the
Greek *polis*, with which Homeric epic was contemporary.

The bibliography on Homer is immense. The few titles listed may especially
attract those interested in ancient religions.

BOOKS BY HOMER

Homeric Hymns. Trans. by Charles Boer. Spring Pubns. 1970 $13.50. ISBN 0-88214-210-0.
    A translation into short, pithy modern verse of important hymns to the Homeric
    gods.
The Iliad. Trans. by Robert Fagles. Viking Penguin 1991 $8.95. ISBN 0-14-044592-7. An
    energetic new translation that may become the translation of choice.
The Iliad of Homer. Trans. by Richmond Lattimore. U. Ch. Pr. 1975 $8.95. ISBN 0-226-
    46940-9. An elegant verse translation that has been the choice of a generation, a
    classic rendering of a classic.

The Odyssey. Trans. by Robert Fitzgerald. Knopf 1992 $20.00. ISBN 0-679-41047-3. A translation of what is probably the more popular of the Homeric epics into highly readable verse.

Odyssey: Critical Edition. Ed. and trans. by Albert Cook. Norton 1974 $12.95. ISBN 0-393-09971-7. A verse translation and then some; the critical essays will be invaluable to beginning students of the poem.

BOOKS ABOUT HOMER

Edwards, Mark W. *Homer: Poet of the Iliad.* Johns Hopkins 1987 $48.00. ISBN 0-8018-3329-9. Probably the most accessible, up-to-date introduction to Homer for the general reader; strongly recommended.

Ehnmark, Erland. *The Idea of God in Homer.* Gordon Pr. 1980 $59.95. ISBN 0-8490-3182-6. An older work, first published in 1935, that can still be used with profit by those who can identify outmoded theories of religion on sight.

Griffen, Jasper. *Homer on Life and Death.* OUP 1980 $18.95. ISBN 0-19-814026-6. A scholarly account of the significance of living and dying for gods, men, and heroes, focusing primarily on the *Iliad*.

Lamberton, Robert. *Homer the Theologian: Allegorical Reading and the Growth of the Epic Tradition.* U. CA Pr. 1986 $14.95. ISBN 0-520-06607-3. A rich account of how Homer came to be read as a fountain of truth in later Greek and Roman antiquity.

Scully, Stephen. *Homer and the Sacred City.* Cornell Univ. Pr. 1991 $32.95. ISBN 0-8014-2364-X. A study that identifies Troy as a sacred city, as distinct from the households depicted in the *Odyssey*, and sees in the *Iliad* a conflict between civilization and chaos.

JUNG, C. G. 1875–1961

[SEE Volume 5.]

KERÉNYI, KÁROLY. 1897–1973

Those interested in Jungian psychology and ancient religions should look carefully at the work of Károly (or Karl) Kerényi. Kerényi was a friend of, and coauthor with, CARL JUNG (see Vol. 5), a cofounder of the Jung Institute in Zurich, and a regular participant in the Eranos conferences in Ascona, Switzerland. His work is not, however, Jungian in the strictest sense of the word.

Trained as a classical philologist, Kerényi attempted to transcend the limits of historical study and to reveal the "theological" or contemporary significance of ancient myths. In doing so, he relied not solely on literary and archaeological documentation but also invoked a relationship of sympathy between the scholar and the evidence. Among an incredible number of publications, Kerényi pursued this agenda in a series of volumes devoted to the mythologies of individual Greek gods and goddesses. Throughout, his writing is accessible to the general reader.

The dangers of Kerényi's approach should be clear. Under the guise of a sympathetic recovery of authentic significance, one projects one's own convictions and desires back onto the past. The question is: Do less "theological" studies (in Kerényi's sense of the term) avoid this danger, or merely disguise it?

BOOKS BY KERÉNYI

Archetypal Images in Greek Religion. Trans. by Ralph Manheim. 5 vols. Princeton U. Pr. 1959 $47.50. ISBN 0-691-09703-8. Includes the author's well-known studies of Prometheus, Dionysos, Asklepios, Eleusis, Zeus, and Hera.

Eleusis: Archetypal Image of Mother and Daughter. Trans. by Ralph Manheim. Princeton U. Pr. 1991 $47.50. ISBN 0-691-01915-0. Part four of *Archetypal Images*: eventually reads the most famous ancient mysteries in terms of the beautific vision.

Essays on a Science of Mythology: The Myths of the Divine Child and the Mysteries of Eleusis. (coauthored with Carl G. Jung). Princeton U. Pr. 1985 $22.95. ISBN 0-691-09899-9. Eleusis as providing the intersection of two archetypes, divine child and mother-daughter; an introduction sets the essays in methodological context.

Goddesses of Sun and Moon: Circe, Aphrodite, Medea, Niobe. Trans. by Murray Stein. Spring Pubns. 1979 $9.00. ISBN 0-88214-211-9. Explores daughters of the sun (Circe, Medea, Aphrodite) as well as the more common connection between the feminine and the lunar (Niobe).

The Gods of the Greeks. Thames Hudson 1980 $10.95. ISBN 0-500-27048-1. Presents the major Greek myths and aims to demonstrate the "vital relationship between the mythology and the society."

The Religion of the Greeks and Romans. Greenwood 1973 repr. of 1962 ed. $35.00. ISBN 0-8371-6605-5. An attempt to characterize the "style" of Greek and Roman religion as a whole.

LUCIAN OF SAMOSATA. c.120 c.e.–after 180 c.e.

Lucian of Samosata (now Samsat, Turkey) was a rhetorician and later a philosopher whose works are highly satirical. During his earlier, rhetorical period, Lucian traveled, earning his keep by giving public performances as far west as the Roman province of Gaul (now France). During his philosophical period, Lucian resided and wrote mainly in Athens, although he also spent some time in Carthage.

Among the butts of Lucian's satire is religion in its various aspects. For example, his "Dialogues of the Gods" pokes fun at Greek mythology, while his "Alexander, or the False Prophet," is an exposé of a popular miracle-worker, Alexander the Paphlagonian. Similarly, the "Peregrinus" ridicules a religious fanatic.

For the study of ancient religions, Lucian's most important work is probably "On the Syrian Goddess" (*De dea syria*). It details the mysteries of the Syrian goddess Atargatis as well as the Phrygian Great Mother, Cybele, and includes a notorious account of the public, ritual autocastration of Cybele's priests and their subsequent, cross-sexual practices.

Books by Lucian

Dialogues. 8 vols. HUP $15.50 ea. ISBNs 0-674-99015-3, 0-674-99060-9, 0-674-99144-3, 0-674-99179-6, 0-674-99333-0, 0-674-99474-4, 0-674-99475-2, 0-674-99476-0. The Loeb Classical Library translation; unfortunately, the translation of "The Goddesse of Surrye" imitates a fourteenth-century English satirist and is very hard to use.

Satirical Sketches. Trans. by Paul Turner. Ind. U. Pr. 1990 $29.95. ISBN 0-253-36097-8. Free, fun translations, many from the "Dialogues of the Dead"; includes "Alexander."

Selected Satires of Lucian. Ed. and trans. by Lionel Casson. Norton 1968 $10.95. ISBN 0-393-00443-0. Not so frolicking as Turner's translations, but a larger selection, including "Alexander," "Peregrinus," and "Lucius, or the Ass."

Selected Works. Trans. by B. P. Reardon. Macmillan 1965 $5.65. ISBN 0-672-60385-3. Selected dialogues on a wide range of subjects, including some that ridicule popular religion and the pretensions of philosophers.

The Syrian Goddess (De Dea Syria). Trans. by Harold W. Attridge and Robert A. Oden. o.p. A much more satisfactory translation of this important dialogue than the one in the Loeb Classical Library.

BOOKS ABOUT LUCIAN

Branham, Robert Bracht. *Unruly Eloquence: Lucian and the Comedy of Traditions.* HUP 1989 $27.50. ISBN 0-674-93035-5. Strategies of humor in Lucian's "Dialogues"; how Lucian addressed a sophisticated audience conscious of classical tradition and its relation to it.

Jones, C. P. *Culture and Society in Lucian.* HUP 1986 $28.00. ISBN 0-674-17974-9. A descriptive book, on occasion simply summarizing Lucian, with accessible chapters on philosophy, religion, and Alexander.

Oden, Robert A. *Studies in Lucian's De Syria Dea.* Scholars Pr. GA 1976 $11.50. ISBN 0-89130-123-2. A scholarly study arguing that Lucian's *De Syria Dea* is historically reliable and reveals a close relationship between the Syrian goddess and Canaanite goddesses; presumes minimal Greek.

Robinson, Christopher. *Lucian and His Influence in Europe.* U. of NC Pr. 1979 $32.50. ISBN 0-8078-1404-0. One fourth on Lucian, three fourths of his influence, culminating with his influence on Erasmus and Henry Fielding; accessible but entirely literary in focus.

MALINOWSKI, BRONISLAW. 1884–1942

The anthropologist Bronislaw Malinowski is important to the study of religions both for his pioneering example of fieldwork and his theoretical reflections. Polish by nationality and originally educated in physics and mathematics, Malinowski ascribed his interest in anthropology to reading JAMES G. FRAZER's *The Golden Bough.* During World War I, he spent 21 months with the inhabitants of the Trobriand Islands in the Pacific. Ever since, students of anthropology have been expected to work from field observations.

Malinowski's general position is known as "functionalism." As he once put it, "every custom, material object, idea and belief fulfills some vital function, has some task to accomplish, represents an indispensable part within a working whole" (*Encyclopedia Britannica*, 13th ed.). Malinowski rejected simply identifying cultural artifacts as evolutionary "survivals" or "borrowings" from neighbors. Myth, Malinowski said, does not explain the inexplicable but validates social order. Magic supplements practical activity in situations of technical uncertainty by addressing individual anxiety and the need for social integration. Religious practices, unlike magical ones, are ends in themselves. In Malinowski's view, religion consoles human beings when they encounter tragedy and uncertainty.

More recent anthropologists tend to view religion not in terms of function so much as the symbolic construction of meaning. Biographical research has also cast doubt on how much what Malinowski actually did corresponded to what he claimed. Nevertheless, his example remains significant.

BOOKS BY MALINOWSKI

Argonauts of the Western Pacific. Waveland Pr. 1984 $12.95. ISBN 0-88133-084-1. A detailed ethnographic account that focuses on an interisland system of economic exchange known as *kula.*

Coral Gardens and their Magic. o.p. An account of agricultural practices in the Trobriand Islands; has an important discussion of the magical rituals used.

The Early Writings of Bronislaw Malinowski. Ed. by Robert Thornton and Peter Skalnik. Cambridge U. Pr. 1992 $74.95. ISBN 0-521-38300-5. A collection of early writings that helps situate Malinowski against the cultural and intellectual background of the late nineteenth century.

Magic, Science and Religion and Other Essays. Waveland Pr. 1992 $9.95. ISBN 0-88133-675-2. Malinowski's classical statement on "Magic, Science and Religion," together with "Myth in Primitive Psychology" and an article on "Spirits of the Dead."

Malinowski and the Work of Myth. Ed. by Ivan Strenski. Princeton U. Pr. 1992 $35.00.
ISBN 0-691-07414-3. Selected essays by Malinowski on myth that explore psychoanalytic and especially functionalist interpretations; includes a helpful introduction.

Myth in Primitive Psychology. Greenwood 1972 repr. of 1926 ed. $35.00. ISBN 0-8371-
5954-7. Uses native categories to distinguish myth from fairy tale, legend, and
history: Myth has a sacred character and justifies social and moral behavior.

Sex and Repression in Savage Society. U. Ch. Pr. 1985 $12.95. ISBN 0-226-50287-2.
Compares sexual life, with an eye on Freud, in the Trobriands and Europe to show
that many psychological disturbances are not universal but derive from the
structures of European society.

BOOKS ABOUT MALINOWSKI

Ellen, Roy, et al, eds. *Malinowski Between Two Worlds: The Polish Roots of an
Anthropological Tradition*. Cambridge U. Pr. 1989 $49.95. ISBN 0-521-34566-9.
Malinowski's work viewed against his background.

Firth, Raymond, ed. *Man and Culture: An Evaluation of the Work of Bronislaw
Malinowski*. o.p. Critical essays on Malinowski by a variety of well-known scholars of
an earlier generation, including Talcott Parsons, E. R. Leach, Meyer Fortes, S. F.
Nagel, Firth, and others.

Leach, Jerry W., and Edmund Leach, eds. *The Kula: New Perspectives on Massim
Exchange*. Cambridge U. Pr. 1983 $110.00. ISBN 0-521-23202-3. Several anthropolo-
gists revisit and update a topic that Malinowski introduced to the scholarly world.

NILSSON, MARTIN P. 1874–1967

MIRCEA ELIADE once called Martin Nilsson the Nestor of the historians of
Greek religions. The metaphor justly described not only Nilsson's age but the
respect in which he was universally held.

A Swedish scholar who studied, then taught at the University of Lund for
many years, Nilsson exercised a profound influence on the study of the religions
of ancient Greece. In many respects he appears the archetypal historian, who
carefully threshes the theories of other writers, sharply rejecting what he finds
to be unsubstantiated and unsound. But Nilsson's work is not without positions
of its own that others would find dubious. He was a staunch adherent of
evolutionary theory, which states that religions have evolved from a primitive
substrate, leaving detectable survivals in historical data. He also adopted a
"dynamistic" conception of "primitive religion"; that is, he believed that
religion was originally a husbanding of *mana*, or supernatural power, although
that power was not likely conceived of as such. This belief led Nilsson to take
the Greek *daimon* to be impersonal power, a view that is certainly wrong.

Perhaps Nilsson's most original contribution is his work on the survival of
Minoan and Mycenaean religions in the later religions of ancient Greece.
Nilsson did not speak the last word on the subject, but no scholar ever does.

BOOKS BY NILSSON

The Dionysiac Mysteries of the Hellenistic and Roman Age. Ayer 1976 repr. of 1957 ed.
$15.95. ISBN 0-405-07261-0. Descriptive account of the mysteries of Dionysos as
distinctively Greek, not oriental.

Greek Folk Religion. U. of Pa. Pr. 1972 $16.95. ISBN 0-8122-1034-4. Pays particular
attention to the religion of farmers, herders, and ordinary town-dwellers, in other
words, the vast majority of ancient Greeks.

A History of Greek Religion. Trans. by F. J. Fielden. Greenwood 1980 repr. of 1949 ed.
$52.50. ISBN 0-313-22466-8. Until Burkert's *Greek Religion*, the standard (though
old) survey of Greek religion.

The Minoan-Mycenaean Religion. Biblo 1950 $20.00. ISBN 0-8196-0273-6. Part 1: a careful review of Minoan-Mycenaean evidence according to broad types (columns, pillars, tree cults, etc.); part 2: relation of that evidence to later Greek religion.

The Mycenaean Origins of Greek Mythology. U. CA Pr. 1973 $11.95. ISBN 0-520-05073-8. Compares Mycenaean and mythological sites to show that Greek myths descended from the Mycenaean period.

NOCK, ARTHUR DARBY. 1902–1963

For years, Arthur Darby Nock ranked as "the world's leading authority on the religion of later antiquity," as MARTIN NILSSON is reputed to have said. The range of Nock's scholarship is immense. He wrote on early Christianity and the magical papyri, Greek and Roman religion, Zoroastrianism, Mithraism, Gnosticism, and the Hermetic corpus. But he is a scholar's scholar, and the general reader may find him difficult.

Nock was not entirely adverse to general statement. He once wrote, "The history of religion is a history of feeling rather than a reason." Recently JONATHAN Z. SMITH has pointed out how Protestant convictions influenced some of Nock's other claims. But consciously, at least, Nock was a "minimizer"; that is, he disliked hasty theorizing, bold generalizations, and speculation. He preferred to rest firmly with the evidence, and he insisted that all evidence needs to be examined and interpreted against the background of its context. What results is a scholar's dream, but it may often be less than satisfying for the general reader. Nock's scholarly papers are wonderful compendia of evidence carefully and critically assessed, at times the only full compendia available on a given subject. But his expositions are often intricate and, for a more general audience, overburdened with qualifications. Nevertheless, readers who are seriously interested in ancient religions cannot afford to forego Nock's work.

BOOKS BY NOCK

Conversion: The Old and the New in Religion from Alexander the Great to Augustine of Hippo. o.p. How and why people in the ancient Mediterranean world switched religions, culminating in a consideration of Christianity.

Early Gentile Christianity and its Hellenistic Background. o.p. Emphasizes differences between Christianity and its context and, in contrast to scholars at the turn of the century, downplays "pagan" influences on Christianity.

Essays on Religion and the Ancient World. Ed. by Zeph Stewart. OUP 1986 set $145.00. ISBN 0-19-814282-X. A wide-ranging anthology of Nock's essays, arranged in chronological order; also includes a complete bibliography of his publications.

OTTO, RUDOLF. 1869–1937

Rudolf Otto is best known today for his description of religious experience in a widely read study, *The Idea of the Holy*, first published in 1917. A Christian theologian by training and profession, Otto was intensely concerned with defending the autonomy of religion, indeed, with maintaining the superiority of a religious worldview, in opposition to the naturalistic, materialistic, scientistic perspective that he saw gaining ground in early twentieth-century Germany. At the same time, Otto was well traveled and had great respect for the many religions he encountered, especially Zen Buddhism and Hinduism. As a result, he was not satisfied with a confessional Christianity that cited supernatural revelation to claim an exclusive patent on religious truth.

Otto's classic book develops an analysis of the "holy" or the "sacred" as a complex category uniting two poles, the nonrational and the rational. The nonrational pole is an experience of what Otto calls "the numinous," the sacred minus metaphysical and moral content. Otto identified three sides to this experience: *mysterium*, the numinous as "wholly other"; *tremendum*, the numinous as frightening and overwhelming; and *fascinans*, the numinous as attractive and gracious. Although essentially nonpropositional, these experiences are generally found in a fixed relation with specific ideas. Otto borrowed the Kantian term "schematization" to designate this relationship, but his analysis of it is not very clear. In any case, Otto was convinced that both poles, the nonrational and the rational, as well as the moment unifying them into a complex category, constituted the "religious a priori." They are given in the structure of human experience rather than subject to verification by it. With this assertion Otto achieved two important aims. He insulated religion from scientific criticism, and he eliminated a question that was a burning issue at the time: How has religion evolved? As "a priori," Otto says, religion could not have evolved from anything else.

Although Otto's thought is complex and rich, the unfortunate tendency has been to simplify it to one basic idea, the analysis of numinous experience. Serious analysis of his thought has lagged. In the last two decades, a concern with internal religious experience has given way to analyzing religious symbols and representations. Recently, however, some have begun to take religion's experiental and emotional side more seriously.

BOOKS BY OTTO

Idea of the Holy. Trans. by John W. Harvey. OUP 1950 $8.95. ISBN 0-19-500210-5. Otto's classic study of religious experience as an encounter with a numen that is "wholly other" (*mysterium*), both terrifying (*tremendum*) and attractive (*fascinans*).

India's Religion of Grace and Christianity Compared and Contrasted. o.p. Compares Indian *bhakti*, especially in the tradition of Ramanuja, with Christian devotional religion.

Mysticism East and West. Trans. by Bertha L. Bracey and Richendra C. Payne. Theos. Pub. Hse. 1987 $8.75. ISBN 0-8356-0619-8. A comparison of the German mystic Meister Eckhardt and the great Indian advaitin philosopher Śaṅkara.

Religious Essays: A Supplement to "The Idea of the Holy." OUP 1931 o.p. A set of wide-ranging essays selected to supplement the analysis in *The Idea of the Holy*; on both theological and religio-historical subjects.

BOOKS ABOUT OTTO

Almond, Philip C. *Rudolf Otto: An Introduction to His Philosophical Theology*. U. of NC Pr. 1984 o.p. The best introduction to Otto in English; successfully places Otto in his philosophical context.

Davidson, Robert F. *Rudolf Otto's Interpretation of Religion*. Princeton U. Pr. 1947 o.p. The first book-length study of Otto in English, centered on Otto's idea that religion is autonomous.

PAUSANIAS (of Lydia?). fl. c.150 C.E.

Pausanias traveled through Greece in the middle of the second century A.D. On the way, he wrote about his travels in 10 rich books, beginning at Athens and ending up at Delphi, the site of Apollo's ancient oracle. From his writings, it is clear that Pausanias also knew Palestine, Syria, Asia Minor (now Turkey), Egypt, and parts of Italy, including Rome.

Pausanias liked especially to describe monumental art and architecture, much of it religious in nature. "Without him," JAMES G. FRAZER once wrote, "the ruins of Greece would for the most part be . . . a riddle without an answer." Pausanias routinely gave attention to the history and topography of the most important cities he visited. His descriptions of the wonders of nature reveal his own attitude of personal curiosity. Especially significant for the study of religions are his accounts of local ceremonies, superstitions, legends, and folklore. These are often not as detailed as one might like, but they are invaluable clues to the religious life of Greece in the middle of the second century.

BOOKS BY PAUSANIAS

Description of Greece. Trans. by J. G. Frazer. 6 vols. Biblo 1897 set $150.00. ISBN 0-8196-0144-6. A classic edition of Pausanias, most of it commentary by Frazier, a master anthropologist of an earlier era.

Description of Greece. 5 vols. HUP 1918–1935 $15.50 ea. ISBN 0-674-99104-4, 0-674-99207-4, 0-674-99300-4, 0-674-99328-4, 0-674-99329-2. Greek text and facing page translations in the well-known Loeb Classical Library.

Guide to Greece. 2 vols. Trans. by Peter Levi. Viking Penguin 1984 $7.95–$8.95. ISBNs 0-14-044225-1, 0-14-044226-X. Probably the most accessible translation of Pausanias for the general reader.

PHILO JUDAEUS. c.20 B.C.E.–50 C.E.

[SEE Chapter 13 in this volume.]

PLOTINUS. 205 B.C.E.–270 C.E.

[SEE Chapter 3 in this volume.]

PLUTARCH. Before 50 C.E.–after 120 C.E.

Today Plutarch is remembered most as the author of the "Parallel Lives" of Greeks and Romans," but he is also an indispensable source on religion in the ancient world.

Plutarch was born and resided at Chaeronea in Boeotia (central Greece). He held several posts there, including that of chief magistrate. He was also director of a school whose instruction focused heavily on ethics, and he had ties with the Athenian Academy. From about 95 C.E. until his death, he was a priest of the oracle of Apollo at Delphi and was involved in the revival of the oracle that was then current. Plutarch was a prolific writer: One ancient catalogue ascribes 227 works to his name.

Plutarch's writings are divided into two groups. The first group, the "Lives," pairs biographies of famous Greeks and Romans. Fifty of the lives are still in existence today, 23 pairs and 4 individual biographies. Material from individual lives can often be useful in the study of ancient religions, but the second group of writings contains essays that are of direct significance to the study of ancient religions.

The second group is a loose collection known as the *Moralia* (or, in Greek, the *Ethica*). It contains everything Plutarch wrote that is not biographical. Included are rhetorical works, short essays on moral philosophy, essays on Platonic philosophy, and dialogues.

Plutarch's involvement with the oracle at Delphi is quite apparent from three mature dialogues in the *Moralia*. "On the Failure of the Oracles" grapples with the question of why the oracles declined. "On the Pythian Responses" tries to revive the credibility of the oracle. Finally, "On 'E' at Delphi" explicates the word "EI" inscribed at the entrance to the Delphic temple. In the eyes of some, these three dialogues constitute Plutarch's most important religio-philosophical thought.

Equally important for the study of ancient religions is Plutarch's tractate, "On Isis and Osiris." The work essentially recounts the double murder of Osiris by his brother and rival, Typhon or Set. The first murder occurs when Osiris tries out a beautiful chest to see if it fits and finds himself entombed and floating down the Nile. Isis, Osiris's sister and wife, finds the chest in a tree in Byblos, cuts it out, and bring it back home. The second murder occurs when Set finds Osiris's sarcophagus erected as a pillar. He chops it into 14 pieces and scatters them widely. Isis again travels in search of Osiris and finds every piece but his phallos. She crafts a replica of the phallos, a homologue to the cultic pillar. As a result of these efforts, Isis establishes her mysteries, which were extremely popular in the urban environment of the early Roman Empire.

Critical writing on Plutarch in English, as opposed to other European languages, has been scanty.

BOOK BY PLUTARCH

Moralia. 15 vols. HUP $14.50 ea. ISBNs 0-674-99217-2, 0-674-99245-8, 0-674-99270-9, 0-674-99336-5, 0-674-99337-3, 0-674-99371-3, 0-674-99446-9, 0-674-99466-3, 0-674-99467-1, 0-674-99354-3, 0-674-99469-8, 0-674-99447-7, 0-674-99470-7, 0-674-99472-8, 0-674-99473-6. All of Plutarch's writings except the "Parallel Lives" in the Loeb Classic Library edition.

BOOKS ABOUT PLUTARCH

Barrow, Reginald H. *Plutarch and His Times*. AMS Pr. repr. of 1967 ed. $19.00. ISBN 0-404-15276-7. Plutarch as Roman citizen as well as native Greek; readable and informative, but little about religion.

Betz, Hans Dieter, ed. *Plutarch's Ethical Writings and Early Christian Literature*. Brill 1978 o.p.

———. *Plutarch's Theological Writings and Early Christian Literature*. Brill 1975 o.p. Essays written by a team of scholars that introduce individual works in general terms, then comment on individual words, phrases, and sentences, often citing them in Greek; for the most serious readers only.

Russell, D. A. *Plutarch*. Duckworth 1972 o.p. Not a biography but a discussion of several aspects of Plutarch that may help readers understand him better.

SMITH, JONATHAN Z. 1938–

Jonathan Z. Smith is perhaps the leading theorist working in the study of religions today; he is also a scholar who specializes in Hellenistic and late Antique religions. Trained at Yale University, where he wrote a thesis examining the methods employed in JAMES G. FRAZER's mammoth classic, *The Golden Bough*, Smith has been particularly interested in using the ideas and methods of sociology and anthropology to study religions. Through unrelenting criticism and detailed historical investigations, he has called into question many of the conclusions that an older generation of scholars had reached. His acumen has been directed particularly at the work of MIRCEA ELIADE, who was for years Smith's colleague at the University of Chicago. His recent book, *Drudgery Divine*, aims to expose the sectarian purposes that led Protestant historians to isolate "primitive Christianity" from its contexts in ancient religions, an exposé that Smith's own background in Judaism makes him ideally suited to carry out.

As a theorist, Smith emphasizes the active role of intellection in all scholarly enterprises. He insists that the aim of religious studies is distinct from that of religions ("map is not territory"), that "religion" is a category "imagined" by Western scholars to accomplish certain academic purposes, and that theoretical questions and purposes should explicitly guide all investigations. For example,

Smith states that when scholars compare religions, their immediate concern should not be with finding similarities that pervade a large body of data (cp. Eliade), nor should it be to determine who borrowed what from whom (historical diffusion). Instead, the purpose of comparison is to identify individual differences that assume significance because they elucidate specific theoretical issues. Smith's distinction between locative religions—religions that pertain to specific places—and utopian ones—religions that have broken their bonds with place—is especially helpful in considering the history of religions in the Hellenistic and late Antique periods.

Smith's work is itself too recent to have been the subject of a scholarly monograph, but readers will find Smith's influence extending widely through the study of ancient religions. Those who want critical assessments may wish to consult book review indexes.

BOOKS BY JONATHAN Z. SMITH

Drudgery Divine: On the Comparison of Early Christianities and the Religions of Late Antiquity. U. Ch. Pr. 1990 $24.95. ISBN 0-226-76362-5. Searching theoretical reflection on what scholarly comparison means, as well as an attempt to reinsert early Christianities alongside other contemporary religions.

Imagining Religion: From Babylon to Jonestown. U. Ch. Pr. 1988 $17.50. ISBN 0-226-76358-7. A collection that in many ways continues the project of *Map Is Not Territory*; the essay on the Jonestown suicide should not be missed.

Map Is Not Territory. o.p. Smith's first collection of essays that both initiates his critique of what had become common ideas in religious studies and introduces the distinction between locative and utopian religions.

To Take Place: Toward Theory in Ritual. U. Ch. Pr. 1987 $27.50. ISBN 0-226-76359-5. An extended reflection on ritual space, centering its attention on Jerusalem, that emphasizes the construction of meaning.

SMITH, WILLIAM ROBERTSON. 1846–1894

William Robertson Smith achieved fame and notoriety as a scholar of Semitic religions. A minister of the Free Church of Scotland and a professor at the Church's college in Aberdeen, Smith was dismissed from both after a much publicized heresy trial. He eventually found an academic home at Cambridge University, where he became editor-in-chief of the *Encyclopedia Britannica*.

Smith's troubles began when he published views that were inspired by the biblical criticism then current on the European continent. Today his reputation depends on his creative *Lectures on the Religion of the Semites*. Smith distinguished true religion, which is social and oriented toward action rather than belief, from magic and taboo, which for him are individualistic. He also adopted an evolutionary perspective, which claims that what is essential appears in the most primitive form. For Semitic religion, the most primitive is found in the religion of nomadic bedouins. In elucidating this religion, Smith made heavy use of ethnographic reports and theories, most notably the theory of totemism advanced by his fellow Scot, J. F. M'Lennan. In this view, the social grouping is symbolically represented by an animal or totem that is periodically sacrificed and then eaten in a communal meal. For Smith, these observances were the ultimate source of Christian practice.

Smith's views on religion influenced the important French sociologist, ÉMILE DURKHEIM (see Vol. 3), British anthropologist JAMES GEORGE FRAZER, and the Cambridge Ritualists, led by JANE E. HARRISON.

BOOKS BY WILLIAM ROBERTSON SMITH

Kinship and Marriage in Early Arabia. St. Mut. 1988 $135.00. ISBN 1-85077-188-X. Pre-Islamic Arabian society, indeed all Semitic society, and its connection with totemism; a precursor to the *Lectures.*

Lectures on the Religion of the Semites. o.p. The work on which Smith's current reputation depends.

The Prophets of Israel and Their Place in History: To the Close of the 8th Century. Black 1882 o.p. Designed to popularize then current historical criticism of the Bible; exemplifies the work that got Smith in trouble.

BOOK ABOUT WILLIAM ROBERTSON SMITH

Beidelman, Thomas O. *W. Robertson Smith and the Sociological Study of Religion.* Bks. Demand repr. of 1974 ed. $27.60. ISBN 0-685-3212-6. A very sophisticated study of Smith's thought.

STRABO. c.64? B.C.E.–after 21 C.E.

A native of Pontus (today central northern Turkey along the Black Sea), Strabo is the author of a multivolume *Geography* that gives a full sense of geographical knowledge of the Roman Empire at the time of Augustus.

Although a native of Asia Minor, Strabo spent many years in Rome in circles close to the imperial family. During the course of his Roman stay, he adopted tenets of the Stoic philosophy.

Strabo's first work, "Historical Sketches," is almost entirely lost. It is said to have recounted known history from the middle of the second century B.C. to the founding of the Roman Empire.

Strabo's second work, the *Geography*, is extant in its entirety. In composing it, Strabo relied heavily on secondary sources, even for areas that he himself knew. He described the world from Spain and Mauritania in the West to India and Persia in the East. Strabo knew next to nothing of northern Europe and Asia or sub-Saharan Africa. In describing the eastern Mediterranean, Strabo was particularly concerned with identifying sites mentioned in HOMER (see also Vol. 2), a topic that has fascinated several modern writers, too.

Among the many topics in the *Geography*, Strabo discusses the religious customs of the various areas he describes.

BOOK BY STRABO

Geography. 8 vols. HUP $14.50 ea. ISBNs 0-674-99055-2, 0-674-99056-0, 0-674-99201-6, 0-674-99216-4, 0-674-99233-4, 0-674-99246-6, 0-674-99266-0, 0-674-99295-4. The Loeb Classical Library edition with Greek on the left, English on the right; reasonable translation with some help for the reader, but not much.

VERNANT, JEAN-PIERRE. 1914–

Jean-Pierre Vernant is a leading French scholar of ancient Greece who attempts to elucidate Greek religions, especially mythology, through the development of a historical anthropology. In 1984 he retired from his position as professor of the comparative study of ancient religion at the College de France. Among his earlier accomplishments, Vernant received the Croix de Guerre and the Croix de la Liberation for his service in the French army in World War II; he was also made an officer in the French Legion of Honor.

Vernant is a writer of essays more than of books. As anthropologist JAMES REDFIELD (see Vol. 3) puts it, "His forte . . . has been the informal, slightly rambling essay. . .; he does not collect evidence in order to make a case but rather cites the material in order to illustrate his ideas." Vernant's career has been distinguished by his collaboration with other scholars, most notably with Marcel Detienne and Pierre Vidal-Naquet. His interest in applying anthropological study to ancient Greece derives from his teacher, Louis Gernet, a member of ÉMILE DURKHEIM's (see Vol. 3) school of *L'Année Sociologique*. Vernant also adapts ideas from structuralist anthropology, without, however, surrendering a historical perspective. He works most often on materials from Greece of the fifth century B.C.

Classicists often resist Vernant's approach because it is so heavily informed by theory. Nevertheless, it provides a wonderfully rich and complex vision of the ancient world and is worth serious and prolonged consideration.

BOOKS BY VERNANT

The Cuisine of Sacrifice among the Greeks. (coauthored with Marcel Detienne). Trans. by Paula Wissing. U. Ch. Pr. 1989 $39.95. ISBN 0-226-14351-1. Insightful essays on Greek sacrifice by several French scholars, contains a full (but not comprehensive) bibliography on the subject.

Cunning Intelligence in Greek Culture and Society. (coauthored with Marcel Detienne). Trans. by Janet Lloyd. U. Ch. Pr. 1991 $16.95. ISBN 0-226-14347-3. Groundbreaking study of *mētis* (cunning intelligence) as a mental category in ancient Greece.

Mortals and Immortals: Collected Essays. Ed. by Froma I. Zeitlin. Princeton U. Pr. 1992 $39.50. ISBN 0-691-06831-3. Essays that highlight several current topics: bodies, death, gender, images, and theory (including "Greek Religion, Ancient Religions"); also includes a sophisticated introduction by the editor.

Myth and Society in Ancient Greece. Trans. by Janet Lloyd. Zone Bks. 1988 $26.95. ISBN 0-942299-16-7. Begins with class, warfare, and marriage and ends with spices, Prometheus, and more general reflections; the connecting thread? The reciprocal but not simple relations between society and myth.

Myth and Thought Among the Greeks. Routledge 1983 $42.50. ISBN 0-7100-9544-9. Essays on mythic structure, memory and time, space, work and technology, the double, personal identity, and the shift from religion to reason.

Myth and Tragedy in Ancient Greece. (coauthored with Pierre Vidal-Naquet). Trans. by Janet Lloyd. Zone Bks. 1988 $32.95. ISBN 0-942299-18-3. Two books in one, beginning with essays on the relations between tragedy and social and political institutions and moving on to a series of fascinating topics.

The Origins of Greek Thought. Cornell U. Pr. 1982 $7.95. ISBN 0-8014-9293-9. Contrasts Mycenaean and later Greek cultures in a hunt for the twin births of the polis (city-state) and rational thought.

WACH, JOACHIM. 1898–1955

Joachim Wach is most important for having conceived of a study of religions as a discipline, independent of theology and the philosophy of religion on the one hand and of the social sciences on the other.

Wach was born and worked in Germany until 1935, when the Nazis expelled him because of his Jewish ancestry. (He was descended from the great Jewish philosopher MOSES MENDELSSOHN and his son FELIX MENDELSSOHN [see Vol. 3], the composer, who converted to Christianity). From 1935 until his death, Wach taught in the United States, first at Brown University, than at the University of Chicago.

Wach envisioned the study of religion in terms of a model of experience, expression, and understanding. In his view, religious phenomena are expressions of religious experience in three specific areas of life—the theoretical, the practical, and the sociological. The aim of the study of religions is to understand the meanings of these expressions.

Wach's work during the German period laid the philosophical foundations for this endeavor. He identified two fundamental components in an independent study of religions: historical study and systematics, in other words, a comparative study of general religious forms and patterns. His American works pay particular attention to the systematic study of the sociological dimension of religion, making particular use of the typological method often associated with MAX WEBER (see Vol. 3).

BOOKS BY WACH

The Comparative Study of Religion. o.p. Compiled by Wach's student, Joseph Kitagawa, after Wach's death; a complete and accessible overview of the phenomena of religion.

Introduction to the History of Religions. o.p. English translation of programmatic *Habilitationsschrift* from 1924, setting forth the philosophical foundations for an independent study of religions.

Sociology of Religion. o.p. A thick, rich account that discusses both kinds of religious communities and structures of authority.

Types of Religious Experience: Christian and Non-Christian. U. Ch. Pr. 1972 $2.45. ISBN 0-226-86710-2. A collected series of Wach's essays; see especially "Universals in Religion" for a brief introduction to his thought.

BOOK ABOUT WACH

Wood, Charles M. *Theory and Religious Understanding: A Critique of the Hermeneutics of Joachim Wach.* Scholars Pr. GA 1975 $14.95. ISBN 0-89130-026-0. Good source for an analysis of Wach's general methodological theories.

WEBER, MAX. 1864–1920

[SEE Volume 3.]

CHAPTER 11

Eastern Religions

Catherine Wessinger

May those who seek the path of peace and happiness find it.
—TENZIN GYATSO (THE 14TH DALAI LAMA), *The Buddhism of Tibet*

Do you remember the day
    our Mother first brought me here?
Through the five rivers, I have come to you.
But one day, when you no longer see me,
    smile, and quietly look for me
    in all the things that come and go.
You will find that I am
    that which never comes
    and never goes.
I am that reality beyond time,
    beyond perception.

—THICH NHAT HANH, *The Moon Bamboo*

Eastern religions and philosophies participate in the universal human search for peace and happiness. In their various ways, all of the world's religions search for human contentment and happiness, and those of the East are no exception. The East has made significant contributions to this search, and these will be delineated in the following pages, along with recommendations for further reading.

The religions and philosophies of the East are diverse. There are some perspectives that are polytheistic, others that are monotheistic or even atheistic. There are philosophies that are monistic; they perceive the ultimate as impersonal but as one and inclusive of the manifested world. All of this diversity has its origins in the animistic religions that are native to various Eastern countries. Animism is the belief that the material world is pervaded and made alive by the presence of unseen forces and personal spirits or gods. Animism is the oldest human outlook, and it is found all over the world. An animistic religion, despite its particularities, will have features in common with other animistic religions. Foremost is a concern to be in harmony with the unseen sacred forces and spirits. If this harmony is lacking, there can be no survival or well-being. Harmony with the sacred unseen reality is sought by: sacrificing to the spirits and gods; practicing magic; making offerings to the ancestors and ensuring their well-being in the afterlife; various acts of divination or fortune-telling; utilizing charms or other objects believed to have magic power; the prohibition (taboo) of contact with what is believed to be harmful; and consulting shamans. A shaman is an individual who is believed able to communicate with the unseen spirits, whether they are conceptualized as being the gods or the ancestors or lower spirits. Sometimes the shaman functions as a medium and allows the spirits to utilize his or her body and speak through his or her mouth. Other shamans are believed to be able to take out-of-body journeys to consult with the spirits. What the shaman says is authoritative, and the shaman's instructions will be followed to restore harmony with the unseen sacred forces and spirits. The shaman might make statements about the future or specialize in healing physical and spiritual ills. In the East there are many animistic traditions, and it is important to realize that animism is found not only among preliterate peoples. Shinto in Japan is a beautiful example of an animistic religion that is being practiced today by a people with advanced technology. The Hindu tradition in India also has its roots in animism and remains an animistic religion as it is practiced by Indian villagers today. However, the Hindu tradition includes monistic and monotheistic aspects as well. In this chapter, East Asian animistic traditions are treated in sections entitled Popular Religion.

Animism is the context for other religious developments as well. Within an animistic tradition, if focus is on one god above all others, that tradition will tend toward monotheism. This can be found in Hindu *bhakti* (devotionalism) or in the sect of Buddhism known as Pure Land. Zoroaster developed his monotheism out of the animism of ancient Iran. A number of new Japanese religions have their origins in this manner. Within an animistic tradition, if focus is not on the personal gods and spirits but on an unseen impersonal force, a more philosophical outlook will develop. This can be seen in philosophical Daoism (Taoism) in China or in the Hindu thought found in or based on the Upanishads. The authors whose thoughts are recorded in the Upanishads were searching for the one concept that leads to immortality. They called this one concept Brahman, but Brahman is not accurately called a force because it is an impersonal absolute that is permanent and unchanging. The thought of Gautama Buddha, which was developed within the complex Hindu tradition, is basically atheistic and psychological in orientation. But the Buddhist tradition after Gautama Buddha would develop monistic, monotheistic, and polytheistic tendencies, and Buddhism would accommodate itself very well to the animistic traditions of Central and East Asia. Much of this philosophical search in the East is directed toward the discovery of "that reality beyond time, beyond perception." The poetic statement of THICH NHAT HANH that introduces this chapter reveals a blending of Buddhist outlook with the Daoist tradition that tends to regard the ultimate unmanifest Source as "Mother." The "five rivers" to which he refers are the five *skandhas* of Buddhism, the five constantly changing components of the human personality. Other Eastern systems of thought, such as that of Confucius, are more concerned with social order and personal conduct, but more religious elements eventually crept back into the subsequent Confucian tradition.

The central thread that runs through the diversity of Eastern religions—and Western religions as well—is contained in the DALAI LAMA's wish that all sentient beings who seek the path of peace and happiness find it. This peace and happiness might be believed to be found in this world, or in heaven, or in escaping the cycle of rebirth, but it is sought nonetheless by all.

The great religious founders are featured in introductory sections to the various Eastern religions and philosophies and not in separate profiles. Such great religious founders as Zoroaster, Gautama Buddha, Mahavira, Confucius, and Laozi (Lao Tzu) either did not write and their teachings were passed down orally, or if they did write, it is not possible to conclusively point to a text or a portion of a text as theirs. Furthermore, it usually is not possible to know with detail and precision the facts of their lives. Therefore, the biographical profiles in this chapter are of recent religious figures within the Eastern religious and philosophical traditions who are fascinating exemplars of the issues that arise in the encounter of East and West.

SOUTH ASIAN TRADITIONS

The designation South Asia refers to the Indian subcontinent countries now known as Pakistan, India, Bangladesh, and the island country Sri Lanka (formerly Ceylon), southeast of India. The focus of this section will be on the religions of India because the influence of religious and cultural systems developed originally in India is pervasive throughout this region. India is the birthplace of a variety of religions that have been exported to other parts of Asia. Books relating to Sri Lanka can be found in the listings for Buddhism.

The language in which most major Indian scriptures have been composed is Sanskrit, which demonstrates linguistic relations to such European languages as Latin, German, and the Romance languages. Sanskrit no longer is a commonly spoken language in India, but it is the mother of the primary dialects spoken in northern India. In southern India, Dravidian languages are spoken that appear to have an origin independent of Sanskrit but nevertheless demonstrate Sanskrit influence. Very often the Sanskrit-based dominant religion will act as a canopy under which regional religions expressed in vernacular languages exist and relate to the dominant tradition in various ways. In India, as is the case elsewhere in Asia, diversity of religious expression is the rule.

The primary religious traditions having their origins in India are Hinduism, Buddhism, Jainism, and Sikhism. Zoroastrianism is a significant component of the Indian religious landscape that was brought by immigrants from Persia, called Parsis (Persians), who arrived in eastern India beginning in the seventh century C.E. Islam is another very important part of the Indian religious scene but is treated elsewhere in this volume. The following bibliography for South Asia begins with listings for general works on the religions of India, followed by listings for Hinduism, Buddhism, Jainism, Sikhism, and Zoroastrianism.

Reference Works and Anthologies

Bhattacharyya, Narendra Nath. *A Glossary of Indian Religious Terms and Concepts*. S. Asia Pubs. 1990 $34.00. ISBN 0-685-48705-9. Useful glossary of terms in Sanskrit, Pali, and Prakrit for beginners.

Coward, Harold, Eva Dargyay, and Ronald Neufeldt, eds. *Readings in Eastern Religions*. Wilfred Laurier U. Pr. 1988 $29.95. ISBN 0-88920-955-3. Fine collection of selections from original Hindu, Buddhist, Jain, and Sikh texts, which would benefit from more explanatory materials.

De Bary, William Theodore, ed. *Sources of Indian Tradition*. Col. U. Pr. 1964 $26.00. ISBN 0-231-08600-8

Eliade, Mircea. *A History of Religious Ideas*. U. Ch. Pr. 1985 $18.95. ISBN 0-226-20403-0. Concise coverage of basic religious themes, persons, and sects from a comparative perspective.

_____, ed. *Encyclopedia of Religion*. Macmillan 1986 $1,400.00. ISBN 0-02-909480-1. Up-to-date and authoritative general entries on the most important aspects of Indian tradition.

Feuerstein, Georg. *Encyclopedic Dictionary of Yoga*. Paragon Hse. 1990 $24.95. ISBN 1-55778-245-8. Explains the vocabulary used within the Yoga traditions of India in a manner suitable for beginners.

Grimes, John. *A Concise Dictionary of Indian Philosophy: Sanskrit Terms Defined in English.* State U. NY Pr. 1989 $39.50. ISBN 0-7914-0100-6. Covers Hinduism, Buddhism, and Jainism.

Kitagawa, Joseph M. *The Religious Traditions of Asia.* Macmillan 1989 $12.95. ISBN 0-02-897211-2. Articles excerpted from the *Encyclopedia of Religion.* Part 1 on Hinduism, Buddhism in India and Southeast Asia, Jainism, the Sikhs, and Islam; Part 2 on Tibetan Buddhism, Bon, and Islam in Central Asia; Part 3 on religions in China, Japan, and Korea.

Koller, John M., and Patricia Koller. *A Sourcebook in Asian Philosophy.* Macmillan 1991. ISBN 0-02-365811-8. Collection of English translations of basic texts by experienced teachers of introductory courses in Asian philosophy; introductory materials as well as Hindu and Buddhist texts.

Radhakrishnan, Sarvepalli, and Charles A. Moore, eds. *Sourcebook in Indian Philosophy.* Princeton U. Pr. 1957 $18.95. ISBN 0-691-01958-4

Sharma, Jagdish. *Encyclopedia of India.* 30 vols. S. Asia 1992 $1750.00. ISBN 0-8364-2750-5. Concise entries on basic aspects of religion and philosophy.

General Works

Ames, Roger T., ed. *Nature in Asian Traditions of Thought: Essays in Environmental Philosophy.* State U. NY Pr. 1989 $39.50. ISBN 0-88706-950-9. Collection of essays by foremost scholars of Asian philosophy on the issue of how Asian thought views the environment; accessible to beginning students of Eastern thought.

Basham, A. L. *The Origins and Development of Classical Hinduism.* Ed. by Kenneth G. Zysk. Beacon Pr. 1989 $18.95. ISBN 0-8070-7300-8. Fine general survey of the development of Brahmanical thought, ending with consideration of the *Bhagavad Gita.*

———, ed. *A Cultural History of India.* OUP 1984 $36.50. ISBN 0-19-561520-4. Succinctly written and authoritative discussion of the interrelationship of religion and culture.

———, ed. *The Wonder That Was India: A Survey of the Culture of the Indian Subcontinent Before the Coming of the Muslims.* Grove Pr. 1959 o.p. Classic introduction to pre-Muslim India. Indian tradition treated as a whole, integrating the different cultural elements of religion, society, art, and language.

Berry, Thomas. *Buddhism.* Anima Pubns. 1967 $9.95. ISBN 0-89012-017-X. Highly accessible general introduction to the Buddhist tradition and its expansion in Asia as well as the West.

———. *Religions of India.* Anima Pubns. 1992 $12.95. ISBN 0-89012-067-6. Excellent introduction to Hinduism, Yoga philosophy and practice, and Buddhism and their relevance in today's world.

Bhattacharyya, and others, eds. *The Cultural Heritage of India.* Vedanta Pr. 1937 $270.00. ISBN 0-87481-558-4. Volumes 3 and 4 focus on philosophy and religion.

Burghart, Richard, and Audrey Cantlie, eds. *Indian Religion.* St. Martin 1985 $29.95. ISBN 0-312-41400-5. Good recent topical overview of Indian traditions.

Dasgupta, S. N. *A History of Indian Philosophy.* Orient Bk. Dist. 1975 ISBN 0-8426-0963-6. Authoritative survey of Indian philosophical systems from the Vedas to the modern period. Discusses the Jain and Buddhist philosophies as well as the six orthodox philosophical systems of Hinduism.

Forman, Robert K. C., ed. *Religions of Asia.* St. Martin 1993 $26.70. ISBN 0-312-05753-9. Up-to-date and academically solid presentation of Asian religions, with chapters on South Asia treating Hinduism, Jainism, Sikhism, and Buddhism.

Hinnells, John R., ed. *A Handbook of Living Religions.* Viking Penguin 1984 o.p. The sections on Hinduism, Sikhism, Jainism, and Buddhism are excellent and up-to-date survey discussions

Hopkins, Edward W. *The Religions of India.* Longwood 1979 repr. of 1895 ed. o.p. Informative early work that surveys the major religious traditions.

Koller, John M. *The Indian Way.* Macmillan 1982 $16.00. ISBN 0-02-365800-2. Excellent interpretive introduction to religious and philosophical aspects of Indian tradition.

Morgan, Kenneth W. *Reaching for the Moon: On Asian Religious Paths.* Anima Pubns. 1990 $18.95. ISBN 0-89012-059-5. A scholar of religious studies reflects on the Western attempt to understand Eastern religiosity.

Smart, Ninian. *Religions of Asia.* P-H 1993. ISBN 0-13-772427-6. Presents Asian religions in terms of doctrinal, mythical, institutional, ritual, ethical, experiential, and material dimensions; discusses responses of Asian religions to the West and modernization as well as the role of Asian religions in the global community.

The Ancient Heritage: Pre-Vedic and Vedic Traditions

The Indus Valley civilization that has been uncovered by archaeologists is thought to date to about 3000 B.C.E. and earlier. The Indus Valley area around the Indus River system located now in the political entity of Pakistan was an early site for the development of agriculture, towns, and cities. Excavations of the ancient sites of Harappa and Mohenjo-Daro reveal these to have been planned cities with straight and intersecting streets. The houses were built of fine baked brick and included a system of drains for the removal of sewage.

The common scholarly assumption has been that the Indus Valley civilization was Dravidian-speaking. Clay seals have been found that bear a script, although this language has not been deciphered. The prevailing theory suggests that the Dravidians were dark-skinned inhabitants of India, displaced and pushed to southern India by invading light-skinned Aryans, who originated from the area of the Black Sea and who traveled over the mountains of Afghanistan to enter into the Indian subcontinent. However, the Indus Valley script has not been identified as Dravidian, and some contemporary Indian philologists claim that the script is Sanskrit, the language spoken by the peoples who identified themselves as Aryans, "noble ones" or "people of culture." Because the theory of Aryan invasions into Europe is beginning to be questioned by archaeologists, the theory soon might be questioned in relation to India as well.

The outlines of the religion of the Indus Valley civilization are just as unclear as the ethnic and linguistic origins of its peoples, but there are intriguing hints of continuity with the subsequent Hindu tradition. The clay seals mentioned above often depict bulls who seem to have been regarded as sacred, suggestive of the sacred cow of the later Hinduism. Several seals depict a man wearing a horned headdress seated in a cross-legged posture surrounded by male creatures, such as rhinoceros, elephant, tiger. He is ithyphallic, meaning that his penis is erect. This figure bears a strong resemblance to the later Hindu god Shiva, who is a yogi and is identified as the Lord of Creatures. The erect penis of Shiva is symbolic of his ascetic practices, which include the retention of semen, resulting in the accumulation of immense spiritual power. Shiva in contemporary Hinduism is venerated in a stone object called a *lingam*, which consists of a phallic-shaped pillar set in a base representing his wife's *yoni* or genitalia. The male figure found on the Indus Valley seals is speculated to be an early version of the later god Shiva, a "proto-Shiva." This speculation is supported by discovery of Indus artifacts made of stone that resemble Shiva *lingams*. Goddess worship in the Hindu tradition often is focused on various aspects of Shiva's wife, and the discovery of clay female figures in the Indus Valley archaeological record might indicate that the veneration of goddesses dates back to that time. However, the female figures might not all be goddesses. The presence of clay figures representing animals and carts suggests that some of these items might have been simply children's toys.

There is more certainty about the religion of the Sanskrit-speaking peoples who called themselves Aryans. They composed hymns and texts that were handed down orally but also were written to form a body of literature known as the Vedas ("knowledge"). These written texts tell us more about the roots of the Hindu tradition than the mysterious archaeological artifacts of the Indus Valley civilization.

The earliest portions of the Vedas are called the *samhitas* ("collections"). We can place an approximate date on the *samhitas* of about 1000 B.C.E., remembering that any attempt to date the Vedic texts can be only an approximation. The first three *samhitas*, the Rig Veda, the Yajur Veda, and the Sama Veda, are collections of hymns (*mantras*) addressed to the *devas* (gods associated with various natural forces). The fourth *samhita*, the Arthava Veda, is a collection of magic spells. The religion of the *samhitas*, or the early Vedic religion, was focused on the performance of sacrifice to the *devas*. The sacrifice of food was made on outdoor altars constructed of earth on which fires were built. Fire, itself the *deva* Agni (cognate with the Latin word *ignis*), was considered the mouth of the gods. The universe was seen as an interdependent whole in which the *devas* relied on sacrifice for their nourishment. Once strengthened, the *devas* ensured the functions of nature necessary for the growth of crops and cattle that sustained human beings. The priests who specialized in these sacrifices, the Brahmins (or more correctly, the Brahmanas), came to be regarded as having tremendous power. The maintenance of the universe depended on the proper performance of the sacrifice by the Brahmins. This accounts for their top position in the social hierarchy known as the four *varnas*, which in subsequent centuries developed into the multitude of Hindu castes. The four *varnas* consist of the Brahmins, priests; the Kshatriyas, kings and warriors; the Vaishyas, merchants and farmers; and the Shudras, laborers who were to serve the higher *varnas*. The first three *varnas* were considered "aryan," or "noble," "cultured."

The second portion of the Vedas consists of texts called the Brahmanas, dated approximately 1000–800 B.C.E. These are prose texts composed by the Brahmins, containing myths, philosophical speculation, and details on the proper performance of the sacrifices. The third portion of the Vedas consists of texts called the Aranyakas, "forest texts," composed approximately 800–600 B.C.E. The Aranyakas are transitional to the subsequent body of texts known as the Upanishads. The Aranyakas suggest that it is not necessary to perform the complex fire sacrifice but that the same results can be derived from its mental performance, or visualization in meditation.

The fourth and last body of literature in the Vedas are the Upanishads, composed approximately 600–300 B.C.E. Upanishad means "to sit nearby," and these texts consist of the philosophical instruction of gurus (teachers) to students who sat at their feet. The outlook of the Upanishads is very different from the outlook found in the four early *samhitas*. The Upanishads introduce the idea of reincarnation, which became an established part of the Hindu tradition. The cycle of life, death, and rebirth is termed *samsara*. One constantly is coming and going. *Samsara* is viewed as a trap from which one must escape, a merry-go-round that one must try to get off. Karma is described as a natural law of cause and effect; it is the force of one's actions, and all actions produce results, either in the current lifetime or in a future lifetime. Karma, when combined with the emerging Hindu caste structure, came to justify one's current status in life as the result of actions performed in previous lifetimes. The ultimate goal, according to the Upanishads, is termed *moksha*, the liberation from *samsara* and the effects of karma when one has eliminated desire and come to the direct experiential knowledge that the self, *atman*, is one with the ultimate, termed *Brahman*. *Brahman* is indescribable, but it is the reality that is permanent, unmanifest, and unchanging. The material world is described as *maya*, but the Upanishads are ambiguous as to whether this term indicates that the world is illusory or real but temporary. Later Hindu philosophers, such as Shankara (788–820 C.E.) and Ramanuja (1017–1137), would draw different conclusions from the Upanishads. The Upanishads and the philosophies based on them are called Vedanta, meaning "end of the Vedas."

Bahadur, K. P. *The Wisdom of the Upanishads.* Sterling 1989 o.p. Good general introduction to the Upanishads for the beginner.

Bhagat, M. G. *Ancient Indian Asceticism.* Orient Bk. Dist. 1976 $24.00. ISBN 0-89684-476-5. Study of the development of the dominant ascetic tendencies within early Indian tradition.

Das, A. C. *Rigvedic India.* 2 vols. Orient Bk. Dist. 1971 o.p. Scholarly presentation of Vedic culture and religion.

Drekmeier, Charles. *Kingship and Community in Early India.* Bks. Demand repr. of 1962 ed. $30.00. ISBN 0-7837-0005-9. Analysis of the traditions of sacral kingship. Scholarly format.

Gonda, Jan. *The Indra Hymns of the Rigveda.* E. J. Brill 1989 ISBN 90-04-09139-4. Study of the features of the Rig Vedic hymns addressed to Indra and how these hymns were related to the Rig Vedic sacrifices.

———. *Vision of the Vedic Poets.* Mouton 1963 $48.00. ISBN 90-2790-034-5. Excellent scholarly analysis of the visionary core of Vedic religion.

Heesterman, J. C. *The Inner Conflict of Tradition: Essays in Indian Ritual, Kingship and Society.* U. Ch. Pr. 1985 $14.95. ISBN 0-226-32299-8. Significant scholarly study of the interrelationship between religion and society.

Hume, Robert E., trans. *The Thirteen Principal Upanishads.* OUP 1931 $16.95. ISBN 0-19-561641-3. Important early translation of the principal Upanishads.

Jacobson, Jerome. *Studies in the Archaeology of India and Pakistan.* OUP 1986 $45.00. ISBN 81-204-00852. New theoretical papers on prehistorical India; the chapter by Shaffer suggests the Aryan invasion never took place.

Jamison, Stephanie W. *The Ravenous Hyenas and the Wounded Sun: Myth and Ritual in Ancient India.* Cornell Univ. Pr. 1991 $52.50. ISBN 0-8014-2433-X. Groundbreaking study of Vedic literature assuming that Vedic myths must be understood in the context of the Vedic rituals.

Keith, Arthur B. *The Religion and Philosophy of the Veda and Upanishads.* S. Asia 1989 $62.50. ISBN 81-208-0646-8. Classic authoritative analysis by one of the greatest of the early Indologists. Copious technical annotations.

Mascaro, Juan, trans. *Upanishads.* Viking Penguin 1965 o.p. Effective modern translation of seven Upanishads and portions of others. Helpful introduction.

O'Flaherty, Wendy D. *The Rig Veda: An Anthology.* Viking Penguin 1982 $9.95. ISBN 0-14-044402-5. Readable, reliable, and representative collection of Vedic hymns with excellent introductory discussions.

Panikkar, Raimundo, ed. and trans. *The Vedic Experience: Mantramanjari.* U. CA Pr. 1977 $15.00. ISBN 0-520-02854-0. Translation of selections from the Vedas, arranged by topic, with commentaries intended to make the passages relevant to modern life.

Smith, Brian K. *Reflections on Resemblance, Ritual, and Religion.* OUP 1989 $32.50. ISBN 0-19-505545-4. Outstanding study, arguing that Vedic ritual was based on the imaginative search for resemblances.

Wood, Thomas E. *The Mandukya Upanishad and the Agama Sastra.* UH Pr. 1990 $14.00. ISBN 0-8248-1310-3. Challenges many interpretations of two of India's most important philosophical and religious texts, presenting a new theory of the historical influence of Buddhism on the Shankara school.

Zaehner, R. C., trans. *Hindu Scriptures.* J. M. Dent 1966 $15.00. ISBN 0-460-10944-8. Translations of selections from the Rig Veda, Atharva Veda, Upanishads, and the *Bhagavad Gita* in its entirety.

Hinduism

The term *Hinduism* is notoriously difficult to define. The word actually derives from Muslim invaders coming into the Indian subcontinent over the mountains of Afghanistan. The Sanskrit word for "river" is *sindhu*, and this term as spoken by these foreigners gave rise to the name of the Indus River as well as Hindu as the name of the religion of the inhabitants of the subcontinent. The Hindu tradition itself is extremely diverse and contains within it animism (the belief that the natural world is filled with unseen spirits and forces), philosophical monism, and monotheism.

Hinduism can be seen as a kaleidoscope containing basic elements that are common to the entire tradition. These basic elements include concepts that are expressed in such words as *karma, moksha, yoga, atman, Brahman*. The exact meaning placed on these words will vary, as will the particular way the basic pieces are put together. However, the basic elements are combined by different groups and thinkers in different ways against a backdrop of ideas and practices that are common to the entire Hindu tradition. A very simple definition is that Hinduism designates a religious tradition that has its origin in India and that acknowledges the Vedas to be sacred scripture. Hinduism no longer is confined to the Indian subcontinent; Hindu immigrants are found all over the world, and a number of Westerners have adopted Hindu outlooks and practices or even joined Hindu sects. In order to be a Hindu, a person must acknowledge that the Vedas are sacred, even if the Vedas are not the main focus of that person's religious outlook. In Hinduism, rejection of the Vedas is the primary indicator of heterodoxy.

The Hindu tradition accepts the Vedas as *shruti*, "that which is heard," or divine revelation, but the Hindu tradition is by no means confined to the Vedic literature. Important scriptures that fall outside the Vedas are termed *smriti*, "that which is remembered." *Smriti* includes philosophical speculation, mythology, and epic tales. The *Ramayana* and the *Mahabharata* are the two great Hindu epics, which include characterizations of the two primary *avatars* ("descents," or divine incarnations) of Vishnu, Rama, and Krishna. The *Bhagavad Gita* ("the Song of the Lord"), in which Krishna is revealed to be the one God, is set into the larger *Mahabharata*. The *Bhagavad Gita* is an extremely important Hindu text that presents the important methods of *karma yoga* (discipline of action) and *bhakti yoga* (intense love and devotion to God conceived as personal). Much of the later Hindu tradition consists of various manifestations of devotionalism, or *bhakti*. God can be regarded as Vishnu or one of his *avatars*, as the fearsome yogi Shiva, or as the Great Goddess in a variety of manifestations. The Puranas are a vast body of literature containing the lively Hindu mythology.

The caste system, with its innumerable social groupings, is an integral part of the Hindu tradition. It is believed that one's current caste and sex are the result of actions performed in previous lifetimes and that members of different caste groups should not intermarry or share food. Traditionally, one's occupation in life is determined by the caste into which one is born. The caste system, officially illegal in contemporary India, remains an important force in Hindu life. The ultimate demise of the caste system probably will be caused by the forces of industrialization and urbanization, not by legal measures.

Ames, Roger T., ed. *Nature in Asian Traditions of Thought: Essays in Environmental Philosophy*. State U. NY Pr. 1989 $39.50. ISBN 0-88706-950-9. Collection of essays by foremost scholars of Asian philosophy on the issue of how Asian thought views the environment; accessible to beginning students of Eastern thought.

Amore, Roy C. *Lustful Maidens and Ascetic Kings: Buddhist and Hindu Stories of Life.* OUP 1981 $9.95. ISBN 0-19-502839-2. Engaging popular collection of significant folktales and themes. Helpful contextual introductions.

Apparadurai, Arjun, Frank J. Korom, and Margaret A. Mills, eds. *Gender, Genre, and Power in South Asian Expressive Traditions.* U. of Pa. Pr. 1991 $47.95. ISBN 0-8122-3082-5. Eighteen scholars write on issues of gender, genre, and power in popular religious performances in South Asia, providing illuminating articles from the perspective of anthropology, theater, linguistics, literature, and folklore.

Babb, Lawrence A. *The Divine Hierarchy: Popular Hinduism in Central India.* Col. U. Pr. 1975 $43.00. ISBN 0-231-03882-8. Classic and influential study of Hinduism.

Beals, Alan R. *Gopalpur: A South Indian Village.* HR&W 1962 o.p. Case study of Hindu life in a south Indian village.

Brown, C. Mackenzie. *The Triumph of the Goddess: The Canonical Models and the Theological Visions of the Devi-Bhagavata Purana.* State U. NY Pr. 1990 $59.50. ISBN 0-7914-0363-7. Excellent treatment of the Devi Bhagavata Purana, a text of devotion to the Goddess, and how it relates to other Hindu scriptures.

Brown, Robert L. *Ganesh: Studies of an Asian God.* State U. NY Pr. 1991 $59.50. ISBN 0-7914-0656-3. Eleven essays on the significance of a very popular god in Hindu art, ritual, and Sanskrit literature, bringing to light the significance of Ganesh in Hindu Tantra as well as in the cultures of Tibet, southeast Asia, China, and Japan.

Carpenter, K. *Theism in Medieval India.* Orient Bk. Dist. 1977 $22.50. ISBN 0-89684-457-9. Interesting historical analysis of Hindu devotional doctrine of god.

Chaudhuri, Nirad C. *Hinduism: A Religion to Live By.* OUP 1979 $9.95. ISBN 0-19-520221-X. Engaging and sensitive portrait of Hinduism as a practical way of life. Popular format.

Clothey, Fred W. *Rhythm and Intent.* S. Asia 1984 o.p. Interpretive analysis of popular ritual traditions.

Coburn, Thomas B. *Encountering the Goddess: A Translation of the Devi-Mahatmya and a Study of Its Interpretation.* State U. NY Pr. 1991 $19.95. ISBN 0-7914-0445-5. Outstanding translation and interpretation of this Hindu scripture devoted to the Goddess, as well as description of how this text relates to popular Hinduism.

Coomaraswamy, Ananda K., and M. E. Noble. *Myths of the Hindus and Buddhists.* Dover 1967 repr. of 1913 ed. $7.95. ISBN 0-486-21759. Popular representation of some of the most widespread myths and folktales.

Courtright, Paul B. *Ganesa: Lord of Obstacles, Lord of Beginnings.* OUP 1985 $14.95. ISBN 0-19-505742-2. Overview of the origins, mythology, psychology, and worship of a most popular Hindu deity.

Coward, Harold, and David Goa. *Mantra: Hearing the Divine in India.* Anima Pubns. 1991 $9.95. ISBN 0-89012-062-5. Fine discussion of the philosophy and practice of mantra.

Darian, Steven G. *The Ganges in Myth and History.* UH Pr. 1978 o.p. The human experience and the myths of India's most sacred river.

Dumont, Louis. *Homo Hierarchicus: The Caste System.* U. Ch. Pr. 1981 $18.50. ISBN 0-226-16963-4. Brilliant sociological analysis of the caste system.

Eck, Diana L. *Banaras: City of Lights.* Princeton U. Pr. 1982 $14.95. ISBN 0-691-02023-X. Classic study of the most sacred Hindu city.

———. *Darsan: Seeing the Divine Image in India.* Anima Pubns. 1985 $8.95. ISBN 0-89012-042-0. Engaging popular study of Hindu iconology.

Eliade, Mircea. *Yoga: Immortality and Freedom.* Princeton U. Pr. 1991 $14.95. ISBN 0-691-01764-6. Classic study of the development and significance of yoga by the famous historian of religions.

Embree, Ainslie T., ed. *The Hindu Tradition—Readings in Oriental Thought.* Random 1976 $7.10. ISBN 0-394-71702-3. Representative collection of primary sources showing religious and cultural developments of the Hindu religion arranged chronologically.

Erndl, Kathleen M. *Victory to the Mother: The Hindu Goddess of Northwest India in Myth, Ritual, and Symbol.* OUP 1993 $35.00. ISBN 0-19-507014-3. Groundbreaking study of the significance and understanding of the Goddess in northwest India.

Falk, Nancy Auer, and Rita M. Gross, eds. *Unspoken Worlds: Women's Religious Lives.* Wadsworth Pub. 1989. ISBN 0-534-09852-5. Groundbreaking collection on religion in women's lives, including Charles S. J. White on a woman guru, Jnanananda; Doranne Jacobson on Hindu childbirth rituals in central India; Susan S. Wadley on Hindu women's family and household rituals; and James M. Freeman on rituals of middle-aged women devotees of Krishna in eastern India.

Freeman, James. *Untouchable: An Indian Life History.* Stanford U. Pr. 1979 $16.95. ISBN 0-8047-1103-8. Important presentation of "untouchability" in Hinduism.

Freitag, Sandra B., ed. *Culture and Power in Banaras: Community, Performance and Environment. 1800–1980.* U. CA Pr. 1989 $40.00. ISBN 0-520-06367-8. Scholarly essays on the variety of cultural activities and influences in Hinduism's most sacred city.

Fuller, C. J. *The Camphor Flame: Popular Hinduism and Society in India.* Princeton U. Pr. 1992 $45.00. ISBN 0-691-07404-6. Excellent presentation of Hinduism from the perspective of anthropology. Some chapters are appropriate for beginners; others are written for experts.

Goldman, Robert P., ed. *The Ramayana of Valmika.* 3 vols. Princeton U. Pr. Vol. 1 Trans. by Robert P. Goldman. 1984 $69.50. ISBN 0-691-06561-6. Vol. 2 Trans. by Sheldon I. Pollock. 1986 $79.00. ISBN 0-691-06654-X. Vol. 3 Trans. by Sheldon I. Pollock. 1990 $67.50. ISBN 0-691-06660-4. The major English translation of this most influential epic in Indian culture and religion; to appear in seven volumes.

Gonda, J. *Visnuism and Sivaism: A Comparison.* Orient Bk. Dist. 1976 $19.50. ISBN 0-89684-465-X. Scholarly study of the two major forms of Hindu devotion.

Haddad, Yvonne Yazbeck, and Ellison Banks Findly, eds. *Women, Religion and Social Change.* State U. NY Pr. 1985 $59.50. ISBN 0-88706-068-4. Fine scholarship on women and religion, including Ellison Banks Findly on women philosophers in Ancient India; Sandra P. Robinson on Hindu views of women; Donna Marie Wulff on Bengali women's devotional singing; and Lou Ratte on women in the Indian nationalist movement.

Hawley, John Stratton, and Donna Marie Wulff, eds. *The Divine Consort: Radha and the Goddesses of India.* Beacon Pr. 1987 $14.95. ISBN 0-8070-1303-X. Collection of articles on Hindu goddesses by top scholars.

Hawley, John Stratton, and Mark Juergensmeyer. *Songs of the Saints of India.* OUP 1988 $35.00. ISBN 0-19-505220-X. Highly accessible presentation of the devotional songs/poems of great Indian saints.

Herman, A. L. *A Brief Introduction to Hinduism: Religion, Philosophy and Ways of Liberation.* Westview 1991 $42.50. ISBN 0-8133-8109-6. Good general introduction to Hinduism for beginners.

Hiltebeitel, Alf. *Criminal Gods and Demon Devotees: Essays on the Guardians of Popular Hinduism.* State U. NY Pr. 1989 $74.50. ISBN 0-88706-981-9. Textual, ethnographic, and iconographic studies of guardian figures in popular Hinduism.

———. *The Cult of Draupadi.* 2 vols. U. Ch. Pr. Vol. 1 *Mythologies: From Gingee to Kuruksetra.* 1988 $74.95. ISBN 0-226-34045-7. Vol. 2 *On Hindu Ritual and the Goddess.* 1991 $74.95. ISBN 0-226-34047-3. Vol. 1 is an extensive study of myths of the *Mahabharata* heroine Draupadi; and Vol. 2 provides an excellent ethnographic and textual study of the ritual cult of the south Indian goddess Draupadi.

———. *The Ritual of Battle: Krishna in the Mahabharata.* State U. NY Pr. 1990 $49.50. ISBN 0-7914-0249-5. Draws on the theories of Indo-European mythology.

Hopkins, Thomas J. *The Hindu Religious Tradition.* Wadsworth Pub. 1971. ISBN 0-8221-0022-3. Concise textbook discussion of the diverse elements of the Indian tradition from the early Aryans to modern Hindu reform. Stresses the ritual structure of Hindu tradition.

Katz, Ruth Cecily. *Arjuna in the Mahabharata: Where Krishna Is, There Is Victory*. U. of SC Pr. 1989 $34.95. ISBN 0-87249-542-6. Study of the hero Arjuna in the great Hindu epic the *Mahabharata*, in comparison with epic heroes from other traditions.

Kieckhefer, Richard, and George D. Bond, eds. *Sainthood: Its Manifestations in World Religions*. U. of SC Pr. 1988 $42.50. ISBN 0-520-05154-8. Collection of excellent essays on sainthood in world religions, with an essay by C. White on Hinduism.

Kinsley, David R. *The Goddesses' Mirror: Visions of the Divine from East and West*. State U. NY Pr. 1989 $39.50. ISBN 0-88706-835-9. Scholarly and accessible accounts of great goddesses, treating the Hindu goddesses Durga, Lakshmi, and Sita.

_____. *Hindu Goddesses: Visions of the Divine Feminine in the Hindu Religious Tradition*. U. CA Pr. 1985 $50.00. ISBN 0-520-05393-1. Important scholarly presentation of the Hindu goddesses.

_____. *Hinduism: A Cultural Perspective*. P-H 1992 $18.00. ISBN 0-13-395732-2. Fine introductory text that views religion as a cultural system that interacts with historical, intellectual, and social forms.

_____. *The Sword and the Flute*. U. CA Pr. 1975 $14.00. ISBN 0-520-03510-0. Fascinating study of the deities Krishna and Kali.

Klostermeier, Klaus K. *Mythologies and Philosophies of Salvation in the Theistic Traditions of India*. Humanities 1984 o.p. Excellent, though technical, study of Hindu theism.

_____. *A Survey of Hinduism*. State U. NY Pr. 1989 $59.50. ISBN 0-88706-807-3. Excellent introductory presentation of the Hindu tradition.

Knipe, David M. *Hinduism: Experiments in the Sacred*. HarpC 1991 $9.95. ISBN 0-06-064780-9. Expert general treatment of the Hindu tradition.

Lutgendorf, Phillip. *The Life of a Text: Performing the Ramacaritamanas of Tulsi-Das*. U. CA Pr. 1990 $39.95. ISBN 0-520-06690-1. Superb elucidation of the annual performance of Tulsidas's Ramayana in Benares.

Lynch, Owen M., ed. *Divine Passions: The Social Construction of Emotion in India*. U. CA Pr. 1990 $42.50. ISBN 0-520-06647-2. Provocative collection of essays exploring the social construction of emotion in the Hindu *bhakti* (devotional) tradition.

McDaniel, June. *The Madness of the Saints: Ecstatic Religion in Bengal*. U. Ch. Pr. 1989 $45.00. ISBN 0-226-55722-7. Illuminating study of saints in the Bengali devotional tradition.

Madan, T. N. *Non-Renunciation: Themes and Interpretations in Hindu Culture*. OUP 1988 $22.50. ISBN 0-19-562040-2. Study of the world-affirming aspects of Hinduism.

Marglin, Frederique Apffel. *Wives of the God-King: The Rituals of Devadasis of Puri*. OUP 1985 $32.50. ISBN 0-19-561731-2. Significant study of the dying breed of women dedicated to dance for the god—the so-called temple prostitutes.

Meyer, J. J. *Sexual Life in Ancient India*. Orient Bk. Dist. 1971 o.p. Discusses sexual customs in relation to religious tradition.

Michaell, George. *The Hindu Temple: An Introduction to Its Meaning and Forms*. U. Ch. Pr. 1988 $14.95. ISBN 0-226-53250-5. Very general introduction to Hindu temples.

Miller, Barbara Stoler, trans. *The Bhagavad-Gita: Krishna's Counsel in Time of War*. Col. U. Pr. 1986 $28.00. ISBN 0-231-06468-3. Highly readable translation of the *Bhagavad Gita*, with an introduction discussing the context and text, plus an afterword discussing the influence of the *Bhagavad Gita* on Henry David Thoreau.

O'Flaherty, Wendy Doniger. *Karma and Rebirth in Classical Indian Traditions*. U. CA Pr. 1980 $47.50. ISBN 0-520-03923-0. Delightful collection of tales about Hindu gods and demons. Convenient source for the most important myths of the major and minor gods of classical Hinduism.

_____. *Siva: The Erotic Ascetic*. OUP 1973 $12.95. ISBN 0-19-520250-3. Analysis of a wide range of myths about the Hindu deity Shiva.

_____. *Women, Androgynes and Other Mythical Beasts*. U. Ch. Pr. 1982 $27.50. ISBN 0-226-61849-8. Interpretations of Hindu myths reflective of attitudes toward gender.

_____, trans. *Hindu Myths: A Sourcebook Translated from the Sanskrit*. Viking Penguin 1975 $8.95. ISBN 0-14-044306-1

Olson, Carl, ed. *The Book of the Goddess Past and Present*. Crossroad NY 1985 $12.95. ISBN 0-8245-0689-8. Solid and accessible articles by experts in their respective fields, including chapters on Kali, Lakshmi, and Radha, as well as Rita M. Gross's article "Hindu Female Deities as a Resource for Contemporary Rediscovery of the Goddess."

Richman, Paula, ed. *Many Ramayanas: The Diversity of a Narrative Tradition in South Asia*. U. CA Pr. 1991 $40.00. ISBN 0-520-07281-2. Excellent collection of essays describing the pervasive importance of the epic *Ramayana* in South Asian culture.

Sargeant, Winthrop, trans. *The Bhagavad Gita*. State U. NY Pr. 1984 $14.95. ISBN 0-87395-830-6. Very useful translation; each verse is given in the devanagari script, transliteration, and English translation, with a glossary of the relevant Sanskrit words on the same page.

Sharma, Arvind, ed. *Essays on the Mahabharata*. E. J. Brill 1991 $160.00. ISBN 90-04-09211-0. Collection of illuminating essays on the great Hindu epic.

————, ed. *Women in World Religions*. State U. NY Pr. 1987 $14.95. ISBN 0-88706-375-6. Articles that are sound in scholarship and accessible to the general reader; Katherine Young contributes the chapter on Hinduism.

Sharma, B. N. *Festivals of India*. S. Asia 1978 o.p. Descriptive discussion of the background and nature of some of the most common festival traditions.

Sheridan, Daniel P. *The Advaitic Theism of the Bhagavata Purana*. S. Asia 1986 $14.00. ISBN 81-208-0179-2. Expert analysis of the thought of the Bhagavata Purana, an important scripture for Krishna devotionalism.

Singer, Milton B., ed. *Krishna: Myths, Rites, and Attitudes*. U. Ch. Pr. 1969 $12.00. ISBN 0-226-76101-0. Accessible anthropological study of Bhakti devotion and the Krishna/Vaishnava religious movements down to the present. Bhakti is the key idea of "loving devotion" toward a savior deity (especially Krishna as an *avatar* of the god Vishnu) found especially among the Vaishnavas or followers of Vishnu. The American Hari Krishna movement is a contemporary descendant of these traditions.

Sullivan, Lawrence, ed. *Healing and Restoring: Health and Medicine in the World's Religious Traditions*. Macmillan 1989 $35.00. ISBN 0-02-923791-2. Interdisciplinary and multicultural study of the topic of healing and health in the world's religions; David Knipe and Sudhir Kakar deal with the Hindu medical tradition, Ayurveda.

Sutherland, Gail Hinich. *The Disguises of the Demon: The Development of the Yaksa in Hinduism and Buddhism*. State U. NY Pr. 1991 $57.50. ISBN 0-7914-0621-0. Explores the meaning of the figure of the Yaksa "demon" or "nature spirit" as it appears in Hindu, Buddhist, and Jain literature and sculpture.

Timm, Jeffrey R., ed. *Texts in Context: Traditional Hermeneuctics in South Asia*. State U NY Pr. 1991 $59.50. ISBN 0-7914-0796-9. Articles by experts in the interpretation of Hindu, Buddhist, Jain, and Sikh texts.

Trawick, Margaret. *Notes on Love in a Tamil Family*. U. CA Pr. 1990 $45.00. ISBN 0-520-06636-7. Ethnographic study of Hindu devotionalism as it relates to one south Indian family's understanding of love.

Tyler, Stephen A. *India: An Anthropological Perspective*. Waveland Pr. 1986 $10.95. ISBN 0-88133-245-3. Overview of the Hindu tradition, culture, and peoples by an anthropologist.

van Buitenan, J.A.B., trans. *The Bhagavadgita in the Mahabharata*. U. Ch. Pr. 1981 $19.00. ISBN 0-226-84600-1. Features an English translation, transliteration from the Devanagari script, and analysis of the text.

Wadley, Susan Snow. *Shakti: Power in the Conceptual Structure of Karimpur Religion*. Dept. of Anthropology, U. Ch. Pr. 1975 o.p. Fascinating description of religion practiced in the village of Karimpur, and as such, an important book to read in conjunction with *Behind Mud Walls* by the Wisers.

Waghorne, Joanne Punzo, and Norman Cutler, eds. *Gods of Flesh and Gods of Stone: The Embodiment of Divinity in India*. Anima Pubns. o.p. Experts explore Hindu concepts and practices revolving around the embodiment of the divine.

Welbon, Guy, and Glen Yocum, eds. *Festivals in South India and Sri Lanka*. S. Asia 1982 $25.00. ISBN 0-8364-0900-0. Important topical collection of articles by leading scholars.

Whitehead, Henry. *The Village Gods of South India*. S. Asia 1986 $15.00. ISBN 0-8364-1709-7. Interesting presentation of beliefs concerning local deities.

Wood, Thomas E. *The Mandukya Upanisad and the Agama Sastra*. UH Pr. 1990 $14.00. ISBN 0-8248-1310-3. Challenges many interpretations of two of India's most important philosophical and religious texts and presents a new theory of the historical influence of Buddhism on the Shankara school.

FOREIGN INFLUENCES AND THE MODERN ERA

The Hindu response in the late nineteenth century to the encounter with Western ideas and religions often is termed the Hindu Renaissance. In the medieval period, Muslim invaders entered into northern India from the northwest and established control of north central India until the eighteenth century C.E. Much of India came under British domination from the eighteenth century until Indian independence in 1947. With British imperialism came Christian missionaries, who criticized Hinduism as a heathen and immoral religion. The Hindu Renaissance from the nineteenth century onward can be seen as consisting of a variety of Hindu responses to Western science, technology, philosophy, and religion. The authors and religious figures profiled below were concerned to reconcile this meeting of East and West, and they all addressed issues that arose when means of rapid communications and travel began to create a global culture.

Ashby, Philip H. *Modern Trends in Hinduism*. Col. U. Pr. 1974 o.p. Helpful discussion of religious and philosophical developments in relation to social change.

Babb, Lawrence A. *Redemptive Encounters: Three Modern Styles in the Hindu Tradition*. U. CA Pr. 1987 $40.00. ISBN 0-520-05645-0. Expert examination of three contemporary manifestations of Hinduism—Radhasoami, Brahma Kumaris, and Sathya Sai Baba.

Baird, Robert D., ed. *Religion in Modern India*. S. Asia 2nd rev. ed. 1989 $36.00. ISBN 81-85054-64-9. The best treatment of modern Indian thinkers and religious movements.

Barnes, Michael, ed. *An Ecology of the Spirit: Religious Reflection and Environmental Consciousness*. U. Pr. of Amer. 1993 $52.00. ISBN 0-8191-8959-6. Includes an article by Christopher Chapple on "Contemporary Jaina and Hindu Responses to the Ecological Crisis."

Bassuk, Daniel E. *Incarnation in Hinduism and Christianity*. Humanities 1987 $45.00. ISBN 0-391-03452-9. Fascinating description of Hindu *avatars*, classical and modern, and comparison with the concept of Christ.

Bjorkman, James Warner, ed. *Fundamentalism, Revivalists and Violence in South Asia*. Riverdale Co. 1988 $29.00. ISBN 0-913215-06-6. Collection of articles on South Asian fundamentalism and its relation to politics, including Jones on women in the Arya Samaj and other nineteenth-century revivalist groups; Surjit Mansingh on political function of religious identities in British India; and Rudolphs on secularism.

Bonner, Arthur. *Averting the Apocalypse: Social Movements in India Today*. Duke 1990 $52.50. ISBN 0-8223-1029-5. Searing picture of the social and religious problems of India and the people working for social change.

Borden, Carla M., ed. *Contemporary Indian Tradition*. Smithsonian 1988 $35.00. ISBN 0-87474-258-7. Scholarly but highly accessible essays on aspects of contemporary Indian culture that were lectures delivered at a symposium in conjunction with the Festival of India hosted by the Smithsonian Institution.

Brooks, Charles R. *The Hare Krishnas in India*. Princeton U. Pr. 1989 $47.50. ISBN 0-691-03135-5. Fascinating anthropological study of the interaction of Western devotees of Krishna with Indian Hindus.

Bumiller, Elisabeth. *May You Be the Mother of a Hundred Sons: A Journey among the Women of India*. Random 1990 $19.45. ISBN 0-449-90614-0. Reporter's honest and sympathetic account of the problems and violence endured by Indian women.

Datta, V. N. *Sati: Widow Burning*. Riverdale Co. 1988 $29.00. ISBN 0-913215-31-7. Examination of British and Indian attitudes toward "sati" or "suttee," the burning of a widow on the funeral pyre of her husband.

Fenton, John Y. *Transplanting Religious Traditions: Asian Indians in America*. Praeger 1988 $45.00. ISBN 0-295-92676-1. Analysis of religious practices of an Asian Indian community in Atlanta from 1984 to 1985.

Ghadially, Rehana, ed. *Women in Indian Society: A Reader*. Sage 1988 $30.00. ISBN 0-8039-9564-4. Twenty-one articles on images of women in Indian myths, textbooks, and movies, on gender roles in India, Indian feminism, and violence against women in India.

Graham, Bruce. *Hindu Nationalism and Indian Politics: The Origins and Development of the Bharatiya Jana Sangh*. Cambridge U. Pr. 1990 $54.95. ISBN 0-521-38348-X. Examination of the development of the Hindu political party Bharatiya Jana Sangh (Indian People's Party), which sought, between 1951 and 1967, to make India a Hindu state and why it so far has failed to achieve its goal.

Halbfass, Wilhelm. *India and Europe*. State U. NY Pr. 1988 $19.95. ISBN 0-88706-794-8. Explores the reciprocal influences between Indian and European philosophy.

Jackson, Carl T. *The Oriental Religions and American Thought: Nineteenth-Century Explorations*. Greenwood 1988 $38.50. ISBN 0-313-22491-9. Superb treatment of the American discovery of Asian thought—Hindu, Buddhist, and East Asian.

Jones, Kenneth W. *Socio-Religious Reform Movements in British India*. Cambridge U. Pr. 1989 $44.95. ISBN 0-521-24986-4. Highly competent survey of Hindu, Muslim, Sikh, Christian, and Zoroastrian religious movements in nineteenth- and twentieth-century India.

Juergensmeyer, Mark. *Radhasoami Reality: The Logic of a Modern Faith*. Princeton U. Pr. 1991 $29.95. ISBN 0-691-07378-3. Comprehensive study of a Hindu sect that is now an international religion and how it deals with modern tensions, such as those between religion and science, as well as individual transformation and community.

———. *Religion as a Social Vision: The Movement Against Untouchability in 20th-Century Punjab*. U. CA Pr. 1982 $47.50. ISBN 0-520-04301-4. Helpful in learning about the "untouchable" experience and views.

Kishwar, Madhu, and Ruth Vanita, eds. *In Search of Answers: Indian Women's Voices from Manushi*. Zed Bks. 1984 o.p. Excellent collection from the New Delhi journal about Indian women and society; Madhu Kishwar and Ruth Vanita offer penetrating analysis of the conditions of Indian women.

Kumar, Nita. *The Artisans of Banaras: Popular Culture and Identity, 1880–1986*. Princeton U. Pr. 1988 $29.50. ISBN 0-691-05531-9. Study of the relations between Hindu and Muslim artisans in the ancient Hindu holy city of Benares.

Minor, Robert. *Radhakrishnan: A Religious Biography*. State U. NY Pr. 1987 $19.95. ISBN 0-88076-555-4

———, ed. *Modern Indian Interpreters of the Bhagavad Gita*. State U. NY Pr. 1986 $59.50. ISBN 0-88706-297-0. Sound scholarship on modern Hindu thought, including chapters on theosophy, Bankim Candra Chatterji, Tilak, Sri Aurobindo, Gandhi, Vinoba Bhave, Swami Vivekananda, Radhakrishnan, Swami Sivananda, and Swami Bhaktivedanta.

Mitter, Sara S. *Dharma's Daughters: Contemporary Indian Women and Hindu Culture*. Rutgers U. Pr. 1991 $32.00. ISBN 0-8135-1678-1. Description of the lives of middle and lower class women in Bombay, examining the influence of Hindu goddess imagery on real women and looking at efforts of contemporary Indian women to improve their lot.

Neill, Stephen. *A History of Christianity in India 1707–1858*. Cambridge U. Pr. 1985 $115.00. ISBN 0-521-30376-1. Authoritative discussion of the important impact of Christianity on Indian tradition.

Sharma, Arvind, ed. *Neo-Hindu Views of Christianity*. E. J. Brill 1988 o.p. Collection of essays on how important modern Hindu thinkers viewed Christianity, treating Ram Mohan Roy, Ramakrishna, Vivekananda, Keshub Chandra Sen, Dayananda Saraswati, Mahatma Gandhi, Radhakrishnan, and Sri Aurobindo.

Sharma, Arvind, Ajit Ray, Alaka Hejib, and Katherine K. Young. *Sati: Historical and Phenomenological Essays*. S. Asia 1988 $8.75. ISBN 0-685-22787-1. Twelve essays, nine by Sharma, on the issue of "sati" or "suttee," the immolation of a widow on her husband's funeral pyre; good introduction to the topic with both Hindu and British viewpoints.

Thomas, P. M. *Twentieth Century Indian Interpretations of Bhagavad Gita: Tilak, Gandhi, and Aurobindo*. ISPCK 1987 o.p. Analysis of how modern Hindus have interpreted the *Bhagavad Gita* to meet the challenges of contact with Western religion and culture.

Williams, Raymond B. *A New Face of Hinduism: The Swaminarayan Religion*. Cambridge U. Pr. 1984 $18.95. ISBN 0-521-25454-X. Historical, sociological, and theological study of an international Hindu sect originating in Gujarat.

Williams, Raymond Brady, ed. *A Sacred Thread: Modern Transmission of Hindu Traditions in India and Abroad*. Anima Pubns. 1992 $24.95. ISBN 0-89012-065-X. Articles by experts on contemporary developments in Hinduism, including its presence outside India.

Wiser, William, and Charlotte Wiser. *Behind Mud Walls 1930–1960, with a Sequel: The Village in 1970 and a New Chapter by Susan S. Wadley: The Village in 1984*. U. CA Pr. rev. ed. 1989 $14.00. ISBN 0-520-02101-0. In its most recent edition, fascinating firsthand account of life in a village in northern India over a period of more than 50 years, exploring the ramifications of caste, religion, and gender and depicting the changes wrought by Indian contact with the West and industrialization.

Jainism

Both Jainism and Buddhism have their origins in the India of the sixth century B.C.E., the time of the composition of the Upanishads. Jainism was founded by a man known as Mahavira, or "great hero," whose era traditionally is thought to be 540–468 B.C.E. Mahavira stressed extreme ascetic practices, with special emphasis on *ahimsa*, nonviolence toward all living beings. Jainism sees its tradition as growing out of the teachings of 24 Jinas ("conquerors") or Tirthankaras ("makers of the ford"), with Mahavira being the most recent of these. Jains see karma as a substance that weights down the soul. The goal is to free oneself from karma, and this is done by practicing asceticism and nonviolence.

Barnes, Michael, ed. *An Ecology of the Spirit: Religious Reflection and Environmental Consciousness*. U. Pr. of Amer. 1993 $52.00. ISBN 0-8191-8959-6. Includes an article by Christopher Chapple on "Contemporary Jaina and Hindu Responses to the Ecological Crisis."

Carrithers, Michael, and Caroline Humphrey, eds. *The Assembly of Listeners: Jains in Society*. Cambridge U. Pr. 1991 $64.95. ISBN 0-521-36505-8. The first sociological treatment of Jainism.

Jaini, Padmanabh S. *Jaina Debates on the Spiritual Liberation of Women*. U. CA Pr. 1991 $32.50. ISBN 0-520-06820-3. Translation of Jain texts that discuss whether women can achieve the Jain ultimate goal; introduced by helpful historical material.

Kitagawa, Joseph M. *The Religious Traditions of Asia*. Macmillan 1989 $12.95. ISBN 0-02-897211-2. Articles excerpted from the *Encyclopedia of Religion*. Includes article on Jainism.

Kulkarni, V. M. *The Story of Rama in Jain Literature*. Saraswati Pustak Bhander 1990 o.p. Scholarly study of the Jain version of the epic *Ramayana*.

Levering, Miriam. *Rethinking Scripture: Essays from Comparative Perspective*. State U. NY Pr. 1989 $44.50. ISBN 0-88706-614-3. Excellent comparative study of scriptures, with a chapter on Jainism by Kendall Folkert.

Settar, S. *Inviting Death: Indian Attitude towards the Ritual Death*. E. J. Brill 1989 $85.75. ISBN 90-04-08790-7. Important study of the Jain ritual of fasting to death practiced by Jain ascetics; very technical, with photos.

Shri Priyadarsha. *Jain Ramayan*. 3 vols. Trans. by K. Ramappa. o.p. English translation of a lengthy retelling of the Jain *Ramayana* by a Shvetambar monk.

Sutherland, Gail Hinich. *The Disguises of the Demon: The Development of the Yaksa in Hinduism and Buddhism*. State U. NY Pr. 1991 $44.50. ISBN 0-7914-0622-9. The history of the figure of the Yaksa "demon" or "nature spirit" as it appears in Hindu, Buddhist, and Jain literature and sculpture.

Timm, Jeffrey R., ed. *Texts in Context: Traditional Hermeneutics in South Asia*. State U. NY Pr. 1992 $49.50. ISBN 0-7914-0796-9. Including articles by experts in the interpretation of Hindu, Buddhist, Jain, and Sikh texts, including "Svetambar Murtipujak Jain Scripture in a Performative Context, by John E. Cort.

Tiwari, M. N. *Ambika in Jaina Art and Literature*. Bharatiya Jnanpith 1989 o.p. Study of the Jain goddess Ambika based on textual and artistic sources.

Tobias, Michael. *Life Force: The World of Jainism*. Jain Pub. Co. 1991 $12.00. ISBN 0-89581-899-X. Good general introduction to Jainism by an ecologist and filmmmaker who sees in Jainism a worldview that is respectful of the natural environment.

Williams, R. *Jaina Yoga: A Survey of the Mediaeval Sravakacaras*. S. Asia 1968 $16.50. ISBN 0-89581-967-8. Very technical study of Jaina texts known as *Sravakacaras*.

Wiltshire, Martin G. *Ascetic Figures before and in Early Buddhism: The Emergence of Gautama as the Buddha*. Mouton 1990 $120.00. ISBN 3-11-009896-2. Study of the Pali Canon, and secondarily Jain literature, for references to ascetic figures that elucidate the context within which Gautama Buddha rose to prominence.

Buddhism

Buddhism originated with the life of Siddhartha Gautama (563–483 B.C.E.), who was known as Gautama Buddha after his enlightenment. Gautama Buddha taught a "Middle Way" between extreme asceticism and extreme sensual indulgence. The Buddhist ultimate goal is *nirvana*, "the blowing out" of all desires, which results in ending the cycle of rebirth. Gautama's emphasis that nothing whatsoever is permanent led him to teach that there is no permanent self or soul (*atman*), nor a permanent ultimate source to be termed God. Therefore, the Buddha's system can be seen as an atheistic religion. Gautama Buddha taught that anyone can achieve *nirvana* but that it is easier to accomplish if one is a member of the Buddhist monastic order, or *sangha*. Gautama Buddha admitted women into the *sangha*, but in the centuries after his death the status of Buddhist nuns declined greatly. By about the thirteenth century C.E., Buddhism had virtually disappeared in India but was found as a living tradition in other Asian countries.

Theravada Buddhism is regarded as being the type of Buddhism that is closest to the original teachings of Gautama Buddha. Its scriptures are known as the Pali Canon because they were written in a Sanskrit dialect known as Pali. Theravada Buddhism is found in the southeast Asian countries of Sri Lanka (formerly Ceylon), Myanmar (Burma), Thailand, Cambodia, and Laos. Although trends can be identified to the contrary, the overriding emphasis in Theravada Buddhism is that one must rely only on oneself for the achievement of *nirvana* and that Gautama Buddha was simply an extraordinary man who achieved the ultimate goal.

Mahayana Buddhism, or the Buddhism of the "great vehicle," has its origins in developments in northern India from about 200 C.E. Mahayana as a living tradition is found in China, Taiwan, Korea, Japan, Tibet, Mongolia, Nepal, Bhutan, and Vietnam. Mahayana Buddhism is a tradition that is just as diverse in practice and outlook as the Hindu tradition. Generally, however, Mahayana views Gautama Buddha as a superhuman being. Further, in Mahayana Buddhism, there are thought to be many Buddhas, who reside in various heavens, and compassionate enlightened beings called *bodhisattvas*, who possess supernatural powers. One can pray to these beings for salvation or assistance in one's daily life. All *bodhisattvas* are seen as having taken a vow to refrain from entering into the state of *nirvana* so that they can respond to the suffering of all living beings and assist them to reach the farther shore. In the Mahayana tradition, many new scriptures called *sutras* were composed in Sanskrit, all purporting to present the secret teachings of Gautama Buddha.

The Mahayana philosophical concepts are extremely complex. The two Indian schools that have had significant impact on Buddhist thought in other Asian countries are Madhyamika, formulated by Nagarjuna (second or third century C.E.), and Yogacara, formulated by two brothers, Asanga and Vasubandhu, in the fourth century C.E.

Underlying the variety of Mahayana schools is a cosmology that is stated in the doctrine of the *trikaya*, or three bodies of the Buddha. This doctrine states that the reality that is the Buddha exists on three levels. The ultimate level is the Dharmakaya, the "body of the dharma" or the absolute Buddha. This is regarded as the ground of all being, a totally unconditioned reality, that is indicated by such terms as emptiness, or the Void (*shunya* or *shunyata*). Mahayana Buddhist understanding of this first level tends toward monism, in which reality is seen as one impersonal whole. The second level is the Sambhogakaya, the "enjoyment body," or the body of bliss. This is the level of the celestial Buddhas and *bodhisattvas*. This level of reality is conditioned, but it is above the terrestrial and therefore heavenly. Mahayana Buddhist understanding of this second level tends toward theism in its worship of the various Buddhas and *bodhisattvas*. If there is particular emphasis on one celestial Buddha, a type of monotheism develops, as is found in Pure Land Buddhism. The third level is the Nirmanakaya, the "body of manifestation," in other words, the level of earthly existence in which the historical Gautama Buddha appeared.

Nagajuna focused on the first level and taught that ultimate reality is indescribable, and he utilized logical criticism to show the inadequacy of all views of reality. His intent was that, by demolishing all views, reality would appear of itself. This immediate perception of reality is *prajnaparamita*, the perfection of wisdom or pure understanding. It is direct perception of *tathata* (thatness, suchness) or *shunya* or *shunyata* (the Void or emptiness). Nagarjuna taught that all Buddhist doctrines purporting to describe reality are simply *upaya*, "skill in means," or devices to enable one to arrive at the perception of *shunyata*.

Asanga and Vasubandhu taught Yogacara or Vijnanavada, "the doctrine of only consciousness is real." They called the Void *vijnana* (consciousness). Everything is pure mind, and material existence is illusion projected by erroneous thoughts. Yogacarins used yogic techniques to purify the mind of thoughts and perceptions to reach pure consciousness.

Another Mahayana line of thought that originated in India but developed into a flourishing religion in China, Korea, and Japan, is Pure Land Buddhism, in which the focus is on the second level of the *trikaya* and particularly on

Amitabha Buddha, who resides in a heavenly paradise called the Pure Land.
Amitabha is believed to have vowed to respond to all who call his name with
faith by taking them into the Pure Land at death. The worshipper must have
faith in Amitabha, and this faith is expressed in the recitation of Amitabha's
name and in his worship. Amitabha responds by offering his grace, the means by
which one enters the Pure Land. The ultimate goal of Pure Land Buddhism is
really about going to heaven, but it is said that in the Pure Land *nirvana* is easy
to achieve. Amitabha's name is pronounced in Chinese in a variety of ways, and
in Japanese he is known as Amida Buddha. Amitabha is assisted by a
bodhisattva, originally of Indian origin but who has had an illustrious career in
East Asian countries. In Sanskrit he is known as Avalokiteshwara, the lord who
looks down from above and responds to the cries of people in the world. In
China, Avalokiteshwara became known as Gwan Yin (Kwan Yin), and in Japan
as Kannon. Gwan Yin or Kannon has come to be depicted as either a male or
female *bodhisattva*. In recent centuries she usually is depicted as female. Gwan
Yin responds to people in need and assists them with their worldly crises, such
as childbirth, shipwreck, bandits, and illness.

Akira, Hirakawa. *A History of Indian Buddhism: From Sakyamuni to Early Mahayana*. Ed.
   and trans. by Paul Groner. UH Pr. 1990 $35.00. ISBN 0-8248-1203-4. Exceptionally
   comprehensive and detailed survey of the first six centuries of Indian Buddhism.

Ames, Roger T., ed. *Nature in Asian Traditions of Thought: Essays in Environmental
   Philosophy*. State U. NY Pr. 1989 $39.50. ISBN 0-88706-950-9. Collection of
   introductory essays by foremost scholars of Asian philosophy on the issue of how
   Asian thought views the environment.

Amore, Roy C. *Lustful Maidens and Ascetic Kings: Buddhist and Hindu Stories of Life*.
   OUP 1981 $29.95. ISBN 0-19-502838-4. Engaging popular collection of significant
   folktales and themes. Helpful contextual introductions.

Berry, Thomas. *Buddhism*. Anima Pubns. 1967 $9.95. ISBN 0-89012-017-X. Highly
   accessible general introduction to the Buddhist tradition as well as its expansion in
   Asia and the West.

Boucher, Sandy. *Turning the Wheel: American Women Creating the New Buddhism*.
   HarpC 1988. ISBN 0-06-250097-X. Feminist American Buddhist women confront
   authoritarianism and sexism within the Buddhist tradition.

Carrithers, Michael, Raymond Dawson, Humphrey Carpenter, and Michael Cook.
   Founders of Faith. OUP 1989 $10.95. ISBN 0-19-283066-X. Good introduction to four
   important religious founders, with Michael Carrithers writing on Gautama Buddha.

Conze, Edward. *Buddhist Thought in India*. U. of Mich. Pr. 1967 $16.95. ISBN 0-472-
   06129-1. Technical discussion of archaic Buddhist philosophy, the Sthavira, and the
   Mahayana schools of philosophy.

Dharmasiri, Gunapala. *Fundamentals of Buddhist Ethics*. Golden Leaves Pub. 1989
   $11.95. ISBN 0-942353-02-1. Engaging introduction to Buddhist ethics.

Falk, Nancy Auer, and Rita M. Gross, eds. *Unspoken Worlds: Women's Religious Lives*.
   Wadsworth Pub. 1989. ISBN 0-534-09852-5. Groundbreaking collection on religion
   in women's lives; Nancy Auer Falk writes on the vanishing of Buddhist nuns in India,
   and Reginald A. Ray writes on women practitioners of Tantric Buddhism in
   medieval India and Tibet.

Fox, Douglas A. *The Heart of Buddhist Wisdom: A Translation of the Heart Sutra with
   Historical Introduction and Commentary*. E. Mellen 1985 $79.95. ISBN 0-88946-
   053-1. Translation and explanation of the most famous of the prajnaparamita sutras
   in Mahayana Buddhism.

Fryba, Mirko. *The Art of Happiness: Teachings of Buddhist Psychology*. Trans. by Michael
   H. Kohn. Shambhala 1989 $15.95. ISBN 0-87773-466-6. Written by a Swiss
   psychotherapist who has received Buddhist monastic training in Sri Lanka from
   Nyanaponika Thera, this book interprets Theravada Buddhism as relevant to the
   contemporary world.

Gombrich, Richard. *Theravada Buddhism: A Social History from Ancient Benares to Modern Colombo.* Routledge 1988 $7.95. ISBN 0-7102-1319-0. Introductory history of Buddhism in India and Sri Lanka.

Haddad, Yvonne Yazbeck, and Ellison Banks Findley, eds. *Women, Religion and Social Change.* State U. NY Pr. 1985 $59.50. ISBN 0-88706-068-4. Fine scholarship on women and religion; Janice D. Willis writes on women in early Buddhism in India.

Hookham, S. K. *The Buddha Within: Tathagatagarbha Doctrine According to the Shentong Interpretation of the Ratnagotravibhava.* State U. NY Pr. 1991 $59.50. ISBN 0-7914-0357-2. History and explanation of the Indian Mahayana Buddhist *tathagatagarbha* doctrine, which has been translated as "Buddha nature," and its influence in Tibet; a book on an abstract subject that is accessible to the beginner.

Huntington, C. W., and Geshe Namgyal Wangchen. *The Emptiness of Emptiness: An Introduction to Early Indian Madhyamika.* UH Pr. 1989 $35.00. ISBN 0-8248-1165-8. Translation and explanation of the *Madhyamakavatara* (The Entry into the Middle Way) of seventh-century C.E. Madhyamika philosopher Candrakirti.

Kalupahana, David J. *A History of Buddhist Philosophy: Continuities and Discontinuities.* UH Pr. 1992 $14.95. ISBN 0-8248-1402-9. Kalupahana builds upon his earlier work, *Buddhist Philosophy,* to present in a new volume a completely reconstructed and detailed analysis of both early and later Buddhism.

Kennedy, Alex. *A Buddhist Vision: An Introduction to the Theory and Practice of Modern Buddhism.* Weiser 1987 $8.95. ISBN 0-87728-620-5. Good general introduction to Buddhist thought and practice.

Kieckhefer, Richard, and George D. Bond, eds. *Sainthood: Its Manifestations in World Religions.* U. CA Pr. 1988 $42.50. ISBN 0-520-05154-8. Collection of excellent essays on sainthood in world religions; G. Bond and D. Lopez write on Theravada and Mahayana Buddhism.

King, Sallie B. *Buddha Nature.* State U. NY Pr. 1990 $49.50. ISBN 0-7914-0427-7. Good introductory analysis of the *Buddha Nature Treatise* ascribed to the Indian Buddhist philosopher Vasubandhu but that exists now only in its sixth-century Chinese translation.

Kitagawa, Joseph M. *The Religious Traditions of Asia.* Macmillan 1989 $12.95. ISBN 0-02-897211-2. Articles excerpted from the *Encyclopedia of Religion*: Part 1 on Hinduism, Buddhism in India and Southeast Asia, Jainism, the Sikhs, and Islam; Part 2 on Tibetan Buddhism, Bon, and Islam in Central Asia; Part 3 on religions in China, Japan, and Korea.

Kitagawa, Joseph M., and Mark D. Cummings, eds. *Buddhism and Asian History.* Macmillan 1989 $12.95. ISBN 0-02-897212-0. Excellent reference work on Buddhism, consisting of articles taken from the *Encyclopedia of Religion* on the "Foundations of the Tradition," Buddhism in Southeast Asia, Central Asia, China, Korea, Japan, Tibet, and Mongolia; the major Buddhist schools within the Theravada, Mahayana, and Vajrayana traditions; Buddhist practices, art, and popular Buddhism; and such major concepts as *nirvana* and the *bodhisattva*.

LaFleur, William R. *Buddhism: A Cultural Perspective.* P-H 1988 o.p. Presentation of Buddhism in its multifaceted cultural entirety, including a general discussion of history of Buddhism; Buddhist poetry; controversial issues, including the status of women; Buddhist doctrine and philosophy; descriptions of rituals, meditation practices, and monastic life; and analysis of the sociological expression of Buddhism.

Lamotte, Etienne. *History of Indian Buddhism: From the Origins to the Saka Era.* Trans. by Sara Webb-Boin. Peeters Pr. 1988 o.p. English translation of the definitive history of Buddhism in India.

Lindtner, Charles, trans. *Master of Wisdom: Writings of the Buddhist Master Nagarjuna.* Dharma Pub. 1986 $35.95. ISBN 0-89800-139-0. English translation from Tibetan texts attributed to the great Buddhist philosopher Nagarjuna.

Lopez, Donald S., Jr. *Buddhist Hermeneutics.* UH Pr. 1988 $35.00. ISBN 0-8248-1161-5. Important scholarly essays on the principles utilized by Buddhist communities in interpreting Buddhist texts.

Martin, Rafe. *The Hungry Tigress: Buddhist Legends and Jataka Tales*. Parallax Pr. 1990 $15.00. ISBN 0-938077-25-2. Buddhist legends and jataka tales (stories of Buddha's earlier incarnations) retold in appealing form by a master storyteller, with appropriate historical and explanatory material provided.

Paul, Diana Y. *Women in Buddhism: Images of the Feminine in the Mahayana Tradition*. U. CA Pr. 1985 $15.00. ISBN 0-520-05445-8. Examination of Mahayana Buddhist egalitarianism and sexism as reflected in texts.

Richman, Paula. *Women, Branch Stories, and Religious Rhetoric in a Tamil Buddhist Text*. Syracuse U. Pr. 1988 $19.00. ISBN 0-915984-90-3. Study of a document produced by sixth-century C.E. Tamil Buddhists that recounts how a woman converted from Hinduism to Buddhism.

Robinson, Richard H., and Willard L. Johnson. *The Buddhist Religion: A Historical Introduction*. Wadsworth Pub. 1982. ISBN 0-534-01027-X. Solid presentation of the origins of Buddhism, Indian Buddhism—including the origins of Mahayana and Buddhist Tantra—Buddhism in Southeast Asia, in Tibetan cultural area, in East Asia, and in the West.

Sharma, Arvind, ed. *Women in World Religions*. State U. NY Pr. 1987 $44.50. ISBN 0-88706-374-8. Articles sound in scholarship and accessible to the general reader; Nancy Schuster Barnes contributes the article on Buddhism.

Sizemore, Russell R., and Donald K. Swearer. *Ethics, Wealth and Salvation: A Study in Buddhist Social Ethics*. U. of SC Pr. 1990 $18.95. ISBN 0-87249-612-0. Contributors address the question of how individual spiritual perfection is related to social well-being in Theravada tradition.

Sullivan, Lawrence, ed. *Healing and Restoring: Health and Medicine in the World's Religious Traditions*. Macmillan 1989 $35.00. ISBN 0-02-923791-2. Interdisciplinary and multicultural study of the topic of healing and health in the world's religions; Joseph Kitagawa and Raoul Birnbaum write on healing generally in Buddhism and specifically in China; and Gananath and Obeyesekere write on healing in Sri Lanka.

Sutherland, Gail Hinich. *The Disguises of the Demon: The Development of the Yaksa in Hinduism and Buddhism*. State U. NY Pr. 1991 $44.50. ISBN 0-7916-0621-0. The history of the Yaksha "demon" or "nature spirit" as it appears in Hindu, Buddhist, and Jain literature and sculpture.

Timm, Jeffrey R., ed. *Texts in Context: Traditional Hermeneutics in South Asia*. State U. NY Pr. 1992 $59.50. ISBN 0-7914-0796-9. Articles by experts in the interpretation of Hindu, Buddhist, Jain, and Sikh texts; Frank J. Hoffmann writes on the oral tradition in Nikaya Buddhism, and José Ignácio Cabezon writes on Vasubandhu's *Vyakhya-yukti*, on the authenticity of the Mahayana sutras.

Walshe, Maurice, trans. *Thus Have I Heard: The Long Discourses of the Buddha*. Wisdom MA 1987 $34.95. ISBN 0-86171-030-4. English translation of the discourses of Gautama Buddha presented in the Pali text *Digha Nikaya*.

Wayman, Alex, and Hideko Wayman. *The Lion's Roar of Queen Srimala*. S. Asia 1990 $20.00. ISBN 81-208-0731-6. Translation of and introduction to a Mahayana text featuring a female Buddha.

Williams, Paul. *Mahayana Buddhism: The Doctrinal Foundations*. Routledge 1989 $55.00. ISBN 0-415-02536-2. Important handbook for advanced students of Mahayana Buddhism that discusses Prajnaparamita, Madhyamaka, Cittamatra, Tathagata-garbha, and Avatamsaka texts; the Lotus Sutra, Buddha-body teachings, the *bodhi-sattva* path, and worship of various Buddhas and *bodhisattvas*, including Pure Land Buddhism.

Wiltshire, Martin G. *Ascetic Figures before and in Early Buddhism: The Emergence of Gautama as the Buddha*. Mouton 1990 $120.00. ISBN 3-11-009896-2. Study of the Pali Canon, and secondarily Jain literature, for references to ascetic figures that elucidate the context within which Gautama Buddha rose to prominence.

Wood, Thomas E. *Mind Only: A Philosophical and Doctrinal Analysis of the Vijnanavada*. UH Pr. 1990 $18.00. ISBN 0-8248-1356-1. Investigates the extent to which the Vijnanavadins believed in an Absolute, demonstrating that they were in fact ambivalent in their philosophical views on this point.

Zwalf, W., ed. *Buddhism: Art and Faith*. Macmillan 1985 $19.95. ISBN 0-02-934500-6. Photographs of Buddhist works of art, with commentary.

MODERN DEVELOPMENTS IN BUDDHISM

Bjorkman, James Warner, ed. *Fundamentalism, Revivalists and Violence in South Asia*. Riverdale Co. 1988 $29.00. ISBN 0-913215-06-6. Collection of articles on South Asian fundamentalism and its relation to politics; K. M. deSilva gives a history of Buddhist politics in Sri Lanka.

Bond, George D. *The Buddhist Revival in Sri Lanka: Religious Tradition, Reinterpretation and Response*. U. of SC Pr. 1988 $34.95. ISBN 0-87249-557-4. Examination of how twentieth-century Sri Lankans have reinterpreted their Buddhist tradition in light of pluralism, individualism, and urbanism.

Friedman, Lenore. *Meetings with Remarkable Women: Buddhist Teachers in America*. Shambhala 1987 $19.00. ISBN 0-87773-366-X. Vignettes of significant Buddhist women teachers in America.

Gombrich, Richard, and Gananath Obeyesekere. *Buddhism Transformed: Religious Change in Sri Lanka*. Princeton U. Pr. 1988 $60.00. ISBN 0-691-07333-3. Presentation of Sri Lankan Buddhist responses to colonialism and contact with Christian missionaries, including what is termed Protestant Buddhism.

Kapferer, Bruce. *A Celebration of Demons: Exorcism and the Aesthetics of Healing in Sri Lanka*. Ind. U. Pr. 1983 $29.95. ISBN 0-253-31326-0. Study of shamanistic popular religion in Sri Lanka.

Taylor, Robert H. *The State in Burma*. UH Pr. 1988 $32.00. ISBN 0-8248-1141-0. Includes a study of Buddhism as part of this social history of modern Burma (now Myanmar).

Tsomo, Karma Lekshe, ed. *Sakyadhita: Daughters of the Buddha*. Snow Lion 1988 $14.95. ISBN 0-937938-72-6. Papers presented at the first international conference on Buddhist nuns, representing the first time information has been published on the status of Buddhist nuns in Asian countries.

Sikhism

Sikhism results from the sixteenth-century synthesis of Hinduism and Islam in north India by Guru Nanak, the founder of the Sikh tradition. The word *Sikh* means "disciple." Sikhism combines the *bhakti*, or devotional tradition, of Hinduism with elements from Islam. Guru Nanak's emphasis that there is no need for conflict between Hinduism and Islam is expressed in his famous statement: "There is no Hindu; there is no Muslim." Nanak's poems are contained in the Sikh scripture known as the Holy Granth, which also contains the writings of the subsequent Sikh gurus (teachers). There is a lineage of 10 gurus within Sikhism. The fifth guru, Arjuna (1563–1606), compiled the writings that make up the Holy Granth, and it is enshrined in the foremost Sikh place of worship, the Golden Temple in Amritsar, in the Punjab state of north India.

Although the Sikhs originally were founded to demonstrate the harmony of Hinduism and Islam, they have found themselves increasingly in conflict with those two religions. During the centuries after Guru Nanak, the Mughal emperors, who were Muslims and who controlled much of north India, persecuted the Sikhs, causing the martyrdom of Sikh gurus and massacres of Sikhs. The tenth guru, Gobind Rai (1666–1708), responded to these pressures by instituting a Sikh fraternity known as the Khalsa. Male Sikhs who are members of the Khalsa take the surname Singh, which means "lion," and they are characterized by uncut hair, which should be clean and kept neat in a turban. They always should have on their persons a comb for their long hair, a steel bracelet symbolizing strength, shorts or an undergarment giving mobility in battle, and a *kirpan*, or dagger. After the death of the tenth guru, the Holy Granth is regarded as the Sikh guru.

In recent years, Sikhism has found itself increasingly in conflict with the predominantly Hindu secular state of India. The Sikhs were caught between the Hindus and Muslims during the partition of the Indian subcontinent in 1947 that produced the independent states of Pakistan (Muslim) and India. Many Sikhs died during the communal conflicts that accompanied partition. In recent years, militant Sikhs in India have begun to demand the creation of a separate and independent Sikh country in the Punjab. The activities of militant Sikhs resulted in the storming of the Golden Temple in Amritsar in 1984 by the Indian military. In retaliation, the prime minister of India, Indira Gandhi, was assassinated by her Sikh bodyguards. Militant Sikhs continue to be a volatile factor in the communal tensions that still threaten to rip apart the state of India.

Baird, Robert D., ed. *Religion in Modern India*. S. Asia 1989 $36.00. ISBN 81-85054-64-9. The best treatment of modern Indian thinkers and religious movements; N. Gerald Barrier writes on "The Singh Sabhas and the Evolution of Modern Sikhism, 1875–1925."

Barrer, N. Gerald, and Verne A. Dusenbery, eds. *The Sikh Diaspora: Migration and the Experience beyond the Punjab*. S. Asia 1989 $44.00. ISBN 0-685-35370-2. Excellent collection of essays on contemporary Sikhism, with four articles treating Sikhs in North America, one article on Sikhs in Great Britain, one on Sikhs in East Africa, and three articles on Sikhs in the Punjab and the continuing influences on Sikhs outside the Punjab.

Dass, Nirmal, trans. *Songs of Kabir from the Adi Granth*. State U. NY Pr. 1991 $44.50. ISBN 0-7914-0560-5. Translation of and introduction to the poems of Kabir, which have been included in the Sikh scripture.

Fox, Richard G. *Lions of the Punjab: Culture in the Making*. U. CA Pr. 1985 $45.00. ISBN 0-520-05491-1. Examines the complexities of Sikh reactions to British imperialism culminating in the Third Sikh War, 1920–25.

Jones, Kenneth W. *Socio-Religious Reform Movements in British India*. Cambridge U. Pr. 1989 $44.95. ISBN 0-521-24986-4. Highly competent survey of Hindu, Muslim, Sikh, Christian, and Zoroastrian religious movements in nineteenth- and twentieth-century India.

Juergensmeyer, Mark. *Sikh Studies: Comparative Perspectives on a Changing Tradition*. Graduate Theological Union 1979 o.p. Wide-ranging collection of essays that includes treatment of Sikhs outside India.

Juergensmeyer, Mark, and John Stratton Hawley. *Songs of the Saints of India*. OUP 1988 $35.00. ISBN 0-19-505220-X. Includes a section on Guru Nanak.

Kapur, Rajiv A. *Sikh Separatism: The Politics of a Faith*. Routledge Chapman & Hall 1986 $34.95. ISBN 0-04-320179-2. Study of the emergence of Sikh separatism and its characteristics.

Kitagawa, Joseph M. *The Religious Traditions of Asia*. Macmillan 1989 $12.95. ISBN 0-02-897211-2. Articles excerpted from the *Encyclopedia of Religion*, with an article on Sikhism in Part 1.

McLeod, W. H. *The Evolution of the Sikh Community: Five Essays*. OUP 1976 $36.00. ISBN 0-19-826529-8. Classic examination of the history and scripture of the Sikhs to understand the transition to a martial religion.

_____. *Guru Nanak and the Sikh Religion*. OUP 1968 o.p. Very important work on Sikhism.

_____. *The Sikhs: History of Religion and Society*. Col. U. Pr. 1989 $42.00. ISBN 0-231-06814-X. Excellent brief introduction to Sikhism.

_____. *Textual Sources for the Study of Sikhism*. U. Ch. Pr. 1990 $12.95. ISBN 0-226-56085-6. Very useful translations from Sikh scripture.

_____. *Who Is a Sikh? The Problem of Sikh Identity*. OUP 1989 $39.95. ISBN 0-19-826548-4. Excellent discussion of Sikhism, as distinct from Hinduism.

O'Connell, Joseph T., Milton Israel, Willard G. Oxtoby, W. H. McLeod, and J. S. Grewal, eds. *Sikh History and Religion in the Twentieth Century*. S. Asia 1988 $34.00. ISBN 0-

9692907-4-8. Twenty-five articles on Sikhism in the twentieth century by major scholars.

Rai, Priya Muhar. *Sikhism and the Sikhs: An Annotated Bibliography.* Greenwood 1989 $49.95. ISBN 0-313-26130-X. Helpful annotated bibliography of books and articles on Sikhism published since 1965.

Schomer, Karine, and W. H. McLeod, eds. *The Sants: Studies in a Devotional Tradition of India. Berkeley Religious Studies Ser.* S. Asia 1987 $50.00. ISBN 0-9612208-0-5. Includes three articles on Sikhism.

Singh, Khushwant. *A History of the Sikhs.* 2 vols. Princeton U. Pr. 1991 $11.95. ISBN 0-19-562643-5. Complete history of the Sikh tradition.

Timm, Jeffrey R., ed. *Texts in Context: Traditional Hermeneutics in South Asia.* State U. NY Pr. 1992 $49.50. ISBN 07914-0796-9. Articles by experts in the interpretation of Hindu, Buddhist, Jain, and Sikh texts; Nikky-Guninder Kaur Singh writes on "Poetics as a Hermeneutic Technique in Sikhism."

Tully, Mark, and Satish Jacob. *Amritsar: Mrs. Gandhi's Last Battle.* S. Asia 1985 $6.00. ISBN 0-8364-2826-9. Describes the conflict between the Sikhs and the Indian government that resulted in the assassination of Indira Gandhi.

Parsis (Zoroastrians in India)

Only about 10,000 Zoroastrians remain today in their land of origin, Iran, where they are a persecuted minority. When Iran was conquered by Muslims in the seventh century C.E., Zoroastrians began to migrate to India, where they are known as Parsis (Persians). The largest community of Zoroastrians today resides in India, numbering approximately 120,000. Most Parsis are found in western India around Bombay, where they are a prosperous and highly educated community. In the center of Bombay, Parsis have built a *dakhma,* or "tower of silence," for the purpose of disposing of human corpses in the traditional Zoroastrian manner. The *dakhma* in Bombay is surrounded by a beautiful park with many trees, so that the casual visitor never actually sees the *dakhma* or what takes place there. According to Zoroastrian belief, a corpse represents the triumph of evil forces and is contaminated by those forces, so it should not be placed in contact with the sacred earth, fire, or water. Therefore, the corpse is deposited in a cubicle in the circular *dakhma,* which is open to the air. When the corpse bearers leave, vultures and other birds of prey devour the corpse. Once the bones have crumbled from exposure to the purifying air, rain, and sunshine, the residue is washed down into a central drain. (For more information, see the entry on Persian Zoroastrianism in the section on Non-Islamic and Non-Jewish Traditions of the Middle East and North Africa.)

Baird, Robert D., ed. *Religion in Modern India.* S. Asia 1989 $36.00. ISBN 81-85054-64-9. The best treatment of modern Indian thinkers and religious movements; John R. Hinnells writes on "The Parsi Community."

Choksky, Jamsheed K. *Triumph Over Evil: Purity and Pollution in Zoroastrianism.* U. of Tex. Pr. 1989 $25.00. ISBN 0-292-79802-4. Very useful study of the Zoroastrian purification rituals of the past and present, demonstrating the influence of Zoroastrianism on Islam and Hinduism; written by a Zoroastrian.

Hinnells, John R. *Zoroastrianism and the Parsis.* Sterling 1981 o.p. Concise general introduction to history, beliefs, and practice of Zoroastrianism in India.

Jones, Kenneth W. *Socio-Religious Reform Movements in British India.* Cambridge U. Pr. 1989 $44.95. ISBN 0-521-24986-4. Highly competent survey of Hindu, Muslim, Sikh, Christian, and Zoroastrian religious movements in nineteenth- and twentieth-century India.

Kotwal, Firoze M., and James W. Boyd, eds. and trans. *A Guide to the Zoroastrian Religion: A Nineteenth Century Catechism with Modern Commentary.* Scholars Pr. GA 1982 $18.75. ISBN 0-89130-573-4. English translation from Gujarati of a Zoroastrian catechism written by a Zoroastrian priest in 1869 C.E. in India, accompanied by the commentary of a contemporary Zoroastrian high priest, Dastur Dr. Firoze M. Kotwal.

Kulke, Eckehard. *The Parsees in India: A Minority as Agent of Social Change.* Vikas Pub. Hse. India 1978 o.p. Analysis of the social position of the Parsi community in India, the Parsi relation to Indian politics, and the Parsi as determinants of social change.

Pangborn, Cyrus R. *Zoroastrianism: A Beleaguered Faith.* Advent NY 1983 $25.00. ISBN 0-89891-006-4. Historical treatment of the development of Zoroastrianism and the issues facing Zoroastrians in the modern world.

SOUTHEAST ASIAN TRADITIONS

The designation Southeast Asia refers to the geographical areas now known as Myanmar (Burma), Thailand, Laos, Kampuchea (Cambodia), Malaysia, Indonesia, Philippines, and Vietnam. India and China have had important cultural and religious influences throughout the region. Vietnam is the only Southeast Asian country that will receive separate treatment in this section.

General Works

Cadet, J. M. *Ramakien: The Thai Epic.* Kodansha 1970 o.p. Readable and competent translation of an important religious and political work.

Desai, Santosh N. *Hinduism in Thai Life.* Asia Bk. Corp. 1980 $23.95. ISBN 0-940500-66-3. Descriptive study of the important influence of Hinduism on Thai tradition.

Ginsburg, Henry. *Thai Manuscript Painting.* UH Pr. 1989 $34.00. ISBN 0-8248-1295-6. Beautifully illustrated book on Thai manuscript painting, which reveals the Thai cosmology.

Heine-Geldern, Robert. *Conceptions of State and Kingship in Southeast Asia.* Cornell SE Asia 1956 $3.50. ISBN 0-87727-018-X. Important brief discussion of the interrelationship between religion and politics from the standpoint of comparative cultural history.

Hooker, A. Thomas, ed. *Islam in South East Asia.* Humanities 1983 o.p. Collection of scholarly articles on the role and significance of Islam in Southeast Asia.

Kitagawa, Joseph M. *The Religious Traditions of Asia.* Macmillan 1989 $12.95. ISBN 0-02-897211-2. Articles excerpted from the *Encyclopedia of Religion.* Part 1 on Hinduism, Buddhism in India and Southeast Asia, Jainism, the Sikhs, and Islam; Part 2 on Tibetan Buddhism, Bon, and Islam in Central Asia; Part 3 on religions in China, Japan, and Korea.

Matthews, Bruce, and Judith Nagata, eds. *Religion, Values, and Development in Southeast Asia.* Inst. SE Asian Studies 1986 $9.00. ISBN 9971-988-20-8. Collection of 10 papers on a variety of issues relating to Malaysia, the Phillipines, Thailand, and Myanmar from the perspectives of anthropology, economics, linguistics, law, and history; the symbology of Angkor Wat is treated, as is the relation of traditional religions to modernization.

Smith, Bardwell L., ed. *Religion and Legitimation of Power in Thailand, Laos, and Burma.* Anima Pubns. 1978 $5.95. ISBN 0-89012-009-9. Valuable symposium on various historical and thematic aspects of religion and politics. Scholarly format.

Von der Mehden, Fred. *Religion and Modernization in Southeast Asia.* Syracuse U. Pr. 1986 $34.95. ISBN 0-8156-2360-7. Scholarly analysis of the modern significance of religion.

Popular Religion

Ackerman, Susan E., and Raymond L. M. Lee. *Heaven in Transition: Non-Muslim Religious Innovation and Ethnic Identity in Malaysia.* UH Pr. 1988 $22.00. ISBN 0-

8248-1121-6. Anthropological study of the minority non-Muslim religions in Malaysia and their reaction to state politics.

Htin, Aung U. *Folk Elements in Burmese Buddhism*. Greenwood 1978 $38.50. ISBN 0-313-20275-3. Important descriptive study of popularized Buddhism.

Kirsch, Thomas. *Feasting and Social Oscillation*. Cornell SE Asia 1973 $5.00. ISBN 0-87727-092-9. Interpretive analysis of feasting ritual from a social-anthropological perspective.

Rajadhon, Phya Anuman. *Popular Buddhism in Siam and Other Essays on Thai Studies*. Sathirakoses Nagapradipa Foundation 1986 o.p. Provides a wealth of information on Buddhist and non-Buddhist popular religion in Thailand.

_____. *Some Traditions of the Thai*. Sathirakoses Nagapradipa Foundation 1986 o.p. Record of fast-disappearing Thai traditions: folk beliefs, including belief in spirits; Thai shamanism; ritual to remove evil spirits; and ceremony for preparing the bridal bed.

Scanlon, Phil, Jr. *Southeast Asia: A Cultural Study through Celebration*. Cornell SE Asia 1985 $15.00. ISBN 1-877979-73-2. Interesting study of the ritual context for Southeast Asian tradition. Scholarly format.

Tambiah, S. J. *Buddhism and the Spirit Cults in Northeast Thailand*. Cambridge U. Pr. 1970 o.p. Excellent anthropological study of popular Buddhist practices. Technical, yet very readable, scholarship.

_____. *The Buddhist Saints of the Forest and the Cult of Amulets*. Cambridge U. Pr. 1984 $27.95. ISBN 0-521-27787-6. Insightful reflections on the interactions between Buddhism and popular tradition.

Buddhist Traditions

Bunnay, Jane. *Buddhist Monk, Buddhist Layman*. Cambridge U. Pr. 1973 o.p. A basic source for understanding Buddhist life in Thailand from the perspectives of the monastic and lay communities.

Goldstein, Joseph. *The Experience of Insight*. Shambhala 1987 $14.00. ISBN 0-87773-226-4. Lucid popular exposition of the Burmese method of Vipassana meditation (a kind of self-insight technique).

Ishii, Yoneo. *Sangha, State and Society: Thai Buddhism in History*. UH Pr. 1986 $25.00. ISBN 0-8248-0994-7. Important scholarly study that stresses the social and political role of Buddhism.

Kitagawa, Joseph M., and Mark D. Cummings, eds. *Buddhism and Asian History*. Macmillan 1989 $12.95. ISBN 0-02-897212-0. Excellent reference work on Buddhism consisting of articles taken from the *Encyclopedia of Religion* on the "Foundations of the Tradition"; Buddhism in Southeast Asia, Central Asia, China, Korea, Japan, Tibet, and Mongolia; the major Buddhist schools within the Theravada, Mahayana, and Vajrana traditions; Buddhist practices, art, and popular Buddhism; and such major concepts as *nirvana* and the *bodhisattva*.

Lester, Robert C. *Theravada Buddhism in Southeast Asia*. U. of Mich. Pr. 1973 $14.95. ISBN 0-472-06184-4. Effective overview of Buddhism stressing its social organization and cultural life. Includes a helpful general exposition of Buddhist philosophy.

Pe, Hla. *Burma: Literature, Historiography, Scholarship, Language, Life, and Buddhism*. Inst. SE Asian Studies 1985 $15.00. ISBN 9971-988-00-3. Highly personal presentation of Buddhism in Burma (Myanmar).

Ray, Nihar Ranjan. *An Introduction to the Study of Theravada Buddhism in Burma*. AMS Pr. 1946 $25.00. ISBN 0-404-16853-1. Authoritative descriptive presentation of Burmese Buddhist tradition.

Spiro, Melford E. *Buddhism and Society: A Great Tradition and Its Burmese Vicissitudes*. U. CA. Pr. 1982 $14.95. ISBN 0-520-04672-2. Significant sociological analysis of the transformations of Buddhism within Burmese tradition. Scholarly, yet accessible.

Strachan, Paul. *Pagan: Art and Architecture of Old Burma*. Arran 1989 $60.00. ISBN 1-870838-20-3. Fascinating study of the Buddhist art and architecture of the ancient capital of Burma.

Suksamran, Somboon. *Buddhism and Politics in Thailand.* Gower 1982 o.p. Knowledgeable discussion of the modern political significance of Buddhism.
————. *Political Buddhism in Southeast Asia.* St. Martin 1977 $20.00. ISBN 0-312-
62137-X. Informed analysis by a leading scholar.
Swearer, Donald K. *Buddhism and Society in Southeast Asia.* Anima Pubns. 1981 $6.95.
ISBN 0-89012-023-4. Insightful discussion of Buddhism in a Southeast Asian village
and urban traditions. Popular format.
————. *Secrets of the Lotus.* Ed. by C. Alexandre. Macmillan 1971 o.p. Informed and
sensitive introduction to Buddhist meditation as practiced in Burma.
Wells, Kenneth E. *Thai Buddhism.* AMS Pr. 1960 $34.50. ISBN 0-404-16876-0. Competent
descriptive overview of the distinctive aspects of ritual practice.

Vietnamese Traditions

Formerly part of French Indo-China, Vietnam was divided into two states in
1954, with North Vietnam under Communist control. During the 1960s and
early 1970s, North Vietnam was supported by the former Soviet Union, and
American troops were deployed to fight on the side of South Vietnam. When the
war ended in 1973, Vietnam became a united socialist republic. At that time,
many South Vietnamese attempted to leave the country, and in that effort many
became "boat people" who drowned, starved, or were raped or murdered by
pirates.

Vietnam is unique among the Southeast Asian countries in that it combines
the Theravada and Mahayana heritages of Buddhism. There is a strong Zen
tradition in Vietnam that is called Thien. The Pure Land form of Buddhism also
is strong in Vietnam, where it is called Tinh-do. Additionally, there are Roman
Catholic Vietnamese, many of whom fled the country when the Catholic-
controlled government in Saigon fell. An indigenous religion that developed in
the early part of the twentieth century is called Cao Dai, and it might have about
two million adherents. Cao Dai combines influences from Catholicism, Buddhism, Daoism, and the popular religion of spirits and ancestors, but Western
scholarship has little knowledge of it.

Beaver, R. Pierce, and others, eds. *Eerdman's Handbook to the World Religions.*
Eerdmans 1982 $29.99. ISBN 0-8028-3563-5. Useful and colorful handbook on the
world religions containing one of the few scholarly descriptions of Cao Dai.
LaFleur, William R. *Buddhism: A Cultural Perspective.* P-H 1988 o.p. Contains an
excellent section on Buddhism in Vietnam that adequately explains the phenomenon of Buddhist monks immolating themselves during the war.
Stein, Rolf A. *The World in Miniature: Container Gardens and Dwellings in Far Eastern
Religious Thought.* Trans. by Phyllis Brooks. Stanford U. Pr. 1990 $39.50. ISBN 0-
8047-1674-9. Analysis and elucidation of the cosmology that underlies the miniature
gardens of China, Japan, and Vietnam; the cosmology underlying the architecture of
homes in China, Tibet, and north and northeast Asia; and the concept of mountains
(Sumeru and K'un-lun) as axes of communication between heaven and earth.

EAST ASIAN TRADITIONS

The designation East Asia is used in this section to refer to the geographical
areas known as the People's Republic of China, Taiwan, North and South Korea,
Japan, and the trading centers of Hong Kong, Macao, and Singapore. Chinese
culture has been an important influence in the entire area, particularly in the
forms of Confucianism and Chinese Buddhism.

Chinese Traditions

China was a location for the early development of agriculture during the Neolithic period. Therefore, Chinese culture dates at least to the third millennium B.C.E. and might well be older. The earliest historical Chinese dynasty was the Shang, which usually is dated from about 1500 to about 1000 B.C.E. The distinctive patterns of Chinese religiosity date from this time. These patterns include concern for the veneration of ancestral spirits, maintaining harmony with good spirits and keeping away evil spirits, divination practices to predict the future, the concept of an unseen impersonal force underlying all of nature termed the Dao (Tao), or the Way, and the two polar forces within the Dao termed Yin and Yang. The period from about the sixth century B.C.E. until the first century B.C.E. saw from this animistic popular religion the emergence of the earliest forms of Confucianism and Daoism. Mahayana Buddhism was brought to China from India perhaps as early as the third century B.C.E. In China, Mahayana Buddhism developed distinctively Chinese forms. Confucianism, Daoism, Buddhism, and the Chinese popular religion are the main components of the overall Chinese religious and philosophical tradition. Although scholars treat these as separate, in the lives of the people there is no hard and fast division between these four religious streams.

The Communist People's Republic of China, established in 1949, initially attempted to eradicate the old practices and ways of thought, particularly during the Great Cultural Revolution, 1966–69. Under the Communist government, the old ways are stigmatized as "feudal" or "superstitious." However, the Chinese religions continue to constitute a living tradition in Taiwan, Hong Kong, and Singapore or wherever there are Chinese populations outside China. In recent years there have been increasing signs that the old Chinese outlook is alive and well in the People's Republic of China, especially in the form of Chinese medicine that utilizes the basic concepts of Yin and Yang.

In this section on Chinese religions and philosophy, the more recent Pinyin System of transliterating Chinese characters into English will be used primarily. However, because many of the books listed here use the older Wade-Giles method of transliteration, that spelling will be given in parentheses in the annotations.

REFERENCE WORKS AND ANTHOLOGIES

Chan, Wing-tsit. *Source Book in Chinese Philosophy*. Princeton U. Pr. 1963 $18.95. ISBN 0-691-01964-9. An excellent compilation of primary source readings from the major philosophical and religious traditions by the dean of contemporary commentators on Chinese philosophy. Faithful translations and helpful introductions to the various texts.

Coward, Harold, Eva Dargyay, and Ronald Neufeldt, eds. *Readings in Eastern Religions*. Humanities 1988 $29.95. ISBN 0-88920-955-3. Fine collection of selections from original texts, which would benefit from more explanatory materials; selections from early Chinese thought, Confucianism, Daoism (Taoism), and Mao Zedong (Mao Tse-tung).

de Bary, William Theodore, and others, eds. *Sources of Chinese Traditions*. Col. U. Pr. 1964 $18.00. ISBN 0-231-08603-2. Along with Chan's *Source Book*, the best collection of primary readings on Chinese philosophy and religion. Introductory discussions to the various texts and traditions are especially valuable.

Eberhard, Wolfram. *A Dictionary of Chinese Symbols*. Routledge 1988 $16.95. ISBN 0-415-0228-1. Useful for the beginning student of Chinese characters.

Ebrey, Patricia. *Chinese Civilization: A Source Book*. Free Pr. 1981 $19.95. ISBN 0-02-908752-X. Contains excellent selections on family regulations and Chinese popular religion.

Eliade, Mircea, ed. *Encyclopedia of Religion*. Macmillan 1986 $1,400.00. ISBN 0-02-909480-1. Entries on various aspects of Chinese religious tradition represent accessible surveys of recent scholarship. Most authoritative and up-to-date general reference source.

Fu, Charles Wei-hsun, and Wing-tsit Chan. *Guide to Chinese Philosophy*. G. K. Hall 1978 o.p. Though skewed in the direction of Confucian and neo-Confucian thought, this work is an authoritative and useful annotated bibliography of Chinese philosophical tradition.

Graham, A. C. *Chuang Tzu, The Seven Inner Chapters*. Routledge 1981 o.p. Authoritative translation of Zhuangzi (Chuang Tzu).

Kitagawa, Joseph M. *The Religious Traditions of Asia*. Macmillan 1989 $12.95. ISBN 0-02-897211-2. Articles excerpted from the *Encyclopedia of Religion*; Part 3 covers religions in China, Japan, and Korea.

Kitagawa, Joseph M., and Mark D. Cummings, eds. *Buddhism and Asian History*. Macmillan 1989 $12.95. ISBN 0-02-897212-0. Excellent reference work on Buddhism, consisting of articles taken from the *Encyclopedia of Religion* on the "Foundations of the Tradition"; Buddhism in Southeast Asia, central Asia, China, Korea, Japan, Tibet, and Mongolia; the major Buddhist schools within the Theravada, Mahayana, and Vajrana traditions; Buddhist practices, art, and popular Buddhism; and such major concepts as *nirvana* and the *bodhisattva*.

Koller, John M., and Patricia Koller. *A Sourcebook in Asian Philosophy*. Macmillan 1991. ISBN 0-02-365811-8. Collection of English translations of basic texts by experienced teachers of introductory courses in Asian philosophy, including introductory materials and selections from Buddhist and Chinese texts.

Thompson, Laurence. *Chinese Religions in Western Languages*. U. of Ariz. Pr. 1985 o.p. Very useful bibliography.

———. *The Chinese Way in Religion*. Wadsworth Pub. 1973. ISBN 0-8221-0109-2. Interesting and worthwhile compilation of primary and secondary source readings with excellent contextual discussions. In contrast with the Chan and De Bary sourcebooks, this work includes important materials on popular tradition. Companion volume to *Chinese Religion in Western Languages* (above).

Yanchi, Liu. *The Essential Book of Traditional Chinese Medicine*. 2 vols. Trans. by Fang Tingyu and Chen Laidi. Col. U. Pr. 1988 $107.00. ISBN 0-231-06518-3. Vol. 1 *Theory*; Vol. 2 *Clinical Practice*. Readable basic books on Chinese medicine based on restoring the harmony of yin and yang, wind, water, fire, and earth.

Yu, David C. *Guide to Chinese Religion*. Macmillan 1985 $55.00. ISBN 0-8161-7902-6. Somewhat eccentric in its organization and annotations, but covers many important, and relatively ignored, studies found in specialized journals. Complements Fu and Chan's *Guide to Chinese Philosophy*.

GENERAL WORKS

Allinson, Robert E., ed. *Understanding the Chinese Mind: The Philosophical Roots*. OUP 1989 $29.95. ISBN 0-685-47313-9. Nine helpful essays on various aspects of Chinese thought.

Ames, Roger T., ed. *Nature in Asian Traditions of Thought: Essays in Environmental Philosophy*. State U. NY Pr. 1989 $39.50. ISBN 0-88706-951-7. Collection of accessible essays by foremost scholars of Asian philosophy on the issue of how Asian thought views the environment.

Christie, Anthony. *Chinese Mythology*. P. Bedrick Bks. 1985 o.p. Fascinating nonscholarly discussion of both classical and popular mythology.

Creel, Herrlee G. *Chinese Thought from Confucius to Mao Tse-tung*. U. Ch. Pr. 1971 $10.95. ISBN 0-226-12030-9. Readable and generally reliable popular discussion that reflects Creel's special strengths in the ancient period.

de Bary, William Theodore. *East Asian Civilizations: A Dialogue in Five Stages*. HUP 1988 $9.95. ISBN 0-674-22406-X. Interpretation by an eminent scholar of East Asian— particularly Chinese—religion and philosophy, with chapters entitled "The Classical Legacy" of ancient China, "The Buddhist Age," The Neo-Confucian Stage," "East Asia's Modern Transformation," "The Post-Confucian Era," and "East Asia and the West: Catching Up with Each Other."

Feibleman, James K. *Understanding Oriental Philosophy*. NAL-Dutton 1984 $9.95. ISBN 0-452-00710-0. Competent introductory discussion that places Eastern thought in relation to Western philosophical issues.

Forman, Robert K. C., ed. *Religions of Asia*. St. Martin 1993 $27.60. ISBN 0-312-05753-9. Up-to-date and academically solid presentation of Asian religions, with Chinese religions presented, as well as the Communist challenge.

Hackett, Stuart C. *Oriental Philosophy: A Westerner's Guide to Eastern Thought*. Bks. Demand repr. of 1979 ed. $65.30. ISBN 0-8357-4748-4. Concise introduction to the philosophical implications of Eastern thought.

Hinnells, John R., ed. *A Handbook of Living Religions*. Viking Penguin 1984 o.p. The chapter on "Chinese Religions" by Michael Saso is a good general introduction to the overall tradition.

Jochim, Christian. *Chinese Religions*. P-H 1986 o.p. Thematic introduction to Chinese religious traditions as related to a broad cultural framework. Synthetically draws on recent specialized scholarship.

Koller, John M. *Oriental Philosophies*. Macmillan 1985. ISBN 0-02-365810-X. Good introductory analysis from a comparative philosophical point of view.

Laufer, Berthold. *Jade: Its History and Symbolism in China*. Dover 1989 o.p. Fascinating cultural history of China tracing the uses and symbolism of jade.

Morgan, Kenneth W. *Reaching for the Moon: On Asian Religious Paths*. Anima Pubns. 1990 $18.95. ISBN 0-89012-059-5. A scholar of religious studies reflects on the Western attempt to understand Eastern religiosity.

Needham, Joseph. *Science and Civilisation in China*. 6 vols. Cambridge U. Pr. 1956-84 $89.95–$185.00. ISBNs 0-521-05799-X–0-521-25076-5. A modern classic that traces the history of Chinese science in its close relationship to religious and philosophical thought. Especially provocative and controversial with respect to its discussions of Taoism. Technical and scholarly, though written with graceful style and telling insight.

Overmyer, Daniel L. *The Religions of China*. HarpC 1986 o.p. Brief, and sometimes overly terse, synthetic history that is noteworthy for its integrated discussion of popular religious currents. Digests the best of current specialized research.

Smart, Ninian. *Religions of Asia*. P-H 1993. ISBN 0-13-772427-6. Presents Asian religions in terms of doctrinal, mythical, institutional, ritual, ethical, experiential, and material dimensions; discusses responses of Asian religions to the West and modernization, Asian religions in the global community, and Confucianism, Daoism (Taoism), and New Chinese State Ideology.

Stein, Rolf A. *The World in Miniature: Container Gardens and Dwellings in Far Eastern Religious Thought*. Trans. by Phyllis Brooks. Stanford U. Pr. 1990 $39.50. ISBN 0-8047-1674-9. Analysis and elucidation of the cosmology that underlies the miniature gardens of China, Japan, and Vietnam; the cosmology underlying the architecture of homes in China, Tibet, and north and northeast Asia; and the concept of mountains (Sumeru and K'un-lun) as axes of communication between heaven and earth.

Thompson, Laurence G. *Chinese Religion: An Introduction*. Wadsworth Pub. 1979 o.p. Probably the best general introductory text specifically devoted to Chinese religion. Thematically organized and based on available scholarship. Effectively integrates elite and popular traditions within the total Chinese cultural milieu.

Waldron, Arthur. *The Great Wall of China: From History to Myth*. Cambridge U. Pr. 1990 $39.50. ISBN 0-521-36518-X. Study of the Great Wall demonstrating that it was built during the Ming dynasty (1363–1644 C.E.) and dispelling many twentieth-century myths about the Wall.

Weidner, Marsha, ed. *Flowering in the Shadows: Women in the History of Chinese and Japanese Painting*. UH Pr. 1990 $35.00. ISBN 0-8248-1149-6. Ten essays that break new ground on the role of Chinese and Japanese women as painters, calligraphers, collectors, and patrons.

Yang, C. K. *Religion in Chinese Society*. U. CA Pr. 1961 o.p. Neo-Weberian sociological discussion that is important for its revisionist demonstration of the religious nature of Confucianism and the general Chinese tradition.

ANCIENT TRADITION AND THE CLASSICS

The ancient religious tradition primarily refers to the various beliefs and practices associated with the development of a coherent Chinese civilization during the first millennium B.C.E. It is in this period that ancestral ritual, along with its related ideas of the afterlife and divination practices of communication with the dead and other spirits, takes shape as a fundamental expression of Chinese tradition. Also evident in the earliest periods are the characteristic Chinese understanding of the bureaucratic ordering of life on earth and in the heavens and the basic emphasis on the king or emperor's interrelated political and religious responsibilities for ensuring the harmonious relation between the human and spirit realms.

It is, in fact, the so-called Classics—those semisacred scriptures that primarily included the *Book of History, Book of Songs, Spring and Autumn Annals, Book of Rites,* and the *Book of Changes*—that record the righteous ways of past sage kings and constitute a kind of permanent guide to civic life (especially as it came to be interpreted by the Confucian tradition). The Classics, therefore, represent an attempt to determine and inculcate a standardized understanding of the meaning of human existence and can be said to be concerned with three basic principles: (1) the importance of a common ritualized pattern of life, (2) the significance of the political-theological theory of the "mandate of Heaven," which ensured the divine legitimacy of a ruling house (and in the early Zhou [Chou] period probably involved quasimonotheistic belief in an all powerful sky deity known as Tian [T'ien] or Shang Di [Shang Ti]), and (3) the dynamic interrelatedness of all aspects of space and time as expressed by the key ideas of Dao (Tao) as the ultimate principle and of *yin* and *yang* as the complementary opposites of existence.

Eliade, Mircea. *From Gautama Buddha to the Triumph of Christianity*. Volume 2 in *A History of Religious Ideas*. Trans. by William R. Trask. U. Ch. Pr. 1982 o.p. See particularly the chapter "The Religions of Ancient China." Compact general discussion of the historical development of ancient Chinese religion from the standpoint of Eliade's distinctive comparative concern for the paradigmatic nature of myth, ritual, and symbol. Sometimes too reliant on the speculative scholarship of C. Hentze and Marcel Granet.

Field, Stephen, trans. *Tian Wen: A Chinese Book of Origins*. New Dir. Pr. 1986 $8.95. ISBN 0-8112-1011-1. Important, although enigmatic and terse, collection of ancient mythic fragments in interrogatory form. Skillfully translated and supplemented with notes sensitive to the mythological and ritual background.

Jing-Nuan, Wu. *Yi Jing*. UH Pr. 1991 $30.00. ISBN 0-8248-1362-6. Landmark translation of the ancient book of divination *Yi Jing* (*I Ching*), based on inscriptions on oracle bones discovered in China at the turn of the century and examining the Chinese characters as they were written approximately 3,000 years ago.

Loewe, Michael. *Chinese Ideas of Life and Death*. Allen & Unwin 1982 o.p.

Munro, Donald J. *The Concept of Man in Early China*. Stanford U. Pr. 1969 $32.50. ISBN 0-8047-0682-4. Technically proficient and deftly written analysis of early Confucian and Taoist thought that is notable for its reference to comparable Western ideas.

Rubin, Vitaly A. *Individual and State in Ancient China*. Bks. Demand repr. of 1976 ed. $46.60. ISBN 0-8357-7779-0. Concise and readable account of Confucius, Zhuangzi (Chuang Tzu), Mo-tzu, and Shang Yang as related to political philosophy by an accomplished Russian scholar.

Schwartz, Benjamin I. *The World of Thought in Ancient China*. HUP 1985 $32.50. ISBN 0-674-96190-0. Impressive, and elegantly written, recent synthesis by one of the most respected intellectual historians of China. Incorporates the best of contemporary sinological scholarship but tends to neglect perspectives coming from the comparative history of religions.

Van Over, Raymond, ed. *I Ching*. Viking Penguin o.p. Condensed edition of the Legge translation of the Yi Jing (I Ching), including a discussion of the Yi Jing's history and philosophy and of its popularity in the West.

Waley, Arthur. *Three Ways of Thought in Ancient China*. Stanford U. Pr. 1939 $10.95. ISBN 0-8067-1169-0. Felicitous translations of, and brief commentary on, Mencius, Zhuangzi (Chuang Tzu), and Legalist (or "Realist" as Waley prefers) texts.

———, trans. *The Nine Songs: A Study of Shamanism in Ancient China*. City Lights 1973 o.p. Important early observations on ecstatic practices in the ancient southern state of Ch'u.

Wilhelm, Richard, and C. F. Baynes, trans. *The I Ching or Book of Changes*. Princeton U. Pr. 1967 $18.50. ISBN 0-691-09750-X. Long considered the most insightful translation, with a foreword by C. G. Jung.

CONFUCIUS AND CONFUCIANISM

Confucius (traditional dates, 551–479? B.C.) was born during the Zhou (Chou) period, when the feudal order was disintegrating. It was Confucius's genius as China's "first teacher" and greatest sage to establish a method for bringing harmony and stability back into political and personal life. He stressed, therefore, an education in the ritual principles (*li*) and moral principles (especially *ren* [*jen*], or "benevolence") as codified in the ancient Classics. Through the propriety of ritual and the progressive cultivation of morality within the family and state, all persons could achieve the nobility of a virtuous (*te*) life.

Although Confucius himself was not successful in impressing his ideas on the ruling powers of his day, his later disciples—especially the "second sage" known as Mencius (who emphasized the original goodness of human nature) and others like the tough-minded Xunzi (H'sun Tzu)—went on to develop and apply his thought in ways that ultimately would influence all of Chinese tradition. The triumph of the tradition, in fact, came about initially during the early Han dynasty (first two centuries B.C.E.), when Confucianism was established as official state doctrine.

Neo-Confucianism is an important philosophical tradition dating from the eleventh and twelfth centuries C.E. that demonstrates the influence of Daoist (Taoist) and Buddhist ideas. The leading Neo-Confucian thinkers were Zhu Xi (Chu Hsi, 1130–1200) and Wang Yangming (Wang Shouren, 1472–1529). Zhu Xi was concerned with *qi*, vital or physical force, and *li*, law or rational principle. This rational principle in its operation he called Tai Ji (T'ai Chi), or Great Ultimate. The Tai Ji impels the vital force *qi* to movement, which produces the two polar energies *yang* (a rapidly vibrating energy) and *yin* (a slowly vibrating energy). The interaction of *yang* and *yin* produces the five elements that give rise to the manifested universe: water, fire, wood, metal, and earth. Every manifested thing is ultimately a product of the ordering rational principle (*li*), or the Tai Ji. Zhu Xi practiced meditation in order to discover the unity of all beings. Wang Yangming taught that the mind distorts all perceptions of reality, that the mind is like a clouded or dirty mirror and must be polished through the practice of meditation to eliminate the selfish desires that inhibit the direct perception of reality.

Carrithers, Michael, and others. *Founders of Faith*. OUP 1989 $10.95. ISBN 0-19-283066-X. Good study of four important religious founders, with Raymond Dawson writing on Confucius.

Chan, Wing-tsit. *Chu Hsi: New Studies*. UH Pr. 1989 $40.00. ISBN 0-8248-1201-8. Important new information presented by an eminent Chinese scholar about the Neo-Confucian Zhu Xi (Chu Hsi) that includes material on Zhu Xi's life, his thought, and his students and associates.

————, ed. *Chu Hsi and Neo-Confucianism*. UH Pr. 1986 $30.00. ISBN 0-8248-0961-0. "This book will long stand as a monument to classical statements of most of the major senior authorities on Zhu Xi (Chu Hsi) and mainstream Confucianism" (*Philosophy East & West*).

de Bary, William Theodore, and John W. Chaffee, eds. *Neo-Confucian Education: The Formative Stage*. U. CA Pr. 1989 $65.00. ISBN 0-520-06393-7. Seventeen articles on the development of education in Sung dynasty Neo-Confucianism, with special attention to the role of Zhu Xi (Chu Hsi); one paper treats Zhu Xi's denial of education to women.

Graham, A. C. *Chuang Tzu, The Seven Inner Chapters*. Routledge 1981 o.p. Authoritative translation of Chuang Tzu.

Kieckhefer, Richard, and George D. Bond, eds. *Sainthood: Its Manifestations in the World Religions*. U. CA. Pr. 1988 $42.50. ISBN 0-520-05154-8. Collection of excellent essays on sainthood in world religions, with R. Taylor writing on Confucianism.

Sharma, Arvind, ed. *Women in World Religions*. State U. NY Pr. 1987 $14.95. ISBN 0-88706-374-8. Articles that are sound in scholarship and accessible to the general reader; Theresa Kelleher contributes the chapter on women in Confucianism.

Spiro, Audrey. *Contemplating the Ancients: Aesthetic and Social Issues in Early Chinese Portraiture*. U. CA Pr. 1990 $35.00. ISBN 0-520-06567-0. Study of fourth- and fifth-century Chinese portraiture depicting the Seven Worthies of the Bamboo Grove as exemplars of the "cultivated gentleman."

Taylor, Rodney L. *The Cultivation of Sagehood as a Religious Goal in Neo-Confucianism*. Scholars Pr. GA 1978 o.p.

————. *The Way of Heaven: An Introduction to the Confucian Religious Life*. E. J. Brill 1986 $41.25. ISBN 90-04-07423-6. This and the title above are important for their innovative delineation of the religious nature of Confucianism as a system of "self-transformation."

Tillman, Hoyt Cleveland. *Confucian Discourse and Chu Hsi's Ascendancy*. UH Pr. 1992 $38.00. ISBN 0-8248-1416-9. Integrated intellectual history of the development of Neo-Confucianism that for the first time places Zhu Xi (Chu Hsi) within the context of his contemporaries.

Tu, Wei-ming. *Confucian Thought: Selfhood as Creative Transformation*. State U. NY Pr. 1985 $49.50. ISBN 0-88706-005-6

————. *Humanity and Self-Cultivation: Essays in Confucian Thought*. Jain Pub. Co. 1980 $30.00. ISBN 0-89581-600-8. Tu is perhaps the most knowledgeable and sensitive contemporary interpreter of the Confucian tradition. Many of these collected essays here and the book above represent minor classics in the modern reassessment of Confucianism. Balanced appreciation of the philosophical, ethical, and religious implications.

Waley, Arthur D. *The Analects of Confucius*. Random 1989 $9.00. ISBN 0-679-72296-3. Very readable, and generally trustworthy, translations of Confucius—although Waley is sometimes too confident in his attempt to determine the "original" *Analects*. Also to be recommended for its introductory discussion of the cultural and intellectual context.

EARLY DAOIST (TAOIST) CLASSICS AND THE DAOIST (TAOIST) RELIGION

The ultimate roots of the Daoist (Taoist) tradition go back to the turmoil of the late Zhou (Chou) period (sixth through third centuries B.C.E.) and are especially associated with the semihistorical figure known as Laozi (Lao Tzu), or the "Old Master." At more or less the same time, another shadowy sage known as Zhuangzi (Chuang Tzu) also was teaching, like Laozi, an enigmatic philosophy that challenged the ritualized public morality of the Confucians. Early so-called classical or philosophical Daoism is, then, not so much a distinct school of thought but rather a convenient label for the basically similar mystical visions found in the ancient texts attributed to Laozi (the *Dao de jing* [*Tao Te Ching*], or the Classic of the Tao and its Power) and Zhuangzi (the composite text known as the *Zhuangzi*). These texts generally emphasized the need for a mystical return to a union with the unsullied dynamic principle of natural life known as the Dao (*Tao*). Rejecting the ritual propriety and civic righteousness of Confucianism, they recommended the method of *Wu-wei* ("non[competitive] action," or "nonstriving") as the way to reactivate the inner power *de (te)* and spontaneous freedom of the Dao.

In the early Han period (second and first centuries B.C.E.) the thought of Laozi and Zhuangzi was incorporated loosely into popular movements that stressed the salvational goal of physical immortality as associated with the figure of the *xian (hsien)* (Daoist immortal or saint.) It was, therefore, the popular cult of immortality, and various messianic movements during the breakup of the later Han dynasty (especially the movements identified with the new revelations of the semilegendary Zhang Ling—the first "heavenly master" of religious Daoism), that gave rise to the organized Daoist religion. The Six Dynasties Period of political disunity (second through sixth centuries C.E.) saw the greatest efflorescence of sectarian forms of religious Daoism and produced various complex ecclesiastical, theological, liturgical, and scriptural forms. What scholarship designates Religious Daoism or Popular Daoism to distinguish it from the earlier philosophical texts attributed to Laozi and Zhuangzi retained some of the ancient mystical and individualistic spirit of Laozi and Zhuangzi. Laozi, in fact, became a kind of salvational deity associated with the highest trinity of Daoist gods. But more fundamentally, religious Daoism functioned as a popular vehicle for ritually ensuring the periodic renewal of corporate life, especially at the village level.

Benn, Charles D. *The Cavern-Mystery Transmission: A Taoist Ordination Rite of A.D. 711.* UH Pr. 1991 $25.00. ISBN 0-8248-1359-6. Rare account of the Daoist (Taoist) ordination rite for two Tang princesses, describing the mechanism by which the Daoist priesthood ordered and perpetuated itself.

Blofeld, John. *Taoism: The Road to Immortality.* Shambhala 1978 o.p. Knowledgeable and fascinating, though rather uncritical, popular discussion of religious Taoism. As a self-styled insider, Blofeld reinforces the hermetic "magic garden" image of religious Taoism.

Chang, Chung-yuan. *Creativity and Taoism.* HarpC 1982 $11.00. ISBN 0-06-131968-6. Informed and graceful essays on the various cultural and artistic embodiments of the Taoist tradition. Written for a general audience.

Cleary, Thomas, ed. and trans. *Immortal Sisters: Secrets of Taoist Women.* Shambhala Pubns. 1989 $8.95. ISBN 0-87773-481-X. Translation and explanation in popular format, of mysterious practices of Daoist women to achieve immortality representing a correction to androcentric bias of scholarship on popular Daoism.

_____, trans. *The Inner Teachings of Taoism.* Shambhala Pubns. 1986 $14.00. ISBN 0-87773-363-5. Knowledgeable translation of, and brief contextual commentary on, some of the esoteric texts of religious Daoism (Taoism). Popular format.

Feng, Gia-Fu, and Jane English, trans. *Lao Tzu: Tao Te Ching.* Random 1989 $7.00. ISBN 0-679-72434-6. Fluent new translation that is noteworthy for its use of images that complement the text. Popular format.

Girardot, N. J. *Myth and Meaning in Early Taoism.* U. CA Pr. 1983 $55.00. ISBN 0-520-04330-8. Comparative analysis of the mythological and symbolic context for understanding the early Daoist (Taoist) texts.

Graham, A. C., ed. and trans. *Chuang Tzu: The Inner Chapters.* Allen & Unwin 1987 o.p. Innovative scholarly translation and sinuously intelligent commentary by one of the most gifted of contemporary scholars. Along with Watson's rendition (see below), the best available modern translation.

Henricks, Robert G., trans. *Lao-Tzu: Te-Tao Ching.* Ballantine 1989 $19.95. ISBN 0-345-37099-6. Excellent translation and treatment of the Dao De Jing (Tao Te Ching) for beginners and specialists based on a 168 B.C.E. text discovered in 1973 in the tomb of a Chinese nobleman.

Hoff, Benjamin. *The Tao of Pooh.* Routledge Chapman & Hall 1987 $1.50. ISBN 0-416-46960-4. Pooh bear as Laozi (Lao Tzu)! Introduction to Daoist (Taoist) philosophy via the medium of the popular children's story. Often effective and entertaining, but in places overly precious and misleading.

———. *The Te of Piglet.* NAL-Dutton 1992 $16.00. ISBN 0-525-93496-0. Explores the Daoist concept of De (Te), or "virtue," as embodied in Piglet, a Very Small Animal who proved to be so Useful after all.

I-ming, Liu. *Awakening to the Tao.* Ed. by Thomas Cleary. Shambhala Pubns. 1988 $9.95. ISBN 0-87773-447-X. Translation of the teachings of a Daoist sage.

Kohn, Livia, ed. *Taoist Meditation and Longevity Techniques.* Ctr. Chinese Studies 1989 $16.50. ISBN 0-89264-85-5. Collection of 11 articles by Japanese and European scholars on the Daoist techniques to achieve immortality or longevity.

LaFargue, Michael. *The Tao of the Tao Te Ching: A Translation and Commentary.* State U. NY Pr. 1992 $12.95. ISBN 0-7914-0986-4. Translation of the Dao De Jing (Tao Te Ching), with explanation showing its relevance to contemporary situations, followed by an explanation of the approach to translating this text, its sociohistorical origins, and a detailed topical glossary.

Lau, D. C., trans. *Lao Tzu: Tao Te Ching.* Coronet Bks. 1982 $39.50. ISBN 962-201-252-3. Excellent modern scholarly translation that stresses the philosophical-political implications of the text more than the religious-mystical aspects.

Little, Stephen. *Realm of the Immortals: Daoism in the Arts of China.* Cleveland Mus. Art 1988 $14.95. ISBN 0-910386-92-7. The catalog of a 1988 exhibit of Daoist art that serves as an excellent general introduction to a very difficult topic.

Maspero, Henri. *Taoism and Chinese Religion.* Trans. by Frank A. Kierman, Jr. U. of Mass. Pr. 1981 o.p. Important collection of scholarly essays by the eminent French sinologue. Includes Maspero's groundbreaking early work on religious Daoism (Taoism).

Po-tuan, Chang. *Understanding Reality: A Taoist Alchemical Classic.* Trans. by Thomas Cleary. UH Pr. 1987 $25.00. ISBN 0-8248-1139-9. "A welcome contribution to our sparse repertoire of translations of Daoist primary works" (*Religious Studies Review*).

Saso, Michael R. *Blue Dragon White Tiger: Taoist Rites of Passage.* UH Pr. 1990 $16.00. ISBN 0-8248-1361-8. This view of Chinese religion from the Daoist (Taoist) perspective is based on the Daoist hypothesis that all Chinese rites of passage and festivals are structured by Yin-Yang Five-Element cosmology.

———. *Taoism and the Rite of Cosmic Renewal.* Wash. St. U. Pr. 1990 $20.00. ISBN 0-87422-054-8. Short ethnographic discussion of the living tradition of liturgical Daoism (Taoism) on Taiwan by one of the leading scholars of religious Taoism. Semipopular in format, but sometimes overly technical and confusing.

Sharma, Arvind, ed. *Women in World Religions.* State U. NY Pr. 1987 $14.95. ISBN 0-88706-374-8. Articles that are sound in scholarship and accessible to the general reader; Barbara Reed contributes the chapter on women in Daoism.

Waley, Arthur. *The Way and Its Power.* Grove-Atltic. 1988 $10.95. ISBN 0-8021-5085-3. Valuable translation, interpretive commentary, and introduction that emphasize the mystical (or early "Daoist [Taoist] yoga") implications of the text.

Ware, James R., trans. *Chinese Alchemy, Medicine, and Religion in the China of A.D. 320: The Nei P'ien of Ko Hung (Pao-p'u tzu)*. Dover 1981 o.p. Complete accurate translation of an important Daoist (Taoist) text that stresses the esoteric methods of alchemical "immortality." The translation of individual terms are sometimes idiosyncratic and misleading.

Watson, Burton, trans. *Chuang Tzu: Basic Writings*. Col. U. Pr. 1964 $12.00. ISBN 0-231-08606-7. Along with Graham's version (see above), the best available modern translation.

Wilhelm, Richard, trans. *Lao Tzu: Tao Te Ching*. Methuen 1985 o.p. Good scholarly translation, helpful notes, general introduction, and contextual essay that stress the metaphysical and religious implications of the text.

Wu, Kuang-Ming. *Chuang Tzu: World Philospher at Play*. Scholars Pr. GA 1989 $22.95. ISBN 0-89130-537-8. Engaging phenomenological analysis of the interrelated philosophical, religious, and social meaning of Chuang Tzu.

CHINESE BUDDHISM

Buddhism entered China during the second century C.E. and during the Six Dynasties period (second through sixth centuries C.E.) became fully integrated within Chinese tradition (e.g., the idea of karma or moral retribution became an accepted part of popular Chinese tradition at this time). The development of Buddhism during this period primarily concerns the intellectual and practical adaptation of Buddhism to its Chinese environment, its struggle with the indigenous traditions of Daoism and Confucianism, and the emergence of various synthetic scriptural schools (such as Tiantai [T'ien-T'ai] and Hua Yen Buddhism) and the more popular, influential, and uniquely Chinese forms known as Pure Land and Chan (Zen) Buddhism.

In general, it was the Mahayana form of Buddhism that entered China and such distinctive Mahayana doctrines as the role of the bodhisattva and the "emptiness" of existence are especially prominent in the Pure Land and Chan traditions.

Pure Land was especially the religion of the masses and promised salvation in a heavenly paradise called the Pure Land through faith and devotion to the celestial Buddha Emiduo (A-mi-t'o-fo, or Amitabha in Sanskrit, or Amida in Japanese). Chan Buddhism, showing the influence of Daoism, stressed the discipline of meditation as the basic way to experience the Buddha-nature in the ever-present moment of everyday life.

Chang, Chung-yuan, ed. *The Original Teachings of Ch'an Buddhism*. Grove Pr. 1982 o.p. Helpful contextual discussion and good translations of important, yet little known, works associated with the Chinese origins of Ch'an (or Zen) Buddhism.

Ch'en, Kenneth. *Buddhism in China*. Princeton U. Pr. 1974 o.p. Scholarly, though not overly technical, discussion of Chinese Buddhism by one of the leading modern experts. Most reliable general historical survey.

Cleary, Thomas, trans. *Entry into the Realm of Reality: The Text*. Shambhala Pubns. 1989 o.p. English translation in popular format of the Chinese translation of the Sanskrit Mahayana text *Gandavyuha*, which is the final chapter in the larger *Avatamsaka Sutra*.

Falk, Nancy Auer, and Rita M. Gross. *Unspoken Worlds: Women's Religious Lives*. Wadsworth Pub. 1989. ISBN 0-534-09852-5. Groundbreaking collection on religion in women's lives; Diana Paul writes on Empress Wu, the only woman emperor of China, and her relation to Buddhism.

Gregory, Peter N. *Traditions of Meditation in Chinese Buddhism*. UH Pr. 1987 $16.00. ISBN 0-8248-1088-0. "An important contribution to the literature on Buddhist meditation" (*Journal of Asian Studies*).

Haddad, Yvonne Yazbeck, and Ellison Banks Findly, eds. *Women, Religion and Social Change*. State U. NY Pr. 1985 $59.50. ISBN 0-88706-068-4. Fine scholarship on women and religion, with Nancy Schuster writing on women in early Chinese Buddhism.

Howard, Angela Falco. *The Imagery of the Cosmological Buddha*. E. J. Brill 1986 $68.50. ISBN 90-04-07612-3. Iconographical and textual study of depictions of the "cosmological Buddha" in East Asian Mahayana Buddhism.

King, Sallie B. *Buddha Nature*. State U. NY Pr. 1991 $49.50. ISBN 0-7914-0427-7. Analysis of the *Buddha Nature Treatise* ascribed to the Indian Buddhist philosopher Vasubandhu but now existing only in its sixth-century Chinese translation, providing a good introduction to the Buddha-nature/Yogacara tradition in India and China.

Kinsley, David. *The Goddesses' Mirror: Visions of the Divine from East and West*. State U. NY Pr. 1988 $38.50. ISBN 0-88706-835-9. Scholarly and accessible accounts of great goddesses, treating the female bodhisattva Guan Yin (Kuan Yin).

Kitagawa, Joseph M., and Mark D. Cummings, eds. *Buddhism and Asian History*. Macmillan 1989 $12.95. ISBN 0-02-897212-0. Excellent reference work on Buddhism consisting of articles taken from the *Encyclopedia of Religion*.

Levering, Miriam. *Rethinking Scripture: Essays from a Comparative Perspective*. State U. NY Pr. 1989 $59.50. ISBN 0-88706-613-5. Excellent comparative study of scriptures; Levering writes the chapter on Chinese Buddhism.

McRae, John R. *The Northern School of and the Formation of Early Ch'an Buddhism*. UH Pr. 1987 $40.00. ISBN 0-8248-1056-2. Expert history of the Northern School of Chan Buddhism.

Olson, Carl, ed. *The Book of the Goddess Past and Present*. Crossroad NY 1986 $12.95. ISBN 0-8245-0689-8. Solid and accessible articles by experts in their respective fields, including a chapter on Guan Yin.

Robinson, Richard H., and Willard L. Johnson. *The Buddhist Religion: A Historical Introduction*. Wadsworth Pub. 1982. ISBN 0-534-01027-X. Informative introductory text to overall tradition with good concise chapters on East Asian Buddhism. Digests best of modern technical scholarship.

Sullivan, Lawrence, ed. *Healing and Restoring: Health and Medicine in the World's Religious Traditions*. Macmillan 1989 $35.00. ISBN 0-02-923791-2. Interdisciplinary and multicultural study of the topic of healing and health in the world's religions; Joseph Kitagawa and Raoul Birnbaum write on healing generally in Buddhism and specifically in China.

Swanson, Paul L. *Foundations of T'ien-T'ai Philosophy: The Flowering of the Two Truths Theory in Chinese Buddhism*. Jain Pub. Co. 1989 $60.00. ISBN 0-89581-918-X. Study of the thought of Chih-i, the founder of the T'ien-t'ai Buddhism.

Welch, Holmes. *The Practice of Chinese Buddhism 1900–1950*. HUP 1967 $15.95. ISBN 0-674-69701-4. Definitive descriptive presentation of modern Chinese Buddhist customs. Scholarly format.

Wright, Arthur F. *Studies in Chinese Buddhism*. Ed. by Robert M. Somers. Yale U. Pr. 1990 $25.00. ISBN 0-300-04717-7. Very accessible essays on Chinese Buddhism published by Wright from 1948 and 1957.

CHINESE POPULAR RELIGION

The term Chinese popular religion is used here to designate the animistic elements of the Chinese tradition. These include ancestor veneration, the practice of magic, divination, shamanism, use of charms and amulets, and belief in unseen spirits, gods, and ghosts. However, it is important to remember that what is designated here as the Chinese popular religion is not separate in the lives of the Chinese people from the other religions that have been treated above.

Ahern, Emily M. *Cult of the Dead in a Chinese Village*. Stanford U. Pr. 1973 $32.50. ISBN 0-8047-0835-5. Important interpretive study of modern ancestral practices from an anthropological perspective.

DeVos, George A., and Takao Sofue, eds. *Religion and the Family in East Asia*. U. CA Pr. 1986 $17.00. ISBN 0-520-05762-7. Enlightening essays on religion in the Asian family contexts, with topics ranging from ancestral veneration to shamanism.

Jordan, David K. *Gods, Ghosts and Ancestors: The Folk Religion of a Taiwanese Village*. U. CA Pr. 1972 o.p. Notable anthropological study of current practices on Taiwan.

Jordan, David K., and Daniel L. Overmyer. *The Flying Phoenix: Aspects of Chinese Sectarianism in Taiwan*. Princeton U. Pr. 1986 o.p. Effectively integrated scholarly study of the historical and ethnographic aspects of contemporary Taiwanese sects.

Meyer, Jeffrey F. *The Dragons of Tiananmen: Beijing as a Sacred City*. U. of SC Pr. 1986 $47.00. ISBN 0-691-07304-X. "Deciphers the city's code through the last half-millennium, while subtly discriminating between the perceptual frameworks of different classes of inhabitants" (Paul Wheatley).

Palmer, Martin, trans. *T'ung Shu*. Shambhala 1986 o.p. Intriguing discussion and partial translation of a typical folk almanac. Popular format that follows illustrative style of a traditional almanac.

Sangren, Steven. *History and Magical Power in a Chinese Community*. Stanford U. Pr. 1987 $42.50. ISBN 0-8047-1344-8. Fascinating anthropological study of religion in a Taiwanese community.

Teiser, Stephen F. *The Ghost Festival in Medieval China*. Princeton U. Pr. 1988 $42.50. ISBN 0-691-05525-4. Highly readable study of Chinese ideas of the afterlife, shamanism, and popular religiosity.

Wagner, Rudolf G. *Reenacting the Heavenly Vision: The Role of Religion in the Taiping Rebellion*. U. CA Pr. 1984 o.p. Short, lucid, scholarly analysis of the religious nature of the most important nineteenth-century revolutionary movement.

Watson, James L., and Evelyn S. Rawski, eds. *Death Ritual in Late Imperial and Modern China*. U. CA Pr. 1988 $47.50. ISBN 0-520-06081-4. Very valuable collection of essays on Chinese ancestor veneration in the past and present, with attention to the relation of Chinese ancestor veneration to the People's Republic of China's attempt to discontinue the practice.

Wolf, Arthur, ed. *Religion and Ritual in Chinese Society*. Stanford U. Pr. 1974 $47.50. ISBN 0-8047-0858-4. Excellent collection of anthropological articles on Chinese ritual and popular religion.

Yu, Anthony. *The Journey to the West*. U. Ch. Pr. 1984 $37.50. ISBN 0-226-97147-3. Elegant and authoritative complete translation of *Monkey*, the great folk classic that describes the fantastic travels of a motley group of Buddhist pilgrims searching for salvation.

FOREIGN INFLUENCES AND THE MODERN ERA

MARCO POLO (see Vol. 3) traveled to China in the thirteenth century, but the first extensive contacts that the Chinese had with Westerners were the result of Spanish and Portuguese explorations in the sixteenth century. Jesuits were able to attract Chinese converts to Christianity by adapting and blending into Chinese culture, but at the beginning of the eighteenth century the Jesuits were expelled from China. In the nineteenth century, China was faced with Western imperialistic incursions into Chinese territory, accompanied by Western modes of thought, technology, science, and culture. Christian missionaries from the United States and Great Britain were active in China during this time. A fusion of Christian and Daoist elements produced the revitalization movement known as the Tai Ping Rebellion, an armed revolution against the Manchu emperor from 1850 to 1864. The rebellion's prophet was Hong Xiuchuan (1814–1864), who claimed that he was Jesus' younger brother sent to destroy the evil influences of Confucianism and to establish God's kingdom on earth. This millennial condition would be the Tai Ping (Great Peace). Millions of people were killed before the rebellion finally was subdued.

Chinese imperial rule was replaced at the beginning of the twentieth century by a short-lived nationalist republic led by Jiang Jieshi (Chiang Kai-shek, 1887–1975). By 1949, the Communists had established the People's Republic of China, and Taiwan became home to the nationalists exiled from the mainland. MAO ZEDONG (Mao Tse-tung, 1893–1976) led the Chinese Communist government until his death. As a Communist state, the People's Republic of China treated religion as the "opiate of the people," which was to be eradicated. Aspects of Confucianism, Buddhism, Daoism, and of Chinese popular religion were labeled as feudal or superstitious. Particularly during the Cultural Revolution of 1966–69, Chinese Communists aggressively attempted to eliminate any presence of the old Chinese culture and outlook. In their place, Marxism became the vaunted ideology, the Chinese were expected to pursue the Marxist ultimate goal, Mao Zedong was the Marxist prophet to the Chinese people, and his "little red book" was their scripture. Greater openness to the West and greater leniency toward religious practice have characterized the People's Republic of China in the 1980s and early 1990s, but students' demands for greater democracy were quashed violently at Tiananmen Square in November 1989.

Bush, Richard C. *Religion in Communist China*. Abingdon 1970 o.p. Informed general appraisal of religion, both traditional and non-Chinese, during the Maoist period. Needs revision in light of the post-Maoist era.

Chan, Wing-tsit. *Religious Trends in Modern China*. Hippocrene Bks. 1970 repr. of 1953 ed. o.p. Interesting and still important discussion of the impact of Western ideas and modernization.

Cohen, Paul A. *China and Christianity*. HUP 1963 $35.00. ISBN 0-674-11701-8. Important for its descriptive analysis of the nineteenth-century antimissionary movements. Scholarly format.

Crouch, Archie R., Steven Agoratus, Arthur Emerson, and Debra E. Soled, eds. *Christianity in China: A Scholar's Guide to Resources in the Libraries and Archives in the United States*. M. E. Sharpe 1989 $135.00. ISBN 0-87332-419-6. Valuable resource recording the archival materials available in the United States on Christianity in China.

Fairbank, John K., ed. *The Missionary Enterprise in China and America*. HUP 1974 $28.00. ISBN 0-674-57655-1. Significant scholarly essays on various nineteenth- and early twentieth-century missionary topics.

Gernet, Jacques. *China and the Christian Impact*. Cambridge U. Pr. 1985 $69.95. ISBN 0-521-26681-5. Fascinating study in the clash of cultures.

Haddad, Yvonne Yazbeck, and Ellison Banks Findly, eds. *Women, Religion and Social Change*. State U. NY Pr. 1985 $59.50. ISBN 0-88706-068-4. Fine scholarship on women and religion; Michael E. Lestz writes on the Soony sisters and China's revolutions, 1911–1936.

Levenson, Joseph R. *Confucian China and Its Modern Fate*. U. CA Pr. 1968 $49.95. ISBN 0-520-00736-0. Minor scholarly classic by one of the great modern exponents of Chinese intellectual history.

Lifton, Robert J. *Revolutionary Immortality: Mao Tse-tung and the Chinese Revolution*. Peter Smith o.p. Fascinating psychological interpretation of the religious functionality of Maoism.

Metzger, Thomas A. *Escape from Predicament: Neo-Confucianism and China's Evolving Political Culture*. Col. U. Pr. 1986 $16.00. ISBN 0-231-03980-8. Controversial revisionist discussion of the role of neo-Confucianism in the modern period.

Ronan, Charles E., and Bonnie B. C. Oh, eds. *East Meets West: The Jesuits in China, 1582–1773*. Loyola 1988 $19.95. ISBN 0-8294-0572-0. Essays on the Jesuits in China that address the issue of enculturation.

Saso, Michael R., ed. and trans. *Buddhist Studies in the People's Republic of China*. UH Pr. 1993 $14.00. ISBN 0-8248-1464-9. Vignette of contemporary scholarship on

Buddhist studies taking place in the People's Republic of China today; four scholars discuss Chan (Zen), ethnic minorities and Buddhism, Zhuangzi (Chuang-tzu), and Buddhist-influenced art.

Watson, James L., and Evelyn S. Rawski, eds. *Death Ritual in Late Imperial and Modern China*. U. CA Pr. 1988 $47.50. ISBN 0-520-06081-4. Very valuable collection of essays on Chinese ancestor veneration in the past and present, with a couple of articles studying the relation of Chinese ancestor veneration to the People's Republic of China's attempt to discontinue the practice.

Weiming, Tu, Milan G. Hejtmanek, and Alan Wachman, eds. *The Confucian World Observed: A Contemporary Discussion of Confucian Humanism in East Asia*. UH Pr. 1992 $12.95. ISBN 0-8248-1435-5. Seeks to illuminate claims that Confucian ethics have provided the necessary background and a powerful motivation for the rise of the industrial Asia.

Wiest, Jean-Paul. *Maryknoll in China: A History 1918–1955*. M. E. Sharpe 1988 $35.00. ISBN 0-87332-418-8. Chronicle of the social impact of the Maryknoll mission in China.

Japanese and Korean Traditions

Japan and Korea, though each represents a distinctive tradition, may be linked because of certain shared linguistic similarities (i.e., common affinities with the Altaic language family) and because of their interrelated history of cultural borrowings from the more ancient Chinese legacy. In fact, many of the appropriations from China, particularly Confucian political and ethical thought and Buddhism, were initially transmitted to Japan through the medium of early Korean tradition. Given the impact of China on these traditions, it is especially important to examine the manner in which Chinese elements (e.g., the Chinese written script, Confucian political and social institutions, the *yin-yang* cosmological system, and various Buddhist sectarian traditions) were adapted and transformed by the unique cultural geniuses of Japan and Korea. Another critical consideration concerns the way indigenous pre-Chinese religious elements developed in the face of the foreign influx—that is, the continuation of ancient shamanistic practices of Korea, the emergence of Shinto in Japan, and, finally, the overall nature and significance of folk practices in both Korea and Japan.

In the modern period, the influence of Western tradition must be taken into account, especially in relation to the spectacular rise of "new religions" and the Westernization of philosophical, social, and political thought. Finally, it should be noted that Korean religious and intellectual tradition has still not been sufficiently studied.

REFERENCE WORKS AND ANTHOLOGIES

Adams, Charles J., ed. *A Reader's Guide to the Great Religions*. Free Pr. 1977 o.p. See especially Joseph M. Kitagawa's chapter, "The Religions of Japan." Excellent annotated compilation of scholarly books and articles.

Coward, Harold, Eva Dargyay, and Ronald Neufeldt, eds. *Readings in Eastern Religions*. Humanities 1988 $29.95. ISBN 0-88920-955-3. Fine collection of selections from original texts, which would benefit from more explanatory materials.

Earhart, H. Byron. *Religion in the Japanese Experience*. Wadsworth Pub. 1974. ISBN 0-8221-0104-1. Interesting popular collection of primary and secondary source readings that complements Earhart's *Japanese Religion* (see next section under General Works).

Grayson, James Huntley. *Korea: A Religious History*. OUP 1989 $74.00. ISBN 0-19-826186-1. Comprehensive history of religion in Korea.

Itasaka, Gen, and Maurits Dekker, eds. *Encyclopedia of Japan*. 9 vols. Kodansha 1983 o.p. Concise, authoritative, and up-to-date basic reference source for many topics related to both religion and philosophy.

Kitagawa, Joseph M. *The Religious Traditions of Asia*. Macmillan 1989 $12.95. ISBN 0-02-897211-2. Articles excerpted from the *Encyclopedia of Religion*; Part 3 on religions in China, Japan, and Korea.

Kitagawa, Joseph M., and Mark D. Cummings, eds. *Buddhism and Asian History*. Macmillan 1989 $12.95. ISBN 0-02-897212-0. Excellent reference work on Buddhism consisting of articles taken from the *Encyclopedia of Religion*.

Lancaster, Lewis R., ed. *The Korean Buddhist Canon*. U. CA Pr. 1980 $80.00. ISBN 0-520-03159-8. First Western presentation of the overall contents and distinctive features of the Buddhist patrology within Korean religious history.

Schwade, Arcadio. *Shinto-Bibliography in Western Languages*. E. J. Brill 1986 $33.25. ISBN 90-04-08173-9. Helpful, recent compilation that includes many obscure, yet valuable, scholarly publications.

Stein, Rolf A. *The World in Miniature: Container Gardens and Dwellings in Far Eastern Religious Thought*. Trans. by Phyllis Brooks. Stanford U. Pr. 1990 $39.50. ISBN 0-8047-1674-9. Analysis and elucidation of the cosmology that underlies the miniature gardens of China, Japan, and Vietnam; the cosmology underlying the architecture of homes in China, Tibet, and north and northeast Asia; and the concept of mountains (Sumeru and K'un-lun) as axes of communication between heaven and earth.

Tsunoda, Ryusaku, and others. *Sources of Japanese Tradition*. Col. U. Pr. 1964 $89.00. SBN 0-231-02254-9. Like De Bary's *Sources of Chinese Tradition* (see under East Asian Traditions, Chinese Traditions, Reference Works and Anthologies, in this chapter). This is an expertly produced anthology of representative primary texts accompanied by succinct introductory discussions.

Yu, Chai-Shin, ed. *Korean and Asian Religious Tradition*. Korean and Related Studies Pr. 1977 o.p. Contains articles on Korean shamanism and popular religion, Confucianism, Daoism, and Chan (Zen).

GENERAL WORKS

Ames, Roger T., ed. *Nature in Asian Traditions of Thought: Essays in Environmental Philosophy*. State U. NY Pr. 1989 $39.50. ISBN 0-88706-951-7. Collection of accessible essays by foremost scholars of Asian philosophy on the issue of how Asian thought views the environment.

Anesaki, Masaharu. *History of Japanese Religion*. C. E. Tuttle 1963 repr. of 1930 ed. o.p. General historical overview by one of Japan's leading scholars. Still an important source, but somewhat stilted in style and dated in content and method.

Benedict, Ruth. *Chrysanthemum and the Sword*. HM 1989 $10.95. ISBN 0-395-50075-3. Fascinating and controversial World War II analysis of Japanese tradition by a leading cultural anthropologist that includes many topics directly bearing on religious issues.

Cleary, Thomas, trans. *Shobogenzo: Zen Essays by Dogen*. UH Pr. 1992 $12.95. ISBN 0-8248-1401-0. Translation of a Zen classic for the general audience.

Davis, Winston. *Japanese Religion and Society: Paradigms of Structure and Change*. State U. NY Pr. 1992 $18.95. ISBN 0-7914-0840-X. Sociological analysis of religion in Japan.

Earhart, H. Byron. *Japanese Religion: Unity and Diversity*. Wadsworth Pub. 1982. ISBN 0-534-01028-8. "Suitable for an undergraduate survey course or for an introductory approach to religious thought and practice. Excellent footnotes; annotated bibliography; and index. The table of religious history, introduction, and presentation of themes prepare the reader for the history and themes of three major periods" (*Choice*).

———. *Religions of Japan*. Harper SF 1984 $10.00. ISBN 0-06-062112-5. Balanced introductory appraisals of religion that draw on the best of specialized scholarship. Popular textbook format.

Ellwood, Robert S., Jr. *An Invitation to Japanese Civilization*. Wadsworth Pub. 1980 o.p. Well-written general introduction that brings out the diffuse interrelation of culture, religion, and philosophy in Japan.

Forman, Robert K. C., ed. *Religions of Asia*. St. Martin 1993 $26.70. ISBN 0-312-05753-9. Up-to-date and academically solid presentation of Asian religions, with a presentation of Japanese religions from prehistory to the contemporary period.

Hinnells, John R., ed. *A Handbook of Living Religions*. Viking Penguin 1984 o.p. The chapter devoted to Japanese religions provides an excellent, concise overview of the tradition.

ll-ch'ol Sin, and others. *Main Currents of Korean Thought*. Pace Intl. Res. 1983 $25.00. ISBN 0-89209-020-0. Collection of diverse articles on philosophical and religious topics by leading authorities.

Kitagawa, Joseph M. *Religion in Japanese History*. Col. U. Pr. 1966 $52.50. ISBN 0-231-02834-2. Scholarly study that stresses the sociological significance of the history of Japanese religions. Especially strong on Buddhist tradition.

Morgan, Kenneth W. *Reaching for the Moon: On Asian Religious Paths*. Anima 1990 $18.95. ISBN 0-89012-059-5. A scholar of religious studies reflects on the Western attempt to understand Eastern religiosity.

Piggot, Juliet. *Japanese Mythology*. P. Bedrick Bks. 1983 $24.95. ISBN 0-911745-09-2. Good semipopular presentation of both elite and popular mythology.

Reader, Ian. *Religion in Contemporary Japan*. UH Pr. 1991 $16.00. ISBN 0-8248-1354-5. Survey of Japanese religion as practiced in daily life.

Smart, Ninian. *Religions of Asia*. P-H 1993 ISBN 0-13-772427-6. Presents Asian religions in terms of doctrinal, mythical, institutional, ritual, ethical, experiential, and material dimensions, discussing responses of Asian religions to the West and modernization, Asian religions in the global community, and Buddhism and Shinto.

Weidner, Marsha, ed. *Flowering in the Shadows: Women in the History of Chinese and Japanese Painting*. UH Pr. 1990 $35.00. ISBN 0-8248-1149-6. Ten essays that break new ground on the role of Chinese and Japanese women as painters, calligraphers, collectors, and patrons.

Yun, Sasson. *Critical Issues in Neo-Confucian Thought*. Trans. by Michael C. Kalton. UH Pr. o.p. Study of Yi Hwang (1501–1570), Korea's outstanding Neo-Confucian thinker.

ANCIENT TRADITION AND SHINTO IN JAPAN

After a long period of prehistoric development, Japanese civilization starts to emerge as a self-consciously coherent tradition in the sixth century C.E. Through the coalescence of various clans under a single ruling house, the ancient Japanese tradition was clearly influenced via Korea by Confucianism concerning state polity and public morality and by Buddhism concerning religious matters. The most important expression of the ancient imperial tradition is found in the composite texts known as the *Nihongi* and *Kojiki* (dating to roughly the eighth century C.E., but drawing on earlier oral tradition) that articulate the official story of the divine origins of Japan. From the mythic perspective of these works (much of it adapted from Chinese and other sources), Japanese imperial tradition was understood as a direct inheritance from the sacred foundational actions of the gods (the *kami* spirits), especially the sun goddess Amaterasu-omi-kami. Shinto as the "Way of the Kami" represents the semi-organized and syncretistic expression (institutionalized Shinto clearly betrays Buddhist influence) of the national mythology and primarily involves ritual traditions of purification and worship designed to maintain a balanced and reciprocal relationship with the *kami* spirits. During World War II, Shinto became the nationalistic state religion; but even after its official disestablishment in 1945, it continues as a significant expression of Japanese indigenous culture and tradition.

Aston, W. G. *Nihongi*. C. E. Tuttle 1971 $18.95. ISBN 0-8048-0984-4. Only available complete rendition of the ancient sacred classic of Shinto and the imperial cult. Dated, but reliable scholarly translation.

Chamberlain, Basil Hall, trans. *Ko-ji-ki*. C. E. Tuttle 1982 $16.95. ISBN 0-8048-1639-2. Still helpful, though methodologically dated, early study by a leading scholar of the time.

Ebersole, Gary L. *Ritual Poetry and the Politics of Death in Early Japan*. Princeton U. Pr. 1989 $35.00. ISBN 0-691-01929-0. Fine presentation of ancient Japanese religion that discusses burial practices, court poetry, Shinto mythology, mourning rituals, Shinto festivals, and politics relating to the emperor.

Kinsley, David. *The Goddesses' Mirror: Visions of the Divine from East and West*. State U. NY Pr. 1989 $39.50. ISBN 0-88706-835-9. Scholarly and accessible accounts of great goddesses, treating the Shinto sun goddess, Amaterasu.

Olson, Carl, ed. *The Book of the Goddess Past and Present*. Crossroad NY 1986 $12.95. ISBN 0-8245-0689-8. Solid and accessible articles by experts in their respective fields, including a chapter on Amaterasu.

Ono, Sokyo. *Shinto: The Kami Way*. C. E. Tuttle 1962 $12.95. ISBN 0-8048-0525-3. Interesting popular introductory treatment by a Shinto priest.

Philippi, Donald, trans. *Norito: A Translation of the Ancient Japanese Ritual Prayers*. Princeton U. Pr. 1990 $9.95. ISBN 0-691-01489-2. English translation of prayers from Shinto ceremony as found in the Engi-shiki, with an introductory preface by Joseph Kitagawa.

Picken, Stuart D. B. *Shinto: Japan's Spiritual Roots*. Kodansha 1980 o.p. Vivid photographs of Japanese religious life and shrines, with commentary, plus an introduction by Edwin O. Reischauer.

Ross, Floyd H. *Shinto: The Way of Japan*. Greenwood 1983 repr. of 1965 ed. o.p. Semipopular and readable thematic history.

Sullivan, Lawrence, ed. *Healing and Restoring: Health and Medicine in the World's Religious Traditions*. Macmillan 1989 $35.00. ISBN 0-02-923791-2. Interdisciplinary and multicultural study of the topic of healing and health in the world's religions; Emiko Ohnuki-Tierney writes on healing in Shintoism.

JAPANESE AND KOREAN BUDDHISM

Buddhism, particularly sinified forms of Mahayana coming from Korea, entered Japan during the formative period of the sixth century C.E. and by the Nara period (710–784) was primarily represented by six philosophical and monastic centers closely associated with the imperial tradition. Later in the Heian and Kamakura periods (eighth to fourteenth centuries), Buddhism became more fully assimilated into the native tradition in ways that resulted in such syncretistic forms as Ryobu Shinto. More important, however, were the important Bajrayana esoteric sect of Shingon founded by the brilliant Kobo Daishi (also known as Kukai), the philosophical school of Tendai (= the Chinese T'ien-t'ai), and the more popular Pure Land (Jodo) traditions of Honen and Shinran, the Rinzai (stressing *koan* practice) and Soto (stressing sitting meditation) Zen traditions, and the evangelical *Lotus Sutra* sect founded by the messianic Nichiren (1222–1282). Given its powerful appeal to the common people, Pure Land tradition and its devotion to the Bodhisattva Amida Buddha was the most popular of these developments; but Zen Buddhism, especially in relation to the distinctive Soto Zen thought of Dogen, had a pervasive impact on Japanese art and culture (e.g., such characteristic "do" arts as the tea ceremony, gardening, theater, haiku poetry, and so on).

Anesaki, Masaharu. *Nichiren: The Buddhist Prophet*. Peter Smith 1916 o.p. General historical study of the founder of one of the most important, and distinctive, Buddhist sects.

Bielefeldt, Carl. *Dogen's Manuals of Zen Meditation.* U. CA Pr. 1988 $35.00. ISBN 0-520-06056-3. Study of the thirteenth-century founder of the Japanese Soto Zen School and his instructions on meditation as "just sitting."

Bloom Alfred. *Shinran's Gospel of Pure Grace.* U. of Ariz. Pr. 1965 o.p. Short, interestingly written, scholarly study of the founder of the pietist True Pure Land sect. Pure Land Buddhism is a kind of Mahayana that stresses the salvation of the common person through faith in the power of the Bodhisattva deity known as Amida Buddha.

Bodiford, William. *Soto Zen in a Japanese Town.* UH Pr. o.p. Examines the development of Soto Zen Buddhism in rural Japan from the fourteenth to the sixteenth century.

Buswell, Robert E. *The Korean Approach to Zen.* UH Pr. 1983 o.p. Valuable scholarly study of the distinctive, and little known, aspects of Korean Zen as expressed in the work of the monk Chinul.

Buswell, Robert E., Jr. *The Formation of Ch'an Ideology in China and Korea: The Vajrasamadhisutra. A Buddhist Apocryphon.* Princeton U. Pr. 1989 $47.00. ISBN 0-691-07336-8. Study of a Mahayana text composed in Korea.

_____. *Tracing Back the Radiance: Chinul's Korean Way of Zen.* UH Pr. 1983 $15.95. ISBN 0-8248-0785-5. Abridgment of Buswell's *The Korean Approach to Zen*, the first major work in English to deal with the philosophical and meditative traditions of Korean Zen Buddhism.

Castile, Rand. *The Way of Tea.* Weatherhill 1971 o.p. Excellent semipopular description of the tea cult that treats its historical, religious, philosophical, and aesthetic aspects.

Cleary, J. C., trans. *A Buddha from Korea: The Zen Teachings of T'aego.* Shambhala 1988 o.p. Translation of the sayings of the Korean Son (Zen) Master T'aego (1301–1382), with a lengthy introduction.

Dumoulin, Heinrich. *A History of Zen Buddhism.* Trans. by Paul Peachery. Beacon Pr. 1963 o.p. History of Zen and its emergence from early and Mahayana Buddhism.

_____. *Zen Buddhism in the Twentieth Century.* Trans. by Joseph S. O'Leary. Weatherhill 1992 $14.95. ISBN 0-8348-0247-3. Presentation of the encounter of Zen with the West and Christianity; also Zen psychology.

Dykstra, Yoshiko, trans. *Miraculous Tales of the Lotus Sutra from Ancient Japan: The Dainihonkoku Hokekyokenki of Priest Chingen.* UH Pr. 1984 $25.00. ISBN 0-8248-0967-X. "Supplies valuable information about medieval views of holy men, karma and rebirth, and the miracle-working efficacy of the Lotus Sutra" *(Journal of Asian Studies).*

Hyers, Conrad. *Once-Born, Twice-Born Zen: The Soto and Rinzai Schools of Japan.* Hollowbrook 1989 $12.50. ISBN 0-89341-524-3. Very useful comparative treatment of the two Japanese schools of Zen, utilizing William James's categories of once-born and twice-born religious experiences.

Ives, Christopher. *Zen Awakening and Society.* UH Pr. 1992 $14.95. ISBN 0-8248-1453-3. Considers the relationship between Zen and social ethics by examining ethical facets of Zen practice and *satori*, the traditional sociopolitical role of Zen in Japan, and the possible avenues along which Zen Buddhists could begin to formulate a self-critical, systematic social ethic.

Kapleau, Philip. *The Three Pillars of Zen.* Doubleday 1989 $10.95. ISBN 0-385-26093-8. Intelligent and well-written discussion of the nature of Rinzai Zen by a leading American master. Rinzai Zen stresses sudden enlightenment by means of *koan* practice.

Kasulis, T. P. *Zen Action/Zen Person.* UH Pr. 1985 $7.95. ISBN 0-8248-1023-6. "For the thoughtful Westerner this must be one of the most clear and perceptive accounts of Zen available" *(Times Literary Supplement).*

Kitagawa, Joseph M., and Mark D. Cummings, eds. *Buddhism and Asian History.* Macmillan 1989 $12.95. ISBN 0-02-897212-0. Excellent reference work on Buddhism consisting of articles taken from the *Encyclopedia of Religion.*

Kraft, Kenneth. *Eloquent Zen: Daito and Early Japanese Zen.* UH Pr. 1992 $34.00. ISBN 0-8248-1383-9. Daito Kukushi (1282–1337) played a major role in transmission of

Zen (Ch'an) from China to Japan, founding one of the most influential monasteries, interpreting Chinese texts, and composing a body of Zen writing.

Kraft, Kenneth, ed. *Zen: Traditions and Transition.* Grove Pr. 1988 $8.95. ISBN 0-8021-3162-X. Collection of very accessible essays on Zen by Asian and North American scholars.

Masunaga, Reiho. *A Primer of Soto Zen: A Translation of Dogen's Shobogenzo Zuimoniki.* UH Pr. 1975 $5.95. ISBN 0-8248-0357-4. "A good introductory text to main Zen themes and ideas for those who desire to practice Zen" *(Philosophy East & West).*

O'Neil, Kevin. *An Introduction to Nichiren Shoshu Buddhism.* Crises Res. Pr. 1980 $5.00. ISBN 0-86627-002-7. Popular discussion of the history of Nichiren sectarian Buddhism with an emphasis on the modern period. Nichiren emphasized the importance of the *Lotus Sutra* and the relationship between the state and religion.

Robinson, Richard, and Willard L. Johnson. *The Buddhist Religion.* Wadsworth Pub. 1982. ISBN 0-534-01027-X. Informative textbook introduction to the overall tradition with good concise chapters on East Asian Buddhism. Digests best of modern technical scholarship.

Saso, Michael. *Tantric Art and Meditation: The Tendai Tradition.* UH Pr. 1991 $16.00. ISBN 0-8248-1363-4. Illustrated with woodblock prints and line art, this book describes the four meditations of Japanese Tantric Buddhism: the Eighteen-path Mandala, the Lotus-womb Mandala, the Vajra-thunder Mandala, and the Goma Rite of Fire.

Sato, Giei. *Unsui: A Diary of Zen Monastic Life.* Text by Eshin Nishimura. Ed. by Bardwell L. Smith. UH Pr. 1973 $14.95. ISBN 0-8248-0272-1. Charming and informative illustrated book on Zen monasticism.

Sen, Soshitsu. *Tea Life, Tea Mind.* Weatherhill 1979 $12.50. ISBN 0-8348-0142-6. Interesting reflections on the philosophical and religious nature of the tea cult.

Snodgrass, Adrian. *The Matrix and Diamond World Mandalas in Shingon Buddhism.* 2 vols. S. Asia 1988 $148.50. ISBN 81-85179-27-1. Helpful reference work on mandala symbolism in the Japanese Tantric Buddhist school known as Shingon.

Stambaugh, Joan. *Impermanence Is Buddha-Nature: Dogen's Understanding of Temporality.* UH Pr. 1990 $18.95. ISBN 0-8248-1257-3. Grapples with Dogen's understanding of temporality through a dialogical approach to such Western thinkers as Plato, Aristotle, Leibniz, Nietzsche, and Heidegger.

Sunim, Kusan. *The Way of Korean Zen.* Weatherhill 1985 $12.50. ISBN 0-8348-0201-5. Knowledgeable descriptive presentation.

Suzuki, Shunryu. *Zen Mind, Beginner's Mind. Informal Talks on Zen Meditation and Practice.* Ed. by Trudy Dixon. Weatherhill 1973 $14.95. ISBN 0-8348-0052-7. Introductory talks by the teacher who established Soto Zen in the United States.

Tanabe, George J., Jr., and Willa Jane Tanabe, eds. *The Lotus Sutra in Japanese Culture.* UH Pr. 1989 $25.00. ISBN 0-8248-1198-4. Collection of essays on the importance of the Mahayana text and the Lotus Sutra in Japanese culture.

Varley, Paul, and Kumakura Isao, eds. *Tea in Japan: Essays on the History of Chanoyu.* UH Pr. 1989 $25.00. ISBN 0-824-8-1218-2. "Precisely because it is *not* only about tea, this book is, by far, the best book about tea in any Western language" *(Chanoyu Quarterly).*

Yampolsky, Philip B., ed. *Selected Writings of Nichiren.* Trans. by Burton Watson and others. Col. U. Pr. 1990 $47.50. ISBN 0-231-07260-0. English introduction to the influential writings of the thirteenth-century Japanese Buddhist priest Nichiren.

POPULAR TRADITIONS IN JAPAN AND KOREA

As in the section on Chinese Popular Religion above, this section lists books that treat the animistic religious traditions of Japan and Korea. The native animistic religion of Japan is Shinto, which received its own section above. However, here Shinto and the popular religion of Korea are treated as they most intimately affect the lives of people, in their shamanism, religious festivals, pilgrimages, ancestor veneration, mythology, and so on.

Ashkenazi, Michael. *Matsuri: Festivals of a Japanese Town*. UH Pr. 1993 $36.00. ISBN 0-8248-1385-5. Examines the numerous festivals, or *matsuri*, that take place in a small Japanese town and shows how they relate to Japanese religion and culture.

Blacker, Carmen. *The Catalpa Bow: A Study of Shamanistic Practices in Japan*. Routledge Chapman & Hall 1986 $19.95. ISBN 0-04-398008-2. Brilliant interpretive study, from both a historical and ethnographic point of view, of the important role of shamanism in Japan.

Buruma, Ian. *Behind the Mask: On Sexual Demons, Sacred Mothers, Transvestites, Gangsters, and Other Japanese Cultural Heroes*. NAL-Dutton 1985 $8.95. ISBN 0-452-00738-0. Fascinating popular study of the archetypal and mythic context for contemporary Japanese popular culture.

Covell, Alan C. *Ecstasy: Shamanism in Korea*. Hollym Intl. 1983 $22.50. ISBN 0-930878-33-7. General analysis of the nature and function of shamanistic practices within Korean tradition.

DeVos, George A., and Takao Sofue, eds. *Religion and the Family in East Asia*. U. CA Pr. 1984 $17.00. ISBN 0-520-05762-7. Enlightening essays on religion in the Asian family contexts, with topics ranging from ancestor veneration to shamanism.

Dorson, Richard M., ed. *Studies in Japanese Folklore*. Ayer repr. of 1963 ed. $36.50. ISBN 0-405-13310-3. Important collection of varied articles by leading authorities. Especially helpful for drawing out the religious implications of folklore.

Falk, Nancy Auer, and Rita M. Gross, eds. *Unspoken Worlds: Women's Religious Lives*. Wadsworth Pub. 1989. ISBN 0-534-09852-5. Groundbreaking collection on religion in women's lives; Kyoko Motomochi Nakamura writes on a woman founder, Sayo Kitamura, of a new Japanese religion, and Youngsook Kim Harvey writes on women shamans in Korea.

Hearn, Lafcadio. *Kokoro*. Greenwood 1970 repr. of 1896 ed. o.p. Engaging meditations by the famous literary eccentric. Hearn (1850–1904) was a journalist, essayist, and novelist of Irish-Greek extraction who emigrated to the United States and then to Japan in 1890. Fascinated with the exotic and strange, he wrote extensively on Japanese culture, religion, and legends. Known as Koizumi Yakumo in Japan, he taught literature at the Imperial University in Tokyo from 1896 to 1903.

Hori, Ichiro. *Folk Religion in Japan*. U. Ch. Pr. 1983 $16.95. ISBN 0-226-35335-4. Compilation of important articles by one of the leading Japanese historians of religion.

Janelli, Roger L., and Dawnhee Y. Janelli. *Ancestor Worship and Korean Society*. Stanford U. Pr. 1982 $35.00. ISBN 0-8047-1135-6. Social-scientific study of a rural Korean village that stresses the relationship of kinship and ancestral traditions. Helpful is the description of the role of neo-Confucian institutions and indigenous shamanistic type rituals.

Kendall, Laurel. *The Life and Hard Times of a Korean Shaman*. UH Pr. 1988 $23.00. ISBN 0-8248-1136-4. Engaging account of the life of a Korean woman shaman as told to an anthropologist, illuminating the hardships of women in a patriarchy.

———. *Shamans, Housewives and Other Restless Spirits*. UH Pr. 1987 $9.95. ISBN 0-8248-1142-9. An ethnographic study of feminine and shamanistic village practices that raises important issues concerning the nature and significance of the role of women in the history of Korean religion.

Kendall, Laurel, and Griffin Dix, eds. *Religion and Ritual in Korean Society*. Institute of East Asian Studies, U. CA Pr. 1987 o.p. Interesting articles on Korean popular religion.

Mayer, Fanny H., ed and trans. *Ancient Tales in Modern Japan*. Bks. Demand repr. of 1985 ed. $99.10. ISBN 0-8357-3940-6. Well-translated collection of exemplary folktales.

Statler, Oliver. *Japanese Pilgrimage*. UH Pr. o.p. Account of walking the Shikoku Pilgrimage, a 1,000-mile trek around the fourth largest island in Japan following the path of an ancient Buddhist master.

Yu, Chai-shin, and R. Guisso, eds. *Shamanism: The Spirit World of Korea*. Jain Pub. Co. 1988 $30.00. ISBN 0-89581-875-2. Collection of essays by Korean scholars on Korean popular religion.

FOREIGN INFLUENCES AND THE MODERN ERA

Japan began its confrontation with the West during the Tokugawa period, dating from 1600 to 1867. Particularly after 1867, Shinto developed into a nationalistic religion that supported Japan's military effort during World War II. At the war's end in 1945, because of American pressure, Shinto was declared no longer the official state religion of Japan. A variety of Japanese "new religions" have their origins in the period after World War II, and some date even earlier. These Japanese new religions draw on Buddhism and Shinto and often are focused on a charismatic leader. The Japanese new religions seem particularly designed to assist Japanese in coping with the meaning of life in modernity.

The vast majority of the books listed below deal with Japan's reaction to foreign influences and the modern era in terms of religion. Much more scholarly work in English remains to be done on Korea's religious reactions to foreign influences and modernity.

Bellah, Robert N. *Tokagawa Religion*. Free Pr. 1985 $12.95. ISBN 0-02-902460-9. Minor modern classic study from the standpoint of the sociology of religion.

Boxer, C. R. *The Christian Century in Japan 1549–1650*. U. CA Pr. 1974 repr. of 1967 ed. o.p. Historical survey of Roman Catholicism in Japan with translated documents.

Clark, Donald N. *Christianity in Modern Japan*. U. Pr. of Amer. 1986 o.p. Descriptive study of the influential role of Christian groups on modern day Korea.

Davis, Winston. *Dojo: Magic and Exorcism in Modern Japan*. Stanford U. Pr. 1980 $45.00. ISBN 0-8047-1053-8. Fascinating sociological analysis of a new religion known as Sukyo Mahikari that stresses Meuling magic and ritual.

de Bary, William Theodore, and Jahyuan K. Haboush, eds. *The Rise of Neo-Confucianism in Korea*. Col. U. Pr. 1985 $63.00. ISBN 0-231-06052-1. Collection of articles by a group of international scholars on the generally neglected topic of neo-Confucianism in Korean tradition. Technical and topically fragmented in nature, but important as an initial survey of issues related to Korean neo-Confucianism.

Earhart, H. Byron. *Gedatsu-kai and Religion in Contemporary Japan*. Ind. U. Pr. 1989 $57.50. ISBN 0-253-35007-7. In-depth study of a Japanese new religion, Gedatsu-kai, its founder, history and growth, and its relation to the context of contemporary Japan.

Edwards, Walter. *Modern Japan through Its Weddings: Gender, Person, and Society in Ritual Portrayal*. Stanford U. Pr. 1989 $27.50. ISBN 0-8047-1815-6. Illuminating study of the meanings found in contemporary Japanese wedding practices, by an anthropologist who worked for several years in a Japanese wedding palace.

Endo, Shusoku. *Silence*. Taplinger 1980 $9.95. ISBN 0-8008-7186-3. Haunting historical novel of the clash between traditional Japanese values and Christianity.

Guthrie, Stewart. *A Japanese New Religion: Rissho Kosei-kai in a Mountain Village*. U. of Mich. Pr. 1988 $21.95. ISBN 0-939512-33-5. Excellent ethnographic study of why Japanese join the new religion of Rissho Kosei-kai.

―――――. *The Religion of Japan's Korean Minority*. U. CA Pr. 1985 $6.00. ISBN 0-912966-67-X

―――――. *Shinto and the State 1968–1988*. Princeton U. Pr. 1989 $29.50. ISBN 0-691-07348-1. History of the Japanese government's sponsorship of Shinto prior to and during World War II, Shinto's subsequent disestablishment, and its contemporary status.

Hardacre, Helen. *Kurozumikyo and the New Religions of Japan*. Princeton U. Pr. 1986 $30.00. ISBN 0-691-006675-2. Provides a general historical overview of Japanese new religions and the Shinto Kurozumikyo specifically, based on Hardacre's participant observation.

―――――. *Lay Buddhism in Contemporary Japan: Reiyukai Kyodan*. Princeton U. Pr. 1984 $45.00. ISBN 0-691-07284-1. Study of one of Japan's largest new religions—three million members—based on four years of ethnographic research.

McFarland, H. Neill. *Rush Hour of the Gods: A Study of New Religious Movements in Japan.* Macmillan 1967 o.p. Balanced popular appraisal of five new religions.

Metraux, Daniel. *The History and Theology of Soka Gakkai: A Japanese New Religion.* E. Mellen 1988 $89.95. ISBN 0-88946-055-8. Study of the history of Soka Gakkai, its outlook and eschatology, its activities, and motivation for membership, in Japan and elsewhere.

Murakami, Shigeyoshi. *Japanese Religion in the Modern Century.* Trans. by H. Byron Earhart. U. of Tokyo Pr. 1980 $24.50. ISBN 0-86008-260-1. Analysis of Japanese religion relative to political, economic, and social conditions.

Nishitani, Keiji. *Religion and Nothingness.* U. CA. Pr. 1982 $45.00. ISBN 0-520-04329-4. Translation of one of the key works of the most famous contemporary Japanese philosopher. Existentialist and Buddhist in tone.

Nosco, Peter, ed. *Confucianism and Tokugawa Culture.* Princeton U. Pr. 1989 $17.95. ISBN 0-691-00839-6. Significant compilation of scholarly articles on neo-Confucianism's broad influence during the Tokugawa period.

Phillips, James M. *From the Rising of the Sun: Christians and Society in Contemporary Japan.* Bks. Demand repr. of 1981 ed. $86.40. ISBN 0-8357-2687-8. Popular study of the place of Christianity in contemporary Japan.

Piovesana, G. *Recent Japanese Philosophical Thought.* Sophia Univ. Pr. 1968 o.p. Competent survey of the diverse influence of Western thought on modern Japanese philosophy.

Reader, Ian. *Religion in Contemporary Japan.* UH Pr. 1991 $16.00. ISBN 0-8248-1354-5. Presentation of Japanese religion today from sociological and anthropological perspectives.

Stoesz, William, ed. *Kurozumi Shinto: An American Dialogue.* Anima Pubns. 1989 $19.95. ISBN 0-89012-049-X. Study of the Shinto new religion Kurozumikyo and comparison with Christianity.

Thomsen, Harry. *The New Religions of Japan.* Greenwood 1963 $35.00. ISBN 0-8371-9878-X. General study of Tenrikyo, Kurozumikyo, Konkyo, Soka Gakkai, Reiyukai, Rissho Kosei-kai, Omoto, and other Japanese new religions.

Taylor, Rodney L. *The Confucian Way of Contemplation: Okada Takehiko and the Tradition of Quiet-Sitting.* U. of SC Pr. 1988 $34.95. ISBN 0-87249-532-9. Study of the thought and practice of a modern Japanese Neo-Confucian.

CENTRAL ASIAN TRADITIONS

The designation Central Asia is used in this section to refer to Mongolia, Siberia, the Himalayan countries of Tibet (which now is part of the People's Republic of China), Nepal, and Bhutan, and areas part of the former U.S.S.R., including Kazakhstan, Krygyzstan, Tajikistan, Uzbekistan, Turkmenistan, Azerbaijan, and Armenia. These remote areas have received little Western scholarly treatment, but because there is a significant body of recent scholarship on Tibet, this country's religious and philosophical traditions will be treated separately.

Dharmatala, Damcho Gyatsho. *Rosary of the White Lotuses, Being the Clear Account of How the Precious Teachings of Buddha Appeared and Spread in the Great Hor Country.* Trans. by Piotr Klafkowski. Otto Harrassowitz 1987 o.p. English translation of a document produced by a Mongolian monastery in 1889 that purports to give the history of Buddhism's origins in Japan and its spread to China, Tibet, and Mongolia.

Dioszegi, V., ed. *Popular Beliefs and Folklore Tradition in Siberia.* Mouton 1968 $68.00. ISBN 0-686-22621-6. Collection of scholarly articles that stress important aspects of traditional Siberian religion.

Heissig, Walther. *The Religions of Mongolia.* U. CA Pr. 1980 $42.50. ISBN 0-520-03857-6. Accessible scholarly presentation of Mongolian religious history.

Holmberg, David H. *Order in Paradox: Myth, Ritual, and Exchange among Nepal's Tamang.* Cornell Univ. Pr. 1989 $29.95. ISBN 0-8014-2247-7. Anthropological study of the Tamang, a Buddhist people speaking a Tibeto-Burman language, in central Nepal.

Hyer, Paul, and Sechin Jagchid. *A Mongolian Living Buddha: Biography of the Kanjurwa Khutughtu*. State U. NY Pr. 1983 $10.95. ISBN 0-87395-714-8. Biography of a Mongolian teacher (born 1914) who was selected and raised as a child to be a "living Buddha."

Kitagawa, Joseph M. *The Religious Traditions of Asia*. Macmillan 1989 $12.95. ISBN 0-02-897211-2. Articles excerpted from the *Encyclopedia of Religion*; Part 2 on Tibetan Buddhism, Bon, and Islam in Central Asia.

Kitagawa, Joseph M., and Mark D. Cummings, eds. *Buddhism and Asian History*. Macmillan 1989 $12.95. ISBN 0-02-897212-0. Excellent reference work on Buddhism consisting of articles taken from the *Encyclopedia of Religion*.

Lang, David Marshall. *The Armenians: A People in Exile*. Unwin Hyman 1989 o.p. Reprint of Lang's 1981 book, providing a general introduction to the Armenian people and their history that helps to explain the relationship of Christian Armenians to Muslims, including the Turkish genocidal campaign against the Armenians.

Moses, Larry, and Stephen A. Halkovic, Jr. *Introduction to Mongolian History*. Reg. Inst. Inner Asian Studies 1985 $20.00. ISBN 0-933070-18-7. Recent scholarly overview of Mongolian tradition that includes useful discussions of religion.

Tibetan Traditions

The Tibetan plateau north of India is a huge expanse of land equal to the size of western Europe. This area is home to a highly developed but endangered cultural and religious tradition. Owing to its location among the highest mountain peaks of the world, its virtual inaccessibility for many centuries caused outsiders to regard Tibet as shrouded in mystery. Tibet possesses a highly developed Tantric Buddhist culture that has combined with features native to Tibet, including the animistic religion called Bon. Tibet was annexed by the People's Republic of China in 1950. When the Chinese used force to suppress a Tibetan revolt in 1959, the religious and temporal ruler of Tibet, the young DALAI LAMA, fled to India. Since that time, the Chinese have ruthlessly attempted to eradicate the Tibetan identity and religiosity. Prior to 1950 there were over 6,000 Buddhist monasteries in Tibet. As of 1980, only 12 monasteries existed intact. Over a million Tibetans, one-sixth of the population, have died as a result of the Chinese occupation of their country. In addition to stripping the Tibetan natural environment of its resources and decimating Tibetan wildlife, most recently the Chinese government has been bringing in Chinese settlers, so that the Chinese population in Tibet now outnumbers the ethnic Tibetans. Refugees continue to leave Tibet for Nepal and India, heading particularly for Dharmsala, where the Dalai Lama has established a Tibetan community. The Dalai Lama, at once the political and spiritual leader of Tibetans, continues to work for the nonviolent emancipation of Tibet. In so doing, he has become an internationally known and highly regarded voice for peace in the world. However, the Tibetan situation receives little media coverage because of the concern of the United States for good relations with the People's Republic of China. Since 1979, there has been a little more freedom for Tibetans to practice their religion.

The native religion of Tibet is an animistic religion called Bon. The form of Mahayana Buddhism that was taken into Tibet from India was Tantric, which has a highly esoteric side to it. In combination with the native tradition, Tibetan Buddhism took on a unique form known as Vajrayana Buddhism. Tibetan Buddhists meditate on colorful depictions of Buddhist deities, both benign and wrathful, whose deep meaning is only beginning to be understood by Western scholars. In Tibetan Buddhism, Tantric sexual spiritual practices coexist with the celibate community of Buddhist monks (lamas) and nuns. Prayer flags and prayer wheels are ubiquitous in the everyday world of Tibetan Buddhists. A Tibetan text well known in the West is the *Bardol Thodol,* or The Tibetan *Book of the Dead,* which contains information about the afterlife and instructions for the soul either to escape rebirth or to achieve a favorable rebirth. A significant body of scholarship on Tibetan Buddhism—long incomprehensible to Westerners—now is beginning to emerge.

Allione, Tsultrim. *Women of Wisdom.* Viking Penguin 1986 $8.95. ISBN 1-85063-044-5. An American woman presents the stories of six Tibetan women mystics.

Aris, Michael. *Hidden Treasures and Secret Lives: A Study of Pemalingpa (1450–1521) and the Sixth Dalai Lama (1683–1706).* Routledge Chapman & Hall. 1989 $45.00. ISBN 0-7103-0328-9. Fascinating study of two important figures in Tibetan Buddhism: Pemalingpa, who purported to discover hidden texts, and the Sixth Dalai Lama, who in adulthood refused to become a monk.

Eliade, Mircea. *From Muhammad to the Age of Reforms.* Trans. by Alf Hiltebeitel and Diane Apostolos-Cappadona. U. of Ch. Pr. 1985 o.p. See especially the chapter on "Tibetan Religions." Helpful overview of Tibetan religious history from Eliade's comparative perspective. Good annotated bibliography.

Forman, Robert K. C., ed. *Religions of Asia.* St. Martin 1993 $26.70. ISBN 0-312-05753-9. Up-to-date and academically solid presentation of Asian religions, with a good general treatment of Buddhism in Tibet.

Goldstein, Melvyn C. *A History of Modern Tibet, 1913–1951.* U. CA Pr. 1989 $75.00. ISBN 0-520-07590-0. Excellent study of Tibet's political history leading to annexation by the People's Republic of China.

Guenther, Herbert V. *Tibetan Buddhism in Western Perspective.* Dharma Pubs. 1989 $12.95. ISBN 0-913546-49-6. General descriptive analysis that is, at times, overly technical.

Gyatso, Geshe. *Buddhism in the Tibetan Tradition.* Viking Penguin 1988 $8.95. ISBN 0-14-019333-2. Semipopular historical survey.

Hoffman, Helmut. *The Religions of Tibet.* U. CA Pr. 1988 $30.00. ISBN 0-520-03856-8. Distinguished scholarly study that covers pre-Buddhist, as well as Buddhist, traditions.

Hoog, Constance, trans. *Prince Jin-Gim's Textbook of Tibetan Buddhism, the "Sesbya Rab-Gsal (Jneya-Prakasa)."* E. J. Brill 1983 o.p. This translation of a thirteenth-century C.E. text is a concise introduction to Tibetan Buddhism.

Hookham, S. K. *The Buddha Within: Tathagatagarbha Doctrine according to the Shentong Interpretation of the Ratnagotravibhava.* State U. NY Pr. 1991 $59.50. ISBN 0-7914-0357-2. History and explanation of the Indian Mahayana Buddhist *tathagatagarbha* doctrine, which has been translated as "Buddha-nature," and its influence in Tibet; a book on an abstract subject that is accessible to the beginner.

Hopkins, Jeffrey, and Ann Klein. *Compassion in Tibetan Buddhism.* Snow Lion 1980 o.p. Semipopular account of the principle of compassion by two leading Buddhist scholars.

Kitagawa, Joseph M. *The Religious Traditions of Asia.* Macmillan 1989 $12.95. ISBN 0-02-897211-2. Articles excerpted from the *Encyclopedia of Religion*; Part 2 on Tibetan Buddhism, Bon, and Islam in Central Asia.

Kitagawa, Joseph M., and Mark D. Cummings, eds. *Buddhism and Asian History.* Macmillan 1989 $12.95. ISBN 0-02-897212-0. Excellent reference work on Buddhism consisting of articles taken from the *Encyclopedia of Religion.*

Kvaerne, Per. *Tibet Bon Religion: A Death Ritual of the Tibetan Bonpos.* E. J. Brill 1985 o.p. Study, with lots of black-and-white photos, of the death rituals of adherents to Bon, the native Tibetan animistic religion.

Lizhong, Liu. *Buddhist Art of the Tibetan Plateau.* China Bks. 1988 $100.00. ISBN 0-8351-2128-3. Outstanding photographs of Tibetan works of art taken in the mid-1980s with permission from the People's Republic of China, as well as separate chapters on architecture, sculpture, painting, culture objects, and monasticism.

Middleton, Ruth. *Alexandra David-Neel: Portrait of an Adventurer.* Shambhala 1989 $12.95. ISBN 0-87773-413-5. Fascinating biography of David-Neel (1868–1969), who traveled extensively throughout Tibet, China, India, and Sikkim and wrote some of the first books on Tibetan Buddhism.

Mullin, Glenn H. *Death and Dying: The Tibetan Tradition.* Viking Penguin o.p. Based on Tibetan texts, including the Tibetan *Book of the Dead*, Mullin discusses meditation techniques of preparation for death and stories of the deaths of Tibetan saints.

Rangdrol, Tsele Natsok. *Lamp of Mahamudra.* Trans. by Erik Pema Kunsang. Shambhala 1989 $9.95. ISBN 0-87773-487-9. Translation of a work by the seventeenth-century C.E. Kagyu (combination of Yogacara and Madhyamaka) teacher Tsele Natsok Rangdrol, suitable for advanced students.

Sopa, Geshe Lhundup, and Jeffrey Hopkins. *The Practice and Theory of Tibetan Buddhism.* Grove Pr. 1976 o.p. Useful popular introduction by two authoritative commentators.

Stein, Rolf A. *The World in Miniature: Container Gardens and Dwellings in Far Eastern Religious Thought.* Trans. by Phyllis Brooks. Stanford U. Pr. 1990 $39.50. ISBN 0-8047-1674-9. Analysis and elucidation of the cosmology that underlies the miniature gardens of China, Japan, and Vietnam, the cosmology underlying the architecture of homes in China, Tibet, and north and northeast Asia, and the concept of mountains (Sumeru and K'un-lun) as axes of communication between heaven and earth.

Trungpa, Chogyam. *Cutting through Spiritual Materialism.* Shambhala 1987 $16.00. ISBN 0-87773-050-4. Transcriptions of lectures applying Buddhist thought to modern American life by a noted Tibetan master.

Tucci, Giuseppe. *To Lhasa and Beyond: Diary of the Expedition to Tibet in the Year 1948.* Snow Lion 1985 $14.95. ISBN 0-937938-57-2. This diary of Tucci's six months in Tibet prior to the Chinese takeover in 1959 is an excellent introduction to Tibetan religion and culture.

Wentz, Walter Yeeling Evans, trans. *Bardo Thodol.* OUP 1957 o.p. Complete translation of the celebrated esoteric Buddhist text that recounts the journeys of the soul after death.

Willis, Janice D., ed. *Feminine Ground: Essays on Women and Tibet.* Snow Lion 1989 $11.95. ISBN 0-937938-73-4. Top-notch essays on Tibetan women and the complex female imagery in Tibetan Buddhism.

NON-ISLAMIC AND NON-JEWISH TRADITIONS OF THE MIDDLE EAST AND NORTH AFRICA

The designation Middle East refers to the southwest Asian countries now known as Turkey, Cyprus, Syria, Lebanon, Israel, Jordan, Saudi Arabia, Yemen, southern Yemen or the People's Democratic Republic, Oman, Qatar, United Arab Emirates, Kuwait, Bahrain, Iraq, Iran, and Afghanistan. The North African countries of Egypt, Sudan, and Somalia have strong cultural ties with the Middle East. Islam is the dominant religious influence throughout the area, excepting, of course, the Jewish state of Israel. Because Judaism and Islam are treated in separate sections, this section will attempt to treat only the Middle Eastern and North African religions present in the area prior to Islam and separate from Judaism.

Assyro-Babylonian and Semitic Traditions

Collon, Dominique. *First Impressions: Cylinder Seals in the Ancient Near East.* U. Ch. Pr. 1988 $29.95. ISBN 0-226-11388-4. Very accessible general introduction to information to be gleaned from cylinder seals used in the ancient Near East.

Dalley, Stephanie. *Myths from Mesopotamia: Creation, the Flood, Gilgamesh, and Others.* OUP 1989 $69.00. ISBN 0-19-814397-4. Excellent translation and presentation of major Akkadian myths suitable for the general reader.

de Moor, Johanes C. *An Anthology of Religious Texts from Ugarit.* E. J. Brill 1987 o.p. Translation of texts from Ugarit for students.

Eliade, Mircea. *From the Stone Age to the Eleusinian Mysteries.* Trans. by Willard R. Trask. U. Ch. Pr. 1979 o.p. Readable and up-to-date surveys with valuable bibliographic essays.

Farnell, Lewis R. *Greece and Babylon: A Comparative Sketch.* Gordon Pr. 1977 $59.95. ISBN 0-8490-1906-0. Authoritative comparative study by a brilliant classical scholar.

Gibson, John C. *Canaanite Myths and Legends.* Bks. Intl. VA 1978 $39.95. ISBN 0-567-02351-6. Accessible and reliable scholarly presentation that digests specialized research.

Grayson, A. Kirk. 2 vols. U. of Toronto Pr. Vol. 1 *Assyrian Rulers of the Third and Second Millennia B.C. (to 1115).* 1987 $90.00. ISBN 0-8020-2605-2. Vol. 2 *Assyrian Rulers of the Early First Millennium B.C. (1114–859).* 1991 $150.00. ISBN 0-08020-2605-2. Collection of primary documents found on monumental inscriptions and cylinder seals, with information on each document.

Grosz, Katarzyna. *The Archives of the Wullu Family.* Museum Tusculanums Forlag 1988 o.p. Reconstruction of cuneiform records kept by a wealthy Upper Mesopotamian family during fifteenth and fourteenth centuries B.C.E. and interpretation of the kinship system that they reveal.

Hoffner, Harry A., Jr. *Hittite Myths.* Scholars Pr. GA 1990 $19.95. ISBN 1-55540-482-0. Fine translation, with some commentary, of Hittite myths, suitable for the general reader.

Hooke, S. H. *Babylonian and Assyrian Religion.* U. of Okla. Pr. 1963 o.p. Good introductory text.

Jacobsen, Thorkild. *The Treasures of Darkness: A History of Mesopotamian Religion.* Yale U. Pr. 1976 $14.00. ISBN 0-300-02291-3. Fascinating interpretations by one of the leading experts in Mesopotamian tradition.

Kovacs, Maureen Gallery. *The Epic of Gilgamesh.* Stanford U. Pr. 1989 $29.50. ISBN 0 8047-1589-0. Excellent translation and presentation of the first-millennium B.C.E. epic, including a very helpful introduction, glossary of places and names, explanation about cuneiform writing, and recommended bibliography for further reading.

Kramer, Samuel N. *Sumerian Mythology.* Greenwood 1972 $55.00. ISBN 0-313-26363-9. Authoritative translations and discussions of the most important myths concerning the origin of man, the great flood, and the descent to the underworld.

Leick, Gwendolyn. *A Dictionary of Ancient Near Eastern Mythology.* Routledge 1991 $59.95. ISBN 0-415-00240-0. Useful descriptions of the deities and heroes of ancient Mesopotamia, Anatolia, Elam, Canaan.

Livingstone, Alasdair. *Mystical and Mythological Explanatory Works of Assyrian and Babylonian Scholars.* OUP Pr. 1986 $85.00. ISBN 0-19-815462-3. Accessible presentation of writings on Assyrian and Babylonian myths and divination by first-millennium B.C.E. Assyrian and Babylonian scholars serving at royal courts.

Maier, Walter A., III. *Aserah: Extrabiblical Evidence.* Scholars Pr. GA 1986 $23.95. ISBN 1-55540-046-9. Good collection of extrabiblical evidence for the goddess Asherah, rival to Yahweh.

Michalowski, Piotr. *The Lamentation over the Destruction of Sumer and Ur.* Eisenbrauns 1989 $36.50. ISBN 0-931464-43-9. Translation of a Sumerian text describing the fall of Ur.

Olyan, Saul M. *Asherah and the Cult of Yahweh in Israel.* Scholars Pr. GA 1988 $19.95. ISBN 1-55540-253-4. Study of the biblical evidence concerning the goddess Asherah and her worship.

Parpola, Simo, and Kazuko Watanabe. *The Correspondence of Sargon II, Part I: Letters from Assyria and the West.* Eisenbrauns 1987 $55.00. ISBN 951-570-004-3

_____. *Neo-Assyrian Treaties and Loyalty Oaths.* Eisenbrauns 1988 $45.00. ISBN 951-570-034-5. The first two volumes in a series consisting of the translations of materials found in the royal archives of Nineveh.

Sanders, N. K. *The Epic of Gilgamesh.* Viking Penguin 1960 $4.95. ISBN 0-14-044100-X. Readable semipopular redacted translation with helpful introduction and notes.

Wolkstein, Diane, and Samuel Noah Kramer. *Inanna, Queen of Heaven and Earth: Her Stories and Hymns from Sumer.* HarpC 1983 $16.95. ISBN 0-06-014713-X. Attractive and scholarly presentation of the Sumerian and Akkadian myth of Inanna.

Yoffee, Norman, and George L. Cowgill, eds. *The Collapse of Ancient States and Civilizations.* U. of Ariz. Pr. 1988 $45.00. ISBN 0-8165-1049-0. Though not solely about ancient Middle Eastern civilizations, this book is a helpful examination of the possible causes of the decline of Mesopotamia and the rise and fall of the Neo-Assyrian and Neo-Babylonian empires.

Persian Zoroastrianism

Zoroastrianism is a religion that originated with the life of Zoroaster in that part of the world now known as Iran. The exact dates for Zoroaster's life are unknown, but it can be estimated that he lived about 1000 B.C.E. He was a priest of the pre-Zoroastrian polytheistic and animistic religion (related to India's Rig Vedic religion), but he began to preach that he had received a new revelation that only one God should be worshipped and that was Ahura Mazda (the Wise Lord, later known as Ormazd). Zoroaster asserted that the *daevas,* nature deities of the pre-Zoroastrian religion, were not gods at all but actually were devils and servants of Ahura Mazda's opponent, Angra Mainyu (later known as Ahriman). Little is known about the details of Zoroaster's life, but Zoroastrian scripture preserves 17 hymns (*gathas*) composed by him. Zoroastrianism might be the first monotheistic religion, and it has had an important influence on Judaism, Christianity, and Islam in its belief in Heaven and Hell, stress on the expectation of a messiahlike figure, a dualism depicting God (Ahura Mazda) in a pitched battle for control of the universe against a powerful Satanlike figure (Angra Mainyu), an eschatology involving the destruction of the world as we know it, a resurrection of the dead, a final judgment, and the defeat of the powers of evil so that the Kingdom of God will be created on earth. The Jews first encountered Zoroastrianism when they were liberated from the Babylonian captivity in 538 B.C.E., when Cyrus, the king of Persia, defeated the Babylonians. Prior to this time, the ancient Hebrew religion did not have the concepts of Heaven and Hell, but references to these new ideas and a Zoroastrianlike eschatology gradually were incorporated into Jewish scriptures after 538 B.C.E. Of course, Zoroastrian influence on Christianity and even Islam was mediated primarily through Judaism.

Zoroastrianism was the official religion of two great Iranian dynasties, the Achaemenids (550–330 B.C.E.) and the Sasanians (224–651 C.E.). Since the dominance of Islam, beginning in the seventh century C.E., Zoroastrianism has become a persecuted minority in Iran. In the ninth century C.E., Iranian Zoroastrians began migrating to refuge in India, where they are known as PARSIS (or Parsees, Persians), and the largest community of Zoroastrians in the world now is located in western India around Bombay. [See the sub-section on Parsis (Zoroastrians in India) in the section in this chapter on South and Southeast Asia.]

Zoroastrianism addresses the question of the origin of evil by postulating the existence of two eternal and uncreated spirits, Ahura Mazda (or Spenta Mainyu, Benevolent Spirit) and Angra Mainyu (Evil Spirit). Ahura Mazda and Angra

Mainyu are twins but opposites. Zoroastrianism is a monotheistic religion because it affirms that only one of these spirits is God, Ahura Mazda, the benevolent spirit that created the universe, which is good, like its creator. Only Ahura Mazda should be worshipped as God. Angra Mainyu became jealous when he beheld his brother's good creation. Evil, impurity, and suffering came into the good universe when Angra Mainyu entered the universe in order to take it over and spoil it. Zoroastrianism sees Ahura Mazda and Angra Mainyu locked in battle over who will be the master of the universe. Human beings were created by Ahura Mazda to assist him in the battle against Angra Mainyu. However, humans have free will to choose either to support Ahura Mazda with their good thoughts, words, and deeds or to support Angra Mainyu with their evil thoughts, words, and deeds. At death the soul is judged according to how the earthly life was lived and goes either to Heaven or to Hell. In Zoroastrianism, Hell is not a place of fire, because fire is the Zoroastrian symbol of Ahura Mazda's purity as well as one of the four basic elements of God's good creation. Zoroastrianism's Hell is a place of immense impurity—filled with all of the possible bodily excrements, noxious insects, and unclean beasts. According to the Zoroastrian eschatology, the earth ultimately will be purified of the sinfulness and impurity caused by Angra Mainyu in a catastrophic conflagration; Angra Mainyu will be defeated and cast out of the universe; and subsequently there will be a universal salvation in Ahura Mazda's perfect kingdom on earth.

Boyce, Mary. *A History of Zoroastrianism*. E. J. Brill repr. of 1975 ed. $94.25. ISBN 90-04-08847-4

_____. *A Persian Stronghold of Zoroastrianism*. OUP 1977 $35.00. ISBN 0-19-826531-X. Ethnographic study of an Iranian Zoroastrian village that has the oldest sacred fires (perhaps 2,000 years).

_____. *Zoroastrianism: The Rediscovery of Missing Chapters in Man's Religious History*. Ind. U. Pr. Asian Studies Research Institute 1977 o.p. Prepared as a teaching aid, this is a very helpful discussion of the issue of whether Zoroastrianism influenced Judaism and Christianity or vice versa.

_____. *Zoroastrians: Their Religious Beliefs and Practices*. Routledge 1986 $17.95. ISBN 0-7102-0156-7. Comprehensive presentation that draws on the best of current scholarship. Scholarly, yet accessible.

Boyce, Mary, ed. and trans. *Textual Sources for the Study of Zoroastrianism*. U. Ch. Pr. 1990 $12.95. ISBN 0-226-06930-3. The best collection of Zoroastrian texts available.

Choksky, Jamsheed K. *Purity and Pollution in Zoroastrianism: Triumph over Evil*. U. of Tex. Pr. 1989 $25.00. ISBN 0-292-79802-4. Very useful study of the Zoroastrian purification rituals of the past and present that demonstrates the influence of Zoroastrianism on Islam and Hinduism; written by a Zoroastrian.

Eliade, Mircea. *A History of Religious Ideas*. U. Ch. Pr. 1985 $18.95. ISBN 0-226-20403-0. Helpful overview that stresses the general significance of Zoroastrian tradition within the history of world religions.

Hinnells, John R. *Persian Mythology*. P. Bedrick Bks. 1985 $24.95. ISBN 0-87226-017-8. Semipopular presentation that includes translated mythic materials and contextual discussion.

Kotwal, Firoze M., and James W. Boyd, eds. and trans. *A Guide to the Zoroastrian Religion: A Nineteenth Century Catechism with Modern Commentary*. Scholars Pr. GA 1982 $12.50. ISBN 0-89130-573-4. English translation from Gujarati of a Zoroastrian catechism written by a Zoroastrian priest in 1869 C.E. in India, accompanied by the commentary of a contemporary Zoroastrian high priest, Dastur Dr. Firoze M. Kotwal; good comparison of Zoroastrianism as practiced in Iran and India.

Malandra, William W. *An Introduction to Ancient Iranian Religion: Readings from the Avesta and Achaemenid Inscriptions*. U. of Minn. Pr. 1983 $29.95. ISBN 0-8166-

1114-9. Comprehensive introduction to Zoroastrianism, including modern English translations of the sacred texts.

Pangborn, Cyrus R. *Zoroastrianism: A Beleaguered Faith.* Advent NY 1983 o.p. Historical treatment of the development of Zoroastrianism and the issues facing Zoroastrians in the modern world.

Zaehner, R. C. *The Teachings of the Magi: A Compendium of Zoroastrian Beliefs.* OUP 1956 $7.95. ISBN 0-19-519857. Introduction to Zoroastrian beliefs based on interpretations of Zoroastrian scriptures.

North African Traditions: Ancient Egypt

Allen, George, trans. *Book of the Dead.* U. Ch. Pr. 1974 o.p. Recent authoritative translation and discussion. Scholarly, yet accessible.

Armour, Robert. *Gods and Myths of Ancient Egypt.* Col. U. Pr. 1986 o.p. Scholarly analysis that draws on current specialized research.

David, A. Rosalie. *The Ancient Egyptians: Religious Beliefs and Practices.* Routledge 1982 $19.95. ISBN 0-7100-0878-3. Good up-to-date scholarly study.

Eliade, Mircea. *From the Stone Age to the Eleusinian Mysteries.* U. Ch. Pr. 1981 $27.50. ISBN 0-226-20401-4. Readable synthesis along with helpful annotated bibliography.

Frankfort, Henri. *Ancient Egyptian Religion: An Interpretation.* HarpC 1961 $12.00. ISBN 0-06-130077-2. Valuable semipopular work by a leading expert.

Ions, Veronica. *Egyptian Mythology.* P. Bedrick Bks. 1983 $24.95. ISBN 0-911745-07-6. Convenient and generally reliable collection with helpful commentary.

Morenz, Siegfried. *Egyptian Religion.* Cornell Univ. Pr. 1992 $15.95. ISBN 0-8014-8029-9. Brilliant synthetic work. Scholarly yet accessible format that sets Egyptian religion within the context of the overall history of religions.

Murnane, William J. *The Penguin Guide to Ancient Egypt.* Viking Penguin 1983 $12.95. ISBN 0-14-046326-7. Semipopular and comprehensive work that includes excellent discussions of religion.

Shorter, A. W. *The Egyptian Gods: A Handbook.* Borgo Pr. 1993 $25.00. ISBN 0-89370-682-5. Recent survey of basic information on the Egyptian pantheon.

CHRONOLOGY OF AUTHORS

Besant, Annie. 1847–1933
Vivekananda. 1863–1902
Gandhi, Mohandas K(aramchand). 1869–1948
Suzuki, D(aisetz) T(eitaro). 1870–1966

Paramahansa Yogananda. 1893–1952
Krishnamurti, Jiddu. 1895–1986
Thich Nhat Hanh. 1926–
Tenzin Gyatso, the Dalai Lama. 1935–

BESANT, ANNIE. 1847–1933

Annie Besant in the 1870s already had gained notoriety as an estranged Anglican priest's wife who had rejected Christianity and embraced atheism. She was a famous orator who spoke on behalf of the Freethought movement, social reform, the right to publish information on contraception, improved education, and Fabian socialism. However, Besant perplexed her critics and admirers when, in 1889, she abandoned her atheistic stance and embraced Theosophy. The Theosophical Society had been founded in 1875 by Madame HELENA BLAVATSKY and Colonel Henry S. Olcott and had its international headquarters in India. Theosophy's outlook affirmed the mystical components of each of the world's religions, but it was influenced especially by Hindu and Buddhist thought. By the mid-1890s, Annie Besant had made India her home, and she was elected the second president of the Theosophical Society subsequent to the death of Olcott in 1907. In India, Besant made it her special mission to uplift Hindu self-esteem, which had been severely battered by British imperialism and Christian missionaries. She founded the Central Hindu College, which later was incorporated into the new Benares Hindu University. She spoke out for social reform, and from 1913 onward she undertook political agitation for Indian home rule. She was elected president of the Indian National Congress in 1918, and she was the first person to make that position an active, year-round job. Immediately thereafter, she lost her popularity because of the rise to prominence in Indian politics of MOHANDAS K. GANDHI. Until the end of her life, Besant increasingly turned her attention to the promotion of a young Indian boy, JIDDU KRISHNAMURTI, as the coming World-Teacher, a messiah who would bring about a collective human transformation resulting in unity and peace among all peoples.

Despite the apparently contradictory stages of Besant's life, continuity can be detected in her consistent attempts to discover the means by which human suffering could be eliminated to achieve an earthly millennial condition. Besant's books and lectures were an important factor in the popularization of Eastern, particularly Hindu, religious and philosophical thought in the West. Besant's books continue to have an international impact, and several of them are kept in print by the Theosophical Publishing House, which is known in the United States as Quest Books.

BOOKS BY BESANT

The Ancient Wisdom. Theos. Pub. Hse. 9th ed. 1972 $9.95. ISBN 0-8356-7038-4. Introductory text on Theosophical cosmology and view of human nature, discussing reincarnation and karma, subtle sheaths that are vehicles for the soul, the planes on which the sheaths are operative, and the imperative to service that Besant calls the Law of Sacrifice.

Annie Besant: An Autobiography. Theos. Pub. Hse. 1939 $19.50. ISBN 0-8356-7568-8. First published in 1893, this is written from her perspective as a Theosophist.

Autobiographical Sketches. Gordon Pr. 1972 $59.95. ISBN 0-87968-683-9

Avataras. East School Pr. 1983 $5.95. ISBN 0-912181-06-0. Besant elucidates the Hindu doctrine of *avatars* (the descent of the Divine that takes on a form in the material world) from her Theosophical perspective.

Death and After. Theos. Pub. Hse. 1972 $4.75. ISBN 0-8356-7039-2. Popular Theosophical treatment of what happens after death.

Dharma. Theos. Pub. Hse. 1986 $3.95. ISBN 0-8356-7116-X. Explains the Hindu concept of *dharma,* one's duties to perform in life.

Doctrine of the Heart. Theos. Pub. Hse. 1988 $5.95. ISBN 0-8356-7189-5. Extracts from letters to Hindus encouraging them to understand discipleship under the Theosophical Masters in terms of the Hindu devotional tradition (*bhakti*) as well as other Hindu concepts.

Esoteric Christianity. Theos. Pub. Hse. 8th ed. 1986 $12.95. ISBN 0-8356-7052-X. Very popular presentation of Christianity in the light of Theosophy.

From the Outer Court to the Inner Sanctum. Ed. by Shirley Nicholson. Theos. Pub. Hse. 1983 $4.50. ISBN 0-8356-0574-4. Consists of five lectures given in 1895 delineating the Theosophical view of personal spiritual development.

Hints on the Study of the Bhagavad Gita. Theos. Pub. Hse. 1984 $7.95. ISBN 0-8356-7079-1. Besant's four lectures on the Hindu scripture that were delivered in India and first published in 1906.

The Inner Government of the World. Sun Pub. 1981 $7.00. ISBN 0-89540-092-8. Explains the Theosophical cosmology that includes the concept of Masters who psychically direct human evolution according to a "Divine Plan."

Introduction to Yoga. Theo. Pub. Hse. 1972 $6.50. ISBN 0-8356-7120-8. Commentary on the *Yoga Sutras* of Patanjali for the practice of yoga.

Karma. 1895. Theos. Pub. Hse. 1975 $5.95. ISBN 0-8356-7035-X. Explains the Hindu doctrine of karma, the cosmic law of cause and effect, from her Theosophical perspective.

Man and His Bodies. Theos. Pub. Hse. 12th ed. 1967 $4.95. ISBN 0-8356-7083-X. Elucidation of the Theosophical view of the human being (based on Hinduism) as possessing subtle sheaths or "bodies" that are operative on various planes of existence.

Path of Discipleship. Theos. Pub. Hse. 1980 $6.95. ISBN 0-8356-7044-9. Discusses the path of discipleship under the Theosophical Masters and its implications for human evolution.

Reincarnation. Theos. Pub. Hse. 1975 $5.95. ISBN 0-8356-7019-8. Introductory presentation of the Theosophical understanding of reincarnation.

Seven Great Religions. Theos. Pub. Hse. 1990 $7.25. ISBN 0-8356-7218-2. Popular expositions of seven world religions, all of which are found in India: Hinduism, Zoroastrianism, Jainism, Buddhism, Christianity, Islam, Sikhism.

Seven Principles of Man. Theos. Pub. Hse. 1987 $5.25. ISBN 0-8356-7321-9. Very influential elucidation of the Theosophical concept of each human having seven "sheaths" or subtle bodies.

The Spiritual Life. Theos. Pub. Hse. 1991 $8.95. ISBN 0-8356-0666-X. A collection of talks and writings, most of which were originally published in the journal *The Theosophical Review*, of which Besant was coeditor. Clearly expresses Besant's conviction that altruism is the cornerstone of spirituality.

Study in Consciousness. Theos. Pub. Hse. 6th ed. 1972 $9.75. ISBN 0-8356-7287-5. Drawing on the writings of Helena P. Blavatsky, Besant's exposition of the Theosophical understanding of human nature—its psychology and physiology.

Thought Forms. (coauthored with Charles W. Leadbeater). Theos. Pub. Hse. 1969 $7.50. ISBN 0-8356-0008-4. Very influential book asserting that thought takes on forms in subtle matter that can be discerned with psychic senses; the color plates of paintings depicting thought forms are regarded as a stimulus to the development of modern abstract art.

Thought Power: Its Control and Culture. Theos. Pub. Hse. 1967 $5.95. ISBN 0-8356-0312-1. Highly influential book on the power of thought to effect changes in the material world.

Wisdom of the Upanishads. Theos. Pub. Hse. 1986 $5.95. ISBN 0-8356-7092-9. Four Theosophical Society convention lectures delivered in 1906 on the philosophy of the Upanishads, which come at the end of the Hindu Vedas, and addressing the Upanishadic concepts of the impersonal and permanent Absolute, the Lord, the immortal Self, and the round of birth and death.

Books about Besant

Nethercot, Arthur H. *The First Five Lives of Annie Besant.* U. Ch. Pr. 1960 $107.80. ISBN 0-8357-9645-0. Annie Besant's life and activities prior to her conversion to Theosophy; excellent on her activities, but there is little attempt to understand her thought.

———. *The Last Four Lives of Annie Besant.* U. Ch. Pr. 1963 $124.80. ISBN 0-317-28137-2. Focuses on Besant's life and activities after her conversion to Theosophy, especially her work in India for Hindu self-esteem and Hindu education, social reform, and Indian home rule; very useful detailing of Besant's adversarial relationship with Mohandas Gandhi, but no attempt to read her speeches and writings in order to understand her thought.

Wessinger, Catherine Lowman. *Annie Besant and Progressive Messianism.* E. Mellen 1988 o.p. In-depth study of Besant's thought and intellectual development throughout her life, tracing her development from young Anglican to atheist, Freethinker, materialist, and Fabian socialist, and then to her espousal of Theosophy, and finally her move to messianism and the promoting of J. Krishnamurti as the World-Teacher.

GANDHI, MOHANDAS K(ARAMCHAND). 1869–1948

Mohandas K. Gandhi was an Indian of the merchant caste who became known as Mahatma ("great soul") because he played such a prominent role in the struggle for Indian independence from Great Britain, and he emphasized traditional modes of lifestyle and spirituality. Married to Kasturba at age 13, in 1888 the young Gandhi left India alone to study law in London. There his contact with Theosophists introduced him to an appreciation of his Hindu heritage and its great texts. Also in London he came to appreciate the gospel accounts of Jesus, especially the Sermon on the Mount, which preaches pacifism. Returning to India in 1891, Gandhi spent a couple of years attempting to find a job and finally found employment in South Africa in 1893. While in South Africa, he found himself called upon to combat discrimination against Indians. Influenced by his reading of RUSKIN (see Vol. 1), TOLSTOY (see Vol. 2), and THOREAU (see Vol. 1), Gandhi formulated his technique for the nonviolent resolution of conflict that he termed Satyagraha, most simply translated as "holding onto Truth."

Gandhi's Satyagraha had three stages. First was the attempt to persuade the opponent through reason. If this failed, the second stage was persuasion of the opponent through one's own suffering. By suffering, one dramatized the issues and attempted to get the opponent to listen to rational argument. If this failed, the third stage was nonviolent civil disobedience, or what Gandhi termed noncooperation or passive resistance. Gandhi stressed that at all times the protest should be characterized by *ahimsa*, nonviolence or harmlessness. The practitioner of Satyagraha, the Satyagrahi, must never strike back against the oppressor and must be willing to take on suffering, even death, in order to urge the opponent to negotiate a resolution meeting the needs of all concerned.

Gandhi returned to India in 1914, and by 1919 he was an important force in the Indian struggle for home rule. In India, Satyagraha took the form of general strikes, boycott of British-made cloth, picketing of liquor shops, dramatic protest against the British monopoly and tax on salt, and other acts of noncooperation with the British government. Gandhi simplified his lifestyle and dress to correspond to that of the poorest Indian peasant, thus provoking WINSTON CHURCHILL's (see Vol. 3) contemptuous remark that he was a half-naked *faqir*. The positive side of Gandhi's Satyagraha in India was what he termed his constructive program, which included: the removal of untouchability; the uplift of Indian women, entailing the eradication of child marriage, ending the giving of dowry to the groom's family by the bride's family, and the movement of women out of seclusion in the home; education of Indians in health and hygiene; and the promotion of village self-government, agriculture, and cottage industries. Gandhi's fasts, which became a hallmark of his methodology, were undertaken to persuade people who loved him, the Indians themselves.

When Indian independence in 1947 came with the partition of the subcontinent into the states of India and East and West Pakistan, this event was marred by the migrations of twelve million Hindus, Muslims, and Sikhs and massacres of one community by another. Gandhi's fast for peace in Calcutta managed to stop the communal riots there and in east and west Bengal. Gandhi then moved to the Indian capital city of Delhi, which contained Hindu and Sikh refugees from West Pakistan, Indian Muslims preparing to go to Pakistan, and Muslims who intended to continue to make Delhi their home. There he undertook a fast until Delhi leaders promised that they would end all communal violence.

Therefore, violence on the most massive scale occurred on and around the India-West Pakistan border. Gandhi was unable to turn his peace efforts to this area because he was assassinated on January 30, 1948, by a Hindu who believed that Gandhi was making too many concessions to the Muslims.

Gandhi's nonviolent stand against racism, sexism, imperialism, and all forms of violence remains relevant today. A prolific writer, his works remain in print thanks to Navajivan Publishing House in Ahmadabad, India. Many of these books are distributed in the United States by Greenleaf Books. Numerous books have been written about Gandhi, and only a partial list of the most significant works are cited below.

BOOKS BY GANDHI

An Autobiography of Mahatma Gandhi: Or the Story of My Experiments with Truth. Trans. by Mahadev Desai. Greenleaf 1983 $12.00. ISBN 0-934676-40-2. Provides important insight into Ghandi's social and philosophical outlook.

The Bhagavad Gita: An Interpretation. Ed. by D. Narahari Parikh. Greenleaf 1984 $10.00. ISBN 0-934676-65-8. Gandhi's exposition of his understanding of the Hindu scripture that was so influential in his life and work.

The Collected Works of Mahatma Gandhi. 90 vols. Greenleaf 1983 $1,400.00. ISBN 0-934676-35-6. The comprehensive collection of Gandhi's writings.

The Essential Gandhi, His Life, Work and Ideas: An Anthology. Ed. by Louis Fischer. Vint. 1983 o.p. Classic selection of Gandhi's writings on Indian independence, civil disobedience and Satyagraha, nonviolence, racism, war, sexuality, and sanitation.

Gandhi in India, in His Own Words. Ed. by Martin Green. U. Pr. of New Eng. 1987 $35.00. ISBN 0-87451-390-1

Gandhi Reader: A Source Book of His Life and Writings. Ed. by Homer Jack. AMS Pr. 1970 $34.00. ISBN 0-404-03540-X

Hind Swaraj, or Indian Home Rule. Greenleaf 1981 $2.50. ISBN 0-934676-25-9. English translation of an essay written in 1908 that first was published in a South African Indian newspaper, presenting Gandhi's understanding of India's condition of oppression under British rule and proposing nonviolent means of working for Indian independence.

Letters to Mirabehn. Ed. by Madeleine Slade. Greenleaf 1983 $9.50. ISBN 0-934676-53-4.

The Message of Jesus Christ. Ed. by A. T. Hingorani. Greenleaf 1980 $1.25. ISBN 0-934676-20-8. Gandhi's reflections on the teachings of Jesus and Christian mission work.

The Mind of Mahatma Gandhi. Ed. by R. K. Prabhu and U. R. Rao. Greenleaf 1988 $30.00. ISBN 0-934676-54-2. Collection of Gandhi's thoughts on himself, his search for Truth, fearlessness, faith, nonviolence, Satyagraha, nonpossession, labor, Sarvodaya, trusteeship, celibacy (*brahmacharya*), freedom and democracy, promoting and using Indian-made products (*swadeshi*), and human brotherhood.

The Moral and Political Writings of Mahatma Gandhi. 3 vols. Ed. by R. N. Iyer. OUP 1986–87 $115.00. ISBN 0-19-824756-0. Valuable collection of Gandhi's writings on moral and political topics.

My Religion. Ed. by B. Kumarappa. Greenleaf 1983 $9.50. ISBN 0-934676-54-2. Extracts of speeches and writings showing how Gandhi viewed and practiced religion and on the relation of religion to his life's work.

Sarvodaya: The Welfare of All. Ed. by B. Kumarappa. Greenleaf $8.50. ISBN 0-686-87486-2

Satyagraha in South Africa. Trans. by Valji Govindji Desai. Greenleaf 1980 $12.00. ISBN 0-934676-15-1. Gandhi's account of his formative experiences in South Africa relating to the development of Satyagraha; the translation from Gujarati was approved by Gandhi.

The Selected Works of Mahatma Gandhi. Ed. by Shriman Narayan. Navajivan Publishing Hse. o.p. Vols. 1 and 2 *An Autobiography or the Story of My Experiments with Truth.* Trans. by Mahadev Desai. 1927. Vol. 3 *Satyagraha in South Africa.* Trans. by Valji

Govindji Desai. 1928. Vol. 4 *The Basic Works*. 1968. Vol. 5 *Selected Letters*. 1968. Vol. 6 *The Voice of Truth*. 1968. Helpful selection of Gandhi's basic writings.

BOOKS ABOUT GANDHI

Bondurant, J. *Conquest of Violence: The Gandhian Philosophy of Conflict*. Princeton U. Pr. 1988 $9.95. ISBN 0-691-02281-X. Reprint of the most helpful explanation and analysis of Gandhi's technique of Satyagraha.

Borman, William. *Gandhi and Non-Violence*. State U. NY Pr. 1986 $49.50. ISBN 0-88706-330-6. Practical analysis of Gandhi's philosophy on nonviolence and the technique of Satyagraha.

Brown, Judith M. *Gandhi and Civil Disobedience: The Mahatma in Indian Politics 1928–34*. Col. U. Pr. 1977 o.p. Details Gandhi's role in the middle years of the Indian agitation for home rule.

―――――. *Gandhi: Prisoner of Hope*. Yale U. Pr. 1989 $17.00. ISBN 0-300-04595-6. Realistic and comprehensive history and analysis of Gandhi and his strengths and weaknesses that successfully avoids hagiography.

―――――. *Gandhi's Rise to Power: Indian Politics 1915–1922*. Col. U. Pr. 1972 o.p. Details Gandhi's rise to prominence in the Indian struggle for home rule.

Chatterjee, Margaret. *Gandhi's Religious Thought*. U. of Notre Dame Pr. 1986 $11.95. ISBN 0-268-01011-0. Important new study that brings out the Hindu and Christian aspects of Gandhi's thought.

Copley, A. *Gandhi: Against the Tide*. Blackwell Pubs. 1987 o.p. Succinct presentation of Gandhi's life and thought.

Datta, Dhirendra M. *Philosophy of Mahatma Gandhi*. U. of Wis. Pr. 1953 $10.95. ISBN 0-299-01014-7. Brief readable descriptive study.

Erikson, Erik. *Gandhi's Truth: On the Origins of Militant Nonviolence*. Norton 1993 $9.95. ISBN 0-393-31634-5. Psychological interpretation of Gandhi's life.

Fox, Richard G. *Gandhian Utopia: Experiments with Culture*. Beacon Pr. 1989 $27.50. ISBN 0-8070-4100-9. Interesting "culture history" to account for the utopianism of Gandhi.

Gracie, David M., ed. *Gandhi and Charlie*. Cowley Pubns. 1989 $9.95. ISBN 0-936384-71-9. Illuminating collection of the letters and other writings exchanged between Gandhi and his friend and colleague Rev. Charles Freer Andrews.

Green, Martin. *The Origins of Nonviolence: Tolstoy and Gandhi in Their Historical Settings*. Pa. State U. Pr. 1985 $27.50. ISBN 0-271-00414-2. Examines the lives of Tolstoy and Gandhi and their formulation of a philosophy of nonviolence within the context of expanding modern democratic culture.

Hunt, James D. *Gandhi and the Nonconformists: Encounters in South Africa*. S. Asia 1986 ISBN 81-85002-03-7. Fine biography focusing on Gandhi's years in South Africa.

Juergensmeyer, Mark. *Fighting with Gandhi*. HarpC 1984 o.p. Engaging and insightful discussion of Gandhi's idea of nonviolence and the methods of *satyagraha* or "grasping onto principles." Popular format.

Mehta, V. *Mahatma Gandhi and His Apostles*. Yale U. Pr. 1993 $15.00. ISBN 0-300-05539-0

Nanda, B. R. *Gandhi and His Critics*. OUP 1985 $22.50. ISBN 0-19-561722 3. Sympathetic general presentation of Gandhi's life, his views, his critics, and the scholarship on Gandhi.

Rao, K. L. *Mahatma Gandhi and Comparative Religion*. S. Asia 1990 $15.00. ISBN 81-208-0755-3. Interesting study of Gandhi in relation to the history of religions.

Sharma, Arvind, ed. *Neo-Hindu Views of Christianity*. E. J. Brill 1988 o.p. Collection of essays on how important modern Hindu thinkers viewed Christianity, including a chapter on Gandhi.

Shepard, Mark. *Gandhi Today: The Story of Mahatma Gandhi's Successors*. Seven Locks Pr. 1987 $20.00. ISBN 0-932020-51-8. California journalist explores the ways Gandhi's legacy is continued in India today.

Shirer, William L. *Gandhi, A Memoir*. S. Asia 1993 $6.00. ISBN 0-8364-2838-2

Swan, Maureen. *Gandhi: The South African Experience*. Ohio U. Pr. 1985 $19.95. ISBN 0-86975-232-4. Scholarly in-depth examination of Gandhi's formative experiences in South Africa.

Thomas, P. M. *Twentieth Century Indian Interpretations of Bhagavad Gita: Tilak, Gandhi, and Aurobindo*. ISPCK 1987 o.p. Analysis of how modern Hindus, including Gandhi, have interpreted the *Bhagavad Gita* to meet the challenges of contact with Western religion and culture.

KRISHNAMURTI, JIDDU. 1895–1986

As a boy, Jiddu Krishnamurti was taken by ANNIE BESANT from obscure and impoverished Indian origins to become the physical vehicle for a spiritual master whom she termed the World-Teacher, identical to the Christ or the Buddhist Lord Maitreya. As such, Krishnamurti and his brother were taken to England for education and looked after by wealthy Theosophists. After the death of his brother from tuberculosis in 1925, Krishnamurti gradually began to speak as the World-Teacher. He developed his teachings, which emphasized personal responsibility for one's enlightenment and stated that there should be no reliance on external authority. Contrary to many scholarly accounts, Krishnamurti did not deny that he was the World-Teacher, but he did deny the usefulness of such a concept. He rejected Besant's idea that a new religion would be centered around him and his teachings, and he taught that all organizations limited truth. He urged his listeners not to be concerned about his identity but to judge his message on its own merits. In 1929, in Besant's presence, Krishnamurti dissolved the Order of the Star, the international organization (30,000 members) that Besant had built around him. He was particularly critical of the idea of reincarnation that is so prominent in Theosophy, and although he did not deny the reality of reincarnation, he taught that preoccupation with the doctrine could impede liberation, which consisted of living fully in the present moment. In his mature years, Krishnamurti became an internationally noted speaker on the possibility of achieving what he termed constant voluntary awareness or choiceless awareness, which ended all thought processes, entailed the perception of universal unity, and generated spontaneous and appropriate action. Krishnamurti refused to speculate publicly on whether he was the World-Teacher, because that concept was irrelevant to individual transformation. His teachings were attractive to Western and Indian intelligentsia, as well as to numerous Theosophists, and have been recorded in about 40 books translated into 47 languages.

BOOKS BY KRISHNAMURTI

The Awakening of Intelligence. HarpC 1973 $16.00. ISBN 0-06-064834-1. Includes Krishnamurti's dialogues with Jacob Needleman, Alan Naude, Swami Venkatesananda, and David Bohm.

The Collected Works of J. Krishnamurti. 17 vols. Kendall-Hunt 1992 $14.95 ea. ISBNs 0-8403-6235-8–0-8403-6314-1. Important collection of Krishnamurti's talks in the United States, Europe, India, New Zealand, and South America from 1933 to 1967.

Commentaries on Living. 3 vols. Theos. Pub. Hse. $8.95 ea. ISBNs 0-8356-0390-3, 0-8356-0415-2, 0-8356-0402-0. Krishnamurti's early teachings on the human condition.

Education and the Significance of Life. HarpC 1953 $9.00. ISBN 0-06-064876-7. Krishnamurti's classic statement of his views on education.

The Ending of Time. HarpC 1985 $9.00. ISBN 0-06-064796-5. Dialogue of Krishnamurti and physicist David Bohm on human existence.

The First and Last Freedom. HarpC 1954 $10.95. ISBN 0-06-064831-7. Early and highly popular record of Krishnamurti's teachings that has sold more than 63,000 copies since 1975; foreword is by his friend Aldous Huxley.

Freedom from the Known. HarpC 1969 $9.95. ISBN 0-06-064808-2. Another classic statement, selling more than 85,000 copies since 1969.

The Future is Now: Last Talks in India. HarpC 1989 o.p. Krishnamurti's final talks in India in 1985, when he was 90 years old.

The Future of Humanity. Mirananda 1986 o.p. Krishnamurti discusses the future of humanity with David Bohm.

Krishnamurti at Los Alamos 1984. Krishnamurti 1984 o.p. An eight-page booklet containing Krishnamurti's conversation with scientists at the National Laboratory Research Center at Los Alamos, New Mexico.

Krishnamurti on Freedom. Harper SF 1992 $10.00. ISBN 0-06-250535-1. Explains that freedom is fearlessness.

Krishnamurti on God. Harper SF 1992 $10.00. ISBN 0-06-250607-2. Explains the futility of seeking knowledge of what is ultimately unknowable and that freedom is the cessation of seeking.

Krishnamurti on Living and Dying. Harper SF 1991 $10.00. ISBN 0-06-250610-2. Examines the human fear of death and how death is linked with living.

Krishnamurti on Nature and the Environment. Harper SF 1991 $8.95. ISBN 0-06-250534-3. Explains how the human interior life is linked with the environment.

Krishnamurti on Relationship. Harper SF 1992 $10.00. ISBN 0-06-250608-0. Compilation of Krishnamurti's teachings on relationships, personal and international.

Krishnamurti on Right Livelihood. Harper SF 1992 $10.00. ISBN 0-06-250609-9. Discusses work as expression of liberation.

Krishnamurti on Social Responsibility. Krishnamurti 1992 o.p. Explains that social problems can be addressed only when there is personal transformation.

Krishnamurti's Journal. HarpC 1982 o.p. Personal reflections recorded from 1973 to 1975.

Krishnamurti's Notebook. HarpC 1976 $11.00. ISBN 0-06-064795-7. Record of Krishnamurti's awareness over a period of seven months.

Last Talks at Saanen. HarpC 1985 o.p. Krishnamurti's last talks at Saanen, Switzerland, in which he emphasizes that he is not a guru.

Meditations. Krishnamurti o.p. Compilation of statements on meditation.

The Second Penguin Krishnamurti Reader. Viking Penguin 1970 o.p. Includes "The Urgency of Change" and "The Only Revolution."

Think on These Things. HarpC 1964 $10.00. ISBN 0-06-091609-5. The most popular of the Krishnamurti books, selling more than 500,000 copies.

Truth and Actuality. HarpC 1978 $10.00. ISBN 0-06-06-4875-9. Contains three dialogues with physicist David Bohm on reality and truth.

The Wholeness of Life. HarpC 1978 $10.95. ISBN 0-06-064868-6. Krishnamurti's discussions with physicist David Bohm and David Shainberg, M.D.

You Are the World. HarpC 1972 $7.95. ISBN 0-06-080303-7. Krishnamurti's talks on the campuses of Brandeis, University of California at Berkeley and Santa Cruz, and Stanford.

BOOKS ABOUT KRISHNAMURTI

Field, Sydney, and Peter Hay. *Krishnamurti: The Reluctant Messiah*. Paragon Hse. 1989 o.p. Personal memoir of Sydney Field's relationship with and perceptions of Krishnamurti.

Holroyd, Stuart. *Krishnamurti: The Man, the Mystery and the Message*. Element MA 1991 $14.95. ISBN 1-85230-200-3. Scholarly examination of Krishnamurti's life and thought.

———. *The Quest of the Quiet Mind: The Philosophy of Krishnamurti*. Aquarian Pr. UK 1980 o.p. Very useful analysis of the mature thought of Krishnamurti, focusing on the topics of human bondage; mind, consciousness and the self; religion and the religious life; life and death; and the psychological revolution.

Jayakar, Pupul. *Krishnamurti: A Biography*. HarpC 1986 $17.95. ISBN 0-06-250401-0. Biography that highlights his importance in India from an Indian perspective.

Lutyens, Mary. *Krishnamurti: His Life and Death*. St. Martin 1991 $19.95. ISBN 0-312-05455-6. General treatment of Krishnamurti's biography.

———. *Krishnamurti: The Open Door*. Avon 1988 $7.95. ISBN 0-380-70971-6. Account of the conclusion of Krishnamurti's life.

———. *Krishnamurti: The Years of Awakening*. Avon 1983 $9.95. ISBN 0-380-71113-3. Account of Krishnamurti's early years and experiences within the fold of the Theosophical Society by an author who is the daughter of Lady Emily Lutyens, an important surrogate mother-figure for Krishnamurti during those years.

———. *Krishnamurti: The Years of Fulfillment*. Avon 1983 $8.95. ISBN 0-380-71112-5. Covers Krishnamurti's life from 1930 through 1980 as a lecturer speaking in the United States, Europe, and India.

Sloss, Radha Rajogopal. *Lives in the Shadow with J Krishnamurti*. Addison-Wesley 1993 $25.00. ISBN 0-201-63211-X. Thoughtful account of Krishnamurti's life by the woman who was the child at the center of a love triangle formed by Krishnamurti, Rosalind Rajogopal, and her husband, D. Rajagopal; important reading for anyone inclined to idealize Krishnamurti as the World-Teacher.

PARAMAHANSA YOGANANDA. 1893–1952

Swami Yogananda, a young Hindu monk, delivered his first address, "The Science of Religion," to the International Congress of Religious Liberals meeting in Boston on October 6, 1920. He remained in America and began to attract thousands to his public lectures. In 1925, Yogananda established the headquarters of his organization, the Self-Realization Fellowship, on Mount Washington in Los Angeles. (One of his most distinguished disciples was the horticulturist Luther Burbank.) His *Autobiography of a Yogi* was published in 1946 and has been translated into 18 languages. Yogananda and the Self-Realization Fellowship have been the means by which many Americans have been introduced to and have adopted Hindu modes of thought and religious practice. Yogananda taught that Hindu mysticism was compatible with and similar to Western and Christian mysticism. In 1935 his guru gave Yogananda the title Paramahansa, which means "supreme swan" and is a title indicating the highest spiritual attainment. His disciples regard the manner of Yogananda's death—he expired immediately after addressing a banquet in honor of the ambassador from India—as a demonstration of his supreme yogic bodily control. The Self-Realization Fellowship continues to be an important alternative religion in America, and it has a strong institutional presence in and around the Los Angeles area.

Books by Paramahansa Yogananda

Autobiography of a Yogi. 1946. Self Realization 1990 $15.00. ISBN 0-87612-079-6. Yogananda's widely read autobiography was published first in 1946 and has been translated into 18 languages. It provides the account of his life and his encounters with saints, Eastern and Western, plus his core teachings.

The Divine Romance. Self Realization 1986 $12.00. ISBN 0-87612-240-3. Collection of Yogananda's teachings on life and the spiritual life, with photographs.

How You Can Talk with God. 1957. Self Realization 1990 $2.00. ISBN 0-87612-160-1. Booklet containing Yogananda's exposition on how one can communicate with the ultimate.

The Law of Success. Self Realization 1990. ISBN 0-87612-150-4. Widely influential booklet first published in 1944 on how to achieve success by directing one's thought.

Metaphysical Meditations. 1964. Self Realization 1989 $1.95. ISBN 0-87612-041-9. Collection of Yogananda's sayings on the spiritual life, the nature of reality, and the power of thought.

The Science of Religion. Self Realization 1982 $6.00. ISBN 0-87612-004-4. Expanded
   version of Yogananda's first American speech, delivered to the International
   Congress of Religious Liberals in 1920.
Scientific Healing Affirmations: Theory and Practice of Concentration. 1958. Self
   Realization 1987 $1.95. ISBN 0-87612-144-X. Widely influential little book on the
   power of thought.
Where There is Light: Insight Inspiration for Meeting Life's Challenges. Self Realization
   1988 $4.95. ISBN 0-87612-275-6. Selections from Yogananda's teachings.

BOOKS ABOUT PARAMAHANSA YOGANANDA

Paramahansa Yogananda: In Memoriam. Self Realization 1989 $3.00. ISBN 0-87612-
   170-9. Includes accounts of Yogananda's final days and departure from the physical
   body on March 7, 1952, after giving a speech at a banquet; from India a letter from
   the Mortuary Director attests to the nondecay of the body for 16 days before being
   sealed in a casket. Includes photographs.
Rosser, Brenda Lewis. *Treasures against Time: Paramahansa Yogananda with Doctor and
   Mrs. Lewis.* Borrego Pubns. 1991 o.p. Includes letters of Yogananda to two early
   American disciples and their reminiscences of him.
Walters, J. Donald (Swami Kriyananda). *The Path: A Spiritual Autobiography.* Crystal
   Clarity 1989 $6.95. ISBN 0-916124-12-6. Autobiography of an American direct
   disciple of Yogananda containing many accounts of his interaction with Yogananda.

SUZUKI, D(AISETZ) T(EITARD). 1870–1966

A student of the Zen master Shaku Soen, who addressed the 1893 World's
Parliament of Religions held in Chicago, D. T. Suzuki did more to introduce Zen
to Westerners than any other representative of that tradition. Shaku Soen sent
the young Suzuki to America in 1897 to help Paul Carus translate the Chinese
text the Dao De Jing. Suzuki remained in America for about a decade, working
at Carus' Open Court Publishing Company outside Chicago. After Suzuki
returned to Japan, he married an American woman, Beatrice Lane, in 1911, and
they began publishing an English journal, *The Eastern Buddhist*, in 1921. During
this time in Japan, Suzuki translated into Japanese a number of Swedenborgian
texts. He traveled to China in 1934, and he went to London in 1936 to attend the
World Congress of Faiths. Suzuki recognized that the West had much to offer
the East, but like SWAMI VIVEKANANDA, he was convinced that the East had much
to offer the West in its religion and philosophy. On this basis he was motivated
to write about Zen in English. Suzuki wrote about 30 books in English and many
more in Japanese. Suzuki's first books in English were a translation of
Ashvaghosha's *Discourse on the Awakening of Faith in the Mahayana* (1900) and
Outlines of Mahayana Buddhism (1907).

A practitioner of Rinzai Zen Buddhism, Suzuki, in his writings about the
ultimate experience of *satori* and the meditative use of *koans*, made Zen terms
almost household words in the United States. In the early part of the twentieth
century, Suzuki devoted himself to the propagation of Zen via his writings. After
World War II he became a noted lecturer on Zen at American and European
universities. That Suzuki's work was effective can be seen in the fact that Zen
was picked up in the 1950s by California beatniks, producing what was termed
Beat Zen. From that time on, Americans increasingly began to go to Japan to
study Zen, and more Zen masters began to come to the United States to teach.
The earliest institutions devoted to the practice of Zen in America were
established in San Francisco in 1928, in Los Angeles in 1929, and in New York
City in 1931. Zen centers remain an important part of the American urban
scene, and several of them have established rural Zen retreat centers.

BOOKS BY SUZUKI

An Introduction to Zen Buddhism. Grove-Atltic. 1959 $4.95. ISBN 0-8021-3055-0

Japanese Spirituality. Trans. by Norman Waddell. Greenwood 1972 $45.00. ISBN 0-313-26554-2. Explains that this book was written first in Japanese between trips to the air raid shelter and was directed to the Japanese during the war in order to point them to their greatness in spirituality.

Manual of Zen Buddhism. Grove-Atltic. 1987 $10.95. ISBN 0-8021-3065-8

Mysticism: Christian and Buddhist. Ed. by Ruth Nanda Anshen. HarpC 1982 $8.95. ISBN 0-04-149053-3. Collection of Suzuki's essays.

Outlines of Mahayana Buddhism. 1900. Schocken 1963 o.p. Suzuki's first book on Buddhism in English that was not a translation of a text: introductory essay by Alan Watts.

Shin Buddhism. HarpC 1970 o.p. Exposition of Japanese Pure Land Buddhism.

Studies in Zen. Ed. by Christmas Humphreys. Delta 1955 o.p. C. G. Jung characterized this book as being among "the best contributions to the knowledge of living Buddhism."

The Training of the Zen Buddhist Monk. Globe Pr. Bks. 1991 $9.95. ISBN 0-936385-23-5. Highly illuminating treatment of life in a Zen monastery. Includes 43 paintings of Zen monastic life by Zenchu Sato who, like Suzuki, drew on his personal experience of Zen monasticism.

Zen Buddhism. Ed. by William Barrett. Doubleday 1962 o.p.

Zen Buddhism and Psychoanalysis. (coauthored with Erich Fromm and Richard DeMartino). HarpC 1960 $7.95. ISBN 0-06-090175-6

Zen and Japanese Culture. Princeton U. Pr. 1993 $16.95. ISBN 0-691-01770-0

BOOKS ABOUT SUZUKI

Abe, Masao, ed. *A Zen Life: D. T. Suzuki Remembered.* Weatherhill 1986 $19.95. ISBN 0-8348-0213-9. Includes two autobiographical accounts by Suzuki and his essay "Satori," as well as contributions by Christmas Humphreys, Thomas Merton, Erich Fromm, Alan Watts, Philip Kapleau, Gary Snyder, Robert Aitken, and Masao Abe. Includes a complete bibliography.

Dumoulin, Heinrich. *Zen Buddhism in the Twentieth Century.* Trans. by Joseph S. O'Leary. Weatherhill 1992 $14.95. ISBN 0-8348-0247-3. Portions of this book address Suzuki's contributions in bringing Zen to the West.

TENZIN GYATSO, THE DALAI LAMA. 1935– (NOBEL PRIZE 1989)

Tenzin Gyatso is the fourteenth Dalai Lama in a lineage that goes back to the fourteenth century C.E. The title Dalai Lama comes from the Mongolian word for ocean and the Tibetan term for guru, or teacher. The Dalai Lama is the foremost of what Tibetans call *tulkus* (incarnations). These are beings who can choose their rebirth so as to be of the most help to others. Prior to the Chinese invasion of Tibet, there were several thousand *tulkus*; now there are but a few hundred. (It is interesting to note that Westerners are beginning to be identified as *tulkus*.) The Dalai Lama is believed to be the incarnation of the foremost *bodhisattva* of compassion, known as Avalokiteshwara in Sanskrit or Chenrezi in Tibetan. In Mahayana Buddhism, *Bodhisattvas* are believed to delay their own ultimate salvation out of compassion for the suffering of others.

The fourteenth Dalai Lama was born July 5, 1935, in the northeastern province of Tibet named Amdo. He was the ninth of 16 children, 7 of whom survived. At the time of his discovery in 1938, an elder brother already had been recognized as being a *tulku* and had been taken to a monastery. After the death of the thirteenth Dalai Lama in 1933, a complicated search was undertaken to discover his reincarnation. The corpse of the thirteenth Dalai Lama sitting in state was believed to indicate by the inclination of the head the direction in which the rebirth would take place. Officials traveled to a sacred lake and received visions in its waters providing additional clues as to where the next incarnation could be found. Many children were interviewed until the child was found who recognized the thirteenth Dalai Lama's former companions and belongings. So at an early age the child who would be regarded as the fourteenth Dalai Lama was taken to reside in a monastery, and ultimately he was taken, along with his parents and an older brother, to the capital city of Lhasa. In 1940, at age 4, he was installed as the Dalai Lama on the Lion Throne in the Lhasa castle known as the Potala. At age 15, he was invested as the head of the Tibetan state. The young Dalai Lama was given monastic training and an education. From an early age he displayed a mechanical talent, and he continues to enjoy repairing watches, clocks, and other small machines. In his youth he discovered an old movie projector that belonged to the thirteenth Dalai Lama, repaired it, and used it to watch Tarzan movies.

In 1959, as a result of the Chinese takeover of his country, the Dalai Lama was forced to hastily make a two-week journey to asylum in India. In Dharmsala, the Dalai Lama has built a Tibetan community complete with health and educational institutions. His government-in-exile is democratic, and its constitution contains provisions for the possibility of impeaching the Dalai Lama, even though his followers did not desire this. The Dalai Lama uses Dharmsala as a base from which he attempts to make the world aware of the Tibetan plight. He has traveled internationally, speaking on behalf of Tibet and world peace generally. An admirer of MOHANDAS GANDHI, the Dalai Lama emphasizes that Tibetan freedom must be obtained nonviolently. As an incarnation of a *bodhisattva* and a teacher of Mahayana Buddhism, he says that he has compassion for all beings who suffer, including the Chinese. The Dalai Lama says that he is working for Tibetan freedom with "the powerful weapons of truth and determination."

Whenever living in Dharmsala, the Dalai Lama keeps track of world events by listening to the morning news broadcast on radio by the BBC World Service. He likes to read in Western philosophy and science, especially nuclear physics, astronomy, and neurobiology. He enjoys discussions with scientists and states that he is not interested in proselytizing for Buddhism. He is interested, instead, in how Buddhists can contribute to a peaceful world. The Dalai Lama is not dogmatic and thinks that the diversity of religious views is useful for the variety of human beings. He also believes that religious teachings should be tested and evaluated scientifically, even the teachings of Gautama Buddha, and if found lacking in basis, discarded.

In September 1987, the Dalai Lama proposed a five-point peace plan for the resolution of the Tibetan situation, but the People's Republic of China has not responded favorably. In the plan, the Dalai Lama proposed: (1) to make Tibet into a "Zone of Ahimsa" (nonviolence); (2) a cessation of the influx of Chinese settlers into Tibet; (3) that there be respect for the human and democratic rights of Tibetans; (4) to restore and protect Tibet's natural environment; and (5) to begin negotiations between Tibet and China about their future relations. In proposing Tibet as a Zone of Ahimsa, the Dalai Lama envisions his country as a "peace sanctuary" or refuge, where there will be harmony between human beings and nature. Tibet would be a place where people from all over the world could go for spiritual retreat and spiritual nourishment to enhance their work in the world. In the Tibetan Zone of Ahimsa there would be no arms of any sort. The manufacture, testing, and stockpiling of nuclear weapons would be prohibited. Tibet would extend support to all organizations working for human rights in the world.

The Dalai Lama received the Nobel Peace Prize in 1989, and he continues his international work for peace. As a Buddhist, he teaches that the Buddhist doctrine of interdependence is relevant to life in today's world in which the interdependence of all peoples and nations is becoming more and more obvious. He acknowledges that he likes his role as the Dalai Lama because it gives him the opportunity to help others. As a *bodhisattva*, he is concerned to help all who suffer. He is considering other means of perpetuating authority among Tibetans, especially by democratic means, and thus he might be the last Dalai Lama. However, he states that he will take rebirth wherever he can be of the most help to sentient beings. The Dalai Lama states, "my true religion is kindness," and he often repeats a *bodhisattva*'s prayer:

> For as long as space endures,
> And for as long as living beings remain,
> Until then may I, too, abide
> To dispel the misery of the world.

Books by Tenzin Gyatso

The Bodhgaya Interviews. Ed. by José Ignácio Cabezon. Snow Lion 1988 $8.95. ISBN 0-937938-62-9. Transcripts of question-and-answer sessions of the Dalai Lama with Western Buddhists at annual gatherings from 1981 to 1984 at Bodhgaya, the place of Gautama Buddha's enlightenment.

The Buddhism of Tibet. Ed. and trans. by Jeffrey Hopkins. Snow Lion 1975 $12.95. ISBN 0-937938-48-3. Introduction to Buddhist principles and their relevance to modern life, with special emphasis on Tibetan Buddhism.

The Dalai Lama at Harvard: Lectures on the Buddhist Path to Peace. Ed. by Jeffrey Hopkins. Snow Lion 1984 $14.95. ISBN 0-937938-70-X. Lectures and question-and-answer sessions given in 1981 at Harvard, constituting a complex introduction to Tibetan Buddhist philosophy and practice.

Freedom in Exile: The Autobiography of the Dalai Lama. HarpC 1990 o.p. Written by the Dalai Lama at age 56, a straightforward and fascinating account of his life.

Kindness, Clarity, and Insight. Trans. by Jeffrey Hopkins. (coedited with Elizabeth Napper). Snow Lion 1984 $12.95. ISBN 0-937938-18-1. Twenty lectures given by the Dalai Lama in the United States and Canada, 1979–81, including general talks on Buddhism, explanatory talks on Tibetan Buddhism and culture, need for compassion in global politics—alway enlightening.

My Tibet. (coauthored with Galen Rowell). U. CA Pr. 1990 $40.00. ISBN 0-520-07109-3. Beautiful book consisting of Rowell's color photographs of Tibetan landscape and people, accompanied by the Dalai Lama's comments and reflections.

Ocean of Wisdom: Guidelines for Living. Harper SF 1989 $8.95. ISBN 0-940666-09-X. Collection of simple but profound sayings of the Dalai Lama and his answers to questions, with color photographs.

A Policy of Kindness: An Anthology of Writings by and about the Dalai Lama. Ed. by Sidney Piburn. Snow Lion 1990 $6.95. ISBN 0-937938-91-2. Includes the Dalai Lama's Nobel Peace Prize lecture and essays demonstrating his friendship toward all people and his intelligent analysis of the world situation.

Tantra in Tibet. Ed. and trans. by Jeffrey Hopkins. Snow Lion 1977 $14.95. ISBN 0-937938-49-1. The Dalai Lama's exposition of Tantric Buddhism, a translation of "The Great Exposition Mantra" of Tsong-ka-pa (1357–1419), and supplemental commentaries gathered by Jeffrey Hopkins; prior general knowledge of Mahayana and Tibetan Buddhism necessary for understanding these treatises.

The Union of Bliss and Emptiness: A Commentary on the Lama Choepa Guru Yoga Practice. Trans. by Thupten Jinpa. Snow Lion 1988 $12.95. ISBN 0-937938-69-6. The Dalai Lama's commentary on the complexities of the Tantric practice of *Lama Choepa*, or *guru yoga*, involving visualization.

BOOK ABOUT TENZIN GYATSO

Goodman, Michael Harris. *The Last Dalai Lama: A Biography*. Shambhala 1986 o.p. Vivid account of the life of the fourteenth Dalai Lama and of the colorful Tibetan culture, focusing on the period from the Dalai Lama's birth until his flight from Tibet in 1959.

THICH NHAT HANH. 1926–

Thich Nhat Hanh was born in central Vietnam and became a Buddhist monk when he was 16 years old. In the 1950s he founded the first Buddhist high school in his country and assisted in the founding of Van Hanh Buddhist University in Saigon. During the war he organized the School of Youth for Social Service to rebuild villages and resettle thousands of people displaced by the war. In 1966 he traveled to the United States and Europe to make people aware of the intense suffering caused by the war. Like many other Buddhist monks, he did not take sides during the war but spoke out for peace. During his visit, he met with Robert McNamara—at that time U.S. Secretary of Defense— along with members of the U.S. Congress, officials at the United Nations, MARTIN LUTHER KING, JR., THOMAS MERTON, and Pope Paul VI. Martin Luther King, Jr., subsequently nominated Thich Nhat Hanh for the Nobel Peace Prize in 1967. Because of his outspokenness against the war, Thich Nhat Hanh was not allowed to return to Vietnam, and he was granted asylum in France. At the Paris peace talks, he served as chairperson of the Vietnamese Buddhist Peace Delegation. Thich Nhat Hanh continues to reside in France in a community called Plum Village, but he travels frequently to the United States and elsewhere to present his teachings on peace and the spiritual life. In the United States he has had an important impact on Americans associated with the Buddhist Peace Fellowship. His teachings reflect his Mahayana Buddhist heritage, which includes the Vietnamese tradition that corresponds to Chan or Zen Buddhism. As a Zen Master, he advocates what he calls engaged Buddhism, working for social justice and alleviating suffering. Thich Nhat Hanh stresses that Americans will develop their uniquely American form of Buddhism, which will be primarily laic rather than monastic.

BOOKS BY THICH NHAT HANH

Being Peace. Ed. by Arnold Kotter. Parallax Pr. 1987 $9.00. ISBN 0-938077-00-7. Collection of talks given to peaceworkers and students of meditation in American Buddhist centers in fall 1985, including some beautiful and profound insights.

The Heart of Understanding. Ed. by Peter Levitt. Parallax Pr. 1988 $6.00. ISBN 0-938077-11-2. Translation and commentary on the Mahayana text and the Prajnaparamita Heart Sutra; profound but simple introduction of abstract Buddhist doctrines suitable for beginners.

Interbeing: Commentaries on the Tiep Hein Precepts. Parallax Pr. 1987 $8.00. Explains the precepts for living to be followed by lay and monastic members of a Buddhist order dedicated to promoting peace.

Lotus in a Sea of Fire. Hill & Wang 1967 o.p. Record of Thich Nhat Hanh's talks in the West revealing the conditions of the war in Vietnam.

The Miracle of Mindfulness! A Manual on Meditation. Trans. by Mobi Warren. Beacon Pr. 1976 $10.00. ISBN 0-8070-1118-5. Elementary instruction in Buddhist meditation/breathing/constant mindfulness.

The Moon Bamboo. Trans. by Vo-Dinh Mai and Mobi Ho. Parallax Pr. 1989 $12.00. ISBN 0-938077-20-1. Four short stories that unflinchingly confront human brutality and suffering while conveying the depth of human spirit in lyrical and simple prose; immediately accessible to any reader.

The Raft Is Not the Shore. (coauthored with Daniel Berrigan). Beacon Pr. 1975 o.p.
  Conversations with the American peace activist and Catholic priest Daniel Berrigan
  on a variety of topics, including eucharist and death, religion, exile, Jesus and
  Buddha, communities of resistance, and a particularly intriguing discussion of self-
  immolation (by Buddhists and Catholics) out of the desire to alleviate the suffering of
  others.

The Sun My Heart: From Mindfulness to Insight Contemplation. Parallax Pr. 1988 $10.00.
  ISBN 0-938077-12-0. Flowing series of reflections—drawing on everyday life—on
  Buddhist thought and practice and their relevance to the modern world.

Touching Peace: Practicing the Art of Mindful Living. Parallax Pr. 1992 $9.50. ISBN 0-
  938077-57-0. Recent talks in North America and Europe on the practice of
  mindfulness, the roots of war and violence, alcoholism and drug abuse, social
  alienation, and how to go about the rebuilding of society and family.

VIVEKANANDA. 1863–1902

Swami Vivekananda, a Hindu monk whose guru was RAMAKRISHNA
PARAMAHANSA (1836–1886), was the first Hindu to attract widespread attention
in the United States and Europe. He first came to America in 1893 to address the
World's Parliament of Religions, which was being held in conjunction with the
Columbian Exposition in Chicago. He was said to have been the most popular
speaker to address the Parliament. Vivekananda emerged as a vigorous
defender of Hinduism against the slanders of Christian missionaries, and he
continued lecturing in America after the conclusion of the Parliament. His
message, which he termed Vedanta, was that each individual is able to achieve
the direct experience of God-realization and that the diversity of various
religions and sects merely meant that they were different paths to the same goal.
He taught that the genius of the West was in the realm of technology and
organization and that the genius of the East was in religion and philosophy.
When Vivekananda returned to India in 1896, he was welcomed as a hero who
had reversed the tide of Christian proselytization by winning Western converts
to Hinduism. He and his brother monks formed the Ramakrishna Math
(monastic order) and Mission (to deliver aid to the poor). Vivekananda returned
to the United States in 1899–1900 and lectured, particularly in Los Angeles and
San Francisco. After returning to India, Vivekananda passed away on July 4,
1902. Other monks from the Ramakrishna order came to the United States, and
Ramakrishna swamis continue to run the various Vedanta centers located in
major urban areas in America.

BOOKS BY VIVEKANANDA

The Complete Works of Swami Vivekananda. 8 vols. Vedanta Pr. 1989 $78.00. ISBN 0-
  87481-092-2. Includes Vivekananda's addresses, his famous teachings, reports from
  American newspapers, epistles, interviews, notes from lectures and discourses,
  prose writings, and poems.

Inspired Talks, My Master, and Other Writings. Ramakrishna 1987 $12.50. ISBN 0-911206-
  24-8. The notes recording Vivekananda's lessons to a small group of American
  disciples at Thousand Island Park and other lectures, as well as selected poems and
  letters.

What Religion Is in the Words of Swami Vivekananda. Ed. by Swami Vidyatmananda.
  Vedanta Pr. 1985 o.p. Collection of Vivekananda's thoughts on religion compiled by
  the American John Yale, who became a swami in the Ramakrishna order;
  introductory biographical essay by Christopher Isherwood.

BOOKS ABOUT VIVEKANANDA

Baird, Robert D., ed. *Religion in Modern India*. S. Asia 1989 $36.00. ISBN 0-945921-03-9.
  Includes two fine articles by George M. Williams on Vivekananda, "The Rama-

krishna Movement: A Study in Religious Change," and "Swami Vivekananda: Archetypal Hero or Doubting Saint?"

Burke, Marie Louise. *Swami Vivekananda in the West: New Discoveries.* 6 vols. Vedanta Pr. Ashrama 1985 $8.95 ea. ISBN 0-87481-219-4. The record of Swami Vivekananda's visits to the West, found in newspaper reports and letters arranged in chronological order.

Isherwood, Christopher. *Ramakrishna and His Disciples.* S&S Trade 1965 $10.95. ISBN 0-87481-037-X. Account of Ramakrishna's life and his relationship to Vivekananda and other disciples, prepared for Westerners.

Reminiscences of Swami Vivekananda. Vedanta Pr. 1983 $5.95. ISBN 0-87481-232-1. Fascinating collection of reminiscences of Swami Vivekananda by a variety of people.

Sharma, Arvind, ed. *Neo-Hindu Views of Christianity.* E. J. Brill 1988 o.p. Collection of essays on how important modern Hindu thinkers, including Vivekananda, viewed Christianity.

Sister Nivedita. *Swamiji and His Message.* Vedanta Pr. 1983 o.p. Booklet containing the reminiscences of Swami Vivekananda by his Irish disciple Margaret E. Noble.

Swami Atulananda. *With the Swamis in America and India.* Vedanta Pr. 1988 $9.95. ISBN 0-87481-233-X. Reminiscences of Swami Vivekananda and other swamis of the Ramakrishna order by a Western disciple who became a swami.

Thomas, P. M. *Twentieth Century Indian Interpretations of Bhagavad Gita: Tilak, Gandhi, and Aurobindo.* ISPCK 1987 o.p. Analysis of how modern Hindus have interpreted the *Bhagavad Gita* to meet the challenges of contact with Western religion and culture; treats Vivekananda as well as the thinkers listed in the title.

Williams, George M. *The Quest for Meaning of Swami Vivekananda: A Study of Religious Change.* New Horizons o.p. Scholarly and reliable presentation and analysis of Vivekananda's thought.

CHAPTER 12

Islam

Leo Hamalian

> Islam is not just a religion: It is also a civilization. In the areas of its greatest concentration in Asia and Africa it has produced a shared cultural heritage, which is often more important than regional or ethnic elements. It has given rise to societies having distinct political institutions and military and legal traditions peculiar to the Muslim world.
> —JULIAN BALDICK, *Mystical Islam*

By a conservative estimate, more than a billion people profess the faith of Islam, with the number steadily increasing. Through warfare, proselytizing, and the influence of its great medieval scholars, the religion founded by MUHAMMAD has had, from its very beginning in the seventh century to the present, an enormous impact on the Western world.

Islam emphasizes a strict monotheism and uncompromising adherence to certain religious practices. Although the history of Islam produced many sects and movements, its followers (known as Muslims or Mussulmen) were traditionally bound by a common faith and a sense of belonging to a single community. In our time the political strife and armed clashes between Sunni and Shiite sects throughout the Muslim world have shaken that sense of common unity to its very foundation. These unfolding disturbances, along with a militant "reawakening" among the religious, especially in parts of the Middle East, both threaten and strengthen Islam anew.

Islam began as a political entity with laws based on the Koran and modifications of the Koran's canon law devised by Muhammad's successors. The Islamic state developed at the expense of the Byzantine and Persian empires, the two great powers in the Middle East during the period of Islamic expansion. At its peak, the Muslim Empire exceeded Rome in scope.

According to authorities, Islam is not essentially an Arabic invention. Although it spread through the Arabic language, it is compounded of other cultures—ancient Semitic, classical Greek, and medieval Indo-Persian. PHILIP KHURI HITTI (see Vol. 3), a leading scholar in the field, maintains that the culture of Islam was formulated largely by the peoples it conquered. For a period of about 400 years, from midway through the eighth century to the twelfth century, the achievements of this synthesized culture were perhaps unsurpassed. In fact, certain facets of the science and literature of the European Renaissance were inspired by Islamic models.

The basic beliefs necessary to the faithful are contained in the Five Doctrines: (1) There is only one true God, Allah; (2) there are angels, including Gabriel and a fallen angel, *iblis* (Satan or Shatin), whose minions are the *djinn* (demons or genies) with supernatural power over human beings; (3) there are four inspired books—the Torah, the Psalms of David, the Evangel of Jesus, and the Koran (Qur'an), which contains Allah's final message and which is therefore supreme among the four; (4) there are 28 prophets, including Adam, Noah, Abraham, Moses, Jesus, and John the Baptist, but the greatest and the last is Muhammad; (5) there will be an end of this world, a bodily resurrection, and a final judgment (in some sects salvation is immediately available to anyone who falls in defense of the faith). The doctrine of *kismet* (fate, or whatever is destined or inevitably decreed) is also taught, but not as necessary to faith.

The faithful believer responds to Allah by the Five Pillars of Faith: (1) the profession of faith—"There is no god but Allah and Muhammad is his Prophet" recited correctly and feelingly at least once in his or her lifetime; (2) praying five times a day facing Mecca; (3) giving alms to the needy; (4) fasting from daybreak to sundown during the holy month of Ramadan; and (5) making a pilgrimage (*hadj*) to Mecca, through which one becomes a *hadji*, or a person of honor. Prayer is at the heart of Muslim religious life, and the faithful are called to prayer five times a day by the *muezzin*, crying out in a loud voice (nowadays amplified electronically) from a minaret of the local mosque. The most commonly repeated prayer is the short first *sura*, or section, of the Koran, beginning, "Praise be to Allah, Lord of the Creation, the compassionate, the merciful." The worshiper may chant this prayer at home or wherever he or she happens to be, alone or in a group. Whether in a group or in a mosque, there must be an *imam*, or leader, so that order is kept. Services are held on Fridays, with a sermon by the imam.

The development of Muslim thought has been marked by countless complex theological differences, often accentuated by bitter political dissension intensified by many factors—politics toward Israel, expanding populations, economic pressures created by fluctuating petroleum prices, and the influence of revolutionary thought and modern technology on traditional mores and customs.

The major schism has been between the Sunni orthodoxy (the term *sunnah* refers to the "well-trodden path of the consolidated majority") and the Shiah, the followers of Ali, the fourth caliph and son-in-law of the Prophet, who was murdered by the Kharijites (a secessionist sect in favor of a radically democratic and puritanical reform community) for accepting arbitration with Muawiya, the founder of the Umayyad dynasty. In contrast to the open profession, pragmatism, and consensual nature of Sunni belief, the Shiah emphasize transcendentalism, dissimulation, and emotionalism. The violent demise of Husayn (in 680), son of Ali, is celebrated, especially in Iran, with orations, passion plays (known in Afghanistan and on the Indian subcontinent as *ta'zihays*), and processions in which the celebrants, worked up to a frenzy, beat themselves with heavy chains and sharp instruments, inflicting bodily wounds in imitation of Husayn's death at the hands of Umayyad troops (these ceremonies are not practiced in Egypt or elsewhere in North Africa). While Shiism claims only about 50 million adherents (mainly in Iran, where it has been the official religion since the sixteenth century), its doctrines have profoundly influenced Sunni Muslims, especially in the way they venerate Ali and his family, and in the respect they show his descendants, known as *sayyids* in the East and *asharifs* in North Africa.

Shiism has produced several "extremist" sects, most notably the Ismailis (found mainly in East Africa, Pakistan, India, and Yemen), who instead of recognizing Musa as the seventh imam (spiritual leader) as do most Shiites, upheld the claims of his elder brother Ismail. Another subdivision of the Shiites is that of the Imamites, or "Twelvers," who supported the descendants of al-Kadim, brother of Ismail the seventh imam. Ever since their twelfth imam, al-Mahdi, reportedly disappeared, they have believed that he is still living and that he will appear again to restore justice to the world. Sufism, or Islamic mysticism, which emerged out of Shiism, stresses asceticism, ecstasy, and intuitive knowledge as bulwarks against the overworldliness and legalist tendencies that constantly endanger the Muslim community. The Mawlawiyah order of Muslims, founded by the famed Persian mystic RUMI and now popularly known in the West as the Dancing or Whirling Dervishes, is a Turkish version of Sufism, in which the symbolism of the dancer's robes and headdress is as central to the mysteries of the order as its texts are.

One of the most pressing questions in the Islamic world today is the extent to which Westernization should be accepted. The Muslim brotherhood, a fundamentalist religio-political organization founded in 1928 in Egypt, has been steadily advocating a return to Koranic teaching and the Hadith (accounts of the deeds and the sayings of the Prophet), at times leading to conflict with the governments of Arab countries. Many other Muslim groups are also demanding a return to strict Islamic law. Disagreement over what this would mean is agitating Muslim communities all over the world.

In Pakistan in 1988, Benazir Bhutto became the first woman to lead an Islamic country but was dismissed in 1990 for alleged incompetence, setting back the feminist cause in Islam and throwing Pakistan into political turmoil. Since the Islamic revolution in 1979, liberal trends in Iran have been reversed: All political parties are now banned, and women must observe strict codes of dress and behavior.

Still Islam has been revitalized in many parts of the world in the last third of this century and is attracting new adherents, especially in places distant from its traditional centers, such as the Philippines, Indonesia, central Asia, black Africa, and black America. The Nation of Islam was started as a separatist movement among disillusioned African Americans by Wali Fard Mohammad around the time of World War I and remained such during its expansion under the direction of Elijah Muhammad between 1934 and 1975. Its most famous convert was MALCOLM X, who by the end of his life, however, had embraced a more orthodox Islam that welcomed all races. Elijah Muhammad's son, Wallace, has changed the leadership, organization, and doctrine of the movement to conform to orthodox Islam.

The study of Islam has been receiving greater attention in the United States in recent years, partly for geopolitical reasons and partly because of the influx of Muslim immigrants. In 1993 Harvard Law School was given a gift of $5 million to establish a center for the study of Islamic law that is expected to become the nation's most extensive program in that area.

DICTIONARIES, ENCYCLOPEDIAS, AND LITERATURE

Gibb, Hamilton A., and J. H. Kramers, eds. *The Shorter Encyclopedia of Islam*. E. J. Brill 1993 $63.00. ISBN 90-04-00681-8. Emphasis on religion and canonical law.

Glasse, Cyril. *The Concise Encyclopedia of Islam*. Harper SF 1989 $59.95. ISBN 0-06-063123-6. Includes historical maps, genealogical, dynastic, and sectarian charts, and a chronology.

Hughes, Thomas P. *A Dictionary of Islam*. 2 vols. Gordon Pr. 1980 repr. of 1885 ed. $199.95. ISBN 0-8490-3121-4. As its subtitle says, an "encyclopedia of the doctrines, rites, ceremonies, and customs, together with the technical and theological terms of the Muhammedan religion."

Jeffery, Arthur. *A Reader on Islam*. Ayer 1980 repr. of 1962 ed. $57.50. ISBN 0-8369-9264-4. Substantial study from original sources illustrating beliefs and practices.

Kirtzeck, James, ed. *Anthology of Islamic Literature: From the Rise of Islam to Modern Times*. NAL-Dutton 1975 $10.95. ISBN 0-452-00783-6. Includes newly translated sections of the Koran and essays, poetry, and proverbs on the favorite Islamic themes of love, beauty, death, and God.

———. *Modern Islamic Literature: From 1800 to the Present*. NAL-Dutton 1972 o.p. Provides excerpts from works by "the best and most important Moslem writers of modern times," including masterpieces of fiction by Tewfiq al-Hakim, Mahmud Taymur, and Sadegh Hedayat.

Lewis, Bernard, and others. *The Encyclopaedia of Islam*. 5 vols. to date. Macmillan 1965–1986 o.p. Brings together in a projected 10-volume set the religious and political life of the Islamic community.

Netton, Ian Richard. *A Popular Dictionary of Islam*. Humanities 1992 $17.50. ISBN 0-391-03756-0. Both a dictionary and a glossary, covering the entire field of Islam, especially terms likely to appear in current reading. Also contains brief biographies of eminent Muslims and Islamic scholars throughout the ages.

Rahman, Habib U. *Chronology of Islamic History*. Macmillan 1989 $45.00. ISBN 0-8161-9067-4. Chronological history from c.570 to c.1000 Excellent sketch maps and genealogical charts.

Robinson, Francis. *Atlas of the Islamic World Since 1500*. Facts on File 1982 $45.00. ISBN 0-87196-629-8. Best collection of maps available.

GENERAL HISTORIES AND COMPARATIVE STUDIES

Ahmad, Aziz. *Islamic Modernism in India and Pakistan*. OUP 1967 o.p. General introduction to the landmarks of political thought in Islamic India and Pakistan, dealing mainly with individual thinkers and their works.

Ajami, Fouad. *The Vanished Imam: Musa al Sadr and the Shia of Lebanon*. Cornell Univ. Pr. 1986 $17.95. ISBN 0-8014-1910-7. A fascinating analysis and clarification of the religious and political issues at stake in the recent civil war in Lebanon, written by a Lebanese Shiite.

Akhavi, Shahrough. *Religion and Politics in Contemporary Iran*. State U. NY Pr. 1980 $47.50. ISBN 0-87395-4564. Along with studies of Keddie and Mottahedeh, presents a good picture of the Islamic revolution in Iran during the 1970s.

Aletrino, L. *Six World Religions*. Trans. by Mary Foran. Morehouse 1969 o.p. "An objective analysis by a well-known Dutch journalist of the major non-Christian religions of the world" (*Publishers Weekly*).

Amir, Ali Syed. *The Spirit of Islam: A History of the Evolution and Ideals of Islam with a Life of the Prophet*. Methuen 1865 o.p.

Arnold, Thomas W. *The Preaching of Islam: A History of Propagation of the Muslim Faith*. 1896. *Mid-East Studies* S. Asia 1990 repr. of 1913 ed. $15.00. ISBN 81-85395-60-8

Arnold, Thomas W., and Alfred Guillaume, eds. *The Legacy of Islam*. Gordon Pr. 1976 repr. of 1960 ed. $250.00. ISBN 0-8490-2141-3. A collection of scholarly essays on the worldwide influence of Islam.

Bennigsen, Alexandre. *Mystics and Commissars*. U. CA Pr. 1986 $45.00. ISBN 0-520-05576-4. Emphasizes the struggle of Sufism in the former Soviet Union and gives considerable space to the conflict of cultures in the Afghanistan War.

Bishai, Wilson B. *Islamic History of the Middle East*. Allyn 1968 o.p. Provides discussion and speculation on Islamic historical events as well as useful glossaries and bibliography.

Blunt, Wilfred Scawen. *The Future of Islam*. Kegan Paul 1882 o.p. A classic and sympathetic collection of essays by a brilliant English writer who lived among the Muslims and traveled throughout Saudi Arabia.

Boer, Tjize J. De. *The History of Philosophy in Islam*. Scholarly repr. of 1903 ed. $55.00. ISBN 0-403-00525-6. A valuable, brief account

Bouquet, A. C. *Comparative Religion*. Viking Penguin 1973 o.p. A fine study by an outstanding authority in the field.

Bowker, John. *Problems of Suffering in the Religions of the World.* Cambridge U. Pr. 1975 $17.95. ISBN 0-521-09903-X. According to *Library Journal,* a "penetrating and moving study" that devotes a chapter to how Islam copes with anguish in the lives of its devotees.

Braude, Benjamin, and Bernard Lewis, eds. *Christians and Jews in the Ottoman Empire: The Functioning of a Plural Society.* 2 vols. Holmes & Meier 1982 $94.50. ISBN 0-685-02331-1. Examines the political and social arrangements that made possible the effective functioning of a polyethnic, multireligious society for more than 400 years, assessing the fundamental issue of religion and community in the Middle East.

Bravmann, Rene A. *African Islam.* Smithsonian 1984 $17.95. ISBN 0-87474-281-1. Selection of essays exploring the social and historical dynamics as well as the aesthetic response of Africans to the appearance of Islam south of the Mediterranean littoral.

Brockelmann, C. *History of the Islamic Peoples.* Routledge 1980 $17.95. ISBN 0-7100-0521-0. A general introduction, useful for identifying many people and groups.

Cash, Wilson W. *The Expansion of Islam: An Arab Religion in the Non-Arab World.* Columbia U. Pr. 1928 o.p. A general history of Islam as it related to other cultures and responded to Western ideas.

Cavendish, Richard. *The Great Religions.* Arco Pub. 1980 o.p. Contains an excellent illustrated introduction to the history of Islam.

Cohn-Sherbok, Don, ed. *Islam in a World of Diverse Faiths.* St. Martin 1991 $45.00. ISBN 0-312-05348-7. Seeks to provide "a framework for understanding Islam in a world of diverse faiths."

Cragg, Kenneth. *The Call of the Minaret.* Orbis Bks. 1985 $16.95. ISBN 0-88344-207-8. Interesting study of the contrast between Christianity and Islam.

———. *The House of Islam. Religious Life of Man Ser.* Wadsworth Pub. 1988 $10.95. ISBN 0-534-08736-1. "A valuable supplementary text . . . strongly recommended as a follow-up to Gibb" (*Choice*).

Curtis, Michael, ed. *Religion and Politics in the Middle East. Westview Special Studies on the Middle East.* Westview 1982 o.p. Reliable and reasonably current collection of essays by authorities in the field.

Daniel, Norman A. *Islam and the West.* One Wrld Pubns. 1993 $33.95. ISBN 1-85168-043-8. Seeks to correct erroneous ideas many Europeans have about Islam.

Dann, Uriel, ed. *The Great Powers in the Middle East, 1919–1939.* Holmes & Meier 1988 $75.00. ISBN 0-8419-0875-3. Essays by a distinguished roster of international contributors, providing an account of how the great powers acted to advance their own national interests in the Middle East and how those actions influenced the nations and issues in the area so that they still hold center stage in world politics today.

Dekmejian, Hrair. *Islam in Revolution: Fundamentalism in the Arab World. Contemporary Issues in the Middle East Ser.* Syracuse U. Pr. 1985 $34.95. ISBN 0-8156-2329-1. Presents fundamentalist movements from the very beginning of Islam as a world religion and emphasizes that the present Islamic resurgence is a historically familiar reappropriation of Islam for purposes of political protest.

Donner, Fred M. *The Early Islamic Conquests. Princeton Studies on the Near East.* Princeton U. Pr. 1981 $21.95. ISBN 0-691-05327-8. "This book represents a description and interpretation of the early Islamic conquest movement, from its beginning under the Prophet Mohammad . . . through the conquest of the Fertile Crescent" (Preface).

Endress, Gerhard. *An Introduction to Islam.* Trans. by Carole Hillenbrand. Columbia U. Pr. 1988 o.p. Provides a "history of Muslim peoples, an introduction to basic concepts and problems," and an extensive and convenient chronology of important dates.

Esslemont, J. E. *Baha'u'llah and the New Era: An Introduction to the Baha'i Faith.* Baha'i 5th rev. ed. 1980 $5.75. ISBN 0-87743-160-4. The classic introduction to the Baha'i faith, a revolutionary offshoot of Shiah Islam, giving a general view of its history and teachings. (For Baha'i, see Chapter 17 in this volume.)

Franzius, Enno. *The History of the Order of Assassins*. Funk & Wagnalls 1969 o.p. Discusses the members of the Ismaili sect founded by Hasan Sabbah, who was determined to conquer the entire Middle East.

Gabrieli, Francesco. *The Arab Revival*. Random 1961 o.p. Useful opening chapter on "The Glorious Past."

Gaer, Joseph. *What the Great Religions Believe*. NAL-Dutton 1964 $4.99. ISBN 0-451-15529-7. Explains the major beliefs of 11 religions, Islam prominent among them, and presents selections from their sacred literature.

Gaudefroy-Demombynes, Maurice. *Muslim Institutions*. Greenwood 1984 repr. of 1950 ed. o.p. Describes principal institutions of Islam, using original sources.

Geertz, Clifford. *Islam Observed: Religious Development in Morocco and Indonesia*. U. Chi. Pr. 1971 repr. of 1968 ed. $6.95. ISBN 0-226-28511-1. An influential study that establishes a general framework for the comparative analysis of religion and applies it to the development of the supposedly single creed of Islam as it influences two contrasting civilizations.

Gibb, Hamilton A. *Modern Trends in Islam*. Hippocrene Bks. 1971 repr. of 1947 ed. o.p. A critique of Islamic modernist thought by a world-renowned authority on Islam that shaped both Muslim and non-Muslim views in the following years.

———. *Mohammedanism: An Historical Survey*. OUP 1962 repr. of 1953 ed. $7.95. ISBN 0-19-500245-8. A penetrating study of Islam, regarded by many as the classic exposition by a Western author.

———. *Studies in the Civilization of Islam*. Ed. by William R. Polk and Stanford J. Shaw. Princeton U. Pr. 1982 repr. of 1962 ed. $11.95. o.p. Contains 15 major essays on Islamic history and culture, including an important essay by Gibb, "Arab-Byzantine Relations under the Umayyad Caliphate."

Gibb, Hamilton A., and Harold Bowen. *Islamic Society and the West*. 2 vols. OUP 1957 o.p. A controversial study of the impact of Western civilization on Muslim culture in the Near East.

Glubb, John Bagot. *The Great Arab Conquests*. P-H 1963 o.p. Glubb, who once served as commander of the Jordanian Army, describes how Islam followed wherever the Arabs went.

Haddad, Robert M. *Syrian Christians in Muslim Society: An Interpretation*. Princeton Studies on the Near East. Greenwood 1991 repr. of 1970 ed. $38.50. ISBN 0-313-23054-4. "A significant contribution to several areas. The summing-up is an interpretive essay which will be well used by those studying minority groups, whether within or without the Middle East" (*Choice*).

Haddad, Yvonne Yazbeck. *Contemporary Islam and the Challenge of History*. State U. NY Pr. 1982 $59.50. ISBN 0-87395-544-7. Analyzes "the forces and events of the twentieth century, both within and without the Islamic community, that have made it necessary for Muslims to redefine and articulate their understanding of Islam" (Prologue).

Hawting, G. R. *The First Dynasty of Islam: The Umayyad Caliphate A.D. 661–750*. S. Ill. U. Pr. 1986 $24.95. ISBN 0-8093-1324-3. Provides an introductory survey of the Umayyad period and enters the continuing debate about the place of the Umayyads in Islamic history.

Hayes, John R. *The Genius of Arab Civilization: Source of Renaissance*. NYU Pr. 1992 $50.00. ISBN 0-8147-3985-5. Aims to introduce the general reader to "the cultural achievements and heritage of the Arabs" through more than 80 full-color illustrations and a group of scholarly essays by outstanding authorities on the subject.

Hick, John, and Edmund Meltzer. *Three Faiths, One God*. State U. NY Pr. 1989 $59.50. ISBN 0-7914-0042-5. Describes the interaction of Islam, Judaism, and Christianity.

Hitti, Philip K. *History of the Arabs*. St. Martin 1970 o.p. Among the best references on the historical development of Islam.

———. *Islam: A Way of Life*. Regnery 1971 o.p. A readable, little volume by one of the world's experts in Arab affairs.

Hodgson, Marshall G. *The Order of Assassins*. AMS Pr. repr. of 1955 ed. $46.00. ISBN 0-404-17018-8. A collection of translations of various authors, perhaps the most complete on the subject.

————. *Venture of Islam: Conscience and History in World Civilization*. 3 vols. U. Ch. Pr. 1975 $30.00 ea. ISBN 0-226-34680-3. A highly regarded historical overview.

Holt, P. M., and others, eds. *Cambridge History of Islam*. 2 vols. Cambridge U. Pr. 1977–78 $250.00. ISBN 0-521-07567-X. An authoritative survey of the society and civilization of the central Islamic lands and the further Islamic lands. Particularly good are three chapters on Islam in Southeast Asia.

Israeli, Raphael, ed. *The Crescent in the East: Islam in Asia Major*. St. Mut. 1981 $45.00. ISBN 0-7007-0143-5. An anthology created around the idea that, although the political, spiritual, and economic core of Islam is located in the Middle East, the numerical heartland is farther to the east in Asia.

Itzkowitz, Norman. *Ottoman Empire and Islamic Tradition*. U. Chi. Pr. 1980 repr. of 1972 ed. $6.95. ISBN 0-226-38806-9. A brief, clear, and precise history of the pre-nineteenth-century Ottoman Empire and its interaction with Islam.

Jansen, Godfrey. *Militant Islam*. Harper 1980 o.p. Examines the militancy of Islam from 1800 to the present, emphasizing its resurgence in the last few decades.

Kaba, Lansine. *Wahhabiyya: Islamic Reform and Politics in French West Africa. Studies in African Religion*. Northwestern U. Pr. 1974 o.p. "A significant addition to the literature on African Islam" (*Choice*).

Kahn, Margaret. *Children of the Jinn: In Search of the Kurds and Their Country*. Putnam 1980 o.p. A popular introduction to contemporary Islamic societies.

Katsh, Abraham I. *Judaism and the Koran*. A. S. Barnes 1962 o.p. The biblical and Talmudic backgrounds of Surahs 2 and 3 of the Koran.

Keddie, Nikki R. *Religion and Politics in Iran: Shi'ism from Quietism to Revolution*. Yale U. Pr. 1983 $35.00. ISBN 0-300-02874-4. An excellent study, complementing studies by Akhavi and Mottahedeh.

Kelly, Marjorie. *Islam: The Religious and Political Life of a World Community*. Greenwood 1984 $75.00. ISBN 0-275-91204-3. A collection of essays that seeks to reveal "the dynamism and diversity of Islam in today's world" (Preface).

Kelsey, John, and James Turner Johnson, eds. *Just War and Jihad*. Greenwood 1991 $49.95. ISBN 0-313-27347-2. Historical and theoretical perspectives on war and peace in Western and Islamic traditions by eight specialists.

Kepel, Gilles. *Muslim Extremism in Egypt: The Prophet and the Pharaoh*. U. CA Pr. 1986 $37.50. ISBN 0-520-05687-6. Using chiefly Arab and French sources, Kepel takes up "the challenge to Western categories of thought posed by contemporary Islam in its most spectacular, most monstrous manifestations" (Introduction).

Kettani, M. Ali. *Muslim Minorities in the World Today*. Mansell 1986 o.p. Recount of "the long, continuous and glorious epic of the struggle for survival against heavy odds of minority Muslim communities in the different parts of the world."

Kitagawa, Joseph M. *Religions of the East*. Westminster 1960 o.p.

Kitagawa, Joseph M., and Charles H. Long, eds. *History of Religions: Essays on the Problem of Understanding*. U. Chi. Pr. 1967 o.p. Contains 11 essays on the study of sacred texts, including those of Islam, by specialists in the history of religions.

Koller, John M. *Oriental Philosophies*. Macmillan 1985 $12.95. ISBN 0-02-365810-X. "While a certain exuberance allied with an over-reliance on Western or 'Westernized' Asian source material flaws the author's attempt at a complete summary of Asian philosophical-religious thought. Koller's approach has nobility and a valuable distinction—he has a gift for succinct definition that most readers will appreciate" (*Publishers Weekly*).

Lane-Poole, S. *The Mohammadan Dynasties*. London. 1893 o.p. A concise, clear exposition of the dynastic history of Islam.

Lapidus, Ira M. *Contemporary Islamic Movements in Historical Perspective. Policy Papers in International Affairs*. U. CA IAS 1983 $6.50. ISBN 0-87725-518-0. Policy papers in international affairs involving Islam.

Laroui, Abdallah. *The History of the Maghrib: An Interpretive Essay.* Trans. by Ralph Manheim. *Studies on the Near East.* Princeton U. Pr. 1977 o.p. Useful and thought-provoking interpretation of Islam's role in North Africa by an authority in the studies of the area.

Levonian, Lufty. *Islam and Christianity.* Allen & Unwin 1941 o.p. A study of the relationship to two major religions, in psychological and historical terms, by an authority who was dean of the School of Theology in Beirut.

Levtzion, Nehemia, ed. *Conversion to Islam.* Holmes & Meier 1979 $39.50. ISBN 0-8419-0343-3. Essays span the 13 centuries of Islamic history, ranging from analyses of historical processes to a review of modern European and Muslim interpretations of conversions and from anthropological studies to literary analyses of local myths, chronicles, and didactic literature.

Lewis, Bernard. *The Assassins: A Radical Sect in Islam.* OUP 1987 $9.95. ISBN 0-19-520550-2. Fascinating account of the mystery surrounding the origins and identity of the legendary sect, debunking the proper legend of Assassins as hashish addicts.

———. *The Jews of Islam.* Princeton U. Pr. 1987 $42.50. ISBN 0-691-05419-3. Lectures delivered at Hebrew Union College in Cincinnati developed into a definitive analysis of the Jewish preserve in the Arab world.

———. *Race and Color in Islam.* Hippocrene Bks. 1980 o.p. Lewis writes in his preface: "Describing the evidence of prejudice and discrimination in the Islamic countries, I have tried to correct the false pictures drawn by the myth makers, the picture of the total absence of such evils. [But] at no time did the Islamic world ever practice the kind of racial discrimination which we find in the Republic of South Africa or which existed until recently in parts of the United States."

———. *Semites and Anti-Semites: An Inquiry into Conflict and Prejudice.* Norton 1987 $7.95. ISBN 0-393-30420-5. A Princeton specialist in the Near East, Lewis explains that for centuries Christian and Muslim attitudes toward Jews diverged: Christians vilified Jews as people who had refused Christ, while Muslims regarded Jews as insignificant losers (Muhammad had beaten three Jewish tribes) and focused their hostility on Christians. Lewis, after tracing its evolution in Europe, shows how anti-Semitism was imported into the Middle East. At present, the media in the Muslim Middle East claim that John Wilkes Booth and Al Capone were Jews and evoke the memory of "that great man Hitler." Even so, Lewis contends that this insanity has not permeated Islamic society. A peaceful settlement between Israel and its neighbors would arrest the spread of the disease, says Lewis.

———, ed. and trans. *Islam: From the Prophet Muhammad to the Capture of Constantinople.* 3 vols. OUP 1987 Vol. 1 *Politics and War.* $13.95. ISBN 0-19-505087-8. Vol. 2 o.p. Vol. 3 *Religion and Society.* $14.95. ISBN 0-19-505088-6. Selections from the original sources for the history of Islam in the Middle Ages.

Lewis, I. M., ed. *Islam in Tropical Africa.* Ind. U. Pr. 1980 $10.95. ISBN 0-253-28514-3. A classic text in a revised, updated edition that presents 14 specialist studies on the history and sociology of the Muslim communities of sub-Saharan Africa.

Lichtenstadter, Ilse. *Islam and the Modern Age.* Irvington 1958 $29.00. ISBN 0-8290-0179-4. Appraisal of the problems and perplexities that confront Muslims at the opening of the atomic age.

Lincoln, C. Eric. *The Black Muslims in America.* Beacon 1961 o.p. A study of the Black Muslim movement in America.

Ling, Trevor. *A History of Religion East and West: An Introduction and Interpretation.* Harper 1970 o.p. Most helpful to the nonspecialist. "What it lacks in depth and variety of interpretation it provides in scope and general information" (*Choice*).

Mahmud, S. F. *A Short History of Islam.* OUP 1989 $17.95. ISBN 0-19-577884-5. Designed to appeal to demands of secondary- and college-level students; provides an understanding of the rich religious and cultural heritage of the Islamic world.

Margoliouth, David S. *The Early Development of Mohammedanism.* AMS Pr. 1979 repr. of 1914 ed. $22.50. ISBN 0-404-60415-3. Helpful study of the formulation of Islamic doctrine by an Oxford University don and author of the primer *Mohammedanism.*

Marshall, Richard H., Jr., and others, eds. *Aspects of Religion in the Soviet Union, 1917–1967.* U. Chi. Pr. 1971 o.p. Collection of essays intended to enhance the reader's understanding of religion in the former Soviet Union, especially of the growing Muslim population in the Adzhar Republic.

Masse, Henri. *Islam.* Trans. by Halide Edib. Putnam 1938 o.p. Intended as a corrective to the "limited aims" and "dogmatic accounts" of earlier writers.

Metcalf, Barbara Daly. *Islamic Revival in British India: Deoband, 1860–1900.* Princeton U. Pr. 1982 $47.00. ISBN 0-691-05343-X. Describes one of the major movements of religious renewal in British India—that of the reformist *'ulama* (the religious scholars) of the late nineteenth century.

Mitchell, Richard P. *Society of the Muslim Brothers. Middle Eastern Monographs Ser.* OUP 1969 o.p. The standard authority on the history of the organization.

Morris, James. *Islam Inflamed.* Pantheon, 1957. o.p. Seeks to present "a picture [of the Middle East] as it was on that day [in November 1956 during the war between Israel and Egypt], frozen for a moment in all its varied attitudes before the hot breath of history melted the tableau" (Introduction).

Mottahedeh, Roy. *The Mantle of the Prophet: Religion and Politics in Modern Iran.* Pantheon 1986 $14.95. ISBN 0-394-74865-4. Highly recommended work discussing the revival of religious enthusiasm in late-twentieth-century Iran.

Naff, Thomas, and Roger Owen, eds. *Studies in Eighteenth-Century Islamic History.* So. Ill. U. Pr. 1977 $24.95. ISBN 0-8093-0819-3. Perhaps the best collection of materials illustrating the main lines of contemporary scholarship on the eighteenth century.

Oded, Arye. *Islam in Uganda.* Transaction Pubs. 1974 $24.95. ISBN 0-87855-171-9. Studies Islamization in a centralized state in pre-colonial East Africa.

Parrinder, Edward G. *Book of World Religions.* St. Mut. 1965 $70.00. ISBN 0-7175-0443-3. Comparative study covering four parts—"Men at Prayer," "The Founders," "Holy Books and Their Teachings," and "Growth and Present State of Religions"—and featuring several maps, charts, outlines, and photographs.

Payne, Robert. *The History of Islam.* Dorset Pr. 1990. ISBN 0-88029-562-7. Colorful, dramatic presentation of Islamic history originally published by Harper in 1959 as *The Holy Sword.*

Pinault, David. *The Shi'ites.* St. Martin 1992 $35.00. ISBN 0-312-07953-2. Outlines the defining events of early Shi'ite history—the struggle for the caliphate after Muhammad's death, the battle of Karbala, and the persecution of the imams—and explains how these events were later interpreted by Muslim religious authorities to form a distinctive Shi'ite theology.

Pullapilly, Cyriac K., ed. *Islam in the Contemporary World.* Crossroad 1980 o.p. Short but perceptive discussions of the major Islamic minorities.

Rice, Edward. *The Five Great Religions.* Four Winds Pr. 1977 o.p. Includes a 30-page chapter, distilling the author's personal experiences with Islam, especially its rituals.

Ruthven, Malise. *Islam in the World.* OUP 1984 $27.95. ISBN 0-19-520453-0. Shows how Islam's "continuous political manifestations fall within the tradition of political activism going back nearly fourteen hundred years" (Preface).

Said, Edward W. *Covering Islam: How the Media and the Experts Determine How We See the Rest of the World.* Pantheon 1981 $8.95. ISBN 0-685-03936-6. Brilliant, often controversial interpretation by a Palestinian scholar.

Savory, Roger M., ed. *Introduction to Islamic Civilization.* Cambridge U. Pr. 1976 $54.95. ISBN 0-521-20777-0. Illustrated collection of essays ranging from the pre-Islamic to the modern era and showing the interaction between Christian West and Islamic East from the Crusades down to the encroachment of the West on the Muslim world.

Schact, Joseph, and C. E. Bosworth, eds. *The Legacy of Islam.* OUP 1974 $45.00. ISBN 0-19-821913-X. This work "has a two-fold purpose: to analyze the contribution of Islamic civilization to the achievements of mankind and to depict the contacts of Islam with the non-Islamic world" (*Choice*).

Schimmel, Annemarie, and Abdolajawad Falaturi, eds. *We Believe in One God: The Experience of God in Christianity and Islam.* Crossroad 1979 o.p. Nine leading

Christian and Muslim theologians exchange ideas on a broad range of theological, social, and political issues.

Schoeps, Hans-Joachim. *The Religions of Mankind*. Trans. by Richard Winston and Clara Winston. Doubleday 1966 o.p. General overview by a widely recognized authority in the field of comparative religion.

Schuon, Frithjof. *Dimensions of Islam*. Trans. by P. N. Townsend. Allen & Unwin 1970 o.p. Seeks to make "transparent the religious forms and practices of the most diverse traditions, thereby revealing the transcendent unity that lies behind their forms" (Preface).

————. *Understanding Islam*. Trans. by D. M. Matheson. Allen & Unwin Mandala Edition, 1986 $5.95. ISBN 0-04-2970-35-0. A closely argued commentary designed to explain Muslim beliefs.

Sivan, Emanuel. *Interpretations of Islam: Past and Present*. Darwin Pr. 1985 $19.95. ISBN 0-87850-049-9. Demonstrates the relationship between the Islamic past and present.

Slater, Robert H. *World Religions and World Community. Lectures on the History of Religions*. Col. U. Pr. 1963 $43.00. ISBN 0-231-02615-3. Examines the major religions, their common elements and differences, and the contributions they may make toward the survival of the race.

Smith, Wilfred C. *Islam in Modern History*. Bks. Demand repr. of 1957 ed. $88.70. ISBN 0-8357-3427-7. A challenging, controversial study of Islam in a state of flux.

Spencer, Robert F., ed. *Religion and Change in Contemporary Asia*. Bks. Demand repr. of 1971 ed. $49.20. ISBN 0-318-39666-1. In-depth approach.

Stewart, Desmond. *Early Islam. Great Ages of Man*. Silver Burdett Pr. 1967 o.p. Traces the development of early Islam and discusses its culture, science, and arts.

Stoddard, Lothrop. *The New World of Islam*. Scribner 1921 o.p. Calling the rise of Islam "the most amazing event in human history," the author provides a good picture of Islamic dynamism during and immediately after World War I.

Stoddard, Philip, and others, eds. *Change and the Muslim World. Contemporary Issues in the Middle East Ser*. Syracuse U. Pr. 1981 $12.95. ISBN 0-8156-2251-6. Based on papers presented at a two-day conference in Washington, D.C., in 1980, this volume discusses religious and political issues that concern the Islamic world from Morocco to Indonesia.

Sweetman, James W. *Islam and Christian Theology: A Study of Interpretations of Theological Ideas in the Two Religions*. 3 vols. Gordon Pr. 1980 $229.95. ISBN 0-8490-3136-2. An instructive aid to the serious student who wishes to understand Islamic thought in relation to that of the West.

Trimingham, J. Spencer. *The Influence of Islam upon Africa*. Praeger 1968 o.p. Describes the influence of Islam in Africa in a revised and condensed version of Trimingham's previous books about Islam in the Sudan, Ethiopia, and West Africa.

Voll, John O. *Islam: Continuity and Change in the Modern World*. Westview 1983 o.p. Explores the vitality of the faith across the centuries, finding the basis of today's Islamic resurgence in the continuing interaction of varying styles of Islam—fundamentalist, conservative, and individualist—and in the way each meets the challenge of the modern era.

Von Grunebaum, Gustave E, *Medieval Islam: A Study in Cultural Orientation*. U. Ch. Pr. 1961 o.p. A general overview of Muslim culture during the Middle Ages by an outstanding scholar in the field.

Watt, W. M. *The Influence of Islam upon Medieval Europe*. Col. U. Pr. 1973 $10.00. ISBN 0-85224-439-8. Fine short history of an important crossing of cultures.

Wright, Robin. *Sacred Rage: The Crusade of Modern Islam*. S&S Trade 1986 o.p. Especially candid and useful in covering the religious aspects of terrorism and violence in the Middle East.

Ye'or, Bat. *The Dhimmi: Jews and Christians under Islam* Trans. by David Maisel and others. Fairleigh Dickinson 1985 $32.50. ISBN 0-8386-3233-5. Ye'or, an Egyptian Jew, analyzes the historical realities faced by the *dhimmi*, people (Jews and Christians) who were subjected to Muslim domination.

Zaehner, Robert C. *Concordant Discord: The Interdependence of Faiths*. OUP 1970 o.p. "Zaehner's jumping from one cultural-religious expression to another is fascinating although sometimes disconcerting. His radical interpretations are refreshing and intriguing" (*Choice*).

ISLAMIC MYSTICISM, PHILOSOPHY, AND THEOLOGY

Arberry, Arthur J. *The Doctrine of the Sufis*. Cambridge U. Pr. 1977 $17.95. ISBN 0-521-29218-2. A brief account of Sufism, the name commonly given to the mystical tradition in Islam that arose from Shiite belief, by a leading Western expert on Sufism.

———. *Revelation and Reason in Islam*. AMS Pr. 1982 repr. of 1957 ed. $20.00. ISBN 0-404-18952-0. Challenging and comprehensive treatment of the problem of the "sublime dilemma" as it affects Islam.

Arnold, T. W. *The Preaching of Islam*. Kazi Pubns. 1956 $35.00. ISBN 1-56744-185-8. A history of the propagation of the Muslim faith, emphasizing its missionary nature.

Attar, Farid. *Muslim Saints and Mystics: Episodes from the Tadhkirat Al-Auliya (Memorial of the Saints)*. Trans. by Arthur J. Arberry. Viking Penguin 1990 $9.95. ISBN 0-14-019264-6. Prose work by one of the great poets of thirteenth-century Islamic literature.

Baldick, Julian. *Mystical Islam: An Introduction to Sufism*. NYU Pr. 1989 $40.00. ISBN 0-8147-1138-3. Examines the development of Sufi doctrines and practices over the 14 centuries of Islam. Useful bibliography.

Birge, John K. *The Bektashi Order of Dervishes*. AMS Pr. 1982 repr. of 1937 ed. $35.00. ISBN 0-404-16400-5. Detailed full treatment of the order, history, and doctrine.

Bravmann, M. M. *The Spiritual Background of Islam*. E. J. Brill 1972 o.p. The customs and concepts of the ancient Arabs that were absorbed into later religious doctrine.

Brown, J. P. *The Dervishes, or Oriental Spiritualism*. Ed. by H. A. Rose. F. Cass 1968 o.p. Originally published in 1868, this book remains one of the best treatments of the various orders—the Rifa'ia (Howling Dervishes), the Baqtashis, the Malamiyun (Hamzawis), the Malavi (Whirling Dervishes), the Naqshbandis, the hashish-imbibing dervishes of northern Iran (Hashshashin), the wandering dervishes of India, and the real and false dervishes.

Copleston, Frederick. *Religion and the One: Philosophies East and West. Gifford Lectures*. Crossroad NY 1981 o.p. A study of the idea, in Eastern metaphysics, of the One as the source of the many and as the ultimate reality.

Cragg, Kenneth. *The Pen and the Faith: Eight Modern Muslim Writers and the Qur'an*. Routledge Chapman & Hall 1985 $24.95. ISBN 0-04-297044-X. A selection from contemporary Muslim writers who wish to illuminate "the diversity of Quaranic understanding and to indicate how Quaranic guidance is discerned and applied to critical situations in the modern world."

Craig, William L. *The Kalam Cosmological Argument*. B & N Imports 1979 o.p. Examines one particular "proof" for the existence of God: the Kalam cosmological argument, originated with medieval Arab theologians and bequeathed to the West, where it became the center of a hotly disputed controversy (more or less over free will).

Donaldson, Dwight M. *The Shi'ite Religion: A History of Islam in Persia and Iraq*. AMS Pr. 1980 repr. of 1933 ed. $49.50. ISBN 0-404-18959-8. A thorough but not critical study.

Fakhry, Majid. *A History of Islamic Philosophy*. U. Ch. Pr. 1983 $44.50. ISBN 0-231-05532-3. An excellent account of the historical unfolding, rather than of the conceptual complexities, of Islamic thought.

Farah, Caesar E. *Islam: Beliefs and Observances*. Barron 1987 $10.95. ISBN 0-8120-3799-5. A simplified explanation of the most important components of the Islamic religion. Contains a useful glossary and annotated bibliography.

al Faruqi, Isma'il Ragi. *Islam*. Argus 1979 o.p. Among the best introductions to Islam, by a Sunni thinker with considerable teaching experience in the West.

Goldhizer, Ignaz. *Introduction to Islamic Theology and Law.* Trans. by Andras Hamori and Ruth Hamori. Princeton U. Pr. 1981 o.p. A classic introduction to the intellectual content of Islam.

Guillaume, Alfred. *Islam.* Viking Penguin 1961 o.p. Published in 1954 as *Traditions of Islam*; an excellent brief survey for the reader new to the subject.

Hitti, Philip K. *The Origins of the Druze People and Religion, with Extracts from Their Sacred Writings.* AMS Pr. 1981 repr. of 1928 ed. o.p. Though written 60 years ago, this study of a Muslim sect remains authoritative and revealing.

Hourani, George F. *Reason and Tradition in Islamic Ethics.* Cambridge U. Pr. 1985 o.p. Deals with an aspect of Islamic traditionalism's longstanding contest with a powerful current of potentially corrosive philosophical rationalism.

————., ed. *Essays on Islamic Philosophy and Science.* Bks. Demand repr. of 1975 ed. $70.00. ISBN 0-8357-6583-0. A first-rate collection that illuminates many aspects of Muslim thought by one of the great Arab scholars in the world.

Kasravi, Ahmad. *On Religion.* Trans. by M. R. Ghanoonparvar. Ed. by Mohammad Ali Jazayery. U. of Tex. Pr. 1986 o.p. The first of several volumes devoted to Kasravi's religious proclamations, introducing two of his most celebrated and controversial works: *On Islam* and *Shi'ism.*

Katz, Steven, ed. *Mysticism and Religious Tradition.* OUP 1983 $19.95. ISBN 0-19-503313-2. Contains several essays, including a concise and reliable account of the passionate piety of an Islamic sect—"Sufism and the Islamic Tradition" by Annemarie Schimmel.

Keddie, Nikki R., ed. *Scholars, Saints, and Sufis: Muslim Religious Institutions Since 1500.* U. CA Pr. 1972 $11.95. ISBN 0-520-03644-1. Anthology on Muslim religious institutions in the modern Middle East, in which B. G. Martin's "A Short History of the Khalwati Order of Dervishes" is outstanding.

Lammens, Henri. *Islam: Beliefs and Institutions.* Trans. by E. Denison Ross. Gordon Pr. 1976 $59.95. ISBN 0-8490-2080-8. Despite its hypocritical skepticism, one of the early classics on the subject and an indispensable reference book.

Leaman, Oliver. *An Introduction to Medieval Islamic Philosophy.* Cambridge U. Pr. 1985 $19.95. ISBN 0-521-28911-4. Intelligent, thorough, and highly recommended; perhaps the best work of its kind available.

Lewis, Bernard. *The Origins of Isma'ilism: A Study of the Historical Background of the Fatimid Caliphate.* AMS Pr. 1974 repr. of 1940 ed. $22.50. ISBN 0-404-56289-2. Basic work on this important sect.

Lings, Martin A. *A Sufi Saint of the Twentieth Century: Shaikh Ahmed al-'Alawi, His Spiritual Heritage and Legacy.* U. CA Pr. 1972 $11.95. ISBN 0-520-02486-9. A thorough, intimate account.

————. *What Is Sufism?* U. CA Pr. 1975 o.p. General introduction to the history and beliefs of Sufism.

Macdonald, Duncan B. *Religious Attitude and Life in Islam.* AMS Pr. 1970 repr. of 1909 ed. $20.50. ISBN 0-404-04125-6. These Haskell lectures in comparative religion delivered at the University of Chicago in 1906 remain an excellent insight into Islam at work.

Malik Charles, ed. *God and Man in Contemporary Islamic Thought.* Syracuse U. Pr. 1972 $24.95. ISBN 0-8156-6035-9. A presentation of reflections on some of the deepest themes concerning Islamic thought and life by several distinguished scholars.

Maududi, Abdul A. *Towards Understanding Islam.* Trans. by Khurshid Ahmad. New Era Pubns. MI 1985 $5.95. ISBN 0-86037-053-4. Basic introduction by a leading South Asian Muslim fundamentalist thinker of the twentieth century.

Maulana Muhammad Ali. *The Religion of Islam.* Ahmadiyya Anjuman 1992 repr. of 1936 ed. $19.95. ISBN 0-913321-32-X. Comprehensive discussion of the sources, principles, and practices of Islam, containing more than 2,000 references to 50 authoritative sources.

Metcalf, Barbara Daly, ed. *Moral Conduct and Authority: The Place of Adab in South Asian Islam.* U. CA Pr. 1984 $52.50. ISBN 0-520-04660-9. Essays exploring *adab*, the Muslim ideal of the harmonious life, consisting of knowledge of one's proper relationship to God, to others, and to oneself.

Morewidge, Parviz, ed. *Islamic Philosophical Theology*. State U. NY Pr. 1979 $64.50. ISBN 0-87395-242-1. Features essays by noted authorities on the subject.

_____. *Islamic Philosophy and Mysticism. Studies in Islamic Philosophy and Science*. Caravan Bks. 1981 $50.00. ISBN 0-88206-302-2. Contains a number of excellent essays.

_____. *Neoplatonism and Islamic Thought*. State U. NY Pr. 1992 $49.50. ISBN 0-7914-1335-7. Islamic, Jewish, and Christian scholars explore Neoplatonism as a framework for philosophical reflection in the Islamic world.

Morgan, Kenneth W., ed. *Islam: The Straight Path—Islam Interpreted by Muslims*. S. Asia 1987 $26.00. ISBN 81-208-0403-1. Skillfully meshed interpretations of various aspects of Islam by 11 outstanding scholars.

Nasr, Seyyed H. *Ideals and Realities of Islam*. Allen & Unwin 1983 o.p. An introduction written from the perspective of modern philosophical Sufism within the Shiite tradition.

_____. *Knowledge and the Sacred*. State U. NY Pr. 1989 $44.50. ISBN 0-7914-0176-6. A series of lectures by a specialist in Sufi doctrines that explores the intellectual and spiritual chaos of modern times.

Nicholson, Reynold A. *The Mystics of Islam: An Introduction to Sufism*. Viking Penguin 1990 $7.95. ISBN 0-14-019168-2. Among the finest analyses of the subject.

Qutb, Sayyid. *This Religion of Islam*. New Era Pubns. 1977 $2.95. ISBN 0-939830-08-6. An introduction by one of the major scholars in the Muslim Brotherhood of Egypt. Widely read in Egypt and throughout the Islamic world.

Rahman, Fazlur. *Islam*. U. Ch. Pr. 1979 $9.95. ISBN 0-226-70281-2. Discussion of Islamic practices and beliefs by a contemporary scholar.

Renard, John. *In the Footsteps of Muhammed: Understanding the Islamic Experience*. Paulist Pr. 1992 $9.95. ISBN 0-8091-5316-4. Multifaceted view of Islam that attempts to erase media stereotypes.

Rescher, Nicholas. *The Development of Arabic Logic*. U. of Pittsburgh Pr. 1964 o.p. An instructive history of the subject.

Roberts, Denis. *Islam: A Concise Introduction*. Harper SF 1982 $7.95. ISBN 0-06-066880-6. Covers Muhammad's life, his marriage, Islamic law, society, politics, family and domestic relations, and theology.

Schuon, Frithjof. *Dimensions of Islam*. Trans. by P. N. Townsend. Allen & Unwin 1970 o.p. Seeks to make "transparent the religious forms and practices of the most diverse traditions, thereby revealing the transcendent unity that lies behind their forms."

_____. *Understanding Islam*. Trans. by D. M. Matheson. Routledge Chapman & Hall 1989 $9.00. ISBN 0-04-297035-0. A closely argued commentary designed to explain Muslim beliefs.

Shafii, Mohammed. *Freedom from the Self: Sufism, Meditation, and Psychotherapy*. Human Sci. Pr. 1988 $32.95. ISBN 0-89885-231-5. Compares modern psychoanalytic theory with Sufism, maintaining that, as the spiritual and psychological core of Islam, Sufism has evolved a holistic concept of human development built on basic personality structures strikingly similar to those in psychoanalysis and ego psychology.

Shah, Idries. *The Sufis*. Inst. Study Human 1983 repr. of 1963 ed. $24.00. ISBN 0-86304-020-9. A popular treatment, with a wonderful introduction by the English poet Robert Graves.

_____. *Tales of the Dervishes: Teaching-Stories of the Sufi Masters over the Past Thousand Years*. Inst. Study Human 1967 $25.00. ISBN 0-900860-47-2. Features translations of entertaining and instructive religious stories.

Taha, Mahmud Mohamed. *The Second Message of Islam*. Trans. by Abdullah Ahmed An-Na'im. Syracuse U. Pr. 1987 $29.95. ISBN 0-8156-2407-7. Main text of the liberal movement started by Taha, the Muslim reformer who was executed in 1985.

Tikku, Girdhari, ed. *Islam and Its Cultural Divergence*. Bks. Demand repr. of 1971 ed. $66.50. ISBN 0-8357-9685-X. Among the more interesting essays in this collection honoring Gustav von Grunebaum is Fritz Meier's "The Ultimate Origin and Hereafter in Islam," which identifies parallels between Calvinism and Islam.

Trimingham, J. Spencer. *The Sufi Orders in Islam*. OUP 1973 o.p. Valuable historical account.

Tritton, Arthur S. *Islam: Belief and Practice*. Hutchinson Hse. 1951 o.p. A short account of the essentials of Islam.

_____. *Muslim Theology*. Hyperion Conn. 1980 repr. of 1947 ed. $25.00. ISBN 0-8305-0052-9. Useful reference to various aspects of doctrinal development.

Watt, W. M. *The Formative Period of Islamic Thought*. Col. U. Pr. 1973 o.p. Provides an excellent treatment of the Kharijite movement and the development of its doctrines as well as a detailed analysis of the chief Sunnite theologians.

_____. *Islamic Philosophy and Theology*. Aldine de Gruyter 1962 o.p. Provides an excellent introduction to Islamic speculation, with a necessarily strong emphasis on its theological side, stressing in particular the early opposition between the Sunnite orthodoxy and the rationalist Mutazilites.

Wensinck, Arent J. *The Muslim Creed: Its Genesis and Historical Development*. Coronet Bks. repr. of 1932 ed. $24.00. ISBN 0-685-13805-4. Critical study of the rise of the orthodox view.

Williams, John Alden. *Islam*. Braziller 1962 o.p. A coherent and comprehensive anthology covering important aspects of Islam.

ISLAMIC SOCIETY AND POLITICS

MUHAMMAD's social and political legacy has been developed and transformed over the generations. Islam was, from the start, a law-centered religion, and parts of Muhammad's politics are alive to this day, although the nature of the Islamic state has undergone great revisions from the simple model developed for a tribal society. The ideal of the fusion of religion and politics, however, has lasted and informs current Islamic fundamentalism from Egypt to Pakistan. The incorporation of aspects of Western law into Muslim societies is being increasingly challenged.

There is, however, a great variety of Muslim social worlds, from the feudal aristocracy of the Gulf states to the striving new bourgeoisie of North Africa. For this reason, Muslim movements are far more complex and diverse than a simplistic division between "Westerners" and "fundamentalists" would suggest. The titles listed here give some idea of the present diversity of viewpoints and experiences, as well as of Islamic social and political history.

Abraham, Antoine J., and George Haddad. *The Warriors of God: Jihad and the Fundamentalism of Islam*. Cloverdale Lib. 1990 $24.95. ISBN 0-55605-123-9. Background to and explanation of the Muslim concept of "holy war."

Ahmad, Aziz. *Islamic Modernism in India and Pakistan*. OUP 1967 o.p. General introduction to the landmarks of political thought in Islamic India and Pakistan dealing mainly with individual thinkers and their works.

Ajami, Fouad. *The Vanished Imam: Musa al Sadr and the Shia of Lebanon*. Cornell Univ. Pr. 1992 $24.50. ISBN 0-8014-1910-7. A fascinating analysis and clarification of the religious and political issues at stake in the recent civil war in Lebanon, written by a Lebanese Shiite.

Akhavi, Shahrough. *Religion and Politics in Contemporary Iran*. State U. NY Pr. 1980 $57.50. ISBN 0-87395-456-4. Along with Keddie and Mottahedeh, presents a good picture of the Islamic revolution in Iran during the 1970s.

Allen, Henry E. *Turkish Transformation: A Study in Social and Religious Development*. Greenwood 1968 repr. of 1935 ed. $35.00. ISBN 0-8371-0284-7. Studies the impact of modernism on the Islamic tradition in Turkey.

Arjomand, Said A. *The Shadow of God and the Hidden Imam: Religion, Political Order and Societal Change in Shi'ite Iran from the Beginning to 1890.* U. Ch. Pr. 1987 $14.95. ISBN 0-226-02784-8. A study of the intellectual, historical, theological, and social foundations of Shi'ite Islam in Iran.

Bakhash, Shaul. *The Reign of the Ayatollahs: Iran and the Islamic Revolution.* Basic 1986 $11.95. ISBN 0-465-06889-8. Deals with the problems of the anti-Shah movement and its economic aftermath.

Batatu, John. *The Old Social Classes and the Revolutionary Movements of Iraq.* Princeton U. Pr. 1979 $55.00. ISBN 0-691-02198-8. Impressive work, using Iraq as a case study for exploring the relationship among ideology, social structure, and tradition in the Arab-Islamic context.

Bingham, Marjorie Wall, and Susan Hill Gross. *Women in Islam.* UM Womens Hist. 1980 $7.95. ISBN 0-86596-000-3. An account of women's place in Middle Eastern culture from ancient to modern times. Includes a section entitled "Four Aspects of the Islamic View of Women" discussing property rights, polygyny, divorce, and veiling.

Boulares, Habib. *Islam: The Fear and the Hope.* Humanities 1990 $45.00. ISBN 0-86232-944-2. Examines the variety of Islamic experiences and militancy throughout the Muslim world to provide an understanding of why Islam has emerged as such a strong political force in the last quarter of the twentieth century.

Burke, Edmond, and Ira Lapidus. *Islam, Politics, and Social Movements.* U. CA Pr. 1988 $49.95. ISBN 0-520-06868-8. Fifteen scholars focus on the resurgence of Islamic activism, particularly in its Shi'ite form; Hamid Algaz's piece, "Imam Khomeini, 1902–1963: The Pre-Revolution Years" is required reading for understanding modern Iranian politics.

Coulson, Noel J. *Conflicts and Tensions in Islamic Jurisprudence.* U. Ch. Pr. 1969 $12.00. ISBN 0-226-11610-7. Examines the conflict between traditional Islamic law and the changing standards and values of society.

Esposito, John L., ed. *Islam and Development: Religion and Sociopolitical Change. Contemporary Issues in the Middle East Ser.* Bks. Demand 1980 $76.00. ISBN 0-685-20510-X. A helpful and basically reliable collection.

_____. *Islam and Politics.* Syracuse U. Pr. 1991 $16.95. ISBN 0-8156-2544-8. Deals with events and developments since 1979, when the Islamic storm broke in full fury with the birth of the Islamic republic in Iran.

_____. *The Islamic Threat: Myth or Reality?* OUP 1992 $22.00. ISBN 0-19-507184-0. "A much-needed and highly valuable account of an ancient and widespread culture too often presented only in terms of villainous stereotypes" (*Kirkus Review*).

Ewing, Katherine P., ed. *Shari'at and Ambiguity in South Asian Islam.* U. CA Pr. 1988 $45.00. ISBN 0-520-05575-6. Examines diverse Muslim communities in India, Pakistan, Bangladesh, and Malaysia, analyzing codes of behavior derived from Islamic principles and juxtaposing them with alternative codes in specific local settings.

Gilsenan, Michael. *Recognizing Islam.* Pantheon 1982 o.p. Explores a variety of social worlds that claim Islamic affiliation, ranging from the feudal aristocracy of Lebanon to the new bourgeoisie of northern Africa.

Haddad, Yvonne Yazbeck. *Contemporary Islam and the Challenge of History.* State U. NY Pr. 1982 $59.50. ISBN 0-87395-543-9. Chapter 3 ("The Zionist Challenge") and Chapter 5 ("The Case of the Feminist Movement") provide useful background for understanding two important issues facing modern Islam.

Haddad, Yvonne, Byron Haines, and Ellison Findly. *The Islamic Impact.* Syracuse U. Pr. 1984 $15.95. ISBN 0-8156-2299-6. A collection of essays by eminent scholars, analyzing "the manner in which Muslims in the past have attempted to nurture, synthesize, and implement the prescriptions of the faith in fashioning their world."

Hiro, Dilys. *Holy Wars.* Routledge 1989 $42.00. ISBN 0-415-90207-X. Provides a context for understanding the outbreak of Islamic fundamentalism in the Gulf region, Afghanistan, Libya, Egypt, Syria, and other countries.

Hussain, Asaf. *Islamic Iran: Revolution and Counter-revolution.* St. Martin 1985 $35.00. ISBN 0-19-825473-3. A study that sets out to correct what the author sees as a mistaken Western view of Iran by presenting a sociopolitical analysis, reflecting what Islam means to the Iranians.

Jansen, G. H. *Militant Islam*. HarpC 1979 o.p. Examines the militancy of Islam from 1800 to the present, emphasizing the resurgence of that militancy in recent times.

Khomeini, Imam. *Practical Laws of Islam*. Tahrike Tarsile Quran 1983 $9.00. ISBN 0-940368-25-0. Required reading for students of contemporary Iranian society.

Lawrence, Bruce. *Defenders of God*. Harp SF 1992 repr. of 1989 ed. $15.00. ISBN 0-06-250539-4. In four parts: assesses Islamic fundamentalism since the Iranian Revolution; confronts the gap between the rhetoric of Islamic activists and the reality of Muslim politics; surveys Islamic fundamentalism in Indonesia, Egypt, and Pakistan; and inquires into the unique circumstances of Shi'ite Iran and its accommodation to the Age of Technology.

Lewis, Bernard. *The Political Language of Islam*. U. Ch. Pr. 1991 $9.95. ISBN 0-226-47693-6. Investigates the semantics of Islamic political language and how Western misunderstanding of that language has led to seriously erroneous interpretations of events.

Loeffler, Reinhold. *Islam in Practice*. State U. NY Pr. 1988 $59.50. ISBN 0-88706-678-X. Through interviews, documents how Islam is practiced as an individual belief system in a Shi'ite Iranian village.

MacEoin, Denis, and Ahmed al-Shahi, eds. *Islam in the Modern World*. St. Martin 1983 $29.95. ISBN 0-312-43740-4. Eleven essays, giving a comprehensive overview and clear explanation of current religiopolitical concerns in the Muslim world.

Marsh, Clifton. *From Black Muslims to Muslims: The Transition from Separatism to Islam, 1930–1980*. Scarecrow 1984 $24.00. ISBN 0-8108-1705-5. Focuses on the origin and development of the Nation of Islam from black separatism to orthodox Islam.

Marsot, A. L., ed. *Society and the Sexes in Medieval Islam*. Undena Pubns. 1979 o.p. Of particular interest is J. C. Burgal's study, "Love, Lust and Longing: Eroticism in Early Islam as Reflected in Literary Sources."

Mehdi, Rubya. *The Islamization of Laws in Pakistan*. Humanities 1993 $35.00. ISBN 0-7007-0236-9. A detailed study of reforms made since 1977 to bring Pakistani law into accord with the requirements of Islam.

Mernessi, Fatima. *Islam and Democracy: Fear of the Modern World*. Trans. by Mary Jo Lakeland. Addison-Wesley 1993. ISBN 0-201-60883-9. Considers the impact of the Gulf War on Muslim life and asserts that women can lead the Muslim world to freedom from fears (of free thought, individualism, democracy, the imams, the past and the present) that make democracy so elusive.

Mohammad, Imam W. *Al-Islam: Unity and Leadership*. Sense Maker 1992 $7.95. ISBN 1-879698-00-5. Surveys the growth of Al-Islam in the United States from the conception of the movement by Elijah Muhammad (the author's father) to the present-day community of Muslim Americans, concentrating on the principles that unite Muslims worldwide.

Mortimer, Edward. *Faith and Power: The Politics of Islam*. Random 1982 $11.96. ISBN 0-394-71173-4. Argues that Islam provides the form and vocabulary of political action but does not determine its content, which is why Muslim movements are complex and diverse.

Naipaul, V. S. *Among the Believers: An Islamic Journey*. Random 1982 $14.00. ISBN 0-394-71195-5. Especially good descriptions of the holy cities of Qum and Mashad in Iran and of Muslim society in Malaysia and Indonesia. A valiant attempt by a prominent novelist to understand the Islamic faith.

Peretz, Don, Sofia Mohsen, and Richard W. Moench. *Islam: Legacy of the Past, Challenge of the Future*. New Horizon NJ 1984 $12.95. ISBN 0-88477-048-3. Modern developments in Islam and their relationship to civil law, socialism, and education.

Peronal-Hugoz, Jean-Pierre. *The Raft of Muhammad*. Trans. by George Holoch. Paragon Hse. 1988 o.p. Considers the rise of Muslim fundamentalism and its attitude toward minorities in Islam.

Rodinson, Maxime. *Islam and Capitalism*. Trans. by Brian Pierce. Pantheon Bks. 1973 o.p. An intellectually challenging work by a Marxist sociologist specializing in

Islamic studies, investigating why capitalism triumphed in modern Europe and not in Muslim countries and why it penetrated the Muslim world so easily.

Roff, William R., ed. *Islam and the Political Economy of Meaning*. U. CA Pr. 1987 $47.50. ISBN 0-520-05956-5-5. Discusses the meaning and prospects of Islam and its relation to the political and social world.

Rohr, Janelle, ed. *The Middle East*. Greenhaven 1988 o.p. Several specialists take opposing views on whether resurgent Islam has been useful to the Iranian people and whether Islam can avoid Western influences.

Rosenthal, Edwin J. *Islam in the Modern National State*. Cambridge U. Pr. 1966 o.p. "A thorough, competent study based upon firsthand acquaintance with people, leaders, and native scholars in each country. For the specialist and advanced student" (*Library Journal*).

———. *Political Thought in Medieval Islam: An Introductory Outline*. Greenwood 1985 repr. of 1958 ed. $55.50. ISBN 0-313-25094-4. An excellent study of the ways in which Islamic political thought has developed and the reasons for the course it took.

Tahiri, Amin. *Holy Terror: Inside the World of Islamic Terrorism*. Adler & Adler 1987 o.p. Explores the question, "Is Islam a religion of terror?"; after investigating Islamic terrorism, concludes, "No more than other major religions."

Walther, Wiebke. *Women in Islam*. Wiener Pub. 1993 $34.95. ISBN 1-55876-052-0. Of current interest are two chapters: "Women in Islamic Law, in the Koran, and in Tradition," and "Women in Islamic History."

Williams, John A., ed. *Themes of Islamic Civilization*. U. CA Pr. 1971 $45.00. ISBN 0-520-4514-9. Examines Islamic ideas on the community, political and individual freedom, law, holy war, and mysticism, using original texts.

CHRONOLOGY OF AUTHORS

Muhammad. 570?–632	Ibn al-Arabi. 1165–1240
Avicenna. 980–1037	Rumi. 1207–1273
Ibn Hazm. 994–1064	Ibn Khallikan. 1211–1281
Ghazālī, al-. 1058–1111	Ibn Khaldun. 1332–1406
Ibn Tufayl. ?–1185	Jami. 1414–1492
Averroës. 1126–1198	Jalal al-Din al-Suyuti. 1445–1505

AVERROËS. 1126–1198

Averroës is the name in the West of Abu al-Walid Muhammed ibn-Ahmad ibn-Rushd al-Qurtubi, an influential Muslim thinker who integrated Islamic tradition with Greek philosophy. Educated in Muslim religious, medical, and philosophical studies, he became the chief judge of Córdoba (where he was born) and later personal physician to two caliphs. He wrote a series of summaries and commentaries on ARISTOTLE (see also Vol. 3) and on PLATO's (see also Vol. 3) *Republic*, as well as attacks on AVICENNA's view of existence. Western Christian philosophers drew inspiration from his interpretation of Aristotle, especially his assertion that reason and philosophy are superior to faith and knowledge founded on faith. He died in Marrakesh in Morocco.

BOOKS BY AVERROËS

Averroës Corduhensis Compendia Librorum Aristotelis Qui Parva Naturala Vocantur. Ed. by Harry Blumberg. Medieval Acad. 1972 $30.00. ISBN 0-910956-54-5.

Averroës Destructio Destructorum Philosophiae Algazelis in the Latin Version of Calo Calonymos. Ed. by Beatrice H. Zedler. Marquette 1961 $14.95. ISBN 0-87462-421-5

Averroës on Plato's "Republic." Trans. by Ralph Lerner. Cornell Univ. Pr. 1974 o.p. Particularly interesting for the light it sheds on the problems encountered by an Islamic thinker as he tries to come to terms with early Western political thought.

BOOKS ABOUT AVERROËS

Kogan, Barry S. *Averroës and the Metaphysics of Causation.* State U. NY Pr. 1985 $64.50. ISBN 0-88706-065-X. A study of Averroës's response to the philosophical views of the Ash'arites.

Mohammad, Ovey N. *Averroës' Doctrine of Immortality: A Matter of Controversy.* Humanities 1984 o.p. Argues against the view that Averroës did not believe in the survival of the individual self after death, though he did hold that our being also consists of immortal, immaterial intelligence, resembling the soul in Plato. An interesting, if unconventional, reading of Averroës.

Urvoy, Dominque. *Ibn Rushd: Averroes.* Routledge 1991 $55.00. ISBN 0-415-02141-3. Comprehensive introduction to Ibn Rushd, known in the West as Averroës.

AVICENNA. 980–1037

The most famous of the philosopher-scientists of Islam, Abu Ali al-Husayn ibn-Abd Allah ibn-Sina, known in the West as Avicenna, was born in Bukhara, Persia, and died in Hamadan. After a long period of wandering through Persia, he became the court physician of Shams al-Dawlah in Hamadan and composed the *Kitab ash-shifa* (The Book of Healing), a vast philosophical and scientific encyclopedia, and the *Canon of Medicine*, among the most famous books in the history of medicine. He was also a Neoplatonic thinker whose influence was felt throughout the Christian West during the Middle Ages. Medieval thought reacted powerfully to the rediscovery, in the twelfth and thirteenth centuries, of the work of ARISTOTLE (see also Vol. 3), which had been exercising the intellects of Islamic thinkers for some time already. Hence, many of the doctrinal disputes that arose in Europe in the course of the late thirteenth and early fourteenth centuries reflect the opposing views of Arab thinkers, notably those of AVERROËS and Avicenna. Avicenna's thought had developed out of a variety of sources. In addition to PLATO (see also Vol. 3) there were influences of Stoic logic and earlier Islamic theological philosophers. One of his more important beliefs was that God is the "Necessary Existent," the necessary ground from which all existent things proceed. In themselves, he argued, no things that exist do so necessarily; that is, they may or may not be. Everything that exists must therefore have a cause, and the chain of such causality would be an infinite regression without God, the one necessary being. God is thus the cause of all existence and of all things being as they are. This "necessitarian" limitation provoked a severe reaction among Western thinkers, who saw it as a limitation placed on God's freedom.

BOOKS BY AVICENNA

Avicenna's Psychology. Ed. by F. Rahman. Hyperion Conn. 1990 repr. of 1952 ed. $19.50. ISBN 0-8305-0024-3. As in much early Greek philosophy, "psychology" refers to the soul, not the mind.

The Metaphysics. Trans. by Parviz Morewedge. Col. U. Pr. 1973 o.p. The "Book of the Wisdom of Allah."

BOOKS ABOUT AVICENNA

Afnan, Soheil M. *Avicenna: His Life and Works.* Greenwood 1980 repr. of 1958 ed. $38.50. ISBN 0-313-22198-7. The place to start for a first approach to Avicenna.

Corbin, Henry. *Avicenna and the Visionary Recital.* Trans. by Willard R. Trask. Spring
    Pub. 1980 o.p. Avicenna's mystical doctrines and their development in the context of
    the Sufi tradition.
Gohlman, William. *The Life of the Sina.* State U. NY Pr. 1974 o.p. A critical edition and
    annotated translation.
Heath, Peter. *Allegory and Philosophy in Avicenna: Ibn Sina.* U. PA Pr. 1992 $28.95. ISBN
    0-8122-3151-1. Explores Avicenna's use of allegory.
Nasr, Seyyed H. *Three Muslim Sages: Avicenna, Suhwardi, Ibn-'Arabi.* Caravan Bks. 1976
    repr. of 1969 ed. $10.00. ISBN 0-88206-500-9. Views of Islamic thought in its
    mystical and rationalist aspects.
Wickens, G. M., ed. *Avicenna: Scientist and Philosopher.* Luzac 1952 o.p. A collection of
    authoritative studies of the Persian thinker.

GHAZĀLĪ, AL-. 1058–1111

Abu Hamid Muhammed ibn-Muhammed a-Tusi al-Ghazālī began an academic
career in Baghdad but abandoned it after a spiritual crisis in 1095. He became a
Sufi mystic and, after years of wandering, settled in Tus, Persia (his birthplace),
where he and his followers took up a monastic life. After visiting Mecca,
Alexandria, and Jerusalem (which he left just before it was captured by the
Crusaders), he resumed teaching in Nishapur until his death. Ironically
considered by Europeans as the disciple of AVICENNA (because he was best
known in the West through a translation of his detailed presentation of
Avicenna's philosophy), al-Ghazālī had actually summarized and explained
Avicenna in order to attack him. In keeping with his mystical point of view, al-
Ghazālī contested Avicenna's rationalist emphasis on the superiority of philosophical knowledge to religious belief, a disagreement that found multiple
echoes in Western medieval debates over the relative place of faith and reason.
It was through his writing that Sufism, long regarded as a heretical doctrine in
Iran, was made acceptable to the orthodox. Though his works are not widely
available in translation, they exerted a tremendous influence on all later Persian
thought.

Books by al-Ghazālī

The Book of Knowledge. Orientalia 1970 $15.00. ISBN 0-87902-106-3. A translation of al-
    Ghazālī's *Book of Fear and Hope,* which was his most influential work.
The Faith and Practice of al-Ghazālī. Trans. by W. Montgomery Watt. Longman 1963 o.p.
    Al-Ghazālī describes how he examined Kalam (orthodox Muslim scholasticism),
    Falsafa (metaphysics based on Greek thought), and T'lim (the doctrine of those who
    accept uncritically the teaching of an infallible imam) before choosing Sufism.
The Incoherence of the Philosophers (Tahāfut al-Falāsifah). Orientalia 1971 o.p. All
    philosophical systems are attacked, from those of Plato and Aristotle to those of his
    own day.

Books about al-Ghazālī

Ormsby, Eric. *Theodicy in Islamic Thought.* Princeton U. Pr. 1984 $47.00. ISBN 0-691-
    07278-7. Explores the controversy stirred up by al-Ghazālī's belief that the world,
    being the creation of a perfect god, must itself necessarily be the best of all possible
    worlds—a point of view that found Western expression during the Enlightenment
    and that Voltaire mocked in *Candide.*
Watt, W. Montgomery. *Muslim Intellectual: A Study of al-Ghazālī.* Edinburgh U. Pr. 1963
    o.p. The most informative study of the man and his environment.

IBN AL-ARABI. 1165–1240

Muhammad ibn-'Ali ibn al-Arabi, also called Muhyi al-Din, was the celebrated
Muslim philosopher who first formulated the esoteric mystical dimension of

Islamic thought. Born in Murcia, Spain, he devoted 30 years to the study of traditional Islamic sciences in Seville. After travelling extensively in the East, he settled in Damascus, where he spent his last days in contemplation, teaching, and writing. Ibn al-Arabi composed two great mystical treatises, *The Meccan Revelations* and *Wisdom of the Prophets (Fusus al-Hikam)*. Completed in Damascus, *The Meccan Revelations* is a personal encyclopedia of 560 chapters extending over all the esoteric sciences in Islam as he knew them, combined with valuable autobiographical information. *Wisdom* contains only 27 chapters, but, as the mature expression of ibn al-Arabi's mystical thought, it is regarded as one of the most important documents of its kind. However, he is best known for his mystical odes, wherein, like all Sufis, he expresses his longing for union with God in terms of passionate human love (in Mecca, he fell in love with a young beauty who came to personify wisdom for him). It is not clear whether his poetry is religious or erotic, an ambiguity also characteristic of the work of the great Persian lyricst HAFIZ (see Vol. 2). Critics have found in ibn al-Arabi's poetry, as in most Sufi verse, elements of Muslim orthodoxy, Manichaeanism, Gnosticism, Neoplatonism, and Christianity.

BOOKS BY IBN AL-ARABI

Philosophy of Plato and Aristotle. Free Pr. 1962 o.p.
Tarjuma'n Al-Ashwa'q. Theosophical Pub. Hse. o.p.
Wisdom of the Prophets. Trans. by Titus Burckardt. Weiser 1976 o.p.

BOOKS ABOUT IBN AL-ARABI

Affifi, Abul E. *The Mystical Philosophy of Muhyid Din-Ibnul 'Arabi*. AMS pr. 1977 repr. of 1939 ed. $12.00. ISBN 0-404-56205-1. Courageous attempt to reduce a difficult subject to order.
Nicholson, Reynold A. *Studies in Islamic Mysticism*. Humanities 1993 $19.95. ISBN 0-7007-0278-4

IBN HAZM. 994–1064

'Ali ibn-Ahmad, known in the West as ibn Hazm, is among the greatest Arab writers. The grandson of a Spanish convert to Islam, he served as the chief minister at Córdoba until forced to withdraw from public life as a result of the odium created by his bitter attacks on his theological opponents. Though he began as a poet, he developed into the outstanding figure in eleventh-century Hispano-Arab prose through his renowned book on chivalric love, *Tauq al-Hamama (The Ring of the Dove)*. This vivid picture of life in Muslim Spain, describing some of the more intimate experiences of ibn Hazm himself, is thought to have had an important influence on Provençal poetry. Ibn Hazm belonged to the Zahiri school of Islamic thought, a strict sect that interpreted the Koran literally, recognizing no precedent except that based either on the Koran or well-verified customs of the Prophet. He wrote an influential tract on comparative religion, *The Book of Religious and Philosophical Sects*, wherein he analyzes and rejects the claims made by the various non-Muslim faiths, exposing at some length the inconsistencies in the Old and New Testaments. Because he attacked many of the most revered authorities of Islam, his books were once publicly burned in Seville.

BOOK BY IBN HAZM

The Ring of the Dove: A Treatise on the Art and Practice of Arab Love. Trans. by Arthur J. Arberry. AMS Pr. 1978 repr. of 1953 ed. $34.50. ISBN 0-404-17148-6

BOOK ABOUT IBN HAZM

Nicholson, L. H. *The Heterdoxies of the Shi'ites According to Ibn Hazm*. Yale U. Pr. 1909
o.p.

IBN KHALDUN. 1332–1406

'Abd al-Rahman ibn-Muhammad, known as ibn Khaldun, the Arab philosopher and historian, was born in Tunis to an aristocratic family long resident in
Muslim Spain. He was educated well and given various official posts in North
Africa and Spain. After serving as the sultan of Granada's ambassador to the
court of Pedro the Cruel in Castile, he retired to Egypt, where be became chief
judge. Before he died in Cairo, he went on an embassy to Tamerlane, described
in his autobiography. *The Book of Examples*, a general history of the Muslims,
especially the North African dynasties, is regarded as his principal work, but his
reputation really rests on his introduction to it—the first systematic treatise on
the philosophy of history.

BOOK BY IBN KHALDUN

The Muqaddimah. Ed. by N. J. Dawood, trans. by Franz Rosenthal. *Bollingen Ser.*3 vols.
Princeton U. Pr. 1967 $160.00. ISBN 0-691-01754-9. In the introduction to his
multivolume history, ibn Khaldun criticizes the view that history is a mere record of
events, and presents his own view of how it must be pursued and of how societies
have developed.

BOOKS ABOUT IBN KHALDUN

Al-Azmeh, Ariz. *Ibn Khaldun: An Essay in Reinterpretation*. Routledge 1990 $14.95. ISBN
0-415-03598-8. Reverses the established order of priorities given to ibn Khaldun's
thought, emphasizing historical factors that determine the subject matter of the
famous *Muqaddima* instead of the philosophy that informs it.
Fischel, W. J. *Ibn Khaldun and Tamerlane: Their Historic Meeting in Damascus*. U. CA Pr.
1952 o.p.
Mahdi, Muhsin. *Ibn Khaldun's Philosophy of History: A Study in the Philosophic
Foundation of the Science of Culture*. U. Ch. Pr. 1964 o.p.

IBN KHALLIKAN. 1211–1281

The great biographer Ahmad ibn-Muhammad, known as ibn Khallikan, was
born in Arbela (in present-day Iraq), studied there and in Aleppo, and then went
to Egypt, where he became deputy judge and professor. In 1261 he was
promoted to chief judge of Damascus, but after 10 years was dismissed and
returned to his professorship in Egypt. He was reappointed to Damascus about 7
years later but was again dismissed shortly before his death. In studies of the
Prophet, great importance had been attached from the start to the men who
reported, directly or indirectly, his words and acts. Muslim historians also
included information concerning notable men of Islam in their chronicles,
inasmuch as they were the spiritual heirs of the Prophet. Frequently they added
obituaries of those who had died in a given year as an appendix to the annals of
that year. Often such information was arranged in separate biographical
dictionaries dealing with specific professions. Ibn Khallikan occupied the
leading place in this literary genre.

BOOK BY IBN KHALLIKAN

Ibn Khallikan's Biographical Dictionary. 4 vols. Intl. Bk. Ctr. 1976 $110.00. ISBN 0-86685-
129-1. Most comprehensive biographical dictionary in Arab literature, with hundreds

of entries arranged alphabetically, relating to rulers, soldiers, scholars, judges, statesmen, and poets.

IBN TUFAYL. ?–1185

Although known in his day as a philosopher, some of whose views were criticized by AVERROËS, ibn Tufayl is today remembered as the author of the philosophical novel *Hayy ibn Yaqzan*. An allegory of the conflict between reason and religion, the story traces the intellectual development of a man secluded on a desert island who, through his own unaided efforts, arrives at knowledge of the divine. Later, he encounters a wise man of religion, who is astonished to discover that, despite all his training and knowledge of doctrine, he knows no more than the untutored hermit.

BOOK BY IBN TUFAYL

Hayy ibn Yaqzan. Trans. by Lenn. E. Goodman. Gee Tee Bee 1983 o.p. Ibn Tufayl's novel on man and nature was widely translated in Europe during the seventeenth century and enjoyed considerable popularity, often with some such title as *The Self-Taught Philosopher*.

IQBAL, SIR MUHAMMAD. 1873–1938

[SEE Chapter 8 in this volume.]

JALAL AL-DIN AL-SUYUTI. 1445–1505

Abd-Fadl Abd-Arrahman ibn-Abu Bakr Jalal al-Din al-Suyuti was an Egyptian author who wrote about everything of importance to Islam, especially the religious sciences. The son of a judge, he was tutored by a Sufi friend of his father. In 1486 he was given a chair in the mosque of Baybars in Cairo. His attempt to reduce the stipends of Sufi scholars at the mosque precipitated a revolt in which he was almost killed. He was placed on trial and afterward was put under house arrest on the island of Rawda, where he worked in seclusion until his death. With Jalal ad-Din al-Mahalli, he coauthored a word-by-word commentary on the Koran.

BOOK ABOUT JALAL

Sartain, E. M. *Jalal Al-Din Al-Suyuti*. 2 vols. Cambridge U. Pr. 1975 o.p. Volume 1 is a biographical and intellectual study with notes on Jalal's autobiography, while Volume 2 is the Arabic text of the autobiography, appearing here in complete form for the first time.

JAMI. 1414–1492

Nur ad-Din Abd ar-Rahman, known as Jami, was a Persian poet, scholar, and mystic, and the last great figure of the Golden Age of Persian literature. He studied for a theological career in Samarkand before entering the mystical life. Sultan Hysayn Bayqara, the Timurid ruler of Herat, founded a college especially for him, where he achieved enormous fame and authority as teacher, writer, and proponent of the mystical way.

BOOK BY JAMI

Edward FitzGerald's Salaman and Absal. Trans. by Arthur J. Arberry. Cambridge U. Pr. 1956 o.p. Jami's *Haft Aurang* (*The Seven Thrones*) is a set of seven long poems, one of which is *Salaman and Absal*, which expounds through allegorical love stories the mystic's quest for God.

BOOK ABOUT JAMI

Davis, F. Hadland. *Jami: The Persian Mystic and Poet*. Kaz. Pubns. 1985 $3.95. ISBN 1-56744-315-X

MUHAMMAD (or MOHAMMED). 570?–632

The Arabs of pre-Islamic times needed a hero capable of assuming a tripartite role. First, he had to be a political leader in order to establish a united Arab nation; second, he had to be a military genius who could transform the Arab raiding capacity into a fighting force capable of advancing the Arabs as a whole; and third, he had to be a religious leader with divine authority to receive support beyond tribal boundaries.

When Muhammad was born in Mecca, that great trade center was already the focus of religious piety attached to the Kaaba, the Holy Rock, and its pantheon of tribal deities, of whom Allah was one. The future Prophet of Islam was orphaned at an early age and was raised by his grandfather and uncle, both of whom were prominent members of the Quraysh, the tribe responsible for maintaining the Kaaba and its lands and sacred well. Under their guardianship, Muhammad grew up in an atmosphere of religious excitement.

Possibly from Jews and Christians who visited or dwelt in Mecca, possibly from contacts made with them on his travels, Muhammad learned something of the biblical faith. In his twenties, he married the wealthy widow Khadijah, who freed him from financial concern, supported his meditations, bore him seven children, and became his first and most fervent follower. In a cave on Mount Hira near Mecca, where Muhammad often withdrew for meditation, he experienced a vision of the angel Gabriel calling him to prophesy. When he felt convinced that the revelation was genuine, Muhammad began to preach, proclaiming Allah as the one true God, the same God who had revealed himself to Abraham, Moses, and Jesus. It was his monotheism that aroused the fury of the inhabitants of Mecca, whose livelihood depended in part on pilgrims who came to worship the gods of the Kaaba.

Muhammad was forced to flee Mecca in 622. From this event, known as the Hegira, Islam dates its calendar. It marks the beginning of the Muhammadan era. The Prophet found refuge in Medina and there established his theocracy. There, too, he began to develop his theory of Holy War (*jihad*). He assembled an army and in 630 marched against Mecca. He easily conquered the city, purged the Kaaba of pagan gods, and pronounced the brotherhood of all who became Muslims. He was well on his way to unifying the divergent Arab tribes when he died suddenly of an unknown cause (according to one legend, poisoned by a woman who sought to test his ability to prophesy the future).

The sacred book of Islam, the Koran, is written in classical Arabic and considered to be the most influential book in the world after the Bible. The faithful believe that it was revealed by God to his Prophet Muhammad, who in turn revealed it to his adherents. The 114 separate surahs, or chapters, which make up the book are said to have been written down first on pieces of paper (papyrus), stones, palm leaves, rib bones, pieces of leather, "as well as upon the hearts of men." After the Prophet's death, the book was edited and arranged by Muhammad's secretary, Zaid ibn Thabit, on the orders of the caliph Abu Bakr.

BOOKS BY MUHAMMAD

The Koran. Trans. by George Sale. Warne 1983 o.p. Sale's translation first appeared in 1734 and has passed through many editions, becoming something of a classic that is still regarded as useful in many respects, though later translations have more or less supplanted it.

The Quran. Ed. by E. H. Palmer. 2 vols. Asian Humanities Pr. o.p. An early translation that supplements Sale's of 1734.

The Meaning of the Glorious Koran. Trans. by M. M. Pickthall. NAL-Dutton 1953 $5.99. ISBN 0-451-62745-8. For the first time, the sacred book of Islam, translated by an Englishman who became a Muslim, is true to the spirit and meaning of the Arabic. With a foreword by Pickthall.

The Quran. Trans. by Muhammad Zafrulla Khan. Curzon Pr. 1992 o.p. Arabic text and English translation in parallel columns. Combines Arabic scholarship and Islamic learning with felicitous fluency in English.

The Qur'an: A New Translation with a Critical Rearrangement of the Surahs. Trans. by N. J. Dawood. Viking Penguin 1956 o.p. The Dawood translation is for those who only want a taste of the whole; the text, although a radical departure from the traditional arrangement, is perhaps more appealing to the average non-Muslim Western reader.

BOOKS ABOUT THE KORAN

Arberry, Arthur J. *The Koran Interpreted.* Macmillan 1964 $13.95. ISBN 0-02-083260-5. Professor Arberry of Cambridge University aims "to present to English readers what Muslims the world over hold to be the meaning of the words of the Koran, and the nature of that Book, in not unworthy language and concisely, with a view to the requirements of English Muslims."

Ayoub, Mahmoud M. *The Qur'an and Its Interpreters.* State U. NY Pr. 1992 $59.50. ISBN 0-7914-0993-7. First of a series of commentaries covering the entire Koran, the purpose of which is to introduce English readers to the Koran as Muslims have understood it.

Bell, Richard. *Introduction to the Qur'an.* Edinburgh U. Pr. 1958 o.p. Intended to accompany Bell's translation of the Koran, this work clarifies his sometimes misunderstood views of the Surahs on which his analysis was based.

Cragg, Kenneth. *The Event of the Koran: Islam and Its Scripture.* Allen & Unwin 1972 o.p. Examines the Koran as "a fusion, unique in history, of personal *charisma*, literary fascination, corporate possession, and imperative religion" (Introduction).

Jeffery, Arthur. *Materials for the History of the Text of the Qur'an.* AMS Pr. 1979 repr. of 1937 ed. $57.50. ISBN 0-404-56282-5. Handy for a critical study of the Koran.

———. *The Qur'an as Scripture.* AMS Pr. 1980 repr. of 1952 ed. $18.00. ISBN 0-404-18970-9. Deals with the Koran's view of its own function.

Kassis, Hanna E. *A Concordance of the Qur'an.* U. CA Pr. 1984 $134.00. ISBN 0-520-04327-8. Comprises the *Concordance* proper and an extensive index of all the English words that occur as translations of the Arabic in the Koran.

Stanton, H. V. *The Teaching of the Qur'an.* St. Mut. 1987 $190.00. ISBN 1-85077-157-X. Summarizes the essence of Koranic doctrine.

Watt, W. M., and R. Bell. *An Introduction to the Qur'an.* Col. U. Pr. 1990. $15.00. ISBN 0-85224-335-9. A recent printing of the revised edition (1970) of Richard's Bell's book about the Koran that rearranges some of the material.

BOOKS ABOUT MUHAMMAD

Abbott, Nabia. *Aishah: The Beloved of Muhammad.* Ayer 1973 repr. of 1942 ed. $18.00. ISBN 0-405-05318-5. The Prophet married many women after his move to Medina, not limiting himself to four (a variety of motives are given—some political, some personal, some humanitarian), but while his beloved Aisha was alive, he took no other woman. This is an account of that remarkable relationship.

Ali, Syed A. *The Spirit of Islam: A History of the Evolution and Ideals of Islam with a Life of the Prophet.* Hilary Hse. Pub. 1922 o.p. "An account of the history and evolution of Islam as a world religion, its rapid spread and remarkable hold it obtained over the conscience and minds of millions of people within a short space of time" (Preface).

588 THE READER'S ADVISER

Andrae, Tor. *Muhammad: The Man and His Faith*. Trans. by T. Menzel. Ayer 1979 repr. of 1936 ed. $19.95. ISBN 0-8369-5821-7. Standard biography by a Lutheran bishop, scholarly yet simple and vital.

Archer, John Clark. *Mystical Elements in Muhammad*. AMS Pr. 1981 repr. of 1924 ed. $22.50. ISBN 0-404-60281-9. Stresses that "we have not chosen to examine herein either the Faith or the record of its development. Mohammad alone engages us. Nor is the whole of his life our present concern, but only an aspect and portion which seems not yet to be understood in full measure . . . Mohammad the mystic" (Preface).

Azzam, Abd-al-Rahman. *The Eternal Message of Muhammad*. Devin 1964 o.p. This study, by the former first secretary general of the Arab League, emphasizes Islam as both a culture and a religion; a life of the Prophet is included.

Balyuzi, M. M. *Mohammad and the Course of Islam*. OUP 1976 o.p. Balyuzi candidly states his belief in the God-given mission of Muhammad and thinks such belief is a necessary antidote to Western scholars whose skepticism precludes the recognition of Muhammad as the messenger of God.

Bey, Essad. *Mohammad*. Trans. by Helmut Ripperger. St. Mut. 1984 $250.00. ISBN 1-85077-019-0. "Mohammad launched the idea of a state of God into the world. What happened to the idea?" Bey asks and attempts to answer the question by providing a historical context for the development of the idea.

Carlyle, Thomas. *On Heroes, Hero Worship, and the Heroic in History*. Ed. by Carl Niemeyer. U. of Nebr. Pr. 1966 $6.95. ISBN 0-8032-5030-4. Assessment of Muhammad is contained in the second chapter of this classic.

_____. *Readings in the Qur'an*. Trans. by Kenneth Cragg. Harper SF 1988 $14.00. ISBN 0-00-599087-9. A new translation into lucid, modern English that opens the way to a fuller understanding of the Qur'an, for beginners and scholars.

Cook, Michael. *Muhammad*. OUP 1983 $14.95. ISBN 0-19-287606-6. Incisive account of the man who inspired the faith of more than one-sixth of the world's population. Cook attempts to go beyond the traditional understanding of the Prophet to question how much of it is historically justified.

Dibble, R. F. *Mohammad*. Viking Penguin 1926 o.p. A popular and readable biography, sympathetic and often witty.

Gabrieli, Francesco. *Muhammad and the Conquests of Islam*. Trans. by Virginia Luling and Rosamund Linell. McGraw 1968 o.p. Historical study by an Italian specialist on Islam, featuring a substantial bibliography and illustrations.

Glubb, John B. *The Life and Times of Muhammad*. Stein & Day 1970 o.p. An especially interesting biography by one who lived much of his life among the Bedouin Arabs.

Guillaume, Alfred. *The Life of Muhammad*. OUP 1955 o.p. A translation of Is'haq's *'Sīrat Rasūl Allah*, one of the three chief Arabic biographies of the Prophet.

Haykal, Muhammad Husayn. *The Life of Muhammad*. Trans. by Isma'il Raqi A. al Faruqi. No. Am. Trust Pub. 1976 $15.95. ISBN 0-685-42966-5. A controversial biography by an Arab writer that, according to some scholars, lacks balance.

Ibn-Hisham. *The Life of Muhammad*. Trans. by Alfred Guillaume. OUP 1955 o.p. The standard original account with useful notes.

Irving, Washington. *Mohamet and His Successors*. 2 vols. G. P. Putnam's Sons 1868 o.p. Traces the progress of Muslim dynasties from the death of Muhammad to the invasions of Spain in 710 A.D., when Muslims extended their empire and faith over wide regions of the world.

Lings, Martin. *Muhammad*. Inner Tradit. Intl. 1987 $14.95. ISBN 0-89281-170-6. A thorough, scholarly work based on the writings of Muslim historians of the eighth and ninth centuries.

Margoliouth, David S. *Muhammad and the Rise of Islam*. AMP Pr. 1973 repr. of 1905 ed. $30.00. ISBN 0-404-58273-7. Margoliouth regards Muhammad as "a great man who solved a political problem of appalling difficulty—the construction of a state and an empire out of the Arab tribes" (Preface).

Muir, William. *The Life of Muhammad from Original Sources*. Ed. by Thomas H. Weir. AMS Pr. 1979 repr. of 1923 ed. $57.50. ISBN 0-404-56306-6. Detailed and thorough.

Rodinson, Maxime. *Muhammad*. Trans. by Anne Carter. Pantheon 1980 $5.95. ISBN 0-394-47110-5. A French version of the Prophet who "turned the world upside down."

Schimmel, Annemarie. *And Muhammad Is His Messenger: The Veneration of the Prophet in Islamic Piety*. U. of NC Pr. 1985 $39.95. ISBN 0-8078-1639-6. Explores the nature of Muhammad's importance to Muslims.

Watt, W. Montgomery. *Muhammad at Mecca*. OUP 1953 o.p. Deals with the first part of the Prophet's career, paying special attention to the economic and sociological background.

———. *Muhammad at Medina*. OUP 1981 repr. of 1956 ed. o.p. Studies the second part of the Prophet's career from the standpoint of a modern historian.

———. *Muhammad: Prophet and Statesman*. OUP 1961 $9.95. ISBN 0-19-881078-4. Essentially an abridgment of the author's *Muhammad at Mecca* and *Muhammad at Medina*.

RUMI. 1207–1273

Rumi is the West's name for Jalal ud-Din, known also as Mawlana or Our Master, the great Persian mystic and founder of the Mawlawiyah, or Mevlevi, order of the so-called Dancing Dervishes. Born in Balkh in northern Afghanistan, an important center of Arab learning, Rumi fled, while still young, with his father before the Mongol invasion of Jenghiz Khan. After much wandering, they settled in Konya (formerly called Iconium or Rum, from which his name derives), capital of a Seljuk sultanate in Asia Minor. Rumi succeeded his father as professor of theology and like him became a renowned public preacher. He first probed the secrets of the mystic way under the guidance of an old student of his father, but his real conversion did not come until his encounter with the spiritual director Shams al-Din of Tabriz, to whom he became passionately devoted. This relationship unleashed a series of rapturous lyrics, many inspired by al-Din, whom Rumi saw as the reflection of the Godhead. Rumi was buried alongside his father in Konya, and his shrine remains a revered place of pilgrimage in modern-day Turkey.

BOOKS BY RUMI

The Discourses of Rumi. Ed. by Arthur J. Arberry. Weiser 1977 o.p. Seventy-one of his short prose meditations on the mystical life, recorded by one of his disciples.

The Mathnawi of Jalalu'ddin Rumi. Trans. by R. A. Nicholson. 3 vols. David Brown 1982 $99.00. ISBN 0-906094-27-5. Recent translation of Rumi's great work in some 27,000 couplets.

Mystical Poems of Rumi. Trans. by Arthur J. Arberry. U. Ch. Pr. 1974 $10.95. ISBN 0-226-73151-0

Mystical Poems of Rumi: Second Selection. Trans. by Arthur J. Arberry. Mazula Pubs. 1983 $19.50. ISBN 0-89158-477-3. A reprint of the pioneering, inexpensive edition of 1974 published by the University of Chicago Press (see above).

One-Handed Basket Weaving: Poems on the Theme of Work. Trans. by Coleman Barks. Maypop Pr. 1992 $9.00. ISBN 0-9618916-3-7. The great Sufi master says that genuine work involves friendship with the invisible world and attention to that place where the visible and invisible worlds touch.

Open Secret: Versions of Rumi. Trans. by Coleman Barks and John Moyne. Threshold VT 1984 $9.00. ISBN 0-939660-06-7. "Barks and Moyne offer felicitous new translations of Rumi. . . . These reflections on love, the dance of selves, happiness, acceptance of life's sorrows, and the transitory nature of joy are touchingly sensitive in their search for philosophical peace of mind" (*Library Journal*).

Rumi: Poet and Mystic. Trans. by R. A. Nicholson. Allen & Unwin 1978 o.p.

BOOKS ABOUT RUMI

Chittick, William C. *The Sufi Path of Love: The Spiritual Teachings of Rumi.* State U. NY Pr. 1984. $44.50. ISBN 0-87395-723-7. Divides Rumi's message into three aspects: knowledge or theory; works or practice; and attainment of God, or "spiritual psychology."

Iqbal, Afzal. *The Life and Work of Muhammad Jalal-ud Din Rumi.* Ins. Study Human 1983 $30.00. ISBN 0-86304-33-0. This promises to become the standard scholarly work on the great poet.

CHAPTER 13

Judaism

Jacob Neusner and Alan J. Avery-Peck

> If you have learned much Torah, do not claim credit for it, since it was for
> that purpose that you were created.
> —RABBAN YOHANAN BEN ZAKKAI, *Mishnah Abot* 2:8

When we speak of "Judaism," we refer to a religious account of a social system—the way of life of a social group, its worldview, and its theory of itself as a social entity—that appeals to the Pentateuch, or Five Books of Moses (Genesis, Exodus, Leviticus, Numbers, and Deuteronomy), as the exhaustive account of God's self-manifestation to humanity and that calls itself "Israel," meaning the group in the here and now to which the Pentateuch and other parts of ancient Israel's Scripture refer. Through time, there have been many such Judaic systems or Judaisms. It follows that Judaism encompasses a complex religious world. The Jews themselves form one of humanity's older enduring groups. In the nature of things, the longer a group exists, the more interesting is its history, the more diverse is its culture, and the more complex is its society. In the case of the Jews, who look back on 4,000 years of continuous history, matters are still further complicated by dispersion throughout Europe, Asia, North and South Africa, North and Latin America, and Australasia. No single history of a given group of people in a single territory encompasses all of the histories that Jews in many parts of the world have written for themselves, so one cannot speak of a single, unitary, linear, harmonious, and incremental Jewish history, any more than one can define a single Judaism, emerging everywhere through space and time. Because Christianity and Islam share the Hebrew Scriptures, or Old Testament, and because all parties take for granted that today's Jews form the descendants of the "Israel" of those Scriptures, considerable interest attaches to Jews and what they do and are.

The more we know, the more complicated we realize are both the history of the Jews and the history of Judaism. The complication is the same for both religion and society. Jews from 586 B.C. onward have lived, not in a single country, but in many lands. The condition of dispersion is normal. Furthermore, although Jews appeal to the Hebrew Bible as the authority and source of theology and law alike, nonetheless, through time, Jews have formed a variety of Judaic religious systems—not one Judaism but many Judaisms—each autonomous, each identifying an urgent question and offering a self-evidently valid answer. These Judaisms are not coherent with one another and do not form a linear chain back to Scripture. In antiquity, we realize, a range of Judaic systems—worldviews, ways of life, each addressed to a distinct definition of a social entity called an "Israel"—flourished. The Essene community of Qumran, for example, constitutes one such Judaic religious system, not to be treated as harmonious with, or a linear development of, any other Judaism either

contemporary with, or prior to, itself. Because every Judaic system takes up a
distinctive, urgent question and presents an answer found by its adherents to be
self-evidently true, we realize that the questions that are found to be urgent and
the answers that are deemed to be self-evident will prove diverse among the
various Judaisms. Along these same lines, there has been no one linear and
unitary "Jewish history." Because Jews lived in various places, in diverse
political and cultural circumstances, they also have worked out various
histories. Jews' histories are not continuous with one another and do not form a
single linear chain, a unitary "Jewish history," any more than the various
Judaisms all grow out of one another, or all together, out of Scripture (except
after the fact). It follows that, the more we know about the Jews as a group and
about their religion, the more complex matters appear to be.

   This bibliography lays forth the history, religion, and culture of Judaism in all
its complexity. It distinguishes between the history of the Jews as a group of
people and the history of Judaism as a religion. Within the category of Judaism,
it distinguishes between personal ideology and institutionalized movements.
The bibliography begins with general works; subsequent subsections divide
Judaism into ancient, medieval, and modern historical periods, with subsections devoted to specific aspects of Jewish life and experience.

GENERAL WORKS

   Although people take for granted that there is a single Jewish "people" with
one unitary history, the Jews have, in fact, formed diverse groups over time,
each such group in its particular location living out a distinct history of its own.
The Jews in ancient Egypt had their own history, which moved along its own
lines, different from the history of the Jews in the Land of Israel ("Palestine"),
and the Jews in Babylonia had yet another distinct history. In a few ways, these
historical entities shared common traits, but they do not present a single
history. Hence, one-volume histories of the Jews, although popular, give a sense
of unity and cogency that, in fact, the evidence does not support. Still, these
histories are an excellent way of gaining a perspective on the long and diverse
histories of Jews in various places and times, and they provide a good
introduction to a subject that is far more complex than people realize.
Comprehensive works propose to link Jews' histories in different times and
places into the history of the Jews, treating as one the various diverse groups.
These works tend to take a diachronic view, joining data from a long time span,
but selecting only facts deemed continuous and understood as incremental. The
alternative (the synchronic) view sees Jews in particular times and places and
describes them within the encompassing framework of the age under discussion. The former approach is more popular, because it tells a sustained
narrative, beginning to end, and gives readers the sense that they know almost
the whole story. The latter approach presents difficulties, because it maintains
that there really is no "whole story." The general works listed here carefully
define and delineate matters so that there is no oversimplification or harmoni-
zation of diverse acts into a single fictive picture. The histories that follow,
whether by one author or many, tend to telescope much into a small
framework. Nonetheless, all provide valuable introductions to individual topics
and problems. Furthermore, in the case of the Jews and Judaism, efforts to
interpret facts into meaningful patterns fall into the category of theology, and

thus histories of the Jews, which teach lessons and draw meaningful conclusions, form the counterpart, for Judaism, of theology in Christianity.

Two large and important encyclopedias, one of which is outdated but still useful, should be consulted also. *The Jewish Encyclopedia* (1901–06) contains many classic articles, even though knowledge has grown and the twentieth century is omitted. The *Encyclopedia Judaica* (1972), though flawed, is the single best introduction to most of the topics it covers, and it can be read sequentially for the vast information that it contains. The histories of Jews in various times and places are well narrated there, and the events of the Holocaust—the destruction of most of the Jews in continental Europe by the Germans from 1933 through 1945—are recorded place by place and event by event.

Ausubel, Nathan, and David C. Gross. *Pictorial History of the Jewish People from Biblical Times to Our Own Day throughout the World*. Crown Pub. Group 1984 $19.95. ISBN 0-517-55283-3. An update of Ausubel's one-volume work, originally published in 1953, including more than 1,000 photographs and short essays covering many details of Jewish history from biblical events to the present.

Barnavi, Eli, ed. *A Historical Atlas of the Jewish People: From the Time of the Patriarchs to the Present*. Knopf 1992 $49.50. ISBN 0-679-40332-9. Covering three millenia of Jewish history and culture through a concise text, accurate well-drawn maps, and a sumptuous array of photographs, diagrams, and reproductions of paintings.

Baron, Salo W. *The Jewish Community: Its History and Structure to the American Revolution*. 3 vols. Greenwood 1972 repr. of 1942 ed. o.p. Detailed study of Jewish political and religious institutions from antiquity until the early modern period.

———. *A Social and Religious History of the Jews*. 15 vols. Col. U. Pr. 1958–73 $65.00 ea. ISBN 0-231-08838-8. A monumental work of scholarship, covering all aspects of Jewish history from antiquity through the medieval period, and an indispensable reference work for any major library.

Baron, Salo W., and others. *Economic History of the Jews*. Ed. by Nahum Gross. Schocken 1976 o.p. A broad range of articles, originally published in the *Encyclopedia Judaica*, on Jewish economic history, from agriculture in ancient Israel to department stores in America.

Ben-Sasson, Haim, ed. *A History of the Jewish People*. HUP 1976 $22.95. ISBN 0-674-39731-2. A comprehensive survey with articles written by scholars at the Hebrew University of Jerusalem, often reflecting an Israeli perspective.

Biale, David. *Power and Powerlessness in Jewish History*. Schocken 1986 $18.95. ISBN 0-805-20841-0. Seeks to dispel the myth of Jewish political passivity and ineptitude through consideration of activities and ideologies of the Jewish community from the Middle Ages to the present.

Bridger, David, and Samuel Wolk, eds. *The New Jewish Encyclopedia*. Behrman 1976 $19.95. ISBN 0-874-41120-3. A good one-volume encyclopedia, designed for young readers.

Conway, Joan. *The Diaspora Story: The Epic of the Jewish People among the Nations*. Random 1980 o.p. An overview of Jewish history, full of photos, paintings, maps, and charts.

Eban, Abba. *Heritage: Civilization and the Jews*. Summit 1984 $40.00. ISBN 0-671-44103-5. Attractive coffee-table book, with photographs, illustrations, and maps, providing a superficial account of Jewish history and culture through the ages, based on the popular Public Broadcasting System television series.

———. *My People: Story of the Jews*. Random 1968 $14.95. ISBN 0-874-41294-3. A sounder treatment of Jewish history than the preceding work, especially the sections on modern Israeli politics.

Eisenstadt, Schmuel N. *Jewish Civilization: The Jewish Historical Experience in a Comparative Perspective*. State U. NY Pr. 1992 $74.50. ISBN 0-79141-1095-1. Begins with ancient Israel and concludes with contemporary Judaism and the modern state of Israel, arguing that Jewish historical experience is best understood when the Jews are seen not as a religious or ethnic group alone, but as bearers of a civilization.

Encyclopedia Judaica. 16 vols. Macmillan 1972 o.p. Excellent articles by important scholars on every imaginable topic concerning Jews and Judaism.

Feingold, Henry L., ed. *Jewish People in America.* 5 vols. Johns Hopkins 1992 $145.00. ISBN 0-8018-4486-X. The primary theme connecting these five volumes is the tension between accommodation and group survival as Jews attempted to maintain their group identity through succeeding generations.

Finkelstein, Louis, ed. *The Jews: Their History, Culture, and Religion.* 2 vols. Greenwood 1979 repr. of 1960 ed. o.p. Collection of articles, of the highest quality, on the history of Jews and Judaism.

Fischel, Jack, and Sanford Pinsker, eds. *Jewish-American History and Culture: An Encyclopedia.* 2 vols. Garland 1992 $95.00. ISBN 0-8240-6622-7. Emphasis is on the significant impact that Jews have had on American life and culture. An expansive treatment of serious topics such as Black-Jewish relations, Jewish organizations, and important Jewish figures.

Grayzel, Solomon. *A History of the Jews.* NAL-Dutton 1968 repr. of 1947 ed. $14.95. ISBN 0-452-00694-5. A popular and readable one-volume history of the Jews that is frequently uncritical and apologetic.

Gribetz, Judah, and others. *The Timetables of Jewish History: A Chronology of the Most Important People and Events in Jewish History.* S&S Trade 1993 $35.00. ISBN 0-671-64007-0. Covers a span of time from prehistory through 1991 arranged in tabular form under the headings of General History, Jewish History, and Jewish Culture.

The Jewish Encyclopedia. 12 vols. Gordon Pr. 1976 repr. of 1901–06 ed. $2,400.00. ISBN 0-849-02101-4. Documents the state of Jewish knowledge at the turn of the century and includes many articles that are still the authoritative statements on their subjects.

Kedourie, Elie, ed. *The Jewish World: History and Culture of the Jewish People.* Abrams 1979 o.p. A richly illustrated introduction to Jewish civilization by various scholars.

Kellerman, Aharon. *Society and Settlement: Jewish Land of Israel in the Twentieth Century.* State U. NY Pr. 1993 $59.50. ISBN 0-7914-1295-4. Scrutinizes the interrelationships between Jewish spatial organization and social structure and change in Palestine/Israel.

Kobler, Franz, ed. *Letters of Jews through the Ages.* 2 vols. Hebrew Pub. 1978 $7.95 ea. ISBN 0-852-22212-2. Vol. 1, *From Biblical Times to the Renaissance to the Emancipation.* Reprints and provides introductions to private letters that give a view of the everyday world of Jews, often very different from the view afforded by religious texts and public documents.

Lewis, Bernard. *The Jews of Islam.* Princeton U. Pr. 1984 $42.50. ISBN 0-691-05419-3. A scholarly analysis of the close cultural interchange between Arabs and Jews over 14 centuries, by one of the foremost authorities on Islam.

Margolis, Max, and Alexander Marx. *History of the Jewish People.* Atheneum 1969 o.p. A collection of the basic facts about the Jews' histories in various times and places.

Meyer, Michael A., ed. *Ideas of Jewish History. Lib. of Jewish Studies.* Wayne St. U. Pr. 1987 $15.95. ISBN 0-814-31950-5. Documents the various ways Jews throughout the ages have understood their own particular historical experience.

Neusner, Jacob. *Self-Fulfilling Prophecy: Exile and Return as the History of Judaism. South Florida Studies in the History of Judaism.* Scholars Pr. GA 1990 $25.00. ISBN 1-555-40494-4. Suggests that all Judaic systems refer back to the pattern of exile and return.

Raphael, Chaim. *The Road from Babylon: The Story of Sephardic and Oriental Jews.* HarpC 1986 $22.45. ISBN 0-06-039048-4. An attractive and readable overview of the history of Jewish communities in non-Western countries, from their origins to the twentieth century.

Roth, Cecil. *A History of the Jews: From Earliest Times through the Six-Day War.* Schocken 1970 $16.00. ISBN 0-805-20009-6. A concise and readable survey that views the Jews in relationship to their cultural and historical backgrounds.

Schwarz, Leo W., ed. *Great Ages and Ideas of the Jewish People*. Random 1977 $17.00. ISBN 0-394-60413-X. A popular collection of essays by noted scholars emphasizing the cultural and religious history of the Jews in each period, from ancient Israel to the "American Experience."

Seltzer, Robert M. *Jewish People, Jewish Thought: The Jewish Experience in History*. Macmillan 1982 $29.95. ISBN 0-024-08940-0. Surveys Jewish religious and intellectual development in the contexts of changing social and political circumstances.

Shenker, Israel. *Coat of Many Colors: Pages from Jewish Life*. Doubleday 1985 o.p. Discusses with wit and insight the features of religion, language, and attitudes that make Jews a distinct group.

Sigal, Phillip. *Judaism: The Evolution of a Faith*. Rev. and ed. by Lillian Sigal. Eerdmans 1989 o.p. Discusses the history of Judaism and features an appendix by Lillian Sigal on "images of women in Judaism."

Silver, Daniel J., and Bernard Martin. *A History of Judaism*. 2 vols. Basic 1974 o.p. A good introduction to the history of Judaism that occasionally touches on the social and political history of the Jews.

Werblowsky, Zwi, and Geoffrey Wigoder, eds. *The Encyclopedia of the Jewish Religion*. Modan-Adama 1986 $39.95. ISBN 0-915-36153-1. Nontechnical, one-volume encyclopedia of Jewish beliefs and practices and key figures in the history of Judaism.

Yerushalmi, Yosef H. *Zakhor: Jewish History and Jewish Memory*. Stroum Lectures in Jewish Studies. U. of Wash. Pr. 1982 $17.50. ISBN 0-295-95939-8. A philosophic history of Jewish historiography, arguing that memory always has held a central place in Judaism but that historians have played an uncertain and ambiguous role.

Judaism

Judaism comprises a sizable family of related but essentially independent Judaic systems. For a long time, only a single system existed, variously called "Rabbinic Judaism," "classical Judaism," or "the Judaism of the dual Torah." This single paramount system drew its meaning from the myth that God revealed the Torah to Moses at Sinai in two media—writing and memory. The system defines the canon on the basis of which people write books on the philosophy and theology of Judaism, the ethics of Judaism, the religious practices (including the liturgy) of Judaism, and the like.

There is, of course, no such thing as a single, uniform "Judaism." Quite to the contrary, history yields many Judaisms, each with its own worldview, way of life, and definition of who and what constitutes "Israel." Any system that claims to encompass all Jews and to deal with every important document is, by definition, making selections—selections that are guided by a prior criterion for what is important. That is why, to understand the Jewish worldview, the reader moves from history to theology and to efforts to explain and account for the whole of Jewish experience, viewed all together and all at once. Theology in the form of reflection on the past, present, and future character and condition of the Jews need not deal in particular with the proof and definition of God; rather, much of it addresses the condition of "Israel," the holy people, and can incorporate sociology and even ethnography. The main thrust of works on the Jewish worldview, however, is the effort to see things whole and in a cogent way.

What has been said about the Jewish worldview applies equally to the Judaic way of life. It is true that Scripture assigns to Israel and the Jewish people certain religious duties. As diverse Judaisms read Scripture, however, each one makes choices concerning which selected truths of Scripture prove relevant to the system at hand. Any account of the Jewish way of life today will address the way of life required by the Judaism of the dual Torah (oral and written), will cover the liturgy and holy way of life of that particular Judaism, and will describe the holy days and festivals as these are designated and observed by the Judaism. Such an account will not take up issues of the sociology of Jews in the modern world, indicators of behavior that today are deemed distinctive to Jews. Judaism in the form of the dual Torah is what tells us about the Judaic way of life.

GENERAL

Bamberger, Bernard J. *The Story of Judaism*. Schocken 1964 $17.95. ISBN 0-805-20077-0. A well-written history of Jewish ideas, practice, and institutions.

Baron, Salo W. *A Social and Religious History of the Jews*. Col. U. Pr. 1993. ISBN 0-231-08856-6. An index to the final 10 volumes of the revised and enlarged second edition of Baron's history of the Jews since ancient times. Picks up with Volume 9, *Late Middle Ages and Era of European Expansion, 1200–1650: On the Empire's Periphery*.

Birnbaum, Philip. *Encyclopedia of Jewish Concepts (A Book of Jewish Concepts)*. Hebrew Pub. 1979 $27.50. ISBN 0-884-82930-8. A useful resource with short articles on Jewish terms and concepts, listed alphabetically by transliterated Hebrew words.

Davies, W. D., ed. *The Cambridge History of Judaism*. Cambridge U. Pr. 1984 $84.95. ISBN 0-521-21880-2. Collections of essays of uneven quality on various topics.

Glatzer, Nahum N. *The Judaic Tradition*. Behrman 1982 $9.95. ISBN 0-87441-334-3

Himelstein, Shamvel. *The Jewish Primer*. Facts on File 1992 repr. of 1991 ed. ISBN 0-8160-2849-4. An introductory guide to all facets of Judaism, composed in question-and-answer form.

Jacobs, Louis. *The Book of Jewish Belief*. Behrman 1984 $8.95. ISBN 0-874-41379-6. Very basic and at times superficial introduction to Jewish thought, with illustrations.

Kaufman, William E. *Contemporary Jewish Philosophies*. Wayne St. U. Pr. 1992 repr. of 1976 ed. $14.95. ISBN 0-8143-2429-0. A systematic critique of the theological and philosophical views of the major Jewish thinkers of the twentieth century.

Lewisohn, Ludwig. *What Is This Jewish Heritage?* B'nai B'rith Bk. 1954 o.p. A powerful, brief statement of why young Jews should affirm their Jewish roots.

Neusner, Jacob. *Between Time and Eternity: The Essentials of Judaism*. Wadsworth Pub. 1975 ISBN 0-822-0160-2. An introduction to the fundamentals of Judaism.

———. *An Introduction to Judaism. Textbook and Anthology*. Westminster John Knox 1992 $24.99. ISBN 0-664-25348-2

———. *Life of Torah: Readings in the Jewish Religious Experience*. Wadsworth Pub. 1974 o.p. An anthology of modern classical writings on the principal aspects of Judaic religious life.

———. *The Way of Torah. An Introduction to Judaism. Living Religion of Man Ser.* Ed. by Frederick Streng. Wadsworth Pub. rev. ed. 1993. ISBN 0-534-16938-4. A simple introduction to the history and beliefs of Judaism, from the beginning to the present; the most widely used textbook for the academic study of Judaism.

Petuchowski, Jacob J. *Heirs of the Pharisees*. U. Pr. of Amer. 1986 repr. of 1970 ed. $22.00. ISBN 0-819-15256-0. Examines the worldview and way of life of the ancient Pharisees as a model for contemporary Judaism.

Prager, Dennis, and Joseph Telushkin. *The Nine Questions People Ask about Judaism*. S & S Trade 1981 $14.95. ISBN 0-671-62261-7. Written for skeptical Jews and curious Christians, this book answers, in a controversial style, such common questions as "How can I believe in God after the Holocaust?" and "Why shouldn't I intermarry?"

Roth, Leon. *Judaism: A Portrait*. Schocken 1972 repr. of 1961 ed. o.p. A fluent introduction to Judaism by a traditionally minded philosopher.

Seeskin, Kenneth. *Jewish Philosophy in a Secular Age*. State U. NY Pr. 1990 $59.50. ISBN 0-7914-0104-9. A dialogue concentrating on selected texts and themes pertaining to Jewish philosophy.

Steinberg, Milton. *Basic Judaism*. Aronson 1987 $20.00. ISBN 0-876-68975-6. This compact book remains one of the best elementary introductions to Jewish thought, practice, and institutions.

Wouk, Herman. *This Is My God*. Doubleday 1991 $15.95. ISBN 0-8027-2643-7. For those interested in a readable, one-volume introduction to Judaism.

ART AND MUSIC

Although many people suppose that the commandment against making a graven image prevented Jews from developing an artistic tradition, the opposite is true. From antiquity to the present, Jews have decorated synagogues, made objects for cultic and ritual use, and otherwise fostered a graphic and tactile artistic tradition. Moreover, a musical tradition began with the requirement that synagogue liturgy be sung, and, still more important, for the Torah to be read aloud in accord with a fixed pattern of cantillation. Thus, in both art and music, a long tradition of expression has marked the history of Judaism.

Frankel, Ellen, and Betsy P. Teutsch. *Encyclopedia of Jewish Symbols*. Aronson 1992 $35.00. ISBN 0-87668-594-7. Around 250 entries trace the history and meaning of symbols important to Jewish ideas and experience.

Kanof, Abram. *Jewish Art and Religious Observance*. Abrams 1980 o.p. Historical, pictorial overview of Jewish observance at home and in the synagogue, featuring a beautiful presentation of ceremonial art objects with an analysis of their relationship to Judaism.

Krinsky, Carol Herselle. *Synagogues of Europe: Architecture, History, Meaning*. Architectural Hist. Found. 1985 $60.00. ISBN 0-262-11097-0. An attractive and thorough treatment of the architecture, history, and meaning of the synagogue, from antiquity to the twentieth century.

Landsberger, Franz. *A History of Jewish Art*. Kennikat 1973 o.p. An excellent introduction to Jewish art through the ages.

Levine, Lee I., ed. *The Synagogue in Late Antiquity*. Jewish Sem. 1987 $26.95. ISBN 0-317-64344-4. Thirteen essays on a variety of loosely linked subjects.

Neusner, Jacob, ed. *Goodenough's Jewish Symbols: An Abridged Edition*. Princeton U. Pr. 1988 $44.50. ISBN 0-691-09967-7. The most important portions of Goodenough's classic 13-volume work.

Roth, Cecil. *Jewish Art: An Illustrated History*. NY Graphic Soc. 1971 o.p. Revised and updated by Bezalel Narkiss. Survey of Jewish art culled from many contexts.

Shiloah, Amnon. *Jewish Musical Traditions*. Jewish Folklore and Anthropology Ser. Wayne St. U. Pr. 1992 $39.95. ISBN 0-8143-2234-4. Discusses how the 2,000-year-old Jewish musical heritage meshes with the complex web of Jewish history.

Ungerleider-Mayerson, Joy. *Jewish Folk Art: From Biblical Days to Modern Times*. Summit 1986 o.p. A contemporary scholar of Jewish art presents a survey of the creations of folk artists.

Werner, Eric. *The Sacred Bridge: Liturgical Parallels in Synagogue and Early Church*. Music Repr. Ser. Da Capo 1979 repr. of 1959 ed. $65.00. ISBN 0-306-79581-7. The classic account of the music of Judaism and of the synagogue and the cross-influences of Jewish and Christian liturgical music over the centuries, by the leading musicologist of Judaism in the twentieth century.

Wigoder, Geoffrey, ed. *Jewish Art and Civilization*. Walker 1972 o.p. Richly illustrated survey of Jewish civilization arranged chronologically by country.

———, ed. *The Story of the Synagogue: A Diaspora Museum Book*. HarpC 1986 o.p. Coffee-table book displaying the art and architecture of the synagogues throughout the world and throughout history, from the remnants and replicas in Tel Aviv's Diaspora Museum.

ETHICS

The ethics of Judaism is a complex subject encompassing various ways of thinking about ethical problems, from the Scripture's prophetic injunction through the philosopher's efforts at generalization and the defense of inclusive principles of conduct. Although the importance of ethics to Judaism makes the subject urgent, systemization of thought always has competed with more fragmentary ways of stating matters, such as the use of apothegms, or sayings. The ethical tradition reaches expression at every period in the history of Judaism—scriptural, Talmudic, medieval, and modern—and in every medium of Judaic discourse, from the received holy books through the liturgy.

Bleich, J. David. *Contemporary Halakhic Problems. Lib. of Jewish Law and Ethics.* 3 vols. Ktav $29.50. Vol. 1 ISBN 0-685-02912-3. Vol. 2 ISBN 0-87068-451-5. Vol. 3 ISBN 0-88125-315-4. Recommended as a view of the typical Orthodox mode of discussing Jewish law.

Bloch, Abraham P. *A Book of Jewish Ethical Concepts.* Ktav 1984 $25.00. ISBN 0-88125-039-2

Borowitz, Eugene B. *Choosing a Sex Ethic: A Jewish Inquiry.* Schocken 1970 o.p. A Reform rabbi outlines his approach to sexuality and ethical decisions in general, suggesting four levels of sexual ethics, the highest of which is abstinence before marriage.

Dan, Joseph. *Jewish Mysticism and Jewish Ethics.* U. of Wash. Pr. 1986 $20.00. ISBN 0-295-96265-8. Explains how the Jewish mystical tradition has informed, and should continue to inform, Jewish ethics.

Feldman, David M. *Birth Control in Jewish Law: Marital Relations, Contraception, and Abortion as Set Forth in the Classic Texts of Jewish Law.* Greenwood 1980 repr. of 1968 ed. $27.50. ISBN 0-313-21297-X. An analysis of traditional Jewish mores concerning sexuality and contraception with a comparison to Christianity; the discussion on abortion provides a good introduction to the way rabbis and scholars approach issues of Jewish law (Halakhah).

———. *Health and Medicine in the Jewish Tradition: The Pursuit of Wholeness.* Crossroad NY 1986 $15.95. ISBN 0-824-50707-X. Short book on traditional Jewish mores concerning health and medical practice.

Fox, Marvin, ed. *Modern Jewish Ethics: Theory and Practice.* Ohio St. U. Pr. 1975 $34.50. ISBN 0-8142-0192-X

Freehof, Solomon Benner. *New Reform Responsa.* Hebrew Union Col. Pr. 1980 o.p. Part of a series of volumes in which a Reform rabbi responds to such ethical questions as conversion, burial, and artificial insemination.

Gordis, Robert. *Judaic Ethics for a Lawless World.* Jewish Sem. 1986 $20.00. ISBN 0-87334-034-5. Fourteen essays emphasizing significant realities in democracy, freedom of conscience, and nuclear age coexistence.

Kellner, Menachem Marc, ed. *Contemporary Jewish Ethics.* Sanhedrin 1978 o.p. Somewhat dated collection of essays by various authors, reprinted from other sources, that reflects mainstream and traditional perspectives.

Klagsbrun, Francine. *Voices of Wisdom: Jewish Ideals and Ethics for Everyday Living.* Jonathan David 1986 $16.95. ISBN 0-87923-656-6. An anthology of inspiring Jewish quotations from sources ranging from the Bible to twentieth-century works, selected for a contemporary audience and arranged by topic.

Leiman, Sid Z., ed. *Jewish Moral Philosophy.* Behrman 1979 o.p. A collection of essays on the theory of Jewish ethics.

Novak, David, ed. *Halakhah in a Theological Dimension: Essays on the Interpretation of Law and Theology in Judaism.* Scholars Pr. GA 1985 $19.75. ISBN 0-891-30757-5. Derives theological principles from Jewish law and looks to these principles, rather than to the details of Jewish law, for answers to such contemporary ethical and religious issues as drug abuse, nuclear disarmament, and whether women should be ordained as rabbis.

Silver, Daniel J. *Judaism and Ethics.* Ktav 1970 $25.00. ISBN 0-87068-010-2

LITURGY

The liturgy of Judaism is received and classic; that is, Judaic worship conforms to received patterns. It is not subject to daily invention, and it does not require a direct and immediate revelation from God or a call from God to say prayers. Judaic liturgy is divided into two parts—one covering ordinary

days, Sabbaths, and festivals, and another covering the Days of Awe, or High
Holy Days (the New Year and the Day of Atonement) in autumn. The liturgical
prayer book follows a fixed pattern of worship, although all modern Judaic
religious groups have made additions, revisions, and deletions.

Agnon, S. Y. *Days of Awe*. Schocken 1948 o.p. The great novelist here introduces the
   High Holy Days, guiding the reader through the main beliefs in a compelling
   manner.

Appel, Gersion. *The Concise Code of Jewish Law: A Guide to Prayer and Religious
   Observance on the Sabbath*. Vol. 2 Ktav $22.50. ISBN 0-88125-314-6

Arzt, Max. *Justice and Mercy*. Hartmore 1963 o.p. An introduction to the liturgy for the
   High Holy Days that leads the reader through the principal prayers.

Birnbaum, Philip, ed. and trans. *The Birnbaum Haggadah*. Hebrew Pub. 1976 o.p. A good
   translation of the Passover Haggadah, with Hebrew and English on facing pages and
   a running English commentary.

_____. *Hasiddur Hashalem: Daily Prayer Book*. Hebrew Pub. 1977 $14.00. ISBN 0-88482-
   054-8. A version of the traditional weekly prayer book in which the English
   translation faces the original Hebrew and Aramaic and footnotes give biblical
   references and background information for the most important prayers.

_____. *Mahzor Hashalem: High Holyday Prayer Book*. 5 vols. Hebrew Pub. 1971 $82.00.
   ISBN 0-88482-169-2. This traditional prayer book for the High Holy Days is designed
   for practical use as well as for study.

Bronstein, Herbert, ed. *A Passover Haggadah*. Central Conf. 1982 $30.00. ISBN 0-916694-
   06-2. Published by the Reform movement, this Haggadah avoids sexist language.

Cardozo, Arlene Rossen. *Jewish Family Celebrations: Shabbat Festivals and Traditional
   Ceremonies*. St. Martin 1982 $17.50. ISBN 0-312-44231-9. A guidebook for beginners,
   dealing with Jewish holidays, Bar/Bat Mitzvahs, weddings, and births.

Donin, Hayim II. *To Pray as a Jew*. Basic 1980 $19.95. ISBN 0-465-08628-4. Walks readers
   through a traditional synagogue service, part by part, presenting historical background and practical instructions.

Edwards, Michelle. *Blessed Are You: Traditional Jewish Prayers for Children*. Lothrop
   1993. ISBN 0-688-10759-1. Thirteen tableaux, each typifying an occasion for offering
   a particular Hebrew prayer.

Fruchtenbaum, Arnold G. *A Passover Haggadah for Jewish Believers*. Ariel Pr. CA repr. of
   1970 ed. $5.00. ISBN 0-914863-04-5

Gaster, Theodor H. *Festivals of the Jewish Year: A Modern Interpretation and Guide*.
   Morrow 1971 $9.95. ISBN 0-688-06008-0. A simple account of the festivals of
   Judaism, what they mean, and how they are observed.

Goodman, Philip, ed. *Hanukkah Anthology*. JPS Phila. 1976 o.p. This and the following
   books edited by Goodman provide useful guides for the celebration of the major
   Jewish festivals. Each volume contains approximately 400 pages of readings from
   biblical, rabbinic, and modern sources as well as information on related art, music,
   children's stories, and activities.

_____. *Passover Anthology*. JPS Phila. 1961 $14.95. ISBN 0-827-60019-4

_____. *Purim Anthology*. JPS Phila. 1949 $12.95. ISBN 0-8276-0319-3

_____. *Rosh Hashanah Anthology*. JPS Phila. 1970 o.p.

_____. *The Shavuot Anthology*. JPS Phila. 1975 $12.95. ISBN 0-8276-0391-6

_____. *The Sukkot and Simhat Torah Anthology*. JPS Phila. 1973 o.p.

_____. *Yom Kippur Anthology*. JPS Phila. 1971 o.p.

Greenberg, Irving. *The Jewish Way: Living the Holidays*. Summit 1988 $24.95. ISBN 0-
   67149-399-X. A lovely and accessible interpretation of the meaning of the holidays
   within Orthodox Judaism.

Idelsohn, A. Z. *Jewish Liturgy and Its Development*. H. Holt & Co. 1932 o.p. A classic
   account of the development of Jewish liturgy from antiquity through the nineteenth
   century.

Kadushin, Max. *Worship and Ethics: A Study in Rabbinic Judaism.* Bloch 1978 $8.95. ISBN 0-313-20217-6. Explains the theory that Judaic liturgy expresses principles of ethical behavior.

Martin, Bernard. *Prayer in Judaism.* Basic 1968 o.p. A good introduction to the content of Jewish liturgy and its function in Jewish life.

Millgram, Abraham E. *Jewish Worship.* JPS Phila. 1971 $18.95. ISBN 0-8276-0003-8

Neusner, Jacob. *The Enchantments of Judaism. Rites of Transformation from Birth through Death.* Basic 1987 $15.95. ISBN 0-465-01964-7. A theology of Judaism based on the liturgical life of observance, showing how life is transformed through the right words said in the right way.

Petuchowski, Jakob J., ed. *Understanding Jewish Prayer.* Ktav 1972 $7.95. ISBN 0-870-68186-9. An introduction to the Judaic prayer book and its main prayers.

Raphael, Chaim. *A Feast of History: Passover through the Ages as a Key to Jewish Experience.* S & S Trade 1972 $12.50. ISBN 0-910250-26-X. A popular book on the historical development of the Passover seder, enhanced by a beautiful collection of photographs and a presentation of the entire Hebrew Haggadah with an English translation.

Schauss, Hayyim. *The Jewish Festivals: From Their Beginnings to Our Own Day.* UAHC rev. ed. 1969 $10.00. ISBN 0-8074-0095-5. A classic introduction to the High Holy Days and how they are observed.

———. *The Lifetime of a Jew: Throughout the Ages of Jewish History.* UAHC 1976 $9.95. ISBN 0-8074-0096-3. Reviews the life-cycle celebrations of Judaism, birth through death, and delineates the practices and their meanings.

Stern, Chaim, ed. *Gates of Prayer for Weekdays and at a House of Mourning.* Central Conf. 1975 $2.50. ISBN 0-88123-039-1. The recently revised daily prayer book of the Reform movement, providing an interesting contrast to the Birnbaum version in terms of style and content.

———. *Gates of Repentance.* Central Conf. 1978 $18.50. ISBN 0-916694-39-9. The most recent High Holy Day prayer book of the Reform movement.

Strassfeld, Michael. *The Jewish Holidays.* HarpC 1985 $24.45. ISBN 0-06-015406-3. Traditional approaches and contemporary reinterpretations of Jewish holidays, by a leader of the Havurah fellowship movement, designed for observant Jews interested in keeping holidays in the fullness of tradition.

Waskow, Arthur I. *Seasons of Our Joy: A Handbook of Jewish Festivals.* Summit 1991 $12.95. ISBN 0-8070-3611-0. Traditional and innovative approaches to Jewish holidays, with practical information on how to prepare for each festival and discussion of the special prayers, songs, food, and background readings for each holiday.

Wolpe, David J. *In Speech and in Silence: The Jewish Quest for God.* H. Holt & Co. 1992 $19.95. ISBN 0-8050-1678-3. Explores biblical aspects of language, prayer, and the Torah arriving at the conclusion that some silences speak more deeply than words, and that a listening God does not need language to hear.

PHILOSOPHY

Jewish philosophy is primarily a medieval phenomenon that began with the Muslim conquest of the Middle East and the introduction of the tradition of Greek philosophy into the world of Judaism (and later, Christianity). Judaic thinkers, starting with SAADIA GAON in ninth-century Baghdad, thus faced the problem of harmonizing rationalism with revelation and reason with Scripture. The next 500 years saw a continuous Jewish philosophical tradition, mainly among the Judaic thinkers of the Muslim world. Then, in the nineteenth century, a new philosophical tradition began in Germany, a tradition whereby Reform Judaic thinkers accommodated Judaic thought to the systems of IMMANUEL KANT and GEORGE HEGEL (see also Vol. 3). This tradition has continued to the present in Europe, the United States, and elsewhere.

Blau, Joseph L. *The Story of Jewish Philosophy.* Ktav 1962 $8.95. ISBN 0-870-68174-5. Presents an overview of Jewish thought throughout the ages for readers without a background in philosophy.

Guttmann, Julius. *Philosophy of Judaism: The History of Jewish Philosophy from Biblical Times to Franz Rosenzweig.* Avonson 1988 $35.00. ISBN 0-87668-872-5. A good, descriptive introduction to the major philosophical systems of medieval and modern Judaism.

Katz, Steven T. *Jewish Philosophers.* Bloch 1975 $10.95. ISBN 0-819-70387-7. A summary of Jewish thought from antiquity to the present, primarily adapted from articles appearing in the *Encyclopedia Judaica,* with individual essays on more than 30 major figures.

Neusner, Jacob. *Judaism as Philosophy. The Method and Message of the Mishnah.* U. of SC Pr. 1991 $39.95. ISBN 0-87249-736-4

Petuchowski, Jakob J. *Ever since Sinai: A Modern View of Torah.* Arbit 1979 $7.95. ISBN 0-930038-11-8. A popular introductory textbook on the theology of Judaism.

RELIGIOUS LITERATURE

These books offer an introduction to Judaic religious literature from biblical times to the present. Constant study of the classic writings is regarded as a religious duty. There is nothing secular in the literary act of writing a holy book.

Frank, Ruth S., and William Wolheim. *The Book of Jewish Books: A Reader's Guide to Judaism.* HarpC 1986 o.p. A useful reference book containing reviews on all types of literature, from Jewish history and philosophy to children's books, cookbooks, and introductory essays for the uninitiated.

Holtz, Barry, ed. *Back to the Sources: Reading the Classic Jewish Texts.* Summit 1984 $19.95. ISBN 0-671-45467-6. A readable introduction with chapters on 10 different forms of Jewish religious literature, from biblical narrative, law, and poetry to the teachings of Hasidic masters, as well as extensive citations, commentaries, and a bibliography.

Zinberg, Israel. *A History of Jewish Literature.* 12 vols. Ktav 1971–78 $315.00. ISBN 0-685-5636-X. Comprehensive survey of Jewish literature, with emphasis on the medieval period.

RELIGIOUS PRACTICE

Judaic religious practice involves a variety of religious duties that sanctify the Jewish people and make their lives conform to God's will. These religious duties, called *mitzvot* (often translated as commandments), require Jews to either do or not do certain things. Such duties affect every aspect of life, from eating to sexual conduct; they also order the division of time into ordinary days and holy days and prescribe conduct for the latter. The following books present diverse authoritative accounts of the religious practices of Judaism.

Bial, Morrison D. *Liberal Judaism at Home: The Practices of Modern Reform Judaism.* UAHC 1971 $5.95. ISBN 0-8074-0075-0. Provides an introduction to Reform ritual for both Orthodox and Conservative Jews.

Diamant, Anita. *The New Jewish Wedding.* Summit 1985 $16.95. ISBN 0-671-62882-8. Both a practical guide for planning a wedding and a historical study of the development of Jewish marriage customs.

Dobrinsky, Herbert. *A Treasury of Sephardic Laws and Customs.* Ktav 1986 $29.50. ISBN 0-881-25031-7. A comprehensive compendium of laws and customs of the four main Sephardic Jewish communities of North America—Syrian, Moroccan, Judeo-Spanish, and Spanish-Portuguese.

Donin, Hayim. *To Be a Jew: A Guide to Jewish Observance in Contemporary Life.* Basic 1972 $17.95. ISBN 0-465-08624-1. Detailed reference on Orthodox practice, daily life, holidays, and rites of passage.

Fox, Karen L., and Phyllis Z. Miller. *Seasons for Celebration: A Contemporary Guide to the Joys, Practices, and Traditions of the Jewish Holidays.* Putnam Pub. Group 1992

$12.95. ISBN 0-399-51764-2. A straightforward guide to major Jewish holidays intended for use in the religious school classroom and in the home.

Klein, Isaac. *A Guide to Jewish Religious Practice. Moreshet Ser.* Basic 1991 $25.00. ISBN 0-665-08632-2. A comprehensive code of Jewish law designed for Conservative Jews, dealing with daily prayers, the holidays, dietary laws, and marriage.

Lamm, Maurice. *Jewish Way in Death and Mourning.* Jonathan David 1972 $11.95. ISBN 0-8246-0126-2. A historical account and practical guide to the traditional Jewish understanding of and customs relating to death and mourning.

_____. *The Jewish Way in Love and Marriage.* HarpC 1982 $13.00. ISBN 0-8246-0353-2. An Orthodox perspective on sexual ethics and marital customs.

Maslin, Simeon J., ed. *Shaarei Mitzvah: Gates of Mitzvah.* Central Conf. 1979 $9.95. ISBN 0-916-694337-2. Guide to Reform Jewish practices at each rite of passage from birth to death.

Plotch, Batia, and Patricia Cobe, eds. *The International Kosher Cookbook: The Ninety-Second Street Cooking School.* Fawcett 1992 $22.00. ISBN 0-449-90366-4. For cooks without a lot of training or ambition; an attractive, varied, broadening, and handy collection.

Silverstein, Y. *Jewish Laws of Childbirth.* Feldheim 1990 $17.95. ISBN 0-685-45563-7

Strassfeld, Michael, and Richard Siegel, comps. *The Jewish Catalog: A Do-It-Yourself Kit.* JPS Phila. 1973 $8.95. ISBN 0-827-60042-9. An introduction for the uninitiated and a reference book for the well informed, full of interesting information and playful illustrations on traditional Jewish observance.

_____. *The Second Jewish Catalogue: Sources and Resources.* JPS Phila. 1976 $8.95. ISBN 0-827-60084-4. Companion volume to the preceding book, providing background information and readings on various aspects of Jewish observance.

Strassfeld, Michael, and Sharon Strassfeld, eds. *The Third Jewish Catalogue: Building Community.* JPS Phila. 1980 $9.95. ISBN 0-827-60183-2. The final volume of the trilogy focuses on Jewish communal responsibility, discussing charity, social action, ecology, Zioism, and much more. Includes an index to all three volumes.

Trepp, Leo. *The Complete Book Jewish Observance.* Summit 1980 $25.00. ISBN 0-671-41797-5. A comprehensive guide to Orthodox, Conservative, and Reform practices, with discussion of the theories behind each custom.

Zinner, Gauriel. *The Laws and Custom of the Jewish Wedding.* CIS Comm. 1992. ISBN 1-56062-119-2

Judaism and Christianity through the Ages

Because it generally is taken for granted that Christianity emerged from the Judaism of its day, it is common to take an interest in the relationships between those two religious traditions. Over time, theologians have compared and contrasted the two faiths, conducted dialogues between them, and formulated a considerable body of writings on how the two religions that share the Old Testament (written Torah) relate to each other.

Buber, Martin. *Two Types of Faith: The Interpretation of Judaism and Christianity.* Macmillan 1986 $8.95. ISBN 0-02-084180-9

Chilton, Bruce D., and Jacob Neusner. *Christianity and Judaism: The Formative Categories.* I. *Revelation. The Torah and the Bible.* TPI PA 1995

_____. *Christianity and Judaism: The Formative Categories.* II. With Bruce D. Chilton. *The Body of Faith: Israel and Church.* TPI PA 1996

_____. *Christianity and Judaism: The Formative Categories.* III. *God in the World.* TPI PA 1997

_____. *Judaeo-Christian Debates. Communion with God, the Kingdom of God, the Mystery of the Messiah.* Fortress Pr. 1997

Neusner, Jacob. *Jesus: A Jewish Dissent.* Doubleday 1993. ISBN 0-385-42466-3. An imagined response of a first-century rabbi who hears the Sermon on the Mount and other teachings of Jesus as reported in the Gospel of Matthew.

_____ *Jews and Christians: The Myth of a Common Tradition.* TPI PA 1991 $14.95. ISBN 0-334-02465-X

_____. *Telling Tales: Making Sense of Christian and Judaic Nonsense. The Urgency and Basis for Judaeo-Christian Dialogue.* Westminster John Knox Pr. 1993 $10.95. ISBN 0-664-25371-7. A convincing argument that what is called Jewish-Christian dialogue is in fact an exchange of monologues, in which each religion views the other in inauthentic terms.

Schoeps, Hans Joachim. *The Jewish-Christian Argument: A History of Theologies in Conflict.* H. Holt & Co. 1963 o.p. Covers both sides of the dispute from the beginnings of the church until the twentieth century.

Talmage, Frank, ed. *Disputation and Dialogue: Readings in the Jewish-Christian Encounter.* Ktav 1975 $14.95. ISBN 0-870-68284-9. An excellent anthology of theological disputes between Jews and Christians during the last two millennia, arranged by topic with clearly written introductions.

ANCIENT JUDAISM

Ancient Judaism covers the period from the formation of the Pentateuch—the Five Books of Moses, as we now have it—in the fifth century B.C. (c.450), to the Muslim conquest of the Near and Middle East in the middle of the seventh century A.D. (c.640). During that period of 1,000 years, Jews in the Roman Empire witnessed three important turning points: (1) the incorporation of the Land of Israel into the Roman Empire in the century from 140 to 40 B.C., (2) the destruction of the Temple in Jerusalem in A.D. 70, and (3) the establishment of Christianity as the religion of the Roman Empire in the fourth century (from the edict of toleration of 312 to the conversion of Constantine just before his death in 337). The first of these events joined the Jews of the Land of Israel to the larger world of cosmopolitan Rome. The second marked a massive change in the religious world in which Judaism would flourish. The third redefined the political conditions in which Jews would live from the fourth to the nineteenth century. The meaning of the first—the inclusion of the Land of Israel in the Roman Empire—was that Jews would participate in the cultural life of the Greco-Roman world as part of the Greek- and Aramaic-speaking East. The weight of the second—the destruction of the Temple—bore heavily through the next century, and a new mode of worship of and relationship to God had to be worked out. The meaning of the establishment of Christianity as the definitive force in the politics and culture of the West was ambiguous. On the one hand, Jews lost their long-established rights and immunities, being merely tolerated (and sometimes not even tolerated), pending the second coming of Christ and their final conversion. On the other hand, Jews' fundamental view of themselves, as stated by their Holy Scriptures, found reinforcement in Christianity's adoption of those same Scriptures. A shared reading of the revelation, or Torah, of ancient Israel lent to Jews' holy books a new importance and general currency. As a result, Jews' sense of themselves as a special and distinctive group was confirmed by the politics and culture of the West.

History of the Jews

SECOND TEMPLE PERIOD

The Jews between 450 B.C. and A.D. 70 lived throughout the Roman Empire, in the Land of Israel, Egypt, Syria, Asia Minor, Greece, and Italy, as well as in Babylonia, the western satrapy of the Iranian Empire, at the confluence of the

Tigris and Euphrates rivers in present-day Iraq. Although much information is available on the Jews in the Land of Israel and Egypt, we know less of their histories in other parts of the Roman and Iranian empires. The sole continuous history concerns the Jews in the Land of Israel and rests on the narrative composed by a Jewish general and historian, JOSEPHUS, who wrote after the destruction of the Temple in A.D. 70 in order to explain the tragic event and to provide, for ancient readers, a positive view of the Jews as loyal citizens, despite the actions of those he represented as a radical and extreme group. Histories of Jews in other parts of the world, even in Egypt, where Greek-speaking Jews produced a sizable corpus of writings, are episodic and not continuous. For the Jews in the Iranian Empire, we have only bits and pieces of stories.

Alon, Gedalyahu. *Jews, Judaism and the Classical World: Studies in Jewish History in the Times of the Second Empire and Talmud.* Trans. by Israel Abrahams. Humanities 1977 o.p. Original and important studies on religion and history.

Bickerman, Elias. *From Ezra to the Last of the Maccabees: Foundations of Post-Biblical Judaism.* Schocken 1962 $5.95. ISBN 0-8052-0036-3. A classic, concise account pulling together the major trends in Judaism and the Jews' history in the Land of Israel in a brief and insightful account.

Bickerman, Elias, and Morton Smith. *The Ancient History of Western Civilization.* HarpC 1976 o.p. A comprehensive textbook considering the Jews and the Land of Israel in the much broader context of ancient history and culture from the beginnings to the end of antiquity.

Borgen, Peder. *Philo, John and Paul: New Perspectives on Judaism and Early Christianity.* Scholars Pr. GA 1987 o.p. A collection of essays focused upon the proposition that no sharp distinction existed between Palestinian Judaism and non-Palestinian, Hellenistic Judaism.

Büchler, Adolph. *Studies in Jewish History.* OUP 1956 o.p. Essays representing the finest work of the foremost specialist on Talmudic Judaism of the early part of the twentieth century.

Cohen, Shaye J. D. *From the Maccabees to the Mishnah.* Westminster John Knox 1987 $20.00. ISBN 0-664-21911-X. An attempt to locate unity within the diverse religious expressions of Judaism in Second Temple and early rabbinic times.

Feldman, Louis. *Jew and Gentile in the Ancient World: Attitudes and Interactions from Alexander to Justinian.* De Gruyter 1993 $59.50. ISBN 0-691-07416-X. Examines why gentiles in the ancient world were attracted to Judaism.

Grabbe, Lester. *Judaism from Cyrus to Hadrian.* Vol. 1 *The Persian and Greek Periods.* Vol. 2 *The Roman Period.* Fortress Pr. 1992 $57.00. ISBN 0-8006-2619-2. A thorough account of the state of the important questions of research through ancient times; the best available picture of what we now know.

Hengel, Martin. *Judaism and Hellenism: Studies in Their Encounter in Palestine during the Early Hellenistic Period.* Trans. by John Bowden. Fortress Pr. 1981 o.p. The definitive work on the relationship between Judaism and the surrounding Hellenistic world, this is a judicious, compelling account.

Jagersma, Henk. *A History of Israel from Alexander the Great to Bar Kochba.* Fortress Pr. 1986 $9.50. ISBN 0-334-02049-2. A good, reliable one-volume history.

Jeremias, Joachim. *Jerusalem in the Time of Jesus: An Investigation into Economic and Social Conditions during the New Testament Period.* Fortress Pr. 1975 $14.00. ISBN 0-8006-1136-5. A colorful and engaging work focusing on aspects of social life and culture, desribing the everyday life of the time and place.

Klausner, Joseph. *The Messianic Idea in Israel.* Macmillan 1955 o.p. A classic survey of the doctrines concerning the Messiah stated in various Judaic writings from biblical times to the end of antiquity.

Linder, Amnon, ed. *The Jews in Roman Imperial Legislation.* Wayne St. U. Pr. 1987 $44.95. ISBN 0-81431-809-6. An important research source for the legal status of Jews in the Roman Empire in the second through sixth centuries A.D.

Neusner, Jacob. *First-Century Judaism in Crisis: Yohanan ben Zakkai and the Renaissance of Torah.* Ktav 1981 $14.95. ISBN 0-870-68728-X. A popular account of what happened in Judaism before and after the destruction of the Temple. Very readable.

———. *A History of the Jews in Babylonia.* 5 vols. E. J. Brill 1965–1970. Vol. 1 *The Parthian Period.* Scholars Pr. GA repr. 1984 ISBN 0-89130-738-9. A detailed account of the Jewish community that produced the Talmud of Babylonia, from its beginnings to the Muslim conquest.

———, ed. *The Origins of Judaism: Religion, History, and Literature in Late Antiquity.* 20 vols. With William Scott Green. Garland 1991 $1,625.00. ISBN 0-8240-7499-8. Twenty volumes of reprinted scholarly essays, with introductions, constituting a broad survey of available, important articles on all aspects of ancient Judaism from a variety of viewpoints and perspectives.

Oesterley, William O. *From the Fall of Jerusalem: 586 B.C. to the Bar-Kakhba Revolt, A.D. 135.* Vol. 2 in *A History of Israel.* OUP 1932 o.p. An old, but still useful, detailed survey.

Pfeiffer, Robert H. *History of New Testament Times.* Greenwood 1972 repr. of 1949 ed. o.p. Presents essays on many important topics and provides a detailed bibliography.

Radin, Max. *The Jews among the Greeks and Romans.* Ayer 1973 repr. of 1915 ed. $33.00. ISBN 0-405-05286-3. A valuable, pioneering work on its subject.

Reicke, Bo. *The New Testament Era: The World of the Bible from 500 B.C. to A.D. 100.* ISBN 0-8006-1080-6. Fortress Pr. 1974 $12.00. A reliable one-volume history of the Jews and Judaism in the setting of the interests of the New Testament.

Reinhold, Meyer. *Diaspora: The Jews among the Greeks and Romans.* Samuel-Stevens 1983 o.p. A useful and attractively presented short collection of primary sources describing all aspects of Jewish life outside the Land of Israel during the Greek and Roman periods.

Russell, David S. *Between the Testaments.* Fortress Pr. 1960 o.p. A brief account of the Judaisms of the period between Ezra and the first century.

———. *The Jews from Alexander to Herod.* OUP 1967 $15.95. ISBN 0-19-836913-1. A history of the Jews in the period from the third to the first century B.C.

Sandmel, Samuel. *Herod: A Profile of a Tyrant.* Lippincott 1967 o.p. A biography, restating the received narratives of Josephus, together with materials deriving from Roman writings and archeology, on the most important Jewish ruler in the first century B.C.

Schürer, Emil. *The History of the Jewish People in the Age of Jesus Christ: A New English Edition.* Ed. and rev. by Geza Vermes, Fergus Millar, and Pamela Vermes. 4 vols. Bks. Intl. VA 1973–86 $34.95–$64.95 ea. ISBNs 0-567-02242-0, 0-567-02243-9, 0-567-09373-5. Covers all topics of history, politics, religion, and culture, with thorough updating of bibliographies as well as scholarly presentation; these are the starting point for all research on ancient Judaism.

Segal, Alan F. *Rebecca's Children: Judaism and Christianity in the Roman World.* HUP 1986 $20.00. ISBN 0-674-7075-6. A well-written summary of recent scholarship on Judaism and Christianity from the destruction of the first Temple to the end of the first century of the common era, with anthropological comparisons to present-day religions.

Sievers, Joseph. *The Hasmoneans and Their Supporters. From Mattathias to the Death of John Hyrcanus I.* Scholars Pr. GA 1990 $49.95. ISBN 1-55540-449-9. A history of the Hasmoneans focused upon the nature of the group and its relationship with other parties within Judaism and the Roman world.

Tcherikover, Victor. *Hellenistic Civilization and the Jews.* Atheneum 1970 repr. of 1959 ed. $9.95. ISBN 0-689-70248-5. A classic English work, second only to Hengel's, covering the relationship of Jews to the larger Greek-speaking world in which they lived.

Whittaker, Molly. *Jews and Christians: Graeco-Roman Views.* Cambridge U. Pr. 1984 $47.50. ISBN 0-521-24251-7. Collects Greek and Latin sources from 200 B.C.E. to 200 C.E. on Jews and Christians written by others.

Zeitlin, Solomon. *The Rise and Fall of the Judean State: A Political, Social and Religious History of the Second Commonwealth.* 3 vols. JPS Phila. 1968–78 o.p. An idiosyncratic work based on the theory that the Dead Sea Scrolls were a medieval forgery, important only for completeness in large research collections.

_____. *Studies in the Early History of Judaism.* 4 vols. Ktav 1973–78 $49.50–$59.50 ea. ISBNs 0-87068-208-3, 0-87068-209-1, 0-87068-278-4, 0-87068-454-X. Erudite but uncritical studies, important only for completeness in large collections.

RABBINIC PERIOD

The Rabbinic period is so named because during that time, from 70 to 640, the Jewish leaders in both the Land of Israel and Babylonia bore the title *rabbi*, meaning "my lord" or "sir." Rabbis were sages who mastered the Torah, written and oral, and participated in the Jews' government—autonomous regimes recognized by the two world empires (Rome for the Land of Israel, Iran for Babylonia) as part of their systems of governing diverse populations, so far as possible, under their own local authorities. For the Land of Israel, Jewish self-government came to an end in the early fifth century, as the now-Christian Roman government withdrew recognition from the autonomous administration that had flourished for 400 years. For Babylonia, the same pattern was repeated in the sixth century. By the rise of Islam in the seventh century, Jews in both empires found themselves in far less suitable circumstances than they had known earlier.

Avi-Yonah, Michael. *The Holy Land from the Persian to the Arab Conquests 536 B.C.–A.D. 640: A Historical Geography.* Baker 1966 o.p. An important complement to the next entry, necessary for the study of history and politics.

_____. *The Jews under Roman and Byzantine Rule: A Political History of Palestine from the Bar-Kokhba War to the Arab Conquest.* Schocken 1984 $23.00. ISBN 0-805-23580-9. The best single one-volume history of the Jews in the Land of Israel from the second through the seventh centuries; reliable and complete.

Goodman, Martin. *State and Society in Roman Galilee, A.D. 132–212.* Rowman 1983 $33.95. ISBN 0-865-98089-6. Extensively notated study of Jewish communal and political institutions.

Lieberman, Saul. *Greek in Jewish Palestine: Studies in the Life and Manners of Jewish Palestine in the II–IV Centuries C.E.* Feldheim 1965 o.p. A general collection of discrete observations on Greek words and phrases in Talmudic literature, important for lexicographical purposes.

_____. *Hellenism in Jewish Palestine: Studies in the Literary Transmission, Beliefs and Manners of Palestine in the I Century B.C.E.–IV Century B.C.E.* Ktav 1962 o.p. Another collection like the foregoing.

Neusner, Jacob. *Ancient Israel after Catastrophe. The Religious World-View of the Mishnah. The Richard Lectures for 1982.* Bks. Demand 1983 $25.00. ISBN 0-813-90980-5. Summary of basic traits of the Mishnah's Judaism.

_____. *Death and Birth of Judaism. The Impact of Christianity, Secularism, and the Holocaust on Jewish Faith.* Basic 1987 $21.95. ISBN 0-465-01577-8. Argues that Judaism succeeded in the West so long as the challenge of Christianity remained the paramount issue facing Jews, because that Judaism took shape to meet the challenge.

_____. *Economics of the Mishnah.* U. Ch. Pr. 1990 $45.00. ISBN 0-226-57655-8. Explains how the Mishnah sets forth a classical system of economics and tells why economics was an important medium for the Mishnah's message.

_____. *Formation of the Jewish Intellect: Making Connections and Drawing Conclusions in the Traditional System of Judaism. Brown Judaic Studies.* Scholars Pr. GA 1988 $46.95. ISBN 1-555-40255-0. Identifies the logics of coherent discourse that animate thought in Rabbinic literature.

_____. *Foundations of Judaism: Method, Teleology, Doctrine.* Fortress Pr. 1983–85 Vol. 1 *Midrash in Context: Exegesis in Formative Judaism.* o.p. Accounts for the collection of Midrash exegeses within Rabbinic Judaism in particular.

———. *Foundations of Judaism: Method, Teleology, Doctrine*. Fortress Pr. 1983–85 Vol. 2 *Messiah in Context: Israel's History and Destiny in Formative Judaism*. o.p. Discusses the documents in which the Messiah theme plays a role and identifies those in which it is absent.

———. *Foundations of Judaism: Method, Teleology, Doctrine*. Fortress Pr. 1983–85 Vol. 3 *Torah: From Scroll to Symbol in Formative Judaism*. o.p. Identifies the various meanings assigned to the word and symbol Torah.

———. *Incarnation of God: The Character of Divinity in Formative Judaism*. Fortress Pr. 1988 o.p. Traces the perception of God in the writings of Rabbinic Judaism.

———. *Judaism and Its Social Metaphors: Israel in the History of Jewish Thought*. Cambridge U. Pr. 1989 $49.95. ISBN 0-521-35471-4. Traces the history of the metaphorization of "Israel" in Rabbinic Judaism.

———. *Judaism and Scripture: The Evidence of Leviticus Rabbah*. U. Ch. Pr. 1986 $45.00. ISBN 0-226-57614-0. Fresh translation of Margulies' text and systematic analysis of problems of composition and redaction.

———. *Judaism and Story: The Evidence of the Fathers According to Rabbi Nathan*. U. Ch. Pr. 1992 $49.00. ISBN 0-226-57630-2. Shows how tractate Abot was supplied with stories and classifies the types of stories that were important in the *Fathers According to Rabbi Nathan*.

———. *Judaism in Society: The Evidence of the Yerushalmi. Toward the Natural History of a Religion*. U. Ch. Pr. 1983 $69.95. ISBN 0-226-57616-7. Shows the correspondence between the literary traits of the Talmud of the Land of Israel and the social world designed by that document.

———. *Judaism: The Classical Statement: The Evidence of the Bavli*. U. of Ch. Pr. 1986 $37.00. ISBN 0-226-57620-5. Spells out the Judaism put forth by the Mishnah.

———. *Rabbinic Political Theory: Religion and Politics in the Mishnah*. U. Ch. Pr. 1991 $49.95. ISBN 0-226-57650-7. Shows how the political theory of the Mishnah conveys an important component of the Mishnah's larger theological scheme.

———. *Torah through the Ages: A Short History of Judaism*. TPI PA 1990 $21.95. ISBN 0-334-02456-0. Summarizes the history of Judaism by reference to its formulations of the idea of the Torah.

———. *Transformation of Judaism from Philosophy to Religion*. U. of Ill. Pr. 1992 $36.95. ISBN 0-252-01805-2. Traces the history of Judaism as laid out in the documents from the Mishnah to the Talmud of the Land of Israel.

———. *Vanquished Nation, Broken Spirit: The Virtues of the Heart in Formative Judaism*. Cambridge U. Pr. 1987 $39.95. ISBN 0-521-32832-2. Argues that Judaism put forth a doctrine of virtue, including virtuous emotions, corresponding to the political necessities of the life of a defeated people.

———. *Writing with Scripture: The Authority and Uses of the Hebrew Bible in the Torah of Formative Judaism*. Fortress Pr. 1989 o.p. Explains how the sages of the Rabbinic writings turned Scripture into a medium for their own writing.

Literature

JEWISH LITERATURE IN GREEK

During the Hellenistic period, the Jewish cultural elite was thoroughly conversant with Greek language and thought. Greek was the language of commerce, politics, and culture for Jews in the Land of Israel and the Diaspora (itself a Greek word). In fact, many faithful Jews relied on the Septuagint, the Greek translation of the Bible (third century B.C.), because they did not understand Hebrew. The extant Jewish literature in Greek is limited primarily to the works of two authors, PHILO and JOSEPHUS. For the influence of Greek language and thought on Palestinian Jewish religious literature, see the works by Saul Lieberman listed above.

Belkin, Samuel. *In His Image: The Jewish Philosophy of Man as Expressed in Rabbinic Tradition*. Greenwood 1979 repr. of 1960 ed. $27.50. ISBN 0-313-21234-1. A thoughtful introduction to the life and system of Philo.

Feldman, Louis H. *Scholarship on Philo and Josephus, 1937–1962*. Studies in Judaica Ser. Bloch 1962 o.p. The classic bibliography by the leading bibliographer of Philo and Josephus and the foremost Josephus scholar of the day.

Jews in the Hellenistic World: Josephus, Aristeas, The Sibylline Oracles, Eupolemus. Cambridge U. Pr. 1989 $69.95. ISBN 0-521-30511-X. An illustrated presentation of Greek literature dealing with Hellenistic Jewish life.

TRANSLATIONS OF SCRIPTURE INTO ARAMAIC, OR TARGUMS

Targums are translations of the Hebrew Bible into Aramaic, the language common among Jews in Palestine, Syria, and lands east. The best-known targums were preserved among Jewish scholars down through the centuries: These include Targum Onkelos, the so-called Fragmentary Targums, and Targum (Pseudo-) Jonathan—all translations of the Pentateuch as well as Targum Jonathan to the Prophets and the Writings. These texts, along with Targum Neofiti to the Pentateuch, probably were completed between A.D. 300 and 700, but scholars are certain that they also contain some material that reflects the thinking of earlier periods. In general, targums provide a fairly literal rendering of the Hebrew text into Aramaic. They tend to follow the Hebrew text closely, although the translators often add a word or two to the literal rendition. In addition to the trend of literal translation, however, the targums occasionally contain sizable augmentations to the literal text. These expansions—and to a lesser extent, the translation material—reveal information concerning the use of Scripture by the translators. This information is used by modern scholars—most frequently New Testament scholars—to discover the way Scripture was understood by the Jews in Palestine.

Bowker, John W. *The Targums and Rabbinic Literature*. Cambridge U. Pr. 1969 o.p. An introduction to some of the targums together with an account of some Rabbinic writings; not very well informed on the latter subject.

Chilton, Bruce D. *A Galilean Rabbi and His Bible: Jesus' Use of the Interpreted Scripture of His Time*. Good News Studies Ser. Liturgical Pr. 1984 o.p. A thoughtful attempt to use the later targums to illuminate the interpretations of the Hebrew Scriptures.

———. *The Glory of Israel*. JSOT Pr. 1983 o.p.

———. *Targumic Approaches to the Gospels: Essays in the Mutual Definition of Judaism and Christianity*. U. Pr. of Amer. 1987 $24.75. ISBN 0-819-15731-7. An engaging collection of essays on targumic interpretations of Scripture and their relationship to interpretations found in the Gospels.

Etheridge, J. W., trans. *Targums of Onkelos and Jonathan Ben Uzziel on the Pentateuch with the Fragments of the Jerusalem Targum from the Chaldee*. Ktav 1969 repr. of 1865 ed. o.p. The only complete English translation of either targum.

Grossfeld, B. *A Bibliography of Targum Literature*. Hermon 1990 $39.95. ISBN 0-87203-132-2.

Hayward, Robert. *Divine Name and Presence: The Memra*. Allanheld 1981 $25.50. ISBN 0-865-18067-5. An interesting and readable study of the targumic term *memra*, which is used by the targums instead of God's name.

———. *The Targum of Jeremiah*. Liturgical Pr. 1987 $47.95. ISBN 0-8146-5481-9.

Levey, Samson H. *The Messiah: An Aramaic Interpretation*. Ktav 1974 $20.00. ISBN 0-872-80402-4. A collection and discussion of passages from many different targums that concern the Messiah.

Levine, Ethan. *The Aramaic Version of Lamentations*. Hermon 1976 o.p.

McNamara, Martin. *From Targum to Testament*. Eerdmans 1972 o.p. An outdated introduction to the targums by a New Testament scholar who has a strong interest in linking targum materials to sayings of Jesus.

McNamara, M., and D.R.G. Beattie, eds. *The Aramaic Bible: Targums in their Historical Context*. Sheffield Acad. Pr. 1993 o.p.

Smolar, Leivy, and Pinchas Churgin. *Studies in Targum Jonathan to the Prophets*. Ktav 1983 $39.50. ISBN 0-870-68109-5. Philologically based studies of the history, geographical allusions, and matters of Jewish law found in the targum to the prophets.

RABBINIC LITERATURE: THE MISHNAH, TOSEFTA, MIDRASH COMPILATIONS, AND TALMUDS

From the second to the seventh century, Jewish sages, who addressed one another by the title *rabbi*, composed a number of documents in Palestine and Babylonia. These books, which came to be called Rabbinic literature, became canonized as a sacred body of literature, along with the Hebrew Bible. This corpus contains a variety of literary genres, including legal codes, biblical interpretation, legends, moral exhortations, and philosophic discussions. The documents were written at different times, in different places, in different languages (Hebrew and Aramaic), by different people, for different purposes. Each document has unique characteristics that distinguish it from other documents, but all books of the Rabbinic canon exhibit certain common features, such as the frequent reference to the statements and actions of rabbis and the division of the text into discrete and compact discussions.

The earliest extant document of the Rabbinic corpus is the Mishnah, a philosophic law code, compiled at the beginning of the third century but also containing material from the previous two centuries. In large part, the Mishnah provides a utopian picture of the way in which Jews should act in a perfect world. It is a sizable document, consisting of 6 divisions, divided into 63 tractates, each containing a number of chapters. The Mishnah represents the first statement of Rabbinic Judaism, the movement that provided the foundation of practically all subsequent forms of Judaism. The Tosefta (c.300) is a commentary on the Mishnah. Like the Mishnah, it contains material presumably preserved from the preceding centuries. In general, the Tosefta is less tightly reasoned and composed than the Mishnah.

Midrash, meaning "investigation," refers to the interpretation of the Hebrew Bible. The word also has come to describe those documents composed from the third century on that contain discussion of Scripture. These documents discuss the Bible through paraphrase, exegesis, philological analysis, and imaginative embellishment. The documents arrange material in a variety of ways. For example, Genesis Rabbah provides a verse-by-verse analysis of the book of Genesis, whereas Pesikta deRab Kahana presents topical discussions related to the weekly lections.

Two vast commentaries to the Mishnah, called Talmuds, were created: one in the Land of Israel (c.400), bearing the title of the Talmud of the Land of Israel, or the Palestinian Talmud (in Hebrew, the Yerushalmi), and the other in Babylonia (c.600), called the Talmud of Babylonia (in Hebrew, the Bavli). The latter is a larger work containing a significant amount of Midrashic material, as well as commentary on the Mishnah. The Talmud of Babylonia is assumed to be the consummate text of Rabbinic Judaism, melding together the various strains of material into one conclusive statement.

Avery-Peck, Alan J. *Mishnah's Division of Agriculture: A History and Theology of Seder Zeraim*. Scholars Pr. GA 1985 $39.25. ISBN 0-891-30888-1. A history of the formation of the Mishnah's agricultural law.

Blackman, P., trans. *Mishnayoth*. 6 vols. Judaica Pr. 1964 o.p. A popular collection that juxtaposes the original Hebrew text and the English translation.

Braude, William G., and Israel J. Kapstein, trans. *Pesikta De-Rab Kahana: R. Kahana's Compilation of Discourses for Sabbath and Festival Days.* JPS Phila. 1975 $23.95. ISBN 0-827-60051-8. A literate and attractive rendition, not at all close to the Hebrew text.

Danby, Herbert, trans. *The Mishnah.* OUP 1933 $69.00. ISBN 0-19-815402-X. The first English translation and a generally reliable, handy one-volume work.

Fishbane, Michael. *The Garments of Torah: Essays in Biblical Hermeneutics. Indiana Studies in Biblical Literature.* Ed. by Herbert Marks and Robert Polzin. Ind. U. Pr. 1989 $29.95. ISBN 0-253-32217-0. Includes essays on hermeneutics of Scripture in formation; two papers on scriptural hermeneutics and the forms of culture; and "hermeneutics, Scripture, and the present hour."

Fraade, Steven D. *From Tradition to Commentary: Torah and Its Interpretation in the Midrash Sifre to Deuteronomy.* State U. NY Pr. 1991 $59.50. ISBN 0-791-40495-1. Intended for beginners and scholars; presents "a series of critical commentaries to the earliest extant commentary to the biblical Book of Deuteronomy."

Ginzberg, Louis. *Legends of the Jews.* 7 vols. JPS Phila. 1956–62 set $150.00. ISBN 0-8276-0148-4. Anthologizes rabbinic comments on the Hebrew Scriptures from a variety of books and periods.

Glatzer, Nahum N., ed. *Hammer on the Rock: A Midrash Reader.* Schocken 1962 $4.95. ISBN 0-805-20032-0. An anthology of Midrashic literature accomplished with taste and charm.

Goldin, Judah. *The Living Talmud: The Wisdom of the Fathers.* NAL-Dutton 1957 $4.95. ISBN 0-452-00961-8. A translation of "The Fathers" (Mishnah Tractate Avot), together with a commentary, readily accessible to the American reader.

———. *The Song at the Sea.* Yale U. Pr. 1971 o.p. A translation of part of a rabbinic commentary on the book of Exodus, rich in erudite observations.

———, trans. *The Fathers According to Rabbi Nathan.* Schocken 1974. ISBN 0-805-20465-2

Green, William S. *Approaches to Ancient Judaism: Theory and Practice.* 3 vols. Scholars Pr. GA 1983–85 $15.00–$17.25 ea. ISBN 0-891-30130-5. Collections of original and important articles on ancient Judaism.

Hammer, Reuven, trans. *Sifre: A Tannaitic Commentary on the Book of Deuteronomy. Judaica Ser.* Yale U. Pr. 1986 $45.00. ISBN 0-300-03345-1. A good translation but lacking a reference system and critical apparatus, it can be used only to survey the contents—not to conduct studies—of the original text.

Handelman, Susan A. *The Slayers of Moses: The Emergence of Rabbinic Interpretation in Modern Literary Theory. Modern Jewish Lit. and Culture Ser.* State U. NY Pr. 1982 $49.50. ISBN 0-873-95576-5. Argues that modern Jewish scholars—Freud, Derrida, and Bloom—advocate approaches akin to the supposed "intertextuality" of Midrash, a dubious, unproven assumption about the character of Rabbinic literature.

Hartman, Geoffrey, and Sanford Budick. *Midrash and Literature.* Yale U. Pr. 1986 $28.50. ISBN 0-300-03453-9. A collection of essays on the relationship between Judaic biblical exegesis and contemporary literary criticism.

Kalmin, Richard. *The Redaction of the Babylonian Talmud: Amoraic or Saboraic?* Hebrew Union Col. Pr. 1989 $30.00. ISBN 0-87820-411-3. Argues, sometimes unsuccessfully, that the Talmud was put together by authorities later than the final generation of Talmudic rabbis.

Lauterbach, Jacob Z., trans. *Mekilta Derabbi Ishmael. Lib. of Jewish Class.* 3 vols. JPS Phila. 1976 o.p. A model of first-class translation and presentation of an important document with a complete analytical program.

Mielziner, Moses. *Introduction to the Talmud.* Bloch 1969 repr. of 1925 ed. $27.50. ISBN 0-8197-0015-0. With a new bibliography (1925–67), by Alexander Guttmann. An old but still useful bibliographic study, together with a summary of basic facts about Talmudic literature.

Montefiore, C. G., and H. Loewe, eds. *A Rabbinic Anthology.* Schocken 1970 o.p. The best single anthology of Talmudic and Midrashic writings, organized around topics of theological interest.

Neusner, Jacob. *The Bavli: The Talmud of Babylonia. An Introduction. South Florida Studies in the History of Judaism.* Scholars Pr. GA 1992 $59.95. ISBN 1-55540-697-1. An anthological introduction to the most important document of Judaism.

———. *Esther Rabbath I: An Analytical Translation. Brown Judaic Studies.* Scholars Pr. GA 1989 $49.95. ISBN 1-555-40382-4. The first analytical translation of the document.

———. *Fathers According to Rabbi Nathan: An Analytical Translation and Explanation. Brown Judaic Studies.* Scholars Pr. GA 1986 $41.95. ISBN 1-555-40051-5. The first analytical translation.

———. *Genesis Rabbah: The Judaic Commentary on Genesis: A New American Translation. Brown Judaic Studies.* Scholars Pr. GA 1985 $33.95. ISBN 0-891-30935-7. A three-volume translation, the first analytical one.

———. *Invitation to Midrash: The Working of Rabbinic Bible Interpretation: A Teaching Book.* HarpC 1988 $28.95. ISBN 0-060-66107-0. A systematic introduction to the types of Midrash-compilations.

———. *Invitation to the Talmud: A Teaching Book.* HarpC rev. ed. 1985 $13.95. ISBN 0-060-66099-6. The finest teaching book available on this topic.

———. *Judaism and Scripture: The Evidence of Leviticus Rabbah.* U. Ch. Pr. 1986 $50.00. ISBN 0-226-57614-0. An account of how the Rabbinic mode of interpreting Scripture presents not merely comments on verses but also systematic propositions and arguments.

———. *Judaism in Society: The Evidence of the Yerushalmi: Toward the Natural History of a Religion. Chicago Studies in the History of Judaism.* U. Ch. Pr. 1986 $69.95. ISBN 0-226-57616-7. How the Talmud of the Land of Israel portrays the society of the Jews of its time and place.

———. *Judaism: The Classical Statement, the Evidence of the Bavli.* U. Ch. Pr. 1987 $37.00. ISBN 0-226-57620-5. Why the Talmud of Babylonia turned out to define Judaism.

———. *Judaism: The Evidence of the Mishnah. Brown Judaic Studies.* Scholars Pr. GA 1987 $59.95. ISBN 1-555-40181-3. How the Mishnah sets forth the principal parts of a Judaic religious system.

———. *Lamentations Rabbah: An Analytical Translation. Brown Judaic Studies.* Scholars Pr. GA 1989 o.p.

———. *Making the Classics in Judaism: The Three Stages of Literary Formation. Brown Judaic Studies.* Scholars Pr. GA 1990 $50.95. ISBN 1-555-40377-8. How to delineate the history of the formation of the various rabbinic documents.

———. *Mekhilta According to R. Ishmael: An Analytical Translation.* I. *Pisha, Beshallah, Shirata, and Vayassa.* II. *Amalek, Bahodesh, Neziqin, Kaspa, and Shabbata. Brown Judaic Studies.* Scholars Pr. GA 1988 $44.95. ISBN 1-555-40237-2. The first analytical translation.

———. *Mekhilta According to R. Ishmael: An Introduction to Judaism's First Scriptural Encyclopaedia. Brown Judaic Studies.* Scholars Pr. GA 1988 $40.95. ISBN 1-55540-262-3

———. *Midrash Compilations of the Sixth and Seventh Centuries: An Introduction to the Rhetorical, Logical, and Topical Program.* Vol. 1 *Lamentations Rabbah.* Vol. 2 *Esther Rabbah I.* Vol. 3 *Ruth Rabbah.* Vol. 4 *Song of Songs Rabbah. Brown Judaic Studies.* Scholars Pr. GA 1990 o.p. Introduction to the Midrash-compilation.

———. *Midrash: An Introduction.* Aronson 1990 $30.00. ISBN 0-876-68814-8. An introduction to the types of Midrash-exegesis and the documents that compile them.

———. *Midrash Reader.* Augsburg-Fortress 1990 $12.00. ISBN 0-800-62453-5. Introductions and selections.

———. *Mishnah: Introduction and Reader: An Anthology. Library of Rabbinic Literature.* TPI PA Intl. 1992 $16.95. ISBN 1-56338-021-8. Explains how the Mishnah treats fundamental topics in designing the social order of its Israel.

———. *Mishnah: A New Translation.* Yale U. Pr. 1988 $75.00. ISBN 0-300-03065-7. The first analytical translation of the document, showing the exact traits of language and formulation in the English.

Neusner, Jacob. *Oral Torah: The Sacred Books of Judaism: An Introduction.* HarpC 1985 $19.45. ISBN 0-060-66103-8. An introduction to principal documents of the oral Torah, together with an account of the theory of how these writings form part of the Torah.

––––––. *Our Sages, God, and Israel: An Anthology of the Jerusalem Talmud.* Rossel Bks. 1985 $19.95. ISBN 0-940646-18-8. Introduces the Jerusalem Talmud.

––––––. *Pesiqta deRab Kahana: An Analytical Translation and Explanation.* 2 pts. Scholars Pr. GA 1987 $34.95. ISBN 1-555-40072-8. The first translation of the critical text, *With an Introduction to Pesiqta deRab Kahana.*

––––––. *Ruth Rabbah: An Analytical Translation. Brown Judaic Studies.* Scholars Pr. GA 1989 o.p. The first analytical translation.

––––––. *Sifra: An Analytical Translation.* 3 vols. Scholars Pr. GA 1988 Vol. 1 *Introduction* and *Vayyiqra Dibura Denedabah* and *Vayiqqra Dibura Dehobah.* $37.95. ISBN 1-55540-205-4. Vol. 2 *Sav, Shemini, Tazria, Negaim, Mesora,* and *Zabim.* $41.95. ISBN 1-55540-206-2. Vol. 3 *Aharé Mot, Qedoshim, Emor, Behar,* and *Behuqotai.* $49.95. ISBN 1-55540-207-0. The first translation of this important Midrash-compilation.

––––––. *Sifra in Perspective: The Documentary Comparison of the Midrashim of Ancient Judaism. Brown Judaic Studies.* Scholars Pr. GA 1988 $39.95. ISBN 1-555-40232-1

––––––. *Sifré to Deuteronomy: An Analytical Translation. Brown Judaic Studies.* Scholars Pr. GA 1987 $29.95. ISBN 1-55540-145-7. The first analytical translation.

––––––. *Sifré to Deuteronomy: An Introduction to the Rhetorical, Logical, and Topical Program. Brown Judaic Studies.* Scholars Pr. GA 1987 $24.95. ISBN 1-555-40168-6

––––––. *Sifré to Numbers: An American Translation.* With William Scott Green. *Brown Judaic Studies.* Scholars Pr. GA 1986 Pt. 1 1–58. $22.95. ISBN 1-55540-009-4. Pt. 2 59–115. $19.95. ISBN 1-55540-011-6. The first translation of this text.

––––––. *Song of Songs Rabbah: An Analytical Translation.* Vol. 1 *Song of Songs Rabbah to Song Chapters One through Three.* Vol. 2 *Song of Songs Rabbah to Song Chapters Four through Eight. Brown Judaic Studies.* Scholars Pr. GA 1990 o.p. The first analytical translation.

––––––. *Study of Ancient Judaism.* Vol. 1, *Mishnah, Midrash, Siddur;* Vol. 2, *The Palestinian and Babylonian Talmuds.* Ktav 1982 $37.50 ea. ISBN 0-870-68892-8. Bibliographic essays by various scholars, introducing studies of the named documents, including essays on the two Talmuds, by Baruch M. Bokser and David Goodblatt, respectively, that are regarded as classics in the genre of bibliographic essays and cover all topics pertinent to Talmudic literature, history, and exegesis.

––––––. *Talmud of Babylonia: An American Translation. Brown Judaic Studies.* Scholars Pr. GA 1984–1993 $24.95–$69.95 ea. In 75 volumes.

––––––. *Talmud: A Close Encounter.* Fortress Pr. 1991 $13.00. ISBN 0-8006-2498-X

––––––. *Talmud of the Land of Israel: A Preliminary Translation and Explanation.* 35 vols. U. Ch. Pr. 1982–1993 $19.00–75.00 ea. The first complete and reliable translation of this fundamental document.

––––––. *Torah from Our Sages: Pirke Avot.* Rossel Bks. 1986 $18.95. ISBN 0-940-64605-6. A new commentary to the classic, stressing issues of an intellectual character.

––––––. *Tosefta: An Introduction. South Florida Studies in the History of Judaism.* Scholars Pr. GA 1992 $89.95. ISBN 1-55540-713-7

––––––. *Tosefta: Translated from the Hebrew.* 6 vols. Ktav 1977–1986 $59.50 ea. ISBNs 0-87068-693-3, 0-87068-691-7, 0-87068-684-4, 0-87068-692-5, 0-87068-340-3, 0-87068-430-2. The first translation of this fundamental document.

––––––. *Translating the Classics of Judaism: In Theory and in Practice. Brown Judaic Studies.* Scholars Pr. GA 1989 $44.95. ISBN 1-555-40353-0. An explanation of the theory of analytical translation.

––––––. *Uniting the Dual Torah: Sifra and the Problem of the Mishnah.* Cambridge U. Pr. 1989 $64.95. ISBN 0-521-38125-8. An account of how Sifra deals with the Mishnah's indifference to the written Torah.

––––––. *What Is Midrash?* Augsburg Fortress 1987 $7.00. ISBN 0-8006-0472-5. Presents helpful definitions, Midrash's biblical origins, and the basis for comparative analysis.

_____. *Yerushalmi: The Talmud of the Land of Israel: An Introduction.* Aronson 1993
$30.00. ISBN 0-87668-812-1

Nickelsburg, George W. E. *Jewish Literature between the Bible and the Mishnah: A
Historical and Literary Introduction.* Augsburg Fortress 1981 $19.00. ISBN 0-8006-
1980-3. A good introduction to the Jewish literature of the Hellenistic and early
Roman periods organized according to historical occurrences.

Petuchowski, Jakob J. *Our Masters Taught Rabbinic Stories and Sayings.* Crossroad NY
1982 $10.95. ISBN 0-824-50521-2. A short collection of citations arranged by topic
on theological and ethical subjects.

Porton, Gary G. *Understanding Rabbinic Midrash: Texts and Commentary.* Ktav 1985
$16.95. ISBN 0-88125-056-2. A fine introduction that exemplifies the diverse genres
of Midrashic literature.

Saldarini, Anthony J. *Scholastic Rabbinism: A Literary Study of the Fathers According to
Rabbi Nathan.* Scholars Pr. GA 1982 $12.00. ISBN 0-891-30523-8. On the function of
and message conveyed by Pirke Avot, viewed as a tractate of the Mishnah.

Sanders, James A. *Torah and Canon.* Augsburg Fortress 1972 $9.00. ISBN 0-800-60105-X.
Traces the events that gave rise to the Hebrew Bible and explains the significance
this collection had for Jews in the period of the Babylonian exile.

Steinsaltz, Adin. *The Talmud. The Steinsaltz Edition. Vol. I. Tractate Bava Metzia. Part I.*
Random 1989 $45.00. ISBN 0-394-57666-7. A good and useful piece of work, and
when brought to completion in 40 volumes, will serve synagogue study groups,
Yeshiva and Hebrew day school classes, and others interested in serious intellectual
encounter in Judaism.

Stern, David. *Parables in Midrash: Narrative and Exegesis in Rabbinic Literature.* HUP
1991 $34.95. ISBN 0-674-65447-1. Argues unconvincingly that, over time, the literary
character of Midrashic discourse was formalized. Examines king-parables in ancient
through modern Hebrew and Near Eastern literatures.

Strack, H. L., and G. Stemberger. *Introduction to the Talmud and Midrash.* Augsburg
Fortress 1992 $22.00. ISBN 0-8006-2524-2. A complete bibliography, dating from
1987, on the state of research on the classical writings of Judaism, with foreword by
Jacob Neusner.

Zlotnick, Dov. *The Iron Pillar—The Mishnah: Redaction, Form, and Intent.* Ktav 1988
$39.50. ISBN 0-88125-327-8. Writing on the theme of "Rabbi's Mishnah and the
development of Jewish law," Zlotnick covers various topics, such as the editorial
activity of Rabbi Judah the Patriarch, memory and the integrity of the oral tradition,
some aspects of Mishnaic repetition, conservatism in the making of law, strengthening the oral law, the inoperative Halakhah, and whether the Mishnah is a code.

Material Evidence: Art and Archaeology

Art and archaeology frequently provide a perspective on the world of late
antiquity very different from that of the written sources. Literary evidence
presents a harmonious and homogenous picture of a religious system. In reality,
however, religious practices and beliefs vary even within a small community of
coreligionists. The visual evidence of wall paintings, mosaics, and decorative
arts focuses on a range of symbols different from those we find in the extant
literature. For example, the artwork on the wall of the synagogue at Dura-
Europos (on the Euphrates in Babylonia) from the middle of the third century
portrays Greco-Roman images banned in Rabbinic literature. Archaeology also
provides information on the daily life, economy, and social structure of Jewish
communities. In upper Galilee, for example, archaeologists recently unearthed
some information that corroborates the view of Jewish life found in the Talmud
(e.g., ritual baths and study houses) and some information that calls it into
question (e.g., pig bones and burial tombs).

Brooten, Bernadette J. *Women Leaders in the Ancient Synagogue: Inscriptional Evidence and Background Issues. Brown Judaic Studies.* Scholars Pr. GA 1982 $29.95. ISBN 0-891-30587-4. Argues that the inscriptions point to women as well as men in positions of synagogue authority.

Chiat, Marilyn. *Handbook of Synagogue Architecture. Brown Judaic Studies.* Scholars Pr. GA 1982 $20.00. ISBN 0-891-30524-6. Lists the various sites and their traits.

Goldman, Bernard. *The Sacred Portal: A Primary Symbol in Ancient Judaic Art.* U. Pr. of Amer. 1986 repr. of 1966 ed. $26.50. ISBN 0-8191-5269-2. An examination of "some of the most important thematic motifs that dominate the art of the ancient Jews."

Gutmann, Joseph. *Beauty in Holiness: Studies in Jewish Ceremonial Art and Customs.* o.p.

———. *The Synagogue: Studies in Origins, Archaeology, and Architecture.* Ktav 1974 $35.00. ISBN 0-870-68331-4. Reproduction of scholarly articles on the material and literary evidence of ancient synagogues.

———, ed. *Ancient Synagogues: The State of Research.* Scholars Pr. GA 1981 $14.00. ISBN 0-89130-467-3. A collection of clearly written articles on the symbolism, architecture, and function of ancient synagogues.

Kraeling, Carl H. *The Synagogue.* Ktav rev. ed. 1979 $100.00. ISBN 0-870-68331-4. An illustrated report on the art and architecture of the synagogue excavated at Dura-Europos, Mesopotamia (present-day Syria), the most important synagogue find in modern times; one wall was completely intact and covered with representational art.

Levine, L. I. *Ancient Synagogues Revealed.* Wayne St. U. Pr. 1982 o.p. A survey of known discoveries, conveniently summarized, with essays by noted scholars.

Neusner, Jacob. *Symbol and Theology in Early Judaism.* Augsburg Fortress 1991 o.p. Explains the diverse discourse, verbal and nonverbal, in Rabbinic literature, ed.

———, ed. *Goodenough's Jewish Symbols. An Abridged Edition.* Princeton U. Pr. 1988 o.p. Provides a summary of the main points of the great work on artistic symbols in ancient Judaism.

Yadin, Yigael. *Massada: Herod's Last Fortress and the Zealots' Last Stand.* Random 1966 o.p. A vivid depiction of the Zealots' last stand and collective suicide of 73 C.E. in the war against Rome.

Religious Movements

FIRST-CENTURY SECTS

No single orthodoxy in the early centuries A.D. characterized all Jews throughout the world. Those in Egypt spoke Greek; those in the Land of Israel, Greek and Aramaic and possibly Hebrew; those in Babylonia, one kind of Aramaic; those in the Land of Israel, a different kind of Aramaic. Scripture was read in different languages and interpreted in different ways. Furthermore, the Greek-speaking Jews, represented by PHILO of Alexandria, read Scripture within the categories of the Greek-speaking world, whereas those who spoke Hebrew produced a different reading altogether. Still, in the common theology of the Jews in late antiquity, we should point to important—indeed definitive—components, such as Scripture, read in diverse ways, to be sure; reverence for the Temple and its sacrificial system—more important to those nearby, less so for those at a distance; and above all, identification within a common social entity, "Israel." That identification bore so many differing elements among diverse groups, however, that to seek a single orthodox "Judaism" produces frustration. Harmonizing all of the different viewpoints into a single orthodoxy distorts the evidence and yields only misinterpretation, out of all context. Against the background of a common culture prevailing in one place, namely, the Land of Israel, however, a number of small groups, each with its own special points of emphasis and interest, can be described. These are called sects.

GENERAL WORKS

Kraft, Robert A., and George W. E. Nickelsburg. *Early Judaism and Its Modern Interpreters.* Scholars Pr. GA 1986 $24.95. ISBN 0-891-30921-7. A systematic, thorough, and reliable presentation of recent scholarship on the Judaisms of the period from 500 B.C. to A.D. 70.

Neusner, Jacob. *Judaism in the Beginning of Christianity.* Augsburg Fortress 1984 $5.95. ISBN 0-800-61750-9. A brief and popular account of what is known about first-century Judaism in the Land of Israel.

Nickelsburg, George W. E., and Michael E. Stone. *Faith and Piety in Early Judaism: Texts and Documents.* Augsburg Fortress 1983 $19.95. ISBN 0-800-60679-5. An excellent collection of sources in translation, introduced and properly presented.

Simon, Marcal. *Jewish Sects at the Time of Jesus.* Trans. by James H. Farley. Augsburg Fortress 1980 o.p. A good summary of what is known about the sects mentioned in the New Testament and in the writings of Josephus.

Stone, Michael E. *Scripture, Sects and Visions: A Profile of Judaism from Ezra to the Jewish Revolts.* Augsburg Fortress 1980 $11.95. ISBN 0-529-05711-5. A collection of essays, not sustained or systematic but interesting in parts.

PHARISEES

The Pharisees, well known because of their prominent position in the Gospels of Matthew, Mark, and Luke, are described in two further bodies of sources: the writings of JOSEPHUS and the Rabbinic literature of the second and later centuries. The writings of Josephus, first in order of composition, identify the Pharisees as a political party in the time of the Hasmonean rulers of the first century B.C. and also as a philosophical group with certain distinctive ideas concerning, for example, free will, the life of the soul after death, and so forth. Next in line, the Gospels represent the Pharisees in part as a political group, in part as a people who kept certain aspects of the law with special care. These aspects of the law cover three main matters: Sabbath observance, purity laws, and tithing of foods. Purity laws applied in the Temple and protected the cult and the priesthood and the offering from those sources of contamination specified in the books of Leviticus and Numbers. Pharisees—as the Gospels portray them—kept those same laws at home. They therefore sought to live a holy way of life even outside the Temple and to identify the table of the family at home with the cult and the priesthood. Tithing laws affect the disposition of crops and the preparation of food and hence were also a kind of dietary rule. The later Rabbinic writings include many sayings assigned to authorities before 70 B.C., and some of those authorities are identified by Josephus or New Testament writers with Pharisees. These sayings assigned to pre-70 B.C. figures who might have been Pharisees deal with the same issues that are prominent in the Gospels' accounts of the matter.

Baeck, Leo. *Pharisaism in the Making: Selected Essays.* Ktav 1972 o.p. An apologetic work, reacting to the Christian prejudices against the Pharisees.

————. *The Pharisees.* Schocken 1947 o.p. A theological work in which the historical Pharisees are not the center of interest.

Büchler, Adolph. *Studies in Sin and Atonement. Lib. of Biblical Studies Ser.* Ktav 1967 o.p. Büchler's theological studies rest on the premise that whatever is assigned to a given authority really was said by that authority and that whatever anyone said, without regard to that person's dates, represents opinion held in the first century.

Finkelstein, Louis. *The Pharisees: The Social Background of Their Faith.* 2 vols. Jewish Pubns. 1962 o.p. A socioeconomic interpretation of the Pharisees as plebeians, against upperclass Sadducees; very popular in its day, long since rendered a mere curiosity.

Mason, Steve. *Flavius Josephus on the Pharisees: A Composition-Critical Study.* E. J. Brill 1990 $120.00. ISBN 9-00409-181-5. Detailed interpretation of all passages in which Josephus mentions the Pharisees, showing that, overall, Josephus disliked the group.

Neusner, Jacob. *From Politics to Piety: The Emergence of Pharisaic Judaism.* Ktav 1978 $9.95. ISBN 0-87068-677-1. A summary of the distinct sources that refer to the Pharisees and an analysis of the viewpoint of each.

————. *The Rabbinic Traditions about the Pharisees before 70.* 3 vols. E. J. Brill 1971 o.p. An account of what various Rabbinic documents say about authorities cited therein who are believed to have lived before 70 B.C. and to have belonged to the Pharisaic group.

Saldarini, Anthony J. *Pharisees, Scribes and Sadducees in Palestinian Society: A Sociological Approach.* Liturgical Pr. 1988 $19.95. ISBN 0-8146-5744-3. The sociological approach addresses issues of social classes in Palestinian Jewish society and the Roman Empire and social relations and groups in Palestine.

ESSENES

The Essenes, another small group or sect, are known from references among ancient writers—in particular, JOSEPHUS—and also from the Dead Sea Scrolls found at Qumran. Josephus portrays them within the same pattern that applies to the Pharisees, but the Dead Sea Scrolls present a much more elaborate and detailed picture. In that picture the Essenes bear affinities to the Pharisees, in their interest in sanctification in general and the holy meal in particular, and also to the Christians, in their concern for salvation overall and the meaning of history and the end of time. Later on, in the writings on Rabbinic Judaism of the fourth through seventh centuries, these same concerns—for sanctification now, attained through living a holy way of life, and salvation at the end of time—would come to a fresh statement. The structure, however, remained constant.

Ringgren, H. *The Faith of Qumran.* Crossroad NY 1993 $16.95. ISBN 0-8245-1258-8. A systematic account of the religious viewpoint of the Judaism of Qumran.

Vermes, Geza. *The Dead Sea Scrolls in English: Qumran in Perspective.* Augsburg Fortress 1981 repr. of 1978 ed. $25.00. ISBN 1-850-75151-X. The classic survey of the first 25 years of research; the starting point for all work.

SADDUCEES

What is known about the Sadducees comes from the Gospels' references and from statements in JOSEPHUS' writings. No writings deriving from Sadducees come down from ancient times, with the result that knowledge of the group and its place in the larger Judaic world is slight. Josephus represents the group within his established pattern—as a political party of philosophical opinion— and the Gospels' references conform also to their larger scheme, presenting an organized group, with some political influence, opposed to Jesus.

Saldarini, Anthony J. *Pharisees, Scribes and Sadducees in Palestinian Society: A Sociological Approach.* Liturgical Pr. 1988 $19.95. ISBN 0-8146-5744-3. Addresses issues of social classes in Palestinian Jewish society and the Roman Empire and social relations and groups in Palestine.

Simon, Marcal. *Jewish Sects at the Time of Jesus.* Trans. by James H. Farley. Augsburg Fortress 1980 o.p. A good summary of what is known about the sects mentioned in the New Testament and in the writings of Josephus.

Stone, Michael E. *Scripture, Sects and Visions: A Profile of Judaism from Ezra to the Jewish Revolts.* Augsburg Fortress 1980 $11.95. ISBN 0-529-05711-5. A collection of essays, some of which are quite interesting.

EARLY CHRISTIANS

A sizable and important literature treats Christianity within the Judaic context in which it came to original expression. Because all of the earliest Christians were Jews and saw their community as an "Israel," the prevailing approach is sensible. Just what it means to see Christianity as a Judaism, however, is not entirely worked out as yet. The important continuities between the earliest Christian writings and the Hebrew Scriptures, or Old Testament, registered forcefully by the First Gospel, for example, form an important starting point. Vast tracts of the Gospels cannot be grasped without a detailed knowledge of Judaic belief and behavior, and, we also stress, the Gospels form the principal source (along with JOSEPHUS) for our understanding of Jews' worldviews and ways of life in the Land of Israel in the first century.

Barrett, C. K. *The Gospel of John and Judaism.* Trans. by D. M. Smith. Bks. Demand repr. of 1975 ed. $27.80. ISBN 0-685-15523-4. A fine example of how knowledge derived from various Judaic documents facilitates the understanding of a Gospel.

————, ed. *New Testament Background: Selected Documents.* HarpC SF 1989 $16.00. ISBN 0-06-060553-7. Among the documents are samples of Judaic writings.

Bultmann, Rudolf. *Primitive Christianity: In Its Contemporary Setting.* Trans. by Reginald H. Fuller. Augsburg Fortress 1980 repr. of 1956 ed. $13.00. ISBN 0-8006-1408-9. Survey of the various groups that constitute Judaism, representing an ignorant and bigoted work by a good scholar.

Davies, W. D. *Jewish and Pauline Studies.* Bks. Demand repr. of 1984 ed. $112.10. ISBN 0-318-34893-4. Pioneer on Paul's Judaic roots.

————. *Paul and Rabbinic Judaism: Some Rabbinic Elements in Pauline Theology.* Augsburg Fortress 1983 o.p. Best account of how knowledge of Judaic studies illuminates the thought of Paul.

Kee, Howard C. *Christian Origins in Sociologic Perspective: Methods and Resources.* Westminster John Knox 1980 o.p. The Judaic setting in which earliest Christianity took shape.

————. *The Origins of Christianity: Sources and Documents.* P-H 1973 ISBN 0-13-642553-4. Reader encompassing the Judaic sources of Christianity.

Neusner, Jacob. *Are There Really Tannaitic Parallels to the Gospels? A Refutation of Morton Smith. South Florida Studies in the History of Judaism.* Scholars Pr. GA 1993 $59.95. ISBN 1-55540-867-2. Rejection of the claim that Tannaite documents relate to each other in the same way that the Synoptic Gospels do.

————. *Judaic Law from Jesus to the Mishnah: A Systematic Reply to Professor E. P. Sanders. South Florida Studies in the History of Judaism.* Scholars Pr. GA 1993 $89.95. ISBN 1-55540-873-7. Argues that a prominent New Testament scholar has misunderstood the complexity of Judaism.

————. *What We Cannot Show, We Do Not Know: Rabbinic Literature and the New Testament.* TPI PA 1993 o.p. Systematic account of errors of New Testament scholarship in the reading of Rabbinic literature.

Overman, J. Andrew, and Robert S. MacLennan, eds. *Diaspora Jews and Judaism: Essays in Honor of, and in Dialogue with, A. Thomas Kraabel.* Scholars Pr. GA 1992 $74.95. ISBN 1-555-40696-3. Studies on the relationship between diaspora Jews and Christianity as well as diaspora Jews, Judaism, and the Roman world.

Sanders, E. P. *Jesus and Judaism.* Augsburg Fortress 1985 $18.00. ISBN 0-334-02091-3. Best account of the relationship of certain sayings and actions of Jesus to the Judaism of the time and place.

————. *Paul and Palestinian Judaism: A Comparison of Patterns of Religion.* Augsburg Fortress 1977 $26.00. ISBN 0-8006-1899-8. Comparison of the religious systems of Paul, the Essene Judaism of Qumran, and Rabbinic Judaism to demonstrate that the Judaism of the day was a religion of covenantal nomism.

Stendahl, Krister. *Paul among the Jews and Gentiles.* Augsburg Fortress 1976 o.p. Argues that Paul's primary concern was the relationship between Jews and gentiles and that his idea of justification by faith can be understood only as a reflection of this concern.

Theissen, Gerd. *The Social Setting of Pauline Christianity: Essays on Corinth*. Trans. by John H. Schultz. Augsburg Fortress 1982 $19.95. ISBN 0-800-60669-8. Includes much about Judaism, but the sources are used uncritically and the author knows very little about the problems of studying ancient Judaisms or about the sociology of the Jewish world.

————. *The Sociology of Early Palestinian Christianity*. Trans. by John Bowden. Augsburg Fortress 1978 $12.00. ISBN 0-8006-1330-9. The same criticism applies to this work as to the previous entry.

Vermes, Geza. *Jesus and the World of Judaism*. Augsburg Fortress 1984 $10.95. ISBN 0-334-02094-8. Collection of essays on Jesus in the Jewish cultural milieu, with emphasis on the evidence of the Dead Sea Scrolls.

————. *Jesus the Jew: A Historian's Reading of the Gospels*. Augsburg Fortress 1981 repr. of 1973 ed. $13.00. ISBN 0-8006-1443-7. A rather private vision of Jesus, in which a highly selective view of what he really did and said produces the picture of a Galilean pietist.

SAMARITANS

After the reigns of David and Solomon, the ancient people of Israel split in two—the northern kingdom comprising 10 tribes in Samaria and the southern kingdom comprising 2 tribes in Judea. In 722 B.C., the Assyrians conquered the north and forced the deportation of the 10 tribes (the famous 10 lost tribes of Israel). The leadership of the Judeans, centered in Jerusalem, subsequently warned against contact with the Israelites from Samaria, arguing that the Samaritans had intermarried with non-Israelites and had forgotten the Torah. The Samaritans continued, too, as a distinct group in the Land of Israel parallel to, and part of, the Jewish people. Unlike the Jews, who ceased conducting sacrifices after the destruction of the Temple in Jerusalem, the Samaritans continued cultic practices at their temple at Mount Gezirim. Another difference is that the Samaritans knew of no oral Torah to supplement their Scriptures, which are almost identical to the Jewish Pentateuch. A small community of Samaritans remains today in the State of Israel.

Bowman, John. *The Samaritan Problem: Studies in the Relationship of Samaritanism, Judaism, and Early Christianity*. Trans. by Alfred M. Johnson, Jr. *Pittsburgh Theological Monographs*. Pickwick 1975 $5.95. ISBN 0-915-13804-2. Study of the Samaritans in antiquity and their relationship to the New Testament Gospels and the Dead Sea Scrolls.

————, ed. and trans. *Samaritan Documents: Relating to Their History, Religion and Life*. *Pittsburgh Original Texts and Translations Ser.* Pickwick 1977 $7.95. ISBN 0-915-13827-1. The standard anthology of extant Samaritan writings.

Coggins, R. J. *Samaritans and Jews: The Origins of Samaritanism Reconsidered*. Westminster John Knox Pr. 1975 o.p. Argues that the relations of Samaritans and Jews prior to the Christian era were closer and more complex than previously believed.

Gaster, Moses. *The Samaritans: History, Doctrines and Literature*. Gordon Pr. 1976 $134.95. ISBN 0-8490-2563-X. This work remains a good general survey.

Purvis, James D. *The Samaritan Pentateuch and the Origin of the Samaritan Sect*. HUP 1968 o.p. The classic introduction to the origin of the Samaritans.

Wright, G. E. *Shechem: Biography of a Biblical City*. McGraw 1965 o.p. Follows the development of Shechem and its central place in early Samaritan history.

RABBINIC JUDAISM

Rabbinic Judaism is the Judaism that maintains the story of the dual Torah. Specifically, when Moses ascended Mount Sinai to receive the Torah, it came to him in two media, writing and memory. The written Torah comprises the five Books of Moses, or Pentateuch—that is, Genesis, Exodus, Leviticus, Numbers, and Deuteronomy. The oral Torah consisted of sayings, or "traditions," handed on, not in writing, but through oral formulation and oral transmission—hence, memory. This oral, or memorized, Torah then came to be written down in diverse documents produced by sages, or rabbis, in late antiquity. To spell out these matters in some detail, the writings produced by sages, or rabbis, of late antiquity in the Land of Israel ("Palestine") and Babylonia fall into two groups, each of which had its own plan and program: One was produced in the second and third centuries; the second was produced in the fourth and fifth centuries. The first of these groups of writings begins with the Mishnah, a philosophical law book brought to closure in A.D. 200 and later called the first statement of the oral Torah. In its wake, the Mishnah drew tractate Abot, C.A.D. 250, a statement concluded a generation after the Mishnah on the standing of the authorities of the Mishnah; Tosefta, C.A.D. 300, a compilation of supplements of various kinds to the Mishnah; and three systematic exegeses of books of Scripture, or the written Torah—Sifre to Leviticus, Sifre to Numbers, and Sifre to Deuteronomy (of indeterminate date but possibly concluded by A.D. 300). Overall, these books form one stage in the unfolding of the Judaism of the dual Torah, a stage that stressed issues of sanctification of the life of Israel, the people, in the aftermath of the destruction of the Temple of Jerusalem in A.D. 70, during which, it was commonly held, Israel's sanctification came to full realization in the bloody rites of sacrifice to God on high. We call this system a Judaism without Christianity, because the issues found urgent in the documents representative of this phase address questions not pertinent to the Christian challenge of Israel.

The second set of these writings begins with the Talmud of the Land of Israel, or Yerushalmi, generally supposed to have come to a conclusion around A.D. 400; Genesis Rabbah, assigned to about the next half-century; Leviticus Rabbah, C.A.D. 450; Pesiqta deRab Kahana, C.A.D. 450–500; and, finally, the Talmud of Babylonia, or Bavli, assigned to the late sixth or early seventh century, C.A.D. 600. The two Talmuds systematically interpret passages of the Mishnah, and the other documents, it is clear, do the same for books of the written Torah. Some other treatments of biblical books important in synagogue liturgy, particularly the Five Scrolls—for example, Lamentations Rabbati, Esther Rabbah, and the like—are supposed also to have reached closure at this time. This second set of writings introduces, alongside the paramount issue of Israel's sanctification, the matter of Israel's salvation, with doctrines of history and the Messiah given prominence in the larger systemic statement.

The first of the two stages in the formation of the Judaism of the dual Torah exhibits no sign of interest in, or response to, the advent of Christianity. The second, from the Yerushalmi forward, lays points of stress and emphasis that, in retrospect, appear to respond to and counter the challenge of Christianity. The point of difference, of course, is that, from the beginning of the legalization of Christianity in the early fourth century to the establishment of Christianity at the end of that same century, Jews in the Land of Israel found themselves facing a challenge that, prior to Constantine, they had no compelling reason to consider. The specific crisis came when the Christians pointed to the success of the church in the politics of the Roman state as evidence that Jesus Christ was king of the world and that his claim to be Messiah and King of Israel now had found vindication. When the Emperor Julian, A.D. 361–363, apostatized and renewed state patronage of paganism, he permitted the Jews to begin to rebuild the Temple, part of his large plan of humiliating Christianity. His prompt death on an Iranian battlefield supplied further evidence for heaven's choice of the church and the truth of the church's allegations concerning the standing and authority of Jesus as the Christ. The Judaic documents that reached closure in the century after these events attended to those questions of salvation—for example, the doctrine of history and of the Messiah, the authority of the sages' reading of Scripture as against the Christians' interpretation, and the like—that had not enjoyed extensive consideration earlier. In all, this second Judaism, which the author characterizes as a Judaism despite Christianity, met the challenge of the events of the fourth century. The Judaic system of the dual Torah—expressed in its main outlines in the Yerushalmi and associated compilations of biblical exegeses concerning Genesis, Leviticus, and some other scriptural books—culminated in the Bavli, which emerged as the authoritative document of the Judaism of the dual Torah from then to now.

Adler, Morris. *The World of the Talmud*. Pantheon 1987 $5.95. ISBN 0-394-20058-6. A very brief and popular description of Talmudic beliefs.

Bamberger, Bernard. *Proselytism in the Talmudic Period*. Hebrew Union Col. Pr. 1939 o.p. A survey of references in Talmudic literature to conversion to Judaism.

Bonsirven, Joseph. *Palestinian Judaism in the Time of Jesus Christ*. H. Holt & Co. 1964 o.p. Originally published in French (1934–35). An informed and thoughtful counterpart, by a French Jesuit, to Moore's picture of the Judaism of the Land of Israel in the first centuries B.C. and A.D.

Boyarin, Daniel. *Intertextuality and the Reading of Midrash. Indiana Studies in Biblical Literature*. Ind. U. Pr. 1990 $27.50. ISBN 0-253-31251-5. Proposes to clarify the nature of Midrash through examining a tiny segment of the anomalous and probably medieval exegetical text, Mekhilta.

Brooks, Roger. *The Spirit of the Ten Commandments: Shattering the Myth of Rabbinic Legalism*. HarpC 1990 $21.95. ISBN 0-06-061132-4. An excellent account of the religious power of law in Judaism, demolishing the myth of vacant legalism and replacing it with a picture of Judaism's true spirituality.

Cohen, Abraham. *Everyman's Talmud*. Schocken 1975 $17.00. ISBN 0-8052-0497-0. An early and still useful topical anthology of Talmudic literature.

Finkelstein, Louis. *Akiba: Scholar, Saint and Martyr*. Atheneum 1970 $6.95. ISBN 0-689-70230-2. An imaginative, semifictional biography, paraphrasing and amplifying stories in the Talmudic literature about the most important rabbi of the founding generation of Judaism.

Gillman, Neil. *Sacred Fragments: Recovering Theology for the Modern Jew*. JPS Phila. 1992 $14.95. ISBN 0-827-60352-5. Theological questions—such as why does God allow suffering? why do we need ritual?—are given philosophical answers.

Ginzberg, Louis. *Students, Scholars, and Saints*. U. Pr. of Amer. 1985 o.p. Classic and masterful essays on fundamental topics in the biography of important Judaic sages.

Glatzer, Nahum N. *Hillel the Elder: The Emergence of Classical Judaism*. B'nai B'rith Bk. 1959 o.p. A brief retelling of Talmudic tales about Hillel in the form of a semifictional biography.

Goldberg, Hillel. *Between Berlin and Slobodka: Jewish Transition Figures from Eastern Europe*. Ktav 1989 $14.95. ISBN 0-881-25142-9. Looks at several significant East European intellectuals and follows them on their journey to the West, a journey that was in part biographical, in part intellectual.

Jacobs, Louis. *Structure and Form in the Babylonian Talmud*. Cambridge U. Pr. 1992 $49.95. ISBN 0-521-40345-6. Uncovers the basic form and structure of the Babylonian Talmud.

Kadushin, Max. *Worship and Ethics: A Study in Rabbinic Judaism*. Bloch 1975 $8.95. ISBN 0-313-20217-6. A brilliant and systematic effort to show the value system implicit in the liturgy of Judaism; the most successful study on its subject ever written.

Kraemer, David. *The Mind of the Talmud: An Intellectual History of the Bavli*. OUP 1990 $35.00. ISBN 0-19-506290-6. Traces the development of the literary forms and conventions of the Babylonian Talmud and analyzes those forms as expressions of emergent rabbinic ideology.

Landman, Leo, ed. *Messianism in the Talmudic Era*. Ktav 1979 $35.00. ISBN 0-870-68445-0. A survey of writings on the topic of the Messiah.

Levine, Lee I. *The Rabbinic Class of Roman Palestine in Late Antiquity*. Yad Ishak Ben-Zvi and Jewish Theol. Sem. of Amer. 1989 o.p. Treats the status of the Rabbinic class, with attention to the ideal of Torah study, the uniqueness and privileges of the sages, the social and economic support system of the rabbis, the sages within Jewish society, and other topics.

Marmorstein, Arthur. *Doctrine of Merits in Old Rabbinical Literature*. Ktav 1969 o.p. A collection of sayings and stories relevant to the doctrine that the merits of one's ancestors serve as a treasury of virtue against which one can draw, for example, for forgiveness in time of suffering.

———. *The Old Rabbinic Doctrine of God*. Gregg Intl. 1968 repr. of 1937 ed. $130.00. ISBN 0-576-80134-8. A collection of sayings and stories on the conception of God in various Rabbinic writings, topically organized.

Moore, George Foot. *Judaism in the First Centuries of the Christian Era*. HUP 1954 o.p. The classic work of historical theology on Judaism in late antiquity, organized in accord with the categories of Protestant theology.

Neusner, Jacob. *From Testament to Torah: An Introduction to Judaism in Its Formative Age*. P-H 1988 $20.00. ISBN 0-13-331620-3. A summary of the author's general theory of the formation of Judaism in late antiquity, for college students.

———. *Judaism and Christianity in the Age of Constantine: Issues of the Initial Confrontation*. U. Ch. Pr. 1987 $29.95. ISBN 0-226-57652-3. A general theory of the formative history of Judaism, arguing that important doctrines of the Judaic system put forth in the Talmud of the Land of Israel and related writings met head-on the challenge of Christian doctrines on those same topics.

———. *Judaism in the Matrix of Christianity*. Augsburg Fortress 1986 $12.95. ISBN 0-800-61897-1. A series of essays that collectively focus on the fourth century as the point at which the indicator traits of the Judaism of the dual Torah first reached literary expression.

———. *Talmudic Thinking: Language, Logic, and Law*. U. of SC Pr. 1992 $34.95. ISBN 0-872-49825-5

———, ed. *Judaisms and Their Messiahs in the Beginning of Christianity*. Cambridge U. Pr. 1988 $54.95. ISBN 0-521-34146-9. A dozen scholars discuss the role of the Messiah in various Judaic systems in antiquity, including Christianity.

Sanders, E. P. *Judaism: Practice and Belief 63 B.C.E.–66 C.E.* TPI PA 1991 $29.95. ISBN 1-56338-015-3. A systematic account of how various sources are combined to portray a single Judaism.

Schechter, Solomon. *Some Aspects of Rabbinic Theology*. Behrman 1936 o.p. A classic and elegant essay on basic theological beliefs of the Judaism of the dual Torah; best of its genre.

Schiffman, Lawrence H. *From Text to Tradition: A History of Second Temple and Rabbinic Judaism*. Ktav 1991 $16.95. ISBN 0-88125-372-3. Argues that various approaches to Judaism represent aspects of a single, encompassing religious civilization.

———. *Who Was a Jew: Rabbinic and Halakhic Perspectives on the Jewish/Christian Schism*. Ktav 1985 $14.95. ISBN 0-881-25084-6. Discusses Jewish self-definition during the early years of Christianity, uncritically assuming that documents from the third to seventh century accurately report the situation in the first century.

Spiegel, Shalom. *The Last Trial: On the Legend and Lore of the Command to Abraham to Offer Isaac as a Sacrifice—The Akedah. Jewish Legacy Ser.* Jewish Lights 1993 repr. of 1973 ed. $17.95. ISBN 1-879045-29-X. An account of how Judaism read and interpreted the story of the binding of Isaac.

Steinberg, Milton. *As a Driven Leaf*. Behrman 1939 o.p. Historical fiction, based on Talmudic literature, about Rabbi Elisha ben Abuyah and his search for faith.

MEDIEVAL JUDAISM

History of the Jews

The beginning of medieval history for Jews in Christendom is marked by the recognition, in the fourth century, that Christianity was the religion of the state. Henceforth, the West became Christian, and the conditions in which Jews would work out their histories were defined. In the case of the territories conquered in the seventh and later centuries by Muslim armies, medieval history begins with the rise of Islam. For Jews, medieval history in the Christian West ended with the secularization of politics, beginning first with the U.S. Constitution in 1787 and the French Revolution in 1789. From the fourth to the nineteenth centuries, no important political changes essentially reshaped the conditions of the histories of Jews. For Jews in the Muslim world, the turning point came in 1948, with the creation of the State of Israel. Until that time, whatever political changes took place in Muslim countries, the situation and position of the Jews remained generally constant. Jews in various countries and regions—in western and eastern Europe, North Africa, and the Middle East—participated in the history of those areas. No single or linear path joins the discrete histories of various groups of Jews into a single unified history. Certain problems do, however, find a place in common among those histories. For example, Jews were minorities in both Muslim and Christian countries, although the rules for treating minorities differed from country to country, as well as from Christendom to Islam. Furthermore, Jews maintained contact with one another, forming one important means by which trade and culture were mediated between the two worlds of medieval times. Many important books trace the history of Jews in particular countries or regions—Spain and North Africa, for example, or France or England. Others survey matters of culture, as these proved uniform for Jews in Christian or in Muslim countries. Still others treat ideas that shaped peoples' thinking throughout the Jewish world, both Christian and Islamic.

GENERAL

Abrahams, Israel. *Jewish Life in the Middle Ages*. JPS Phila. 1993 $9.95. ISBN 0-8276-0479-3. Remains a good introduction to the social life of Jews in medieval Christendom, including discussions of economics, home life, slave trade, social mores, synagogue activities, and much more.

Blumenthal, David R. *Approaches to Judaism in Medieval Times*. 2 vols. Scholars Pr. GA 1984–85 $14.95–$23.95. ISBNs 0-891-30659-5, 0-89130-848-2. Essays on medieval Jewish literature, philosophy, and religion.

Chazan, Robert, ed. *Medieval Jewish Life: Studies from the Proceedings of the American Academy for Jewish Research*. Ktav 1974 o.p. Eclectic collection of essays by noted scholars on political, social, and intellectual history.

Cohen, Gerson D. *Studies in the Variety of Rabbinic Cultures*. JPS Phila. 1990 $37.50. ISBN 0-82760-383-5. A collection of previously published essays on diverse topics relating to medieval and modern Rabbinic ideology.

Finkelstein, Louis. *Jewish Self-Government in the Middle Ages*. Jewish Theol. Sem. 1924 o.p. The classic study of medieval Jewish political institutions.

Kanarfogel, Ephraim. *Jewish Education and Society in the High Middle Ages*. Wayne St. U. Pr. 1991 $19.95. ISBN 0-81432-164-X. A thorough study of the educational institutions of medieval Rabbinic scholarship, with particular attention to the Tosafists and German Pietists.

Lazar, Moshe. *The Sephardic Tradition: Ladino and Spanish-Jewish Literature*. Norton 1972 o.p. Presents English translations of Spanish and Ladino (a Spanish dialect written with Hebrew characters) literature from Jewish communities in Muslim and Christian countries of the fifteenth to nineteenth century.

Marcus, Jacob R., ed. *The Jew in the Medieval World: A Source Book 315–1791*. Greenwood 1975 repr. of 1938 ed. $35.00. ISBN 0-8371-2619-3. Extensive collection of documents from late antiquity to the early modern period, on the social, political, and religious history of the Jews in Islamic and Christian countries.

JEWS IN CHRISTIAN LANDS

The Latin Christian West began in Italy, Spain, and France, and only gradually made its way into Germany, Poland, and southeastern Europe, meeting the Greek-speaking Christian East as it came north and west from Byzantium into the Ukraine and Russia, Greece and Bulgaria, and what was the former nation of Yugoslavia. The two great Christian civilizations encompassed large Jewish populations. The histories of Jews in those Christian kingdoms and empires varied. From the Crusades onward, the Western Latin kingdoms—Spain, France, Germany, and England—became less and less tenable for Jewish life. The advances toward the east, particularly in Poland, Lithuania, and White Russia, by contrast, opened new territories for Jewish settlement, and the (relative) toleration accorded by the Polish and Lithuanian monarchies attracted Jews driven out of England, France, and Germany from the twelfth century onward.

Baer, Yitzhak. *History of the Jews in Christian Spain*. 2 vols. JPS Phila. 1993 repr. of 1961 ed. $37.50. ISBN 0-8276-0431-9. In-depth study of Spanish Jewry from the Christian reconquest of the Iberian peninsula to the expulsion and forced conversion of the Jews.

Berger, David, ed. and trans. *The Jewish-Christian Debate in the High Middle Ages*. JPS Phila. 1978 o.p. Translation (with the original Hebrew) of an anonymous Jewish polemic against Christianity.

Bowman, Steven B. *The Jews of Byzantium, 1204–1453*. Judaic Studies Ser. U. of Ala. Pr. 1985 $42.50. ISBN 0-817-30198-4. Detailed studies of the internal structure of the medieval Jewish community in Asia Minor and its relationship to other Jewish communities.

Chazan, Robert. *Medieval Jewry in Northern France: A Political and Social History*. Johns Hopkins 1973 o.p. The standard work on the political and social history of medieval French Jewry.

———, ed. *Church, State and Jew in the Middle Ages*. Lib. of Jewish Studies. Behrman 1979 $9.95. ISBN 0-874-41301-X. Discusses how religious and political officials frequently condoned the persecution of the Jews, from the eleventh to the thirteenth century, even when official church and state policy guaranteed protection to the Jewish community.

Cohen, Jeremy. *The Friars and the Jews: The Evolution of Medieval Anti-Judaism*. Cornell Univ. Pr. 1984 $10.95. ISBN 0-801-41406-7. Careful analysis of church history and the complex role the Jews and Judaism played in medieval Christian theology.

Cutler, Allan H., and Helen E. Cutler. *The Jew as Ally of the Muslim: Medieval Roots of Anti-Semitism*. U. of Notre Dame Pr. 1985 $50.00. ISBN 0-268-01190-7. Well-documented study of how Christians portrayed Jews as an internal threat, allied with the powerful Muslim empire beyond the borders, from the eleventh to fourteenth century.

Eidelberg, Shlomo, ed. and trans. *The Jews and the Crusaders: The Hebrew Chronicles of the First and Second Crusades*. U. of Wis. Pr. 1977 $15.00. ISBN 0-299-07060-3. Eyewitness accounts of the devastation inflicted by Christian zealots.

Gluckel of Hamelin. *The Memoirs of Gluckel of Hamelin*. Trans. by Marvin Lowenthal. Schocken 1977 $15.00. ISBN 0-8052-0572-1. Written by a seventeenth-century woman to inform her children about her personal, familial, and communal background as a German Jew. Introduction by Robert Rosen.

Grayzel, Solomon. *The Church and the Jews in the Thirteenth Century: A Study of Their Relations during the Years 1198–1254 Based on the Papal Letters and the Conciliar Decrees of the Period.* Dropsie Col. 1933 o.p. Collection of more than 100 official documents of the Catholic Church from a century in which Jews took on new roles in European society as the social, political, and religious order shifted from feudal to more centralized organization.

Hanover, Nathan. *The Abyss of Despair.* Transaction Pubs. 1983 $14.95. ISBN 0-878-55927-2. Eyewitness accounts of the Chmielnicki Massacres of 1648 to 1652, which had a devastating effect on East European Jewry. Introduction by William B. Helmreich.

Katz, Jacob. *Exclusiveness and Tolerance: Studies in Jewish-Gentile Relations in Medieval and Modern Times.* OUP 1961 o.p. Widely cited study of the position of Jews in European society during a period of radical change.

———. *Tradition and Crisis: Jewish Society at the End of the Middle Ages.* Free Pr. 1961 o.p. Excellent discussion of the Jewish community and cultural trends in eastern and central Europe from 1500 to 1800.

Maccoby, Hyam, ed. *Judaism on Trial: Jewish-Christian Disputations in the Middle Ages.* Littman Lib. of Jewish Civilization. OUP 1982 $34.00. ISBN 0-838-63053-7. The best account of the medieval "disputations," in which Judaic and Christian theologians would defend their own faith, respectively, and criticize the other.

Pollack, Herman. *Jewish Folkways in Germanic Lands (1648–1806): Studies in Aspects of Daily Life.* MIT Pr. 1971 o.p. An illustrated and well-documented study of everyday life, with chapters on folk medicine, synagogue activity, rites of passage, and dietary habits.

Richardson, Henry G. *The English Jewry under Angevin Kings.* Greenwood 1983 repr. of 1960 ed. $55.00. ISBN 0-313-24247-X. Details state policy toward the Jews and the actual circumstances of Jewish life in England until the expulsion of the Jews in 1290.

Roth, Cecil. *A History of the Jews in England.* OUP 1979 $13.50. ISBN 0-19-822488-5. Continuous story from the earliest Jewish settlement in Roman times through the expulsion in 1290 and down to the readmission of the Jews in 1654 and their life in Britain to recent times.

———. *A History of the Jews in Venice.* Jewish Pubns. 1930 o.p. Classic study of the Jews of Venice, a small population of less than 5,000 that had an important impact on that city for centuries.

———. *A History of the Jews of Italy.* JPS Phila. 1946 o.p. The first history ever written on the Jews in Italy as a whole, covering the period from late antiquity to World War I.

———. *A History of the Marranos.* Modern Jewish Experience. Ayer 1975 repr. of 1932 ed. $35.50. ISBN 0-405-06742-9. The classic scholarly treatment of the "Marranos" (probably derived from the word for "pig"), the Jews forced to hide their identity during the Spanish Inquisition.

———. *The Jews of the Renaissance.* JPS Phila. 1959 o.p. Traces the influence the Jews had on the Italian Renaissance in art, medicine, music, literature, ethics, and biblical studies.

Ruderman, David B. *The World of a Renaissance Jew: The Life and Thought of Abraham ben Mordecai Farissol.* Ktav 1981 $20.00. ISBN 0-878-20405-9. The intellectual biography of a prominent Jewish man who lived in Renaissance Italy from 1452 to 1528.

Schoenfeld, Joachim. *Shtetl Memories: Jewish Life in Galicia under the Austro-Hungarian Empire and in the Reborn Poland, 1898–1938.* Ktav 1985 $17.50. ISBN 0-881-25075-9. Standard collection of first-person accounts.

Trachtenberg, Joshua. *The Devil and the Jews: The Medieval Conception of the Jew and Its Relation to Modern Anti-Semitism.* JPS Phila. 1983 $6.95. ISBN 0-827-60227-8. An important book tracing the development of the mythology of Jews as demons, sorcerers, and heretics, derived in part from a misconception of Jewish mysticism.

Twersky, Isadore, ed. *Studies in Medieval Jewish History and Literature. Judaic Monographs.* Harvard U. Center Jewish 1985 $25.00. ISBN 0-674-85192-7. Technical essays on Jewish religious life and literature.

Weinryb, Bernard. *The Jews of Poland: A Social and Economic History of the Jewish Community in Poland from 1100 to 1800.* JPS Phila. 1973 o.p. Traces the growth of the Polish Jewish population from a few individuals to over a million.

Yerushalmi, Yosef Hayim. *From Spanish Court to Italian Ghetto: Isaac Cardoso: A Study in Seventeenth-Century Marranism and Jewish Apologetics.* U. of Wash. Pr. 1981 repr. of 1971 ed. $12.50. ISBN 0-295-95824-3. In-depth biography of an individual who lived as a nominal Christian in Spain at a time when anti-Judaism forced Jews underground and then moved to Italy in 1648, becoming a prominent member and defender of the Jewish community.

Zborowski, Mark, and Elizabeth Herzog. *Life Is with People: The Culture of the Shtetl.* Schocken 1962 $12.76. ISBN 0-8052-0020-7. Popular and sentimental account of the daily life and spirituality of small-town Jews in eastern Europe, with an introduction by Margaret Mead.

JEWS IN MUSLIM LANDS

The Muslim conquest encompassed large Jewish populations in Babylonia (present-day Iraq), settled there from 586 B.C. The end of Iranian (Zoroastrian) rule was greeted with relief, because its final century had been marked by unstable government. Muslim conquest of Syria, Palestine, and much of Asia Minor drove out the Roman (Christian) government, and, as the Muslim armies swept into Egypt and what is now Libya, Tunisia, Algeria, and Morocco, the old Roman colonies rapidly gave up Christianity and adopted Islam. The Jewish communities remained stable. Islam accorded to Jews the status of *dhimmi*, protected "people of the book"; Jews were tolerated and not required to accept Islam, although they also were treated as subordinate persons. The general policy of toleration occasionally was set aside here and there, but overall, no sustained attacks, expulsions of entire populations, or vigorous persecution of Jews characterized Muslim rule.

Adler, Elkan N., ed. *Jewish Travellers in the Middle Ages: Nineteen Firsthand Accounts.* Dover 1987 repr. of 1930 ed. $8.95. ISBN 0-486-25397-X. A good source of information about the everyday life of Jews throughout the medieval world.

Ashtor, Eliyahu. *The Jews of Moslem Spain.* Trans. by Jenny M. Klein. 2 vols. JPS Phila. 1985 $37.50. ISBN 0-8276-0432-7. In-depth social, political, religious, and cultural history of the prosperous Spanish Jewish community in its "Golden Age," from 711 until the Christian conquest of the Iberian peninsula, making extensive use of Jewish and Muslim sources.

Brinner, William M, and Stephen D. Richs. *Studies in Islamic and Judaic Traditions.* 2 vols. Scholars Pr. GA 1986–1989 $29.95–$53.95. ISBNs 1-555-40048-5, 1-55540-373-5. Conference papers examining the impact of Islam on Judaism and of Judaism on early Muslim scholars.

Cohen, Amnon. *Jewish Life under Islam: Jerusalem in the Sixteenth Century.* HUP 1984 $30.00. ISBN 0-674-47436-8. Well-documented, clearly written study of the Jews in Jerusalem, at the beginning of Ottoman rule, who were tolerated as a "protected people" under Islam.

Cohen, Mark R. *Jewish Self-Government in Medieval Egypt: The Origins of the Office of Head of the Jews. Princeton Studies on the Near East.* Princeton U. Pr. 1981 $41.00. ISBN 0-691-05307-3. A study of the establishment of centralized Jewish communal institutions in Egypt at a time of cultural and economic prosperity, based on the analysis of 200 *geniza* documents.

Goitein, Shlomo Dov. *Jews and Arabs: Their Contacts through the Ages.* Schocken 1974 $2.95. ISBN 0-805-20464-4. Excellent short introduction to the social and intellectual interaction of the two communities from before the advent of Islam through the thirteenth century.

———. *Letters of Medieval Jewish Traders.* Princeton U. Pr. 1974 o.p. Reprints selections from a huge depository of literature (called a *geniza*), which was discovered in a Cairo synagogue in the nineteenth century and included letters from traders that reveal details about the economic activity of Mediterranean Jews during the medieval period.

———. *A Mediterranean Society: The Jewish Communities of the Arab World as Portrayed in the Documents of the Cairo Geniza.* 5 vols. U. CA Pr. 1968–88 $65.00 ea. ISBNs 0-520-00484-1, 0-520-01867-2, 0-520-03265-9, 0-520-04869-5, 0-520-05647-7. Vol. 1, *Economic Foundations*; Vol. 2, *Community*; Vol. 3, *Family*; Vol. 4, *Daily Life*; Vol. 5, *The Individual.* Makes some of the voluminous finds of the Cairo synagogue accessible to those interested in everyday Jewish life during the medieval period.

Mann, Jacob. *The Jews in Egypt and in Palestine under the Fatimid Caliphs, with Preface and Reader's Guide to Shlomo Dov Goitein.* Ktav 1970 o.p. Analyzes the Cairo synagogue *geniza* fragments to paint a picture of Jewish political and communal life in Egypt and Palestine from 969 to 1204.

Nettler, Ron. *Studies in Muslim-Jewish Relations.* Harwood Acad. Pubs. 1992 o.p. Collection of essays on the encounter between Islam and Judaism from the seventh century to the present.

Nini, Yehuda. *The Jews of Yemen, 1800–1914.* Harwood Acad. Pubs. 1991 $48.00. ISBN 3-718-65041-X. A vivid description of a now almost extinct Sephardic community, by one of the top scholars in the field.

Stillman, Norman A. *The Jews of Arab Lands: A History and Source Book.* JPS Phila. 1979 $10.95. ISBN 0-827-60116-6. An extensive collection of Jewish and Muslim documents from the origins of Islam through the nineteenth century, providing a balanced display of the mix of prosperity and persecution Jews faced under Islamic rule.

Jewish Thought

In contrast to the widely diverse Jewish movements and philosophies of ancient and modern times, during the medieval period Judaism remained relatively uniform. Except for the major schism with the Karaites (see under "Religious Movements" later in this chapter), all Jewish movements and thinkers followed the Judaism of the dual Torah established in late antiquity. Judaism, however, did not stand still. Jewish thinkers established new modes of thought—often in dialogue or disputation with their Muslim and Christian counterparts—in legal codification, biblical commentary, philosophy, and mysticism. These categories frequently overlap, but we shall treat them separately for the sake of convenience.

LEGAL CODIFICATION AND COMMENTARY

The compilation of the Babylonian Talmud marked the culmination of the development of the oral Torah. The medieval Jewish authorities who saw themselves as the continuators of this tradition faced the task of adapting and interpreting this body of literature in order to address new circumstances and problems. During the latter part of the first millennium, Jews from throughout the world appealed to the Geonim, legal experts in Babylonia, for advice in applying the laws of the Talmuds to everyday life. This exchange of letters is called the Responsa Literature. The codifications of Jewish law, compiled during the first centuries of the second millennium, represent the other major body of legal literature from the medieval period. These codifications arranged laws according to topics in order to provide a convenient reference manual. The authoritarian code of religious law for Orthodox Jewry was the product of

Joseph Karo (c.1488–1574). Born in the Spanish city of Toledo, Karo moved with his family to Turkey after the 1492 expulsion of Jews from Spain. He eventually settled in Safed, Palestine, where he wrote the Shulhan Arukh, the systematic compilation of Jewish law—from Rabbinic sources and subsequent tradition—that remains centrally important to this day. When published in 1864, Solomon Ganzfried's abridgment of the Shulhan Arukh soon gained widespread acceptance among Orthodox Jews. It remains the only version translated into English that contains all parts of the code.

Abraham, Ibn Daud. *Sefer ha-Qabbalah: The Book of Tradition.* Trans. by Gerson D. Cohen. Jewish Pubns. 1967 o.p. Written in 1161 to disprove the claims of the Karaites, this historical narrative attempts to establish the continuity of the Rabbinic legal tradition from the biblical period until the twelfth century.

Appel, Gersion. *The Concise Code of Jewish Law: Daily Prayers and Religious Observances in the Life-Cycle of the Jew.* Ktav 1977 $14.95. ISBN 0-87068-298-9. An abridgment of the Shulhan Arukh, which collects the legal material relevant to present-day Orthodox practice, on such topics as prayer, dietary laws, and Torah study.

Birnbaum, Philip, trans. *Mishneh Torah: Maimonides' Code of Law and Ethics.* Hebrew Pub. 1974 o.p. A readable translation of Maimonides' important code of Jewish law.

Carmichael, Calum M. *The Origins of Biblical Law: The Decalogues and the Book of the Covenant.* Cornell Univ. Pr. 1992 $28.50. ISBN 0-8014-2712-6. Assumes that the writer of a biblical law may have some contemporary social problem in mind, but nonetheless argues that the form, language, and order of the laws reflects the narratives of the Bible itself.

Elon, Menachem. *Jewish Law: History, Sources, Principles: Ha-Mishpat Ha-Ivri.* 4 vols. JPS Phila. 1993 $300.00. ISBN 0-8276-0389-4

Freehof, Solomon B. *The Responsa Literature and a Treasury of Responsa.* JPS Phila. 1963 o.p. Collection of the legal opinions written by Jewish authorities in response to queries from Jewish communities throughout the medieval and early modern world.

Ganzfried, Solomon. *Code of Jewish Law (Kitzur Shulhan Arukh).* Trans. by Hyam E. Goldin. Hebrew Pub. 1963 $23.50. ISBN 0-88482-779-8. An 1864 abridgment of the Shulhan Arukh that soon gained widespread acceptance among Orthodox Jews and remains the only version translated into English that contains all parts of the code.

Hurwitz, Simon. *The Responsa of Solomon Luria.* Bloch 1969 $10.00. ISBN 0-8197-0096-7. The legal decisions by a sixteenth-century Talmudic authority in Poland, anthologized in plain English but lacking commentary and notation.

Jacob, Walter, and Mosche Zemer, eds. *Rabbinic Lay Confrontations in Jewish Law.* Rodef Shalom Pr. 1993 $9.50. ISBN 0-929699-04-1

Jacobs, Louis. *A Tree of Life: Diversity, Flexibility, and Creativity in Jewish Law.* OUP 1984 $29.95. ISBN 0-197-10039-2. Argues that Jewish law grew organically during the medieval and modern periods in response to changing attitudes and needs.

Kraemer, David. *The Mind of the Talmud: An Intellectual History of the Bavli.* OUP 1990 $35.00. ISBN 0-19-506290-6. Argues that between the time the Mishnah was compiled and the completion of the Babylonian Talmud a fundamental transformation took place in rabbinic thinking.

Lampel, Zvi L., trans. *Maimonides: Introduction to the Talmud.* Judaica Pr. 1975 o.p. Translation of Maimonides' systematic commentary to the Talmud.

Twersky, Isadore. *Introduction to the Code of Maimonides (Mishneh Torah).* Yale U. Pr. 1980 $50.00. ISBN 0-300-02319-7. An impressive work of scholarship considering Maimonides' legal code from a variety of angles, analyzing the content and form of the Mishneh Torah, and placing it in the context of Jewish philosophic and legal history.

_____. *Rabad of Posquieres: A Twelfth-Century Talmudist.* Semitic Ser. HUP 1962 $22.50. ISBN 0-827-60123-9. Intellectual biography that places Abraham ben David (1125–98) in the context of the Jewish religious elite in southern France of the twelfth century.

_____. *Studies in Jewish Law and Philosophy*. Ktav 1982 $39.50. ISBN 0-870-68335-7. A
    collection of essays providing a good introduction to the scholarship of Twersky on
    medieval Jewish law and philosophy; although some articles are quite technical and
    others are in Hebrew, those on the legal codes of Maimonides and Joseph Karo are
    excellent introductions to the topics.
Werblowsky, J. Z. *Joseph Karo: Lawyer and Mystic*. OUP 1962 o.p. Study of Karo's diary,
    Maggid Mesharim, to show that the author of the standard code of Jewish law lived
    an ascetic and mystical life.

BIBLICAL COMMENTARY

After the Rabbinic period, Jewish scholars continued to compile commentaries on the Hebrew Bible. These commentaries often took the form of line-by-
line explanations of verses of Scripture. The medieval commentators, such as
NAHMANIDES and RASHI, frequently borrowed from, and elaborated on, the
interpretations of the Bible found in Rabbinic Midrash.

Casper, Bernard. *Introduction to Jewish Bible Commentary*. Thomas Yoseloff 1960 o.p. An
    adequate introduction.
Jacobs, Louis. *Jewish Biblical Exegesis*. *Chain of Tradition Ser*. Behrman 1975 o.p. A good
    collection of primary sources, with clear explanations.
Saperstein, Marc. *Decoding the Rabbis: A Thirteenth-Century Commentary on the
    Aggadah*. *Judaic Monographs*. HUP 1980 $20.00. ISBN 0-674-19445-4. A readable and
    well-documented study of Isaac ben Yedaiah, a biblical commentator and populariz-
    er of philosophy to those who did not speak Arabic.
Smalley, Beryl. *The Study of the Bible in the Middle Ages*. U. of Notre Dame Pr. 1964
    $9.95. ISBN 0-631-13168-X. The best and most popular introduction to the mode of
    Jewish biblical commentary developed in northern and western Europe through
    1300.

PHILOSOPHY

Medieval Jewish intellectuals learned about classical Greek philosophy,
especially neo-Aristotelianism, from their Muslim counterparts. Jewish philosophers presented rational arguments proving the existence of God and the
reasonableness of Jewish law. The controversies with the Karaites, who did not
accept the authority of the oral Torah, provoked the so-called Rabbanites to
vigorously defend the legitimacy of the Rabbinic tradition. In many ways,
BARUCH SPINOZA's philosophy marks the transition from the medieval to the
modern world. His ideas provoked a strong reaction during his day but have
since become commonplace. He questioned whether Moses actually wrote the
Pentateuch and whether the Genesis story of creation is historically accurate.
He argued that rationally derived natural law should take precedence over the
received Torah.

Abraham Ibn Daud. *The Exalted Faith*. Fairleigh Dickinson 1986 $90.00. ISBN 0-8386-
    3185-1. A twelfth-century work by the first Jewish Aristotelian philosopher, dealing
    with scientific disciplines and pure philosophy.
Abrahams, Israel, ed. *Hebrew Ethical Wills*. *Lib. of Jewish Class*. JPS Phila. 1976 $10.95.
    ISBN 0-827-60082-8. An anthology of Jewish wills, especially from the medieval
    period, which sometimes provided moral guidance to survivors rather than
    bequeathing property. Foreword by Judah Goldin.
Altmann, Alexander, and others, eds. *Three Jewish Philosophers*. JPS Phila. 1960 o.p.
    Introduction and selections of writings from Philo, Saadia Gaon, and Judah HaLevi.
Bakan, David. *Sigmund Freud and the Jewish Mystical Tradition*. Beacon Pr. 1975 o.p.
    Seeks to link Freud's psychological theories to the Jewish mystical tradition,
    showing that Freud got important ideas from that tradition.

Bleich, J. David. *With Perfect Faith: The Foundations of Jewish Belief*. Ktav 1982 $22.95. ISBN 0-685-42233-X. Collection of over 600 pages of writings by medieval Jewish philosophers, arranged according to Maimonides' 13 principles of faith.

Cooperman, Bernard, ed. *Jewish Thought in the Sixteenth Century*. HUP 1983 $30.00. ISBN 0-674-47461-9. Collection of academic essays.

Glatzer, Nahum N., ed. *Faith and Knowledge: The Jew in the Medieval World*. Beacon Pr. 1963 o.p. Collection of sources by medieval religious authorities.

Husik, Isaac. *A History of Mediaeval Jewish Philosophy*. JPS Phila. 1948 o.p. The best introduction to medieval Jewish thought. Gives a synopsis of the thought of each major figure, placed in the context of medieval Arabic and classic Greek philosophy.

Jacobs, Louis. *Jewish Ethics, Philosophy and Mysticism*. Behrman 1969 o.p. Short anthology of medieval Jewish thought, in three parts, according to the title.

_____. *Theology in the Responsa*. B'nai B'rith Bk. 1975 $37.00. ISBN 0-19-710022-8. Analyzes the theological underpinnings of the legal opinions of rabbis from the medieval and modern periods.

Kane, Israel. *In Quest of the Truth: A Survey of Medieval Jewish Thought*. Random 1985 o.p. A brief and uncritical introduction to some of the main thinkers and issues of medieval philosophy.

Lasker, Daniel J. *Jewish Philosophic Polemics against Christianity in the Middle Ages*. Ktav 1977 $29.50. ISBN 0-87068-498-1. Surveys the various modes of argumentation used to criticize Christianity.

Septimus, Bernard. *Hispano-Jewish Culture in Transition: The Career and Controversies of Ramah*. HUP 1982 $20.00. ISBN 0-674-3230-2. Study of the thought of Meir haLevi Abulafia (c.1165–1244), who lived in Toledo during the transition from Arab to Christian rule, placing him in the context of antirationalism and the controversies provoked by Maimonides' philosophy.

Sirat, Colette. *A History of Jewish Philosophy in the Middle Ages*. Cambridge U. Pr. 1985 $59.50. ISBN 0-521-26087-6

Twersky, Isadore, and Bernard Septimus, eds. *Jewish Thought in the Seventeenth Century*. HUP 1987 $25.00. ISBN 0-674-47465-1. Eclectic collection of old academic essays.

MYSTICISM

In addition to the development of legal codification, biblical commentary, and philosophy, the medieval period witnessed new strains of Jewish mysticism. Medieval Hasidism, a popular folk movement, stressed communal charity and personal asceticism. The *Zohar*, or *Book of Splendor*, compiled in the thirteenth century but written in the style of Rabbinic literature, led to the development of an esoteric mystical tradition called the Cabala. New modes of biblical interpretation emerged that found deeper levels of meaning hidden in the sacred text. The Cabalists reflected on God's various attributes and emanations, and saw their spirituality and ethics as bringing unity and redemption to a world marked by disunity and strife.

Abelson, Joshua. *Jewish Mysticism: An Introduction to Kabbalah*. Hermon 1981 $7.95. ISBN 0-87203-096-2. A classic work treating selected topics rather than attempting a comprehensive account of the topic.

Bension, Ariel. *The Zohar in Moslem and Christian Spain*. Hermon repr. 1974 o.p. Gives a synopsis of the *Zohar* and shows its relationship to Christian and Muslim mystics in medieval Spain. Introduction by Denison Ross.

Ben Zion, Raphael. *The Way of the Faithful: An Anthology of Jewish Mysticism*. Judaica Pr. 1981 o.p. Translations claiming to "transmit the spirit of the work, even at the occasional sacrifice of scientific precision."

Blumenthal, D. R. *Understanding Jewish Mysticism: A Source Reader. Lib. of Jewish Learning*. 2 vols. Ktav 1978–82 $20.00 ea. ISBN 0-870-68334-9. Vol. 1, *The Merkabah Tradition and the Zoharic Tradition*; Vol. 2, *The Philosophic Mystical Tradition and Hasidic Tradition*. The best introduction and overview of Jewish mysticism.

Bokser, Ben Zion. *The Jewish Mystical Tradition*. Pilgrim Bks. 1981 o.p. An anthology of mysticism through the ages, with introductions to each major figure and text.

Dan, Joseph, and Ronald C. Kiener, eds. *The Early Kabbalah. Class. of Western Spirituality*. Paulist Pr. 1986 $13.95. ISBN 0-915-93803-0. Readable translations of works by mystics from Safed, with a preface by Moshe Idel.

Dan, Joseph, and Frank Talmage, eds. *Studies in Jewish Mysticism*. Ktav 1982 $25.00. ISBN 0-87068-803-0. Eclectic collection of academic papers, accessible to a lay audience.

Fine, Lawrence, trans. *Safed Spirituality, Rules of Mystical Piety and Elijah de Vidas' Beginning of Wisdom. Class. of Western Spirituality*. Paulist Pr. 1984 $12.95. ISBN 0-809-12612-5. Excellent collection of teachings by six mystics from sixteenth-century Safed.

Green, Arthur. *Jewish Spirituality from the Bible through the Middle Ages*. Paulist Pr. 1985 o.p. Historical account of Jewish mysticism that views mysticism as part of the core of Judaism, not as an appended curiosity.

Hyamson, Moses, trans. *Duties of the Heart by R. Bachya ibn Paquda*. Feldheim 1968 o.p. A mystical instruction manual bearing the influence of medieval Sufi piety, originally published in Arabic in the eleventh century.

Jacobs, Louis, ed. *Jewish Mystical Testimonies*. Schocken 1987 $17.00. ISBN 0-8052-0585-3. Anthology of personal testimonies of mystical experiences from the biblical to the modern period, with an introduction, commentaries, and bibliography.

Kushner, Lawrence. *God Was in This Place & I, I Did Not Know*. Jewish Lights 1993 $16.95. ISBN 1-879045-33-8. A sustained essay on theological themes, taking as its title Genesis 28:16, which reports what Jacob says when he woke up after dreaming of the ladder that joins heaven and earth.

Matt, Daniel Chanah, ed. and trans. *Zohar: The Book of Enlightenment. Class. of Western Spirituality*. Paulist Pr. 1982 $12.95. ISBN 0-809-10320-6. An excellent introduction that places the *Zohar* in the context of prior Jewish mysticism and traces its influence on later Judaism.

Meltzer, David, ed. *The Secret Garden: An Anthology on the Kabbalah*. Seabury 1976 o.p. A source book of Cabalistic texts.

Rosenberg, Roy A. *The Anatomy of God*. Ktav 1973 o.p. Translated selections of the *Zohar* not included in the Soncino Pr. edition translated by Simon and Levertoff.

Safran, Alexandre. *The Kabbala: Law and Mysticism in the Jewish Tradition*. Feldheim 1975 o.p. A theological treatise that attempts to show that Jewish mysticism and legal observance derive from the same principles.

Sharot, Stephen. *Messianism, Mysticism, and Magic: A Sociological Analysis of Jewish Religious Movements. Studies in Religion*. U. of NC Pr. 1987 repr. of 1982 ed. $12.95. ISBN 0-807-81491-1. Analysis of medieval and modern popular charismatic movements and their relationship to political and economic conditions.

Simon, Maurice, and Paul Levertoff, trans. *The Zohar*. 5 vols. Bloch 1934 $90.00. ISBN 0-900689-38-0. A complete translation, except for the section appearing in Rosenberg's translation.

Trachtenberg, Joshua. *Jewish Magic and Superstition*. Macmillan 1970 $14.00. ISBN 0-689-70234-5. An extensively documented, yet readable, study of Jewish folk religion through 1600.

Weiner, Herbert. *Nine and a Half Mystics: The Kabbala Today*. Macmillan 1986 $8.95. ISBN 0-020-68140-2. A popular, personal account of a present-day Jewish mystical movement based on the Kabbala.

Religious Movements

KARAISM

Karaism was a Judaism formed in reaction against the Judaism of the dual Torah, or Rabbinic Judaism. It denied the belief that at Sinai God had revealed the Torah in two media, oral and written. Karaites accepted the revealed status of the written Torah only. They therefore rejected the authority of the rabbis, who taught and applied the law of the Talmud and related writings. Karaite Judaism flourished in the Byzantine Empire, the Middle East, and in southern Russia and the Ukraine, producing its own literature of biblical exegesis and other religious writings. It was regarded as heresy by the proponents of the Judaism of the dual Torah, which predominated.

Ankori, Zvi. *Karaites in Byzantium: The Formative Years, 970–1100. Columbia Univ. Studies in the Social Sciences.* AMS Pr. 1977 repr. of 1959 ed. $28.50. ISBN 0-404-51597-5. A social and religious history of the Karaites that follows the efforts of the group to adjust to the shift from Islamic to Orthodox Christian rule in Asia Minor.

Birnbaum, Philip. *Karaite Studies.* Hermon 1971 o.p. A collection of technical articles, including reproductions from the beginning of the century, that discuss both sides of the Karaite-Rabbinite controversy.

Isaac ben Abraham of Troki. *Faith Strengthened.* Trans. by Moses Mocatta. Hermon 1975 $12.50. ISBN 0-87203-062-8. A polemic against Christianity and an attack on the New Testament by a Lithuanian Karaite who lived from 1533 to 1594.

Mann, Jacob. *Texts and Studies in Jewish History and Literature.* 2 vols. Ktav rev. ed. 1970 $99.50. ISBN 0-870-6085-4. Massive collection (some 1,600 pages) of Karaite literature from the Near East, Asia Minor, and Eastern Europe.

Nemoy, Leon, trans. *Karaite Anthology: Excerpts from the Early Literature. Judaica Ser.* Yale U. Pr. 1952 $45.00. ISBN 0-300-03929-8. This standard reference for Karaism presents translations of Arabic, Hebrew, and Aramaic writings, arranged by author, as well as a collection of Karaite liturgy.

SABBATEANISM

Between 1665 and 1666 a messiah, Sabbatai Zevi, made himself known through his prophet, Nathan of Gaza, and won the recognition of a sizable part of the Jewish world in both Islamic and Christian countries, with supporters from Egypt in the south to Poland in the north, from Turkey in the east to the Netherlands in the west. Sabbatai Zevi preached the doctrine that the Messiah would inaugurate an age in which the laws of the Torah would no longer apply. Therefore, a mark of his messianic status would be the violation of the laws of the Torah. The Judaism of the dual Torah always had maintained that the Messiah would keep and not violate the law, teaching the doctrine of the Messiah as a sage and rabbi. Sabbatai Zevi ultimately converted to Islam, and most of his followers returned to the Jewish community led by the sages of the day.

Scholem, Gershom. *Sabbatai Sevi: The Mystical Messiah.* Trans. by R. Zwi Werblowski *Bollingen Ser.* Princeton U. Pr. 1973 $67.50. ISBN 0-691-09916-2. A massive work gathering and analyzing the primary source material for the first time and explaining the cultural and religious environment in which this messianic movement became popular.

HASIDISM

A movement of intense piety, Hasidism began in the person and teachings of a wonder-worker, BA'AL SHEM TOV, Master of the Good Name, who died in A.D. 1760. Hasidism taught that the Torah called for rejoicing in God and in creation, and furthermore, that the Zaddik, or holy man, was an instrument of God's sanctification and salvation. The deeds and doings of the Zaddik, therefore, served as a medium of revelation, much as the Torah itself had served. Opposed by sages who saw in the dual Torah the media of revelation, Hasidism brought schism to the Jewish communities of Poland, the Ukraine, and White Russia. Three generations beyond the time of the Master of the Good Name, the Hasidim began to write down stories of the great Zaddikim, or holy men, and these stories served to express a yearning for sanctification in the here and now and for salvation in the coming of the Messiah. Hasidic communities continue to thrive in the United States and the State of Israel.

Buber, Martin. *Hasidism and Modern Man.* Ed. and trans. by Maurice Friedman. Humanities 1988 repr. of 1951 ed. $15.00. ISBN 0-391-03550-9. Writings on the contemporary relevance of Hasidism by the man responsible for bringing its message to an audience outside eastern Europe.

————. *The Origin and Meaning of Hasidism.* Trans. by Maurice Friedman. Horizon Pr. AZ 1972 $15.00. ISBN 0-391-03549-5. A more analytic treatment of Hasidism, in which Buber traces the history of the movement and compares it with biblical prophecy, Spinoza, Freud, Shankara, Meister Eckhart, Gnosticism, Christianity, Zionism, and Zen Buddhism.

————. *Tales of the Hasidim.* Pantheon 1991 $20.00. ISBN 0-8052-0995-6. A creative retelling of tales by and about various Hasidic masters.

————. *Ten Rungs: Hasidic Sayings.* Trans. by Olga Marx. Schocken 1962 o.p. Short collection of witty and inspirational sayings related to everyday life.

Dan, Joseph, ed. *The Teachings of Hasidism.* Behrman 1983 $12.95. ISBN 0-87441-346-X. Anthology of writings by the first generation of Hasidic masters (1780–1811), arranged by topic but sometimes seeming disjointed because the editor does not clearly identify the author or the original literary context of each citation.

Dresner, Samuel H. *Zaddik: The Doctrine of the Zaddik According to the Writings of Rabbi Yaakov Yosef of Polnoy.* Schocken 1974 o.p. Discussion of the role of the Zaddik as the charismatic link between God and the community of followers, based on writings of Rabbi Yaakov Joseph of Polnoy. With preface by Abraham J. Heschel.

Foxbrunner, Roman A. *Habad: The Hasidism of R. Shneur Zalman of Lyady. Judaic Studies Series.* U. of Ala. Pr. 1992 $49.95. ISBN 0-817-30558-0. An attempt at a systematic presentation of the thought of the founder of Habad Hasidism, based upon all of his extant teachings.

Green, Arthur, trans. *Upright Practices: The Light of the Eyes. Class. of Western Spirituality.* Paulist Pr. 1982 o.p. Translation of the works of Nahum of Chernobyl on spiritual depth and on the book of Genesis.

Green, Arthur, and Barry Holtz, eds. *Your Word Is Fire: The Hasidic Masters on Contemplative Prayer. Spiritual Masters Ser.* Paulist Pr. 1977 o.p. An anthology of Hasidic prayer intended as "devotional rather than academic."

Harris, Lis. *Holy Days: The World of a Hasidic Family.* Macmillan 1986 $7.95. ISBN 0-671-46296-2. A staff writer from *The New Yorker* magazine explores the Hasidic religious fervor, the role of women, and the history of the Lubavitcher Hasidic movement, through many visits to a Lubavitcher family.

Heinemann, Benno. *The Maggid of Dubno and His Parables.* Feldheim rev. ed. 1978 $14.95. ISBN 0-87306-156-X. Anthology, with a brief biography of a Hasidic master who lived from 1741 to 1804 and was noted for imaginative interpretations of biblical verse in order to answer ethical and religious questions.

Jacobs, Louis. *Hasidic Prayer.* OUP 1972 $17.95. ISBN 0-805-20604-3. Describes the unusual theory of prayer developed by Hasidic masters.

————. *Hasidic Thought.* Behrman 1976 o.p. Collects short pieces of writing from 35 Hasidic masters, providing introductions and thought-provoking commentary.

Langer, Jiri. *Nine Gates to the Chassidic Mysteries.* Ed. by Seymoure Rossel. Trans. by Stephen Jolly. Aronson 1993 $30.00. ISBN 0-87668-249-2. Popular introduction to Hasidic thought.

Mahler, Raphael, trans. *Hasidism and the Jewish Enlightenment: Their Confrontation in Galicia and Poland in the First Half of the Nineteenth Century.* JPS Phila. 1985 $29.95. ISBN 0-827-60233-2. Places Hasidism not only against the background of its more traditional opponents (the Mitnagdim) but also against the background of the secularists (the Maskilim).

Menahem Nahum of Chernobyl. *The Light of the Eyes: Homilies to Genesis.* Trans. by Arthur Green. *Class. of Western Spirituality.* Paulist Pr. 1982 o.p. Collection of homilies on the book of Genesis appearing in English for the first time.

Mintz, Jerome R. *Legends of the Hasidim: An Introduction to Hasidic Culture and Oral Tradition in the New World.* U. Ch. Pr. 1968 $14.95. ISBN 0-226-53103-1. Studies American Hasidism since the arrival of followers in New York during the 1940s and 1950s, collecting almost 400 tales, many of which refer to the early years of Hasidism, and discussing the social function of storytelling in the contemporary Hasidic community.

Netanyahu, B. *Don Isaac Abravanel: Statesman and Philosopher.* JPS Phila. 1972 $7.95. ISBN 0-8276-0213-8. Study of "an encyclopedic scholar, a philosophic thinker, a noted exegete, and a brilliant writer."

Newman, Louis I. *The Hasidic Anthology.* Schocken 1975 o.p. Originally published in 1934, this anthology collects over 500 pages of short sayings on every imaginable topic.

Rabinowitsch, Wolf Zeev. *Lithuanian Hasidism.* Schocken 1971 o.p. Detailed historical study of the early Hasidic movement, tracing the development and demise of family dynasties.

Rotenberg, Mordecai. *Dialogue with Deviance: The Hasidic Ethic and the Theory of Social Contraction.* U. Pr. of Amer. 1993 repr. of 1983 ed. $27.50. ISBN 0-8191-8975-8. Attempts to define the religious ethic of eighteenth-century Hasidism using sociological and psychological categories.

Uffenheimer, Rivka. *Hasidism as Mysticism: Quietistic Elements in Eighteenth-Century Hasidic Thought.* Trans. by Jonathan Chipman. Princeton U. Pr. 1993 $39.50. ISBN 0-691-023223-8. A classic phenomenological study of Hasidism's theoretical texts, translated from the original Hebrew.

Wiesel, Elie. *Four Hasidic Masters and Their Struggle against Melancholy. Ward-Phillips Lectures in Eng. Language and Lit. Ser.* U. of Notre Dame Pr. 1978 $9.95. ISBN 0-268-00944-9. Four moving lectures on four lesser-known Hasidic masters, by the famous novelist and recipient of the Nobel Prize for peace. Foreword by Theodore Hesburgh.

_____. *Somewhere a Master: Further Tales of the Hasidic Masters.* Summit Bks. 1984 $7.95. ISBN 0-671-50823-7. Biographies of nine Hasidic masters.

_____. *Souls on Fire: Portraits and Legends of Hasidic Masters.* Summit Bks. 1982 $17.50. ISBN 0-394-46437-0. A popular introduction to the spirit of early Hasidism, written passionately and poetically.

MODERN JUDAISM

History of the Jews

The Jews' histories naturally followed diverse paths. Modern history began in the West with the secularization of politics in the late eighteenth and nineteenth centuries, moving from the westernmost fringes of the United States, France, Britain, and Holland eastward into Germany, Hungary, and beyond. Through the nineteenth century, Jews acquired rights as citizens, but they also lost the right to govern their own affairs and to live in their own segregated world and by their own law. As Christianity lost its hold on the politics of the West, other political movements succeeded, with nationalism becoming one of the most powerful. Nationalism as a principle of politics brought with it the conception of the nation-state, in which all citizens conformed to a single law, and that made difficult the Jews' explanation of the ways in which they preserved a difference from others.

GENERAL

DeLange, Nicholas. *Atlas of the Jewish World*. Facts on File 1984 $45.00. ISBN 0-87196-043-5. A fact-filled coffee-table book surveying the history and culture of modern Jewry by country.

Eisen, Arnold M. *The Chosen People in America: A Study in Jewish Religious Ideology. Modern Jewish Experience Ser*. Ind. U. Pr. 1983 $25.00. ISBN 0-253-31365-1

Goldscheider, Calvin, and Alan Zuckerman. *The Transformation of the Jews*. U. Ch. Pr. 1986 $25.00. ISBN 0-226-30147-8. A comparative study of processes of modernization in Jewish communities throughout the world, showing that sociological factors, rather than ideology, were the primary motivations for change.

Grayzel, Solomon. *History of the Contemporary Jews from 1900 to the Present*. Atheneum 1969 $4.95. ISBN 0-689-70080-6. A useful survey of the facts of the matter.

Mahler, Raphael. *A History of Modern Jewry*. Schocken 1971 o.p. An argumentative and engaging socialist discussion of class struggle in the modernization of Jewry.

Mendes-Flohr, Paul R., and Jehuda Reinharz. *The Jew in the Modern World: A Documentary History*. OUP 1980 $35.00. ISBN 0-195-02631-4. An anthology of important primary sources about Jews and Judaism written from many angles.

Meyer, Michael A. *The Origins of the Modern Jew: Jewish Identity and European Culture in Germany, 1749–1824*. Wayne St. U. Pr. 1972 repr. of 1967 ed. $7.95. ISBN 0-814-31470-8. An account of the modernization of Jewish thought and culture and the founding of Reform Judaism in Germany.

Morgan, Michael L. *Dilemmas in Modern Jewish Thought: The Dialectics of Revelation and History*. Ind. U. Pr. 1992 $35.00. ISBN 0-253-33878-6. Explores intellectual and religious conflicts of the modern Jew through an in-depth philosophical study of a number of key thinkers.

Raphael, Marc L., ed. *Approaches to Modern Judaism*. Vol. 2 Scholars Pr. GA 1985 $19.95. ISBN 0-89130-793-1

Sachar, Howard M. *The Course of Modern Jewish History*. Random 1990 $21.00. ISBN 0-679-72746-9. Engaging narrative, well written and easy to read, covering all the important topics in a highly competent way.

Sharot, Stephen. *Judaism: A Sociology*. Holmes & Meier 1976 o.p. A comparative study of Judaism and Jewish life, with special attention to how and why Jews did and did not become acculturated in the various environments in which they lived.

Steinberg, Milton. *The Making of the Modern Jew*. U. Pr. of Amer. 1987 $14.50. ISBN 0-819-14492-4. The best analysis of the situation of Jews in modern culture, as penetrating now as when it was written more than 50 years ago.

EUROPE

Although Jews in the West argued that people could be different in religion while sharing the nationalism of the country in which they lived (whether French or German or British or Italian), not everyone agreed. Some viewed Jews as alien, regardless of how long they had lived in their places of birth and residence. Doctrines of Jew hatred, developing from secular sources and reinforced by long centuries in which Jews had been portrayed by Christianity as deicides, yielded a political movement known as anti-Semitism. Political parties took shape around Jew hatred, teaching the doctrine that the solution to social problems lay in the segregation, expulsion, and ultimately the murder of the Jews. The history of the Jews in modern Europe is the story of the ultimate success of those political parties. The largest Jewish population in the world in the nineteenth century existed in the Russian Empire, which had acquired Poland and its ancient Jewish community, as well as Lithuania, White Russia, and the Ukraine. The Austro-Hungarian Empire and the German Empire also ruled over Jewish communities in eastern Europe. The history of the Jews in nineteenth-century Europe is the story of the breakup of that massive population, its movement to great cities in Germany and the West, its processes of industrialization and modernization, and its migration to the far West—the United States and Canada, in particular. The history of those who stayed in Poland and Russia came to an end, along with the histories of the Jews in all other continental European countries, in the murder of nearly 6 million Jews by the German government and its allies from 1933 to 1945. Since the end of World War II, Jewish presence in much of Europe has remained small, and contemporary Jewish history is centered in North America and Israel.

Adler, Hans G. *The Jews in Germany from the Enlightenment to National Socialism.* U. of Notre Dame Pr. 1969 o.p. A history of the Jews in nineteenth- and twentieth-century Germany.

Albert, Phyllis Cohen. *The Modernization of French Jewry: Consistory and Community in the Nineteenth Century.* U. Pr. of New Eng. 1977 $40.00. ISBN 0-874-51139-9. A sociological and demographic account of the institutions of French Jewry from Napoleon to the Dreyfus affair and how they adapted to modernization.

Avni, Haim. *Spain, the Jews and Franco.* Trans. by Emanuel Shimoni. JPS Phila. 1981 $19.95. ISBN 0-827-60188-3. Argues that Franco saved Jews' lives during the Nazi period.

Baron, Salo W. *The Russian Jew under Tsars and Soviets.* Macmillan rev. ed. 1976 o.p. An excellent survey of the history of the Jews in Russia from the end of the eighteenth century to our own time.

Bauer, Yehuda. *The Holocaust in Historical Perspective.* U. of Wash. Pr. 1978 $18.00. ISBN 0-295-95606-2. A set of lectures on the historical lessons of the Holocaust by one of the pioneers in historical research in that subject.

Bermant, Chaim. *Troubled Eden: An Anatomy of British Jewry.* Basic 1970 o.p. A penetrating and acute social commentary on the Jews in Britain in the contemporary period.

Cowen, Anne, and Roger Cowen. *Victorian Jews through British Eyes.* OUP 1987 $45.00. ISBN 0-19-710042-2. Reproductions from Victorian illustrated magazines reflect attitudes toward Jews and Judaism.

Dawidowicz, Lucy S. *The Golden Tradition: Jewish Life and Thought in Eastern Europe.* Schocken 1984 o.p. An anthology of memoirs, letters, and other documents covering the cultural life of eastern European Jews from the nineteenth century; the best treatment of its subject.

———. *The War against the Jews, 1933–1945.* H. Holt & Co. 1975 $15.00. ISBN 0-03-013661-X. One of the best histories of the mass murder of Jews in World War II, arguing for the centrality of anti-Semitism in Hitler's program.

———, ed. *A Holocaust Reader.* Behrman 1975 $9.95. ISBN 0-874-41219-6. An anthology of primary sources on the subject, designed as a companion volume to the author's *The War against the Jews.*

Doblin, Alfred. *Journey to Poland.* Paragon Hse. 1991 repr. of 1968 ed. $21.95. ISBN 1-55778-267-9. An account of Eastern European Jews in Poland in 1924.

Dobroszycki, Lucjan, and Barbara Kirshenblatt-Gimblett. *Image before My Eyes: A Photographic History of Jewish Life in Poland, 1864–1939.* Schocken 1977 $29.95. ISBN 0-805-23607-4. A collection of photographs—street scenes, family portraits, people at work—giving a vivid picture of Jewish life in Poland before it was destroyed by the Holocaust.

The Drama of the European Jews. Judaica Ser. Gordon Pr. 1992 $79.95. ISBN 0-8490-5448-6

Dwork, Deborah. *Children with a Star: Jewish Youth in Nazi Europe.* Yale U. Pr. 1993 repr. of 1991 ed. $16.00. ISBN 0-300-05447-5

Flannery, Edward. *The Anguish of the Jews: Twenty-three Centuries of Antisemitism.* Paulist Pr. 1985 rev. ed. repr. of 1964 ed. $12.95. ISBN 0-809-12702-4. A history and analysis of anti-Semitism, showing the various sources of Jew-hatred over time.

Gay, Peter. *Freud, Jews and Other Germans: Masters and Victims in Modernist Culture.* OUP 1978 $22.50. ISBN 0-19-502258-0. An account of the development of Jewish culture in the context of the modernization of German society.

Gellert, Charles L., comp. *The Holocaust, Israel, and the Jews: Motion Pictures in the National Archives*. Natl. Archives & Records 1989 $17.00. ISBN 0-911-33378-9. A list of motion pictures, primarily newsreels, found in the National Archives concerning the Holocaust and the founding and early settlement of the State of Israel.

Gilbert, Martin. *The Holocaust: A History of the Jews of Europe during the Second World War*. H. Holt & Co. 1987 $24.95. ISBN 0-03-062416-9. A very human account, through the words of victims themselves, of what happened in Europe, combining historical fact with personal reminiscence.

_____. *The Jews of Hope*. Viking Penguin 1985 $6.95. ISBN 0-333-36625-5. Documents the contemporary struggle of many Soviet Jews to maintain their ethnic identity and to emigrate and features illustrations and personal accounts along with a brief history of Jewish life in Russia over the centuries.

Gilboa, Yehoshua. *The Black Years of Soviet Jewry: 1939–1953*. Little 1971 o.p. Examines the devastating effect of Stalin's purges on the Jewish community.

Gilman, Sander L. *Jewish Self-Hatred: Anti-Semitism and the Hidden Language of the Jews*. Johns Hopkins 1986 $28.50. ISBN 0-8018-3276-4. A highly recommended sociological, psychological, and literary study of how a group responds to negative stereotypes through an analysis of the language of Jews from Karl Marx to Anne Frank.

Glatstein, Jacob, and others. *Anthology of Holocaust Literature*. Atheneum 1972 repr. of 1968 ed. $11.95. ISBN 0-689-70343-0. A useful anthology on the stated subject.

Gordon, Sarah. *Hitler, Germans, and the "Jewish Question."* Princeton U. Pr. 1984 $40.00. ISBN 0-691-05412-6. Detailed analysis of Hitler's conception of the Jews.

Greenberg, Louis. *Jews in Russia: The Struggle for Emancipation*. Ed. by Mark Wishnitzer. 2 vols. AMS Pr. 1982 repr. of 1965 ed. $27.50. ISBN 0-805-20525-X. A classic study of the movement for civil rights by Russian Jews in the second half of the nineteenth century. Foreword by Alfred Levin.

Heller, Celia S. *On the Edge of Destruction: Jews of Poland between the Two World Wars*. Col. U. Pr. 1977 $34.00. ISBN 0-231-03819-4. A scholarly account of Jewish history from World War I to the eve of World War II in Poland, now superseded by Ezra Mendelsohn's *The Jews of East Central Europe*.

Hilberg, Raul. *The Destruction of the European Jews*. 3 vols. Holmes & Meier rev. ed. 1985 $100.00. ISBN 0-841-90832-X. A pioneering and candid discussion, and still the single best account, of how Jews occasionally were drawn into cooperating with the Nazis.

Hyman, Paula. *From Dreyfus to Vichy: The Remaking of French Jewry 1906–1939*. Col. U. Pr. 1979 $28.00. ISBN 0-231-04722-3. A successful monograph on the social and religious history of French Jews in the early part of this century.

Kahn, Lothar. *Mirrors of the Jewish Mind: A Gallery of Portraits of European Jewish Writers of Our Time*. Thomas Yoseloff 1968 o.p. Excellent introduction to important European Jewish writers, introducing a variety of central European figures in particular.

Katz, Jacob. *Out of the Ghetto: The Social Background of Jewish Emancipation, 1770–1870*. HUP 1973 $18.50. ISBN 0-674-64775-0. A history of the impact of the social and political changes that overtook the Jews in the nineteenth century as the corporate community gave way to individual citizenship.

Klepfiscz, Heszel. *Culture of Compassion: The Spirit of Polish Jewry from Hasidism to the Holocaust*. Ktav 1983 $25.00. ISBN 0-88125-037-6. A collection of articles originally published in Yiddish that give a sympathetic account of the religious and cultural life of Polish Jewry.

Kobler, Franz. *Napoleon and the Jews*. Schocken 1976 o.p. Readable account of Napoleon's efforts to liberate the Jews from the ghetto and to restore a modern form of ancient Jewish nationalism.

Kochan, Lionel, ed. *The Jews in Soviet Russia since 1917*. OUP 1978 $9.95. ISBN 0-19-21-5173-8. An objective and comprehensive survey, covering events through 1976.

Malino, Francis, and Bernard Wasserstein, eds. *The Jews in Modern France.* U. Pr. of New Eng. 1985 $32.50. ISBN 0-874-51324-3. A history of the Jews of France in the last two centuries.

Marcus, Jacob R. *The Rise and Destiny of the German Jew.* Ktav rev. ed. 1971 o.p. A good history of the Jews in the nineteenth century, surveying their political progress and achievements in the period immediately preceding nazism and the destruction of the Jewish community.

Marrus, Michael R. *The Politics of Assimilation: The French Jewish Community at the Time of the Dreyfus Affair.* OUP 1980 repr. of 1971 ed. $19.95. ISBN 0-19-821482-0. An analysis of the Jewish response to the anti-Semitism generated by the conviction of Dreyfus, a Jewish military officer falsely charged with treason.

Mendelsohn, Ezra. *The Jews of East Central Europe: Between the World Wars.* Ind. U. Pr. 1983 $27.50. ISBN 0-253-33160-9. The definitive treatment of the interbellum European Jewish community.

Parkes, James W. *The Emergence of the Jewish Problem, 1878–1939.* Greenwood 1971 repr. of 1946 ed. o.p. An excellent account of the rise of modern anti-Semitism as a political movement, especially in eastern Europe, and suggested solutions to the so-called Jewish problem, such as the Balfour Declaration.

Poliakov, Leon. *Harvest of Hate: The Nazi Program for the Destruction of the Jews of Europe.* Greenwood 1971 repr. of 1954 ed. $22.50. ISBN 0-8960-4006-2. Links anti-Semitic doctrine and thought to the Holocaust and spells out the story of the destruction of European Jewry. Foreword by R. Niebuhr.

Reinharz, Jehuda. *Fatherland or Promised Land: The Dilemma of the German Jew 1893–1914.* U. of Mich. Pr. 1975 o.p. Analyzes the choices in politics and ideology that confronted German Jewry at the time of political emancipation.

Rozenblit, Marsha L. *The Jews of Vienna, 1867–1914: Assimilation and Identity. Modern Jewish History Ser.* State U. NY Pr. 1984 $44.50. ISBN 0-873-95844-6. Utilizes demographic information to tell the story of the various means of social integration used by the Jews as they moved from small towns to the cosmopolitan world of Vienna at the turn of the century.

Schwarzfuchs, Simon. *Napoleon, the Jews and the Sanhedrin. Littman Lib. of Jewish Civilization.* Fairleigh Dickinson 1979 o.p. The best study of Napoleon's "Sanhedrin," a group of rabbis of whom Napoleon asked whether the Jews were loyal citizens of France or belonged to some other country.

Sebag-Montefiore, Ruth. *A Family Patchwork: Five Generations of an Anglo-Jewish Family.* Weidenfeld & Nicolson 1987 o.p. A history of the well-known Anglo-Jewish merchant family.

Sichronovsky, Peter. *Strangers in Their Own Lands: Young Jews in Germany and Austria Today.* Basic 1986 $14.95. ISBN 0-710-08955-4. Discusses the attitudes and situation of the remnant of the Jewish community left in Germany and Austria after the Holocaust.

Spiegelman, Art. *Maus: A Survivor's Tale.* Pantheon 1986 $12.00. ISBN 0-394-74723-2. The story of one man's experience in the Holocaust as told by his son, skillfully using the medium of the cartoon; the Jews are represented as mice, the Nazis as cats, and the Poles as pigs.

Stenberg, Peter. *Journey to Oblivion: The End of the East European Yiddish and German Worlds.* U. of Toronto Pr. 1991 $35.00. ISBN 0-8020-5861-2. Traces the extinction of Yiddish-speaking and German-speaking communities in eastern Europe in the twentieth century.

Suhl, Yuri, ed. *They Fought Back: The Story of the Jewish Resistance in Nazi Europe.* ADL repr. of 1975 ed. $7.95. ISBN 0-686-95093-3. Tells the story of the Jewish underground during World War II.

Tal, Uriel. *Christians and Jews in Germany: Religion, Politics, and Ideology in the Second Reich, 1870–1914.* Trans. by Noah J. Jacobs. Cornell Univ. Pr. 1975 $35.00. ISBN 0-805-20479-2. Explains how the theological confrontation between Judaism and Christianity spilled over into politics and shows the limits of German liberalism vis-à-vis the Jews.

Tec, Nechama. *When Light Pierced the Darkness: Christian Rescue of Jews in Nazi-Occupied Poland.* OUP 1986 $19.95. ISBN 0-195-03643-3. Analyzes the psychological and ethical motivations of the "righteous gentiles" in Poland who acted to save Jews during the Holocaust.

Wasserstein, Bernard. *Britain and the Jews of Europe 1939–1945.* OUP 1979 $25.00. ISBN 0-198-22600-4. Surveys the efforts of Britain to help save the Jews during the period of the mass murders and shows that the matter was given a very low priority.

Weinberg, David H. *A Community on Trial: The Jews of Paris in the 1930's.* U. Ch. Pr. 1977 o.p. An account of the political pressures of anti-Semitism on Parisian Jews before World War II, helping account for the extensive collaboration of the French in carrying out the mass murder of French Jewry.

Weisbord, Robert G., and Wallace P. Sillanpoa. *The Chief Rabbi, the Pope, and the Holocaust: An Era in Vatican-Jewish Relations.* Transaction Pubs. 1991 $34.95. ISBN 0-887-38416-1. A study of the conduct during World War II of Pope Pius XII and Israele Zolli, the chief rabbi of Rome, who, in 1945, converted to Catholicism.

Wyszkowski, Charles. *A Community in Conflict: American Jewry During the Great European Immigration.* U. Pr. of Amer. 1991 $49.00. ISBN 0-8191-8263-X. Evaluates American Jewish attitudes toward Jewish communal events, issues, and personalities during the late nineteenth and early twentieth centuries.

Zipperstein, Steven J. *The Jews of Odessa: A Cultural History, 1794–1881.* Stanford U. Pr. 1986 $32.50. ISBN 0-804-71251-4. An account of a Jewish community in Russia during its period of modernization.

NORTH AMERICA

Since the middle of the nineteenth century Jews have come to the United States in large numbers. They were part of a large wave of migration from central Europe, particularly Germany, and settled in the opening territories of the South and the Middle West. At the end of the nineteenth century, a still larger wave of Jews migrated from eastern Europe, particularly White Russia, the Ukraine, Poland, Rumania, Hungary, and Lithuania. Numbering in the millions, those Jews settled in the cities in which their labor was needed, creating vast communities in the large metropolitan areas of the Northeast and Midwest. From the early twentieth century, the children of immigrant Jews entered politics, professions, business, and various cultural ventures and came to form an important component of American life. Their presence in contemporary American society can be felt in all areas of endeavor.

Altshuler, David, ed. *The Jews of Washington.* Rossel Bks. 1986 $17.95. ISBN 0-940646-23-4. An illustrated anthology on the Jewish community in the nation's capital.

Belth, Nathan C. *A Promise to Keep: The American Encounter with Anti-Semitism.* NY Times Bks. 1979 $7.95. ISBN 0-812-90814-7. Tells the history of anti-Semitism as a political and cultural force in America and the effort to combat it by the Anti-Defamation League of B'nai B'rith.

Cohen, Naomi W. *Encounter with Emancipation: The German Jews in the United States, 1830–1914.* JPS Phila. 1984 $25.95. ISBN 0-827-60236-7. A very readable social history describing the struggle of German-Jewish immigrants to make a life for themselves in the United States.

———. *Not Free to Desist: The American Jewish Committee 1906–1966.* JPS Phila. 1972 o.p. History of an important American Jewish political organization.

Cohen, Steven M. *American Assimilation or Jewish Revival?* Ind. U. Pr. 1988 $29.95. ISBN 0-253-3068-6. A fine overview of the interplay between assimilation and the maintenance of a Judaic ethos.

———. *American Modernity and Jewish Identity.* Methuen 1983 $24.00. ISBN 0-422-77740-4. An analysis of the cultural history of American Jews in the recent past and the formation of their identity.

Dalin, David G. *American Jews and the Separationist Faith*. Ethics & Public Policy 1992 $19.95. ISBN 0-89633-176-8. Challenging and stimulating examination of the practical consequences of seemingly abstract constitutional conflicts between the pejorative majority and minority groups of all creeds.

Ehrman, Eliezer L., ed. *Readings in Modern Jewish History: From the American Revolution to the Present*. Ktav 1977 o.p. Anthology on American Jewish history.

Elazar, Daniel J. *Community and Polity: The Organizational Dynamics of American Jewry*. JPS Phila. 1976 $9.95. ISBN 0-827-60068-2. Analyzes the organizational and institutional structure of American Jewry.

Feingold, Henry L. *Zion in America*. Amer. Immigrant Ser. Hippocrene Bks. rev. ed. 1981 $10.95. ISBN 0-882-54307-5. Solid narrative history of U.S. Jews.

Forster, Arnold, and Benjamin Epstein. *The New Anti-Semitism*. McGraw 1974 o.p. Defines new forms of intellectual anti-Semitism in the United States.

Gerber, David A., ed. *Anti-Semitism in American History*. U. of Ill. Pr. 1987 $13.95. ISBN 0-252-01477-4. Some of the finest scholarship in the field. Superb 50-page introductory essay by Gerber.

Glazer, Nathan. *American Judaism*. U. Ch. Pr. ref. ed. 1972 $12.50. ISBN 0-226-29839-6. A classic history of Judaism in America, with particular attention given to the social foundations of Judaic religious life and expression.

Goldscheider, Calvin. *Jewish Continuity and Change: Emerging Patterns in America*. Jewish Political and Social Studies. Ind. U. Pr. 1986 $24.95. ISBN 0-253-33157-9. Brilliant analysis of the principles of communal coherence and the strength of the ethnic ties within Jewry; interprets change and shows continuity.

Goldstein, Sidney, and Calvin Goldscheider. *Jewish Americans: Three Generations in a Jewish Community*. U. Pr. of Amer. 1985 repr. of 1968 ed. o.p. Model demographic study of Jews' social, economic, and religious life.

Handlin, Oscar. *Adventure in Freedom: Three Hundred Years of Jewish Life in America*. McGraw 1954 o.p. Interpretation of the history of the Jews in America within the setting of American life.

Herberg, Will. *Protestant, Catholic, Jew: An Essay in American Religious Sociology*. U. Ch. Pr. 1983 repr. of 1955 ed. $11.95. ISBN 0-226-32734-5. Argues that there is a civil religion or religious style affecting all religions in America and shows how the three religions of democracy grow more and more like one another.

Hertzberg, Arthur. *Being Jewish in America: The Modern Experience*. Schocken 1980 $7.95. ISBN 0-805-23692-9. A set of episodic essays and reflections by a controversial rabbi.

Higham, John. *Send These to Me: Jews and Other Immigrants in Urban America*. Johns Hopkins 1984 $22.50. ISBN 0-689-10617-3. An account of the experience of the Jews and other groups in American cities; among the best histories of the immigrant generations.

Himmelfarb, Milton. *The Jews of Modernity*. Basic 1973 o.p. A set of random thoughts by an acute observer.

Howe, Irving, and others. *Bridges and Boundaries: African American and American Jews*. Braziller 1992 $45.00. ISBN 0-8076-1279-0. Collaborative effort between the NAACP and New York's Jewish Museum. Fifteen essays by noted political and religious leaders, historians, and scholars. Over 100 historically significant visual images.

_____. *World of Our Fathers: The Journey of the East European Jews to America and the Life They Found and Made*. S & S Trade 1983 $12.95. ISBN 0-151-46353-0. A much acclaimed, illustrated account of the cultural life of the immigrant generations.

Janowsky, Oscar I., ed. *American Jew*. Essay Index Repr. Ser. Ayer 1977 repr. of 1942 ed. $18.00. ISBN 0-8369-2166-6. Essays on the state and condition of American Jews.

Joselit, Jenna W. *Our Gang: Jewish Crime and the New York Jewish Community, 1900–1940*. Ind. U. Pr. 1983 $19.95. ISBN 0-253-15845-1. A well-documented study of crime as a means of upward mobility for Jewish immigrants in New York.

Karp, Abraham J. *Haven and Home: A History of the Jews in America*. Schocken 1985 $24.95. ISBN 0-805-23920-0. An optimistic portrayal of American Jewish history from 1654 to the present, emphasizing the diversity of Jewish communities and experiences.

_____, ed. *The Jewish Experience in America: Selected Studies from the Publications of the American Jewish Historical Society*. 5 vols. Ktav 1969 o.p. Anthology of American Jewish history.

Kessner, Thomas. *The Golden Door: Italian and Jewish Immigrant Mobility in New York City, 1880–1915*. OUP 1977 $22.50. ISBN 0-19-502116-9. Readable demographic study of the impoverished Jewish and Italian immigrants in New York.

Klayman, Richard. *The First Jew: Prejudice and Politics in an American Community, 1900–1932*. Old Suffolk 1985 $29.95. ISBN 0-932247-00-8. Briefly depicts the demographic structure of the Malden, Massachusetts, Jewish community and of the Irish community, contrasting their socioeconomic standing and political behavior.

Kohn, Gary J. *The Jewish Experience: A Guide to Manuscript Sources in the Library of Congress*. Ktav 1986 $29.50. ISBN 0-87820-014-2. Offers a concise and easy-to-use means for locating manuscript sources at the Library of Congress.

Learsi, Rufus. *The Jew in America: A History*. Ktav rev. ed. 1972 o.p. One of the earliest histories of American Jews; still readable.

Libo, Kenneth, and Irving Howe. *We Lived There Too: A Documentary History of Pioneer Jews and the Westward Movement of America, 1630–1930*. St. Martin 1984 $24.95. ISBN 0-312-85866-3. A documentary history of the role of Jews in the western expansion of the British colonies and the United States, with many interesting illustrations and stories about little-known people.

Liebman, Charles. *The Ambivalent American Jew*. JPS Phila. 1973 o.p. Penetrating sociological analysis of the attitudes of American Jews.

Marcus, Jacob R. *Early American Jewry*. 2 vols. Ktav 1953 o.p. Anthology of materials on the Jews in colonial times by the leading historian of the period.

_____, ed. *Memoirs of American Jews: 1775–1865*. Ktav 1955 o.p. Anthology of memoirs; quite readable.

Moore, Deborah D. *At Home in America: Second Generation New York Jews*. Col. U. Pr. 1981 $26.50. ISBN 0-231-05062-3. Major study of the children of the immigrants as they made their way in New York City.

Morse, Arthur D. *While Six Million Died: A Chronicle of American Apathy*. Overlook Pr. 1983 repr. of 1966 ed. o.p. Describes the indifference of the Roosevelt administration to the murder of European Jews while the Holocaust was taking place.

Neusner, Jacob. *Israel in America: A Too-Comfortable Exile?* Beacon Pr. 1985 $14.95. ISBN 0-807-03602-1. Relates the history of Judaism in America to the social experience of American Jews.

_____, ed. *Judaism in Cold War America: 1945–1990*. 10 vols. Garland 1993 Vol. 1 *The Challenge of America: Can Judaism Survive in Freedom?* $53.00. ISBN 0-8153-0074-3. Vol. 2 *In the Aftermath of the Holocaust*. $44.00. ISBN 0-8153-0079-4. Vol. 3 *Israel and Zion in American Judaism: The Zionist Fulfillment*. $40.00. ISBN 0-8153-0073-5. Vol. 4 *Judaism and Christianity: The New Relationship*. $38.00. ISBN 0-8153-0075-1. Vol. 5 *The Religious Renewal of Jewry*. $56.00. ISBN 0-8153-0080-8. Vol. 6 *The Reformation of Reform Judaism*. $47.00. ISBN 0-815-30076-X. Vol. 7 *Conserving Conservative Judaism*. $59.00. ISBN 0-8153-0078-6. Vol. 8 *The Alteration of Orthodoxy*. $46.00. ISBN 0-8153-0077-8. Vol. 9 *The Academy and Traditions of Jewish Learning*. $56.00. ISBN 0-8153-0081-6. Vol. 10 *The Rabbinate in America: Reshaping an Ancient Calling*. $42.00. ISBN 0-8153-0082-4. Reprinted scholarly essays with introductions.

Oren, Dan A. *Joining the Club: A History of Jews and Yale*. Yale U. Pr. 1986 $29.95. ISBN 0-300-03330-3. Documents the long history of anti-Semitism at Yale University.

Perlmutter, Nathan, and Ruth Ann Perlmutter. *The Real Anti-Semitism in America*. Arbor Hse. 1982 o.p. A past national director of the Anti-Defamation League and his wife express less concern for the Ku Klux Klan and the neo-Nazis than for the anti-Semitism and anti-Zionism of intellectuals, diplomats, and other people in powerful positions.

Raphael, Marc Lee. *Abba Hillel Silver: A Profile in American Judaism.* Holmes & Meier 1989 $49.50. ISBN 0-841-91059-6. An authoritative biography of one of the last American rabbinic giants, Abba Hillel Silver (1893–1963). Introduction by Alexander M. Schindler.

Rieder, Jonathan. *Canarsie: The Jews and Italians of Brooklyn against Liberalism.* HUP 1985 $22.50. ISBN 0-674-09360-7. Analyzes the recent trend toward political conservatism among lower-middle-class Jews and Italians in Brooklyn.

Rischin, Moses. *The Promised City: New York's Jews. 1870–1914.* HUP 1962 $25.50. ISBN 0-674-71502-0. Best history of the Jews in New York City ever written.

Rochlin, Harriett. *Pioneer Jews: A New Life in the Far West.* HM 1984 $17.95. ISBN 0-395-31832-7. Large-format book with photos on every page and narrative on Jewish participation in the development of the American frontier through 1912.

Rosenberg, Stuart E. *The Search for Jewish Identity in America.* Doubleday 1965 o.p. Classic essays by a leading rabbi on the formation of Jewish identity.

Rothchild, Sylvia. *A Special Legacy: An Oral History of Soviet Jewish Emigres in the United States.* S & S Trade 1985 $17.95. ISBN 0-671-47325-5. Recent interviews with refugees from the Soviet Union who have come to America.

Schoem, David. *Ethnic Survival in America: An Ethnography of a Jewish Afternoon School.* Scholars Pr. GA 1989 $44.95. ISBN 1-555-40265-8. Sociological study identifies a loss of substance and authenticity in American Jewish life.

Schoener, Allon. *The American Jewish Album: 1654 to the Present.* Rizzoli Intl. 1985 $45.00. ISBN 0-847-80500-X. Beautiful coffee-table book with an interesting collection of photographs, essays, and first-person accounts.

Sidorsky, David, ed. *The Future of the Jewish Community in America.* Jewish Pubns. 1973 o.p. A collection of solid essays on the culture and society of U.S. Jewry.

Silberman, Charles E. *A Certain People: American Jews and Their Lives Today.* Summit Bks. 1985 $19.95. ISBN 0-671-44761-0. Argues that Jews have found general acceptance and no longer are oppressed by anti-Semitism in America.

Sklare, Marshall. *America's Jews.* Random 1971 o.p. A systematic account of American Jewry.

———. *The Sociology of the American Jew.* 2 vols. Behrman 1976 o.p. An anthology of valuable essays.

———. *Understanding American Jewry.* Transaction Pubs. 1982 $21.95. ISBN 0-878-55454-8. The great sociologist introduces the sociology of U.S. Jewry.

———, ed. *The Jews: Social Patterns of an American Group.* Greenwood 1977 repr. of 1955 ed. o.p. Classic essays on various aspects of the sociology of American Jewry.

Sklare, Marshall, and Joseph Greenblum. *Jewish Identity on the Suburban Frontier: A Study of Group Survival in the Open Society.* U. Ch. Pr. 2nd ed. 1979 $27.50. ISBN 0-226-76175-4. Studies the attitudes of Jews in suburbs, particularly the children and grandchildren of immigrants.

Sleeper, James A., and Alan L. Mintz, eds. *The New Jews.* Random 1971 o.p. An account of the nascent fourth generation of American Jews and their trend toward the political left in the 1960s.

Waxman, Chaim I. *American Jews in Transition.* Temple U. Pr. 1983 $24.95. ISBN 0-877-22321-1. Scholarly study of American Jewish sociology.

Woocher, Jonathan S. *Sacred Survival: The Civil Religion of American Jews. Jewish Political and Social Studies.* Ind. U. Pr. 1986 $25.00. ISBN 0-253-35041-7. Argues that the most influential ideology of American Jews is the commitment to common social institutions—federations, volunteerism, fundraising, and education.

Wyman, David S. *The Abandonment of the Jews.* Pantheon 1986 $8.95. ISBN 0-394-42813-7. Documents the failure of the American Jewish community and the American government to come to the aid of Jews under Nazi control.

STATE OF ISRAEL

The history of Jews in what was then Palestine became joined to the Zionist movement at the end of the nineteenth century. In 1897 the Zionist Organization was established in Basel, and European and American Jews began to work for the creation of a Jewish state in Palestine. In 1917 the British assumed the government of Palestine and issued the Balfour Declaration. This statement supported the establishment of a Jewish "homeland" in Palestine and respected the rights of the present inhabitants. Between 1917 and 1947, hundreds of thousands of Jews settled in Palestine. But from 1933 to 1945, the Jews in Europe, although facing the threat of murder by the German government under the Nazi party, were officially prohibited from entering the country in sizable numbers. In the aftermath of World War II, many of the Jews who had survived wanted to go to Palestine, and in 1947 the United Nations voted to create a Jewish and an Arab state in Palestine. In 1948 the Jewish state declared independence. Since that time, the state of Israel has survived several wars with its Arab neighbors. Today over 3½ million Jews reside in the State of Israel, along with almost 900,000 Arabs. Conflicts still remain between Israel and its Arab neighbors, particularly in regard to the Palestinians and Palestinian autonomy in the West Bank and Gaza Strip. Israeli and Arab leaders are attempting to resolve these differences and bring peace to the region.

Begin, Menachem. *The Revolt*. Nash repr. 1977 $12.95. ISBN 0-840-21370-0. A memoir by the leader of a Jewish underground in the years leading up to Israel's independence, describing his violent and courageous struggle against the British military and the mainstream Jewish organizations.

Black, Edwin. *The Transfer Agreement: The Untold Story of the Secret Pact between the Third Reich and Jewish Palestine*. Macmillan 1984 $19.95. ISBN 0-02-511130-2. A well-documented account of the secret deal in 1933 between the World Zionist Organization and Nazi Germany to allow 60,000 Jews to emigrate to Palestine in return for a complicated reimbursement scheme.

Collins, Larry, and Dominique Lapierre. *O Jerusalem!* S & S Trade 1988 $14.00. ISBN 0-671-66241-4. The story of Israel's War of Independence is captured in this popular work of historical fiction.

Elon, Amos. *The Israelis: Founders and Sons*. Viking Penguin 1983 $7.95. ISBN 0-140-22476-9. A great writer recaptures the history of the State of Israel from its founding until the present, through the biographies of major figures.

Fein, Leonard J. *Israel: Politics and People*. Beacon Pr. 1967 o.p. A political scientist describes the politics of the new state.

Hazan, Haim. *Managing Change in Old Age: The Control of Meaning in an Institutional Setting*. State U. NY Pr. 1992 $44.50. ISBN 0-7914-1063-3. Illuminates aspects of the existential experience of elderly retirees, through an ethnographic study of an old-age home.

Heilman, Samuel. *The Gate Behind the Wall: A Pilgrimage to Jerusalem*. Viking Penguin 1986 $5.95. ISBN 0-14-008467-3. Vignettes of religious life in contemporary Jerusalem, by an Orthodox Jewish sociologist.

Kellerman, Aharon. *Society and Settlement: Jewish Land of Israel in the Twentieth Century*. State U. NY Pr. 1993 $59.50. ISBN 0-7914-1295-4. Scrutinizes the interrelationships between Jewish spatial organization and social structure and change in Palestine/Israel.

Lehman-Wilzig, Sam. *Wildfire: Grassroots Revolts in Israel in the Post-Socialist Era*. State U. NY Pr. 1992 $44.50. ISBN 0-7914-0871-X. Describes Israeli grassroots extraparliamentarianism and analyzes the impact of the most important alternative systems—illegal settlement activity, a huge underground economy; pirate cable TV stations, "gray" education, Black medicine, anti-religious as well as anti-secular activity, and a growing demand for electoral reform and constitutionalization of the Israeli polity.

Liebman, Charles S., and Eliezer Don Yehiya. *Religion and Politics in Israel. Jewish Political and Social Studies*. Ind. U. Pr. 1984 $17.50. ISBN 0-253-34497-2. The first systematic work on the relationship between state-supported Orthodox Judaism and the politics of the Jewish state.

Naamani, Israel T., David Rudavsky, and Abraham I. Katsch. *Israel: Its Politics and Philosophy*. Behrman 1977 o.p. A standard account of the Zionist ideology and political reality in the State of Israel.

Nisan, Mordechai. *Towards a New Israel: The Jewish State and the Arab Question*. AMS Pr. 1992 $42.50. ISBN 0-404-61631-3. A religious/political manifesto for Israel in the guise of scholarly discourse.

Oz, Amos. *In the Land of Israel*. Trans. by Maurice Bartura Goldberg. HarBraceJ 1983 $12.95. ISBN 0-701-13923-4. A great novelist interviews Arabs and Jews in Israel and clearly records the diversity and increasing divergence of opinion.

Sachar, Abram. *The Redemption of the Unwanted: From the Liberation of the Death Camps to the Founding of Israel*. St. Martin 1983 $19.95. ISBN 0-312-66729-9. The story of the survivors of the concentration camps and how they were brought to what was then Palestine and given new lives.

Sachar, Howard M. *A History of Israel: From the Rise of Zionism to Our Time*. Knopf 1979 $12.95. ISBN 0-394-48564-5. A great historian tells the story of Zionism and the State of Israel in a vivid and compelling narrative.

Said, Edward W. *The Question of Palestine*. Random 1992 $11.00. ISBN 0-679-73988-2. An articulate analysis of the history and politics of the Arab-Israeli conflict from a Palestinian Arab point of view.

Sanders, Ronald. *The High Walls of Jerusalem: A History of the Balfour Declaration and the Birth of the British Mandate for Palestine*. H. Holt & Co. 1983 $24.95. ISBN 0-03-053971-4. The best and most recent book on the Balfour Declaration.

Schenker, Hillel, ed. *After Lebanon: The Israeli-Palestinian Connection*. Pilgrim Bks. 1983 o.p. During and after the Israeli invasion of Lebanon in 1982, Israeli Jews and Arabs, in the middle and left of the political spectrum, discuss the consequences of the war and the future prospects for peace.

Silberstein, Laurence J., ed. *New Perspectives on Israeli History: The Early Years of the State*. NYU Pr. 1991 $45.00. ISBN 0-8147-7929-8. Draws upon recent Israeli and North American historiography to shed light on fundamental social, political, and cultural issues surrounding the emergence of the state of Israel.

Sobel, Zvi, and Benjamin Beit-Hallahmi, eds. *Tradition, Innovation, Conflict: Jewishness and Judaism in Contemporary Israel*. State U. NY Pr. 1991 $64.50. ISBN 0-7914-0554-0. Essays on the centrality of religion in Israeli society, focusing on what Israelis believe and how they behave in religious contexts.

Spiro, Melford E. *Kibbutz: Venture in Utopia*. HUP 1975 $12.00. ISBN 0-674-50331-7. Popular account of the collective communities and how they experimented in new forms of social life.

Sykes, Christopher. *Crossroads to Israel 1917–1948*. Ind. U. Pr. 1973 repr. of 1965 ed. $8.95. ISBN 0-253-20165-9. Excellent book on the period of the British Mandate.

Vital, David. *Zionism: The Formative Years*. OUP 1982 $34.50. ISBN 0-198-27443-2. The best detailed history of the beginnings of Zionism, both as ideology and as organization.

Weiner, Eugene, and Anita Weiner. *Israel—A Precarious Sanctuary: War, Death and the Jewish People*. U. Pr. of Amer. 1989 $34.25. ISBN 0-819-17441-6. A philosophical and deeply moving examination of the precariousness of life in modern Israel and evaluation of options for living with war and death.

Weiner, Herbert. *The Wild Goats of Ein Gedi*. Atheneum 1970 o.p. The story of the mystical side of Judaism in general, with much attention to mystical Judaism in the State of Israel today.

OTHER COUNTRIES

Histories of Jews in other countries tend to conform to a fairly simple pattern. As the vast Jewish settlement in eastern Europe began to send forth emigrants from the mid-nineteenth century onward, small streams found their way to those parts of the world in which European settlement was getting under way. Communities took shape in Australia, South Africa, Canada, and Argentina.

Secondary settlements of Jews from Muslim countries also took root in a few places, particularly Brazil. From 1933 to 1945, small numbers of Jews were admitted to other Latin American countries as well. In the years since World War II, Jewish settlements throughout much of the world have continued to grow and prosper. With the breakup of the Soviet Union, in particular, many Jews from Russia and Eastern Europe have emigrated to other nations.

Arndt, Judy, and Joseph Aron. *A History of Melbourne's Hebrew Congregation.* Intl. Spec. Bk. 1992 $49.95. ISBN 0-522-84479-0

Arni, Haim. *Argentina and the Jews: A History of Jewish Immigration.* U. of Ala. Pr. 1991 $32.95. ISBN 0-8173-0554-8. Extends from the beginning of Argentine independence in 1810 through the establishment and consolidation of the state of Israel in 1950. Translated from the Hebrew.

De Felice, Renzo. *Jews in an Arab Land: Libya, 1835–1970.* Trans. by Judith Roumani. U. of Tex. Pr. 1985 $27.50. ISBN 0-292-74016-6. The ups and downs of a Jewish community in North Africa.

Deshen, Shlomo, and Walter P. Zenner. *Jewish Societies in the Middle East: Community, Culture, and Authority.* U. Pr. of Amer. 1982 $30.50. ISBN 0-819-12578-4. Sociological and anthropological studies of Middle Eastern Jewish communities by various authors.

Diaz-Mas, Paloma. *Sephardim: The Jews from Spain.* U. Ch. Pr. 1992 $27.50. ISBN 0-226-14483-6. A comprehensive history for the general reader.

Elazar, Daniel J. *Jewish Communities in Frontier Societies: Argentina, Australia, and South Africa.* Holmes & Meier 1983 $44.50. ISBN 0-841-90449-9. Social studies of Jewish communities in former European colonies by a well-known political scientist.

Elkin, Judith. *Jews of Latin American Republics.* U. of NC Pr. 1980 o.p. Account of the Jews in the Spanish- and Portuguese-speaking countries of the Western Hemisphere.

Haddad, Heskel M. *The Jews of Arab and Islamic Countries: History, Problems, and Solutions.* Shengold 1984 16.95. ISBN 0-88400-100-8. A good brief historical, sociological, and demographic survey of Sephardic Jews from the medieval period to the present, featuring a study of the relations between Ashkenazi and Sephardic Jews in Israel today.

Kessler, David. *The Falashas: The Forgotten Jews of Ethiopia.* Schocken 1985 o.p. The story of the Jews of Ethiopia, descendants of Israelites who settled in pre-Christian times, who preserved their traditions for thousands of years and only recently returned to the Land of Israel.

Landau, Jacob M. *Jews in Nineteenth-Century Egypt. Studies in Near Eastern Civilization.* NYU Pr. 1969 o.p. A scholarly account of the inner life of the Jewish community in Egypt in the imperial period, with a large collection of documents.

Langlais, Jacques, and David Rone. *Jews and French Quehecers: Two Hundred Years of Shared History.* Humanities 1991 $29.95. ISBN 0-88920-998-7. Confronts honestly the roots of antisemitism in Francophone insecurities, challenging and engaging the readers in issues that transcend the limits of Canadian, Jewish, or Quebec history.

Leslau, Wolf, trans. *Falasha Anthology. Judaica Ser.* Yale U. Pr. 1951 $26.00. ISBN 0-300-03927-1. Collects the ancient writings of the Falashas, some as old as the ninth century, and also contains a 40-page introduction on Falasha history, literature, and religion.

Ozeri, Zion M. *Yemenite Jews: A Photographic Essay.* Schocken 1985 $19.95. ISBN 0-805-23980-4. Pictures of a colorful Jewish community, now settled in the State of Israel.

Pollak, Michael. *Mandarins, Jews and Missionaries: The Jewish Experience in the Chinese Empire.* JPS Phila. 1983 $12.95. ISBN 0-8276-0229-40. Portrays the experience of Jews in a non-Christian and non-Islamic environment, through an examination of the ancient Jewish community of China, which maintained a separate identity through the nineteenth century.

Rejwan, Nissim. *The Jews of Iraq: 3000 Years of History and Culture.* Westview 1985 $16.95. ISBN 0-297-78713-6. Descended from the Jews who settled in Babylonia in

586 B.C., Jews in Iraq went through a turbulent history, until they collectively fled to the State of Israel in the 1950s.

Ross, Dan. *Acts of Faith: A Journey to the Fringes of Jewish Identity*. St. Martin 1982 $15.95. ISBN 0-312-00400-1. Describes various groups on the boundary of the Jewish people—either geographically or theologically—including the Falashas of Ethiopia, the Chuetas of Majorca, the Bene Israel of India, the Samaritans, and the Karaites and explores the perennial question of who is and is not a Jew. Foreword by Raphael Patai.

Sachar, Howard M. *Diaspora: An Inquiry into the Contemporary Jewish World*. HarpC 1985 $27.00. ISBN 0-060-15403-9. Comprehensive treatment of the Jewish communities outside North America and the State of Israel since 1945.

Saron, Gustav, and Louis Hotz, eds. *The Jews in South Africa: A History*. OUP 1955 o.p. A reliable history of the sizable Jewish community that settled in South America in the nineteenth century.

Serels, M. Mitchell. *A History of the Jews of Tangier in the Nineteenth and Twentieth Centuries*. Hermon 1991 $35.00. ISBN 0-87203-136-5. Traces the evolution of this group of less than 800 Jews at the start of the nineteenth century, to its peak of some 15,000 in 1952, to its present status of some 400 largely elderly persons.

Stillman, Norman A. *Jews of Arab Lands in Modern Times*. JPS Phila. 1991 $39.95. ISBN 0-8276-0370-3. Chronicles the demise of Jewish communities of the Arab world. From the time of Muhammad when relative peace and tolerance was enjoyed, to the present day conflict between Arab nationalism and Zionism.

Strizower, Schifra. *The Bene Israel of Bombay: A Study of a Jewish Community*. *Pavilion Social Anthropology Ser*. Schocken 1971 o.p. A social anthropological study of the small Jewish community in India.

Weisbrot, Robert. *The Jews of Argentina. From the Inquisition to Peron*. JPS Phila. 1979 $12.50. ISBN 0-827-60114-X. The history of the large Jewish community in Buenos Aires and smaller communities in the pampas in Argentina, which contains the world's fifth largest Jewish population.

Wiznitzer, Arnold. *Jews in Colonial Brazil*. Col. U. Pr. 1960 o.p. An account of the earliest Jewish settlements in the Western Hemisphere.

Jewish Thought

The intellectual side to the life of Judaism covers both religious and secular matters. Religious issues are addressed in "theology of Judaism," a systematic effort at thinking rigorously and rationally about the truths revealed in the Torah and an effort to mediate between eternal truth and the acutely contemporary issues of the hour. "Philosophy of Judaism" is a term that covers systematic thought about Judaic religious issues that is not grounded in the revealed Torah of Sinai; it forms an arena for explanation and apologetics on the frontier between the religious and the secular worlds, often with a strong tendency to appeal to secular Jews to adopt a religious viewpoint. These religious modes of thought are joined by thinking about secular topics, generally called "Jewish thought." Secular "Jewish thought" covers a variety of subjects. Some attends to political issues, inquiring what sort of social entity the Jews are. Other thought treats what it means to be a believing Jew under the conditions of contemporary culture and society. Still other thought covers the histories of Jews, treating those histories as a single unitary and harmonious history and proposing to specify the "lessons" taught by that history. In these and other ways, Jewish thought forms the intellectual component of the existence of the Jewish people. Nearly all Jewish thought before World War II took place in European settings; there is no important literature of thought deriving from Jews in the Muslim world before 1948. Much of the Jewish thought in Muslim countries was carried on in French—and in France, after the massive migration of those Jews from North Africa to France in the late 1950s. Since the end of the war, the center of Jewish thought has shifted to both the United States and Israel. Israeli contributions to "Jewish thought" cover issues of Zionist ideology and arguments about why the Diaspora is dying and only the State of Israel is thriving. American contributions include consideration of Judaism and the modern world and the role of women in Judaism.

GENERAL

Bergmen, Samuel Hugo. *Faith and Reason: An Introduction to Modern Jewish Thought.* B'nai B'rith Bks. 1961 o.p. A brief and well-presented outline of how some important Jewish thinkers have reconciled the perceived conflict between faith and reason.

Berkovits, Eliezer. *Major Themes in Modern Philosophies of Judaism.* Ktav 1974 $25.00. ISBN 0-87068-264-4. An Orthodox rabbi's account of topics in modern Judaism.

Cohen, Arthur A. *The Natural and the Supernatural Jew: An Historical and Theological Introduction.* Behrman 1979 repr. of 1962 ed. o.p. An account of a number of modern systems of Judaic thought, together with the author's own reflections on some basic issues of religiosity.

Eisen, Arnold M. *The Chosen People in America: A Study in Jewish Religious Ideology. Modern Jewish Experience.* Ind. U. Pr. 1983 $20.00. ISBN 0-253-31365-1. Traces the concept of the chosen in American Jewish intellectual history through 1980, showing how the notion of ethnic distinctiveness conflicts with the desire for assimilation into American society.

Frank, Daniel H., ed. *Autonomy and Judaism: The Individual and Community in Jewish Philosophical Thought.* State U. NY Pr. 1992 $57.50. ISBN 0-7914-1209-1. Eight revised papers from the June 1989 annual conference of the Academy of Jewish Philosophy. Explores Biblical ideas of human fulfillment, medieval ideas of the human good, and engagement in the modern pluralistic state.

Goodman, Lenn E., ed. *Neoplatonism and Jewish Thought.* State U. NY Pr. 1992 $59.50. ISBN 0-7914-1339-X. Shows how major Jewish thinkers dealt with issues such as the definition of the divine, man, and nature, and their proper relations, and the meanings of time, history, and worship.

Katz, Steven T. *Historicism, the Holocaust, and Zionism.* NYU Pr. 1992 $50.00. ISBN 0-8147-4616-0. Twelve well-crafted essays including studies on Franz Rosenzweig, Martin Buber's work, and critical evaluations on the Holocaust.

Neusner, Jacob. *Stranger at Home: Zionism, "The Holocaust," and American Judaism.* U. Ch. Pr. 1981. ISBN 0-226-57629-9. Deals with the issues of Zionism and the Holocaust as these affect American Jewry.

——. *Understanding Jewish Theology: Classical Issues and Modern Perspective.* Ktav 1973 $16.95. ISBN 0-87068-215-6. Anthology on the themes of God, Torah, and Israel and the people of God, in classical and modern Judaic thought.

Rawidowicz, Simon. *Studies in Jewish Thought.* Jewish Pubns. 1975 o.p. Brilliant and original thinker on Jewish social philosophy and history presents his best ideas. Introduction by Benjamin Ravid.

Rotenstreich, Nathan. *Jewish Philosophy in Modern Times.* Wayne St. U. Pr. repr. of 1968 ed. $19.95. ISBN 0-8143-2439-8. The German Judaic tradition of thought presented by a master.

Sandmel, Samuel. *The Several Israels, and an Essay: Religion and Modern Man.* Ktav 1971 o.p. Leading Reform Judaic theologian presents elegant essays on Judaic thought.

ENLIGHTENMENT

The French and German Enlightenment produced a heritage of skepticism and rationalism that affected some Jewish thinkers as well. They turned to the Jewish community with a program of intellectual reform, specifically proposing that Jews enter European culture, learn to read and speak European languages instead of their own Jewish language (Yiddish), and bring to their holy books and their religion the rationalist values of the age. Although not numerous, the Jewish disciples of the Enlightenment exercised considerable influence. They began to write in Hebrew, producing secular as well as religious writings; they took an interest in science and politics; and they brought to the Jewish community some of those secularizing ideas that were reshaping European culture and politics.

Hadas, Moses, ed. *Solomon Maimon: An Autobiography*. Schocken 1967 o.p. A basic account of a critical figure in the eighteenth-century Enlightenment with a wealth of information about the contemporary cultural and social setting.

Hertzberg, Arthur. *The French Enlightenment and the Jews*. Col. U. Pr. 1990 $18.50. ISBN 0-231-07385-2. An excellent history of eighteenth-century French Jewry argues that Voltaire was an anti-Semite and that the French Enlightenment was a source of Jew-hatred.

Jospe, Alfred, ed. *Jerusalem and Other Jewish Writings by Moses Mendelssohn*. Schocken 1969 o.p. The founder of modern Judaic thought and of Reform Judaism is presented here in a fine anthology.

SCIENCE OF JUDAISM (*WISSENSCHAFT DES JUDENTUMS*)

In the German universities of the early nineteenth century, a new approach to learning took shape, called *Wissenschaft*, translated into English as "science." *Wissenschaft* referred to learning that was systematic, critical, encompassing, and not merely a repetition of received information but a search for explanation and theory. The earliest reformers in Judaism looked to scientific method, or *Wissenschaft*, as the correct means for the reformation of Judaism. This they wished to accomplish by a critical rereading of the sources of Judaism and a reconstruction of the history of the Jews along lines of science, rather than credibility or theology. *Wissenschaft des Judentums*, or "science of Judaism," also took hold among Conservative Jews, and, in the twentieth century, in western Orthodoxy as well. At stake among all these groups was a factual and informed knowledge, based on criticism and philological learning, of the Jews' past. (See also "Conservative Judaism" below.)

Geiger, Abraham. *Judaism and Its History: In Two Parts*. Trans. by Charles Newburgh. U. Pr. of Amer. 1985 repr. of 1911 ed. o.p. A series of popular lectures on the nature of Jewish history given in 1865 in Frankfurt by an important figure in the development of Reform Judaism and Jewish historiography.

Graetz, Heinrich. *The Structure of Jewish History and Other Essays*. Ktav 1975 $25.00. ISBN 0-87068-466-3. Essays on Jewish history and historiography by one of the founders of the field; Ismar Schorsch's introduction is the best guide to the system of the founder of Jewish historiography in modern times.

Jospe, Alfred, ed. *Studies in Jewish Thought: An Anthology of German Jewish Scholarship*. Bks. Demand repr. of 1981 ed. $112.90. ISBN 0-685-20907-5. An eclectic collection of writings by important figures in the *Wissenschaft des Judentums* movement on Rabbinic literature, mysticism, and medieval and modern theology.

POST-HOLOCAUST THEOLOGY

Beginning in the late 1960s, Jewish thinkers began to come to terms with the theological dilemma of the Holocaust. Age-old questions of theodicy emerged with an acute sense of urgency. The responses have been varied and contradictory. On one side, Richard Rubenstein asked how Jews could remain faithful to a God who could allow such a tragedy to occur. On the other side, EMIL FACKENHEIM responded that for Jews to give up faith after the Holocaust would give Hitler a posthumous victory.

Berkovitz, Eliezer. *Faith after the Holocaust.* Ktav 1973 $9.95. ISBN 0-87068-193-1. An Orthodox Judaic theologian affirms the received faith of Sinai and argues that the Holocaust is not unique, but rather an extension of typical Christian anti-Semitism.

Cohen, Arthur A. *The Tremendum: A Theological Interpretation of the Holocaust.* Crossroad NY 1981 o.p. Effort at original thought on the subject, marked by absence of clarity.

————, ed. *Arguments and Doctrines: A Reader of Jewish Thinking in the Aftermath of the Holocaust.* JPS Phila. 1970 o.p. An important anthology of contemporary theology on the problem of evil and other issues raised by the Holocaust.

Haynes, Stephen. *Prospects for Post-Holocaust Theology.* Scholars Pr. GA 1991 $29.95. ISBN 1-55540-651-3

Katz, Stephen. *Post-Holocaust Dialogues: Critical Studies in Modern Jewish Thought.* NYU Pr. 1985 $18.50. ISBN 0-8147-4587-3

Neusner, Jacob. *The Jewish War against the Jews: Reflections on Golah, Shoah, and Torah.* Ktav 1984 $12.95. ISBN 0-88125-050-3. Argues against the centrality of the Holocaust in the formation of contemporary Judaic consciousness.

Roskies, David G. *Against the Apocalypse: Responses to Catastrophe in Modern Jewish Culture.* HUP 1984 $12.95. ISBN 0-674-00916-9. Challenges the view that the Holocaust is without precedent or analogy in Jewish thought, comparing the Jewish response to the Holocaust with the way Jews have responded to over a century of European persecutions and pogroms.

CONTEMPORARY THEOLOGY

Axelrad, Albert S. *Meditations of a Maverick Rabbi.* Rossel Bks. 1985 $8.95. ISBN 0-940-64612-9. Beloved Hillel rabbi at Brandeis University and left-wing activist states his religious convictions and his opinions on a wide range of topics.

Bamberger, Bernard J. *The Search for Jewish Theology.* Behrman 1978 o.p. The construction of a new system of Jewish theology by a Reform rabbi.

Berkovitz, Eliezer. *Not in Heaven: The Nature and Function of Halachah.* Ktav 1983 $9.95. ISBN 0-88125-003-1. Discusses the dynamic interaction of traditional Jewish law and the changing situation of Jewish life, focusing on contemporary issues—including conversion and the status of women—that arise in a pluralistic, democratic environment.

Breslauer, S. Daniel. *A New Jewish Ethics.* E. Mellen 1983 $16.95. ISBN 0-88946-700-5. The construction of a pluralistic and ecumenical theology of ethics and interpersonal relations, inspired by the writings of Martin Buber.

Brooks, Roger, ed. *Unanswered Questions: Theological Views of Jewish-Catholic Relations.* U. of Notre Dame Pr. 1988 o.p. Interesting though diverse papers from a conference on Jewish-Catholic relations.

Cohen, Arthur A. *The Myth of the Judeo-Christian Tradition.* HarpC 1970 o.p. This iconoclastic study challenges the common assumption that Jews and Christians share a uniform tradition, arguing for "the invigoration of prophetic radicalism, a dissent from the harmonious conservatism of inherited religion."

The Condition of Jewish Belief: A Symposium Compiled by the Editors of Commentary Magazine. Macmillan 1966 o.p. The answer of over 30 prominent rabbis to 5 burning questions of the day—such as "is God dead?" and "are the Jews the chosen people?"—reflecting the thinking of the mainstream rabbinical establishment in the 1960s.

Finkel, Avraham Y. *Responsa Anthology.* Aronson 1991 $45.00. ISBN 0-87668-773-7. Over 250 she'eilot, life questions, and teshuvot, detailed responses, spanning the entire spectrum of Jewish life.

Green, Arthur. *Seek My Face, Speak My Name: A Contemporary Jewish Theology.* Aronson 1992 $29.95. ISBN 0-87668-592-0. Written by a scholar of Jewish mysticism and the president of the Reconstructionist Rabbinical College. Reflects contemporary concerns such as feminism and ecology. A rewarding and "prayerful" text.

Hartman, David. *A Living Covenant: The Innovative Spirit in Traditional Judaism.* Free Pr. 1985 $29.95. ISBN 0-02-914140-0. Looks to Jewish tradition to establish a "covenantal religious anthropology capable of participating adequately in the challenges of modernity."

Herberg, Will. *Judaism and Modern Man*. Atheneum 1970 o.p. An analysis of how American Jews have responded and should respond to the challenges and opportunities of modern society.

Kaufman, William E. *Contemporary Jewish Philosophies*. Wayne St. U. Pr. 1992 repr. of 1976 ed. $14.95. ISBN 0-8143-2429-0. A good survey of modern thinkers, carefully introduced, with the author's own proposals as well. Preface by Jacob Neusner.

Morgan, Michael. *Dilemmas in Modern Jewish Thought: The Dialectics of Revelation and History*. Ind. U. Pr. 1992 $35.00. ISBN 0-253-33878-6. A study of seventeenth-century through present-day Jewish theologians, intended to shed light on the contemporary Jew's historical and theological situation.

Neusner, Jacob. *Stranger at Home: "The Holocaust," Zionism, and American Judaism*. U. Ch. Pr. 1985 $12.95. ISBN 0-226-57628-0. On the relationship of American Jewry and the State of Israel.

Rosenthal, Gilbert S. *Four Paths to One God*. Bloch 1973 $8.95. ISBN 0-898-85277-3. A Conservative rabbi judges other peoples' Judaisms.

Schacter-Shalom, Zalman, and Donald Gropman. *The First Step: A Guide for the New Jewish Spirit*. Bantam 1983 o.p. A great Jewish spiritual leader proposes creative new models for Jewish practice.

Singer, Howard. *Bring Forth the Mighty Men: On Violence and the Jewish Character*. Funk & Wagnalls 1969 o.p. Reflections on the nature of "being Jewish" by a brilliant writer and social critic.

Stone, Ira F. *Seeking the Path to Life*. Jewish Lights 1993 $19.95. ISBN 1-879045-17-6. Collection of brief, lyrical, personal meditations by a Jewish conservative rabbi.

Wine, Sherwin T. *Judaism beyond God: A Radical Need to be Jewish*. Prometheus Bks. 1986 $13.95. ISBN 0-912-64508-3. Argues that Judaism and Jewish ritual still can be meaningful to Jews who do not believe in God, emphasizing rather the intellectual and ethical dimensions of Jewish tradition.

Wolf, Arnold Jacob, ed. *Rediscovering Judaism: Reflections on New Theology*. Quadrangle 1965 o.p. Reform rabbis reflecting on the renewal of Judaism.

Wyschogrod, Michael. *The Body of Faith: Judaism as Corporeal Election*. Seabury 1983 o.p. A philosophic argument for the chosenness of Israel, the Jewish people, in a corporeal framework.

FEMINISM AND WOMEN'S STUDIES

One of the most lively issues facing Judaism today is the reevaluation of Jewish history, theology, and practice in the light of changing attitudes and roles of women and men. Now that women have been ordained by the Reform, Conservative, and Reconstructionist movements, they are bringing new perspectives into a tradition that has been defined predominantly by men. Traditionalists among feminist theologians claim that there is no reason for change. Conservatives believe that the tradition can adapt to accommodate new concerns. Radicals argue that Judaism must be transformed completely.

Aschkenasy, Nehama. *Eve's Journey: Feminine Images in Hebraic Literary Tradition*. U. of Pa. Pr. 1996 $40.95. ISBN 0-8122-8033-4. Traces the migration of female images through the Jewish tradition, concentrating on the Bible and recent literature and giving special attention to two recurrent images—the "deadly seductress" and the "formidable giver of life."

Baskin, Judith, ed. *Jewish Women in Historical Perspective*. Wayne St. U. Pr. 1991 $19.95. ISBN 0-8143-2091-0. Studies on the place and role of women in Jewish society from biblical times to the present.

Baum, Charlotte, and Sonya Michel. *The Jewish Woman in America*. Dial 1976 o.p. Collection of essays on various aspects of the history of American Jewish women.

Biale, Rachel. *Women and Jewish Law: An Exploration of Women's Issues in Halakhic Sources*. Schocken 1984 $15.00. ISBN 0-8052-3887-5. An attempt to reconcile contemporary concerns of women with the traditional sources of Jewish law.

Brayer, Menachem M. *Jewish Women in Rabbinic Literature*. 2 vols. Ktav 1986 o.p. Vol. 1, *A Psychohistorical Perspective*; Vol. 2, *A Psychosocial Perspective*. An important compendium of sources from the Talmud to modern Orthodoxy that examines woman's role in Judaism as wife, mother, educator, guide, martyr, and religious leader, usually defending the traditional viewpoint against feminism.

Christ, Carol P., and Judith Plaskow. *Womanspirit Rising: A Feminist Reader in Religion*. Harper SF 1992 repr. of 1979 ed. $12.00. ISBN 0-06-061385-8. A collection of essays that place Jewish feminist thought in the context of general efforts to create new traditions of women's spirituality.

Fishman, Sylvia B. *A Breath of Life: Feminism in the American Jewish Community*. Free Pr. 1993 $22.95. ISBN 0-02-910342-8. Successfully renders the ongoing tension between feminism and traditional, especially Orthodox, Judaism.

Greenberg, Blu. *On Women and Judaism: A View from Tradition*. JPS Phila. 1983 $9.95. ISBN 0-8276-0195-6. The best explanation of the Orthodox position on women's issues.

Henry, Sondra, and Emily Taitz. *Written Out of History: Our Jewish Foremothers*. Biblio NY 1990 $15.95. ISBN 0-930395-10-7. An interesting but not always reliable look at the women who have been pushed to the margins of Jewish history and forgotten, from the Bible to the present.

Heschel, Susannah, ed. *On Being a Jewish Feminist*. Schocken 1983 $13.95. ISBN 0-8052-0745-7. A collection of 24 feminist essays by men and women, many of which have been published previously, with a good introduction by the editor.

Kaplan, Marion. *The Jewish Feminist Movement in Germany*. Greenwood 1979 $42.95. ISBN 0-313-20736-4

Koltun, Elizabeth, ed. *The Jewish Woman: New Perspectives*. Schocken 1987 $15.00. ISBN 0-8052-0532-2. A collection of essays on women, written from a variety of perspectives, that originally were published in a special issue of *Response* magazine in 1973.

Marcus, Jacob Rader. *The American Jewish Woman: A Documentary History*. Ktav 1981 $45.00. ISBN 0-87068-752-2. The first volume is a comprehensive history of Jewish women in America, covering social, political, and religious topics; the second volume collects relevant documents, letters, memoirs, and essays.

Meiselman, Moshe. *Jewish Woman in Jewish Law*. *Lib. of Jewish Law and Ethics*. Ktav 1978 $12.95. ISBN 0-87068-329-2. An antifeminist polemic that defends the traditional images and roles of woman.

Morton, Leah (pseud. Elizabeth G. Stern). *I Am a Woman and a Jew*. Rprt. Serv. 1991 repr. of 1926 ed. $79.00. ISBN 0-7812-8364-7. Autobiography of a professional woman in a man's world of journalism and management who, having given up her Jewishness, later develops a passionate pride in her tradition. Introduction by Ellen Umansky.

Rogow, Faith. *Gone to Another Meeting: The National Council of Jewish Women, 1893-1993*. U. of Ala. Pr. 1993 $24.95. ISBN 0-8173-0671-4. Comprehensive history of the oldest religious Jewish women's organization in the U.S.

Ruether, Rosemary R. *Religion and Sexism: Images of Women in the Jewish and Christian Tradition*. S & S Trade 1974 o.p. An important collection of articles by various scholars on the view of women expressed by the Hebrew Bible, New Testament, Church Fathers, Talmud, Canon Law, the Reformation, and German Protestantism.

Schneider, Susan. *Jewish and Female: Choices and Changes in Our Lives Today*. S & S Trade 1984 o.p. A guide for Jewish women, full of practical information and essays encouraging women to take on new roles.

Religious Movements

Each Judaic religious movement has claimed that it continues the entire history of Judaism and represents the natural and logical next step from Sinai to the present day. Orthodoxy alleges that the sole legitimate and authentic Judaism, deriving from Sinai, is Orthodox Judaism. Reform Judaism links itself to reforming movements in the past and holds that Reform Judaism today stands for the authentic and true Judaism as the prophets had set it forth in their day. Conservative Judaism appeals to the processes of scholarship to identify in the past the necessary and essential Judaism that, in the present day, Conservative Judaism would embody. In these and in other ways, each Judaism has alleged that it forms the increment of the past and stands in a linear relationship to Sinai. This mode of legitimation in theological terms has affirmed, on behalf of each Judaism, the authority of Sinai (for Orthodoxy) or of Sinai and of history (for Reform and Conservative Judaisms).

GENERAL

Blau, Joseph L. *Judaism in America: From Curiosity to Third Faith.* U. Ch. Pr. 1976 o.p. A simple and clear introduction to the major movements of Judaism in America— Orthodox, Reform, Conservative, and the like.

_____. *Modern Varieties of Judaism. Lectures on the History of Religions.* Col. U. Pr. 1966 $16.50. ISBN 0-231-08668-7. Good account of the modern Judaisms of the West.

Cohen, Elliot E., ed. *Commentary on the American Scene.* Knopf 1953 o.p. Selected essays from *Commentary*, when the magazine concerned itself with Judaic rather than mainly political-conservative themes.

Cohen, Steven M. *American Modernity and Jewish Identity.* Routledge Chapman Hall 1983 $14.95. ISBN 0-422-77740-4. Examines how various Judaic systems responded to modernity, including Reform and Conservative Judaism, as well as Jewish political liberalism and American Zionism.

Goodman, Saul L., ed. *The Faith of Secular Jews. Lib. of Jewish Learning.* Ktav 1976 $25.00. ISBN 0-87068-489-2. Explains the position of Jews who are Jewish but not Judaic or religious.

Isaacs, Harold R. *Idols of the Tribe: Group Identity and Political Change.* HUP 1989 $9.95. ISBN 0-674-44315-2. Includes attention to American Jews in Israel as an example of how political change affects new definitions in religion.

Mor, Menachem. *Jewish Sects, Religious Movements, and Political Parties.* Creighton U. Pr. 1993 $30.00. ISBN 1-881871-04-5

Neusner, Jacob. *American Judaism: Adventure in Modernity.* Ktav repr. of 1978 ed. $9.95. ISBN 0-87068-681-X. Introduces the issues of history of religion to describe and interpret Judaism in America.

_____. *The Death and Birth of Judaism: The Impact of Christianity, Secularism and the Holocaust on Jewish Faith.* Basic 1987 $21.95. ISBN 0-465-01577-8. Explains the modernization of Judaism in consequence of political change and interprets seven modern Judaisms against the background of contemporary history.

_____, ed. *Understanding American Judaism: Toward the Description of Modern Religion.* 2 vols. ADL 1975 $9.95. ISBN 0-686-95149-2. Vol. 1, *Toward the Description of a Modern Religion: The Synagogue and the Rabbi*; Vol. 2, *The Sectors of American Judaism: Reform, Orthodoxy, Conservatism, and Reconstructionism.* Anthology of diverse writings about the three Judaisms of America, the rabbi, the synagogue, the community, and the consciousness of ordinary Jews.

Raphael, Marc Lee. *Profiles in American Judaism: The Reform, Conservative, Orthodox and Reconstructionist Traditions in Historical Perspective.* HarpC 1984 o.p. A clearly written survey of the history, ideology, and institutions of Reform, Conservative, Orthodox, and Reconstructionist Judaism.

Rudavsky, David. *Modern Jewish Religious Movements.* Behrman 1979 repr. of 1967 ed. o.p. Account of the modernization of Judaism. Foreword by Abraham Kalsch.

Sharot, Stephen. *Messianism, Mysticism, and Magic: A Sociological Analysis of Jewish Religious Movements.* U. of NC Pr. 1987 repr. of 1982 ed. $13.95. ISBN 0-8078-4170-6

REFORM JUDAISM

Reform Judaism, which was founded in early nineteenth-century Germany and enjoys enormous success in twentieth-century America, takes the position that change is legitimate and necessary and that each generation has the task of finding a Judaism that is suitable to its circumstances. As a means of preserving strong links and loyalties between a Judaism and the many Jews who wish to live a secular life and also a Judaic life, Reform Judaism solves the problem of making possible a Judaic life segregated from the politics and culture of the Western nations in which Jews live. Reform Judaism maintains that certain aspects of Judaism (concerning ethics and morality, for example) take priority. To be a good Jew, one does not have to keep dietary laws but does have to practice justice and mercy and live an ethical life. Reform Judaism therefore acts as the instrument for accommodating the desire of large numbers of Jews to live in a mixed society, not in a ghetto, and to live like their gentile neighbors in some ways but different from them in other ways.

Blau, Joseph L., ed. *Reform Judaism: A Historical Perspective.* Central Conf. of Amer. Rabbis 1973 o.p. Anthology of writings by Reform rabbis, spanning a period of 80 years.

Borowitz, Eugene B. *Reform Judaism Today. 1973–77.* Behrman 1983 $14.95. ISBN 0-87441-364-8. Thought-provoking essays designed to facilitate discussion among Reform Jews.

Borowitz, Eugene B., and Joseph L. Blau, eds. *Reform Judaism, A Historical Perspective: Essays from the Yearbook of the Central Conference of American Rabbis.* Ktav 1973 o.p. Anthology of rabbis' writings.

Freehof, Solomon B. *Reform Responsa for Our Time.* Hebrew Union Coll. Pr. 1977 $15.00. ISBN 0-87820-111-4

Goldman, Edward A., ed. *Jews in a Free Society: Challenges and Opportunities.* Hebrew Union Col. Pr. 1976 $15.00. ISBN 0-87820-112-2. Eclectic collection of essays celebrating the centennial of the Reform rabbinical school, on Jewish life in America and the purpose and potential of Reform Judaism.

Jacob, Walter. *Contemporary American Reform Responsa.* Central Conf. 1987 $15.00. ISBN 0-88123-003-0. The author's answers to 202 questions regarding contemporary Jewish ritual and ethics.

Levy, Beryl Harold. *Reform Judaism in America: A Study in Religious Adaptation.* Bloch 1933 o.p. Early account of the history of Reform Judaism.

Marcus, Jacob R. *Israel Jacobson: The Founder of the Reform Movement in Judaism.* Hebrew Union Col. Pr. 1972 $10.00. ISBN 0-878-20000-2. Standard biography of an early Reformer.

Marcus, Jacob R., and Abraham J. Peck, eds. *The American Rabbinate: A Century of Continuity and Change, 1883–1983.* Ktav 1985 $25.00. ISBN 0-88125-076-7. Important picture of the character of the Reform rabbinate.

Martin, Bernard, ed. *Contemporary Reform Jewish Thought.* Quadrangle 1968 o.p. Account of important Reform theological positions by their authors.

Meyer, Michael A. *Response to Modernity: A History of the Reform Movement in Judaism. Studies in Jewish History.* Ed. by Jehuda Reinharz. Vol. 4 OUP 1990 repr. of 1988 ed. $49.95. ISBN 0-19-506342-2. The first full-scale history of Reform Judaism since the beginning of the twentieth century.

Neusner, Jacob, ed. *The Reformation of Reform Judaism.* Garland 1993 $47.00. ISBN 0-8153-0076-X

Olitzky, Kerry M., ed. *Reform Judaism in America.* Greenwood 1993 $75.00. ISBN 0-313-24628-9

Petuchowski, Jakob J. *Prayerbook Reform in Europe: The Liturgy of European Liberal and Reform Judaism.* UAHC 1969 $13.50. ISBN 0-8074-0091-2. The story of how the prayer book became an arena for the reform of Judaism and how Reform Judaism reached the liturgy it currently follows.

JUDAISM 653

Philipson, David. *Reform Movement in Judaism*. Ktav rev. ed. 1967 o.p. The classic history of the nineteenth-century European phase of Reform Judaism, with presentation of primary source material.

Plaut, W. Gunther, ed. *The Growth of Reform Judaism: American and European Sources until 1948*. UAHC 1965 o.p. Continuation of the following listing.

————. *The Rise of Reform Judaism: A Sourcebook of Its European Origins*. UAHC 1963 $10.00 ISBN 0-8074-0089-0. The best anthology on the origin of Reform Judaism.

Temkin, Sefton D. *Isaac Mayer Wise: Shaping American Judaism*. OUP 1992. ISBN 0-19710-059-7. A thorough and extremely competent biography of the founder of the major institutions of American Reform Judaism.

Umansky, Ellen M. *Lily Montagu and the Advancement of Liberal Judaism: From Vision to Vocation*. E. Mellen 1983 $89.95. ISBN 0-88946-537-1. Biography of an important figure in early twentieth-century Liberal Judaism—the British equivalent of American Reform.

Weiner, Max. *Abraham Geiger and Liberal Judaism: The Challenge of the Nineteenth Century*. Hebrew Union Col. Pr. 1981 repr. 1962 ed. $9.95. ISBN 0-87820-800-3. The founder of Reform Judaic theology and scholarship in its Western and modern mode is given his best biography and anthology in English.

ORTHODOX JUDAISM

In Germany and the United States, Orthodox Judaism took shape as a self-conscious reaction to Reform Judaism. It maintained that change could not be declared in response to transient problems and that Jews had to obey the Torah because God had revealed the Torah at Sinai. No knowledge and no science stood in judgment on the Torah, which was eternal, unchanging, and divine in origin and authority. At the same time, Orthodoxy held that Jews could get a secular education and engage in life in close association with gentiles. In preserving the way of life and worldview of the received Judaism of the dual Torah, Orthodoxy recognized that Judaism would constitute a religion, rather than a completely encompassing politics and culture. The Judaism of the dual Torah, with its definition of the Jews as a holy people living a holy life essentially separate from everyone else, can be called traditional. That is because it was a received way of life that did not involve self-conscious affirmation, but simply an ongoing participation in patterns of life and thought that were received as unchanging and eternal. In this sense, we should regard the Judaism of the dual Torah as it flourished in eastern Europe before World War II and as it flourishes in the State of Israel today, as well as in the United States and western Europe, as different from the Orthodoxy that came to expression in nineteenth-century Germany and twentieth-century America. This Judaism of the dual Torah held, and still holds, that the Jews do not need to accommodate themselves to the requirements of Western civilization, should not waste time better devoted to study of the Torah by learning Western science and culture, and should form an essentially segregated and self-contained world, as (so it is maintained) the Jews did for all the centuries since Sinai. Dominating the world of yeshivas (centers for the full-time study of the Talmud and related sacred sciences) this kind of Judaism, although closely related to Orthodoxy, should be seen as an essentially separate Judaism, with its own social policy, and its own types of institutions, and its own politics and culture, distinct from that of the Westernized and modernized Orthodoxy.

Breuer, Mordechai. *Modernity Within Tradition: The Social History of Orthodox Jewry in Imperial Germany*. Trans. by Elizabeth Petuchowski. Col. U. Pr. 1992 $45.00. ISBN 0-231-07470-0. Thoroughly researched study draws on periodicals, personal memoirs, and religious literature.

Bulka, Reuven P. *Dimensions of Orthodox Judaism.* Ktav 1983 $25.00. ISBN 0-87068-894-3. Large collection of essays by various authors describing the ideology of modern Orthodoxy.

Fishman, Aryei. *Judaism and Modernization on the Religious Kibbutz.* Cambridge U. Pr. 1992 $54.95. ISBN 0-521-40388-X. Examines the tension between secular ideology and the religious culture of the Torah in the lives of Orthodox Jews of the Religious Kibbutz Federation.

Friedmann, Thomas. *Damaged Goods.* Permanent Pr. 1985 $21.95. ISBN 0-932966-39-X. An informative and humorous account of second-generation Holocaust survivors in Brooklyn yeshivas (Orthodox religious schools) during the 1960s.

Glenn, Menahem G. *Israel Salanter: The Story of a Religious-Ethical Current in Nineteenth-Century Judaism.* Bloch 1953 o.p. The first biography in English of a leading ethical thinker of nineteenth-century Orthodoxy.

Goldberg, Hillel. *Israel Salanter: Text, Structure, Idea.* Ktav 1982 $29.95. ISBN 0-87068-709-3. Biography of the founder of the Musar movement (nineteenth-century movement that focused on the traditional and ethical component of Judaism), who emerges as a creative thinker interested in understanding and altering the unconscious as well as in the study of the Talmud.

Heilman, Samuel. *Defenders of the Faith: Inside Ultra-Orthodox Jewry.* Schocken 1992 $27.00. ISBN 0-8052-4095-0. Takes us inside the ritual baths, study halls, synagogues, kitchens, and bedrooms of these half-a-million singular denizens of Jerusalem and Brooklyn.

———. *The Gate Behind the Wall: A Pilgrimage to Jerusalem.* Viking Penguin 1986 $5.95. ISBN 0-14-008467-3. An Orthodox Jew offers an insider's sociological study of Talmud study groups in Jerusalem.

———. *Synagogue Life: A Study in Symbolic Interaction.* U. Ch. Pr. 1979 $12.95. ISBN 0-226-32488-5. Description by a close observer of an Orthodox synagogue and its everyday life.

Helmreich, William B. *World of the Yeshiva.* Macmillan 1982 $24.95. ISBN 0-02-914640-2. Close observations of an Orthodox yeshiva on an everyday basis, together with a large-scale study of the entire movement.

Kurzweil, Zvi. *The Modern Impulse of Traditional Judaism.* Ktav 1985 $16.95. ISBN 0-88125-068-6. Outlines the position of centrist Orthodoxy, in contradistinction to more extreme perspectives, in essays on tolerance, democracy, and the equality of women.

Liberles, Robert. *Religious Conflict in Social Context: The Resurgence of Orthodox Judaism in Frankfurt-Am-Main, 1838–1877. Contributions to the Study of Religion Ser.* Greenwood 1985 $42.95. ISBN 0-313-24806-0. A sociological analysis of early Orthodoxy that demonstrates that the movement was not on the verge of collapse prior to Hirsch, as many people assume.

Liebman, Charles S. *Orthodoxy in American Jewish Life.* Am. Jewish Comm. 1966 o.p. A sociological description of the religious and communal institutions of American Orthodoxy.

CONSERVATIVE JUDAISM

Conservative Judaism was born in Germany in the middle of the nineteenth century as a mediating movement between Reform Judaism and Orthodox Judaism. It shared the affirmation of Judaic religious observance of Orthodox Judaism and the critical and scholarly policies of Reform Judaism. As in Reform Judaism, Conservative Judaism permitted change, but change only in accord with the historically valid patterns by which the Judaism of the dual Torah always had produced change. In America, Conservative Judaism attained substantial success as a movement of the Judaic center. For the most part, it involved essentially observant and Orthodox rabbis preaching a middle-of-the-road Conservative Judaism to members made up of unobservant and therefore fundamentally Reform Jews. From 1920 to 1970, Conservative Judaism was the most populous of American Judaisms. Today, however, it is giving way to a strong trend toward Reform Judaism on the one side and a resurgent Orthodox Judaism on the other.

Davis, Moshe. *The Emergence of Conservative Judaism: The Historical School in 19th-Century America.* Greenwood 1977 repr. of 1965 ed. o.p. Account of the beginnings of Conservative Judaism in America (1840–1902).

Feder, Don. *A Jewish Conservative Looks at Pagan America.* Huntington Hse. 1992 $19.99. ISBN 1-56384-037-5

Gillman, Neil. *Conservative Judaism: The New Century.* Behrman 1993. ISBN 0-87441-547-0

Nadell, Pamela S. *Conservative Judaism in America.* Greenwood 1988 $59.95. ISBN 0-313-24205-4

Siegel, Seymour, and Elliot Gertel. *God in the Teachings of Conservative Judaism.* Ktav 1985 $20.00. ISBN 0-88125-066-X. Anthology of theological writings by Conservative rabbis.

Sigal, Phillip. *The Emergence of Contemporary Judaism: The Foundation of Judaism from Biblical Origins to the Sixth Century A.D.* Pickwick 1986 $20.00. ISBN 0-915138-57-3. Conservative rabbi describes the beginnings of Conservative Judaism.

Sklare, Marshall. *Conservative Judaism: An American Religious Movement.* U. Pr. of Amer. 1985 repr. of 1972 ed. $20.25. ISBN 0-8191-4480-0. Sociology of Conservative Judaism as the religion of the second generation of American Jews.

Steinberg, Milton. *A Partisan Guide to the Jewish Problem.* U. Pr. of Amer. 1986 repr. of 1945 ed. o.p. Leading thinker of Conservative Judaism lays out the Jewish problems as he sees them.

Waxman, Mordecai, ed. *Tradition and Change.* United Synagogue Bk. 1958 o.p. The best anthology of Conservative Judaism.

SOCIALISM

During the latter part of the nineteenth century in eastern Europe, thousands of working-class Jews, along with the members of the Jewish intelligentsia, turned to socialism in response to the continual persecution of Jews. These individuals considered anti-Semitism to be a consequence of socioeconomic injustice and therefore advocated Communist revolution. The first Jewish socialist party, the Bund, was established in Vilna and quickly spread from Lithuania to Poland and the Ukraine. While the early socialists advocated universal goals, during the last decade of the century a Jewish movement emerged that emphasized the particular experience and culture of the Jews. Zionist socialism, which incorporated the doctrine of territorialism, developed as an offshoot of Jewish socialism. When Russian-Jewish radicals arrived in the United States during the 1880s, Yiddish-language workers' parties, newspapers, and organizations flourished. Immigrant Jews populated the sweatshops of the Lower East Side of Manhattan, producing a situation ripe for union organizing. Within a short time, Jewish activists had organized the United Garment Workers of America (1891) and other important unions. Most of these unions had a socialist ideology, but one Jew, Samuel Gompers, who helped establish the American Federation of Labor in 1886, sought to keep his union apolitical.

Avineri, Shlomo. *Moses Hess: Prophet of Communism and Zionism.* Modern Jewish Masters Ser. NYU Pr. 1987 $15.00. ISBN 0-8147-0584-7. Examines the thought of Moses Hess (1812–75) and its relationship to Zionist socialism of the early twentieth century.

Buber, Martin. *Paths in Utopia.* Macmillan 1988 $8.95. ISBN 0-02-084190-6. The idealist version of socialism laid out by the great social philosopher.

Deutscher, Isaac. *The Non-Jewish Jew and Other Essays.* OUP 1968 o.p. Jewish socialist figure describes the position of secular Jews attracted to socialism.

Epstein, Melech. *Profiles of Eleven*. U. Pr. of Amer. 1987 repr. of 1965 ed. $16.75. ISBN 0-8191-5493-8. Biographies of 11 men who figured prominently in the Jewish socialist movement among the immigrant generation of 1880–1920, with an introduction by Jacob Neusner.

Fishman, William J. *Jewish Radicals, 1875–1914: From Czarist Stetl to London Ghetto*. Pantheon repr. 1975 o.p. A detailed study of the various Jewish radical movements from 1870 until World War I.

Frankel, Jonathan. *Prophecy and Politics: Socialism, Nationalism, and the Russian Jews, 1862–1917*. Cambridge U. Pr. 1981 o.p. Classic account of the Jews and socialism in eastern Europe.

Goodman, Saul L., ed. *The Faith of Secular Jews*. Lib. of Jewish Learning. Ktav 1976 $14.95. ISBN 0-685-02914-X. Secular, socialist Jews express their deepest convictions.

Green, Nancy L. *Pletzl of Paris: Jewish Immigrant Workers in the Belle Époque*. Holmes & Meier 1985 $42.95. ISBN 0-8419-0995-4. Analysis of the Jewish immigrant labor movement in Paris during the Gay Nineties.

Jacobs, Jack. *On Socialists and "The Jewish Question" after Marx*. NYU Pr. 1992 $50.00. ISBN 0-8147-4178-9. Explores attitudes and ideologies of late nineteenth and early twentieth-century Marxist and social democratic intellectuals toward Zionism, anti-Semitism, Jewish socialist movements, and the nature and future of Jewry.

Johnpoll, Bernard K. *The Politics of Futility: The General Jewish Workers Bund of Poland, 1917–1943*. Cornell Univ. Pr. 1967 o.p. The story of the Jewish socialist movement in Poland.

Levin, Nora. *Jewish Socialist Movements, 1871–1917: While the Messiah Tarried*. Littman Lib. of Jewish Civilization. OUP 1978 $32.00. ISBN 0-19-710029-5. Popular account of Jewish socialism that traces the history of the Bund in prerevolutionary Russia and the development of the American Jewish labor movement and socialist Zionism.

Liebman, Arthur. *The Jews and the Left*. Contemporary Religious Movements. Wiley 1979 o.p. Political science study of the Jews in the left-wing movements of the twentieth century.

Mendelsohn, Ezra. *Class Struggle in the Pale*. Cambridge U. Pr. 1970 o.p. The founding, in competition with Zionism, of the Jewish socialist movement in Russia and Russian Poland.

Portnoy, Samuel A., ed. and trans. *Vladimir Medem: The Life and Soul of a Legendary Jewish Socialist*. Ktav 1979 o.p. The most important intellectual figure in the Jewish socialist movement.

Sorin, Gerald. *The Prophetic Minority: American Jewish Immigrant Radicals, 1880–1920*. Modern Jewish Experience. Ind. U. Pr. 1985 $24.95. ISBN 0-253-34618-5. Engaging account of the Jewish labor activists and socialists, emphasizing ethnicity as a motivation for their ideology.

Tobias, Henry J. *Jewish Bund in Russia from Its Origins to 1905*. Stanford U. Pr. 1972 $52.50. ISBN 0-8047-0764-2. The earliest years of the Jewish socialist movement in Russia and Russian Poland.

Wistrich, Robert S. *Revolutionary Jews from Marx to Trotsky*. B & N Imports 1976 o.p. Socialists who happened to be Jews, as distinct from Jewish socialists, described in biographical studies, with a foreword by James Joll.

_____. *Socialism and the Jews: The Dilemmas of Assimilation in Germany and Austria-Hungary*. Littman Lib. of Jewish Civilization. B'nai B'rith Bk. 1982 $37.50. ISBN 0-19-710053-8. Analyzes the role the Jewish question played in the politics of the German and Austrian Social Democratic parties before 1914, considering the issue of Jewish emancipation, the problem of political anti-Semitism, and the emergence of Jewish nationalism.

YIDDISHISM

Yiddishism was a language-oriented movement allied with Jewish socialism that identified the Yiddish language as the instrument by which Jews would express their culture and collective consciousness. Because most Jews in eastern Europe and a great many in the United States spoke Yiddish, the movement achieved considerable influence for a time. The movement fostered the writing of fiction and serious nonfiction in Yiddish, the development of instruments of education and culture for the propagation of the Yiddish language. Jewish socialists made use of Yiddish as the means of reaching the Jewish masses, and they identified Yiddishism as the cultural dimension of their movement.

Ansky, S. *The Dybbuk and Other Writings*. Pantheon 1992 $24.50. ISBN 0-8052-4111-6. Excellent introduction to the brilliant, brooding works of a Yiddish master.

Blumberg, Arnold B. *Zion Before Zionism*. Syracuse U. Pr. 1985 $29.95. ISBN 0-8156-2336-4. Makes use of British, German, Austrian, US, and Vatican archival sources. Excellent glossary, bibliography, index, illustrations, and 30 pages of notes.

Epstein, Melech. *Profiles of Eleven*. U. Pr. of Amer. 1987 repr. of 1965 ed. $26.50. ISBN 0-8191-5493-8. Account of the earliest Yiddish-speaking socialists, with an introduction by Jacob Neusner.

Goldsmith, Emanuel S. *Architects of Yiddishism at the Beginning of the Twentieth Century*. Fairleigh Dickinson 1976 $32.50. ISBN 0-8386-1384-5

Hoberman, J. *Bridge of Light: Yiddish Film Between Two Worlds*. Pantheon 1991 $40.00. ISBN 0-8052-4107-8. Extends from about 1881 to 1948. Retells the history of each film and recounts the political, economic, and artistic circumstances of the Jewish communities of the era.

Howe, Irving, and Eliezer Greenberg, eds. *Voices from the Yiddish: Essays, Memoirs, Diaries*. U. of Mich. Pr. 1972 o.p. The best anthology of the Yiddishist movement.

ZIONISM

Founded in 1897, Zionism declared that the Jews are a people and require their own state. The Zionist movement thus identified Jews as a political group rather than solely a religious one, and maintained that the Jews' problem was political. Zionists held that anti-Semitism was deeply embedded in Europe and that the Jews had to evacuate Europe in order to save their own lives. The principal goal of political Zionism was to establish a Jewish state in Palestine, a goal that was achieved in 1948. Zionist thought also extended to political questions on the definition of the Jewish people and the description and meaning of their history. During the first half of the twentieth century, Zionism formed one of the principal sources for the definition of Jewish thought and scholarship. Today, Zionism supports various projects in Israel and acts as a cultural bridge between Israel and Jews in other nations.

Agus, Jacob. *Banner of Jerusalem: The Life, Times, and Thought of Abraham Isaac Kuk*. Bloch 1946 o.p. Biography of an Orthodox rabbi who also was a leading Zionist figure.

Ahad Ha'am. *Nationalism and the Jewish Ethic: Basic Writings of Ahad Ha'am*. Ed. by Hans Kohn. Schocken 1962 o.p. A good anthology of Asher Zvi Ginsberg—who took the name Ahad Ha'am (meaning "one of the people")—a leading Zionist theoretician of the early twentieth century, with strong interest in cultural issues.

Avineri, Shlomo. *The Making of Modern Zionism: Intellectual Origins of the Jewish State*. Basic 1984 $14.00. ISBN 0-465-04331-3. History of Zionism by an important political figure and scholar.

Blumberg, Arnold B. *Zion Before Zionism*. Syracuse U. Pr. 1985 $29.95. ISBN 0-8156-2336-4. Makes use of British, German, Austrian, American, and Vatican archival sources. Excellent glossary, bibliography, index, illustrations, and 30 pages of notes.

Cohen, Naomi. *American Jews and the Zionist Idea*. Ktav 1975 $9.95. ISBN 0-87068-272-5. Account of the development of Zionist ideology among American Jewry.

Dubnow, Simon. *Nationalism and History: Essays on Old and New Judaism*. Ed. by Koppel S. Pinson. Atheneum 1970 repr. of 1958 ed. o.p. Account of a Jewish nationalist who did not favor moving all the Jews to the Land of Israel but wished the Diaspora communities to survive.

Elon, Amos. *Herzl*. Schocken 1985 $12.95. ISBN 0-8052-0790-2. Stunning biography of the founder of modern Zionism; by far the best work ever done on the subject.

Halkin, Hillel. *Letters to an American Jewish Friend: A Zionist's Polemic*. JPS Phila. 1977 o.p. Polemic against Jews living in the Diaspora.

Halpern, Ben. *The American Jew: A Zionist Analysis*. Wiener Pub Inc. 1988 repr. of 1956 ed. $6.95. ISBN 0-8052-0742-2. Powerful analysis of the weakness of the American Jewish commitment to Zionism.

————. *The Idea of the Jewish State*. *Middle Eastern Studies*. Bks. Demand 1969 $138.80. ISBN 0-7837-2266-4. Profound analysis of the political foundations of Zionist thought.

Hertzberg, Arthur, ed. *Zionist Idea: A Historical Analysis and Reader*. Macmillan 1972 $17.00. ISBN 0-689-70093-8. Classic anthology of writings about Zionism from the beginnings to the mid-1950s.

Herzl, Theodor. *The Jewish State*. Trans. by Harry Zohn. Herzl 1970 o.p. The influential book by the founder of political Zionism, who argued that Jews will never be accepted into Western society and that the only real solution to their economic and social problems would be the founding of a Jewish state.

Kaplan, Mordecai. *A New Zionism*. Herzl 1955 o.p. New theory of Zionism, deriving from Ahad Ha'am's ideas on Jewish culture, making room for the notion of Jews living outside of the Land of Israel.

Kolsky, Thomas A. *Jews Against Zionism: The American Council For Judaism, 1942-1948*. Temple U. Pr. 1992 $19.95. ISBN 1-56639-009-5. Story of Jewish opposition to Zionism in the 1940s.

Laqueur, Walter. *A History of Zionism*. Schocken 1989 $16.95. ISBN 0-8052-0899-2. The best history of Zionism, from the beginning to the present.

Lilker, Shalom. *Kibbutz Judaism: A New Tradition in the Making*. Assoc. Univ. Prs. 1982 o.p. Argues that the lifestyle and ideology of the secular kibbutz represents a Jewish religion, even if the members do not actually consider themselves religious.

Mendelsohn, Ezra. *Zionism in Poland: The Formative Years 1915–1926*. Bks. Demand repr. of 1981 ed. $103.70. ISBN 0-7837-3324-0. An excellent in-depth account of the rapid growth of Zionism in Poland.

Meyer, Isidore S., ed. *Early History of Zionism in America*. Ayer 1977 repr. of 1958 ed. 1958 o.p. Monograph on the early history of Zionism.

Poppel, Stephen M. *Zionism in Germany, 1897–1933: The Shaping of a Jewish Identity*. JPL Phila. 1977 o.p. Analytic study of the Zionist movement in Germany, its ideas and leadership, before Hitler.

Rabinowicz, Harry M. *Hasidism and the State of Israel*. Littman Lib. of Jewish Civilization. B'nai B'rith Bk. 1982 $24.95. ISBN 0-19-710049-X. Discusses the Hasidic movement and its transplantation to the State of Israel after the Holocaust.

Rubenstein, Amnon. *The Zionist Dream Revisited: From Herzl to Gush Emunim and Back*. Schocken 1984 o.p. The leader of an Israeli centrist party contrasts the old-line labor Zionism, dominant in the early twentieth century, with the contemporary right-wing hawks of the Gush Emunim movement.

Selkitar, Ofira. *New Zionism and the Foreign Policy System of Israel*. S. Ill. U. Pr. 1986 $34.50. ISBN 0-8093-1287-5. Best description so far of New Zionism and religious-nationlist trends in Israel during the last 20 years.

Shapira, Anita. *Land and Power: The Zionist Resort to Force, 1881–1948*. OUP 1992 $59.00. ISBN 0-19-506104-7. By a premier historian of Zionism. Purports to trace the unfolding, multidimensional attitudes to power and the use of force in Palestine. An arresting and indispensible work.

Urofsky, Melvin I. *American Zionism from Herzl to the Holocaust*. Doubleday 1976 o.p. Tells the story of the Zionist institutions and ideology among American Jews during the first half of this century.

Vital, David. *Zionism: The Crucial Phase*. OUP 1987 $79.00. ISBN 0-19-821932-6. Probing and persuasive for the political history of the earlier period.

RECONSTRUCTIONISM

Reconstructionism, an offshoot of Conservative Judaism, began in the twentieth century. It established itself within a naturalist (rather than a supernatural) theology and emphasized the idea of God as the power that makes for salvation. Reconstructionism laid great stress on Jewish peoplehood and emphasized the keeping of religious rites as an expression of loyalty to the people, rather than as obedience to God's will. In America today, Reconstructionist Judaism has its own seminary, the Reconstructionist Rabbinical College in Philadelphia, an organization of rabbis and of synagogues, and it is a fully articulated form of Judaism.

Alpert, Rebecca T., and Jacob J. Staub. *Exploring Judaism: A Reconstructionist Approach.* Reconstructionist Pr. 1985 $11.95. ISBN 0-935457-01-1. A brief introduction to Kaplan's thought and the contemporary practice and institutions of the Reconstructionist movement.

Eisenstein, Ira. *Reconstructing Judaism: An Autobiography.* Reconstructionist Pr. 1986 $17.95. ISBN 0-935457-37-2. An autobiography by a key figure in the development of Reconstructionism as a movement.

Miller, Alan W. *God of Daniel S. in Search of the American Jew. Brown Class. in Judaica Ser.* U. Pr. of Amer. 1986 repr. of 1969 ed. $22.50. ISBN 0-8191-5047-9. Review of all modern theologies of Judaism from the perspective of Reconstructionism.

REVERSIONARY JUDAISM

Since World War II, and particularly in recent decades, large numbers of formerly secular Jews in Israel, America, and Europe have become part of a movement of reversion to Judaism. This movement does not constitute a single Judaism; rather, it is expressed by a higher standard of adherence to Judaic religious practices within Reform congregations as well as by a conversion of secular Jews to Orthodoxy. The pattern of change is relative, therefore, and often involves one step toward a more traditional pattern, rather than a complete revolution in the believer's life and thought. Reversionary Judaism has, however, received its most effective institutional expression within Israeli Orthodoxy. Israeli yeshivas and communities of the pious have undertaken vigorous efforts to receive Jews of little or no background and to educate and train them into the Judaism of the dual Torah. Reversionary Judaism has also found expression in the United States. In the United States, Orthodox Judaism has received and assimilated less observant Orthodox and Reformed and Conservative Jews, not to mention formerly quite secular Jews. These returnees have formed large and vigorous communities of newly-observant persons.

Aviad, Janet. *Return to Judaism: Religious Renewal in Israel.* U. Ch. Pr. 1983 $20.00. ISBN 0-226-03236-1. Solid sociological study of the reversionists in the context of the institutions of Israeli Orthodoxy.

Borowitz, Eugene B. *Renewing the Covenant: A Theology for Postmodern Jews.* JPS Phila 1991 $24.95. ISBN 0-8276-0400-9. Examines theological trends in contemporary Jewish faith.

Danzger, Murray. *Returning to Tradition: The Contemporary Revival of Orthodox Judaism.* Yale U. Pr. 1989 $35.00. ISBN 0-300-03947-6. A thorough sociological study of the reversionist phenomenon in the United States and Israel that serves as a very fine update to Aviad.

Kurzweil, Zvi. *The Modern Impulse of Traditional Judaism.* Ktav 1985 $16.95. ISBN 0-88125-068-6. An excellent, albeit concise, study of the evolution of neo-Orthodoxy.

Levin, Michael Graubart. *Journey to Tradition: The Odyssey of a Born-Again Jew.* Ktav 1986 $14.95. ISBN 0-881-25093-7. The personal story of a young Jew who moved from a null position to Orthodoxy but subsequently left Orthodoxy because, despite ample learning and strict observance, he could not find acceptance there.

CHRONOLOGY OF AUTHORS

Philo Judaeus. c.20 B.C.–C.A.D. 50
Josephus, Flavius. C.A.D. 38–100
Saadia Gaon. 882–942
Rashi. 1040–1105
Judah Halevi. c.1075-1141
Maimonides. 1135–1204
Nahmanides. 1194–c.1270
Gersonides. 1288–1344
Ba'al Shem Tov. c.1700–1760
Nahman of Bratslav. 1772–1811
Hirsch, Samson Raphael. 1808–1888

Cohen, Hermann. 1842–1918
Baeck, Leo. 1873–1956
Buber, Martin. 1878–1965
Kaplan, Mordecai Menahem.
    1881–1983
Rosenzweig, Franz. 1886–1929
Scholem, Gershom. 1897–1982
Soloveitchik, Joseph. 1903–1993
Heschel, Abraham Joshua. 1907–1972
Fackenheim, Emil. 1916–
Borowitz, Eugene. 1924–

BA'AL SHEM TOV (ISRAEL BEN ELIEZER). c.1700–1760

According to Hasidic tradition, Israel ben Eliezer, more commonly known as Ba'al Shem Tov, revealed himself as a healer and leader on his thirty-sixth birthday. His following expanded rapidly and soon encompassed a large part of eastern European Jewry. He employed Cabalistic categories and terminology but emphasized personal experience and salvation over the redemption of the world. The Ba'al Shem Tov spoke of a God directly accessible to human beings through prayer and joyous celebration. Many legends developed during his lifetime and afterward about his miracles and charismatic personality.

BOOKS ABOUT BA'AL SHEM TOV

Buber, Martin. *The Legend of the Baal Shem.* Schocken 1987 repr. of 1955 ed. $14.00. ISBN 0-8052-0233-1. A theological introduction to Hasidism and a creative retelling of the legends concerning the charismatic founder of Hasidism.
Heschel, Abraham J. *The Circle of Baal Shem Tov: Studies in Hasidism.* Ed. by Samuel Dresner. U. Ch. Pr. 1985 $24.95. ISBN 0-226-32960-7. Lucid and passionate essays on four figures from the inner circle of the founder of Hasidism: Pinchas of Korzec, Nahman of Kosov, Gershon Kutover, and Isaac of Drohobyez.

BAECK, LEO. 1873–1956

Leo Baeck was born in Lissa (now Leszno), Poland, to a family of distinguished rabbis. He studied at the Conservative Jewish Theological Seminary of Breslau and then at the Hochschule für die Wissenschaft des Judentums in Berlin. In 1905 he wrote *The Essence of Judaism* in response to Adolf von Harnack's *The Essence of Christianity* and to the general mood of Christian chauvinism and anti-Semitism. Baeck was the most prominent Jewish leader in Germany when the Nazis came to power in 1933. He remained as the outspoken leader of the Berlin Jewish community until he was deported to the Theresienstadt concentration camp in 1943. After the war, he became the chair of the World Union of Progressive Judaism in London and occasionally taught at the Reform seminary in Cincinnati.

BOOKS BY BAECK

The Essence of Judaism. 1905. Schocken rev. ed. 1961 o.p. Defends Judaism against criticism from insiders and outsiders and explains Judaism as a coherent ethical system.
Judaism and Christianity: Essays. Trans. by Walter Kaufmann. Atheneum 1970 repr. of 1958 ed. o.p. Baeck agrees with Hermann Cohen that Judaism constitutes "ethical monotheism" and that this form of religion is superior to Christian "romanticism."
This People Israel. 1955. H. Holt & Co. 1964 o.p. Philosophy of Jewish peoplehood.

BOOKS ABOUT BAECK

Baker, Leonard. *Days of Sorrow and Pain: Leo Baeck and the Berlin Jews.* OUP 1980 $9.95. ISBN 0-025-06340-5. The best account of Leo Baeck's heroic and inspiring leadership of the Berlin Jewish community during the period of its demise at the hands of the Nazis.

Friedlander, Albert H. *Leo Baeck: Teacher of Theresienstadt.* H. Holt & Co. 1968 o.p. A good book on the leading German Judaic Reform theologian of the twentieth century.

BOROWITZ, EUGENE. 1924–

Borowitz is the most original and influential Reform Jewish thinker of today. A Reform rabbi and professor at Columbia University and the Hebrew Union College in New York, he is the founder and editor of *Sh'ma: A Journal of Jewish Responsibility*, a lively publication that promotes open discussion of controversial topics from all Judaic perspectives. He rejects the notion that Judaism is based on a heteronomous tradition or Jewish law; instead, he stresses the importance of autonomous choice and personal faith. Borowitz claims that a covenantal relationship with God forms the core of Reform Jewish theology and ethics.

BOOKS BY BOROWITZ

Choices in Modern Jewish Thought: A Partisan Guide. Behrman 1983 $9.95. ISBN 0-874-41343-5. An analysis and subjective appraisal of the thought of the major Jewish philosophers of the twentieth century, from Hermann Cohen to Joseph Soloveitchik.

Contemporary Christologies: A Jewish Response. Paulist Pr. 1980 $7.95. ISBN 0-809-12305-3. An original, highly recommended examination of and response to contemporary Christian doctrines of Christ—Catholic, Protestant, liberal, neo-Orthodox, evangelical, and postmodern.

Exploring Jewish Ethics: Papers on Covenant Responsibility. Wayne St. U. Pr. 1990 $49.95. ISBN 0-814-32199-2. Jewish applied ethics for twentieth-century America.

Liberal Judaism. UAHC 1984 $8.95. ISBN 0-807-40264-8. Constructs a theological system, expressing Reform attitudes toward the Jewish people, God, the Bible, ethics, and Jewish lifestyle, while emphasizing a covenantal relationship with God and the importance of autonomous choice in Reform Judaism.

The Masks Jews Wear: Self-Deceptions of American Jewry. S & S Trade 1973 o.p. Provocative and timely challenge to American Jews to come to terms with Jewish identity as an internal spiritual and ethical commitment.

A New Jewish Theology in the Making. Westminster John Knox 1968 o.p. The first articulation of Borowitz's theological system.

BUBER, MARTIN. 1878–1965

Martin Buber was born in Vienna, the son of Solomon Buber, an important scholar of Midrashic and medieval literature. Martin Buber studied at the universities of Vienna, Leipzig, Zurich, and Berlin, under WILHELM DILTHEY and Georg Simmel. As a young student, he joined the Zionist movement, advocating the renewal of Jewish culture as opposed to Theodor Herzl's political Zionism. At age 26 he became interested in Hasidic thought and translated the tales of NAHMAN OF BRATSLAV. Buber is responsible for bringing Hasidism to the attention of young German intellectuals who previously had scorned it as the product of ignorant eastern European Jewish peasants. Hasidism had a profound impact on Buber's thought. He credits it as being the inspiration for his theories of spirituality, community, and dialogue. Buber also wrote about utopian socialism, education, Zionism, and respect for the Palestinian Arabs, and, with FRANZ ROSENZWEIG, he translated the Bible. He was appointed to a professorship at the University of Frankfurt in 1925, but, when the Nazis came to power, he received an appointment at the Hebrew University of Jerusalem.

BOOKS BY BUBER

Between Man and Man. 1947. Trans. by Ronald Gregor Smith. Macmillan 1985 $12.00. ISBN 0-02-084210-4. An elaboration of the principles presented in *I and Thou*, with discussions of the theory of education and the thoughts of Kierkegaard, Kant, and others.

I and Thou. 1936. Trans. by S. G. Smith. Macmillan 1978 $35.00. ISBN 0-684-15575-3. The most important single work, developing a theory of interpersonal relations based on openness and respect and maintaining that God exists in the genuine encounter of one person with another.

On Judaism. Ed. by Nahum Glatzer. Schocken 1972 $12.00. ISBN 0-8052-0343-5. A collection of important essays on the nature of Judaism.

The Prophetic Faith. 1942. Peter Smith 1986 o.p. Buber's interpretations of the religion of the prophets.

Two Types of Faith: The Interpretation of Judaism and Christianity. 1961. Macmillan 1986 $8.95. ISBN 0-02-084180-9. Buber's openminded encounter with Jesus, Paul, and the teachings of Christianity.

The Writings of Martin Buber. Ed. by Will Herberg. NAL-Dutton 1974 o.p. Anthology presenting Buber's principal writings.

BOOKS ABOUT BUBER

Berry, Donald L. *Mutuality: The Vision of Martin Buber*. State U. NY Pr. 1985 $39.50. ISBN 0-873-95929-9. A short discussion of Buber's philosophy of dialogue.

Breslauer, S. Daniel. *Martin Buber on Myth: An Introduction*. Garland 1990 $44.00. ISBN 0-82403-721-9. Analyzes "the contribution of Martin Buber as a theorist on myth."

Diamond, Malcolm L. *Martin Buber: Jewish Existentialist*. Gannon U. Pr. 1968 o.p. The single most accessible account of Buber's thought seen as a whole system.

Friedman, Maurice S. *Encounter on the Narrow Ridge: A Life of Martin Buber*. Paragon Hse. 1991 $31.95. ISBN 1-557-78453-1. The first authoritative biography of Martin Buber.

———. *Martin Buber: The Life of Dialogue*. U. Ch. Pr. 3rd rev. ed. 1976 $13.00. ISBN 0-226-26356-8. Important scholarly account of the relationship between Buber's life and thought.

Kepnes, Steven. *The Text as Thou: Martin Buber's Dialogical Hermeneutics and Narrative Theology*. Ind. U. Pr. 1992 $35.00. ISBN 0-253-33127-7

Mendes-Flohr, Paul R. *From Mysticism to Dialogue: Martin Buber's Transformation of German Social Thought*. Wayne St. U. Pr. 1989 $32.95. ISBN 0-814-32028-7. A study of Buber from the perspective of the "romantic discontent" with modernity found in the thought of many central European intellectuals of the turn of the century.

Rotenstreich, Nathan. *Immediacy and Its Limits: A Study in Martin Buber's Thought*. Harwood Acad. Pub. 1991 o.p.

Silberstein, Laurence. *Martin Buber's Social and Religious Thought: Alienation and the Quest for Meaning*. NYU Pr. 1989 $35.00. ISBN 0-814-77886-0. An elucidation of Buber's intellectual enterprise, focusing upon the often overlooked theme of alienation.

COHEN, HERMANN. 1842–1918

The son of a cantor, Hermann Cohen studied at the Jewish Theological Seminary at Breslau but gave up a rabbinical career to study philosophy. He devoted himself to the analysis of Platonic and Kantian idealism and became full professor at the University of Marburg at the young age of 34. His personal philosophy placed ethics at the center of human experience. Late in life he left

Marburg to teach at the Hochschule für die Wissenschaft des Judentums in Berlin. Whereas his early writings located the realm of ethics within autonomous human reason, his work in Berlin saw God as the foundation for any ethical system.

BOOKS BY COHEN

Reason and Hope: Selections from the Jewish Writings of Hermann Cohen. Ed. and trans. by Eva Jospe. Norton 1971 o.p. Anthology of writings by the important German Jewish philosopher.

Religion of Reason out of the Sources of Judaism. 1919. Trans. by Simon Kaplan. Continuum 1971 o.p. First published posthumously, this classic text develops the doctrine of the uniqueness of God, maintaining that Judaism is rooted in reason and therefore can be logically derived and systematically explained; with an introduction by Leo Strauss.

BOOKS ABOUT COHEN

Kaplan, Mordecai. *The Purpose and Meaning of Jewish Existence.* JPS Phila. 1964 o.p. An epitome of and commentary on Hermann Cohen's *Religion of Reason out of the Sources of Judaism.*

Kluback, William. *The Legacy of Hermann Cohen.* Scholars Pr. GA 1989 $44.95. ISBN 1-555-40322-0. A collection of essays exploring Cohen's synthesis of reason and belief, highlighting in particular the place of socialism in Cohen's thought.

Melber, Jehuda. *Hermann Cohen's Philosophy of Judaism.* Jonathan David 1968 o.p. Good introduction to Cohen's difficult philosophy, showing the influences of classical Jewish sources and Kantian philosophy on his philosophic system.

FACKENHEIM, EMIL. 1916–

Fackenheim was born in Halle, Germany, and ordained at the Hochschule für die Wissenschaft des Judentums in Berlin in 1939. In 1940 he went to Canada, narrowly escaping the devastation of the Holocaust. Fackenheim became a professor at the University of Toronto, where he made important contributions to the study of HEGEL (see also Vol. 3) and German idealism. The 1960s saw a radical change in his philosophy, as he attempted to come to terms with the horror of the Holocaust. Arguing that the murder of Jews by the Nazis was qualitatively unique, a "novum" in history, he found that he no longer could think in terms of timeless and abstract philosophic systems, which do not account for the possibility of this radical evil. Fackenheim claims that Jews must not allow the Holocaust to weaken their faith, lest Hitler be given a posthumous victory. He sees the establishment of the State of Israel as a testimony to Jewish defiance in the face of Nazi oppression. Fackenheim recently moved to Jerusalem, where he articulates a Zionist view that Jewish life can be lived authentically once one is in the State of Israel.

BOOKS BY FACKENHEIM

Encounters between Judaism and Modern Philosophy: A Preface to Future Jewish Thought. Schocken 1980 repr. of 1973 ed. $7.95. ISBN 0-80520-656-6. Uses philosophic categories to refine Jewish thought in the aftermath of the Holocaust and discusses the implications of Kant, Hegel, Sartre, and Heidegger for contemporary Judaism.

God's Presence in History: Jewish Affirmations and Philosophical Reflections. HarpC 1973 $9.95. ISBN 0-06-131690-3. The most important statement of the leading Holocaust theologian in Reform Judaism.

The Jewish Bible after the Holocaust: A Re-Reading. Ind. U. Pr. 1991 $27.50. ISBN 0-719-03030-7. A moving theological interpretation of the Bible in light of the themes of Holocaust, identity, and survival.

The Jewish Thought of Emil Fackenheim: A Reader. Ed. and intro. by Michael L. Morgan.
   Wayne St. U. Pr. 1987 $39.95. ISBN 0-814-31820-7. A very good introduction to
   Fackenheim's thought, distilled from 40 years of writing, focusing on Fackenheim's
   shift in thinking about the Holocaust in the 1960s and on the systematic nature of his
   work.
To Mend the World: Foundations of Future Jewish Thought. Schocken 2nd ed. 1989
   $13.95. ISBN 0-80520-938-7. A reformulation and explanation of Fackenheim's post-
   Holocaust and Zionist theology, with a new preface by the author.

GERSONIDES (LEVI BEN GERSHON). 1288–1344

Levi ben Gershon, or Gersonides, wrote 16 major works on religious,
philosophic, mathematical, and medical topics. He spent most of his life in the
major papal cultural centers of southern France and maintained extensive
relations with Christian intellectuals. Gersonides was a supreme rationalist in
the tradition of MAIMONIDES, although they disagreed on a number of key points.
Gersonides held that humans can attain certain positive knowledge of God and
that humans possess a speculative intellect that permits the perception of truth
and the attainment of immortality.

BOOKS BY GERSONIDES

The Creation of the World According to Gersonides. Trans. by Jacob J. Staub. Scholars Pr.
   GA 1982 $20.00. ISBN 0-89130-526-2. Part 6 of *The War of the Lord*; it rejects
   Maimonides's contention that the creation of the world can be known philosophically.
Providence in the Philosophy of Gersonides. Trans. by David J. Bleich. Feldheim 1982 o.p.
   Translation of Part 4 of Gersonides' *The War of the Lord.*

HESCHEL, ABRAHAM JOSHUA. 1907–1972

Heschel received his doctorate at the Hochschule für die Wissenschaft des
Judentums in Berlin but was deported to Poland by the Nazis in 1938. He went
to London in 1940 and after the war accepted a professorship in ethics and
mysticism at the Jewish Theological Seminary in New York. Heschel articulated
a depth theology, arguing that the divine-human encounter takes place at a
deeper level than is attainable by the rational mind. Reaching out to skeptical
Jews and seeking to make Judaism accessible and meaningful in the modern
world, Heschel stressed the interdependence of God and humanity, and
maintained that God recognizes and supports ethical human action and that
humans express their faith through their actions. Heschel lived according to his
word and played an active role in social change, including the civil rights
movement.

BOOKS BY HESCHEL

Between God and Man: An Interpretation of Judaism. 1959. Ed. by Fritz Rothschild. Free
   Pr. 1965 $12.95. ISBN 0-02-914510-4. Anthology of 41 essays by Heschel, providing
   the best introduction to Heschel's philosophy of religion.
The Earth Is the Lord's: The Inner World of the Jew in Eastern Europe. 1950. FS&G 1978
   $8.95. ISBN 0-374-14613-6. Contends that the world of eastern European Jewry from
   the seventeenth through the nineteenth centuries was a "Golden Age," noting that
   these Jews sanctified time, rather than space, thereby making the Sabbath and the
   holy days the center of their spirituality.
God in Search of Man: A Philosophy of Judaism. Aronson 1987 repr. of 1955 ed. $30.00.
   ISBN 0-87668-955-1. Heschel's most important work, a full-scale theology of
   Judaism, covering all aspects of the faith as Heschel reads them.

I Asked for Wonder: A Spiritual Anthology. Ed. by Samuel H. Dresner. Crossroad NY 1983
    $8.95. ISBN 0-824-50542-5. A short collection of brief selections of Heschel's
    writings, unfortunately presented out of context.
The Insecurity of Freedom: Essays on Human Existence. Schocken 1985 repr. of 1966 ed.
    o.p. A collection of Heschel's political, ethical, and religious writings, on religion in
    a free society, civil rights, Zionism, and many other topics.
Israel: An Echo of Eternity. FS&G 1969 o.p. Discusses the role of Jerusalem and the Land
    of Israel in Jewish theology, with a chapter on the contemporary Arab-Israeli
    conflict.
A Passion for Truth. 1973. FS&G 1986 $9.95. ISBN 0-374-22992-9. Tour de force
    comparison of a Hasidic rabbi, the Kotzker, and Kierkegaard.
The Sabbath: Its Meaning for Modern Man. FS&G 1975 o.p. A profound and poetic book
    on the meaning of the Sabbath and the sacredness of time in Judaism.

BOOKS ABOUT HESCHEL

Fierman, Morton. *Leap of Action: Ideas in the Theology of Abraham Joshua Heschel.* U. Pr.
    of Amer. 1989 $40.00. ISBN 0-819-17567-6. An easy, though somewhat superficial,
    guide to Heschel's thought on freedom, peace, racism, justice, Israel, Sabbath,
    commandments.
Merkle, John C. *The Genesis of Faith: The Depth Psychology of Abraham Joshua Heschel.*
    Macmillan 1985 $19.95. ISBN 0-02-920990-0. Traces the influences on Heschel's
    thought, such as the spiritual sources of faith, the mystery of creation, and the
    literary sources of Judaism.
Moore, Donald. *The Human and the Holy: The Spirituality of Abraham Joshua Heschel.*
    Fordham 1989 $29.95. ISBN 0-823-21235-1. Helpful introduction concentrating on
    Heschel's religious anthropology.
Perlman, Lawrence. *Abraham Heschel's Idea of Revelation.* Scholars Pr. GA 1989 $44.95.
    ISBN 1-555-40350-6. How to read Heschel's works so as to identify theological and
    philosophical coherence.
Sherwin, Byron L. *Abraham Joshua Heschel.* Westminster John Knox 1978 o.p. Short (50-
    page) discussion of 10 important themes that pervade Heschel's work and of the
    actual and potential influence of his writings on Judaism and Christianity.

HIRSCH, SAMSON (BEN) RAPHAEL. 1808–1888

The foremost leader of nineteenth-century German Orthodoxy, Hirsch had a
background in Talmud in addition to some study of Greek and Roman classics
at the University of Bonn. He is best known for his passionate advocacy of
Orthodoxy and his polemics against the new Reform movement. He opposed
any notion of historical development of Jewish laws and customs. Hirsch's ideas
and methods continue to shape the lives of many contemporary Jews.

BOOKS BY HIRSCH

The Collected Writings. 3 vols. Feldheim 1984–85 $18.95 ea. ISBNs 0-87306-364-3, 0-
    87306-951-X, 0-87306-924-2
Horeb: A Philosophy of Jewish Laws and Observances. Trans. by I. Grunfled. Bloch 1962
    $19.95. ISBN 1-871055-01-6. An important and detailed account of Jewish obser-
    vance, explaining the ideas and values behind each law.
The Nineteen Letters of Ben Uziel on Judaism. Trans. by Bernard Drachman. Shalom 1969
    $27.50. ISBN 0-87559-076-4. A classic attack on the early Reform movement, written
    in the form of fictional letters between a young intellectual with religious doubts and
    a passionate young Orthodox rabbi.

BOOK ABOUT HIRSCH

Rosenbloom, Noah H. *Tradition in an Age of Reform: The Religious Philosophy of Samson
    Raphael Hirsch.* JPS Phila. 1976 o.p. Authoritative intellectual biography of the
    founder of German Orthodox Judaism.

JOSEPHUS, FLAVIUS. c.a.d. 38–100

Josephus claimed to embody personally many strains of first-century Judaism: His family lineage connected him to the Hasmonean rulers and the priestly caste, his education and religious quest gave him experience with the three major sects of first-century Judaism, and his military command and defeat landed him on both sides of the Jewish war against Rome (A.D. 66–73). His unusual life makes his autobiography, *The Life*, interesting reading. More important, his historical works, *The Jewish War* and *The Jewish Antiquities*, record information about Jewish life in Palestine during the first century. His accounts are frequently subjective and apologetic, but they represent the only extant sources on many significant details of this pivotal century. Even though he became a Roman citizen, Josephus remained a committed Jew. His *Against Apion* (not published separately) is a polemical defense of Judaism that attacks anti-Jewish arguments and asserts the ethical superiority of Judaism over Hellenism.

Books by Josephus

Flavius Josephus: Selections from His Works. Ed. by Abraham Hasserstein. Viking Penguin 1974 o.p. Readable translation from the full range of Josephus' works, designed for the nonspecialist.

The Jewish War. Trans. by G. A. Williamson. Ed. by E. Mary Smallwood. *Penguin Class. Ser.* Viking Penguin 1984 $9.95. ISBN 0-14-044420-3. An alternative translation, not to be ignored, that includes a glossary, maps, and appendices.

Josephus. 9 vols. HUP 1926–65 o.p. This is the standard translation of the *War, History,* and other works.

Books about Josephus

Rajak, Tessa. *Josephus: The Historian and His Society.* Augsburg Fortress 1984 $24.95. ISBN 0-800-60717-1. The best contemporary biography of Josephus, judicious, informed, lucid, and well argued.

Rhoads, David M. *Israel in Revolution 6–74 c.e.: A Political History Based on the Writings of Josephus.* Augsburg Fortress 1976 o.p. A good account, but superseded by Rajak.

Schwartz, Seth. *Josephus and Judaean Politics. Columbia Studies in the Classical Tradition, Vol. 18.* E. J. Brill 1990 $57.00. ISBN 9-004-09230-7. Argues that "by determining who constituted the Jewish part of Josephus' social environment and analyzing the content of his Jewish political propaganda and polemics, we shall be able to recover a great deal of the history of Jewish politics in the 30 years after the destruction of Jerusalem."

Thackeray, Henry. *Josephus: The Man and the Historian.* Ktav 1968 $20.00. ISBN 0-87068-115-X. A brief and somewhat dated but well-written and interesting biography, by a great Josephus scholar.

Williamson, G. A. *The World of Josephus.* Little 1960 o.p. This readable biography places Josephus in historical context, offering a good way to learn about the political and cultural circumstances of the first century.

JUDAH HALEVI. c.1075–1141

Judah Halevi, a Spanish-born poet, philosopher, and physician, left a large volume of writings. His major philosophic work, *The Kuzari*, takes the form of a dialogue with a pagan king of the Khazars who seeks spiritual direction. Judah Halevi asserts the superiority of Rabbinic Judaism over Christianity and Islam. He claims that the God of Israel is known through the received tradition and not through philosophy, with its syllogisms and mathematical reasoning.

BOOK BY JUDAH HALEVI

The Kuzari: An Argument for the Faith of Israel. 1964. Trans. by H. Hirschfeld. Schocken 1987 $14.95. ISBN 0-8052-0075-4. Originally published in 1905, this clearly written translation remains the standard English edition and features a new introduction by Henry Slonimsky.

KAPLAN, MORDECAI MENAHEIM. 1881–1983

Kaplan emigrated to the United States from Lithuania at the age of 8. After graduating from Columbia University in 1902, he was ordained a Conservative rabbi by the Jewish Theological Seminary of America, where he taught for the next 50 years. His attempts to adapt Judaism to the modern world—particularly to the American situation—led to the establishment of a new movement, Reconstructionism. He saw Judaism as representing, first and foremost, a religious civilization and proposed a Jewish theology shaped by Jewish experience and Jewish ethics.

BOOKS BY KAPLAN

Dynamic Judaism: The Essential Writings of Mordecai M. Kaplan. Ed. by Emanuel S. Goldsmith and Mel Scult. Schocken 1985 $22.00. ISBN 0-805-23997-9. Short pieces arranged by topic, with an introduction on Kaplan's life and his view of Judaism.
The Future of the American Jew. 1948. Reconstructionist Pr. 1981 $13.95. ISBN 0-935457-13-5. Classic work of the founder of Reconstructionism on the nature of the American Jewish community.
Judaism as a Civilization: Toward a Reconstruction of American-Jewish Life. 1934. JPS Phila. 1981 $25.00. ISBN 0-827-60193-X. Most important theological statement of Reconstructionism.

BOOKS ABOUT KAPLAN

Goldsmith, Emanuel S., Mel Scult, and Robert Seltzer, eds. *The American Judaism of Mordecai M. Kaplan. Reappraisals in Jewish Social and Intellectual History Ser.* NYU Pr. 1990 $45.00. ISBN 0-814-73024-8. A collection of essays placing Kaplan's thought within the formation of American Judaism as a religion and culture.
Libowitz, Richard. *Mordecai M. Kaplan and the Development of Reconstructionism. Studies in Amer. Religion.* E. Mellen 1984 $49.95. ISBN 0-889-46651-3. Monograph on Kaplan that analyzes each of his many writings and describes the various figures who influenced his thought.

MAIMONIDES (MOSES BEN MAIMON). 1135–1204

Maimonides (Moses ben Maimon) was born in Cordoba, Spain, but spent his most productive years in Cairo, where he served as a royal physician. The Arabic cultural environment brought him into contact with classical Greek philosophy. Maimonides fused neo-Aristotelian philosophy with the Jewish legal tradition into a systemic whole. His main philosophic work, *The Guide for the Perplexed*, is an apologetic appeal to rationalists troubled by the corporeality of God in the biblical accounts. He proposes a philosophic interpretation of the Bible that emphasizes abstract and spiritual meaning over literal interpretation. Maimonides formulated the 13 principles of faith that represent the irreducible core of Judaism.

BOOKS BY MAIMONIDES

The Book of Knowledge. Trans. by Moses Hyamson. Edinburgh 1981 $13.95. ISBN 0-854-05038-8. Translation of the first book of the *Mishnah Torah*, which is devoted to ethical issues, unlike the rest of the document.

Ethical Writings of Maimonides. Ed. and trans. by Raymond L. Weiss and Charles E.
    Butterworth. Dover 1983 $4.50. ISBN 0-486-24522-5. Anthology of seven passages on
    various ethical and philosophic topics.
The Guide for the Perplexed. Ed. and trans. by S. Pines. Peter Smith repr. of 1904 ed.
    $20.00. ISBN 0-8446-2512-4
Treatise on Resurrection. Trans. by Fred Rosner. Ktav 1982 o.p. Annotated translation of
    a treatise, attributed to Maimonides, on the problem of God's unity, the messianic
    age, resurrection, and the world to come.

BOOKS ABOUT MAIMONIDES

Dienstag, Jacob I., ed. *Eschatology in Maimonidean Thought: Messianism, Resurrection
    and the World to Come*. Ktav 1983 $39.50. ISBN 0-870-68706-9. Philosophic essays
    on medieval views of the Messiah, immortality, and resurrection, with selections
    from Maimonides and an extensively annotated bibliography.
Fox, Marvin. *Interpreting Maimonides: Studies in Methodology, Metaphysics, and Moral
    Philosophy*. U. Ch. Pr. 1990 $27.00. ISBN 0-226-25941-2. A good general reference
    work for nonspecialists.
Goldfield, Lea Naomi. *An Inquiry into the Authenticity of Moses Maimonides' Treatise on
    Resurrection*. Ktav 1985 $29.95. ISBN 0-88125-088-0. Convincingly argues that the
    "Treatise on the Resurrection" has been falsely attributed to Maimonides.
Goodman, Lenn E., ed. and trans. *Readings in the Philosophy of Moses Maimonides*. Gee
    Tee Bee 1978 o.p. Good one-volume anthology by a brilliant scholar of medieval
    Jewish and Arab philosophy.
Hartman, David. *Maimonides: Torah and Philosophic Quest*. JPS Phila. 1976 o.p. Effort to
    reconstruct Maimonides' philosophic system so as to integrate his philosophic
    writing, namely, *The Guide to the Perplexed*, and his legal writings.
Heschel, Abraham Joshua. *Maimonides*. Trans. by Joachim Neugroschel. FS&G 1982
    $15.00. ISBN 0-374-19874-8. An engaging intellectual biography, originally pub-
    lished in German in 1935, that brings to life Maimonides' faith and the pressing
    questions of his age.
Kravitz, Leonard. *The Hidden Doctrine of Maimonides' Guide for the Perplexed:
    Philosophical and Religious God-Language in Tension*. E. Mellen 1988 $59.95. ISBN
    0-889-46253-4. An introduction to the *Guide to the Perplexed*. Difficult reading.
Rosner, Fred. *Sex Ethics in the Writings of Moses Maimonides*. Bloch 1974 o.p.
    Description of Maimonides' legal rulings and philosophic writings on sexuality and
    sex roles.
Twersky, Isadore. *A Maimonides Reader*. Behrman 1972 $9.95. ISBN 0-874-41200-5. An
    anthology of Maimonides' philosophic and legal writings, with a strong introduction
    by Twersky.
Weiss, Raymond. *Maimonides Ethics: The Encounter of Philosophic and Religious
    Morality*. U. Ch. Pr. 1991 $29.95. ISBN 0-226-89152-6. An exhaustive review of the
    virtues treated by Maimonides.

NAHMAN OF BRATSLAV. 1772–1811

The great-grandson of BA'AL SHEM TOV, Nahman of Bratslav attracted
attention from an early age. He continually provoked the ire of important anti-
Hasidic and Hasidic figures and advocated a theory of "controversy" as a test of
faith. He tells of the incredible obstacles he endured on a journey to Palestine as
evidence of his being the Messiah. Much of what we know about Nahman comes
from Nathan, his disciple and scribe. Nathan helped to establish the Bratslaver
Hasidic movement that continues to flourish today in Jerusalem. Nathan
records 13 tales, whose meaning is so powerful yet obscure that many authors
have embellished them to make them accessible.

BOOK BY NAHMAN OF BRATSLAV

The Tales of Rabbi Nahman of Bratslav. Trans. by Arnold Band. *Classics of Western Spirituality*. Paulist Pr. 1980 o.p. The only direct translation, without embellishment, of the strange and powerful stories of Nahman of Bratslav, introduced by a short but excellent essay that places Nahman in the context of Hasidic storytelling.

BOOKS ABOUT NAHMAN OF BRATSLAV

Buber, Martin. *Tales of Rabbi Nachman*. Trans. by Maurice Friedman. Humanities 1988 $15.00. ISBN 0-391-03548-7. Buber wrote in 1956, "I have not translated these tales, but retold them with full freedom, yet out of his spirit as it is present to me."

Green, Arthur. *Tormented Master: A Life of Rabbi Nahman of Bratslav*. Schocken 1981 $11.95. ISBN 0-817-36907-4. One of the few academic treatments of the Hasidic movement; Green uses psychoanalytic categories to explain the unusual life and writings of this self-proclaimed "suffering Messiah."

Kaplan, Aryeh. *Until the Mashiach: Rabbi Nachman's Biography, An Annotated Chronology*. Breslov Rsch. Inst. 1985 o.p. A detailed but uncritical study of the life of Nahman, by a leader in the contemporary Bratslav movement.

Schwartz, Howard. *The Captive Soul of the Messiah: New Tales about Reb Nachman*. Schocken 1983 $17.95. ISBN 0-805-23873-5. Another creative retelling of the life of Nahman—this time by a contemporary Jewish poet.

Steinsaltz, Adin. *Beggars and Prayers: Adin Steinsaltz Retells the Tales of Rabbi Nahman of Bratslav*. Trans. by Yehuda Hanegbi. Basic 1985 $9.95. ISBN 0-465-00581-0. Here is yet another adaptation of six of Nahman's stories.

NAHMANIDES (MOSES BEN NAHMAN, also RAMBAN). 1194–c.1270

Moses ben Nahman, also known as the Ramban, was an important Spanish philosopher, mystic, biblical exegete, and poet. His commentaries on the Hebrew Bible were written late in life, in the Land of Israel, after he was expelled from Spain because of his frequent anti-Christian polemics. He focused on the deeper meanings of biblical passages as opposed to the surface meanings of words. He frequently cited Rabbinic and medieval commentaries but took an independent stance that was sometimes critical of these works. Nahmanides's many comments on the Talmud and on Cabala, when taken as a whole, reflect an original mind that had considerable influence on the development of Jewish thought in Spain.

BOOK BY NAHMANIDES

Ramban (Nahmanides) Commentary on the Torah. Trans. by Charles B. Chavel. 5 vols. Shilo Pub. Hse. 1971 $99.75. ISBN 0-686-86743-2. Collection of Nahmanides's commentaries to the Pentateuch, from Genesis to Numbers.

BOOKS ABOUT NAHMANIDES

Chavel, Charles B. *Ramban: His Life and His Teachings*. Feldheim 1963 o.p. A general introduction to the life, thought, and writings of Nahmanides, with extensive translations of his biblical commentaries.

Chazan, Robert. *Barcelona and Beyond: The Disputation of 1263 and Its Aftermath*. U. CA Pr. 1992 o.p. A careful study of Nahmanides's disputation regarding the truth of Christianity.

Twersky, Isadore, ed. *Rabbi Moses Nahmanides: Explorations in His Religious and Literary Virtuosity*. HUP 1983 $9.50. ISBN 0-674-74560-4. Collection of essays, often quite technical, on Nahmanides's philosophy, mysticism, and biblical commentary.

PHILO JUDAEUS. c.20 B.C.–c.A.D. 50

Philo was born to a prominent family in the large and prosperous Jewish community of Alexandria, Egypt, and received an education in classical Greek philosophy. He interpreted Jewish tradition from the point of view of contemporary Hellenistic culture, by employing an original, allegorical method to synthesize biblical theology with Greek philosophy. His etymologies of biblical terms are philologically dubious but highly imaginative. Philo represents the first Jewish thinker known to us who articulated a systematic theology, and his philosophic writings had an enormous influence on the early Christian church and on medieval philosophy in general.

BOOK BY PHILO

Philo. Ed. and trans. by F. H. Colson. 5 vols. HUP 1929–62 o.p. The accepted translation.

BOOKS ABOUT PHILO

Berchman, Robert M. *From Philo to Origen: Middle Platonism in Transition. Brown Judaic Studies.* Scholars Pr. GA 1985 $29.95. ISBN 0891307508. An original thesis on the links between Philo and Origen, the Church Father.

Goodenough, Erwin R. *By Light, Light: The Mystic Gospel of Hellenistic Judaism.* Yale U. Pr. 1935 o.p. Links the thought and system of Philo to the Hellenistic philosophy of the time and place, interpreting Philo's thought as a system of a profoundly mystical character within the Platonic thought-world.

———. *An Introduction to Philo Judaeus.* U. Pr. of Amer. 1986 o.p. The best introduction to the subject.

———. *The Politics of Philo Judaeus: Practice and Theory.* Elliots Bks. 1938 $100.00. ISBN 0-685-69822-X. An original and important account of the political system of Philo and of the Jews of Alexandria, the most important Diaspora community in their day.

Mendelson, Alan. *Secular Education in Philo of Alexandria.* Ktav 1982 $20.00. ISBN 0-878-20406-7. Assesses Philo's appropriation of Hellenistic culture "alien" to his Jewish background.

Sandmel, Samuel. *Philo of Alexandria: An Introduction.* OUP 1979 $9.95. ISBN 0-19-502514-8. A useful introduction to the subject, not up to the masterful standard of Goodenough, but not to be forgotten.

Winston, David, and John Dillon. *Two Treatises of Philo of Alexandria: A Commentary on De Gigantibus and Quod Deus Sit Immutabilis.* Scholars Pr. GA 1983 $15.00. ISBN 0-891-30563-7. A fresh translation and commentary on two important tractates.

Wolfson, Harry A. *Philo: Foundations of Religious Philosophy in Judaism, Christianity and Islam.* 2 vols. HUP rev. ed. 1962 $65.00. ISBN 0-674-66450-7. Links the thought and system of Philo to the Judaic philosophy of a later time and different place, interpreting Philo's thought as a system of a profoundly rational, philosophical character within the Judaic-Rabbinic thought-world.

RASHI (SOLOMON BEN ISAAC). 1040–1105

Rashi (from the acronym for his full name, Rabbi Solomon ben Isaac) of Troyes, France, wrote the most famous medieval commentaries to the Hebrew Bible. His commentaries are written in a simple, lucid, and uniform style. He provides a synthesis of Rabbinic interpretation, altering and abridging Midrashic citations, as well as adding his own insightful comments. Rashi utilized the so-called peshat method of exegesis, which interpreted the Bible in terms of the world of ancient Israel. In this way, he explained complex and ambiguous passages by adducing details from the biblical world and by analyzing the Hebrew language. Rashi also produced the most influential commentary to the Babylonian Talmud—no edition of this Talmud has been printed without it.

BOOKS ABOUT RASHI

Halperin, Herman. *Rashi and the Christian Scholars*. U. of Pittsburgh Pr. 1963 o.p. Compares the writings of Rashi and Nichlaus de Lyra to show the relationship between Jewish and Christian biblical exegesis during the medieval period.

Liber, Maurice. *Rashi: His Life and Works*. Trans. by Adele Szold. Hermon 1971 repr. of 1906 ed. o.p. This in-depth study remains the best introduction to Rashi's thought.

Shereshevsky, Esra. *Rashi: The Man and His World*. Hermon 1982 $22.50. ISBN 0-87203-101-2. Comprehensive biography that places Rashi's work in the context of the Jewish world in which he lived and contains chapters on "the world through Rashi's eyes" that gather remarks from his biblical and Talmudic commentaries in order to reconstruct details about daily life in the medieval world.

ROSENZWEIG, FRANZ. 1886–1929

Rosenzweig was born in 1886 to intellectual and assimilated parents. He studied philosophy, history, and classics. While he was at university, many of his friends and relatives converted to Christianity, and he came close to converting, until a visit to an Orthodox synagogue on the eve of Yom Kippur inspired him to "return" to Judaism. His doctoral thesis, *Hegel and the State*, was published in 1920, and he then began to devote his energies to the construction of a Jewish philosophic system. The result, *The Star of Redemption* (1921), has become a classic, combining German idealism, existentialism, and Jewish tradition into a complex and enduring system. In 1921 a progressive paralysis set in and, although he soon lost his mobility and power of speech, he continued his intellectual activities for seven years. Rosenzweig's wife deciphered his signals, and, among other activities, he began a new translation of the Hebrew Bible (with MARTIN BUBER, who finished it in the 1950s), utilizing a style of German that attempted to retain the spirit of the original Hebrew.

BOOKS BY ROSENZWEIG

Judaism Despite Christianity: The "Letters on Christianity and Judaism" between Eugen Rosenstock-Huessy and Franz Rosenzweig. U. of Ala. Pr. 1969 $16.50. ISBN 0-817-36606-7. Classic exchange of letters between two German soldiers during World War I, a German Christian of Jewish descent and a German Jew.

The Star of Redemption. 1921. U. of Notre Dame Pr. 1985 repr. of 1971 ed. $30.00. ISBN 0-268-01717-4. Assumes a great deal of knowledge about German philosophy. Foreword by Nahum N. Glatzer.

BOOKS ABOUT ROSENZWEIG

Gibbs, Robert. *Correlations in Rosenzweig and Levinas*. Princeton U. Pr. 1992 $29.95. ISBN 0-691-07415-1. A new interpretation of the key figures in modern Jewish philosophy argues that Levinas has much to say about Judaism, and Rosenzweig, about universally accessible concepts.

Glatzer, Nahum N. *Franz Rosenzweig: His Life and Thought*. Schocken 2nd ed. 1962 o.p. An engaging biography and anthology of his writings by a former colleague.

Miller, Ronald Henry. *Dialogue and Disagreement: Franz Rosenzweig's Relevance to Contemporary Jewish-Christian Understanding*. U. Pr. of Amer. 1990 $57.00. ISBN 0-819-17539-0. Foreword by Ycchiel Eckstein.

Moses, Stephane. *System and Revelation: The Philosophy of Franz Rosenzweig*. Trans. by Catherine Tihanyi. Wayne St. U. Pr. 1992 $39.95. ISBN 0-814-32128-3. Foreword by Emmanuel Levinas.

SAADIA GAON (SAADIA BEN JOSEPH AL-FAYUMI). 882–942

Born in Egypt, Saadia ben Joseph al-Fayumi became the leader, or "Gaon," of the Babylonian Jewish community. He issued virulent attacks against the powerful Karaite movement, which rejected the authority of Rabbinic Judaism. Saadia is reputed to be the first medieval philosopher to write monographs on topics of Jewish law and the first to write in Arabic. Saadia also was the first Jew to elaborate systematic and formal proofs of the existence of God. He took an interest in liturgy, grammar, and astrology. His theological and mystical writings on the shekinah (divine presence) and the Ruah ha-Kodesh (holy spirit) influenced medieval Hasidism and Cabala.

BOOK BY SAADIA GAON

The Book of Beliefs and Opinions. Trans. by Samuel Rosenblatt. Yale U. Pr. 1948 o.p. The standard translation of Saadia's major philosophic work, with a brief introduction and extensive notation.

BOOK ABOUT SAADIA GAON

Malter, Henry. *Saadia Gaon: His Life and Works.* Hermon 1969 o.p. A detailed biography examining Saadia's philosophic, liturgical, and philological writings.

SCHOLEM, GERSHOM. 1897–1982

Gershom Scholem's contribution to the understanding of Jewish mysticism is so dramatic that it warrants a separate introduction. As a young student of mathematics, he became a Zionist and his interest shifted to Jewish history. Scholem moved from Germany to become the librarian of the new University and National Library in Jerusalem in 1923 and served as a professor at Hebrew University from 1935 to 1965. Before him, Jewish historians during the nineteenth and early twentieth centuries scorned the ignored mystical dimension of Judaism as a relic of premodern superstition and ignorance. Scholem's erudition and deep insight gave Cabala a scholarly audience. His writings are often difficult to read, but they are indispensable for any thorough knowledge of the subject of Jewish mysticism.

BOOKS BY SCHOLEM

Major Trends in Jewish Mysticism. 1941. Schocken 1988 repr. of 1961 ed. $8.95. ISBN 0-805-20005-3. The classic book on the topic, which integrates a great deal of material to show the development and continuity of Jewish mysticism over the last two millennia.

The Messianic Idea in Judaism and Other Essays on Jewish Spirituality. ADL 1972 $7.95. ISBN 0-686-95141-7. Another important collection of essays on topics spanning the entire history of Judaism.

On Jews and Judaism in Crisis: Selected Essays. Ed. by Werner J. Dannháuser. Schocken 1978 $16.50. ISBN 0-805-23613-9. Episodic observations on twentieth-century German and Israeli Jewry; not his most important book.

On the Kabbalah and Its Symbolism. 1965. Schocken 1969 $12.00. ISBN 0-8052-0235-8. Collection of essays focused on the symbolism, ritual, and ideas of medieval Cabala.

Origins of the Kabbalah. Trans. by Allan Arkush, ed. by R. J. Zwi Weblowsky. Princeton U. Pr. 1987 $47.50. ISBN 0-691-07314-7. This in-depth study demonstrates that Cabala existed in southern France in the twelfth century, prior to the composition of the *Zohar* in Spain at the end of the thirteenth century.

Zohar—The Book of Splendor: Basic Readings from the Kabbalah. (ed.) Schocken 1963 $11.00. ISBN 0-8052-0045-2. A short anthology without adequate annotation or explanation.

BOOKS ABOUT SCHOLEM

Biale, David. *Gershom Scholem: Kabbalah and Counter-history.* HUP 2nd ed. 1982 $7.95. ISBN 0-674-36330-2. A good introduction to Scholem's thought and scholarship that places him in the context of the historical Science of Judaism movement and developments in German Jewish philosophy.

Schweid, Eliezer. *Judaism and Mysticism According to Gershom Scholem: A Critical Analysis and Programmatic Discussion.* Trans. by David A. Weiner. Scholars Pr. GA 1985 $22.95. ISBN 0-891-30887-3. A complex critical reappraisal of Scholem's understanding of Jewish philosophy and mysticism.

SOLOVEITCHIK, JOSEPH. 1903–1993

Born to a family of important rabbis, Soloveitchik has become the most important twentieth-century philosopher of Orthodox Judaism. He resides in Boston but serves as the head of the Theology Seminary of Yeshiva University in New York. Soloveitchik is well schooled in modern philosophy; his doctoral dissertation at the University of Berlin was on HERMANN COHEN's epistemology. His knowledge of Jewish law is unsurpassed. He brings together existentialism, neo-Kantian rationalism, and Orthodox faith into a complex system of thought.

BOOKS BY SOLOVEITCHIK

Halakhic Man. 1944. Trans. by Lawrence Kaplan. JPS Phila. 1984 $12.95. ISBN 0-827-60222-7. Classic statement of Orthodox rationalism in an excellent translation with notes and obervations. Here Soloveitchik presents his famous existentialist typology of humanity based on the two personalities of Adam in the book of Genesis.

The Halakhic Mind: An Essay on Jewish Tradition and Modern Thought. Free Pr. 1985 $16.95. ISBN 0-02-930040-1. Originally written in 1944, and here published for the first time, this monograph argues that Orthodox Judaism represents a valid metaphysical and epistemological system but liberal (i.e., non-Orthodox) Judaism does not. Here Soloveitchik defies the usual label given to him of neo-Kantianism. Difficult reading.

SPINOZA, BARUCH (or BENEDICT).

[SEE Chapter 6 in this volume.]

CHAPTER 14

Early and Medieval Christianity

Maureen A. Tilley

> Our current events will someday become ancient history indispensable to
> those who are our successors.
>
> —*The Passion of Perpetua*

Christianity has been an enormously influential religious tradition in the history
of the Western world. Understanding this tradition is important in comprehend-
ing the history, art, architecture, and literature of much of the West. The pages
that follow provide the reader with some of the more important resources for
unlocking the tradition and understanding its influence.

In the first century of the Common Era (C.E.), Christianity emerged from its
status as a sect of Judaism into an independent religion. Rooted in Judaism, it
developed under several influences in the Greco-Roman world: worship of the
emperor as a divine being, mystery religions with their impressive rituals, the
panoply of polytheistic state religion. In striving for an identity, Christians
pondered and debated many issues. Key among them was the nature of the
divine. Whereas in Judaism, a being was considered divine—or not—and there
was only one God, in the larger world, people believed in degrees of divinity,
from the One above all to heroes like Hercules. Christians wrestled with
articulating the nature of Jesus in that light. They also struggled to define their
participation in the larger world, whether as ascetics, martyrs, or participants in
Roman government. In addition, Christians needed to define themselves as an
autonomous society—one with organized, hierarchically structured communities, with well-defined borders. The final concern that can be traced through
this period involved the relation between reason and revelation. ST. AUGUSTINE
OF HIPPO once said that "understanding is the reward of faith. Therefore seek
not to understand that thou mayest believe, but believe that thou mayest
understand." This quote characterizes one prevalent attitude toward this issue
during the ancient and medieval Church, but this view was by no means the
only one. Some Christians discounted the necessity of the intellect in matters of
faith; others viewed philosophical proof of theological issues as not only
possible but necessary. Yet Christianity is not simply a single religious tradition.
One might more properly speak of *Christianities*. Throughout any study one
must keep in mind that Christianity was a worldwide entity. Nevertheless, its
manifestations, even in the present, reflect the particular societies in which
Christians find themselves.

Much of what occurs in later Christianity has its antecedents in the ancient
and medieval Church, the period covered in this chapter. Christianity did
change, and change dramatically, in the period beginning with the Reformation
and after, but the changes that occurred were not molded out of an entirely new
piece of clay inasmuch as they were primarily reshaped from existing material.

The events and developments of Christianity in the modern period need to be understood in light of the ideas, events, and personalities discussed in this chapter.

GENERAL REFERENCES

Reference Works

Attwater, Donald. *The Penguin Dictionary of Saints*. Ed. by Catherine R. John. Viking Penguin rev. ed. 1984 $8.95. ISBN 0-14-051123-7. "This book is a work of quick reference to the lives and legends of the more important and interesting people among the Christian saints."

Brauer, Jerald C, ed. *Westminster Dictionary of Church History*. Westminster John Knox 1971 $32.00. ISBN 0-664-21285-9. A brief, reliable, one-volume dictionary giving "an immediate, accurate, introductory definition and explanation concerning the major persons, events, facts, and movements in the history of Christianity."

Butler, Alban. *Lives of the Saints*. Ed. by Herbert K. Thurston and Donald Attwater. 4 vols. Chr. Classics 1956 $140.00. ISBN 0-870610-137-2. Short biographies of over 2,500 saints organized according to the church calendar.

Cross, F. L, and Elizabeth A. Livingstone. *The Oxford Dictionary of the Christian Church*. OUP 1974 $65.00. ISBN 0-19-211545-6. The best one-volume encyclopedia in the field, particularly strong in the areas of doctrine, biography, and worship.

Davies, J. G., ed. *The New Westminster Dictionary of Liturgy and Worship*. Westminster John Knox 1986 $30.00. ISBN 0-664-21270-0. Good basic information and up-to-date bibliography on a large number of items in a restricted subject area.

Douglas, J. D., and Earle E. Cairns, eds. *The New International Dictionary of the Christian Church*. Zondervan 1988 $34.99. ISBN 0-310-23830-7. Quick orientation to the entire sweep of church history, especially strong on biography.

Harvey, Van A. *A Handbook of Theological Terms*. Macmillan 1964 $5.95. ISBN 0-02-085430-7. An explanation of over 300 theological terms that illumine the history of doctrine and help to differentiate Roman Catholic, Protestant, and Eastern Orthodox viewpoints.

Kelly, J. N. *The Oxford Dictionary of Popes*. OUP 1989 $29.95. ISBN 0-19-213964-6. A useful reference tool covering the biographies of all popes through John Paul II in concise articles that reflect painstaking scholarship and fulfill the needs of the general reader.

Livingstone, E. A., ed. *The Concise Oxford Dictionary of the Christian Church*. OUP 1980 $11.95. ISBN 0-19-283014-7. Excerpts from the larger volume (see Cross and Livingstone above); no bibliographies.

Macdonald, W. J., and others, eds. *The New Catholic Encyclopedia*. 15 vols. plus 3 supp. vols. J. Heraty Assocs. 1981 $875.00. ISBN 0-07-010235-X. A comprehensive multivolume religious encyclopedia containing 17,000 articles "on subjects ranging from the Doctrine of Atonement and St. Paul to Comic Books and International Trade."

McManners, John, ed. *The Oxford Illustrated History of Christianity*. OUP 1990 $45.00. ISBN 0-19-822-928-3. Popular history, written by 18 scholars; includes essays arranged chronologically.

O'Carroll, Michael. *Corpus Christi: A Theological Encyclopedia of the Eucharist*. Liturgical Pr. 1988 $42.00. ISBN 0-8146-5687-0. Articles and full bibliographies on the history and theology of one of the more important Christian doctrines.

_____. *Theotokos: A Theological Encyclopedia of the Blessed Virgin Mary*. Liturgical Pr. 1982 $24.95. ISBN 0-8146-5268-9. Entries written in a crisp, clear prose and supplied with the latest bibliography comprising a standard tool for readers interested in any aspect of Mariology (the study of the Virgin Mary).

_____. *Trinitas: A Theological Encyclopedia of the Holy Trinity*. Liturgical 1986 $35.00. ISBN 0-8146-5595-5. The same quality and coverage as the *Theotokos* volume.

Rahner, Karl, ed. *Encyclopedia of Theology: The Concise Sacramentum Mundi.* Crossroad NY rev. ed. 1975 $49.50. ISBN 0-8245-0303-1. A one-volume condensation of a major international Catholic theological dictionary featuring general survey articles on broad subjects.

Richardson, Alan, and John Bowden, eds. *The Westminster Dictionary of Christian Theology.* Westminster John Knox 1983 $30.00. ISBN 0-664-21398-7. Revised edition of editor Alan Richardson's *A Dictionary of Christian Theology* (Westminster 1969 o.p.).

Wakefield, Gordon S., ed. *The Westminster Dictionary of Christian Spirituality.* Westminster John Knox 1983 $28.00. ISBN 0-664-21396-0. A modern ecumenical dictionary on the spiritual life and prayer.

Walsh, Michael, ed. *Butler's Lives of the Saints.* HarpC 1985 $21.95. ISBN 0-06-069251-0. A one-volume abbreviated version of the above Butler work.

Histories

Aland, Kurt. *From the Beginnings to the Threshold of the Reformation.* Trans. by James L. Schaaf. Vol. 1 in *A History of Christianity.* Augsburg Fortress 1985 $31.95. ISBN 0-8006-0725-2. An admirably organized narrative of the sweep of early church history, edited from the classroom lectures of a renowned German expert, supplemented by 33 pages of useful "chronological tables."

Atiya, Aziz S. *History of Eastern Christianity.* Kraus 1980 $65.00. ISBN 0-527-03703-6. A comprehensive critical survey of the history, ancient and modern, of the non-Greek churches of the Near East.

Bainton, Roland H. *To the Reformation.* Vol. 1 in *Christendom: A Short History of Christianity and Its Impact on Western Civilization.* HarpC 1966 o.p. A masterful survey for the general reader—exceptionally readable and uncompromisingly scholarly—providing a clear, coherent story and carefully selected illustrations with full explanations.

Bouyer, Louis, Jean Leclercq, and others. *History of Christian Spirituality.* 3 vols. Winston Pr. 1982 o.p. Vol. 1 *The Spirituality of the New Testament and the Fathers*, by Louis Bouyer and others. Vol. 2 *The Spirituality of the Middle Ages*, by Jean Leclercq and others. Vol. 3 *Orthodox Spirituality, and Protestant and Anglican Spirituality*, by Louis Bouyer and others. Provides a full overview of the major figures, movements, concerns, and lifestyles connected with the Christian spiritual endeavor.

The Cambridge History of the Bible. Ed. by Peter R. Ackroyd and others. 3 vols. Cambridge U. Pr. 1963–70. $39.95 ea. ISBN 0-521-29018-X. Vol. 1 *From the Beginnings to Jerome.* Vol. 2 *The West from the Fathers to the Reformation.* Vol. 3 *The West from the Reformation to the Present Day.* Provides a complete picture of all aspects of Bible history: text, translations, interpretation, distribution, and manuscript illumination.

Chadwick, Henry, and G. R. Evans, eds. *Atlas of the Christian Church.* Facts on File 1987 $40.00. ISBN 0-8160-1643-7. A lavishly illustrated history of Christianity as a worldwide movement, supplemented by many maps.

Copleston, Frederick C. *A History of Philosophy.* 3 vols. in 4. 1975 Doubleday $21.00. Vol. 1 *Greece and Rome.* ISBN 0-38-50211-4. Vol. 2 *Medieval Philosophy: Augustine to Scotus.* ISBN 0-38-51631-X. Vol. 3 *Ockham to Suarez.* ISBN 0-38-03235-8. The standard work in the history of philosophy, dealing extensively with the early Christian contribution to philosophical thought.

Dowley, Tim. *Eerdmans' Handbook to the History of Christianity.* Eerdmans 1977 $29.95. ISBN 0-8028-3450-7. A popular survey written mainly by evangelical Protestant scholars presenting church history as a lively story highlighted by quotations from primary sources, color photographs, maps, and diagrams.

Ferguson, Everett, and others. ed. *Encyclopedia of Early Christianity.* 2 vols. Trans. by Adrian Walford. Garland 1992 $95.00. ISBN 0-8240-5745-7. General study of all aspects of early Christianity, including archaeology, theology, doctrine, and daily life.

Frankiel, Sandra S. *Christianity: A Way of Salvation.* HarpC 1985 $8.95. ISBN 0-06-063015-9. An engagingly written, very basic introduction to Christianity emphasizing the broad lines of historical development and the analysis of fundamental themes.

González, Justo L. *The Early Church to the Dawn of the Reformation.* Vol. 1 in *The Story of Christianity.* HarpC 1983 o.p. College and seminary textbook written by a Latin American historian teaching in the United States.

———. *A History of Christian Thought.* 3 vols. Abingdon 1975 rev. ed. $64.95. ISBN 0-687-17185-9. Vol. 1 *From the Beginnings to the Council of Chalcedon in A.D. 451.* Vol. 2 *From Augustine to the Eve of the Reformation.* Vol. 3 *From the Protestant Reformation to the Twentieth Century.* A concise, comprehensive account of the development of Christian thought.

Harnack, Adolf. *History of Dogma.* Trans. by Neil Buchanan. 7 vols. in 4. Peter Smith repr. of 1895–1900 ed. o.p. A classic in its field, this work substantiates Harnack's famous thesis that the development of Christian dogma is a consequence of the "Hellenization" of the earliest Christianity.

Hefele, Karl J. *A History of the Councils of the Church from the Original Documents.* Ed. and trans. by William R. Clark. 5 vols. AMS Pr. 1974 repr. of 1896 ed. $172.50. ISBN 0-404-3260-5. An English translation of Hefele's standard treatment, which, unfortunately, follows the original German, not the revised and enlarged French version by Henri Leclercq and others (1907–52).

Holmes, J. Derek, and Bernard Bickers. *A Short History of the Catholic Church.* Paulist Pr. 1983 o.p. A solid history and good bibliography of the early and medieval periods in the first third of the book.

Jedin, Hubert, and John P. Dolan, eds. *History of the Church.* Trans. by Anselm Biggs and others. 3 vols. Crossroad NY 1992 $50.00 ea. Vol. 1 *The Early Church.* ISBN 0-8245-1253-7. Vol. 2 *The Medieval and Reformation Church.* ISBN 0-8245-1245-5. Vol. 3 *The Church in the Modern World.* ISBN 0-8245-1255-3. The best modern multivolume treatment of the entire period, representing a broad scholarly consensus on the Continent.

Latourette, Kenneth Scott. *A History of Christianity.* 2 vols. HarpC rev. ed. 1975 $18.00. ISBNs 0-06-064952-2, 0-06-064953-4. Volume 1, *Beginnings to 1500,* is a standard textbook of church history, emphasizing the expansion of Christianity, the cultural setting, and fringe movements.

Lohse, Bernhard. *A Short History of Christian Doctrine: From the First Century to the Present.* Trans. by Ernest F. Stoeffer. Augsburg Fortress rev. ed. 1978 $13.95. ISBN 0-8006-1341-4. A well-written, authoritative account organizing the material by major doctrinal themes: canon and creed, the Trinity, Christology, sin and grace, word and sacrament, and so forth.

Manschreck, Clyde L. *A History of Christianity in the World: From Persecution to Uncertainty.* P-H 1985 $38.00. ISBN 0-13-389354-5. A reissuing of a popular 1974 book, half of which deals with the early and medieval church.

Moffett, Samuel Hugh. *A History of Christianity in Asia.* Vol. 1 *Beginnings to 1500.* HarpC 1992 $45.00. ISBN 0-06-065779-0. Cultural and political concerns from earliest Christianity in Palestine to Persia and China.

Pelikan, Jaroslav. *The History of Christian Doctrine.* 5 vols. U. Ch. Pr. Vol. 1 *The Emergence of the Catholic Tradition (100–600).* 1971 $30.00. ISBN 0-226-65370-6. Vol. 2 *The Spirit of Eastern Christendom (600–1700).* 1974 $30.00. ISBN 0-226-65372-2. Vol. 3 *The Growth of Medieval Theology (600–1300).* 1978 $35.00. ISBN 0-226-65374-9. Vol. 4 *Reformation of Church and Dogma (1300–1700).* 1985 $27.50. ISBN 0-226-65376-5. Vol. 5 *Christian Doctrine and Modern Culture (Since 1700).* 1989 $29.95. ISBN 0-226-65378-1. A solid detailed history with frequent references to primary texts and good bibliography.

The Penguin History of the Church. Ed. by Owen Chadwick. 3 vols. Viking Penguin 1964–70. Vol. 1 *The Early Church,* by Henry Chadwick. 1968. Vol. 2 *Western Society and the Church in the Middle Ages,* by R. W. Southern. 1970. Vol. 3 *The Reformation,* by Owen Chadwick. 1964 o.p. All of the volumes in this series are superb achievements of historical analysis and appealing presentation for the general reader as well as the specialist.

Schaff, Philip. *History of the Christian Church.* 8 vols. Eerdmans 1960 $175.60. ISBN 0-8028-8054-1. The most extensive, though somewhat outdated, treatment of the history of the Christian Church written by an American scholar between 1880 and 1910.

Tillich, Paul. *A History of Christian Thought.* S&S Trade 1972 $18.00. ISBN 0-671-21426-8. Edited from the great Protestant theologian's famous classroom lectures at Union Theological Seminary in New York, this book traces the main lines of doctrinal development in generally accessible language.

Walker, Williston. *A History of the Christian Church.* Macmillan 1985 $35.00. ISBN 0-02-423870-8. The fourth edition of the classic one-volume textbook, thoroughly revised and brought up to date by Robert T. Handy, still preserves the virtues of the original version: precise information, clear organization, and readable style.

Williams, Rowan. *Christian Spirituality: A Theological History from the New Testament to Luther and St. John of the Cross.* Bks. Demand repr. of 1980 ed. $50.30. ISBN 0-685-15262-6. An excellent, informative introduction that emphasizes the connections between theology and the spiritual life.

Topical Studies

Aulen, Gustav. *Christus Victor.* Macmillan 1969 $10.95. ISBN 0-02-083400-4. A seminal study by an eminent Swedish theologian challenging the common understanding of atonement as objective satisfaction and proposing the patristic theology of "recapitulation" as the proper alternative. With an introduction by Jaroslov Pelikan.

Bailey, D. Sherwin. *Homosexuality and the Western Christian Tradition.* Shoe String 1975 repr. of 1955 ed. $25.00. ISBN 0-208-01492-6. Written in 1954 by an Anglican scholar as background for a comprehensive report on the issue by the Church of England, this reliable survey concentrates on biblical, historical, and legal aspects of the question.

Bainton, Roland H. *Christian Attitudes toward War and Peace: A Historical Survey and Critical Reevaluation.* Abingdon 1979 $9.95. ISBN 0-687-07027-9. Compellingly written, masterful essay tracing Christian attitudes toward war and peace from the "just-war" theory through the modern peace movement.

Boswell, John. *Christianity, Social Tolerance, and Homosexuality: Gay People in Western Europe from the Beginning of the Christian Era to the Fourteenth Century.* U. Ch. Pr. 1981 $18.95. ISBN 0-226-06711-4. The most authoritative treatment of its subject available today; with an appendix presenting several relevant texts and translations.

Clark, Elizabeth A. *Women in the Early Church. Message of the Fathers Ser.* Liturgical Pr. 1983 $12.95. ISBN 0-89453-332-0. General history mixed with primary source materials.

Delehaye, Hippolyte. *The Legends of the Saints.* Trans. by Donald Attawater. Bks. Demand repr. of 1907 ed. $37.50. ISBN 0-7837-0442-9. One of the founders of scientific hagiography explains the laws by which legends develop.

Graef, Hilda. *Mary: A History of Doctrine and Devotion.* 2 vols. in 1. Chr. Classics 1985 repr. of 1965 ed. $23.00. ISBN 0-87061-113-5. The best brief account in English of the historical development of Mariology written for a general readership.

Jones, Cheslyn, and Edward Yarnold, eds. *The Study of Liturgy.* OUP 1978 $17.95. ISBN 0-19-520076-14. An excellent new standard work in this field, covering the early and medieval period thoroughly, written by three well-known Oxford scholars.

Kelly, J. N. D. *The Oxford History of the Popes.* OUP 1986 $29.95. ISBN 0-19-213964-9. Succinct chronological entries and bibliographies on each pope.

Klauser, Theodor. *A Short History of the Western Liturgy.* Trans. by John Halliburton. OUP 1979 $12.95. ISBN 0-19-213223-7. Probably the best introduction to all aspects of Western worship available in English today.

Laporte, Jean. *The Role of Women in Early Christianity. Studies in Women and Religion.* E. Mellen 1982 $79.95. ISBN 0-88946-549-5. An informative but very conservative interpretation of the evidence from the first three centuries.

McGinley, Phyllis. *Saint Watchings. Crossroad Paperback Ser.* Crossroad NY 1982 $9.95. ISBN 0-8245-0450-X. "A warm, humorous, and affectionate book of prose about the saints she likes. . . . Here is an ecumenical book written for all people who like people" (*Library Journal*).

McGinn, Bernard, and John Meyendorff, eds. *Christian Spirituality from the Apostolic Fathers to the Twelfth Century.* Crossroad NY 1987 $49.50. ISBN 0-8245-0681-2. A valuable collection of scholarly yet clearly written essays forming Volume 16 of a new publication venture: *World Spirituality: An Encyclopedic History of the Religious Quest.*

McGrath, Alister E. *Iustitia Dei: A History of the Doctrine of Justification.* Cambridge U. Pr. 1986 $59.50. ISBN 0-521-30887-9. The first full history of this important doctrine and a careful study of considerable ecumenical significance.

Meyendorff, John. *Christ in Eastern Christian Thought (Le Christ dans la théologie Byzantine).* St. Vladimirs 1975 $10.95. ISBN 0-91-3836-27-3. A clearly written, lucid introduction to the theological answer given by the Eastern Orthodox Fathers to the question: Who was Jesus Christ?

_____. *The Orthodox Church: Its Past and Its Role in the World Today.* St. Vladimirs 1981 repr. of 1962 ed. o.p. An ecumenically oriented introduction to the tradition of the Eastern Church, giving considerable attention to the Russian Church and modern Eastern Orthodox churches.

Niebuhr, H. Richard, and Daniel D. Williams. *The Ministry in Historical Perspective.* HarpC 1983 repr. of 1956 ed. o.p. An important collection of essays on the historical development of the Christian priesthood and ministry.

Ruether, Rosemary R. *Religion and Sexism.* S&S Trade 1974 o.p. An excellent introduction to the issue of sexism in Christian history, challenging stereotypes and raising new questions.

Ruether, Rosemary R., and Eleanor McLaughlin. *Women of Spirit: Female Leadership in the Jewish and Christian Tradition.* S&S Trade 1979 o.p. Going beyond the mere documentation of the marginal role of women in the two traditions, the 13 essays of this volume want to contribute "both toward the recovery of important chapters in women's history and toward the charting of the paradigms of female leadership."

Spidlik, Tomas. *The Spirituality of the Christian East: A Systematic Handbook.* Trans. by Anthony P. Gythiel. *Cistercian Studies Ser.* Cistercian Pubns. 1986 $48.95. ISBN 0-87907-879-0. A rather ambitious, but competently composed, manual systematizing all important topics connected with the theology of the spiritual life in the Christian East.

Tavard, George H. *Woman in Christian Tradition.* Bks. Demand repr. of 1973 ed. $67.30. ISBN 0-394-71155-6. A theological treatment of the topic by a leading Catholic ecumenical scholar thoroughly familiar with the historical background.

Underhill, Evelyn. *The Mystics of the Church.* Attic Pr. 1975 repr. of 1925 ed. o.p. A concise introduction to the vast literature of Christian mysticism by a recognized authority.

Warner, Marina. *Alone of All Her Sex: The Myth and the Cult of the Virgin Mary.* Knopf 1983 $16.00. ISBN 0-394-71155-6. A very readable, thoughtful exploration of the background, development, and function of Marian devotion, drawing on history, mythology, psychology, and the visual arts.

White, R. E. *Christian Ethics: The Historical Development.* Westminster John Knox 1981 o.p. An extensive survey meant "to bring the student reasonably equipped to the threshold of the current debate," and featuring eight chapters on early Christianity up to Erasmus.

Source Collections

Ancient Christian Writers: The Works of the Fathers in Translation. Paulist Pr. 1946–present. Over 50 vols. to date. $10.95–$26.95 ea. A well-established series, begun under the auspices of the Catholic University of America in 1946, presenting authoritative translations of a wide range of early Christian writings.

The Ante-Nicene Fathers: Translations of the Writings of the Fathers down to A.D. 325. Ed. by Alexander Roberts and James Donaldson. 10 vols. Eerdmans 1951 repr. of 1884–97 ed. $29.95 ea. Presents the older standard English translations of the earliest church fathers' major works, for many of which no other English translation is available.

Barry, Colman J., ed. *Readings in Church History.* 3 vols. in 1. Chr. Classics 1985 o.p. A very useful documentary sourcebook that presents substantial excerpts of texts illustrating the various aspects of church history with special emphasis on thought and doctrine.

Bettenson, Henry, ed. *Documents of the Christian Church.* OUP 1970 $10.95. ISBN 0-19-501293-3. The best brief anthology of important documents from the history of the church; more than half of the material comes from the early and medieval period.

_____. *Early Christian Fathers: A Selection from the Writings of the Fathers from St. Clement of Rome to St. Athanasius.* OUP 1969 repr. of 1956 ed. $13.95. ISBN 0-19-283009-0. For each author, the excerpts are topically arranged, illustrating his thinking on a rich variety of doctrinal themes.

_____. *The Later Christian Fathers: A Selection from the Writings of the Fathers from St. Cyril of Jerusalem to St. Leo the Great.* OUP 1972 $12.95. ISBN 0-19-283012-0. A continuation of the preceding volume, covering the period from the early fourth century to c. A.D. 460.

Cistercian Father Series. Ed. by Basil M. Pennington. Cistercian Pubns. 1970–present. Over 47 vols. to date. $7.95–$26.95 ea. Begun in 1970, this rapidly expanding series offers excellent modern translations, many for the first time, of the works of medieval Cistercian writers, notably St. Bernard of Clairvaux, but also lesser-known figures.

Classics of Western Spirituality. Paulist Pr. 1974–present. Over 66 vols. to date. $11.95–$37.95 ea. A series of original translations from the works of the Western spiritual and mystical tradition, which has turned out to be very successful and popular.

The Fathers of the Church. Cath. U. Pr. 1947–present. $14.95–$37.95 ea. The series of new translations, founded by Ludwig Schopp in 1947 and originally published by its own corporation, continues to present reliable English translations of patristic literature; of approximately 100 projected volumes, 83 have been published, following no particular order.

Leith, John H., ed. *Creeds of the Churches: A Reader in Christian Doctrine from the Bible to the Present.* Westminster John Knox 1982 $16.99. ISBN 0-8042-0526-4. The documents in this weighty little volume make for fascinating reading. The first 60 pages present major doctrinal affirmations from the New Testament to the Council of Florence (1438–65).

The Library of Christian Classics. 19 vols. Westminster John Knox 1950–present. $14.99–$16.99 ea. Translations of major Christian writings before 1600 under the editorship of an acknowledged authority and containing superbly written introductions along with the texts.

Neuner, J., and J. Dupuis, eds. *The Christian Faith.* Alba House rev. ed. 1983 $15.95. ISBN 0-8189-0453-4. A classic compendium of authoritative documents from all periods of church history defining the official teaching of the Roman Catholic Church on major topics of Christian doctrine.

A Select Library of the Nicene and Post-Nicene Fathers of the Christian Church. Ed. by Philip Schaff and others. 28 vols. Eerdmans 1956 Ser. 1 and 2 $29.95 ea. Continues the *Ante-Nicene Fathers* in two series, one on the works of St. Augustine (Vols. 1–8) and St. Chrysostom (Vols. 9–14) and the other in 14 volumes on works by Eusebius, Athanasius, Basil the Great, Gregory of Nyssa, Ephrem the Syrian, Hilary, Jerome, Gregory the Great, and others.

Thompson, Bard, ed. *Liturgies of the Western Church*. Augsburg Fortress 1980 repr. of 1962 ed. $14.95. ISBN 0-8006-1428-3. A very useful collection of orders of worship and similar materials from various traditions, especially the Protestant Reformation.

THE EARLY CENTURIES (to circa A.D. 600)

The early centuries of Christianity were witness to the gradual Christianization of the Roman Empire. Beginning as a small sect within Judaism, Christianity quickly found converts among members of various classes of Greco-Roman society. At the end of its first 300 years, it is estimated that 10 percent of the inhabitants of the empire were Christian. With Constantine's edict of toleration (313) and later Theodosius I's establishment of Christianity as the imperial religion (390), conversions to Christianity increased greatly. There was great political advantage in being a member of the official religion of the empire. Missionaries converted people outside the empire, including the tribal groups migrating from the Russian steppe into Western Europe, such as the Vandals, Huns, and Goths.

The growth of Christianity, however, was not accomplished without difficulties. Christians faced not only external threats, philosophical condemnation, and sporadic instances of violence and persecution from their neighbors, but also internal division. Groups propounded differing, often contradictory, doctrines and beliefs, each group believing itself to have the correct understanding, to be "orthodox." Many of the more important issues, such as the Trinity and the nature of Christ, were settled at a series of councils, most important during this period being those of Nicea (325), Constantinople (381), and Chalcedon (451). By the end of this period, two major centers of Christianity emerged: Rome, which, as the church founded (according to tradition) by the Apostle Peter, became the center of the Roman Catholic church; and Constantinople, the center for the Orthodox Church.

Special Histories

Bainton, Roland H. *Early Christianity*. Krieger 1984 repr. of 1960 ed. $9.50. ISBN 0-89874-735-X. Combines one of the best brief accounts of early church history with an excellent selection of "Documents and Readings" in English translation.

Frend, W. H. *The Rise of Christianity*. Augsburg Fortress 1984 $25.95. ISBN 0-8006-1931-5. A learned, but lively, account of Christianity's victory to A.D. 604, modeled after Harnack's *Expansion of Christianity* (see below), but including new archaeological and literary evidence.

Grant, Robert M. *Augustus to Constantine: The Rise and Triumph of Christianity in the Roman World*. Harper SF 1990 $12.95. ISBN 0-06-250350-2. An excellent survey by one of the foremost authorities in early Christian studies on the political and religious conditions of the Roman Empire and their impact on Christianity.

Harnack, Adolf. *The Expansion of Christianity in the First Three Centuries*. 2 vols. Trans. by James Moffatt. *Select Bibliographies Repr. Ser.* Ayer 1972 repr. of 1904–05 ed. $64.00. ISBN 0-8369-6882-4. The classic study of the early spread of Christianity in the Roman Empire.

Kidd, Beresford J. *A History of the Church to A.D. 461*. 3 vols. AMS Pr. 1976 repr. of 1922 ed. $135.00. ISBN 0-404-15010-1. In its time the most detailed standard history of the first four centuries written by an English scholar.

Lebreton, Jules, and Jacques Zeiller. *The History of the Primitive Church*. Gordon Pr. 1973 $80.00. Vol. 1 *The Church in the New Testament: From the Death of St. John to the End of the Second Century*. Vol. 2 *The Church in the Third Century*. The first two volumes in the English translation of the famous French series *Histoire de l'Eglise*, edited by Fliche and Martin.

Lietzmann, Hans. *A History of the Early Church*. 4 vols. in 2. Meridian Bks. 1961 o.p. Vol. 1 *The Beginnings of the Christian Church*. Vol. 2 *The Founding of the Church Universal*. Vol. 3 *From Constantine to Julian*. Vol. 4 *The Era of the Church Fathers*. True classics in the field, telling the story in a lively and readable style and representing the harvest of decades of scholarly work on the major themes of early Christian history by the author and his generation.

MacMullen, Ramsey, and Eugene N. Lane. *Paganism and Christianity, 100–425: A Sourcebook*. Augsburg Fortress 1992 $14.95. ISBN 0-8006-2647-8. A judiciously chosen collection of documents with minimal commentary exploring the non-Judaic matrix of early Christianity.

Wand, J. W. C. *History of the Early Church from A.D. 500*. Routledge Chapman & Hall 1975 $14.95. ISBN 0-416-18110-4. A concise summary, written in 1934 by a well-known Anglican churchman and former bishop of London, that remains a favorite textbook because of its reliable information and its balanced judgment.

Christianity in the World of the Roman Empire

In the famous correspondence between the Emperor Trajan and PLINY THE YOUNGER (see Vol. 2), then governor of Bithynia, Trajan informed Pliny that Christians who refused to recant their allegiance by making the proper sacrifices and oaths should be punished but that they should not be sought out actively. This policy set the tone for the relations between Christians and the imperial government up to the middle of the third century. The sporadic acts of violence against Christians that did occur during this period were usually popular hostility and not imperial policy. In 250 Decius was the first emperor to sanction a general persecution of Christians. The persecution lasted intermittently for several years, after which came a period of 40 years of relative peace. In 303 the persecutions were resumed by Diocletian. Churches were destroyed, sacred books were confiscated, and clergy were imprisoned and compelled to offer sacrifice. This official policy ended in 313, when Constantine, who in the previous year had, at least nominally, converted to Christianity, issued the "Edict of Milan" ending the persecution and officially recognizing the Christian churches. Finally, in 390 Theodosius I made Christianity the official imperial religion.

Barker, John W. *Justinian and the Later Roman Empire*. U. of Wis. Pr. 1975 $12.95. ISBN 0-299-03944-7. A general, responsible account of politics and religion during a crucial time of transition between antiquity and the Christian Middle Ages.

Baynes, Norman H. *Constantine the Great and the Christian Church*. World History Ser. Gordon Pr. 1972 repr. of 1930 ed. $75.00. ISBN 0-838-0131-2. The classic statement of the view that the early sources depicting Constantine as a convinced Christian are trustworthy, reissued with preface that traces the debate over Baynes's thesis in the past few decades.

Benko, Stephen. *Pagan Rome and the Early Christians*. Midland Book Ser. Ind. U. Pr. 1985 $25.00. ISBN 0-253-34286-4. Tries to show that pagan suspicions about early Christians were often not as unfounded as many people believe.

Browning, Robert. *The Emperor Julian*. U. CA Pr. 1976 o.p. The most recent full-length biography of the fourth-century Roman Emperor whom Christians call "the Apostate."

Burckhardt, Jacob. *The Age of Constantine the Great*. Trans. by Moses Hadas. U. CA Pr. 1983 $12.95. ISBN 0-520-04680-3. The classic interpretation of the Constantinian era as an age of disturbing transition by the greatest cultural historian of the nineteenth century.

Cochrane, Charles N. *Christianity and Classical Culture: A Study of Thought and Action from Augustus to Augustine.* OUP 1957 repr. of 1944 ed. $12.95. ISBN 0-19-500207-5. First published in 1941, one of the most intriguing interpretations of the history of ideas both "pagan" and Christian and their interaction during the first four centuries of our era.

Cunningham, Agnes. *The Early Church and the State. Sources of Early Christian Thought Ser.* Augsburg Fortress 1982 o.p. A collection of fresh translations of key documents from the second to the end of the fourth century, with a brief introduction.

Dodds, E. R. *Pagan and Christian in an Age of Anxiety: Some Aspects of Religious Experience from Marcus Aurelius to Constantine.* Cambridge U. Pr. 1970 $15.95. ISBN 0-521-38599-7. Famous but controversial study of the religious mood of the early Christian centuries using the Christian and pagan images of each other as illustrations of a common world of religious experience.

Doerries, Hermann. *Constantine and Religious Liberty.* Elliots Bks. 1960 $49.50. ISBN 0-686-51363-0. The Terry Lectures delivered at Yale in 1959, translated by Roland Bainton, the foremost church historian of his generation in the United States.

Fox, Robin L. *Pagans and Christians.* Knopf 1987 $45.00. ISBN 0-394-55495-7. Links the story of early Christianity through the fourth century to the religious world of the Roman Empire at every point, making full use of recent advances in historical method and archaeology.

Gager, John. *Kingdom and Community: The Social World of Early Christianity.* P-H 1975 $14.95. ISBN 0-13-516203-3. Attempts to understand early Christianity as one religious cult among others in the empire and includes essays on "Religion and Society in the Early Roman Empire" and "The Success of Christianity."

Grant, Robert M. *Gods and the One God. Library of Early Christianity.* Westminster John Knox 1986 $20.00. ISBN 0-664-21905-5. An introduction to the religious conflict between Christians and their neighbors in the empire, discussing not only the mutual image of the two sides but also the influence of pagan religious concepts on distinctive Christian doctrines such as those of God, Christ, and the Holy Spirit.

———. *Greek Apologists of the Second Century.* Westminster John Knox 1990 $20.00. ISBN 0-664-21915-2. A well-written analysis of the works of the writers who sought to make Christianity intelligible to Greco-Roman intellectuals.

Green, Michael. *Evangelism in the Early Church.* Eerdmans 1970 $18.95. ISBN 0-8028-1612-6. The methods, motives, and strategies of Christian evangelism as a proclamation of salvation and an invitation to conversion.

Greenslade, Stanley L. *Church and State from Constantine to Theodosius.* Greenwood 1981 repr. of 1954 ed. $39.75. ISBN 0-313-20793-3. Three lectures by the celebrated author of *Schism in the Early Church* given before a general audience and tracing the main development of Christianity as a state religion during the decisive century.

Hillgarth, J. N., ed. *Christianity and Paganism, 350–750: The Conversion of Western Europe.* U. of Pa. Pr. rev. ed. 1986 $16.95. ISBN 0-8122-1213-4. A revision of *The Conversion of Europe, 350–750* (1969). Presents an excellent anthology of relatively inaccessible sources that illustrate the slow penetration of Christianity into the changing society of Western Europe.

Hinson, E. Glenn. *The Evangelization of the Roman Empire: Identity and Adaptability.* Mercer Univ. Pr. 1981 $22.00. ISBN 0-86554-244-9. A good, broadly conceived study written by a church historian in the Free Church Tradition, beginning with the assumption of the missionary nature of the church and seeking to describe the contribution of theology and Christian lifestyles to the missionary task.

Hoffman, R. Joseph, trans. *Celsus: On the True Doctrine.* OUP 1987 o.p. A brief study and new translation of the fragments of a famous anti-Christian treatise preserved in its rebuttal by the church father Origen.

Jaeger, Werner. *Early Christianity and Greek Paideia.* Balknap Pr. 1961 $7.95. ISBN 0-674-22052-8. The Carl Newell Jackson Lectures at Harvard for 1960 presenting an outstanding classicist's view of the reception of Greek learning into early Christianity.

Jones, A. H. *Constantine and the Conversion of Europe. Medieval Academy Repr. for Teaching Ser.* U. of Toronto Pr. 1979 repr. of 1948 ed. $9.95. ISBN 0-8020-6369-1. Gives a clear, straightforward account of the Constantinople turn, skeptical of doubts about Constantine's serious Christian intentions.

Krautheimer, Richard. *Three Christian Capitals: Topography and Politics. Una's Lectures.* U. CA Pr. 1983 $42.50. ISBN 0-520-04541-6. Rich insights into the architectural features of Christian Rome, Milan, and Constantinople against the general background of fourth- and fifth-century politics.

McCullough, W. Stewart. *A Short History of Syriac Christianity to the Rise of Islam.* Scholars Pr. GA 1982 $23.95. ISBN 0-891-30454-1. The only general introduction in English to a field of study that finds great interest among church historians today.

McMullen, Ramsey. *Christianizing the Roman Empire, A.D. 100–400.* Yale U. Pr. 1984 $25.00. ISBN 0-300-03216-1. A clear account of the way the common people heard and assimilated the Christian message.

Mattingly, Harold. *Christianity in the Roman Empire.* Norton 1967 o.p. A popular survey of church-state relations during the first three centuries in six brief chapters, with pertinent passages from primary sources, explanatory notes, and illustrations of imperial coins.

Ruether, Rosemary R. *Faith and Fratricide: The Theological Roots of Anti-Semitism.* Winston Pr. 1974 o.p. An important book whose author argues that the historical roots of modern anti-Semitism reach deep into classical history, including the New Testament and the church fathers.

Sordi, Marta. *The Christians and the Roman Empire.* Trans. by Annabel Bedini. U. of Okla. Pr. 1986 $27.95. ISBN 0-8061-2011-8. A major study of the changing status of Christians in the Roman Empire, describing the persecutions and social conflicts and accenting the religious rather than the political sphere.

Wilken, Robert L. *The Christians as the Romans Saw Them.* Yale U. Pr. 1984 $25.00. ISBN 0-300-03066-5. A fresh look at early Christianity from the outside, written with a thorough knowledge of the sources yet unencumbered by technical discussions, opening up new and often surprising vistas that every reader will enjoy.

———. *John Chrysostom and the Jews: Rhetoric and Reality in the Late Fourth Century. The Transformation of the Classical Heritage.* U. CA Pr. 1983 $40.00. ISBN 0-520-04757-5. A scholarly study of the social relations between Christians and the vigorous Jewish community of the city of Antioch, based on an analysis of eight sermons against the Jews by the church father Chrysostom.

Christian Doctrine and Heresies

During the early centuries of Christianity, numerous beliefs developed that attempted to answer questions that were fundamental to the religion. What is the nature of God, and how is the relation among the members of the Trinity—the Father, the Son, and the Holy Spirit—understood? What is the relation between the earthly Jesus and the divine Christ? How are the sacraments, such as baptism and the Eucharist, to be understood and performed? What is Christian Scripture, and how should it be interpreted? What is the human condition, and do free will and grace affect that condition? There were several differing, sometimes contradictory, positions for each question. It took several centuries for the demarcation between "orthodox" doctrine and "heretical" belief to be clearly established, and the winners in the dispute rewrote history each time. During this period, there were several important groups, including Gnostics, who taught, among other things, that it was not the Creator but the true God, God the Father, who sent Jesus, and that salvation was given to an elect group through the knowledge (Greek *gnosis*) of revealed truths. Other great controversies of the early centuries included Donatism, which divided the church over who had the authority to administer the sacraments; Arianism, which debated whether Christ is coeternal with the Father or created; and Pelagianism, which was concerned with whether human salvation could be affected by human free will and the role of God's grace.

Armstrong, D. M., ed. *The Cambridge History of Later Greek and Early Medieval Philosophy.* Cambridge U. Pr. 1967 $110.00. ISBN 0-521-04054. Massive handbook authored by a team of specialists containing a wealth of basic information and bibliography on Christian thought and thinkers to the early Middle Ages.

Bauer, Walter. *Orthodoxy and Heresy in Earliest Christianity.* Ed. by Robert A. Kraft and Gerhard Krodel. Bks. Demand 1979 $88.00. ISBN 0-68517039-X. A seminal work advancing the thesis that orthodox Christianity in many places was preceded by heretical forms of the faith so that the boundaries between orthodoxy and heresy must be seen as rather fluid in earliest times.

Brown, Raymond E. *The Virginal Conception and Bodily Resurrection of Jesus.* Paulist Pr. 1973 $7.95. ISBN 0-8091-1768-1. A clear, concise study of two early Christian doctrines giving full weight to the biblical material.

Burkitt, Francis C. *The Religion of the Manichees: Donnellan Lectures for 1924.* AMS Pr. 1979 repr. of 1925 ed. $29.00. ISBN 0-404-16105-7. Burkitt's masterful study, which is based on three Donnellan Lectures given at Dublin in 1924, ranks as the best general introduction to Manichaeism, addressing all major questions, such as sources, history, and teachings of this fascinating religion, remnants of which survived for many centuries.

Burns, J. Patout, ed. *Theological Anthropology. Sources of Early Christian Thought Ser.* Fortress Pr. 1981 $9.95. ISBN 0-8006-1412-7. A valuable sourcebook featuring new translations of patristic texts with an emphasis on the Pelagian controversy in which Saint Augustine was involved.

Burns, J. Patout, and Gerald Fagin. *The Holy Spirit. Message of the Fathers Ser.* Liturgical Pr. 1984 $16.95. ISBN 0-8146-5343-X. Expertly chosen extracts from primary source documents woven together with brief commentary trace the history of the doctrine of the Holy Spirit from the Apostolic Fathers to the fifth century.

Chadwick, Henry. *Early Christian Thought and the Classical Tradition: Studies in Justin, Clement, and Origen.* OUP 1984 $19.95. ISBN 0-19-82667-3. Based on four lectures delivered in 1962, these delightful essays interpret the main themes of early Christian apologetics with great subtlety but in a language accessible to the general reader.

Filoramo, Giovanni. *A History of Gnosticism.* Trans. by Anthony Alcock. Blackwell Pubs. 1990 $39.95. ISBN 0-631-15756-5. A sympathetic, well-documented portrayal of Gnostic doctrines and ethics.

Frend, W. H. *The Donatist Church: A Movement of Protest in Roman North Africa. Orthodoxies and Heresies in the Early Church Ser.* repr. of 1972 ed. $49.50. ISBN 0-404-62383-2. Detailed and scholarly standard history of the schismatic Donatist church of North Africa.

———. *The Rise of the Monophysite Movement: Chapters in the History of the Church in the Fifth and Sixth Centuries.* Cambridge U. Pr. 1972 o.p. Lively exploration of the history of the most important group of Christological dissidents after the Council of Chalcedon (451) down to the Arab conquest.

Grant, Robert M., ed. *Gnosticism: A Source Book of Heretical Writings from the Early Christian Period.* AMS Pr. 1985 repr. of 1961 ed. $32.50. ISBN 0-404-16108-1. Contains a standard collection of primary sources on Gnosticism in reliable English translations with brief introductory notes.

Gregg, Robert C., and Dennis E. Groh. *Early Arianism: A View of Salvation.* Fortress Pr. 1981 o.p. Controversial attempt at revising the image of the Arian heresy, arguing that Arius was less concerned with the question of God and the Trinity than with Christ as the model of a redeemed, mature humanity exemplified in the Christian Church.

Grillmeier, Aloys. *Christ in the Christian Tradition.* Westminster John Knox. Vol. 1 *From the Apostolic Age to Chalcedon.* rev. ed. Trans. by John S. Bowden. 1975 $38.00. ISBN 0-8042-0492-6. Vol. 2 Part 1: *From Chalcedon to Justinian.* Trans. by Pauline

Allen and John Cawte. 1987 $38.00. ISBN 0-8042-0493-4. The best detailed history of Christology in the ancient Church, providing precise explanations and excellent documentation.

Hall, Stewart G. *Doctrine and Practice in the Early Church.* Eerdmans 1991 $16.95. ISBN 0-2810-4521-6. Traces the development of the Christian tradition to 451, emphasizing the continuity of theology with biblical materials.

Harnack, Adolf. *Marcion: The Gospel of the Alien God.* Trans. by John E. Steely and Lyle D. Bierma. Labyrinth Pr. 1987 $30.00. A monumental study of Marcion, the second-century heretic, which is based on the full range of early sources.

Jonas, Hans. *Gnostic Religion: The Message of the Alien God and the Beginnings of Christianity.* Peter Smith 2nd rev. ed. 1963 $18.95. ISBN 0-582-49219-X. One of the best-known books on Gnosticism, analyzing the religion in terms of the existentialist movement.

Kelly, J. N. *Early Christian Creeds.* Longman 1981 $18.95. ISBN 0-582-49219-X. The most recent edition of a widely used textbook that explains clearly and thoroughly the text, the history, and the meaning of all the important Christian creeds from the New Testament to the so-called Apostles' Creed, which, in its modern form, probably originated in early medieval France.

————. *Early Christian Doctrines.* HarpC rev. ed. 1978 $10.95. ISBN 0-06-064334-X. Kelly's masterly survey, organized by doctrinal themes within a chronologically ordered basic framework, remains undoubtedly the standard text in the field.

Lieu, Samuel N. *Manichaeism in the Later Roman Empire and Medieval China. Wiss UNT Neuen Testament Ser.* Coronet Bks. 1992 $117.50. ISBN 0-7190-1088-8. Pioneering scholarly study of Manichaeism that not only discusses Mani and the beginnings of the movement, taking into account recent discoveries, but traces the religion's development in China.

Norris, Richard A., Jr., ed. and trans. *The Christological Controversy. Sources of Early Christian Thought Ser.* Fortress Pr. 1980 $10.95. ISBN 0-8006-1411-9. A selection of essential primary texts in new translations, furnished with a concise introductory sketch.

Pagels, Elaine. *Adam, Eve and the Serpent.* Random 1988 $17.95. ISBN 0-394-52140-4. A somewhat controversial assessment of the roots of sexism within Christianity.

————. *The Gnostic Gospels.* Random 1980 $5.95. ISBN 0-394-74043-2. Draws on the new Nag Hammadi writings in a spirited plea for justice on behalf of Gnostic Christianity, which, Pagels argues, was suppressed because it challenged the power structures of an authoritarian church.

Prestige, George L. *Fathers and Heretics. Bampton Lectures.* Allenson 1940 o.p. An engaging account of some important theological controversies and personalities of the third and fourth centuries: Bishop Callistus of Rome, Origen, Athanasius, Apollinaris, Nestorius, Cyril of Alexandria.

————. *A God in Patristic Thought.* Fortress Pr. 1952 o.p. An old classic (1936) by a master historian tracing the development of the doctrine of God and of the Trinity in a comprehensive fashion without becoming shallow.

Robinson, James M. *The Nag Hammadi Library in English.* Trans. by members of the Coptic Gnostic Library Project of the Institute for Antiquity and Christianity. Harper SF 1990 repr. of 1978 ed. $18.00. ISBN 0-06-066935-7. The first complete and authoritative English translation of the Gnostic books from the early Christian era that were found in Egypt shortly after World War II.

Rudolph, Kurt. *Gnosis: The Nature and History of Gnosticism.* Harper SF 1987 $16.95. ISBN 0-06-067018-5. Probably the most comprehensive historical investigation to date of the entire Gnostic movement in the ancient world, featuring sections on Manichaeism and the Mandaeans.

Rusch, William G., ed. *The Trinitarian Controversy. Sources of Early Christian Thought Ser.* Fortress Pr. 1980 $10.95. ISBN 0-8006-1410-0. An excellent selection of primary sources, mainly from the Arian controversy of the fourth century, which is also useful through its concise introduction to the persons and issues involved.

Russell, Jeffrey B. *Satan: The Early Christian Tradition*. Cornell Univ. Pr. 1981 $36.50. ISBN 0-8014-1267-6. A sequel to the same author's *The Devil* (Cornell Univ. Pr. 1977 $32.50) carefully documenting the theology and symbolism connected with evil from the second to the fifth century.

Turner, Henry E. *The Pattern of Christian Truth: A Study in the Relations between Orthodoxy and Heresy in the Early Church. Bampton Lectures*. AMS Pr. 1977 repr. of 1954 ed. ISBN 0-404-16114-6. Traces the pattern of doctrinal orthodoxy with particular reference to the three principal sources of theology—Scripture, tradition, and reason in answer to the thesis of Walter Bauer.

Wallace-Hadrill, D. S. *Christian Antioch: A Study of Early Christian Thought in the East*. Cambridge U. Pr. 1982 o.p. The first intensive study of the great center of Christian antiquity whose "school" helped in shaping Christian doctrine and controversy, comprising a well-written and thoroughly documented examination of what the label *Antiochian* meant in the early church.

Wand, John W. *The Four Great Heresies: Heresies of the Early Christian*. AMS Pr. 1985 repr. of 1955 ed. $29.00. ISBN 0-404-16189-8. The former Bishop of London discusses clearly and succinctly the main tenets of the Arian, Apollinarian, Nestorian, and Eutychian heresies.

Wiles, Maurice F. *Making of Christian Doctrine*. Cambridge U. Pr. 1967 o.p. Outlines convincingly the fundamental factors that contributed to the formulation of early Christian doctrine: Scripture, the experience of worship, and specific theological convictions concerning salvation.

Wiles, Maurice F., and M. Santer, eds. *Documents in Early Christian Thought*. Cambridge U. Pr. 1977 $16.95. ISBN 0-521-09915-3. A very helpful sourcebook featuring excerpts from the major church fathers on doctrinal topics such as God, Trinity, Christ, Holy Spirit, sin and grace, tradition and Scripture, and church.

Wolfson, Harry A. *The Philosophy of the Church Fathers: Faith, Trinity, Incarnation*. HUP 3rd rev. ed. 1970 $34.95. ISBN 0-674-66551. Following the method of his classic study on Philo the Jew, the famous Harvard historian of philosophy develops the thesis that early Christian doctrines were the result of a recasting of Christian beliefs in the form of a Greek philosophy.

Young, Frances. *From Nicaea to Chalcedon: A Guide to the Literature and Its Background*. Bks. Demand repr. of 1983 ed. $108.20. ISBN 0-685-24167-X. Examines doctrinal developments between 325 and 451 in the context of the lives of the era's principal theologians.

_____. *The Making of the Creeds*. TPI PA 1991 $10.95. ISBN 0-334-02488-9. Clearly written with background materials for the development of credal formulae.

Life in the Christian Church

In addition to the developments in doctrine, the church paid great attention to matters affecting the Christian life, including church structure, prayer, liturgy, and such ethical issues as Christian participation in military service and human sexuality. One important facet of this life was monasticism. From the deserts of Egypt and Syria, Christians both individually and in groups set themselves off from the rest of the world and pursued a life of perfection. Most of our knowledge of early Christian life comes from literary sources but is greatly enhanced by the numerous remains from the ancient catacombs, churches, and various pieces of iconography.

Bradshaw, Paul F. *The Search for the Origins of Christian Worship: Sources and Methodology for the Study of Early Liturgy*. OUP 1992 $35.00. ISBN 0-19-908050-5. Applies advances in the methodology for the history of liturgy, finding not one but several trajectories in the development of patristic liturgies.

Brown, Peter. *The Cult of the Saints: Its Rise and Function in Latin Christianity*. U. Ch. Pr. 1982 $8.95. ISBN 0-22-07622-9. Surveys changes in piety between the New

Testament and the medieval period as tomb, relics, and saints loomed ever larger in Christian religiosity.

Cadoux, C. John. *The Early Christian Attitude to War: A Contribution to the History of Christian Ethics*. Gordon Pr. 1974 $250.00. ISBN 0-87968-198-5. Standard treatment of the subject covering the period before Constantine and arguing the thesis that Jews and early Christians "closely identified their religion with peace" and therefore disapproved of war.

Chitty, Derwas J. *The Desert a City*. St. Vladimirs 1977 $11.95. ISBN 0-913836-45-1. An important contribution to its field, tracing the details of the earliest history of Christian monasticism in an imaginative synthesis of the literary and archaeological sources.

Cunningham, Agnes. *The Bishop in the Church: Patristic Texts on the Role of the Episkopos*. *Theology and Life Ser*. Liturgical Pr. 1985 $3.95. ISBN 0-8146-5469. Texts and commentary on the development of episcopal office between the New Testament and the medieval period.

De Vogue, Adalbert. *The Rule of Saint Benedict: A Doctrinal and Spiritual Commentary*. Trans. by John B. Hasbrouck. *Cistercian Studies Ser*. Cistercian Pubns. 1983 $25.95. ISBN 0-87907-845-6. Contains a fascinating and eminently readable discussion of this foundational document of Western monasticism.

Dix, Dom G. *The Shape of the Liturgy*. HarpC 1982 o.p. A classic of long standing on the revival of liturgical studies since 1945, touching on many aspects of liturgical life but concentrating on the Eucharist, and stressing the Jewish roots of the central act of Christian worship.

Eno, Robert B. *The Rise of the Papacy*. *Theology and Life Ser*. Liturgical Pr. 1986 $12.95. ISBN 0-8146-5802-4. The development of papal power and theology to the beginning of the seventh century.

———. *Teaching Authority in the Early Church*. *Message of the Fathers Ser*. Liturgical Pr. 1984 $9.95. ISBN 0-8146-5325-1. A carefully selected and annotated volume of readings on a crucial question that covers such issues as the canon of Scripture, apostolic tradition, creeds, councils, and the authority of the Roman bishops through the fifth century.

Forell, George W. *History of Christian Ethics: From the New Testament to Augustine*. Fortress Pr. 1979 o.p. The first major effort at a synthesis of this kind in decades, this volume by a well-known Lutheran ethicist presents a very informative, balanced survey that takes into account historical advances and contemporary interests.

Giles, Edward, ed. *Documents Illustrating Papal Authority, A.D. 96–454*. Hyperion Conn. 1979 repr. of 1952 ed. $28.00. ISBN 0-88355-696-0. The standard collection in English of the primary texts that allow the reader to trace in great detail the development of the idea of papal primacy in the early church.

Grabar, Andre. *Christian Iconography: A Study of Its Origins*. *A. W. Mellon Lectures in the Fine Arts*. Princeton U. Pr. 1980 $24.00. ISBN 0-691-01830-8. Richly illustrated essay by one of the best-known interpreters of early Christian art, focusing on the way early Christian imagery was composed and used.

Greer, Rowan A. *Broken Lights and Mended Lives: Theology and Common Life in the Early Church*. Pa. St. U. Pr. 1986 $25.00. ISBN 0-271-00422-3. Studies the impact of theology on the Christian life in the early centuries, stressing the complexity of early Christianity.

Harnack, Adolf. *Militia Christi: The Christian Religion and the Military in the First Three Centuries (Militia Christi: Die Christliche Religion Und Der Soldatenstand In Den Ersten Drei Jahrhunderten)*. Trans. by David M. Grace. Fortress Pr. 1981 o.p. The first English edition of Harnack's brief but important essay in two parts ("The Christian as Soldier" and "The Christian Religion and the Military Profession") enhanced by a short introduction tracing the impact of Harnack's book.

Helgeland, John, and others. *Christians and the Military: The Early Experience*. Fortress Pr. 1985 o.p. Analyzes the historical situation combining extensive quotations from the sources with interpretation and a brief narrative framework and concluding that "early Christian attitudes toward military service seem to be at least ambiguous."

Jungmann, Josef A. *The Early Liturgy to the Time of Gregory the Great.* Trans. by Francis A. Brunner. *Liturgical Studies Ser.* U. of Notre Dame Pr. 1959 $14.95. ISBN 0-268-00083-2. Traces the development of Christian worship up to the seventh century in clear nontechnical prose and includes the liturgical calendar, hymns, and doctrinal controversies affecting liturgy.

———. *The Mass of the Roman Rite: Its Origins and Development.* Trans. by Francis A. Brunner. 2 vols. Chr. Classics $39.95. ISBN 0-87061-129-1. A major modern in-depth analysis of the Roman Mass, following the outline of the traditional worship service and tracing the history of each component through the centuries.

Kannengiesser, Charles, ed. *Early Christian Spirituality.* Trans. by Pamela Bright. *Sources of Early Christian Thought Ser.* Fortress Pr. 1986 $9.95. ISBN 0-8006-1416-X. Ten representative texts from the Eastern and Western traditions are preceded by an introduction placing the selections in their historical context.

Kee, Howard C. *Miracle in the Early Christian World: A Study in Sociohistorical Method.* Yale U. Pr. 1983 $12.95. ISBN 0-300-03008-8. A serious attempt to read early Christian miracle stories in the framework of the general religious attitudes and practices in the Roman Empire.

Laeuchli, Samuel. *Power and Sexuality: The Emergence of Canon Law at the Synod of Elvira.* Temple U. Pr. 1972 o.p. An engaging study seeking to uncover the human drama behind the language of the laws passed by a fourth-century church synod.

Louth, Andrew. *The Origins of the Christian Mystical Tradition: From Plato to Denys.* OUP 1981 $19.95. ISBN 0-19-826668-5. A thorough, very sympathetic introduction to early Christian mystical theology, weaving extensive quotations from primary sources into the interpretive narrative.

McNamara, Jo Ann. *A New Song: Celibate Women in the First Three Christian Centuries.* Haworth Pr. 1983 $29.95. ISBN 0-86656-249-4. An excellent study by a feminist historian who tries to draw a more adequate picture of the role of communities of celibate women in early Christianity who "carved out a new niche for themselves in the social structure" and were the pioneers of a Christian freedom achieved by asceticism.

Mancinelli, Fabrizio. *Catacombs and Basilicas: The Early Christians in Rome.* Scala Books 1981 o.p. Particularly valuable for its superb pictures in full color, which give the reader a vivid impression of the most ancient monuments of Christian Rome.

Musurillo, Herbert. *The Acts of the Christian Martyrs: Text and Translations.* OUP 1972 o.p. The best recent collection of the early reports on Christian martyrdom, usable both by the specialist and the general reader.

Phan, Peter C. *Social Thought. Message of the Fathers Ser.* Liturgical Pr. 1984 $15.95. ISBN 0-8146-5360-X. A good collection of excerpts from the fathers of the first five centuries, together with a brief general introduction.

Quasten, Johannes. *Music and Worship in Pagan and Christian Antiquity.* Trans. by Boniface Ramsey. Pastoral Pr. 1983 $11.95. ISBN 0-9602378-7-9. Translated from the second German edition (1973), a fascinating, comprehensive treatment of the subject.

Rader, Rosemary. *Breaking Boundaries: Male-Female Friendship in Early Christian Communities.* Paulist Pr. 1983 o.p. Investigates a major early Christian alternative to marriage in the relation between men and women.

Snyder, Graydon F. *Ante Pacem: Archaeological Evidence of Church Life before Constantine.* Mercer Univ. Pr. 1985 o.p. A scholarly but straightforward introduction to the archaeological remains of early Christianity giving accurate information, bibliography, and English translations of inscriptions.

Stevenson, J. *The Catacombs: Rediscovered Monuments of Early Christianity. Ancient People and Places Ser.* Thames Hudson 1978 $19.95. ISBN 0-500-02091-4. The best recent introduction to all aspects of the Christian catacombs in Rome and elsewhere, beautifully laid out and profusely illustrated.

Swift, Louis J. *The Early Fathers on War and Military Service. Message of the Fathers Ser.* Liturgical Pr. 1984 $9.95. ISBN 0-8146-5359-6. Judiciously chosen brief excerpts from the Christian literature of the early centuries within the framework of a narrative that stresses the variety of viewpoints and the changes.

Veilleux, Armand, trans. *Pachomian Koinonia. Cistercian Studies Ser.* Cistercian Pubs. Vol. 45 *The Life of St. Pachomius.* 1981 $12.95. ISBN 0-97907-945-2. Vol. 47 *Letters, Instructions, and Other Writings.* 1983 $26.95. ISBN 0-87907-847-2. The first comprehensive collection of the sources from the circle of the founder of the communal religious life in fourth-century Egypt.

Von Campenhausen, Hans. *Ecclesiastical Authority and Spiritual Power in the Church of the First Three Centuries.* Trans. by J. A. Baker. Stanford U. Pr. 1969 $35.00. ISBN 0-8047-0665-4. A penetrating analysis by an eminent church historian discussing the conflict over authority among early Christians: Who has authority and why? Which tradition is authoritative?

Waddell, Helen. *The Desert Fathers.* U. of Mich. Pr. 1957 $13.95. ISBN 0-472-06008-2. A classic selection from the wisdom of the early monks culled from the *vitae patrum,* the standard Latin translation of the "Sayings of the Fathers."

Wimbush, Vincent L., ed. *Ascetic Behavior in Greco Roman Antiquity. Studies in Antiquity and Christianity.* Fortress Pr. 1990 $41.95. ISBN 0-8006-3105-6. A documentary record of a wide variety of ascetic movements seen through the prism of social history.

Womer, Jan L. *Morality and Ethics in Early Christianity. Sources of Early Christian Thought Ser.* Fortress Pr. 1987 $9.95. ISBN 0-8006-1417-8. Representative texts from early Christian and patristic writings that are ably introduced by the editor-translator.

Church Fathers and Writers

Goodspeed, Edgar J. *A History of Early Christian Literature.* Ed. by Robert M. Grant. *Midway Repr. Ser.* U. Ch. Pr. rev. ed. 1966 o.p. The masterly survey from the beginning to A.D. 325, which one of the most distinguished American scholars authored in the 1930s.

Quasten, Johannes, ed. *Patrology.* Trans. by Placid Solari. 4 vols. Chr. Classics 1983–86 $85.00. ISBN 0-87061-2691-5. Indispensable repertory of the fathers and of all early Christian literature, providing, for each author, a brief biography, a detailed analysis of the literary legacy with a listing of English translations and bibliography, and an overview of the main teachings.

Ramsey, Boniface. *Beginning to Read the Fathers.* Paulist Pr. 1985 $9.95. ISBN 0-8091-2691-5. Adaptations from lectures given before the monks of Gethsemani Abbey in Kentucky, skillfully introducing the reader into the thought world of the fathers.

Squire, Aelred, ed. *Fathers Talking: An Anthology.* Cistercian Pubns. 1986 $12.95. ISBN 0-87907-893-6. Offers a thoughtful selection of excerpts from Origen, Popes Leo I and Gregory I, Augustine, and Cyril of Jerusalem for meditative reading.

Von Campenhausen, Hans. *The Fathers of the Greek Church.* Pantheon 1959 o.p.

————. *The Fathers of the Latin Church.* Stanford U. Pr. 1964 $37.50. ISBN 0-8047-0685-9. Two classic volumes by one of the best German church historians, containing excellent and lively biographies of the major church fathers from the second through the fifth centuries.

Wiles, Maurice. *The Christian Fathers.* OUP 1982 repr. of 1966 ed. $9.95. ISBN 0-19-520260-0. A topical introduction to the teaching of the fathers covering the image of God; the divinity of Christ; the Incarnation, sin, and salvation; sacraments; church; and ethics.

MEDIEVAL CHRISTIANITY

Special Histories

The study of Christianity in this period, roughly 600 to 1500, is practically inseparable from the study of Western civilization in general. Although church and state could often function as one, there was a recurring conflict between the two, especially over the question of what power each had in the other's affairs. The period saw the development of Christianity in several areas, especially ecclesiastical, spiritual, liturgical, theological, doctrinal, monastic, and architectural. This time also witnessed the growing division between the Eastern and Western churches and the Crusades, which initially were aimed at recapturing Jerusalem from the Muslims.

Despite the almost universal allegiance to the authority of the church, based on its interpretation of Scripture and ecclesiastical traditions, individuals and groups continually challenged the established doctrines and structures. Various attempts were made to reform the church. Some of the reformers, such as the Cathari in France and JOHN HUS in Czechoslovakia, were thought to go beyond the bounds of reform and were deemed heretical. These attempts to reform the church, attempts both within the established structure and outside of it, paved the way for the Protestant Reformation, which would permanently change the face of Christianity.

Bainton, Roland H. *The Medieval Church*. Anvil Ser. Krieger 1979 repr. of 1962 ed. $9.50. ISBN 0-88275-786-5. A very brief introduction to the history and thought of the church in the medieval period followed by primary documents that correspond to and illuminate the historical narrative.

Barraclough, Geoffrey. *The Crucible of Europe: The Ninth and Tenth Centuries in European History*. U. CA Pr. 1976. A very readable study of the political history of the ninth and tenth centuries in Europe, with special attention to the Carolingian empire.

Bolton, Brenda. *Medieval Reformation*. *Foundations of Medieval History Ser.* Holmes & Meier 1983 $22.50. ISBN 0-8419-0874-6. A general introduction to the Renaissance of the twelfth century, providing an "account of the varied attempts which were made in the period to transform the life of the Church and the way the hierarchy responded to them."

Deanesly, Margaret. *History of the Medieval Church, 590–1500*. Routledge Chapman & Hall 1969 $14.95. ISBN 0-416-18100-7. A very well-written short study of the church in this period, with particular emphasis on the social and personal aspects of church history.

Hamilton, Bernard. *Religion in the Medieval West*. Arnold 1986 o.p. General study of the interaction between the church and lay society in three sections exploring the faith taught by the institutional church, the extent to which the laity understood and practiced this faith, and noninstitutional faiths that existed between the sixth and sixteenth centuries.

Huizinga, Johan. *The Waning of the Middle Ages: A Study of the Forms of Life, Thought, and Art in France and the Netherlands in the XIVth and XVth Centuries*. Doubleday 1954 repr. of 1924 ed. $8.95. ISBN 0-385-09288-1. A classic examination of the forms of life and thought in France and the Netherlands in the fourteenth and fifteenth centuries.

Oakley, Francis. *The Western Church in the Later Middle Ages*. Cornell Univ. Pr. $39.95. ISBN 0-8014-1208-0. An examination of the late medieval period, discussing political history, the institutional church, liturgy, devotional practice, canon law, mysticism, and monasticism.

Southern, R. W. *Western Society and the Church in the Middle Ages*. Viking Penguin 1970 $8.95. ISBN 0-14-020503-9. Comprehensive and well-written history of Western Christianity emphasizing its political context.

Spitz, Lewis W. *Renaissance and Reformation*. 2 vols. Concordia 1980 $16.95 ea. ISBNs 0-570-3818-9, 0-570-3819-7. A very readable intellectual history of two crucial periods in history, paying particular attention to ecclesiastical developments of the Reformation era.

Wallace-Hadrill, John Michael. *The Frankish Church*. OUP 1983 $98.00. ISBN 0-19-826906-4. Collection of essays on various subjects dealing with the Frankish Church, which, taken together, provide an excellent account of the church in the Merovingian and Carolingian periods.

Eastern Churches and Crusades

The Orthodox Church began in the eastern part of the Roman Empire, spread to Russia and other parts of eastern Europe, and today consists of several churches independent in their administration, but sharing a common faith. Differences between the Western and Eastern churches can be traced back to the Middle Ages, when the two churches grew increasingly estranged from one another until their disagreements finally erupted into an open and lasting schism. Two dates have been suggested as the beginning of the schism: 1054, when the Roman church excommunicated Michael Caerularius, Patriarch of Constantinople, and the patriarch excommunicated legates of the Roman church; and 1204, when crusading forces from the West sacked Constantinople. The causes of the schism, however, developed over centuries and therefore cannot be dated exactly. One particular difference between the two traditions is the veneration of icons in the Orthodox church. Icons, flat pictures with representations of Jesus, Mary, or the saints, are used in public and private worship, and are believed to provide access to the Divine. During the eighth and ninth centuries, a factious, sometimes violent, debate was waged over whether the worship of icons should be permitted. The struggle, referred to as the iconoclastic controversy, failed, however, to dislodge their use in the East or in the West, for that matter.

Part of the history of the Eastern church and its relations with the West is the phenomenon of the Crusades. The first Crusade was preached by Pope Urban II in 1095 with the original objective of recovering the Holy Land from Islam. This was accomplished in 1099, but the Holy Land was lost back to the Muslims very soon. The causes of the Crusades were complex, including ideological, social, and economic factors. Later Crusades were also directed against non-Christians outside the Holy Land and against Christian heretics, such as the Albigensian Crusade of the thirteenth century, which was aimed at a group of Cathari in southern France.

Atiya, Aziz S. *The Crusade: Historiography and Bibliography*. Greenwood 1976 o.p. Provides extensive bibliographical information on the literature of the Crusades from both Christian and Muslim worlds.

Cowdrey, H. E. *Popes, Monks and Crusaders*. Hambledon Press 1983 $55.00. ISBN 0-907628-34-6. A collection of scholarly articles written over a period of 13 years, about half of which are on issues and events concerning the Crusades.

Dvornik, Francis. *Byzantium and the Roman Primacy*. Fordham rev. ed. 1979 $15.00. ISBN 0-8232-0701-3. A general study of the political history to the background of the division between Eastern and Western Christianity.

―――――. *Early Christian and Byzantine Political Philosophy: Origins and Background*. 2 vols. Dumbarton Oaks 1966 o.p. A scholarly and thorough study of political philosophy over two millennia in the Ancient Near East, Ancient Greece, the Hellenistic world, the world of Judaism, the Roman Empire, and early Christian and Byzantine societies.

Erdman, Carl. *The Origin of the Idea of Crusade*. Trans. by Marshall W. Baldwin and Walter Goffart. Princeton U. Pr. 1977 o.p. Originally published in 1935, an important and erudite investigation of the history of the Crusade, arguing that it was a culmination of a centuries-long development based on holy war and Christian knighthood, whose true aim was the liberation of the entire Eastern Church by a holy war.

Geanakoplos, Deno J. *Byzantine Church, Society, and Civilization Seen through Contemporary Eyes.* U. Ch. Pr. 1986 $32.50. ISBN 0-226-28460-3. A very useful sourcebook of texts arranged topically concerning Byzantine ecclesiastical, social, and political history as well as several helpful chronological lists and maps.

———. *Emperor Michael Palaeologus and the West, 1258–1282: A Study in Byzantine-Latin Relations.* Shoe String 1973 repr. of 1959 ed. o.p. In the words of the author, "examines the relations between Eastern and Western Christendom during the reign of the thirteenth century Byzantine Emperor Michael VIII Palaeologus."

———. *The Interaction of the "Sibling" Byzantine and Western Cultures in the Middle Ages and Italian Renaissance (330–1600).* Bks. Demand repr. of 1976 ed. $114.00. ISBN 0-8357-8186-0. "This collection of essays is tied together by the common theme of Byzantine-Latin cultural relations" (Alice-Mary Talbot, *Journal of the Amer. Academy of Religion*).

Hopko, Thomas, ed. *Women and the Priesthood: Essays from the Orthodox Tradition.* St. Vladimirs 1983 o.p. Essays in a scriptural, historical, and theological context presenting various reasons against allowing women to become Orthodox priests.

Hussey, J. M. *The Orthodox Church in the Byzantine Empire. History of the Christian Church Ser.* OUP 1990 $29.95. ISBN 0-19-826456-9. General treatment of both internal and external affairs of the Byzantine Church from the seventh through the fifteenth centuries.

Kazhdan, Alexander P., ed. *The Oxford Dictionary of Byzantium.* 3 vols. OUP 1991 ISBN 0-19-504652-8. Comprehensive in-depth articles on all aspects of Byzantine life, indicating the integration of religion, politics, and everyday life.

Lossky, Vladimir. *Orthodox Theology: An Introduction.* St. Vladimirs 1978 $8.95. ISBN 0-913836-43-5. Includes an English translation of a series of related articles concerning various doctrinal issues important to the Orthodox Church, including the Trinity, creation, and Christology.

Magoulias, Harry J. *Byzantine Christianity: Emperor, Church and the West.* Wayne St. U. Pr. 1982 $22.50. ISBN 0-8143-1704-9. A general survey of Christianity in the Byzantine Empire focusing on four topics: the relation between Christianity and the emperor, various fringe and heretical groups in the East, types of mysticism, and relations with the West.

Meyendorff, John. *Byzantine Theology: Historical Trends and Doctrinal Themes.* Fordham 2nd rev. ed. 1987 $15.00. ISBN 0-8232-0967-9. A very useful introduction to Byzantine religious thought, discussing Byzantine theology within its historical context from the fifth through the fifteenth centuries and various doctrines important to the theology including creation, man, Jesus Christ, the Holy Spirit, God, and the Eucharist.

———. *Byzantium and the Rise of Russia.* Cambridge U. Pr. 1981 $82.50. A detailed and scholarly examination of the complex ecclesiastical and cultural relations between Byzantium and Russia in the twelfth through fourteenth centuries and the diplomatic activity of the fourteenth-century ecclesiastical leaders.

Nicol, D. M. *Church and Society in the Last Centuries of Byzantium. Birkbeck Lectures.* Cambridge U. Pr. 1979 o.p. Analyzes three situations that particularly marked the internal life of the empire: the Arsemite schism, Palamite controversies, and the question of union with Rome, attempting to show that despite the fall of the empire, the spirit of Byzantium was preserved by the Orthodox Church.

Ouspensky, Leonid, and Vladimir Lossky. *The Meaning of Icons.* Trans. by G. E. Palmar and E. Kadlovbousky. St. Vladimirs rev. ed. $39.95. A valuable theological and art historical study of the iconography in the Orthodox Church, with most attention devoted to Russian icons.

Peters, Edward. *The First Crusade: The Chronicle of Fulcher of Chartres and Other Source Materials.* U. of Pa. Pr. 1971 $28.95. ISBN 0-8122-7643-4. A social history of the eleventh-century church reform and the development of the theology of the Crusades through the eyes of participants.

Queller, Donald E. *The Fourth Crusade. Middle Ages Ser.* U. of Pa. Pr. 1977 $10.95. A valuable, detailed account of how the Fourth Crusaders came to conquer Constantinople.

Riley-Smith, Jonathan S. C. *The First Crusade and the Idea of Crusading. Middle Ages Ser.* U. of Pa. Pr. 1986 $18.95. ISBN 0-8122-1363-7. Shows how the idea of crusading was transformed by the dreadful experiences of the army on the march and the euphoria that followed the capture of Jerusalem into a new association of ideas that found its way into the narrative accounts of eyewitnesses.

Runciman, Steven. *The Byzantine Theocracy. Weil Lecture Ser.* Cambridge U. Pr. 1977 $34.95. ISBN 0-521-21401-7. Lectures on the church and state in Byzantium.

———. *The Eastern Schism.* AMS Pr. 1983 repr. of 1956 ed. $24.50. ISBN 0-404-16247-9. Discusses the historical background of the schism between the Western and Eastern churches, focusing on the impact the Crusades had on this division.

———. *History of the Crusades.* 3 vols. Cambridge U. Pr. 1987 $125.00. ISBN 0-521-06163-6. A masterful treatment of all of the religious and political aspects of the Crusades.

Schulz, Hans Joachim. *The Byzantine Liturgy.* Liturgical Pr. 1986 $17.50. ISBN 0-8146-607-2. A discussion of specific authors and documents important for understanding Byzantine liturgy between the fourth and fifteenth centuries. Introduction by Robert Taft.

Ware, Timothy. *Orthodox Church.* Viking Penguin 1963 $6.95. ISBN 0-14-020592-6. A simple, balanced, irenic introduction to the Orthodox Church, providing a general history from the fourth century to the present and discussing such topics as God and humans, the sacraments, ecclesiology, and liturgy.

Emperors, Popes, and Councils

The Middle Ages witnessed several important events that influenced the internal workings of the church and the relation between the church and secular authorities. In the investiture controversy, the church and secular leaders battled over whether the secular leaders had the authority to appoint persons to religious posts. Lay investiture was prohibited in 1075 by Pope Gregory VII, although such practices continued to varying degrees in certain parts of western Europe. A severe test to the institution of the papacy came during the fourteenth century, when, for a time, two, and later, three, men claimed the title of pope. This Great Schism, as it is sometimes called, lasted until 1417, when the Council of Constance elected Martin V as sole pope. The schism of the papacy provided fuel to the conciliar theorists who believed the supreme authority in the church lies not with the pope, but with a general council. Although later papal decrees significantly curtailed the power of the councils, the conciliar movement can be viewed as an important influence leading to the Reformation.

Barraclough, Geoffrey. *The Medieval Papacy. Lib. of World Civilization.* Norton 1979 $9.95. ISBN 0-393-951006. A well-written and richly illustrated introduction for the general reader in which the author describes the "various factors which historically helped to shape the develement of the medieval papacy."

Crowder, Christopher. *Unity, Heresy, and Reform, 1378–1460.* Limestone Pr. 1987 $12.50. ISBN 0-919642-10-1. A history of medieval attempts to end the split between eastern and western Christianity, providing introductory comments to the documents that comprise the heart of the book.

Gill, Joseph. *The Council of Florence.* AMS Pr. 1981 repr. of 1959 ed. $37.50. ISBN 0-404-17016-1. A detailed study of the fifteenth-century council, which "dealt a death-blow to Conciliarism" and attempted to unite the separated churches of East and West.

Izbicki, Thomas M. *Protector of the Faith: Cardinal Johannes de Turrecremata and the Defense of the Institutional Church.* Bks. Demand repr. of 1981 ed. $55.00. ISBN 0-

685-17842-0. A scholarly volume focusing on the ecclesiology of Turrecremata, the Dominican cardinal who was a dominant papal apologist of the fifteenth century.

Morris, Colin. *The Papal Monarchy: The Western Church from 1050 to 1250*. OUP 1989 $84.00. ISBN 0-19-826907-2. A detailed investigation of the evolution of the papacy against the backdrop of the emerging institutions of late medieval culture.

Noble, Thomas F. X. *The Republic of St. Peter, 680–825*. U. of Pa. Pr. $19.95. ISBN 0-8122-1239-8. A thorough study of the critical period when the bishop of Rome became a pawn and then a major player in regional and international politics.

Swanson, R. N. *University, Academics, and the Great Schism*. Cambridge U. Pr. 1979 o.p. Examines university participation in the post-1378 schism and the theories that were developed in academic circles to help heal the schism and restore a united papacy.

Thomson, J. A. *Popes and Princes 1417–1517: Politics and Polity in Late Medieval Church. Early Modern Europe Today Ser.* Unwin Hyman 1980 $16.95. ISBN 0-04-901027-1. Papal history between the Council of Constance and the Lutheran Reformation, arguing that "the various princes of Europe holding threat of another general council over the Popes, asserted their authority in their own national churches and reduced the relatively passive, politically reactive papacy to a mere principality itself."

Tierney, Brian. *The Crisis of Church and State, 1050–1300*. U. of Toronto Pr. 1988 $19.95. ISBN 0-8020-6701-8. Extracts from various documents revealing ideas behind the conflict between the church and the secular authority, prefaced by a very helpful introduction providing the historical background of the documents.

Ullmann, Walter. *A Short History of the Papacy in the Middle Ages*. Methuen 1974 o.p. How the papacy as an institution developed from the end of the Roman empire into the medieval period.

Christian Thought and Doctrine

Much of Christian thought during the Middle Ages was devoted to an inquiry into the relation between reason and revelation. Is it necessary, or even possible, for reason to prove the Christian truths that are known through faith or revelation? Two major developments played a significant role in these debates. First was the rise of Scholasticism, the application of logical and dialectical principles to philosophical and theological problems. The culmination of this intellectual development was the theological syntheses ("summae"), the most famous being the *Summa Theologica* of THOMAS AQUINAS, written during the second half of the thirteenth century. The second important influence on Christian thought was the translation of ARISTOTLE's (see also Vol. 3) works into Latin and their dissemination in western Europe beginning in the twelfth century. These writings had a great impact on the thinkers of this period, most notably Aquinas. Not all of the developments in Christian thought during the Middle Ages were based on rational thought. Several individuals and groups emphasized mystical elements within Christianity.

Baldwin, John W. *The Scholastic Culture of the Middle Ages: 1000–1300. Civilization and Society Ser.* Heath 1990 $10.50. ISBN 0-669-62059-9. Very good textbook description of early Scholasticism, beginning with an overview of medieval society in the eleventh through nineteenth centuries.

Bynum, Caroline W. *Jesus as Mother: Studies in the Spirituality of the High Middle Ages*. U. CA Pr. 1982 $12.95. ISBN 0-520-05222-6. Studies the complex relations between the individual and the community and women and clerical authority.

Cassirer, Ernst, and others, eds. *The Renaissance Philosophy of Man*. U. Ch. Pr. 1956 $12.95. ISBN 0-226-09604-1. Seeks to "acquaint the informed student with certain major thinkers of the early Italian Renaissance through translations of some of their more important works."

Chenu, M. D. *Nature, Man, and Society in the Twelfth Century: Essays on New Theological Perspectives in the Latin West.* Ed. and trans. by Jerome Taylor and Lester K. Little. *Midway Repr. Ser.* U. Ch. Pr. 1983 $21.95. ISBN 0-226-10256-4. Nine essays that together represent a "classic study in the medieval interrelationships of theology and history" (Ray Petry, *Church History*).

Cohen, Jeremy. *The Friars and the Jews: The Evolution of Medieval Anti-Judaism.* Cornell Univ. Pr. 1984 $12.95. ISBN 0-8014-9266-1. Focuses on "the friars' attack upon the Jews, the basic ideas and theological considerations that underlay their anti-Jewish activities and polemics" during the period between the fourth Lateran Council (1215) and the Black Death (1347–50).

Evans, G. R. *The Language and Logic of the Bible: The Earlier Middle Ages.* Cambridge U. Pr. 1984 $49.95. ISBN 0-521-26371-9. Examines how the study of the Bible was transformed in the Middle Ages by the penetration of grammatical and dialectical studies.

_____. *Old Arts and New Theology: The Beginnings of Theology as an Academic Discipline.* OUP 1980 o.p. An examination of the interaction between theology and the liberal arts and the development of theology into an academic discipline during the twelfth century, when the methods of investigation used in teaching the liberal arts began to be applied to theology.

Gilmore, Myron P. *The World of Humanism, 1453–1517. Rise of Modern Europe Ser.* Greenwood 1983 repr. of 1952 ed. $52.50. General survey of the social, economic, religious, scientific, and artistic developments, and the relation among them, at the end of the medieval period and the beginning of the Renaissance, a period that saw, among other things, the flowering of humanism.

Gilson, Étienne. *History of Christian Philosophy in the Middle Ages.* Random 1955 o.p. "Provides the general reader with an introduction to the history of Christian philosophy from Justin Martyr in the second century up to Nicholas of Cusa in the fifteenth century whose work stands on the border line of a new historical period," according to the author.

_____. *The Spirit of Medieval Philosophy.* U. of Notre Dame Pr. 1991 $12.95. ISBN 0-268-01740-9. In lectures that present a recognizable phenomenon of Christian philosophy, Gilson states that the "spirit of Medieval philosophy is the spirit of Christianity penetrating the Greek tradition, working within it, drawing out of it a certain view of the world specifically Christian."

Kantorowicz, Ernest H. *The King's Two Bodies: A Study of Medieval Political Theology.* Princeton U. Pr. 1957 $19.95. ISBN 0-691-02018-3. A scholarly study examining a religious strand within the political theory of later medieval England, showing how jurists in England worked out a political theory of "two bodies of the king" from the Christological doctrine of the two natures of Christ.

Kieckhefer, Richard. *Unquiet Souls: Fourteenth Century Saints and Their Religious Milieu.* U. Ch. Pr. 1984 o.p. Valuable analysis of the theological assumptions of the hagiography of fourteenth-century saints. The dominant motifs are found to be "patience, extraordinary identification with the Passion, extreme self-perception of oneself as a sinner," and inner spirituality as seen in experiences of rapture and relevation.

Knowles, David. *The Evolution of Medieval Thought.* Ed. by D. E. Luscombe. Trans. by C. N. Brooke. Longman 1988 $19.95. ISBN 0-582-49426-5. Very good account of what the author calls "the rise and decline of a great and ambitious intellectual structure which the thirteenth century brought to a precariously stable apogee and which the fourteenth century saw disintegrate."

Kretzmann, Norman. *The Cambridge History of Later Medieval Philosophy: From the Rediscovery of Aristotle to the Disintegration of Scholasticism 1100–1600.* Cambridge U. Pr. 1982 o.p. Contains the collaborative efforts of 41 scholars whose work provides up-to-date research on numerous areas of the history of medieval philosophy, including literature, logic, metaphysics and epistemology, natural philosophy, ethics, and political theory.

Kristeller, Paul O. *Renaissance Thought: The Classic, Scholastic and Humanistic Strains.* Ed. by Michael Mooney. Col. U. Pr. 1981 $55.00. ISBN 0-231-04512-3. Attempts to demonstrate "the impact and influence of classical studies and of ancient sources upon the philosophical and general thought of the Renaissance period."

Lasker, Daniel J. *Jewish Philosophical Polemics against Christianity in the Middle Ages.* ADL $15.00. ISBN 0-686-95177-8. Examines the rise of philosophical Jewish anti-Christian materials in the twelfth century, documents that were later a common feature of medieval Jewish literature.

Leff, Gordon. *Medieval Thought from Saint Augustine to Ockham.* Humanities 1978 repr. of 1958 ed. o.p. A general introduction to the philosophical thinking of the Middle Ages.

Le Goff, Jacques. *The Birth of Purgatory.* Trans. by Arthur Goldhammer. U. Ch. Pr. 1986 $17.95. ISBN 0-226-47083-0. "Traces the formation of the idea of purgatory from its Judeo-Christian antiquity to its emergence in the second half of the twelfth century."

———. *The Medieval Imagination.* Trans. by Arthur Goldhammer. U. Ch. Pr. 1988 $29.95. ISBN 0-226-470849. Well-written and documented study of the medieval concepts of miracles, time and space, the body, imagination and literature, and dreams.

Oberman, Heiko A. *Forerunners of the Reformation: The Shape of Late Medieval Thought.* Trans. by Paul L. Nyhus. Bks. Demand repr. of 1981 ed. $86.80. ISBN 0-685-17052-7. Designed for the nonspecialist, in Oberman's words, the book "introduces the reader to aspects of such major themes as conciliarism, curialism, mysticism, scholasticism, 'devotio moderna,' and the impact of Renaissance humanism."

———. *The Harvest of Medieval Theology: Gabriel Biel and Late Medieval Nominalism.* Labyrinth Pr. 1983 repr. of 1963 ed. $18.50. ISBN 0-939464-05-5. A complex and detailed work that examines nominalist thought, especially that of Gabriel Biel, a fifteenth-century Scholastic philosopher.

Ozment, Steven E. *The Age of Reform 1250–1550: An Intellectual and Religious History of Late Medieval and Reformation Europe.* Yale U. Pr. 1980 $17.00. ISBN 0-300-02760-5. A very good general account of the intellectual and religious history of the period.

Petry, Ray C. *Late Medieval Mysticism. Lib. of Christian Class.* Westminster John Knox 1980 $14.99. ISBN 0-664-24163-8. Selections from the writings of persons important to the mystical thought of medieval Christianity.

Rubin, Miri. *Corpus Christi: The Eucharist in Late Medieval Culture.* OUP 1991 $69.95. ISBN 0-19-35605-9. A thorough study of the one subject that brings into focus philosophical, theological, and practical problems of medieval Christianity.

Russell, Jeffrey B. *Lucifer: The Devil in the Middle Ages.* Cornell Univ. Pr. 1984 $36.50. ISBN 0-8014-1503-9. A study of the disparate views of the devil in the Middle Ages and the relation of the devil to evil as seen from theology, philosophy, literature, drama, homiletics, hagiography, folklore, and the visual arts.

Smalley, Beryl. *Study of the Bible in the Middle Ages.* U. of Notre Dame Pr. 1964 $13.95. ISBN 0-268-00267-3. A general survey of biblical studies during the Middle Ages, with most attention paid to the studies in universities and monastic communities.

Szarmach, Paul E., ed. *An Introduction to the Medieval Mystics of Europe.* State U. NY Pr. 1985 $49.50. ISBN 0-87395-835-7. Fourteen essays on various topics including Augustine, St. Bernard, Jewish mysticism, Aquinas as mystic, Juliana of Norwich, women mystics, Meister Eckhart, and Nicholas of Cusa.

Tavard, George H. *Holy Writ or Holy Church: The Crisis of the Protestant Reformation.* Greenwood 1978 repr. of 1959 ed. $35.00. ISBN 0-313-2058-4. A brief study of patristic and early medieval treatments of the relation between the attitudes toward Scripture and tradition, and "a more detailed account of the positions taken by numerous writers from the fourteenth century . . . through the Elizabethan period in England" (John Cobb, *Interpretation*).

Trinkaus, Charles. *The Scope of Renaissance Humanism.* U. of Mich. Pr. 1983 $39.50. ISBN 0-472-10031-9. Contains essays written over a period of 40 years, centering on an "effort to evaluate the historical importance of Renaissance humanism both in the context of Italian and Northern Renaissance and in the larger perspective of its place in the history of Western Civilization."

Weinberg, Julius R. *A Short History of Medieval Philosophy*. Princeton U. Pr. 1964 $12.95.
  ISBN 0-691-01956-8. A general introduction to the major figures and philosophical
  ideas of the period, including sections on Islamic and Jewish thought.

Christian Life and Culture

In western Europe, Christian life and culture was for most people synonymous with life and culture in general. The titles in this section discuss some of
the more important and interesting aspects of this culture, including the making
of pilgrimages; the veneration of relics; miracles; the rise of various heretical
groups, such as the Cathari, Waldensians, and Lollards; and the attempt by
ecclesiastical authorities to control and eliminate such groups, often through
the use of inquisitions, the practice of penance and indulgences, and the
expansion of monastic and other religious orders, such as the Dominicans and
Franciscans.

Atkinson, Clarissa W. *Mystic and Pilgrim: The "Book" and the World of Margery Kempe*.
  Cornell Univ. Pr. 1983 $31.95. ISBN 0-8014-1521-7. Begins with an epitome of the
  "Book" of Kempe and then traces the familial and social relations and those with the
  church and clergy of this fifteenth-century mystic.
Baldwin, John W. *Masters, Princes, and Merchants: The Social Views and Reforms of
  Peter the Chanter and His Circle*. 2 vols. Princeton U. Pr. 1970 o.p. Solid study, rich in
  documentation, providing an "analysis of the ideas of the circle of Peter the
  Chanter," a group of teachers in Paris whose central concern was individual
  righteousness.
Bell, Rudolph M. *Holy Anorexia*. U. Ch. Pr. 1985 $11.95. ISBN 0-226-04205-7. Traces
  medieval women's attempt to control their lives through anorexia, revealing much
  about family life during the era.
Brooke, Rosalind, and Christopher Brooke. *Popular Religion in the Middle Ages*. Thames
  Hudson 1985 $10.95. ISBN 0-500-27381-2. General appraisal of Christianity as
  understood and practiced by the laity, evidenced largely by relics, church buildings,
  and other religious objects.
Bynum, Caroline W. *Holy Feast and Holy Fast: The Religious Significance of Food to
  Medieval Women. The New Historian: Studies in Cultural Poetics*. U. CA Pr. 1987
  $37.50. ISBN 0-520-05722-8. Discusses how religiously shaped images of food
  functioned in the lives of medieval women, from anorexics to those who were
  refused the Eucharist.
Cohn, Norman. *Pursuit of the Millennium: Revolutionary Millenarians and Mystical
  Anarchists of the Middle Ages*. OUP rev. ed. 1970 $11.95. ISBN 0-19-500456-6. Traces
  the history of millennial sects of Europe, groups that believed, in Cohn's words, in a
  "miraculous event in which the world would be utterly transformed."
Davies, Horton, and Marie Helene Davies. *Holy Days and Holidays: The Medieval
  Pilgrimage to Compostela*. Bucknell U. Pr. 1982 $37.50. ISBN 0-8387-5018-4. A
  scholarly but very readable description of the sacred and secular aspects of "the
  medieval pilgrimage to Compostela, the third most important pilgrimage site after
  Jerusalem and Rome" (Howard Happ, *Theology Today*).
Dronke, Peter. *Women Writers of the Middle Ages: A Critical Study of Texts from Perpetua
  (203) to Marguerite Porete (1310)*. Cambridge U. Pr. 1984 $15.95. ISBN 0-521-27573-3.
  Seeks to explore the ways women helped to shape the earliest Christian writing in a
  Western language and to observe their particular contributions to Western literature
  over a millennium."
Ferrante, Joan M. *Woman as Image in Medieval Literature from the Twelfth Century to
  Dante*. Labyrinth Pr. 1985 repr. of 1975 ed. $8.95. ISBN 0-939464-43-8. Focuses on
  the symbolic treatment of women in the literature of the twelfth and thirteenth
  centuries, concluding with the writings of Dante.

Fleming, John V. *An Introduction to the Franciscan Literature of the Middle Ages.* Franciscan Pr. 1977 $10.95. ISBN 0-8199-0651-4. A general discussion of the major literary works written by Franciscans during the thirteenth and fourteenth centuries.

Geary, Patrick J. *Furta Sacra: Thefts of Relics in the Central Middle Ages.* Princeton U. Pr. 1990 $12.95. ISBN 0-691-00862-0. Reviews accounts from the ninth to the twelfth centuries that told of and often condoned the theft of sacred relics.

Gies, Joseph, and Frances Gies. *Women in the Middle Ages.* HarpC 1979 $6.95. ISBN 0-06-464037-X. A general discussion of women in the Middle Ages, followed by more specific studies on women in various states of life and professions.

Hamilton, Bernard. *The Medieval Inquisition: Foundations of Medieval History.* Holmes & Meier 1981 o.p. A general introduction to the actions undertaken by the inquisitions of the Middle Ages, which began in the thirteenth century.

Hardison, O. B. *Christian Rite and Christian Drama in the Middle Ages: Essays in the Origin and Early History of Modern Drama.* Greenwood 1983 repr. of 1965 ed. $65.00. ISBN 0-313-24121-X. A detailed analysis examining the close connection between religious ritual and drama, the emergence of liturgical drama, and the origins of medieval drama.

Haskins, Charles H. *The Renaissance of the Twelfth Century.* HUP 1971 $12.50. ISBN 0-674-76075-1. A very readable general examination of the twelfth-century revival of the "Latin classics and their influence, the new jurisprudence and the more varied historiography, the new knowledge of the Greeks and Arabs and its effects upon Western science and philosophy, and the new institutions of learning."

Hunt, Noreen, ed. *Cluniac Monasticism in the Central Middle Ages.* Shoe String 1971 o.p. A collection of 10 valuable essays surveying the principal area of Cluniac scholarship, including Cluniac spirituality, the expansion and influence of Cluniac monasticism, and the role of the Cluniacs in the Crusades.

Johnson, Penelope. *Equal in Monastic Profession: Religious Women in Medieval France.* Women in Culture and Society Ser. U. Ch. Pr. 1991 $39.95. ISBN 0-226-40185-5. Analysis of nuns' lives and roles in society contrasted with the lives and power of monks.

Knowles, David. *The Religious Orders in England.* 3 vols. Cambridge U. Pr. 1948–79 o.p. A thorough investigation of the organizational history of the religious orders from the thirteenth century until their dissolution in the sixteenth century.

Laistner, Max. *Thought and Letters in Western Europe, A.D. 500–900.* Gordon Pr. 1972 $59.95. ISBN 0-8490-1207-4. A general survey of the literature and the study of literature in western Europe from the fifth through the ninth centuries.

Lambert, Malcolm. *Medieval Heresy: Popular Movements from Bogomil to Hus.* Blackwell Pubs. rev. ed. 1992. ISBN 0-631-17432-X. A general introduction to the popular heretical movements between the eighth and fifteenth centuries, movements with a substantial following among laypeople that deviated from papal teachings.

Lawrence, C. H. *Medieval Monasticism: Forms of Religious Life, Western Europe in the Middle Ages.* Longman 1989 text ed. $19.95. ISBN 0-582-01727-0. A short but detailed and very readable survey of monasticism, tracing the "growth of the monastic tradition as a whole in its social context from its origins in late antiquity down to the later Middle Ages."

Lea, Henry C. *History of Auricular Confession and Indulgences in the Latin Church.* 3 vols. Greenwood 1968 repr. of 1896 ed. $67.25. ISBN 0-8371-0140-9. A scholarly and detailed study of the origin and development of the practice of confession and indulgences.

Leclerq, Jean. *The Love of Learning and the Desire for God: A Study of Monastic Culture.* Trans. by C. Mishrashi. Fordham 1985 $14.00. ISBN 0-8232-0407-3. Explores the relation between learning and study and spirituality in monastic communities of the Middle Ages.

Leroy-Ladurie, Emmanuel. *Montaillou: The Promised Land of Error.* Trans. by Barbara Bray. Random 1979 $11.96. ISBN 0-394-72964-1. A detailed study of Montaillou, a small French village that actively supported the Cathar heresy.

Leyser, Henrietta. *Hermits and the New Monasticism: A Study of Religious Communities in Western Europe, 1000–1150.* St. Martin 1984 $29.95. ISBN 0-312-36999-9. Surveys the phenomenon of hermitism or solitary monastic life and focuses on its eventual fusion with monasticism through the emergence of new communal forms of the hermitic lifestyle.

Little, Lester K. *Religious Poverty and the Profit Economy in Medieval Europe.* Cornell Univ. Pr. 1983 $12.95. ISBN 0-8014-9247-5. Traces the relationship between the church and the newly emergent profit economy of medieval Europe, especially in Italy and France, between 1000 and 1300.

McGinn, Bernard. *Visions of the End: Apocalyptic Traditions in the Middle Ages. Records of Civilization Sources and Studies.* Col. U. Pr. 1979 o.p. A very helpful anthology of texts accompanied by substantial introductions placing each selection in its historical context, providing a useful introduction to medieval apocalypticism.

McNeil, John T., and Helena M. Gamer. *Medieval Handbooks of Penance: A Translation of the Principal* Libri Poenitenitales. *Records of Western Civilization Ser.* Col. U. Pr. 1990 $58.00. ISBN 0-231-00889-9. Introductory essays and translations that reveal the preoccupations of medieval confessors and penitents.

Moore, R. I., ed. *The Birth of Popular Heresy. Documents of Medieval History Ser.* St. Martin 1976 $25.00. ISBN 0-231-08190-1. A selection of texts relating to heresy in the eleventh and twelfth centuries, including such topics as popular dissent in the eleventh century, the emergence of anticlericalism in the twelfth century, the infiltration of Eastern dualism in the West, and the establishment of the Cathari.

Nichols, John A, and M. Thomas Shank, eds. *Medieval Religious Women I: Distant Echoes. Cistercian Studies Ser.* Cistercian Pubns. 1984 $29.95. ISBN 0-87907-5. The first of three projected volumes on medieval religious women presents in a historical vein the variety of lifestyles open to religious women from the fourth to the fifteenth centuries.

Payer, Pierre J. *Sex and the Penitentials: The Development of a Sexual Code 550–1150.* U. of Toronto Pr. 1984 $35.00. ISBN 0-8020-5649-0. An examination of the church's attitude toward sexuality as found in medieval penitential literature.

Pennington, Basil. *The Last of the Fathers.* St. Bedes Pubns. 1983 o.p. A discussion of the writings and thoughts of the major figures in this monastic community, particularly Bernard of Clairvaux, William of St. Thierry, Guerrie of Igny, and St. Aelred of Rievaulx.

Peters, Edward, ed. *Monks, Bishops, and Pagans: Christian Culture in Gaul and Italy. Middle Ages Ser.* U. of Pa. Pr. 1975 o.p. Pertinent sources in translation, including *The World of Gregory of Tours,* translated by W. C. McDermott.

Power, Eileen, and M. Poston. *Medieval Women.* Cambridge U. Pr. 1976 $12.95. ISBN 0-521-09946-3. Essays on medieval women, including mistresses of great households, heiresses, owners of businesses, scholars, and nuns.

Russell, Jeffrey B. *Dissent and Reform in the Early Middle Ages.* AMS Pr. 1982 repr. of 1965 ed. $36.00. ISBN 0-404-16196-0. A thorough examination of the dissenting and heretical groups that appeared in western Europe up to the thirteenth century, claiming that these groups were exaggerations of or reactions against reform movements of the Western Church.

_____. *A History of Witchcraft: Sorcerers, Heretics and Pagans.* Peter Smith 1983 $22.50. ISBN 0-8446-6052-3. "The author continues to argue that witchcraft during the witch-craze era (14th–17th centuries) derived from heretical groups and individuals rebelling against Christian authoritarianism. . . . Strikes a nice balance between scholarship and readability" (*Library Journal*).

_____. *Witchcraft in the Middle Ages.* Cornell Univ. Pr. 1984 $39.95. ISBN 0-8014-0697-8. A scholarly "demonstration of how the political, social, economic, religious, and intellectual developments during the Middle Ages either fostered or militated against the growth of witchcraft" (Walter Bense, *Church History*).

Shannon, Albert C. *The Medieval Inquisition.* Augustinian Coll. Pr. 1983 $15.00. ISBN 0-9612336-0-5. Traces the growth of the repression of heresy to its culmination in the Inquisition.

Tentler, T. *Sin and Confession on the Eve of the Reformation.* Princeton U. Pr. 1977 o.p. Explores the theology of penance implicit in the practical manuals for confessors.

Thurston, Herbert. *The Holy Year of Jubilee: An Account of the History and Ceremonial of the Roman Jubilee.* AMS Pr. 1980 repr. of 1900 ed. $38.50. ISBN 0-404-16547-8. A comprehensive history of the Jubilee Year, the practice of granting to those who make the pilgrimage to Rome during the proclaimed year a complete remission from punishment of their sins, from its beginning in 1300 to the end of the nineteenth century.

Tuchman, Barbara W. *A Distant Mirror: The Calamitous Fourteenth Century.* Knopf 1978 $45.00. ISBN 0-394-40026-7. A Pulitzer Prize-winning account of the fourteenth century, concentrating on French chivalry, constructed around the figure of Euguerrand de Coucy VII, whom the author describes as "the most skilled and experienced of all the knights of France."

Vogel, Cyrille. *Medieval Liturgy: An Introduction to the Sources.* Trans. and rev. by William G. Storey and Niels Krogh Rasmussen. Pastoral Pr. 1987 $25.95. ISBN 0-912405-10-4. An indispensable introduction to resources and scholarly literature of medieval liturgy.

Von Simson, Otto G. *The Gothic Cathedral: Origins of Gothic Architecture and the Medieval Concept of Order.* Bollingen Ser. Princeton U. Pr. 1988 $14.95. ISBN 0-691-01867-7. Examines what early Gothic architecture tells us about the religious thought of that period.

Voragine, Jacobus de. *The Golden Legend.* Trans. by William Granger Ryan. 2 vols. Princeton U. Pr. 1993 $90.00. ISBN 0-691-00894-9. The most popular collections of saints' lives in the middle ages, shedding light on daily life and popular beliefs.

Wakefield, Walter L. *Heresy, Crusade, and Inquisition in Southern France, 1100–1250.* U. CA Pr. 1974 o.p. A solid account of the rise of the heretical groups—the Cathari and Waldensians—in southern France, the prosecution of the heresy, including the Albigensian Crusade fought in the thirteenth century, and the inquisition that stemmed from it.

Ward, Benedicta. *Miracles and the Medieval Mind: Theory, Record, and Event, 1000–1215.* U. of Pa. Pr. 1982 $19.95. ISBN 0-8122-1228-2. Examines transformations in medieval views of miracles from folk tales to genres controlled by church officials.

Weinstein, Donald, and Rudolph Bell. *Saints and Society: The Two Worlds of Western Christendom, 1000 to 1700.* U. Ch. Pr. 1986 $16.95. ISBN 0-226-89056-2. An investigation of what the legends of the saints tell us about medieval religious values, especially the life stages of childhood, adolescence, and adulthood, and notions of sanctity, for the period 1000 through 1700.

Wemple, Suzanne F. *Women in Frankish Society: Marriage and the Cloister, 500–900.* Univ. of Pa. Pr. 1985 repr. of 1980 ed. $24.95. ISBN 0-8122-1209-6. Focuses on the legal and economic position of women in Frankish religious and secular society during the early Middle Ages, showing how "medieval women were far more visible, vocal, and powerful than their sisters in antiquity."

CHRONOLOGY OF AUTHORS

Apostolic Fathers. c.1st century A.D.
Tertullian. c.160–c.230
Cyprian of Carthage, St. c.200?–258
Eusebius of Caesarea. c.260–c.340
Basil of Caesarea, St. c.330–379
Ambrose, St. 340?–397
Jerome, St. c.347–419
Chrysostom, St. John. c.354–407
Cassian, St. John. c.365–435
Patrick, St. c.390–460
Benedict of Nursia, St. c.480–540

Gregory the Great (Pope Gregory I). c.540–604
Anselm of Canterbury, St. 1033?–1109
Joachim of Fiore. c.1132–1202
Alan of Lille. d.1203
Francis of Assisi, St. c.1181?–1226
Eckhart, Meister. c.1260–c.1328
Wyclif, John. c.1330–1384
Julian of Norwich. c.1342–c.1416
Catherine of Siena, St. c.1347–1380
Hus, John. c.1372–1415

ALAN OF LILLE. d.1203

Alan of Lille was a poet, theologian, and preacher who combined vast intellectual energy with a passion for poetry. He held an almost mystical view of learning and study, believing that rational powers, along with spiritual ones, should be employed in a search for God.

BOOKS ABOUT ALAN OF LILLE

Evans, G. R. *Alan of Lille: The Frontiers of Theology in the Twelfth Century.* Cambridge U. Pr. 1983 o.p. An examination of Alan's work in terms of his work as a theologian.
Ziolkowski, Jan. *Alan of Lille's Grammar of Sex: The Making of Grammar to a Twelfth-Century Intellectual. Speculum Anniversary Monographs.* Medieval Acad. 1985 $20.00. ISBN 0-910956-85-5. Insightful examination of theology from the point of view of a participant.

AMBROSE, ST. 340?–397

Ambrose was bishop of Milan during the last quarter of the fourth century. His work as bishop had a lasting influence on the relation between the church and secular authority. He was a counselor to several emperors and sought an alliance between the Roman state and Christianity, perceiving "the Emperor to be in the Church and not above it." The most significant demonstration of this belief was his demand for penance and excommunication of Roman Emperor Theodosius I for ordering a massacre of civilians in Thessalonica. Ambrose was well known for his preaching and defense of orthodoxy, and was in part responsible for the conversion of AUGUSTINE OF HIPPO. His writings include sermons and hymns and treatises on the sacraments, ethics, and ascetical subjects. He was a supporter of monasticism in northern Italy and is ranked as one of the four doctors of the Latin Church.

BOOKS BY ST. AMBROSE

Hexameron, Paradise, Cain and Abel. Trans. by John J. Savage. *Fathers of the Church Ser.* Cath. U. Pr. 1961 $34.95. ISBN 0-8132-0042-3. The "Hexameron" contains nine homilies concerning the scriptural account of the six days of creation, while "Paradise" and "Cain and Abel" are early homiletical works.
A Select Library of the Nicene and Post-Nicene Fathers. Ed. by Philip Schaff. Eerdmans 1974 $29.95. ISBN 0-8028-8124-6. Volume 10 includes "Duties of the Clergy," "Holy Spirit," "Death of Satyrus," "Belief in the Resurrection," "Christian Faith," "Mysteries," "Repentance," "Virgins," "Widows," and selected letters.
Seven Exegetical Works. Trans. by Michael P. McHugh. *Fathers of the Church Ser.* Cath. U. Pr. 1972 $34.95. ISBN 0-8132-0065-2. The exegetical works contained in this volume are "Isaac or the Soul," "Death as a Good," "Jacob and the Happy Life," "Joseph," "Patriarchs," "Flight from the World," "Prayer of Job and David."
Theological and Dogmatic Works. Trans. by Roy J. Deferrari. *Fathers of the Church Ser.* Cath. U. Pr. 1963 $34.95. ISBN 0-8132-0044-X. "Mysteries" represents addresses given to the newly baptized during Easter week; "Holy Spirit" is an attack on the Macedonians, a semi-Arian heresy; "Sacrament of the Incarnation of our Lord" and "Sacraments" address the issue of the sacraments especially as they were taught to the newly baptized Christians.

BOOK ABOUT ST. AMBROSE

Paredi, Angela. *St. Ambrose: His Life and Times.* Bks. Demand repr. of 1964 ed. $123.80. ISBN 0-317-26143-6. A very readable exploration both of the life of Ambrose and relevant Church history of the fourth and fifth centuries.

ANSELM OF CANTERBURY, ST. 1033?–1109

Anselm was Archbishop of Canterbury and one of the foremost thinkers among the earlier Scholastics. He broke with most earlier theologians by defending the faith with intellectual reasoning instead of employing arguments built on scripture and other written authorities. It is Anselm who first elaborated the ontological argument for the existence of God.

BOOKS BY ST. ANSELM OF CANTERBURY

Anselm of Canterbury: Complete Treatises. Ed. by Jasper Hopkins. Trans. by Herbert Richardson. 4 vols. E. Mellen 1974 $124.95. ISBN 0-88946-977.

St. Anselm's Proslogion. Ed. by M. J. Charlesworth. U. of Notre Dame Pr. 1979 repr. of 1965 ed. $9.95. ISBN 0-268-01697-6. Contains the *Proslogion, Gaunilo's Reply*, and the *Reply to Gaunilo* in Latin with an English translation on facing pages.

BOOKS ABOUT ST. ANSELM OF CANTERBURY

Eadmer. *The Life of St. Anselm, Archbishop of Canterbury*. Ed. and trans. by R. W. Southern, 1972

Evans, G. R. *Anselm and a New Generation. Outstanding Christian Thinkers Ser*. Morehouse Pub. 1989 $15.95. ISBN 0-819201484-1. Shows Anselm among his contemporaries and as trailblazer for a new generation.

———. *Anselm and Talking about God*. Oxford 1978 o.p. An examination of Anselm's thought about God and his intellectual processes.

Hopkins, Jasper. *A Companion to the Study of St. Anselm*. U. of Minnesota Pr. 1972 o.p. A clear synthesis of Anselm's philosophical and theological thought, discussing his basic writings and the sources that influenced him.

Southern, R. W. *St. Anselm: A Portrait in a Landscape*. Cambridge U. Pr. 1991 $59.50. ISBN 0-521-3626-2-8. A detailed biography of Anselm in his context with special emphasis on his theological innovations.

APOSTOLIC FATHERS. c.1st century A.D.

The name "Apostolic Fathers" was given in the seventeenth century to a group of Christian writers from the earliest times who may have been contemporary to the apostles and their immediate successors but whose writings were not accepted into the New Testament canon, even though some early biblical manuscripts contain one or two of them along with other New Testament writings. Normally, the group comprises First Clement (Clement of Rome), Second Clement, the letters of Ignatius and Polycarp, the Martyrdom of Polycarp, the Didache or Teaching of the Apostles, the Epistle of Barnabas, the Letter to Diognetus, and the Shepherd of Hermas.

BOOKS ABOUT THE APOSTOLIC FATHERS

Barnard, L. W. *Studies in the Apostolic Fathers and Their Background*. Schocken 1966 o.p. One of the best collections of essays on various works of the Apostolic Fathers, with major emphasis on the "Letter of Barnabas" and aspects of the development of early Christianity.

Goodspeed, Edgar J, trans. *The Apostolic Fathers: An American Translation*. HarpC 1950 o.p. Contains "Doctrina," "Didache," the "Letter of Barnabas," "First Clement," "Second Clement," "Hermas," "Letters of Ignatius," "Letter of Polycarp to the Philippians," "Martyrdom of Polycarp," "Apology of Quadratus," "Fragments of Papias," and "Diognetus."

Grant, Robert M., ed. *The Apostolic Fathers: A New Translation and Commentary*. 6 vols. Nelson-Hall 1964–68 o.p. Vol. 1 *An Introduction*, by Robert M. Grant. Vol. 2 *First and Second Clement*, by Robert M. Grant and Holt H. Graham. Vol. 3 *The Didache and Barnabas*, by Robert A. Kraft. Vol. 4 *Ignatius of Antioch*, by Robert M. Grant. Vol. 5

Polycarp, Martyrdom of Polycarp, Fragments of Papias, by William Schoedel. Vol. 6
Hermas, by Graydon F. Snyder. Each volume contains a substantial introduction to
the relevant texts, translation, detailed commentary, and helpful bibliography.

Lake, Kirsopp. *The Apostolic Fathers. Loeb Class. Lib.* 2 vols. HUP repr. of 1912–13 ed.
o.p. These volumes contain Greek-English facing pages of the "Letter of Barnabas,"
"First Clement," "Second Clement," "Letters of Ignatius," "The Letter of Polycarp
to the Philippians," "Didache," "Shepherd of Hermas," "Martyrdom of Polycarp,"
and "Epistle to Diognetus."

Lawson, John. *A Theological and Historical Introduction to the Apostolic Fathers.*
Macmillan 1961 o.p. A primarily theological and spiritual introduction to these
writings, with chapter-by-chapter brief commentaries on "First Clement," "Second
Clement," "Didache," "Letters of Ignatius," "Martyrdom of Polycarp," "Letter of
Barnabas," "Hermas," and "Diognetus."

Lightfoot, J. B., ed. *The Apostolic Fathers. Twin Brooks Ser.* Baker Bk. 1990 repr. of 1891
ed. $17.95. ISBN 0-8010-5655-1. Contains only the English translations from
Lightfoot's major study (see below).

————. *The Apostolic Fathers, Clement, Ignatius, and Polycarp: Revised Texts with
Introductions, Notes, Dissertations, and Translations.* 2 pts. in 5. Hendrickson MA
1981 repr. of 1889–90 ed. $99.95. ISBN 0-943575-27-3. Lightfoot's famous volumes
present the fullest scholarly discussion of the Apostolic Fathers in any language.

Schoedel, William. *Ignatius of Antioch: A Commentary on the Seven Letters of Ignatius.
Hermeneia Ser.* Fortress Pr. 1985 $34.95. ISBN 0-8006-6016-1. A scholarly commen-
tary on the authentic writings of Ignatius.

Staniforth, Maxwell, trans. *Early Christian Writings: The Apostolic Fathers.* Viking
Penguin 1987 $5.95. ISBN 0-14-044475-0. The brief introduction and texts by
Andrew Louth to "First Clement," "Letters of Ignatius," "Letter of Polycarp to the
Philippians," "Martyrdom of Polycarp," "Diognetus," "Letter of Barnabas," and
"Didache."

AUGUSTINE OF HIPPO, ST. 354–430

[SEE Chapter 4 in this volume.]

BASIL OF CAESAREA, ST. c.330–379

Basil, also known as Basil the Great, is included as one of the Cappadocian
Fathers, the leaders of philosophical Christian orthodoxy in the later fourth
century. Basil was born in Cappadocia (in present-day southeastern Turkey) and
educated according to the best Christian and non-Christian culture of his day.
He briefly pursued the monastic life in Syria and Egypt. Although he returned to
his homeland, he remained influential in the monastic life of Asia Minor. In 370
he succeeded Eusebius as bishop of Caesarea, a post he held until his death.
Basil was continuously involved in defending orthodoxy against many of the
significant controversies of the fourth century. His most important work was as
leader in the intellectual defense of Nicene Christianity. He was a champion of
the term *homoiousios* ("like in substance to the Father") and argued that it had
the same implications as the Nicene *homoousios* ("of one substance"). One of
his most important treatises, "On the Holy Spirit," argued against the belief of
those denying the divinity of the Holy Spirit.

BOOKS BY ST. BASIL OF CAESAREA

Ascetical Works. Trans. by M. Monica Wagner. *Fathers of the Church Ser.* Cath. U. Pr.
1950 $26.95. ISBN 0-8132-0009-1. Contains 16 treatises addressed to ascetics, rules
based on teaching of the Gospel directed at the laity, monastic problems, and various
homilies on ascetical questions.

Exegetic Homilies. Trans. by Agnes C. Way. *Fathers of the Church Ser.* Cath. U. Pr. 1963 $19.95. ISBN 0-8132-0046-6. Contains 9 homilies on the "Hexaemeron" and 13 on various Psalms.

Letters. Trans. by Roy J. Deferrari and M. R. P. McGuire. *Loeb Class. Lib.* 4 vols. HUP 1926–34 $15.50 ea. ISBNs 0-674-99209-1, 0-674-99237-7, 0-674-9968-7, 0-674-99298-9. The complete letters are included with a Greek text, and Volume 4 also includes the "Address to Young Men on How They Might Derive Benefit from Greek Culture."

A Select Library of Nicene and Post-Nicene Fathers. Ed. by Philip Schaff. Eerdmans 1974 $29.95. ISBN 0-8028-8122-X. Volume 8 contains "On the Holy Spirit," the "Hexaemeron," and the letters.

BOOK ABOUT ST. BASIL OF CAESAREA

Murphy, M. Gertrude. *Saint Basil and Monasticism.* AMS Pr. 1982 repr. of 1930 ed. $14.75. ISBN 0-404-0454-3. Good, solid biography.

BENEDICT OF NURSIA, ST. c.480–540

Born in Nursia and educated in Rome, Benedict retreated from the uproar of the city to a cave at Subiaco in the hills outside Rome c.500, where he lived as a hermit for several years. Gradually, over 100 ascetics established themselves nearby. Around 525 he and some of his associates moved south to Monte Cassino, where he served as abbot until his death. Benedict's genius for organization inspired the *Rule of St. Benedict,* the charter document for monasticism in Western Christianity. Benedict began with the presupposition that communal or coenobitic life was the best preparation for the life of the anchorite or solitary hermit. His rules for communal life stand in the tradition of monastic regulations, such as those of BASIL OF CAESAREA, JOHN CASSIAN, and AUGUSTINE OF HIPPO. Benedict's rules include commitment to poverty, chastity, obedience to the abbot, and stability, that is, staying at one monastery for one's lifetime unless ordered to move by the abbot. His particular talent was the composition of rules both spiritually and practically oriented, and his discipline was comparatively mild and open to a variety of temperaments. The abbot was a firm but kindly father figure who challenged each monk to advance in the spiritual life. Benedictine monasteries were expected to be self-supporting, to join both manual labor and the recitation of the Divine Office in a daily routine. Though he never sought to establish a religious order, his rule became the governing document, in whole or in part, for monastic foundations in England and Ireland during the sixth century. In an attempt to regulate religious practice, Charlemagne made the *Rule of St. Benedict* the standard for all monastic communities in his realm. From that point, *Benedict's Rule* became the most influential monastic document of the medieval world.

BOOKS BY ST. BENEDICT OF NURSIA

The Rule of St. Benedict in Latin and English with Notes. Ed. by T. Fry and Imogene Baker. Liturgical Pr. 1982 $2.00. ISBN 0-8146-1272-5

The Rule of the Master. Trans. by L. Eberle and C. Philippi. *Cistercian Studies Ser.* Cistercian Pubns. 1977. $12.95. ISBN 0-87907-806-5. An early, extended version of the *Rule,* less edited by the later tradition and more insistent on community life.

BOOKS ABOUT ST. BENEDICT OF NURSIA

Butler, Edward Cuthbert. *Benedictine Monasticism.* Longman 1924 o.p. A classic not yet surpassed.

Gregory the Great. *Dialogues.* Ed. by O. Zimmermann. *Fathers of the Church Ser.* Cath. U. Pr. 1959. ISBN 0-8132-0039-3. A highly embroidered account, written in the sixth century, providing the earliest and almost only information about Benedict.

Kardong, T. *Commentaries on Benedict's Rule.* Assumption Abbey 1987 o.p. A step-by-step explanation of the rules.

BERNARD OF CLAIRVAUX, ST. 1090?–1153

[SEE Chapter 4 in this volume.]

BONAVENTURE, ST. 1221–1274

[SEE Chapter 4 in this volume.]

CASSIAN, ST. JOHN. c.365–c.435

John Cassian, an important figure in the early history of monasticism, can be considered "one of the principal architects of the western monastic system." He joined a monastery at Bethlehem but left soon after to study monasticism in Egypt. Eventually he found his way west, spending a short time in Rome and settling in Marseilles, where he founded two monasteries. He collected much of his knowledge on monastics and monasticism in his *Institutes* and *Conferences.* The former work was used by Benedict of Nursia in his famous monastic *Rule.* Cassian's theological importance and legacy comes in his disagreement with the Augustinian views of grace and predestination. He maintained that "the first steps towards the Christian life were ordinarily taken by the human will and that Grace supervened only later." His views, traditionally described as "Semi-Pelagianist," received widespread support in the monasteries in the West.

BOOKS BY ST. JOHN CASSIAN

John Cassian: Conferences. Trans. by Colm Luibhed. *Class. of Western Spirituality Ser.* Paulist Pr. 1985 $15.95. ISBN 0-8091-0361. An authoritative source for monastic rules and spiritual direction.

A Select Library of the Nicene and Post-Nicene Fathers. Ed. by Philip Schaff. Eerdmans 1979 o.p. Volume 11 contains the "Institutes," "Conferences," and "Incarnation of the Lord."

BOOK ABOUT ST. JOHN CASSIAN

Chadwick, Owen. *John Cassian.* Cambridge U. Pr. 1968 o.p. A very readable introduction to the life and thought of John Cassian.

CATHERINE OF SIENA, ST. c.1347–1380

Born into a relatively comfortable family of Siena, Catherine opted for the life of asceticism from an early age. She became a Dominican tertiary at 16, refused to marry, and became a recluse. Beginning in 1370 she devoted herself to charitable works in her city, including a ministry to lepers. Gradually, she developed a reputation as a woman who used her personal charismatic authority in resolving conflict. She is credited with encouraging the pope to return to Rome after the Avignon "Captivity," as well as with helping to resolve the Great Western Schism. Her asceticism and personal magnetism attracted many followers.

BOOKS BY ST. CATHERINE OF SIENA

Catherine of Siena: The Dialogue. Ed. by Suzanne Noffke. *Class. of Western Spirituality Ser.* Paulist Pr. 1980 $16.95. ISBN 0-8091-2233-2. Catherine's most famous work, with a general introduction to her life and work.

The Letters of St. Catherine of Siena. Trans. by Suzanne Noffke. *Medieval and Renaissance Tests and Studies.* Vol. 1 MRTS 1988 $28.00. ISBN 0-86698-036-9. The first of a proposed 4-volume set and the only critical edition/translation of her letters; a valuable resource for church historians because she corresponded with many influential figures.

BOOK ABOUT ST. CATHERINE OF SIENA

Fatula, Mary Ann. *Catherine of Siena's Way. Class. of Western Spirituality Ser.* Liturgical Pr. 1987 $14.95. ISBN 0-8146-5589-0. Combines information from Raymond of Capua's untranslated biography with extracts from Catherine's work and the author's perceptive analysis, comprising one of the best volumes in this series.

CHRYSOSTOM, ST. JOHN. c.354–407

John Chrysostom, whose life and career center around Antioch and Constantinople, is noted for his preaching, exegesis, and liturgical reforms. He was interested in monasticism and the life of the ascetic. For a period of some years, he lived as a hermit. He was especially gifted in his powers of oratory (Chrysostom means "golden mouthed"). His skills were especially directed to the instruction and moral reformation of the people of Antioch. In terms of scriptural exegesis, he spoke for a literal interpretation of the text against the allegorical school that was prominent in Alexandria. In 398 he became Patriarch of Constantinople. During his tenure he seriously angered the Patriarch of Alexandria and the empress, who eventually had Chrysostom removed from office in 403 and later exiled, first to Antioch and later to Pontus, where he died.

BOOKS BY ST. JOHN CHRYSOSTOM

Baptismal Instructions. Trans. by Paul Harkins. Newman 1963 o.p. A complete series of eight instructions on baptism.

Homilies on Genesis. Trans. by Robert C. Hill. *Fathers of the Church Ser.* Cath. U. Pr. 1985 $29.95. The volume contains Homilies 1–17.

On Virginity: Against Remarriage. Trans. by Sally R. Shore. E. Mellen 1984 $49.95. Contains two treatises important for understanding Chrysostom's views on women, virginity, asceticism, and marriage, and an introduction to the translations provides a helpful discussion of these views.

Palladius: Dialogue on the Life of St. John Chrysostom. Ed. by Robert T. Meyer. *Ancient Christian Writers Ser.* Paulist Pr. 1985 $16.95. ISBN 0-8091-0358-3. One of the earliest biographies of Chrysostom with an excellent introduction.

A Select Library of the Nicene and Post-Nicene Fathers. Ed. by Philip Schaff. Eerdmans 1979 o.p. Vol. 9 Letters, Homilies, "On Priesthood," "Instructions to Candidates for Baptism." Vol. 10 Homilies on the Gospel of Matthew. Vol. 11 Homilies on Acts of the Apostles. Vol. 12 Homilies on First and Second Corinthians. Vol. 13 Homilies on Galatians and Ephesians. Vol. 14 Homilies on the Gospel of John and Hebrews.

CYPRIAN OF CARTHAGE, ST. c.200?/210?–258

Cyprian was born and educated in traditional Roman religion. Two years after his conversion in 246, he became bishop of Carthage, the provincial capital. Beginning in 250, his diocese was faced with the Decian persecutions (250–251). Cyprian fled the city, subjecting himself to intense criticism and ruled his diocese from exile. During his absence many Christians lapsed from their faith, and many more obtained *libelli pacis*, government-issued certificates stating that they had sacrificed to the Roman divinities to avoid punishment. Much of Cyprian's extant correspondence deals with the reconciliation between the church and these *lapsi* (apostates). Critical issues included the necessity for re-baptism and the status of reconciled clergy. The most important principle was that a cleric who had apostatized was regarded as not in communion with the larger church and could not baptize or ordain. This issue was to haunt Christianity in North Africa and in Egypt (a separate Roman province) and lead to the Donatist and Melitian schisms, in their respective provinces, in the fourth and fifth centuries. Cyprian's intransigence regarding unity with the church led to his dictum: "Outside the Church there is no salvation." During the Valerianic persecutions in 258, he was martyred at Carthage. His writings are known for their attention to martyrs, ministry, and the sacraments.

BOOKS BY ST. CYPRIAN OF CARTHAGE

Ante-Nicene Fathers. Ed. by Alexander Roberts and James Donaldson. Rev. by A. C. Coxe. Eerdmans 1978 o.p. Volume 5 contains Cyprian's letters and several treatises.

The Lapsed. Trans. by Maurice Bevenot. OUP 1971 o.p. The Latin text of this treatise is given with an English translation.

The Letters of St. Cyprian of Carthage. Trans. by G. W. Clarke. *Ancient Christian Writers Ser.* Paulist Pr. 1984–89 $24.95 ea. ISBNs 0-8091-0341-9, 0-8091-0342-7, 0-8091-0369-9, 0-8091-0341-9. Details of Cyprian's entire career, especially issues raised by persecution.

Treatises. Trans. by Roy D. Ferrari and others. *Fathers of the Church Ser.* Cath. U. Pr. 1957 $29.95. Contains 13 treatises written by Cyprian, including "On the Unity of the Church" and "The Lapsed."

BOOKS ABOUT ST. CYPRIAN OF CARTHAGE

Hinchcliff, Peter. *Cyprian of Carthage and the Unity of the Christian Church*. Chapman 1974 o.p. A scholarly, yet nontechnical, biography of the third-century Bishop of Carthage.

Sage, Michael. *Cyprian*. Philadelphia Patristic Foundation 1975 o.p. Treats the background for and chronology of Cyrian's episcopate.

DUNS SCOTUS, JOHN. c.1265–1308

[SEE Chapter 4 in this volume.]

ECKHART, (JOHANNES) MEISTER. c.1260–c.1328

Born in Hochheim near Gotha, Meister Eckhart was a German Dominican mystic whose central concern was the relation of the soul to God. He regarded "the innermost essence of the soul as something uncreated, not only 'like' God in a creaturely resemblance, but truly 'one' with God" (Bernard McGinn, *Meister Eckhart*). Eckhart's thinking offended orthodox sensibilities as pantheistic, and he was accused of heretical teachings by the archbishop of Cologne. Two years after his death, Eckhart's writings were condemned by Pope John XXII. Nevertheless, Eckhart's teaching influenced later religious mysticism and speculative philosophy..

BOOKS BY MEISTER ECKHART

Meister Eckhart: The Essential Sermons, Commentaries, Treatises, and Defense. Trans. and ed. by Bernard McGinn and Edmund College. Paulist Pr. 1981 $15.95. ISBN 0-8091-2370-3

Meister Eckhart: A Modern Translation. Trans. by Raymond B. Blakney. HarpC. 1957 $12.00. ISBN 0-06-130008-X.

BOOKS ABOUT MEISTER ECKHART

McGinn, Bernard, ed. *Meister Eckhart: Teacher and Preacher*. *Class. of Western Spirituality Ser.* Paulist Pr. 1986 $13.95. ISBN 0-8091-0377-X. Preface by Kenneth J.

Northcott. "Texts that illustrate the diversity of one of the most enigmatic and influential mystics of the Western Christian Traditions" (Publisher's catalog).

Tobin, Frank. *Meister Eckhart: Thought and Language.* U. of Pa. Pr. 1986 $40.95. ISBN 0-8122-8009-1. "The best full-length study of this thirteenth century Dominican mystic convicted of heresy so far published in English" (*Journal of Medieval History*).

ERASMUS OF ROTTERDAM. 1466?–1536

[SEE Chapter 5 in this volume.]

EUSEBIUS OF CAESAREA. c.260–c.340

Eusebius is best remembered for his important writings. His most celebrated, *Ecclesiastical History*, provides a history of Christianity, sometimes without critical judgment of the veracity of certain events, from the apostolic age down to the early fourth century. It is primarily this work that earned Eusebius the title of the "Father of Church History." His other writings, including *Preparation for the Gospel*, *Onomasticon*, *Commentaries on the Psalms*, and *Isaiah*, contain quotations from classical authors now lost, allegorical interpretations of biblical texts, and a valuable work on biblical topography. Theologically, Eusebius is remembered for his retelling of Christian history to include a positive role for the "good" Roman emperors as instruments of God's will. He held the position of bishop of Caesarea beginning around 315 until his death c.340.

BOOKS BY EUSEBIUS OF CAESAREA

Ecclesiastical History. Trans. by Roy J. Deferrari. *Fathers of the Church Ser.* Cath. U. Pr. Vol. 19 (Books 1–5) 1953 $18.95. ISBN 0-8132-0019-9. Vol. 29 (Books 6 10) 1955 $39.95. ISBN 0-8132-0029-6. An important source, although not always historically accurate, for our knowledge of early church history.

A Select Library of the Nicene and Post-Nicene Fathers. Ed. by Philip Schaff. Eerdmans 1979 $29.95. ISBN 0-8028-8115-7. Volume 1 contains "Ecclesiastical History" and the "Life of Constantine."

BOOKS ABOUT EUSEBIUS OF CAESAREA

Attridge, Harold W., and Gohei Hata, eds. *Eusebius, Christianity and Judaism.* Wayne St. U. Pr. 1992 $49.95. ISBN 0-8143-2361-8. The evidence for the relationship between Christianity and Judaism found between the lines in the writings of Eusebius.

Barnes, Timothy D. *Constantine and Eusebius.* HUP 1984 $14.95. ISBN 0-674-16531-4. A scholarly study of "the history of the Constantinian age and the personalities of two of that period's most important figures" (Gerald Virna, *Anglican Theological Review*), including an extensive bibliography.

Chesnut, Glenn F. *The First Christian Histories: Eusebius, Socrates, Sozomen, Theodoret, and Evagrius.* Mercer Univ. Pr. rev. ed. 1986 $19.95. ISBN 0-86654-201-1. A learned study that focuses on how Christian historians, particularly Eusebius, dealt with the motifs of fate and fortune in Rome and the Roman emperors.

FRANCIS OF ASSISI, ST. c.1181–1226

Raised in a wealthy household in Assisi, Francis was trained in the family business and expected to follow the profession of his father, a cloth merchant. However, the high-spirited young man was more attuned to a life of adventure, and after capture in a local military conflict (1202) and a subsequent pilgrimage to Rome, he broke with his family and adopted an ascetic life. In 1208 he began a common life with a group of followers and wrote a rule of life based on the Gospels and consecrated especially to poverty. The Franciscan rule received papal approval by 1210 and was extended to a women's group headed by St. Clare in 1212.

Francis is famous for his devotion to Lady Poverty, for his reception of the stigmata (the marks of Christ's passion) on his own body, and for his evangelistic fervor that, legend has it, extended to preaching to animals.

BOOKS BY ST. FRANCIS OF ASSISI

Brother Francis: An Anthology of Writings by and about St. Francis of Assisi. Ed. by Lawrence Cunningham. HarpC 1972 o.p. A judiciously chosen collection that captures the spirit of Francis.

Little Flowers of St. Francis. Trans. by Raphael Brown. Doubleday 1971 $5.95. ISBN 0-385-07544-8. A clear and readable translation revealing Francis's mystical bent.

BOOKS ABOUT ST. FRANCIS OF ASSISI

Cook, William R. *Francis of Assisi. Way of the Christian Mystics Ser.* Vol. 8 Liturgical Pr. 1989 $8.95. ISBN 0-8146-5626-9. An examination of Francis's mysticism with an eye toward its utility for contemporary Christianity.

Cunningham, Lawrence. *Francis of Assisi.* HarpC 1989 $5.00. ISBN 0-06-061657-1. A popularly accessible yet rich treatment of the life of Francis.

GREGORY THE GREAT (POPE GREGORY I). c.540–604

Gregory, who became pope in 590, oversaw great changes in the church. He was an able pastor and theologian, a promoter of monasticism, and, most significantly, a reformer of the Western church who expanded the prestige and the authority of the papacy. Most of his activities were concerned with the practical shape of the Christian life. He made important changes in the liturgy; wrote an influential treatise, "Pastoral Rule," that set out directives for the pastoral life of a bishop; developed a doctrine of purgatory; wrote treatises, such as his *Morals on the Book of Job*, that contributed to monastic spirituality. He also promoted the conversion of the Arian Visogoths to Catholicism, initiated the conversion of the Anglo-Saxons in England, and reformed the administration and expenditure of the revenues of the landed estates that supported orphanages, schools, and hospitals. Notwithstanding the great influence that Gregory had on the church as it entered into the Middle Ages, he is remembered for his humility. He rejected the suggestion of the patriarch of Constantinople to style himself the "Universal Patriarch"; rather, he referred to himself as "the servant of the servants of God."

BOOKS BY GREGORY THE GREAT

Pastoral Care. Trans. by Henry Davies. Newman 1950 o.p. The translator states that the treatise "sets forth the awesome character and difficulties of the office of the priesthood," and shows "how to fulfill the duties that go with it as they should be fulfilled."

A Select Library of the Nicene and Post-Nicene Fathers. Ed. by Philip Schaff. Eerdmans 1979 o.p. Volume 12 contains selected letters and the "Book of Pastoral Rule," in which, according to Schaff, Gregory "sets out the directives for the pastoral life of a bishop" and letters, while Volume 13 contains the remainder of Gregory's letters.

BOOKS ABOUT GREGORY THE GREAT

Evans, G. R. *The Thought of Gregory the Great. Cambridge Studies on Medieval Life and Thought Ser.* Cambridge U. Pr. 1988 $13.95. ISBN 0-521-36826-X. A brief study of Gregory's thought, in particular (in the author's words) "his attempt to bring active and contemplative together and his theology."

Straw, Carol. *Gregory the Great: Perfection in Imperfection. The Transformation of the Classical Heritage Ser.* Vol. 14. U. CA Pr. 1988 $42.50. ISBN 0-520-5767-8. A searching analysis of Gregory's theology with an accent on the dynamics of the spiritual life.

HUS, JOHN. c.1372–1415

John Hus was a Bohemian reformer and a well-known preacher in Prague. His thinking was influenced by the Czech reform movement and the writings of JOHN WYCLIF. He taught that the true church consists only of the predestined and that the "only law of the Church is the Bible, above all the New Testament, and, like Wyclif, ruled out the extrabiblical traditions of canon law but did not deny the teaching authority of the ancient fathers and doctors." Hus was excommunicated in 1411 for his teachings, and in 1415, at the Council of Constance, he was tried and convicted of heresy. He suffered death at the stake. Popular in Bohemia during his life, Hus became a national hero.

BOOKS ABOUT JOHN HUS

Spinka, Matthew. *John Hus: A Biography.* Greenwood 1978 repr. of 1968 ed. $41.50. ISBN 0-313-21050-0. Scholarly portrait of Hus's life and its dramatic end at the Council of Constance in 1415.
————. *John Hus at the Council of Constance.* Col. U. Pr. 1965 o.p. Primarily a translation of Peter of Mladonovice's eyewitness account of Hus's execution at Constance but also a useful introduction concerning the conciliar movement, including some of Hus's letters and documents relating to the final years of his life.

JEROME, ST. c.347–419

Jerome was the greatest scholar of the ancient church. Most of his mature life was spent in study in various parts of the Eastern Mediterranean. In approximately 372, he set out for the East and stayed in Antioch for a short period, eventually settling as a hermit in the Syrian desert for four or five years. He then spent some time in Constantinople and in 382 returned to Rome, where he became secretary to Pope Damasus. During his brief residence in Rome, he began his revision of the Bible into Latin translated from the original languages. The culmination of his work, which took over two decades, was known as the Vulgate, a Latin translation of the Bible. He returned to the East in 385 and eventually settled in Bethlehem, where he ruled a newly founded monastery and devoted the rest of his life to study and writing.

In addition to the Vulgate, his writings include biblical commentaries and treatises concerning linguistic and topographical material written in order to help in the interpretation of Scripture.

BOOKS BY ST. JEROME

Dogmatic and Polemical Works. Trans. by John Hritzu. *Fathers of the Church Ser.* Cath. U. Pr. 1965 $21.95. ISBN 0-8132-0053-9. The volume contains "On the Perpetual Virginity of the Blessed Virgin against Helvidius," "Apology against the Books of Rufinius," and "Dialogue against the Pelagians."
Homilies on Psalms. Trans. by Marie L. Ewald. *Fathers of the Church Ser.* Cath. U. Pr. 1964 o.p. Fifty-nine homilies on various Psalms.
Homilies on Psalms and Other Texts. Trans. by Marie L. Ewald. *Fathers of the Church Ser.* Cath. U. Pr. 1966 o.p. Contains 15 homilies on the Psalms, 10 on the Gospel of Mark, and 12 more on various writings and topics.
Select Letters. Trans. by E. A. Wright. *Loeb Class. Lib.* HUP 1980 repr. of 1933 ed. $15.50. ISBN 0-674-99288-1. A selection of letters of various types and contents, with a Latin text on facing pages.

A Select Library of the Nicene and Post-Nicene Fathers. Ed. by Philip Schaff. Eerdmans
    1979 $29.95 ea. ISBN 0-8028-8120-3, 0-8028-8120-6. Volume 3 contains "Lives of
    Illustrious Men," short biographies of Christian writers from the apostles to himself,
    while Volume 6 contains treatises and prefaces to his biblical commentaries and the
    letters.

BOOKS ABOUT ST. JEROME

Clark, Elizabeth A. *Jerome, Chrysostom and Friends: Essays and Translations. Studies in
    Women and Religion.* Vol. 2. E. Mellen 1983 repr. of 1979 ed. $59.95. ISBN 0-88946-
    548-7. Contains two essays on the attitude toward male-female relationships in
    fourth-century Christianity as well as translations of relevant primary texts.
Kelly, J. N. *Jerome: His Life, Writings and Controversies.* Christian Classics 1980 repr. of
    1975 ed. o.p. A comprehensive and scholarly biography dealing with Jerome's
    personality and multifaceted career.

JOACHIM OF FIORE. c.1132–1202

In a series of works known as *The Everlasting Gospel*, the mystic Joachim of
Fiore put forth the view of a Trinitarian conception of history. The first period,
that of the Father, is the age when humans lived under the Law until the end of
the Old Testament dispensation. The second, that of the Son, is lived under
grace and covers the New Testament dispensation. Joachim thought that this
period lasted for 42 generations of 30 years each. The final age, that of the Holy
Spirit, was to be inaugurated in 1260 and would see "the rise of new religious
orders destined to convert the whole world." Joachim's apocalytpic thinking
was very influential among the Franciscan Spirituals.

BOOKS ABOUT JOACHIM OF FIORE

McGinn, Bernard. *The Calabrian Abbot: Joachim of Fiore in the History of Thought.*
    Macmillan 1985 ISBN 0-317-18119-X. Examines the background, thought, and later
    influence on medieval writers of Joachim of Fiore, an important apocalyptic figure
    of the Middle Ages.
West, Selno C., and Sandra Zimdars-Swartz. *Joachim of Fiore: A Study in Spiritual
    Perception and History.* Bks. Demand 1983 $40.80. ISBN 0-7837-1763-6. A good
    introduction to Joachim's thought, examining his use of patristic and medieval
    sources, his exegetical method, and his interpretation of the Incarnation and the
    relation between Christ and the Holy Spirit.

JULIAN OF NORWICH. c.1342–c.1416

Little is known about this mystic writer who took up residence in St. Julian's
Church, Norwich, England. The *Showings* are her meditations on her mystical
experiences of May 8, 1373. Influenced by Neo-Platonism, she sees evil as less
real than good. She focuses on the love of God and the care of Christ as mother
for those who are devoted to him.

BOOK BY AND ABOUT JULIAN OF NORWICH

Julian of Norwich: "Showings." Trans. by Edmund College and James Walsh. Paulist Pr.
    1978 $16.95. ISBN 0-8091-0234-X. Clearly written modern translations of the long
    and short versions of the *Showings*, with an introduction by Jean Leclercq that is the
    best summary of Julian's theology in print (1993).

NICHOLAS OF CUSA. c.1401–1464

[SEE Chapter 5 in this volume.]

ORIGEN. 185?–254?

[SEE Chapter 4 in this volume.]

PATRICK, ST. c.390–460

St. Patrick, the "Apostle of Ireland," was born in Britain. At age 16 he was captured by Irish pirates and carried into slavery in Ireland, where he labored in bondage for several years. He eventually escaped and returned to Britain, where he trained for the Christian ministry. At some point Patrick was sent to Ireland, where he spent the rest of his life evangelizing, conciliating local chieftains, ordaining clergy, and organizing the common life of monks and nuns. The few facts known about Patrick were embellished by his biographers in the Middle Ages.

BOOK ABOUT ST. PATRICK

Hanson, R. *The Life and Writings of the Historical St. Patrick.* Winston Pr. 1983. Contains Patrick's "Letter to Coroticus" and "Confession," with accompanying commentaries to each, and a general introduction to the life and thought of Patrick; the best book in print on Patrick (1993).

TERTULLIAN. c.160–c.230

Tertullian, a convert to Christianity, lived and wrote in the North African city of Carthage. Although he never held a clerical post, his influence on Christianity, especially in the West, was enormous. His writings include apologetic, theological, controversial, and ascetic works. He never shied away from discoursing against those he believed to be expounding against the "rule of faith." He is the first major Christian author to write in Latin and to provide Latin terminology for trinitarian theology. Tertullian's theological interests centered around his concern for the purity and holiness of the church. The importance of these issues eventually led Tertullian to join the Montanist sect, which emphasized the immediacy of the spirit, ecstatic prophecy, and a moral strictness.

BOOKS BY TERTULLIAN

Ante-Nicene Fathers. Ed. by A. Clevland Coxe. Eerdmans 1978 o.p. Volumes 3 and 4 contain apologetic, antiheretical, and ethical treatises.

Adversus Marcionem (Against Marcion). Ed. and trans. by Ernst Evans. 2 vols. OUP 1972 o.p. A Latin text accompanies the translation.

Apologetical Works. Trans. by Rudolph Arbesmann, Emily Daly, and Edwin Quain. *Fathers of the Church Ser.* Cath. U. Pr. 1950 $34.95. ISBN 0-8132-0010-5. Contains "Apology," "Testimony of the Soul," "To Scapula," and "On the Soul."

Apology and Spectacles. Trans. by Gerald H. Renall. *Loeb Class. Lib.* HUP 1977 repr. of 1931 ed. o.p. A Latin text accompanies the translation of these two treatises.

Disciplinary, Moral, and Ascetical Works. Trans. by Rudolph Arbesmann, Emily Daly, and Edwin Quain. *Fathers of the Church Ser.* Cath. U. Pr. 1959 $34.95. ISBN 0-8132-0040-7. Contains "To Martyrs," "Spectacles," "Apparel of Women," "Prayer," "Patience," "Chaplet," "Flight in Time of Persecution."

Treatise against Hermogenes. Trans. by J. H. Waszink. Newman 1956 o.p. The introduction briefly explains Hermogenes' views on creation and matter, which Tertullian rejected.

Treatises on Marriage and Remarriage. Trans. by William Le Saint. Newman 1951 o.p. The volume contains "To His Wife," "Exhortation to Chastity," and "Monogamy." In these documents Tertullian speaks against remarriage and shows signs of sympathies with Montanist beliefs in purity.

Treatises on Penance. Trans. by William Le Saint. Newman 1959 o.p. Contains "On Patience" and "On Purity," the latter document being written during Tertullian's Montanist period.

BOOKS ABOUT TERTULLIAN

Barnes, Timothy D. *Tertullian: A Historical and Literary Study.* OUP 1985 $49.95. ISBN 0-19-814362-1. A scholarly study of Tertullian and the sources that depict him, considering Tertullian in his pagan and Christian historical context and providing appendixes on specific issues relating to Jerome, Tertullian, African Christianity, and Roman history.

Bray, Gerald L. *Holiness and the Will of God: Perspectives on the Theology of Tertullian.* Westminster John Knox 1980 o.p. Focuses on sanctification, asceticism, and Scripture in a study accessible to a general audience.

THOMAS AQUINAS, ST. 1225?–1274

[SEE Chapter 4 in this volume.]

WYCLIF, JOHN. c.1330–1384

John Wyclif was an English philosopher, theologian, and reformer. Many of his beliefs varied from traditional Church teachings, and some views put him outside of the orthodox fold. He argued, for instance, that ecclesiastical authorities not in a state of grace could be deprived of their endowments by civil authority and that there was no scriptural foundation for the religious orders. He also argued against the doctrine of transubstantiation, desiring rather to emphasize the moral and spiritual effects of the Eucharist, a position later condemned by the English church. Wyclif's greatest influence was, interestingly, not in England but in Bohemia, where JOHN HUS preached Wyclif's theology.

BOOKS BY JOHN WYCLIF

An Apology for Lollard Doctrines Attributed to Wicliffe. Ed. by James H. Todd. AMS Pr. 1983 repr. of 1842 ed. $28.00. ISBN 0-404-50120-6.

The English Works of Wyclif. Ed. by F. D. Matthew. Kraus repr. of 1880 ed. $75.00. ISBN 0-527-0073-6.

On Universals: The Tractatus de universalibus. Ed. by Ivan Mueller. Trans. by Anthony Kenny. OUP $62.00. ISBN 0-19-842681-1

Select English Writings. Ed. by Herbert E. Winn. AMS Pr. 1978 repr. of 1929 ed. o.p.

BOOKS ABOUT JOHN WYCLIF

Dahmus, Joseph H. *The Prosecution of John Wyclif.* Shoe String 1970 repr. of 1952 ed. o.p. A study of Wyclif's career in general and his struggle with the church in particular.

Hall, Louis B. *The Perilous Vision of John Wyclif.* Nelson-Hall 1983 o.p. A popular account of the life and times of Wyclif.

Hudson, Anne, ed. *Selections from English Wycliffite Writings.* Cambridge U. Pr. 1981 $21.95. ISBN 0-521-28258-6. A representative anthology of 27 passages with commentaries "of Lollard ideas and preoccupations and the different types of Lollard tracts, sermons, satire, and biblical translation."

Mudroch, Vaclav. *The Wyclyf Tradition.* Ed. by Albert C. Reeves. Ohio U. Pr. 1979 $15.00. ISBN 0-8214-0403-2. An analysis of the judgments and evaluations of Wyclif made in the sixteenth and seventeenth centuries.

Stacey, John. *John Wyclif and Reform.* AMS Pr. 1979 repr. of 1964 ed. $24.50. ISBN 0-404-16239-8. In the author's words, a readable "assessment of Wyclif's place as a forerunner of the reformers of the sixteenth century."

CHAPTER 15

Late Christianity, 1500 to the Present

W. Fred Graham and David G. Murphy

> Christian faith is, it seems to me, most basically a claim that the universe is neither indifferent nor malevolent but that there is a power (and a personal power at that) which is on the side of life and its fulfillment. . . . [E]ach generation must venture, through an analysis of what fulfillment could and must mean for its own time, the best way to express that claim.
>
> —SALLIE MCFAGUE, *Models of God: Theology for*
> *an Ecological Nuclear Age*

Beginning at about the year 1500 and continuing to the present day, the history of Christianity can be seen as the story of the gradual relaxation of the religious impulse among the peoples of Western Europe and North America. Or it can be understood as the era in which Christianity moved out of the backwaters of Europe into the newly discovered parts of the globe, growing from a parochial religion to its present status as the most populous faith on earth.

Probably both readings are correct. Few will deny that in Europe and the Americas the religious permeation of society that obtained in the fifteenth century has declined. In Western Europe, all art was once Christian art, all economics Christian economics. The great buildings and the great wars were cathedrals and crusades, while today the public square seems largely untouched by the dictates of prophet or priest. The common term for this desacralizing of society is *secularization*. But a long view of history also finds Christianity globally vibrant. Jesus's birthday and his resurrection are celebrated in every nation on earth, even in militantly atheist Albania and militantly Muslim Pakistan. If the splitting of the church in the West into Roman Catholic and Protestant served to hasten the secularizing of society, the resulting revivals of sectarian Christianity sparked missionary movements of heroic proportions. And where Protestant and Catholic have foundered, the stepchild, Pentecostalism, bids fair to root out pagan vestiges within the endemic Christianity of South and Central America, and to cooperate with those same tendencies in tribal Africa, making that continent the largest Christian continent on earth.

The story of Christianity has become more complex, making the detecting of patterns even more difficult. The vast majority of Americans profess to be Christians, and American political figures freely appeal to Christianity. Christianity played a vital role in the reorganization of Eastern Europe in the early 1990s. At the same time, signs of the decline of traditional Christianity in the West are plentiful. The response of many of our authors to these confusing signals is not to seek clear patterns but rather to uncover complexity after complexity in an attempt to do justice to reality. The attempt to grasp specific events adequately sometimes has the surprising effect of prompting scholars to form new generalizations about trends in Christianity. In the following pages, the reader will not only find some maps of the entire territory of Christianity since the Reformation, but also numerous guides to specific points of interest.

Although the following pages could be arranged in a number of ways, the editors have followed a consciously historical outline, beginning with the Reformation—Protestant and Roman Catholic—and moving through the Enlightenment and the nineteenth century, and on to the present time. A number of movements—institutional and theological, as well as popular—are noted within each epoch, and they and their leaders serve as the gathering points for the bibliography that follows.

GENERAL REFERENCE WORKS

Brosse, Jacques. *Religious Leaders.* Chambers 1992 $9.95. ISBN 0-550-17006-5
Gorman, G. E., and Lyn Gorman. *Theological and Religious Reference Materials.* 3 vols. Greenwood. Vol. 1 *General Resources and Biblical Studies.* 1984 $65.00. ISBN 0-313-20924-3. Vol. 2 *Systematic Theology and Church History.* 1985 $75.00. ISBN 0-313-24779-X. Vol. 3 *Practical Theology.* 1986 $55.00. ISBN 0-313-25397-8. Takes an extremely complicated and gigantic body of material and makes it useful to scholars in religion of every level.
Religious and Inspirational Books and Serials in Print, 1985. Bowker 1985 $79.95. o.p. A comprehensive listing of nearly 60,000 books (arranged by author, title, and subject) and 3,600 serials (by subject and title) of currently available American publications in religion, metaphysics, theology, ethics, and related subjects.
Religious Reading: The Annual Guide. McGrath 1975–86 o.p. Each volume provides a current and accurate listing of all religious publications for the year from all American publishers, with entries arranged by subject area.
Sheehy, Eugene P., and others, eds. *Guide to Reference Books.* ALA 10th ed. 1986 $80.00. ISBN 0-8389-0390-8. Devotes 50 pages to works on religion divided into subject categories with subdivisions. The *Supplement* covers works published through 1990.
West, Edward N. *Outward Signs: The Language of Christian Symbolism.* Walker 1989 $30.00. ISBN 0-8027-1073-5. Discusses the origin and meaning of Christian symbols used in architecture, liturgy, and vestments. Includes drawings, index, and a bibliography.
Wilson, John F. *Research Guide to Religious Studies.* Ed. by Thomas P. Slavens. *Sources of Information in the Humanities Ser.* ALA 1982 o.p. Useful for finding direction in conducting preliminary searches.

DICTIONARIES, ENCYCLOPEDIAS, HANDBOOKS

The Church

Barrett, David. ed. *World Christian Encyclopedia: A Comparative Survey of Churches and Religions in the Modern World, A.D. 1900 to 2000.* OUP 1982 $195.00. ISBN 0-19-572435-6. Probably the only comprehensive survey of all branches of Christianity worldwide, with special attention given to church growth and to fringe groups.
Broderick, Robert C., ed. *The Catholic Encyclopedia.* Nelson rev. ed. 1987 o.p. A one-volume dictionary for the nonspecialist.
Cross, Frank L., and Elizabeth A. Livingstone, eds. *The Oxford Dictionary of the Christian Church.* OUP 1974 $65.00. ISBN 0-19-211545-6. Standard work that includes Eastern Christianity and Vatican II changes in Catholicism; referred to as "the most representative general dictionary of the church" (*Theological and Religious Reference Materials*).

Douglas, J. D., and Earle Cairns, eds. *The New International Dictionary of the Christian Church.* Zondervan rev. ed. 1988 $34.99. ISBN 0-310-23830-7. A useful, general reference source, wide in scope and evangelical in outlook.

Douglas, J. D., ed. *New Twentieth Century Encyclopedia of Religious Knowledge.* Baker Bk. 1991 $39.99. ISBN 0-8010-3002-1. Contains 2,100 topical and biographical entries on theology, biblical studies, church history, and comparative religion from an evangelical perspective.

Eliade, Mircea, ed. *The Encyclopedia of Religion.* 16 vols. Macmillan 1986 $1,400.00. ISBN 0-02-909480-1. An outstanding work intended to replace the Hastings *Encyclopedia of Religion and Ethics* (see below), influenced heavily by the history of religions approach of its editor and including work by many of the best scholars in nearly every field of religious study.

Hardon, John A. *A Modern Catholic Dictionary.* Doubleday 1980 $22.50. ISBN 0-385-12162-8. A modern, up-to-date dictionary with Roman Catholic orientation.

Hastings, James, ed. *Encyclopedia of Religion and Ethics.* 13 vols. Bks. Intl. VA 1926 $1,250.00. ISBN 0-567-09489-8. Found in many libraries, this is old but comprehensive and still very useful.

Jackson, Samuel M., and others, eds. *The New Schaff-Herzog Encyclopedia of Religious Knowledge.* 13 vols. Baker Bk. 1949–50 repr. of 1908–14 ed. o.p. Based on an original German publication, this is especially valuable for biography and for ancient and modern religions.

Livingstone, Elizabeth A., ed. *The Concise Oxford Dictionary of the Christian Church.* OUP 1980 $11.95. ISBN 0-19-283014-7. The abridged version of *The Oxford Dictionary of the Christian Church*, referred to as "probably the most adequate single volume dictionary in its field" (*Theological and Religious Reference Materials*).

Loetscher, Lefferts A., and others, eds. *Twentieth Century Encyclopedia of Religious Knowledge: An Extension of the New Schaff-Herzog Encyclopedia of Religious Knowledge.* 2 vols. Baker Bk. 1955 o.p. Brings Schaff-Herzog into the middle of the present century, especially in church history.

Ludlow, Daniel, ed. *Encyclopedia of Mormonism.* 5 vols. Macmillan 1992 $340.00. ISBN 0-02-904040-X. An impressively produced, comprehensive description of Mormonism that includes the spread of Mormonism overseas but focuses on the history of Mormonism in the United States.

McDonald, William J., and others, eds. *New Catholic Encyclopedia.* 18 vols. J. Heraty Assocs. 1989 $875.00. ISBN 0-07-0102335-X. Ecumenical in scope and nontechnical for the most part; good emphasis on biography.

MacGregor, Geddes. *Dictionary of Religion and Philosophy.* Paragon Hse. 1989 $35.00. ISBN 1-55778-019-6. Brief articles in alphabetical order; includes a classified bibliography.

Mead, Frank S., and Samuel S. Hill. *Handbook of Denominations in the United States.* Abingdon 9th rev. ed. 1990 $13.95. ISBN 0-687-16572-5. Brief history, doctrines, governance, and statistics of more than 200 American denominations; handy for reference or for beginning study.

Melton, J. Gordon, and James V. Geisendorfer. *A Directory of Religious Bodies in the United States.* Garland 1977 o.p. Nearly 1,300 religious groups are listed and clustered into families: e.g., the Lutheran family, as well as under such headings as mail-order churches, neopaganism.

————. *The Encyclopedia of American Religions.* 3 vols. Liguori Pubns. 1992 $14.95 ea. Compares more than 1,000 groups with Catholics, Baptists, and Lutherans.

————. *The Encyclopedia of American Religions, First Edition Supplement.* Gale 1991 $85.00. ISBN 0-8103-6903-6

Piepkorn, Arthur C. *Profiles in Belief: The Religious Bodies of the United States and Canada.* 4 vols. HarpC. Vol. 1 1977 o.p. Vol. 2 1978 $30.00. ISBN 0-06-066582-3. Vols. 3 and 4 1990 $24.95. ISBN 0-06-066581-5. An objective, comprehensive, and invaluable tool from a Lutheran-Ecumenical perspective.

Reid, Daniel G., ed. *Dictionary of Christianity in America*. InterVarsity 1990 $44.99. ISBN 0-8308-1776-X. Authoritative articles by 500 scholars, covering religious bodies, movements, individuals, etc.

Wakefield, Gordon S. *The Westminster Dictionary of Christian Spirituality*. Westminster Pr. 1983 $20.95. ISBN 0-664-21396-0. More than 150 contributors have compiled concise articles that are ecumenical in perspective and international in scope.

Ethics and Theology

Berkhof, Hendrikus. *Two Hundred Years of Theology: Report of a Personal Journey*. Trans. by John Vriend. Eerdmans 1989 o.p. Points out the transition during the past two centuries from one type of theology to another, tracing with great historical knowledge and theological acumen the movement from Schleiermacher to Barth to post-Barthian theology.

Childress, James, and John MacQuarrie, eds. *The Westminster Dictionary of Christian Ethics*. Westminster John Knox 1986 $35.00. ISBN 0-664-20940-8. An excellent starting point for topics ranging from "Abandonment" to "Zoroastrian Ethics," edited by Christian scholars of renown.

Cobb, John B. *Varieties of Protestantism*. Westminster John Knox 1960 o.p. Outline of nine basic Protestant theologies.

Ferm, Deane W. *Contemporary American Theologies: A Critical Survey*. HarpC 1981 $8.95. ISBN 0-8164-2341-5. Brief and clear introductions to the main features of modern theologies in America, including Roman Catholic and conservative Protestant.

Ford, David, ed. *The Modern Theologians*. 2 vols. Blackwell Pubs. 1989 $55.00 ea. ISBNs 0-631-15371-3, 0-631-16807-9. A good introduction, with essays by experts on Paul Tillich, Asian theology, and postliberal theology.

Gaynor, Frank. *Dictionary of Mysticism*. Carol Pub. Group 1973 $2.45. ISBN 0-8065-0172-3. Alphabetically arranged definitions of 2,200 terms used in religious mysticism and psychical research, and so on.

Gonzalez, Justo L. *History of Christian Thought*. 3 vols. Abingdon rev. ed. 1988 $64.95. ISBN 0-687-17185-7. Like his earlier volumes, an amazingly surefooted survey from a Protestant but objective point of view.

Häring, Bernard. *The Law of Christ*. Trans. by Edwin G. Kaiser. 3 vols. Paulist Pr. 1961–66 o.p. Recognized as a watershed in Roman Catholic moral theology and annotated to make a handbook.

Harrison, Everett F., ed. *Baker's Dictionary of Theology*. Baker Bk. 1985 $18.95. ISBN 0-8010-4289-5. Acquaints readers with areas of disagreement in modern theology from conservative standpoint, with helpful bibliographies.

Harrison, R. K., ed. *Encyclopedia of Biblical and Christian Ethics*. Nelson-Hall 1987 o.p. Discusses such topics as television, nihilism, and euthanasia, including not only descriptions but also prescriptions from evangelical perspectives. Brief bibliographies.

Harvey, Van A. *Handbook of Theological Terms*. Macmillan 1964 $5.95. ISBN 0-02-085430-7. Useful in comparing the traditions since both Protestant and Catholic views are given on use of terms.

Henry, Carl F. H., ed. *Baker's Dictionary of Christian Ethics*. Baker Bk. 1978 o.p. Signed articles on ethical issues with brief bibliographies from a conservative Protestant perspective.

Hordern, William E. *Layman's Guide to Protestant Thought*. Macmillan rev. ed. 1968 $5.95. ISBN 0-02-085470-6. Clearly written account of theological movement from the Protestant reformers to the twentieth century, with particular attention to twentieth-century theologians, the major ones examined carefully.

Keeley, Robin, ed. *Eerdmans' Handbook to Christian Belief*. Eerdmans 1982 o.p. Evangelical, clear, and careful.

Kliever, Lonnie D. *The Shattered Spectrum: A Survey of Contemporary Theology.* Westminster John Knox 1981 o.p. Picks up six prominent theological schools of thought since World War II and examines each carefully and in fairly easy style.

Leith, John, ed. *Reformed Reader: A Sourcebook in Christian Theology.* 2 vols. Westminster John Knox 1993. Vol. 1 *Classical Beginnings, 1519–1799.* $30.00. ISBN 0-664-21957-8. Vol. 2 *Contemporary Trajectories, 1799–Present.* $25.00. ISBN 0-664-21958-6. A valuable collection of excerpts from major Protestant theologians, arranged thematically.

McKim, Donald, ed. *Encyclopedia of the Reformed Faith.* Westminster John Knox 1992 $37.00. ISBN 0-664-21882-2. Excellent in what it presents; one reviewed noted, however, that the book underplays the role of women in the Reformed faith.

Macquarrie, John. *Principles of Christian Theology.* Macmillan 1977 $39.75. ISBN 0-02-3745-10-X. A large book, presenting in ecumenical fashion current theological directions and issues.

Placher, William C. *A History of Christian Theology: An Introduction.* Westminster John Knox 1983 $16.99. ISBN 0-664-24496-3. Excellent one-volume survey of history of Christian thought, with the last seven chapters covering the Reformation to the present.

———, ed. *Readings in the History of Christian Theology, Vol. 2: From the Reformation to the Present.* Westminster John Knox 1988 $16.99. ISBN 0-664-24058-5. Beginning with Martin Luther and concluding with Rosemary Radford Ruether, this volume of readings gives short excerpts from numerous authors.

Rahner, Karl, and Herbert Vorgrimler. *Concise Theological Dictionary.* St. Mut. 1982 o.p. Short articles on Roman Catholic theology, incorporating material generated by Vatican II, with excellent reference data.

Rahner, Karl, and others, eds. *Encyclopedia of Theology: The Concise Sacramentum Mundi.* Crossroad NY rev. ed. 1975 $49.50. ISBN 0-8245-0303-1. The single-volume edition of the six-volume work with some revision and bibliographies.

———. *Sacramentum Mundi: An Encyclopedia of Theology.* 6 vols. Fr. & Eur. 1968–70 o.p. A widely popular book that has appeared in five other European languages. Based on the work of more than 600 Roman Catholic theologians, it attempts to present current developments and differences in all areas of theology.

Richardson, Alan, and John Bowden, eds. *Dictionary of Christian Theology.* Westminster John Knox 1983 $30.00. ISBN 0-664-21398-7. Alphabetically arranged short articles for students.

Church History

Barry, Colman J., ed. *Readings in Church History.* 3 vols. Chr. Classics 1985 o.p. Collection of primary materials illustrating important events, movements, and thinkers from the Reformation to the modern period.

The Book of Saints: A Dictionary of Persons Canonized or Beatified by the Catholic Church. T. Y. Crowell 5th ed. 1966 o.p. A 740-page dictionary providing concise biographical data on some 2,200 saints.

Bowden, Henry W., and Edwin S. Gaustad, eds. *Dictionary of American Religious Biography.* Greenwood 1977 $45.00. ISBN 0-8371-8906-3. Contains 425 well-annotated biographical sketches of people who have helped shape America's religious traditions.

Brauer, Jerald C., ed. *Westminster Dictionary of Church History.* Westminster John Knox 1971 $32.00. ISBN 0-664-21285-9. An 887-page resource for definitions and explanations of facts, movements, events, and persons in church history.

Caldwell, Sandra M., and Ronald J. Caldwell. *History of the Episcopal Church in America, 1607–1991: A Bibliography.* Garland 1993 $82.00. ISBN 0-8153-0936-8

Delaney, John J. *A Dictionary of Saints.* Doubleday 1980 $29.95. ISBN 0-385-13594-7. Up-to-date compendium of 5,000 saints.

———. *Pocket Dictionary of Saints.* Doubleday 1983 $8.00. ISBN 0-385-18274-0

Dowley, Tim, ed. *Eerdmans' Handbook to the History of Christianity*. Eerdmans 1977 $29.95. ISBN 0-8028-3450-7. Seventy scholars have contributed to this handy description of the history of Christianity, which provides popular but good scholarship with many aids but no bibliography.

Eberhardt, Vernon C. *A Summary of Catholic History*. 2 vols. Fr. & Eur. 1961–62 o.p. The second volume begins with 1453 and carries the story to modern times, filling the gap between one-volume summaries and Jedin's massive work (see below).

Jedin, Hubert, and John Patrick Dolan, gen. eds. *The History of the Church*. 10 vols. Crossroad NY 1980 $595.00. ISBN 0-8245-0318-X. Translation of Jedin's *Handbuch der Kirchengeschichte*, a solid history from a Catholic viewpoint with bibliography and index for each volume.

Latourette, Kenneth S. *A History of Christianity*. 2 vols. HarpC 1975 $18.00 ea. ISBNs 0-06-064952-6, 0-06-064953-4. Dean of American church historians summarizes his life's work in these accurate and ecumenical volumes.

Littell, Franklin H. *The Macmillan Atlas History of Christianity*. Macmillan 1976 o.p. Excellent set of 197 maps and commentary focusing on intellectual, ethical, and expansionist aspects of Christianity from beginning to present. Illustrated by E. Hausman.

Manschreck, Clyde L. *A History of Christianity in the World: From Persecution to Uncertainty*. P-H 2nd ed. 1985 $38.00. ISBN 0-13-389354-5. Moderate Protestant view of history of church.

Moyer, Elgin, and Earle Cairns. *Wycliffe Biographical Dictionary of the Church*. Moody 1982 o.p. Formerly entitled *Who Was Who in Church History*, this volume, Protestant in emphasis, includes brief biographical sketches of 2,000 religious leaders, Christian and non-Christian.

Neill, Stephen C., and others. *Concise Dictionary of the Christian World Mission*. Abingdon 1971 o.p. Indispensable coverage of all aspects of missions from ecumenical perspective; brief articles by 200 specialists treat the spread of Christianity in various lands, discuss topics relating to missionary work, and provide biographies of leaders.

Pelikan, Jaroslav. *The Christian Tradition: A History of the Development of Doctrine*. Vol. 5 *Christian Doctrine and Modern Culture (Since 1700)*. U. Ch. Pr. 1989 $29.95. ISBN 0-226-65378-1. Concluding with the Vatican II Council, Pelikan completes his astonishing piece of research on Christian doctrine, published in five volumes.

Walker, Williston. *A History of the Christian Church*. Rev. by Robert T. Handy. Macmillan 4th ed. 1985 $35.00. ISBN 0-02-423870-8. First published in 1918, its steady and fair coverage is continued in Handy's revision, which features index and maps.

THE REFORMATION OF THE SIXTEENTH CENTURY: 1500–1560

The Reformation has been alternately characterized as "that infamous sundering of the Body of Christ" and "the rediscovery of the pure bride of Christ." Not limited to the Protestant movements, it also involved a reformation in church practice and morality by the Roman Catholic church and a fixing of Roman Catholic theology in a form that lasted until the Second Vatican Council (1962–65). At one time the Protestant reformers were vilified by Roman Catholic historians, but in recent decades a number of such historians have acknowledged good cause for the Protestant zeal while still lamenting the end of unified Western Christianity. The Orthodox churches of the East escaped the divisiveness that has characterized Christianity in the West since the beginning of the Reformation.

Background: Before the Reformation

Cohn, Norman. *The Pursuit of the Millennium.* OUP rev. ed. 1970 $11.95. ISBN 0-19-500456-6. The left wing, or "stepchildren," of the Middle Ages comes to the surface—sometimes violently—after Luther. See also listings under The Radical Reformation for Leonard Verduin and George Williams.

Erasmus, Desiderius. *The Essential Erasmus.* Ed. and trans. by John Dolan. NAL-Dutton 1989 $4.95. ISBN 0-452-00914-6. A marvelous collection of writings of Erasmus of Rotterdam, the influential humanist who saw serious problems in the church but argued that love forbade the church's fragmentation.

Gilson, Étienne. *History of Christian Philosophy in the Middle Ages.* Chr. Classics 1955 o.p. In about 830 pages, all anyone wants to know about the subject. Some of Luther's rejection of philosophy, the "devil's whore," can be seen here.

Halkin, Léon-E. *Erasmus: A Critical Biography.* Trans. by John Tonkin. Blackwell Pubs. 1993 $39.95. ISBN 0-631-16929-6. Halkin, praised by *Le Monde* as the leading authority on Erasmus, ably addresses many of the facets of Erasmus's life that have remained obscure, including the date of his birth.

Hudson, Anne, ed. *Selections from English Wycliffite Writings.* Cambridge U. Pr. 1981 $21.95. ISBN 0-521-28258-6. Addresses the problem of whether the English Reformation existed already as a primarily underground movement when Henry VIII rejected papal ecclesiastical control over England in order to get his divorce.

Knowles, David. *The English Mystical Tradition.* HarpC 1961 o.p. Small volume, broad in scholarship and even wisdom, by the dean of English students of monasticism.

Lambert, Malcolm. *Medieval Heresy: Popular Movements from Bogomil to Hus.* Holmes & Meier 1977 $54.50. ISBN 0-8419-0298-4. Good, clear account of various medieval movements, such as Albigensian, Waldensian, Hussite, and others.

Lerner, Robert E. *The Heresy of the Free Spirit in the Later Middle Ages.* U. of Notre Dame Pr. 1991 $15.95. ISBN 0-268-01094-3. Brief, but careful, study of a wider sort of heresy than the title suggests.

McFarlane, Kenneth B. *John Wycliffe and the Beginnings of English Nonconformity.* Verry 1952 o.p. Small, fine study that has held its own with later studies of Wycliffe and his followers.

McNiven, Peter. *Heresy and Politics in the Reign of Henry IV: The Burning of John Badby.* Boydell & Brewer 1987 $70.00. ISBN 0-85115-467-0

Oakley, Francis. *The Western Church in the Later Middle Ages.* Cornell Univ. Pr. 1985 $39.95. ISBN 0-8014-1208-0. Good survey by top scholar.

Oberman, Heiko. *Forerunners of the Reformation: The Shape of Late Medieval Thought.* Trans. by Paul Nyhus. Bks. Demand repr. of 1981 ed. $86.80. ISBN 0-685-17052-7. Selections from religious reformers before Luther.

———. *The Harvest of Medieval Theology: Gabriel Biel and Late Medieval Nominalism.* Labyrinth Pr. 1983 repr. of 1963 ed. $18.50. ISBN 0-939464-05-5. Although focused on the nominalist theologian Gabriel Biel, this is a good survey of late medieval theology and philosophy.

Ozment, Steven E. *The Age of Reform 1250–1550: An Intellectual and Religious History of Late Medieval and Early Reformation Europe.* Yale U. Pr. 1980 $17.00. ISBN 0-300-02760-5. Defies usual periodization in order to put the Reformation into a medieval perspective and to show that Luther stood in a line of reformers.

———, ed. *The Reformation in Medieval Perspective.* New Viewpoints 1971 o.p. Concentrates on the pre-Luther period but shows continuities and radical breaks with the reforming tradition.

Peters, Edward. *Heresy and Authority in Medieval Europe.* U. of Pa. Pr. 1980 $19.95. ISBN 0-8122-1103-0

Spinka, Matthew. *John Hus: A Biography.* Greenwood 1978 repr. of 1968 ed. $41.50. ISBN 0-313-21050-0. Brief and enjoyable.

———, ed. *Advocates of Reform: From Wyclif to Erasmus.* Westminster John Knox 1953 o.p. Useful selections from major works of pre-Reformation critics of church and society, Wycliffe, Hus, and others.

General Studies of the Reformation

Chadwick, Owen. *The Reformation.* Viking Penguin 1964 $6.95. ISBN 0-14-020-504-7. Balanced study by one of the leaders in British history; includes indexes and bibliographies.

Dickens, A. G. *Reformation and Society in Sixteenth-Century Europe.* HarBraceJ 1966 o.p. Good on preconditions for reform; has glossary of theological terms and a reading list.

Durant, Will. *The Reformation.* Fine Comms. 1993. ISBN 1-56731-017-6

Elton, G. R. *Reformation Europe, 1517–1559.* HarpC 1968 o.p. An unbiased book that very clearly sets the Reformation in its broader context.

Gerrish, Brian. *Reformers in Profile.* Fortress Pr. 1967 o.p. A handy introduction to several prereformers, Erasmus, and major reform leaders such as Luther, Zwingli, Calvin, Cranmer, Simons, and (for Catholicism) Loyola.

Green, Robert W., ed. *Protestantism and Capitalism and Social Science: The Weber Thesis Controversy.* Heath 2nd ed. 1973 $8.50. ISBN 0-669-81737-6. Presents in handy fashion arguments for and against the thesis that Protestantism was responsible for the rise of capitalism.

Grimm, Harold J. *The Reformation Era: 1500–1650.* Macmillan 2nd ed. 1973 o.p. Excellent treatment, supplemented by 65 pages of bibliography.

Hillerbrand, Hans J., ed. *The Protestant Reformation.* HarpC 1968 $12.00. ISBN 0-06-131342-4. Lively account making good use of pamphlet literature as well as major works on all sides. Good bibliography.

———. *The Reformation: A Narrative History Related by Contemporary Observers and Participants.* Baker Bk. 1978 $19.95. ISBN 0-8010-4185-6. Quotations and illustrations made before and during the Reformation, with brief commentary, providing sharp flavor absent in objective accounts.

Hsia, R. Po-Chia, ed. *The German People and the Reformation.* Cornell Univ. Pr. 1988 $12.95. ISBN 0-8014-9485-0. Interesting results follow from historians' attempts to focus on the lives of ordinary people rather than on ideas.

Hughes, Philip. *A Popular History of the Reformation.* Hanover Hse. 1957 o.p. Although this work by a Catholic historian has the *nihil obstat* and the *imprimatur,* it is not anti-Protestant.

Lortz, Joseph. *The Reformation in Germany.* Trans. by Ronald Walls. Fr. & Eur. 1968 o.p. Lortz was the first Catholic historian to present Luther in a favorable light; originally published in 1939.

McGrath, Alister. *The Intellectual Origins of the European Reformation.* Blackwell Pubs. 1993 $19.95. ISBN 0-631-18688-3. Contends that the Reformation was not a radical break from the past and that, in fact, intellectual trends before Luther made some kind of upheaval likely.

———. *Reformation Thought: An Introduction.* Blackwell Pubs. 1988 $14.95. ISBN 0-631-15803-0. Returning to a topic on which he has written several books, McGrath introduces, explains, and contextualizes the ideas of the Reformation.

Moeller, Bernd. *Imperial Cities and the Reformation.* Ed. by H. C. Erik Midelfort and Mark U. Edwards, Jr. Labyrinth Pr. 1982 repr. of 1972 ed. $6.95. ISBN 0-939464-04-7. Three essays that appeared separately in German, studying problems in research on the era, the role of the German humanists, and imperial cities.

Mosse, George L. *The Reformation.* Peter Smith rev. ed. 1991 $2.25. ISBN 1-877891-02-9. Viewpoint of author, well known for studies of nazism and Jewry, makes this a unique study.

Ozment, Steven E. *Protestants: Birth of a Revolution.* Doubleday 1993 $12.00. ISBN 0-385-47101-7

———. *Reformation Europe: A Guide to Research.* Center Reform. 1982 $18.50. ISBN 0-910345-01-5. Essays by experts in various facets of Reformation history; a must for the serious student or researcher.

———. *The Reformation in the Cities: The Appeal of Protestantism to Sixteenth-Century Germany and Switzerland.* Yale U. Pr. 1975 $32.50. ISBN 0-300-01898-3. Necessary study of humanists as well as city councils, with smooth narrative flow and 70 pages of notes.

Raitt, Jill. *The Colloquy of Montbéliard: Religion and Politics in the Sixteenth Century.* OUP 1993 $45.00. ISBN 0-19-507566-8. Concentrates on a theological debate between Lutherans and Calvinists; demonstrates that theological discussions in the Reformation were shaped by political circumstances.

Spitz, Lewis W. *The Protestant Reformation 1517–1559.* HarpC 1987 $12.00. ISBN 0-06-132069-2. By a noted historian. The 45-page bibliography is useful.

Todd, John M. *Reformation.* Doubleday 1971 o.p. Balanced study by a Catholic biographer of Luther, with bibliography and index.

The Radical Reformation: Anabaptists, Spiritualists, and Evangelical Rationalists

It is difficult to group all the left-wing, radical reformers under one name. Some historians use the three headings employed above—Anabaptists, Spiritualists, and Evangelical Rationalists—and perhaps that is the best that can be done to cover the fantastic array of religious nonconformists of the sixteenth century. The major reformers—MARTIN LUTHER, HULDRYCH ZWINGLI, JOHN CALVIN, leaders of the English Reformation—all concurred with Roman Catholics in believing that church and state, religion and society, should be one. Indeed, it seemed to all of them *"frénétique et fantastique"* to think that a society could hold together if not bound by the ties of a common religion.

This was not so with the radical reformers. Although they disagreed among themselves, all of the radical reformers wanted a clear separation of state and church, believing that the former belonged to Satan and the latter to Christ. The radical reformers all wanted to restore the primitive church, the small band of true believers whose light shone in a dark world. Some are denoted Anabaptists to show that their detractors identified them primarily by their insistence on the baptism of all believers, which, in practice, meant the rebaptism of those already baptized as infants. Others are called Spiritualists, for they held the activity of the Holy Spirit within the believer to be even more important than the Bible. In the next century, the Quakers (Society of Friends) institutionalized that position in the form we recognize today. The Evangelical Rationalists were Evangelical because, like Luther, they held to justification by faith alone, but their rationalism led them to deny doctrines that had to be accepted on faith, like the deity of Christ and the Trinity. Their existence in Poland lasted scarcely two generations, but they have cast a long shadow down the history of Christianity.

Armour, Rollin S. *Anabaptist Baptism.* Herald Pr. 1966 $16.95. ISBN 0-8361-1178-8. Studies views of baptism on part of Anabaptist leaders and finds that they differ in many respects.

Bak, Janos, ed. *The German Peasant War of 1525.* Biblio NY 1976 $26.00. ISBN 0-7146-3063-2. Contains essays that set forth various conflicting opinions on Thomas Müntzer, a religious radical before he was led by divine inspiration into heading the folk rebellion in middle Germany.

Clasen, Claus-Peter. *Anabaptism: A Social History, 1525–1618.* Cornell Univ. Pr. 1972 o.p. Clearly written, with a large bibliography, by an author who believes one can quantitatively assess Anabaptist social history.

———. *The Anabaptist in South and Central Germany, Switzerland, and Austria.* Mennonite Hist. Soc. 1978 o.p. Has been called the "major research achievement of twentieth-century Anabaptist studies"; it omits the radicals of northern Germany and the Netherlands.

Davis, Kenneth R. *Anabaptism and Asceticism: A Study in Intellectual Origins.* Herald Pr. 1974 $19.95. ISBN 0-8361-1195-8. Good intellectual history arguing that there are spiritual and intellectual ties between medieval monks and the Anabaptists.

Durnbaugh, Donald F. *Believer's Church: The History and Character of Radical Protestantism.* Herald Pr. 1985 repr. of 1968 ed. $14.95. ISBN 0-8361-1271-7. Brings the stress of radical Protestants on church-state separation and pacifism into this century in an excellent study.

Gross, Leonard. *The Golden Years of the Hutterites.* Bks. Demand repr. of 1980 ed. $72.10. ISBN 0-8357-2663-0. Primarily a study of second-generation Anabaptists in southern and eastern Europe, just before their savage persecution by the Austrian Empire.

Klaassen, Walter. *Anabaptism in Outline: Selected Primary Sources.* Bks. Demand repr. of 1981 ed. $14.95. ISBN 0-8361-1241-5. Writings from major leaders, as well as confessional statements and debate materials.

_____. *Living at the End of the Ages: Apocalyptic Expectation in the Radical Reformation.* U. Pr. of Amer. 1992 $41.00. ISBN 0-8191-8506-X

Littell, Franklin H. *The Anabaptist View of the Church.* Starr King 1958 o.p. Nearly a classic, this centers on the restoration of the primitive church from its Constantinian "Fall" and the pacifism of the Anabaptists.

Ozment, Steven E. *Mysticism and Dissent: Religious Ideology and Social Protest in the Sixteenth Century.* Yale U. Pr. 1973 o.p. Traces mystical belief from pre-Reformation German thought through left wingers of the Reformation, such as Müntzer and others; shows the link between them and social protest, e.g., the Peasants' War.

Packull, Werner O. *Mysticism and the Early South German-Austrian Anabaptist Movement, 1525-1531.* Herald Pr. 1977 $19.95. ISBN 0-8361-1130-3. Too obviously a doctoral dissertation, but still a readable way to see the origins of southern radicals.

Rupp, Gordon. *Patterns of Reformation.* Fortress Pr. 1969 o.p. Rupp, dean of English Reformation historians, is always enjoyable; this is described as an "entertaining study of two wayward radicals, Müntzer and Carlstadt" (Lewis Spitz).

Ruth, John L. *Conrad Grebel: Son of Zurich.* Herald Pr. 1975 $12.95. ISBN 0-8361-1767-0. Admiring but not uncritical.

Stayer, James M. *Anabaptists and the Sword.* Coronado Pr. 2nd rev. ed. 1976 $20.00. ISBN 0-87291-081-4. Argues that the one unifying idea was not theological but political—namely, the Anabaptists' attitude toward government authority (the sword).

Stayer, James M., and Werner O. Packull, eds. *The Anabaptists and Thomas Müntzer.* Kendall-Hunt 1980 o.p. An anthology and a good introduction.

Verduin, Leonard. *The Stepchildren of the Reformation.* Eerdmans 1964 o.p. By a Calvinist who sees the radicals as existing long before the Reformation but only coming into the open with Luther.

Waite, Gary K. *Anabaptist Writings of David Jovis, 1535-1543.* Herald Pr. 1993 $39.95. ISBN 0-8361-3113-4

Wilbur, Earl M. *A History of Unitarianism.* 2 vols. HUP 1947-52 o.p. Vol 1 *A History of Unitarianism, Socinianism and Its Antecedents.* Vol. 2 *In Transylvania, England, and America.* This is the work most frequently cited, but appears to do more with later Unitarianism than the serious scholar of the Reformation might want.

Williams, George H. *Radical Reformation.* Sixteenth Cent. 1992 $100.00. ISBN 0-940474-15-8. The first major study by an unbiased scholar, providing a good section on what he calls the Evangelical Rationalists, and including information of Socinus and his uncle Laelius Socinus, who promulgated Unitarian ideas in Italy.

Williams, George H., and Angel M. Mergal, eds. *Spiritual and Anabaptist Writers.* Westminster John Knox 1977 $14.99. ISBN 0-664-24150-6. The radicals were prolific writers, but this is about the only good-sized English translation of some major writings; the second part of this edition is on Evangelical Catholicism, especially the Spaniard humanist writer Juan Valdes.

Zuck, Lowell H., ed. *Christianity and Revolution: Radical Christian Testimonies, 1520–1650*. Temple U. Pr. 1975 o.p. Excerpts from various radicals, especially reflecting their relationship with their enemies; long end notes serve as bibliography.

The English Reformation: From Henry VIII to the Elizabethan Settlement

In recent years, it has been said that English historians still do not fully understand their Reformation. Some historians present the view that it was essentially a political matter, concentrating on the consolidation of religious and political power under Henry VIII, whose religious contribution was to reject papal claims in England and burn overzealous Protestants. Others hold that it was basically a religious fermentation that destroyed the old church, for which Henry's policies happened to allow some grudging measure of freedom. Certainly the resulting Church of England was more like the Roman Catholic church than the churches of MARTIN LUTHER, the Reformed or the left wing, at least in deliberately retaining the governing role of bishops. Indeed, it was this episcopal rule that drew the ire of Puritans after the Elizabethan Settlement and provided most of the fireworks for the later history of church reform in England.

It should be noted that Henry VIII not only rejected the pope's control of the English church, but also closed the monasteries, which resulted in an enormous amount of land and money reverting to the crown. These lands were often given or sold cheaply to local nobles, thus strengthening the power of the king. A fuller Reformation ensued under the rule of Henry's young son, Edward VI, and through the genius of THOMAS CRANMER, archbishop of Canterbury (the chief church official in England), who guided this essentially Reformed movement and wrote the justly renowned *Book of Common Prayer*, the order for worship in England. A brief return to Roman Catholicism took place under Henry's daughter Mary, whom the Protestants dubbed "Bloody" because of her killing of Protestants, including Cranmer. But Protestantism of the Anglican variety returned for good under Elizabeth I, the daughter conceived by Henry and Anne Boleyn. It was Henry's desire to marry Anne Boleyn that prompted him to seek more earnestly the divorce from Catherine of Aragon and that first moved him to break with the pope.

Baker, Derek, ed. *Reform and Reformation: England and the Continent 1500–1750*. Blackwell Pubs. 1980 $65.00. ISBN 0-631-19270-0. Helpful articles on various aspects of the Reformation in England.

Brigden, Susan. *London and the Reformation*. OUP 1990 $130.00. ISBN 0-19-822774-4. Wonderfully comprehensive, massive, and monumental. Based on manuscripts, public records, and printed sources. Includes special analyses of London wills and of London martyrs.

Bromiley, G. W. *Thomas Cranmer*. Attic Pr. repr. of 1956 ed. o.p. Definitive but brief 100-page study by a recognized scholar.

Capp, Bernard. *English Almanacs, 1500–1800: Astrology and the Popular Press*. Cornell Univ. Pr. 1979 $57.50. ISBN 0-8014-1229-3. A much more important form of popular literature than it is today and therefore offers insights into popular religious beliefs at the time of the Reformation.

Christianson, Paul K. *Reformers and Babylon: Apocalyptic Visions in England from the Reformation to the Outbreak of the Civil War*. U. of Toronto Pr. 1978 o.p. Many of the English thought that Christ was about to begin his 1,000-year rule with England as its center, a view that became common in nineteenth-century America and is reflected in theologies as diverse as the Millerites, the Oneida Community, and the Mormons.

Clebsch, William A. *England's Earliest Protestants, 1520–1535*. Greenwood 1980 repr. of 1964 ed. $38.50. ISBN 0-313-22420-X. The best single volume on the pioneers of reform in England, with attention to Barnes, Firth, Tyndale, as well as to the reforming aspirations of Thomas More.

Cranmer, Thomas. *The Work of Thomas Cranmer*. Ed. by G. E. Duffield. Fortress Pr. 1965 o.p. Omits *The Book of Common Prayer*, which was largely Cranmer's work, but his other writings are here and are commented on expertly.

Cross, Claire. *Church and People, 1450–1600*. Humanities 1976 o.p. There is a good bibliography attached to this work, which argues that the Reformation was the defeat of churchly powers by the laity.

Dickens, Arthur G. *The English Reformation*. Schocken 1991 $19.95. ISBN 0-271-00798-2. Dickens is always good, and many regard this as the best single book on the English Reformation, showing it in all its delightful confusion.

Duffield, G. E. *The Work of William Tyndale*. Fortress Pr. 1965 o.p. Tyndale lost his life because he translated the Bible into English and had it smuggled into Henry VIII's England.

Elton, G. R. *England under the Tudors*. Methuen 3rd rev. ed. 1991 $19.95. ISBN 0-415-06533-X. Elton is dean of English scholars of the Reformation and always good; makes perhaps more of politics and less of religion than Dickens.

―――. *Reform and Reformation: England 1509–1558*. HUP 1979 $30.50. ISBN 0-674-75245-7. Draws together 25 years of research.

Erickson, Carolly. *Bloody Mary*. St. Martin 1985 $10.95. ISBN 0-312-08508-7. Like Antonia Fraser and Barbara Tuchman, Erickson writes large but nontechnical books for the general public; see also Richardson and Ridley for more on Mary Tudor.

―――. *Mistress Anne: The Exceptional Life of Anne Boleyn*. Summit Bks. 1985 $12.95. ISBN 0-671-60651-4. Good nontechnical account of the second wife of Henry VIII, who lost her head over him but produced the girl, Elizabeth, who would knit the nation together.

Finucane, Ronald C. *Miracles and Pilgrims: Popular Beliefs in Medieval England*. Rowman 1977 o.p. Plates, bibliography, and a useful look at popular religion as the Reformation approaches.

Firth, Katherine R. *The Apocalyptic Tradition in Reformation Britain 1530–1645*. OUP 1979 o.p. Gives insight into the wild side of the Reformation (see also Christianson above.)

Haigh, Christopher. *English Reformations: Religion, Politics and Society Under the Tudors*. OUP 1993 $55.00. ISBN 0-19-822162-2

Heal, Felicity, and Rosemary O'Day. *Church and Society in England: Henry VIII to James I*. Shoe String 1977 o.p. Helpful articles on a plethora of topics about both church and society in a revolutionary age.

Hughes, Philip E. *Theology of the English Reformers*. Baker Bk. rev. ed. 1980 o.p. Good study by one who agrees with Reformist theology.

Hunt, Ernest W. *Dean Colet and His Theology*. A. R. Allenson 1956 o.p. A small study of Erasmus's friend, whose reforming views were realized more violently than he would have wanted.

Jordan, Wilbur K. *Edward VI: The Threshold of Power*. Allen & Unwin 1970 o.p.

―――. *Edward VI: The Young King*. Allen & Unwin 1968 o.p. Together these two volumes tell most readers everything they want to know about the boy king in whose name Protestantism was fully established through the politics of his governors and the religious genius of Thomas Cranmer.

Kendall, R. T. *Calvin and English Calvinism to 1649*. OUP 1979 o.p. Small but useful study of those who were later called Puritans and the problems predestination gave them as pastors.

King, John N. *Spenser's Poetry and the Reformation Tradition*. Princeton U. Pr. 1990 $41.50. ISBN 0-691-06800-3. Examines Spenser's work as a contemporary social commentary of Reformation England. Presented with expert clarity, precision, and thoroughness.

O'Day, Rosemary. *The Debate on the English Reformation*. Routledge Chapman & Hall 1986 $12.95. ISBN 0-416-72680-1. Study of various commentators of the Reformation; from its sixteenth-century contemporaries to the twentieth century academic.

Ozment, Steven. *Protestants*. Doubleday 1992 $20.00. ISBN 0-385-42172-9. Examines Protestantism as an ideological whole, as well as the judgments and viewpoints of laypeople and scholars alike toward the Reform. A worthwhile study by a Harvard specialist on the Reformation.

Parker, Thomas H. L. *English Reformers*. Westminster John Knox 1966 o.p. Vignettes of Tyndale, Ridley, Latimer, Cranmer, and others, providing a good place for a beginner to start, for Parker is trustworthy.

Powicke, Maurice R. *The Reformation in England*. OUP 1941 o.p. Old and very brief, therefore oversimplifies the scene, but in a way that the student is not misled very much. Read Powicke, then Dickens (above), and then smaller studies of individuals.

Reynolds, Ernest E. *Thomas More and Erasmus*. Fordham 1966 $35.00. ISBN 0-8232-0670-X. Correspondence between the two humanist scholars with their somewhat different responses to the Reformation.

Richardson, Walter C. *Mary Tudor, the White Queen*. U. of Wash. Pr. 1969 o.p. Praised as a good account of her life, her marriage to Philip of Spain, and the tragedy of her reign.

Ridley, Jasper. *The Life and Times of Mary Tudor*. Weidenfeld & Nicolson 1973 o.p. An easy-to-read coffee-table book about Mary and her times.

_____. *Thomas Cranmer*. Darby Pub. 1983 repr. of 1962 ed. o.p. This is the basic biography that Ridley excels in: easy to read and thoroughly researched.

Rupp, Ernest G. *Six Makers of English Religion, 1500–1700. Essay Index Repr. Ser.* Ayer repr. of 1957 ed. $16.75. ISBN 0-518-10159-2. Discusses Tyndale, Cranmer, and John Foxe, author of the *Book of Martyrs*, as well as Milton, Bunyan, and Isaac Watts, the hymnwriter.

_____. *Studies in the Making of the English Protestant Tradition*. Cambridge U. Pr. 1947 o.p. The first part fits this period in a solid way.

Scarisbrick, J. J. *Henry VIII*. U. CA Pr. 1968 $13.95. ISBN 0-520-01130-9. Best modern biography but a bit daunting at 560 pages.

Thomas, Keith. *Religion and the Decline of Magic*. Macmillan 1975 $24.00. ISBN 0-684-14542-1. Surveys English folk religion during this period. A long book, but so well organized that it makes it easy to study particular aspects of religion or magic, e.g., astrology, witchcraft.

Whiting, Robert. *The Blind Devotion of the People: Religion and the English Reformation*. Cambridge U. Pr. 1989 $59.95. ISBN 0-521-35606-7. Detailed account of religion in Devon and Cornwall between 1530 and 1570. A painstaking analysis of wills, church wardens' accounts, and related documents.

The Catholic Reformation: From 1500 through the Council of Trent

The Catholic Reformation or the Counter-Reformation? In the sense that the Roman Catholic church had the resources within itself to purge the institution of the corruptions of simony, nepotism, and a host of feudal ills, it was certainly a Catholic Reformation. But in the sense that the strongest stirrings for change came from men like MARTIN LUTHER and others, who were either excommunicated by the church or who rejected the Roman communion and established churches outside Roman Catholic jurisdiction, it was necessarily a Counter-Reformation. Even the Council of Trent, the chief expounder of Catholic reform that met intermittently from 1545 until 1563, can be seen either as summarizing and clarifying the church's long traditional theology and practice or as a means of stating theology in opposition to the Protestants.

The great leaders of the Catholic Reformation were not popes and bishops, but people like ST. IGNATIUS OF LOYOLA, founder of the Society of Jesus (Jesuits), or St. Teresa of Avila, who combined obedience with a radical spirituality centered on the Passion of Christ. It was the Jesuits, especially, who produced the theologians and built the schools to produce an educated ministry, the strongest challenge the Church of Rome faced from the scholarly Protestants. Jesuits tutored the bishops in theology at the Council of Trent. Jesuits saved a remnant for the church in England and encouraged kings and emperors to remain true to the faith in many lands. Jesuits stormed the rapidly opening lands in the Americas for the gospel, almost as fast as Portuguese and Spanish conquistadors searched those lands for their wealth. Companions to the early explorers were Jesuit missionaries, men like Father Louis Hennepin and Jacques Marquette, whose names are known even to schoolchildren in America.

Bireley, Robert. *The Counter-Reformation Prince: Anti-Machiavellianism or Catholic Statecraft in Early Modern Europe.* U. of NC Pr. 1990 $39.95. ISBN 0-8078-1925-5. Recuperation of six Catholic political theorists who argue against Machiavelli that virtuous princes will be rewarded.

Brodrick, James. *St. Francis Xavier, 1506–1552.* Wicklow Pr. 1952 o.p. Good-sized tome on a man who took the gospel to India, China, and Japan; a great explorer and observer, as well as missionary.

————. *St. Peter Canisius.* Loyola 1962 $19.95. ISBN 0-8294-0008-7. Canisius is often regarded as the one who saved half of Germany from the Lutherans; Brodrick is always inclined to "see no evil" in his heroes.

Chatellier, Louis. *The Europe of the Devout: The Catholic Reformation and the Formation of a New Society.* Cambridge U. Pr. 1989 $59.95. ISBN 0-521-36333-0. Focusing on the Jesuits as the principal force, the author examines the profound change in Catholic society during the two centuries after the Council of Trent.

Christian, William A., Jr. *Local Religion in Sixteenth-Century Spain.* Princeton U. Pr. 1989 $14.95. ISBN 0-691-00827-2. The sort of solid story we need for more lands. Some modern scholars believe that the masses of rural folk were largely un-Christianized during the Middle Ages. This was not true of Spain, Christian shows.

Delumeau, Jean. *Catholicism between Luther and Voltaire: A New View of the Counter-Reformation.* Trans. by Jeremy Moiser. Westminster John Knox 1977 o.p. Argues that most people were not Christianized in the Middle Ages and that the Reformation and Catholic Reformation accomplished the conversion of the masses of Europeans to Christianity.

Dickens, A. G. *The Counter Reformation.* Norton 1979 $9.95. ISBN 0-393-95086-7. Solid book by a noted Reformation historian.

Douglas, Richard M. *Jacopo Sadoleto, 1477–1547: Humanist and Reformer.* HUP 1959 o.p. Sadoleto and Calvin had a published correspondence over the validity of the Reformation.

Evennet, H. O. *The Spirit of the Counter Reformation.* U. of Notre Dame Pr. 1970 $7.95. ISBN 0-268-00425-0. A positive evaluation of the Catholic Reformation, especially of the Council of Trent, which many historians, both Catholic and Protestant, have understood as a narrowing and hardening of the church's theology and practice.

Gleason, Elizabeth G. *Reform Thought in Sixteenth Century Italy.* Ed. by James A. Massey. Scholars Pr. GA 1981 $15.95. ISBN 0-89130-498-3. Features translated and edited reforming documents from Italy—some by those who broke with Rome (Ochino) and others by men who led reform (G. Carafa, who became Pope Paul IV)—a handy sourcebook with clear introductions.

Iggers, Georg G. *New Directions in European Historiography.* U. Pr. of New Eng. rev. ed. 1984 $16.00. ISBN 0-8195-6071-5. Obviously for those who want to know how history is written, with the chapter on changes in writing about the Catholic Reformation very clearly set forth.

Janelle, Pierre. *The Catholic Reformation.* Bruce 1949 o.p. Rather a classic telling of the story, with special emphasis on the Catholic humanist as key to the success of the Catholic Reformation.

Jedin, Hubert. *A History of the Council of Trent.* 5 vols. Nelson 1957–63 o.p. The standard history that all scholars have used as point of departure.

McNally, Robert E. *The Unreformed Church.* Sheed & Ward MO 1965 o.p. McNally, a Jesuit, argues that the late medieval church was unreformed in worship, in its view and use of Scripture, in its administration, and in its spirituality; he claims that the Reformation was inevitable.

Minnich, Nelson H. *The Catholic Reformation: Council, Churchmen, Controversies.* Ashgate Pub. Co. 1993 $97.95. ISBN 0-86078-350-2

Olin, J. C. *The Catholic Reformation: Savonarola to Ignatius Loyola.* Chr. Classics 1969 o.p. A collection of reforming epistles, speeches, confessions, rules for new orders, and the like, all introduced within the context of the Reformation. Not the first book one would consult, but very useful for seeing firsthand what people thought needed reforming.

Schenk, Wilhelm. *Reginald Pole: Cardinal of England.* Longman 1950 o.p. Long the standard biography of Mary Tudor's chief churchman, a humanist, and a reformer in his own right.

Schroeder, H. J., trans. *Canons and Decrees of the Council of Trent.* TAN Bks. Pubs. 1978 repr. of 1941 ed. $12.00. ISBN 0-89555-074-1. The older printing had Latin on one side and English on the other; a recent printing eliminated the Latin. No commentary, but simply the decision of the bishops as finally promulgated.

THE REFORMATION IN ITS LATER DEVELOPMENTS: 1560–1648

One of the frustrations of historians is dividing history into periods, a necessity for teaching courses that end when the semester ends and writing books with beginnings and endings. One way to periodize the Reformation Era is to characterize the period from 1517, when MARTIN LUTHER posted his Ninety-five Theses (whether he nailed them or mailed them, we can at least say that he "posted" them), until about 1560 as the formative stage of the Reformation. The period from 1560 to 1648, when the Treaty of Westphalia ended the Thirty Years' War in Germany and pretty much set the present Catholic-Protestant boundaries, can thus be categorized as the Later Period, or the consolidation, or (in Lewis Spitz's term) its Second Surge.

A number of deaths and settlements makes 1560 an attractive date to distinguish the fresh movements for reform from its Consolidation in both Catholic and Protestant circles. In 1564 the reforming Catholic Council of Trent finished its work of internal reform, but most of the reforming had yet to be done. Luther died in 1546, the year after the council began; and JOHN CALVIN died in 1564, the year before it ended. In England, the Elizabethan Settlement was ratified by Parliament in 1559, and that same year JOHN KNOX came to Scotland and introduced the Reformation there, that great "spider that sat down beside her" (Mary Queen of Scots).

This periodization, however, does not fit in every region. France became embroiled in its terrible Wars of Religion soon after 1560, and peace did not come conclusively until the Protestant Henry of Navarre, who later became Henry IV of France and converted to Catholicism, granted his former fellow Protestants partial freedom in his Edict of Nantes in 1598. In Ireland one can hardly say that the Reformation was over in 1648, for it was not until 1690 that the Catholic James II, deposed as King of England the year before, was defeated by his Protestant son-in-law, William III, at the Boyne. It was this victory that sealed Ireland in its present mold, with Ulster largely a Protestant enclave in a Catholic island.

Post-Luther Lutheranism in Germany and Scandinavia

Theologically, Lutherans were faced with the challenge of formulating some type of coherent system out of MARTIN LUTHER's somewhat sprawling theology. Most historians of theology think that issues such as Christ's presence in Holy Communion were quite well solidified by 1580, when the Formula of Concord became the norm for Lutheran theology. By the end of the century, reforms had expanded and the various Scandinavian countries had all become predominantly Lutheran. This was fortunate, for it was only the intervention by Sweden's King Gustavus Adolphus in the Thirty Years' War (1618–48) that saved Protestantism in Germany from being destroyed or exiled by the Hapsburg Empire. The Treaty of Westphalia (1648) is regarded by German historians as marking the end of the Reformation era, since it required the various principalities of Germany to take on the religion of the local ruler. Even today, areas of Germany are primarily Lutheran or Catholic or (in a few places) Reformed on the basis of that treaty.

Bergendoff, Conrad J. *Olavus Petri and the Ecclesiastical Transformation in Sweden (1521–1552): A Study in the Swedish Reformation.* AMS Pr. 1985 repr. of 1928 ed. $32.50. ISBN 0-404-19868-6. It is difficult to find good work in English on the Reformation in Sweden and Finland. (See Michael Roberts below.)

Dunkley, Ernest H. *The Reformation in Denmark.* A. R. Allenson 1948 o.p. Brief, clear, and concise. The brief bibliography—almost every work written in Danish—shows how hard it is to find sustained studies of the Reformation in Denmark.

Elert, Werner. *The Structure of Lutheranism: The Theology and Philosophy of Life of Lutheranism, 16th and 17th Centuries.* Trans. by Walter A. Hansen. Concordia 1974 o.p. Discusses the arguments before and after the Formula of Concord (1580), which united German Lutheranism in one line of thought.

Klug, Eugene F. *From Luther to Chemnitz on Scripture and the Word.* Eerdmans 1971 o.p. Lutheranism grew much more conservative in its understanding of Scripture after Luther, who had a tendency to dismiss Scriptures that "preached not Christ."

Larsen, Karen. *A History of Norway.* Princeton U. Pr. 1948 o.p. A large work, but only two chapters on the Reformation in Norway, with much of it concerning the Vikings.

Lohff, Wenzel, and Lewis Spitz, eds. *Discord, Dialogue, and Concord: Studies in the Lutheran Reformation's Formula of Concord.* Fortress Pr. 1977 o.p. Excellent study of the formation of Lutheran Orthodoxy after Luther, highlighting Melanchthon's role in several of the articles.

Manschreck, Clyde L. *Melanchthon: The Quiet Reformer.* Greenwood 1975 repr. of 1958 ed. $38.50. ISBN 0-8371-6131-2. A classic study of Luther's friend and colleague that is careful and trustworthy.

Midelfort, H. C. Erik. *Witch Hunting in Southwest Germany, 1562–1684: The Social and Intellectual Foundations.* Stanford U. Pr. 1972 $37.50. ISBN 0-8047-0805-3. This book, with its big bibliography on witchcraft during the period, is highly regarded by those historians who focus on fear, superstition, alienation, and death as a part of religion.

Moeller, Bernd. *Imperial Cities and the Reformation: Three Essays.* Ed. and trans. by H. C. Erik Midelfort and Mark U. Edwards, Jr. Labyrinth Pr. 1982 repr. of 1972 ed. $6.95. ISBN 0-939464-04-7. An early study of how the cities that hosted officials of the Hapsburg Empire tended to go Protestant.

Pauck, Wilhelm. *The Heritage of the Reformation.* Free Pr. 1961 o.p. Good summary of the positive and negative effects of the Reformation Era.

Preus, Robert D. *The Theology of Post-Reformation Lutheranism.* Concordia 1972 o.p. Comprehensive on Lutheran thought and struggle from the late sixteenth to the early eighteenth century, by an author sympathetic to the dogmatics of Lutheran Orthodoxy. Excellent coverage for Lutheran argument and post-Luther personalities.

Roberts, Michael. *The Early Vasas: A History of Sweden, 1523–1611*. Cambridge U. Pr. 1986 $29.95. ISBN 0-521-31182-9. A new edition is planned of this good, comprehensive study of both religion and politics as Sweden became Protestant.

Scharlemann, Robert. *Thomas Aquinas and John Gerhard*. Yale U. Pr. 1964 o.p. Studies Gerhard (1582–1637), the greatest theologian of post-Lutheran Orthodoxy, and Aquinas in order to see how scholastic later Lutheran theology became, since Aquinas was the dean of the medieval schoolmen.

Strauss, Gerald. *Luther's House of Learning: Indoctrination of the Young in the German Reformation*. Bks. Demand repr. of 1979 ed. $101.30. ISBN 0-317-20464-5. Controversial work arguing that Luther's Reformation penetrated into the faith of the people very, very slowly.

Waddams, Herbert M. *The Swedish Church*. Greenwood 1981 repr. of 1946 ed. $39.75. ISBN 0-313-22184-7. Helps put the Reformation in perspective by looking at later church history.

Zeeden, Ernest W. *The Legacy of Luther: Martin Luther and the Reformation in the Estimation of the German Lutherans from Luther's Death to the Beginning of the Age of Goethe*. AMS Pr. repr. of 1954 ed. $30.00. ISBN 0-404-19865-1

Reformed Struggle after Calvin

The struggles in the Reformed branch were of two kinds: fighting political and religious enemies without and fighting antipredestinarians within, especially the Arminians in the Netherlands and England. (The struggle between Calvinism—usually in its Puritan form—and Arminianism in England will be dealt with in the next section.) The second struggle was for the very life of Protestantism in France, the Low Countries, the Palatine region of present-day Germany, Hungary, Poland, Rumania, and England. In each of these places, Calvinism was identified as a subversion of the social order, and political and military efforts were made to destroy it. For information on some of these areas, the reader might consult general works such as Menno Prestwich's *International Calvinism*. For places such as Hungary or Romania, the person who reads English only may need to be content with the sketchy chapters to be found in general histories of the epoch.

Armstrong, Brian G. *Calvinism and the Amyraut Heresy: Protestant Scholasticism and Humanism in Seventeenth-Century France*. U. of Wis. Pr. 1969 $92.10. ISBN 0-8357-4741-7. Armstrong argues that under Theodore Beza's leadership, Reformed theology became scholastic and hair-splitting, defending points like predestination and missing the evangelical core of Calvin's own thought.

Baird, Henry M. *History of the Rise of the Huguenots of France*. 2 vols. AMS 1970 repr. of 1879 ed. $90.00. ISBN 0-404-00520-4. A classic, with much information, but dated because of its partisanship.

Bangs, Carl. *Arminius: A Study in the Dutch Reformation*. Ed. by Joseph D. Allison. Zondervan rev. ed. 1985 o.p. A solid study of the man and the theology that split Calvinism over the issue of predestination and election.

Bray, John. *Theodore Beza's Doctrine of Predestination*. Humanities 1975 o.p. Balanced and judicious study of the doctrine that came to be regarded as both norm and fighting center of Reformed theology.

Davis, Natalie Z. *Society and Culture in Early Modern France: Eight Essays by Natalie Zemon Davis*. Stanford U. Pr. 1975 $42.50. ISBN 0-8047-0868-1. Eight separate essays, all useful, by one who knows French archives like no other American scholar.

Duke, Alastair, Gillian Lewis, and Andrew Pettegree, eds. *Calvinism in Europe, 1555–1620: A Collection of Documents*. St. Martin 1992 $24.95. ISBN 0-7190-3552-X

Geyl, Pieter. *The Revolt of the Netherlands 1555–1609*. B & N Imports 1980 repr. of 1958 ed. $14.25. ISBN 0-06-492383-5. The true story of the Dutch revolt against Spanish

rule—cutting dikes to keep enemy troops at bay, as well as less dramatic episodes in
Dutch history—by a noted European scholar.

Kingdon, Robert M. *Myths about St. Bartholomew's Day Massacres, 1572–1576.* HUP
1988 $30.00. ISBN 0-674-59831-8. Includes accounts of the Huguenot massacres,
both Protestant and Catholic reactions to the massacres, and treatises on politics and
religion arising from the atrocities.

Mattingly, Garrett. *The Armada.* HM 1962 $29.45. ISBN 0-395-48682-3. A great story,
linking the execution of Mary Queen of Scots with the determination of the Spanish
king Philip II to do a "Bay of Pigs" on England. Court intrigue in France, the killing
of the Protestant nobility on St. Bartholomew's Day—a thundering history written by
an outstanding scholar.

Parker, Geoffrey. *The Dutch Revolt.* Viking Penguin rev. ed. 1989 $8.95. ISBN 0-14-
055233-2. A good account.

Prestwich, Menno, ed. *International Calvinism.* OUP 1985 $26.00. ISBN 0-19-822874-0.
Excellent study of various aspects of later Calvinism with three chapters following
Huguenots in their diaspora after the revocation of the Edict of Nantes (1685); there
is a chapter on Scotland, one on Hungary, and other excellent material.

Raitt, Jill. *The Eucharistic Theology of Theodore Beza: Development of the Reformed
Doctrine.* Scholars Pr. GA 1974 $14.95. ISBN 0-89130-156-9. Raitt explores Beza's
beliefs in a brief work (90 pages) with some comparisons to other major thinkers.

Reid, W. Stanford, ed. *John Calvin: His Influence in the Western World.* Zondervan 1982
o.p. Comprehensive coverage of Calvinistic influence on various Western nations.

Rothrock, George A. *The Huguenots: A Biography of a Minority.* Nelson-Hall 1979 $27.95.
ISBN 0-88229-277-3. This 200-page work is good for beginning study, with some
plates and bibliography.

Salmon, J. H. *Society in Crisis: France in the Sixteenth Century.* St. Martin 1975 o.p. Much
good material in this compilation.

Sutherland, N. M. *The Huguenot Struggle for Recognition.* Yale U. Pr. 1980 o.p. Very
scholarly tome in which the author argues that with Protestantism existing as an
aggressive enclave within the body of the nation, it was difficult for France to remain
united.

Zoff, O. *The Huguenots.* Trans. by E. B. Ashton and Jo Mayo. Allen & Unwin 1943 o.p.
Stimulating work by a Catholic writer who obviously likes the Huguenots.

The Radical Reformation after the Death of Menno Simons, 1561

Historians generally have not paid much attention to the Anabaptists and
other radical reform groups after their early struggles in Switzerland and
northern Germany. And much of what has been written is found only in
denominational histories (some of which may be found in the section "Christian
Religion in America"). Persecuted for their beliefs by both Catholics and
Protestants, many of the radical reform movements went underground. Some
were unable to survive as organized entities. Other less aggressive groups, such
as the Anabaptist group founded by Dutch reformer Menno Simons, were able
to survive. Some of the surviving groups later emigrated to America, where
their unique religious ideas and the societies based on those ideas were
tolerated. The Mennonites (named after Menno Simons but not founded by
him) and Moravian brethren are among the direct descendants of the sixteenth-
century Anabaptists.

Bittinger, Emmert F. *Heritage and Promise: Perspectives on the Church of the Brethren.*
Brethren rev. ed. 1983 $6.95. ISBN 0-87178-357-6. Basic historical survey, with
attention to doctrinal controversies and lifestyle changes.

Durnbaugh, Donald F. *The Believers' Church.* Herald Pr. 1985 repr. of 1968 ed. $14.95.
ISBN 0-8361-1271-7. Contains historical sketches of a number of leaders and groups,

such as Brethren, Mennonites, Hutterites, and others and connects them with American churches today.

Estep, William R. *The Anabaptist Story*. Eerdmans 1975 $14.95. ISBN 0-8028-1594-4. Basic and accurate on most forms of the left wing of the Reformation and its modern descendants.

Horsch, John. *Hutterian Brethren, 1528-1931*. Plough 1931 $11.00. ISBN 0-87486-055-5

Williams, George H. *The Radical Reformation*. Sixteenth Cent. 1992 $125.00. ISBN 0-94047-15-8. Revised and expanded. Extensive bibliography.

Yoder, Paton. *Tradition and Transition: Amish Mennonites and Old Order Amish 1800-1900*. Herald Pr. 1991 $28.95. ISBN 0-8361-3108-8. Documents one strand of the legacy of the radical reformation.

The Reformation in Great Britain: From the Elizabethan Settlement to 1700

By the time Elizabeth I had settled on a uniform policy for religion in England, she was disturbed by radicals of two sorts. On one side were the Catholic *récusants* (refusers), who refused to sign the oath acknowledging that she was governor of the church in England; on the other side were militant Calvinists, the Puritans, who objected to ceremonialism in worship and to the bishops she appointed to rule the church. These disaffections led in two directions: Catholics were implicated in plots to replace Elizabeth with Mary Stuart, Queen of Scots, who had fled to England in the 1560s when her marital scandals turned the Scots against her. Elizabeth eventually felt forced to execute Mary, who was her cousin, in 1587. The radical Protestants, on the other hand, grew in numbers until they finally rebelled against Charles I and, led by Oliver Cromwell, established a decade of quasi-religious rule in England. The rise, triumph, and fall of Puritanism has occasioned as vast a body of literature as has MARTIN LUTHER's revolt, and only a little of it can be listed below.

Between Elizabeth I and the unfortunate Charles I—whom Cromwell had beheaded—was the rule of James VI of Scotland, son of poor Mary Stuart. In 1603 he became James I of England and united the two realms, had a Bible translation named for him, and began the Plantation of Ulster, which led to British control over Ireland until 1921.

ENGLAND

Arnott, Anne. *Valiant for Truth: The Story of John Bunyan*. Eerdmans 1986 o.p. A popular biography of the author of *Pilgrim's Progress*, sympathetic and challenging. Foreword by Blanche Stuart.

Ashton, Robert. *Reformation and Revolution 1558-1660*. OUP 1984 $39.95. ISBN 0-19-520444-1

Barbour, Hugh. *The Quakers in Puritan England*. Friends United 1985 repr. of 1964 ed. $14.95. ISBN 0-913408-87-5. Solid study that includes George Fox and also the environment against which his movement demands to be studied.

Collinson, Patrick. *The Elizabethan Puritan Movement*. OUP 1990 $24.95. ISBN 0-19-822298-X. A straightforward account by a dependable historian.

Foxe, John. *Foxe's Book of Martyrs*. Ed. by W. Grinton Berry. Baker Bk. 1978 $9.95. ISBN 0-8010-3483-3. This book labeled Mary Tudor as "Bloody Mary" for her killing of Protestants and is the first Protestant martyrology, to be followed by many more.

Fraser, Antonia. *Cromwell: The Lord Protector*. D. I. Fine 1986 repr. of 1973 ed. $14.95. ISBN 0-917657-90-X. In more than 700 pages, this popular historian has included about all that is known of the doughty Puritan soldier and regicide.

_____. *King Charles I*. Weidenfeld & Nicolson 1978 o.p. A book on the king Cromwell beheaded.

―――――. *Royal Charles: Charles II and the Restoration*. Dell 1986 o.p. On Charles's son, who came to the throne when Richard Cromwell, inheritor of the Commonwealth on his father's death, proved inadequate to the task.

Greaves, Richard L. *Society and Religion in Elizabethan England*. Bks. Demand repr. of 1981 ed. $160.00. ISBN 0-685-15913-3. In more than 900 pages Greaves gives the reader all she or he ever wanted to know about religion, including Puritans and Catholics, in the time of Elizabeth.

Greaves, Richard L., and R. Zaller, eds. *Biographical Dictionary of British Radicals in the Seventeenth Century*. Humanities 1984 o.p. Just what the beginning scholar needs to locate all of the English left-wing Puritans.

Grell, Ole P., Jonathan Israel, and Nicholas Tyacke, eds. *From Persecution to Toleration: The Glorious Revolution and Religion in England*. OUP 1991 $69.00. ISBN 0-19-820196-6

Haller, William. *The Rise of Puritanism*. U. of Pa. Pr. 1972 repr. of 1938 ed. o.p. Moderate-sized book by a recognized historian, whose reputation for this solid work remains firm despite later studies.

Hill, Christopher. *Change and Continuity in Seventeenth-Century England*. Yale U. Pr. 1991 $20.00. ISBN 0-300-05044-5. Tends to let socialism interpret his historiography, but can be relied on for the facts.

―――――. *God's Englishman: Oliver Cromwell and the English Revolution*. HarpC 1972 $12.00. ISBN 0-06-131666-0. In about half as many pages as Fraser, Hill discloses Cromwell, leader of a socioreligious revolution.

Hooker, Richard. *Of the Laws of Ecclesiastical Polity*. 4 vols. Ed. by P. G. Stanwood. HUP Vols. 1 and 2 1977 $110.00. ISBN 0-674-63205-2. Vol. 3 1981 $76.00. ISBN 0-674-63210-9. Vol. 4 1982 $48.00. ISBN 0-674-63216-8. Hooker's "laws" have always been regarded by Anglicans as the "middle way" between the extremes of Roman Catholicism and Calvinism.

Jones, Rufus M. *George Fox: Seeker and Friend*. Allen & Unwin 1930 o.p. The best of the old biographies.

Kingdon, Robert M., ed. *"The Execution of Justice in England," by William Cecil, and "A True, Sincere, and Modest Defense of English Catholics," by William Allen*. Cornell Univ. Pr. 1965 o.p. Cecil, premier adviser to Elizabeth I, argues the legitimacy of prosecuting Catholic missionaries to England, while Allen, director of the Catholic seminary in Douai, France argues that it was legally right for Mary Tudor to kill heretics but not right for Elizabeth; a marvelous study of intolerance from the original documents, expertly edited.

Meyer, Arnold Oskar. *England and the Catholic Church under Queen Elizabeth*. Trans. by J. R. McKee. Routledge 1967 o.p. This reprint of an older edition is still regarded as remarkably accurate and dispassionate, as John Bossy says in his introduction to this edition.

Morgan, John. *Godly Learning: Puritan Attitudes towards Reason, Learning, and Education, 1560–1640*. Cambridge U. Pr. 1988 $22.95. ISBN 0-521-35700-4. A very useful book in getting at the heart of Puritan concepts; includes education of the ministers, the "godly household," the role of the teacher, and more.

Noble, Wilfred Vernon. *The Man in Leather Breeches: The Life and Times of George Fox*. Philos. Lib. 1953 o.p. "This popular biography will be enjoyed by readers who like a well-told tale, with plenty of adventure and pathos" (*New Statesman & Nation*).

O'Day, Rosemary. *The English Clergy: The Emergence and Consolidation of a Profession, 1558–1642*. Humanities 1979 o.p. Excellent study of a sometimes privileged and sometimes embattled elite.

Paul, Robert. *The Lord Protector*. Eerdmans 1964 o.p. Of the three books listed on Cromwell himself, this is the only one by an author who sympathizes with his basic commitments; despite that, it is the harshest in its judgment.

Seaver, Paul S. *The Puritan Lectureships: The Politics of Religious Dissent, 1560–1662*. Stanford U. Pr. 1970 $45.00. ISBN 0-8047-0711-1. Hugh bibliography is attached to an important study of the way merchants and others got around laws against Puritan preachers by hiring them to present lectures.

Stannard, David E. *The Puritan Way of Death: A Study in Religion, Culture, and Social Change.* OUP 1977 $24.95. ISBN 0-19-502226-2. The kind of study that gets the reader deep into the mind of a culture.

Stone, Lawrence. *The Family, Sex, and Marriage: England 1500–1800.* HarpC 1983 $13.00. ISBN 0-06-131979-1. A thorough and well-known charting of the rise of the modern family.

Wallace, Dewey D., Jr. *Puritans and Predestination: Grace in English Protestant Theology, 1525–1695.* Bks. Demand repr. of 1982 ed. $79.10. ISBN 0-8357-3904-X. All the theological issues between Puritan and Anglican, Calvinist and Archbishop Laud's style of Arminianism are dealt with carefully in this excellent work.

Walzer, Michael. *The Revolution of the Saints: A Study in the Origins of Radical Politics.* HUP 1982 $10.95. ISBN 0-674-76786-1. A seminal work that argues that the Puritan revolt expressed the Western world's conviction that the political realm belongs to people, not to inheritors of privilege.

Watkins, Owen. *The Puritan Experience.* Schocken 1972 o.p. The Puritans are explored through their diaries.

SCOTLAND

The list that follows contains works that cover the whole of the Scottish Reformation. In some of these works, readers can find notes and bibliographies that may prove helpful in providing direction for further research.

Bardgett, Frank D. *Scotland Reformed: The Reformation in Angus and the Mearns.* Humanities 1989 $55.00. ISBN 0-85976-261-0

Cowan, I. B. *Blast and Counterblast: Contemporary Writings on the Scottish Reformation.* St. Mut. 1986 $20.00. ISBN 0-85411-008-9

———. *The Scottish Covenanters, 1660–1688)* Verry 1976 o.p. These are the folk whose rejection of Charles I's prayer book sparked a war between Scotland and England, a war that the Puritans in Parliament took advantage of to mount an army against the king, led by Oliver Cromwell.

———. *The Scottish Reformation: Church and Society in Sixteenth-Century Scotland.* St. Martin 1982 $26.50. ISBN 0-312-70519-0 By one of the two leading (Donaldson is the other) Scottish historians.

———, ed. *The Enigma of Mary Stuart.* St. Martin 1971 o.p. Examines all the materials that relate to the decisive points in Mary's reign, where scandal and tragedy conspired to cost her both her son and the throne, and eventually her life.

Donaldson, Gordon. *All the Queen's Men: Power and Politics in Mary Stewart's Scotland.* St. Martin 1983 o.p. Scotland's emeritus church historian gives us an overview of the duplicity of Scotland's nobility at the time of Mary.

———. *Mary Queen of Scots.* Verry 1974 o.p.

———. *Scotland: The Shaping of a Nation.* David & Charles 1975 o.p. Donaldson is always clear and sometimes argumentative, particularly when he claims that Knox wanted a church run by bishops.

Donnachie, Ian, and George Hewitt. *A Companion to Scottish History: From the Reformation to the Present.* Facts on File 1990 $27.50. ISBN 0-8160-2398-0. Contains more than 500 articles. Includes a chronology, 17 maps, genealogies, and census figures.

Fraser, Antonia. *Mary Queen of Scots.* Dell 1984 $6.95. ISBN 0-440-35476-5. Fraser's work is always popular and balanced, though the reader gets more Mary and somewhat less social scenery than in the scholarly works about people like Mary, her son James I, and Cromwell.

Henderson, G. D. *Religious Life in Seventeenth-Century Scotland.* Cambridge U. Pr. 1937 o.p. Classic study ranging from royalty and nobility and General Assembly of the Kirk, to the way the faith was practiced in those turbulent times.

Knox, John. *The History of the Reformation in Scotland.* Banner of Truth 1982 $10.95. ISBN 0-85151-358-1. This book, which has had several earlier editions, is the place to go for understanding Knox's prophetic self-image as an "Elijah" sent to destroy the religion of "Baal" (Romanism) in Scotland.

McGregor, Geddes. *The Thundering Scot: A Portrait of John Knox.* Westminster John Knox 1957 o.p. The briefest of the biographies, written by a man who has distinguished himself in writing theology.

Reid, W. Stanford. *Trumpeter of God: A Biography of John Knox.* Baker Bk. 1982 repr. of 1974 ed. o.p. This is the most positive depiction of the Scottish reformer and is based on a thorough study of the basic sources.

Ridley, Jasper. *John Knox.* OUP 1968 o.p. This, the most detailed of the books on Knox listed here, is written by the biographer of many of the great names in the Reformation period in Great Britain.

Wormald, Jenny. *Court, Kirk, and Community: Scotland, 1470–1625. New History of Scotland Ser.* Bks. Demand repr. of 1981 ed. $56.00. ISBN 0-685-15912-4. Highly praised look at three levels of Scottish society during the turbulent years of religious and social revolution.

The Catholic Reformation after the Council of Trent

Probably the best place to begin searching for information about the progress of the Catholic Reformation after the Council of Trent is in general histories of Christianity or of Christian thought. Some of these can be found in this chapter in the section on Dictionaries, Encyclopedias, Handbooks: The Church, Church History. The book *History of Christian Throught* by Justo Gonzalez is highly recommended (see under Dictionaries, Encyclopedias, Handbooks: Ethics and Theology). The studies listed below tend either to be regional or to deal with such individuals as St. Teresa of Avila or St. John of the Cross (see Vol. 2).

Bilinkoff, Jodi. *The Avila of Saint Teresa: Religious Reform in a Sixteenth Century City.* Cornell Univ. Pr. 1992 $10.95. ISBN 0-8014-8052-3. Offers fresh insights. Feminist critique of the historical era of the reformation.

Bossy, John. *The English Catholic Community, 1570–1850.* OUP 1976 o.p. Although covering a greater span than our U.S. period, a valuable study especially because it compares Catholic and Protestant groups that were legislated against in Great Britain.

Brodrick, James. *Robert Bellarmine, Saint and Scholar.* Newman Pr. 1961 o.p. A rewriting of an earlier two-volume work about a theologian and political thinker who has sometimes been credited with providing part of the theoretical basis for the development of democratic thought.

Chatellier, Louis. *Europe of the Devout: Catholic Reformation and the Formation of a New Society.* Cambridge U. Pr. 1989 $59.95. ISBN 0-521-36333-0. An examination of the profound change in Catholic society during the two centuries after the Council of Trent.

Copleston, Frederick. *Ockham to Suarez.* Vol. 3 in *The History of Philosophy.* Paulist Pr. $19.95. ISBN 0-8091-0066-5. Contains a clear account of the thought of the Jesuit Suarez, whose theology most clearly guided the church both at Trent and afterward.

Dombrowski, Daniel. *St. John of the Cross: An Appreciation.* State U. NY Pr. 1992 $16.95. ISBN 0-7914-0888-4. Perhaps accounting for some of the current surge of interest in mysticism, Dombrowski relates St. John of the Cross to several issues being debated today.

Dunn, Richard S. *The Age of Religious Wars, 1559–1689.* Norton 1979 $10.95. ISBN 0-393-09021-8. One means of pushing back Protestantism was the use of force, of which the Thirty Years' War is the best or worst example. Dunn looks at the whole age through the spectacles of warfare.

Garstein, Oskar. *Rome and the Counter-Reformation in Scandinavia.* E. D. Brill 1992 $125.75. ISBN 90-04-09393-1. Massive scholarship in a neglected area.

John of the Cross, St. *The Collected Works of St. John of the Cross.* Trans. by Kieran Kavanaugh and Otilio Rodriquez. ICS Pubns. 1991 $24.95. ISBN 0-9352216-15-4. The writings of Saint John of the Cross and his friend Teresa of Avila established a "norm for spirituality" for Catholics that retains its power to inspire.

Knox, Ronald A. *Enthusiasm: A Chapter in the History of Religion with Special Reference to the Seventeenth and Eighteenth Centuries.* Chr. Classics 1983 o.p. Entertaining in its discussion of two French Catholic movements, Jansenism and Quietism.

O'Connell, Marvin R. *The Counter Reformation: 1599–1610.* Ed. by William L. Lange. HarpC 1974 o.p. Described as the best work on the Catholic Reformation after the Council of Trent.

Parker, Geoffrey. *Europe in Crisis, 1589–1648.* Cornell Univ. Pr. 1980 o.p. Covers all phases of the Hapsburg emperors' nearly successful attempts to eliminate Protestantism in Germany by military force.

———. *Philip II.* Little 1978 o.p. Compact study of the Spanish king who managed to bankrupt the richest nation in Europe because of his efforts to overcome Protestants by intrigue and because of his failed Armada.

———, ed. *The Thirty Years War.* Routledge Chapman & Hall 1988 $15.95. ISBN 0-7102-1181-3. Articles by various well-known scholars about the last of the great religious wars in which probably one in every three Germans died.

Sedgwick, Alexander. *Jansenism in Seventeenth-Century France: Voices from the Wilderness.* U. of Va. Pr. 1977 $27.50. ISBN 0-8139-0702-0. Jansenism, sometimes called Catholic Calvinism, was a strong force in France and Ireland, and the Jesuits bent every effort to destroy it at Port Royal and in the schools.

Art and the Reformation

A few works on this subject seem appropriate here. Some of the Protestant reform groups had a strong Hebrew flavor in their rejection of the graphic and plastics arts in worship and devotion. Here Lutheranism and, in general, Anglicanism demurred. All the churches, Protestant and Catholic, thought highly of music and developed it in various ways; the Protestants, in particular, developed large bodies of congregational hymnody and, in Germany, reformers developed the chorale.

Andersson, Christiane. *From a Mighty Fortress: Prints, Drawings, and Books in the Age of Luther, 1483–1546.* Detroit Inst. Arts 1983 o.p. A 400-page catalog of a large exhibition, with an index that should be useful to art historians interested in the Reformation Era in Germany. Preface by Frederick Cummings.

Christensen, Carl C. *Art and the Reformation in Germany.* Ohio U. Pr. 1981 o.p. Examines both theory and practice among the German reformers, radicals as well as Luther.

Crew, P. Mack. *Calvinist Preaching and Iconoclasm in the Netherlands, 1544–1569.* Cambridge U. Pr. 1978 o.p. Not only a good study of image-breaking and the role (or nonrole) of the Calvinist preachers in that, but also of the essentially conservative nature of the early Calvinists in the Low Countries.

Eire, Carlos M. *War against the Idols: The Reformation of Worship from Erasmus to Calvin.* Cambridge U. Pr. 1989 $49.95. ISBN 0-521-30685-X. After a thorough look at Luther and his response to iconoclasm, the story switches to Geneva and Calvin, where idolatry is seen as the Calvinist "shibboleth."

Garside, Charles, Jr. *The Origins of Calvin's Theology of Music, 1536–1553.* Am. Philos. 1979 o.p. This tiny study distinguishes Luther and Calvin on music.

———. *Zwingli and the Arts.* Da Capo 1981 repr. of 1966 ed. $29.50. ISBN 0-306-76018-5. Examines why of all the major reformers Zwingli was the most thoroughly indoctrinated into humanism, yet had the reputation of being the one most averse to painting, sculpture, and music.

Lang, Paul H., ed. *Music in Western Civilization.* Norton 1940 $35.95. ISBN 0-393-09428-6. Has an excellent discussion of Luther's contribution.

LeHurray, Peter. *Music and the Reformation in England: 1549-1660.* Bks. Demand repr. of 1978 ed. $121.00. ISBN 0-685-15583-8

Liemohn, E. *The Chorale*. Muhlenberg Pr. 1953 o.p. A classic study of the German chorale, especially as developed by J. S. Bach, as the epitome of liturgical music.

Nettl, Paul. *Luther and Music*. Trans. by Ralph Wood. Russell Sage 1967 repr. of 1948 ed. o.p. Straightforward study by one who knows the era well.

Panofsky, Erwin. *The Life and Art of Albrecht Dürer*. Princeton U. Pr. 1955 $29.95. ISBN 0-691-00303-3. A well-known art historian examines Dürer's work and the theological background, including some study of other reformers and their attitudes toward art in religious observance.

Phillips, John R. *The Reformation of Images: Destruction of Art in England, 1535–1669*. U. CA Pr. 1974 $37.50. ISBN 0-520-02424-9. Moves the reader right through the English Reformation, from Henry VIII through the English Civil War and the temporary victory of the Puritans.

THE AGE OF REASON: CHRISTIANITY IN THE EIGHTEENTH CENTURY

The Age of Reason is usually dated from the publication of NEWTON's (see also Vol. 5) *Principia Mathematica* in 1689 and ends with the revolutions near the end of the century, especially the French Revolution in 1789. It is marked economically as the age of colonial expansion and of the Industrial Revolution. In religion, especially Protestantism, there was a tearing asunder of the Christian soul: on the one hand were those who felt the strong demands of rational religion, allegiance to a God who made nature's laws and let them be, and a religious spirit that found the Bible incredibly crude, primitive, and superstitious; on the other hand were those who centered on the indwelling Spirit of God—the German and Reformed Pietists on the Continent, and the Methodists and Quakers in Great Britain. Catholicism experienced a weakened papacy, so servile to the rules of the "Catholic bastions" that Jesuits, attempting to bring a measure of humanity to slaves and people oppressed by colonialism, were suppressed in 1764. This was also the period of JOHN WESLEY, whose revivals began Methodism and in whose own experimental spirituality and love for the new sciences of experimentation the sundered soul was reknit.

Aaron, Richard I. *John Locke*. OUP 3rd ed. 1971 o.p. If historians of the political process look to Locke as the champion of constitutionalism, those in religious history see him as a major force for "natural" or deistic religion, as contrasted with "revealed" or biblical religion.

Bradley, James E. *Religion, Revolution and English Radicalism*. Cambridge U. Pr. 1990 $59.95. ISBN 0-521-38010-3. Relates religious and economic divisions in society to radical ideology. Extensive footnotes.

Chadwick, Owen. *The Popes and European Revolution*. OUP 1981 $95.00. ISBN 0-19-826919-6. The first six chapters are an excellent overview of the work of the popes during this period.

Chilcote, Paul W. *John Wesley and the Women Preachers of Early Methodism*. Scarecrow 1991 $42.50. ISBN 0-8108-2414-0. Attempts to rediscover the lost history of the early women preachers of Methodism. Reconstructs more than 100 portraits in a narrative interweaving biographical, historical, and theological concerns.

Corrigan, John. *The Prism of Piety: Catholic Congregational Clergy at the Beginning of the Enlightenment*. OUP 1991 $32.50. ISBN 0-19-506758-4-6326. Focuses on a select group of early-eighteenth-century Boston congregationalists who comfortably appropriated Enlightenment ideas into their theology.

Cragg, Gerald R. *The Church and the Age of Reason*. Viking Penguin 1961 $6.95. ISBN 0-14-020505-5. Probably the surest guide to this period, with all the major figures discussed, whether Catholic or Protestant, philosopher or church leader.

_____. *From Puritanism to the Age of Reason*. Cambridge U. Pr. 1966 o.p. Spans the brief period from the end of Cromwell's Puritan theocracy to this age of skepticism.

_____. *Reason and Authority in the Eighteenth Century*. Cambridge U. Pr. 1964 o.p. Thoroughly explores the "battle for the Bible" conflict between natural and revealed faith.

Daniel-Rops, Henri. *The Church in the Eighteenth Century*. Vol. 7 in *The History of the Church of Christ*. Trans. by John Warrington. NAL-Dutton 1964 o.p. A Roman Catholic viewpoint is interesting for the light it casts on the struggles of Protestantism.

Frei, Hans W. *The Eclipse of Biblical Narrative: A Study in Eighteenth- and Nineteenth-Century Hermeneutics*. Yale U. Pr. 1974 $14.00. ISBN 0-300-02602-1. "Discusses with unusual sensitivity changes in the way people read the Bible" (Placher).

Gay, Peter. *The Enlightenment: An Interpretation*. 2 vols. Norton 1977 repr. of 1966 ed. Vol. 1 *The Rise of Modern Paganism*. $14.95. ISBN 0-393-00870-3. Vol. 2 *The Science of Freedom*. $16.95. ISBN 0-393-00875-4. Volume 1 focuses on religion and the philosophic issues that contributed to the rise of skepticism, deism, and the like.

Haskins, James. *The Methodists*. Hippocrene Bks. 1992 $14.95. ISBN 0-7818-0029-3. Traces the formation of today's loosely connected worldwide fellowship of churches from its founding in eighteenth-century England by John and Charles Wesley.

Henry, S. C. *George Whitefield: Wayfaring Witness*. Abingdon 1957 o.p. Whitefield, John Wesley's Calvinistic friend, evangelized in England and the colonies and even won the praise of the worldly Ben Franklin.

Hume, David. *A Treatise of Human Nature*. Ed. by Ernest G. Mossner. OUP 1978 $13.95. ISBN 0-19-842488-2. This tough-minded Scot woke Kant from his "dogmatic slumbers" and his understanding of how knowledge is gained undermined both religion and science.

_____. *Dialogues Concerning Natural Religion*. Prometheus Bks. 1989 $4.95. ISBN 0-87975-527-X. A highly influential book, full of issues for the reader to ponder—for example, is Hume justly called an atheist even though his characters do not profess atheism?

Kant, Immanuel. *Critique of Practical Reason*. Trans. by Lewis W. Beck. Bobbs 1956 o.p. Kant argued that there are tenets that must be regarded as true because they are basic to the moral life, such as that God exists, that God rewards and punishes in the afterlife, and that the self is free to do right and wrong.

_____. *Religion within the Limits of Reason Alone*. Trans. by Theodore Greene and Hoyt H. Hudson. HarpC 1960 $13.00. ISBN 0-06-130067-5. He equated grace, so important to Luther, not with knowledge of the way of salvation, or with trusting Christ, but with the soul's becoming worthy of God's favor. Here salvation is turned into a free act of the person, thus reversing Luther's stress on God's initiative.

Lessing, Gotthold. *Lessing's Theological Writings: Selections in Translation*. Trans. by Henry Chadwick. Stanford U. Pr. 1957 $8.95. ISBN 0-8047-0335-3. His optimistic and rational Christianity was influential on educated Protestants everywhere.

Locke, John. *An Essay Concerning Human Understanding*. Ed. by A. O. Woozley. NAL-Dutton 1974 $8.95. ISBN 0-452-00835-2. He argued that the mind begins as a clear slate, a *tabula rasa*, with no inborn ideas; so moral and religious belief must not be argued on the basis of such ideas, but on the basis of experience, from which comes reality and truth.

_____. *The Reasonableness of Christianity and a Discourse on Miracles*. Ed. by I. T. Ramsey. Stanford U. Pr. 1958 $8.95. ISBN 0-8047-0341-8. Locke's predeist rationalism was a prelude to American constitutionalism and to draining the supernatural out of religious thought, with the result being a simple and rational Christianity, one available outside the Scripture, as well as an end to mystical and theological speculation; in a word, deism.

Nichols, James H. *History of Christianity, 1650–1950: Secularization of the West*. Wiley 1956 o.p. Very surefooted guide through this period.

Orr, James. *English Deism: Its Roots and Its Fruits*. Eerdmans 1934 o.p. Somewhat dated but comprehensive and succinct.

Schweitzer, Albert. *J. S. Bach.* 2 vols. Trans. by Ernest Newman. Paganiniana Pubns. 1980 $24.95. ISBN 0-87666-612-8. Here is a great soul, *le grand docteur*, writing about Luther's music, soul, Bach.

Weinlick, J. R. *Count Zinzendorf.* Abingdon 1956 o.p. A German noble and churchman, Zinzendorf rescued persecuted Moravians from Bohemia at his estate, Herrnhut, and then brought a colony to Pennsylvania that became part of the Pennsylvania Dutch.

Wesley, John. *The Journal of John Wesley.* Ed. by Elisabeth Jay. OUP 1987 $45.00. ISBN 0-19-212268-1. Selections from Wesley's journal which he kept from 1735 through 1790.

Yolton, John W, ed. *Philosophy, Religion and Science in the Seventeenth and Eighteenth Centuries.* Univ. Rochester Pr. 1990 $49.50. ISBN 1-878822-01-2. Essays illustrating the interrelationship between science, religion, and philosophy in the seventeenth and eighteenth centuries.

THE AGE OF REVOLUTION: CHRISTIANITY IN THE NINETEENTH CENTURY

If we follow the custom of historians by beginning the century with the French Revolution (1789), and if we think of the enormous changes that people experienced during the 1800s, with all authority seemingly demolished and human thought and expectations turned upside down, we shall capture the spirit of the age in a nutshell: revolution. This revolution took all forms. In France the royal couple was beheaded; in England CHARLES DARWIN (see Vol. 5) traced the less than divine descent of man. KARL MARX (see also Vol. 3) set the stage for international communism. Missionaries, both Catholic and Protestant, left the relative safety of Europe and America and took the gospel almost everywhere. Popes wrote defensive works and great social encyclicals and in 1870 were declared infallible—under certain conditions. In the bibliography that follows, the so-called warfare between science and religion has been ignored, for that topic is covered elsewhere in this series. The expansion of Western Christianity through missionary labors has a separate section later in this chapter. And American Christianity is covered in the next section.

Altholz, Josef L. *Churches in the Nineteenth Century.* Bobbs 1967 o.p. Covers in a brief survey all the churches, including the Eastern Orthodox, and all the movements.

Barry, Colman J., ed. *Readings in Church History.* 3 vols. in 1. Chr. Classics 1985 o.p. Almost everything is covered here in succinct summaries, with each section loaded with major statements or excerpts from major writers.

Cashdollar, Charles. *The Transformation of Theology, 1830–1890: Positivism and Protestant Throught in Britain and America.* Princeton U. Pr. 1989 $45.00. ISBN 0-691-05555-6. A painstakingly researched book, tracing the theme of positivism and successfully organizing a mass of diverse materials.

Chadwick, Owen. *The Popes and European Revolution.* OUP 1981 $95.00. ISBN 0-19-826919-6. Chapters 7 and 8 give a fine survey of this period.

———, ed. *The Mind of the Oxford Movement.* Stanford U. Pr. 1961 o.p. This High Church or medievalist movement among Anglicans produced great scholarship as well as a few notable converts to Rome. (See also the various listings for Cardinal Newman in this chapter.)

Collier, Richard. *The General Next to God: The Story of William Booth and the Salvation Army.* NAL-Dutton 1965 o.p. A good size and style for this readable study.

Feuerbach, Ludwig. *The Essence of Christianity.* 1854. HarpC 1957 $12.00. ISBN 0-06-130011-X. The introductory essay of Karl Barth makes this special: the great modern theologian of God's transcendence and the theologian of God's absence under one cover. Foreword by Richard Niebuhr.

Gargan, E. T. *Leo XIII and the Modern World.* Sheed & Ward MO 1961 o.p. Short pieces illustrative of Leo's work, with helpful introductions by the editor.

Gerrish, B. A. *The Old Protestantism and the New: Essays on the Reformatio Heritage.* U. Ch. Pr. 1982 $38.00 ISBN 0-226-28869-2. After essays on Erasmus and the reformers, Gerrish turns to the rise of science and the theologies that respond, those of Friedrich Schleiermacher and of Ernst Troeltsch.

Hales, E. E. *The Catholic Church in the Modern World.* Doubleday 1958 o.p. A sure guide from the French Revolution through the pontificate of Pius XII, John XXIII's predecessor. Especially good on relations between church and state.

Harnack, Adolph. *What Is Christianity?* Fortress Pr. 1986 $14.95. ISBN 0-8006-3201-X. Greatest nineteenth-century church historian Harnack followed Hegel in patterning his work on the early church, finding that Catholic Orthodoxy was a synthesis of Petrine and Jamesian legalism or Jewish Christianity and its opposite, Pauline and Johannine Hellenism. Introduction by Rudolf Bultmann.

Latourette, Kenneth S. *Christianity in a Revolutionary Age.* 5 vols. Greenwood 1973 repr. of 1958 ed. $160.50. ISBN 0-8371-5700-5. By the man who was dean of American church historians for the first half century.

Nietzsche, Friedrich. *The Portable Nietzsche.* Ed. by Walter Kaufmann. Viking Penguin 1977 $10.95. ISBN 0-14-015062-5. The German atheist had a profound influence on theologies much more orthodox.

O'Mahony, Christopher, ed. and trans. *St. Thérèse of Lisieux: By Those Who Knew Her.* Ignatius Pr. 1975 $14.95. ISBN 0-901810-84-3. Contains not only testimony by Thérèse's sisters but also by a woman disliked by Thérèse. Provides insights not only into Thérèse's life but also into the process of canonization.

Petry, M. D. *Alfred Loisy: His Religious Significance.* Cambridge U. Pr. 1944 o.p. Loisy was perhaps the greatest of the modernist thinkers condemned by the pope just as the period ended (1907).

Phillips, Charles S. *The Church in France, 1848–1907.* Russell Sage 1967 repr. of 1936 ed. o.p. The Catholic church in France between the revolutions of the bourgeoisie and the proletariat.

Ranchetti, Michele. *The Catholic Modernists: A Study of the Religious Reform Movements, 1864–1907.* Trans. by Isabel Quigly. OUP 1969 o.p. Scholars regard this as a fair and definitive study of Catholic modernism.

Reardon, Bernard M. *Religion in the Age of Romanticism: Studies in Early Nineteenth Century Thought.* Cambridge U. Pr. 1985 $66.95. ISBN 0-521-31745-2. Exploration of the intersection of religious ideas and Romanticism in nine early nineteenth-century figures.

———. *Religious Thought in the Nineteenth Century.* Cambridge U. Pr. 1966 o.p. Features the words of the great thinkers of the century in a very useful source for the student who has some of the names straight and perhaps a slight grasp of intellectual movement through the period.

———, ed. *Roman Catholic Modernism.* Stanford U. Pr. 1970 $29.50. ISBN 0-8047-0750-2. Glance at the works by Ranchetti and Vidler and the reader can see that by about 1970 the winds of change from Vatican II were causing some to ask if there were precedents for change in the monolithic thought that had characterized Romanism.

Redeker, Martin, ed. *Schleiermacher: Life and Thought.* Trans. by John Wallhausser. Fortress Pr. 1973 o.p. An excellent way to get into the Father of Liberal Theology is through this translation of his own *apologia,* edited and introduced ably here.

Smart, Ninian, and others, eds. *Nineteenth Century Religious Thought in the West.* 3 vols. Cambridge U. Pr. 1985 $74.95 ea. ISBNs 0-521-22831-X, 0-521-22832-8, 0-521-30114-9. All the thinkers of the century are given chapters of about 40 pages, from Kant to Troeltsch, including nontheologians like Marx. Also contains introductions to schools.

Stearns, Peter N. *Priest and Revolutionary.* HarpC 1967 o.p. A sympathetic study of Lamennais, priest turned revolutionary thinker, and one of the odd ones of Catholic modernism.

Troeltsch, Ernst. *The Christian Faith*. Ed. by Gertrud von le Fort. Trans. by Garrett Paul. Augsburg Fortress 1991 $19.95. ISBN 0-8006-3209-5. Once thought to have been refuted, Troeltsch continues to hold the admiration of Protestant liberals with his masterful German theology of the classical style.

Vidler, Alexander R. *The Modernist Movement in the Roman Church*. Gordon Pr. 1976 $250.00. ISBN 0-8490-0889-1. Vidler's 1930s study of Catholic modernism won awards when it was published, and it has stood the test of time.

————. *A Variety of Catholic Modernists*. Cambridge U. Pr. 1970 o.p. Earlier work than Ranchetti's, but also good.

Welch, Claude. *Protestant Thought in the Nineteenth Century*. 2 vols. Yale U. Pr. 1986 $16.00 ea. ISBNs 0-300-04200-0, 0-300-04201-9. The bibliography contains everything useful, and the commentary is excellent.

CHRISTIANITY IN THE TWENTIETH CENTURY: 1914 TO THE PRESENT

One way to describe Christianity in our present century is to say that in the global arena Christian adherents have grown by exponential leaps, whereas in its homeland of Europe its members have shrunk and its energies have faltered. Already, peoples who have been evangelized only a generation or two are talking of sending missionaries to Europe, where in Protestant and Catholic nations alike the faith seems to speak strongly neither to the intelligentsia nor to the common people. In America the strength of Christian practice, and maybe even theology, seems to have passed from the old denominations and is now in the hands of more evangelical groups.

Theologically, something of the same picture holds, though not so clearly. Theology has always been the forte of the Germans, and from KARL BARTH's massive protest against liberalism's optimism after World War I, until the 1970s, one could still talk of theology being made in Germany, processed in England, and sold in America. But with the controversy over the short-lived death of God theologies in the mid-1960s and the advent of new liberation theologies in former colonial regions, Christian theology too has taken on a non-European complexion.

General Religion and Theology

The books below were chosen to illustrate the thought or career of some major figures who do not receive separate biographical treatment in profiles and to give surveys of various kinds, either in theology or ethics.

Barrett, David, ed. *World Christian Encyclopedia: A Comparative Survey of Churches and Religions in the Modern World, A.D. 1900 to 2000*. OUP 1982 $195.00. ISBN 0-19-572435-6. The only comprehensive survey of all branches of Christendom everywhere; special attention to church growth; statistics abound.

Bianci, Eugene, and Rosemary Radford Ruether, eds. *A Democratic Catholic Church: The Reconstruction of Roman Catholicism*. Crossroad NY 1992 $22.50. ISBN 0-8245-1186-7. Thirteen scholars speak on what it means that the church is, as Vatican II states, "the People of God."

Blazynski, George. *John Paul II: A Man from Krakow*. Weidenfeld & Nicolson 1979 o.p. As soon as Karol Wojtyla became the first non-Italian pope since the sixteenth century, a flood of books came out, most by Polish authors; this one is compact and reads well.

Bloesch, Donald. *The Future of Evangelical Theology*. Doubleday 1983 o.p. The author is one of the major voices in modern Evangelicalism and a mainline churchman who has written many books; this one allows him to summarize, reflect, and plead for Evangelical unity.

Brümmer, Vincent. *Speaking of a Personal God: An Essay in Philosophical Theology.* Cambridge U. Pr. 1992 $44.95. ISBN 0-521-430532-6. Contends that systematic theology is, in the main, a form of philosophy, using philosophical tools to clarify questions such as, Can God act in the way that humans can?

Bultmann, Rudolf. *Kerygma and Myth.* Ed. by Hans Bartsch. Trans. by Reginald H. Fuller. HarpC 1961 o.p. Bultmann, apostle of demythologizing the gospels, is criticized and responds to his critics.

———. *The New Testament and Mythology, and Other Basic Writings.* Ed. and trans. by Schubert M. Ogden. Augsburg Fortress 1984 $11.95. ISBN 0-8006-2442-4. Bultmann died in 1976, and here a disciple has collected materials that are accessible to the ordinary reader.

Carmody, John. *Toward a Male Spirituality.* Twenty-Third 1989 $7.95. ISBN 0-89622-410-4. Starting not with generalizations but with personal experiences, Carmody ruminates about male spirituality, a topic gaining attention in the current men's movement.

Cobb, John. *Sustainability: Economics, Ecology, and Justice.* Orbis Bks. 1992 $39.95. ISBN 0-88344-823-8. Lucid descriptions of complex issues, by famous Process theologian who says that Christians need not be anthropocentric.

Cobb, John B., Jr., and David R. Griffin. *Process Theology: An Introductory Exposition.* Westminster John Knox 1976 $9.95. ISBN 0-664-24743-1. A good introduction to process theology, with its developing deity and its Whiteheadian language.

Curran, Charles. *Critical Concerns in Moral Theology.* Bks. Demand repr. of 1984 ed. $72.80. ISBN 0-318-34709-1. Although it is the general tenor of his approach to ethics that cost Curran his teaching position at Catholic University, probably the sharpest disagreements are found in this book, with matters sexual heading the list.

———. *Directions in Catholic Social Ethics.* U. of Notre Dame Pr. 1985 $11.95. ISBN 0-268-00853-1. Various articles by the Catholic church's most controversial ethicist on population control, peace and war, health care, and more.

Devaney, Sheila Greeve, ed. *Theology at the End of Modernity.* TPI PA 1991 $39.95. ISBN 1-56338-011-0. Sallie MaFague, James Gustafson, and Mark C. Taylor are among the leading contemporary theologians who have contributed essays to this noteworthy collection.

Doig, Desmond. *Mother Teresa: Her Work and Her People.* HarpC 1980 $11.95. ISBN 0-06-061941-4. Small text with many pictures, some of them in color. Illustrated by Rahgu Rai.

Dowley, Tim, ed. *Eerdmans' Handbook to the History of Christianity.* Eerdmans 1977 $29.95. ISBN 0-8028-3450-7. Seventy scholars have contributed to this, and the twentieth century is handled very adroitly.

Du Boulay, Shirley. *Tutu: Voice of the Voiceless.* Eerdmans 1988 $22.50. ISBN 0-8028-3649-6. An admiring portrait of this admirable protester against injustice in South Africa.

Ferm, Deane W. *Contemporary American Theologies: A Critical Survey.* HarpC 1981 $8.95. ISBN 0-8164-2341-5. Brief and clear introductions to the main features of modern theologies in America, including Catholic and conservative Protestant.

Flannery, Austin, ed. *Vatican Council II: The Conciliar and Post-Conciliar Documents.* 2 vols. Vol. 1 St. Paul Books 1988 $9.95. ISBN 0-317-67497-8. Vol. 2 Liturgical Pr. 1983. ISBN 0-8146-1299-7. These volumes contain the 16 constitutions and decrees of Vatican II, with many subsequent clarifying and implementing documents.

Ford, John, Germain Grisez, Joseph Boyle, John Finnis, and William May. *The Teaching of Humanae Vitae: A Defense.* Ignatius Pr. 1988 $12.95. ISBN 0-89870-214-3. Addresses misinterpretations of church teaching.

Frei, Hans. *Types of Christian Theology.* Ed. by George Hunsinger and William Placher. Yale U. Pr. 1992 $26.50. ISBN 0-300-05104-2. Published posthumously, the book presents Frei's unfinished but brilliant classification of modern Christian theology.

Gilkey, Langdon. *Naming the Whirlwind: The Renewal of God-Language*. Bobbs 1969 o.p. The author is probably the dean of American theologians, Protestant and Catholic, and this is probably his major work.

Gustafson, James. *Ethics from a Theocentric Perspective*. 2 vols. U. Ch. Pr. Vol. 1 *Theology and Ethics*. 1983 $14.95. ISBN 0-226-31111-2. Vol. 2 *Ethics and Theology*. 1992 $17.95. ISBN 0-226-31113-9. The foremost religious ethician in the United States argues that a wide array of proposals are prone to the error of anthropocentrism, and draws from the Christian tradition in support of theocentrism, at the same time offering a radical critique of that tradition.

Hastings, Adrian, ed. *Modern Catholicism*. OUP 1991. ISBN 0-19-520657-6. Intended as informative rather than polemical, this book is likely to become a standard reference work on Vatican II and the ensuing quarter of a century.

Hauerwas, Stanley. *Against the Nations: War and Survival in a Liberal Society*. U. of Notre Dame Pr. 1992. ISBN 0-268-00638-5. An influential and controversial ethicist illustrates what a postliberal ethic looks like pertaining to specific issues like Jonestown and disarmament.

Hebblethwaite, Peter. *The Year of Three Popes*. HarpC 1979 o.p. Gives the reader an idea of the uproar in Rome when Pope Paul VI died and was followed by John Paul I, who lived in office but 30 days (yes, you can find books that say he was murdered), and was succeeded by the present John Paul II.

Hebblethwaite, Peter, and Ludwig Kaufmann. *John Paul II: A Pictorial Biography*. McGraw 1979 o.p. Lots of colored photos and a good text.

Henry, Carl F. *God, Revelation and Authority: God Who Speaks and Shows*. 6 vols. Word Bks. 1976–79 o.p. Henry and Bloesch are Evangelicalism's major theologians; Bloesch (see above) is relatively easy to read, while Henry requires deep plowing.

Herbstrith, Waltraud. *Edith Stein: A Biography*. Trans. by Bernard Bonowitz. Ignatius Pr. 1992 $11.98. ISBN 0-89870-410-3. Reports on the early stages of the canonization of the mystic and philosopher Edith Stein, who converted from Judaism to become a Carmelite nun and was murdered in Auschwitz.

Hordern, William E. *A Layman's Guide to Protestant Theology*. Macmillan rev. ed. 1968 $5.95. ISBN 0-02-085470-6. A clearly written account of theological movements from the Protestant reformers to the twentieth century, with particular attention to twentieth-century theologians, the major ones examined carefully.

Jüngel, Eberhard. *Theological Essays*. Trans. by J. B. Webster. Bks. Intl. VA 1989 $35.95. ISBN 0-567-09502-9. Jüngel, perhaps Germany's foremost contemporary theologian, produced writings deeply influenced by Karl Barth and reflecting an astonishing knowledge of exegetical, theological, and philosophical literature.

Kaufman, Gordon. *In Face of Mystery: A Constructive Theology*. HUP 1993 $39.95. ISBN 0-674-44575-9. The Harvard theologian shows how a concept of God can be constructed that provides a center of value without conflicting with scientific findings.

Keeley, Robin. ed. *Christianity in Today's World: An Eerdmans Handbook*. Eerdmans 1985 o.p. Many scholars look at the astonishing variety of Christians in Africa, Asia, and Latin America.

Kuitert, H. M. *I Have My Doubts: How to Become a Christian without being a Fundamentalist*. Trans. by John Bowden. TPI PA 1993 $19.00. ISBN 1-56338-057-9. A number-one bestseller in the Netherlands and an outspoken and controversial work that invites the reader to think honestly about issues such as resurrection, prayer, and the nature of faith.

Lamb, Matthew L. *Creativity and Method: Studies in Honor of Rev. Bernard Lonergan, S.J.* Marquette 1981 $19.95. ISBN 0-685-03299-X. Lonergan is the epitome of Catholic theology but nearly impossible to get hold of. Here his disciples explain him to each other and to the reader.

Long, Edward, Jr. *A Survey of Recent Christian Ethics*. OUP 1982 $14.95. ISBN 0-19-503160-1. A readable and reliable survey that nicely introduces topics such as character ethics and comparative religious ethics.

McBrien, Richard P. *Catholicism Study Edition*. Winston Pr. 1981 $30.00. ISBN 0-86683-601-2

McCormick, Richard A., and Paul Ramsey, eds. *Doing Evil to Achieve Good: Moral Choice in Conflict Situations*. Loyola 1978 $12.95. ISBN 0-8294-0285-3. Introduces the reader to the major Protestant ethicists.

McFague, Sallie. *Models of God: Theology for an Ecological, Nuclear Age*. Augsburg Fortress 1987 $12.95. ISBN 0-8006-2051-8. Proposes that speaking of God as mother, lover, and friend can help move theology beyond its patriarchal tradition.

Macquarrie, John. *Twentieth Century Religious Thought: The Frontiers of Philosophy and Theology*. Trinity Press International $19.95. ISBN 0-334-01709-2. A handbook with summaries of about 150 theologians and philosophers that make it a handy reference tool for beginner and practitioner alike.

Muggeridge, Malcolm. *Something Beautiful for God: Mother Teresa of Calcutta*. HarpC 1971 $18.45. ISBN 0-06-066041-4. Brief, full of photos and conversations with Muggeridge, who was the first one to "discover" Mother Teresa for the West.

Nash, James. *Loving Nature: Ecological Integrity and Christian Responsibility*. Abingdon 1991 $16.95. ISBN 0-687-22824-7. One of the first places to turn for insights on Christianity and the environment, featuring an impressive response to charges that Christianity is to blame for the ecological crisis.

Neill, Stephen C., and others, eds. *Concise Dictionary of the Christian World Mission*. Abingdon 1971 o.p. International and ecumenical in scope, this excellent source covers all facets of missions with brief articles by more than 200 specialists that treat the missionary work and provide biographies of missionary leaders; an "indispensable reference work in its field" (Gorman).

Niebuhr, H. Richard. *Faith on Earth*. Ed. by Richard R. Niebuhr. Yale U. Pr. 1991 $12.00. ISBN 0-300-05122-0. A posthumously published collection of writings edited by Niebuhr's son, who teaches theology at Harvard.

O'Brien, David, and Thomas Shannon. eds. *Catholic Social Thought: The Documentary Heritage*. Orbis Bks. 1992. ISBN 0-88344-787-8. An unequaled collection of Catholic social teachings in the century following Pope Leo XIII's historical encyclical *Rerum Novarum*.

Ogletree, Thomas W. *The Death of God Controversy*. Abingdon 1966 o.p. Here three of the major proponents argue their case for the death of God, and the editor provides a good introduction.

Pannenberg, Wolfhart. *Systematic Theology*. Vol. 1 Trans. by Geoffrey Bromiley. Eerdmans 1988. ISBN 0-8028-3656-9. The first volume of the magnum opus of Pannenberg, one of today's foremost theologians.

Pinches, Charles, and Jay McDaniel, eds. *Good News for Animals? Christian Approaches to Animal Well-Being*. Orbis Bks. 1993 $24.95. ISBN 0-88344-787-8. Collection of essays on what Christians have said about animals in the past and what they should say today.

Rahner, Karl. *The Christian Commitment: Essays in Pastoral Theology*. Trans. by Cecily Hastings. Sheed & Ward 1963 o.p. Rahner at his pastoral best, when his theology sounds less Germanic than usual.

————. *Foundations of Christian Faith: An Introduction to the Idea of Christianity*. Crossroad NY 1982 $16.95. ISBN 0-8245-0523-9. Usually regarded as the best brief exposition of his theology; the longer statement is in the 20 volumes of *Theological Investigations*.

————. *Karl Rahner in Dialogue*. Crossroad NY 1986 $22.50. ISBN 0-8245-0749-5. Reviewers say the essential Rahner is here, including comments on Hans Küng's conflict with the church and modifications on his church of the future.

————. *A Rahner Reader*. Ed. by Gerald McCool. Crossroad NY 1975 o.p. Excerpts and shorter materials; about 375 pages.

Ramsey, Paul. *Basic Christian Doctrine*. Westminster John Knox 1993. ISBN 0-664-25324-5. A republication of the most important book by Paul Ramsey, a giant among Protestant theological ethicists.

Ratzinger, John Cardinal. *Principles of Catholic Theology: Building Stones for a Fundamental Theology.* Ignatius Pr. 1987 $29.95. ISBN 0-89870-133-3. As the Prefect for the Congregation for a Doctrine of the Faith, Ratzinger has been at the center of many a theological debate, and his interpretation of the Catholic faith is, therefore, worth noting.

Robinson, John A. *Honest to God.* Westminster John Knox 1963 $8.99. ISBN 0-664-24465-3. A concise and thoroughly bad book that had an enormous impact.

Rouse, Ruth, and Stephen C. Neill, eds. *A History of the Ecumenical Movement, 1517–1948.* 2 vols. Westminster John Knox rev. ed. 1970 o.p. An indispensable book on the ecumenical movement, formation of the World Council of Churches, and Vatican relations.

Santmire, H. Paul. *The Travail of Nature: The Ambiguous Ecological Promise of Christian Theology.* Augsberg Fortress 1991 $14.95. ISBN 0-8006-1806-8. Discusses whether Christianity is the cause of the current environmental crisis.

Schillebeeckx, Edward. *God and Man.* Trans. by Edward Fitzgerald and Peter Tomlinson. Sheed & Ward 1969 o.p. Although not the Dutch Catholic theologian's latest book, it indicates some of the reasons he got in trouble with the Vatican.

Spink, Kathryn. *The Miracle of Love: Mother Teresa of Calcutta, Her Missionaries of Charity, and Her Coworkers.* HarpC 1982 o.p. Twice as long as Muggeridge's work (see above), with many color photos and what almost amounts to a biography.

Spong, John. *Fundamentalism: A Bishop Rethinks the Meaning of Scripture.* Harper SF 1992 $10.00. ISBN 0-06-067518-7. Spong, a Episcopalian bishop, tries to wrest Christianity from the grip of racists, sexists, and homophobes and speculates that Paul may have been homosexual.

Tanner, Kathryn. *The Politics of God: Christian Theologies and Social Justice.* Augsberg Fortress 1992. ISBN 0-8006-2613-3. Tanner, quickly establishing herself as a major figure on the American theological scene, argues that theology need not undergird the status quo.

Thielicke, Helmut. *Modern Faith and Thought.* Trans. by G. Bromiley. Eerdmans 1990 $39.99. ISBN 0-8028-3685-2. Engaging with the major modern European thinkers, Thielicke eruditely addresses questions such as What is truth?

Thiemann, Ronald, ed. *The Legacy of H. Richard Niebuhr.* Augsberg Fortress 1991 $13.95. ISBN 0-8006-7084-1. Among the essayists—Niebuhr's former students—are such prominent figures as Hans Frei, Gordon Kaufman, and James Gustafson.

Tracy, David. *Analogical Imagination.* Crossroad NY 1985 $19.95. ISBN 0-8245-0694-4. Wrestles with the pluralism in thought-worlds today, showing the importance of the "classical writings" in each tradition (e.g., Bible Augustine, etc., for Christianity; Qu'ran for Islam), and argues their abiding importance rather than the official interpreters of the faith.

———. *Blessed Rage for Order: The New Pluralism in Theology.* HarpC 1985 $19.95. ISBN 0-8164-2202-8. Catholic theologian lays out the philosophic grounds on which theology can be built in an age that is not religiously literate.

Vecchione, Patrice, and Amber Coverdale Sumrall, eds. *Catholic Girls.* Plume 1992 $11.00. ISBN 0-452-26842-7. A fascinating collection of stories and recollections by 52 authors; Mary Gordon, for example, speaks of the "comedy of Catholic life," recounting failed attempts to become a saint.

Verhey, Allen. *The Great Reversal: Ethics and the New Testament.* Eerdmans 1984 $13.95. ISBN 0-8028-0004-1. A refreshing work, easy to read and thoughtful for any level of student.

Wainwright, Geoffrey, ed. *Dictionary of the Ecumenical Movement.* Eerdmans 1991 $79.99. ISBN 0-8028-2428-5. Well over a thousand pages of compactly presented, reliable information.

Weger, Karl-Heinz. *Karl Rahner: An Introduction to His Theology.* Crossroad NY 1980 o.p. Best English-language summary, with some attention to Rahner's life.

Wilkinson, Loren, ed. *Earthkeeping in the Nineties: Stewardship of Creation.* Eerdmans 1991 $19.99. ISBN 0-8028-0534-5. An evangelical, interdisciplinary response to environmental issues, written not only for the scholar but also for the general reader.

Williams, George H. *The Mind of John Paul II: Origins of His Thought and Action*. HarpC 1981 $26.95. ISBN 0-8164-0473-9. This book is unusual because it was written by a Protestant Reformation scholar who came to know Cardinal Wojtyla before anyone had an idea he would become pope.

Wojtyla, Karol. *Love and Responsibility*. Trans. by H. T. Willetts. FS&G 1981 o.p. The present pope begins his study of human love with "the sexual urge" and goes on with a thorough scholar's analysis of sex, love, chastity, and marriage, with a section on birth control.

Wuthnow, Robert. *Christianity in the Twenty-First Century: Reflections on the Challenges Ahead*. OUP 1993 $25.00. ISBN 0-19-507957-4. Praised by Mark Noll as the best person to describe Christianity in the next century, Wuthnow asks questions such as Will fundamentalism continue to set the agenda for liberal Christianity?

Liberation Theologies

Liberation theology, arising in the 1970s, appears to have a few major themes. First, it is theology "from below," that is, from the standpoint of oppressed people, not from college and seminary professors who are attacking or defending established literary positions. Next, it readily admits its debt to the Marxist "scientific" analysis of the ills of capitalism and colonialism. (See Novak's work below for criticism.) Finally, it differs according to the place of its origin: Latin American liberationists and middle-class American women liberationists do not always see the same issues as important. The books listed are generally recent ones that will not only state a case but will also lead the reader back through earlier works in a rapidly changing field.

GENERAL

Brown, Robert McAfee. *Liberation Theology: An Introductory Guide*. Westminster John Knox 1993 $9.99. ISBN 0-664-25424-1. Focuses on Catholic Latin American theology but does not neglect the wide variety of liberation movements.

Cadorette, Curt, and others, eds. *Liberation Theology: An Introductory Reader*. Orbis Bks. 1992 $16.95. ISBN 0-88344-801-7. A magnificent, thematically arranged introduction to liberation theology that contains contributions from across the world by thinkers such as James Cone, Gustavo Gutierrez, Sallie McFague.

Smith, Christian. *The Emergence of Liberation Theology: Radical Religion and Social Movement Theory*. U. Ch. Pr. 1991 $14.95. ISBN 0-226-76410-9. A refreshing approach to theology from the vantage point of a sociologist, in which Smith accounts for liberation theology's emergence.

LATIN AMERICAN LIBERATION THEOLOGY

Alves, Rubem. *What Is Religion?* Trans. by Don Vinzant. Orbis Bks. 1984 o.p. Most of the liberationists are Roman Catholic, but Alves and José Miguez Bonino are noted Protestant authors.

Berryman, Philip. *The Religious Roots of Rebellion: Christians in Central American Revolutions*. Orbis Bks. 1984 $19.95. ISBN 0-88344-105-5. Tells the story of recent revolutionary activity from a Christian perspective and in great detail.

Boff, Leonardo. *The Path to Hope: Fragments from a Theologian's Journey*. Orbis Bks. 1993 repr. of 1991 ed. $12.95. ISBN 0-88344-815-7. The embattled Brazilian theologian explains why he is leaving the Franciscan order and the priesthood.

Brockman, James R. *The Word Remains: A Life of Oscar Romero*. Bks. Demand repr. of 1982 ed. $67.50. ISBN 0-8357-2668-1. "This is not a complete biography of El Salvador's martyred archbishop but rather the story of the last few years of Romero's life and work . . . highly recommended, both as a biography and as an insightful account of the situation in Central America" (*Library Journal*).

Dussel, Enrique. *A History of the Church in Latin America: Colonialism to Liberation.* Bks. Demand repr. of 1981 ed. $99.90. ISBN 0-685-23454-1. Best one-volume treatment of the subject of colonialism and the church, including recent revolutions (e.g., El Salvador, Nicaragua).

Erdozain, Placido. *Archbishop Romero: Martyr of Salvador.* Trans. by John M. McFadden and Ruth Warner. Bks. Demand repr. of 1981 ed. $33.30. ISBN 0-8357-8805-9. Oscar Romero, shot to death at the altar, is examined and eulogized as a fighter for liberation, albeit a peaceful one (his writings are listed below).

Freire, Paulo. *Pedagogy of the Oppressed.* Trans. by Myra B. Raymos. Continuum rev. ed. 1992 $11.95. ISBN 0-8264-0611-4. Remains a sort of liberationist classic, although that term had hardly been coined when he wrote it.

Gutierrez, Gustavo. *A Theology of Liberation.* Ed. and trans. by Sister Caridad Inda and John Eagleson, Sr. Orbis Bks. 1988 $34.95. ISBN 0-88344-543-3. The basic theology of the movement—the author is careful to dialogue at length with European theology—with a foreword by a noted American theologian.

Hall, Mary. *The Impossible Dream: The Spirituality of Dom Helder Camara.* Bks. Demand repr. of 1979 ed. $26.00. ISBN 0-8357-2675-4. This Brazilian leader is one of the patron saints of the oppressed in Latin America, a scrappy yet irenic battler for the poor, the Indians, and all who lack freedom.

Lernoux, Penny. *Cry of the People: The Struggle for Human Rights in Latin America—The Catholic Church in Conflict with U.S. Policy.* Viking Penguin 1982 $9.95. ISBN 0-14-006047-2. Particularly readable because the author is a journalist who can write the story without neglecting the research.

Novak, Michael. *Freedom with Justice: Catholic Social Thought and Liberal Institutions.* HarpC 1984 o.p. A spirited and learned attack on all leftward leaning within his church, by an articulate spokesman for the so-called New Right.

Romero, Oscar. *Voice of the Voiceless: The Four Pastoral Letters and Other Statements.* Trans. by Michael J. Walsh. Orbis Bks. 1985 $14.95. ISBN 0-88344-525-5. In addition to the pastoral letters to the faithful of El Salvador, the Salvadorian liberationist churchman writes to the American Protestants of the National Council of Churches, and even to President Carter.

BLACK LIBERATION THEOLOGIES

Cone, James H. *A Black Theology of Liberation: Twentieth Anniversary with Critical Responses.* Orbis Bks. 1990 $14.95. ISBN 0-88344-685-5. Cone allows that in the face of womanist theology, he would revise his classic work somewhat; this is a good introduction that includes Cone's rejoinders to critical responses.

Hopkins, Dwight. *Black Theology: U.S.A. and South Africa.* Orbis Bks. 1989 $16.95. ISBN 0-88344-639-1. After providing brief introductions to several black theologians in the United States and South Africa, Hopkins identifies a common denominator: a shared interpretation of the gospel and its societal significance.

Lincoln, C. Eric, and Lawrence Mamiya. *The Black Church in the African American Experience.* Duke 1990 $19.95. ISBN 0-8223-1073-2. More than 1,800 interviews with African American religious leaders make up only one part of the prodigious research that helps make this a major contribution to the field.

Nelsen, Hart M., ed. *The Black Church in America.* Basic 1971 o.p. Articles and book chapters, old and more recent, including materials from about every major writer, including all the ones listed in this bibliography.

Paris, Peter. *Black Religious Leaders: Conflict in Unity.* Westminster John Knox 1991 $15.99. ISBN 0-664-25145-5. Reviewing the work of Martin Luther King, Jr., Malcolm X, Joseph Jackson, and Adam Clayton Powell, Paris concludes that each is needed as part of a fully adequate description of and response to racism.

Roberts, J. Deotis. *Black Theology in Dialogue.* Westminster John Knox 1987 $12.99. ISBN 0-664-24022-4. Roberts shows how black theology of liberation can enter into dialogue with Jewish theology of liberation.

Roberts, James D. *Black Theology Today: Liberation and Contextualization.* E. Mellen 1984 $89.95. ISBN 0-88946-755-2. Articles written at different times, edited together into a good analysis of movements in black theology, with some ties to Latin American theology.

Washington, Joseph R., Jr. *Black Sects and Cults*. U. Pr. of Amer. 1984 repr. of 1973 ed. o.p. A major theologian looks at the side of black Christianity that is most visible when viewed from the street but gets very little attention in print. Their intention, he argues, is to be power communities.

West, Cornel. *Prophecy Deliverance! An Afro-American Revolutionary Christianity*. Westminster John Knox 1982 $11.99. ISBN 0-664-24447-5. Draws from Marxism and prophetic African American Christianity to forge his impressive proposal.

Wilmore, Gayraud S., and James H. Cone, eds. *Black Theology: A Documentary History, 1966–1979*. Orbis Bks. $18.95. ISBN 0-88344-042-3. Good collection, chosen for breadth and related well to central issues.

WOMEN'S LIBERATION THEOLOGIES

Bainton, Roland W. *Women in the Reformation in France and England*. Beacon Pr. 1975 o.p. If Bainton did it, it is good Reformation history.

Bührig, Marga. *Woman Invisible: A Personal Odyssey in Christian Feminism*. Trinity Press International 1993 ISBN 1-56338-056-0. Bührig, formerly the Ecumenical President of the World Council of Churches, reflects on the invisibility of women in the church.

Carmody, Denise Lardner. *Virtuous Woman: Reflections on Christian Feminist Ethics*. Orbis Bks. 1992 $16.95. ISBN 0-88344-817-3. Ruminations on assorted contemporary sources, emphasizing the *Christian* character of Christian feminist ethics.

Carson, Anne, ed. *Feminist Spirituality and the Feminine Divine: An Annotated Bibliography. Feminist Ser.* Crossing Pr. 1986 o.p. Probably the best catalog of materials in the field, with an annotation toward the "goddess" ideal in feminist religious matters.

Chopp, Rebecca. *The Power to Speak: Feminism, Language, God*. Crossroad NY 1991 repr. of 1989 ed. $17.95. ISBN 0-8245-0940-4. A compact and well-documented presentation discussing feminist theologies as "discourses of emancipatory transformation."

Daly, Mary. *Beyond God the Father: Toward a Philosophy of Women's Liberation*. Beacon Pr. 2nd rev. ed. 1985 $13.00. ISBN 0-8070-1503-2. Although the author has done later work (this was originally published in 1973), nothing exploded on the scene like this bitter, careful analysis and attack on patriarchy in Christian thought and practice.

Davis Finson, Shelley. *A Bibliographic Guide to Christian Feminist Liberation Theology*. U. of Toronto Pr. 1991 $70.00. ISBN 0-8020-5881-7. An invaluable resource on the topic, containing helpful sections on Judaism and Wicca.

Dickey Young, Pamela. *Feminist Theology/Christian Theology: In Search of Method*. Augsberg Fortress 1990 $8.95. ISBN 0-8006-2402-5. Describes the debate in feminist theology over whether it is possible to be both a feminist and a Christian and makes a constructive proposal.

Greaves, Richard L., ed. *Triumph over Silence: Women in Protestant History. Contributions to the Study of Religion Ser.* Greenwood 1985 $42.95. ISBN 0-313-24799-4. This 300-page work carefully summarizes the struggles of women to be heard or to lead.

McHaffie, Barbara J. *Her Story: Women in Christian Tradition*. Augsberg Fortress 1986 $11.95. ISBN 0-8006-1893-9. Amazingly able survey of women in the early church, medieval, Reformation, and Puritan attitudes, and the struggle by women in these epochs.

Mollenkott, Virginia R. *Women, Men, and the Bible*. Abingdon 1977 o.p. The author is a literary scholar and an Evangelical and thus is able to throw light from several directions on the women's struggle.

Ruether, Rosemary Radford. *Gaia and God: An Ecofeminist Theology of Earth Healing*. Harper SF 1992 $22.00. ISBN 0-06-067022-3. Critiques Christianity but also draws from it as well from "pagan" sources to construct an ecofeminist theology.

Ruether, Rosemary R., and Rosemary S. Keller. *Women and Religion in America*. 3 vols. HarpC 1982–86. Vols. 1 and 2 o.p. Vol. 3 $15.95. ISBN 0-06-066838-5. Excellent introductions to a myriad of studies of women in America, Protestant and Catholic, liberal and Evangelical, social movers and church reformers.

Scanzoni, Letha, and Virginia R. Mollenkott. *Is the Homosexual My Neighbor? Another Christian View*. HarpC 1980 $9.95. ISBN 0-06-067076-2. Here Mollenkott is teamed with another Evangelical, a sociologist, and their convictions on the rights of the homosexual have helped split the Evangelical community in this regard and thus in the whole area of women in the church.

Schüssler Fiorenza, Elisabeth. *Discipleship of Equals: A Critical Feminist Ecclesia-logy of Liberation*. Crossroad NY 1993 $18.95. ISBN 0-8245-1244-8. Having gained fame as a biblical scholar, Schüssler Fiorenza turns her attention to the church; note her crucial altered spelling of *ecclesiology*.

Soelle, Dorothee. *Thinking About God: An Introduction to Theology*. TPI PA 1990 $15.95. ISBN 0-334-02476-5. Moves adeptly from typologies of theology to literary allusions to personal experiences.

CHRISTIAN RELIGION IN AMERICA

An English writer who visited the United States in the 1830s wrote: "The almost universal profession in America of the adoption of Christianity . . . compels the inquiry . . . what sort of Christianity it is that is professed, and how it is come by. There is no evading the conviction that it is to a vast extent a monstrous superstition that is thus embraced by the tyrant, the profligate, the wordling, the bigot, the coward, and the slave; a superstition which offers little molestation to their vices, little rectification to their errors; a superstition which is but the spurious offspring of . . . divine Christianity" (Harriet Martineau, *Society in America*).

Certainly, of all the aspects of religious life that fascinated the European visitor in the last century, the separation of state and church, with its corollary, the voluntary church, was the one that interested them most. All European lands had an established church. In some, no other church could exist, but in all of them the nonestablished bodies were scorned or feared, and regarded as aberrations. To be properly Spanish was to be Catholic; the name for Romanians is the same as adherents to the Romanian Orthodox church; all important Englishmen were Anglicans, even if—as CHURCHILL (see Vol. 3) said later—it meant to be like a flying buttress, supporting the church from the outside.

In the bibliographies that follow, no attempt has been made to be exhaustive. However, the reader who needs information on persons, periods, movements, or schools of thought will find plentiful guidance, either in the bibliographies or the general works listed below. Almost no facet of religious America has gone unresearched, and the diligent student can find what is wanted with a little perseverance.

Bibliographies

Ahlstrom, S. E. *A Religious History of the American People*. Yale U. Pr. 1972 $24.95. ISBN 0-300-01762-4. For the beginning student this is a handy, well-written guide to the whole history of religion in America, with superb material for a great number of Christian denominations, as well as for groups that have made a conscious split with historic Christianity.

Burr, Nelson R., ed. *Critical Bibliography of Religion in America*. 2 vols. Princeton U. Pr. 1961 o.p. Burr's bibliography, as it is always called, is the basic bibliography, providing in its table of contents a helpful organization of vast amounts of material.

_____. *Religion in Amer. Life. Goldentree Bibliographies in Amer. History Ser.* Harlan Davidson 1971 $14.95. ISBN 0-88295-507-1. A condensation of and supplement to the preceding entry.

General Studies

Dean, William. *American Religious Empiricism.* State U. NY Pr. 1986 $19.95. ISBN 0-88706-281-4. In a remarkable achievement, Dean links American thinkers from Jonathan Edwards in the eighteenth century to Chicago School thinkers today.

Dolan, Jay. *The American Catholic Experience: A History from Colonial Times to the Present.* U. of Notre Dame Pr. 1992 repr. of 1985 ed. $15.95. ISBN 0-268-00639-3. Gives an indispensable account of what life has been like for ordinary Catholics in America.

Ellis, John Tracy. *American Catholicism.* Ed. by Daniel J. Boorstin. U. Ch. Pr. 2nd ed. 1969 $13.95. ISBN 0-226-20556-8. Ellis invented the field and is still its master.

_____. *Documents of American Catholic History.* 3 vols. Liturgical Pr. 1987 $75.00. ISBN 0-8146-5610-2. Volume 1 covers the churches, including the Spanish colonies, to 1866; Volume 2 covers from then until 1966; Volume 3 covers 1966–86.

Ellis, John Tracy, and Robert Trisco. *A Guide to American Catholic History.* ABC-CLIO 2nd rev. ed. 1982 o.p. An early work, but still useful. Shows the church before Vatican II had any influence on the church or on the historian.

Gausted, Edwin S. *Historical Atlas of Religion in America.* HarpC rev. ed. 1976 o.p. Maps, charts, tables, and text provide an excellent guide to the expansion and development of religious institutions in America.

_____. *A Religious History of America.* Harper SF 1990 $19.95. ISBN 0-06-063094-9. A revised version of the much-praised history that was published 25 years earlier; an accessible book that is fair in every respect.

_____, ed. *A Documentary History of Religion in America since 1865.* Eerdmans 1983 $19.95. ISBN 0-8028-1874-9. Skillfully edited primary sources that are placed together to tell the story.

Greeley, Andrew M. *The Catholic Experience: An Interpretation of American Catholicism.* Doubleday 1967 o.p. People forget that Greeley, tarred by the brush of his recent flashy novels, has always been and is a trenchant, insightful, and faithful exponent of the faith. This is a very good book.

Hatch, Nathan. *The Democratization of American Christianity.* Yale U. Pr. 1991 $13.95. ISBN 0-300-05060-7. Prize-winning study of the early republic illustrates that American Christianity cannot be understood without recognizing its democratization.

Hudson, Wintrop, and John Corrigan. *Religion in America.* Macmillan 5th ed. 1992 ISBN 0-02-357830-0. An updated version of what has long been recognized as a standard account of American religious history.

Mead, Frank S., and Samuel S. Hill. *Handbook of Denominations in the United States.* Abingdon 9th rev. ed. 1990 $13.95. ISBN 0-687-16572-5. Brief history, doctrinal views, polity, and statistics on more than 200 American denominations.

Melton, James G. *The Encyclopedia of American Religions.* 3 vols. Liguori Pubns. 1992 $14.95 ea. Surveys about 1,200 distinct religious groups, comparing practices and beliefs with Roman Catholic, Lutheran, and Baptist practice and belief.

Melton, James G., and James V. Geisendorfer. *A Directory of Religious Bodies in the United States.* Garland 1977 o.p. Nearly 1,300 religious groups, some not in Mead (see above), are listed, including such headings as mail-order churches and neopaganism.

Noll, Mark A., and others, eds. *Eerdmans' Handbook to Christianity in America.* Eerdmans 1983 o.p. Judicious, fair, and succinctly written, with many illustrations.

Piepkorn, Arthur C. *Profiles in Belief: The Religious Bodies of the United States and Canada.* 4 vols. HarpC 1977–79 o.p. An invaluable reference tool for the reader who wants to dive in more deeply than the handbooks above allow.

Smith, H. Shelton, and others, eds. *American Christianity: An Historical Interpretation with Representative Documents.* 2 vols. Scribner 1960 o.p. Fine collection of sources and documents with 1607–1820 covered in the first volume.

Smith, James W., and A. Leland Jamison, eds. *Religion in American Life.* 4 vols. Princeton U. Pr. 1961 o.p. Volumes 1 and 2 are interpretive essays; for Volumes 3 and 4, see above under Bibliographies for Burr, *Critical Bibliography of Religion in America.*

Vollmar, Edward R. *The Catholic Church in America: An Historical Bibliography.* Scarecrow 1963 o.p. Full bibliography until its publication date; after that the reader must rely on Ahlstrom's briefer bibliography.

The Yearbook of American and Canadian Churches. Ed. by Constant H. Jacquet, Jr. Abingdon 1991 $28.95. ISBN 0-687-46646-6. A handy annual guide to everything about churches: their names, seminaries, church-related schools, religious periodicals, and statistics for membership and finances.

French and Spanish Colonies

Most readers forget that the Spanish and French beat the English, Swedish, and Dutch to what is now the continental United States by about a century. Along with the early French and Spanish explorers came missionaries who sought to bring their faith to the New World and convert the "heathens" to Christianity. These missionaries played an especially crucial role in those colonies established in the name of France and Spain.

Kennedy, John H. *Jesuit and Savage in New France.* Yale U. Pr. 1950 o.p. Good account of brave people who, for the most part, failed because of the white pressure on the native American.

Picon-Salas, Mariano. *A Cultural History of Spanish America from Conquest to Independence.* Trans. by Irving A. Leonard. Greenwood 1982 repr. of 1962 ed. $38.50. ISBN 0-313-23454-X. Covers a great deal of material in a reasonable amount of space.

Other Useful Books

What follows is the editor's choice for some of the most helpful interpretations of the religious experience in America.

Balmer, Randall. *Mine Eyes Have Seen the Glory: A Journey into the Evangelical Subculture of America.* OUP 1992 ISBN 0-19-507985-X. A nicely written book both critical and enthusiastic about the evangelical subculture.

Bellah, Robert N. *Habits of the Heart: Individualism and Commitment in American Life.* HarpC 1986 $12.00. ISBN 0-06-097027-8. A follow-up and extension of the earlier work, listed immediately below.

Bellah, Robert N., and Philip E. Hammond. *Varieties of Civil Religion.* HarpC 1982 o.p. Develops the famous construct of Bellah, a sociologist of religion, on the unacknowledged civil religion, which is part of, yet transcends, any particular faith or denomination.

Bianco, Frank. *Voices of Silence: Lives of the Trappists Today.* Paragon Hse. 1991 $18.95. ISBN 1-55778-305-5. Conversations with Trappists and descriptions of their lives shed light on their communities without removing all traces of mystery.

Bratt, James D. *Dutch Calvinism in Modern America: A History of a Conservative Subculture.* Bks. Demand repr. of 1984 ed. $95.20. ISBN 0-8357-4356-X. Someone has called the Dutch the Jews of Christian America, and their emergence from the ethnic cocoon is interesting, as well as promising for religion in America.

Byrnes, Timothy. *Catholic Bishops in American Politics.* Princeton U. Pr. 1993 $29.95. ISBN 0-691-07876-9. A political scientist examines not only the goals of recent Catholic bishops but also how politicians selectively appropriate themes for their own purposes.

Cohen, Norman, ed. *The Fundamentalist Phenomenon: A View from Within; A Response from Without.* Eerdmans 1990 $14.95. ISBN 0-8028-0447-0. Includes both hostile and sympathetic answers to questions about fundamentalism.

Epstein, Daniel Mark. *Sister Aimee: The Life of Aimee Semple McPherson.* HarBraceJ 1993 $27.95. ISBN 0-15-182688-9. Miracles, fame, and sex scandals all find their place in this well-told story of the life of the charismatic evangelist.

Hadden, Jeffrey K. *Gathering Storm in the Churches.* Doubleday 1969 o.p. In what begins as a study of the race issue, Hadden concludes that clergy and laity are split over the meaning of the church, over the Christian message, and over the issue of authority.

Heimert, Alan, and Andrew Delbanc, eds. *The Puritans in America: A Narrative Anthology.* HUP 1985 $11.95. ISBN 0-674-74066-1. Argues that Puritanism was a more varied phenomenon than is often thought; the book contains both a lively interrogation of a woman accused of witchcraft and excerpts from famous theologians.

Herberg, Will. *Protestant, Catholic, Jew: An Essay in American Religious Sociology.* U. Ch. Pr. 1983 repr. of 1955 ed. $11.95. ISBN 0-226-32734-5. Seminal work on self-understanding in America by a scholar who invented his own credentials.

Hill, Samuel S., Jr. *Southern Churches in Crisis.* H. Holt & Co. 1967 o.p. First major historical study of the southern churches entering the modern era.

Hochfield, George, ed. *Selected Writings of the New England Transcendentalists.* NAL-Dutton 1966 o.p. The basic writings of authors like Emerson and Thoreau, with enough annotation to set the stage.

Hutchison, William R., ed. *American Protestant Thought in the Liberal Era.* U. Pr. of Amer. 1985 repr. of 1968 ed. $20.50. ISBN 0-8191-4336-7. The liberal mind in America existed prior to the Social Gospel, which is its finest flowering.

McLoughlin, William G. *Modern Revivalism: Charles Grandison Finney to Billy Graham.* Ronald Pr. 1959 o.p. The author is *the* historian of that old American institution, the religious revival.

Marsden, George M. *Fundamentalism and American Culture: The Shaping of Twentieth-Century Evangelicalism, 1870–1925.* OUP 1980 $10.95. ISBN 0-19-503083-4. Written by a staunch conservative, it is the best book in the field.

Marshall, Bruce, ed. *Theology and Dialogue: Essays in Conversation with George Lindbeck.* U. of Notre Dame Pr. 1990 ISBN 0-268-01874-X. Contains appreciative essays by Lindbeck's close colleagues David Kelsey and Hans Frei.

Marty, Martin. *Modern American Religion.* U. Ch. Pr. Vol. 1 *The Irony of It All, 1893–1919.* 1986 $24.95. ISBN 0-226-50893-5. Vol. 2 *The Noise of Conflict.* 1991 $27.50. ISBN 0-226-50895-1. The first two of four planned volumes covering an amazing array of materials, presented clearly by an esteemed scholar of American religious history.

——. *A Nation of Behavers.* U. Ch. Pr. 1980 $9.95. ISBN 0-226-50892-7. Expert presentation of six new maps of religious allegiance in America: mainline and Evangelical churches, fundamentalism, pentecostal-charismatic religion, the new religions, ethnic religions, and civil religion.

Mead, Sidney E. *The Lively Experiment: The Shaping of Christianity in America.* HarpC 1963 o.p. Develops a view of the Religion of the Republic, which transcends particular faiths; a variant on civil religion pursued acutely.

Meyer, Donald. *The Positive Thinkers: Religion as Pop Psychology from Mary Baker Eddy to Norman Vincent Peale and Ronald Reagan.* Wesleyan Univ. Pr. $17.95. ISBN 0-8195-6166-5. Good background and analysis of this perennial version of faith, represented today by an increasing number of television preachers.

Miller, Perry. *The New England Mind: From Colony to Province.* HUP 1983 $13.95. ISBN 0-674-61301-5. Miller practically discovered the Puritans and their enduring importance for understanding religion in America.

Niebuhr, H. Richard. *The Kingdom of God in America.* Wesleyan Univ. Pr. 1988 $12.95. ISBN 0-8195-6222-X. Seminal work in which he traces the movement from the seventeenth century's passion for God through the passion to change the social order for God.

O'Dea, Thomas F. *The Catholic Crisis*. Beacon Pr. 1968 o.p. Finds that American Catholics approve of the changes brought about by Vatican II but are estranged by them as well.

Powell, Milton B. *The Voluntary Church: American Religious Life Seen through the Eyes of Its European Visitors*. Macmillan 1967 o.p. One can only really see the radical newness of American denominationalism by seeing it through the eyes of wondering Europeans.

Prelinger, Catherine, ed. *Episcopal Women: Gender, Spirituality and Commitment in an American Mainline Denomination*. OUP 1992 $24.95. ISBN 0-19-507433-5. A collection of essays on the roles of women in the Episcopal Church, past and present; Marjorie Nichols Farmer's essay "Different Voices: African American Women in the Episcopal Church" is particularly noteworthy.

Redmont, Jane. *Generous Lives: American Catholic Women Today*. Morrow 1992 $23.00. ISBN 0-688-06707-7. Conversations with over 110 women give a fascinating inside picture of Catholicism today.

Sandeen, Ernest R. *The Roots of Fundamentalism*. U. Ch. Pr. 1970 o.p. Along with Marsden's, one of the best studies of the conservative Protestant tradition.

Smith, Timothy. *Revivalism and Social Reform: American Protestantism on the Eve of the Civil War*. Johns Hopkins 1980 $13.95. ISBN 0-8018-2477-X. American Evangelical passion to change society, of which the abolition of slavery was a chief part, and why they lose it.

Stein, Stephen. *The Shaker Experience in America: A History of the United Society of Believers*. Yale U. Pr. 1992 $40.00. ISBN 0-300-05139-5. In this definitive historical study of Shakerism, Stein takes the reader well beyond the popular, sentimental picture of the Shakers.

Sweet, Leonard I., ed. *The Evangelical Tradition in America*. Mercer Univ. Pr. 1984 $25.95. ISBN 0-86554-092-6. The editor's 85-page introduction "makes the volume well worth the price for any student of the subject."

Wilson, John F. *Public Religion in American Culture*. Temple U. Pr. 1981 $14.95. ISBN 0-87722-226-6. A wise study of the way religion operates in America even when it appears to be hidden in the churches.

Wilson, John F., and John M. Mulder, eds. *Religion in American History: Interpretive Essays*. P-H 1978 ISBN 0-13-771980-9. Twenty-seven essays that have had an impact on the reinterpretation of America's religious past. A rich source for the reader who already knows something about religious history in America.

Wuthnow, Robert. *The Restructuring of American Religion: Society and Faith since World War II*. Princeton U. Pr. 1988 ISBN 0-691-07759-2. Highly praised sociological account of recent American religious life, full of facts, yet readable, and including an excellent account of the evolving role of women in churches.

EASTERN ORTHODOX CHRISTIANITY

From the very beginning of Christian history, all the major Christian centers—save Rome—were in the eastern Mediterranean region, places like Jerusalem, Ephesus, Alexandria, and Constantinople. Throughout the centuries several barriers arose to what had at one time been easy communication between the churches of the East and those within the orbit of Rome. Language changed, as the Western churches turned to Latin, where their ancestors in faith had used the common Greek of trade around the Mediterranean basin. The Eastern churches tended to stick with the languages of the people—Greek for the Greek-speaking, Arabic, Coptic, Armenian, and a dozen more. Politically, power centered in Constantinople (modern Istanbul), Turkey, and the Eastern churches may have lost some spiritual power vis-à-vis the state in the Caesaropapism that developed there. And ecclesiastically Rome's bishop began to demand acknowledgment that his jurisdiction was a universal one, a claim the Eastern churches found aggrandizing, and not rooted in the histories they have ever been fond of. Indeed, a slogan of the Eastern churches toward Rome is that "St. Peter had primacy of honor, but not of jurisdiction."

One can find several dates to mark the final surrendering of relations between Eastern churches and the one Western church, but 1054 is the date usually accepted. Among various language groups different liturgies developed, and within regions different systems of hierarchy were established—where they had not been established almost from the beginning, as, for example, in Greece. Moscow received its own patriarch, second in the Eastern churches only to the patriarch of Constantinople. The Crusades sometimes ravaged the Eastern churches more than they did Turkish-dominated Islam; indeed, the cruelties of the Crusaders' empire in the Holy Land were responsible for the church there losing thousands of converts to Islam, for Suleiman was a more compassionate ruler over Christians than were the barbarian Christians from the West.

In the East, the major religious event of the modern era was a nonevent: the Eastern churches experienced no Protestant Reformation. No MARTIN LUTHER arose to challenge the hierarchy; no Reformed tradition produced Puritans intent on painting over the icons on the screen before the altar. Perhaps because of this, a fairly unbroken tradition stretches back as far as the historical eye can see, losing itself somewhere in the dimness surrounding the church of the first or second century.

Archbishop Paul of Finland. *Feast of Faith*. Trans. by Ester Williams. St. Vladimir's 1988 $6.95. ISBN 0-88141-072-1. The Archbishop of the Orthodox church clearly expounds the meaning of the eucharist as the central ritual of the church.

Attwater, Donald. *The Christian Churches of the East*. 2 vols. Bruce rev. ed. 1961 o.p. Volume 1 covers churches in communion with Rome (Melkite, Maronite, etc.), with a chapter on monasticism in the East. Volume 2 surveys the Orthodox churches, the Nestorians and Monophysites.

Bacovcin, Helen. *The Way of the Pilgrim and The Pilgrim Continues His Way*. Doubleday 1978 $8.00. ISBN 0-385-46814-8. Can a Christian pray without ceasing? Following the pilgrim, we learn the answer in this classic of mysticism.

Bolshakoff, Sergius. *Russian Mystics*. Cisterian Pubns. 1981 repr. of 1977 ed. ISBN 0-87907-926-6. Includes a portrait of St. Tikhon of Zadonsk—who served as model for Zosima in Dostoevsky's *The Brothers Karamazov*—with a preface by Thomas Merton.

Chadwick, Owen. *The Christian Church in the Cold War*. Viking Penguin 1992 $25.00. ISBN 0-713-99046-5. Among the accomplishments of this book is the clarification it provides of the delicate position of Eastern European Orthodox Christianity after World War I.

Ellis, Jane. *The Russian Orthodox Church: A Contemporary History*. Ind. U. Pr. 1986 o.p. This work sticks to the Russian scene from the mid-1960s, so its more than 500-page length allows for considerable depth and interpretation.

Fortescue, Adrian. *The Orthodox Eastern Church*. Ayer repr. of 1920 ed. $26.50. ISBN 0-8369-6649-X. "Frequently reprinted, this work covers the history, theology, liturgical structure of the Orthodox Church before and after the Great Schism to modern times" (Gorman).

Fouyas, Methodius. *Orthodoxy, Roman Catholicism and Anglicanism*. OUP 1972 o.p. Describes the beliefs and practices of the three churches and examines the prospects for their reunion.

Fries, Paul, and Tivan Nersoyan, eds. *Christ in East and West*. Mercer Univ. Pr. 1987 $14.95. ISBN 0-86554-277-5. Reflects conversations on Christology between representatives of various Orthodox churches and representatives of Protestant and Catholic churches. Contains good descriptions of historical Orthodox positions.

Lossky, Vladimir. *Orthodox Theology: An Introduction.* St. Vladimir's 1978 $8.95. ISBN 0-913836-43-5. A textbook that provides fundamental concepts in Orthodox theology.

Maloney, George A. *A History of Orthodox Theology since 1453.* Nordland 1976 o.p. This nearly 400-page book soundly examines developments since the fall of Constantinople to the Turks in five of the Orthodox traditions: Russian, Greek, Serbian, Bulgarian, and Rumanian.

Meehan, Brenda. *Holy Women of Russia: The Lives of Five Orthodox Women Offer Spiritual Guidance for Today.* Harper SF 1993 $17.00. ISBN 0-06-065472-4. Included is the story of the hermit Anastasiia, who remained in prayer even when bleeding from wounds caused by ants that covered her.

Meyendorff, John. *Byzantine Theology: Historical Trends and Doctrinal Themes.* Fordham 2nd rev. ed. 1987 $15.00. ISBN 0-8232-0967-9. Excellent study by one of Orthodoxy's best historians of theology.

———. *The Orthodox Church: Its Past and Its Role in the World Today.* St. Vladimir's 1981 o.p. A useful introduction, but Ware (below) is probably better for the new reader in this field.

Meyendorff, John, J. Breck, and E. Silk. eds. *The Legacy of St. Vladimir.* St. Vladimir's 1990 $10.95. ISBN 0-88141-078-0. Twenty papers by internationally acclaimed scholars on various aspects of Orthodoxy.

Nichols, Aidan. *Theology in the Russian Diaspora: Church, Fathers, Eucharist in Nikoai Afanas'ev, 1893–1966.* Cambridge U. Pr. 1990 $39.95. ISBN 0-521-36543-0. The author sees Afanas'ev's relatively sympathetic views of the pope as opening up ecumenical possibilities.

Nicodemos. *Nicodemos of the Holy Mountain: A Handbook of Spiritual Counsel.* Trans. by Peter Chamberas. Paulist Pr. 1989 $12.95. ISBN 0-8091-3038-6. Few Orthodox writers in the past two centuries can rival the influence of St. Nicodemos; this book exemplifies the mysticism that pervades the Orthodox church.

Nielsen, Niels. *Revolutions in Eastern Europe: The Religious Roots.* Orbis Bks. 1991 $16.95. ISBN 0-88344-764-9. The portion of the book on the Russian Orthodox church tells, for example, about the renewed interest in the philosopher Nicolas Berdyaev, a critic of both communism and capitalism.

Schmemann, Alexander. *Russian Theology, 1920–1965: A Bibliographic Survey.* Union Theological Seminary (Virginia) 1969 o.p. Excellent introduction to Orthodox theology since 1920, and not confined to Russian.

Tolstoy, Leo. *The Gospel According to Tolstoy.* Ed. and trans. by David Patterson. U. of Ala. Pr. 1992 ISBN 0-8173-0590-4. In retelling a New Testament story, Tolstoy substituted Orthodox officials for Pharisees, and, not surprisingly, the radical Christian novelist was eventually excommunicated from the Russian Orthodox church.

Ugolnik, Anthony. *The Illuminating Icon.* Eerdmans 1989 $18.95. ISBN 0-8028-3652-6. Ugolnik, a member of the Greek Orthodox church, clears up misperceptions that Americans have about the Orthodox, the practices of which, says Ugolnik, can revitalize American Christianity.

Ware, Timothy. *Orthodox Church.* Viking Penguin 1963 $6.95. ISBN 0-14-020592-6. Highly regarded because, as a convert, he knows the stumbling blocks to Western appreciation of the ornate and "Byzantine" character of Orthodoxy.

CHRONOLOGY OF AUTHORS

Luther, Martin. 1483–1546
Zwingli, Huldrych. 1484–1531
Cranmer, Thomas. 1489–1556
Ignatius of Loyola, St. 1491–1556
Menno Simons. 1496?–1561
Knox, John. c.1505–1572

Calvin, John. 1509–1564
Teresa of Avila, St. 1515–1582
Edwards, Jonathan. 1703–1758
Wesley, John. 1703–1791
Newman, John Henry, Cardinal. 1801–1890

Berdyaev, Nikolai A. 1874–1948
John XXIII, Pope. 1881–1963
Barth, Karl. 1886–1968
Tillich, Paul Johannes. 1886–1965
Niebuhr, Reinhold. 1892–1971
Day, Dorothy. 1897–1980
Lewis, C(live) S(taples). 1898–1963
Bonhoeffer, Dietrich. 1906–1945
Weil, Simone. 1909–1943

Merton, Thomas. 1915–1968
Graham, William Franklin. 1918–
Daly, Mary. 1928–
Gutierrez, Gustavo. 1928–
Küng, Hans. 1928–
King, Martin Luther, Jr. 1929–1968
Ruether, Rosemary Radford. 1936–
Cone, James H. 1938–

BARTH, KARL. 1886–1968

Up every morning to the strains of WOLFGANG AMADEUS MOZART (see Vol. 3), to bed each night after an evening of beer and cigars with his students—it is hard to believe that the Basel theologian was probably the most prolific writer Christendom has ever produced. His gigantic *Church Dogmatics* runs well over 12,000 pages in English translation, yet there is also a great body of occasional writing, tossed off in his spare time, it would seem. Indeed, Barth would be worthy of mention if only for his first published work, a commentary on "The Epistle to the Romans."

In 1918, when he published this study, Barth was a young pastor in his native Switzerland. The guns of World War I could still be heard, their angry shells destroying, perhaps forever, the liberal optimism of Continental theology. Where was the progress young Barth had learned about from Harnack in Berlin? Where was human rationality, dispelling the noisome holes of ignorance and superstition, when the great leaders of Christendom descended to the barbarity of trench warfare? Turning to St. Paul's greatest epistle, as ST. AUGUSTINE OF HIPPO and MARTIN LUTHER had before him, Barth clutched it, he said, like a man clutching at a rope when he is falling, only to discover that the rope is attached to the church bell and he has just awakened the city from its slumbers.

He secured a post at the University of Bonn, but Hitler objected to his work with the Confessing Church (see DIETRICH BONHOEFFER), and he was forced to return to his own country, there to produce all his great tomes. Turning theologians from their rational optimism, Barth has driven them to consider again the power of the Word of God: that acted, spoken, inscripturated, incarnated Word was always his chief theme. Against it, all human pride and pretension, all schemes for utopian societies, all theologies based on anything other than the Bible and Christ have proved transient. His objectors reply that his God is too far away (like SØREN KIERKEGAARD, he spoke of the "infinite qualitative distinction" between God and man), that he ignores scientific advances, that he cares little for dialogue with other religions. But they never complain of lack of erudition or ecumenical concern. To some he is the greatest theologian the church has produced. He died as he had hoped, with his *Dogmatics* still unfinished.

BOOKS BY BARTH

Church Dogmatics: The Doctrine of God. 1936–69. Trans. by Geoffrey W. Bormiley and others. 12 vols. Bks. Intl. VA 1956–1977 $44.95 ea. This is a portion of Barth's major work, occupying his whole life, even as he churned out volume after volume of occasional writings.

The Epistle to the Romans. 1919. Trans. by Edwyn C. Hoskyns. OUP 6th ed. 1968 $14.95.
ISBN 0-19-500294-6. Neo-orthodox theology began with this volume, just as the
Protestant Reformation began with Luther's studies on Romans.

The Humanity of God. 1956. Trans. by John N. Thomas and Thomas Weiser. Westminster
John Knox 1960 $6.99. ISBN 0-8042-0612-0. A helpful corrective to some of the
Church Dogmatics.

A Karl Barth Reader. Ed. by Rolf Erler and Reiner Marquard. Trans. by Geoffrey
Bromiley. Eerdmans 1986 $10.99. ISBN 0-8028-0190-0. This short introduction to
Barth's work contains some pieces that are otherwise not easily accessible to those
who do not read German.

BOOKS ABOUT BARTH

Bromiley, Geoffrey W. *An Introduction to the Theology of Karl Barth.* Eerdmans 1979
$24.95. ISBN 0-567-29054-9. Who better to interpret Barth than his faithful
translator, a theologian in his own right?

Busch, Eberhard. *Karl Barth: His Life from Letters and Autobiographical Texts.* Trans. by
John Bowden. Fortress Pr. 1979 o.p. In his declining years Barth chose Busch for
this work, and he has performed it well.

Hunsinger, George. *How to Read Karl Barth: The Shape of His Theology.* OUP 1993 repr.
of 1990 ed. $14.95. ISBN 0-19-508369-5. Barth would have been taken aback at the
notion of an "authoritative" reading of his work, but this *is* a reliable, clear, and
insightful interpretation by a longtime Barth interpreter.

McKim, Donald, ed. *How Karl Barth Changed My Mind.* Bks. Demand repr. of 1986 ed.
$51.00. ISBN 0-8357-4365-9. This collection of essays demonstrates the enormous
influence of Barth, extending as it does even to theologians in fundamental
disagreement with his work.

BERDYAEV, NIKOLAI A. 1874–1948

The Russian philosopher and spiritual thinker Nikolai A. Berdyaev was born
in Kiev in the Ukraine, the scion of a privileged family with French royal blood
on his mother's side. Early in his youth, Berdyaev began to regard the world
about him as illusory, and he considered himself part of another, "real" world.
The consciousness of his spiritual aptitude—an eschatological and mystical
yearning—found expression in later writing.

Berdyaev became interested in Marxism while attending Kiev University and
eventually was expelled and banished to northern Russia because of his radical
political activities. In the north, he abandoned Marxism and began religious
study, continuing this pursuit in Heidelberg, Germany, after he was released. In
1905 he returned to Russia and became a leading intellectual in St. Petersburg.
He soon fell into disfavor with the czarist government, however, because of his
criticism of the Russian Orthodox church.

Following the Russian Revolution, Berdyaev was named professor of philosophy at the University of Moscow. However, because he continued to uphold
religious beliefs and began to criticize the Communist regime, he was
imprisoned and then exiled. In exile, he traveled first to Berlin and then to
Paris, where he lived the rest of his life and wrote many of his greatest works,
including *The Bourgeois Mind and Other Essays* (1934), *Freedom and the Spirit*
(1935), *The Fate of Man in the Modern World* (1935), *The Destiny of Man* (1937),
and *The Realm of Spirit and the Realm of Caesar* (1951).

Berdyaev believed that life in one world was flat; he sought transcendence
and believed that the human spirit strives toward the unlimited and the infinite.
He held that to live only in the secular realm is to deny the realm of the spirit,
and such restriction was contrary to his ideas of freedom, creativity, and hope.
Only a Christian outlook, as embodied in his Russian Orthodox tradition, could

embrace both heaven and earth and lead toward an understanding of the kingdom of God. The truth, he asserted, was not the result of a rational quest but the result of "a light which breaks through from the transcendent world of the spirit." Berdyaev viewed the task of humans as stewardship toward God's end— a view that called for a total reevaluation of present values and lifestyle. Thus, for him, the Christian outlook was far more revolutionary than Marxism. According to Berdyaev, the Christian gospel pointed to an ethic of redemption culminating in the coming of the kingdom of God, a kingdom based on love rather than rights and rules. He felt that the truth of the spiritual life cannot conform completely to earthly life. As a result, there never was or could be a Christian state, Christian family, or Christian learning, because in the kingdom of God there is no state, no family, no teaching, nor any other aspects of life governed by law.

The basic idealism in Berdyaev's thinking led him to a serious devaluation of this world. Nevertheless, his lasting influence as a Christian philosopher lies in his ability to stimulate dialogue among different cultures and patterns of thought.

BOOKS BY BERDYAEV

The Destiny of Man. Ayer 1937 o.p.
Dream and Reality: An Essay in Autobiography. Trans. by Katherine Lampert. Macmillan 1951 o.p.

BOOK ABOUT BERDYAEV

Calian, Carnegie Samule. *Berdyaev's Philosophy of Hope: A Contribution to Marxist-Christian Dialogue.* Minneapolis 1968 o.p. Contains a complete list of Berdyaev's works.

BONHOEFFER, DIETRICH. 1906–1945

Born in Breslau, Germany, now part of Poland, Dietrich and his twin sister, Sabine, were raised in a home where the intellect was encouraged. His father was a physician and professor of psychiatry at the University of Berlin. Scholars like the famous church historian Adolph von Harnack, Ernst Troeltsch, theologian and sociohistorian, and MAX WEBER (see Vol. 3), a founder of modern sociology, were guests of his parents. A precocious student, he decided early on the church and theology as his life's work, evidencing a degree of independence of thought that was at odds with the reverence in which his fellow students held their professors. He was a product of liberal studies, but was much influenced by KARL BARTH's recovery of Orthodoxy, an influence evident all through his writings.

IIis doctoral dissertation, *Sanctorum Communio: A Dogmatic Investigation of the Sociology of the Church*, was published in 1930, by which time he was teaching theology at the University of Berlin. Then followed a year's study in the United States (he liked the social concern of American students, but not their disdain of theology) and leadership of the World Alliance of Churches, where his flair for languages and his genial disposition won him many friends. These American and British friends tried unsuccessfully to dissuade him from returning to Germany after the rise of Hitler in 1932. But he went back, and, joining the so-called Confessing Church of those who resisted "Germanizing" the church, he conducted an illegal seminary in Finkenwalde. Out of this experience came his *Life Together*, and out of his struggles to encourage

Christians to resist the Nazis came his study of the Sermon on the Mount, *The Cost of Discipleship* (trans. 1948).

Although he escaped military duty by joining the intelligence service, he was eventually arrested and imprisoned by the gestapo and was linked to the attempt on Hitler's life, as were his brother Klaus and friends of the family who occupied high posts in the military. His *Letters and Papers from Prison* (trans. 1953), his testimony of faith, gave the American death of God movement the term "religionless Christianity." Together with a few others, he was killed at Flössenburg prison, where the prison doctor wrote of him: "I have hardly ever seen a man die so entirely submissive to the will of God." Although some interpreters of his work concentrate on his undeveloped idea of religionless Christianity, he is probably best understood as a radical theologian of the Word of God.

BOOKS BY BONHOEFFER

The Cost of Discipleship. Peter Smith 1984 $19.25. ISBN 0-8446-5960-6. His major work on the Sermon on the Mount.

Letters and Papers from Prison. Macmillan 1972 $8.95. ISBN 0-02-083420-0. Here are his thoughts from the concentration camp on religionless Christianity.

Life Together. HarpC 1976 $7.95. ISBN 0-06-060851-X. Only 120 pages, but it allows the new reader to see the radical commitment that Hitler caused Christians to make.

Meditating on the Word. Ed. and trans. by David McI.Gracie. Cowley Pubns. 1986 $8.95. ISBN 0-936384-41-7. Illustrates how Bonhoeffer's approach to the Bible poses a vital alternative to the biblicist and historical critic alike.

BOOKS ABOUT BONHOEFFER

Bethge, Eberhard. *Costly Grace: An Illustrated Biography of Dietrich Bonhoeffer.* Trans. by Rosaleen Ockenden. HarpC 1979 $4.95. ISBN 0-06-060773-4. An abbreviated version of Bethge's magisterial biography of Bonhoeffer.

————. *Dietrich Bonhoeffer.* HarpC 1977 o.p. This is the definitive biography of the scholar, martyr, and friend, by one who knew Bonhoeffer well and has edited most of his works.

Morris, Kenneth. *Bonhoeffer's Ethic of Discipleship: A Study in Social Psychology, Political Thought, and Religion.* Pa. St. U. Pr. 1986 $22.50. ISBN 0-271-00428-2. Argues that the ambivalence towards authority demonstrated by Bonhoeffer within the context of his family is reflected in his later emphasis on Christian discipleship and his opposition to Nazi tyranny.

CALVIN, JOHN. 1509–1564

Born Jean Cauvin in Noyon, Picardy, France, John Calvin was only a boy when MARTIN LUTHER first raised his challenge concerning Indulgences. Calvin was enrolled at the age of 14 at the University of Paris, where he received preliminary training in theology and became an elegant Latinist. However, following the dictates of his father, he left Paris at the age of 19 and went to study law, first at Orléans, then at Bourges, in both of which centers the ideas of Luther were already creating a stir.

On his father's death, Calvin returned to Paris, began to study Greek, the language of the New Testament, and decided to devote his life to scholarship. In 1532 he published a commentary on SENECA's *De Clementia*, but the following year, after experiencing a "sudden conversion," he was forced to flee Paris for his religious views. The next year was given to the study of Hebrew in Basel and to writing the first version of his famous *Institutes of the Christian Religion*, which he gave to the printer in 1535.

The rest of his life—except for a forced exile of three years—he spent in Geneva, where he became chief pastor, without ever being ordained. When he died, the city was solidly on his side, having almost become what one critic called a "theocracy." By then the fourth and much-revised edition of his *Institutes* had been published in Latin and French, commentaries had appeared on almost the whole Bible, treatises had been written on the Lord's Supper, on the Anabaptists, and on secret Protestants under persecution in France. Thousands of refugees had come to Geneva, and the city—energized by religious fervor—had found room and work for them. Though Calvin was sometimes bitter in his denunciation of those who disagreed with him, intolerant of other points of view, and absolutely sure he was right on the matter of predestination, he was nonetheless one of the great expounders of the faith. From his work the Reformed tradition had its genesis, and from his genius continues to refresh itself.

BOOKS BY CALVIN

Calvin: Institutes of the Christian Religion. Ed. by John T. McNeill. Trans. by Ford Lewis Battles. 2 vols. Westminster John Knox 1960 $40.00. ISBN 0-664-22028-2. Calvin's major theological work.

Calvin: Theological Treatises. Ed. by J.K.S. Reid. Westminster John Knox 1978 o.p. Most shorter writings, translated with notes, including church ordinances, catechisms, church visitation orders, his reply to Cardinal Sadoleto, and more.

Calvin's Commentaries. 22 vols. Baker Bk. repr. 1979 $595.00. ISBN 0-8010-2440-4. For the Old Testament only, nineteenth-century translations of the commentaries are available in English.

Calvin's New Testament Commentaries. Ed. by David W. Torrance and Thomas F. Torrance. 12 vols. Eerdmans 1960 $260.00. ISBN 0-8028-2053-0. Unlike the case with Luther, there is no English compendium of all of Calvin's works, thus the multiple listings.

Tracts and Treatises of the Reformed Faith. Ed. and trans. by Thomas F. Torrance and Henry Beveridge. 3 vols. Eerdmans 1958 o.p. A larger selection than Reid's work (see below).

BOOKS ABOUT CALVIN

Armstrong, Brian G. *Calvinism and the Amyraut Heresy: Protestant Scholasticism and Humanism in Seventeenth-Century France.* U. of Wis. Pr. 1969 $92.10. ISBN 0-8357-4741-7. Very early the tensions in predestinarian theology began to surface, as did questions of how the new Protestantism should be expressed theologically.

Balke, Willem. *Calvin and the Anabaptist Radicals.* Trans. by William J. Heynen. Bks. Demand repr. of 1982 ed. $87.50. ISBN 0-8357-7977-7. Examination of Calvin's polemics against religious left-wingers, somewhat biased toward Calvin.

Bouwsma, William. *John Calvin: A Sixteenth Century Portrait.* OUP 1987 $12.95. ISBN 0-19-505951-4. Shows how complexities and tensions in Calvin were played out with great sensitivity to the contemporary situation as well as with deference to Christian and humanist traditions; draws a wealth of information together to build a compelling thesis.

Cochrane, Arthur C. *Reformed Confessions of the Sixteenth Century.* Westminster John Knox 1966 o.p. Confessions from Switzerland, Germany, France, and Belgium influenced by Zwingli and Calvin.

Douglass, Jane D. *Women, Freedom, and Calvin.* Westminster John Knox 1985 o.p. Only serious study of Calvin from a feminist perspective by a major historian.

Dowey, Edward A. *The Knowledge of God in Calvin's Theology.* Col. U. Pr. 1952 o.p. Classic work on how God is known in Calvin's thought.

Duffield, Gervase, ed. *John Calvin.* Eerdmans 1966 o.p. Articles by major Calvin scholars on various aspects of his thought and activity.

Gerrish, Brian. *Grace and Gratitude: The Eucharistic Theology of John Calvin.* Augsburg Fortress 1992 $7.95. ISBN 0 8006 2368 4. One of the most astute Calvin scholars maintains that the whole of Calvin's theology has a eucharistic shape.

Graham, W. Fred. *The Constructive Revolutionary: John Calvin and His Socio-Economic Impact.* Mich. St. U. Pr. 1987 $9.95. ISBN 0-87013-249-0. After a brief history of Calvin in Geneva, this work summarizes Calvin's social and economic thought and assesses its influence.

Höpfl, Harro. *The Christian Polity of John Calvin.* Cambridge U. Pr. 1985 $19.95. ISBN 0-521-31638-3. Best work on Calvin's understanding of church and state.

Innes, William C. *Social Concern in Calvin's Geneva.* Pickwick 1983 $15.00. ISBN 0-915138-33-6. Less Calvin and more Geneva than in the work by Graham (above).

Leith, John H. *Introduction to the Reformed Tradition: A Way of Being in the Christian Community.* Westminster John Knox rev. ed. 1981 $13.99. ISBN 0-8042-0479-9. Complements McNeill (below) with more on theological development, liturgy, and impact on culture.

McDonnell, Kilian, *John Calvin, the Church and the Eucharist.* Bks. Demand repr. of 1967 ed. $105.00. ISBN 0-317-08461-5. Roman Catholic priest sympathetically examines doctrines of the church and of Christ's presence in Holy Communion.

McGrath, Alister. *A Life of John Calvin: A Study in the Shaping of Western Culture.* Blackwell Pubs. 1990 $29.95. ISBN 0-631-16398-0. A comprehensive introduction to the thought of Calvin and the impact of his ideas that impressively refers to contemporary interpretations, for example, on Calvinism and human rights.

McNeill, J. T. *The History and Character of Calvinism.* OUP 1979 $13.95. ISBN 0-19-500743-3. This is the simple best overview of Calvinism's later history, including Huguenots, Presbyterians, and others in the Reformed churches.

Monter, E. William. *Calvin's Geneva.* Krieger 1975 repr. of 1967 ed. o.p. Good for relations between church and state, Calvin and city government in Geneva.

Muller, Richard A. *Christ and the Decree: Christology and Predestination in Reformed Theology from Calvin to Perkins.* Labyrinth Pr. 1986 $30.00. ISBN 0-8010-6231-4. Best place to examine predestination in Calvin and his followers.

Parker, T. H. *John Calvin: A Biography.* Westminster John Knox 1976 $10.95. ISBN 0-939464-39-X. By all accounts a top-flight biography.

Reid, W. S., ed. *John Calvin: His Influence in the Western World. Contemporary Evangelical Perspectives Ser.* Zondervan 1982 o.p. Unique collection of articles on Calvinistic influence on various Western nations.

Richard, Lucien J. *The Spirituality of John Calvin.* Westminster John Knox 1974 o.p. By a Roman Catholic, a careful study of Calvin's piety or Christian "lifestyle."

Selinger, Suzanne. *Calvin against Himself: An Inquiry in Intellectual History.* Shoe String 1984 $32.50. ISBN 0-208-01948-0. A psychological study of Calvin by an art historian that has raised controversy.

Wendel, François. *Calvin: Origins and Development of His Religious Thought.* Trans. by Philip Mairet. Labyrinth Pr. 1987 $14.95. ISBN 0-939464-44-6. Classic study and one of the first works a student should read on Calvin, along with Parker's biography (see above).

Wolterstorff, Nicholas. *Until Justice and Peace Embrace.* Eerdmans 1983 $14.95. ISBN 0-8028-1980-X. Although a philosophy of economics in the modern world, this gives an excellent account of Calvin's social thought and its economic consequences.

CONE, JAMES H. 1938–

A leading African American theologian and the preeminent advocate of black theology, James H. Cone was born in Fordyce, Arkansas. Cone came of age during the civil rights movement, and he was drawn to the black power movement that gained prominence in the late 1960s. Rejecting the nonviolence of MARTIN LUTHER KING, JR., Cone moved to join theology with the militant, separatist vision of MALCOLM X, with its espousal of forceful societal change to achieve racial equality. Cone's book *Black Theology and Black Power* (1969) eloquently equated black power with the political and spiritual liberation of black Americans. In it, he equated blackness as symbolic of oppression and whiteness as symbolic of the oppressors. Cone continued his teachings of what soon became known as "black theology" in a second book, *A Black Theology of Liberation* (1971), which strongly condemned racism and oppression.

During the 1970s, Cone became a seminal force in the development of liberation theologies in Third World countries. Their concern for involving churches and church leadership in social and political movements aimed at mitigating the poverty and misery of people in developing nations closely paralleled Cone's own philosophy. Beginning in 1976, he became an important figure in the Ecumenical Association of Third World Theologians.

Cone's association with liberation theologies also broadened and transformed his vision of Christian theology. In *Crosscurrents*, published in 1977, he strongly articulated the view that Christian theology must move beyond reaction to white racism in America. It must, indeed, encompass all of humanity, undifferentiated by race or national groupings.

Cone joined the faculty of Union Theological Seminary in 1969 and was appointed to the distinguished Charles A. Biggs chair of systematic theology in 1977.

BOOKS BY CONE

Black Theology and Black Power. Harper SF 1969 $5.95. ISBN 0-8164-2003-3
A Black Theology of Liberation. Orbis Bks. 1990 $14.95. ISBN 0-88394-685-5
For My People. Orbis Bks. 1984 $16.95. ISBN 0-88344-106-3
God of the Oppressed. Harper SF 1984 $14.00. ISBN 0-8164-2607-4
Martin and Malcolm in America. Orbis Bks. 1991 $22.95. ISBN 0-88344-721-5. Martin Luther King, Jr., and Malcolm X as complementary and converging modes of political thought and liberation philosophy.
My Soul Looks Back. Orbis Bks. 1986 $11.95. ISBN 0-88344-355-4
The Spirituals and the Blues: An Interpretation. Orbis Bks. 1991 repr. of 1972 ed. $13.95. ISBN 0-88344-747-9. The African American experience through their music.

CRANMER, THOMAS. 1489–1556

Thomas Cranmer, the English prelate and archbishop of Canterbury, was born in Aslacton in Nottinghamshire. In 1503 he was sent to study at Jesus College, Cambridge University, where he obtained a fellowship. Forced to forfeit this fellowship because of his marriage to "black Joan" of the Dolphin Tavern, he regained it within a year when she died.

Cranmer took holy orders in 1523. Six years later, he left Cambridge because of the plague and went to Waltham, where he came to the attention of King Henry VIII because of his suggestion that Henry submit the question of his divorce from Catherine of Aragon to a debate by universities throughout Christian Europe. Cranmer subsequently became a counsel in this suit and was then appointed royal chaplain and archdeacon of Taunton. In 1533 he was made archbishop of Canterbury and soon after declared Catherine's marriage to Henry null and void. Throughout the remainder of Henry's reign, he was subservient to the will of the king, annulling Henry's marriage to Anne Boleyn, divorcing him from Anne of Cleves, and informing the king of Catherine Howard's premarital affairs.

Under Henry VIII, Cranmer had been slowly drifting into Protestantism; upon the king's death, he was quickly swept into great religious changes. While serving as archbishop under Edward VI, Cranmer shaped the doctrinal and liturgical transformation of the Church of England, placing the English Bible in churches and, in 1552, revising the *Book of Common Prayer*. Shortly after the Roman Catholic queen Mary I assumed the throne, however, Cranmer was tried and convicted of treason and heresy and condemned to be burned at the stake. Before being put to death, he recanted his errors and retracted all he had written. While on the stake, he reportedly thrust his right hand into the flame and cried, "This hath offended! Oh this unworthy hand!"

In addition to *The Book of Common Prayer*, Cranmer wrote a number of other works, including the *Reformatio Legum Ecclesiasticarum* (1571) and *A Defence of the Doctrine of the Sacrament* (1550).

BOOK BY CRANMER

The Work of Thomas Cranmer. Ed. by G. E. Duffield. Fortress Pr. 1965 o.p.

BOOKS ABOUT CRANMER

Hughes, Philip E. *Faith and Works: Cranmer and Hooker on Justification*. Morehouse Pubs. 1982 $7.95. ISBN 0-8192-1315-2
Pollard, Albert F. *Thomas Cranmer and the English Reformation 1489–1556*. AMS Pr. repr. of 1927 ed. $42.50. ISBN 0-404-19905-4

DALY, MARY. 1928–

America's leading feminist theologian, Mary Daly was born in Schenectady, New York. After receiving her Ph.D. from St. Mary's College/Notre Dame University in 1954, she taught at the University of Fribourg in Switzerland, where she also earned doctorates in theology and philosophy. Since 1966 she has been a member of Boston College's theology department.

Daly was a pioneer in the feminist movement that began in the late 1960s. As a theologian and polemicist, she articulated what she termed "the spiritual dimension of women's liberation." In *The Church and the Second Sex* (1968), she targeted the patriarchal dominance of Catholicism and the Catholic church, decrying its oppression of the true nature of women and demanding an end to its androcentric (male gender) teachings and theology. Unsurprisingly, the Church condemned her work, and she was granted tenure at Boston College only after pressures generated by student protests and the media. Radicalized by her experiences, she evolved from being a reformist Catholic to a post-Christian radical feminist.

Daly's *Beyond God the Father* (1973) openly challenged the patriarchal structure of all religions as defining the universal oppression of women in all societies. She rejected the gender attribution of God and reinterpreted the Second Coming as reference to women's newfound roles in societal affairs. She also insistently identified the women's movement as key to eliminating the sexist society created by patriarchal religion.

Increasingly, Daly's focus shifted from religion to society as the determining force in defining women's enforced "inferiority." With this shift came an investigation and reinvention of language to combat gender discrimination. For example, in *Gyn-Ecology* (1978) and *Pure Lust* (1984), Daly explored language usage and what she regarded as the myths by which patriarchal thinking had long held women hostage. In these writings, she invented a new feminist vocabulary, which she effectively invoked to strengthen feminist philosophy.

BOOKS BY DALY

Beyond God the Father: Toward a Philosophy of Women's Liberation. Beacon Pr. 1985 $13.00. ISBN 0-8070-1503-2. A bitter, careful analysis and attack on patriarchy in Christian thought and practice.

The Church and the Second Sex. Beacon Pr. 1985 repr. of 1968 ed. $13.00. ISBN 0-8070-1101-0

Gyn-Ecology: The Metaethics of Radical Feminism. Beacon Pr. 1990 $16.00. ISBN 0-8070-1511-3. Characterized by Daly as "a Thunderbolt of Rage I hurled into the world . . ."

Natural Knowledge of God in the Philosophy of Jacques Maritain. Catholic Book Agency 1966 o.p.

Pure Lust: Elemental Feminist Philosophy. Harper SF 1992 $16.00. ISBN 0-06-250208-5

Webster's First New Intergalactic Wickedary of the English Language. Ed. by Jane Caputi. Beacon Pr. 1987 $18.00. ISBN 0-8070-6733-4. A lexicon that revamps the English language in the light of nonpatriarchal consciousness.

DAY, DOROTHY. 1897–1980

Dorothy Day has been described as "the most significant, interesting, and influential person in the history of American Catholicism" (David O'Brien, *Commonweal*). After leading a bohemian life as a young woman, Day turned to the Catholic church knowing it meant the end for her common-law marriage to a devout atheist. As a woman with socialistic, anarchistic leanings, Day met Peter Maurin, a man rooted in Catholic traditions, and together they founded the *Catholic Worker.* As a journalist, Day wrote about topics ranging from labor disputes to pacifism to motherhood. A social activist, she was last arrested at the age of 75 as a participant in a strike by the United Farm Workers. As part of the Catholic Worker movement, she helped to establish over a hundred Houses of Hospitality. Living in poverty among the poor, Day detested being called a saint. As a saint she could be dismissed as embodying an impossible ideal; Day simply believed that the world could change for the better if people would practice Christian love.

BOOKS BY DAY

Dorothy Day: Selected Writings. Ed. by Robert Ellsberg. Orbis Bks. 1992 repr. of 1984 ed. $15.95. ISBN 0-88344-802-5. A sizable anthology that draws both from Day's journalistic articles and her books; contains, for example, her account of a brief stay in jail.

From Union Square to Rome. Ayer 1978 repr. of 1938 ed. $17.00. ISBN 0-405-10815-X. A brief story of her conversion from atheistic Marxism to Catholic communism.

The Long Loneliness: An Autobiography. HarpC 1981 $12.00. ISBN 0-06-061751-9. Her autobiography, although written a bit early in her life. Introduction by Daniel Berrigan.

Therese. Templegate 1979 $9.95. ISBN 0-87243-090-1. Not a scholarly biography, but a loving yet sober account of the life of a nineteenth-century saint, Thérèse of Lisieux. Day suggests that the appeal of the "little Flower" lies in her ordinariness and that Thérèse's simple spirituality is a key to social transformation.

BOOKS ABOUT DAY

Coles, Robert. *Dorothy Day: A Radical Devotion.* Addison-Wesley 1989 $9.57. ISBN 0-201-07974-7. Draws heavily from over 50 hours of taped conversations with Day, presenting a wide array of questions, such as What was it like to raise a daughter in a hospitality house? How would Day, a pacifist, deal with Hitler? What novels help us to understand Day?

Ellis, Marc H. *Peter Maurin: Prophet in the Twentieth Century.* Paulist Pr. 1981 o.p. This Saint Francis in modern times was Day's right hand in their House of Hospitality; Day's words on his death must be read.

Klejment, Anne, and Alice Klejment. *Dorothy Day and the Catholic Worker: Bibliography and Index.* Garland 1985 $62.00. ISBN 0-8240-9045-4. Simply a listing of all her editorials and articles, cross-indexed, for the specialist.

Miller, William D. *Dorothy Day: A Biography.* HarpC 1984 o.p. Justly praised biography.

————. *A Harsh and Dreadful Love*. Doubleday 1974 o.p. The story of the Catholic
   Worker movement, of which Day and Peter Maurin were the spark and the drive.
O'Connor, June. *The Moral Vision of Dorothy Day: A Feminist Perspective*. Crossroad NY
   1991 $16.95. ISBN 0-8245-1080-1. Clearly written reflections on connections
   between Day and (later) feminism. Noting Day's criticisms of some forms of
   feminism, O'Connor nevertheless contends that there are significant affinities, e.g.,
   in Day's commitment to an ethic of care.
Roberts, Nancy. *Dorothy Day and the Catholic Worker*. State U. NY Pr. 1985 $14.95. ISBN
   0-87395-939-6. Gives a detailed and insightful picture not only of issues addressed by
   Day as primary journalist of the newspaper, but also of dynamics within the *Catholic
   Worker* as a movement.

EDWARDS, JONATHAN. 1703–1758

American theologian and metaphysician Jonathan Edwards was born in
Windsor, Connecticut. Often called "the last Calvinist," he is widely regarded
among scholars as one of the most creative minds ever grown on American soil.
At the age of 13, Edwards entered Yale University and four years later had a
mystical religious experience, which he described much later in his "Personal
Narrative" (1740). In 1729 he took charge of a Puritan congregation in
Northampton, Massachusetts, and he soon gained a wide following as a result of
his forceful preaching. Among his most famous sermons was *Sinners in the
Hands of an Angry God* (1741), which exhorted the necessity of salvation and
reminded listeners of the eternal torments that awaited sinners.

Influenced by thinkers such as ISAAC NEWTON (see also Vol. 5) and JOHN
LOCKE, Edwards saw the world in terms of sense impressions from which ideas
are derived and in terms of natural and immutable laws reflecting the
perfection and absolute sovereignty of God. He believed that, since ideas are a
result of sense impressions, humans achieve moral grace through the senses
rather than through will or reason. In his "Treatise on Grace," (published
posthumously in 1865), he distinguishes between "common grace" and
"supernatural grace"; the latter accompanies religious conversion and bestows
a new sense of spiritual awareness. This doctrine proposed a radical idea in
Puritan thought: conversion was a clear and obvious event that involved
emotions more than reason. At the time, membership in the Puritan church and
communion were open to anyone who wished to join, a policy that reflected the
belief that communion was a means of grace even for individuals who were not
yet renewed in heart or reborn in spirit. Edwards, however, believed that
communion should be administered cnly to those who had already experienced
conversion. This belief brought him into conflict with his parish in Northampton and, in 1750, he was forced to resign. His beliefs about the place of the
emotions in religious experience made him one of the most important figures in
the Great Awakening, a period of religious revival that swept through colonial
America in the middle of the eighteenth century.

The latter part of Edwards's life was spent as a missionary to Native
Americans in New England's frontier region and, for a very brief time before his
death, as president of the College of New Jersey (now Princeton University).
During this time, he wrote some of his most important works, including *A
Careful and Strict Enquiry into the Freedom of Will* (1754), which set forth
metaphysical and ethical arguments for determinism, and *The Great Christian
Doctrine of Original Sin Defended* (1758).

BOOKS BY EDWARDS

A Careful and Strict Enquiry into the Freedom of Will. 1754. Rprt. Serv. 1992 $75.00. ISBN
   0-7812-2771-2

The Great Christian Doctrine of Original Sin Defended. 1758. Rprt. Serv. 1992 $75.00.
   ISBN 0-7812-2772-0

Sinners in the Hands of an Angry God. 1741. Rprt. Serv. 1992 $75.00. ISBN 0-7812-2765-8

The Works of Jonathan Edwards. 2 vols. Banner of Truth 1979 $99.95. ISBN 0-85151-216-X. Includes parts of Edwards's work that have been available only to archivists who could decipher his faded handwriting.

BOOKS ABOUT EDWARDS

Aldridge, Alfred Owen. *Jonathan Edwards. Great Amer. Thinkers Ser.* Twayne 1966 o.p. Short and readable introduction in which the author manages to capture the flavor of the man and his work.

Cherry, Conrad. *The Theology of Jonathan Edwards: A Reappraisal.* Ind. U. Pr. 1990 $12.95. ISBN 0-253-20559-X. Comprehensive study of Edwards's theology; contests the image of Edwards as dour and fanatical and puts Edwards's failure in Northampton in the context of broader developments in American religion.

Davidson, Edward H. *Jonathan Edwards: The Narrative of a Puritan Mind.* Bks. Demand repr. of 1968 ed. $43.80. ISBN 0-317-07848-8. Tells the story of the development of Edwards's thought by relating it to his biography.

De Lattre, Roland. *A Beauty and Sensibility in the Thought of Jonathan Edwards.* Bks. Demand repr. of 1968 ed. $66.10. ISBN 0-8357-8701-X. The new reader should read Aldridge (above) or Winslow (below) before tackling this book.

Hatch, Nathan, and Harry Stout. *Jonathan Edwards and the American Experience.* OUP 1988 $34.50. ISBN 0-19-506077-6. Surprisingly, perhaps, academic interest in Edwards has been steadily increasing during the past several decades; this volume contains work by several prominent Edwards scholars.

Holbrook, Clyde A. *The Ethics of Jonathan Edwards: Morality and Aesthetics.* U. of Mich. Pr. 1973 o.p. Edwards never separated beauty or morality from each other, or from God, giver of both; Holbrook digs deeply here, carrying on a debate with the other best book on the subject, Roland De Lattre's (see above).

Jenson, Robert. *America's Theologian: A Recommendation of Jonathan Edwards.* OUP 1988 $38.00. ISBN 0-19-504941-1. Proclaims Edwards as America's theologian because he goes beyond a dualism posed by Puritanism and Enlightenment.

Levin, David, ed. *Jonathan Edwards: A Profile.* Hill & Wang 1969 o.p. A curious book in a way, yet useful in that Levin allows Edwards to speak for himself, from diary extracts, and then prints some excellent articles by other writers, including some in this list.

Miller, Perry. *Jonathan Edwards. Amer. Men of Letters Ser.* Greenwood 1973 repr. of 1949 ed. $35.00. ISBN 0-8371-6551-2. Miller rediscovered the "New England mind," and he calls this the biography of the life of a mind.

Smith, Jonathan E. *Jonathan Edwards: Puritan, Preacher, Philosopher.* U. of Notre Dame Pr. 1993 $23.95. ISBN 0-268-01192-3. Particularly illuminating in describing Edwards's relationship to John Locke, written by a prominent expert on American philosophy.

Tracy, Patricia. *Jonathan Edwards, Pastor: Religion and Society in Eighteenth-Century Northampton. Amer. Century Ser.* Hill & Wang 1980 o.p. Here is the Northampton story told expertly, providing a slice of social history, full of real people.

Winslow, Ola E. *Jonathan Edwards, 1703–1758: A Biography.* Macmillan 1940 o.p. Though not devoid of theology, this is nonetheless a popular telling, and the book the general reader might begin with.

GRAHAM, WILLIAM FRANKLIN (BILLY). 1918–

Billy Graham has been America's foremost evangelist since the 1950s, and he is still going strong in the 1990s. Born in Charlotte, North Carolina, Graham studied at Florida Bible Institute (which is now Trinity College) and became an ordained minister of the Southern Baptist Church in 1940. He went to study anthropology at Wheaton College for a year in 1943, the same year that he was married to Ruth Bell. In 1944 Graham became the "first evangelist" of Youth for Christ. His first notable preaching crusade was in 1949. Since that time, he has conducted his religious crusades in many nations on all continents. His fiery and persuasive preaching and his great facility with mass audiences and the media have brought great success, fame, and international recognition. The Billy Graham Evangelical Association, which serves as a base of his worldwide crusades, publishes *Decision* magazine and produces printed material as well as material for radio, television, and film. Through his crusades and this association, Graham has helped to bring millions of people into the Christian fold. Graham's high visibility has also made him a friend and counselor for many high government officials. Although in recent years many evangelical figures have been plagued with scandal, Graham has remained a person of high integrity. His books include *Peace with God* (1952), *World Aflame* (1965), and *Angels* (1975).

BOOKS BY GRAHAM

Angels. Word Inc. 1991 $4.99. ISBN 0-8499-3299-8
Peace with God. Word Inc. 1984 o.p.
World Aflame. Word Inc. 1965 o.p.

BOOKS ABOUT GRAHAM

Ashman, Chuck. *The Gospel According to Billy.* Carol Pub. Group 1977 $8.95. ISBN 0-8184-0251-2. A journalistic look at the Graham message and the techniques used by Graham's evangelistic team, by an author who does not like Graham, nor what he terms the Jeu Bu$ine$$.
Bishop, Mary. *Billy Graham: America's Evangelist.* Putnam Pub. Group 1978 o.p. Lots of pictures and just enough text to tell the story.
Cornwell, Patricia. *A Time for Remembering: The Story of Ruth Bell Graham.* Walker & Co. 1985 $16.95. ISBN 0-8027-2501-5. Offers details of the Grahams' life together, such as how Ruth Graham managed their financial affairs.
Frady, Marshall. *Billy Graham: A Parable of American Righteousness.* Little 1979 o.p. A fairer and more able analysis than Ashman's (see above), because while Frady doesn't like many things Graham says, he likes and respects the man.
McLoughlin, William G. *Billy Graham: Revivalist in a Secular Age.* Ronald Pr. 1960 o.p. A historian of revivalism discusses Graham's place within that tradition; some of the author's judgments were made of necessity before Graham became somewhat of a statesman, more responsible in his dictates, especially after his entanglement in the Nixon affair.
Pollock, John. *To All Nations: The Billy Graham Story.* HarpC 1985 o.p. An authorized biography, a follow-up of an earlier volume by the same author.

GUTIERREZ, GUSTAVO. 1928–

A Peruvian Catholic priest, Gustavo Gutierrez was born to mestizo parents in a barrio of Lima, Peru. Often called the founder of liberation theology in Latin America, he studied philosophy at the University of Louvain in Belgium and took his doctorate in theology at the University of Lyon in France in 1959.

Returning to Lima in 1960, Gutierrez taught theology at the Catholic University in Lima. His own background and identification with the poor soon prompted him to work among the dispossessed peasant families crowding Lima's barrios. His experiences led to a break with the Catholic hierarchy and traditional church teachings in the 1960s and 1970s.

Gutierrez rejects the existing Catholic view of poverty. In his view, while God regarded all people as equals, he held a special concern for the impoverished and disinherited. Gutierrez believes that God not only supports the poor's struggle for justice but also wishes the teachings of his church to ensure their liberation. In theological terms, this entails liberation from unjust social classes, from a sense of fate, and from personal sin and guilt. Therefore, Gutierrez fiercely argues, the church has a duty to take the lead in redeeming society and helping end the social, political, and economic conditions that entrap Latin Americans in poverty. His forthright explication of these views in *A Theology of Liberation* (1971) brought him worldwide attention. Almost overnight, these beliefs helped shape both a religious and a political agenda known as "liberation theology," which has spread throughout Latin America.

Even as Gutierrez was criticized by church leaders and his ideas were labeled as Marxist-inspired by the dominant classes, liberation theology strengthened its hold. By the end of the 1980s the spread of democracy and improving social conditions in many Latin American countries seemed to validate Gutierrez's espousal of the church's activist role in society.

BOOKS BY GUTIERREZ

Liberation and Change (coauthored with Richard M. Shaull). Ed. by Ronald H. Stone. Westminster John Knox 1977 o.p.
On Job: God-Talk and the Suffering of the Innocent. Orbis Bks. 1987 o.p.
The Power of the Poor in History. Orbis Bks. 1983 $15.95. ISBN 0-88344-388-0
Praxis of Liberation and Christian Faith. Mex. Am. Cult. 1976 o.p.
A Theology of Liberation: History, Politics, and Salvation. Orbis Bks. 1988 $34.95. ISBN 0-88344-543-3
We Drink from Our Own Wells: The Spiritual Journey of a People. Orbis Bks. 1989 $13.95. ISBN 0-88344-707-X

BOOKS ABOUT GUTIERREZ

Brown, Robert McAfee. *Gustavo Gutierrez.* Orbis Bks. 1990 $16.95. ISBN 0-88344-597-2. A fascinating look at Gutierrez, his life, and his philosophy.
Cadoretti, Curt. *From the Heart of the People: The Theology of Gustavo Gutierrez.* Meyer Stone Bks. 1988 $14.95. ISBN 0-940989-18-2. Thoughtful study of Gutierrez in his Peruvian context, carefully elaborating the complex use of Marxism in his theology.
Ellis, Marc, and Otto Moduro, eds. *Expanding the View: Gustavo Gutierrez and the Future of Liberation Theology.* Orbis Bks. 1990 $16.95. ISBN 0-88344-690-1

IGNATIUS OF LOYOLA, ST. 1491–1556

Inigo Lopez de Loyola was born into a wealthy Basque family in northern Spain. Small but quick of mind and body, he won appointment as a page to a wealthy confidant and treasurer to King Ferdinand. Filling his mind with chivalrous and amorous adventures from popular books, he was fired with a militant ardor that was later to transfer readily from secular to religious activities. As a young man, he was cited several times for acts of violence. When the French invaded Navarre in 1521 and attacked Pamplona, Loyola counseled defense to the death, and during the subsequent bombardment one of his legs was broken and the other injured by a cannonball. The small garrison surrendered; Loyola's life changed abruptly.

Recovering from his wounds and the operations undergone to lengthen his broken leg, Ignatius (as he now began to call himself) turned to reading stories of the saints and of Christ. He quickly developed an aversion to worldly ideals and resolved to serve and imitate Christ alone. He lived in a cave in Manresa for 11 months in total poverty and there finished the first edition of his *Spiritual Exercises.* Though they were not finished to his satisfaction until 1541, he soon began to use them to help retreat leaders and penitents to structure their days of devotion.

After a brief visit to Jerusalem, he returned to Spain, where he continually fell afoul of the Inquisition. To escape its restrictions, he traveled to the University of Paris, took a master's degree in philosophy, and gathered a company of nine companions who, in 1540, were canonically confirmed by Pope Pius III as the Society of Jesus, which became known as the Jesuits. The next year he was elected superior-general for life. Loyola's amazing abilities as spiritual director, organizer, and money raiser are revealed in his massive correspondence and in the instant success of his new order. By the time of his death, the society numbered nearly 1,000 members. Already they were leaders in the Catholic Reformation, missionaries wherever Spanish and Portuguese ships sailed, and faculty for the many seminaries the church set up to counter the Protestant insistence on an educated ministry. Ignatius was canonized in 1622.

BOOKS BY ST. IGNATIUS

The Autobiography of St. Ignatius Loyola, with Related Documents. Trans. by Joseph F. O'Callaghan. Peter Smith 1974 o.p. His own account, well edited and translated.
Spiritual Exercises. Trans. by Louis J. Puhl. Loyola 1968 o.p. Many translations of and commentaries on this spiritual classic have been published over the years; these are fairly recent and readable.

BOOKS ABOUT ST. IGNATIUS

Brodrick, James. *The Origin of the Jesuits.* Greenwood 1971 repr. of 1940 ed. $45.00. ISBN 0-8371-5523-1. Good introduction for beginning students because the author curbs himself to about 275 pages of material on Loyola and his small band of proto-Jesuits.
_____. *St. Ignatius Loyola: The Pilgrim Years, 1491–1538.* FS&G 1956 o.p. Solid and adulatory, as befits one Jesuit writing about the founder of the Society of Jesus.
De Nicolas, Antonio. *Powers of Imagining: Ignatius de Loyola.* State U. NY Pr. 1986 $7.95. ISBN 0-88706-110-9. Contains translations of Ignatius's *Spiritual Exercises, Spiritual Diary, Autobiography,* as well as of his letters, and a lengthy introduction describing the hermeneutic of Ignatius, using his concentration on memory and on imagining as a focal point.
Rahner, Karl, and Paul Imhof. *Ignatius of Loyola.* HarpC 1979 o.p. An interpretive essay with splendid old engravings and color photographs.

JOHN XXIII, POPE. 1881–1963

Born Angelo Giuseppe Roncalli, the son of peasants who rented land as sharecroppers, Pope John XXIII early demonstrated intellectual abilities that saw him through seminary studies in Bergamo, near his home, and on to his ordination in 1904. For a number of years he worked with Catholic women's and youth organizations under the bishop of Bergamo. In World War I he served as a medical sergeant and as a chaplain and after the war was active in the Society for the Propagation of the Faith, with its headquarters in Rome. In 1925 he was appointed to the first of several diplomatic missions, first among the Catholic minority in Bulgaria, then in Turkey, where he set the precedent of introducing Turkish into the Mass, and in Greece, where during World War II military operations destroyed any opportunity he might have had to work with the Orthodox majority and confronted him with a hatred of Italians fueled by the Italian army's occupation of the country.

As the war began to heat up on French soil, he was appointed papal nuncio to France and arrived in Paris at the very end of 1944. There, for almost a decade, he worked with first the Germans and then the French government to heal the wounds of warfare, to keep the church intact through rapid changes of government, to keep Catholic schools alive, and to deal with the French bishops who saw the increasing secularization of the nation and the failing religious allegiance of the people as signs pointing to the need for radical new measures to propagate the faith. Nevertheless, it is true that the worker-priest movement, which he watched at first with approval, received its deathblow during his pontificate.

After serving as patriarch of Venice and being made cardinal (1953), he was elected by the College of Cardinals in 1958 to succeed Pius XII. The major accomplishment of his pontificate was the calling of the Second Vatican Council, whose arguments and decrees seemed revolutionary in their time (1962–65) and whose ripples continue to move the barque of Rome to this day. Thirty-nine non-Catholic observers attended with his blessing, special provision being made for translation from Latin documents and speeches, and it is perhaps not surprising that one of the first conciliar decrees was to allow the vernacular to replace Latin in the liturgy. He died of a gastric ulcer on June 3, 1963.

Books by Pope John XXIII

Journal of a Soul. Trans. by Dorothy White. Doubleday 1980 repr. of 1965 ed. o.p. His diary is necessary reading for those who want to understand the saintly revolutionary.

The Teachings of Pope John XXIII. Ed. by Michael Cinigo. Trans. by Arthur A. Coppotelli. Putnam Pub. Group 1967 o.p. All the essential encyclicals, letters, occasional teaching.

Books about Pope John XXIII

Bolton, R. *Living Peter: A Biographical Study of Pope John XXIII.* Humanities 1961 o.p. An unusual study, for it follows the pope in his earlier career and shows his relationships to Orthodoxy and to the Anglican Church.

Calvez, Jean-Yves. *The Social Thought of John XXIII: Mater et Magistra.* Trans. by George McKenzie. Greenwood 1977 $38.50. ISBN 0-8371-8711-7. Stresses the novelty of Pope John's teaching without neglecting its continuity with tradition.

Hebblethwaite, Peter. *Pope John XXIII: Shepherd of the Modern World.* Doubleday 1987 $10.95. ISBN 0-385-23537-2. The largest and most recent of the many studies of the great pope, and the author is a skilled interpreter of things Roman to English-speaking audiences.

Lercano, Giacomo, and Gabriele DeRosa. *John XXIII: Simpleton or Saint?* Trans. by Dorothy White. Franciscan Pr. 1968 $4.95. ISBN 0-8199-0055-9. Beginning with the premise that if the pope was a simpleton then he was not a saint, the authors demonstrate that the pope was not a simpleton but, in fact, had a good sense of the magnitude of the changes that his call for a council provoked.

KANT, IMMANUEL. 1724–1804

[See Chapter 6 in this volume.]

KIERKEGAARD, SØREN. 1813–1855

[See Chapter 6 in this volume.]

KING, MARTIN LUTHER, JR. 1929–1968 (Nobel Prize 1964)

Son and grandson of Baptist preachers, Martin Luther King, Jr., was born into a middle-class black family in Atlanta, Georgia. At Morehouse College his early concerns for social justice for African Americans were deepened by reading Henry David Thoreau's (see Vol. 1) essay "Civil Disobedience." He enrolled in Crozer Theological Seminary and there became acquainted with the Social

Gospel movement and the works of its chief spokesman, Walter Rauschen-busch. Mohandas Gandhi's practice of nonviolent resistance (*ahimsa*) became for him later a tactic for transforming love into social change.

After seminary, he postponed his ministry vocation by first earning a doctorate at Boston University School of Theology. There he discovered the works of Reinhold Niebuhr and was especially struck by Niebuhr's insistence that the powerless must somehow gain power if they are to achieve what is theirs by right. In the Montgomery bus boycott, it was by economic clout that African Americans broke down the walls separating the races, for without African American riders, the city's transportation system nearly collapsed.

The bus boycott took place in 1954, the year King and his bride, Coretta Scott, went to Montgomery, where he had been called to serve as pastor of the Dexter Avenue Baptist Church. Following the boycott, he founded the Southern Christian Leadership Conference (SCLC) to coordinate civil rights organizations. Working through African American churches, activists led demonstrations all over the South and drew attention, through television and newspaper reports, to the fact that nonviolent demonstrations by blacks were being suppressed violently by white police and state troopers. The federal government was finally forced to intervene and pass legislation protecting the right of African Americans to vote and desegregating public accommodations. For his nonviolent activism, King received the Nobel Peace Prize in 1964.

While organizing a "poor people's campaign" to persuade Congress to take action against poverty, King accepted an invitation to visit Memphis, Tennessee, where sanitation workers were on strike. There, on April 4, 1968, he was gunned down while standing on the balcony of his hotel. Though today King is the only religious leader, save Jesus, who has an "official day" in most states, and his nonviolent strategy to win racial equality was the major cause for rewriting the laws of the nation, not everyone admired him, as the reader can see from the bibliography below.

Book by King

A Testament of Hope: The Essential Writings of Martin Luther King, Jr. Ed. by James M. Washington. Harper SF 1986 $18.00. ISBN 0-06-064691-8. This really does have most of the essential writings: King's *Strength to Love* and *Stride toward Freedom* appear to be intact in this recent collection.

Books about King

Baldwin, Lewis. *To Make the Wounded Whole: Cultural Legacy of Martin Luther King, Jr.* Augsburg Fortress 1992 $16.95. ISBN 0-8006-2543-9. Includes a valuable discussion of King's influence on contemporary American theologians and ethicists, observes that King's message became more encompassing as time passed.

Bennett, Lerone, Jr. *What Manner of Man: A Biography of Martin Luther King, Jr., 1929–1968.* Johnson Chi. 1968 $17.95. ISBN 0-87485-027-4. This is the coffee-table King. There is also a nonillustrated paperback, same author, title, publisher, and date, but with more text.

Cone, James. *Martin and Malcolm and America: A Dream or a Nightmare.* Orbis Bks. 1991 $22.95. ISBN 0-88344-721-5. A fascinating comparison of King and Malcolm X that contends that their differences are often overstated.

Garrow, David J. *The FBI and Martin Luther King, Jr.* Viking Penguin 1983 $11.00. ISBN 0-14-006486-4. A trifle garish for serious scholarship, but seems to verify the conviction of King's followers that J. Edgar Hoover hated King more than he hated the Mafia.

King, Coretta S. *My Life with Martin Luther King, Jr.* H. Holt & Co. rev. ed. 1993 $16.95. ISBN 0-8050-2445-X. Published very hastily after King's assassination, this nevertheless catches the intimate King, although critics say it glosses over his weaknesses.

Lewis, David L. *King: A Biography. Blacks in the New World Ser.* U. of Ill. Pr. 2nd ed. 1978 $11.95. ISBN 0-252-00680-1. Very good, but written in the heat of the controversies immediately following his death; the reader might want to check Oates (below) for a more reflective account as well.

Lokos, Lionel. *House Divided: The Life and Legacy of Martin Luther King.* Arlington Pr. 1969 o.p. The death of King made him a martyr just as Lokos was researching and writing the great exposé of King, whom he considered a communist. Criticizes the man, his tactics, and his impact on the laws of the nation.

Oates, Stephen B. *Let the Trumpet Sound: The Life of Martin Luther King, Jr.* NAL-Dutton 1988 $5.99. ISBN 0-451-62350-9. This book is big at 500 pages, but reads well, by a sound scholar and biographer.

KNOX, JOHN. c.1505–1572

Scottish theologian and leader of the Reformation in Scotland, John Knox was born near Haddington in Lothian. After attending university, probably at St. Andrews, Knox returned to Haddington, where he entered the Catholic priesthood in about 1540. He also became tutor to the sons of several influential families with political ties to Protestant reformers.

Knox's sympathies for Reformation doctrines soon were revealed by his support of George Wishart, a Scottish Reformer who was put to death for heresy in 1546. During the years of political and religious turmoil in Scotland, Knox was captured by French forces in 1547 and held prisoner until 1549. From this experience, he emerged as the voice of the Scottish Reformation, convinced of his calling to defeat the Catholic church, which he now termed "the synagogue of Satan." After his release from prison, he worked with the Protestant regency ruling for Edward IV in England and helped shape *The Book of Common Prayer*. When the Catholic Mary Tudor came to the English throne in 1553, Knox left England and eventually moved to Geneva, where his strong Presbyterian beliefs were finally forged from the teachings of JOHN CALVIN.

In Calvin's "Bible Commonwealth" at Geneva, Knox had found the ideals of the true Protestant church. His mission became one of wiping out the vestiges of Catholicism in Scotland by leading the true church to enforce its strict religious beliefs and rules of conduct on individuals. To achieve this, Knox reasserted Calvin's conviction of the people's right to overthrow any ruler who attempts to enforce the supremacy of false doctrine (Catholicism) on their subjects.

In 1559 Knox returned to Scotland, where he led a group of Protestant nobles intent on ending the power of the Roman Catholic church and overthrowing Mary Stuart. He was now recognized as the leader of the Reform movement. Even before this, however, he had begun to encourage the organization of reformed congregations that assumed the authority to choose their own ministers and elders. Backed by the Scottish Parliament, which outlawed the celebration of Mass, he framed the Confession of Faith and summoned the first General Assembly of the Reformed Church. The articles of the Presbyterian faith that were established were modeled on Calvin's views on theology and church governance.

The arrival of Mary Queen of Scots in 1561 touched off years of conflict in Scotland that ended only with her forced abdication in 1567. During this period, Knox defied Mary's authority, denounced her private masses as a disguised attempt to restore outlawed Catholic worship, and tirelessly championed the doctrines of the Reformed church. By the time of Knox's death in 1572, Catholicism in Scotland had been vanquished. Knox's Reformed church now prevailed, resting firmly on the Calvinistic doctrine of predestination and the elect of God. And its severe strictures of right conduct and morality were permanently joined to the ascendant role of the congregation in church government.

BOOK BY KNOX

The Works of John Knox. 1846–64. 6 vols. Ed. by David Laing. AMS Pr. repr. of 1864 ed. $345.00. ISBN 0-404-52880-5. A work of distinguished scholarship that comprises the collected writings of the Reformer. *The History of the Reformation in Scotland* remains Knox's most important literary work.

BOOKS ABOUT KNOX

Cowan, Henry. *John Knox: The Hero of the Scottish Reformation.* AMS Pr. repr. of 1905 ed. $27.50. ISBN 0-404-01788-6

Dickinson, W. Croft, ed. *John Knox's History of the Reformation in Scotland.* 1979 o.p. An annotated edition of Knox's important book in modern English.

McEwen, James S. *The Faith of John Knox.* Westminster John Knox 1957 o.p. Analyzes Knox's religious views and their relation to those of other Reformers.

McCrie, Thomas. *The Life of John Knox.* AMS Pr. repr. of 1898 ed. $57.50. ISBN 0-404-19902-X

McGregor, Geddes. *The Thundering Scot.* Westminster Pr. 1957 o.p.

Muir, Edwin. *John Knox: Portrait of a Calvinist.* Ayer repr. of 1929 ed. $21.00. ISBN 0-8369-5656-7

Percy, Eustace. *John Knox.* Westminster Pr. 1965 o.p.

Reid, William S. *Trumpeter of God: A Biography of John Knox.* Macmillan 1982 o.p.

Ridley, Jasper G. *John Knox.* 1968 o.p. A well-researched biography, with a valuable bibliography.

KÜNG, HANS. 1928–

Hans Küng is Swiss and was born into a middle-class family. He studied in Rome for seven years, obtaining his licentiate in philosophy and theology from the Gregorian University there, and then receiving his doctorate in theology from the Catholic Institute in Paris. Since 1960 he has been a professor at Tübingen University, where he taught dogmatic and ecumenical theology until his permission to teach Catholic theology was removed as a consequence of statements judged to be contrary to official doctrine. Since 1980 he has taught at the University of Chicago and the University of Michigan, and occasionally in Europe as well.

His difficulties with the church began with the publication *The Church* (1967) and became very hot with the publication of *Infallible? An Inquiry* (1971). More recently, his *On Being Christian* (1977) has raised the question of whether his theology is not simply rational Protestant theology of the turn of the century. Official inquiries were held, statements were exchanged between Küng and the Conference of German Bishops, and the Rome-based Congregation for the Doctrine of the Faith, but no agreement was to be had. Küng continues to declare himself a loyal member of the Roman Catholic church and seems unlikely to leave its priesthood or to be excommunicated.

BOOKS BY KÜNG

The Church. Doubleday 1976 $6.95. ISBN 0-385-11367-6

The Christian Challenge. Trans. by Edward Quinn. Doubleday 1979 o.p. Since Küng is given to writing long books, it is good to have a shortened version of *On Being Christian,* one of his major theological works.

Does God Exist? An Answer for Today. Crossroad NY 1991 $22.95. ISBN 0-8245-1119-0. More than 800 pages of Küngiana, in which the reader can see how mightily the theologian wrestles with major nonreligious spokespersons.

Eternal Life? Life after Death as a Medical, Philosophical, and Theological Problem. Crossroad NY 1991 $16.95. ISBN 0-8245-1120-4. More temperate in space at 270 pages.

Global Responsibility: In Search of a New World Ethics. Trans. by John Bowden. Crossroad NY 1991 $18.95. ISBN 0-8245-1102-6. Drawing from his phenomenal knowledge, Küng argues against the view that all ethics are relative, maintaining that the magnitude of the problems facing us demands a renewed quest for a world ethic.

Infallible? An Inquiry. Doubleday 1983 o.p. It was this book that brought Küng into conflict with Rome, since he argues that Paul VI's encyclical against birth control, which was meant to be infallible teaching, has since been rejected by the church.

Küng in Conflict. Ed. and trans. by Leonard Swidler. Doubleday 1981 o.p. Here, in more than 600 pages, is the story of Küng's conflict with Rome.

Mozart: Traces of Transcendence. Eerdmans 1993 $9.99. ISBN 0-8028-0688-0. Like his mentor Karl Barth, Küng lovingly applies his theological acumen to Mozart.

Paradigm Change in Theology: A Symposium for the Future. (coauthored with David Tracy). Trans. by Margaret Köhl. Crossroad NY 1989 $34.50. ISBN 0-8245-0925-0. Includes several contributors from the University of Chicago and the University of Tübingen, perhaps the two main centers for academic theology at the time of the symposium.

Theology for the Third Millennium. Doubleday 1990 $12.95. ISBN 0-385-41125-1. Küng not only situates his proposals in relation to the conditions of "post-modernity" but also reflects anew on the work of Karl Barth, a theologian mistakenly thought of by some as premodern.

BOOK ABOUT KÜNG

LaCugna, Catherine M. *The Theological Methodology of Hans Küng.* Scholars Pr. GA 1982 $18.95. ISBN 0-89130-546-7

LESSING, GOTTHOLD EPHRAIM. 1729–1781

[SEE Chapter 6 in this volume.]

LEWIS, C(LIVE) S(TAPLES) (pseud. of Clive Hamilton). 1898–1963

C. S. (Jack) Lewis was born in Belfast, Northern Ireland, to a middle-class Protestant family. His father was a lawyer, his mother the daughter of an Anglican clergyman. Flora Hamilton Lewis died when Jack was 9 years old, but not before she had taught him the rudiments of Greek and Latin. He and his brother Warren had their early schooling at public (private) schools in England, but Jack persuaded his father to allow him to be privately educated by William Kirkpatrick, who, while preparing him rigorously in logic and languages, told Lewis's father that he had no talents except those of a scholar.

His schooling at Oxford was interrupted by military duty in World War I. Lewis served in the trenches and was wounded, as he says, by an English shell that fell short. Mustered out, he returned to Oxford and plunged into his studies, receiving "firsts" in Greats (classics and philosophy) and in English. He was then offered a fellowship in English at Magdalen College and thereafter crowded his writing into a busy schedule of lecturing and tutoring students who were facing exams.

Lewis became a believing Christian and re-entered the Anglican Church in 1931. Among those who helped him through atheism to theism and finally to classical Christian doctrine were the author and fellow scholar J.R.R. TOLKIEN (see Vol. 1), author of *The Hobbit* and *The Lord of the Rings*, and Owen Barfield, lawyer, theosophist, scholar, and author of many influential books. Not long after his conversion, Lewis's defenses of the faith began to appear: *Pilgrim's Regress* (1933) and *The Problem of Pain* (1940) were followed by the work that established his reputation as a shrewd observer of human nature, *The Screwtape Letters* (1942). Largely on the basis of that and other apologetical works, *Time* magazine placed him on its cover with the legend: "Oxford's C. S. Lewis, His Heresy: Christianity."

In 1954 Lewis was appointed professor of medieval and Renaissance literature at Cambridge, a post he held until his death. In 1956 he married an American, Joy Davidman, who died of cancer in 1961. Lewis himself was stricken with a series of illnesses and died on November 22, 1963, the same day as ALDOUS HUXLEY (see Vol. 1), and also the day John F. Kennedy was assassinated.

BOOKS BY LEWIS

All My Road Before Me: The Diary of C. S. Lewis, 1922–1927. HarBraceJ 1991 $24.95. ISBN 0-15-104609-3. Many details of varying degrees of interest are contained in Lewis's student diary.

The Chronicles of Narnia. 7 vols. Macmillan 1988 $89.95. ISBN 0-02-758801-7. These popular children's stories were originally published separately, each with its own title.

The Screwtape Letters. 1942. Macmillan rev. ed. 1982 $2.95. ISBN 0-02-086740-9. Published in many editions, these are letters from Uncle Wormwood, very low in the Lowerarchy of Hell, to his nephew Screwtape on how to tempt an Englishman.

BOOKS ABOUT LEWIS

Barfield, Owen. *Owen Barfield on C. S. Lewis.* Ed. by G. B. Tennyson. U. Pr. of New Eng. 1989 $19.95. ISBN 0-8195-5233-X. The material collected in this volume includes essays by Barfield on his friend Lewis, interviews with Barfield, and even a fictional depiction of Lewis.

Beversluis, John. *C. S. Lewis and the Search for Rational Religion.* Eerdmans 1985 o.p. Beversluis avoids both adulation and invective against Lewis, his nuanced account showing that Lewis significantly modified the apologetic for which he has become known.

Carpenter, Humphrey. *The Inklings.* Ballantine 1981 o.p. The beautiful thing about this work is that it includes J.R.R. Tolkien and Charles Williams and their friends, while concentrating on Lewis.

Christensen, Michael. *C. S. Lewis on Scripture.* Abingdon 1989 $7.95. ISBN 0-687-04559-2. With the "battle for the Bible" as backdrop, Christensen contends that Lewis's commitment to the truth of the Bible and his expertise on literary genres can help move debates on the Bible forward.

Gibb, Jocelyn. *Light on C. S. Lewis.* Macmillan 1965 o.p. Although this is a series of essays on Lewis by people who knew him or have critiqued his work, the best thing here is the complete bibliography of Lewisiana.

Green, Robert L., and Walter Hooper. *C. S. Lewis: A Biography.* HarBraceJ 1976 o.p. To date this is the definitive biography; in about 300 pages the authors catch the Lewis most people knew. Hooper is the official curator of Lewis's papers.

Holbrook, David. *The Skeleton in the Wardrobe: C. S. Lewis's Fantasies: A Phenomenological Study.* Bucknell U. Pr. 1991. ISBN 0-8387-5183-0. Employing psychoanalytic approaches, Holbrook finds even in the oft-praised *Chronicles of Narnia* thinly veiled sadism and hatred, claiming that Lewis rejected not only sex but also the body and the world.

Holmer, Paul. *C. S. Lewis: The Shape of His Faith and Thought.* HarpC 1976 o.p. An original thinker gives an original interpretation of Lewis.

Kreeft, Peter. *C. S. Lewis: A Critical Essay.* Christendom Pr. 1988 $5.95. ISBN 0-931888-26-3. A brief but insightful exposition of Lewis's apologetic by someone who is himself an important Christian apologist.

Walsh, Chad. *The Literary Legacy of C. S. Lewis.* HarBraceJ 1979 $4.95. ISBN 0-15-152725-3. Concerns the flood of critical studies of Lewis's work.

Wilson, A. N. *C. S. Lewis: A Biography.* Norton 1990 $22.50. ISBN 0-393-02813-5. A widely praised biography that moves behind the myth of C. S. Lewis to uncover a complex person, and describes Lewis's tangled relationships with women.

LUTHER, MARTIN. 1483–1546

At the age of 22, the young Luther, destined for a career in law, was so terrified during an electrical storm that he vowed to become a monk. Two years later he was ordained a priest, but this did not quiet the storms raging in his soul. Despite incessant prayer, fasting, self-flagellation, and a journey to Rome for his Augustinian order, the fear of hell clung to him, causing bitter depressions that he called *Anfechtungen* (onslaughts). His superior, John Staupitz, pushed him into studying for a doctorate in theology, a degree he earned at Wittenberg a year after going there to teach in 1511.

At Wittenberg, a university founded in 1502 by the prince elector of Saxony, Frederick the Wise, he worked through the letters of Paul, finally understanding—in what he afterward called his "tower experience"—that being right with God (justification) is a matter of faith or trust in the death of Christ for one's sins, not a matter of performing enough meritorious works to induce God to be merciful. However, no sooner had he begun to experience the release and joy of sins forgiven than he felt compelled to fight the traffic in Indulgences in Germany. Indulgences, paper writs promising release from purgatory, which were being hawked across the river from Wittenberg and were attracting people from the city, seemed to Luther to promise salvation upon the payment of money. In protest, he posted his Ninety-five Theses (whether by nailing or mailing is not clear), which soon led to trouble with Rome. It was by the sale of Indulgences that the archbishop of Mainz was recouping the vast sums he had paid the pope to secure a second princedom within the church. When the popularity of Luther's attack led to decreased sales, the church was forced to take notice, and a series of debates over church authority ensued that further radicalized the priest-professor. In 1520 Luther was excommunicated by the pope, and he began seriously that same year to urge reformation of church and society in three treatises: *An Address to the German Nobility*, *The Babylonian Captivity* (in which he argued that there are but two sacraments), and *The Freedom of the Christian Man*.

Outlawed by the Emperor Charles V after his appearance at the imperial Diet of Worms ("Here I stand, I can do no other"), he was given protection by Frederick and spent his remaining years translating the Bible from the original languages into German (completed in 1534), reforming the church in those parts of Germany where the rulers were favorable, preaching, engaging in doctrinal debate, and teaching his beloved students at the University of Wittenberg. In 1525 he married a former nun, Katherina von Bora, and they raised six children.

Luther is credited—or blamed—for the origin of Protestantism and praised for his translation of the Bible and for setting in his home life the ideal for the

Lutheran pastor's family. He died while visiting churches, and his work was carried forward by his young friend and scholar Philip Melanchthon. Perhaps the most noteworthy item in modern scholarship about Luther is the high praise he now receives from many Roman Catholic scholars, who admire his courage and his theology, while deploring the split he created in Western Christendom.

BOOKS BY LUTHER

Martin Luther's Basic Theological Writings. Ed. by Timothy Lull. Augsberg Fortress 1989 ISBN 0-8006-2327-4. A collection that should prove to be an effective entry to Luther's writings for years to come.

Three Treatises. Trans. by C. M. Jacobs and others. Fortress Pr. rev. ed. 1970 $7.95. ISBN 0-8006-1639-1. Luther's three treatises of 1520 drew widespread support for him in Germany; his excommunication followed.

Works. Concordia 55 vols. 1955– $19.95 ea. The German edition of Luther's writings now stands at 110 volumes and the count is still rising; the English translation gives students a chance to read much of Luther, although there are still gaps in the offerings.

BOOKS ABOUT LUTHER

Althaus, Paul. *The Theology of Martin Luther.* Trans. by Robert C. Schultz. Fortress Pr. 1966 $17.95. ISBN 0-8006-1855-6. Sympathetic discussion by the dean of German Luther scholars.

Atkinson, James. *Martin Luther and the Birth of Protestantism.* Westminster John Knox 1981 repr. of 1968 ed. $11.99. ISBN 0-8042-0941-3. Deals with both his life and theology in readable style.

Bainton, Roland H. *Here I Stand: A Life of Martin Luther.* 1950. Peter Smith $18.00. ISBN 0-8446-6225-9. Superb and popular study with many illustrations; has gone through many printings and still fascinates.

Boehmer, Heinrich. *Martin Luther: Road to Reform.* Trans. by John W. Doberstein and Theodore G. Tappert. Meridian 1957 o.p. Shows the young Luther and his development toward the role of reformer.

Dickens, A. G. *Martin Luther and the Reformation.* HarpC 1969 o.p. Useful for beginning students.

Edwards, Mark U. *Luther's Last Battles: Politics and Polemics, 1531–1546.* 1983 $12.95. ISBN 0-8014-9393-5. While biographers have tended to overlook Luther's last 15 years, Edwards deals with his anger and frustration, relationship with Jews, his hopes, fears, and his death.

Erikson, Erik H. *Young Man Luther.* Norton 1962 $5.95. ISBN 0-393-00170-9. Neo-Freudian interpretation of Luther's conversion experience; on this study John Osborne based his play *Luther.*

Gerrish, Brian A. *Grace and Reason: A Study in the Theology of Luther.* U. Ch. Pr. 1979 o.p. Clear and useful in the controversy over Luther's use of philosophy.

Gritsch, Eric. *Martin—God's Court Jester: Luther in Retrospect.* Sigler Pr. 1991 $19.95. ISBN 0-9623642-1-5. A reader-friendly introduction to Luther's work, containing helpful parallel chronologies on Luther and events in the surrounding world.

Harran, Marilyn J. *Luther on Conversion: The Early Years.* Cornell Univ. Pr. 1983 $34.95. ISBN 0-8014-1566-7. Analyzes Luther's thoughts on conversion with a final word on his own; read this with Erikson (see above).

Hendrix, Scott H. *Luther and the Papacy: Stages in a Reformation Conflict.* Fortress Pr. 1981 $56.30. ISBN 0-685-17044-6. Definitive work on Luther's gradual disenchantment with the papacy and his final dismissal of the pope as Antichrist.

Lohse, Bernard. *Martin Luther: An Introduction to His Life and Work.* Trans. by Robert Schulz. Augsberg Fortress 1986 $17.95. ISBN 0-8006-1964-1. An overview that effectively and comprehensively covers the history of interpretation of Luther.

McGrath, Alister. *Luther's Theology of the Cross: Martin Luther's Theological Breakthrough.* Blackwell Pubs. 1985 $14.95. ISBN 0-631-13855-2. Traces the development of the theology of the cross from 1509 to 1519, regarding Luther's notion of the "crucified God" as both old and new.

Oberman, Heiko. *Luther: Man between God and the Devil*. Trans. by Eileen Walliser-Schwarzbart. Yale U. Pr. 1989 $29.95. ISBN 0-300-03794-5. Highlights themes that are sometimes muffled in contemporary Luther scholarship and features descriptions of Luther's vitalizing battle with the devil—for example, in his decision to marry.

Olin, John C., and others, eds. *Luther, Erasmus and the Reformation: A Catholic-Protestant Reappraisal*. Greenwood 1982 repr. of 1969 ed. $39.75. ISBN 0-313-23652-6. Has articles by some of the best-known scholars on the two Reformation figures and on the aftermath of their polemics concerning the freedom or bondage of the human will.

Olivier, Daniel. *Luther's Faith: The Cause of the Gospel in the Church*. Concordia 1982 $13.95. ISBN 0-570-03868-5. Outstanding Roman Catholic interpretation of Luther's theology published by the most conservative Lutheran publisher.

Prenter, Reginald. *Spiritus Creator*. Muhlenberg Pr. 1953 o.p. Classic study of the Holy Spirit as corollary to Luther's insistence on the centrality of the Bible.

Rupp, Gordon. *Luther's Progress to the Diet of Worms*. HarpC 1964 o.p. By the dean of Luther scholars, very useful for Luther's earlier thought and work.

Rupp, E. Gordon, and Philip S. Watson, eds. *Luther and Erasmus: Free Will and Salvation*. Westminster John Knox 1978 $14.99. ISBN 0-664-24158-1. Luther insisted that the human will is not free, and Erasmus publicly disagreed. This confirmed Erasmus in his determination not to follow Luther's revolt. Both their treatises on the freedom and bondage of the will are edited and translated in this useful volume.

Schwiebert, Ernest G. *Luther and His Times: The Reformation from a New Perspective*. Concordia 1950 $26.95. ISBN 0-570-03246-6. In 900 pages, the most exhaustive study of Luther and his environment, including Wittenberg, its ruler, and its university.

Steinmetz, David C. *Luther and Staupitz: An Essay in the Intellectual Origins of the Protestant Reformation*. Duke 1980 o.p. A necessary study in the origins of Luther's thought.

————. *Luther in Context*. Ind. U. Pr. 1986 $7.95. ISBN 0-253-33647-3. What did Luther say about the drunkenness of Noah? What did Luther and Calvin think of each other? This collection of essays answers these and other questions.

Tappert, Theodore G., ed. and trans. *The Book of Concord: The Confessions of the Evangelical Lutheran Church*. Augsberg Fortress 1959 $24.95. ISBN 0-8006-0825-9. This book amounts to the confessional digest of Lutheran theology and contains some of Luther's own works, such as his *Small Catechism*, the Augsburg Confession (1530), and the Formula of Concord (1580), which capped Lutheran theology a generation after Luther.

Von Loewenich, Walter. *Martin Luther: The Man and His Work*. Trans. by Lawrence Denet. Augsburg Fortress 1986 $29.99. ISBN 0-8066-2019-6. With over 1,500 quotations from Luther's work, the book provides an excellent introduction to Luther's life, theology, and the impact of Luther's controversial marriage to Katharina von Bora.

MENNO SIMONS. 1496?–1561

Little is known of Menno Simons' early life except that he was of peasant stock, went to monastic schools, and that he was ordained a Praemonstratensian Order priest in 1524 and served several parishes in his native Friesland. His religious struggles began while he was relatively young, according to his own accounts, and centered on the sacraments. That he had difficulty affirming the real presence of Christ in the bread and wine of the Mass does not necessarily mean that the influence of MARTIN LUTHER had reached his North Sea region, for antisacramentarian views had long permeated the Low Countries. He also rejected the validity of infant baptism, but this seems to have come after he began serious study of the Bible.

By 1528 he had become known as an Evangelical preacher, and by 1536 he found it prudent to go into hiding. The next year he became the leader of some scattered Anabaptist groups, and at about the same time he married. No doubt many of his followers were people who had been confused over the Anabaptist takeover of the city of Münster, the institution of polygamy and religious terror there, and the destruction of the conspiracy by combined Lutheran and Catholic forces in 1535.

Although one can fruitfully study Menno's thought by examining his views on the sacraments, or pacifism, or even the "heavenly flesh" of Jesus (a view found in some of the church fathers), it is really his doctrine of the church that anchors his thought and that of the Mennonites, followers who took his name to define themselves. Luther and JOHN CALVIN worked for a pure church, but Menno insisted on one. Since the church is the pure bride of Christ, it must be pure; thus, excommunication and the ban (exclusion from the church and shunning of those excluded) became marks of the true church. Unfortunately, such rigor produces division, and, to combat it, Menno's writings took on a harshness that had not been there in the beginning. Harried, persecuted, a price on his head, he finally settled in Holstein and continued to guide Anabaptist thought and practice by his pen until his death.

BOOK BY MENNO SIMONS

The Complete Writings of Menno Simons. Ed. by John C. Wenger. Trans. by Leonard Verduin. Mennonite Pub. 1983 o.p. A basic English source that includes a brief biography by Harold S. Bender.

BOOKS ABOUT MENNO SIMONS

Krahn, Cornelius. *Dutch Anabaptism.* Herald Pr. 1981 o.p. Devotes considerable attention to Menno Simons, as well as examining proto-Anabaptism in the Netherlands.

Littell, Franklin H. *A Tribute to Menno Simons: A Discussion of the Theology of Menno Simons, and Its Significance for Today.* Herald Pr. 1971 o.p. Highly adulatory and by a non-Anabaptist.

MERTON, THOMAS. 1915–1968

Born in France, Thomas Merton was the son of an American artist and poet and her New Zealander husband, a painter. Merton lost both parents before he had finished high school, and his younger brother was killed in World War II. Something of the ephemeral character of human endeavor marked all his works, deepening the pathos of his writings and drawing him close to Eastern, especially Buddhist, forms of monasticism.

After an initial education in the United States, France, and England, he completed his undergraduate degree at Columbia University. His parents, nominally Friends, had given him little religious guidance, and in 1938 he converted to Roman Catholicism. The following year he received an M.A. from Columbia University and in 1941 he entered Gethsemani Abbey in Kentucky, where he remained until a short time before his death.

His working life was spent as a Trappist monk. At Gethsemani he wrote his famous autobiography, *The Seven Storey Mountain* (1948); there he labored and prayed through the days and years of a constant regimen that began with daily prayer at 2:00 A.M. As his contemplative life developed, he still maintained contact with the outside world, his many books and articles increasing steadily as the years went by. Reading them, it is hard to think of him as only a "guilty bystander," to use the title of one of his many collections of essays. He was vehement in his opposition to the Vietnam War, to the nuclear arms race, to racial oppression.

Having received permission to leave his monastery, he went on a journey to confer with mystics of the Hindu and Buddhist traditions; he was accidentally electrocuted in a hotel in Bangkok, Thailand, on December 10, 1968.

BOOKS BY MERTON

The Asian Journal of Thomas Merton. Ed. by Naomi B. Stone and others. New Dir. Pr. 1973 $12.95. ISBN 0-8112-0570-3. In these 445 pages, some of them introductions and commentary, the reader catches a glimpse of a lively mind wrestling with Eastern spirituality, comparing it with the great Benedictine tradition.

Conjectures of a Guilty Bystander. Doubleday 1968 $10.00. ISBN 0-385-01018-4. Comments on racism, the heroism of Martin Luther King and his nonviolent activists, growing concern over Vietnam.

Geography of Holiness: The Photography of Thomas Merton. Ed. by Debra Prasad Patnaik. Pilgrim Bks. 1980 o.p. One hundred pages of pictures, most taken by Merton.

The Literary Essays of Thomas Merton. Ed. by Patrick Hart. New Dir. Pr. 1985 $18.95. ISBN 0-8112-0931-8. Fine essays introduced by a careful friend and critic of Merton.

Mystics and Zen Masters. FS&G 1986 $9.95. ISBN 0-374-52001-1. Merton relates his expectations when he went to Asia; a good companion to what he actually found, as recorded in *The Asian Journal.*

The Secular Journal of Thomas Merton. FS&G 1959 o.p. Provides background for his biography, *The Seven Storey Mountain.*

The Seven Storey Mountain. Harvest Bks. 1978 $9.95. ISBN 0-15-680679-7. His most-read classic. Many of the extreme positions he took not too long after entering the Trappists he modified later.

A Thomas Merton Reader. Ed. by Thomas P. McDonnell. Doubleday 1974 o.p. More than 500 pages, containing much of his important writing that is not included elsewhere in this listing.

Thomas Merton: Spiritual Master: The Essential Writings. Ed. by Lawrence Cunningham. Paulist Pr. 1992. ISBN 0-8091-3314-8. Provides a comprehensive introduction to Merton's works.

BOOKS ABOUT MERTON

Carr, Anne. *A Search for Wisdom and Spirit: Thomas Merton's Theology of the Self.* U. of Notre Dame Pr. 1989 $9.95. ISBN 0-268-01735-2. A prominent Catholic feminist theologian uses Merton's notion of the true self as a key to interpreting his theological work.

Furlong, Monica. *Merton: A Biography.* HarBraceJ 1985 $6.95. ISBN 0-15-656960-4. Furlong does not discount the bitterness Merton felt toward authority at the monastery, or the spiritual struggles he went through, but she accentuates his turn outward when this "desert" (as he called it) had been traversed. A good book.

Griffin, John Howard. *Follow the Ecstasy: The Hermitage Years of Thomas Merton.* Orbis Bks. 1993 repr. of 1985 ed. $12.95. ISBN 0-88344-847-5. Poignant descriptions of Merton's difficulty in finding solitude, of his relationship with Margie Smith, and of his final trip to Asia make this a book not to be missed by those interested in Merton.

Rice, Edward. *The Man in the Sycamore Tree: The Good Life and Hard Times of Thomas Merton.* HarBraceJ 1985 $6.95. ISBN 0-15-656960-4. Rice, an old and enduring friend of Merton's, believes that Merton's life would have been more joyful and positive had he not spent most of it in a monastery.

Wilkes, Paul, ed. *Merton: By Those Who Knew Him Best.* HarpC 1990 $11.00. ISBN 0-06-069418-1. Like *C. S. Lewis at the Breakfast Table,* this is an appreciation and personal-glimpse collection.

NEWMAN, JOHN HENRY, CARDINAL. 1801–1890

Born in London, John Henry Newman had an evangelical experience in 1816, the same year he enrolled at Trinity College, Oxford. In 1822 he was elected a fellow of Oriel College and slowly began to be drawn toward the High Church tradition, partly because of a personal bereavement and partly because of friendships with Hurrell Froude, John Keble, and Edward Pusey. Ordained an Anglican priest in 1825, he was vicar of the university church of Saint Mary the Virgin, where he gained fame as a preacher. In 1833, with the publication of the first *Tract for the Times*, Newman launched the Oxford movement, a High Church movement within Anglicanism that emphasized Catholic elements in the Church of England and within the early church. During this period he argued for the traditional *via media*, which held that the Anglican church was the only true representative of the unbroken tradition of the church fathers, both Rome and the Protestants falling to either side.

However, through further research into the early church, he came finally to believe that his own church was schismatic; he resigned from his parish and his university fellowship and, in 1845, converted to Roman Catholicism. After study in Rome, he founded an oratory (a Catholic religious society of diocesan priests) in Birmingham. It was later moved to nearby Edgbaston, where he remained for the rest of his life, except for nearly a decade of teaching at the Catholic University of Dublin.

Controversy was Newman's great delight. He argued for development of doctrine against Catholic theologians, a viewpoint now commonplace. He defended Rome against Protestant attack in work after work. His editorship of the *Rambler*, which published lay opinion, earned him the animosity of his bishop. And he refused to attend the First Vatican Council, at which papal infallibility was declared, because he thought its definition was unripe and misplaced for the time. But he weathered all these controversies, earned the respect of his opponents, Protestant and Roman Catholic, and was awarded the cardinal's hat in 1879. Among his works, his *Apologia Pro Vita Sua* (1864) and *The Idea of a University* (1873) are regarded as classics in religion and intellectual education.

BOOKS BY NEWMAN

Apologia Pro Vita Sua. 1864. Ed. by A. D. Culler. HM 1956 $9.16. ISBN 0-395-05109-6. Newman's autobiographical defense of his movement into Orthodoxy and then into Roman Catholicism.

The Idea of a University. 1873. Ed. by Martin J. Svaglic. U. of Notre Dame Pr. 1982 $10.95. ISBN 0-268-01150-8. Newman's most famous work on education.

Letters of John Henry Newman: A Selection. Ed. by Derek Stanford and Muriel Spark. Newman Pr. 1957 o.p. "An admirable introduction to John Henry the man" (*New Statesman*).

Newman the Theologian: A Reader. Ed. by Ian Ker. U. of Notre Dame Pr. 1990 $9.95. ISBN 0-268-01469-8. An ideal point of entry for study of Newman, featuring a substantial introduction to Newman's writings on topics like papal infallibility.

A Packet of Letters: A Selection from the Correspondence of John Henry Newman. Ed. by Joyce Suggs. OUP 1983 o.p. The scholar will know, and the beginning student not care, about the 31-volume Birmingham Oratory edition of *The Letters and Diaries of John Henry Newman*, with various dates and published by several houses.

BOOKS ABOUT NEWMAN

Blehl, Vincent. *John Henry Newman: A Bibliographical Catalogue*. U. Pr. of Va. 1978 $25.00. ISBN 0-8139-0738-1. A remarkable attempt to list not only all of Newman's work but also "all the editions and reprints published during his lifetime."

Bouyer, Louis. *Newman: His Life and Spirituality.* Kennedy 1958 o.p. The life of an English convert written by a French convert. Excellent handling of some of the tender spots in Newman's human relationships.

Chadwick, Owen. *Newman.* OUP 1983 $6.95. ISBN 0-19-287567-1. For the student who wants great scholarship.

D'Arcy, Martin. *The Nature of Belief.* Ayer repr. of 1931 ed. $21.00. ISBN 0-8369-5930-2. D'Arcy uses his analysis of Newman to further his claim that acceptance of Christianity is rational.

Dawson, Christopher H. *The Spirit of the Oxford Movement.* AMS Pr. 1976 repr. of 1934 ed. $29.50. ISBN 0-404-14025-4. A Catholic intellectual of the twentieth century examines Newman's greatest contribution to Anglican religious thought in the nineteenth, the Oxford movement.

Harrold, Charles F. *John Henry Newman: An Expository and Critical Study of His Mind, Thought, and Art.* Shoe String 1966 repr. of 1945 ed. o.p. Sympathetic approach by a non-Catholic, with special attention to his conversion and to his literary efforts.

Ker, Ian. *The Achievement of John Henry Newman.* U. of Notre Dame Pr. 1991 $9.95. ISBN 0-268-00631-8. Noting Newman's denial that he was a theologian, Ker nevertheless focuses on Newman's achievement as a theologian, noting that as an educator Newman opposed excessive reliance on lecturing.

Ker, Ian, and Alan Hill, eds. *Newman after a Hundred Years.* OUP 1990. ISBN 0-19-812891-6. Essays of high scholarly caliber on a variety of topics pertaining to Newman.

Weatherby, Harold L. *Cardinal Newman in His Age: His Place in English Theology and Literature.* Vanderbilt U. Pr. 1973 $16.50. ISBN 0-8265-1182-1. Good study of Newman's place in theology and literature.

NIEBUHR, REINHOLD. 1892–1971

Walter Lippmann (see Vol. 3) once called Reinhold Niebuhr the greatest mind America had produced since Jonathan Edwards. It was fitting, then, that Niebuhr died at home in Stockbridge, Massachusetts, in the town where Edwards had preached. He was born in Wright City, Missouri, and his father was a German immigrant who served those German-speaking churches that preserved both the Lutheran and Reformed (Calvinist) traditions and piety. After seminary in St. Louis, he studied for two years at Yale University, and the M.A. he received there was the highest degree he earned. Rather than work for a doctorate, he became a pastor in Detroit, where in his 13 years of service a tiny congregation grew to one of 800 members. Part of his diary from those years was published in 1929 as *Leaves from the Notebook of a Tamed Cynic.*

During that time he began to attract attention through articles on social issues; as he said, he "cut [his] eyeteeth fighting [Henry] Ford." But the socialism to which he was attracted soon seemed naive to him: human problems could not be solved just by appealing to the good in people or by promulgating programs for change. Power, economic clout, was needed to change the systems set up by sinful groups, a position expressed in his 1932 book, *Moral Man and Immoral Society.* Tough and brash, it exposed the shallow optimism of liberal thought and was in its way as revolutionary as Karl Barth's commentary on Romans a decade earlier was for German theology. By this time Niebuhr was teaching at Union Theological Seminary in New York, where he spent the rest of his career. His wife, Ursula, became head of the religion department at Barnard College; his brother H. Richard, who became nearly as famous as Reinhold, taught at Yale.

Niebuhr's theology always took second place to ethics. He ran for office as a socialist, rescued Paul Tillich from Germany, became a strong supporter of Israel, gave up pacifism, and was often too orthodox for the liberals, too liberal for the orthodox. His *The Nature and Destiny of Man* is one of the few seminal theological books written by an American. In it he reiterates a theme that led some to place him in the Barthian camp of Neo-orthodoxy: the radical sinfulness of the human creature. But he was never as interested in Christ as God's unique response to human sin as others in the Augustine-Luther-Calvin-Barth continuum, and the label probably fits him less than it does Barth or DIETRICH BONHOEFFER. The human condition as illumined by the Christian tradition—that was always the arena in which he worked.

BOOKS BY NIEBUHR

The Essential Reinhold Niebuhr: Selected Essays and Addresses. Ed. by Robert M. Brown. Yale U. Pr. 1986 o.p. Includes bibliography of his work and works about him. Edited by a colleague and a theologian nearly as celebrated as his subject, so the introduction is valuable too.

Leaves from the Notebook of a Tamed Cynic. HarpC 1980 $5.95. ISBN 0-06-066231-X. Written as Niebuhr left a 13-year pastorate in Detroit to become America's most celebrated home-grown theologian.

Moral Man and Immoral Society: A Study in Ethics and Politics. 1932. Scribner 1960 $11.95. ISBN 0-684-71857-X. This is an amazingly acute evisceration of philosophies of progress and reason, and almost a blueprint of later struggles for equality among minority people.

The Nature and Destiny of Man. 1941–43. 2 vols. Scribner 1949 o.p. His major theological work.

A Reinhold Niebuhr Reader: Selected Essays, Articles, and Book Reviews. Ed. by Charles Brown. TPI Pr. 1992 $18.95. ISBN 1-56338-043-9. Collects shorter pieces by Niebuhr that otherwise would not be accessible to many readers.

BOOKS ABOUT NIEBUHR

Brown, Charles. *Niebuhr and His Age: Reinhold Niebuhr's Prophetic Role in the Twentieth Century.* TPI PA 1992 $34.95. ISBN 1-56338-042-0. Langdon Gilkey predicts that this will be the "definitive" intellectual biography of Niebuhr.

Fox, Richard W. *Reinhold Niebuhr: A Biography.* Pantheon 1986 o.p. We are fortunate to have this full-blown study of the man, his life and thought, in readable form; it contains judicious evaluations of earlier works and a very good bibliography.

Harries, Richard, ed. *Reinhold Niebuhr and Issues of Our Time.* Eerdmans 1986 $10.95. ISBN 0-8028-0232-X. A collection of essays by distinguished scholars like Richard Fox, James Gustafson, and Langdon Gilkey.

Patterson, Bob E. *Reinhold Niebuhr.* Hendrickson 1991 $15.95. ISBN 0-943575-66-4. The quickest way into Niebuhr's mind and thought.

Plaskow, Judith. *Sex, Sin and Grace: Women's Experience and the Theologies of Reinhold Niebuhr and Paul Tillich.* U. Pr. of Amer. 1980 $18.25. ISBN 0-8191-0882-0. Argues that Niebuhr's analysis of sin is of more limited applicability than he claims and that Niebuhr's focus on the sin of pride is more appropriate for men than it is for women.

RUETHER, ROSEMARY RADFORD. 1936–

American feminist theologian Rosemary Radford Ruether was born in St. Paul, Minnesota. Ruether graduated from Scripps College in 1958 and received her doctorate in classics and patristics from Claremont Graduate School in 1956. In 1976 she became Georgia Harkness Professor of Theology at Garrett-Evangelical Theological Seminary, a position she continues to hold.

An activist in the civil rights and peace movements of the 1960s, Ruether turned her energies to the emerging women's movement. During the 1970s and successive decades, feminist concerns impelled her to rethink historical theology, analyzing the patriarchal biases in both Christianity and Judaism that elevated male gender at the expense of women. Her rigorous scholarship has challenged many of the assumptions of traditionally male-dominated Christian theology. Recognized as one of the most prolific and readable Catholic writers, Ruether's work represents a significant contribution to contemporary theology, and her views have influenced a generation of scholars and theologians. Her imprint on feminist theology has been reenforced by her lectureships at a number of universities in the United States and abroad.

BOOKS BY RUETHER

The Church against Itself. B. Herder 1967 o.p.

Contemporary Roman Catholicism: Crises and Challenges. Sheed and Ward MO 1987 o.p.

Disputed Questions: On Being a Christian. Orbis Bks. 1989 $13.95. ISBN 0-88344-549-2

Faith and Fratricide: The Theological Roots of Anti-Semitism. Harper SF 1974 o.p.

From Machismo to Mutuality: Essays on Sexism and Woman-Man Liberation. (coauthored with Eugene Bianchi). Paulist Pr. 1975 o.p.

Gaia and God: Ecofeminist Theology of Earth Healing. Harper SF 1992 $22.00. ISBN 0-06-067022-3. Comprehensive discussion of the three main myths of creation, destruction, and domination.

Gregory Nazianzus: Rhetor and Philosopher. OUP 1969 o.p.

Liberation Theology: Human Hope Confronts Christian History and American Power. Harper SF 1972 o.p.

Mary: The Feminine Face of the Church. Westminster John Knox 1977 $8.99. ISBN 0-664-24759-8

The New Woman/New Earth: Sexist Ideologies and Human Liberation. Harper SF 1975 o.p.

The Radical Kingdom: The Western Experience of Messianic Hope. HarpC 1970 o.p.

Sexism and God-Talk: Toward a Feminist Theology. Beacon Pr. 1993 $14.00. ISBN 0-8070-1205-X

To Change the World: Christology and Cultural Criticism. Crossroad NY 1983 $9.95. ISBN 0-8245-0573-5

Womanguides: Readings toward a Feminist Theology. Beacon Pr. 1986 $14.00. ISBN 0-8070-1203-3

Women-Church: Theology and Practice of Feminist Liturgical Communities. Harper SF 1988 $11.95. ISBN 0-06-066835-0. Develops the historical framework of Women-Church, a movement composed of bases of feminist culture and celebrational communities.

Women of Spirit: Female Leadership in the Jewish and Christian Traditions. (coauthored with Eleanor McLaughlin). S&S Trade 1978 o.p.

BOOKS ABOUT RUETHER

Ramsay, William M. *Four Modern Prophets: Walter Rauschenbusch, Martin Luther King, Jr., Gustavo Gutierrez, Rosemary Radford Ruether.* Westminster John Knox 1986 $8.99. ISBN 0-8042-0811-5. Explorations of the thought of four religious thinkers and activists who have foregrounded the radical social message of the Gospel.

Snyder, Mary H. *The Christology of Rosemary Radford Ruether: A Critical Introduction.* Twenty Third 1988 $12.95. ISBN 0-89622-358-2. Celebrates the liberation theology of Ruether and emphasizes both the politically radical nature of her thought and her significance as a Christian theologian.

SCHLEIERMACHER, FRIEDRICH DANIEL ERNST. 1768-1834

[SEE Chapter 6 in this volume.]

TERESA OF AVILA, ST. 1515-1582

At the age of seven, Teresa ran away from her home in Avila, hoping to be martyred at the hands of the Moors. As a teen, she secretly enjoyed reading novels of chivalry. Taught by Augustinian nuns, Teresa acquired a sense of religious vocation only gradually. Deciding to become a nun, she professed as a Carmelite of Avila in 1537. Although she became ill to the point of having wax applied to her eyes in preparation of death, she did not die, but she did leave the convent. Teresa later returned to the convent and, upon reading ST. AUGUSTINE's *Confessions*, experienced a conversion at the age of 40. When she experienced visions and heard voices, she wondered at first if it was the work of the devil. She found comfort in Peter of Alcantara's assessment that her experiences were of a divine origin.

Life as a Carmelite nun tended to be comfortable, but not dissolute. Inspired by her mystical experiences, Teresa took practical steps to reform the Carmelite order. In 1562 she founded a convent with a stricter regime of discipline than was common. She also organized a Discalced Carmelite monastery for men. In doing so, she met Juan de Yepes y Alvarez, known to us as the mystic ST. JOHN OF THE CROSS, who became a fellow reformer. In all, she founded 16 reformed convents. Teresa's spirituality cannot be characterized in a word, but humility rather than honor was at its center. Her life of contemplation led to active service. Upon her death in 1582, her body remained preserved. This, along with other signs of saintliness, led to her canonization in 1622. In 1970, she was declared a "Doctor of the Church," the first woman in the history of the Catholic church to receive that honor.

BOOKS BY ST. TERESA

The Conquest of the Perfect Love. 2 vols. Am. Classical Coll. Pr. 1986 o.p. Contains a number of her writings, including *The Way of Perfection*, justly regarded as a classic of spiritual devotion.

The Interior Castle. Trans. by Kieran Kavanaugh and Otilio Rodriguez. Paulist Pr. 1979 $9.95. ISBN 0-8091-2254-5. Written late in her life to describe the soul's progress through seven mansions to the inmost chamber where it is united to God.

The Life of Teresa of Jesus. Ed. and trans. by E. Allison Peers. Doubleday 1991 $12.00. ISBN 0-385-01109-1. Ranges from ruminations on her awakening to discussion of the best way of scaring off devils; this book continues to draw attention centuries after it was written.

BOOKS ABOUT ST. TERESA

Bilinkoff, Jodi. *The Avila of Saint Teresa: Religious Reform in a Sixteenth-Century City.* Cornell Univ. Pr. 1989 $8.95. ISBN 0-8014-2203-5. Places Teresa in the context of changes in the Europe of her day.

Chorpenning, Joseph. *The Divine Romance: Teresa of Avila's Narrative Theology.* Loyola 1992 $15.95. ISBN 0-8294-0732-4. Chorpenning productively focuses on narrative to illumine the theology of Saint Teresa.

Clissold, Stephen. *St. Teresa of Avila.* Harper SF 1982 $18.95. ISBN 0-8164-2621-X. An easily accessible retelling of the story of St. Teresa, which popularizes without trivializing.

Haneman, Mary. *The Spirituality of St. Teresa of Avila.* St. Paul Bks. 1988 $3.95. ISBN 0-8198-6844-2. A commendable account of Teresa's life and work. Contains a helpful comparison of Teresa and John of the Cross.

Lincoln, Victoria. *Teresa: A Woman: A Biography of Teresa of Avila.* State U. NY Pr. 1984 $59.50. ISBN 0-87395-937-X. Described by the editor as a "novel-like biography," the author presents her research in a fluent, literary manner, rejecting hagiography and creating a realistic portrait as a result.

Luti, J. Mary. *Teresa of Avila's Way.* Liturgical Pr. 1991 $14.95. ISBN 0-8146-5548-3. What difference should it make to our interpretation of Teresa as a mystic that she is a woman? Luti's nuanced answer is but one of the features of the book that should interest the reader.

Papasogli, Giorgio. *St. Teresa of Avila*. St. Paul Bks. 1958 o.p. More than 400 pages of good old-fashioned storytelling about the life of a saint.

Weber, Alison. *Teresa of Avila and the Rhetoric of Femininity*. Princeton U. Pr. 1990 $22.50. ISBN 0-691-06812-7. Weber takes a novel approach that undercuts conventional interpretations of Teresa.

Williams, Rowan. *Teresa of Avila*. Morehouse Pub. 1991 $19.95. ISBN 0-8192-1496-5. A clear and comprehensive account of Teresa's life and thought. Lifts out the theme of friendship with God as central to her devotion.

TILLICH, PAUL JOHANNES. 1886–1965

Paul Johannes Tillich was born into a German Lutheran pastor's family in that part of Germany that is now Poland. He attended several universities, earning the doctorate in philosophy in 1910, then taught at several more from 1919 to 1933. Removed from his professorate at Frankfurt by the Nazi government, he emigrated to the United States, with the encouragement of REINHOLD NIEBUHR, and taught at Union Theological Seminary in New York (1933–55), Harvard University (1955–62), and the University of Chicago (1962–65). The fullest biography, including some fairly lurid material of a psychosexual nature, can be found in the appreciative work by Wilhelm and Marion Pauck.

The student who wants to encounter Tillich at his most succinct might turn to *The Courage To Be* (1952) or *The Theology of Paul Tillich* (1982). He is sometimes classified as Neo-orthodox, but that label does not fit him as well as it does KARL BARTH, who had small regard for Tillich's "theology of correlation," where responding to the world's questions is seen as the proper way of practicing theology.

BOOKS BY TILLICH

The Courage to Be. Yale U. Pr. 1952 $11.00. ISBN 0-300-00241-6. As suggested in the biographical narrative, this is perhaps the best place to begin reading Tillich.

The Essential Tillich: An Anthology of the Writings of Paul Tillich. Ed. by F. Forrester Church. Macmillan 1988 $9.95. ISBN 0-02-018920-6. Carefully selected excerpts from Tillich's work, introduced by his daughter, Mutie Tillich Farris.

The New Being. Macmillan 1950 $9.95. ISBN 0-684-71908-8. Some of his shorter essays and sermons, in which the power of the prophetic preacher is clear and urgent.

The Shaking of the Foundations. Macmillan 1940 $9.95. ISBN 0-684-71910-X. Should be read with *The New Being*, for *Shaking* has a good deal of the prophetic "no," while *The New Being* is more positive.

Systematic Theology: Life and the Spirit, History and the Kingdom of God. 1951–63. 3 vols. U. Ch. Pr. 1973–76 $55.00. ISBN 0-226-80336-8. Here is Tillich's summary of the method and material of his work. The first-time reader should begin with one of the books listed above.

The Theology of Paul Tillich. Ed. by Charles W. Kegley. Pilgrim Bks. rev. ed. 1982 o.p. Includes 15 short critiques of his theology by noted writers (not all of them theologians), and his own 20-page reply as well as a list of all of Tillich's voluminous writings, great and obscure.

BOOKS ABOUT TILLICH

Gilkey, Langdon. *Gilkey on Tillich*. Crossroad NY 1990 $24.95. ISBN 0-8245-0991-9. Decades of engagement with Tillich's work are reflected in this affectionate and incisive analysis.

Grigg, Richard. *Symbol and Empowerment: Paul Tillich's Post-Theistic System*. Mercer Univ. Pr. 1985. ISBN 0-86554-163-9. Discusses Tillich's "God above the God of theism" and his reliance on German idealism, which turns away many contemporary readers who otherwise share Tillich's interests.

Pauck, Wilhelm, and Marion Pauck. *Paul Tillich: His Life and Thought*. HarpC 1976 o.p.
    Very good study that shows Tillich in all his intellectual glory and with all his moral
    dilemmas.
Tavard, George H. *Paul Tillich and the Christian Message*. Scribner 1962 o.p. A major
    American Catholic theologian assesses the positive and negative consequences of
    Tillich's Christology.
Tillich, Hannah. *From Time to Time*. Stein and Day 1973 o.p. The author's revelations
    about the sexual activities of her husband have caused some to reevaluate Paul
    Tillich's work as a theologian.

WEIL, SIMONE. 1909–1943

French thinker, political activist, and religious mystic Simone Weil was born
in Paris. Her parents were secularized Jews and intellectuals, and Weil attended
the prestigious École Normale. A brilliant and unusual student, Weil was held in
awe by some of her peers and mocked by others for her radical political
opinions. After her graduation in 1931, she taught philosophy for several years
in provincial lycees for girls.

During the early 1930s, the plight of the working class began to command
Weil's attention. The poverty and despair inflicted by the worldwide depression
riveted her search for social justice. In an effort to understand how workers had
become victimized by society, she herself labored at factory jobs. During this
period, she also displayed an intense interest in Marxism, and even briefly
fought on the Loyalist side in the Spanish Revolution. These experiences,
however, left her increasingly disillusioned, unable to find answers to her
consuming concerns about absolute truth and social justice in the dogmas of
the political Left.

In the late 1930s, Weil abandoned her agnosticism, and after several mystical
experiences she turned to Christianity. Although she never formally embraced
Catholicism, its tenets were central in her religious thought. Her faith was in the
tradition of the fourteenth-century German mystics MEISTER ECKHART and ST.
JOHN OF THE CROSS. She upheld the centrality of love and beauty in the world,
rejecting materialism and self as anathema to the human spirit. Religion now
became the focus of her thinking, as is clearly reflected in her essays, letters,
notebooks, and journals.

In poor health for much of her life, Weil died at age 34 in England, where she
had fled after Hitler's takeover of France. During her lifetime, she was known
primarily as an essayist. Although she wrote no books, her writings were
collected and published during the 1950s and 1960s, and she soon gained
recognition as one of the leading figures in twentieth-century religious thought.

BOOKS BY WEIL

Gravity and Grace. Putnam Pub. Group 1952 o.p.
The Need for Roots. 1952. HarpC 1971 o.p.
Oppression and Liberty. 1958. Ed. by A. Wills and J. Petrie. U. of Mass. Pr. 1973 $13.95.
    ISBN 0-87023-251-7
Selected Essays. 1962. Trans. by Richard Rees. OUP 1962 o.p.
Simone Weil Reader. Ed. by George Panichas. Moyer Bell 1985 $10.95. ISBN 0-918825-
    01-6
Waiting for God. 1951. Borgo Pr. 1991 $20.00. ISBN 0-8095-9093-X

BOOK ABOUT WEIL

Coles, Robert. *Simone Weil: A Modern Pilgrim*. Addison-Wesley 1989 $9.57. ISBN 0-201-
    07964-X

WESLEY, JOHN. 1703–1791

John Wesley's life, begun in a poor parish at Epworth in Lincolnshire, spanned the century of the Enlightenment, during which human happiness, based on the new sciences, was confidently predicted. It was also the century of the Industrial Revolution, whose factories swallowed up the new cities' teeming masses, imprisoning them in lives that were brutish and short. Wesley's father, Samuel, was a pastor so hated that his parishioners once set their home ablaze; his mother, Susanna, bore 19 children in 21 years, of whom only 9 survived infancy. At the age of 11, John was sent away to school in London and was soon at Oxford University, of which all his memories were pleasant. He left Oxford briefly to be his father's assistant, but in 1729 returned to lecture on Greek and philosophy. There he and his younger brother Charles founded an informal club, which was dubbed by its detractors the Holy Club, and its members derided, because of their dutiful religious observances, as Methodists.

After their father's death, the two Wesleys went to Georgia, to the colony of imprisoned debtors settled by James Oglethorpe. On the voyage they were impressed by the simple faith of some German Moravians who exhibited no fear when their ship was tossed by storms that sent terror to the hearts of the two pious brothers. Things worked out badly in Georgia—there is some mystery about a failed romance there—and the brothers returned to England, where John underwent a period he referred to as his dark night of the soul. In 1738 it ended when, as he recorded in his journal, "I felt my heart strangely warmed."

The rest of his life John spent in spreading the gospel of the wondrous grace of God throughout Great Britain, including Scotland and Ireland. He rode thousands of miles, organized religious societies in every major center, insisted on loyalty to the Church of England (he was, after all, a priest), wrote copiously, and with Charles published hymnbooks for the societies. There was in John Wesley none of the ignorant ranting of the evangelical preachers. He was an Oxford man, faithful to the church. It was only with the greatest reluctance that he ordained men to preach in the colonies. Above all, he was an organizer of talent and power. Wherever the population was growing and people uprooted from the countryside and thrust into the cities needed a warmhearted message and a practical ministry to help debtors, miners, and the out-of-work, there his ministry made a profound impression. His own failed marriage, his refusal to take the side of the colonies in their just grievances against England, the refusal of the Anglican church to accept his societies as part of its churches—none of these failures dim the brilliance of "this man sent from God, whose name was John."

BOOKS BY WESLEY

A Plain Account of Christian Perfection. TPI PA 1952 $9.95. ISBN 0-7162-0081-3. After defending the possibility of Christian perfection, Wesley professes bewilderment as to why his claim is disconcerting to other Christians.

The Journal of John Wesley. Ed. by Percy L. Parker. Moody 1974 o.p. A condensation of all four volumes of Wesley's journals, which were published during his lifetime, even as he wrote them.

The Works of John Wesley. Ed. by Albert Outler. OUP 1964 o.p. Outler, a scholar who usually works with the ancient fathers of the church, here edited Wesley's works expertly for the person who wants Wesley's life and thought in his own words.

BOOKS ABOUT WESLEY

Abelone, Henry. *Evangelist of Desire: John Wesley and the Methodists.* Stanford U. Pr. 1990 $25.00. ISBN 0-8047-1826-1. Shows a complex interplay between leader and community in which Wesley's charisma played a pivotal role in coaxing the community into desired patterns of behavior.

Green, Vivian H. *The Young Mr. Wesley*. St. Martin 1965 o.p. A detailed account of Wesley's years as a student at Oxford.

Harmon, Rebecca Lamar. *Susanna, Mother of the Wesleys*. Abingdon 1991 $5.95. ISBN 0-687-40767-2. One of several available popular studies of John and Charles Wesley's mother.

Heitzenrater, Richard P. *The Elusive Mr. Wesley: John Wesley His Own Biographer*. 2 vols. Abingdon 1984 o.p. Allows Wesley to tell in his own words the story of his life, with minimal input from the author.

Lindstrom, Harold. *Wesley and Sanctification: A Study in the Doctrine of Salvation*. Zondervan 1984 repr. of 1946 ed. o.p. This study focuses on the doctrine that has helped split American Methodists into Wesleyan and plain Methodists. Foreword by Timothy L. Smith.

Marquardt, Manfred. *John Wesley's Social Ethics: Praxis and Principles*. Trans. by John Steely and W. Stephen Gunter. Abingdon 1992 $19.95. ISBN 0-687-20494-1. Marquardt ably explains pertinent theoretical issues but shows that these, taken in isolation, cannot allow us to grasp Wesley's work. An outstanding introduction.

Pudney, John. *John Wesley and His World*. Scribner 1978 o.p. Richly illustrated.

Schmidt, M. *John Wesley: A Theological Biography*. 2 vols. Abingdon 1962–73 o.p. The definitive theological study of Wesley.

ZWINGLI, HULDRYCH (also HULDREICH). 1484–1531

Although of peasant stock, Huldrych Zwingli's family was well off, and he received a first-rate education, culminating in a master's degree at the University of Basel in 1506. In that year he became parish priest in Glarus, where his pastoral duties led him to question the sending of Swiss youth as mercenary soldiers to Italy. Despite his doubts, he served as chaplain to the Glarus contingent of the pope's armies in 1513 and 1515 and earned a papal pension for his good work. Because he was in the good graces of Rome, his earliest movements for reform were not opposed by the church.

He pursued his interests in classical studies and music, corresponded with the famous humanist ERASMUS, and by 1516—a year before MARTIN LUTHER wrote his Ninety-five Theses against the traffic in Indulgences—had probably reached what came to be Protestant convictions about the role of Scripture and justification by faith. After serving for two years as pastor in Einsiedeln, he was called to the office of people's priest at the Great Minster in Zurich, although some objected to his passion for music, and others to his passion for a young girl he was said to have seduced (and probably had). In 1520, his reforming views having become stronger, he persuaded the city council to back him in a move requiring scriptural support for all the affairs of the church. Since the Bible does not explicitly require celibacy for church leaders, Zwingli was free to marry, which he did in 1524.

As it became clearer that Zwingli, like Luther, was breaking with Rome, opposition to him began to harden. On the one hand, some former supporters now wanted more radical reformation: they wished to sever connections between church and state and insisted on believers' baptism. After many debates, a number of such opponents were arrested and one even put to death, ironically, by drowning. On the other hand were those Swiss cantons that wanted to remain Roman Catholic. Their opposition led to military conflict, and Zwingli, once more acting as chaplain, was killed during an intercantonal battle at Kappel in 1531. He was succeeded as pastor by his son-in-law Heinrich

Bullinger, whose writings probably had a much greater influence on the subsequent progress of the Reformation, especially on its Reformed side.

In 1529, two years before his death, Zwingli had met at Marburg with Luther and other reformers in an attempt to mend their differences. Only the question of the Eucharist proved beyond agreement. Luther insisted that the risen Jesus gives his flesh to those who receive Communion, taking the words "This is my body" with a literalism that Zwingli, ever the rational humanist, could not accept. The break was unmendable.

BOOKS BY ZWINGLI

Commentary on True and False Religion. Ed. by Samuel M. Jackson. Labyrinth Pr. 1981 $15.95. ISBN 0-939464-00-4. Argues that philosophy is worthless when attempting to discern the shape of the life of faith and that reliance on tradition leads to the "false religion" of Catholicism.

Selected Works. Ed. by Samuel M. Jackson. Bks. Demand repr. of 1972 ed. $77.80. ISBN 0-8122-7670-1. Illustrates Zwingli's battles on two sides. As a Catholic, Zwingli advocated that the church allow priests to marry; as a Protestant, Zwingli fiercely argued against Baptists that the (Catholic) practice of child baptism be retained.

Selected Writings of Huldrych Zwingli. Trans. by E. J. Furcha and H. Wayne Pipkin. *Pittsburgh Theological Monographs: New Ser.* 2 vols. Pickwick 1984 o.p. Vol. 1 *The Defense of the Reformed Faith.* Vol. 2 *In Search of True Religion: Reformation, Pastoral, and Eucharistic Writings.*

BOOKS ABOUT ZWINGLI

Bromiley, G. W., ed. *Zwingli and Bullinger.* Westminster John Knox 1979 $14.99. ISBN 0-664-24159-X. Lengthy excerpts from the writings of the two churchmen, with solid translation, editing, and commentary.

Courvoisier, Jacques. *Zwingli: A Reformed Theologian.* Westminster John Knox 1963 o.p. Accurate but very brief and therefore suitable for the beginning student.

Farner, Oskar. *Zwingli the Reformer: His Life and Work.* Shoe String 1968 o.p. About 100 pages, very readable and, like Courvoisier, accurate.

Pipkin, H. Wayne, ed. *A Zwingli Bibliography.* Pitts. Theolog. 1972 $7.00. ISBN 0-931222-06-0. In spite of its age, this is still a helpful resource, containing over 1,600 entries and an index.

Potter, G. R. *Zwingli.* Cambridge U. Pr. 1984 o.p. Very careful, readable, and probably the best single work, with maps and bibliography. Not to be confused with the author's *Ulrich Zwingli* (1977), which is a bibliography on the Swiss reformer, published in London by the Historical Association.

Rilliet, Jean. *Zwingli: Third Man of the Reformation.* Trans. by Harold Knight. Westminster John Knox 1964 o.p. A standard work that reads easily and is more popular than Potter, less so than Courvoisier or Farner (see their entries above).

Stephens, W. P. *Zwingli: An Introduction to His Thought.* OUP 1992 $45.00. ISBN 0-19-826329-5. Places Zwingli's theology in the context of the dramatic story of his life, giving a good sense of the development of Zwingli's thought.

CHAPTER 16

The Bible and Related Literature

J. Kenneth Kuntz

> It may be only for a minority that Scripture remains unambiguously
> authoritative, yet most of us continue to feel the pressure of authority exerted
> by this extraordinary collection of ancient writings. From the humanist
> perspective, and; indeed, from many religious perspectives as well, Scripture
> no longer speaks in one clearly prescriptive voice, but its resonances still
> carry into the recesses of our spiritual and political imagination. The Bible
> has been a central force of coherence and continuity in our culture, and so it
> may not be, after all, surprising that many are now impelled to discover how
> they might close the gap that modernity has interposed between themselves
> and the biblical texts.
>
> —ROBERT ALTER, *The World of Biblical Literature*

Our English noun *bible* owes its existence to the Greek noun *biblia*, which
means "books." As a repository of diverse pieces of literature, the Bible is no
single book but a vast collection of writings. Although the earliest sources for
the Bible surely reflect previously existing oral traditions, what lies before us
today is the product of a sustained written effort that has spanned no less than
13 centuries. A few poetic fragments in the Pentateuch (the first five books of
the Old Testament), such as the Song of Miriam in Exodus 15:21, may trace back
to the thirteenth century B.C. Final editions of the books of Amos, 1–2 Kings,
and Ruth likely date to the eighth, sixth, and fourth centuries B.C., respectively,
and a majority of the books comprising the New Testament doubtlessly emerged
during the second half of the first century A.D.

As we approach this body of literature in all of its remoteness and complexity,
we should recognize that it is the work of a few known and many unknown
authors. Depicting a world that is not altogether congenial with our own, these
authors have bequeathed to us a remarkable assemblage of texts that Jewish and
Christian communities have come to embrace as revered scripture. No museum
in our times boasts within its collections any original biblical manuscript. Even
the celebrated presence of a Daniel text among the Qumran (Dead Sea) Scrolls
that may well date within a century of the book's origin does not alter the
conclusion firmly held by critical scholars that, at best, the biblical manuscripts
we have in hand are copies of copies and translations. Thus, the majority of
those Hebrew manuscripts that lie behind what we know as the Old Testament,
or Hebrew Bible (the designation preferred by most Jewish readers), date from
the ninth to eleventh centuries A.D., and the earliest complete Greek manuscripts of the New Testament only reach back to the fourth century A.D.

Since a well-stocked bookstore is likely to have available a number of
attractive and highly readable Bible translations, those who are newly initiated
into serious scriptural study may easily lose sight of the fact that the text was not
originally written in English. Indeed, the spoken languages of the ancient
biblical authors—Hebrew, Aramaic, and Koiné ("common") Greek—bear only

a modest resemblance to their more recent counterparts. It is not unusual, therefore, for instructors of classical Hebrew to tell their students, "In Old Testament Hebrew, we confront a dead language but a living tradition!" The classical Hebrew of the Old Testament books belongs to those centuries prior to the Babylonian exile in the sixth century B.C. A few late portions of Jewish scripture found in the books of Ezra and Daniel are cast in Aramaic, a related Semitic language that was in vogue in Palestine around the time of Jesus. Koiné Greek, the language of the New Testament, is not the Attic prose of classical Greek, but a "common" Greek that dominated the Greek world language between roughly 300 B.C. and A.D. 500.

Since contemporary readers of the Bible find themselves radically distanced from the above-mentioned trilingual biblical heritage, it is almost impossible to exaggerate the importance of sensitive, responsible translation. It is sometimes argued that biblical translators and interpreters perform entirely separate tasks—the former tell us what the text *says*, whereas the latter tells us what it *means*. Such a distinction is bound to falter, since translation necessarily entails interpretation. Translation activity is not simply a process of word substitution. It is a far more subtle endeavor that takes account of nuances, hyperbole, irony, and the like. Moreover, biblical translators dare not limit their attention to the original writings themselves, which are called "texts" in our arrangement. They must be conversant with the classical translations, called "versions" here, which, in large measure, became the models of modern-language versions.

Even a cursory inspection of the bibliography in this chapter should impress on the reader that serious biblical scholarship is a multifaceted endeavor. It employs literary, historical, and theological methods that are basically interdependent. The method of literary criticism, closely associated with that of historical criticism, involves analytical study of biblical documents and is designed to aid in a more accurate understanding of concepts contained in them. Careful examination of the documents indicates that most of them have had a long, complex literary history. The analysis involves observations regarding variant styles, diction, literary forms and structure, divergent concepts, and historical allusions contained within each of the documents. Historical criticism, in turn, seeks to reconstruct the matrix of events, personalities, and ideas that produced the literature and thought of the Bible. Here it becomes quite apparent that neither the biblical Israel of the Old Testament nor the early church of the New Testament pursued its existence in a vacuum. Both were part of a real world that significantly shaped the life and thought of the religious community in question. Finally, theological interpretation operates on the assumption that the biblical writers persistently set forth a view of reality essentially religious or theological in character. Such interpretation seeks both to understand the ancient biblical perspective and to reflect on its relevance and meaning for present-day humanity.

GENERAL WORKS

In the lists that follow, the principal "critical editions" of the original texts of both the Old and New Testaments are given first; then the most authoritative access tools, grammars, and dictionaries, which assist any reading of the original; and, finally, bibliographies. Critical editions are those that list variant manuscript readings for uncertain passages in an accompanying annotation footnoted to the text.

Critical Editions of Original Texts

The Hebrew text of the Old Testament emerged in increasingly standardized form during the earliest age of rabbinical scholarship, the second to the fifth centuries A.D., and received remarkable standardization during the sixth to eighth centuries A.D. through the work of scholars called the Masoretes, who copied with rigid discipline, painstakingly evaluated the manuscripts on hand, and introduced vowel signs to a language previously written with consonants only. New manuscripts of some Hebrew Scriptures were found among the famous Dead Sea Scrolls from Qumran, beginning in 1947, and, although these go back hundreds of years before the Masoretes, their readings evaluated so far roundly endorse the accuracy and fidelity of the Masoretic text.

Aland, Kurt, ed. *Synopsis of the Four Gospels.* United Bible 1983 $7.95. ISBN 0-8267-0500-6. An indispensable tool of Gospel study featuring Greek and English translations in columns on facing pages.

Aland, Kurt, and others, eds. *The Greek New Testament.* Am. Bible 1983 $13.50. ISBN 3-438-05110-9. Fundamentally the same text as that of Nestle and Aland (below), but includes captions for English-speaking readers and a simplified critical notation.

Elliger, K., ed. *Twelve Prophets. Biblia Hebraica Stuttgartensia Ser.* Am. Bible 1970 $6.95. ISBN 3-438-05210-5. A greatly improved critical edition of the Masoretic text, meaning one that lists divergent manuscript readings for each unstable passage in footnotes to the sacred text established by the editors.

The Holy Scriptures of the Old Testament: Hebrew and English. Am. Bible 1982 o.p. A useful edition of the Hebrew text, without critical notes, alongside columns containing the venerable King James Version.

Nestle, E., and Kurt Aland. *Novum Testamentum Graece.* Am. Bible 1987 $13.95. ISBN 3-438-05110-9. The work of an international committee of foremost textual scholars represents the most authoritative text of the Greek New Testament and most complete presentation of variant readings.

Principal Access Tools

Bauer, W., F. W. Gingrich, and F. W. Danker. *A Greek-English Lexicon of the New Testament and Other Early Christian Literatures.* Trans. by William F. Arndt. U. Ch. Pr. rev. ed. 1979 $47.50. ISBN 0-226-03932-3. An English adaptation of the fourth edition of the celebrated German work, widely recognized as the finest New Testament dictionary.

Blass, F., and A. Debrunner. *A Greek Grammar of the New Testament and Other Early Christian Literature.* Trans. by Robert W. Funk. U. Ch. Pr. 1990 $54.99. ISBN 0-310-24780-2. This German work in English translation is first among New Testament Greek grammars, of which there are many, in varying degrees of depth.

Funk, Robert W. *A Beginning-Intermediate Grammar of Hellenistic Greek.* 3 vols. Scholars Pr. GA rev. ed. 1973 o.p. Explains the morphology and grammar of the common tongue as it emerged from the classical and includes appendixes, paradigms, and an index.

Gesenius, William. *Hebrew and Chaldee Lexicon to the Old Testament.* Trans. by S. P. Tregelles. Baker Bk. 1984 $29.95. ISBN 0-8010-3801-4. Originally published in the nineteenth century, through several revisions this remains the most convenient unabridged Hebrew-Aramaic dictionary, with surveys of usage accompanying each definition.

Gesenius, William, and E. Kautzsch. *Gesenius' Hebrew Grammar.* Trans. by A. E. Cowley. OUP 1910 $32.00. ISBN 0-19-815406-2. Though some of its treatments are out of date, this exhaustively documented and illustrated grammar is still the best reference tool available in English.

Greenlee, J. Harold. *A Concise Exegetical Grammar of New Testament Greek.* Eerdmans rev. ed. 1987 $7.95. ISBN 0-8028-0173-0. This is a thorough revision of a popular, "user-friendly" instrument recommended for students in early stages of New Testament textual study.

Holladay, William L. *A Concise Hebrew and Aramaic Lexicon of the Old Testament.* Eerdmans 1971 $32.95. ISBN 0-8028-3413-2. This condensed version of the foremost Hebrew-Aramaic lexicon (L. Koehler and W. Baumgartner, *Lexicon in Veteris Testamenti Libros*) is well suited for students beginning their study of the two Old Testament languages.

Johns, Alger F. *A Short Grammar of Biblical Aramaic.* Andrews Univ. Pr. 1972 repr. of 1963 ed. $10.95. ISBN 0-943872-01-4. A beginner's tool, presupposing knowledge of biblical Hebrew.

Liddell, H. G., and R. Scott. *A Greek-English Lexicon.* OUP repr. of 1968 ed. $98.00. ISBN 0-19-864214-8. An immense lexicon, devoted mainly to classical Greek but including word usages from the Old and New Testaments, intended for the specialist.

Waltke, Bruce K., and M. O'Connor. *An Introduction to Biblical Hebrew Syntax.* Eisenbrauns 1990 $42.50. ISBN 0-931464-31-5. An outstanding intermediary grammar that is structured more on topical than pedagogical lines and focusing on the interaction of syntax and semantics; emphasizes the meaning of various Hebrew forms. A rich bibliography of Biblical Hebrew studies is included.

Weingreen, Jacob. *A Practical Grammar for Classical Hebrew.* OUP 1959 $18.95. ISBN 0-19-815422-4. This is the most popular beginner's grammar, offering only the most basic information together with exercises, tables of forms, and a short vocabulary.

Zerwick, Max. *A Grammatical Analysis of Greek New Testament.* Loyola 1974 $22.50. ISBN 88-7653-553-5. A valuable companion for the beginner, identifying Greek forms and finely shaded word meanings verse by verse throughout the New Testament.

Bibliographies

Included in this category are several bibliographies that appear continuously and therefore could also be classified as serials. Listed here are only those items considered most helpful for the person striking out in Scripture study. In addition, the reader should consult articles in such periodicals as *The Bible Today, The Biblical Archaeologist, Biblical Theology Bulletin, Catholic Biblical Quarterly, Interpretation: A Journal of Bible and Theology, Journal of Biblical Literature, Semeia: An Experimental Journal for Biblical Criticism*, and *Vetus Testamentum.*

Aune, David E. *Jesus and the Synoptic Gospels: A Bibliographic Study Guide.* Ed. by Mark L. Branson. Inter Varsity 1981 $6.95. ISBN 0-8308-5498-3. Includes an introduction that lists basic reference works, literary criticism, traditional criticism, historical criticism, and theological study of the Gospels. Entries are annotated; guidance is very sound.

Childs, Brevard S. *Old Testament Books for Pastor and Teacher.* Westminster John Knox 1977 o.p. For the Protestant pastor-teacher; includes Old Testament text and translations, commentaries extensively evaluated, introductions to the Old Testament, history, theology.

Danker, Frederick W. *Multipurpose Tools for Bible Study.* Concordia 1970 o.p. An extensive and valuable listing of the main resources needed for serious study of both Testaments, together with explanations of their use and relationship to the interpretive enterprise as a whole.

Fitzmyer, Joseph A. *An Introductory Bibliography for the Study of Scripture.* Loyola 1981 o.p. One of the very finest bibliographies of its kind, extensively and incisively annotated, with bibliographies, periodicals, texts and versions, introductions, lexica, grammars, concordances, dictionaries, commentaries, archaeology, history, theology, apocryphal and other contemporary writings, and religious milieu of the Bible.

Hurd, John C., Jr., ed. *Bibliography of New Testament Bibliographies*. A. R. Allenson 1966 o.p. Directs the student quickly to the bibliographies available on individual books, sections, and topics pertaining to New Testament study.

New Testament Abstracts. Weston School of Theology triannual 1956–present $24.00 per year. This very important service abstracts the most important articles and books that have appeared in Catholic, Protestant, and Jewish periodicals, on topics and texts in the New Testament. Also offers short précis in English of materials published in all major European languages, as well as English.

Nober, Petrus, and J. Swetnam. *Elenchus Bibliographies Biblicus*. Loyola 1972 o.p. Biblical studies, both books and articles, are listed in the thousands, from many countries and languages, under both topical and biblical headings (Latin), embracing biblical exegesis and all its associated disciplines.

Old Testament Abstracts. Catholic Bibl. Assn. triannual 1978–present $14.00. Modeled after *New Testament Abstracts* (see above) and offering a parallel service, this publication, under the auspices of the Catholic Biblical Association of America, extends to the most important publications in Old Testament and related disciplines, which it extracts competently and clearly.

TEXTS AND VERSIONS OF THE BIBLE

Ancient Versions

The oldest translations, or "versions," of the Hebrew Bible were products of both the Jewish Diaspora, following the Babylonian exile (586–539 B.C.), and the great institution that linked far-flung Jewish communities with their tradition, the Synagogue. The Greek translation was undertaken in Alexandria, Egypt, in the third century B.C. and bears a name, the "Septuagint," that echoes the legend of its accomplishment by a symbolic "70" translators. The Aramaic paraphrases grew out of the practice of the Palestinian synagogues and are called "targums" (translations). Out of reverence for the original Hebrew, the Aramaic paraphrases were never written down until the fifth century A.D., but there were undoubtedly a fixed oral tradition of Aramaic renderings of the Hebrew by the time of Jesus.

Brenton L. L. *The Septuagint Version of the Old Testament and Apocrypha*. Am. Bible 1986 $44.95. ISBN 0-913573-44-2. A convenient edition with facing English columns, but both Greek and English are dated and flawed.

Jellicoe, Sidney. *The Septuagint and Modern Study*. Eisenbrauns 1989 repr. of 1968 ed. $22.50. ISBN 0-931464-00-5. A survey of this century's Septuagint research, covering its origins and transmission, then questions of its text and language.

McNamara, Martin, ed. *The Targum Neofiti to Genesis. Aramaic Bible Ser.* Liturgical Pr. 1992 $65.00. ISBN 0-8146-5476-2. A professional translation of the targums with critical annotations. Shows relationships between the English and Aramaic original.

Rahlfs, A., ed. *Septuaginta*. Am. Bible 1979 repr. of 1935 ed. $30.95. ISBN 3-438-05120-6. The Greek text is the editor's reconstruction from major manuscripts, but its critical foundation and textual apparatus are inadequate.

Sperber, A. *The Bible in Aramaic Based on Old Manuscripts and Printed Texts*. 4 vols. E. J. Brill 1992 $271.50. ISBN 90-04-09580-2. The best available critical edition of various targums, concluding with a study of the relationship of the targum to the Hebrew Bible (Vol. 4B).

Weber, R., ed. *Biblia sacra iuxta vulgatam versionem*. Am. Bible 1990 $40.00. A manual edition of the Vulgate Latin version of the St. Jerome (fourth century) based on the major critical editions.

English Versions

From the introduction of Christianity into Britain until the late fourteenth century, translation of the Bible into English was fragmentary and sporadic, being held back by the Western church's wariness of lay use of Scripture and the "profane" vernacular dialects (as against the officially sanctioned Latin Vulgate). The Oxford scholar JOHN WYCLIF, precursor of the Reformation in England, supervised the first complete English translation (1382–84), and this began a tradition of English renderings, including those of William Tyndale (1525–31) and Miles Coverdale (1535), that produced the authorized Bibles of the Church of England under Henry VIII (1539), Elizabeth I (1568), and, most enduring, the "authorized version" commissioned by James of Scotland in 1611. Even at this stage, however, study of the Hebrew and Greek originals was still in its infancy, and the more adequate foundation of the English Bible in them would have to await much later revisions, the Revised Version of 1881 to 1885 and the celebrated Revised Standard Version (see below) of 1946 to 1952. As for the routed Roman Catholics of England, their scholars in exile produced a New Testament at Rheims in 1582, then the Old Testament at Douay (1609–10), but both were slavishly dependent on the Latin Vulgate and desperately needed the considerable revision given them under Bishop Richard Challoner (1749–63). English bibles for Catholics could not be fully based on the original texts until the pontificate of Pius XII, in the middle of the twentieth century, and the recent New American Bible (see below) is among the first fruits of that revolution.

Bruce, F. F. *History of the Bible in English.* OUP 1978 $9.95. ISBN 0-19-520088-8. Effectively attunes its reader to the complexity and the marvelous consistency of the tradition of English renderings.

The Complete Bible: An American Translation. U. Ch. Pr. 1939 o.p. An American effort, better known as the "Chicago Bible," spearheaded by E. J. Goodspeed's initiative to bring the New Testament out from under the shroud of archaic "biblical" English. This bible is one of the first to accomplish the shift to attractive contemporary idiom.

The Holy Bible: King James Version. NAL-Dutton 1974 $7.95. ISBN 0-452-00617-1. The "authorized version" of 1611, which continues in diligent use among more conservative, "evangelical" Christians who abhor any modernizing of the biblical language; although it was a towering literary achievement justly celebrated for the depth of its interpretative insight by seventeenth-century standards, the King James Version speaks an English that is often opaque to even cultivated readers today and the translators' access to the texts was obviously obstructed by the primitive philology and historical science practiced in their era. This honored version remains in widespread use, but many users seem to relish its hieratic spell while failing to comprehend what it says. The King James version (Nelson 1982) presents the old text with stylistic revisions aimed at narrowing the gap between the King James Version and modern English usage. It does not, however, surmount the critical weaknesses nor the basic idiomatic barriers of its ancestor.

The Holy Bible: New International Version, Containing the Old Testament and New Testament. Zondervan 1984 $17.99. ISBN 0-310-90326-2. A conservative, but respectable, translation into modern English by an interdenominational team of Protestant scholars of "evangelical" persuasion.

The Holy Bible: The New Revised Standard Version. Nelson-Hall 1990 $17.95. ISBN 0-8407-1383-5. As explained in the preface, this is "an authorized revision of the Revised Standard Version, published in 1952, which was a revision of the American Standard Version, published in 1901, which, in turn, embodied earlier revisions of the King James Version, published in 1611."

Kubo, Sakae, and Walter Specht. *So Many Versions?* Zondervan 1983 $16.99. ISBN 0-310-45691-6. An incisive critical review of 15 English versions produced in this century.

Metzger, Bruce, and Roland E. Murphy, eds. *The New Oxford Annotated Bible with the Apocryphal/Deuterocanonical Books.* OUP 1991 $39.95. ISBN 0-19-528356-2. One of the best of the annotated editions, presenting the New Revised Standard Version with introductions to each biblical book and footnoted explanations of points in the text. It enjoys broad interconfessional endorsement and is a truly first-class study bible.

The New American Bible: Revised New Testament. Eerdmans 1988 $4.95. ISBN 0-8028-0417-9. See also Donald Senior, ed., *The Catholic Study Bible.*

The New American Bible: Translated from the Original Languages with Critical Use of All the Ancient Sources; with Textual Notes on Old Testament Readings. 2 vols. in 1. St. Anthony Guild o.p. A fresh translation replacing earlier Catholic translations bound to the Latin Vulgate and the old Douay-Rheims version from the Counter-Reformation.

The New Jerusalem Bible. Ed. by A. Jones. Doubleday 1990 $35.00. ISBN 0-385-14264-1. A highly attractive and successful Roman Catholic annotated version, based on a critically acclaimed French vernacular translation.

The Revised English Bible with the Apocrypha. OUP 1989 $21.95. ISBN 0-19-529408-4. A revision of the *New English Bible* that, like its predecessor, is both extremely readable and reliable in the sense that it reflects the latest stages of biblical and textual scholarship.

Senior, Donald, ed. *The Catholic Study Bible.* OUP 1990 $29.95. ISBN 0-685-45424-X. Offers the text of *The New American Bible,* including the revised New Testament, along with over 600 pages of study guide. Introductory articles, as well as reading guides to specific books in both testaments span roughly the first quarter of this more than 2,000 page book. Following the text of the Old and New Testaments is a series of helpful reference articles. The reference material in this hefty publication is written with the novice in mind and is remarkably comprehensive.

Suggs, M. Jack, and others, eds. *The Oxford Study Bible: Revised English Bible with the Apocrypha.* OUP 1992 $37.95. ISBN 0-19-529000-3. Excellent modern English rendering with annotations from Jewish, Catholic, and Protestant scholars, make this a perfect companion resource to *The Revised English Bible with the Apocrypha* (see above).

Tanakh, of The Holy Scriptures: A New Translation According to the Traditional Hebrew Text. JPS Phila. 1985 $23.95. ISBN 0-8276-0252-9. A fresh translation by leading American Jewish scholars that adheres closely to the received Hebrew text but provides ample notes on textual problems and variant readings. Since 1985 both Jewish and non-Jewish readers have been favored with the funneling of these texts with revisions into a single volume. This most recent link in a long chain of Jewish Bible translations enjoys the benefit of the translators' exposure to wide-ranging biblical interpretation, as well as their tenacity in employing a graceful contemporary English idiom

Throckmorton, B. H. *Gospel Parallels: A Synopsis of the First Three Gospels.* Van Nos. Reinhold 1979 $43.95. ISBN 0-442-30683-0. English (Revised Standard Version) edition of the Huck-Lietzmann gospel synopsis offering a less complicated and cheaper alternative to the Aland *Synopsis of the Four Gospels* (see above under Critical Editions of Original Texts) that is also available in wholly English format and includes John's Gospel, whereas Throckmorton restricts John to pertinent footnote citation.

Weigle, L. A. *The New Testament Octapla: Eight English Versions of the New Testament in the Tyndale-King James Tradition.* Nelson-Hall 1962 o.p. The interested student can compare eight older English versions, including the King James Version and the Revised Standard Version, which represent milestones in the history of the English Bible.

Chronology of Principal Versions

1382. WYCLIF BIBLE

JOHN WYCLIF (or Wycliffe, Wiclif, Wickliffe) (c. 1330–1384) initiated the first complete translation of the Bible from the Vulgate into English in order to reach the people directly. He himself translated the Gospels and probably the rest of the New Testament and part of the Old Testament. He entrusted the editing to John Purvey, who completed the translation (c.1388).

1525–1566. TYNDALE BIBLE

The first printed English Bible was William Tyndale's New Testament. His translation of the Pentateuch was issued in 1530 with revisions of both in 1534–1535. Tyndale began his translation of the New Testament from Greek into the vernacular and, finding publication impossible in England, left for Hamburg (1525); he completed at Worms the printing of 3,000 New Testaments in small octavo, which were smuggled into England and there suppressed by bishops (only five or six copies are now extant). Constantly harassed, he was finally imprisoned, strangled, and burned at the stake, in spite of intercession by Thomas Cromwell.

1535–1537. COVERDALE BIBLE

Miles Coverdale was a former colleague of Tyndale who completed the work left unfinished by Tyndale's death. It was produced in Germany in 1535.

1537. MATTHEW'S BIBLE

With the royal approval of Henry VIII in 1537, a new translation appeared. Supposedly the work of Thomas Matthew, it is more likely that it was the work of John Rodgers, another colleague of Tyndale. To avoid the embarrassment of official sponsorship of work most decidedly that of the executed Tyndale and of Coverdale, a fictitious translator's name may have been used.

1539. THE GREAT BIBLE

Authorized by Henry VIII in 1538, this was a revision of the text of Matthew's Bible. Every parish was ordered to have a copy of this bible in its church, with half the cost to be borne by the parishioners. It was known as the Great Bible because of its massive size. The Psalms in the Protestant Episcopal Prayer Book through the revision of 1928 followed this translation. A long preface by Archbishop Cranmer in the second edition of 1540 explains why it is sometimes referred to as the Cranmer Bible.

1560–1644. THE GENEVA BIBLE

As the first Bible in Roman type, it became quite popular. It was also the first English Bible to use marginal notes and verse divisions. It is often known as the "Breeches" Bible because of the rendering of Genesis 3:7: "They sewed figge-tree leaves together, and made thcmselves breeches." It was published by English exiles in Geneva and brought to America by the Pilgrims. An edition of this version was the first Bible printed at the Cambridge University Press in 1591; its publication broke the monopoly in Bible production in England, held up to that time by the king's printer in London. It was the favored Bible in England for half a century because of its excellent translation, though its Calvinist slant was a source of irritation to King James I.

1568–1606. THE BISHOP'S BIBLE

A revision of the Great Bible; each book bears the initials of the bishop who translated it. The 1602 edition was made the basis of the King James Version.

1582–1610. DOUAY VERSION

This was a translation published at the English College in the town of Douai in northern France. Modern editions differ somewhat from the original, but the Bible used by Roman Catholics at the present day is, on the whole, the Douay translation. The Confraternity Version (see below) was intended to replace the Douay Version in the United States. The Roman Catholic Bible differs from the Protestant Bible not only in rendering but also in the order of the books, the titles of the books, and the number of the books. The books of the Apocrypha are accepted as canonical and appear in the Roman Catholic Bible scattered among the various books of the Old and New Testaments. The peculiarity of the Douay Version, also known as the Douay-Rheims Bible, by which it is distinguished from Protestant versions, is the fact that it was translated from a Latin manuscript. The earliest manuscripts of the Old Testament are in Hebrew, and of the New Testament in Greek. When Rome conquered the world, and Latin became the speech of the people, there was need of a translation of the Bible into Latin, into the vulgar language—the language of the *vulgus*, the crowd. The Douay Version is a translation of the Latin Translation called the Vulgate. The Vulgate (c.383–405) was the work of SAINT JEROME (Eusebius Hieronymous, c.340–420), one of the four doctors of the church, who spent most of his life in a monastery in Bethlehem writing several ecclesiastical works.

1611. KING JAMES VERSION

The King James Version is known as the Authorized Version, although, as a matter of fact, it was never authorized by the king. It was, however, initiated by him as the result of a Puritan complaint that the Coverdale Authorized Version, revised as the Bishop's Bible (1568), was inaccurate. He appointed a group of scholars to undertake the task of fresh translation. Later editions had printed on their title pages, "Appointed to be read in the churches," which probably gave rise to the legend of authorization. The King James Version was made between 1607 and 1611, during the lifetime of Shakespeare (see Vol. 1)—the Golden Age of English literature. It was translated by 54 scholars and remains the most famous English Bible. The late Dwight Macdonald (1906–1982) (like many who value the Bible as literature) regretted the fact that those who, with justice, set out to correct this translation usually went too far and bowdlerized great passages. For many, the King James Version, with all its imperfections, can never be surpassed for poetry, religious feeling, and majesty and loveliness of utterance. In *Against the American Grain* (1952), in his essay on the Revised Standard Version called "Updating the Bible," Macdonald writes: "The King James Version is probably the greatest translation ever made. It is certainly 'The Noblest Monument of English Prose,' as the late John Livingston Lowes called his essay on the subject. 'Its phraseology,' he wrote, 'has become part and parcel of our common tongue. . . . Its rhythms and cadences, its turns of speech, its familiar imagery, its very words are woven into the texture of our literature. . . . The English of the Bible . . . is characterized not merely by a homely vigor and pithiness of phrase but also by a singular nobility of diction and by a rhythmic quality which is, I think, unrivalled in its beauty.' . . . The speed with which it was accomplished was possible only because it was not so much a translation as a synthesis of earlier efforts, the final form given to a continuous process of creation, the climax to the great century of English Bible translation." The *New King James Version* was published in 1982.

1661–1663. THE ALGONQUIAN BIBLE

The first Bible printed in America was not the King James Version but a translation by John Eliot for the Algonquian Indians called the Up-Biblum God.

1881–1885. THE ENGLISH REVISED VERSION

The Revised Version of the King James was begun in 1870 at the Convocation of Canterbury by two committees, British and American, the latter advisory only. The New Testament was issued in 1881, the Old Testament in 1885, and the Apocrypha in 1895, by the Oxford and Cambridge University Presses. In 1901 the surviving members of the American Committee published through Thomas Nelson Publishing Company, then of New York, the American Revised Version embodying the readings they had previously suggested and other improvements. The revisions had been undertaken for two reasons:

1. The discovery of fresh Bible manuscripts spurred revision. When the King James Version of the Bible was made, there had not yet been discovered three early manuscripts of the Bible: the Vatican manuscript, fourth century (in the Vatican library, Rome); the Sinaitic manuscript, fourth century (discovered on Mount Sinai, and long in Leningrad, purchased in 1934 by the Trustees of the British Museum for £100,000 from the Soviet government, the highest price ever paid for a manuscript or printed book); the Alexandrian manuscript, fifth century (in the British Museum). The discovery of these three manuscripts gave to translators a Bible text older and more accurate than any they had had before, and so much new light was thrown on obscure passages in the Scriptures that a fresh translation was not only warranted but demanded.

2. The second reason for revision was the archaic character of the language of the King James Version; so many words in the King James Version are obsolete, or have lost their original meaning, that contemporary readers no longer understand them in their intended sense. For instance, David prays that the Lord may enlarge his feet. In the Revised Version, the word *enlarge* is changed to *set free*. This original meaning of the word survives today in the phrase *at large*, meaning "free."

The translators of the Revised Version did not put the Bible into modern English—other translators have done that—but they did revise archaic words that are misleading in sense in the present day, and they corrected many mistranslations. An updated edition of the American Standard Version was published as *The New American Standard Bible* in 1971.

1917. THE JEWISH VERSION

Published by the Jewish Publication Society of America, *The Holy Scriptures According to the Masoretic Text* was produced in "Bible English." An earlier translation, made by Isaac Leeser in 1853, in Philadelphia, was a single-handed effort and never claimed a wide Jewish readership. Up to this time, the English Bible used by those professing Judaism has been either the King James Version or the Revised Version. Orthodox Jews have preferred the King James Version because it does not use the name Jehovah, the ineffable divine name that never occurs in the Jewish version. The Hebrew Bible (Old Testament only) is not called the Holy Bible, but the Holy Scriptures. Actually, in fact, the word *bible* does not occur in the Bible itself. It came from the Latin *biblia*, from the Greek *biblia*, plural of *biblion*, the diminutive of *biblos*, "book"—"little book."

The paragraphing of the Jewish version follows that of the Revised Version. Verse divisions, uniform with those of the King James Version, are indicated in small type. The correspondence is in some cases approximate rather than identical, because the Jews divide the Old Testament into 24 books, while the Protestants divide it into 39 books. Moreover, the order of the Hebrew Bible is at several junctures different from the order of the Protestant. The Hebrew Bible ends with an incomplete sentence, the twenty-third verse of 2 Chronicles, "let him go up." In the Protestant Bible the Book of Ezra follows after 2 Chronicles and completes the sentence, "let him go up to Jerusalem which is in Judah."

The Revised Translation of the Holy Scriptures for Jews was undertaken in 1955 by the Jewish Publication Society. It is a complete revision of the 1917 version and embodies all the latest findings of modern biblical scholarship for all people, together with a modern text that is free from all archaism of language and therefore is more understandable to Jewish laymen. The first volume of *A New Translation of the Holy Scriptures According to the Masoretic Text* is the *Torah*, which appeared in 1963; in 1978 the second volume, *The Prophets*, was published; and in 1982 *The Writings* appeared. In 1985 all three volumes were first published as a one-volume Jewish Bible.

1945–1949. THE KNOX VERSION

This Roman Catholic version was translated into modern English by Monsignor Ronald Knox in England and is officially approved by the Roman Catholic church.

1946–1952. THE REVISED STANDARD VERSION

This is the authorized revision of the American Standard Version. Important manuscripts and fragments became available that were not known in 1611 or even in 1901 when the American Standard Version appeared. An old Syrian version of the Gospels, probably of the second century, was found in a monastery on Mount Sinai; in 1933 a fragment of Tatian's Harmony of the Four Gospels was discovered at Dura on the Euphrates; and most important of all was the discovery of fragments of 12 manuscripts, now known as the Chester Beatty manuscripts, 3 of them from the New Testament, which may date as early as the first half of the third century. In addition to the biblical documents, a great number of Greek papyri and papyrus fragments were unearthed in Egypt. These writings were contemporary with the New Testament and, together with inscriptions, furnished new meaning to Greek words and phrases as they were used in the years when the New Testament was written.

In 1928 a committee of 15 scholars was appointed by the International Council of Religious Education, with which the educational boards of 44 of the major Protestant denominations of the United States and Canada are associated, and to which the copyright of the American Standard Version had been transferred. Although lack of funds delayed the work, it was finally begun in 1937. The committee was divided into two sections, one for the Old Testament and one for the New. Dean Luther A. Weigle of the Yale Divinity School served as chair of the whole committee, and JAMES MOFFATT was the executive secretary from 1937 until his death in 1944. The New Testament appeared in 1946, the Old Testament in 1952, and the Apocrypha in 1957.

The publication of the Revised Standard Version of the Holy Bible in September 1952 aroused great public interest and a new sales record was set: 1,600,000 copies in the first six weeks after publication.

1961–1970. THE NEW ENGLISH BIBLE
(SOMETIMES CALLED THE OXFORD BIBLE)

An entirely new translation from the original Greek into current English, this version was prepared under the direction of all leading Protestant churches in the British Isles. The New Testament appeared first in 1961 and was published in its second edition in 1970. A new translation of the Old Testament and the Apocrypha was published in 1970. Scholars of different denominations and from a number of British universities took part in the work, providing a faithful rendering of the best available Greek texts that reflected the most recent biblical scholarship. The new translation was directed by the Joint Committee of the Churches, which consisted of representatives of the Church of England, the Church of Scotland, the Methodist Church, the Congregational Union, the Baptist Union, the Presbyterian Church of England, the Churches in Wales, the Churches in Ireland, the Society of Friends, the British and Foreign Bible Society, and the National Bible Society of Scotland. The university presses at Oxford and Cambridge published the new translation, which was released simultaneously worldwide. The introduction states, "In assessing the evidence, the translators have taken into account (a) ancient manuscripts of the New Testament in Greek, (b) manuscripts of early translations into other languages, and (c) quotations from the New Testament by early Christian writers. . . . In particular, our knowledge of the kind of Greek used by most of the New Testament writers has been greatly enriched since 1881 by the discovery of many thousands of papyrus documents in popular or nonliterary Greek of about the same period as the New Testament. . . . Taken as a whole, our version claims to be a translation, free, it may be, rather than literal, but a faithful translation nevertheless, so far as we could compass it. . . . But always the overriding aims were accuracy and clarity. . . . The translators are as conscious as anyone can be of the limitations and imperfections of their work. No one who has not tried it can know how impossible an art translation is. . . . Yet we may hope that we have been able to convey to our readers something at least of what the New Testament has said to us during these years of work, and trust that under the providence of Almighty God this translation may open the truth of the scriptures to many who have been hindered in their approach to it by barriers of language."

1966. THE JERUSALEM BIBLE

Originally a modern translation in French prepared by Dominican scholars in Jerusalem (1956), La Bible de Jerusalem became The Jerusalem Bible when it was translated into English in 1966. A new edition titled *The New Jerusalem Bible* was published in 1985.

1970. CONFRATERNITY VERSION

Generally known as the Confraternity Edition, the Confraternity Version is a new translation, the first made from the original Hebrew and Greek languages for Roman Catholics, and intended to replace the Douay Version for public reading in the United States. The Confraternity revision of the New Testament translation was made in 1941.

The new translation of the Old Testament, made in accordance with directives of the late Pope Pius XII in his encyclical letter of September 30, 1943, was sponsored by the Bishops' Committee of the Confraternity of Christian Doctrine. These translations made their first appearance in 1952, with the work completed in 1970 and published as *The New American Bible*. The *N.Y.*

Times Book Review said: "It was a stroke of genius to give a new name to the awkwardly designated 'Confraternity Version of the Bible' and call it, in its final definitive edition, 'The New American Bible.' . . . The English of the new version is simple and natural and exhibits none of the painful Latinity of the Douay version. While they were putting the Bible into standard modern English, the translators were also able to take advantage of the remarkable achievements of recent Catholic, Protestant and Jewish scholarship."

1989. THE REVISED ENGLISH BIBLE

In large measure, the New English Bible (NEB), completed in 1970, had succeeded in making accessible to contemporary British and non-British readers well-known biblical narratives, proverbs, parables, and ideals that had long since become domesticated in Western culture. As was true of its predecessor, the Revised English Bible (REB) committee of translators consist-ed of British scholars selected for their scholarly talent rather than for their church affiliation. As it set about revising what was widely regarded as a pioneering modern language translation, the new committee was mindful of recent contributions made to biblical scholarship as well as the more legitimate criticisms leveled against the NEB.

For example, the NEB committee had not expected that its product would be used in public readings, and, when its popularity with general readers led to such usage, it was found wanting. Thus, the REB committee modified some of the idiomatic English of the NEB in order to confer on the new product "appropriate dignity for liturgical use." If the REB is less idiomatic than its predecessor, the price paid for alleged dignity is not so high that it actually jeopardizes the committee's goal to offer the public a truly comprehensible and precise English translation. Finally, it should be noted that, in addition to carefully reviewing available Hebrew, Aramaic, and Greek texts, the translation committee invited a number of writers and poets to assess the new translation from a literary perspective.

1990. THE NEW REVISED STANDARD VERSION

The New Revised Standard Version (NRSV) presents itself as the most recent link in a chain of tradition tracing back to 1611, when the King James Version, long celebrated for its lofty cadences, was first issued and became the authorized translation of English-speaking people. Since 1952, when it was initially published in its entirety, the Revised Standard Version (RSV), under the sponsorship of the National Council of Churches of Christ in the USA, has become the mainstay Bible translation of American Protestants. Moreover, it is no stranger to other segments of American Christianity that recognized its usefulness in private reading, public worship, and the classroom. Though the RSV is expected to continue in publication until 1995, a revised edition was issued in 1990 and was promptly endorsed by Protestants, Orthodox, and Roman Catholic theologians. Again, under the auspices of the National Council of Churches, a committee of highly competent biblical scholars worked in close collaboration for more than a decade as they gave shape to the final product. As a widely representative body of male and female translators associated with Protestant, Orthodox, Roman Catholic, and Jewish traditions, the 30-member committee labored diligently to produce an accurate, unbiased, and readable translation. It operated under the maxim, "as *literal* as possible, as *free* as necessary."

During the past three decades, interest in translating the Bible has been especially intense. Clearly, several crucial factors argued for a replacement of the RSV. Since 1952, scholarly perceptions of the biblical text have been sharpened both by virtue of impressive archaeological discoveries and an ever-improving command of ancient biblical languages. Furthermore, the English language has recently experienced dramatic changes, including the advent of new words, shifting meanings of known terms, and the commitment of increasing numbers of persons to avoid gender-exclusive language when possible. As it renders the ancient biblical languages of Hebrew, Aramaic, and Greek into English, the NRSV is predominantly a literal translation. Nevertheless, since a word-for-word rendering often yields a poorly understood product, the committee was not timid about resorting to free translation if that appeared to be the sole mechanism for replicating in English the meaning of an ancient word or phrase. Given its predilection for contemporary idiom that, among other things, eliminates many male-centered terms and all of the archaic *thees* and *thous*, the NRSV makes itself readily understood by a general readership. Moreover, it addresses certain infelicities that plagued its parent (e.g., the phrase "I will accept no bull from your house" in the RSV of Psalm 50:9 is rendered in the NRSV as "I will not accept a bull from your house"). Compensating for the absence of a common gender third-person singular pronoun in English, ancient singular discourse is often transformed into the plural (e.g., "Happy are those who" replaces the RSV "Blessed is the man who" in Psalm 1:1). Admittedly, such shifts do not please all readers. Even so, the NRSV promises to be a definitive translation for several decades to come.

Textual Criticism

The original texts of the Bible came down through handwritten (manuscript) copying, long before the invention of the printing press. The variations of reading, both deliberate and accidental, that transmission by hand inevitably entailed create the need for a complex discipline for restoring the original text. The highly refined norms of this discipline, and the typical procedures of its application to disputed passages, are the subject of works listed below. One must remember that textual criticism cannot achieve conclusive results operating by itself, apart from the other methods of interpreting the sacred writers' thoughts. All component disciplines of biblical interpretation must be in communication and cooperation with one another, since determining what was *written* and what was *meant* are complementary and interacting pursuits.

Aland, Kurt, and Barbara Aland. *The Text of the New Testament*. Trans. by Erroll F. Rhodes. Eerdmans 1990 $34.95. ISBN 0-8028-3662-3. An excellent introduction to the critical editions of the New Testament and to the theory and practice of modern textual criticism by the most authoritative practitioners of the discipline.

Cambridge History of the Bible. 3 vols. Cambridge U. Pr. Vol. 1 *From the Beginnings to Jerome*. Ed. by P. R. Ackroyd and C. F. Evans. 1975 $39.95. ISBN 0-521-09973-0. Vol. 2 *The West from the Fathers to the Reformation*. Ed. by G. W. Lampe. 1975 $74.95. ISBN 0-521-04255-0. Vol. 3 *The West from the Reformation to the Present Day*. Ed. by S. L. Greenslade. 1975 $39.95. ISBN 0-521-29016-3

Metzger, Bruce M. *The Canon of the New Testament: Its Origin, Development, and Significance*. OUP 1987 $59.00. ISBN 0-19-826180-2. Offers a full-scale survey of biblical literature published from the seventeenth through the twentieth centuries; after spelling out his own understanding of the canonization process in detail, the author reflects on certain historical and theological issues (e.g., inspiration, criteria defining canonicity, the plurality of the Gospels).

———. *The Early Versions of the New Testament.* OUP 1977 $29.95. ISBN 0-19-826170-5. Indispensable witnesses to the scriptural text, the ancient translations, Eastern and Western, including the ancestor languages of those currently spoken, are introduced and evaluated as mediators of the Greek text of the New Testament.

———. *Text of the New Testament: Its Transmission, Corruption, and Restoration.* OUP 1992 $16.95. ISBN 0-19-507297-9. General study for the nonspecialist by one of the foremost practitioners of New Testament textual criticism; especially good for students.

———, ed. *A Textual Commentary on the Greek New Testament.* Am. Bible 1975 $14.95. ISBN 3-438-06010-8. A unique reference tool intended for use with Aland, *The Greek New Testament* (see above under Reference Works, Critical Editions of Original Texts), offering a brief documentation and explanation of the editors' decisions on major variant readings.

Wurthwein, Ernst. *The Text of the Old Testament (Text Des Alten Testaments).* Trans. by Erroll F. Rhodes. Eerdmans 1980 $19.95. ISBN 0-8028-3530-9. An indispensable workbook for the study of the Hebrew text, introducing both the many witnesses to the text and the steps in the procedure for restoring it in the presence of conflicting variant readings.

HISTORICAL BACKGROUND OF THE BIBLE

Histories of Judaism and Early Christianity

Recognition that the writings of the Bible came from specific locations in the distant human past and were essentially conditioned by their time and place has been the intellectual foundation of modern biblical studies. Three periods should be studied as indispensable background for the sacred books: the history of Israel from the period of the Hebrew ancestors (patriarchs, c.1750 B.C.) through the Babylonian exile (586–539 B.C.), the history of the intertestamental period from after the exile through the time of Christ, and the history of the New Testament period (reaching into the early second century A.D.). These are the broad and very unequal periods to which most historical-background titles are devoted.

HISTORY OF ISRAEL

Albright, William Foxwell. *From the Stone Age to Christianity: Monotheism and the Historical Process.* Johns Hopkins 1957 o.p. Admittedly conservative by present standards, this classic explains in engaging prose Albright's thesis that monotheism is the driving force behind the history of Western civilization.

Bright, John. *A History of Israel.* Westminster John Knox 1981 $26.99. ISBN 0-664-21381-2. Although this presentation is still within the relatively conservative principles of the Albright school, it deserves the high praise it has drawn from many reviewers and teachers who have used it.

Edwards, I. E., and N. G. Hammond, eds. *The Cambridge Ancient History.* 12 vols. Cambridge U. Pr. 1927–1992 $63.00–$145.00. Wide coverage of the world of the Old and New Testament. With companion volumes of illustration plates.

Hayes, John H., and J. Maxwell Miller, eds. *Israelite and Judaean History. Old Testament Lib.* Westminster John Knox 1990 $29.95. ISBN 0-334-02435-8. A collection of 11 major essays, offering a wide-ranging critical assessment of the contributions of major schools of thought through the Roman era.

Miller J. Maxwell, and John H. Hayes. *A History of Ancient Israel and Judah.* Westminster John Knox 1986 $30.00. ISBN 0-664-21262-X. A balanced and comprehensive survey of biblical history from the era of the Judges to the post-exilic era of Ezra–Nehemiah. Fully investigates the available resources of Israelite and Judean history. Regularly penetrates through the theoretical overlay of the bible in order to come more fully to terms with social, political, and economic dimensions of biblical Israel's history.

Noth, Martin. *A History of Israel: Biblical History.* HarpC 1960 $16.95. ISBN 0-06-066310-3. This classic formulation of the history of biblical Israel is informed by the German-based Alt-Noth school, which is more skeptical in its handling of early Israelite history than is the American-based school of Albright-Bright.

Rogerson, John, and Philip Davies. *The Old Testament World.* P-H 1989 $39.00. ISBN 0-13-634049-0. A richly illustrated text that sketches the geography, ecology, social, and political organization of biblical Israel, surveying main developments in its history and religion, considering diverse literary and sociological influences on individual books in the Old Testament canon, and reflecting on the literary unity of the Old Testament. The authors have the general reader in mind.

INTERTESTAMENTAL PERIOD

Foerster, Werner. *From the Exile to Christ: A Historical Introduction to Palestinian Judaism.* Trans. by G. E. Harris. Fortress Pr. 1964 o.p. This account is as competent and comprehensive as it can be given the gaps in the source material. The main source is the Jewish historian Flavius Josephus.

Hengel, Martin. *Judaism and Hellenism: Studies in Their Encounter in Palestine during the Early Hellenistic Period.* Trans. by John Bowden. 2 vols. 1992 $24.95. ISBN 0-8006-1495-X. One volume of text and one of notes provide a rich fund of information on the intertestamental period and are indispensable to students of that period as well as students of the New Testament.

Koester, Helmut. *History, Culture, and Religion of the Hellenistic Age.* Vol. 1 in *Introduction to the New Testament.* De Gruyter 1987 $19.95. ISBN 0-89925-351-2. A survey of the age beginning with the conquests of Alexander the Great, equipped with maps, photos, and a glossary, dedicated to setting the proximate historical context for New Testament study.

Sanders, E. P. *Judaism: Practice and Belief 63BCE–66CE.* TPI PA 1991 $39.95. ISBN 1-56338-016-1. An appealing and wide-ranging survey of Judaism during that eventful century-and-a-half interval between the Roman conquest of Palestine in 63 B.C. and the onset of the Jewish revolt against Rome leading to the destruction of the Second Jerusalem Temple in A.D. 70.

NEW TESTAMENT PERIOD

Bultmann, Rudolf. *Primitive Christianity: In Its Contemporary Setting.* Trans. by Reginald H. Fuller. Fortress Pr. 1980 repr. of 1956 ed. $12.95. ISBN 0-8006-1408-9. A persuasive study of how late Judaism, Greek paganism, Stoicism, and Gnosticism significantly shaped early Christian beliefs and practices.

Court, John, and Kathleen Court. *The New Testament World.* P-H 1990 $40.00. ISBN 0-13-538992-5. Drawing on the contributions of various archaeologists, historians, and sociologists, this richly illustrated volume clearly portrays human culture in the time of Jesus and is especially recommended for the nonspecialist.

Ferguson, Everett. *Backgrounds of Early Christianity.* Eerdmans 1987 $24.95. ISBN 0-8028-0292-3. A broadly conceived yet compactly written volume spelling out the historical origins of Christianity in a manner that is advantageous for both experienced and inexperienced scholars of the Bible.

Jeremias, Joachim. *Jerusalem in the Time of Jesus: An Investigation into Economic and Social Conditions during the New Testament Period.* Trans. by F. H. Cave and C. H. Cave. Fortress Pr. 1975 $13.95. ISBN 0-8006-1136-5. Since less than half of this competent volume focuses on Jerusalem as such, it is better characterized as a survey of prevailing social conditions in all of Palestine that were contemporary with Jesus.

Kee, Howard Clark. *Jesus in History.* HarBraceJ 1977 $15.50. ISBN 0-15-547382-4. A fascinating survey of both biblical and extrabiblical sources for our knowledge of Jesus, providing a balanced analysis of gospel traditions about Jesus as well as noncanonical traditions.

Lohse, Edward. *The New Testament Environment*. Trans. by John E. Steely. Abingdon 1976 $12.95. ISBN 0-687-27944-5. Divided into Jewish and Hellenistic Roman "environments," this work sketches both contemporary political history and currents in religion and culture in a convenient reference work for the casual student and beginners in the field.

Schürer, Emil. *A History of the Jewish People in the Age of Jesus Christ (175 B.C.–135 A.D.): A New English Version*. Ed. by Matthew Black and Martin Goodman. 3 vols. in 4. Fortress Pr. 1973–86 $59.95–$64.95. ISBN 0-567-02242-0. This nineteenth-century classic is given a new adaptation, with new information and up-to-date bibliographies, to maintain its stature as an irreplaceable authority on the subject.

Biblical Archaeology

Although archaeology is among the younger sciences, scarcely yet 150 years old, it has made a significant impact on twentieth-century biblical interpretation. The investigation of ancient sites and of the literatures found at them, or near them, has given us exciting new terms of comparison for what we read in the Bible. For example, the excavations of the ancient Babylonian civilization at Mari, and the discovery of written tablets at places like Amarna on the Nile and Ras Shamra in coastal Syria, shed fresh light on many features of lore and language previously considered unique to the Old Testament. If the artifactual and epigraphic data unearthed by field archaeologists seldom prove the "truth" of the Bible, they do much in the way of supplementing the text. Spectacular sites in Israel itself, including Hazor and Tel Dan in the North, Caesarea on the coast, Megiddo on the central plain, Gezer in the Judean hills, Jericho and Qumran near the Dead Sea, and the sector of the temple-mount in Jerusalem, have illumined the whole course of the region's history, from the distant beginnings of civilization down through the successive conquests of the Arabs, the Crusaders, and the Turks. The following titles are selected from among the most seminal works in this rapidly expanding field.

Albright, William F. *The Archaeology of Palestine*. Peter Smith 1976 $19.00. ISBN 0-8446-0003-2. A useful volume explaining how archaeologists execute their field work, identifying significant twentieth-century accomplishments in Syro-Palestinian archaeology, and commenting on the occupants and customs of that region in light of the artifactual data uncovered.

Avi-Yonah, Michael, ed. *Encyclopedia of Archaeological Excavations in the Holy Land*. 4 vols. P-H 1975 o.p. A comprehensive survey of 155 sites and topics drawn from the contributions of 68 scholars, many of whom led the excavations on which they report.

Dever, William G. *Recent Archaeological Discoveries and Biblical Research*. U. of Wash. Pr. 1990 $14.95. ISBN 0-295-96588-6. A generously illustrated volume, reflecting realistically on the relationship between excavated evidence and the biblical text and showing no patience whatsoever with the tendentious use of archaeological data to endorse notions about biblical inerrancy.

Finegan, Jack. *Archaeology of the New Testament: The Life of Jesus and the Beginning of the Early Church*. Princeton U. Pr. 1970 $29.95. ISBN 0-691-00220-7. One of the better discussions of sites and symbols connected with Christian beginnings, culling the best information and presenting it in highly readable prose.

Mazar, Amihai. *Archaeology of the Land of the Bible: 10,000–586 B.C.E. Anchor Bible Reference Lib*. Doubleday 1990 $20.00. ISBN 0-385-23970-X. Buttressed by many illustrations and extensive citations, this commanding volume focuses on materials gleaned from cultures in and around the land of Canaan from the Neolithic period down to the end of the Iron Age.

Moorey, Roger. *A Century of Biblical Archaeology*. Westminster John Knox 1992 $14.99. ISBN 0-664-25392-X. Provides a concise historical survey of major archaeological undertakings in Israel and the Near East between 1890 (when Syro-Palestinian archaeology under Sir Flinders Petrie truly began to be driven by scientific principles) and 1990, focusing on the attempt by archaeologists in the last 30 years to establish the methods and goals of "biblical archaeology."

Murphy-O'Connor, Jerome. *The Holy Land: An Archaeological Guide from Earliest Times to 1700*. OUP 1992 $14.95. ISBN 0-19-285269-8. More a studious tourist's guide than a primer in archaeological science, this small volume is nevertheless a wonderful companion for Holy Land visits, elegantly written and lightly seasoned with the author's native humour and long experience on the scene.

Biblical Geography

To any historical investigation, geography is one of the principal coordinates, together with chronology. An appreciation of the location and natural circumstances of biblical sites adds appreciably, sometimes substantively, to the understanding of biblical texts. The features of the land the Israelite invaders coveted as they approached from the east, the stark contrasts between the fertile and barren regions different tribes obtained, the bucolic hills of Galilee, the stunning beauty of the Jordan Valley, the obvious sparseness of the Negev desert, and what it so clearly meant to "go *up* to Jerusalem," are only a few among the many points where biblical geography impinges on the biblical text.

Aharoni, Yohanan. *The Land of the Bible: A Historical Geography*. Trans. by A. F. Rainey. Westminster John Knox 1980 $19.99. ISBN 0-664-24266-9. A first-class expository work, giving first the setting and historic features of the Holy Land, then its historical development from the Canaanite period through the early post-exile.

Aharoni, Yohanan, and Michael Avi-Yonah. *The Macmillan Bible Atlas*. Macmillan 1977 $34.95. ISBN 0-02-500590-1. An excellent joint effort of two premier archaeologists with map specialists, featuring 264 maps pertaining to every period of biblical history, each accompanied by full and effective explanation.

May, Herbert G., and G. H. Hunt, eds. *Oxford Bible Atlas*. OUP 1985 $27.95. ISBN 0-19-143452-3. A small and succinct atlas, with 26 maps, accompanied by explanations of biblical history from the Patriarchs through the travels of Paul.

Pritchard, James B., ed. *The Harper Atlas of the Bible*. HarpC 1987 $44.95. ISBN 0-06-181883-6. Work of 50 international scholars; provides maps, charts, graphs, and text, supported by a useful index. A colorful and attractive book.

Roaf, Michael. *Cultural Atlas of Mesopotamia and the Ancient Near East*. Facts on File 1990 $45.00. ISBN 0-8160-2218-6. A helpful survey of ancient civilizations in the fertile crescent, lucidly written, nicely illustrated, and organized under three headings: Villages, Cities, Empires.

Vogel E. K., ed. *Bibliography of Holy Land Sites*. Vol. 42 in *Hebrew Union College Annual*. Am. Schls. Oriental 1982 $5.00. ISBN 0-87820-626-4. A valuable listing according to biblical sites, arranged alphabetically.

Biblical Backgrounds and Extracanonical Materials

Sound biblical interpretation operates on the assumption that the Jewish and Christian scriptures should not be considered apart from their larger literary context. This textual environment may be identified according to the two different categories of materials. First are the contemporary writings of Jewish and Christian authors that were never gathered into the biblical canon. Second are the diverse literary products of neighboring cultures that often help to illumine the biblical text.

A central element in the first category is the Apocrypha. That name is given to 14 books written between 200 B.C. and A.D. 100. This period between the Old and New Testaments is often termed the "intertestamental period." The word *apocrypha* comes from a Greek word meaning "hidden." In time the term was also thought to designate that which was "spurious," since those who were not conversant with this literature dismissed it as being riddled with esoteric and even heretical elements. In our day, Roman Catholicism accepts the books of the Apocrypha as of like inspiration with the other books of the Bible. Since both Judaism and Protestantism deem them of lesser inspiration, they deny them canonical status. If one but reads a portion of the following list, he or she should develop a fuller appreciation for the often fascinating larger literary environment of biblical texts.

Barnstone, Willis, ed. *The Other Bible.* HarpC 1984 $20.00. ISBN 0-06-250030-9. A wide-ranging collection of manifestly esoteric passages from the Pseudepigrapha, the Dead Sea Scrolls, the early Kabbalah, the Nag Hammadi Gnostic literature, and so forth, with brief introductions acquainting the neophyte with the kinds of Jewish and Christian literature that never became official, "sacred" literature.

Barrett, Charles K., ed. *New Testament Background: Selected Documents.* HarpC 1989 $14.95. ISBN 0-06-060553-7. A wide selection of documents—Roman, Hellenistic, and Jewish—including interesting specimens of the Greek papyrus manuscripts presented in excerpts keyed to the interpretation of the New Testament.

Beyerlin, Walter, ed. *Near Eastern Religious Texts Relating to the Old Testament.* Trans. by John Bowden. *Old Testament Lib.* Westminster John Knox 1978 o.p. Texts from five cultures that touched ancient Israel—Egyptian, Mesopotamian, Hittite, Ugaritic, and North Semitic—are arranged under subheadings to assist their comparison with the Bible.

Charlesworth, James H., ed. *The Old Testament Pseudepigrapha.* 2 vols. Doubleday 1983–85 $40.00 ea. ISBN 0-385-19491-9. Vol. 1 *Apocalyptic Literature and Testaments.* Vol. 2 *Expansions of the Old Testament and Legends, Wisdom and Philosophical Literature, Prayers, Psalms and Odes, Fragments of Lost Judaeo-Hellenistic Works.* Fresh translations, by an international team of scholars, of a vast literature produced by Jews and Christians between 200 B.C. and A.D. 200, predominantly attributed to ideal figures of the Old Testament and claiming to contain God's revelation. The 52 writings are accompanied by a detailed introduction and footnoted commentary; they do not include the so-called Apocrypha, which were part of the Greek Bible's (Septuagint's) Old Testament and have been considered "biblical" in the Roman Catholic tradition.

———, ed. *The Pseudepigrapha and Modern Research with a Supplement.* Scholars Pr. GA 1981 $14.95. ISBN 0-89130-441-X. A brief but useful introduction to each document in the field followed by discussion of scholarly views of its background and message.

Colson, F. H., and G. H. Whitaker. *Philo with an English Translation. Loeb Class. Lib.* 10 vols. HUP 1929–62 $16.25 ea. ISBNs 0-674-99249-0, 0-674-99250-4, 0-674-99272-5, 0-674-99287-3, 0-674-99303-9, 0-674-99319-5, 0-674-99353-5, 0-674-99376-4, 0-674-99400-0, 0-674-99417-5. The Loeb collection of the writings, Greek original with facing English, of Philo Judaeus, the great Hellenistic-Jewish expositor of the Scriptures who was a contemporary of Jesus.

Cross, Frank M. *The Ancient Library of Qumran and Modern Biblical Studies. Haskell Lectures Ser.* Greenwood 1976 repr. of 1958 ed. $41.50. ISBN 0-8371-9281-1. A highly informative introduction, including an account of the discoveries and their investigation, by a major participant in the process.

Danby, Herbert, trans. *The Mishnah.* OUP 1933 $69.00. ISBN 0-19-815402-X. A full translation of the earliest body of rabbinical literature, collected around A.D. 200 and representing schools that grew up after the Jewish revolt and ensuing fall of Jerusalem in A.D. 70.

Dupont-Sommer, A. *The Essene Writings from Qumran.* Trans. by G. Vermes. Peter Smith 1973 $24.75. ISBN 0-8446-2012-2. Joseph Fitzmyer considers this the best translation of the Qumran scrolls in English, supplying the original column and line numbers for easy location of passages under discussion.

Finegan, Jack. *Myth and Mystery: An Introduction to the Pagan Religions of the Biblical World.* Baker Bk. 1989 $24.95. ISBN 0-8010-3555-4. Technical analysis of the religions of ancient Mesopotamia, Egypt, Canaan, Persia, Greece, and Rome, along with Gnosticism, Mandaeanism, and Manichaeanism, in a volume replete with archaeological data, biblical references, and scholarly citations; will better serve seasoned readers than novice ones, owing to the manifestly technical tenor of its prose.

Fitzmyer, Joseph A. *The Dead Sea Scrolls: Major Publications and Tools for Study.* Scholars Pr. GA 1990 $25.95. ISBN 1-55540-510-X. An excellent, classified bibliography furnishes guided access to the famous discoveries of Khirbet Qumran, near the Dead Sea, beginning in 1947, comprising a Jewish sectarian literature spanning the period from c.200 B.C. to A.D. 70.

————. *Responses to 101 Questions on the Dead Sea Scrolls.* Paulist Pr. 1992 $8.95. ISBN 0-8091-3348-2. Through a format that is undeniably reader-friendly, Fitzmyer has much to say about the discovery, contents, significance, and delayed publication of these Qumran finds.

Foerster, W. *Gnosis: A Selection of Gnostic Texts.* 12 vols. Trans. by R. M. Wilson. OUP 1972–74 o.p. Vol. 1 *Patristic Evidence.* Vol. 2 *Coptic and Mandean Sources.* An important collection of Christian (and post-Christian) testimonies to the mysterious phenomenon of Gnosticism, a late-Hellenistic religious movement, probably of pre-Christian origin, whose influence on the Christian sources remains among the liveliest debates of biblical studies.

Gaster, Theodor H. *The Dead Sea Scriptures.* Doubleday 1976 $12.00. ISBN 0-385-08859-0. A highly readable and popular translation of most of the scrolls with introductions and a useful analytical index.

Grant, Robert M., ed. *The Apostolic Fathers: A Translation and Commentary.* 6 vols. Nelson-Hall 1964–68 o.p. Authoritative expositions of the honored writings that followed directly upon the New Testament books in the esteem and usage of the early church, and also coincided in time with the later New Testament books.

Hengel, Martin. *Judaism and Hellenism: Studies in Their Encounter in Palestine in the Early Hellenistic Period.* Trans. by John Bowden. Fortress Pr. 1992 $24.95. ISBN 0-8006-1495-X. A comprehensive and competent treatment of those political, economic, intellectual, and religious factors that shaped Judaism's response to the challenge of encroaching Greek thought and society.

Hennecke, Edgar. *New Testament Apocrypha.* 2 vols. Westminster John Knox 1963–66 o.p. An authoritative presentation of the numerous "gospels" and apostles' "acts," "instructions," and so on, which proliferated in early Christianity, with excellent introductions and bibliographies.

James, Montague R., trans. *Apocryphal New Testament.* OUP 1924 $66.50. ISBN 0-19-826121-7. A convenient, one-volume collection now almost 70 years old and lacking more recent discoveries and scholarly perspective.

Jonas, Hans. *The Gnostic Religion: The Message of the Alien God and the Beginnings of Christianity.* Peter Smith 1958 $24.25. ISBN 0-8446-2339-3. A fascinating introduction that helps to promote a clearer understanding of the declining Hellenistic culture in which Christianity, among other religious movements from the East, achieved its rapid expansion.

Kee, Howard Clark. *The Origins of Christianity: Sources and Documents.* P-H 1973. ISBN 0-13-642553-4. Excerpts from contemporary documents illustrate political and religious history, religious and philosophical currents, and literary conventions pertinent to Christian beginnings.

Nickelsburg, George W. E. *Jewish Literature Between the Bible and the Mishnah.* Fortress Pr. 1981 $17.95. ISBN 0-8006-1980-3. Intended as a primer to the Jewish literature of the so-called intertestamental period, this volume scrutinizes Jewish texts that originated during those centuries immediately before and after the birth of Jesus.

Pritchard, James B., ed. *The Ancient Near East in Pictures Relating to the Old Testament.* Princeton U. Pr. 1969 $99.50. ISBN 0-691-03502-4. More than 750 pictures, with explanatory text, illustrate various aspects of ancient Near Eastern life and religion, especially helpful when used as a companion to the following entry.

————. *Ancient Near Eastern Texts Relating to the Old Testament.* Princeton U. Pr. 1969 $160.00. ISBN 0-8357-8001-6. The collection of absolutely first importance for Old Testament study that has grown through successive editions as the Near Eastern library itself has grown through successive discoveries.

Robinson, James M. *The Nag Hammadi Library.* HarpC 1989 $25.95. ISBN 0-06-066934-9. A crucial translation of Coptic manuscripts discovered in Egypt in 1945, which document a mostly Gnosticized, often wildly heterodox, Christianity of the second and third centuries A.D.

Sandmel, Samuel. *Philo of Alexandria: An Introduction.* OUP 1979 o.p. A convenient and informative primer for the student beginning an acquaintance with this important Jewish voice.

Schiffman, Lawrence H. *From Text to Tradition: A History of Second Temple and Rabbinic Judaism.* Ktav 1991 $16.95. ISBN 0-88125-372-3. Analyzes those changes that unfolded in Judaism between 538 B.C. and A.D. 500, discussing important methodological issues, summarizing earlier religious traditions that Judaism has inherited at the outset of the Second Temple era, and focusing generally on particular periods, places, and texts.

Smelik, K.A.D. *Writings from Ancient Israel: A Handbook of Historical and Religious Documents.* Westminster John Knox 1991 $19.99. ISBN 0-664-25308-3. Offers a lucid translation and sensitive exposition of those Palestinian texts, *ostraca* (inscribed potsherds), and seals dating between 1000 and 500 B.C. that cast significant light on the Old Testament.

Strack, H. L. *Introduction to the Talmud and Midrash.* Atheneum 1992 $21.95. ISBN 0-8006-2524-2. An old, but still useful, primer for the student seeking access to the vast rabbinic literature.

Thackeray, H. St. J. *Josephus: The Man and the Historian.* Ktav 1968 $20.00. ISBN 0-87068-115-X. This is an introduction by the historians' master translator.

Thackeray, H. St. J., and others. *Josephus with an English Translation. Loeb Class. Lib.* 10 vols. HUP 1926–65 $17.95 ea. ISBNs 0-674-99205-9, 0-674-99223-7, 0-674-99232-6, 0-674-99267-9, 0-674-99310-1, 0-674-99360-8, 0-674-99402-7, 0-674-99451-5, 0-674-99477-9, 0-674-99502-3. Furnishes a good Greek text and facing English translation of the *Jewish Antiquities* and *Wars of the Jews,* two works by the Palestinian-Jewish historian Josephus, who offers a record of events in the period between the Testaments and the New Testament period, much of which cannot be found elsewhere.

Vermes, Geza. *The Dead Sea Scrolls in English.* Viking Penguin 1988 $7.95. ISBN 0-14-022779-2. Regarded by many as the standard English translation of the nonbiblical Qumran scrolls, providing much in the way of helpful orientation, including a portrayal of the Qumran community in the light of its historical context and religious ideas.

HISTORY, METHOD, AND EXAMPLES OF MODERN BIBLICAL STUDY

The field of biblical study is as vast and diverse as the Bible's human constituency. Thus, any survey of literature in this field has to depend at least partially on the bibliographer's own background and perspective for its principles of selection. We shall try to list only what is important and widely influential in anyone's judgment in a field of study that is growing increasingly "ecumenical."

Histories of Biblical Interpretation

To include this heading in the bibliography is to recognize that the way the Bible is interpreted assuredly depends on where in the history of human knowledge and culture the interpreter stands. After the patristic and medieval periods of church history, when biblical interpretation remained strictly subordinate to church tradition and tilted more and more in favor of figurative and moralistic senses of the sacred text, MARTIN LUTHER (see also Vol. 2) raised a clarion cry for the literal sense and the manifest intention of the written word, which was to become the first recourse in pursuit of Christian revelation. Luther's call germinated during the continental Renaissance and bore its fruits, sometimes bitter for the Protestant churches, in the historical and critical study of Scripture unleashed by the Enlightenment (roughly 1775 onward). When we speak of "biblical criticism" today, we mean that trend of analytical interpretation, rooted in the Reformation, slowly modulated and warily embraced by the mainline churches (now including Roman Catholicism), which seeks to understand the biblical text through exacting research of the author's original intention, grounded in the full social and linguistic context of the writing. Admittedly, some very recent trends of interpretation point away from this historical sense again toward the inherent features and aesthetic impressions of the text.

Obviously the long history sketched here so lightly attests to the fact that the meanings found in the Bible depend on the questions put to it and the shifting vantage points of the questioners. The following titles are recommended for the purpose of researching that complex and often colorful history.

Cambridge History of the Bible. 3 vols. Cambridge U. Pr. 1975 $100.00. ISBN 0-521-29018-X. See above under Texts and Versions of the Bible, Textual Criticism.

Clements, Ronald E. *One Hundred Years of Old Testament Interpretation.* Westminster John Knox 1976 o.p. Selecting major currents and figures in modern Old Testament criticism, this survey covers the Pentateuch and historical books, Prophets, Psalms, Wisdom, and Old Testament theology.

Epp, Eldon J., and George W. MacRae, eds. *The New Testament and Its Modern Interpreters.* Scholars Pr. GA 1989 $24.95. ISBN 0-89130-882-2. Essays providing an overview of major accomplishments in all areas of New Testament studies since the 1940s.

Grant, Robert M., and David Tracy. *A Short History of the Interpretation of the Bible.* Fortress Pr. 1984 $12.95. ISBN 0-8006-1762-2. A most engaging short sketch of the long and tortuous story, with three chapters by David Tracy added to the new edition under the promise of bringing the book "into its new port" of modern interpretive theory and agenda.

Hatch, Nathan O., and Mark A. Noll, eds. *The Bible in America: Essays in Cultural History.* OUP 1982 $7.95. ISBN 0-19-503100-8. Eight essays that trace the changing assumptions regarding the unity and authority of the Bible.

Johnson, Luke Timothy. *The Writings of the New Testament: An Interpretation.* Fortress Pr. 1986 $21.95. ISBN 0-8006-0886-0. "A sustained interpretation of the origins and functions of the documents in the early church. Among the most significant interpretative chapters are those that survey the individual books, chapters on the claims of the first Christians, on resurrection faith, and on the memory of Jesus in the church . . ." (*Choice*).

Kraeling, E. G. *The Old Testament Since the Reformation.* Schocken 1969 o.p. First published in 1955, this is an instructive history of theological attitudes toward the Old Testament in the Reformed churches from Luther through the twentieth century.

Kugel, James L., and Rowan A. Greer. *Early Biblical Interpretation. Lib. of Early Christianity.* Westminster John Knox 1988 $12.99. ISBN 0-664-24013-0. This survey fills an unfortunate gap in scholarly coverage of the history of biblical interpretation, the exegesis of Scripture by the Fathers of the church.

Kümmel, Werner G. *The New Testament: The History of the Investigations of Its Problems.* Trans. by S. MacLean Gilmour and Howard Clark Kee. Abingdon 1972 o.p. A truly valuable survey for the New Testament, covering pace-setting continental scholarship from the Enlightenment through 1930, and offering salient passages from landmark works as well as introductions to them.

Neill, Stephen. *Interpretation of the New Testament, 1861–1961.* OUP 1964 $13.95. ISBN 0-19-283057-0. Easier and more engaging than Kümmel's work, which Neill counterbalances with his greater critical reserve and fuller coverage of British contributions.

Nickelsburg, George W., and Robert A. Kraft, eds. *Early Judaism and Its Modern Interpreters.* Fortress Pr. 1986 $34.95. ISBN 0-8006-0772-8. A collection of essays covering Judaism as society, culture, and religion in the Greco-Roman context, treating recent scholarship and recent discoveries pertaining to its history and literature.

Tucker, Gene M., and Douglas A. Knight. *The Hebrew Bible and Its Modern Interpreters.* Scholars Pr. GA 1985 $15.95. ISBN 0-89130-784-2. Contains 15 articles covering developments in the study of the major segments of the Old Testament from around 1945 to the present.

Von Campenhausen, Hans. *The Formation of the Christian Bible.* Trans. by J. A. Baker. Fortress Pr. 1977 o.p. A competently told and fascinating story of the emergence of a Scripture comprised of "Old" and "New" Testaments as the outcome of a fierce struggle against Christian renunciation of the Hebrew Scriptures.

Methods and Principles of Biblical Exegesis

The student wishing to locate a mainstream of biblical study, in which a momentum of cooperative and progressive investigation of the biblical books has been built up in the twentieth century, might look to the following titles for guidance on accepted methods and principles of interpretation.

Dodd, Charles H. *The Bible Today.* Cambridge U. Pr. 1946 $19.95. ISBN 0-521-04844-3. Discusses with stylistic clarity and simplicity the nature, origins, and meaning of the Bible as well as its role in religious history.

Fee, Gordon D. *New Testament Exegesis: A Handbook for Students and Pastors.* Westminster John Knox rev. ed. 1993 $11.99. ISBN 0-664-25442-X. A step-by-step analysis of sound exegetical procedure, the revised edition of which takes serious account of the ever-expanding secondary literature in the discipline, the availability of computer-aided research materials, and the insights that rhetorical criticism has recently brought to the biblical text.

Fiorenza, Elisabeth Schüssler. *Bread Not Stone: The Challenge of Feminist Biblical Interpretation.* Beacon Pr. 1986 $13.00. ISBN 0-8070-1103-7. Recognizing that throughout history the Bible has been subjected to the interpretive prism of communities that read it, the author argues that objective historical scholarship is impossible and advances a new paradigm of interpretation (the "pastoral-theological"), which maintains that the Bible must be read through the eyes of the oppressed.

Guides to Biblical Scholarship. Ed. by D. O. Via, Jr., and G. M. Tucker. Fortress Pr. 1969–92 o.p. A series of small, attractive paperbacks offering explanations and paradigms of the component methodologies employed by modern biblical criticism. Listed here are titles considered most useful, arranged in the order a newcomer might wish to follow: *Canon and Community.* James A. Sanders. 1984. ISBN 0-8006-0468-7. *Form Criticism of the Old Testament.* Gene Tucker. 1971. ISBN 0-8006-0177-7. *The Historical Critical Method.* Edgar Krentz. 1975. ISBN 0-8006-0460-1. *Literary Criticism of the Old Testament.* Norman C. Habel. 1971. ISBN 0-8006-0176-9.

Tradition History and the Old Testament. Walter E. Rast. 1972. ISBN 0-8006-1460-7. *The Old Testament and the Archaeologist.* H. Darrell Lance. 1981. ISBN 0-8006-0467-9. *The Old Testament and the Historian.* J. Maxwell Miller. 1976. ISBN 0-8006-0461-X. *Sociological Approaches to the Old Testament.* Robert R. Wilson. 1984. ISBN 0-8006-0469-8. *What Is Form Criticism?* Edgar V. McKnight. 1969. ISBN 0-8006-0180-7. *What Is Narrative Criticism?* Mark Allan Powell. 1990 $8.95. ISBN 0-8006-0473-3. *What Is Redaction Criticism?* Norman Perrin. 1969. ISBN 0-8006-0181-5. *Rhetoric and the New Testament.* Burton Mack. 1989. ISBN 0-8006-2395-9. *Structural Exegesis for New Testament Critics.* Daniel Patte. 1989 $8.95. ISBN 0-8006-2396-7

Kaiser, Otto, and Werner G. Kümmell. *Exegetical Method: A Student's Handbook.* Trans. by E. V. Goetchius and M. J. O'Connell. Seabury rev. ed. 1981 o.p. A convenient and readable guide to the historico-critical method of Old Testament (Kaiser) and New Testament (Kümmell) exegesis, detailing the steps to reaching a comprehensive interpretation of a passage.

Kee, Howard C. *Christian Origins in Sociological Perspective: Methods and Resources.* Westminster John Knox 1980 o.p. Introduces the recent trend of applying the social sciences to the reconstruction of a more adequate social context for interpreting the New Testament writings.

Koch, Klaus. *Growth of the Biblical Tradition.* Scribner 1975 $24.50. ISBN 0-684-14524-3. An excellent introduction to the twentieth century's dominant methodology of scriptural exegesis, divided between exposition of the method and selected examples of its application.

Levenson, Jon D. *The Hebrew Bible, the Old Testament, and Historical Criticism: Jews and Christians in Biblical Studies.* Westminster John Knox 1993 $14.99. ISBN 0-664-25407-1. Analyzes the relationships between two interpretive communities, one involving contemporary scholars who rely heavily on historical-critical methods of biblical interpretation, and one involving those ancients who were responsible for the canonization and preservation of the Hebrew Bible.

Lohfink, Gerhard. *The Bible, Now I Get It: A Form Criticism Handbook.* Doubleday 1979 o.p. A truly delightful primer in the concept and application of form criticism, adorned with clever cartoons that tell much of the story by themselves. It is a "natural" for neophytes who wish to know more about the discipline.

Russell, Letty M., ed. *Feminist Interpretation of the Bible.* Westminster John Knox 1985 $10.99. ISBN 0-664-24639-7. Contains 11 diverse essays uniformly sensitive to reading Jewish and Christian scripture from the perspective of the oppressed, intent on raising tough questions about biblical authority and seeking to define a viable feminist hermeneutic.

Soulen, Richard N. *Handbook of Biblical Criticism.* Westminster John Knox 1985 $12.99. ISBN 0-8042-0045-9. A very useful handbook of technical terms and tools for biblical study, highly recommended as a standby for beginners in the field.

Stuhlmacher, Peter. *Historical Criticism and Theological Interpretation of Scripture: Towards a Hermeneutics of Consent.* Trans. by Roy A. Harrisville. Fortress Pr. 1977 o.p. An important essay by a foremost New Testament exegete, signaling new trends in the agenda of Scripture scholarship in Germany and taking a new and independent direction in assessing the responsibility of criticism to the Bible's roots in history and in the life of the church. With an introduction by the translator.

Westermann, Claus. *Essays on Old Testament Hermeneutics.* Trans. by J. L. Mays. Westminster John Knox 1979 o.p. Contributions by prominent Christian scholars explore different aspects of the quest for meaning in Old Testament texts, mainly in pursuit of the message and authority of the Old Testament for the Christian believer.

Introduction to the Two Testaments

The genre of biblical "introduction" involves a special kind of book, which is ordinarily arranged in the order of the biblical books and systematically unfolds the historical background, authorship, and salient literary features of each, at least so far as these are matters of current consensus or debate. The student consults these books for the underpinnings of interpretation, rather than for interpretation itself. They give information to start with, but also assumptions in need of further testing, in any new work of exegesis on a given biblical book.

Alter, Robert, and Frank Kermode, eds. *The Literary Guide to the Bible*. HUP 1987 $35.00. ISBN 0-674-87530-3. "The authors utilize the full range of critical tools to analyze structure, thematic patterns, narrative techniques, poetic form, and symbolic systems of the books of both Old and New Testaments" (*Booklist*).

Anderson, Bernhard W. *Understanding the Old Testament*. P-H 1986 $39.00. ISBN 0-13-935925-7. A mainstay of Old Testament courses for more than 35 years, this thorough and balanced introduction is adorned with attractive maps, charts, and illustrations and remains one of the best manuals for nonspecialized instruction. Specific biblical narratives, the unfolding history of Israelite tradition, and final literary formulations are regularly interrelated in highly readable prose.

Anderson, G. W. *Tradition and Interpretation*. OUP 1979 o.p. Thirteen essays offer a detailed "state of the question" in the major segments of Old Testament study, quite useful for those who wish to delve deeper into the business of scientific exegesis.

Brown, Raymond E. *Responses to 101 Questions on the Bible*. Paulist Pr. 1990 $6.95. ISBN 0-8091-3188-9. A highly respected New Testament scholar intently reflects on the nature of biblical interpretation, declaring that the deeper meaning of biblical texts is often lost on those who insist on a literalist approach. A treasure for readers who are new to biblical studies.

Eissfeldt, Otto. *The Old Testament: An Introduction*. HarpC 1965 $14.95. ISBN 0-06-062171-0. A classic introduction, still unsurpassed in its scope and depth, and especially valuable for the attention it gives to the prehistory of the books in oral tradition and literary sources.

Fohrer, Georg. *Introduction to the Old Testament*. Trans. by D. E. Green. Abingdon 1968 o.p. The scope and technical detail of this introduction nearly match those of the preceding entry. The two are indispensable tools of the professional student.

Gottwald, Norman K. *The Hebrew Bible: A Socio-Literary Introduction*. Fortress Pr. 1985 $24.95. ISBN 0-8006-1853-X. Boldly executed introductory textbook to the Old Testament instructs its readers in both established critical methods and in innovative literary and social scientific methods that in recent years have been increasingly employed by Old Testament interpreters.

Josipovici, Gabriel. *The Book of God: A Response to the Bible*. Yale U. Pr. 1990 $15.00. ISBN 0-300-04865-3. Taking up such issues as the rhythms of biblical literature, varieties of discourse, character portrayal, and the relation of canonical order and meaning, the author engages the Bible not on historical or theological terms, but on literary terms.

Kee, Howard Clark. *Understanding the New Testament*. P-H 1983 $40.00. ISBN 0-13-948266-0. A lucid introduction to the literature of emerging Christianity, which has long enjoyed widespread classroom use.

Koester, Helmut. *History and Literature of Early Christianity*. Vol. 2 in *Introduction to the New Testament*. De Gruyter 1987 $19.95. ISBN 0-89925-352-0. Places the New Testament books within a broadly reconstructed history of the early churches and a literary context enlarged by the Nag Hammadi papyrus discoveries.

Kümmel, Werner G. *Introduction to the New Testament*. Trans. by Howard C. Kee. Abingdon rev. ed. 1975 o.p. A classic New Testament introduction in terms of scope and authority, accredited by its author's thorough acquaintance with the literature and his judicious, moderate stance on issues of dispute.

Lohse, Edward. *The Formation of the New Testament*. Trans. by Eugene M. Boring. Abingdon 1981 $9.95. ISBN 0-687-13294-0. A convenient, readable treatment of the development of the writings, beginning with the oral traditions that preceded them, written by a popular and authoritative scholar.

Perrin, Norman, and Dennis C. Duling. *The New Testament: An Introduction*. HarBraceJ 1982 $16.50. ISBN 0-15-565726-7. The author was among the most influential

American biblical scholars, and his approach here illustrates the legacy of literary criticism and comparative religion that he left in his works on the New Testament.

Rendtorff, Rolf. *The Old Testament: An Introduction.* Trans. by John Bowden. Fortress Pr. 1986 $14.95. ISBN 0-8006-2544-7. A well-written and balanced treatment of contemporary literary and sociological approaches to the biblical text. The author's prose is succinct and easy to follow.

Rosenberg, Joel. *King and Kin: Political Allegory in the Hebrew Bible.* Ind. U. Pr. 1986 $29.95. ISBN 0-253-14624-0. "Focusing on the Garden story, the Abraham cycle, and the Davidic history, Rosenberg contributes a detailed study of the complexity and richness of allegory as a fundamental form of the art of biblical narrative" (*Choice*).

Schmidt, Werner H. *Old Testament Introduction.* Trans. by M. J. O'Connell. Crossroad NY 1984 $16.95. ISBN 0-8245-1051-8. "The book gives insight after insight into the meaning of individual passages and even whole collections of texts" (*Choice*).

Tyson, Joseph B. *The New Testament and Early Christianity.* Macmillan 1984. ISBN 0-02-421890-1. Provides a helpful sketch of the Greco-Roman and Jewish contexts out of which Christianity emerged as well as an informed discussion of the New Testament that takes serious account of its social, political, religious, and literary milieu.

Bible Dictionaries and Concordances

A concordance is an alphabetical index of principal words in partial contexts, showing the places where the words occur in their full contexts, and is sometimes limited to common words, exclusive of proper names. One Bible concordance may differ from another in completeness, in the version of the Bible concorded, and in the inclusion or exclusion of the books of the Apocrypha.

A Bible dictionary contains short descriptive articles about people, places, things, and customs mentioned in the Bible. It explains the meaning of such terms as *phylactery, prophet, ark, Nazarite, Apocalypse,* and so on. A Bible dictionary differs from a concordance in that it lists many words and phrases that do not occur in the Bible itself, such as *Bible, Subbatical Year, Ten Commandments, Lord's Prayer.* A dictionary defines; a concordance locates words.

Both tools are indispensable for biblical interpretation, and both develop into extensive, scientific enterprises the ancient marginal notations on biblical manuscripts that offered word statistics, keyword meanings, and interpretive cross-references.

Achtemeier, Paul J., ed. *Harper's Bible Dictionary.* HarpC 1985 $37.95. ISBN 0-06-069862-4. A comprehensive, richly illustrated, and entirely readable volume presenting the contributions of 179 members of the Society of Biblical Literature, whose expertise in their assigned topics is widely recognized.

Aland, Kurt. *Vollständige Konkordanz zum griechischen Neuen Testament.* 2 vols. De Gruyter 1975–78 $174.25. ISBNs 3-11-009698-6, 3-11-007349-8. This is the "state of the art" in biblical concordances of the original text, giving all the Greek words, down to conjunctions and particles, with their contexts in alphabetical listing (Volume 1), then offering statistical and analytical surveys of word usage by each New Testament author (Volume 2).

Barr, James. *Semantics of Biblical Language.* OUP 1961 $17.95. ISBN 1-56338-023-4. Stresses the need to determine word meanings from an attentive study of context rather than abstract etymologies and contoured histories of usage.

Botterweck, G. Johannes, and Helmer Ringgren, eds. *Theological Dictionary of the Old Testament.* Trans. by J. T. Willis and D. E. Green. 6 vols. Eerdmans 1977–90 $39.95 ea. ISBNs 0-8028-2325-4, 0-8028-2326-2, 0-8028-2327-0, 0-8028-2328-9, 0-8028-2329-7, 0-8028-2330-0. An invaluable reference work on the Hebrew vocabulary of the Old Testament, which reached its sixth volume in 1990 and is not quite halfway through the Hebrew alphabet.

Brown, Colin, ed. *New International Dictionary of New Testament Theology*. 4 vols. Zondervan 1975–86 $149.99. ISBN 0-310-33238-9. Groups words according to related ideas and concentrates on their theological significance, thereby providing a pastoral resource for preachers and catechists.

Buttrick, George A., and Keith R. Crim, eds. *The Interpreter's Dictionary of the Bible*. 5 vols. Abingdon 1976 $159.95. ISBN 0-687-19268-4. Although this multivolume work maintains its reputation as a significant tool for serious biblical studies, it is expected to be partially eclipsed by the recently published *Anchor Bible Dictionary* (see the Freedman entry that follows).

Freedman, David Noel, ed. *The Anchor Bible Dictionary*. 6 vols. Doubleday 1992 $360.00. ISBNs 0-385-19351-3, 0-385-19360-2, 0-385-19361-0, 0-385-19362-9, 0-385-19363-7, 0-385-26190-X. This up-to-date and wide-ranging endeavor cannot be called anything less than definitive, with 6,200 entries covering a wide range of biblical subjects. Six years of work by nearly 1,000 authors.

Gentz, William H., ed. *The Dictionary of Bible and Religion*. Abingdon 1986 $26.95. ISBN 0-687-10757-1. In addition to serving as a Bible dictionary, this volume also addresses numerous related religious topics that are of interest to students of contemporary religion, history of Christianity, Christian doctrine, and world religions. Twenty-eight scholars have authored more than 2,800 entries.

Goodrick, Edward W., ed. *NIV Exhaustive Concordance*. Zondervan 1990 $39.99. ISBN 0-310-43690-7. Expands the 1981 edition, by identifying all original-language words in the *NIV Bible*, including articles, conjunctions, particles, prepositions, and pronouns.

Hammond, N. G., and H. H. Scullard, eds. *Oxford Classical Dictionary*. OUP 1970 $55.00. ISBN 0-19-869117-3. Handy in its one-volume, concise format, this is an authoritative reference book for the Greco-Roman antiquity, thus important background for part of the Bible.

Hatch, Edwin, and Henry A. Redpath. *A Concordance to the Septuagint and Other Greek Versions of the Old Testament (including the Apocryphal Books)*. 3 vols. in 2. Baker Bk. 1983 repr. of 1906 ed. $94.99. ISBN 0-8010-4270-4. As the only concordance to the Greek Old Testament, this is an extremely valuable tool, though its authority is limited by the fact that it was based on only four major biblical manuscripts and has not the benefit of up-to-date textual criticism.

Kittel, Gerhard, ed. *Theological Dictionary of the New Testament*. Trans. by Gerhard Friedrich. 10 vols. Eerdmans $499.50. ISBN 0-8028-2324-6. A monumental resource, of which Volume 10 is a massive index, following the Greek alphabet with the most significant vocabulary of the New Testament, grouped by root word.

Mandelkern, Solomon. *Heichal Hakodesh Concordance to the Old Testament*. Shalom $95.00. ISBN 0-87559-163-9

————. *Veteris Testamenti concordantiae Hebraicae atque Chaldaicae*. Schocken 1971 o.p. Although numerous corrections and additions have accrued to this work, it is still the best concordance to the Hebrew and Aramaic text of the Old Testament, divided by word forms within the section devoted to each word.

Metzger, Bruce M., and Michael D. Coogan, eds. *The Oxford Companion to the Bible*. OUP 1993 $45.00. ISBN 0-19-504645-5. More than 250 scholars from 20 countries provide more than 700 entries that pursue diverse goals, addressing biblical literature and history in conventional ways, while also taking into account such matters as the Bible's role in the arts and its place in popular culture.

Mills, Watson E., ed. *Mercer Dictionary of the Bible*. Mercer Univ. Pr. 1990 $35.00. ISBN 0-86554-373-9. The product of four years of research and writing, this up-to-date scholarly reference work is quite accessible to the general reader.

Morrison, Clinton. *An Analytical Concordance to the Revised Standard Version of the New Testament*. Westminster John Knox 1979 $20.00. ISBN 0-664-20773-1. This is a concordance for students unable to investigate the Greek vocabulary; listing English words in alphabetical order with their occurrences, it also groups them according to the original Greek words they translate.

Moulton, W. F., and A. S. Geden, eds. *A Concordance to the Greek Testament*. Bks. Intl. VA 1978 $59.95. ISBN 0-567-01021-X. This was the most popular concordance of the Greek New Testament before the publication of the Aland (see above) concordance, which has wholly surpassed it in textual foundation and completeness.

The New Westminster Dictionary of the Bible. Ed. by Henry Snyder Gehman. Westminster John Knox 1982 $32.00. ISBN 0-664-21388-X. "Like its earlier edition, this is an excellent work destined to become the study companion of all students of the Bible. . . . The new volume includes more than 5,000 entries . . . including biblical books, persons, places, and themes" (*ADRIS Newsletter*).

Schmoller, A. *Concordance to the Greek New Testament*. United Bible 1989 o.p. Although it does not pretend total coverage of every Greek word in the New Testament, this handy instrument is worth mentioning because of its convenient format.

Walker, William O., ed. *Harper's Bible Pronunciation Guide*. HarpC 1989 $15.95. ISBN 0-06-068951-X. With its inclusion of more than 7,000 entries, this comprehensive and handsome volume should greatly assist American readers in the formidable task of pronounciation.

Commentaries

The most comprehensive guide to biblical interpretation is the verse-by-verse commentary, in which the author assembles all the philological, historical, and contextual data on each passage to support his or her understanding of its meaning. Scholarly commentaries ordinarily furnish an introduction to the book at the beginning, with discussions similar to those found in the Introductions listed above, after which specific explanations follow the order of the biblical text by chapter and verse. The entries below will follow this order: (1) one-volume commentaries on the whole Bible; (2) prominent commentary series, in which single volumes on individual books might be sought; (3) a few particularly excellent commentaries on popular books about the Bible that appear outside of series.

ONE-VOLUME COMMENTARIES

Black, Matthew, and H. H. Rowley. *Peake's Commentary on the Bible*. Nelson-Hall 1962 o.p. Gives a reliable introduction and explanation for all the sacred books (not including the Old Testament Apocrypha), together with some excellent introductory articles on biblical topics, a section of maps, and a fine index.

Brown, Raymond E., ed. *The New Jerome Biblical Commentary*. P-H 1990 $69.95. ISBN 0-13-614934-0. This effort of U.S. Roman Catholic scholars parallels *Peake's Commentary* but adds more extensive topical articles and commentary on the Apocrypha.

Laymon, Charles M., ed. *The Interpreter's One-Volume Commentary on the Bible*. Abingdon 1971 $34.95. ISBN 0-687-19299-4. "It is slated not so much to the specialist or to the theological student as to the layman, the Sunday school teacher, and the busy parish minister. It has a profusion of pictorial illustrations, some forty-eight general articles on a wider range of topics than is normally covered" (*Theology Today*).

Mays, James L., ed. *Harper's Bible Commentary*. HarpC 1988 $39.95. ISBN 0-06-065541-0. All books of the Hebrew scriptures, Apocrypha, and New Testament are covered, with balanced introductions, interpretations, and several fascinating articles that relate the Bible to several important historical, literary, and interpretive contexts.

Newsom, Carol A., and Sharon H. Ringe, eds. *The Woman's Bible Commentary*. Westminster John Knox 1992 $20.00. ISBN 0-664-21922-5. Focuses on passages that depict female characters, that symbolize the feminine, that reflect on aspects of Israelite life and institutions (be they social or religious) bearing directly on women, and that sketch male-female relationships. A critical volume for those interested in sound feminist biblical interpretation.

MULTIVOLUME COMMENTARIES

These commentaries are multivolume series. In some cases, the series are still ongoing; in others, only some of the titles are still in print. Within a series, the price of each volume may not be the same. Because of these differences, the reader should consult the publisher or *Books in Print* for information concerning availability and prices of particular titles.

Anchor Bible Dictionary. 6 vols. Doubleday 1992 $60.00 ea. ISBNs 0-385-19351-3, 0-385-19360-2, 0-385-19361-0, 0-385-19362-9, 0-385-19363-7, 0-385-26190-X. Represents the most comprehensive collection of scholarly articles on biblical studies; represents work of nearly 1,000 contributors from varying religious and scholarly backgrounds.

Augsburg Commentary on the New Testament. 10 vols. Augsburg Fortress 1980–88 $8.95–$19.95 ea. ISBNs 0-8066-8874-2, 0-8066-8862-9, 0-8066-8886-X, 0-8066-2165-6, 0-8066-2166-4, 0-8066-8876-9, 0-8066-8866-1, 0-8066-1937-6, 0-8066-8860-2, 0-8066-8858-0, 0-8066-8856-4, 0-8066-8856-8, 0-8066-8880-7, 0-8066-8864-5, 0-8066-8868-8. This series, about half complete (mostly in the epistles, but now including Acts and John), consists of succinct commentaries, with minimum technical and bibliographic detail, based on the English Revised Standard text and geared to laypeople, students, and pastors.

Augsburg Commentary on the Old Testament. 7 vols. Augsburg Fortress o.p. This is at the same level and quality as its New Testament counterpart (above) but is as yet less than one-quarter underway.

Cambridge Bible Commentary. Ed. by Peter R. Ackroyd. 17 vols. *New Testament Ser.* Cambridge U. Pr. 1963 o.p. Small volumes, succinct and geared for the general reader, now include all of the New Testament and much of the Old, based on the New English Bible with the Apocrypha.

Harper's New Testament Commentaries. Ed. by H. Chadwick and others. HarpC o.p. Provides a basic understanding, not in-depth criticism, for the reader who does not know Greek.

Hermeneia: A Critical and Historical Commentary on the Bible. Ed. by F. M. Cross and Helmut Koester. 22 vols. to date. Fortress Pr. 1971–present. Promises the most up-to-date and technically sophisticated level of commentary available to the English-speaking reader. A large, visually attractive format separates the rich, technical, and bibliographic annotation from the main expository line and quotations from the original texts. Entries thus far are mostly translated and updated works by foremost German Protestant scholars.

The Interpreter's Bible. Ed. by George A. Buttrick. 12 vols. Abingdon 1957 $414.95. ISBN 0-686-76914-7. Covers both Testaments and includes extensive introductions and background essays as well as exegetical and homiletic commentary. King James and English Revised Standard texts are printed in parallel columns accompanying the textual comment. The series is dated and uneven, but much of its informational content remains useful.

The New Century Bible Commentary. Ed. by Ronald E. Clements and Matthew Black. 30 vols. Eerdmans 1981–present. $14.99–$19.99 ea. ISBN 0-685-05545-0. A nontechnical series on both Testaments, featuring brief introductions and interspersed commentary with lead phrases from the English Revised Standard version.

The New International Commentary on the New Testament. Ed. by F. F. Bruce. Eerdmans 1978 $22.99. ISBN 0-8028-2189-8. This series and the one following are twins, both featuring moderately technical commentary for serious students, and both hewing to a strongly conservative Protestant-evangelical platform of "the Scriptures as the infallible Word of God."

The New International Commentary on the Old Testament. Ed. by E. J. Young. 12 vols. Eerdmans 1984 $360.00. ISBN 0-8028-2350-5

The New International Greek Testament Commentary. Ed. by W. W. Gasque and H. H. Marshall. 3 vols. Eerdmans 1979 o.p. Based on the latest Greek text (Nestle and Aland), provides scholarly, detailed comment for serious, professional students of the original writings.

New Testament Message: A Biblical Theological Commentary. Ed. by W. Harrington and D. Senior. 22 vols. M. Glazier 1980–82 o.p. A series for the general reader by Roman Catholic scholars that uses the Revised Standard Version and explains the argument of larger sections rather than commenting verse by verse.

Old Testament Library. Ed. by Peter R. Ackroyd and others. Westminster John Knox 1962–present. Includes both commentaries and topical treatises and now boasts 22 distinguished commentaries on Old Testament books, many being translated German works, and all at a high scholarly level without exceeding the grasp of the nonspecialist.

Old Testament Message. 23 vols. Liturgical Pr. 1981 $240.00. ISBN 0-8146-5235-2. Companion project to the *New Testament Message* (above), following the same procedure under the same auspices.

Pelican New Testament Commentaries. Viking Penguin 1963 o.p. An unfinished series of small, compact paperback volumes for beginners and outsiders to biblical study, based on Revised Standard Version, with the critical standard rather rudimentary.

Proclamation Commentaries: The New Testament Witnesses for Preaching. Ed. by Gerhard Krodel. Fortress Pr. 1978–81 $9.95 ea. ISBNs 0-8006-0596-9, 0-8006-2340-1, 0-8006-0585-3, 0-8006-1917-X, 0-8006-1916-1. A counterpart of the *New Testament Message* (above) under Protestant auspices and at mostly higher quality; includes sectional introductions (Synoptics, Paul) as well as individual verses.

Proclamation Commentaries: The Old Testament Witnesses for Preaching. Fortress Pr. 1978–81 o.p. Much the same can be said of the Old Testament companion series, which is newer.

IMPORTANT COMMENTARIES OUTSIDE OF SERIES

Bultmann, Rudolf. *The Gospel of John: A Commentary.* Trans. by G. R. Beasley-Murray, R.W.N. Hoare, and J. K. Riches. Westminster John Knox 1971 $27.00. ISBN 0-664-20893-2. The isolation of a "signs source" and a thorough consideration of Gnostic backgrounds are among the more prominent features of this volume, which offers a major interpretation of Johannine theology.

Ebeling, Gerhard. *Truth of the Gospel: An Exposition of Galatians.* Fortress Pr. 1985 o.p. A master expositor gives a wide audience his best in this work on Paul's sharpest controversial response to his critics.

Gordis, Robert. *The Book of Job: Commentary, New Translation and Special Studies.* Moreshet Ser. Ktav 1977 $59.50. ISBN 0-87334-003-5. A lifetime of work on one of the Bible's perennial fascinations comes to fruition in this magisterial commentary.

Haenchen, Ernst. *The Acts of the Apostles: A Commentary.* Westminster John Knox 1971 $30.00. ISBN 0-664-20919-X. Representing roughly two decades of labor by a leading New Testament scholar, this erudite volume provides accurate translation and judicious commentary, and is truly the standard commentary for advanced study of the book of Acts.

Käsemann, Ernst. *Commentary on Romans.* Trans. by Geoffrey W. Bromiley. Eerdmans 1978 $25.95. ISBN 0-8028-3499-X. An infelicitous mingling of exposition and bibliographic annotation suggests that this massive work on Paul's monumental letter is for the specialist. Nevertheless, the nonspecialist will be richly rewarded.

Kraus, Hans-Joachim. *Psalms 1–59: A Commentary; Psalms 60–150: A Commentary.* Trans. by Hilton C. Oswald. 2 vols. Augsburg Fortress 1987–89 $39.95 ea. ISBNs 0-8066-2284-9, 0-8066-2425-6. A magisterial two-volume work, offering a rather literal rendering of the Hebrew text to which is appended useful linguistic, textual, and form-critical remarks. After discussing the discrete units of a given psalm, the author concludes with informed remarks about "purpose and trust" that seeks to embrace the text holistically. Although present in abundance, detailed critical information is not permitted to take over in a way that might overwhelm the reader.

North, Christopher R. *The Second Isaiah Introduction, Translation and Commentary to Chapters 40–55*. OUP 1964 o.p. A foundational English-language work on one of the most fascinating and influential voices in all the Bible (Chapters 40 to 55 of the book of Isaiah).

Schnackenburg, Rudolf. *The Gospel According to St. John*. 2 vols. Crossroad NY 1982 $39.50 ea. ISBN 0-86012-110-0. This is the last word in scientific and theologically nutritious commentary, unquestionably the finest on the Gospel of John in any language. The topical excursus sections repay the steep price of the set by themselves.

Schweizer, Eduard. *The Good News According to Luke*. Trans. by David E. Green. Westminster John Knox 1984 $20.00. ISBN 0-8042-0249-4. This and the following two entries form a fine trio of Synoptic Gospel commentaries that combines this author's solid scholarship with a generous outreach to the general reader, and the result is a model of informative and stimulating commentary.

_____. *The Good News According to Mark*. Trans. by Donald Madvig. Westminster John Knox 1970 $20.00. ISBN 0-8042-0250-8

_____. *The Good News According to Matthew*. Trans. by David E. Green. Westminster John Knox 1975 $23.00. ISBN 0-8042-0251-6

Westermann, Claus. *Genesis: A Commentary*. Trans. by John J. Scullion. 3 vols. Augsburg Fortress 1984–86. Vol. 1 $39.95. ISBN 0-8006-9500-3. Vol. 2 $39.95. ISBN 0-8006-9501-1. Vol. 3 $29.95. ISBN 0-8006-9502-X. Monumental in both size and stature, this outstanding commentary rewards the specialist with its dense detail and the hungry spirit with its steadfast theological stewardship. Its translation for English-speaking readers is a taxing but welcome public service, which well deserves first mention here among the outstanding commentaries published outside of series.

Selected Masterworks on Biblical Topics and Authors

The principal authors and literary categories of the Bible all have their pathfinding works in modern biblical research. The titles in his section have been chosen either because they have won pathfinder status in their area or because they uniquely capture the spirit and fruits of current study in the area. The fact that so many of the works are translated from the German is testimony to the leadership of German scholars in this field, but also to the fact that ongoing work often responds to, and modifies, the lead taken by the Germans.

OLD TESTAMENT

Albright, William F. *Yahweh and the Gods of Canaan: A Historical Analysis of Two Contrasting Faiths*. Eisenbrauns 1990 repr. of 1968 ed. $18.50. ISBN 0-9131464-01-3. Portrays Canaanite religion in the Bronze Age and assesses its impact on the ensuing Israelite religion that took root in ancient Palestine.

Alter, Robert. *The Art of Biblical Narrative*. Basic 1983 $11.95. ISBN 0-465-00427-X. Operates on the assumption that historically-oriented questions about text, source, and form, which so often preoccupy biblical scholars, should be set aside in favor of more specifically literary questions so that the interpretation of biblical narrative will not get in the way of reading it in much the same way that works of classical literature are read. A compelling volume.

_____. *The Art of Biblical Poetry*. Basic 1987 $12.00. ISBN 0-465-00431-8. An artistically sensitive companion volume to the work listed immediately above, providing a highly readable study that explains the mysteries of biblical poetics and demonstrates that poetic form and meaning are inextricably linked.

_____. *The World of Biblical Literature*. Basic 1991 $23.00. ISBN 0-465-09255-1. Continues to focus on "the formal articulations of the literary texts" through an engaging style and insightful close readings of specific passages that readily foster in the reader a fresh appreciation of the literary talents of the biblical writers and the bearing of those talents on emerging Israelite faith and culture.

Berlin, Adele. *The Dynamics of Biblical Parallelism.* Ind. U. Pr. 1988 $10.95. ISBN 0-253-20765-7. A lucid, scholarly investigation into the intricate structure of biblical poetry, which claims that parallelism is *the* fundamental feature of Hebrew verse.

Crenshaw, James L. *Studies in Ancient Israelite Wisdom.* Ktav 1974 $69.50. ISBN 0-87-068-255-5. A major addition to the author's masterful survey of *Old Testament Wisdom* traditions and Wisdom books. A superb set of essays on this biblical stratum.

Fishbane, Michael. *Biblical Interpretation in Ancient Israel.* OUP 1989 $24.95. ISBN 0-19-826699-5. An admittedly technical but pioneering work developing the thesis that the origins of biblical interpretation trace back to the Bible itself. Taking note that later texts in the Hebrew Bible (Old Testament) interpret earlier ones, the author spells out four categories of interpretation: scribal, legal, homiletic, and interpretations of divine revelations through dreams, omens, and prophecy itself.

Gunkel, Hermann. *The Legends of Genesis: The Biblical Saga and History.* Trans. by W. H. Carruth. Schocken 1987 $5.50. ISBN 0-8052-0086-X. A translation of the introduction to Gunkel's epoch-making Genesis commentary, which concerns itself with classifying and describing the diverse literary forms employed by the writers of the biblical text. With an introduction by William F. Albright.

_____. *The Psalms: A Form-Critical Introduction.* Trans. by Thomas M. Horner. Augsburg Fortress 1967 $4.95. ISBN 0-8006-3043-2. A groundbreaking form-critical analysis of the Psalms in terms of their diverse literary types and respective settings in the ongoing life of biblical Israel. Introduction by James Muilenburg.

Hanson, Paul D. *The Dawn of Apocalyptic: The Historical and Sociological Roots of Jewish Apocalyptic Eschatology.* Fortress Pr. 1979 $16.95. ISBN 0-8009-1809-2. Here, from the most widely quoted author on the movement, is a rewarding study of the outlook and literature that form a major link between the two Testaments.

Koch, Klaus. *The Prophets.* Trans. by Margaret Kohl. 2 vols. Fortress Pr. 1982–84 $13.95 ea. Vol. 1 *The Assyrian Period.* ISBN 0-8006-1648-0. Vol. 2 *The Babylonian and Persian Periods.* ISBN 8006-1756-8. An excellent introduction to the thought of the individual prophets of the Bible by one of the leading scholars of their literature and periods. It occasionally makes heavy demands on the reader.

Kraus, Hans-Joachim. *Theology of the Psalms.* Trans. by Keith Crim. Augsburg Fortress 1986 $29.95. ISBN 0-8006-2225-3. A systematic statement of the faith content and religious significance of the Old Testament's songbook, most of which derived from the liturgical rites of the temple at Jerusalem.

Miller, Patrick D., Jr. *Interpreting the Psalms.* Augsburg Fortress 1986 $12.95. ISBN 0-8006-1896-3. Intended for serious inquirers, this bipartite volume contains five helpful essays devoted to foundational aspects of psalms interpretation and ten thoughtful expositions of representative psalms.

Mowinckel, Sigmund. *The Psalms in Israel's Worship.* Trans. by D. R. Ap-Thomas. Abingdon 1962 o.p. The Norwegian scholar's towering achievement in psalm study modified and complemented Gunkel's (see above). Moreover, his expository talent and his translator's charism make this the best handbook for psalm study currently in the marketplace.

Noth, Martin. *A History of Pentateuchal Traditions.* Trans. by Bernhard Anderson. P-H 1972 o.p. A classic traditio-critical analysis that traces the history of principal themes from their spoken origins (oral tradition) to the written form they assumed at the point of the books' composition.

_____. *The Laws in the Pentateuch and Other Studies.* Trans. by D. R. Ap-Thomas. Augsburg Fortress 1966 $18.95. ISBN 0-334-00870-0. A useful collection of Noth's truly seminal essays; those on "The Laws in the Pentateuch" and "God, King, and Nation in the Old Testament" have been particularly influential on ensuing biblical scholarship.

Rad, Gerhard von. *The Message of the Prophets.* Trans. by D.M.G. Stalker. HarpC 1965 $13.95. ISBN 0-06-068929-3. Provides incisive summaries of the proclamations of biblical Israel's prophets, prefaced by helpful chapters that clarify the manner, concerns, and scope of prophetic thought in the Old Testament.

————. *The Problem of the Hexateuch and Other Essays.* Trans. by E. Trueman Dicken. Fortress Pr. 1966 o.p. Several of the essays join forces with the title essay in spelling out the author's critical understanding of the Pentateuch.

Russell, D. S. *The Method and Message of Jewish Apocalyptic. Old Testament Lib.* Westminster John Knox 1964 $24.00. ISBN 0-664-20543-7. Among his several writings on this topic, the author's larger treatise, well written and documented, will prove most rewarding for the serious inquirer.

Seybold, Klaus. *Introducing the Psalms.* Trans. by R. Graeme Dunphy. Bks. Intl. VA 1990 $19.95. ISBN 0-567-29174-X. This wide-ranging yet succinct discussion of the book of Psalms is intended for a diverse audience and includes 11 well-organized chapters investigating such matters as the origins and transmission of the psalms, their poetic construal, their occasional indebtedness to ancient Near Eastern psalmody, and their religious outlook.

Smith, Mark S. *The Early History of God: Yahweh and the Other Deities in Ancient Israel.* HarpC 1990 $26.95. ISBN 0-06-067416-4. Presents a synthesis of contemporary scholarly perceptions of the history of the Israelite concept of God, discussing the Canaanite heritage of the Israelite religion, diverse Israelite ritual practices in the light of their Canaanite setting, and the history of Israelite monotheism.

Westermann, Claus. *Basic Forms of Prophetic Speech.* Trans. by H. C. White. Westminster John Knox 1991 $18.99. ISBN 0-664-25244-3. An indispensable key to understanding the prophets by a premier Old Testament scholar, who maintains that the key is the set speech forms in which the prophets expressed themselves—now familiar trademarks of their books.

————. *Praise and Lament in the Psalms.* Trans. by Keith Crim and Richard Soulen. John Knox 1981 repr. of 1965 ed. $9.95. ISBN 0-8042-1792-0. An important and influential contribution to the same field travels in a different direction from Mowinckel (see above) with Gunkel's (see above) heritage.

Wilson, Robert R. *Prophecy and Society in Ancient Israel.* Fortress Pr. 1980 $15.95. ISBN 0-8006-1814-9. Pioneering study that corrects the lingering romantic portrait of the prophets as isolated free spirits, warring against their society from outside its institutions. The author's perception of sociological dimensions in biblical prophetic texts is notably acute.

NEW TESTAMENT

Becker, Jürgen. *Paul: Apostle to the Gentiles.* Trans. by O. C. Dean, Jr. Westminster John Knox 1993 $30.00. ISBN 0-664-21930-6. Offers a lucid and comprehensive treatment of the person, world, letters, and thinking of Paul that takes full account of the Hellenistic setting in which the apostle functioned.

Beker, J. Christian. *Paul the Apostle: The Triumph of God in Life and Thought.* Fortress Pr. 1980 $16.95. ISBN 0-8006-1811-4. Already celebrated as the most important book on Paul in recent years, this wordy treatise systematically applies the character of Paul's letters to the search for a coherent center of his thought.

Bornkamm, Günther. *Jesus of Nazareth.* Trans. by I. MacLuskey and F. MacLuskey. HarpC 1975 $10.95. ISBN 0-06-060932-X. Focuses on the mission and teachings of Jesus, maintaining the New Testament Gospels yield a hard core of authentic sayings.

————. *Paul.* Trans. by D. M. Stalker. HarpC 1971 o.p. In this major work, novice but well-educated readers will find ready access to Paul's life and thought as well as historical backgrounds and theological issues.

Brown, Raymond E. *The Churches the Apostles Left Behind.* Paulist Pr. 1984 $7.95. ISBN 0-8091-2611-7. A short, well-written survey of the "subapostolic period," covering the books written in apostles' names after their deaths (Pastoral epistles, Colossians/Ephesians, I Peter, and so on) and the early church concerns reflected in this enterprise.

Bultmann, Rudolf. *The History of the Synoptic Tradition.* Trans. by John Marsh. HarpC 1972 o.p. A foundational form-critical analysis of the New Testament Gospels of

Matthew, Mark, and Luke, which has exerted a marked influence on subsequent serious investigations into the composition and theology of the Gospels.

————. *Jesus and the Word.* Trans. by Louise Pettibone Smith and Erminie Huntress Lantero. *Hudson River Ed. Ser.* Macmillan 1982 repr. of 1975 ed. $40.00. ISBN 0-684-17586-7. An investigation into the teachings of Jesus that affords excellent access into Bultmann's critical handling of the Gospel traditions as well as his understanding of history.

————. *Jesus Christ and Mythology.* Macmillan 1981. ISBN 0-684-17228-3. Series of lectures, originally written in English and delivered at Yale and Vanderbilt Universities in 1951, that disclose Bultmann's most characteristic views and concerns as a Gospel critic.

————. *New Testament and Mythology and Other Basic Writings.* Ed. and trans. by Schubert M. Ogden. Augsburg Fortress 1984 $11.95. ISBN 0-8006-2442-4. Seven essays imparting Bultmann's thought as a Christian theologian and New Testament critic for whom demythologizing is the requisite methodology for a twentieth-century grasp of the Gospel proclamation.

Conzelmann, Hans. *The Theology of St. Luke.* Trans. by G. Buswell. Augsburg Fortress 1982 $13.95. ISBN 0-8006-1650-2. The first stroke in the most recent trend of compositional study of Luke-Acts. It is not easy to read.

Cullmann, Oscar. *The Christology of the New Testament.* Trans. by Shirley C. Guthrie and Charles A. M. Hall. Westminster John Knox rev. ed. 1980 $14.99. ISBN 0-664-24351-7. Discusses Christology's place in the theological deliberations of earliest Christianity and provides a systematic treatment of the many Christological titles in the New Testament that refer to the present and future work of Jesus as well as to his pre-existence.

Dibelius, Martin. *From Tradition to Gospel.* Trans. by Bertram L. Wooff. Attic Pr. 1971 o.p. This pioneering work of form criticism, complementing Bultmann's (above) is more concise and readable, though less comprehensive and conclusive, than the latter's treatise.

Dodd, Charles H. *The Interpretation of the Fourth Gospel.* Cambridge U. Pr. 1976 repr. of 1953 ed. $27.95. ISBN 0-521-09517-4. Inspects the historical setting of the Gospel of John and clearly spells out its leading ideas, giving special attention to the actual course of the evangelist's argument.

Grant, Robert M. *Heresy and Criticism: The Search for Authenticity in Early Christian Literature.* Westminster John Knox 1993 $17.00. ISBN 0-664-21971-3. Authoritatively argues that so-called Christian heretics were the first to subject Christian books to literary criticism, claiming that the heretics' methods were identical to those of their pagan contemporaries, and that, as time passed, orthodox critics were well served by the same methods.

Käsemann, Ernst. *Essays on New Testament Themes.* Augsburg Fortress 1982 o.p. This collection, by a foremost Bultmann student, includes a trend-setting essay on the historical Jesus that moderated his master's skepticism on the subject.

————. *Perspectives on Paul.* Bks. Demand 1982 repr. of 1971 ed. $45.80. ISBN 0-317-55776-9. Seminal essays by one of the most stimulating Pauline interpreters of our day make engrossing and demanding fare for the very serious student of Paul.

Keck, Leander E., and J. Louis Martyn, eds. *Studies in Luke-Acts.* Fortress Pr. 1980 o.p. Widely quoted, watershed essays are included in this collection of studies on both larger issues and individual passages.

Koester, Helmut. *Ancient Christian Gospels: Their History and Development.* TPI PA 1990 $19.95. ISBN 0-334-02450-1. Complex and technical discussion of the history and development of both canonical and non-canonical gospel literature, which will assuredly shape subsequent scholarly proposals about ancient Christian gospels and their respective settings.

Marxsen, Willi. *Mark the Evangelist.* Trans. by Roy A. Harrisville. Abingdon 1977 o.p. These essays inaugurated the compositional criticism of the Gospel of Mark, currently a significant field of exegetical output.

Sanders, E. P. *Paul and Palestinian Judaism: A Comparison of Patterns of Religion.*
    Fortress Pr. 1977 $24.95. ISBN 0-8006-1899-8. A controversial but widely admired
    and richly documented treatment of the understanding of the Mosaic Law presumed
    in Paul's writing that includes a survey of views on Paul's central concept of divine
    "righteousness" by M. T. Brauch.

Schweitzer, Albert. *Paul and His Interpreters: A Critical History.* Trans. by W. Mont-
    gomery. Schocken 1964 o.p. Announces for Paul a liberation from nineteenth-
    century liberal theology in favor of the native Jewish apocalyptic thinking that
    nourished the Apostle.

————. *The Quest of the Historical Jesus.* Trans. by W. Montgomery. Macmillan rev. ed.
    1968 $16.95. ISBN 0-02-089240-3. A classic chronicle of the many failures and the
    unsuspected successes of the nineteenth century's "gold rush" in pursuit of the real
    Jesus. It is a "must" for every serious inquirer in this field.

Schweizer, Eduard. *Church Order in the New Testament.* Trans. by Frank Clarke. *Student
    Christian Movement Pr. Ser.* OUP 1961 o.p. A widely quoted survey of the New
    Testament books for the community organization they reflect brings out, with clarity
    and consistency, a pivotal criterion for discerning the later, postapostolic writings.

Smith, D. Moody. *Johannine Christianity: Essays on Its Setting, Sources, and Theology.*
    U. of SC Pr. 1989 $13.95. ISBN 0-87249-672-4. A distinguished career in the research
    of John's Gospel (and letters) is epitomized in these fine essays, whose moderation in
    assessing and employing current trends recommends them to the serious
    Johannine student.

Stuhlmacher, Peter. *Reconciliation, Law and Righteousness: Essays in Biblical Theology.*
    Trans. by Everett R. Kalin. Fortress Pr. 1986 o.p. Included are very important essays
    on Paul's thought by one of his best and most influential present-day interpreters.

Taylor, Vincent. *The Formation of the Gospel Tradition.* St. Martin 1968 o.p. A highly
    respected British voice reacts to the early work of the form critics in Germany,
    providing a warmly recommended example of the conservative slant on that
    momentous movement.

Theissen, Gerd. *The Social Setting of Pauline Christianity: Essays on Corinth.* Trans. by J.
    H. Schütz. Augsburg Fortress 1982 $11.95. ISBN 0-8006-2095-X. An outstanding
    collection of original essays depicting the type of society in which the first Christians
    lived, the tensions within the church that they faced, and the new types of social
    relationships that they forged.

Tuckett, Christopher, ed. *The Messianic Secret. Issues in Religion and Theology Ser.*
    Fortress Pr. 1983 o.p. Important essays attack the crucial issue raised in Wrede
    (below) and should be read with it.

Weiss, Johannes. *Jesus' Proclamation of the Kingdom of God.* Trans. by David L. Holland.
    Scholars Pr. GA 1985 $14.95. ISBN 0-89130-859-8. The monumental treatise of 1892
    that changed a whole generation's view of Jesus' basic message and set the stage for
    all approaches to it in this century.

Wrede, William. *The Messianic Secret.* Trans. by J. C. Greig. Attic Pr. 1971 o.p. This turn-
    of-the-century work, together with that of Weiss (above), shattered the idealistic
    Jesus portraits of the preceding generation and prescribed a radically new approach
    to the Gospel's documentation of Jesus' life.

Biblical Theologies

This genre, usually in the form of a "Theology of the Old Testament" or a
"Theology of the New Testament," attempts to organize the vast contents of
either Testament in a systematic fashion, either according to the guiding ideas
or as illustration and orchestration of a historical process. Whether one chooses
a concept or a view of history as the guiding principle, the project is very risky,
and modern research has tended to discourage it by revealing the complexity
and diversity of the biblical testimonies. Nevertheless, biblical studies do not
lack a theological dimension, even if it is not unanimously perceived.

Bultmann, Rudolf. *The Theology of the New Testament.* Trans. by Kendrick Grobel. *Contemporary Theology Ser.* Scribner 1970. ISBN 0-02-305580-4. A monumental treatment of the message and meaning of the New Testament, with special emphasis on the theology of Paul and theology of the Gospel of John and the Johannine epistles.

Childs, Brevard S. *Biblical Theology of the Old and New Testaments.* Augsburg Fortress 1993 $39.95. ISBN 0-8006-2675-3. Considers the witnesses of both testaments, examining such major themes of the Christian Bible as the identity of God, the covenant, humanity old and new, and providing a holistic reading of Christian scripture.

Conzelmann, Hans. *An Outline of the Theology of the New Testament.* Trans. by John Bowden. HarpC 1969 o.p. A work of modest ambition in the Bultmann tradition but a step forward from the master in terms of scholarly currency and flexibility. A rich reference for all serious students of the New Testament.

Eichrodt, Walther. *Theology of the Old Testament.* Trans. by J. Baker. *Old Testament Lib.* 2 vols. Westminster John Knox 1961–67 $25.00 ea. ISBNs 0-664-20352-3, 0-664-20769-3. A classic work arguing that the covenant theme stands at the very center of the Old Testament thought and organizing the biblical data around three rubrics: God and People, God and the World, God and Man.

Hasel, Gerhard F. *New Testament Theology: Basic Issues in the Current Debate.* Eerdmans 1978 $12.95. ISBN 0-8028-1733-5. Offers a well-written, comprehensive survey of diverse approaches to the discipline discussing problems relating to the center and unity in New Testament theology before setting forth a "multiplex" approach.

———. *Old Testament Theology: Basic Issues in the Current Debate.* Eerdmans 1991 $14.95. ISBN 0-8028-0537-X. Manifests a special interest in debating the existence of a "center" for Old Testament theology and in advancing several proposals of his own.

Jeremias, Joachim. *New Testament Theology.* Trans. by J. Bowden. Scribner 1977 $40.00. ISBN 0-684-15157-X. The highly respected author never got beyond this first volume of his theology, but everyone can benefit from its erudition, and many will appreciate its more conservative stance on the recovery of Jesus' authentic words.

Rad, Gerhard von. *Old Testament Theology.* Trans. by D.M.G. Stalker. 2 vols. HarpC 1962–65 $21.95–$22.95. ISBN 0-06-068931-5. A compelling treatment of emerging historical and poetic traditions that celebrates the diversity of the Old Testament witness.

CHRONOLOGY OF AUTHORS

Gunkel, Hermann. 1862–1932
Moffatt, James. 1870–1944
Bultmann, Rudolf. 1884–1976
Dodd, Charles Harold. 1884–1973
Eichrodt, Walther. 1890–1978

Albright, William F. 1891–1971
Rad, Gerhard von. 1901–1971
Cullmann, Oscar. 1902–
Noth, Martin. 1902–1968
Bornkamm, Günther. 1905–

ALBRIGHT, WILLIAM F. 1891–1971

Born in Coquimbo, Chile, William F. Albright, a preeminent orientalist, was the son of American missionary parents. By 1903 the family returned to the United States, where they would spend their next years in several drab small-town parsonages in the Midwest. At 16, as a student at the Senior Academy preparatory department of Upper Iowa University in Fayette, Iowa, the precocious Albright taught himself Hebrew, using his father's inductive grammar. After receiving his A.B. from Upper Iowa in 1912 and serving one year as a high school principal, Albright embarked on a graduate program in

Semitic Studies at Johns Hopkins University. Given his previous voracious reading of ancient history, as well as his aptitude for foreign languages, he was ripe for the challenge. At Johns Hopkins, Albright came under the influence of the well-established German-trained orientalist, Paul Haupt. From him Albright learned to appreciate the role that Babylonian texts might play in solving biblical cruxes. Even so, he eventually came to distance himself from Haupt's radical biblical scholarship.

Receiving his Ph.D. in 1916, Albright remained at Johns Hopkins until called into military service. His lengthy tenure in Palestine began in 1919, when he was invited to engage in postdoctoral research at the American School of Oriental Research in Jerusalem. From 1920 to 1929, and again from 1933 to 1936, he functioned as director of the school. Recognized for his remarkable linguistic talent and passion for ancient texts, Albright was designated W. W. Spence Professor of Semitic Languages at Johns Hopkins in 1929. His command of Assyriology, Egyptology, Northwest Semitic philology, and ancient Near Eastern history was phenomenal. For an entire generation, Albright's contributions to American biblical scholarship and Syro-Palestinian archaeology were legion. His academic breadth led to his elections as president of the American Oriental Society (1935) and the Society of Biblical Literature (1939).

During his residency in Palestine, Albright became fully exposed to its history, pottery, and customs, both ancient and modern. He truly experienced Palestine as the land of the Bible. Between 1926 and 1932, he directed four seasons of excavation at Tell Beit Mirsim in southern Judah. So fully did Albright master its pottery and stratigraphy that his ceramic chronology for the Bronze and Iron Ages (c.3500–600 B.C.) remains in use even today. Also, largely under Albright's tutelage, the first Jewish archaeologists in Palestine became active in the field. Thus, Albright helped to lay the foundations of the later "Israeli School" of archaeology.

Albright was no fundamentalist, but he often reacted against the excesses of an earlier European-style literary criticism that discredited the Bible as a viable source of history. This gifted historian of religion was capable of perceiving sweeping vistas. His well-known volumes, *The Archaeology of Palestine* and *From the Stone Age to Christianity*, are two among many that effectively interpret the Bible in relation to its multifaceted environment.

BOOKS BY ALBRIGHT

The Archaeology of Palestine. Peter Smith 1976 $19.00. ISBN 0-8446-0003-2. Explains how archaeologists execute their field work, identifies significant twentieth-century accomplishments in Syro-Palestinian archaeology, and comments on the occupants and customs of that region in light of the artifactual data uncovered.

From the Stone Age to Christianity: Monotheism and the Historical Process. Johns Hopkins 1957 o.p. Admittedly conservative by present standards, this classic explains, in engaging prose, Albright's thesis that monotheism is the driving force behind the history of Western civilization.

Yahweh and the Gods of Canaan: A Historical Analysis of Two Contrasting Faiths. Eisenbrauns 1990 repr. of 1968 ed. $18.50. ISBN 0-931464-01-3. Portrays Canaanite religion in the Bronze Age and assesses its impact on the ensuing Israelite religion that took root in ancient Palestine.

BOOK ABOUT ALBRIGHT

Running, Leona Glidden, and David Noel Freedman. *William Foxwell Albright: A Twentieth-Century Genius.* Palo Verde Pr. 1975 $15.00. ISBN 0-8467-0071-9. An engaging biography, discussing the main events in Albright's life as well as his formative impact on Syro-Palestinian archaeology.

BORNKAMM, GÜNTHER. 1905–

Günther Bornkamm, a pioneering German New Testament scholar, made significant contributions in the allied areas of form criticism and redaction criticism. As a young academic, he taught in the theological school at Bethel until 1939, when it was shut down by the Nazis. After brief pastorates in Münster and Dortmund, Bornkamm joined the Germany army in 1943. Following World War II, he resumed his academic career, first at the University of Göttingen, and then (in 1949) at the University of Heidelberg, where he taught until his retirement.

As a redaction critic, Bornkamm pressed upon biblical scholars the importance of reading the Gospels again as wholes and grasping their theology. As this pupil of RUDOLF BULTMANN analyzed the Gospel of Matthew, he raised important form-critical questions. In addition, he sought to grasp Matthew's distinctive theological perspective and intention as this might be inferred from his handling of traditional material. The resulting volume, *Tradition and Interpretation in Matthew* (1963), called attention to the actual structuring of the discourses of Jesus in Matthew that appeared to be driven by the evangelist's own perception of the church, the eschaton, the law, and Jesus himself. Bornkamm insisted that Matthew was no mere transmitter of traditions about Jesus; rather, he was a theological commentator on that tradition.

Bornkamm's name is also associated with what has come to be known as the "new quest" of the historical Jesus. He agreed with Bultmann that the writing of a comprehensive biography of Jesus is an impossibility. Even so, he was more positive in his assessment of the historical data in the Gospel texts than was his teacher. In his widely read book, *Jesus of Nazareth* (1960), Bornkamm argued that, despite the interpretive bias of the early church, the primary figure of Jesus of Nazareth is knowable through the parables that he taught, the controversies in which he engaged, and the steady progression in the narrative to its climax on the cross.

BOOKS BY BORNKAMM

Jesus of Nazareth. Trans. by I. MacLuskey and F. MacLuskey. HarpC 1975 $10.95. ISBN 0-06-060932-X. Focuses on the mission and teachings of Jesus, maintaining that the New Testament Gospels yield a hard core of authentic sayings.

The New Testament: A Guide to Its Writings. Trans. by Reginald H. Fuller and Ilse Fuller. Bks. Demand 1973 $45.30. ISBN 0-317-58196-1. Offers a helpful depiction of the diverse history and rich variety of the writings of the New Testament canon, focusing on the relation of these texts to the emergence and development of earliest Christianity.

Paul. Trans. by D.M.G. Stalker. HarpC 1971 o.p. In this major work, novice but well-educated readers will find ready access to Paul's life and thought as well as historical backgrounds and theological issues.

BULTMANN, RUDOLF. 1884–1976

Rudolf Bultmann, a highly acclaimed New Testament scholar, was born in the former German state of Oldenburg and reared in the home of an Evangelical Lutheran pastor. His theological training, which began at the University of Tübingen in 1903, was subsequently carried out at the Universities of Marburg and Berlin. Adolf von Harnack, Wilhelm Herrmann, and Johannes Weiss, who taught in the areas of church history, systematic theology, and New Testament, respectively, rank high among professors who most influenced Bultmann. In the course of his distinguished teaching career, brief appointments at the Universities of Marburg (1912–16), Breslau (1916–20), and Giessen (1920–21) were followed by a lengthy tenure at Marburg (1921–51) that put him in close association with the existentialist philosopher MARTIN HEIDEGGER (see also Vol. 5). Already enamored of Herrmann's insight that theology must engage experience as well as concepts, Bultmann was drawn to Heidegger's understanding of existence with its distinctive emphasis on two modes of being—authenticity and inauthenticity. That perception of the human struggle significantly informed Bultmann's understanding of the New Testament message as a clarion summons to authentic existence. In his biblical scholarship, Bultmann did not slight the writings of Paul, but most of his publications centered on the Gospels.

During his residency in Breslau, Bultmann completed his first major work (1921), whose English translation appeared in 1963 under the title *The History of the Synoptic Tradition*. This epoch-making analysis quickly established Bultmann as a leading biblical scholar. Bultmann endorsed Martin Dibelius's recently expressed judgment that, if New Testament scholars were to further their understanding of the Gospel traditions, they would do well to adopt the form-critical methodology that HERMANN GUNKEL had successfully applied to Old Testament traditions. Focusing on diverse literary forms as the starting point of his investigation into the nature of the earliest Christian communities, Bultmann seriously questioned the assumptions of liberal theology that the historical Jesus was, in fact, knowable in the Gospel narrative. He regarded as untenable Harnach's view that the Gospel traditions contained the necessary data for constructing a trustworthy biographical portrait of Jesus. Thus, Bultmann insisted that the early church's apologetic, catechetical, and liturgical activities primarily dictated the shaping of the written Gospels. It was the Christ of faith who was being confessed in the various apophthegms attributed to Jesus (sayings set into a brief secondary context), in stories about his miracles that drew upon popular folk tales, and in legends more concerned about serving the needs of religious edification than satisfying the canons of historical accuracy. Although Bultmann's assertions evoked much opposition, they continue to influence how New Testament specialists perceive the Gospel.

In his provocative essay, "New Testament and Mythology," published in 1941, Bultmann sets forth his program for demythologizing the New Testament. He argues that the biblical message is mediated through a mythological framework that is alien to the worldview of modern humanity. For example, notions about supernatural interventions in this world, a three-storied universe, ascensions into heaven, and descents into hell may be the stuff of New Testament mythology, but they warrant no place in contemporary scientific discourse. Recognizing that humanity is not afforded the luxury of selecting its worldview at will, Bultmann avers that Christianity can remain viable only if it develops its capacity to distance itself from primitive mythology. He explains that the framers of New Testament myth were not attempting to describe the world objectively; rather, they were seeking to understand themselves within it. Thus, the demythologizing task that is incumbent on twentieth-century biblical interpreters is not to eliminate the myth but to perceive it existentially. This insight induces Bultmann to issue a creative restatement of the New Testament faith in existentialist categories drawn from Heidegger. If that procedure has not endeared him to readers who are less enthusiastic about Heidegger than he, few have faulted Bultmann's claim that the Christian gospel stands independent of the worldview in which it was originally shaped. The form criticism and demythologizing that are so central in Bultmann's hermeneutical agenda are, of course, readily discernible in his *Theology of the New Testament*.

BOOKS BY BULTMANN

The Gospel of John: A Commentary. Trans. by G. R. Beasley-Murray, R.W.N. Hoare, and J. K. Riches. Westminster John Knox 1971 $27.00. ISBN 0-664-20893-2. The isolation of a "signs source" and a thorough consideration of Gnostic backgrounds are among the more prominent features of this volume, which offers a major interpretation of Johannine theology.

The History of the Synoptic Tradition. Trans. by John Marsh. HarpC 1972 repr. of 1968 ed. o.p. A foundational form-critical analysis of the New Testament Gospels of Matthew, Mark, and Luke, which has exerted a marked influence on subsequent serious investigations into the composition and theology of the Gospels.

Jesus and the Word. Trans. by Louise Pettibone Smith and Erminie Huntress Lantero. Macmillan 1982 repr. of 1975 ed. $40.00. ISBN 0-684-17586-7. An investigation into the teachings of Jesus that affords excellent access into Bultmann's critical handling of the Gospel traditions as well as his understanding of history.

Jesus Christ and Mythology. Macmillan 1981 $18.00. ISBN 0-02-305570-7. Lectures originally written in English and delivered at Yale and Vanderbilt universities in 1951, disclosing Bultmann's most characteristic views and concerns as a Gospel critic.

New Testament and Mythology and Other Basic Writings. Ed. and trans. by Schubert M. Ogden. Augsburg Fortress 1984 $11.95. ISBN 0-8006-2442-4. Seven essays imparting Bultmann's thought as a Christian theologian and New Testament critic for whom demythologizing is the requisite methodology for a twentieth-century grasp of the Gospel proclamation.

Primitive Christianity: In Its Contemporary Setting. Trans. by Reginald H. Fuller. Augsburg Fortress 1980 repr. of 1956 ed. $12.95. ISBN 0-8006-1408-9. A persuasive study of how late Judaism, Greek paganism, Stoicism, and Gnosticism significantly shaped early Christian beliefs and practices.

Theology of the New Testament. Trans. by Kendrick Grobel. *Contemporary Theology Ser.* Scribner 1970 repr. of 1951 ed. ISBN 0-02-305580-4. A monumental treatment of the message and meaning of the New Testament, with special emphasis on the theology of Paul and the theology of the Gospel of John and the Johannine epistles.

BOOKS ABOUT BULTMANN

Ashcraft, Morris. *Rudolf Bultmann*. *Makers of the Modern Theological Mind Ser.* Hendrickson MA 1991 repr. of 1972 ed. ISBN 0-943575-60-5. A helpful presentation of Bultmann's form-critical and existentialist perception of the New Testament and his marked impact on developing twentieth-century Christian theology.

Jones, Gareth. *Bultmann: Towards a Critical Theology*. Blackwell Pubs. 1991 $44.95. ISBN 0-7456-0697-0. A lucid inspection of Bultman's theology, with special reference to the philosophical foundations and impact on subsequent hermeneutic reflection.

Ogden, Schubert M. *Christ Without Myth: A Study Based on the Theology of Rudolf Bultmann*. SMU Pr. 1991 $9.95. ISBN 0-87074-172-1. A critical evaluation of Bultmann's theology that is primarily driven by the desire to assist contemporary Protestant theology as it goes about setting its own constructive agenda.

CULLMANN, OSCAR. 1902–

Oscar Cullmann, a prominent Lutheran theologian and New Testament scholar, was born in Strasbourg, France, and held membership in the Lutheran church of Alsace. He earned three academic degrees at the University of Strasbourg, including a doctorate in theology in 1930. He pursued further studies at the Sorbonne, University of Paris. Cullmann taught at the Universities of Strasbourg (1927–38) and Basel, Switzerland (1938–72), and also offered courses at the Sorbonne (1951–72). Quite active in Protestant-Roman Catholic dialogue, he was cofounder of the Ecumenical Institute at Jerusalem.

For more than a generation, Cullmann took the lead in advocating a salvation-historical interpretation of the New Testament. Partly in reaction to RUDOLF BULTMANN's existentialist approach to the New Testament, Cullmann insisted that biblical texts be studied inductively. Thus, he argued that those postbiblical suppositions favored by nineteenth-century historicism and twentieth-century existentialism must be consciously set aside if the New Testament authors are to be heard on their own terms.

In Cullmann's view, *Heilsgeschichte* (i.e., the story of God's self-revelation and saving action) is the unifying thematic center of the entire Bible. The midpoint and consummation of salvation history is discernible in the life, death, and resurrection of Jesus. This "Christ event" establishes meaning for all that comes before (the period of Israel) and all that follows (the period of the church). The coming eschaton, says Cullmann, is the fulfillment of the decisive eschatological event in the death and resurrection of Christ. Cullmann's views are best known from his influential volume, *Christ and Time* (1950). Some scholars question Cullmann's identification of the Christ event as history's midpoint, because many early Christians understood Christ to be the end of history. Since the New Testament perceives the end in different ways, it appears that Cullmann has favored the way that is most congenial to his own theology.

BOOKS BY CULLMANN

Christ and Time: The Primitive Christian Conception of Time and History. Trans. by Floyd V. Filson. Westminster John Knox 1950 o.p. An influential theological study fully reflecting on the meaning of the New Testament claim that the appearance of Jesus of Nazareth is history's most decisive turning point.

The Christology of the New Testament. Trans. by Shirley C. Guthrie and Charles A. M. Hall. Westminster John Knox 1980 $14.99. ISBN 0-664-24351-7. Discusses Christology's place in the theological deliberations of earliest Christianity and provides a systematic treatment of the many Christological titles in the New Testament that refer to the present and future work of Jesus as well as to his pre-existence.

Salvation in History. Trans. by Sidney G. Sowers. HarpC 1967 o.p. A detailed consideration of the salvation-historical orientation of the New Testament and its significance for post-biblical Christianity.

DODD, CHARLES HAROLD. 1884–1973

Charles Harold Dodd, a leading British New Testament scholar, was born in Wrexham, North Wales. Awarded a B.A. degree in classics at University College, Oxford, in 1906, Dodd engaged in further studies at the University of Berlin, where he pursued a research program in ancient history and archaeology, and at Mansfield College, Oxford, where he prepared himself in theology. After serving as minister of the Independent (Congregational) Church at Warwick (1912–15, 1918–19), he returned to Mansfield College as Yates Lecturer in New Testament. In 1930 he moved to Manchester University to become professor of biblical criticism and exegesis. Five years later he assumed the Norris-Hulse professorship at Cambridge University, where he taught until his retirement in 1949. In the following year, he embarked on a 15-year directorship of the New English Bible translation project. In recognition of his achievements, Dodd received from Queen Elizabeth the Companionship of Honour in 1963.

In his slender but weighty study, *The Apostolic Preaching and Its Developments* (1936), Dodd discerns within the diverse strata of the New Testament a common unifying core, namely, the *kerygma* (preaching) of the primitive church. This core consisted of a sequence of events—the life, death, and resurrection of Jesus of Nazareth—in which God's glory was declared to have been disclosed. Thus, emerging Christianity embraced this as the decisive deed of God for humanity's salvation. For Dodd this *kerygma* theology *is* the theology of the New Testament.

Dodd also advanced the study of biblical eschatology by uncovering in the parables of Jesus not an apocalyptic but a realized eschatology. Here he challenged Albert Schweitzer's claim that Jesus made no room for either apocalyptic or traditional eschatological ideas in his teaching. According to Dodd's reading of the New Testament, no future cataclysmic event would inaugurate the long-awaited kingdom of God. Rather, the kingdom was manifested in Jesus' own life. Thus, in Dodd's analysis of realized eschatology, the New Testament attests a God who has acted in a manner that has not shattered history but has instead made known in the life and teaching of the historical Jesus his eternal will.

BOOKS BY DODD

The Bible Today. Cambridge U. Pr. 1946 $19.95. ISBN 0-521-04844-3. With stylistic clarity and simplicity, the author discusses the nature, origins, and meaning of the Bible as well as its role in religious history.

Historical Tradition in the Fourth Gospel. Cambridge U. Pr. 1976 repr. of 1963 ed. $29.95. ISBN 0-521-29123-2. A sequel to the book next enumerated, arguing that, despite its strong theological cast, the Gospel of John embodies important narrative elements that readily stand in the service of historical revelation.

The Interpretation of the Fourth Gospel. Cambridge U. Pr. 1976 repr. of 1953 ed. $27.95. ISBN 0-521-09517-4. After inspecting the historical setting of the Gospel of John, Dodd clearly spells out its leading ideas, giving special attention to the actual course of the evangelist's argument.

The Parables of the Kingdom. Scribner 1961 o.p. Reflects on the nature and purpose of the Gospel parables in a manner that supports the claim that it was through this medium that Jesus taught a "realized eschatology."

BOOK ABOUT DODD

Dillistone, Frederick W. *C. H. Dodd: Interpreter of the New Testament.* Eerdmans 1977 o.p. A quite readable volume that appreciates Dodd's brilliance as lecturer and author as well as his humanity and sensitivity to human need. Although he does not make light of them, the author is not foremost concerned with Dodd's historical reconstructions and theological interpretations.

EICHRODT, WALTHER. 1890–1978

Walther Eichrodt, an eminent German biblical scholar, was born in Gernsbach, Baden. After his introduction into theological studies at the seminary in Bethel, Eichrodt continued his training at the Universities of Griefswald and Heidelberg. He taught for a brief period at the University of Erlangen (1918–21). A 40-year career then ensued at the University of Basel, Switzerland (1921–61), where Eichrodt was designated professor of Old Testament and the history of religion in 1934. Moreover, from 1953 he was rector of the theological faculty at Basel. Eichrodt's wide-ranging publications include a dissertation on the priestly stratum in Genesis and commentaries on Ezekiel and Isaiah, as well as studies in eschatology, anthropology, and the history of Israelite religion.

As a pioneer in what is known as the biblical theology movement, Eichrodt devoted his major effort to writing a monumental three-volume *Theology of the Old Testament*, which appeared in 1933, 1935, and 1939 (the two-volume English translation was published in 1961 and 1967). It is a magisterial, though controversial, integration of historically diverse biblical ideas about God, humanity, and the world under the quasi-comprehensive category of the covenant relationship binding Yahweh, the God of Israel, and Israel, the people of Yahweh. It is written on the supposition that, whereas Old Testament theology is admittedly a normative and not a simply descriptive undertaking, it is driven by scientific rather than confessional concerns. Moreover, as he crafts his exposition, Eichrodt remains in touch with biblical Israel's Near Eastern environment and the later New Testament, on the one hand, and Old Testament belief in its distinctive structural unity, on the other.

BOOKS BY EICHRODT

Ezekiel: A Commentary. Trans. by Cosslett Quin. Westminster John Knox 1971 $28.00. ISBN 0-664-20872-X. Despite the author's heavy style and sometimes unconvincing textual rearrangement, his theological insights into the prophet's message are most instructive.

Theology of the Old Testament. 2 vols. Trans. by J. A. Baker. Westminster John Knox 1961–67 $25.00 ea. ISBNs 0-664-20352-3, 0-664-20769-3. A classic work arguing that the covenant theme stands at the very center of the Old Testament thought and organizing biblical data around three rubrics: God and People, God and the World, God and Man.

BOOK ABOUT EICHRODT

Spriggs, D. G. *Two Old Testament Theologies. Studies in Biblical Theology Ser*. Allenson 1974 o.p. Comparative evaluation of the respective biblical theologies of Eichrodt and Gerhard von Rad, commenting lucidly on the configurations of Eichrodt's theological agenda and the centrality of the covenant theme.

GUNKEL, HERMANN. 1862–1932

Hermann Gunkel, a high-ranking biblical scholar, was born in Springe, Germany, near Hanover, and obtained his formal education at the Universities of Göttingen, Giessen, and Leipzig. After teaching New Testament for one year at Göttingen in 1888, Gunkel devoted the rest of his academic career to Old Testament studies at Halle (1889–93), Berlin (1894–1907), and Giessen (1907–20) before returning to Halle (1920–27).

As a pioneering investigator of literary genres in the Bible, Gunkel significantly shaped the form-critical and history-of-religions agenda in which a vast number of twentieth-century biblical scholars have engaged. Although, during his lifetime, Gunkel's form-critical findings did not command the attention that Julius Wellhausen's source-critical findings commanded, Gunkel's methodology and claims are more fully embraced by contemporary biblical scholarship than are those of Wellhausen. Gunkel focused much of his attention on the preliterary history of the Old Testament. He was especially sensitive to the distinctive rhythms of the biblical texts in which ongoing individual and communal life was reflected. He therefore posited the *Sitz im Leben* (life setting) that triggered specific oral formulations. As an inveterate collector of specimens of a given *Gattung* (literary type), Gunkel frequently drew from extant ancient Near Eastern texts.

Gunkel's methodological insights and conclusions are most readily evident in two masterful commentaries on Genesis (1901) and Psalms (1926). Above all,

Gunkel emphasized the significance of the community as opposed to individual biblical authors and spelled out the ways in which tradition is handed down orally within the community. His isolation of various family and cultic legends in the book of Genesis and his identification of different types of psalmic composition—such as the psalm of individual thanksgiving, royal psalm, and hymn—in the book of Psalms has assuredly shaped subsequent scholarly treatment of not only these two key Old Testament books but also other books in the biblical canon.

BOOKS BY GUNKEL

The Legends of Genesis: The Biblical Saga and History. Trans. by W. H. Carruth. Schocken 1987 $5.50. ISBN 0-8052-0086-X. A translation of the introduction to Gunkel's epoch-making Genesis commentary, which concerns itself with classifying and describing the diverse literary forms employed by the writers of the biblical text. With an introduction by William F. Albright.

The Psalms: A Form-Critical Introduction. Trans. by Thomas M. Horner. Augsburg Fortress 1967 $4.95. ISBN 0-8006-3043-2. A groundbreaking form-critical analysis of the Psalms in terms of their diverse literary types and respective settings in the ongoing life of biblical Israel. With an introduction by James Muilenburg.

MOFFATT, JAMES. 1870–1944

James Moffatt, a leading scholar of the New Testament and early Christianity, was a native of Glasgow, Scotland. After obtaining his education at the university of Free Church College there, he served as minister in several Presbyterian churches (1896–1912). During that interval, Moffatt published several books that amply demonstrated his capacity as a serious scholar. In due course, he filled three academic posts, two in Great Britain and one in America. He was Yates Professor of Greek and New Testament Exegesis at Mansfield College, Oxford (1912–15), then professor of church history at United Free College in Glasgow (1915–27), and, finally, Washburn Professor of Church History at Union Theological Seminary in New York City (1927–44).

This energetic and undeniably erudite scholar is best remembered for the translation of the Bible (the New Testament in 1913 and the entire Bible in 1925) that bears his name. Rigorous in its use of free-style contemporary speech, it accords well with Moffatt's commitment to make major scholarly insights about the biblical text available to laypersons. After his retirement in 1938, Moffatt was most faithful in his service as executive secretary to the committee that ultimately published the Revised Standard Version translation of the Bible. Moffatt's name is also attached to a 17-volume New Testament Commentary series (1928–50) that is mainly designed to spell out the religious message of the New Testament writings for intelligent novice readers.

BOOKS BY MOFFATT

The Approach to the New Testament. Hibbert Lectures, 1921. AMS Pr. repr. of 1921 ed. $28.00. ISBN 0-404-60420-X. A thoughtful, lucid treatment of the New Testament as both a historical document and the medium of a timeless spiritual and social message.

A Critical and Exegetical Commentary on the Epistle to the Hebrews. International Critical Commentary Ser. Bks. Intl. VA 1924 $34.95 ISBN 0-567-06034-3. An outstanding, if somewhat outdated, close reading of the Greek text.

NOTH, MARTIN. 1902–1968

Martin Noth, a most resourceful biblical historian, was a native of Dresden, Germany. On the completion of his studies at the Universities of Erlangen,

Leipzig, and Rostock, he initiated his teaching career at the University of Griefswald (1927–30). Noth then taught Old Testament studies at the University of Königsberg (1930–45) before moving to the University of Bonn, where he was Distinguished Professor of New Testament Exegesis and president of its evangelical theological seminary (1945–65). From 1965 until his death three years later, Noth was director of the Institute for the Study of the Holy Land in Jerusalem, a position once held by his teacher, Albrecht Alt.

In addition to his pioneering tradition-critical work on the Pentateuch (*A History of Pentateuchal Traditions*, made available in English in 1972), Noth authored perceptive commentaries on the books of Exodus, Leviticus, and Numbers (whose English translations appeared in 1962, 1965, and 1968, respectively). Noth is mainly known to English-speaking readers through his classic, *The History of Israel* (1960). Though Noth's innovative historical reconstruction of pre-monarchical Israel as a tribal and cultic "amphictyony," an analogy to early Greek society, has suffered criticism in recent years, related ideas regarding ancient Israel's gradual settlement in the land of Canaan have proven useful. Moreover, many scholars have been influenced by Noth's theory that the book of Deuteronomy is no appendage to the Tetrateuch (Genesis–Numbers), but is instead the initial component of a large, complex literary work known as the Deuteronomistic History, which incorporates the Old Testament books of Joshua, Judges, 1–2 Samuel, and 1–2 Kings. This historical witness, says Noth, received its final editing in the sixth century B.C. after the dual monarchies of Israel and Judah had fallen to the enemy.

BOOKS BY NOTH

The History of Israel: Biblical History. HarpC 1960 $16.95. ISBN 0-06-066310-3. This classic formulation of the history of biblical Israel is informed by the German-based Alt-Noth school, which is more skeptical in its handling of early Israelite history than is the American-based school of Albright-Bright.

A History of Pentateuchal Traditions. Trans. by Bernhard Anderson. P-H 1972 o.p. A classic traditio-critical analysis that traces the history of principal themes from their spoken origins (oral tradition) to the written form they assumed at the point of the books' composition.

The Laws in the Pentateuch and Other Studies. Trans. by D. R. Ap-Thomas. Fortress Pr. 1966 $18.95. ISBN 0-334-00870-0. A useful collection of Noth's truly seminal essays; those on "The Laws in the Pentateuch" and "God, King, and Nation in the Old Testament" have been particularly influential on ensuing biblical scholarship.

RAD, GERHARD VON. 1901–1971

Gerhard von Rad, a renowned Old Testament scholar, was born in Nürnberg. In 1925, upon completion of his theological studies at the Universities of Erlangen and Tübingen, he became a curate in the *Landeskirche* (Lutheran church) in Bavaria. Distressed by increasing signs of antisemitism among his people, von Rad soon took a leave of absence from the pastorate in order to define with greater precision the bearing of the Old Testament on the Christian church. Further studies equipped him for an appointment as a *privatdozent* (private lecturer) in Leipzig in 1930, where he enjoyed a stimulating association with Albrecht Alt, a prominent Israelite historian. Subsequently, von Rad held professorial appointments at the Universities of Jena (1934–45), Göttingen (1945–49), and Heidelberg (1949–67). During his tenure at Heidelberg, his reputation as a leading Old Testament theologian became well established.

Convinced that source criticism, which had long held the high ground in biblical studies, was now yielding diminishing returns, von Rad turned to form criticism as a viable way of engaging the biblical text and linking it with the ongoing life of the ancient Israelites. In developing his methodology, von Rad furthered the pioneering work of the famous German biblical-form critic, HERMANN GUNKEL. He shared Gunkel's interest in ascertaining the life settings of individual texts in a manner that still took into account some of source criticism's best insights (notably in the work of Julius Wellhausen). However, von Rad went beyond Gunkel in his zeal to grasp the thematic unity of more expansive literary blocks.

Most of von Rad's early scholarship focused on the manner in which the Hexateuch (the Pentateuch plus the book of Joshua) had attained its final shape. Perceiving it as a thematic whole that celebrated the history of Israel's redemption, Rad identified three short historical credos—Deuteronomy 6:20–25, 26:5–10, and Joshua 24:2–13—as its nucleus. These texts attest to the descent of the Genesis patriarchs into Egypt, the cruel enslavement of their descendants there, and their divinely sponsored liberation to new life in the land of Canaan. Associating these disclosures with Israel's earliest period, von Rad held that the distinctive thematic unity of the Hexateuch is the product of the Yahwist who fleshed out the schema of the ancient cultic credo with blocks of tradition that had hitherto been imparted orally in certain cultic festivals that transpired at various Israelite sanctuaries. Here von Rad argued for the existence of two independent blocks of tradition—an Exodus–Conquest tradition, focusing on Israel's transformation from enslavement in Egypt to independent settlement in the Land of Promise, and a Sinai tradition, focusing on God's self-revelation and giving of the law. It was the genius of the Yahwist, held von Rad, to fuse these two blocks into a uniform theology of history. Then, by affixing to that material various cycles of patriarchal and primeval legend now preserved in the book of Genesis, the Yahwist ensured that the resulting salvation history reached back to creation itself. Moreover, von Rad claimed that subsequent literary accretions by the Elohist (E) and Priestly (P) writers did not diminish the continuing impact of the Yahwist's grand narrative epic.

By embracing that epic in all its engaging attentiveness to salvation history as the foundation on which the faith of biblical Israel is truly structured, von Rad sets the course for his *Old Testament Theology*. Pursuing a diachronic method that is committed to exposing the successive layers of the fixed text of the Old Testament, von Rad insists that, above all else, Old Testament theology must interact with biblical Israel's explicit, and admittedly diverse, assertions about its God Yahweh. Convinced that the Old Testament, unlike the New Testament, lacks a unity, von Rad refused to organize his theology around a single concept or organizing principle. Keenly aware that biblical Israel regularly confessed its faith by means of historical statements, he contends that the retelling or rehearsal of these statements is the Old Testament theologian's most fundamental task. In this manner, ancient biblical traditions might achieve a welcome contemporary actualization. By the actualization of significant divine-human encounters, von Rad claims that the human past and present can be effectively bridged. Thus, the witness to God's action in history, which has its origin in Israel's earliest traditions, is perceived to extend through God's revelation in Jesus Christ and even to reach into the present.

BOOKS BY VON RAD

Deuteronomy: A Commentary. Trans. by Dorothea Barton. Westminster John Knox 1966 $19.00. ISBN 0-664-20734-0. Introductory disclosures about the origin, purpose, and literary form of Deuteronomy preface a detailed analysis of its 34 chapters.

Genesis: A Commentary. Trans. by John H. Marks. Westminster John Knox 1973 $24.00.
ISBN 0-664-20957-2. Introductory remarks about the sources and dominant theological currents in Genesis preface extensive comment on its 50 chapters.

Holy War in Ancient Israel. Trans. by Marva J. Dawn. Eerdmans 1991 $14.95. ISBN 0-
8028-0528-0. A persuasive, classical treatment of holy war as a sacred institution
unfolding as a cultic enterprise involving the early religious community of biblical
Israel.

The Message of the Prophets. Trans. by D.M.G. Stalker. HarpC 1965 $13.95. ISBN 0-06-
068929-3. Provides incisive summaries of the proclamations of biblical Israel's
prophets, prefaced by helpful chapters that clarify the manner, concerns, and scope
of prophetic thought in the Old Testament.

The Problem of the Hexateuch and Other Essays. Trans. by E. Trueman Dicken. Augsburg
Fortress 1966 o.p. Several of the essays join forces with the title essay in spelling out
the author's critical understanding of the Pentateuch.

Old Testament Theology. Trans. by D.M.G. Stalker. 2 vols. HarpC 1962–65 $21.95–$22.95.
ISBN 0-06-068931-5. A compelling treatment of emerging historical and prophetic
traditions that celebrates the diversity of the Old Testament witness.

BOOKS ABOUT VON RAD

Crenshaw, James L. *Gerhard von Rad. Makers of the Modern Theological Mind Ser.*
Hendrickson MA 1991 repr. of 1978 ed. ISBN 0-943575-69-9. An engaging portrait of
Rad's thought as it addresses both the worldview of biblical Israel and the ancient
confessional traditions of the Old Testament along with their transmitters.

Spriggs, D. G. *Two Old Testament Theologies. Studies in Biblical Theology Ser.* Allenson
1974 o.p. Comparative evaluation of the respective biblical theologies of Rad and
Walther Eichrodt, thoroughly considering the grounding of Rad's theology in
Heilsgeschichte (salvation history).

CHAPTER 17

Minority Religions and Contemporary Religious Movements

Robert S. Ellwood

> There is no religion higher than Truth.
> —MOTTO OF THE THEOSOPHICAL SOCIETY

> Thus every individual is, as it were, God in disguise, playing hide-and-seek with himself through the ages of eternity.
> —ALAN WATTS, *Cloud-Hidden, Whereabouts Unknown*

Minority religious movements in the United States received a powerful impetus in the turbulent decade of the 1960s, and in the minds of many are largely identified with the Hare Krishnas, Moonies, meditators, and neopagans spawned in those colorful times. But America's spiritual diversity has roots deep in the nineteenth century.

Religious America has long presented two spectacles to the world and to itself. In one, it is a "Christian nation," established by devoutly believing Founding Fathers and patriots, endowed with a sacred mission, and generally righteous in its dealings. In this picture, valid pluralism at the most embraces the conventional "three faiths" to which the great majority of Americans adhere: Catholicism, Protestantism, and Judaism. However much it may involve a mythologizing of the American past, this view is undoubtedly reinforced today by the fact that the rate of church attendance in America, mostly, of course, in conventional churches and synagogues, is among the highest in the world. According to public opinion polls, an extraordinarily high percentage of Americans claim that they are believers and that religion is important to them.

We must, however, not forget the other image of religious America, also remarked on by the world and, gladly or grudgingly, admitted by most Americans as well. That is the America of riotous religious diversity, hosting virtually every spiritual option in the world, spawning new sects and cults profligately. This perspective, too, has its truth. Owing both to immigration and domestic creativity, nearly every major American city boasts not only its traditional American places of worship but also its Buddhist temples, Hindu centers, Muslim mosques, and sanctuaries of a congeries of exceptional faiths old and new, whether Spiritualist churches with their deep nineteenth-century roots or "New Age" products exhibiting the spiritual exuberance of our times.

This chapter deals with a part of the diverse spectrum. The bibliography features works concerning religious movements in the United States (though a few important works on European background will be cited) outside conventional Judaism and Christianity and not primarily ethnic in character (i.e., it does not include Japanese-American Buddhist churches, ethnic Muslims, predominantly African American and Native American groups). It includes studies of groups from nineteenth- and twentieth-century America in the esoteric, communal, Eastern traditions that have drawn followers from several sectors and of American society and that have had a certain impact on American life generally. The limiting definition of groups covered is "bent" in a few instances to include Christian and ethnic groups such as Jehovah's Witnesses and the "Black Muslims," about which there is widespread interest and significant literature. Listings on individual movements essentially consist of a limited number of basic texts and current works of independent scholarship on the group.

NINETEENTH-CENTURY MOVEMENTS

The young American republic was a fertile field both for Christianity in its various forms and for unconventional spiritual movements. Broadly speaking, these movements had roots in a European philosophical tradition that can be traced back to ancient Neoplatonism, and even before, and flourished in the Renaissance, but with the rise of modern science had been in recession as a dominant worldview. This Western Neoplatonism and its progeny emphasized the unity of the cosmos, the priority of mind and spirit to matter, the concept of "correspondences" (i.e., relationships between different planes of reality, as between signs of the Zodiac and human personality), and the "Great Chain of Being" idea that ranks of angelic or spiritual beings greater and lesser than humans lie between the lowest levels of creation and God. It was easy to move from theoretical acceptance of this outlook to belief in such concrete manifestations of it, as spirits and magic. Though adherence to objective manifestations of the older worldview, such as the earth-centered Ptolemaic astronomy, dwindled to virtually nothing in the seventeenth and eighteenth centuries, some people continued to affirm the spiritual significance of such ideas as correspondences and the Great Chain of Being. Increasingly, though, they found themselves marginal to mainstream science and religion alike.

By the early nineteenth century, however, something of the spiritual side of the old worldview was being revived under the powerful impetus of several new movements that gave it a contemporary face and sociological grounding. These include Swedenborgianism and Mesmerism (discussed later), and Freemasonry, with its image of lodges in which one was initiated into ancient and secret wisdom. In the background was the vogue for romanticism, with its exaltation of feeling and inner experience as ways of knowing, and its idealization of the past, and for philosophical idealism not far removed from Neoplatonism. In America, on one level the new mix produced the Transcendentalism of RALPH WALDO EMERSON (see Vol. 1) and HENRY DAVID THOREAU (see Vol. 1). On another, vivid movements such as Spiritualism, which has been called "Swedenborgianism Americanized," and later Theosophy, Christian Science, and "New Thought" emerged.

The young American nation was also fascinated by social and even sexual experimentation. It was dotted with utopian communities, often based on unconventional religious doctrines, testing new forms of social organization and sexual arrangements, from celibacy to polygamy. We will present such groups as the Oneida community, the Shakers, and the Latter-Day Saints (Mormons). Some groups that were considered radical in the nineteenth century have now become well established and conventional, while others have disappeared. All, however, help demonstrate the importance of religious diversity and experimentation in the United States.

General Works

Albanese, Catherine. *Nature Religion in America: From the Algonkian Indians to the New Age.* U. Ch. Pr. 1991 $11.95. ISBN 0-534-16488-9. Highly original and fascinating study of a facet of religious life important to the alternative tradition.

Bednorowski, Mary F. *New Religions and the Theological Imagination in America.* Ind. U. Pr. 1989 $25.00. ISBN 0-253-31137-3. An innovative book that emphasizes the theological creativity of new religious movements, particularly in their relationship to nature and the feminine.

Cross, Whitney R. *The Burned-Over District: The Social and Intellectual History of Enthusiastic Religion in Western New York, 1800-1850.* Cornell Univ. Pr. 1982 $14.95. ISBN 0-8014-9232-7. Classic study of the matrix out of which Spiritualism, Mormonism, and other movements of the nineteenth century emerged.

Ellwood, Robert S. *Alternative Altars: Unconventional and Eastern Spirituality in America. Chicago History of Amer. Religion Ser.* U. Ch. Pr. 1979 $5.50. ISBN 0-226-20620-3. A theoretical and historical study, focusing on the concept of an ongoing pattern of "emergent religion" in American life and citing Spiritualism, Theosophy, and Zen as major examples.

Foster, Lawrence. *Religion and Sexuality: The Shakers, the Mormons, and the Oneida Community.* OUP 1984 $38.00. ISBN 19-502794-9. An excellent study of three nineteenth-century movements, emphasizing their highly individual perspectives on sexuality, while considering them in the larger context of ideology, religious experience, and cultural environment.

Fuller, Robert C. *Alternative Medicine and American Religious Life.* OUP 1989 $24.95. ISBN 0-19-505775-9. A balanced and authoritative study of a tradition closely intertwined with new religious movements.

———. *America and the Unconscious.* OUP 1986 $35.00. ISBN 0-19-504027-9. A history of the "unconscious mind" in the United States, including its role in such movements as Spiritualism, Christian Science, and psychoanalysis.

Jackson, Carl T. *The Oriental Religions and American Thought: Nineteenth-Century Explorations.* Greenwood 1981 $38.50. ISBN 0-313-224-91-9. An exceptionally fine piece of scholarship that emphasizes the impact of Hinduism and Buddhism on American writers and that provides invaluable background for understanding the popularity of Eastern-based groups and movements in the spiritual life of the United States.

Judah, J. Stillson. *The History and Philosophy of the Metaphysical Movements in America.* Westminster John Knox 1967 o.p. Comprehensive treatment of Spiritualism, Theosophy, Christian Science, and the "New Thought" groups in American culture, emphasizing the healing aspects of these movements and the ways in which they are varied expressions of a single "metaphysical" theme.

Kyle, Richard. *The Religious Fringe: A History of Alternative Religions in America.* InterVarsity 1993 $17.99. ISBN 0-8308-1766-2

Kerr, Howard, and Charles L. Crow, eds. *The Occult in America: New Historical Perspectives.* U. of Ill. Pr. 1983 $24.95. ISBN 0-252-01360-3. Collection of historical essays by various authorities, covering such topics as Spiritualism, Theosophy, Christian Science, and "Women in Occult America."

Leventhal, Herbert. *In the Shadow of the Enlightenment: Occultism and Renaissance Science in Eighteenth-Century America.* NYU Pr. 1976 o.p. Provides invaluable background for understanding religion in the nineteenth century, particularly how European occultism and the Renaissance worldview took root in America and influenced later movements.

Mandelker, Ira L. *Religion, Society and Utopia in Nineteenth Century America.* U. of Mass. Pr. 1984 $22.50. ISBN 0-87023-436-6

Miller, Timothy. *American Communes, 1860–1960.* Garland 1990 $44.00. ISBN 0-8240-8470-5

Moore, R. Laurence. *Religious Outsiders and the Making of America.* OUP 1987 $13.95. ISBN 0-19-505188-2. The importance of alternative religions in the making of American history.

Tamney, Joseph B. *American Society in the Buddhist Mirror.* Garland 1992 $33.00. ISBN 0-8153-0721-7. A study of why Buddhism has been popular in America from the nineteenth century to the present, and in turn how the American experience has changed Buddhism.

Tweed, Thomas A. *The American Encounter with Buddhism, 1844–1912: Victorian Culture and the Limits of Dissent.* Ind. U. Pr. 1992 $29.95. ISBN 0-253-36099-4. A stimulating discussion of the kinds of people who responded to Buddhism in the nineteenth and early twentieth centuries and how they interpreted the religion to fit the leading concerns of the times.

Webb, James. *The Occult Underground.* Open Court 1974 $18.95. ISBN 0-912-050-46-2. A discussion of nineteenth-century Theosophy, Christian Science, secret societies, and so on, in Europe and America, interpreting these movements as fearful reactions against modern reason and science.

Individual Religious Movements

CHRISTIAN SCIENCE

The Church of Christ, Scientist, was founded by MARY BAKER EDDY (1821–1910), a New England woman who believed that she had been healed of a grave injury in a remarkable manner in 1866; she later referred to that event as her discovery of Christian Science. After effecting a number of healings of others, Eddy published the first edition of her major book, *Science and Health with Key to the Scriptures*, in 1875. The Church was incorporated in Boston in 1879. Healing through treatments that inculcate belief in the ultimate unreality of evil and disease has always been important to Christian Science. Basic doctrine presents God as the sole true reality, the "divine Principle of all that really is," and regards sin and sickness, like matter, as objects of erroneous belief; healing means attaining the spiritual understanding that disease is not real. The Christian Science church has no clergy, but "practitioners" exercise leadership roles, especially in healing treatments. Worship is simple and centers around readings from the Bible and *Science and Health*.

In the late 1980s and the 1990s, the Church of Christ, Scientist, endured a series of troubles. Several convictions of parents who attempted to use Christian Science healing on their children brought unfavorable publicity. Ill-advised media ventures resulted in enormous financial losses to the Mother Church. In 1992 the church republished an old and long-forgotten controversial book by Bliss Knapp, *The Destiny of the Mother Church*, which was seen by some as virtually deifying Mary Baker Eddy, contrary to established doctrine. Although church governing officials stated that the volume was being presented simply as part of a historical reprint series, a large bequest was attached to the publication and distribution of the work, and the Christian Science movement was deeply divided by the actions.

Braden, Charles S. *Christian Science Today: Power, Policy, Practice.* Bks. Demand repr. of 1958 ed. $120.70. ISBN 0-8357-8846-6. An important study, though now somewhat dated.

Eddy, Mary B. *Church Manual of the Mother Church*. Christian Sci. repr. of 1895 ed. $11.95. ISBN 0-87952-061-2. More than merely a book of operating procedures, the *Manual* offers important insights into ideas and their applications.

———. *Health and Medicine in the Christian Science Tradition*. Crossroad NY 1988 $19.95. ISBN 0-8245-0895-5. A summary of Christian Science's most distinctive practice by a leading scholar within the church.

———. *Mary Baker Eddy*. 3 vols. Christian Sci. 1966–77 $24.95 ea. Vol. 1 *The Years of Discovery*. ISBN 0-87510-085-6. Vol. 2 *The Years of Trial*. ISBN 0-87510-118-6. Vol. 3 *The Years of Authority*. ISBN 0-87510-142-9. By far the most comprehensive biography of the founder of Christian Science.

———. *Prose Works*. Christian Sci. 1925 o.p. Essential works, apart from *Science and Health*, by the founder of Christian Science.

———. *Science and Health with Key to the Scriptures*. Christian Sci. 1875 $14.95. ISBN 0-87452-034-5. The basic text.

Gottschalk, Stephen. *The Emergence of Christian Science in American Religious Life*. U. CA Pr. 1974 $27.50. ISBN 0-520-02308-0. The most comprehensive treatment of Christian Science history and teaching in the nineteenth century.

Knapp, Bliss. *The Destiny of the Mother Church*. Christian Sci. 1992 $14.95. ISBN 0-87510-231-X. Controversial book that inspired a crisis in Christian Science.

Peel, Robert. *Christian Science: Its Encounter with American Culture*. Doubleday 1965 o.p. A basic work on the rise of Christian Science and its place in American life.

COMMUNAL GROUPS

Communal groups, separatist associations based on religious, ideological, or political affiliations, have long attracted people in search of a perfect society. Among communal groups with a religious basis in nineteenth-century America were the Oneida community, a long-prosperous settlement in upstate New York celebrated for its practice of "complex marriage"; Fountain Grove in California, founded by the intriguing mystic and former Spiritualist and Swedenborgian Thomas Lake Harris; and Amana in Iowa, which (like Oneida) eventually moved from sect to successful corporation.

Of particular interest is the succession of spiritual communes in New Harmony, Indiana. The original commune was founded in 1814 as a celibate, pietistic settlement by George Rapp, a German immigrant and former Lutheran who believed, on the basis of the first chapter of Genesis, that God was both male and female. In 1825 it was sold to Robert Owen, the celebrated British industrialist and philanthropist, who established a cooperative community along his own utopian lines, which included decent working conditions, sickness and old age insurance, and educational and recreational facilities. The experiment cost him most of his fortune, however, and Owen returned to England in 1828, where he became a Spiritualist in his old age. One of his sons who remained in America, Robert Dale Owen, pursued an interesting and varied life of romance, politics (he was a member of the U.S. House of Representatives for four years in the 1840s and later an abolitionist), communalism, and Spiritualism.

Barthel, Diane L. *Amana: From Pietist Sect to American Community*. Bks. Demand repr. of 1984 ed. $64.30. ISBN 0-7837-1900-0. The most extensive study of this important community.

Chmielewski, Wendy, and others, eds. *Women in Spiritual Communitarian Societies in the United States*. Syracuse U. Pr. 1992 $39.95. ISBN 0-8156-2568-5. An important gender-based study.

Dare, Philip N. *American Communes to 1860: An Annotated Bibliography*. Garland 1986 $32.00. ISBN 0-8240-8572-8. A valuable bibliographical resource, with brief summaries of each group's history.

Demaria, Richard. *Communal Love at Oneida: A Perfectionist Vision of Authority, Property and Sexual Order. Texts and Studies in Religion*. E. Mellen 1983 $89.95. ISBN 0-88946-986-5. A valuable study of Oneida's exceptional theology of love and its sexual practice.

Fellman, Michael. *The Unbounded Frame: Freedom and Community in Nineteenth Century American Utopianism*. Greenwood 1973 $38.50. ISBN 0-8371-6369-2. An examination of the basic paradox in utopian groups.

Fogarty, Robert S. *All Things New: American Communes and Utopian Movements, 1860–1914*. U. Ch. Pr. 1990 $34.50. ISBN 0-226-25654-5. An examination of communalism during an important period generally neglected by scholarship.

_____. *The Righteous Remnant: The House of David*. Kent St. U. Pr. 1989 $12.50. ISBN 0-87338-395-2. Study of a male commune noted for its baseball team.

Hinds, William A. *American Communities. Amer. Utopian Adventure Ser.* Porcupine Pr. 1975 repr. of 1908 ed. $49.50. ISBN 0-87991-017-8. Classic account based largely on personal observation of such celebrated nineteenth-century American utopias as Economy, Zoar, Bethel, Aurora, Icaria, the Shakers, and Oneida.

Hine, Robert V. *California's Utopian Colonies*. U. CA Pr. 1983 $35.00. ISBN 0-520-04865-2. An account of Fountain Grove, the Theosophical community at Point Loma, and other early California spiritual and utopian communities.

Kolmerten, Carol A. *Women in Utopia: The Ideology of Gender in the American Owenite Communities*. Ind. U. Pr. 1990 $29.50. ISBN 0-253-33192-7. A study of women's experience in one of the major strands of American communalism in the nineteenth century.

Kring, Hilda A. *The Harmonists: A Folk-Cultural Approach*. Scarecrow 1973 o.p. The best modern study of the Rappites, properly called the Harmony community, a Protestant celibate movement that lasted in several locations, including New Harmony, Indiana, from 1805 to 1905.

Leopold, Richard W. *Robert Dale Owen*. Hippocrene Bks. 1969 repr. of 1940 ed. $31.50. ISBN 0-374-94940-9. A substantial biography of Robert Owen's distinguished son, who continued his father's communalist and spiritualist work.

Lockwood, George B. *The New Harmony Communities*. AMS Pr. 1975 repr. of 1902 ed. $34.50. ISBN 0-404-08456-7. Still the most comprehensive history of these planned communities, giving extensive attention to the Rappites and the work of Robert Owen.

Mandelker, Ira L. *Religion, Society, and Utopia in Nineteenth-Century America*. U. of Mass. Pr. 1984 $22.50. ISBN 0-87023-436-6. A sociological study of utopian communities and their relation to the outside world, focusing on the Oneida community.

Miller, Timothy. *American Communes, 1860–1960: A Bibliography*. Garland 1990 $44.00. ISBN 0-8240-8470-5. A highly recommended bibliographical guide to communes.

Nordhoff, Charles. *Communistic Societies of the United States: From Personal Visit and Observation*. Corner Hse. 1978 repr. of 1875 ed. $24.00. ISBN 0-87928-092-1. Classic firsthand account of Amana, Harmony, Zoar, the Shakers, and Oneida, among others, with emphasis on the religious creed of each and an introduction by Mark Holloway.

Oved, Yaacov. *Two Hundred Years of American Communes*. Transaction Pubs. 1992 $24.95. ISBN 1-56000-647-1

Thomas, Robert D. *The Man Who Would Be Perfect: John Humphrey Noyes and the Utopian Impulse*. U. of Pa. Pr. 1977 o.p. A life of the visionary who founded the Oneida community.

Veysey, Laurence R. *The Communal Experience: Anarchist and Mystical Communities in Twentieth Century America*. U. Ch. Pr. 1978 $7.95. ISBN 0-226-85458-2. A detailed and valuable study of several spiritual communities, including a Vedanta and a Gurdjieff group.

THE LATTER-DAY SAINTS (MORMONS)

The Church of Jesus Christ of Latter-Day Saints, or the Mormon Church as it is popularly called, has been the most successful of distinctive new religious movements originating in the United States. The recipient of the revelation that inaugurated Mormonism was JOSEPH SMITH (1805–44), who in 1822 was told in a vision by the angel Moroni where to find certain buried tablets. These golden plates engraved with strange hieroglyphics were retrieved, translated, and published by Smith in 1830 as the *Book of Mormon*, which Mormons regard as a major supplement to the biblical scriptures. The *Book of Mormon* tells the history of Near Eastern peoples who brought the Torah to America in ancient times and describes sacred events, including an appearance by the resurrected Christ, to their descendants. Citing these revelations, Smith called on the faithful to abandon apostate churches and restore pure religion.

Many vicissitudes followed, including violent mob action against Mormons and Smith's murder, leading up to the settlement of Utah by Mormons under Brigham Young (1801–77), beginning in 1847. During this time the controversial practice of polygamy commenced. It was formally abandoned in 1890, in order to meet conditions laid down by the U.S. government for Utah's admission to statehood, but reportedly the practice continues secretly in some places to this day.

Mormon theology accepts some conventional Christian doctrines, such as belief in God, the work of Christ, and free will, but includes such distinctive ideas as the concept of God as a finite being with a material body who has attained his exalted position through evolution and the eternal progression of human beings toward godhead. Mormonism is led by a president or high priest to whom, Mormons believe, God speaks in a continuing revelation. Virtually all male Mormons hold priesthood rank. Faithful Mormons tithe their incomes to the Church and believe in the resurrection of the dead and a final, eternal judgment.

Several LDS churches exist, the largest of which is headquartered in Salt Lake City, is highly organized and well known for its effective missionary work. The Reorganized Church of Jesus Christ of Latter-Day Saints, formed in 1860 by groups opposed to Brigham Young, is headquartered in Independence, Missouri.

Alexander, Thomas G. *Mormonism in Transition: The Latter-Day Saints and Their Church, 1890–1930*. U. of Ill. Pr. 1986 $24.95. ISBN 0-252-01185-6. An important historical work on the development of the LDS church.

Anderson, Scott. *The Four O'Clock Murders: A True Story of a Mormon Family's Vengence*. Doubleday 1993 $20.00. ISBN 0-385-41904-X. Lurid tale of renegade Mormon family's bloody criminal empire and their indulgence in "blood atonement."

Arrington, Leonard J., and Davis Bitton. *The Mormon Experience: A History of the Latter-Day Saints*. U. of Ill. Pr. 1992 $14.95. ISBN 0-232-06236-2. A rich introductory, historical account of Mormonism by members of the LDS church.

Bernotas, Bob. *Brigham Young*. Chelsea Hse. 1993 $17.95. ISBN 0-7910-1642-0. Biography of Joseph Smith's successor detailing the ways that Young ensured the religion's survival.

Brodie, Fawn M. *No Man Knows My History: The Life of Joseph Smith*. Knopf 1971 $35.00. ISBN 0-394-46967-4. An important, though controversial, investigation of Smith.

Bushman, Richard L. *Joseph Smith and the Beginnings of Mormonism*. U. of Ill. Pr. 1984 $24.95. ISBN 0-252-01143-0. A comprehensive, well-written introduction to the LDS perspective on the origins of the religion.

Flake, Chad J., and Larry W. Draper, eds. *A Mormon Bibliography, 1830–1930: Books, Pamphlets, Periodicals, and Broadsides Relating to the First Century of Mormonism*. U. of Utah Pr. 1990 $30.00. ISBN 0-87480-338-1. A basic resource for students of Mormonism.

Leone, Mark P. *Roots of Modern Mormonism.* HUP 1979 $19.50. ISBN 0-674-77970-3. An unconventional look at the development of Mormonism, emphasizing economic factors as well as diversity and conformity in the Mormon world.

Ludlow, Daniel, ed. *Encyclopedia of Mormonism.* 5 vols. Macmillan 1991 $340.00. ISBN 0-02-904040-X. An invaluable resource, edited from a perspective basically sympathetic to the faith. The last volume contains the *Book of Mormon, The Pearl of Great Price,* and other basic texts.

Mangum, Garth, and Bruce Blumell. *The Mormon's War on Poverty. A History of L.D.S. Welfare, 1830–1990.* U. of Utah Pr. 1993 $29.95. ISBN 0-87480-414-0

O'Dea, Thomas F. *Mormons.* U. Ch. Pr. 1964 $10.00. ISBN 0-226-61744-0. Still the best overall introduction by a sociologist of religion.

Shields, Steven L. *The Latter Day Saints Churches: An Annotated Bibliography.* Garland 1987 $54.00. ISBN 0-8240-8582-5. Covers material from 1931 through 1986 on the LDS, the Reorganized Church of Latter-Day Saints, and smaller groups in the Mormon tradition.

Shipps, Jan. *Mormonism: The Story of a New Religious Tradition.* U. of Ill. Pr. 1985 $12.95. ISBN 0-256-01417-0. A new, compact, and insightful study of the religion by a non-Mormon, emphasizing its originality as a new religion.

Shupe, Anson. *The Darker Side of Virtue: Corruption, Scandal and the Mormon Empire.* Prometheus Bks. 1991 $23.95. ISBN 0-87975-654-3. An analysis of recent controversial events in the LSD church.

Smith, Joseph, Jr. *Book of Mormon, 1830. Heritage Repr. Ser.* Herald Hse. 1973 repr. of 1966 ed. $7.25. ISBN 0-8309-0273-2. The book translated by Joseph Smith from the tablets known as the Golden Plates.

————. *Doctrine and Covenants of the Church of Jesus Christ of Latter-Day Saints: Containing the Revelations Given to Joseph Smith, Jun, the Prophet, for the Building Up of the Kingdom of God in the Last Days.* Ed. by Orson Pratt. Greenwood 1971 repr. of 1880 ed. $49.75. ISBN 0-8371-4101-X. A fundamental Mormon scriptural text. Inexpensive editions, often bound with a companion work, *The Pearl of Great Price,* are widely available through the LDS church.

MESMERISM

The Viennese-educated physician Franz Anton Mesmer (1734–1815), whose practice in Paris during the 1780s attracted many wealthy people and aristocrats, including Marie Antoinette, and aroused great controversy, is considered the modern father of Mesmerism, or hypnotism. His experiments indirectly contributed greatly to the development of psychotherapy and psychosomatic medicine. He also substantially influenced nineteenth-century Spiritualism and occultism.

Mesmer believed that healing could be effected by "animal magnetism," a universal force that can be transmitted from one person to another by stroking gestures. After his patients were placed in a large wooden tub filled with water and iron filings, Mesmer, dressed in a long silk robe and accompanied by slow music, would stroke their ailing body parts with his iron wand. These operations could easily put patients into a hypnotic trance in which suggestibility was high; thus, such treatments "cured" a variety of ailments and also permitted material from the unconscious to rise to the surface. Mesmer came to believe that animal magnetism could awaken latent powers of extrasensory perception, healing, and wisdom.

In the 1830s and 1840s, Mesmerism became in vogue in America, with Mesmerist experimentation, medical healings, and stage performances popular. When Mesmerist trance was combined with Swedenborgian cosmology to produce the trance mediumship of discarnate spirits, the result was Spiritualism.

Buranelli, Vincent. *Wizard from Vienna: Franz Anton Mesmer*. Putnam Pub. Group 1975 o.p. A good, readable biography of Mesmer.

Crabtree, Adam. *Magnetic Sleep: Mesmer and the Roots of Psychological Healing*. Yale U. Pr. 1993 $45.00. ISBN 0-300-05588-9

Fuller, Robert C. *Mesmerism and the American Cure of Souls*. U. of Pa. Pr. 1982 $40.95. ISBN 0-8122-7847-X. Despite an occasionally arch tone, the best book on the subject.

Tatar, Maria M. *Spellbound: Studies on Mesmerism and Literature*. Princeton U. Pr. 1978 o.p. Affords important insights into the cultural significance of Mesmerism in Europe and America.

NEW THOUGHT

The New Thought movement was centered on ideas, related to those of Christian Science, that God is all, mind is basic, good thoughts create good realities, and evil and sickness are the result of false beliefs. A major source of this teaching was PHINEAS P. QUIMBY (1802–66) of Maine, a onetime student of Mesmerism and mentor of MARY BAKER EDDY and early New Thought teachers, such as Warren Felt Evans and Julius Dresser. The principal doctrinal difference between New Thought and Christian Science is that the former believes in directing the power of mind toward healing, whereas the latter affirms that disease does not exist on the deepest level. There are also organizational differences: the Christian Science Church is a highly structured institution, whereas New Thought has been a diverse movement of individuals, independent churches, and often loosely organized denominations. Among the New Thought groups are Unity, the Church of Divine Science, and the Church of Religious Science. Although relatively small, these denominations continue to exist in the 1990s, often exerting an influence greater than their numbers would suggest because of the wide distribution of their inspirational literature. The most successful of them has probably been Unity, which emphasizes the power of prayer to produce not only inner harmony and good health but also worldly success and which teaches that salvation is attainable through a series of progressive reincarnations that culminate in a Christlike state of perfection. The New Thought ideology, sometimes spoken of as "positive thinking," has also been widely adapted and popularized by prominent clergy of traditional churches, such as Norman Vincent Peale and Robert Schuller.

Anderson, C. Alan. *Healing Hypotheses: Horatio W. Dresser and the Philosophy of New Thought*. Garland 1993 $110.00. ISBN 0-8153-0778-0. Study of Dresser and other important founders of the New Thought tradition.

Braden, Charles S. *Spirits in Rebellion: The Rise and Development of New Thought*. SMU Pr. 1963 $15.95. ISBN 0-87074-025-3. The best scholarly study of this movement.

Dresser, Horatio W., ed. *The Quimby Manuscripts*. Carol Pub. Group 1984 o.p. Edited material by and about the principal founder of New Thought.

Fox, Emmet. *The Emmet Fox Treasury*. 5 vols. HarpC repr. of 1979 ed. $22.00. ISBN 0-06-062860-X. Basic works by one of the most articulate New Thought teachers, providing a good introductory sample.

Holmes, Fenwick. *Ernest Holmes: His Life and Times*. Putnam Pub. Group 1989 $16.95. ISBN 0-396-06054-4. The story of the founder of the Church of Religious Science—a major New Thought denomination—written by his brother.

Holmes, Ernest. *A Dictionary of New Thought Terms*. DeVorss 1991 $8.95. ISBN 0-87516-632-6

Wilcox, Ella. W. *The Heart of the New Thought*. Sun Pub. 1993 $8.00. ISBN 0-89540-268-8

ROSICRUCIANISM

The term *Rosicrucian* (from the Latin for the tradition's symbol: the rose and the cross) alludes to a body of esoteric wisdom and an ancient order that allegedly possesses it. The wisdom is essentially based on the worldview of Neoplatonism that resurfaced during the Renaissance with the rediscovery of classical sources and interest in the new science sources. The name and the concept of a secret order first appeared in Germany in the famous tract *Fama Fraternitatis* (1614), which purported to be an account of a secret order founded to advance piety and scientific and magical studies by Christian Rosenkreutz, a German knight who was supposed to have learned the mystic and esoteric arts, along with Arabic philosophy and the Jewish cabala, in the Near East. It invited men of learning to join this Order of the Rosy Cross and excited a good deal of interest, but the mystical brotherhood could not be found. Most scholars today regard the tract as an allegorical work by a theologian named Johann Valentin Andrea (1586–1654).

The name, however, stuck, and it is now used loosely for a body of occult learning in the Renaissance style. Modern Rosicrucianism claims to be descended from an ancient Egyptian mystery school whose members through the ages have included such luminaries as PLATO (see also Vol. 3), Jesus, FRANCIS BACON, and BENJAMIN FRANKLIN (see Vol. 1). The literature speaks of the separate destiny of the inner self from the physical body, astrological correspondences, heavenly hierarchies, and the unity of all human beings; the pyramid and the rose-garlanded cross are common symbols. A Rosicrucian society was established in Pennsylvania in 1694, and, both in America and elsewhere, numerous groups called themselves by that designation in the eighteenth and nineteenth centuries. At least five such orders are extant in America today, the oldest being the Fraternitas Rosae Crucis founded in 1868. The best known is undoubtedly the international Ancient Mystical Order Rosae Crucis, headquartered in San Jose, California, which advertises widely. Little independent literature on modern Rosicrucianism exists.

Jennings, Hargrove. *The Rosicrucians: Their Rites and Mysteries.* Ayer repr. of 1907 ed. $36.50. ISBN 0-405-07957-5. A curious and somewhat influential occult classic.
Lewis, H. Spencer. *Behold the Sign.* 1972 o.p.
_____. *Rosicrucian Questions and Answers.* AMORC 17th ed. 1993 $18.95. ISBN 0-912057-59-9
McIntosh, Christopher. *The Rosy Cross Unveiled: The History, Mythology, and Rituals of an Occult Order.* Borgo Pr. 1989 o.p. A basic work by the leading historian of Rosicrucianism.
Melton, J. Gordon, ed. *Rosicrucianism in America.* Garland 1990 $103.00. ISBN 0-8240-4365-0. Facsimile edition of rare texts, with an introduction by Melton.
Roberts, Marie E. *Gothic Immortals: The Fiction of the Brotherhood of the Rosy Cross.* Routledge 1990 $35.00. ISBN 0-415-02368-8. Summarizes and interprets a mysterious and secretive order that has long fascinated writers of speculative fiction.
Waik, A. E. *The Brotherhood of the Rosy Cross.* Kessinger Pub. 1992 $36.50. ISBN 1-56459-100-X
Yates, Frances. *The Rosicrucian Enlightenment.* 1972 o.p.

THE SHAKERS

The United Society of Believers in Christ's Second Appearing, commonly known as the Shakers, was a significant presence in nineteenth-century American spiritual life. Clustered in celibate rural communes from Maine to Kentucky, the Shakers combined an outward life of hard work and plain living with an inner world of sacred dance and ecstatic visions. They received their name from the trembling produced by strong religious emotion. Their numerous practical inventions, simple, well-made furniture, and lively songs are now parts of American lore.

The movement actually originated in a Quaker revival in England in 1747 and was known as the "Shaking Quakers." However, it was strengthened by its leader, Ann Lee (1736–84). Raised in the slums of Manchester, England, she experienced a religious transformation among the "Shaking Quakers" and came to America with a few other believers in 1774. Two years later, Lee established the first community near Albany, New York. At its peak, around 1830, Shakerism had some 19 communal houses of several hundred members each. The Shaker way of life involved celibacy, open confession of sins, pacifism, and consecrated work. Believers who joined a Shaker community donated their services and possessions to the group, but they were always free to leave whenever they wished. Because of the principle of celibacy, the communities eventually died out and there are very few Shakers left today.

Shaker belief centered on the dual nature of God. Male and female principles were perceived as equally present in the divine, and, as the male aspect had appeared in Jesus Christ, so had the female in Lee, who came to be known as Mother Ann. Thus, the "Second Appearing" had already come. The Society was called to live the life of the new age of perfection following that event, when men and women would be absolutely equal and the lower passions transcended, and human beings could pursue lives of free cooperation together. To this ideal the quiet empire of Shaker communities testified.

Shaker worship was elaborate, combining precision marches and dances with spontaneous gifts of tongues and song. In 1837 a great Spiritualistic movement swept through the Shaker world, with many reports of visits by past worthies, from biblical figures to Mother Ann. Despite emotional excess, these manifestations led to the fine Shaker art that endeavors to capture glimpses of another world on paper.

Both primary and secondary literature on the Shakers is extensive and growing. Below are a few books that may serve as starting points.

Andrews, Edward D. *The Gift to Be Simple: Songs, Dances, and Rituals of the American Shakers*. Dover 1940 $4.50. ISBN 0-486-20022-1. Valuable insights into Shaker forms of expression.

_____. *People Called Shakers: A Search for the Perfect Society*. Dover 1953 $6.95. ISBN 0-486-21081-2. A standard introduction by an eminent student of Shakerism.

Bolick, Nancy O., and Sallie G. Randolph. *Shaker Villages*. Walker & Co. 1993 $12.95. ISBN 0-8027-8210-8. Outlines basic tenets of the Shaker Faith, worship services, and village organization and architecture.

Brewer, Priscilla J. *Shaker Communities, Shaker Lives*. U. Pr. of New Eng. 1986 $15.95. ISBN 0-87451-400-2. A good study based on primary documents.

Evans, Frederick W. *Autobiography of a Shaker and Revelation of the Apocalypse. Amer. Utopian Adventure Ser.* AMS Pr. 1986 repr. of 1888 ed. $19.50. ISBN 0-404-10748-6. Classic autobiography and statement of a leading nineteenth-century Shaker and social radical.

Humez, Jean M., ed. *Mother's First-Born Daughters: Early Shaker Writings on Women and Religion*. Ind. U. Pr. 1993 $39.95. ISBN 0-253-20744-4. Articles emphasizing the ambiguous role of women in the Shaker movement.

Melcher, Marguerite F. *The Shaker Adventure*. Shaker Mus. 1980 $9.75. ISBN 0-937942-08-1. A good, popular introduction.

Procter-Smith, Marjorie. *Women in Shaker Community and Worship: A Feminist Analysis of the Uses of Religious Symbolism. Studies in Women and Religion*. E. Mellen 1985 o.p. A well-researched feminist examination of the unique faith and society of the Shakers.

Richmond, Mary L., ed. *Shaker Literature: A Bibliography*. U. Pr. of New Eng. 1976 o.p. An exhaustive resource for primary and secondary materials on the Shakers.

Sasson, Sarah D. *The Shaker Spiritual Narrative.* U. of Tenn. Pr. 1983 $26.95. ISBN 0-
   87049-392-2. A fascinating look at the Shaker experience, with its visions and
   spiritual journeys, through the intimate journals of community members.
Stein, Stephen J. *The Shaker Experience in America.* Yale. U. Pr. 1992 $40.00. ISBN 0-
   300-05139-5. A large-scale scholarly history of the movement that will surely become
   the standard.
Whitson, Robley E., ed. *The Shakers: Two Centuries of Spiritual Reflection. Classics of
   Western Spirituality Ser.* Paulist Pr. 1983 $11.95. ISBN 0-8091-2373-8. An excellent,
   well-introduced collection of writings by Shakers.

SPIRITUALISM

The formal beginning of the Spiritualist movement is generally attributed to
the famous "Rochester rappings," messages tapped in code first heard in
upstate New York in 1848 by Margaret and Kate Fox, two girls of humble
background. The way had been abundantly prepared. Not only were Swedenborgianism and Mesmerism at hand, but just the year before Andrew Jackson
Davis (1826–1910), the chief philosopher of nineteenth-century American
Spiritualism, had published his major work, *The Principles of Nature: Her Divine
Revelation and a Voice to Mankind* (1847). A practicing Mesmerist, Davis had
dictated the manuscript of some 800 pages while in a trance to several scribes.
Philosophically, much of it is little more than SWEDENBORG paraphrased, but it
adds to Swedenborg's metaphysics an exuberant optimism, characteristic of
America at this juncture, full of faith in progress and ever-brighter democratic
futures without end.

The primary belief of Spiritualism is that the human personality continues to
exist after death and can communicate with the living through the efforts of a
"medium" or a "psychic."

For a decade or so after 1848, when sensational newspaper articles about the
Fox sisters' encounter provoked a thousand imitative attempts at contacting the
Other Side, Spiritualism was an enthusiasm, both vigorously attacked and
defended. Trance mediumship, seances, listening for rappings, and even
"physical phenomena," such as the manifestation of spirit trumpets and
levitation, were widely reported. Its ideology was Swedenborgian and Mesmerist, often joined to Davis's progressivist social idealism. After the Civil War,
despite occasional revivals, Spiritualism maintained a much quieter existence,
but it persists to this day. In upper New York State, the community of Lily Dale,
a center for mediums and conferences of Spiritualists, remains active. Spiritualism's direct and indirect influence on later movements, such as Theosophy and
New Thought, as well as on the rise of scientific psychical research, is
significant. The literature about Spiritualism still tends to be either highly
sympathetic or antagonistic, reflecting the strong feelings this colorful American movement has always evoked.

Brandon, Ruth. *The Spiritualists: The Passion for the Occult in the Nineteenth and
   Twentieth Centuries.* Prometheus Bks. 1984 $19.95. ISBN 0-87975-269-6. A general
   history written from a skeptical viewpoint.
Braude, Ann. *Radical Spirits: Spiritualism and Women's Rights in Nineteenth-Century
   America.* Beacon Pr. 1989 $24.95. ISBN 0-8070-7500-0. A splendid study that
   considers the important issue of Spiritualism as largely a women's religious
   movement.
Doyle, Arthur Conan. *The History of Spiritualism. Perspectives in Psychical Research Ser.*
   Ayer 1975 repr. of 1926 ed. $22.00. ISBN 0-405-07025-X. A classic history by the
   creator of Sherlock Holmes; Doyle was himself a Spiritualist believer and writes
   sympathetically.

Fornell, Earl W. *The Unhappy Medium: Spiritualism and the Life of Margaret Fox*. U. of Tex. Pr. 1964 o.p. ISBN 0-317-10609-0. Though limited in its treatment of the religious and cultural background of Spiritualism, this is an interesting biographical introduction to the troubled life of one of its inciters.

Goldfarb, Russell M., and Clare R. Goldfarb. *Spiritualism and Nineteenth-Century Letters*. Fairleigh Dickinson 1978 $25.00. ISBN 0-8386-2025-6. A summary of nineteenth-century Spiritualism and references to it in British and American literature.

Hardinge, Emma. *Modern American Spiritualism: A Twenty Years' Record of the Communion Between Earth and the World of Spirits*. Univ. Bks. 1970 o.p. An incomparable original source of much of the lore of early American Spiritualism.

Kerr, Howard. *Mediums, and Spirit-Rappers, and Roaring Radicals*. Bks Demand repr. of 1972 ed. $67.80. ISBN 0-317-41918-8. A comprehensive study of Spiritualism in nineteenth-century American literature and social movements.

Moore, R. Laurance. *In Search of White Crows: Spiritualism, Parapsychology, and American Culture*. OUP 1977 o.p. A rich, well-documented investigation of spiritualism and the scientific studies of psychic phenomena that it inspired.

Nelson, G. K. *Spiritualism and Society*. Schocken 1969 o.p. A study of Spiritualism from a sociological perspective; emphasizes the movement in Britain.

Oppenheim, Janet. *The Other World: Spiritualism and Psychical Research in England, 1850–1914*. Cambridge U. Pr. 1988 $69.95. ISBN 0-521-34767-X. Account of the relation between spiritualism and psychic research in the context of the conflict between the claims of

SWEDENBORGIANISM

EMANUEL SWEDENBORG (1688-1772), the Swedish scientist and mystic, had a profound impact on unconventional nineteenth-century spiritual movements. Of brilliant intellect, Swedenborg began his career in science and engineering. In midlife, however, after the onset of a remarkable series of visions, he turned to religion. His experiences included spiritual journeys to the realms of departed spirits, which he saw as educative rather than dedicated to reward and punishment. Applying his extraordinary mind to the philosophical and theological understanding of what he had seen, Swedenborg revived not only the Neoplatonist doctrine of the separate destiny of the soul from the body in an eternity of growth and glory but also the concept of correspondences. He held that appearances in our time and space are reflections of realities and events in the spiritual world.

A small but influential church, the Church of the New Jerusalem, commonly called the "New Church," was founded in England based on the teachings of the Swedish sage and was established in America as early as 1792. It has kept the ideas of Swedenborg alive to play a role on the larger stage of American intellectual life. Their influence can be seen in movements like Transcendentalism, Spiritualism, Theosophy, and New Thought. Indeed, the 1840s, seminal for that collection of interwoven causes, has been called the decade of the "Swedenborgian wave."

Swedenborgianism affected both common people and intellectuals in the New World. John Chapman ("Johnny Appleseed," 1774–1845) was a convinced apostle of that cause and spread tracts popularizing it (as well as apple orchards) on the upper frontier. Given Swedenborg's vivid portrayals of the life of the departed, it is little wonder that Spiritualism was soon advocating conversation with them.

Block, Marguerite. *The New Church in the New World*. Swedenborg 1984 $12.95. ISBN 0-877865-126-3. The best treatment to date of Swedenborgianism in America.

Brock, Erland J., and others. *Swedenborg and His Influence.* Acad. New Church 1988 $24.95. ISBN 0-910557-23-3. A highly informative collection of papers on the intellectual influence of Swedenborg on the nineteenth and twentieth centuries.

Dole, George, and Robert Kirven. *A Scientist Explores Spirit.* Swedenborg 1992 $9.95. ISBN 0-87785-143-3. Outlines key concepts of the theology in relation to Swedenborg's biography and social context.

Larsen, Robin, ed. *Emanuel Swedenborg: A Continuing Vision.* Swedenborg 1988 $75.00. ISBN 0-87785-136-0. A large, lavishly illustrated study of the visionary thinker and his ideas.

Meyers, Mary A. *A New World Jerusalem: The Swedenborgian Experience in Community Construction. Contributions in Amer. Studies.* Greenwood 1983 $42.95. ISBN 0-313-23602-X. A study of Bryn Athyn, Pennslyvania, the center of the General Church of the New Jerusalem and one of the two Swedenborgian churches in America.

Price, Robert. *Johnny Appleseed, Man and Myth.* Peter Smith 1967 $18.50. ISBN 0-8446-1366-5. The classic study of a legendary figure who was a Swedenborgian and who carried that message, as well as apple seeds, to the western frontier.

Swedenborg, Emanuel. *True Christian Religion.* Trans. by J. Ager. 2 vols. Swedenborg 1906 $20.00. ISBN 0-87785-086-0. Perhaps the most lucid and comprehensive of Swedenborg's numerous theological writings.

Toksvig, Signe. *Emanuel Swedenborg, Scientist and Mystic. Biography Index Repr. Ser.* Ayer 1972 repr. of 1948 ed. $25.00. ISBN 0-8369-8140-5. A standard biography of Swedenborg.

Trobridge, George. *Swedenborg: Life and Teaching.* Swedenborg 1992 $15.95. ISBN 0-87785-139-5. Entirely sympathetic portrait of the man and his refusal to separate science and religion.

THEOSOPHY

The Theosophical Society was founded in 1875 in New York by, HELENA P. BLAVATSKY (1831–91), the author of the basic Theosophical literature; Henry Steel Olcott (1832–1907), its first president, and others. The major works of Blavatsky, *Isis Unveiled* (1877) and *The Secret Doctrine* (1888), postulate an ancient, primordial wisdom underlying all religions preserved through the ages in esoteric circles, whose tenets can now be presented as an alternative to modern dogmatic religion and materialistic science. They include the eternal interaction of consciousness and matter to shape the manifested universe, the existence of advanced souls (called Masters or Mahatmas) as teachers of humankind and the evolution of the world and of individuals ("pilgrims") through many cycles of existence. After the publication of *Isis Unveiled,* Blavatsky and Olcott went to India, where the movement became influential and certain Eastern ideas, such as karma and reincarnation, became more central to its ideology. In turn, Theosophy, despite a tumultuous history, has played an important role in popularizing Eastern religion and philosophy in the West. Its own distinctive teaching, however, is founded as much on the Western Neoplatonist and occultist tradition as on oriental lore, although it sees a fundamental unity between the two. A breakaway movement, known as Anthroposophy, was founded in 1912 by RUDOLF STEINER.

Blavatsky, Helena P. *Isis Unveiled: A Master-Key to the Mysteries of Ancient and Modern Science and Theology.* 2 vols. Theos. U. Pr. 1976 repr. of 1877 ed. $30.00. ISBN 0-911500-02-2. Blavatsky's first major work.

————. *The Secret Doctrine: The Synthesis of Science, Religion, and Philosophy.* Ed. by Boris De Zirkoff. Theosophy 1925 repr. of 1888 ed. $18.50. ISBN 0-938998-00-5. The most important Theosophical text.

Campbell, Bruce F. *Ancient Wisdom Revived: A History of the Theosophical Movement.* U. CA Pr. 1980 $29.95. ISBN 0-520-03968-8. The fullest independent scholarly history.

Cranston, Sylvia. *H.P.B.: The Extraordinary Life and Influence of Helena Blavatsky.* Putnam Pub. Group 1993 $30.00. ISBN 0-87477-688-0. A large-scale sympathetic biography of the founder of the modern Theosophical movement, using much new material and emphasizing her impact on her times and after.

Elior, Rachel. *The Paradoxical Ascent to God: The Kabbalistic Theosophy of Habad Hasidism.* Trans. by Jeffrey M. Green. State U. NY Pr. 1992 $49.50. ISBN 0-7914-1045-5. Concentrates on the central Theosophical ideas that energize Habad, from a discussion of man's contemplative consciousness to the denial of true reality to anything but God.

Gomes, Michael. *Dawning of the Theosophical Movement.* Theosophical Pub. Hse. 1987 $8.95. ISBN 0-8356-0023-6. A new scholarly study of the movement's origins in the nineteenth century.

———. *Theosophy in the Nineteenth Century: An Annotated Bibliography.* Garland 1993 $65.00. A necessary tool for serious scholarship in Theosophical history.

Kingsland, William. *The Esoteric Basis of Christianity or Theosophy and Christian Doctrine.* Kessinger Pub. 1993 $18.95. ISBN 1-56459-358-4. Details the often suppressed shared origins and common themes in theosophy and more orthodox Christian traditions.

Mills, Joy. *One Hundred Years of Theosophy.* Theosophical Pub. Hse. 1987 $9.95. ISBN 0-8356-0235-4. A history of the Theosophical Society in the United States.

Olcott, Henry S. *Old Diary Leaves.* 6 vols. Theosophical Pub. Hse. 1973 $9.50 ea. ISBN 0-8356-7106-2. Fascinating personal account of Blavatsky and the early American life of the Theosophical Society by its first president; the volumes carry Olcott's recollections of Blavatsky and Theosophy up to 1898.

TWENTIETH-CENTURY MOVEMENTS

Most of the new religious movements already cited that appeared in nineteenth-century America have continued into the late twentieth century, albeit less in the public eye. However, certain new stages in unconventional spiritual life have also been reached.

Oriental religion packaged in specific denominational forms for occidentals first made its appearance at the very end of the nineteenth century in the wake of the celebrated World's Parliament of Religions, held in Chicago in 1893 in conjunction with the Columbian Exposition. There, for the first time, swamis, Zen masters, and other Eastern religious representatives, well prepared for the task, addressed, and often very favorably impressed, Western audiences. Some, such as Swami Vivekananda of Vedanta and the Zen teacher Soyen Shaku, were soon instrumental in founding centers of their tradition in America for Western students. These increased in numbers and influence throughout the first half of the twentieth century.

Many other Eastern teachers came as well. Indeed, a dominant feature of such movements, beginning perhaps in the decade following World War I, has been a great emphasis on the role of charismatic individuals—swamis, gurus, masters—rather than of more abstract teachings. The same could be said of new movements more in the Western tradition, too, such as "I Am," or Scientology.

After World War II, this strand of American spirituality deepened through the popular philosophical writings of such eclectics as ALDOUS HUXLEY (see Vol. 1) and ALAN WILSON WATTS, and explored new lifestyles in the "Beatnik" Zen associated with writers like JACK KEROUAC (see Vol. 1) and GARY SNYDER (see Vol. 1). The next great phase, however, was the much-discussed "countercul-ture" of the 1960s, when enthusiasm for the East, the occult, and spiritual adventure seemed to go hand-in-hand with emerging "youth culture." Many new unconventional religious groups appeared, some growing phenomenally in that decade and the early 1970s. Much controversy was engendered, but by the late 1970s, most of the 1960s-generation new religions had become more institutionally stabilized and were enjoying only modest rates of growth. Some continue, however, to exhibit a salient feature of the groups of the 1960s: a desire to embrace not only new ideas and the leadership of a charismatic individual but also a total lifestyle, expressed in dress, diet, career values, and perhaps communalism. As we have seen, these characteristics are by no means novel in America, having rich nineteenth-century precedents, yet during the 1960s they were often displayed with a flamboyance and a special emphasis on youth that made them highly visible, to the excitement of some and the acute discomfort of others.

By the 1990s, movements of the 1960s generation were for the most part stable or declining. In the general population, "New Age" spirituality was in vogue. This movement revived some themes of the 1960s and earlier mysticism and occultism, such as reincarnation and alternative healing methods, but was generally more eclectic, individualistic, and noninstitutional. There was a diffuse, yet pervasive, interest in ecological and feminist spirituality, including the worship of nature or the earth as a goddess. Additionally, there was a new wave of ethnic minority religions, largely Asian and Afro-Caribbean.

Directories, Encyclopedias, and Bibliographies

This section includes reference works—directories, encyclopedias, and general bibliographies—covering several different twentieth-century groups.

Choquette, Diane, comp. *New Religious Movements in the United States and Canada: A Critical Assessment and Annotated Bibliography. Bibliographies and Indexes in Religious Studies Ser.* Greenwood 1985 $49.95. ISBN 0-313-23772-7. A comprehensive research tool. Mostly covers movements from the 1960s through 1983 in North America. Lists 738 items and includes useful indexes.

Lacoff, Cheryl Klein. *Parapsychology, New Age and the Occult: A Source Encyclopedia.* Reference Pr. Intl. 1993 $24.95. ISBN 1-879583-00-2. A useful and fascinating encyclopedia of groups, centers, outlets, and bibliography on the subject topics, including many new religious and spiritual movements.

Mather, George A., and Larry A. Nichols. *Dictionary of Cults, Sects, Religions and the Occult.* Zondervan 1993 $24.95. ISBN 0-310-53100-4. Thousands of short articles on terms, concepts, or individuals are cross-referenced to the religions they represent.

Melton, J. Gordon. *Biographical Dictionary of American Cult and Sect Leaders. Lib. of Social Sciences.* Garland 1986 $50.00. ISBN 0-8240-9037-3. Fundamental information on individuals important in minority religions. Contains sketches of 213 persons connected with the development of minority religious groups in the United States. Only leaders who died before 1983 are included.

———. *Cults and New Religions: Sources for the Study of Nonconventional Religious Groups in Nineteenth and Twentieth Century America.* 22 vols. Garland 1992 $2,420.00. ISBN 0-8153-000-X

———, ed. *Encyclopedia of American Religions.* Gale 1992 $165.00. ISBN 0-8103-6904-4. Comprehensive reference work, especially in the area of new and unconventional groups. An essential resource for the study of minority religions.

———. *The Encyclopedic Handbook of Cults in America. Lib. of Social Sciences.* Garland 1992 $55.00. ISBN 0-8153-0502-8. Essential information on a number of groups; a "cult" is defined nonpejoratively as a "first-generation religion."

———. *Religious Bodies in the United States, A Directory. Reference Lib. of the Humanities.* Garland 1992 $55.00. ISBN 0-8153-9402-2. Supplements Melton's *Encyclopedia of American Religions* with addresses.

General Descriptive and Historical Works

This section presents books covering several twentieth-century new religious movements in historical or descriptive form.

Barker, Eileen, ed. *New Religious Movements: A Perspective for Understanding Society. Studies in Religion and Society*. E. Mellen 1982 $99.95. ISBN 0-88946-864-8. Useful collection of essays.

———. *New Religious Movements: A Practical Introduction*. E. Mellen 1982 $99.95. ISBN 0-88946-864-8. Though based on the British rather than the U.S. scene, a valuable overview of movements and controversies by a prominent and sociological observer of new religions.

Braden, Charles S. *These Also Believe*. Macmillan 1949 o.p. Still a valuable resource on older groups, such as Theosophy, "I Am," New Thought, Father Divine, and others.

Bromley, David, and Anson Shupe. *Strange Gods: The Great American Cult Scare*. Beacon Pr. 1982 $13.00. ISBN 0-8070-1109-6. A book for the general reader that summarizes major groups while seeking to dispel popular misconceptions about "cults." Critical of the "anticult" stance.

Bromley, David, and Phillip E. Hammond, eds. *The Future of New Religious Movements*. Mercer Univ. Pr. 1987 $19.95. ISBN 0-86554-238-4. Essays by sociologists and historians of religion on the future prospects of many of the most talked about "cults" and new religions.

Ellwood, Robert S., and Harry Partin. *Religious and Spiritual Groups in Modern America*. P-H 1988 $28.00. ISBN 0-13-773045-4. A survey of unconventional and Eastern groups in America.

Glock, Charles, and Robert N. Bellah, eds. *The New Religious Consciousness*. U. CA Pr. 1976 $49.95. ISBN 0-520-03083-4. Valuable collection of papers based on field research on a number of groups; well introduced by the editors, both prominent sociologists of religion.

Needleman, Jacob. *New Religions*. Crossroad NY 1984 o.p. A readable introduction based on the 1960s experience.

Pavlos, Andrew J. *The Cult Experience. Contributions to the Study of Religion*. Greenwood 1982 $45.00. ISBN 0-313-23164-8. An often helpful introductory study, though sometimes overgeneralized and based on secondhand material.

Robbins, Thomas. *Cults, Converts and Charisma: The Sociology of New Religious Movements*. Russell Sage 1988 $45.00. ISBN 0-8039-8158-9. An important discussion by a leading sociologist in the field.

Shupe, Anson D., Jr. *Six Perspectives on New Religions: A Case Study Approach. Studies in Religion and Society*. E. Mellen 1981 $89.95. ISBN 0-889436-983-0. Criminological, philosophical, anthropological, psychological, sociological, and historical approaches to new religions. Includes reading lists and discussion questions.

Stark, Rodney, and William Sims Bainbridge. *The Future of Religion: Secularization, Revival and Cult Formation*. U. CA Pr. 1985 $49.95. ISBN 0-520-05731-7. A sociological study of religion that gives much attention to data and theories about cults and sects.

Tipton, Steven M. *Getting Saved from the Sixties: Moral Meaning in Conversion and Cultural Change*. U. CA Pr. 1982 $35.00. ISBN 0-520-05228-5. Excellent sociological study centering on three movements—EST, a Zen Center, and a youth-oriented fundamentalist Christian center—arguing that such groups channeled and tamed the spiritual energies of the 1960s.

Ungerleider, J. Thomas. *The New Religions: Insights into the Cult Phenomenon*. Merck-Sharp-Dohme 1979 o.p. Balanced report based on psychological investigations.

Wagner, Melinda B. *Metaphysics in Midwestern America*. Ohio St. U. Pr. 1983 $29.00. ISBN 0-8142-0346-9. The history and sociology of the Spiritual Frontiers Fellowship, an interdenominational group that promotes openness to psychic phenomena and other "New Age" perspectives.

Webb, James. *The Occult Establishment*. Open Court 1976 $9.95. ISBN 0-87548-434-4. Study of the occult in twentieth-century political and social life in Europe and America. Interesting material, though the author's hypotheses may not be convincing to all.

Wuthnow, Robert. *Experimentation in American Religion: The New Mysticisms and Their Implications for the Churches*. U. CA Pr. 1978 $45.00. ISBN 0-520-03446-5. Scholarly sociological study based on groups in the San Francisco Bay Area, illuminating spiritual trends that underlie new religious movements.

Zaretsky, Irving I., and Mark P. Leone, eds. *Religious Movements in Contemporary America*. Princeton U. Pr. 1974 o.p. Excellent essays on a variety of groups.

General Works on Controversial Issues

Understandably, new religious movements have brought controversy, and this has been expressed in full-length books as well as articles. Indeed, there has arisen an "anticult" set of groups and publications that some observers perceive as a movement in its own right. Arguments have involved charges that intensive religious groups, often labeled *cults*, "brainwash" initiates to make them psychologically unable to leave. Countercharges assert that such rhetoric is exaggerated and inflammatory and disregards the rights of individuals to make their own religious choices. The practice of "deprogramming"—the intentional removal and deconversion of "cult" members—has likewise spawned vehement debate between proponents and those who see it as kidnapping and a gross violation of religious freedom. Behind these debates lie far-reaching issues concerning the psychology of religious movements, their legal status, and their relation to the larger society. This section will not deal with philosophical and theological responses to new religions, but to controversies regarding their psychological and legal position vis-à-vis the lives of individuals.

Beckford, James A. *Cult Controversies*. Routledge 1985 o.p. Excellent sociological study of new religious movements and public response to them, especially in Europe.

Bromley, David G., and James T. Richardson, eds. *The Brainwashing/Deprogramming Controversy: Sociological, Psychological, Legal and Historical Perspectives*. E. Mellen 1983 $99.95. ISBN 0-88996-868-0. A valuable collection of essays from a variety of perspectives by leading scholars; invaluable for the serious student.

Galanter, Marc, ed. *Cults: Faith, Healing and Coercion*. OUP 1989 $30.00. ISBN 0-19-505631-0. Models and case histories of "charismatic" groups by a psychologist who spent 15 years studying them.

Jacobs, Janet L. *Divine Disenchantment: Deconverting from New Religions*. Ind. U. Pr. 1990 $22.95. ISBN 0-253-32396-7. A sociological study of a number of persons who have defected from new religious movements.

Lane, David Christopher. *Exposing Cults: Understanding the Rise of Gurus in North America*. Garland 1993 o.p. A critical history of several new movements and their leaders, with an extensive bibliography.

Levine, Saul. *Radical Departures: Desperate Detours to Growing Up*. HarBraceJ 1984 $4.95. ISBN 0-15-675799-0. Case studies by a medical doctor who has dealt with cult members and their families.

Melton, J. Gordon. *The Cult Controversy: A Guide to Sources*. Garland 1992 $65.00. ISBN 0-8153-0860-4

Richardson, Herbert W., ed. *New Religions and Mental Health: Understanding the Issues*. *Symposium Ser.* E. Mellen 1980 $79.95. ISBN 0-88946-910-5. Essays by 15 writers generally opposed to "deprogramming" and "brainwashing" theories; contains such important pieces as Richard Rubenstein's "Who Shall Define Reality for Us?" and "Jews Against 'Messianic' Jews" by David Rausch.

Richardson, James T., ed. *Money and Power in the New Religions*. E. Mellen 1988 o.p. A collection of essays about how the new religions collect and use money, a topic often raised but seldom so well documented and discussed.

Robbins, Thomas. *Civil Liberties, "Brainwashing" and "Cults": A Select Annotated Bibliography*. Graduate Theological Union of Berkeley 1981 o.p. A useful guide to the complex, interrelated issues suggested in the title.

———. *Cults, Culture and the Law: Perspectives on New Religious Movements*. Scholars Pr. GA 1985 $14.95. ISBN 0-89130-833-4. Balanced discussion by a leading scholar of new religious movements or "cults."

Robbins, Thomas, and Dick Anthony, eds. *In Gods We Trust: New Patterns of Religious Pluralism in America*. Transaction Pubs. 1980 $22.95. ISBN 0-88738-800-0. Useful collection of scholarly essays.

Ross, Joan Carol, and Michael D. Langone. *Cults: What Parents Should Know: A Practical Guide to Help Parents with Children in Destructive Groups*. Am. Family Foun. 1988 $9.95. ISBN 0-931337-00-3. A good example of material written from the perspective that cults are destructive.

Rudin, Marcia R. *Cults on Campus: Continuing Challenge*. Am. Family Foun. 1991 $12.00. ISBN 0-685-48002-X. A recent work from an "anticult" perspective.

Saliba, John A. *Psychiatry and the Cults: An Annotated Bibliography*. Garland 1986 $91.00. ISBN 0-8240-3719-7. Highly recommended sourcebook.

Shepherd, William C. *To Secure the Blessings of Liberty: American Constitutional Law and the New Religious Movements*. Scholars Pr. GA 1984 $23.95. ISBN 0-89130-733-8. A thorough discussion of the legal issues, based on the premise that "the law knows no heresy."

Shupe, Anson D., Jr., and others. *The Anti-Cult Movement in America: A Bibliographic History*. Garland 1984 o.p. An important introduction to the nature and literature of the opposition evoked by the new religions.

Stark, Rodney, ed. *Religious Movements: Genesis, Exodus, and Numbers*. Paragon Hse. 1985 o.p. Significant essays, including some on such important aspects as defection from "cults," the revival of astrology in the United States, and the Rajneesh movement.

Theological and Philosophical Responses to the New Religions

A vast amount of writing has attempted to assess new religious movements and the overall worldview many of them imply from philosophical or theological perspectives. Such works were particularly prolific during the 1960s, 1970s, and 1980s, as controversy swirled around "cults" and the "New Age" movement. Some of the assessments have been basically sympathetic, perceiving the movements as harbingers of important cultural and spiritual change or as signifying the opening up of new and positive kinds of experience. Others have seen disturbing signs of narcissism or even totalitarianism in them. Still other critics have challenged these new religious movements from the standpoint of different beliefs, especially those of conservative Christianity. Only a sampling of this literature is presented here, emphasizing those works of general rather than highly partisan or denominational character.

Burnett, David. *Clash of Worlds: A Christian's Handbook on Cultures, World Religions, and Evangelism*. Nelson Comm. 1992 $12.99. ISBN 0-8407-9592-0

Cox, Harvey. *Turning East: The Promise and Peril of the New Orientalism*. S&S Trade 1977 o.p. A sensitive, sometimes critical, interpretation by a liberal Christian theologian.

Enroth, Ronald. *A Guide to Cults and New Religions*. InterVarsity 1983 $9.99. ISBN 0-87784-837-8. Descriptions together with evangelical Christian responses by a sociologist of religion.

Hexham, Irving, and Karla Poewe. *Understanding Cults and New Religions*. Eerdmans 1986 $9.95. ISBN 0-8028-0710-6. A fresh, insightful book written from an evangelical perspective, regarding new religious movements as neither new nor religious, but as primarily magical and therapeutic in nature.

Isser, Natalie, and Lita L. Schwartz. *The History of Conversion and Contemporary Cults.* P. Lang Pubs. 1988 $36.50. ISBN 0-8204-06457

Johnston, William. *The Inner Eye of Love: Mysticism and Religion.* HarpC 1978 $8.95. ISBN 0-06-064195-9. Written by a distinguished Jesuit theologian interested in dialogue between the mystical traditions of all religions; offers deep understanding of new religious movements of Eastern or mystical orientation.

Martin, Walter. *The New Cults.* Vision Hse. 1980 $8.95. ISBN 0-88449-016-5. The perspective of a well-informed evangelical writer.

Toolan, David. *Facing West from California's Shores: A Jesuit's Journey into New Age Consciousness.* Crossroad NY 1987 $19.95. ISBN 0-8245-0805-X. A meditative consideration of the new vogues for Eastern, nature, and polytheistic religion.

Modern Theosophical Groups

The Theosophical movement has continued to be a vital force in the alternative spirituality of the twentieth century. Three major Theosophical societies have existed throughout the century; one of them was centered in an important utopian community in Point Loma, San Diego, until 1942. The largest, the Theosophical Society headquartered in Adyar, Madras, India, experienced several vicissitudes until the 1930s under the brilliant but controversial leadership of ANNIE BESANT and C. W. Leadbeater, who professed psychic powers and whose further refinements of the doctrines of the Masters produced a "second generation" of Theosophical literature. Above all, Besant and Leadbeater sponsored the career of JIDDU KRISHNAMURTI (1895–1986), who was first hailed as a Theosophical "World Teacher" but who later broke with all organized groups to establish a major independent career as a spiritual teacher.

Other movements that sprang out of a Theosophical background in the twentieth century can only be named: the Anthroposophy of the remarkable philosopher and visionary RUDOLF STEINER, the teachings and meditation groups of Alice Bailey, the "I Am" activity, modern Gnostic churches, and the Liberal Catholic church. The following list contains biographies and other works on persons and institutions connected with twentieth-century Theosophy and related groups. For general books on Theosophical teaching and history, see the bibliography under Nineteenth-Century Movements, Theosophy.

Bailey, Alice A. *Unfinished Autobiography.* Lucis 1951 $24.00. ISBN 0-85330-624-0. The life of the founder of a distinctive set of meditation groups based on Theosophical principles.

Easton, Stewart C. *Man and World in the Light of Anthroposophy.* Anthroposophic 1989 $18.00. ISBN 0-88010-272-1. A good introduction to this tradition.

––––––. *Rudolf Steiner: Herald of a New Epoch.* Anthroposophic 1980 $10.95. ISBN 0-910142-93-9. A study of the founder of Anthroposophy.

Greenwalt, Emmett A. *The Point Loma Community in California, 1897–1942: A Theosophical Experiment.* AMS Pr. 1979 repr. of 1955 ed. $26.00. ISBN 0-404-60068-9. Ample historical and sociological account.

Holroyd, Stuart. *Krishnamurti: The Man, the Mystery and the Message.* Element MA 1991 $14.95. ISBN 1-85230-200-3

Lutyens, Mary. *Krishnamurti: The Years of Awakening.* Avon 1991 $9.95. ISBN 0-308-71113-3. The first volume of a standard biography of Krishnamurti by one of his disciples.

––––––. *Krishnamurti: The Years of Fulfillment.* Avon 1991 $8.95. ISBN 0-380-68007-6. The life and times of the mature Krishnamurti.

McDermott, Robert A., ed. *The Essential Rudolf Steiner*. HarpC 1983 $15.95. ISBN 0-06-065345-0. Basic writings by the founder of Anthroposophy.

Nethercot, Arthur H. *The First Five Lives of Annie Besant*. U. Ch. Pr. 1960 o.p. The first volume of the major biography of Besant, one of the most attractive and colorful figures in the "second generation" of Theosophy.

————. *The Last Four Lives of Annie Besant*. U. Ch. Pr. 1963 o.p. A continuation of the preceding work.

Pruter, Karl, and J. Gordon Melton. *The Old Catholic Sourcebook*. Garland 1983 o.p. Brief descriptions and full bibliographies on churches in the modern Gnostic and Liberal Catholic traditions, among others.

Sheehan, Edmund W. *Teaching and Worship of the Liberal Catholic Church*. Ed. by William H. Pitkin. St. Alban Pr. 1978 $2.90. ISBN 0-91890-07-0. A standard summary issued by the church.

Individual Religious Movements

AMERICAN ZEN AND OTHER BUDDHISM

Buddhism in the United States has two traditions, ethnic and occidental. The former is represented by the temples and churches of Japanese Americans, Thai Americans, and others from largely Buddhist countries. Our concern will be with the latter—Buddhist centers serving Americans of occidental background who have found Buddhism through a personal spiritual quest. Many occidental Buddhists have been attracted to one of three forms of the religion: Zen, Nichiren Shoshu, and Tibetan (Vajrayana) Buddhism. Zen is known for its quiet seated meditations, its emphasis on simplicity and immediacy of life, and its rich cultural expressions. Nichiren Shoshu, also from Japan, has prospered since midcentury both in Japan and abroad through the vigorous efforts of its lay missionary arm, Soka Gakkai; it is a modern Buddhism that stresses chanting and dynamic living. Tibetan Buddhism, complex, colorful, and psychologically profound, has drawn a highly dedicated following. A growing interest in the southern or Theravada school of Buddhism, especially its meditation method called *vipassana*, can also be discerned.

Thus far, books on American Buddhism are largely limited to general accounts and personal narratives. As background, a vast literature exists on Buddhism in general, and especially on Zen and Tibetan religion. Much material can also be found on the "Beat" Zen of the American 1950s from biographical and literary perspectives.

Anderson, Walt. *Open Secrets*. J. P. Tarcher 1989 o.p. Excellent, popular introduction to the practice of Tibetan Buddhism for Westerners.

Ames, Van Meter. *Zen and American Thought*. Greenwood 1978 repr. of 1962 ed. $35.00. ISBN 0-313-20066-1. A classic study of parallels between Zen and American thought.

Berry, Scott. *A Stranger in Tibet: The Adventures of a Wandering Zen Monk*. Kodansha 1989 $19.95. ISBN 0-87011-891-9. Story of a Japanese monk in contemporary Tibet.

Fields, Rick. *How the Swans Came to the Lake: A Narrative History of Buddhism in America*. Shambhala Pubns. 1992 $20.00. ISBN 0-87773-631-6. A full and interesting history of all schools of American Buddhism.

Furlong, Monica. *Zen Effects: The Life of Alan Watts*. HM 1986 o.p. A highly readable life of Alan Watts, the brilliant but controversial "philosophical entertainer" who did much to publicize Zen and other forms of Eastern spirituality in America during the mid-twentieth century.

Hurst, Jane D. *Nichiren Shoshu Buddhism and the Soka Gakkai in America: The Ethos of a New Religious Movement*. Garland 1992 $81.00. ISBN 0-8153-0776-4. A sociological study of the life and history of the largest religious movement ever brought from the East to the United States.

Kapleau, Philip. *The Three Pillars of Zen: Teaching, Practice, Enlightenment.* Doubleday 1989 $10.95. ISBN 0-385-26093-8. A standard text on the theory and practice of Zen for Westerners, with lectures by Zen Masters and valuable narratives of Zen experiences by both Eastern and Western students.

Kerouac, Jack. *Dharma Bums.* Buccaneer Bks. 1976 $21.95. ISBN 0-451-15275-1. A very influential novel from the 1950s "Beat" Zen epoch.

Layman, Emma M. *Buddhism in America.* Nelson-Hall 1976 $21.95. ISBN 0-88229-436-9. A basic history, with considerable material on ethnic Buddhism.

Prebish, Charles. *American Buddhism.* Duxbury 1979 o.p. A good overview, emphasizing Buddhist movements appealing to Occidentals.

Snow, David A. *Shakubuku: A Study of the Nichiren Shoshu Buddhist Movement in America, 1960–1975.* Garland 1993 $76.00. ISBN 0-8153-1137-0. The early years of this proselytizing Buddhist movement from a sociological and historical perspective.

Tamney, Joseph B. *American Society in the Buddhist Mirror.* Garland 1992 $33.00. ISBN 0-8153-0721-7. Investigates the appeal of Buddhism to Americans, connecting early nineteenth-century transcendentalism to 1980s New Agers.

Watts, Alan W. *Way of Zen.* Random 1965 $4.95. ISBN 0-394-70298-0. Classic work from the 1950s; an important introduction of Zen to the West by a noted interpreter of it in the tradition of D. T. Suzuki.

ASTROLOGY AND OTHER OCCULTISM

Astrology represents a movement or sphere of influence popular worldwide rather than among particular groups, though a few small astrological churches and institutions have arisen. Its main influence is on the millions who read astrological books, periodicals, or newspaper columns, or the smaller but still large numbers who have professional horoscopes cast or do their own. Many explanations have been offered for this continuing interest in the ancient art, both by believers and nonbelievers. However, serious independent studies of astrology as a social phenomenon are few.

Although also seldom institutionalized, other forms of occultism ("hidden wisdom"), such as palmistry, interpreting tarot cards, and numerology, are practiced in contemporary America, both by paid "readers" and by private individuals. As in the case of astrology, those employing these mystic arts seek insight into their futures and, probably no less significantly, their personalities and the meaning of their lives. In addition to the works listed below, general histories of occultism and related topics will contain information on the history and practice of astrology and other occult traditions.

Adams, Evangeline. *The Bowl of Heaven.* Sun Pub. 1992 $18.00. ISBN 0-89540-1967. Reprint of a classic work by a founder of modern American astrology.

Edmondson, Edna. *A Fifty Year History of the American Federation of Astrologers.* Am. Fed. Astrologers 1990 $19.00. ISBN 0-86690-366-6

Jorgensen, Danny. *The Esoteric Scene: Cultic Milieu and Occult Tarot.* Garland 1992 $75.00. ISBN 0-815-30769-1. Sociological study of a Texas spiritual group that views occult practices as important.

Kaplan, Stuart B. *The Encyclopedia of Tarot.* 2 vols. US Games Syst. Vol. 1 1978 $25.00. ISBN 0-913866-11-3. Vol. 2 1985 $35.00. ISBN 0-9138660-36-9. Comprehensive information on the tarot cards, a staple of modern esoterica.

Lewis, James R., ed. *The Beginnings of Astrology in America: Astrology and the Re-Emergence of Cosmic Religion.* Garland 1990 $101.00. ISBN 0-8240-4364-2. Facsimile reproduction of classic astrological texts, with an introduction by the editor.

Omarr, Sydney. *My World of Astrology.* Wilshire 1976 $7.00. ISBN 0-87980-103-4. Anecdotal autobiography and philosophy of one of America's leading astrologers.

BAHA'I

The Baha'i faith originated in Persia (Iran) in the mid-nineteenth century when Baha'u'llah (1817–92), believed by his followers to be the major prophet of the age, proclaimed a new universal religion. Having roots in Islam, Baha'i also believes in a continuing succession of prophets, including the founders of the great religions. It differs from Islam in its belief that MUHAMMAD was not the last prophet, but that the list has continued past Muhammad to include its founder. Baha'i is monotheistic and affirms immortality, but the emphasis tends to be ethical and social; the new age inaugurated by the prophet Baha'u'llah will be one in which humanity will realize its unity, overcoming the prejudice, inequality, and war that set people against one another, and to these ends Bahaists dedicate themselves. Worship is simple, and the sense of community among Bahaists is strong. The faith first came to America around 1892 and has become well established, as may be seen by its headquarters in the United States, the beautiful Baha'i temple on the shores of Lake Michigan in Wilmette, Illinois. By 1992 there were about 110,000 Baha'is in the United States, many of them driven from Iran by religious persecution.

Baha'u'llah. *Gleanings for the Writings of Baha'u'llah.* Trans. by Shaghi Effendi. Bahai 1983 $8.50. ISBN 0-87743-187-6. A basic introduction to the founder of Baha'i and his writings.

Bjorling, Joel. *The Baha'i Faith: An Historical Bibliography.* Garland 1985 o.p. A valuable resource for the student of Baha'i.

Cole, Juan R., and Moojan Momen, eds. *From Iran East and West.* Vol. 2 in *Studies in Babi and Baha'i History.* Kalimat 1984 $32.50. ISBN 0-933770-40-5. Example of modern historical scholarship within the Baha'i movement.

Collins, William P., ed. *Bibliography of English Language Works on the Babi and Bahai Faiths 1844–1985.* G. Ronald Pubs. 1991 $65.00. ISBN 0-85398-315-1. Important listing of sources for the study of Baha'i, divided into primary and secondary sources.

Esslemont, J. E. *Baha'u'llah and the New Era: An Introduction to the Baha'i Faith.* Bahai 1980 $5.75. ISBN 0-87743-160-4. A very readable introductory study of the faith.

Hatcher, William S., and Martin J. Douglas. *The Bahai Faith: The Emerging Global Religion.* HarpC 1985 o.p. Explains the wide range of the teachings of Baha'i, emphasizing its independence of Islam.

Lee, Anthony A., ed. *Circle of Unity: Baha'i Approaches to Current Social Issues.* Kalimat 1984 $11.95. ISBN 0-933770-28-6. A good examination of modern Baha'i thought.

Sheppherd, Joseph. *Elements of the Bahai Faith.* Element MA 1992 $8.95. ISBN 1-85230-372-7. An introduction to the basic tenets.

Smith, Peter. *The Bahai Religion: A Short Introduction to Its History and Teachings.* G. Ronald Pubs. 1988 $5.95. ISBN 0-85398-277-5

THE BLACK MUSLIMS

The "Black Muslims," originally called the Nation of Islam and later the World Community of Islam in the West and finally American Muslim Mission, began as a movement expressing alienation and nationalism among African Americans. Although the founder was W. D. Fard, the most effective organizer was Elijah Muhammad (Elijah Poole, 1897–1975), who shaped it into a militant, separatist community with distinctive features centering in the special divine destiny of the black race. After the death of Elijah Muhammad, leadership was assumed by his son Wallace Muhammad, who has led the movement to accept white members and adopt a more orthodox Islamic faith and practice, including prayer, study of the Koran, fasting during the holy month of Ramadan, tithing, and making pilgrimages to Mecca. Despite a strict moral and dietary code, the Black Muslims have enjoyed considerable success in attracting converts. Among the best-known converts was Malcolm Little, better known as MALCOLM X, an influential political leader who was assassinated in 1965.

Baldwin, James. *The Fire Next Time.* Dell 1985 $5.99. ISBN 0-440-32542-0. Two impassioned letters on the destructive estrangement of blacks and whites in America.

Halasa, Malu. *Elijah Muhammad.* Chelsea Hse. 1990 $17.95. ISBN 1-55546-602-8. Traces the life of the leader of the Nation of Islam in terms of the social and religious impact this group had on American culture.

Hall, Raymond L. *Black Separatism in the United States.* Bks Demand repr. of 1978 ed. $79.50. ISBN 0-8357-7297-7. Background and accounts of the movement.

Lincoln, C. Eric. *The Black Muslims in America.* Greenwood 1982 o.p. A classic though now dated account that first brought the group to the attention of the general public in the 1960s.

Lomax, Louis E. *When the Word Is Given: A Report on Elijah Muhammad, Malcolm X, and the Black Muslim World.* Greenwood 1979 repr. of 1964 ed. $45.00. ISBN 0-313-21002-0. A major study.

Malcolm X. *Autobiography of Malcolm X as Told to Alex Haley.* Ballantine 1977 $20.00. ISBN 0-345-37975-6. A much-read and discussed book by a prominent Black Muslim.

Marsh, Clifton E. *From Black Muslims to Muslims: The Transition from Separatism to Islam, 1930–1980.* Scarecrow 1984 $24.00. ISBN 0-8108-1705-5. Historical narrative of a major development, toward normative Islam, in the movement's growth.

Mohammed, Imam W. *Al-Islam: Unity and Leadership.* Sense Maker 1992 $7.95. ISBN 1-879698-00-5. Brings to focus the Islamic perspective given by an indigenous Muslim African American.

THE HARE KRISHNA MOVEMENT

Among the most colorful and controversial of the new religious movements is the Hare Krishna, properly the International Society for Krishna Consciousness. It was founded by Swami Bhaktivedanta (1896–1977), who came to the United States in 1965 to promote the practice of bhakti, or devotional Hinduism. The movement's object of worship is Krishna, regarded as the "Supreme Personality of Godhead." Its ecstatic devotionalism and insistence on strictly traditional "Vedic" dress, diet, and way of life, as well as the widespread scale of its literature, have attracted much attention. The ornate and opulent temples of the movement have become showplaces in a number of cities and rural areas. At the same time, the communalism and interesting life histories of many occidental adherents have made the Hare Krishnas the subject of several good sociological studies.

At the end of the 1980s, the Hare Krishnas suffered legal problems, divisions, and some decline in numbers in the United States, although the movement was doing well overseas. In the early 1990s, the movement went through some changes, taking on a looser, more family-oriented structure.

Bhaktivedanta, Swami A. C. *Krsna: The Supreme Personality of Godhead.* Bhaktivedanta $8.95. ISBN 0-89213-136-5. A good introduction by the founder.

Bromley, David G. and Larry D. Shinn, eds. *Krishna Consciousness in the West.* Bucknell U. Pr. 1989 $39.50. ISBN 0-8387-5144-X. A collection of scholarly papers on the American movement.

Brooks, Charles R. *The Hare Krishnas in India.* Princeton U. Pr. 1989 $47.50. ISBN 0-691-03135-5. Fascinating social history of the establishment by foreigners of a Hare Krishna temple in a traditional Indian town.

Burr, Angela. *I Am Not My Body: A Study of the International Hare Krishna Sect.* Advent NY 1984 o.p. A good sociological study, using attitudes toward the body as a touchstone of interpretation.

Gelberg, Steven. *The Hare Krishna Movement.* Garland 1994 $27.00. ISBN 0-8240-8751-8. A social study of the movement by one of its most scholarly adherents.

Hubner, John, and Lindsey Gruson. *Monkey on a Stick.* HarBraceJ 1988 $19.95. ISBN 0-15-162086-5. A controversial journalistic account of scandals in the movement.

Judah, J. Stillson. *Hare Krishna and the Counterculture. Contemporary Religious Movements Ser.* Bks. Demand repr. of 1974 ed. $80.00. ISBN 0-317-07867-4. Valuable, first major study of the movement.

Rochford, E. Burke. *Hare Krishna in America.* Rutgers U. Pr. 1985 $32.00. ISBN 0-8135-1113-5. A lively and valuable participant-observer sociological study.

Shinn, Larry D. *The Dark Lord.* Westminster John Knox 1987 $16.99. ISBN 0-664-24170-0. An important study of Krishnaism in India and America, based in part on extensive interviews with adherents.

JEHOVAH'S WITNESSES

The Jehovah's Witnesses are a controversial Christian denomination noted for biblical literalism, streetcorner and door-to-door evangelism, and expectations for the imminent return of Christ and Judgment. From time to time, the movement has encountered difficulties over such issues as the refusal of its members to salute the flag or the acceptance of blood transfusions for themselves or their children. While the organization has also faced internal defections because of unfulfilled prophecies and its authoritarian character, losses have been made good by new recruits.

The organizer of the movement, Charles Taze Russell (1852–1916), founded its well-known magazine *The Watchtower* in 1879 and preached and wrote widely on his interpretations of the Bible. These included the idea that the Second Coming of Christ had already happened invisibly in 1874 and that the world has been in a Millennial Age that will be fulfilled with the establishment of God's kingdom on earth. Gradually a denomination emerged out of the various groups and informal followings attracted to Russell's message. Joseph Franklin Rutherford (1869–1942) succeeded Russell as head of the movement and gave it the name Jehovah's Witnesses and a worldwide proselytizing mission in 1931. Today the movement is highly organized, and members are expected to give primary loyalty to it. They shun political activities (even to the point of not voting), military service, and all unnecessary participation in the activities of the present world. They are also obliged to do a certain amount of door-to-door proselytizing every month to announce the coming kingdom of God.

Bergman, Jerry. *Jehovah's Witnesses and Kindred Groups: A Historical Compendium and Bibliography. Social Science Ser.* Garland 1985 $69.00. ISBN 0-8240-9109-4. An important scholarly tool.

Botting, Gary. *Fundamental Freedoms and Jehovah's Witnesses.* Paul & Co. Pubs. 1993 $14.95. ISBN 1-895176-06-9. Critical study of the restrictions that Jehovah's Witnesses subject themselves to.

Botting, Heather, and Gary Botting. *The Orwellian World of Jehovah's Witnesses.* U. of Toronto Pr. 1984 $16.95. ISBN 0-8020-6545-7. A social study.

Curry, Melvin D. *Jehovah's Witnesses: The Effects of Millenarianism on the Maintenance of a Religious Sect.* Garland 1992 $63.00. ISBN 0-8153-0773-X. Provides background on the Witnesses and discusses their reactions when various prophecies did not come true.

Harrison, Barbara G. *Visions of Glory: A History and a Memory of Jehovah's Witnesses.* S&S Trade 1978 o.p. A sensitive, scholarly, and personal account by a former member.

Penton, M. James. *Apocalypse Delayed: The Story of Jehovah's Witnesses.* U. of Toronto Pr. 1985 $19.95. ISBN 0-8020-6721-2. The seminal work on the subject.

Reed, David A. *Jehovah's Witness Literature: A Critical Guide to Publications from the Watchtower.* Baker Bk. 1993 $8.99. ISBN 0-8010-7768-0. Notes on the movement's publication.

THE "JESUS MOVEMENT"

A much-discussed American religious phenomenon in the early 1970s was the "Jesus Movement," a trend toward evangelical Christianity among young people, particularly many who had been involved in the drugs, mysticism, and protest of the 1960s. The movement took many forms, from highly intensive communal groups like the Children of God to normative evangelical churches and collegiate organizations. Observers tended to see the movement as a way of coming to terms with the personal chaos often engendered by the 1960s experience and of reintegrating into the mainstream of American life. As the 1970s drew to a close, the movement had subsided as a distinct social phenomenon but, without doubt, was reflected in the fresh vigor apparent in evangelical Christianity.

The "Jews for Jesus" movement, or "Messianic Judaism," because of its initially largely youthful character, is often regarded as a part of the "Jesus Movement." It was founded, as an organized activity aimed at leading Jews to Jesus as the Messiah while still retaining their Judaic character, by Moishe Rosen in 1973. By the 1990s, however, this movement had lost much of its visibility, although it still lives in the Union of Messianic Jewish Congregations.

Enroth, Ronald M. *The Story of the Jesus People: A Factual Survey.* Attic Pr. 1972 $4.95. ISBN 0-85364-131-5. Now dated, but an interesting and important overview, with descriptions of various groups and centers as they were during the movement's heyday.

Horsley, Richard. *Sociology and the Jesus Movement.* Crossroad NY 1990. ISBN 0-8245-0992-7

Mills, Watson E. *Charismatic Religion in Modern Research: A Bibliography.* Ed. by David M. Scholer. NABPR 1985 $16.95. ISBN 0-86554-143-4. A research bibliography, including works on the "Jesus Movement."

Pritchett, W. Douglas. *The Children of God/Family of Love: An Annotated Bibliography.* Garland 1984 o.p. A basic resource on one of the most talked about "Jesus Movement" groups.

Rausch, David A. *Messianic Judaism.* E. Mellen 1983 $89.95. ISBN 0-88946-802-8. A scholarly, historical, and sociological study of the "Jews for Jesus" movement.

Richardson, James T., and others. *Organized Miracles: A Study of a Contemporary Youth, Communal, Fundamentalist Organization.* Transaction Pubs. 1979 $29.95. ISBN 0-87855-284-7. A careful, fascinating account of a "Jesus Movement" commune.

Sobel, B. Zvi. *Hebrew Christianity: The Thirteenth Tribe.* Wiley 1974 o.p. An important study of the modern "Jews for Jesus" movement around the time of its institutional origin.

Van Zandt, David E. *Living with the Children of God.* Princeton U. Pr. 1991 $24.95. ISBN 0-691-09463-2. A social study.

Wangerin, Ruth. *The Children of God: A Make-Believe Revolution.* Greenwood 1993. ISBN 0-89789-352-2. A critical assessment of the beliefs and aspirations of the movement.

NEOPAGANISM, WITCHCRAFT, AND MAGIC

Among the most interesting, and possibly the most significant, developments in alternative religion since the mid-twentieth century has been a marked rise in the number of groups practicing paganism, witchcraft, and ceremonial magic. Although related, these three phenomena are not identical. Pagans, or neopagans, are concerned with reviving polytheistic religions of the pre-Christian past, such as those of the ancient Celts, Greeks, Egyptians, or Norsemen, or with creating fresh religions in their spirit. Modern witchcraft, or Wicca, as its followers often call it, shares neopaganism's pluralistic and harmony-with-nature mood but has certain ritual traditions of its own, with a special emphasis on a supreme God and Goddess. The role of the Goddess in Wicca has particularly attracted persons interested in feminist spirituality. Followers of modern witchcraft in Europe and America insist it should not be confused, as it sometimes is, with Satanism. Workers of ritual or ceremonial magic perform elaborate evocations of deities in rites that owe much to medieval cabalism and Renaissance occultism.

Reliable literature on these fascinating groups by independent scholars is sparse. Few books can be found on neopaganism and witchcraft; the best current sources of information are the periodicals of the movement itself. On ceremonial magic in America there is virtually nothing of book length, although a number of studies exist of its English precursors, the famous turn-of-the-century Order of the Golden Dawn, and the career of the celebrated Aleister Crowley.

Adler, Margot. *Drawing Down the Moon: Witches, Druids, Goddess-Worshippers and Other Pagans in America Today*. Beacon Pr. 1987 $16.95. ISBN 0-8070-3253-0. By far the best book on the subject.

Clifton, Chas S., ed. *Witchcraft Today. Bk 1: The Modern Craft Movement*. Llewellyn Pubns. 1992 $9.95. ISBN 0-87542-377-9. An excellent collection of historical and practical essays on various aspects of contemporary witchcraft by informed practicioners; introduced by the editor with a fine discussion of the theoretical background and worldview of the craft.

Faber, M. D. *Modern Witchcraft and Psychoanalysis*. Farleigh Dickinson 1993 $29.50. ISBN 0-8386-3488-5. Scholarly look at Wicca, a growing cult emphasizing a female-centered universe and ecology, which is set in contrast to the phallocentrism of Freud.

Farrar, Janet, and Stewart Farrar. *The Witches' Way: Principles, Rituals and Beliefs of Modern Witchcraft*. Phoenix WA 1986 repr. of 1984 ed. $22.95. ISBN 0-919345-71-9. A complete summary of attitudes and practice in modern witchcraft.

Jorgensen, Danny L. *The Esoteric Scene, Cultic Milieu, and Occult Tarot*. Garland 1992 $75.00. ISBN 0-8153-0769-1. A sociological study of a contemporary American occult group.

Kelly, Aidan. *Crafting the Art of Magic, Bk 1: A History of Modern Witchcraft 1939–1964*. Llewellyn Pubns. 1991 $10.95. ISBN 0-87542-370-1. A landmark attempt to delineate the complicated paths by which modern Wicca has developed and to separate fact from legend in magic's lore.

Luhrman, T. M. *Persuasions of the Witch's Craft*. HUP 1989 $25.00. ISBN 0-674-66323-3. Based on fieldwork in England by an American scholar, the first major sociological study of modern magicians and Wiccans, affording invaluable insights into their thought.

Melton, J. Gordon, and Isotta Poggi. *Magic, Witchcraft and Paganism in America: A Bibliography. Philosophy and Religion Ser*. Garland 1992 $65.00. ISBN 0-8153-0859-0. Basic bibliography plus an introduction, providing a valuable historical perspective. A fundamental resource.

Scott, Gini G. *The Magicians: A Study of the Use of Power in a Black Magic Group*. Irvington 1984 o.p. A rare and interesting study based on participant observation.

Starhawk. *Dreaming the Dark: Magic, Sex, and Politics*. Beacon Pr. 1989 $12.95. ISBN 0-8070-1025-1. Statement by a leading figure in contemporary witchcraft.

———. *The Spiral Dance: Rebirth of the Ancient Religion of the Goddess*. HarpC 1979 $14.00. ISBN 0-06-250814-8. The basic ritual and rationale of modern witchcraft and goddess worship.

THE NEW AGE

One of the most discussed spiritual phenomena of the late twentieth century has been the so-called New Age movement, a diverse collection of attitudes and practices that has in common an interest in the religion of nature, alternative methods of healing (such as the use of "crystals"), life after death, and reincarnation. Included in this movement is channeling, in which an entity from another plane of existence communicates spiritual advice or other information through an individual known as a "channeler." While few of the practices are truly new—and some are as old as paleolithic shamanism—the particular conjunction of them in the contemporary world is seen by adherents as a sign of shifting spiritual attitudes. The movement has produced a vast literature, of which only a sampling can be presented here.

Basford, Terry K. *Near-Death Experiences: An Annotated Bibliography*. Garland 1990 $28.00. ISBN 0-8240-6349-X. A burgeoning interest in these experiences has been a feature of the New Age movement; an indispensable research tool in their study.

Basil, Robert, ed. *Not Necessarily the New Age: Critical Essays*. Prometheus Bks. 1988 $24.95. ISBN 0-87975-490-7. A collection of essays generally written from a skeptical, traditionally scientific perspective; introduced by an excellent, objective historical summary of the movement by J. Gordon Melton.

Bjorling, Joel. *Channeling: A Bibliographic Exploration*. Garland 1992 $57.00. ISBN 0-8240-5691-4. A summary of the beliefs and practices of the channelers and a historical background of such channeled modern scriptures as *Oahspe, The Urantia Book*, and *The Aquarian Gospel of Jesus the Christ*.

Capra, Fritjof. *Uncommon Wisdom*. Bantam 1989 $12.00. ISBN 0-553-3400-5. A good summary of the scientific philosophy underlying New Age thinking.

Chandler, Russell. *Understanding the New Age*. Zondervan 1993 $10.99. ISBN 0-310-38564-X. A fair and balanced summary with critique from a Christian perspective.

D'Antonio, Michael. *Heaven on Earth: Dispatches from America's Spiritual Frontier*. Crown Pub. Group 1992 $20.00. ISBN 0-517-57802-6. A readable encounter with many persons and places important to the New Age movement.

Gardner, Martin. *The New Age: Notes of a Fringewatcher*. Prometheus Bks. 1991 $15.95. ISBN 0-87975-644-6. A skeptic's view of the New Age.

Klimo, Jon. *Channeling: Investigations on Receiving Information from Paranormal Sources*. J. P. Tarcher 1988 $10.95. ISBN 0-87477-477-2. A psychological study of one of the New Age's most characteristic phenomena.

Lewin, Roger. *Complexity: Life on the Edge of Chaos*. Macmillan 1992 $22.00. ISBN 0-02-570485-0. Science for the New Age; interdisciplinary study of complex systems.

Lewis, James R., and J. Gordon Melton, eds. *Perspectives on the New Age*. State U. NY Pr. 1992 $59.50. ISBN 0-7914-1214-8. A collection of articles on the subject by distinguished scholars.

Melton, J. Gordon. *The New Age Encyclopedia: A Compendium of Information on the Beliefs, Concepts, Terms, People and Organizations Related to Higher Consciousness, Spiritual Development, Holistic Health and Other Topics*. Gale 1990 $59.50. ISBN 0-8103-7159-6. A useful summary of all facets of the movement with names, addresses, and bibliography.

Moody, Raymond. *Life After Life*. Mockingbird Bks. 1981 $14.95. ISBN 0-89176-037-7. A slim volume that, in its original 1975 edition, prompted much of the current interest in near-death experiences.

Plumb, Lawrence D. *Critique of the Human Potential Movement*. Garland 1993 $62.00. ISBN 0-8153-0777-2. A study of the philosophical background and leading figures in this New Age movement.

Ross, Andrew. *Strange Weather: Culture, Science and Technology in the Age of Limits*. Routledge Chapman & Hall 1991 $59.95. ISBN 0-86091-356-6. Fascinating discussion of new cultural phenomena such as the New Age in relation to the social deployment of science and technology.

Scott, Gini Graham. *Cult and Countercult: A Study of a Spiritual Growth Group and a Witchcraft Order*. Greenwood 1980 $42.95. ISBN 0-313-22074-3. A lively, though controversial, comparative sociological study of two groups associated with the New Age.

THE PEOPLE'S TEMPLE

The People's Temple first came to dramatic world attention on November 18, 1978, when over 900 members of the movement committed suicide or, in a few cases, were killed in Jonestown, its settlement in the jungles of the small South American nation of Guyana. The People's Temple had been founded by the Rev. Jim Jones (1931–78), who started out as a fairly conservative white "mainline" Protestant minister but later, as he worked with inner-city, largely African American congregations in Indianapolis and then San Francisco, became increasingly radical in politics and apocalyptic in religion. His social work was highly respected, but, at the same time, disturbing rumors surfaced concerning the personal loyalty and sexual favors he demanded and the regimentation of his flock. After an exposé article in the magazine *New West*, Jones took his followers in August 1977 to the Guyana location, where he intended to establish an agricultural commune and sit out the nuclear holocaust he was expecting. By this time he allegedly combined his vision of a Christian socialist state with extreme ego-inflation, identifying himself with God and Christ. The mass suicide followed an investigation and charges by a U.S. congressman and journalists that people were being held against their wills at Jones's isolated sanctuary.

Most literature on the People's Temple centers on the enigmatic personality of Jim Jones and on attempts to understand the shocking and tragic event of November 18, 1978.

Chidester, David. *Salvation and Suicide: An Interpretation of Jim Jones, The Peoples Temple, and Jonestown*. Ind. U. Pr. 1988 $29.95. ISBN 0-253-35056-5. Offers the first account of Jim Jones, The Peoples Temple, and the Jonestown mass suicide written from a history-of-religions perspective.

Hall, John R. *Gone from the Promised Land: Jonestown as American Cultural History*. Transaction Pubs. 1987 $34.95. ISBN 0-88738-124-3. Exceptionally sophisticated understanding of the sociology of religion underlies this exposition of the wide range of social and religious factors that produced the tragedy of Jonestown.

Levi, Ken, ed. *Violence and Religious Commitment: Implications of Jim Jones's People's Temple Movement*. Pa. St. U. Pr. 1982 $22.50. ISBN 0-271-00296-4. Interpretations of the group and the suicides by a number of scholars.

Moore, Rebecca. *In Defense of People's Temple*. E. Mellen 1988 $69.95. ISBN 0-88946-676-9. Attempt to reach beyond the sensationalism and assess the appeal and achievements of the movement.

Naipaul, Shiva. *Journey to Nowhere: A New World Tragedy*. Viking Penguin 1982 $8.95. ISBN 0-14-006189-4. An overview of the tragedy and its meaning.

Weightman, Judith M. *Making Sense of the Jonestown Suicides: A Sociological History of People's Temple*. Studies in Religion and Society. E. Mellen 1984 $89.95. ISBN 0-88946-87-0. The most important scholarly study.

SANTERÍA, VOUDON, AND KINDRED MOVEMENTS

The United States has long been home to religious movements of non-European background, that often combine Christian elements with those of other religious and cultural derivation. These movements have particularly flourished among Americans of African, Latin American, and Asian backgrounds and have attracted attention in the late twentieth century because of the rising interest in multiculturalism. Among the best known are Voudon from Haiti, long established in New Orleans, as well as among more recent Haitian immigrants, and Santería, practiced among Cubans, Puerto Ricans, and others. Both incorporate elements from Catholicism and African religions. Several others, including Umbanda from Brazil and Cao Dai from Vietnam, can also be found in America, but have been less written about. Although they vary in many colorful details, these religions are all basically spiritualistic, emphasizing the possession of priests and priestesses by the deities they serve, and magical practices. Serious practicioners undergo initiations. Some controversy was generated in the 1990s by the use of animal sacrifice by Santería, a practice the U.S. Supreme Court ruled was protected under the First Amendment.

Brandon, George. *Santería from Africa to the New World*. Ind. U. Pr. 1993 $29.95. ISBN 0-253-31257. Places the development of the religion in the context of the African diaspora.

Brown, Karen M. *Mama Lola: A Vodoo Priestess in Brooklyn*. U. CA Pr. 1991 $24.95. ISBN 0-520-07073-9. An innovative and much-discussed participant-observer study.

Gonzales-Wippler, Migene. *The Santería Experience: A Journey into the Miraculous*. Llewellyn Pubns. 1991 $3.95. ISBN 0-87542-257-8. A sensitive account of the faith from the inside.

_____. *Santería: The Religion*. Crown Pub. Group 1989 $19.95. ISBN 0-517-57154-4. Presentation of the religion's basic beliefs and practices.

Murphy, Joseph A. *Santería: African Spirits in America*. Beacon Pr. 1993 $14.00. ISBN 0-8070-1021-9. A sympathetic, scholarly account.

Tallant, Robert. *Voodoo in New Orleans*. Pelican 1983 $3.95. ISBN 0-88289-336-X. An older, largely anecdotal, and engrossing story of this tradition and its legendary "Voodoo Queens."

SATANISM

Satanism must be clearly distinguished from such practices as neopaganism and witchcraft, since it is not concerned with reviving pre-Christian or non-Christian worship, but rather with honoring precisely that entity that for the Judeo-Christian tradition supremely epitomizes evil and antoganism to God. Thus it has overtones of ultimate rebellion. Satanists can, however, be divided into two groups: those persons, often sociopathic, for whom Satan is truly evil and will reward those who serve him by doing evil, and those for whom Satan is actually a benign God, encouraging no more than the indulgence of "natural" drives that the other God would have us repress. The best-known example of the latter is the Church of Satan in San Francisco.

During the late 1980s, allegations of widespread Satanism in the United States drew much attention. Highly secretive Satanic groups were accused of animal sacrifice, child abuse, and other "ritual crimes." Such accounts prompted several books and articles which maintained that most of these rumors could not be substantiated.

Hicks, Robert D. *In Pursuit of Satan: The Police and the Occult*. Prometheus Bks. 1991 $24.95. ISBN 0-87975-604-7. A thoroughly researched study of alleged Satanism and "occult crime" that debunks claims that either is widespread in America.

LaVey, Anton S. *Satanic Bible*. Avon 1969 $5.95. ISBN 0-380-01539-0. Basic text of the famous Church of Satan in San Francisco.

_____. *The Satanic Rituals*. Avon 1972 $4.75. ISBN 0-380-01392-4. Rites of the Church of Satan.

Lyons, Arthur. *Satan Wants You! The Cult of Devil Worship in America*. Warner Bks. 1989 $4.50. ISBN 0-445-40822-7. An updating of Lyons's earlier book; responsible journalistic writing, despite the sensational title.

_____. *The Second Coming: Satanism in America*. Dodd 1970 o.p. The first independent book on the subject, chronicling the emergence of LaVey's Church of Satan.

Richardson, James T., and others, eds. *The Satanism Scare*. Aldine de Gruyter 1991 $46.95. ISBN 0-202-30378-0. A collection of essays by leading scholars suggesting that the notion of Satanism's prevalence in America is a "modern myth."

SCIENTOLOGY

Few modern movements have generated the success or controversy of Scientology. It was founded by the science fiction writer L. Ron Hubbard (1911–86), who began his psychospiritual work in the early 1950s with the teaching called Dianetics; Scientology was established in 1952 and grew rapidly as a part of the 1960s subculture. The basic teaching is a highly dualistic view of the soul, or "thetan," as separate from the body but trapped in it and in the matter-energy-space-time universe. Scientological "processing" involves ways to "go clear"—delete the "engrams" implanted in the mind by previous negative events, often in past lives—and then to become an "operating thetan." A "clear" person is said to be "at cause" of his or her life and totally free. Controversy has surrounded the fees Scientologists charge for "processing," their alleged tactics against critics, and their ongoing battles with governments regarding such issues as their tax status.

Despite the popularity of Scientology, there are few independent studies of it, though a vast amount of in-house publications and journalistic literature remains to be mined.

Atack, Jon. *A Piece of Blue Sky: Scientology, Dianetics and L. Ron Hubbard Exposed.* Carol Pub. Group 1990 $19.95. ISBN 0-685-45110-0. A devastating critique of the religion and its methods in autobiographical form by a former member.

Croydon, Bent, and L. Ron Hubbard, Jr. *L. Ron Hubbard: Madman or Messiah.* Carol Pub. Group 1987 $20.00. ISBN 0-8184-25286-8. A generally negative biography.

Hubbard, L. Ron. *Dianetics: The Modern Science of Mental Health.* Bridge Pubns. Inc. 1986 $25.00. ISBN 0-88404-258-8. The basic text that started the movement.

————. *Scientology: The Fundamentals of Thought.* Bridge Pubns. Inc. 1990 $4.95. ISBN 0-88404-503-X. One of L. Ron Hubbard's voluminous publications; a good, basic introduction to the philosophy of Scientology.

Littler, June D. *The Church of Scientology and L. Ron Hubbard: A Bibliography.* Garland 1993 $60.00. ISBN 0-8240-4345-6. A comprehensive bibliography, including the works of Hubbard on Scientology and Dianetics, those of other movements influenced by them, and material on the organization's legal suits.

Miller, Russell. *Bare-Faced Messiah: A Biography of L. Ron Hubbard.* H. Holt & Co. 1988 o.p. A fascinating, though controversial and largely negative, story of a life that, as the author states, was in fact more unbelievable than most of the legends about it.

Wallis, Roy. *The Road to Total Freedom.* Col. U. Pr. 1977 $49.50. ISBN 0-231-04200-0. The preeminent, independent account.

UFO RELIGIONS

Since the modern series of reported sightings began in 1947, UFOs (Unidentified Flying Objects; also called flying saucers) have attracted religious as well as scientific and popular attention. Within a few years, certain individuals, often called contactees, claimed communication from beings aboard the mysterious objects. Such communications sometimes took the form of visits from aliens and even rides on UFOs to distant planets for the contactee; at other times it was only mediumistic communication reminiscent of Spiritualism. In those contacts of religious significance, inevitably the space beings were portrayed as morally and spiritually superior to humans, and bearers of important messages to humanity by the contactee. We were urged to reform, to put aside war, and to join a galaxy full of advanced and happy worlds. Out of these communications emerged a set of small but interesting religious groups. Literature on them is uneven in quality, but the following diverse sources should serve to introduce the reader to the world of UFO religions.

Adamski, George. *Inside the Spaceships: UFO Experiences of George Adamski 1952–1955.* GAF Intl. repr. of 1955 ed. $9.95. ISBN 0-942176-01-4. One of the classic "contactee" accounts; Adamski was the first and most influential person to claim communication and a religious message from UFO beings.

Clark, Jerome. *The Emergence of a Phenomenon: UFOs from the Beginning through 1959.* Omnigraphics Inc. 1992 $95.00. ISBN 1-55888-741-5. An ongoing, comprehensive work that gives considerable attention to the colorful movements and personalities of UFO religion. Contains 113 articles with extensive bibliographies.

———. *UFOs in the 1980s.* Omnigraphics Inc. 1990 $95.00. ISBN 1-55888-301-0. First volume of a projected three-volume work that includes *The Emergence of a Phenomenon: UFOs from the Beginning through 1959.* Contains 84 articles covering a variety of UFO issues and personalities.

Curran, Douglas. *In Advance of the Landing.* Abbeville Pr. 1986 o.p. Readable, informative, and well-illustrated survey of UFO beliefs.

Festinger, Leon. *When Prophecy Fails: A Social and Psychological Study of a Modern Group that Predicted the Destruction of the World.* HarpC 1964 $11.00. ISBN 0-06-131132-4. A much-discussed sociological study based on participant observation of a UFO group; interesting not only for the account of the group and its response to the failure of its prophecy but also for the issues of sociological ethics and methods it raises.

Jacobs, David M. *The UFO Controversy in America.* Bks. Demand repr. of 1975 ed. $99.99. ISBN 0-8357-3962-7. A good, readable, and scholarly history, containing a chapter on contactees and religious groups.

Jung, C. G. *Flying Saucers: A Modern Myth of Things Seen in the Sky.* Princeton U. Pr. 1978 $8.95. ISBN 0-691-01822-7. A much-cited book by a world-renowed analytic psychologist on the archetypal or symbolic meaning of UFOs and the reasons why they easily become religiously significant.

Kannenburg, Ida. *The Alien Book of Truth: Who Am I? What Am I? Why Am I Here?* Blue Water Pub. 1993 $7.95. ISBN 0-926524-15-1

Rasmussen, Richard M. *The UFO Literature: A Comprehensive Annotated Bibliography of Works of English.* McFarland & Co. 1985 $29.95. ISBN 0-89950-136-2. A valuable resource for the whole field through 1985.

Ring, Kenneth. *Omega Project: Near Death Experiences, UFO Encounters, and Mind at Large.* Morrow 1992 $20.00. ISBN 0-688-10729-X. Compares the experiences of UFO abductees and the out-of-body journeys of those near death.

Strieber, Whitley. *Communion: A True Story.* Outlook Bk. Co. 1991 $4.99. ISBN 0-517-05750-5. Reprint of a best-seller by a well-known novelist, chronicling his personal encounters with aliens; this book did much to spark recent interest in abduction accounts.

Thompson, Keith. *Angels and Aliens: UFOs and the Mythic Imagination.* Addison-Wesley 1991 $19.95. ISBN 0-201-63227-6. A fascinating and generally excellent study of the meaning of UFOism as mythology and in popular culture.

UNIFICATION CHURCH

Officially named the Holy Spirit Association for the Unification of World Christianity, the Unification Church was founded in Korea in 1954 by the Rev. SUN MYUNG MOON (1920–). Rev. Moon declared that Jesus had appeared to him in 1936 and asked him to take on the task of establishing the Kingdom of God on earth by reordering human society in accordance with hierarchical, puritanical principles. These are presented in the faith's basic text, *Divine Principle*, which also shows elaborate parallels between history before and since the time of Jesus, suggesting that the world is ready for a new messianic figure, a role that many "Moonies," as Unificationists are popularly called, see fulfilled in Rev. Moon.

The Unification Church has received much criticism for authoritarianism and allegedly deceptive recruiting practices. Members are expected to raise funds steadily, work to expiate personal and general world sins, recruit others, and remain celibate for several years until they are matched by Rev. Moon with a mate they may never have seen before. In 1982, at a widely publicized ceremony in New York's Madison Square Garden, over 2,000 couples so engaged were wed en masse; all the brides wore identical dresses, and the grooms wore dark blue suits and maroon ties. The fund-raising has enabled the movement to establish a multibillion-dollar empire of businesses, real estate, and newspapers. Moon received a brief prison term for income tax evasion in the 1980s. And, although it has been accused of avoiding income taxes on its businesses, the movement sees itself as victimized by hostile propaganda and illegal kidnapping of its members by families intent on reclaiming them. In recent years the Unification Church has steadily endeavored to enhance its intellectual credentials by improving the education of leaders and sponsoring scholarly conferences. The literature on the Unification Church reflects highly varied perceptions of its nature and role in American and world society.

Barker, Eileen. *The Making of a Moonie: Choice or Brainwashing?* Blackwell Pubs. 1984 $39.95. ISBN 0-031-13246-5. A highly regarded sociological study.

Bromley, David G., and Anson D. Shupe. *Moonies in America: Cult, Church and Crusade.* Bks. Demand repr. of 1979 ed. $70.00. ISBN 0-8357-4771-9. A study by two leading sociologists specializing in new religious movements.

Chryssides, George D. *The Advent of Sun Myung Moon: The Origins, Beliefs and Practices of the Unification Church.* St. Martin 1991 $35.00. ISBN 0-312-05347-9. A good, independent, and noncontroversial study of the church and its background.

Dean, Roger A. *The Moonies: A Psychological Analysis of the Unification Church.* Garland 1992 $54.00. ISBN 0-8153-0774-8. Study that challenges some common assumptions, presenting adherents to the Unification Church as rational people who see themselves as engaged in a desperate struggle against evil.

Fichter, Joseph H. *The Holy Family of Father Moon.* Leaven Pr. 1985 o.p. Written by a prominent Catholic sociologist.

Lofland, John. *Doomsday Cult: A Study of Conversion, Proselytization, and Maintenance of Faith.* Irvington 1981 $29.00. ISBN 0-8290-0095-X. An early study of the Unification Church that has become a sociological classic.

Lowney, Kathleen S. *Passport to Heaven: Gender Roles in the Unification Church.* Garland 1992 $60.00. ISBN 0-8153-0075-6. A critical study that views Unificationism as a perpetuation of patriarchal attitudes toward male and female roles, in the process affording much insight into the church and the sociology of gender.

Mickler, Michael. *A History of the Unification Church in the San Francisco Bay Area, 1960–1974.* Garland 1993 $69.00 o.p. A revealing study of the church in an area where its presence has been highly visible and controversial.

_____. *The Unification Church in America: Sects and Cults in America. Bibliographical Guides Ser.* Garland 1986 o.p. An invaluable resource.

VEDANTA

Among the oldest of Eastern movements in America are those sponsored by the Ramakrishna Mission, frequently called the Vedanta Societies. Its origins go back to the life and teaching of RAMAKRISHNA (1834–86), a saintly modern Hindu mystic who emphasized the unity of all religions as paths to God-realization. Swami Vivekananda (1863–1902), a disciple of Ramakrishna, established Vedanta Societies in 1897 in several American cities to offer philosophical Hinduism and certain devotional practices to Westerners. The spiritual leadership of these societies is in the hands of swamis who are monks of the Ramakrishna Order, originally established among students of Ramakrishna. The teaching, which is basically in the advaita (nondualist) Vedanta tradition, emphasizes the oneness of all things as manifestations of the Brahman or God and the presence of the divine within each individual as the true Self. The Vedanta Societies have not grown dramatically but, by presenting an intellectually sophisticated version of Eastern lore, have attracted a complement of writers and thinkers and have had a significant role in the spread of Eastern ideas in the West.

Clooney, Francis X. *Theology after Vedanta: An Experiment in Comparative Theology.* State U. NY Pr. 1993 $44.50. ISBN 0-7914-1366-7. A reexamination of Christian comparative theology as rethought in the light of Vedanta insights.

Damrell, Joseph D. *Seeking Spiritual Meaning: The World of Vedanta. Sociological Observations Ser.* Russell Sage 1977 o.p. An excellent sociological document.

French, Harold W. *The Swan's Wide Waters: Ramakrishna and Western Culture.* Assoc. Faculty Pr. 1974 o.p. A useful, historical account.

Isherwood, Christopher. *My Guru and His Disciple.* FS&G 1988 $8.95. ISBN 0-374-52087-9. A beautifully written and candid account of Swami Prabhavananda of the Vedanta Society of Southern California by one of his most prominent disciples, the distinguished novelist and playwright Christopher Isherwood.

————, ed. *Vedanta for the Western World: A Symposium on Vedanta.* Vedanta Pr. 1945 $10.95. ISBN 0-8741-000-0. Interpretation of Vedanta by literate adherents, addressing European and American seekers.

Torwesten, Hans. *Vedanta: Heart of Hinduism.* Grove-Atltic. 1992 $10.95. ISBN 0-8021-3262-6. Scholarly introduction to central tenets of Hindu philosophy, exploring parallels between Eastern mysticism and Christianity.

OTHER GROUPS OF EASTERN BACKGROUND

A number of groups of Eastern derivation have flourished in America, although most have not received sustained outside study. We have already considered Buddhist groups. Here we consider Hindu and other groups that are significant parts of the spiritual scene. Of yoga groups, one of the best known is the Self-Realization Fellowship, founded by PARAMAHANSA YOGANANDA (1893–1952). An important modern spiritual teacher was Meher Baba (1894–1969), noted for a long period of smiling silence, whose doctrine combined ideas from Hinduism and Sufism of mystical Islam. Many people both in India and the West consider Satya Sai Baba (1926–), a Hindu teacher celebrated for his reputed miracles, an avatar or appearance of God in the world. Transcendental Meditation, a simple technique offered by the Maharishi Mahesh Yogi (1911?–), was sensationalized in the 1960s through its temporary endorsement by the Beatles and other stellar entertainment figures: it became in vogue in the 1970s and still maintains a significant following. A smaller but likewise interesting group is Eckankar, founded by Paul Twitchell (1910?–1971), presenting techniques of "soul travel" and divine realization. The Divine Light Mission had a meteoric rise and fall in the early 1970s under its "teenage guru," Maharaj Ji (1958–).

Baba, Meher. *The Everything and the Nothing.* Meher Baba Info. 1963 $4.95. ISBN 0-940700-00-X. The fundamental spiritual philosophy of Meher Baba.

Downton, James V., Jr. *Sacred Journeys: Conversion and Commitment to Divine Light Mission.* Col. U. Pr. 1979 $42.00. ISBN 0-231-04198-5. A sociological study of the Divine Light Mission.

Klass, Morton. *Singing with Sai Baba: The Politics of Revitalization in Trinidad.* Westview 1990 $28.00. ISBN 0-8133-7969-5. Study of the formation of religious identity in a post-colonial context, revealing the different impact a religion may have in terms of socio-political contexts.

Lane, David C. *The Making of a Spiritual Movement: The Untold Story of Paul Twitchell and Eckankar. Understanding Cults and Spiritual Movements Ser.* Garland 1993

$38.00. ISBN 0-685-26797-0. An illuminating, objective study of Eckankar and its founder.

Mahesh Yogi, Maharishi. *Transcendental Meditation*. NAL-Dutton 1973 $4.95. ISBN 0-451-1481-8. A basic presentation by the founder of Transcendental Meditation.

Purdom, C. D. *The God-Man: The Life, Journeys, and Work of Meher Baba*. Sheriar Pr. 1971 o.p. The major biography of Meher Baba, from a believer's perspective.

Rofé, Hosein. *The Path of Subud*. Undiscovd. Worlds Pr. 1988 $8.95. ISBN 0-945126-03-4. An account of the religion through the personal narrative of an early convert.

Russel, Peter. *The TM Technique: An Introduction to Transcendental Meditation and the Teachings of Maharishi Mahesh Yogi*. Viking Penguin 1990 $8.95. ISBN 0-14-019229-8. A TM primer by an adherent.

Sandweiss, Samuel H. *Sai Baba: The Holy Man and the Psychiatrist*. Birth Day 1975 $9.00. ISBN 0-9600958-1-0. A good introduction to the world of Sai Baba by a Western convert.

Twitchell, Paul. *The Tiger's Fang*. Illum. Way Pub. 1988 $10.95. ISBN 0-88155-063-9. An introduction to basic concepts of Eckankar by its founder.

Yogananda, Paramahansa. *Autobiography of a Yogi*. Self Realization 1981 $15.00. ISBN 0-87612-080-X. The influential autobiography of the founder of the Self-Realization Fellowship.

CHRONOLOGY OF AUTHORS

Swedenborg, Emanuel. 1688–1772
Quimby, Phineas P. 1802–1866
Smith, Joseph, Jr. 1805–1844
Eddy, Mary Baker. 1821–1910
Blavatsky, Helena P. 1831–1891
Steiner, Rudolf. 1861–1925

Gurdjieff, G(eorge) I(vanovich). 1877–1949
Watts, Alan Wilson. 1915–1973
Moon, Sun Myung. 1920–
Malcolm X. 1925–1965

BLAVATSKY, HELENA P. 1831–1891

A cofounder in 1875 of the Theosophical Society and its principal catalyst and intellectual force, Helena Blavatsky has had perhaps a greater influence than any other single person on modern occultism and alternative spirituality. Born Helena de Hahn of an aristocratic Russian family, she married Nikofor Blavatsky in 1848 but soon left him to travel widely. While the details of her wandering years are not entirely clear, it is evident that she augmented natural psychic and spiritualist interests with much esoteric lore. In 1874 she came to New York, where she met Henry Steel Olcott, who became the first president of the Theosophical Society upon its establishment in the following year as a vehicle for the study of arcane wisdom and the promotion of human brotherhood. In 1877 Blavatsky published her first book, *Isis Unveiled*. In 1878–79, she and Olcott moved to India, where the new movement met with both success and controversy. Returning to Europe, she settled in London in 1887, where her major work, *The Secret Doctrine*, was published in 1888. Combining shamanistic, Hindu, Buddhist, Neoplatonist, and Cabalistic lore to reconstruct what she considered to be the primordial human wisdom, Blavatsky forcefully engaged its concepts with those of the science and religion of her day. A woman of independent and colorful character, she evoked strong responses, both positive and negative, and left a permanent legacy whose influence on modern cultural movements in both India and the West is increasingly recognized.

BOOKS BY BLAVATSKY

Collected Writings. Ed. by Boris de Zirkoff. 1874–1891. 14 vols. Theos. Pub. Hse. $21.95.
    Essential for the serious student and for anyone who enjoys Helena Blavatsky's
    inimitable, pungent style.

Isis Unveiled: A Master-Key to the Mysteries of Ancient and Modern Science and Theology.
    Theosophy 1931 $17.00. ISBN 0-938998-01-3. Blavatsky's first major work.

The Key to Theosophy. Theosophy 1930 repr. of 1889 ed. $6.00. ISBN 0-938998-03-X.
    Though dated in some respects, still a valuable treatment of key Theosophical terms
    and concepts with applications to contemporary life.

The Secret Doctrine: The Synthesis of Science, Religion, and Philosophy. Ed. by Boris de
    Zirkoff. Theosophy 1925 repr. of 1888 ed. $18.50. ISBN 0-938998-00-5. The most
    important Theosophical text.

The Voice of the Silence. Theos. Pub. Hse. 1992 $15.95. ISBN 0-8356-0681-3. A short
    meditation said to be based on ancient mystical sources.

BOOKS ABOUT BLAVATSKY

Caldwell, Daniel H., ed. *The Occult World of Madame Blavatsky: Reminiscences and
    Impressions by Those Who Knew Her.* Impossible Dream 1991 $13.95. ISBN 0-
    941657-04-3. An interesting, generally sympathetic collection of firsthand accounts
    of this unforgettable personality.

Cranston, Sylvia. *H.P.B.: The Extraordinary Life and Influence of Helena Blavatsky.*
    Putnam Pub. Group 1992 $30.00. ISBN 0-87477-688-0. A large-scale biography, using
    much new material and emphasizing her impact on her own and later times.

Mead, Marion. *Madame Blavatsky: The Woman Behind the Myth.* Putnam Pub. Group
    1980 o.p. An interesting study, though somewhat speculative.

Murphet, Howard. *When Daylight Comes.* Theos. Pub. Hse. 1975 $17.95. ISBN 0-8356-
    0459-4. A biography of Helena Blavatsky from a traditional Theosophical per-
    spective.

Neff, Mary K. *Personal Memoirs of H. P. Blavatsky.* Theos. Pub. Hse. 1967 o.p. A
    reconstruction of Blavatsky's life based on her own scattered accounts.

EDDY, MARY BAKER. 1821–1910

Mary Baker Eddy was the discoverer of Christian Science and the founder of
one of the most influential of American new religious movements, the Church
of Christ, Scientist. Experiencing prolonged ill health after the birth of her first
child, Eddy visited a "mind-cure" teacher, PHINEAS P. QUIMBY of Portland,
Maine, in 1862; she obtained some relief and began to study Quimby's teachings
extensively. Although ultimately her doctrine differed from Quimby's on key
points, particularly the understanding of Scripture, this association was an
important milestone in her development. In 1866, while reading the Bible, she
perceived that evil and sickness are nonexistent in God's eyes and subsequently
experienced complete healing from an injury resulting from a fall. Soon she was
healing others as well in accordance with her newly discovered principle. The
first edition of Eddy's major book, *Science and Health*, was published in 1875,
and she founded the Church three years later. It was reorganized in 1892, and in
the 1890s Eddy worked on the Church Manual that governs the denomination's
life. Although Eddy and Christian Science were influential on the broader New
Thought and "positive thinking" movements, her belief in the unreality of evil
and the tight organization of her church remain unique.

BOOKS BY EDDY

Church Manual of the Mother Church. Christian Sci. repr. of 1895 ed. $12.95. ISBN 0-
    87952-084-1. More than merely a book of operating procedures, the manual offers
    important insights into Christian Science ideas and their application.

Prose Works. Christian Sci. repr. of 1925 ed. $44.95. ISBN 0-87452-074-4. Essential works, apart from *Science and Health*, by Eddy.

Science and Health with Key to the Scriptures. Christian Sci. repr. of 1875 ed. $29.95. ISBN 0-87452-034-5. The basic text.

BOOKS ABOUT EDDY

Peel, Robert. *Mary Baker Eddy.* 3 vols. Christian Sci. 1966–1977 $24.95 ea. Vol. 1 *The Years of Discovery.* ISBN 0-87510-085-6. Vol. 2 *The Years of Trial.* ISBN 0-87510-118-6. Vol. 3 *The Years of Authority.* ISBN 0-87510-142-9. By far the most comprehensive biography of the discoverer of Christian Science.

Powell, Lyman P. *Mary Baker Eddy: A Life-Sized Portrait.* Christian Sci. 1992 $17.95. ISBN 0-87510-108-9. A sympathetic biography.

Silberger, Julius. *Mary Baker Eddy: An Interpretive Biography of the Founder of Christian Science.* Little 1980 o.p. A critical, independent look at the subject involving some psychological analysis.

GURDJIEFF, G(EORGE) I(VANOVICH). 1877–1949

George Gurdjieff was a modern magus who was born in Alexandropol, Armenia, and traveled widely as a young man, spending several years in Central Asia and Tibet. His experiences during this time led to his famous book *Meetings with Remarkable Men*, an account of his alleged encounters with Eastern spiritual teachers that was published posthumously in 1963.

Gurdjieff's system draws on diverse sources, including Sufism, Buddhism, and the Cabala. He taught that human beings have neither soul nor true will and must strive to cure these defects by work and suffering. The ordinary person is asleep, acting merely according to habit, and needs the shock of awakening. To this end he sponsored experiences of dance, exercise, hard labor, and sometimes surprises or acute frustration.

Gurdjieff, like so many notable spiritual teachers, had a powerful personality and attracted devoted followers. The following is a sample of books, mostly by former students, about this enigmatic man.

BOOKS BY GURDJIEFF

Beelzebub's Tales to His Grandson. NAL-Dutton 1973 $30.00. ISBN 0-525-47351-3. A massive work, outlining Gurdjieff's teachings through colorful parables and accounts of human folly.

Life is Real Only Then, When "I Am." Viking Penguin 1991 $19.95. ISBN 0-670-83563-3

Meetings with Remarkable Men. Trans. by Alfred R. Orage. 1963. NAL-Dutton 1969 repr. of 1963 ed. $7.95. ISBN 0-525-48498-1. One of Gurdjieff's principal works; describes his alleged encounters with Eastern spiritual teachers, mostly Sufi.

BOOKS ABOUT GURDJIEFF

Anderson, Margaret. *The Unknowable Gurdjieff.* Viking Penguin 1991 $9.95. ISBN 0-14-019139-9. An interesting memoir.

Bennett, John G. *Gurdjieff: Making a New World.* HarpC 1973 o.p. A substantial biography and interpretation by one of Gurdjieff's leading British disciples.

Byrd, Rudolph P. *Jean Toomer's Years with Gurdjieff: Portrait of an Artist 1923–36.* U. of Ga. Pr. 1990 $30.00. ISBN 0-8203-1248-7. Examination of Toomer's largely unknown later work.

De Hartmann, Thomas, and Olga De Hartmann. *Our Life with Mr. Gurdjieff.* Cooper Sq. 1964 $51.25. ISBN 0-8154-0058-6. Readable account by a couple who shared Gurdjieff's adventurous escape from revolutionary Russia and his work in the West.

Gurdjieff Foundation of California, and J. Walter Driscoll. *Gurdjieff: An Annotated Bibliography. Lib. of Social Sciences.* Garland 1984 $60.00. ISBN 0-8240-8972-3. A basic resource.

McCorkle, Beth. *The Gurdjieff Years: 1929–1949.* Work Study Assn. 1990. ISBN 0-9626729-0-4. Recollections of Louise Mardi, a onetime adherent.

Moore, James. *Gurdjieff: The Anatomy of a Myth.* Element MA 1991 $27.95. ISBN 1-85230-114-7. A recent reinterpretation of Gurdjieff's life and thought.

Ouspensky, P. D. *Fourth Way.* Random 1971 $10.00. ISBN 0-394-71672-8. Study of the path to enlightenment by Gurdjieff's major philosophical disciple.

———. *In Search of the Miraculous: Fragments of an Unknown Teaching.* HarBraceJ 1965 $14.95. ISBN 0-15-644508-5. A large-scale treatise by a philosopher and sometime associate of Gurdjieff who was deeply influenced by his ideas.

Peters, Fritz. *Boyhood with Gurdjieff.* Capra Pr. 1980 o.p. Compelling narrative of a childhood influenced by the mysterious master.

Webb, James. *The Harmonious Circle: The Lives and Work of G. I. Gurdjieff, P. D. Ouspensky, and Their Followers.* Putnam Pub. Group 1980 o.p. One of the few studies of this movement by an outsider. Well researched and documented.

Wilson, Colin. *Gurdjieff: War Against Sleep.* Thorsons SF o.p. A brief summary of Gurdjieff by a British writer long interested in the occult.

MALCOLM X (MALCOLM LITTLE). 1925–1965

Born in Omaha, Nebraska, and the son of a Baptist minister, Malcolm Little grew up with violence. Several members of his family, including his father, were killed by whites. As a youngster, he went to live with a sister in Boston, where he started a career of crime that he continued in New York's Harlem as a drug peddler and pimp. While serving a prison term for burglary in 1952, he converted to Islam and undertook an intensive program of study and self-improvement, movingly detailed in *Autobiography of Malcolm X.* He wrote constantly to Elijah Muhammad (Elijah Poole, 1897–1975), head of the black separatist Nation of Islam, which already claimed the loyalty of several of his brothers and sisters. Upon release from prison, Little went to Detroit, met with Elijah Muhammad, and dropped the last name *Little,* adopting *X* to symbolize the unknown African name his ancestors had been robbed of when they were enslaved.

Soon he was actively speaking and organizing as a Muslim minister. In his angry and articulate preaching, he condemned white America for its treatment of blacks, denounced the integration movement as black self-delusion, and advocated black control of black communities. During the turbulent 1960s, he was seen as inflammatory and dangerous.

In 1963 a storm broke out when he called President Kennedy's assassination a case of "chickens coming home to roost," meaning that white violence, long directed against blacks, had now turned on itself. The statement was received with fury, and Elijah Muhammad denounced him publicly. Shocked and already disillusioned with the leader because of his reputed involvement with several women, Malcolm X went on a pilgrimage to Mecca and then traveled to several African countries, where he was received as a fellow Muslim. When he returned home, he was bearing a new message: Islam is a religion that welcomes and unites people of all races in the Oneness of Allah. On the night of February 21, 1965, as he was preaching at Harlem's Audubon Ballroom, he was assassinated.

Books by Malcolm X

Autobiography of Malcolm X. Ballantine 1977 $20.00. ISBN 0-345-37975-6

By Any Means Necessary. Ed. by George Brectman. Pathfinder NY 1992 $13.95. ISBN 0-87348-754-0

Malcolm X Speaks. Ed. by George Brectman. Grove-Atltic. 1990 $8.95. ISBN 0-8021-3213-8

BOOKS ABOUT MALCOLM X

Diamond, Arthur. *Malcolm X—A Voice for Black America*. Enslow Pubs. 1994. ISBN 0-89490-435-3

Goldman, Peter. *The Death and Life of Malcolm X*. U. of Ill. Pr. 1979 $12.95. ISBN 0-252-00774-3

Marable, Manning, ed. *The Malcolm X Reader: His Life, His Thought, His Legacy*. NAL-Dutton 1993 $12.00. ISBN 0-452-26750-1. Important collection of articles by and about Malcolm X.

Wolfenstein, E. Victor. *The Victims of Democracy*. Guilford Pr. 1993 $19.95. ISBN 0-89862-133-X

MOON, SUN MYUNG. 1920–

The founder of the Unification Church bases his theology on a vision that he says he received on Easter Day 1936, in which it was revealed to him that he was divinely appointed to complete the mission of Christ that was cut short by his Crucifixion; that mission was to establish the Kingdom of God on earth. After being ordained a Presbyterian minister, Rev. Moon began his mission in 1945 in North Korea, where he was born, but was soon arrested and imprisoned by Communist authorities. He came to regard the two-and-a-half years he spent in a labor camp as a Christlike indemnity for the sins of Adam and Eve and their descendants.

Upon his release, he traveled to South Korea, where in 1954 he started his movement to establish a unified Christian church, according to his interpretation of the Bible and his special revelations. The movement spread to Japan in the late 1950s but did not have much success in the West until the late 1960s, when "Moonies," as adherents are commonly known, started appearing in significant numbers on the streets of American cities to solicit funds and to witness (proselytize). Rev. Moon himself came to the United States in the 1970s to lecture on his messianic teachings. He spent heavily for publicity, entertainment of public figures, and conferences designed to attract neutral scholars. Nevertheless, his movement remained controversial, especially for its intense methods of recruitment, arranged marriages, and alleged attempts to buy political influence. In 1982 Rev. Moon was convicted of income tax evasion and served a 13-month prison term in 1984–85.

Hostility toward Rev. Moon was quite high during the 1970s and early 1980s but appears to have subsided somewhat since then as the Unification Church has attempted to become more mainstream. He remains the sole head of his church, which he characterizes as a "Unified Family."

BOOK BY MOON

The Divine Principle and Its Application. o.p. Not properly speaking the bible for church members, but rather an interpretation of the Christian Bible.

BOOK ABOUT MOON

Gullery, Jonathan G. *The Path of a Pioneer: Early Days of Sun Myung Moon and the Unification Church*. HSA Pubns. 1986 $3.95. ISBN 0-910621-50-0

QUIMBY, PHINEAS P. 1802–1866

Although he had practically no formal education, Phineas Quimby had a keen mind and a streak of inventive genius. Before he took up his career as a faith healer, he worked as a clockmaker and daguerreotype artist, and produced several useful inventions, including an apparatus for boat steering.

Quimby was born in Lebanon, New Hampshire, but moved with his family at the age of 2 to Belfast, Maine. Thirty-two years later, he attended an exhibition of Mesmerism there that changed his life. Finding that he possessed mesmeric powers himself, Quimby shortly thereafter was giving exhibitions of his own. He was so successful that he became a professional lecturer throughout New England, working with a "medium" who, in hypnotic trance, gave people advice that apparently cured their illnesses. However, Quimby was troubled by the theatricality of this routine and came to believe that the cures arose from the patients' faith rather than the medium's advice.

He gave up Mesmerism in 1847 and began to practice mental healing, moving to Portland in 1859, where he gained many patients. His thinking developed along with his practice, and by the 1860s he was convinced that each human soul was linked to God in an intimate relationship that gave human beings access to divine wisdom. Disease was a purely mental concept that could be removed through realization of this truth.

In 1862 came his celebrated meeting with MARY BAKER EDDY (1821–1910), then the chronically ailing Mrs. Patterson (she had not yet married her third husband or discovered the principles of Christian Science). He told her that her family and physician were holding her in bondage and that the grief this caused her was reflected in physical illness. After several visits, during which Quimby imparted "healthy electricity" into her, she pronounced herself cured and became, for a while, his disciple.

Quimby ended his practice in 1865, suffering from an abdominal tumor that did not respond to mental treatment. He returned to Belfast and busied himself in revising his manuscripts until his death in January 1866.

BOOK BY QUIMBY

The Quimby Manuscripts. Ed. by H. W. Dresser. Carol Pub. Group 1984 $9.95. ISBN 0-8065-0913-9

BOOKS ABOUT QUIMBY

Bates, E. S., and J. V. Dittemore. *Mary Baker Eddy.* o.p.
Dresser, A. G., ed. *The Philosophy of Phineas P. Quimby.* o.p.

SMITH, JOSEPH, JR. 1805–1844

Founder of the Church of Jesus Christ of Latter-Day Saints, or the Mormons, Joseph Smith was raised in rural New England and upstate New York. In 1820 he began experiencing a series of visions that led him away from conventional churches. According to Smith, three years later the angel Moroni showed him golden plates buried in a hillside, allowing him to obtain and begin translating them in 1827. The translation was published in 1830 as the *Book of Mormon*; it tells the story of ancient Israelites who had settled in America and were subsequently visited by Jesus Christ. In 1830 the church was founded as a restoration of the original priesthood and church of Christ on the basis of these texts and other visions. The new church attracted members and also almost immediate persecution, leading Smith to move his band of followers to Kirkland, Ohio, then to Missouri and finally to Nauvoo, Illinois. There a community with several distinctive and controversial practices, including polygamy, was established. Smith was arrested in 1844 and imprisoned in Carthage, Illinois, where he was killed by a mob. After his death, a large group of Mormons under Brigham Young migrated to Utah.

BOOKS BY SMITH

Book of Mormon, 1830. Heritage Repr. Ser. Herald Hse. 1973 $7.25. ISBN 0-8309-0273-2. The book translated from the golden plates by Joseph Smith.

Doctrine and Covenants of the Church of Jesus Christ of Latter-Day Saints: Containing the Revelations Given to Joseph Smith, Jun, the Prophet, for the Building Up of the Kingdom of God in the Last Days. Ed. by Orson Pratt. Greenwood 1971 repr. of 1880 ed. $49.75. ISBN 0-8371-4101-X. A fundamental, Mormon scriptural text. Inexpensive editions, often bound with a companion work, *The Pearl of Great Price,* are widely available through the LDS church.

History of the Church. 8 vols. Deseret Bk. 1991 $49.95. ISBN 0-87579-486-6. Compiled and annotated by B. H. Robinson. A narrative of Smith's life and early Mormonism based on his own journals and correspondences.

BOOKS ABOUT SMITH

Brodie, Fawn M. *No Man Knows My History: The Life of Joseph Smith.* Knopf 1971 $35.00. ISBN 0-394-46967-4. An important, though controversial, investigation of Smith.

Bushman, Richard L. *Joseph Smith and the Beginnings of Mormonism.* U. of Ill. Pr. 1984 $24.95. ISBN 0-252-01143-0. A comprehensive, well-written summary of early Mormonism, based on the acceptance of Mormon documents at face value. A good introduction to the LDS perspective on the origins of the religion.

Hill, Donna. *Joseph Smith, The First Mormon.* Doubleday 1977 o.p. A sympathetic portrait of the inspired prophet.

STEINER, RUDOLF. 1861–1925

Austrian-born Rudolf Steiner was a noted GOETHE (see Vol. 2) scholar and private student of the occult who became involved with Theosophy in Germany in 1902, when he met ANNIE BESANT (1847–1933), a devoted follower of Madame HELENA P. BLAVATSKY (1831–1891). In 1912 he broke with the Theosophists because of what he regarded as their oriental bias and established a system of his own, which he called Anthroposophy (*anthro* meaning "man"; *sophia* meaning "wisdom"), a "spiritual science" he hoped would restore humanism to a materialistic world. In 1923 he set up headquarters for the Society of Anthroposophy in New York City.

Steiner believed that human beings had evolved to the point where material existence had obscured spiritual capacities and that Christ had come to reverse that trend and to inaugurate an age of spiritual reintegration. He advocated that education, art, agriculture, and science be based on spiritual principles and infused with the psychic powers he believed were latent in everyone.

The world center of the Anhthroposophical Society today is in Dornach, Switzerland, in a building designed by Steiner. The nonproselytizing society is noted for its schools.

BOOKS BY STEINER

Curative Eurythmy. Anthroposophic 1990 $14.95. ISBN 0-85440-398-1. Outlines Steiner's theory and practice in the connecting of movement and sound.

New Spirituality and the Christ Experience of the Twenty-First Century. Anthroposophic 1990 $20.00. ISBN 0-88010-213-6

Social Issues: Meditative Thinking and the Threefold Social Order. Anthroposophic 1991 $24.95. ISBN 0-8810-359-0. Steiner's holistic and psychical strategies applied to social and community issues and problems.

BOOKS ABOUT STEINER

Furness, C. J. *Lotus Petals: The Life and Work of Rudolph Steiner.* 1972 $59.95. ISBN 0-8490-0557-4

Hiebel, Friedrich. *Time of Decision with Rudolf Steiner: Experience and Encounter*. Anthroposophic 1989 $19.95. ISBN 0-88010-274-8

Shepherd, A. P. *Rudolph Steiner: Scientist of the Invisible*. Inner Tradit. 1987 $10.95. ISBN 0-89281-174-9

SWEDENBORG, EMANUEL. 1688–1772

The son of a Swedish Lutheran pastor, professor, and court chaplain, Emanuel Swedenborg first became a scientist and mining engineer. Of brilliant intellect and wide-ranging interests, he explored many areas of nature, doing pioneering work in several fields. In 1743 he began to experience a series of visions of the spiritual world. Over subsequent years he maintained that he held conversations with angels, the departed, and even God, and that he had visited heaven and hell. Swedenborg penned a lengthy series of writings inspired by these encounters, based on the concept of a spiritual cosmos as model for the physical, an educative view of the afterlife, and the allegorical interpretation of Scripture. In 1774 the small Church of the New Jerusalem was founded explicitly on the basis of his revelations. Swedenborg's influence has been much wider than its membership. His teachings entered American culture generally through the popularity of several of his books and his impact on Spiritualism and the New England Transcendentalists.

BOOKS BY SWEDENBORG

This list presents only a few of Swedenborg's numerous religious works.

Four Doctrines. Swedenborg 1904 repr. of 1857 ed. $10.00. ISBN 0-87785-065-8. Generally considered the most basic of Swedenborg's theological works.

Heaven and Hell. Swedenborg 1982 $8.25. ISBN 0-87785-130-1. The classic account of Swedenborg's visits to the realms of departed spirits.

Marital Love. Swedenborg 1974 $12.00. ISBN 0-87785-150-6. Considered very daring and controversial at the time of its first publication; this almost modern-sounding treatment of marriage has long been Swedenborg's most popular work.

True Christian Religion. 2 vols. Swedenborg 1906 $20.00. ISBN 0-87785-086-0. Perhaps the most lucid and comprehensive of Swedenborg's numerous theological writings.

BOOKS ABOUT SWEDENBORG

Larsen, Robin, ed. *Emanuel Swedenborg: A Continuing Vision*. Swedenborg 1988 $75.00. ISBN 0-87785-137-9. A large, lavishly illustrated study of the visionary thinker and his ideas.

Spalding, J. Howard. *Introduction of Swedenborg's Religious Thought*. Swedenborg 1973 $4.50. ISBN 0-87785-121-2. A good, brief presentation of the basic concepts.

Toksvig, Signe. *Emanuel Swedenborg, Scientist and Mystic*. Biography Index Repr. Ser. Ayer 1972 repr. of 1948 ed. $25.00. ISBN 0-8369-8140-5. A standard biography of Swedenborg.

Trobridge, George. *Swedenborg: Life and Teachings*. Swedenborg 1992 $10.95. ISBN 0-87785-139-5. Still the best, single introduction.

WATTS, ALAN WILSON. 1915–1973

Alan Watts had an unparalled role in the popularization of Eastern philosophical and spiritual concepts in the West in the crucial decades of the 1950s and 1960s, when interest in these ideas grew remarkably. Born in England, he was raised an Anglican, but acquired an interest in Buddhism early in life, publishing his first book on Zen as early as 1932. He was, however, ordained a priest in the Episcopal church in 1944, after marrying an American woman and coming to the United States on the eve of World War II. As an Episcopalian, he published two well-regarded books integrating Christian and Eastern thought, *Behold the Spirit* (1947) and *The Supreme Identity* (1950). In 1950, however, his marriage and priesthood ended. Watts subsequently made a career as an independent writer and lecturer, popularizing with considerable literary grace basic themes from Zen, Daoism, and other Eastern sources.

BOOKS BY WATTS

The Book: On the Taboo Against Knowing Who You Are. Random 1989 $8.00. ISBN 0-679-72300-5. Vedanta-type philosophy of "universal oneness" as our true identity.

The Essential Alan Watts. Celestial Arts 1984 $7.95. ISBN 0-89087-403-4. Collection of major articles and excerpts.

Myth and Ritual in Christianity. Beacon Pr. 1968 $14.00. ISBN 0-8070-1375-7. A still-provocative study of traditional, largely Catholic-type Christianity interpreted from a mystical point of view.

Psychotherapy East and West. Random 1974 $4.50. ISBN 0-394-71609-4. A popular comparison of Western psychotherapy and the insights of Eastern spiritual guidance.

This Is It. Random 1973 $7.00. ISBN 0-394-71904-2. A short meditation on universal oneness.

Way of Zen. Random 1965 $4.95. ISBN 0-394-70298-0. Classic work from the 1950s; an important introduction of Zen to the West in the tradition of D. T. Suzuki.

Wisdom of Insecurity. Random 1968 $7.00. ISBN 0-394-70468. A work on accepting uncertainty and living in the moment that was prompted by the author's own vocational and marital crises.

BOOKS ABOUT WATTS

Brannigan, Michael C. *Everywhere and Nowhere: The Path of Alan Watts*. P. Lang Pubs. 1988 o.p. A philosophical inspection of Watts's ideas.

Furlong, Monica. *Zen Effects: The Life of Alan Watts*. HM 1986 o.p. A highly readable life of Watts, sympathetic to his spiritual quest but also honest about his human flaws.

CHAPTER 18

Contemporary Issues in Religious Thought

James J. Buckley

> What a given religion is—its specific content—is embodied in the images and metaphors its adherents use to characterize reality. . . . But such a religion's career—its historical course—rests in turn upon the institutions which render these images and metaphors available to those who thus employ them.
> —CLIFFORD GEERTZ, *Islam Observed*

Like all thought, religious thought is undertaken by persons in particular social and historical contexts. Both the participant in, and the observer of, religious thought need to take into account a religion's "specific content" as well as its "historical course." This list of suggested readings in contemporary issues in religious thought concentrates on the former, although always with the latter in mind.

What makes thought "religious"? There is no consensus on the answer to this question. For much of the history of the West, religion was part of the virtue of justice, consisting of doing what we owe to the Divinity. Italian religious figure and philosopher ST. THOMAS AQUINAS offered a synthesis of Greek, Roman, and Christian traditions on the virtue of religion in the Second Part of his *Summa Theologiae*, written in the late 1260s.

By the nineteenth century, however, particularly after the publication of FRIEDRICH SCHLEIERMACHER's *On Religion* (1799), religion came to be regarded in broader terms. First, it came to embrace not only particular beliefs and ceremonies but also lifestyles, attitudes as well as ritual and moral actions. Second, it also came to involve ways of life and thought, not only in relation to deities, but also in relationship to other concepts and objects of unrestricted importance. Similarly, "religious thought" came to embrace not simply ways of living and thinking about God or the gods, as in Judaism, Christianity, Islam, and varieties of Hinduism, but also such various concepts as the state of nirvana achieved in Buddhism, the belief in a nation or land as divine, and even the notion that religion is a personal experience defined by the individual.

Some members of religious communities object to being characterized as religious in the traditional or modern sense, maintaining that the term suggests a separation of spiritual and everyday life. Such individuals find that the tenets and practices of Judaism, Christianity, Islam, or Buddhism are not merely "religious" but are truths informing entire cultures and even the world. Therefore, the reader of texts in religious thought needs to ask whether specific texts are or are not "religious" in such traditional or modern senses. The following bibliography reflects this diverse and often conflicting variety of religious thought.

This bibliography includes more works on Christianity than Judaism or other religions simply because more English-language literature exists on the subject. However, contemporary issues are constantly changing, because religious thought not only has a history handed down from the past but also has a specific content shaped by attitudes and actions of individuals and religious communities. Members of large religious communities must often struggle with how to address such contemporary issues without ignoring their past traditions or their future goals. Movements that seem to be odd and extreme (e.g., the various "fundamentalisms" and "postmodernisms" mentioned later) are often warnings to religious communities that they are focusing on contemporary issues at the expense of their authentic identity. However, the problem is that, more often than not, we are only able to discern trends in contemporary thought decades after the fact. Will future generations think of this era as one in which one or more traditional religions took on new life? Will they say that not only God but also religion died in our time? Or will they view our contemporary ecological, psychological, and liberation movements as the seeds of new religions? Such questions remind us that any advice about reading in "contemporary issues in religious thought" ought to be regarded as tentative and fallible.

INTRODUCTIONS TO RELIGIONS

One can find introductions to various religions in almost any encyclopedia. (For general reference works pertaining to religion, refer also to Chapter 1.) For contemporary issues in the religious thought of particular religions, readers should first consult encyclopedias specific to many of these religions, such as *Encyclopedia of Buddhism*, *Encyclopedia Judaica*, *Encyclopedia of Islam*, and *New Catholic Encyclopedia*. The following texts, which include sections on contemporary issues in religious thought, represent only a sampling of the overviews available on religions.

Carrasco, David. *Religions of Mesoamerica. Religious Traditions of the World Ser.* Harper SF 1990 $10.00. ISBN 0-06-061325-4

Denny, Frederick. *Islam. Religious Traditions of the World Ser.* Harper SF 1988 $8.95. ISBN 0-06-061875-2

Earhart, H. Byron. *Religions of Japan. Religious Traditions of the World Ser.* Harper SF 1990 $10.00. ISBN 0-06-062112-5

——, ed. *Religious Traditions of the World. A Journey Through Africa, North America, Mesoamerica, Judaism, Christianity, Islam, Hinduism, Buddhism, China, and Japan.* Harper SF 1992 $39.00. ISBN 0-06-062115-X. A single-volume edition of a series on religions of the world written by scholars for a lay audience. The volumes are also available individually; see the entries by Carrasco, Denny, Earhart, Fishbane, Frankiel, Hultkrantz, Knipe, Lawson, Lester, and Overmyer.

Ellwood, Robert W. *Introducing Religion. From Inside and Outside.* P-H 1993 ISBN 0-13-5035-66-X. A good introduction to the academic study of religion, including a useful appendix on various ways to study a religion.

Fishbane, Michael. *Judaism. Religious Traditions of the World Ser.* Harper SF 1987 $8.00. ISBN 0-06-062655-0

Frankiel, Sandra S. *Christianity. Religious Traditions of the World Ser.* Harper SF 1985 $8.95. ISBN 0-06-063015-9

Hultkrantz, Ake. *Native Religions of North America. Religious Traditions of the World Ser.* Harper SF 1988 $10.00. ISBN 0-06-064061-8

Karpinski, Leszek M. *The Religious Life of Man: Guide to the Basic Literature.* Scarecrow 1978 $27.50. ISBN 0-8108-1110-3. Solidly annotated bibliography of books and journals on major religions.

Knipe, Daniel M. *Hinduism. Religious Traditions of the World Ser.* Harper SF 1991 $9.95. ISBN 0-06-064780-9

Lawson, E. Thomas. *Religions of Africa. Religious Traditions of the World Ser.* Harper SF 1985 $9.00. ISBN 0-06-065211-X

Lester, Robert C. *Buddhism. Religious Traditions of the World Ser.* Harper SF 1987 $8.95. ISBN 0-06-065243-8

Overmyer, Daniel L. *Religions of China. Religious Traditions of the World Ser.* Harper SF 1986 $8.95. ISBN 0-06-066401-0

Smart, Ninian. *The Religious Experience.* Macmillan 1991 $30.00. ISBN 0-02-412735-3. A good overview of the history and current state of religions.

THE CURRENT STATE OF TRADITIONAL RELIGIOUS AND THEOLOGICAL ISSUES

Traditional religious and theological issues are issues that have been handed down from one generation to another and that have remained relevant within particular religious communities. Nevertheless, such traditional religious communities as Judaism, Christianity, Islam, Hinduism, and Buddhism have rarely been satisfied with simply observing traditions; rather, they have generally worked to bring tradition to bear on their lives and their world, with the result that these traditions sometimes are preserved, sometimes revised, and occasionally abrogated.

God

The word *God* is used in many different and often incompatible ways by many different sorts of people. Some understand God as representing the central precepts of a religion, that is, whatever or whoever any individual or group takes to be of unrestricted importance. God is most often thought of, however, in more specific ways by members of traditional religious communities. For example, traditional Jewish, Christian, and Muslim theologies center on the God of Israel, the God of Jesus Christ, and Allah, respectively. The following section focuses on such traditional communities. For information on those modern and postmodern religious thinkers who sometimes reject these alternatives, see the sections "Postmodernism and Deconstruction" and "Interreligious Dialogue" in this chapter.

Buckley, Michael, S. J. *At the Origins of Modern Atheism.* Yale U. Pr. repr. of 1987 ed. $14.95. ISBN 0-300-03719-8. Shows how the notion of "atheism" developed, finding the concept ambiguous because its meaning depends on which "god" is denied.

Burrell, David, C. S. C. *Knowing the Unknowable God: Ibn-Sina, Maimonides, Aquinas.* U. Notre Dame Pr. 1986 $9.45. ISBN 0-268-01225-3. Explores how theologians— medieval Muslim, Jewish, and Christian—think we know the unknowable God.

Dharmasiri, Gunapala. *A Buddhist Critique of the Christian Concept of God.* Glden Leaves Pub. 1988 $42.85. ISBN 0-942353-01-3. A Buddhist criticizes the concept of God in favor of the quest for Nirvana.

Heschel, Abraham Joseph. *God in Search of Man.* Aronson 1955 $30.00. ISBN 087668-955-1. One of many texts by a major Jewish religious thinker.

Jacobs, Louis. *Jewish Thought Today.* Behrman Hse. 1970 o.p. An anthology that includes a section of 16 chapters by major Jewish thinkers on the concept of God.

McFague, Sally. *Models of God. Theology for an Ecological Nuclear Age.* Fortress Pr. 1987 $12.95. ISBN 0-8006-2051-8. A deconstruction of the Judaeo-Christian tradition's patriarchal model of God and the construction of models of God as mother, lover, and friend.

Nasr, Seyyed Hossein, ed. *Islamic Spirituality: Foundations.* Crossroad NY 1991 $49.50. ISBN 0-8245-0767. Essays on Islam, including an essay on God (with further bibliography) by the editor.

Oden, Thomas. *The Living God. Systematic Theology.* Vol. I. Harper SF 1987 $20.00. ISBN 0-06-066363-4. A summary of the "consensus" of the Christian tradition on the triune God.

van der Leeuw, Gerardus. *Religion in Essence and Manifestation: A Study in Phenomenology.* 2 vols. Trans. by J. E. Turner. Princeton U. Pr. 1986 $80.00. ISBN 0-691-07272-8. Although few would accept van der Leeuw's notion that all religions center on power, these volumes, originally published in 1933, are a goldmine of the diverse "objects" and "subjects" of various religions.

Incarnation

The notion of incarnation is used in reference to life after death and has been recently reclaimed by some Jewish theologians. However, the most singular use of the notion has been by Christians who have traditionally believed that Jesus Christ is God's word become flesh or incarnate. Thus, a theology of the Incarnation refers to reflection on Jesus as God incarnate; in a broader sense, a theology of the Incarnation is reflection on the entire narrative of Jesus Christ, from preexistence through his life and death and resurrection to his presence and promised return.

Borowitz, Eugene. *Contemporary Christologies: A Jewish Response.* Paulist Pr. 1980 o.p. Responds to Christian reflection on Jesus Christ.

Frei, Hans. *The Identity of Jesus Christ: The Hermeneutical Bases of Dogmatic Theology.* Fortress Pr. 1975 o.p. An influential work arguing that if we read the Gospels as narratives (and not as simply reports of isolated facts), we "cannot not" think Jesus Christ risen.

Goulder, Michael, ed. *Incarnation and Myth: The Debate Continued.* Bks. Demand repr. of 1979 ed. $67.30. ISBN 0-8028-1199-X. Essays responding to issues raised in *The Myth of God Incarnate.*

Hick, John, ed. *The Myth of God Incarnate.* Westminster John Knox 1977 o.p. A collection of essays debating whether describing Jesus Christ as God Incarnate is appropriate or is a myth.

Marshall, Bruce. *Christology in Conflict: The Identity of a Saviour in Barth and Rahner.* Blackwell Pubs. 1987 $45.00. ISBN 0-631-15465-5. A difficult but rewarding study of one of the key issues of modern Christian theology, concerning Jesus Christ's role as a saviour.

Oden, Thomas. *The Word of Life. Systematic Theology.* Vol. 2. Harper SF 1989 $32.95. ISBN 0-06-066348. An effort to summarize the consensus about Jesus Christ from the Christian tradition.

Parrinder, Geoffrey. *Avatar and Incarnation.* Faber and Faber 1970 o.p. A comparison of avatars in Hinduism, buddhas in Buddhism, and incarnation in Christianity.

Wyschogrod, Michael. *The Body of Faith: God in the People Israel.* Harper SF 1983 $14.95. ISBN 0-06-069706-07. A Jewish philosopher's overview of Judaism, reappropriating the concept of incarnation for Judaism.

Atonement

A theology of atonement describes how "at-one-ment" or oneness is brought about after persons or groups have been divided from each other and God. Theologies of atonement differ according to one's views on the physical and human world, what divides persons from each other in that world, and what religions contribute to overcoming those divisions. Theologies of atonement may also be called theologies of salvation, redemption, reconciliation, and liberation. However, no one of these concepts seems to be common to all religions, much less to all religious thinkers. The concept of atonement has been most often associated with Jewish holy days of Rosh Hashana and Yom Kippur and the Christian Easter holiday, for which the central issue has been how the death of Jesus was a redemption for the sins of humankind and gave the promise of eternal salvation.

Agnon, S. Y. *Days of Awe. A Treasury of Traditions, Legends, and Learned Commentaries Concerning Rosh Ha-Shanah, Yom Kippur, and the Days Between.* Schocken 1965 $14.00. ISBN 0-8052-0100-9. Abridged version of a Hebrew text, with a wealth of traditions on atonement, the 1966 Nobel Prize-winner for Literature.

Aulen, Gustaf. *Christus Victor: An Historical Study of the Three Main Types of the Idea of the Atonement.* Trans. by A. G. Hebert. Macmillan 1986 $20.00. ISBN 0-02-083400-4. Originally published in Swedish in 1931; studies the interaction of "objective," "subjective," and "classic" views of atonement.

Bowker, John. *Problems of Suffering in the Religions of the World.* Cambridge U. Pr. 1970 $17.95. ISBN 0-521-09903-X. A good survey of the problem of suffering, including views of suffering as atonement.

Cohen, Arthur Allen, ed. *Arguments and Doctrines: A Reader of Jewish Thinking in the Aftermath of the Holocaust.* HarpC 1970 o.p. Essays on the *Shoah*, considered one of the greatest evils of the twentieth century.

Feenstra, Ronald J., and Cornelius Plantinga, Jr., eds. *Trinity, Incarnation, and Atonement. Philosophical and Theological Essays.* U. Notre Dame Pr. 1989 $29.95. ISBN 0-268-01870-7. Includes three essays on philosophical problems with the Christian doctrine of atonement.

Ricoeur, Paul. *The Symbolism of Evil.* Trans. by Emerson Buchanan. Beacon Pr. 1967 $17.00. ISBN 0-8070-1567-9. A philosopher emphasizes the way that speculation about evil (e.g., theories of atonement) depends on stories about evil which in turn depend on more basic experiences.

Rosenzweig, Franz. *The Star of Redemption.* Trans. by William W. Hallo. U. Notre Dame Pr. 1985 $12.95. ISBN 0-268-01717-4. A major Jewish thinker proposes a new reading of Judaism and Christianity; originally published in 1921.

Soloveitchik, Joseph. *Soloveitchik on Repentance.* Trans. by Pinchas Peli. Paulist Pr. 1984 $11.95. ISBN 0-8091-2604-4. Lectures on repentance, expiation, and redemption by a major Orthodox rabbi.

Surin, Kenneth. *Theology and the Problem of Evil.* Blackwell Pubs. 1986 $39.95. ISBN 0-631-14664-4. Maintains that "the Christian who takes the atonement seriously has no real need for a theodicy [i.e., a defense of God in the face of evil]."

Swinburne, Richard. *Responsibility and Atonement.* OUP 1989 $62.00. ISBN 0-19-824839-3. Argues that we first need to define the role of atonement in relations between people before considering how it applies to God and people.

Life after Death

What, some religious thinkers ask, is the ultimate end of life? Death, of course, is one answer. However, some religions hold a belief in immortality, and that we, or some part of us, such as our soul, will not die. Insofar as we or part of us dies, is there life after death? The doctrine of reincarnation (in Hinduism, Jainism, and Buddhism) teaches that we will live another life after death, being reborn again and again until we attain liberation. The doctrine of the resurrection (which plays an important role in Zoroastrianism, Orthodox Judaism, Islam, and Christianity) teaches that, for there to be life after death, we will have to be "raised" from the dead. The central reason that life after death is important in traditional theistic religions is because it represents life with God and does not simply represent an extension of this life. Similarly, reincarnation is important in Buddhism, not because it is another life after death but because it is part of the path to achieving nirvana.

DEATH

Badham, Paul, and Linda Badham, eds. *Death and Immortality in the Religions of the World*. Paragon Hse. 1987 o.p. Fifteen essays on life after death, ranging from African religions through traditional Eastern and Western religions and modern skeptics.

Bowker, John. *The Meanings of Death*. Cambridge U. Pr. 1991 $27.95. ISBN 0-521-39117-2. A survey of death in various world religions, concluding with reflections on death as sacrifice.

Brandon, S. G. F. *The Judgment of the Dead: The Idea of Life After Death in the Major Religions*. Scribner 1967 o.p. A useful historical and comparative study, although it makes no attempt "to evaluate the metaphysical or theological credentials of the concept" of life after death.

Davis, Stephen T., ed. *Death and Afterlife*. St. Martin 1989 $35.00. ISBN 0-312-03537. A useful collection of essays on immortality, resurrection, reincarnation, and annihilation.

Kung, Hans. *Eternal Life?: Life After Death as a Medical, Philosophical, and Theological Problem*. Trans. by Edward Quinn. Crossroad NY 1991 $19.95. ISBN 0-8245-1100-9. A Christian theologian goes through the secular and religious opinions on life after death, presenting his own faith in eternal life.

Reynolds, Frank, and Earle H. Waugh, eds. *Religious Encounters with Death*. Pa. St. U. Pr. 1977 o.p. Essays on death from ancient myth to the Holocaust.

REINCARNATION

Collins, Steven. *Selfless Persons: Imagery and Thought in Theravada Buddhism*. Cambridge U. Pr. 1990 $19.95. ISBN 0-521-39726-X. Although not an introductory text, this is perhaps the best Western analysis of the Buddhist "doctrine of the no-self."

Head, Joseph, and S. L. Cranston, eds. *Reincarnation: The Phoenix Fire Mystery*. Point Loma Pub. 1977 $14.95. ISBN 0-913004-71-5. Concerned more with the similarities than differences in convictions about reincarnation in different religions.

Neufeldt, Ronald W., ed. *Karma and Rebirth: Post Classical Developments*. State U. NY Pr. 1986 $21.95. ISBN 0-87395-990-6. Essays on karma and rebirth in the Hindu context, the Buddhist context, and the Western context.

Rinbochay, Lati, and Jeffrey Hopkins. *Death, Intermediate State and Rebirth in Tibetan Buddhism*. Snow Lion 1985 $7.95. ISBN 0-937938-00-9. A translation of and commentary on a classic text of Buddhism by the eighteenth-century thinker Yang-Jen-ga-way-lo-dro on how to purify oneself of death, the intermediate state, and rebirth.

RESURRECTION

Benoit, Pierre, and Roland Murphy. *Immortality and Resurrection*. Herder and Herder 1970 o.p. Articles on an important dispute among Christians about whether their common belief in Jesus' resurrection implies a belief in the immortality of the soul.

Brown, Raymond. *The Virginal Conception and Bodily Resurrection of Jesus*. Paulist Pr. 1973 $7.95. ISBN 0-8091-1768-1. A good overview of the historical data on Jesus' resurrection.

Carnley, Peter. *The Structure of Resurrection Belief*. OUP 1987 $85.00. ISBN 0-19-826679-0. Careful analysis of twentieth-century Christian theologies of the resurrection, centering on the resurrection as a liturgical experience.

Smith, J. I., and Y. Y. Haddad. *The Islamic Understanding of Death and Resurrection*. State U. NY Pr. 1981 $59.50. ISBN 0-87395-506-4. A very readable attempt "to give as broad an overview as possible of the Islamic eschatological narrative."

Spirituality

The term "spirituality" is used in diverse ways. Here it simply represents a convenient term referring to an individual's religious thought and experience—

that "spirit" which is irreducibly unique to each person. Various religions disagree, of course, on what makes each individual irreducibly unique, and on the inner character that enables the individual to express that uniqueness.

Cousins, Ewert, ed. *World Spirituality: An Encyclopedic History of the Religious Quest.* 25 vols. planned. Crossroad NY 1980–present. A planned multivolume treatment of the history and contemporary spiritual life of a variety of religious communities; the first three volumes cover Christian, Islam, and Jewish spirituality.

Cummings, Charles. *Eco-Spirituality: Toward a Reverent Life.* Paulist Pr. 1991 $8.95. ISBN 0-8091-3251-6. A succinctly argued examination of ecology's current role in the "physical as well as the spiritual world. A somewhat theological solution to the environmental crisis at hand."

Evans, Donald. *Spirituality and Human Nature.* State U. of NY Pr. 1992 $44.50. ISBN 0-7914-1279-2. Discusses spirituality and depth psychology, positivism, humanism and morality, religion, and social action.

O'Brien, Theresa K., ed. *The Spiral Path: Essays and Interviews on Women's Spirituality.* Yes Intl. 1988 $13.95. ISBN 0-936663-01-4. Focuses on representatives from the major world religions, East and West, and covers all dimensions of women's spirituality.

CURRENT THEOLOGICAL METHOD

In its broadest sense, theological method concerns whether and how one might go about practicing theology today; in its narrowest sense, theological method is about what some logicians call the "truth conditions" of theology (e.g., the conditions under which the claims theologians make might be true).

Religion, Language, and Knowledge

In modernity, issues of truth are closely related to issues of knowledge, and both are generally regarded as inseparable from the language or languages we speak. However, for those who think that we are or ought to be "postmodern," the connections between truth, knowledge, and language are not as clear.

Audi, Robert, and William J. Wainright, eds. *Rationality, Religious Belief and Moral Commitment.* Cornell Univ. Pr. 1986 $49.50. ISBN 0-8014-1856-9. A collection of essays representative of how some Anglo-American philosophers approach religious belief.

Cohen, A., and P. Mendes-Flohr, eds. *Contemporary Jewish Religious Thought: Original Essays on Critical Concepts, Movements, and Beliefs.* Free Pr. 1987 $24.95. ISBN 0-684-18628-4. A dictionary of Judaism from aesthetics to Zionism; a good starting point for brief essays on contemporary Jewish thought.

Ford, David F., ed. *The Modern Theologians. An Introduction to Christian Theology in the Twentieth Century.* 2 vols. Blackwell Pubs. 1989. $55.00. ISBNs 0-631-15371-3, 0-631-16807-9. Essays on the major Christian theologians and theological movements and methods in the twentieth century.

Nasr, Seyyed Hossein, ed. *Islamic Spirituality*, Vol. 2 Crossroad NY 1991 $49.50. ISBN 0-8245-0768-5. Essays on Sufism, Islamic literature, art, and thought, including an essay by the editor on "Theology, Philosophy, and Spirituality."

Nishida, Kitaro. *Last Writings: Nothingness and the Religious Worldview.* Trans. by D. A. Dilworth. UH Pr. 1987 $18.00. ISBN 0-8248-1040-6. Essays originally written in 1949 and 1966 by the major Japanese philosopher of East-West religious thought of this century. With an introduction by D. A. Dilworth.

Thurman, Robert A. F. *The Central Philosophy of Tibet: A Study and Translation of Jey Tsong Khapa's Essence of True Eloquence.* Princeton U. Pr. 1984 $18.95. ISBN 0-691-

02067-1. A translation of Tibet's greatest philosopher, with a lengthy introduction to the background in Buddhism.

Tracy, David. *Plurality and Ambiguity: Hermeneutics, Religion, Hope.* HarpC 1987 $14.95. ISBN 0-06-254742-9. An argument by a revisionist Christian theologian that, despite our diverse and ambiguous world, we can believe in an ultimate reality.

Postmodernism and Deconstruction

Postmodernism suggests disillusionment with modernity, whether in its religious or nonreligious forms; while deconstruction represents a specific critical practice among the postmodernists. While some postmodernists aim at reaffirmation of their traditional religion, others suggest that we must invent our own religion. It must be noted that both postmodernism and deconstruction are difficult terms to define, and that texts written from this perspective are frequently very complex, since they quite intentionally transgress normal ways of communication.

Bloom, Harold. *The American Religion: The Emergence of the Post-Christian Nation.* S & S Trade 1992 $22.00. ISBN 0-671-67997-X. A prolific literary critic argues that the peculiarly American religions are really religions celebrating freedom as "total inward solitude."

Keiji, Nishitani. *Religion and Nothingness.* Trans. by Jan van Bragt. U. CA Pr. 1982 o.p. A Japanese philosopher reflects on Buddhism, particularly Buddhist teaching on *sunyata* (emptiness or absolute nothingness), in relation to Western philosophy and religion.

Lindbeck, George. *The Nature of Doctrine: Religion and Theology in a Postliberal Age.* Westminster John Knox 1984 $18.00. ISBN 0-664-21829. A useful summary of three contemporary theories of religion, one focused on propositions, another on experience, and the third, on Lindbeck's own "cultural-linguistic" theory of religion.

Marion, Jean-Luc. *God Without Being. Hors-Texte.* Trans. by Thomas A. Carlson. *Religion and Postmodernism Ser.* Ed. by Mark C. Taylor. U. Ch. Pr. 1991 $32.00. ISBN 0-226-50540-5. A difficult but rewarding set of essays by a French Catholic philosopher arguing against the ways believers and nonbelievers reduce God's gift of love to a human idol.

Scharlemann, Robert. *The Reason of Following: Christology and the Ecstatic I. Religion and Postmodernism Ser.* Ed. by Mark C. Taylor. U. Ch. Pr. 1991 $22.50. ISBN 0-226-73659-8. Maintains that there is a structure of reasoning entailed in following Christ, much as there is a structure of reasoning for all the particular activities of reason.

Taylor, Mark C. *Erring: A Postmodern A/theology.* U. Ch. Pr. 1984 $11.95. ISBN 0-226-79192-4. Studies how the death of God leads to the death of the self, history, and the book, as well as to the life of "writing" as the "divine milieu."

THE SOCIAL SCIENCES AND RELIGION

One of the major changes in religious thinking in modernity is that religion is no longer thought about only by members of religious communities using the tools provided by philosophy, theology, or even history. Instead, what is called the field of religious studies relies on psychology, sociology, cultural anthropology, and other fields to understand religious ways of life and thought. It is crucial to remember, however, that not all thought about religion is religious thought; we can think about religion in various ways without actually being religious.

Psychology of Religion

Capps, Donald, Lewis Rambo, and Paul Ransohoff. *Psychology of Religion: A Guide to Information Sources*. Gale 1976 o.p. Bibliography of general works on religion as well as the psychological aspects of the mythical, ritual, experiential, dispositional, social, and "directional" dimensions of religion.

Clifford, Terry. *Tibetan Buddhist Medicine and Psychiatry: The Diamond Healing*. Weiser 1984 $15.95. ISBN 0-87728-528-4. An intriguing history and analysis of medicine's use, especially that of psychiatry, in the Buddhism of Tibet as well as some comparison to Western psychiatries.

Kakar, Sudhir. *Shamans, Mystics, and Doctors: A Psychological Inquiry into India and Its Healing Traditions*. U. Ch. Pr. 1990 $14.95. ISBN 0-226-42279-8. A study of religious healing in India, compared with healing in modern psychotherapy.

Maloney, H. Newton, ed. *Current Perspectives in the Psychology of Religion*. Eerdmans 1977 o.p. Good essays, largely by Western psychologists on Western religions; includes a chapter on "the religion of psychologists."

O'Flaherty, Wendy Doniger. *Women, Androgynes, and Other Mythical Beasts*. U. Ch. Pr. 1980 $27.50. ISBN 0-226-61849-8. Uses history, linguistics, and psychology to develop an analysis of the symbols of Indian mythology.

Spero, Moshe Halevi. *Judaism and Psychology: Halakhic Perspectives*. Ktav 1980 $25.00. ISBN 0-87068-703-4. Good essays on philosophical and clinical issues; *Halakha* is a law or custom established or ratified by authoritative rabbinic teachers in Orthodox Judaism.

Sociology of Religion

Bellah, Robert N., and others. *The Good Society*. Knopf 1991 $25.00. ISBN 0-679-40098-2. Rejecting a separation between the social sciences, philosophy, and public life, the authors make proposals about the role of "biblical religion" in America.

Berger, Peter. *Sacred Canopy: Elements of a Sociological Theory of Religion*. Doubleday 1990 $8.95. ISBN 0-385-07305-4. An influential theory centered on holding together "dialectically" such competing sociological theorists as Emile Durkheim and Max Weber.

Marty, Martin E., and R. Scott Appleby, eds. *Fundamentalisms Observed. The Fundamentalism Project*. Vol. 1. U. Ch. Pr. 1991 $40.00. ISBN 0-226-50877-3. The first of several planned volumes on fundamentalism in the major religions, featuring a very readable text with excellent bibliography.

Milbank, John. *Theology and Social Theory. Beyond Secular Reason*. Blackwell Pubs. 1990 $75.00. ISBN 0-631-14573-7. A very difficult book with an important argument that all secular social theories contain implicit theologies aptly characterized as neopagan.

O'Dea, Thomas. *The Sociology of Religion*. P-H $26.00. ISBN 0-13-821066-7. A good introduction, with test cases of American Catholicism and Mormonism.

Spiro, Melford E. *Buddhism and Society*. U. CA Pr. 1982 $14.95. ISBN 0-520-04672-2. Buddhism in Burmese society, with attention to the differences between the religious thought of Buddhist intellectual elites and that of the majority of Buddhists.

CONTEMPORARY ROMAN CATHOLIC THOUGHT

Contemporary Roman Catholic thought is quite diverse. It includes trends in traditionalism, postmodernism, liberation theologies, and others. What follows are topics in Roman Catholic religious thought that do not merely repeat examples in other sections of this chapter—official documents, select theologians, and introductions.

Introductions

Cunningham, Lawrence. *The Catholic Experience*. Crossroad NY 1987 $10.95. ISBN 0-8245-0811-4. Clear, readable essays on the Catholic experience.

Dulles, Avery. *The Catholicity of the Church*. OUP 1987 $14.95. ISBN 0-19-826695-2. A set of essays on Catholicism by a premier North American Catholic theologian.

Happel, Stephen, and David Tracy. *A Catholic Vision*. Fortress Pr. 1984 o.p. An introduction to the history of Catholic Christianity by Catholic liberal or revisionist theologians.

McCabe, Herbert. *The Teaching of the Catholic Church*. Liturgical Pr. 1986 $3.95. ISBN 0-8146-5608-0. A brief, clear exposition of essential Catholic teachings.

Strange, Roderick. *The Catholic Faith*. OUP 1986 $35.10. ISBN 0-19-826685-5. A series of lectures on Catholic faith as a way to know and love God.

Official Documents

Carlen, Claudia, IHM. *The Papal Encyclicals*. 5 vols. Pierian 1990 $495.00. ISBN 0-8434-0765-4. A collection of the English translations of official encyclicals (letters) from the bishops of Rome from 1740 to 1981.

Catechism of the Catholic Church. Paulist Pr. 1993 $19.95. ISBN 0-8091-3434-9. Addressed to Catholic bishops, this is the first official Catholic catechism proposed for worldwide use since the sixteenth century.

Flannery, Austin P., O.P., ed. *The Documents of Vatican II*. Eerdmans 1981 $13.95. ISBN 0-8434-0765-4. The key documents of probably the most important contemporary event for Catholics, Vatican II, a meeting or council of bishops and theologians and non-Catholic observers at the Vatican from 1962 to 1965.

Tanner, Norman, S.J., ed. *Decrees of the Ecumenical Councils*. 2 vols. Georgetown U. Pr. 1990 $210.00. ISBN 0-87840-490-2. The first complete collection (original languages with English translation) of about two dozen meetings of Christians to resolve various controversies.

Select Theologians

von Balthasar, Hans Urs. *The Von Balthasar Reader*. Ed. by Medard Kehl, S.J., and Werner Loser, S.J. Trans. by Robert J. Daly and Fred Lawrence. Crossroad NY 1982 $19.95. ISBN 0-8245-0468-2. An anthology of the writings of an important theological guardian of the Roman Catholic tradition in the twentieth century.

Fiorenza, Francis Schussler, and John P. Galvin. *Systematic Theology: Roman Catholic Perspectives*. 2 vols. Augsburg Fortress Pr. 1991 $42.95. ISBNs 0-8006-2460-2, 0-8006-2461-0. Essays with good bibliographies by Catholic theologians on central theological topics.

Rahner, Karl. *The Content of Faith: The Best of Karl Rahner's Theological Writings*. Ed. by Karl Lehmann and Albert Raffelt. Trans. by Harvey D. Egan, S.J. Crossroad NY 1992 $42.50. ISBN 0-8245-1221-9. Excellent anthology of the writings of perhaps the most important liberal Catholic theologian of this century, with references to primary and secondary literature.

Ratzinger, Joseph Cardinal. *Principles of Catholic Theology: Building Stones for a Fundamental Theology*. 1982 Trans. by Sister Mary Frances McCarthy, S.N.D. Ignatius Pr. 1987 $29.95. ISBN 0-89870-133-3. A set of theological essays by a major theological voice in Rome.

WOMEN'S ISSUES

Few issues have generated as much interesting and controversial reading in English as issues of women and religion. Various sections in this chapter

Sexuality

Becher, Jeanne, ed. *Women, Religion, and Sexuality: Studies on the Impact of Religious Teaching on Women.* TPI PA 1991 $16.95. ISBN 1-56338-013-7

Bogle, Darlene. *Strangers in a Christian Land.* Baker Bk. 1990 $7.99. ISBN 0-8007-9160-6

Bouhdiba, Abdelwahab. *Sexuality in Islam.* Trans. by Alan Sheridan. Routledge 1985 $55.00. ISBN 0-7100-9608-9. An "attempt to think through the mutual relationship of the sexual and the sacral within the Arabo-Muslim societies."

Cabezon, José Ignacio, ed. *Buddhism, Sexuality, and Gender.* State U. NY Pr. 1992 $59.50. ISBN 0-7914-0757-8. Explores questions relating to the position and experience of women and gay people in the Buddhist world focusing on Buddhist history, contemporary culture, Buddhist symbols, and homosexuality.

Cahill, Lisa Sowle. *Between the Sexes: Foundations for a Christian Ethics of Sexuality.* Paulist Pr. 1985 $9.95. ISBN 0-8006-1834-3. A clear statement of a moderately liberal Roman Catholic position on crucial issues.

Dynes, Wayne R., and Stephen Donaldson, eds. *Homosexuality and Religion and Philosophy. Studies in Homosexuality.* Vol. XII. Garland 1992 $60.00. ISBN 0-8153-0767-5. One of a series of volumes on homosexuality, focusing on Judeo-Christian religious traditions.

Grace, James H. *God, Sex, and the Social Project: The Glassboro Papers on Religion and Human Sexuality. Symposium Ser.* Vol. 2. E. Mellen 1978 $89.95. ISBN 0-88946-900-8

Hanigan, James P. *Homosexuality: The Test Case for Christian Social Ethics.* Paulist Pr. 1988 $9.95. ISBN 0-8091-2944-2. Deals with both the "homosexual situation" and the "biblical and theological tradition" laying the groundwork for discussion on topics such as sin and human freedom, chastity, and the relationship between sexuality and vocation.

Nelson, James B. *Between Two Gardens: Reflections on Sexuality and Religious Experience.* Pilgrim OH 1983 $9.95. ISBN 0-8298-0681-4

Parrinder, Geoffrey. *Sex in the World's Religions.* OUP 1980 $13.95. ISBN 0-1952-0202-3. A reliable overview.

Sapp, Stephen. *Sexuality, the Bible, and Science.* Bks. Demand repr. of 1977 ed. $38.00. ISBN 0-685-16263-X

Schmitt, Arno, and Tehoeda Sofer. *Sexuality and Eroticism among Males in Moslem Societies.* Harrington Pk. 1991 $26.95. ISBN 1-56024-047-4. Nineteen essays on male homosexuality among Moslems including personal accounts, historical and legal treatments, and reviews of literature and film.

Abortion

Blanchard, Dallas A., and Terry J. Prewitt. *Religious Violence and Abortion: The Gideon Project.* U. Press Fla. $39.95. ISBN 0-8130-1193-0. Examines the anti-abortion movement through the case study of the bombings of three abortion clinics in 1984. Deals with the links between religious ideology, political action, social isolation, and violence.

Burtchaell, James. *Rachel Weeping: The Case Against Abortion.* HarpC 1984 o.p. A Catholic theologian argues that abortion is wrong except for "the rare, rare instance when [pregnancy] is a mortal threat to the mother's life."

Callahan, Sidney, and Daniel Callahan, eds. *Abortion: Understanding Differences.* Plenum 1984 $49.50. ISBN 0-306-41640-9. The authors, one pro-life and one pro-choice, gather essays on the question, "How can it be . . . that intelligent people of good will . . . come down on different sides of the controversy?"

Coughlan, Michael J. *The Vatican, the Law, and the Human Embryo.* U. of Iowa Pr. 1990 $10.95. ISBN 0-87745-304-7. Draws on Catholic writings and history to explore the Vatican's positions on human life and abortion.

Coward, Harold G., Julius J. Lipner, and Katherine K. Young. *Hindu Ethics: Purity, Abortion, and Euthanasia.* State U. NY Pr. 1989 $49.50. ISBN 0-88706-763-8. An essay on the classical Hindu view on abortion and the moral status of the unborn, aimed at opening up a discussion "by and large taboo."

Fedoryka, Damian. *Abortion and the Ransom of the Sacred.* Christendom Pr. 1991 $3.95. ISBN 0-931888-40-9

Feldman, David M. *Birth Control in Jewish Law: Marital Relations, Contraception, and Abortion as Set Forth in the Classic Texts of Jewish Law.* NYU Pr. 1968 o.p. An important text on the necessary links between the topics in the title.

Glendon, Mary Ann. *Abortion and Divorce in Western Law: American Failures, European Challenges.* HUP 1987 $11.95. ISBN 0-674-00161-3. A comparative study of abortion and divorce laws in western countries. Argues that American laws are usually extreme relative to other western countries because of American individualism.

Harrison, B. W. *Our Right to Choose: Toward a New Ethic of Abortion.* Beacon Pr. 1983 $12.95. ISBN 0-8070-1415-X. A Christian, pro-choice argument seeking a "strategy that will simultaneously bring about both less reliance on abortion and less resort to coercion of women and enforced childbearing."

Kogan, Barry S., ed. *A Time to be Born and a Time to Die: The Ethics of Choice.* Aldine de Gruyter 1991 $44.95. ISBN 0-202-30388-8. Presents a broad range of religious perspectives and discussions on bioethical issues as they pertain to abortion.

Melton, J. Gordan, ed., and Gary L. Ward, contrib. ed. *The Churches Speak On: Abortion. Official Statements from Religious Bodies and Ecumenical Organizations.* Gale 1991 $32.00. ISBN 0-8103-7219-3. Part of series *The Churches Speak On*, useful for a variety of topics in ethics. The volumes include Christian churches, Jewish synagogues, and other religious bodies.

Stallsworth, Paul. *The Church and Abortion.* Abingdon 1993 $10.95. ISBN 0-687-07852-0. Examines the Church's stance on abortion from an historical and theological perspective.

Swyhart, Barbara A. *Bioethical Decision-making: Releasing Religion from the Spiritual.* Bks. Demand repr. of 1975 ed. $35.00. ISBN 0-8357-7223-3. Examines a number of issues, including abortion, in ways that seek to find a middle ground of opinion.

Welton, K. B. *Abortion Is Not a Sin: A New-Age Look at an Age-Old Problem.* Pandit Pr. 1988 $9.95. ISBN 0-944361-00-5. Three abortion studies focus on the recent history of abortion in the United States, revealing both the ongoing debate and a broad division based on religious, moral, medical, and feminist grounds.

Wenz, Peter S. *Abortion Rights As Religious Freedom.* Temple U. Pr. 1991 $49.95. ISBN 0-87722-857-4. Presents an interesting perspective on this most controversial issue.

WAR AND PEACE

Religious thought on war embraces absolute nonviolence and holy wars, as well as arguments that some wars are just and some are unjust.

Ferguson, John. *War and Peace in the World's Religions.* OUP 1978 $5.95. ISBN 0-19-520073-X. A good, brief introduction to war and peace in many religions.

Khadduri, M. *War and Peace in the Law of Islam.* AMS Pr. 1955 $29.50. ISBN 0-4464-10925-X. Remains the best reconstruction of the classical legal theory of Islam.

Ling, Trevor. *Buddhism, Imperialism, and War. Burma and Thailand in Modern History.* Humanities 1979 o.p. How Buddhist nations are no strangers to the battlefield.

Merton, Thomas, ed. *Gandhi on Non-Violence. Selected Texts from Gandhi's Non-Violence in Peace and War.* New Dir. Pr. 1965 $4.95. ISBN 0-8112-0097-3. Selections from *Non-Violence*, a two-volume work, published in 1942 and 1949, by Gandhi, the most important advocate of nonviolence in the twentieth century.

Peters, Rudolph. *Islam and Colonialism: The Doctrine of Jihad in Modern History.* Mouton 1979 $29.95. ISBN 3-11-010022-3. The doctrine of *jihad* (struggle, not always armed), reinterpreted by modern Muslims as a response to Western colonialism.

Ramsey, Paul. *The Just War: Force and Political Responsibility*. Littlefield 1991 $19.95. ISBN 0-8226-3014-1. A Christian theologian discusses the conditions under which war can be "just."

United States Catholic Conference. *The Challenge of Peace: God's Promise and Our Response*. US Catholic 1983. $3.95. ISBN 1-55586-863-0. A "Pastoral Letter on War and Peace" from the American Catholic Bishops, rearticulating the classic notion that there are just wars, while leaving room for some individuals to conscientiously object.

World Council of Churches. *Peace and Disarmament. Documents of the World Council of Churches and the Roman Catholic Church*. The Commission of the Churches on International Affairs of the World Council of Churches, and the Pontifical Commission "Iustitia et Pax" 1982 o.p. A statement by a fellowship of Christian churches.

Yoder, John Howard. *Nevertheless: The Varieties and Shortcomings of Religious Pacifism*. Herald Pr. 1971 $9.95. ISBN 0-8361-1661-5. A Mennonite Christian theologian sorts out the differences among over a dozen forms of pacifism.

LIBERATION THEOLOGY

Liberation theology grew out of movements in Latin America during the 1960s centering on the importance of revolutionary action on behalf of the poor. The term is now used to refer to any theology centered on revolutionary action on behalf of any oppressed group (e.g., African, African American, or Black theology; Feminist theology; Gay or Lesbian theology, etc.). While the label liberation theology is used primarily by Christians, comparable issues in other religions could be studied by reading books on the social ethics of these religions (see the section on "Religious Ethics Today").

Ateek, Naim S., Marc H. Ellis, and Rosemary Radford Ruether, eds. *Faith and the Intifada: Palestinian Christian Voices*. Orbis Bks. 1992 $13.95. ISBN 0-88344-808-4. A collection of papers from a 1990 conference in Tantur, Israel, on Palestinian Liberation Theology.

Boff, Leonardo, and Clodovis Boff. *Introducing Liberation Theology*. Trans. by Paul Burns. Orbis Bks. 1987 $24.95. ISBN 0-88344-575-1. A brief, excellent introduction to Christian liberation theology.

Chopp, Rebecca S. *The Praxis of Suffering: An Interpretation of Liberation and Political Theologies*. Orbis Bks. 1986 $16.95. ISBN 0-88344-256-6. An introduction to several major political (European, especially German) and liberation (Latin American) theologies.

Cone, James H., and Gayraud Wilmore, eds. *Black Theology: A Documentary History*. 2 vols. Orbis Bks. 1993 $18.95 ea. ISBNs 0-88344-853-X, 0-88344-773-8. Vol. 1 *1966–1979*. Vol. 2 *1980–1992*. An anthology of texts, including texts in what is sometimes called "black theology of liberation."

Guttierrez, Gustavo. *A Theology of Liberation: History, Politics, and Salvation*. Trans. and ed. by Sister Caridad Inda and John Eagleson. Orbis Bks. 1988 $34.95. ISBN 0-88344-543-3. Originally published in Peru in 1971, this is the revised version of the definitive work on liberation theology. With a new introduction.

Loades, Ann. *Feminist Theology: A Reader*. Westminster John Knox 1990 $19.99. ISBN 0-664-25129-3. Good representative essays with a helpful bibliography from an important movement struggling with conflicts from within and without.

McGovern, Art. *Liberation Theology and Its Critics: Toward an Assessment*. Orbis Bks. 1989 $16.95. ISBN 0-88344-595-6. An account of the theological, political, and ecclesiastical criticisms of liberation theology.

Sizemore, Russell F., and Donald K. Swearer. *Ethics, Wealth, and Salvation: A Study in Buddhist Social Ethics*. U. of SC Pr. 1990 $34.95. ISBN 0-87249-612-0. Although Buddhists do not practice theology or, therefore, liberation theology, these are good essays on Buddhist social ethics, largely by non-Buddhist scholars.

CHARACTER, AFFECTIONS, AND VIRTUES

It is tempting to think that ethics is primarily about decisions we make or that it consists of religions addressing practical issues. A major way to resist this temptation has been to develop an ethics that takes seriously the proposal that ethics concerns who we are (our character) rather than the decisions we make. This requires thinking about the way in which different religious communities nurture different sorts of affections (emotions, passions, and feelings) and virtues (dispositions and powers). The comparative study of this issue in different religious communities has barely begun.

Hauerwas, Stanley. *Character and the Christian Life: A Study in Theological Ethics*. U. of Notre Dame Pr. 1989 $11.95. ISBN 0-268-00772-1. A good overview of the issue of character and the virtues in Aristotle and Aquinas by a Christian theologian critical of other Christian theologians for ignoring these issues.

MacIntyre, Alasdair. *After Virtue: A Study in Moral Theory*. U. of Notre Dame Pr. 1984 $11.95. ISBN 0-268-00611-3. A very influential philosophical study, centered on a narrative of the eclipse of issues of virtue in modernity.

Yearley, Lee. *Mensius and Aquinas: Theories of Virtue and Conceptions of Courage*. State U. NY Pr. 1990 $49.50. ISBN 0-7914-0431-5. Very good comparison between a Confucian master (born around 372 B.C.) and a medieval Christian theologian.

PERSPECTIVES ON RITUAL, WORSHIP, AND RELIGIOUS COMMUNITY

Religious communities encourage their members to mark a variety of special occasions in life. Such occasions can embrace common human events (birth and death, waking up and going to sleep, seasonal transitions, etc.) as well as special festivals in particular religions (Passover for Jews, Easter for Christians, Ramadan for Muslims, etc.). The repeated patterns of action on such occasions are sometimes called "rituals." For surveys of the rituals of diverse religions, see the section "Introductions to Religions" found at the beginning of this chapter. The best texts to read are, of course, books of meditation, prayer, song, and worship relating to actual rituals. The following are select commentaries about these rituals.

Conze, E. *Buddhist Meditation*. St. Mut. 1959 $70.00. ISBN 0-317-94192-5. The most important Buddhist rituals are discussed in this still-useful book, originally published in 1953.

Eliade, Mircea. *Rites and Symbols of Initiation: The Mysteries of Birth and Rebirth*. Trans. by Willard R. Trask. HarpC 1965 $10.00. ISBN 0-06-131236-3. One of many texts by an important student of religions, emphasizing the contrast between the initiatory rites of archaic societies and the lack thereof in modern societies.

Grimes, Ronald L. *Beginnings in Ritual Studies*. U. Pr. of Amer. 1982 $54.75. ISBN 0-8191-2210-6. Sketches of a theory of ritual, emphasizing "the priority of persons in action" in rituals.

Jones, Cheslyn, Geoffrey Wainwright, and Edward Yarnold, eds. *The Study of Liturgy*. OUP 1978 $17.96. ISBN 0-19-520076-4. Dozens of essays on major aspects of Christian worship.

Lessa, William, and Evon Z. Vogt. *Reader in Comparative Religion: An Anthropological Approach*. HarpC 1971 $45.00. ISBN 0-06-043-991-2. A good anthology, including a section on the anthropological study of rituals.

Millgram, Abraham. *Jewish Worship*. JPS Phila. 1971 $18.95. ISBN 0-8276-0003-8. The history of Jewish worship, with useful index and English bibliography.

Parrinder, Geoffrey. *Worship in the World's Religions.* Littlefield 1976 $14.25. ISBN 0-8226-0316-0. A survey of the world's religions.

Ray, Benjamin C. *African Religions: Symbol, Ritual, and Community. Prentice-Hall Studies in Religion Ser.* Ed. by John P. Reeder and John F. Wilson. P-H 1976 ISBN 0-13-018630-9. Includes a chapter on ritual that discusses the practice of animal sacrifice.

Turner, Victor W. *The Ritual Process: Structure and Anti-Structure.* Cornell Univ. Press 1977 $10.95. ISBN 0-8014-9163-0. Begins with a description of the religion and rituals of the Ndembu of northwestern Zambia in Africa and goes on to develop a theory of ritual centered on "liminality."

Wainwright, Geoffrey. *Doxology: The Praise of God in Worship, Doctrine, and Life: A Systematic Theology.* OUP 1980 $35.00. ISBN 0-19-520192-2. The major treatment of ritual, worship, and community by a Christian theologian.

INTERRELIGIOUS DIALOGUE

While religious wars continue in many parts of the world, modernity has also brought more diverse and competing forms of religious thought into closer contact under conditions of peace than any previous era. One question this raises for each religion is: What shall be our beliefs about, as well as attitudes and policies toward, these other religions, their individual members, their practices, and their teachings? There is no consensus on how to answer such questions within (much less among) any of the larger religions. A few religious thinkers propose that religions are so different that no real dialogue is possible between them—or that religions basically "all say the same thing" so that no dialogue and debate are really necessary. Many more thinkers reject these alternatives and seek for ways in which to preserve their own religion's identity while seeking the truths and good in other religions.

Christian, William A. *Oppositions of Religious Doctrines: A Study of the Logic of Dialogue among Religions.* Herder and Herder 1972 o.p. An advanced study of the different sorts of oppositions that might emerge in interreligious dialogue, featuring a description of the notion of "unrestricted importance."

Coward, Harold, ed. *Modern Indian Responses to Religious Pluralism.* State U. NY Pr. 1987 $49.50. ISBN 0-88706-571-6. Representative essays on responses from within Hinduism as well as from other religions within India, such as Parsi, Muslim, Sikh, Christian, and Buddhist.

Croner, Helga, and Leon Klenicki, eds. *Issues in the Jewish-Christian Dialogue: Jewish Perspectives on Covenant, Mission and Witness.* ADL 1983 $7.95. ISBN 0-686-95172-7. A set of essays by Jewish scholars on the problems of the day and in response to various statements of Christian churches on Jewish-Christian relations.

D'Costa, Gavin, ed. *Christian Uniqueness Reconsidered: The Myth of a Pluralistic Theology of Religions.* Orbis Bks. 1990 $39.95. ISBN 0-88344-687-1. A set of essays (in debate with Hick and Knitter below) arguing that the contribution Christians must make to interreligious dialogue is to be authentic Christians.

Hick, John. *God Has Many Names.* Westminster John Knox 1982 $10.99. ISBN 0-664-24419-X. A major advocate of the claim that all religions are equal and valid paths to the one divine reality.

Hick, John, and Paul Knitter, eds. *The Myth of Christian Uniqueness.* Orbis Bks. 1987 $16.95. ISBN 0-88344-602-2. A set of essays suggesting that participating in interreligious dialogue will require changing fundamental Christian convictions.

Jayatilleke, K. N. *The Buddhist Attitude to Other Religions.* Wisdom MA 1975 o.p. A brief essay by an important Buddhist scholar arguing that Buddhism has been able to combine "missionary zeal" and "critical tolerance" of other religions.

World Council of Churches. *Guidelines on Dialogue with People of Living Faiths and Ideologies.* Wrld Coun. Churches 1979 o.p. Proposals on interreligious dialogue from a major fellowship of Christian churches and communions.

CHRONOLOGY OF AUTHORS

Rahner, Karl. 1904–1984
Levinas, Emmanuel. 1906–
Gustafson, James M. 1925–
Nasr, Seyyed Hossein. 1933–

Tenzin Gyatso, The Dalai Lama. 1935–
Ruether, Rosemary Radford. 1936–

GUSTAFSON, JAMES M. 1925–

James M. Gustafson grew up in what he has called "an immigrant sectarian community" in Michigan. He served in Burma and India during World War II and received a B.S. from Northwestern University (1948), a B.D. from the University of Chicago (1951), and a Ph.D. from Yale University (1955). After serving as a pastor of a Congregational church, he taught at Yale from 1955 to 1972 and at the University of Chicago Divinity School from 1972 to 1987. Since then he has been Henry R. Luce Professor of Humanities and Comparative Studies at Emory University in Atlanta, Georgia.

Gustafson's life in diverse cultures, as well as the lessons he learned from such thinkers as James Luther Adams, brother of Reinhold Niebuhr H. RICHARD NIEBUHR, and ERNST TROELTSCH prompted him to prefer relativism to objectivism in his approach to religion. Under relativism, moral good is relative to particular eras or social groups, while objectivism maintains that there is some ultimate and unchanging moral good or truth that any disinterested agent can realize and attain. However, Gustafson was dissatisfied with the tendency of relativism to yield to subjectivism, the notion that moral good is simply whatever particular persons or subjects decide it is. In matters ethical, such subjectivism requires that the world exists only for the benefit of the human species; in matters religious, subjectivism turns God into an instrument for satisfying human wants. Both are variants of what Gustafson calls "anthropocentrism" (i.e. the notion that human beings, *anthropoi*, are at the center of things).

Gustafson therefore developed a strategy for handling this problem of taking seriously the relative and the objective without succumbing to relativism or objectivism. He found that theology must relate four "base points": an interpretation of God, of the world, of persons as moral agents, and of how such persons should make moral choices. One's interpretation of these base points should be judged in relation to four "sources": the Christian tradition, philosophy, science, and human experience. A theocentric perspective holds all these together by showing that religion is basically a matter of the affections (in the sense that JONATHAN EDWARDS used the term) and that these affections intimate a sovereign power who holds sway over us, even and especially in the face of the unresolved ambiguities and tragedies of our lives. In his work, *Ethics from a Theocentric Perspective* (1981), Gustafson expresses his belief that the leitmotif of a theocentric ethics is that "we are to conduct life so as to relate all things in a manner appropriate to their relations to God." While his theological critics have argued that he pays more attention to philosophy, science, and experience than to Christian tradition, his philosophical critics might find that his religiosity escapes the standard criticisms of religious thought, for Gustafson takes modern science very seriously.

BOOKS BY GUSTAFSON

Christ and the Moral Life. HarpC 1968 o.p. An analysis of the diverse roles that Jesus Christ plays in the thought of different ethicians.

Ethics from a Theocentric Perspective. Vol. 1 *Theology and Ethics.* U. Ch. Pr. 1981 $14.95. ISBN 0-226-31113-9. The nature of ethics, Gustafson's preference for the Reformed tradition, and the nature of the relations between God and humanity.

Ethics from a Theocentric Perspective. Vol. 2. *Ethics and Theology.* U. Ch. Pr. 1984 $17.95. ISBN 0-226-31111-2. An analysis of some particular theologians and philosophers as well as select issues in ethics, such as marriage and family, suicide, population and nutrition, and biomedical funding.

Protestant and Roman Catholic Ethics: Prospects for Rapprochement. U. Ch. Pr. 1978 $10.95. ISBN 0-226-31107-4. Mediates between Catholics and Protestants on some "persistent polarities": being and becoming, order and dynamics, continuity and change, nature and grace, law and gospel.

BOOK ABOUT GUSTAFSON

Beckley, Harlan R., and Charles M. Swezey. *James M. Gustafson's Theocentric Ethics: Interpretations and Assessments.* Mercer Univ. Pr. 1988 $34.95. ISBN 0-86554-307-0. Papers from a 1985 symposium on Gustafson's ethics.

LEVINAS, EMMANUEL. 1906–

Emmanuel Levinas was born in Kovno, Lithuania, to an Orthodox Jewish family. Hebrew was the first language that he learned to read; he also acquired a love of the Russian classics, particularly works by PUSHKIN (see Vol. 2) and TOLSTOY (see Vol. 2), which first stirred his philosophical interests. Levinas studied in Strasbourg, Freiburg, and Paris, developing a particular interest in the philosophers HENRI BERGSON, EDMUND HUSSERL, and MARTIN HEIDEGGER (see also Vol. 5). He became a French citizen and eventually a prisoner during World War II, at which time his entire family was exterminated. After the war, Levinas taught at Poitiers, Nanterre, and eventually became professor of philosophy at the Sorbonne in 1973. He has also been deeply involved in the problems of Western Jews, including active membership in the Alliance Israelite Universelle, an organization established in 1860 to promote Jewish emancipation.

The experience of the ravages of totalitarianism during World War II convinced Levinas that only a rediscovery of the specificity of Judaism could deliver the modern world from itself. Levinas's central concern is with "the other"—not the self or the cosmos, but the faces of other persons who make a claim on us and provide traces of the working of an infinite other. *Totality and Infinity* (1961) is a central but very difficult text. In it Levinas argues that Western philosophy has been captured by a notion of totality from which nothing is distant, exterior, or other and that, thus, when persons who are different confront such totalistic ways of living and thinking, they go to war. Moving beyond totality and war requires a notion of transcendence or infinity, which can bring peace. In fact, religion is, according to Levinas, "the bond that is established between the same and the other without constituting a totality." Levinas maintains that "the existence of God is not a question of an individual soul's uttering logical syllogisms. It cannot be proved. The existence of God . . . is sacred history itself, the sacredness of man's relation to man through which God may pass. God's existence is the story of his revelation in biblical history."

Levinas has said that the most common objection to his thought is that it is utopian, for people are always asking, "Where did you ever see the ethical relation [with the other] practiced?" But Levinas is convinced that, although concern for the other is "always other than the 'ways of the world,'" there are "many examples of it in the world." This is the reason that his writings on Judaism, such as *Difficult Freedom* (1963) and *Nine Talmudic Essays* (1968), are at least as important as his philosophical texts.

BOOKS BY LEVINAS

Difficult Freedom: Essays on Judaism. 1963. Trans. by Sean Hand. Johns Hopkins 1990 $29.95. ISBN 0-8018-4074-0. Essays from the 1950s to the 1970s, including an autobiographical essay entitled "Signatures."

Ethics and Infinity. Trans. by Richard A. Cohen. Duquesne 1985 $12.00. ISBN 0-8207-0178-5. A collection of radio interviews from 1981, which provide a very good introduction to Levinas.

The Levinas Reader. Ed. by Sean Hand. Blackwell Pubs. 1989 $16.95. ISBN 0-631-16446-4. An excellent anthology of Levinas's books and essays. A good starting point after reading the "dialogue" with Levinas in Richard Cohen's *Face to Face with Levinas*.

Nine Talmudic Readings. 1968. Trans. by Annette Aronowicz. Ind. U. Pr. 1990 $29.95. ISBN 0-253-33379-2. Levinas not only provides readings of the Talmud (teachings of the rabbis) but also tries to recover a Talmudic way of reading such texts for our time.

Otherwise than Being or Beyond Essence. 1974. Trans. by Alphonso Lingis. Kluwer Ac. 1981 $55.00. ISBN 90-247-2374-4. Dedicated to victims of the Nazis, this sequel to *Totality and Infinity* analyzes our relations to the other as responsibility, substitution, and expiation for an other.

Totality and Infinity: An Essay on Exteriority. 1961. Trans. by Alphonso Lingis. Duquesne 1979. $12.95. ISBN 0-391-01004-2.

BOOKS ABOUT LEVINAS

van Beeck, Frans Jozef, S.J. *Loving the Torah More than God? Towards a Catholic Appreciation of Judaism*. Loyola 1989 $9.95. ISBN 0-8294-0620-4. Includes Levinas's "To Love the Torah More than God" and a response.

Bernasconi, Robert, and Simon Critchley, eds. *Re-reading Levinas*. Ind. U. Pr. 1991 $37.50. ISBN 0-253-31179-9. Although most of these essays are not explicitly on issues of religious thought, the book's index entries "God" and "Judaism" are a guide to these themes throughout the book.

Cohen, Richard A., ed. *Face to Face with Levinas*. State U. NY Pr. 1986 $19.95. ISBN 0-887606258-X. Includes a very clear and helpful "Dialogue with Emmanuel Levinas" as well as essays on Levinas's philosophy.

NASR, SEYYED HOSSEIN. 1933–

Nasr was born in Tehran, Iran, in 1933 to a family of religious scholars and traditional physicians. His endeavor to live in the tension between East and West began early. He attended high school in the United States, and he received a B.S. from the Massachusetts Institute of Technology in 1954 and a Ph.D. from Harvard University in the history of science and learning (with special concentration in Islamic science and philosophy) in 1958. During this time Nasr was influenced not only by his teachers but also by the writings of such Eastern scholars as Rene Gueron, A. K. Coomaraswamy, and Frithjof Schuon. In 1958 he returned to Iran as professor of the history of science and philosophy at Tehran University; he also became dean and vice-chancellor of Tehran University and rector of Arymehr University. Here Nasr renewed his training in

Islam under a number of religious authorities, including some leading philosophers. Because of the turmoil of the Iranian Revolution, Nasr returned to the United States to teach at Temple University from 1979 to 1984. Since 1984 he has been university professor of Islamic studies at George Washington University.

The breadth of these spiritual, political, and academic experiences of East and West forms the background to Nasr's many writings in philosophy, theology, metaphysics, science, art, and spirituality. *Ideals and Realities of Islam* (1966) shows Nasr as a religious thinker, concerned with studying Islam "from its own point of view, from within the tradition." He aims to undertake such study in a way that is intelligible to a Western audience but that does not yield to the "desacralization" of knowledge that has taken place in the modern West. The way to do this, Nasr suggests in *Knowledge and the Sacred* (1966), is to recognize that there is a traditional sacred or "principal" knowledge of the sacred in which each religion is "*the* religion and *a* religion," a vision of the Absolute in its relatively absolute forms. The central form for attaining this knowledge is prayer, not primarily the prayer of people to God, but the prayer in which God "invokes His own Name in the temple of the purified body and soul of his theomorphic creature." For Nasr, the climax of the Islamic tradition is the form of Muslim mysticism generally known as Sufism (derived from the word *Sufi*, meaning "one who wears undyed wool," indicating the simplicity involved).

Books by Nasr

Ideals and Realities of Islam. 1966. Unwin Hyman 1988 o.p. Six lectures on key features of Islam—The Qur'an, the Prophet, the *Shari'ah*, the *Tariqah*, and the relations between Sunni and Shi'ite Islam.

Islamic Spirituality: Foundations. World Spirituality: An Encyclopedic History of the Religious Quest Ser. Vol. 19 Crossroad NY 1991 $49.50. ISBN 0-8245-0767-3. Covers the origins and traditions of Islam, along with sections on Sufism and knowledge.

Islamic Spirituality: Manifestations. World Spirituality: An Encyclopedic History of the Religious Quest Ser. Vol. 20 Crossroad NY 1991 $49.50. ISBN 0-8245-0767-3. Covers Islamic spirituality as manifest in history and culture (arts and literature, architecture and poetry, philosophy and the sciences).

Knowledge and the Sacred: The Gifford Lectures, 1981. State U. of NY Pr. 1981 $44.50. ISBN 0-7914-0176-6

Man and Nature: The Spiritual Crisis in Modern Man. 1968. Thorsons SF 1991 $12.95. ISBN 0-04-440620-7. An early diagnosis of the ecological crisis.

Sufi Essays. State U. of NY Pr. 1991 $16.95. ISBN 0-87395-389-4. A collection of essays on the history and contemporary relevance of the Islamic mystical quest.

Book about Nasr

Chittick, William C. *The Works of Seyyed Hossein Nasr Through His Fortieth Birthday.* Univ. Utah (Middle East Center) 1977 o.p. Nasr's writings through 1977, with a helpful biographical preface.

RAHNER, KARL. 1904–1984

Karl Rahner was born in Freiburg in Breisgau, Germany, the fourth of seven brothers and sisters. In 1922 he entered the Jesuits, a Roman Catholic religious order founded during the sixteenth century Catholic Reformation, and was ordained a priest in 1932. Rahner began his academic career as a student of the history of philosophy and took courses under MARTIN HEIDEGGER (see also Vol. 5). However, his dissertation—now regarded as a classic for bringing ST.

THOMAS AQUINAS and modern philosophy into dialogue—was not accepted by Heidegger. Rahner next pursued and received his Ph.D. in theology at the University of Innsbruck in 1936 and spent his life teaching at various German universities. Rahner was centrally concerned with addressing the pastoral problems of Catholics (especially in Germany) from World War II through the reforms in Catholic life and thought brought about by the Second Vatican Council (1962–1965) to the situation of the new "world church" during the 1970s and 1980s.

Rahner's thought is sometimes divided into three stages. In the earliest stage, he studied and wrote on the traditional sources of Catholic theology, particularly the theologians of early Christianity and the school theology or scholasticism that had become important for Catholic theology. In the second stage, Rahner expanded and deepened a question he had asked since his early days as a student of philosophy: What are the conditions of the possibility for God's revelation to speak to the experiences of modern men and women? This is sometimes called Rahner's transcendental theology, or, more accurately, the transcendental moment of his theology. This stage roughly coincided with the massive reforms that took place in Catholic life and thought as a result of the Second Vatican Council. Rahner wrote many of his approximately 4,000 publications during this period, writing on relations with non-Catholic churches, other religions, and the philosophical world of unbelief. The third stage of Rahner's thought consisted of contemplating the wintry season in which he thought the church was living after Vatican II. He responded to his critics, some of whom thought that his transcendental theology distracted from the proclamation of God's all-consuming love and some of whom thought that it distracted from the political tasks called for by the existence of oppressed human beings. Most important, he continued his effort to speak to the concrete situation of believers in modernity.

BOOKS BY RAHNER

The Content of Faith: The Best of Karl Rahner's Theological Writings. Ed. by Karl Lehmann and Albert Raffelt. Trans. by Harvey D. Egan, Crossroad NY 1982 $42.50. ISBN 0-8245-1221-9. Excellent anthology, with further references to primary and secondary literature.

Foundations of Christian Faith: An Introduction to the Idea of Christianity. Trans. by William V. Dych. Crossroad NY 1982 $16.95. ISBN 0-8245-0523-9. Perhaps Rahner's most important book, although very difficult reading for the beginner.

Karl Rahner in Dialogue: Conversations and Interviews 1965–1982. Ed. by Paul Imhof and Hubert Biallowons. Trans. by Harvey D. Egan. Crossroad NY 1986 $22.50. ISBN 0-8245-0749. A good sampling of what it was like to hear Rahner answer questions about God, life, and his theology. Abridged by Egan.

Karl Rahner: Theologian of the Graced Search for Meaning. Ed. by Geffrey B. Kelly. Fortress Pr. 1992 $19.95. ISBN 0-8006-3400-4. Another good selection of texts, with useful commentary by the editor.

Theological Investigations. 1954–84. Vols. 1-17, 20, 22, 23. Crossroad NY $29.50. ea. Vol. 1 1975 ISBN 0-8245-0377-5. Vol. 2 *Man and the Church.* 1975 ISBN 0-8245-0378-3. Vol. 3 *Theology of the Spiritual Life.* ISBN 0-8245-0379-1. Vol. 4 *More Recent Writings.* ISBN 0-8245-0380-5. Vol. 5 *Later Writings.* ISBN 0-8245-0381-3. Vol. 6 *Concerning Vatican Council II.* ISBN 0-8245-0382-1. Vol. 7 *Further Theology of the Spiritual Life I.* ISBN 0-8245-0382-1. Vol. 8 *Further Theology of the Spiritual Life II.* ISBN 0-8245-0383-X. Vol. 9 *Writings of 1965-1967, I.* ISBN 0-8245-0384-8. Vol. 10 *Writings of 1965-1967, II.* ISBN 0-8245-0385-6. Vol. 11 *Confrontation I.* ISBN 0-8245-0386-4. Vol. 12 *Confrontation II.* ISBN 0-8245-0387-2. Vol. 13 *Theology, Anthropology, Christology.* ISBN 0-8245-0388-0. Vol. 14 *In Dialogue with the Future.* ISBN 0-

8245-0389-9. Vol. 15 *Penance in the Early Church*. ISBN 0-8245-0390-2. Vol. 16 *Experience of the Spirit: Source of Theology*. ISBN 0-8245-0025-3. Vol. 17 *Jesus, Man and Church*. ISBN 0-8245-0392-9. Vol. 22 *Humane Society and the Church of Tomorrow*. ISBN 0-8245-0924-2. Vol. 23 *Final Writings*. 1992 ISBN 0-8245-1165-4. Rahner's major theological essays, some written for academic audiences but many accessible to the general reader.

BOOKS ABOUT RAHNER

von Balthasar, Hans Urs. *The Moment of Christian Witness*. Trans. by Richard Beckley. Newman 1969 o.p. A polemic partly directed against Rahner (or, perhaps, abuses of Rahner's thought) for downplaying the primacy of God's revelation.

Dych, William V., S.J. *Karl Rahner*. Liturgical Pr. 1992 $11.95. ISBN 0-8146-5053-8. A good introduction with further bibliography.

Metz, Johannes. *Faith in History and Society: Toward a Practical Fundamental Theology*. Trans. by David Smith. Seabury 1980 o.p. A sympathetic student of Rahner, criticizes Rahner's transcendental method for downplaying the importance of the political.

O'Donovan, Leo, ed. *A World of Grace: An Introduction to the Themes and Foundations of Karl Rahner's Theology*. Crossroad NY 1980 $11.95. ISBN 0-8245-0406-2. Introductory essays on various topics in Rahner's theology.

RUETHER, ROSEMARY RADFORD. 1936–

Rosemary Radford Ruether was born in St. Paul, Minnesota, in 1936. She grew up in what she called "a relatively privileged, patriotic, and pious family." She began her college work at Scripps College in Claremont, California, and was interested in becoming an artist. In part provoked by a teacher in a medieval history class who mentioned that the Church did not oppose slavery or serfdom, Ruether developed an interest in early Christianity. She received her Ph.D. in history from Claremont Graduate School in 1965. During this time she became interested in the Second Vatican Council's reforms of the Roman Catholic church, as well as the civil rights movement (working, for example, as a Delta Ministry volunteer in Mississippi in 1965). Ruether taught at the School of Religion of Howard University, a black divinity school in Washington D.C., from 1965 to 1976. She has also been visiting professor at the divinity schools at Harvard and Yale universities. Since 1976 Ruether has been Georgia Harkness Professor at Garrett-Evangelical Theological Seminary in Evanston, Illinois.

Like her biography, Ruether's religious thought moves between two poles. She finds the legacy of the Christian and Western cultural heritage a story of both unjust domination (of nature and animals by people, of slaves by masters, of women by men, of poor by rich, of black by white, of Jews by Christians) and a struggle against such sin. Her books aim to expose these patterns of domination in the Christian and Western tradition, to explore the alternatives also present in this tradition (especially the prophets in the Hebrew Scriptures and the New Testament's vision of a universal redemptive community); and to bring these alternatives to bear on our contemporary circumstances. In *Sexism and God-Talk* (1983) her writing focuses on feminist theology, the "critical principle" of which is "the promotion of the full humanity of women"; but her interests range from anti-Semitism, as well as Palestinian Christian criticisms of Israel, to ecology.

Ruether's major political critics are conservatives as well as liberals who claim that her political socialism is utopian. Her major theological critics are radical feminists, who view Christianity as intrinsically sexist, and conservatives, who argue that the Christianity she conserves from the tradition bears

little resemblance to the central claims Christians need to make about Jesus
Christ and the triune God.

BOOKS BY RUETHER

Beyond Occupation: American, Jewish, and Palestinian Voices for Peace. Ed. by
Rosemary Ruether and Marc H. Ellis. Beacon Bks. 1990 o.p. A collection of essays on
one of the great intractable issues of our time. (Includes two essays by Ruether, "The
Occupation Must End" and "Beyond Anti-Semitism and Philo-Semitism").

Gaia & God. An Ecofeminist Theology of Earth Healing. HarpC 1992 $22.00. ISBN 0-06-
067022-3. Examines the Western tradition on the creation, destruction, and healing
of the world.

Gregory of Nazianzus. Rhetor and Philosopher. OUP 1969 o.p. A historical study of an
early Christian theologian.

Sexism and God-Talk: Toward a Feminist Theology. Beacon Pr. 1983 $14.00. ISBN 0-8070-
1104-5. A classic in feminist theology and excellent overview of Ruether's position
on topics ranging from God and Christ to Mariology and eschatology.

Womenguides: Readings Toward a Feminist Theology. Beacon Pr. 1985 $14.00. ISBN 0-
8070-1203-3. A collection of readings from old and new religions, with a commentary by Ruether.

BOOKS ABOUT RUETHER

Kimel, Alvin F., ed. *Speaking the Christian God: The Holy Trinity and the Challenge of
Feminism.* Eerdmans 1992 $21.95. ISBN 0-8028-0612-0. A collection of essays critical
of feminist theology, sometimes stridently so, with several references to Ruether.

Ramsey, William M. *Four Modern Prophets: Walter Rauschenbusch, Martin Luther King,
Jr., Gustavo Gutierrez, Rosemary Radford Ruether.* Westminster John Knox 1986 o.p.
A brief introduction with some study suggestions.

Snyder, Mary Hembrow. *The Christology of Rosemary Radford Ruether. A Critical
Introduction.* Twenty-Third 1988 $12.95. ISBN 0-89622-358-2. A sympathetic intro-
duction, with comparison of Ruether to those less skeptical of traditional theology.

TENZIN GYATSO, THE (14th) DALAI LAMA. 1935– (NOBEL PRIZE 1989)

The Dalai Lama was born in 1935 in Tibet, where the traditional religion is
Buddhism. Dalai Lama (which loosely translates into "Ocean of Wisdom") is an
office in this Tibetan Buddhism dating to the fourteenth century. When Lhamo
Thondup (as he was named at birth) was almost 3 years old, he was discovered
to be an incarnation of the Dalai Lama and was taken to a monastery and
installed. The Dalai Lama is thought by some to be a living Buddha or even a
god-king. However, His Holiness the Dalai Lama XIV says that he is "just a
human being, and incidentally a Tibetan, who chooses to be a Buddhist monk";
"Dalai Lama" is merely a title that signifies an office he holds, although, as he
states in his autobiography *Freedom in Exile* (1990), he sees himself "spiritually
connected both to the thirteen previous Dalai Lamas, to Chenrezig [Bodhisattva
of Compassion], and to the Buddha himself."

In 1950 Chinese Communists invaded Tibet. His Holiness the Dalai Lama was
receptive to the Communists, finding that "a synthesis of Buddhist and pure
Marxist doctrines . . . really would prove to be an effective way of conducting
politics." But he gradually became convinced that the Chinese Communists
were more nationalists than Marxists and escaped into exile in India in 1959. He
was awarded the Noble Peace Prize in 1989.

The Dalai Lama has said that he tries to live his life pursuing the Bodhisattva
ideal, that is, practicing "infinite compassion with infinite wisdom." He
frequently travels abroad, stressing three themes: the responsibility that human
beings have for each other, for all sentient beings, and for all of nature; the

harmony among all religions; and the cause of justice in Tibet. His many collections of essays in English stress these themes, as do his interpretations of the classic texts and traditions of Buddhism.

BOOKS BY TENZIN GYATSO

The Dalai Lama at Harvard: Lectures on the Buddhist Path to Peace. Trans. and ed. by Jeffrey Hopkins. Snow Lion 1988 $22.95. ISBN 0-937938-70-X. An introduction to Buddhist thought and practice prompted by a visit to the United States in 1981.
Freedom in Exile: The Autobiography of the Dalai Lama. Harper SF 1990 $22.95. ISBN 0-06-039116-2. The most recent autobiography.
Kindness, Clarity, and Insight. Trans. by Jeffrey Hopkins. Ed. by Jeffrey Hopkins and Elizabeth Napper. Snow Lion 1984 $10.95. ISBN 0-937938-18-1. A collection of the talks the Dalai Lama gave in his visits to Canada and the United States from 1979 to 1981.

BOOK ABOUT TENZIN GYATSO

Avedon, John. *In Exile from the Land of Snows.* Random 1985 $14.95. ISBN 0-394-74071-8. A clear, reliable biography.

Name Index

In addition to authors of books, this index includes the names of persons mentioned in introductory essays, section introductions, biographical profiles, general bibliographic entries, and "Books about" sections. Throughout, however, persons mentioned only in passing—to indicate friendships, relationships, and so on—are generally not indexed. Editors, translators, and compilers are not indexed unless there is no specific author given for the work in question. Writers of the introductions, forewords, afterwords, and similar parts of works are not indexed. The names of individuals who are represented by separate biographical profiles appear in boldface, as do the page numbers on which their profiles appear.

Aaron, Richard I., 179, 738
Aaronson, Jerrold L., 384
Abbott, Nabia, 587
Abduh, Muhammad, 374, 375
Abel, Reuben, 19
Abelard, Peter, 93, 101, **105,** 111
Abelone, Henry, 789
Abelson, Joshua, 629
Abelson, Raziel, 19
Abe Masao, 363, 558
Aberle, David F., 467
Aboulafia, Mitchell, 308
Abraham, Antoine J., 577
Abraham of Troki, Isaac ben, 631
Abrahams, Israel, 622, 628
Achtemeier, Paul J., 817
Ackerman, Robert, 246, 477, 479
Ackerman, Susan E., 518
Ackrill, J. L., 66
Adams, Charles C., 374
Adams, Charles J., 5, 533
Adams, Evangeline, 860
Adams, Frederick, 22
Adams, Marilyn McCord, 120
Adams, Robert, 438
Adams, Robert M., 177
Adamski, George, 870
Adelmann, F. J., 30
Adkins, Arthur W., 47
Adler, Elkan N., 625
Adler, Hans G., 635
Adler, Margot, 865

Adler, Morris, 620
Adler, Mortimer J., 66, 260, **269**
Adorno, Theodor W., 271, 386, 390, **392,** 403
Aelred of Reivaulx, 101
Aeschylus, 474
Affifi, Abul E., 583
Afnan, Soheil M., 581
Agassiz, Louis, 235
Agera, Cassian R., 37
Agnon, S. Y., 599, 886
Agoratus, Steven, 532
Agrippa of Nettesheim, Henry Cornelius, 133
Agus, Jacob, 657
Ahad Ha'am, 657
Aharoni, Yohanan, 809
Ahern, Emily M., 530
Ahlstrom, S. E., 750
Ahmad, Aziz, 372, 567, 577
Aiken, Henry D., 159
Ajami, Fouad, 567, 577
Akeroyd, Richard H., 27
Akhavi, Shahrough, 567, 577
Akira, Hirakawa, 512
Aland, Barbara, 805
Aland, Kurt, 676, 794, 805, 817
Alan of Lille, 702
Albanese, Catherine, 841
Albert, Phyllis Cohen, 635
Albert the Great, 106
Albright, William F., 445, 806, 808, 822, **827**
Aldridge, Alfred Owen, 767

Alegria, Ricardo E., 466
Aletrino, L., 567
Alexander, Ian W., 27
Alexander, Peter, 179
Alexander, Robert L., 444
Alexander, Thomas G., 845
Alford, C. Fred, 408
Ali, Ameer, 372
Ali, Syed A., 587
Aliotta, Antonio, 271
Allan, D. F., 66
Allard, Jean-Louis, 307
Allen, Don C., 123
Allen, George, 548
Allen, Henry E., 577
Allen, H. J., 71
Allen, Michael J. B., 141
Allen, Percy S., 139
Allen, R. E., 50, 89
Allinson, Robert E., 522
Allione, Tsultrim, 543
Allison, David, 246
Allison, Henry E., 187, 206, 208
Almond, Philip C., 488
Alon, Gedalyahu, 604
Alpern, Henry, 16
Alpers, Anthony, 461
Alpert, Rebecca T., 659
Alston, William P., 19
Alter, Robert, 816, 822
Althaus, Paul, 778
Altholz, Josef L., 740
Althusser, Louis, 242
Altizer, Thomas J., 474
Altmann, Alexander, 209, 628

Altshuler, David, 638
Alves, Rubem, 747
Ambrose, A., 22
Ambrose, St., 702
Ames, Roger T., 498, 502, 512, 522, 534
Ames, Van Meter, 33, 859
Amir, Ali Syed, 567
Amore, Roy C., 503, 512
Amundsen, Darrel W., 893
Anderson, Bernhard W., 816
Anderson, C. Alan, 847
Anderson, C. Anthony, 324
Anderson, Fulton H., 165
Anderson, G. W., 816
Anderson, J. K., 91
Anderson, Margaret, 875
Anderson, Paul R., 34
Anderson, Scott, 845
Anderson, Walt, 859
Andersson, Christiane, 737
Andrae, Tor, 588
Andrews, Edward D., 849
Anesaki, Masaharu, 534, 536
Angeles, Peter A., 2, 12
Ankori, Zvi, 631
Annas, Julia, 55, 58, 66, 78
Anscombe, G.E.M., 344
Anselm of Canterbury, St., 93, 100, **107, 703**
Ansky, S., 657
Anthony, Dick, 857
Anton, John P., 47, 66, 78
Anyanwu, K. C., 369
Apel, Karl-Otto, 249
Apollodoros of Athens, 468
Apostel, L., 26
Apostolic Fathers, 703
Apparadurai, Arjun, 503
Appel, Gersion, 599, 627
Appiah, Anthony, 19
Appignanesi, Lisa, 27
Appleby, R. Scott, 890
Apuleius, 60, **469**
Aquila, Richard E., 16
Aquinas, St. Thomas, 19, 93, 101, 106, 108, 112, 113, **117,** 122, 136, 154, 260, 285, 305, 388, 695, 714, 882, 902
Aqvist, Lennart, 211
Arac, Jonathan, 400
Arbaugh, George E., 239
Arberry, Arthur J., 574, 587
Archer, John Clark, 588
Arendt, Hannah, 271, 299, 386, **394**
Arens, W., 466
Aris, Michael, 543
Aristophanes, 91, 474
Aristotle, 1, 44, 54, **64,** 76, 90, 93, 96, 98, 101, 103, 112, 115, 123, 136, 141,

150, 152, 153, 164, 221, 320, 363, 376, 401, 407, 580, 581, 695
Arjomand, Said A., 578
Arlen, Shelley, 479
Armour, Robert, 548
Armour, Rollin S., 723
Armstrong, Arthur H., 46, 55, 86
Armstrong, Brian G., 731, 761
Armstrong, D. M., 93, 685
Arnauld, Antoine, 163, 176, 181
Arndt, Judy, 644
Arnett, Willard Eugene, 327
Arni, Haim, 644
Arnold, E. Vernon, 59
Arnold, Thomas W., 567, 574
Arnott, Anne, 733
Aron, Joseph, 644
Aronson, Ronald, 330
Arrington, Leonard J., 845
Artz, Frederick B., 96
Arzt, Max, 599
Asante, Molefi Kete, 368
Aschkenasy, Nehama, 649
Ashby, Philip H., 507
Ashcraft, Morris, 831
Ashe, Geoffrey, 352
Ashkenazi, Michael, 539
Ashman, Chuck, 768
Ashmore, Jerome, 327
Ashton, Robert, 733
Ashtor, Eliyahu, 625
Ashworth, E. J., 123
Asmis, Elizabeth, 73
Ast, Freidrich, 79
Aston, W. G., 536
Atack, Jon, 869
Atanasijevic, Ksenija, 135
Ateek, Naim S., 896
Atherton, Margaret, 191
Atiya, Aziz S., 676, 692
Atkinson, Clarissa W., 698
Atkinson, James, 778
Atkinson, M. J., 86
Attar, Farid, 574
Attridge, Harold W., 709
Attwater, Donald, 275, 675, 755
Atulananda, Swami, 563
Auden, W. H., 47
Audi, Robert, 888
Augustine of Hippo, St., 63, 93, 98, 107, **108,** 114, 116, 150, 155, 674, 702, 704, 705, 757, 786
Aulen, Gustaf, 678, 886
Aune, Bruce A., 206, 262, 380
Aune, David E., 795
Aurelius, Marcus, 56, 59

Austin, John Langshaw, 261, **271**
Austin, M. M., 449
Austin, Norman, 428
Austin, Scott, 52
Ausubel, Nathan, 593
Avedon, John, 906
Aveni, Anthony F., 455, 457
Averroës, 96, 101, **580,** 581, 585
Avery-Peck, Alan J., 609
Aviad, Janet, 659
Avicenna, 96, 101, 149, 580, **581,** 582
Avineri, Shlomo, 232, 242, 655, 657
Avi-Yonah, Michael, 606, 808, 809
Avni, Haim, 635
Axelrad, Albert S., 648
Axinn, Sidney, 388
Ayer, Michael, 179
Ayer, Sir Alfred Jules, 41, 201, 237, 249, 262, **272,** 312, 324, 343, 344, 370
Ayers, Michael, 162
Ayoub, Mahmoud M., 587
Azad, Abu-l-Kalam, 372
Azmeh, Ariz al-, 584
Azzam, Abd-al-Rahman, 588

Ba'al Shem Tov (Israel Ben Eliezer), 660
Baba, Meher, 872
Babb, Lawrence A., 503, 507
Bachelard, Gaston, 273
Bachelard, Suzanne, 234
Bacon, Francis, 164, 173, 848
Bacon, Roger, 110, 115
Bacovcin, Helen, 755
Badham, Linda, 887
Badham, Paul, 887
Baeck, Leo, 615, **660**
Baer, Yitzhak, 623
Bagnell, Roger, 449
Baha'u'llah, 861
Bahadur, K. P., 501
Bahm, Archie J., 5
Bahn, Paul, 432, 436
Baier, Annette, 201
Bailey, Alice A., 858
Bailey, Cyril, 53, 73
Bailey, D. R., 72
Bailey, D. Sherwin, 678
Bain, Alexander, 244
Bainbridge, William Sims, 855
Bainton, Roland H., 139, 676, 678, 681, 691, 749, 778
Baird, Forrest, 23

Baird, Henry M., 731
Baird, Robert D., 422, 507, 516, 517, 562
Bak, Janos, 723
Bakan, David, 628
Baker, Derek, 725
Baker, G. P., 229
Baker, Leonard, 661
Bakhash, Shaul, 578
Bakhtiar, Laleh, 375
Bakhurst, David, 30
Baldick, Julian, 574
Baldry, H. C., 47
Baldwin, James, 862
Baldwin, James M., 13
Baldwin, John D., 309
Baldwin, John W., 695, 698
Baldwin, Lewis, 772
Baldwin, Thomas, 312
Bales, Eugene F., 13
Balibar, Etienne, 242
Balke, Willem, 761
Ball, Terence, 242
Ballard, Bruce W., 292
Ballestrem, K. G., 30
Ballou, Robert O., 5
Balmer, Randall, 752
Balthasar, Hans Urs von, 63, 891, 904
Balyuzi, M. M., 588
Balz, Albert G., 169, 187
Balzer, Marjorie M., 430
Bamberger, Bernard J., 596, 620, 648
Bangs, Carl, 731
Banton, Michael, 422
Baqir As-Sadr, Muhammad, 373
Barber, W. H., 177
Barbour, Hugh, 733
Barbour, Ian, 388
Bardgett, Frank D., 735
Barfield, Owen, 776
Barineau, R. Maurice, 341
Barker, Eileen, 855, 871
Barker, Ernest, 66, 79
Barker, John W., 682
Barnard, Frederick, 199
Barnard, L. W., 703
Barnavi, Eli, 593
Barnes, Barry, 406
Barnes, Hazel E., 262, 330
Barnes, Jonathan, 50, 56, 58, 66, 108
Barnes, Michael, 507, 509
Barnes, Timothy D., 709, 714
Barnstone, Willis, 810
Baron, Hans, 29, 123, 151
Baron, Salo W., 593, 596, 635
Barr, James, 817
Barraclough, Geoffrey, 691, 694

Barral, Mary R., 311
Barrer, N. Gerald, 516
Barrett, Charles K., 810
Barrett, C. K., 617
Barrett, Cyril, 344
Barrett, David B., 3, 716, 742
Barrett, Leonard E., 467
Barrett, William, 262
Barrow, Reginald H., 490
Barry, Colman J., 680, 719, 740
Bars, Henry, 307
Barth, Else M., 391
Barth, Karl, 254, 742, **757**, 759, 783, 787
Barthel, Diane L., 843
Bary, William Theodore de, 358, 497, 521, 523, 526, 540
Barzun, Jacques, 237
Bascom, William, 462
Basford, Terry K., 866
Basham, A. L., 351, 498
Basil, Robert, 866
Basil of Caesarea, St., 704, 705
Baskin, Judith, 649
Bassuk, Daniel E., 507
Batatu, John, 578
Bates, E. S., 878
Bateson, Gregory, 461
Batley, Edward, 208
Baudelaire, Charles, 329
Baudry, Leon, 104
Bauer, Walter, 98, 685, 794
Bauer, Yehuda, 635
Baum, Alan, 210
Baum, Charlotte, 649
Bauschatz, Paul C., 437
Bayle, Malebranche, 176
Bayle, Pierre, 166, 173
Baynes, C. F., 525
Baynes, Kenneth, 316, 378
Baynes, Norman H., 682
Beals, Alan R., 503
Beare, J. I., 47
Beattie, D.R.G., 609
Beauchamp, Tom L., 19, 201
Beaumont, Ernest V., 34
Beauvoir, Simone de, 309, 329
Beaver, R. Pierce, 520
Becher, Jeanne, 894
Bechtel, William, 384
Beck, Leslie J., 169
Beck, Lewis White, 159, 206, 209, 219
Beck, Robert N., 19
Becker, Carl, 159
Becker, Charlotte B., 2, 13
Becker, Jürgen, 824
Becker, Lawrence C., 2, 13

Becker, Reinhard P., 124
Beckford, James A., 856
Beckley, Harlan R., 900
Bedani, Gino, 216
Bedau, Hugo, 386
Bedell, Gary, 19
Bedell, Kenneth B., 5
Bednorowski, Mary F., 841
Beers, William, 892
Begin, Menachem, 642
Behler, Ernest, 292
Beidelman, Thomas O., 492
Beiser, Frederick C., 16, 159, 209, 233
Beit-Hallahmi, Benjamin, 643
Beker, J. Christian, 824
Belfiore, Elizabeth, 67
Belier, Wouter W., 472
Belkin, Samuel, 608
Bell, Catherine, 426
Bell, David, 229, 234
Bell, Diane, 461
Bell, Richard, 587
Bell, Rudolph M., 698, 701
Bellah, Robert N., 422, 424, 540, 752, 855, 890
Belth, Nathan C., 638
Benardete, Seth, 89
Benedict, Ruth, 477, 534
Benedict of Nursia, St., 705
Benhabib, Seyla, 404
Benko, Stephen, 682
Benn, Charles D., 527
Bennett, John G., 875
Bennett, Jonathan, 187, 206
Bennett, Lerone, Jr., 772
Bennigsen, Alexandre, 567
Benoit, Pierre, 887
Ben-Sasson, Haim, 593
Bension, Ariel, 629
Benson, Hugh H., 89
Bentham, Jeremy, 158, **190**, 243, 256
Bentley, Jerry H., 124
Benveniste, Emile, 435
Ben Zion, Raphael, 629
Berchman, Robert M., 670
Berdyaev, Nikolai A., 274, 334, **758**
Berg, Alban, 392
Bergendoff, Conrad J., 730
Berger, David, 623
Berger, Peter L., 424, 890
Bergin, Thomas G., 151
Bergman, Jerry, 863
Bergmann, Gustav, 222
Bergmen, Samuel Hugo, 646
Bergson, Henri, 219, 305, 314, 900
Berkeley, George, 12, 158, 166, 182, **191**, 211, 255
Berkhof, Hendrikus, 718
Berkovits, Eliezer, 646, 648

Berkson, William, 409
Berlin, Adele, 823
Berlin, Isaiah, 199, 216, 242
Berlo, Janet C., 457
Berman, A. K., 20
Bermant, Chaim, 635
Bernal, Ignacio, 455
Bernal, Martin, 446
Bernard of Clairvaux, St.,
    106, **111**, 706
Bernasconi, Robert, 292, 901
Bernauer, James W., 400
Berndt, Catherine H., 461
Berndt, Ronald M., 461
Bernotas, Bob, 845
Bernstein, Eckhard, 124
Bernstein, Richard, 404
Bernstein, Richard J., 225,
    249, 262, 292, 378
Berrin, Kathleen, 457
Berry, Christopher J., 201
Berry, Donald L., 662
Berry, Scott, 859
Berry, Thomas, 498, 512
Berryman, Philip, 747
Bertocci, Peter A., 34, 262
Besant, Annie, 548, 554,
    858, 879
Bethge, Eberhard, 760
Bett, Henry, 149
Bettelheim, Bruno, 430
Bettenson, Henry, 680
Bettini, Maurizio, 448
Betz, Hans Dieter, 451, 490
Bevan, E., 55
Beversluis, John, 776
Bey, Essad, 588
Beyerlin, Walter, 810
Bhagat, M. G., 501
Bhaktivedanta, Swami A. C.,
    862
Bhaskar, Roy, 413
Bhattacharyya, Narendra
    Nath, 497, 498
Bial, Morrison D., 601
Biale, David, 593, 672
Biale, Rachel, 650
Bianci, Eugene, 742
Bianco, Frank, 752
Bickerman, Elias, 604
Bickers, Bernard, 677
Bielefeldt, Carl, 537
Bigg, Charles, 63, 116
Bilinkoff, Jodi, 786
Billings, Thomas H., 60
Bingham, Marjorie Wall, 578
Bird, Charles S., 462
Bird, Graham, 206, 237
Bireley, Robert, 728
Birge, John K., 574
Birnbaum, Philip, 596, 599,
    627, 631
Birx, H. James, 336

Bishai, Wilson B., 567
Bishop, Mary, 768
Bittinger, Emmert F., 732
Bitton, Davis, 845
Bjork, Daniel W., 237
Bjorkman, James Warner,
    507, 515
Bjorling, Joel, 861, 866
Black, Edwin, 642
Black, Matthew, 819
Black, Max, 344
Black Elk, 464
Blacker, Carmen, 539
Blackham, Harold John, 262
Blackman, P., 609
Blackstone, William, 203
Blackwell, Richard J., 142
Blackwood, R. T., 37
Blake, William, 235
Blakeley, T. J., 30, 31, 34
Blanchard, Dallas A., 894
Bland, Kalman P., 130
Blanshard, Brand, 275, 297
Blasi, Anthony J., 425
Blass, F., 794
Blau, Joseph L., 124, 601,
    651, 652
Blavatsky, Helena P., 548,
    852, **873**, 879
Blazynski, George, 742
Blehl, Vincent, 782
Bleich, J. David, 598, 629
Blewett, John, 225
Blinkoff, Jodi, 736
Bloch, Abraham P., 598
Bloch, Ernst, 276
Block, Marguerite, 851
Blocker, H. Gene, 24, 316
Bloesch, Donald, 742
Blofeld, John, 527
Blom, John J., 169
Bloom, Alfred, 537
Bloom, Harold, 889
Blumberg, Arnold B., 657
Blumell, Bruce, 846
Blumenthal, David R., 622,
    629
Blumenthal, Henry, 66
Blumenthal, H. J., 61
Blunt, Wilfred Scawen, 567
Blyth, John W., 341
Boardman, John, 446
Boas, Marie, 124
Boccaccio, 469
Bochenski, Innocentius
    Marie, 20, 27, 31, 262
Bodiford, William, 537
Bodin, Jean, 133
Bodunrin, P. O., 368
Boehmer, Heinrich, 778
Boehner, Philotheus, 97, 120
Boethius, 93, 96, 98, 100,
    112, 155

Boff, Clodovis, 896
Boff, Leonardo, 747, 896
Bogdan, Radu J., 395
Boggs, Carl, 287
Bogle, Darlene, 894
Bohman, James, 378
Böhme, Gernot, 384
Bokser, Ben Zion, 630
Bolick, Nancy O., 849
Bolshakoff, Sergius, 755
Bolton, Brenda, 691
Bolton, R., 771
Bonansea, Bernardino M.,
    114, 137
Bonaventure of Bagnorea,
    St., 112, 706
Bond, George D., 505, 513,
    515, 526
Bondurant, Joan V., 352, 553
Bonevac, Daniel, 349
Bonhoeffer, Dietrich, 757,
    759, 784
Bonjour, Laurence, 380
Bonnefoy, Yves, 428
Bonner, Arthur, 507
Bonner, Gerald, 109
Bonser, Wilfrid, 431
Bonsirven, Joseph, 620
Bonsor, Jack A., 292
Boolos, George, 411
Booth, Newell S., 462
Borden, Carla M., 507
Borgen, Peder, 604
Borman, William, 553
Bornkamm, Günther, 824,
    829
Borowitz, Eugene, 598, 652,
    661, 885
Bosanquet, Bernard, 303
Boscherini, Emilia Giancotti,
    187
Boschetti, Ann, 330
Bossy, John, 736
Boswell, John, 678
Bosworth, C. E., 572
Botero, Giovanni, 124
Botterweck, G. Johannes,
    817
Botting, Gary, 863
Botting, Heather, 863
Boucher, Sandy, 512
Boudouris, C., 47
Bouhdiba, Abdelwahab, 894
Boulares, Habib, 578
Bouquet, A. C., 567
Bourdieu, Pierre, 292
Bourgeois, Patrick L., 309,
    311
Bouwsma, O. K., 345
Bouwsma, William J., 124,
    761
Bouyer, Louis, 139, 676, 783
Bowden, Henry W., 719

Bowden, John, 676, 719
Bowen, Alan C., 47
Bowen, Harold, 569
Bowen-Moore, Patricia, 394
Bowes, Pratima, 37
Bowie, G. Lee, 20
Bowie, Norman, 388
Bowker, John W., 568, 608, 886, 887
Bowman, John, 618
Bowman, Steven B., 623
Boxer, C. R., 540
Boyarin, Daniel, 620
Boyce, Mary, 443, 444, 547
Boyd, Gregory A., 289
Boyd, James W., 517, 547
Boydston, Jo Ann, 225
Boyer, David L., 263
Boyle, Joseph, 743
Boyle, Marjorie O., 139, 151
Braaten, Jane, 404
Bracken, Harry M., 191
Braden, Charles S., 842, 847, 855
Bradley, Francis Herbert, 220, 260, 303
Bradley, James E., 738
Bradley, Raymond, 345
Bradshaw, Leah, 395
Bradshaw, Paul F., 687
Brandes, Georg, 246
Brandon, George, 868
Brandon, Ruth, 850
Brandon, S. G., 3, 887
Brandt, Reinhard, 179
Brandt, Richard, 19, 254
Brandwood, Leonard, 79
Branham, Robert Bracht, 485
Brannigan, Michael C., 881
Bratman, Michael, 23
Bratt, James D., 752
Braude, Ann, 850
Braude, Benjamin, 568
Braude, William G., 610
Brauer, Jerald C., 675, 719
Bravmann, M. M., 574
Bravmann, Rene A., 568
Bray, Gerald L., 714
Bray, John, 731
Brayer, Menachem M., 650
Breck, J., 756
Bregman, Jay, 62, 63
Bréhier, Emile, 16, 86, 124, 159
Brenner, Geoffrey, 196
Brentano, Franz, 67, **221,** 234, 395
Brenton L. L., 796
Breslauer, S. Daniel, 648, 662
Breuer, Mordechai, 653
Breuil, Henri, 432

Brewer, Priscilla J., 849
Bricker, Phillip, 184
Brickhouse, Thomas C., 89
Bridger, David, 593
Bridges, John H., 111
Brière, O., 358
Brigden, Susan, 725
Bright, John, 806
Brinner, William M, 625
Broad, Charles Dunbar, 192, **277,** 303, 304
Broadie, Alexander, 32
Broadie, Sarah, 67
Brock, Dan W., 25
Brock, Erland J., 852
Brockelmann, C., 568
Brockhaus, Richard R., 345
Brockman, James R., 747
Brockman, John, 18
Broda, Johanna, 457
Broderick, Robert C., 716
Brodie, Fawn M., 845, 879
Brodie, Howard, 388
Brodrick, James, 728, 736, 770
Bromiley, Geoffrey W., 725, 758, 791
Bromley, David G., 855, 856, 862, 871
Bronowski, Jacob, 159
Bronstein, Herbert, 599
Brooke, Christopher, 698
Brooke, Rosalind, 698
Brooks, Charles R., 507, 862
Brooks, Richard, 218
Brooks, Roger, 620, 648
Brooten, Bernadette J., 614
Brosman, Catherine, 330
Brosse, Jacques, 716
Brown, Charles, 784
Brown, C. Mackenzie, 503
Brown, Colin, 818
Brown, Curtis, 21
Brown, Hanbury, 384
Brown, Harold I., 384
Brown, Joseph E., 464
Brown, J. P., 574
Brown, Judith M., 553
Brown, Karen M., 868
Brown, K. C., 174
Brown, Michael F., 465
Brown, Peter, 109, 449, 687
Brown, Raymond E., 685, 816, 819, 824, 887
Brown, Robert F., 252
Brown, Robert L., 503
Brown, Robert McAfee, 747, 769
Brown, S. C., 263
Brown, Stuart C., 177
Browne, Lewis, 5
Browning, Robert, 682
Bruce, F. F., 797

Brues, Guy de, 124
Brumbaugh, Robert S., 46, 79, 341
Brümmer, Vincent, 743
Brundage, Burr C., 457
Brundell, Barry, 173
Bruni, Leonardo, 124
Bruno, Giordano, 123, 133, **134,** 137, 148
Bruns, Gerald L., 292
Brush, Craig, 146
Bruteau, Beatrice, 353
Bruyne, Edgar de, 95
Bryson, Gladys, 32
Buber, Martin, 304, 334, 602, 632, 655, 660, **661,** 669, 671
Bubner, R., 28
Büchler, Adolph, 604, 615
Buchler, Justus, 249
Buckley, George T., 124
Buckley, Michael, S. J., 884
Budd, Malcolm, 345
Budick, Sanford, 610
Buford, Thomas O., 20
Bührig, Marga, 749
Bulka, Reuven P., 654
Bullock, Marcus, 253
Bultmann, Rudolf, 366, 617, 743, 807, 821, 824, 827, **829,** 832
Bumiller, Elisabeth, 508
Bunnay, Jane, 519
Buranelli, Vincent, 250, 847
Burbidge, John, 233
Burckhardt, Jacob, 682
Bürger, Peter, 379
Burger, Ronna, 79
Burghart, Richard, 498
Burian, Peter, 475
Burian, Richard, 381
Buridan, John, 103
Burke, Edmund, 192, 210, 578
Burke, Marie Louise, 563
Burke, T. E., 410
Burkert, Walter, 87, 429, 450, **470**
Burkhardt, Hans, 159
Burkitt, Francis C., 685
Burley, Walter, 16
Burnet, John, 50, 79
Burnett, David, 857
Burns, Allan F., 465
Burns, J. H., 98
Burns, John, 219
Burns, J. Patout, 685
Burnyeat, Myles, 56, 58
Burr, Angela, 862
Burr, David, 101
Burr, John R., 6, 37, 263
Burr, Nelson R., 750
Burrell, David, C.S.C., 884

Burridge, Kenelm, 467
Bursill-Hall, G. L., 101
Burtchaell, James, 894
Burton, John H., 201
Burtt, Edwin A., 29, 124, 159
Buruma, Ian, 539
Busch, Eberhard, 758
Busch, Thomas W., 330
Bush, Douglas, 124
Bush, Richard C., 532
Bushman, Richard L., 845, 879
Bussanich, John, 86
Bussell, Frederick W., 76
Buswell, Robert E., 537
Butcher, S. H., 67
Butler, Alban, 675
Butler, C., 111
Butler, Christopher, 263, 391
Butler, Edward Cuthbert, 705
Butler, Joseph, 158, **193**
Butrick, Richard, Jr., 279
Buttrick, George A., 818
Butts, Robert E., 143
Buytaert, Eligius, 120
Bynagle, Hans E., 6, 13
Bynum, Caroline Walker, 695, 698, 892
Byrd, Rudolph P., 875
Byrnes, Timothy, 752
Bywater, Ingram, 67

Cabezon, José Ignacio, 894
Cacoullos, Ann, 230
Cadet, J. M., 518
Cadorette, Curt, 747, 769
Cadoux, C. John, 688
Caesar, Julius, 75, 436, 452
Cahill, Lisa Sowle, 894
Cahn, Steven M., 20
Cain, Seymour, 305
Caird, Edward, 223
Caird, John, 187
Cairns, Earle E., 675, 717, 720
Cajetan, Cardinal, 136
Calder, William M., 479
Caldwell, Daniel H., 874
Caldwell, Richard, 446
Caldwell, Ronald J., 719
Caldwell, Sandra M., 719
Calhoun, Craig, 404
Calian, Carnegie Samuel, 759
Callahan, Daniel, 894
Callahan, John F., 47
Callahan, Sidney, 894
Callinicos, Alex, 263, 379, 391
Callus, D. A., 115
Calvez, Jean-Yves, 771

Calvin, John, 1, 729, **760,** 773, 780
Cammett, John M., 287
Campanella, Tommaso, 123, **137**
Campbell, Bruce F., 852
Campbell, Joseph, 428
Campbell, Lewis, 79
Campbell, Robert, 388
Campbell, T. D., 215
Campenhausen, Hans von, 98, 690, 814
Camurati, Mireya, 33
Camus, Albert, 329
Canfield, John Y., 345
Cannon, Betty, 330
Canovan, Margaret, 395
Cantlie, Audrey, 498
Capaldi, Nicholas, 20, 201
Capek, M., 220
Caponigri, A. Robert, 124, 159, 216
Capp, Bernard, 725
Capps, Donald, 890
Capra, Fritjof, 866
Caputo, John D., 292
Cardozo, Arlene Rossen, 599
Carlen, Claudia, 891
Carlsson, Percy, 194
Carlyle, Thomas, 588
Carman, John, 26, 892
Carmichael, Calum M., 627
Carmody, Denise Lardner, 749, 892
Carmody, John, 743
Carnap, Rudolf, 261, **278,** 279, 313, 332, 411
Carnley, Peter, 887
Carpenter, Humphrey, 512, 776
Carpenter, K., 503
Carr, Anne, 781
Carr, David, 234, 391
Carrasco, David, 454, 457, 474, 883
Carrithers, Michael, 509, 512, 526
Carruthers, Peter, 345, 382
Carson, Anne, 749
Carter, Robert E., 365
Carver, Terrell, 227, 242
Cash, Wilson W., 568
Cashdollar, Charles, 740
Casper, Bernard, 628
Cassian, St. John, 705, **706**
Cassiodorus, 98
Cassirer, Ernst, 124, 153, 155, 156, 160, 206, 261, **279,** 331, 695
Cassuto, Umberto, 445
Castile, Rand, 537
Castro, Eduardo Viveiros de, 466

Catalano, Joseph S., 330
Catherine of Siena, St., 706
Caton, Charles E., 263
Cavalier, Robert, 160
Cavarnos, Constantine, 29, 312
Cave, John D., 474
Cavell, Stanley, 345
Cavendish, Richard, 568
Caws, Peter, 34, 330
Cerny, Jaroslav, 442
Ch'en, Kenneth, 529
Chadwick, Henry, 63, 99, 110, 112, 676, 685
Chadwick, J., 446
Chadwick, Owen, 706, 722, 738, 740, 755, 783
Chaffee, John W., 526
Chamberlain, Basil Hall, 536
Chambers, Raymond W., 147
Chan, Román Piña, 455
Chan, Wing-tsit, 358, 521, 522, 526, 532
Chance, Thomas H., 79
Chandler, Russell, 866
Chang, Chung-yuan, 527, 529
Chang, Hao, 361
Chappell, Vere, 27, 160, 170
Charles, David, 67
Charlesworth, James H., 810
Charlesworth, Max, 461
Charlton, D. G., 28
Charron, Jean D., 125
Charron, Pierre, 125
Chatellier, Louis, 728, 736
Chatterjee, Margaret, 352, 553
Chattopadhyaya, D. P., 353
Chaucer, Geoffrey, 469
Chaudhuri, Nirad C., 503
Chavel, Charles B., 669
Chazan, Robert, 622, 623, 669
Chekhov, Anton, 335
Chenu, M. D., 101, 696
Cheny, David, 24
Cherniss, Harold F., 67, 79
Cherry, Conrad, 767
Chesnut, Glenn F., 709
Chiari, Joseph, 28, 263
Chiat, Marilyn, 614
Chidester, David, 867, 893
Chilcote, Paul W, 738
Childe, V. Gordon, 438
Childress, James F., 2, 718, 893
Childs, Brevard S., 795, 827
Chilton, Bruce D., 602, 608
Chinnici, Rosemary, 892
Chisholm, Roderick M., 222, 261, 263, 280 **395**
Chittick, William C., 590, 902

Chitty, Derwas J., 688
Chmielewski, Wendy, 843
Choksky, Jamsheed K., 517, 547
Chomsky, Noam, 170
Chopp, Rebecca S., 749, 896
Choquette, Diane, 3, 854
Chorpenning, Joseph, 786
Chou, Min-chih, 360
Christ, Carol P., 650
Christensen, Carl C., 737
Christensen, Darrel E., 28, 263, 341, 379
Christensen, Michael, 776
Christian, William A., 342, 728, 898
Christianson, Gale E., 184
Christianson, Paul K., 725
Christie, Anthony, 522
Christophersen, Hans O., 179
Chrysostom, St. John, 707
Chryssides, George D., 871
Church, Ralph W., 201
Churchill, Winston, 551, 750
Churchland, Patricia Smith, 382
Churgin, Pinchas, 609
Chuvin, Pierre, 449
Cicero, 59, 72, 75, 150
Clark, Donald N., 540
Clark, Elizabeth A., 678, 712
Clark, Jerome, 870
Clark, J. G., 433
Clark, Martin L., 59
Clark, Robert, 199
Clark, Ronald, 324
Clark, Stephen R., 67
Clarke, Samuel, 158, 194, 203, 210
Clasen, Claus-Peter, 723
Clavelin, Maurice, 143
Clay, Diskin, 73, 75
Cleary, J. C., 537
Cleary, John, 47, 67
Cleary, Thomas, 527, 529, 534
Clebsch, William A., 726
Clegg, Jerry S., 79
Clements, Ronald E., 813
Clendenning, John, 250
Clendinnen, Inga, 457
Clifford, James, 426
Clifford, Terry, 890
Clifton, Chas S., 865
Clissold, Stephen, 786
Clive, Geoffrey, 247
Clooney, Francis X., 872
Clothey, Fred W., 503
Clulee, Nicholas H., 125
Cobb, John, 743
Cobb, John B., Jr., 263, 289, 294, 379, 718, 743
Cobb, William S., 79

Cobban, A. B., 101
Cobe, Patricia, 602
Cobo, Bernabe, 458
Coburn, Robert C., 380
Coburn, Thomas B., 503
Cochrane, Arthur C., 761
Cochrane, Charles N., 99, 683
Code, Lorraine, 391
Coe, Michael D., 455
Coggins, R. J., 618
Cohen, A., 888
Cohen, Abraham, 620
Cohen, Amnon, 625
Cohen, Arthur Allen, 646, 648, 886
Cohen, Elliot E., 651
Cohen, G. A., 242
Cohen, Gerson D., 622
Cohen, Hermann, 662, 673
Cohen, Jeremy, 623, 696
Cohen, Mark R., 625
Cohen, Morris Raphael, 280, 297, 313
Cohen, Naomi W., 638, 657
Cohen, Norman, 753
Cohen, Paul A., 532
Cohen, Richard A., 901
Cohen, Shaye J. D., 604
Cohen, Steven M., 638, 651
Cohen-Solal, Annie, 330
Cohn, Norman, 698, 721
Cohn-Sherbok, Don, 568
Cole, Juan R., 861
Coleman, Francis, 185
Coles, Robert, 765, 788
Colie, Rosalie, 168
Collier, Richard, 740
Collingwood, Robin George, 281
Collins, Ardis B., 141
Collins, James, 187, 239
Collins, James D., 160
Collins, Larry, 642
Collins, Steven, 887
Collins, William P., 861
Collinson, Diane, 13, 388
Collinson, Patrick, 733
Collon, Dominique, 544
Colson, F. H., 810
Comaroff, Jean, 467
Comaroff, John L., 467
Comte, Auguste, 159, 222
Condillac, Étienne Bonnot de, 157, 194
Cone, James H., 748, 749, 762, 772, 896
Confucius, 360, 363
Connell, Desmond, 182
Connor, W. R., 448
Conrad, Geoffrey W., 457
Conrad, Joseph, 321
Conway, Anne, 166

Conway, Joan, 593
Conze, E., 897
Conze, Edward, 512
Conzelmann, Hans, 825, 827
Coogan, Michael D., 445, 818
Cook, Michael, 512, 588
Cook, William R., 710
Coomaraswamy, Ananda K., 503
Cooper, Barry, 311, 400
Cooper, John M., 67
Cooper, Lane, 67
Cooperman, Bernard, 629
Copeland, Jack, 382
Copenhaver, Brian P., 125
Copernicus, 135, 406
Copleston, Frederick Charles, 2, 38, 94, 118, 125, 160, 247, 256, 263, 574, 676, 736
Copley, A., 553
Corbin, Henry, 16, 582
Corlett, J. Angelo, 316
Cormier, Ramona, 6
Cornford, Francis M., 46, 50, 79
Cornman, James W., 20
Cornwell, Patricia, 768
Corrigan, John, 738, 751
Corrington, Gail Peterson, 451
Corti, Walter R., 309
Costello, Frank B., 125
Cotkin, George, 237
Cottingham, John, 170
Coughlan, Michael J., 894
Coughlan, Neil, 225
Couliano, Ioan P., 125
Coulson, Noel J., 578
Coulton, G. G., 96
Court, John, 807
Court, Kathleen, 807
Courtenay, William J., 103
Courtright, Paul B., 503
Courvoisier, Jacques, 791
Cousins, Ewert, 888
Couvalis, George, 399
Covell, Alan C., 539
Cowan, Henry, 774
Cowan, I. B., 735
Coward, Harold G., 398, 497, 503, 521, 533, 894, 898
Cowdrey, H. E., 692
Cowen, Anne, 635
Cowen, Roger, 635
Cowgill, George L., 546
Cox, Gary, 388
Cox, Harvey, 857
Crabtree, Adam, 847
Cragg, Gerald R., 738
Cragg, Kenneth, 373, 568, 574, 587
Craig, Albert, 358

Craig, William L., 574
Craik, George L., 165
Cranmer, Thomas, 725, 726, **763**
Cranston, Maurice, 179, 213
Cranston, S. L., 887
Cranston, Sylvia, 853, 874
Crawford, Donald, 206
Crawford, S. Cromwell, 355
Creegan, Charles L., 345
Creel, Herrlee G., 358, 522
Crenshaw, James L., 823, 838
Crew, P. Mack, 737
Crim, Keith R., 3, 818
Crimmins, James, 190
Critchley, Simon, 901
Croce, Benedetto, 271, 281
Crocker, Lester G., 160
Crombie, A. C., 97
Crombie, I. M., 79
Croner, Helga, 898
Cronk, George, 309
Cross, Claire, 726
Cross, Frank L., 675, 716
Cross, Frank M., 810
Cross, Whitney R., 841
Crouch, Archie R., 532
Crow, Charles L., 841
Crowder, Christopher, 694
Crownfield, David, 892
Croydon, Bent, 869
Cru, R. Loyalty, 196
Cudworth, Ralph, 167, 178
Cullmann, Oscar, 825, **831**
Cummings, Charles, 888
Cummings, Mark D., 513, 519, 522, 530, 534, 537, 542, 543
Cumont, Franz, 450, 451
Cuneo, Michael W., 425
Cunliffe, Christopher, 194
Cunningham, Agnes, 683, 688
Cunningham, Gustavus W., 263
Cunningham, Lawrence, 710, 891
Curley, E. M., 56, 170
Curran, Charles, 743
Curran, Douglas, 870
Curry, Melvin D., 863
Curtis, Michael, 568
Cushman, Robert E., 80
Cutler, Allan H., 623
Cutler, Helen E., 623
Cutler, Norman, 506
Cyprian of Carthage, St., 707

Dabashi, Hamid, 373
Dahlberg, Frances, 431

Dahlbom, Bo, 396
Dahmus, Joseph H., 714
Dalgarno, Melvin, 211
Dalin, David G., 639
Dalley, Stephanie, 545
Dallmayr, Fred, 292
Daly, Lowrie J., 103
Daly, Mary, 423, 749, **764**
Damrell, Joseph D., 872
Dan, Joseph, 598, 630, 632
Danby, Herbert, 610, 810
Dancy, Jonathan, 192
Dancy, R. M., 67, 80
Danford, John W., 345
Daniel, Glyn, 432, 436
Daniel, Norman A., 568
Daniel-Rops, Henri, 739
Daniels, Norman, 211, 388
Danker, Frederick W., 794, 795
Dann, Uriel, 568
Dannhauser, Werner J., 89
Danto, Arthur, 247
D'Antonio, Michael, 866
Danzger, Murray, 659
D'Arcy, Martin, 783
Dare, Philip N., 843
Dargyay, Eva, 497, 521, 533
Darian, Steven G., 503
Darwin, Charles, 281, 406, 740
Das, A. C., 501
Dasgupta, Surendranath, 351, 498
Dass, Nirmal, 516
Datta, Dhirendra M., 553
Datta, V. N., 508
Dauer, Dorothea W., 256
David, A. Rosalie, 442, 548
Davidson, Donald Herbert, 282, 380, 396
Davidson, Edward H., 767
Davidson, Gustav, 3
Davidson, Herbert A., 96
Davidson, Hilda R. Ellis, 437
Davidson, Hugh M., 185
Davidson, Robert F., 20, 488
Davies, Horton, 698
Davies, J. G., 675
Davies, Marie Helene, 698
Davies, Nigel, 457
Davies, Philip, 807
Davies, W. D., 596, 617
Davis, F. Hadland, 586
Davis, Harold E., 33
Davis, J. C., 125
Davis, Kenneth R., 724
Davis, Moshe, 655
Davis, Natalie Z., 731
Davis, Stephen T., 887
Davis, Thomas D., 20
Davis, Winston, 534, 540
Dawidoff, Robert, 327

Dawidowicz, Lucy S., 635
Dawsey, James, 6
Dawson, Christopher H., 783
Dawson, Jerry, 254
Dawson, M. M., 89
Dawson, Raymond, 512
Day, Dorothy, 765
Day, Sebastian, 114
D'Costa, Gavin, 898
Dean, Roger A., 871
Dean, William, 751
Deane, Herbert A., 110
Deanesly, Margaret, 691
DeArmey, Michael, 290
De Boer, Tjize J., 567
Debrunner, A., 794
Debus, Allen G., 125, 128, 150
De Felice, Renzo, 644
DeGeorge, Richard R., 388
De George, Richard T., 13
De Hartmann, Thomas, 875
De Heusch, Luc, 429
Dekker, Maurits, 534
Dekmejian, Hrair, 568
Delahunty, R. J., 187
Delaney, C. F., 334
Delaney, Cornelius, 281
Delaney, John J., 719
DeLange, Nicholas, 634
De la Torre, Teodoro, 16
De Lattre, Roland, 767
Delbanc, Andrew, 753
Delehaye, Hippolyte, 678
Deleuze, Gilles, 400
Deloria, Vine, Jr., 464
Delumeau, Jean, 728
Demarest, Arthur A., 457
Demaria, Richard, 844
de Moor, Johanes C., 545
Deng, Francis Mading, 462
De Nicolas, Antonio, 770
Denis, Numa, 438
Dennett, Daniel C., 382, **396**
Denny, Frederick, 883
Dent, N.J.H., 213
Depew, David J., 47
De Romilly, Jacqueline, 54
DeRosa, Gabriele, 771
Derow, Peter, 449
Derrida, Jacques, 262, 283, 390, **396,** 414
Desai, Santosh N., 518
Descartes, René, 12, 122, 146, 157, 164, 167, **168,** 171, 172, 173, 181, 183, 186, 199, 314, 381
Deshen, Shlomo, 644
Desjardins, Rosemary, 80
Detienne, Marcel, 429, 446
Detmer, David, 330
Deutsch, Eliot, 349

Deutscher, Isaac, 655
Devaney, Sheila Greeve, 289, 743
Dever, William G., 808
De Vogue, Adalbert, 688
DeVos, George A., 531, 539
DeVries, Jan, 420
DeVries, Willem A., 16, 233
Dewey, John, 28, **223**, 260, 297, 301, 308, 324, 360
Dewhurst, Kenneth, 179
De Witt, Norman W., 73
Dews, Peter, 391
Dharmasiri, Gunapala, 512, 884
Dharmatala, Damcho Gyatsho, 541
Diamant, Anita, 601
Diamond, Arthur, 877
Diamond, Cora, 345
Diamond, Irene, 391
Diamond, Malcolm L., 662
Diaz-Mas, Paloma, 644
Dibble, R. F., 588
Dibelius, Martin, 825
Dickens, Arthur G., 722, 726, 728, 778
Dickey, Laurence, 233
Dickinson, W. Croft, 774
Dicks, D. R., 48
Dickson, D. Bruce, 433
Diderot, Denis, 195, 212
Diehl, Richard A., 455, 457
Dienstag, Jacob I., 668
Dijksterhuis, E. J., 125
Dillistone, Frederick W., 833
Dillon, J. M., 55
Dillon, John M., 60, 62, 670
Dilman, Ilham, 412
Dilthey, Wilhelm, 158, **226**, 254, 661
Dilworth, David, 37, 263
Dinwiddy, John, 191
Diogenes Laertius, 46
Diop, Cheik Anta, 368
Dioszegi, V., 541
Dittemore, J. V., 878
Dix, Dom G., 688
Dix, Griffin, 539
Dixon, E. James, 454
Dobbs, Betty J., 184
Doblin, Alfred, 635
Dobrinsky, Herbert, 601
Dobrolyubov, N. A., 31
Dobroszycki, Lucjan, 635
Dobson, Andrew, 315
Dodd, Charles Harold, 814, 825, **832**
Dodds, Eric R., 48, 61, 63, 446, 449, 683
Dodson, E. O., 337
Dodson, George R., 220
Doering, Bernard, 307

Doerries, Hermann, 683
Doig, Desmond, 743
Dolan, Jay, 751
Dolan, John Patrick, 677, 720
Dolan, Walter, 13
Dole, George, 852
Dole, Nathan H., 76
Dombrowski, Daniel, 736
Donagan, Alan, 187, 282
Donahue, John J., 373
Donaldson, Dwight M., 574
Donaldson, Gordon, 735
Donaldson, James, 100
Donaldson, Stephen, 894
Doney, Willis, 170
Donin, Hayim H., 599, 601
Donnachie, Ian, 735
Donner, Fred M., 568
Dooling, D. M., 464
Dorey, T. A., 139
Doria, Charles, 439
Dorson, Richard M., 539
Dostoevsky, Fyodor, 335
Doty, William G., 428
Double, Richard, 380
Douglas, Andrew H., 154
Douglas, J. D., 3, 675, 717
Douglas, Martin J., 861
Douglas, Mary, 477
Douglas, Richard M., 728
Douglass, Jane D., 761
Dow, James, 465
Dowey, Edward A., 761
Dowley, Tim, 676, 720, 743
Downing, Christine, 424
Downton, James V., Jr., 872
Doyle, Arthur Conan, 850
Drabkin, I. E., 125
Drake, Stillman, 125, 143, 172
Drandl, Johannes, 345
Draper, Hal, 242
Draper, Larry W., 845
Drekmeier, Charles, 501
Dresner, Samuel H., 632
Dresser, A. G., 878
Dresser, Horatio W., 847
Dreyfus, Hubert L., 234, 292, 400
Driscoll, J. Walter, 875
Driver, G. R., 445
Driver, Harold E., 464
Dronke, Peter, 16, 94, 698
Dubnow, Simon, 657
Du Boulay, Shirley, 743
Duchesne-Guillemin, Jacques, 443, 444
Dudley, D. R., 55
Duerr, Hans P., 430
Duff, Robert A., 187
Duffield, G. E., 726
Duffield, Gervase, 761

Duhem, Pierre, 97
Duke, Alastair, 731
Duling, Dennis C., 816
Dulles, Avery, 153, 891
Dumézil, Georges, 435, 437, 443, **471**
Dummett, Michael, 229, 382
Dumont, Louis, 503
Dumoulin, Heinrich, 537, 558
Duncan, G., 244
Dundes, Alan, 428
Dunkley, Ernest H., 730
Dunn, John, 179
Dunn, Richard S., 736
Duns Scotus, John, **113**, 708
Dupont-Sommer, A., 810
Dupuis, J., 680
Duran, Jane, 391
Durant, Will, 15, 16, 722
Durfee, Harold A., 264
During, Ingemar, 67, 80
Durkheim, Émile, 210, 424, 425, 427, 472, 491, 493
Durnbaugh, Donald F., 724, 732
Dusenbery, Verne A., 516
Duska, Ronald, 388
Dussel, Enrique, 748
Dvornik, Francis, 692
Dworetz, Steven, 180
Dwork, Deborah, 635
Dworkin, Ronald, 386
Dwyer, Philip, 311
Dych, William V., 904
Dykhuizen, George, 225
Dykstra, Yoshiko, 537
Dynes, Wayne R., 894

Eadmer, 703
Earhart, H. Byron, 533, 534, 540, 883
Easterling, P. E., 46
Easthope, Anthony, 29
Easton, Stewart C., 111, 858
Eban, Abba, 593
Ebeling, Gerhard, 821
Eberhard, Wolfram, 521
Eberhardt, Vernon C., 720
Ebersole, Gary L., 536
Ebrey, Patricia, 522
Eck, Diana L., 503
Eckhart, Meister, 708, 788
Eco, Umberto, 95, 118
Eddy, Mary Baker, 842, 843, 847, **874**, 878
Edel, Abraham, 67
Edelstein, Ludwig, 48, 56
Edie, James M., 31, 235
Edmondson, Edna, 860
Edwards, I. E., 806

Edwards, James C., 20
Edwards, Jonathan, 766,
   783, 899
Edwards, Mark U., 778
Edwards, Mark W., 483
Edwards, Michelle, 599
Edwards, Paul, 2, 13, 20, 94,
   160
Edwards, Rem B., 34
Edwards, Walter, 540
Egan, Howard T., 173
Ehnmark, Erland, 483
Ehrman, Eliezer L., 639
Eichner, Hans, 253
Eichrodt, Walther, 827, 833
Eidelberg, Shlomo, 623
Eire, Carlos M., 737
Eisen, Arnold M., 634, 646
Eisenbichler, Konrad, 141
Eisendrath, Craig R., 342
Eisenstadt, Schmuel N., 593
Eisenstein, Ira, 659
Eissfeldt, Otto, 816
Elazar, Daniel J., 639, 644
Elders, L., 67
Elert, Werner, 730
Elgin, Catherine Z., 382, 403
Eliade, Mircea, 2, 4, 425,
   427, 430, 431, 461, **472**,
   486, 490, 497, 503, 522,
   524, 543, 545, 547, 548,
   717, 897
Elias, Julius A., 80
Elior, Rachel, 853
Eliot, T. S., 88, 305, 476
Elkin, Judith, 644
Ellen, Roy, 486
Ellery, John B., 244
Elliger, K., 794
Ellis, Jane, 755
Ellis, John Tracy, 751
Ellis, Marc H., 765, 769, 896
Ellwood, Robert S., 4, 535,
   841, 855
Ellwood, Robert W., 883
El Madhy, Christine, 442
Elon, Amos, 642, 658
Elon, Menachem, 627
Elrod, J. W., 239
Else, Gerald Frank, 68
Elster, Jon, 242
Elton, G. R., 722, 726
Embree, Ainslie T., 503
Emerson, Arthur, 532
Emerson, Ralph Waldo, 840
Emilsson, Eyjolfur Kjalar, 86
Emmet, Dorothy, 342
Endo, Shusoku, 540
Endress, Gerhard, 568
Engels, Friedrich, 226, 228,
   241
English, Jane, 527
Eno, Robert B., 688

Enroth, Ronald M., 857, 864
Entwistle, Harold, 287
Epicurus, 53, 73, 75, 89,
   172
Epp, Eldon J., 813
Epp, Ronald, 57
Epstein, Benjamin, 639
Epstein, Daniel Mark, 753
Epstein, Melech, 656, 657
Erasmus, Desiderius, 133,
   138, 147, 155, 709, 721,
   790
Erdman, Carl, 692
Erdozain, Placido, 748
Eribon, Didier, 401
Erickson, Carolly, 726
Erigena, Johannes Scotus,
   93, 100, **114**
Erikson, Erik, 553
Erikson, Erik H., 778
Erndl, Kathleen M., 504
Erskine, Andrew, 55, 57
Esposito, John L., 373, 578
Esposito, Joseph L., 252
Esslemont, J. E., 568, 861
Estep, William R., 733
Etheridge, J. W., 608
Euben, J. Peter, 48
Euripides, 474
Eusebius of Caesarea, 709
Evangeliou, Christos, 61
Evans, Donald, 888
Evans, Frederick W., 849
Evans, Gillian Rosemary, 16,
   108, 110, 112, 676, 696,
   702, 703, 710
Evans, J.A.S., 480
Evans, J. D., 68
Evans, Joseph Claude, Jr.,
   334
Evans-Pritchard, E(dward)
   E(van), 475
Evennet, H. O., 728
Ewing, Alfred C., 20
Ewing, Katherine P., 578
Eynine, Simon, 283

Faber, M. D., 865
Fackenheim, Emil, 647, 663
Fagan, Brian M., 432, 454
Fagin, Gerald, 685
Fairbank, John King, 358,
   532
Fairweather, Eugene R., 94
Fakhry, Majid, 97, 373, 574
Falaturi, Abdolajawad, 572
Falcone, Vincent J., 20
Falk, Nancy Auer, 504, 512,
   529, 539
Fallico, Arturo, 126
Fann, K. T., 272
Farah, Caesar E., 574

Faraone, Christopher A., 451
Farber, Marvin, 34
Farcy, Robert S., 337
Farnell, Lewis R., 545
Farner, Oskar, 791
Farquharson, Arthur, 76
Farr, James, 242
Farrar, Janet, 865
Farrar, Stewart, 865
Farrias, Victor, 293
Farrington, Benjamin, 165
Faruqi, Isma'il Ragi al-, 574
Fash, William L., 455
Fatula, Mary Ann, 707
Faulkner, Raymond O., 442
Faulkner, William, 321
Fears, J. Rufus, 452
Febvre, Lucien, 126
Feder, Don, 655
Fedoryka, Damian, 895
Fee, Gordon D., 814
Feenstra, Ronald J., 886
Feibleman, James Kern,
   283, 523
Feigl, Herbert, 264
Fein, Leonard J., 642
Feinberg, Joel, 19, 20, 386
Feinberg, Paul, 21
Feingold, Henry L., 594, 639
Feldman, David M., 598, 895
Feldman, Louis H., 604, 608
Fell, Joseph P., III, 330
Fellman, Michael, 844
Fellows, Otis, 196
Feng, Gia-Fu, 527
Fenton, John Y., 508
Ferejohn, Michael, 68
Ferguson, Everett, 676, 807
Ferguson, James, 194
Ferguson, John, 48, 68, 110,
   446, 449, 895
Ferguson, Sinclair B., 5
Ferm, Deane W., 718, 743
Ferm, Vergilius, 16
Fernandez, James W., 426
Fernia, Joseph V., 287
Ferrante, Joan M., 698
Ferrari, G.R.F., 80
Ferry, Luc, 293
Festinger, Leon, 870
Feuer, Lewis S., 187
Feuerbach, Ludwig
   Andreas, 227, 740
Feuerstein, Georg, 497
Feyerabend, Paul K., 160,
   398, 409
Fichte, Johann Gottlieb,
   158, **197**, 231, 251, 252,
   254
Fichter, Joseph Henry, 154,
   871
Ficino, Marsilio, 80, 123,
   140, 152

Fieg, Eugene C., 6
Field, Arthur, 126
Field, G. C., 80
Field, Stephen, 524
Field, Sydney, 555
Fields, Rick, 859
Fierman, Morton, 665
Fierz, Markus, 126
Figgis, John N., 126
Filoramo, Giovanni, 60, 685
Finamore, John, 61
Findly, Ellison Banks, 426, 504, 513, 529, 532, 578
Fine, Gail, 68
Fine, Lawrence, 630
Finegan, Jack, 439, 808, 811
Fink, Eugen, 74
Finkel, Avraham Y., 648
Finkelstein, Louis, 594, 615, 620, 622
Finn, David, 446
Finnegan, Ruth, 460
Finnis, John, 743
Finocchiaro, Maurice A., 143, 172
Finson, Shelley Davis, 749
Finucane, Ronald C., 726
Fiorenza, Elisabeth Schüssler, 750, 814
Fiorenza, Francis Schüssler, 891
Firth, Katherine R., 726
Firth, Raymond, 461, 486
Fisch, Max H., 34, 34
Fisch, Menachem, 258
Fischel, Jack, 594
Fischel, W. J., 584
Fischer, Michael F. J., 426
Fishbane, Michael, 610, 823, 883
Fishman, Aryei, 654
Fishman, Sylvia B., 650
Fishman, William J., 656
Fitzmyer, Joseph A., 795, 811
Flage, Daniel, 201
Flake, Chad J., 845
Flanagan, Owen, 382, 388
Flannery, Austin P., 743, 891
Flannery, Edward, 635
Flaubert, Gustave, 329
Fleming, John V., 699
Fletcher, George P., 389
Flew, Antony G., 3, 13, 21, 202, 264
Floistad, Guttorm, 264
Flournoy, T., 237
Flower, Elizabeth, 160
Foerster, Werner, 807, 811
Fogarty, Robert S., 844
Fogelin, Robert J., 202, 345
Fogg, Walter L., 23
Fohrer, Georg, 816
Foley, Helene P., 475

Fontenrose, Joseph, 446
Force, James, 184
Ford, David F., 718, 888
Ford, John, 743
Ford, Lewis S., 342
Ford, Marcus P., 237
Forell, George W., 688
Forman, Robert K. C., 498, 523, 535, 543
Formigari, Lia, 29
Fornell, Earl W., 851
Forster, Arnold, 639
Forster, Michael, 233
Fortenbaugh, William W., 90, 91
Fortescue, Adrian, 755
Foshay, Toby, 398
Foster, John, 273
Foster, Kenelm, 151
Foster, Lawrence, 841
Foster, M. B., 233
Foti, Veronique M., 293
Foucault, Michel, 262, 284, 390, 399
Fouyas, Methodius, 755
Fowler, D. H., 80
Fowler, W. Warde, 448
Fox, Alistair, 126, 147
Fox, Douglas A., 512
Fox, Emmet, 847
Fox, Karen L., 601
Fox, Marvin, 598, 668
Fox, Michael Allen, 389
Fox, Richard G., 516, 553
Fox, Richard W., 784
Fox, Robin L., 683
Foxbrunner, Roman A., 632
Foxe, John, 733
Fraade, Steven D., 610
Frady, Marshall, 768
Frame, Donald M., 146
France, Peter, 196, 213
Francis of Assisi, St., 709
Franck, Frederick, 363
Frank, Daniel H., 646
Frank, Ruth S., 601
Frankel, Charles, 160
Frankel, Ellen, 597
Frankel, Jonathan, 656
Frankfort, Henri, 439, 441, 442, 548
Frankfurt, Harry, 170
Frankiel, Sandra S., 677, 883
Franklin, Benjamin, 200, 210, 848
Franklin, Julian H., 134, 180
Franzius, Enno, 569
Fraser, Alexander C., 180
Fraser, Antonia, 733, 735
Fraser, Robert, 477
Frazer, James George, 421, 476, 479, 485, 488, 490, 491

Frede, Michael, 48
Freedman, David Noel, 4, 818, 828
Freehof, Solomon Benner, 598, 627, 652
Freeman, Eugene, 187, 249
Freeman, James, 504
Frege, Gottlob, 228, 234
Frei, Hans W., 739, 743, 885
Freidman, George, 408
Freire, Paulo, 748
Freitag, Sandra B., 504
French, Harold W., 872
French, Peter A., 21, 389
Frend, W. H., 681, 685
Freppert, Lucan, 120
Freud, Sigmund, 255, 423, 424, 427, 477
Freund, E. Hans, 22
Friedlander, Albert H., 661
Friedlander, Paul, 80
Friedman, George, 264, 394
Friedman, Jerome, 126
Friedman, Lenore, 515
Friedman, Maurice S., 264, 662
Friedman, Michael, 206, 384
Friedman, Milton, 387
Friedmann, Thomas, 654
Fries, Paul, 755
Fritz, Kurt von, 71
Frolov, Ivan, 3, 13
Frost, S. E., Jr., 16
Fruchtenbaum, Arnold G., 599
Fryba, Mirko, 512
Fu, Charles Wei-hsun, 349, 358, 522
Fuchs, Oswald, 120
Fuchs, Stephan, 384
Fuhrman, Manfred, 72
Fuller, C. J., 504
Fuller, Robert C., 841, 847
Fung Yu-Lan (Feng You-Lan), 358, 359
Funk, Robert W., 794
Funkenstein, Amos, 126, 160
Furbank, Philip, 196
Furley, David J., 48, 50, 74
Furlong, Monica, 781, 859, 881
Furness, C. J., 879
Furse, Margaret, 296
Fuss, Peter L., 250
Fustel de Coulanges, Numa Denis, 438
Fynsk, Christopher, 293
Fyzee, A. A., 373

Gabriel, Ralph H., 34
Gabrieli, Francesco, 569, 588
Gadamer, Hans-Georg, 80,

226, 262, 284, 318, 390, **401**
Gaer, Joseph, 569
Gager, John, 683
Galanter, Marc, 856
Galen, 58
Galilei, Galileo, 123, 135, **141**, **171**, 173, 406
Gallagher, Kenneth T., 305
Gallie, Roger, 212
Gallie, W. B., 249
Gallop, David, 52
Galvin, John P., 891
Gamer, Helena M., 700
Gandhi, Mohandas K(aramchand), 321, 351, 549, **551**, 559, 772
Ganzfried, Solomon, 627
Gaon, Saadia, 600
Garber, Daniel, 170
Garcia, Jorge J., 264, 379
Gard, Richard A., 6
Gardiner, Patrick, 160, 240
Gardner, Martin, 866
Gargan, E. T., 741
Garin, Eugenio, 126
Garland, Robert, 447
Garrow, David J., 772
Garry, Ann, 391
Garside, Charles, Jr., 737
Garstein, Oskar, 736
Gasche, Rodolphe, 398
Gaskell, G. A., 4
Gassendi, Pierre, 171, **172**
Gasset, José Ortega y, 177, 261, **314**, 331
Gaster, Moses, 618
Gaster, Theodor H., 439, 477, 599, 811
Gatti, Hilary, 135
Gaudefroy-Demombynes, Maurice, 569
Gaukroger, Stephen, 170
Gausted, Edwin S., 719, 751
Gauthier, David P., 174
Gavin, William J., 31, 34
Gay, Peter, 160, 218, 635, 739
Gaynor, Frank, 718
Geach, P. T., 304
Geanakoplos, Deno J., 693
Geary, Patrick J., 699
Geden, A. S., 819
Geertz, Clifford, 477, 569
Geiger, Abraham, 647
Geisendorfer, James V., 717, 751
Geisler, Norman L., 21
Gelberg, Steven, 862
Gellert, Charles L., 636
Gelven, Michael, 293
Genet, Jean, 329
Gennep, Arnold van, 430

Gentile, Giovanni, 271, **284**
Gentz, William H., 818
Gerber, David A., 639
Gernet, Jacques, 358, 532
Gerrish, Brian A., 254, 722, 741, 762, 778
Gersh, Stephen, 60
Gerson, Lloyd, 55
Gersonides, 664
Gerstenblith, Patty, 445
Gertel, Elliot, 655
Gervais, Karen G., 389
Gesenius, William, 794
Geuss, R., 264, 404
Gewirth, Alan, 386
Geyl, Pieter, 731
Geymonat, Ludovico, 143, 172
Ghadegesin, Segun, 368
Ghadially, Rehana, 508
Ghazālī, Al-, 582
Ghose, Aurobindo, 352
Giancotti, Emilia, 188
Gibb, Hamilton A., 373, 566, 569
Gibb, Jocelyn, 776
Gibbs, Robert, 671
Gibson, James, 180
Gibson, John C., 545
Gibson, Roger F., 412
Gies, Frances, 699
Gies, Joseph, 699
Gilbert, A. H., 145
Gilbert, Alan, 242
Gilbert, Felix, 145
Gilbert, Martin, 636
Gilbert, Neal Ward, 126
Gilboa, Yehoshua, 636
Gilby, Thomas, 118
Gildin, Hilail, 213
Giles, Edward, 688
Giles of Rome, 103
Gilkey, Langdon, 744, 787
Gill, Jerry H., 311
Gill, Joseph, 694
Gill, Mary Louise, 68
Gill, Sam D., 464
Gillies, Alexander, 199
Gillman, Neil, 620, 655
Gilman, Sander L., 247, 636
Gilmore, Myron P., 696
Gilsenan, Michael, 578
Gilson, Étienne, 94, 95, 104, 110, 112, 113, 118, 126, 170, 260, **285**, 696, 721
Gimbutas, Marija, 434
Gingrich, F. W., 794
Ginsburg, Henry, 518
Ginzberg, Louis, 610, 620
Ginzburg, Carlo, 431
Girard, Rene, 429
Girardot, N. J., 528
Glasse, Cyril, 4, 566

Glatstein, Jacob, 636
Glatzer, Nahum N., 596, 610, 620, 629, 671
Glazer, Nathan, 639
Gleason, Elizabeth G., 728
Gleason, John B., 126
Glendon, Mary Ann, 895
Glenn, Menachem G., 654
Glock, Charles, 855
Glubb, John Bagot, 569, 588
Gluckel of Hamelin, 623
Goa, David, 503
Gochet, Paul, 412
Godelier, Maurice, 242
Godwin, Joscelyn, 450
Goethe, Johann Wolfgang von, 198, 254, 879
Gohlman, William, 582
Goitein, Shlomo Dov, 625
Gokalp, Ziya, 373
Goldberg, Hillel, 620, 654
Golden, Leon, 68
Goldfarb, Clare R., 851
Goldfarb, Russell M., 851
Goldfield, Lea Naomi, 668
Goldhizer, Ignaz, 575
Goldin, Judah, 610
Goldman, Alvin, 380
Goldman, Bernard, 614
Goldman, Edward A., 652
Goldman, Peter, 877
Goldman, Robert P., 504
Goldmann, Lucien, 185
Goldscheider, Calvin, 634, 639
Goldsmith, Emanuel S., 657, 667
Goldsmith, Maurice, 174
Goldstein, Joseph, 519
Goldstein, Melvyn C., 543
Goldstein, Sidney, 639
Golino, Carlo L., 143, 172
Gombrich, Richard, 513, 515
Gomes, Michael, 853
Gomperz, Theodor, 46
Gonda, Jan, 501, 504
Gonzales-Wippler, Migene, 868
González, Justo L., 677, 718
Goodenough, Erwin R., 60, 670
Goodman, Lenn E., 646, 668
Goodman, Martin, 606
Goodman, Michael Harris, 357, 561
Goodman, Nelson, 286, 380, **402**
Goodman, Philip, 599
Goodman, Russell B., 34
Goodman, Saul L., 651, 656
Goodrick, Edward W., 818
Goodspeed, Edgar J., 690, 703

Goodwin, George L., 289
Goody, Jack, 460
Gopal, Sarvepalli, 354
Gordis, Robert, 598, 821
Gordon, Cyrus H., 439
Gordon, Douglas H., 196
Gordon, Sarah, 636
Gorman, G. E., 716
Gorman, Lyn, 716
Gosling, J. C., 80
Gotthelf, Allan, 68
Gottschalk, Stephen, 843
Gottwald, Norman K., 816
Gouinlock, James, 160, 225
Gould, James A., 20, 21
Gould, John, 480
Gould, Josiah B., 57
Gould, Thomas, 48
Goulder, Michael, 885
Grabar, Andre, 688
Grabbe, Lester, 604
Grace, James H., 894
Gracia, Jorge J. E., 33, 101
Gracie, David M., 553
Graef, Hilda, 678
Graetz, Heinrich, 647
Grafton, Anthony, 126
Graham, A. C., 522, 526, 528
Graham, Bruce, 508
Graham, Daniel W., 68
Graham, George, 382
Graham, W. Fred, 762
Graham, William Franklin (Billy), 767
Gramsci, Antonio, 286
Gramwell, Franklin I., 289
Grant, Edward, 94, 97, 126
Grant, Frederick C., 448
Grant, Michael, 439
Grant, Robert M., 99, 116, 453, 681, 683, 685, 703, 811, 813, 825
Grant, Ruth, 180
Grassi, Ernesto, 127
Grassian, Victor, 21
Grattan-Guinness, I., 324
Grau, Joseph A., 337
Grave, S. A., 32, 212
Gray, Donald P., 337
Gray, Rockwell, 315
Graybeal, Jean, 293
Grayling, A. C., 192, 345
Grayson, A. Kirk, 545
Grayson, James Huntley, 533
Grayzel, Solomon, 594, 624, 634
Grean, Stanley, 214
Greaves, Richard L., 734, 749
Greeley, Andrew M., 751
Green, Arthur, 630, 632, 648, 669
Green, Martin, 553

Green, Michael, 683
Green, Nancy L., 656
Green, Robert L., 776
Green, Robert W., 722
Green, Thomas Hill, 180, 230
Green, Vivian H., 790
Green, William S., 610
Greenawalt, Kent, 386
Greenberg, Blu, 650
Greenberg, Eliezer, 657
Greenberg, Irving, 599
Greenberg, Louis, 636
Greenberg, Sidney, 136
Greenblum, Joseph, 641
Greene, Norman N., 330
Greenlee, J. Harold, 794
Greenslade, Stanley L., 683
Greenwalt, Emmett A., 858
Greer, Rowan A., 688, 814
Gregg, Robert C., 685
Gregory, Peter N., 529
Gregory, Richard L., 382
Gregory the Great (Pope Gregory I), 706, 710
Grell, Ole P., 734
Grene, David, 80
Grene, Marjorie, 68, 163, 188, 264
Grewal, J. S., 516
Gribetz, Judah, 594
Grice, Paul, 287
Griffen, Jasper, 483
Griffin, David Ray, 384, 743
Griffin, James, 389
Griffin, John Howard, 307, 781
Griffin, Miriam D., 88
Griffin, Nicholas, 324
Griffiths, A. Phillips, 273, 345
Griffiths, Morwenna, 391
Grigg, Richard, 787
Grillmeier, Aloys, 685
Grim, John, 337
Grim, Mary E., 337
Grimaldi, Alfonsina A., 216
Grimes, John A., 3, 13, 498
Grimes, Ronald L., 897
Grimm, Harold J., 722
Grimshaw, Jean, 391
Grimsley, Ronald, 213
Grisez, Germain, 743
Griswold, Charles L., Jr., 81
Gritsch, Eric, 778
Grogin, R. C., 220
Groh, Dennis E., 685
Gropman, Donald, 649
Gross, David C., 593
Gross, Leonard, 724
Gross, Rita M., 504, 512, 529, 539
Gross, Susan Hill, 578
Grosseteste, Robert, 115

Grossfeld, B., 608
Grossman, Reinhardt, 230
Grossman, Susan, 892
Grosz, Katarzyna, 545
Grote, George, 68
Grote, Harriet, 29
Grove, David C., 455
Grube, G. M., 81
Grunebaum, Gustave E. von, 573
Gruson, Lindsey, 862
Guenther, Herbert V., 543
Gueroult, Martial, 170
Guerry, Herbert, 13
Guignon, Charles B., 293
Guillaume, Alfred, 567, 575, 588
Guisso, R., 539
Gullery, Jonathan G., 877
Gulley, Norman, 81
Gummere, Richard M., 88
Gundersheimer, Werner L., 127
Gunkel, Hermann, 823, 830, 834, 837
Gunnell, John G., 81
Gunter, Pete A., 309
Guppy, Robert, 247
Gurdjieff, G(eorge) I(vanovich), 875
Gurney, O. R., 445
Gurwitsch, Aron, 235
Guss, David M., 465
Gustafson, James M., 744, 893, 899
Guthrie, K. S., 87
Guthrie, Stewart, 540
Guthrie, William K., 46, 54, 89
Gutierrez, Gustavo, 748, 768, 896
Gutmann, Joseph, 614
Gutting, Gary, 401, 406
Guttmann, Julius, 601
Guy, John, 126
Guyer, Paul, 206
Gyatso, Geshe, 543
Gyekye, Kwame, 26, 369
Gysi, Lydia, 168

Haaparanta, Leila, 230
Habermas, Jürgen, 288, 386, 390, 403
Habicht, Christian, 72
Haboush, Jahyuan K., 540
Hacker, P.M.S., 229, 345
Hackett, Stuart C., 523
Hacking, Ian, 160
Hadas, Moses, 57, 451, 647
Haddad, George, 577
Haddad, Heskel M., 644
Haddad, Robert M., 569

Haddad, Yvonne Yazbeck, 426, 504, 513, 529, 532, 569, 578, 887
Hadden, Jeffrey K., 753
Haddox, John H., 33
Hadreas, Peter J., 311
Hadzsits, George D., 75
Haenchen, Ernst, 821
Hafiz, 583
Hahm, David E., 55
Hahn, Lewis E., 273, 289, 305, 338, 412
Haigh, Christopher, 726
Haight, Elizabeth H., 469
Haines, Byron, 578
Hajime, Tanabe, 365
Hakim, Albert, 21
Halasa, Malu, 862
Halbfass, Wilhelm, 508
Hale, Frederick, 15
Hales, E. E., 741
Halevy, Elie, 245
Halkin, Hillel, 658
Halkin, Léon-E., 721
Halkovic, Stephen A., 542
Hall, David L., 342
Hall, Harrison, 234
Hall, John R., 867
Hall, Louis B., 714
Hall, Mary, 748
Hall, Raymond L., 862
Hall, Robert W, 81
Hall, Roland, 180, 202
Hall, Stewart G., 686
Haller, Rudolf, 345
Haller, William, 734
Halliburton, David, 293
Hallie, Philip P., 58, 146
Halliwell, S., 68
Halper, Edward C., 68
Halperin, Herman, 671
Halpern, Ben, 658
Halverson, William H., 21
Hamann, J. G., 216
Hamerton-Kelly, Robert G., 429
Hamidullah, M., 373
Hamilton, Bernard, 691, 699
Hamilton, Peter, 309
Hamilton, Richard, 481
Hamlyn, David W., 2, 16, 256
Hammer, Reuven, 610
Hammond, Mason, 439
Hammond, N. G., 806, 818
Hammond, Norman, 455
Hammond, Philip E., 752, 855
Hampshire, Stuart, 160, 188
Hampson, Norman, 210
Hampton, Cynthia, 81
Hampton, Jean, 174
Handelman, Susan A., 610

Handlin, Oscar, 225, 639
Haneman, Mary, 786
Hanfling, Oswald, 264, 345
Hanh, Thich Nhat, 496
Hanigan, James P., 894
Hankey, W. J., 118
Hankins, James, 127
Hanks, Maxine, 892
Hanover, Nathan, 624
Hans, James S., 293
Hanson, Paul D., 823
Hanson, R., 713
Happel, Stephen, 891
Hardacre, Helen, 540
Hardie, W. F., 68
Hardimon, Michael, 233
Harding, Sandra G., 36, **39**, 391
Hardinge, Emma, 851
Hardison, O. B., Jr., 68, 699
Hardon, John A., 717
Hardwick, Charles S., 345
Hardy, Godfrey H., 324
Hardy, Thomas, 255
Hare, Peter, 16
Hare, R. M., 81
Häring, Bernard, 718
Harlow, Victor E., 264
Harman, Gilbert, 380
Harmon, Rebecca Lamar, 790
Harnack, Adolf, 95, 677, 681, 686, 688, 741
Harran, Marilyn J., 778
Harre, Rom, 384
Harrell, Stevan, 892
Harries, Richard, 784
Harris, Errol E., 188
Harris, H. S., 233
Harris, Leonard, 386
Harris, Lis, 632
Harris, R. Baine, 61
Harris, William T., 21
Harrison, Barbara G., 863
Harrison, B. W., 895
Harrison, Everett F., 718
Harrison, Jane E., 478, 491
Harrison, R. K., 718
Harrison, Ross, 191
Harrold, Charles F., 783
Hartman, David, 648, 668
Hartman, Geoffrey, 610
Hartmann, Klaus, 330
Hartmann, Olga De, 875
Hartnack, Justus, 345
Hartog, Francois, 480
Hartshorne, Charles, 17, 34, 41, 161, 260, **288**, 338, 342
Harvey, Elizabeth D., 391
Harvey, Irene E., 398
Harvey, Robert, 330
Harvey, Van A., 675, 718

Hasel, Gerhard F., 827
Haskins, Charles H., 101, 699
Haskins, James, 739
Hastings, Adrian, 744
Hastings, James, 4, 717
Hata, Gohei, 709
Hatab, Lawrence J., 37
Hatch, Edwin, 63, 99, 818
Hatch, Nathan O., 751, 767, 813
Hatcher, William S., 861
Hathaway, Baxter, 127
Hauerwas, Stanley, 744, 897
Haugeland, John, 382
Haut, Rivka, 892
Havard, W. C., 257
Havelock, Eric A., 48, 81, 460
Hawkes, Jacquetta, 432
Hawley, John Stratton, 504, 516
Hawting, G. R., 569
Hay, Peter, 555
Hayek, Friedrich A. von, 245
Hayes, John H., 806
Hayes, John R., 569
Haykal, Muhammad Husayn, 588
Hayman, Ronald, 331
Haynes, Stephen, 648
Hayward, Robert, 608
Hazan, Haim, 642
Hazard, Paul, 161
Head, Joseph, 887
Heal, Felicity, 726
Healan, Dan M., 457
Hearn, Lafcadio, 539
Heath, Peter, 582
Heath, Thomas, 68
Hebblethwaite, Peter, 744, 771
Hedrick, Charles W., 453
Heehs, Peter, 353
Heesterman, J. C., 501
Hefele, Karl J., 677
Hegel, Georg Wilhelm Friedrich, 12, 17, 158, 197, 198, 216, 227, 230, **231**, 238, 249, 251, 254, 259, 279, 281, 303, 366, 385, 393, 401, 409, 600, 663
Heidegger, Martin, 50, 74, 206, 226, 234, 252, 261, **290**, 299, 304, 309, 318, 328, 331, 334, 363, 365, 367, 376, 390, 393, 394, 396, 401, 830, 900, 902
Heidel, Alexander, 440
Heilman, Samuel, 642, 654
Heimert, Alan, 753
Heine-Geldern, Robert, 518

Heinemann, Benno, 632
Heisig, James W., 366
Heissig, Walther, 541
Heitzenrater, Richard P., 790
Hejib, Alaka, 509
Hejtmanek, Milan G., 533
Held, David, 264, 404, 405
Helgeland, John, 688
Heller, Agnes, 127
Heller, Celia S., 636
Helmreich, William B., 654
Hempel, Carl Gustav, 383, 384
Hendel, Charles W., 202
Henderson, G. D., 735
Henderson, John S., 455
Hendley, Brian, 324, 342
Hendley, Steve, 331
Hendrix, Scott H., 778
Hengel, Martin, 604, 807, 811
Henig, Martin, 448
Henige, David, 460
Henley, Tracey B., 237
Hennecke, Edgar, 811
Henninger, Mark G., 104
Henricks, Robert G., 528
Henry, Carl F. H., 718, 744
Henry, D. P., 88, 108
Henry, E., 88
Henry, S. C., 739
Henry, Sondra, 650
Heraclitus of Ephesus, 50, 52, 56, **74**
Herberg, Will, 639, 649, 753
Herbstrith, Waltraud, 744
Herder, Johann Gottfried, 158, **198**, 204, 216, 459
Herdt, Gilbert H., 430
Herman, A. L., 37, 504
Herodotus, 419, **479**
Hertzberg, Arthur, 161, 639, 647, 658
Herzl, Theodor, 658
Herzog, Elizabeth, 625
Heschel, Abraham Joshua, **664**, 660, 668, 884
Heschel, Susannah, 650
Hesiod, 446, **481**
Hesse, Mary B., **405**
Hessing, Siegfried, 188
Hetherington, Norriss S., 13
Hewitt, George, 735
Hexham, Irving, 857
Hexter, Jack H., 147
Hick, John Harwood, 36, **40**, 117, 380, 569, 885, 898
Hickman, Larry A., 225
Hicks, Robert D., 55, 868
Hiebel, Friedrich, 880
Higgins, Kathleen, 247, 248
Higgins, W. E., 91

Higham, John, 639
Hijmans, B. L., Jr., 469
Hilberg, Raul, 636
Hill, Alan, 783
Hill, Christopher, 734
Hill, Claire O., 324
Hill, Donna, 879
Hill, Jonathan D., 454
Hill, Samuel S., 717, 751, 753
Hill, Thomas E., Jr., 206
Hillerbrand, Hans J., 722
Hillgarth, J. N., 683
Hiltebeitel, Alf, 504
Himelstein, Shamvel, 596
Himmelfarb, Milton, 639
Himsworth, Harold, 384
Hinchcliff, Peter, 708
Hindery, Roderick, 893
Hinds, William A., 844
Hine, Ellen, 195
Hine, Robert V., 844
Hinnant, Charles H., 174
Hinnells, John R., 4, 444, 498, 517, 523, 535, 547
Hinson, E. Glenn, 683
Hintikka, Jaakko, 68, 230
Hintikka, Merrill B., 283
Hiro, Dilys, 578
Hirsch, Samson Raphael, **665**
Hirsch, Steven W., 91
Hitti, Philip Khuri, 564, 569, 575
Hobbes, Thomas, 158, 167, **173**, 185, 193, 214
Hoberman, J., 657
Hobsbawn, E. J., 242
Hochberg, Herbert, 312
Hochfield, George, 753
Hocking, William Ernest, **295**
Hocutt, Max, 21
Hodder, Ian, 434
Hodges, Herbert A., 226
Hodges, Michael P., 346
Hodgson, Marshall G., 570
Hodgson, Robert, 453
Hoff, Benjamin, 528
Höffding, Harald, 161
Hoffman, Helmut, 543
Hoffman, R. Joseph, 683
Hoffner, Harry A., Jr., 545
Holbrook, Clyde A., 767
Holbrook, David, 776
Hölderlin, Friedrich, 231, 251
Holladay, William L., 795
Hollinger, Robert, 413
Hollis, Martin, 21, 405
Holmberg, David H., 541
Holmer, Paul, 777
Holmes, Ernest, 847

Holmes, Fenwick, 847
Holmes, J. Derek, 677
Holmes, Robert L., 389
Holmes, Roger W., 285
Holroyd, Stuart, 555, 858
Holt, Edwin B., 264
Holt, P. M., 570
Holtz, Barry, 601, 632
Holub, Robert C., 404
Holzman, Donald, 363
Homans, Peter, 424
Homer, 446, 481, **482**, 492
Honer, Stanley M., 21
Hoog, Constance, 543
Hook, Sidney, 34, 225, 260, 264, 265, **297**, 321
Hooke, S. H., 441, 545
Hooker, A. Thomas, 518
Hooker, Michael, 170, 177
Hooker, Richard, 734
Hookham, S. K., 513, 543
Hookway, Christopher, 249, 382, 412
Hooper, Walter, 776
Hope, Vincent, 32, 212
Höpfl, Harro, 762
Hopkins, Dwight, 748
Hopkins, Edward W., 498
Hopkins, Jasper, 108, 149, 703
Hopkins, Jeffrey, 356, 543, 544, 887
Hopkins, Thomas J., 504
Hopko, Thomas, 693
Hordern, William E., 718, 744
Hori, Ichiro, 539
Hornell, W., 100
Hornum, M., 61
Hornung, Erik, 442
Horsch, John, 733
Horsley, Richard, 864
Hotz, Louis, 645
Houlgate, Stephen, 233
Hountondji, Paulin J., 26, **369**
Hourani, Albert, 373
Hourani, George F., 575
Howard, Angela Falco, 530
Howe, Irving, 639, 640, 657
Howell, Wilbur S., 127
Hoy, David C., 401
Hsia, R. Po-Chia, 722
Hsiao, Kung-Chuan, 361
Htin, Aung U., 519
Hubbard, L. Ron, Jr., 869
Hubert, Henri, 429
Hubner, John, 862
Hudson, Anne, 714, 721
Hudson, C. Wayne, 277
Hudson, Deal W., 307
Hudson, William, 211
Hudson, Wintrop, 751

Hughes, Philip E., 127, 722, 726, 764
Hughes, Thomas P., 566
Hugh of St. Victor, 101
Huizinga, Johan, 139, 691
Hull, David, 384
Hultkrantz, Ake, 464
Hume, David, 12, 58, 157, 158, 166, 182, 194, 195, **199**, 203, 210, 211, 212, 214, 230, 255, 272, 410, 739
Hume, Robert E., 501
Humez, Jean M., 849
Humphrey, Caroline, 509
Humphrey, Derek, 389
Hunnings, Gordon, 346
Hunsinger, George, 758
Hunt, Ernest W., 726
Hunt, G. H., 809
Hunt, James D., 553
Hunt, Noreen, 699
Hunt, Thomas C., 21
Hunter, J. M., 346
Huntington, C. W., 513
Huntington, Richard, 430
Huppert, George, 127
Hurd, John C., Jr., 796
Hurlbutt, Robert H., 184, 202
Hurst, Jane D., 859
Hurwitz, Simon, 627
Hus, John, 691, **711**, 714
Husain, Taha, 374
Hu Shih, 360
Husik, Isaac, 629
Hussain, Asaf, 578
Husserl, Edmund, 159, 221, **233**, 261, 290, 309, 318, 328, 331, 334, 366, 376, 396, 900
Hussey, Edward, 50
Hussey, J. M., 693
Hutcheson, Francis, 158, **203**, 210, 214
Hutchins, Robert Maynard, 269
Hutchison, John A., 37
Hutchison, William R., 753
Hutton, Sarah, 183
Huxley, Aldous, 776, 853
Hyamson, Moses, 630
Hyer, Paul, 542
Hyers, Conrad, 537
Hyim, Gila J., 331
Hyland, D., 50
Hyman, Arthur, 94
Hyman, Paula, 636

Ibn Al-Arabi, 582
Ibn Daud Abraham, 627, 628
Ibn Hazm, 583

Ibn-Hisham, 588
Ibn Khaldun, 584
Ibn Khallikan, 584
Ibn Tufayl, 585
Idelsohn, A. Z., 599
Iggers, Georg G., 728
Ignatius of Loyola, St., 727, 769
Ihde, Don, 267, 392
Il-ch'ol Sin, 535
Imhof, Paul, 770
I-ming, Liu, 528
Immerwahr, Henry R., 480
Inada, Kenneth K., 6
Ingarden, Ramon, 235
Inge, W. R., 86
Ingram, David B., 405
Ingram, Paul O., 423
Innes, William C., 762
Inwood, Brad, 53, 55
Inwood, Michael, 233
Ions, Veronica, 548
Iorio, Dominick A., 30
Iqbal, Afzal, 590
Iqbal, Sir Muhammad, 374, 375, 585
Irving, Washington, 588
Irwin, Terence, 46, 68
Irwin, William A., 439
Isaacs, Harold R., 651
Isao, Kumakura, 538
Isherwood, Christopher, 354, 563, 872
Ishii, Yoneo, 519
Israel, Jonathan, 734
Israel, Milton, 516
Israeli, Raphael, 570
Isser, Natalie, 858
Itasaka, Gen, 534
Itzkoff, Seymour W., 280
Itzkowitz, Norman, 570
Ives, Christopher, 537
Iyer, Raghavan Narasimhan, 352
Izbicki, Thomas M., 694

Jackson, Carl T., 508, 841
Jackson, Samuel M., 717
Jacob, Satish, 517
Jacob, Walter, 627, 652
Jacobs, David M., 870
Jacobs, Jack, 656
Jacobs, Janet L., 856
Jacobs, Louis, 596, 620, 627, 628, 629, 630, 632, 884
Jacobsen, Thorkild, 440, 441, 545
Jacobson, Jerome, 501
Jaeger, Werner, 48, 50, 63, 69, 683
Jagchid, Sechin, 542
Jagersma, Henk, 604

Jaini, Padmanabh S., 509
Jalal Al-Din Al-Suyuti, 585
James, D. G., 257
James, Frank M., III, 129
James, Henry, 235
James, Montague R., 811
James, William, 223, **235**, 237, 248, 249, 260, 295, 301, 364, 423, 424
Jami, 585
Jamison, A. Leland, 752
Jamison, Stephanie W., 501
Janaway, Christopher, 256
Janelle, Pierre, 728
Janelli, Dawnhee Y., 539
Janelli, Roger L., 539
Janowsky, Oscar I., 639
Jansen, Godfrey H., 570, 579
Jardine, Lisa, 126, 165
Jaspers, Karl, 17, 21, 188, 247, 261, **298**, 304, 318, 349, 377, 394
Jay, Martin, 394
Jayakar, Pupul, 555
Jayatilleke, K. N., 898
Jayne, Sears R., 141
Jedin, Hubert, 677, 720, 729
Jeffery, Arthur, 566, 587
Jellicoe, Sidney, 796
Jenkins, J. J., 180
Jennings, Hargrove, 848
Jensen, Adolf E., 429, 432
Jensen, Henning, 203
Jenson, Robert, 767
Jeremias, Joachim, 604, 807, 827
Jerome, St., 711, 800
Jervolino, Domenico, 319
Jessop, Thomas E., 192, 202, 212
Jing-Nuan, Wu, 524
Joachim, Harold L., 170
Joachim, H. H., 69
Joachim of Fiore, 712
Joad, Cyril E., 21
Jochim, Christian, 523
Joergensen, Joergen, 265
John of Paris, 101
John of Salisbury, 115
John of the Cross, St., 736, 786, 788
Johnpoll, Bernard K., 656
Johns, Alger F., 795
Johnson, Galen A., 311
Johnson, Harold J., 98
Johnson, James Turner, 570
Johnson, Luke Timothy, 813
Johnson, Michael G., 237
Johnson, Oliver A., 21
Johnson, Penelope, 699
Johnson, Willard L., 514, 530, 538
Johnston, G. A., 32

Johnston, William, 858
John XXIII, Pope, 770
Joll, James, 287
Jolley, Nicholas, 177, 180, 182
Jonas, Hans, 63, 453, 686, 811
Jones, Adam L., 34
Jones, A. H., 684
Jones, Cheslyn, 678, 897
Jones, C. P., 485
Jones, Gareth, 831
Jones, Howard, 74
Jones, John, 69, 328
Jones, Kenneth W., 508, 516, 517
Jones, Mary M., 274
Jones, O. R., 383
Jones, Peter, 32
Jones, Rufus M., 734
Jones, W. T., 17, 46, 161
Jordak, Francis E., 13
Jordan, David K., 531
Jordan, Louis Henry, 420
Jordan, Wilbur K., 726
Jordan, William, 50
Jordan, Z. A., 30
Jordan-Smith, Paul, 464
Jorgensen, Danny L., 860, 865
Jorgenson, Joseph G., 467
Joselit, Jenna W., 639
Joseph, Horace W., 81
Josephus, Flavius, 604, 607, 615, 616, 617, **666**
Josipovici, Gabriel, 816
Jospe, Alfred, 647
Jourdan, Eric, 307
Judaeus, Philo, 45, 60
Judah, J. Stillson, 841, 863
Judah Halevi, 666
Judson, Lindsay, 69
Juergensmeyer, Mark, 504, 508, 516, 553, 892
Julian of Norwich, 712
Jung, Carl G., 423, 424, 427, 473, 483, 870
Jung, Hwa Jol, 307
Jüngel, Eberhard, 744
Jungmann, Josef A., 689
Justin Martyr, 99

Kaba, Lansine, 570
Kaberry, Phyllis M., 461
Kadushin, Max, 600, 620
Kaelin, E. F., 293
Kahn, Charles H., 51, 74
Kahn, Lothar, 636
Kahn, Margaret, 570
Kahn, Victoria, 127
Kaiser, Otto, 815
Kakar, Sudhir, 424, 890

Kallen, H. M., 324
Kallen, Horace M., 34, 237, 265
Kalmin, Richard, 610
Kalupahana, David J., 513
Kamenka, Eugene, 243
Kamuf, Peggy, 398
Kanarfogel, Ephraim, 622
Kane, Israel, 629
Kang, W., 309
K'ang Yu-Wei, 360
Kannenburg, Ida, 870
Kannengiesser, Charles, 689
Kanof, Abram, 597
Kant, Immanuel, 158, 197, 198, 200, 203, **204,** 208, 216, 219, 229, 230, 231, 253, 255, 279, 301, 318, 333, 363, 387, 413, 600, 739, 771
Kantorowicz, Ernst H., 98, 696
Kapferer, Bruce, 515
Kaplan, Aryeh, 669
Kaplan, Gisela, 395
Kaplan, Marion, 650
Kaplan, Mordecai Mena-heim, 658, 663, **667**
Kaplan, Stuart B., 860
Kapleau, Philip, 537, 860
Kaplon, Morton, 172
Kapur, Rajiv A., 516
Kardong, T., 706
Karp, Abraham J., 639
Karp, Ivan, 462
Karpinski, Leszek M., 883
Käsemann, Ernst, 821, 825
Kashap, S. Paul, 188
Kasravi, Ahmad, 575
Kassis, Hanna E., 587
Kasulis, T. P., 537
Kateb, George, 395
Katsh, Abraham I., 570, 643
Katz, Jacob, 624, 636
Katz, Ruth Cecily, 505
Katz, Stephen, 648
Katz, Steven, 575
Katz, Steven T., 601, 646
Kaufman, Gordon, 744
Kaufman, William E., 596, 649
Kaufmann, Ludwig, 744
Kaufmann, Walter, 161, 247, 265
Kautsky, Karl, 147
Kautzsch, E., 794
Kazhdan, Alexander P., 693
Keaney, John J., 69
Kearney, Richard, 27
Keat, Russell, 405
Keck, Leander E., 825
Keddie, Nikki R., 570, 575

Kedourie, Elie, 594
Kee, Howard Clark, 617, 689, 807, 811, 815, 816
Keeley, Robin, 718, 744
Keiji, Nishitani, 363, 365, 889
Keith, Arthur B., 501
Kekes, John, 389
Keller, Rosemary S., 749
Kellerman, Aharon, 594, 642
Kelley, Donald R., 127
Kellner, Douglas, 17, 408
Kellner, Menachem Marc, 598
Kelly, Aidan, 865
Kelly, J. N. D., 675, 678, 686, 712
Kelly, Marjorie, 570
Kelsey, John, 570
Kendall, Laurel, 539
Kendall, R. T., 726
Kendall, Willmoore, 180
Kennedy, Alex, 513
Kennedy, John H., 752
Kennedy, Leonard A., 104, 127
Kennington, Richard, 188
Kenny, Anthony, 17, 69, 119, 147, 170, 346, 386
Kent, Rosamond, 54
Kepel, Gilles, 570
Kepler, Clive, 395
Kepnes, Steven, 662
Kepple, Robert J., 6
Ker, Ian, 783
Kerényi, Károly, 470, **483**
Kermode, Frank, 816
Kerner, George C., 331
Kerns, Virginia, 466
Kerouac, Jack, 853, 860
Kerr, Fergus, 346
Kerr, Howard, 841, 851
Kerr, H. T., 63
Kerr, Malcolm H., 374
Kersey, Ethel M., 6, 161
Kessler, David, 644
Kessner, Thomas, 640
Ketner, Kenneth L., 249, 282
Kettani, M. Ali, 570
Kettering, Emil, 294
Keynes, John Maynard, 321
Keyt, David, 69
Khadduri, M., 895
Khomeini, Imam, 579
Kibre, Pearl, 153
Kidd, Beresford J., 681
Kidd, I. G., 56
Kieckhefer, Richard, 505, 513, 526, 696
Kiener, Ronald C., 630
Kierkegaard, Søren, 207, **238,** 261, 299, 328, 334, 366, 757, 771

Kiernan, Thomas P., 14
Kilcullen, John, 164, 166
Kilmister, C. W., 324
Kilvington, Richard, 104
Kimel, Alvin F., 905
King, Coretta S., 773
King, H. H., 100
King, John N, 726
King, Karen L., 453
King, Martin Luther, Jr., 561, 762, **771**
King, Peter, 180
King, Preston T., 134
King, Sallie B., 513, 530
King, Thomas H., 337
Kingdon, Robert M., 732, 734
Kingsland, William, 853
Kingston, Frederick T., 265
Kinsley, David R., 505, 530, 536
Kirk, G. S., 50, 75
Kirk, Robert, 412
Kirkham, Richard L., 381
Kirkwood, Mossie M., 327
Kirmmse, Bruce, 240
Kirsch, Thomas, 519
Kirshenblatt-Gimblett, Barbara, 635
Kirtzeck, James, 567
Kirven, Robert, 852
Kirwan, Christopher, 110
Kishwar, Madhu, 508
Kitagawa, Joseph M., 498, 509, 513, 516, 518, 519, 522, 530, 534, 535, 537, 542, 543, 570
Kitarō, Nishida, 348, 365, 366
Kitchen, Philip, 385
Kitchener, Richard F., 383
Kitcher, Patricia, 206
Kittel, Gerhard, 818
Kitzinger, Rachel, 439
Kivy, Peter, 203
Klaassen, Walter, 724
Klagsbrun, Francine, 598
Klass, Morton, 872
Klauder, Francis J., 21
Klauser, Theodor, 678
Klausner, Joseph, 604
Klayman, Richard, 640
Klein, Ann, 543
Klein, Isaac, 602
Klein, Jacob, 81
Kleinz, J., 102
Klejment, Alice, 765
Klejment, Anne, 765
Klemke, E. D., 22, 312
Klemm, David E., 319
Klenicki, Leon, 898
Klepfiscz, Heszel, 636
Kliever, Lonnie D., 719

Klimo, Jon, 866
Kline, George L., 188, 342
Kloesel, Christian, 249
Klostermeier, Klaus K., 505
Kluback, William, 663
Klug, Eugene F., 730
Knapp, Bliss, 843
Kneale, Martha, 97
Kneale, William, 97
Knight, Douglas A., 814
Knipe, Daniel M., 884
Knipe, David M., 505
Knitter, Paul, 898
Knowles, David, 94, 696, 699, 721
Knox, B.M.W., 46
Knox, John, 729, 735, **773**
Knox, Ronald A., 737
Kobler, Franz, 594, 636
Koch, Klaus, 815, 823
Kochan, Lionel, 636
Kockelmans, Joseph J., 235, 293
Koenigsberger, Dorothy, 127
Koepke, Wulf, 199
Koester, Helmut, 449, 807, 816, 825
Koestler, Arthur, 161
Kogan, Barry S., 581, 895
Kohl, Benjamin G., 127
Kohn, Gary J., 640
Kohn, Livia, 528
Kojève, Alexandre, 233
Kolakowski, Leszek, 220
Kolb, David, 293
Kolenda, Konstantin, 17, 34, 325, 413
Kolig, Erich, 467
Koller, John M., 349, 351, 498, 522, 523, 570
Koller, Patricia, 498, 522
Kolmerten, Carol A., 844
Kolsky, Thomas A., 658
Koltun, Elizabeth, 650
Komonchak, Joseph, 4
Konecsni, Johnemery, 22
Kopf, David, 355
Korom, Frank J., 503
Korsch, Karl, 243
Koszegi, Michael A., 6, 7
Kotwal, Firoze M., 517, 547
Kovach, Francis, 107
Kovacs, Maureen Gallery, 545
Koyré, Alexandre, 81, 128, 143, 161
Kraeling, Carl H., 614
Kraeling, E. G., 813
Kraemer, David, 620, 627
Kraemer, Ross S., 449, 892
Kraft, Kenneth, 537, 538
Kraft, Robert A., 615, 814
Kraft, R. Wayne, 337

Krahn, Cornelius, 780
Krämer, Hans Joachim, 81
Kramer, Samuel Noah, 428, 439, 440, 441, 545, 546
Kramers, J. H., 566
Kraus, Hans-Joachim, 821, 823
Kraus, Michael, 282
Kraussz, Michael, 381
Kraut, Richard, 69, 81, 89
Krautheimer, Richard, 684
Kravitz, Leonard, 668
Kreeft, Peter J., 23, 777
Krell, David F., 293
Krettek, Thomas, 340
Kretzmann, Norman, 94, 95, 104, 119, 696
Kreyche, Gerald F., 17
Krieger, Leonard, 186
Krikorian, Yervant H., 265
Kring, Hilda A., 844
Krinsky, Carol Herselle, 597
Kripke, Saul, **300**
Krishnamurti, Jiddu, 549, **554**, 858
Kristeller, Paul Oskar, 30, 55, 128, 141, 697
Krois, John M., 280
Kropf, Richard W., 337
Krupp, E. C., 434
Kubo, Sakae, 798
Kugel, James L., 814
Kuhn, Thomas S., 383, 399, **406**, 409
Kuitert, H. M., 744
Kukathas, Chandran, 316
Kuklick, Bruce, 34, 265
Kulkarni, V. M., 509
Kulke, Eckehard, 518
Kumar, Nita, 508
Kümmel, Werner G., 814, 815, 816
Küng, Hans, 423, **774**, 887
Kuntz, Marian Leathers, 128
Kuntz, Marion, 303
Kuntz, Paul G., 303, 324, 342
Kurtz, Paul, 298
Kurzweil, Zvi, 654
Kushner, David Z., 277
Kushner, Lawrence, 630
Kustas, George L., 47
Kvaerne, Per, 543
Kwame, Safro, 369
Kyle, Richard, 841

LaBarre, Weston, 467
Laboucheix, Henri, 211
Labrousse, Elizabeth, 166
Lacey, A. R., 3, 14, 220
La Charité, Raymond, 146
Lachs, John, 22

Lacoff, Cheryl Klein, 854
Lacoue-Labarthe, Phillippe, 293
LaCugna, Catherine M, 775
Ladd, George T., 22
Laeuchli, Samuel, 689
LaFargue, Michael, 528
LaFleur, William R., 513, 520
Laistner, Max, 100, 699
Laitin, David D., 467
Lake, Kirsopp, 704
Lama, Dalai, 496
Lamb, Matthew L., 744
Lamberg-Karlovsky, C. C., 439, 454
Lambert, Malcolm, 699, 721
Lamberton, Robert, 482, 483
Lamm, Maurice, 602
Lammens, Henri, 575
Lammers, Stephen E., 893
Lamont, Corliss, 225
Lamotte, Etienne, 513
Lampel, Zvi L., 627
Lampert, Laurence, 247
Lamprecht, Sterling P., 17, 161
Lancaster, Lewis R., 534
Land, Stephen K., 29
Landau, Jacob M., 644
Lander, Mary K., 91
Landman, Leo, 621
Landsberger, Franz, 597
Lane, David Christopher, 856, 872
Lane, Eugene N., 449, 682
Lane, Michael, 245
Lane-Poole, S., 570
Lang, David Marshall, 542
Lang, Mabel, 480
Lang, Paul H., 737
Langan, Thomas, 294
Langer, Jiri, 632
Langlais, Jacques, 644
Lango, John W., 342
Langone, Michael D., 857
Lanson, Gustav, 218
Lantier, Raymond, 432
Lapidus, Ira M., 570, 578
Lapierre, Dominique, 642
Lapointe, François H., 331, 346
Laporte, Jean, 679
Laqueur, Walter, 658
Laroui, Abdallah, 571
Larsen, Karen, 730
Larsen, Robin, 852, 880
Larson, Gerald James, 349
Lasker, Daniel J., 629, 697
Laszlo, Ervin, 31, 265
Latourette, Kenneth Scott, 677, 720, 741
Lau, D. C., 528

Lauer, Rosemary, 218
Laufer, Berthold, 523
Lauterbach, Jacob Z., 610
LaVey, Anton S., 868
Lawrance, Alan, 362
Lawrence, Bruce, 579
Lawrence, C. H., 699
Lawrence, D. H., 321, 334
Lawrence, Nathaniel, 342
Lawrence, Peter, 467
Lawson, E. Thomas, 884
Lawson, John, 704
Layman, Emma M., 860
Laymon, Charles M., 819
Layton, Bentley, 453
Lazar, Moshe, 622
Lazerowitz, M., 22
Lea, Henry C., 699
Leach, Edmund, 486
Leach, Jerry W., 486
Leaman, Oliver, 97, 575
Lear, Jonathan, 69
Learsi, Rufus., 640
Leatherbarrow, William J., 31
Lebowitz, Naomi, 240
Lebreton, Jules, 681
Leclercq, Jean, 676, 699
Ledger, Gerald R., 81
Lee, Anthony A., 861
Lee, H.D.P., 52
Lee, Raymond L. M., 518
Leeming, David A., 427
Leff, Gordon, 102, 104, 697
Lefkowitz, Mary R., 447
Le Goff, Jacques, 697
Lehman-Wilzig, Sam, 642
Lehrer, Keith, 20, 22, 212, 381
LeHurray, Peter, 737
Leibniz, Gottfried Wilhelm, Baron von, 12, 154, 155, 158, 164, 167, **175**, 183, 186, 194, 218, 229, 317
Leick, Gwendolyn, 545
Leighton, Walter L., 28
Leiman, Sid Z., 598
Leith, John H., 680, 719, 762
Lennon, Thomas, 183
Lennox, James, 68
Lenowitz, Harris, 439
Leone, Mark P., 846, 856
Leon-Portilla, Miguel, 457
Leopold, Richard W., 844
LePore, Ernest, 283, 381
Lercano, Giacomo, 771
Lerner, Ralph, 95
Lerner, Robert E., 721
Lernoux, Penny, 748
LeRoi-Gourhan, André, 433
Leroy, Andre L., 202
Leroy-Ladurie, Emmanuel, 699

Lesher, J. H., 52
Leslau, Wolf, 644
Lessa, William A., 426, 897
Lessing, Gotthold Ephraim, 197, **207**, 208, 739, 775
Lester, Robert C., 519, 884
Levenson, Jon D., 815
Levenson, Joseph R., 532
Leventhal, Herbert, 841
Levering, Miriam, 510, 530
Levertoff, Paul, 630
Levey, Samson H., 608
Levi, A., 128
Levi, Albert W., 22, 161
Levi, Ken, 867
Levin, David, 767
Levin, Michael Graubart, 659
Levin, Nora, 656
Levinas, Emmanuel, 235, **900**
Levine, Ethan, 608
Levine, Lee I., 597, 614, 621
Levine, Saul, 856
Levinger, Elma, 172
Levinson, Henry S., 237, 328
Lévi-Strauss, Claude, 426, 427, 428, 465
Levonian, Lufty, 571
Levtzion, Nehemia, 571
Levy, Beryl Harold, 652
Levy, Paul, 29
Levy-Bruhl, Lucien, 223
Lewes, George H., 17, 161
Lewin, Roger, 866
Lewis, Bernard, 567, 568, 571, 575, 579, 594
Lewis, Clarence Irving, 260, **301**, 317
Lewis, C(live) S(taples), 99, **775**
Lewis, David K., 381
Lewis, David L., 773
Lewis, Ewart, 98
Lewis, Frank A., 69
Lewis, Gillian, 731
Lewis, H. Spencer., 848
Lewis, I. M., 431, 571
Lewis, James R., 860, 866
Lewisohn, Ludwig, 596
Leyden, W. von, 175, 181
Leyser, Henrietta, 700
Liaqat, M. Muntaz, 375
Liber, Maurice, 671
Liberles, Robert, 654
Libo, Kenneth, 640
Libowitz, Richard, 667
Lichtenstadter, Ilse, 571
Lichtheim, Miriam, 442
Liddell, H. G., 795
Lieberman, Saul, 606
Liebeschuetz, J. H. W. G., 448
Liebman, Arthur, 656

Liebman, Charles S., 640, 642, 654
Liemohn, E., 738
Lienhardt, Godfrey, 462
Lietzmann, Hans, 682
Lieu, Samuel N., 686
Lifton, Robert J., 532
Light, Stephen, 331
Lightfoot, J. B., 704
Lilker, Shalom, 658
Lilla, Salvatore R., 63
Lincoln, Bruce, 426, 430, 435, 472
Lincoln, C. Eric, 571, 748, 862
Lincoln, Victoria, 786
Lind, Peter, 408
Lindbeck, George, 889
Lindberg, David, 128
Lindberg, David C., 97
Linder, Amnon, 604
Lindgren, J. Ralph, 215
Lindhardt, Jan, 128
Lindstrom, Harold, 790
Lindtner, Charles, 513
Lineback, Richard H., 5, 6, 14
Linforth, Ivan M., 447
Ling, Trevor, 571, 895
Lings, Martin A., 575, 588
Lipner, Julius J., 894
Lipp, Solomon, 33
Lippmann, Walter, 783
Lippy, Charles H., 4
Lipshires, Sidney, 408
Liszka, James J., 428
Littell, Franklin H., 720, 724, 780
Little, Daniel, 243, 385
Little, David, 893
Little, Lester K., 700
Little, Stephen, 528
Littler, June D., 869
Littleton, C. Scott, 472
Livingston, Donald W., 202
Livingstone, Alasdair, 545
Livingstone, Elizabeth A., 675, 716, 717
Lizhong, Liu, 543
Llewelyn, John, 294, 391, 398
Lloyd, A. C., 61
Lloyd, Genevieve, 17
Lloyd, Geoffrey E., 69
Lloyd, G.E.R., 48
Llull, Ramon, 102
Loades, Ann, 896
Locke, John, 12, 122, 157, 168, 173, 176, 178, 193, 195, 211, 214, 217, 739, 766
Lockwood, Dean P., 128
Lockwood, George B., 844

Lockwood, Michael, 19
Lodge, R. C., 81
Loeb, Louis E., 161
Loeffler, Reinhold, 579
Loemker, Leroy E., 177
Loetscher, Lefferts A., 717
Loewe, H., 610
Loewe, Michael, 524
Loewenich, Walter von, 779
Lofland, John, 871
Loftin, John D., 465
Logan, George M., 147
Lohff, Wenzel, 730
Lohfink, Gerhard, 815
Lohse, Bernhard, 677, 778
Lohse, Edward, 808, 816
Lo Jung-pang, 361
Lokos, Lionel, 773
Lomax, Louis E., 862
Lonergan, Bernard, 119
Long, A. A., 55, 55
Long, Charles H., 426, 427, 570
Long, Edward, Jr., 744
Lopez, Donald S., Jr., 513
Lord, Albert B., 460
Lord, Carnes, 69
Lortz, Joseph, 722
Lossky, Nicholas O., 31, 161
Lossky, Vladimir, 693, 756
Lotze, Rudolf Hermann, 229, 240
Lough, John, 180
Louis, Kam, 358
Louth, Andrew, 63, 689
Loux, Michael J., 69
Lovejoy, Arthur Oncken, 95, 161, 302
Low, Douglas B., 311
Lowe, Victor, 342
Lowney, Kathleen S., 871
Lowrie, Donald A., 275
Lowrie, Walter, 240
Lucas, George R., 342
Lucas, Jean M., 188
Luce, A. A., 182, 192
Lucey, Kenneth, 14, 265, 386
Lucian of Samosata, 484
Luck, Georg, 451
Lucretius, 59, 73, 75
Ludlow, Daniel, 4, 717, 846
Luhrman, T. M., 865
Lukàcs, Georg, 162
Lukas, Ellen, 337
Lukas, Mary, 337
Lukasiewicz, Jan, 69
Lukes, Steven, 243, 405
Lukes, Timothy J., 408
Luscombe, D. E., 106
Lutgendorf, Phillip, 505
Luther, Martin, 133, 136, 138, 725, 727, 729, 730,

733, 755, 757, 760, 777, 779, 790, 813
Luti, J. Mary, 786
Lutoslawski, Wincenty, 82
Lutyens, Mary, 556, 858
Lynch, John E., 102
Lynch, John Patrick, 70
Lynch, Owen M., 505
Lynch, William F., 82
Lyons, Arthur, 868
Lyons, David, 191
Lyons, J. A., 337
Lyons, Kimon, 82
Lyons, William, 325
Lyotard, Jean F., 265

McAfee, Ward, 2
McAlister, Linda, 222
McAllester, Mary, 274
McBride, William L., 331
McBrien, Richard P., 745
McCabe, Herbert, 891
McCabe, James Patrick, 6
MacCana, Proinsias, 436
McCarthy, Thomas A., 378, 405
MacClintock, S., 97
McCloskey, H. J., 389
Maccoby, Hyam, 624
McCorkle, Beth, 876
MacCormack, Sabine, 449, 458
McCormick, John, 328
McCormick, Richard A., 745
McCormick, Thomas W., 319
McCosh, James, 32, 212
McCown, Joe, 305
McCracken, Charles, 182
McCrie, Thomas, 774
McCullough, W. Stewart, 684
Maccuun, John, 193
McDaniel, Jay, 745
McDaniel, June, 505
McDermott, Charlene, 37
McDermott, Emily A., 475
McDermott, Robert A., 353, 859
MacDonald, Douglas, 20
MacDonald, Duncan B., 575
McDonald, William J., 675, 717
McDonnell, Kilian, 762
McDonough, Richard, 346
McEachran, F., 199
MacEoin, Denis, 579
McEvoy, James, 115
McEwen, James S., 774
McFague, Sallie, 745, 884
McFarland, H. Neill, 541
McFarland, J. D., 206
McFarlane, Kenneth B., 721
MacGaffey, Wyatt, 462, 467

McGinley, Phyllis, 679
McGinn, Bernard, 679, 700, 708, 712
McGovern, Art, 896
McGrade, A. S., 121
McGrath, Alister E., 679, 722, 762, 778
MacGregor, Geddes, 4, 14, 717, 736, 774
McGuinness, Brian, 333, 346
McHaffie, Barbara J., 749
Machan, Tibor, 14, 265, 386
McHenry, Leemon, 22
Machiavelli, Niccolo, 144
McInerny, Ralph M., 119, 307
McIntosh, Christopher, 848
McIntrye, J. L., 136
MacIntyre, Alasdair C., 387, **406**, 408, 897
Mack, M. P., 191
Mack, Robert D., 342
MacKendrick, Paul, 59
MacKenzie, Patrick T., 22
McKeon, C. K., 102
McKeon, Richard, 95, 189
Mackie, J. L., 180, 202
McKim, Donald, 719, 758
McKinnon, Alastair, 240
MacKinnon, Barbara, 35
McKirahan, Richard D., Jr., 46, 70, 82
McLaughlin, Brian, 283, 381
McLaughlin, Eleanor, 679
McLellan, David, 227, 243
MacLennan, Robert S., 617
McLeod, W. H., 516, 517
McLoughlin, William G., 753, 768
McLuhan, Marshall, 459
McMahon, Gregory, 445
McManners, John, 2, 675
MacMullen, Ramsay, 449, 682, 684
McMullin, Ernan, 48, 143
McNally, Robert E., 729
McNamara, Jo Ann, 689
McNamara, Martin, 608, 609, 796
McNay, Lois, 401
McNeill, John T., 94, 700, 762
MacNiven, Don, 221
McNiven, Peter, 721
MacPherson, Crawford B., 174, 180, 193
Macpherson, James, 459
Macquarrie, John, 2, 265, 718, 719, 745, 893
Macqueen, J. G., 445
MacRae, George W., 813
McRae, John R., 530

McTaggart, John McTaggart Ellis, 259, **303**
McWhorter, La Delle, 294
Madan, T. N., 505
Madden, Edward H., 35
Maddock, Kenneth, 461
Magee, Bryan, 256, 410
Magill, Frank N., 2, 266
Magnus, Bernd, 247
Magoulias, Harry J., 693
Mahdi, Muhsin, 95, 584
Mahesh Yogi, Maharishi, 873
Mahler, Raphael, 632, 634
Mahmud, S. F., 571
Mahoney, Edward P., 128
Mahowald, Mary B., 17
Maier, Anneliese, 97
Maier, Walter A., III., 545
Maimonides, 208, 664, **667**
Makinde, M. Akin, 26, 369
Makkreel, Rudolf A., 226
Malachowski, Alan, 413
Malandra, William W., 443, 547
Malcolm, John, 82
Malcolm, Norman, 346
Malebranche, Nicolas, 157, 164, **181**
Malik, Charles, 373, 575
Malino, Francis, 637
Malinowski, Bronislaw, 485
Maloney, George A., 756
Maloney, H. Newton, 890
Malpas, J. E., 283
Malter, Henry, 672
Maly, Kenneth, 75
Mamiya, Lawrence, 748
Mancinelli, Fabrizio, 689
Mandelbaum, Maurice, 22, 162, 187
Mandelker, Ira L., 842, 844
Mandelkern, Solomon, 818
Mandrou, Robert, 162
Manganaro, Marc, 477
Mangum, Garth, 846
Mann, Heinrich, 247
Mann, Jacob, 626, 631
Mann, Nicholas, 151
Mann, Thomas, 255, 256
Manning, Rita, 391
Manschreck, Clyde L., 677, 720, 730
Manser, Anthony, 221, 331
Mansfield, Harvey C., Jr., 145
Manson, Richard, 216
Manuel, Frank E., 128, 184
Manuel, Fritzie P., 128
Marable, Manning, 877
Marcel, Gabriel, 250, **304**, 318, 331
Marcell, David W., 237
Marcil-Lacoste, Louise, 212

Marcus, George E., 426
Marcus, Jacob Rader, 623, 637, 640, 650, 652
Marcuse, Herbert, 245, 297, 305, 386, 390, 403, **407**
Marenbon, John, 94, 100
Marglin, Frederique Apffel, 505
Margoliouth, David S., 571, 588
Margolis, Joseph, 294, 381
Margolis, Max, 594
Marias, Julian, 17, 22, 162, 315
Maringer, Johannes, 432
Marion, Jean-Luc, 889
Maritain, Jacques, 22, 220, 260, 285, **305**
Marius, Richard, 148
Mark, Thomas C., 189
Markman, Peter T., 465
Markman, Roberta H., 465
Markovic, Mihailo, 33
Markus, Robert A., 110
Marmorstein, Arthur, 621
Marquardt, Manfred, 790
Marrone, Steven P., 115
Marrou, H. I., 110
Marrus, Michael R., 637
Marsden, George M., 753
Marsh, Clifton E., 579, 862
Marshack, Alexander, 434
Marshall, Bruce, 753, 885
Marshall, Richard H., Jr., 572
Marsot, A. L., 579
Martin, Bernard, 595, 600, 652
Martin, Bill, 398
Martin, Gottfried, 177, 206
Martin, Luther H., 450
Martin, Mike W., 389
Martin, Rafe, 514
Martin, Richard M., 403
Martin, Robert M., 14, 383
Martin, Terence, 32, 35
Martin, Walter, 858
Martindale, Joanna, 128
Martinich, A. P., 22
Marty, Martin E., 753, 890, 893
Martyn, J. Louis, 825
Martz, Louis L., 148
Marx, Alexander, 594
Marx, Karl Heinrich, 12, 158, 216, 227, 228, **241**, 261, 297, 309, 377, 385, 399, 407, 409, 424, 425, 740
Marx, Werner, 252
Marxsen, Willi, 825
Mascaro, Juan, 501
Maslin, Simeon J., 602

Mason, H. T., 218
Mason, S. M., 210
Mason, Steve, 616
Maspero, Henri, 528
Masse, Henri, 572
Masson, Michel C., 359
Masters, Roger, 213
Masud, Muhammad K., 375
Masunaga, Reiho, 538
Matczak, Sebastian A., 14
Mates, Benson, 57
Mather, George A., 854
Matsen, Herbert S., 128
Matt, Daniel Chanah, 630
Matthews, Bruce, 518
Matthews, Eric, 211
Mattingly, Garrett, 732
Mattingly, Harold, 684
Maucini, Matthew J., 307
Maududi, Abdul A., 575
Maulana, Muhammad Ali,
   575
Maurer, Armand, 119
May, Herbert G., 809
May, William, 743
Mayer, Fanny H., 539
Mayer, J. P., 134
Mays, James L., 819
Mays, Wolf, 263
Mazar, Amihai, 808
Mazlish, Bruce, 159
Mbiti, John S(amuel), 370,
   463
Mead, Frank S., 6, 717, 751
Mead, George Herbert, 260,
   308
Mead, G. R., 87
Mead, Hunter, 22
Mead, Marion, 874
Mead, Sidney E., 753
Meagher, Robert, 475
Medawar, Peter, 385
Meehan, Brenda, 756
Megill, Allan, 398
Mehden, Fred von der, 518
Mehdi, Rubya, 579
Mehta, Ved, 266, 553
Meigs, Anna S., 462
Meinwald, Constance C., 82
Meiselman, Moshe, 650
Melber, Jehuda, 663
Melcher, Marguerite F., 849
Mellaart, J., 434
Melnick, Arthur, 206
Melton, J. Gordon, 4, 6, 7,
   717, 751, 848, 854, 856,
   859, 865, 866, 895
Meltzer, David, 630
Meltzer, Edmund, 569
Mencken, Henry L., 247
Mendelsohn, Ezra, 637, 656,
   658
Mendelson, Alan, 670

Mendelssohn, Felix, 209, 493
Mendelssohn, Moses, 204,
   208, 219, 252, 493
Mendes-Flohr, Paul R., 634,
   662, 888
Menges, M. C., 121
Menno Simons, 779
Mepham, John, 243
Merchant, Carolyn, 167
Mergal, Angel M., 724
Merkel, Ingrid, 128
Merkle, John C., 665
Merlan, Philip, 61
Merleau-Ponty, Maurice,
   234, 261, 309, 329
Mernessi, Fatima, 579
Merrell, Floyd, 266, 391
Merrill, Kenneth R., 35, 202
Merton, Thomas, 561, 780,
   895
Merz, John Theodore, 162,
   177
Metcalf, Barbara Daly, 572,
   575
Metcalf, Peter, 430
Metraux, Alfred, 467
Metraux, Daniel, 541
Metz, Johannes, 904
Metzger, Bruce M., 798, 805,
   818
Metzger, Thomas A., 532
Meyendorff, John, 679, 693,
   756
Meyer, Arnold Oskar, 734
Meyer, B. E., 161
Meyer, Donald, 753
Meyer, Isidore S., 658
Meyer, Jeffrey F., 531
Meyer, J. J., 505
Meyer, Marvin, 450
Meyer, Michael A., 594, 634,
   652
Meyer, R. W., 177
Meyers, Mary A., 852
Michael, George, 505
Michaels, Meredith W., 20
Michalos, Alex C., 381
Michalowski, Piotr, 545
Michaud, Regis, 28
Michel, Paul-Henri, 136
Michel, Sonya, 649
Michell, John, 434
Mickler, Michael, 871
Middleton, Ruth, 544
Midelfort, H. C. Erik, 730
Midgley, Mary, 389
Mielziner, Moses, 610
Milbank, John, 890
Mill, John Stuart, 158, 223,
   243, 257, 385
Millar, Fergus, 452
Miller, Alan W., 659
Miller, Barbara Stoler, 505

Miller, David L., 309
Miller, Fred, 24, 69
Miller, James, 214, 401
Miller, J. Maxwell, 806
Miller, Mary E., 454
Miller, Mitchell H., Jr., 82
Miller, Patrick D., Jr., 823
Miller, Perry G., 35, 753, 767
Miller, Phyllis Z., 601
Miller, Richard, 243
Miller, Richard W., 389
Miller, Ronald Henry, 671
Miller, Russell, 869
Miller, Timothy, 842, 844
Miller, William D., 765
Millerd, Clara E., 53
Miller J. Maxwell, 806
Millgram, Abraham E., 600,
   897
Mills, Joy, 853
Mills, Margaret A., 503
Mills, Patricia J., 391
Mills, Watson E., 5, 818, 864
Minadeo, Richard, 75
Minar, Edwin L., Jr., 87
Mink, Louis O., 282
Minnich, Nelson H., 729
Minor, Robert Neil, 354, 508
Minton, Arthur J., 22
Mintz, Alan L., 641
Mintz, Jerome R., 633
Mirandola, Giovanni Pico
   della, 140, 147, 151
Mitchell, Richard P., 572
Mitchell, Thomas N., 72
Mitsis, Phillip, 74
Mitter, Sara S., 508
Moctezuma, Eduardo M., 457
Modrak, Deborah K. W., 70
Moduro, Otto, 769
Moeller, Bernd, 722, 730
Moench, Richard W., 579
Moffatt, James, 802, 835
Moffett, Samuel Hugh, 677
Mohammad, Ovey N., 581
Mohammed, Imam W., 579,
   862
Mohanty, J. N., 295
Mohsen, Sofia, 579
Moked, Gabriel, 192
Moline, Jon, 82
Mollenkott, Virginia R., 749,
   750
Momen, Moojan, 861
Monan, J. D., 70
Monk, Ray, 346
Montaigne, Michel Eyquem
   de, 145
Montefiore, Alan, 28, 266,
   379
Montefiore, C. G., 610
Monter, E. William, 762
Montesquieu, Charles-Louis

Secondat, Baron de, 158, **209**
Moody, Ernest Addison, 121
Moody, Raymond, 866
Moon, Sun Myung, 870, **877**
Mooney, Michael, 217
Moore, Charles A., 37, 351, 358, 363, 498
Moore, Deborah D., 640
Moore, Donald, 665
Moore, Edward C., 225, 238, 249
Moore, George Edward, 211, 221, 260, **311,** 325, 343, 395
Moore, George Foot, 621
Moore, James, 876
Moore, Rebecca, 867
Moore, R. I., 700
Moore, R. Laurence, 842, 851
Moorey, Roger, 808
Mor, Menachem, 651
Moravcsik, Julius, 82
Moravscik, Michael, 385
More, Henry, 166, 168, **182,** 184
More, Paul Elmer, 55, 82
More, Sir Thomas, 138, **147**
Morenz, Siegfried, 442, 548
Morewedge, Parviz, 61, 576
Morgan, George A., Jr., 247
Morgan, John, 734
Morgan, Kenneth W., 499, 523, 535, 576
Morgan, Michael L., 82, 634, 649
Morganbesser, Sidney, 225
Morley, Henry, 133
Morley, John, 196
Morrall, John B., 98
Morreale, Don, 7
Morris, Brian, 422
Morris, Charles R., 180, 266
Morris, Colin, 695
Morris, George S., 29
Morris, James, 572
Morris, Kenneth, 760
Morris, Phyllis S., 331
Morris, Randall C., 289
Morrison, Clinton, 818
Morrison, Donald R., 91
Morrow, Glenn R., 62, 82
Morse, Arthur D., 640
Mortimer, Edward, 579
Mortley, Raoul, 28, 266
Morton, Leah, 650
Moseley, Michael E., 458
Moses, Larry, 542
Moses, Stephane, 671
Moskop, John C., 289
Mosse, George L., 722
Mossner, Ernest C., 202

Motoyama, Yukihiko, 363
Mottahedeh, Roy, 572
Motto, A. L., 88
Moulton, W. F., 819
Mounce, H. O., 346
Mourant, John A., 22
Mourelatos, Alexander P. D., 51, 52
Mowinckel, Sigmund, 823
Moyer, Elgin, 720
Mozart, Wolfgang Amadeus, 757
Mudimbe, V. Y., 369
Mudroch, Vaclav, 714
Mueller, Friedrich Max, 354
Mueller-Vollmer, Kurt, 28
Muether, John R., 6
Muggeridge, Malcolm, 745
Muhammad (or Mohammed), 374, 564, 577, **586,** 861
Muir, Edwin, 774
Muir, William, 588
Muirhead, John Henry, 29, 351
Mulder, John M., 754
Mulgan, R. G., 70
Mulhall, Stephen, 294, 346
Mulholland, Leslie, 206
Mulkay, M. J., 406
Mullaney, T., 154
Muller, Jerry, 215
Muller, Richard A., 762
Mullin, Glenn H., 544
Munevar, Gonzalo, 399
Mungello, David E., 177
Munitz, Milton K., 23
Munro, Donald J., 359, 524
Munson, T. N., 328
Munz, Peter, 410
Murakami, Shigeyoshi, 541
Murdoch, Iris, 83, 331
Mure, G.R.G., 70, 233
Murnane, William J., 548
Murphet, Howard, 874
Murphey, Murray G., 160, 249
Murphy, Joseph A., 868
Murphy, M. Gertrude., 705
Murphy, Roland E., 798, 887
Murphy-O'Connor, Jerome, 809
Murray, Gilbert, 48
Murty, K. Satchidananda, 354
Musurillo, Herbert, 689
Mutahhari, Ayatollah M., 373
Myerhoff, Barbara, 465
Myers, Gerald, 238

Naamani, Israel T., 643
Nadell, Pamela S., 655
Nadler, Steven, 164, 182

Naess, Arne, 189
Naff, Thomas, 572
Nagata, Judith, 518
Nagel, Ernest, 313, 385
Nagel, Thomas, 379
Nagy, Joseph Falaky, 436
Nahmanides, 628, **669**
Nahman of Bratslav, 661, **668**
Nails, Debra, 188
Naipaul, Shiva, 867
Naipaul, V. S., 579
Nakamura, Hajime, 37, 349
Nakhnikian, George, 23
Nanda, B. R., 553
Narayanan, Vasudha, 26
Narveson, Jan, 386
Nash, James, 745
Nasr, Seyyed Hossein, 375, 576, 582, 885, 888, **901**
Natanson, Maurice, 235, 331
Nathanson, Jerome, 225
Nauert, Charles G., Jr., 133
Nauman, St. Elmo, Jr., 3, 14
Navia, Luis E., 51
Needham, Joseph, 523
Needleman, Jacob, 855
Neff, Emery, 245
Neff, Mary K., 874
Negri, Antonio, 189
Nehemas, Alexander, 247
Neill, Stephen C., 508, 720, 745, 746, 814
Neilsen, Kai, 386
Neilson, Francis, 337
Nelsen, Hart M., 748
Nelson, G. K., 851
Nelson, James B., 894
Nelson, John C, 136
Nemoy, Leon, 631
Nersoyan, Tivan, 755
Neske, Gunther, 294
Nestle, E., 794
Netanyahu, B., 633
Nethercot, Arthur H., 550, 859
Nettl, Paul, 738
Nettler, Ron, 626
Nettleship, Richard L., 83
Netton, Ian Richard, 567
Neufeldt, Ronald W., 497, 521, 533, 887
Neuhouser, Fred, 198
Neuner, J., 680
Neusner, Jacob, 594, 596, 597, 600, 601, 602, 605, 606, 611, 612, 614, 615, 616, 617, 621, 640, 646, 648, 649, 651, 652
Neville, Robert Cummings, 391
Newman, John Henry, Cardinal, 782

Newman, Louis I., 633
Newsom, Carol A., 819
Newton, Sir Isaac, 157, 176, **183**, 194, 195, 383, 406, 738, 766
Nicholas of Autrecourt, 104
Nicholas of Cusa, 116, 138, **148**, 712
Nichols, Aidan, 756
Nichols, James H., Jr., 75, 739
Nichols, John A, 700
Nichols, Larry A., 854
Nichols, Mary P., 90
Nicholson, Graeme, 294
Nicholson, H. B., 455
Nicholson, L. H., 584
Nicholson, Reynold A., 576, 583
Nickelsburg, George W. E., 613, 615, 811, 814
Nicodemos, 756
Nicol, D. M., 693
Niebuhr, H. Richard, 679, 745, 753, 899
Niebuhr, Reinhold, 772, **783**, 787
Niebuhr, Richard, 254
Nieli, Russell, 346
Nielsen, Kai, 413
Nielsen, Niels, 756
Nietzsche, Friedrich Wilhelm, 38, 159, **245**, 255, 256, 261, 314, 334, 367, 390, 399, 407, 741
Nilsson, Martin P., 450, 470, **486**, 487
Nini, Yehuda, 626
Nisan, Mordechai, 643
Nisbet, Hugh Barr, 199
Nishida Kitarō, 364, 888
Nishitani Keiji, 365, 541
Nissen, Hans, 434, 441
Nkrumah, Kwame, 26, **370**
Nober, Petrus, 796
Noble, M. E., 503
Noble, Thomas F. X., 695
Noble, Wilfred Vernon, 734
Nobo, Jorge L., 342
Nock, Arthur Darby, 470, **487**
Noddings, Nel, 391
Noer, Deliar, 373
Noll, Mark A., 751, 813
Nordhoff, Charles, 844
Nordquist, Joan, 277, 294, 395, 398, 401
Noreña, Carlos G., 128, 156
Norris, Christopher, 266, 391, 398
Norris, John, 180
Norris, Richard A., Jr., 99, 686

North, Christopher R., 822
North, Helen, 48
Norton, David F., 202
Nosco, Peter, 541
Noss, David S., 2
Nota, John H., 332
Noth, Martin, 807, 823, **835**
Novak, David, 598
Novak, Michael, 748
Noxon, James, 202
Nozick, Robert, 313
Nuchelmans, G., 97
Numbers, Ronald L., 893
Nussbaum, Martha C., 48, 70
Nye, Andrea, 392

Oakeshott, Michael, 174
Oakley, Francis, 105, 691, 721
Oates, Stephen B., 773
Oates, Whitney J., 56, 70
Obbink, Dirk, 451
Oberman, Heiko A., 105, 128, 129, 697, 721, 779
Obeyesekere, Gananath, 424, 462, 515
O'Brien, David, 745
O'Brien, Denis, 53
O'Brien, Michael J., 90
O'Brien, Theresa K., 888
O'Carroll, Michael, 675
Ochshorn, Judith, 439
O'Connell, Joseph T., 516
O'Connell, Marvin R., 737
O'Connell, Robert J., 110
O'Connor, Bernard F., 300
O'Connor, Daniel J., 162
O'Connor, David, 69, 312
O'Connor, June, 353, 766
O'Connor, M., 795
O'Day, Rosemary, 726, 727, 734
O'Dea, Thomas F., 754, 846, 890
Oded, Arye, 572
Oden, Robert A., 485
Oden, Thomas, 885
O'Donovan, Leo, 904
Oesterley, William O., 605
Oestreich, Gerhard, 129
Offord, D. C., 31
O'Flaherty, Wendy Doniger, 428, 501, 505, 890
Ogden, Schubert M., 831
Ogilvie, R. M., 448
Ogletree, Thomas W., 745
O'Gorman, Frank, 193
Oh, Bonnie B. C., 532
O'Hear, Anthony, 385, 410
Oizerman, Theodor, 18
Oizerman, T. I., 23
Okadigbo, Chuba, 371

Okere, Theophilus, 26, 369
Oko, Adolph S., 189
Okrent, Mark, 294
Okruhlik, Kathleen, 391
Olcott, Henry S., 853
Oldfather, W. A., 57
Olen, Jeffrey, 23
Olin, John C., 729, 779
Olitzky, Kerry M., 652
Oliver, Douglas L., 462
Oliver, James H., 76
Olivier, Daniel, 779
Olscamp, Paul J., 23
Olsen, Fred, 466
Olson, Carl, 355, 506, 530, 536
Olson, David R., 460
Olson, Raymond E., 31
Olupona, Jacob K., 463
Olyan, Saul M., 545
O'Mahony, Christopher, 741
Omarr, Sydney, 860
O'Meara, Dominic J., 62, 87, 99
O'Meara, John J., 115
Ong, Walter J., 129, 460
O'Neil, Charles J., 286
O'Neil, Kevin, 538
O'Neill, John, 311
O'Neill, Onora, 206, 387
Onians, Richard B., 49
Ono, Sokyo, 536
Ophir, Adi, 83
Oppenheim, A. Leo, 441
Oppenheim, Frank, 250
Oppenheim, Janet, 851
Oren, Dan A, 640
Organ, Troy Wilson, 70, 354
Orieux, Jean, 218
Origen, 62, 93, 98, **116**
Ormsby, Eric, 582
Orr, James, 739
Oruka, J. Odera, 26, **371**
Osborn, E. F., 63
Osborne, Catherine, 49
Osborne, Harold, 465
Osler, Margaret J., 56
Otten, Willemien, 115
Otto, Rudolf, 487
Ourmette, Victor, 315
Ouspensky, Leonid, 693
Ouspensky, P. D., 876
Outka, Gene, 893
Oved, Yaacov, 844
Overfield, James H., 129
Overman, J. Andrew, 617
Overmyer, Daniel L., 523, 531, 884
Overzee, Anne H., 337
Owen, G. E., 49, 67, 80
Owen, Roger, 572
Owens, Joseph, 46, 70
Oxtoby, Willard G., 516

Oz, Amos, 643
Ozeri, Zion M., 644
Ozment, Steven E., 129, 697, 721, 722, 724, 727
Ozmon, H., 18

Paardt, R. T. Van der, 469
Pachter, Henry M., 150
Packer, J. I., 5
Packull, Werner O., 724
Paden, William E., 422
Padley, G. A., 129
Pagel, Walter, 129, 150
Pagels, Elaine, 453, 686
Pallis, Svend A., 441
Palmer, Martin, 531
Palmer, Richard E., 402
Pangborn, Cyrus R., 518, 548
Pangle, Thomas, 210
Panichas, George A., 74
Panikkar, Raimundo, 501
Pannenberg, Wolfhart, 99, 745
Panofsky, Erwin, 738
Pap, Arthur, 20
Papasogli, Giorgio, 787
Pappas, George S., 20
Paracelsus, Philippus Aureolus, 123, 149
Paramahansa, Ramakrishna, 562
Paramahansa Yogananda, 556
Paredi, Angela, 702
Parel, Anthony J., 145
Parent, David, 247
Paringer, William, 225
Paris, Peter, 748
Parke, H. W., 447
Parker, Geoffrey, 732, 737
Parker, Thomas H. L., 727, 762
Parkes, Graham, 294, 350
Parkes, James W., 637
Parkinson, G.H.R., 162, 177
Parpola, Simo, 545
Parrinder, Edward G., 572
Parrinder, Geoffrey, 5, 463, 885, 894, 898
Parrington, Vernon L., 35
Parry, Milman, 460
Partee, Charles, 129
Partin, Harry, 855
Pascal, Blaise, 164, 185
Passmore, John, 168, 202, 266, 379
Pater, Walter H., 83
Paterson, Antoinette M., 136
Paton, H. J., 207
Patrick, Mary Mills, 58
Patrick, St., 713

Patterson, Bob E., 784
Patterson, Richard, 83
Pattison, George, 240
Pauck, Marion, 788
Pauck, Wilhelm, 730, 788
Paul, Anthony M., 31
Paul, Diana Y., 514
Paul, Robert, 734
Paul of Finland, Archbishop, 755
Paul of Venice, 129
Pausanias, 488
Pavlos, Andrew J., 855
Payer, Pierre J., 700
Payne, Robert, 572
Payne, Wardell, J., 7
Pazstory, Esther, 457
Pe, Hla, 519
Peacock, Sandra J., 479
Pears, David, 346
Pearson, Birger A., 453
Peck, Abraham J., 652
Peel, Robert, 843, 875
Peirce, Charles Sanders, 211, 235, 248, 260, 317, 333
Pelikan, Jaroslav, 99, 677, 720
Pellegrin, Pierre, 70
Pelletier, Francis Jeffrey, 83
Penelhum, Terence, 202
Pennington, M. Basil, 112, 700
Penton, M. James, 863
Percesepe, Gary J., 398
Percy, Eustace, 774
Peretz, Don, 579
Perkins, Merle, 214
Perkins, Robert L., 240
Perlman, Lawrence, 665
Perlmutter, Nathan, 640
Perlmutter, Ruth Ann, 640
Peronal-Hugoz, Jean-Pierre, 579
Perreiah, Alan R., 130
Perrin, Norman, 816
Perrin, Ron, 332
Perry, John, 23
Perry, Ralph Barton, 27, 35, 238, 266
Persall, Marilyn, 391
Peter of Spain, 102
Peters, Edward, 693, 700, 721
Peters, Fritz, 876
Peters, Hans F., 247
Peters, Richard S., 174
Peters, Rudolph, 895
Petersen, Michael, 381
Peterson, Donald, 346
Petersson, Torsten, 72
Petit, Philip, 316
Petrarch, 145, 150

Petrovic, Gajo, 33
Petry, M. D., 741
Petry, Ray C., 697
Pettegree, Andrew, 731
Pettinato, Giovanni, 445
Petuchowski, Jakob J., 596, 600, 601, 613, 652
Pfeiffer, Robert H., 605
Pfuetze, Paul, 309
Phan, Peter C., 689
Philip, James A., 87
Philippi, Donald, 536
Philipson, David, 653
Phillips, Charles S., 741
Phillips, James M., 541
Phillips, John R., 738
Phillips, Margaret M., 139
Phillips, Stephen H., 349, 353
Philo Judaeus, 489, 607, 614, 670
Picken, Stuart D. B., 536
Pico Della Mirandola, Gianfrancesco, 151
Pico Della Mirandola, Giovanni, 152, 156
Picon-Salas, Mariano, 752
Piepkorn, Arthur C., 717, 751
Piggot, Juliet, 535
Piggott, Stuart, 436
Pilkington, A. E., 220
Pinault, David, 572
Pinches, Charles, 745
Pinsker, Sanford, 594
Piovesana, Gino K., 363, 541
Pipkin, H. Wayne, 791
Pippin, Robert, 207, 233, 408
Pitkin, Hanna F., 145
Pitt, Joseph C., 143, 334
Placher, William C., 719
Planck, Max, 332
Plantinga, Cornelius, 886
Planty-Bonjour, G., 31
Plaskow, Judith, 650, 784
Plato, 11, 44, 52, 54, 58, 64, 76, 88, 91, 123, 140, 150, 152, 208, 253, 257, 281, 283, 401, 409, 414, 482, 580, 581, 848
Plaut, W. Gunther, 653
Pliny the Younger, 682
Plochmann, George Kimball, 83
Plotch, Batia, 602
Plotinus, 61, 85, 116, 123, 140, 489
Plumb, Lawrence D., 866
Plutarch, 60, 489
Pocock, J.G.A., 145
Poewe, Karla, 857
Pogge, Thomas W., 316

Poggi, Isotta, 865
Pojman, Louis P., 23
Polansky, Ronald M., 83
Poliakov, Leon, 637
Pollack, Frederick, 189
Pollack, Herman, 624
Pollak, Michael, 644
Pollard, Albert F., 764
Pollock, John, 768
Polome, Edgar C., 436, 472
Pomeroy, Sarah B., 447
Pompa, Leon, 217
Pomponazzi, Pietro, 123,
153
Popkin, Richard H., 18, 23,
24, 130, 162, 202
Poppel, Stephen M., 658
Popper, Sir Karl Raimund,
315, **408**
Porphyry, 62
Portnoy, Samuel A., 656
Porton, Gary G., 613
Poster, Mark, 266, 331
Poston, M., 700
Potter, G. R., 791
Potts, D. C., 28
Potts, T. C., 95
Po-tuan, Chang, 528
Powell, Lyman P., 875
Powell, Milton B., 754
Powell, T.G.E., 436
Power, Eileen, 700
Powicke, Maurice R., 727
Prager, Dennis, 596
Prebish, Charles, 860
Prelinger, Catherine, 754
Prenter, Reginald, 779
Prestige, George L., 686
Prestwich, Menno, 732
Preus, Anthony, 47, 66, 78
Preus, J. Samuel, 420
Preus, Robert D., 730
Price, A. W., 83
Price, Henry H., 202
Price, Richard, 203, **210**
Price, Robert, 852
Price, S.R.F., 452
Priestley, Joseph, 210, 212
Primoratz, Igor, 387
Prior, William J., 83
Pritchard, James B., 7, 439,
809, 812
Pritchett, W. Douglas, 864
Proclus, 62
Procter-Smith, Marjorie, 849
Proust, Marcel, 255
Pruter, Karl, 859
Pudney, John, 790
Pufendorf, Samuel, 185
Pugliese, Olga Z., 141
Puhvel, Jaan, 436
Pullapilly, Cyriac K., 572
Purdom, C. D., 873

Purtill, Richard L., 23
Purvis, James D., 618
Pushkin, Aleksandr, 900
Pustilnik, Jack, 23
Putnam, Hilary, 288, 315,
379, **410**
Pythagoras of Samos, 87

Quadir, C. A., 373
Quasten, Johannes, 689, 690
Queller, Donald E., 694
Quimby, Phineas P., 847,
874, **877**
Quinby, Lee, 391
Quine, Willard Van Orman,
14, 279, 282, 315, 317,
379, 410, **411**
Qutb, Sayyid, 576

Rabil, Albert, Jr., 130, 139
Rabinowicz, Harry M., 658
Rabinowitsch, Wolf Zeev,
633
Rad, Gerhard von, 823, 827,
836
Rader, Melvin, 23
Rader, Rosemary, 689
Radhakrishnan, Sarvepalli,
350, 351, **353**, 498
Radin, Max, 605
Radner, Daisie, 182
Rahlfs, A., 796
Rahman, Fazlur, 373, 576
Rahman, Habib U., 567
Rahman, Razlur, 893
Rahner, Karl, 423, 676, 719,
745, 770, 891, **902**
Rai, Priya Muhar, 417
Rainbow, Paul, 400
Raitt, Jill, 723, 732
Rajadhon, Phya Anuman, 519
Rajak, Tessa, 666
Rajchman, John, 267, 379,
401
Raju, P. T., 38
Raley, Harold, 315
Ramakrishna, 354, 871
Rambo, Lewis, 890
**Rammohun Roy (Roy, Ram
Mohan), 355**
Ramsay, William M., 785,
905
Ramsey, Boniface, 690
Ramsey, Paul, 745, 896
Ranchetti, Michele, 741
Rand, Benjamin, 192
Rand, Edward K., 99
Randall, John Herman, 55,
70, 83, 130, 162, 267
Randolph, Sallie G., 849
Rangdrol, Tsele Natsok, 544

Ransohoff, Paul, 890
Rao, K. L., 553
Rapaport, Herman, 294
Raphael, Chaim, 594, 600
Raphael, D. D., 174, 204,
215
Raphael, Marc Lee, 634, 641,
651
Rashi (Solomon Ben Isaac),
628, **670**
Rasmussen, David M., 400,
405
Rasmussen, Richard M., 870
Ratzinger, Joseph Cardinal,
746, 891
Rausch, David A., 864
Raven, J. E., 50, 83, 87
Rawidowicz, Simon, 646
Rawls, John, 313, **315,** 385,
412
Rawski, Evelyn S., 531, 533
Rawson, Beryl, 72
Rawson, Elizabeth, 72
Ray, Ajit, 509
Ray, Benjamin C., 463, 898
Ray, Nihar Ranjan, 519
Reader, Ian, 535, 541
Reader, John P., 893
Reale, Giovanni, 46, 55, 70
Reardon, Bernard M., 741
Reck, Andrew J., 238, 267
Redeker, Martin, 741
Redfield, James, 492
Redfield, Robert, 477
Redford, Donald B., 442
Redmont, Jane, 754
Redondi, Pietro, 143
Redpath, Henry A., 818
Redpath, Peter, 308
Rée, Jonathan, 18, 162
Reed, David A., 863
Rees, John, 245
Reese, William L., 14
Reesor, Margaret E., 57
Reeves, Marjorie, 102
Regan, Tom, 312, 389
Regosin, Richard, 146
Reich, Warren T., 893
Reichenbach, Hans, 278, 385
Reicke, Bo, 605
Reid, Daniel G., 5, 718
Reid, Thomas, 211, 259, 395
Reid, W. Stanford, 732, 736,
762, 774
Reik, Miriam, 175
Reinharz, Jehuda, 130, 634,
637
Reinhold, K. L., 204
Reinhold, Meyer, 605
Reischauer, Edwin O., 358
Reiss, Edmund, 112
Rejwan, Nissim, 644
Renard, John, 576

Renault, Alain, 293
Rendtorff, Rolf, 817
Renfrew, Colin, 432, 434, 436, 472
Rescher, Nicholas, 177, 185, **316**, 385, 389, 576
Resnik, Michael, 230
Reuchlin, Johann, 130
Reynolds, Ernest E., 727
Reynolds, Frank, 887
Reynolds, Frank E., 428
Rhees, Rush, 346
Rhoads, David M., 666
Rhodes, P. J., 70
Rice, David G., 446
Rice, Edward, 572, 781
Rice, Eugene F., Jr., 130
Richard, Lucien J., 762
Richardson, Alan, 676, 719
Richardson, Henry G., 624
Richardson, Herbert W., 856
Richardson, Hugh E., 356
Richardson, James T., 856, 857, 864, 868
Richardson, John T., 346
Richardson, Joseph, 294
Richardson, Walter C., 727
Richman, Paula, 506, 514, 892
Richmond, Mary L., 849
Richs, Stephen D., 625
Richter, Melvin, 230
Richter, Peyton E., 23
Ricketts, Mac L., 474
Rickman, H. P., 226
Ricoeur, Paul, 18, 267, **318**, 426, 886
Ridley, Jasper G., 727, 736, 774
Ridolfi, Roberto, 145
Rieder, Jonathan, 641
Riedl, John O., 130
Riepe, Dale, 23
Rigby, S. H., 227
Riley, Isaac W., 35
Riley-Smith, Jonathan S. C., 694
Rilke, Rainer Maria, 255
Rilliet, Jean, 791
Rinbochay, Lati, 887
Ring, Kenneth, 870
Ringe, Sharon H., 819
Ringgren, Helmer, 441, 445, 616, 817
Rischin, Moses, 641
Rist, John M., 57, 74, 87
Roaf, Michael, 809
Robb, Kevin, 49
Robb, Nesca A., 130
Robbins, Thomas, 855, 857
Roberts, Alexander, 100
Roberts, Denis, 576
Roberts, James D., 748

Roberts, J. Deotis, 748
Roberts, Julian, 28
Roberts, Marie E., 848
Roberts, Michael, 731
Roberts, Nancy, 766
Roberts, Richard H., 277
Robinson, Christopher, 485
Robinson, Daniel N., 70
Robinson, Daniel S., 32, 250
Robinson, Francis, 567
Robinson, Franklin E., 83
Robinson, Howard, 66
Robinson, James M., 294, 453, 686, 812
Robinson, John A., 746
Robinson, John M., 47
Robinson, Richard H., 83, 514, 530, 538
Robinson, T. M., 75, 83
Robson, John A., 104
Rochelle, Gerald, 304
Rochford, E. Burke, 863
Rochlin, Harriett, 641
Rockefeller, Steven C., 225
Rockmore, Tom, 294
Rodinson, Maxime, 579, 589
Roemer, John, 243
Roensch, Frederick J., 119
Rofé, Hosein, 873
Roff, William R., 580
Rogers, G.A.J., 175
Rogers, Jack B., 23
Rogerson, John, 807
Rogow, Arnold A., 175
Rogow, Faith, 650
Rohatyn, Dennis, 312
Rohde, Erwin, 49
Rohr, Janelle, 580
Rolfe, John C., 73
Romanell, Patrick, 33, 285
Rome, Beatrice, 182
Romer, John, 442
Romero, Oscar, 748
Ronan, Charles E., 532
Ronan, Colin A., 144
Rone, David, 644
Rorem, Paul, 63
Rorty, Amelie Oksenberg, 70, 170
Rorty, Richard McKay, 35, 267, 294, 320, 376, 390, **412**
Rosaldo, Renate, 426
Rosen, Allen, 207
Rosen, Michael, 233
Rosen, Stanley, 83, 381
Rosenberg, Alexander, 201, 385
Rosenberg, Alfred, 247
Rosenberg, Jay, 23
Rosenberg, Joel, 817
Rosenberg, Roy A., 630
Rosenberg, Stuart E., 641

Rosenbloom, Noah H., 665
Rosenfield, Leonora, 162, 170
Rosenmeyer, Thomas G., 59, 88
Rosenthal, Edwin J., 580
Rosenthal, Gilbert S., 649
Rosenthal, Sandra B., 302, 309, 311
Rosenzweig, Franz, 662, **671**, 886
Roskies, David G., 648
Rosner, Fred, 668
Ross, Andrew, 866
Ross, Dan, 645
Ross, Floyd H., 536
Ross, G. MacDonald, 177
Ross, Joan Carol, 857
Ross, Sir David, 207
Ross, Stephen D., 342
Ross, W. D., 71, 84
Rosser, Brenda Lewis, 557
Rossi, Paolo, 130, 166
Rotenberg, Mordecai, 633
Rotenstreich, Nathan, 646, 662
Roth, Cecil, 5, 594, 597, 624
Roth, John, 2
Roth, Leon, 170, 189, 596
Rothchild, Sylvia, 641
Rothrock, George A., 732
Rouner, Leroy S., 297
Rouse, Ruth, 746
Rousseau, Jean-Jacques, 195, 200, **212**
Rowe, William, 194, 212
Rowley, H. H., 819
Royce, Josiah, 248, **249**, 260, 295, 301, 304
Rozenblit, Marsha L., 637
Ruben, David-Hillel, 227, 243
Ruben, Douglas H., 14
Rubenstein, Amnon, 658
Rubin, Miri, 697
Rubin, Vitaly A., 525
Ruch, E. A., 369
Rudavsky, David, 643, 651
Ruderman, David B., 624
Rudin, Marcia R., 857
Rudolph, Kurt, 453, 686
Ruether, Rosemary Radford, 650, 679, 684, 742, 749, **784**, 896, **904**
Ruf, Henry L., 38
Ruffo-Fiore, Silvia, 145
Rumi, 566, **589**
Runciman, Steven, 694
Rundle, Bede, 346
Runes, Dagobert D., 3, 15, 18
Running, Leona Glidden, 828
Rupp, Ernest Gordon, 727, 779

Rupp, Gordon, 724, 779
Rusch, William G., 686
Ruse, Michael, 385
Ruskin, John 551
Russel, Peter, 873
Russell, Bertrand Arthur William, 18, 23, 38, 162, 177, 220, 221, 229, 236, 260, 272, 278, 301, 302, **320**, 333, 340, 343, 377, 379
Russell, D. A., 490
Russell, David S., 605, 824
Russell, Jeffrey B., 687, 697, 700
Russell, Letty M., 815
Ruth, John L., 724
Rutherford, R. B., 59, 76
Ruthven, Malise, 572
Ryan, Alan, 175
Ryan, John K., 114
Ryan, Michael, 267, 392
Ryle, Gilbert, 84, 261, **325**, 381

Saadia Gaon, 671
Saatkamp, Herman J., Jr., 328
Sabloff, Jeremy A., 439, 454, 456
Sachar, Abram, 643
Sachar, Howard M., 634, 643, 645
Sacksteder, William, 175
Saddhatissa, Hammalava, 893
Safran, Alexandre, 630
Safranski, Rudiger, 256
Sage, Michael, 708
Saggs, H.W.F., 440
Sahlins, Marshall, 462
Said, Edward W., 572, 643
Sainsbury, Mark, 324
Saldarini, Anthony J., 613, 616
Saliba, John A., 857
Salkever, Stephen G., 71
Sallis, John, 75, 294, 398
Salmon, J. H., 732
Salmon, Nathan U., 411
Salomé, Lou A., 247
Sambursky, Samuel, 49, 57
Sandars, Nancy K., 445
Sandbach, F. H., 57
Sandberg, Karl, 166
Sandeen, Ernest R., 15, 754
Sanders, E. P., 617, 621, 807, 826
Sanders, James A., 613
Sanders, N. K., 546
Sanders, Ronald, 643
Sanders, Steven, 24

Sandmel, Samuel, 60, 100, 605, 646, 670, 812
Sandweiss, Samuel H., 873
Sangren, Steven, 531
Sankhdher, B. M., 355
Santas, Gerasimos X., 90
Santayana, George, 29, 75, 241, 296, **325**
Santer, M., 687
Santillana, Giorgio de, 130, 144
Santmire, H. Paul, 746
Saperstein, Marc, 628
Sapir, Edward, 477
Sapp, Stephen, 894
Sargeant, Winthrop, 506
Saron, Gustav, 645
Sartain, E. M., 585
Sartre, Jean-Paul, 39, 234, 261, 299, 301, 309, 318, **328**, 377
Saso, Michael R., 528, 532, 538
Sasson, Sarah D., 850
Sassoon, Anne S., 287
Sato, Giei, 538
Saunders, Jason L., 130
Saunders, Trevor J., 84
Savage, C. Wade, 324
Savory, Roger M., 572
Sawicki, Jana, 401
Saxonhouse, Arlene W., 49
Sayce, R. A., 146
Sayre, Kenneth M., 84
Scanlon, Phil, Jr., 519
Scanzoni, Letha, 750
Scarborough, Vernon L., 456
Scarisbrick, J. J., 727
Schacht, Richard, 247
Schact, Joseph, 572
Schacter-Shalom, Zalman, 649
Schaff, Philip, 100, 678
Schaffer, Simon, 175, 258
Schaper, Eva, 207
Scharfstein, Ben-Ami, 18, 37, 350
Scharlemann, Robert, 731, 889
Schaupp, Zora, 195
Schauss, Hayyim, 600
Schechter, Solomon, 621
Scheffler, Israel, 385
Scheler, Max Ferdinand, 261, **331**
Schellenberg, James A., 309
Schelling, Friedrich Wilhelm Joseph, 158, 197, 231, **250**
Schenk, Wilhelm, 729
Schenker, Hillel, 643
Scherer, Donald, 24

Schiffman, Lawrence H., 621, 812
Schillebeeckx, Edward, 746
Schilpp, Paul Arthur, 41, 276, 277, 280, 300, 302, 305, 312, 324, 331, 338, 343, 354, 410, 412
Schimmel, Annemarie, 375, 572, 589
Schlam, Carl C., 469
Schlegel, August, 251
Schlegel, Friedrich, 252, 253
Schleiermacher, Friedrich Daniel Ernst, 253, 254, 421, 785, 882
Schlick, Moritz, 272, 278, **332**
Schlipp, P. A., 279
Schlossberg, Edwin, 18
Schmemann, Alexander, 756
Schmidt, Dennis J., 295
Schmidt, M., 790
Schmidt, Werner H., 817
Schmitt, Arno, 894
Schmitt, Charles B., 71, 125, 130, 152
Schmitt, Richard, 243
Schmoller, A., 819
Schnackenburg, Rudolf, 822
Schneewind, Jerome, 257
Schneider, Herbert W., 35, 267
Schneider, Susan, 650
Schoeck, Richard J., 139
Schoedel, William, 704
Schoem, David, 641
Schoener, Allon, 641
Schoenfeld, Joachim, 624
Schoenfield, M., 50
Schoeps, Hans-Joachim, 573, 603
Schofield, Malcolm, 53, 56, 57
Scholem, Gershom, 631, **672**
Schomer, Karine, 517
Schoolman, Morton, 408
Schopenhauer, Arthur, 38, 245, **254**
Schouls, Peter A., 180
Schowalter, Daniel N., 452
Schram, Stuart R., 362
Schrift, Alan, 295
Schroeder, Frederic M., 87
Schroeder, H. J., 729
Schroeder, W. Widick, 263, 379
Schulte, Joachin, 347
Schultz, Bart, 257
Schulz, Hans Joachim, 694
Schuon, Frithjof, 373, 573, 576
Schürer, Emil, 605, 808

Schurman, Reiner, 295
Schurts, Mary M., 5
Schwade, Arcadio, 534
Schwartz, Benjamin I., 359, 525
Schwartz, Howard, 669
Schwartz, Leon, 196
Schwartz, Lita L., 858
Schwartz, Seth, 666
Schwartzbach, Bertram, 218
Schwarz, Leo W., 595
Schwarzfuchs, Simon, 637
Schweid, Eliezer, 673
Schweitzer, Albert, 740, 826
Schweizer, Eduard, 822, 826
Schwertner, Thomas M., 107
Schwiebert, Ernest G., 779
Sciacca, Michele F., 267
Scott, Alan, 63
Scott, Charles E., 22
Scott, Gini Graham, 865, 866
Scott, R., 795
Scotus, John Duns, 93, 103
Screech, M. A., 139, 146
Scriven, Michael, 24, 331
Scruton, Roger, 189
Scullard, H. H., 448, 818
Scully, Stephen, 483
Scult, Mel, 667
Searle, John, 383
Seaver, G., 275
Seaver, Paul S., 734
Sebag-Montefiore, Ruth, 637
Sebba, Gregor, 170
Sedgwick, Alexander, 737
Sedgwick, Henry D., 74, 76
Sedley, D. N., 55
Seeskin, Kenneth, 90, 596
Segal, Alan F., 605
Segal, Charles, 75, 475
Seigel, J. E., 131
Seigfried, Charlene H., 238
Seligman, Paul, 51
Selinger, Suzanne, 762
Selkitar, Ofira, 658
Sellars, Wilfrid, 162, 264, **333**
Sellars, W. V. Quine, 261
Seltzer, Robert M., 440, 595, 667
Sen, Soshitsu, 538
Seneca, Lucius Annaeus, 12, 59, **87**, 150, 760
Senior, Donald, 798
Septimus, Bernard, 629
Serels, M. Mitchell, 645
Serequeberhan, Tsenay, 26, 369
Sergeant, John, 180
Seth, Andrew, 32, 203
Sethna, K. D., 337
Settar, S., 510
Sextus Empiricus, 58

Seybold, Klaus, 824
Shackleton, Robert, 210
Shafer, Byron E., 442
Shaffer, Jerome A., 383
Shafii, Mohammed, 576
Shaftesbury, Anthony Ashley Cooper, 158, 203, **214**
Shah, Idries, 576
Shahan, Robert, 107
Shahan, Robert G., 412
Shahan, Robert W., 35, 202, 295
Shahi, Ahmed al-, 579
Shakabpa, W. D., 356
Shank, Michael H., 105
Shank, M. Thomas, 700
Shanker, S. G., 347
Shannon, Albert C., 700
Shannon, Thomas, 745
Shapere, Dudley, 144
Shapin, Steven, 175
Shapira, Anita, 658
Shapiro, H., 56
Shapiro, Herman, 121, 126
Shapiro, Ian, 387
Sharer, Robert J., 455
Sharma, Arvind, 355, 506, 509, 514, 526, 528, 553, 563, 892
Sharma, B. N., 506
Sharma, Jagdish, 498
Sharot, Stephen, 630, 634, 651
Sharpe, Eric J., 420, 422
Sharples, R., 90
Shea, William R., 144, 172
Sheehan, Edmund W., 859
Sheehy, Eugene P., 716
Shein, Louis J., 31, 335
Shenker, Israel, 595
Shepard, Mark, 553
Shepherd, A. P., 880
Shepherd, William C., 857
Sheppherd, Joseph, 861
Sherburne, Donald W., 343
Shereshevsky, Esra, 671
Sheridan, Daniel P., 506
Shermis, Michael, 5
Sherwin, Byron L., 665
Shestov, Lev, 247, **334**
Shields, Steven L., 846
Shiloah, Amnon, 597
Shimron Binyamin, 480
Shinn, Larry D., 862, 863
Shipka, Thomas A., 22
Shipps, Jan, 846
Shirer, William L., 553
Shook, Lawrence K., 286
Shorey, Paul, 84
Shorter, A. W., 548
Shri Priyadarsha, 510
Shumway, David R., 401

Shupe, Anson D., Jr., 846, 855, 857, 871
Sichronovsky, Peter, 637
Sidgwick, Henry, 158, **256**
Sidorsky, David, 641
Siebt, Johanna, 334
Siegel, Richard, 602
Siegel, Seymour, 655
Sievers, Joseph, 605
Sigal, Phillip, 595, 655
Sigmund, Paul E., 149
Sikes, J. G., 106
Silberger, Julius, 875
Silberman, Charles E., 641
Silberstein, Laurence J., 643, 662
Silk, E., 756
Sillanpoa, Wallace P., 638
Silver, Daniel J., 595, 598
Silverblatt, Irene, 458
Silverman, Hugh J., 267, 392, 398, 402
Silverstein, Y., 602
Simon, Marcal, 615, 616
Simon, Maurice, 630
Simon, Yves R., 71, 307
Simoneau, Karin, 466
Simpson, George E., 468
Simpson, William K., 442
Simson, Otto G. von, 701
Sinaiko, Herman L., 84
Singer, Beth, 328
Singer, Dorothea W., 136
Singer, Howard, 649
Singer, Milton B., 506
Singer, Peter Albert David, 37, **43**, 389
Singh, Bhagwan B., 250
Singh, Karen Lee, 59
Singh, Khushwant, 517
Sirat, Colette, 629
Sister Nivedita, 563
Sivan, Emanuel, 573
Sizemore, Russell F., 896
Sizemore, Russell R., 514
Skemp, J. B., 84
Skinner, Andrew, 215
Skinner, Quentin, 105, 131
Skirbekk, Gunnar, 32
Sklare, Marshall, 641, 655
Skolimowski, Henryk, 38
Skomal, Susan S., 436
Skorupski, John, 245
Slater, Robert H., 573
Slavens, Thomas P., 15
Sleeper, James A., 641
Sleeper, R. W., 225
Sleigh, Robert, 164, 178
Sloss, Radha Rajogopal, 556
Slote, Michael, 389
Sluga, Hans, 230
Smalley, Beryl, 102, 628, 697

Smart, Ninian, 422, 426, 499, 523, 535, 741, 884
Smelik, K.A.D., 812
Smith, Adam, 158, 200, **214**
Smith, Bardwell L., 518
Smith, Brian K., 501
Smith, Christian, 747
Smith, Colin, 28
Smith, D. Moody, 826
Smith, Elizabeth H., 316
Smith, Gerard, 131
Smith, H. Shelton, 752
Smith, James W., 752
Smith, J. I., 887
Smith, John E., 35, 250, 267
Smith, Jonathan E., 767
Smith, Jonathan Z., 438, 451, 470, 473, 487, **490**
Smith, Joseph, Jr., 845, 846, **878**
Smith, Marilyn, 25
Smith, Mark S., 824
Smith, Michael B., 311
Smith, Morton, 451, 604
Smith, Nicholas D., 89
Smith, Norman Kemp, 171, 202, 206
Smith, Peter, 383, 861
Smith, Preserved, 139
Smith, Roch C., 274
Smith, Steven, 233
Smith, Thomas V., 36, 163
Smith, Timothy, 754
Smith, Wilfred Cantwell, 422, 423, 427, 573
Smith, William A., 285
Smith, William Robertson, 428, **491**
Smolar, Leivy, 609
Snell, Bruno, 49
Snellgrove, David L., 356
Snodgrass, Adrian, 538
Snow, David A., 860
Snyder, Gary, 853
Snyder, Graydon F., 689
Snyder, Mary Hembrow, 785, 905
Snyder, William S., 24
Sobel, B. Zvi, 643, 864
Soccio, Douglas J., 24
Socrates, 11, 44, 50, 52, 53, 76, **88,** 91, 238, 314
Soelle, Dorothee, 750
Sofer, Tehoeda, 894
Soffer, Olga, 433
Sofue, Takao, 531, 539
Sokoloff, Boris, 223
Sokolowski, Robert, 235
Soled, Debra E., 532
Solmsen, Friedrich, 71, 84
Solomon, Robert C., 20, 24, 248, 267

Soloveitchik, Joseph, 673, 886
Somerville, John, 31
Sontag, Frederick, 240
Sopa, Geshe Lhundup, 544
Sophocles, 474
Sorabji, Richard, 66, 71
Sordi, Marta, 684
Sorensen, Roy A., 385
Sorin, Gerald, 656
Sorrell, Tom, 175
Sosa, Ernest, 192
Soulen, Richard N., 815
Soustelle, Jacques, 455
Southern, Richard W., 96, 108, 691, 703
Spade, Paul Vincent, 104
Spalding, J. Howard, 880
Spargo, Emma J., 113
Specht, Walter, 798
Speigler, Gerhard, 254
Spencer, Herbert, 245
Spencer, Robert F., 573
Spenser, Edmund, 182
Sperber, A., 796
Spero, Moshe Halevi, 890
Spidlik, Tomas, 679
Spiegel, Shalom, 621
Spiegelberg, Herbert, 235, 267
Spiegelman, Art, 637
Spiegler, Gerhard E., 349
Spink, John S., 28, 163
Spink, Kathryn, 746
Spinka, Matthew, 711, 721
Spinoza, Baruch, 12, 158, 167, 171, 175, **186,** 197, 208, 209, 628, 673
Spiro, Audrey, 526
Spiro, Melford E., 519, 643, 890
Spitz, Lewis W., 691, 723, 730
Spong, John, 746
Sprague, Rosamond Kent, 54
Sprigge, Timothy, 328
Spriggs, D. G., 834, 838
Sprintzen, David A., 24
Sproul, Barbara C., 427
Squadrito, Kathleen M., 181
Squire, Aelred, 690
Srzednicki, J., 222
Stacey, John., 714
Stack, George J., 240
Stalin, Joseph, 321
Stalley, R. F., 84
Stallsworth, Paul, 895
Stambaugh, Joan, 295, 538
Stambaugh, John E., 446
Standish, Paul, 295
Staniforth, Maxwell, 704
Stannard, David E., 735
Stanton, H. V., 587

Starhawk, 865
Stark, Rodney, 855, 857
Starkey, Edward D., 7
Starr, John Bryan, 362
Staten, Henry, 398
Statler, Oliver, 539
Staub, Jacob J., 659
Staude, J. R., 332
Stayer, James M., 724
Stearns, Peter N., 741
Steenbergen, G. J., 15
Steenberghen, F. van, 97, 119
Stegmueller, Wolfgang, 29, 268
Stein, Rolf A., 356, 520, 523, 534, 544
Stein, Stephen J., 754, 850
Steinbeck, Bonnie, 389
Steinberg, Jules, 181
Steinberg, Milton, 596, 621, 634, 655
Steiner, George, 295
Steiner, Rudolf, 248, 852, 858, **879**
Steinkraus, Warren E., 192
Steinmetz, David C., 779
Steinsaltz, Adin, 613, 669
Stemberger, G., 613
Stenberg, Peter, 637
Stendahl, Krister, 617
Stenius, Erik, 347
Stephen, Sir Leslie, 175, 245
Stephens, W. P., 791
Stephenson, Charles L., 217
Sterba, James, 160
Stern, Chaim, 600
Stern, David, 613
Stern, J. P., 248
Stevenson, J., 689
Stewart, David, 24
Stewart, Desmond, 573
Stewart, J. A., 71
Stewart, M. A., 32
Stillman, John M., 150
Stillman, Norman A., 626, 645
Stocks, John L., 71
Stoddard, Lothrop, 573
Stoddard, Philip, 573
Stoesz, William, 541
Stokes, Michael C., 51
Stone, Ira F., 649
Stone, Lawrence, 735
Stone, Michael E., 615, 616
Stough, Charlotte L., 58
Stout, Harry, 767
Stout, Jeffrey, 893
Stove, D. C., 203
Strabo, 492
Strachan, Paul, 519
Strack, H. L., 613, 812
Strange, Roderick, 891

Strassfeld, Michael, 600, 602
Strassfeld, Sharon, 602
Stratton, G. M., 91
Strauss, Gerald, 731
Strauss, Leo, 90, 91, 145, 175, 189
Straw, Carol, 711
Strawson, Galen, 203
Strawson, Peter F., 207, 261, 321, 335, 379, **413**
Strayer, Joseph R., 94
Streng, Frederick J., 423
Strenski, Ivan, 420, 427, 428
Strieber, Whitley, 870
Striker, Gisela, 56
Strizower, Schifra, 645
Stroll, Avrum, 23, 24
Stromberg, Roland N., 27
Stroud, Barry, 203
Strozier, Robert M., 74
Struhl, Karsten J., 24
Struhl, Paula R., 24
Stuart, J. A., 84
Stuhlmacher, Peter, 815, 826
Stuhr, John J., 36
Stump, Eleonore, 95, 119
Stumpf, Samuel E., 18, 24
Stunkel, Kenneth R., 38
Sturluson, Snorri, 437
Suárez, Francisco, 105, **154**
Suggs, M. Jack, 798
Suhl, Benjamin, 331
Suhl, Yuri, 637
Suksamran, Somboon, 520
Sullivan, Lawrence, 506, 514, 530, 536
Sullivan, Lawrence E., 465, 466
Sullivan, Robert R., 402
Sullivan, Roger, 207
Sumrall, Amber Coverdale, 746
Sundaram, K., 280
Sundkler, Bengt, 468
Sunim, Kusan, 538
Surin, Kenneth, 886
Surtz, Edward L., 148
Suter, Ronald, 347
Sutherland, Gail Hinich, 506, 510, 514
Sutherland, N. M., 732
Suzuki, D(aisetz) T(eitard), 363, 364, **557**
Suzuki, Shunryu, 538
Swain, Tony, 461
Swami Atulananda, 563
Swan, Maureen, 554
Swanberg, Jane M., 474
Swanson, Paul L., 530
Swanson, R. N., 695
Swearer, Donald K., 514, 520, 896

Swedenborg, Emanuel, 850, 851, 852, **880**
Sweeney, Amin, 460
Sweeney, Leo, 51
Sweet, Leonard I., 754
Sweetman, James W., 573
Swetnam, J., 796
Swezey, Charles M., 900
Swiderski, Edward M., 31
Swidler, Leonard, 423
Swift, Louis J., 689
Swinburne, Richard, 886
Swoyer, Chris, 412
Swyhart, Barbara A., 895
Sykes, Christopher, 643
Sylvester, Robert D., 312
Szarmach, Paul E., 697
Szonyi, David M., 7

Tachau, Katherine, 121
Tacitus, 437
Taggart, James M., 465
Tagliacozzo, Giorgio, 217
Tagore, Sir Rabindranath, 355
Taha, Mahmud Mohamed, 576
Tahiri, Amin, 580
Taitz, Emily, 650
Takeuchi Yoshinori, 365
Tal, Uriel, 637
Tallant, Robert, 868
Talmage, Frank, 603, 630
Talmor, Ezra, 203
Tambiah, S. J., 519
Tamineaux, Jacques, 295
Tamney, Joseph B., 842, 860
Tanabe, George J., 538
Tanabe, Willa Jane, 538
Tanabe Hajime, 366
Tanner, Kathryn, 746
Tanner, Norman, 891
Tappert, Theodore G., 779
Taran, Leonardo, 52
Tarnas, Richard, 18
Tarrant, Harold, 58
Tatar, Maria M., 847
Tatarkiewicz, Wladislaw, 131
Tatum, James, 469
Taussig, Michael, 431
Tavard, George H., 679, 697, 788
Taylor, A. E., 84, 90, 203
Taylor, Charles, 233, **414**
Taylor, Henry Osborn, 96, 131
Taylor, Lily R., 452
Taylor, Mark C., 268, 392, 889
Taylor, Richard, 381
Taylor, Robert H., 515
Taylor, Rodney L., 526, 541

Taylor, Vincent, 826
Tcherikover, Victor, 605
Tec, Nechama, 638
Tedlock, Barbara, 456, 465
Tedlock, Dennis, 456, 465
Teilhard de Chardin, Pierre, 335
Teiser, Stephen F., 531
Telushkin, Joseph, 596
Temkin, Sefton D., 653
Tempels, Placide, 369
Tentler, T., 701
Tenzin Gyatso, 356, 558, 905
Teodorsson, Sven Tage, 53
Teresa of Avila, St., 728, 736, **785**
Terry, Patricia, 437
Tertullian, 713
Tetsurō, Watsuji, 367
Teutsch, Betsy P., 597
Thackeray, Henry, 666, 812
Thayer, Horace S., 225, 268
Theissen, Gerd, 618, 826
Theophrastus of Eresus, 65, 90
Thich Nhat Hanh, 561
Thielicke, Helmut, 746
Thiemann, Ronald, 746
Thomas, Charles, 437
Thomas, David, 211
Thomas, E. E., 241
Thomas, Geoffrey, 230
Thomas, Julian, 434
Thomas, Keith, 727
Thomas, Milton H., 225
Thomas, P. M., 509, 554, 563
Thomas, Robert D., 844
Thomas, Rosalind, 460
Thompson, Bard, 681
Thompson, J. Eric S., 456
Thompson, John B., 405
Thompson, Josiah, 240
Thompson, Keith, 870
Thompson, Laurence G., 522, 523
Thompson, Robert F., 26
Thomsen, Harry, 541
Thomson, J. A., 695
Thomson, Judith J., 387
Thoreau, Henry David, 551, 771, 840
Thorndike, Lynn, 98, 102, 131
Throckmorton, B. H., 798
Thulstrup, Niels, 240
Thurman, Robert A. F., 888
Thurston, Herbert, 701
Tice, Terrence N., 15
Tierney, Brian, 695
Tighman, B. R., 347
Tikku, Girdhari, 576
Tiles, J. E., 226, 414

Tiles, Mary, 274
Tillich, Hannah, 788
Tillich, Paul Johannes, 252,
    366, 422, 678, 783, **787**
Tillman, Hoyt Cleveland, 526
Timm, Jeffrey R., 506, 510,
    514, 517
Tipton, Steven M., 855
Titus, Harold, 25
Tiwari, M. N., 510
Tmeko, Phillip, 82
Tobias, Henry J., 656
Tobias, Michael, 510
Tobin, Frank, 102, 709
Tobriner, Marian Leona, 156
Todd, John M., 723
Todd, William B., 203
Toews, John, 233
Toffanin, G., 131
Toksvig, Signe, 852, 880
Tolkien, J.R.R., 776
Tolstoy, Leo, 255, 551, 756,
    900
Toolan, David, 858
Torrance, Nancy, 460
Torre, Michael D., 271, 308
Torrey, Norman L., 196, 218
Torwesten, Hans, 872
Toulmin, Stephen, 25
Tov, Ba'al Shem, 631, 668
Townsend, H. G., 36
Toynbee, Arnold Joseph, 337
Trachtenberg, Joshua, 624,
    630
Tracy, David, 99, 428, 746,
    813, 889, 891
Tracy, Patricia, 767
Tracy, Theodore J., 84
Trawick, Margaret, 506
Trepp, Leo, 602
Trigg, Joseph W., 117
Trimingham, J. Spencer, 573,
    577
Trinkaus, Charles, 131, 151,
    697
Tripolitis, Antonia, 63
Trisco, Robert, 751
Tritton, Arthur S., 577
Trobridge, George, 852, 880
Troeltsch, Ernst, 95, 742,
    899
Trollope, Anthony, 73
Trompf, G. W., 468
Tropea, Gregory, 295
Troxell, Eugene A., 24
Trueblood, Elton, 25
Trungpa, Chögyam, 357,
    544
Tse-tung, Mao (also Mao
    Zedong), 359, 361
Tsomo, Karma Lekshe, 515
Tsunoda, Ryusaku, 534
Tu, Wei-ming, 526

Tucci, Giuseppe, 356, 544
Tuchman, Barbara W., 701
Tuck, Richard, 175
Tucker, Gene M., 814
Tucker, Mary E., 337
Tucker, Robert C., 243
Tuckett, Christopher, 826
Tully, Mark, 517
Turbayne, Colin M., 192
Turner, Harold W., 468
Turner, Henry E., 100, 687
Turner, Victor Witter, 429,
    430, 463, 477, 898
Tursman, Richard, 249
Turville-Petre, E.O.G., 437
Tu Wei-Ming, 362, 533
Tweed, Thomas A., 842
Tweedale, M., 106
Twersky, Isadore, 625, 627,
    629, 668, 669
Twiss, Sumner B., 893
Twitchell, Paul, 873
Tyacke, Nicholas, 734
Tyler, Stephen A., 506
Tyson, Joseph B., 817

Ueberweg, Friedrich, 18, 163
Uffenheimer, Rivka, 633
Ugolnik, Anthony, 756
Ugrinsky, Alexej, 208
Ulansey, David, 450
Ullmann, Walter, 695
Umansky, Ellen M., 653
Unamuno, Miguel de, 261,
    337
Underhill, Evelyn, 679
Underhill, Ruth M., 465
Ungerleider, J. Thomas, 855
Ungerleider-Mayerson, Joy,
    597
Unno, Taitetsu, 365, 366
Urbach, Peter, 166
Urmson, J. O., 15, 192, 268
Urofsky, Melvin I., 658
Urton, Gary, 458, 466
Urvoy, Dominque, 581

Valla, Lorenzo, 154
van Beeck, Frans Jozef, 901
van Buitenan, J.A.B., 506
Van Croonenburg, Englebert
    J., 25
Vanden Burgt, Robert J., 238
van der Leeuw, Gerardus,
    427, 885
Van der Linden, Harry, 207
Van Doren, Charles, 2
Van Herik, Judith, 424
Vanhoozer, Kevin J., 320
Vanita, Ruth, 508
Van Over, Raymond, 525

Van Straaten, Zak, 414
Van Zandt, David E., 864
Varley, Paul, 538
Vartanian, Aram, 197
Vaughn, Karen I., 181
Vaux, Kenneth L., 893
Veatch, Henry B., 71
Vecchione, Patrice, 746
Vecsey, Christopher, 7
Veilleux, Armand, 690
Velkley, Richard, 207
Vellacott, Jo, 325
Vendler, Zeno, 171
Vento, Arnold C., 33
Verbeke, Gerald, 57
Verduin, Leonard, 724
Verene, Donald P., 217
Verhey, Allen, 746, 893
Vermazen, Bruce, 283
Vermes, Geza, 616, 618, 812
Vernant, Jean-Pierre, 49,
    429, **492**
Versényi, Laszlo, 54, 84, 295
Vesey, Godfrey, 25
Veysey, Laurence R., 844
Vickers, Brian, 166
Vickery, John B., 477
Vico, Giambattista, 30, 158,
    215
Vidal-Naquet, Pierre, 447
Vidler, Alexander R., 742
Viney, Donald W., 289
Viroli, Maurizio, 214
Vital, David, 643, 658
Vivekananda, Swami, 355,
    557, **562**
Vives, Juan Luis, 155
Vlastos, Gregory, 85, 90
Voegelin, Eric, 85
Vogel, Cyrille, 701
Vogel, E. K., 809
Vogt, Evon Z., 426, 465, 897
Vohra, Ashok, 354
Voll, John O., 573
Vollmar, Edward R., 752
Voltaire, 12, 15, 166, 173,
    195, **217**
Voragine, Jacobus de, 701
Vorgrimler, Herbert, 719
Voss, Stephen, 171

Waardenburg, Jacques, 422
Wach, Joachim, 493
Wachman, Alan, 533
Wachterhauser, Brice R.,
    268, 392
Waddams, Herbert M., 731
Waddell, Helen, 690
Wade, Ira O., 28, 218
Wadley, Susan Snow, 506
Waghorne, Joanne Punzo,
    506

Wagner, Melinda B., 855
Wagner, Richard, 245, 255
Wagner, Rudolf G., 531
Wahl, Jean A., 268
Waik, A. E., 848
Wainright, William J., 888
Wainwright, Geoffrey, 5, 746, 897, 898
Waite, Gary K., 724
Waithe, Mary Ellen, 163
Wakefield, Gordon S., 676, 718
Wakefield, Walter L., 701
Wakeman, Frederic E., 362
Walcott, P., 482
Waldenfels, Hans, 365
Waldron, Arthur, 523
Waley, Arthur D., 525, 526, 528
Walicki, Andrzej, 30
Walker, D. P., 131
Walker, Ralph, 207
Walker, William O., 819
Walker, Williston, 678, 720
Wallace, Dewey D., 735
Wallace, Karl R., 166
Wallace, Ruth A, 892
Wallace, William A., 25, 74, 102, 132, 144, 256
Wallace-Hadrill, D. S., 687
Wallace-Hadrill, John Michael, 692
Wallach, Luitpold, 100
Wallack, F. Bradford, 343
Wallis, Richard T., 62, 63
Wallis, Roy, 869
Wallraff, Charles F., 300
Walsh, Chad, 777
Walsh, James J., 71, 94
Walsh, Michael, 676
Walshe, Maurice, 514
Walters, Gregory J., 300
Walters, J. Donald (Swami Kriyananda), 557
Walther, Wiebke, 580
Waltke, Bruce K., 795
Walton, Craig, 182
Walton, Douglas, 381
Walzer, Michael, 735
Wand, John W., 682, 687
Wangchen, Geshe Namgyal, 513
Wangerin, Ruth, 864
Warburton, Nigel, 25
Ward, Benedicta, 701
Ward, Gary L., 895
Ware, James R., 529
Ware, Timothy, 694, 756
Warner, Marina, 679
Warner, Stephen, 197
Warnke, Georgia, 402
Warnock, Geoffrey J., 192, 268, 272

Warnock, Mary, 268
Warrender, Howard, 175
Wartofsky, Marx, 228
Washington, Joseph R., Jr., 749
Waskow, Arthur I., 600
Wasserstein, Bernard, 637, 638
Waswo, Richard, 132
Watanabe, Kazuko, 545
Waterfield, Robin, 51
Waterlow, Sarah, 71
Waterman, Amy, 218
Watkins, J.W.N, 175
Watkins, Owen, 735
Watson, Burton, 358, 529
Watson, James L., 531, 533
Watson, Philip S., 779
Watson, Richard A., 171
Watsuji Tetsurō, 366
Watt, William Montgomery, 97, 373, 573, 577, 582, 587, 589
Watts, Alan Wilson, 853, 860, 880
Watts, Pauline Moffit, 149
Waugh, Earle H., 887
Waxman, Chaim I., 641
Waxman, Mordecai, 655
Wayman, Alex, 514
Wayman, Hideko, 514
Weatherby, Harold L., 783
Webb, Clement C. J., 18, 116
Webb, Eugene, 320
Webb, James, 842, 856, 876
Weber, Alison, 787
Weber, Max, 424, 425, 494, 759
Weber, R., 796
Webering, Damascene, 121
Wedberg, Anders, 18, 85, 268
Wedin, Michael V., 71
Wegener, Charles, 381
Weger, Karl-Heinz, 746
Weidner, Marsha, 524, 535
Weightman, Judith M., 867
Weigle, L. A., 798
Weil, Simone, 788
Weinberg, David H., 638
Weinberg, Julius R., 94, 163, 698
Weinberg, R. J., 104
Weinberger, Jerry, 166
Weiner, Anita, 643
Weiner, David A., 347
Weiner, Eugene, 643
Weiner, Herbert, 630, 643
Weiner, Joan, 230
Weiner, Max, 653
Weingart, Richard E., 106
Weingreen, Jacob, 795
Weinlick, J. R., 740

Weinryb, Bernard, 625
Weinsheimer, Joel, 402
Weinstein, Donald, 701
Weinstein, Michael A., 33, 36
Weisbord, Robert G., 638
Weisbrot, Robert, 645
Weisheipl, James A., 107, 119
Weiss, Johannes, 826
Weiss, Paul, 262, 288, 338
Weiss, Raymond, 668
Weiss, Roberto, 132
Weitz, Morris, 268
Welbon, Guy, 507
Welch, Claude, 742
Welch, Holmes, 530
Wells, Kenneth E., 520
Welton, K. B., 895
Wemple, Suzanne F., 701
Wendel, François, 762
Wenke, Robert J., 432, 439
Wensinck, Arent J., 577
Wentz, Walter Yeeling Evans, 544
Wenz, Peter S., 389, 895
Werblowsky, J. Z., 628
Werblowsky, Zwi, 595
Werhane, Patricia H., 347
Werkmeister, William H., 36
Werner, Eric, 597
Wernham, James C., 335
Wertheimer, Alan, 387
Wesley, John, 738, 740, 789
Wessinger, Catherine Lowman, 550
West, Cornel, 267, 268, 379, 749
West, Edward N., 716
West, Selno C., 712
West, Thomas H., 277
Westbrook, Robert B., 226
Westermann, Claus, 815, 822, 824
Westfall, Richard S., 184
Westoby, Adam, 18, 162
Westphal, Fred A., 25
Westphal, Jonathan, 347
Westphal, Kenneth, 233
Wetlesen, Jon, 189
Wetter, Gustav A., 31
Wettersten, John, 409
Whaling, Frank, 422
Wheatley, Paul, 439
Wheelwright, Phillip E., 75
Whewell, William, 257
Whitaker, G. H., 810
White, Alan, 252
White, Alan R., 312, 387
White, David A., 85, 295
White, Morton G., 36, 226, 268
White, Nicholas P., 85
White, R. E., 679

White, Stephen K., 405
Whitehead, Alfred North,
  260, 288, 301, 302, 320,
  338, **340**, 377, 379, 411
Whitehead, Henry, 507
Whiten, Andrew, 383
Whiteside, Kerry H., 311
Whiting, Robert, 727
Whitman, Cedric, 475
Whitmarsh, Katherine, 355
Whitney, Barry L., 289
Whitson, Robley E., 850
Whittaker, Molly, 605
Whittaker, Thomas, 62
Whittemore, Robert C., 284
Wickens, G. M., 582
Wickett, Ann, 389
Wiener, Philip P., 3, 15, 163
Wienpahl, Paul, 189
Wiesel, Elie, 633
Wiest, Jean-Paul, 533
Wigoder, Geoffrey, 5, 595,
  597
Wilbert, Johannes, 466
Wilbur, Earl M., 724
Wilbur, J. B., 71
Wilcox, David R., 456
Wilcox, Ella W., 847
Wild, John D., 85, 238
Wiles, Maurice F., 687, 690
Wilhelm, Richard, 525, 529
Wilken, Robert L., 100, 684
Wilkes, Paul, 781
Wilkins, Burleigh, 193
Wilkins, Ernest H., 151
Wilkinson, Loren, 746
Wilks, Michael J., 116
Willard, Dallas, 235
William Douglas E., 410
William of Ockham, 93,
  103, 113, **119**
William of Sherwood, 103
William of St. Thierry, 102
Williams, Bernard, 171
Williams, Daniel D., 679
Williams, George H., 724,
  733, 747
Williams, George M., 563
Williams, John Alden, 577,
  580
Williams, Paul, 514
Williams, Peter W., 4
Williams, Raymond Brady,
  509, 510
Williams, Rowan, 678, 787
Williamson, G. A., 666
Willis, Janice D., 544
Willis, R., 189
Wills, Gary, 36
Wilmore, Gayraud S., 749,
  896
Wilson, A. N., 777
Wilson, Bryan, 425

Wilson, Catherine, 178
Wilson, Charles, 228
Wilson, Colin, 876
Wilson, Curtis, 104
Wilson, Daniel J., 303
Wilson, John, 379, 389
Wilson, John F., 716, 754
Wilson, Margaret, 25, 171
Wilson, Robert R., 824
Wilson, Thomas, 215
Wiltshire, Martin G., 510,
  514
Wimbush, Vincent L., 690
Windelband, Wilhelm, 18,
  163
Windt, Peter Y., 25
Wine, Sherwin T., 649
Winkler, John J., 469
Winn, Ralph B., 36
Winslow, Ola E., 767
Winston, David, 60, 670
Wippel, John F., 95, 103,
  119
Wiredu, Kwasi, 27, **371**
Wirszubski, Chaim, 153
Wiser, Charlotte, 509
Wiser, William, 509
Wistrich, Robert S., 656
Witt, Charlotte, 72
Witt, R. E., 60
Witt, Ronald G., 127, 132
Wittgenstein, Ludwig Josef
  Johann, 12, 261, 271, 272,
  278, 320, 325, 332, 333,
  337, **343**, 377, 381
Wiznitzer, Arnold, 645
Wojtyla, Karol, 747
Wolf, Abraham, 189
Wolf, Albert, 132
Wolf, Arnold Jacob, 649
Wolf, Arthur, 531
Wolfenstein, E. Victor, 877
Wolff, Christian, 207, **218**
Wolff, Philippe, 100
Wolff, Robert P., 25
Wolfson, Harry Austryn, 60,
  63, 100, 189, 670, 687
Wolheim, William, 601
Wolin, Richard, 295
Wolk, Samuel, 593
Wolkstein, Diane, 440, 546
Wolpe, David J., 600
Wolpert, Stanley A., 351
Wolter, Allan B., 95, 114
Wolterstorff, Nicholas, 762
Womack, Brantly, 362
Womer, Jan L., 690
Woocher, Jonathan S., 641
Wood, Allen W., 207, 233,
  243
Wood, Charles M., 494
Wood, David, 398
Wood, Forrest, Jr., 290

Wood, John, 215
Wood, Neal, 59, 181
Wood, Thomas E., 501, 507,
  514
Woodbridge, Frederick J.,
  72, 85
Woodhouse, Mark B., 25
Woodhouse, Roger, 180
Woodward, Anthony, 328
Woodward, William H., 132
Woolhouse, R. S., 181
Wormald, Jenny, 736
Wouk, Herman, 597
Wrede, William, 826
Wright, Arthur F., 530
Wright, David F., 5
Wright, G. E., 618
Wright, Georg H. von, 337
Wright, Kathleen, 402
Wright, Larry, 415
Wright, M. R., 53
Wright, Richard A., 27, 369
Wright, Robin, 573
Wu, Kuang-Ming, 529
Wulff, Donna Marie, 504
Wurthwein, Ernst, 806
Wuthnow, Robert, 747, 754,
  856
Wyclif, John, 711, **714,** 797,
  799
Wyman, David S., 641
Wymer, J. J., 433
Wyschogrod, Edith, 295, 392
Wyschogrod, Michael, 649,
  885
Wyszkowski, Charles, 638

X, Malcolm (Malcolm Lit-
  tle), 566, 762, 861, 862,
  876
Xenophon, 88, **91**

Yadin, Yigael, 614
Yampolsky, Philip B., 538
Yanchi, Liu, 522
Yang, C. K., 524
Yarnold, Edward, 678, 897
Yates, Frances A., 132, 136,
  848
Ye'or, Bat, 573
Yearley, Lee, 897
Yehiya, Eliezer Don, 642
Yerushalmi, Yosef Hayim,
  595, 625
Yocum, Glen, 507
Yoder, John Howard, 896
Yoder, Paton, 733
Yoffee, Norman, 546
Yogananda, Paramahansa,
  872, 873

Yolton, John W., 163, 181, 740
Yost, Robert, 178
Young, Frances, 687
Young, Gordon Davis, 445
Young, John, 25
Young, Julian, 248, 256
Young, Katherine K., 509, 892, 894
Young, Pamela Dickey, 749
Young, Serinity, 892
Young-Bruehl, Elisabeth, 300, 395
Yovel, Yirmiahu, 207
Yu, Anthony, 531
Yu, Chai-Shin, 534, 539
Yu, David C., 522

Yuasa Yasuo, 367
Yun, Sasson, 535

Zaehner, Robert C., 5, 501, 548, 574
Zahan, Dominique, 463
Zaller, R., 734
Zangwill, O. L., 382
Zaretsky, Irving I., 856
Zborowski, Mark, 625
Zea, Leopoldo, 33
Zeeden, Ernest W., 731
Zeiller, Jacques, 681
Zeitlin, Solomon, 605
Zemer, Mosche, 627
Zenner, Walter P., 644

Zerwick, Max, 795
Zimdars-Swartz, Sandra, 712
Zimmer, Heinrich, 351
Zimmerman, Michael, 295
Zinberg, Israel, 601
Zinn, William V., 38
Zinner, Gauriel, 602
Ziolkowski, Jan, 702
Zipperstein, Steven J., 638
Zlotnick, Dov, 613
Zoff, O., 732
Zuck, Lowell H., 725
Zuckerman, Alan, 634
Zuesse, Evan, 463
Zuidema, R. Tom, 458
Zwalf, W., 515
Zwingli, Huldrych, 790

Title Index

Titles of all books discussed in *The Reader's Adviser* are indexed here, except broad generic titles such as "Complete Works," "Selections," "Poems," "Correspondence." Also omitted is any title written by a profiled author that also includes that author's full name or last name as part of the title, such as *The Collected Works of Jeremy Bentham*. The only exception to this is Shakespeare (Volume 1), where *all* works by and about him are indexed. To locate all titles by and about a profiled author, the user should refer to the Name Index for the author's primary listing (given in boldface). In general, subtitles are omitted unless two or more works have the same main title, or the main title consists of an author's full or last name (e.g., *John Calvin: A Biography)*. When two or more works by different authors have the same title, the authors' last names will appear in parentheses following the title.

Abailard on Universals, 106
The Abandonment of the Jews, 641
Abba Hillel Silver: A Profile in American Judaism, 641
The ABC of Relativity, 322
Abingdon Dictionary of Living Religions, 3
Aboriginal Religions in Australia: A Bibliographical Survey, 461
Aboriginal Women, Sacred and Profane, 461
Abortion: Understanding Differences, 894
Abortion and Divorce in Western Law, 895
Abortion and the Ransom of the Sacred, 895
Abortion Is Not a Sin: A New-Age Look at an Age-Old Problem, 895
Abortion Rights as Religious Freedom, 895
About Philosophy, 25
Abraham Geiger and Liberal Judaism: The Challenge of the Nineteenth Century, 653
Abraham Heschel's Idea of Revelation, 665
Abraham Joshua Heschel, 665
Absolute Nothingness: Foundations for a Buddhist-Christian Dialogue, 365
Abstract of a Treatise of Human Nature, 1740: A Pamphlet Hitherto Unknown, 200
The Abyss of Despair, 624
The Achievement of John Henry Newman, 783
Acting and Thinking: The Political Thought of Hannah Arendt, 395
Acting on Principle, 206
Actions and Events, 381
Actions and Events: Perspectives on the Philosophy of Donald Davidson, 283, 381
Activation of Energy, 336
Activity of Philosophy: A Concise Introduction, 25
Acts of Faith: A Journey to the Fringes of Jewish Identity, 645
Acts of Literature, 397
The Acts of the Christian Martyrs: Text and Translations, 689
Adages, 138
Adam, Eve and the Serpent, 686
Adam Smith, 215
Adam Smith: Critical Assessments, 215
Adam Smith in His Time and Ours, 215
Adam Smith's Science of Morals, 215
Adaptive Knowing, 284
Addresses to the German Nation, 197
An Address to the German Nobility, the Babylonian Captivity, 777
Adieux: A Farewell to Sartre, 330
Adorno, 394
The Advaitic Theism of the Bhagavata Purana, 506
The Advancement of Learning, 165
The Advent of Sun Myung Moon, 871
Adventure in Freedom: Three Hundred Years of Jewish Life in America, 639
Adventures of Ideas, 341
Adventures of the Dialectic, 310
Adversity's Noblemen, 131
Adversus Marcionem, 713
Advocates of Reform: From Wyclif to Erasmus, 721
The Aesthetic and Miscellaneous Works, 253
The Aesthetic Dimension, 408
The Aesthetics of Thomas Aquinas, 118
Aesthetic Theory, 393

Africa Must Unite, 370
African Islam, 568
African Mythology, 463
The African Origin of Civilization: Myth or Reality, 368
African Philosophy: A Historico-Hermeneutical Investigation of the Conditions of Its Possibility, 26, 369
African Philosophy: An Introduction, 27, 369
African Philosophy: An Introduction to the Main Philosophical Trends in Contemporary Africa, 369
African Philosophy: Myth and Reality, 26, 369
African Philosophy: The Essential Readings, 26, 369
African Philosophy: Traditional Yoruba Philosophy and Contemporary African Realities, 368
African Philosophy—Myth or Reality, 26
African Philosophy, Culture, and Traditional Medicine, 26, 369
African Religions: A Symposium, 462
African Religions: Symbol, Ritual, and Community, 898
African Religions and Philosophy, 370
African Traditional Religion, 463
African Traditional Religion in Contemporary Society, 463
The Afroasiatic Roots of Classical Civilization, 446
The Afrocentric Idea, 368
After Foucault Humanistic Knowledge, Postmodern Challenges, 400
After Lebanon: The Israeli-Palestinian Connection, 643
After Marx, 242
After Philosophy, 378
After the Demise of the Tradition, 413
After Virtue: A Study in Moral Theory, 406, 407, 897
Against Epistemology—A Metacritique, 393
Against Method, 399
Against Post-Modernism, 391
Against the Academicians, 109

Against the American Grain, 800
Against the Apocalypse: Responses to Catastrophe in Modern Jewish Culture, 648
Against the Musicians, 58
Against the Nations: War and Survival in a Liberal Society, 744
Against the Self-Images of the Age, 407
The Age of Adventure: The Renaissance Philosophers, 130
Age of Analysis: Twentieth-Century Philosophers, 268
The Age of Constantine the Great, 682
An Age of Crisis: Man and World in Eighteenth-Century French Thought, 160
The Age of Criticism: The Late Renaissance in Italy, 127
Age of Erasmus, 139
The Age of Ideology: The Nineteenth-Century Philosophers, 159
Age of Reason: The Seventeenth-Century Philosophers, 160
The Age of Reform 1250–1550, 129, 697, 721
The Age of Religious Wars, 1559–1689, 736
The Ages of the World, 251
Agrippa and the Crisis of Renaissance Thought, 133
The Aims of Education, 341
Air and Dreams: An Essay on the Imagination of Movement, 274
Aishah: The Beloved of Muhammad, 587
Akhenaton: The Heretic King, 442
Akiba: Scholar, Saint and Martyr, 620
Alan of Lille: The Frontiers of Theology in the Twelfth Century, 702
Alan of Lille's Grammar of Sex, 702
Alban Berg: Master of the Smallest Link, 393
Albert Einstein: Philosopher-Scientist, 41
Albert the Great: Commemorative Essays, 107
Albertus Magnus and the Sciences, 107

Albinus and the History of Middle Platonism, 60
Alcuin and Charlemagne: Studies in Carolingian History and Literature, 100
Alessandro Achillini (1463–1512) and His Doctrine of Universals and Transcendentals, 128
Alexandra David-Neel: Portrait of an Adventurer, 544
Alfarabi, Avicenna and Averroës, 96
Alfred Loisy: His Religious Significance, 741
Alfred North Whitehead: The Man and His Work, Vol. I: 1861–1910, 342
Alfred North Whitehead: The Man and His Work, Vol. II: 1910–1947, 342
Algebraic Calculations of the Rainbow and the Calculation of Chances, 187
The Alien Book of Truth: Who Am I? What Am I? Why Am I Here?, 870
Al-Islam: Unity and Leadership, 579, 862
Allegory and Philosophy in Avicenna: Ibn Sina, 582
All My Road Before Me: The Diary of C. S. Lewis, 1922–1927, 776
All the Queen's Men: Power and Politics in Mary Stewart's Scotland, 735
All Things Are Possible and Penultimate Words and Other Essays, 335
All Things New: American Communes and Utopian Movements, 1860–1914, 844
Alone of All Her Sex: The Myth and the Cult of the Virgin Mary, 679
Alpha: The Myths of Creation, 427
Alpha and Omega, 479
Alternative Altars: Unconventional and Eastern Spirituality in America, 841
Alternative Medicine and American Religious Life, 841
Amana: From Pietist Sect to American Community, 843
Ambika in Jaina Art and Literature, 510
The Ambivalent American Jew, 640

America and the Unconscious, 841
American Assimilation or Jewish Revival, 638
American Buddhism, 860
The American Catholic Experience, 751
American Catholicism, 751
American Christianity, 752
American Communes, 1860-1960: A Bibliography, 842, 844
American Communes to 1860: An Annotated Bibliography, 843
American Communities, 844
The American Encounter with Buddhism, 1844-1912, 842
The American Evasion of Philosophy: A Genealogy of Pragmatism, 268
American Jew, 639
The American Jew: A Zionist Analysis, 658
The American Jewish Album: 1654 to the Present, 641
The American Jewish Woman: A Documentary History, 650
American Jews and the Separationist Faith, 639
American Jews and the Zionist Idea, 657
American Jews in Transition, 641
American Judaism, 639
American Judaism: Adventure in Modernity, 651
The American Judaism of Mordecai M. Kaplan, 667
American Modernity and Jewish Identity, 638, 651
American Philosophers at Work, 34
American Philosophy: A Historical Anthology, 35
American Philosophy: From Edwards to Quine, 35
American Philosophy and the Romantic Tradition, 34
American Philosophy Today and Tomorrow, 34, 265
American Pragmatism: Peirce, James and Dewey, 225, 238, 249
American Protestant Thought in the Liberal Era, 753
The American Rabbinate: A Century of Continuity and Change, 1883-1983, 652
The American Religion: The Emergence of the Post-Christian Nation, 889
American Religion and Philosophy: A Guide to Information Sources, 15
American Religious Empiricism, 751
American Society in the Buddhist Mirror, 842, 860
American Thought from Puritanism to Pragmatism and Beyond, 35
American Values: Continuity and Change, 34
American Zionism from Herzl to the Holocaust, 658
America's Jews, 641
America's Philosophical Vision, 35, 267
America's Theologian: A Recommendation of Jonathan Edwards, 767
Am I My Parents' Keeper?, 388
Among the Believers: An Islamic Journey, 579
Among the Gods: An Archaeological Exploration of Ancient Greek Religion, 446
Amritsar: Mrs. Gandhi's Last Battle, 517
Anabaptism: A Social History, 1525-1618, 723
Anabaptism and Asceticism: A Study in Intellectual Origins, 724
Anabaptism in Outline: Selected Primary Sources, 724
Anabaptist Baptism, 723
The Anabaptist in South and Central Germany, Switzerland, and Austria, 723
Anabaptists and the Sword, 724
The Anabaptists and Thomas Müntzer, 724
The Anabaptist Story, 733
The Anabaptist View of the Church, 724
Anabaptist Writings of David Jovis, 1535-1543, 724
Analects, 526
The Analects of Confucius, 526
Analogical Imagination, 746
Analogy, 193
The Analogy of Names and the Concept of Being, 136
The Analogy of Religion, 193
Analysis and Metaphysics, 414
Analysis of Knowledge and Valuation, 302
The Analysis of Mind, 322
The Analyst and the Mystic, 424
An Analytical Concordance to the Revised Standard Version of the New Testament, 818
Analytical Marxism, 243
Analyzing Marx, 243
Anarchy, State and Utopia, 314
The Anatomy of God, 630
The Anatomy of Neoplatonism, 61
Anaxagoras' Theory of Matter, 53
Anaximander and the Origins of Greek Cosmology, 51
Ancestor Worship and Korean Society, 539
The Anchor Bible Dictionary, 4, 818, 820
Ancient Christian Gospels: Their History and Development, 825
Ancient Christian Writers: The Works of the Fathers in Translation, 679
The Ancient City, 438
Ancient Civilizations: The Near East and Mesoamerica, 439, 454
Ancient Concepts of Philosophy, 50
The Ancient Egyptian Book of the Dead, 442
Ancient Egyptian Literature: A Book of Readings, 442
Ancient Egyptian Religion: An Interpretation, 442, 548
The Ancient Egyptians: Religious Beliefs and Practices, 442, 548
The Ancient History of Western Civilization, 604
Ancient Indian Asceticism, 501
Ancient Israel after Catastrophe. The Religious World-View of the Mishnah, 606
The Ancient Library of Qumran and Modern Biblical Studies, 810
Ancient Lives: Daily Life in Egypt of the Pharaohs, 442
Ancient Maya Civilization, 455

Ancient Mesopotamia: Portrait of a Dead Civilization, 441
The Ancient Mysteries: A Sourcebook, 450
Ancient Mystery Cults, 450, 470
Ancient Near East, 439
Ancient Near Eastern Texts Relating to the Old Testament, 812
Ancient Near Eastern Texts Relating to the Old Testament with Supplement, 439
The Ancient Near East in Pictures Relating to the Old Testament, 812
Ancient Near East in Pictures with Supplement, 439
Ancient Places: The Prehistoric and Celtic Sites of Britain, 436
The Ancient Quarrel between Poetry and Philosophy, 48
Ancient Roman Religion, 448
Ancient Synagogues: The State of Research, 614
Ancient Synagogues Revealed, 614
Ancient Tales in Modern Japan, 539
The Ancient Theology, 131
The Ancient Wisdom, 549
Ancient Wisdom Revived: A History of the Theosophical Movement, 852
And Muhammad Is His Messenger, 589
Angels, 768
Angels and Aliens: UFOs and the Mythic Imagination, 870
The Angels and Us, 269
The Anguish of the Jews: Twenty-three Centuries of Antisemitism, 635
Animadversiones, 172
Animal Liberation, 43
Animal Myths and Metaphors in South America, 466
Animal Rights and Human Obligations, 389
Animals and Why They Matter, 389
Annie Besant and Progressive Messianism, 550
Annotated Bibliography of the Writings of William James, 238
Annual Review of Women in World Religions, Vol. II: Heroic Women, 892
Anselm, 108
Anselm and a New Generation, 703
Anselm and Talking about God, 703
Anselm of Canterbury: Complete Treatises, 703
Anselm's Discovery, 288
The Ante-Nicene Fathers, 100, 680, 708, 713
Ante Pacem: Archaeological Evidence of Church Life before Constantine, 689
Anthology of Holocaust Literature, 636
Anthology of Islamic Literature: From the Rise of Islam to Modern Times, 567
An Anthology of Religious Texts from Ugarit, 545
An Anthology of Sacred Texts by and about Women, 892
Anthropological Approaches to the Study of Religion, 422
Anthropological Studies of Religion: An Introductory Text, 422
Anthropology and Roman Culture: Kinship, Time, Images of the Soul, 448
Anthropology as Cultural Critique, 426
Anthropology from a Pragmatic Point of View, 205
The Anthropology of Johannes Scottus Eriugena, 115
The Antichrist, 245, 246
The Anti-Cult Movement in America: A Bibliographic History, 857
Anti-Semite and Jew, 329
Anti-Semitism in American History, 639
Antonio Caso: Philosopher of Mexico, 33
Antonio Gramsci, 287
Antonio Gramsci: Conservative Schooling for Radical Politics, 287
Antonio Gramsci and the Origins of Italian Communism, 287
The "Apeiron" of Anaximander, 51
Apocalypse Delayed: The Story of Jehovah's Witnesses, 863
The Apocalyptic Tradition in Reformation Britain 1530–1645, 726
Apocryphal New Testament, 811
Apologetical Works, 713
Apologia and Florida of Apuleius of Madaura, 469
Apologia Pro Vita Sua, 782
Apology, 89, 152
Apology and Spectacles, 713
Apology for Raymond Sebonde, 146
The Apostolic Fathers, 704
The Apostolic Fathers: An American Translation, 703
The Apostolic Fathers: A New Translation and Commentary, 703, 811
The Apostolic Fathers, Clement, Ignatius, and Polycarp, 704
The Apostolic Preaching and Its Developments, 833
The Apotheosis of Captain Cook: European Myth-Making in the Pacific, 462
Appeal to Immediate Experience, 342
Appearance and Reality: A Metaphysical Essay, 220, 221
Applications of Inductive Logic, 405
Approaches to Ancient Judaism: Theory and Practice, 610
Approaches to God, 306
Approaches to Gramsci, 287
Approaches to Judaism in Medieval Times, 622
Approaches to Modern Judaism, 634
Approach to the Metaphysics of Plato through the Parmenides, 82
The Approach to the New Testament. Hibbert Lectures, 1921, 835
Apuleius and His Influence, 469
Apuleius and the Golden Ass, 469
Aquinas (Copleston), 39
Aquinas (Kenny), 119
Aquinas: A Collection of Critical Essays, 119
Aquinas against the Averroists, 119
Aquinas on Human Action, 119
An Aquinas Reader, 117
Aquinas to Whitehead: Seven

Centuries of Metaphysics of Religion, 288

Arabic Thought in the Liberal Age 1798–1939, 373

The Arab Revival, 569

The Aramaic Bible: Targums in their Historical Context, 609

The Aramaic Version of Lamentations, 608

Arcana Mundi: Magic and the Occult in the Greek and Roman Worlds, 451

The Archaeological and Documentary Evidence, 446

Archaeological History of the Ancient Middle East, 439

Archaeology: Theories, Methods and Practice, 432

Archaeology and Language: The Puzzle of Indo-European Origins, 436, 472

The Archaeology of Knowledge, 400

The Archaeology of Palestine, 808, 828

The Archaeology of the Frivolous, 397

Archaeology of the Land of the Bible: 10,000–586 B.C.E., 808

Archaeology of the New Testament, 808

Archaic Roman Religion, 471

Archbishop Romero: Martyr of Salvador, 748

Archetypal Images in Greek Religion, 483

The Archetypes and the Collective Unconscious, 424

Archetypes of Wisdom: An Introduction to Philosophy, 24

The Archidoxes of Magic, 149

Architects of Yiddishism at the Beginning of the Twentieth Century, 657

The Architecture of Hesiodic Poetry, 481

The Architecture of the Intelligible Universe in the Philosophy of Plotinus, 86

The Archives of the Wullu Family, 545

Are There Really Tannaitic Parallels to the Gospels?, 617

Argentina and the Jews: A History of Jewish Immigration, 644

Argonauts of the Western Pacific, 485

The Argument of the "Tractatus," 346

Arguments and Doctrines, 648, 886

The Aristotelian Ethics, 69

Aristotelianism, 71

The Aristotelians of Renaissance Italy: A Philosophical Exposition, 30

Aristotelian Theory of Comedy, 67

The Aristotelian Tradition and Renaissance Universities, 130

Aristotle (Barnes), 66

Aristotle (Ferguson), 68

Aristotle (Grote), 68

Aristotle (Mure), 70

Aristotle (Randall), 70

Aristotle (Ross), 71

Aristotle: A Contemporary Appreciation, 71

Aristotle: Fundamentals of the History of His Development, 69

Aristotle: Growth and Structure of His Thought, 69

Aristotle: Selections, 71

Aristotle: The Collected Papers of Joseph Owens, 70

Aristotle: The Desire to Understand, 69

Aristotle: The Nicomachean Ethics: A Commentary, 69

Aristotle: The Power of Perception, 70

Aristotle and His Philosophy, 67

Aristotle and His World View, 67, 221

Aristotle and Logical Theory, 69

Aristotle and Plato in the Mid-Fourth Century, 67, 80

Aristotle and the Human Good, 69

Aristotle and the Later Tradition, 66

Aristotle and the Problem of Value, 70

Aristotle and the Renaissance, 71, 131

Aristotle Dictionary, 13

Aristotle for Everybody, 66, 270

Aristotle on Eudaimonia, 66

Aristotle on Interpretation: Commentary by St. Thomas and Cajetan, 137

Aristotle on Memory, 71

Aristotle on Substance: The Paradox of Unity, 68

Aristotle on the Art of Poetry, 67

Aristotle on the Many Senses of Priority, 67

Aristotle on the Perfect Life, 69

Aristotle's Categories and Porphyry, 61

Aristotle's Classification of Animals, 70

Aristotle's Conception of Moral Weakness, 71

Aristotle's Concept of Dialectic, 68

Aristotle's Contribution to the Practice and Theology of Historiography, 71

Aristotle's Criticism of Plato and the Academy, 79

Aristotle's Criticism of Presocratic Philosophy, 67

Aristotle's "De Motu Animalium," 70

Aristotle's Ethical Theory, 68

Aristotle's First Principles, 68

Aristotle's Man: Speculations upon Aristotelian Anthropology, 67

Aristotle's Ontology: Essays in Ancient Greek Philosophy, V, 66

Aristotle's Philosophy of Action, 67

Aristotle's Physics, 69

Aristotle's Poetics, 68

Aristotle's Poetics: A Translation and Commentary for Students, 68

Aristotle's Poetics: The Argument, 68

Aristotle's Political Theory: An Introduction for Students of Political Theory, 70

Aristotle's Prior and Posterior Analytics, 71

Aristotle's Psychology, 70

Aristotle's School: A Study of a Greek Educational Institution, 70

Aristotle's Syllogistic: From the Standpoint of Modern Formal Logic, 69

Aristotle's System of the Physical World, 71

Aristotle's Theology: A Commentary on the Book of Metaphysics, 67

Aristotle's Theory of Contrariety, 66

Aristotle's Theory of Poetry and Fine Art, 67

Aristotle's Two Systems, 68

Aristotle's Vision of Nature, 72
Aristotle the Philosopher, 66
Arjuna in the Mahabharata: Where Krishna Is, There Is Victory, 505
The Armada, 732
The Armenians: A People in Exile, 542
Arminius: A Study in the Dutch Reformation, 731
Arnauld and the Cartesian Philosophy of Ideas, 164
Art: Beauty in the Middle Ages, 95
Art, Ideology, and the City of Teotihuacan, 457
Art and Ceremony in Late Antiquity, 449
Art and Morality, 364
Art and Philosophy: A Symposium, 264
Art and Prudence, 270
Art and Prudence: Studies in the Thought of Jacques Maritain, 307
Art and Scholasticism: With Other Essays, 306
Art and the Reformation in Germany, 737
The Art and Thought of Heraclitus, 74
Arthur O. Lovejoy: An Annotated Bibliography, 303
Arthur O. Lovejoy and the Quest for Intelligibility, 303
Arthur Schopenhauer: Philosopher of Pessimism, 256
Articles on Aristotle, 66
Artificial Intelligence, 382
The Artisans of Banaras: Popular Culture and Identity, 1880–1986, 508
The Art of Biblical Narrative, 822
The Art of Biblical Poetry, 822
The Art of Happiness: Teachings of Buddhist Psychology, 512
Art of Happiness or the Teachings of Epicurus, 74
The Art of Memory, 136
The Art of Mesoamerica, 454
The Art of Philosophizing and Other Essays, 322
The Art of Thinking, 164
The Art of War, 144, 145
The Arts of Orpheus, 447
The Arts of the Beautiful, 285
As a Driven Leaf, 621

The Ascent of Mount Ventoux, 150
Ascent to Truth, 412
Ascetical Works, 704
Ascetic Behavior in Greco Roman Antiquity, 690
Ascetic Figures before and in Early Buddhism, 510, 514
Aserah: Extrabiblical Evidence, 545
Asherah and the Cult of Yahweh in Israel, 545
The Ash Wednesday Supper, 135
The Asian Journal of Thomas Merton, 781
Aspects of Apuleius' Golden Ass, 469
Aspects of Religion in the Soviet Union, 1917–1967, 572
The Assassins: A Radical Sect in Islam, 571
The Assembly of Listeners: Jains in Society, 509
Assyrian Rulers of the Early First Millennium B.C. (1114–859), 545
Assyrian Rulers of the Third and Second Millennia B.C. (to 1115), 545
Astrology and Religion among the Greeks and Romans, 451
Astrology in the Renaissance: The Zodiac of Life, 126
Atheism: Collected Essays, 1943–1949, 322
Atheism in the English Renaissance, 124
Athenaeum, 252
Athens and Jerusalem, 335
At Home in America: Second Generation New York Jews, 640
Atlas of Ancient Archaeology, 432
Atlas of the Christian Church, 676
Atlas of the Islamic World since 1500, 567
Atlas of the Jewish World, 634
The Atom Bomb and the Future of Man, 299
Atoms, Pneuma, and Tranquility, 56
Attack upon "Christendom," 239
Attempt at a Critique of All Revelation, 197
At the Crossroads of Faith

and Reason: An Essay on Pierre Bayle, 166
At the Crossroads of the Earth and the Sky: An Andean Cosmology, 458
At the Origins of Modern Atheism, 884
At the Threshold of Exact Science, 97
Auctor and Actor: A Narratological Reading of Apuleius' Golden Ass, 469
Augsburg Commentary on the New Testament, 820
Augsburg Commentary on the Old Testament, 820
Auguste Comte, Vol. 1: An Intellectual Biography, 223
Auguste Comte and Positivism, 223
Augustine (Chadwick), 110
Augustine (Kirwan), 110
Augustine: A Collection of Critical Essays, 110
Augustine and His Influence through the Ages, 110
Augustine of Hippo: A Biography, 109
Augustine on Evil, 110
Augustine to Galileo, 97
Augustus to Constantine, 681
Aurobindo's Philosophy of Brahman, 353
The Aurora of the Philosophers, 149
Australian Religions: An Introduction, 461
The Authoritarian Personality, 393
Authority and the Individual, 322
Autobiographical Sketches, 549
An Autobiography (Collingwood), 281
Autobiography (Eliade), 473
Autobiography (Nkrumah), 370
Autobiography: The Story of My Experiments with Truth, 352
Autobiography of a Shaker and Revelation of the Apocalypse, 849
Autobiography of a Yogi, 556, 873
The Autobiography of John Stuart Mill, 243, 244
An Autobiography of Mahatma Gandhi, 552
Autobiography of Malcolm X, 876

Autobiography of Malcolm X as Told to Alex Haley, 862

The Autobiography of St. Ignatius Loyola, with Related Documents, 770

Autonomy and Judaism, 646

Availability: Gabriel Marcel and the Phenomenology of Human Openness, 305

Avatamsaka Sutra, 529

Avatar and Incarnation, 885

Avataras, 549

Averroës and His Philosophy, 97

Averroës and the Metaphysics of Causation, 581

Averroës' Doctrine of Immortality: A Matter of Controversy, 581

Averting the Apocalypse: Social Movements in India Today, 507

Avesta. The Hymns of Zarathustra, 443

Avicenna: His Life and Works, 581

Avicenna: Scientist and Philosopher, 582

Avicenna and the Visionary Recital, 582

The Avila of Saint Teresa: Religious Reform in a Sixteenth-Century City, 736, 786

The Awakening of Europe, 100

The Awakening of Intelligence, 554

Awakening to the Tao, 528

Ayer, 273

Aztec Image of Self and Society: An Introduction to Nahua Culture, 457

The Aztecs: A History, 457

Aztecs: An Interpretation, 457

The Babylonian Akitu Festival, 441

Babylonian and Assyrian Religion, 441, 545

The Babylonian Genesis: The Story of Creation, 440

Bacchae, 474

Bachelard: Modern European Philosophy, 274

Backgrounds of Early Christianity, 807

Back to the Sources: Reading the Classic Jewish Texts, 601

Bacon: His Writings and His Philosophy, 165

Baffling Phenomena, 317

The Baha'i Faith: An Historical Bibliography, 861

The Bahai Faith: The Emerging Global Religion, 861

The Bahai Religion: A Short Introduction to Its History and Teachings, 861

Baha'u'llah and the New Era: An Introduction to the Baha'i Faith, 861, 568

Baker's Dictionary of Christian Ethics, 718

Baker's Dictionary of Theology, 718

Ball Courts and Ceremonial Plazas in the West Indies, 466

Banaras: City of Lights, 503

Banner of Jerusalem: The Life, Times, and Thought of Abraham Isaac Kuk, 657

Bantu Philosophy, 367, 369

Bantu Prophets in South Africa, 468

Baptismal Instructions, 707

Barcelona and Beyond: The Disputation of 1263 and Its Aftermath, 669

Bardo Thodol, 544

Bare-Faced Messiah: A Biography of L. Ron Hubbard, 869

Basic Christian Doctrine, 745

Basic Forms of Prophetic Speech, 824

Basic Judaism, 596

The Basic Problems of Phenomenology, 290

Basic Questions in Theology: Collected Essays, 99

The Basic Teachings of the Great Philosophers, 16

The Basic Works, 553

The Basic Works of Aristotle, 45

Basic Writings, 291

The Basic Writings of Bertrand Russell 1903–1959, 322

Basic Writings of St. Augustine, 109

Basic Writings of St. Thomas Aquinas, 117

The Basis of Morality According to William of Ockham, 120

The Bavli: The Talmud of Babylonia. An Introduction, 611

Bayle, 166

A Beauty and Sensibility in the Thought of Jonathan Edwards, 767

Beauty in Holiness: Studies in Jewish Ceremonial Art and Customs, 614

The Becket Conflict and the Schools, 102

Beelzebub's Tales to His Grandson, 875

Before and after Socrates, 46

Before Eureka: The Presocratics and Their Science, 51

Beggars and Prayers, 669

The Beginning and the End, 275

A Beginning-Intermediate Grammar of Hellenistic Greek, 794

Beginnings in Ritual Studies, 897

The Beginnings of Astrology in America, 860

Beginning to Read the Fathers, 690

Begriffschrift, 229

Behemoth: or the Long Parliament, 173

Behind Mud Walls 1930–1960, with a Sequel, 506, 509

Behind the Mask, 539

Behold the Sign, 848

Behold the Spirit, 881

Being and Existence in Kierkegaard's Pseudonymous Works, 239

Being and Having: An Existentialist Diary, 304

Being and Knowing, 119

Being and Nothingness, 329

Being and Time, 291, 367

Being a Philosopher: The History of a Practice, 2

Being-in-the-World, 292

Being Jewish in America: The Modern Experience, 639

Being Peace, 561

The Bektashi Order of Dervishes, 574

Belief and History, 427

Belief and Worship in Native North America, 464

Believer's Church: The History and Character of Radical Protestantism, 724, 732

Benedict De Spinoza, 187

Benedictine Monasticism, 705

The Bene Israel of Bombay:

A Study of a Jewish Community, 645
Bentham, 191
Berdyaev's Philosophy of Hope: A Contribution to Marxist-Christian Dialogue, 759
Bergson, 220
Bergson and His Influence, 220
Bergson and Modern Physics: A Reinterpretation and Reevaluation, 220
Bergson and the Modern Spirit, 220
The Bergsonian Controversy in France, 1900–1914, 220
Bergsonian Philosophy and Thomism, 220, 306
Bergson to Sartre, 263
Berkeley (Bracken), 191
Berkeley (Urmson), 192
Berkeley (Warnock), 192
Berkeley: An Introduction, 192
Berkeley: The Central Arguments, 192
Berkeley and Malebranche, 182
Berkeley's American Sojourn, 192
Berkeley's Argument, 192, 277
Berkeley's Revolution in Vision, 191
Bertrand Russell, 272, 324
Bertrand Russell and the Pacifists in the First World War, 325
Bertrand Russell and Trinity: A College Controversy of the Last War, 324
The Bertrand Russell Case, 324
Bertrand Russell's Best, 322
Between Berlin and Slobodka, 620
Between Cultures, 37
Between Frieburg and Frankfurt: Toward a Critical Ontology, 292
Between God and Man: An Interpretation of Judaism, 664
Between Man and Man, 662
Between Past and Future, 394
Between the Sexes: Foundations for a Christian Ethics of Sexuality, 894
Between the Testaments, 605
Between Time and Eternity:

The Essentials of Judaism, 596
Between Two Gardens: Reflections on Sexuality and Religious Experience, 894
Beyond All Appearances, 338, 339
Beyond Belief: Essays on Religion in a Post-Traditional World, 424
Beyond God the Father: Toward a Philosophy of Women's Liberation, 749, 764
Beyond Good and Evil, 245, 246
Beyond Humanism: Essays in the Philosophy of Nature, 288
Beyond Metaphor: The Theory of Tropes in Anthropology, 426
Beyond Metaphysics?, 391
Beyond Objectivity and Relativism, 378
Beyond Occupation: American, Jewish, and Palestinian Voices for Peace, 905
Beyond Reason, 399
Beyond the Self: Wittgenstein, Heidegger, and the Limits of Language, 295
The Bhagavad Gita, 502, 506
The Bhagavad Gita: An Interpretation, 552
The Bhagavad-Gita: Krishna's Counsel in Time of War, 505
The Bhagavadgita in the Mahabharata, 506
The Bible, Now I Get It: A Form Criticism Handbook, 815
The Bible in America: Essays in Cultural History, 813
The Bible in Aramaic Based on Old Manuscripts and Printed Texts, 796
The Bible Today, 814, 833
Biblia sacra iuxta vulgatam versionem, 796
Biblical Interpretation in Ancient Israel, 823
Biblical Narrative in the Philosophy of Paul Ricoeur, 320
Biblical Theology of the Old and New Testaments, 827
Bibliographia Cartesiana, 170
Bibliographical Introduction to the Study of John Locke, 179
A Bibliographical Survey for

a Foundation in Philosophy, 13
A Bibliographic Guide to Christian Feminist Liberation Theology, 749
A Bibliographic Guide to the Comparative Study of Ethics, 892
Bibliography and Genetic Study of American Realism, 264
A Bibliography of David Hume and of Scottish Philosophy from Francis Hutcheson to Lord Balfour, 202, 212
Bibliography of Editions, Translations, and Commentary on Xenophon's Socratic Writings, 1600 to Present, 91
Bibliography of English Language Works on the Babi and Bahai Faiths 1844–1985, 861
A Bibliography of Epictetus, 57
Bibliography of George Berkeley, 192
Bibliography of Holy Land Sites, 809
Bibliography of New Religious Movements in Primal Societies, 468
Bibliography of New Testament Bibliographies, 796
A Bibliography of Philosophical Bibliographies, 13
A Bibliography of Targum Literature, 608
Bibliography of the Works of John Stuart Mill, 245
Bibliography on Plato's Laws 1920–1970, with Additional Citations through May 1975, 84
Bibliotheka, 468
The Big Questions: A Short Introduction to Philosophy, 24
Billy Graham: America's Evangelist, 768
Billy Graham: A Parable of American Righteousness, 768
Billy Graham: Revivalist in a Secular Age, 768
Bioethical Decision-making: Releasing Religion from the Spiritual, 895
Biographical Dictionary of American Cult and Sect Leaders, 6, 854

Biographical Dictionary of British Radicals in the Seventeenth Century, 734

The Biographical History of Philosophy from Its Origin in Greece down to the Present Day, 17, 161

A Biography of Philosophy, 17

The Birnbaum Haggadah, 599

Birth Control in Jewish Law, 598, 895

The Birth of Popular Heresy, 700

The Birth of Purgatory, 697

Birth of Reason and Other Essays, 326

Birth of the Clinic, 400

The Birth of Tragedy (and The Genealogy of Morals), 246

The Birth of Tragedy Out of the Spirit of Music, 245

The Bishop in the Church: Patristic Texts on the Role of the Episkopos, 688

Black Athena, 446

Black-Body Theory and the Quantum Discontinuity, 1894–1912, 406

The Black Church in America, 748

The Black Church in the African American Experience, 748

The Black Hunter: Forms of Thought and Forms of Society in the Greek World, 447

The Black Muslims in America, 571, 862

Black Religions in the New World, 468

Black Religious Leaders: Conflict in Unity, 748

Black Sects and Cults, 749

Black Separatism in the United States, 862

Black Theology: A Documentary History, 1966–1979, 749, 896

Black Theology: U.S.A. and South Africa, 748

Black Theology and Black Power, 763

Black Theology in Dialogue, 748

A Black Theology of Liberation: Twentieth Anniversary with Critical Responses, 748, 763

Black Theology Today: Liber-

ation and Contextualization, 748

The Black Years of Soviet Jewry: 1939–1953, 636

Blaise Pascal, 185

Blast and Counterblast: Contemporary Writings on the Scottish Reformation, 735

Blessed Are You: Traditional Jewish Prayers for Children, 599

Blessed Rage for Order: The New Pluralism in Theology, 746

The Blind Devotion of the People: Religion and the English Reformation, 727

Bloody Mary, 726

Bloomsbury's Prophet, 312

The Blue and Brown Books, 343

Blue Dragon White Tiger: Taoist Rites of Passage, 528

The Bodhgaya Interviews, 560

Bodin: On Sovereignty, 134

The Body: Toward an Eastern Mind-Body Theory, 367

The Body Divine, 337

The Body in Interpersonal Relations: Merleau-Ponty, 311

The Body of Faith: God in the People Israel, 885

The Body of Faith: Judaism as Corporeal Election, 649

Body-Text in Julia Kristeva: Religion, Women, and Psychoanalysis, 892

Boethius, 112

Boethius: The Consolations of Music, Logic, Theology and Philosophy, 112

Bolshevism: Practice and Theory, 322

Bonhoeffer's Ethic of Discipleship, 760

The Book: On the Taboo Against Knowing Who You Are, 881

The Book of Beliefs and Opinions, 672

Book of Changes, 524

The Book of Common Prayer, 764, 773

The Book of Concord: The Confessions of the Evangelical Lutheran Church, 779

The Book of Examples, 584

The Book of God: A Response to the Bible, 816

Book of History, Book of Songs, Spring and Autumn Annals, Book of Rites, 524

The Book of Jewish Belief, 596

The Book of Jewish Books: A Reader's Guide to Judaism, 601

A Book of Jewish Ethical Concepts, 598

The Book of Job: Commentary, New Translation and Special Studies, 821

The Book of Knowledge, 582, 667

The Book of Life, 140

Book of Mormon, 1830, 845, 846, 878, 879

The Book of Religious and Philosophical Sects, 583

The Book of Saints, 719

Book of the Dead, 548

The Book of the Goddess Past and Present, 506, 530, 536

Book of the Universal Concord, 361

Book of World Religions, 572

Born in Tibet, 357

Born to Sing: An Interpretation and World Survey of Bird Song, 288

The Bounds of Sense, 207, 414

The Bourgeois Mind and Other Essays, 758

The Bowl of Heaven, 860

Boyhood with Gurdjieff, 876

Bradley's Moral Psychology, 221

Bradwardine and the Pelagians, 104

Brahma Sutra: The Philosophy of Spiritual Life, 353

The Brahmo Samaj and the Shaping of the Modern Indian Mind, 355

Brainstorms, 396

The Brainwashing/Deprogramming Controversy, 856

Bread Not Stone: The Challenge of Feminist Biblical Interpretation, 814

The Breakdown of Cartesian Metaphysics, 171

Breaking Boundaries: Male-Female Friendship in Early Christian Communities, 689

A Breath of Life: Feminism in the American Jewish Community, 650
Brentano and Intrinsic Value, 222, 395
Brentano and Meinong Studies, 222, 395
Breviloquium, 113
Bridge of Light: Yiddish Film between Two Worlds, 657
Bridges and Boundaries: African Americans and American Jews, 639
A Brief Introduction to Hinduism, 504
Brigham Young, 845
Bring Forth the Mighty Men: On Violence and the Jewish Character, 649
Britain and the Jews of Europe 1939–1945, 638
British Post-Structuralism: since 1968, 29
British Thought and Thinkers, 29
Broken Lights and Mended Lives, 688
Brother Francis: An Anthology of Writings by and about St. Francis of Assisi, 710
The Brotherhood of the Rosy Cross, 848
Bruno, or On the Natural and Divine Principle of Things, 251
The Buddha Eye: An Anthology of the Kyoto School, 363
A Buddha from Korea: The Zen Teachings of T'aego, 537
Buddha Nature, 513, 530
The Buddha Within, 513, 543
Buddhism (Berry), 498, 512
Buddhism (Lester), 884
Buddhism: A Cultural Perspective, 513, 520
Buddhism: Art and Faith, 515
Buddhism, Imperialism, and War. Burma and Thailand in Modern History, 895
Buddhism, Sexuality, and Gender, 894
Buddhism and Asian History, 513, 519, 522, 530, 534, 537, 542, 543
Buddhism and Politics in Thailand, 520
Buddhism and Society: A Great Tradition and Its

Burmese Vicissitudes, 519, 890
Buddhism and Society in Southeast Asia, 520
Buddhism and the Spirit Cults in Northeast Thailand, 519
Buddhism in America, 860
Buddhism in China, 529
Buddhism in the Tibetan Tradition, 543
The Buddhism of Tibet, 356, 560
Buddhism Transformed: Religious Change in Sri Lanka, 515
Buddhist America: Centers, Retreats, Practices, 7
Buddhist Art of the Tibetan Plateau, 543
The Buddhist Attitude to Other Religions, 898
Buddhist-Christian Dialogue: Mutual Renewal and Transformation, 423
A Buddhist Critique of the Christian Concept of God, 884
Buddhist Ethics: The Path to Nirvana, 893
Buddhist Hermeneutics, 513
Buddhist Meditation, 897
Buddhist Monk, Buddhist Layman, 519
Buddhist Philosophy, 513
The Buddhist Religion: A Historical Introduction, 514, 530, 538
The Buddhist Revival in Sri Lanka, 515
The Buddhist Saints of the Forest and the Cult of Amulets, 519
Buddhist Studies in the People's Republic of China, 532
Buddhist Thought in India, 512
A Buddhist Vision, 513
Bultmann: Towards a Critical Theology, 831
Burke, 193
Burma, 519
The Burned-over District, 841
Business Ethics, 388
Butler's Ethics, 194
Butler's Lives of the Saints, 676
By Any Means Necessary, 876
By Light, Light: The Mystic

Gospel of Hellenistic Judaism, 670
Byzantine Christianity: Emperor, Church and the West, 693
Byzantine Church, Society, and Civilization Seen through Contemporary Eyes, 693
The Byzantine Liturgy, 694
The Byzantine Theocracy, 694
Byzantine Theology: Historical Trends and Doctrinal Themes, 693, 756
Byzantium and the Rise of Russia, 693
Byzantium and the Roman Primacy, 692

C. H. Dodd: Interpreter of the New Testament, 833
C. S. Lewis: A Biography, 776, 777
C. S. Lewis: A Critical Essay, 777
C. S. Lewis: The Shape of His Faith and Thought, 777
C. S. Lewis and the Search for Rational Religion, 776
C. S. Lewis at the Breakfast Table, 781
C. S. Lewis on Scripture, 776
The Calabrian Abbot: Joachim of Fiore in the History of Thought, 712
California's Utopian Colonies, 844
The Call of the Minaret, 568
Calvin: Institutes of the Christian Religion, 761
Calvin: Origins and Development of His Religious Thought, 762
Calvin: Theological Treatises, 761
Calvin against Himself: An Inquiry in Intellectual History, 762
Calvin and Classical Philosophy, 129
Calvin and English Calvinism to 1649, 726
Calvin and the Anabaptist Radicals, 761
Calvinism and the Amyraut Heresy, 731, 761
Calvinism in Europe, 1555–1620: A Collection of Documents, 731

Calvinist Preaching and Icon-
oclasm in the Netherlands,
1544–1569, 737
Calvin's Commentaries, 761
Calvin's Geneva, 762
Calvin's New Testament
Commentaries, 761
The Cambridge Ancient His-
tory, 806
Cambridge Bible Commen-
tary, 820
The Cambridge Companion
to Aquinas, 119
The Cambridge Companion
to Descartes, 170
The Cambridge Companion
to Hegel, 233
The Cambridge Companion
to Kant, 206
The Cambridge Companion
to Marx, 242
The Cambridge Companion
to Plato, 81
Cambridge Essays 1888–1889,
322
The Cambridge History of
Classical Literature, 46
Cambridge History of Islam,
570
The Cambridge History of
Judaism, 596
The Cambridge History of
Later Greek and Early Me-
dieval Philosophy, 55, 93,
685
The Cambridge History of
Later Medieval Philosophy,
94, 696
The Cambridge History of
Medieval Political
Thought, c.350–c.1450, 98
The Cambridge History of
the Bible, 676, 805, 813
The Cambridge Platonists,
168
Cambridge Ritualists, 479
Cambridge Ritualists Recon-
sidered, 479
The Cambridge Translations
of Medieval Philosophical
Texts, 95
Camillus: A Study of Indo-
European Religion as Ro-
man History, 471
The Camphor Flame: Popular
Hinduism and Society in
India, 504
Canaanite Myths and Leg-
ends, 445, 545
Canarsie: The Jews and Ital-
ians of Brooklyn against
Liberalism, 641
Candide, or Optimism, 217

Candide and Other Stories,
217
The Canon of the New Tes-
tament: Its Origin, Devel-
opment, and Significance,
805
Canons and Decrees of the
Council of Trent, 729
Can't We Make Moral Judg-
ments?, 389
Can Women Re-Image the
Church?, 892
Capital, 227, 241, 242
The Capitalist Manifesto, 270
The Captive Soul of the Mes-
siah: New Tales about Reb
Nachman, 669
Cardinal Cajetan Responds: A
Reader in Reformation
Controversy, 137
Cardinal Newman in His
Age: His Place in English
Theology and Literature,
783
The Career of Philosophy,
162
A Careful and Strict Enquiry
into the Freedom of Will,
766
Cargo Cults and Millennarian
Movements, 468
Caring, 391
Caring and Curing: Health
and Medicine in the West-
ern Religious Traditions,
893
Carlyle and Mill, 245
Carnap on Meaning and Ana-
lyticity, 279
Cartesian Linguistics: A
Chapter in the History of
Rationalist Thought, 170
Cartesian Meditations: An In-
troduction to a Phenome-
nology, 234
The Case for Animal Experi-
mentation, 389
The Case for Animal Rights,
389
Cassirer, Symbolic Forms
and History, 280
Cassirer's Conception of Cau-
sality, 280
The Catacombs: Rediscov-
ered Monuments of Early
Christianity, 689
Catacombs and Basilicas:
The Early Christians in
Rome, 689
Catalog of the Hoose Library
of Philosophy, 15
A Catalogue of Renaissance

Philosophers: 1350–1650,
130
The Catalpa Bow: A Study of
Shamanistic Practices in
Japan, 539
Catalyst of the Enlighten-
ment: Gotthold Ephraim
Lessing, 208
Catechism of the Catholic
Church, 891
The Categorical Imperative,
207
The Categories of Dialectical
Materialism: Contemporary
Soviet Ontology, 31
Category Formation and the
History of Religions, 422
The Category of the Aesthet-
ic in the Philosophy of St.
Bonaventure, 113
Catherine of Siena: The Dia-
logue, 706
Catherine of Siena's Way,
707
Catholic Bishops in Ameri-
can Politics, 752
The Catholic Church in
America: An Historical
Bibliography, 752
The Catholic Church in the
Modern World, 741
The Catholic Crisis, 754
The Catholic Encyclopedia,
716
The Catholic Experience, 751
The Catholic Experience: An
Interpretation of American
Catholicism, 891
The Catholic Faith, 891
Catholic Girls, 746
Catholicism between Luther
and Voltaire, 728
Catholicism Study Edition,
745
The Catholicity of the
Church, 891
The Catholic Modernists, 741
The Catholic Periodical, 7
The Catholic Reformation,
728
The Catholic Reformation:
Council, Churchmen, Con-
troversies, 729
The Catholic Reformation:
Savonarola to Ignatius
Loyola, 729
Catholic Social Thought: The
Documentary Heritage,
745
The Catholic Study Bible,
798
A Catholic Vision, 891
Catholic Worker, 765

Causality and Scientific Explanation: Medieval and Early Classical Science, 102, 132
Cause, Experiment and Science, 143
Cause, Principle, and Unity: Five Dialogues, 135
The Cavern-Mystery Transmission: A Taoist Ordination Rite of A.D. 711, 527
A Celebration of Demons, 515
Celebrations of Death: The Anthropology of Mortuary Ritual, 430
Celsus: On the True Doctrine, 683
Celtic Britain, 437
Celtic Mythology, 436
The Celts, 436
The Censoring of Diderot's Encyclopedia and the Reestablished Text, 196
Centrality and Commonality: An Essay on Confucian Religiousness, 362
Centrality and Commonality (1989), Humanity and Self-Cultivation, 362
The Central Philosophy of Tibet, 888
A Century of Biblical Archaeology, 808
A Certain People: American Jews and Their Lives Today, 641
The Challenge of Peace: God's Promise and Our Response, 896
Chance, Love, and Logic, 248
Change and Continuity in Seventeenth-Century England, 734
Change and the Muslim World, 573
Change in View, 380
Channeling: A Bibliographic Exploration, 866
Channeling: Investigations on Receiving Information from Paranormal Sources, 866
Character and Opinion in the United States 1920, 326
Character and the Christian Life: A Study in Theological Ethics, 897
Characteristics of Men, Manners, Opinions, Times, 214
Characters, 90

Charismatic Religion in Modern Research: A Bibliography, 864
Charles Hartshorne and the Existence of God, 289
Charles Peirce's Empiricism, 249
Charles Sanders Peirce: From Pragmatism to Pragmaticism, 249
Chekhov and Other Essays, 335
The Chemical Philosophy, 150
Chemistry, Alchemy and the New Philosophy, 1550–1700, 125
The Chief Rabbi, the Pope, and the Holocaust, 638
The Chief Works and Others, 145
The Children of God: A Make-Believe Revolution, 864
The Children of God/Family of Love: An Annotated Bibliography, 864
Children of the Jinn: In Search of the Kurds and Their Country, 570
Children with a Star: Jewish Youth in Nazi Europe, 635
China and Christianity, 532
China and the Christian Impact, 532
China's Own Critics: A Selection of Essays, 360
Chinese Alchemy, Medicine, and Religion in the China of A.D. 320, 529
Chinese Civilization: A Source Book, 522
Chinese Ideas of Life and Death, 524
Chinese Intellectuals in Crisis: Search for Order and Meaning (1890–1911), 361
The Chinese Mind: Essentials of Chinese Philosophy and Culture, 358
Chinese Mythology, 522
Chinese Religion: An Introduction, 523
Chinese Religion in Western Languages, 522
Chinese Religions, 523
The Chinese Renaissance, 360
Chinese Thought: From Confucius to Mao Tse-tung, 358, 522

The Chinese Way in Religion, 522
Choices in Modern Jewish Thought: A Partisan Guide, 661
Choosing a Sex Ethic: A Jewish Inquiry, 598
The Chorale, 738
The Chosen People in America: A Study in Jewish Religious Ideology, 634, 646
Chrestomathia, 190
Christ and the Decree, 762
Christ and the Moral Life, 900
Christ and Time: The Primitive Christian Conception of Time and History, 832
Christening Pagan Mysteries: Erasmus in Pursuit of Wisdom, 139
Christian Antioch: A Study of Early Christian Thought in the East, 687
Christian Attitudes toward War and Peace, 678
Christian Blessedness, with Reflections upon a Late Essay Concerning Human Understanding, 180
The Christian Century in Japan 1549–1650, 540
The Christian Challenge, 775
The Christian Churches of the East, 755
The Christian Church in the Cold War, 755
The Christian Commitment: Essays in Pastoral Theology, 745
Christian Discourses, 239
Christian Ethics: The Historical Development, 679
The Christian Faith, 253, 680, 742
The Christian Fathers, 690
Christian Iconography: A Study of Its Origins, 688
The Christian Interpretation of the Cabala in the Renaissance, 124
Christianity: A Way of Salvation, 677, 883
Christianity, Communism, and the Ideal Society, 284
Christianity, Social Tolerance, and Homosexuality, 678
Christianity and Classical Culture, 99, 683
Christianity and Democracy, 306

Christianity and Evolution, 336

Christianity and Judaism: The Formative Categories, 602

Christianity and Paganism, 350–750: The Conversion of Western Europe, 683

Christianity and Revolution: Radical Christian Testimonies, 1520–1650, 725

Christianity and World Religion, 423

Christianity in a Revolutionary Age, 741

Christianity in China, 532

Christianity in Modern Japan, 540

Christianity in the Roman Empire, 684

Christianity in the Twenty-First Century: Reflections on the Challenges Ahead, 747

Christianity in Today's World: An Eerdmans Handbook, 744

Christianizing the Roman Empire, A.D. 100–400, 684

A Christian Looks at the Jewish Question, 306

Christian Origins in Sociologic Perspective: Methods and Resources, 617, 815

Christian Periodical Index, 7

The Christian Philosophy of St. Augustine, 110

The Christian Platonists of Alexandria: Eight Lectures, 63, 116

The Christian Polity of John Calvin, 762

Christian Rite and Christian Drama in the Middle Ages, 699

Christians and Jews in Germany, 637

Christians and Jews in the Ottoman Empire, 568

Christians and the Military: The Early Experience, 688

The Christians and the Roman Empire, 684

The Christians as the Romans Saw Them, 100, 684

Christian Science: Its Encounter with American Culture, 843

Christian Science Today: Power, Policy, Practice, 842

Christian Spirituality, 678

Christian Spirituality from the Apostolic Fathers to the Twelfth Century, 679

The Christian Tradition: A History of the Development of Doctrine, 99, 720

Christian Uniqueness Reconsidered, 898

Christ in East and West, 755

Christ in Eastern Christian Thought, 679

Christ in the Christian Tradition, 685

The Christological Controversy, 686

Christology in Conflict: The Identity of a Saviour in Barth and Rahner, 885

The Christology of Rosemary Radford Ruether: A Critical Introduction, 785, 905

The Christology of the New Testament, 825, 832

Christus Victor, 678, 886

Christ without Myth: A Study Based on the Theology of Rudolf Bultmann, 831

A Chronicle of the Last Pagans, 449

The Chronicles of Narnia, 776

Chronika, 468

Chronology of Islamic History, 567

The Chronology of Plato's Dialogues, 79

Chrysanthemum and the Sword, 534

Chuang Tzu: A New Selected Translation with an Exposition of the Philosophy of Kuo Hsiang, 359

Chuang Tzu: Basic Writings, 529

Chuang Tzu: The Inner Chapters, 528

Chuang Tzu: World Philospher at Play, 529

Chuang Tzu, The Seven Inner Chapters, 522, 526

Chu Hsi: New Studies, 526

Chu Hsi and Neo-Confucianism, 526

The Church, 774

Church, State and Jew in the Middle Ages, 623

The Church against Itself, 785

The Church and Abortion, 895

Church and People, 1450–1600, 726

Church and Society in England: Henry VIII to James I, 726

Church and Society in the Last Centuries of Byzantium, 693

Church and State from Constantine to Theodosius, 683

The Church and the Age of Reason, 738

The Church and the Jews in the Thirteenth Century, 624

The Church and the Second Sex, 764, 765

Church Dogmatics: The Doctrine of God, 757

Churches in the Nineteenth Century, 740

The Churches Speak On: Abortion, 895

The Churches the Apostles Left Behind, 824

The Church in France, 1848–1907, 741

The Church in the Eighteenth Century, 739

Church Manual of the Mother Church, 843, 874

The Church of Scientology and L. Ron Hubbard: A Bibliography, 869

Church Order in the New Testament, 826

Cicero, 72

Cicero: A Biography, 72

Cicero: A Portrait, 72

Cicero, the Senior Statesman, 72

Cicero and His Influence, 73

Cicero and the Roman Republic, 72

Ciceronianus: Or, A Dialogue on the Best Style of Speaking, 138

Cicero Scepticus, 131

Cicero's Social and Political Thought: An Introduction, 59

Cicero the Politician, 72

Cinders, 397

Cinematics, 339

The Circle of Baal Shem Tov: Studies in Hasidism, 660

Circle of Unity: Baha'i Approaches to Current Social Issues, 861

Cistercian Father Series, 680

The City in the Ancient World, 439

The City of God against the Pagans, 109

The City of the Sun: A Poetical Dialogue, 137
Civil Disobedience and Moral Law in Nineteenth-Century American Philosophy, 35
Civilization before Greece and Rome, 440
The Civilization of Experience: A Whiteheadian Theory of Culture, 342
Civilization of the Ancient Mediterranean, 439
The Civilization of the Goddess: The World of Old Europe, 434
Civil Liberties, "Brainwashing" and "Cults": A Select Annotated Bibliography, 857
The Claim of Reason: Wittgenstein, Skepticism, Morality, and Tragedy, 345
Clash of Worlds, 857
Classical American Philosophy: Essential Readings and Interpretive Essays, 36
Classical Approaches to the Study of Religion, 422
Classical Thought, 46
The Classical World Bibliography of Philosophy, Religion, and Rhetoric, 13
Classic American Philosophers, 34
Classic Philosophical Questions, 21
Classics of Western Philosophy, 20
Classics of Western Spirituality, 680
Class Struggle in the Pale, 656
Claude Buffier and Thomas Reid: Two Common Sense Philosophers, 212
Clement of Alexandria: A Study in Christian Platonism and Gnosticism, 63
Climate and Culture: A Philosophical Study, 367
Cluniac Monasticism in the Central Middle Ages, 699
Coat of Many Colors: Pages from Jewish Life, 595
Code of Jewish Law, 627
Coelum Philosophorum: Or, the Book of Vexations, 149
Coercion, 387
The Cogito and Hermeneutics: The Question of the Subject in Ricoeur, 319
Cognitive Economy: The

Economic Dimension of the Theory of Knowledge, 317
The Collapse of Ancient States and Civilizations, 546
Collected Articles on Ockham, 120
The Collected Dialogues of Plato, 45
Collected Essays and Reviews, 236
Colloquies, 138
Colloquium of the Seven about Secrets of the Sublime, 134
The Colloquy of Montbéliard: Religion and Politics in the Sixteenth Century, 723
Colour: Some Philosophical Problems from Wittgenstein, 347
Commemorative Issue, 120
Commentaries on Benedict's Rule, 706
Commentaries on Living, 554
Commentaries on the Psalms, 709
Commentary on a Canzone of Benivieni, 152
Commentary on Being and Essence, 137
Commentary on "De Grammatico," 108
Commentary on Hegel's Logic, 303
A Commentary on Heidegger's Being and Time, 293
Commentary on Jean-Paul Sartre's Being and Nothingness, 330
A Commentary on Jean-Paul Sartre's Critique of Dialectical Reason, 330
A Commentary on Kant's Critique of Practical Reason, 206
A Commentary on Kant's Critique of Pure Reason, 206
A Commentary on Plato's Meno, 81
Commentary on Plato's Symposium on Love, 80, 140
Commentary on Plato's Timaeus, 84
A Commentary on Plotinus: Ennead, 86
Commentary on Romans, 821
Commentary on the American Scene, 651
A Commentary on the Aris-

totelian Athenaion Politeia, 70
Commentary on True and False Religion, 791
Commerce and Government, 195
A Common Faith, 224
Common Sense and Nuclear Warfare, 322
Common Sense and the Fifth Amendment, 298
The Communal Experience, 844
Communal Love at Oneida, 844
Communication and the Evolution of Society, 403
Communion: A True Story, 870
Communism and China: Ideology in Flux, 359
Communistic Societies of the United States, 844
Community and Polity: The Organizational Dynamics of American Jewry, 639
A Community in Conflict, 638
A Community on Trial: The Jews of Paris in the 1930's, 638
A Companion to Aristotle's Politics, 69
A Companion to Plato's Republic, 85
A Companion to Scottish History: From the Reformation to the Present, 735
A Companion to the Study of St. Anselm, 108, 703
A Companion to Wittgenstein's "Tractatus," 344
Comparative Ethics in Hindu and Buddhist Traditions, 893
A Comparative History of Ideas, 37, 349
Comparative Philosophy: Selected Essays, 37
Comparative Religion, 567
Comparative Religion: A History, 420
Comparative Religion: Its Genesis and Growth, 420
Comparative Religious Ethics, 893
The Comparative Study of Religion, 494
Compassion in Tibetan Buddhism, 543
Compendium of the Study of Theology, 111

The Complete Bible: An American Translation, 797

The Complete Book of Jewish Observance, 602

Complexity: Life on the Edge of Chaos, 866

The Composition of Aristotle's Athenaion Politeia, 69

Computational Analysis of Kierkegaard's Samlede Vaerker, 240

Concept and Empathy: Essays in the Study of Religion, 426

The Conception of Immortality, 250

The Conception of Value, 288

Conceptions of God in Ancient Egypt, 442

Conceptions of State and Kingship in Southeast Asia, 518

The Concept of Anxiety, 239

The Concept of First Philosophy and the Unity of the Metaphysics of Aristotle, 70

The Concept of Irony: With Constant Reference to Socrates, 239

The Concept of Judgment in Montaigne, 146

The Concept of Man in Contemporary China, 359

The Concept of Man in Early China, 524

The Concept of Matter in Greek and Medieval Philosophy, 48

The Concept of Mind, 325

The Concept of Nature, 341

The Concept of Univocity Regarding the Predication of God and Creature According to William of Ockham, 121

Conceptual Notation and Related Articles, 229

Concerning Consciousness, 382

Concerning Vatican Council II, 423

The Concise Code of Jewish Law: A Guide to Prayer and Religious Observance on the Sabbath, 599

The Concise Code of Jewish Law: Daily Prayers and Religious Observances in the Life-Cycle of the Jew, 627

A Concise Dictionary of Indi-

an Philosophy: Sanskrit Terms Defined in English, 3, 13, 498

Concise Dictionary of the Christian World Mission, 720, 745

The Concise Encyclopedia of Islam, 4, 566

Concise Encyclopedia of Living Faiths, 5

The Concise Encyclopedia of Western Philosophy and Philosophers, 2, 15

A Concise Exegetical Grammar of New Testament Greek, 794

A Concise Hebrew and Aramaic Lexicon of the Old Testament, 795

A Concise Introduction to Philosophy, 21

A Concise Introduction to the Philosophy of Nicholas of Cusa, 149

The Concise Oxford Dictionary of the Christian Church, 675, 717

Concise Readings in Philosophy, 21

Concise Theological Dictionary, 719

The Concluding Unscientific Postscript, 239

A Concordance of the Qur'an, 587

Concordance to the Gospel of Sri Ramakrishna, 355

A Concordance to the Greek Testament, 819

A Concordance to the Septuagint and Other Greek Versions of the Old Testament (Including the Apocryphal Books), 818

Concordant Discord: The Interdependence of Faiths, 574

Concordia Mundi: The Career and Thought of Guillaume Postel, 1510–1581, 124

The Condition of Jewish Belief, 648

Condition of the Working Class in England, 227

The Confessions, 109, 213, 786

The Conflict of Interpretations: Essays on Hermeneutics, 318

Conflict of the Faculties, 205

Conflicts and Tensions in Islamic Jurisprudence, 578

Confrontations: Derrida-Heidegger-Nietzsche, 292

Confucian China and Its Modern Fate, 532

Confucian Discourse and Chu Hsi's Ascendancy, 526

Confucianism and Tokugawa Culture, 541

Confucian Thought: Selfhood as Creative Transformation, 362, 526

The Confucian Way of Contemplation, 541

The Confucian World Observed, 533

Conjectures and Refutations, 409

Conjectures of a Guilty Bystander, 781

The Connection between Scientific Method and Metaphysics, or Logic and Mysticism, 322

The Conquest of Happiness, 322

The Conquest of the Perfect Love, 786

Conquest of Violence: The Gandhian Philosophy of Conflict, 352, 553

Conrad Grebel: Son of Zurich, 724

Conscience in Medieval Philosophy, 95

Consciencism—Philosophy and Ideology for Decolonization and Development with Particular Reference to the African Revolution, 26, 371

Consciencism in African Political Philosophy, 371

Consciousness, Introspection and the Operation of the Mind, 322

Consciousness and Revolution in Soviet Philosophy, 30

Consciousness and the Acquisition of Language, 310

Consciousness Explained, 396

Consequences of Pragmatism: Essays 1972–1980, 35, 413

Conservative Judaism: An American Religious Movement, 655

Conservative Judaism: The New Century, 655

Conservative Judaism in America, 655

Considerations on Representative Government, 244

The Consolation of Philosophy, 112
Constantine and Eusebius, 709
Constantine and Religious Liberty, 683
Constantine and the Conversion of Europe, 684
Constantine the Great and the Christian Church, 682
Constitutional Code, 190
The Construction of Reality, 405
The Constructive Revolutionary: John Calvin and His Socio-Economic Impact, 762
Contemplating the Ancients, 526
Contemporary American Philosophy: Second Series, 36, 267
Contemporary American Reform Responsa, 652
Contemporary American Theologies: A Critical Survey, 718, 743
Contemporary Approaches to the Study of Religion, 422
Contemporary Christologies: A Jewish Response, 661, 885
Contemporary European Philosophy, 27, 262
Contemporary French Philosophy: A Study in Norms and Values, 28
Contemporary German Philosophy, 28, 263, 379
Contemporary Halakhic Problems, 598
Contemporary Indian Philosophy, 351
Contemporary Indian Tradition, 507
Contemporary Islam and the Challenge of History, 569, 578
Contemporary Islamic Movements in Historical Perspective, 570
Contemporary Japanese Philosophical Thought, 363
Contemporary Jewish Ethics, 598
Contemporary Jewish Philosophies, 596, 649
Contemporary Jewish Religious Thought, 888
Contemporary Philosophy: A New Survey, 264
Contemporary Philosophy in Scandinavia, 31

Contemporary Reform Jewish Thought, 652
Contemporary Roman Catholicism: Crises and Challenges, 785
Content and Consciousness, 396
The Content of Faith: The Best of Karl Rahner's Theological Writings, 891, 903
The Contest of Faculties: Deconstruction, Philosophy and Theory, 266, 391, 398
The Context of the Phenomenological Movement, 235
Contingency, Irony and Solidarity, 413
Continuing the Revolution: The Political Thought of Mao, 362
Continuity and Change in Roman Religion, 448
Contra Celsum, 116
Contributions towards a Bibliography of Epictetus: A Supplement, 57
Conversations with Nietzsche: A Life in the Words of His Contemporaries, 247
Conversion, 487
Conversion to Islam, 571
Convictions, 298
The Copernican Revolution, 406
Coping with Science, 384
Coral Gardens and their Magic, 485
Cornelius Agrippa: The Life of Henry Cornelius Agrippa von Nettesheim, 133
Corporations in the Moral Community, 389
Corpus Christi: A Theological Encyclopedia of the Eucharist, 675
Corpus Christi: The Eucharist in Late Medieval Culture, 697
Correlations in Rosenzweig and Levinas, 671
Correspondence of Benedict De Spinoza, 189
The Correspondence of Sargon II, Part I, 545
The Cosmic Christ in Origen and Teilhard de Chardin, 337
The Cosmological Argument, 194
The Cosmology of Giordano Bruno, 136
Costly Grace: An Illustrated

Biography of Dietrich Bonhoeffer, 760
The Cost of Discipleship, 760
The Council of Florence, 694
Counsels and Maxims, 255
Counsels in Contemporary Islam, 373
The Counter Reformation, 728
The Counter Reformation: 1599–1610, 737
The Counter-Reformation Prince, 728
Counterrevolution and Revolt, 408
Count Zinzendorf, 740
The Courage to Be, 787
The Course of Modern Jewish History, 634
Court, Kirk, and Community: Scotland, 1470–1625, 736
Covering Islam, 572
Crafting the Art of Magic, Bk. 1: A History of Modern Witchcraft 1939–1964, 865
The Creation of Mythology, 446
The Creation of the World According to Gersonides, 664
Creative Evolution, 220
Creative Intuition in Art and Poetry, 306
The Creative Mind: An Introduction to Metaphysics, 220
Creative Ventures, 338, 339
Creativity and Common Sense: Essays in Honor of Paul Weiss, 340
Creativity and Method: Studies in Honor of Rev. Bernard Lonergan, S.J., 744
Creativity and Taoism, 527
Creativity in American Philosophy, 34, 288
Creativity in George Herbert Mead, 309
Creeds of the Churches, 680
The Crescent in the East: Islam in Asia Major, 570
The Crime of Galileo, 144
Criminal Gods and Demon Devotees, 504
Crises of the Republic, 394
The Crisis of Church and State, 1050–1300, 695
The Crisis of European Sciences and Transcendental Phenomenology, 234
Crisis of the Early Italian Renaissance, 123

Crisis of the European Sciences, 234

A Critical and Exegetical Commentary on the Epistle to the Hebrews, 835

Critical and Interpretive Essays, 192

Critical Bibliography of Religion in America, 750, 752

Critical Concerns in Moral Theology, 743

Critical Essays in the Philosophy of Robin George Collingwood, 282

A Critical Exposition of the Philosophy of Leibniz, 177

Critical Guide to Catholic Reference Books, 6

A Critical History of Western Philosophy, 162

Critical Issues in Neo-Confucian Thought, 535

A Critical Study of Condillac's Traite des Systemes, 195

Critical Theory and Post-Structuralism: In Search of a Context, 266

The Critical Theory of Jürgen Habermas, 405

Critique, Norm, and Utopia, 404

Critique of Dialectical Reason, 329

A Critique of Jean-Paul Sartre's Ontology, 331

Critique of Judgment, 204, 205

Critique of Practical Reason, 204, 205, 739

The Critique of Pure Modernity: Hegel, Heidegger, and After, 293

Critique of Pure Reason, 204, 205, 206

A Critique of Pure Tolerance, 245, 408

Critique of the Human Potential Movement, 866

Critiques of Confucius in Contemporary China, 358

Crito, 89

Croce versus Gentile: A Dialogue on Contemporary Italian Philosophy, 285

Cromwell: The Lord Protector, 733

Crosscurrents, 763

Crossroads to Israel 1917–1948, 643

The Crucible of Europe: The Ninth and Tenth Centuries in European History, 691

The Crusade: Historiography and Bibliography, 692

Cry of the People, 748

The Cuisine of Sacrifice among the Greeks, 429, 493

Cult and Countercult, 866

Cult Controversies, 856

The Cult Controversy: A Guide to Sources, 856

The Cult Experience, 855

The Cultivation of Sagehood as a Religious Goal in Neo-Confucianism, 526

The Cult of Draupadi, 504

Cult of the Dead in a Chinese Village, 530

The Cult of the Saints: Its Rise and Function in Latin Christianity, 687

Cults: Faith, Healing and Coercion, 856

Cults: What Parents Should Know, 857

Cults, Converts and Charisma: The Sociology of New Religious Movements, 855

Cults, Culture and the Law: Perspectives on New Religious Movements, 857

Cults and New Religions, 854

Cults on Campus: Continuing Challenge, 857

Cultural Atlas of Mesopotamia and the Ancient Near East, 809

The Cultural Heritage of India, 498

A Cultural History of India, 498

A Cultural History of Spanish America from Conquest to Independence, 752

A Cultural History of Tibet, 356

Culture and Modernity: East-West Perspectives, 349

Culture and Power in Banaras, 504

Culture and Society in Lucian, 485

Culture and Truth: The Remaking of Social Analysis, 426

Culture and Value, 343

Culture of Compassion, 636

The Culture of Renaissance Humanism, 124

Cunning Intelligence in Greek Culture and Society, 493

Cupid and Psyche, 469

Curative Eurythmy, 879

Current Perspectives in the Psychology of Religion, 890

Cutting through Spiritual Materialism, 357, 544

Cyprian, 708

Cyprian of Carthage and the Unity of the Christian Church, 708

Daimon Life: Heidegger and Life-Philosophy, 293

The Dalai Lama at Harvard: Lectures on the Buddhist Path to Peace, 560, 906

Damaged Goods, 654

Dante and Philosophy, 104

Dante the Philosopher, 286

The Darker Side of Virtue: Corruption, Scandal and the Mormon Empire, 846

The Dark Lord, 863

The Darkness and the Light, 288

Darsan: Seeing the Divine Image in India, 503

Daughters of the Dreaming, 461

Daughters of the King: Women and the Synagogue, 892

David Hume, 202

David Hume: An Introduction to His Philosophical System, 202

David Hume: Common Sense Moralist, Sceptical Metaphysician, 202

David Hume: Many-Sided Genius, 202

David Hume: Philosopher of Moral Science, 202

David Hume: The Newtonian Philosopher, 201

David Hume: The Philosophical Works, 230

David Hume and the Miraculous, 203

David Hume's Theory of Mind, 201

Dawning of the Theosophical Movement, 853

The Dawn of Apocalyptic, 823

The Dawn of Belief: Religion in the Upper Paleolithic of Southwestern Europe, 433

The Dawn of European Art: An Introduction to Palaeolithic Cave Painting, 433

Dawn of Humanism in Italy, 132

Days of Awe, 599, 886

Days of Sorrow and Pain: Leo Baeck and the Berlin Jews, 661

The Dead Sea Scriptures, 811

The Dead Sea Scrolls: Major Publications and Tools for Study, 811

The Dead Sea Scrolls in English: Qumran in Perspective, 616, 812

Dean Colet and His Theology, 726

Dear Carnap, Dear Van: The Quine-Carnap Correspondence and Related Work, 279

Dear Russell—Dear Jourdain, 324

Death, Intermediate State and Rebirth in Tibetan Buddhism, 887

Death, War, and Sacrifice: Studies in Ideology and Practice, 426, 472

Death and After, 549

Death and Afterlife, 887

The Death and Birth of Judaism, 606, 651

Death and Dying: The Tibetan Tradition, 544

Death and Immortality in the Religions of the World, 887

The Death and Life of Malcolm X, 877

Death and the Labyrinth, 400

Death Is Different, 386

The Death of God Controversy, 745

The Death of Nature, 167

Death or Dialogue? From the Age of Monologue to the Age of Dialogue, 423

Death Ritual in Late Imperial and Modern China, 531, 533

The Debate on the English Reformation, 727

Decayed Gods, 472

De Cive or the Citizen, 173

De Clementia, 760

The Decline of Modernism, 379

Decoding the Rabbis: A Thirteenth-Century Commentary on the Aggadah, 628

De conscribendis epistolis, 156

Deconstruction: Theory and Practice, 266, 391

Deconstruction and Philosophy, 398

Deconstruction and the Interests of Theory, 266

Deconstruction in Context: Literature and Philosophy, 268, 392

Deconstruction Reframed, 266, 391

The Deconstructive Turn: Essays in the Rhetoric of Philosophy, 266, 392

Decrees of the Ecumenical Councils, 891

De Dialectica, 109

De erroribus philosophorum, 103

Defenders of God, 579

Defenders of the Faith: Inside Ultra-Orthodox Jewry, 654

The Defense of Galileo, 137

The Definition of Moral Virtue, 71

De la recherche du bien: A Study of Malebranche's Science of Ethics, 182

De ludo globi: The Game of Spheres, 148

Democracy and Education: An Introduction to the Philosophy of Education, 224

A Democratic Catholic Church, 742

The Democratization of American Christianity, 751

Demons, Dreamers and Madmen, 170

Dennett and His Critics, 396

De Officiis, 72

Deontology, 190

De Partibus Animalium, Book I, and De Generatione Animalium, Book I, with Passages from Book II, 1–3, 65

De reductione artium ad theologiam, 113

De Rerum Natura, 75

Derrida, 398

Derrida: A Critical Reader, 398

Derrida and Deconstruction, 398

Derrida and Negative Theology, 398

Derrida and the Economy of Difference, 398

Derrida on the Threshold of Sense, 398

A Derrida Reader: Between the Blinds, 398

The Dervishes, or Oriental Spiritualism, 574

Descartes, 171

Descartes: A Study of His Philosophy, 170

Descartes: Critical and Interpretive Essays, 170

Descartes: His Moral Philosophy and Psychology, 169

Descartes: Philosophy, Mathematics and Physics, 170

Descartes: The Project of Pure Enquiry, 171

Descartes against the Skeptics, 170

Descartes and Hume, 203

Descartes and the Modern Mind, 169

Descartes' Discourse on Method, 170

Descartes' Metaphysical Physics, 170

Descartes' Philosophy Interpreted According to the Order of Reasons, 170

Descartes' Rules for the Direction of the Mind, 170

Description of Greece, 489

The Desert a City, 688

The Desert Fathers, 690

Desires, Right and Wrong: The Ethics of Enough, 270

Destiny of a King, 471

The Destiny of Man, 275, 758, 759

The Destiny of the Mother Church, 842, 843

The Destroyers: The Underside of Human Nature, 284

The Destruction of the European Jews, 636

Determinism and Freedom in the Age of Modern Science, 264

Deuteronomy: A Commentary, 837

The Development of Arabic Logic, 317, 576

The Development of Franz Brentano's Ethics, 222

The Development of Logic, 97

Development of Logical Empiricism, 265

The Development of Logical Method in Ancient China, 360

Development of Peirce's Philosophy, 249

The Devil and the Jews, 624

De voluptate, 155
Dewey, 226
Dewey, Russell, Whitehead: Philosophers as Educators, 324, 342
Dewey and His Critics, 225
Dharma, 549
Dharma Bums, 860
Dharma's Daughters: Contemporary Indian Women and Hindu Culture, 508
The Dhimmi: Jews and Christians under Islam, 573
Dialectical Disputations, 155
Dialectical Materialism, 31
Dialectic of Enlightenment, 393
Dialectics: A Controversy-Oriented Approach to the Theory of Knowledge, 317
Dialectics of Nature, 227
Dialogue and Dialectic: Eight Hermeneutical Studies on Plato, 80, 401
Dialogue and Disagreement, 671
Dialogue and Discovery: A Study in Socratic Method, 90
Dialogue between a Philosopher and a Student of the Common Laws of England, 174
A Dialogue between Philosophy and Religion, 300
Dialogue Concerning the Two Chief World Systems, Ptolemaic and Copernican, 142, 171
A Dialogue of a Philosopher with a Jew and a Christian, 106
A Dialogue of Comfort against Tribulation, 147
A Dialogue on G. E. Moore's Ethical Philsophy, 312
Dialogue on John Dewey, 225
Dialogue on Poetry and Literary Aphorisms, 253
Dialogues, 200, 706
Dialogues Concerning Natural Religion, 194, 200, 739
Dialogues Concerning the Two Chief World Systems, Ptolemaic and Copernican, 172
Dialogues Concerning Two New Sciences, 172
The Dialogues of Alfred North Whitehead, 341

The Dialogues of Guy de Brues, 124
Dialogues on Metaphysics, 182
Dialogues on Metaphysics and on Religion, 181
Dialogue with Deviance, 633
Dianetics: The Modern Science of Mental Health, 869
Diaspora: An Inquiry into the Contemporary Jewish World, 645
Diaspora: The Jews among the Greeks and Romans, 605
Diaspora Jews and Judaism, 617
The Diaspora Story: The Epic of the Jewish People among the Nations, 593
Dictionary of All Scriptures and Myths, 4
Dictionary of American Philosophy, 3, 14
Dictionary of American Religious Biography, 719
A Dictionary of Ancient Near Eastern Mythology, 545
A Dictionary of Angels: Including the Fallen Angels, 3
Dictionary of Asian Philosophies, 3, 14
The Dictionary of Bible and Religion, 818
A Dictionary of Chinese Symbols, 521
Dictionary of Christianity in America, 5, 718
Dictionary of Christian Theology, 719
A Dictionary of Comparative Religion, 3
Dictionary of Cults, Sects, Religions and the Occult, 854
A Dictionary of Islam, 566
Dictionary of Mysticism, 718
A Dictionary of New Thought Terms, 847
A Dictionary of Non-Christian Religions, 3, 5
Dictionary of Philosophy (Angeles), 2, 12
Dictionary of Philosophy (Frolov), 3, 13
Dictionary of Philosophy (Runes), 3, 15
A Dictionary of Philosophy (Flew), 3, 13
A Dictionary of Philosophy (Lacey), 3, 14

Dictionary of Philosophy and Psychology, 13
Dictionary of Philosophy and Religion: Eastern and Western Thought, 14
Dictionary of Religion and Philosophy, 4, 14, 717
A Dictionary of Saints, 719
Dictionary of the Ecumenical Movement, 5, 746
Dictionary of the History of Ideas, 3, 15, 163
Dictionary of the Middle Ages, 94
Diderot, 196
Diderot: A Critical Biography, 196
Diderot and Descartes, 197
Diderot and the Encyclopedists, 196
Diderot and the Jews, 196
Diderot as a Disciple of English Thought, 196
Didyma: Apollo's Oracle, Cult, and Companions, 446
Die Philosophie Franz Brentanos, 222
Dietrich Bonhoeffer, 760
The Difference between Fichte's and Schelling's System of Philosophy, 198, 232
Difficult Freedom: Essays on Judaism, 901
Digha Nikaya, 514
Dignity and Practical Reason, 206
Dilemmas, 325
Dilemmas in Modern Jewish Thought: The Dialectics of Revelation and History, 634, 649
Dilthey: Philosopher of the Human Studies, 226
Dilthey Today, 226
Dimensions of Islam, 573, 576
Dimensions of Orthodox Judaism, 654
Dinka Folktales: African Stories from the Sudan, 462
The Dionysiac Mysteries of the Hellenistic and Roman Age, 450, 486
Dionysiac Poetics and Euripides' Bacchae, 475
Directions in Catholic Social Ethics, 743
Directions in Euripidean Criticism: A Collection of Essays, 475

Directory of African American Religious Bodies, 7

Directory of American Philosophers, 5

A Directory of Religious Bodies in the United States, 717, 751

The Discarded Image, 99

Discascalicon: A Medieval Guide to the Arts, 101

Discipleship of Equals: A Critical Feminist Ecclesiology of Liberation, 750

Disciplinary, Moral, and Ascetical Works, 713

Discipline and Punish, 400

The Discipline of Taste and Feeling, 381

Disciplining Foucault: Feminism, Power, and the Body, 401

Discord, Dialogue, and Concord, 730

A Discourse Concerning the Being and Attributes of God, 194

Discourse on Free Will, 138

Discourse on Metaphysics, Correspondence with Arnauld, Monadology, 164, 176

Discourse on Method, 168, 169

Discourse on the Awakening of Faith in the Mahayana, 557

Discourse on the Natural Theology of the Chinese, 176

Discourse on the Origin of Inequality, 212

Discourse on the Sciences and Arts, 212

Discourse on Thinking, 291

The Discourses, 145

The Discourses of Rumi, 589

Discourses on Livy, 144

Discourses on Two New Sciences, 142

Discovering Plato, 81

Discovering Reality, 40

The Discovery of the Mind in Early Greek Philosophy and Literature, 49

Discrimination and Reverse Discrimination, 386

The Disguises of the Demon, 506, 510, 514

Disputation against Astrology, 152

Disputation and Dialogue: Readings in the Jewish-Christian Encounter, 603

Disputed Questions: On Being a Christian, 785

Disputed Questions in Theology and the Philosophy of Religion, 380

Disputed Questions on the Mystery of the Trinity, 113

Dissemination, 397

Dissent and Reform in the Early Middle Ages, 700

The Dissolution of the Medieval Outlook, 104

A Distant Mirror: The Calamitous Fourteenth Century, 701

The Divine Consort: Radha and the Goddesses of India, 504

Divine Dialogues, 183

Divine Disenchantment: Deconverting from New Religions, 856

The Divine Hierarchy: Popular Hinduism in Central India, 503

The "Divine Man": His Origin and Function in Hellenistic Popular Religion, 451

Divine Milieu: An Essay on the Interior Life, 336

Divine Name and Presence: The Memra, 608

Divine Omniscience and Human Freedom, 289

Divine Passions: The Social Construction of Emotion in India, 505

Divine Power: A Study of Karl Barth and Charles Hartshorne, 289

The Divine Principle and Its Application, 877

The Divine Relativity: A Social Conception of God, 289

The Divine Romance, 556

The Divine Romance: Teresa of Avila's Narrative Theology, 786

Divinity and Experience: The Religion of the Dinka, 462

The Divinity of the Roman Emperor, 452

The Divisions and Methods of the Sciences, 117

Doctrine and Covenants of the Church of Jesus Christ of Latter-Day Saints, 846, 879

Doctrine and Practice in the Early Church, 686

Doctrine of Merits in Old Rabbinical Literature, 621

Doctrine of the Heart, 549

The Doctrine of the Soul in the Thought of Plotinus and Origen, 63

The Doctrine of the Sufis, 574

A Documentary History of Religion in America since 1865, 751

A Documentary History of Russian Thought, 31

Documents Illustrating Papal Authority, A.D. 96–454, 688

Documents in Early Christian Thought, 687

Documents in the History of American Philosophy, 36

Documents of American Catholic History, 751

Documents of the Christian Church, 680

The Documents of Vatican II, 891

Does God Exist? An Answer for Today, 775

Dogen's Manuals of Zen Meditation, 537

Dogmatic and Polemical Works, 711

The Dogmatic Principles of Soviet Philosophy (as of 1958), 31

Doing Evil to Achieve Good: Moral Choice in Conflict Situations, 745

Doing Philosophy Historically, 16

Dojo: Magic and Exorcism in Modern Japan, 540

The Domestication of Europe, 434

The Domestication of the Savage Mind, 460

Dominations and Powers: Reflections on Liberty, Society and Government, 326

Donald Davidson, 283

The Donatist Church: A Movement of Protest in Roman North Africa, 685

Don Isaac Abravanel: Statesman and Philosopher, 633

Doomsday Cult, 871

Dorothy Day: A Biography, 765

Dorothy Day: A Radical Devotion, 765

Dorothy Day: Selected Writings, 765

Dorothy Day and the Catholic Worker: Bibliography and Index, 765

Dorothy Day and the Catholic Worker, 766

Dostoyevsky, Tolstoy and Nietzsche, 247, 335

Doubt and Dogmatism: Studies in Hellenistic Epistemology, 56

Doubt's Boundless Sea, 123

Downfall of Cartesianism, 171

Doxology: The Praise of God in Worship, Doctrine, and Life, 898

Dr. Samuel Clarke: An Eighteenth Century Heretic, 194

Drafts for the Essay Concerning Human Understanding and Other Philosophical Writings, 179

The Dragons of Tiananmen: Beijing as a Sacred City, 531

The Drama of the European Jews, 635

The Drama of Thought, 24

Drawing Down the Moon, 865

Dream and Reality: An Essay in Autobiography, 759

A Dreamer's Journey: The Autobiography of Morris Raphael Cohen, 280

Dreaming the Dark: Magic, Sex, and Politics, 865

The Dream of d'Alembert, 195

Dreamtime: Concerning the Boundary between Wilderness and Civilization, 430

Drudgery Divine, 490, 491

The Druids, 436

Dutch Anabaptism, 780

Dutch Calvinism in Modern America: A History of a Conservative Subculture, 752

The Dutch Revolt, 732

Duties of the Heart by R. Bachya ibn Paquda, 630

The Duty of Genius, 346

The Dybbuk and Other Writings, 657

Dynamic Judaism: The Essential Writings of Mordecai M. Kaplan, 667

The Dynamics of Biblical Parallelism, 823

Dynamism in the Cosmology of Christian Wolff, 219

Earlier Philosophical Writings, 187

Early American Jewry, 640

Early American Philosophers, 34

Early Arianism: A View of Salvation, 685

Early Biblical Interpretation, 814

Early Christian and Byzantine Political Philosophy: Origins and Background, 692

The Early Christian Attitude to War, 688

Early Christian Creeds, 686

The Early Christian Doctrine of God, 99

Early Christian Doctrines, 686

Early Christian Fathers, 680

Early Christianity, 681

Early Christianity and Greek Paideia, 63, 683

Early Christian Spirituality, 689

Early Christian Thought and the Classical Tradition: Studies in Justin, Clement, and Origen, 99, 685

Early Christian Thoughts and the Classical Tradition, 63

Early Christian Writings: The Apostolic Fathers, 704

The Early Church and the State, 683

The Early Church to the Dawn of the Reformation, 677

The Early Development of Mohammedanism, 571

Early Essays, 312

The Early Fathers on War and Military Service, 689

Early Gentile Christianity and Its Hellenistic Background, 487

Early German Philosophy: Kant and His Predecessors, 209, 219

Early Greek Astronomy to Aristotle, 48

Early Greek Philosophy, 50

Early Greek Thinking: The Dawn of Western Philosophy, 50, 291

The Early History of God: Yahweh and the Other Deities in Ancient Israel, 824

The Early History of the Ancient Near East, 9000–2000 B.C., 434, 441

Early History of Zionism in America, 658

Early Islam, 573

The Early Islamic Conquests, 568

Early Judaism and Its Modern Interpreters, 615, 814

The Early Kabbalah, 630

The Early Liturgy to the Time of Gregory the Great, 689

Early Man in China, 336

Early Medieval Philosophy, 480–1150: An Introduction, 94

Early Philosophical Writings, 198

Early Pythagorean Politics in Practice and Theory, 87

The Early Reception of Berkeley, 1710–1733, 191

Early Theological Writings, 232

Early Thomistic School, 119

The Early Vasas: A History of Sweden, 1523–1611, 731

The Early Versions of the New Testament, 806

Early Writings, 242

The Ear of the Other, 397

The Earth Is the Lord's: The Inner World of the Jew in Eastern Europe, 664

Earthkeeping in the Nineties: Stewardship of Creation, 746

The Earthly Republic: Italian Humanists on Government and Society, 127

East Asia: The Modern Transformation, 358

East Asian Civilizations: A Dialogue in Five Stages, 523

The Eastern Buddhist, 557

Eastern Religions and Western Thought, 353

The Eastern Schism, 694

East Meets West: The Jesuits in China, 1582–1773, 532

Ebla: A New Look at History, 445

Ecce Homo, 246

Ecclesiastical Authority and Spiritual Power in the Church of the First Three Centuries, 690

Ecclesiastical History, 709

Echoes: After Heidegger, 294

The Eclipse of Biblical Narrative, 739

Ecological Ethics and Politics, 389
The Ecological Spirituality of Teilhard, 337
An Ecology of the Spirit, 507, 509
Economic History of the Jews, 593
Economics of the Mishnah, 606
Eco-Philosophy, 38
Eco-Spirituality: Toward a Reverent Life, 888
Ecstasies: Deciphering the Witches' Sabbath, 431
Ecstasy: Shamanism in Korea, 539
Ecstatic Religion, 431
Edifying Discourses, 238
Edith Stein: A Biography, 744
Edmund Burke: His Political Philosophy, 193
Edmund Husserl: Philosopher of Infinite Tasks, 235
Edmund Husserl's "Origin of Geometry," 397
Edmund Husserl's Phenomenological Psychology, 235
Edmund Husserl's Phenomenology: A Critical Commentary, 235
Education and Civilization, 284
Education and Culture in the Political Thought of Aristotle, 69
Education and the Significance of Life, 554
Education at the Crossroads, 306
Education for Freedom: The Philosophy of Education of Jacques Maritain, 307
Education in the Age of Science, 276
Education of a Christian Prince, 139
The Education of Man: Educational Philosophy, 306
The Education of the Human Race, 208
Edward FitzGerald's Salaman and Absal, 585
Edward VI: The Threshold of Power, 726
Edward VI: The Young King, 726
Eerdmans' Handbook to Christian Belief, 718
Eerdmans' Handbook to Christianity in America, 751

Eerdmans' Handbook to the History of Christianity, 676, 720, 743
Eerdman's Handbook to the World Religions, 520
Egotism in German Philosophy, 29, 326
The Egyptian Gods: A Handbook, 548
Egyptian Mythology, 548
Egyptian Religion, 442, 548
Eichmann in Jerusalem, 394
Eighteenth-Century Philosophy, 159
Eight Philosophers of the Italian Renaissance, 30, 128
Eighty Years of Locke Scholarship, 1900–1980: A Bibliographic Guide, 180
Elbow Room, 396
The Elementary Forms of the Religious Life, 425
Elementary Logic, 411
Elements of Christian Philosophy, 286
The Elements of Ethics, 312
Elements of Law: Natural and Politic, 174
Elements of Morality Including Polity, 257
Elements of Newton's Philosophy, 217
The Elements of Philosophy: A Compendium for Philosophers and Theologians, 24, 25
Elements of the Bahai Faith, 861
The Elements of Theology, 62
Elements of the Philosophy of Newton, 195
Elements of the Philosophy of Right, 231, 232
Elenchus Bibliographies Biblicus, 796
Eleusis: Archetypal Image of Mother and Daughter, 484
El Hijo Prodijo: A Critical Index of Twentieth-Century Mexican Thought, 33
Elijah Muhammad, 862
The Elizabethan Puritan Movement, 733
Eloquent Zen: Daito and Early Japanese Zen, 537
Elucidations of the Search after Truth, 181
The Elusive Mr. Wesley: John Wesley His Own Biographer, 790
Emanuel Swedenborg: A

Continuing Vision, 852, 880
Emanuel Swedenborg, Scientist and Mystic, 852, 880
An Emendation of Collingwood's Doctrine of Absolute Presuppositions, 282
The Emergence of Christian Science in American Religious Life, 843
The Emergence of Conservative Judaism, 655
The Emergence of Contemporary Judaism, 655
The Emergence of Liberation Theology, 747
The Emergence of Probability, 160
The Emergence of the Jewish Problem, 1878–1939, 637
The Emergence of Whitehead's Metaphysics, 1925–29, 342
Emerging from the Chrysalis: Studies in Rituals of Women's Initiation, 430
Emile, 212, 213
The Emmet Fox Treasury, 847
Emotion in the Thought of Sartre, 330
The Emotions: Outline of a Theory, 329
Empedocles: The Extant Fragments, 53
Empedocles' Cosmic Cycle, 53
The Emperor and the Gods: Images from the Time of Trojan, 452
The Emperor in the Roman World, 452
The Emperor Julian, 682
Emperor Michael Palaeologus and the West, 1258–1282, 693
The Emptiness of Emptiness: An Introduction to Early Indian Madhyamika, 513
The Enchantments of Judaism, 600
Enchiridion Ethicum, 183
Enchiridion Metaphysicum, 183
Enchiridion of Erasmus, 139
Encountering the Goddess, 503
Encounter on the Narrow Ridge: A Life of Martin Buber, 662
Encounters between Judaism

and Modern Philosophy, 663

Encounter with Emancipation, 638

The Encyclopaedia of Islam, 567

Encyclopedia Judaica, 5, 594

The Encyclopedia of American Religions, 4, 717, 751, 854

Encyclopedia of Archaeological Excavations in the Holy Land, 808

Encyclopedia of Biblical and Christian Ethics, 718

Encyclopedia of Bioethics, 893

Encyclopedia of Cosmology, 13

Encyclopedia of Early Christianity, 676

Encyclopedia of Eastern Philosophy and Religion, 4

The Encyclopedia of Ethics, 2, 13

Encyclopedia of India, 498

Encyclopedia of Japan, 534

Encyclopedia of Jewish Concepts (A Book of Jewish Concepts), 596

Encyclopedia of Jewish Symbols, 597

Encyclopedia of Judaism, 5

The Encyclopedia of Logic, 232

Encyclopedia of Mormonism, 4, 717, 846

The Encyclopedia of Philosophy, 2, 13, 94, 160, 231

The Encyclopedia of Religion, 4, 497, 522, 717

Encyclopedia of Religion and Ethics, 4, 717

The Encyclopedia of Tarot, 860

Encyclopedia of the American Religious Experience, 4

The Encyclopedia of the Jewish Religion, 595

Encyclopedia of Theology: The Concise Sacramentum Mundi, 676, 719

Encyclopedia of the Reformed Faith, 719

Encyclopedic Dictionary of Yoga, 497

The Encyclopedic Handbook of Cults in America, 4, 854

Ending Lives, 388

The Ending of Time, 554

The Enduring Questions, 23

Engels and the Formation of Marxism, 227

England and the Catholic Church under Queen Elizabeth, 734

England's Earliest Protestants, 1520–1535, 726

England under the Tudors, 726

English Almanacs, 1500–1800: Astrology and the Popular Press, 725

The English Catholic Community, 1570–1850, 736

The English Clergy, 734

English Deism: Its Roots and Its Fruits, 739

English Humanism: Wyatt to Cowley, 128

The English Jewry under Angevin Kings, 624

The English Mystical Tradition, 721

The English Philosophers from Bacon to Mill, 29, 159

English Philosophy since 1900, 268

The English Reformation, 726

English Reformations: Religion, Politics and Society under the Tudors, 726

English Reformers, 727

The English Utilitarians: Jeremy Bentham, James Mill, John Stuart Mill, 245

The Enigma of Faith, 102

The Enigma of Mary Stuart, 735

The Enlightenment: An Interpretation, 160, 739

Enlightenment, Revolution and Romanticism, 159

Enquiries Concerning Human Understanding and Concerning the Principles of Morals, 99, 200

An Enquiry Concerning Human Understanding: And Letter from a Gentleman to His Friend in Edinburgh, 199, 200

An Enquiry Concerning the Principles of Morals, 200

An Enquiry Concerning the Principles of Natural Knowledge, 341

Enquiry into Plants, 90

Enthusiasm, 737

Entry into the Realm of Reality: The Text, 529

Enuma Elish, 440

Environmental Justice, 389

The Epic of Gilgamesh, 545, 546

Epicurea, 73

Epicureanism: Chief Ancient Philosophies, 74

Epicurean Political Philosophy: The "De Rerum Natura" of Lucretius, 75

The Epicurean Tradition, 74

Epicurus, 74

Epicurus: An Introduction, 74

Epicurus and Hellenistic Philosophy, 74

Epicurus and His Philosophy, 73

Epicurus' Ethical Theory: The Pleasures of Invulnerability, 74

Epicurus' Scientific Method, 73

Epilegomena to the Study of Greek Religion, 479

Episcopal Women, 754

Epistemology and Cognition, 380

Epistemology of G. E. Moore, 312

The Epistle to the Romans, 758

The Epochal Nature of Process in Whitehead's Metaphysics, 343

An Epoch of Miracles: Oral Literature of the Yucatec Maya, 465

Equal in Monastic Profession: Religious Women in Medieval France, 699

Equality and Liberty: Analyzing Rawls and Nozick, 316

Equality and Liberty, 386

Erasmus, 139

Erasmus: A Critical Biography, 721

Erasmus: A Study of His Life, Ideals and Place in History, 139

Erasmus: Ecstasy and the Praise of Folly, 139

Erasmus: Lectures and Wayfaring Sketches, 139

Erasmus and His Times, 139

Erasmus and the Age of Reformation, 139

Erasmus and the New Testament: The Mind of a Christian Humanist, 139

Erasmus and the Northern Renaissance, 139

Erasmus grandescens: The

Growth of a Humanist's Mind and Spirituality, 139
Erasmus of Christendom, 139
Erasmus of Europe: The Making of a Humanist, 139
Erasmus on Language and Method in Theology, 139
Eriugena, 115
Ernest Holmes: His Life and Times, 847
Ernst Bloch, 277
Ernst Bloch: A Bibliography, 277
Ernst Cassirer: An Annotated Bibliography, 280
Ernst Cassirer: Scientific Knowledge and the Concept of Man, 280
Eros and Civilization, 408
Eros and Magic in the Renaissance, 125
Eros and Psyche: Studies in Plato, Plotinus, and Origen, 87
Errand into the Wilderness, 35
Erring: A Postmodern A/theology, 889
Escape from Predicament, 532
Eschatology in Maimonidean Thought, 668
The Esoteric Basis of Christianity or Theosophy and Christian Doctrine, 853
Esoteric Christianity, 549
The Esoteric Scene: Cultic Milieu and Occult Tarot, 860, 865
An Essay Concerning Human Understanding, 178, 179, 739
The Essayes or Counsels, Civill and Morall, 165
An Essay on African Philosophical Thought: The Akan Conceptual Scheme, 26, 369
An Essay on Anaxagoras, 53
An Essay on Liberation, 408
An Essay on Man: An Introduction to a Philosophy of Human Culture, 279
An Essay on Metaphysics, 281
Essay on Morals, 217
An Essay on Philosophical Method, 281
Essay on the Active Powers of Man, 211
Essay on the Intellectual Powers of Man, 211

An Essay on the Origin of Human Knowledge, 195
Essays in Aesthetics, 329
Essays in Ancient Greek Philosophy (Anton and Kustas), 47
Essays in Ancient Greek Philosophy (Anton and Preus), 47, 66, 78
Essays in Ancient Philosophy, 48
Essays in Existentialism, 329
Essays in Political Philosophy, 282
Essays in Pragmatism, 236
Essays in Psychology, 236
Essays in Radical Empiricism and a Pluralistic Universe, 236
Essays in Religion and Morality, 236
Essays in Science and Philosophy, 341
Essays in the History of Ideas, 302
Essays in the Philosophy of History, 282
The Essays of Montaigne: A Critical Exploration, 146
Essays on Actions and Events, 283, 396
Essays on Adam Smith, 215
Essays on Aristotle's De Anima, 70
Essays on Aristotle's Ethics, 70
Essays on Aristotle's Poetics, 71
Essays on a Science of Mythology, 484
Essays on Biblical Interpretation, 318
Essays on Davidson: Actions and Events, 283
Essays on Descartes' Meditations, 170
Essays on Early Modern Philosophers, 27, 160
Essays on Heidegger and Others: Philosophical Papers, 294
Essays on Henry Sidgwick, 257
Essays on Islamic Philosophy and Science, 575
Essays on Language, Mind and Matter, 1919–1926, 322
Essays on New Testament Themes, 825
Essays on Old Testament Hermeneutics, 815

Essays on Philosophical Subjects, 215
Essays on Religion and the Ancient World, 487
Essays on the Active Powers of Man, 211
Essays on the Active Powers of the Human Mind, 211
Essays on the Context, Nature, and Influence of Isaac Newton's Theology, 184
Essays on the Foundations of Aristotelian Political Science, 69
Essays on the Mahabharata, 506
Essays on the Philosophy and Science of René Descartes, 171
Essays on the Philosophy of George Berkeley, 192
Essays on the Philosophy of Leibniz, 177
Essays on the Philosophy of Music, 277
Essays on the Philosophy of Socrates, 89
Essays on the Philosophy of W. V. Quine, 412
Essay towards a New Theory of Vision, 191
The Essence of Christianity, 228, 660, 740
The Essence of Judaism, 660
The Essence of Philosophy, 226
The Essence of Religion, 228
The Essene Writings from Qumran, 810
The Essential Alan Watts, 881
Essential Articles for the Study of Francis Bacon, 166
The Essential Augustine, 109
The Essential Aurobindo, 352
The Essential Book of Traditional Chinese Medicine, 522
The Essential Erasmus, 721
Essential Marxism in Postwar France: From Sartre to Althusser, 267
Essential Readings in Logical Positivism, 264
The Essential Reinhold Niebuhr: Selected Essays and Addresses, 784
The Essential Rudolf Steiner, 859
Essential Sacred Writings

from around the World, 2, 473

The Essential Tension, 406

The Essential Tillich: An Anthology of the Writings of Paul Tillich, 787

The Essential Wisdom of George Santayana, 328

The Essential Works of Stoicism, 57

The Essential Writings of Fritjof Schuon, 375

Esther Rabbath I: An Analytical Translation, 611

The Esthetics of the Middle Ages, 95

The Eternal Covenant, 254

Eternal Life?, 775, 887

The Eternal Message of Muhammad, 588

Eternal Truths and the Cartesian Circle, 170

Ethica, 489

Ethica Eudemia, 65

The Ethical Foundations of Marxism, 243

Ethical Idealism: An Inquiry into the Nature and Function of Ideals, 317, 389

Ethical Studies, 220

Ethical Writings of Maimonides, 668

Ethics (Abelard), 106

Ethics (Broad), 277

Ethics (Spinoza), 186

Ethics: A Bibliography, 14

Ethics, Wealth and Salvation: A Study in Buddhist Social Ethics, 514, 896

Ethics after Babel: The Languages of Morals and Their Discontents, 893

Ethics and Infinity, 901

The Ethics and Selected Letters, 187

Ethics and the History of Philosophy: Selected Essays, 277

Ethics from a Theocentric Perspective, 744, 900

Ethics in an Age of Technology, 388

Ethics in the History of Western Philosophy, 160

The Ethics of Authenticity, 414

The Ethics of Jonathan Edwards: Morality and Aesthetics, 767

The Ethics of Socrates: A Compilation, 89

Ethics since Nineteen Hundred, 268

Ethics with Aristotle, 67

Ethnic Survival in America: An Ethnography of a Jewish Afternoon School, 641

Étienne Gilson, 286

An Étienne Gilson Tribute, 286

The Eucharistic Theology of Theodore Beza, 732

Eugen Duhring's Revolution in Science, 227

Euripides and the Full Circle of Myth, 475

Euripides' Medea: The Incarnation of Disorder, 475

European Intellectual History since Seventeen Eighty-Nine, 27

European Thought in the Eighteenth Century: From Montesquieu to Lessing, 161

Europe in Crisis, 1589–1648, 737

Europe of the Devout, 728, 736

Eusebius, Christianity and Judaism, 709

Euthyphro, 89

The Evangelical Tradition in America, 754

Evangelism in the Early Church, 683

Evangelist of Desire: John Wesley and the Methodists, 789

The Evangelization of the Roman Empire: Identity and Adaptability, 683

The Event of the Koran: Islam and Its Scripture, 587

Ever since Sinai: A Modern View of Torah, 601

Everyman's Talmud, 620

The Everything and the Nothing, 872

Everywhere and Nowhere: The Path of Alan Watts, 881

Eve's Journey: Feminine Images in Hebraic Literary Tradition, 649

Evil and the God of Love, 117

Evil and the Process God, 289

Evolution and the Founders of Pragmatism, 163

The Evolution of Medieval Thought, 94, 696

The Evolution of Rights in Liberal Theory, 387

The Evolution of the Sikh Community: Five Essays, 516

Evolution of Urban Society: Early Mesopotamia and Prehispanic Mexico, 438

The Exalted Faith, 628

An Examination of Dr. Reid's Inquiry into the Human Mind, 212

Examination of McTaggart's Philosophy, 277, 304

An Examination of Plato's Doctrines, 79

An Examination of Sir William Hamilton's Philosophy, 244

The Examined Life: Philosophical Meditations, 314, 389

Exclusiveness and Tolerance, 624

"The Execution of Justice in England," by William Cecil, and "A True, Sincere, and Modest Defense of English Catholics," by William Allen, 734

Exegetical Method: A Student's Handbook, 815

Exegetic Homilies, 705

Existence and Actuality: Conversations with Charles Hartshorne, 289

Existence and Being, 291

The Existential Dialectic of Marx and Merleau-Ponty, 311

Existentialism (Macquarrie), 265

Existentialism (Solomon), 267

Existentialism (Warnock), 268

Existentialism and Human Emotions, 329

Existentialism and Humanism, 329

Existentialist Ethics, 262

Existential Psychoanalysis, 329

The Existential Sociology of Jean-Paul Sartre, 331

Expanding the View: Gustavo Gutierrez and the Future of Liberation Theology, 769

The Expansion of Christianity in the First Three Centuries, 681

The Expansion of Islam: An Arab Religion in the Non-Arab World, 568

Experience and Certainty, 296
Experience and Education, 224
Experience and Nature, 224
The Experience of Insight, 519
Experimentation in American Religion, 856
Explaining Religion: Criticism and Theory from Bodin to Freud, 420
Explanation and Understanding, 338
The Explanation of Behavior, 414
Explorations in African Systems of Thought, 462
Explorations in Whitehead's Philosophy, 342
Exploring Jewish Ethics: Papers on Covenant Responsibility, 661
Exploring Judaism: A Reconstructionist Approach, 659
Exposing Cults: Understanding the Rise of Gurus in North America, 856
The Expulsion of the Triumphant Beast, 135
Ezekiel: A Commentary, 834

Fable about Man, 156
Faces of Hunger, 387
Face to Face with Levinas, 901
Facing West from California's Shores, 858
Fact, Fiction and Forecast, 403
Faith, Prayer and Grace: A Comparative Study in Ramanuja and Kierkegaard, 37
Faith, Reason and Theology, 117
Faith, Trinity, Incarnation, 63
Faith after the Holocaust, 648
Faith and Fratricide: The Theological Roots of Anti-Semitism, 684, 785
Faith and Knowledge: The Jew in the Medieval World, 629
Faith and Piety in Early Judaism: Texts and Documents, 615
Faith and Power: The Politics of Islam, 579
Faith and Reason: An Intro-

duction to Modern Jewish Thought, 646
Faith and the Intifada: Palestinian Christian Voices, 896
Faith and Works: Cranmer and Hooker on Justification, 764
Faith in History and Society: Toward a Practical Fundamental Theology, 904
The Faith of a Liberal, 280
The Faith of John Knox, 774
The Faith of Qumran, 616
The Faith of Reason, 160
The Faith of Secular Jews, 651, 656
Faith on Earth, 745
Faith Strengthened, 631
Falasha Anthology, 644
The Falashas: The Forgotten Jews of Ethiopia, 644
Fallible Man: Philosophy of the Will, 318
The False Prison: A Study of the Development of Wittgenstein's Philosophy, 346
The Family, Sex, and Marriage: England 1500–1800, 735
A Family Patchwork: Five Generations of an Anglo-Jewish Family, 637
Farewell to Reason, 399
The Fate of Man in the Modern World, 758
The Fate of Reason: German Philosophy from Kant to Fichte, 16, 159, 209
Fatherland or Promised Land: The Dilemma of the German Jew 1893–1914, 637
The Fathers According to Rabbi Nathan, 610, 611
Fathers and Heretics, 686
The Fathers of the Church, 680
The Fathers of the Greek Church, 98, 690
The Fathers of the Latin Church, 98, 690
Fathers Talking: An Anthology, 690
The FBI and Martin Luther King, Jr., 772
Fear of Diversity: The Birth of Political Science in Ancient Greek Thought, 49
The Fear of the Dead in Primitive Religion, 476
Feasting and Social Oscillation, 519

Feast of Faith, 755
A Feast of History: Passover through the Ages as a Key to Jewish Experience, 600
The Female Experience and the Nature of the Divine, 439
Feminine Ground: Essays on Women and Tibet, 544
Feminism and Foucault, 391
Feminist Interpretation of the Bible, 815
Feminist Perspectives in Philosophy, 391
Feminist Spirituality and the Feminine Divine: An Annotated Bibliography, 749
Feminist Theology: A Reader, 896
Feminist Theology/Christian Theology: In Search of Method, 749
Feminist Theory and the Philosophies of Man, 392
Festivals and Calendars of the Roman Republic, 448
Festivals in South India and Sri Lanka, 507
Festivals of India, 506
Festivals of Interpretation, 402
Festivals of the Athenians, 447
Festivals of the Jewish Year: A Modern Interpretation and Guide, 599
Feuerbach: Opposition of Materialistic and Idealistic Outlook, 228
Feuerbach and the Search for Otherness, 228
Feyerabend's Critique of Foundationalism, 399
Fichte's Theory of Subjectivity, 198
Ficino and Renaissance Neoplatonism, 141
Fifteen Sermons, 193
The Fifth Sun: Aztec Gods, Aztec World, 457
Fifty Major Philosophers: A Reference Guide, 13
A Fifty-Year History of the American Federation of Astrologers, 860
Fifty Years of Chinese Philosophy 1898–1950, 358
Fifty Years of Hume Scholarship, 202
Fighting with Gandhi, 553
The Final Foucault, 400
Finding the Mean: Theory

and Practice in Aristotelian Political Philosophy, 71
The Finitude of Being, 295
The Fire and the Sun: Why Plato Banished the Artists, 83
The Fire Next Time, 862
The First and Last Freedom, 554
First-Century Judaism in Crisis, 605
The First Christian Histories, 709
First Considerations: An Examination of Philosophical Evidence, 338, 339
The First Crusade, 693
The First Crusade and the Idea of Crusading, 694
The First Dynasty of Islam: The Umayyad Caliphate A.D. 661–750, 569
The First Five Lives of Annie Besant, 550, 859
A First Glance at St. Thomas, 119
First Impressions: Cylinder Seals in the Ancient Near East, 544
The First International and After, 242
The First Jew: Prejudice and Politics in an American Community, 1900–1932, 640
First Letter Concerning Toleration, 178
The First Person, 395
First Philosophy: An Introduction to Philosophical Issues, 21
The First Step: A Guide for the New Jewish Spirit, 649
The First Systematic Theologian, Origen of Alexandria, 63
The First Thirteen Centuries, 98
Five Essays on Philosophy, 361
The Five Great Religions, 572
Five Sermons, 193
Five Stages of Greek Religion, 48
Five Types of Ethical Theory, 277
The Five Ways: St. Thomas Aquinas' Proofs of God's Existence, 119
The Flame of the Candle, 274

Flash of the Spirit: African and Afro-American Art and Philosophy, 26
Flavius Josephus: Selections from His Works, 666
Flavius Josephus on the Pharisees: A Composition-Critical Study, 616
The Flayed God: The Mythology of Mesoamerica, 465
The Flight into Inwardness, 408
Flowering in the Shadows, 524, 535
Fly and the Fly-Bottle: Encounters with British Intellectuals, 266
The Flying Phoenix: Aspects of Chinese Sectarianism in Taiwan, 531
Flying Saucers: A Modern Myth of Things Seen in the Sky, 870
Folk Elements in Burmese Buddhism, 519
Folk Literature of the Tehuelche Indians, 466
Folk Religion in Japan, 539
Follow the Ecstasy: The Hermitage Years of Thomas Merton, 781
Food, Sex and Pollution: A New Guinea Religion, 462
Forbidden Knowledge, 317
Forces and Fields, 405
Forerunners of the Reformation: The Shape of Late Medieval Thought, 128, 697, 721
The Forest of Symbols: Aspects of Ndembu Ritual, 463
The Forgotten Hume, Le Bon David, 202
Formal and Transcendental Logic, 234
Formalism in Ethics and Non-Formal Ethics of Values, 332
Form and Thought in Herodotus, 480
Form and Transformation: A Study in the Philosophy of Plotinus, 87
For Marx, 242
The Formation of Ch'an Ideology in China and Korea: The Vajrasamadhisutra, 537
The Formation of the Atomic Theory and Its Earliest Critics, 48

The Formation of the Christian Bible, 814
The Formation of the Gospel Tradition, 826
Formation of the Jewish Intellect, 606
The Formation of the New Testament, 816
The Formative Period of Islamic Thought, 577
For My People, 763
Fortune Is a Woman, 145
Foucault, 400
Foucault: A Critical Reader, 401
Foucault and Feminism, 401
Foucault's Archaeology: Science and the History of Reason, 401
Foundational Reflections: Studies in Contemporary Philosophy, 264
The Foundation of Jacques Maritain's Political Philosophy, 307
Foundation of Space-Time Physics, 384
The Foundations of Arithmetic, 229
Foundations of Christian Faith: An Introduction to the Idea of Christianity, 745, 903
Foundations of Judaism: Method, Teleology, Doctrine, 606, 607
The Foundations of Knowing, 395
The Foundations of Mao Zedong's Political Thought, 1917–1935, 362
The Foundations of Modern Political Thought: The Renaissance, 105, 131
The Foundations of Newton's Alchemy: Or "The Hunting of the Greene Lyon," 184
Foundations of the Metaphysics of Morals, 204, 205
Foundations of T'ien-T'ai Philosophy, 530
Founders of Faith, 512, 526
The Founders of the Middle Ages, 99
Four Dissertations, 210
Four Doctrines, 880
The Fourfold Root of the Principle of Sufficient Reason, 254
The Four Great Heresies, 687
Four Hasidic Masters and

Their Struggle against Melancholy, 633
Four Modern Prophets, 785, 905
The Four O'Clock Murders: A True Story of a Mormon Family's Vengeance, 845
Four Paths to One God, 649
Four Reasonable Men: Aurelius, Mill, Renan, Sidgwick, 276
The Fourth Crusade, 694
Four Theories of Myth in Twentieth-Century History, 420, 428
Fourth Way, 876
Four Tragedies, nos. 1–4, Three Tragedies, no. 5, 474
Four Tragedies and Octavia, 88
Four Views of Time in Ancient Philosophy, 47
Foxe's Book of Martyrs, 733
The Fragility of Goodness: Luck and Ethics in Greek Tragedy and Philosophy, 48
Fragments of a Poetics of Fire, 274
Francis Bacon: Discovery and the Art of Discourse, 165
Francis Bacon: From Magic to Science, 166
Francis Bacon: His Career and His Thought, 165
Francis Bacon: Philosopher of Industrial Science, 165
Francis Bacon and Renaissance Prose, 166
Francis Bacon on the Nature of Man, 166
Francis Bacon's Philosophy of Science: An Account and Reappraisal, 166
Francis Hutcheson and Contemporary Ethical Theory, 203
Francis of Assisi, 710
The Frankish Church, 692
Franz Brentano's Analysis of Truth, 222
Franz Rosenzweig: His Life and Thought, 671
A Free Discussion of the Doctrines of Materialism and Philosophical Necessity, 210
Freedom, 270
Freedom, Emotion and Self-Substance, 189

Freedom and Karl Jaspers' Philosophy, 300
Freedom and Morality and Other Essays, 272
Freedom and Nature: The Voluntary and Involuntary, 319
Freedom and Politics in Ethical Behaviour, 230
Freedom and Resentment, 414
Freedom and the End of Reason, 207
Freedom and the Modern World, 306
Freedom and the Spirit, 758
Freedom as a Value: A Critique of the Ethical Theory of Jean-Paul Sartre, 330
Freedom from the Known, 555
Freedom from the Self: Sufism, Meditation, and Psychotherapy, 576
Freedom in Exile: The Autobiography of the Dalai Lama, 356, 560, 906
Freedom in the Modern World, 271, 308
The Freedom of the Christian Man, 777
Freedom of the Press, 296
Freedom with Justice: Catholic Social Thought and Liberal Institutions, 748
Free Will and the Theory of the Moral Desire, 230
Frege: Logical Excavations, 229
Frege: Philosophy of Language, 229
Frege: Philosophy of Mathematics, 229
Frege and the Philosophy of Mathematics, 230
Frege in Perspective, 230
Frege's Theory of Judgment, 229
Frege Synthesized, 230
The French Enlightenment and the Jews, 161, 647
French Existentialism: A Christian Critique, 265
French Free Thought from Gassendi to Voltaire, 28, 163
French Humanism: 1470–1600, 127
French Literature and the Philosophy of Consciousness, 27
French Moralists: The Theory

of the Passions 1585–1649, 128
The French Paracelsians, 150
French Philosophers—New England Transcendentalism, 28
French Philosophers in Conversation, 28, 266
French Thought since Sixteen Hundred, 28
Freud, Jews and Other Germans: Masters and Victims in Modernist Culture, 635
Freud and Philosophy: An Essay on Interpretation, 319
Freud on Femininity and Faith, 424
The Friars and the Jews: The Evolution of Medieval Anti-Judaism, 623, 696
Friar Thomas D'Aquino: His Life, Thought, and Work, 119
Friedrich Engels, 227
Friedrich Engels: His Life and Thought, 227
Friedrich Nietzsche, 246
Friedrich Nietzsche: Fighter for Freedom, 248
Friedrich Nietzsche: Philosopher of Culture, 247
Friedrich Schlegel, 253
Friedrich Schleiermacher: The Evolution of a Nationalist, 254
A Friendly Companion to Plato's "Gorgias," 83
The Friendship of the Barbarians: Xenophon and the Persians, 91
From a Logical Point of View, 411
From a Mighty Fortress, 737
From Beast Machine to Man Machine, 162, 170
From Black Muslims to Muslims, 579, 862
From Descartes to Hume, 161
From Dreyfus to Vichy: The Remaking of French Jewry 1906–1939, 636
From Ezra to the Last of the Maccabees: Foundations of Post-Biblical Judaism, 604
From Gautama Buddha to the Triumph of Christianity, 524
From Hegel to Marx: Studies in the Intellectual Development of Karl Marx, 298
From Honey to Ashes: Intro-

duction to a Science of Mythology, 428, 465

From Humanism to Science, 1480 to 1700, 162

From Humanism to the Humanities, 126

From Iran East and West, 861

From Luther to Chemnitz on Scripture and the Word, 730

From Luther to Popper, 408

From Machismo to Mutuality: Essays on Sexism and Woman-Man Liberation, 785

From Morality to Virtue, 389

From Muhammad to the Age of Reforms, 543

From Mysticism to Dialogue: Martin Buber's Transformation of German Social Thought, 662

From Myth to Fiction, 471

From Nicaea to Chalcedon: A Guide to the Literature and Its Background, 687

From Paracelsus to Van Helmont, 150

From Persecution to Toleration, 734

From Philo to Origen: Middle Platonism in Transition, 670

From Platonism to Neoplatonism, 61

From Politics to Piety: The Emergence of Pharisaic Judaism, 616

From Primitives to Zen, 472

From Puritanism to the Age of Reason, 739

From Religion to Philosophy: A Study of the Origins of Western Speculation, 50

From Shakespeare to Existentialism, 161, 265

From Spanish Court to Italian Ghetto, 625

From Targum to Testament, 608

From Testament to Torah: An Introduction to Judaism in Its Formative Age, 621

From Text to Action, 319

From Text to Tradition: A History of Second Temple and Rabbinic Judaism, 621, 812

From the Beginnings to the Threshold of the Reformation, 676

From the Circle of Alcuin to the School of Auxerre, 100

From the Closed World to the Infinite Universe, 128, 161

From the Enemy's Point of View, 466

From the Exile to Christ: A Historical Introduction to Palestinian Judaism, 807

From the Fall of Jerusalem, 586 B.C. to the Bar-Kakhba Revolt, A.D. 135, 605

From the Heart of the People: The Theology of Gustavo Gutierrez, 769

From the Maccabees to the Mishnah, 604

From the Many to the One, 47

From the Middle Ages to the Enlightenment, 130

From the Outer Court to the Inner Sanctum, 549

From the Poetry of Sumer: Creation, Glorification, Adoration, 441

From the Rising of the Sun: Christians and Society in Contemporary Japan, 541

From the Stone Age to Christianity: Monotheism and the Historical Process, 806, 828

From the Stone Age to the Eleusinian Mysteries, 545, 548

From Time to Time, 788

From Tradition to Commentary, 610

From Tradition to Gospel, 825

From Twilight to Dawn: The Cultural Vision of Jacques Maritain, 308

From Union Square to Rome, 765

Fugitive Essays, 250

A Full Hearing: Orality and Literacy in the Malay World, 460

The Function of Reason, 341

Fundamental Freedoms and Jehovah's Witnesses, 863

Fundamentalism: A Bishop Rethinks the Meaning of Scripture, 746

Fundamentalism, Revivalists and Violence in South Asia, 507, 515

Fundamentalism and American Culture, 753

Fundamentalisms Observed. The Fundamentalism Project, 890

The Fundamentalist Phenomenon, 753

Fundamental Laws of Arithmetic, 229

Fundamental Problems of Philosophy, 364

The Fundamental Questions of Philosophy, 20

Fundamentals of Buddhist Ethics, 512

Fundamentals of Islamic Thought: God, Man and the Universe, 373

Fundamentals of Philosophy, 24

Fundamental Studies of Jean Bodin: An Original Anthology, 134

Furta Sacra: Thefts of Relics in the Central Middle Ages, 699

Future(s) of Philosophy: The Marginal Thinking of Jacques Derrida, 398

The Future Is Now: Last Talks in India, 555

The Future of an Illusion, 424

The Future of Evangelical Theology, 742

The Future of Humanity, 555

The Future of Islam, 567

Future of Man, 336

The Future of New Religious Movements, 855

The Future of Religion: Secularization, Revival and Cult Formation, 855

The Future of the American Jew, 667

The Future of the Jewish Community in America, 641

G. E. Moore, 312

G. E. Moore: A Critical Exposition, 312

G. H. Mead's Concept of Rationality, 309

Gabriel Marcel, 305

Gabriel's Wing: A Study into the Religious Ideas of Sir Muhammad Iqbal, 375

Gadamer: Hermeneutics, Tradition, and Reason, 402

Gadamer and Hermeneutics, 402

Gadamer's Hermeneutics, 402

Gaia and God: An Ecofeminist Theology of Earth Healing, 749, 785, 905
A Galilean Rabbi and His Bible, 608
Galileo (Drake), 143
Galileo (Ronan), 144
Galileo: A Philosophical Study, 144
Galileo: Pioneer Scientist, 143, 172
Galileo, Bellarmine and the Bible, 142
Galileo, First Observer of Marvelous Things, 172
Galileo, Human Knowledge, and the Book of Nature, 143
Galileo, the Jesuits and the Medieval Aristotle, 144
The Galileo Affair: A Documentary History, 143, 172
Galileo and His Sources, 144
Galileo and the Art of Reasoning, 143
Galileo at Work, 172
Galileo at Work: His Scientific Biography, 143
Galileo Galilei: A Biography and Inquiry into His Philosophy of Science, 143, 172
Galileo Heretic, 143
Galileo Man of Science, 143
Galileo Reappraised, 143, 172
Galileo's Intellectual Revolution, 172
Galileo's Intellectual Revolution: Middle Period, 1610–1632, 144
Galileo's Logical Treatises, 144
Galileo's Logic of Discovery and Proof, 144
Galileo Studies: Personality, Tradition, and Revolution, 143, 172
Gandavyuha, 529
Gandhi, 352
Gandhi: Against the Tide, 553
Gandhi: Prisoner of Hope, 553
Gandhi: The South African Experience, 554
Gandhi, A Memoir, 553
Gandhi and Charlie, 553
Gandhi and Civil Disobedience: The Mahatma in Indian Politics 1928–34, 553
Gandhi and His Critics, 553

Gandhi and Non-Violence, 553
Gandhi and the Nonconformists: Encounters in South Africa, 553
Gandhian Utopia: Experiments with Culture, 553
Gandhi on Non-Violence. Selected Texts from Gandhi's Non-Violence in Peace and War, 895
Gandhi's Religious Thought, 352, 553
Gandhi's Rise to Power: Indian Politics 1915–1922, 553
Gandhi's Truth: On the Origins of Militant Nonviolence, 553
Gandhi Today: The Story of Mahatma Gandhi's Successors, 553
Ganesa: Lord of Obstacles, Lord of Beginnings, 503
Ganesh: Studies of an Asian God, 503
The Ganges in Myth and History, 503
The Garments of Torah: Essays in Biblical Hermeneutics, 610
Gassendi's View of Knowledge, 173
Gaston Bachelard, 274
Gaston Bachelard, Subversive Humanist, 274
The Gate behind the Wall: A Pilgrimage to Jerusalem, 642, 654
Gates of Prayer for Weekdays and at a House of Mourning, 600
Gates of Repentance, 600
Gateway to Reality: An Introduction to Philosophy, 25
Gathering Storm in the Churches, 753
The Gay Science, 245, 246
Gedatsu-kai and Religion in Contemporary Japan, 540
Gender, Genre, and Power in South Asian Expressive Traditions, 503
Gender and Religion: On the Complexity of Symbols, 892
The General Next to God, 740
General Philosophy, 25
General Psychopathology, 299
General Theory of Knowledge, 333

A General View of Positivism, 222
Generous Lives: American Catholic Women Today, 754
Genesis: A Commentary, 822, 838
Genesis and Structure of Society, 285
The Genesis of Faith: The Depth Psychology of Abraham Joshua Heschel, 665
Genesis Rabbah: The Judaic Commentary on Genesis, 611
Genius and Talent, 347
The Genius of Arab Civilization: Source of Renaissance, 569
The Genteel Tradition and the Sacred Rage, 327
The Genteel Tradition at Bay, 326
Gentle Bridges: Conversations with the Dalai Lama on the Sciences of Mind, 356
Geography, 492
Geography of Holiness: The Photography of Thomas Merton, 781
George Fox: Seeker and Friend, 734
George Herbert Mead: A Unifying Theory for Sociology, 309
George Herbert Mead: Critical Assessments, 309
George Herbert Mead: Self Language and the World, 309
George Herbert Mead on Social Psychology, 308
George Santayana: A Bibliographical Checklist, 1880–1980, 328
George Santayana: A Biography, 328
George Whitefield: Wayfaring Witness, 739
Gerhard von Rad, 838
German-French Annals, 228
German Humanism, 124
German Humanism and Reformation: Selected Writings, 124
The German Peasant War of 1525, 723
The German People and the Reformation, 722
German Philosophy: An Introduction, 28

German Philosophy and Politics, 28
Gershom Scholem: Kabbalah and Counter-History, 672
Gesenius' Hebrew Grammar, 794
Getting Saved from the Sixties, 855
The Ghost Festival in Medieval China, 531
Giambattista Vico and the Foundations of a Science of the Philosophy of History, 217
Giambattista Vico's Science of Humanity, 217
Gianfrancesco Pico della Mirandola (1469–1533) and His Critique of Aristotle, 152
The Gift to Be Simple: Songs, Dances, and Rituals of the American Shakers, 849
Gilbert Ryle: An Introduction to His Philosophy, 325
Giles of Rome on Ecclesiastical Power, 103
Gilgamesh, 440
Gilkey on Tillich, 787
Giordano Bruno, 136
Giordano Bruno, His Life and Thought, 136
Giordano Bruno and the Hermetic Tradition, 136
Giovanni Gentile on the Existence of God, 285
Girolamo Cardano, 1501–1576, 126
Glas, 397
Gleanings for the Writings of Baha'u'llah, 861
The Global Philosophy, 38
Global Responsibility: In Search of a New World Ethics, 775
The Glory of Israel, 608
A Glossary of Indian Religious Terms and Concepts, 497
Gnosis: A Selection of Gnostic Texts, 811
Gnosis: The Nature and History of Gnosticism, 453, 686
The Gnostic Gospels, 453, 686
Gnosticism: A Source Book of Heretical Writings from the Early Christian Period, 453, 685
Gnosticism, Judaism, and Egyptian Christianity, 453

The Gnostic Religion, 63, 453, 686, 811
The Gnostic Scriptures: A New Translation with Annotations, 453
God, Revelation and Authority: God Who Speaks and Shows, 744
God, Sex, and the Social Project, 894
God, Some Conversations, 199
God and Creatures: The Quodlibetal Questions, 114
God and Man, 746
God and Man in Contemporary Islamic Thought, 373, 575
God and Philosophy, 286
God and World in Early Christian Theology, 99
The Goddess: Mythological Images of the Feminine, 424
The Goddess Anath: Canaanite Epics of the Patriarchal Age, 445
Goddesses, Whores, Wives and Slaves, 447
The Goddesses' Mirror: Visions of the Divine from East and West, 505, 530, 536
Goddesses of Sun and Moon: Circe, Aphrodite, Medea, Niobe, 484
Godet's Proof, 313
God Has Many Names, 40, 898
God in Himself, 118
God in Modern Philosophy, 160
A God in Patristic Thought, 686
God in Search of Man: A Philosophy of Judaism, 664, 884
God in the Teachings of Conservative Judaism, 655
God Is Red: A Native View of Religion, 464
Godly Learning, 734
The God-Man: The Life, Journeys, and Work of Meher Baba, 873
God of Daniel S. in Search of the American Jew, 659
God of the Oppressed, 763
Gods, Ghosts and Ancestors: The Folk Religion of a Taiwanese Village, 531
Gods and Myths of Ancient Egypt, 548

Gods and Myths of Northern Europe, 437
Gods and the One God, 683
God's Englishman: Oliver Cromwell and the English Revolution, 734
Gods of Flesh and Gods of Stone: The Embodiment of Divinity in India, 506
The Gods of Prehistoric Man, 432
Gods of the Ancient Northmen, 437, 471
The Gods of the Greeks, 484
God's Presence in History: Jewish Affirmations and Philosophical Reflections, 663
God Was in This Place and I, I Did Not Know, 630
God We Seek, 339
God without Being, 889
The Golden Bough, 476, 485, 490
The Golden Door, 640
The Golden Epistle: A Letter to the Brethren at Mont Dieu, 102
The Golden Lands of Thomas Hobbes, 175
The Golden Legend, 701
The Golden Tradition: Jewish Life and Thought in Eastern Europe, 635
The Golden Years of the Hutterites, 724
Gone from the Promised Land: Jonestown as American Cultural History, 867
Gone to Another Meeting: The National Council of Jewish Women, 1893-1993, 650
Goodenough's Jewish Symbols: An Abridged Edition, 597, 614
The Good News According to Luke, 822
The Good News According to Mark, 822
The Good News According to Matthew, 822
Good News for Animals? Christian Approaches to Animal Well-Being, 745
The Good Society, 890
Gopalpur: A South Indian Village, 503
The Gospel According to Billy, 768
The Gospel According to St. John, 822

The Gospel According to Tolstoy, 756
The Gospel of John: A Commentary, 821, 831
The Gospel of John and Judaism, 617
Gospel Parallels: A Synopsis of the First Three Gospels, 798
The Gothic Cathedral, 701
Gothic Immortals: The Fiction of the Brotherhood of the Rosy Cross, 848
Gottlob Frege, 230
Grace and Gratitude: The Eucharistic Theology of John Calvin, 762
Grace and Reason: A Study in the Theology of Luther, 778
The Grammar of Justification, 346
A Grammatical Analysis of Greek New Testament, 795
Grammatical Theory in Western Europe 1500–1700, 129
Gramsci's Marxism, 287
Gramsci's Political Thought, 287
Gramsci's Politics, 287
Gravity and Grace, 788
Great Ages and Ideas of the Jewish People, 595
Great Ages of Man, 573
The Great Arab Conquests, 569
Great Books of the Western World, 270
The Great Chain of Being: A Study of the History of an Idea, 95, 161, 303
The Great Christian Doctrine of Original Sin Defended, 766, 767
The Great Ideas: One Hundred Two Essays, 270
The Great Ideas Anthologies, 270
The Great Instauration, 165
Great Instauration and New Atlantis, 165
The Great Philosophers, 299
The Great Powers in the Middle East, 1919–1939, 568
The Great Religions, 568
Great Religions of Modern Man, 6
The Great Reversal: Ethics and the New Testament, 746

The Great Sophists in Periclean Athens, 54
The Great Temple of Tenochtitlan, 457
Great Thinkers, Great Ideas: An Introduction to Western Thought, 20
Great Treasury of Western Thought, 270
The Great Wall of China: From History to Myth, 523
Greece and Babylon: A Comparative Sketch, 545
Greek Apologists of the Second Century, 683
Greek Atomists and Epicurus, 53, 73
The Greek Concept of Justice, 48
The Greek Cosmologists, 48
A Greek-English Lexicon, 795
A Greek-English Lexicon of the New Testament and Other Early Christian Literatures, 794
Greek Folk Religion, 486
A Greek Grammar of the New Testament and Other Early Christian Literature, 794
Greek Historical Documents: The Hellenistic Period, 449
Greek in Jewish Palestine, 606
Greek Literature, 46
The Greek Magical Papyri in Translation, Including the Demotic Spells, 451
The Greek New Testament, 794
Greek Philosophers: From Thales to Aristotle, 46
Greek Philosophers of the Hellenistic Age, 55
Greek Political Theory: The Image of Man in Thucydides and Plato, 80
Greek Religion, 470
The Greeks and the Good Life, 47
The Greeks and the Irrational, 48, 446
The Greek Sceptics, 58
Greek Skepticism: A Study in Epistemology, 58
Greek Theories of Elementary Cognition from Alcmaeon to Aristotle, 47
Greek Thinkers: A History of Ancient Philosophy, 46
Greek Tragedy and Political Theory, 48

Gregory Nazianzus: Rhetor and Philosopher, 785, 905
Gregory the Great: Perfection in Imperfection, 711
The Growth of Philosophical Radicalism, 245
The Growth of Reform Judaism: American and European Sources until 1948, 653
Growth of the Biblical Tradition, 815
Grundrisse, 242
The Guide for the Perplexed, 667, 668
Guidelines on Dialogue with People of Living Faiths and Ideologies, 899
Guides to Biblical Scholarship, 814
A Guide to American Catholic History, 751
Guide to Buddhist Philosophy, 6
Guide to Chinese Philosophy, 358, 522
Guide to Chinese Religion, 522
A Guide to Cults and New Religions, 857
Guide to Greece, 489
A Guide to Jewish Religious Practice, 602
Guide to Philosophy, 21
Guide to Reference Books, 716
A Guide to the Works of John Dewey, 225
A Guide to the Zoroastrian Religion, 517, 547
Guillaume Postel, Prophet of the Restitution of All Things, 128
Gurdjieff: An Annotated Bibliography, 875
Gurdjieff: Making a New World, 875
Gurdjieff: The Anatomy of a Myth, 876
Gurdjieff: War against Sleep, 876
The Gurdjieff Years: 1929–1949, 876
Guru Nanak and the Sikh Religion, 516
Gustavo Gutierrez, 769
Gyn-Ecology: The Metaethics of Radical Feminism, 423, 765

H.P.B.: The Extraordinary

Life and Influence of Helena Blavatsky, 853, 874
Habad: The Hasidism of R. Shneur Zalman of Lyady, 632
Habermas: Critical Debates, 405
Habermas and Modernity, 404
Habermas and the Dialectic of Reason, 405
Habermas and the Public Sphere, 404
Habermas's Critical Theory of Society, 404
Habits of the Heart: Individualism and Commitment in American Life, 752
Halakhah in a Theological Dimension, 598
Halakhic Man, 673
The Halakhic Mind: An Essay on Jewish Tradition and Modern Thought, 673
Hammer on the Rock: A Midrash Reader, 610
The Handbook of a Christian Soldier, 138
Handbook of Biblical Criticism, 815
Handbook of Denominations in the United States, 6, 717, 751
A Handbook of Living Religions, 498, 523, 535
Handbook of Metaphysics and Ontology, 159
Handbook of Middle American Indians, 465
Handbook of Synagogue Architecture, 614
A Handbook of Theological Terms, 675, 718
Handbook of Western Philosophy, 162
Handbook of World Philosophy: Contemporary Developments since 1945, 6, 37, 263
Hannah Arendt, 395
Hannah Arendt: A Bibliography, 395
Hannah Arendt: Thinking, Judging, Freedom, 395
Hannah Arendt's Philosophy of Natality, 394
Hanukkah Anthology, 599
Hare Krishna and the Counterculture, 863
Hare Krishna in America, 863
The Hare Krishna Movement, 862

The Hare Krishnas in India, 507, 862
The Harmonious Circle, 876
The Harmonists: A Folk-Cultural Approach, 844
The Harper Atlas of the Bible, 7, 809
Harper's Bible Commentary, 819
Harper's Bible Dictionary, 817
Harper's Bible Pronunciation Guide, 819
Harper's New Testament Commentaries, 820
The Harps That Once: Sumerian Poetry in Translation, 440
A Harsh and Dreadful Love, 766
Hartshorne's Neo-Classical Theology, 290
Harvest of Hate, 637
The Harvest of Medieval Theology, 105, 129, 697, 721
Hasiddur Hashalem: Daily Prayer Book, 599
The Hasidic Anthology, 633
Hasidic Prayer, 632
Hasidic Thought, 632
Hasidism and Modern Man, 632
Hasidism and the Jewish Enlightenment, 632
Hasidism and the State of Israel, 658
Hasidism as Mysticism, 633
Has Man a Future?, 322
The Hasmoneans and Their Supporters, 605
Haven and Home: A History of the Jews in America, 639
Have without Have-Nots: Six Essays on Democracy and Socialism, 270
Hayy ibn Yaqzan, 585
The Healer's Power, 388
Healing and Restoring, 506, 514, 530, 536
Healing Hypotheses: Horatio W. Dresser and the Philosophy of New Thought, 847
Health and Medicine in the Christian Science Tradition, 843
Health and Medicine in the Islamic Tradition, 893
Health and Medicine in the Jewish Tradition: The Pursuit of Wholeness, 598

Health/Medicine and the Faith Traditions, 893
The Heart of Buddhism, 366
The Heart of Buddhist Wisdom, 512
The Heart of the Matter, 336
The Heart of the New Thought, 847
The Heart of Understanding, 561
Heaven and Hell, 880
Heaven in Transition, 518
The Heavenly City of the Eighteenth-Century Philosophers, 159
Heaven on Earth: Dispatches from America's Spiritual Frontier, 866
Hebrew and Chaldee Lexicon to the Old Testament, 794
The Hebrew Bible: A Socio-Literary Introduction, 816
The Hebrew Bible, the Old Testament, and Historical Criticism, 815
The Hebrew Bible and Its Modern Interpreters, 814
Hebrew Christianity: The Thirteenth Tribe, 864
Hebrew Ethical Wills, 628
Hegel (Inwood), 233
Hegel (Taylor), 233, 414
Hegel: Religion, Economics and Politics of the Spirit, 1770–1807, 233
Hegel, Nietzsche and the Criticism of Metaphysics, 233
Hegel and Modern Society, 414
Hegel and Skepticism, 233
Hegel and the State, 671
Hegelianism, 233
Hegelian-Whiteheadian Perspectives, 341
Hegel's Critique of Liberalism, 233
Hegel's Development: Night Thoughts, 233
Hegel's Development: Toward the Sunlight, 233
Hegel's Dialectic, 402
Hegel's Dialectic and its Criticism, 233
Hegel's Epistemological Realism, 233
Hegel's Ethical Thought, 233
Hegel's Idealism, 233
Hegel's Idea of a Phenomenology of Spirit, 233
Hegel's Ontology, 408
Hegel's Phenomenology of Spirit, 291

Hegel's Theory of Mental Activity, 233
Hegel's Theory of the Modern State, 232
Hegemony and Culture: Politics and Religious Change among the Yoruba, 467
Heichal Hakodesh Concordance to the Old Testament, 818
Heidegger, 294
Heidegger: Thought and Historicity, 293
Heidegger, Art and Politics: The Fiction of the Political, 293
Heidegger, Being, and Truth, 295
Heidegger and Asian Thought, 294, 350
Heidegger and Derrida: Reflections on Time and Language, 294
Heidegger and Modernity, 293
Heidegger and Nazism, 293
Heidegger and the Earth: Issues in Environmental Philosophy, 294
Heidegger and the Language of Poetry, 295
Heidegger and the Poets: Poiesis/Sophia/Techné, 293
Heidegger and the Problem of Knowledge, 293
Heidegger and the Project of Fundamental Ontology, 295
Heidegger and the Question of Renaissance Humanism: Four Studies, 127
The Heidegger Case: On Philosophy and Ethics, 294
Heidegger on Being and Acting: From Principles to Anarchy, 295
Heidegger's Being and Time: A Reading for Readers, 293
Heidegger's Being and Time: The Analytic of Dasein as Fundamental Ontology, 293
Heidegger's Confrontation with Modernity: Technology, Politics, and Art, 295
Heidegger's Estrangements, 292
Heidegger's Pragmatism: Understanding Being and the Critique of Metaphysics, 294
Heirs of the Pharisees, 596

Hellenika: I-II 3.10, 91
Hellenism in Jewish Palestine, 606
Hellenistic Civilization and the Jews, 605
The Hellenistic Philosophers, 55
Hellenistic Philosophies, 55
Hellenistic Philosophy: Introductory Readings, 55
Hellenistic Philosophy: Selections from Epicureanism, Skepticism, and Neoplatonism, 56
Hellenistic Philosophy: Stoics, Epicureans, Skeptics, 55
Hellenistic Philosophy of Mind, 55
Hellenistic Religions: An Introduction, 450
The Hellenistic Stoa: Political Thought and Action, 55, 57
Hellenistic Ways of Deliverance and the Making of the Christian Synthesis, 55
The Hellenistic World from Alexander to the Roman Conquest, 449
Heloïse and Abelard, 286
Henry More (1614–1687) Tercentenary Studies, 183
Henry Sidgwick: Science and Faith in Victorian England, 257
Henry Sidgwick and Later Utilitarian Political Philosophy, 257
Henry VIII, 727
Heptaplus, or Discourse on the Seven Days of Creation, 152, 153
Heraclitean Fragments: A Comparison Volume to the Heidegger-Fink Seminar on Heraclitus, 75
Heraclitus, 75
Heraclitus: Fragments: A Text and Translation with a Commentary, 75
Heraclitus: The Cosmic Fragments, 75
Heraclitus Seminar, 1966–1967, 74, 291
Herbert Marcuse, 407, 408
Herbert Marcuse and the Crisis of Marxism, 408
Hercules at the Crossroads: The Life, Works, Thought of Coluccio Salutati, 132
Herder, 199

Herder: His Life and Thought, 199
Herder and the Philosophy and History of Science, 199
Herder's Social and Political Thought: From Enlightenment to Nationalism, 199
Here I Stand: A Life of Martin Luther, 778
Heresy, Crusade, and Inquisition in Southern France, 1100–1250, 701
Heresy and Authority in Medieval Europe, 721
Heresy and Criticism: The Search for Authenticity in Early Christian Literature, 825
Heresy and Politics in the Reign of Henry IV: The Burning of John Badby, 721
The Heresy of the Free Spirit in the Later Middle Ages, 721
Heritage: Civilization and the Jews, 593
Heritage and Promise: Perspectives on the Church of the Brethren, 732
Heritage of Our Times, 277
The Heritage of the Reformation, 730
The Heritage of Wisdom: Essays in the History of Philosophy, 17
Hermann Cohen's Philosophy of Judaism, 663
Hermeneia: A Critical and Historical Commentary on the Bible, 820
The Hermeneutical Theory of Paul Ricoeur: A Constructive Analysis, 319
Hermeneutics, 402
Hermeneutics: The Handwritten Manuscripts, 254
Hermeneutics and Deconstruction, 267, 392
Hermeneutics and Modern Philosophy, 268, 392
Hermeneutics and Praxis, 413
Hermeneutics and the Human Sciences, 319
The Hermeneutics Reader, 28
Hermetic Astronomy, 149
Hermeticism and the Renaissance, 128
The Hermit of Carmel, and Other Poems, 326

Hermits and the New Monasticism, 700

Herod: A Profile of a Tyrant, 605

Herodotean Narrative and Discourses, 480

Herodotus, 480

Herodotus, Explorer of the Past: Three Essays, 480

Heroes and Gods: Spiritual Biographies in Antiquity, 451

The Heroic Enthusiasts, 135

The Hero in History: A Study in Limitation and Possibility, 298

Her Share of Blessings, 449, 892

Her Story: Women in Christian Tradition, 749

Herzl, 658

Hesiod, 482

Hesiod and the Near East, 482

The Heterdoxies of the Shi'ites According to Ibn Hazm, 584

Hexameron, Paradise, Cain and Abel, 702

The Hidden Doctrine of Maimonides' Guide for the Perplexed, 668

Hidden God, 185

Hidden Treasures and Secret Lives, 543

The Highroad around Modernism, 391

The High Road to Pyrrhonism, 162, 202

The High Walls of Jerusalem, 643

Hillel the Elder: The Emergence of Classical Judaism, 620

Hind Swaraj, or Indian Home Rule, 552

Hindu Ethics: Purity, Abortion, and Euthanasia, 894

Hindu Goddesses, 505

Hinduism, 884

Hinduism: A Cultural Perspective, 505

Hinduism: A Religion to Live By, 503

Hinduism: Experiments in the Sacred, 505

Hinduism in Thai Life, 518

Hindu Myths: A Sourcebook Translated from the Sanskrit, 505

Hindu Nationalism and Indian Politics, 508

The Hindu Religious Tradition, 504

Hindu Scriptures, 501

The Hindu Temple: An Introduction to Its Meaning and Forms, 505

The Hindu Tradition—Readings in Oriental Thought, 503

Hints on the Study of the Bhagavad Gita, 549

Hippias Major, 78

Hispano-Jewish Culture in Transition: The Career and Controversies of Ramah, 629

Historical and Critical Dictionary: Selections, 166

Historical Atlas of Religion in America, 751

A Historical Atlas of the Jewish People, 593

Historical Atlas of the Religions of the World, 4

Historical Criticism and Theological Interpretation of Scripture, 815

Historical Introduction to Philosophy, 21

Historical Tradition in the Fourth Gospel, 833

Historicism, the Holocaust, and Zionism, 646

Histories, 480

The History, 480

History: Written and Lived, 339

History, Culture and Religion of the Hellenistic Age, 449, 807

History, Man, and Reason: A Study in Nineteenth-Century Thought, 162

The History and Character of Calvinism, 762

History and Class Consciousness, 162

History and Literature of Early Christianity, 816

History and Magical Power in a Chinese Community, 531

The History and Philosophy of the Metaphysical Movements in America, 841

The History and Theology of Soka Gakkai: A Japanese New Religion, 541

History and Truth, 319

History and Will: Philosophical Perspectives of Mao Tse-tung's Thought, 362

History as a System, 314

History Begins at Sumer: Thirty-Nine Firsts in Man's Recorded History, 441

A History of American Philosophy, 35

A History of Ancient Israel and Judah, 806

A History of Ancient Philosophy, 46

History of Ancient Western Philosophy, 46

History of Auricular Confession and Indulgences in the Latin Church, 699

A History of Buddhist Philosophy: Continuities and Discontinuities, 513

A History of Chinese Civilization, 358

A History of Chinese Philosophy, 358, 359

The History of Christian Doctrine, 677

History of Christian Ethics: From the New Testament to Augustine, 688

A History of Christianity, 677, 720

History of Christianity, 1650–1950: Secularization of the West, 739

A History of Christianity in Asia, 677

A History of Christianity in India 1707–1858, 508

A History of Christianity in the World: From Persecution to Uncertainty, 677, 720

History of Christian Philosophy in the Middle Ages, 94, 126, 696, 721

History of Christian Spirituality, 676

A History of Christian Theology: An Introduction, 719

A History of Christian Thought (González), 677, 718

A History of Christian Thought (Tillich), 678

The History of Conversion and Contemporary Cults, 858

A History of Cynicism from Diogenes to the Sixth Century A.D., 55

History of Dogma, 95, 677

A History of Early Christian Literature, 690

History of Eastern Christianity, 676

History of England: From

the Invasion of Julius Caesar to the Revolution of 1688, 201
History of England from the Roman Invasion to the Glorious Revolution, 199
A History of European Thought in the Nineteenth Century, 162
History of Florence, 144
A History of Gnosticism, 60, 685
A History of Greek Philosophy, 46
A History of Greek Religion, 486
History of Humanism, 131
A History of Indian Buddhism: From Sakyamuni to Early Mahayana, 512
History of Indian Buddhism: From the Origins to the Saka Era, 513
A History of Indian Philosophy, 351, 498
The History of Islam, 572
A History of Islamic Philosophy, 16, 97, 574
A History of Israel, 806
The History of Israel: Biblical History, 836
A History of Israel: From the Rise of Zionism to Our Time, 643
A History of Israel from Alexander the Great to Bar Kochba, 604
History of Japanese Religion, 534
History of Japan's Ethical Thought, 367
A History of Jewish Art, 597
A History of Jewish Literature, 601
A History of Jewish Philosophy in the Middle Ages, 629
A History of Judaism, 595
A History of Knowledge: Past, Present, and Future, 2
A History of Magic and Experimental Science, 131
The History of Marxism, 242
A History of Mediaeval Jewish Philosophy, 629
A History of Medieval Philosophy, 39, 94
A History of Melbourne's Hebrew Congregation, 644
A History of Modern Jewry, 634

A History of Modern Philosophy, 161
A History of Modern Tibet, 1913–1951, 543
History of New Testament Times, 605
A History of Norway, 730
A History of Orthodox Theology since 1453, 756
A History of Pentateuchal Traditions, 823, 836
A History of Philosophical Ideas in America, 36
History of Philosophical Systems, 16
History of Philosophy (Bréhier), 16, 159
History of Philosophy (Copleston), 2, 39, 94, 676
History of Philosophy (Marias), 162
A History of Philosophy (Ueberweg), 18, 163
History of Philosophy: Eastern and Western, 350
A History of Philosophy: From Bolzano to Wittgenstein, 268
History of Philosophy: Late Medieval and Renaissance Philosophy, 125
A History of Philosophy: With Especial Reference to the Formation and Development of Its Problems and Conceptions, 163
History of Philosophy and Philosophical Education, 286
A History of Philosophy in America, 160
History of Philosophy in Islam (De Boer), 373
The History of Philosophy in Islam (Fakry), 567
A History of Religion East and West: An Introduction and Interpretation, 571
History of Religions: Essays on the Problem of Understanding, 570
A History of Religious Ideas, 2, 473, 497, 524, 547
The History of Russian Philosophy, 31, 161
The History of Scepticism from Erasmus to Spinoza, 130, 162
A History of Science, Technology and Philosophy in the Sixteenth and Seventeenth Centuries, 132
The History of Sexuality, 400

The History of Spiritualism, 850
History of the Arabs, 569
History of the Bible in English, 797
A History of the Christian Church, 678, 720
The History of the Church (Jedin), 677, 720
History of the Church (Smith), 879
A History of the Church in Latin America: Colonialism to Liberation, 748
A History of the Church to A.D. 461, 681
History of the Concept of Time: Prolegomena, 291
History of the Contemporary Jews from 1900 to the Present, 634
A History of the Council of Trent, 729
A History of the Councils of the Church from the Original Documents, 677
History of the Crusades, 694
A History of the Early Church, 682
History of the Early Church from A.D. 500, 682
A History of the Ecumenical Movement, 1517–1948, 746
History of the Episcopal Church in America, 1607–1991, 719
History of the Inductive Sciences, 257, 258
History of the Islamic Peoples, 568
A History of the Jewish People (Ben-Sasson), 593
History of the Jewish People (Margolis and Marx), 594
A History of the Jewish People in the Age of Jesus Christ (175 B.C.–135 A.D.), 808
The History of the Jewish People in the Age of Jesus Christ: A New English Edition, 605
A History of the Jews, 594
A History of the Jews: From Earliest Times through the Six-Day War, 594
A History of the Jews in Babylonia, 605
History of the Jews in Christian Spain, 623
A History of the Jews in England, 624

A History of the Jews in Venice, 624
A History of the Jews of Italy, 624
A History of the Jews of Tangier in the Nineteenth and Twentieth Centuries, 645
The History of the Maghrib: An Interpretive Essay, 571
A History of the Marranos, 624
History of the Medieval Church, 590–1500, 691
The History of the Order of Assassins, 569
History of the Persian Wars, 480
The History of the Primitive Church, 681
The History of the Reformation in Scotland, 735
History of the Rise of the Huguenots of France, 731
A History of the Sikhs, 517
The History of the Synoptic Tradition, 824, 830, 831
A History of the Unification Church in the San Francisco Bay Area, 1960–1974, 871
A History of the World's Great Religions, 2
A History of Twelfth-Century Western Philosophy, 16, 94
A History of Unitarianism, 724
A History of Western Philosophy (Hamlyn), 16
A History of Western Philosophy (Jones), 17, 46
A History of Western Philosophy (Russell), 18, 162, 322
A History of Witchcraft: Sorcerers, Heretics and Pagans, 700
A History of Women Philosophers, 163
A History of Zen Buddhism, 537
A History of Zionism, 658
A History of Zoroastrianism, 444, 547
Hitler, Germans, and the "Jewish Question," 636
Hittite Myths, 545
The Hittites, 445
The Hittites and Their Contemporaries in Asia Minor, 445

The Hittite State Cult of the Tutelary Deities, 445
Hobbes (Peters), 174
Hobbes (Sorrell), 175
Hobbes (Stephen), 175
Hobbes (Tuck), 175
Hobbes: Morals and Politics, 174
Hobbes and Locke: The Politics of Freedom and Obligation, 175, 181
Hobbes and the Social Contract Tradition, 174
Hobbes on Civil Association, 174
Hobbes's Science of Politics, 174
Hobbes's System of Ideas, 175
Hobbes Studies, 174
Hobbes Studies Bibliography: 1879–1979, 175
Hobbes to Hume, 161
The Hobbit, 776
Holiness and Justice: An Interpretation of Plato's "Euthyphro," 84
Holiness and the Will of God: Perspectives on the Theology of Tertullian, 714
Holiness of Life, 113
The Holocaust: A History of the Jews of Europe during the Second World War, 636
The Holocaust: An Annotated Bibliography and Resource Guide, 7
The Holocaust, Israel, and the Jews: Motion Pictures in the National Archives, 636
The Holocaust in Historical Perspective, 635
A Holocaust Reader, 635
Holy Anorexia, 698
The Holy Bible: King James Version, 797
The Holy Bible: New International Version, Containing the Old Testament and New Testament, 797
The Holy Bible: The New Revised Standard Version, 797
Holy Days: The World of a Hasidic Family, 632
Holy Days and Holidays: The Medieval Pilgrimage to Compostela, 698
The Holy Family of Father Moon, 871

Holy Feast and Holy Fast, 698
The Holy Land: An Archaeological Guide from Earliest Times to 1700, 809
The Holy Land from the Persian to the Arab Conquests 536 B.C.–A.D. 640, 606
The Holy Scriptures According to the Masoretic Text, 801
The Holy Scriptures of the Old Testament: Hebrew and English, 794
The Holy Spirit, 685
Holy Terror: Inside the World of Islamic Terrorism, 580
Holy War in Ancient Israel, 838
Holy Wars, 578
Holy Women of Russia, 756
Holy Writ or Holy Church: The Crisis of the Protestant Reformation, 697
The Holy Year of Jubilee, 701
Homage to Galileo, 172
Homage to Georges Dumézil, 472
Homer: Poet of the Iliad, 483
Homer and the Sacred City, 483
Homeric Hymns, 482
Homer on Life and Death, 483
Homer the Theologian, 483
Homilies on Genesis, 707
Homilies on Psalms, 711
Homilies on Psalms and Other Texts, 711
Homo Hierarchicus: The Caste System, 503
Homo Necans, 429, 470
Homosexuality: The Test Case for Christian Social Ethics, 894
Homosexuality and Religion and Philosophy, 894
Homosexuality and the Western Christian Tradition, 678
Homo Viator: Introduction to a Metaphysic of Hope, 304
The Honest Mind: The Thought and Work of Richard Price, 211
Honest to God, 746
Hope and Its Hieroglyph, 277

Horeb: A Philosophy of Jewish Laws and Observances, 665

House Divided: The Life and Legacy of Martin Luther King, 773

The House of Islam, 568

How Karl Barth Changed My Mind, 758

How the Swans Came to the Lake: A Narrative History of Buddhism in America, 859

How to Do Things with Words, 272

How to Get the Most Out of Philosophy, 24

How to Grow Science, 385

How to Read a Book, 270

How to Read Karl Barth: The Shape of His Theology, 758

How to Think about God: A Guide for the Twentieth-Century Pagan, 270

How We Think, 224

How You Can Talk with God, 556

The Huguenots, 732

The Huguenots: A Biography of a Minority, 732

The Huguenot Struggle for Recognition, 732

The Human and the Holy: The Spirituality of Abraham Joshua Heschel, 665

The Human Condition, 394

Human Energy, 336

Human Immortality and Pre-Existence, 303

Human Interests: Reflections on Philosophical Anthropology, 317

Humanism and Scholasticism in Late Medieval Germany, 129

Humanism and Terror: An Essay on the Communist Problem, 310

Humanism in England during the Fifteenth Century, 132

The Humanism of Leonardo Bruni: Selected Texts, 124

Humanists and Holy Writ: New Testament Scholarship in the Renaissance, 124

Humanity and Self-Cultivation: Essays in Confucian Thought, 362, 526

The Humanity of God, 758

Human Nature and Conduct, 224

Human Nature and Human History, 282

Human Nature and Its Remaking, 296

Human Rights, 386

The Human Search: An Introduction to Philosophy, 22

Human Values and Economic Policy: A Symposium, 265

Hume (Ayer), 201, 272

Hume (Stroud), 203

Hume, Hegel and Human Nature, 201

Hume, Newton, and the Design Argument, 184, 202

Hume and Locke, 180

Hume and the Enlightenment: Essays Presented to Ernest Campbell Mossner, 203

Hume and the Problem of Causation, 201

Hume's Intentions, 202

Hume's Moral Theory, 202

Hume's Philosophical Development: A Study of His Methods, 202

Hume's Philosophy of Common Life, 202

Hume's Skepticism in the Treatise of Human Nature, 202

Hume's Theory of the External World, 202

Hume's Theory of the Understanding, 201

A Hundred Years of Philosophy, 266

The Hungry Tigress: Buddhist Legends and Jataka Tales, 514

Hu Shih and the Intellectual Choice in Modern China, 360

Husserl, 234

Husserl: An Analysis of His Phenomenology, 319

Husserl: Intentionality and Cognitive Science, 234

Husserlian Meditations: How Words Present Things, 235

Hutterian Brethren, 1528–1931, 733

Hymn of the Universe, 336

Hymns of Zarathustra, 443

I Am a Woman and a Jew, 650

Iamblichus and the Theory of the Vehicle of the Soul, 61

I Am Not My Body: A Study of the International Hare Krishna Sect, 862

I and Thou, 662

I Asked for Wonder: A Spiritual Anthology, 665

I Became Part of It: Sacred Dimensions in Native American Life, 464

Ibn Khaldun: An Essay in Reinterpretation, 584

Ibn Khaldun and Tamerlane: Their Historic Meeting in Damascus, 584

Ibn Khaldun's Philosophy of History, 584

Ibn Rushd: Averroes, 581

Icanchu's Drum: An Orientation to the Meaning in South American Religions, 466

Icastes: Marsilio Ficino's Interpretation of Plato's "Sophist," 141

I Ching, 525

The I Ching or Book of Changes, 525

Idea and Essence in the Philosophies of Hobbes and Spinoza, 187

The Idealism of Giovanni Gentile, 285

Idealistic Argument in Recent British and American Philosophy, 263

The Idealistic Reaction against Science, 271

An Idealist View of Life, 354

Ideals and Realities of Islam, 375, 576, 902

The Idea of a Critical Theory: Habermas and the Frankfurt School, 264, 404

The Idea of a University, 782

The Idea of Christ in the Gospels; or God in Man, a Critical Essay, 326

The Idea of God in Homer, 483

The Idea of History, 282

The Idea of Nature, 282

The Idea of Perfect History: Historical Erudition and Historical Philosophy in Renaissance France, 127

The Idea of Prehistory, 432

The Idea of Principle in Leibnitz and the Evolution of Deductive Theory, 177

The Idea of Progress in Classical Antiquity, 48

The Idea of the Good in Platonic-Aristotelian Philosophy, 80, 402

The Idea of the Holy, 487, 488

The Idea of the Jewish State, 658

Ideas, Qualities and Corpuscles, 179

Ideas and Ideals in the North European Renaissance, 132

Ideas for a Philosophy of Nature, 251

Ideas from France: The Legacy of French Theory, 27

Ideas of Jewish History, 594

Ideas Pertaining to a Pure Phenomenology and to a Phenomenological Philosophy, 234

Ideas toward a Pure Phenomenology, 234

Ideas toward the Philosophy of History of Humanity, 198

The Identity of Jesus Christ: The Hermeneutical Bases of Dogmatic Theology, 885

The Ideology of Order, 134

Idiota de mente, 148

The Idler and His Works, 326

Idols of the Tribe: Group Identity and Political Change, 651

Ifa Divination: Communication between Gods and Men in West Africa, 462

If I Could Preach Just Once, 322

Ignatius of Antioch: A Commentary on the Seven Letters of Ignatius, 704

Ignatius of Loyola, 770

I Have My Doubts, 744

The Iliad, 482

The Illuminating Icon, 756

The Illusion of Technique: A Search for Meaning in a Technological Civilization, 262

Illustrations of Being: Drawing upon Heidegger and upon Metaphysics, 294

Illustrations on the Moral Sense, 203

Image and Reality in Plato's Metaphysics, 83

Image before My Eyes, 635

The Imagery of the Cosmological Buddha, 530

Images of the Feminine in Gnosticism, 453

The Imaginary Witness, 408

Imagination: A Philosophical Critique, 329

Imagination and Metaphysics in St. Augustine, 110

Imagining Religion: From Babylon to Jonestown, 491

Immediacy and Its Limits: A Study in Martin Buber's Thought, 662

Immortality and Resurrection, 887

The Immortality of the Soul, 183

Immortal Sisters: Secrets of Taoist Women, 527

Impact of Science on Society, 322

The Imperative of Modernity: An Intellectual Biography of José Ortega y Gassett, 315

Imperial Cities and the Reformation: Three Essays, 722, 730

Impermanence Is Buddha-Nature: Dogen's Understanding of Temporality, 538

The Imposition of Method: A Study of Descartes and Locke, 180

The Impossible Dream: The Spirituality of Dom Helder Camara, 748

Improving Your Reasoning, 381

In Advance of the Landing, 870

Inanna, Queen of Heaven and Earth: Her Stories and Hymns from Sumer, 440, 546

Inca Civilization in Cuzco, 458

Inca Religion and Customs, 458

Incarnation and Myth: The Debate Continued, 885

Incarnation in Hinduism and Christianity, 507

Incarnation of God: The Character of Divinity in Formative Judaism, 607

The Incas and Their Ancestors: The Archaeology of Peru, 458

The Incoherence of the Phi-

losophers (Tahāfut al-Falāsifah), 582

In Commemoration of William James, 1842–1942, 237

In Defense of Animals, 43

In Defense of People's Temple, 867

Index of Xenophontis Memorabilia, 91

Index Scholastico-Cartesian, 170

Index to Aristotle, 70

Index to Book Reviews in Religion, 7

Index to Jewish Periodicals, 8

Index to Nietzsche, 247

India: An Anthropological Perspective, 506

India and Europe, 508

The Indian Mind: Essentials of Indian Philosophy and Culture, 351

Indian Philosophy, 351

Indian Religion, 498

Indians of North America, 464

The Indian Way, 351, 498

India's Religion of Grace and Christianity Compared and Contrasted, 488

Individual and State in Ancient China, 525

The Individual and the Cosmos in Renaissance Philosophy, 124

The Individual and the Social Self, 308

The Individual and the Universe: An Introduction to Philosophy, 21

Individuals, 414

Indo-European Language and Society, 435

The Indra Hymns of the Rigveda, 501

Induction, 317

Induction, Probability and Causation: Selected Papers, 277

In Exile from the Land of Snows, 906

In Face of Mystery: A Constructive Theology, 744

Infallible? An Inquiry, 774, 775

The Infinite in Giordano Bruno, 136

The Infinite Worlds of Giordano Bruno, 136

Infinity and Continuity in

Ancient and Medieval Thought, 104

Infinity in the Presocratics, 51

The Influence of Darwin on Philosophy and Other Essays, 224

The Influence of Greek Ideas on Christianity, 63, 99

The Influence of Islam upon Africa, 573

The Influence of Islam upon Medieval Europe, 573

The Influence of Prophecy in the Later Middle Ages: A Study of Joachimism, 102

In Gods We Trust: New Patterns of Religious Pluralism in America, 857

In His Image, 608

In Job's Balances: On the Sources of Eternal Truths, 335

The Inklings, 776

The Inner Conflict of Tradition: Essays in Indian Ritual, Kingship and Society, 501

The Inner Eye of Love: Mysticism and Religion, 858

The Inner Government of the World, 549

The Inner Teachings of Taoism, 527

In Our Image and Likeness, 131

In Place of the Flawed Diamond, 311

In Praise of Idleness and Other Essays, 322

In Praise of Philosophy, 310

In Pursuit of Satan: The Police and the Occult, 868

In Quest of the Truth: A Survey of Medieval Jewish Thought, 629

Inquiries into Truth and Interpretation, 283, 380

An Inquiry Concerning Beauty, Order, Harmony, Design, 203

An Inquiry into Meaning and Truth, 322

An Inquiry into the Authenticity of Moses Maimonides' Treatise on Resurrection, 668

An Inquiry into the Good, 364

An Inquiry into the Human Mind on the Principles of Common Sense, 211

Inquiry into the Original of Our Ideas of Beauty and Virtue, 203

In Search of a Better World, 409

In Search of Ancient Astronomies, 434

In Search of Answers: Indian Women's Voices from Manushi, 508

In Search of Florentine Civic Humanism, 29, 123

In Search of the Miraculous: Fragments of an Unknown Teaching, 876

In Search of Wagner, 393

In Search of White Crows: Spiritualism, Parapsychology, and American Culture, 851

The Insecurity of Freedom: Essays on Human Existence, 665

Inside the Spaceships: UFO Experiences of George Adamski 1952–1955, 870

Insights and Oversights of Great Thinkers, 17, 161, 289

In Speech and in Silence: The Jewish Quest for God, 600

Inspired Talks, My Master, and Other Writings, 562

Institutes of the Christian Religion, 760

Instructed Vision, 32, 35

The Intellectual Adventure of Ancient Man, 439

The Intellectual Cowardice of the American Philosophers, 34

Intellectual Development of Voltaire, 218

The Intellectual Enterprise: Sartre and Les Temps Modernes, 330

An Intellectual History of Islamic India, 372

The Intellectual Origins of the European Reformation, 722

Intellectual Origins of the French Enlightenment, 28

Intelligibility and the Philosophy of Nothingness, 364

Intentionality, 383

Intentions and Uncertainty, 288

The Interaction of the "Sibling" Byzantine and Western Cultures in the Middle

Ages and Italian Renaissance (330–1600), 693

Interbeing: Commentaries on the Tiep Hein Precepts, 561

The Interior Castle, 786

The Internal Stance, 396

International Calvinism, 732

International Directory of Philosophy and Philosophers, 1990–92, 6

The International Kosher Cookbook, 602

Interpretation, Deconstruction, and Ideology, 391

The Interpretation of Cultures, 263, 477, 478

An Interpretation of Religion: Human Responses to the Transcendent, 40

The Interpretation of the Fourth Gospel, 825, 833

Interpretation of the New Testament, 1861–1961, 814

An Interpretation of Universal History, 314

An Interpretation of Whitehead's Metaphysics, 342

Interpretations of Islam: Past and Present, 573

Interpretations of Poetry and Religion: Critical Edition, 326

Interpretation Theory: Discourse and the Surplus of Meaning, 319, 426

The Interpreter's Bible, 820

The Interpreter's Dictionary of the Bible, 818

The Interpreter's One-Volume Commentary on the Bible, 819

Interpreting across Boundaries: New Essays in Comparative Philosophy, 349

Interpreting Husserl: Critical and Comparative Studies, 234

Interpreting Maimonides, 668

Interpreting Modern Philosophy, 160

Interpreting the Psalms, 823

Interpreting the Sacred: Ways of Viewing Religion, 422

Interpreting Wittgenstein: A Cloud of Philosophy, a Drop of Grammar, 347

Intertextuality and the Reading of Midrash, 620

In the Footsteps of Muhammed: Understanding

the Islamic Experience, 576

In the Interest of the Governed, 191

In the Land of Israel, 643

In the Land of the Olmec, 455

In the Presence of the Creator: Isaac Newton and His Times, 184

In the Shadow of the Enlightenment, 841

In the World of Sumer: An Autobiography, 441

Intimations of Mortality, 293

Introducing Liberation Theology, 896

Introducing New Gods: The Politics of Athenian Religion, 447

Introducing Persons, 382

Introducing Philosophy: A Text with Integrated Writings, 24

Introducing Religion: From Inside and Outside, 883

Introducing the Existentialists, 267

Introducing the Psalms, 824

Introduction of Logic, 103

Introduction of Swedenborg's Religious Thought, 880

Introduction to African Religion, 370, 463

An Introduction to Ancient Iranian Religions, 443, 547

An Introduction to Ancient Philosophy, 46

An Introduction to Biblical Hebrew Syntax, 795

Introduction to Comparative Philosophy, 38

Introduction to Critical Theory: Horkheimer to Habermas, 264, 404

An Introduction to Divine and Human Readings, 98

Introduction to Early Greek Philosophy, 47

Introduction to Existentialism, 264

An Introduction to Hegel, 233

An Introduction to Islam, 568

Introduction to Islamic Civilization, 572

Introduction to Islamic Theology and Law, 575

Introduction to Jewish Bible Commentary, 628

An Introduction to Judaism.

Textbook and Anthology, 596

Introduction to Logical Theory, 414

Introduction to Marx and Engels, 243

Introduction to Mathematical Philosophy, 323

Introduction to Mathematics, 341

An Introduction to Medieval Islamic Philosophy, 97, 575

An Introduction to Metaphysics, 291

Introduction to Mongolian History, 542

An Introduction to Nichiren Shoshu Buddhism, 538

An Introduction to Philo Judaeus, 60, 670

Introduction to Philosophy (Geisler), 21

An Introduction to Philosophy (Maritain), 22, 306

An Introduction to Philosophy (Nakhnikian), 23

An Introduction to Philosophy (Olscamp), 23

Introduction to Philosophy (Stroll and Popkin), 24

Introduction to Philosophy: A Case Study Approach, 23

Introduction to Philosophy: An Inquiry after a Rational System of Scientific Principles in the Relation to the Ultimate Reality, 22

Introduction to Philosophy: Classical and Contemporary Readings, 23

Introduction to Philosophy: From Wonder to World View, 24

An Introduction to Philosophy: Ideas in Conflict, 25

An Introduction to Plato's Laws, 84

An Introduction to Plato's Republic, 78

Introduction to Positive Philosophy, 222

Introduction to St. Thomas Aquinas, 117

Introduction to Symbolic Logic and Its Applications, 278

Introduction to Systems Philosophy—Toward a New Paradigm of Contemporary Thought, 265

Introduction to the Code of

Maimonides (Mishneh Torah), 627

An Introduction to the Franciscan Literature of the Middle Ages, 699

Introduction to the History of Religions, 494

Introduction to the Human Sciences, 226

An Introduction to the Logic of the Sciences, 384

An Introduction to the Medieval Mystics of Europe, 697

Introduction to the New Testament, 449, 816

Introduction to the Old Testament, 816

Introduction to the Philosophy of Science, 385

An Introduction to the Politics and Philosophy of José Ortega y Gasset, 315

Introduction to the Principles of Morals and Legislation, 190

Introduction to the Problem of Individuation in the Early Middle Ages, 101

Introduction to the Qur'an (Bell), 587

An Introduction to the Qur'an (Watt), 587

Introduction to the Reading of Hegel, 233

Introduction to the Reformed Tradition, 762

Introduction to the Sociology of Music, 393

Introduction to the Study of Philosophy, 21

An Introduction to the Study of Theravada Buddhism in Burma, 519

Introduction to the Talmud, 610

Introduction to the Talmud and Midrash, 613, 812

An Introduction to the Theology of Karl Barth, 758

Introduction to Value Theory, 317

Introduction to William James: An Essay and Selected Texts, 238

Introduction to Wittgenstein's Tractatus, 344

Introduction to Yoga, 550

An Introduction to Zen Buddhism, 558

An Introductory Bibliography for the Study of Scripture, 795

Introductory Philosophy, 25
Introductory Readings in
    Philosophy, 24
Intuition and Reflection in
    Self-Consciousness, 364,
    365
Intuitive Cognition: A Key to
    the Significance of the
    Later Scholastics, 114
Invention of Africa: Gnosis,
    Philosophy, and the Order
    of Knowledge, 369
Investigating Philosophy, 38
An Invitation to Japanese
    Civilization, 535
Invitation to Midrash, 611
An Invitation to Philosophy
    (Capaldi), 20
Invitation to Philosophy
    (Hollis), 21
Invitation to Philosophy
    (Honer and Hunt), 21
Invitation to the Talmud: A
    Teaching Book, 611
Inviting Death: Indian Atti-
    tude towards the Ritual
    Death, 510
Ionian Philosophy, 47
Iqbal: Manifestation of the
    Islamic Spirit, 375
Iqbal through Western Eyes,
    375
The Iron Pillar—The Mish-
    nah: Redaction, Form, and
    Intent, 613
Irrational Man: A Study in
    Existential Philosophy, 262
Isaac Mayer Wise: Shaping
    American Judaism, 653
Isaiah, 709
Isis Unveiled, 852, 873, 874
Islam (Denny), 883
Islam (al Faruqi), 574
Islam (Guillaume), 575
Islam (Masse), 572
Islam (Rahman), 576
Islam (Williams), 577
Islam: A Concise Introduc-
    tion, 576
Islam: A Way of Life, 569
Islam: Belief and Practice,
    577
Islam: Beliefs and Institu-
    tions, 575
Islam: Beliefs and Obser-
    vances, 574
Islam: Continuity and
    Change in the Modern
    World, 573
Islam: From the Prophet Mu-
    hammad to the Capture of
    Constantinople, 571
Islam: Legacy of the Past,

Challenge of the Future,
    579
Islam: The Fear and the
    Hope, 578
Islam: The Religious and Po-
    litical Life of a World
    Community, 570
Islam: The Straight Path—
    Islam Interpreted by Mus-
    lims, 576
Islam, Philosophy and Sci-
    ence, 373
Islam, Politics, and Social
    Movements, 578
Islam and Capitalism, 579
Islam and Christianity, 571
Islam and Christian Theolo-
    gy, 573
Islam and Colonialism: The
    Doctrine of Jihad in Mo-
    dern History, 895
Islam and Democracy: Fear
    of the Modern World, 579
Islam and Development: Re-
    ligion and Sociopolitical
    Change, 578
Islam and Its Cultural Diver-
    gence, 576
Islam and Modernism in
    Egypt, 374
Islam and Modernity: Trans-
    formation of an Intellectu-
    al Tradition, 373
Islam and Nationalism, 372
Islam and Politics, 578
Islam and the Modern Age,
    571
Islam and the Plight of Mo-
    dern Man, 375
Islam and the Political Econ-
    omy of Meaning, 580
Islam and the West, 568
Islamic Fundamentalism and
    Modernity, 373
Islamic History of the Mid-
    dle East, 567
The Islamic Impact, 578
Islamic Iran: Revolution and
    Counterrevolution, 578
Islamic Modernism in India
    and Pakistan, 567, 577
Islamic Philosophical Theolo-
    gy, 576
Islamic Philosophy and Mys-
    ticism, 576
Islamic Philosophy and The-
    ology, 97, 577
Islamic Reform, 374
Islamic Revival in British In-
    dia: Deoband, 1860–1900,
    572
Islamic Society and the
    West, 569

Islamic Spirituality, 885, 888,
    902
The Islamic Threat: Myth or
    Reality?, 578
The Islamic Understanding of
    Death and Resurrection,
    887
Islam in a World of Diverse
    Faiths, 568
Islam Inflamed, 572
Islam in Modern History,
    573
Islam in North America: A
    Sourcebook, 6
Islam in Practice, 579
Islam in Revolution: Funda-
    mentalism in the Arab
    World, 568
Islam in South East Asia,
    518
Islam in the Contemporary
    World, 572
Islam in the Modern Nation-
    al State, 580
Islam in the Modern World,
    579
Islam in the World, 572
Islam in Transition: Muslim
    Perspectives, 373
Islam in Tropical Africa, 571
Islam in Uganda, 572
The Islamization of Laws in
    Pakistan, 579
Islam Observed: Religious
    Development in Morocco
    and Indonesia, 478, 569
Island of History, 462
Israel: An Echo of Eternity,
    665
Israel: Its Politics and Philos-
    ophy, 643
Israel: Politics and People,
    642
Israel in America: A Too-
    Comfortable Exile, 640
Israel in Revolution 6–74
    C.E., 666
The Israelis: Founders and
    Sons, 642
Israelite and Judaean His-
    tory, 806
Israel Jacobson: The Found-
    er of the Reform Move-
    ment in Judaism, 652
Israel Salanter: Text, Struc-
    ture, Idea, 654
Israel Salanter: The Story of
    a Religious-Ethical Current
    in Nineteenth-Century Ju-
    daism, 654
Israel—A Precarious Sanctu-
    ary: War, Death and the
    Jewish People, 643

Issues in Marxist Philosophy, 243

Issues in the Jewish-Christian Dialogue, 898

Issues in the Sociology of Religion: A Bibliography, 425

Is the Homosexual My Neighbor? Another Christian View, 750

Italian Humanism: Philosophy and Civic Life in the Renaissance, 126

The Ivory Tower, 386

J. G. Frazer: His Life and Work, 477

J. L. Austin, 272

J. S. Bach, 740

Jacob's Ladder and the Tree of Life, 303

Jacopo Sadoleto, 1477–1547: Humanist and Reformer, 728

Jacques Derrida: A Bibliography, 398

Jacques Maritain: Homage in Words and Pictures, 307

Jacques Maritain and the French Catholic Intellectuals, 307

Jacques the Fatalist, 195

Jade: Its History and Symbolism in China, 523

The Jade Steps: A Ritual Life of the Aztecs, 457

Jaina Debates on the Spiritual Liberation of Women, 509

Jaina Yoga: A Survey of the Mediaeval Sravakacaras, 510

Jain Ramayan, 510

Jalal Al-Din Al-Suyuti, 585

James M. Gustafson's Theocentric Ethics: Interpretations and Assessments, 900

Jami: The Persian Mystic and Poet, 586

Jane Ellen Harrison: The Mask and the Self, 479

Jansenism in Seventeenth-Century France: Voices from the Wilderness, 737

The Japanese Mind: Essentials of Japanese Philosophy and Culture, 363

Japanese Mythology, 535

A Japanese New Religion: Rissho Kosei-kai in a Mountain Village, 540

Japanese Pilgrimage, 539

Japanese Religion: Unity and Diversity, 534

Japanese Religion and Philosophy, 363

Japanese Religion and Society: Paradigms of Structure and Change, 534

Japanese Religion in the Modern Century, 541

Japanese Spirituality, 558

The Jargon of Authenticity, 393

Jean Baudrillard: From Marxism to Postmodernism and Beyond, 17

Jean Bodin and the Rise of Absolutist Theory, 134

Jean Bodin and the Sixteenth-Century Revolution in the Methodology of Law and History, 134

Jean-Jacques: The Early Life and Work of Jean-Jacques Rousseau, 1712–1754, 213

Jean-Jacques Rousseau, 213

Jean-Jacques Rousseau and the Well-Ordered Society, 214

Jean-Paul Sartre, 330

Jean-Paul Sartre: The Existentialist Ethic, 330

Jean-Paul Sartre: The Philosopher as a Literary Critic, 331

Jean-Paul Sartre and His Critics, 331

Jean Toomer's Years with Gurdjieff: Portrait of an Artist 1923–36, 875

Jehovah's Witnesses, 863

Jehovah's Witnesses and Kindred Groups, 863

Jehovah's Witness Literature, 863

Jeremy Bentham: An Odyssey of Ideas, 191

Jerome: His Life, Writings and Controversies, 712

Jerome, Chrysostom and Friends: Essays and Translations, 712

Jerusalem; or, on Religious Power and Judaism, 208, 209

Jerusalem and Other Jewish Writings by Moses Mendelssohn, 647

Jerusalem in the Time of Jesus, 604, 807

Jesuit and Savage in New France, 752

Jesuit Thinkers of the Renaissance, 131

Jesus: A Jewish Dissent, 602

Jesus and Judaism, 617

Jesus and the Synoptic Gospels: A Bibliographic Study Guide, 795

Jesus and the Word, 825, 831

Jesus and the World of Judaism, 618

Jesus as Mother: Studies in the Spirituality of the High Middle Ages, 695

Jesus Christ and Mythology, 825, 831

Jesus in History, 807

Jesus of Nazareth, 824, 829

Jesus' Proclamation of the Kingdom of God, 826

Jesus the Jew: A Historian's Reading of the Gospels, 618

Jew and Gentile in the Ancient World, 604

The Jew as Ally of the Muslim: Medieval Roots of Anti-Semitism, 623

The Jew in America: A History, 640

The Jew in the Medieval World: A Source Book 315–1791, 623

The Jew in the Modern World: A Documentary History, 634

Jewish-American History and Culture: An Encyclopedia, 594

Jewish Americans: Three Generations in a Jewish Community, 639

Jewish and Female: Choices and Changes in Our Lives Today, 650

Jewish and Pauline Studies, 617

The Jewish Antiquities, 666

Jewish Art: An Illustrated History, 597

Jewish Art and Civilization, 597

Jewish Art and Religious Observance, 597

The Jewish Bible after the Holocaust: A Re-Reading, 663

Jewish Biblical Exegesis, 628

Jewish Bund in Russia from Its Origins to 1905, 656

The Jewish Catalog: A Do-It-Yourself Kit, 602

The Jewish-Christian Argument: A History of Theologies in Conflict, 603

The Jewish-Christian Debate in the High Middle Ages, 623

Jewish-Christian Relations: An Annotated Bibliography and Resource Guide, 5

Jewish Civilization, 593

Jewish Communities in Frontier Societies: Argentina, Australia, and South Africa, 644

The Jewish Community: Its History and Structure to the American Revolution, 593

A Jewish Conservative Looks at Pagan America, 655

Jewish Continuity and Change: Emerging Patterns in America, 639

Jewish Education and Society in the High Middle Ages, 622

The Jewish Encyclopedia, 594

Jewish Ethics, Philosophy and Mysticism, 629

The Jewish Experience, 640

The Jewish Experience in America, 640

Jewish Family Celebrations: Shabbat Festivals and Traditional Ceremonies, 599

The Jewish Feminist Movement in Germany, 650

The Jewish Festivals: From Their Beginnings to Our Own Day, 600

Jewish Folk Art: From Biblical Days to Modern Times, 597

Jewish Folkways in Germanic Lands (1648–1806), 624

The Jewish Holidays, 600

Jewish Identity on the Suburban Frontier, 641

Jewish Law: History, Sources, Principles: Ha-Mishpat Ha-Ivri, 627

Jewish Laws of Childbirth, 602

Jewish Life in the Middle Ages, 622

Jewish Life under Islam: Jerusalem in the Sixteenth Century, 625

Jewish Literature Between the Bible and the Mishnah, 613, 811

Jewish Liturgy and Its Development, 599

Jewish Magic and Superstition, 630

Jewish Moral Philosophy, 598

Jewish Musical Traditions, 597

Jewish Mystical Testimonies, 630

The Jewish Mystical Tradition, 630

Jewish Mysticism: An Introduction to Kabbalah, 629

Jewish Mysticism and Jewish Ethics, 598

Jewish People, Jewish Thought: The Jewish Experience in History, 595

Jewish People in America, 594

Jewish Philosophers, 601

Jewish Philosophical Polemics against Christianity in the Middle Ages, 629, 697

Jewish Philosophy in a Secular Age, 596

Jewish Philosophy in Modern Times, 646

The Jewish Primer, 596

Jewish Radicals, 1875–1914: From Czarist Stetl to London Ghetto, 656

Jewish Sects, Religious Movements, and Political Parties, 651

Jewish Sects at the Time of Jesus, 615, 616

Jewish Self-Government in Medieval Egypt, 625

Jewish Self-Government in the Middle Ages, 622

Jewish Self-Hatred: Anti-Semitism and the Hidden Language of the Jews, 636

Jewish Socialist Movements, 1871–1917: While the Messiah Tarried, 656

Jewish Societies in the Middle East: Community, Culture, and Authority, 644

Jewish Spirituality from the Bible through the Middle Ages, 630

The Jewish State, 658

Jewish Thought in the Seventeenth Century, 629

Jewish Thought in the Sixteenth Century, 629

The Jewish Thought of Emil Fackenheim: A Reader, 664

Jewish Thought Today, 884

Jewish Travellers in the Middle Ages: Nineteen Firsthand Accounts, 625

The Jewish War, 666

The Jewish War against the Jews: Reflections on Golah, Shoah, and Torah, 648

The Jewish Way: Living the Holidays, 599

Jewish Way in Death and Mourning, 602

The Jewish Way in Love and Marriage, 602

The Jewish Woman: New Perspectives, 650

The Jewish Woman in America, 649

Jewish Woman in Jewish Law, 650

Jewish Women in Historical Perspective, 649

Jewish Women in Rabbinic Literature, 650

The Jewish World: History and Culture of the Jewish People, 594

Jewish Worship, 600, 897

The Jews: Social Patterns of an American Group, 641

The Jews: Their History, Culture, and Religion, 594

Jews, Judaism and the Classical World, 604

Jews Against Zionism: The American Council for Judaism, 1942-1948, 658

The Jews among the Greeks and Romans, 605

Jews and Arabs: Their Contacts through the Ages, 625

Jews and Christians: Graeco-Roman Views, 605

Jews and Christians: The Myth of a Common Tradition, 603

Jews and French Quehecers: Two Hundred Years of Shared History, 644

The Jews and the Crusaders, 623

The Jews and the Left, 656

The Jews from Alexander to Herod, 605

Jews in a Free Society: Challenges and Opportunities, 652

Jews in an Arab Land: Libya, 1835–1970, 644

Jews in Colonial Brazil, 645

The Jews in Egypt and in Palestine under the Fatimid Caliphs, with Preface and Reader's Guide to Shlomo Dov Goitein, 626

The Jews in Germany from

the Enlightenment to National Socialism, 635
The Jews in Modern France, 637
Jews in Nineteenth-Century Egypt, 644
The Jews in Roman Imperial Legislation, 604
Jews in Russia: The Struggle for Emancipation, 636
The Jews in South Africa: A History, 645
The Jews in Soviet Russia since 1917, 636
Jews in the Hellenistic World, 608
The Jews of Arab and Islamic Countries: History, Problems, and Solutions, 644
The Jews of Arab Lands: A History and Source Book, 626
Jews of Arab Lands in Modern Times, 645
The Jews of Argentina. From the Inquisition to Peron, 645
The Jews of Byzantium, 1204–1453, 623
The Jews of East Central Europe: Between the World Wars, 637
The Jews of Hope, 636
The Jews of Iraq: 3000 Years of History and Culture, 644
The Jews of Islam, 571, 594
Jews of Latin American Republics, 644
The Jews of Modernity, 639
The Jews of Moslem Spain, 625
The Jews of Odessa: A Cultural History, 1794–1881, 638
The Jews of Poland, 625
The Jews of the Renaissance, 624
The Jews of Vienna, 1867–1914: Assimilation and Identity, 637
The Jews of Washington, 638
The Jews of Yemen, 1800–1914, 626
The Jews under Roman and Byzantine Rule, 606
Joachim of Fiore: A Study in Spiritual Perception and History, 712
Johann Gottfried Herder, 199
Johannine Christianity: Essays on Its Setting,

Sources, and Theology, 826
John Calvin, 761
John Calvin: A Biography, 762
John Calvin: A Sixteenth Century Portrait, 761
John Calvin: His Influence in the Western World, 732, 762
John Calvin, the Church and the Eucharist, 762
John Case and Aristotelianism in Renaissance England, 71, 131
John Cassian: Conferences, 706
John Chrysostom and the Jews, 684
John Colet, 126
John Colet and Marsilio Ficino, 141
John Dee: The Mathematical Preface, 125
John Dee's Natural Philosophy: Between Science and Religion, 125
John Dewey, 225
John Dewey: A Centennial Bibliography, 225
John Dewey: An Intellectual Portrait, 225, 298
John Dewey: His Thought and Influence, 225
John Dewey: Religious Faith and Democratic Humanism, 225
John Dewey: The Reconstruction of the Democratic Life, 225
John Dewey and American Democracy, 226
John Dewey and the Paradox of Liberal Reform, 225
John Dewey's Challenge to Education, 225
John Dewey's Philosophy of Value, 225
John Dewey's Pragmatic Technology, 225
John Duns Scotus, 1265–1965, 114
John Henry Newman, 783
John Henry Newman: A Bibliographical Catalogue, 782
John Hus: A Biography, 711, 721
John Hus at the Council of Constance, 711
John Knox (Percy), 774
John Knox (Ridley), 736
John Knox: Portrait of a Calvinist, 774

John Knox: The Hero of the Scottish Reformation, 774
John Knox's History of the Reformation in Scotland, 774
John Locke (Aaron), 179, 738
John Locke (Squadrito), 181
John Locke: A Biography, 179
John Locke: An Introduction, 181
John Locke: Economist and Social Scientist, 181
John Locke: Physician and Philosopher, 179
John Locke and the Doctrine of Majority Rule, 180
John Locke and the Theory of Sovereignty, 180
John Locke and the Way of Ideas, 181
John Locke's Liberalism, 180
John Locke Symposium, 179
Johnny Appleseed, Man and Myth, 852
John of Paris on Royal and Papal Power, 101
John of Salisbury, 116
John Paul II: A Man from Krakow, 742
John Paul II: A Pictorial Biography, 744
John Rawls' Theory of Social Justice: An Introduction, 316
John Stuart Mill (Ellery), 244
John Stuart Mill (Skorupski), 245
John Stuart Mill: A Criticism with Personal Recollections, 244
John Stuart Mill: His Life and Works, 245
John Stuart Mill and Harriet Taylor: Their Friendship and Subsequent Marriage, 245
John Stuart Mill's "On Liberty," 245
John XXIII: Simpleton or Saint?, 771
John Wesley: A Theological Biography, 790
John Wesley and His World, 790
John Wesley and the Women Preachers of Early Methodism, 738
John Wesley's Social Ethics: Praxis and Principles, 790
John Wyclif and Reform, 714
John Wycliffe and the Begin-

nings of English Noncon-
formity, 721
Joining the Club: A History
of Jews and Yale, 640
Jonathan Edwards (Aldridge),
767
Jonathan Edwards (Miller),
767
Jonathan Edwards: A Profile,
767
Jonathan Edwards: Puritan,
Preacher, Philosopher, 767
Jonathan Edwards: The Nar-
rative of a Puritan Mind,
767
Jonathan Edwards, Pastor:
Religion and Society in
Eighteenth-Century North-
ampton, 767
Jonathan Edwards, 1703–1758:
A Biography, 767
Jonathan Edwards and the
American Experience, 767
José Ortega y Gasset, 315
José Ortega y Gasset: Philos-
ophy of European Unity,
315
Joseph Butler's Moral and
Religious Thought: Tercen-
tenary Essays, 194
Joseph Karo: Lawyer and
Mystic, 628
Joseph Smith, the First Mor-
mon, 879
Joseph Smith and the Begin-
nings of Mormonism, 845,
879
Josephus: The Historian and
His Society, 666
Josephus: The Man and the
Historian, 666, 812
Josephus and Judaean Poli-
tics, 666
Josephus with an English
Translation, 812
Josiah Royce, 250
Journal of a Soul, 771
The Journal of John Wesley,
740, 789
Journeys through Philosophy,
20
Journey to Nowhere: A New
World Tragedy, 867
Journey to Oblivion, 637
Journey to Poland, 635
The Journey to the West,
531
Journey to Tradition: The
Odyssey of a Born-Again
Jew, 659
The Joyful Wisdom, 246
Juan Luis Vives, 156

Juan Luis Vives and the
Emotions, 156
Judaeo-Christian Debates, 602
Judaic Ethics for a Lawless
World, 598
Judaic Law from Jesus to
the Mishnah, 617
The Judaic Tradition, 596
Judaism, 883
Judaism: A Portrait, 596
Judaism: A Sociology, 634
Judaism: Practice and Belief
63 B.C.E.–66 C.E., 621, 807
Judaism: The Classical State-
ment: The Evidence of the
Bavli, 607, 611
Judaism: The Evidence of
the Mishnah, 611
Judaism: The Evolution of a
Faith, 595
Judaism and Christianity: A
Guide to the Reference
Literature, 7
Judaism and Christianity: Es-
says, 660
Judaism and Christianity in
the Age of Constantine,
621
Judaism and Ethics, 598
Judaism and Hellenism, 604,
807
Judaism and Its History: In
Two Parts, 647
Judaism and Its Social Meta-
phors, 607
Judaism and Modernization
on the Religious Kibbutz,
654
Judaism and Modern Man,
649
Judaism and Mysticism Ac-
cording to Gershom Scho-
lem, 673
Judaism and Psychology: Ha-
lakhic Perspectives, 890
Judaism and Scripture: The
Evidence of Leviticus Rab-
bah, 607, 611
Judaism and Story: The Evidence of the Fathers Ac-
cording to Rabbi Nathan,
607
Judaism and the Koran, 570
Judaism as a Civilization:
Toward a Reconstruction
of American-Jewish Life,
667
Judaism as Philosophy: The
Method and Message of
the Mishnah, 601
Judaism beyond God: A Radical Need to Be Jewish,
649

Judaism Despite Christianity,
671
Judaism from Cyrus to Had-
rian, 604
Judaism in America: From
Curiosity to Third Faith,
651
Judaism in Cold War Ameri-
ca: 1945–1990, 640
Judaism in Society, 607, 611
Judaism in the Beginning of
Christianity, 615
Judaism in the First Centu-
ries of the Christian Era,
621
Judaism in the Matrix of
Christianity, 621
Judaism on Trial: Jewish-
Christian Disputations in
the Middle Ages, 624
Judaisms and Their Messiahs
in the Beginning of Chris-
tianity, 621
The Judgment of the Dead,
887
Jürgen Habermas, 404
Jürgen Habermas on Society
and Politics: A Reader,
404
Just Business, 389
Just Health Care, 388
Justice, Law, and Culture,
284
Justice and Mercy, 599
Justice as Fairness, 316
Justice in Wartime, 323
Justifying Legal Punishment,
387
Justinian and the Later Ro-
man Empire, 682
Justus Lipsius: The Philoso-
phy of Renaissance Stoi-
cism, 130
The Just War: Force and Po-
litical Responsibility, 896
Just War and Jihad, 570

The Kabbala: Law and Mysti-
cism in the Jewish Tradi-
tion, 630
The Kalam Cosmological Ar-
gument, 574
Kang Yu-wei: A Biography
and a Symposium, 361
Kant, 207, 299
Kant and the Claims of
Knowledge, 206
Kant and the Claims of
Taste, 206
Kant and the Exact Sciences,
206

Kant and the Experience of Freedom, 206
Kant and the Nineteenth Century, 161
Kant and the Philosophy of History, 207
Kant and the Problem of Metaphysics, 206, 291
Kantian Ethics and Socialism, 207
Kant's Aesthetic Theory, 206
Kant's Analogies of Experience, 206
Kant's Analytic, 206
Kant's Concept of Teleology, 206
Kant's Dialectic, 206
Kant's Ethical Theory, 207
Kant's Life and Thought, 206, 279
Kant's Metaphysics and Theory of Science, 206
Kant's Metaphysics of Experience, 207
Kant's Moral Religion, 207
Kant's Moral Theory, 207
Kant's Rational Theology, 207
Kant's Theory of Form, 207
Kant's Theory of Freedom, 206
Kant's Theory of Justice, 207
Kant's Theory of Knowledge, 206
Kant's Theory of Morals, 206
Kant's Theory of Rights, 206
Kant's Transcendental Psychology, 206
Karaite Anthology: Excerpts from the Early Literature, 631
Karaites in Byzantium: The Formative Years, 970–1100, 631
Karaite Studies, 631
Karl Barth: His Life from Letters and Autobiographical Texts, 758
A Karl Barth Reader, 758
Karl Jaspers: An Introduction to His Philosophy, 300
Karl Jaspers: Basic Philosophical Writings, 299
Karl Jaspers and the Role of "Conversion" in the Nuclear Age, 300
Karl Marx, 242, 243
Karl Marx: His Life and Thought, 243
Karl Marx's Theory of History: A Defense, 242

Karl Marx's Theory of Revolution, 242
Karl Popper, 410
Karl Rahner, 904
Karl Rahner: An Introduction to His Theology, 746
Karl Rahner: Theologian of the Graced Search for Meaning, 903
Karl Rahner in Dialogue: Conversations and Interviews 1965–1982, 745, 903
Karma, 550
Karma and Rebirth: Post Classical Developments, 887
Karma and Rebirth in Classical Indian Traditions, 505
Kerygma and Myth, 743
The Key to Theosophy, 874
A Key to Whitehead's "Process and Reality," 343
Kibbutz: Venture in Utopia, 643
Kibbutz Judaism: A New Tradition in the Making, 658
Kierkegaard (Gardiner), 240
Kierkegaard (Thompson), 240
Kierkegaard: A Collection of Critical Essays, 240
Kierkegaard: A Life of Allegory, 240
Kierkegaard: Construction of the Aesthetic, 393
Kierkegaard: The Aesthetic and the Religious, 240
Kierkegaard and Christendom, 240
A Kierkegaard Handbook, 240
Kierkegaard in Golden Age of Denmark, 240
Kierkegaard's Authorship: A Guide to the Writings of Kierkegaard, 239
Kierkegaard's Concluding Unscientific Postscript, 240
Kierkegaard's Existential Ethics, 240
Kierkegaard's Fear and Trembling: Critical Appraisals, 240
Kierkegaard's Relation to Hegel, 240
Kindness, Clarity, and Insight, 560, 906
King: A Biography, 773
King and Kin: Political Allegory in the Hebrew Bible, 817
King Charles I, 733
Kingdom and Community:

The Social World of Early Christianity, 683
The Kingdom of God in America, 753
Kingdoms of Gold, Kingdoms of Jade: The Americas before Columbus, 454
Kingship and Community in Early India, 501
Kingship and the Gods, 441, 442
The King's Two Bodies: A Study of Medieval Political Theology, 98, 696
Kinship and Marriage in Early Arabia, 492
Knowing and Acting: An Invitation to Philosophy, 25
Knowing and the Known, 224
Knowing the Unknowable God: Ibn-Sina, Maimonides, Aquinas, 884
Knowledge, Goodness and Power, 130
Knowledge and Human Interests, 404
Knowledge and the Good in Plato's Republic, 81
Knowledge and the Sacred: The Gifford Lectures, 1981, 375, 576, 902
The Knowledge of God in Calvin's Theology, 761
Ko-ji-ki, 536
Kokoro, 539
The Koran, 586
The Koran Interpreted, 587
Korea: A Religious History, 533
Korean and Asian Religious Tradition, 534
The Korean Approach to Zen, 537
The Korean Buddhist Canon, 534
Krishna: Myths, Rites, and Attitudes, 506
Krishna Consciousness in the West, 862
Krishnamurti: A Biography, 555
Krishnamurti: His Life and Death, 556
Krishnamurti: The Man, the Mystery and the Message, 555, 858
Krishnamurti: The Open Door, 556
Krishnamurti: The Reluctant Messiah, 555
Krishnamurti: The Years of Awakening, 556, 858

Krishnamurti: The Years of Fulfillment, 556, 858
Krsna: The Supreme Personality of Godhead, 862
The Kula: New Perspectives on Massim Exchange, 486
Küng in Conflict, 775
Kurozumikyo and the New Religions of Japan, 540
Kurozumi Shinto: An American Dialogue, 541
The Kuzari: An Argument for the Faith of Israel, 666, 667

L. Ron Hubbard: Madman or Messiah, 869
La Mandragola, 144
The Lamentation over the Destruction of Sumer and Ur, 545
Lamentations Rabbah: An Analytical Translation, 611
Lamp of Mahamudra, 544
Land and Power: The Zionist Resort to Force, 1881–1948, 658
The Land of the Bible: A Historical Geography, 809
Language, Counter-Memory, Practice, 400
Language, Society, and Paleoculture:, 436
Language, Truth and Logic, 273
Language and Experience in Seventeenth Century British Philosophy, 29
Language and Logic in the Post Medieval Period, 123
The Language and Logic of the Bible: The Earlier Middle Ages, 696
Language and Meaning in the Renaissance, 132
Language and Myth, 279
Language and Philosophy: A Symposium, 265
Language and the "Feminine" in Nietzsche and Heidegger, 293
Language and Thought in Early Greek Philosophy, 49
Language in Dispute, 102
Language in Wittgenstein's Later Philosophy, 345
Language of the Goddess, 434
Languages of Art, 403
Laocoon, Nathan the Wise, Minna von Barnhelm, 208

Laocoon, or the Bounds of Painting and Poesy, 207
Lao Tzu: Tao Te Ching, 527, 528, 529
Lao-Tzu: Te-Tao Ching, 528
The Lapsed, 708
The Last Dalai Lama: A Biography, 357, 561
The Last Days of Socrates, 78
The Last Four Lives of Annie Besant, 550, 859
The Lasting Elements of Individualism, 296
The Last of the Fathers, 700
The Last Puritan: A Memoir in the Form of a Novel, 327
Last Talks at Saanen, 555
The Last Trial, 621
Last Writings: Nothingness and the Religious Worldview, 365, 888
Last Writings Vol. 1: Preliminary Studies for Part III of Philosophical Investigations, 343
Late Medieval Mysticism, 697
The Later Christian Fathers, 680
The Later Heidegger and Theology, 294
Later Medieval Philosophy (1150–1350): An Introduction, 94
The Later Philosophy of R. G. Collingwood, 282
The Later Philosophy of Schelling, 252
Latin American Mind, 33
Latin American Thought: A Historical Introduction, 33
The Latter Day Saints Churches: An Annotated Bibliography, 846
Laughter: An Essay on the Meaning of the Comic, 220
Lautreamont, 274
Law and Philosophy: A Symposium, 265
Law and the Social Order: Essays in Legal Philosophy, 280
The Law of Christ, 718
The Law of Success, 556
The Laws: History, 78
The Laws and Custom of the Jewish Wedding, 602
The Laws in the Pentateuch and Other Studies, 823, 836
Lay Buddhism in Contempo-

rary Japan: Reiyukai Kyodan, 540
A Layman's Guide to Protestant Theology, 744
Layman's Guide to Protestant Thought, 718
Leap of Action: Ideas in the Theology of Abraham Joshua Heschel, 665
Learning from Error, 409
Leaves from the Notebook of a Tamed Cynic, 783, 784
Lectures in Logic, 205
Lectures on Ethics, 205
Lectures on Ideology and Utopia, 319
Lectures on Kant's Political Philosophy, 394
Lectures on Philosophical Theology, 205
Lectures on the Ethics of T. H. Green, Herbert Spencer, and J. Martineau, 257
Lectures on the History of Philosophy, 17, 232
Lectures on the History of Religions, 573
Lectures on the Philosophy of Kant and Other Philosophical Lectures and Essays, 257
Lectures on the Philosophy of Religion, 232
Lectures on the Philosophy of World History: Introduction, 232
Lectures on the Principles of Political Obligation, 230
Lectures on the Religion of the Semites, 491, 492
Lectures on the Republic of Plato, 83
Le Devin du village, 212
Lefèvre: Pioneer of Ecclesiastical Renewal in France, 127
The Legacy of H. Richard Niebuhr, 746
The Legacy of Hermann Cohen, 663
The Legacy of Islam, 567, 572
The Legacy of Luther, 731
The Legacy of St. Vladimir, 756
The Legacy of Wittgenstein, 346
The Legend of the Baal Shem, 660
The Legends of Genesis: The Biblical Saga and History, 823, 835

Legends of the Hasidim, 633
Legends of the Jews, 610
The Legends of the Saints, 678
Legitimation Crisis, 404
Leibnitz and Locke: A Study of the New Essay and Human Understanding, 177, 180
Leibniz, 177
Leibniz: An Introduction to His Philosophy, 177
Leibniz: Critical and Interpretive Essays, 177
Leibniz: Logic and Metaphysics, 177
Leibniz and Arnauld, 164, 178
Leibniz and Confucianism: The Search for Accord, 177
Leibniz and Philosophical Analysis, 178
Leibniz and the Seventeenth-Century Revolution, 177
Leibniz in France—From Arnauld to Voltaire, 177
Leibniz's Metaphysics: A Historical and Comparative Study, 178
Leibniz's Monadology: An Edition for Students, 317
Leo Baeck: Teacher of Theresienstadt, 661
Leontiev, 275
Leo XIII and the Modern World, 741
Lessing and the Enlightenment, 208
Lessing's Theological Writings: Selections in Translation, 739
The Letter and the Spirit, 116
A Letter Concerning Toleration, 179
The Letter on the Blind for the Benefit of Those Who See, 196
The Letters and Diaries of John Henry Newman, 782
Letters and Papers from Prison, 760
Letters of Jews through the Ages, 594
Letters of John Henry Newman: A Selection, 782
Letters of Medieval Jewish Traders, 626
The Letters of St. Catherine of Siena, 707
The Letters of St. Cyprian of Carthage, 708

The Letters of William James, 236
Letters on Familiar Matters: Rerum Familiarum Libri, 150
Letters to an American Jewish Friend: A Zionist's Polemic, 658
Letters to Mirabehn, 552
Letter to the Grand Duchess Christina, 142
Let the Trumpet Sound: The Life of Martin Luther King, Jr., 773
The Levant at the Beginning of the Middle Bronze Age, 445
Leviathan, 174
Leviathan and the Air Pump: Hobbes, Bayle, and the Experimental Life, 175
The Levinas Reader, 901
Lexicon Plantonicum Sive Vacum Platonicarum Index, 1835–1838, 79
Lexicon Spinozanum, 187
Liberal Judaism, 661
Liberal Judaism at Home: The Practices of Modern Reform Judaism, 601
Liberation and Change, 769
Liberation Theology: An Introductory Guide, 747
Liberation Theology: An Introductory Reader, 747
Liberation Theology: Human Hope Confronts Christian History and American Power, 785
Liberation Theology and Its Critics: Toward an Assessment, 896
The Libertarian Idea, 386
The Library, 469
The Library of Christian Classics, 680
The Library of Pico della Mirandola, 153
Lies, Language, and Logic in the Late Middle Ages, 104
Life after Life, 866
The Life and Art of Albrecht Dürer, 738
The Life and Correspondence of David Hume, 201
The Life and Hard Times of a Korean Shaman, 539
The Life and Letters of John Locke, with Extracts from His Journals and Common-place Books, 180
Life and Mind of John Dewey, 225

The Life and Philosophy of J. McT. E. McTaggart, 1866–1925, 304
The Life and Philosophy of Johann Gottfried Herder, 199
The Life and Thought of Josiah Royce, 250
The Life and Times of Mary Tudor, 727
The Life and Times of Muhammad, 588
The Life and Work of Muhammad Jalal-ud Din Rumi, 590
The Life and Work of Roger Bacon: An Introduction to the Opus Majus, 111
The Life and Writings of the Historical St. Patrick, 713
Life before Birth, 389
The Life Divine, 352, 353
Life Force: The World of Jainism, 510
Life Is Real Only Then, When "I Am," 875
Life Is with People: The Culture of the Shtetl, 625
The Life of a Jewish Woman, 394
Life of Arthur Schopenhauer, 256
The Life of a Text: Performing the Ramacaritamanas of Tulsi-Das, 505
The Life of Bertrand Russell, 324
The Life of Cicero, 73
The Life of David Hume, 202
The Life of George Berkeley, Bishop of Cloyne, 192
The Life of Jesus, 254
A Life of John Calvin: A Study in the Shaping of Western Culture, 762
The Life of John Knox, 774
The Life of Muhammad, 588
The Life of Muhammad from Original Sources, 588
The Life of Niccolò Machiavelli, 145
The Life of Plotinus, 85
The Life of Reason, 327
The Life of Solitude, 150
The Life of St. Anselm, Archbishop of Canterbury, 703
The Life of Teresa of Jesus, 786
The Life of the Mind, 394
The Life of the Sina, 582
Life of Torah: Readings in the Jewish Religious Experience, 596

The Lifetime of a Jew: Throughout the Ages of Jewish History, 600
Life Together, 759, 760
Light and Enlightenment, 168
The Light of the Eyes: Homilies to Genesis, 633
The Light of the Soul, 182
Light on C. S. Lewis, 776
Lily Montagu and the Advancement of Liberal Judaism, 653
Limited, Inc., 397
The Limits of Analysis, 381
The Limits of Science, 317, 385
Linguistic Analysis and Phenomenology, 263
The Linguistic Turn: Recent Essays in Philosophical Method, 267, 413
Lions of the Punjab: Culture in the Making, 516
The Lion's Roar of Queen Srimala, 514
Listening to the Cicadas: A Study of Plato's Phaedrus, 80
Literacy and Orality, 460
Literacy and Orality in Ancient Greece, 460
The Literary Essays of Thomas Merton, 781
The Literary Guide to the Bible, 816
The Literary Impact of the Golden Bough, 477
The Literary Legacy of C. S. Lewis, 777
Literature and Existentialism, 329
The Literature of Ancient Egypt, 442
Lithuanian Hasidism, 633
Little Flowers of St. Francis, 710
Liturgies of the Western Church, 681
The Lively Experiment: The Shaping of Christianity in America, 753
Lives in the Shadow with J. Krishnamurti, 556
Lives of Eminent Philosophers, 46
Lives of the Saints, 675
Living at the End of the Ages, 724
A Living Covenant: The Innovative Spirit in Traditional Judaism, 648

The Living God: Systematic Theology, 885
Living in the Eternal: A Study of George Santayana, 328
Living Issues in Philosophy, 25
Living Options in World Philosophy, 37
Living Peter: A Biographical Study of Pope John XXIII, 771
Living Religions and a World Faith, 296
The Living Talmud: The Wisdom of the Fathers, 610
The Living Thoughts of Nietzsche, 247
The Living Thoughts of Schopenhauer, 256
The Living Thoughts of St. Paul, 306
Living with the Children of God, 864
Local Knowledge: Further Essays in Interpretive Anthropology, 478
Local Religion in Sixteenth-Century Spain, 728
Locke (Ayer), 179
Locke (Fraser), 180
Locke (Woolhouse), 181
Locke, Berkeley, Hume, 180
Locke, Rousseau, and the Idea of Consent, 181
Locke's Theory of Knowledge and Its Historical Relations, 180
Locke's Travels in France, 1675–1679, 180
Logic, 240
Logic: Theory of Inquiry, 224
Logic, Science, and Dialectic, 49
Logical and Philosophical Papers, 1909–1913, 323
The Logical Basis of Metaphysics, 382
A Logical Introduction to Philosophy, 23
Logical Investigations, 229, 234
Logical Papers: A Selection, 176
Logical Positivism, Pragmatism and Scientific Empiricism, 266
Logical Positivism (Ayer), 262, 273
Logical Positivism (Hanfling), 264
The Logical Structure of the

World and Pseudoproblems in Philosophy, 278
Logica Magna. Part I Fascicule 8, 129
Logica Magna. Part II Fascicule 3, 129
Logica Magna, Tractatus De Suppositione, 129
Logic and Knowledge: Essays 1901–50, 323
Logic and Language Second Series, 264
Logic and Ontology in Heidegger, 295
Logic and Philosophy, 338
Logic and Reality in Leibniz's Metaphysics, 177
Logic and Rhetoric in England, 1500–1700, 127
Logic and the Objectivity of Knowledge: Studies in Husserl's Early Philosophy, 235
Logica Parva, 129
Logic in Three Books: Of Thought, of Investigation, and of Knowledge, 241
The Logic of Decision and Action, 317
The Logic of Divine Love, 106
Logic of Leviathan: The Moral and Political Theory of Thomas Hobbes, 174
The Logic of Perfection and Other Essays in Neoclassical Metaphysics, 289
Logic of Pragmatism: An Examination of John Dewey's Logic, 225
The Logic of Reflection: German Philosophy in the Twentieth Century, 28
The Logic of Scientific Discovery, 409
The Logic of St. Anselm, 108
The Logic of William of Ockham, 121
Logico-Linguistic Papers, 414
Logics of Disintegration, 391
London and the Reformation, 725
The Long Loneliness: An Autobiography, 765
The Lord of the Rings, 776
The Lord Protector, 734
Lore and Science in Ancient Pythagoreanism, 470
Lotus in a Sea of Fire, 561
Lotus Petals: The Life and Work of Rudolph Steiner, 879
Lotus Sutra, 538

The Lotus Sutra in Japanese Culture, 538

Lotze's System of Philosophy, 241, 327

Lotze's Theory of Reality, 241

Love, Knowledge, and Discourse in Plato, 84

Love and Friendship in Plato and Aristotle, 83

Love and Responsibility, 747

Love and Science in Ancient Pythagoreanism, 87

The Love of Learning and the Desire for God: A Study of Monastic Culture, 699

Loving Nature: Ecological Integrity and Christian Responsibility, 745

Loving the Torah More Than God? Towards a Catholic Appreciation of Judaism, 901

Loyalty, 389

Lucian and His Influence in Europe, 485

Lucifer: A Theological Tragedy, 327

Lucifer: The Devil in the Middle Ages, 697

Lucinde, 252

Lucinde and Fragments, 253

Lucretius and Epicurus, 73, 75

Lucretius and His Influence, 75

Lucretius on Death and Anxiety: Poetry and Philosophy in De Rerum Natura, 75

Ludwig Feuerbach and the Outcome of Classical German Philosophy, 228

Ludwig Wittgenstein: A Comprehensive Bibliography, 346

Ludwig Wittgenstein: Critical Assessments, 347

Ludwig Wittgenstein: Personal Recollections, 346

Lull and Bruno: Collected Essays, Vol. 1, 136

Lustful Maidens and Ascetic Kings: Buddhist and Hindu Stories of Life, 503, 512

Luther: Man between God and the Devil, 779

Luther, Erasmus and the Reformation: A Catholic-Protestant Reappraisal, 779

Luther and Erasmus: Free Will and Salvation, 779

Luther and His Times: The Reformation from a New Perspective, 779

Luther and Music, 738

Luther and Staupitz, 779

Luther and the Papacy: Stages in a Reformation Conflict, 778

Luther in Context, 779

Luther on Conversion: The Early Years, 778

Luther's Faith: The Cause of the Gospel in the Church, 779

Luther's House of Learning: Indoctrination of the Young in the German Reformation, 731

Luther's Last Battles: Politics and Polemics, 1531–1546, 778

Luther's Progress to the Diet of Worms, 779

Luther's Theology of the Cross: Martin Luther's Theological Breakthrough, 778

The Lyre of Science: Form and Meaning in Lucretius's De Rerum Natura, 75

The Machiavellian Cosmos, 145

Machiavelli and Guicciardini, 145

The Machiavellian Moment, 145

Machiavelli's New Modes and Orders: A Study of the "Discourses on Livy," 145

Machiavelli's "Prince" and Its Forerunners, 145

The Macmillan Atlas History of Christianity, 720

The Macmillan Bible Atlas, 809

Madame Blavatsky: The Woman behind the Myth, 874

Madness and Civilization, 400

The Madness of the Saints: Ecstatic Religion in Bengal, 505

The Mad Philosopher: Auguste Comte, 223

Maenads, Martyrs, Matrons, Monastics, 449

The Maggid of Dubno and His Parables, 632

Magic, Reason and Experience, 48

Magic, Science and Religion and Other Essays, 485

Magic, Witchcraft and Paganism in America: A Bibliography, 865

The Magicians: A Study of the Use of Power in a Black Magic Group, 865

Magic into Science: The Story of Paracelsus, 150

Magika Hiera: Ancient Greek Magic and Religion, 451

Magnetic Sleep: Mesmer and the Roots of Psychological Healing, 847

Mahabharata, 502, 505

Mahatma Gandhi and Comparative Religion, 553

Mahatma Gandhi and His Apostles, 553

Mahayana Buddhism: The Doctrinal Foundations, 514

Mahler: A Musical Physiognomy, 393

Mahzor Hashalem: High Holyday Prayer Book, 599

Maimonides, 668

Maimonides: Introduction to the Talmud, 627

Maimonides: Torah and Philosophic Quest, 668

Maimonides Ethics: The Encounter of Philosophic and Religious Morality, 668

A Maimonides Reader, 668

Main Currents in American Thought, 35

Main Currents in Contemporary German, British, and American Philosophy, 29, 268

Main Currents of Korean Thought, 535

Main Trends in Philosophy, 18, 23, 267, 319

Major Themes in Modern Philosophies of Judaism, 646

Major Trends in Jewish Mysticism, 672

The Making of a Moonie: Choice or Brainwashing?, 871

The Making of a Spiritual Movement, 872

Making of Christian Doctrine, 687

The Making of Homeric Verse, 460

Making of Men, 339

The Making of Modern Zionism: Intellectual Origins of the Jewish State, 657
The Making of the "Canzoniere" and Other Petrarchan Studies, 151
The Making of the Creeds, 687
The Making of "The Golden Bough": The Origins and Growth of an Argument, 477
Making of the Mexican Mind: A Study in Recent Mexican Thought, 33
The Making of the Modern Jew, 634
The Making of the Modern Mind, 162
Making Sense of Marx, 242
Making Sense of the Jonestown Suicides, 867
Making Sense of Things: An Invitation to Philosophy, 24
Making the Classics in Judaism: The Three Stages of Literary Formation, 611
The Malaise of Modernity, 415
Malcolm X—A Voice for Black America, 877
The Malcolm X Reader: His Life, His Thought, His Legacy, 877
Malebranche: A Study of a Cartesian System, 182
Malebranche and British Philosophy, 182
Malebranche and Ideas, 182
Malinowski and the Work of Myth, 486
Malinowski between Two Worlds, 486
Mama Lola: A Vodoo Priestess in Brooklyn, 868
Man, 174
Man, Land and Myth in North Australia: The Gunwinggu People, 461
Managing Change in Old Age, 642
Man and Crisis, 314
Man and Culture, 486
Man and His Approach to God in John Duns Scotus, 114
Man and His Bodies, 550
Man and Nature: The Spiritual Crisis in Modern Man, 902
Man and Nature in the Renaissance, 125

Man and People, 315
Man and Society: The Scottish Inquiry of the Eighteenth Century, 32
Man and the State, 296, 306
Man and World in the Light of Anthroposophy, 858
Mandarins, Jews and Missionaries, 644
The Mandukya Upanishad and the Agama Sastra, 501, 507
The Man-Eating Myth: Anthropology and Anthropophagy, 466
Manichaeism in the Later Roman Empire and Medieval China, 686
The Man in Leather Breeches: The Life and Times of George Fox, 734
Man in the Modern Age, 299
The Man in the Sycamore Tree, 781
Man Is the Measure, 19
The Man of Reason: Male and Female in Western Philosophy, 17
Man of Spain: A Biography of Francis Suárez, 154
Man's Freedom, 338, 339
Man's Place in Nature, 332
The Mantle of the Prophet: Religion and Politics in Modern Iran, 572
Mantra: Hearing the Divine in India, 503
Manual of Zen Buddhism, 558
The Man Who Would Be Perfect, 844
Many Faces of Realism, 410
Many Ramayanas: The Diversity of a Narrative Tradition in South Asia, 506
Mao Zedong: A Bibliography, 362
Map Is Not Territory, 491
March of Philosophy, 16
Marcion: The Gospel of the Alien God, 686
Marcus Aurelius: A Biography, 76
Marcus Aurelius: Aspects of Civic and Cultural Policy in the East, 76
Marcus Aurelius: His Life and His World, 76
Marcus Aurelius and the Later Stoics, 76
Marcuse: Critical Theory and the Promise of Utopia, 408

Marcuse and Freedom, 408
Marcuse's Dilemma, 408
Margins of Philosophy, 397
Marital Love, 880
Mark the Evangelist, 825
Marriage and Morals, 323
Martin and Malcolm and America: A Dream or a Nightmare, 763, 772
Martin Buber: Jewish Existentialist, 662
Martin Buber: The Life of Dialogue, 662
Martin Buber on Myth: An Introduction, 662
Martin Buber's Social and Religious Thought, 662
Martin Heidegger, 295
Martin Heidegger: A Bibliography, 294
Martin Heidegger and National Socialism: Questions and Answers, 294
Martin Luther: An Introduction to His Life and Work, 778
Martin Luther: Knowledge and Mediation in the Renaissance, 128
Martin Luther: Road to Reform, 778
Martin Luther: The Man and His Work, 779
Martin Luther and the Birth of Protestantism, 778
Martin Luther and the Reformation, 778
Martin Luther's Basic Theological Writings, 778
Martin—God's Court Jester: Luther in Retrospect, 778
Marx and Engels: The Intellectual Relationship, 227
Marx and Mill: Two Views of Social Conflict and Social Harmony, 244
Marx and the Marxists: The Ambiguous Legacy, 298
The Marxian Revolutionary Idea, 243
Marxism and Christianity, 407
Marxism and Deconstruction: A Critical Articulation, 267, 392
Marxism and Materialism, 227
Marxism and Morality, 243
Marxism and Philosophy (Callinicos), 263, 379
Marxism and Philosophy (Korsch), 243

The Marxist Philosophy of Ernst Bloch, 277

Marx's Politics, 242

Marx's Social Theory, 242

Mary: A History of Doctrine and Devotion, 678

Mary: The Feminine Face of the Church, 785

Mary Baker Eddy (Bates), 878

Mary Baker Eddy (Eddy), 843

Mary Baker Eddy (Peel), 875

Mary Baker Eddy: A Life-Sized Portrait, 875

Mary Baker Eddy: An Interpretive Biography of the Founder of Christian Science, 875

Maryknoll in China: A History 1918–1955, 533

Mary Queen of Scots, 735

Mary Tudor, the White Queen, 727

The Mask of Power: Seneca's Tragedies and Imperial Power, 88

The Masks Jews Wear: Self-Deceptions of American Jewry, 661

The Masks of God, 428

Masada: Herod's Last Fortress and the Zealots' Last Stand, 614

The Mass of the Roman Rite: Its Origins and Development, 689

Master of Wisdom: Writings of the Buddhist Master Nagarjuna, 513

Masterpieces of World Philosophy, 2

Masters, Princes, and Merchants, 698

Masters of Social Philosophy: Freud, Mead, Lewin, and Skinner, 309

Materials for the History of the Text of the Qur'an, 587

Mathematical Logic, 411

Mathematical Principles of Natural Philosophy, 183

Mathematics, Metaphysics and the Power of the Scientific Mind, 323

Mathematics in Aristotle, 68

The Mathematics of Plato's Academy, 80

The Mathnawi of Jalalu'ddin Rumi, 589

The Matrix and Diamond

World Mandalas in Shingon Buddhism, 538

Matrix and Line: Derrida and the Possibilities of Postmodern Social Theory, 398

Matsuri: Festivals of a Japanese Town, 539

Matter and Memory, 220

The Matter of My Book: Montaigne's "Essais" as the Book of the Self, 146

A Matter of Principle, 386

Maus: A Survivor's Tale, 637

Max Scheler: The Man and His Works, 332

Max Scheler, 1874–1928: An Intellectual Portrait, 332

Max Scheler's Concept of the Person: An Ethics of Humanism, 332

Maya History and Religion, 456

May You Be the Mother of a Hundred Sons, 508

Mead and Merleau-Ponty: Toward a Common Vision, 309, 311

Meaning and Action: A Critical History of Pragmatism, 268

Meaning and Being in Myth, 428

The Meaning and End of Religion, 422

Meaning and Method, 411

Meaning and Necessity: A Study in Semantics and Modal Logic, 278

The Meaning of God in Human Experience, 296

The Meaning of Heidegger, 294

The Meaning of Human History, 281

The Meaning of Icons, 693

The Meaning of Immortality in Human Experience, Including Thoughts on Life and Death, 296

The Meaning of Language, 383

The Meaning of Life: Essays by the Author of Language, Truth and Logic, 273

The Meaning of Life: Questions, Answers, and Analysis, 24

The Meaning of More's Utopia, 147

The Meaning of Stoicism, 56

The Meaning of the Glorious Koran, 587

The Meaning of Truth: A Sequel to Pragmatism, 236

The Meanings of Death, 887

Mechanics in Sixteenth-Century Italy, 125

The Mechanization of the World Picture: Pythagoras to Newton, 125

The Mediating Self: Mead, Sartre, and Self-Determination, 308

Medieval Aspects of Renaissance Learning: Three Essays, 128

The Medieval Church, 691

Medieval Cosmology, Theories of Infinity, Place, Time, Void and the Plurality of Worlds, 97

Medieval Handbooks of Penance, 700

Medieval Heresy: Popular Movements from Bogomil to Hus, 699, 721

Medieval Humanism and Other Studies, 96

The Medieval Imagination, 697

The Medieval Inquisition, 700

The Medieval Inquisition: Foundations of Medieval History, 699

Medieval Islam: A Study in Cultural Orientation, 573

Medieval Jewish Life, 622

Medieval Jewry in Northern France: A Political and Social History, 623

Medieval Liturgy: An Introduction to the Sources, 701

Medieval Logic: An Outline of Its Development from 1250–1400, 97

The Medieval Mind, 96

Medieval Monasticism, 699

The Medieval Papacy, 694

Medieval Philosophy, 39

Medieval Philosophy: From St. Augustine to Nicholas of Cusa, 95

Medieval Political Ideas, 98

Medieval Political Philosophy: A Sourcebook, 95

Medieval Reformation, 691

Medieval Religious Women I: Distant Echoes, 700

Medieval Thought from Saint Augustine to Ockham, 697

The Medieval Tradition of Natural Law, 98
The Medieval Universities, 101
Medieval Women, 700
Meditating on the Word, 760
Meditation in Action, 357
Meditations (Aurelius), 76
Meditations (Krishnamurti), 555
Meditations of a Maverick Rabbi, 648
The Meditations of Marcus Aurelius: A Study, 59, 76
Meditations on First Philosophy, 168, 169
Meditations on Hunting, 315
A Mediterranean Society, 626
Mediums, and Spirit-Rappers, and Roaring Radicals, 851
Medusa's Hair: An Essay on Personal Symbols and Religious Experience, 424
Meetings with Remarkable Men, 875
Meetings with Remarkable Women: Buddhist Teachers in America, 515
The Megalithic Monuments of Western Europe: The Latest Evidence, 434
Megalithomania, 434
Meister Eckhart: A Modern Translation, 708
Meister Eckhart: Teacher and Preacher, 708
Meister Eckhart: The Essential Sermons, Commentaries, Treatises, and Defense, 708
Meister Eckhart: Thought and Language, 102, 709
Mekhilta According to R. Ishmael: An Analytical Translation, 611
Mekhilta According to R. Ishmael: An Introduction to Judaism's First Scriptural Encyclopaedia, 611
Mekilta Derabbi Ishmael, 610
Melanchthon: The Quiet Reformer, 730
Memoirs of American Jews: 1775–1865, 640
The Memoirs of Gluckel of Hamelin, 623
Memorabilia, 91
Memorial Essays, 273
Memories and Studies, 236
Memories for Paul de Man, 397
Men in Dark Times, 394
The Men of the Old Stone

Age: Palaeolithic and Mesolithic, 432
Mensius and Aquinas: Theories of Virtue and Conceptions of Courage, 897
Mental Illness and Psychology, 400
Mercer Dictionary of the Bible, 5, 818
Merit and Responsibility: A Study in Greek Values, 47
Merleau-Ponty and Marxism: From Terror to Reform, 311
Merleau-Ponty and Metaphor, 311
Merleau-Ponty and the Foundation of an Existential Politic, 311
Merton: A Biography, 781
Merton: By Those Who Knew Him Best, 781
Mesmerism and the American Cure of Souls, 847
The Mesoamerican Ballgame, 456
Mesolithic Prelude, 433
The Message of Jesus Christ, 552
The Message of the Gita: With Text, Translation and Notes, 353
The Message of the Prophets, 823, 838
The Messiah: An Aramaic Interpretation, 608
The Messianic Idea in Israel, 604
The Messianic Idea in Judaism and Other Essays on Jewish Spirituality, 672
Messianic Judaism, 864
The Messianic Secret, 826
Messianism, Mysticism, and Magic, 630, 651
Messianism in the Talmudic Era, 621
Messias, 167
The Metalogicon of John of Salisbury, 116
Metamorphoses, 469
The Metamorphoses of Apuleius: On Making an Ass of Oneself, 469
The Metaphysical and Geometrical Doctrine of Bruno as Given in His Work "De triplici minimo," 135
Metaphysical Disputations, 154
The Metaphysical Foundations of Logic, 291
The Metaphysical Founda-

tions of Modern Physical Science, 124, 159
Metaphysical Foundations of Natural Science, 205
Metaphysical Meditations, 556
Metaphysical Themes in Thomas Aquinas, 119
The Metaphysical Thought of Godfrey of Fontaines, 103
Metaphysics (Aune), 380
The Metaphysics (Avicenna), 581
Metaphysics (Lotze), 240
Metaphysics (Taylor), 381
Metaphysics in Midwestern America, 855
Metaphysics in Three Books: Ontology, Cosmology, and Psychology, 241
The Metaphysics of Descartes: A Study of the Meditations, 169
The Metaphysics of Education, 323
The Metaphysics of Epistemology: Lectures by Wilfred Sellars, 333
The Metaphysics of G. E. Moore, 312
The Metaphysics of Good and Evil According to Suárez, 105
Metaphysics of Morals, 204, 205
The Metaphysics of Pragmatism, 298
The Metaphysics of Tractatus, 345
The Metaphysics of Transcendental Subjectivity, 334
The Method and Message of Jewish Apocalyptic, 824
Method for the Easy Comprehension of History, 133, 134
Methodical Realism, 286
The Methodists, 739
Methods and Problems in Greek Science, 48
The Methods of Ethics, 256, 257
Methods of Logic, 411
Michel Foucault (Eribon), 401
Michel Foucault (Shumway), 401
Michel Foucault: A Bibliography, 401
Michel Foucault: An Introductory Study of His Thought, 400
Michel Foucault: Beyond

Structuralism and Hermeneutics, 400
Michel Foucault: The Freedom of Philosophy, 401
Michel Foucault's Force of Flight, 400
The Middle Ages and the Renaissance, 124
The Middle East, 580
Middle Platonism and Neoplatonism, 60
The Middle Platonists 80 B.C. to A.D. 220, 60
The Middle Voice of Ecological Conscience, 294
Mid-Journey: An Unfinished Autobiography, 317
Midrash: An Introduction, 611
Midrash and Literature, 610
Midrash Compilations of the Sixth and Seventh Centuries, 611
Midrash Reader, 611
Mid-Twentieth Century American Philosophy: Personal Statements, 34, 262
Mikrokosmos, 240
Militant Islam, 570, 579
Militia Christi, 688
Mind, History, and Dialectic: The Philosophy of R. G. Collingwood, 282
Mind, Self, and Society: From the Standpoint of a Social Behaviorist, 308
Mind and Imagination in Aristotle, 71
Mind and Nature, 281
Mind and the World-Order: Outline of a Theory of Knowledge, 302
The Mind of John Paul II: Origins of His Thought and Action, 747
The Mind of Kierkegaard, 239
The Mind of St. Bernard of Clairvaux, 112
The Mind of the Middle Ages: An Historical Survey, A.D. 200–1500, 96
The Mind of the Oxford Movement, 740
The Mind of the Talmud: An Intellectual History of the Bavli, 620, 627
The Mind of Voltaire, 218
Mind Only: A Philosophical and Doctrinal Analysis of the Vijnanavada, 514
Minds, Machines, and Evolution, 382

The Mind's I, 396
The Mind's Journey to God, 113
Mine Eyes Have Seen the Glory, 752
Minima Moralia, 393
The Ministry in Historical Perspective, 679
The Minoan-Mycenaean Religion, 487
Miracle and Natural Law in Graeco-Roman and Early Christian Thought, 99
Miracle in the Early Christian World: A Study in Sociohistorical Method, 689
The Miracle of Love, 746
The Miracle of Mindfulness! A Manual on Meditation, 561
Miracles and Pilgrims: Popular Beliefs in Medieval England, 726
Miracles and the Medieval Mind: Theory, Record, and Event, 1000–1215, 701
Miraculous Tales of the Lotus Sutra from Ancient Japan, 537
Mircea Eliade: The Romanian Roots, 1907–1945, 474
Mircea Eliade and the Dialectic of the Sacred, 474
Mircea Eliade's Vision for a New Humanism, 474
The Mirror of Faith, 103
The Mirror of Herodotus, 480
The Mirror of Meaning: Donald Davidson and the Theory of Interpretation, 283
Mirrors of the Jewish Mind, 636
The Mishnah, 610, 810
Mishnah: A New Translation, 611
Mishnah: Introduction and Reader: An Anthology, 611
Mishnah's Division of Agriculture: A History and Theology of Seder Zeraim, 609
Mishnayoth, 609
Mishneh Torah: Maimonides' Code of Law and Ethics, 627
The Missionary Enterprise in China and America, 532
Mistress Anne: The Exceptional Life of Anne Boleyn, 726

Mitra-Varuna: An Essay on Two Indo-European Representations of Sovereignty, 471
Models and Analogies in Science, 405
Models of God: Theology for an Ecological Nuclear Age, 745, 884
The Mode of Information: Poststructuralism and Social Context, 267
Modern Aesthetics, 131
Modern American Religion, 753
Modern American Spiritualism, 851
A Modern Approach to Islam, 373
A Modern Catholic Dictionary, 717
Modern Catholicism, 744
A Modern China and a New World, 361
Modern Christian Thinkers, 275
Modern Congo Prophets: Religion in a Plural Society, 467
Modern Faith and Thought, 746
Modern German Philosophy, 28
Modern Greek Philosophers on the Human Soul, 29
Modern Greek Thought, 29
The Modern Impulse of Traditional Judaism, 654
Modern Indian Interpreters of the Bhagavad Gita, 508
Modern Indian Responses to Religious Pluralism, 898
Modern Introduction to Philosophy, 20
Modern Islamic Literature: From 1800 to the Present, 567
The Modernist Movement in the Roman Church, 742
The Modernist Muslim Movement in Indonesia, 1900–1942, 373
Modernity within Tradition, 653
The Modernization of French Jewry, 635
Modern Japan through Its Weddings, 540
Modern Jewish Ethics: Theory and Practice, 598
Modern Jewish Religious Movements, 651

Modern Movements in European Philosophy, 27
Modern Philosophy: The French Enlightenment to Kant, 160
The Modern Prince and Other Writings, 287
Modern Revivalism: Charles Grandison Finney to Billy Graham, 753
The Modern Theme, 315
The Modern Theologians, 718, 888
Modern Thought and Literature in France, 28
Modern Trends in Hinduism, 507
Modern Trends in Islam, 373, 569
Modern Varieties of Judaism, 651
Modern Witchcraft and Psychoanalysis, 865
Modes of Being, 338, 339
The Modes of Scepticism: Ancient Texts and Modern Interpretations, 58
Modes of Thought, 341
Mohamet and His Successors, 588
Mohammad (Bey), 588
Mohammad (Dibble), 588
Mohammad and the Course of Islam, 588
The Mohammadan Dynasties, 570
Mohammedanism: An Historical Survey, 569
The Moment of Christian Witness, 904
Monadology, 167
The Monadology and Other Philosophical Writings, 176
Money and Power in the New Religions, 857
A Mongolian Living Buddha: Biography of the Kanjurwa Khutughtu, 542
Monkey on a Stick, 862
Monks, Bishops, and Pagans: Christian Culture in Gaul and Italy, 700
Montaigne: A Biography, 146
Montaigne and Bayle: Variations on the Theme of Skepticism, 146
Montaigne and Melancholy: The Wisdom of the Essays, 146
Montaigne's Discovery of Man: The Humanization of a Humanist, 146

Montaillou: The Promised Land of Error, 699
Montesquieu: A Critical Biography, 210
Montesquieu and Rousseau: Forerunners of Sociology, 210
Montesquieu and Social Theory, 210
Montesquieu's Idea of Justice, 210
Montesquieu's Philosophy of Liberalism: A Commentary on the Spirit of the Laws, 210
Moon, Sun and Witches, 458
The Moon Bamboo, 561
The Moonies: A Psychological Analysis of the Unification Church, 871
Moonies in America: Cult, Church and Crusade, 871
Moore: G. E. Moore and the Cambridge Apostles, 29
Moral Absolute: An Essay on the Nature and Rationale of Morality, 317
The Moral and Political Thought of Mahatma Gandhi, 352
Moral Conduct and Authority: The Place of Adab in South Asian Islam, 575
Moral Consciousness and Communicative Action, 404
Moral Differences, 389
Moralia, 489, 490
Morality and Ethics in Early Christianity, 690
Morality and the Human Future in the Thought of Teilhard de Chardin, 337
Moral Knowledge and Its Methodology in Aristotle, 70
The Moral Limits of the Criminal Law, 386
Moral Man and Immoral Society: A Study in Ethics and Politics, 783, 784
A Moral Military, 388
The Moral Philosophy of Josiah Royce, 250
The Moral Philosophy of Richard Price, 211
The Moral Philosophy of T. H. Green, 230
The Moral Philsophy of G. E. Moore, 312
The Moral Sense, 204
Morals on the Book of Job, 710

Moral Values in the Ancient World, 48
The Moral Vision of Dorothy Day: A Feminist Perspective, 766
Mordecai M. Kaplan and the Development of Reconstructionism, 667
More of My Life, 273
More's Utopia: The Biography of an Idea, 147
A Mormon Bibliography, 1830–1930, 845
The Mormon Experience: A History of the Latter-Day Saints, 845
Mormonism: The Story of a New Religious Tradition, 846
Mormonism in Transition: The Latter-Day Saints and Their Church, 1890–1930, 845
Mormons, 846
The Mormon's War on Poverty: A History of L.D.S. Welfare, 1830–1990, 846
Morning Hours, 209
Morritz Schlick, 333
Mortals and Immortals: Collected Essays, 493
Mortal Vision: The Wisdom of Euripides, 475
Moses and Monotheism, 424
Moses Hess: Prophet of Communism and Zionism, 655
Moses Mendelssohn: A Biographical Study, 209
The Most Ancient Testimony, 126
Mother Earth: An American Story, 464
Mother's First-Born Daughters: Early Shaker Writings on Women and Religion, 849
Mother Teresa: Her Work and Her People, 743
Motivation and the Moral Sense in Francis Hutcheson's Ethical Theory, 203
Movements and Issues in World Religions, 349
Mozart: Traces of Transcendence, 775
Much Ado about Nothing, 126
Muhammad (Cook), 588
Muhammad (Lings), 588
Muhammad (Rodinson), 589
Muhammad: Prophet and Statesman, 589

Muhammad: The Man and His Faith, 588
Muhammad and the Conquests of Islam, 588
Muhammad and the Rise of Islam, 588
Muhammad at Mecca, 589
Muhammad at Medina, 589
Multiculturalism and "The Politics of Recognition," 415
Multipurpose Tools for Bible Study, 795
Mummies, Myth and Magic: In Ancient Egypt, 442
The Muqaddimah, 584
The Muse Learns to Write, 460
Music, Spirit and Language in the Renaissance, 132
Music and the Reformation in England: 1549-1660, 737
Music and Worship in Pagan and Christian Antiquity, 689
Music in Western Civilization, 737
The Muslim Creed: Its Genesis and Historical Development, 577
Muslim Extremism in Egypt: The Prophet and the Pharaoh, 570
Muslim Institutions, 569
Muslim Intellectual: A Study of al-Ghazālī, 582
Muslim Minorities in the World Today, 570
Muslim Saints and Mystics, 574
Muslim Theology, 577
Mutuality: The Vision of Martin Buber, 662
The Mycenaean Origins of Greek Mythology, 487
The Mycenaean World, 446
My Guru and His Disciple, 872
My Land and My People, 356
My Life with Martin Luther King, Jr., 773
My People: Story of the Jews, 593
My Philosophical Development, 323
My Religion, 552
My Soul Looks Back, 763
The Mysteries of Mithra, 450
The Mysteries of Selflessness, 374
The Mysterious Play of Kali:

An Interpretive Study of Ramakrishna, 355
The Mystery of Being, 304
Mystery Religions in the Ancient World, 450
Mystical and Mythological Explanatory Works of Assyrian and Babylonian Scholars, 545
The Mystical Element in Heidegger's Thought, 292
Mystical Elements in Muhammad, 588
Mystical Islam: An Introduction to Sufism, 574
The Mystical Philosophy of Muhyid Din-Ibnul 'Arabi, 583
Mystical Poems of Rumi: Second Selection, 589
The Mystical Theology of St. Bernard, 112, 286
Mystic and Pilgrim: The "Book" and the World of Margery Kempe, 698
Mysticism: Christian and Buddhist, 558
Mysticism and Dissent, 724
Mysticism and Guilt-Consciousness in Schelling's Philosophical Development, 252
Mysticism and Logic and Other Essays, 323
Mysticism and Religious Tradition, 575
Mysticism and the Early South German-Austrian Anabaptist Movement, 1525-1531, 724
Mysticism East and West, 488
Mystics, Philosophers, and Politicians, 130
Mystics and Commissars, 567
Mystics and Zen Masters, 781
The Mystics of Islam: An Introduction to Sufism, 576
The Mystics of the Church, 679
Myth, Cosmos, and Society: Indo-European Themes of Creation and Destruction, 435
Myth, Legend and Custom in the Old Testament, 477
Myth, Rhetoric, and the Voice of Authority, 477
Myth, Ritual, and Kingship in Buganda, 463
Myth and Cult among Primitive Peoples, 429, 432

Myth and Law among the Indo-Europeans, 436
Myth and Meaning in Early Taoism, 528
Myth and Mystery, 811
Myth and Philosophy: A Contest of Truths, 37, 428
Myth and Religion of the North, 437
Myth and Ritual in Christianity, 881
The Myth and Ritual School: J. G. Frazer and the Cambridge Ritualists, 479
Myth and Society in Ancient Greece, 493
Myth and Thought among the Greeks, 49, 493
Myth and Tragedy in Ancient Greece, 493
Myth in Primitive Psychology, 486
The Myth of Christian Uniqueness, 898
The Myth of God Incarnate, 885
Myth of the Eternal Return, 473
The Myth of the Judeo-Christian Tradition, 648
The Myth of the State, 279
Mythography: The Study of Myths and Rituals, 428
Mythologies, 428
Mythologies: From Gingee to Kuruksetra, 504
Mythologies and Philosophies of Salvation in the Theistic Traditions of India, 505
Mythologies of the Ancient World, 428, 439
Mythologiques, 428
Myths about St. Bartholomew's Day Massacres, 1572-1576, 732
Myths from Mesopotamia: Creation, the Flood, Gilgamesh, and Others, 545
The Myths of Plato, 84
Myths of the Hindus and Buddhists, 503
My Tibet, 560
My World and Its Value, 345
My World of Astrology, 860

Nag Hammadi, Gnosticism, and Early Christianity, 453
The Nag Hammadi Library, 812
The Nag Hammadi Library in English, 453, 686

Nahuat Myth and Social Structure, 465
Naming and Necessity, 301
Naming the Whirlwind: The Renewal of God-Language, 744
Napoleon, the Jews and the Sanhedrin, 637
Napoleon and the Jews, 636
Nathan the Wise, 208
Nationalism and History: Essays on Old and New Judaism, 657
Nationalism and the Jewish Ethic: Basic Writings of Ahad Ha'am, 657
A Nation of Behavers, 753
Native American Religions: An Introduction, 464
Native American Religions: North America, 465
Native American Traditions: Sources and Interpretations, 464
Native Religions of North America, 464
The Natural and the Supernatural Jew, 646
The Natural History of Religion, 201
Naturalism and Ontology, 333
Naturalism and the Human Spirit, 265
The Naturalism of Condillac, 195
Natural Knowledge of God in the Philosophy of Jacques Maritain, 765
Natural Law, 232
Natural Law and Human Dignity, 277
The Natural Philosophy of Galileo, 143
A Natural Theology for Our Time, 289
Natural Theories of Mind, 383
Nature, Change and Agency in Aristotle's Physics: A Philosophical Study, 71
Nature, Man, and Society in the Twelfth Century, 101, 696
The Nature and Destiny of Man, 784
Nature and Life, 341
Nature and Man, 338, 339
Nature in Asian Traditions of Thought: Essays in Environmental Philosophy, 498, 502, 512, 522, 534
The Nature of All Being: A

Study of Wittgenstein's Modal Atomism, 345
The Nature of Belief, 783
The Nature of Doctrine: Religion and Theology in a Postliberal Age, 889
The Nature of Existence, 303
The Nature of Man and His Relation with the Universe, 323
The Nature of Man in Early Stoic Philosophy, 57
The Nature of the Gods, 72
The Nature of Thought, 276
Nature Religion in America: From the Algonkian Indians to the New Age, 841
Nature's Nation, 35
Naven, 461
Near-Death Experiences: An Annotated Bibliography, 866
Near Eastern Religious Texts Relating to the Old Testament, 810
Necessary Questions: An Introduction to Philosophy, 19
Necessity, Cause and Blame: Perspectives on Aristotle's Theory, 71
The Necessity of Pragmatism: John Dewey's Conception of Philosophy, 225
The Need for Roots, 788
Negara: Theatre-State in 19th Century Bali, 478
Negative Dialectics, 393
Neither Angel nor Beast: The Life and Work of Blaise Pascal, 185
Neo-Assyrian Treaties and Loyalty Oaths, 546
Neo-Confucian Education: The Formative Stage, 526
Neo-Confucian Thought in Action: Wang Yang-ming's Youth, 362
Neo-Hindu Views of Christianity, 509, 553, 563
The Neolithic of the Near East, 434
Neoplatonism, 62
Neoplatonism and Christian Thought, 62, 99
Neoplatonism and Gnosticism, 62, 63
Neoplatonism and Islamic Thought, 61, 576
Neoplatonism and Jewish Thought, 646
Neoplatonism of the Italian Renaissance, 130

Neo-Platonists, 62
Neostoicism and the Early Modern State, 129
Neurophilosophy, 382
Never at Rest: A Biography of Isaac Newton, 184
Nevertheless: The Varieties and Shortcomings of Religious Pacifism, 896
The New Age: Notes of a Fringewatcher, 866
The New Age Encyclopedia, 4, 866
The New American Bible: Revised New Testament, 798
The New American Bible: Translated from the Original Languages with Critical Use of All the Ancient Sources, 798, 803
The New American Bible, 803
The New American Philosophers, 267
The New American Standard Bible, 801
The New Anti-Semitism, 639
The New Archaeology and the Ancient Maya, 456
The New Being, 787
The New Capitalists, 270
The New Catholic Encyclopedia, 5, 93, 675
The New Century Bible Commentary, 820
The New Church in the New World, 851
The New Comparative Mythology, 472
The New Conservatism, 404
The New Constellation, 262, 292
A New Creation Story: The Creative Spirituality of Teilhard de Chardin, 337
The New Cults, 858
The New Dictionary of Existentialism, 3, 14
New Dictionary of Theology, 4, 5
New Directions in European Historiography, 728
New Encyclopedia of Philosophy, 15
The New England Mind: From Colony to Province, 753
New Essays Concerning Human Understanding, 176
A New Face of Hinduism: The Swaminarayan Religion, 509

The New Golden Bough, 476
The New Harmony Communities, 844
New Heaven, New Earth: A Study of Millenarian Activities, 467
The New Héloise, 212
A New History of India, 351
The New International Commentary on the New Testament, 820
The New International Commentary on the Old Testament, 820
New International Dictionary of New Testament Theology, 818
The New International Dictionary of the Christian Church, 675, 717
The New International Greek Testament Commentary, 821
A New Introduction to Philosophy, 20
The New Jerome Biblical Commentary, 819
The New Jerusalem Bible, 798, 803
The New Jewish Encyclopedia, 593
A New Jewish Ethics, 648
A New Jewish Theology in the Making, 661
The New Jewish Wedding, 601
The New Jews, 641
The New Leviathan: Man, Society, Civilization and Barbarism, 282
New Light on the Most Ancient East, 438
Newman, 783
Newman: His Life and Spirituality, 783
Newman after a Hundred Years, 783
Newman the Theologian: A Reader, 782
The New Nietzsche, 246
The New Oxford Annotated Bible with the Apocryphal/Deuterocanonical Books, 798
New Perspectives on Galileo, 143
New Perspectives on Israeli History: The Early Years of the State, 643
New Realism: Cooperative Studies in Philosophy, 264
New Reform Responsa, 598
The New Religions: Insights into the Cult Phenomenon, 855
New Religions, 855
New Religions and Mental Health: Understanding the Issues, 856
New Religions and the Theological Imagination in America, 841
The New Religions of Japan, 541
The New Religious Consciousness, 855
New Religious Movements: A Perspective for Understanding Society, 855
New Religious Movements: A Practical Introduction, 855
New Religious Movements in the United States and Canada, 3, 854
The New Schaff-Herzog Encyclopedia of Religious Knowledge, 717
The New Science, 215
The New Scientific Spirit, 274
A New Song: Celibate Women in the First Three Christian Centuries, 689
New Spirituality and the Christ Experience of the Twenty-First Century, 879
New Studies in Berkeley's Philosophy, 192
The New Testament: A Guide to Its Writings, 829
The New Testament: An Introduction, 816
The New Testament: The History of the Investigations of Its Problems, 814
New Testament Abstracts: A Record of Current Periodical Literature, 8, 796
The New Testament and Early Christianity, 817
The New Testament and Its Modern Interpreters, 813
The New Testament and Mythology, and Other Basic Writings, 743, 825, 831
New Testament Apocrypha, 811
New Testament Background: Selected Documents, 617, 810
The New Testament Environment, 808
The New Testament Era: The World of the Bible from 500 B.C. to A.D. 100, 605
New Testament Exegesis: A Handbook for Students and Pastors, 814
New Testament Message: A Biblical Theological Commentary, 821
The New Testament Octapla, 798
New Testament Theology: Basic Issues in the Current Debate, 827
The New Testament World, 807
New Twentieth-Century Encyclopedia of Religious Knowledge, 3, 717
New Vico Studies, 217
The New Westminster Dictionary of Liturgy and Worship, 675
The New Westminster Dictionary of the Bible, 819
The New Woman/New Earth: Sexist Ideologies and Human Liberation, 785
A New World Jerusalem, 852
The New World of Islam, 573
A New Zionism, 658
New Zionism and the Foreign Policy System of Israel, 658
Niccolò Machiavelli, 145
Nichiren: The Buddhist Prophet, 536
Nichiren Shoshu Buddhism and the Soka Gakkai in America, 859
Nicholas of Autrecourt, 104
Nicholas of Cusa, 149
Nicholas of Cusa and Medieval Political Thought, 149
Nicholaus Cusanus: A Fifteenth-Century Vision of Man, 149
Nicodemos of the Holy Mountain: A Handbook of Spiritual Counsel, 756
Nicolas Berdyaev, 275
Nicomachean Ethics, 66
Niebuhr and His Age, 784
Nietzsche (Heidegger), 291
Nietzsche (Rosenberg), 247
Nietzsche (Salomé), 247
Nietzsche (Schacht), 247
Nietzsche: A Collection of Critical Essays, 248
Nietzsche: A Frenzied Look, 246
Nietzsche: An Introduction to His Philosophical Activity, 247

Nietzsche: A Self-Portrait from His Letters, 246
Nietzsche: Life as Literature, 247
Nietzsche: Philosopher, Psychologist, Antichrist, 247
Nietzsche and Asian Thought, 350
Nietzsche and the Question of Interpretation, 295
Nietzsche as Philosopher, 247
Nietzsche's Existential Imperative, 247
Nietzsche's Philosophy of Art, 248
Nietzsche's Teaching: An Interpretation of Thus Spoke Zarathustra, 247
Nietzsche's View of Socrates, 89
Nietzsche's Zarathustra, 247
Nihongi, 536
Nihon Kodai Bunka, 366
Nihon Seishin-shi Kenkyū, 366
Nine and a Half Mystics: The Kabbala Today, 630
Nine Gates to the Chassidic Mysteries, 632
The Nine Questions People Ask about Judaism, 596
The Nine Songs: A Study of Shamanism in Ancient China, 525
Nine Talmudic Readings, 901
The Nineteen Letters of Ben Uziel on Judaism, 665
Nineteenth-Century Philosophy, 160
Nineteenth-Century Religious Thought in the West, 741
Nishida Kitarō, 365
NIV Exhaustive Concordance, 818
The Nobel Peace Prize and the Dalai Lama, 357
The Noble Savage: Jean-Jacques Rousseau, 1754–1762, 213
No Man Knows My History: The Life of Joseph Smith, 845, 879
The Non-Jewish Jew and Other Essays, 655
The Non-Reality of Free Will, 380
Non-Renunciation: Themes and Interpretations in Hindu Culture, 505
Norito: A Translation of the Ancient Japanese Ritual Prayers, 536

The Normative Grounds of Social Criticism: Kant, Rawls, and Habermas, 316
The Normative Theory of Individual Choice, 314
The Norms of Nature: Studies in Hellenistic Ethics, 56
The Northern School of and the Formation of Early Ch'an Buddhism, 530
Notebooks, 306
Notebooks 1914–1916, 344
Notebooks for an Ethics, 329
Notes on Love in a Tamil Family, 506
Notes on the Nicomanchean Ethics of Aristotle, 71
Notes to Literature, 393
Not Free to Desist: The American Jewish Committee 1906–1966, 638
Nothing Is Hidden: Wittgenstein's Criticism of His Early Thought, 346
The Nothingness beyond God, 365
Not in Heaven: The Nature and Function of Halachah, 648
Not Necessarily the New Age: Critical Essays, 866
Novum Organum and Related Writings, 165
Novum Testamentum Graece, 794
Nuer Religion, 475

Objective Knowledge, 409
Objectivity, Realism, and Truth: Philosophical Papers, 413
Observation and Objectivity, 384
Occasions for Philosophy, 20
The Occult Establishment, 856
The Occult in America: New Historical Perspectives, 841
The Occult Philosophy, 133
Occult Philosophy in the Elizabethan Age, 132
The Occult Underground, 842
The Occult World of Madame Blavatsky, 874
Oceania: The Native Cultures of Australia and the Pacific Islands, 462
Ocean of Wisdom: Guidelines for Living, 560

Ockham, Descartes, and Hume: Self-Knowledge, Substance, and Causality, 163
Ockham's Theory of Propositions: Part II of the Summa Logicae, 120
Ockham's Theory of Terms: Part I of the Summa Logicae, 120
Ockham to Suarez, 736
The Odyssey, 482, 483
Of Being and Unity, 153
Of Grammatology, 397
Of Human Freedom, 251
Of Mind and Other Matters, 403
Of Revelation and Revolution, Vol. 1, 467
Of Spirit: Heidegger and the Question, 397
Of the Laws of Ecclesiastical Polity, 734
Of the Standard of Taste and Other Essays, 201
Of the Vanitie and Uncertaintie of Artes and Sciences, 133
Of Wisdome, 125
O Jerusalem, 642
Olavus Petri and the Ecclesiastical Transformation in Sweden (1521–1552), 730
Old Arts and New Theology, 696
The Old Catholic Sourcebook, 859
Old Diary Leaves, 853
The Older Sophists, 54
The Oldest Biography of Spinoza, 188
The Old Protestantism and the New: Essays on the Reformation Heritage, 741
The Old Rabbinic Doctrine of God, 621
The Old Social Classes and the Revolutionary Movements of Iraq, 578
The Old Testament: An Introduction, 816, 817
Old Testament Abstracts, 8, 796
Old Testament Books for Pastor and Teacher, 795
Old Testament Introduction, 817
Old Testament Library, 821
Old Testament Message, 821
The Old Testament Pseudepigrapha, 810
The Old Testament since the Reformation, 813

Old Testament Theology: Basic Issues in the Current Debate, 827, 838

The Old Testament World, 807

The Olmec: Mother Culture of Mesoamerica, 455

The Olmecs: The Oldest Civilization in Mexico, 455

The Olmec World, 455

Omega Project: Near Death Experiences, UFO Encounters, and Mind at Large, 870

Omnipotence and Other Theological Mistakes, 289

On Aristotle and Greek Tragedy, 69

On Aristotle's Categories, 62

On Being a Jewish Feminist, 650

On Being and the One, 152

On Being Christian, 774

On Being in the World: Wittgenstein and Heidegger on Seeing Aspects, 294, 346

Once-Born, Twice-Born Zen: The Soto and Rinzai Schools of Japan, 537

On Certainty, 344

On Christian Doctrine, 109

On Conjectures, 148

On Copia of Words and Ideas, 139

The One and Its Relation to Intellect in Plotinus, 86

One and Many in Aristotle's Metaphysics: The Central Books, 68

One and Many in Presocratic Philosophy, 51

One-Dimensional Man, 408

On Education, 224

One-Handed Basket Weaving: Poems on the Theme of Work, 589

One Hundred Years of Old Testament Interpretation, 813

One Hundred Years of Theosophy, 853

On Enchantments, 153

Oneself as Another, 319

On Fate, Free Will and Predestination, 153

On Feeling, Knowing, and Valuing: Selected Writings, 332

On First Principles: Being Koetschau's Text of the De Principiis, 116

On Formal and Universal Unity, 105, 154

On Free Choice of the Will, 109

On Free Will, 138, 155

Ongoing Journey, 317

On Hegel's Logic, 233

On Heroes, Hero Worship, and the Heroic in History, 588

On Hindu Ritual and the Goddess, 504

On His Own Ignorance and That of Many Others, 150

On Ideas: Aristotle's Criticism of Plato's Theory of Forms, 68

On Jews and Judaism in Crisis: Selected Essays, 672

On Job: God-Talk and the Suffering of the Innocent, 769

On Judaism, 662

On Kingship to the King of Cyprus, 117

On Law, Morality, and Politics, 118

On Learned Ignorance, 148, 149

On Liberty, 244

On Love and Happiness, 336

On Metaphysics, 395

On Moral Medicine: Theological Perspectives in Medical Ethics, 893

On Motion and on Mechanics, 142

On Old Age and on Friendship, 72

Onomasticon, 709

On Philosophical Style, 276

On Poetic Imagination and Reverie, 274

On Religion, 425, 575

On Religion: Speeches to Its Cultured Despisers, 253, 254

On Revolution, 394

On Rhetoric, 66

On Socialists and "The Jewish Question" after Marx, 656

On the Art of the Kabbalah, 130

On the Basis of Morality, 255

On the Cause, Principle and One, 135

On the Causes of Plants, 90

On the Church of Christ: The Person of the Church and Her Personnel, 306

On the Composition of Images, Signs and Ideas, 135

On the Dignity of Man, on Being and the One, Heptaplus, 153

On the Duty of Man and Citizen According to Natural Law, 186

On the Edge of Destruction: Jews of Poland between the Two World Wars, 636

On the Essence of Finite Being as Such, on the Existence of the Essence, and Their Distinction, 105, 154

On the Eternal in Man, 332

On the Eternity of the World, 118

On the Existence of God, 221

On the Fourfold Root of the Principle of Sufficient Reason, 255

On the Genealogy of Morals, 245, 246

On the Glaubenslehre: Two Letters to Dr. Leucke, 254

On the Imagination, 152

On the Infinite, the Universe and Worlds, 135

On the Interpretation of Empedocles, 53

On the Kabbalah and Its Symbolism, 672

On the Law of Nature and Nations, 186

On the Lives and Characters of the Philosophers, 16

On the Logic of the Social Sciences, 404

On the Most Ancient Wisdom of the Italians, 30, 216

On the Motives Which Led Husserl to Transcendental Idealism, 235

On the Natural State of Men, 186

On the Nature of Things, 75

On the Philosophy of History, 306

On the Plurality of Worlds, 381

On the Power of God, 118

On the Proof by Spirit and Power, 207

On the Remedies of Good and Bad Fortune, 150

On the Secret Conflict of My Worries, 150

On the Several Senses of Being in Aristotle, 67, 221

On the Solitary Life, 150

On the Soul and Life, 156
On the Study Methods of
    Our Time, 215, 216
On the Sublime and Beauti-
    ful, 192
On the Supreme Good, 96
On the Trial of the Arawaks,
    466
On the True Good, 155
On the Truth of Being: Re-
    flections on Heidegger's
    Later Philosophy, 293
On the Truth of the Catholic
    Faith, 118
On the Unity of the Intellect,
    118
On the Use of Philosophy:
    Three Essays, 306
On the Vanity of Pagan
    Learning, 151
On the Various Kinds of Dis-
    tinctions, 105, 154
On the Way to Language,
    291
On Thinking, 325
On Time and Being, 291
The Ontological Argument,
    108
The Ontological Argument of
    Charles Hartshorne, 289
Ontological Relativity, 411
Ontology, 284
Ontology and Alterity in
    Merleau-Ponty, 311
On True and False Ideas,
    164
On Truth, 118
On Universals: The Tractatus
    de Universalibus, 714
On University Studies, 252
On Virginity: Against Remar-
    riage, 707
On Vision and Colors, 254
On War and Morality, 389
On Women and Judaism: A
    View from Tradition, 650
Open Secret: Versions of
    Rumi, 589
Open Secrets, 859
The Open Society and Its
    Enemies, 409
The Open Universe, 409
Opera, 77
Opera: Enneades, 86
Opera Posthuma, 186
Operations of the Geometric
    and Military Compass, 142
Oppositions of Religious
    Doctrines, 898
Oppression and Liberty, 788
Opus Maius, 111
Opus Postumum, 204, 205
Oral Historiography, 460

Orality and Literacy: The
    Technologizing of the
    World, 460
Oral Poetry: Its Nature, Sig-
    nificance and Social Con-
    text, 460
Oral Torah: The Sacred
    Books of Judaism: An In-
    troduction, 612
Oration on the Dignity of
    Man, 153
Ordeal by Labyrinth: Conver-
    sations with Claude-Henri
    Rocquet, 473
Order and Chance: The Pat-
    tern of Diderot's Thought,
    196
Order in Paradox: Myth, Rit-
    ual, and Exchange among
    Nepal's Tamang, 541
Orderly Chaos: The Mandala
    Principle, 357
The Order of Assassins, 570
The Order of Things, 400
The Organization of Thought,
    Educational and Scientific,
    341
Organized Miracles, 864
The Orientalizing Revolution,
    471
Oriental Philosophies, 349,
    523, 570
Oriental Philosophy: A West-
    erner's Guide to Eastern
    Thought, 523
The Oriental Religions and
    American Thought, 508,
    841
Origen: Spirit and Fire: A
    Thematic Anthology of His
    Writings, 63
Origen: The Bible and Phi-
    losophy in the Third Cen-
    tury Church, 117
Origen and the Life of the
    Stars: A History of an
    Idea, 63
The Original Teachings of
    Ch'an Buddhism, 529
The Origin and Goal of His-
    tory, 299
The Origin and Growth of
    Plato's Logic, 82
The Origin and Meaning of
    Hasidism, 632
Origin of Dewey's Instrumen-
    talism, 226
The Origin of Our Knowl-
    edge of Right and Wrong,
    222
The Origin of Philosophy,
    315
The Origin of the Gods: A

Psychoanalytic Study of
    Greek Theogonic Myth,
    446
The Origin of the Idea of
    Crusade, 692
The Origin of the Jesuits,
    770
The Origin of the Soul in St.
    Augustine's Later Works,
    110
Origins: Creation Texts from
    the Ancient Mediterra-
    nean, 439
The Origins and Develop-
    ment of Classical Hin-
    duism, 498
The Origins of Aristotelian
    Science, 68
The Origins of Biblical Law:
    The Decalogues and the
    Book of the Covenant, 627
The Origins of Calvin's The-
    ology of Music,
    1536–1553, 737
The Origins of Certainty:
    Means and Meanings in
    Pascal's Pensées, 185
The Origins of Christianity:
    Sources and Documents,
    617, 811
The Origins of European
    Thought about the Body,
    the Mind, the Soul, the
    World, Time and Fate, 49
The Origins of Greek
    Thought, 49, 493
The Origins of Isma'ilism,
    575
The Origins of Judaism: Reli-
    gion, History, and Litera-
    ture in Late Antiquity, 605
The Origins of Nonviolence:
    Tolstoy and Gandhi in
    Their Historical Settings,
    553
The Origins of Philosophy,
    50
Origins of Pragmatism, 237,
    249, 273
Origins of Religious Art and
    Iconography in Preclassic
    Mesoamerica, 455
The Origins of Stoic Cosmol-
    ogy, 55
The Origins of the Christian
    Mystical Tradition: From
    Plato to Denys, 63, 689
The Origins of the Druze
    People and Religion, with
    Extracts from Their Sa-
    cred Writings, 575
The Origins of the Family,

Private Property and the State, 227

Origins of the Kabbalah, 672

The Origins of the Mithraic Mysteries, 450

The Origins of the Modern Jew, 634

The Origins of the Platonic Academy of Florence, 126

The Origins of Totalitarianism, 394

Orthodox Church, 694, 756

The Orthodox Church: Its Past and Its Role in the World Today, 679, 756

The Orthodox Church in the Byzantine Empire, 693

The Orthodox Eastern Church, 755

Orthodox Theology: An Introduction, 693, 756

Orthodoxy, Roman Catholicism and Anglicanism, 755

Orthodoxy and Heresy in Earliest Christianity, 98, 685

Orthodoxy in American Jewish Life, 654

The Orwellian World of Jehovah's Witnesses, 863

The Other Bible, 810

The Other Heading, 397

Other People's Myths: The Cave of Echoes, 428

Otherwise Than Being or Beyond Essence, 901

The Other World, 851

Ottoman Empire and Islamic Tradition, 570

"O un Amy!" Essays on Montaigne in Honor of Donald M. Frame, 146

Our Gang: Jewish Crime and the New York Jewish Community, 1900–1940, 639

Our Knowledge of the External World, 323

Our Knowledge of the Growth of Knowledge, 410

Our Life with Mr. Gurdjieff, 875

Our Masters Taught Rabbinic Stories and Sayings, 613

Our Philosophical Traditions, 17, 161

Our Philosophy, 373

Our Public Life, 339

Our Right to Choose: Toward a New Ethic of Abortion, 895

Our Sages, God, and Israel:

An Anthology of the Jerusalem Talmud, 612

An Outline of Philosophy, 23

An Outline of the Theology of the New Testament, 827

Outlines of a Philosophy of Art, 282

Outlines of Mahayana Buddhism, 557, 558

Outlines of the History of Ethics, 257

Out of Step: An Unquiet Life in the Twentieth Century, 298

Out of the Ghetto: The Social Background of Jewish Emancipation, 1770–1870, 636

Outward Signs: The Language of Christian Symbolism, 716

Owen Barfield on C. S. Lewis, 776

Oxford Bible Atlas, 809

Oxford Classical Dictionary, 818

The Oxford Companion to the Bible, 818

The Oxford Companion to the Mind, 382

The Oxford Dictionary of Byzantium, 693

The Oxford Dictionary of Popes, 675

The Oxford Dictionary of the Christian Church, 675, 716

The Oxford History of the Popes, 678

The Oxford Illustrated History of Christianity, 2, 675

The Oxford Study Bible: Revised English Bible with the Apocrypha, 798

Pachomian Koinonia, 690

A Packet of Letters, 782

Pagan: Art and Architecture of Old Burma, 519

Pagan and Christian in an Age of Anxiety, 63, 449, 683

Paganism and Christianity, 100–425 C.E.: A Sourcebook, 449, 682

Paganism in the Roman Empire, 449

Pagan Rome and the Early Christians, 682

Pagans and Christians, 683

Paideia: The Ideals of Greek Culture, 48

Paideia Problems and Possibilities, 270

The Paideia Program: An Educational Syllabus, 270

The Paideia Proposal: An Educational Manifesto, 270

The Paleolithic Age, 433

Palestinian Judaism in the Time of Jesus Christ, 620

Palladius: Dialogue on the Life of St. John Chrysostom, 707

The Papal Encyclicals, 891

The Papal Monarchy: The Western Church from 1050 to 1250, 695

Parables in Midrash: Narrative and Exegesis in Rabbinic Literature, 613

The Parables of the Kingdom, 833

Paracelsus, 150

Paradigm Change in Theology: A Symposium for the Future, 775

Paradigms and Revolutions, 406

The Paradoxes of Freedom, 298

The Paradoxical Ascent to God, 853

Paramahansa Yogananda: In Memoriam, 557

Parapsychology, New Age and the Occult: A Source Encyclopedia, 854

Parerga and Paralipomena: Short Philosophical Essays, 255

Paris and Oxford Universities in the 13th and 14th Centuries, 102

Parmenides, 291

Parmenides: A Text with Translation, Commentary and Critical Essays, 52

Parmenides: Being, Bounds and Logic, 52

Parmenides, Plato and the Semantics of Not-Being, 83

Parmenides of Elea: Fragments, 52

The Parsees in India: A Minority as Agent of Social Change, 518

The Parthenon and Its Sculptures, 446

Particles and Ideas: Bishop Berkeley's Corpuscularian Philosophy, 192

A Partisan Guide to the Jewish Problem, 655

Part of My Life, 273
Pascal's Wager: A Study of Practical Reasoning in Philosophical Theology, 185, 317
The Passage of Nature, 342
A Passion for Truth, 665
The Passion of Michael Foucault, 401
The Passion of the Western Mind, 18
The Passions of the Soul: The Third Book of "De anima et vita," 156
Passover Anthology, 599
A Passover Haggadah, 599
A Passover Haggadah for Jewish Believers, 599
Passport to Heaven: Gender Roles in the Unification Church, 871
Pastoral Care, 710
The Path: A Spiritual Autobiography, 557
The Path of a Pioneer, 877
Path of Discipleship, 550
The Path of Subud, 873
Paths in Utopia, 655
The Path to Hope: Fragments from a Theologian's Journey, 747
Patrology, 690
The Pattern of Christian Truth, 100, 687
Pattern of Politics, 415
Patterns in Comparative Religion, 472
Patterns in Prehistory: Humankind's First Three Million Years, 432, 439
Patterns of Action: Religion and Ethics in Comparative Perspective, 893
Patterns of Reformation, 724
Paul, 824, 829
Paul: Apostle to the Gentiles, 824
Paul among the Jews and Gentiles, 617
Paul and His Interpreters: A Critical History, 826
Paul and Palestinian Judaism: A Comparison of Patterns of Religion, 617, 826
Paul and Rabbinic Judaism: Some Rabbinic Elements in Pauline Theology, 617
Paul of Venice: A Bibliographical Guide, 130
Paul the Apostle: The Triumph of God in Life and Thought, 824

Paul Tillich: His Life and Thought, 788
Paul Tillich and the Christian Message, 788
Peace and Disarmament, 896
Peace with God, 768
Peake's Commentary on the Bible, 819
Pedagogy of the Oppressed, 748
Peirce, 249
Peirce, Semiotic, and Pragmatism: Essays by Max H. Fisch, 249
Peirce and Pragmatism, 249
Peirce's Philosophy of Science, 317
Peirce's Theory of Scientific Discovery, 249
Pelagius: A Historical and Theological Study, 110
Pelican New Testament Commentaries, 821
The Pen and the Faith: Eight Modern Muslim Writers and the Qur'an, 574
The Penguin Dictionary of Religions, 4
The Penguin Dictionary of Saints, 675
The Penguin Guide to Ancient Egypt, 548
The Penguin History of the Church, 677
Pensées, 185
People Called Shakers: A Search for the Perfect Society, 849
Perceiving, 395
Perception, Expression and History, 311
Perceptual Acquaintance from Descartes to Reid, 163
Perennial Philosophical Issues, 21
The Perilous Vision of John Wyclif, 714
Periphyseon: The Division of Nature, 115
Peri theōn, 468
The Persecution of Peter Olivi, 101
Persian Letters, 209
Persian Mythology, 444, 547
A Persian Stronghold of Zoroastrianism, 547
Personal Memoirs of H. P. Blavatsky, 874
Personal Philosophy: The Art of Living, 20
Person and Community: Gha-

naian Philosophical Studies I, 371
Person and Community in American Philosophy, 34
Person and Object, 395
The Person and the Common Good, 306
Persons and Places: The Autobiography of George Santayana, 327
Persons and Their World: An Introduction to Philosophy, 23
Perspective in Whitehead's Metaphysics, 342
Perspectives in Philosophy: A Book of Readings, 19
Perspectives in the History of Religions, 420
Perspectives on Paul, 825
Perspectives on Peirce: Critical Essays on Charles Sanders Peirce, 249
Perspectives on the New Age, 866
Perspectives on Thomas Hobbes, 175
Persuasions of the Witch's Craft, 865
Perversity and Error, 97
Pesikta De-Rab Kahana, 610
Pesiqta deRab Kahana: An Analytical Translation and Explanation, 612
Peter Abelard, 106
Peter Maurin: Prophet in the Twentieth Century, 765
Peter of Ailly and the Harvest of Fourteenth-Century Philosophy, 104, 127
Petrarch (Bergin), 151
Petrarch (Mann), 151
Petrarch: An Introduction to the Canzoniere, 151
Petrarch: Poet and Humanist, 151
Petrarch's Eight Years in Milan, 151
Petrarch's Genius: Pentimento and Prophecy, 151
Petrarch's Later Years, 151
Petrarch's "Secretum": Its Making and Its Meaning, 151
The Peyote Cult, 467
Peyote Hunt: The Sacred Journey of the Huichol Indians, 465
The Peyote Religion among the Navaho, 467
Phaedo, 89
The Phaedo: A Platonic Labyrinth, 79

Phaedo, or on the Immortality of the Soul, 208
Phaedon; or, the Death of Socrates, 209
Pharisaism in the Making: Selected Essays, 615
The Pharisees, 615
The Pharisees: The Social Background of Their Faith, 615
Pharisees, Scribes and Sadducees in Palestinian Society: A Sociological Approach, 616
The Phenomenological Movement: An Historical Introduction, 235, 267
Phenomenology and the Foundation of the Sciences, 234
The Phenomenology of Perception, 310
The Phenomenology of Spirit, 231, 232
Phenomenon of Man, 336
The Phenomenon of Man Revisited, 337
Philip II, 737
Philo: Foundations of Religious Philosophy in Judaism, Christianity and Islam, 60, 100, 670
Philo, John and Paul: New Perspectives on Judaism and Early Christianity, 604
Philo of Alexandria: An Introduction, 60, 100, 670, 812
Philosopher at Large: An Intellectual Autobiography, 270
The Philosophers: Life and Thought, 18
Philosophers Ancient and Modern, 25
The Philosopher's Annual, 263
The Philosopher's Dictionary, 14
The Philosopher's Game, 18
The Philosopher's Guide to Sources, Research Tools, Professional Life, and Related Fields, 13
The Philosopher's Index, 14
Philosopher's Index: An International Index to Philosophical Periodicals, 8
The Philosopher's Index Thesaurus, 14
Philosophers Lead Sheltered Lives: A First Volume of Memoirs, 284

Philosophers of Consciousness, 320
Philosophers of the Scottish Enlightenment, 32, 212
Philosophers Speak for Themselves: Berkeley, Hume, and Kant, 163
Philosophers Speak for Themselves: From Descartes to Locke, 163
Philosophers Speak of God, 289
Philosophiae Moralis Institutio, 203
Philosophical Analysis: Its Development between the Two World Wars, 268
Philosophical Analysis in Latin America, 264, 379
The Philosophical Anthropology of George Herbert Mead, 309
Philosophical Apprenticeships, 402
The Philosophical Books of Cicero, 59
Philosophical Correspondence, 205
Philosophical Dictionary, 15, 217, 218
The Philosophical Discourse of Modernity, 404
Philosophical Essays, 176, 273
Philosophical Explanations, 314
Philosophical Foundations of Soviet Aesthetics, 31
Philosophical Fragments (Kierkegaard), 239
Philosophical Fragments (Schlegel), 253
Philosophical Fragments: 1901–1914 and the Philosopher and Peace, 304
Philosophical Grammar, 344
Philosophical Hermeneutics, 402
Philosophical Ideas in the United States, 36
The Philosophical Imagination: An Introduction to Philosophy, 19
Philosophical Investigations in the U.S.S.R., 30
Philosophical Issues in Aristotle's Biology, 68
Philosophical Letters, 169, 217, 218
The Philosophical Movement in the Thirteenth Century, 97

Philosophical Papers (Austin), 272
Philosophical Papers (Feyerbend), 399
Philosophical Papers (Moore), 312
Philosophical Papers (Putnam), 410
Philosophical Papers (Rorty), 413
Philosophical Papers (Taylor), 415
Philosophical Papers (von Wright), 338
Philosophical Papers 1896–1899 (Russell), 323
Philosophical Papers and Letters, 176
Philosophical Perspectives: History of Philosophy, 162, 333
Philosophical Perspectives: Metaphysics and Epistemology, 333
Philosophical Perspectives on Newtonian Science, 184
Philosophical Problems, 24
Philosophical Problems and Arguments: An Introduction, 20
Philosophical Profiles: Essays in a Pragmatic Mode, 262, 379
The Philosophical Propaedeutic, 232
Philosophical Questions: An Introductory Anthology, 23
Philosophical Radicals of 1832, 29
Philosophical Remarks, 344
Philosophical Studies, 304
Philosophical Subjects, 414
The Philosophical Theology of Duns Scotus, 114
Philosophical Theories, 22
Philosophical Thought in America, 33
Philosophical Thoughts, 195
Philosophical Trends in the Contemporary World, 267
Philosophical Works, 201
Philosophical Works Including the Works of Vision, 191
Philosophical Writing: An Introduction, 22
Philosophical Writings (Berkeley), 191
Philosophical Writings (Duns Scotus), 114
Philosophical Writings (William of Ockham), 120
Philosophic Problems, 22

Philosophic Thought in France and the United States, 34
Philosophic Way of Life in America, 36
Philosophies and Cultures, 39
Philosophies Men Live By, 20
Philosophies of India, 351
The Philosophies of Science, 384
Philosophizing with Socrates: An Introduction to the Study of Philosophy, 19
Philosophy, 300
Philosophy: A Guide to the Reference Literature, 6, 13
Philosophy: A Modern Encounter, 25
Philosophy: An Introduction, 20, 21, 25
Philosophy: An Introduction through Original Fiction, Discussion and Readings, 20
Philosophy: A Select, Classified Bibliography of Ethics, Economics, Law, Politics, Sociology, 14
Philosophy: East and West, 37
Philosophy: Paradox and Discovery, 22
Philosophy: The Basic Issues, 22
Philosophy: The Basics, 25
Philosophy, Religion and Science in the Seventeenth and Eighteenth Centuries, 740
Philosophy, Social Theory, and the Thought of George Herbert Mead, 308
Philosophy, Technology and the Arts in the Early Modern Era, 130
Philosophy after Darwin, 162, 267
Philosophy and an African Culture, 27, 372
Philosophy and Contemporary Problems: A Reader, 23
Philosophy and Culture, East and West: East-West Philosophy in Practical Perspective, 37
Philosophy and Feminist Thinking, 391
Philosophy and History: A Symposium, 265

Philosophy and Humanism, 128
Philosophy and Ideology, 30
Philosophy and Its Past, 18, 162
Philosophy and Knowledge: A Commentary on Plato's Theaetetus, 83
Philosophy and Literature in Latin America, 33
Philosophy and Logical Syntax, 278
Philosophy and Ordinary Language, 263
The Philosophy and Poetics of Gaston Bachelard, 274
The Philosophy and Psychology of Pietro Pomponazzi, 154
The Philosophy and Psychology of Sensation, 289
Philosophy and Public Policy, 298
Philosophy and Romantic Nationalism: The Case of Poland, 30
Philosophy and Science in the Islamic World, 373
Philosophy and Science in the Scottish Enlightenment, 32
Philosophy and the Human Condition, 19
Philosophy and the Idea of Freedom, 413
Philosophy and the Mirror of Nature, 378, 413
Philosophy and the Modern World, 161
Philosophy and Theology in the Middle Ages, 16
Philosophy and the Real World, 410
Philosophy and the World, 300
Philosophy and Tradition, 359
Philosophy as Metanoetics, 366
Philosophy before Socrates, 46
Philosophy Born of Struggle, 386
Philosophy East/Philosophy West, 37, 350
Philosophy for a New Generation, 20
Philosophy for Everyman: From Socrates to Sartre, 18
A Philosophy for Living: A Sketch of Aquinate Philosophy, 22

Philosophy from the Renaissance to the Romantic Age, 124
Philosophy from the Romantic Age to the Age of Reason, 159
Philosophy in Africa: Trends and Perspectives, 368
Philosophy in America, 35
Philosophy in America from Puritans to James, 34
Philosophy in and out of Europe, 264
Philosophy in France Today, 28, 266, 379
Philosophy in Process, 339
Philosophy in Russia: From Herzen to Lenin and Berdyaev, 39
Philosophy in the Middle Ages: The Christian, Islamic and Jewish Traditions, 94
Philosophy in the Soviet Union: A Survey of the Mid-Sixties, 31, 265
Philosophy in the Twentieth Century, 262, 273
Philosophy in World Perspective, 37, 263
Philosophy Journals and Serials: An Analytical Guide, 14
Philosophy Looks to the Future: Confrontation, Commitment and Utopia, 23
Philosophy Now, 24
The Philosophy of A. J. Ayer, 273
The Philosophy of Alfred North Whitehead, 41, 343
Philosophy of Aristotle, 66
Philosophy of Arithmetic, 234
The Philosophy of Art, 252
The Philosophy of Atomism and Other Essays, 1914–1919, 323
The Philosophy of Auguste Comte, 223
The Philosophy of Baruch Spinoza, 188
The Philosophy of Bergson, 220
The Philosophy of Bertrand Russell, 42, 324
Philosophy of Biological Science, 384
Philosophy of Biology Today, 385
The Philosophy of Brand Blanshard, 42, 276

The Philosophy of C. D. Broad, 42, 277

The Philosophy of C. I. Lewis, 42, 302

The Philosophy of Charles Hartshorne, 289

The Philosophy of Chrysippus, 57

The Philosophy of Clement of Alexandria, 63

The Philosophy of David Hume, 202

The Philosophy of Dr. Samuel Clarke and Its Critics, 194

Philosophy of Education, 224

The Philosophy of Ernst Cassirer, 42, 280

Philosophy of Existence, 300, 304

The Philosophy of Existentialism, 305

The Philosophy of F. H. Bradley, 221

The Philosophy of F.W.J. Schelling: History, System, and Freedom, 252

The Philosophy of Franz Brentano, 222

The Philosophy of Friedrich Nietzsche, 247

The Philosophy of G. E. Moore, 42, 312

The Philosophy of Gabriel Marcel, 42, 305

The Philosophy of George Herbert Mead, 309

The Philosophy of George Santayana, 42

The Philosophy of Georg Henrik von Wright, 42, 338

Philosophy of History, 218, 253

The Philosophy of Jean-Paul Sartre, 42, 331

The Philosophy of John Dewey, 42

Philosophy of Judaism, 601

The Philosophy of Karl Jaspers, 42, 300

The Philosophy of Karl Popper, 42, 410

The Philosophy of Language in Britain, 29

The Philosophy of Leibniz, 323

The Philosophy of Lev Shestov, 1866–1938: A Russian Religious Existentialist, 335

The Philosophy of Life, and Philosophy of Language, in a Course of Lectures, 253

Philosophy of Logic, 410, 411

The Philosophy of Loyalty, 250

Philosophy of Mahatma Gandhi, 553

The Philosophy of Malebranche, 182

The Philosophy of Marsilio Ficino, 141

The Philosophy of Martin Buber, 42

Philosophy of Mathematics, 410

The Philosophy of Mind, 232, 382, 383

Philosophy of Modern Music, 393

The Philosophy of Natural Magic, 133

Philosophy of Natural Science, 384

Philosophy of Nature, 232

The Philosophy of Nietzsche, 247

The Philosophy of Paul Ricoeur: An Anthology of His Work, 319

The Philosophy of Phineas P. Quimby, 878

Philosophy of Plato and Aristotle, 583

Philosophy of Plotinus: The Gifford Lectures at St. Andrews, 1917–1918, 86

The Philosophy of Popper, 410

The Philosophy of Robert Grosseteste, 115

The Philosophy of Rousseau, 213

The Philosophy of Rudolph Carnap, 42, 279

The Philosophy of Sarvepalli Radhakrishnan, 43, 354

The Philosophy of Schleiermacher, 254

The Philosophy of Schopenhauer, 256

Philosophy of Science, 384

Philosophy of Social Science, 385

The Philosophy of Socrates: A Collection of Critical Essays, 90

The Philosophy of Spinoza: The Unity of His Thought, 189

The Philosophy of Spinoza: Unfolding the Latent Processes of His Reasoning, 189

The Philosophy of St. Bonaventure, 113, 286

The Philosophy of St. Thomas Aquinas, 118, 286

Philosophy of Subjective Spirit, 232

The Philosophy of Symbolic Forms, 279

The Philosophy of the Act, 308

The Philosophy of the American Revolution, 36

The Philosophy of the Church Fathers: Faith, Trinity, Incarnation, 63, 100, 687

The Philosophy of the Enlightenment, 160, 279

The Philosophy of the Inductive Sciences, 257, 258

The Philosophy of the Present, 308

Philosophy of the Recent Past, 27, 35, 266

Philosophy of the Sixteenth and Seventeenth Centuries, 130, 162

The Philosophy of Thomas Reid, 211

The Philosophy of W. V. Quine, 43, 412

The Philosophy of Wilhelm Dilthey, 226

Philosophy of William James, 237

Philosophy of Woman: An Anthology of Classic and Current Concepts, 17

Philosophy's Journey: From the Presocratics to the Present, 17

Philo with an English Translation, 810

Physical Opinions, 90

Physical Order and Moral Liberty, 327

Physical Science in the Middle Ages, 97

Physical World of the Greeks, 49

Physics and the Ultimate Significance of Time, 384

Physics of the Stoics, 57

Physiological Theory and the Doctrine of the Mean in Plato and Aristotle, 84

Piaget's Theory of Knowledge, 383

Pico della Mirandola's Encounter with Jewish Mysticism, 153

A Pictorial Encyclopedia of Trades and Industry, 196
Pictorial History of the Jewish People from Biblical Times to Our Own Day throughout the World, 593
Pictures, Images and Conceptual Change, 334
A Piece of Blue Sky: Scientology, Dianetics and L. Ron Hubbard Exposed, 869
Pierre Bayle and Voltaire, 218
Pierre Gassendi: From Aristotelianism to a New Natural Philosophy, 173
Pierre Teilhard de Chardin's Philosophy of Evolution, 336
The Pilgrimage of Eternity, 374
Pilgrim's Regress, 776
Pioneer Jews: A New Life in the Far West, 641
Pivot of the Four Quarters, 439
The Place of Emotion in Argument, 381
The Place of St. Thomas More in English Literature and History, 147
A Plain Account of Christian Perfection, 789
Plato (Hall), 81
Plato (Hare), 81
Plato: An Introduction, 80
Plato: Dramatist of the Life of Reason, 83
Plato: The Man and His Work, 84
Plato: The Midwife's Apprentice, 80
Plato, One: Metaphysics and Epistemology; a Collection of Critical Essays, 85
Plato, Two: Ethics, Politics, and Philosophy of Art and Religion; a Collection of Critical Essays, 85
Plato and Aristotle, 85
Plato and Aristotle on Poetry, 68
Plato and Augustine, 300
Plato and His Contemporaries, 80
Plato and Parmenides, 79
Plato and Platonism, 82, 83
Plato and Socrates: A Comprehensive Bibliography, 1958–1973, 82
Plato and the Foundations of Metaphysics, 81

Plato in the Italian Renaissance, 127
The Platonic Epistles, 78
Platonic Piety: Philosophy and Ritual in Fourth-Century Athens, 82
The Platonic Renaissance in England, 279
Platonic Studies, 85
Platonic Studies of Greek Philosophy: Form, Arts, Gadgets, and Hemlock, 46
The Platonic Theology (Six Books of Proclus on the Theology of Plato), 62
Platonic Theology, 140
Platonic Tradition in Anglo-Saxon Philosophy, 29
Platonism, 79, 82
Platonism and Cartesianism in the Philosophy of Ralph Cudworth, 168
The Platonism of Marsilio Ficino, 141
The Platonism of Philo Judaeus, 60
Plato on Beauty, Wisdom and the Arts, 82
Plato on Justice and Power: Reading Book I of Plato's Republic, 82
Plato on Knowledge and Reality, 85
Plato on the Self-Prediction of Forms, 82
Plato's Analytic Method, 84
Plato's Cosmology, 79
Plato's Defence of Poetry, 80
Plato's Dialectical Ethics, 402
Plato's Earlier Dialectic, 83
Plato's Euthydemus: Analysis of What Is and Is Not Philosophy, 79
Plato's Invisible Cities: Discourse and Power in the Republic, 83
Plato's Mathematical Imagination, 79
Plato's Parmenides: The Conversion of the Soul, 82
Plato's Penal Code, 84
Plato's Philebus, 283
Plato's Philosophy of Mathematics, 85
Plato's Progress, 84, 325
Plato's Psychology, 83
Plato's Slavery in Its Relation to Greek Law, 82
Plato's Sophist: The Drama of Original and Image, 79, 83
Plato's Symposium, 84
Plato's Theology, 84

Plato's Theory of Art, 81
Plato's Theory of Education, 82
Plato's Theory of Ethics: The Moral Criterion and the Highest Good, 82
Plato's Theory of Ideas, 84
Plato's Theory of Knowledge: The Theaetetus and the Sophist of Plato, 79, 81
Plato's Theory of Man, 85
Plato's Theory of Understanding, 82
Plato's Thought, 81
Plato's Thought in the Making, 83
Plato's Trilogy: Theaetetus, the Sophist, and the Statesman, 81
Plato's Universe, 85
Pleasure, Knowledge, and Being: An Analysis of Plato's Philebus, 81
Pletzl of Paris: Jewish Immigrant Workers in the Belle Époque, 656
Plotinus, 87
Plotinus: The Road to Reality, 87
Plotinus on Sense-Perception: A Philosophical Study, 86
A Pluralistic Universe, 236
Plurality and Ambiguity: Hermeneutics, Religion, Hope, 889
Plutarch, 490
Plutarch and His Times, 490
Plutarch's Ethical Writings and Early Christian Literature, 490
Pocket Dictionary of Saints, 719
The Poem of Empedocles: A Text and Translation with an Introduction, 53
Poem of the Elder Edda, 437
The Poet as Philosopher, 151
Poetics of Aristotle, 67
Poetics of Reverie: Childhood, Language and Cosmos, 274
Poetics of Space, 274
Poetic Thinking: An Approach to Heidegger, 293
Poetry, Language, Thought, 291
Poetry and Experience, 226
The Poet's Testament: Poems and Two Plays, 327
The Point Loma Community in California, 1897–1942, 858

Point of View for My Work as an Author, 238

The Polarity of Mexican Thought, 33

Policraticus: The Statesman's Book, 116

A Policy of Kindness: An Anthology of Writings by and about the Dalai Lama, 560

Policy Papers in International Affairs, 570

The Political and Social Ideas of Saint Augustine, 110

Political Buddhism in Southeast Asia, 520

Political Hermeneutics: The Early Thinking of Hans-Georg Gadamer, 402

Political Ideals, 323

The Political Language of Islam, 579

The Political Ontology of Martin Heidegger, 292

The Political Philosophies of Plato and Hegel, 233

Political Philosophy and Time: Plato and the Origins of Political Vision, 81

The Political Philosophy of Burke, 193

The Political Philosophy of Hobbes: His Theory of Obligation, 175

Political Philosophy of Hobbes: Its Basis and Its Genesis, 175

The Political Philosophy of Luis De Molina, S. J., 125

The Political Philosophy of Rousseau, 213

The Political Philosophy of the Frankfurt School, 264, 394, 408

The Political Theory of John Wyclif, 103

The Political Theory of Possessive Individualism: Hobbes to Locke, 174, 180

Political Thought from Gerson to Grotius: 1414–1625, 126

Political Thought in Medieval Islam: An Introductory Outline, 580

Political Thought in Medieval Times, 98

The Political Thought of John Locke, 179

The Political Thought of Pierre D'Ailly, 105

Political Thought of Plato and Aristotle, 66, 79

The Political Thought of Thomas Aquinas, 118

The Political Thought of William of Ockham, 121

Political Writings, 196, 205, 232

Politics, Philosophy, Culture, 400

Politics and Belief in Herodotus, 480

The Politics of Assimilation, 637

The Politics of Being: The Political Thought of Martin Heidegger, 295

The Politics of Conscience: T. H. Green and His Age, 230

The Politics of Discretion: Pufendorf and the Acceptance of Natural Law, 186

The Politics of Friendship: Pompey and Cicero, 72

The Politics of Futility, 656

The Politics of God: Christian Theologies and Social Justice, 746

The Politics of Locke's Philosophy, 181

The Politics of Philo Judaeus: Practice and Theory, 670

The Politics of Social Theory, 405

Pope John XXIII: Shepherd of the Modern World, 771

Popes, Monks and Crusaders, 692

The Popes and European Revolution, 738, 740

Popes and Princes 1417–1517, 695

Popol Vuh, 456

Popper Selections, 409

Popular Beliefs and Folklore Tradition in Siberia, 541

Popular Buddhism in Siam and Other Essays on Thai Studies, 519

A Popular Dictionary of Islam, 567

Popular History of Philosophy, 16

A Popular History of the Reformation, 722

Popular Religion in the Middle Ages, 698

Popular Works, 198

Porphyry's Isagoge, 62

Porphyry's Launching-Points to the Realm of the Mind, 61

The Portable Greek Reader, 47

The Portable Nietzsche, 246, 741

Portable Voltaire, 218

The Portable World Bible, 5

A Portrait of Aristotle, 68

A Portrait of Wittgenstein as a Young Man, 338

Posidonius: The Fragments, 56

Positions, 397

The Positive Analysis of Social Phenomena, 222

Positive History of the New Social Order and Historical Analysis of Social Phenomena, 222

Positive Philosophy, 222

The Positive Thinkers, 753

The Positivist Dispute in German Sociology, 393

Post-Analytic Philosophy, 267, 379

The Post Card, 397

Post-Holocaust Dialogues: Critical Studies in Modern Jewish Thought, 648

Post Metaphysical Thinking, 404

The Postmodern Explained: Correspondence 1982–85, 265

Potestas Calvium, 335

The Poverty of Historicism, 409

Power, 323

Power and Powerlessness in Jewish History, 593

Power and Sexuality: The Emergence of Canon Law at the Synod of Elvira, 689

Power-Knowledge, 400

The Power of Consciousness and the Force of Circumstances in Sartre's Philosophy, 330

The Power of the Poor in History, 769

Powers of Imagining: Ignatius de Loyola, 770

The Power to Speak: Feminism, Language, God, 749

Practical Ethics, 211

A Practical Grammar for Classical Hebrew, 795

Practical Laws of Islam, 579

The Practice and Theory of Tibetan Buddhism, 544

The Practice of Chinese Buddhism 1900–1950, 530

The Practice of Philosophy:

A Handbook for Beginners, 23
The Pragmatic, 302
The Pragmatic Movement in American Philosophy, 266
Pragmatics, Truth, and Language, 403
Pragmatism, 236
Pragmatism: A New Name for Some Old Ways of Thinking, 236
Pragmatism: The Classic Writings, 268
Pragmatism and Other Essays, 236
Pragmatism and the American Mind, 268
Pragmatism and the Meaning of Truth, 236
Praise and Lament in the Psalms, 824
The Praise of Folly, 138, 139, 147
The Praise of Pleasure, 148
Praxeology: An Anthology, 32
Praxis, 33
Praxis of Liberation and Christian Faith, 769
The Praxis of Suffering, 896
Prayerbook Reform in Europe, 652
Prayer in Judaism, 600
The Preaching of Islam: A History of Propagation of the Muslim Faith, 567, 574
Predestination, God's Foreknowledge, and Future Contingents, 120
A Preface to Metaphysics: Seven Lectures on Being, 307
A Preface to Morality, 389
A Preface to Philosophy, 25
Preface to Plato, 81
A Prehistoric Bibliography, 431
Preliminary Discourse on Philosophy in General, 219
Prelude to Galileo, 144
Preparation for the Gospel, 709
The Presence of Stoicism in Medieval Thought, 57
Present Philosophical Tendencies, 266
Present Status of the Philosophy of Law and of Rights, 296
The Presocratic Philosophers, 50
The Presocratic Philosophers:

A Critical History with a Selection of Texts, 50
The Presocratic Philosophers: An Annotated Bibliography, 51
The Presocratics, 50
The Pre-Socratics: A Collection of Critical Essays, 51
Priest and Revolutionary, 741
Priests, Warriors and Cattle: A Study in the Ecology of Religions, 435
The Primacy of Perception, 310
Primal Myths: Creating the World, 427
Primary Ousia: An Essay on Aristotle's Metaphysics Z and H, 69
Primary Philosophy, 24
A Primer of Soto Zen: A Translation of Dogen's Shobogenzo Zuimoniki, 538
Primitive Christianity: In Its Contemporary Setting, 617, 807, 831
The Prince, 144, 145
Prince Jin-Gim's Textbook of Tibetan Buddhism, the "Sesbya Rab-Gsal," 543
A Prince of the Church, 254
Princeps a Diis Electus, 452
Princeps Concordiae: Pico della Mirandola and the Scholastic Tradition, 153
Princeton Studies on the Near East, 569
The Principal Upanishads, 354
Principia Ethica, 312
Principia Mathematica, 323, 341, 738
Principium Sapientiae: The Origins of Greek Philosophical Thought, 50
The Principle of Hope, 277
The Principle of Reason, 291
Principles, Dialogues and Philosophical Correspondence, 191
Principles and Proofs: Aristotle's Theory of Demonstrative Science, 70
The Principles of Art, 282
Principles of Catholic Theology: Building Stones for a Fundamental Theology, 746, 891
Principles of Christian Theology, 719
The Principles of Descartes' Philosophy, 171, 186

Principles of Logic, 220
The Principles of Mathematics, 323
The Principles of Nature: Her Divine Revelation and a Voice to Mankind, 850
Principles of Philosophy, 168, 169
Principles of Political Economy, 244
The Principles of Psychology, 235, 236
The Principles of the Most Ancient and Modern Philosophy, 167
Principles of the Philosophy of the Future, 228
Prior Analytics, 66, 164
The Prism of Piety, 738
Prisms, 393
Prison Notebooks: Selections, 287
Privacy, 339
Probability and Hume's Inductive Skepticism, 203
The Problem of Burke's Political Philosophy, 193
The Problem of Knowledge: Philosophy, Science, and History since Hegel, 273, 279
The Problem of Pain, 776
The Problem of the Criterion, 395
The Problem of the Hexateuch and Other Essays, 824, 838
The Problem of Unbelief in the Sixteenth Century: The Religion of Rabelais, 126
Problems and Projects, 403
Problems from Locke, 180
Problems in Philosophy: West and East, 37
Problems in the History of Philosophy, 18
Problems of a Sociology of Knowledge, 332
Problems of Cartesianism, 183
The Problems of China, 323
The Problems of Christianity, 250
The Problems of Consciousness, 364
Problems of Men, 224
The Problems of Philosophers: An Introduction, 22
The Problems of Philosophy: Introductory Readings, 19, 22, 23, 323
The Problems of Philosophy

in Their Interconnection, 333

Problems of Religious Pluralism, 41

Problems of Suffering in the Religions of the World, 568, 886

Proceedings of the Boston Area Colloquium in Ancient Philosophy, 47

Proceedings of the First Italian International Congress on Spinoza, 188

Process and Reality: An Essay in Cosmology, 341

Process Philosophy and Political Ideology, 289

Process Philosophy and Social Thought, 263, 379

Process Theology: An Introductory Exposition, 743

Proclamation Commentaries: The New Testament Witnesses for Preaching, 821

Proclamation Commentaries: The Old Testament Witnesses for Preaching, 821

Proclus: A Commentary on the First Book of Euclid's Elements, 62

Proclus' Commentary on Plato's Parmenides, 62

The Professional Quest for Truth, 384

"The Profession of the Religious" and the Principal Arguments from "The Falsely-Believed and Forged Donation of Constantine," 155

Profiles in American Judaism, 651

Profiles in Belief: The Religious Bodies of the United States and Canada, 717, 751

Profiles of Eleven, 656, 657

Progress and Pragmatism, 237

A Progress of Sentiments: Reflections on Hume's Treatise, 201

The Project of Reconciliation, 233

Prolegomena to Any Future Metaphysics, 204, 205

Prolegomena to Ethics, 230

Prolegomena to the Study of Greek Religion, 479

The Promised City: New York's Jews, 1870–1914, 641

A Promise to Keep: The

American Encounter with Anti-Semitism, 638

Properties as Processes: A Synoptic Study of Wilfred Sellars' Nominalism, 334

Prophecy and Politics, 656

Prophecy and Society in Ancient Israel, 824

Prophecy Deliverance! An Afro-American Revolutionary Christianity, 749

The Prophetic Faith, 662

The Prophetic Minority: American Jewish Immigrant Radicals, 1880–1920, 656

The Prophets, 823

Prophets of Extremity, 398

The Prophets of Israel and Their Place in History, 492

The Prosecution of John Wyclif, 714

The Prose Edda of Snorri Sturluson: Tales from Norse Mythology, 437

Proselytism in the Talmudic Period, 620

The Prose of the World, 310

Prose Works, 843, 875

Prospects for a Common Morality, 893

Prospects for Post-Holocaust Theology, 648

Protagoras, 78

Protector of the Faith, 694

Protestant, Catholic, Jew: An Essay in American Religious Sociology, 639, 753

Protestant and Roman Catholic Ethics: Prospects for Rapprochement, 893, 900

The Protestant Ethic and the Spirit of Capitalism, 425

Protestantism and Capitalism and Social Science: The Weber Thesis Controversy, 722

The Protestant Reformation 1517–1559, 722, 723

Protestants: Birth of a Revolution, 722

Protestant Thought in the Nineteenth Century, 742

Proto-Indo-European: The Archaeology of a Linguistic Problem, 436

Providence in the Philosophy of Gersonides, 664

The Provincial Letters, 185

The Psalms: A Form-Critical Introduction, 823, 835

Psalms 1–59: A Commentary;

Psalms 60–150: A Commentary, 821

The Psalms in Israel's Worship, 823

The Pseudepigrapha and Modern Research with a Supplement, 810

Pseudo-Dionysius, 63

Psyche: The Cult of Souls and Belief in Immortality among the Greeks, 49

Psyche and Symbol, 424

Psychiatry and the Cults: An Annotated Bibliography, 857

Psychoanalysis, Scientific Method and Philosophy: A Symposium, 265

Psychoanalysis of Fire, 274

Psychological Investigations, 315

Psychology from an Empirical Standpoint, 222

The Psychology of Aristotle, 67

The Psychology of Habit According to William Ockham, 120

Psychology of Imagination, 329

Psychology of Religion: A Guide to Information Sources, 890

Psychotherapy East and West, 881

The Public and Its Problems: An Essay in Political Inquiry, 224

Public Religion in American Culture, 754

Pulling Up the Ladder: The Metaphysical Roots of Wittgenstein's Tractatus, 345

Pure Lust: Elemental Feminist Philosophy, 764, 765

Pure Pragmatics and Possible Worlds: The Early Essays of Wilfrid Sellars, 333

Purim Anthology, 599

The Puritan Experience, 735

The Puritan Lectureships: The Politics of Religious Dissent, 1560–1662, 734

Puritans and Predestination: Grace in English Protestant Theology, 1525–1695, 735

The Puritans in America: A Narrative Anthology, 753

The Puritan Way of Death: A Study in Religion, Culture, and Social Change, 735

Purity and Pollution in Zo-
roastrianism: Triumph
over Evil, 547
Purity of Heart, 239
The Purpose and Meaning of
Jewish Existence, 663
Pursuit of the Millennium,
698, 721
Pursuit of Truth, 411
Puzzles, Paradoxes and Prob-
lems: A Reader for Intro-
ductory Philosophy, 21
Pythagoras and Early Pytha-
goreanism, 87
Pythagoreans and Elatics, 87
The Pythagorean Sourcebook
and Library, 87

The Quakers in Puritan Eng-
land, 733
Quantum Theory and the
Schism in Physics, 409
The Quarrel over Future
Contingents (Louvain,
1465–1475), 104
Quasi Una Fantasia: Essays
on Music and Culture, 393
The Quest: History and
Meaning in Religion, 474
The Quest for Being and
Other Studies in Natural-
ism and Humanism, 298
The Quest for Certainty, 223
The Quest for Meaning of
Swami Vivekananda: A
Study of Religious Change,
563
The Quest for Political and
Spiritual Liberation, 353
Quest for the Origins of the
First Americans, 454
The Question Concerning
Technology and Other Es-
says, 292
The Question of Being, 291
The Question of "Eclecti-
cism": Studies in Later
Greek Philosophy, 55
The Question of Jean-Jacques
Rousseau, 279
The Question of Language in
Heidegger's History of Be-
ing, 292
The Question of Palestine,
643
The Question of Value, 293
Questions on Wittgenstein,
345
The Quest of the Historical
Jesus, 826
The Quest of the Quiet

Mind: The Philosophy of
Krishnamurti, 555
Quiddities: An Intermittently
Philosophical Dictionary,
14, 411
The Quimby Manuscripts,
847
Quine: Language, Experience,
and Reality, 412
Quine on Ontology, Necessi-
ty, and Experience, 412
Quodlibetal Questions, 120
The Qur'an: A New Transla-
tion with a Critical Rear-
rangement of the Surahs,
587
The Quran (Khan), 587
The Quran (Palmer), 587
The Qur'an and Its Interpret-
ers, 587
The Qur'an as Scripture, 587

Rabad of Posquieres: A
Twelfth-Century Talmudist,
627
Rabbi Moses Nahmanides,
669
A Rabbinic Anthology, 610
The Rabbinic Class of Ro-
man Palestine in Late An-
tiquity, 621
Rabbinic Lay Confrontations
in Jewish Law, 627
Rabbinic Political Theory:
Religion and Politics in
the Mishnah, 607
The Rabbinic Traditions
about the Pharisees before
70, 616
Race and Color in Islam,
571
Rachel Vernhagen: The Life
of a Jewish Woman, 394
Rachel Weeping: The Case
against Abortion, 894
Radhakrishnan: A Biography,
354
Radhakrishnan: A Religious
Biography, 354, 508
Radhakrishnan: His Life and
Ideas, 354
Radhakrishnan and the Ways
to Oneness of East and
West, 354
Radhasoami Reality: The
Logic of a Modern Faith,
508
Radical Departures: Desper-
ate Detours to Growing
Up, 856
The Radical Empiricism of
William James, 238

The Radical Kingdom: The
Western Experience of
Messianic Hope, 785
The Radical Reformation,
724, 733
The Radical Spinoza, 189
Radical Spirits, 850
The Raft Is Not the Shore,
562
The Raft of Muhammad, 579
Rahner, Heidegger and
Truth, 292
A Rahner Reader, 745
Ralph Cudworth: An Inter-
pretation, 168
Ramakien: The Thai Epic,
518
Ramakrishna: His Life and
Sayings, 354
Ramakrishna and His Disci-
ples, 354, 563
Ramakrishna and His Mes-
sage, 355
Ramakrishna and Vivekanan-
da: New Essays, 355
Ramayana, 502, 509
The Ramayana of Valmika,
504
Ramban (Nahmanides) Com-
mentary on the Torah,
669
Ramban: His Life and His
Teachings, 669
Rameau's Nephew, 195
Rameau's Nephew and
D'Alembert's Dream, 196
Ram Mohan Roy: Social, Po-
litical, and Religious Re-
form in 19th Century In-
dia, 355
Ram Mohan Roy, the Apostle
of Indian Awakening, 355
Ramus, Method, and the De-
cay of Dialogue, 129
Ransoming the Time, 307
Rashi: His Life and Works,
671
Rashi: The Man and His
World, 671
Rashi and the Christian
Scholars, 671
The Rastafarians: Sounds of
Cultural Dissonance, 467
The Rational Enterprise:
Logos in Plato's Theaete-
tus, 80
Rationalism, Empiricism, and
Pragmatism, 262, 380
Rationality: A Philosophical
Inquiry into the Nature
and Rationale of Reason,
317

Rationality, Relativism and the Human Sciences, 381

Rationality, Religious Belief and Moral Commitment, 888

Rationality and Irrationality in Economics, 242

Rationality and Relativism, 405

The Rational Society: A Critical Reading of Santayana's Social Thought, 328

The Ravenous Hyenas and the Wounded Sun, 501

Rawls: A Theory of Justice and Its Critics, 316

Reaching for the Moon: On Asian Religious Paths, 499, 523, 535

The Reach of Philosophy, Essays in Honor of James Kern Feibleman, 284

Reader in Comparative Religion: An Anthropological Approach, 426, 897

A Reader on Islam, 566

The Reader's Adviser, 419

A Reader's Guide to the Great Religions, 5, 533

Reading Capital, 242

Reading Habermas, 405

Reading Heidegger: Commemorations, 294

Reading Nietzsche, 248

Reading Rorty: Critical Response to Philosophy and the Mirror of Nature, 413

Readings in African Philosophy: An Akan Collection, 369

Readings in Church History, 680, 719, 740

Readings in Eastern Religions, 497, 521, 533

Readings in Ethical Theory, 334

Readings in Modern Jewish History, 639

Readings in Philosophical Analysis, 264, 334

Readings in Russian Philosophical Thought, 31

Readings in the History of Christian Theology, Vol. 2, 719

Readings in the Philosophy of Moses Maimonides, 668

Readings in the Qur'an, 588

A Ready Reference to Philosophy East and West, 13

The Real Anti-Semitism in America, 640

Realism: A Critique of Brentano and Meinong, 222

Realism and the Aim of Science, 409

Realism and the Background of Phenomenology, 263, 395

Realism with a Human Face, 410

The Realistic Spirit: Wittgenstein, Philosophy and the Mind, 345

A Realist Philosophy of Science, 384

Reality, 338, 339

Reality, Knowledge and the Good Life: A Historical Introduction to Philosophy, 16

The Reality of the Historical Past, 319

Realizing Rawls, 316

The Realm of Rights, 387

The Realm of Spirit and the Realm of Caesar, 275, 758

Realm of the Immortals: Daoism in the Arts of China, 528

Reappraisals in Renaissance Thought, 131

The Reason, the Understanding, and the Time, 303

The Reasonableness of Christianity and a Discourse on Miracles, 178, 179, 739

Reason and Analysis, 276

Reason and Authority in the Eighteenth Century, 739

Reason and Belief, 276

Reason and Goodness, 276

Reason and Hope: Selections from the Jewish Writings of Hermann Cohen, 663

Reason and Human Good in Aristotle, 67

Reason and Life: The Introduction to Philosophy, 22

Reason and Nature: An Essay on the Meaning of Scientific Method, 281

Reason and Rationality in Natural Science: A Group of Essays, 317

Reason and Relativism: A Sartrean Investigation, 331

Reason and Religious Belief, 381

Reason and Responsibility, 20

Reason and Revelation: From Paul to Pascal, 27

Reason and Revolution, 408

Reason and Right: A Critical Examination of Richard Price's Moral Philosophy, 211

Reason and Tradition in Islamic Ethics, 575

Reason in Art, 327

Reasoning and the Logic of Things, 248

Reasoning Things Out, 25

Reason in Science, 327

Reason in Society, 327

Reason in the Age of Science, 402

The Reason of Following: Christology and the Ecstatic I, 889

The Reason of State and the Greatness of Cities, 124

Reason to Hope, 337

Reassessing the Henrician Age: Humanism, Politics and Reform, 1500–1550, 126

Rebecca's Children: Judaism and Christianity in the Roman World, 605

A Rebellious Prophet: A Life of Nicolai Berdyaev, 275

Recent American Philosophy: Studies of Ten Representative Thinkers, 267

Recent Archaeological Discoveries and Biblical Research, 808

Recent Japanese Philosophical Thought, 541

Recent Philosophers, 266, 379

Recent Work in Philosophy, 14, 265, 386

The Recent Work of Jürgen Habermas, 405

Recognizing Islam, 578

Reconciliation, Law and Righteousness: Essays in Biblical Theology, 826

Reconstructing Judaism: An Autobiography, 659

Reconstruction in Philosophy, 223, 224

The Reconstruction of Religious Thought in Islam, 375

Re-Counting Plato, 81

Recovering the Stoics: The Spindel Conference 1984, 57

The Redaction of the Babylonian Talmud: Amoraic or Saboraic, 610

Redefining Death, 389

The Redemption of the Unwanted, 643

Redemptive Encounters:
Three Modern Styles in
the Hindu Tradition, 507
Rediscovering Judaism: Re-
flections on New Theolo-
gy, 649
Red Man's Religion: Beliefs
and Practices of the Indi-
ans North of Mexico, 465
Reenacting the Heavenly Vi-
sion: The Role of Religion
in the Taiping Rebellion,
531
Reference and Essence, 411
Reference Works for Theo-
logical Research, 6
Reflections on America, 307
Reflections on Frege's Philos-
ophy, 230
Reflections on Human Na-
ture, 303
Reflections on Philosophy:
Introductory Essays, 22
Reflections on Resemblance,
Ritual, and Religion, 501
Reflections on the Philoso-
phy of the History of Man-
kind, 199
Reflections on the Revolu-
tion in France, 192, 210
Reform and Reformation:
England 1509–1558, 726
Reform and Reformation:
England and the Continent
1500–1750, 725
The Reformation (Chadwick),
722
The Reformation (Durant),
722
The Reformation (Mosse),
722
Reformation (Todd), 723
The Reformation: A Narra-
tive History Related by
Contemporary Observers
and Participants, 722
Reformation and Revolution
1558–1660, 733
Reformation and Society in
Sixteenth-Century Europe,
722
The Reformation Era:
1500–1650, 722
Reformation Europe: A
Guide to Research, 722
Reformation Europe,
1517–1559, 722
The Reformation in Den-
mark, 730
The Reformation in England,
727
The Reformation in Germa-
ny, 722

The Reformation in Medieval
Perspective, 721
The Reformation in the Cit-
ies, 722
The Reformation of Images:
Destruction of Art in Eng-
land, 1535–1669, 738
The Reformation of Reform
Judaism, 652
Reformation Thought: An In-
troduction, 722
Reformed Confessions of the
Sixteenth Century, 761
Reformed Reader: A Source-
book in Christian Theolo-
gy, 719
Reformers and Babylon, 725
Reformers in Profile, 722
Reforming American Educa-
tion, 270
Reform Judaism: A Historical
Perspective, 652
Reform Judaism, a Historical
Perspective: Essays from
the Yearbook of the Cen-
tral Conference of Ameri-
can Rabbis, 652
Reform Judaism in America:
A Study in Religious
Adaptation, 652
Reform Judaism in America,
652
Reform Judaism Today,
1973–77, 652
Reform Movement in Juda-
ism, 653
Reform of Education, 285
Reform Responsa for Our
Time, 652
Reform Thought in Six-
teenth-Century Italy, 728
Refutation of Helvetius, 195
Reginald Pole: Cardinal of
England, 729
Regional Perspectives on the
Olmec, 455
Regulae, 164
The Reign of the Ayatollahs:
Iran and the Islamic Revo-
lution, 578
Reincarnation, 550
Reincarnation: The Phoenix
Fire Mystery, 887
Reinhold Niebuhr, 784
Reinhold Niebuhr: A Biogra-
phy, 784
Reinhold Niebuhr and Issues
of Our Time, 784
A Reinhold Niebuhr Reader:
Selected Essays, Articles,
and Book Reviews, 784
Relations: Medieval Theories,
1250–1325, 104

Relations of Indian, Greek
and Christian Thought in
Antiquity, 38
The Relevance of Charles
Peirce, 249
The Relevance of the Beauti-
ful, 402
Religion: A Dialogue, and
Other Essays, 255
Religion, Ideology and Hei-
degger's Concept of Fall-
ing, 295
Religion, Revolution and Eng-
lish Radicalism, 738
Religion, Society, and Utopia
in Nineteenth-Century
America, 842, 844
The Religion, Spirituality,
and Thought of Traditional
Africa, 463
Religion, Values, and Devel-
opment in Southeast Asia,
518
Religion and Art, 340
Religion and Change in Con-
temporary Asia, 573
Religion and Empire: The
Dynamics of Aztec and
Inca Expansion, 457
Religion and Hopi Life in
the Twentieth Century,
465
Religion and Legitimation of
Power in Thailand, Laos,
and Burma, 518
Religion and Modernization
in Southeast Asia, 518
Religion and Neoplatonism
in Renaissance Medicine,
129
Religion and Nothingness,
365, 541, 889
The Religion and Philosophy
of the Veda and Upani-
shads, 501
Religion and Politics in Con-
temporary Iran, 567, 577
Religion and Politics in Iran:
Shi'ism from Quietism to
Revolution, 570
Religion and Politics in Isra-
el, 642
Religion and Politics in the
Middle East, 568
Religion and Ritual in Chi-
nese Society, 531
Religion and Ritual in Kore-
an Society, 539
Religion and Science, 323
Religion and Sexism: Images
of Women in the Jewish
and Christian Tradition,
650, 679

Religion and Sexuality: The Shakers, the Mormons, and the Oneida Community, 841

Religion and Society in Central Africa: The Bakongo of Lower Zaire, 462

Religion and the Decline of Magic, 727

Religion and the Family in East Asia, 531, 539

Religion and the One: Philosophies East and West, 574

Religion as a Social Vision, 508

Religion in Aboriginal Australia: An Anthology, 461

Religion in America, 751

Religion in American History: Interpretive Essays, 754

Religion in American Life, 751, 752

Religion in Ancient Egypt: Gods, Myths, and Personal Practice, 442

Religion in Chinese Society, 524

Religion in Communist China, 532

Religion in Contemporary Japan, 535, 541

Religion Index One: Periodicals, 8

Religion Index Two: Multi-Author Works, 8

Religion in Essence and Manifestation: A Study in Phenomenology, 427, 885

Religion in Japanese History, 535

Religion in Modern India, 507, 516, 517, 562

Religion in Native North America, 7

Religion in Relation: Method, Application, and Moral Location, 427

Religion in Roman Britain, 448

Religion in Sociological Perspective, 425

Religion in the Age of Romanticism, 741

Religion in the Andes: Vision and Imagination in Early Colonial Peru, 458

Religion in the Japanese Experience, 533

Religion in the Making, 341

Religion in the Medieval West, 691

Religion Journals and Serials: An Analytical Guide, 6

The Religion of Isaac Newton: The Fremantle Lectures 1973, 184

The Religion of Islam, 575

The Religion of Japan's Korean Minority, 540

The Religion of Java, 478

Religion of Reason out of the Sources of Judaism, 663

The Religion of the Greeks and Romans, 484

The Religion of the Manichees: Donnellan Lectures for 1924, 685

Religions of Africa, 884

Religions of Antiquity, 440

Religions of Asia, 498, 499, 523, 535, 543

The Religions of China, 523, 884

The Religions of India, 498

Religions of Japan, 534, 883

The Religions of Mankind, 573

Religions of Mesoamerica, 454, 883

The Religions of Mongolia, 541

Religions of the Ancient Near East, 441, 445

Religions of the East, 570

The Religions of the Roman Empire, 449

The Religions of Tibet, 356, 543

Religion within the Bounds of Plain Reason, 204

Religion within the Limits of Reason Alone, 205, 739

Religious and Inspirational Books and Serials in Print, 1985, 716

Religious and Spiritual Groups in Modern America, 855

Religious and Theological Abstracts, 8

Religious Attitude and Life in Islam, 575

Religious Bodies in the United States: A Directory, 6, 854

Religious Conflict in Social Context, 654

Religious Encounters with Death, 887

Religious Essays: A Supplement to "The Idea of the Holy," 488

Religious Evolution, 422

The Religious Experience, 884

Religious Experience and Truth: A Symposium, 265

The Religious Experience of Mankind, 422

The Religious Fringe: A History of Alternative Religions in America, 841

A Religious History of America, 751

A Religious History of the American People, 750

Religious Information Sources: A Worldwide Guide, 7

The Religious Investigations of William James, 237

Religious Leaders, 716

Religious Leaders of America, 7

Religious Life in Seventeenth-Century Scotland, 735

The Religious Life of Man: Guide to the Basic Literature, 883

Religious Movements: Genesis, Exodus, and Numbers, 857

Religious Movements in Contemporary America, 856

The Religious Orders in England, 699

Religious Outsiders and the Making of America, 842

The Religious Philosophy of Nishitani Keiji, 365

The Religious Philosophy of Plotinus and Some Modern Philosophies of Religion, 86

The Religious Philosophy of Tanabe Hajime, 366

The Religious Philosophy of William James, 238

Religious Platonism, 284

Religious Poverty and the Profit Economy in Medieval Europe, 700

Religious Reading: The Annual Guide, 716

The Religious Roots of Rebellion: Christians in Central American Revolutions, 747

Religious Thought in the Nineteenth Century, 741

The Religious Traditions of Asia, 498, 509, 513, 516, 518, 522, 534, 542, 543

Religious Traditions of the World, 883

Religious Trends in Modern
China, 532
Religious Violence and Abor-
tion: The Gideon Project,
894
The Reluctant Naturalist: A
Study of G. E. Moore's
Principia Ethica, 312
Remarks on Colour, 344
Remarks on Frazer's Golden
Bough, 344
Remarks on Marx, 400
Remarks on the Foundations
of Mathematics, 344
Remarks on the Philosophy
of Psychology, 344
Reminiscences of Swami
Vivekananda, 563
The Renaissance, the Refor-
mation and the Erratic
Behavior of Desiderius
Erasmus, 140
The Renaissance and English
Humanism, 124
Renaissance and Reforma-
tion, 691
Renaissance Concepts of
Method, 126
The Renaissance Drama of
Knowledge: Giordano Bru-
no in England, 135
Renaissance Humanism, 127
Renaissance Humanism:
Studies in Philosophy and
Poetics, 127
Renaissance Humanism,
Vols. 1–3: Foundations,
Forms and Legacy, 130
Renaissance Humanism
1300–1550: A Bibliography
of Materials in English,
127
The Renaissance Idea of
Wisdom, 130
Renaissance Man, 127
Renaissance Man and Crea-
tive Thinking, 127
The Renaissance of the
Twelfth Century, 101, 699
Renaissance Philosophy (Co-
penhaver), 125
Renaissance Philosophy (Fal-
lico), 126
Renaissance Philosophy: New
Translations of Lorenzo
Valla, Paul Cortese, Caje-
tan, T. Bacciliere, Juan
Luis Vives, Peter Ramus,
127
The Renaissance Philosophy
of Man, 125, 153, 155,
156, 279, 695
Renaissance Theory of Love:

The Context of Giordano
Bruno's "Eroici Furori,"
136
Renaissance Thought: The
Classic, Scholastic and Hu-
manistic Strains, 697
Renaissance Thought and Its
Sources, 128
Renaissance Thought and the
Arts: Collected Essays, 128
Renewing Philosophy, 410
Representation and Reality,
411
Representative Government
and the Degeneration of
Democracy, 244
The Republic, 78
The Republic of Plato, 79
The Republic of St. Peter,
680–825, 695
Re-reading Levinas, 901
Rereading Russell: Essays on
Bertrand Russell's Meta-
physics and Epistemology,
324
Res Cogitans: An Essay in
Rational Psychology, 171
Research Guide to Philoso-
phy, 15
Research Guide to Religious
Studies, 716
Responsa Anthology, 648
The Responsa Literature and
a Treasury of Responsa,
627
The Responsa of Solomon
Luria, 627
Responses to 101 Questions
on the Bible, 816
Responses to 101 Questions
on the Dead Sea Scrolls,
811
Response to Modernity: A
History of the Reform
Movement in Judaism, 652
Responsibility and Atone-
ment, 886
The Responsibility of the Art-
ist, 307
The Restructuring of Ameri-
can Religion: Society and
Faith since World War II,
754
Rethinking Early Greek Phi-
losophy, 49
Rethinking History and Myth,
454
Rethinking Scripture: Essays
from a Comparative Per-
spective, 510, 530
Rethinking the Neolithic, 434
Returning to Tradition: The

Contemporary Revival of
Orthodox Judaism, 659
Return to Judaism: Religious
Renewal in Israel, 659
A Return to Moral and Reli-
gious Philosophy in Early
America, 34
Revelation and Reason in
Islam, 574
The Reveries of the Solitary
Walker, 213
The Revised English Bible
with the Apocrypha, 798
Revivalism and Social Re-
form, 754
The Revolt, 642
The Revolt against Dualism:
An Inquiry Concerning the
Existence of Ideas, 303
The Revolt of the Masses,
315
The Revolt of the Nether-
lands 1555–1609, 731
Revolutionary Immortality:
Mao Tse-tung and the Chi-
nese Revolution, 532
Revolutionary Jews from
Marx to Trotsky, 656
The Revolution of the Saints:
A Study in the Origins of
Radical Politics, 735
Revolution or Reform, 408
Revolutions and Reconstruc-
tions in the Philosophy of
Science, 405
Revolutions in Eastern Eu-
rope: The Religious Roots,
756
The Revolutions of 1848, 242
Rhetoric, Prudence and
Skepticism in the Renais-
sance, 127
Rhetoric and Philosophy in
Renaissance Humanism,
131
Rhetoric and Reality in Pla-
to's Phaedrus, 85
Rhetoric and Reform: Eras-
mus' Civil Dispute with
Luther, 139
Rhetoric as Philosophy: The
Humanist Tradition, 127
The Rhetoric of Alcuin and
Charlemagne, 100
The Rhetoric of Morality and
Philosophy, 89
Rhyme or Reason: A Limer-
ick History of Philosophy,
16
Rhythm and Intent, 503
Richard Price as Moral Phi-
losopher and Political
Theorist, 211

The Ricoeur Reader: Reflection and Imagination, 319
The Riddle of the Early Academy, 79
Right and Wrong: A Philosophical Dialogue between Father and Son, 340
The Righteous Remnant: The House of David, 844
Rights, 387
Rights, Restitution, and Risk, 387
Rights of Man and Natural Law, 307
The Right to Die, 389
The Right to Dream, 274
The Rig Veda: An Anthology, 501
Rigvedic India, 501
The Ring of the Dove: A Treatise on the Art and Practice of Arab Love, 583
Risalāt al-Tauhīd, 374
The Rise and Destiny of the German Jew, 637
The Rise and Fall of the Judean State, 605
The Rise of American Philosophy: Cambridge, Massachusetts, 1860–1930, 34, 265
The Rise of Christianity, 681
The Rise of Neo-Confucianism in Korea, 540
The Rise of Puritanism, 734
The Rise of Reform Judaism: A Sourcebook of Its European Origins, 653
The Rise of Scientific Philosophy, 385
The Rise of the Monophysite Movement, 685
The Rise of the Papacy, 688
The Rise of Universities, 101
The Rise of Western Rationalism, 160
Risk, 317
Rites and Symbols of Initiation: The Mysteries of Birth and Rebirth, 430, 897
The Rites of Passage, 430
Ritual Cosmos: The Santification of Life in African Religions, 463
Ritual Irony: Poetry and Sacrifice in Euripides, 475
The Ritual of Battle: Krishna in the Mahabharata, 504
Ritual Poetry and the Politics of Death in Early Japan, 536
The Ritual Process: Structure

and Anti-Structure, 430, 898
Rituals and Power: The Roman Imperial Cult in Asia Minor, 452
Rituals of Manhood: Male Initiation in Papua New Guinea, 430
Ritual Theory, Ritual Practice, 426
Road Belong Cargo, 467
The Road from Babylon: The Story of Sephardic and Oriental Jews, 594
Roads to Freedom: Socialism, Anarchism and Syndication, 323
The Road to Total Freedom, 869
Robert Bellarmine, Saint and Scholar, 736
Robert Dale Owen, 844
Robert Grosseteste: Scholar and Bishop, 115
Roderick M. Chisholm, 395
Roger Bacon and His Search for a Universal Science, 111
Roger Bacon's Letter Concerning the Marvelous Power of Art and of Nature and Concerning the Nullity of Magic, 111
The Role of Mood in Heidegger's Ontology, 292
The Role of the Emotions and the Will in the Process of Mental Phenomena, 323
The Role of Women in Early Christianity, 679
Roman Augury and Etruscan Divination, 448
Roman Catholic Modernism, 741
The Roman Festivals of the Period of the Republic, 448
The Roman Mind, 59
The Romans and Their Gods in the Age of Augustus, 448
Roman Stoicism: Being Lectures, 59
Romanticism and Marxism, 253
Rome and the Counter-Reformation in Scandinavia, 736
The Roots of Civilization, 434
The Roots of Fundamentalism, 754

Roots of Modern Mormonism, 846
The Roots of Reference, 411
Rorty's Humanistic Pragmatism, 413
Rosary of the White Lotuses, Being the Clear Account of How the Precious Teachings of Buddha Appeared and Spread in the Great Hor Country, 541
Rosh Hashanah Anthology, 599
The Rosicrucian Enlightenment, 848
Rosicrucianism in America, 848
Rosicrucian Questions and Answers, 848
The Rosicrucians: Their Rites and Mysteries, 848
The Rosy Cross Unveiled, 848
Rousseau: An Introduction to His Psychological, Social and Political Theory, 213
Rousseau: Confessions, 213
Rousseau: Dreamer of Democracy, 214
Rousseau, Judge of Jean-Jacques, 213
Rousseau and the Religious Quest, 214
Rousseau's Social Contract: The Design of the Argument, 213
The Route of Parmenides, 52
Royal Charles: Charles II and the Restoration, 734
Royce and Hocking: American Idealists, 250
Royce's Logical Essays, 250
Royce's Mature Philosophy of Religion, 250
Royce's Metaphysics, 250, 305
Royce's Social Infinite: The Community of Interpretation, 250
Rudolf Bultmann. Makers of the Modern Theological Mind Ser., 831
Rudolf Otto: An Introduction to His Philosophical Theology, 488
Rudolf Otto's Interpretation of Religion, 488
Rudolf Steiner: Herald of a New Epoch, 858
Rudolph Steiner: Scientist of the Invisible, 880
The Rule of Metaphor, 319
The Rule of Saint Benedict:

A Doctrinal and Spiritual
  Commentary, 688
The Rule of St. Benedict in
  Latin and English with
  Notes, 705
The Rule of the Master, 705
Rumi: Poet and Mystic, 589
Rush Hour of the Gods: A
  Study of New Religious
  Movements in Japan, 541
Russell, 324
Russell and Moore: The Ana-
  lytical Heritage, 273, 312,
  324
Russell's Idealist Apprentice-
  ship, 324
Russia and America: A Philo-
  sophical Comparison, 31,
  34
The Russian Idea, 275
The Russian Jew under Tsars
  and Soviets, 635
Russian Mystics, 755
The Russian Orthodox
  Church: A Contemporary
  History, 755
Russian Philosophical Termi-
  nology, 30
Russian Philosophy, 31
The Russian Revolution, 275
Russian Theology, 1920–1965:
  A Bibliographic Survey,
  756
Ruth Rabbah: An Analytical
  Translation, 612

Saadia Gaon: His Life and
  Works, 672
Sabbatai Sevi: The Mystical
  Messiah, 631
The Sabbath: Its Meaning for
  Modern Man, 665
Sacramentum Mundi: An En-
  cyclopedia of Theology,
  719
The Sacred and the Profane:
  The Nature of Religion,
  472, 474
The Sacred Bridge: Liturgical
  Parallels in Synagogue and
  Early Church, 597
Sacred Canopy: Elements of
  a Sociological Theory of
  Religion, 424, 890
Sacred Fragments: Recovering
  Theology for the Modern
  Jew, 620
Sacred Journeys: Conversion
  and Commitment to Di-
  vine Light Mission, 872
Sacred Narrative: Reading in
  the Theory of Myth, 428

The Sacred Pipe: Black Elk's
  Account of the Seven
  Rites of the Oglala Sioux,
  464
The Sacred Portal: A Pri-
  mary Symbol in Ancient
  Judaic Art, 614
Sacred Rage: The Crusade of
  Modern Islam, 573
Sacred Survival: The Civil
  Religion of American
  Jews, 641
A Sacred Thread, 509
Sacrifice: Its Nature and
  Function, 429
Sacrifice in Africa: A Struc-
  turalist Approach, 429
Saeculum: History and Soci-
  ety in the Theology of St.
  Augustine, 110
Safed Spirituality, Rules of
  Mystical Piety and Elijah
  de Vidas' Beginning of
  Wisdom, 630
The Sage and the Way: Stud-
  ies in Spinoza's Ethics of
  Freedom, 189
Sage Philosophy, 26, 371
Sai Baba: The Holy Man and
  the Psychiatrist, 873
Saint Anselm and His Biog-
  rapher, 108
Saint Basil and Monasticism,
  705
Sainthood: Its Manifestations
  in World Religions, 505,
  513, 526
Saints and Postmodernism,
  392
Saints and Society: The Two
  Worlds of Western Chris-
  tendom, 1000 to 1700, 701
Saint Thomas and the Prob-
  lem of Evil, 307
Saint Watchings, 679
Sakyadhita: Daughters of the
  Buddha, 515
Salvation and Suicide, 867
Salvation in History, 832
Samaritan Documents: Relat-
  ing to Their History, Reli-
  gion and Life, 618
The Samaritan Pentateuch
  and the Origin of the Sa-
  maritan Sect, 618
The Samaritan Problem, 618
The Samaritans: History,
  Doctrines and Literature,
  618
Samaritans and Jews: The
  Origins of Samaritanism
  Reconsidered, 618
Sanctorum Communio, 759

Sangha, State and Society:
  Thai Buddhism in History,
  519
Santayana: An Examination
  of His Philosophy, 328
Santayana: Saint of the Imag-
  ination, 327
Santayana, Art, and Aesthet-
  ics, 327
Santayana, Pragmatism and
  the Spiritual Life, 328
Santayana and the Sense of
  Beauty, 327
Santería: African Spirits in
  America, 868
Santería: The Religion, 868
The Santería Experience: A
  Journey into the Miracu-
  lous, 868
Santería from Africa to the
  New World, 868
The Sants: Studies in a De-
  votional Tradition of In-
  dia, 517
Sartre (Caws), 330
Sartre (Hayman), 331
Sartre: A Life, 330
Sartre: A Philosophic Study,
  331
Sartre: Romantic Moralist,
  331
Sartre and Flaubert, 330
Sartre and Psychoanalysis:
  An Existentialist Challenge
  to Clinical Metatheory,
  330
Sartre's Concept of a Person,
  331
Sartre's Existential Biogra-
  phies, 331
Sartre's Marxism, 331
Sartre's Ontology: A Study of
  Being and Nothingness in
  the Light of Hegel's Logic,
  330
Sartre's Political Theory, 331
Sartre's Second Critique, 330
Sarvodaya: The Welfare of
  All, 552
Satan: The Early Christian
  Tradition, 687
Satanic Bible, 868
The Satanic Rituals, 868
The Satanism Scare, 868
Satan Wants You! The Cult
  of Devil Worship in Amer-
  ica, 868
Sati: Historical and Phenom-
  enological Essays, 509
Sati: Widow Burning, 508
Satirical Sketches, 484
Satyagraha in South Africa,
  552

The Savage Anomaly: The Power of Spinoza's Metaphysics and Politics, 189

The Scar of Montaigne: An Essay in Personal Philosophy, 146

Sceptical Essays, 323

Scepticism, Man and God: Selections from the Writings of Sextus Empiricus, 58

Scepticism, Rules, and Private Languages, 347

Scepticism and Animal Faith: Introduction to a System of Philosophy, 327

Scepticism or Platonism: The Philosophy of the Fourth Academy, 58

Schelling: An Introduction to His System of Freedom, 252

Schelling's Idealism and Philosophy of Nature, 252

Schelling's Treatise on the Essence of Human Freedom, 252, 292

Schleiermacher: Life and Thought, 741

Schleiermacher on Christ and Religion, 254

Scholars, Saints, and Sufis: Muslim Religious Institutions since 1500, 575

A Scholar's Guide to Academic Journals in Religion, 6

Scholarship on Philo and Josephus, 1937–1962, 608

The Scholastic Culture of the Middle Ages: 1000–1300, 695

Scholasticism and Politics, 307

Scholastic Miscellany: Anselm to Ockham, 94

Scholastic Rabbinism, 613

The School and Society, 224

The School of Peter Abelard, 106

Schools and Scholars in Fourteenth-Century England, 103

Schopenhauer, 256

Schopenhauer and the Wild Years of Philosophy, 256

Schopenhauer as Educator, 256

Schopenhauer as Transmitter of Buddhist Ideas, 256

Science, Faith, and Politics, 166

Science, Perception and Reality, 334

Science and Civic Life in the Italian Renaissance, 126

Science and Civilisation in China, 523

Science and Health with Key to the Scriptures, 842, 843, 874, 875

Science and Metaphysics: Variations on Kantian Themes, 334

Science and Philosophy in Classical Greece, 47

Science and Sentiment in America, 36

Science and Subjectivity, 385

Science and Synthesis, 337

Science and the Human Imagination, 405

Science and the Modern World, 341

Science and the Revenge of Nature, 408

Science and the Sociology of Knowledge, 406

Science and Thought in the Fifteenth Century, 131

Science and Wisdom, 307

Science as a Process, 384

Science in a Free Society, 399

Science in the Middle Ages, 97

The Science of Ethics, 198

The Science of Knowledge, 198

Science of Logic, 231, 232

The Science of Religion, 557

The Science of Rights, 198

The Science of the Mind, 382

The Science Question in Feminism, 40, 391

Scientific Healing Affirmations: Theory and Practice of Concentration, 557

Scientific Knowledge and Philosophic Thought, 384

The Scientific Marx, 243

Scientific Progress, 318

The Scientific Renaissance 1450–1630, 124

A Scientist Explores Spirit, 852

Scientology: The Fundamentals of Thought, 869

The Scope of Renaissance Humanism, 131, 697

Scotland: The Shaping of a Nation, 735

Scotland Reformed: The Reformation in Angus and the Mearns, 735

The Scottish Covenanters, 1660–1688, 735

Scottish Philosophy, 32, 203

The Scottish Philosophy, Biographical, Expository, Critical, from Hutcheson to Hamilton, 32, 212

The Scottish Philosophy of Common Sense, 32, 212

The Scottish Reformation, 735

The Screwtape Letters, 776

Scribes, Warriors and Kings: The City of Copan and the Ancient Maya, 455

Scripture, Sects and Visions, 615, 616

The Sculpture and Sculptors of Yazilikava, 444

The Sea Peoples: Warriors of the Ancient Mediterranean, 1250 to 1150, 445

The Search after Truth and Elucidations of the Search after Truth, 181, 182

Search for a Father: Sartre, Paternity, and the Question of Ethics, 330

Search for a Method, 329

The Search for Concreteness—Reflections on Hegel and Whitehead, 341

The Search for Jewish Identity in America, 641

The Search for Jewish Theology, 648

The Search for the Origins of Christian Worship, 687

A Search for Wisdom and Spirit: Thomas Merton's Theology of the Self, 781

Seasons for Celebration, 601

Seasons of Our Joy: A Handbook of Jewish Festivals, 600

The Second Coming: Satanism in America, 868

The Second Isaiah Introduction, Translation and Commentary to Chapters 40–55, 822

The Second Jewish Catalogue: Sources and Resources, 602

A Second Look in the Rear-View Mirror, 270

The Second Message of Islam, 576

The Second Treatise of Civil Government, 179

The Secret Connexion: Cau-

sation, Realism, and David Hume, 203
The Secret Doctrine: The Synthesis of Science, Religion, and Philosophy, 852, 873, 874
The Secret Garden: An Anthology on the Kabbalah, 630
Secrets of the Lotus, 520
Secrets of the Self, 375
Secular Education in Philo of Alexandria, 670
The Secular Is Sacred, 141
Secularization and Moral Change, 407
The Secular Journal of Thomas Merton, 781
Secular Utilitarianism, 190
Seeking Spiritual Meaning: The World of Vedanta, 872
Seeking the Path to Life, 649
Seek My Face, Speak My Name: A Contemporary Jewish Theology, 648
Sefer ha-Qabbalah: The Book of Tradition, 627
Selected Critical Writings of George Santayana, 327
The Selected Letters of Bertrand Russell, Vol. 1: The Private Years, 1884–1914, 324
Selected Philosophical Essays, 332
Selected Philosophical Russian Contemporary Essays, 31
Selected Political Writings, 209
Selected Works of Ramon Llull (1232–1316), 102
Selected Writings of Huldrych Zwingli, 791
Selected Writings of Nichiren, 538
Selected Writings of the New England Transcendentalists, 753
Selected Writings of Thomas Aquinas, 118
Selected Writings on the History of Science, 258
Select English Writings, 714
Selections from Cultural Writings, 287
Selections from English Wycliffite Writings, 714, 721
Selections from Medieval Philosophers, 95
Selections from Political Writings, 1910–1920, 287

Selections from Political Writings, 1921–1926, 287
Selections from the Scottish Philosophy of Common Sense, 32
Selections from Three Works of Francisco Suárez, 154
Select Letters, 72, 711
A Select Library of the Nicene and Post-Nicene Fathers of the Christian Church, 100, 680, 702, 705, 706, 707, 709, 710, 712
Select Passages Illustrating Neoplatonism, 61
The Self, Its Body, and Freedom, 296
Self, Society, Existence, Human Nature and Dialogue in the Thought of George Herbert Mead and Martin Buber, 309
The Self and Its Brain, 409
Self and Nature in Kant's Philosophy, 207
The Self and the World in the Philosophy of Josiah Royce, 250
Self and World in Schopenhauer's Philosophy, 256
Self-Deception and Morality, 389
Self-Direction and Political Legitimacy: Rousseau and Herder, 199
Self-Fulfilling Prophecy: Exile and Return as the History of Judaism, 594
Self-Knowledge in Plato's Phaedrus, 81
Selfless Persons: Imagery and Thought in Theravada Buddhism, 887
The Self-Overcoming of Nihilism, 365
Semantics of Biblical Language, 817
The Semiotic of Myth: A Critical Study of the Symbol, 428
Semites and Anti-Semites: An Inquiry into Conflict and Prejudice, 571
Send These to Me: Jews and Other Immigrants in Urban America, 639
Seneca, 88
Seneca: A Philosopher in Politics, 88
Senecan Drama and Stoic Cosmology, 59, 88

Seneca the Philosopher and His Modern Message, 88
Sensations and Images and the Strange Deviations of the Mind, 323
Sense and Contradiction: A Study in Aristotle, 67
Sense and Non-Sense, 310
Sense and Sensibilia, 272
Sense and Subjectivity: A Study of Wittgenstein and Merleau-Ponty, 311
The Sense of Beauty: Critical Edition, 327
The Sephardic Tradition: Ladino and Spanish-Jewish Literature, 622
Sephardim: The Jews from Spain, 644
Septuaginta, 796
The Septuagint and Modern Study, 796
The Septuagint Version of the Old Testament and Apocrypha, 796
Sermons, 193
Set Theory and Its Logic, 411
Seven Exegetical Works, 702
Seven Great Religions, 550
Seven Principles of Man, 550
The Seven Storey Mountain, 780, 781
Seventeenth and Eighteenth Century British Philosophers, 160
The Seventh Sense, 203
The Several Israels, and an Essay: Religion and Modern Man, 646
Sex, Sin and Grace, 784
Sex and Repression in Savage Society, 486
Sex and the Penitentials: The Development of a Sexual Code 550–1150, 700
Sex Ethics in the Writings of Moses Maimonides, 668
Sex in the World's Religions, 894
Sexism and God-Talk: Toward a Feminist Theology, 785, 905
Sexuality, the Bible, and Science, 894
Sexuality and Eroticism among Males in Moslem Societies, 894
Sexuality in Islam, 894
Sexual Life in Ancient India, 505
Shaarei Mitzvah: Gates of Mitzvah, 602

The Shadow of God and the Hidden Imam, 578

Shaftesbury's Philosophy of Religion and Ethics, 214

The Shaker Adventure, 849

Shaker Communities, Shaker Lives, 849

The Shaker Experience in America, 754, 850

Shaker Literature: A Bibliography, 849

The Shakers: Two Centuries of Spiritual Reflection, 850

The Shaker Spiritual Narrative, 850

Shaker Villages, 849

Shakespeare and the Stoicism of Seneca, 88

The Shaking of the Foundations, 787

Shakti: Power in the Conceptual Structure of Karimpur Religion, 506

Shakubuku, 860

Shamanism: Archaic Techniques of Ecstasy, 431, 474

Shamanism: Soviet Studies of Traditional Religion in Siberia and Central Asia, 430

Shamanism: The Spirit World of Korea, 539

Shamanism, Colonialism, and the Wild Man: A Study in Terror and Healing, 431

Shamans, Housewives and Other Restless Spirits, 539

Shamans, Mystics, and Doctors, 890

The Shaman's Touch: Otomi Indian Symbolic Healing, 465

The Shape of Death: Life, Death, and Immortality in the Early Fathers, 99

The Shape of the Liturgy, 688

Shari'at and Ambiguity in South Asian Islam, 578

The Shattered Spectrum: A Survey of Contemporary Theology, 719

The Shavuot Anthology, 599

Shechem: Biography of a Biblical City, 618

The Shi'ite Religion: A History of Islam in Persia and Iraq, 574

The Shi'ites, 572

Shin Buddhism, 558

Shinran's Gospel of Pure Grace, 537

Shinto: Japan's Spiritual Roots, 536

Shinto: The Kami Way, 536

Shinto: The Way of Japan, 536

Shinto and the State 1968–1988, 540

Shinto-Bibliography in Western Languages, 534

Shobogenzo: Zen Essays by Dogen, 534

The Shorter Encyclopedia of Islam, 566

A Short Grammar of Biblical Aramaic, 795

A Short History of Christian Doctrine: From the First Century to the Present, 677

A Short History of Ethics, 407

A Short History of Existentialism, 268

A Short History of Islam, 571

A Short History of Medieval Philosophy, 94, 698

A Short History of Syriac Christianity to the Rise of Islam, 684

A Short History of the Catholic Church, 677

A Short History of the Interpretation of the Bible, 99, 813

A Short History of the Papacy in the Middle Ages, 695

A Short History of the Western Liturgy, 678

A Short Introduction to Moral Philosophy, 203

Short Life of Kierkegaard, 240

Shtetl Memories, 624

Shuzo Kuki and Jean-Paul Sartre, 331

Sic et non: A Critical Edition, 106

The Sickness unto Death, 239

Sidgwick's Ethics and Victorian Moral Philosophy, 257

Sidney Hook: Philosopher of Democracy and Humanism, 298

Sidney Hook and the Contemporary World, 298

Sifra: An Analytical Translation, 612

Sifra in Perspective, 612

Sifre: A Tannaitic Commentary on the Book of Deuteronomy, 610

Sifré to Deuteronomy: An Analytical Translation, 612

Sifré to Deuteronomy: An Introduction to the Rhetorical, Logical, and Topical Program, 612

Sifré to Numbers: An American Translation, 612

Sigmund Freud and the Jewish Mystical Tradition, 628

Signeponge-Signeponge, 397

The Significance of Neoplatonism, 61

Significations: Signs, Symbols, and Images in the Interpretation of Religion, 426

Signs, 310

The Sikh Diaspora: Migration and the Experience beyond the Punjab, 516

Sikh History and Religion in the Twentieth Century, 516

Sikhism and the Sikhs: An Annotated Bibliography, 517

The Sikhs: History of Religion and Society, 516

Sikh Separatism: The Politics of a Faith, 516

Sikh Studies: Comparative Perspectives on a Changing Tradition, 516

Silence, 540

Silent Revolution, 467

Simone Weil: A Modern Pilgrim, 788

Simone Weil Reader, 788

Sin and Confession on the Eve of the Reformation, 701

Sincerity and Truth: Essays on Arnauld, Bayle, and Toleration, 164, 166

The Singer of Tales, 460

Singing with Sai Baba: The Politics of Revitalization in Trinidad, 872

Sinners in the Hands of an Angry God, 766, 767

Sir James Frazer and the Literary Imagination: Essays in Affinity and Influence, 477

Sister Aimee: The Life of Aimee Semple McPherson, 753

Siva: The Erotic Ascetic, 505

The Six Bookes of a Commonweale, 133, 134

Six Existentialist Thinkers, 262

Six Great Ideas: Truth, Goodness, Beauty, Liberty, Equality, Justice, 270

Six Makers of English Religion, 1500–1700, 727

Six Perspectives on New Religions: A Case Study Approach, 855

Six Pillars: Introduction to the Major Works of Sri Aurobindo, 353

Six World Religions, 567

The Skeleton in the Wardrobe, 776

The Skeptical Tradition, 58

Skepticism: A Critical Appraisal, 318

Skepticism and Naturalism, 414

Skywatchers of Ancient Mexico, 455, 457

The Slayers of Moses, 610

Sleepwalkers, 161

The Social and Political Thought of Karl Marx, 242

A Social and Religious History of the Jews, 593, 596

Social Concern in Calvin's Geneva, 762

Social Contract, 212

Social Contract and Discourses, 213

Socialism and the Jews: The Dilemmas of Assimilation in Germany and Austria-Hungary, 656

Social Issues: Meditative Thinking and the Threefold Social Order, 879

Social Philosophy and Religion of Comte, 223

The Social Philosophy of Adam Smith, 215

The Social Setting of Pauline Christianity: Essays on Corinth, 618, 826

The Social Teaching of the Christian Churches, 95

Social Thought, 689

The Social Thought of John XXIII: Mater et Magistra, 771

Society and Culture in Early Modern France, 731

Society and Religion in Elizabethan England, 734

Society and Settlement: Jewish Land of Israel in the Twentieth Century, 594, 642

Society and the Holy in Late Antiquity, 449

Society and the Sexes in Medieval Islam, 579

Society in Crisis: France in the Sixteenth Century, 732

Society of the Muslim Brothers, 572

Sociology and the Jesus Movement, 864

The Sociology of Early Palestinian Christianity, 618

The Sociology of Religion, 494, 890

The Sociology of the American Jew, 641

Socio-Religious Reform Movements in British India, 508, 516, 517

Socrates, 89, 90

Socrates, Buddha, Confucius and Jesus, 17, 300, 349

Socrates, Ironist and Moral Philosopher, 90

Socrates and Aristophanes, 90

Socrates and Legal Obligation, 89

Socrates and the Political Community: An Ancient Debate, 90

Socrates and the State, 89

Socrates on Trial, 89

Socrates to Sartre: A History of Philosophy, 18

Socratic Humanism, 54

The Socratic Paradoxes and the Greek Mind, 90

Socratic Satire: An Essay on Diderot and Le Neveu de Rameau, 197

Solid Philosophy, 180

Soliloquies in England and Later Soliloquies, 327

Solitude and Society, 275

Solomon Maimon: An Autobiography, 647

Soloveitchik on Repentance, 886

So Many Versions?, 798

Some Aspects of Hittite Religion, 445

Some Aspects of Rabbinic Theology, 621

Some Dogmas of Religion, 304

Some Problems of Philosophy, 236

Some Questions about Language, 271

Something Beautiful for God: Mother Teresa of Calcutta, 745

Some Thoughts Concerning Education, 178

Some Traditions of the Thai, 519

Some Turns of Thought in Modern Philosophy, 327

Somewhere a Master: Further Tales of the Hasidic Masters, 633

Somnium et vigilia in Somnium Scipionis, 156

The Song at the Sea, 610

Song of Songs Rabbah: An Analytical Translation, 612

Songs of Kabir from the Adi Granth, 516

Songs of the Saints of India, 504, 516

The Son of Apollo: Themes of Plato, 85

The Sophismata of Richard Kilvington, 104

Sophisms on Meaning and Truth, 103

The Sophists, 54

Sophrosyne: Self-Knowledge and Self-Restraint in Greek Literature, 48

Soto Zen in a Japanese Town, 537

Souls and the Structure of Being in Late Neoplatonism—Syrianus, Proclus and Simplicius, 61

Souls on Fire: Portraits and Legends of Hasidic Masters, 633

A Sourcebook in Asian Philosophy, 498, 522

Source Book in Chinese Philosophy, 358, 521

Sourcebook in Indian Philosophy, 351, 498

A Source Book in Medieval Science, 94

Sources for the Study of Greek Religion, 446

Sources of Chinese Tradition, 358, 521

Sources of Contemporary Philosophical Realism in America, 35, 267

Sources of Indian Tradition, 497

Sources of Japanese Tradition, 534

Sources of the Self, 415

South American Mythology, 465

Southeast Asia: A Cultural Study through Celebration, 519

Southern Churches in Crisis, 753

Soviet Ideology, 31

Soviet Marxism, 408

Soviet Philosophy: A General Introduction to Contemporary Soviet Thought, 30

Soviet Philosophy: A Study of Theory and Practice, 31

Soviet Russian Dialectical Materialism, 31

Soviet Scholasticism, 30

Spain, the Jews and Franco, 635

Speaking from the Heart, 391

Speaking of a Personal God: An Essay in Philosophical Theology, 743

Speaking the Christian God: The Holy Trinity and the Challenge of Feminism, 905

A Special Legacy, 641

Speculation and Revelation, 335

Speculative Grammars of the Middle Ages, 101

Speculum Mentis, or the Map of Knowledge, 282

Speculum Spinozanum: 1677–1977, 188

Speech and Phenomena, 397

Spellbound: Studies on Mesmerism and Literature, 847

Spenser's Poetry and the Reformation Tradition, 726

Spinoza (Caird), 187

Spinoza (Jaspers), 188

Spinoza (Scruton), 189

Spinoza: A Collection of Critical Essays, 188

Spinoza: Dictionary, 15

Spinoza: Essays in Interpretation, 187

Spinoza: His Life, Correspondence and Ethics, 189

Spinoza: His Life and Philosophy, 189

Spinoza, Descartes and Maimonides, 189

Spinoza and the Rise of Liberalism, 187

Spinoza and the Sciences, 188

A Spinoza Bibliography, 189

Spinoza in Soviet Philosophy: A Series of Essays, 188

Spinoza on Nature, 187

Spinoza's Critique of Religion, 189

Spinoza's Philosophy: An Outline, 188

Spinoza's Political and Ethical Philosophy, 187

Spinoza's Theory of Truth, 189

The Spiral Dance: Rebirth of the Ancient Religion of the Goddess, 865

The Spiral Path: Essays and Interviews on Women's Spirituality, 888

Spirit in Ashes: Hegel, Heidegger, and Man-Made Mass Death, 295

The Spirit of American Philosophy, 36

The Spirit of Chinese Philosophy, 358, 359

The Spirit of Islam, 372, 567, 587

The Spirit of M. Spinoza, or the Three Imposters, Moses, Jesus, and Mohammed, 188

The Spirit of Medieval Philosophy, 95, 286, 696

The Spirit of Modern Philosophy, 250

The Spirit of the Counter Reformation, 728

The Spirit of the Laws, 209, 210

The Spirit of the Oxford Movement, 783

The Spirit of the Ten Commandments, 620

Spirits in Rebellion: The Rise and Development of New Thought, 847

Spiritual and Anabaptist Writers, 724

Spiritual and Demonic Magic from Ficino to Campanella, 132

The Spiritual Background of Islam, 574

Spiritual Exercises, Spiritual Diary, Autobiography, 769, 770

Spiritual Friendship, 101

Spiritualism and Nineteenth-Century Letters, 851

Spiritualism and Society, 851

The Spiritualists, 850

Spirituality and Human Nature, 888

The Spirituality of John Calvin, 762

The Spirituality of St. Teresa of Avila, 786

The Spirituality of Teilhard de Chardin, 337

The Spirituality of the Christian East: A Systematic Handbook, 679

The Spirituality of the Future, 337

The Spiritual Life, 550

The Spirituals and the Blues: An Interpretation, 763

Spiritus Creator, 779

Sport: A Philosophic Inquiry, 340

Spurs: Nietzsche's Styles, 397

Sri Aurobindo: A Brief Biography, 353

Sri Aurobindo and Karl Marx: Integral Sociology and Dialectical Sociology, 353

St. Albert the Great, 107

St. Ambrose: His Life and Times, 702

St. Anselm: A Portrait in a Landscape, 703

St. Anselm's Proslogion, 703

St. Augustine of Hippo: Life and Controversies, 109

St. Augustine's Early Theory of Man, A.D. 386–391, 110

St. Augustine's Platonism, 110

St. Bernard of Clairvaux, 112

St. Francis Xavier, 1506–1552, 728

St. Ignatius Loyola: The Pilgrim Years, 1491–1538, 770

St. John of the Cross: An Appreciation, 736

St. Peter Canisius, 728

St. Teresa of Avila, 786, 787

St. Thérèse of Lisieux: By Those Who Knew Her, 741

St. Thomas and the Gentiles, 270

St. Thomas Aquinas: On Charity, 118

St. Thomas Aquinas: On Spiritual Creatures, 118

St. Thomas Aquinas: Philosophical Texts, 118

St. Thomas Aquinas: Theological Texts, 118

The Stakes of the Warrior, 472

The Star of Redemption, 671, 886

Starry Messenger, 142

State and Society in Roman Galilee, A.D. 132–212, 606

The State in Burma, 515

The Stepchildren of the Reformation, 724

Stoic and Epicurean, 55
The Stoic and Epicurean
    Philosophers, 56
The Stoic Idea of the City,
    57
Stoic Logic, 57
Stoic Philosophy, 57
The Stoics, 57
Stoics and Skeptics, 55
Stories from Ancient Canaan,
    445
The Story of Jewish Philoso-
    phy, 601
The Story of Judaism, 596
Story of Philosophy, 15, 16
The Story of Rama in Jain
    Literature, 509
The Story of Scottish Philos-
    ophy, 32
The Story of the Jesus Peo-
    ple: A Factual Survey, 864
The Story of the Synagogue:
    A Diaspora Museum Book,
    597
The Story of Two Souls: The
    Correspondence of Jac-
    ques Maritain and Julien
    Green, 307
Strange Gods: The Great
    American Cult Scare, 855
The Strangeness of the Ordi-
    nary, 380
Stranger at Home: "The Ho-
    locaust," Zionism, and
    American Judaism, 646,
    649
A Stranger in Tibet: The Ad-
    ventures of a Wandering
    Zen Monk, 859
Strangers in a Christian
    Land, 894
Strangers in Their Own
    Lands, 637
Strange Weather: Culture,
    Science and Technology
    in the Age of Limits, 866
The Strife of Systems, 318
A Stroll with William James,
    237
Structural Anthropology, 426
The Structural Transforma-
    tion of the Public Sphere,
    404
Structure and Form in the
    Babylonian Talmud, 620
Structure and History in
    Greek Mythology and Ritu-
    al, 470, 471
The Structure of Appearance,
    403
The Structure of Behavior,
    310
The Structure of Being: A

Neoplatonic Interpretation,
    61
The Structure of Empirical
    Knowledge, 380
The Structure of Jewish His-
    tory and Other Essays, 647
The Structure of Lutheran-
    ism, 730
The Structure of Philosophy,
    23
The Structure of Plato's Phi-
    losophy, 79
The Structure of Resurrec-
    tion Belief, 887
The Structure of Science,
    313, 385
The Structure of Scientific
    Inference, 405
The Structure of Scientific
    Revolutions, 406
The Structure of Society, 315
Struggle for Synthesis, 177
A Student at the Azhar, 374
Students, Scholars, and
    Saints, 620
Studies in African Religion,
    570
Studies in Ancient Israelite
    Wisdom, 823
Studies in Chinese Bud-
    dhism, 530
Studies in Eighteenth-Century
    Islamic History, 572
Studies in Hegelian Cosmol-
    ogy, 304
Studies in Hegelian Dialectic,
    304
Studies in Islamic and Juda-
    ic Traditions, 625
Studies in Islamic Mysticism,
    583
Studies in Islamic Philosophy
    and Science, 576
Studies in Japanese Folklore,
    539
Studies in Jewish History,
    604
Studies in Jewish Law and
    Philosophy, 628
Studies in Jewish Mysticism,
    630
Studies in Jewish Thought:
    An Anthology of German
    Jewish Scholarship, 646,
    647
Studies in Kant's Aesthetics,
    207
Studies in Logical Theory,
    225
Studies in Lucian's De Syria
    Dea, 485
Studies in Luke—Acts, 825
Studies in Medieval Jewish

History and Literature,
    625
Studies in Medieval Philoso-
    phy, Science, and Logic,
    121
Studies in Medieval Thought,
    96
Studies in Muslim-Jewish Re-
    lations, 626
Studies in Pessimism, 256
Studies in Phenomenological
    Psychology, 235
Studies in Philosophy: A
    Symposium on Gilbert
    Ryle, 325
Studies in Post-Medieval Se-
    mantics, 123
Studies in Pre-Socratic Phi-
    losophy, 50
Studies in Renaissance Phi-
    losophy and Science, 131
Studies in Sin and Atone-
    ment, 615
Studies in Soviet Thought,
    31
Studies in Spanish Renais-
    sance Thought, 128
Studies in Spinoza: Critical
    and Interpretive Essays,
    188
Studies in Targum Jonathan
    to the Prophets, 609
Studies in the Apostolic Fa-
    thers and Their Back-
    ground, 703
Studies in the Archaeology
    of India and Pakistan, 501
Studies in the Cartesian Phi-
    losophy, 171
Studies in the Civilization of
    Islam, 569
Studies in the Early History
    of Judaism, 606
Studies in the History of Ar-
    abic Logic, 318
Studies in the Life and
    Works of Petrarch, 151
Studies in the Making of the
    English Protestant Tradi-
    tion, 727
Studies in the Philosophy of
    David Hume, 202
Studies in the Philosophy of
    Kant, 206
Studies in the Philosophy of
    the Scottish Enlighten-
    ment, 32
Studies in the Theory of Ide-
    ology, 405
Studies in the Variety of
    Rabbinic Cultures, 622
Studies in the Ways of
    Words, 288

Studies in Zen, 558
Studies on the Near East, 571
Studies on Voltaire, 218
Study in Consciousness, 550
The Study of American Indian Religions, 465
Study of Ancient Judaism, 612
A Study of Dōgen: His Philosophy and Religion, 364
Study of Husserl's Formal and Transcendental Logic, 234
The Study of Liturgy, 678, 897
A Study of Nietzsche, 248
A Study of Spinoza's Ethics, 187
The Study of the Bible in the Middle Ages, 628, 697
A Study of the "Summa philosophiae" of the Pseudo-Grosseteste, 102
Suárez on Human Freedom, 154
Suárez on Individuation, 105
Subject and Predicate in Logic and Grammar, 414
The Subjection of Women, 244
Substance and Essence in Aristotle: An Interpretation of Metaphysics VII–IX, 72
Substance and Function and Einstein's Theory of Relativity, 279
Substance and Predication in Aristotle, 69
The Subtle Connection between the Theory of Experience and the Logic of Science, 409
Sufi Essays, 902
The Sufi Orders in Islam, 577
The Sufi Path of Love: The Spiritual Teachings of Rumi, 590
The Sufis, 576
A Sufi Saint of the Twentieth Century, 575
The Sukkot and Simhat Torah Anthology, 599
Sumerian Mythology, 441, 545
A Summary of Catholic History, 720
The Sun Dance Religion: Power for the Powerless, 467
The Sun My Heart: From

Mindfulness to Insight Contemplation, 562
The Supreme Identity, 881
Survey of American Philosophy, 36
A Survey of Hinduism, 505
A Survey of Recent Christian Ethics, 744
Surveys from Exile, 242
Susanna, Mother of the Wesleys, 790
Sustainability: Economics, Ecology, and Justice, 743
Swamiji and His Message, 563
Swami Vivekananda in the West: New Discoveries, 563
The Swan's Wide Waters: Ramakrishna and Western Culture, 872
Swedenborg: Life and Teachings, 852, 880
Swedenborg and His Influence, 852
The Swedish Church, 731
The Sword and the Flute, 505
Symbol, Myth, and Culture: Essays and Lectures by Ernst Cassirer 1935–1945, 280
Symbol and Empowerment: Paul Tillich's Post-Theistic System, 787
Symbol and Theology in Early Judaism, 614
Symbolic Wounds: Puberty Rites and the Envious Male, 430
Symbolism: Its Meaning and Effect, 341
The Symbolism of Evil, 319, 886
Symphorien Champier and the Reception of the Occultist Tradition in Renaissance France, 125
The Symposium, 78, 91
Symposium on J. L. Austin, 272
The Synagogue: Studies in Origins, Archaeology, and Architecture, 614
The Synagogue in Late Antiquity, 597
Synagogue Life: A Study in Symbolic Interaction, 654
Synagogues of Europe: Architecture, History, Meaning, 597
Synopsis of the Four Gospels, 794

The Synoptic Vision: Essays on the Philosophy of Wilfrid Sellars, 334
Syntagma philosophicum, 173
Syrian Christians in Muslim Society: An Interpretation, 569
The Syrian Goddess, 484
System and Revelation: The Philosophy of Franz Rosenzweig, 671
Systematic Theology: Life and the Spirit, History and the Kingdom of God, 787
Systematic Theology: Roman Catholic Perspectives, 422, 745, 891
System of Logic: Ratiocinative and Inductive, 243, 244
System of Moral Philosophy, 203
System of Natural Philosophy, 194
System of Positive Polity, 223
A System of Pragmatic Idealism, 318
System of Transcendental Idealism, 251, 252
The Systems of the Hellenistic Age: A History of Ancient Philosophy, 55

T. S. Kuhn and Social Sciences, 406
The Tain of the Mirror, 398
Tales of Rabbi Nachman, 669
The Tales of Rabbi Nahman of Bratslav, 669
Tales of the Dervishes, 576
Tales of the Hasidim, 632
Tales of the Sacred and the Supernatural, 474
Talmud: A Close Encounter, 612
The Talmud: The Steinsaltz Edition, Vol. I, 613
Talmudic Thinking: Language, Logic, and Law, 621
Talmud of Babylonia: An American Translation, 612
Talmud of the Land of Israel: A Preliminary Translation and Explanation, 612
The Tamil Veda: Pillan's Interpretation of the Tiruvaymoli, 26

Tanakh, of the Holy Scriptures, 798
Tantra in Tibet, 560
Tantric Art and Meditation: The Tendai Tradition, 538
The Tantric Distinction: An Introduction to Tibetan Buddhism, 356
Taoism: The Road to Immortality, 527
Taoism and Chinese Religion, 528
Taoism and the Rite of Cosmic Renewal, 528
Taoist Meditation and Longevity Techniques, 528
The Tao of Pooh, 528
The Tao of the Tao Te Ching: A Translation and Commentary, 528
Targumic Approaches to the Gospels, 608
The Targum Neofiti to Genesis, 796
The Targum of Jeremiah, 608
The Targums and Rabbinic Literature, 608
Targums of Onkelos and Jonathan Ben Uzziel on the Pentateuch with the Fragments of the Jerusalem Targum from the Chaldee, 608
Tarjuma'n Al-Ashwa'q, 583
Ta T'ung Shu, The One-World Philosophy of K'ang Yu-Wei, 361
Tauq al-Hamama, 583
The Teacher. The Free Choice of the Will. Grace and Free Will, 109
Teaching and Research in Philosophy: Africa, 26
Teaching and Worship of the Liberal Catholic Church, 859
Teaching Authority in the Early Church, 688
The Teaching of Humanae Vitae: A Defense, 743
The Teaching of the Catholic Church, 891
The Teaching of the Qur'an, 587
Teachings from the American Earth: Indian Religion and Philosophy, 465
The Teachings of Hasidism, 632
The Teachings of Pope John XXIII, 771
The Teachings of the Magi:

A Compendium of Zoroastrian Beliefs, 548
Tea in Japan: Essays on the History of Chanoyu, 538
Tea Life, Tea Mind, 538
Teilhard, 337
Teilhard, Scripture and Revelation, 337
Teilhard de Chardin, 337
Teilhard de Chardin: A Short Biography, 337
Teilhard de Chardin's Vision of the Future, 337
Teleological Explanations, 415
Teleology Revisited and Other Essays in the Philosophy and History of Science, 313
Telescopes, Tides and Tactics, 143
Telling Tales, 603
Temporal Modalities in Arabic Logic, 318
Ten Colloquies, 139
Ten Philosophical Mistakes, 271
Ten Rungs: Hasidic Sayings, 632
The Te of Piglet, 528
Teotihuacan, 457
Teotihuacan: The City of Gods, 457
Teresa: A Woman; A Biography of Teresa of Avila, 786
Teresa of Avila, 787
Teresa of Avila and the Rhetoric of Femininity, 787
Teresa of Avila's Way, 786
Tertullian: A Historical and Literary Study, 714
A Testament of Hope: The Essential Writings of Martin Luther King, Jr., 772
The Text as Thou, 662
The Text of the New Testament: Its Transmission, Corruption, and Restoration, 805, 806
The Text of the Old Testament, 806
Texts, Hebrew Translation, Commentary, and Introduction, 445
Texts and Dialogues, 310
Texts and Studies in Jewish History and Literature, 631
Texts in Context: Traditional Hermeneutics in South Asia, 506, 510, 514, 517

A Textual Commentary on the Greek New Testament, 806
Textual Sources for the Study of Sikhism, 516
Textual Sources for the Study of Zoroastrianism, 443, 547
Thai Buddhism, 520
Thai Manuscript Painting, 518
The Theaetetus of Plato, 79
Theatre of Nature, 134
Theism in Medieval India, 503
Themes in Soviet Marxist Philosophy, 30
Themes of Islamic Civilization, 580
Themis: A Study of the Social Origins of Greek Religion, 479
Theodicy in Islamic Thought, 582
Theodore Beza's Doctrine of Predestination, 731
Theogony: Translated with Introduction, Commentary and Interpretative Essay, 228, 481
Theogony and Works and Days, 481
Theological and Dogmatic Works, 702
A Theological and Historical Introduction to the Apostolic Fathers, 704
Theological and Religious Reference Materials, 716
Theological Anthropology, 685
Theological Dictionary of the New Testament, 818
Theological Dictionary of the Old Testament, 817
Theological Essays, 744
Theological Investigations, 423, 903
The Theological Methodology of Hans Küng, 775
Theological Political Tractatus, 186
Theology after Freud: An Interpretive Inquiry, 424
Theology after Vedanta: An Experiment in Comparative Theology, 872
Theology after Wittgenstein, 346
Theology and Dialogue: Essays in Conversation with George Lindbeck, 753
Theology and Social Theory.

Beyond Secular Reason, 890

Theology and the Problem of Evil, 886

Theology and the Scientific Imagination from the Middle Ages to the Seventeenth Century, 126, 160

Theology at the End of Modernity, 743

Theology for the Third Millennium, 775

Theology in the Responsa, 629

Theology in the Russian Diaspora, 756

Theology of Discontent, 373

The Theology of Jonathan Edwards: A Reappraisal, 767

A Theology of Liberation: History, Politics, and Salvation, 748, 769, 896

The Theology of Martin Luther, 778

The Theology of Paul Tillich, 787

The Theology of Post-Reformation Lutheranism, 730

The Theology of Schleiermacher, 254

The Theology of St. Luke, 825

The Theology of the Early Greek Philosophers: The Gifford Lectures, 1936, 50

Theology of the English Reformers, 726

The Theology of the New Testament, 827, 831

Theology of the Old Testament, 827, 834

Theology of the Psalms, 823

The Theology of Unity, 374

Theophrastean Studies, on Natural Science, Physics and Metaphysics, Ethics, Religion and Rhetoric, 90

Theophrastus and the Greek Physiological Psychology before Aristotle, 91

Theophrastus Bombastus von Hohenheim Called Paracelsus, 150

Theophrastus of Eresus: On His Life and Work, 91

Theorems on Essence and Existence, 103

Theoretical Philosophy 1755–1770, 205

Theories and Things, 411

Theories of Primitive Religion, 475

Theories of Reading in Dialogue: An Interdisciplinary Study, 319

Theories of the Proposition, 97

Theories of Truth, 381

Theories of Vision from al-Kindi to Kepler, 128

Theory and Practice, 404

Theory and Religious Understanding, 494

The Theory of Alfred North Whitehead: A Logical and Ethical Vindication, 341

The Theory of Categories, 222

The Theory of Communicative Action, 404

Theory of Demonstration According to William Ockham, 121

The Theory of Intuition in Husserl's Phenomenology, 235

A Theory of Justice, 316

Theory of Knowledge (Chisholm), 395

Theory of Knowledge (Lehrer), 22, 381

Theory of Knowledge: The 1913 Manuscript, 22, 323, 381, 395

Theory of Knowledge of Giambattista Vico, 216

The Theory of Knowledge of Hugh of St. Victor, 102

The Theory of Knowledge of Vital du Four, 102

The Theory of Moral Life, 225

Theory of Moral Sentiments, 214, 215

The Theory of Motion in Plato's Later Dialogues, 84

Theory of Science, 197

Theory of the Spirit and the Egocentric Propensities of Man, 285

Theory of Valuation, 225

Theosophy in the Nineteenth Century: An Annotated Bibliography, 853

Theotokos: A Theological Encyclopedia of the Blessed Virgin Mary, 675

Therapeia: Plato's Conception of Philosophy, 80

Theravada Buddhism, 513

Theravada Buddhism in Southeast Asia, 519

Therese, 765

These Also Believe, 855

Thespis: Ritual, Myth, and Drama in the Ancient Near East, 439

They Call Her Pastor: A New Role for Catholic Women, 892

They Fought Back: The Story of the Jewish Resistance in Nazi Europe, 637

The Things That Are Not Caesar's, 307

Things That Happen, 414

Thinking about Being: Aspects of Heidegger's Thought, 295

Thinking about God: An Introduction to Theology, 750

Thinking Matter: Materialism in Eighteenth-Century Britain, 163

Think on These Things, 555

The Third Force in Seventeenth-Century Thought, 18, 162

The Third Jewish Catalogue: Building Community, 602

The Thirteen Pragmatisms and Other Essays, 303

The Thirteen Principal Upanishads, 501

Thirteen Thinkers: A Sampler of Great Philosophers, 17

The Thirty Years War, 737

This Is It, 881

This Is My God, 597

This Is Not a Pipe, 400

This People Israel, 660

This Religion of Islam, 576

Thomas Aquinas, 118

Thomas Aquinas and John Gerhard, 731

Thomas Aquinas and Radical Aristotelianism, 119

Thomas Cranmer, 725, 727

Thomas Cranmer and the English Reformation 1489–1556, 764

Thomas Hill Green: Philosopher of Rights, 230

Thomas Hobbes, 174

Thomas Hobbes: Radical in the Service of Reaction, 175

Thomas Merton: Spiritual Master: The Essential Writings, 781

A Thomas Merton Reader, 781

Thomas More, 147

Thomas More: A Biography, 148

Thomas More: History and Providence, 147

Thomas More: The Search for the Inner Man, 148
Thomas More and Erasmus, 727
Thomas More and His Utopia, 147
Thomas Paine, 273
Thomas Reid, 212
Thomas Reid and the "Way of Ideas," 212
Thomas Reid on Freedom and Morality, 212
Thomas Reid's Inquiry: The Geometry of Visibles and the Case for Realism, 211
Thomas White's De Mundo Examined in First English Translation, 174
Thomist Realism, 286
Thought, Fact, and Reference: The Origins and Ontology of Logical Atomism, 312
The Thought and Character of William James, 238
Thought and Expression in the Sixteenth Century, 131
Thought and Letters in Western Europe, A.D. 500–900, 100, 699
Thought Experiments, 385
Thought Forms, 550
The Thought of Gregory the Great, 710
The Thought of Mao Tsetung, 362
Thought Power: Its Control and Culture, 550
Thoughts on Death and Immortality, 227, 228
Thoughts on Machiavelli, 145
Three Argentine Thinkers, 33
Three Books of Occult Philosophy or Magic, 133
Three Books on Life, 141
Three Chilean Thinkers, 33
Three Christian Capitals: Topography and Politics, 684
Three Dialogues between Hylas and Philonous, 191
Three Dialogues on Knowledge, 399
Three Discourses on Imagined Occasions, 239
Three Essays on Religion, 244
Three Faiths—One God: A Jewish, Christian, Muslim Encounter, 41, 569
Three Jewish Philosophers, 628
Three Muslim Sages: Avicen-
na, Suhwardi, Ibn-'Arabi, 582
Three Philosophical Moralists: Mill, Kant, and Sartre, 331
Three Philosophical Poets, 75, 327
The Three Pillars of Zen: Teaching, Practice, Enlightenment, 537, 860
Three Reformers: Luther, Descartes, Rousseau, 307
Three Rival Versions of Moral Enquiry, 407
Three Studies in Current Philosophical Questions, 303
Three Treatises, 778
Three Treatises on the Nature of Science, 58
Three Treatments of Universals by Roger Bacon, 111
Three Ways of Thought in Ancient China, 525
The Thundering Scot: A Portrait of John Knox, 736, 774
Thus Have I Heard: The Long Discourses of the Buddha, 514
Thus Spake Zarathustra, 245, 246
Tian Wen: A Chinese Book of Origins, 524
Tibet: A Political History, 356
Tibetan Buddhism in Western Perspective, 543
Tibetan Buddhist Medicine and Psychiatry: The Diamond Healing, 890
Tibetan Civilization, 356
Tibet Bon Religion: A Death Ritual of the Tibetan Bonpos, 543
The Tiger's Fang, 873
Time, Narrative, and History, 391
Time and Free Will, 220
Time and Idea: The Theory of History in Giambattista Vico, 216
Time and Narrative, 319
Time and Necessity: Studies in Aristotle's Theory of Modality, 68
Time and the Highland Maya, 456, 465
A Time for Remembering: The Story of Ruth Bell Graham, 768
Time of Decision with Ru-
dolf Steiner: Experience and Encounter, 880
The Time of My Life, 412
The Timetables of Jewish History, 594
A Time to Be Born and a Time to Die: The Ethics of Choice, 895
The TM Technique, 873
To All Nations: The Billy Graham Story, 768
To Be a Jew: A Guide to Jewish Observance in Contemporary Life, 601
To Change Place: Aztec Ceremonial Landscapes, 457
To Change the World: Christology and Cultural Criticism, 785
The Toils of Scepticism, 58
Tokagawa Religion, 540
To Lhasa and Beyond: Diary of the Expedition to Tibet in the Year 1948, 544
The Toltec Heritage: From the Fall of Tula to the Rise of Tenochtitlan, 457
The Toltecs, until the Fall of Tula, 457
To Make the Wounded Whole: Cultural Legacy of Martin Luther King, Jr., 772
To Mend the World: Foundations of Future Jewish Thought, 664
Tommaso Campanella: Renaissance Pioneer of Modern Thought, 137
To Pray as a Jew, 599
Torah and Canon, 613
Torah from Our Sages: Pirke Avot, 612
Torah through the Ages: A Short History of Judaism, 607
Tormented Master: A Life of Rabbi Nahman of Bratslav, 669
Tortillas for the Gods: A Symbolic Analysis of Zinacanteco Rituals, 465
To Secure the Blessings of Liberty, 857
Tosefta: An Introduction, 612
Tosefta: Translated from the Hebrew, 612
To Take Place: Toward Theory in Ritual, 491
Totality and Infinity: An Essay on Exteriority, 901
The Totality of Man's Philosophical System, 323

Totem and Taboo, 424
Totemism and Exogamy, 476
To the Reformation, 676
Touching Peace: Practicing the Art of Mindful Living, 562
Toward a Feminist Epistemology, 391
Toward a Male Spirituality, 743
Toward a Perfected State, 340
Toward a Rational Society, 404
Toward Reunion in Philosophy, 268
Towards a New Israel: The Jewish State and the Arab Question, 643
Towards a World Theology: Faith and the Comparative History of Religion, 423
Towards Understanding Islam, 575
Toward the Future, 336
To Weave and Sing, 465
Tracing Back the Radiance: Chinul's Korean Way of Zen, 537
Tractates, De consolatione philosophiae, 112
Tractatus Logico-Philosophicus: German Text with English Translation, 344
Tractatus Theologico-Politicus, 189
Tract for the Times, 782
Tracts and Treatises of the Reformed Faith, 761
Tradition, Innovation, Conflict, 643
Traditional Islam in the Modern World, 375
Tradition and Change, 655
Tradition and Crisis: Jewish Society at the End of the Middle Ages, 624
Tradition and Interpretation, 816
Tradition and Interpretation in Matthew, 829
Tradition and Transition, 733
Tradition in an Age of Reform, 665
The Tradition of Scottish Philosophy, 32
Traditions of Meditation in Chinese Buddhism, 529
Tragic Pleasures: Aristotle on Plot and Emotion, 67
Tragic Wisdom and Beyond, 305
Training in Christianity, 239

The Training of the Zen Buddhist Monk, 558
Transcendence and Wittgenstein's Tractatus, 346
The Transcendence of the Ego: An Existentialist Theory of Consciousness, 329
Transcendental Meditation, 873
Transcending Madness: The Experience of the Six Bardos, 357
The Transfer Agreement, 642
Transformation of Judaism from Philosophy to Religion, 607
The Transformation of the Jews, 634
The Transformation of Theology, 1830–1890, 740
Translating the Classics of Judaism: In Theory and in Practice, 612
Translation Determined, 412
Transplanting Religious Traditions: Asian Indians in America, 508
The Travail of Nature, 746
Treasures against Time: Paramahansa Yogananda with Doctor and Mrs. Lewis, 557
The Treasures of Darkness: A History of Mesopotamian Religion, 441, 545
A Treasury of Sephardic Laws and Customs, 601
A Treatise, Concerning the Causes of the Magnificence and Greatness of Cities, 124
Treatise against Hermogenes, 713
A Treatise Concerning Eternal and Immutable Morality, 168
A Treatise Concerning the Principles of Human Knowledge, 191
A Treatise of Human Nature, 199, 201, 739
Treatise of Man, 169
A Treatise on Free Will, 168
Treatise on God as First Principle, 114
Treatise on Nature and Grace, 181, 182
Treatise on Resurrection, 668
Treatise on Sensations, 195
Treatise on Separate Substances, 118

A Treatise on Systems, 195
Treatise on the Immortality of the Soul, 153
Treatises, 708
Treatises on Marriage and Remarriage, 713
Treatises on Penance, 714
Treatises II: The Steps of Humility and Pride, on Loving God, 111
A Tree of Life: Diversity, Flexibility, and Creativity in Jewish Law, 627
The Tremendum: A Theological Interpretation of the Holocaust, 648
The Trial and Death of Socrates, 78
A Tribute to Menno Simons, 780
The Trinitarian Controversy, 686
Trinitas: A Theological Encyclopedia of the Holy Trinity, 675
Trinity, Incarnation, and Atonement, 886
Trinity, Incarnation and Redemption, 108
Trinity and Process, 289
The Triumph of the Goddess, 503
Triumph over Evil: Purity and Pollution in Zoroastrianism, 517
Triumph over Silence: Women in Protestant History, 749
Troubled Eden: An Anatomy of British Jewry, 635
True Christian Religion, 852, 880
True Humanism, 307
The True Intellectual System of the Universe, 168
Trumpeter of God: A Biography of John Knox, 736, 774
Truth, Freedom, and Evil: Three Philosophical Dialogues, 108
Truth, Hope, and Power, 410
Truth, Knowledge, and Modality: Philosophical Papers, 338
Truth, Love, and Immortality: An Introduction to McTaggart's Philosophy, 304
Truth and Actuality, 555
Truth and Existence, 329
Truth and Interpretation: Perspectives on the Philos-

ophy of Donald Davidson, 283

Truth and Method, 402

Truth and Symbol, 300

The Truth in Painting, 398

Truth in Religion: The Plurality of Religions and the Unity of Truth, 271

Truth of the Gospel: An Exposition of Galatians, 821

Tsewa's Gift: Magic and Meaning in an Amazonian Society, 465

Tudor School Boy Life, 156

Tula: The Toltec Capital of Ancient Mexico, 457

Tula of the Toltecs: Excavations and Survey, 457

T'ung Shu, 531

Turkish National and Western Civilization: Selected Essays of Ziya Gokalp, 373

Turkish Transformation: A Study in Social and Religious Development, 577

Turning East: The Promise and Peril of the New Orientalism, 857

Turning the Wheel: American Women Creating the New Buddhism, 512

Tutu: Voice of the Voiceless, 743

Twelve Great Western Philosophers, 18

Twentieth-Century Encyclopedia of Religious Knowledge, 717

Twentieth-Century French Thought: From Bergson to Levi-Strauss, 28, 263

Twentieth-Century Indian Interpretations of Bhagavad Gita, 509, 554, 563

Twentieth-Century Philosophy: The Analytic Tradition, 268

Twentieth-Century Religious Thought: The Frontiers of Philosophy and Theology, 266, 745

Twenty-Five Years of Descartes Scholarship, 1960–1984, 170

Twenty Questions: An Introduction to Philosophy, 20

Twilight of the Idols, 245

Two Ages: The Age of Revolution and the Present Age, 239

Two Centuries of Philosophy, 34

Two Concepts of Rules, 316

Two Essays on Entropy, 278

Two Hundred Years of American Communes, 844

Two Hundred Years of Theology: Report of a Personal Journey, 718

Two New Sciences, 142, 171

Two Old Testament Theologies, 834, 838

The Two Revolutions: Antonio Gramsci and the Dilemmas of Marxism, 287

Two Russian Thinkers: An Essay in Berdyaev and Shestov, 335

The Two Sources of Morality and Religion, 220

Two Studies in the Early Academy, 80

Two Studies in the Greek Atomists, 74

Two Tracts on Government, 179

Two Treatises of Government, 178, 179

Two Treatises of Philo of Alexandria, 60, 670

Two Types of Faith: The Interpretation of Judaism and Christianity, 602, 662

Two Views of Freedom in Process and Thought, 342

Types and Problems of Philosophy, 22

Types of Christian Theology, 743

Types of Religious Experience: Christian and Non-Christian, 494

The Ubiquity of the Finite, 295

The UFO Controversy in America, 870

The UFO Literature, 870

Ugarit in Retrospect: Fifty Years of Ugarit and Ugaritic, 445

Ugo Bénzi, Medieval Philosopher and Physician 1376–1439, 128

Ultimate Hope without God: The Atheistic Eschatology of Ernst Bloch, 277

Unanswered Questions: Theological Views of Jewish-Catholic Relations, 648

The Unbounded Frame, 844

Uncommon Wisdom, 866

The Unconditioned in Human Knowledge: Four

Early Essays, 1794–1796, 252

The Unconscious, 407

Understanding American Jewry, 641

Understanding American Judaism, 651

Understanding Cults and New Religions, 857

Understanding Islam, 373, 573, 576

Understanding Jewish Mysticism: A Source Reader, 629

Understanding Jewish Prayer, 600

Understanding Jewish Theology: Classical Issues and Modern Perspective, 646

Understanding Locke, 180

Understanding Maritain: Philosopher and Friend, 307

Understanding Non-Western Philosophy: Introductory Readings, 349

Understanding Oriental Philosophy, 284, 523

Understanding Rabbinic Midrash: Texts and Commentary, 613

Understanding Reality: A Taoist Alchemical Classic, 528

Understanding Religion, 422

Understanding the Chinese Mind: The Philosophical Roots, 522

Understanding the New Age, 866

Understanding the New Testament, 816

Understanding the Old Testament, 816

Understanding Whitehead, 342

Understanding Wittgenstein: Studies of Philosophical Investigations, 346

Unended Quest, 409

Unfinished Autobiography, 858

The Unhappy Medium: Spiritualism and the Life of Margaret Fox, 851

The Unification Church in America: Sects and Cults in America, 871

Unifying Moment, 342

The Union of Bliss and Emptiness, 560

Uniting the Dual Torah: Sifra and the Problem of the Mishnah, 612

Unity, Heresy, and Reform, 1378–1460, 694

Unity and Development in Plato's Metaphysics, 83

The Unity of Mankind in Greek Thought, 47

The Unity of Plato's Thought, 84

Universal Elements of Jurisprudence, 186

The Universal Humanity of Giambattista Vico, 216

The Universals Treatise of Nicholas of Autrecourt, 104

University, Academics, and the Great Schism, 695

University Records and Life in the Middle Ages, 102

The Unknowable Gurdjieff, 875

"Unless You Believe, You Shall Not Understand," 105

Unpopular Essays on Technological Progress, 318

Unquiet Souls: Fourteenth-Century Saints and Their Religious Milieu, 696

The Unreformed Church, 729

Unruly Eloquence: Lucian and the Comedy of Traditions, 485

Unselfishness, 318

Unspoken Worlds: Women's Religious Lives, 504, 512, 529, 539

Unsui: A Diary of Zen Monastic Life, 538

Until Justice and Peace Embrace, 762

Until the Mashiach: Rabbi Nachman's Biography, an Annotated Chronology, 669

Untouchable: An Indian Life History, 504

The Unvarnished Doctrine: Locke, Liberalism, and the American Revolution, 180

Upanishads, 501

Upbuilding Discourses in Various Spirits, 239

The Upper Paleolithic of the Central Russian Plain, 433

Upright Practices: The Light of the Eyes, 632

A Useful Inheritance: Evolutionary Aspects of the Theory of Knowledge, 318

Utilitarianism, 244

Utopia, 147

Utopia: An Elusive Vision, 147

Utopia and the Ideal Society: A Study of English Utopian Writing, 1516–1700, 125

The Utopian Function of Art and Literature: Selected Essays, 277

Utopian Thought in the Western World, 128

Valiant for Truth: The Story of John Bunyan, 733

The Validity of Values—A Normative Theory of Evaluative Rationality, 318

The Valley of the Kings: Horizon of Eternity, 442

Values Americans Live By, 36

Values and Imperatives: Studies in Ethics, 302

The Vanished Imam: Musa al Sadr and the Shia of Lebanon, 567, 577

Vanquished Nation, Broken Spirit, 607

Varieties of Civil Religion, 752

Varieties of Experience: An Introduction to Philosophy, 22

Varieties of Moral Personality, 388

Varieties of Protestantism, 718

The Varieties of Religious Experience: A Study in Human Nature, 236, 237, 424

Varieties of Social Explanation, 385

A Variety of Catholic Modernists, 742

The Vatican, the Law, and the Human Embryo, 894

Vatican Council II: The Conciliar and Post-Conciliar Documents, 743

Vaulting Ambition, 385

Vedanta: Heart of Hinduism, 872

Vedanta for the Western World: A Symposium on Vedanta, 872

The Vedic Experience: Mantramanjari, 501

Venture of Islam: Conscience and History in World Civilization, 570

Verbum: Word and Idea in Aquinas, 119

Veteris Testamenti concor-

dantiae Hebraicae atque Chaldaicae, 818

Via Augustini, 129

Vico: A Study of the New Science, 217

Vico: Past and Present, 217

Vico and Contemporary Thought, 217

Vico and Herder: Two Studies in the History of Ideas, 216

Vico and Herder: Two Studies in the Philosophy of History, 199

Vico and Marx, 217

Vico in the Tradition of Rhetoric, 217

Vico Revisited: Orthodoxy, Naturalism and Science in the Scienzia Nuova, 216

Vico's Science of Imagination, 217

The Victims of Democracy, 877

Victorian Jews through British Eyes, 635

Victory to the Mother, 504

The View from Nowhere, 379

The Village Gods of South India, 507

Violence and Religious Commitment, 867

Violence and the Sacred, 429

Violent Origins, 429

The Virginal Conception and Bodily Resurrection of Jesus, 685, 887

Virtuous Woman: Reflections on Christian Feminist Ethics, 749

The Visible and the Invisible, 311

Vision and Certitude in the Age of Ockham, 121

The Vision in God: Malebranche's Scholastic Sources, 182

Vision of the Vedic Poets, 501

Visions of Glory: A History and a Memory of Jehovah's Witnesses, 863

Visions of the End: Apocalyptic Traditions in the Middle Ages, 700

Visnuism and Sivaism: A Comparison, 504

Vittorino Da Feltre and Other Humanist Educators, 132

A Vives Bibliography, 156

Vives' Introduction to Wisdom: A Renaissance Textbook, 156
Vladimir Medem: The Life and Soul of a Legendary Jewish Socialist, 656
The Vocation of Man, 198
The Voice of the Silence, 874
Voice of the Voiceless: The Four Pastoral Letters and Other Statements, 748
The Voice of Truth, 553
Voices from the Yiddish: Essays, Memoirs, Diaries, 657
Voices of Silence: Lives of the Trappists Today, 752
Voices of Wisdom: Jewish Ideals and Ethics for Everyday Living, 598
Vollständige Konkordanz zum griechischen Neuen Testament, 817
Voltaire, 218, 273
Voltaire, Pascal, and Human Destiny, 218
Voltaire and Leibniz, 218
Voltaire and the English Deists, 218
Voltaire's Old Testament Criticism, 218
Voltaire's Politics, 218
The Voluntary Church, 754
The Von Balthasar Reader, 891
Voodoo in Haiti, 467
Voodoo in New Orleans, 868
Vyakhyayukti, 514

W. Robertson Smith and the Sociological Study of Religion, 492
Wahhabiyya: Islamic Reform and Politics in French West Africa, 570
Waiting for God, 788
Waiting for the Dawn: Mircea Eliade in Perspective, 474
The Waning of the Middle Ages, 691
War against the Idols: The Reformation of Worship from Erasmus to Calvin, 737
The War against the Jews, 1933–1945, 635
War and Peace in the Law of Islam, 895
War and Peace in the World's Religions, 895

War Crimes in Vietnam, 324
The Warriors of God: Jihad and the Fundamentalism of Islam, 577
Water and Dreams: An Essay on Imagination of Matter, 274
The Watershed: A Biography of Johannes Kepler, 161
The Way and Its Power, 528
The Way of Heaven: An Introduction to the Confucian Religious Life, 526
The Way of Korean Zen, 538
The Way of Tea, 537
The Way of the Faithful: An Anthology of Jewish Mysticism, 629
The Way of the Pilgrim and the Pilgrim Continues His Way, 755
The Way of Torah. An Introduction to Judaism, 596
Way of Zen, 860, 881
The Ways of Paradox, 412
The Ways of Peace, 388
The Ways of Philosophy, 23
Ways of Thinking of Eastern Peoples: India, China, Tibet, Japan, 350
Ways of Worldmaking, 403
The Way to Wisdom: An Introduction to Philosophy, 21, 300
The Wealth of Nations, 215
We Believe in One God: The Experience of God in Christianity and Islam, 572
The Web of Belief, 412
Webster's First New Intergalactic Wickedary of the English Language, 765
We Drink from Our Own Wells: The Spiritual Journey of a People, 769
We Hold These Truths, 271
Welfare: The Social Issues in Philosophical Perspective, 318
We Lived There Too, 1630–1930, 640
The Well and the Tree: World and Time in Early Germanic Culture, 437
Well-Being, 389
Wesley and Sanctification: A Study in the Doctrine of Salvation, 790
The Western Church in the Later Middle Ages, 691, 721
The Western Intellectual Tra-

dition: From Leonardo to Hegel, 159
Western Mysticism: Neglected Chapters in the History of Religion, 111
The Western Response to Zoroaster, 444
Western Society and the Church in the Middle Ages, 691
The Westminster Dictionary of Christian Ethics, 2, 718, 893
The Westminster Dictionary of Christian Spirituality, 676, 718
The Westminster Dictionary of Christian Theology, 676
Westminster Dictionary of Church History, 675, 719
Westminster Review, 190
Westview Special Studies on the Middle East, 568
What Can She Know?, 391
What I Believe, 324
What Is a Thing?, 292
What Is Called Thinking?, 292
What Is Christianity?, 741
What Is Literature?, 329
What Is Midrash?, 612
What Is Philosophy?, 292, 315
What Is Religion?, 747
What Is Sufism?, 575
What Is This Jewish Heritage?, 596
What Man Can Make of Man, 296
What Manner of Man: A Biography of Martin Luther King, Jr., 1929–1968, 772
What Nietzsche Means, 247
What Philosophy Can Do, 379
What the Great Religions Believe, 569
What We Cannot Show, We Do Not Know, 617
When Daylight Comes, 874
When Light Pierced the Darkness, 638
When Prophecy Fails, 870
When the Word Is Given, 862
Where There Is Light: Insight Inspiration for Meeting Life's Challenges, 557
While Six Million Died: A Chronicle of American Apathy, 640
Whitehead, Process Philosophy, and Education, 341

Whitehead and the Modern World: Science, Metaphysics, and Civilization, 342

Whitehead's American Essays in Social Philosophy, 341

Whitehead's Metaphysics of Extension and Solidarity, 342

Whitehead's Ontology, 342

Whitehead's Philosophical Development, 342

Whitehead's Philosophy: Selected Essays, 1935–1970, 289, 342

Whitehead's Theory of Knowledge, 341

Who Is a Sikh? The Problem of Sikh Identity, 516

The Wholeness of Life, 555

Whose Justice? Which Rationality?, 407

Whose Science? Whose Knowledge? Thinking from Women's Lives, 40

Who's Who in Religion, 1992–93, 7

The Who's Who in the History of Philosophy, 14

Who Was a Jew, 621

Why God Became Man and the Virgin Conception and Original Sin, 108

Why I Am Not a Christian and Other Essays on Religion and Related Subjects, 324

Why Men Fight: A Method of Abolishing the International Duel, 324

The Wilderness and the City: American Classical Philosophy as a Moral Quest, 36

Wildfire: Grassroots Revolts in Israel in the Post-Socialist Era, 642

The Wild Goats of Ein Gedi, 643

Will and Circumstance: Montesquieu, Rousseau and the French Revolution, 210

William Auvergne and Robert Grosseteste, 115

William Foxwell Albright: A Twentieth-Century Genius, 828

William Heytesbury: Medieval Logic and the Rise of Mathematical Physics, 104

William James, 237

William James: His Life and Thought, 238

William James: The Center of His Vision, 237

William James, Public Philosopher, 237

William James and Henri Bergson: A Study in Contrasting Theories, 237

William James's Philosophy: A New Perspective, 237

William James's Radical Reconstruction of Philosophy, 238

William Ockham, 120

William of Sherwood's Treatise on Syncategorematic Words, 103

William Whewell: A Composite Portrait, 258

William Whewell, Philosopher of Science, 258

Willing and Unwilling: A Study in the Philosophy of Arthur Schopenhauer, 256

The Will to Believe and Human Immortality, 237

The Will to Power, 245, 246

Wisdom and Love in St. Thomas Aquinas, 286

Wisdom as Moderation: A Philosophy of the Middle Way, 289

Wisdom of Insecurity, 881

The Wisdom of Life: Being the First Part of Aphorismen zur Lebensweisheit, 256

The Wisdom of Marcus Aurelius, 76

The Wisdom of Pierre Charron: An Original and Orthodox Code of Morality, 125

The Wisdom of Science, 384

The Wisdom of the Outlaw, 436

Wisdom of the Prophets, 583

The Wisdom of the Upanishads, 501, 550

Wisdom of the West, 324

The Wissenschaftslehre nova methodo, 198

Witchcraft, Oracles, and Magic among the Azande, 475, 476

Witchcraft in the Middle Ages, 700

Witchcraft Today. Bk 1: The Modern Craft Movement, 865

The Witches' Way: Principles, Rituals and Beliefs of Modern Witchcraft, 865

Witch Hunting in Southwest Germany, 1562–1684, 730

Within Human Experience: The Philosophy of William Ernest Hocking, 297

With Perfect Faith: The Foundations of Jewish Belief, 629

With Reference to Reference, 382, 403

With the Swamis in America and India, 563

Wittgenstein (Ayer), 273, 344

Wittgenstein (Grayling), 245

Wittgenstein (Von Wright), 338

Wittgenstein: A Life: Young Ludwig, 1889–1921, 346

Wittgenstein: An Introduction, 347

Wittgenstein: Conversations, 1949–1951, 345

Wittgenstein: From Mysticism to Ordinary Language, 346

Wittgenstein: Language and World, 345

Wittgenstein: Lectures and Conversations on Aesthetics, Psychology, and Religious Belief, 344

Wittgenstein: Meaning and Mind, 345

Wittgenstein—Toward a Re-Evaluation, 345

Wittgenstein, Ethics and Aesthetics: The View from Eternity, 347

Wittgenstein and Derrida, 398

Wittgenstein and His Times, 346

Wittgenstein and Kierkegaard, 345

Wittgenstein and Modern Philosophy, 345

Wittgenstein and Political Philosophy, 345

Wittgenstein and the Turning Point in the History of Mathematics, 347

Wittgenstein Centenary Essays, 345

Wittgenstein on Ethics and Religious Belief, 344

Wittgenstein on Language: Meaning, Use, and Truth, 346

Wittgenstein on Rules and Private Language, 301

Wittgenstein's Early Philosophy: Three Sides of the Mirror, 346

Wittgenstein's Later Philosophy, 345
Wittgenstein's Philosophy of Psychology, 345
Wittgenstein's Tractatus: A Critical Exposition of Its Main Lines on Thought, 347
Wittgenstein's Tractatus: An Introduction, 346
Wives of the God-King: The Rituals of Devadasis of Puri, 505
Wizard from Vienna: Franz Anton Mesmer, 847
Woman as Image in Medieval Literature from the Twelfth Century to Dante, 698
Womanguides: Readings toward a Feminist Theology, 785, 905
Woman in Christian Tradition, 679
Woman Invisible: A Personal Odyssey in Christian Feminism, 749
The Woman's Bible Commentary, 819
Womanspirit Rising: A Feminist Reader in Religion, 650
Woman the Gatherer, 431
Women, Androgynes, and Other Mythical Beasts, 505, 890
Women, Branch Stories, and Religious Rhetoric in a Tamil Buddhist Text, 514
Women, Freedom, and Calvin, 761
Women, Knowledge, and Reality, 391
Women, Men, and the Bible, 749
Women, Nature, and Psyche, 391
Women, Religion, and Sexuality, 894
Women, Religion, and Social Change, 426, 504, 513, 529, 532
Women and Authority: Re-emerging Mormon Feminism, 892
Women and Jewish Law, 650
Women and Reason, 391
Women and Religion in America, 749
Women and Sacrifice: Male Narcissism and the Psychology of Religion, 892
Women and the Ancestors:

Black Carib Kinship and Ritual, 466
Women and the Priesthood: Essays from the Orthodox Tradition, 693
Women and World Religions, 892
Women-Church: Theology and Practice of Feminist Liturgical Communities, 785
Women in Buddhism: Images of the Feminine in the Mahayana Tradition, 514
Women in Frankish Society: Marriage and the Cloister, 500–900, 701
Women in Greek Myth, 447
Women in Indian Society: A Reader, 508
Women in Islam, 578, 580
Women in Shaker Community and Worship, 849
Women in Spiritual Communitarian Societies in the United States, 843
Women in the Early Church, 678
Women in the Middle Ages, 699
Women in the Reformation in France and England, 749
Women in Utopia, 844
Women in World Religions, 506, 514, 526, 528, 892
Women Leaders in the Ancient Synagogue, 614
Women of Spirit: Female Leadership in the Jewish and Christian Traditions, 679, 785
Women of Wisdom, 543
Women Philosophers, 391
Women Philosophers: A Bio-Critical Sourcebook, 6, 161
Women Writers of the Middle Ages, 698
The Wonder of Philosophy, 21
The Wonder That Was India, 351, 498
Word and Object, 412
Word and Object in Husserl, Frege, and Russell, 324
The Word of Life. Systematic Theology, 885
The Word Remains: A Life of Oscar Romero, 747
The Work of the Gods in Tikopia, 461

Works and Days, 481
Works and Lives: The Anthropologist as Author, 478
Works of Love: Some Christian Reflections in the Form of Discourses, 239
The Works of Seyyed Hossein Nasr through His Fortieth Birthday, 902
Works on Vision, 191
World Aflame, 768
The World and Language in Wittgenstein's Philosophy, 346
The World and the Individual, 249, 250
The World as Will and Idea, 254
The World as Will and Representation, 256
World Christian Encyclopedia, 3, 716, 742
The World in Miniature, 520, 523, 534, 544
The World of a Renaissance Jew, 624
World of Art, 340
The World of Biblical Literature, 822
A World of Grace, 904
The World of Humanism, 1453–1517, 696
The World of John of Salisbury, 116
The World of Josephus, 666
The World of Myth: An Anthology, 427
World of Our Fathers, 639
The World of the Ancient Maya, 455
The World of the Polynesians Seen through Their Myths and Legends, Poetry, and Art, 461
The World of the Talmud, 620
World of the Yeshiva, 654
The World of Thought in Ancient China, 525
World Philosophy, 7, 38
World Philosophy: Essays and Reviews of 225 Major Works, 266
World Prehistory: A Brief Introduction, 432
World Religions and World Community, 573
The World's Greatest Scriptures, 5
The World's Great Religions, 6

The Worlds of Existentialism: A Critical Reader, 264
The Worlds of Plato and Aristotle, 71
World Spirituality: An Encyclopedic History of the Religious Quest, 888
Worship and Ethics: A Study in Rabbinic Judaism, 600, 620
Worship in the World's Religions, 898
The Worship of Nature, 477
Writing and Difference, 398
Writing Culture: The Poetics and Politics of Ethnography, 426
Writings from Ancient Israel: A Handbook of Historical and Religious Documents, 812
The Writings of Jean-Paul Sartre, 330
The Writings of Martin Buber, 662
The Writings of the New Testament: An Interpretation, 813
Writings on Economics, 201
Writing with Scripture, 607
Written Out of History: Our Jewish Foremothers, 650
Wyclif and the Oxford Schools, 104
Wycliffe Biographical Dictionary of the Church, 720
The Wyclyf Tradition, 714

Xenophanes of Colophon: Fragments, 52
Xenophon, 91
Xenophon's Socratic Discourse: An Interpretation of the Oeconomicus, 91
Xenophon the Athenian, 91

Yahweh and the Gods of Canaan, 445, 822, 828
The Yearbook of American and Canadian Churches, 5, 752

The Year of Three Popes, 744
Yemenite Jews: A Photographic Essay, 644
Yerushalmi: The Talmud of the Land of Israel: An Introduction, 613
Yi Jing, 524
Yoga: Immortality and Freedom, 474, 503
Yoga Sutras, 550
Yom Kippur Anthology, 599
You, I, and the Others, 340
You Are the World, 555
Young John Dewey: An Essay in American Intellectual History, 225
Young Man Luther, 778
The Young Mr. Wesley, 790
Your Word Is Fire: The Hasidic Masters on Contemplative Prayer, 632

Zaddik, 632
Zadig, or Destiny, 217
Zakhor: Jewish History and Jewish Memory, 595
Zarathustra's Sister: The Case of Elizabeth and Friedrich Nietzsche, 247
Zen: Traditions and Transition, 538
Zen Action/Zen Person, 537
Zen and American Thought, 33, 859
Zen and Japanese Culture, 558
Zen and Western Thought, 364
Zen Awakening and Society, 537
Zen Buddhism, 558
Zen Buddhism and Psychoanalysis, 558
Zen Buddhism in the Twentieth Century, 537, 558
Zen Effects: The Life of Alan Watts, 859, 881
A Zen Life: D. T. Suzuki Remembered, 558

Zen Mind, Beginner's Mind. Informal Talks on Zen Meditation and Practice, 538
Zeno of Elea: A Text with Translation and Notes, 52
Zettel, 344
Zion before Zionism, 657
Zion in America, 639
Zionism: The Crucial Phase, 658
Zionism: The Formative Years, 643
Zionism in Germany, 1897–1933: The Shaping of a Jewish Identity, 658
Zionism in Poland: The Formative Years 1915–1926, 658
The Zionist Dream Revisited: From Herzl to Gush Emunim and Back, 658
Zionist Idea: A Historical Analysis and Reader, 658
Zohar: The Book of Enlightenment, 630
Zohar—The Book of Splendor: Basic Readings from the Kabbalah, 672
The Zohar in Moslem and Christian Spain, 629
Zoroastrianism: A Beleaguered Faith, 518, 548
Zoroastrianism: The Rediscovery of Missing Chapters in Man's Religious History, 547
Zoroastrianism and the Parsis, 444, 517
Zoroastrians, 444
Zoroastrians: Their Religious Beliefs and Practices, 547
Zwingli, 791
Zwingli: An Introduction to His Thought, 791
Zwingli: A Reformed Theologian, 791
Zwingli: Third Man of the Reformation, 791
Zwingli and Bullinger, 791
Zwingli and the Arts, 737
A Zwingli Bibliography, 791
Zwingli the Reformer: His Life and Work, 791

Subject Index

This index provides detailed, multiple-approach access to the subject content of the volume. Arrangement is alphabetical. The names of profiled, main-entry authors are not included in this index; the reader is reminded to use the Name Index to locate these individuals. For additional information, the reader should refer to the detailed Table of Contents at the front of the volume.

Abortion, contemporary religious issues, 894
Absolute idealism, 249
Absolute nothing, 290
Academic life, contemporary philosophical issues, 378
Academy, Greek. See Greek Academy
Action theory, Western philosophy, twentieth-century, 282
Actual idealism, Western philosophy, twentieth-century, 284
Aesthetics
  contemporary philosophical issues, 392
  Western philosophy, 1700–1800, 192, 203, 204, 207
  Western philosophy, 1800–1900, 253, 255
  Western philosophy, twentieth-century, 326
African Americans
  Islam, 566, 876
  late Christianity, 762, 771
  liberation theology, 748
  religious movements, twentieth-century, 861, 867
African philosophy, 26, 367–71
  authors, 369–71
  authors, chronology, 350
  general works, 368
African religions, indigenous, 459, 462
Age of Reason, Christianity in the eighteenth century, 738–40

Age of Revolution, Christianity in the nineteenth century, 740–42
Albany, New York, Shakers, 849
Alchemy, Renaissance philosophy, 149
Alexandrian school, 61
  medieval philosophy, 116
Algonquian Bible, 801
Amana community, 843
America. See also United States
  Christian religion, 750–54
  French and Spanish colonies, 752–54
American civilization, ancient religions and philosophies, 453–58
American Philosophical Association, 378
Americas, indigenous religions, 463–66
Anabaptists, 723, 732
Analytic geometry, Western philosophy, 1600–1700, 168
Analytic philosophy
  contemporary issues, 376, 377, 381, 395, 410, 412
  Western philosophy, twentieth-century, 261, 262, 271, 282, 311, 333
Ancestor worship
  Chinese religion, 521
  indigenous religions, 462
  Mediterranean ancient urban civilization, 438
Ancient civilizations, urban

Mediterranean religions, 419, 438–53
New World religions, 419, 453–58
Ancient religions and philosophies, 419–94
  authors, 468–94
  authors, chronology, 468
  Canaanite, 444
  Egyptian, 441
  Greek, 445
  Hittite, 444
  indigenous, 419, 458–66
  Iranian, 443
  prehistoric religions, 431–37
  Roman, 447
  study of, 420–31
  urban civilizations, Mediterranean, 419, 438–53
  urban civilizations, New World, 419, 453–58
  women authors, 478
Anglican Church, 776
Animal behavior. See Ethology
Animal rights, 43
Animism
  ancient religion, 421
  Chinese religion, 521
  Eastern religions, 495, 496
  Hinduism, 502
  Japan and Korea popular religion, 538
Anonymous works
  Western philosophy, 1600–1700, 178
  Western philosophy, 1700–1800, 197

Anonymous works (*cont.*)
  Western philosophy,
    1800–1900, 227
Anthropocentricity, 43
Anthropology
  study of religion, 425, 426
  Western philosophy, twen-
    tieth-century, 335
Anthroposophy, 852, 858,
  880
Anti-Semitism
  contemporary issues, 394
  European Jews, 634
  modern Judaism, 655
  Western philosophy,
    1800–1900, 220
  Zionism, 657
Apocrypha
  extracanonical materials,
    809–10
  historical background, 806,
    807
Apologists, 62
Apothegms. *See* Proverbs
Argument, contemporary is-
  sues, 379
Arianism, early Christianity,
  684
Aristotelianism
  books, 66–72
  medieval philosophy, 93,
    112, 117
  Renaissance philosophy,
    123, 152, 153
Arminianism, 731
Art, philosophy of, contem-
  porary issues, 403, 407
Artificial intelligence, con-
  temporary philosophi-
  cal issue, 382
Asceticism
  early and medieval Chris-
    tianity, 674
  Jainism, 509
  medieval Judaism, 629
  Western philosophy, twen-
    tieth-century, 305
Asian philosophy, modern,
  348–67, 372–75
  Chinese, 357–62
  general works, 349
  Indian, 350–55
  Islam, 372–75
  Japanese, 363–67
  Tibetan, 355–57
Assyro-Babylonian religious
  tradition, 544
Astrology
  oikoumene world, 451
  religious movements, twen-
    tieth-century, 860
Atheism, Western philosophy,
  twentieth-century, 328

Atomism
  Greek philosophy, 73
  modern Western philoso-
    phy, 158
  pre-Socratic philosophy, 52
  Roman philosophy, 75
  Western philosophy,
    1600–1700, 172
  Western philosophy, twen-
    tieth-century, 320, 333,
    343
Atonement, traditional issues,
  885
Augustinians
  medieval philosophy, 108
  Renaissance philosophy,
    138
Australia, indigenous reli-
  gions, 460, 461
Autobiography
  Western philosophy, twen-
    tieth-century, 272, 280,
    320, 321, 329
Averroism, medieval philoso-
  phy, 96
Aztecs, 456, 457

Baha'i faith, religious movements, twentieth-cen-
  tury, 860
Beat generation, religious
  movements, twentieth-
  century, 853, 859
Behaviorism, Western philosophy, twentieth-cen-
  tury, 309
Being, Western philosophy,
  twentieth-century, 290,
  304
Belief
  African philosophy, 371
  early Christianity, 684–87
  Islamic philosophy, 372
  Islamic religion, 564
Bible, 792–838
  authors, 827–38
  authors, chronology, 827
  books of. *See* individual
    books
  general works, 793–96
    access tools, 794
    bibliographies, 795
    critical editions of origi-
      nal texts, 794
  historical background,
    806–12
    archaeology, 808
    extracanonical materials,
      809–12
    geography, 809
    Judaism and early Chris-
      tianity, 806–8

  languages, 792–93
  New Testament. *See* New
    Testament
  Old Testament. *See* Old
    Testament
  study of, 793, 812–27
    commentaries, 819–22
    dictionaries and concor-
      dances, 817–19
    interpretation histories,
      813
    introduction, 815–17
    methods and principles,
      814
    theologies, 826
    topic and author master-
      works, 822–26
    versions. *See* Versions of
      the Bible
Biology, contemporary philo-
  sophical issues, 384
Bishop's Bible, 800
Black Muslims, religious
  movements, twentieth-
  century, 566, 861
Blacks, liberation theology,
  748
Bloomsbury group, 312
Bon religion, 542
Brahmanism, 496
Buddha, 511, 512
Buddhism
  Chinese religion, 521, 529
  Eastern religions, 496
  Japanese philosophy, 365
  Japanese religion, 536–38,
    540
  Korean religion, 536–38,
    540
  modern developments, 515
  religious movements, twen-
    tieth-century, 859
  South Asian religion,
    510–15
  Southeast Asian religion,
    519
  Tibet, 542
  Tibetan philosophy, 356,
    357
  Vietnam, 520
Business ethics, contempo-
  rary philosophical is-
  sues, 387

Cabala
  medieval Judaism, 629
  Renaissance philosophy,
    152
  Western philosophy,
    1600–1700, 167

Calculus, Western philosophy, 1600–1700, 176, 183
Calvinism, 731
Cambridge Platonism
  modern Western philosophy, 157
  Western philosophy, 1600–1700, 166, 167, 182
Canaanite religions, 444
Cao Dai religion, 520
  religious movements, twentieth-century, 867
Cargo cults, 466, 467
Caribbean religions, indigenous, 464, 466
Cartesianism
  modern Western philosophy, 157, 158
  Western philosophy, 1600–1700, 164, 181
Carvings, prehistoric religion, 432, 433
Caste
  Hinduism, 502
  South Asian religions, 500
Catacombs, early Christianity, 687
Causality, modern Western philosophy, 157–58
Cave art, prehistoric religion, 432
Celibacy
  Shakers, 848, 849
  Unification Church, 870
Celtic religion, prehistoric, 436
Censorship
  Renaissance philosophy, 142
  Western philosophy, 1600–1700, 171, 182
  Western philosophy, 1800–1900, 231
Central Asian religion, 541–44
  Tibetan, 542–44
Ceremonials, primitive, Mediterranean ancient urban civilization, 438
Channeling, 865. See also Correspondences
Chinese philosophy, 357–62
  authors, 359–62
  authors, chronology, 350
  general works, 358
Chinese religion
  ancient tradition and classics, 524
  Buddhism, 529
  Confucianism, 521, 525
  East Asia, 521–33

general works, 522–24
popular, 530
reference works and anthologies, 521
Taoism, 521, 526–29
Western influence and modern era, 531–33
Christian Church
  early centuries, 687–90
  late centuries, 716–18, 719
Christian Churches of the East
  Crusades, 692–94
  medieval Christianity, 691
Christianity
  Age of Reason, 738–40
  Age of Revolution, 740–42
  ancient Judaism, 616, 619
  atonement, 886
  contemporary issues, 883
  early and medieval, 674–714
    authors, 702–14
    authors, chronology, 701
    histories, 676–78, 681
    reference works, 675
    source collections, 679–81
    topical studies, 678
    women authors, 706
  early thinkers, 62
    general works, 63
  Greek and Roman philosophy, 45
  historical background, 806–8
  indigenous religions, 463
  Judaism and, 602
  late, 1500 to the present, 715–91
    authors, 757–91
    authors, chronology, 756–57
    dictionaries, encyclopedias, handbooks, 716–20
    ethics and theology, 718
    general reference works, 716
    women authors, 764–65, 784–85, 788
  late, 1914 to the present, 742–50
    liberation theology, 747–50
  medieval, 690–701
    Eastern churches and Crusades, 692–94
    emperors, popes, and councils, 694
    life and culture, 698–701
    special histories, 690–92

thought and doctrine, 695–98
medieval Judaism, 623–25
medieval philosophy, 92–121
mystery cults, 450
theological study of religion, 422
Western philosophy, 1800–1900, 238, 253
Christian Science, 842
Church and state
  late Christianity, 1500–1560, 723
  medieval Christianity, 690
Church Fathers. See Fathers of the Church
Church of England, 725, 763
Cistercians, medieval philosophy, 111
City life. See Urban life
City-state, Greek civilization, 446
Cognition
  contemporary philosophical issues, 381, 382, 396
  modern Western philosophy, 157
Collegiants, Western philosophy, 1600–1700, 186
Colonialism
  African philosophy, 348
  Asian philosophy, modern, 348
  Indian philosophy, 350
  indigenous religions affected by, 466
  religion in America, 752–54
Commonsense school, Western philosophy, 1700–1800, 211
Communal groups, religious movements, nineteenth-century, 843
Communism
  Chinese philosophy, 361
  Western philosophy, twentieth-century, 286
Comparative philosophy, 36–38
  East-West, 37
  general, 37
  Indian, 353
Conceptual pragmatism, Western philosophy, twentieth-century, 301
Confessing Church, 757, 759
Confraternity Version. See New American Bible
Confucianism, 496
  Chinese philosophy, 358, 359, 360, 362

Confucianism (*cont.*)
  Chinese religion, 521, 525
Consciencism
  African philosophy, 370
Consciousness, Japanese phi-
    losophy, 364
Conservative Judaism, 651,
    654
Contemplation, late Chris-
    tianity, 780, 786
Cooperative communities.
    See Communal groups
Copernican system, Renais-
    sance philosophy, 134,
    135, 141, 142
Correspondences, religious
    movements, nine-
    teenth-century, 840.
    See also Channeling
Cosmogony, Western philoso-
    phy, 1600–1700, 167
Cosmology, philosophical
  Renaissance philosophy,
    134, 135, 148
  Western philosophy, twen-
    tieth-century, 260, 340
Council of Trent. *See* Trent,
    Council of
Councils of the Church
  early Christianity, 681
  medieval Christianity, 694
Counter Reformation,
    727–29, 736
Court life, medieval philoso-
    phy, 115
Coverdale Bible, 799
Critical idealism, Western
    philosophy, twentieth-
    century, 274
Critical realism, Western phi-
    losophy, twentieth-cen-
    tury, 260, 302, 326
Crusades
  Eastern Orthodox Church,
    755
  medieval Christianity,
    692–94
Crystallography, 257
Cults
  cargo, 466, 467
  imperial, 451
  mystery, 446, 450
  prehistoric religion, 433
  religious movements, twen-
    tieth-century, 856, 857
Culture, philosophy of. *See*
    Historicism
Cuneiform writing, Mesopota-
    mian ancient urban
    civilization, 440
Cynicism, Greek philosophy,
    89
Cyrenaic school, 89

Dalai Lama, 356, 558
  contemporary religious is-
    sues, 905
Dancing Dervishes. *See*
    Whirling Dervishes
Dead Sea Scrolls, 792, 794
Death customs and rites
  Egypt, ancient religion,
    441
  indigenous religions, 461
  prehistoric religion, 432
  Zoroastrianism, 517
Deconstructionism
  contemporary philosophical
    issues, 390–92, 396
  current theological meth-
    od, 889
  Western philosophy, twen-
    tieth-century, 262
Democratic socialism, West-
    ern philosophy, twenti-
    eth-century, 297
Dialectic
  Greek philosophy, 88
  medieval philosophy, 107
  Western philosophy, twen-
    tieth-century, 269, 281
Dialectical materialism, West-
    ern philosophy,
    1800–1900, 227
Dialogues
  Plato, 77–78, 89
  Socrates, 89
Dianetics, 869
Diaspora
  Hebrew Bible, 796
  Jews, 591, 607
Dionysiac movements, Greek
    ancient religion, 446
Divine Light Mission, 872
Doctrine
  early Christianity, 681,
    684–87
  medieval Christianity,
    695–98
Dominicans, Renaissance phi-
    losophy, 134, 136, 137
Donatism, early Christianity,
    684
Douay Version, 800
Dreaming, the, 460, 461
Drugs, indigenous religions,
    464
Druids, Celtic religion, 436
Dualism
  contemporary philosophical
    issues, 396
  gnosticism, 453
  Iranian ancient religions,
    443
  Western philosophy,
    1600–1700, 168

Western philosophy, twen-
    tieth-century, 277, 302,
    320, 325
Dunamis, 339

East Asian religion, 520–41
  Chinese, 521–33
  Japanese and Korean,
    533–41
Eastern churches. *See* Chris-
    tian Churches of the
    East; Eastern Orthodox
    Church
Eastern Orthodox Church
  Crusades, 692–94, 755
  early Christianity, 681
  late Christianity, 754–56
Eastern religions
  authors, 548–63
  authors, chronology, 548
  Central Asia, 541–44
  East Asia, 520–41
  non-Islamic and non-Jew-
    ish of the Middle East
    and North Africa,
    544–48
  religious movements, twen-
    tieth-century, 853, 871,
    872, 880
  South Asia, 497–518
  Southeast Asia, 518–20
  women authors, 548
Eckankar, 872
Eclecticism, 59
Economics, Western philoso-
    phy, 1800–1900, 227,
    241, 244
Ecophilosophy, 38
Ecstasy
  Shakers, 848
  shamanism, 430
Ecumenical movement
  Bible study, 812, 832
  late Christianity, 774
  theological study of reli-
    gion, 423
Education, philosophy of,
    Western philosophy,
    1800–1900, 223
Egypt
  ancient, North African tra-
    dition, 548
  ancient religion, 441
Eleatic school, 51
Elitism, Western philosophy,
    twentieth-century, 314
Empiricism
  contemporary issues, 408,
    411
  modern Western philoso-
    phy, 157

Western philosophy,
1600–1700, 164, 169
Western philosophy,
1700–1800, 195
Western philosophy,
1800–1900, 244
Encyclopedists, Western philosophy, 1700–1800,
195
England, Reformation,
725–27, 733–35
English Revised Version, 801
Enlightenment
late Christianity, 716
modern Judaism, 646
modern Western philosophy, 158
Western philosophy,
1600–1700, 166
Western philosophy,
1700–1800, 198, 204,
208
Environmental degradation
contemporary philosophical
issues, 388
religious movements, twentieth-century, 854
Epicureanism, 54
Greek philosophy, 73
Roman philosophy, 58, 75
Epistemology
contemporary issues, 380,
395, 399, 403, 411
medieval philosophy, 98
Western philosophy,
1600–1700, 178
Western philosophy, twentieth-century, 275, 302,
312, 320, 332
Essenes, 616
Ethics
animal rights, 43
contemporary issues, 406
contemporary philosophical
issues, 387–89
contemporary religious issues, 892–95, 897
Islamic philosophy, 374
Japanese philosophy, 367
Judaism, 597
late Christianity, 718
late Christianity, 1914 to
present, 742–47
Modern Western philosophy, 158
Renaissance philosophy,
122
Western philosophy,
1700–1800, 193, 194,
196, 204, 210, 211,
214, 215

Western philosophy,
1800–1900, 230, 244,
253, 256
Western philosophy, twentieth-century, 301, 311,
316, 332, 338
Ethnography, study of religion, 425
Ethnophilosophy, African,
367, 369, 370, 371
Ethology, ancient religion,
421
Europe
modern Judaism, 634–38
modern philosophy, 157
philosophy, 27–33
Evangelical groups, 742, 780
religious movements, twentieth-century, 864
Evangelical Rationalists, 723
Evangelism, 767
religious movements, twentieth-century, 863
Evidence, philosophical,
Western philosophy,
1700–1800, 208
Evil, problem of
medieval philosophy, 116
Western philosophy,
1700–1800, 217
Evolution
Western philosophy,
1800–1900, 219
Western philosophy, twentieth century, 336
Excommunication
late Christianity, 727, 777,
780
medieval Christianity, 692
medieval philosophy, 119
Western philosophy,
1600–1700, 186
Existentialism
contemporary issues, 376
Western philosophy, twentieth-century, 261, 290,
298, 299, 304, 309,
328, 334
Experimental psychology, 382
Extraterrestial life, 257
Extremism, Islamic religion,
565

Fairy, Germanic religion, 437
Faith
early and medieval Christianity, 674, 695
medieval philosophy, 107,
108
Renaissance philosophy,
151, 153

Western philosophy, twentieth-century, 285
Faith healing
Christian Science, 842
indigenous religions, 462
Mesmerism, 846
oikoumene world, 450
shamanism, 430
Fathers of the Church
early Christianity, 690
medieval philosophy, 93,
108, 112
patristic period, 98–100
Feasts and festivals
Greek ancient religion, 446
Hittite and Canaanite religions, 444
Feeling
Western philosophy,
1700–1800, 215
Western philosophy,
1800–1900, 253
Feminism
contemporary philosophical
issues, 390
contemporary religious issues, 891, 904
late Christianity, 764, 784
liberation theology, 749
modern Judaism, 649
philosophy, 40
religious movements, twentieth-century, 854, 865
theological study of religion, 423
Western philosophy,
1800–1900, 244
Florentine Academy, 140
Flying saucers. See UFO
Folklore, indigenous religions, 459
Forgery, Renaissance philosophy, 155
Fortune telling and
divination
Chinese religion, 521
Hittite and Canaanite religions, 444
Inca religion, 458
indigenous religions, 461
Mesopotamian ancient urban civilization, 440
oikoumene world, 450
religious movements, twentieth-century, 860
Fountain Grove community,
843
France, philosophy, 27
Franciscans, medieval philosophy, 93, 110, 112,
119
Frankfurt School, 262, 392,
403, 407

Freemasons, 840
Free will
    medieval philosophy, 108,
        113, 114, 116
    Renaissance philosophy,
        122, 152, 155
    Western philosophy,
        1600–1700, 168
    Western philosophy,
        1700–1800, 210
    Western philosophy,
        1800–1900, 254
Friends, Religious Society of
    Shakers, 849
    Western philosophy,
        1600–1700, 167
Fundamentalism
    Islamic philosophy, 372
    Islamic religion, 566, 577
Future life, beliefs in
    mystery cults, 450
    Tibetan Buddhism, 543

Gauls. See Celtic religion
Generalization, contemporary
    issues, 383
Geneva Bible, 799
Genocide, European Jews,
    634, 635
Germanic religion, prehis-
    toric, 437
Germany
    Lutheranism, late Christian-
        ity, 730
    philosophy, 28
Gift of tongues. See Glossola-
    lia
Glossolalia, Shakers, 849
Gnosticism
    early Christianity, 684
    oikoumene world, 452
God. See also Theism
    early Christianity, 684
    medieval philosophy, 113,
        116
    traditional issues, 884, 900
    Western philosophy,
        1600–1700, 167, 169,
        181, 182
    Western philosophy,
        1700–1800, 194
    Western philosophy, twen-
        tieth-century, 285, 288
Gods
    Aztecs, 456
    Celtic religion, 436
    Egypt, ancient religion,
        441
    Germanic religion, 437
    Greek ancient religion, 445
    Hinduism, 502

Hittite and Canaanite reli-
    gions, 444
Inca religion, 458
indigenous religions, 461,
    463
Iranian ancient religions,
    443
Japanese religion, 535
Mediterranean ancient ur-
    ban civilization, 438,
    440
mystery cults, 450
religious movements, twen-
    tieth-century, 868
Roman religion, 447
South Asian religions, 499,
    500
Taoism, 527
Good
    Western philosophy,
        1600–1700, 168
    Western philosophy,
        1800–1900, 241
Gospels
    ancient Judaism, 615, 616,
        617
    Bible study, 829
Grace, Western philosophy,
    1600–1700, 181
Great Bible, 799
Great books series, 269
Great Britain
    philosophy, 29
    Reformation, 733–36
Great Chain of Being, reli-
    gious movements,
    nineteenth-century, 840
Greek Academy, 77
    books, 78–85
Greek civilization
    Minoans and Mycenaeans,
        445
    oikoumene world, 448
    Western philosophy,
        1800–1900, 245
Greek philosophy, 29, 44–91
    authors, 64–91
    authors, chronology, 64
    general works, 46–49
    pre-Socratic, 49–53
    Sophists, 53–54
    Western philosophy,
        1800–1900, 221
Greek religion, ancient, 445
Guru
    religious movements, twen-
        tieth-century, 853, 872
    Sikhism, 515
    South Asian religions, 500

Hare Krishna movement, 862

Harmony
    Chinese religion, 524
    Eastern religions, 495, 496
Haruspicy, 450
Hasidism, 631–33
    medieval Judaism, 629
Hebrew Bible, 792, 793, 801,
        802
    ancient Judaism, 608
    commentaries, 628
    Hittites and Canaanites,
        444
    versions, 796
Hebrew literature, 647. See
    also Jewish literature
Hegelianism, Western philos-
    ophy, twentieth-cen-
    tury, 303
Hellenistic Age
    Greek philosophy, 44, 45
    Jewish literature, 607
    oikoumene world, 448–53
    philosophies, 54–58
    Skepticism, 57
    Stoicism, 56
Hepatoscopy, 440
Heresy
    early Christianity, 684–87
    late Christianity, 764
    medieval Christianity, 691,
        698
    medieval philosophy, 119
    Renaissance philosophy,
        133, 135, 137
Hermeneutics
    contemporary issues, 401
    Western philosophy,
        1800–1900, 226
    Western philosophy, twen-
        tieth-century, 262, 283,
        290, 318
Hinduism, 502–9
    animism, 496
    Indian philosophy, 351,
        353, 354, 355
    religious movements, twen-
        tieth-century, 862, 871,
        872
    Western influences, 507–9
Historical-interpretive ap-
    proach, study of reli-
    gion, 425
Historicism
    modern Western philoso-
        phy, 158
    Western philosophy,
        1800–1900, 226
    Western philosophy, twen-
        tieth-century, 261, 279,
        340
History, philosophy of
    contemporary issues, 401

Western philosophy,
1700–1800, 204, 216
Hittite religions, 444
Holism
contemporary philosophical
issues, 411
Western philosophy,
1700–1800, 198
Western philosophy,
1800–1900, 221, 226
Holocaust
contemporary philosophical
issues, 386
contemporary religious issues, 900
European Jews, 635
Jewish history, 593
Jewish literature, 663
theology after, 647
Humanism
Chinese philosophy, 362
Renaissance philosophy,
122, 138, 145, 147,
148, 150, 152, 154,
155
Western philosophy,
1800–1900, 222
Hypnotism. See Mesmerism

Iconoclastic controversy, 692
Iconography
early Christianity, 687
medieval Christianity, 692
Idealism
modern Western philoso-
phy, 158
Western philosophy,
1700–1800, 191, 197
Western philosophy,
1800–1900, 220, 230,
231, 249, 251, 252,
255
Western philosophy, twen-
tieth-century, 259, 281,
284, 303, 304, 317
Ideas, history of
medieval philosophy, 96
Western philosophy, twen-
tieth-century, 302
Immanence, modern Western
philosophy, 157, 158
Immortality. See also Life after death
Renaissance philosophy,
140
Western philosophy,
1700–1800, 208
Imperial cult, oikoumene
world, 451
Inca calendar, 458
Inca religion, New World,
458

Incarnation, traditional is-
sues, 885
Indian philosophy, 350–55
authors, 351–55
authors, chronology, 350
general works, 351
Indian religion
South Asian traditions,
497–518
Western philosophy,
1800–1900, 255
Indigenous religions, 419,
458–66
Africa, 459, 462
Americas, 463–66
Australia, 460, 461
Caribbean, 464, 466
Mesoamerica, 463, 465
North America, 463, 464
Oceania, 461
South America, 464, 465
Western influence, 466
Individualism
medieval philosophy, 93,
113
modern Western philoso-
phy, 158
Renaissance philosophy,
122
Western philosophy, twen-
tieth century, 275, 303
Indo-European religions, pre-
historic, 434
Indus Valley civilization,
South Asian religions,
499
Infinity, Renaissance philoso-
phy, 135
Initiation rites. See also
Rites of passage
mystery cults, 450
religious movements, twentieth-century, 868
shamanism, 430
Instrumentalism, 223
Intentionality, theory of, 221
Intertestamental period of
the Bible. See Apocry-
pha
Investiture controversy, 694
Iranian religions, ancient,
443
Islamic culture and society
philosophy, 372
religion, 577–80
Islamic law, 564, 566
Islamic philosophy, 372–75
authors, 374–75
authors, chronology, 350
general works, 372
medieval philosophy, 96
Islamic religion, 564–90
authors, 580–90

authors, chronology, 580
contemporary religious issues, 902
dictionaries, encyclopedias,
and literature, 566
general histories and comparative studies,
567–74
Jews in Muslim lands, 625
mysticism, philosophy, and
theology, 574–77
philosophy, 374, 375
Israel, land of
history of, 806, 836
Judaism, 595
ancient, 603, 604, 606,
614
sites of the Bible, 808, 809
Israel, state of
modern Judaism, 641–43
Zionism, 657
Italy, philosophy, 29

Jainism, 509
Jansenism, Western philosophy, 1600–1700, 163,
185
Japanese philosophy, 363–67
authors, 363–67
authors, chronology, 350
general works, 363
Japanese religion, 496,
533–41
ancient tradition and
Shinto, 535
Buddhism, 536–38, 540
general works, 534
popular, 538–40
reference works and an-
thologies, 533
Western influence, 533,
540
Jehovah's Witnesses, 863
Jena period system
Western philosophy,
1700–1800, 197, 218
Western philosophy,
1800–1900, 228, 231,
251, 252
Western philosophy, twen-
tieth-century, 278
Jerusalem Bible, 803
Jesuits
late Christianity, 728, 770
Renaissance philosophy,
154
Jesus Christ
ancient Judaism, 619
early and medieval Chris-
tianity, 674
early Christianity, 684

Jesus Christ (*cont.*)
  incarnation, traditional issues, 885
  religious movements, twentieth-century, 864
Jesus movement, 864
Jewish Bible. *See* Hebrew Bible
Jewish law, codes of
  medieval Judaism, 626
  Rabbinic literature, 609
Jewish literature. *See also* Hebrew literature
  ancient Judaism, 607–13
  religious, 601
Jewish philosophy
  Judaism, 600
  medieval Judaism, 628
  modern Judaism, 645
  Rabbinic literature, 609
  Western philosophy, 1700–1800, 208
Jewish religion. *See* Judaism
Jewish Version, 801
Jews, history of
  Judaism, 591–673
    ancient, 603–7
    medieval, 622–26
    modern, 633–45
Judaism, 591–673
  ancient, 603–21
    art and archaeology, 613
    Jews, history of, 603–7
    literature, 607–13
    religious movements, 614–21
  art and music, 597
  atonement, 886
  authors, 660–73
  authors, chronology, 660
  Bible, 801
  and Christianity, 602
  contemporary religious issues, 900
  ethics, 597
  historical background, 806–8
  liturgy, 598–600
  medieval, 622–33
    Jews, history of, 622–26
    religious movements, 630–33
    thought, 626–30
  modern, 633–59
    Jews, history of, 633–45
    religious movements, 650–59
    thought, 645–50
  practice, 601
  religious movements, twentieth-century, 864
  Western philosophy, 1700–1800, 208

Justice
  contemporary issues, 385–87
  Western philosophy, twentieth-century, 315

Kantianism, Western philosophy, 1700–1800, 197
Karaites, 628, 630
Karma
  Buddhism, 529
  South Asian religions, 500
King James Version, 800
Knowledge. *See also* Epistemology
  medieval philosophy, 108, 117
  Renaissance philosophy, 148
  Western philosophy, 1700–1800, 199
Knox Version, 802
Koran
  Islamic philosophy, 374
  Islamic religion, 564, 587
Korean religion, 533–41
  Buddhism, 536–38, 540
  general works, 534
  popular, 538–40
  reference works and anthologies, 533
  Western influence, 540
Kyoto School, 363, 364, 365, 366

Language, contemporary philosophical issues, 390, 396, 402, 411, 413
Language, philosophy of, Western philosophy, 1700–1800, 190
Latin America
  liberation theology, 747, 768
  modern Judaism, 644
  philosophy, 33
  religious movements, twentieth-century, 867
Latter-Day Saints, 844–46
Law, philosophy of
  Renaissance, 154
  Western philosophy, 1600–1700, 186
  Western philosophy, 1700–1800, 190, 209
Liberalism, Islamic philosophy, 372
Liberation theology, 467, 747–50
  authors, 763, 764, 768

contemporary issues, 896
study of religion, 423
Life after death, 886–87. *See also* Immortality; Incarnation
Life experience, Western philosophy, 1800–1900, 226
Linear B script, Greek civilization, 445
Linguistic analysis, Western philosophy, twentieth-century, 261, 271, 278, 282, 325
Lingustics, history of, Western philosophy, 1700–1800, 198
Logic
  contemporary issues, 379, 380
  medieval philosophy, 97, 107, 120
  Western philosophy, 1600–1700, 164, 176
  Western philosophy, 1800–1900, 228, 243, 248
  Western philosophy, twentieth-century, 261
Logical empiricism, Western philosophy, twentieth-century, 261, 272, 278, 313, 343
Logical positivism, Western philosophy, twentieth-century, 261, 272, 278, 332, 337, 343
Lutherans, late Christianity, 730
Lyceum, Athens. *See* Peripatetic school

Magic
  oikoumene world, 448, 450, 451
  religious movements, nineteenth-century, 840
  religious movements, twentieth-century, 864
  Renaissance philosophy, 133, 134, 135, 137, 149
  shamanism, 430
  South Asian religions, 500
Mahayana Buddhism, 511
Manichaeism, 443
Maoism, 358, 359, 361
Martyrdom
  early and medieval Christianity, 674
  Renaissance philosopher, 135, 147

Marxism
  African philosophy, 370
  contemporary philosophical
    issues, 393, 407
  Western philosophy,
    1800–1900, 227, 241
  Western philosophy, twen-
    tieth-century, 261
Masoretes, 794
Materialism, modern Western
  philosophy, 159
Mathematics, history of
  contemporary philosophical
    issues, 410
  Greek philosophy, 87
  Western philosophy,
    1600–1700, 183, 185
  Western philosophy,
    1800–1900, 229, 257
  Western philosophy, twen-
    tieth-century, 260–61,
    320
Matthew's Bible, 799
Maya, 454, 455
Maya calendar, 455
Meaning
  contemporary issues, 376
  Western philosophy, twen-
    tieth-century, 310
Mechanism, modern Western
  philosophy, 157, 158
Medical ethics
  contemporary philosophical
    issues, 387
  contemporary religious is-
    sues, 893
Medici circle, Renaissance
  philosophy, 140, 144,
    152
Medicine men. See Shaman-
  ism
Medieval philosophy, 92–121
  authors, 105–21
  authors, chronology, 105
  Averroism, 96
  fourteenth and fifteenth
    centuries, 103–5
  general works, 93
  ideas, history, 96
  Islamic thought, 96
  method of study, 95
  special topics, 95–98
  text collections, 94
  twelfth and thirteenth cen-
    turies, 101–3
  Western philosophy, twen-
    tieth-century, 285
Meditation
  Buddhism, Chinese, 529
  Confucianism, 525
  Indian philosophy, 352

religious movements, twen-
    tieth-century, 858, 859,
    872
Tibetan Buddhism, 542
Tibetan philosophy, 357
Western philosophy, twen-
    tieth-century, 313
Mediterranean world
  ancient religions and phi-
    losophies, 419, 438–53
  Eastern Orthodox Church,
    754
Megalithic monuments, pre-
    historic religion, 433
Megarian school, 89
Mennonites, 780
Mesmerism, 846
Mesoamerica religions
  indigenous, 463, 465
  Maya, 454, 455
  New World, 454–57
  Olmecs, 454, 455
Mesopotamian religions,
    Mediterranean ancient
    urban civilization, 440
Messiah
  ancient Judaism, 620
  religious movements, twen-
    tieth-century, 864
  Sabbateanism, 631
Meta-ethics, contemporary
    philosophical issues,
    387
Metaphysics
  Greek philosophy, 64
  medieval philosophy, 120
  Renaissance philosophy,
    135, 154
  Western philosophy,
    1600–1700, 168
  Western philosophy,
    1700–1800, 219
  Western philosophy, twen-
    tieth-century, 302, 305,
    314, 333, 338
Methodism, 738
Mexico, Mesoamerica reli-
    gions, 456
Middle Ages
  Christianity, 690–701
  Judaism, 622–33
  medieval philosophy,
    92–121
  Western philosophy,
    1800–1900, 253
Middle America. See Me-
  soamerica
Middle East, non-Islamic and
    non-Jewish tradition,
    544–48
Middle Platonism, 59
Midrash, 609
Milesian school, 51

Militancy
  Islamic religion, 564
  late Christianity, 762
  religious movements, twen-
    tieth-century, 861, 876
  Sikhism, 516
Military ethics, contemporary
    philosophical issues,
    388
Mind, nature of. See also
    Dualism
  contemporary issues, 395,
    396
  contemporary philosophical
    issues, 381–83
Minority religions
  religious movements,
    839–81
    authors, 873–81
    authors, chronology, 873
    women authors, 873–74
  religious movements, nine-
    teenth-century, 840–53
  religious movements, twen-
    tieth-century, 853–73
    controversial issues, 856
    descriptive and historical
      works, 855
    directories, encyclope-
      dias, and bibliogra-
      phies, 854
    theological and philo-
      sophical response, 857
    Theosophy, 858
Mishnah, 609, 619
Missionaries
  American colonies, 752
  early Christianity, 681
  late Christianity, 715, 728,
    740, 770
Mithraism, 443
Modal logic, Western philos-
    ophy, twentieth-cen-
    tury, 300, 301
Molecular genetics, contem-
    porary philosophical is-
    sues, 384
Monad, Western philosophy,
    1600–1700, 167
Monasticism
  early Christianity, 687
  medieval Christianity, 698
  medieval philosophy, 111
Monism
  Hinduism, 502
  Western philosophy,
    1800–1900, 221
  Western philosophy, twen-
    tieth-century, 283, 320
Monotheism
  ancient religion, 421
  Eastern religions, 496

Monotheism (cont.)
  Egypt, ancient religion, 442
  Hinduism, 502
  Iranian ancient religions, 443
  Islamic religion, 564
  Zoroastrianism, 546, 547
Moonies. See Unification Church
Morality. See also Ethics
  modern Western philosophy, 158
  Western philosophy, 1700–1800, 193, 203
  Western philosophy, 1800–1900, 254
  Western philosophy, twentieth-century, 277, 299
Mormons. See Latter-Day Saints
Multidisciplinary approach, contemporary philosophical issues, 376
Music, contemporary philosophical issues, 392
Muslims
  Islamic religion, 564, 565, 566
  medieval Judaism, 625
  society and politics, 577
Mystery cults
  Greek ancient religion, 446
  oikoumene world, 450
Mysticism. See also Sufism
  Islamic philosophy, 375
  Islamic religion, 574–77
  late Christianity, 786, 788
  medieval Christianity, 695
  medieval Judaism, 629
  medieval philosophy, 111, 112
  Renaissance philosophy, 133, 149
  Western philosophy, 1600–1700, 185
Myth
  Germanic religion, 437
  gnosticism, 453
  Hinduism, 502
  Hittite and Canaanite religions, 444
  indigenous religions, 460, 461, 463
  Japanese religion, 535
  Mesopotamian ancient urban civilization, 440
  Mexico, 456
  study of religion, 427

Naropa Institute, Colorado, 357

Nation of Islam. See Black Muslims
Native Americans
  Bible, 801
  indigenous religions, 463–66
Naturalism, Western philosophy, twentieth-century, 259
Natural philosophy, modern Western philosophy, 157
Natural rights, Western philosophy, 1600–1700, 186
Nature, philosophies of, Renaissance philosophy, 123, 133, 137
Nazism
  Christian authors affected by, 757, 759, 787, 788
  European Jews affected by, 635, 642
  German philosopher association with, 290
  German philosophers affected by, 298, 299
  German philosophers escaping, 392, 394, 407
  Jewish authors affected by, 660, 663, 664, 900
  Jewish philosophers affected by, 220, 234
  Jewish scholars affected by, 493
Neo-Kantianism
  modern Western philosophy, 159
  Western philosophy, twentieth-century, 279
Neolithic period, prehistoric religion, 433
Neoplatonism, 60–62
  Greek philosophy, 77
  medieval philosophy, 114
  Roman philosophy, 86
Neo-Thomism, Western philosophy, twentieth-century, 260, 269, 285
New Age movement, religious movements, twentieth-century, 854, 857, 865
New American Bible, 803–4
New English Bible, 803, 804
New Harmony, Indiana, communal groups, 843
New Realism, Western philosophy, twentieth-century, 260
New Revised Standard Version, 804
New Testament, 792

historical background, 806, 807
introduction to study of, 815–17
theological study, 826, 829–34
topic and author masterworks, 824–26
New Thought movement, 847
Newtonianism, modern Western philosophy, 157
New World civilization. See American civilization
New World religions
  ancient urban civilization, 419, 453–58
  Inca, 458
  Mesoamerica, 454–57
Nihilism
  Japanese philosophy, 365
  Western philosophy, 1800–1900, 246
Nirvana, Buddhism, 510
Nobel Prize
  contemporary religious issues, 905
  Eastern religions, 558
  late Christianity, 771
  Tibetan philosophy, 356
  Western philosophy, 1800–1900, 219
  Western philosophy, twentieth-century, 320, 321, 328
Nominalism
  contemporary philosophical issues, 402
  medieval philosophy, 93, 120
  Western philosophy, 1700–1800, 190
Nonviolence
  contemporary religious issues, 895
  Indian philosophy, 351
  Jainism, 509
  late Christianity, 772
Noogenesis, 336
Norse mythology, Germanic religion, 437
North Africa, non-Islamic and non-Jewish tradition, 544–48
North America
  indigenous religions, 459, 463, 464
  modern Judaism, 638–41
Numbers, theory of, 229

Occasionalism, Western philosophy, 1600–1700, 181

Occult
  religious movements, twentieth-century, 853, 854, 860
  Rosicrucianism, 848
Oceania, indigenous religions, 461
Oikoumene world
  faith healing, 450
  gnosticism, 452
  Hellenistic world, 448–53
  imperial cult, 451
  magic, 448, 450, 451
  mystery cults, 450
  Roman Empire, 448–53
Old Stone Age. See Paleolithic period
Old Testament, 792
  introduction to study of, 815–17
  texts, 794
  theological study, 826, 834, 837
  topic and author masterworks, 822–24
Olmecs, 454, 455
Oneida community, 843
Ontological argument, Western philosophy, twentieth-century, 288
Ontology
  contemporary issues, 380
  Western philosophy, twentieth-century, 283
Oral tradition
  Bible, 792, 796, 835
  Celtic religion, 436
  Eastern religions, 496
  indigenous religions, 459
  Japanese religion, 535
  Rabbinic Judaism, 619
Oratory, Roman philosophy, 72
Oriental philosophy. See Asian philosophy; Chinese philosophy; Indian philosophy; Islamic philosophy
Orphism, Greek ancient religion, 446
Orthodox Church, Eastern. See Eastern Orthodox Church
Orthodox Judaism, 651, 653
  medieval period, 626, 627
Oxford Bible. See New English Bible

Pacifism
  Indian philosophy, 351
  Western philosophy, twentieth-century, 320, 321

Paganism
  religious movements, twentieth-century, 864
  Renaissance philosophy, 150, 151
Paleolithic period, prehistoric religions, 432
Paleontology, Western philosophy, twentieth-century, 335
Panpsychism, Western philosophy, twentieth-century, 288
Pantheism
  Western philosophy, 1600–1700, 186
  Western philosophy, twentieth-century, 288
Papacy
  late Christianity, 740, 770
  medieval Christianity, 694
Paradigm, 406
Parapsychology
  Spiritualism, 850
  Theosophy, 858
Parmenidean absolute, Western philosophy, 1800–1900, 221
Patristic philosophy, medieval thought, 98–100
Pelagianism, early Christianity, 685
Pentateuch, 792, 836
Pentecostal movements, 467
  late Christianity, 715
People's Temple, 867
Perception
  contemporary issues, 395
  contemporary philosophical issues, 382
  medieval philosophy, 108
  Western philosophy, 1600–1700, 164
  Western philosophy, 1700–1800, 211
  Western philosophy, 1800–1900, 254
  Western philosophy, twentieth-century, 277, 309
Peripatetic school, 64, 65
  books, 66–72
  membership, 90
Personalism, Western philosophy, twentieth-century, 259, 299
Pessimism
  Western philosophy, 1700–1800, 192, 217
  Western philosophy, twentieth-century, 281
Pharisees, 615

Phenomenalism, Western philosophy, twentieth-century, 320
Phenomenology
  contemporary issues, 376
  modern Western philosophy, 159
  Western philosophy, 1800–1900, 234
  Western philosophy, twentieth-century, 261, 290, 309, 318, 331
Philosophical Radicals, 190
Philosophy
  African, modern, 367–71
  ancient religion and, 419–94
  Asian, modern, 348–67, 372–75
  contemporary issues, 376–415
    authors, 392–415
    authors, chronology, 392
    deconstruction and postmodernism, 390–92
    ethics, 387–89
    general works, 378–79
    mind, nature of, 381–83
    problems, state of, 379–81
    rights and justice, 385–87
    science, philosophy of, 383–85
    women authors, 394, 405
  encyclopedias and dictionaries, 2, 12–15
  general, 11–43
    authors, 38–43
    authors, chronology, 38
    women authors, 39
  general histories and surveys, 2
  general reference, 1–8
  geographic area, 25–36
  Greek and Roman, 44–91
  handbooks, sourcebooks, and guides, 5–7
  histories, 15–18
  indexes, 7, 12–15
  introductions, 19–25
  Islam, modern, 372–75
  Islamic religion, 574–77
  medieval, 92–121
  Renaissance, 122–56
  Western, modern, 1600–1900, 157–258
  Western, twentieth-century, 259–347
Philosophy, comparative. See Comparative philosophy

Planetary motion, Western
    philosophy, 1600–1700,
    171
Platonism
    books, 77–85
    Middle Platonism, 59
    Neoplatonism, 60–62
    Renaissance philosophy,
        122–23, 140
Pleasure
    Greek philosophy, 73
    Renaissance philosophy,
        155
    Roman philosophy, 75
Pluralism
    contemporary philosophical
        issues, 377, 380
    pre-Socratic philosophy, 52
Poland, philosophy, 30
Political science and
        philosophy
    contemporary issues, 377,
        386, 394, 407
    medieval thought, 98
    modern Western philoso-
        phy, 158
    Renaissance, 133–34, 144
    Western philosophy,
        1600–1700, 173, 178
    Western philosophy,
        1700–1800, 204, 210,
        213
    Western philosophy,
        1800–1900, 227, 230,
        231, 241
    Western philosophy, twen-
        tieth-century, 313
Polygamy, Latter-Day Saints,
    845
Pope. See Papacy
Positive thinking. See New
    Thought movement
Positivism
    modern Western philoso-
        phy, 159
    Western philosophy,
        1800–1900, 222
Posthumous works
    contemporary philosophical
        issues, 377
    Renaissance philosophy,
        144, 153
    Western philosophy,
        1600–1700, 168, 173
    Western philosophy,
        1700–1800, 195, 200,
        213
    Western philosophy,
        1800–1900, 227, 230,
        238, 244, 248
    Western philosophy, twen-
        tieth-century, 280, 308,
        336

Postmodernism
    contemporary philosophical
        issues, 390–92, 399,
        412
    current theological meth-
        od, 889
Pragmatism
    Chinese philosophy, 360
    modern Western philoso-
        phy, 159
    Western philosophy,
        1800–1900, 223, 235
    Western philosophy, twen-
        tieth-century, 260, 308,
        317
Prayer, Islamic religion, 565
Prayer wheels, 543
Preanimism, ancient religion,
    421
Prehistoric religions, 419,
    431–37
    Celtic, 436
    Germanic, 437
    Indo-European, 434
    Neolithic period, 433
    Paleolithic period, 432
    Proto-Indo-European, 434,
        435
Presbyterianism, late Chris-
    tianity, 773
Pre-Socratic philosophy,
    49–53
    Atomism, 52
    Eleatic school, 51
    general works, 50
    Milesian school, 51
    pluralism, 52
Primitive religions. See Pre-
    historic religions
Prison experience
    Christian author, 759
    Renaissance philosophy,
        147
    Western philosophy, twen-
        tieth-century, 286
Prizes and awards
    Western philosophy, twen-
        tieth-century, 282, 297,
        299, 301, 305, 313,
        314, 338
Process philosophy
    Western philosophy, twen-
        tieth-century, 260, 275,
        288, 340
Protestantism
    Bible, 802, 803, 804
    late Christianity,
        1500–1560, 720, 725
    theological study of reli-
        gion, 423
Proto-Indo-European reli-
    gions, prehistoric, 434,
    435

Proverbs
    Judaism, 598
    ancient, 615, 619
Pseudonym
    Western philosophy,
        1700–1800, 217
    Western philosophy,
        1800–1900, 238
Psychologism, Western phi-
    losophy, 1800–1900,
    229, 234
Psychology
    study of religion, 423, 424
    contemporary issues, 890
Publishing, contemporary
    philosophical issues,
    378
Punishment, contemporary
    issues, 386
Pure Land Buddhism, 511,
    512
    Chinese religion, 529
    Eastern religions, 496
    Japan and Korea, 536
    Vietnam, 520
Puritans
    late Christianity, 766
    Reformation, 733
Pyramids, 441
    Mexico, 456
Pyrrhonism, 58

Quakers. See Friends, Reli-
    gious Society of

Rabbi
    ancient Judaism, 606
    Rabbinic Judaism, 619
    Rabbinic literature, 609–13
Rabbinic Judaism, 618–21
Rabbinic literature, 609–13
    Midrash, 609
    Mishnah, 609, 619
    Talmuds, 609, 619
    Tosefta, 609, 619
Rabbinic period, ancient Ju-
    daism, 606
Ramakrishna Mission, 354,
    871
Rationalism
    Jewish thought, 646
    modern Western philoso-
        phy, 158
    Western philosophy,
        1700–1800, 209, 218
    Western philosophy, twen-
        tieth-century, 280
Realism
    Western philosophy, twen-
        tieth-century, 259, 280,
        283, 312, 332

Reality
  Western philosophy,
    1800–1900, 251
  Western philosophy, twen-
    tieth-century, 259
Reason
  early and medieval Chris-
    tianity, 674, 695
  modern Western philoso-
    phy, 158
  Western philosophy,
    1700–1800, 205, 210
  Western philosophy, twen-
    tieth-century, 276, 285
Reasoning
  Japanese philosophy, 366
  Western philosophy,
    1700–1800, 199
Reconstructionism, 659
Reformation
  late Christianity, 716
  late Christianity,
    1500–1560, 720–29
    English, 725–27
    radical elements, 723–25
    Roman Catholic, 727–29
  late Christianity,
    1560–1648, 729–38
    after Calvin, 731
    art and music, 737
    Great Britain, 733–36
    Lutheranism in Germany
      and Scandinavia, 730
    radical elements, 732
Reform Judaism, 600, 651,
    652
Reincarnation. See Trans-
    migration
Religion
  ancient, and philosophies,
    419–94
  Bible, 792–838
  Christianity, early and me-
    dieval, 674–714
  Christianity, late, 1500 to
    the present, 715–91
  contemporary issues,
    882–906
  authors, 899–906
  authors, chronology, 899
  character, affections, and
    virtues, 897
  ethics, 892–95
  interreligious dialogue,
    898
  liberation theology, 896
  ritual, worship, and reli-
    gious community, 897
  Roman Catholic thought,
    890–91
  social sciences, 889–90
  theological method,
    888–89

  traditional, 884–88
  women, 891
  women authors, 904
  Eastern, 495–563
  encyclopedias, dictionaries,
    and atlases, 2–5
  general histories and sur-
    veys, 2
  general reference, 1–8
  handbooks, sourcebooks,
    and guides, 5–7
  indexes, 7
  introductions to, 883
  Islamic, 564–90
  Judaism, 591–673
  medieval philosophy,
    92–121
  Western philosophy,
    1700–1800, 208
  Western philosophy,
    1800–1900, 241, 253
Religion, philosophy of
  contemporary issues,
    882–906
  contemporary philosophical
    issues, 380
  Western philosophy,
    1700–1800, 200
Religious movements
  ancient Judaism, 614–21
  contemporary issues, 883
  Indian philosophy, 354
  indigenous religions, 466
  late Christianity, 716
  medieval Judaism, 630–33
  minority religions, 839–81
  authors, 873–81
  authors, chronology, 873
  women authors, 873–74
  modern Judaism, 650–59
  nineteenth-century, 840–53
  twentieth-century, 853–73
  controversial issues, 856
  descriptive and historical
    works, 855
  directories, encyclope-
    dias, and bibliogra-
    phies, 854
  theological and philo-
    sophical response, 857
  Theosophy, 858
Religious sects
  ancient Judaism, 614
  Islamic religion, 565
Renaissance philosophy,
    122–56
  authors, 133–56
  authors, chronology, 132
  general works, 123–32
Responsa literature, 626
Resurrection, traditional is-
    sues, 886, 887

Revelation
  early and medieval Chris-
    tianity, 674, 695
  Western philosophy, twen-
    tieth-century, 285
Reversionary Judaism, 659
Revised English Bible, 804
Revised Standard Version,
    802
Rights, contemporary issues,
    385–87
Rites of passage
  indigenous religions, 462
  study of religion, 429
Ritual
  Aztecs, 456
  contemporary religious is-
    sues, 897
  Egypt, ancient religion,
    441
  indigenous religions, 460,
    461, 463, 464
  Islamic religion, 565, 566
  Japanese religion, 535
  Maya, 455
  medieval Christianity, 698
  Mediterranean ancient ur-
    ban civilization, 438
  prehistoric religion, 432
  study of religion, 427–30
Roman Catholic Church
  Apocrypha, 810
  Bible, 800, 802, 803
  contemporary issues,
    890–91, 902, 904
  early Christianity, 681
  late Christianity,
    1500–1560, 720,
    727–29
  theological study of reli-
    gion, 423
Roman Empire
  early Christianity, 681,
    682–84
  oikoumene world, 448–53
Roman philosophy
  authors, 64–91
  authors, chronology, 64
  Epicureanism, 58
  Greek influence, 44–91
  general works, 46–49
  Stoicism, 56, 58, 59
Roman religion, ancient, 447
Romanticism
  religious movements, nine-
    teenth-century, 840
  Western philosophy,
    1800–1900, 252, 253
Rosicrucianism, 847
Runic inscriptions, Germanic
    religion, 437
Russell Paradox, 229
Russia, philosophy, 30

Russian literature, Western philosophy, twentieth-century, 335

Sabbateanism, 631
Sacrament, early Christianity, 684
Sacrifice
  Aztecs, 456
  Celtic religion, 436
  Inca religion, 458
  Mesopotamian ancient urban civilization, 440
  prehistoric religion, 432
  South Asian religions, 500
  study of religion, 428
Sadducees, 616
Sage philosophy
  African, 371
  Chinese religion, 524, 525, 527
Salt Lake City, Utah, Latter-Day Saints, 845
Salvation
  Western philosophy, 1800–1900, 253, 255
  Western philosophy, twentieth-century, 305
Samaritans, 618
Sanskrit, Indian religion, 497
Santería
  religious movements, twentieth-century, 867
  sacrifice, 428, 868
Satanism, 868
Satire
  Renaissance philosophy, 138
  Western philosophy, 1700–1800, 209, 217
Scandinavia
  Lutheranism, late Christianity, 730
  philosophy, 31
Schism, medieval Christianity, 692, 694
Scholasticism
  medieval Christianity, 695
  Renaissance philosophy, 136, 152
  Western philosophy, twentieth-century, 305
Science, history of
  medieval philosophy, 97
  Renaissance philosophy, 134, 141
Science, philosophy of
  contemporary issues, 383–85, 398, 405, 406, 409
  Greek philosophy, 64, 65
  medieval philosophy, 110

modern Western philosophy, 159
Western philosophy, 1600–1700, 164
Western philosophy, 1800–1900, 257
Western philosophy, twentieth-century, 273, 313, 340
Science, Western philosophy, 1600–1700, 169, 171, 172
Science of Judaism, 647
Scientific method
  contemporary philosophical issues, 383, 402, 405
  Greek philosophy, 64
  Judaism, 647
  Renaissance philosophy, 141, 142
  Western philosophy, 1600–1700, 165
  Western philosophy, twentieth-century, 259, 261, 280
Scientific theory, contemporary issues, 383
Scientology, 869
Scotland
  philosophy, 32
  Reformation, 735, 773
Seance, 850
Second Temple period, ancient Judaism, 603–6
Seers, Celtic religion, 436
Self-Realization Fellowship, 872
Sensation, Western philosophy, 1700–1800, 195
Septuagint, 796
Sexism
  late Christianity, 764
  philosophy, 40
Sexuality
  contemporary religious issues, 894
  prehistoric religion, 433
  religious movements, twentieth-century, 867
  Western philosophy, 1800–1900, 228, 255
Shakers, 848–50
Shamanism
  Eastern religions, 495, 496
  indigenous religions, 463, 464
  study of religion, 430
Shiite sect, Islamic religion, 564, 565
Shinto, Japanese religion, 535, 538, 540
Shrine, prehistoric religion, 433

Sikhism, 515–17
Sin, doctrines of, medieval philosophy, 116
Skepticism
  contemporary philosophical issues, 384
  Hellenistic Age, 57
  Jewish thought, 646
  Renaissance philosophy, 133, 146, 151
  Western philosophy, 1600–1700, 166, 172
  Western philosophy, 1700–1800, 199, 200
Social behaviorism, 308
  contemporary philosophical issues, 414
Social contract, contemporary issues, 385–87
Social philosophy
  modern Judaism, 655
  Renaissance, 136
  Western philosophy, twentieth-century, 313, 314, 316
Social sciences
  contemporary philosophical issues, 384
  contemporary religious issues, 889–90
  study of religion, 423
Sociology
  study of religion, 423, 424
  contemporary issues, 890
  Western philosophy, 1800–1900, 222, 223, 228, 241
  Western philosophy, twentieth-century, 331
Solar system
  Western philosophy, 1600–1700, 169, 184
  Western philosophy, 1700–1800, 204
Sophists, 53–54
Soul
  medieval philosophy, 117
  Renaissance philosophy, 134, 140
  Western philosophy, 1600–1700, 169, 182
South America, indigenous religions, 464, 465
South Asian religions, 497–518
  ancient heritage, 499–501
  Buddhism, 510–15
  general works, 498
  Hinduism, 502–9
  Jainism, 509
  reference works and anthologies, 497
  Sikhism, 515–17

Zoroastrianism, 517
Southeast Asian religion,
    518–20
  Buddhism, 519
  general works, 518
  popular, 518
  Vietnam, 520
Space and time
  Western philosophy,
    1600–1700, 184
  Western philosophy, twen-
    tieth-century, 302
Speculative philosophy
  contemporary issues, 377
  Western philosophy, twen-
    tieth-century, 338, 340
Spinozism, Western philoso-
    phy, 1700–1800, 208
Spirits
  indigenous religions, 463
  Japanese religion, 535
  religious movements, nine-
    teenth-century, 840
  Renaissance philosophy,
    134
  shamanism, 430
  Western philosophy,
    1600–1700, 167
Spiritualism
  communal groups, 843
  Mesmerism, 846
  religious movements, nine-
    teenth-century, 840,
    850
  religious movements, twen-
    tieth-century, 868
  Shakers, 849
  Swedenborgianism, 851
Spiritualists, 723
Spirituality
  religious movements, twen-
    tieth-century, 853, 854
  traditional issues, 887
Stoicism
  Hellenistic Age, 56
  Roman philosophy, 58, 59,
    76, 88
Stonehenge, 433
Structuralism, study of reli-
    gion, 426
Sufism
  Islamic philosophy, 375
  Islamic religion, 566
Suicide
  Greek philosopher, 89
  religious movements, twen-
    tieth-century, 867
  Roman philosopher, 88
Sunni sect, Islamic religion,
    564, 565
Swami, religious movements,
    twentieth-century, 853,
    862, 871

Swedenborgianism, 851
Symbolic forms, theory of,
    Western philosophy,
    twentieth-century, 279
Symbolic logic, Western phi-
    losophy, twentieth-cen-
    tury, 301, 320
Synagogue, 796

Talmuds, 609, 619
Tantric Buddhism, 542
Taoism, 496
  Chinese religion, 521,
    526–29
Targums, 608, 796
Teleology
  modern Western philoso-
    phy, 158
  Western philosophy,
    1700–1800, 204
Temples
  Hittite and Canaanite reli-
    gions, 444
  Inca religion, 458
  Maya, 455
  Mediterranean ancient ur-
    ban civilization, 438,
    440
  Mexico, 456
  religious movements, twen-
    tieth-century, 862
Teotihuacan, Mexico, 456,
    457
Theism
  Western philosophy,
    1600–1700, 168
  Western philosophy, twen-
    tieth-century, 260, 271,
    332
Theology
  Bible study, 826
  Christian, study of religion,
    422
  contemporary traditional
    issues, 884–88
  current method, 888–89
  postmodernism and de-
    construction, 889
  religion, language, and
    knowledge, 888
  Islamic religion, 574–77
  Judaism, 592, 595
  late Christianity, 718
  late Christianity, 1914 to
    present, 742–47
  medieval philosophy,
    92–121
  modern Judaism, 645, 648
  modern Western philoso-
    phy, 157
  post-Holocaust, 647

Western philosophy,
    1700–1800, 207
Theosophy
  religious movements, nine-
    teenth-century, 852
  religious movements, twen-
    tieth-century, 858
Theravada Buddhism
  Eastern religions, 510
  religious movements, twen-
    tieth-century, 859
Thomism
  contemporary issues, 376
  medieval philosophy, 93
  Renaissance philosophy,
    136
  Western philosophy, twen-
    tieth-century, 260, 305
Tibetan philosophy, 355–57
  authors, 356–57
  authors, chronology, 350
  general works, 356
Tibetan religion, 542–44
Toltecs, 456, 457
Torah, 593, 597
  Orthodox Judaism, 653
  Rabbinic Judaism, 618–20
Tosefta, 609, 619
Totemism, ancient religion,
    421, 429
Trance
  Mesmerism, 846
  shamanism, 430
  Spiritualism, 850
Transcendentalism, religious
    movements, nine-
    teenth-century, 840
Transcendental meditation,
    872
Translations of the Bible.
    See Versions of the
    Bible
Transmigration
  South Asian religions, 500
  traditional issues, 886, 887
Trent, Council of, 727, 728
Tribal religions. See Indige-
    nous religions
Trinity
  early Christianity, 684
  Western philosophy,
    1600–1700, 167
Truth
  contemporary philosophical
    issues, 376
  Western philosophy, twen-
    tieth-century, 276
Tyndale Bible, 799

UFO, 869
Umbanda, 867

Unidentified Flying Objects. *See* UFO
Unification Church, 870, 877
United States. *See also* America
  minority religious movements, 839–81
  philosophy, 33–36
Unity of science movement. *See* Logical positivism
Upanishads, Vedanta religion, 500, 501
Up-Biblum God, 801
Urban life
  Mediterranean world, ancient civilizations, 438–53
  New World, ancient civilizations, 419, 453–58
Utilitarianism
  modern Western philosophy, 158
  Western philosophy, 1700–1800, 190
  Western philosophy, 1800–1900, 243, 244, 256
Utopian views
  Chinese philosophy, 360, 361
  communal groups, 843
  Indian philosophy, 352
  religious movements, nineteenth-century, 840
  Renaissance philosophy, 137, 147
  Theosophy, 858
  Western philosophy, twentieth-century, 276

Vedanta, Indian philosophy, 353
Vedanta religion
  religious movements, twentieth-century, 871
  Upanishads, 501
Vedic literature
  Aranyakas, 500
  Brahmanas, 500
  Hinduism, 502
  Upanishads, 500, 501
  Vedas, 500
Vedic religion, 500
Versions of the Bible
  ancient, 796–806
  chronology, 799–805

English, 797–98
  textual criticism, 805
Vienna Circle, 409
  Western philosophy, twentieth-century, 272, 278, 332, 337, 343
Vietnamese religious traditions, 520
Voudon, 867

Wall paintings, ancient Judaism, 613
Warfare
  contemporary philosophical issues, 388
  contemporary religious issues, 895, 900
Western civilization, Western philosophy, 158
Western influence
  Chinese philosophy, 360
  Chinese religion, 531
  Hinduism, 507–9
  indigenous religions, 466
  Islamic philosophy, 372
  Japanese philosophy, 363
  Japanese religion, 533, 540
  Korean religion, 540
Westernization
  African philosophy, 348
  Asian philosophy, modern, 348
  Indian philosophy, 350
Western philosophy, 1600–1900, 157–258
  1600–1700, 157
    authors, 163–89
    authors, chronology, 163
    women authors, 166
  1700–1800, 157, 158
    authors, 190–219
    authors, chronology, 190
  1800–1900, 158, 159
    authors, 219–58
    authors, chronology, 219
    general bibliography, 159–63
Western philosophy, twentieth-century, 259–347
  authors, 269–349
  authors, chronology, 269
  general works, 262–68
Whirling Dervishes, 566, 589
Wicca. *See* Witchcraft

Witchcraft, religious movements, twentieth-century, 864
Working-class movement, Western philosophy, 1800–1900, 227, 241
Worship
  Celtic religion, 436
  contemporary religious issues, 897
  Islamic religion, 565
  Judaism, 598–600
  medieval Christianity, 698
  Roman religion, 447
Wyclif Bible, 799

Yeshiva, Orthodox Judaism, 653
Yiddish literature, 655, 656. *See also* Hebrew literature; Jewish literature
Yin and Yang, Chinese religion, 521, 524, 525
Yoga
  Buddhism, 511
  Hinduism, 502
  Indian philosophy, 352
  religious movements, twentieth-century, 872
Yogacara, 511
Young Hegelians, Western philosophy, 1800–1900, 227, 228, 241
Youth culture, religious movements, twentieth-century, 853–54
Yugoslavia (former), philosophy, 33

Zen
  Chinese Buddhism, 529
  Japan and Korea, 536
  Japanese philosophy, 364
  religious movements, twentieth-century, 853, 859
  Vietnam, 520
Ziggurat, 440
  Inca religion, 458
Zionism, 641, 655, 657
Zoroastrianism
  Indian religion, 497
  Parsis, 517, 546
  Iran, 546–48
  Iranian ancient religions, 443